Oxford
WORDPOWER
Dictionary

Oxford WORDPOWER Dictionary

edited by
Sally Wehmeier

Oxford University Press

Oxford University Press
Walton Street, Oxford OX2 6DP

Oxford New York
Athens Auckland Bangkok Bogota Bombay
Buenos Aires Calcutta Cape Town Dar es Salaam
Delhi Florence Hong Kong Istanbul Karachi
Kuala Lumpur Madras Madrid Melbourne
Mexico City Nairobi Paris Singapore
Taipei Tokyo Toronto

and associated companies in
Berlin Ibadan

OXFORD and OXFORD ENGLISH are
trade marks of Oxford University Press

ISBN 0 19 431138 4
© Oxford University Press 1993

First published 1993
Tenth impression 1996

No unauthorized photocopying

All rights reserved. No part of this publication may be
reproduced, stored in a retrieval system, or transmitted,
in any form or by any means, electronic, mechanical,
photocopying, recording, or otherwise, without the
prior written permission of Oxford University Press.

This book is sold subject to the condition that it shall
not, by way of trade or otherwise, be lent, re-sold, hired
out or otherwise circulated without the publisher's prior
consent in any form of binding or cover other than that
in which it is published and without a similar condition
including this condition being imposed on the
subsequent purchaser.

This book includes some words which are or are
asserted to be proprietary names. The presence or
absence of such assertions should not be regarded as
affecting the legal status of any proprietary name or
trade mark.

Illustrators
Kevin Baverstock, Anna Brookes, Martin Cox, Angelika Elsebach,
Gay Galsworthy, Margaret Jones, Richard Lewington,
Martin Lonsdale/Hardlines, Vanessa Luff, Coral Mura,
Oxford Illustrators, Martin Shovel, Technical Graphics
Department OUP, Harry Venning, Michael Woods
Maps © Oxford Practical Atlas

Typeset in Great Britain by
Tradespools Ltd., Frome, Somerset

Printed in Great Britain by
Caledonian International Book Manufacturing Ltd

Contents

Short forms and symbols used in the dictionary	inside front cover
Preface	vii
A short guide to the dictionary	ix
Dictionary A–Z	1–716

Study pages (with blue edges)

Using the Wordpower Dictionary

Dictionary quiz	A2
Words that go together	A4
Checking your work	A6

Vocabulary pages

Health and fitness	A8
The Family	A9
Clothes	A10
Houses	A12
Computers	A13
Education	A14
Government	A16
The Environment	A18
Keeping vocabulary records	A20

Study notes

Word formation	A22
List of prefixes and suffixes	A24
Phrasal verbs	A26
Punctuation	A28
Letter-writing	A30
American English	A32

Appendices

Irregular verbs	719
Expressions with numbers	723
Common first names	729
Abbreviations	731
Geographical names and maps	737

Phonetic spelling and Pronunciation	inside back cover

Preface

This new dictionary has been written with the intention of opening up the world of words to the intermediate learner of English. Everyone who has worked on the text with me is a teacher or ex-teacher of English, and I hope that our experience of teaching at the intermediate level is reflected in the clarity of our definitions, choice of illustrative examples, and the practical help that we give in the many notes throughout the dictionary. I am confident that the Oxford Wordpower Dictionary will prove to be an extremely useful resource, both in the classroom and for self-study.

My special thanks go to Margaret Deuter and Fiona Mills, who edited the text with me and worked on the illustrations, study pages and appendices. Their constructive comments were always welcome as was their cheerful support. I am grateful to the following lexicographers for their dedicated work over a long period: Evadne Adrian-Vallance, Chris Cowley, Mark Harrison, Julia Marshall, and Christine Rickards. Thanks are due also to Jane Walsh who helped out with the editing at a late stage in the project. I should also like to acknowledge the work of the large team that made the production of the book possible once the text of the dictionary was complete.

Oxford, 1993   Sally Wehmeier

The information in the dictionary

FINDING AND SPELLING WORDS

☆ **power** /'paʊə(r)/ *noun* **1** [C,U] the ability to do sth: *The minister promised to do everything in her power to make sure the hostages were not*

star showing **important words**

☆ **organize** (*also* **organise**) /'ɔːɡənaɪz/ *verb* **1** [T] to plan or arrange an event, an activity,

alternative spelling given in brackets

bark¹ /bɑːk/ *noun* [U] the hard outer covering of a tree
☆ **bark²** /bɑːk/ *verb* **1** [I] **bark (at sb/sth)** (used about dogs) to make a loud, short noise or

Words with the **same spelling** have different numbers.

☆ **centre** (*US* **center**) /'sentə(r)/ *noun* **1** [C, usually sing] the middle point or part of sth:

American spelling

WORDS AND PHRASES RELATED TO THE MAIN WORD

(IDIOMS) **a breath of fresh air** ⇨ BREATH
in the air probably going to happen soon: *A feeling of change was in the air.*
in the open air ⇨ OPEN¹

idioms
(The arrow ⇨ shows that the meaning of the idiom is explained at the word following the arrow.)

(PHRASAL VERBS) **set sb/sth back** to delay sb/sth: *The bad weather has set our plans back six weeks.*
set in to arrive and remain for a period of time: *I'm afraid that the bad weather has set in.*

phrasal verbs
(Look at page A26 for an explanation of how to use them.)

☆ **deaf** /def/ *adj* **1** unable to hear anything or unable to hear very well: *You'll have to speak louder. My father's a bit deaf.* **2 deaf to sth** not wanting to listen to sth: *I've told her what I think but she's deaf to my advice.*
the deaf *noun* [plural] deaf people: *sign language for the deaf*
deafness *noun* [U] the state of being deaf
deaf-and-'dumb *adj* unable to hear or speak

derivatives of the main word (words with the same spelling but a different part of speech; or the main word plus an ending such as -*ly*, -*ness*, etc)

compounds (formed from the main word and one or more other words)

MEANING

banger /ˈbæŋə(r)/ *noun* [C] (*Brit informal*) **1** a sausage **2** an old car that is in very bad condition **3** a small firework that explodes with a short loud noise

The **meaning** of words and phrases is given in simple English using the words which have stars. If there is more than one meaning, all the meanings are listed after numbers.

☆ **below** /bɪˈləʊ/ *prep* at or to a lower position or level than sb/sth: *Do not write below this line.* ○ *It hurts here – just below my knee.* ○ *The temperature fell below freezing during the night.* ○ *Her marks in the exam were below average.* ○

The **example sentences** help you understand the word and show how it is used.

discontent /ˌdɪskənˈtent/ (*also* **discontentment** /ˌdɪskənˈtentmənt/) *noun* [U] the state

a word which has the **same meaning**

nappy /ˈnæpɪ/ *noun* [C] (*pl* **nappies**) (*US* **diaper**) a piece of soft thick cloth or paper that

an **American word** with the **same meaning**

dog² /dɒg; *US* dɔːg/ *verb* [T] (**dogg**ing; **dogg**ed) to follow closely: *A shadowy figure was dogging their every move.* ○ (*figurative*) *Bad luck and illness has dogged her career from the start.*

a **figurative** use of the word (= not using a word in its true sense, but in an imaginative way, in order to give a special effect)

GRAMMAR

bellow /ˈbeləʊ/ *verb* **1** [I] to make a deep low sound, like a bull **2** [I,T] to shout in a loud deep voice —**bellow** *noun* [C]
belly /ˈbelɪ/ *noun* [C] (*pl* **bellies**) the stomach

the **part of speech** of a word (whether it is a noun, verb, etc)

glare /gleə(r)/ *noun* **1** [U] strong light that hurts your eyes: *the glare of the sun on snow* ○ *the glare of a car's headlights* **2** [C] a (long) angry look

countable and uncountable nouns
These letters tell you whether the noun can be counted [C] or not [U].

☆ **think²** /θɪŋk/ *noun* [sing] an act of thinking: *I'm not sure. I'll have to have a think about it.*

a **singular noun**

premises /ˈpremɪsɪz/ *noun* [plural] (*formal*) a building and the land that surrounds it: *The*

a **plural noun**

☆ **committee** /kəˈmɪtɪ/ *noun* [C, with sing or pl verb] a group of people who have been chosen

a noun that can be used with either **a singular or a plural verb**

☆ **tomato** /təˈmɑːtəʊ; *US* təˈmeɪtəʊ/ *noun* [C] (*pl* **tomatoes**) a soft red fruit that is often eaten

irregular plural

xi

☆**hide¹** /haɪd/ *verb* (*pt* **hid** /hɪd/; *pp* **hidden** /'hɪdn/) **1** [T] to put or keep sb/sth in a place where he/she/it cannot be seen: *Where shall I hide the money?* ○ *You couldn't see Bill in the photo – he was hidden behind John.* ○ *The trees hid the house from view.* **2** [I] to be or get in a place where you cannot be seen or found: *Quick, run and hide!* ○ *The child was hiding under the bed.*

transitive and intransitive verbs
These letters tell you whether a verb is transitive [T] (= followed by an object) or intransitive [I] (= never followed by an object).

☆**take** /teɪk/ *verb* [T] (*pt* **took** /tʊk/; *pp* **taken** /'teɪkən/) **1** to carry sb/sth or to go with sb

irregular forms of verbs

hum /hʌm/ *verb* (hu**mm**ing; hu**mm**ed) **1** [I] to make a continuous low noise like the noise

The **last letter** of the word **is doubled** before you add *-ed* or *-ing*.

☆**good¹** /gʊd/ *adj* (**better** /'betə(r)/, **best** /best/) **1** of a high quality or standard: *a good*

the **comparative and superlative forms** (regular forms are not given)

☆**happy** /'hæpi/ *adj* (**happier; happiest**) **1** feeling, showing or giving pleasure or satis-

☆**trousers** /'traʊzəz/ (*US* **pants**) *noun* [plural] a piece of clothing that covers both legs and reaches from your waist to your ankles ☞ Notice that, because **trousers** is a plural word, we cannot say, for example, 'a new trouser'. The following are possible: *I need some new trousers.* ○ *I need a new pair of trousers.* Before another noun the form **trouser** is used: *a trouser leg.*

a note giving **grammatical information**

USING WORDS

☆**consider** /kən'sɪdə(r)/ *verb* [T] **1 consider sb/sth (for/as sth); consider doing sth** to think about sb/sth, often before making a de-

how a word is used in a sentence (sb = somebody; sth = something)

dependent /dɪ'pendənt/ *adj* **1 dependent (on sb/sth)** needing sb/sth to support you:

the particular **preposition** that is used after a word

☆**awake²** /ə'weɪk/ *adj* (not before a noun) not sleeping: *I was awake most of the night, worrying.*

The adjective cannot be used before a noun; it must always follow a verb like *be, seem*, etc.

☆**lone** /ləʊn/ *adj* (only *before* a noun) without any other people; alone: *a lone swimmer on the beach*

The adjective can only be used before a noun.

beast /biːst/ *noun* [C] **1** (*formal*) an animal, especially a large one: *a wild beast* **2** (*informal*) an unpleasant or cruel person

words used in **particular situations**
Words may be labelled *formal* (used in formal written English), *informal* (used in informal conversation and not usually written in an essay, etc) or *slang* (very informal).

xii

CHOOSING THE RIGHT WORD/VOCABULARY BUILDING

> ☆ **contain** /kən'teɪn/ verb [T] **1** to have sth inside (or as part of) itself: *Each box contains 24 tins.* ○ *petrol containing lead* **2** to keep sth within limits: *efforts to contain inflation* ○ *The children couldn't contain themselves – they burst out laughing.* ○ *She found it hard to contain her anger.* ☞ **Contain** or **include**? **Contain** is used when we are talking about objects which have other things inside them: *a jar containing olives* ○ *The parcel contained six books.* **Include** is used to show that several things are part of a whole or thought to belong to something: *The price of the holiday includes accommodation and evening meals but not lunch.* ○ *a team of seven people including a cameraman and a doctor*

a note explaining the **difference between words** that might be confused

> ☞ You book a **double**, **single** or **twin-bedded** room at a hotel. When you arrive you **check in** or register and when you leave you **check out**. Look at the note at **inn**.

a note giving **related vocabulary**

> ☆ **grateful** /'greɪtfl/ adj **grateful (to sb) (for sth)**; **grateful (that...)** feeling or showing thanks (to sb): *We are very grateful to you for all the help you have given us.* ○ *He was very grateful that you did as he asked.* ○ *I should be very grateful if you could send me a copy of your brochure.* ☞ The opposite is **ungrateful**. The noun is **gratitude**.

members of a **word family**

PRONUNCIATION

> ☆ **serviette** /ˌsɜːvɪ'et/ noun [C] a square of cloth or paper that you use when you are eating to

the **pronunciation** of each word

> ˌgrass 'roots noun [plural] the ordinary people in an organization and not those who

where the **stress** falls on a word or phrase

Oxford
WORDPOWER
Dictionary

A,a

A, a¹ /eɪ/ noun [C] (pl **A's; a's** /eɪz/) **1** the first letter of the English alphabet: *'Andy' begins with (an) 'A'.* **2** the highest grade given for an exam or piece of work: *I got an 'A' for my essay.*
'A-road noun [C] (*Brit*) a major road, usually not as wide as a motorway

☆ **a²** /ə/; strong form eɪ/ (*also* **an** /ən/; strong form æn/) *indefinite article* ☞ The form **an** is used before a vowel sound. **1** one: *A cup of coffee, please.* o *an apple and a pear* **2** (used when you are talking about sth in general, not one particular example of it): *A lion is a dangerous animal.* **3** (used with sb's name to show that the speaker does not know the person): *There's a Ms Mills to see you.* **4** (used for showing that sb/sth is a member of a group, class or profession): *She's a Muslim.* o *Their car's a Metro.* o *He's a doctor.* o *She's an MP.* **5** (used with some expressions of quantity): *a lot of money* o *a few cars* **6** (used with prices, rates, measurements) each: *They cost 50p a pound.* o *twice a week* o *He was travelling at about 80 miles an hour.*

aback /ə'bæk/ *adv*
(PHRASAL VERB) **take sb aback** ⇨ TAKE

☆ **abandon** /ə'bændən/ *verb* [T] **1** to leave sb/sth that you are responsible for, usually permanently: *an abandoned car* **2** to stop doing sth without finishing it or without achieving what you wanted to do: *The search for the missing sailors was abandoned after two days.* —**abandonment** *noun* [U]

abashed /ə'bæʃt/ *adj* ashamed and embarrassed because of having done sth bad

abattoir /'æbətwɑː(r)/; *US* ˌæbə'twɑːr/ *noun* [C] = SLAUGHTERHOUSE

abbess /'æbes/ *noun* [C] a woman who is the head of a religious community for women (**nuns**)

abbey /'æbɪ/ *noun* [C] a building where monks or nuns live or used to live

abbot /'æbət/ *noun* [C] a man who is the head of a religious community for men (**monks**)

abbreviate /ə'briːvɪeɪt/ *verb* [T] **1** to make a word or phrase shorter by leaving out some letters **2** to make a story or a piece of writing or speech shorter: *the abbreviated version of the story*

abbreviation /əˌbriːvɪ'eɪʃn/ *noun* [C] a short form of a word or phrase: *In this dictionary 'sth' is the abbreviation for 'something'.*

ABC /ˌeɪbiː'siː/ *noun* [sing] **1** the alphabet; the letters of English from A to Z **2** the simple facts about sth: *the ABC of Gardening*

abdicate /'æbdɪkeɪt/ *verb* **1** [I] to give up being King or Queen: *The Queen abdicated and her son became King.* **2** [T] to give sth up, especially power or a position: *to abdicate responsibility* (= to refuse to be responsible for sth) —**abdication** /ˌæbdɪ'keɪʃn/ *noun* [C,U]

abdomen /'æbdəmən/ *noun* [C] a part of the body below the chest, in which the stomach is contained —**abdominal** /æb'dɒmɪnl/ *adj*

abduct /əb'dʌkt; æb-/ *verb* [T] to take hold of sb and take him/her away illegally: *He has been abducted by a terrorist group.* —**abduction** /əb'dʌkʃn; æb-/ *noun* [C,U]

abet /ə'bet/ *verb* [T] (**abetting; abetted**)
(IDIOM) **aid and abet** ⇨ AID

abhor /əb'hɔː(r)/ *verb* [T] (**abhorring; abhorred**) to hate sth very much: *All civilized people abhor the use of torture.* —**abhorrence** /əb'hɒrəns; *US* -'hɔːr-/ *noun* [U] —**abhorrent** /əb'hɒrənt; *US* 'hɔːr-/ *adj*

abide /ə'baɪd/ *verb*
(IDIOM) **can't/couldn't abide sb/sth/doing sth** to dislike sth very much: *I can't abide getting up early.*
(PHRASAL VERB) **abide by sth** to obey a law, etc; to do what you have agreed or decided: *You must abide by the rules of the game.*

☆ **ability** /ə'bɪlətɪ/ *noun* [C,U] (pl **abilities**) the mental or physical power or skill that makes it possible to do sth: *A person of his ability will have no difficulty getting a job.* o *an ability to make decisions*

ablaze /ə'bleɪz/ *adj* (not before a noun) burning strongly; completely on fire: *Within ten minutes, the whole house was ablaze.*

☆ **able¹** /'eɪbl/ *adj* **be able to do sth** (used as a modal verb) to have the ability, power, opportunity, time, etc to do sth: *Will you be able to come to a meeting next week?* o *I'll be able to give you the money back in a few days.* o *I was able to solve the problem quickly.* ☞ In the passive **can/could** are used, not **be able**: *The arrangement can't be changed.*

able² /'eɪbl/ *adj* clever; doing your job well: *one of the ablest students in the class* o *an able politician* —**ably** *adv*

abnormal /æb'nɔːml/ *adj* different from what is normal or usual, in a way that worries you or that is unpleasant: *I don't want to have children. Is that abnormal?* o *abnormal weather conditions* —**abnormality** /ˌæbnɔː'mælətɪ/ *noun* [C,U] (pl **abnormalities**) —**abnormally** /æb'nɔːməlɪ/ *adv*

aboard /ə'bɔːd/ *adv, prep* on or into a train, ship, aircraft or bus: *We went aboard the boat and found our cabins.* o *Welcome aboard this flight to Caracas.*

abode /ə'bəʊd/ *noun* [sing] (*formal*) the place where you live: *They have the right of abode in Hong Kong* (= they are officially allowed to live there).

s	z	ʃ	ʒ	h	m	n	ŋ	l	r	j	w
so	zoo	she	vision	how	man	no	sing	leg	red	yes	wet

(IDIOM) **(of) no fixed abode/address** ⇨ FIXED

abolish /əˈbɒlɪʃ/ verb [T] to put an end to or stop a law or system officially: *When was capital punishment abolished here?* —**abolition** /ˌæbəˈlɪʃn/ noun [U]: *the abolition of slavery in the US*

abominable /əˈbɒmɪnəbl; *US* -mən-/ adj very unpleasant; very bad: *abominable behaviour* ○ *abominable weather* —**abominably** /əˈbɒmɪnəbli; *US* -mən-/ adv

Aboriginal /ˌæbəˈrɪdʒənl/ (also **Aborigine** /ˌæbəˈrɪdʒəni/) noun [C] a member of the race of people who were the original inhabitants of Australia —**Aboriginal** (also **Aborigine**) adj: *Aboriginal traditions*

abort /əˈbɔːt/ verb [I,T] **1** to end a pregnancy intentionally and cause the baby inside to die **2** to end sth before it is complete

abortion /əˈbɔːʃn/ noun [C,U] an operation to end a pregnancy intentionally, causing the baby inside to die: *to have an abortion* ○ *Abortion is illegal in that country.*

abortive /əˈbɔːtɪv/ adj not completed successfully: *an abortive attempt*

abound /əˈbaʊnd/ verb [I] **1** to exist in large numbers: *Restaurants abound in this part of the city.* **2 abound with sth** to contain large numbers of sth

☆ **about¹** /əˈbaʊt/ adv **1** (*especially US* **around**) a little more or less than; approximately: *It's about three miles from here to the city centre.* ○ *I got home at about half past seven.* **2** (*informal*) almost; nearly: *Dinner's just about ready.* **3** (*also* **around**) in many directions or places: *I could hear people moving about upstairs.* **4** (*also* **around**) here and there, in different positions: *clothes lying about all over the floor* **5** (*also* **around**) (used after certain verbs) without doing anything in particular: *People were standing about in the street.* **6** (*also* **around**) present in a place; existing: *It was very late and there were few people about.*
(IDIOM) **be about to do sth** to be going to do sth very soon: *The film's about to start.* ○ *I was just about to explain when she interrupted me.*

a.bout-'turn (*US* **a.bout-'face**) noun [C] a turn in the opposite direction; a change of opinion

☆ **about²** /əˈbaʊt/ prep **1** on the subject of: *a book about Spain* ○ *Let's talk about something else.* ○ *I don't like it, but there's nothing I can do about it.* **2** (*also* **around**) in many directions or places; in different parts of sth: *We wandered about the town for an hour or two.* **3** in the character of sb: *There's something about him that I don't quite trust.*
(IDIOM) **how/what about…?** **1** (used when asking for information about sb/sth or for sb's opinion or wish): *How about Ruth? Have you heard from her lately?* ○ *I'm going to have chicken. What about you?* **2** (used when making a suggestion): *What about going to a film tonight?*

☆ **above** /əˈbʌv/ adv, prep **1** in a higher place: *The people in the flat above make a lot of noise.* ○ *I live in a small house above the village.* ○ *He looked up at the sky above.* ☛ picture at **over**.

2 in an earlier part (of sth written): *When replying, quote the reference number above.* **3** more than a number, amount, price, etc: *children aged 11 and above* ○ *A score of 70 and above will get you a grade B.* ○ *You must get above 50% to pass.* ○ *above-average temperatures* **4** too good, etc to do sth: *She's not above telling a few lies, if it makes life easier.* **5** with a higher rank: *The person above me is the department manager.*
(IDIOMS) **above all** most importantly: *Above all, stay calm!*
(be) above board (used especially about a business deal, etc) honest and open

abrasive /əˈbreɪsɪv/ adj **1** rough and likely to scratch: *Do not use abrasive cleaners on the bath.* **2** (used about a person) rude and rather aggressive

abreast /əˈbrest/ adv **abreast (of sb/sth)** next to or level with and going in the same direction: *The soldiers marched two abreast.*
(IDIOM) **be/keep abreast of sth** to have all the most recent information about sth

abridge /əˈbrɪdʒ/ verb [T] to make sth (usually a book) shorter by removing parts of it: *an abridged version of a novel* —**abridgement** (*also* **abridgment**) noun [C,U]

☆ **abroad** /əˈbrɔːd/ adv in or to another country or countries: *My mother has never been abroad.* ○ *They found it difficult to get used to living abroad.*

abrupt /əˈbrʌpt/ adj **1** sudden and unexpected: *an abrupt change of plan* **2** (used about a person's behaviour) rather rude and unfriendly —**abruptly** adv —**abruptness** noun [U]

abscess /ˈæbses/ noun [C] a swelling on or in the body, containing a poisonous liquid (**pus**)

abscond /əbˈskɒnd/ verb [I] (*formal*) to run away from a place where you should stay, sometimes with sth that you should not take: *She absconded with all the company's money.*

☆ **absence** /ˈæbsəns/ noun **1** [C,U] a time when sb is away from somewhere; the fact of being away from somewhere: *Frequent absences due to illness meant he was behind with his work.* ○ *His absence from the team will greatly weaken it.* **2** [U] the fact of sth not being there; lack: *The first thing I noticed about the place was the absence of noise.*

☆ **absent** /ˈæbsənt/ adj **1** not present somewhere: *He was absent from work because of illness.* ○ *absent friends* **2** thinking about sth else, and so not paying attention: *an absent stare* —**absently** adv

absent-'minded adj often forgetting or not noticing things, because you are thinking about sth else —**absent-'mindedly** adv —**absent-'mindedness** noun [U]

absentee /ˌæbsənˈtiː/ noun [C] a person who is absent and should be present

☆ **absolute** /ˈæbsəluːt/ adj **1** complete; total: *We are aiming at absolute perfection!* ○ *The whole trip was an absolute disaster.* ○ *None of the parties had an absolute majority* (= more votes, etc than all the other parties together). **2** not measured in comparison with sth else: *Spend-*

iː	ɪ	e	æ	ɑː	ɒ	ɔː	ʊ	uː	ʌ
see	sit	ten	hat	arm	got	saw	put	too	cup

ing on the Health Service has increased in absolute terms.

☆ **absolutely** *adv* **1** /'æbsəlu:tlɪ/ completely; totally: *What you're saying is absolutely wrong.* ○ *I absolutely refuse to believe that.* ○ *He made absolutely no effort* (= no effort at all) *to help me.* **2** /ˌæbsə'lu:tlɪ/ (used when you are agreeing with sb) yes; certainly: *'It is a good idea, isn't it?' 'Oh, absolutely!'*

absolve /əb'zɒlv/ *verb* [T] **absolve sb (from/of sth)** to state formally that sb is free from guilt or blame: *The driver was absolved from any responsibility for the train crash.*

absorb /əb'sɔ:b/ *verb* [T] **1** to take in and hold sth (a liquid, heat, etc): *a drug that is quickly absorbed into the bloodstream* **2** to take sth into the mind and understand it: *I found it impossible to absorb so much information so quickly.* **3** to take sth into sth larger, so that it becomes part of it: *Over the years many villages have been absorbed into the city.* **4** to hold sb's attention completely or interest sb greatly: *History is a subject that absorbs her.*

absorbed *adj* with sb's attention completely held: *He was absorbed in his work and didn't hear me come in.*

absorbent /-ənt/ *adj* able to take in and hold liquid: *an absorbent cloth*

absorbing *adj* holding the attention completely: *an absorbing story* —**absorption** /əb'sɔ:pʃn/ *noun* [U]

abstain /əb'steɪn/ *verb* [I] **abstain (from sth) 1** to stop yourself from doing sth that you enjoy: *to abstain from eating fattening food* ☛ The noun is **abstinence**. **2** (in a vote) to say that you are not voting either for or against sth: *Two people voted in favour, two voted against and one abstained.* ☛ The noun is **abstention**.

abstention /əb'stenʃn/ *noun* [C,U] the act of not voting either for or against sth

abstinence /'æbstɪnəns/ *noun* [U] stopping yourself from having or doing sth that you enjoy: *The doctor advised total abstinence from alcohol.*

abstract[1] /'æbstrækt/ *adj* **1** existing only as an idea, not as a physical or real thing: *I find it hard to think about abstract ideas like the meaning of life.* **2** (used about art) not showing things as they really look: *an abstract painting*

abstract[2] /'æbstrækt/ *noun* [C] an example of abstract art: *an exhibition of abstracts by Braque*

(IDIOM) **in the abstract** without mentioning particular people, objects, etc: *I find it hard to think about the problem in the abstract.*

absurd /əb'sɜ:d/ *adj* that should be laughed at; ridiculous; not seeming sensible: *You look absurd in that hat.* ○ *Don't be absurd! I can't possibly do all this work in one day.* —**absurdity** *noun* [C,U] (*pl* **absurdities**) —**absurdly** *adv*: *The rules of the game are absurdly complicated.*

abundance /ə'bʌndəns/ *noun* [U,sing] a very large quantity of sth

abundant /ə'bʌndənt/ *adj* existing in very large quantities; more than enough: *abundant supplies of food* —**abundantly** *adv*

abuse[1] /ə'bju:z/ *verb* [T] **1** to use sth in the wrong way, eg dishonestly: *He was accused of abusing his position for personal gain.* **2** to say rude things to sb **3** to treat sb badly, often violently: *Social workers discovered that the girl had been sexually abused by her father.*

abuse[2] /ə'bju:s/ *noun* **1** [C,U] using sth in the wrong way: *an abuse of power* ○ *the dangers of drug abuse* **2** [U] rude words, used to insult another person: *The other driver leaned out of the car and hurled abuse at me.* **3** [U] bad, usually violent treatment of sb: *child abuse*

abusive /ə'bju:sɪv/ *adj* using rude language to insult sb: *an abusive remark*

abysmal /ə'bɪzməl/ *adj* very bad; of very poor quality —**abysmally** *adv*

academic /ˌækə'demɪk/ *adj* **1** connected with the educational activities of schools, colleges and universities: *The academic year begins in September.* **2** connected with subjects of interest to the mind rather than technical or practical subjects: *academic subjects such as History* **3** not connected with reality; not affecting the facts of a situation: *It's academic which one I prefer because I can't have either of them.*

academic *noun* [C] a person who teaches and/or does research at a university or college —**academically** /-klɪ/ *adv*

academy /ə'kædəmɪ/ *noun* [C] (*pl* **academies**) **1** a school for special training: *a military academy* **2** (*also* **Academy**) a society of people who are important in art, science or literature: *the Royal Academy of Arts*

☆ **accelerate** /ək'seləreɪt/ *verb* [I,T] to go faster; to make sth go faster or happen more quickly: *I accelerated and left the other cars behind.* —**acceleration** /əkˌselə'reɪʃn/ *noun* [U]

accelerator /ək'seləreɪtə(r)/ *noun* [C] the pedal in a car, etc that you press in order to increase speed

☆ **accent** /'æksent; 'æksənt/ *noun* **1** [C,U] a particular way of pronouncing words that is connected with the country, area or social class that you come from: *a strong Scottish accent* **2** [C] the act of emphasizing a word or part of a word by pronouncing it with greater force: *In the word 'because' the accent is on the second syllable.* **3** [C] (in writing) a mark, usually above a letter, that shows that it has to be pronounced in a certain way **4** [C, usually sing] the particular importance that is given to sth: *In all our products the accent is on quality.*

accentuate /ək'sentʃʊeɪt/ *verb* [T] to make sth easier to notice

☆ **accept** /ək'sept/ *verb* **1** [I,T] to take sth willingly that sb offers you: *Please accept this small gift.* ○ *Do I have to pay in cash or will you accept a cheque?* ○ *Why won't you accept my advice?* **2** [I,T] to say yes to sth or to agree to sth: *Thank you for your invitation. I am happy to accept.* ○ *He asked her to marry him and she accepted him.* ○ *I'd be pleased to accept your offer.* **3** [T] to admit or recognize that sth unpleasant is true: *They refused to accept responsibility for the accident.* **4** [T] to recognize that sth cannot be changed: *It is hard to accept the death of a child.* **5** [T] to believe sth: *I'm afraid I don't accept* that, it simply isn't true. ○ She didn't accept that I was telling the truth. **6** [T] to decide that sb/sth is suitable: *I had a letter from the university saying that I had been accepted on the course.*

acceptable /ək'septəbl/ *adj* **1** allowed, often by people in general: *One or two mistakes are acceptable but no more than that.* **2** satisfactory; good enough: *We hope that you will consider our offer acceptable.* ☛ The opposite is **unacceptable**. —**acceptability** /ək,septə'bɪləti/ *noun* [U] —**acceptably** /-bli/ *adv*

acceptance /ək'septəns/ *noun* [C,U] the act of accepting or being accepted: *a letter of acceptance from the university* ○ *the acceptance of a difficult situation* (= seeing that it cannot be changed) ○ *He quickly gained acceptance in the group* (= the other people thought of him as equal to them).

access /'ækses/ *noun* [U] **1 access (to sth)** a way of entering or reaching a place: *Access to the garden is through the kitchen.* **2 access (to sth)** the chance or right to use or have sth: *Do you have access to a personal computer?* **3 access (to sb)** permission, especially legal or official, to see sb: *They are divorced, but he has regular access to the children.*

accessible /ək'sesəbl/ *adj* **1** possible to be reached or entered: *Because of the snow, the village was not accessible by car.* **2** easy to get, use or understand ☛ The opposite is **inaccessible**. —**accessibility** /ək,sesə'bɪləti/ *noun* [U]

accession /æk'seʃn/ *noun* [U] the act of taking a very high position or rank, especially as ruler of a country or head of sth: *the accession of Queen Elizabeth to the throne in 1952*

accessory /ək'sesəri/ *noun* [C] (*pl* **accessories**) **1** an extra item that is added to sth and is useful or attractive but not essential: *The car has accessories such as an electronic alarm.* **2** [usually pl] a small item that is worn or carried with the main items of clothing (eg shoes, a bag, etc) **3 accessory (to sth)** (in law) a person who helps sb to do sth illegal

☆ **accident** /'æksɪdənt/ *noun* [C] an unpleasant event that happens unexpectedly and causes damage, injury or death: *I hope they haven't had an accident.* ○ *a fatal accident* (= when sb is killed) ○ *I didn't mean to kick you, it was an accident.*

(IDIOM) **by accident** by chance; without being planned: *We met each other again completely by accident.*

'**accident-prone** *adj* frequently having accidents, and therefore more likely to have them than other people

accidental /,æksɪ'dentl/ *adj* happening by chance; not having been planned —**accidentally** /-təli/ *adv*

acclaim /ə'kleɪm/ *verb* [T] to praise sb/sth greatly: *The novel has been acclaimed as a modern classic.* —**acclaim** *noun* [U]: *The film received widespread critical acclaim.*

acclimatize (*also* **acclimatise**) /ə'klaɪmətaɪz/ *verb* [I,T] **acclimatize (yourself/sb/sth) (to sth)** to get used to a new climate, a new situation, etc so that it is not a problem any more: *It took me a long time to get acclimatized to the heat when I went to live in Africa.* —**acclimatization** (*also* **acclimatisation**) /ə,klaɪmətaɪ'zeɪʃn/; *US* -tɪ'z-/ *noun* [U]

accommodate /ə'kɒmədeɪt/ *verb* [T] **1** to have enough space for sb/sth (especially a certain number of people): *Each apartment can accommodate up to six people.* **2** to provide sb with a place to stay, live or work: *During the conference, you will be accommodated in a nearby hotel.* **3** to do or provide what sb wants or needs: *Should you have any special requirements, our staff will do their best to accommodate you.*

accommodating *adj* (used about a person) willing to do or provide what sb wants

☆ **accommodation** /ə,kɒmə'deɪʃn/ *noun* [U] a place for sb to live or stay: *We lived in rented accommodation before buying this house.* ○ *The price of the holiday includes flights and accommodation.* ☛ **Accommodation** is uncountable. We cannot say, 'I will help you to find an accommodation.' In this case we could say, 'I will help you to find somewhere to live.'

accompaniment /ə'kʌmpənɪmənt/ *noun* **1** [C] something that naturally or pleasantly goes with sth else (especially food or drink): *He only drinks wine as an accompaniment to a meal.* **2** [C,U] music that is played with singing or the main instrument: *a violin piece with a piano accompaniment*

☆ **accompany** /ə'kʌmpəni/ *verb* [T] (*pres part* **accompanying**; *3rd pers sing pres* **accompanies**; *pt, pp* **accompanied**) **1** to go with sb to a place: *Children must be accompanied by an adult.* **2** to happen or exist at the same time as, or because of, sth: *Massive publicity accompanied the film's release.* **3** to give or send sth together with sth else, in addition to it: *The letter was accompanied by a cheque for £50.* **4** to play music for a singer or another instrument: *She accompanied him on the guitar.*

accomplice /ə'kʌmplɪs; *US* ə'kɒm-/ *noun* [C] a person who helps sb to do sth bad, especially a crime

accomplish /ə'kʌmplɪʃ; *US* ə'kɒm-/ *verb* [T] to succeed in doing sth requiring effort and/or skill; to achieve: *Very little was accomplished in the meeting.*

accomplished *adj* skilled: *an accomplished pianist*

accomplishment /ə'kʌmplɪʃmənt; *US* ə'kɒm-/ *noun* **1** [U] the act of completing sth successfully **2** [C] something impressive that sb has achieved; a skill that sb has

accord[1] /ə'kɔːd/ *noun* [C] an agreement, eg between countries: *the Helsinki accords on human rights*

(IDIOMS) **in accord** in agreement about sth

of your own accord without being forced or asked: *He wasn't sacked from his job, he left of his own accord.*

accord[2] /ə'kɔːd/ *verb* **1** [T] to give sth to sb: *The diplomats were accorded very respect during their visit.* **2** [I] (*formal*) to match; to agree with: *The information did not accord with what I had been told previously.*

accordance /ə'kɔːdəns/ *noun*

p	b	t	d	k	g	tʃ	dʒ	f	v	θ	ð
pen	bad	tea	did	cat	got	chin	June	fall	van	thin	then

accordingly 5 **achieve**

(IDIOM) **in accordance with sth** in a way that follows or obeys sth: *to act in accordance with instructions*

accordingly /əˈkɔːdɪŋli/ *adv* **1** in a way that is suitable after what has happened: *I realized that I was in danger and acted accordingly.* **2** (*formal*) therefore; for that reason: *We accept that the mistake was ours and, accordingly, have pleasure in refunding your money.*

☆ **according to** /əˈkɔːdɪŋ tə/ *prep* **1** as stated by sb; as shown by sth: *According to Mick, it's a brilliant film.* ○ *More people now have a high standard of living, according to the statistics.* **2** in a way that matches, follows or depends on sth: *Everything went off according to plan* (= as we had planned it). ○ *The salary will be fixed according to age and experience.*

accordion /əˈkɔːdɪən/ *noun* [C] a musical instrument that you hold in both hands and play by pulling the two sides apart and then pushing them together, while pressing the keys with your fingers

accost /əˈkɒst; *US* əˈkɔːst/ *verb* [T] to approach and talk to a stranger in a way that is considered unpleasant or frightening

account¹ /əˈkaʊnt/ *noun* [C] **1** a report or description of sth that has happened: *She gave the police a full account of the robbery.* **2** the arrangement by which a bank looks after your money for you: *to open/close an account on an account with Barclays* ○ *My salary is paid into my bank account.* ○ *How much money have I got left in my account?* ○ *Can I withdraw £500 from my account?* ☛ *We use a* **current** *account to pay for things with a* **cheque**. *We can save money in a* **deposit** *or* **savings** *account.* **3** [usually pl] a record of all the money that a person or business has received or paid out: *He takes care of the business and his wife keeps the accounts.* **4** an arrangement with a shop, etc that allows you to pay for goods or services at a later date: *Could you charge that to my account?*

(IDIOMS) **by all accounts** according to what everyone says: *By all accounts, she's a very good doctor.*

on account of because of: *Our flight was delayed on account of bad weather.*

on no account; not on any account not for any reason: *On no account should you walk home by yourself.*

take account of sth; take sth into account to consider sth, especially when deciding or judging sth: *We'll take account of your comments.*

account² /əˈkaʊnt/ *verb*

(PHRASAL VERB) **account for sth 1** to explain or give a reason for sth: *How can we account for these changes?* ○ *I was asked by my boss to account for all the money I had spent* (= to say what I had spent it on). **2** to supply the amount that is mentioned: *Sales to Europe accounted for 80% of our total sales last year.*

accountable /əˈkaʊntəbl/ *adj* expected to give an explanation of your actions, etc; responsible: *She is too young to be held accountable for what she did.* —**accountability** /-əbɪlətɪ/ *noun* [U]: *The new law requires greater accountability from the police.*

accountant /əˈkaʊntənt/ *noun* [C] a person whose job is to keep or examine the financial accounts of a business, etc

accountancy /əˈkaʊntənsɪ/ *noun* [U] the profession of an accountant: *a career in accountancy*

accumulate /əˈkjuːmjʊleɪt/ *verb* **1** [T] to collect a number or quantity of sth over a period of time: *Over the years, I've accumulated hundreds of records.* **2** [I] to increase over a period of time: *Dust soon accumulates if you don't clean the house for a week or so.* —**accumulation** /əˌkjuːmjʊˈleɪʃn/ *noun* [C,U]

accuracy /ˈækjərəsɪ/ *noun* [U] the quality of being exact and correct ☛ The opposite is **inaccuracy**.

☆ **accurate** /ˈækjərət/ *adj* careful and exact; without mistakes: *an accurate description of the house* ○ *That clock isn't very accurate.* ☛ The opposite is **inaccurate**. —**accurately** *adv*

accusation /ˌækjuːˈzeɪʃn/ *noun* [C,U] a statement that says that sb has done sth wrong: *He said that a false accusation had been made against him.* ○ *There was a note of accusation in her voice* (= she sounded critical).

☆ **accuse** /əˈkjuːz/ *verb* [T] **accuse sb (of sth)** to say that sb has done wrong or broken the law: *I accused her of cheating.* ○ *He was accused of murder and sent for trial.*

the accused *noun* [C] (*pl* **the accused**) (used in a court of law) the person who is said to have broken a law: *Will the accused please stand.*

accusing /əˈkjuːzɪŋ/ *adj* that shows that you think sb has done sth wrong: *He gave me an accusing look.* —**accusingly** /əˈkjuːzɪŋlɪ/ *adv*

accustomed /əˈkʌstəmd/ *adj* **1 accustomed to sth** if you are accustomed to sth, you are used to it and it is not strange for you: *She's accustomed to travelling a lot in her job.* ○ *It took a while for my eyes to get accustomed to the dark room.* **2** (*formal*) usual; regular: *He took his accustomed walk after lunch.*

ace /eɪs/ *noun* [C] **1** a playing card which has a single shape on it. An ace has either the lowest or the highest value in a game of cards: *the ace of spades* ☛ Look at the note at **card**. **2** (in tennis) the first stroke of a game (**serve**) that the person playing against you cannot hit back

☆ **ache** /eɪk/ *noun* [C,U] a pain that lasts for a long time: *to have toothache, earache, stomach-ache, etc* ☛ **Ache** is often used in compounds. In British English it is usually used without 'a' or 'an': *I've got toothache.* But we always use 'a' with 'headache': *I've got a headache.* In American English, ache is usually used with 'a' or 'an', especially when talking about a particular attack of pain: *I have an awful toothache.*

ache *verb* [I] to feel a continuous pain: *His legs ached after playing football for two hours.* ○ *She was aching all over.*

☆ **achieve** /əˈtʃiːv/ *verb* [T] **1** to gain sth, usually by effort or skill: *You have achieved the success you deserve.* **2** to get sth done; to complete: *They have achieved a lot in a short time.*

achievement *noun* **1** [C] something that is done successfully, especially through hard

---

s	z	ʃ	ʒ	h	m	n	ŋ	l	r	j	w
so	zoo	she	vision	how	man	no	sing	leg	red	yes	wet

work or skill: *She felt that the book was her greatest achievement.* **2** [U] the act of finishing sth successfully; the feeling that you get when you have finished sth successfully: *Climbing the mountain gave him a sense of achievement.*

☆ **acid** /'æsɪd/ *noun* [C,U] (in chemistry) a liquid substance that can dissolve metal and may burn your skin or clothes: *sulphuric acid* ☞ Look at **alkali**.

acid *adj* **1** (used about a fruit, etc) having a sharp, sour taste **2** (*also* **acidic**) containing an acid: *an acid solution* ☞ Look at **alkaline**.

acidity /ə'sɪdətɪ/ *noun* [U] the quality of being acid

‚acid 'rain *noun* [U] rain that is polluted by acid substances from the chimneys of factories and that causes damage to trees, buildings and rivers

☆ **acknowledge** /ək'nɒlɪdʒ/ *verb* [T] **1** to accept or admit that sth is true or exists: *He acknowledged the fact that he had been wrong.* ○ *They wouldn't acknowledge defeat.* ○ *It is acknowledged that he is the country's greatest writer.* ○ *He is acknowledged to be the country's greatest writer.* **2** to show that you have seen sb by raising your hand, smiling, etc: *She refused to acknowledge him and walked straight past.* **3** to say that you have received a letter, etc: *I would be grateful if you could acknowledge my letter.* **4** to show or say that you are grateful for sth: *I should like to acknowledge all the help I have received from my family.*

acknowledgement (*also* **acknowledgment**) *noun* **1** [U] the act of acknowledging: *I have received no acknowledgement for all the work I did.* **2** [C] a letter, etc stating that sth has been received **3** [C] a few words of thanks that an author writes at the beginning or end of a book to the people who have helped him/her

acne /'æknɪ/ *noun* [U] a type of skin disease, usually affecting young people, that causes a lot of spots on the face and neck

acorn /'eɪkɔːn/ *noun* [C] a small nut that is the fruit of the oak tree

acoustic /ə'kuːstɪk/ *adj* **1** connected with sound or the sense of hearing **2** (of a musical instrument) not electric: *an acoustic guitar*

acoustics *noun* [plural] **1** the qualities of a room, etc that make it good or bad for you to hear music, etc: *The theatre has excellent acoustics.* **2** [with sing verb] the scientific study of sound

acquaintance /ə'kweɪntəns/ *noun* **1** [C] a person that you know but who is not a close friend **2** [U] **acquaintance with sb/sth** a slight knowledge of sb/sth: *I made his acquaintance* (= got to know him) *at a party in London.*

acquainted /ə'kweɪntɪd/ *adj* (*formal*) **1 acquainted with sth** knowing sth: *Are you acquainted with the facts?* **2 acquainted (with sb)** knowing sb, but usually not very closely: *The two women had been acquainted since they were children.*

acquiesce /ˌækwɪ'es/ *verb* [I] (*formal*) to accept sth without argument, although you may not agree with it —**acquiescence** /ˌækwɪ'esns/ *noun* [U]

☆ **acquire** /ə'kwaɪə(r)/ *verb* [T] to get or obtain sth: *The company has acquired shares in a rival business.* ○ *Children do not automatically acquire British citizenship if they are born in this country.* ○ *She acquired an American accent while living in New York.* ○ *He's acquired a reputation for being difficult to work with.*

acquisition /ˌækwɪ'zɪʃn/ *noun* **1** [C] something that you have obtained or bought, especially sth you are pleased with: *This painting is my latest acquisition.* **2** [U] the act of obtaining sth: *the acquisition of wealth*

acquit /ə'kwɪt/ *verb* [T] (acquitting; acquitted) **1 acquit sb (of sth)** to declare formally that a person is not guilty of a crime: *The jury acquitted her of murder.* ☞ The opposite is **convict**. **2 acquit yourself...** (*formal*) to behave in the way that is mentioned: *He acquitted himself quite well in his first match as a professional.* —**acquittal** /ə'kwɪtl/ *noun* [C, U]

acre /'eɪkə(r)/ *noun* [C] a measure of land; 0·405 of a hectare: *a farm of 20 acres/a 20-acre farm*

acrobat /'ækrəbæt/ *noun* [C] a person who performs difficult movements of the body or difficult balancing acts (eg walking on a wire), especially in a circus —**acrobatic** /ˌækrə'bætɪk/ *adj*

acrobatics *noun* [U] (the art of performing) acrobatic acts

acronym /'ækrənɪm/ *noun* [C] a short word that is made from the first letters of a group of words: *TEFL is an acronym for Teaching English as a Foreign Language.*

☆ **across** /ə'krɒs; *US* ə'krɔːs/ *adv, prep* **1** from one side of sth to the other: *The stream was too wide to jump across.* ○ *He walked across the field.* ○ *I drew a line across the page.* ○ *A smile spread across his face.* **2** on the other side of sth: *There's a bank just across the road.* ☞ We can use **across** or **over** to mean 'on or to the other side ': *I ran across/over the road.* But when we talk about crossing something high, we usually use **over**: *I can't climb over that wall.* With 'room' we usually use **across**: *I walked across the room to the door.* **3** measuring from side to side: *The river was about 20 metres across.*

(IDIOM) **across the board** involving or affecting all groups, members, cases, etc: *a 10% pay increase across the board*

acrylic /ə'krɪlɪk/ *adj* of a material that is made artificially by a chemical process and used in making sweaters and other clothes

☆ **act¹** /ækt/ *verb* **1** [I] to do sth; to take action: *There's no time to lose – you must act now.* ○ *The government were slow to act over the problem of dangerous dogs.* ○ *The man we met on the plane to Tokyo was kind enough to act as our guide* (= to perform the function of guide). **2** [I] to behave in the manner stated: *Don't act like a fool.* **3** [I,T] to perform or have a part in a play or film: *I've never acted before.* ○ *He's always wanted to act the part of Hamlet.*

acting *noun* [U] the art or profession of performing in plays or films.

☆ **act²** /ækt/ *noun* **1** [C] a thing that you do: *In a typical act of generosity they refused to accept*

iː	ɪ	e	æ	ɑː	ɒ	ɔː	ʊ	uː	ʌ
see	sit	ten	hat	arm	got	saw	put	too	cup

any money. ☞ **Act** and **action** can have the same meaning: *It was a brave act/action.* **Act**, not **action** can be followed by **of**: *It was an act of bravery.* **Activity** is used for something that is done regularly: *I like outdoor activities such as walking and gardening.* **Deed** is a formal and rather old-fashioned word and often refers to very important acts: *Robin Hood was famous for his brave deeds.* It is the word usually used with **good**: *I wanted to pay back the good deed he had done.* **2** often **Act** [C] one of the main divisions of a play or opera: *How many scenes are there in Act 4?* **3** [C] a short piece of entertainment that is usually part of a show or circus: *Ladies and gentlemen, please welcome our next act, the Roncalli brothers.* **4** often **Act** [C] a law made by a government: *the Prevention of Terrorism Act* **5** [C] (*informal*) a piece of behaviour that hides your true feelings: *She seems very happy but she's just putting on an act.*
(IDIOMS) **get your act together** to get organized so that you can do sth properly
in the act (of doing sth) while doing sth, especially sth wrong: *He was looking through the papers on her desk and she caught him in the act.*

acting *adj* doing the job mentioned for a short time: *Helen will be the acting director of studies while Susan White is away.*

☆ **action** /ˈækʃn/ *noun* **1** [U] doing things, often for a particular purpose: *Now is the time for action.* o *I didn't like the film, there wasn't much action in it.* **2** [C] something that you do: *The doctor's quick action saved the child's life.* o *They should be judged by their actions, not by what they say.* ☞ Look at the note at **act²**. **3** [sing] the most important events in a story or play: *The action is set in London during the Second World War.* **4** [sing] the effect that one substance has on another: *The building has been damaged by the action of acid rain.* **5** [U] the fighting that takes place in battle: *Their son was killed in action.*
(IDIOMS) **course of action** ⇨ COURSE
in action in operation; while working or doing sth: *We shall have a chance to see their new team in action next week.*
into action into operation: *We'll put the plan into action immediately.*
out of action not working; unable to function as normal: *The coffee machine's out of action again.*
take action to do sth, in order to solve a problem, etc: *The government must take action over unemployment.*

activate /ˈæktɪveɪt/ *verb* [T] to make sth start working: *A slight movement can activate the car alarm.*

☆ **active** /ˈæktɪv/ *adj* **1** able and willing to do things; energetic: *My grandfather is very active for his age.* o *Students should take an active part in college life.* o *He was on active service for five years during the war* (= he served in the armed forces). **2** that produces an effect; that is in operation: *What is the active ingredient in this medicine?* o *an active volcano* (= one that can still erupt) **3** (used about the form of a verb or a

sentence when the subject of the sentence performs the action of the verb): *In the sentence 'The dog bit him', the verb is active.* ☞ You can also say: 'The verb is in the active'. Look at **passive**.

☆ **activity** /ækˈtɪvəti/ *noun* (*pl* **activities**) **1** [U] a situation in which there is a lot of action or movement: *The house was full of activity on the morning of the wedding.* ☞ The opposite is **inactivity**. **2** [C] something that you do, usually regularly and for enjoyment: *The hotel offers a range of leisure activities.* ☞ Look at the note at **act²**.

☆ **actor** /ˈæktə(r)/ *noun* [C] a person whose job is to act in a play, film or television programme

☆ **actress** /ˈæktrɪs/ *noun* [C] a woman whose job is to act in a play, film or television programme

☆ **actual** /ˈæktʃuəl/ *adj* real; that happened, etc in fact: *The actual damage to the car was not as great as we had feared.* o *They seemed to be good friends but in actual fact they hated each other.*

actually /ˈæktʃuəli/ *adv* **1** really; in fact: *You don't actually believe her, do you?* o *I can't believe that I'm actually going to America!* **2** although it may seem strange: *He actually expected me to cook his meal for him!* ☞ **Actually** is often used in conversation to get somebody's attention or to correct somebody politely: *Actually, I wanted to show you something. Have you got a minute?* o *We aren't married, actually.* o *I don't agree about the book. I think it's rather good, actually.* In English **actual** and **actually** do not mean '(existing) at the present time'. We use **currently** or **at present** instead: *He's currently working for the government.* o *I'm studying for my exams at present.*

acupuncture /ˈækjupʌŋktʃə(r)/ *noun* [U] a way of treating an illness or stopping pain by putting thin needles into parts of the body

acute /əˈkjuːt/ *adj* **1** severe; very great: *an acute shortage of food* o *acute pain* **2** (used about an illness) reaching a dangerous stage quickly: *acute appendicitis* ☞ The opposite is **chronic**. **3** (used about feelings or the senses) very strong: *Dogs have an acute sense of smell.* **4** showing that you are able to understand things easily: *The report contains some acute observations on the situation.* —**acutely** *adv*: *They are acutely aware of the problem.*

acute ˈangle *noun* [C] an angle of less than 90°

ad /æd/ *noun* (*informal*) = ADVERTISEMENT: *I saw your ad in the local paper.*

adamant /ˈædəmənt/ *adj* (*formal*) (used about a person) very sure; not willing to change your mind: *He was adamant that he had not made a mistake.* —**adamantly** *adv*

☆ **adapt** /əˈdæpt/ *verb* **1** [I] **adapt (to sth)** to change your behaviour because the situation you are in has changed: *He was quick to adapt to the new system.* **2** [T] **adapt sth (for sth)** to change sth so that you can use it in a different situation: *The car was adapted for use as a taxi.* **3** [T] to change a book, etc so that it can be shown as a film, etc: *Tonight's play has been adapted for radio from the novel by Charles Dickens.*

adaptable *adj* able and willing to change to

ɜː	ə	eɪ	əʊ	aɪ	aʊ	ɔɪ	ɪə	eə	ʊə
fur	ago	pay	home	five	now	join	near	hair	pure

suit new conditions: *You have to be adaptable if you want to live in a foreign country.*

adaptation /ˌædæpˈteɪʃn/ *noun* [C] **1** a play or film that is based on a novel, etc: *a television adaptation of 'Wuthering Heights'* **2** the state or process of adapting: *a period of adaptation*

adaptor (*also* **adapter**) *noun* [C] **1** a device that allows more than one plug to be connected to an electricity supply point (**socket**) **2** a device that fits on an electrical plug and allows you to use a piece of electrical equipment with a different type of socket: *You'll need an adaptor to use your hair-drier in Spain.*

☆ **add** /æd/ *verb* **1** [I,T] **add (sth) (to sth)** to put sth together with sth else, so that you increase the size, number, value, etc: *Next, add some milk to the mixture.* ○ *He wanted to add his name to the letter.* ○ *They had invited an entertainer to the party, just to add to the fun.* **2** [T] to put numbers or amounts together so that you get a total: *If you add 3 and 3 together, you get 6.* ○ *Add £8 to the total, to cover postage and packing.* ☛ We often use the word **plus** when we add two numbers: *2 plus 2 is 4.* **3** [T] to say sth more: *'Don't forget to write to us,' she added.*

(PHRASAL VERBS) **add sth on (to sth)** to include: *10% will be added on to your bill as a service charge.*

add up to seem as if it could be true: *I'm sorry, but your story just doesn't add up.*

add (sth) up to find the total of several numbers: *The waiter hadn't added up the bill correctly.*

add up to sth to have as a total: *The bill should add up to about £40.*

adder /ˈædə(r)/ *noun* [C] a small poisonous snake

addict /ˈædɪkt/ *noun* [C] a person who cannot stop taking or doing sth harmful: *a drug addict.*

addicted /əˈdɪktɪd/ *adj* **addicted (to sth)** unable to stop taking or doing sth harmful: *He is addicted to heroin.* ○ *He's addicted to football.* —**addiction** /əˈdɪkʃn/ *noun* [C,U]: *the problem of teenage drug addiction* —**addictive** /əˈdɪktɪv/ *adj*: *addictive drugs*

☆ **addition** /əˈdɪʃn/ *noun* **1** [U] the process of adding sth, especially of adding up two or more numbers ☛ Look at **subtraction**. **2** [C] **addition (to sth)** a person or thing that is added to sth: *They've got a new addition to the family* (= another child).

(IDIOM) **in addition (to sth)** as well as: *She speaks five foreign languages in addition to English.*

additional /-ʃənl/ *adj* added; extra: *a small additional charge for the use of the swimming-pool* —**additionally** /-ʃənəli/ *adv*

additive /ˈædɪtɪv/ *noun* a substance that is added in small amounts for a special purpose: *food additives* (= to add colour or flavour)

☆ **address**[1] /əˈdres/; *US* ˈædres/ *noun* [C] **1** the number of the house and the name of the street and town, where you live or work: *Let me give you my home/business address.* ○ *She no longer lives at this address.* ○ *Please inform the office of any change of address.* ○ *an address book* (= a small book that you keep the addresses of people you know in) **2** a formal speech that is given to an audience

address[2] /əˈdres/ *verb* [T] **1 address sth (to sb/sth)** to write (on a letter, etc) the name and address of the person you are sending it to: *The parcel was returned because it had been wrongly addressed.* **2** to make an important or formal speech to a crowd or audience **3 address sth to sb** (*formal*) make a remark, etc to sb: *Would you kindly address any complaints you have to the manager.* **4** to talk or write to sb using a particular name or title: *She prefers to be addressed as 'Ms'.* **5 address yourself to sth** (*formal*) to try to deal with a problem, etc: *He had to address himself to the task of finding a new job.*

adept /ˈædept; əˈdept/ *adj* **adept (at sth)** very good or skilful at sth

☆ **adequate** /ˈædɪkwət/ *adj* **1** enough for what you need: *The food they eat is barely adequate to keep them alive.* **2** good enough; acceptable: *Your work is adequate but I'm sure you could do better.* ☛ The opposite is **inadequate**. —**adequacy** /ˈædɪkwəsi/ *noun* [U] —**adequately** *adv*: *The work has been done adequately, but not well.* ○ *The mystery has never been adequately explained.*

adhere /ədˈhɪə(r)/ *verb* [I] (*formal*) **1 adhere (to sth)** to stick firmly: *Make sure that the paper adheres firmly to the wall.* **2 adhere to sth** to continue to support an idea, etc; to follow a rule: *This rule has never been strictly adhered to by members of staff.*

adherent *noun* [C] somebody who supports a particular idea —**adherence** *noun* [U]: *His adherence to his principles cost him his job.*

adhesive /ədˈhiːsɪv/ *noun* [C] a substance that makes things stick together: *a fast-drying adhesive*

adhesive *adj* that can stick, or can cause two things to stick together: *He sealed the parcel with adhesive tape.*

ad hoc /ˌæd ˈhɒk/ *adj* made or formed for a particular purpose: *They set up an ad hoc committee to discuss the matter.*

adjacent /əˈdʒeɪsnt/ *adj* situated next to or close to sth: *There was a fire in the adjacent building.* ○ *She works in the office adjacent to mine.*

☆ **adjective** /ˈædʒɪktɪv/ *noun* [C] (*grammar*) a word used with a noun that tells you more about it: *The adjective 'hot' can come either before or after a noun, ie you can say 'that is hot soup' or 'that soup is hot'.*

adjectival /ˌædʒekˈtaɪvl/ *adj* that contains or is used like an adjective: *an adjectival phrase*

adjoining /əˈdʒɔɪnɪŋ/ *adj* joining sth or situated next or nearest to sth: *A scream came from the adjoining room.*

adjourn /əˈdʒɜːn/ *verb* [I,T] to stop sth (a meeting, a trial, etc) for a short period of time and start it again later: *This court will adjourn until tomorrow.* ○ *The meeting was adjourned until the following week.* —**adjournment** *noun* [C]: *The lawyers asked for an adjournment.*

adjudicate /əˈdʒuːdɪkeɪt/ *verb* [I,T] (*formal*) to act as an official judge in a competition or to

p	b	t	d	k	g	tʃ	dʒ	f	v	θ	ð
pen	bad	tea	did	cat	got	chin	June	fall	van	thin	then

adjust /əˈdʒʌst/ verb **1** [T] to change sth slightly, especially because it is not in the right position: *There's something wrong with the brakes on the car – they need adjusting.* ○ *The figures have been adjusted to take account of inflation.* **2** [I] **adjust (to sth)** to get used to new conditions or a new situation: *She found it hard to adjust to working at night.*

adjustable *adj* that can be adjusted: *an adjustable mirror* —**adjustment** *noun* [C,U]

ad lib /ˌæd ˈlɪb/ *adj, adv* done or spoken without preparation: *She had to speak ad lib because she couldn't find her notes.* —**ad lib** *verb* [I] (ad li**bb**ing; ad li**bb**ed)

administer /ədˈmɪnɪstə(r)/ *verb* [T] **1** to control or manage sth: *The system is very complicated and difficult to administer.* **2** (*formal*) to make sb suffer sth (especially medicine): *The doctor administered a pain-killing drug.*

administration /ədˌmɪnɪˈstreɪʃn/ *noun* **1** [U] the control or management of sth (eg a system, an organization or a business): *The administration of a large project like this is very complicated.* **2** [sing] the group of people who organize or control sth: *the hospital administration* **3** often **the Administration** [C] the government of a country, especially the USA: *the Bush Administration*

administrative /ədˈmɪnɪstrətɪv; *US* -streɪtɪv/ *adj* connected with the organization and management of a country or business, etc: *London is still the most important administrative centre.* ○ *an administrative assistant*

administrator /ədˈmɪnɪstreɪtə(r)/ *noun* [C] a person whose job is to organize or manage a system, a business, etc

admirable /ˈædmərəbl/ *adj* deserving admiration or praise: *an admirable example of good planning* —**admirably** /-əblɪ/ *adv*: *She dealt with the problem admirably.*

admiral /ˈædmərəl/ *noun* [C] an officer of very high rank in the navy who commands a group (**fleet**) of ships

☆ **admiration** /ˌædməˈreɪʃn/ *noun* [U] a feeling that you have when you like and respect sb/sth very much: *I have great admiration for his work.*

☆ **admire** /ədˈmaɪə(r)/ *verb* [T] to respect or like sb/sth very much; to look at sb/sth with pleasure: *Everyone admired the way he dealt with the problem.* ○ *I've always admired her for being such a wonderful mother.* ○ *We walked round the house, admiring the furniture and decorations.*

admirer *noun* [C] a person who admires sb/sth

admiring *adj* feeling or expressing admiration: *an admiring look* —**admiringly** *adv*

☆ **admission** /ədˈmɪʃn/ *noun* **1** [C,U] permission to enter a school, club, public place, etc: *All those who were not wearing a tie were refused admission to the club.* ○ *Admissions to British universities have increased by 15% this year.* **2** [U] the amount of money that you pay to enter a place: *The museum charges £3 admission.* **3** [C] a statement that something, usually unpleasant, is true: *I viewed her silence as an admission of guilt.*

☆ **admit** /ədˈmɪt/ *verb* (admi**tt**ing; admi**tt**ed) **1** [I,T] **admit to sth/doing sth**; **admit (that**...) to agree, often without wanting to, that sth is true: *He refused to admit to the theft.* ○ *You should admit your mistake.* ○ *I have to admit that I was wrong.* ○ *'I was wrong,' he admitted.* ○ *She admitted having broken the computer.* **2** [T] **admit sb/sth (into/to sth)** to allow sb/sth to enter; to take sb into a place: *I have a ticket that admits a member plus one guest to the gardens.* ○ *He was admitted to hospital with suspected appendicitis.*

admittedly *adv* it must be admitted (that): *The work is very interesting. Admittedly, I do get rather tired.*

admittance /ədˈmɪtns/ *noun* [U] being allowed to enter a place (especially a private one); the right to enter: *The journalist tried to gain admittance to the minister's office.* ○ *No admittance* (= as a warning on a door that people should keep out).

adolescence /ˌædəˈlesns/ *noun* [U] the period of a person's life between being a child and becoming an adult, ie between the ages of about 13 and 17

adolescent /ˌædəˈlesnt/ *noun* [C] a young person who is no longer a child and not yet an adult: *the problems of adolescents* ○ *an adolescent daughter* ☛ Look at **teenager**.

☆ **adopt** /əˈdɒpt/ *verb* **1** [I,T] to take a child into your family and treat him/her as your own child by law **2** [T] to take and use sth: *She decided not to adopt her husband's name when she got married.* ○ *All his suggestions have been adopted.* —**adopted** *adj*: *an adopted child* —**adoption** /əˈdɒpʃn/ *noun* [C,U]: *The party is considering the adoption of a new transport policy.* ○ *We can't have children so we're interested in adoption.* ○ *The number of adoptions has risen in the past year* (= the number of children being adopted).

adorable /əˈdɔːrəbl/ *adj* (used for expressing affection for a child or animal) very attractive

adore /əˈdɔː(r)/ *verb* [T] **1** to love and admire sb/sth very much: *Kim adores her older sister.* **2** (*informal*) to like sth very much: *I adore strawberries.* —**adoration** /ˌædəˈreɪʃn/ *noun* [U]

adorn /əˈdɔːn/ *verb* [T] to add sth in order to make a thing or person more attractive or beautiful: *a building adorned with flags*

adrenalin /əˈdrenəlɪn/ *noun* [U] a substance that your body produces when you are very angry, frightened or excited and that makes your heart beat faster

adrift /əˈdrɪft/ *adj* (not before a noun) not tied to anything or controlled by anybody (used about a boat)

☆ **adult** /ˈædʌlt; əˈdʌlt/ *noun* [C] a person or animal that is fully grown: *This film is suitable for both adults and children.* —**adult** *adj*: *She was born here but has spent her adult life in Chile.*

adultery /əˈdʌltərɪ/ *noun* [U] sexual relations

☆ **advance**[1] /əd'vɑːns; US -'væns/ verb **1** [I] to move forward: *The army advanced towards the city.* ☞ Look at **retreat**. **2** [I,T] to make progress or help sth make progress: *Our research has not advanced much recently.*

advanced adj **1** of a high level: *an advanced English class* **2** highly developed: *a country that is not very advanced industrially*

Advanced level = A LEVEL

☆ **advance**[2] /əd'vɑːns; US -'væns/ noun **1** [C, usually sing] forward movement: *the army's advance towards the border* **2** [C,U] progress in sth: *advances in computer technology* **3** [C] an amount of money that is paid to sb before the time when it is usually paid
(IDIOM) **in advance (of sth)** before a particular time or event: *You should book tickets for the concert well in advance.*

☆ **advantage** /əd'vɑːntɪdʒ; US -'væn-/ noun **1** [C] **an advantage (over sb)** something that may help you to do better than other people: *Her secretarial experience gave her an advantage over the other people applying for the job.* ○ *Our team had the advantage of playing at our home ground.* **2** [C,U] something that helps you or that will bring you a good result: *the advantages and disadvantages of a plan* ○ *There's no advantage in driving into London. There won't be anywhere to park.* ☞ The opposite is **disadvantage**.
(IDIOM) **take advantage of sth 1** to make good or full use of sth: *Take advantage of the cheap prices while they last.* **2** to make unfair use of sb or of sb's kindness, etc in order to get what you want: *You shouldn't let him take advantage of you like this.*

advantageous /ˌædvənˈteɪdʒəs/ adj that will help you or bring you a good result

advent /'ædvənt/ noun [sing] **1** (*formal*) the arrival or coming of sb/sth: *This area was very isolated before the advent of the railway.* **2** **Advent** (in the Christian year) the four weeks before Christmas

☆ **adventure** /ədˈventʃə(r)/ noun [C,U] an experience or event that is very unusual, exciting or dangerous: *She left home to travel, hoping for excitement and adventure.* ○ *an adventure story*

adventurous adj **1** (used about a person) liking to try new things or have adventures **2** involving adventure: *For a more adventurous holiday try mountain climbing.*

☆ **adverb** /'ædvɜːb/ noun [C] a word that adds information to a verb, adjective, phrase or another adverb: *In the sentence 'Please speak slowly', 'slowly' is an adverb.* ○ *'Happily', 'well', 'always', 'very' and 'too' are all adverbs.*

adverbial /ædˈvɜːbɪəl/ adj used like an adverb: *an adverbial phrase (eg 'in the afternoon')*

adversary /'ædvəsəri; US -seri/ noun [C] (pl **adversaries**) (*formal*) an enemy, or an opponent in a competition

adverse /'ædvɜːs/ adj (*formal*) making sth difficult for sb; not favourable: *Our flight was cancelled because of adverse weather conditions.*

—**adversely** adv

adversity /ədˈvɜːsəti/ noun [C,U] (pl **adversities**) (*formal*) difficulties or problems: *to show strength in the face of adversity*

advert /'ædvɜːt/ noun [C] (Brit informal) = ADVERTISEMENT

☆ **advertise** /'ædvətaɪz/ verb **1** [I, T] to put information in a newspaper, on television, on a poster, etc in order to persuade people to buy sth, apply for a job, etc: *a poster advertising a new type of biscuit* ○ *The job was advertised in the local newspapers.* ○ *It's very expensive to advertise on television.* **2** [I] **advertise for sb/sth** to say publicly in a newspaper, on a noticeboard, etc that you need sb to do a particular job, want to buy sth, etc: *The shop is advertising for a part-time sales assistant.*

advertisement /əd'vɜːtɪsmənt; US ˌædvərˈtaɪzmənt/ noun [C] (*also* **advert**; **ad**) a piece of information in a newspaper, on television, on a poster, etc that tries to persuade people to buy sth, apply for a job, etc: *a television advert for a new brand of washing powder* ○ *If you want to sell your car, why don't you put an advertisement in the local newspaper?*

—**advertising** noun [U]: *The magazine gets a lot of money from advertising.* ○ *an advertising campaign*

☆ **advice** /əd'vaɪs/ noun [U] an opinion that you give sb about what he/she should do or how he/she should behave: *She took her doctor's advice and gave up smoking.* ○ *You should get some legal advice (= ask a lawyer to tell you what to do).* ○ *Let me give you some advice ...* ☞ **Advice** is an uncountable noun, so we cannot say 'an advice' or 'some advices'. We can say: *a piece of advice* and: *a lot of advice.*

advisable /ədˈvaɪzəbl/ adj (*formal*) that sb would recommend you to do; sensible: *It is advisable to reserve a seat.*

☆ **advise** /əd'vaɪz/ verb **1** [I,T] **advise (sb) (to do sth)**; **advise (sb) (against sth/against doing sth)** to tell sb what you think he/she should do: *I would strongly advise you to take the job.* ○ *They advised us not to travel on a Friday.* ○ *The newspaper article advised against buying a house in that area.* ○ *He did what the doctor advised.* ○ *She advises the Government on economic affairs.* **2** [T] (*formal*) to inform sb: *We would like to advise you that the goods are now ready for collection.*

adviser (*US* **advisor**) noun [C] a person who gives advice to a company, government, etc: *an adviser on economic affairs*

advisory /ədˈvaɪzəri/ adj giving advice only; not having the power to make decisions: *an advisory committee*

advocate /'ædvəkeɪt/ verb [T] (*formal*) to recommend or say that you support a particular plan or action: *The Minister advocated a reform of the tax system.*

advocate /'ædvəkət/ noun [C] **1** **advocate (of sth)** a person who supports a particular plan or action, especially in public: *an advocate of nuclear disarmament* **2** a lawyer who defends sb in a court of law

aerial[1] /'eəriəl/ (*US* **antenna**) noun [C] a long

iː	ɪ	e	æ	ɑː	ɒ	ɔː	ʊ	uː	ʌ
see	sit	ten	hat	arm	got	saw	put	too	cup

metal stick on a building, car, etc that receives radio or television signals

aerial² /ˈeərɪəl/ *adj* **1** from or in the air: *an aerial attack on the city* ○ *aerial warfare* **2** taken from an aircraft: *an aerial photograph of the village*

aerobics /eəˈrəʊbɪks/ *noun* [U] energetic physical exercises that increase the amount of oxygen in your blood. Aerobics is often done to music: *I do aerobics twice a week to keep fit.*

aerodynamics /ˌeərəʊdaɪˈnæmɪks/ *noun* [plural, with sing verb] the scientific study of the way that things move through the air —**aerodynamic** *adj*

☆ **aeroplane** /ˈeərəpleɪn/ (*also* **plane**; *US* **airplane**) *noun* [C] a vehicle with wings and one or more engines that can fly through the air: *the noise of an aeroplane flying overhead* ○ *I went to Berlin by plane.*

aerosol /ˈeərəsɒl; *US* -sɔːl/ *noun* [C] a container in which a liquid substance is kept under pressure. When you press a button the liquid comes out in a fine spray: *an aerosol deodorant*

aesthetic /iːsˈθetɪk/ (*US also* **esthetic** /esˈθetɪk/) *adj* involving people's sense of beauty: *The columns are there for purely aesthetic reasons* (= only to look beautiful). —**aesthetically** (*US also* **esthetically**) /-klɪ/ *adv*: *to be aesthetically pleasing*

afar /əˈfɑː(r)/ *adv* (*formal*)
(IDIOM) **from afar** from a long distance away: *The lights of the city were visible from afar.*

☆ **affair** /əˈfeə(r)/ *noun* **1** [C] an event or situation: *The wedding was a very grand affair.* ○ *The whole affair has been extremely unpleasant.* **2 affairs** [plural] important personal, business, national, etc matters: *The organization should have control of its own financial affairs.* ○ *the Irish minister for foreign affairs* ○ *current affairs* (= the political and social events that are happening at the present time) **3** [sing] something private that you do not want other people to know about: *What happened between us is my affair. I don't want to discuss it.* **4** [C] a sexual relationship between two people who are not married to each other: *He's having an affair with his boss.*
(IDIOM) **state of affairs** ⇨ STATE¹

☆ **affect** /əˈfekt/ *verb* [T] **1** to influence or cause sb/sth to change in a particular way: *Her personal problems seem to be affecting her work.* ○ *Loud music can affect your hearing.* ☛ Look at the note at **influence**. **2** to cause sb to feel very sad, angry, etc: *The whole community was affected by the terrible tragedy.* ☛ Notice that **affect** is a verb and **effect** is a noun: *Smoking can affect your health.* ○ *Smoking can have a bad effect on your health.*

affected /əˈfektɪd/ *adj* (used about a person or a person's behaviour) not natural or sincere —**affectation** /ˌæfekˈteɪʃn/ *noun* [C,U]

☆ **affection** /əˈfekʃn/ *noun* [U] **affection (for/towards sb/sth)** a feeling of loving or liking sb/sth: *Mark felt great affection for his sister.*

affectionate /əˈfekʃənət/ *adj* showing that you love or like sb very much: *a very affectionate child* —**affectionately** *adv*: *He looked at her affectionately.*

affiliate /əˈfɪlɪeɪt/ *verb* [T] (*usually passive*) **affiliate sth (to sth)** to connect an organization to a larger organization: *Our local club is affiliated to the national association.* —**affiliated** *adj*: *the NUJ and other affiliated unions* —**affiliation** /əˌfɪlɪˈeɪʃn/ *noun* [C,U] a connection made by affiliating: *The group has affiliations with the Conservative Party.*

affinity /əˈfɪnəti/ *noun* [C,U] (*pl* **affinities**) **1 affinity (for/with sb/sth)** a strong feeling that you like and understand sb/sth, usually because you feel similar to him/her in some way: *He had always had an affinity for wild and lonely places.* **2 affinity (with sb/sth); affinity (between A and B)** a similar quality in two or more people or things: *His music has certain affinities with Brahms.*

affirm /əˈfɜːm/ *verb* [T] (*formal*) **1** to say clearly that you hold a particular belief: *The people affirmed their country's right to independence.* **2** to say that sth is a fact: *She affirmed that he would resign.* —**affirmation** /ˌæfəˈmeɪʃn/ *noun* [C,U]

affirmative /əˈfɜːmətɪv/ *adj* (*formal*) meaning 'yes': *an affirmative answer* ☛ We can also say 'an answer in the affirmative'. The opposite is **negative**.

afflict /əˈflɪkt/ *verb* [T] (*usually passive*) (*formal*) to cause sb/sth to suffer pain, sadness, etc: *He had been afflicted with a serious illness since childhood.*

affliction /əˈflɪkʃn/ *noun* [C,U] a thing that causes suffering: *Poor sight and hearing are common afflictions of old age.*

affluent /ˈæfluənt/ *adj* having a lot of money —**affluence** *noun* [U]

☆ **afford** /əˈfɔːd/ *verb* [T] **1** (*usually after can, could or be able to*) to have enough money or time to be able to do sth: *We couldn't afford a television in those days.* ○ *There's a lot to do. We can't afford to waste any time.* **2 can't/couldn't afford** to not be able to do sth or let sth happen because it would have a bad result for you: *We can't afford to lose this contract. The future of the company depends on it.*

affront /əˈfrʌnt/ *noun* [C] something that you say or do that is insulting to another person or thing

afield /əˈfiːld/ *adv*
(IDIOM) **far afield** ⇨ FAR²

afloat /əˈfləʊt/ *adj* (not before a noun) **1** on the surface of the water; not sinking **2** (used about a business, an economy, etc) having enough money to survive: *We will need to borrow ten million pounds to keep the company afloat.*

afoot /əˈfʊt/ *adj* (not before a noun) being planned or prepared: *There was a plan afoot to build a new theatre.*

☆ **afraid** /əˈfreɪd/ *adj* (not before a noun) **1 afraid (of sb/sth); afraid (of doing sth/to do sth)** having or showing fear; frightened: *Why are some people afraid of spiders?* ○ *Sue is afraid of going out after dark.* ○ *I was too afraid to answer the door.* **2 afraid (that...); afraid (of doing sth)** worried about sth: *We were*

afraid that you would be angry. ○ *to be afraid of offending sb*
(IDIOM) **I'm afraid (that...)** (used for saying politely that you are sorry about sth): *I'm afraid I can't come on Sunday.* ☛ Compare **afraid** and **frightened**. You can only use **afraid** after a noun, but you can use **frightened** before or after a noun: *a frightened animal* ○ *The animal was afraid/frightened.*

afresh /əˈfreʃ/ *adv* (*formal*) again, in a new way: *to start afresh*

African-American /ˌæfrɪkən əˈmerɪkən/ (*also* **Afro-American** /ˌæfrəʊ əˈmerɪkən/) *noun* [C] an American citizen whose family was originally from Africa —**African-American** (*also* **Afro-American**) *adj*

Afro-Caribbean /ˌæfrəʊ kærɪˈbiːən; *US* -kəˈrɪbiən/ (*also* **African-Caribbean**) *noun* [C] **1** a person from the Caribbean whose family was originally from Africa **2** a person from a different country whose family was originally Afro-Caribbean(1) —**Afro-Caribbean** (*also* **African-Caribbean**) *adj*: *the Afro-Caribbean community in West London*

☆ **after¹** /ˈɑːftə(r); *US* æf-/ *prep* **1** later than sth: *Ian phoned just after six o'clock.* ○ *the week, month, year, etc after next* ○ *I hope to arrive some time after lunch.* ○ *We spent three days in Edinburgh and after that we went to Glasgow.* ○ *After doing my homework, I went out for a walk.* **2** ...**after**... repeated many times or continuing for a long time: *day after day of hot weather* ○ *I've told the children time after time not to do that.* **3** following or behind sb/sth: *Shut the door after you.* ○ *The dog ran after its master.* ○ *After you* (= used for politely allowing sb to use sth, go through a door, etc first) **4** following in order: *C comes after B in the alphabet.* **5** because of sth: *After the way he behaved I won't invite him here again.* **6** looking for or trying to catch or get sb/sth: *The police were after him.* ○ *Nicky is after a job in advertising.* **7** (used when sb/sth is given the name of another person or thing): *The street is called Wellington Street, after the famous general.*
(IDIOM) **after all 1** (used when sth happens that you did not expect to happen, or when you discover that sth that you thought was not true is, in fact, true): *So you decided to come after all!* (= I thought you weren't going to come) ○ *Maybe he's not so stupid after all.* **2** (used for reminding sb of a certain fact): *She can't understand. After all, she's only two.*

☆ **after²** /ˈɑːftə(r); *US* æf-/ *conj* at a time later than sth: *They arrived at the station after the train had left.* ○ *After we had finished our dinner, we went into the garden.*

☆ **after³** /ˈɑːftə(r); *US* æf-/ *adv* at a later time: *That was in 1986. Soon after, I heard that he was ill.* ○ *They lived happily ever after* (= for ever). ☛ It is more common to use **afterwards** at the end of a sentence: *We played tennis and then went to Angela's house afterwards.*

ˈafter-effect *noun* [C] an unpleasant result of sth that comes some time after it has happened: *the after-effects of a serious illness*

aftermath /ˈɑːftəmæθ/ *noun* [sing] a situation that is the result of an important or unpleasant event: *the aftermath of a war*

☆ **afternoon** /ˌɑːftəˈnuːn; *US* ˌæf-/ *noun* [C,U] the part of a day between midday and about six o'clock: *I'll see you tomorrow afternoon.* ○ *We sat in the garden all afternoon.* ○ *He goes swimming every afternoon.* ○ *She arrived at four o'clock in the afternoon.* ○ *Tom works two afternoons a week.* ○ *Are you busy on Friday afternoon?* ○ *afternoon tea* ○ *Where were you on the afternoon of February 26th?*
(IDIOM) **good afternoon** (used when you see sb for the first time in the afternoon) ☛ Look at the note at **morning**.

aftershave /ˈɑːftəʃeɪv/ *noun* [C,U] a liquid with a pleasant smell that men put on their faces after shaving

afterthought /ˈɑːftəθɔːt/ *noun* [C, usually sing] something that you think of or add to sth else at a later time: *He did the shopping, and then bought some flowers on the way home as an afterthought.*

☆ **afterwards** /ˈɑːftəwədz; *US* æf-/ (*US also* **afterward**) *adv* at a later time: *I met her at a party and saw her again soon afterwards.* ○ *Afterwards, Nick said he hadn't enjoyed the film.*

☆ **again** /əˈgen; əˈgeɪn/ *adv* **1** once more; another time: *Could you say that again, please?* ○ *She was out. I'll phone again later.* ○ *Don't ever do that again!* **2** in the place or condition that sb/sth was in before: *It's great to be home again.* ○ *I hope you'll soon be well again.* **3** (used for expressing that sth that you have just said may not happen or be true): *She might pass her test, but then again she might not.* **4** in addition: *'Is that enough?' 'No, I'd like half as much again, please'* (= one-and-a-half times the original amount).
(IDIOMS) **again and again** many times: *He said he was sorry again and again.*
yet again ⇒ YET

☆ **against** /əˈgenst; əˈgeɪnst/ *prep* **1** touching or leaning on sb/sth for support: *Put the cupboard over there against the wall.* **2** in the opposite direction to sth: *We had to cycle against the wind.* **3** opposing sb/sth in a game, competition, war, etc: *Leeds are playing against Everton on Saturday.* **4** not agreeing with or supporting sb/sth: *Are you for or against the plan?* ○ *She felt that everybody was against her.* **5** what a law, rule, etc says you must not do: *It's against the law to buy cigarettes before you are sixteen.* **6** to protect yourself from sb/sth: *Take these pills as a precaution against malaria.*

☆ **age¹** /eɪdʒ/ *noun* **1** [C,U] the length of time that sb has lived or that sth has existed: *Nigel is seventeen years of age.* ○ *She left school at the age of sixteen.* ○ *When I was your age I never did anything like that!* ○ *Children of all ages will enjoy this film.* ○ *He needs some friends of his own age.* ☛ When you want to ask about somebody's age, you usually say: *How old is she?* and the answer can be: *She's eighteen* or: *She's eighteen years old* but NOT: *She's eighteen years.* Here are some examples of other ways of talking about age: *I'm nearly nineteen.* ○ *a girl*

p	b	t	d	k	g	tʃ	dʒ	f	v	θ	ð
pen	bad	tea	did	cat	got	chin	June	fall	van	thin	then

of eighteen ○ *an eighteen-year-old girl* ○ *The girl, aged 18, said she came from Perth* ○ *I first went abroad when I was fifteen.* **2** [U] one of the periods of sb's life: *a problem that often develops in middle age* **3** [U] the state of being old: *a face lined with age* ☛ Look at **youth**. **4** [C] a particular period of history: *We are now living in the computer age.* ○ *the history of art through the ages* **5 ages** [plural] (*informal*) a very long time: *We had to wait ages at the hospital.*
(IDIOM) **under age** not old enough by law to do sth

'age group *noun* [C] people of a particular age (1): *This club is very popular with the 20-30 age group.*

☆ **age²** /eɪdʒ/ *verb* [I,T] (*pres part* **ageing** or **aging**; *pt, pp* **aged** /eɪdʒd/) to become or look old; to cause sb to look old: *My father seems to have aged a lot recently.*

aged /eɪdʒd/ *adj* (not before a noun) of a particular age(1): *The woman, aged 26, was last seen at Victoria Station.*

the aged /ˈeɪdʒɪd/ *noun* [plural] old people

☆ **agency** /ˈeɪdʒənsi/ *noun* [C] (*pl* **agencies**) **1** a business that provides a particular service: *an advertising agency* **2** (*US*) a government department: *the Central Intelligence Agency*

agenda /əˈdʒendə/ *noun* [C] a list of all the subjects that are to be discussed at a meeting

☆ **agent** /ˈeɪdʒənt/ *noun* [C] **1** a person whose job is to do business for a company or for another person: *Our company's agent in Rio will meet you at the airport.* ○ *Most actors and musicians have their own agents.* ○ *a travel agent* ○ *an estate agent* **2** = SECRET AGENT

aggravate /ˈægrəveɪt/ *verb* [T] **1** to make sth worse or more serious: *The country's food problems were aggravated by the hot dry summer.* **2** (*informal*) to make sb angry or annoyed —**aggravation** /ˌægrəˈveɪʃn/ *noun* [C,U]

aggregate /ˈægrɪɡət/ *noun*
(IDIOM) **on aggregate** in total: *Our team won 3-1 on aggregate.*

aggression /əˈɡreʃn/ *noun* [U] **1** the act of starting a fight or war without reasonable cause: *This is an intolerable act of aggression against my country.* **2** angry feelings or behaviour that make you want to attack other people: *People often react to this kind of situation with fear or aggression.*

aggressor /əˈɡresə(r)/ *noun* [C] a person or country that attacks sb/sth or starts fighting first

☆ **aggressive** /əˈɡresɪv/ *adj* **1** ready or likely to fight or argue: *an aggressive dog* ○ *Some people get aggressive after drinking alcohol.* **2** using or showing force or pressure in order to succeed: *an aggressive salesman* —**aggressively** *adv*

aggrieved /əˈɡriːvd/ *adj* (*formal*) upset or angry

agile /ˈædʒaɪl; *US* ædʒl/ *adj* able to move quickly and easily —**agility** /əˈdʒɪləti/ *noun* [U]

agitate /ˈædʒɪteɪt/ *verb* [I] **agitate (for/against sth)** to make other people feel very strongly about sth so that they want to do sth to help you achieve it: *to agitate for reform*

agitated *adj* worried or excited: *She became more and more agitated when her son did not appear.* —**agitation** /ˌædʒɪˈteɪʃn/ *noun* [U]

agnostic /æɡˈnɒstɪk/ *noun* [C] a person who believes that you cannot know whether or not God exists

☆ **ago** /əˈɡəʊ/ *adv* in the past; back in time from now: *Patrick left ten minutes ago* (= if it is twelve o'clock now, he left at ten to twelve). ○ *That was a long time ago.* ○ *How long ago did this happen?* ☛ **Ago** is used with the simple past tense and not the present perfect tense: *I arrived in Britain three months ago.* Compare **ago** and **before**. **Ago** means 'before now' and **before** means 'before then' (ie before a particular time in the past): *Anne married Simon two years ago.* ○ *She had left her first husband six years before* (= six months before she married Simon).

agonize (*also* **agonise**) /ˈæɡənaɪz/ *verb* [I] to worry or think about sth for a long time: *to agonize over a difficult decision*

agonized (*also* **agonised**) *adj* showing extreme pain or worry: *an agonized cry*

agonizing (*also* **agonising**) *adj* causing extreme worry or pain: *an agonizing choice* ○ *an agonizing headache*

agony /ˈæɡəni/ *noun* [C,U] (*pl* **agonies**) great pain or suffering: *to scream in agony*

☆ **agree** /əˈɡriː/ *verb* **1** [I,T] **agree (with sb/sth)**; **agree (that**...) to have the same opinion as sb/sth: '*I think we should talk to the manager about this.' 'Yes, I agree.'* ○ *I agree with Paul.* ○ *Do you agree that we should travel by train?* ○ *I'm afraid I don't agree.* ☛ Look at **disagree**. **2** [I] **agree (to sth)** to say yes to sth: *I asked if I could go home early and she agreed.* ○ *Andrew has agreed to lend me his car for the weekend.* ☛ Look at **refuse¹**. **3** [I,T] **agree (to do sth)**; **agree (on) (sth)** to make an arrangement or agreement with sb: *They agreed to meet again the following day.* ○ *Can we agree on a price?* ○ *We agreed a price of £500.* **4** [I] **agree with sth** to think that sth is right: *I don't agree with experiments on animals.* **5** [I] to be the same as sth: *The two accounts of the accident do not agree.*

agreeable /əˈɡriːəbl/ *adj* **1** pleasant; nice ☛ The opposite is **disagreeable**. **2** (*formal*) ready to agree: *If you are agreeable, we would like to visit your offices on 21 May.* —**agreeably** /-əbli/ *adv*

☆ **agreement** /əˈɡriːmənt/ *noun* **1** [C] a contract or decision that two or more people have made together: *Please sign the agreement and return it to us.* ○ *The leaders reached an agreement after five days of talks.* **2** [U] the state of agreeing with sb/sth: *She nodded her head in agreement.* ☛ The opposite is **disagreement**.

☆ **agriculture** /ˈæɡrɪkʌltʃə(r)/ *noun* [U] keeping animals and growing crops for food; farming: *the Minister of Agriculture* —**agricultural** /ˌæɡrɪˈkʌltʃərəl/ *adj*: *agricultural land*

ah /ɑː/ *interj* (used for expressing surprise, pleasure, sympathy, etc): *Ah, there you are.* ○ *Ah well, never mind.*

aha /ɑːˈhɑː/ *interj* (used when you suddenly

s	z	ʃ	ʒ	h	m	n	ŋ	l	r	j	w
so	zoo	she	vision	how	man	no	sing	leg	red	yes	wet

find or understand sth): *Aha! Now I understand.*

☆ **ahead** /ə'hed/ *adv, adj* **ahead (of sb/sth) 1** in front of sb/sth: *I could see the other car about half a mile ahead of us.* ○ *The path ahead looked narrow and steep.* ○ *Look straight ahead and don't turn round!* **2** before or in advance of sb/sth: *Jane and Nicky arrived a few minutes ahead of us.* ○ *London is about five hours ahead of New York.* **3** into the future: *He's got a difficult time ahead of him.* ○ *We must think ahead and make a plan.* **4** doing better than another person or team in a game, competition, etc: *The third goal put Italy ahead.* **5** more advanced than sb/sth else: *The Japanese are way ahead of us in their research.*
(IDIOM) **streets ahead** ⇨ STREET

aid /eɪd/ *noun* **1** [U] help: *to walk with the aid of a stick* ○ *to go to sb's aid* (= to go and help sb) ☛ Look at **first aid**. **2** [C] a person or thing that helps you: *a hearing aid* **3** [U] money, food, etc that is sent to a country or people in order to help them: *aid to the Third World* ○ *Oxfam and other aid agencies*
(IDIOM) **in aid of sb/sth** in order to raise money for sb/sth: *a concert in aid of Children in Need*

aid *verb* [T] (*formal*) to help sb
(IDIOM) **aid and abet** to help sb to do sth that is against the law

aide /eɪd/ *noun* [C] a person who is an assistant to sb important in the government, etc

Aids (*also* **AIDS**) /eɪdz/ *noun* [U] an illness which destroys the body's ability to fight infection: *an AIDS victim* ○ *Thousands of people have died of Aids.* ☛ **Aids** is short for **Acquired Immune Deficiency Syndrome**.

ailing /'eɪlɪŋ/ *adj* not in good health; weak: (*figurative*) *an ailing economy*

ailment /'eɪlmənt/ *noun* [C] (*formal*) an illness (that is not very serious)

☆ **aim¹** /eɪm/ *noun* **1** [C] something that you intend to do or achieve: *Our aim is to open offices in Paris and Rome before the end of the year.* ○ *His only aim in life is to make money.* **2** [U] the act of pointing sth at sb/sth before trying to hit him/her/it with it: *Get ready to shoot. Take aim – fire!* ○ *Her aim was good and she hit the target.*
aimless *adj* having no purpose: *an aimless discussion* — **aimlessly** *adv*

☆ **aim²** /eɪm/ *verb* **1** [I] **aim to do sth**; **aim at/for sth** to intend to do or achieve sth: *We aim to leave after breakfast.* ○ *The company is aiming at a 25% increase in profit.* ○ *You should always aim for perfection in your work.* **2** [T] **aim sth at sb/sth** to direct sth at a particular person or group: *The advertising campaign is aimed at young people.* **3** [I,T] **aim (sth) (at sb/sth)** to point sth at sb/sth before trying to hit him/her/it with it: *She picked up the gun, aimed, and fired.*
(IDIOM) **be aimed at sth** to be intended to achieve sth: *The new laws are aimed at reducing heavy traffic in cities.*

ain't /eɪnt/ (*informal*) short for AM NOT, IS NOT, ARE NOT, HAS NOT, HAVE NOT ☛ **Ain't** is considered to be incorrect English.

☆ **air¹** /eə(r)/ *noun* **1** [U] the mixture of gases that surrounds the earth and that people, animals and plants breathe: *the pure mountain air* ○ *The air was polluted by smoke from the factory.* **2** [U] the space around and above things: *to throw a ball high into the air* ○ *in the open air* (= outside) **3** [U] travel or transport in an aircraft: *to travel by air* ○ *an air ticket* **4** [C] **an air (of sth)** the impression that sb gives or the impression you get of a place, event, etc: *a confident air* ○ *There was a general air of confusion outside the President's palace.*
(IDIOMS) **a breath of fresh air** ⇨ BREATH
in the air probably going to happen soon: *A feeling of change was in the air.*
in the open air ⇨ OPEN¹
on (the) air broadcasting on the radio or television: *This radio station is on the air 24 hours a day.*
vanish, etc into thin air ⇨ THIN

'airbase *noun* [C] an airport for military aeroplanes

'air-conditioned *adj* having air-conditioning: *air-conditioned offices*

'air-conditioning *noun* [U] the system that keeps the air in a room, building, etc cool and dry

'airfield *noun* [C] an area of land where aeroplanes can land or take off. An airfield is smaller than an airport.

'air force *noun* [C, with sing or pl verb] the part of a country's military organization that fights in the air ☛ Look at **army** and **navy**.

'air-hostess (*also* **hostess**) *noun* [C] a woman who looks after the passengers on an aeroplane

'airline *noun* [C] a company that provides regular flights for people or goods in aeroplanes: *an airline pilot*

'airliner *noun* [C] a large aeroplane that carries passengers

'airmail *noun* [U] the system for sending letters, parcels, etc by aeroplane

'airplane *noun* [C] (*US*) = AEROPLANE

'airport *noun* [C] a place where aircraft can land and take off and that has buildings for passengers to wait in

'air raid *noun* [C] an attack by military aeroplanes

'airspace *noun* [U] the part of the sky that is above a country and that belongs to that country by law

'airtight *adj* that air cannot get into or out of

,air traffic con'troller *noun* [C] a person whose job is to organize routes for aeroplanes, and to tell pilots by radio when they can land and take off

air² /eə(r)/ *verb* **1** [I,T] to put clothes, etc in a warm place or outside in the fresh air to make sure they are completely dry; to be put in this place: ○ *Put the sleeping-bag on the washing-line to air.* **2** [I,T] to make a room, etc fresh by letting air into it; to become fresh in this way: *Open the window to air the room.* **3** [T] to tell people what you think about sth: *The discussion gave people a chance to air their views.*

i:	ɪ	e	æ	ɑ:	ɒ	ɔ:	ʊ	u:	ʌ
see	sit	ten	hat	arm	got	saw	put	too	cup

airborne — **alienate**

'airing cupboard *noun* [C] a warm cupboard that you use for airing(1) clothes in

airborne /'eəbɔ:n/ *adj* flying in the air: *airborne missiles*

☆ **aircraft** /'eəkrɑ:ft/ *noun* [C] (*pl* **aircraft**) any vehicle that can fly in the air, eg an aeroplane, a helicopter, etc

'aircraft carrier *noun* [C] a ship that carries military aircraft and that has a long flat area where they can take off and land

airless /'eəlɪs/ *adj* not having enough fresh air: *The room was hot and airless.*

airy /'eərɪ/ *adj* (**airier**; **airiest**) having a lot of fresh air: *a light and airy room*

aisle /aɪl/ *noun* [C] a passage between the rows of seats in a church, theatre, etc

ajar /ə'dʒɑ:(r)/ *adj* (not before a noun) slightly open (used about a door)

akin /ə'kɪn/ *adj* **akin to sth** similar to or like sth

à la carte /ˌɑː lɑː 'kɑːt/ *adj, adv* (used about a meal in a restaurant) where each dish on the menu has a separate price and there is not a fixed price for a complete meal

☆ **alarm** /ə'lɑːm/ *noun* **1** [U] a sudden feeling of fear or worry: *She jumped up in alarm.* **2** [sing] a warning of danger: *A small boy saw the smoke and raised the alarm.* **3** [C] a machine that warns you of danger, eg by ringing a loud bell: *a burglar alarm* ○ *a fire alarm* **4** [C] = ALARM CLOCK
(IDIOM) **a false alarm** ⇨ FALSE

alarm *verb* [T] to make sb/sth feel suddenly frightened or worried: *The news of the escaped prisoner alarmed the local people.*

alarmed *adj* **alarmed (at/by sth)** frightened or worried: *Government ministers are alarmed at the recent rise in unemployment.*

alarming *adj* that makes you frightened or worried: *The population of the world is increasing at an alarming rate.* —**alarmingly** *adv*

a'larm clock (*also* **alarm**) *noun* [C] a clock that you can set to make a noise at a particular time to wake you up: *She set the alarm clock for half past six.* ○ *My alarm clock goes off at seven o'clock.* ☛ picture at **clock**.

alas /ə'læs/ *interj* (*formal*) (used for expressing sadness about sth)

albino /æl'biːnəʊ; *US* -'baɪ-/ *noun* [C] (*pl* **albinos**) a person or animal with very white skin, white hair and pink eyes

album /'ælbəm/ *noun* [C] **1** a record that has about 25 minutes of music or speech on each side ☛ Look at **single** and **LP**. **2** a book in which you can keep stamps, photographs, etc that you have collected

☆ **alcohol** /'ælkəhɒl; *US* -hɔːl/ *noun* [U] **1** the colourless liquid in drinks such as beer, whisky and wine that can make you drunk **2** drinks (eg beer, whisky, wine) that contain alcohol —**alcoholic** /ˌælkə'hɒlɪk; *US* -'hɔːl-/ *adj*: *alcoholic drinks* ☛ The opposite is **non-alcoholic**. Drinks without alcohol are also called **soft drinks**.

alcoholic *noun* [C] a person who is dependent on alcohol and drinks a large amount of it every day ☛ A person who does not drink alcohol at all is a **teetotaller**.

alcoholism /-ɪzəm/ *noun* [U] the medical condition that is caused by regularly drinking a large amount of alcohol

alcove /'ælkəʊv/ *noun* [C] a small area in a room where one part of the wall is further back than the rest of the wall

ale /eɪl/ *noun* [U] beer ☛ In modern English we use the word **beer**, not **ale**, except when we are talking about certain types of beer.

alert /ə'lɜːt/ *adj* **alert (to sth)** watching, listening, etc for sth with full attention: *Security guards must be alert at all times.* ○ *to be alert to possible changes*

alert *noun* [C] a warning of possible danger: *a bomb alert*
(IDIOM) **on the alert (for sth)** ready or prepared for danger or an attack: *The public were warned to be on the alert for possible terrorist attacks.*

alert *verb* [T] **alert sb (to sth)** to warn sb of danger or a problem

A level /'eɪ levl/ (*also formal* **Advanced level**) *noun* [C] an examination that schoolchildren in England, Wales and Northern Ireland take when they are about eighteen. You usually take A levels in two or three subjects and you need good grades if you want to go to university: *How many A levels have you got?* ○ *I'm doing my A levels this summer.* ☛ Look at **AS level** and **GCSE**.

> In Scotland the examination system is different. Schoolchildren take the Higher grade of the Scottish Certificate of Education (SCE) when they are seventeen and the Certificate of Sixth Year Studies (CSYS) when they are eighteen.

algae /'ældʒi:; 'ælgaɪ/ *noun* [plural, with sing or pl verb] very simple plants that grow mainly in water: *During the hot summer algae spread to levels which made it impossible to swim at some beaches.*

algebra /'ældʒɪbrə/ *noun* [U] a type of mathematics in which letters and symbols are used to represent numbers

alias /'eɪlɪəs/ *noun* [C] a false name, eg one that is used by a criminal

alias *adv* (used for giving sb's false name): *Mrs Phillips, alias Maria Jones*

alibi /'ælɪbaɪ/ *noun* [C] (*pl* **alibis**) a statement by sb that says you were in a different place at the time of a crime and so cannot be guilty of the crime: *He had a good alibi for the night of the robbery.*

alien /'eɪlɪən/ *noun* [C] **1** (*formal*) a person who comes from another country **2** a creature that comes from another planet

alien *adj* **1** of another country; foreign: *an alien land* **2** very strange and completely different from your normal experience: *The idea of eating meat was alien to her.*

alienate /'eɪlɪəneɪt/ *verb* [T] **1** to make people feel that they cannot share your opinions any more: *The Prime Minister's new policies on defence have alienated many of his supporters.* **2 alienate sb (from sb/sth)** to make sb feel that he/she does not belong somewhere or is not part of sth: *Many*

ɜː	ə	eɪ	əʊ	aɪ	aʊ	ɔɪ	ɪə	eə	ʊə
fur	ago	pay	home	five	now	join	near	hair	pure

young unemployed people feel completely alienated from the rest of society. —**alienation** /ˌeɪliəˈneɪʃn/ *noun* [U]

alight[1] /əˈlaɪt/ *adj* on fire; burning: *The petrol had been set alight* (= made to start burning) *by a cigarette.* ☛ Alight can only be used after a noun, but you can use **burning** before a noun: *The whole building was alight.* ○ *a burning building.*

alight[2] /əˈlaɪt/ *verb* [I] (*formal*) **alight (from sth)** to get off a bus, train, etc

align /əˈlaɪn/ *verb* [T] **1 align sth (with sth)** to arrange things in a straight line or so that they are parallel to sth else: *to align the wheels of a car* **2 align yourself with sb** to say that you support the opinions of a particular group, country, etc: *The Green Party has aligned itself with the Socialists over this issue.* ☛ Look at **non-aligned**.

alignment /əˈlaɪnmənt/ *noun* **1** [U] arrangement in a straight line or parallel to sth else **2** [C,U] an agreement between political parties, countries, etc to support the same thing: *the alignment of Japan with the West*

☆ **alike** /əˈlaɪk/ *adj* like one another; the same: *The two children are very alike.* ☛ Alike can only be used after a noun, but you can use **similar-looking** before a noun: *The houses in this street are all alike.* ○ *a street of similar-looking houses.*

alike *adv* in the same way: *We try to treat women and men alike in this company.* ○ *The musical has been a success with adults and children alike.*

alimony /ˈælɪməni; *US* -məʊni/ *noun* [U] money that you have to pay by law to your former wife or husband after a divorce

☆ **alive** /əˈlaɪv/ *adj* **1** not dead; living: *The young woman was still alive when the ambulance reached the hospital.* ○ *He kept the little cat alive by feeding it warm milk.* ☛ Alive can only be used after a noun, but you can use **living** before a noun: *Are her parents still alive?* ○ *Does she have any living relatives?* **2** full of life: *In the evening the town really comes alive.* **3** continuing to exist: *Many old traditions are very much alive in this area of Britain.*

alkali /ˈælkəlaɪ/ *noun* [C,U] any of the chemical substances with a pH value of more than 7 ☛ Look at **acid**. —**alkaline** *adj*

☆ **all**[1] /ɔːl/ *det, pron* **1** the whole of a thing: *All (of) the food has gone.* ○ *They've eaten all of it.* ○ *They've eaten it all.* ○ *This money is all yours.* ○ *All of it is yours.* **2** the whole of the period of time: *It rained all day.* ○ *all week/month/year* ○ *He worked hard all his life.* **3** every one of a group: *All cats are animals but not all animals are cats.* ○ *All (of) my children can swim.* ○ *My children can all swim.* ○ *She's read all (of) these books.* ○ *She's read them all.* ○ *The people at the meeting all voted against the plan.* ○ *All of them voted against the plan.* **4** everything that; the only thing that: *I wrote down all I could remember.* ○ *All I've eaten is a slice of toast.*

(IDIOMS) **above all** ⇒ ABOVE

after all ⇒ AFTER[1]

in all in total: *There were ten of us in all.*

not all that... not very: *The film wasn't all that good.*

(not) at all in any way: *I didn't enjoy it at all.*
☛ We can say **not at all** as a reply when somebody thanks us for something.

☆ **all**[2] /ɔːl/ *adv* **1** completely; very: *He has lived all alone since his wife died.* ○ *I didn't watch that programme – I forgot all about it.* ○ *They got all excited about it.* **2** (in sport) for each side: *The score was two all.*

(IDIOMS) **all along** from the beginning: *I knew you were joking all along.*

all right; alright 1 good or good enough: *Is everything all right?* **2** safe; not hurt; well: *The children are all right. Don't worry.* ○ *Do you feel all right?* **3** (showing you agree): '*You go on ahead.' 'Oh, all right.*'

all the better, harder, etc better, harder, etc than before: *It will be all the more difficult with two people missing.*

the ˌall-ˈclear *noun* [sing] a signal telling you that danger is over

ˌall-ˈin *adj* including everything: *an all-in price*
ˌall ˈout *adj, adv* using all your strength, etc: *We're going all out for the Cup.* ○ *an all-out effort*

ˌall-ˈrounder *noun* [C] a person who can do many different things well

Allah /ˈælə/ the Muslim name for God

allay /əˈleɪ/ *verb* [T] (*formal*) to make sth less strong: *to allay sb's fears*

allege /əˈledʒ/ *verb* [T] (*formal*) to say that sb has done sth wrong, but without proving that this is true: *The woman alleged that Williams had attacked her with a knife.* —**allegation** /ˌæləˈgeɪʃn/ *noun* [C]: *to make allegations of police corruption* —**alleged** /əˈledʒd/ *adj*: *the alleged criminal* (= people say this person is a criminal but nobody has proved that this is true) —**allegedly** /əˈledʒɪdli/ *adv*: *The man was allegedly shot while trying to escape.*

allegiance /əˈliːdʒəns/ *noun* [U] (*formal*) support for or loyalty towards a leader, government, belief, etc: *to swear your allegiance to the Queen*

allergy /ˈælədʒi/ *noun* [C] (*pl* **allergies**) **an allergy (to sth)** a medical condition that makes you ill when you eat, touch or breathe sth that does not normally make other people ill: *an allergy to cats, shellfish, pollen, etc*

allergic /əˈlɜːdʒɪk/ *adj* **1 allergic (to sth)** having an allergy: *I can't drink cow's milk. I'm allergic to it.* **2** caused by an allergy: *an allergic reaction to house dust*

alleviate /əˈliːvieɪt/ *verb* [T] to make sth less strong or bad: *The doctor gave me an injection to alleviate the pain.* —**alleviation** /əˌliːviˈeɪʃn/ *noun* [U]

alley /ˈæli/ (*also* **alley-way**) *noun* [C] a narrow passage between buildings

alliance /əˈlaɪəns/ *noun* [C] an agreement between people, groups, countries, etc to work together and support each other: *the country's military alliance with France* ☛ Look at **ally**.

allied ⇒ ALLY

alligator /ˈælɪgeɪtə(r)/ *noun* [C] a large animal with a long body and sharp teeth that lives in the lakes and rivers of the southern United

p	b	t	d	k	g	tʃ	dʒ	f	v	θ	ð
pen	bad	tea	did	cat	got	chin	June	fall	van	thin	then

allocate /ˈæləkeɪt/ verb [T] **allocate sth (to sb/sth)** to give sth to sb as his/her share or to decide to use sth for a particular purpose: *6 000 seats for next Saturday's football match have been allocated to Liverpool supporters.* ○ *The BBC has allocated £160 000 for each new programme.*

allocation /ˌæləˈkeɪʃn/ noun [C,U] giving sth for a particular purpose; the amount that is given: *the allocation of resources for health care*

allot /əˈlɒt/ verb [T] (allo**tt**ing; allo**tt**ed) **allot sth (to sb/sth)** to give sb money, a piece of work, etc as his/her share or to decide to allow a certain amount of time for sth: *Different tasks were allotted to each member of the class.* ○ *We all finished the exam in the allotted time.*

allotment /əˈlɒtmənt/ noun [C] (*Brit*) a small area of land in a town that you can rent for growing vegetables on

☆**allow** /əˈlaʊ/ verb [T] **1 allow sb/sth to do sth; allow sth** to give permission for sb/sth to do sth or for sth to happen: *Children under eighteen are not allowed to buy alcohol.* ○ *I'm afraid we don't allow people to bring dogs into this restaurant.* ○ *Photography is not allowed inside the cathedral.* ☞ Compare **allow, permit** and **let. Allow** can be used in both formal and informal English. The passive form **be allowed to** is especially common. **Permit** is a formal word and is usually used only in written English. **Let** is an informal word, and very common in spoken English. You **allow sb to do sth** but **let sb do sth** (no 'to'). **Let** cannot be used in the passive: *Visitors are not allowed/permitted to smoke in this area.* ○ *Smoking is not allowed/permitted.* ○ *I'm not allowed to smoke in my bedroom.* ○ *My Dad won't let me smoke in my bedroom.* **2** to give permission for sb/sth to be or go somewhere: *No dogs allowed.* ○ *I'm only allowed out on Friday and Saturday nights.* **3 allow sb sth** to let sb have sth: *My contract allows me four weeks' holiday a year.* **4 allow sb/sth to do sth** to make it possible for sb/sth to do sth: *Working part-time would allow me to spend more time with my family.* **5 allow sth (for sb/sth)** to provide money, time, etc for sth: *You should allow about 30 minutes for each examination question.*

(PHRASAL VERB) **allow for sb/sth** to think about possible problems when you are planning sth and include extra time, money, etc for them: *The journey should take about two hours, allowing for heavy traffic.*

allowance /əˈlaʊəns/ noun [C] **1** an amount of sth that you are allowed: *Most flights have a 20 kg baggage allowance.* **2** an amount of money that you receive regularly to help you pay for sth that you need.

(IDIOM) **make allowances for sb/sth** to judge a person or a person's actions more kindly because he/she has a particular problem or disadvantage: *You really should make allowances for her. She's very inexperienced.*

allude /əˈluːd/ verb [I] **allude to sb/sth** (*formal*) to speak about sb/sth in an indirect way: *He mentioned no names but we all knew who he was alluding to.*

allusion /əˈluːʒn/ noun [C,U] an act of speaking about sth indirectly: *The play is full of allusions to classical mythology.*

ally /əˈlaɪ/ noun [C] (*pl* **allies**) **1** a country that has an agreement to support another country, especially in a war: *France and its European allies* ☞ Look at **alliance. 2** a person who helps and supports you, especially when other people are against you: *the Prime Minister's political allies*

allied /ˈælaɪd; əˈlaɪd/ adj **1** (used about organizations, countries, etc) having an agreement to work together and support each other: *allied forces* ○ *Allied Irish Banks* **2 allied (to sth)** connected with; similar: *coalmining and allied industries*

almighty /ɔːlˈmaɪti/ adj **1** having the power to do anything: *Almighty God* **2** (only *before* a noun) (*informal*) very great: *Suddenly we heard the most almighty crash.*

almond /ˈɑːmənd/ noun [C] an oval nut that is often used in cooking: *trout with almonds* ☞ picture at **nut.**

☆**almost** /ˈɔːlməʊst/ adv not quite; very nearly: *By nine o'clock almost everybody had arrived.* ○ *Careful! I almost fell into the water then!* ○ *The film has almost finished.* ○ *She almost always cycles to school.* ○ *There's almost nothing left.*

☆**alone** /əˈləʊn/ adj, adv **1** without any other person: *The old man lives alone.* ○ *Are you alone? Can I speak to you for a moment?* ○ *I don't like walking home alone after dark.* ☞ **Alone** and **lonely** both mean that you are not with other people. **Lonely** (*US* **lonesome**) means that you are unhappy about this, but **alone** does not usually suggest either happiness or unhappiness. **Alone** cannot be used before a noun. You can also use **on your own** and **by yourself** to mean 'alone'. These expressions are more informal and very common in spoken English. **2** (after a noun or pronoun) only: *You alone can help us.* ○ *The food alone cost £40. The wine was extra.*

(IDIOMS) **leave sb/sth alone** ⇒ LEAVE¹
let alone ⇒ LET¹

☆**along** /əˈlɒŋ; *US* əˈlɔːŋ/ prep **1** from one end to or towards the other end of sth: *I walked slowly along the road.* ○ *David looked along the corridor to see if anyone was coming.* ○ *Carry on along this street until you get to the traffic lights.* **2** in a line that follows the side of sth long: *Wild flowers grew along both sides of the river.* **3** at a particular point on or beside sth long: *Our house is about halfway along Hope Street.*

along adv **1** forward: *We moved along slowly with the crowd.* **2** (*informal*) with sb: *We're going to the pub. Why don't you come along too?*

(IDIOMS) **all along** ⇒ ALL²

along with sb/sth together with sb/sth: *Along with hundreds of others, she lost her job when the factory closed.*

alongside /əˌlɒŋˈsaɪd; *US* əˌlɔːŋˈsaɪd/ adv, prep **1** next to or along the side of sth: *a garden with a small river running alongside* ○ *The boat moored alongside the quay.* **2** together with sb/

sth: *the opportunity to work alongside experienced musicians*

aloof /ə'lu:f/ *adj* **1** not friendly or open to other people; distant **2** not involved in sth; apart: *The President can no longer remain aloof from the problem.*

☆ **aloud** /ə'laʊd/ (*also* **out loud**) *adv* in a normal speaking voice that other people can hear; not silently: *to read aloud from a book*

☆ **alphabet** /'ælfəbet/ *noun* [C] the set of letters that you use when you are writing a particular language, especially when they are arranged in a fixed order: *There are 26 letters in the English alphabet.*

alphabetical /ˌælfə'betɪkl/ *adj* arranged in the same order as the letters of the alphabet: *The poems are listed in alphabetical order.* —**alphabetically** /-kli/ *adv*

alpine /'ælpaɪn/ *adj* of or found in high mountains: *alpine flowers*

☆ **already** /ɔ:l'redi/ *adv* **1** (used for talking about sth that has happened before now or before a particular time in the past, especially if it happened earlier than you expected): *'Would you like some lunch?' 'No, I've already eaten, thanks.'* o *We got there at 6.30 but Martin had already left.* o *Sarah was already awake when I went into her room.* **2** (used in negative sentences and questions for expressing surprise) so early; as soon as this: *Have you finished already?* o *Surely you're not going already!*

alright /ɔ:l'raɪt/ *adv* (*informal*) = ALL RIGHT

☆ **also** /'ɔ:lsəʊ/ *adv* (not with negative verbs) in addition; too: *Mark Wilson paints and writes novels in his spare time. He also speaks Chinese.* o *Please bring some paper, a pen and also a calculator.* o *The food is wonderful, and also very cheap.* ☞ **Too** and **as well** are less formal than **also** and are very common in spoken English. **Also** usually goes before a main verb or after 'is', 'are', 'were', etc: *He also enjoys reading.* o *He has also been to Australia.* o *He is also intelligent.* **Too** and **as well** usually go at the end of a phrase or sentence: *I really love this song, and I liked the first one too/as well.* Do not confuse **also** with **even**: *Even (NOT also) in the middle of summer, the nights can be cold.*
(IDIOM) **not only ... but also** ⇨ ONLY²

altar /'ɔ:ltə(r)/ *noun* [C] the holy table in a church or temple

☆ **alter** /'ɔ:ltə(r)/ *verb* [I,T] to make sth different in some way, but without changing it completely; to become different: *They've altered the plan for the new building. The main entrance will now be in Queen Street.* o *This does not alter the fact that the company is in serious financial difficulty.* o *This skirt is too big for me now. I'll have to alter it* (= make it smaller by sewing it). o *The village seems to have altered very little in the last twenty years.*

alteration /ˌɔ:ltə'reɪʃn/ *noun* [C,U] a small change in sb/sth: *We want to make a few alterations to the house before we move in.* o *The travel company will inform you of any alteration in the time of departure.*

alternate¹ /ɔ:l'tɜ:nət; *US* 'ɔ:ltərnət/ *adj* **1** (used about two types of events, things, etc) happening or following regularly one after the other: *Helen and Nick take the children to school on alternate days* (= Helen takes them on Monday, Nick on Tuesday, Helen on Wednesday, etc). **2** one of every two: *He works alternate weeks* (= he works the first week, he doesn't work the second week, he works again the third week, etc). —**alternately** *adv*

alternate² /'ɔ:ltəneɪt/ *verb* **1** [I] **alternate with sth**; **alternate between A and B** (used about two types of events, things, etc) to happen or follow regularly one after the other: *It's exciting music. Quiet violin passages alternate with sudden bursts of trumpet sound.* o *She seemed to alternate between hating him and loving him.* **2** [T] **alternate A with B** to cause two types of events or things to happen or follow regularly one after the other: *He alternated periods of work with periods of rest.* —**alternation** /ˌɔ:ltə'neɪʃn/ *noun* [C,U]

☆ **alternative** /ɔ:l'tɜ:nətɪv/ *adj* (only *before* a noun) that you can use, do, etc instead of sth else: *There is heavy traffic on the A34. Drivers are advised to find an alternative route.*

alternative *noun* [C] one of two things that you can choose between: *The Minister suggested community service as an alternative to imprisonment.* ☞ **Alternative** is now often used for talking about more than two things: *There are several alternatives open to us at the moment.* —**alternatively** *adv*: *Trains leave London Paddington every half hour. Alternatively, there is a regular coach service from Victoria Coach Station.*

☆ **although** /ɔ:l'ðəʊ/ *conj* **1** (used for introducing a statement that makes the main statement in a sentence seem surprising): *Although she was tired, she stayed up to watch the late night film on television.* **2** (used for introducing a statement that modifies the main statement) and yet; but: *There will be heavy rain in many parts of Britain tonight, although it is unlikely to reach the South West until morning.* ☞ You can also use **though** but it is less formal than **although**. **Even** can be used with **though** for emphasis, but not with **although**: *She didn't want to go to the party, although/though/even though she knew all her friends would be there.* **Though**, but not **although** can be used at the end of a sentence: *She knew all her friends would be there. She didn't want to go, though.*

altitude /'æltɪtju:d; *US* -tu:d/ *noun* **1** [sing] the height of sth above sea level: *The plane climbed to an altitude of 10 000 metres.* **2** [usually pl] a place that is high above sea level: *You need to carry oxygen when you are climbing at high altitudes.*

alto /'æltəʊ/ *noun* [C] (*pl* **altos**) the lowest normal singing voice for a woman, the highest for a man; a woman or man with this voice

altogether /ˌɔ:ltə'geðə(r)/ *adv* **1** completely: *I don't altogether agree with you.* o *At the age of 55 he stopped working altogether.* **2** including everything: *We've got about £65 altogether.* **3** when you consider everything; generally: *Altogether, Oxford is a pleasant place to live.* ☞ **Altogether** is not the same as **all together**. **All together** means 'everything or everybody

i:	ɪ	e	æ	ɑ:	ɒ	ɔ:	ʊ	u:	ʌ
see	sit	ten	hat	arm	got	saw	put	too	cup

aluminium /ˌæljʊˈmɪniəm/ (US **aluminum** /əˈluːmɪnəm/) (symbol **Al**) noun [U] a light silver-coloured metal that is used for making cooking equipment, etc: *aluminium foil*

☆ **always** /ˈɔːlweɪz/ adv **1** at all times; regularly: *We almost always go to Scotland for our holidays.* ○ *Why is the train always late when I'm in a hurry?* **2** all through the past until now: *Tom has always been shy.* ○ *I've always liked music.* **3** for ever: *I shall always remember this moment.* **4** (with continuous tenses) again and again, usually in an annoying way: *She's always complaining about something.* **5** (used with 'can' or 'could' for suggesting sth that sb could do, especially if nothing else is possible): *If you haven't got enough money, I could always lend you some.* ☛ **Always** does not usually go at the beginning of a sentence. It usually goes before the main verb or after 'is', 'are', 'were', etc: *He always wears those shoes.* ○ *I have always wanted to visit Egypt.* ○ *Fiona is always late.* However, **always** can go at the beginning of a sentence when you are telling somebody to do something: *Always stop and look before you cross the road.*

am ⇒ BE

amalgamate /əˈmælɡəmeɪt/ verb [I,T] (used especially about organizations, groups, etc) to join together to form a single organization, group, etc: *If the two unions amalgamated, they would be much more powerful.* —**amalgamation** /əˌmælɡəˈmeɪʃn/ noun [C,U]

amass /əˈmæs/ verb [T] to gather together a large quantity of sth: *We've amassed a lot of information on the subject.*

amateur /ˈæmətə(r)/ noun [C] **1** a person who takes part in a sport or an activity for pleasure, not for money as a job: *Only amateurs can take part in the tournament; no professionals will be allowed.* **2** (usually used when being critical) a person who does not have skill or experience when doing sth: *The repair work on this house was clearly done by a bunch of amateurs.*

amateur adj done, or doing sth, for pleasure (not for money as a job): *an amateur photographer* **2** (also **amateurish**) done without skill or experience

☆ **amaze** /əˈmeɪz/ verb [T] to surprise sb very much; to seem incredible to sb: *Sometimes your behaviour amazes me!* ○ *It amazes me that anyone could be so stupid!*

amazed adj extremely surprised; feeling that you cannot believe sth: *She was amazed to discover the truth about her husband.* ○ *I was amazed by the change in his attitude.* —**amazement** noun [U]: *He looked at me in amazement.* ○ *To my amazement, I passed the test easily.*

amazing adj causing you to be very surprised: *She has shown amazing courage.* ○ *I've got an amazing story to tell you.* —**amazingly** adv: *It's an amazingly pleasant country to visit.*

ambassador /æmˈbæsədə(r)/ noun [C] a diplomat of high rank who represents his/her country in a foreign country: *the Spanish Ambassador to Britain* ☛ *The ambassador lives and works in an embassy.*

amber /ˈæmbə(r)/ noun [U] **1** a hard clear yellow-brown substance used for making jewellery or ornaments **2** a yellow-brown colour: *The three colours in traffic-lights are red, amber and green.* —**amber** adj

ambiguity /ˌæmbɪˈɡjuːəti/ noun [C,U] (pl **ambiguities**) the possibility of being understood in more than one way; sth that can be understood in more than one way

ambiguous /æmˈbɪɡjuəs/ adj having more than one possible meaning: *That's a rather ambiguous remark – what exactly do you mean?* —**ambiguously** adv

☆ **ambition** /æmˈbɪʃn/ noun **1 ambition (to be/do sth)** [U] strong desire to be successful, to have power, etc: *One problem of young people today is their lack of ambition.* **2** [C] something that you very much want to have or do: *It has always been her ambition to travel the world.*

☆ **ambitious** /æmˈbɪʃəs/ adj **1 ambitious (to be/do sth)** having a strong desire to be successful, to have power, etc: *I'm not particularly ambitious – I'm content with my life the way it is.* **2** difficult to achieve or do because it takes a lot of work or effort: *The company have ambitious plans for expansion.*

ambivalent /æmˈbɪvələnt/ adj having or showing a mixture of feelings or opinions about sth or sb: *I have always felt rather ambivalent about having children.* —**ambivalence** noun [U]

☆ **ambulance** /ˈæmbjʊləns/ noun [C] a special motor vehicle for taking ill or injured people to and from hospital

ambush /ˈæmbʊʃ/ noun [C] a surprise attack from a hidden position —**ambush** verb [T]

amen /ɑːˈmen; US eɪˈmen/ interj (used at the end of a prayer by Christians) let this be so: *In the name of the Father, the Son and the Holy Ghost. Amen.*

amenable /əˈmiːnəbl/ adj willing to accept sth; willing to be guided: *I'm amenable to any suggestions you may have.*

amend /əˈmend/ verb [T] to change sth slightly, often in order to make it better: *The law needs to be amended.*

amendment noun **1** [C] a part that is added or a small change that is made to a piece of writing, especially to a law **2** [U] an act of amending: *The bill was passed without amendment.*

amends /əˈmendz/ noun [plural]
(IDIOM) **make amends** to do sth for sb, that shows that you are sorry for sth bad that you have done before: *I bought her a present to make amends for the horrible things I had said to her.*

amenity /əˈmiːnəti; US əˈmenəti/ noun [C] (pl **amenities**) something in a place that helps to make living there pleasant or easy: *Among the town's amenities are two cinemas and a sports centre.*

☆ **American** /əˈmerɪkən/ adj from or connected with the USA: *Have you met Bob? He's Amer-*

ɜː	ə	eɪ	əʊ	aɪ	aʊ	ɔɪ	ɪə	eə	ʊə
fur	ago	pay	home	five	now	join	near	hair	pure

ican. ○ *an American accent* ○ *In American English 'theatre' is spelt 'theater'.*

American *noun* [C] a person who comes from the USA: *His wife is an American.*

American 'football (*US* **football**) *noun* [U] a form of football played in the USA with an oval-shaped ball. The players wear helmets and other protective clothing and are allowed to pick up and carry, as well as kick, the ball.

American 'Indian = NATIVE AMERICAN

amiable /ˈeɪmɪəbl/ *adj* friendly and pleasant —**amiably** *adv*

amicable /ˈæmɪkəbl/ *adj* made or done in a friendly way, without argument: *I'm sure we can find an amicable way of settling the dispute.* —**amicably** *adv*

amid /əˈmɪd/ (*also* **amidst** /əˈmɪdst/) *prep* (*formal*) in the middle of; among: *Amid all the confusion, the thieves got away.*

amiss /əˈmɪs/ *adj, adv* wrong; not as it should be: *When I walked into the room I could sense that something was amiss.*
(IDIOMS) **not come/go amiss** to be welcome: *Things are fine, although a bit more money wouldn't come amiss.* ○ *An apology wouldn't go amiss.*

take sth amiss to be upset by sth, perhaps because you have understood it in the wrong way: *Please don't take my remarks amiss.*

ammunition /ˌæmjʊˈnɪʃn/ *noun* [U] **1** the supply of bullets, etc that you need to fire from a weapon: *The troops surrendered because they had run out of ammunition.* **2** (*figurative*) facts or information that can be used against sb/sth

amnesty /ˈæmnəsti/ *noun* [C] (*pl* **amnesties**) **1** a time when a government forgives political crimes **2** a time when people can give in illegal weapons

☆ **among** /əˈmʌŋ/ (*also* **amongst** /əˈmʌŋst/) *prep* **1** surrounded by; in the middle of: *I often feel nervous when I'm among strangers.* ○ *The modern block looks wrong among all the old buildings.* ○ *I found the missing letter amongst a heap of old newspapers.* ☞ picture at **between**. **2** in the group or number of: *She is among the nicest people I have ever met.* ○ *Among the city's attractions are its museums and art galleries.* **3** to each one (of a group): *On his death, his money will be divided among his children.* **4** inside (a group): *Discuss it amongst yourselves and let me know your decision.* ☞ Look at the note at **between**.

☆ **amount** /əˈmaʊnt/ *noun* [C] **1** the amount of sth is how much of it there is; quantity: *I spent an enormous amount of time preparing for the exam.* ○ *I have a certain amount of sympathy with her.* **2** total or sum of money: *You are requested to pay the full amount within seven days.*

amount *verb* [I] **amount to sth 1** to add up to; to total: *The cost of the repairs amounted to £5 000.* **2** to be the same as: *Whether I tell her today or tomorrow, it amounts to the same thing.*

amp /æmp/ (*also formal* **ampere** /ˈæmpeə(r); *US* ˈæmpɪər/) *noun* [C] a unit for measuring electric current

ample /ˈæmpl/ *adj* **1** enough or more than enough: *We've got ample time to make a decision.* ○ *I'm not sure how much the trip will cost, but I should think £500 will be ample.* **2** large; having a great deal of space: *There is space for an ample car park.* —**amply** /ˈæmpli/ *adv*: *The report makes it amply clear whose mistake it was.*

amplify /ˈæmplɪfaɪ/ *verb* [T] (*pres part* **amplifying**; *3rd pers sing pres* **amplifies**; *pt, pp* **amplified**) **1** to increase the strength of a sound, using electrical equipment **2** to add details to sth in order to explain it more fully: *Would you like to amplify your recent comments, Minister?* —**amplification** /ˌæmplɪfɪˈkeɪʃn/ *noun* [U]: *These comments need further amplification.*

amplifier *noun* [C] a piece of electrical equipment for making sounds louder or signals stronger

amputate /ˈæmpjʊteɪt/ *verb* [I,T] to cut off a person's arm or leg (or part of it) for medical reasons: *His leg was so badly injured that it had to be amputated.* —**amputation** /ˌæmpjʊˈteɪʃn/ *noun* [C,U]

☆ **amuse** /əˈmjuːz/ *verb* [T] **1** to make sb laugh or smile; to seem funny to sb: *Everybody laughed but I couldn't understand what had amused them.* **2** to make time pass pleasantly for sb; to stop sb from getting bored: *I did some crosswords to amuse myself on the journey.* ○ *I've brought a few toys to amuse the children.*

amused *adj* **1** if you are amused you think that sth is funny and it makes you want to laugh or smile: *You may think it's funny, but I'm not amused.* ○ *I was amused to hear his account of what happened.* **2** if sth keeps you amused it makes you pass the time pleasantly, without getting bored.

amusement *noun* **1** [U] the feeling caused by sth that makes you laugh or smile, or by sth that entertains you and that stops you from being bored: *There was a look of amusement on his face.* ○ *Much to the pupils' amusement, the teacher fell off his chair.* **2** [C] something that makes time pass pleasantly; an entertainment: *The holiday centre offers a wide range of amusements, including golf and tennis.*

amusing *adj* causing you to laugh or smile: *He's a very amusing person and he makes me laugh a lot.* ○ *an amusing story*

an ⇨ A²

anaemia (*US* **anemia**) /əˈniːmiə/ *noun* [U] a medical condition in which there are not enough red cells in the blood

anaemic (*US* **anemic**) /əˈniːmɪk/ *adj* suffering from anaemia

anaesthetic (*US* **anesthetic**) /ˌænɪsˈθetɪk/ *noun* [C,U] a substance that stops you feeling pain, eg when a doctor is performing an operation on you: *You'll need to be under anaesthetic for the operation.* ○ *a local anaesthetic* (= one that only affects part of the body and does not make you unconscious) ○ *a general anaesthetic* (= one that makes you unconscious)

anaesthetist (*US* **anesthetist**) /əˈniːsθətɪst/ *noun* [C] a person who is qualified to give anaesthetics to patients

p	b	t	d	k	g	tʃ	dʒ	f	v	θ	ð
pen	bad	tea	did	cat	got	chin	June	fall	van	thin	then

anaesthetize (*also* **anaesthetise**; *US* **anesthetize**) /əˈniːsθətaɪz/ *verb* [T] to give an anaesthetic to sb

anagram /ˈænəgræm/ *noun* [C] a word or phrase that is made by arranging the letters of another word or phrase in a different order: *'Worth' is an anagram of 'throw'.*

analogous /əˈnæləgəs/ *adj* (*formal*) **analogous (to/with sth)** similar in some way; that you can compare

analogy /əˈnælədʒi/ *noun* [C] (*pl* **analogies**) **an analogy (between sth and sth)** a comparison between two things that shows a way in which they are similar: *You could make an analogy between the human body and a car engine.*

(IDIOM) **by analogy** If you explain sth by analogy to sth else you compare it to the other thing and show how it is similar.

☆**analyse** (*US* **analyze**) /ˈænəlaɪz/ *verb* [T] to look at or think about the different parts or details of sth carefully in order to understand or explain it: *The water samples are now being analysed in a laboratory.* ○ *to analyse statistics* ○ *She analysed the situation and then decided what to do.*

☆**analysis** /əˈnæləsɪs/ *noun* (*pl* **analyses** /-əsiːz/) **1** [C,U] the careful examination of the different parts or details of sth: *Some samples of the water were sent to a laboratory for analysis.* ○ *They carried out an analysis of the causes of the problem.* **2** [C] the result of such an examination: *Your analysis of the situation is different from mine.*

analytic /ˌænəˈlɪtɪk/ (*also* **analytical** /-kl/) *adj* looking carefully at the different parts of sth in order to understand or explain it: *analytic techniques*

analyst /ˈænəlɪst/ *noun* [C] a person whose job is to analyse things as an expert: *a food analyst*

anarchy /ˈænəki/ *noun* [U] a situation in which people do not obey rules and laws; a situation in which there is no government in a country: *While the civil war went on, the country was in a state of anarchy.*

anarchic /əˈnɑːkɪk/ *adj* without rules or laws

anarchism /ˈænəkɪzəm/ *noun* [U] the political theory that there should be no government or laws in a country

anarchist *noun* [C] a person who believes in this theory, especially one who takes action to achieve it

anatomy /əˈnætəmi/ *noun* (*pl* **anatomies**) **1** [U] the scientific study of the structure of human or animal bodies **2** [C] the structure of a living thing: *the anatomy of the frog* —**anatomical** /ˌænəˈtɒmɪkl/ *adj*

ancestor /ˈænsestə(r)/ *noun* [C] a person in your family who lived a long time before you, from whom you are descended: *My ancestors settled in this country a hundred years ago.*

ancestry /ˈænsestri/ *noun* [C,U] (*pl* **ancestries**) all of a person's ancestors, when you think of them as a group: *He was of Irish ancestry.*

anchor /ˈæŋkə(r)/ *noun* [C] a heavy metal object at the end of a chain that you drop into the water from a boat in order to keep the boat in one place

anchor *verb* **1** [I,T] to drop an anchor; to stop a boat moving by using an anchor: *We anchored the boat in the harbour and went ashore.* **2** [T] to fix sth firmly so that it is held in a place and cannot move: *They anchored the tent with strong ropes.*

☆**ancient** /ˈeɪnʃənt/ *adj* **1** belonging to or connected with the distant past: *ancient civilizations* **2** having existed for a long time: *The annual festival is one of the ancient traditions of the region.* **3** (*informal*) very old: *I can't believe he's only 30, he looks ancient!*

☆**and** /ənd; ən; strong form ænd/ *conj* **1** (used to connect words or parts of sentences) also; in addition to: *bread and butter* ○ *one woman, two men and three children* ○ *a boy and a girl* ○ *an apple and a pear* ○ *Do it slowly and carefully.* ○ *We were singing and dancing all evening.* ☛ When the two things are closely linked, you do not need to repeat the 'a', etc: *a knife and fork* ○ *my father and mother* **2** (used when you are saying numbers) plus: *Twelve and six is eighteen.* ○ *It cost me a hundred and sixty pounds.* ☛ When you are saying large numbers *and* is used after the word 'hundred ': *We say 2264 as two thousand, two hundred and sixty-four.* **3** then; following this or that: *Come in and sit down.* **4** as a result of this or that; because of this or that: *It was a terrible shock and he was very upset.* ○ *Say that again and I'll lose my temper.* **5** (used between repeated words to show that sth is increasing or continuing): *The situation is getting worse and worse.* ○ *I shouted and shouted but nobody answered.* **6** (used between repeated words for saying that there are important differences between things of the same kind): *City life can be very exciting but there are cities and cities.* **7** (used instead of 'to' after certain verbs eg 'go', 'come', 'try'): *Go and answer the door for me, will you?* ○ *I'll try and find out what's going on.* ○ *Why don't you come and stay with us one weekend?*

anecdote /ˈænɪkdəʊt/ *noun* [C] a short interesting story about a real person or event

anemia, anemic (*US*) = ANAEMIA, ANAEMIC

anesthetic (*US*) = ANAESTHETIC

anew /əˈnjuː; *US* əˈnuː/ *adv* (*formal*) again; in a new or different way: *I wish I could start my life anew!*

angel /ˈeɪndʒl/ *noun* [C] **1** a servant of God: *In pictures angels are usually dressed in white, with wings.* **2** a person who is very kind: *Be an angel and wash these clothes for me, will you?*

angelic /ænˈdʒelɪk/ *adj* looking or acting like an angel —**angelically** *adv*

☆**anger** /ˈæŋgə(r)/ *noun* [U] the strong feeling that you have when sth has happened or sb has done sth that you do not like: *He could not hide his anger at the news.* ○ *She was shaking with anger.*

anger *verb* [T] to cause sb to become angry: *It angers me that such things can be allowed to happen.*

☆**angle¹** /ˈæŋgl/ *noun* [C] **1** the space between two lines or surfaces that meet, measured in

s	z	ʃ	ʒ	h	m	n	ŋ	l	r	j	w
so	zoo	she	vision	how	man	no	sing	leg	red	yes	wet

angles

a right angle | an angle of 40°

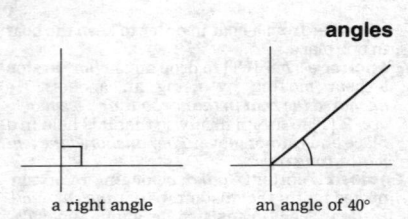

degrees: *a right angle* (= an angle of 90°) o *at an angle of 40°* o *The three angles of a triangle add up to 180°.* **2** the direction from which you look at sth: *Viewed from this angle, the building looks bigger than it really is.* o *If we look at the problem from another angle, it might be easier to solve it.*

(IDIOM) **at an angle** not straight: *This hat is meant to be worn at an angle.*

angle *verb* [T] **angle sth (at/to/towards sb)** to present sth from a particular point of view; to aim sth at a particular person: *The new magazine is angled at young professional people.*

angle² /'æŋgl/ *verb* [I] to try and make sb give you sth, without asking for it directly: *She was angling for a free ticket to the match.*

angler /'æŋglə(r)/ *noun* [C] a person who catches fish as a hobby

angling *noun* [U] the sport of fishing as a hobby: *He goes angling at weekends.*

Anglican /'æŋglɪkən/ *noun* [C] a member of the Church of England, or of a related church in another English-speaking country

Anglo- /æŋgləʊ/ (in compounds) English or British; connected with England or Britain (and another country or countries): *Anglo-American relations*

☆**angry** /'æŋgri/ *adj* (**angrier; angriest**) **angry (with sb) (at/about sth)** feeling or showing anger: *Calm down, there's no need to get angry.* o *My parents will be angry with me if I get home late.* o *I'm very angry with them for letting me down at the last moment.* o *He's always getting angry about something.* —**angrily** /-əli/ *adv*

anguish /'æŋgwɪʃ/ *noun* [U] great pain or suffering, especially of a mental kind: *The newspaper told of the mother's anguish at the death of her son.* —**anguished** *adj*: *There was an anguished expression in his eyes.*

angular /'æŋgjʊlə(r)/ *adj* with sharp points or corners: *an angular face* (= one where you can see the bones clearly)

☆**animal** /'ænɪml/ *noun* [C] **1** a living creature that is not a plant: *the animal kingdom* o *Man is a social animal.* **2** a living creature of this kind, but not including humans: *She thinks that zoos are cruel to animals.* o *They keep cows, chickens and other animals on their farm.* **3** a living creature that is not a human, bird, fish, insect or reptile: *He studied the animals and birds of Southern Africa.* o *Domestic animals such as cats and dogs are not very popular in my country.*

animated /'ænɪmeɪtɪd/ *adj* **1** lively and interesting: *an animated discussion* **2** (used about films) using a technique by which drawings appear to move: *an animated cartoon*

animation /,ænɪ'meɪʃn/ *noun* [U] **1** the state of being lively: *She spoke with great animation on the subject.* **2** the technique of making films, videos and computer games with drawings that appear to move

☆**ankle** /'æŋkl/ *noun* [C] the part of the body where the foot joins the leg: *The water only came up to my ankles.* o *I tripped and sprained my ankle.* ☞ picture on page A8.

annex /ə'neks/ *verb* [T] to take possession and control of another country or region: *Many people feel that the dictator plans to annex the two neighbouring countries.* —**annexation** /,ænek'seɪʃn/ *noun* [C,U]: *the annexation of Austria*

annexe (*especially US* **annex**) /'æneks/ *noun* [C] a building that is joined to or near a larger one

annihilate /ə'naɪəleɪt/ *verb* [T] to destroy or defeat sb/sth completely: *The army was annihilated in the battle.* o *They weren't just beaten in the match, they were annihilated.* —**annihilation** /ə,naɪə'leɪʃn/ *noun* [U]: *Modern weapons have placed mankind in danger of annihilation.*

anniversary /,ænɪ'vɜːsəri/ *noun* [C] (*pl* **anniversaries**) a day that is exactly a year or a number of years after a special or important event: *the hundredth anniversary of the country's independence* o *a twenty-fifth wedding anniversary* ☞ Look at **birthday**.

annotated /'ænəteɪtɪd/ *adj* (used about a book, etc) with notes added to it that explain and give extra information about the contents

☆**announce** /ə'naʊns/ *verb* [T] **1** to make sth known publicly, in an official way: *We are pleased to announce the opening of our new department store.* o *The winners will be announced in next week's paper.* o *The champion was defeated and announced his retirement from the sport.* **2** to say sth in a loud voice or in an aggressive way: *She stormed into my office and announced that she was leaving.*

announcement *noun* **1** [sing] an act of telling people about sth: *The announcement of the election results takes place at the Town Hall.* **2** [C] a statement that tells people about sth: *Ladies and gentlemen, may I have your attention. I have an important announcement to make.*

announcer *noun* [C] a person who introduces or gives information about programmes on radio or television

☆**annoy** /ə'nɔɪ/ *verb* [T] to make sb quite angry: *It really annoys me when you act so selfishly.* o *Close the door if the noise is annoying you.*

annoyance /-əns/ *noun* **1** [U] the feeling of being annoyed: *Much to my annoyance, the train had just left when I got to the station.* **2** [C] something that annoys: *Low-flying planes are an annoyance in this area.*

annoyed *adj* angry or fairly angry: *I shall be extremely annoyed if he turns up late again.* o *She's annoyed with herself for making such a stupid mistake.* o *He's annoyed that nobody*

iː	ɪ	e	æ	ɑː	ɒ	ɔː	ʊ	uː	ʌ
see	sit	ten	hat	arm	got	saw	put	too	cup

believes him. ○ I was annoyed to see that they had left the door open.

annoying adj making you feel rather angry: Oh, how annoying! I've left my money at home.

☆**annual** /'ænjuəl/ adj **1** happening or done once a year or every year: the company's annual report ○ an annual festival **2** for the period of one year: Her annual income is £20 000. ○ the annual sales figures

annual noun [C] a book or magazine that is published once a year, with the same title but different contents: the 1993 Football Annual —**annually** adv: Payment will be made annually. ○ China produces about 60 tonnes of gold annually.

anonymity /ˌænə'nɪməti/ noun [U] the situation where a person's name is not known

anonymous /ə'nɒnɪməs/ adj **1** (used about a person) with a name that is not known or made public: An anonymous caller told the police that the robbery was going to take place. **2** done, written, given, etc by sb whose name is not known or made public: He received an anonymous letter. —**anonymously** adv

anorak /'ænəræk/ noun [C] a short coat with a hood that protects you from rain, wind and cold

☆**another** /ə'nʌðə(r)/ det, pron **1** one more; an additional thing or person: Would you like another drink? ○ 'Have you finished yet?' 'No, I've still got another three questions to do.' ○ They've got three children already and they're having another. ○ Is this another of your silly jokes? **2** a different thing or person: I'm afraid I can't see you tomorrow, could we arrange another day? ○ She discovered that he was having an affair with another woman. ○ If you've already seen that film, we can go and see another.

(IDIOMS) **one after another/the other** ⇨ ONE¹

one another ⇨ ONE³

☆**answer¹** /'ɑːnsə(r); US 'ænsər/ verb [I,T] **1** to say or write sth back to sb who has asked you sth: I asked her what the matter was but she didn't answer. ○ I've asked you a question, now please answer me. ○ Answer all the questions on the form. ○ When I asked him how much he earned, he answered that it was none of my business. ☛ **Answer** and **reply** are the most common verbs used for speaking or writing in reaction to questions, letters, etc: I asked him a question but he didn't answer. ○ I sent my application but they haven't replied yet. Note that you **answer** a person, a question or a letter (no 'to') but you **reply to** a letter. **Respond** is less common and more formal with this meaning: Applicants must respond within seven days. It is more commonly used with the meaning of 'reacting in a way that is desired': Despite all the doctor's efforts the patient did not respond to treatment. **2** to do sth as a reply: Can you answer the phone for me, please? (= pick up the receiver). ○ I rang their doorbell but nobody answered. ○ He hasn't answered my letter yet (= written a letter back to me).

(PHRASAL VERBS) **answer back** to defend yourself against sth bad that has been written or said about you: It's wrong to write things like that about people who can't answer back.

answer (sb) back to reply rudely to sb

answer for sb/sth 1 to accept responsibility or blame for: Somebody will have to answer for all the damage that has been caused. **2** to speak in support of sb/sth: I can certainly answer for her honesty.

answerable /'ɑːnsərəbl/ **answerable to sb (for sth)** having to explain and give good reasons for your actions to sb; responsible to sb

☆**answer²** /'ɑːnsə(r); US 'ænsər/ noun [C] **answer (to sb/sth) 1** something that you say, write or do as a reply: The answer to your question is that I don't know. ○ They've made me an offer and I have to give them an answer by Friday. ○ I wrote to them two weeks ago and I'm still waiting for an answer. ○ I knocked on the door and waited but there was no answer. **2** a solution to a problem: I didn't have any money so the only answer was to borrow some. **3** something that is written or said, trying to give the correct information asked for in a test or exam: What was the answer to question 4?

(IDIOM) **in answer (to sth)** as a reply (to sth): They sent me some leaflets in answer to my request for information.

answerphone /'ɑːnsəfəʊn; US 'æns-/ noun [C] a machine that answers the telephone and records messages from callers: I rang him and left a message on his answerphone.

ant /ænt/ noun [C] a very small insect that lives in large groups and works very hard: an army of ants ☛ picture at **insect**.

antagonism /æn'tægənɪzəm/ noun [U] **antagonism (towards sb/sth); antagonism (between A and B)** a feeling of hate and of being opposed to sb/sth.

antagonize (also **antagonise**) /æn'tægənaɪz/ verb [T] to make sb angry or to annoy sb: She tends to antagonize people with her outspoken remarks.

Antarctic /æn'tɑːktɪk/ adj connected with the coldest, most southern parts of the world: an Antarctic expedition ☛ Look at **Arctic**.

the Antarctic noun [sing] the most southern part of the world ☛ picture at **earth**.

antelope /'æntɪləʊp/ noun [C] (pl **antelope** or **antelopes**) an animal with horns that has long, thin legs, looks like a deer and can run very fast. It is found especially in Africa.

antenatal /ˌæntɪ'neɪtl/ adj happening or existing before birth: an antenatal clinic (= for pregnant women)

antenna /æn'tenə/ noun [C] **1** (pl **antennae** /-niː/) one of the two long thin parts on the heads of insects and some animals that live in shells. It is used for feeling things with. **2** (pl **antennas**) (US) = AERIAL¹

anthem /'ænθəm/ noun [C] a song, especially one that is sung in church or on special occasions: the national anthem (= the special song of a country)

anthology /æn'θɒlədʒi/ noun [C] (pl **anthologies**) a book that contains pieces of written work or poems, often on the same subject, by different authors: an anthology of love poetry

anthropology /ˌænθrə'pɒlədʒi/ noun [U] the

study of human beings, especially of their origin, development, customs and beliefs

antibiotic /ˌæntɪbaɪˈɒtɪk/ *noun* [C] a medicine which is used for destroying bacteria and curing infections: *The doctor gave me some antibiotics for a chest infection.*

anticipate /ænˈtɪsɪpeɪt/ *verb* [T] to expect sth to happen (and to prepare for it): *to anticipate a problem* ○ *Traffic jams are anticipated on all coastal roads this weekend.* ○ *I anticipate that the situation will get worse.* ○ *We anticipate an increase in sales over the next few months.*

anticipation /ænˌtɪsɪˈpeɪʃn/ *noun* [U] **1** the state of expecting sth to happen (and preparing for it): *The government has reduced tax in anticipation of an early general election.* **2** the state of feeling excited about sth that is going to happen: *They queued outside the cinema in excited anticipation.*

anticlimax /ˌæntɪˈklaɪmæks/ *noun* [C,U] an event, etc that is less exciting than you had expected or than what has already happened: *a mood/feeling of anticlimax* ○ *The ending of the film was a dreadful anticlimax.*

anticlockwise /ˌæntɪˈklɒkwaɪz/ *adv, adj* in the opposite direction to the movement of the hands of a clock: *Turn the lid anticlockwise/in an anticlockwise direction.*

antics /ˈæntɪks/ *noun* [plural] funny, strange or silly ways of behaving: *The children roared with laughter at the clown's antics.*

antidote /ˈæntɪdəʊt/ *noun* [C] **1** a medical substance that is used to prevent a poison or a disease from having an effect: *an antidote to snake-bites* **2** anything that helps you to deal with sth unpleasant: *Many people find music a marvellous antidote to stress.*

antipathy /ænˈtɪpəθi/ *noun* [U] **antipathy (to/towards sb/sth)** (a strong feeling of) dislike: *I experienced a feeling of antipathy towards the speaker.*

antiperspirant /ˌæntɪˈpɜːspərənt/ *noun* [C,U] a liquid, cream, etc that you use to reduce sweating, especially under the arms

antique /ænˈtiːk/ *adj* very old and therefore unusual and valuable: *an antique vase, table, etc* ○ *antique furniture, jewellery, etc*

antique *noun* [C] an old and valuable object, eg a piece of furniture: *He collects antiques.* ○ *an antique shop* (= one that sells antiques) ○ *That vase is an antique.*

antiquity /ænˈtɪkwəti/ *noun* (*pl* **antiquities**) **1** [U] ancient times, especially those of the Egyptians, Greeks and Romans: *myths and legends from antiquity* **2** [C, usually pl] a building, work of art or other object that remains from ancient times: *Greek, Roman, etc antiquities* **3** [U] great age: *priceless objects of great antiquity*

anti-Semitism /ˌæntɪ ˈsemɪtɪzəm/ *noun* [U] prejudice against Jewish people

antiseptic /ˌæntɪˈseptɪk/ *noun* [C,U] a liquid or cream that prevents a cut, etc from becoming infected: *Put an antiseptic/some antiseptic on that scratch.* —**antiseptic** *adj*: *antiseptic cream*

antisocial /ˌæntɪˈsəʊʃl/ *adj* **1** not willing to be with other people; unfriendly: *We don't go out much. I suppose we're rather antisocial.* **2** not considered acceptable by other people or the rest of society: *antisocial behaviour/activities* ○ *Some people regard smoking as antisocial.*

antler /ˈæntlə(r)/ *noun* [C, usually pl] a horn on the head of a male deer: *a pair of antlers* ☛ picture at **deer**.

anus /ˈeɪnəs/ *noun* [C] (*pl* **anuses**) the hole through which solid waste substances leave the body

☆ **anxiety** /æŋˈzaɪəti/ *noun* [C,U] (*pl* **anxieties**) a feeling of worry or fear, especially about the future: *a feeling/a state of anxiety* ○ *There are anxieties over the effects of unemployment.*

☆ **anxious** /ˈæŋkʃəs/ *adj* **1 anxious (about/for sb/sth)** worried and afraid: *I began to get anxious when they still hadn't arrived at 9 o'clock.* ○ *an anxious look, expression, etc* **2** causing worry and fear: *For a few anxious moments we thought we'd missed the train.* **3 anxious to do sth** wanting sth very much; eager for sth: *Police are anxious to find the owner of the white car.* —**anxiously** *adv*

☆ **any** /ˈeni/ *det, pron* **1** (used in negative sentences and in questions, also after *if/whether*) some: *We didn't have any lunch.* ○ *I speak hardly any Spanish.* ○ *I don't know any Canadians.* ○ *He asked if we had any questions.* ○ *I wanted chips but there aren't any.* ○ *I don't like any of his books.* ☛ Look at the note at **some**. **2** (used for saying that it does not matter which thing or person you choose): *Take any book you want.* ○ *Any teacher would say the same.* ○ *Come round any time – I'm usually in.* ○ *I'll take any that you don't want.*

any *adv* (used in negative sentences and questions) at all; to any degree: *I can't run any faster.* ○ *Is your father any better?*

☆ **anybody** /ˈenibɒdi/ (*also* **anyone**) *pron* **1** (usually in questions or negative statements) any person: *I didn't know anybody at the party.* ○ *Is there anybody here who can speak Japanese?* ○ *Would anybody else* (= any other person) *like to come with me?* ☛ The difference between **somebody** and **anybody** is the same as the difference between **some** and **any**. Look at the notes at **some** and **somebody**. **2** any person, it does not matter who: *Anybody* (= all people) *can learn to swim.* ○ *Can anybody come? Or are there special invitations?*

☆ **anyhow** /ˈenihaʊ/ *adv* **1** (*also* **anyway**) (used to add an extra point or reason) in any case: *Spain will be terribly hot in August and anyhow we can't afford a holiday abroad.* **2** (*also* **anyway**) (used when saying or writing sth which contrasts in some way with what has gone before) however: *It's a very difficult exam but anyway you can try.* ○ *I'm afraid I can't come to your party, but thanks anyway.* **3** (*also* **anyway**) (used for correcting sth you have just said and making it more accurate) at least: *Everybody wants to be rich – well, most people anyhow.* **4** (*also* **anyway**) (used after a pause in order to change the subject or go back to a subject being discussed before): *Anyway, that's enough about my problems. How are you?* **5** in a

p	b	t	d	k	g	tʃ	dʒ	f	v	θ	ð
pen	bad	tea	did	cat	got	chin	June	fall	van	thin	then

careless way; with no order: *She threw her clothes on anyhow and dashed out of the door.*

☆ **anyone** /'enɪwʌn/ *pron* = ANYBODY

anyplace (*US*) = ANYWHERE

☆ **anything** /'enɪθɪŋ/ *pron* **1** (usually in questions or negative statements) one thing (of any kind): *The fog was so thick that I couldn't see anything at all.* ○ *There isn't anything interesting in the newspaper today.* ○ *Did you buy anything?* ○ *'I'd like a pound of apples please.' 'Anything else?'* (= any other thing?) ☛ The difference between **something** and **anything** is the same as the difference between **some** and **any**. Look at the note at **some**. **2** any thing or things: it does not matter what: *I'm starving. I'll eat anything.* ○ *I'll do anything you say.*
(IDIOMS) **anything like sb/sth** at all similar to sb/sth; nearly: *She isn't anything like her sister, is she?* ○ *This car isn't anything like as fast as mine.*

like anything ⇨ LIKE²

not come to anything ⇨ COME

☆ **anyway** /'enɪweɪ/ *adv* = ANYHOW

☆ **anywhere** /'enɪweə(r)/; *US* -hweər/ (*US* **anyplace**) *adv* **1** (usually in questions or negative statements) in, at or to any place: *I can't find my keys anywhere.* ○ *Is there a post-office anywhere near here?* ○ *You can't buy the book anywhere else* (= in another place). ○ *If we want to go anywhere in August we'd better book it now.* ☛ The difference between **somewhere** and **anywhere** is the same as the difference between **some** and **any**. Look at the note at **some**. **2** any place; it does not matter where: *'Where shall we go to eat?' 'Oh, anywhere will do.'*

☆ **apart** /ə'pɑːt/ *adv* **1** away from sb/sth or each other; not together: *The doors slowly slid apart.* ○ *They always quarrel so it's best to keep them apart.* **2** away from each other by the distance mentioned: *Plant the potatoes two feet apart.* ○ *I'm afraid our ideas are too far apart.* **3** into pieces: *to fall apart* ○ *The material was so old that it just fell/came apart in my hands.* ○ *Their relationship was clearly falling apart* (= about to end).
(IDIOMS) **take sth apart** to separate sth into pieces: *He took the whole bicycle apart.*

tell A and B apart to see the difference between A and B: *It's very difficult to tell the twins apart.*

a'part from (*especially US* **aside from**) *prep* **1** except for: *I've finished my homework apart from some reading we have to do.* ○ *There's nobody here apart from me.* **2** as well as; in addition to: *Apart from their house in the country they've got a flat in London.* **3** (used to add an extra point or anyway) in addition; anyway: *You've got to help me. Apart from anything else you're my brother.*

apartheid /ə'pɑːtheɪt; *US* -heɪt/ *noun* [U] the former official government policy in South Africa of separating people of different races and making them live apart

apartment /ə'pɑːtmənt/ *noun* [C] **1** (*especially US*) = FLAT¹ **2** (usually pl) one of a number of rooms in a large house, used by an important person: *the Duke's private apartments*

apathy /'æpəθi/ *noun* [U] a lack of interest in things or of a desire to do anything

apathetic /ˌæpə'θetɪk/ *adj* lacking interest or a desire to act: *Don't be so apathetic!*

ape /eɪp/ *noun* [C] a type of animal like a large monkey with no tail or only a very short tail: *Chimpanzees and gorillas are apes.*

ape *verb* [T] to copy sb/sth

aperitif /ə'perətɪf; *US* əˌperə'tiːf/ *noun* [C] a drink of alcohol that you have before a meal

apiece /ə'piːs/ *adv* each: *He gave the children £1 apiece.*

apologetic /əˌpɒlə'dʒetɪk/ *adj* feeling or showing that you are sorry for sth you have done: *He was most apologetic about his son's bad behaviour.* ○ *I wrote him an apologetic letter.* —**apologetically** /-klɪ/ *adv*

☆ **apologize** (*also* **apologise**) /ə'pɒlədʒaɪz/ *verb* [I] **apologize (to sb) (for sth)** to say that you are sorry for sth you have done: *I do apologize for taking so long to reply to your letter.* ○ *You'll have to apologize to your teacher for forgetting to do your homework.*

☛ When you apologize, the actual words you use are usually **'I'm sorry'**.

☆ **apology** /ə'pɒlədʒi/ *noun* [C,U] (*pl* **apologies**) **apology (to sb) (for sth)** a spoken or written statement that you are sorry for sth you have done, etc: *Please accept our apologies for the problems you experienced during your stay in the hotel.* ○ *He was full of apology for having missed my birthday.*

apostle /ə'pɒsl/ *noun* [C] one of the twelve men chosen by Christ to spread his teaching

apostrophe /ə'pɒstrəfi/ *noun* [C] **1** the sign (') used for showing that you have left a letter or number out of a word (as in 'I'm', 'can't', 'we'll', etc) **2** the sign (') used for showing who or what sth belongs or relates to as in 'John's chair', 'the boy's room' or 'the book's title'.

appal (*US* **appall**) /ə'pɔːl/ *verb* [T] (**appalling**; **appalled**) (usually passive) to shock sb deeply: *We were appalled by the poverty and starvation we saw everywhere.*

appalling *adj* shocking or terrible: *appalling cruelty* ○ *The food is appalling.* —**appallingly** *adv*

☆ **apparatus** /ˌæpə'reɪtəs; *US* -'rætəs/ *noun* [U] a set of tools, instruments or equipment used for doing a job or an activity: *the scientific apparatus necessary for carrying out experiments*

☆ **apparent** /ə'pærənt/ *adj* **1** (only *before* a noun) perhaps not true or real although seeming to be so: *His apparent interest in the proposal didn't last very long.* **2 apparent to sb** clear; easy to see: *It was apparent to everyone that the man could not be trusted.* ○ *For no apparent reason she suddenly burst into tears.*

apparently *adv* **1** according to what people say (but perhaps not true): *Apparently, he's already been married twice.* **2** according to how sth seems or appears (but perhaps not true): *He was apparently undisturbed by the news.*

☆ **appeal** /ə'piːl/ *verb* [I] **1 appeal to sb (for sth); appeal for sth** to make a serious request for sth you need or want very much: *Relief workers in the disaster area are appealing for*

s	z	ʃ	ʒ	h	m	n	ŋ	l	r	j	w
so	zoo	she	vision	how	man	no	sing	leg	red	yes	wet

more help and supplies. ○ She appeared on television to appeal to the men for her child's safe return. **2 appeal (to sb)** to be attractive or interesting (to sb): *The idea of living in the country doesn't appeal to me at all.* **3 appeal to sth** to influence sb's feelings or thoughts so that he/she will do sth you want: *to appeal to sb's honour, sense of justice, etc* ○ *We aim to appeal to people's generosity.* **4 appeal (to sb) (for/against sth)** to ask sb in authority to change a decision: *He decided to appeal against his conviction.* ○ *The team decided to appeal against the referee's decision.*

appeal *noun* **1** [C] a serious request for sth you need or want very much: *The police have made an urgent appeal for witnesses to come forward.* ○ *a television, radio, etc appeal* (= a television or radio programme asking for help or money for a particular cause) **2** [C] **appeal to sth** a written or spoken statement that tries to influence sb's feelings or thoughts so that he/she will do what you want: *a powerful appeal to our sense of loyalty* **3** [C] a formal request to sb in authority to change a decision: *The judge turned down the defendant's appeal.* **4** [U] attraction or interest: *I can't understand the appeal of stamp collecting.*

appealing *adj* **1** attractive or interesting: *The idea of a Greek holiday sounds very appealing!* **2** showing that you need help, etc: *an appealing glance in my direction* —**appealingly** *adv*

☆ **appear** /əˈpɪə(r)/ *verb* [I] **1** to be seen; to come into sight: *The bus appeared round the corner.* **2** to begin to exist: *The disease is thought to have appeared in Africa.* **3** to be published or printed: *The article appeared in the 'Daily Mail' on Friday.* **4** to present yourself in public to speak, perform, act, etc: *to appear on television* ○ *I've been asked to appear in court.* ○ *She is currently appearing in 'Macbeth'.* **5** to seem: *She appears to be very happy in her job.* ○ *It appears that you were given the wrong information.* ○ *'Do you think there will be an election?' 'It appears so/not.'* ☞ The adjective is **apparent**.

☆ **appearance** /əˈpɪərəns/ *noun* **1** [sing] the arrival of sb/sth: *I was surprised by her unexpected appearance at the party.* **2** [sing] the beginning (of sth never seen or used before): *the appearance of television in the home in the 1950s* **3** [C] an act of appearing in public, especially on stage, television, etc: *His last appearance before his death was as 'Julius Caesar'.* **4** [U] the way that sb/sth looks: *A different hairstyle can completely change your appearance.* ○ *He gives the appearance of being extremely confident.*

appendicitis /əˌpendɪˈsaɪtɪs/ *noun* [U] an illness in which your appendix becomes extremely painful and usually has to be removed

appendix /əˈpendɪks/ *noun* [C] **1** (*pl* **appendixes**) a small tube inside your body which is attached to the intestine **2** (*pl* **appendices** /-dɪsiːz/) a section at the end of a book, etc that gives extra information

appetite /ˈæpɪtaɪt/ *noun* **1** [C,U] the desire for food: *a good/healthy appetite* ○ *My two teenage sons have enormous appetites!* ○ *Some fresh air and exercise should give you an appetite* (= make you hungry). **2** [C,U] a natural desire: *sexual appetites*
(IDIOM) **whet sb's appetite** ⇨ WHET

appetizing (*also* **appetising**) /ˈæpɪtaɪzɪŋ/ *adj* (used about food, etc) attractive and tempting: *an appetizing smell*

applaud /əˈplɔːd/ *verb* **1** [I,T] to clap your hands in order to show that you like sb/sth: *The audience applauded loudly.* ○ *The team was applauded as it left the field.* **2** [T] (usually passive) to praise sb/sth: *The decision was applauded by everybody.*

☆ **applause** /əˈplɔːz/ *noun* [U] the pleasure and approval of a group of people, shown by them clapping their hands: *The performance got terrific applause from the audience.* ○ *The actor was greeted by a round of applause.*

☆ **apple** /ˈæpl/ *noun* [C] a hard, round fruit with a smooth green, red or yellow skin: *cooking/eating apples* ○ *an apple pie*

appliance /əˈplaɪəns/ *noun* [C] a piece of equipment for a particular purpose in the house: *electrical appliances*

applicable /ˈæplɪkəbl; əˈplɪkəbl/ *adj* (not before a noun) **applicable (to sb/sth)** that concerns or relates to: *This part of the form is only applicable to married women.*

☆ **applicant** /ˈæplɪkənt/ *noun* [C] a person who applies for sth, especially a job

☆ **application** /ˌæplɪˈkeɪʃn/ *noun* **1** [C,U] **application (to sb) (for sth)** a formal written request, especially for a job or a place in a school, club, etc: *Applications for the job should be made to the Personnel Manager.* ○ *an application form* (= a special form on which you apply for a job, etc) **2** [C,U] a/the practical use (of sth): *The lecture was about the application of educational theory to the classroom.* **3** [U] hard work; effort

☆ **apply** /əˈplaɪ/ *verb* (*pres part* **applying**; *3rd pers sing pres* **applies**; *pt, pp* **applied**) **1** [I] **apply (to sb) (for sth)** to ask for sth in writing: *I'm going to apply for that job they advertised.* ○ *My daughter's applying for a place at university.* **2** [T] **apply yourself/sth (to sth/to doing sth)** to make yourself concentrate on sth: *to apply your mind to sth* ○ *He applied himself to his studies.* **3** [I] **apply (to sb/sth)** to concern or relate to sb/sth): *This information applies to all children born after 1983.* **4** [T] **apply sth (to sth)** to make practical use of sth: *new technology which can be applied to solving problems in industry* **5** [T] (usually passive) to use a word, a name, etc to refer to sb/sth: *I don't think the word 'antique' can be applied to this old table, do you?* **6** [T] **apply sth (to sth)** to put or spread sth (onto sth): *Apply the cream to the infected area twice a day.*

applied *adj* (used about a subject) having a practical use: *applied mathematics* (eg as used in engineering)

☆ **appoint** /əˈpɔɪnt/ *verb* [T] **1 appoint sb (to sth)** to choose sb for a job, etc: *The committee have appointed a new chairperson.* ○ *He's been appointed (as) Assistant Secretary to the Minis-*

ter of Education. **2 appoint sth (for sth)** (*formal*) to arrange or decide on sth: *the date appointed for the next meeting*

☆ **appointment** /əˈpɔɪntmənt/ *noun* **1** [C,U] **appointment (with sb)** an arrangement to see sb at a particular time: *a doctor's, dentist's, hairdresser's, etc appointment* ○ *I'd like to make an appointment to see the manager.* ○ *I'm afraid I won't be able to keep our appointment on Monday.* ○ *to cancel an appointment* ○ *visits are by appointment only* (= at a time that has been arranged in advance). **2** [C] a job or position of responsibility: *a temporary/permanent appointment* **3** [U] **appointment (to sth)** the act of choosing sb for a job: *Many people criticized the appointment of such a young man to the post.*

appraise /əˈpreɪz/ *verb* [T] to form an opinion about the value or quality of sb/sth

appraisal /əˈpreɪzl/ *noun* [C,U] an opinion about the value or quality of sb/sth; a judgement

appreciable /əˈpriːʃəbl/ *adj* noticeable or important: *There has been an appreciable drop in the rate of inflation.*

☆ **appreciate** /əˈpriːʃieɪt/ *verb* **1** [T] to enjoy sth or to understand the value of sth: *The art of Van Gogh was not appreciated during his own lifetime.* **2** [T] to understand sth (a problem, situation, etc): *I don't think you appreciate how serious this situation is.* **3** [T] to be grateful for sth: *Thanks for your help. We did appreciate it.* **4** [I] to increase in value: *Houses in this area have appreciated faster than elsewhere.*

appreciative /əˈpriːʃətɪv/ *adj* **1** feeling or showing pleasure or admiration: *'You look lovely,' he said, with an appreciative smile.* **2 appreciative (of sth)** grateful for sth: *He was very appreciative of our efforts to help.*

appreciation /əˌpriːʃiˈeɪʃn/ *noun* **1** [U] understanding and enjoyment of the value of sth): *I'm afraid I have little appreciation of modern architecture.* **2** [U] the feeling of being grateful for sth: *We bought him a present to show our appreciation for all the work he had done.* ○ *Please accept these flowers as a token* (= a sign) *of my appreciation.* **3** [U] understanding of what sth involves: *None of us had the slightest appreciation of the seriousness of the situation.* **4** [U] increase in value: *the appreciation of antiques and works of art*

apprehension /ˌæprɪˈhenʃn/ *noun* [C,U] (*formal*) worry or fear about sth in the future: *feelings of apprehension*

apprehensive /ˌæprɪˈhensɪv/ *adj* worried or afraid: *to be/feel apprehensive* ○ *The students were apprehensive about their forthcoming exams.*

apprentice /əˈprentɪs/ *noun* [C] a person who works for sb for low wages, in order to learn an occupation or skill: *an apprentice electrician*

apprenticeship /-tɪʃɪp/ *noun* [C,U] the state or time of being an apprentice

☆ **approach** /əˈprəʊtʃ/ *verb* **1** [I,T] to come near or nearer to sb/sth: *The day of her wedding approached.* ○ *When you approach the village you will see a garage on your left.* ○ *And now as we approach a new century* ... **2** [T] to speak to sb usually in order to ask for sth: *I'm going to approach my bank manager about a loan.* **3** [T] to begin to deal with sth (a problem, a situation, etc): *What is the best way to approach this problem?* **4** [T] to almost reach sth (a certain standard, level, etc): *at a depth approaching 50 feet under water*

approach *noun* **1** [sing] the act of coming nearer (to sb/sth): *The children stopped talking at the teacher's approach.* **2** [C] a discussion about getting sth; a request for sth: *The company has made an approach to us for financial assistance.* **3** [C] a road or path, etc leading to sth: *the approach to the village* **4** [C] a way of dealing with sb/sth: *Parents don't always know what approach to take with teenage children.*

approachable *adj* **1** friendly and easy to talk to: *She's nice but her husband's not very approachable.* ☛ The opposite is **unapproachable**. **2** (not before a noun) able to be reached: *The area was easily approachable by bus.*

☆ **appropriate** /əˈprəʊpriət/ *adj* **appropriate (for/to sth)** suitable or right: *The matter will be dealt with by the appropriate authorities.* ○ *This card is rather appropriate for the occasion, isn't it?* ○ *Please take whatever action you think is appropriate.* ☛ The opposite is **inappropriate**. —**appropriately** *adv*

☆ **approval** /əˈpruːvl/ *noun* [U] feeling, showing or saying that you think sth is good; agreement: *Everybody gave their approval to the proposal.* ○ *I'm afraid I can't sign these papers without my partner's approval.* ○ *She was always anxious to win her mother's approval.*

☆ **approve** /əˈpruːv/ *verb* **1** [I] **approve (of sb/sth)** to be pleased about sth; to like sb/sth: *His father didn't approve of his leaving school at 16.* ○ *Her parents don't approve of her friends.* ☛ The opposite is **disapprove**. **2** [T] to agree to sth or to accept sth as correct: *We need to get an accountant to approve these figures.*

approving *adj* showing support or admiration for sth: *'I agree entirely,' he said with an approving smile.* —**approvingly** *adv*

☆ **approximate** /əˈprɒksɪmət/ *adj* almost correct but not completely accurate: *The approximate time of arrival is 3 o'clock.* ○ *I can only give you an approximate idea of the cost.*

approximately *adv* about: *It's approximately fifty miles from here.*

approximation /əˌprɒksɪˈmeɪʃn/ *noun* [C] a number, answer, etc which is nearly, but not exactly, right

apricot /ˈeɪprɪkɒt/ *noun* [C] a small, round, yellow or orange fruit with soft flesh and a stone inside

☆ **April** /ˈeɪprəl/ *noun* [C,U] (*abbr* Apr) the fourth month of the year, coming before May ☛ For examples of the use of the months in sentences, look at **January**.

,**April 'Fool** *noun* [C] a person who has a joke or trick played on him/her on 1 April

,**April 'Fool's Day** *noun* [sing] 1 April

ɜː	ə	eɪ	əʊ	aɪ	aʊ	ɔɪ	ɪə	eə	ʊə
fur	ago	pay	home	five	now	join	near	hair	pure

☛ On this day it is traditional for people to play tricks on each other, especially by inventing silly stories and trying to persuade other people that they are true. If somebody believes such a story he/she is called an April Fool.

apron /'eɪprən/ noun [C] a piece of clothing that you wear over the front of your usual clothes in order to keep them clean, especially when cooking ☛ picture at **overall**.

apt /æpt/ adj **1** suitable: *a very apt reply* **2 apt to do sth** having a tendency to do sth; likely: *You'd better remind me. I'm rather apt to forget.*
aptly adv suitably: *The house was aptly named 'Sea View'* (= because it had a view of the sea).

aptitude /'æptɪtjuːd; US -tuːd/ noun [C,U] **aptitude (for sth/for doing sth)** (a) natural ability: *She has an aptitude for learning languages.* ○ *He's shown no aptitude for music.*

aquarium /ə'kweəriəm/ noun [C] (pl **aquariums** or **aquaria** /-rɪə/) **1** a glass container filled with water, in which fish and water animals are kept **2** a building, often in a zoo, where fish and water animals are kept

Aquarius /ə'kweərɪəs/ noun [C,U] the eleventh sign of the zodiac, the Water-carrier; a person who was born under this sign ☛ picture at **zodiac**.

aquatic /ə'kwætɪk/ adj **1** (used about an animal or a plant) living in water **2** (used about a sport) performed on or in water

☆**Arab** /'ærəb/ noun [C] a member of a people who lived originally in Arabia and who now live in many parts of the Middle East and North Africa —**Arab** adj: *Arab countries*

Arabic /'ærəbɪk/ noun [sing] **1** the language that is spoken by Arab people **2** the religious language of Islam

arable /'ærəbl/ adj (in farming) connected with growing crops for sale, not keeping animals

arbitrary /'ɑːbɪtrəri; US 'ɑːrbɪtreri/ adj not based on any principle or reason; not thinking about the wishes of the other people involved: *The choice he made seemed completely arbitrary. I couldn't see any reason for it, anyway.* —**arbitrarily** adv

arbitrate /'ɑːbɪtreɪt/ verb [I,T] to settle an argument between two people or groups by finding a solution that both can accept

arbitration /ˌɑːbɪ'treɪʃn/ noun [U] the process of settling an argument between two people or groups by a third person (who has been chosen by them): *The union and the management decided to go to arbitration.*

arc /ɑːk/ noun [C] a curved line, part of a circle

arcade /ɑː'keɪd/ noun [C] a large covered passage or area with shops along one or both sides; a passage with arches: *a shopping arcade*

arch /ɑːtʃ/ noun [C] **1** a structure made with two columns joined over the top in a curve. An arch may support a bridge or the roof of a large building or it may be above a door or a window. ☛ Look at **archway**. **2** a monument in the shape of an arch: *Marble Arch in London* **3** the middle part of the inside of your foot

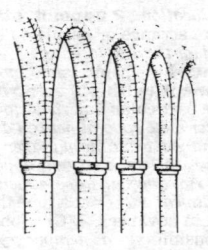

arch

arch verb [I,T] to make a curve: *The cat arched its back and hissed.*

archaeology (*especially US* **archeology**) /ˌɑːki'ɒlədʒi/ noun [U] the study of ancient civilizations, based on objects or parts of buildings that are found in the ground
archaeological (*especially US* **archeological**) adj connected with archaeology
archaeologist (*especially US* **archeologist**) noun [C] an expert in archaeology

archaic /ɑː'keɪɪk/ adj old-fashioned; no longer in common use

archbishop /ˌɑːtʃ'bɪʃəp/ noun [C] a priest in some branches of the Christian church who is in charge of all the bishops, priests and churches in a large area of a country: *the Archbishop of Canterbury*

archer /'ɑːtʃə(r)/ noun [C] a person who shoots with a bow and arrow

archery noun [U] the sport of shooting with a bow and arrow

☆**architect** /'ɑːkɪtekt/ noun [C] a person whose job is to design buildings

architecture /'ɑːkɪtektʃə(r)/ noun [U] **1** the study of how buildings are planned and constructed **2** the style or design of a building or buildings: *the architecture of the fifteenth century* ○ *modern architecture*
architectural /ˌɑːkɪ'tektʃərəl/ adj connected with the design of buildings

archives /'ɑːkaɪvz/ noun [plural] (*also* **archive** /'ɑːkaɪv/ noun [C]) a collection of historical documents, etc which record the history of a place or an organization; the place where they are kept: *In the city archives they found letters dating from the Middle Ages.* ○ *archive material on the First World War*

archway /'ɑːtʃweɪ/ noun [C] a passage or entrance with an arch over it

Arctic /'ɑːktɪk/ adj **1** connected with the region round the North Pole (the most northern point of the world) **2 arctic** very cold: *The mountaineers faced arctic conditions near the top of the mountain.*
the Arctic noun [sing] the area round the North Pole ☛ picture at **earth**.
the Arctic 'Circle noun [sing] the line of latitude 66° 30'N ☛ Look at **Antarctic**.

ardent /'ɑːdnt/ adj showing strong feelings, especially a strong liking for sb/sth: *He was an ardent supporter of the Government.* —**ardently** adv

arduous /'ɑːdjuəs; US -dʒu-/ adj full of

p	b	t	d	k	g	tʃ	dʒ	f	v	θ	ð
pen	bad	tea	did	cat	got	chin	June	fall	van	thin	then

difficulties; needing a lot of effort: *an arduous journey*

are, aren't ⇨ BE

☆ **area** /'eərɪə/ *noun* **1** [C] a part of a town, a country or the world: *Housing is very expensive in the London area.* ○ *The wettest areas are in the West of the country.* ○ *Do not sound your horn in a built-up area* (= where there are buildings). ○ *The high winds scattered litter over a wide area.* ☛ Look at the note at **district**. **2** [C,U] the size of a surface, that you can calculate by multiplying the length by the width: *The area of the office is 35 square metres.* ○ *The office is 35 square metres in area.* **3** [C] a space used for a particular activity: *The restaurant has a non-smoking area.* ○ *the penalty area* (= the space in front of the goal, in football) **4** [C] a particular part of a subject or activity: *Training is one area of the business that we could improve.*

arena /ə'ri:nə/ *noun* [C] **1** an area with seats around it where public entertainments (sporting events, concerts, etc) are held **2** where a particular activity happens: *The Foreign Secretary was well-respected in the international political arena.*

arguable /'ɑ:gjuəbl/ *adj* **1** that can be argued; probably true: *It is arguable that no one should have to pay for hospital treatment.* **2** not certain; that you do not accept without question: *Whether it is a good idea to invest so much money is highly arguable.*

arguably *adv* probably; you can argue that: *'King Lear' is arguably Shakespeare's best play.*

☆ **argue** /'ɑ:gju:/ *verb* **1** [I] **argue (with sb) (about/over sth)** to say things (often angrily) that show that you do not agree with sb about sth: *The couple next door are always arguing.* ○ *I never argue with my husband about money.* **2** [I,T] **argue that; argue (for/against sth)** to give reasons that support your opinion about sth: *John argued that buying a new computer was a waste of money.* ○ *He argued against buying a new computer.*

☆ **argument** /'ɑ:gjumənt/ *noun* **1** [C,U] **argument (with sb) (about/over sth)** an angry discussion between two or more people who disagree with each other: *Sue had an argument with her father about politics.* ○ *He accepted the decision without argument.* ☛ A **quarrel** is usually about something less serious. **2** [C] the reason(s) that you give to support your opinion about sth: *His argument was that if they bought a smaller car, they would save money.*

argumentative /ˌɑ:gju'mentətɪv/ *adj* often involved in or enjoying arguments

arid /'ærɪd/ *adj* (used about land or climate) very dry; with little or no rain

Aries /'eəri:z/ *noun* [C,U] the first sign of the zodiac, the Ram; a person who was born under this sign ☛ picture at **zodiac**.

☆ **arise** /ə'raɪz/ *verb* (*pt* **arose** /ə'rəʊz/; *pp* **arisen** /ə'rɪzn/) to begin to exist; to appear: *If any problems arise, let me know.*

aristocracy /ˌærɪ'stɒkrəsɪ/ *noun* [C, with sing or pl verb] (*pl* **aristocracies**) the people of the highest social class who often have special titles

aristocrat /'ærɪstəkræt/; *US* ə'rɪst-/ *noun* [C] a member of the highest social class, often with a special title —**aristocratic** *adj*

☆ **arithmetic** /ə'rɪθmətɪk/ *noun* [U] the branch of mathematics which involves counting with numbers (adding, subtracting, multiplying and dividing).

☆ **arm¹** /ɑ:m/ *noun* [C] **1** the limb at each side of the human body from the shoulder to the hand: *He was carrying a newspaper under his arm.* ○ *They waved their arms in the air and shouted at us.* ○ *I put my arm round her and tried to comfort her.* **2** the part of a piece of clothing that covers your arm; a sleeve: *He had a hole in the arm of his jumper.* **3** something shaped like an arm: *the arm of a chair* (= where you rest your arm)

arm in arm   arms crossed/folded

(IDIOMS) **arm in arm** with your arm linked together with sb else's arm: *The two friends walked arm in arm.*

cross/fold your arms to cross your arms in front of your chest: *She folded her arms and waited.* ○ *James was sitting with his arms crossed.*

twist sb's arm ⇨ TWIST¹

with open arms ⇨ OPEN¹

'arm-band *noun* [C] **1** a piece of material that you wear around your sleeve: *People often used to wear black arm-bands at funerals.* **2** a plastic ring filled with air which you can wear on your arms when you are learning to swim

'armful /'ɑ:mfʊl/ *noun* [C] the amount that you can carry in your arms

'armhole [C] the opening in a piece of clothing where your arm goes through

'armpit [C] the part of the body under the arm at the point where it joins the shoulder ☛ picture on page A8.

arm² /ɑ:m/ *verb* [I,T] to prepare sb/yourself to fight by supplying weapons: *The country is beginning to arm itself for war.* ☛ Look at **armed** and **arms**.

armaments /'ɑ:məmənts/ *noun* [plural] weapons and military equipment

armchair /'ɑ:mtʃeə(r)/ *noun* [C] a soft comfortable chair with sides which support your arms

☆ **armed** /ɑ:md/ *adj* carrying a gun or other weapon; involving weapons: *All the terrorists were armed.* ○ *armed robbery* ○ *the armed forces* (= the army, navy and air force) ○ (*figurative*) *They came to the meeting armed with all the latest information.*

armistice /'ɑ:mɪstɪs/ *noun* [C] an agreement

s	z	ʃ	ʒ	h	m	n	ŋ	l	r	j	w
so	zoo	she	vision	how	man	no	sing	leg	red	yes	wet

armour (*US* **armor**) /ˈɑːmə(r)/ *noun* [U] clothing, often made of metal, that soldiers wore in earlier times to protect themselves: *a suit of armour*

armoured (*US* **armored**) *adj* (used about a vehicle) covered with metal to protect it in an attack

☆ **arms** /ɑːmz/ *noun* [plural] **1** weapons, especially those that are used in war: *a reduction in nuclear arms* **2** = COAT OF ARMS
(IDIOM) **be up in arms** very angry; protesting about sth: *The workers were up in arms over the news that the factory was going to close.*

☆ **army** /ˈɑːmi/ *noun* [C, with sing or pl verb] (*pl* **armies**) the military forces of a country which are trained to fight on land; a large group of soldiers: *the British Army* ○ *She joined the army at the age of eighteen.* ○ *He's a sergeant in the army.* ○ *an army officer* ☛ Look at **air force** and **navy**.

aroma /əˈrəʊmə/ *noun* [C] a smell (usually one that is pleasant)

arose *pt* of ARISE

☆ **around¹** /əˈraʊnd/ *adv* **1** (*also* **about**) in or to various places or directions: *We walked around for hours looking for a café.* ○ *I don't want to buy anything – I'm just looking around.* ○ *This is our office – David will show you around* (= show you the different parts of it). **2** moving so as to face in the opposite direction: *Turn around and go back the way you came.* **3** on all sides; forming a circle: *The garden is very nice with a wall all around.* ○ *Gather around so that you can all see.* ☛ In senses 1, 2 and 3 **round** can be used instead of **around**. **4** (*also* **about**) present or available: *I went to the house but there was nobody around.* ○ *That isn't a new book. It's been around for ages.* **5** (*also* **about**) (used for activities with no real purpose): *'What are you doing?' 'Nothing, just lazing around.'* ○ *John likes messing around with cars.* ○ *I found this pen lying around on the floor.*

☆ **around²** /əˈraʊnd/ *prep* **1** in various directions inside an area; in different places in a particular area: *They wandered around the town, looking at the shops.* **2** in a circle or following a curving path: *We sat down around the table.* ○ *The athlete ran around the track ten times.* ○ *Go around the corner and it's the first house on the left.* ○ *She had a bandage around her leg.* ○ (*figurative*) *There doesn't seem to be any way around the problem.* **3** near a place: *Is there a bank around here?* ☛ In senses 1, 2 and 3 **round** can also be used. **4** (*also* **about**) (at) approximately: *It's around three hours' drive from here.* ○ *I'll see you around seven* (= at about 7 o'clock).

arouse /əˈraʊz/ *verb* [T] to cause a particular reaction in people: *His actions have aroused a lot of criticism.* —**arousal** *noun* [U]

☆ **arrange** /əˈreɪndʒ/ *verb* [T] **1** to put sth in order or in a particular pattern: *The books were arranged in alphabetical order.* ○ *Arrange the chairs in a circle.* ○ *She arranged the flowers in a vase.* **2** to make plans and preparations so that sth can happen in the future: *Isobel's parents arranged a big party for her eighteenth birthday.* ○ *He arranged for Peter to stay with friends in France.* ○ *She arranged to meet Stuart after work.*

☆ **arrangement** /əˈreɪndʒmənt/ *noun* **1** [C, usually pl] plans or preparations for sth that will happen in the future: *We're just making the final arrangements for the concert.* **2** [C,U] something that you have agreed or settled with sb else; the act of doing this: *They made an arrangement to share the cost of the food.* ○ *Under the new arrangement it will be possible to pay monthly instead of weekly.* ○ *Use of the swimming-pool will be by special arrangement only.* **3** [C] a group of things that have been placed in a particular pattern: *a flower arrangement*

array /əˈreɪ/ *noun* [C] a large collection of things, especially one that is impressive and is seen by other people: *There was a colourful array of vegetables on the market stall.*

arrears /əˈrɪəz/ *noun* [plural] money that should have been paid by an earlier date or that is owed for work which has been done: *I'm in arrears with the rent* (= I owe some money). ○ *You will be paid monthly in arrears* (= at the end of month for the work done during the month).

☆ **arrest** /əˈrest/ *verb* [T] when the police arrest sb they take him/her prisoner in order to question him/her about a crime

arrest *noun* [C] the act of arresting sb: *The police made ten arrests after the riot.*
(IDIOM) **be under arrest**: *He was under arrest for murder.*

☆ **arrival** /əˈraɪvl/ *noun* **1** [U] the act of reaching the place to which you were travelling: *On our arrival we were told that our rooms had not been reserved.* ○ *British Rail apologizes for the late arrival of this train.* **2** [C] people or things that have arrived: *We brought in extra chairs for the late arrivals.* ○ *I'll look on the arrivals board to see when the train gets in.*

☆ **arrive** /əˈraɪv/ *verb* [I] **1** to reach the place to which you were travelling: *We arrived home at about midnight.* ○ *What time does the train arrive in Newcastle?* ○ *They arrived at the station ten minutes late.* ○ *Has my letter arrived yet?* **2** to come or happen: *The day of the wedding had finally arrived.* ○ *Paula's baby arrived* (= was born) *two weeks late.*
(PHRASAL VERB) **arrive at** to reach sth: *After months of discussions they finally arrived at a decision.*

arrogant /ˈærəgənt/ *adj* thinking that you are better and more important than other people and not caring about their feelings; proud —**arrogance** /ˈærəgəns/ *noun* [U] —**arrogantly** *adv*

arrow /ˈærəʊ/ *noun* [C] **1** a thin piece of wood or metal, with one pointed end and feathers at the other end, that is shot from a bow: *The Indians fired on the cowboys with bows and arrows.* **2** the sign (→) which is used to show direction: *The arrow is pointing left.*

arsenic /ˈɑːsnɪk/ *noun* [U] a type of very strong poison

arson /ˈɑːsn/ *noun* [U] the crime of setting fire to a building on purpose

iː	ɪ	e	æ	ɑː	ɒ	ɔː	ʊ	uː	ʌ
see	sit	ten	hat	arm	got	saw	put	too	cup

☆ **art** /ɑːt/ noun **1** [U] the producing of beautiful things such as paintings, drawings, etc; the objects that are produced: *an art class* o *She studied History of Art at university.* o *the art of the Italian Renaissance* o *modern art* o *an art gallery* ☛ Look at **work of art**. **2** [U] a skill or sth that requires skill: *There's an art to writing a good letter.* **3 the arts** [plural] activities such as painting, writing literature or writing and performing music: *The government has agreed to spend £2 million extra on the arts next year.* **4 arts** [plural] subjects such as history or languages that you study at school or university ☛ We usually contrast **arts** (or **arts subjects**) with **sciences** (or **science subjects**).

artery /'ɑːtəri/ noun [C] (pl **arteries**) one of the tubes which take blood from the heart to other parts of the body ☛ Look at **vein**.

artful /'ɑːtfl/ adj clever at getting what you want, perhaps by deceiving people

arthritis /ɑː'θraɪtɪs/ noun [U] a disease which causes swelling and pain in the joints of your body (where you bend your arms, fingers, etc)

artichoke /'ɑːtɪtʃəʊk/ (also **globe 'artichoke**) noun [C] a plant whose flower looks like pointed leaves. The bottoms of the leaves and the centre of the flower can be eaten as a vegetable.

☆ **article** /'ɑːtɪkl/ noun [C] **1** a thing or object, especially one of a set: *Articles of clothing were lying all over the room.* **2** a piece of writing in a newspaper or magazine: *There's an article about cycling holidays in today's paper.* **3** (grammar) the words 'a/an' (the indefinite article) or 'the' (the definite article).

articulate¹ /ɑː'tɪkjʊlət/ adj good at expressing your ideas clearly

articulate² /ɑː'tɪkjʊleɪt/ verb [I,T] to say sth clearly or to express your ideas or feelings

articulated /ɑː'tɪkjʊleɪtɪd/ adj (used about a vehicle such as a lorry) made of two sections which are connected in a special way so that the lorry can turn corners easily

☆ **artificial** /ˌɑːtɪ'fɪʃl/ adj not genuine or natural but made by people to seem like something natural: *artificial flowers* o *an artificial lake* —**artificially** adv: *This drug cannot be produced artificially.*

ˌartificial insemi'nation noun [U] a scientific technique to introduce male seed into a female, so that babies or young can be produced without sex

ˌartificial in'telligence noun [U] (the study of) the way in which computers can be made to imitate human thought

artillery /ɑː'tɪləri/ noun [U] a number of large guns on wheels; the part of the army which uses them

☆ **artist** /'ɑːtɪst/ noun [C] somebody who produces art, especially paintings or drawings: *I like that picture – who is the artist?* o *an exhibition of paintings by the English artist, Constable*

artistic /ɑː'tɪstɪk/ adj **1** connected with art: *the artistic director of the theatre* **2** showing a skill in art: *Helen is very artistic – her drawings are excellent.* —**artistically** /-klɪ/ adv: *The garden was laid out very artistically.*

artistry /'ɑːtɪstri/ noun [U] the skill of an artist

☆ **as** /əz; strong form æz/ conj, prep, adv **1** while sth else is happening: *The phone rang just as I was leaving the house.* o *As she walked along the road, she thought about her father.* **2 as... as** (used for comparing people or things): *Tom's almost as tall as me.* o *Tom's almost as tall as I am.* o *It's not as cold as it was yesterday.* o *I'd like an appointment as soon as possible.* **3 as... as** (used with 'much' or 'many' for comparing people or things): *She earns twice as much as her husband.* o *I haven't got as many books as you have.* **4** (used for talking about sb's job): *He works as a train driver for British Rail.* **5** (used for describing sb/sth's role): *Think of me as your friend, not as your boss.* **6** (used for describing sb/sth in an unusual role or function): *I went to the party dressed as a policeman.* o *You could use this white sheet as a tablecloth.* **7** in a particular way, state, etc: *Please do as I tell you.* o *Leave the room as it is. Don't move anything.* **8** (used at the beginning of a comment about what you are saying): *As you know, I've decided to leave at the end of the month.* **9** because: *I didn't buy the dress, as I decided it was too expensive.*

(IDIOMS) **as for**; **as to** (used when you are starting to talk about a different person or thing): *Jane's in Paris at the moment. As for Andrew, I've no idea where he is.*

as if; **as though** (used for saying how sb/sth appears): *She looks as if she's just got out of bed.* o *He behaved as though nothing had happened.*

as it were (used for saying that sth is only true in a certain way): *She felt, as it were, a stranger in her own house.*

as of; **as from** starting from a particular time: *As from next week, Tim Shaw will be managing this department.*

as to about a particular thing: *I was given no instructions as to how to begin.*

asbestos /æs'bestɒs/ noun [U] a soft grey material which does not burn and which is used to protect against heat

ascend /ə'send/ verb [I,T] (formal) to go or come up —**ascending** adj: *The questions are arranged in ascending order of difficulty* (= the most difficult ones are at the end). ☛ Look at **descend**.

Ascension Day /ə'senʃn deɪ/ the day forty days after Easter when Christians remember Christ leaving the earth and going to heaven

ascent /ə'sent/ noun [C] **1** the act of climbing or going up: *Their aim was the ascent of the highest mountains in the Himalayas.* **2** a path or slope leading upwards: *There was a steep ascent before the path became flat again.*

ascertain /ˌæsə'teɪn/ verb [T] (formal) to find out: *It was difficult to ascertain who was telling the truth.*

ascribe /ə'skraɪb/ verb [T] **ascribe sth to sb/sth** to say that sth was written by or belonged to sb, or that sth was caused by sth: *This piece of music was ascribed to Bach, although we now* believe it was written by another composer. ○ He ascribed his forgetfulness to old age.

ash[1] /æʃ/ noun [C] a type of tree that is found in British forests

☆ **ash**[2] /æʃ/ noun **1** [U] (also **ashes** [plural]) the grey or black powder which is left after sth has burned: *cigarette ash* ○ *They found the ring in the ashes of the fire.* **2 ashes** [plural] what remains after a human body has been burned

ashtray noun [C] a small dish for cigarette ash

☆ **ashamed** /əˈʃeɪmd/ adj **ashamed (of sth/sb/yourself); ashamed (that...); ashamed (to...)** (not before a noun) feeling sorry or embarrassed about sb/sth or about yourself or sth you have done: *She was ashamed of her old clothes.* ○ *He was ashamed of himself for having made such an unkind remark.* ○ *How could you be so rude? I'm ashamed of you!* ○ *She felt ashamed that she hadn't visited her aunt more often.* ○ *He knew that it was his fault but he was ashamed to admit his mistake.*

ashore /əˈʃɔː(r)/ adv onto the land: *The passengers went ashore for an hour while the ship was in port.*

☆ **Asian** /ˈeɪʃn; US ˈeɪʒn/ noun [C] a person from Asia or whose family was originally from Asia: *British Asians* —**Asian** adj: *the Asian community in Birmingham*

☆ **aside** /əˈsaɪd/ adv **1** on or to one side; out of the way: *She took Richard aside to tell him her secret.* **2** to be kept separately, for a special purpose: *They are setting aside £50 a month for their summer holiday.*

aside noun [C] something which a character in a play says to the audience, but which the other characters on stage do not hear

aside from prep (especially US) = APART FROM

☆ **ask** /ɑːsk/ verb **1** [I,T] **ask (sb) (about sb/sth)** to put a question to sb in order to find out some information: *We need to ask about the price.* ○ *I'll ask the salesman how much the jacket is.* ○ *Did you ask Sarah about the bike?* ○ *She asked whether I wanted tea or coffee.* ○ *'What's the time?' he asked.* ○ *He asked what the time was.* ○ *He asked me the time.* ○ *She asked the little boy his name.* ○ *I got lost coming here and I had to ask somebody the way.* **2** [I,T] **ask (sb) for sth; ask sth (of sb); ask sb to do sth** to request that sb gives you sth or does sth for you: *She sat down at the table and asked for a cup of coffee.* ○ *Don't ask John for money – he hasn't got any.* ○ *You are asking too much of him – he can't possibly do all that!* ○ *Ring this number and ask for Mrs Smith* (= ask to speak to Mrs Smith). ○ *I asked him if he would drive me home.* ○ *I asked him to drive me home.* **3** [T] to say the price that you want for sth: *They're asking £2 000 for their car.* **4** [I,T] to request permission to do sth: *I'm sure she'll let you go if you ask.* ○ *He asked to use our phone.* ○ *We asked permission to go early.* ○ *We asked if we could go home early.* **5** [T] **ask sb (to sth)** to invite sb: *They asked six friends to dinner.* ○ *He's asked Eileen out on Saturday* (= asked her to go out with him).

(IDIOMS) **ask for trouble/it** to behave in a way that will almost certainly cause trouble: *Not wearing a seat belt is just asking for trouble.*

if you ask me if you want my opinion: *If you ask me, she's too young to travel alone.*

(PHRASAL VERB) **ask after sb** to inquire about sb's health or to ask for news of sb: *I saw Miss Black today. She asked after you.*

askew /əˈskjuː/ adv, adj (not before a noun) not in a straight or level position

☆ **asleep** /əˈsliːp/ adj (not before a noun) not awake; sleeping: *The baby is asleep.* ○ *to be sound/fast asleep* ○ *to fall asleep* ☞ Look at the note at **sleep**[2].

AS level /ˌeɪ ˈesˌlevl/ (also formal **Advanced Supplementary level**) noun [C] an examination that schoolchildren in England, Wales and Northern Ireland take when they are about 18. An AS level is the same standard as an A level but involves only half the amount of work.

asparagus /əˈspærəgəs/ noun [U] a plant with long green stems that you can cook and eat as a vegetable

☆ **aspect** /ˈæspekt/ noun [C] one of the qualities or parts of a situation, idea, problem, etc: *information about many aspects of British life*

asphalt /ˈæsfælt; US -fɔːlt/ noun [U] a thick black substance that is used for making the surface of roads, etc

asphyxiate /əsˈfɪksieɪt/ verb [T] (usually passive) (used about gas, smoke, etc) to cause sb to be unable to breathe: *He was asphyxiated by the smoke while he was asleep.* —**asphyxiation** /əsˌfɪksiˈeɪʃn/ noun [U]

aspiration /ˌæspəˈreɪʃn/ noun [C,U] (often plural) a strong desire to have or do sth: *She has aspirations to become an opera singer.*

aspire /əˈspaɪə(r)/ verb [I] **aspire to sth/to do sth** (formal) to have a strong desire to have or do sth: *She aspired to become managing director.* ○ *an aspiring ballet dancer*

aspirin /ˈæsprɪn; ˈæspərɪn/ noun [C,U] a type of medicine that reduces pain and fever: *I've taken two aspirins* (= two tablets).

ass /æs/ noun [C] **1** = DONKEY **2** (informal) a stupid person

assailant /əˈseɪlənt/ noun [C] a person who attacks sb

assassin /əˈsæsɪn; US -sn/ noun [C] a person who kills a famous or important person for money or for political reasons

assassinate /əˈsæsɪneɪt; US -sən-/ verb [T] to kill a famous or important person for money or for political reasons ☞ Look at the note at **kill**. —**assassination** /əˌsæsɪˈneɪʃn; US əˌsæsəˈneɪʃn/ noun [C,U]: *an assassination attempt*

assault /əˈsɔːlt/ noun [C,U] **assault (on sb/sth)** a sudden attack on sb/sth: *Assaults on the police are becoming more common.* —**assault** verb: [T] *a prison sentence for assaulting a police officer*

assemble /əˈsembl/ verb **1** [I,T] to come together in a group; to gather or collect: *The leaders assembled in Strasbourg for the summit meeting.* ○ *I've assembled all the information I need for my essay.* **2** [T] to fit the parts of sth together: *We spent all day trying to assemble our new bookshelves.*

assembly /əˈsembli/ noun (pl **assemblies**) **1** [C,U] a large group of people who come

p	b	t	d	k	g	tʃ	dʒ	f	v	θ	ð
pen	bad	tea	did	cat	got	chin	June	fall	van	thin	then

together for a particular purpose: *school assembly* (= a regular meeting for all the students and teachers of a school) o *The regional assembly has the power to raise local taxes.* **2** [U] the act of fitting the parts of sth together: *the assembly of cars by robots*

as'sembly line *noun* [C] a line of people and machines in a factory that fit the parts of sth together in a fixed order: *the assembly-line workers at the Toyota car plant*

assent /əˈsent/ *noun* [U] (*formal*) agreement: *The committee gave their assent to the proposed changes.*
▶ **assent** *verb* [I] **assent (to sth)** to say that you agree to sth

assert /əˈsɜːt/ *verb* [T] **1** to say sth clearly and firmly: *He asserted that the allegations were untrue.* **2** to behave in a way that makes other people listen to you and take notice of you: *You ought to assert yourself more.* o *to assert your authority*

assertion /əˈsɜːʃn/ *noun* **1** [U] the act of asserting sth/yourself: *the assertion of power* **2** [C] something that you say firmly and clearly: *his confident assertion that he would win*

assertive /əˈsɜːtɪv/ *adj* expressing your opinion clearly and firmly so that people listen to you and take notice of you: *to speak in an assertive manner* —**assertively** *adv* **assertiveness** *noun* [U]

assess /əˈses/ *verb* [T] **1** to estimate or decide the amount or value of sth: *The value of the house was assessed at £75 000.* o *to assess the cost of repairs* **2** to judge or form an opinion about sth: *It's too early to assess the effects of the price rises.*

assessment *noun* [C,U] the act of judging or forming an opinion about sb/sth: *Students' marks are based on continuous assessment of their work.* o *to make a careful assessment of a situation*

asset /ˈæset/ *noun* [C] **1 an asset (to sb/sth)** a person or thing that is useful to sb/sth: *She's a great asset to the organization.* o *It's an asset to be able to drive.* **2** [usually pl] something of value that a person, company, etc owns: *The company is having to sell its assets.*

assign /əˈsaɪn/ *verb* [T] **1 assign sth to sb** to give sth to sb for him/her to use or do **2 assign sb to sth** to give sb a particular job or type of work to do: *She was assigned to the publicity department.* o *A detective was assigned to the case.*

assignment *noun* [C] a job or type of work that you are given to do: *Kate is on an assignment in Iraq for the BBC.* o *to give pupils an assignment to do during the holidays*

assimilate /əˈsɪməleɪt/ *verb* **1** [I,T] (to allow sb/sth) to become part of a country or social group: *Many immigrants have difficulty in assimilating.* o *to assimilate people from other cultures* **2** [T] to learn and understand sth: *to assimilate new facts/information/ideas* —**assimilation** /əˌsɪməˈleɪʃn/ *noun* [U]

☆ **assist** /əˈsɪst/ *verb* [I,T] **assist (sb) in/with sth; assist (sb) in doing sth** (*formal*) to help: *A man is assisting the police with their inquiries.*

assistance *noun* [U] (*formal*) help: *Can I be of any assistance?* (eg said by a shop assistant) o *financial assistance for poorer families*

assistant *noun* [C] **1** a person who helps sb of higher rank: *The director is away today. Would you like to speak to her assistant?* o *the assistant manager* **2** a person who sells things to people in a shop: *a shop/sales assistant*

associate¹ /əˈsəʊʃiət/ *adj* (only *before* a noun) of a slightly lower rank or status: *associate members of the organization*

associate *noun* [C] a person that you meet and get to know through your work: *a business associate*

☆ **associate**² /əˈsəʊʃieɪt/ *verb* **1** [T] **associate sb/sth (with sb/sth)** to connect sb/sth with sb/sth else (in your mind): *lung cancer and other illnesses associated with smoking* o *Somehow, I don't associate Sweden with skiing.* **2** [I] **associate with sb** to spend time with sb: *I prefer not to associate with colleagues outside work.* **3** [T] **associate yourself with sth** to say that you support sth or agree with sth: *I do not wish to associate myself with any organization that promotes violence.*

association /əˌsəʊsiˈeɪʃn/ *noun* **1** [U] the act of joining or working with another person or group: *We work in association with our New York office.* **2** [C] a group of people or organizations who join or work together for a particular purpose: *a housing association* o *the British Medical Association* o *the Football Association* **3** [C,U] the act of connecting sb/sth to sb/sth else in your mind

assorted /əˈsɔːtɪd/ *adj* of different types; mixed: *a packet of assorted sweets*

assortment /əˈsɔːtmənt/ *noun* [C] a group of different things or of different types of the same thing; a mixture: *You'll find a wide assortment of different gifts in our shop.*

☆ **assume** /əˈsjuːm; *US* əˈsuːm/ *verb* [T] **1** to accept or believe that sth is true even though you have no proof; to expect sth to be true: *I assume that you have the necessary documents.* o *You'll be going to the meeting, I assume?* o *We can assume profits of around 5%.* o *Everyone assumed Ralph was guilty.* o *Everyone assumed Ralph to be guilty.* **2** [T] to falsely pretend to have or be sb/sth: *to assume a false name* **3** [T] to begin to use power or to have a powerful position: *to assume control of sth* o *to assume political power* o *to assume a position of responsibility*

assumption /əˈsʌmpʃn/ *noun* **1** [C] something that you accept is true even though you have no proof: *Our figures are based on the assumption that the rate of inflation will be 5% by the end of the year.* o *a reasonable, false, etc assumption* **2** [U] **assumption of sth** the act of taking power or of starting an important job: *the assumption of power by the army*

assurance /əˈʃɔːrəns; *US* əˈʃʊərəns/ *noun* **1** (*also* **self-assurance**) [U] the belief that you can do or succeed at sth; confidence: *He spoke with assurance* (= confidently). o *the calm assurance that comes from being rich* **2** [C] a

s	z	ʃ	ʒ	h	m	n	ŋ	l	r	j	w
so	zoo	she	vision	how	man	no	sing	leg	red	yes	wet

promise that sth will certainly happen or be true: *They gave me an assurance that the work would be finished by Friday.*

assure /əˈʃɔː(r); US əˈʃʊər/ *verb* [T] **1** to promise sb that sth will certainly happen or be true, especially if he/she is worried: *I assure you that it is perfectly safe.* ○ *Let me assure you of my full support.* **2** to make sth sure or certain: *The survival of the species is assured.*
  assured (*also* **self-assured**) *adj* believing that you can do sth or succeed at sth; confident: *a calm and self-assured young woman*

asterisk /ˈæstərɪsk/ *noun* [C] the sign (*) that you use to call attention to sth in a piece of writing

asthma /ˈæsmə/; US ˈæzmə/ *noun* [U] a medical condition that causes difficulty in breathing
  asthmatic *noun* [C] a person who suffers from asthma

☆ **astonish** /əˈstɒnɪʃ/ *verb* [T] to cause sb to be very surprised: *She astonished everybody by announcing her engagement.* —**astonished** *adj*: *The Prime Minister was said to be astonished by the decision.* —**astonishing** *adj*: *astonishing news* —**astonishingly** *adv*: *an astonishingly high price*

astonishment *noun* [U] very great surprise: *To my absolute astonishment the scheme was a huge success.* ○ *A look of astonishment crossed her face.* ○ *He dropped his book in astonishment.*

astound /əˈstaʊnd/ *verb* [T] (usually passive) to cause sb to be very surprised: *We were astounded at how well he performed.*
  astounding *adj* very surprising: *an astounding success*

astray /əˈstreɪ/ *adv* away from the right way: *The young are easily led astray* (= persuaded to do bad things by other people).
  (IDIOM) **go astray** to become lost: *My new pen seems to have gone astray.*

astride /əˈstraɪd/ *adv, prep* with one leg on each side of sth: *to sit astride a horse*

astrology /əˈstrɒlədʒɪ/ *noun* [U] the study of the positions and movements of the stars and planets and the way that they are supposed to affect people and events ☛ Look at **astronomy** and also at **horoscope** and **zodiac**.
  astrologer /əˈstrɒlədʒə(r)/ *noun* [C] a person who is an expert in astrology

astronaut /ˈæstrənɔːt/ *noun* [C] a person who travels in a spaceship

astronomy /əˈstrɒnəmɪ/ *noun* [U] the scientific study of the sun, moon, stars, etc ☛ Look at **astrology**.
  astronomer /əˈstrɒnəmə(r)/ *noun* [C] a person who studies or is an expert in astronomy
  astronomical /ˌæstrəˈnɒmɪkl/ *adj* **1** connected with astronomy **2** very large, often too large (describing a price, number, amount, etc): *astronomical house prices*

astute /əˈstjuːt; US əˈstuːt/ *adj* very clever

asylum /əˈsaɪləm/ *noun* **1** [U] protection that a government gives to people who have left their own country for political reasons: *The leaders of the coup were given political asylum by the US* (= invited to stay in the US where they would be safe). **2** [C] an old-fashioned word for a hospital for people who are mentally ill

☆ **at** /ət; strong form æt/ *prep* **1** (showing the position of sth or where sth happens): *at the bottom of the page* ○ *at the top of the hill* ○ *He was standing at the door.* ○ *Change trains at Didcot.* ○ *We were at home all weekend.* ○ *Are the children at school?* ○ *at the theatre* ○ *'Where's Peter?' 'He's at Sue's.'* (= at Sue's house) **2** (showing when sth happens): *I start work at 9 o'clock.* ○ *at the weekend* ○ *at night* ○ *at Christmas* ○ *She got married at 18* (= when she was 18). **3** in the direction of sb/sth: *What are you looking at?* ○ *He pointed a gun at the policeman.* ○ *Somebody threw a tomato at the prime minister.* ○ *Don't shout at me!* **4** because of: *I was surprised at her behaviour.* ○ *We laughed at his jokes.* **5** (showing what sb is doing or what is happening): *They were hard at work.* ○ *The two countries were at war.* **6** (showing the price, rate, speed, etc of sth): *What price are you selling at?* ○ *We were travelling at about 50 miles per hour.* **7** (used with adjectives that show how well sb/sth does sth): *She's not very good at French.* ○ *I'm hopeless at hockey.*

ate *pt* of EAT

atheism /ˈeɪθiɪzəm/ *noun* [U] the belief that there is no God

atheist /ˈeɪθiɪst/ *noun* [C] a person who believes that there is no God

athlete /ˈæθliːt/ *noun* [C] a person who can run, jump, etc very well, especially one who takes part in sports competitions, etc

athletic /æθˈletɪk/ *adj* **1** connected with athletes or athletics **2** (used about a person) having a fit, strong, and healthy body

athletics /æθˈletɪks/ *noun* [U] sports such as running, jumping, throwing, etc: *an athletics meeting/track*

atishoo /əˈtɪʃuː/ *interj* (used for expressing the sound that you make when you sneeze)

atlas /ˈætləs/ *noun* [C] (*pl* **atlases**) a book of maps

☆ **atmosphere** /ˈætməsfɪə(r)/ *noun* **1** [C, usually sing] **the atmosphere** the mixture of gases that surrounds the earth or any other star, planet, etc: *the earth's atmosphere* **2** [sing] the air in a place: *a smoky atmosphere* **3** the mood or feeling of a place or situation: *There was a tense atmosphere during the final minutes of the game.*

atmospheric /ˌætməsˈferɪk/ *adj* connected with the atmosphere(1).

☆ **atom** /ˈætəm/ *noun* [C] the smallest part into which an element can be divided: (*figurative*) *She hasn't got an atom of common sense* (= she hasn't got any). ☛ Look at **molecule**.

atomic /əˈtɒmɪk/ *adj* of or concerning an atom or atoms: *atomic physics*
  a,tomic 'bomb (*also* **atom bomb**) *noun* [C] a bomb that explodes using the energy that is produced when an atom or atoms are split
  a,tomic 'energy *noun* [U] the energy that is produced when an atom or atoms are split. Atomic energy can be used to produce electricity.

atrocious /əˈtrəʊʃəs/ *adj* very bad or cruel:

iː	ɪ	e	æ	ɑː	ɒ	ɔː	ʊ	uː	ʌ
see	sit	ten	hat	arm	got	saw	put	too	cup

What atrocious weather! —**atrociously** *adv*: *The children behaved atrociously.*

atrocity /əˈtrɒsəti/ *noun* [C,U] (*pl* **atrocities**) (an act of) great cruelty: *Both sides were guilty of dreadful atrocities during the war.*

☆ **attach** /əˈtætʃ/ *verb* [T] **1 attach sth (to sth)** to fasten or join sth to sth: *A note was attached to the document with a paper-clip.* **2 attach yourself to sb/sth; attach sb to sb/sth** to join another person or group; to make sb do this: *Tom will be attached to the finance department for the next six months.* **3 attach sth to sb/sth** to consider that sth has a particular quality: *Don't attach too much importance to what they say.* ○ *No blame was attached to him.*

(IDIOM) **(with) no strings attached**; **without strings** ⇨ STRING¹

attached *adj* **attached to sb/sth** liking sb/sth very much: *He's become very attached to you.*

attachment *noun* **1** [C] something that can be fitted on sth else: *a bath with a shower attachment* **2** [C,U] **attachment (to/for sb/sth)** the feeling of liking sb/sth very much: *an emotional attachment* ○ *I feel a strong attachment to this house.*

☆ **attack** /əˈtæk/ *noun* **1** [C,U] **an attack (on sb/sth)** an act of trying to hurt or defeat sb/sth by using force: *The rebel forces launched an attack on the capital.* ○ *to be under attack* (= to be attacked by sb/sth) **2** [C,U] **attack (on sb/sth)** an act of saying strongly that you do not like or agree with sb/sth: *an outspoken attack on government policy* **3** [C] a short period when you suffer badly from a disease, medical condition, etc: *an attack of asthma, flu, etc* **4** [C] an act of trying to score a point in a game of sport: *England made several strong attacks but failed to score a goal.* ○ *The home team went on the attack again.*

attack *verb* **1** [I,T] to try to hurt or defeat sb/sth by using force: *The enemy attacked at night.* ○ *to be attacked by a wild animal* **2** [T] to say strongly that you do not like or agree with sb/sth: *The minister attacked the press for misleading the public.* **3** [T] to damage or harm sb/sth: *a virus that attacks the nervous system* **4** [I,T] to try to score a point in a game of sport

attacker *noun* [C] a person who attacks sb/sth

attain /əˈteɪn/ *verb* [T] to succeed in getting or achieving sth, especially after great effort: *to attain a goal*

attainable *adj* that can be attained

attainment *noun* **1** [U] the act of achieving sth: *the attainment of the government's objectives* **2** [C] a skill or achievement: *students with few academic attainments*

☆ **attempt** /əˈtempt/ *verb* [T] to try to do sth that is difficult: *The prisoner was shot while attempting to escape.* ○ *She was accused of attempted murder* (= she didn't succeed). ○ *Don't attempt to argue with him.*

attempt *noun* [C] **1 attempt (to do sth/at doing sth)** an act of trying to do sth: *He managed to hit the target at the first attempt.* ○ *They failed in their attempt to reach the North Pole.* **2 attempt (on sb/sth)** an act of trying to attack or beat sb/sth: *She hopes to make an attempt on the world record in tomorrow's race.* ○ *an attempt on sb's life* (= to kill sb)

☆ **attend** /əˈtend/ *verb* **1** [T] to go to or be present at a place: *Do you attend church regularly?* ○ *I'm afraid I will be unable to attend tonight's meeting.* ○ *The children attend the local school.* **2** [I] **attend to sb/sth** (*formal*) to give your care, thought or attention to sb/sth or look after sb/sth: *Please attend to this matter immediately.*

attendance /əˈtendəns/ *noun* **1** [U] being present somewhere: *Attendance at lectures is not compulsory.* **2** [C,U] the number of people who go to or are present at a place: *There was a large attendance at the meeting.* ○ *Attendance has decreased in recent months.*

attendant /əˈtendənt/ *noun* [C] **1** a person who looks after a public place: *a swimming-pool attendant* **2** a person who looks after an important person: *the Queen's attendants*

attendant *adj* (only *before* a noun) (*formal*) that goes with or results from sth: *unemployment and all its attendant social problems*

☆ **attention** /əˈtenʃn/ *noun* [U] **1** the act of watching, listening to or thinking about sb/sth carefully: *Please pay attention to what I am about to say.* ○ *to call/draw sb's attention to sth* ○ *The bride is always the centre of attention* (= the person that everybody is watching). ○ *I shouted in order to attract her attention.* ○ *to hold sb's attention* (= to keep them interested in sth) **2** special care or action: *The hole in the roof needs urgent attention.* ○ *to require medical attention* **3** a position in which a soldier stands up straight and still: *to come/stand to attention*

(IDIOMS) **catch sb's attention/eye** ⇨ CATCH¹
draw sb's attention to sth ⇨ DRAW²
pay attention ⇨ PAY²

attention *interj* (used for asking people to listen to sth carefully): *Attention, please! The boat will be leaving in five minutes.*

attentive /əˈtentɪv/ *adj* watching, listening to or thinking about sb/sth carefully: *The staff at the hotel were very attentive.* ○ *an attentive audience* —**attentively** *adv*: *to listen attentively to sth*

attic /ˈætɪk/ *noun* [C] the space or room under the roof of a house ☛ Look at **loft**.

☆ **attitude** /ˈætɪtjuːd; *US* -tuːd/ *noun* [C] **attitude (to/towards sb/sth)** the way that you think, feel or behave: *social attitudes and beliefs* ○ *the British attitude to the European Community* ○ *She shows a very positive attitude to her work.*

attorney /əˈtɜːni/ *noun* [C] (*pl* **attorneys**) (*US*) a lawyer

☆ **attract** /əˈtrækt/ *verb* [T] **1** to cause sb/sth to go to or give attention to sth: *to attract sb's attention* ○ *Moths are attracted to light.* ○ *The new film has attracted a lot of publicity.* **2** to cause sb to like sb/sth: *She's attracted to older men.*

attraction /əˈtrækʃn/ *noun* **1** [U] attracting or being attracted: *I can't understand the attraction of fishing.* ○ *sexual attraction* **2** [C] something that attracts sb/sth: *Blackpool offers all kinds of tourist attractions.* ○ *One of the attractions of the job is having a company car.*

☆ **attractive** /əˈtræktɪv/ *adj* **1** that pleases or in-

attribute

terests you; that you like: *an attractive idea* **2** pretty, beautiful or handsome: *an attractive room* ○ *an attractive man/woman* —**attractively** *adv* —**attractiveness** *noun* [U]

attribute¹ /əˈtrɪbjuːt/ *verb* [T] **attribute sth to sb/sth** to believe that sth was caused or done by sb/sth: *Terry attributes his success to hard work.* ○ *a poem attributed to Shakespeare*

attribute² /ˈætrɪbjuːt/ *noun* [C] a quality or feature of sb/sth: *physical attributes*

aubergine /ˈəʊbəʒiːn/ (*especially US* **eggplant**) *noun* [C,U] a long vegetable with dark purple skin

auburn /ˈɔːbən/ *adj* (usually used about hair) reddish-brown

auction /ˈɔːkʃn/ *noun* [C,U] a public sale at which items are sold to the person who offers to pay the most money: *The house will be sold by auction.*

auction *verb* [T] to sell sth at an auction

auctioneer /ˌɔːkʃəˈnɪə(r)/ *noun* [C] a person who organizes the selling at an auction

audible /ˈɔːdəbl/ *adj* that can be heard: *Her speech was only just audible.* ☛ Look at **inaudible**. —**audibly** /-əblɪ/ *adv*: *to sigh audibly*

☆ **audience** /ˈɔːdɪəns/ *noun* [C] **1** [with sing or pl verb] the group of people who are watching or listening to a play, concert, speech, the television, etc: *The audience was/were wild with excitement.* ○ *There were only about 200 people in the audience.* ○ *Television can reach an audience of millions.* **2** a formal meeting with a very important person: *an audience with the Pope*

audiovisual /ˌɔːdɪəʊˈvɪʒuəl/ *adj* using both sound and pictures: *A video recorder is an excellent audiovisual aid in the classroom.*

audition /ɔːˈdɪʃn/ *noun* [C] a short performance by a singer, actor, musician, etc to find out if he/she is good enough to be in a play, show, concert, etc

auditorium /ˌɔːdɪˈtɔːrɪəm/ *noun* [C] (*pl* **auditoriums** or **auditoria**) the part of a theatre, etc where the audience sits

augur /ˈɔːgə(r)/ *verb*
(IDIOM) **augur well/ill for sb/sth** (*formal*) to be a good/bad sign of what will happen in the future: *The opinion polls augur well for the government.*

☆ **August** /ˈɔːgəst/ *noun* [C,U] (*abbr* **Aug**) the eighth month of the year, coming before September ☛ For examples of the use of the months in sentences, look at **January**.

☆ **aunt** /ɑːnt; *US* ænt/ (also *informal* **auntie**; **aunty** /ˈɑːntɪ; *US* ˈæntɪ/) *noun* [C] the sister of your father or mother; the wife of your uncle: *Aunt Ann*

au pair /ˌəʊ ˈpeə(r)/ *noun* [C] a person, usually a girl, from another country who comes to live with a family in order to learn the language. An au pair helps with the housework and looking after the children.

aura /ˈɔːrə/ *noun* [C] (*formal*) the quality that sb/sth seems to have: *The village had an aura of peace and tranquillity.*

aural /ˈɔːrəl/ *adj* of or concerning the ear or hearing: *an aural comprehension test* ☛ Look at **oral**.

auspices /ˈɔːspɪsɪz/ *noun* [plural]

(IDIOM) **under the auspices of sb/sth** with the help and support of sb/sth: *The visit was arranged under the auspices of the local church.*

auspicious /ɔːˈspɪʃəs/ *adj* that seems likely to succeed or be pleasant in the future

austere /ɒˈstɪə(r)/ *adj* **1** not having pleasures or luxuries: *The nuns lead simple and austere lives.* **2** very plain and simple; without decoration

austerity /ɒˈsterətɪ/ *noun* [U] the quality of being austere

authentic /ɔːˈθentɪk/ *adj* that you know is true or genuine: *an authentic Van Gogh painting* —**authenticity** /ˌɔːθenˈtɪsətɪ/ *noun* [U]: *to check the authenticity of a document*

☆ **author** /ˈɔːθə(r)/ *noun* [C] a person who writes a book, play, etc: *a well-known author of detective novels* —**authorship** *noun* [U]: *The authorship of the play is unknown.*

authoritarian /ɔːˌθɒrɪˈteərɪən/ *adj* not allowing people the freedom to decide things for themselves: *The authoritarian government crushed all signs of opposition.* ○ *authoritarian parents*

authoritative /ɔːˈθɒrətətɪv; *US* -teɪtɪv/ *adj* **1** having authority; demanding or expecting that people obey you: *an authoritative tone of voice* **2** that you can trust because it/he/she has a lot of knowledge and information: *They will be able to give you authoritative advice on the problem.*

☆ **authority** /ɔːˈθɒrətɪ/ *noun* (*pl* **authorities**) **1** [C] (often plural) a person, group or government department that has the power to give orders, make official decisions, etc: *Cases of the illness must be reported to the health authority.* ○ *The French authorities refused permission for the hijacked plane to land.* **2** [U] the power and right to give orders and make others obey: *Children often begin to question their parents' authority at a very early age.* ○ *You must get this signed by a person in authority* (= who has a position of power). **3** [U] **authority (to do sth)** the right to act in a particular way: *The police have the authority to question anyone they wish.* **4** [U] a quality that sb has which makes it possible to influence and control other people: *He spoke with authority and everybody listened.* **5** [C] a person with special knowledge: *He's an authority on ancient Egypt.*

authorize (*also* **authorise**) /ˈɔːθəraɪz/ *verb* [T] to give official permission for sth or for sb to do sth: *Any new buildings have to be authorized by the planning department.* ○ *He authorized his secretary to sign letters in his absence.*

authorization (*also* **authorisation**) /ˌɔːθəraɪˈzeɪʃn; *US* -rɪˈz-/ *noun* [U] official permission for sth: *I can't give you the information without authorization from the manager.*

autistic /ɔːˈtɪstɪk/ *adj* having a serious mental illness which makes it very difficult to form relationships with other people: *an autistic child*

autobiography /ˌɔːtəbaɪˈɒgrəfɪ/ *noun* [C,U] (*pl* **autobiographies**) the story of a person's life written by that person ☛ Look at **biography**. —**autobiographical** /ˌɔːtəbaɪəˈgræfɪkl/ *adj*

p	b	t	d	k	g	tʃ	dʒ	f	v	θ	ð
pen	bad	tea	did	cat	got	chin	June	fall	van	thin	then

autograph /'ɔ:təgrɑ:f; *US* -græf/ *noun* [C] the signature of a famous person: *People were waiting at the stage door to get the dancer's autograph.*
autograph *verb* [T] to put your signature on or in sth: *a painting autographed by the artist*

automate /'ɔ:təmeɪt/ *verb* [T] (usually passive) to make sth operate by machine, without needing people: *The system in the factory has been fully automated.*

☆ **automatic** /ˌɔ:tə'mætɪk/ *adj* **1** (used about a machine) that can work by itself without direct human control: *an automatic washing-machine* **2** (used about actions) done without thinking or like a machine; unconscious: *Practise this exercise until it becomes automatic.* **3** certain to happen because it is part of a normal process: *Not everyone with a British passport has the automatic right to live in Britain.*
automatic *noun* [C] an automatic machine, gun or car: *This car is an automatic* (= has automatic gears). —**automatically** /-klɪ/ *adv*: *The lights will come on automatically when it gets dark.* ○ *You will automatically receive a reminder when your next payment is due.*

automation /ˌɔ:tə'meɪʃn/ *noun* [U] the use of machines, instead of people, to do work: *Unemployment is rising because of increased automation.*

automobile /'ɔ:təməbi:l/ *noun* [C] (*especially US*) = CAR(1)

autonomous /ɔ:'tɒnəməs/ *adj* having the right to govern or control its own affairs: *The people in this region want to be completely autonomous.*

autonomy /ɔ:'tɒnəmɪ/ *noun* [U] the right of an organization, region, etc to govern or control its own affairs

autopsy /'ɔ:tɒpsɪ/ *noun* [C] (*pl* **autopsies**) an examination of a dead body to find out the cause of death

☆ **autumn** /'ɔ:təm/ (*US usually* **fall**) *noun* [C,U] the season of the year that comes between summer and winter: *It was a very cold autumn that year.* ○ *In autumn the leaves on the trees begin to fall.* ○ *autumn weather* —**autumnal** /ɔ:'tʌmnəl/ *adj*

auxiliary /ɔ:g'zɪlɪərɪ/ *adj* (only *before* a noun) giving extra help: *auxiliary nurses, troops, etc*
au'xiliary ˌverb *noun* [C] (*grammar*) a verb (eg *be, do* or *have*) that is used with a main verb to show tense, etc or to form questions

avail /ə'veɪl/ *noun* [U]
(IDIOMS) **of little/no avail** not helpful or effective: *All our efforts to persuade her were of little avail.*
to little/no avail; without avail without success: *They had searched everywhere, but to no avail.*

☆ **available** /ə'veɪləbl/ *adj* **1** (used about things) that you can get, buy, use, etc: *Do you know if there are any flats available in this area?* ○ *I'm afraid that material is no longer available, Madam.* ○ *This information is easily available to everyone at the local library.* ○ *Refreshments are available at the snack bar.* **2** (used about people) free to be seen, talked to, etc: *The minister was not available for comment.*

availability /əˌveɪlə'bɪlətɪ/ *noun* [U] the state of being available: *You will receive the colour you order, subject to availability* (= if it is available).

avalanche /'ævəlɑ:nʃ; *US* -læntʃ/ *noun* [C] a very large amount of snow that slides quickly down the side of a mountain: *Two skiers are still missing after yesterday's avalanche.* ○ (*figurative*) *The company received an avalanche of complaints.*

avant-garde /ˌævɒŋ'gɑ:d/ *adj* (used especially about art and literature) extremely new and modern

avenge /ə'vendʒ/ *verb* [T] **avenge sth**; **avenge yourself on sb** to punish sb for hurting you, your family, etc in some way: *He wanted to avenge his father's murder.* ○ *He wanted to avenge himself on his father's murderer.* ☞ Look at **revenge**.

avenue /'ævənju:; *US* -nu:/ *noun* [C] **1** (*abbr* **Ave**) a wide street, especially one with trees or tall buildings on each side: *Pleasant avenues lead out from the centre of the town.* ○ *I live at 12 Tennyson Avenue.* ○ *Fifth Avenue, New York* ☞ Look at the note at **road**. **2** a way of doing or getting sth: *We must explore every avenue open to us* (= try every possibility).

☆ **average** /'ævərɪdʒ/ *noun* **1** [C] the number you get when you add two or more figures together and then divide the total by the number of figures you added: *The average of 14, 3 and 1 is 6* (= 18 divided by 3 is 6). **2** [sing,U] the normal standard, amount or quality: *Only 60% of the students passed the exam. That's well below the national average.*
average *adj* **1** (only *before* a noun) (used about a number) found by calculating the average(1): *What's the average age of your students?* **2** normal or typical: *People on average incomes are finding it hard to manage at the moment.* ○ *children of above/below average intelligence*
average *verb* [T] to do, get, etc a certain amount as an average: *If we average 50 miles an hour we should arrive at about 4 o'clock.*
(PHRASAL VERB) **average out (at sth)** to result in an average (of sth): *The meal averaged out at about £20 each.*

averse /ə'vɜ:s/ *adj* **averse to sth** (*formal*) (often with a negative) against or opposed to sth: *He is not averse to trying out new ideas.*

aversion /ə'vɜ:ʃn; *US* ə'vɜ:rʒn/ *noun* [C] **1** [usually sing] **an aversion (to sb/sth)** a feeling of great dislike: *Some people have an aversion to telephones.* **2** a thing that you greatly dislike: *Mathematics was always one of my particular aversions.*

avert /ə'vɜ:t/ *verb* [T] to prevent sth unpleasant; to avoid: *The accident could have been averted.*

aviary /'eɪvɪərɪ; *US* -vɪerɪ/ *noun* [C] (*pl* **aviaries**) a large cage or area in which birds are kept

aviation /ˌeɪvɪ'eɪʃn/ *noun* [U] the flying or building of aircraft

avid /'ævɪd/ *adj* (only *before* a noun) keen and eager; greedy: *an avid collector of* antiques o *The people crowded round the radio, avid for news.* —**avidly** *adv*: *He read avidly as a child.*

avocado /ˌævəˈkɑːdəʊ/ *noun* [C] (*pl* **avocados**) a fruit shaped like a pear with a tough dark green skin and a large stone inside

☆ **avoid** /əˈvɔɪd/ *verb* [T] **1 avoid (doing sth)** to prevent sth happening: *He always tried to avoid an argument if possible.* o *It was so dark that we managed to avoid being seen.* o *She has to avoid eating fatty food* (= she must make an effort not to eat it). **2** to keep away from (sb/sth): *I leave home at 7 o'clock in order to avoid the rush-hour.* o *Jane is trying to avoid her boyfriend at the moment.*

avoidable *adj* that can be prevented; unnecessary: *We have been asked to cut down on any avoidable expense.* ☛ The opposite is **unavoidable.** —**avoidance** *noun* [U]

await /əˈweɪt/ *verb* [T] (*formal*) **1** (used about people) to wait for sb/sth: *Please await further instructions.* **2** (used about things or events) to be ready or waiting for sb/sth: *We were unaware of the danger that awaited us.*

awake[1] /əˈweɪk/ *verb* (*pt* **awoke** /əˈwəʊk/; *pp* **awoken** /əˈwəʊkən/) **1** [I,T] to wake up; to make sb/sth wake up: *I awoke to find that it was already 9 o'clock.* o *A sudden loud noise awoke us all.* ☛ **Wake up** is more common than **awake**. **2** [T] to make sb have a particular feeling, attitude, etc: *His words awoke fear and hatred in the boy.*

☆ **awake**[2] /əˈweɪk/ *adj* (not before a noun) not sleeping: *I was awake most of the night, worrying.* o *The children are always wide* (= completely) *awake at 6 o'clock in the morning.* o *They were so tired that they found it difficult to keep awake.* ☛ The opposite is **asleep**.

awaken /əˈweɪkən/ *verb* **1** [I,T] (*formal*) to wake up; to make sb/sth wake up: *I awakened to find the others already up.* o *We were awakened by a loud knock at the door.* ☛ **Wake up** is much more common than **awaken**. **2** [T] (*formal*) to produce a particular feeling, attitude, etc in sb: *The film awakened memories of her childhood.*

(PHRASAL VERB) **awaken sb to sth** to make sb become aware of sth: *The letter awakened me to the seriousness of the situation.*

awakening /əˈweɪkənɪŋ/ *noun* [sing] **1** the start (of a feeling, etc): *the awakening of an interest in the opposite sex* **2** an act of realizing: *It was a rude* (= unpleasant) *awakening when I suddenly found that I was unemployed.*

☆ **award** /əˈwɔːd/ *verb* [T] **award sth (to sb)** to give sth to sb as a prize, payment, etc: *She was awarded first prize in the gymnastics competition.* o *The novel was awarded the Booker Prize.* o *The court awarded £10 000 each to the workers injured in the factory accident.*

award *noun* [C] **1** a prize, etc that sb gets for doing sth well: *This year the awards for best actor and actress went to two Americans.* **2** an amount of money given to sb as the result of a court decision: *She received an award of £5 000 for damages.*

☆ **aware** /əˈweə(r)/ *adj* **1 aware (of sb/sth); aware (that)** knowing about or realizing sth; conscious of sb/sth: *I am aware of the difficulties you face.* o *I am aware that you will face difficulties.* o *I suddenly felt aware of somebody watching me.* o *There is no other entrance, as far as I am aware.* ☛ The opposite is **unaware**. **2** interested and informed: *to be politically aware*

awareness *noun* [U] knowledge, consciousness or interest: *People's awareness of healthy eating has increased in recent years.*

awash /əˈwɒʃ/ *adj* (not before a noun) covered with water; flooded: *The bathroom was awash because the bath had overflowed.* o (*figurative*) *The city was awash with rumours.*

☆ **away** /əˈweɪ/ *adj, adv* ☛ Look also at phrasal verbs, eg **give away**, **take away**. **1 away (from sb/sth)** to a different place or in a different direction: *Go away! I'm busy!* o *I asked him a question, but he just looked away.* **2** at a distance from a place: *My parents live five miles away.* o *The village is two miles away from the sea.* **3 away (from sth)** (used about people) not present; absent: *My neighbours are away on holiday at the moment.* o *Tom was away from school for two weeks with measles.* **4 away (from sth)** in the future: *Our summer holiday is only three weeks away.* **5** into a safe place: *Put your books away now.* o *He tidied his clothes away.* o *They cleared the dishes away* (= off the table). ☛ Contrast **throw that away** (= put it in the rubbish bin). **6** (used about a football, etc team) on the other team's ground: *Our team's playing away on Saturday.* o *an away match/game* **7** until it disappears completely: *The crash of thunder slowly died away.* o *The writing has almost faded away.* **8** continuously, without stopping: *They chatted away for hours.*

(IDIOM) **right/straight away** immediately; without any delay: *I'll phone the doctor right away.* o *I understood straight away what she wanted me to do.*

awe /ɔː/ *noun* [U] a feeling of respect and either fear or admiration: *We watched in awe as the rocket took off into space.* o *As a young boy he was very much in awe of his uncle.*

awesome /-səm/ *adj* impressive and rather frightening: *an awesome task*

'awe-inspiring *adj* causing a feeling of respect and fear or admiration

☆ **awful** /ˈɔːfl/ *adj* **1** very bad or unpleasant: *We had an awful holiday. It rained every day.* o *What an awful thing to say!* **2** terrible; very serious: *I'm afraid there's been some awful news.* **3** (only *before* a noun) (*informal*) very great: *I'm in an awful hurry. See you later.* o *We've got an awful lot of work to do.*

awfully /ˈɔːfli/ *adv* (*informal*) very; very much: *I'm awfully sorry.*

awkward /ˈɔːkwəd/ *adj* **1** not convenient, difficult: *My mother always phones at an awkward time.* o *You've put me in an awkward position.* o *That's an awkward question.* o *It's awkward for her to get home by bus.* o *This tin opener is very awkward to clean.* **2** (used about people) causing difficulties; unreasonable: *He keeps asking for different things – he's just being awkward.* **3** embarrassed; not relaxed: *There*

iː	ɪ	e	æ	ɑː	ɒ	ɔː	ʊ	uː	ʌ
see	sit	ten	hat	arm	got	saw	put	too	cup

awoke *pt* of AWAKE
awoken *pp* of AWAKE
awry /ə'raɪ/ *adv* wrong, not in the way that was planned: *Our plans went awry.*
awry *adj* (not before a noun) untidy; in the wrong position: *Her hair was all awry.*
axe (*especially US* **ax**) /æks/ *noun* [C] a tool with a wooden handle and a metal blade used for cutting wood, etc: *He chopped the tree down with an axe.*

was an awkward silence when no one could think of anything to say. **4** without grace or skill: *an awkward gesture* —**awkwardly** *adv*
awkwardness *noun* [U]

axe (*especially US* **ax**) *verb* [T] **1** to remove or end sth: *Hundreds of jobs have been axed.* **2** to reduce sth greatly: *School budgets are to be axed.*
axis /'æksɪs/ *noun* [C] (*pl* **axes** /'æksiːz/) **1** an imaginary line through the middle of an object that turns: *The earth rotates on its axis.* ☞ picture at **earth**. **2** a fixed line used for marking measurements on a graph: *the horizontal/vertical axis*
axle /'æksl/ *noun* [C] a bar that connects a pair of wheels on a vehicle
aye (*also* **ay**) /aɪ/ *interj* yes ☞ **Aye** is common in Scotland and the North of England.

Bb

B, b /biː/ *noun* [C] (*pl* **B's; b's**) the second letter of the English alphabet: *'Billy' begins with (a) 'B'.*
'B-road *noun* [C] (in Britain) a road that is not as wide or important as a motorway or an A-road: *Turn right onto the B427.*
baa /bɑː/ *noun* [C] the sound that a sheep or lamb makes
babble /'bæbl/ *verb* [I] **1** to talk quickly or in a way that is difficult to understand **2** to make the sound of water running over stones
babble *noun* [U] **1** the sound of many voices talking at the same time: *I could hear a babble of voices coming from downstairs.* **2** the sound of water running over stones
babe /beɪb/ *noun* [C] **1** (*old-fashioned*) a baby **2** (*US slang*) (used when talking to sb, especially a girl or young woman): *It's OK, babe.*
☆**baby** /'beɪbi/ *noun* [C] (*pl* **babies**) **1** a very young child: *I've got wonderful news. I'm going to have a baby.* ○ *She's expecting a baby early next year* (= she's pregnant and the baby will be born early next year). ○ *When's the baby due?* (= when will it be born?) ○ *Babies can usually sit up when they are about six months old.* ○ *a baby boy/girl* **2** a very young animal or bird: *a baby rabbit* **3** (*US slang*) a person, especially a girl or young woman that you are fond of
babyish *adj* like or suitable for a baby: *Don't be so babyish – stop crying.* ○ *This book is a bit too babyish for Tom now.*
'baby carriage *noun* [C] (*US*) = PRAM
'babysit *verb* [I] (**babysitting**; *pt, pp* **babysat**) to look after a child for a short time while the parents are out: *We have friends who babysit for us if we go out in the evening.*
'babysitter *noun* [C] *We can't come this evening. We couldn't find a babysitter.*
bachelor /'bætʃələ(r)/ *noun* [C] **1** a man who has not yet married ☞ There is a word

spinster which means 'a woman who has not married' but it is not often used now. **2** a person who has a first university degree: *a Bachelor of Arts* ○ *a Bachelor of Science*
☆**back¹** /bæk/ *noun* [C] **1** the part of a person's or animal's body between the neck and the bottom: *Do you sleep on your back or on your side?* ○ *She was standing with her back to me so I couldn't see her face.* ○ *He swung himself up onto the horse's back.* **2** the part or side of sth that is furthest from the front: *David couldn't see the blackboard because he was sitting at the back of the class.* ○ *Jane sat next to the driver and Anne and I sat in the back of the car.* ○ *The back of the house is much prettier than the front.* ○ *There's some information about the author at the back of the book.* **3** the part of a chair that you lean against when you sit down: *Don't climb on the back of the sofa, children!*
(IDIOMS) **back to front** with the back where the front should be: *Wait a minute – you've got your jumper on back to front.*
behind sb's back without sb's knowledge or agreement: *They criticized her behind her back.*

back to front

get off sb's back (*informal*) to stop bothering or annoying sb: *I wish she'd get off my back!*
know sth inside out/like the back of your hand ⇨ KNOW
a pat on the back ⇨ PAT¹
'backbone *noun* **1** [C] the line of bones down the back of your body ☞ Look at **spine**. **2** [sing] the main strength or support: *Volun-*

ɜː	ə	eɪ	əʊ	aɪ	aʊ	ɔɪ	ɪə	eə	ʊə
fur	ago	pay	home	five	now	join	near	hair	pure

teer workers are the backbone of the organization.

'backpack noun [C] (especially US) = RUCKSACK

'backstroke noun [U] a style of swimming that you do on your back: *Can you do backstroke?*

☆ **back²** /bæk/ adj **1** (only *before* a noun) furthest from the front: *Have you locked the back door?* ○ *the back row of the theatre* ○ *back teeth* **2** owed for a time in the past: *back pay*

,back 'bench noun [C, usually pl] (*Brit*) a seat in the House of Commons for an ordinary member of Parliament: *to sit on the back benches*

,back-'bencher noun [C] (*Brit*) a member of Parliament who does not have an important position in a political party

'backhand noun [sing] a stroke in tennis, etc that is made with the back of your hand facing forward ☛ Look at **forehand**.

'backlog noun [C, usually sing] an amount of work, etc that has not yet been done and needs doing: *I've got an enormous backlog of letters to write.*

'backside noun [C] (*informal*) the part of the body that you sit on; your bottom

'backstage adv behind the stage in a theatre, where the actors get dressed, etc

'backwater noun [C] a place that is not affected by new ideas or outside events

,back'yard noun [C] an area behind a house, usually of concrete or stone, with a wall or fence around it

☆ **back³** /bæk/ adv **1** in or to a place or state that sb/sth was in before: *Bye! I'll be back about 6 o'clock* (= back home again). ○ *When is your brother coming back from Australia?* ○ *Go back to sleep.* ○ *Could I have my pen back, please?* **2** away from the direction you are facing or moving in: *She walked away without looking back.* ○ *Could everyone move back a bit, please?* **3** away from sth; under control: *The police were unable to keep the crowds back.* ○ *She tried to keep back her tears.* **4** in return or in reply: *He said he'd phone me back in half an hour.* **5** in or into the past; ago: *I met him a few years back, in Madrid.* ○ *Think back to your first day at school.*

(IDIOM) **back and forth** from one place to another and back again, all the time: *Travelling back and forth to work takes up quite a bit of time.*

'backdate verb [T] to make sth valid from an earlier date: *The pay rise will be backdated to 1 April.*

'backfire verb [I] to have an unexpected and unwanted result, often the opposite of what was intended

'backlash noun [sing] a strong reaction against a political or social event or development

☆ **back⁴** /bæk/ verb **1** [I,T] to move backwards or to make sth move backwards: *I'll have to back into that parking space.* ○ *He backed the car into the parking space.* **2** [I] to face sth at the back: *Many of the colleges back onto the river.* **3** [T] to give help or support to sb/sth: *We can go ahead with the scheme if the bank will agree to back us.* **4** [T] to bet money that a particular horse, team, etc will win in a race or game: *Which horse are you backing in the 2 o'clock race?*

(PHRASAL VERBS) **back away (from sb/sth)** to move backwards because you are afraid, shocked, etc: *He began to back slowly away from the snake.*

back down to stop insisting that you are right: *I think you are right to demand an apology. Don't back down now.*

back out (of sth) to decide not to do sth that you had promised to do: *You promised you would come with me. You can't back out of it now!*

back sb/sth up to support sb; to say or show that sth is true: *I'm going to say exactly what I think at the meeting. Will you back me up?* ○ *All the evidence backed up what the woman had said.*

back sth up (*computing*) to make a copy of a computer program, etc in case the original one is lost or damaged: *If you don't back up your files you risk losing data.*

'backer noun [C] a person who gives support or money to another person, a scheme, etc

'backing noun [U] help or support to do sth, often in the form of money: *financial backing*

'backup noun **1** [U] extra help or support: *Her success is partly due to the backup she gets from her team.* **2** [C] a copy of a computer disk that you can use if the original one is lost or damaged: *Always make a backup of your files.*

☆ **background** /'bækgraʊnd/ noun **1** [C] the type of family and social class you come from and the education and experience you have: *We get on very well together in spite of our different backgrounds.* ○ *a working-class background* **2** [sing,U] the facts or events that are connected with a situation: *The talks are taking place against a background of increasing tension.* ○ *I need some background information.* **3** [sing] the part of a view, scene, picture, etc which is furthest away from the person looking at it: *You can see the mountains in the background of the photo.* ☛ Look at **foreground**. **4** [sing] a position where sb/sth can be seen/heard, etc but is not the centre of attention: *The film star's husband prefers to stay in the background.* ○ *All the time I was speaking to her, I could hear a child crying in the background.* ○ *The restaurant kept playing the same background music again and again.*

☆ **backward** /'bækwəd/ adj **1** (only *before* a noun) directed towards the back: *a backward step, glance, etc* **2** slow to learn or develop: *Considerable modernization is needed in the more backward areas of the country.*

backwards (also **backward**) adv **1** away from the front; towards the back: *Could everybody take a step backwards?* ○ *He fell backwards and hit the back of his head.* ○ *We seem to be going backwards, not forwards.* **2** the opposite way to usual; with the end first: *It was a very easy code. All the words were written backwards.* **3** towards an earlier time: *The film was about some people who travelled backwards in time.*

p	b	t	d	k	g	tʃ	dʒ	f	v	θ	ð
pen	bad	tea	did	cat	got	chin	June	fall	van	thin	then

(IDIOM) **backward(s) and forward(s)** first in one direction and then in the other, all the time: *The dog ran backwards and forwards, barking loudly.*

bacon /ˈbeɪkən/ *noun* [U] thin pieces of salted or smoked meat from the back or sides of a pig: *a full English breakfast of bacon, eggs, sausage and tomato.* ☛ Look at the note at **meat**.

bacteria /bækˈtɪəriə/ *noun* [plural] very small living things that can only be seen with a microscope. Bacteria exist in large numbers in air, water, soil, plants and the bodies of people and animals. Some bacteria cause disease. ☛ Look at **virus**.

☆ **bad** /bæd/ *adj* (**worse** /wɜːs/, **worst** /wɜːst/) **1** not good or pleasant: *Our family's had rather a bad time recently.* o *The weather forecast for the weekend is very bad.* **2** severe or serious: *The traffic was extremely bad on the way to work.* o *She went home with a bad headache.* o *That was a bad mistake!* **3** of poor quality; of a low standard: *Many accidents are caused by bad driving.* o *Some of the company's problems are the result of bad management.* **4 bad (at sth/at doing sth)** not able to do sth well or easily; not skilful or reliable: *a bad teacher, driver, cook, etc* o *I've always been bad at sport, but Liz is even worse than me.* o *He's very bad at keeping us informed* (= we can't rely on him to give us information). **5** (used about food) not fresh or fit to eat; rotten: *Smell this meat – I think it's gone bad.* **6** (used about parts of the body) not healthy; painful: *He's always had a bad heart.* **7** (used about a person or behaviour) not good; morally wrong: *He was not a bad man, just rather weak.* **8** (not before a noun) **bad for sb/sth** likely to damage or hurt sb/sth: *Too many sweets are bad for you.* **9 bad (for sth/to do sth)** difficult or unsuitable: *This is a bad time to phone – everyone's out to lunch.*

(IDIOMS) **not bad** (*informal*) quite good: *'What was the lecture like?' 'Not bad.'* o *He earned £100 – not bad for four hours' work!*

too bad (*informal*) (used to show that nothing can be done to change a situation): *'I'd much rather stay at home.' 'Well that's just too bad. We've said we'll go.'*

baddy *noun* [C] (*pl* **baddies**) (*informal*) a bad person in a film, book, etc ☛ The opposite is a **goody**.

bad ˈlanguage *noun* [U] words that are used for swearing: *You'll get into trouble if you use bad language.*

bad-ˈtempered *adj* often angry or impatient: *a bad-tempered old man*

bade *pt* of **BID**[1]

☆ **badge** /bædʒ/ *noun* [C] a small piece of metal or cloth with a design or words on it which you pin or sew onto your clothing. A badge can show position, rank, membership of a club, etc, or express a message: *The players all have jackets with the club badge on them.*

badger /ˈbædʒə(r)/ *noun* [C] an animal with black and white stripes on its head that lives in holes in the ground and comes out at night

badly /ˈbædli/ *adv* (**worse**; **worst**) **1** in a way that is not satisfactory; not well: *'Can you speak French?' 'Well, only very badly.'* o *Some modern houses are very badly built.* o *She did badly in the exams.* **2** greatly or severely: *He was badly hurt in the accident.* **3** very much: *He badly needed a holiday.*

(IDIOM) **badly off** poor; not having enough of sth: *They don't seem too badly off – they have smart clothes and a nice house.* ☛ The opposite is **well off**.

badminton /ˈbædmɪntən/ *noun* [U] a game for two or four people in which players hit a type of light ball with feathers (**shuttlecock**) over a high net, using rackets: *to play badminton*

baffle /ˈbæfl/ *verb* [T] to be impossible for sb to understand; to confuse greatly: *His illness baffled the doctors.*

baffled *adj* very confused; unable to understand: *The instructions were so complicated that I was absolutely baffled.* —**baffling** *adj*: *I find English a baffling language.*

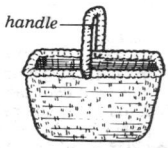

carrier bag   basket   handle

☆ **bag**[1] /bæg/ *noun* [C] **1** a container made of paper, plastic, cloth or leather that is open at the top, often with handles, in which you can carry things: *The assistant took my money and put the book in a paper bag.* o *She brought some sandwiches in a plastic bag.* o *Are carrier bags free in this supermarket?* o *a shopping bag* o *a shoulder bag* o *a sports bag* o *a handbag* o *She took her purse out of her bag* (= handbag). **2** a container made of paper or plastic that is closed at the top; a packet: *a bag of sweets, crisps, sugar, etc* ☛ picture at **container**. **3** a thing that looks like a bag: *bags under the eyes* (= folds of skin under the eyes, often caused by lack of sleep) **4** (*slang*) an unpleasant woman

bag[2] /bæg/ *verb* [T] (**bagging**; **bagged**) (*informal*) to try to reserve sth for yourself so that other people cannot have it: *Somebody's bagged the seats by the pool!* ☛ When we say that we want something, we often say **bags**: *Bags I go first!*

☆ **baggage** /ˈbægɪdʒ/ *noun* [U] = LUGGAGE: *We loaded our baggage into the car.* o *Baggage should be checked in* (= given to an airline employee at a counter) *at least an hour before the flight.* o *excess baggage* (= baggage weighing more than the airline's permitted limit)

baggy /ˈbægi/ *adj* (used about a piece of clothing) hanging loosely on the body: *a baggy pullover*

bagpipes /ˈbægpaɪps/ (*also* **pipes**) *noun* [plural] a musical instrument, popular in Scotland, that is played by blowing air through a pipe into a bag and then pressing the bag so that the air comes out of other pipes ☛ picture on next page.

bagpipes

kilt

bags /bægz/ noun [plural] **bags (of sth)** a lot (of sth); plenty (of sth): *There's no hurry, we've got bags of time.*

bail /beɪl/ noun [U] **1** money that is handed over to a court so that a person accused of a crime can be free until the trial: *She was released on bail of £2 000.* ○ *The judge set bail at £10 000.* **2** permission for sb who is accused of a crime to be free until the trial if a sum of money is handed over to the court: *The judge felt that he was a dangerous man and refused him bail.* ○ *She was granted bail.*
▶ **bail** verb

(PHRASAL VERB) **bail sb out 1** to obtain sb's freedom by paying his/her bail(1): *After she had been charged, her parents bailed her out.* **2** to rescue sb or sth from a difficult situation (especially by providing money)

bailiff /'beɪlɪf/ noun [C] an officer whose job is to make sure that a court order is carried out, especially by taking possession of people's goods when they owe money

bait /beɪt/ noun [U] **1** food or sth that looks like food that is put onto a hook to catch fish, or placed in a trap to catch animals or birds **2** something that is used for tempting or attracting sb: *Free offers are often used as bait to attract customers.*

☆ **bake** /beɪk/ verb [I,T] **1** to cook in an oven in dry heat: *I could smell bread baking in the oven.* ○ *On his birthday she baked him a cake.* ○ *Would you like boiled or baked potatoes?* ☛ Look at the note at **cook**. **2** to become or to make sth hard by heating it: *The hot sun baked the earth.*

baking adj (*informal*) very hot: *The workers complained of the baking heat in the office in the summer.*

☆ **baker** /'beɪkə(r)/ noun [C] a person who bakes and sells bread, cakes, etc: *Get a loaf at the baker's.* ☛ Note that **the baker** is the person who runs the shop and **the baker's** is the shop.

bakery /'beɪkəri/ noun [C] (*pl* **bakeries**) a place where bread, cakes, etc are baked to be sold

☆ **balance**[1] /'bæləns/ verb **1** [I,T] to be or to put sb/sth in a steady position in which weight is evenly spread: *I had to balance on the top step of the ladder to paint the ceiling.* ○ *Carefully, she balanced a glass on top of the pile of plates.* **2** [I,T] to have equal totals of money spent and money received: *I must have made a mistake – the accounts don't balance.* ○ *She is always very careful to balance her weekly budget.* **3** [T] **balance sth (out) (with sth)** to have or give sth equal value, importance, etc in relation to other parts: *It's difficult to balance the demands of a career with caring for an elderly relative.* ○ *The loss in the first half of the year was balanced out by the profit in the second half.* **4** [T] **balance sth against sth** to consider and compare one matter in relation to another: *In planning the new road, we have to balance the benefit to motorists against the damage to the environment.*

balanced adj **1** including all different sides, opinions, etc equally; fair: *I like this newspaper because it gives a balanced view.* **2** consisting of parts that are in the correct or pleasing proportions: *A balanced diet plays an important part in good health.*

☆ **balance**[2] /'bæləns/ noun **1** [U] the state of being in a steady position in which weight is evenly spread: *You need a good sense of balance to ride a motor bike.* **2** [sing] **(a) balance (between A and B)** a situation in which different or opposite things are of equal importance, size, etc or are in the correct proportions: *The course provides a good balance between academic and practical work.* ○ *Man has upset the environmental balance of the world.* **3** [C] (*technical*) an instrument used for weighing things ☛ Look at **scales**. **4** [C] the amount of money in sb's bank account: *While I was in the bank I asked the cashier for my balance.* **5 the balance** [sing] the amount that still has to be paid; the amount that remains after some has been used, taken, etc: *You can pay a 10% deposit now, with the balance due in one month.* ○ *I took most of my annual holiday in the summer and I'm taking the balance over Christmas.*

(IDIOMS) **in the balance** uncertain: *Following poor results, the company's future is in the balance.*

keep/lose your balance to remain/not to remain steady and upright: *It's difficult to keep your balance on this icy path.* ○ *She tripped, lost her balance and fell over.*

(catch/throw sb) off balance (to find or put sb) in an unsteady position from which it is easy to fall: *A strong gust of wind caught me off balance and I nearly fell over.*

on balance having taken all sides, facts, etc into consideration: *On balance, I've had a pretty good year.*

strike a balance ⇨ STRIKE[2]

,**balance of 'payments** noun [sing] the difference between the amount of money one country receives from other countries from exports, etc and the amount it pays to them for imports, etc

,**balance of 'power** noun [sing] **1** a situation in which power is evenly divided among the various sides, parties, groups, etc involved **2** the power that a smaller political party has when the larger parties need its support because they do not have enough votes on their own

'**balance sheet** noun [C] a written record of money received and money paid out, showing the difference between the totals of each

☆ **balcony** /'bælkəni/ noun [C] (*pl* **balconies**) **1** a platform built on an upstairs outside wall of a building, with a wall or rail around it: *Our hotel room had a balcony where we could sit and*

iː	ɪ	e	æ	ɑː	ɒ	ɔː	ʊ	uː	ʌ
see	sit	ten	hat	arm	got	saw	put	too	cup

balcony

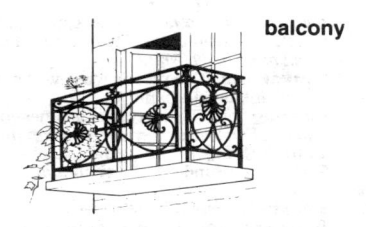

look at the lake. **2** the rows of seats high up and near the back of a theatre

bald /bɔːld/ *adj* **1** (used about people) having little or no hair on the head: *He went bald when he was only 30.* ○ *He has a bald patch on the top of his head.* ☞ picture at **hair**. **2** (used about sth that is said) simple; without extra words: *the bald truth*

balding *adj* becoming bald: *a balding man in his fifties*

bale /beɪl/ *noun* [C] a large quantity of sth (paper, hay, cloth, etc) tied together in a bundle so that it can be transported

balk = BAULK

☆ **ball¹** /bɔːl/ *noun* [C] **1** a round object that you hit, kick, throw, etc in games and sports: *a tennis ball* ○ *a golf ball* ○ *a football* ○ *The children were playing with a ball in the garden.* ○ *The ball bounced over the fence.* **2** any object that has this shape or has been formed into this shape: *a ball of wool* ○ *The cat curled up into a ball and went to sleep.* ○ *The children threw snowballs at each other.* ○ *We had meatballs and pasta for dinner.*

(IDIOMS) **(be) on the ball** (*informal*) (to be) aware of what is happening and able to react to or deal with it quickly: *With so many new developments, you really have to be on the ball.*

set/start the ball rolling to start sth (an activity, conversation, etc) that involves or is done by a group: *I made the first contribution to the collection to set the ball rolling.*

,**ball-'bearing** *noun* [C] one of a number of metal balls put between parts of a machine to make them move smoothly

'**ball game** *noun* **1** [C] any game played with a ball: *Tennis, football, golf – he's good at all ball games.* **2** [C] (*US*) a baseball match **3** [sing] (*informal*) a situation; a set of circumstances: *After living in a village for so long, living in the big city is a whole new ball game for me.*

'**ball-point** (*also* ,**ball-point 'pen**) *noun* [C] a pen with a very small metal ball at the end that rolls ink onto paper ☞ Look at **Biro**.

ball² /bɔːl/ *noun* [C] a large formal party at which people dance

'**ballroom** *noun* [C] a large room used for dancing

,**ballroom 'dancing** *noun* [U] a formal type of dance in which couples dance together using particular steps and movements

ballad /'bæləd/ *noun* [C] a long song or poem in simple language, telling a story

ballerina /ˌbæləˈriːnə/ *noun* [C] a woman who dances in ballets

ballet /'bæleɪ/ *noun* **1** [U] a style of dancing that tells a story with music but without words: *I like opera but I'm not keen on ballet.* **2** [C] a performance or work that consists of this type of dancing: *They went to see a performance of Tchaikovsky's ballet 'The Nutcracker'.*

'**ballet-dancer** *noun* [C] a person who dances in ballets

balloon /bə'luːn/ *noun* [C] **1** a small coloured rubber bag that you blow air into and use as a toy or for decoration: *We hung balloons around the room for the party.* ○ *The child cried when his balloon burst.* **2** (*also* **hot-'air balloon**) a large bag that is filled with gas or hot air so that it can rise into and fly through the air, carrying people in a basket attached below it: *They crossed the Atlantic in a balloon.*

ballot /'bælət/ *noun* [C,U] a secret written vote: *A ballot will be held to elect a new chairman.* ○ *The members of the union voted in a ballot to accept the pay rise.* ○ *The committee are elected by ballot every year.*

ballot *verb* [T] **ballot sb (about/on sth)** to ask sb to vote in a ballot; to arrange and hold a ballot: *The union is balloting its members on strike action.*

bamboo /ˌbæm'buː/ *noun* [C,U] a tall tropical plant of the grass family. Young bamboo shoots can be eaten; the hard, hollow stems are used for making furniture, etc: *a bamboo chair*

☆ **ban** /bæn/ *verb* (**banning; banned**) [T] **1** to forbid officially, often by law: *The government has banned the import of products from that country.* **2 ban sb (from sth/from doing sth)** to officially forbid sb to do sth, often by law: *He was convicted of drunken driving and banned for a year.* —**ban** *noun* [C] **a ban (on sth/sb)**: *There is a ban on smoking in this office.*

banal /bə'nɑːl; *US* 'beɪnl/ *adj* not original or interesting: *a banal comment*

banana /bə'nɑːnə; *US* bə'nænə/ *noun* [C] a long curved fruit that has a yellow skin and that can be eaten: *a bunch of bananas* ○ *a banana milk-shake*

☆ **band** /bænd/ *noun* [C] **1** a thin, flat, narrow piece of material used for fastening sth, or put round sth, often to hold it together: *She rolled up the papers and put an elastic band round them.* ○ *The cards were held together by a rubber band.* ○ *He was wearing a white hat with a black band round it.* **2** a line of a colour or design that is different from the one on either side of it: *She wore a red pullover with a green band across the middle.* **3** [with sing or pl verb] a group of people who have joined together with a common purpose: *The attack was made by a small band of rebels.* **4** a group of musicians: *a brass band* ○ *a jazz band* ○ *a rock band* **5** = WAVEBAND

'**bandwagon** *noun*

(IDIOM) **climb/jump on the bandwagon** to copy what other people are doing because it is fashionable or successful

bandage /'bændɪdʒ/ *noun* [C] a long piece of soft white material that is wrapped round a wound or injury ☞ picture at **plaster**. —**bandage** *verb* [T] **bandage sth/sb (up)**: *She played the game with a bandaged knee.*

ɜː	ə	eɪ	əʊ	aɪ	aʊ	ɔɪ	ɪə	eə	ʊə
fur	ago	pay	home	five	now	join	near	hair	pure

bandit /ˈbændɪt/ noun [C] an armed robber, usually in a wild place

☆ **bang¹** /bæŋ/ verb [I,T] **1** to make a loud noise by hitting sth hard, closing sth, or putting sth down: *The people downstairs banged on their ceiling to complain about the noise.* ○ *Somewhere in the house, I heard a door bang.* ○ *She stormed out of the room, banging the door behind her.* ○ *He banged his fist on the table and started shouting.* **2** to knock against sth by accident: *As I was crossing the room in the dark I banged into a table.* ○ *Be careful not to bang your head on the ceiling. It's quite low.*
(PHRASAL VERB) **bang about/around** to move around a place making loud noises: *I could hear him banging about in the kitchen.*

☆ **bang²** /bæŋ/ noun [C] **1** a sudden, short, very loud noise: *There was an enormous bang when the bomb exploded.* ○ *The balloon burst with a bang.* **2** a short, strong knock or blow, especially one that causes pain and injury: *He received a nasty bang on the head and was unconscious for several minutes.*

bang interj (used to sound like the noise of a gun, etc): *The children were running around with toy guns, shouting, 'Bang! Bang!'*

bang³ /bæŋ/ adv (informal) exactly; directly; right: *She phoned bang in the middle of dinner.* ○ *The shot was bang on target.*
(IDIOM) **bang goes sth** (informal) (used for expressing the idea that sth is now impossible): *'It's raining!' 'Ah well, bang goes our picnic!'*

banger /ˈbæŋə(r)/ noun [C] (Brit informal) **1** a sausage **2** an old car that is in very bad condition **3** a small firework that explodes with a short loud noise

bangle /ˈbæŋgl/ noun [C] a large bracelet or metal band that is worn round the arm for decoration ☛ picture at **jewellery**.

bangs /bæŋz/ noun [plural] (US) = FRINGE(1)

banish /ˈbænɪʃ/ verb [T] **1** to send sb away (especially out of the country), usually as a punishment: *They were banished from the country for demonstrating against the government.* ○ *The children were banished to the garden for making too much noise in the house.* **2** to remove sth completely; to force out: *She banished all hope of winning from her mind.*

banister /ˈbænɪstə(r)/ noun [C] (often plural) a rail supported by upright bars at the side of a staircase, that you hold on to when you are going up- or downstairs

banjo /ˈbændʒəʊ/ noun (pl **banjos**) a musical instrument with a long thin neck, a round body and four or more strings, played with the fingers

☆ **bank¹** /bæŋk/ noun [C] **1** an organization which keeps money safely for its customers; the office or building of such an organization. You can take money out, save, borrow or exchange money at a bank: *Is there a bank near here where I can change some traveller's cheques?* ○ *He went to the bank and got some money out of his account.* ○ *She got a loan from the bank to buy a new car.* **2** a store of things, which you keep to use later: *a data bank* ○ *a blood bank in a hospital*

banker noun [C] a person who owns or has an important job in a bank

banking noun [U] the type of business done by banks: *She decided on a career in banking.*

bank 'holiday noun [C] a public holiday (not a Saturday or Sunday) when banks are officially closed

'**banknote** noun [C] = NOTE¹(4)

'**bank statement** (also **statement**) noun [C] a printed list of all the money going into or out of a bank account during a certain period

☆ **bank²** /bæŋk/ noun [C] **1** the ground along the side of a river or canal: *People were fishing along the banks of the river.* ○ *We rowed to the bank and got out of the boat.* **2** any area of sloping ground: *There were grassy banks on either side of the road.* **3** (used about certain features of weather) a mass of sth: *a bank of cloud*

bank³ /bæŋk/ verb
(PHRASAL VERB) **bank on sb/sth** to expect and trust sb to do sth, or sth to happen: *I suppose you might be lucky but I wouldn't bank on it.* ○ *We haven't booked a hotel – we're banking on finding somewhere to stay when we get there.*

☆ **bankrupt** /ˈbæŋkrʌpt/ adj not having enough money to pay your debts: *The company went bankrupt owing thousands of pounds.*

bankrupt verb [T] to cause sb/sth to become bankrupt

bankruptcy /ˈbæŋkrəpsɪ/ noun [C,U] (pl **bankruptcies**) the state when a person or an organization is bankrupt: *During this period of economic difficulty, bankruptcies are becoming more common.* ○ *Competition from larger companies drove them to bankruptcy.*

banner /ˈbænə(r)/ noun [C] a long piece of cloth with words or signs on it, which can be hung up or carried through the streets on two poles: *The demonstrators carried banners saying 'Stop the War'.*

banquet /ˈbæŋkwɪt/ noun [C] a formal dinner for a large number of people, usually as a special event at which speeches are made

baptism /ˈbæptɪzəm/ noun [C,U] a ceremony in which a person becomes a member of the Christian Church by being placed briefly under water or having drops of water put onto his/her head. Often he/she is also publicly given a name. ☛ Look at **christening**.

baptize (also **baptise**) /bæpˈtaɪz/ verb [T] to perform the ceremony of baptism: *Were you baptized as a child?* ○ *He was baptized 'George David'.*

Baptist /ˈbæptɪst/ noun, adj (a member) of a Protestant Church that believes that baptism should only be for people who are old enough to understand the meaning of the ceremony and should be done by placing the person fully under water

☆ **bar¹** /bɑː(r)/ noun [C] **1** a place where you can buy and drink (especially alcoholic) drinks and sometimes have sth to eat: *They had a drink in the bar before the meal.* ○ *a wine bar* ○ *a coffee bar* ○ *a snack bar*

☛ In Britain, a bar where you can get alcoholic drinks is not a separate building (except a wine bar), but usually found as part of a pub, hotel, restaurant, etc. In a pub there may be two types of bar. The lounge bar is more comfortable (and often more expensive) than the public bar.

2 a long, narrow, high table or counter where drinks are served: *She went to the bar and ordered a drink* ○ *We sat on stools at the bar.* ○ *He works behind the bar in the local pub.* **3** a long, thin, straight piece of metal, often placed across a window or door, etc to make it strong or to prevent people from passing through it: *They escaped by sawing through the bars of their prison cell.* ○ *To open the emergency exit door, push the bar.* **4** a small block of solid material, longer than it is wide: *a bar of soap* ○ *a bar of chocolate* **5** a thing that prevents you from doing sth: *Lack of education is not always a bar to success in business.* **6** one of the short, equal units of time into which music is divided: *If you sing a few bars of the song I might recognize it.*
(IDIOM) **behind bars** (*informal*) in prison

'barmaid *noun* [C] a woman who serves drinks from behind a bar in a pub, etc

'barman /-mən/ *noun* [C] (*pl* **barmen** /-mən/) a man who serves drinks from behind a bar in a pub, etc

bar² /bɑː(r)/ *verb* [T] (**barring**; **barred**) **1** to fasten with a bar(3) or bars: *The heavy door was barred and bolted.* **2** to stop sb going through or into a place: *A line of police barred the entrance to the embassy.* **3 bar sb from sth/ from doing sth** to forbid sb officially to do, use or enter sth: *She was barred from the club for bad behaviour.*

bar³ /bɑː(r)/ *prep* except: *All the seats were taken, bar one.*

barbarian /bɑːˈbeəriən/ *noun* [C] a wild, uncivilized person

barbaric /bɑːˈbærɪk/ (*also* **barbarous**) *adj* very cruel and violent: *barbaric punishments* ○ *barbaric treatment of prisoners* —**barbarism** /ˈbɑːbərɪzəm/ *noun* [U]: *acts of barbarism committed in war*

barbarous /ˈbɑːbərəs/ *adj* **1** = BARBARIC **2** uncivilized; without culture: *a barbarous society*

barbecue /ˈbɑːbɪkjuː/ *noun* [C] **1** a metal frame on which food is cooked over an open fire outdoors **2** an outdoor party at which food is cooked in this way: *Let's have a barbecue.* —**barbecue** *verb* [T]: *barbecued steak*

barbed wire /ˌbɑːbd ˈwaɪə(r)/ *noun* [U] strong wire with sharp points on it: *a barbed wire fence*

barber /ˈbɑːbə(r)/ *noun* [C] a man who cuts men's hair: *Your hair's getting rather long. It's time you went to the barber's.* ☛ Note that the **barber** is the person who runs the shop and the **barber's** is the shop.

☆ **bare** /beə(r)/ *adj* **1** (used about part of the body) not covered by clothing: *bare arms* ○ *a bare chest* ○ *She killed him with her bare hands* (= *without a weapon*). ☛ Look at **naked** and **nude**. **2** without anything covering it: *They had taken the painting down, so the walls were all bare.* **3** empty; without its usual contents: *I looked for some food but the cupboards were bare.* **4** minimum, basic and no more: *We were so poor that we didn't even have the bare necessities of life.* ○ *Just give me the bare facts as quickly as you can.*

barely *adv* only just; hardly; almost not: *You've barely eaten anything – are you feeling all right?* ○ *She's barely older than you.*

'bareback *adj*, *adv* on a horse without a saddle: *bareback riders in the circus* ○ *She likes riding bareback.*

'barefoot (*also* **ˌbareˈfooted**) *adj*, *adv* with nothing (eg shoes, socks, etc) on the feet: *I was barefoot because my shoes and socks had got wet.* ○ *We walked barefoot along the beach.*

bargain /ˈbɑːɡɪn/ *noun* [C] **1** an agreement between people or groups about what each of them will do for the other or others: *'You wash and I'll dry up.' 'Okay, it's a bargain.'* ○ *I hope he keeps his side of the bargain.* **2** something that is cheaper or at a lower price than usual: *At that price, it's an absolute bargain!* ○ *I found a lot of bargains in the sale.*
(IDIOMS) **into the bargain** (used for emphasizing sth) as well; in addition; also: *They gave me free tickets and a free meal into the bargain.* ○ *She's a good manager and a nice person into the bargain.*
strike a bargain ⇨ STRIKE²

bargain *verb* [I] **bargain (with sb) (about/ over/for sth)** to discuss the form of an agreement, a price, etc: *I'm sure that if you bargain with him, he'll drop the price.* ○ *They bargained over the price.*
(PHRASAL VERB) **bargain for/on sth** to expect sth or to be prepared for sth: *When I agreed to help him I didn't bargain for how much it would cost me.*

bargaining *noun* [U] discussion about the form of an agreement, the price for a sale, etc, in which people are trying to get a result that is to their own advantage: *Hours of bargaining failed to produce an agreement.*

barge /bɑːdʒ/ *noun* [C] a long narrow boat with a flat bottom that is used for transporting goods or people on a canal or river

baritone /ˈbærɪtəʊn/ *noun* [C] a singing voice that is fairly low, between tenor and bass

bark¹ /bɑːk/ *noun* [U] the hard outer covering of a tree

☆ **bark²** /bɑːk/ *verb* **1** [I] **bark (at sb/sth)** (used about dogs) to make a loud, short noise or noises: *Their dog always barks at anyone who rings the doorbell.* **2** [I,T] **bark (sth) (out) (at sb)** to speak to sb in a loud voice with an angry or aggressive tone: *The boss came in, barked some orders and left again.* —**bark** *noun* [C]: *The dog next door has a very loud bark.*

barley /ˈbɑːli/ *noun* [U] **1** a plant similar to grass that produces grain that is used for food or for making beer and other drinks **2** the grain produced by this plant

barn /bɑːn/ *noun* [C] a large building on a farm in which crops or animals are kept

barometer /bəˈrɒmɪtə(r)/ *noun* [C] **1** an

instrument that measures air pressure and indicates changes in weather **2** something that indicates the state of sth (a situation, a feeling, etc): *Results of local elections are often a barometer of the government's popularity.*

baron /'bærən/ *noun* [C] **1** a man who belongs to the lowest rank of the aristocracy **2** a person who controls a large part of a particular industry or type of business: *an oil baron*

baroness /'bærənɪs/ *noun* [C] a woman who is of the same rank as a baron or is the wife of a baron

barracks /'bærəks/ *noun* [C, with sing or pl verb] (*pl* **barracks**) a building or group of buildings in which soldiers live: *Guards were on duty at the gate of the barracks.*

barrage /'bærɑːʒ; *US* bə'rɑːʒ/ *noun* [C] **1** a continuous attack with a large number of guns in a particular direction **2** a large number of questions, remarks, etc, aimed at a person very quickly: *The minister faced a barrage of questions from reporters.*

barrel /'bærəl/ *noun* [C] **1** a large, round, often wooden container for liquids, that has a flat top and bottom and is wider in the middle: *a barrel of wine* ○ *The price of oil is usually given per barrel.* **2** the long metal tube of a gun, through which the bullet passes when it is fired

barrel

barren /'bærən/ *adj* **1** (used about land) not good enough to grow crops on **2** (used about trees or plants) not producing fruit or seeds

barricade /,bærɪ'keɪd/ *noun* [C] an object or line of objects that is placed (usually quickly) across a road, entrance, etc to stop people getting through: *The demonstrators put up barricades to keep the police away.*

barricade *verb* [T] to block sth with a barricade: *Rioters barricaded the road with cars.*
(PHRASAL VERB) **barricade yourself in** to defend yourself by putting up a barricade: *Demonstrators took over the university building and barricaded themselves in.*

☆ **barrier** /'bæriə(r)/ *noun* [C] **1** an object that keeps people or things apart or prevents them moving from one place to another: *The police put up barriers along the pavement to stop the crowd getting on to the road.* ○ *You must show your ticket at the barrier before going onto the platform.* **2** something that causes problems or makes it impossible for sth to happen: *Old-fashioned attitudes are a barrier to progress.* ○ *When you live in a foreign country, the language barrier is often the most difficult problem to overcome.* ○ *trade barriers*

barring /'bɑːrɪŋ/ *prep* **1** except for: *Barring one or two small problems, everything's fine at the moment.* **2** if there is/are not: *Barring any unforeseen problems, we'll be moving house in a month.*

barrister /'bærɪstə(r)/ *noun* [C] (in English law) a lawyer who is qualified to speak in the higher courts ☞ Look at the note at **lawyer**.

barrow /'bærəʊ/ *noun* [C] **1** = WHEELBARROW **2** a small cart on which fruit, vegetables, etc are moved or sold in the street, especially in markets

barter /'bɑːtə(r)/ *verb* [I,T] **barter sth (for sth)** to exchange goods for other goods, not for money: *I bartered my watch for a guitar with a man in the street.*

barter *noun* [U] the exchange of goods for other goods, not for money: *Spices were used for barter many years ago.*

☆ **base¹** /beɪs/ *noun* [C] **1** the lowest part of sth, especially the part on which it stands or at which it is attached to sth: *The sculptor's name can be found at the base of the statue.* ○ *I felt a terrible pain at the base of my spine.* **2** a starting point from which sth develops or is made: *With these ingredients as a base, you can create all sorts of interesting dishes.* **3** a strong foundation on which sth is built or maintained: *The country needs a strong economic base.* **4** a place used as a centre from which activities are done or controlled: *This hotel is an ideal base for touring the region.* ○ *Taxi drivers are in contact with their base so that they know where to go to next.* **5** a military centre from which forces operate: *an army base* ○ *an air base* ○ *a naval base*

☆ **base²** /beɪs/ *verb* [T] **1 base sth on sth** to form or develop sth from a particular starting point or source: *This film is based on a true story.* **2** (usually passive) **base sb/sth in...** to make one place the centre from which sb/sth can work or move around: *I'm based in New York, although my job involves a great deal of travel.*

baseball /'beɪsbɔːl/ *noun* [U] a team game that is popular in the USA in which players hit the ball with a bat and run round four points (**bases**). They have to touch all four bases in order to score a point (**run**).

basement /'beɪsmənt/ *noun* [C] the lowest room or rooms of a building which are partly or completely below ground level: *The toy department is in the basement of the store.* ○ *a basement flat*

bases *pl* of BASIS

bash /bæʃ/ *verb* (*informal*) **1** [T] to hit sb/sth very hard **2** [I] **bash against/into sb/sth** to crash into sb/sth

bash *noun* [C] a hard blow
(IDIOM) **have a bash (at sth)** (*informal*) to try: *I don't know whether I can do it, but I'll have a bash.*

bashful /'bæʃfl/ *adj* shy and embarrassed

☆ **basic** /'beɪsɪk/ *adj* **1** forming a starting point or basis on which other ideas rest: *The basic question is, can we afford it?* **2** simplest or most elementary; including only what is most necessary: *This course teaches basic skills in First Aid.* ○ *The basic pay is £100 a week – with extra for overtime.* ○ *The rooms in the cheapest hotels are very basic – they have no bathrooms or televisions.*

basically /-klɪ/ *adv* looking at what is most important or basic in a person or an object or

iː	ɪ	e	æ	ɑː	ɒ	ɔː	ʊ	uː	ʌ
see	sit	ten	hat	arm	got	saw	put	too	cup

in a particular situation: *She seemed to me to be basically a very nice person.* ○ *The design of the new car is basically the same as the old one.* ○ *Basically, all I want is to be left alone.*

basics *noun* [plural] the things that you need most or that are the most important: *You can get all the basics at the local shop.*

☆**basin** /'beɪsn/ *noun* [C] **1** = WASH-BASIN: *a shower room with bidet, basin and WC* **2** a round open bowl often used for mixing or cooking food: *a pudding basin* **3** an area of land from which water flows into a river: *the Congo Basin*

☆**basis** /'beɪsɪs/ *noun* [C] (*pl* **bases** /'beɪsiːz/) **1** the way sth is done or organized: *They meet on a regular basis.* ○ *The changes have been introduced on a voluntary basis this year but will become compulsory next year.* **2** the principle or reason which lies behind sth: *We made our decision on the basis of the reports which you sent us.* **3** a starting point, from which sth can develop: *Her diaries formed the basis of the book she later wrote.*

bask /bɑːsk; *US* bæsk/ *verb* [I] to sit or lie in a place where you can enjoy the warmth: *The snake basked in the sunshine on the rock.* ○ (*figurative*) *He basked in the admiration of his fans.*

☆**basket** /'bɑːskɪt; *US* 'bæskɪt/ *noun* [C] a container for carrying or holding things, made of strips of light material such as cane or wire that are woven together: *a waste-paper basket* ○ *a shopping basket* ○ *a basket of shopping* (= one that is full of shopping) ☛ picture at **bag**.
(IDIOM) **put all your eggs in one basket** ⇨ EGG

basketball

basket

basketball /'bɑːskɪtbɔːl; *US* 'bæs-/ *noun* [U] a game for two teams of five players. There is a net (**basket**) fixed to a metal ring high up at each end of the court and the players try to throw a ball through the other team's net in order to score points (**baskets**).

bass /beɪs/ *noun* **1** [C] the lowest male singing voice; a singer with this kind of voice **2** [U] the lowest part in music **3** [C] = DOUBLE-BASS **4** [C] (*also* **bass guitar**) an electric guitar which plays very low notes ☛ picture at **rock band**.

bass *adj* producing a deep sound; connected with the lowest part in music: *a bass drum* ○ *Can you sing the bass part in this song?*

bassoon /bə'suːn/ *noun* [C] a musical instrument of the woodwind family which makes a very deep sound

bastard /'bɑːstəd; *US* 'bæs-/ *noun* [C] **1** a child whose parents were not married to each other when he/she was born ☛ You may offend people by using this word. A more neutral expression is 'an **illegitimate** child'. **2** (*slang*) (used as an insult) an unpleasant or cruel person

bat¹ /bæt/ *noun* [C] a small animal, like a mouse with wings, which comes out and flies around at night

bat² /bæt/ *noun* [C] a piece of wood for hitting the ball in sports such as table tennis, cricket or baseball: *a cricket bat* ☛ Look at **club²**(2), **racket¹** and **stick¹**(3).

bat

(IDIOM) **off your own bat** without anyone asking you or helping you

bat *verb* [I] (**batting**; **batted**) (used about one player or a whole team) to have a turn hitting the ball in sports such as cricket or baseball

bat³ /bæt/ *verb* (**batting**; **batted**)
(IDIOM) **not bat an eyelid** to show no reaction

batch /bætʃ/ *noun* [C] a number of things or people which belong together as a group: *The bus returned to the airport for the next batch of tourists.*

bated /'beɪtɪd/ *adj*
(IDIOM) **with bated breath** excited or afraid, because you are waiting for sth to happen

☆**bath** /bɑːθ; *US* bæθ/ *noun* (*pl* **baths** /bɑːðz; *US* bæðz/) **1** [C] (*especially US* **'bath-tub**) a large container for water in which you sit to wash your body: *All the rooms have a private bath or shower.* ○ *Can you answer the phone? I'm in the bath!* **2** [sing] an act of washing the whole of your body when you sit or lie in a bath filled with water: *to have a bath* ○ *Would you prefer to take a bath or a shower?* ○ *bath oil* **3 baths** [plural] (*Brit*) an indoor public swimming-pool or a building where you can take a bath

bath *verb* **1** [T] to give sb a bath: *bath the baby* **2** [I] to have a bath: *I prefer to bath in the mornings.*

'bathrobe *noun* [C] = DRESSING-GOWN

'bathroom *noun* [C] **1** a room where there is a bath and usually a wash-basin (and sometimes a toilet) **2** (*US*) a room with a toilet ☛ Look at **toilet**.

'bath-tub *noun* [C] = BATH(1)

bathe /beɪð/ *verb* **1** [I] to swim in the sea or in a lake or river **2** [T] to wash or put part of the body in water, often for medical reasons: *She bathed the wound with antiseptic.*

bathed *adj* (not before a noun) covered with or surrounded by sth: *The room was bathed in light.*

bathing *noun* [U] the act of swimming in the sea, etc (not in a swimming-pool): *Bathing is possible at a number of beaches along the coast.*

baton /'bætn; 'bætɒn; *US* bə'tɒn/ *noun* [C] **1** a

ɜː	ə	eɪ	əʊ	aɪ	aʊ	ɔɪ	ɪə	eə	ʊə
fur	ago	pay	home	five	now	join	near	hair	pure

short thin stick used by the conductor of an orchestra **2** = TRUNCHEON **3** a stick which a runner in a relay race passes to the next person in the team **4** a plastic or rubber bullet

battalion /bəˈtælɪən/ *noun* [C] a large unit of soldiers forming part of another larger unit in the army

batter¹ /ˈbætə(r)/ *verb* [I,T] to hit sb/sth hard, many times: *The wind battered against the window.* ○ *He battered the door down.* ○ *High winds battered Britain again yesterday.* ○ *The parents were accused of battering the child* (= of hitting him/her often and violently).

▶ **battered** *adj* no longer looking new; damaged or out of shape: *a battered old hat*

batter² /ˈbætə(r)/ *noun* [U] a mixture of flour, eggs and milk used to make pancakes, etc or to cover food such as fish before frying

☆ **battery** /ˈbætəri/ *noun* [C] (*pl* **batteries**) **1** a device which provides electricity for a torch, radio, car, etc: *I need a new battery for my Walkman.* ○ *He couldn't start the car because the battery was flat.* ☛ picture at **light**. When a car battery is flat, you need to **recharge** it. **2** a large number of very small cages in which hens are kept: *a battery chicken* ☛ Look at **free-range**.

☆ **battle** /ˈbætl/ *noun* **1** [C,U] a fight, especially between armies in a war: *the battle of Trafalgar* ○ *They won the first battle but still they lost the war.* ○ *to die/be killed in battle* **2** [C] a struggle of any kind: *After three years she lost her battle against cancer.* ○ *the battle against inflation*

(IDIOM) **a losing battle** ➔ LOSE

▶ **battle** *verb* [I] **battle (with/against sb/sth) (for sth); battle (on)** to fight hard; to struggle: *Mark is battling with his maths homework.* ○ *The little boat battled against the wind.* ○ *The two brothers were battling for control of the family business.* ○ *Life is hard at the moment but we're battling on.*

'battlefield, 'battleground *noun* [C] the place where a battle is fought

'battleship *noun* [C] the largest type of ship used in war

baulk (*also* **balk**) /bɔːk/ *verb* [I] **baulk (at sth)** to be unwilling to do or agree to sth because it seems difficult, dangerous or unpleasant: *She liked the flat but she baulked at paying so much for it.*

bawl /bɔːl/ *verb* [I,T] to shout or cry loudly

☆ **bay¹** /beɪ/ *noun* [C] a part of the coast where the land forms a curve inwards: *the Bay of Bengal* ○ *The harbour was in a sheltered bay.*

bay² /beɪ/ *noun* [C] a part of a building, aircraft or area which has a particular purpose: *the loading bay of the factory*

,bay 'window *noun* [C] a window in a part of a room that sticks out from the wall of a house

bay³ /beɪ/ *noun* [C]

(IDIOM) **hold/keep sb at bay** to stop sb who is chasing you from coming near; to stop sb/sth reaching you

bayonet /ˈbeɪənɪt/ *noun* [C] a knife which can be fixed to the end of a gun

bazaar /bəˈzɑː(r)/ *noun* [C] **1** (in Eastern countries) a market **2** a sale where the money that is made goes to charity: *a church bazaar*

☆ **be¹** /bɪ; strong form biː/ *auxiliary verb*

present tense	past tense
I **am** (I**'m**)	I **was**
you **are** (you**'re**)	you **were**
he/she/it **is** (he**'s**/she**'s**/it**'s**)	he/she/it **was**
we **are** (we**'re**)	we **were**
you **are** (you**'re**)	you **were**
they **are** (they**'re**)	they **were**
past participle	**been**
present participle	**being**
negative short forms	**aren't, isn't, wasn't, weren't**

1 (used to form the continuous tense of verbs): *You're sitting on my book.* ○ *We were listening to the radio.* ○ *Is he coming?* ○ *How long have we been waiting?* **2** (used to form the passive): *This cheese is made in France.* ○ *We were taken to the police station.* ○ *The car has been repaired.* **3** (used to show that sth must happen or that sth has been arranged): *You are to leave here at 10 o'clock at the latest.* ○ *They are to be married in June.* **4** (used to show that sth is possible but not very likely): *If they were to offer me the job, I'd probably take it.*

☆ **be²** /bɪ; strong form biː/ *verb* **1** (used with *there* to say that sb/sth exists or is in in a particular place): *Is there a God?* ○ *I tried phoning them but there was no answer.* ○ *There are some people outside.* ○ *There are a lot of trees in our garden.* **2** (used when you are naming people or things, describing them or giving more information about them): *That's Jane over there.* ○ *I'm Alan.* ○ *He's Italian. He's from Milan.* ○ *Sue is 18. She's at university.* ○ *He's a doctor.* ○ *What's that?* ○ *A lion is a mammal.* ○ *Where are the scissors?* ○ *'What colour is your car?' 'It's green.'* ○ *It's 6 o'clock.* ○ *It was Tuesday yesterday.* ○ *How much was your ticket?* ○ *The film was excellent.* ○ *She's very friendly.* **3** (only used in the perfect tenses) to go to a place (and return): *Have you ever been to Japan?* ☛ Compare **has/have gone**: *Julia's gone to the doctor's* (= she hasn't returned yet). ○ *Julia's been to the doctor's today* (= she has returned).

(IDIOMS) **be yourself** to act naturally: *Don't be nervous; just be yourself and the interview will be fine.*

-to-be (in compounds) future: *his wife-to-be*

☆ **beach** /biːtʃ/ *noun* [C] the piece of sandy or rocky land next to the sea: *a nice sandy beach*

beacon /ˈbiːkən/ *noun* [C] a fire or light on a hill, a tower or near the coast, which is used as a signal

bead /biːd/ *noun* [C] **1** a small ball of wood, glass or plastic with a hole in the middle for threading a string through **2 beads** [plural] a necklace made of beads ☛ picture at **jewel-**

beach

[illustration labels: cliff, sand-dunes, waves, beach]

lery. **3** a drop of liquid: *There were beads of sweat on his forehead.*
☆ **beak** /biːk/ *noun* [C] the hard pointed part of a bird's mouth ☞ picture at **bird**.
beaker /ˈbiːkə(r)/ *noun* [C] **1** a tall cup for drinks, sometimes without a handle **2** a glass container used in laboratories for pouring liquids
beam /biːm/ *noun* [C] **1** a long piece of wood, metal, concrete, etc that is used to support weight, eg in the floor or ceiling of a building **2** a line of light: *the beam of a car's headlights* o *a laser beam* **3** a happy smile
beam *verb* **1** [I] to send out light and warmth: *The sun beamed down on them.* **2** [I] to smile happily: *Beaming with pleasure she stepped forward to receive her prize.* **3** [T] to broadcast a signal: *The programme was beamed live by satellite to many different countries.*
☆ **bean** /biːn/ *noun* [C] **1** the seeds or seed containers (**pods**) from a climbing plant which are eaten as vegetables: *broad beans* o *runner beans* o *soya beans* o *a tin of baked beans* (= beans in a tomato sauce) **2** similar seeds from other plants: *coffee beans*
☆ **bear¹** /beə(r)/ *noun* [C] a large, heavy wild animal with thick fur: *a brown bear* o *a polar bear.* ☞ Look at **teddy bear**.
☆ **bear²** /beə(r)/ *verb* [T] (*pt* **bore** /bɔː(r)/; *pp* **borne** /bɔːn/) **1** to support sth: *Twelve pillars bear the weight of the roof.* **2** (*formal*) to carry sth: *The waiters came in bearing trays of food.* o (*figurative*) *In her position as Minister she bears a great responsibility.* o (*figurative*) *Customers will bear the full cost of the improvements.* **3** to suffer sth without complaining or giving in: *She bore her illness bravely.* o *The heat is too much to bear.* o *These figures won't bear close examination* (= when you look closely you will find mistakes). **4** (with *can/could* in negative sentences or in questions) to dislike strongly; to hate: *I can't bear spiders.* o *Joanne can't bear people who are late.* o *She can't bear waiting for people.* o *She can't bear to wait for people.* o *How can you bear to listen to that music?* **5** (*formal*) to give birth to children: *She bore four children, all sons.* ☞ A more common expression is 'She has had four children.' When you talk about a person's own birth you use 'to be born': *Robert was born in 1986.* o *The baby will be born in spring.* **6** to produce flowers or fruit: *The tree in our garden bears more apples than we can eat.* o (*figurative*) *Our plan is beginning to bear fruit — these are the first signs of success.* **7** to show the mark of sth: *The coins bear the date and the Queen's head on them.* o *He still bears the scars of his accident.* o *She bears a strong resemblance to her mother* (= she is very like her). **8** (*formal*) to have a feeling: *I offended him once and he bore me a grudge for years.* **9** to turn or go in the direction that is mentioned: *At the crossroads, bear left.*
(IDIOMS) **bear the brunt of sth** to suffer the main force of sth: *The west bore the brunt of the storm.*
bear in mind (that) to remember that: *You can have something to eat now but bear in mind that there'll be a big meal later.*
bear/keep sb/sth in mind ⇨ **MIND¹**
bear witness (to sth) to show evidence of sth: *The burning buildings and empty streets bore witness to a recent attack.*
(PHRASAL VERBS) **bear sb/sth out** to show that sb is right or that sth is true: *The figures bear him out.* o *The figures bear out what he says.*
bear with sb/sth to be patient with: *Bear with me — I won't be much longer.*
bearable /ˈbeərəbl/ *adj* that you can bear(2): *It was extremely hot but the breeze made it more bearable.* ☞ The opposite is **unbearable**.
☆ **beard** /bɪəd/ *noun* [C,U] the hair which grows on a man's cheeks and chin: *He's got a beard.* o *He's growing a beard.* o *He's had his beard shaved off.* ☞ picture at **moustache**.
bearded *adj* with a beard
bearer /ˈbeərə(r)/ *noun* [C] a person who carries or brings sth: *a cheque payable to the bearer*
bearing /ˈbeərɪŋ/ *noun* **1** [U] **bearing on sth** relation or connection to the subject being discussed: *Her comments had no bearing on our decision.* **2** [C] a direction measured by a compass
(IDIOM) **lose your bearings** to become confused about where you are
beast /biːst/ *noun* [C] **1** (*formal*) an animal, especially a large one: *a wild beast* **2** (*informal*) an unpleasant or cruel person
beastly *adj* (*informal*) very unpleasant
☆ **beat¹** /biːt/ *verb* (*pt* **beat**; *pp* **beaten** /ˈbiːtn/) **1** [I,T] to hit many times, usually very hard: *The man was beating the donkey with a stick.* o *The rain was beating on the roof of the car.* **2** [T] to mix quickly with a fork, etc: *Beat the eggs and sugar together.* **3** [I,T] to make a regular sound or movement: *Her heart beat faster as she ran to pick up her child.* o *We could hear the drums beating as the band marched towards us.* o *The bird beat its wings and tried to fly away.* **4** [T] to defeat sb; to be better than sth: *He always beats me at tennis.* o *We're hoping to beat the world record.* o *You can't beat a nice cup of tea.* o (*informal*) *This question beats me* (= it is too difficult for me).

s	z	ʃ	ʒ	h	m	n	ŋ	l	r	j	w
so	zoo	she	vision	how	man	no	sing	leg	red	yes	wet

(IDIOMS) **beat about the bush** to talk about sth without mentioning the main point
beat time (to sth) to move sth (a stick, your foot or your hand) following the rhythm of a piece of music
off the beaten track in a place where people do not often go
(PHRASAL VERBS) **beat sb/sth off** to fight until sb/sth goes away: *The thieves tried to take his wallet but he beat them off.*
beat sb to sth to get somewhere or do sth before sb else: *She beat me back to the house.* o *I wanted to ring him first but Sheila beat me to it.*
beat sb up to attack sb by hitting or kicking
beating noun [C] **1** a punishment that you give to sb by hitting him/her: *The boys got a beating when they were caught stealing.* **2** a defeat
(IDIOM) **take a lot of/some beating** to be so good that it would be difficult to find sth better: *Mary's cooking takes some beating.*

beat² /biːt/ noun **1** [C] a single stroke or blow that comes at regular intervals in a series; the sound it makes: *a heartbeat* o *the beat of the drums* **2** [sing] the strong rhythm that a piece of (especially pop) music has **3** [sing] the route along which a policeman or woman regularly walks: *Having more policemen on the beat helps reduce crime.*

beautician /bjuːˈtɪʃn/ noun [C] a person whose job is to improve the way people look, eg with beauty treatments and make-up

☆ **beautiful** /ˈbjuːtɪfl/ adj lovely; attractive; giving pleasure to the senses: *The view from the top of the hill was really beautiful.* o *What a beautiful day – the weather's perfect!* o *He has a beautiful voice.* o *A beautiful perfume filled the air.* o *a beautiful woman* ☞ **Beautiful** is usually used for women and girls. It is stronger than **pretty**, which is also used of women and girls only. Men are described as **handsome** or **good-looking**. —**beautifully** /-fli/ adv: *He plays the piano beautifully.* o *She was beautifully dressed.*

☆ **beauty** /ˈbjuːti/ noun (pl **beauties**) **1** [U] the quality which gives pleasure to the senses; the state of being beautiful: *Thousands of tourists are attracted to Cornwall by the beauty of its coast.* o *Brahms wrote music of great beauty.* **2** [C] a beautiful woman: *She grew up to be a beauty.* **3** [C] a particularly good example of sth: *Look at this tomato – it's a beauty!*
'beauty spot noun [C] a place which is famous for its attractive scenery

beaver /ˈbiːvə(r)/ noun [C] an animal with brown fur, a long, broad tail and sharp teeth, with which it cuts branches to make dams across rivers

became pt of BECOME

☆ **because** /bɪˈkɒz; US -kɔːz/ conj for the reason that: *They didn't go for a walk because it was raining.*
because of prep by reason of, as a result of: *They didn't go for a walk because of the rain.*

beck /bek/ noun
(IDIOM) **at sb's beck and call** always ready to obey sb's orders

beckon /ˈbekən/ verb [I,T] to show sb (often with a movement of your finger or hand) that you want him/her to come closer: *She beckoned me over to speak to her.*

☆ **become** /bɪˈkʌm/ verb [I] (pt **became** /bɪˈkeɪm/; pp **become**) to begin to be sth: *John Major became Prime Minister in 1990.* o *She wants to become a pilot.* o *They became friends.* o *She became nervous as the exam date came closer.* o *He is becoming more like you every day.* o *It became clear that she wanted to stay.* ☞ **Get** is also used with adjectives in this sense: *She got nervous as the exam date came closer.* o *He's getting more like you every day.* It is very common in conversation and is less formal than **become**.
(PHRASAL VERB) **become of sb/sth** to happen to sb/sth: *What became of Eileen? – I haven't seen her for years!*

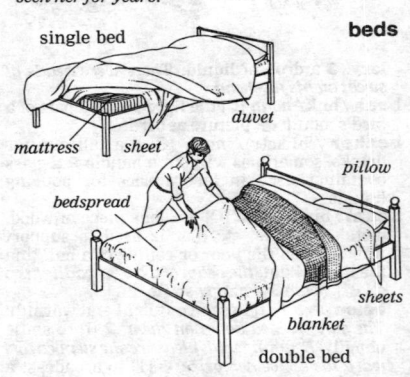

beds
single bed
duvet
mattress   sheet
bedspread
pillow
sheets
blanket
double bed

☆ **bed¹** /bed/ noun **1** [C,U] a piece of furniture that you lie on when you sleep: *a single/double bed* o *twin beds* (= two single beds in one room) o *The children sleep in bunk beds.* o *to make a bed* (= to arrange the sheets, etc so that the bed is tidy and ready for sb to sleep in) o *What time do you usually go to bed?* o *When he rang I was already in bed.* o *It's late. It's time for bed.* o *to get into/out of bed* **2** [C] the ground at the bottom of a river or the sea **3** = FLOWER-BED
(IDIOMS) **bed and breakfast** accommodation in a house or small hotel that consists of a room for the night and breakfast; a place that provides this: *Bed and breakfast costs £23 per night.* o *We stayed in a nice bed and breakfast near Cork.*
go to bed with sb (informal) to have sex with sb

'bedclothes noun [plural] the sheets, etc that you use on a bed
'bedroom noun [C] a room which is used for sleeping in: *You can sleep in the spare bedroom.*
'bedside noun [sing] the area that is next to a bed: *She sat at his bedside all night long.* o *a bedside table*
'bed-sitter (also **'bedsit**) noun [C] (Brit) a room which is used for both living and sleeping in
'bedspread noun [C] an attractive cover for a

bed that you put on top of the sheets and blankets ☞ picture at **bed**.

'bedtime *noun* [C,U] the time that you normally go to bed

bed² /bed/ *verb* [T] to place sth firmly in or on sth

(PHRASAL VERB) **bed down** to make yourself comfortable and sleep somewhere: *We couldn't find a hotel so we bedded down for the night in the back of the van.*

-bedded (in compounds) having the stated type or number of beds: *a twin-bedded room* ○ *a three-bedded room*

bedding *noun* [U] the sheets, etc that are used on a bed, sometimes including the mattress

☆ **bee** /biː/ *noun* [C] a black and yellow striped insect that lives in large groups and that makes honey ☞ picture at **insect**. A large number of bees together is a **swarm**. Bees **buzz** or **hum** when they make a noise. They may **sting** if they are angry.

'beehive (*also* **hive**) *noun* [C] a type of box that people use for keeping bees in

beech /biːtʃ/ (*also* **'beech tree**) *noun* [C,U] a large tree with a smooth trunk that has small three-sided nuts

☆ **beef** /biːf/ *noun* [U] the meat of a cow: *a slice of roast beef* ☞ Look at the note at **meat**.

beefburger /'biːfbɜːɡə(r)/ *noun* [C] minced beef in a flat round shape ☞ Look at **hamburger**.

☆ **been** /biːn/ *pp* of BE, GO ☞ **Been** is used as the past participle of both **be** and **go**: *I've never been seriously ill.* ○ *I've never been to Lisbon.* **Gone** is also a past participle of **go**. Note the difference in meaning: *They've been to the cinema* (= They went and have come back). ○ *They've gone to the cinema* (= They went and have not yet come back).

beep /biːp/ *noun* [C] a short high noise, eg made by the horn of a car

beep *verb* [I] to make a beep

☆ **beer** /bɪə(r)/ *noun* **1** [U] a type of alcoholic drink that is made from grain **2** [C] a type or glass of beer: *This pub serves a wide range of beers.* ○ *We stopped for a couple of beers on the way home.*

☞ **Lager** is a type of light-coloured beer. **Ale** is a type of strong dark beer. **Shandy** is beer mixed with lemonade.

beetle /'biːtl/ *noun* [C] an insect that has hard coverings for its wings and often a black shiny body. There are many different types of beetle. ☞ picture at **insect**.

beetroot /'biːtruːt/ (*US* **beet**) *noun* [C,U] a dark red vegetable which is the root of a plant. Beetroot is cooked and can be eaten hot or cold.

befall /bɪ'fɔːl/ *verb* [I,T] (*pt* **befell** /bɪ'fel/; *pp* **befallen** /bɪ'fɔːlən/) (*formal*) (used about sth bad) to happen to sb

☆ **before¹** /bɪ'fɔː(r)/ *prep* **1** earlier than sb/sth: *You can call me any time before 10 o'clock.* ○ *the week before last* ○ *Ellen worked in Liverpool before moving here.* ○ *They should be here before long* (= soon). **2** in front/ahead of sb/sth (in an order): *'H' comes before 'N' in the alphabet.* ○ (*figurative*) *A very difficult task lies before us.* ○ (*figurative*) *a company that puts profit before safety* **3** when sb is present: *You will appear before the court in the morning.* **4** (*formal*) in a position in front of sb/sth: *They knelt before the throne.*

☆ **before²** /bɪ'fɔː(r)/ *conj* **1** earlier than the time that: *Turn the lights off before you leave.* **2** (*formal*) rather than: *I'd die before I apologized to him!*

☆ **before³** /bɪ'fɔː(r)/ *adv* at an earlier time: *I think we've met somewhere before.* ○ *It was fine yesterday but it rained the day before.*

beforehand /bɪ'fɔːhænd/ *adv* at an earlier time than sth: *We prepared most of the food for the party beforehand.*

befriend /bɪ'frend/ *verb* [T] (*formal*) to act as a friend to sb; to be kind to sb

beg /beɡ/ *verb* [I,T] (**begging**; **begged**) **1 beg (for) sth (from/of sb)** to ask sb for food, money, etc, eg because you are very poor: *There are people begging for food in the streets of London.* ○ *She begged some money for her children's clothes.* **2 beg sth (of sb); beg (sb) for sth** to ask sb for sth strongly, or with great emotion: *He begged for forgiveness.* ○ *Can I beg a favour of you?* ○ *We begged him to let the children go free.*

(IDIOM) **I beg your pardon 1** I'm sorry: *I beg your pardon. I picked up your bag by mistake.* **2** (used for asking sb to repeat sth because you did not hear it properly)

began *pt* of BEGIN

beggar /'beɡə(r)/ *noun* [C] a person who lives by asking people for money, food, etc on the streets

☆ **begin** /bɪ'ɡɪn/ *verb* (*pres part* **beginning**; *pt* **began** /bɪ'ɡæn/; *pp* **begun** /bɪ'ɡʌn/) **1** [I] to take place from a particular time; to start: *What time does the concert begin?* ☞ **Begin** and **start** are very similar in meaning but **start** is more often used in informal speech. They can be followed by *to* or the *-ing* form of a verb: *The baby began/started to cry/crying.* When **begin** or **start** are themselves in the *-ing* form they must be followed by *to*: *The baby was just beginning/starting to cry.* In some meanings only **start** can be used: *I couldn't start the car.* ○ *We'll have to start* (= leave) *early if we want to be in Dover by 8 o'clock.* **Commence** is much more formal than **begin** or **start** and is not usually used in conversation. **2** [I,T] to do or make a start on the first part of sth; to start: *Shall I begin or will you?* ○ *Please begin at page 10.* ○ *I began* (= started reading) *this novel last month and I still haven't finished it.* ○ *When did he begin his speech?* ○ *He began to speak at 11 o'clock.* ○ *When do you begin work?* ○ *Children usually begin school at 9 o'clock.* ○ *Oh no, it's beginning to rain.* ○ *We began writing to each other in 1970.* ○ *The paint is beginning to get dirty.* ○ *I should like to begin by thanking everybody for coming.* **3** [I] to form the first part of sth: *My name begins with 'W' not 'V'.* ○ *This is where our garden begins.*

(IDIOM) **to begin with 1** (used for giving your first reason for sth): *We can't possibly go. To begin with it's too far and we can't afford it*

ɜː	ə	eɪ	əʊ	aɪ	aʊ	ɔɪ	ɪə	eə	ʊə
fur	ago	pay	home	five	now	join	near	hair	pure

either. **2** at first: *To begin with they were very happy.*

beginner *noun* [C] a person who has just begun learning sth

beginning *noun* [C,U] the first part of sth; the time when or place where sth starts: *The beginning of the book is quite interesting but it gets boring towards the end.* ○ *I've read the article from beginning to end.* ○ *We're going away at the beginning of the school holidays.*

begrudge /bɪˈgrʌdʒ/ *verb* [T] **begrudge (sb) sth 1** to feel angry or upset because sb has sth that you think that he/she does not deserve: *He's worked hard. I don't begrudge him his success.* **2** to be unwilling to give sb sth

☆**behalf** /bɪˈhɑːf; *US* -ˈhæf/ *noun*
(IDIOM) **on behalf of sb; on sb's behalf** for sb; as the representative of sb: *Mary couldn't be present so her husband accepted the prize on her behalf.* ○ *I should like to thank you all on behalf of my colleagues and myself.*

☆**behave** /bɪˈheɪv/ *verb* **1** [I] **behave well, badly, etc (towards sb)** to act in a particular way: *Don't you think that Ellen has been behaving very strangely recently?* ○ *I think you behaved very badly towards your father.* ○ *He behaves as if he was the boss.* **2** [I,T] **behave (yourself)** to act in the correct or proper way: *The children behaved themselves very well while we were out.*

-behaved (in compounds) behaving in a particular way: *a well-behaved child*

☆**behaviour** (*US* **behavior**) /bɪˈheɪvjə(r)/ *noun* [U] the way that you act or behave: *Her behaviour has been very strange recently.* ○ *'I will not tolerate this sort of behaviour', said the teacher.*

☆**behind¹** /bɪˈhaɪnd/ *prep* **1** in, at or to the back of sb/sth: *I was sitting behind a very tall woman and I couldn't see anything at all.* ○ *There's a small garden behind the house.* ○ *The sun went behind a cloud.* ○ *Look behind you before you drive off.* ○ (*figurative*) *It's time you put your problems behind you* (= forgot about them). **2** later or less good than sb/sth: *The train is twenty minutes behind schedule.* ○ *Jane is behind the rest of the class in maths.* **3** supporting or agreeing with sb/sth: *Most people are behind the President's policies.* **4** causing or starting sth: *What is the reason behind his sudden change of opinion?*

☆**behind²** /bɪˈhaɪnd/ *adv* **1** in, at or to the back of sb/sth: *You go on ahead. I'll follow on behind.* ○ *Try not to look behind.* ○ *He ran off but the police were close behind.* **2** in the place where sb/sth is or was: *Oh no! I've left the tickets behind* (= at home). **3 behind (in/with sth)** later or less good than sb/sth: *We are a month behind with the rent.* ○ *Arsenal were behind at half-time.* ☞ Look at **ahead**.

behind³ /bɪˈhaɪnd/ *noun* [C] (*informal*) the part of your body that you sit on ☞ Look at **bottom** and **buttocks**.

beige /beɪʒ/ *adj, noun* [U] (of) a light-brown colour

being /ˈbiːɪŋ/ *noun* **1** [U] the state of existing: *When did the organization come into being?* (= when did it start) **2** [C] a living person or thing: *a human being* ○ *a strange being from another planet*

belated /bɪˈleɪtɪd/ *adj* coming late: *a belated apology* —**belatedly** *adv*: *They have realized, rather belatedly, that they have made a big mistake.*

belch /beltʃ/ *verb* **1** [I] to let gas out from your stomach through your mouth with a sudden noise, eg because you have eaten a lot **2** [T] to send out smoke, etc: *The volcano belched smoke and ashes.* —**belch** *noun* [C]: *Julia gave a loud belch.*

belie /bɪˈlaɪ/ *verb* [T] (*pres part* **belying**; *3rd pers sing pres* **belies**; *pt, pp* **belied**) to give a false or untrue idea of sth: *His smiling face belied his true feelings.*

☆**belief** /bɪˈliːf/ *noun* (*pl* **beliefs**) **1** [sing,U] **belief in sb/sth** a feeling that sb/sth is true, good or right, or that sb/sth really exists: *She has lost her belief in God.* ○ *The amount of money we spend has increased beyond belief* (= very much). ☞ Look at **disbelief**. **2** [sing,U] **belief (that...)** (*formal*) something you accept as true; what you believe: *It's my belief that people are basically good.* ○ *There is a general belief that things will soon get better.* ○ *The man was killed in the mistaken belief that he was a member of a terrorist organization.* ○ *Contrary to popular belief* (= in spite of what many people think) *the North of the country is not poorer than the South.* **3** [C] an idea about religion, politics, etc: *Divorce is contrary to their religious beliefs.*

☆**believe** /bɪˈliːv/ *verb* (not in the continuous forms) **1** [T] to feel sure that sth is true or that sb is telling the truth: *He said he hadn't taken any money but I didn't believe him.* ○ *Nobody believes a word she says.* ○ *When they said they were getting married, I just couldn't believe it.* **2** [T] **believe (that)...** to think or suppose: *I believe they have moved to Peterborough.* ○ *Ian has joined the army, I believe.* ○ *The escaped prisoner is believed to be in this area.* **3** [I] to have religious faith
(IDIOMS) **believe it or not** it may be surprising but it is true: *Believe it or not, English food can sometimes be quite good.*

give sb to believe/understand (that) ➪ **GIVE¹**

(PHRASAL VERBS) **believe in sb/sth** to be sure that sb/sth exists: *Do you believe in God?* ○ *Most young children believe in Father Christmas.*

believe in sb/sth; believe in doing sth to think that sb/sth is good or right: *I believe in the value of a good education.* ○ *He doesn't believe in going by car if he can walk.*

believable /-əbl/ *adj* that can be believed ☞ Look at **unbelievable**.

believer *noun* [C] a person who has religious faith
(IDIOM) **be a (great/firm) believer in sth** to think that sth is good or right: *He is a great believer in getting things done on time.*

belittle /bɪˈlɪtl/ *verb* [T] to make sb/sth seem unimportant or not very good

☆**bell¹** /bel/ *noun* [C] **1** a hollow metal object, usually shaped like a cup, that makes a ringing sound when it is hit: *the sound of church bells*

2 an object that makes a ringing sound; the sound that it makes, often used as a signal: *a bicycle bell* o *a doorbell* o *Ring the bell and see if they're in.* o *There's the bell for the end of the lesson.*
(IDIOM) **ring a bell** ⇒ RING²

bellow /'beləʊ/ *verb* **1** [I] to make a deep low sound, like a bull **2** [I,T] to shout in a loud deep voice —**bellow** *noun* [C]

belly /'beli/ *noun* (*pl* **bellies**) the stomach or the part of the body between the chest and the legs: *a full/empty belly*

☆ **belong** /bɪ'lɒŋ; *US* -lɔːŋ/ *verb* [I] **1 belong to sb** to be owned by sb: *Who does this pen belong to?* o *Don't take anything that doesn't belong to you.* **2 belong to sth** to be a member of a group or organization: *Do you belong to any political party?* **3** to have a proper or usual place: *The plates belong in the cupboard over there.* o *I don't think this paragraph really belongs here.* o *It took quite a long time before we felt we belonged in the village* (= until we felt at home).

belongings *noun* [plural] the things that you own that can be moved, ie not land and buildings: *The tourists lost all their belongings in the hotel fire.*

beloved /bɪ'lʌvd; bɪ'lʌvɪd/ *adj* (*formal*) much loved: *He was a man who was beloved by all who knew him.* o *They had always intended to return to their beloved Ireland.*

☞ When 'beloved' comes before a noun, the pronunciation is /bɪ'lʌvɪd/.

☆ **below** /bɪ'ləʊ/ *prep* at or to a lower position or level than sb/sth: *Do not write below this line.* o *It hurts here – just below my knee.* o *The temperature fell below freezing during the night.* o *Her marks in the exam were below average.* o *All of the beaches are below European standards.* o *A sergeant in the police force is below an inspector.* ☞ Look at the picture and note at **under**.

below *adv* at or to a lower position or level: *I don't live on the top floor. I live on the floor below.* o *For further explanation of this point, please see below* (= a later part of the book, etc). o *temperatures of 30° and below*

☆ **belt** /belt/ *noun* [C] **1** a thin piece of cloth, leather, etc that you wear around your waist: *I've lost the belt for this dress.* o *I need a belt to keep these trousers up.* o *to do up/undo a belt* ☞ picture on page A11. Look at **safety-belt** and **seat-belt**. **2** a long strip of rubber, etc in a circle, that is used for carrying things or for making parts of a machine move: *The suitcases were carried round on a conveyor belt.* o *the fan belt of a car* **3** an area of land that has a particular quality: *the Green Belt around London* (= an area of countryside where you are not allowed to build houses, factories, etc)
(IDIOMS) **below the belt** (*informal*) unkind or not fair: *That remark was rather below the belt.*
under your belt (*informal*) that you have already done or achieved: *Faldo has got four tournament wins under his belt.*

belt *verb* [T] (*informal*) **1** to hit sb hard **2** to run or move very fast

(PHRASAL VERB) **belt up 1** to fasten your seatbelt in a car **2** (*informal*) to be quiet: *Belt up! I can't think with all this noise.*

bemused /bɪ'mjuːzd/ *adj* not knowing what to think or do; confused or puzzled

☆ **bench** /bentʃ/ *noun* [C] **1** a long wooden or metal seat for two or more people, often outdoors: *a park bench* **2** (*Brit*) (in the British parliament) the seats where a particular group of Members of Parliament sit: *the Government front bench* o *the Labour benches* **3** a long narrow table that people work at, eg in a factory or laboratory: *a carpenter's bench*

bend

bending down   bending a spoon

☆ **bend¹** /bend/ *verb* (*pt, pp* **bent** /bent/) **1** [T] to make sth that was straight into a curved shape; to make sth that was upright lean forward: *Bend your legs when you pick up something heavy.* o *to bend a piece of wire into an S shape* o *She sat with her head bent forward, thinking about what he had said.* **2** [I] to be or become curved: *The road bends to the left here.* **3** [I] to move your body forwards and downwards: *He bent down to tie up his shoelaces.* o *She had to bend forward to hear what the child was saying.*
(IDIOM) **bend the rules** to change the rules a little in order to allow sth for a particular reason

☆ **bend²** /bend/ *noun* [C] a curve or turn, eg in a road: *a sharp bend in the road*
(IDIOM) **round the bend** (*informal*) mad; crazy: *His behaviour is driving me round the bend* (= annoying me very much).

☆ **beneath** /bɪ'niːθ/ *prep* **1** in, at or to a lower position than sb/sth; under: *The ship disappeared beneath the waves.* o *I love to feel the grass beneath my feet again.* o *He seemed a nice person but there was a lot of anger beneath the surface.* ☞ Look at the note at **under**. **2** not good enough for sb: *She felt that washing up for other people was beneath her.*

beneath *adv* (*formal*) in, at or to a lower position: *From the top of the tower we gazed down on the city beneath.*

benefactor /'benɪfæktə(r)/ *noun* [C] a person who helps or gives money to a person or an organization

beneficial /ˌbenɪ'fɪʃl/ *adj* **beneficial (to sb/sth)** having a good or useful effect: *a beneficial effect/influence on sb/sth*

☆ **benefit** /'benɪfɪt/ *noun* **1** [U] the advantage or good or useful effect of sth: *Most parents want to give their children the benefit of a good education.* o *A change in the law would be to everyone's benefit.* o *I can't see the benefit of doing things this way.* **2** [C] a thing that has a good or useful effect: *the benefits of modern technology* **3** [U] money that the government gives to people

who are ill, poor, unemployed, etc: *I'm not entitled to unemployment benefit.*
(IDIOMS) **for sb's benefit** especially to help, please, etc sb: *For the benefit of the newcomers, I will explain again what we are planning to do.*
give sb the benefit of the doubt to believe that what sb says is true because there is no clear proof that it is not
benefit *verb* (*pt, pp* **benefited**; *US also* **benefitted**) **1** [T] to have a good or useful effect: *The new tax laws will benefit people on low wages.* **2 benefit (from sth)** [I] to receive an advantage from sth: *We've certainly benefited from the changes in the law.*
benevolent /bɪˈnevələnt/ *adj* (*formal*) kind, friendly and helpful to others —**benevolence** /bɪˈnevələns/ *noun* [U]
benign /bɪˈnaɪn/ *adj* **1** (used about people) kind or gentle **2** (used about a disease, etc) not causing death: *a benign tumour* ☞ Look at **malignant**.
bent¹ *pt, pp* of BEND
bent² /bent/ *adj* **1** (*slang*) not honest: *a bent policeman* **2** (used about a person) with a body that is not straight: *The old lady was nearly 90 and was bent with age.* **3 bent on sth/on doing sth** wanting to do sth very much, so that you cannot accept not doing it: *They seem bent on moving house, whatever the difficulties.*
bent³ /bent/ *noun* [C, usually sing] **a bent for sth/doing sth** a natural skill at sth or interest in sth: *She has a bent for music.*
bequeath /bɪˈkwiːð/ *verb* [T] (*formal*) **bequeath sth (to sb)** to arrange for sth to be given to sb after you have died: *He bequeathed £1 000 to his favourite charity.* ☞ **Leave** is a more common word.
bequest /bɪˈkwest/ *noun* [C] (*formal*) something that you arrange to be given to sb after you have died: *He left a bequest to each of his grandchildren.*
bereaved /bɪˈriːvd/ *adj* having had a relative or close friend die
the bereaved *noun* [C] a person whose relative or close friend has died recently ☞ The plural is also **the bereaved**.
bereavement *noun* (*formal*) **1** [U] the state of being bereaved **2** [C] the death of a relative or close friend: *There has been a bereavement in the family.*
beret /ˈbereɪ; *US* bəˈreɪ/ *noun* [C] a soft flat round hat ☞ picture at **hat**.
☆ **berry** /ˈberi/ *noun* [C] (*pl* **berries**) a small soft fruit with seeds: *Those berries are poisonous.* ○ *a raspberry*
berth /bɜːθ/ *noun* [C] **1** a place for sleeping on a ship or train: *a cabin with four berths* **2** a place where a ship can be tied up in a harbour
☆ **beside** /bɪˈsaɪd/ *prep* at the side of, or next to sb/sth: *Come and sit beside me.* ○ *He kept his bag close beside him at all times.*
(IDIOM) **beside yourself (with sth)** not able to control yourself because of a very strong emotion: *Emily was almost beside herself with grief.*
besides /bɪˈsaɪdz/ *prep* in addition to or as well as sb/sth: *There will be six people coming, besides you and David.*

besides *adv* in addition; also: *I thought the hotel was too expensive. Besides, it was very close to the main road.*
besiege /bɪˈsiːdʒ/ *verb* [T] to surround a place with an army: (*figurative*) *The pop singer was besieged by fans and reporters.*
☆ **best¹** /best/ *adj* (the superlative of *good*) of the highest quality or level; most suitable: *Who's your best friend?* ○ *His latest book is by far his best.* ○ *It's best to arrive early if you want a good seat.* ○ *Who in the class is best at maths?* ○ *What's the best way to get to York from here?* ○ *The best thing to do is to forget all about it.*
(IDIOMS) **your best bet** (*informal*) the best thing for you to do in a particular situation: *There's nowhere to park in the city centre. Your best bet is to go in by bus.*
the best/better part of sth ⇨ PART¹
ˌ**best ˈman** *noun* [C] a man who helps and supports the bridegroom at his wedding ☞ Look at the note at **wedding**.
☆ **best²** /best/ *adv* (the superlative of *well*) **1** in the most excellent way: *He works best in the morning.* **2** to the greatest degree; most: *Which of these dresses do you like best?* ○ *one of Britain's best-loved TV stars* ○ *Next week would suit me best.* ○ *Ask Peter. He'll know best what to do.*
(IDIOM) **as best you can** as well as you can even if it is not perfectly
ˌ**best ˈseller** *noun* [C] a book or other product that has been bought by large numbers of people
ˌ**best-ˈselling** *adj* very popular: *Frederick Forsyth has written many best-selling novels.*
☆ **best³** /best/ *noun* [sing] **1** something that is of the highest quality or level: *When you pay that much for a meal you expect the best.* ○ *I'm not in the best of health.* ○ *They are the best of friends.* ○ *The best we can hope for is that the situation doesn't get any worse.* ☞ Look at **second-best**. **2 the best** [with sing or pl verb] a person that is best: *Even the best of us make mistakes sometimes.*
(IDIOMS) **all the best** (*informal*) (used when you are saying goodbye to sb and wishing him/her success): *All the best! Keep in touch, won't you?*
at best if everything is as favourable as possible; taking the most hopeful view: *We won't be able to deliver the goods before March, or, at best, the last week in February.*
at its/your best in its/your best state or condition: *This is an example of Beckett's work at its best.* ○ *No one is at their best first thing in the morning.*
be (all) for the best to be good in the end even if it does not seem good at first: *He didn't go to London after all, but as it turned out it was all for the best* (= because he was able to do something that was better).
bring out the best/worst in sb to show sb's best/worst qualities: *The crisis really brought out the best in Tony.*
do/try your best to do all or the most that you can: *It doesn't matter whether you win or not. The important thing is doing your best.*

i:	ɪ	e	æ	ɑ:	ɒ	ɔ:	ʊ	u:	ʌ
see	sit	ten	hat	arm	got	saw	put	too	cup

look your best to look as beautiful or attractive as possible

make the best of sth/a bad job to accept a difficult situation and try to be as happy as possible

☆ **bet** /bet/ verb [I,T] (pres part **betting**; pt, pp **bet** or **betted**) **bet (sth) (on sth)** to risk some money on the result of sth (eg a horse-race). If you are wrong about the result, you have to pay some money: *Which horse did you bet on?* ○ *I bet him £10 he couldn't stop smoking for a week.*

(IDIOMS) **I bet (that)...** (*informal*) I'm sure that... : *I bet he arrives late – he always does.*

you bet (*informal*) a way of saying, 'Yes, of course!': *'Are you coming too?' 'You bet.'*

bet noun [C] **1** an act of betting: *Did you have a bet on that race?* ○ *to win/lose a bet* **2** an opinion: *My bet is that he's missed the train.*

(IDIOMS) **your best bet** ⇨ BEST¹

hedge your bets ⇨ HEDGE

'betting-shop /'betɪŋ ʃɒp/ noun [C] a shop where you can go to place a bet on a horse-race, etc

betray /bɪ'treɪ/ verb [T] **1** to be disloyal to a person or thing; to harm a person or organization that trusts you: *By taking the money he had betrayed the trust that she had put in him.* ○ *When parents get divorced the children often feel betrayed.* ○ *to betray your country* **2** to make facts about sb/sth known to an enemy; to make a secret known: *She betrayed all the members of the group to the secret police.* ○ *He refused to betray the information.* **3** to show a feeling or quality that you would like to keep hidden: *Her steady voice did not betray the emotion she was feeling.*

betrayal /bɪ'treɪəl/ noun [C,U] the act of betraying sb/sth

☆ **better¹** /'betə(r)/ adj **1** (the comparative of *good*) **better than sth** of a higher quality or level or more suitable: *I think her second novel was much better than her first.* ○ *He's better at Chemistry than Physics.* ○ *It's a long way to drive. It would be better to take the train.* ○ *You'd be better getting the train than driving* (= it would be more suitable or sensible). **2** less ill or fully recovered from an illness: *I feel a bit better today.* ○ *You can't go swimming until you're better.*

☆ **better²** /'betə(r)/ adv (the comparative of *well*) in a better way; to a greater or higher degree: *I think you could have done this better.* ○ *Sylvie speaks English better than I do.* ○ *She is much better known than her sister.*

(IDIOMS) **the best/better part of sth** ⇨ PART¹

(be) better off 1 to be in a more pleasant or suitable situation: *You look terrible. You'd be better off at home in bed.* **2** with more money: *We're much better off now I go out to work.*

you, etc had better you should; you would be wise to: *I think we'd better go before it gets dark.* ○ *You'd better take a pen and paper. You might want to take notes.*

know better ⇨ KNOW

think better of (doing) sth ⇨ THINK¹

☆ **better³** /'betə(r)/ noun [sing] something that is of higher quality: *The hotel wasn't very good. I must say we'd expected better.*

(IDIOM) **get the better of sb/sth** to defeat or be stronger than sb/sth: *When we have an argument she always gets the better of me.*

between/among

a small house **between** two large ones

a house **among** some trees

☆ **between** /bɪ'twi:n/ prep **1** in the space that separates two things, people, etc; somewhere in the middle: *I was sitting between Anne and Derek.* ○ *a village between Cambridge and Ely* **2** from one place to another and back again: *There aren't any direct trains between here and Milton Keynes.* ○ *the journey between home and the office* **3** involving or linking two people, groups or things: *There's some sort of disagreement between them.* ○ *There may be a connection between the two crimes.* **4** (used about two amounts, distances, ages, times, etc) at a point that is greater or later than the first and smaller or earlier than the second; somewhere in the middle: *She must be between about thirty and thirty-five.* ○ *They said they would arrive between 4 and 5 o'clock.* ○ *a cost of between £200 and £300* **5** choosing one and not the other (of two things): *to choose between two jobs* ○ *What's the difference between 'some' and 'any'?* **6** by putting together the actions, efforts, etc of two or more people: *We've got over a thousand pounds saved up between us.* **7** giving each person a share: *The money was divided equally between the two children.* ○ *We ate all the chocolates between us.* ☛ **Between** is usually used of two people or things: *sitting between her mother and father* ○ *between the ages of 12 and 14.* However, **between** can sometimes be used of more than two when the people or things are being considered as individuals, especially when the meaning is that of number 7 (above): *We drank a bottle of wine between the three of us.* **Among** is always used of more than two people or things considered as a group rather than as individuals: *You're among friends here.*

between (*also* **in between**) adv in the space or period of time that separates two things, points, people, times, etc: *We can't get to the beach this way. There's a railway line in between.* ○ *I've got a meeting at 10 and one at 11 but I should manage to see you in between.*

beverage /'bevərɪdʒ/ noun [C] (*formal*) (used especially on menus) a drink

beware /bɪ'weə(r)/ verb [I] (only in the im-

ɜː	ə	eɪ	əʊ	aɪ	aʊ	ɔɪ	ɪə	eə	ʊə
fur	ago	pay	home	five	now	join	near	hair	pure

perative or infinitive) **beware (of sb/sth)** (used for giving a warning) to be careful: *Beware of the dog!* (= written on a sign) ○ *We were told to beware of strong currents in the sea.*

bewilder /bɪˈwɪldə(r)/ *verb* [T] to confuse: *I was completely bewildered by his sudden change of mood.* —**bewildered** *adj: He seemed bewildered by all the fuss.* —**bewildering** /bɪˈwɪldərɪŋ/ *adj: a bewildering experience* —**bewilderment** *noun* [U]: *to stare at sb in bewilderment*

bewitch /bɪˈwɪtʃ/ *verb* [T] to fascinate sb and be very attractive to them

☆**beyond** /bɪˈjɒnd/ *prep* **1** on the other side of: *beyond the distant mountains* **2** further than; later than: *Does the motorway continue beyond Birmingham?* ○ *Most people don't go on working beyond the age of 65.* **3** out of the range or reach of sth (so that sth is not possible): *The house was beyond what I could afford.* ○ *The car was completely beyond repair.* ○ *His success was beyond all our expectations* (= more than we expected). ○ *The fact that she is guilty is beyond doubt* (= there is no doubt about it). **4** except for or apart from: *I haven't heard anything beyond a few rumours.*

(IDIOM) **be beyond sb** (*informal*) to be impossible for sb to understand or imagine: *Why she wants to go and live there is quite beyond me.*

beyond *adv* on the other side or further on: *We could see the mountains and the sea beyond.*

bias /ˈbaɪəs/ *noun* [C,U, usually sing] (*pl* **biases**) **1** [C] an opinion, feeling or attitude that is not fair and not based on facts: *a bias against women drivers* **2** [C,U] giving one side in an argument an advantage over the other; not being neutral: *The BBC has been accused of political bias.*

bias *verb* [T] (**biasing**; **biased** or **biassing**; **biassed**) to influence sb/sth, especially unfairly; to give an advantage to one group, etc: *Good newspapers should not be biased towards a particular point of view.* ○ *Our schools are biased in favour of middle-class children.* ○ *a biased* (= unfair) *report*

bib /bɪb/ *noun* [C] a piece of cloth or plastic that a baby or small child wears under the chin to protect its clothes while it is eating

☆**bible** /ˈbaɪbl/ (*also* **the Bible**) *noun* [C] the holy book of the Christian and Jewish people —**biblical** /ˈbɪblɪkl/ *adj*

bibliography /ˌbɪbliˈɒɡrəfi/ *noun* [C] (*pl* **bibliographies**) **1** a list of the books and articles that a writer used when he/she was writing a particular book **2** a list of books on a particular subject

bicentenary /ˌbaɪsenˈtiːnəri; *US* -ˈsentəneri/ (*US* **bicentennial** /ˌbaɪsenˈteniəl/) *noun* [C] (*pl* **bicentenaries**) the day or year two hundred years after sth happened or began: *the bicentenary of the French Revolution*

biceps /ˈbaɪseps/ *noun* [C] (*pl* **biceps**) the large muscle at the front of the top part of your arms

bicker /ˈbɪkə(r)/ *verb* [I] to quarrel about unimportant things: *The boys were bickering about whose turn it was to play with the train.*

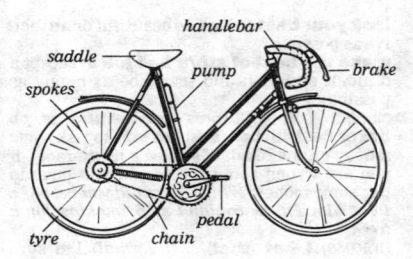

handlebar, saddle, pump, brake, spokes, pedal, tyre, chain

bicycle

☆**bicycle** /ˈbaɪsɪkl/ (*also informal* **bike**) *noun* [C] a vehicle with two wheels, which you sit on and ride by moving your legs: *to ride a bicycle* ○ *to go somewhere by bicycle* ☛ Look at **cycle**. This is usually used as the verb. **Cyclist** is the usual noun.

bid¹ /bɪd/ *verb* (**bidding**; *pt, pp* **bid** or, in sense 2 *pt* **bade** /bæd/; *pp* **bidden** /ˈbɪdn/) **1** [I,T] **bid (sth) (for sth)** to offer a sum of money in order to buy sth: *to bid for sth at an auction* ○ *Somebody bid £5 000 for the painting.* **2** [T] (*old-fashioned formal*) to say as a greeting: *He bade us good-day and got up to leave.*

bidder *noun* [C] a person who offers a sum of money in order to buy sth: *The house was sold to the highest bidder* (= the person who offered the most money).

bid² /bɪd/ *noun* [C] **1** an attempt to do, obtain, etc sth: *a bid to slow down traffic and prevent accidents* ○ *her bid to win the championship* ○ *His bid for power had failed.* **2** an offer of a sum of money in order to buy sth: *We made a bid of £100 for the chair.* **3** (*especially US*) = TENDER²

bide /baɪd/ *verb*

(IDIOM) **bide your time** to wait for a good opportunity: *I'll bide my time until the situation improves.*

bidet /ˈbiːdeɪ; *US* biːˈdeɪ/ *noun* [C] a small bath that you can sit on in order to wash your bottom

☆**big** /bɪɡ/ *adj* (**bigger**; **biggest**) **1** large; not small: *a big house, town, salary, etc* ○ *This dress is too big for me.* **2** great or important: *They had a big argument yesterday.* ○ *That was the biggest decision I've ever had to make.* ○ *some of the big names in Hollywood* **3** (only *before* a noun) (*informal*) older: *a big brother/sister* ☛ **Big** and **large** can both be used when talking about size or number. **Large** is more formal and is not usually used for describing people: *a big/large house* ○ *a big boy.* **Great** is mostly used when talking about the importance, quality, etc of a person or thing. It can also be used with uncountable nouns to mean 'a lot of': *a great occasion* ○ *a great musician* ○ *great happiness, care, etc.*

(IDIOM) **give sb/get a big hand** to clap sb/to be clapped loudly: *The audience gave the little girl a big hand when she finished her song.*

big *adv* (*slang*) in a grand or ambitious way:

p	b	t	d	k	ɡ	tʃ	dʒ	f	v	θ	ð
pen	bad	tea	did	cat	got	chin	June	fall	van	thin	then

You have to think big if you want to be successful.
bigamy /ˈbɪgəmɪ/ *noun* [U] the crime of being married to two people at the same time —**bigamist** *noun* [C]
bigoted /ˈbɪgətɪd/ *adj* having very strong and unreasonable opinions and refusing to change them or to listen to other people
☆**bike** /baɪk/ *noun* [C] (*informal*) a bicycle or a motorcycle: *Mary's just learnt to ride a bike.*
bikini /bɪˈkiːnɪ/ *noun* [C] a piece of clothing, in two pieces, that women wear for swimming
bilingual /ˌbaɪˈlɪŋgwəl/ *adj* **1** having or using two languages: *a bilingual dictionary* **2** able to speak two languages equally well: *Our children are bilingual in English and Spanish.*
☆**bill¹** /bɪl/ *noun* **1** [C] (*US* **check**) a piece of paper that shows how much money you owe for goods or services: *an electricity bill* ○ *Can I have the bill, please* (eg in a restaurant) *?* ○ *to pay a bill* **2** [C] (*US*) = NOTE¹(4): *a ten-dollar bill* **3** [C] a plan for a possible new law: *The bill was discussed in Parliament.* ○ *The bill was passed/defeated.* **4** [sing] the programme of entertainment offered in a show, concert, etc: *Frank Sinatra headed the bill.* ○ *a double bill of 'Swan Lake' and 'The Nutcracker'*
(IDIOM) **foot the bill** ⇨ FOOT²
bill *verb* [T] to announce to the public with an advertisement, etc: *The show is billed as a musical comedy.*
¹**billboard** *noun* [C] (*US*) = HOARDING
¹**billfold** *noun* [C] (*US*) = WALLET
bill² /bɪl/ *noun* [C] a bird's beak
billiards /ˈbɪlɪədz/ *noun* [U] a game played on a big table covered with cloth. You use a long stick (**a cue**) to hit balls into pockets at the corners and sides of the table: *to play billiards* ○ *to have a game of billiards*
billiard- /ˈbɪlɪəd-/ (in compounds) used for billiards: *a billiard-table*
☆**billion** /ˈbɪlɪən/ *number* 1 000 000 000; one thousand million: *billions of dollars* ☛ Formerly, 'billion' was used with the meaning 'one million million'. We now say **trillion** for this. Look at Appendix 2.
billow /ˈbɪləʊ/ *verb* [I] to rise or move slowly in the wind, like waves: *curtains billowing in the breeze*
bin /bɪn/ *noun* [C] **1** a container that you put rubbish in: *to throw sth in the bin* ○ *a litter-bin* ○ *The dustmen come to empty the bins on Wednesdays.* **2** a container, usually with a lid, for storing bread, flour, etc: *a bread bin*
binary system /ˈbaɪnərɪ sɪstəm/ *noun* [sing] (*technical*) a system of numbers using only the numbers 0 and 1. It is used especially with computers.
bind /baɪnd/ *verb* [T] (*pt, pp* **bound** /baʊnd/)
1 bind A (to B); bind A and B (together) to tie or fasten with string or rope: *They bound the prisoner's hands behind his back.* ○ (*figurative*) *The two men were bound together* (= united or held together) *by the strength of their beliefs.*
2 bind sb/yourself (to sth) to cause or force sb to do sth: *to be bound by a law, an agreement, etc* ○ *The contract binds you to completion of the work within two years.* **3** (usually passive) to fasten sheets of paper into a cover to form a book: *The book was bound in leather.*

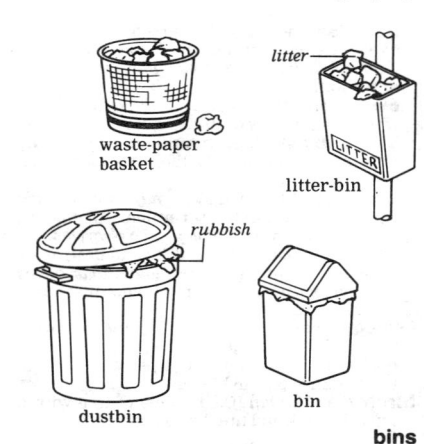

bind *noun* [sing] (*informal*) something that you find boring or annoying; a nuisance: *I find housework a real bind.*

binder *noun* [C] a hard cover for holding loose sheets of paper together

binding *noun* **1** [C] a cover that holds the pages of a book together **2** [U] material that you use for making the edge of sth stronger or more attractive

binding *adj* making it necessary for sb to do sth they have promised or to obey a law, etc: *This contract is legally binding.*

binge /bɪndʒ/ *noun* [C] (*informal*) a period of eating or drinking too much

bingo /ˈbɪŋgəʊ/ *noun* [U] a game in which each player has a different card with numbers on it. The person in charge of the game calls numbers out and the winner is the first player to have all the numbers on their card called out.

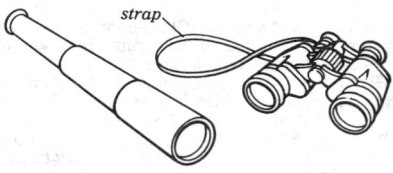

binoculars /bɪˈnɒkjʊləz/ *noun* [plural] an instrument with two lenses which you look through in order to make distant objects seem nearer: *a pair of binoculars* ☛ Look at **telescope**.

biochemistry /ˌbaɪəʊˈkemɪstrɪ/ *noun* [U] the study of the chemistry of living things

biodegradable /ˌbaɪəʊdɪˈgreɪdəbl/ *adj* that can decay naturally: *Most plastic packaging is not biodegradable.*

biography /baɪˈɒgrəfɪ/ *noun* [C,U] (*pl* **bio-**

graphies) the story of a person's life written by sb else: *a biography of Napoleon* ○ *I enjoy reading history and biography.* ☛ Look at **autobiography**.

biographer /baɪˈɒgrəfə(r)/ *noun* [C] a person who writes a story of sb else's life

biographical /ˌbaɪəˈgræfɪkl/ *adj* containing information about sb's life: *interesting biographical details*

biological /ˌbaɪəˈlɒdʒɪkl/ *adj* **1** connected with the scientific study of animals, plants and other living things: *biological research* **2** involving the use of living things to destroy or damage other living things: *biological weapons* ○ *a biological detergent* (= one that uses enzymes to destroy dirt)

biology /baɪˈɒlədʒi/ *noun* [U] the scientific study of living things

biologist /-dʒɪst/ *noun* [C] a person who studies or is an expert in biology

birch /bɜːtʃ/ *noun* [C,U] a type of tree with a smooth trunk and thin branches

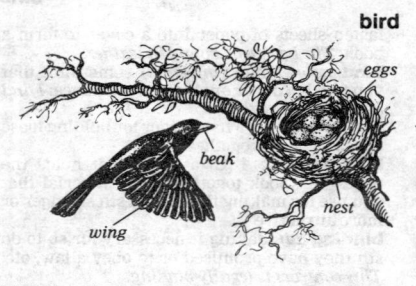

bird

eggs
beak
nest
wing

☆ **bird** /bɜːd/ *noun* [C] **1** a creature with feathers and wings which can (usually) fly ☛ Birds fly and sing. They build nests and lay eggs. **2** (*Brit slang*) a word used by men to refer to a young woman or girl: *a gorgeous blonde bird* ☛ Many women dislike the use of this word. (IDIOM) **kill two birds with one stone** ⇒ KILL

ˌbird of ˈprey *noun* [C] a bird that kills and eats other animals and birds

ˈbird-watcher *noun* [C] a person who studies birds in their natural surroundings ☛ The formal word is **ornithologist**.

Biro /ˈbaɪərəʊ/ *noun* [C] (*pl* **Biros**) (*trade mark*) a type of pen in which ink comes out of a small metal ball at the end ☛ Look at **ball-point**.

☆ **birth** /bɜːθ/ *noun* **1** [C,U] being born; coming out of a mother's body: *It was a difficult birth.* ○ *The baby weighed six pounds at birth* (= when it was born). ○ *She's been slightly deaf since birth.* ○ *What's your date of birth?* (= the date on which you were born) **2** [U] your nationality or your place of birth: *She's always lived in England but she's German by birth.* **3** [sing] the beginning of sth: *the birth of an idea*
(IDIOM) **give birth (to sb/sth)** to produce a baby: *She gave birth to her second child at home.*

ˈbirth certificate *noun* [C] an official piece of paper that states the date and place of a person's birth

ˈbirth control *noun* [U] ways of controlling or limiting the number of children you have ☛ Look at **contraception**.

ˈbirthmark *noun* [C] a permanent mark on your body, that you are born with

ˈbirthplace *noun* **1** [C] the house or area where a person was born **2** [sing] the place where sth began: *in Greece, the birthplace of the Olympic Games*

ˈbirth rate *noun* [C] the number of babies born in a particular group of people during a particular period of time: *The birth rate is falling/rising.*

☆ **birthday** /ˈbɜːθdeɪ/ *noun* [C] the day in each year which is the same date as the one when you were born: *My birthday's (on) November 15th.* ○ *my eighteenth birthday* ○ *a birthday present* ○ *a birthday card* ☛ An **anniversary** is not the same as a **birthday**. It is the day in each year which is the same date as an important past event: *our wedding anniversary* ○ *the fiftieth anniversary of the sinking of the Titanic* (= exactly fifty years after it happened). When it is a person's birthday we say **Happy Birthday!** or **Many happy returns!** If we know the person well we send a special card to them or a present. Your eighteenth birthday is an important occasion when you legally become an adult.

☆ **biscuit** /ˈbɪskɪt/ *noun* [C] (*US* **cookie; cooky**) a type of small cake that is thin, hard and usually sweet: *a chocolate biscuit* ○ *a packet of biscuits* ☛ picture at **cake**.

bisexual /ˌbaɪˈsekʃuəl/ *adj* sexually attracted to both men and women

bishop /ˈbɪʃəp/ *noun* [C] a senior person in the Christian Church, who is in charge of the churches in a city or a district: *the Bishop of Durham* ☛ Look at **archbishop**.

☆ **bit**[1] /bɪt/ *noun* [C] **1** a small piece or amount of sth: *There were bits of broken glass all over the floor.* ○ *I think these strawberries need a bit more sugar.* ○ *Could you give me a bit of advice?* **2** [sing] (especially with *quite*) (*informal*) a lot: *It must have rained quite a bit during the night.* (IDIOMS) **a bit 1** slightly; rather: *I'm afraid I'll be a bit late tonight.* ○ *I was a bit annoyed with him.* **2** a short time or distance: *Could you move forward a bit?*

bit by bit slowly or a little at a time: *Bit by bit we managed to get the information we needed.*

a bit much (*informal*) annoying or unpleasant: *It's a bit much expecting me to work on Sundays.*

a bit of a (*informal*) rather a: *I've got a bit of a problem...* ○ *He's a bit of a tyrant, isn't he?*

bits and pieces (*informal*) small things of different kinds: *I've finished packing except for a few bits and pieces.*

do your bit (*informal*) to do your share of sth; to help with sth: *It won't take long to finish if we all do our bit.*

not a bit not at all: *The holiday was not a bit what we had expected.*

to bits into small pieces: *She angrily tore the letter to bits.*

bitty *adj* made up of lots of parts which do not seem to be connected: *a bitty letter*

bit² /bɪt/ noun [C] a metal bar that you put in a horse's mouth when you ride it ☞ picture at **horse**.

bit³ /bɪt/ noun [C] (*technical*) the smallest unit of information that is stored in a computer's memory, represented by the numbers 0 or 1.

bit⁴ pt of BITE¹

bitch /bɪtʃ/ noun [C] **1** a female dog **2** (*slang*) a very unpleasant woman: *She's a real bitch.* ○ *You bitch!* (= used to insult a woman)

bitchy adj (usually used about women or their behaviour) tending to talk about other people in an unkind way: *a bitchy remark*

☆ **bite¹** /baɪt/ verb (*pt* **bit** /bɪt/; *pp* **bitten** /'bɪtn/) **1** [I,T] **bite (into sth)** to cut or attack with the teeth: *Don't worry about the dog. She never bites.* ○ *The dog bit me.* ○ *He picked up the bread and bit into it hungrily.* ☞ picture at **lick**. **2** [T] (used about insects or snakes) to prick your skin and cause pain: *He was bitten by a snake.* ☞ Wasps and bees do not **bite** you. They **sting** you. **3** [I] to begin to have an effect, usually in an unpleasant way: *In the South the job losses are starting to bite.*

☆ **bite²** /baɪt/ noun **1** [C] a piece of food that you can put into your mouth: *She took a big bite of the apple.* **2** [C] a painful place on the skin made by an insect, snake, dog, etc: *a mosquito bite* **3** [sing] (*informal*) some food: *Would you like a bite to eat before you go?*

bitten pt of BITE¹

☆ **bitter** /'bɪtə(r)/ adj **1** (used about a person) very unhappy or angry about sth that has happened; disappointed: *She was very bitter about the breakup of her marriage.* **2** causing unhappiness or anger for a long time; difficult to accept: *His son has been a bitter disappointment to him.* **3** caused by anger or hatred: *a bitter quarrel* **4** (used about the weather) very cold: *a bitter wind* **5** having a sharp, unpleasant taste; not sweet: *bitter coffee*

bitter noun [U] (*Brit*) a type of dark beer with a bitter taste: *A pint of bitter, please.*

bitterly adv **1** (used for describing strong negative feelings or cold weather) extremely: *bitterly disappointed* ○ *a bitterly cold winter* **2** in a bitter(1) way: *'I've lost everything,' he said bitterly.*

bitterness noun [U] anger and unhappiness as a result of sth bad happening

bizarre /bɪ'zɑː(r)/ adj very strange: *The story had a most bizarre ending.*

☆ **black¹** /blæk/ adj **1** of the darkest colour possible, the colour of the night sky **2** belonging to a race of people with dark skins: *the black population of Britain* ○ *black culture* **3** (used about coffee or tea) without milk or cream: *black coffee with sugar* **4** (used about a situation) without hope; depressing: *The economic outlook for the coming year is rather black.* **5** funny in a cruel or unpleasant way: *The film was a black comedy.* **6** very angry: *a black mood* ○ *to give sb a black look*
(IDIOM) **black and blue** covered with bruises
black and white (used about television, photographs, etc) showing no colours except black, white and grey: *a black and white television*

blacken /'blækən/ verb [T] **1** to make sth black: *The soldiers had to blacken their faces at night.* **2** to make sth seem bad, by saying unpleasant things about it: *to blacken sb's name* —**blackness** noun [U]

blackberry /'blækbri, -beri/ noun [C] (*pl* **blackberries**) a small black fruit that grows wild on bushes

'**blackbird** noun [C] a common European bird. The male is black with a yellow beak and the female is brown.

'**blackboard** (*US* **chalkboard**) noun [C] a piece of dark board used for writing on, especially with chalk and in a classroom

,**blackcurrant** noun [C] a small round black fruit that grows in bunches on bushes

black 'eye noun [C] an eye with dark-coloured skin around it as the result of a blow: *He got a black eye in the fight.*

'**blackhead** noun [C] a small spot on the skin with a black centre

,**black 'magic** noun [U] a type of magic that is used for evil purposes

,**black 'market** noun [C] the buying and selling of goods or foreign money in a way that is not legal: *to buy/sell sth on the black market*

'**blackout** noun [C] **1** a period of time during a war, when all lights must be turned off or covered so that the enemy cannot see them **2** a period when you lose consciousness for a short time: *to have a blackout*

☆ **black²** /blæk/ noun **1** [U] the darkest colour, like the night sky: *People usually wear black* (= black clothes) *at funerals.* **2** usually **Black** [C] a person who belongs to a race of people with dark skins ☞ Look at **African-American**.
(IDIOMS) **be in the black** to have some money in the bank ☞ Look at **in the red**.
in black and white in writing or in print: *I won't believe we've got the contract till I see it in black and white.*

black³ /blæk/ verb
(PHRASAL VERB) **black out** to lose consciousness for a short time: *I remember losing control of the car and then I blacked out.*

blacklist /'blæklɪst/ noun [C] a list of people who are considered bad or dangerous: *to be on sb's blacklist* —**blacklist** verb [T]

blackmail /'blækmeɪl/ noun [U] the crime of forcing a person to give you money or do sth for you, usually by threatening to make known sth which they want to keep secret —**blackmail** verb [T]: *He was blackmailed into paying an enormous amount of money.* —**blackmailer** noun [C]

blacksmith /'blæksmɪθ/ noun [C] a person whose job is to make and repair things made of metal, especially horses' shoes

bladder /'blædə(r)/ noun [C] the part of the body where waste liquid (**urine**) collects before leaving the body

☆ **blade** /bleɪd/ noun [C] **1** the flat, sharp part of a knife, sword, etc ☞ picture at **penknife**. **2** one of the flat, wide parts that spin round on an aeroplane, helicopter, etc **3** a long, thin leaf of grass, wheat, etc: *a blade of grass*

☆ **blame** /bleɪm/ verb [T] **1 blame sb (for sth)**;

blame sth on sb to think or say that a certain person or thing is responsible for sth bad that has happened: *The teacher blamed me for the accident.* ○ *Some people blame the changes in the climate on pollution.* **2 not blame sb (for sth)** to think that sb is not wrong to do sth: *'I'd like to leave school and get a job.' 'I don't blame you.'* (= I can understand why). ○ *I don't blame you for feeling fed up.*
(IDIOM) **be to blame (for sth)** to be responsible for sth bad: *The police say that careless driving was to blame for the accident.*
blame *noun* [U] **blame (for sth)** responsibility for sth bad: *to take the blame for sth* ○ *The report puts the blame on rising prices.*
blameless *adj* deserving no blame; not guilty: *He insisted that his wife was blameless and hadn't known about his activities.*

bland /blænd/ *adj* **1** showing no strong feelings; calm **2** (used about food) mild or lacking in taste **3** ordinary or uninteresting: *a rather bland style of writing* —**blandly** *adv*

☆**blank** /blæŋk/ *adj* **1** without writing or anything else on it: *a blank cassette* ○ *a blank piece of paper* ○ *a blank wall* **2** without feelings, understanding or interest: *a blank expression on his face* ○ *My mind went blank when I saw the exam questions* (= I couldn't think properly or remember anything).
blank *noun* [C] an empty space: *Fill in the blanks in the following exercise.* ○ (*figurative*) *I couldn't remember his name – my mind was a complete blank.*
(IDIOM) **draw a blank** ⇨ DRAW²
blankly *adv* with a blank expression
blank 'cheque *noun* [C] a cheque that has been signed but that has an empty space so that the amount to be paid can be filled in later

☆**blanket** /'blæŋkɪt/ *noun* [C] **1** a cover made of wool, etc that is put on beds to keep people warm ☞ picture at bed. **2** affecting everybody or everything: *a blanket ban on journalists reporting the case*
(IDIOM) **a wet blanket** ⇨ WET
blanket *verb* [T] to cover sth completely: *The countryside was blanketed in snow.*

blare /bleə(r)/ *verb* [I,T] **blare (sth) (out)** to make a loud, unpleasant noise: *The radio was blaring in the room next to ours.* ○ *The loudspeaker blared out a warning.* —**blare** *noun* [U]: *the blare of a siren*

blasphemy /'blæsfəmi/ *noun* [U] writing or speaking about God in a way that shows a lack of respect —**blasphemous** /'blæsfəməs/ *adj*

blast¹ /blɑːst; *US* blæst/ *noun* [C] **1** an explosion, especially one caused by a bomb: *The windows of the nearby shops were shattered in the blast.* **2** a sudden strong rush of air: *a blast of cold air* **3** a loud sound made by a musical instrument such as a horn: *a few blasts on his trumpet*

blast² /blɑːst; *US* blæst/ *verb* [T] to make a hole, a tunnel, etc in sth with an explosion: *They had to blast their way through the mountainside.*
(PHRASAL VERB) **blast off** (used about a spacecraft) to leave the ground; to take off

blast *interj* a mild swear-word, used to show that you are angry: *Blast! I've cut my finger.*
blasted *adj* (*informal*) very annoying: *Can you turn that blasted music down?*
'blast-off *noun* [U] the time when a spacecraft leaves the ground

blatant /'bleɪtnt/ *adj* very clear or obvious: *their blatant dislike for each other* ○ *a blatant lie* ☞ This word is used in a critical way. —**blatantly** *adv*

blaze¹ /bleɪz/ *noun* **1** [C] a large and often dangerous fire: *It took firemen four hours to put out the blaze.* **2** [sing] **a blaze of sth** a very bright display of light or colour: *In the summer the garden was a blaze of colour.* ○ (*figurative*) *The new theatre was opened in a blaze of publicity* (= the newspapers, television, etc gave it a lot of attention).

blaze² /bleɪz/ *verb* [I] **1** to burn with bright strong flames: *a blazing log fire* **2 blaze (with sth)** to be extremely bright; to shine brightly: *I woke up to find that the room was blazing with sunshine.* ○ (*figurative*) *'Get out!' she shouted, her eyes blazing with anger.*

blazer /'bleɪzə(r)/ *noun* [C] a jacket, especially one that has the colours or sign (**badge**) of a school, club, team, etc on it; usually worn by men, or by schoolchildren as part of their uniform: *a school blazer*

bleach /bliːtʃ/ *verb* [T] to make sth white or lighter in colour (by using a chemical or by leaving it in the sun)
bleach *noun* [C,U] a strong chemical substance used for making clothes, etc whiter or for cleaning things

bleak /bliːk/ *adj* **1** (used about a situation) bad; not encouraging or hopeful: *a bleak future for the next generation* **2** (used about a place) cold, bare and grey: *the bleak Yorkshire Moors* **3** (used about the weather) cold and grey: *a bleak winter's day* —**bleakly** *adv* —**bleakness** *noun* [U]

bleary /'blɪəri/ *adj* (used about the eyes) red, tired and unable to see clearly: *We were all rather bleary-eyed after the journey.* —**blearily** *adv*: *'What's the time?' he said blearily, switching on the light.*

bleat /bliːt/ *verb* **1** [I] to make the sound of a sheep or goat **2** [I,T] to speak in a weak, uncertain way —**bleat** *noun* [C]

☆**bleed** /bliːd/ *verb* [I] (*pt, pp* **bled** /bled/) to lose blood: *He was bleeding badly from a cut on his head.* ○ *Is your finger bleeding?*
bleeding *noun* [U] blood flowing from a cut, etc: *He wrapped a scarf around his arm to try to stop the bleeding.*

bleep /bliːp/ *noun* [C] a short, high sound made by an electronic machine
bleep *verb* **1** [I] (used about machines) to make a short high sound: *Why is the computer bleeping?* **2** [T] to attract a person's attention using a bleeper
bleeper *noun* [C] a small piece of equipment that makes bleeps to let a person (eg a doctor) know when sb is trying to contact them

blemish /'blemɪʃ/ *noun* [C] a mark that spoils

p	b	t	d	k	g	tʃ	dʒ	f	v	θ	ð
pen	bad	tea	did	cat	got	chin	June	fall	van	thin	then

the way sth looks: *make-up to hide spots and other blemishes*
blemish *verb* [T] to spoil sth
blend /blend/ *verb* **1** [T] **blend A with B**; **blend A and B (together)** to mix: *First blend the flour and the melted butter together.* **2** [I] **blend with sth** to look or sound good with sth else: *new buildings which don't blend with their surroundings* **3** [I] **blend (into sth)** to be difficult to tell apart from sth else: *These animals' ability to blend into their surroundings provides a natural form of defence.*
(PHRASAL VERB) **blend in (with sth)** to look or sound good with sth else because the two things are similar: *The new room is decorated to blend in with the rest of the house.*
blend *noun* [C] a mixture: *a blend of China and Indian tea* o *He had the right blend of enthusiasm and experience.*
blender /'blendə(r)/ *noun* [C] = LIQUIDIZER
bless /bles/ *verb* [T] (*pt, pp* **blessed** /blest/) to ask for God's help and protection for sb/sth: *At the end of the marriage service, the vicar will bless the young couple.*
(IDIOMS) **be blessed with sth/sb** to be lucky enough to have sth/sb: *The West of Ireland is an area blessed with many fine sandy beaches.*
bless you! what you say to a person who has just sneezed
blessed /'blesɪd/ *adj* **1** (in religious language) holy: *the Blessed Virgin Mary* **2** (in religious language) lucky; fortunate: *Blessed are the pure in heart.* **3** giving great pleasure: *The cool breeze brought blessed relief from the heat.* **4** (used for expressing anger or surprise): *Where's the blessed train?*
blessing /'blesɪŋ/ *noun* [C] **1** a thing that you are grateful for or that brings happiness: *It's a great blessing that we have two healthy children.* o *a blessing in disguise* (= something which seems unlucky but turns out to be a good thing) o *to count your blessings* **2** [usually sing] approval or support: *They got married without their parents' blessing.* **3** [usually sing] (a prayer asking for) God's help and protection: *to ask for God's blessing* o *The priest said a blessing.*
blew *pt* of BLOW[1]
☆ **blind**[1] /blaɪnd/ *adj* **1** unable to see: *a blind person* o *to be completely/partially blind* ☞ We often describe a person as **visually handicapped** rather than **blind**. **2 blind (to sth)** not willing to notice or understand sth: *He was completely blind to her faults.* **3** without reason or thought: *her blind acceptance of fate* o *He drove down the motorway in a blind panic.* **4** impossible to see round: *You should never overtake on a blind corner.*
(IDIOM) **turn a blind eye (to sth)** to pretend not to notice sth
the blind *noun* [plural] people who are blind: *ways of making homes safer for the blind*
—**blindly** *adv* —**blindness** *noun* [U]
,blind 'date *noun* [C] an arranged meeting between a man and a woman who have never met before to see if they like each other enough to begin a romantic relationship
'blind spot *noun* [C] **1** if you have a blind spot about sth, you cannot understand or accept it **2** the part of the road that you cannot see when driving a car, ie the part which is just behind you
blind[2] /blaɪnd/ *verb* [T] **1** to make sb unable to see: *Her grandfather had been blinded in an accident* (= permanently). o *For a minute I was blinded by the lights of the oncoming car* (= for a short time). **2 blind sb (to sth)** to prevent sb from being aware of sth
blind[3] /blaɪnd/ *noun* [C] a piece of cloth or other material that you pull down to cover a window ☞ picture at **curtain**.
blinders /'blaɪndəz/ *noun* [plural] (*US*) = BLINKERS
blindfold /'blaɪndfəʊld/ *verb* [T] to cover a person's eyes with a piece of cloth, etc so that he/she cannot see
blindfold *noun* [C] a piece of cloth, etc that is used for covering sb's eyes
blink /blɪŋk/ *verb* **1** [I,T] to shut your eyes and open them again very quickly: *Oh dear! You blinked just as I took the photograph!* ☞ Look at **wink**. **2** [I] (used about a light) to come on and go off again quickly —**blink** *noun* [C]
blinkers /'blɪŋkəz/ (*US* **blinders**) *noun* [plural] pieces of leather fixed beside a horse's eyes so that it can only look straight in front
blip /blɪp/ *noun* [C] **1** a short sound made by an electronic machine **2** a small point of light on a screen **3** a small problem that does not last for long
bliss /blɪs/ *noun* [U] perfect happiness: *fifteen years of domestic bliss with his wife Mary* —**blissful** /-fl/ *adj* —**blissfully** /-fəli/ *adv*
blister /'blɪstə(r)/ *noun* [C] a small painful area of skin that looks like a bubble and contains clear liquid. Blisters are usually caused by rubbing or burning: *These shoes give me blisters.*
blister *verb* [I,T] to get or cause blisters
blistering /'blɪstərɪŋ/ *adj* **1** very great or severe: *the blistering midday heat* **2** showing great anger: *a blistering attack on his political enemies*
blitz /blɪts/ *noun* [C] **1** a sudden heavy military attack, especially from the air **2 a blitz (on sth)** (*informal*) a sudden great effort: *I had a blitz on the garden and it's looking quite nice now.*
blizzard /'blɪzəd/ *noun* [C] a very bad snowstorm with strong winds ☞ Look at the note at **storm**.
bloated /'bləʊtɪd/ *adj* unusually or uncomfortably large and full because of liquid, food or gas inside: *I felt a bit bloated after all that food.*
blob /blɒb/ *noun* [C] a small piece of a thick liquid: *a blob of paint, cream, etc*
bloc /blɒk/ *noun* [C, with sing or pl verb] a group of countries, political parties, etc who have similar political ideas and who act together: *the Eastern bloc*
☆ **block**[1] /blɒk/ *noun* [C] **1** a large, heavy piece of sth, usually with flat sides: *a block of wood* o *huge concrete blocks* **2** a large building that is divided into separate flats or offices: *a block of flats* o *an office block* ☞ picture on page A12. **3** a group of buildings in a town which has

streets on four sides: *I went for a walk around the block.* **4** [usually sing] a thing that makes movement or progress difficult or impossible: *a block to further progress in the talks*

(IDIOM) **to have a block (about sth)** to be unable to think or understand sth properly: *I had a complete mental block. I just couldn't remember his name.*

,block 'letter (*also* **block 'capital**) *noun* [C, usually pl] a capital letter: *Please write your name in block letters.*

☆ **block²** /blɒk/ *verb* [T] **1 block sth (up)** to make it difficult or impossible for anything or anybody to pass: *Many roads are completely blocked by snow.* ○ *I'm afraid the sink's blocked up.* **2** to prevent sth from being done: *The management tried to block the deal.* **3** to prevent sth from being seen by sb: *Get out of the way, you're blocking the view!*

(PHRASAL VERBS) **block sth off** to separate one area from another with sth solid: *This section of the motorway has been blocked off by the police.*

block sth out to try not to think about sth unpleasant: *She tried to block out the memory of the crash.*

blockage /ˈblɒkɪdʒ/ *noun* [C] a thing that is blocking sth; the state of being blocked: *a blockage in the drainpipe* ○ *blockages on some major roads*

blockade /blɒˈkeɪd/ *noun* [C] a situation in which a place is surrounded by soldiers or ships in order to prevent goods or people from reaching it — **blockade** *verb* [T]

blockbuster /ˈblɒkbʌstə(r)/ *noun* [C] a book or film with an exciting story which is very successful and popular: *the latest Hollywood blockbuster, Robin Hood*

bloke /bləʊk/ *noun* [C] (*Brit informal*) a man: *He's a really nice bloke.* ○ *What does her bloke (= boyfriend) do?*

blond (*also* **blonde**) /blɒnd/ *noun* [C], *adj* (a person) with fair or yellow hair: *Most of our family have blond hair.* ☛ When describing women the spelling **blonde** is used: *She's tall, slim and blonde.* The noun is usually only used of women and is spelt **blonde**: *She's a blonde.*

☆ **blood** /blʌd/ *noun* [U] the red liquid that flows through the body: *Blood was pouring from a cut on his knee.* ○ *The heart pumps blood around the body.*

(IDIOMS) **in your blood** a strong part of your character: *A love of the countryside was in his blood.*

in cold blood ⇒ COLD¹

'blood bath *noun* [C] an act of violently killing many people

'blood-curdling *adj* horrible and frightening: *a blood-curdling scream*

'blood donor *noun* [C] a person who gives his/her blood for use in medical operations

'blood group (*also* **'blood type**) *noun* [C] any of several different types of human blood: *Do you know which blood group you belong to?*

'blood pressure *noun* [U] the force with which the blood travels round the body: *to have high/low blood pressure*

'bloodshed *noun* [U] the killing or wounding of people: *Both sides in the war want to avoid further bloodshed.*

'bloodshot *adj* (used about the white part of the eyes) full of red lines, eg when sb is tired

'blood sport *noun* [C] a sport such as fox-hunting, in which animals are killed

'bloodstained *adj* having marks of blood on it

'bloodstream *noun* [sing] the blood as it flows through the body: *drugs injected straight into the bloodstream*

'blood transfusion *noun* [C] an injection of blood into a person's body: *to have a blood transfusion*

'blood-vessel *noun* [C] any of the tubes in the body which blood flows through

bloodless /ˈblʌdlɪs/ *adj* **1** (used about a part of the body) very pale **2** without killing or violence: *a bloodless coup*

bloodthirsty /ˈblʌdθɜːsti/ *adj* eager to use violence or to watch scenes of violence

bloody¹ /ˈblʌdi/ *adj* (**bloodier**; **bloodiest**) **1** involving a lot of violence and killing: *a bloody war* **2** covered with blood: *a bloody knife*

bloody² /ˈblʌdi/ *adj, adv* (*Brit informal*) (used for emphasizing anger, annoyance or just an opinion): *The bloody train was late again this morning.* ○ *What a bloody stupid idea!* ○ *We had a bloody good time.* ☛ Some people think that it is rude to use this word.

,bloody-'minded *adj* (*Brit informal*) difficult and unhelpful, often on purpose

bloom /bluːm/ *noun* [C] a flower

(IDIOM) **in bloom** with its flowers open: *All the wild plants are in bloom.*

bloom *verb* [I] to produce flowers: *This shrub blooms in May.* ○ (*figurative*) *You look blooming (= very healthy)!*

blossom /ˈblɒsəm/ *noun* [C,U] a flower or a mass of flowers, especially on a fruit tree: *The apple tree is covered in blossom.*

blossom *verb* [I] **1** (used especially about trees) to produce flowers **2 blossom (out) (into sth)** to develop well: *She had blossomed (out) into a lovely young girl.*

blot¹ /blɒt/ *noun* [C] **1** a spot or stain, especially one made by ink on paper **2 a blot on sth** a thing that spoils sb's reputation, character, future, etc

blot² /blɒt/ *verb* [T] (**blotting**; **blotted**) **1** to make a spot or stain on sth, especially one of ink on paper **2** to dry spots of liquid on sth by pressing it with soft paper or cloth

(PHRASAL VERB) **blot sth out** to cover or hide: *Heavy fog blotted out the view completely.* ○ *She kept herself busy, hoping to blot out her unhappy memories (= trying not to think of them).*

'blotting-paper *noun* [U] soft paper that you use for drying wet ink on writing paper, etc

blotch /blɒtʃ/ *noun* [C] a mark or an area of different colour, especially on sb's skin: *The blotches on her face showed that she had been crying.*

blotched (*also* **blotchy**) *adj* covered in blotches

iː	ɪ	e	æ	ɑː	ɒ	ɔː	ʊ	uː	ʌ
see	sit	ten	hat	arm	got	saw	put	too	cup

☆ **blouse** /blaʊz; *US* blaʊs/ *noun* [C] a piece of clothing like a shirt, that women wear

blow/suck

blowing

sucking

☆ **blow¹** /bləʊ/ *verb* (*pt* **blew** /bluː/; *pp* **blown** /bləʊn/) **1** [I] (used about wind, air, etc) to move: *Out at sea, a gentle breeze was blowing.* **2** [I] to send air out of the mouth: *Take a deep breath and then blow.* **3** [T] to make or shape sth by blowing air out of your mouth: *to blow bubbles* **4** [I,T] to produce sound from a musical instrument, whistle, etc by means of air: *I heard the guard's whistle blow as I ran up the station steps.* ○ *He blew a few notes on the trumpet.* ○ *All the drivers behind me were blowing their horns.* **5** [T] (*informal*) to waste an opportunity of succeeding in sth: *I think I've blown my chances of promotion.* **6** [T] **blow sth (on sth)** (*informal*) to spend or waste a lot of money on sth: *She blew all her savings on a trip to China.* **7** [I,T] (*informal*) (used for expressing anger, annoyance or the fact that you do not care about sth): *Oh, blow! It's raining.* ○ *'What will the neighbours think?' 'Oh blow the neighbours* (= I don't care about them)*!'* **8** [I,T] (used about an electric fuse) to stop working suddenly because the electric current is too strong; to make sth do this: *A fuse has blown.* ○ *I think the kettle's blown a fuse.*

(IDIOM) **blow your nose** to clear your nose by blowing strongly through it into a handkerchief, etc

(PHRASAL VERBS) **blow (sb/sth) down, off, over, etc** to move or make sth move through the air in the direction mentioned, because of the wind, etc: *My papers blew all over the garden.* ○ *The balloons blew away into the sky.* ○ *The wind suddenly blew my hat off.*

blow sth out to make sth stop burning by blowing air at it: *to blow out the candles on a birthday cake*

blow over to pass away; to end: *I expect those black clouds will soon blow over.* ○ *We often have arguments but they usually blow over fairly quickly.*

blow up 1 to explode or to be destroyed in an explosion: *A bomb blew up near our Oxford Street this morning.* ○ *The car blew up when the door was opened.* **2** to start suddenly and strongly: *A storm blew up in the night.* ○ *An argument blew up about money.* **3** (*informal*) to become very angry: *The teacher blew up when I said I'd forgotten my homework.*

blow sth up 1 to make sth explode or to destroy sth in an explosion: *The terrorists tried to blow up the plane.* **2** to fill sth with air or gas: *to blow up a balloon*

blow *noun* [C] an act of blowing: *Give your nose a blow!*

ˈ**blow-dry** *verb* [T] (*pt, pp* **blow-dried**) to dry and shape sb's hair using a hairdrier that you hold and a brush —ˈ**blow-dry** *noun* [sing]: *an appointment at the hairdresser's for a cut and blow-dry*

☆ **blow²** /bləʊ/ *noun* [C] **1** a hard knock from your hand, a weapon, etc that hits or is intended to hit sb/sth: *He felt a blow on the back of his head and fell down unconscious.* ○ *She aimed a blow at me.* **2 a blow (to sb/sth)** a sudden shock or disappointment: *It was rather a blow when I heard that I hadn't got the job.*

(IDIOMS) **a blow-by-blow account, description, etc (of sth)** an account, etc of an event that gives all the exact details of it

come to blows (over sth) to start fighting or arguing (about sth): *We always come to blows over where to go for our holiday.*

deal sb/sth a blow; deal a blow to sb/sth ⇨ DEAL²

blown *pp* of BLOW¹

☆ **blue¹** /bluː/ *adj* **1** having the colour of a clear sky on a sunny day: *His eyes were bright blue.* ○ *light/dark blue* **2** (*informal*) (often used in popular songs) sad **3** (used about jokes, films, etc) connected with sex

(IDIOM) **black and blue** ⇨ BLACK

ˌblue-ˈcollar *adj* doing or involving physical work with the hands rather than office work

☆ **blue²** /bluː/ *noun* **1** [C,U] the colour of a clear sky on a sunny day: *I'd like some curtains with some blue in them.* ○ *dressed in blue* (= blue clothes) **2 the blues** [plural, with sing or pl verb] a type of slow sad music similar to jazz: *a blues singer* **3 the blues** [plural] (*informal*) the state of feeling sad or depressed: *to have the blues*

(IDIOMS) **once in a blue moon** ⇨ ONCE

out of the blue suddenly; without being expected: *I didn't hear from him for years and then this letter came out of the blue.*

blueprint /ˈbluːprɪnt/ *noun* [C] a plan or description of how to make, build or achieve sth

bluff /blʌf/ *verb* [I,T] to try to convince people of sth that is not really true, usually by appearing very confident: *Don't take any notice of him, he's just bluffing.* ○ *They tried to bluff their parents into believing there was no school that day.* —**bluff** *noun* [C,U]: *John keeps threatening to leave home but I'm sure it's only bluff!*

bluish (*also* **blueish**) /ˈbluːɪʃ/ *adj* (*informal*) slightly blue: *bluish green*

blunder /ˈblʌndə(r)/ *noun* [C] a silly mistake: *I'm afraid I've made a terrible blunder.*

blunder *verb* to make a blunder

(PHRASAL VERB) **blunder about, around, etc** to move in an uncertain or careless way, as if blind: *We blundered about in the dark, trying to find the light switch.*

ɜː	ə	eɪ	əʊ	aɪ	aʊ	ɔɪ	ɪə	eə	ʊə
fur	ago	pay	home	five	now	join	near	hair	pure

blunt /blʌnt/ *adj* **1** (used about a person, remark, etc) saying exactly what you think in a not very polite way: *I'm sorry to be so blunt, but I'm afraid you're just not good enough.* **2** (used about a knife, pencil, tool, etc) not sharp: *blunt scissors*

blunt *verb* [T] to make sth less sharp or less strong —**bluntly** *adv* —**bluntness** *noun* [U]

blur /blɜː(r)/ *noun* [C, usually sing] something that you cannot see or remember clearly: *Through the window of the train the countryside was just a blur.*

blur *verb* [I,T] (**blur**ring; **blur**red) to become unclear; to make sth less clear: *The words on the page blurred as tears filled her eyes.* o *His thoughts were blurred and confused.*

blurt /blɜːt/ *verb*
(PHRASAL VERB) **blurt sth out** to say sth suddenly or without thinking: *We didn't want to tell Mum but Ann blurted the whole thing out.*

blush /blʌʃ/ *verb* [I] to become red in the face, especially because of shame or embarrassment: *She blushed with embarrassment.* —**blush** *noun* [C, usually sing]: *She admitted, with a blush, that she had been lying.*

boa /ˈbəʊə/ (*also* **ˈboa constrictor**) *noun* [C] a large snake that kills animals by squeezing them

boar /bɔː(r)/ *noun* [C] (*pl* **boar** *or* **boars**) **1** a male pig **2** a wild pig ☞ Look at the note at pig.

☆ **board¹** /bɔːd/ *noun* **1** [C] a long, thin, flat piece of wood used for making floors, walls, etc: *The old house needed new floorboards.* **2** [C] a thin flat piece of wood, etc used for a particular purpose: *an ironing-board* o *a diving-board* o *a blackboard* o *a surfboard* **3** [C] a flat and usually square piece of wood, cardboard, etc that you play certain games on: *a chessboard* o *board games* (= games you play on a board) ☞ picture at **chess**. **4** [C, with sing or pl verb] a group of people who control an organization, company, etc: *The board of directors is/are meeting to discuss the firm's future.* o *the Irish Tourist Board* **5** [U] the meals that are provided when you stay in a hotel, etc: *The prices are for a double room and full board* (= all the meals).
(IDIOMS) **above board** ⇨ ABOVE
across the board ⇨ ACROSS
on board on a ship or aeroplane: *All the passengers were safely on board.*

board² /bɔːd/ *verb* [T] to get on a plane, ship, bus, etc: *We said goodbye and boarded the train.* o *Lufthansa flight LH120 is now boarding* (= ready to take passengers) *at Gate 27.*
(PHRASAL VERB) **board sth up** to cover with boards¹(1): *Nobody lives there now – it's all boarded up.*

boarder *noun* [C] **1** a person who pays to live at sb's house **2** a pupil who lives at a school during term-time

ˈboarding card *noun* [C] a card that you must show in order to board a plane or ship: *Could passengers please have their boarding cards ready for inspection?*

ˈboarding-house *noun* [C] a private house where you can pay to stay and have meals for a period of time

ˈboarding-school *noun* [C] a school that pupils live at during term-time

boardroom /ˈbɔːdruːm; -rʊm/ *noun* [C] the room where a company's board of directors meets

boast /bəʊst/ *verb* **1** [I,T] to talk with too much pride about sth that you have or can do: *I wish she wouldn't boast about her family so much.* o *He's always boasting that he's the fastest runner in the school.* **2** [T] (used about a place) to have sth that it can be proud of: *The town boasts over a dozen restaurants.*

boast *noun* [C] **1** something you say that is too proud: *I didn't believe his boasts about how well he played.* **2** a thing that you are proud of: *It is our proud boast that our city is the most exciting in Europe.*

boastful /-fʊl/ *adj* (used about a person or the things that he/she says) showing too much pride

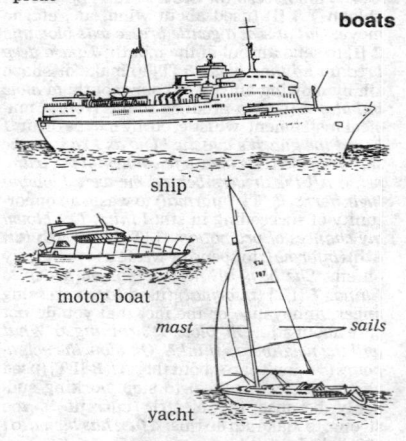

boats

ship

motor boat

mast — sails

yacht

☆ **boat** /bəʊt/ *noun* [C] a small vehicle that is used for travelling across water: *The cave can only be reached by boat/in a boat.* o *a rowing boat* o *a fishing boat* o *a motor boat* ☞ Usually **boat** means a small vessel but it can also be used for a large ship, especially one that carries passengers: *When does the next boat to France sail?*

bob /bɒb/ *verb* (**bob**bing; **bob**bed) [I,T] to move quickly up and down; to make sth do this: *The boats in the harbour were bobbing up and down in the water.*
(PHRASAL VERB) **bob up** to appear suddenly: *He disappeared and then bobbed up again on the other side of the pool.*

bobby /ˈbɒbɪ/ *noun* [C] (*pl* **bobbies**) (*Brit informal*) a policeman

bode /bəʊd/ *verb*
(IDIOM) **bode well/ill (for sb/sth)** to be a good/bad sign for sb/sth

bodily /ˈbɒdɪlɪ/ *adj* of the human body; physical: *First we must attend to their bodily needs*

p	b	t	d	k	g	tʃ	dʒ	f	v	θ	ð
pen	bad	tea	did	cat	got	chin	June	fall	van	thin	then

(= make sure that they have a home, enough to eat, etc).

bodily *adv* by taking hold of the body: *She picked up the child and carried him bodily from the room.*

☆ **body** /'bɒdɪ/ *noun* (*pl* **bodies**) **1** [C] the whole physical form of a person or animal: *the human body* **2** [C] the body apart from the legs, arms and head: *She had injuries to her head and body.* **3** [C] a dead human body: *The police have found a body in the canal.* **4** [sing] the main part of sth: *The main body of the guests will arrive at about 7 o'clock.* **5** [C, with sing or pl verb] a group of people who work or act together, especially in an official way: *The governing body of the college meets/meet once a month.* **6** [C] an object: *Do not remove a foreign body* (= something that should not be there) *from a wound. Leave that to the doctor.*
(IDIOM) **in a body** all together: *The students went in a body to complain to their teacher.*

body-building *noun* [U] making the muscles of the body stronger and larger by exercise

body language *noun* [U] showing how you feel by the way you move, stand, sit, etc, rather than by what you say

body odour *noun* [U] (*abbr* **BO**) the unpleasant smell of a person's body when it is sweating

bodyguard /'bɒdɪgɑːd/ *noun* [C] a person or group of people whose job is to protect sb ☛ When **bodyguard** means a group of people, it can be used with either a singular or plural verb: *His bodyguard is/are armed.*

bog /bɒg/ *noun* **1** [C,U] an area of ground that is very soft and wet: *the peat bogs of central Ireland* **2** [C] (*Brit slang*) a toilet

bogged down *adj* **1** if a vehicle is bogged down, it has sunk into mud, etc and cannot move **2** if a person is bogged down in sth, he/she cannot make any progress: *We got bogged down in a long discussion and didn't have time to make any decisions.*

boggy /'bɒgɪ/ *adj* (used about land) soft and wet, so that your feet sink into it

boggle /'bɒgl/ *verb* [I] to be very surprised at sth, or to find it difficult to imagine: *Bob Brown as headteacher? The mind boggles!*

bogus /'bəʊgəs/ *adj* pretending to be sth that it is not; not genuine: *He made a bogus claim to the insurance company.*

☆ **boil¹** /bɔɪl/ *verb* **1** [I] (used about a liquid) to reach a high temperature where bubbles rise to the surface and the liquid changes to a gas: *Water boils at 100°C.* ○ *The kettle's boiling* (= the water inside the kettle). **2** [T] to heat a liquid until it boils and let it keep boiling: *Boil all drinking water for five minutes.* **3** [I,T] to cook in boiling water: *Put the potatoes on to boil, please.* ○ *He doesn't even know how to boil an egg.* **4** [I] (used about a person) to feel very angry: *She was boiling with rage.*
(PHRASAL VERBS) **boil down to sth** to have sth as the most important point: *What it all boils down to is that you don't want to spend too much money.*

boil over 1 (used about a liquid) to boil and flow over the sides of a pan: *You let the soup boil over.* **2** (used about an argument or sb's feelings) to become more serious or angry

boil *noun* [sing] an act or period of boiling
(IDIOMS) **bring sth to the boil** to heat sth until it boils: *Bring the soup to the boil, then allow to simmer for five minutes.*

come to the boil to begin to boil

boiling (*also* **boiling 'hot**) *adj* (*informal*) very hot: *Open a window – it's boiling hot in here.* ○ *Can I have a drink? I'm boiling.*

boiling-point *noun* [C] the temperature at which a liquid starts to boil

boil² /bɔɪl/ *noun* [C] a painful swelling under your skin, like a large spot: *The boil on my neck has burst.*

boiler /'bɔɪlə(r)/ *noun* [C] **1** a metal container used for providing hot water in a house **2** a large metal container used for producing steam in an engine

boiler suit *noun* [C] a piece of clothing that covers your body, arms and legs, worn especially for dirty work

boisterous /'bɔɪstərəs/ *adj* (used about a person or his/her behaviour) noisy and full of energy: *Their children are very nice but they can get a bit too boisterous.* —**boisterously** *adv*

☆ **bold** /bəʊld/ *adj* **1** (used about a person or his/her behaviour) brave and confident; not afraid: *Not many people are bold enough to say exactly what they think.* ○ *We need somebody with bold new ideas.* **2** that you can see clearly: *The new fashion is for bold, bright colours.* **3** (used about printed letters) in thick, dark type: *The title was written in bold type.* —**boldly** *adv* —**boldness** *noun* [U]

bollard /'bɒlɑːd/ *noun* [C] a short thick concrete post in the middle or at the side of a road. Bollards divide the two sides of the road, or they are used to stop cars passing or parking.

bolster /'bəʊlstə(r)/ *verb* [T] **bolster sb/sth (up)** to support or encourage sb/sth; to make sth stronger: *His remarks did nothing to bolster my confidence.*

bolt¹ /bəʊlt/ *noun* [C] **1** a small piece of metal (shaped like a screw without a point) that is used with another piece of metal (**a nut**) for fastening things together. The nut screws onto the bolt. **2** a bar of metal that you can slide across the inside of the door in order to fasten it

bolt *verb* [T] **1** to fasten one thing to another using a bolt: *All the tables have been bolted to the floor so that nobody can steal them.* **2** to fasten a door, etc with a bolt: *Make sure that the door is locked and bolted.*

bolt² /bəʊlt/ *verb* **1** [I] (used especially about a horse) to run away very suddenly, usually in fear: *The noise of the explosion made the horses bolt.* **2** [T] **bolt sth (down)** to eat sth very quickly: *She bolted down a sandwich and dashed out of the house.*

bolt³ /bəʊlt/ *adv*
(IDIOM) **bolt upright** (sitting or standing) very straight

☆ **bomb** /bɒm/ *noun* **1** [C] a container that is filled with material that will explode when it is thrown or dropped, or when a device inside it

s	z	ʃ	ʒ	h	m	n	ŋ	l	r	j	w
so	zoo	she	vision	how	man	no	sing	leg	red	yes	wet

sets it off: *There are reports that a bomb has gone off at the station.* ○ *The terrorists planted the bomb in a wastebin.* ○ *Several tons of bombs were dropped on the city.* **2 the bomb** [sing] nuclear weapons: *How many countries have the bomb now?* **3 a bomb** [sing] (*informal*) a lot of money: *That coat must have cost you a bomb!*

bomb *verb* [T] to attack a city, etc with bombs: *Enemy forces have bombed the bridge.*

(PHRASAL VERB) **bomb along, down, up**, etc (*Brit informal*) to move along very fast in the direction mentioned, especially in a vehicle: *He was bombing along at 90 miles an hour when the police stopped him.*

'bomb-disposal *noun* [U] the removing or exploding of bombs in order to make an area safe: *a bomb-disposal expert*

bombard /bɒmˈbɑːd/ *verb* [T] to attack a place with bombs or guns: *They bombarded the city until the enemy surrendered.* ○ (*figurative*) *The reporters bombarded the minister with questions.*

bombardment /bɒmˈbɑːdmənt/ *noun* [C,U] an attack with bombs or guns: *The main radio station has come under enemy bombardment.*

bomber /ˈbɒmə(r)/ *noun* [C] **1** a type of aeroplane that drops bombs **2** a person who throws bombs or leaves them to explode in a public place

bombshell /ˈbɒmʃel/ *noun* [C, usually sing] an unexpected piece of news, usually about sth unpleasant

bona fide /ˌbəʊnə ˈfaɪdi/ *adj, adv* real or genuine: *This car park is for the use of bona fide customers only.*

bond /bɒnd/ *noun* **1** [C] (often plural) something that links two or more people or groups of people together, such as a feeling of friendship: *Our two countries are united by bonds of friendship.* **2** [C] a certificate that you can buy from a government or company that promises to pay you interest on the money you have lent: *National Savings Bonds*

☆ **bone** /bəʊn/ *noun* **1** [C] one of the hard parts inside the body of a person or animal that is covered with flesh and skin: *He's broken a bone in his hand.* ○ *Mind the dog – it's eating a bone.* ○ *This fish has got a lot of bones in it.* **2** [U] the substance that bones are made of

(IDIOMS) **have a bone to pick with sb** to have sth that you want to complain to sb about

make no bones about (doing) sth to do sth without hesitating or feeling worried about it: *She made no bones about telling him exactly what she thought about him.*

bone *verb* [T] to take the bones out of sth: *to bone a fish, chicken, etc*

bone-'dry *adj* completely dry: *Give that plant some water. It's bone-dry.*

'bone marrow (also **marrow**) *noun* [U] the soft substance that is inside the bones of a person or animal

bonfire /ˈbɒnfaɪə(r)/ *noun* [C] a large fire that you build outside to burn rubbish, etc

'Bonfire Night *noun* [C] the night of 5 November. On this day people in Britain light bonfires and fireworks to celebrate the failure of Guy Fawkes to blow up the Houses of Parliament in the seventeenth century.

bonkers /ˈbɒŋkəz/ *adj* (*slang*) mad; crazy

bonnet /ˈbɒnɪt/ *noun* [C] **1** (*US* **hood**) the front part of a car that covers the engine **2** a type of hat which covers the sides of the face and is fastened with strings under the chin

bonus /ˈbəʊnəs/ *noun* (*pl* **bonuses**) **1** a payment that is added to what is usual: *All our employees will receive a Christmas bonus.* **2** something good that you get in addition to what you expect: *As a special bonus, all our holidays will include use of a car for a week.*

bony /ˈbəʊni/ *adj* (**bonier; boniest**) so thin that you can see the shape of the bones: *long bony fingers*

boo /buː/ *interj, noun* [C] (*pl* **boos**) **1** a sound you make to show that you do not like sb/sth: *The minister's speech was met with boos from the audience.* **2** a sound you make to frighten or surprise sb: *He jumped out from behind the door and said 'boo'.* —**boo** *verb* [I,T]: *The crowd booed when they were told that the show had been cancelled.*

boob¹ /buːb/ *noun* [C] (*informal*) a silly mistake: *to make a boob* —**boob** *verb* [I]: *I'm afraid I've boobed again.*

boob² /buːb/ *noun* [C, usually pl] (*slang*) a woman's breast

booby prize /ˈbuːbi praɪz/ (*also* **wooden spoon**) *noun* [C] a prize that is given as a joke to the person who is last in a competition

booby-trap /ˈbuːbi træp/ *noun* [C] something dangerous, like a bomb, which is hidden inside sth that seems harmless —**booby-trap** *verb* [T]: *The car had been booby-trapped.*

☆ **book¹** /bʊk/ *noun* **1** [C] a number of sheets of paper, fastened together inside a cover, with words printed on them for people to read: *I'm reading a book on astrology.* ○ *She's writing a book about her life abroad.* ○ *Do you have any books by William Golding?* ○ *Open your books, please.* ○ *to publish a book* ○ *a library book* ○ *a cookery book* **2** [C] a number of pieces of paper, fastened together inside a cover, for people to write on: *Please write down all the new vocabulary in your exercise books.* **3** [C] a small number of things fastened together in the form of a book: *a book of stamps* **4 books** [plural] the records that a company, etc, keeps of the amount of money it spends or receives: *We employ an accountant to keep the books.*

(IDIOMS) **be in sb's good/bad books** (*informal*) to have someone pleased/angry with you: *He's been in his girlfriend's bad books since he forgot her birthday.*

by the book exactly according to the rules: *A policeman must always do things by the book.*

'bookcase *noun* [C] a piece of furniture with shelves to keep books on

'bookkeeping *noun* [U] keeping the accounts of the money that a company, etc, spends or receives

'bookmaker (also *informal* **bookie**) *noun* [C] a person whose job is to take bets on horse-races, etc

'bookmark *noun* [C] a narrow piece of card,

etc that you put between the pages of a book so that you can find the same place again easily

'bookseller noun [C] a person whose job is selling books

'bookshop (US **'bookstore**) noun [C] a shop that sells books ☛ Look at **library**.

'bookstall (US **'news-stand**) noun [C] a type of small shop, which is open at the front, selling newspapers, magazines and books, eg on a station

'bookworm noun [C] a person who likes reading books very much

☆ **book²** /bʊk/ verb **1** [I,T] to arrange to have or do sth at a particular time: *You must book weeks in advance if you want to travel on Christmas Eve.* ○ *Have you booked a table, sir?* ○ *to book a seat on a plane/train/bus* ○ *I've booked a hotel room for you/I've booked you a hotel room.* ○ *I'm sorry, but this evening's performance is fully booked* (= there are no seats left). **2** [T] to write the name of a person who has done sth wrong in a book: *The police booked her for dangerous driving* (= charged her with dangerous driving). ○ *The player was booked twice during the match and then sent off.*

(PHRASAL VERBS) **book in** to say that you have arrived at a hotel, etc (and sign your name on a list)

book sb in to arrange a room for sb at a hotel, etc in advance: *I've booked you in at the George Hotel.*

booking noun [C,U] the arrangement you make in advance to have a hotel room, a seat on a plane, etc: *Did you manage to make a booking?* ○ *Booking for the new musical does not start until October.*

'booking-office noun [C] an office where you buy tickets

bookie /'bʊki/ noun [C] (*informal*) = BOOKMAKER

booklet /'bʊklɪt/ noun [C] a small thin book, usually with a soft cover, that gives information about sth

boom¹ /buːm/ noun [C] a period in which sth increases or develops very quickly: *There was a boom in car sales in the 1980s.* ○ *a boom year for exports*

boom verb [I] to grow very quickly in size or value: *Business is booming in the Japanese car industry.*

boom² /buːm/ verb [I,T] **boom (sth) (out)** to make a loud, deep, hollow sound: *guns booming in the distance* ○ *The loudspeaker boomed out instructions to the crowd.*

boomerang /'buːməræŋ/ noun [C] a curved piece of wood that returns to you when you throw it in the right way, used for hunting by the first people who lived in Australia

boon /buːn/ noun [C] a thing that is very helpful and that you are grateful for

boost /buːst/ verb [T] to increase sth in number, value or strength: *If we lower the price, that should boost sales.* ○ *The good exam result boosted her confidence.*

boost noun [C] an increase; sth that encourages people: *The fall in the value of the pound has led to a boost in exports.* ○ *The president's visit gave a boost to the soldiers' morale.*

☆ **boot** /buːt/ noun [C] **1** a type of shoe that covers your foot and ankle and sometimes part of your leg: *a pair of ladies' boots* ○ *ski boots* ○ *walking/climbing boots* ○ *football boots* ☛ picture at **shoe**. **2** (US **trunk**) the part of a car where you put luggage, usually at the back

boot verb [T] to kick sth/sb hard: *He booted the ball over the fence.*

booth /buːð; US buːθ/ noun [C] a small enclosed place with thin walls that divide it from the rest of the room or area: *He called from a public phone booth at the station.* ○ *a ticket booth*

booty /'buːti/ noun [U] things that are taken by thieves or captured by soldiers in war

booze /buːz/ verb [I] (*informal*) to drink a lot of alcohol: *He went out boozing with some friends on Saturday.* —**booze** noun [U] (*informal*): *You had too much booze last night.*

'booze-up noun [C] (*Brit informal*) an occasion when people drink a lot of alcohol: *We had a bit of a booze-up after work.*

☆ **border** /'bɔːdə(r)/ noun [C] **1** a line that divides two countries, etc ; the land close to this line: *The refugees escaped across/over the border.* ○ *We crossed the border into Switzerland.* ○ *the Swiss border* ○ *the border between France and Italy* ○ *Italy's border with France* ☛ We use **border** and **frontier** to talk about the line that divides two countries or states. We usually use **border** to talk about natural divisions: *The river forms the border between the two countries.* **Boundary** is usually used for the line that divides smaller areas: *the county boundary.* **2** a band or strip around the edge of sth, often for decoration: *a white tablecloth with a blue border*

border verb [T] to be a border to; to be on the border of: *The road was bordered with trees.* ○ *Which English counties border Scotland?*

(PHRASAL VERB) **border on sth 1** to be next to sth: *Our garden borders on the railway line.* **2** to be almost the same as sth: *The dictator's ideas bordered on madness.*

'borderline noun [sing] the line that marks a division between two different cases, conditions, etc: *The novel is on the borderline between fiction and non-fiction.* ○ *He's a borderline case – he may pass the exam or he may fail.*

☆ **bore¹** /bɔː(r)/ verb [T] to make sb tired and uninterested: *I hope I'm not boring you.* ○ *Those old jokes bore me.*

bore noun **1** [C] a person who talks or behaves in an uninteresting way: *Her husband is such a bore.* **2** [sing] (*informal*) something that you have to do that you find uninteresting: *It's such a bore having to learn these lists of irregular verbs.*

bored adj feeling uninterested and tired because sth is not exciting or because you do not have anything to do: *I'm bored. There's nothing to do at home.* ○ *The children got bored in the long holidays.* ○ *He gave a bored yawn.* ○ *The play was awful. We were bored stiff* (= extremely bored).

boredom /-dəm/ noun [U] the state of being bored: *People say that many young people turn to crime out of boredom.*

ɜː	ə	eɪ	əʊ	aɪ	aʊ	ɔɪ	ɪə	eə	ʊə
fur	ago	pay	home	five	now	join	near	hair	pure

boring /ˈbɔːrɪŋ/ adj uninteresting; dull: *a boring film* ○ *boring work*

bore² /bɔː(r)/ verb [I,T] to make a round hole or passage through sth: *The drill can bore through solid rock.* ○ *They are boring a tunnel through the mountain.*

bore³ /bɔː(r)/ pt of BEAR²

☆ **born** /bɔːn/ verb **be born** to come into the world by birth; to start existing: *Where were you born?* ○ *My parents were born in Wales, but they grew up in England.* ○ *Peter Jones, born 1932, died 1992.* ○ *He was born in Frankfurt, of Italian parents.* ○ *I'm going to give up work after the baby is born.* ○ *Their baby was born deaf.* ○ *The idea of free education for all was born in the nineteenth century.* ○ *His unhappiness was born out of a feeling of frustration.*

born adj having a natural ability to do the task mentioned: *She's a born leader.*

-born (in compounds) born in the place or state mentioned: *Samuel Beckett, the Irish-born writer, lived in Paris most of his life.*

born-a'gain adj having found new, strong faith in a religion: *a born-again Christian*

borne /bɔːn/ pp of BEAR²

borough /ˈbʌrə; US -rəʊ/ noun [C] a town, or an area within a large town, that has some form of local government: *the London Borough of Lambeth*

borrow/lend

She's **lending** her son some money.

He's **borrowing** some money from his mother.

☆ **borrow** /ˈbɒrəʊ/ verb [I,T] **borrow (sth) (from/off sb/sth)** **1** to take or receive sth from sb/sth that you intend to give back, usually after a short time: *I had to borrow from the bank to pay for my car.* ○ *They borrowed £10 000 to buy a new car.* ○ *Could I borrow your pen for a minute?* ○ *Can I borrow £10? I'll pay you back next week.* ○ *He's always borrowing off his mother.* ○ *I borrowed a book from the library.* ☛ Be careful not to confuse **borrow** with its opposite **lend**. **2** to take sth and use it as your own; to copy: *That idea is borrowed from another book.*

borrower noun [C] a person who borrows

bosom /ˈbʊzəm/ noun [C] (formal) [C] (usually singular) a person's chest, especially a woman's breasts: *She clutched the child to her bosom.*

(IDIOM) **in the bosom of sth** close to; with the protection of: *He was glad to be back in the bosom of his family.*

bosom 'friend noun [C] a very close friend

☆ **boss** /bɒs/ noun [C] (*informal*) a person whose job is to give orders to others at work; an employer; a manager: *I'm going to ask the boss for a day off work.* ○ *Who's in charge when the boss is away?* ○ *OK. You're the boss* (= you make the decisions).

boss verb [T] **boss sb (about/around)** to give orders to sb, especially in an annoying way: *I wish you'd stop bossing me around.*

bossy adj (**bossier**; **bossiest**) liking to give orders to other people, often in an annoying way: *His mother was a strong, bossy woman.*
— **bossily** adv — **bossiness** noun [U]

botany /ˈbɒtəni/ noun [U] the scientific study of plants — **botanical** /bəˈtænɪkl/ adj: *botanical gardens* (= a type of park where plants are grown for scientific study)

botanist /ˈbɒtənɪst/ noun [C] a person who studies plants

botch /bɒtʃ/ verb [T] **botch sth (up)** to do or repair sth badly because you are not very skilful: *I've made rather a botched job of this typing, I'm afraid.*

☆ **both¹** /bəʊθ/ det, pron the two; the one as well as the other: *Both women were French.* ○ *Both the women were French.* ○ *Both of the women were French.* ○ *I talked to the women. Both of them were French/They were both French.* ○ *I liked them both.* ○ *We were both very tired.* ○ *Both of us were tired.* ○ *They have both seen the film.* ○ *I've got two sisters. They both live in London/Both of them live in London.* ○ *Both of my sisters live in London.* ☛ Note that we CANNOT say: *the both women* or: *my both sisters.*

☆ **both²** /bəʊθ/ adv **both... and...** not only... but also...: *I like both him and his wife.* ○ *They were both hungry and thirsty.*

☆ **bother** /ˈbɒðə(r)/ verb **1** [T] to disturb or annoy sb: *I'm sorry to bother you, but could I speak to you for a moment?* ○ *Don't bother Sue with that now – she's busy.* **2** [T] to worry sb: *You don't look very happy. Is something bothering you?* **3** [I,T] **bother (to do sth); bother about sth** (usually negative) to make the effort to do sth: *'Shall I make you something to eat?' 'No, don't bother – I'm not hungry.'* ○ *He didn't even bother to say thank you.* ○ *Don't bother about the washing-up. I'll do it later.* ○ *Don't bother waiting for me – I'll catch you up later.*

bother noun [U] trouble or difficulty: *Thanks for all your help. It's saved me a lot of bother.*

bother interj (used when you are annoyed): *Oh bother! I've left my keys in the car!*

bothered adj worried: *I'm a bit bothered about my sister – she doesn't look very well.*

(IDIOMS) **can't be bothered (to do sth)** If sb can't be bothered to do sth, he/she does not want to make the effort and is not going to do it: *I can't be bothered to do my homework now. I'll do it tomorrow.*

I'm not bothered I don't mind: *'What would you like to do this evening?' 'I'm not bothered really.'*

☆ **bottle** /ˈbɒtl/ noun [C] **1** a glass or plastic con-

p	b	t	d	k	g	tʃ	dʒ	f	v	θ	ð
pen	bad	tea	did	cat	got	chin	June	fall	van	thin	then

tainer with a narrow neck for keeping liquids in: *a beer bottle* o *an empty bottle* **2** the amount of liquid in a bottle: *a bottle of beer*

bottle *verb* [T] to put sth into bottles: *After three or four months the wine is bottled.*

bottled *adj* that you can buy in bottles: *bottled water*

'bottle bank *noun* [C] a large container in a public place where people can leave their empty bottles so that the glass can be used again (**recycled**) ☞ picture on page A19.

'bottleneck *noun* [C] a narrow piece of road that causes traffic to slow down or stop

☆ **bottom** /'bɒtəm/ *noun* **1** [C, usually sing] the lowest part of sth: *The house is at the bottom of a hill.* o *Look at the picture at the bottom of page 23.* o *I think I've got a pen in the bottom of my bag.* **2** [C] the flat surface on the outside of an object, on which it stands: *There's a label on the bottom of the box.* **3** [sing] the far end of sth: *The bus stop is at the bottom of the road.* **4** [sing] the least important position in relation to other people: *She started at the bottom and now she's the Managing Director.* **5** [sing] the ground under the sea, a river, a swimming-pool, etc: *The water was so clear that we could see the bottom.* **6** [C] the part of your body that you sit on: *He fell over and landed on his bottom.* **7 bottoms** [plural] the lower part of a piece of clothing that is in two parts: *pyjama bottoms* o *track suit bottoms*

(IDIOMS) **be at the bottom of sth** to be the real cause of sth: *I'm sure Kate Mills is at the bottom of all this.*

get to the bottom of sth to find out the real cause of sth

bottom *adj* in the lowest position: *the bottom shelf* o *I live on the bottom floor of a block of flats.*

bottomless *adj* very deep; without limit

bough /baʊ/ *noun* [C] one of the main branches of a tree

bought /bɔːt/ *pt, pp* of BUY

boulder /'bəʊldə(r)/ *noun* [C] a very large rock

boulevard /'buːləvɑːd; *US* 'bʊl-/ *noun* [C] a wide street in a city with trees on each side

bounce /baʊns/ *verb* **1** [I,T] (used about a ball, etc) to move away quickly after it has hit a hard surface; to make a ball do this: *In tennis, the ball can only bounce once before you hit it back.* o *The stone bounced off the wall and hit her on the head.* o *A small boy came down the street, bouncing a ball.* **2** [I] to jump up and down continuously: *The children were bouncing on their beds.* **3** [I] (used about a cheque) to be returned by a bank without payment because there is not enough money in the account

(PHRASAL VERB) **bounce back** to recover from a failure, disappointment, etc and return quickly to your normal life with the same energy as before—**bounce** *noun* [C]: *I couldn't reach the ball before the second bounce.*

bound¹ /baʊnd/ *adj* **1 bound to do sth** certain to do sth: *You've done so much work that you're bound to pass the exam.* o *There are bound to be problems in a situation like this.* **2** (not before a noun) having a legal or moral duty to do sth: *The company is bound by UK employment law.* o *She felt bound to refuse the offer.*

(IDIOM) **bound up with sth** very closely connected with sth

bound² /baʊnd/ *adj* **bound (for...)** travelling to a particular place: *a ship bound for Australia*

bound³ /baʊnd/ *verb* [I] to run quickly with jumping movements: *She bounded up the stairs in a state of great excitement.* —**bound** *noun* [C]: *With a couple of bounds he had crossed the room.*

bound⁴ *pt, pp* of BIND

☆ **boundary** /'baʊndri/ *noun* [C] (*pl* **boundaries**) **1** a line that marks the limits of a place and divides it from other places: *The main road is the boundary between the two districts.* **2** the farthest limit of sth: *Scientists continue to push back the boundaries of human knowledge.* ☞ Look at the note at **border**.

boundless /'baʊndlɪs/ *adj* having no limit: *boundless energy*

bounds /baʊndz/ *noun* [plural] limits that cannot or should not be passed: *Price rises must be kept within reasonable bounds.*

(IDIOM) **out of bounds** forbidden; not to be entered by sb: *This area is out of bounds to all staff.*

bouquet /bʊ'keɪ/ *noun* [C] a bunch of flowers that is arranged in an attractive way: *The actress received a huge bouquet of roses.*

bourbon /'bɜːbən/ *noun* [C,U] a type of whisky that is made mainly in the USA

bourgeois /'bɔːʒwɑː; *US* ˌbʊər'ʒwɑː/ *adj* typical of fairly rich middle-class people: *bourgeois attitudes, ideas, values, etc*

bourgeoisie /ˌbɔːʒwɑː'ziː; *US* ˌbʊərʒwɑː'ziː/ *noun* [sing, with sing or pl verb] the middle class

bout /baʊt/ *noun* [C] **1** a short period of great activity: *a bout of hard work* **2** a period of illness: *I'm just recovering from a bout of flu.*

boutique /buː'tiːk/ *noun* [C] a small shop that sells fashionable clothes, etc

☆ **bow¹** /baʊ/ *verb* **1** [I,T] to bend your head or

s	z	ʃ	ʒ	h	m	n	ŋ	l	r	j	w
so	zoo	she	vision	how	man	no	sing	leg	red	yes	wet

the upper part of your body forward and down, as a sign of respect: *At the end of the play all the actors came onto the stage and bowed.* ○ *He bowed his head respectfully.* **2 bow to sb/sth** [I] to accept sth: *I do not think the unions should bow to pressure from the Government.*

(PHRASAL VERB) **bow out (of sth)** to retire from an important position or stop taking part in sth: *After 12 years on the committee, she decided to bow out.*

bow *noun* [C] an act of bowing(1): *The audience were still clapping so the actors came back for another bow.*

bow² /bəʊ/ *noun* [C] **1** a knot with two loops and two loose ends that you use when you are tying shoes, ribbons, etc: *He tied the ribbon into a bow.* ○ *She had a black bow in her hair.* ☞ picture at **knot**. **2** a weapon for shooting arrows. A bow is a curved piece of wood that is held in shape by a tight string. **3** a long thin piece of wood with horsehair stretched along it that you use for playing a violin, etc

,bow-'tie *noun* [C] a tie in the shape of a bow(1), that is worn by men, especially on formal occasions

bow³ /baʊ/ *noun* [C] the front part of a ship ☞ Look at **stern**.

☆ **bowel** /'baʊəl/ *noun* [C, usually pl] one of the tubes that takes waste food from the stomach so that it can pass out of the body

☆ **bowl¹** /bəʊl/ *noun* [C] **1** a deep round dish without a lid that is used for holding food or liquid: *a sugar bowl* ○ *a mixing bowl* ☞ picture at **plate**. **2** the amount of sth that is in a bowl: *I usually have a bowl of cereal for breakfast.* **3** a large plastic container that is used for washing up, washing clothes, etc

bowl² /bəʊl/ *verb* [I,T] (in cricket) to throw the ball in the direction of the batsman

(PHRASAL VERB) **bowl sb over 1** to knock sb down when you are moving quickly **2** to astonish sb in a pleasant way: *I was absolutely bowled over by the beautiful scenery.*

bowler /'bəʊlə(r)/ (*also* ,bowler 'hat) (*US* **derby**) *noun* [C] a round hard black hat, usually worn by men ☞ picture at **hat**.

bowling /'bəʊlɪŋ/ *noun* [U] a game in which you roll a ball towards a group of wooden objects and try to knock down as many of them as you can: *tenpin bowling*

bowls /bəʊlz/ *noun* [U] a game in which you try to roll large wooden balls as near as possible to a smaller ball

☆ **box¹** /bɒks/ *noun* **1** [C] a square or rectangular container for solid objects. A box often has a lid: *We opened the lid and looked inside the box.* ○ *I keep the letters in an old shoebox.* **2** [C] a box and the things inside it: *a box of chocolates, matches, tissues, etc* ☞ picture at **container**. **3** [C] an empty square or rectangle on a form in which you have to write sth: *Write your full name in the box below.* **4** [C] an enclosed area that is used for a particular purpose: *a telephone box* ○ *a witness box* (= in a court of law) **5** [C] an enclosed area in a theatre in which a small group of people can sit and watch the play **6 the box** [sing] (*Brit informal*) television: *What's on the box tonight?*

box *verb* [T] to put into a box: *a boxed set of CDs*
'**box number** *noun* [C] a number that is given in a newspaper advertisement as part of the address to which replies should be sent
'**box office** *noun* [C] the place in a cinema, theatre, etc where the tickets are sold

☆ **box²** /bɒks/ *verb* [I,T] to fight in the sport of boxing: *He used to box when he was in the Army.*

boxer *noun* [C] a person who boxes as a sport, often professionally

boxing *noun* [U] a sport in which two people fight by hitting each other with their hands inside large gloves: *the world middleweight boxing champion* ○ *boxing gloves*

'**boxer shorts** *noun* [plural] men's underpants that are similar to shorts

☆ **Boxing Day** /'bɒksɪŋ deɪ/ *noun* [U] the day after Christmas Day; 26 December

☞ In England and Wales Boxing Day is a public holiday.

☆ **boy¹** /bɔɪ/ *noun* **1** [C] a male child: *They've got three children – two boys and a girl.* **2 the boys** [plural] (*informal*) a group of male friends

boyhood *noun* [U] the time of being a boy: *My father told me some of his boyhood memories.*

boyish *adj* like a boy: *a boyish smile*
'**boyfriend** *noun* [C] a man or boy with whom a person has a romantic and/or sexual relationship

Boy 'Scout = SCOUT(2)

boy² /bɔɪ/ *exclamation* (*informal*) (*especially US*) (used for expressing a strong feeling): *Boy, it's hot today!*

boycott /'bɔɪkɒt/ *verb* [T] to refuse to buy things from a particular company, take part in an event, etc because you strongly disapprove of it: *Several countries boycotted the Olympic Games in protest.* —**boycott** *noun* [C]: *a boycott of the local elections*

☆ **bra** /brɑː/ (*also formal* **brassière**) *noun* [C] a piece of clothing that women wear under their other clothes to support their breasts

brace¹ /breɪs/ *noun* **1** [C] a metal frame that is attached to a child's teeth in order to make them straight **2 braces** (*US* **suspenders**) [plural] a pair of straps for holding your trousers up. You put the braces over your shoulders and attach them to the top of your trousers at the front and back.

brace² /breɪs/ *verb* [T] **1 brace sth/yourself** to make your body stiff or press it against sth in order to prepare yourself, eg if sth is going to hit you, or to stop yourself from falling: *He braced himself as the big man came towards him.* **2 brace yourself (for sth)** to prepare yourself for sth difficult or unpleasant: *You'd better brace yourself for some bad news.*

bracing *adj* (used about a type of air, etc) making you feel healthy and lively: *bracing sea air*

☆ **bracelet** /'breɪslɪt/ *noun* [C] a piece of jewellery (eg a metal chain or band) that you wear around your wrist or arm ☞ picture at **jewellery**.

bracket /'brækɪt/ *noun* [C] **1** [usually pl] (es-

| i: | ɪ | e | æ | ɑ: | ɒ | ɔ: | ʊ | u: | ʌ |
| see | sit | ten | hat | arm | got | saw | put | too | cup |

pecially US **parenthesis; parentheses**) one of two marks, ( ) or [ ], that you put round extra information in a piece of writing **2** a piece of metal or wood that is attached to a wall and used as a support for a shelf, lamp, etc **3** a group of people whose ages, incomes, etc are between two limits: *to be in a high income bracket* o *The magazine is aimed at people in the 30-40 age bracket.*

bracket *verb* [T] **1** to put brackets(1) round a word, number, etc **2 bracket A and B (together); bracket A with B** to think of two or more people or things as similar in some way

brag /bræg/ *verb* [I,T] (bragging; bragged) to talk too proudly about sth: *She's always bragging about how clever she is.*

braid /breɪd/ *noun* **1** [U] a narrow piece of material that is used to decorate clothes, curtains, etc: *a uniform with gold braid on it* **2** [C] (*US*) = PLAIT: *You look nice with your hair in braids.*

Braille /breɪl/ *noun* [U] a way of printing for blind people, using raised dots that they read by touching them with their fingers

☆ **brain** /breɪn/ *noun* **1** [C] the part of the body inside the head that controls your thoughts, feelings and movements: *He suffered serious brain damage in a road accident.* o *a brain surgeon* **2** [C,U] the ability to think clearly; intelligence: *She has a very quick brain and learns fast.* o *He hasn't got the brains to be a doctor.* **3** [C] (*informal*) a very clever person: *He's one of the best brains in the country.* **4 the brains** [sing] the person who plans or organizes sth: *She's the real brains in the organization.*
(IDIOMS) **have sth on the brain** (*informal*) to think about sth all the time: *I've had that song on the brain all day.*
rack your brains ⇨ RACK²

brainless *adj* very silly

brainy *adj* (**brainier; brainiest**) (*informal*) clever

'brainchild *noun* [sing] the idea or invention of a particular person: *The music festival was the brainchild of a young teacher.*

brainstorm /'breɪnstɔːm/ *verb* [I,T] to solve problems or make decisions by asking all the members of a group to think of as many ideas as possible

brainwash /'breɪnwɒʃ/ *verb* [T] to force sb to believe sth by using strong mental pressure: *Television advertisements try to brainwash people into buying things that they don't need.* —**brainwashing** *noun* [U]

brainwave /'breɪnweɪv/ (*US* **brainstorm**) *noun* [C] (*informal*) a sudden clever idea

braise /breɪz/ *verb* [T] to cook meat or vegetables slowly in a little liquid in a covered dish

☆ **brake** /breɪk/ *noun* [C] **1** the part of a vehicle that makes it go slower or stop: *She put her foot on the brake and just managed to stop in time.* o *I'm taking my car to the garage today – there's something wrong with the brakes.* **2** something that makes sth else slow down or stop: *The Government must try to put a brake on inflation.*

brake *verb* [I] to make a vehicle go slower or stop by using the brakes: *If the driver hadn't braked in time, the car would have hit me.*

bran /bræn/ *noun* [U] the brown outer parts of wheat grains that have been separated from the flour

☆ **branch** /brɑːntʃ; *US* bræntʃ/ *noun* [C] **1** one of the main parts of a tree that grows from its trunk and often has leaves, flowers or fruit on it: *The little boy climbed the tree and sat on a branch.* ☞ picture at **tree**. **2** an office, shop, etc that is part of a larger organization: *The company I work for has branches in Paris, Milan and New York.* o *the High Street branch of Barclays Bank* **3** a part of an academic subject: *Psychology is a branch of medicine.*

branch *verb*
(PHRASAL VERBS) **branch off** (used about a road) to leave a larger road and go off in another direction: *A bit further on, the road branches off to the left.*

branch out (into sth) to start doing sth new and different from the things you usually do: *The company sells radios and stereo equipment and has recently branched out into computers.*

☆ **brand** /brænd/ *noun* [C] **1** the name of a product that is made by a particular company: *'Nescafé' is a well-known brand of coffee.* **2** a particular type of sth: *a strange brand of humour*

brand *verb* [T] **1** to mark an animal with a hot iron to show who owns it **2 brand sb (as sth)** to say that sb has a bad character so that people have a bad opinion of him/her: *She was branded as a troublemaker after she complained about her long working hours.*

brand-'new *adj* completely new

brandish /'brændɪʃ/ *verb* [T] to wave sth in the air in an aggressive or excited way: *The attacker stood in front of me, brandishing a knife.*

brandy /'brændi/ *noun* [C, U] a strong alcoholic drink that is made from wine

brash /bræʃ/ *adj* too confident and direct: *Her brash manner makes her unpopular with strangers.* —**brashness** *noun* [U]

brass /brɑːs; *US* bræs/ *noun* **1** [U] a yellow metal that is a mixture of copper and zinc: *brass buttons on a uniform* **2** [sing, with sing or pl verb] the group of musical instruments that are made of brass, eg the trumpet, the trombone: *the brass section in an orchestra* o *a brass band*

brassière /'bræsɪə(r); *US* brə'zɪər/ *noun* [C] (*formal*) = BRA

brat /bræt/ *noun* [C] a child who behaves badly and annoys you

bravado /brə'vɑːdəʊ/ *noun* [U] behaviour that makes you appear to be brave and confident when you are not, in order to impress people

☆ **brave** /breɪv/ *adj* ready to do things that are dangerous or difficult without showing fear: *the brave soldiers who fought in the war* o *'This may hurt a little, so try and be brave,'* said the dentist.

brave *verb* [T] to face sth dangerous or difficult without showing fear: *She braved the rain and went out into the street.* —**bravely** *adv*: *The men bravely defended the town for three days.* o

She smiled bravely and continued walking. —**bravery** /ˈbreɪvəri/ *noun* [U]: *After the war he received a medal for bravery.*

bravo /ˌbrɑːˈvəʊ/ *interj* a word that you shout to show that you like sth that sb has done, eg an actor's performance in a play

brawl /brɔːl/ *noun* [C] a noisy fight among a group of people, usually in a public place: *a drunken brawl outside a pub* —**brawl** *verb* [I]: *We saw some football fans brawling in the street.*

breach /briːtʃ/ *noun* **1** [C,U] an act that breaks an agreement, a law, etc: *Giving private information about clients is a breach of confidence.* ○ *She was dismissed from the company for breach of contract.* **2** [C] a break in friendly relations between people, groups, etc: *a breach between two countries* **3** [C] an opening in a wall, etc that defends or protects sb/sth: *The waves made a breach in the sea wall.*

breach *verb* [T] **1** to break an agreement, a law, etc: *He accused the Government of breaching international law.* **2** to make an opening in a wall, etc that defends or protects sb/sth

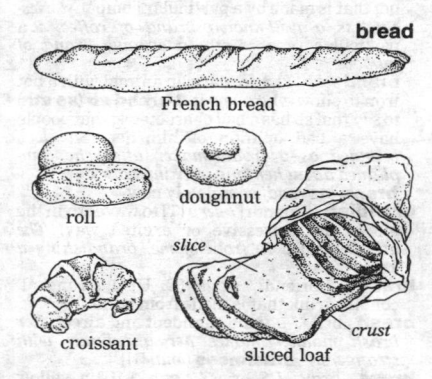

bread

French bread
roll
doughnut
slice
croissant
crust
sliced loaf

☆**bread** /bred/ *noun* [U] a type of food. To make bread you mix together flour and water (and yeast if you want the bread to rise) and bake the mixture in an oven: *a piece/slice of bread* ○ *We had bread and cheese for lunch.* ○ *Would you like some bread and butter?*

☛ A **loaf** of bread is bread that has been shaped and cooked in one piece. **Wholemeal** bread is made from flour that contains all the grain.

ˈbreadcrumbs *noun* [plural] very small bits of bread that are used in cooking

☆**breadth** /bredθ/ *noun* **1** [C,U] the distance between the two sides of sth: *We measured the length and breadth of the garden.* ☛ picture at **length**. **2** [U] the wide range of sth: *I was amazed by the breadth of her knowledge.* ☛ The adjective is **broad**.
(IDIOM) **the length and breadth of sth** ⇒ LENGTH

breadwinner /ˈbredwɪnə(r)/ *noun* [C, usually sing] the person who earns the money that his/her family needs

☆**break¹** /breɪk/ *verb* (*pt* **broke** /brəʊk/; *pp* **broken** /ˈbrəʊkən/) **1** [I,T] to separate, or make sth separate, into two or more pieces: *She dropped the vase onto the floor and it broke.* ○ *I've broken one of your dinner plates.* ○ *He broke his leg in a car accident.* **2** [I,T] (used about a machine, etc) to stop working; to stop a machine, etc working: *The photocopier has broken.* ○ *Be careful with my camera – I don't want you to break it.* **3** [T] to do sth that is against the law, or to not keep a promise, etc: *A policeman told me that I was breaking the law.* ○ *Slow down! You're breaking the speed limit.* ○ *to break a contract* ○ *Don't worry – I never break my promises.* **4** [T] **break a record** to do sth better or faster than anyone has ever done before: *She broke the world record for the 100 metres.* **5** [I,T] to stop doing sth for a short time: *Let's break for coffee now.* ○ *We decided to break the journey by stopping for lunch in Chester.* **6** [T] to interrupt sth so that it ends suddenly: *Suddenly, the silence was broken by the sound of a bird singing.* **7** [T] to make sth end by force or strong action: *It's very difficult to break the habit of smoking.* ○ *Two days of talks failed to break the deadlock between the two countries.* **8** [I] (used about a day or the dawn) to begin: *Dawn was breaking as I walked home after the party.* **9** [I] (used about a storm) to begin suddenly: *We ran indoors when the storm broke.* **10** [I] (used about a wave) to curl over and fall: *I watched the waves breaking on the rocks.* **11** [I] (used about a piece of news) to become known: *When the story broke in the newspapers, nobody could believe it.* **12** [I] (used about a boy's voice) to become permanently deeper, usually at about the age of 13 or 14

☛ For idioms containing **break**, look at the entries for nouns, adjectives, etc. For example, **break even** is at **even**.

(PHRASAL VERBS) **break away (from sb/sth) 1** to escape suddenly from sb who is holding you **2** to leave a political party, state, etc in order to form a new one: *Several politicians broke away from the Labour Party and formed the SDP.*

break down 1 (used about a vehicle or machine) to stop working: *Jill's car broke down on the way to work this morning.* **2** (used about a system, discussion, etc) to fail: *Talks between the two countries have completely broken down.* **3** to lose control of your feelings and start crying: *He broke down in tears when he heard the news.*

break sth down to make a substance separate into parts or change into a different form in a chemical process: *Food is broken down in our bodies by the digestive system.*

break in 1 to enter a building by force, usually in order to steal sth **2** to interrupt when sb else is speaking: *'But that's not true!' she broke in angrily.*

break into sth 1 to enter a building by force, usually in order to steal sth **2** to start doing sth suddenly: *He broke into a smile when he*

p	b	t	d	k	g	tʃ	dʒ	f	v	θ	ð
pen	bad	tea	did	cat	got	chin	June	fall	van	thin	then

heard the good news. ○ She broke into a run and disappeared into the distance.
break off to suddenly stop doing or saying sth: *He started speaking and then broke off in the middle of a sentence.*
break (sth) off to remove a part of sth by force; to come off in this way: *Could you break off another bit of chocolate for me?* ○ *Oh no, part of my tooth has broken off!*
break sth off to end a relationship suddenly: *They broke off their engagement after a bad argument.* ○ *to break off diplomatic relations with another country*
break out (used about fighting, wars, fires, etc) to start suddenly
break out (of sth) to escape from a prison, etc
break up 1 (used about events that involve a group of people) to come to an end: *The meeting broke up just before lunch.* **2** (*Brit*) to start school holidays at the end of a term: *When do you break up for the summer holidays?*
break up (with sb) to end a relationship with a wife, husband, girlfriend or boyfriend: *My marriage broke up when I was 25.* ○ *She's broken up with her boyfriend.*
break (sth) up to separate into parts: *The ship broke up on the rocks.*
break sth up to end an event by separating the people who are involved in it: *The police arrived and broke up the fight.*
break with sth to end a relationship or connection with sb/sth: *to break with tradition, the past, etc*

☆ **break²** /breɪk/ *noun* [C] **1** a place where sth has been broken: *a break in a pipe* **2** an opening or space in sth: *Wait for a break in the traffic before you cross the road.* ○ *a break in the clouds* **3** a short period of rest: *We worked all day without a break.* ○ *to take a break* ○ *a tea/coffee break* ☞ Look at the note at **interval**. **4 break (in sth); break (with sb/sth)** a change from what usually happens or an end to sth: *a break with tradition* ○ *She wanted to make a complete break with the past.* ○ *The incident led to a break in diplomatic relations.* **5** (*informal*) a piece of good luck: *to give sb a break* (= to help sb by giving him/her a chance to be successful).
(IDIOM) **break of day** the time when light first appears in the morning; dawn

breakage /'breɪkɪdʒ/ *noun* [C, usually pl] something that has been broken: *Customers must pay for any breakages* (eg in a shop selling glass).

breakdown /'breɪkdaʊn/ *noun* [C] **1** a time when a vehicle, machine, etc stops working: *We had a breakdown on the motorway.* **2** the failure or end of sth: *The breakdown of the talks means that a strike is likely.* **3** = NERVOUS BREAKDOWN **4** a list of all the details of sth: *I would like a full breakdown of how the money was spent.*

☆ **breakfast** /'brekfəst/ *noun* [C,U] the meal which you have when you get up in the morning: *to have breakfast* ○ *to eat a big breakfast*

☞ In a hotel, etc an **English** breakfast means cereal, fried eggs, bacon, sausages, tomatoes, toast, etc. A **Continental** breakfast means bread and jam with coffee.

(IDIOM) **bed and breakfast** ⇒ BED¹

break-in /'breɪkɪn/ *noun* [C] entering a building by force, especially in order to steal sth: *The police say there have been several break-ins in this area.*

breakthrough /'breɪkθruː/ *noun* [C] an important discovery or development: *Scientists have made a major breakthrough in cancer research.* ○ *The agreement represents a breakthrough in relations between the two countries.*

breakup /'breɪkʌp/ *noun* [C] **1** the end of a relationship between two people: *the breakup of a marriage* **2** the separation of a group or organization into smaller parts: *the breakup of the Soviet Union*

☆ **breast** /brest/ *noun* [C] **1** one of the two soft round parts of a woman's body that can produce milk **2** a word used especially in literature for the upper part of the front of your body: *to clasp sb to your breast* **3** the front part of the body of a bird

'**breast-feed** *verb* [I,T] (*pt, pp* '**breast-fed**) to feed a baby with milk from the breast

'**breast-stroke** *noun* [U] a style of swimming on your front in which you start with your hands together, push both arms forward and then pull them outwards and back through the water

☆ **breath** /breθ/ *noun* **1** [U] the air that you take into and blow out of your lungs: *to have bad breath* (= breath which smells unpleasant) **2** [C] an act of taking air into or blowing air out of your lungs: *Take a deep breath.*
(IDIOMS) **a breath of fresh air** the clean air which you breathe outside, especially when compared to the air inside a room or building: *Let's go for a walk. I need a breath of fresh air.* ○ (*figurative*) *Her happy face is like a breath of fresh air in that miserable place.*
get your breath (again/back) to rest after physical exercise so that your breathing returns to normal
hold your breath to stop breathing for a period of time, eg when swimming underwater or because of fear or excitement: *We all held our breath as we waited for her reply.*
(be) out of/short of breath to be breathing very quickly, eg after physical exercise
say sth, speak, etc under your breath to say sth very quietly, usually because you do not want people to hear what you are saying
take your breath away to surprise sb very much: *The spectacular view took our breath away.* ☞ The adjective is **breathtaking**.
with bated breath ⇒ BATED

'**breath test** *noun* [C] a test by the police on the breath of a driver to measure how much alcohol he/she has drunk

breathalyse /'breθəlaɪz/ *verb* [T] (used about a police officer) to test the breath of a driver with a special machine (**a breathalyser**) to measure how much alcohol he/she has drunk

☆ **breathe** /briːð/ *verb* [I,T] to take air, etc into

s	z	ʃ	ʒ	h	m	n	ŋ	l	r	w
so	zoo	she	vision	how	man	no	sing	leg	red	yes	wet

your lungs and blow it out again: *She was unconscious but still breathing.* o *to breathe in/out* (= to take air in/to blow air out) o *I hate sitting in restaurants breathing in other people's cigarette smoke.*
(IDIOM) **not breathe a word (of/about sth) (to sb)** not tell sb about sth that is secret: *If you breathe a word of this to my mother, I'll never speak to you again!* —**breathing** *noun* [U]: *heavy, irregular, etc breathing*

breather /ˈbriːðə(r)/ *noun* [C] (*informal*) a short rest: *to have/take a breather*

breathless /ˈbreθləs/ *adj* **1** breathing quickly or with difficulty, eg after physical exercise **2** not able to breathe because you are so excited, frightened, etc: *to be breathless with excitement* —**breathlessly** *adv*

breathtaking /ˈbreθteɪkɪŋ/ *adj* very exciting, beautiful, etc: *breathtaking mountain scenery*

breed /briːd/ *verb* (*pt, pp* **bred** /bred/) **1** [I] (used about animals or plants) to produce young animals or plants: *Many animals won't breed in zoos.* **2** [T] to keep animals or plants in order to produce young from them: *cattle which are bred to produce high yields of milk* **3** [T] to cause sth: *This kind of thinking breeds intolerance and violence.*

breed *noun* [C] a type of animal: *a breed of cattle*

breeder *noun* [C] a person who breeds animals or plants: *a dog breeder*

breeding *noun* [U] **1** the act of producing young plants or animals: *The breeding of fighting dogs has been banned.* **2** good manners and behaviour as a result of coming from an upper-class family: *a man and woman of breeding*

ˈbreeding-ground *noun* [C] **1** a place where wild animals go to breed **2** a place where sth can develop: *a breeding-ground for crime*

breeze /briːz/ *noun* [C] a light wind: *A warm breeze was blowing.*

breeze *verb*
(PHRASAL VERB) **breeze along, in, out, etc** (*informal*) to move in a cheerful relaxed way, even when this is not suitable behaviour: *He just breezed in twenty minutes late without a word of apology.*

breezy *adj* (**breezier; breeziest**) **1** a little windy **2** cheerful and relaxed: *You're bright and breezy this morning!*

brevity /ˈbrevəti/ *noun* [U] the state of being short or quick ☛ The adjective is **brief**.

brew /bruː/ *verb* **1** [T] to make beer **2** [T] to make a drink of tea or coffee by adding hot water: *to brew a pot of tea* **3** [I] (used about tea) to stand in hot water before it is ready to drink: *Leave it to brew for a few minutes.*
(IDIOM) **be brewing** (used about sth bad) to develop or grow: *There's trouble brewing.*

brewery /ˈbruːəri/ *noun* [C] (*pl* **breweries**) a place where beer is made

bribe /braɪb/ *noun* [C] money, etc that is given to sb such as an official to persuade him/her to do sth to help you, especially when you want him/her to do sth dishonest: *to offer a bribe to sb* o *to accept/take bribes* —**bribe** *verb* [T] **bribe sb (with sth)**: *They got a visa by bribing an official.* —**bribery** /ˈbraɪbəri/ *noun* [U]

☆**brick** /brɪk/ *noun* [C,U] a hard block of baked clay that is used for building houses, etc: *a house built of red brick* o *a lorry carrying bricks*
ˈbricklayer *noun* [C] a person whose job is to build walls with bricks
ˈbrickwork *noun* [U] the part of a building that is made of bricks

bridal /ˈbraɪdl/ *adj* (only *before* a noun) connected with a bride or a wedding: *the bridal suite in a hotel*

☆**bride** /braɪd/ *noun* [C] a woman on or just before her wedding-day: *the bride and groom* ☛ Look at the note at **wedding**.

☆**bridegroom** /ˈbraɪdɡruːm/ (*also* **groom**) *noun* [C] a man on or just before his wedding-day ☛ Look at the note at **wedding**.

bridesmaid /ˈbraɪdzmeɪd/ *noun* [C] a woman or girl who helps the bride at her wedding ☛ Look at the note at **wedding**.

☆**bridge¹** /brɪdʒ/ *noun* [C] **1** a structure that carries a road or railway, across a river, valley, road or railway: *a bridge over the River Thames* o *a motorway bridge* **2** the high part of a ship where the captain and the people who control the ship stand
bridge *verb* [T] to build a bridge over sth
(IDIOM) **bridge a/the gap** to fill a space between two people, groups or things or to bring them closer together

bridge² /brɪdʒ/ *noun* [U] a card game for four people

bridle /ˈbraɪdl/ *noun* [C] the leather straps that you put over a horse's head so that you can control it when you are riding it ☛ picture at **horse**.

☆**brief¹** /briːf/ *adj* short or quick: *a brief description* o *a brief phone call* o *Please be brief. We don't have much time.* ☛ The noun is **brevity**.
(IDIOM) **in brief** using only a few words: *News in Brief* (= in a newspaper)
briefly *adv* **1** for a short time; quickly: *She glanced briefly at her mother.* o *We met briefly in London yesterday.* **2** using only a few words: *I'd like to comment very briefly on that last statement.*

brief² /briːf/ *noun* [C] instructions or information about a job or task: *When he was appointed he was given the brief of improving the image of the organization.*
brief *verb* [T] to give sb information or instructions about sth: *The minister has been fully briefed on what questions to expect.*
briefing *noun* [C,U] instructions or information that you are given before sth happens: *a press/news briefing* (= where information is given to journalists)

briefcase /ˈbriːfkeɪs/ *noun* [C] a flat case that you use for carrying papers, etc, especially when you go to work ☛ picture at **luggage**.

briefs /briːfs/ *noun* [plural] pants for men or women

brigade /brɪˈɡeɪd/ *noun* [C] **1** a unit of soldiers in the army **2** a group of people who work together for a particular purpose: *the fire brigade*

brigadier /ˌbrɪɡəˈdɪə(r)/ *noun* [C] an officer of high rank in the army

☆**bright** /braɪt/ *adj* **1** having a lot of light: *a*

bright, sunny day ○ eyes bright with happiness **2** (used about a colour) strong: *a bright yellow jumper* **3** clever, or able to learn things quickly: *a bright child* ○ *a bright idea* **4** likely to be pleasant or successful: *The future looks bright.* **5** cheerful, happy: *You seem very bright and cheerful today.*

brighten /'braɪtn/ *verb* [I,T] **brighten (sth) (up)** to become brighter or happier; to make sth brighter: *His face brightened when he saw her.* ○ *to brighten up sb's day* (= make it happier)
—**brightly** *adv*: *brightly-coloured clothes*
—**brightness** *noun* [U]

☆ **brilliant** /'brɪliənt/ *adj* **1** having a lot of light; very bright: *brilliant sunshine* **2** very clever or intelligent: *a brilliant young scientist* **3** very good: *a brilliant performance by Pavarotti*
—**brilliance** /'brɪliəns/ *noun* [U] —**brilliantly** *adv*

brim /brɪm/ *noun* [C] **1** the top edge of a cup, glass, etc: *The cup was full to the brim.* **2** the bottom part of a hat, that is wider than the rest
brim *verb* [I] (bri**mm**ing; bri**mm**ed) **brim (with sth)** to be full of sth: *His eyes were brimming with tears.*
(PHRASAL VERB) **brim over (with sth)** (used about a cup, glass, etc) to have more liquid than it can hold: *The bowl was brimming over with water.* ○ *(figurative) to be brimming over with health/happiness*

bring/take

'Bring me my newspaper!'

'Take it into the kitchen!'

☆ **bring** /brɪŋ/ *verb* [T] (*pt, pp* **brought** /brɔːt/) **1** to come to a place with sb/sth: *We will be out all day so bring some sandwiches with you.* ○ *Is it all right if I bring a friend to the party?* ○ *Bring me two coffees, please.* ○ *The prisoner was brought into the court by two policewomen.* ○ *(figurative) He will bring valuable skills and experience to the team.* **2** to cause or result in sth: *The sight of her brought a smile to his face.* ○ *Money doesn't always bring happiness.* **3** to cause sb/sth to be in a certain place or condition: *Their screams brought people running from all directions.* ○ *Add water to the mixture and bring it to the boil.* ○ *What brings you here? Business or pleasure?* ○ *to bring sth to an end* **4** to force yourself to do sth: *The film was so horrible that I couldn't bring myself to watch it.*
(PHRASAL VERBS) **bring about** to cause sth to happen: *to bring about changes in people's lives*
bring sb/sth back to return sb/sth: *You can borrow the video if you bring it back tomorrow morning.*

bring sth back 1 to cause sth that existed before to be introduced again: *Nobody wants to bring back the days of child labour.* **2** to cause sb to remember sth: *The photographs brought back memories of his childhood.*

bring sb sth back to return with sth for sb: *My sister went to Spain on holiday and brought me back a T-shirt.*

bring sb/sth down to cause sb/sth to be defeated or to lose a position of power: *to bring down a government*

bring sth down to make sth lower in level: *to bring down the price of sth*

bring sth forward 1 to move sth to an earlier time: *The date of the wedding has been brought forward by two weeks.* **2** to suggest sth for discussion

bring sb in to ask or appoint sb to do a particular job: *A specialist was brought in to set up the new computer system.*

bring sth in to introduce sth: *The government have brought in a law on dangerous dogs.*

bring sth off (*informal*) to manage to do sth difficult: *The team brought off an amazing victory.*

bring sth on to cause sth: *Her headaches are brought on by stress.*

bring sth out to produce or cause sth to appear: *When is the company bringing out its next new model?* ○ *A crisis can sometimes bring out the best in people.*

bring sb round to cause sb to become conscious again

bring sb round (to sth) to persuade sb to agree with your opinion: *After a lot of discussion we finally brought them round to our point of view.*

bring sth round to sth to direct a conversation to a particular subject: *I finally brought the conversation round to the subject of money.*

bring sb up to look after a child until he/she is adult and to teach him/her how to behave: *After her parents were killed the child was brought up by her uncle.* ○ *a well-brought up child*

bring sth up 1 to be sick so that food that you have swallowed comes back out of your mouth; to vomit **2** to introduce sth into a discussion or conversation: *I intend to bring the matter up at the next meeting.*

brink /brɪŋk/ *noun* [sing] the edge at the top of a high place: *(figurative) The firm was close to disaster but the new director brought it back from the brink.*
(IDIOM) **be on the brink (of sth/of doing sth)** to be about to do or experience sth exciting or dangerous

3ː	ə	eɪ	əʊ	aɪ	aʊ	ɔɪ	ɪə	eə	ʊə
fur	ago	pay	home	five	now	join	near	hair	pure

brisk /brɪsk/ adj **1** quick or using a lot of energy; busy: *They set off at a brisk pace.* ○ *Trading has been brisk this morning.* **2** confident and efficient; wanting to do things quickly: *a brisk manner* —**briskly** adv **briskness** noun [U]

bristle /'brɪsl/ noun [C] **1** a short thick hair on a person or an animal **2** one of the short thick hairs of a brush

bristle verb [I] **1** (used about hair or an animal's fur) to stand up straight because of fear, anger, cold, etc **2 bristle (with sth)** to show that you are angry
(PHRASAL VERB) **bristle with sth** to be full of sth

Brit /brɪt/ noun [C] (*informal*) a British person

☆ **Britain** /'brɪtn/ = GREAT BRITAIN ☛ Look at the note at **United Kingdom**.

☆ **British** /'brɪtɪʃ/ adj of the United Kingdom, ie Great Britain and Northern Ireland: *British industry* ○ *to hold a British passport*

the British noun [plural] the people of the United Kingdom

Britisher noun [C] (*US*) a person who comes from Great Britain

the ˌBritish ˈIsles noun [plural] Great Britain and Ireland with all the islands that are near their coasts. The British Isles are a geographical but not a political unit.

Briton /'brɪtn/ noun [C] a person who comes from Great Britain ☛ This is normally only used in newspapers, or when talking about the inhabitants of Britain in earlier times: *Three Britons killed in air crash!* ○ *the Ancient Britons*. Otherwise we say 'a British man', 'a British woman'.

brittle /'brɪtl/ adj hard but easily broken: *brittle fingernails*

broach /brəʊtʃ/ verb [T] to start talking about a particular subject, especially one which is difficult or embarrassing: *Have you broached the subject of the money he owes us?*

☆ **broad** /brɔːd/ adj **1** large in size from one side to the other; wide: *a broad river valley* ○ *the broad boulevards of the capital* ☛ **Wide** is more often used than **broad** when you are talking about the distance between one side of something and the other: *The gate is four metres wide.* ○ *The table is too wide to go through the door.* **Broad** is often used about geographical features: *a broad expanse of desert* and in particular phrases such as: *broad shoulders.* The noun from **broad** is **breadth**. The opposite is **narrow**. **2** easily noticeable; very clear: *She spoke with a broad Somerset accent.* **3** without a lot of detail; general: *Just give me a broad outline of your plan.* **4** felt or believed by a lot of people: *There seems to be broad support for stronger anti-pollution laws.*
(IDIOM) **(in) broad daylight** during the day, ie not at night: *He was attacked in broad daylight.*

broaden /'brɔːdn/ verb [I,T] **broaden (out)** to become broader; to make sth broader: *The river broadens out beyond the bridge.* ○ (*figurative*) *Travel broadens the mind* (= it makes you understand other people better).

broadly adv **1** (used to describe a way of smiling): *to smile broadly* (= to have a very big, wide smile) **2** generally: *Broadly speaking, the scheme will work as follows...*

ˌbroad ˈbean noun [C] a type of large flat green bean that can be cooked and eaten as a vegetable

ˌbroad-ˈminded adj willing to listen to and accept beliefs and ways of life that are different from your own; tolerant: *They're very broad-minded about sex.* ☛ The opposite is **narrow-minded**.

☆ **broadcast** /'brɔːdkɑːst; *US* 'brɔːdkæst/ verb (*pt, pp* **broadcast**) **1** [I,T] to send out radio or television programmes: *The BBC World Service broadcasts to most countries in the world.* ○ *The Olympics are broadcast live by satellite.* **2** [I] to speak or appear on radio or on television: *The President broadcasts to the nation at times of crisis.*

broadcast noun [C] something that is sent out by radio or television: *a news broadcast*

broadcaster noun [C] a person who speaks on serious subjects on the radio or on television

broccoli /'brɒkəli/ noun [U] a plant with green or purple flower-heads that can be cooked and eaten as a vegetable ☛ picture at **cabbage**.

brochure /'brəʊʃə(r); *US* brəʊ'ʃʊər/ noun [C] a small book with pictures in it that gives you information about sth: *a holiday brochure*

broil /brɔɪl/ verb [T] (*especially US*) = GRILL

broke¹ *pt* of BREAK¹

broke² /brəʊk/ adj (not before a noun) (*informal*) having no money: *I can't come out tonight. I'm absolutely broke.*

broken¹ *pp* of BREAK¹

☆ **broken²** /'brəʊkən/ adj **1** damaged or in pieces; not working: *The washing-machine's broken.* ○ *Watch out! There's broken glass on the floor.* ○ *a broken leg* ☛ picture at **chip**. **2** not continuous; interrupted: *a broken line* ○ *a broken night's sleep* **3** not kept: *a broken promise* **4** (used about a foreign language) spoken slowly with a lot of mistakes: *to speak in broken English*

ˌbroken-ˈdown adj in a very bad condition: *a broken-down old shed*

ˌbroken-ˈhearted adj = HEARTBROKEN

ˌbroken ˈhome noun [C] a family in which the parents do not live together, eg because they are separated or divorced: *Many of the children came from broken homes.*

ˌbroken ˈmarriage noun [C] a marriage that has ended because the partners have got divorced

broker /'brəʊkə(r)/ noun [C] **1** a person who buys and sells things (eg shares in a business) for other people: *an insurance broker* **2** = STOCKBROKER

bronchitis /brɒŋ'kaɪtɪs/ noun [U] an illness of part of the lungs (**bronchial tubes**) that causes a very bad cough

bronze /brɒnz/ noun **1** [U] a brown-coloured metal that is made from copper and tin **2** [U] the colour of bronze **3** [C] = BRONZE MEDAL

bronze adj of the colour of bronze

ˌbronze ˈmedal noun [C] a round piece of bronze that you get as a prize for coming third in a race or a competition ☛ Look at **gold** and **silver medal**.

p	b	t	d	k	g	tʃ	dʒ	f	v	θ	ð
pen	bad	tea	did	cat	got	chin	June	fall	van	thin	then

brooch /brəʊtʃ/ noun [C] a piece of jewellery with a pin at the back that women wear on a dress, blouse or jacket ☛ picture at **jewellery**.

brood /bruːd/ noun [C] all the young birds that belong to one mother

brood verb [I] **1** (used about a female bird) to sit on her eggs **2 brood (on/over sth)** to worry, or to think a lot about sth that makes you sad: *to brood on a failure*

broody adj **1** (used about a female bird) ready to have or sit on eggs: *a broody hen* **2** (used about a woman) wanting to have a baby

brook /brʊk/ noun [C] a small stream

broom /bruːm/ noun [C] a brush with a long handle that you use for sweeping the floor ☛ picture at **brush**.

'broomstick noun [C] the handle of a broom. In stories witches are sometimes said to fly on broomsticks.

broth /brɒθ; US brɔːθ/ noun [U] thin soup: *chicken broth*

brothel /'brɒθl/ noun [C] a place where men can go and pay to have sex with a woman (**a prostitute**)

☆ **brother** /'brʌðə(r)/ noun [C] **1** a man or boy who has the same parents as another person: *Michael and Jim are brothers.* ○ *Michael is Jim's brother.* ○ *a younger/older brother* ○ *a twin brother* ☛ Look at **half-brother** and **stepbrother**. Notice that there is not a common English word that means 'both brothers and sisters': *Have you got any brothers and sisters?* The word **sibling** is very formal. **2** a man who is a member of a Christian religious community: *Brother John*

brotherhood /-hʊd/ noun **1** [U] a feeling of great friendship and loyalty between people: *the brotherhood of Man* (= a feeling of friendship between all the people in the world) **2** [C, with sing or pl verb] a organization which is formed for a particular, often religious, purpose

brotherly adv of or like a brother: *brotherly love*

brother-in-law /'brʌðər ɪn lɔː/ noun [C] (pl **brothers-in-law**) **1** the brother of your husband or wife **2** the husband of your sister

brought pt, pp of BRING

brow /braʊ/ noun [C] **1** [usually pl] = EYEBROW **2** = FOREHEAD: *Sweat was pouring from his brow.* **3** the top part of a hill or slope: *Suddenly a car came over the brow of the hill.*

☆ **brown** /braʊn/ adj **1** having the colour of soil or wood: *brown eyes* ○ *brown shoes* ○ *dark brown hair* **2** having skin of this colour: *They were very brown when they got back from their holiday.*

brown noun [C,U] the colour brown: *the yellows and browns of the trees in autumn* ○ *You don't look nice in brown* (= in brown clothes).

brown verb [I,T] to become or cause sth to become brown

brownish adj slightly or fairly brown: *She has brownish eyes.*

,brown 'paper noun [U] strong, thick paper used for wrapping parcels, etc

Brownie /'braʊni/ (also **'Brownie Guide**) noun [C] a young girl who is a member of the junior branch of the Girl Guides organization

browse /braʊz/ verb [I] **1** to spend time pleasantly, looking round a shop, without a clear idea of what you are looking for: *I spent hours browsing in the local bookshop.* **2 browse through sth** to look through a book or magazine without reading every part or studying it carefully: *I enjoyed browsing through the catalogue but I didn't order anything.* —**browse** noun [sing]: *I had a browse through the newspapers on the plane.*

☆ **bruise** /bruːz/ noun [C] a dark mark on the skin caused by a blow that injures but does not break the skin: *He didn't break any bones but he suffered cuts and bruises to his face.* ☛ A bruise on your eye is a **black eye**.

bruise verb **1** [T] to cause a bruise or bruises: *I fell over and bruised my arm.* ○ *She had a badly bruised face.* ○ *Handle the fruit carefully or you'll bruise it.* **2** [I] to get a bruise or bruises: *I've got the sort of skin that bruises easily.*

brunette /bruːˈnet/ noun [C] a white woman with dark brown hair ☛ Look at **blond**.

brunt /brʌnt/ noun
(IDIOM) **bear the brunt of sth** ⇨ BEAR²

brushes

hairbrush
nail-brush
brush
dustpan
brush (*also* broom)
paintbrushes
toothbrush

☆ **brush¹** /brʌʃ/ noun **1** [C] an object that is used for cleaning things, painting, tidying your hair, etc: *I took a brush and swept the snow from the path.* ○ *a clothes-brush* ○ *a toothbrush* ○ *a paintbrush* ○ *a hairbrush* **2** [sing] an act of sweeping, cleaning, tidying the hair, etc with a brush: *Your coat needs a brush.* **3** [C] **a brush with sb** a short argument or fight with sb

☆ **brush²** /brʌʃ/ verb **1** [T] to clean, tidy, sweep, etc with a brush: *Make sure you brush your teeth twice a day.* ○ *She was brushing her hair in front of a mirror.* ☛ Look at the note at **clean²**. **2** [I,T] to touch sb/sth lightly when passing: *Her hand brushed his cheek.* ○ *Leaves brushed against the car as we drove along the narrow road.*

(PHRASAL VERBS) **brush sb/sth aside 1** to refuse to pay attention to sb/sth: *She brushed*

s	z	ʃ	ʒ	h	m	n	ŋ	l	r	j	w
so	zoo	she	vision	how	man	no	sing	leg	red	yes	wet

aside the protests and continued with the meeting. **2** to get past sb/sth: *He hurried through the crowd, brushing aside the reporters who tried to stop him.*

brush sth away/off to remove sth with a brush or with the hand, as if using a brush: *I brushed the dust off my jacket.*

brush sth up/brush up on sth to study or practise sth in order to get back knowledge or skill that you had before and have lost: *She took a course to brush up her Spanish.*

'brush-off noun [C] (*informal*) an act of refusing to be friendly to sb: *He asked her to go out with him but she gave him the brush-off.*

brusque /bruːsk; US brʌsk/ adj not taking time to be polite when you are dealing with people: *He gave a brusque 'No comment!' and walked off.* —**brusquely** adv

Brussels sprout /ˌbrʌslz 'spraʊt/ (*also* **sprout**) noun [C, usually pl] a green vegetable that looks like a very small cabbage ☛ picture at **cabbage**.

brutal /'bruːtl/ adj very cruel and violent; without pity: *a brutal murder* ○ *brutal treatment of prisoners* ○ *a brutal dictatorship*

brutality /bruː'tæləti/ noun [C,U] (*pl* **brutalities**) very cruel and violent behaviour; acts that show no pity: *There have been many complaints of police brutality.* —**brutally** adv: *The girl had been brutally attacked.* ○ *He was brutally honest and told her that he didn't love her any more.*

brute /bruːt/ noun [C] **1** a large animal: *That dog of theirs is an absolute brute.* **2** a cruel, violent man: *Don't you dare hit him again, you brute!*

brute adj without the use of thought; using a violent method: *I think you'll have to use brute force to get this window open.*

bubbles

☆ **bubble** /'bʌbl/ noun [C] a hollow ball containing air or gas, in liquid or floating in the air: *The children were blowing bubbles with washing-up liquid.* ○ *the bubbles in a glass of champagne*

bubble verb [I] **1** to produce bubbles or to rise with bubbles: *Cook the pizza until the cheese starts to bubble.* ○ *The clear water bubbled up out of the ground.* **2 bubble (over) (with sth)** to be full of happy feelings

bubbly /'bʌbli/ adj **1** full of bubbles: *a bubbly drink* **2** (used about a person) lively and happy: *She has a naturally bubbly personality.*

'bubble gum noun [U] chewing-gum that can be blown into bubbles out of the mouth

buck¹ /bʌk/ noun [C] (*US informal*) a US dollar: *Could you lend me a few bucks?*

buck² /bʌk/ noun [C] (*pl* **buck** or **bucks**) a male deer or rabbit ☛ Look at the note at **deer**.

buck³ /bʌk/ noun
(IDIOM) **pass the buck** ⇨ PASS²

buck⁴ /bʌk/ verb [I] (used about a horse) to jump into the air with all four feet off the ground: *His horse suddenly bucked and he fell off.*
(PHRASAL VERBS) **buck up** (*informal*) to hurry up: *Come on, buck up! We have to leave in a minute.*

buck (sb) up (*informal*) to become or to make sb more cheerful or less unhappy: *Buck up! It's not the end of the world.*

☆ **bucket** /'bʌkɪt/ noun [C] **1** a round, open container, usually made of metal or plastic, with a handle, that is used for carrying or holding liquids or sand **2** (*also* **bucketful**) the amount that a bucket contains: *How many buckets of cement do you think we'll need?*

buckle /'bʌkl/ noun [C] a piece of metal or plastic at the end of a belt or strap that is used for fastening it

buckle verb [I,T] **1** to fasten or be fastened with a buckle **2** to bend because of heat, force, weakness, etc: *Some railway lines buckled in the heat.*

bud /bʌd/ noun [C] a small lump on a tree or plant that opens and develops into a flower or leaf: *rosebuds* ○ *At this time of year all the trees are in bud* (= have buds on them).

budding adj wanting or starting to develop and be successful: *Have you got any tips for budding young photographers?*

Buddhism /'bʊdɪzəm/ noun [U] an Asian religion that was founded in India by Buddha

Buddhist /'bʊdɪst/ noun [C] a person whose religion is Buddhism —**Buddhist** adj: *a Buddhist temple*

buddy /'bʌdi/ noun [C] (*pl* **buddies**) (*informal*) a friend, especially a male friend of a man

budge /bʌdʒ/ verb [I,T] **1** to move or cause sth to move a little: *I tried as hard as I could to loosen the screw but it simply wouldn't budge.* ○ *We just couldn't budge the car when it got stuck in the mud.* **2** to change or cause sb to change a firm opinion: *Neither side in the dispute is prepared to budge.* ○ *Once he's made up his mind, nothing will budge him.*

budgerigar /'bʌdʒərɪgɑː(r)/ (*also informal* **budgie**) noun [C] a small, brightly-coloured bird that people often keep as a pet in a cage

☆ **budget** /'bʌdʒɪt/ noun [C] **1** a plan of how to spend an amount of money over a particular period of time; the amount of money that is mentioned: *What's your monthly budget for food?* ○ *The government has announced reductions in the country's defence budget.* ○ *The new product was launched with an advertising budget of £2 million.* **2** (*also* **Budget**) a statement by a government saying how much money it plans to spend on particular things in the next year and how it plans to collect money: *Do you think taxes will go up in this year's budget?*

budget verb [I,T] **budget (sth) (for sth)** to plan carefully how much money to spend on sth: *Don't forget to budget for possible increased*

iː	ɪ	e	æ	ɑː	ɒ	ɔː	ʊ	uː	ʌ
see	sit	ten	hat	arm	got	saw	put	too	cup

costs. ○ *Costs for the new building are already far greater than the £10 million originally budgeted.*
budget *adj* (*informal*) (used in advertisements) very cheap
budgie /'bʌdʒɪ/ *noun* [C] (*informal*) = BUDGERIGAR
buff /bʌf/ *noun* [C] (*informal*) a person who knows a lot about a particular subject and is very interested in it: *Film buffs say that 'Citizen Kane' is one of the greatest films ever made.*
buffalo /'bʌfələʊ/ *noun* [C] (*pl* **buffalo** or **buffaloes**) a large wild animal that looks like a cow with long curved horns: *a herd of buffalo*
buffer /'bʌfə(r)/ *noun* [C] **1** a flat round piece of metal with a spring behind it that is put on the front or back of a train or at the end of a railway track. Buffers reduce the shock when sth hits them. **2** a thing or person that reduces the unpleasant effects of sth
buffet[1] /bə'feɪ; 'bʊfeɪ; *US* bə'feɪ/ *noun* [C] **1** a counter where passengers can buy food and drinks on a train; a café at a station: *The buffet car is situated at the rear of the train.* **2** a meal (usually at a party or on a special occasion) at which food is placed on a long table and people serve themselves: *Lunch was a cold buffet.* ○ *a buffet lunch*
buffet[2] /'bʌfɪt/ *verb* [T] to knock or push sth in a rough way from side to side: *The boat was buffeted by the rough sea.*
bug /bʌg/ *noun* **1** [C] a small insect, especially one that causes damage or is found in dirty places **2** [C] an illness that is not very serious and that people get from each other: *I don't feel very well – I think I've got the bug that's going round.* **3** usually **the bug** [sing] (*informal*) a sudden interest in sth: *They've been bitten by the golf bug.* **4** [C] a tiny hidden microphone that secretly records people's conversations **5** [C] something wrong in a system or machine, especially a computer: *There's a bug in the software.*
bug *verb* [T] (**bugging**; **bugged**) **1** to hide a tiny microphone somewhere so that people's conversations can be recorded secretly: *Be careful what you say. This room is bugged.* **2** (*informal*) to annoy or worry sb: *It bugs him that he's not as successful as his brother.*
buggy /'bʌgɪ/ *noun* [C] (*pl* **buggies**) (*Brit*) = PUSHCHAIR
☆ **build** /bɪld/ *verb* (*pt, pp* **built** /bɪlt/) **1** [T] to make sth by putting pieces, materials, etc together: *How long ago was your house built?* ○ *They've built a new bridge across the river.* ○ *The house is built of stone and brick.* **2** [I] to build buildings in a place: *There's plenty of land to build on around here.* **3** [T] to develop or increase sth: *The government is trying to build a more modern society.* ○ *This book claims to help people to build their self-confidence.*
(PHRASAL VERBS) **build sth in; build sth into sth 1** to fix furniture into a wall so that it cannot be moved: *We're going to have new cupboards built in the kitchen.* **2** to make sth a part of sth else: *They've made sure that a large number of checks are built into the system.*

build on sth to use sth as a base from which you can make further progress: *Now that we're beginning to make a profit, we must build on this success.*
build sth on sth to base sth on sth: *a society built on the principle of freedom and democracy*
build up to become greater in amount or number; to increase: *The traffic starts to build up at this time of day.*
build sth up 1 to make sth seem more important or greater than it really is: *I don't think it's a very serious matter, it's just been built up in the newspapers.* **2** to increase or develop sth over a period: *You'll need to build up your strength again slowly after the operation.*
build *noun* [C,U] the shape and size of sb's body: *She has a very athletic build.* ○ *Police are looking for a young man of slim build.* ☛ Compare **build** and **figure**. **Build** usually describes size in connection with strength and muscle and is used for both men and women. **Figure** usually describes shape, especially whether it is attractive or not, and is usually used only for women.
builder *noun* [C] a person whose job is to build houses and other buildings
-built (in compounds) having a body with a particular shape and size: *a tall well-built man*
'build-up *noun* [C, usually sing] **1 a build-up (of sth)** an increase of sth over a period: *The build-up of tension in the area has made war seem more likely.* **2 a build-up (to sth)** a period of preparation or excitement before an event: *The players started to get nervous in the build-up to the big game.*
built-'in *adj* **1** (used about furniture) built so it is fixed into a wall and cannot be moved: *built-in cupboards* **2** made a part of sth else: *There is built-in unfairness in the system.*
built-'up *adj* covered with buildings: *a built-up area*
☆ **building** /'bɪldɪŋ/ *noun* **1** [C] a structure, such as a house, church or school, that has a roof and walls: *There are a lot of very old buildings in this town.* **2** [U] the process or business of making buildings: *building materials* ○ *the building industry*
'building site *noun* [C] an area of land on which a building is being built
'building society *noun* [C] (*Brit*) an organization rather like a bank with which people can save money and get interest on it and which lends money to people who want to buy houses or flats
bulb /bʌlb/ *noun* [C] **1** (also **'light-bulb**) the glass part of an electric lamp that gives out light: *The bulb's gone* (= it no longer works) – *I'll have to put a new one in.* ○ *a 60-watt light-bulb* ☛ picture at **light**. **2** the round part of certain plants: *a tulip bulb*
bulge /bʌldʒ/ *noun* [C] an outward curve or lump on sth that is usually flat
bulge *verb* [I] **1** to stick out from sth that is usually flat; to swell outwards: *My stomach is starting to bulge. I must get more exercise.* **2 bulge with sth** to be full of sth: *His bags were bulging with presents for the children.*
bulging *adj* **1** sticking out: *He had a thin face*

ɜː	ə	eɪ	əʊ	aɪ	aʊ	ɔɪ	ɪə	eə	ʊə
fur	ago	pay	home	five	now	join	near	hair	pure

and rather bulging eyes. **2** very full: *She came home with bulging carrier bags.*

bulk /bʌlk/ *noun* **1** [U] the large size or amount of sth: *The cupboard isn't especially heavy, it's its bulk that makes it hard to move.* **2** [C] a very large body: *He slowly lifted his vast bulk out of the chair.* **3 the bulk (of sth)** [sing] the main part of sth; most of sth: *The bulk of the work has been done, there's only a bit left.*
(IDIOM) **in bulk** in large quantities: *If you buy in bulk, it is 10% cheaper.*
▶ **bulky** *adj* (**bulkier; bulkiest**) large and heavy and therefore difficult to move or carry: *a bulky parcel*

bull /bʊl/ *noun* [C] **1** an adult male of the cow family ☞ Look at the note and picture at **cow**. **2** the male of certain other animals, eg the elephant and the whale

'bullfight *noun* [C] a traditional public entertainment, especially in Spain, Portugal and Latin America, in which a man makes a bull angry, fights it and often kills it

'bullfighter *noun* [C] a man who takes part in a bullfight

'bullfighting *noun* [U] the public entertainment in which men fight bulls in a special stadium (**bullring**)

bulldog /'bʊldɒg/ *noun* [C] a strong dog with short legs, a large head and a short, thick neck

bulldoze /'bʊldəʊz/ *verb* [T] to make ground flat or knock down a building with a bulldozer: *The old buildings were bulldozed and new ones were built.*

bulldozer /'bʊldəʊzə(r)/ *noun* [C] a large, powerful tractor with a broad piece of metal at the front, used for clearing ground or knocking down buildings

☆ **bullet** /'bʊlɪt/ *noun* [C] a small rounded piece of metal with a pointed end that is fired from a gun: *The bullet hit her in the arm.* ○ *a bullet wound* ○ *There were bullet holes in the window.*

'bulletproof *adj* made of a strong material that stops bullets from passing through it

bulletin /'bʊlətɪn/ *noun* [C] **1** a short news report on TV or radio; an official statement about a situation: *The next news bulletin on this channel is at nine o'clock.* ○ *There were regular bulletins on the Prince's progress while he was in hospital.* **2** a short newspaper that a club or an organization produces: *As a member of the fan club, she receives a monthly bulletin.*

'bulletin board *noun*[C] (*US*) = NOTICE-BOARD

bullion /'bʊliən/ *noun* [U] bars of gold or silver: *The dollar price of gold bullion has risen by more than 10%.*

bull's-eye /'bʊlzaɪ/ *noun* [C] **1** the centre of a target that you aim at when you are shooting or throwing sth ☞ picture at **darts**. **2** a shot that hits this target

bully /'bʊli/ *noun* [C] (*pl* **bullies**) a person who uses his/her greater strength or power to hurt or frighten people who are weaker

▶ **bully** *verb* [T] (*pres part* **bullying**; *3rd pers sing pres* **bullies**; *pt, pp* **bullied**) to use your strength or power to hurt or frighten sb who is weaker: *There's a lot of bullying in that school.*
(PHRASAL VERB) **bully sb into doing sth** to force sb to do sth by frightening him/her

bum¹ /bʌm/ *noun* [C] (*informal*) (*Brit*) the part of the body on which you sit; bottom

bum² /bʌm/ *noun* [C] (*informal*) (*especially US*) **1** a person who moves from place to place and lives by begging **2** a lazy or useless person

bump /bʌmp/ *verb* **1** [I] **bump against/into sb/sth** to hit sth solid by accident when you are moving: *She bumped into a lamppost because she wasn't looking where she was going.* **2** [T] **bump sth (against/on sth)** to hit sth against or on sth by accident when moving it: *I bumped my knee on the edge of the table.* **3** [I] to move in an uneven way as if going over bumps: *We bumped along the track to the cottage.*
(PHRASAL VERBS) **bump into sb** to meet sb by chance: *I bumped into a old friend on the bus today.*
bump sb off (*slang*) to kill or murder sb

bump *noun* [C] **1** a sudden strong blow caused by sth hard hitting sth else; the sound of such a blow: *She fell and hit the ground with a bump.* ○ *We heard a loud bump from upstairs. One of the children had fallen out of bed.* **2** a lump on the body, often caused by a blow **3** a part of a flat surface that is raised above the rest of it: *There are a lot of bumps in the road, so drive carefully.*
▶ **bumpy** *adj* (**bumpier; bumpiest**) **1** (used about a surface) having a lot of bumps(3): *We drove along a bumpy road until we reached the farm.* **2** (used about a journey) rough and uncomfortable; not smooth: *Because of the stormy weather, it was a very bumpy flight.*

bumper¹ /'bʌmpə(r)/ *noun* [C] the bar fixed to the front and back of a motor vehicle to reduce the effect if it hits sth

bumper² /'bʌmpə(r)/ *adj* larger than usual: *The unusually fine weather has produced a bumper harvest this year.*

bun /bʌn/ *noun* [C] **1** a small round sweet cake: *a currant bun* **2** hair fastened tightly into a round shape at the back of the head: *She wears her hair in a bun.*

bunch /bʌntʃ/ *noun* **1** [C] a number of things, usually of the same type, fastened or growing together: *He bought her a bunch of flowers for her birthday.* ○ *a bunch of bananas/grapes* ○ *a bunch of keys* **2 bunches** [plural] long hair that is tied on each side of the head ☞ picture at **plait**. **3** [C, with sing or pl verb] (*informal*) a group of people: *My colleagues are the best bunch of people I've ever worked with.*
▶ **bunch** *verb* [I,T] **bunch (sth/sb) (up/together)** to stay together in a group; to form sth into a group or bunch: *The athletes bunched up as they came round the final bend.* ○ *He kept his papers bunched together in his hand.*

bundle /'bʌndl/ *noun* [C] a number of things tied or wrapped together: *a bundle of letters with an elastic band round them*
▶ **bundle** *verb* [T] **1 bundle sth (up)** to make or tie sth into a bundle or bundles: *I bundled up the old newspapers and threw them away.* **2** to put or push sb or sth quickly and in a rough way in a particular direction: *He was arrested and bundled into a police car.*

bung /bʌŋ/ *noun* [C] a round piece of wood or

p	b	t	d	k	g	tʃ	dʒ	f	v	θ	ð
pen	bad	tea	did	cat	got	chin	June	fall	van	thin	then

rubber that is used for closing the hole in certain containers eg a barrel, a jar, etc

bung verb [T] (*Brit informal*) to put or throw sth somewhere in a rough or careless way: *We bunged the suitcases into the car and drove away.*

bunged up adj blocked, so that nothing can get through: *I feel terrible. I've got a cold and my nose is all bunged up.*

bungalow /'bʌŋgələʊ/ noun [C] a house that is all on one level, without an upstairs ☞ picture on page A12.

bungle /'bʌŋgl/ verb [I,T] to do sth badly: *The men fled after bungling a raid on a bank in Oxford Road.*

bunk¹ /bʌŋk/ noun [C] **1** a bed that is fixed to a wall (eg on a ship or train) **2** (*also* **'bunk bed**) one of a pair of single beds built as a unit with one above the other

bunk² /bʌŋk/ noun
(IDIOM) **do a bunk** (*Brit informal*) to run away or escape; to leave without telling anyone

bunker /'bʌŋkə(r)/ noun [C] **1** a strongly built underground shelter that gives protection in a war **2** an area of sand on a golf course, where it is difficult to hit the ball

bunny /'bʌni/ noun [C] (used by and to small children) a rabbit

buoy /bɔɪ/ noun [C] a floating object, fastened to the bottom of the sea or a river, that shows ships and boats where dangerous places are
buoy verb [T] **buoy sb/sth (up) 1** to keep sb cheerful: *His encouragement buoyed her up during that difficult period.* **2** to keep sth high by supporting it: *Share prices were buoyed by news of a takeover.*

buoyant /'bɔɪənt/ adj **1** (used about a material) floating or able to float **2** happy and cheerful: *The team were in buoyant mood after their win.* **3** (used about economic and business life) successful, with a lot of activity: *Despite the recession, the property market remained buoyant.* **4** (used about prices) rising or keeping at a high level —**buoyancy** /-ənsi/ noun [U]: *a buoyancy aid* (= something that helps you float) o *the buoyancy of the German economy*

☆ **burden** /'bɜːdn/ noun [C] **1** a heavy load that is difficult to carry **2** a responsibility or difficult task that causes a lot of work or worry: *Having to make all the decisions is a terrible burden for me.* o *I don't want to be a burden to my children when I'm old.*
burden verb [T] **burden sb/yourself (with sth)** to give sb/yourself a responsibility or task that causes a lot of work or worry: *If I were you, I wouldn't burden myself with other people's problems.*

bureau /'bjʊərəʊ; *US* bjʊ'rəʊ/ noun [C] (pl **bureaux** or **bureaus** /-rəʊz/) **1** (*Brit*) a writing desk with drawers and a lid **2** (*US*) = CHEST OF DRAWERS **3** (*especially US*) one of certain government departments: *the Federal Bureau of Investigation* **4** an organization that provides information: *a tourist information bureau*

bureaucracy /bjʊə'rɒkrəsi/ noun (pl **bureaucracies**) **1** [C,U] a system of government by a large number of officials in various departments **2** [U] (often used in a critical way) the system of official rules that an organization has for doing sth, that people often think are too complicated: *With all the bureaucracy involved, it takes ages to get a visa.*

bureaucrat /'bjʊərəkræt/ noun [C] (often used in a critical way) an official in an organization or government department

bureaucratic /,bjʊərə'krætɪk/ adj connected with a bureaucracy, especially when it follows official rules too closely: *You have to go through a complex bureaucratic procedure if you want to get your money back.*

burger /'bɜːgə(r)/ noun [C] = HAMBURGER
-**burger** (in compounds) **1** a hamburger with sth else on top: *a cheeseburger* **2** something that is cooked like and looks like a hamburger, but made of sth else: *a fishburger*

burglar /'bɜːglə(r)/ noun [C] a person who enters a building illegally in order to steal: *The burglars broke in by smashing a window.* ☞ Look at the note at **thief**.

burglary /'bɜːgləri/ noun [C,U] (pl **burglaries**) the crime of entering a building illegally in order to steal: *There was a burglary at the house next door last week.* o *He is in prison for burglary.*

'burglar-alarm noun [C] a piece of equipment, usually fixed on a wall, that makes a loud noise if a thief enters a building

burgle /'bɜːgl/ verb [T] to enter a building illegally in order to steal from it: *Our flat was burgled while we were out.* o *Lock all doors and windows or you might get burgled.*

burial /'beriəl/ noun [C,U] the ceremony when a dead body is put in the ground (**buried**): *The burial took place on Friday.* o *The victims of the disaster were flown home for burial.* ☞ Look at the note at **funeral**.

burly /'bɜːli/ adj (used about a person or sb's body) strong and heavy

☆ **burn** /bɜːn/ verb (pt, pp **burnt** /bɜːnt/ or **burned** /bɜːnd/) **1** [T] to destroy, damage or injure sb/sth with fire or heat: *We took all the rubbish outside and burned it.* o *It was a terrible fire and the whole building was burnt to the ground* (= completely destroyed). o *The water was so hot that I burned my hands.* o *If you get too close to the fire you'll burn yourself.* o *The people inside the building couldn't get out and they were all burnt to death.* **2** [I] to be destroyed, damaged or injured by fire or heat: *If you leave the cake in the oven for much longer, it will burn.* o *I can't spend too much time in the sun because I burn easily.* o *They were trapped by the flames and they burned to death.* **3** [T] to produce a hole or mark in or on sth by burning: *He dropped his cigarette and it burned a hole in the carpet.* **4** [I] to be on fire: *Firemen raced to the burning building.* **5** [I] to produce light: *I don't think he went to bed at all – I could see his light burning all night.* **6** [I] to feel unpleasantly hot: *You must have a temperature, your forehead's burning.* **7** [I] **burn (with sth)** to be filled with a very strong feeling: *She was burning with indignation.*

(PHRASAL VERBS) **burn (sth) down** (used

burp | 82 | **business**

about a building) to destroy or be destroyed completely by fire: *The fire could not be brought under control and the school burned down.* o *The house was burnt down in a fire some years ago.*

burn sth out (usually passive) to completely destroy sth by burning: *the burnt-out wreck of a car*

burn up to be destroyed by fire or strong heat: *The space capsule burnt up on its re-entry into the earth's atmosphere.*

burn sth up to destroy sth by fire: *When all the rubbish had been burnt up I put out the fire.*

burn *noun* [C] an injury or piece of damage caused by fire or heat: *He has been treated for burns to his face and hands.* o *the burns unit of a hospital*

burp /bɜːp/ *verb* [I] to make a noise with the mouth when air rises from the stomach and is forced out: *He sat back when he had finished his meal and burped loudly.* —**burp** *noun* [C]: *a loud burp*

burrow /'bʌrəʊ/ *noun* [C] a hole in the ground made by certain animals (eg rabbits) in which they live

burrow *verb* **1** [I,T] to dig a hole in the ground **2** [I] to search for sth, using your hands as if you were digging: *She burrowed in her handbag for her keys.*

bursar /'bɜːsə(r)/ *noun* [C] the person who manages the financial matters of a school, college or university

bursary /'bɜːsəri/ *noun* [C] (*pl* **bursaries**) a sum of money given to a specially chosen student to pay for his/her studies at a college or university

☆**burst**[1] /bɜːst/ *verb* (*pt, pp* **burst**) **1** [I,T] to break open suddenly and violently, usually because there is too much pressure inside; to cause this to happen: *My shopping bag burst as I was leaving the supermarket.* o *You'll burst that balloon if you blow it up any more.* o *The balloon burst with a loud bang.* o (figurative) *'Would you like some more to eat?' 'No, thanks. If I have any more I'll burst!'* o *If it rains much more, the river will burst its banks.* **2** [I] **burst (with sth)** (only in the *-ing* forms) to be so full that it is in danger of breaking open: *I packed so many clothes that my suitcases were bursting.* o (figurative) *He was bursting with happiness on his wedding day.*

(IDIOM) **be bursting to do sth** to want to do sth very much: *I'm bursting to tell someone the news but it's a secret.*

(PHRASAL VERBS) **burst in on sb/sth** to interrupt sb/sth by arriving suddenly: *I'm sorry to burst in on you like this but there's an urgent phone call.*

burst into sth to start doing sth suddenly: *On hearing the news she burst into tears* (= started crying). o *The lorry hit a wall and burst into flames* (= started burning).

burst into, out of, through, etc to move suddenly in a particular direction, often using force: *She burst into the manager's office and demanded to speak to him.*

burst out 1 to start doing sth suddenly: *He looked so ridiculous that I burst out laughing.*

2 to say sth suddenly and with strong feeling: *Finally she burst out, 'I can't stand it any more!'*

burst[2] /bɜːst/ *noun* [C] **1** an occasion when sth bursts or explodes; a crack caused by an explosion: *a burst in a water pipe* **2** a short period of a particular activity, that often starts suddenly: *With a burst of speed, she left the other runners behind.* o *He prefers to work in short bursts.* o *There were several bursts of applause during her speech.*

☆**bury** /'beri/ *verb* [T] (*pres part* **burying**; *3rd pers sing pres* **buries**; *pt, pp* **buried**) **1** to put a dead body in a grave: *She wants to be buried in the village graveyard.* o *Anne Brontë is buried in Scarborough.* **2** to put sth in a hole in the ground to cover it up: *Our dog always buries its bones in the garden.* o *They say there's buried treasure somewhere on the island!* **3** (usually passive) to cover or hide: *At last I found the photograph, buried at the bottom of a drawer.* o *After the earthquake, hundreds of people were buried under the rubble.* o (figurative) *Sally didn't hear us come in. She was buried in a book.*

☆**bus** /bʌs/ *noun* [C] (*pl* **buses**; *US also* **busses**) a big public vehicle which takes passengers from one stopping-place to another along a fixed route: *Where do you usually get on/off the bus?* o *We'll have to hurry up if we want to catch the 9 o'clock bus.* o *It's so difficult to park your car in town. It's better to go by bus.*

☛ The **bus driver** may also take the money (your **fare**) and give you your **ticket**, or there may be a **conductor** who collects the fares. You can get on or off at a **bus-stop** and the central point where most buses start is the **bus station**. Note that we travel **by bus**. We can also say **on the bus**: *'How do you get to work?' 'On the bus.'*

☆**bush** /bʊʃ/ *noun* **1** [C] a plant like a small, thick tree with many low branches: *a rose bush* o *The house was surrounded by thick bushes.* **2** often **the bush** [U,sing] wild land that is not cultivated, especially in Africa and Australia

(IDIOM) **beat about the bush** ⇒ BEAT[1]

bushy (**bushier**; **bushiest**) *adj* growing thickly: *bushy hair* o *bushy eyebrows*

busier, busiest, busily ⇒ BUSY

☆**business** /'bɪznɪs/ *noun* **1** [U] buying and selling as a way of earning money; commerce: *She has set up in business as a hairdresser.* o *They are very easy to do business with.* o *He teaches English for Business.* **2** [U] the work that you do as your job: *The manager will be away on business next week.* o *a business trip* **3** [U] the amount of trade done: *Business has been good for the time of year.* **4** [C] a firm, a shop, a factory, etc which produces or sells goods or provides a service: *She started an antique business of her own.* o *Small businesses are finding it hard to survive at the moment.* **5** [U] something that concerns a particular person: *The friends I choose are my business, not yours.* o *Our business is to collect the information, not to comment on it.* o *'How much did it cost?' 'It's none of your business.'* (= I don't want to tell you. It's private.) **6** [sing] a situation or an event: *The*

iː	ɪ	e	æ	ɑː	ɒ	ɔː	ʊ	uː	ʌ
see	sit	ten	hat	arm	got	saw	put	too	cup

divorce was an awful business. ○ I found the whole business very depressing.
(IDIOMS) **get down to business** to start the work that must be done: *Let's just have a cup of coffee before we get down to business.*
go out of business to have to close because there is no more money available: *The shop went out of business because it couldn't compete with the new supermarket.*
have no business to do sth/doing sth to have no right to do sth: *You have no business to read/reading my letters without asking me.*
mind your own business ⇨ MIND²
'**businesslike** *adj* efficient and practical: *She has a very businesslike manner.*
'**businessman**, '**businesswoman** *noun* [C] (*pl* **businessmen**; **businesswomen**) **1** a person who works in business(1) especially in a top position **2** a person who is skilful at dealing with money: *My brother can advise you on your investments – he's a better businessman than I am.*
'**business studies** *noun* [U] the study of how to control and manage a business(4): *a course in business studies*
busk /bʌsk/ *verb* [I] to sing or play music in the street so that people will stop and give you money
busker *noun* [C] a street musician
bust¹ /bʌst/ *noun* [C] **1** a model in stone, etc of a person's head, shoulders and chest **2** a woman's breasts; the measurement round a woman's chest: *Have you got this jumper in a 36 inch bust?*
bust² /bʌst/ *verb* [T] (*pt, pp* **bust** or **busted**) (*informal*) to break or damage sth so that it cannot be used
bust *adj* (not before a noun) (*informal*) broken or not working: *The zip on these trousers is bust.*
(IDIOM) **go bust** (*informal*) (used about a business) to have to close because it has lost so much money: *During the recession thousands of businesses went bust.*
'**bust-up** *noun* [C] (*informal*) a serious quarrel
bustle¹ /'bʌsl/ *verb* [I,T] **1** to move in a busy, noisy or excited way; to make sb move somewhere quickly: *He bustled about the kitchen making tea.* ○ *They bustled her out of the room before she could see the body.* **2 bustle (with sth)** to be full of sth (people, noise, activity, etc): *It was the week before Christmas and the streets were bustling with shoppers.*
bustle *noun* [U] excited and noisy activity: *She loved the bustle of city life.*
☆**busy** /'bɪzi/ *adj* (**busier**; **busiest**) **1 busy (at/with sth)**; **busy (doing sth)** having a lot of work or tasks to do; not free; working on sth: *Mr Smith is busy until 4 o'clock but he could see you after that.* ○ *Don't disturb him. He's busy.* ○ *She's busy with her preparations for the party.* ○ *We're busy decorating the spare room before our visitors arrive.* **2** (used about a period of time) full of activity and things to do: *I've had rather a busy week.* **3** (used about a place) full of people, movement and activity: *Oxford Street was so busy that I could hardly move.* **4** (*US*) =

ENGAGED(2): *The line's busy at the moment. I'll try again later.*
(IDIOM) **get busy** start working: *We'll have to get busy if we're going to be ready in time.*
busy *verb* [T] (*pres part* **busying**; *3rd pers sing pres* **busies**; *pt, pp* **busied**) **busy yourself with sth**; **busy yourself doing sth** to keep yourself busy; to find sth to do —**busily** *adv*: *When I came in she was busily writing something at her desk.*
busybody /'bɪzibɒdi/ *noun* [C] (*pl* **busybodies**) a person who is too interested in other people's affairs
☆**but¹** /bət; strong form bʌt/ *conj* **1** (used for introducing an idea which contrasts with or is different from what has just been said): *The weather will be sunny but cold.* ○ *Theirs is not the first but the second house on the left.* ○ *James hasn't got a car but his sister has.* **2** however; and yet: *She's been learning Italian for five years but she doesn't speak it very well.* ○ *I'd love to come but I can't make it till 8 o'clock.* **3** (used with an apology): *Excuse me, but is your name Peter Watkins?* ○ *I'm sorry, but I can't stay any longer.* **4** (used for introducing a statement that shows that you are surprised or annoyed or that you disagree): *'Here's the money I owe you.' 'But that's not right – it was only £6.'*
(IDIOM) **but then** however; on the other hand: *We could go swimming. But then perhaps it's too cold.* ○ *He's brilliant at the piano. But then so was his father* (= however, this is not surprising because…).
☆**but²** /bət; strong form bʌt/ *prep* except: *I've told no one but you about this.* ○ *We've had nothing but trouble with this washing-machine!*
(IDIOM) **but for sb/sth** except for or without sb/sth: *We wouldn't have managed but for your help.*
☆**butcher** /'bʊtʃə(r)/ *noun* [C] **1** a person who sells meat: *The butcher cut me four lamb chops.* ○ *She went to the butcher's for some sausages.* ☛ Note that the **butcher** is the person who runs the shop and the **butcher's** is the shop. **2** a person who kills many people in a cruel way
butcher *verb* [T] to kill a lot of people in a cruel way
butchery *noun* [U] unnecessary or cruel killing
butler /'bʌtlə(r)/ *noun* [C] the most important male servant in a big house
butt¹ /bʌt/ *noun* [C] **1** the thicker, heavier end of a weapon or tool: *the butt of a rifle* **2** a short piece of a cigarette or cigar which is left when it has been smoked **3** (*especially US informal*) your bottom: *Get up off your butt and do some work!*
butt² /bʌt/ *noun* [C] a person who is often laughed at or talked about unpleasantly: *Fat children are often the butt of other children's jokes.*
butt³ /bʌt/ *verb* [T] to hit or push sb/sth with the head
(PHRASAL VERB) **butt in (on sb/sth)** to interrupt sb/sth or to join in sth without being asked: *I'm sorry to butt in but could I speak to you urgently for a minute?*

ɜː	ə	eɪ	əʊ	aɪ	aʊ	ɔɪ	ɪə	eə	ʊə
fur	ago	pay	home	five	now	join	near	hair	pure

butter /ˈbʌtə(r)/ noun [U] a soft yellow fat that is made from cream and used for spreading on bread, etc or in cooking: *Do you prefer butter or margarine?* ○ *First, melt a little butter in the pan.*

butter verb [T] to spread butter on bread, etc: *I'll cut the bread and you butter it.* ○ *hot buttered toast*

'buttermilk noun [U] the liquid that is left when butter has been separated from milk

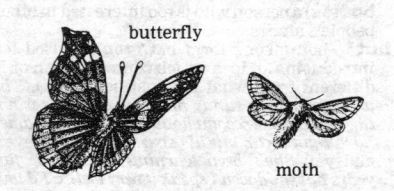

butterfly

moth

butterfly /ˈbʌtəflaɪ/ noun [C] (pl **butterflies**) an insect with a long, thin body and four brightly coloured wings: *Caterpillars develop into butterflies.*

(IDIOM) **to have butterflies (in your stomach)** (informal) to feel very nervous before doing sth

buttock /ˈbʌtək/ noun [C, usually pl] the part of the body which you sit on

button /ˈbʌtn/ noun [C] **1** a small, often round, piece of plastic, wood or metal that you use for fastening your clothes: *One of the buttons on my jacket has come off.* ○ *a coat, shirt, trouser, etc button* ○ *This blouse is too tight. I can't fasten the buttons.* ☛ picture at **zip**. **2** a type of small switch on a machine, etc that you press in order to operate sth: *Press this button to ring the bell.* ○ *Which button turns the volume down?* ○ *the buttons on a telephone* ○ *the fire button on a computer joystick* ☛ picture at **telephone**.

'buttonhole noun [C] **1** a hole in a piece of clothing that you push a button through in order to fasten it ☛ picture at **zip**. **2** (Brit) a flower that you pin to your coat or jacket or push through your buttonhole

'buttonhole verb [T] to make sb stop and listen to what you want to say: *I'll try to buttonhole the headmaster before he goes home.*

buy /baɪ/ verb [T] (pt, pp **bought** /bɔːt/) to get sth by paying money for it: *I'm going to buy a new dress for the party.* ○ *We bought this book for you in London.* ○ *Can I buy you a coffee?* ○ *He bought the car from a friend.* ○ *Did you buy this sofa new?* ○ *He bought the necklace as a present for his wife.*

buy noun [C] an act of buying sth or a thing that you can buy: *I think your house was a very good buy* (= worth the money you paid).

buyer noun [C] **1** a person who is buying sth or may buy sth: *I think we've found a buyer for our house!* **2** a person whose job is to choose and buy goods to be sold in a large shop

buzz /bʌz/ verb **1** [I] to make the sound that bees, etc make when flying: *A large fly was buzzing against the window pane.* **2** [I] **buzz (with sth)** to be full of (talk, thoughts, etc): *Her head was buzzing with questions that she wanted to ask.* ○ *The office was buzzing with rumours about the proposed changes.* **3** [I,T] to call sb by using an electric bell, etc: *The doctor will buzz for you when he's ready.*

buzz noun **1** [C] the sound that a bee, etc makes when flying: *the buzz of insects* **1** [sing] the low sound made by many people talking at the same time: *I could hear the buzz of conversation in the next room.*

(IDIOM) **give sb a buzz** (informal) to telephone sb

buzzer noun [C] a piece of equipment that makes a buzzing sound: *You'll hear the buzzer on the cooker when the meal's ready.*

by¹ /baɪ/ adv **1** past: *We stopped to let the ambulance get by.* ○ *If we sit here we can watch the boats sail by.* ○ *Time seemed to be going by very slowly.* **2** near: *The shops are close by.*

(IDIOMS) **by and large** ⇒ **LARGE**

by² /baɪ/ prep **1** beside; very near: *Come and sit by me.* ○ *We stayed in a cottage by the sea.* **2** past: *He walked straight by me without speaking.* **3** not later than; before: *I'll be home by 7 o'clock.* ○ *He should have telephoned by now/by this time.* ○ *By this time tomorrow you'll be married!* **4** (usually without *the*) during a period of time; in particular circumstances: *By day we covered about thirty miles and by night we rested.* ○ *The electricity went off so we had to work by candlelight.* **5** (of a passive verb) (used for showing who or what did or caused sth): *She was knocked down by a car.* ○ *The event was organized by local people.* ○ *I was deeply shocked by the news.* ○ *The building was designed by Stirling.* ○ *Who was the book written by?/Who is the book by?* **6** through doing sth: *You can get hold of me by phoning this number.* **7** using sth: *Will you be paying by cheque?* ○ *The house is heated by electricity.* ○ *'How do you go to work?' 'By train, usually.'* ○ *by bus, car, plane, bicycle, etc* **8** as a result of; due to: *I got on the wrong bus by mistake/accident.* ○ *I met an old friend by chance.* **9** according to: *It's 8 o'clock by my watch.* ○ *By law you have to attend school from the age of five.* **10** (used for multiplying or dividing): *4 multiplied by 5 is 20.* ○ *6 divided by 2 is 3.* **11** (used for showing the measurements of an area): *The table is six feet by three feet* (= six feet long and three feet wide). **12** (with *the*) in quantities or periods of: *We buy material by the metre.* ○ *You can rent a car by the day, the week or the month.* ○ *Copies of the book have sold by the million.* **13** in groups or units of: *They came in one by one.* ○ *Bit by bit I began to understand.* ○ *Day by day she was getting better.* **14** to the amount of: *Prices have gone up by 10 per cent.* ○ *I missed the bus by a few minutes.* **15** (used with a part of the body or an article of clothing) holding: *He grabbed me by the arm.* **16** with regard to: *She's French by birth.* ○ *He's a doctor by profession.* ○ *By nature she's a very gentle person.*

(IDIOM) **by the way** ⇒ **WAY¹**

bye /baɪ/ (also **bye-bye** /ˌbaɪˈbaɪ/) interj (informal) goodbye: *Bye! See you tomorrow.*

by-election /ˈbaɪɪlekʃn/ noun [C] an election to choose a new Member of Parliament for a

p	b	t	d	k	g	tʃ	dʒ	f	v	θ	ð
pen	bad	tea	did	cat	got	chin	June	fall	van	thin	then

particular town or area (**a constituency**). It is held when the previous member has resigned or died. ☛ Look at **general election**.

bypass /ˈbaɪpɑːs; *US* -pæs/ *noun* [C] a road which traffic can use to go round a town, instead of through it
▶ **bypass** *verb* [T] to go around or to avoid sth using a bypass: *Let's try to bypass the city centre.* ○ *(figurative) It's no good trying to bypass the problem.*

by-product /ˈbaɪprɒdʌkt/ *noun* [C] **1** something that is formed during the making of sth else **2** something that happens as the result of sth else

bystander /ˈbaɪstændə(r)/ *noun* [C] a person who is standing near and sees sth that happens, without being involved in it: *Several innocent bystanders were hurt when the two gangs attacked each other.*

byte /baɪt/ *noun* [C] *(computing)* a unit of information that can represent one item, such as a letter or a number. A byte is usually made up of a series of eight smaller units (**bits**).

Cc

C, c /siː/ *noun* [C] (*pl* **C's**; **c's**) the third letter of the English alphabet: *'Come' begins with (a) 'C'.*

cab /kæb/ *noun* [C] **1** (*especially US*) = TAXI: *Let's take a cab/go by cab.* **2** the part of a lorry, train, bus, etc where the driver sits
'**cab stand** (*US*) = TAXI RANK

cabaret /ˈkæbəreɪ; *US* ˌkæbəˈreɪ/ *noun* [C,U] an entertainment with singing, dancing, etc in a restaurant or night-club

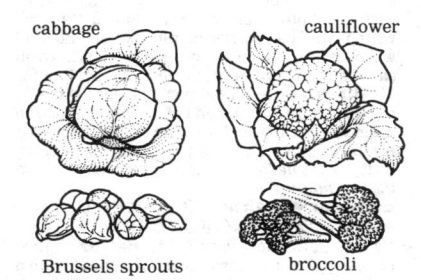

cabbage

cauliflower

Brussels sprouts

broccoli

☆ **cabbage** /ˈkæbɪdʒ/ *noun* [C,U] a large round vegetable with thick green, or sometimes dark red leaves, often eaten cooked: *We've planted cabbages in the garden.* ○ *Shall we have cabbage with the sausages.*

cabin /ˈkæbɪn/ *noun* [C] **1** a small room in a ship or boat, where a passenger sleeps: *We've booked a cabin on the ferry as we'll be travelling overnight.* **2** one of the parts of an aeroplane, at the front or where the passengers sit: *I prefer to have a seat at the front of the cabin.* ○ *the pilot's cabin* **3** a small wooden house or hut: *We stayed in a log cabin in Sweden.*
'**cabin cruiser** *noun* [C] = CRUISER(2)

cabinet /ˈkæbɪnɪt/ *noun* [C] **1** a cupboard with shelves or drawers, used for storing things: *a medicine cabinet* ○ *a filing cabinet* **2** (*also* **the Cabinet**) [with sing or pl verb] the most important ministers in a government, who have regular meetings with the Prime Minister: *The Cabinet is/are meeting today to discuss the crisis.* ○ *a cabinet meeting, minister, etc*

cable /ˈkeɪbl/ *noun* **1** [C] a very strong, thick rope or chain, etc **2** [C,U] a set of wires covered with plastic, etc, for carrying electricity or signals: *an underground electrical cable* ○ *a telephone cable* ○ *fibre-optic cable* **3** [C] (*old-fashioned*) = TELEGRAM **4** [U] = CABLE TELEVISION
'**cable-car** *noun* [C] a carriage that hangs on a moving cable(1) and carries passengers up and down a mountain
cable 'television *noun* [U] a system of broadcasting television programmes by cable(2) instead of by radio signals

cackle /ˈkækl/ *noun* [C] **1** the loud sound that a hen makes after laying an egg **2** a loud, unpleasant laugh —**cackle** *verb* [I]

cactus /ˈkæktəs/ *noun* [C] (*pl* **cactuses** or **cacti** /ˈkæktaɪ/) a type of plant that grows in hot, dry areas, especially deserts. A cactus has a thick stem and sharp points (**prickles**) but no leaves.

cadet /kəˈdet/ *noun* [C] a young person who is training to be in the army, navy, air force or police

cadge /kædʒ/ *verb* [I,T] **cadge (sth) (from/off sb)** (*informal*) to try to persuade sb to give or lend you sth: *He's always cadging meals from people without repaying them!*

Caesarean (*also* **Cesarian, Cesarean**) /sɪˈzeərɪən/ *noun* [C] an operation to remove a baby from its mother's body when a normal birth would be impossible or dangerous

☆ **café** /ˈkæfeɪ; *US* kæˈfeɪ/ *noun* [C] a small restaurant that serves drinks and light meals

s	z	ʃ	ʒ	h	m	n	ŋ	l	r	j	w
so	zoo	she	vision	how	man	no	sing	leg	red	yes	wet

☛ In Britain, a café does not normally serve alcoholic drinks, which are served in a **pub**. A café usually serves morning coffee, light lunches and afternoon tea and normally closes at about 6 o'clock.

cafeteria /ˌkæfəˈtɪərɪə/ noun [C] a restaurant, especially one for staff or workers, where people collect their meals on trays and carry them to their tables ☛ Look at **canteen**.

caffeine /ˈkæfiːn/ noun [U] the substance found in coffee and tea which makes you feel more awake and lively ☛ Look at **decaffeinated**.

☆ **cage** /keɪdʒ/ noun [C] a box made of bars or wire, or a space surrounded by wire or metal bars, in which a bird or animal is kept so that it cannot escape: *The tiger paced up and down its cage.* ○ *The parrot has escaped from its cage.* —**caged** /keɪdʒd/ adj: *He felt like a caged animal in the tiny office.*

cagey /ˈkeɪdʒi/ adj **cagey (about sth)** (*informal*) not wanting to give information or to talk about sth ☛ A more formal word is **secretive**.

cagoule /kəˈguːl/ noun [C] a long waterproof jacket with a hood

cake

cakes

gateau

biscuits

☆ **cake** /keɪk/ noun **1** [C,U] a sweet food made by mixing flour, eggs, butter, sugar, etc together and baking the mixture in the oven: *a birthday cake* ○ *a wedding cake* ○ *a chocolate cake* ○ *a fruit cake* ○ *a sponge cake* ○ *The bride and bridegroom cut the cake.* ○ *Would you like some more cake?* ○ *a piece of birthday cake*

☛ After **making** or **baking** a cake we often **ice** or (*US*) **frost** the top and sides of it.

2 [C] a mixture of other food, cooked in a round, flat shape: *fish cakes* ○ *potato cakes*
(IDIOMS) **have your cake and eat it** to enjoy the advantages of sth without its disadvantages: *You can't go out every night and save for your holiday. You can't have your cake and eat it.*
a piece of cake ⇨ PIECE¹
cake verb [T] (usually passive) to cover sth thickly with a substance that becomes hard when it dries: *boots caked in/with mud*

calamity /kəˈlæməti/ noun [C,U] (*pl* **calamities**) a terrible event that causes a lot of damage or harm

☆ **calculate** /ˈkælkjuleɪt/ verb [T] **1** to find sth out by using mathematics: *I've been calculating the costs involved and it's too expensive.* ○ *It's difficult to calculate how long the project will take.* **2** to consider or expect sth: *We calculated that the advantages would be greater than the disadvantages.*
(IDIOM) **be calculated to do sth** to be intended or designed to do sth: *His remark was clearly calculated to annoy me.*

calculating adj planning things in a very careful and selfish way in order to achieve exactly what you want: *Her cold, calculating approach made her many enemies.*

calculation /ˌkælkjuˈleɪʃn/ noun **1** [C,U] finding an answer by using mathematics: *Several of his calculations are wrong.* ○ *Calculation of the exact cost is impossible.* **2** [U] (*formal*) careful thought and planning in order to achieve your own, selfish aims: *His actions were clearly the result of deliberate calculation.*

calculator /ˈkælkjuleɪtə(r)/ noun [C] a small electronic machine used for calculating figures: *a pocket calculator*

caldron (*especially US*) = CAULDRON

☆ **calendar** /ˈkælɪndə(r)/ noun [C] **1** a list that shows the days, weeks and months of a particular year: *She had ringed the important dates on her calendar in red.* ○ *There was a calendar hanging on the back of the door.* ☛ A **calendar** is often hung on a wall and may have a separate page for each month, sometimes with a picture or photograph. A **diary** is a little book which you can carry around with you and which has spaces next to the dates so that you can write in appointments, etc. **2** a system for dividing time into fixed periods and for marking the beginning and end of a year: *the Muslim calendar* **3** a list of dates and events in a year that are important in a particular area of activity: *Wimbledon is a major event in the sporting calendar.*

ˌcalendar ˈmonth noun [C] = MONTH(1,2)
ˌcalendar ˈyear noun [C] = YEAR(2)

calf¹ /kɑːf; US kæf/ noun [C] (*pl* **calves** /kɑːvz; US kævz/) **1** a young cow ☛ The meat from a calf is called **veal**. Look at the note at **meat**. Look at the note and picture at **cow**. **2** the young of some other animals, eg elephants

calf² /kɑːf; US kæf/ noun [C] (*pl* **calves** /kɑːvz; US kævz/) the back of your leg, below your knee ☛ picture on page A8.

calibre (*US* **caliber**) /ˈkælɪbə(r)/ noun [sing,U] the quality or ability of a person or thing: *The company's employees are of the highest calibre.*

☆ **call¹** /kɔːl/ noun **1** [C] a loud sound that is made to attract attention; a shout: *a call for help* ○ *That bird's call is easy to recognize.* **2** (*also* **ˈphone call**) [C] an act of telephoning or a conversation on the telephone: *Were there any calls for me while I was out?* ○ *I'll give you a call at the weekend.* ○ *The manager is on the line. Will you take the call?* ○ *a local call* ○ *a long-*

iː	ɪ	e	æ	ɑː	ɒ	ɔː	ʊ	uː	ʌ
see	sit	ten	hat	arm	got	saw	put	too	cup

call 87 **camera**

distance call **3** [C] a short visit, especially to sb's house: *We could pay a call on Dave on our way home.* ○ *The doctor has several calls to make this morning.* **4** [C] a request, demand for sth: *There have been calls for the President to resign.* **5** [C,U] **call for sth** a need for sth: *The doctor said there was no call for concern.*
(IDIOMS) **at sb's beck and call** ⇨ BECK
(be) on call to be ready to work if necessary: *Dr Young will be on call this weekend.*
'call-box *noun* [C] = TELEPHONE BOX
'call-in (*US*) = PHONE-IN

☆ **call²** /kɔːl/ *verb* **1** [I,T] **call (out) to sb**; **call (sth) (out)** to say sth loudly or to shout in order to attract attention: *'Hello, is anybody there?' she called.* ○ *I could hear a voice calling for help.* ○ *He called out the names and the winners stepped forward.* ○ *Call the children. Breakfast is ready.* **2** [I,T] (*especially US*) RING²(1): *Who's calling, please?* ○ *Thank you for calling.* ○ *I'll call you tomorrow.* ○ *We're just in the middle of dinner. Can I call you back later?* **3 be called** to have as your name: *What's your wife called?* ○ *What was that village called?* **4** [T] to name or describe a person or thing in a certain way: *They called the baby Martin.* ○ *My name is Elizabeth but I'm often called Liz.* ○ *Can you really call this picture 'art'?* ○ *It was very rude to call her fat.* ○ *Are you calling me a liar?* **5** [T] to order or ask sb to come to a certain place: *Can you call everybody in for lunch?* ○ *The President called his advisers to the White House.* ○ *I think we had better call the doctor.* **6** [T] to arrange for sth to take place at a certain time: *to call a meeting, an election, a strike, etc* **7** [I] **call (in/round) (on sb/at...)** to make a short visit to a person or place: *Can I call in/round after supper?* ○ *We called at his house but there was nobody in.* **8** [I] **call at...** (used about a train, etc) to stop at: *This is the Inter-City service to Poole, calling at Reading and Southampton.*
(IDIOM) **call it a day** (*informal*) to decide to stop doing sth: *Let's call it a day. I'm exhausted.*
(PHRASAL VERBS) **call by** (*informal*) to make a short visit to a place or person as you pass: *I'll call by to pick up the book on my way to work.*
call for sb/sth (*Brit*) to collect: *I'll call for you when it's time to go.*
call for sth to demand or need: *The opposition is calling for an early general election.* ○ *The crisis calls for immediate action.* ○ *This calls for a celebration!* ○ *Their rudeness was not called for* (= there was no need for it).
call sth off to cancel sth: *The football match was called off because of the bad weather.*
call sb out to ask or tell sb to go somewhere: *We had to call out the doctor in the middle of the night.* ○ *The police were called out to control the riot.*
call sb up 1 (*especially US*) to telephone sb: *He called me up to tell me the good news.* **2** to order sb to join the army, navy or air force: *All the men between the ages of 18 and 25 were called up.*

caller *noun* [C] a person who telephones or visits sb: *I don't know who the caller was. He rang off without giving his name.*

callous /'kæləs/ *adj* not caring about the suffering of other people

☆ **calm** /kɑːm; *US* kɑːlm/ *adj* **1** not worried or angry; quiet: *Try to keep calm –there's no need to panic.* ○ *She spoke in a calm voice.* ○ *The city is calm again after last night's riots.* **2** without big waves: *a calm sea* **3** without much wind: *calm weather*

calm *noun* [C,U] a period of time or a state when everything is peaceful: *After living in the city, I enjoyed the calm of country life.*

calm *verb* [I,T] **calm (sb/sth) (down)** to become or to make sb quiet or calm: *Calm down! Shouting at everybody won't help.* ○ *She calmed the horses by talking quietly to them.* ○ *He read the children a story to calm them down.* —**calmly** *adv*: *Len told the police very calmly exactly what he had seen.* —**calmness** *noun* [U]

Calor gas /'kælə gæs/ *noun* [U] (*trade mark*) gas that is kept in special bottles and used for cooking, heating, etc

calorie /'kæləri/ *noun* [C] **1** a unit for measuring the energy that a certain amount of food will produce **2** a unit for measuring heat

calves *pl* of CALF

camcorder /'kæmkɔːdə(r)/ *noun* [C] a camera that you can carry with you and use for recording pictures and sound on a video cassette

came *pt* of COME

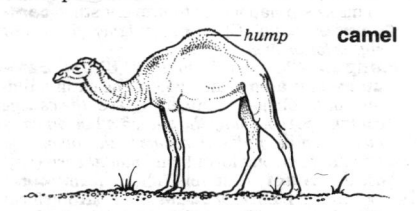

☆ **camel** /'kæml/ *noun* **1** [C] an animal that lives in the desert and has a long neck and either one or two humps on its back. It is used for carrying people and goods. **2** [U] a light brown colour

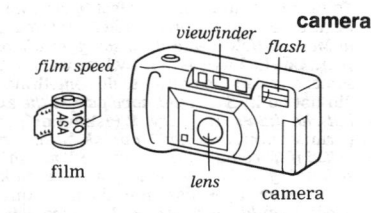

☆ **camera** /'kæmərə/ *noun* [C] a piece of equipment that you use for taking photographs or moving pictures: *I need a new film for my camera.* ○ *a pocket camera* ○ *a television camera* ○ *a video camera*

cameraman /-mæn/ *noun* [C] (*pl* **cameramen**) a person whose job is to operate a camera for a film or a television company

ɜː	ə	eɪ	əʊ	aɪ	aʊ	ɔɪ	ɪə	eə	ʊə
fur	ago	pay	home	five	now	join	near	hair	pure

camouflage /ˈkæməflɑːʒ/ noun [U] materials or colours that soldiers use to make themselves and their equipment less easy to see
camouflage verb [T] to make sb/sth difficult to see in a particular place

☆ **camp** /kæmp/ noun [C,U] a place where people live in tents or huts for a short time: *a scout camp* ○ *a holiday camp* ○ *a training camp* (= for soldiers) ○ *We returned to camp tired after our long hike.* ○ *The climbers set up camp at the foot of the mountain.*
camp verb [I] **camp (out)** to put up a tent and sleep in it: *Where shall we camp tonight?* ○ *The children like to camp out in summer.* ☛ Go **camping** is a common way of talking about camping for pleasure: *They went camping in France last year.*
camper noun [C] **1** a person who camps **2** (US) a caravan
camping noun [U] sleeping or spending a holiday in a tent: *Camping is cheaper than staying in hotels.* ○ *a camping holiday*
'camp-site (also **'camping-site**) noun [C] a place where you can camp

☆ **campaign** /kæmˈpeɪn/ noun [C] **1** a plan to do a number of things in order to achieve a special aim: *an advertising campaign* **2** a planned series of attacks in a war
campaign verb [I] **campaign (for/against sb/sth)** to take part in a campaign(1) in order to make sth happen or to prevent sth —**campaigner** noun [C]: *a campaigner for equal rights for women*

campus /ˈkæmpəs/ noun [C,U] (pl **campuses**) the area of land where the main buildings of a college or university are: *the college campus* ○ *About half the students live on campus – the other half rent rooms in the town.*

☆ **can¹** /kən; strong form kæn/ modal verb (negative **cannot** /ˈkænɒt/ short form **can't** /kɑːnt; US kænt/; pt **could** /kəd/ strong form /kʊd/; negative **could not** short form **couldn't** /ˈkʊdnt/) **1** (used for showing that it is possible for sb/sth to do sth or that sb/sth has the ability to do sth): *I can catch a bus from here.* ○ *Can you ride a bike?* ○ *He can't speak French.* ○ *She couldn't answer the question.* ☛ Can has no infinitive or participle forms. To make the future and perfect tenses, we use **be able to**: *One day people will be able to travel to Mars.* ○ *He's been able to swim for almost a year.* **Could have** is used when we say that somebody had the ability to do something but did not do it: *She could have passed the exam but she didn't really try.* **2** (asking or giving permission): *Can I have a drink, please?* ○ *He asked if he could have a drink.* ○ *You can't go swimming today.* ☛ When we are talking about general permission in the past **could** is used: *I could do anything I wanted when I stayed with my grandma.* When we are talking about one particular occasion we do not use **could**: *They were allowed to visit him in hospital yesterday.* **3** (asking sb to do sth): *Can you help me carry these books?* **4** (offering to do sth): *Can I help at all?* **5** (talking about sb's typical behaviour or of a typical effect): *You can be very annoying.* ○ *Wasp stings can be very painful.* **6** (used in the negative for saying that you are sure sth is not true): *That can't be Mary – she's in London.* ○ *Surely you can't be hungry. You've only just had lunch.* **7** (used with the verbs 'feel', 'hear', 'see', 'smell', 'taste') ☛ These verbs are not used in the continuous tenses. If we want to talk about seeing, hearing, etc at a particular moment, we use **can**: *I can smell something burning.* NOT *I'm smelling…*

☆ **can²** /kæn/ noun [C] **1** a metal or plastic container that is used for holding or carrying liquid: *an oil can* ○ *a can of oil* ○ *a watering can* **2** a metal container for food that is sealed so that the food stays fresh: *a can of sardines* ○ *a can of beer* ☛ picture at **container**.
can verb [T] (**canning**; **canned**) to put food, drink, etc into a can in order to keep it fresh for a long time: *canned fruit*

☆ **canal** /kəˈnæl/ noun [C] a channel that is cut through land so that boats or ships can travel along it or so that water can flow to an area where it is needed: *the Suez Canal*

canary /kəˈneərɪ/ noun [C] (pl **canaries**) a small yellow bird that sings and is often kept in a cage as a pet

☆ **cancel** /ˈkænsl/ verb [T] (**cancelling**; **cancelled**; US **canceling**; **canceled**) **1** to decide that sth that had been planned or arranged will not happen: *Because of the bad weather the picnic was cancelled.* ☛ Look at **postpone**. **2** to stop sth that you asked for or agreed to: *We shall have to cancel the reservation.* ○ *I wish to cancel my order for these books.*
(PHRASAL VERB) **cancel (sth) out** to be equal or have an equal effect: *What I owe you is the same as what you owe me, so our debts cancel each other out.*
cancellation /ˌkænsəˈleɪʃn/ noun [C,U] the act of cancelling sth: *We've had several cancellations for this evening's concert.* ○ *The cancellation of the match was a great disappointment.*

Cancer /ˈkænsə(r)/ noun [C,U] the fourth sign of the zodiac, the Crab; a person who was born under this sign ☛ picture at **zodiac**.

cancer /ˈkænsə(r)/ noun [C,U] a very serious disease in which lumps grow in the body in an uncontrolled way: *She has lung cancer.* ○ *He died of cancer.*

candid /ˈkændɪd/ adj honest and frank; saying exactly what you think ☛ The noun is **candour**. —**candidly** adv

☆ **candidate** /ˈkændɪdət; US -deɪt/ noun [C] **1** a person who applies for a job or wants to be elected to a particular position: *We have some very good candidates for the post.* **2** a person who is taking an examination
candidacy /ˈkændɪdəsɪ/ noun [U] being a candidate

☆ **candle** /ˈkændl/ noun [C] a round stick of wax with a piece of string (**a wick**) through the middle that you can burn to give light: *to light/ blow out a candle*
'candlelight noun [U] the light that a candle produces: *They had dinner by candlelight.*
'candlestick noun [C] a holder for a candle or candles

candour (US **candor**) /ˈkændə(r)/ noun [U]

p	b	t	d	k	g	tʃ	dʒ	f	v	θ	ð
pen	bad	tea	did	cat	got	chin	June	fall	van	thin	then

candle: flame, wick, candle, candlestick

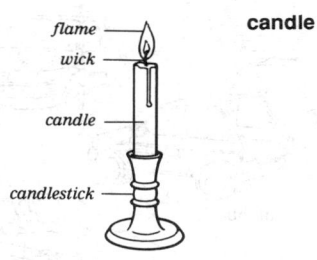

the quality of being honest; saying exactly what you think ☛ The adjective is **candid**.

candy /'kændi/ noun [C,U] (pl **candies**) (US) = SWEET²(1): *You eat too much candy.*

cane /keɪn/ noun **1** [C,U] the long, hollow stem of certain plants, such as the sugar plant **2** [C] a stick, for example a walking stick or a stick used to hit sb with

cane verb [T] to punish sb by hitting him/her with a cane(2)

canine /'keɪnaɪn/ adj connected with dogs or like a dog

canister /'kænɪstə(r)/ noun [C] a small metal container

cannabis /'kænəbɪs/ noun [U] a drug made from a plant (**hemp**) that some people smoke for pleasure, but which is illegal in many countries

cannibal /'kænɪbl/ noun [C] a person who eats other people —**cannibalism** /'kænɪbəlɪzəm/ noun [U]

cannon /'kænən/ noun [C] (pl **cannon** or **cannons**) **1** a large old-fashioned gun that was used for firing stone or metal balls (**cannonballs**) **2** a large modern gun on a ship, tank, aeroplane, etc

cannot /'kænɒt/ = CAN NOT

canoe /kə'nuː/ noun [C] a light, narrow boat for one or two people that you can move through the water using a flat piece of wood (a **paddle**) ☛ Look at **kayak**.

canoe verb [I] (pres part **canoeing**; 3rd pers sing pres **canoes**; pt, pp **canoed**) to travel in a canoe ☛ We can say 'He is learning to canoe' or 'They canoed down the river', but when we are talking about spending time in a canoe it is more usual to say **go canoeing**: *We're going canoeing on the Thames tomorrow.*

canon /'kænən/ noun [C] a Christian priest who works in a cathedral

canopy /'kænəpi/ noun [C] (pl **canopies**) a cover, often a piece of cloth, that hangs above sth: *a throne with a purple silk canopy over it*

can't short for CAN NOT

canteen /kæn'tiːn/ noun [C] the place in a school, factory, office, etc where the people who work there can get meals: *the staff canteen* ☛ Look at **cafeteria**.

canvas /'kænvəs/ noun **1** [U] a type of strong cloth that is used for making tents, sails, bags, etc **2** [C] a piece of canvas for painting a picture on; the painting itself

canvass /'kænvəs/ verb **1** [I,T] to go around an area trying to persuade people to vote for a particular person or political party in an election: *He's canvassing for the Conservative Party.* **2** [T] to find out what people's opinions are about sth

canyon /'kænjən/ noun [C] a deep valley with very steep sides: *the Grand Canyon, Arizona*

☆ **cap** /kæp/ noun [C] **1** a soft flat hat that is usually worn by men or boys ☛ picture at **hat**. **2** a hat that is worn for a particular purpose: *a shower-cap* **3** a covering for the end or top of sth: *Please put the cap back on the bottle.* ○ *Take the lens cap off before you take the photo!* ☛ Look at the note at **top¹**.

cap verb [T] (**capping**; **capped**) **1** to cover the top of sth: *mountains capped with snow* **2** to follow sth with sth bigger or better

(IDIOM) **to cap it all** as a final piece of bad luck: *What a holiday! The plane was delayed for 24 hours, they lost their luggage and to cap it all he broke his leg skiing.*

capability /ˌkeɪpə'bɪləti/ noun [C,U] (pl **capabilities**) the quality of being able to do sth: *How many countries have nuclear capability?* (= have a nuclear bomb) ○ *People are often not aware of their own capabilities.*

☆ **capable** /'keɪpəbl/ adj **1** having a lot of skill; good at doing sth: *She's a very capable teacher.* ○ *We need a capable person to organize the concert.* **2 capable of (doing) sth** able to do sth; having the power to do sth: *He's capable of passing the exam if he tries harder.* ○ *That car is capable of 180 miles per hour.* ○ *I do not believe that she's capable of stealing* (= she is not the sort of person who would steal). ☛ The opposite is **incapable**. —**capably** adv

capacity /kə'pæsəti/ noun (pl **capacities**) **1** [sing,U] the greatest amount that a container or space can hold: *The tank has a capacity of 1 000 litres.* ○ *The stadium was filled to capacity.* **2** [sing,U] the amount that a factory or machine can produce: *The power station is working at full capacity.* **3** [sing] **capacity (for sth)** the ability to understand or do sth: *That book is beyond the capacity of children who are still learning to read.* **4** [C] the official position that a person has: *In his capacity as chairman of the council...*

cape¹ /keɪp/ noun [C] a piece of clothing with no sleeves that hangs from your shoulders ☛ A cape is shorter than a **cloak**.

cape² /keɪp/ noun [C] a piece of land that sticks out into the sea: *the Cape of Good Hope*

☆ **capital¹** /'kæpɪtl/ noun [C] **1** (also **capital city**) the town or city where the government of a country is: *Madrid is the capital of Spain.* **2** (also **capital letter**) the large form of a letter that is used at the beginning of a name or sentence: *Write your name in capitals.*

capital adj (only before a noun) written in the large form that we use at the beginning of a name, a sentence, etc: *'David' begins with a capital 'D'.*

capital² /'kæpɪtl/ adj connected with punishment by death: *a capital offence* (= a crime for which sb can be sentenced to death) ○ *capital punishment* (= punishment by death)

☆ **capital³** /'kæpɪtl/ noun [U] an amount of money that you use to start a business or to

s	z	ʃ	ʒ	h	m	n	ŋ	l	r	j	w
so	zoo	she	vision	how	man	no	sing	leg	red	yes	wet

invest so that you earn more money (**interest**) on it: *When she had enough capital, she bought a shop.* ○ *The firm has been trying to raise extra capital.*
(IDIOM) **make capital (out) of sth** to use a situation to your own advantage

capital in'vestment *noun* [U] money that a business spends on buildings, equipment, etc

capitalism /'kæpɪtəlɪzəm/ *noun* [U] the economic system in which businesses are owned and run for profit by individuals and not by the state ☛ Look at **communism** and **socialism**.
—**capitalist** *noun* [C], *adj*

capitalize (*also* **capitalise**) /'kæpɪtəlaɪz/ *verb*
(PHRASAL VERB) **capitalize on sth** to use sth to your advantage: *We can capitalize on the mistakes that our rivals have made.*

capitulate /kə'pɪtʃuleɪt/ *verb* [I] (*formal*) to stop fighting and say that you have lost; to give in to sb and do what he/she wants —**capitulation** /kə,pɪtʃu'leɪʃn/ *noun* [C,U]

Capricorn /'kæprɪkɔːn/ *noun* [C,U] the tenth sign of the zodiac, the Goat; a person who was born under this sign ☛ picture at **zodiac**.

capsize /kæp'saɪz; *US* 'kæpsaɪz/ *verb* [I,T] (used about boats) to turn over in the water: *The yacht capsized.* ○ *She capsized the yacht.*

capsule /'kæpsjuːl; *US* kæpsl/ *noun* [C] **1** a very small tube containing medicine that you swallow whole **2** the part of a spaceship in which the crew live and work

☆ **captain** /'kæptɪn/ *noun* [C] **1** the person who is in command of a ship or an aeroplane **2** an officer of middle rank in the Army or Navy **3** a person who is the leader of a group or team: *Who's (the) captain of the French team?*
captain *verb* [T] to be the captain of a group or team

caption /'kæpʃn/ *noun* [C] the words that are written above or below a picture, cartoon, etc to explain what it is about

captivate /'kæptɪveɪt/ *verb* [T] to attract and hold sb's attention —**captivating** *adj*

captive /'kæptɪv/ *noun* [C] a prisoner
captive *adj* kept as a prisoner; (of animals) kept in a cage, zoo, etc
(IDIOMS) **hold sb captive** to keep sb as a prisoner and not allow him/her to escape
take sb captive to catch sb and hold him/her as your prisoner ☛ It is also possible to say **hold sb prisoner** and **take sb prisoner**.

captivity /kæp'tɪvəti/ *noun* [U] the state of being kept as a captive: *Wild animals are often unhappy in captivity.*

captor /'kæptə(r)/ *noun* [C] a person who takes or keeps a person as a prisoner

capture /'kæptʃə(r)/ *verb* [T] **1** to take a person or animal prisoner: *The lion was captured and taken back to the zoo.* **2** to take or win sth from your enemy by force: *The town has been captured by the rebels.* **3** to succeed in representing sth in words, pictures, etc: *This poem captures the atmosphere of the carnival.*
capture *noun* [U] a time when a person, animal or thing is captured

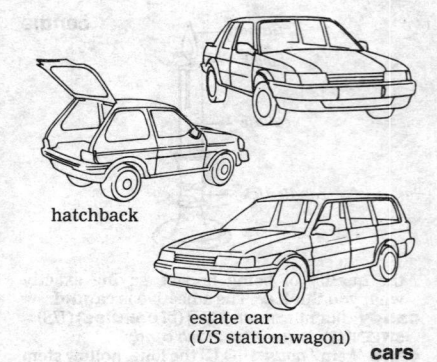

hatchback

estate car
(*US* station-wagon)

cars

☆ **car** /kɑː(r)/ *noun* [C] **1** (*also* **'motor car**) (*especially US* **automobile**) a vehicle with an engine and four wheels that up to four or five people can ride in: *a new/second-hand car* ○ *Where can I park the car?* ○ *He's having the car serviced tomorrow.* ○ *They had a car crash.* ○ *She gave me a lift in her car.* ○ *to get into/out of a car* ○ *an estate car* ☛ Note that we go **by car**. We can also say **in the car**: *Do you prefer going on holiday by coach or by car?* ○ *I come to work in the car.* **2** a railway carriage that is used for a particular purpose: *a dining-car* ○ *a sleeping car*

'car-boot sale *noun* [C] a sale in an outdoor place where people sell things they do not want from the back of their cars ☛ Look at **jumble sale**.

'car park (*US* **parking-lot**) *noun* [C] an area or building where you can leave your car: *a multi-storey car park*

'car phone *noun* [C] a telephone that you can use in a car

caramel /'kærəməl/ *noun* **1** [U] sugar that has been burned so that it is dark brown. It is used in food because of its colour and taste **2** [C,U] a type of sticky sweet that is made from boiled sugar

carat (*US* **karat**) /'kærət/ *noun* [C] a unit of measurement used to describe how pure gold is or how heavy jewels are: *a 20-carat gold ring*

☆ **caravan** /'kærəvæn/ *noun* [C] **1** (*US* **trailer**) a large vehicle that can be pulled by a car or horse. You can sleep, cook, etc in a caravan when you are travelling or on holiday: *They're touring in Wales with a caravan.* ○ *a caravan holiday* ☛ When we are talking about using a caravan for holidays we say **go caravanning**: *We're going caravanning in Scotland this summer.* **2** a group of people and animals that travel together, eg across a desert

carbohydrate /,kɑːbəʊ'haɪdreɪt/ *noun* [C,U] one of the substances in food, eg sugar, that gives your body energy: *Athletes need a diet that is high in carbohydrate and low in fat.* ○ *Bread, potatoes and rice all contain carbohydrates.*

carbon /'kɑːbən/ *noun* [U] (*symbol* **C**) a chemical substance that is found in all living things,

iː	ɪ	e	æ	ɑː	ɒ	ɔː	ʊ	uː	ʌ
see	sit	ten	hat	arm	got	saw	put	too	cup

carbon 'copy noun [C] (pl **carbon copies**) **1** a copy of a letter, etc that was made by using carbon paper **2** an exact copy of sth

carbon di'oxide noun [U] (symbol **CO²**) a gas that has no colour or smell that people and animals breathe out of their lungs

carbon mon'oxide noun [U] (symbol **CO**) the poisonous gas that is produced when carbon is burned in a small amount of air. Motor vehicles produce a lot of carbon monoxide.

'carbon paper noun [U] thin paper with carbon on one side that you put between two pieces of paper. When you write or type on the top piece of paper a copy is produced on the second piece.

carburettor /ˌkɑːbəˈretə(r)/ (US **carburetor** /ˈkɑːrbəreɪtər/) noun [C] the piece of equipment in a car's engine that mixes petrol and air

carcass /ˈkɑːkəs/ noun [C] the dead body of an animal ☛ Look at **corpse**.

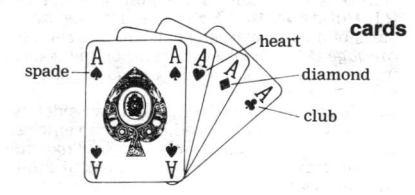

cards

spade — heart
A A A A
♠ ♥ ♦ — diamond
♣ — club

☆ **card** /kɑːd/ noun **1** [U] thick paper that does not bend easily **2** [C] a piece of card or plastic that has information on it: *Here is my business card with my address and telephone number on it.* o *a membership card* o *an identity card* o *a credit card* **3** [C] a piece of card with a picture on it that you use for sending greetings or a message to sb: *a Christmas card* o *a birthday card* o *a get-well card* (= one that you send to sb who is ill) o *We've had a card* (= a postcard) *from Diana in Portugal.* **4** (also **playing-card**) [C] one of a set of 52 small pieces of card with shapes or pictures on them that are used for playing games such as bridge or poker: *a pack of cards* **5** [plural] games that are played with cards: *Let's play cards.* o *Let's have a game of cards.* o *I never win at cards!*

☛ A **pack** of cards is divided into four **suits**, two red (**hearts** and **diamonds**) and two black (**clubs** and **spades**). Each suit has an **ace**, a **king**, a **queen**, a **jack** and nine other cards, numbered from 2 to 10. Before we play cards we **shuffle**, **cut** and **deal** the cards.

'card index noun [C] ⇨ INDEX(2)

☆ **cardboard** /ˈkɑːdbɔːd/ noun [U] very thick paper that is used for making boxes, etc: *The groceries were delivered in large cardboard boxes.*

cardiac /ˈkɑːdiæk/ adj connected with the heart

cardigan /ˈkɑːdɪɡən/ noun [C] a piece of clothing for the top part of the body, often made from wool, that has long sleeves and buttons at the front ☛ picture on page A11. Look at the note at **sweater**.

cardinal¹ /ˈkɑːdɪnl/ noun [C] a priest of high rank in the Roman Catholic church

cardinal² (also **ˌcardinal 'number**) noun [C] a whole number, eg 1, 2, 3 that shows quantity ☛ Look at **ordinal**.

☆ **care¹** /keə(r)/ verb **1** [I,T] **care (about sth)** to be worried about or interested in sth; to mind: *I shall be late and my mother will be cross, but I don't care.* o *Money is the thing that she cares about most.* o *I don't care what you do.* **2** [I] **care for sth**; **care to do sth** (formal) to like or want: *Would you care for a drink?* o *Would you care to leave a message, sir?* ☛ **Care for** in this sense is used in questions and always with 'would'. **3 care for sb/sth** to like: *I don't care for that colour very much.* o *Do you think she still cares for him although he married someone else?*

(IDIOMS) **I, etc couldn't care less** (informal) it does not matter to me, etc at all: *'You don't look very smart.' 'Well, quite honestly, I couldn't care less.'*

who cares? (informal) nobody is interested; it is not important to anyone: *'I wonder who'll win the match.' 'Who cares?'*

(PHRASAL VERB) **care for sb** to look after sb: *Who cared for her while she was ill?*

caring /ˈkeərɪŋ/ adj showing that you care about other people: *We must work towards a more caring society.*

☆ **care²** /keə(r)/ noun **1** [U] **care (over sth/in doing sth)** thinking about what you are doing so that you do it well or do not have an accident: *You should take more care over your homework.* o *This box contains glasses — please handle it with care.* **2** [U] **care (for sb)** looking after people so that they have things they need; responsibility for sb/sth: *All the children in their care were healthy and happy.* o *health care* o *medical care* o *She's in intensive care* (= the part of the hospital for people who are very seriously ill).

☛ Children **in care** live in a home which is organized by the government or the local council.

3 [C,U] worry, anxiety: *She went on holiday to try to forget all her cares.* o *It was a happy life, free from care.*

(IDIOMS) **care of sb** (abbr **c/o**) words used on an envelope when you are writing to sb at another person's address: *Mary Jenkins, c/o Mrs Brown, 10 Riverside Way, Oxford.* o *You can write to the author, care of his publisher.*

take care (that.../to do sth) to be careful: *Goodbye and take care!* o *Take care that you don't spill your tea.* o *He took care not to arrive too early.*

take care of yourself/sb/sth to keep yourself/sb/sth safe from injury, illness, damage, etc: *You should take more care of yourself. You look tired.* o *Could you take care of the cat while we are away on holiday?* o *She always takes great care of her books.*

take care of sb/sth to deal with sb/sth; to

3ː	ə	eɪ	əʊ	aɪ	aʊ	ɔɪ	ɪə	eə	ʊə
fur	ago	pay	home	five	now	join	near	hair	pure

organize or arrange sth: *I'll take care of the food for the party.*

'carefree *adj* happy because you have no problems or worries

☆ **career**¹ /kə'rɪə(r)/ *noun* [C] **1** a job or profession for which you are trained and which you do for a long time, often with the chance to move to a higher position: *Sarah is considering a career in engineering.* ○ *His career was always more important to him than his family.* ○ *a successful career in politics* **2** your working life: *She spent most of her career working in India.*

career² /kə'rɪə(r)/ *verb* [I] to move quickly and dangerously: *The car careered off the road and crashed into a wall.*

☆ **careful** /'keəfl/ *adj* **1 careful (of/with sth)** thinking about what you are doing so that you do not have an accident or make mistakes, etc: *Be careful! There's a car coming.* ○ *Be careful of that knife – it's very sharp.* ○ *Please be very careful with those glasses.* ○ *That ladder doesn't look very safe. Be careful you don't fall.* ○ *I was careful not to say anything about the money.* ○ *Don't worry – she's a careful driver.* **2** showing care and attention to details: *I'll need to give this matter some careful thought.* —**carefully** /'keəfəli/ *adv: Please listen carefully. It's important that you remember all this.* —**carefulness** *noun* [U]

☆ **careless** /'keəlɪs/ *adj* **careless (about/with sth)** not thinking enough about what you are doing so that you make mistakes, lose or damage things, etc: *It was careless of you to go out without locking the door.* ○ *Here's another careless mistake – you've forgotten the full stop at the end of the sentence.* ○ *The accident was caused by careless driving.* —**carelessly** *adv: She threw her coat carelessly on the chair.* —**carelessness** *noun* [U]

caress /kə'res/ *verb* [T] to stroke sb in a gentle and loving way: *He caressed her hand and looked deep into her eyes.* —**caress** *noun* [C]

caretaker /'keəteɪkə(r)/ (*US* **janitor**) *noun* [C] a person whose job is to look after a large building (eg a school or a block of flats) and to do small repairs and other services

☆ **cargo** /'kɑ:gəʊ/ *noun* [C,U] (*pl* **cargoes**; *US also* **cargos**) the goods that are carried in a ship or aircraft: *The ship was carrying a cargo of wheat.*

Caribbean /ˌkærɪ'bi:ən/ (*especially US*) kə'rɪbiən/ *noun* [sing] **the Caribbean** the area in the Caribbean Sea where the group of islands called the West Indies are situated —**Caribbean** *adj: the Caribbean islands*

caricature /'kærɪkətjʊə(r)/ *noun* [C] a picture or description of sb that makes his/her appearance or behaviour funnier and more extreme than it really is: *She drew a very funny caricature of the Prime Minister.* ○ *Many of the people in the book are caricatures of the author's friends.*

carnation /kɑ:'neɪʃn/ *noun* [C] a white, pink or red flower with a pleasant smell

carnival /'kɑ:nɪvl/ *noun* [C] a public festival that takes place outdoors, during which there is a procession in the streets with music and dancing: *the carnival in Rio*

carol /'kærəl/ *noun* [C] a Christian religious song that people sing at Christmas: *carol singers* (= groups of people who sing carols outside people's houses in order to collect money for charity)

carousel /ˌkærə'sel/ *noun* [C] **1** (*US*) = ROUND-ABOUT²(2) **2** (at an airport) a moving belt that carries luggage for passengers to collect

☆ **carpenter** /'kɑ:pəntə(r)/ *noun* [C] a person whose job is to make and repair wooden objects

carpentry /-tri/ *noun* [U] the skill or work of a carpenter

☆ **carpet** /'kɑ:pɪt/ *noun* **1** [C,U] (a piece of) thick, flat material that is used for covering floors and stairs: *We need a new carpet in the bedroom.* ○ *a fitted carpet* (= one that has been cut to the exact shape of a room) ☛ Look at **rug**. **2** [C] a thick layer of sth that covers the ground: *The fields were under a carpet of snow.* —**carpeted** *adj: All the rooms are carpeted.*

☆ **carriage** /'kærɪdʒ/ *noun* **1** [C] (*also* **coach**) a vehicle with wheels that is pulled by horses **2** [C] (*also* **coach**) (*US* **car**) one of the separate parts of a train where people sit: *a first-class carriage* **3** [U] the cost of transporting goods from one place to another: *Carriage must be paid by the receiver.*

'carriageway *noun* [C] one of the two sides of a motorway or major road on which vehicles travel in one direction only: *the southbound carriageway of the motorway* ☛ Look at **dual carriageway**.

carrier /'kæriə(r)/ *noun* [C] **1** (in business) a company that transports people or goods: *the Dutch carrier, KLM* **2** a military vehicle or ship that is used for transporting soldiers, planes, weapons, etc: *an armoured personnel carrier* ○ *an aircraft carrier* **3** a person or animal that can give an infectious disease to others but does not show the signs of the disease: *Some insects are carriers of tropical diseases.* **4** (*Brit also* **'carrier bag**) a plastic or paper bag for carrying shopping

☆ **carrot** /'kærət/ *noun* **1** [C,U] a long thin orange vegetable that grows under the ground: *A pound of carrots, please.* ○ *grated carrot* **2** [C] something attractive that is offered to sb in order to persuade him/her to do sth: *The management have offered them the carrot of a £500 bonus if they agree to work extra hours.*

☆ **carry** /'kæri/ *verb* (*pres part* **carrying**; *3rd pers sing pres* **carries**; *pt, pp* **carried**) **1** [T] to hold sb/sth in your hand, arms or on your back while you are moving from one place to another: *Could you carry this bag for me? It's terribly heavy.* ○ *She was carrying a rucksack on her back.* ☛ You use **wear**, not **carry**, to talk about having clothes, jewellery, etc on your body: *He was wearing a black jacket.* **2** [T] to have with you as you go from place to place: *I never carry much money with me when I go to London.* ○ *Do the police carry guns in your country?* **3** [T] to transport sb/sth from one place to another: *A train carrying hundreds of passengers crashed yesterday.* ○ *The waves carried the boat to the shore.* **4** [T] to have an infectious disease that can be given to others, usually

cart

without showing any signs of the disease yourself: *Rats carry all sorts of diseases.* **5** [T] (usually passive) to accept a proposal in a meeting because a majority of people vote for it: *The motion was carried by 12 votes to 9.* **6** [I] (used about a sound) to reach a long distance: *You'll have to speak louder if you want your voice to carry to the back of the room.*

(IDIOMS) **be/get carried away** to be so excited that you forget what you are doing: *I got so carried away watching the race that I forgot how late it was.*

carry weight to have great influence on the opinion of sb else: *Nick's views carry a lot of weight with our manager.*

(PHRASAL VERBS) **carry it/sth off** to succeed in doing sth difficult: *He felt nervous before he started his speech but he carried it off very well.*

carry on (with sth/doing sth); carry sth on to continue: *How long did the party carry on after I left?* ○ *Carry on* (= continue speaking). *What happened next?* ○ *They ignored me and carried on with their conversation.* ○ *She intends to carry on studying after the course has finished.*

carry sth on to take part in sth: *I can't carry on a normal conversation while you're making that noise.*

carry sth out 1 to do sth that you have been ordered to do: *The soldiers carried out their orders without question.* **2** to do or perform sth, eg a test, repair, etc: *I think we should wait until more tests have been carried out.* ○ *The owner is responsible for carrying out repairs to the building.*

'carry-all noun [C] (*US*) = HOLDALL

'carry-cot noun [C] a small bed, like a box with handles, that you can carry a baby in ☛ picture at **pram**.

cart /kɑːt/ noun [C] a wooden vehicle with wheels that is used for transporting things: *a horse and cart*

cart verb [T] (*informal*) to take or carry sth somewhere, often with difficulty: *We left our luggage at the station because we didn't want to cart it around all day.* ○ *Six of the women were carted off to the police station.*

cartilage /ˈkɑːtɪlɪdʒ/ noun [C,U] a strong substance that surrounds the places where your bones join

carton /ˈkɑːtn/ noun [C] a small container made of cardboard or plastic: *a carton of milk, orange juice, etc* ☛ picture at **container**.

cartoon /kɑːˈtuːn/ noun [C] **1** a funny drawing, especially one in a newspaper or magazine that makes a joke about a current event **2** a film that tells a story by using moving drawings made of real people and places: *a Donald Duck cartoon*

cartoonist noun [C] a person who draws cartoons

cartridge /ˈkɑːtrɪdʒ/ noun [C] **1** a small tube that contains explosive powder and a bullet. You put a cartridge into a gun when you want to fire it. **2** a closed container that holds camera film, typewriter ribbon, ink for a pen, etc. It is easy to change a cartridge when you want to put in a new one.

cash

carve /kɑːv/ verb **1** [I,T] **carve sth (out of sth)** to cut wood or stone in order to make an object or to put a pattern or writing on it: *The statue had been carved out of marble.* ○ *He carved his name on the desk.* **2** [I,T] to cut a piece of cooked meat into slices: *Can you carve while I serve the vegetables?* ○ *to carve a chicken*

carving noun [C,U] an object or design that has been carved: *There are ancient carvings on the walls of the cave.*

cascade /kæˈskeɪd/ noun [C] **1** a waterfall **2** something that hangs or falls in a way that seems similar to a waterfall: *the wall of the villa was covered in a cascade of flowers* —**cascade** verb [I]

☆ **case¹** /keɪs/ noun **1** [C] a particular situation or a situation of a particular type: *In some cases, people have had to wait two weeks for a doctor's appointment.* ○ *Most of us travel to work by tube – or, in Susie's case, by train and tube.* ○ *There's no secret to success in this business. It's just a case of hard work.* **2 the case** [sing] the true situation: *The man said he worked in Cardiff, but we discovered later that this was not the case.* **3** [C] an example of an illness; a person who is suffering from an illness: *Cases of the disease are very unusual in this country.* ○ *The most serious cases were taken to hospital immediately.* **4** [C] a crime that is being investigated by the police: *a murder case* **5** [C] something that is decided in a court of law; a trial: *The case will come to court in a few months.* **6** [C, usually sing] the facts and reasons that support one side in a discussion or legal matter: *She made a case for shorter working hours, but the others disagreed.*

(IDIOMS) **as the case may be** (used when you are not sure which of two or more possibilities will be true in a particular situation): *The money will be received by the husband or wife, as the case may be.*

in any case 1 whatever happens or has happened: *We've decided to go in any case.* **2** anyway: *He didn't say anything about it at the meeting and in any case it's too late now.*

in case because sth might happen: *I think I'll take an umbrella in case it rains.* ○ *Take my number in case you need to phone me.* ○ *I wasn't intending to buy anything but I took my cheque book just in case.*

in case of sth if sth happens: *In case of fire, break this glass.*

in that case if that is the situation: *'I'm busy on Tuesday.' 'Oh well, in that case we'll have to meet another day.'*

prove your/the case/point ⇨ PROVE

'case-study noun [C] a study of the development of a person or group of people, especially in social research

case² /keɪs/ noun [C] **1** (especially in compounds) a container or cover for sth: *a pencil-case* ○ *a pillowcase* ○ *a bookcase* ○ *She put her glasses back in the case.* **2** = SUITCASE: *Would you like me to carry your case?*

☆ **cash** /kæʃ/ noun [U] **1** money in the form of coins or notes and not cheques, credit cards, etc: *Would you prefer me to pay in cash or by cheque?* ○ *How much cash have you got with*

s	z	ʃ	ʒ	h	m	n	ŋ	l	r	j	w
so	zoo	she	vision	how	man	no	sing	leg	red	yes	wet

cashier 94 **catalogue**

you? ☞ picture at **money**. We use **cash** when we are talking about coins and notes, but **change** when we are talking about coins only. **2** (*informal*) money in any form: *I'm a bit short of cash this month so I can't afford to go out much.*

cash *verb* [T] to exchange a cheque, traveller's cheque, etc for coins and notes: *I'm just going to the bank to cash a cheque.*

(PHRASAL VERB) **cash in (on sth)** to take advantage of a situation

'cash desk *noun* [C] the place in a large shop where you pay for things

'cash machine (*also* **'cash dispenser**; **'cash-point**) *noun* [C] a machine inside or outside a bank from which you can get money at any time of day by putting in a special card

cashier /kæˈʃɪə(r)/ *noun* [C] the person in a bank, shop, etc that customers pay money to or get money from

cashmere /ˌkæʃˈmɪə(r)/ *noun* [U] a type of wool that is very fine and soft

casino /kəˈsiːnəʊ/ *noun* [C] (*pl* **casinos**) a place where people play roulette and other games in which you can win or lose money

cask /kɑːsk; *US* kæsk/ *noun* [C] a large wooden container in which alcoholic drinks, etc are stored; barrel

casserole /ˈkæsərəʊl/ *noun* **1** [C,U] a type of food that you make by cooking meat and vegetables in liquid for a long time in the oven: *chicken casserole* **2** [C] a large dish with a lid for cooking casseroles in ☞ picture at **pan**.

☆ **cassette** /kəˈset/ *noun* [C] a flat case with magnetic tape inside that you use for recording and playing music and other sounds: *to put on/play/listen to a cassette* ○ *Paul Simon's new album is available on record, cassette and CD.*

☞ Another word for **cassette** is **tape**. When you want to go back to the beginning of a cassette you **rewind** it. When you want to go forward you **fast forward** it. Look at **video**.

casˈsette recorder *noun* [C] a machine that you use for recording and playing cassettes

cast¹ /kɑːst; *US* kæst/ *noun* [C, with sing or pl verb] all the actors in a play, film, etc: *The film has an excellent cast.*

cast² /kɑːst; *US* kæst/ *verb* [T] (*pt, pp* **cast**) **1** (often passive) to choose an actor for a particular role in a play, film, etc: *She always seems to be cast in the same sort of role.* **2** to make an object by pouring hot liquid metal into a shaped container (**a mould**): *a statue cast in gold* **3** (*old-fashioned*) to throw sth: *She cast a stone into the river.*

(IDIOMS) **cast doubt on sth** to make people unsure about sth: *The newspaper report casts doubts on the truth of the Prime Minister's statement.*

cast an eye/your eye(s) over sb/sth to look at sth quickly

cast light on sth to help to explain sth: *I'd be grateful if you could cast any light on the problem.*

cast a shadow (across/over sth) to cause a shadow to appear somewhere: *The tree cast a long shadow across the garden.* ○ (*figurative*) *The accident cast a shadow over the rest of the holiday* (= stopped people enjoying it fully).

cast a/your vote to vote: *The MPs will cast their votes in the leadership election tomorrow.*

(PHRASAL VERB) **cast sb/sth off** to remove or make yourself free of sb/sth: *He cast off the stress of city life and went to live in the country.*

'castaway *noun* [C] a person who is left in a place far from civilization after a shipwreck

,cast 'iron *noun* [U] a hard type of iron

,cast-'iron *adj* made of cast iron: (*figurative*) *a cast-iron alibi* (= one that people cannot doubt)

'cast-off *noun* [C, usually pl] a piece of clothing that you no longer want and that you give to sb else or throw away: *When I was little I had to wear my sister's cast-offs.*

caste /kɑːst/ *noun* **1** [C] one of the social classes into which Hindus are divided **2** [U] the system of dividing people in this way

☆ **castle** /ˈkɑːsl; *US* ˈkæsl/ *noun* [C] a large building with high walls and towers that was built in the past to defend people against attack: *a medieval castle* ○ *Edinburgh Castle*

castrate /kæsˈtreɪt; *US* ˈkæstreɪt/ *verb* [T] to remove part of the sexual organs of a male animal or person —**castration** /kæˈstreɪʃn/ *noun* [U]

casual /ˈkæʒuəl/ *adj* **1** relaxed and not worried; not showing great effort or interest: *She tried to appear casual as he walked towards her.* ○ *The manager is not happy about your casual attitude to your work.* ○ *It was only a casual remark so I don't know why he got so angry.* **2** (used about clothes) not formal: *I always change into casual clothes as soon as I get home from work.* **3** (used about work) done only for a short period; not regular or permanent: *Most of the building work was done by casual labour.* ○ *She had a number of casual jobs during the university holidays.* —**casually** /ˈkæʒuəli/ *adv*: *She walked in casually and said, 'I'm not late, am I?'* ○ *Dress casually, it won't be a formal party.*

casualty /ˈkæʒuəlti/ *noun* (*pl* **casualties**) **1** [C] a person who is killed or injured in a war or an accident: *After the accident the casualties were taken to hospital.* ○ *The army retreated after suffering heavy casualties.* **2** [C] a person or thing that suffers as a result of sth else: *Many small companies have been casualties of the country's economic problems.* **3** [U] (*also* **'casualty department**) (*US* **emergency room**) the part of a hospital where people who have been injured in accidents are taken for immediate treatment

☆ **cat** /kæt/ *noun* [C] **1** a small furry animal with four legs and a tail. People often keep cats as pets. **2** any larger wild animal that is related to a cat, eg a lion or tiger: *We went to the zoo to see the big cats.*

☞ A young cat is called a **kitten**. A male cat is called a **tom**. When a cat makes a soft sound of pleasure, it **purrs**. When it makes a louder sound, it **miaows**.

catalogue (*US* **catalog** /ˈkætəlɒg; *US* -lɔːg/) *noun* [C] **1** a list of all the things that you can buy from a company, all the books in a library,

iː	ɪ	e	æ	ɑː	ɒ	ɔː	ʊ	uː	ʌ
see	sit	ten	hat	arm	got	saw	put	too	cup

cat: whiskers, paw, kitten, tail

all the paintings in an art exhibition, etc **2** a series, especially of bad things: *a catalogue of disasters*

catalogue *verb* [T] to list things in a catalogue: *She started to catalogue all the new library books.*

catapult /'kætəpʌlt/ *noun* [C] a Y-shaped stick with a piece of elastic attached to each side that is used by children for shooting stones

catapult *verb* [T] **1** to shoot sth from a catapult **2** to throw sb/sth suddenly and with great force: *When the train crashed several people were catapulted through the windows.* o *(figurative) The success of his first film catapulted him to stardom.*

cataract /'kætərækt/ *noun* [C] a diseased area that can grow on a person's eye and cause difficulty in seeing

catarrh /kə'tɑː(r)/ *noun* [U] a thick liquid that forms in the nose and throat when you have a cold

catastrophe /kə'tæstrəfi/ *noun* [C] a sudden event that causes great suffering or damage; disaster: *Major catastrophes like floods and earthquakes happen regularly in that part of the world.* o *a financial catastrophe* —**catastrophic** /ˌkætə'strɒfɪk/ *adj*: *The war had a catastrophic effect on the whole country.*

☆ **catch¹** /kætʃ/ *verb* (*pt, pp* **caught** /kɔːt/) **1** [T] to take hold of sth that is moving, usually with your hand or hands: *She threw the ball and he caught it in one hand.* o *The dog caught the ball in its mouth.* **2** [T] to capture sb/sth that you have been chasing or looking for: *Two policemen ran after the thief and caught him at the end of the street.* o *The murderer still hasn't been caught.* o *to catch a fish* **3** [T] to discover sb who is doing sth bad: *I caught her taking money from my purse.* **4** [T] to get on a form of public transport: *I caught the bus into town.* o *to catch a train, plane, etc* **5** [T] to be in time for sth; not to miss sb/sth: *If I take the letter now, I should catch the post.* o *We arrived just in time to catch the beginning of the film.* o *I'll phone her now. I might just catch her before she leaves the office.* **6** [T] to hear or understand sth that sb says: *I'm sorry, I didn't quite catch what you said. Could you repeat it?* **7** [I,T] to become or cause sth to become accidentally attached to or trapped in sth: *His jacket caught on a nail.* o *I caught my finger in the drawer as I shut it.* o *I'm sorry I'm late. I got caught in the traffic.* **8** [T] to get an illness: *I've got a terrible cold. I must have caught it from someone at work.*

(IDIOMS) **catch sb's attention/eye** to make sb notice sth: *I tried to catch the waiter's eye so that I could get the bill.*

catch fire to start burning, often accidentally: *Nobody knows how the building caught fire.*

catch sb red-handed to find sb just as he/she is doing sth wrong: *A policeman noticed the ladder at the window and caught the burglars red-handed.*

catch sight/a glimpse of sb/sth to see sb/sth for a moment: *I caught sight of the man at the end of the street.* o *We waited outside the theatre, hoping to catch a glimpse of the actress.*

catch the sun to become burned or tanned by the sun: *Your face looks red. You've really caught the sun, haven't you?*

catch/take sb unawares ⇨ UNAWARES

(PHRASAL VERBS) **catch on** (*informal*) **1** to understand or realize sth: *She's sometimes a bit slow to catch on.* **2** to become popular or fashionable: *The idea has never really caught on in this country.*

catch sb out to cause sb to make a mistake by asking a clever question: *Ask me anything you like – you won't catch me out.*

catch up (with sb); catch sb up 1 to reach sb/sth who is ahead of you: *Jackie was walking very fast and I had to run to catch up with her.* o *I'll just finish this letter. You go on and I'll catch you up in a minute.* **2** to reach the same level as sb/sth else: *Our economy is developing fast and we should soon catch up with other countries in the western world.*

catch up on sth to spend time doing sth that you have not been able to do until now: *I'll have to go into the office at the weekend to catch up on my work.*

be/get caught up in sth to be or get involved in sth, usually without intending to: *I seem to have got caught up in a rather complicated situation.*

catch² /kætʃ/ *noun* [C] **1** an act of taking hold of sth that is moving, usually with your hand or hands **2** the amount of fish that sb has caught: *The fishermen brought their catch to the harbour.* **3** a device for fastening sth and keeping it closed: *I can't close my suitcase – the catch is broken.* o *a window catch* **4** a hidden disadvantage to sth that seems attractive: *It looks like a good offer but I'm sure there must be a catch in it.*

catchment area /'kætʃmənt ˌeəriə/ *noun* [C] the area from which a school gets its pupils, a hospital gets its patients, etc

catch-phrase /'kætʃfreɪz/ *noun* [C] a phrase that becomes famous for a while because it is used by a famous person

catchy /'kætʃi/ *adj* (**catchier**; **catchiest**) (used about a tune or song) easy to remember

categorical /ˌkætə'gɒrɪkl; *US* -'gɔːr-/ *adj* completely definite: *The answer was a categorical 'no'.* —**categorically** /-kli/ *adv*: *The Minister categorically denied the rumour.*

category /'kætəgəri; *US* -gɔːri/ *noun* [C] (*pl* **categories**) a group of people or things that are similar to each other: *There were two categories in the competition: children under 5 and 6-8 year-olds.* o *These books are divided into categories according to subject.*

ɜː	ə	eɪ	əʊ	aɪ	aʊ	ɔɪ	ɪə	eə	ʊə
fur	ago	pay	home	five	now	join	near	hair	pure

categorize (*also* **categorise**) /ˈkætəgəraɪz/ *verb* [T] to divide people or things into groups; or to say that sb/sth belongs to a particular group

cater /ˈkeɪtə(r)/ *verb* [I] **1 cater for sb/sth**; **cater to sth** to provide what sb/sth needs or wants: *We need a hotel that caters for small children.* ○ *a newspaper that caters to people's love of sex scandals* **2 cater (for sb/sth)** to provide and serve food and drink for a social event: *the firm that catered at our wedding*

caterer *noun* [C] a person or business that provides food and drink for social events

catering *noun* [U] the activity or business of providing food and drink for social events: *the hotel and catering industry*

caterpillar /ˈkætəpɪlə(r)/ *noun* [C] an animal like a small hairy worm with legs, which changes into a butterfly or moth

cathedral /kəˈθiːdrəl/ *noun* [C] a large church that is the most important one in a district

☆ **Catholic** /ˈkæθəlɪk/ *noun* [C], *adj* = ROMAN CATHOLIC — **Catholicism** /kəˈθɒləsɪzəm/ *noun* [U] = ROMAN CATHOLICISM

cattle /ˈkætl/ *noun* [plural] male and female cows, eg on a farm: *a herd of cattle* (= a group of them) ☛ Look at the note at **cow**.

Caucasian /kɔːˈkeɪziən; kɔːˈkeɪʒn/ *noun, adj* (of) a member of the race of people who have white or light-coloured skin

caught *pt, pp* of CATCH¹

cauldron (*also* **caldron**) /ˈkɔːldrən/ *noun* [C] a large, deep, metal pot that is used for cooking things over a fire

cauliflower /ˈkɒlɪflaʊə(r)/; *US* /ˈkɔːlɪ-/ *noun* [C,U] a large vegetable with green leaves and a round white centre that you eat when it is cooked ☛ picture at **cabbage**.

☆ **cause** /kɔːz/ *noun* **1** [C] a thing or person that makes sth happen: *The police do not know the cause of the accident.* ○ *Smoking is one of the causes of heart disease.* **2** [U] **cause (for sth)** reason: *I don't think you have any real cause for complaint.* **3** [C] an aim or principle that a group of people believe in and support: *We are all committed to the cause of racial equality.* ○ *I don't mind giving money to a good cause.*
(IDIOM) **a lost cause** ⇒ LOST

cause *verb* [T] to make sth happen: *The fire was caused by an electrical fault.* ○ *High winds caused many trees to fall during the night.* ○ *Is your leg causing you any pain?*

caustic /ˈkɔːstɪk/ *adj* **1** (used about a substance) able to burn or destroy things by chemical action **2** (used about a comment or type of humour) cruel and unpleasant

caution /ˈkɔːʃn/ *noun* **1** [U] great care, because of possible danger: *Caution! Falling rocks!* (= on a road sign) **2** [C] a spoken warning that a judge or policeman gives to sb who has committed a small crime

caution *verb* [I,T] to warn sb about sth: *He cautioned me not to believe everything I heard.* ○ *The President's advisers have cautioned against calling an election too early.* ○ *Dixon was cautioned twice by the referee for dangerous tackling.*

cautionary /ˈkɔːʃənəri; *US* ˈkɔːʃəneri/ *adj* giving a warning: *a cautionary tale*

☆ **cautious** /ˈkɔːʃəs/ *adj* taking great care to avoid possible danger: *I'm very cautious about expressing my opinions in public.* —**cautiously** *adv*

cavalry /ˈkævlri/ *noun* [sing, with sing or pl verb] **1** the part of the army which fights in fast, heavily protected vehicles **2** the group of soldiers who fought on horses in the past

☆ **cave** /keɪv/ *noun* [C] a large hole in the side of a cliff or hill, or under the ground: *When it started to rain, we ran to shelter in a cave.*

cave *verb*
(PHRASAL VERB) **cave in** to fall in: *The roof of the tunnel had caved in and we could go no further.* **2** to suddenly stop arguing or opposing sth: *He finally caved in and agreed to the plan.*

cavern /ˈkævən/ *noun* [C] a large, deep cave

caviare (*also* **caviar**) /ˈkæviɑː(r)/ *noun* [U] the eggs of a large fish (**a sturgeon**) that are eaten as food. Caviare is usually very expensive.

cavity /ˈkævəti/ *noun* [C] (*pl* **cavities**) **1** an empty space inside sth solid: *a wall cavity* **2** a hole in a tooth

cease /siːs/ *verb* [I,T] (*formal*) to stop or end: *Fighting in the area has now ceased.* ○ *That organization has ceased to exist.* ○ *500 people lost their jobs when the company ceased trading.*

ceaseless *adj* continuing for a long time without stopping —**ceaselessly** *adv*

cease-ˈfire *noun* [C] an agreement between two groups to stop fighting each other

cede /siːd/ *verb* [T] (*formal*) to give land or control of sth to another country or person

☆ **ceiling** /ˈsiːlɪŋ/ *noun* [C] **1** the top surface of the inside of a room: *We painted the walls pink and the ceiling white.* ○ *a room with a high/low ceiling* **2** a top limit on wages, prices, etc: *The Government has put a 10% ceiling on wage increases.*

☆ **celebrate** /ˈselɪbreɪt/ *verb* **1** [I,T] to do sth special and enjoyable on an important day or because of an important event: *When I got the job we celebrated by opening a bottle of champagne.* ○ *Mrs Halford celebrated her 80th birthday yesterday.* **2** [T] (used about a priest) to lead a religious ceremony: *to celebrate Mass*

celebration /ˌselɪˈbreɪʃn/ *noun* [C,U] the act or occasion of doing sth enjoyable because sth good has happened or because it is a special day: *Christmas celebrations* ○ *I think this is an occasion for celebration!*

celebrated /ˈselɪbreɪtɪd/ *adj* (*formal*) famous: *a celebrated poet*

celebrity /sɪˈlebrəti/ *noun* [C] (*pl* **celebrities**) a famous person

celery /ˈseləri/ *noun* [U] a vegetable with long green stems that is eaten raw in salads and sometimes used in cooking: *a stick of celery* ○ *celery soup*

celibate /ˈselɪbət/ *adj* (*formal*) remaining unmarried or never having sexual relations, often because of religious beliefs —**celibacy** /ˈselɪbəsi/ *noun* [U]

cell /sel/ *noun* [C] **1** the smallest living part of an animal or a plant body: *The human body consists of millions of cells.* ○ *red blood cells* **2** a

p	b	t	d	k	g	tʃ	dʒ	f	v	θ	ð
pen	bad	tea	did	cat	got	chin	June	fall	van	thin	then

cellar 97 **ceremonial**

small room in a prison or police station in which a prisoner is locked

cellar /'selə(r)/ noun [C] an underground room that is used for storing things: *a wine cellar* ☞ Look at **basement**.

cello /'tʃeləʊ/ noun [C] (pl **cellos**) a musical instrument like a large violin. You sit down to play it and hold it between your knees.
cellist /'tʃelɪst/ noun [C] a person who plays the cello

Cellophane /'seləfeɪn/ noun [U] (trade mark) thin transparent material that is used for wrapping things

cellular /'seljʊlə(r)/ adj consisting of cells(1): *cellular tissue*

cellular 'phone noun [C] a telephone that you can carry around with you and that works by using radio signals

☆**Celsius** /'selsiəs/ (also **Centigrade**) adj (abbr **C**) the name of a scale for measuring temperatures, in which water freezes at 0° and boils at 100°: *The temperature tonight will fall to 7°C.* ☞ We say 'seven degrees Celsius'. Look also at **Fahrenheit**.

Celtic /'keltɪk, US 'seltɪk/ adj connected with the people (**the Celts**) who lived in Wales, Scotland Ireland and Brittany in ancient times, or with their culture

cement /sɪ'ment/ noun [U] **1** a grey powder, that becomes hard after it is mixed with water and left to dry. It is used in building for sticking bricks or stones together or for making very hard surfaces. **2** a type of glue
cement verb [T] **1** to cover sth with cement **2** to stick things together **3** to make a relationship very strong: *This agreement has cemented the relationship between our two companies.*

cemetery /'semətri; US 'seməteri/ noun [C] (pl **cemeteries**) a place where dead people are buried (that does not belong to a church) ☞ Look at **graveyard**.

censor /'sensə(r)/ noun [C] an official who examines books, films, plays, etc and removes any parts that might offend people, or who examines letters, newspaper reports, etc and removes any parts which contain secret information: *All films have to be examined by the British Board of Film Censors.* —**censor** verb [T]: *The journalist said that all the information they sent back to Britain was being censored.* —**censorship** noun [U]: *state censorship of radio and television programmes*

censure /'senʃə(r)/ verb [T] (formal) to tell sb, in a strong and formal way, that he/she has done sth wrong: *The minister was censured for not revealing the information earlier.* —**censure** noun [U]: *a vote of censure in parliament*

census /'sensəs/ noun [C] (pl **censuses**) an official count of the people who live in a country, including information about their ages, jobs, etc

☆**cent** /sent/ noun [C] (abbr **c, ct**) a unit of money that is worth 100th part of a US dollar or of the main unit of money in some other countries ☞ Look also at **per cent**.

centenary /sen'ti:nəri; US 'sentəneri/ noun [C] (pl **centenaries**) (US also **centennial** /sen'teniəl/) the year that comes exactly one hundred years after an important event or the beginning of sth: *1982 was the centenary of Darwin's death.* ○ *centenary celebrations*

center /'sentə(r)/ noun [C] (US) = CENTRE

centigrade /'sentɪgreɪd/ adj = CELSIUS

☆**centimetre** (US also **centimeter**) /'sentɪmi:tə(r)/ noun [C] (abbr **cm**) a measure of length. There are 100 centimetres in a metre: *The insect was about two centimetres long.*

☆**central** /'sentrəl/ adj **1** in the centre of sth: *a map of central Europe* ○ *The flat is in Edgware Road, which is very central* (= near the centre of the city and therefore very convenient). **2** (only before a noun) (used about an office, group, etc) having control of all other parts of an organization: *central government* (= the government of a whole country, not local government) ○ *the Conservative Central Office* **3** most important; main: *The film's central character is a fifteen-year-old girl.*

centralize (also **centralise**) /'sentrəlaɪz/ verb [T] (usually passive) to make sth come under central control: *Our educational system is becoming increasingly centralized.* —**centralization** (also **centralisation**) /,sentrəlaɪ'zeɪʃn; US -lɪ'z-/ noun [U]

centrally /'sentrəli/ adv in or from the centre: *a centrally located hotel* (= near the centre of the town) ○ *a centrally heated house*

central 'heating noun [U] a system for heating a building from one main point. Air or water is heated and carried by pipes to all parts of the building: *The house has gas central heating.*

☆**centre** (US **center**) /'sentə(r)/ noun **1** [C, usually sing] the middle point or part of sth: *There was a vase of flowers in the centre of the table.* ○ *I work in the centre of London.* ○ *Which way is the town centre, please?* ☞ Look at the note at **middle**. **2** [C] a building or place where a particular activity or service is based: *a sports, leisure, arts, shopping, etc centre* ○ *a job, information, health, etc centre* **3** [C] a person or thing that receives a lot of attention: *She always likes to be the centre of attention.* **4 the centre** [sing, with sing or pl verb] a political position that is not extreme: *the centre parties*
centre verb
(PHRASAL VERB) **centre on/around sb/sth** to have sb/sth as its centre: *The life of the village centres on the church, the school and the pub.*

☆**century** /'sentʃəri/ noun [C] (pl **centuries**) **1** a particular period of 100 years that is used for giving dates: *We live in the 20th century* (= the period between the years 1901 and 2000). **2** any period of 100 years: *People have been making wine in this area for centuries.*

☆**cereal** /'sɪəriəl/ noun [C,U] **1** a plant such as wheat, rice, etc that is grown to produce grain: *These fields are usually planted with cereals.* ○ *cereal crops* **2** food that is made from the grain of cereals: *10 different varieties of breakfast cereal*

cerebral /'serɪbrəl; US sə'ri:brəl/ adj connected with the brain: *He died of a cerebral haemorrhage.*

ceremonial /,serɪ'məʊniəl/ adj relating to a

s	z	ʃ	ʒ	h	m	n	ŋ	l	r	j	w
so	zoo	she	vision	how	man	no	sing	leg	red	yes	wet

ceremony: *a ceremonial occasion* —**ceremonially** /-nɪəlɪ/ *adv*

☆ **ceremony** /'serɪmənɪ; *US* -məʊnɪ/ *noun* (*pl* **ceremonies**) **1** [C] a formal public or religious event: *the opening ceremony of the Olympic Games* ○ *a wedding ceremony* **2** [U] formal behaviour, speech, actions, etc that are expected on special occasions: *The Queen was welcomed with great ceremony.*

☆ **certain**[1] /'sɜːtn/ *adj* **1** (not before a noun) **certain (that...); certain (of sth)** completely sure; without any doubts: *She's absolutely certain that there was somebody outside her window.* ○ *I think this is the man, but I can't be certain.* ○ *We're not quite certain what time the train leaves.* ○ *I'm certain of one thing – he didn't take the money.* **2 certain (that...); certain (to do sth)** sure to happen or to do sth; definite: *It is almost certain that unemployment will increase this year.* ○ *The Director is certain to agree.* ○ *Nothing is certain at the moment. Wait and see.* ○ *We must rescue them today, or they will face certain death.* ☞ Look at the note at **sure**.

(IDIOMS) **for certain** without doubt: *I don't know for certain what time we'll arrive.*

make certain (that...) to do sth in order to be sure that sth else happens: *They're doing everything they can to make certain that they win.*

certainly *adv* **1** without doubt; definitely: *The number of students will certainly increase after 1995.* ○ *It certainly was a very good party.* ○ *I certainly don't think you should tell him now.* **2** (used in answer to questions) of course: *'Do you think I could borrow your notes?' 'Certainly.'* ○ *'Can I take your car to France?' 'Certainly not!'*

certainty /'sɜːtntɪ/ *noun* (*pl* **certainties**) **1** [U] the state of being completely sure about sth: *We can't say with certainty that there is life on other planets.* ☞ The opposite is **uncertainty**. **2** [C] something that is sure to happen: *It's now almost a certainty that Italy will play in the World Cup Final.*

☆ **certain**[2] /'sɜːtn/ *adj* (only *before* a noun) **1** (used for talking about a particular thing or person without naming them): *You can only contact me at certain times of the day.* ○ *There are certain reasons why I'd prefer not to meet him again.* **2** noticeable but difficult to describe: *There was a certain feeling of autumn in the air.* **3** (used before a person's name to show that you do not know him/her): *I received a letter from a certain Mrs Berry.*

certain *pron* **certain of...** (*formal*) (used for talking about some members of a group of people without giving their names): *Certain of our hotels are only open in the summer months.*

☆ **certificate** /sə'tɪfɪkət/ *noun* [C] an official piece of paper that says that sth is true or correct: *a birth certificate*

certify /'sɜːtɪfaɪ/ *verb* [T] (*pres part* **certifying**; *3rd pers sing pres* **certifies**; *pt, pp* **certified**) **1** to say formally that sth is true or correct: *We need someone to certify that this is her signature.* **2** to give sb a certificate to show that he/she has successfully completed a course of training for a particular profession

Cesarian (*also* **Cesarean**) = CAESAREAN

chain

☆ **chain** /tʃeɪn/ *noun* **1** [C,U] a line of metal rings that are joined together: *They used heavy chains to pull the boat out of the water.* ○ *a bicycle chain* ○ *She was wearing a silver chain round her neck.* ○ *a length of chain* **2** [C] a number of things in a line: *a chain of mountains/a mountain chain* **3** [C] a group of shops, hotels, etc that are owned by the same person or company: *a chain of supermarkets/a supermarket chain* **4** [C] a number of connected events that happen one after another: *The book examines the complex chain of events that led to the Russian Revolution.*

chain *verb* [T] **chain sb/sth (to sth); chain sb/sth (up)** to fasten sb/sth to sth else with a chain: *The prisoners had been chained to the walls.*

'chain-smoker *noun* [C] a person who smokes continuously, lighting one cigarette after another

'chain store *noun* [C] one of a number of similar shops that are owned by the same company

☆ **chair** /tʃeə(r)/ *noun* **1** [C] a piece of furniture for one person to sit on. It has a seat, a back and usually four legs. It sometimes has two arms: *a kitchen chair* ○ *an armchair* ○ *a wheelchair* **2** [sing] the person who is controlling a meeting: *Please address your questions to the chair.* **3** [C] the position of a university professor: *the chair of economics at London University*

chair *verb* [T] to be the chairman or chairwoman of a meeting: *Who's chairing the meeting this evening?*

☆ **chairman** /'tʃeəmən/ *noun* [C] (*pl* **chairmen**) **1** the head of a committee, company or other organization: *the Chairman of IBM* **2** a person who controls a meeting

chairmanship /-ʃɪp/ *noun* [sing] being the chairman of sth; the time during which sb is chairman of sth

chairperson /'tʃeə,pɜːsn/ *noun* [C] (*pl* **chairpersons**) a person who controls a meeting

chairwoman /'tʃeə,wʊmən/ *noun* [C] (*pl* **chairwomen**) a woman who controls a meeting

chalet /'ʃæleɪ/ *noun* [C] a house or hut that is made of wood, especially in a mountain area or holiday camp

☆ **chalk** /tʃɔːk/ *noun* **1** [U] a soft, white rock: *chalk cliffs* **2** [C,U] a small stick of this that is used for writing or drawing on a blackboard: *a piece of chalk*

chalk *verb* [I,T] to write or draw sth with a piece of chalk: *Somebody had chalked a message on the wall.*

(PHRASAL VERB) **chalk sth up** to succeed in

iː	ɪ	e	æ	ɑː	ɒ	ɔː	ʊ	uː	ʌ
see	sit	ten	hat	arm	got	saw	put	too	cup

getting sth: *The team has chalked up five wins this summer.*

chalkboard *noun* [C] (*US*) = BLACKBOARD

☆ **challenge¹** /ˈtʃælɪndʒ/ *noun* **1** [C,U] something new and difficult that forces you to make a lot of effort: *I'm finding my new job an exciting challenge.* ○ *Reducing unemployment will be the main challenge for the new government.* **2** [C] **a challenge (to sb) (to do sth)** an invitation from sb to fight, play, argue, etc against him/her: *The Prime Minister should accept our challenge and call a new election now.*

☆ **challenge²** /ˈtʃælɪndʒ/ *verb* [T] **1 challenge sb (to sth)** to invite sb to fight, play, argue, etc against you: *They've challenged us to a football match this Saturday.* **2** to question whether sth is true or right: *She hates anyone challenging her authority.*

challenger *noun* [C] a person who invites you to take part in a competition, because he/she wants to win a title or position that you already have

challenging *adj* forcing you to make a lot of effort: *a challenging job*

chamber /ˈtʃeɪmbə(r)/ *noun* [C] **1** a large room that is used for formal meetings: *a council chamber* **2** a room that is used for a particular purpose: *a torture chamber*

'chambermaid *noun* [C] a woman whose job is to clean and tidy hotel bedrooms

'chamber music *noun* [U] music that is written for a small group of instruments

champagne /ʃæmˈpeɪn/ *noun* [U] a French white wine which has a lot of bubbles in it and is often very expensive

☆ **champion** /ˈtʃæmpɪən/ *noun* [C] **1** a person, team, etc that has won a competition: *a world champion* ○ *a champion swimmer* **2** a person who speaks and fights for a particular group, idea, etc: *a champion of free speech*

champion *verb* [T] to support or fight for a particular group or idea: *to champion the cause of human rights*

championship *noun* [C] **1** (often plural) a competition or series of competitions to find the best player or team in a sport or game: *to win the world championship* ○ *the World Hockey Championships* **2** the position or title of a champion(1)

☆ **chance¹** /tʃɑːns; *US* tʃæns/ *noun* **1** [C,U] **chance of (doing) sth; chance (that...)** (a) possibility: *The plan didn't really have a chance of succeeding.* ○ *I think there's a good chance that he'll be the next Prime Minister.* ○ *I'm afraid he has very little chance of winning.* ○ *Is there any chance of getting tickets for tonight's concert?* **2** [C] **chance (of doing sth/to do sth)** an opportunity: *If you get the chance of going to America, you should take it!* ○ *Be quiet and give her a chance to explain.* ○ *I think you should tell him now. You may not get another chance.* ☛ Look at the note at **occasion**. **3** [C] a risk: *We may lose some money but that's a chance we'll have to take.* **4** [U] luck or fortune (= sth that you cannot control): *I don't know what will happen – we'll have to leave it to chance.* ○ *We met by chance* (= we had not planned to meet) *as I was walking down the street.*

(IDIOMS) **by any chance** (used for asking sth politely) perhaps or possibly: *Are you, by any chance, going into town this afternoon?*

the chances are (that)... (*informal*) it is probable that...: *The chances are that it will rain tomorrow.*

no chance (*informal*) there is no possibility of that happening: *'Perhaps your mother will give you the money.' 'No chance!'*

on the off chance in the hope that sth might happen, although it is not very likely: *I didn't think you'd be at home, but I just called in on the off chance.*

stand a chance (of sth/of doing sth) to have a possibility of achieving sth: *I think she stands a good chance of winning the competition.*

chance² /tʃɑːns; *US* tʃæns/ *verb* **1** [T] (*informal*) to risk sth: *Shall we take umbrellas or shall we chance it* (= risk getting wet) *?* **2** [I] (*formal*) to do sth without planning or trying to do it: *I chanced to see the letter on his desk.*

chancellor /ˈtʃɑːnsələ(r)/; *US* ˈtʃæns-/ *noun* [C] **1** the head of government in some countries: *the German chancellor* **2** (*also* ˌ**Chancellor of the Ex'chequer**) (*Brit*) the government minister who makes decisions about taxes and government spending

chandelier /ˌʃændəˈlɪə(r)/ *noun* [C] a large light that hangs from the ceiling and that has many light bulbs or candles

☆ **change¹** /tʃeɪndʒ/ *verb* **1** [I,T] to become different or to make sb/sth different: *This town has changed a lot since I was young.* ○ *Our plans have changed. We leave in the morning.* ○ *His fame has not changed him at all.* **2** [I,T] **change (sb/sth) to/into sth**; **change (from sth)** to become sth different; to make sb/sth take a different form: *to change from a caterpillar to a butterfly* ○ *to change water into ice* **3** [T] **change sth (for sth)** to take, have or use sth instead of sth else: *Could I change this blouse for a larger size?* ○ *to change jobs* ○ *to change a light bulb* ○ *to change direction* ○ *Can I change my appointment from Wednesday to Thursday?* **4** [I,T] to get out of one bus, train, etc and get into another: *Does this bus go through to the airport or do we have to change?* ○ *She has to change trains at Reading and Didcot.* **5** [I,T] **change (out of sth) (into sth)** to take off your clothes and put different ones on: *He's changed his shirt.* ○ *I'm going straight to the party from work, so I'll change when I get there.* ○ *She changed out of her gardening clothes and into a clean dress.* ☛ **Get changed** is a common expression meaning 'to change your clothes': *You can get changed in the bedroom.* **6** [T] to put clean things onto sb/sth: *to change the bed* (= to put clean sheets on) ○ *It's time to change the baby's nappy.* **7** [T] **change sth (for/into sth)** to give sb money and receive the same amount back in money of a different type: *Can you change a ten-pound note?* ○ *I'd like to change fifty pounds into Swiss francs.*

(IDIOMS) **change hands** to pass from one owner to another

ɜː	ə	eɪ	əʊ	aɪ	aʊ	ɔɪ	ɪə	eə	ʊə
fur	ago	pay	home	five	now	join	near	hair	pure

change your mind to change your decision or opinion: *I'll have the green one. No, I've changed my mind. I want the red one.*
change/swap places (with sb) ⇨ PLACE¹
change the subject to start talking about sth different
change your tune (*informal*) to change your opinion or feelings about sth
chop and change ⇨ CHOP³
(PHRASAL VERB) **change over (from sth) (to sth)** to stop doing or using one thing and start doing or using sth else: *The theatre has changed over to a computerized booking system.*
changeable /'tʃeɪndʒəbl/ *adj* likely to change; often changing: *English weather is very changeable.*
'change-over *noun* [C] a change from one system to another

☆**change²** /tʃeɪndʒ/ *noun* **1** [C,U] **change (in/to sth)** the process of becoming or making sth different: *There was little change in the patient's condition overnight.* ○ *After two hot summers, people were talking about a change in the climate.* **2** [C] **change (of sth)** something that you take, have or use instead of sth else: *We must notify the bank of our change of address.* **3** [U] coins or notes of lower value that together make up the same value as a larger coin or note: *Have you got change for a pound?* **4** [U] coins of low value: *He needs some change for the phone.* **5** [U] the money that you get back if you pay more than the amount sth costs: *If a cake costs 40p and you pay with a 50p piece, you will get 10p change.*
(IDIOMS) **a change of heart** a change in your opinion or the way that you feel
for a change in order to do sth different from usual: *We always spend our holidays by the sea. Let's go to the mountains for a change this year.*
make a change to be enjoyable or pleasant because it is different from what you usually do

☆**channel** /'tʃænl/ *noun* [C] **1** a television or radio station. Each channel broadcasts on its own frequency or wavelength: *There's an interesting programme on Channel 4 tonight.* ○ *Can I switch over to the other channel?* **2** a narrow area of water between two seas **3 the Channel** = THE ENGLISH CHANNEL **4** an open passage along which liquids can flow: *a drainage channel* **5** the part of a river, etc which is deep enough for boats to pass along **6** a way or route along which news, information, etc is sent: *a channel of communication*
channel *verb* [T] (channelling; channelled; *US also* channeling; channeled) to make sth move along a particular path or route: *Water is channelled from the river to the fields.* ○ (*figurative*) *You should channel your energies into something constructive.*

chant /tʃɑːnt/ *noun* [C] a word or phrase that is sung or shouted many times: *A chant of 'we are the champions' went round the stadium.*
chant *verb* [I,T] to sing or shout a word or phrase many times: *The protestors marched by, chanting slogans.*

chaos /'keɪɒs/ *noun* [U] a state of great disorder; confusion: *The meeting ended in chaos when demonstrators threw tomatoes at the speakers.* ○ *The accident has caused chaos on the M25 motorway.*
chaotic /keɪ'ɒtɪk/ *adj* in a state of chaos: *With no-one in charge the situation became chaotic.*

chap /tʃæp/ *noun* [C] (*especially Brit informal*) a man or boy
chapel /'tʃæpl/ *noun* **1** [C] a small part of a large church that can be used for private prayer **2** [C] a small building or room in a prison, hospital, school, etc that is used as a church **3** [C,U] (*Brit*) a church for some Protestant groups: *a Methodist chapel*
chaperon (*also* **chaperone**) /'ʃæpərəʊn/ *noun* [C] an older person, usually a woman, who goes to public places with a young unmarried woman to look after her and to make sure that she behaves correctly —**chaperon** (*also* **chaperone**) *verb* [T]
chaplain /'tʃæplɪn/ *noun* [C] a priest who works in a hospital, school, prison, army, etc
☆**chapter** /'tʃæptə(r)/ *noun* [C] one of the parts into which a book is divided: *Please read Chapter 2 for homework.* ○ *In the opening chapter, the author sets the scene of the novel.*
☆**character** /'kærəktə(r)/ *noun* **1** [C,U,sing] the quality that makes sb/sth different from other people or things; the nature of sb/sth: *Although they are twins, their characters are quite different.* ○ *The introduction of more practical work has completely changed the character of the science course.* ○ *Modern houses often seem to lack character* (= they all seem the same). **2** [U] a person's inner strength: *The match developed into a test of character rather than just physical strength.* ○ *Military service is said to be character-building.* **3** [C] (*informal*) a person: *There was a suspicious-looking character hanging around outside so I phoned the police.* **4** [C] a person who is very interesting or amusing: *Neil's quite a character.* **5** [C] a person in a book, story, etc: *The main character in the book is a boy who meets an alien.* **6** [C] a letter or sign that you use when you are writing or printing: *Chinese characters*
(IDIOM) **in/out of character** typical/not typical of sb/sth
characteristic /ˌkærəktə'rɪstɪk/ *noun* [C] a quality that is typical of sb/sth and that makes him/her/it different from other people or things: *The chief characteristic of reptiles is that they are cold-blooded.* —**characteristic** *adj*: *Thatched cottages are characteristic of this part of England.* —**characteristically** /-klɪ/ *adv*: *'No' he said, in his characteristically direct manner.* ☛ The opposite is **uncharacteristic**.
characterize (*also* **characterise**) /'kærəktəraɪz/ *verb* [T] **1** (often passive) to be typical of sb/sth: *The 1980s were characterized by the pursuit of money.* **2 characterize sb/sth as sth** to describe the nature of sb/sth or to show a person's character in a particular way: *The President characterized the meeting as friendly and positive.*
charade /ʃə'rɑːd; *US* ʃə'reɪd/ *noun* **1 charades** [U] a game that is played at a party, etc in which one person or team acts out a word for others to guess **2** [C] a situation or event that is

p	b	t	d	k	g	tʃ	dʒ	f	v	θ	ð
pen	bad	tea	did	cat	got	chin	June	fall	van	thin	then

clearly false but in which people pretend to do or be sth: *They pretend to be friends but it's all a charade. Everyone knows they hate each other.*

charcoal /'tʃɑːkəʊl/ *noun* [U] a black substance that is produced when you burn wood in an oven with very little air. Charcoal can be used for drawing with or as a fuel.

☆ **charge¹** /tʃɑːdʒ/ *noun* **1** [C,U] the price that you must pay for sth: *There is no charge for calls to the operator.* o *We deliver free of charge.* o *A small charge is made for admission.* ☛ Look at the note at **price**. **2** [C] an official statement that says that sb has done sth which is against the law: *He was arrested on a charge of theft.* **3** [C] a sudden attack where sb/sth runs directly at sb/sth else: *a cavalry charge*
(IDIOMS) **in charge (of sb/sth)** in control or command (of sb/sth): *Who is in charge of the office while Alan's away?* o *I'd like to speak to the person in charge.*
reverse the charges ⇨ REVERSE³
take charge (of sth) to take control of or responsibility for sth

charge² /tʃɑːdʒ/ *verb* **1** [I,T] **charge (sb/sth) for sth** to ask sb to pay a particular amount of money: *Do you charge for postage and packing?* o *We charge £25 per night for a single room.* o *He charged me 30 pence for the onions.* **2** [T] **charge sb (with sth)** to accuse sb officially of doing sth which is against the law: *Six men are to be charged with attempted robbery.* **3** [I,T] to attack sb/sth by running directly at him/her/it: *The bull put its head down and charged.* o (figurative): *The children charged down the stairs and into the garden.* **4** [T] to put electricity into sth: *to charge a battery*

chariot /'tʃærɪət/ *noun* [C] an open vehicle with two wheels, that was pulled by a horse or horses in ancient times

charisma /kə'rɪzmə/ *noun* [U] the power that some people have to attract and influence people —**charismatic** /ˌkærɪz'mætɪk/ *adj: a charismatic politician*

charitable /'tʃærətəbl/ *adj* **1** kind; generous: *Some people accused him of lying, but a more charitable explanation was that he had made a mistake.* ☛ The opposite is **uncharitable**. **2** connected with a charity(1)

☆ **charity** /'tʃærəti/ *noun* (pl **charities**) **1** [C,U] an organization that collects money to help people who are poor, sick, etc or to do work that will be of benefit to society: *We went on a sponsored walk to raise money for charity.* o *He supports a charity that helps the handicapped.* **2** [U] kindness towards other people: *to act out of charity*

☆ **charm¹** /tʃɑːm/ *noun* **1** [C,U] the quality of being pleasant or attractive: *The charm of the island lies in its unspoilt beauty.* o *One of his charms was his ability to talk amusingly on any topic.* **2** [C] something that you wear because you believe it will bring you good luck: *a necklace with a lucky charm on it*

☆ **charm²** /tʃɑːm/ *verb* [T] to please sb; to influence people by your power to attract them: *Her drawings have charmed children all over the world.*

charming *adj* very pleasing or attractive: *Everyone enjoyed talking to them because they're such a charming couple.* o *What a charming little cottage!* —**charmingly** *adv: She smiled charmingly.*

charred /tʃɑːd/ *adj* black and partly burnt by fire

chart /tʃɑːt/ *noun* **1** [C] a drawing which shows information in the form of a diagram, etc: *a temperature chart* o *a bar chart* **2** [C] a map of the sea or the sky: *navigation charts* **3 the charts** [plural] an official list of the most popular records of pop songs

chart *verb* [T] **1** to make a map of one area of the sea or sky: *an uncharted coastline* **2** to follow or record sth carefully and in detail: *This television series charts the history of the country since independence.*

charter /'tʃɑːtə(r)/ *noun* [C,U] **1** an official written statement of the rights, beliefs and purposes of an organization or a particular group of people: *The club's charter does not permit women to become members.* **2** the hiring of a ship, aeroplane, etc for a particular purpose or for a particular group of people: *a charter airline*

charter *verb* [T] **1** to hire a ship, aeroplane, etc for a particular purpose or for a particular group of people **2** to give a charter(1) to an organization or a particular group of people

chartered /'tʃɑːtəd/ *adj* (only *before* a noun) (used about people in certain professions) fully qualified: *He's training to be a chartered accountant.*

'charter flight *noun* [C] a flight in a chartered(1) aeroplane

☆ **chase¹** /tʃeɪs/ *verb* [I,T] to run after sb/sth in order to catch him/her/it: *The dog chased the cat up a tree.* o *The police car chased the stolen van along the motorway.*

☆ **chase²** /tʃeɪs/ *noun* [C] the act of following sb/sth in order to catch him/her/it; chasing or being chased: *an exciting car chase*
(IDIOM) **give chase** to begin to run after sb/sth in order to try to catch him/her/it: *The robber ran off and the policeman gave chase.*

chasm /'kæzəm/ *noun* [C] **1** a long deep hole in the ground **2** (figurative) a wide difference of feelings, interests, etc

chassis /'ʃæsi/ *noun* [C] (pl **chassis** /'ʃæsiz/) the metal frame of a vehicle onto which the other parts fit

chaste /tʃeɪst/ *adj* **1** never having had a sexual relationship, or only with your husband/wife **2** not involving thoughts and feelings about sex —**chastity** /'tʃæstəti/ *noun* [U]: *The nuns took a vow of chastity.*

chat /tʃæt/ *noun* [C,U] a friendly informal conversation: *Why don't you come in for a cup of coffee and a chat?*

chat *verb* [I] (**chatt**ing; **chatt**ed) to talk to sb in a friendly, informal way: *The two grandmothers sat chatting about the old days.*
(PHRASAL VERB) **chat sb up** (Brit informal) to talk to sb in a friendly way because you are sexually attracted to him/her

chatty *adj* (**chattier**; **chattiest**) **1** fond of talking: *My neighbour's very chatty – she tells*

s	z	ʃ	ʒ	h	m	n	ŋ	l	r	j	w
so	zoo	she	vision	how	man	no	sing	leg	red	yes	wet

'chat show *noun* [C] a television or radio programme on which well-known people are interviewed

chatter /'tʃætə(r)/ *verb* [I] **1** to talk quickly or for a long time about sth unimportant: *The children chattered away continuously.* **2** (used about your teeth) to knock together because you are cold or frightened —**chatter** *noun* [U]: *Stop that chatter and get on with your work.*

chauffeur /'ʃəʊfə(r); *US* ʃəʊ'fɜːr/ *noun* [C] a person whose job is to drive a car for sb else: *a chauffeur-driven limousine* —**chauffeur** *verb* [T]

chauvinism /'ʃəʊvɪnɪzəm/ *noun* [U] **1** a strong belief that your country is better and more important than all others **2** = MALE CHAUVINISM

chauvinist /'ʃəʊvɪnɪst/ *noun* [C] a person who believes in or shows chauvinism

chauvinist, chauvinistic /ˌʃəʊvɪ'nɪstɪk/ *adj* believing in or showing chauvinism

☆ **cheap** /tʃiːp/ *adj* **1** low in price, costing little money: *Oranges are cheap at the moment.* ○ *It's cheaper to buy a return ticket than two singles.* ☛ The opposite is **expensive**. **2** charging low prices: *We are looking for a cheap hotel for the night.*

cheap *adv* (*informal*) for a low price: *I got this coat cheap in the sales.*

(IDIOM) **go cheap** (*informal*) selling at a low price: *They've got strawberries going cheap at the market.*

cheaply *adv* for a low price: *You can travel quickly and cheaply all over the town by bus.*

☆ **cheat** /tʃiːt/ *verb* [I] to act in a dishonest or unfair way in order to get an advantage for yourself: *Len was caught cheating in the exam.* ○ *to cheat at cards*

(PHRASAL VERB) **cheat sb (out) of sth** to take sth from sb in a dishonest or unfair way: *They tried to cheat the old lady out of her savings.*

cheat *noun* [C] a person who cheats

☆ **check¹** /tʃek/ *verb* **1** [I,T] **check (up)** to examine sth in order to make sure that it is safe, correct, in good condition, etc: *He wasn't sure whether he had locked the door, so he went to check.* ○ *I expect they're coming by car but I'll ring them and check up.* ○ *Check your work through for mistakes before you hand it in.* ○ *Can you check that we've got everything that's on the list?* ○ *She looked in her diary to check what time her appointment was.* **2** [T] to stop or go more slowly; to make sb/sth stop or go more slowly: *A tight bandage should check the flow of blood from a wound.* **3** (*US*) to write a cross on a form, etc, to show your choice: *Check the box next to the right answer.* ☛ Look at **tick**.

(PHRASAL VERBS) **check in (at...); check into...** to go to a hotel/airline desk and say that you have arrived: *Passengers should check in two hours before their departure time.*

check sth off to mark names or items on a list: *The boxes were all checked off as they were unloaded.*

check (up) on sb/sth to find out more information about sb/sth: *The boss is checking up on how much work we've done.*

check out (of...) to pay your bill and leave a hotel

check sb/sth out (*especially US*) = CHECK UP ON SB/STH

'check-in *noun* [C] **1** the act of checking in at an airport: *Our check-in time is 10.30 am.* **2** the place where you check in at an airport: *the check-in desk*

'checklist *noun* [C] a list of things that you must do or have

'checkout *noun* [C] the place in a supermarket where you pay for the things you have bought

'checkpoint *noun* [C] a place where all people and vehicles must stop and be checked: *an army checkpoint*

'check-up *noun* [C] a general medical examination to find out whether you are healthy: *You should visit your dentist for a check-up twice a year.*

☆ **check²** /tʃek/ *noun* **1** [C] **a check (on sth)** a close look at sth to make sure that it is safe, correct, in good condition, etc: *We do regular checks on our products to make sure that they are of high quality.* ○ *a security check* **2** [C] an act of going more slowly or stopping or of making sb/sth go more slowly or stop **3** [sing] (in the game of chess) the situation in which a player must move to protect his/her king ☛ Look at **checkmate**. **4** [C] (*US*) = CHEQUE **5** [C] (*US*) = BILL¹(1) **6** [C] (*US*) = TICK(3)

(IDIOM) **hold/keep sth in check** to stop sth from advancing or increasing too quickly: *government measures to keep inflation in check*

'checkbook *noun* [C] (*US*) = CHEQUE-BOOK

'checking account *noun* [C] (*US*) = CURRENT ACCOUNT

check³ /tʃek/ *noun* [C,U] a pattern of squares, often of different colours: *a check jacket* ○ *a pattern of blue and red checks*

checked /tʃekt/ *adj* with a pattern of squares: *a red-and-white checked tablecloth* ☛ picture at **pattern**.

checkers /'tʃekəz/ *noun* [U] (*US*) = DRAUGHTS

checkmate /'tʃekmeɪt/ (*also* **mate**) *noun* [sing] (in the game of chess) the situation in which you cannot protect your king and so have lost the game ☛ Look at **check²**(3).

cheddar /'tʃedə(r)/ *noun* [U] a type of hard yellow cheese that can be eaten cooked or raw

☆ **cheek** /tʃiːk/ *noun* **1** [C] one of the two parts of your face that are on each side of your nose and mouth and below your eyes: *Their cheeks were red when they came in out of the cold.* ○ *Tears rolled down her cheeks.* ☛ picture on page A8. **2** [C,U] (*informal*) rude or impolite behaviour; lack of respect: *What cheek! Asking for my help after saying such horrible things about me.*

(IDIOM) **(with) tongue in cheek** ⇨ TONGUE

cheeky *adj* (**cheekier**; **cheekiest**) impolite; not showing respect: *Don't be so cheeky! Of course I'm not fat!* —**cheekily** *adv*

'cheekbone *noun* [C] the bone that is below your eye

☆ **cheer¹** /tʃɪə(r)/ *verb* [I,T] **1** to shout to show that you like sth or to encourage sb who is tak-

iː	ɪ	e	æ	ɑː	ɒ	ɔː	ʊ	uː	ʌ
see	sit	ten	hat	arm	got	saw	put	too	cup

ing part in competition, sport, etc: *The crowd clapped and cheered.* o *Everyone cheered the winner as he crossed the finishing line.* **2** [T] to make sb happy or more hopeful: *They were all cheered by the good news.*
(PHRASAL VERBS) **cheer sb on** to cheer(1) sb in order to encourage him/her to do better: *As the runners started the last lap the crowd cheered them on.*
cheer (sb/sth) up to become or to make sb happier; to make sth look more attractive: *Cheer up! Things aren't that bad.* o *A few pictures would cheer this room up a bit.*

☆ **cheer²** /tʃɪə(r)/ *noun* [C] a loud shout to show that you like sth or to encourage sb who is taking part in a competition, sport, etc: *Three cheers for the winning team!* (= 'Hip, hip, hurrah' three times)

☆ **cheerful** /'tʃɪəfl/ *adj* happy: *Tom remained cheerful throughout his illness.* o *a cheerful smile* —**cheerfully** /-fəli/ *adv* —**cheerfulness** *noun* [U]

cheerio /ˌtʃɪəri'əʊ/ *interj* (*Brit informal*) goodbye

cheers /tʃɪəz/ *interj* (*especially Brit informal*) **1** (used to express good wishes before you have an alcoholic drink): *'Cheers,' she said, raising her wine glass.* **2** goodbye **3** thank you

☆ **cheese** /tʃiːz/ *noun* **1** [U] a type of solid food that is made from milk. Cheese is white or yellow in colour: *a simple lunch of bread and cheese* o *a cheese sandwich* o *Sprinkle the top of the pizza with grated cheese.* **2** [C] a type of cheese: *a wide selection of cheeses*

cheesecake /'tʃiːzkeɪk/ *noun* [C,U] a type of cake that is made from soft cheese and sugar on a pastry or biscuit base

cheetah /'tʃiːtə/ *noun* [C] a large wild animal of the cat family that comes from Africa and can run very fast

chef /ʃef/ *noun* [C] a person who works as the chief cook in a hotel, restaurant, etc

☆ **chemical** /'kemɪkl/ *adj* connected with chemistry; produced by processes that involve changing the structure of a substance: *a chemical reaction* o *the chemical industry* o *Farmers are using too many chemical fertilizers.*
chemical *noun* [C] a substance that is used or produced in a chemical process: *Sulphuric acid is a dangerous chemical.* —**chemically** /-kli/ *adv*

☆ **chemist** /'kemɪst/ *noun* [C] **1** (*also* **pharmacist**; *US* **druggist**) a person who prepares and sells medicines: *I got my tablets from the chemist's.* o *The doctor gave me a prescription to take to the chemist's.* ☛ A chemist's shop usually sells soap, perfume, etc, as well as medicines. **2** a person who is a specialist in chemistry

chemistry /'kemɪstri/ *noun* [U] **1** the scientific study of the structure of substances and what happens to them in different conditions or mixed with each other: *We did an experiment in the chemistry lesson today.* o *a chemistry laboratory* **2** the structure of a particular substance and the way that it may change under different conditions

☆ **cheque** (*US* **check**) /tʃek/ *noun* [C,U] a piece of paper printed by a bank that you can fill in, sign and use to pay for things: *She wrote out a cheque for £20.* o *I went to the bank to cash a cheque.* o *If there is no money in your account your cheque will bounce* (= your bank will not pay it). o *Can I pay by cheque?* ☛ picture at **money**.

'cheque-book (*US* **'checkbook**) *noun* [C] a book of cheques

'cheque card *noun* [C] a small plastic card that you get from your bank. A cheque card guarantees that any cheques you write will be paid, up to a certain amount

cherish /'tʃerɪʃ/ *verb* [T] **1** to love sb/sth: *The ring was her most cherished possession.* **2** to look after sb/sth carefully **3** to keep a thought, feeling, etc in your mind and think about it often: *a cherished ambition*

cherry /'tʃeri/ *noun* [C] (*pl* **cherries**) **1** a small round black or red fruit that has a stone inside it **2** (*also* **'cherry-tree**) the tree that produces cherries: *a flowering cherry*

cherub /'tʃerəb/ *noun* [C] (*pl* **cherubim** /'tʃerəbɪm/, **cherubs**) a beautiful child often shown in religious paintings as having wings and a round face; a small angel

chess

board
pawn
knight queen king
rook (*also* castle) bishop

chess /tʃes/ *noun* [U] a game for two people that is played on a board with 64 black and white squares (**a chessboard**). Each player has sixteen pieces which can be moved according to fixed rules.

☆ **chest** /tʃest/ *noun* [C] **1** a container, often a large strong one, that is used for storing or transporting things **2** the upper part of the front of your body: *What is your chest measurement?* o *This jacket is a 40-inch chest.* o *to have a hairy chest* o *Linda went to the doctor complaining of chest pains.* ☛ picture on page A8.
(IDIOM) **get sth off your chest** (*informal*) to talk about sth that you have been thinking about or that has been worrying you

ˌchest of 'drawers (*US* **bureau**) *noun* [C] a piece of furniture with drawers in it that is used for storing clothes, etc

chestnut /'tʃesnʌt/ *noun* [C] **1** (*also* **'chestnut tree**) a tree with large leaves that produces smooth reddish-brown nuts in prickly shells **2** one of the nuts from the chestnut tree. You can eat some chestnuts: *roast chestnuts* ☛ Look at **conker**, picture at **nut**.

☆ **chew** /tʃuː/ *verb* [I,T] to break up food in your mouth with your teeth before you swallow it: *You should chew your food thoroughly.*

'chewing gum (*also* **gum**) *noun* [U] a sweet

sticky substance that you chew in your mouth but do not swallow

chic /ʃiːk/ *adj* fashionable; elegant

chick /tʃɪk/ *noun* [C] a young bird, especially a young chicken ☛ picture at **hen**.

☆**chicken** /'tʃɪkɪn/ *noun* **1** [C] a bird that people often keep for its eggs and its meat **2** [U] the meat of this bird: *roast chicken* ○ *cold chicken and salad*

☛ Notice that chicken is the general word for the bird and its meat. A male chicken is called a **cock** (*US* **rooster**), a female is called a **hen** and a young bird is called a **chick**.

chicken *verb*
(PHRASAL VERB) **chicken out (of sth)** (*informal*) to decide not to do sth because you are afraid: *He wanted to swim across the river but he chickened out when he saw how far it was.*

'chickenpox *noun* [U] a disease, especially of children. When you have chickenpox you have a temperature and get red spots on your skin that itch a lot.

chicory /'tʃɪkəri/ (*US* **endive**) *noun* [U] a plant with slightly bitter-tasting leaves that can be eaten in salads

☆**chief** /tʃiːf/ *noun* [C] **1** the leader or ruler of a group of people: *African tribal chiefs* ○ *Indian chiefs* **2** the person who has command or control over an organization: *the chief of police*

chief *adj* (only *before* a noun) **1** most important; main: *One of the chief reasons for his decision was money.* **2** of the highest rank: *the chief executive of a company*

chiefly *adv* mainly; mostly: *His success was due chiefly to hard work.*

chieftain /'tʃiːftən/ *noun* [C] the leader of a tribe

chilblain /'tʃɪlbleɪn/ *noun* [C] a painful red area on your foot, hand, etc that can be caused by cold weather

☆**child** /tʃaɪld/ *noun* [C] (*pl* **children** /'tʃɪldrən/) **1** a boy or girl; a human who is not yet fully grown: *A group of children were playing in the park.* ○ *a six-year-old child* **2** a son or daughter of any age: *She has two children but both are married and have moved away.* ○ *He is married with three children.*

☛ An **only child** is a child who has no brothers or sisters. A couple may **adopt** a child who is not their own son or daughter (for example if the child's parents are dead). A **foster-child** is looked after for a certain period of time by a family that is not his/her own.

childhood /'tʃaɪldhʊd/ *noun* [C,U] the time when you are a child: *Harriet had a very unhappy childhood.* ○ *childhood memories*

childless *adj* having no children: *a childless marriage*

child 'benefit *noun* [U] (*Brit*) a sum of money that is paid every week by the government to parents for each child that they have

'childbirth *noun* [U] the act of giving birth to a baby: *His wife died in childbirth.*

'childlike *adj* like a child ☛ Look at **childish**.

'child-minder *noun* [C] (*Brit*) a person whose job is to look after a child while his/her parents go out to work

childish /'tʃaɪldɪʃ/ *adj* like a child ☛ If you say that people or their behaviour are **childlike**, you mean that they are like children in some way: *childlike innocence* ○ *His childlike enthusiasm delighted us all.* If you say that an adult's behaviour is **childish**, you are criticizing it because you think it is silly and that he/she should be more sensible: *Don't be so childish! You can't always have everything you want.*
—**childishly** *adv*: *to giggle childishly*

chili (*US*) = CHILLI

chill /tʃɪl/ *noun* **1** [sing] an unpleasant coldness: *There's a chill in the air.* ○ (*figurative*) *A chill of fear went down my spine.* **2** [C] an illness like a cold that is caused by being cold or damp: *to catch a chill*

chill *verb* [I,T] to become or to make sb/sth colder: *It's better to chill white wine before you serve it.*

chilling /'tʃɪlɪŋ/ *adj* frightening: *a chilling ghost story*

chilly /'tʃɪli/ *adj* (**chillier**; **chilliest**) unpleasantly cold: *It's a chilly morning. You need a coat on.* ○ (*figurative*) *a chilly reception*

chilli (*US* **chili**) /'tʃɪli/ *noun* [C,U] (*pl* **chillies**; *US* **chilies**) a small green or red vegetable that has a very strong hot taste: *chilli powder*

chime /tʃaɪm/ *verb* **1** [I] (used about a bell) to ring **2** [T] (used about a bell or a clock) to show the time by ringing: *The town-hall clock chimed midnight.*
(PHRASAL VERB) **chime in (with sth)** (*informal*) to interrupt a conversation and add your own comments

chime *noun* [C] the sound of a bell or a clock chiming

☆**chimney** /'tʃɪmni/ *noun* [C] (*pl* **chimneys**) the passage through which smoke, etc can get out of a building. A chimney in a house usually goes up from the fireplace, behind the walls and to a hole in the roof: *The chimney is sooty and needs sweeping.* ○ *Smoke poured out of the factory chimneys.*

'chimney-sweep (*also* **sweep**) *noun* [C] a person whose job is to clean chimneys by sweeping them with long brushes

chimpanzee /ˌtʃɪmpən'ziː, ˌtʃɪmpæn'ziː/ (*also informal* **chimp**) *noun* [C] a type of small ape that lives in Africa

☆**chin** /tʃɪn/ *noun* [C] the part of your face that is below your mouth: *He sat listening, his chin resting on his hand.* ☛ picture on page A8.

china /'tʃaɪnə/ *noun* [U] **1** the substance of which cups, plates, etc can be made. China is made from fine white baked clay: *a china vase* **2** cups, saucers, plates, etc that are made from china: *We only use the best china when we have visitors.*

chink[1] /tʃɪŋk/ *noun* [C] a small narrow opening

chink[2] /tʃɪŋk/ *verb* [I,T] to make a light ringing sound; to cause this sound, eg by knocking two pieces of china or glass together gently
—**chink** *noun* [C]

☆**chip**[1] /tʃɪp/ *noun* [C] **1** a small piece of wood, stone, glass, etc that has broken off sth **2** a

p	b	t	d	k	g	tʃ	dʒ	f	v	θ	ð
pen	bad	tea	did	cat	got	chin	June	fall	van	thin	then

chip

chips
(*US* French fries)

crisps
(*US* chips)

place where a piece has broken off sth: *This dish has a chip in it.* **3** (*US* **French fry**) [usually pl] a thin piece of potato that is fried in hot fat or oil: *Would you like boiled potatoes or chips?* ○ *fish and chips* **4** (*also* **potato chip**) (*US*) = CRISP² **5** a flat round piece of plastic that you use instead of money when you are playing some games **6** = MICROCHIP

(IDIOM) **have a chip on your shoulder** (*informal*) to be angry about sth for a long time, especially because you think you have been treated unfairly

chipped   cracked   broken

chip² /tʃɪp/ *verb* [I,T] (**chipp**ing; **chipp**ed) to lose or to knock a small piece off the edge or surface of sth: *They chipped the paint trying to get the table through the door.*
(PHRASAL VERB) **chip in (with sth)** (*informal*) **1** to interrupt when sb else is talking **2** to give some money as part of the cost of sth: *We all chipped in and bought him a present when he left.*

chiropodist /kɪˈrɒpədɪst/ (*US* **podiatrist**) *noun* [C] a person whose job is to care for people's feet

chirp /tʃɜːp/ *noun* [C] the short high sound that a small bird makes —**chirp** *verb* [I]

chisel /ˈtʃɪzl/ *noun* [C] a tool with a sharp end that is used for cutting or shaping wood, stone, etc ☞ picture at **tool**.

chivalry /ˈʃɪvəlri/ *noun* [U] behaviour which shows particular respect, usually of men towards women —**chivalrous** /ˈʃɪvlrəs/ *adj*

chives /tʃaɪvz/ *noun* [plural] a plant with purple flowers and long thin leaves that are used in cooking. Chives taste similar to onions.

chlorine /ˈklɔːriːn/ *noun* [U] (*symbol* **Cl**) a greenish-yellow gas with a strong smell, that is used for making water safe to drink or to swim in

chock-a-block /ˌtʃɒkəˈblɒk/ *adj* (not before a noun) completely full: *The High Street was chock-a-block with shoppers.*

☆ **chocolate** /ˈtʃɒklət/ *noun* **1** [U] a sweet brown substance that you usually buy in the form of a hard block (**bar**). Chocolate is made from cocoa beans: *milk chocolate* (= sweet and light in colour) ○ *plain chocolate* (= more bitter and darker in colour) **2** [C] a small sweet that is made from chocolate with a nut or another sweet substance inside: *a box of chocolates* **3** [C,U] a drink made from powdered chocolate with hot milk or water: *a mug of hot chocolate*
chocolate *adj* **1** made from or covered with chocolate: *chocolate cake* ○ *a chocolate biscuit* **2** dark brown

☆ **choice** /tʃɔɪs/ *noun* **1** [C] **a choice (between A and B)** an act of choosing between two or more people or things: *to make the right/wrong choice* ○ *David faced a difficult choice between moving house and losing his job.* ○ *You can have first choice of all the cakes* (= you can choose first). **2** [U] the right or chance to choose: *There was a rail strike so we had no choice but to stay on in Paris.* ○ *to have freedom of choice* **3** [C,U] two or more things from which you can or must choose: *This cinema offers a choice of six different films every night.* ○ *You get more choice of vegetables at the market.* **4** [C] a person or thing that has been chosen: *What is your choice of colour?*
(IDIOM) **out of/from choice** because you want to; of your own free will: *I wouldn't have gone to America out of choice. I was sent there on business.*

choice *adj* of very good quality: *choice beef*

choir /ˈkwaɪə(r)/ *noun* [C, with sing or pl verb] a group of people who sing together: *Dennis sings in the church choir.* ○ *The choir meets/meet on Thursday to rehearse.*

☆ **choke** /tʃəʊk/ *verb* **1** [I,T] to be or to make sb unable to breathe because sth is stopping air getting into the lungs: *The child swallowed a pen top and choked to death.* ○ *The smoke choked us.* **2** [T] (usually passive) **choke sth (up) (with sth)** to fill a passage, space, etc, so that nothing can pass through: *The roads to the coast were choked with traffic.*
(PHRASAL VERB) **choke sth back** to hide or control a strong emotion: *to choke back tears*

choke *noun* [C] **1** an act or a sound of choking (1) **2** the piece of equipment in a car, etc that controls the amount of air going into the engine. If you pull out the choke it makes it easier to start the car.

cholera /ˈkɒlərə/ *noun* [U] a serious disease that causes diarrhoea and vomiting. Cholera is most common in hot countries and can be carried by water.

cholesterol /kəˈlestərɒl/ *noun* [U] a substance that is found in the bodies of people and animals, and that helps to carry fats. Too much cholesterol is thought to be a cause of heart disease: *a high/low level of cholesterol*

☆ **choose** /tʃuːz/ *verb* [I,T] (*pt* **chose** /tʃəʊz/; *pp* **chosen** /ˈtʃəʊzn/) **1 choose (between A and/or B); choose (A) (from B); choose sb/ sth as sth** to pick or select the person or thing that you prefer: *Choose carefully before you make a final decision.* ○ *Amy had to choose between getting a job or going to college.* ○ *You can choose three questions from the five on the exam paper.* ○ *The viewers chose this programme as their favourite.* **2** to decide or prefer to do sth: *You are free to leave whenever you choose.* ○

s	z	ʃ	ʒ	h	m	n	ŋ	l	r	j	w
so	zoo	she	vision	how	man	no	sing	leg	red	yes	wet

They chose to resign rather than work for the new manager.

choosy (also **choosey**) /ˈtʃuːzi/ adj (**choosier**; **choosiest**) (informal) careful in choosing; difficult to please

☆ **chop¹** /tʃɒp/ verb [T] (**chop**ping; **chop**ped)
chop sth (up) (into sth) to cut sth into pieces with an axe or knife: *They chopped the logs up.* ○ *finely chopped herbs* ○ *Chop the onions up into small pieces.*
(PHRASAL VERBS) **chop sth down** to cut a tree, etc at the bottom so that it falls down
chop sth off (sth) to remove sth from sth by cutting it with an axe or knife: *to chop a branch off a tree*

chop² /tʃɒp/ noun [C] **1** an act of chopping sth **2** a thick slice of meat with a piece of bone in it ☞ Look at **steak**.

chop³ /tʃɒp/ verb (**chop**ping; **chop**ped)
(IDIOM) **chop and change** to change your plans or opinions several times

chopper /ˈtʃɒpə(r)/ noun [C] **1** a heavy tool that is used for cutting wood, meat, etc **2** (informal) = HELICOPTER

choppy /ˈtʃɒpi/ adj (**choppier**; **choppiest**) (used about the sea) having a lot of small waves, slightly rough

chopsticks /ˈtʃɒpstɪks/ noun [plural] two thin sticks that people in China, Japan, etc use for picking up food

choral /ˈkɔːrəl/ adj written for or involving a group of singers (**a choir**)

chord /kɔːd/ noun [C] two or more musical notes that are played at the same time
(IDIOM) **strike a chord** ⇒ STRIKE²

chore /tʃɔː(r)/ noun [C] a job that is not interesting but that you must do: *household chores*

choreograph /ˈkɒriəɡrɑːf; US ˈkɔːriəɡræf/ verb [T] to design and arrange the movements of a dance

choreographer /ˌkɒriˈɒɡrəfə(r); US ˌkɔːri-/ noun [C] a person whose job is to plan the movements for a dance

choreography /ˌkɒriˈɒɡrəfi; US ˌkɔːri-/ noun [U] the arrangement of movements for a dance, especially ballet

chorus /ˈkɔːrəs/ noun [C] **1** [with sing or pl verb] a large group of people who sing together **2** the part of a song that is repeated at the end of each verse: *The audience joined in with the choruses.* **3** a piece of music for a large group to sing **4** something that a lot of people say together: *a chorus of cheers, boos, criticism, etc* **5** [with sing or pl verb] a group of singers and dancers in a show: *She was always in the chorus, never a star.*

chorus verb [T] (used about a group of people) to sing or say sth together: *'That's not fair!' the children chorused.*

chose pt of CHOOSE
chosen pp of CHOOSE

Christ /kraɪst/ (also **Jesus**; **Jesus Christ** /ˌdʒiːzəs ˈkraɪst/) the man who Christians believe is the son of God and who established the Christian religion

christen /ˈkrɪsn/ verb [T] **1** to give a person, often a child, a name during a Christian ceremony in which he/she is made a member of the Church: *The baby was christened Simon Mark.* ☞ Look at **baptize**. **2** to give sb/sth a name: *People drive so dangerously on this stretch of road that they've christened it 'The Mad Mile'.*

christening /ˈkrɪsnɪŋ/ noun [C] the church ceremony in which a baby is given a name

☆ **Christian** /ˈkrɪstʃən/ noun [C] a person whose religion is Christianity: *Christians all over the world will join in prayers for peace today.*
—**Christian** adj: *the Christian Church, faith, religion, etc*

Christianity /ˌkrɪstiˈænəti/ noun [U] the religion that is based on the teachings of Jesus Christ: *to be converted to Christianity*

ˈChristian name (especially US **ˈgiven name**) noun [C] the name given to a child when he/she is born; first name ☞ Look at the note at **name¹**.

☆ **Christmas** /ˈkrɪsməs/ (also informal **Xmas**) noun [C,U] the period of time before and after Christmas Day: *We wish you a merry Christmas.* ○ *Where are you spending Christmas this year?* ○ *the Christmas holidays*

ˈChristmas card noun [C] a card with a picture on the front and a greeting inside that people send to their friends and relatives at Christmas

ˌChristmas ˈcracker noun [C] = CRACKER(2)

ˌChristmas ˈDay noun [C] the day on which Christians celebrate the birth of Christ each year. For most Christians Christmas Day is 25 December

ˌChristmas ˈdinner noun [C] the traditional meal eaten on Christmas Day, often with roast turkey as the main dish, followed by Christmas pudding

ˌChristmas ˈEve noun [C] the day before Christmas Day, 24 December

ˌChristmas ˈpudding noun [C] a sweet made from dried fruit and eaten hot with sauce at Christmas dinner

ˈChristmas tree noun [C] a tree such as a fir, or an artificial tree, which people bring into their homes and decorate with bright lights and coloured balls

chrome /krəʊm/ (also **chromium** /ˈkrəʊmiəm/) noun [U] a hard shiny metal that is used for covering other metals: *chrome-plated taps*

chromosome /ˈkrəʊməsəʊm/ noun [C] the part of the cells of living things that contains the genes

chronic /ˈkrɒnɪk/ adj (used about a disease or a problem) that continues for a long time: *chronic bronchitis* ○ *There is a chronic shortage of housing in the city.* —**chronically** /ˈkrɒnɪkli/ adv

chronicle /ˈkrɒnɪkl/ noun [C] (often plural) a record of events that happened in the past

chronological /ˌkrɒnəˈlɒdʒɪkl/ adj arranged in the order in which the events happened: *This book describes the main events in his life in chronological order.* —**chronologically** /-kli/ adv

chubby /ˈtʃʌbi/ adj (**chubbier**; **chubbiest**) rather fat; round: *chubby cheeks*

chuck /tʃʌk/ verb [T] (informal) **1** to throw sth

in a careless way: *Chuck that magazine over here.* o *You can chuck those old shoes in the bin.* **2 chuck sth (in)** to give sth up: *He's chucked his job in because he was fed up.*
(PHRASAL VERB) **chuck sb out (of sth)** to force sb to leave a place: *They were chucked out of the cinema for making too much noise.*

chuckle /'tʃʌkl/ *verb* [I] to laugh quietly: *Bruce chuckled to himself as he read the letter.* —**chuckle** *noun* [C]: *He put down the phone with a chuckle.*

chug /tʃʌg/ *verb* [I] (**chugging; chugged**) (used about a machine or engine) to make short repeated knocking sounds while it is working or moving slowly
(PHRASAL VERB) **chug, along, down, up,** etc to move in a particular direction making this sound: *The train chugged out of the station.*

chum /tʃʌm/ *noun* [C] (*informal old-fashioned*) a friend

chunk /tʃʌŋk/ *noun* [C] a large or thick piece of sth: *chunks of bread and cheese*

chunky /'tʃʌŋki/ *adj* (**chunkier; chunkiest**) **1** short and rather fat **2** made of thick material or thick pieces: *chunky jewellery* o *a chunky sweater*

☆ **church** /tʃɜːtʃ/ *noun* **1** [C,U] a building where Christians go to pray: *Services are held in this church every Sunday morning at 10.* o *They are getting married in the village church.* o *the church tower* o *Do you go to church regularly?* ☞ Notice that when you are talking about going to a ceremony (a service) in a church you say 'in church', 'to church' or 'at church' without 'a' or 'the': *Was Mrs Stevens at church today?* **2 Church** [C] a particular group of Christians: *the Anglican, Catholic, Methodist, etc Church*

'**churchgoer** *noun* [C] a person who goes to church regularly

the ˌChurch of 'England *noun* [sing] the Protestant Church which is the official church in England ☞ Look at **Anglican**.

'**churchyard** *noun* [C] the area of land that is around a church ☞ Look at **cemetery** and **graveyard**.

churn /tʃɜːn/ *verb* **1** [T] to beat milk or cream so that it turns into butter **2** [I,T] **churn (sth) (up)** to move, or to make sth move with great force: *The motor boat churned up the water of the lake.*
(PHRASAL VERB) **churn sth out** (*informal*) to produce large numbers of sth very quickly: *Modern factories can churn out cars at an amazing speed.*

chute /ʃuːt/ *noun* [C] a passage down which you can drop or slide things, so that you do not have to carry them: *a laundry chute*

chutney /'tʃʌtni/ *noun* [U] a hot-tasting food that is made from fruit or vegetables with sugar, vinegar and spices. You eat chutney cold with cheese or meat.

cider /'saɪdə(r)/ *noun* [U] an alcoholic drink that is made from apples

cigar /sɪ'gɑː(r)/ *noun* [C] a roll of dried tobacco leaves that people smoke. Cigars are larger and more expensive than cigarettes: *cigar smoke*

☆ **cigarette** /ˌsɪgə'ret; *US* 'sɪgəret/ *noun* [C] a roll of tobacco in a tube of thin white paper that people smoke: *a packet of cigarettes* o *to smoke a cigarette* o *She lit another cigarette.* o *John put out his cigarette.*

ciga'rette lighter (*also* **lighter**) *noun* [C] an object which produces a small flame for lighting cigarettes and cigars

cinder /'sɪndə(r)/ *noun* [C] a very small piece of coal, wood, etc that has been burning and may still be hot

☆ **cinema** /'sɪnəmə:; *US* 'sɪnəmə/ *noun* (*US also* **the movies**) **1** [C] a place where you go to see a film: *Let's go to the cinema this evening* (= go and see a film). o *What's on at the cinema this week?* ☞ In American English, you use **movie theater** to talk about the building where films are shown: *There are five movie theaters in this town.* but **the movies** when you are talking about going to see a film there: *Let's go to the movies this evening.* **2** [U] films in general: *Are you interested in cinema?*

cinnamon /'sɪnəmən/ *noun* [U] a brown powder that is used for giving flavour to sweet food

circa /'sɜːkə/ *prep* (*abbr* **c**) (*formal*) (used with dates) about: *The vase was made circa 600 AD.*

☆ **circle** /'sɜːkl/ *noun* **1** [C] a line which curves round to form the shape of a ring. Every point on the line is the same distance from the centre: *The children were drawing circles and squares on a piece of paper.* o *We all stood in a circle and held hands.* ☞ picture at **shape**. **2** [C] a flat, round area: *She cut out a circle of paper.* **3** [C] a group of people who are friends, or who have the same interest or profession: *He has a large circle of friends.* o *Her name was well known in artistic circles.* **4** [sing] an area of seats that is upstairs in a cinema, theatre, etc: *We've booked seats in the front row of the circle.*
(IDIOM) **a vicious circle** ⇨ **VICIOUS**

circle *verb* **1** [I,T] to move, or to move round sth, in a circle, especially in the air: *The plane circled the town several times before it landed.* **2** [T] to draw a circle round sth, eg on an examination paper: *There are three possible answers to each question. Please circle the correct one.*

circuit /'sɜːkɪt/ *noun* [C] **1** a complete circular path that an electric current can flow around **2** a number of competitions or other events that take place every year in a particular sport. People often take part in all the events, moving round from place to place: *She's one of the best players on the tennis circuit.* **3** a circular journey round sth: *The cars have to complete ten circuits of the track.*

☆ **circular** /'sɜːkjʊlə(r)/ *adj* **1** round and flat; shaped like a circle: *a circular table* **2** (used about a journey, etc) going round in a circle: *The bus will take you on a circular tour of Oxford.* **3** (used about a theory, etc) using the point it is trying to prove as evidence for its conclusion

circular *noun* [C] a printed letter, notice or advertisement that is sent to a large number of people: *'Is there any post?' 'Nothing interesting – just a few circulars.'*

circulate /'sɜːkjʊleɪt/ *verb* **1** [I,T] to go from one person to another; to pass information from one person to another: *Stories were circulating about the Minister's private life.* ○ *We've circulated a copy of the report to each department.* **2** [I,T] (used about a substance) to move or make sth move round continuously: *Blood circulates round the body.*

circulation /ˌsɜːkjʊˈleɪʃn/ *noun* **1** [U] the passing of sth from one person or place to another: *the circulation of news, information, rumours, etc* ○ *Old five pence coins are no longer in circulation* (= being used by people). **2** [C] the number of copies of a newspaper, magazine, etc that are sold each time it is produced: *This newspaper has a circulation of over a million.* **3** [sing] the movement of blood around the body: *If you have bad circulation, your hands and feet get cold easily.*

circumcise /ˈsɜːkəmsaɪz/ *verb* [T] to cut off the skin at the end of a man's penis or a woman's clitoris, for religious or (in the case of a man) medical reasons —**circumcision** /ˌsɜːkəmˈsɪʒn/ *noun* [C,U]

circumference /səˈkʌmfərəns/ *noun* [C,U] the distance round a circle or sth circular: *The circumference of the Earth is about 40 000 kilometres.* ○ *The Earth is about 40 000 kilometres in circumference.*

☆ **circumstance** /ˈsɜːkəmstəns/ *noun* **1** [C, usually pl] the facts and events that affect what happens in a particular situation: *We need to know the exact circumstances surrounding the accident.* ○ *In normal circumstances I would not have accepted the job, but at that time I had very little money.* **2 circumstances** [plural] (*formal*) the amount of money that you have: *The company has promised to repay the money when its financial circumstances improve.*

(IDIOMS) **in/under no circumstances** never, for any reason: *You must in no circumstances mention this subject again.*

in/under the circumstances as the result of a particular situation: *My father was very ill at that time, so under the circumstances I decided not to apply for the job.* ○ *Well, it's not an ideal solution, but it's the best we can do in the circumstances.*

☆ **circus** /ˈsɜːkəs/ *noun* [C] a show performed in a large tent by a company of people and animals: *We saw clowns, acrobats, lions and elephants at the circus.*

cistern /ˈsɪstən/ *noun* [C] a tank for water, especially one that is connected to a toilet

cite /saɪt/ *verb* [T] (*formal*) to mention sth as an example to support what you are saying: *She cited the high unemployment figures as an example of the Government's bad management.*

☆ **citizen** /ˈsɪtɪzn/ *noun* [C] **1** a person who is legally accepted as a member of a particular country: *a British citizen* ○ *She was born in Japan, but became an American citizen in 1981.* **2** a person who lives in a town or city: *Many of the citizens of Paris leave the town for the seaside during the summer.* ☛ Look at **senior citizen**.

citizenship *noun* [U] the state of being a citizen of a particular country: *After living in Spain for twenty years, he decided to apply for Spanish citizenship.*

citrus fruit /ˈsɪtrəs fruːt/ *noun* [C,U] a fruit such as an orange or lemon

☆ **city** /ˈsɪti/ *noun* (*pl* **cities**) **1** [C] a large and important town: *Venice is one of the most beautiful cities in the world.* ○ *Tokyo is the capital city of Japan.* ○ *Many people are worried about housing conditions in Britain's inner cities* (= the central parts where there are often social problems). ○ *the city centre* **2 the City** [sing] the oldest part of London, which is now Britain's financial centre: *She works in a bank in the City.*

civic /ˈsɪvɪk/ *adj* of a city or town: *civic pride* (= feeling proud because you belong to a particular town or city) ○ *Guildford Civic Centre*

civil[1] /ˈsɪvl/ *adj* polite, but not very friendly: *I know you don't like the director, but do try and be civil to him.* —**civilly** /ˈsɪvəli/ *adv*

civil[2] /ˈsɪvl/ *adj* **1** (only *before* a noun) connected with the state, not with the army or the Church: *civil aviation* ○ *civil engineering* (= the designing and building of roads, railways, bridges, etc) ○ *a civil wedding* (= not a religious one) **2** (in law) relating to the rights of ordinary people, and not criminal offences: *civil courts*

ˌcivil ˈrights (*also* ˌcivil ˈliberties) *noun* [plural] a citizen's legal right to freedom and equality whatever his/her sex, race or religion

ˌcivil ˈservant *noun* [C] a person who works in the Civil Service

the ˌCivil ˈService *noun* [sing] all the government departments (except for the armed forces) and all the people who work in them

ˌcivil ˈwar *noun* [C,U] a war between different groups of people who live in the same country

civilian /sɪˈvɪliən/ *noun* [C] a person who is not in the army, navy, air force or police force: *Two soldiers and one civilian were killed when the bomb exploded.* ○ *He left the army and returned to civilian life.*

☆ **civilization** (*also* **civilisation**) /ˌsɪvəlaɪˈzeɪʃn; *US* -əlɪˈz-/ *noun* **1** [C,U] a society which has its own highly developed culture and way of life: *the civilizations of ancient Greece and Rome* ○ *Western civilization* **2** [U] an advanced state of social and cultural development, or the process of reaching this state: *China had reached a higher level of civilization than Europe at that time.* ○ *The civilization of the human race has taken thousands of years.*

civilize (*also* **civilise**) /ˈsɪvəlaɪz/ *verb* [T] to make people or a society develop from a low social and cultural level to a more advanced one

civilized (*also* **civilised**) /ˈsɪvəlaɪzd/ *adj* **1** (used about a society) having a high level of social and cultural development: *In a civilized society there should not be people sleeping on the streets.* **2** polite and reasonable: *a civilized conversation*

clad /klæd/ *adj* (not before a noun) (*old-fashioned formal*) dressed: *The children were warmly clad in coats, hats and scarves.*

☆ **claim**[1] /kleɪm/ *verb* **1** [T] to say that sth is true, without having any proof: *The bus driver claimed that she had not seen the cyclist.* ○ *Colin claims the book belongs to him.* ○ *The woman*

p	b	t	d	k	g	tʃ	dʒ	f	v	θ	ð
pen	bad	tea	did	cat	got	chin	June	fall	van	thin	then

claims to be the oldest person in Britain. ○ *No one has claimed responsibility for the bomb attack.* **2** [I,T] **claim (for sth)** to ask for sth because you think you should have it or that it belongs to you: *The police are keeping the animal until somebody claims it.* ○ *If you are disabled you can claim a special allowance from the Government.* ○ *Don't forget to claim for your travel expenses when you get back.* **3** [T] (*formal*) to cause death: *The earthquake claimed thousands of lives.*

☆ **claim²** /kleɪm/ *noun* [C] **1** a statement that sth is true, that does not have any proof: *I do not believe the Government's claim that they can reduce unemployment by the end of the year.* **2 claim (for sth)** a demand for sth that you think you have a right to: *to make an insurance claim* ○ *After the accident he decided to put in a claim for compensation.* ○ *a pay claim* **3 claim (to sth)** the right to have sth: *You will have to prove your claim to the property in a court of law.*
(IDIOM) **stake a/your claim** ⇨ STAKE¹

clam¹ /klæm/ *noun* [C] a type of shellfish

clam² /klæm/ *verb* (cla**mm**ing; cla**mm**ed)
(PHRASAL VERB) **clam up** (*informal*) to stop talking and refuse to speak: *She always clams up when I ask her about her past.*

clamber /'klæmbə(r)/ *verb* [I] to climb with difficulty, usually using both your hands and feet: *She managed to clamber up the hillside.*

clammy /'klæmi/ *adj* damp and sticky: *clammy hands*

clamour (*US* **clamor**) /'klæmə(r)/ *verb* [I] **clamour for sth** to demand sth in a loud or angry way: *The public are clamouring for an answer to all these questions.* —**clamour** (*US* **clamor** /'klæmə(r)/) *noun* [sing]: *We could hear the clamour of angry voices.*

clamp /klæmp/ *noun* [C] a tool that you use for holding two things together very tightly

clamp *verb* [T] **1** to fasten two things together with a clamp: *The metal rods were clamped together.* ○ *Clamp the wood to the table so that it doesn't move.* **2** to put or hold sth very firmly in a particular place: *He kept his pipe clamped between his teeth.* **3** (*also* **wheelclamp**) to attach a metal object to the wheel of a vehicle that has been parked in an illegal place, so that it cannot move: *Oh no! My car's been clamped.*
(PHRASAL VERB) **clamp down on sb/sth** (*informal*) to take strong action against sb/sth in order to stop or control sth: *The police are clamping down on people who drink and drive.*

'**clamp-down** *noun* [C]: *a clamp-down on tax evasion*

clan /klæn/ *noun* [C, with sing or pl verb] a group of families who are related to each other, especially in Scotland

clandestine /klæn'destɪn/ *adj* (*formal*) secret and often not legal

clang /klæŋ/ *noun* [C] a loud ringing sound that is made when a metal object hits sth: *The huge metal door closed with a clang.*

clang *verb* [I,T] to make or cause sth to make this sound

clank /klæŋk/ *noun* [C] a loud sound that is made when a metal object (eg a heavy chain) hits sth

clank *verb* [I,T] to make or cause sth to make this sound

☆ **clap** /klæp/ *verb* (cla**pp**ing; cla**pp**ed) **1** [I,T] to put your hands together quickly in order to make a loud sound, usually to show that you like sth: *The audience clapped as soon as the singer walked onto the stage.* ○ *Everybody was clapping their hands in time to the music.* **2** [T] to put sth onto sth quickly and firmly: *'Oh no, I shouldn't have said that,' she said, clapping a hand over her mouth.*

clap *noun* [C] **1** an act of clapping: *Let's have a big clap for our next performer!* **2** a sudden loud noise of thunder: *a clap of thunder*

clarify /'klærɪfaɪ/ *verb* [T] (*pres part* **clarifying**; *3rd pers sing pres* **clarifies**; *pt, pp* **clarified**) to make sth become clear and easier to understand: *I hope that what I say will clarify the situation.* —**clarification** /,klærɪfɪ'keɪʃn/ *noun* [U]: *We'd like some clarification of exactly what your company intends to do.*

clarinet /,klærə'net/ *noun* [C] a musical instrument that is made of wood. You play a clarinet by blowing through it.

clarity /'klærəti/ *noun* [U] the quality of being clear and easy to understand: *clarity of expression*

clash /klæʃ/ *verb* **1** [I] **clash (with sb) (over sth)** to fight or disagree seriously about sth: *A group of demonstrators clashed with police outside the Town Hall.* ○ *Conservative and Labour politicians have clashed again over defence cuts.* **2** [I] **clash (with sth)** (used about two events) to happen at the same time: *It's a pity the two concerts clash. I wanted to go to both of them.* **3** [I] **clash (with sth)** (used about colours, etc) not to match or look nice together: *I don't think you should wear that tie – it clashes with your shirt.* **4** [I,T] (used about two metal objects) to hit together with a loud noise; to cause two metal objects to do this: *Their swords clashed.*

clash *noun* [C] **1** a fight or serious disagreement: *a clash between police and demonstrators* **2** a big difference: *a clash of opinions* ○ *There was a personality clash between the two men.* **3** a loud noise, made by two metal objects hitting each other: *the clash of cymbals*

clasp¹ /klɑːsp; *US* klæsp/ *noun* [C] an object, usually of metal, which fastens or holds sth together: *the clasp on a necklace, brooch, handbag, etc*

clasp² /klɑːsp; *US* klæsp/ *verb* [T] to hold sb/sth tightly: *She was clasping a knife.* ○ *Kevin clasped the child in his arms.*

☆ **class** /klɑːs; *US* klæs/ *noun* **1** [C] a group of pupils or students who are taught together: *Jane and I are in the same class at school.* ☛ In the singular **class** can be used with either a singular or a plural verb: *The whole class is/are going to the theatre tonight.* **2** [C,U] a lesson: *Classes begin at 9 o'clock in the morning.* ○ *I go to evening classes in local history on Wednesdays.* ○ *We watched an interesting video in class* (= *during the lesson*) *yesterday.* **3** [U] the way people are divided into social groups: *The idea of class still divides British society.* ○ *class differ-*

s	z	ʃ	ʒ	h	m	n	ŋ	l	r	j	w
so	zoo	she	vision	how	man	no	sing	leg	red	yes	wet

ences 4 [C,U] a group of people who are at the same social and economic level: *the working/middle/upper class* ☞ In the singular **class** can be used with either a singular or a plural verb. **5** [C] a group of things of a similar type: *There are several different classes of insects.* **6** [U] (*informal*) high quality or style: *Lineker is a player of great class.* **7** [C] (especially in compounds) of a certain level of quality or comfort: *a first-class compartment on a train* **8** [C] (*Brit*) (especially in compounds) a grade that you get when you pass your final university examination: *a first-/second-/third-class degree*

class *verb* [T] **class sb/sth (as sth)** to put sb/sth in a particular group or type: *The house has recently been classed as a 'historic building'.*

classy /'klɑːsɪ; *US* 'klæsɪ/ *adj* (**classier**; **classiest**) (*informal*) of high quality or style; expensive: *She took me to a classy restaurant in Soho.*

'classmate *noun* [C] a person who is in the same class as you at school or college

'classroom *noun* [C] a room in a school, college, etc where classes are taught

classic /'klæsɪk/ *adj* **1** typical: *This painting is a classic example of the French Impressionist style.* ○ *It was a classic case of bad management.* **2** (used about a book, play, etc) important and having a value that will last: *the classic film 'Gone With The Wind'*

classic *noun* **1** [C] a famous book, play, etc which has a value that will last: *All of Charles Dickens' novels are classics.* **2 Classics** [U] the study of ancient Greek and Roman language and literature

classical /'klæsɪkl/ *adj* **1** (used about music) serious and having a value that lasts: *I prefer classical music to pop or jazz.* **2** traditional, not modern: *classical ballet* ○ *classical scientific methods* **3** relating to ancient Greece or Rome: *classical architecture* —**classically** /'klæsɪkli/ *adv*

classify /'klæsɪfaɪ/ *verb* [T] (*pres part* **classifying**; *3rd pers sing pres* **classifies**; *pt, pp* **classified**) **classify sb/sth (as sth)** to put sb/sth into a group with other people or things of a similar type: *The books in a library are usually classified according to subject.* —**classification** /ˌklæsɪfɪ'keɪʃn/ *noun* [C,U]: *His job involves the classification of the different species of butterfly.*

classified *adj* officially secret: *classified information*

ˌclassified ad'vertisements (*also Brit informal* **ˌclassified 'ads**; **'small ads**) *noun* [plural] small advertisements that you put in a newspaper if you want to buy or sell sth, employ sb, find a flat, etc

clatter /'klætə(r)/ *noun* [sing] a series of short loud repeated sounds that is made when hard objects hit against each other: *the clatter of knives and forks*

clatter *verb* [I,T] to make or cause sth to make this noise: *The horses clattered down the street.*

clause /klɔːz/ *noun* [C] **1** a paragraph in a legal document **2** (*grammar*) a group of words that includes a subject and a verb. A clause is usually only part of a sentence: *The sentence, 'After we had finished eating, we watched a film on the video' contains two clauses.*

claustrophobia /ˌklɔːstrə'fəʊbiə/ *noun* [U] great fear of being in a small or closed space

claustrophobic /ˌklɔːstrə'fəʊbɪk/ *adj* **1** afraid in this way: *I always feel claustrophobic in lifts.* **2** (used about sth that makes you feel afraid in this way): *a claustrophobic little room*

claw /klɔː/ *noun* [C] **1** one of the pointed nails on the feet of some animals and birds: *Cats have sharp claws.* **2** the part of a leg on some types of insects and sea animals which they use for holding things

clay /kleɪ/ *noun* [U] heavy earth that is soft when it is wet and becomes hard when it is baked or dried: *The students were modelling heads out of clay.* ○ *clay pots*

☆ **clean¹** /kliːn/ *adj* **1** not dirty: *The whole house was beautifully clean.* ○ *Are your hands clean?* ○ *I think I'll change into some clean clothes.* **2** (used about animals and people) having clean habits: *Cats are very clean animals.* **3** (used about humour) not about sex, etc; not dirty: *a clean joke* **4** having no record of offences: *a clean driving-licence*

(IDIOM) **a clean sweep** a complete victory in a sports competition, election, etc that you get by winning all the different parts of it: *The Russians made a clean sweep of all the gymnastics events.*

clean *adv* (*informal*) completely: *The lorry went clean through the wall.* ○ *I clean forgot it was your birthday.*

(IDIOM) **come clean (with sb) (about sth)** (*informal*) to tell the truth about sth that you have been keeping secret: *She decided to come clean with Martin about her relationship with Tom.*

ˌclean-'shaven *adj* (used about men) not having a beard or a moustache

☆ **clean²** /kliːn/ *verb* **1** [T] to remove dirt and marks from sth: *to clean the house, the windows, the kitchen floor, etc* ○ *Don't forget to clean your teeth!* ○ *Oh dear, my shoes need cleaning.* ☞ Clean is a general word for removing dirt from something. If you **wash** something you clean it with water and often soap. You can **wipe** a surface by rubbing it with a wet cloth; you **dust** a surface by rubbing it with a dry cloth. If you **brush** something you clean it with a brush that has a short handle; if you **sweep** the floor you use a brush with a long handle. **2** [I] to make the inside of a house, office, etc free from dust and dirt: *Mr Burrows comes in to clean after office hours.*

(PHRASAL VERBS) **clean sth out** to clean the inside of sth thoroughly: *I'm going to clean out all the kitchen cupboards next week.*

clean (sth) up 1 to remove what is dirty from a place that is particularly dirty: *I'm going to clean up the kitchen before Mum and Dad get back.* **2** to remove sth that has just been spilled: *Oh no, you've spilt coffee on the new carpet! Can you clean it up?*

cleaner /'kliːnə(r)/ *noun* **1** [C] a person whose job is to clean the rooms and furniture inside a

iː	ɪ	e	æ	ɑː	ɒ	ɔː	ʊ	uː	ʌ
see	sit	ten	hat	arm	got	saw	put	too	cup

house or other building: *an office cleaner* **2** [C] a substance or an instrument that you use for cleaning sth: *liquid floor cleaners* ○ *a carpet cleaner* ☛ Look at **vacuum cleaner**. **3 cleaner's** = DRY-CLEANER'S: *Could you take my coat to the cleaner's?*

cleanliness /ˈklenlɪnəs/ *noun* [U] being clean: *High standards of cleanliness are extremely important in a hotel kitchen.*

cleanly /ˈkliːnli/ *adv* easily or smoothly: *The knife cut cleanly through the rope.*

cleanse /klenz/ *verb* [T] to make sth thoroughly clean: *to cleanse a cut*

cleanser *noun* [C] a substance that you use for cleaning sth, especially your skin

☆ **clear¹** /klɪə(r)/ *adj* **1** easy to see through: *clear glass* ○ *The water was so clear that we could see the bottom of the lake.* **2** easy to see, hear or understand: *We get a very clear picture on our new television.* ○ *His voice wasn't very clear on the telephone.* ○ *She gave me clear directions on how to get there.* **3** free from marks: *a clear sky* (= without clouds) ○ *a clear skin* (= without spots) **4** free from things that are blocking the way: *The police say that most roads are now clear of snow.* **5 clear (to sb)** easy to see; obvious: *There are clear advantages to the second plan.* ○ *It was clear to me that he was not telling the truth.* ○ *The answer to the problem is quite clear.* **6 clear (about/on sth)** sure or definite; without any doubts: *I'm not quite clear about the arrangements for tomorrow.* **7** not confused: *Clear thinking is very important in this job.* ○ *We need to get a clear understanding of the situation.* **8** free from guilt: *It wasn't your fault. You can have a completely clear conscience.*

(IDIOM) **make yourself clear; make sth clear/plain (to sb)** to speak so that there can be no doubt about what you mean: *'I do not want you to go to that concert,' said my mother. 'Do I make myself clear?'* ○ *He made it quite clear that he was not happy with the decision.*

clearly *adv* **1** in a way that is easy to see, hear or understand: *It was so foggy that we couldn't see the road clearly.* **2** in a way that is not confused: *I'm so tired that I can't think clearly.* **3** obviously; without doubt: *She clearly doesn't want to speak to you any more.*

˒**clear-ˈheaded** *adj* able to think clearly, especially if there is a problem

˒**clear-ˈsighted** *adj* able to understand situations well and to see what might happen in the future

☆ **clear²** /klɪə(r)/ *adv* **1** = CLEARLY(1): *We can hear the telephone loud and clear from here.* **2 clear (of sth)** away from sth; not touching sth: *stand clear of the doors* (= on a train)

(IDIOM) **keep/stay/steer clear (of sb/sth)** to avoid sb/sth: *It's best to keep clear of the town centre during the rush hour.*

˒**clear-ˈcut** *adj* definite and easy to see or understand: *It was a clear-cut case of police corruption.*

☆ **clear³** /klɪə(r)/ *verb* **1** [T] to remove sth that is not wanted or needed: *to clear the roads of snow/to clear snow from the roads.* ○ *It's your turn to clear the table* (= to take away the dirty plates, etc after a meal). ○ *Shall I help you clear away the plates?* **2** [I] (used about fog, smoke, etc) disappear: *The fog slowly cleared and the sun came out.* **3** [I] (used about the sky, the weather or water) to become free of clouds, rain, or mud: *After a cloudy start, the weather will clear during the afternoon.* **4** [T] to pass over or get past sth without touching it: *The horse cleared the first jump but knocked down the second.* **5** [T] to give permission for sth to happen: *At last the plane was cleared for take-off.* **6** [I] (used about a cheque) to go through the system that transfers money from one account to another: *The cheque will take three days to clear.* **7** [T] **clear sb (of sth)** to prove that sb is not guilty of a crime or mistake: *The man has finally been cleared of murder.*

(IDIOMS) **clear the air** to remove tension by talking openly about worries, doubts, etc: *I'm sure if you discuss your feelings with her it will help to clear the air between you.*

clear your throat to cough slightly in order to make it easier to speak: *He cleared his throat and then began his speech.*

(PHRASAL VERBS) **clear off** (*informal*) (used especially as an order) to go away: *'Clear off,' shouted the farmer, 'you're on my land!'*

clear sth out to tidy sth and throw away things that you do not want: *I really must clear out the kitchen cupboards.*

clear up (used about the weather or an illness) to get better: *We can go out for a walk if it clears up later on.* ○ *The doctor told him to stay at home until his cold cleared up.*

clear (sth) up to make sth tidy: *Make sure you clear up properly before you leave.*

clear sth up to find the solution to a problem, mystery, etc: *There's been a slight misunderstanding but we've cleared it up now.*

clearance /ˈklɪərəns/ *noun* [U] **1** the removing of sth that is old or not wanted: *slum clearance* ○ *The shop is having a clearance sale* (= selling things cheaply in order to get rid of them). **2** the distance between an object and something that is passing under or beside it, eg a ship or vehicle: *There was not enough clearance for the bus to pass under the bridge safely.* **3** official permission for sb/sth to do sth: *clearance to work at the nuclear research establishment*

clearing /ˈklɪərɪŋ/ *noun* [C] a small area without trees in the middle of a wood or forest

cleavage /ˈkliːvɪdʒ/ *noun* [C,U] the space between a woman's breasts

clef /klef/ *noun* [C] (in music) a sign (♭, ♩) at the beginning of a line of written music that shows the range of the notes

clementine /ˈkleməntiːn/ *noun* [C] a type of small orange with a loose skin

clench /klentʃ/ *verb* [T] to close or hold tightly: *He clenched his teeth in pain.* ○ *She clenched her fists and looked as if she was about to hit him.*

clergy /ˈklɜːdʒi/ *noun* [plural] the people who perform religious ceremonies in the Christian church: *a member of the clergy*

clergyman /ˈklɜːdʒimən/ *noun* (*pl* **clergymen** /-mən/) a member of the clergy

clerical /ˈklerɪkl/ *adj* **1** connected with the

3ː	ə	eɪ	əʊ	aɪ	aʊ	ɔɪ	ɪə	eə	ʊə
fur	ago	pay	home	five	now	join	near	hair	pure

work of a clerk in an office: *clerical work* **2** of or concerning the clergy

☆ **clerk** /klɑːk; *US* klɜːrk/ *noun* [C] **1** a person whose job is to do written work or look after records or accounts in an office, bank, court of law, etc **2** (*also* **sales clerk**) (*US*) = SHOP ASSISTANT

☆ **clever** /ˈklevə(r)/ *adj* **1** able to learn, understand or do sth quickly and easily; intelligent: *a clever student* ○ *How clever of you to mend my watch!* ○ *She's so clever with her hands – she makes all her own clothes.* **2** (used about things, ideas, etc) showing skill or intelligence: *a clever device* ○ *a clever plan* —**cleverly** *adv* —**cleverness** *noun* [U]

cliché /ˈkliːʃeɪ; *US* kliːˈʃeɪ/ *noun* [C] a phrase or idea that has been used so many times that it no longer has any real meaning or interest: *the usual cliché of the middle-aged businessman leaving his wife for a twenty-year old girl*

click¹ /klɪk/ *noun* [C] a short sharp sound: *I heard the click of a key in the lock.* ○ *the click of a switch*

click² /klɪk/ *verb* **1** [I,T] to make a short sharp sound; to cause sth to do this: *The door clicked shut.* ○ *He clicked the switch.* ○ *To open a file on the computer, click on the mouse.* **2** [I] (*Brit informal*) (used about two people) to become friendly immediately: *We met at a party and just clicked.* **3** [I] (*informal*) (used about a problem, etc) to become suddenly clear or understood: *Once I'd found the missing letter, everything clicked into place.*

☆ **client** /ˈklaɪənt/ *noun* [C] someone who receives a service from a professional person

clientele /ˌkliːənˈtel; *US* ˌklaɪənˈtel/ *noun* [U] the group of people who regularly go to a particular shop, hotel, etc ☞ This word is more formal than alternatives such as **customers** or **guests**.

☆ **cliff** /klɪf/ *noun* [C] a high, very steep area of rock, especially one next to the sea: *the white cliffs of Dover* ☞ picture at **beach**.

☆ **climate** /ˈklaɪmɪt/ *noun* [C] **1** the normal weather conditions of a particular region: *a dry, humid, tropical, etc climate* ○ *What are the effects of global warming on our climate?* **2** the general opinions, etc that people have at a particular time: *What is the current climate of opinion regarding the death penalty?* ○ *the political climate*

climatic /klaɪˈmætɪk/ *adj* of climate: *a conference to discuss climatic change*

climax /ˈklaɪmæks/ *noun* [C] the most important and exciting part of a book, play, piece of music, event, etc: *the novel's climax in the final chapter* ○ *The election victory marked the climax of his political career.*

climax *verb* [I] to reach a climax

☆ **climb** /klaɪm/ *verb* **1** [I,T] to move up to the top of sth: *The cat managed to climb to the top of the tree.* ○ *to climb a tree, mountain, rope, etc* ○ *She climbed the stairs to bed.* ○ *to climb up a ladder* **2** [I] to move, with difficulty, in the direction mentioned: *I managed to climb out of the window.* **3** [I] to go up mountains, etc as a sport ☞ **Go climbing** is a common way of talking about climbing for pleasure: *I go climbing in the Alps most summers.* **4** [I] to rise to a higher position: *The plane climbed steadily.* ○ *The road climbed steeply up the side of the mountain.* ○ (*figurative*) *The value of the dollar against the pound has climbed to a record level.*

(IDIOM) **climb/jump on the bandwagon** ⇨ BANDWAGON

(PHRASAL VERB) **climb down (over sth)** (*informal*) to admit that you have made a mistake; to change your opinion about sth

climb *noun* [C] an act of climbing or a journey made by climbing: *The monastery could only be reached by a three-hour climb.*

climber *noun* [C] a person who climbs mountains or rocks as a sport

'climb-down *noun* [C] an act of admitting you have been wrong: *a government climb-down*

clinch /klɪntʃ/ *verb* [T] (*informal*) to settle or decide sth finally, eg an argument or business agreement: *to clinch a deal*

cling /klɪŋ/ *verb* [I] (*pt, pp* **clung** /klʌŋ/) **1 cling (on) to sb/sth; cling together** to hold on tightly to sb/sth: *to cling to a rope* ○ *They clung together for warmth.* **2** to continue to believe that sth is true, often when it is not reasonable to do so: *They were still clinging to the hope that the girl would be found alive.* **3** to stick firmly to sth: *Her wet clothes clung to her.*

'cling film *noun* [U] a thin transparent material used for covering food to keep it fresh

clinic /ˈklɪnɪk/ *noun* [C] **1** a small hospital or a part of a hospital where you go to receive special medical treatment: *He's being treated at a private clinic.* ○ *The ante-natal clinic is part of the maternity department.* **2** a time when a doctor in a hospital sees patients and gives special treatment or advice: *Dr Greenall's clinic is from 2 to 4 on Mondays.*

clinical /ˈklɪnɪkl/ *adj* **1** of or relating to the examination and treatment of patients at a clinic or hospital: *Clinical trials of the new drug have proved successful.* **2** (used about a person) cold and not emotional

clinically *adv* **1** according to medical examination: *to be clinically dead* **2** in a clinical(2) way

clink /klɪŋk/ *noun* [sing] the short sharp sound that objects made of glass, metal, etc make when they touch each other: *the clink of glasses* —**clink** *verb* [I,T]

clip¹ /klɪp/ *noun* [C] a small object, usually made of metal or plastic, used for holding things together: *a paper-clip* ○ *a hair-clip*

clip *verb* [I,T] (**clip**ping; **clip**ped) to be fastened with a clip; to fasten sth to sth else with a clip: *Do your earrings clip on?* ○ *Clip the photo to the letter, please.*

clip² /klɪp/ *verb* [T] (**clip**ping; **clip**ped) to cut sth, especially by cutting small parts off: *The hedge needs clipping.*

clip *noun* [C] **1** an act of cutting sth **2** (*informal*) a short sharp blow: *She gave the boy a clip round the ear.* **3** a small section of a film that is shown separately so that people can see what the rest of the film is like —**clipping** (*US*) *noun* [C] = CUTTING¹(2)

clippers /ˈklɪpəz/ *noun* [plural] a small metal

p	b	t	d	k	g	tʃ	dʒ	f	v	θ	ð
pen	bad	tea	did	cat	got	chin	June	fall	van	thin	then

clique /kliːk/ noun [C] a small group of people with the same interests who do not want others to join their group

clitoris /ˈklɪtərɪs/ noun [C] the small part of the female sex organs which becomes larger when a woman is sexually excited

cloak /kləʊk/ noun **1** [C] a type of loose coat without sleeves, more common in former times **2** [sing] a thing that hides sth else

cloakroom /ˈkləʊkrʊm/ noun [C] **1** a room near the entrance to a theatre, school, club, etc where you can leave your coat, bags, etc **2** (Brit) a lavatory in a public building: *Excuse me. Where are the ladies' cloakrooms, please?*

clobber /ˈklɒbə(r)/ verb [T] (Brit informal) to hit sb hard

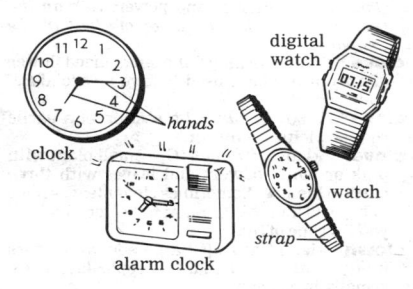

☆ **clock¹** /klɒk/ noun [C] **1** an instrument that shows you what time it is, often found on the wall of a house or building, school, club, etc (not worn like a watch): *an alarm clock* ○ *That clock is five minutes slow* (= it says 10.55 when it is really 11 o'clock). ○ *The clock is five minutes fast* (= it says 6.05 when it is really 6 o'clock). ○ *The clock struck midnight.* **2** an instrument in a car that measures how far it has travelled: *My car has only 10 000 miles on the clock.*

(IDIOMS) **around/round the clock** all day and all night: *They are working round the clock to repair the bridge.*

put the clock/clocks forward/back to change the time, usually by one hour, at the beginning/end of summer

clockwise adv, adj in the same direction as the hands of a clock: *Turn the handle clockwise.* ○ *to move in a clockwise direction* ☛ The opposite is **anticlockwise**.

clock² /klɒk/ verb
(PHRASAL VERBS) **clock in/on; clock off** to record the time that you arrive at or leave work, especially by putting a card into a type of clock

clock sth up to achieve a certain number or total: *Our car clocked up over 2 000 miles while we were on holiday.*

clockwork /ˈklɒkwɜːk/ noun [U] a type of machinery found in certain toys, etc that you operate by winding a key: *a clockwork toy* ○ *The plan went like clockwork* (= smoothly and without any problems).

clog¹ /klɒg/ noun [C] a type of shoe made completely of wood or with a thick wooden bottom: *a pair of clogs*

clog² /klɒg/ verb (**clogging; clogged**) [I,T] **clog (sth) (up) (with sth)** to block or become blocked: *The drain is clogged up with leaves.* ○ *You've clogged up the machine.* ○ *The roads were clogged with traffic.*

clone /kləʊn/ noun [C] an identical copy of a plant or animal that is produced by artificial methods

clone verb [T] to cause sth to grow as a clone

☆ **close¹** /kləʊs/ adj **1** (not before a noun) **close (to sb/sth); close (together)** near: *Is our hotel close to the beach?* ○ *It's close to midnight.* ○ *The edges are quite close together.* **2** (used about a friend, etc) known very well and liked: *They invited only close friends to the wedding.* **3** near in a family relationship: *a close relative* **4** (used about a competition, etc) only won by a small amount: *a close match* **5** careful; thorough: *On close examination, you could see that the banknote was a forgery.* **6** (used about the weather, etc) heavy and with little movement of air: *It's so close today that there might be a storm.*

(IDIOMS) **a close shave/thing** a bad thing that almost happened: *I wasn't injured, but it was a close shave.*

at close quarters at or from a position that is very near

keep a close watch on sb/sth to watch sb/sth very carefully: *The police kept a close watch on the gang.*

closely adv in a close way: *to watch sb closely* ○ *The insect closely resembles a stick.*

closeness noun [U] the state of being close

☆ **close²** /kləʊs/ adv near: *The child stood close to his mother.* ○ *to follow close behind someone* ○ *I held her close* (= tightly).

(IDIOMS) **close by (sb/sth)** at a short distance from sb/sth: *She lives close by.*

close on nearly; almost: *He was born close on a hundred years ago.*

close up (to sb/sth) at or from a very short distance to look at sb/sth: *You can't tell it's a forgery until you look at it close up.*

'close-up noun [C] a photograph or film of sb/sth that you take from a very short distance away: *Here's a close-up of our wedding cake.*

close³ /kləʊs/ noun [C] part of the name of a street, especially one that is closed off at one end: *5 Devon Close*

☆ **close⁴** /kləʊz/ verb [I,T] **1** to shut: *The door closed quietly.* ○ *to close a door, window, cupboard, etc* ○ *Close your eyes – I've got a surprise.* **2** to be, or to make sth, not open to the public: *What time do the shops close?* ○ *The police have closed the road to traffic.* **3** to come or bring sth to an end: *The meeting closed at 10pm.* ○ *Detectives have closed the case on the missing pilot.*

(PHRASAL VERBS) **close (sth) down** to stop all business or work permanently, at a shop or factory: *The factory has had to close down because of the recession.* ○ *Health inspectors have closed the restaurant down.*

close in (on sb/sth) to come nearer and gradually surround sb/sth, especially in order

to attack: *The army is closing in on the enemy troops.*
'closing-time noun [C] the time when a shop, etc closes

☆ **close⁵** /kləʊz/ noun [sing] the end, especially of a period of time or an activity: *the close of trading on the stock market*
(IDIOM) **bring sth/come/draw to a close** to end: *The chairman brought the meeting to a close.* ○ *The guests began to leave as the evening drew to a close.*

☆ **closed** /kləʊzd/ adj not open; shut: *Keep your mouth closed.* ○ *with closed eyes*
,closed-,circuit 'television noun [C,U] a type of television system used inside a building, eg to look for people who are trying to steal things
closet /'klɒzɪt/ noun [C] (US) a large cupboard that is built into a room
closure /'kləʊʒə(r)/ noun [C,U] the permanent closing, eg of a business: *Miners are protesting against pit closures.* ○ *The firm is threatened with closure.*
clot /klɒt/ noun [C] **1** a lump formed by blood as it dries **2** (*Brit informal*) a stupid person
clot verb (clotting; clotted) [I,T] to form or cause sth to form clots
,clotted 'cream noun [U] (*Brit*) a type of thick rich cream

☆ **cloth** /klɒθ; *US* klɔ:θ/ noun (pl **cloths** /klɒθs; *US* klɔ:ðz/) **1** [U] a material made of cotton, wool, etc that you use for making clothes, curtains, etc: *a metre of cloth* **2** [C] a piece of cloth that you use for a particular purpose: *a tablecloth* ○ *Where can I find a cloth to wipe this up?*
clothe /kləʊð/ verb [T] to provide clothes for sb: *to feed and clothe a child*
clothed adj **clothed (in sth)** dressed: *He was clothed in leather from head to foot.* ○ *Luckily I was fully clothed when they arrived.*

☆ **clothes** /kləʊðz; *US* kləʊz/ noun [plural] the things that you wear, eg trousers, shirts, dresses, coats, etc (when thought of all together): *Take off those wet clothes.* ○ *She was wearing new clothes.* ☞ Remember that clothes is always plural. We can use an **item/piece/article of clothing** to describe a single thing that you wear: *A kilt is an item of clothing worn in Scotland.* Look at **garment**.
'clothes-hanger noun [C] = HANGER
'clothes-line noun [C] a thin rope that you hang clothes on so that they can dry ☞ picture at **peg**.
'clothes-peg (*US* **'clothes-pin**) noun [C] = PEG¹(3)

☆ **clothing** /'kləʊðɪŋ/ noun [U] the clothes that you wear: *You will need waterproof clothing.* ☞ **Clothing** is more formal than **clothes**.

☆ **cloud¹** /klaʊd/ noun **1** [C,U] a mass of very small drops of water that floats in the sky and is often grey or white: *The sun disappeared behind a cloud.* ○ *A band of thick cloud is spreading from the west.* **2** [C] a mass of smoke, dust, sand, etc: *Clouds of smoke were pouring from the burning building.*
(IDIOM) **under a cloud** with the disapproval of the people around you: *She left her job under a cloud because she'd been accused of stealing.*

cloudless adj (used about the sky, etc) clear; without any clouds
cloudy adj (**cloudier**; **cloudiest**) **1** (used about the sky, etc) full of clouds **2** (used about liquids, etc) not clear: *cloudy water*
'cloudburst noun [C] a sudden heavy fall of rain
cloud² /klaʊd/ verb **1** [I,T] to become or make sth difficult to see through: *His eyes clouded with tears.* **2** [T] to make sth less clear or easy to understand **3** [T] to make sth less enjoyable; to spoil: *Illness has clouded the last few years of his life.*
(PHRASAL VERB) **cloud over 1** (used about the sky) to become full of clouds **2** (used about a person's face) to start to look sad
clout /klaʊt/ noun (*informal*) **1** [C] a heavy blow, usually with the hand: *to give someone a clout* **2** [U] influence and power: *He's an important man – he has a lot of clout in the company.*
clove¹ /kləʊv/ noun [C] the small dried flower of a tropical plant, used to give a special flavour in cooking
clove² /kləʊv/ noun [C] a section of a garlic root ☞ picture at **onion**.
clover /'kləʊvə(r)/ noun [C] a small plant with pink or white flowers and leaves with three parts to them ☞ Sometimes clover leaves have four parts and it is thought to be very lucky if you find one of these.
clown /klaʊn/ noun [C] a person who wears funny clothes and makes people laugh, especially in a circus
clown verb [I] **clown (about/around)** to act in a funny or foolish way, like a clown: *Stop clowning around and get some work done!*

☆ **club¹** /klʌb/ noun [C] a group of people who meet to share an interest; the place where they meet: *to join a club* ○ *to be a member of a club* ○ *a social club* ○ *a tennis, football, golf, etc club* ☞ Look at **nightclub**.
club verb (clubbing; clubbed)
(PHRASAL VERB) **club together (to do sth)** to share the cost of sth, eg a present: *We clubbed together to buy him a leaving present.*
club² /klʌb/ noun [C] **1** a heavy stick, usually with one end that is thicker than the other, used as a weapon **2** a long stick that is specially shaped at one end and used for hitting a ball when playing golf ☞ Look at **bat²**, **racket¹** and **stick¹**(3).
club verb (clubbing; clubbed) [T] to hit sb/sth hard with a heavy object, especially a club²(1): *to club somebody to death*
club³ /klʌb/ noun **1 clubs** [plural] the group (**suit**) of playing-cards with black three-leafed shapes on them: *the two of clubs* ☞ picture at **card**. **2** [C] a playing-card from this suit: *Haven't you got any clubs?*
cluck /klʌk/ noun [C] the noise made by a hen —**cluck** verb [I]
clue /klu:/ noun [C] a piece of information that helps you solve a problem, answer a question, etc: *The police were looking for clues to his disappearance.* ○ *the clues for solving a crossword puzzle* ☞ picture at **crossword**.
(IDIOM) **not have a clue** (*informal*) to know

clump /klʌmp/ noun [C] a small group of plants or trees, growing together

clumsy /'klʌmzi/ adj (**clumsier**; **clumsiest**) **1** (used about a person) careless or awkward and likely to drop things or do things badly: *I'm afraid I've broken the glass – it was very clumsy of me.* ○ *She undid the parcel with clumsy fingers.* **2** (used about a remark, etc) not showing enough understanding of the feelings of other people; likely to upset or offend people: *He made a clumsy apology.* ○ *her clumsy attempts at humour* **3** large, awkward to use, and not attractive in design: *a clumsy piece of furniture* —**clumsily** adv —**clumsiness** noun [U]

clung pt, pp of CLING

cluster /'klʌstə(r)/ noun [C] a group of people, plants or things that stand or grow close together: *a cluster of schoolchildren* ○ *a cluster of berries*
cluster verb
(PHRASAL VERB) **cluster/be clustered round sb/sth** to form a group around sb/sth: *The tourists clustered around their guide.*

clutch /klʌtʃ/ verb [T] to hold sth tightly, especially because you are afraid or excited: *He clutched his mother's hand in fear.* ○ *The girl ran off, clutching her prize.*
(PHRASAL VERB) **clutch at sth** to try to take hold of sth: *She clutched at the money but the wind blew it away.*
clutch noun **1** [C] an act of seizing or clutching: *to make a clutch at sth* **2 clutches** [plural] the power or control of a person or group: *He fell into the enemy's clutches.* **3** [C] the part of a car that you press with your foot before you change gear; the apparatus that it is connected to: *to press/release the clutch*

clutter /'klʌtə(r)/ noun [U] things that are where they are not wanted or needed and make a place untidy: *Who left all this clutter on the table?* ○ *My desk is in such a clutter* (= so untidy) *that I can't find anything.*
clutter verb [T] **clutter sth (up)** to cover or fill sth with lots of objects in an untidy way: *Don't leave those books there – they're cluttering up the table.* —**cluttered** adj: *a cluttered desk*

☆ **coach¹** /kəʊtʃ/ noun [C] **1** a comfortable bus used for long journeys: *It's cheaper by coach than by train.* ○ *a coach trip* **2** = CARRIAGE **3** a large carriage with four wheels pulled by horses and used especially in former times: *the royal coach*

☆ **coach²** /kəʊtʃ/ noun [C] a person who trains people to compete in certain sports: *a tennis coach*
coach verb [I,T] to train or teach sb, especially to compete in a sport or pass an examination: *She is coached by a former Olympic champion.*

☆ **coal** /kəʊl/ noun **1** [U] a type of black mineral that is dug (**mined**) from the ground and is burned to give heat and energy: *a lump of coal* ○ *a coal fire* **2 coals** [plural] burning pieces of coal

'coalmine (also **pit**) noun [C] a place, usually underground, where coal is dug from the ground ☛ Look at **colliery**.

'coalminer (also **miner**) noun [C] a person whose job is to dig coal in a coalmine

coalition /ˌkəʊə'lɪʃn/ noun [C, with sing or pl verb] the joining of two or more political parties, often for a temporary period, usually in order to form a government: *a coalition between the socialists and the Green Party* ○ *a coalition government*

coarse /kɔːs/ adj **1** consisting of large, not fine pieces; rough, not smooth: *coarse salt* ○ *coarse cloth* **2** (used about a person or sb's behaviour) rude, likely to offend people; having bad manners: *His coarse remarks about women offended her.* —**coarsely** adv: *coarsely chop the onion* (= into pieces which are not too small) ○ *He laughed coarsely.*

coarsen /'kɔːsn/ verb [I,T] to become or to make sth coarse

☆ **coast¹** /kəʊst/ noun [C] the area of land that is next to or close to the sea: *After sailing for an hour we could finally see the coast.* ○ *Holidaymakers reported seeing sharks just off the coast.* ○ *It was a sunny weekend and the roads were full of people going to the coast.* ○ *Scarborough is on the east coast.*

coastal adj at or near a coast: *coastal areas* ○ *fishing in coastal waters*

'coastguard noun [C] a person or group of people whose job is to watch the sea near the coast in order to warn or help ships that are in danger or to stop illegal activities

'coastline noun [C] the edge or shape of a coast: *a rocky coastline*

coast² /kəʊst/ verb [I] **1** to move (especially down a hill) without using power **2** to achieve sth without much effort: *They coasted to victory.*

☆ **coat** /kəʊt/ noun [C] **1** a piece of clothing, usually with long sleeves, that you wear on top of other clothes to keep warm: *Put your coat on – it's cold outside.* ○ *Take off your coat and sit down.* ☛ Look at **overcoat** and **raincoat**. **2** the fur or hair covering an animal's body: *a dog with a smooth coat* **3** a layer of sth covering a surface: *The walls will probably need two coats of paint.*
coat verb [T] **coat sth (with/in sth)** to cover sth with a layer of sth: *biscuits coated with milk chocolate*

coating noun [C] a thin layer of sth that covers sth else: *a coating of dust*

'coat-hanger noun [C] = HANGER

ˌcoat of 'arms (also **arms**) noun [C] a design that is used as the symbol of a family, a town, a university, etc

coax /kəʊks/ verb [T] to persuade sb gently: *The child wasn't hungry, but his mother coaxed him into eating a little.* ○ *They coaxed the cat out of the basket.*
(PHRASAL VERB) **coax sth out of/from sb** to get sth from sb by gently persuading: *At last he coaxed a smile out of her.*

cobble¹ /'kɒbl/ (also **'cobble-stone**) noun [C] a rounded stone used (in the past) for covering

3:	ə	eɪ	əʊ	aɪ	aʊ	ɔɪ	ɪə	eə	ʊə
fur	ago	pay	home	five	now	join	near	hair	pure

the surface of streets —**cobbled** adj: cobbled streets

cobble² /'kɒbl/ verb (PHRASAL VERB) **cobble sth together** to make sth or put sth together quickly and without much care

cobbler /'kɒblə(r)/ noun [C] a person who repairs shoes

cobra /'kəʊbrə/ noun [C] a poisonous snake found in Africa and Asia

cobweb /'kɒbweb/ noun [C] a net of threads made by a spider in order to catch insects

Coca-Cola /,kəʊkə 'kəʊlə/ (also **Coke**) noun [C,U] (trade mark) a brown, sweet, non-alcoholic drink

cocaine /kəʊ'keɪn/ noun [U] a drug that some people take for pleasure but to which they can become addicted (= they cannot stop using it)

☆ **cock¹** /kɒk/ noun [C] **1** (US **rooster**) an adult male chicken: cocks crowing at dawn ☛ picture at **hen**. Look at the note at **chicken**. **2** an adult male bird of any type: a cock sparrow

cock-a-doodle-doo /,kɒk ə ,du:dl 'du:/ interj the noise made by a cock

cock² /kɒk/ verb [T] to raise or move part of the body: The horse cocked its ears on hearing the noise.
(PHRASAL VERB) **cock sth up** (Brit slang) to do something very badly and inefficiently; to spoil sth

'cock-up noun [C] (slang): What a cock-up! You'll have to start again.

cockerel /'kɒkərəl/ noun [C] a young male chicken

cockney /'kɒknɪ/ noun **1** [C] person who was born and grew up in London, especially the East End **2** [U] the way of speaking English that is typical of cockneys —**cockney** adj: a cockney accent

cockpit /'kɒkpɪt/ noun [C] **1** the part of an aircraft where the pilot sits **2** the part of a racing car in which the driver sits

cockroach /'kɒkrəʊtʃ/ (US **roach**) noun [C] a large dark brown insect, often found in dirty rooms or damp places

cocktail /'kɒkteɪl/ noun [C] **1** an alcoholic drink made from a mixture of drinks: a cocktail party **2** a mixture of small pieces of food, usually served as the first part of a meal: a prawn cocktail

cocoa /'kəʊkəʊ/ noun **1** [U] a dark brown powder made from the seeds of a tropical tree and used in making chocolate **2** [C,U] a hot drink made from this powder mixed with milk or water

coconut /'kəʊkənʌt/ noun [C,U] the large brown fruit of a tropical tree. Coconuts have very hard, hairy shells and are filled with a white liquid that you can drink. The white substance inside the shell is often eaten in sweets and cakes.

cod /kɒd/ noun [C,U] (pl **cod**) a large sea fish that you can eat

code /kəʊd/ noun **1** [C,U] a system of words, letters, numbers, etc used instead of other words, letters, etc so that messages, information, etc can be kept secret: They succeeded in breaking/cracking the enemy code (= in finding out what it was). ○ They wrote letters to each other in code. **2** [C] a group of numbers, letters, etc that is used for identifying sth: What's the code (= the telephone number) for Stockholm? ○ a bar code (= a pattern of lines printed on goods, that a computer can read) **3** [C] a set of rules for behaviour: a code of practice (= a set of standards agreed and accepted by a particular profession) ○ the Highway Code (= the rules for driving on the roads)

code verb [T] **1** to put or write sth in code(1): coded messages **2** to use a particular system for identifying things: The files are colour-coded: blue for Europe, green for Africa.

coeducational /,kəʊedʒʊ'keɪʃənl/ adj (used about a school) with both boys and girls together in the same classes

coerce /kəʊ'ɜːs/ verb [T] (formal) to force sb to do sth, eg by threatening him/her —**coercion** /kəʊ'ɜːʃn; US -ʒn/ noun [U]

coexist /,kəʊɪɡ'zɪst/ verb [I] to exist together at the same time or in the same place: Is it possible for these different ethnic groups to coexist peacefully? —**coexistence** noun [U]

☆ **coffee** /'kɒfɪ; US 'kɔːfɪ/ noun **1** [U] the roasted seeds of a tropical tree, made into powder and used for making a drink: Coffee is the country's biggest export. **2** [U] a drink made by adding hot water to this: Would you prefer tea or coffee? ○ a cup of coffee **3** [C] a cup of this drink: Two coffees please.

☛ Black coffee is made without milk; white coffee is with milk. Decaffeinated coffee has had the caffeine taken out. Coffee can be weak or strong. Instant coffee is made by pouring hot water or milk onto coffee powder.

'coffee-table noun [C] a small low table, usually in a living-room

coffin /'kɒfɪn/ noun [C] a box in which a dead body is buried ☛ Look at the note at **funeral**.

cog /kɒɡ/ noun [C] one of the tooth-shaped parts on the edge of a wheel in a piece of machinery. The cogs fit into those on another wheel so that, as it moves, the other wheel moves too.

cognac /'kɒnjæk/ noun **1** [U] a type of brandy (a strong alcoholic drink) made in France **2** [C] a glass of this brandy

cohabit /kəʊ'hæbɪt/ verb [I] (formal) (used about an unmarried couple) to live together as if they were married

coherent /,kəʊ'hɪərənt/ adj connected in a way that makes sense; clear and easy to understand: a coherent plan —**coherence** noun [U] —**coherently** adv

cohesion /kəʊ'hiːʒn/ noun [U] the ability to stay or fit together well: What the team lacks is cohesion—all the players play as individuals.

coil /kɔɪl/ verb [I,T] to wind sth into a round shape: The snake coiled itself round a tree. ○ He coiled up the cable and put it into his tool bag.

coil noun [C] **1** a length of rope, wire, etc that has been wound into a round shape: a coil of rope **2** a small piece of plastic or metal that a woman can wear inside her body to prevent her becoming pregnant

☆ **coin** /kɔɪn/ noun [C] a piece of money made of metal: *a pound coin* ☞ picture at **money**.
coin verb [T] to invent a new word or phrase: *Who was it who coined the phrase 'a week is a long time in politics'?*
coinage noun [U] the system of coins used in a country: *decimal coinage*
coincide /ˌkəʊɪnˈsaɪd/ verb [I] **coincide (with sth) 1** (used about events) to happen at the same time as sth else: *The Queen's visit is timed to coincide with the country's centenary celebrations.* **2** to be exactly the same or very similar: *Our views coincide completely.*
coincidence /kəʊˈɪnsɪdəns/ noun [C,U] the surprising fact of two or more similar things happening at the same time by chance; an occasion when this happens: *By an incredible coincidence I found myself sitting next to someone I hadn't seen for years.* ○ *We hadn't planned to meet, it was just coincidence.*
coincidental /kəʊˌɪnsɪˈdentl/ adj resulting from two similar or related events happening at the same time by chance —**coincidentally** adv
coke /kəʊk/ noun [U] a solid black substance produced from coal and used as a fuel
Coke /kəʊk/ noun [C,U] (trade mark) = COCA-COLA
cola /ˈkəʊlə/ noun [C] a brown, sweet non-alcoholic drink such as Coca-Cola or Pepsi-Cola; a glass, can, etc of this
colander /ˈkʌləndə(r)/ noun [C] a metal or plastic bowl with a lot of small holes in it, used for draining water from food
☆ **cold**[1] /kəʊld/ adj **1** having a low temperature; not hot or warm: *If I were you, I'd put a coat on. It's cold outside.* ○ *I'm not going into the sea, the water's too cold.* ○ *Shall I put the heating on? I'm cold.* ☞ Compare **cold**, **hot**, **cool**, and **warm**. **Cold** indicates a lower temperature than **cool** and may describe a temperature that is unpleasantly low: *a terribly cold winter.* **Cool** means 'fairly cold' and may describe a pleasantly low temperature: *It's terribly hot outside but it's nice and cool in here.* **Hot** indicates a higher temperature than **warm** and may describe a temperature that is unpleasantly high: *I can't drink this yet, it's too hot.* **Warm** means 'fairly hot' and may describe a pleasantly high temperature: *Come and sit by the fire, you'll soon get warm again.* **2** (used about food or drink) not heated or cooked; having become cold after being heated or cooked: *I don't feel like coffee, I'd rather have a cold drink.* ○ *Have your soup before it gets cold.* **3** (used about a person or sb's behaviour) very unfriendly; not showing kindness, sympathy, etc: *She gave him a cold, hard look.*
(IDIOMS) **get/have cold feet** (informal) to become/be afraid to do sth: *She started to get cold feet as her wedding day approached.*
in cold blood cruelly and without pity: *to kill sb in cold blood*
coldly adv in an unfriendly way; in a way that shows no kindness or sympathy: *He looked at her coldly and did not reply.*
coldness noun [U] unfriendliness; a lack of kindness or sympathy

ˌcold-ˈblooded /-ˈblʌdɪd/ adj **1** having a blood temperature that varies with the temperature of the surroundings: *Reptiles are cold-blooded.* **2** cruel; having or showing no pity: *cold-blooded killers*
ˌcold-ˈhearted /-ˈhɑːtɪd/ adj unkind; showing no kindness, sympathy, etc
☆ **cold**[2] /kəʊld/ noun **1** (sing,U) lack of heat; low temperature; cold weather: *We walked home in the snow, shivering with cold.* ○ *He seldom wears a coat because he doesn't feel the cold.* ○ *Come on, let's get out of the cold and go indoors.* **2** [C,U] a common illness of the nose and throat. When you have a cold you sneeze a lot, you have a sore throat and often cannot breathe through your nose: *I think I'm getting a cold.* ○ *Wear some warm clothes when you go out or you'll catch cold.*
colic /ˈkɒlɪk/ noun [U] pain in the stomach area, which especially babies get
collaborate /kəˈlæbəreɪt/ verb [I] **1 collaborate (with sb)(on sth)** to work together (with sb), especially to create or produce sth: *She collaborated with another author on the book.* **2 collaborate (with sb)** to help the enemy forces who have taken control of your country ☞ This word shows disapproval.
collaboration /kəˌlæbəˈreɪʃn/ noun [U] **1** working together to create or produce sth **2** help given to enemy forces who have taken control of your country
collaborator /kəˈlæbəreɪtə(r)/ noun [C] **1** a person who works together with sb else, especially in order to create or produce sth **2** a person who helps the enemy forces who have taken control of his/her country
collage /ˈkɒlɑːʒ; US kəˈlɑːʒ/ noun [C] **1** a picture made by fixing pieces of paper, cloth, photographs, etc onto a surface **2** [U] the art of making these pictures
☆ **collapse** /kəˈlæps/ verb [I] **1** to fall down or inwards suddenly: *A lot of buildings collapsed in the earthquake.* **2** (used about a person) to fall down and perhaps become unconscious: *The winner collapsed at the end of the race.* **3** to fail or break down suddenly or completely: *The company collapsed, leaving hundreds of people out of work.*
collapse noun **1** [sing,U] a sudden fall: *the collapse of the motorway bridge* **2** [sing,U] (used about a person) falling down and perhaps becoming unconscious: *After working for so many hours without a break, I was in a state of collapse.* **3** [C,U] sudden or complete failure: *economic collapse*
collapsible adj able to be folded into a shape that makes it easy to store: *a collapsible chair*
☆ **collar** /ˈkɒlə(r)/ noun [C] **1** the part of a shirt, coat, dress, etc that fits round the neck and is often folded over ☞ picture on page A10. **2** a band of leather that is put round an animal's neck (especially a dog or cat)
collar verb [T] (informal) to catch and keep or hold sb: *She collared me during the party and asked me for advice on her problems.*
ˈcollar-bone noun [C] one of the two bones that connect the chest bones to the shoulder

s	z	ʃ	ʒ	h	m	n	ŋ	l	r	j	w
so	zoo	she	vision	how	man	no	sing	leg	red	yes	wet

☆**colleague** /'kɒli:g/ noun [C] a person that you work with in a job, especially in a profession

☆**collect** /kə'lekt/ verb **1** [T] **collect sth (up)** to bring a number of things together: *All the exam papers will be collected at the end.* **2** [I] to come together; to gather: *A crowd collected to see what was going on.* **3** [I,T] to ask for money from a number of people: *Hello, I'm collecting for a local charity. Would you like to make a contribution?* o *The landlord collects the rent at the end of each month.* **4** [T] to gather a number of objects of a particular type over a period of time as a hobby: *He used to collect stamps.* **5** [T] to go and fetch sb/sth from a particular place: *My daughter's at a party and I have to collect her in half an hour.* **6** [T] **collect yourself/sth** to get control of yourself, your feelings, thoughts, etc: *She collected herself and went back into the room as if nothing had happened.* o *I tried to collect my thoughts before the exam.*

collect adj, adv (US) (used about a telephone call) to be paid for by the person who receives the call: *a collect call* o *She called me collect because she hadn't any money.*

collected adj in control of yourself, your feelings, thoughts, etc; calm

☆**collection** /kə'lekʃn/ noun **1** [C,U] the act of getting sth from a place or from people: *The repairs won't take long and your car will be ready for collection tomorrow.* **2** [C] a group of objects of a particular type that sb has collected as a hobby: *a stamp collection* **3** [C] a number of poems, stories, letters, articles, etc published in one book: *a collection of modern poetry* **4** [C] the act of asking for money from a number of people (for charity, in church, etc): *a collection for the poor* o *The staff had a collection to buy him a present when he retired.* **5** [C] a group of people or things; a pile: *a large collection of papers on the desk*

collective /kə'lektɪv/ adj shared by a group of people together; not individual: *collective responsibility*

collective noun [C, with sing or pl verb] an organization or business that is owned and controlled by the people who work in it —**collectively** adv: *We took the decision collectively at a meeting.*

collector /kə'lektə(r)/ noun [C] (often in compounds) a person who collects things: *a stamp collector* o *a ticket collector*

☆**college** /'kɒlɪdʒ/ noun **1** [C,U] an institution where you can study after you leave school: *an art college* o *a college of education* o *He first got interested in politics when he was at college.* ☛ We talk about **college**, without **the**, when we mean that somebody is attending it as a student: *He's at college in York.* o *She's going to college in October.* but not if somebody goes there for any other reason: *I went to an art exhibition at the college last night.* **2** [C] (in Britain) one of the separate institutions which certain universities are divided: *Kings College, London* **3** [C] (in the US) a university, or part of one, where students can study for a degree

collide /kə'laɪd/ verb [I] **collide (with sb/sth)** to crash; to hit sb/sth very hard while moving: *He ran along the corridor and collided with his teacher.* o *The lorry collided with a coach but fortunately nobody was injured.*

colliery /'kɒlɪəri/ noun [C] (pl **collieries**) (especially Brit) a coalmine and its buildings

collision /kə'lɪʒn/ noun [C,U] a crash; an occasion when things or people collide: *It was a head-on collision and the driver was killed instantly.* o *The two planes were in collision with each other and exploded.*

colloquial /kə'ləʊkwɪəl/ adj (used about words, phrases, etc) used in conversation, not in formal situations or formal writing —**colloquially** /-kwɪəli/ adv

cologne /kə'ləʊn/ noun [U] = EAU-DE-COLOGNE

colon /'kəʊlən/ noun [C] a punctuation mark (:) used before a list, an explanation, an example, etc

colonel /'kɜ:nl/ noun [C] an officer with a high rank in the army

colonial /kə'ləʊnɪəl/ adj connected with or owning a colony(1): *Spain used to be a major colonial power.*

colonialism noun [U] the practice of keeping countries as colonies

colonist /'kɒlənɪst/ noun [C] a person who goes to live in a colony(1) when it is first established as one

colonize (also **colonise**) /'kɒlənaɪz/ verb [T] to take control of a place as a colony; to establish a colony in a place —**colonization** (also **colonisation**) /ˌkɒlənaɪ'zeɪʃn; US -nɪ'z-/ noun [U]: *the colonization of South America by the Spanish*

colony /'kɒləni/ noun (pl **colonies**) **1** [C] a country or area that is ruled by another, more powerful country: *Kenya used to be a British colony.* **2** [C, with sing or pl verb] a group of people from the same country living in a foreign country or city: *the English colony on the Spanish coast* **3** [C, with sing or pl verb] a group of people with the same interests, profession, etc living together in the same place: *an artist's colony* **4** [C] a group of the same type of animals, insects or plants living or growing in the same place: *a colony of ants*

color (US) = COLOUR

colossal /kə'lɒsl/ adj extremely large; huge: *a colossal building* o *a colossal amount*

☆**colour**[1] (US **color**) /'kʌlə(r)/ noun **1** [C,U] the quality that makes sth red, green, yellow, etc: *'What colour is your car?' 'Red.'* o *Brown isn't my favourite colour.* o *What colours do the Swedish team play in?* o *a dark/light colour* o *a bright colour* o *a deep/pale colour* o *Those flowers certainly give the room a bit of colour.* ☛ We say that a thing **is** a certain colour, not that it **has** a colour. **2** [U] the use of all the colours, not just black and white: *All the pictures in the book are in colour.* o *a colour television* **3** [U,sing] redness in your face, particularly showing how healthy you are: *You look much better now, you've got a bit more colour.* **4** [C,U] the colour of a person's skin, showing the person's race: *People of all colours and religions.* o *Discrimination on the grounds of colour is illegal.* **5** [U] interesting or exciting details: *It's a busy area, full of activity and colour.*

i:	ɪ	e	æ	ɑ:	ɒ	ɔ:	ʊ	u:	ʌ
see	sit	ten	hat	arm	got	saw	put	too	cup

(IDIOMS) **off colour** ill: *I didn't go out because I was feeling a bit off colour.*
with flying colours ⇨ FLYING
colourful (*US* **colorful**) /-fl/ *adj* **1** with bright colours; full of colour: *a colourful shirt* **2** full of interest or excitement: *a colourful story* ○ *He has a rather colourful past.*
colourless (*US* **colorless**) *adj* **1** without colour: *a colourless liquid, like water* **2** dull and uninteresting: *a colourless description*
'colour-blind *adj* unable to distinguish between certain colours, especially red and green
'colour scheme *noun* [C] the way in which colours are arranged, especially in a room
☆ **colour²** (*US* **color**) /'kʌlə(r)/ *verb* [T] **1** to put colour on sth, eg by painting it: *Colour the picture with your crayons.* ○ *The area coloured yellow on the map is desert.* **2** to influence thoughts, opinions, etc: *You shouldn't let one bad experience colour your attitude to everything.*
(PHRASAL VERB) **colour sth in** to fill a shape, a picture, etc with colour using pencils, chalk, etc: *The children were colouring in pictures of animals.*
coloured (*US* **colored**) *adj* **1** having colour; a particular colour: *She always writes letters on coloured paper.* ○ *a coffee-coloured dress* ○ *brightly-coloured lights* **2** (used about a person) belonging to a race that does not have white skin ☛ This word is becoming old-fashioned and may offend some people.
colouring (*US* **coloring**) *noun* **1** [U] the colour of a person's hair, skin, etc: *People with such fair colouring get sunburnt easily.* **2** [C,U] a substance that is used for giving a particular colour to sth, especially food
colt /kəʊlt/ *noun* [C] a young male horse
☆ **column** /'kɒləm/ *noun* [C] **1** a tall solid vertical post made of stone, supporting or decorating a building or standing alone **2** something that has the shape of a column: *a column of smoke* **3** one of the vertical sections into which a printed page, especially in a newspaper, is divided **4** a series of numbers written one under the other: *to add up a column of figures* **5** a piece of writing in a newspaper or magazine that is part of a regular series or written by the same writer: *the travel column* **6** a long line of people, vehicles, etc, one following behind another: *a column of troops*
columnist /'kɒləmnɪst/ *noun* [C] a journalist who writes regular articles in a newspaper or magazine: *a gossip columnist* ○ *a political columnist*
coma /'kəʊmə/ *noun* [C] a state of deep unconsciousness, often lasting for a long time and caused by serious illness or injury: *She went into a coma and a few days later she died.*
☆ **comb** /kəʊm/ *noun* **1** [C] a piece of metal or plastic with a row of teeth that you use for making your hair tidy **2** [C, usually sing] an act of combing the hair: *Give your hair a comb before you go out.*
comb *verb* [T] **1** to make the hair tidy using a comb **2 comb (through) sth (for sb/sth)** to search thoroughly: *Police are combing the area for the escaped prisoners.*
combat /'kɒmbæt/ *noun* [C,U] a fight, especially in war: *unarmed combat* (= without weapons) ○ *He got a medal for bravery in combat.*
combat *verb* [T] to fight against sth; to try to stop, reduce or defeat sth: *This government will do everything in its power to combat terrorism.*
combatant /'kɒmbətənt/ *noun* [C] a person who takes part in fighting, especially in war
☆ **combination** /ˌkɒmbɪ'neɪʃn/ *noun* [C,U] a number of people or things mixed or joined together; a mixture: *He left the job for a combination of reasons.* ○ *The team manager still hasn't found the right combination of players.* ○ *On this course, you may study French in combination with Spanish or Italian.*
☆ **combine¹** /kəm'baɪn/ *verb* **1** [I,T] **combine (with sb/sth); combine A and B/A with B** to join or mix two or more things together: *The two organizations combined to form one company.* ○ *Bad planning, combined with bad luck, led to the company's collapse.* **2** [T] **combine A and B/A with B** to do two or more things at the same time or have two or more qualities at the same time: *to combine business with pleasure.* ○ *This car combines speed and reliability.*
combined *adj* done by a number of people joining together; resulting from the joining of two or more things: *The combined efforts of the emergency services prevented a major disaster.* ○ *I use that room as a spare bedroom and office combined* (= it can be used as either).
combine² /'kɒmbaɪn/ (*also* ˌcombine 'harvester) *noun* [C] an agricultural machine that both cuts corn and separates the seed from the stem
combustion /kəm'bʌstʃən/ *noun* [U] the process of burning
☆ **come** /kʌm/ *verb* [I] (*pt* **came** /keɪm/; *pp* **come**) **1** to move to or towards the person who is speaking or the place that sb is talking about: *Come here, please.* ○ *Come and see what I've found.* ○ *I hope you can come to my party.* ○ *They're coming to stay for a week.* ○ *The children came running into the room.* **2** to arrive or reach: *What time are you coming home?* ○ *Has the newspaper come yet?* ○ *The news came as a complete surprise.* ○ *The time has come to say goodbye.* **3** to have a particular position: *March comes after February.* ○ *Charlie came second in the exam.* **4** to be available: *This blouse comes in a choice of four colours.* **5** to be produced by or from sth: *Wool comes from sheep.* **6** to become: *Your blouse has come undone.* **7 come to do sth** (used for talking about how, why or when sth happened): *How did you come to lose your passport?* **8** (used with *to/into* and a noun) to reach a particular state: *We were all sorry when the holiday came to an end.* ○ *The military government came to power in a coup d'état.*
(IDIOMS) **come and go** to be present for a short time and then go away: *The pain in my ear comes and goes.*
come easily, etc to sb to be easy, etc for sb to do: *Apologizing does not come easily to her.*

ɜː	ə	eɪ	əʊ	aɪ	aʊ	ɔɪ	ɪə	eə	ʊə
fur	ago	pay	home	five	now	join	near	hair	pure

come to nothing; not come to anything to be unsuccessful: *Unfortunately, all his efforts came to nothing.*

how come...? (*informal*) why or how: *How come you're back so early?* ○ *How come I didn't get one too?*

to come (used after a noun) in the future: *You'll regret it in years to come.*

when it comes to sth/to doing sth when it is a question of sth: *When it comes to value for money, these prices are hard to beat.*

(PHRASAL VERBS) **come about** to happen: *How did this situation come about?*

come across/over to make an impression of a particular type: *Elizabeth comes across as being rather shy.*

come across sb/sth to meet or find sb/sth by chance: *I came across this book in a second-hand shop.*

come along 1 to arrive or appear: *An old man was coming along the road.* **2** = COME ON(2) **3** = COME ON(3)

come apart to break into pieces: *This old coat is coming apart at the seams.*

come away (from sth) to become loose or unfastened: *The cover of the book is coming away* (= from the pages).

come away with sth to leave a place with a particular opinion or feeling: *We came away with a very favourable impression of Cambridge.*

come back 1 to return: *I don't know what time I'll be coming back.* **2** to become popular or fashionable again: *Flared trousers are coming back again.*

come back (to sb) to be remembered: *When I went to Italy again, my Italian started to come back.*

come before sb/sth to be more important than sb/sth else: *Mark feels his family comes before his career.*

come between sb and sb to damage the relationship between two people: *Arguments over money came between the two brothers.*

come by sth to get sth: *Fresh vegetables are hard to come by in the winter.*

come down 1 to fall down: *The power lines came down in the storm.* **2** (used about an aeroplane, etc) to land: *The helicopter came down in a field.* **3** to become lower: *The price of land has come down in the past year.*

come down to sth/to doing sth (*informal*) to have as the main feature or most important fact: *It all comes down to having the right qualifications.*

come down to sth to reach down to a particular point: *Her hair comes down to her waist.*

come down with sth to become ill with sth: *I think I'm coming down with flu.*

come forward to offer help: *The police are asking witnesses to come forward.*

come from... to live in or have been born in a place: *Where do you come from originally?*

come from (doing) sth to be the result of sth: *'I'm tired.' 'That comes from all the late nights you've had.'*

come in 1 (used about the tide) to move towards the land **2** to become popular or fashionable: *Punk fashions came in in the seventies.* **3** (used about news or information) to be received: *Reports are coming in of fighting in Beirut.*

come in for sth to receive blame, etc: *The government came in for a lot of criticism.*

come of sth/of doing sth to be the result of sth: *We've written to several companies asking for help but nothing has come of it yet.*

come off 1 to be able to be removed: *Does the collar come off?* **2** (*informal*) to be successful: *The deal seems unlikely to come off.* **3** (*informal*) (followed by an adverb) to be in a good, bad, etc situation as a result of sth: *Unfortunately, Dennis came off worst in the fight.*

come off (sth) 1 to fall off sth: *Kim came off her bicycle and broke her leg.* **2** to become removed from sth: *One of the legs has come off this table.*

come off it (*informal*) (used for showing that you do not believe sb/sth or that you strongly disagree with sb): *'I thought it was quite a good performance.' 'Oh, come off it – it was awful!'*

come on 1 to start to act, play in a game of sport, etc: *The audience jeered every time the villain came on.* ○ *The substitute came on in the second half.* **2** (also **come along**) to make progress or to improve: *Your English is coming on nicely.* **3** (also **Come on!; Come along!**) (used for telling sb to hurry up, try harder, etc): *Come on or we'll be late!* ○ *Come on! You can do better work than that.* **4** to begin: *I think I've got a cold coming on.*

come out 1 to appear: *The rain stopped and the sun came out.* ○ *The report came out in 1988.* **2** to become known: *It was only after his death that the truth came out.* **3** (used about a photograph, etc) to be produced successfully: *Only one of our photos came out.*

come out (of sth) to be removed from sth: *Red wine stains don't come out easily.*

come out against sth to say in public that you do not like or agree with sth: *The Prime Minister came out against capital punishment.*

come out in sth to become covered in spots, etc: *Heat makes him come out in a rash.*

come out with sth to say sth: *The children came out with all kinds of stories.*

come over = COME ACROSS

come over (to...) (from...) to move from one place to another: *They've invited us to come over to Australia for a holiday.*

come over sb (used about a feeling) to affect sb: *A feeling of despair came over me.*

come round 1 (used about an event that happens regularly) to happen: *The end of the holidays always comes round very quickly.* **2** (also **come to**) to become conscious again

come round (to...) to visit a person or place: *Why don't you come round to see us on Saturday?*

come round (to sth) to change your opinion so that you agree with sb/sth: *They finally came round to our way of thinking.*

come through (used about news, information, etc) to arrive: *The football results are just coming through.*

come through (sth) to escape injury or death

p	b	t	d	k	g	tʃ	dʒ	f	v	θ	ð
pen	**bad**	**tea**	**did**	**cat**	**got**	**chin**	**June**	**fall**	**van**	**thin**	**then**

in a dangerous situation, illness, etc: *to come through a heart attack*
come to = COME ROUND
come to sth 1 to equal or total a particular amount: *The bill for the meal came to £35.* **2** to reach a bad situation: *We will sell the house to pay our debts if we have to but we hope it won't come to that.*
come under to be included in a particular section, department, etc: *Garages that sell cars come under 'car dealers' in the telephone book.*
come up 1 (used about a plant) to appear above the soil **2** (used about the sun and moon) to rise **3** to be about to happen in the future: *I have an important meeting coming up next week.* **4** to be discussed: *The subject of religion came up.*
come up against sb/sth to find a problem or difficulty that you have to deal with: *The developers came up against a lot of opposition from the local residents.*
come up to sth 1 to reach up as far as a particular point: *The water in the pool came up to our knees.* **2** to be as good as usual or as necessary: *This piece of work does not come up to your usual standard.*
come up with sth to find an answer or solution to sth: *Engineers have come up with new ways of saving energy.*
'comeback *noun* [C] a return to a position of strength or importance that you had before: *The former world champion is hoping to make a comeback.*
'comedown *noun* [C, usually sing] (*informal*) a loss of importance or social position: *It's a bit of a comedown for her having to move to a smaller house.*
comedian /kə'mi:diən/ (*also* **comic**) *noun* [C] a person whose job is to entertain people and make them laugh, eg by telling jokes
comedy /'kɒmədi/ *noun* (*pl* **comedies**) **1** [C] an amusing play, film, etc that has a happy ending ☛ Look at **tragedy**. **2** [U] the quality of being amusing or making people laugh: *There is a hint of comedy in all her novels.*
comet /'kɒmɪt/ *noun* [C] an object that looks like a bright star and that moves around the sun
☆ **comfort** /'kʌmfət/ *noun* **1** [U] the state of having everything your body needs, or of having a pleasant life: *Most people expect to live in comfort in their old age.* **2** [U] the state of being relaxed: *This furniture is not designed for comfort.* **3** [U] help or kindness to sb who is suffering: *I tried to offer a few words of comfort.* **4** [sing] a person or thing that helps you when you are very sad or worried: *You've been a real comfort to me.* **5** [C] something that makes your life easier or more pleasant: *After a week's camping we really appreciated the comforts of home.* ☛ Look at **discomfort**.
comfort *verb* [T] to try to make sb feel less worried or unhappy: *to comfort a crying child*
☆ **comfortable** /'kʌmftəbl/ *US* -fərt-/ (*also informal* **comfy**) *adj* **1** allowing you to feel relaxed and providing you with everything your body needs: *Our hotel room was large and comfortable.* ○ *a comfortable temperature* (= not too hot or too cold) ○ *Sit down and make yourselves comfortable.* ☛ The opposite is **uncomfortable**. **2** not having or causing worry, pain, difficulty, etc: *He did not feel comfortable in the presence of so many women.* **3** having or providing enough money for all your needs: *They are not wealthy but they're quite comfortable.*
comfortably /-təbli/ *adv* in a comfortable way: *You can't live comfortably on such low wages.*
comfy /'kʌmfi/ *adj* (**comfier**; **comfiest**) (*informal*) comfortable(1): *a comfy chair*
comic /'kɒmɪk/ *adj* that makes you laugh; funny: *a comic scene in a serious play*
comic *noun* [C] **1** = COMEDIAN **2** a magazine for children that tells stories through pictures
comical /'kɒmɪkl/ *adj* that makes you laugh
—**comically** /-kli/ *adv*
comic 'strip (*also* **'strip cartoon**) *noun* [C] a series of pictures that tell a story, eg in a newspaper, etc
coming /'kʌmɪŋ/ *noun* [C] the arrival of sth: *The coming of the computer meant the loss of many jobs.*
comma /'kɒmə/ *noun* [C] the punctuation mark (,) used for dividing parts of a sentence or items in a list
☆ **command¹** /kə'mɑ:nd; *US* -'mænd/ *verb* **1** [I,T] to tell or order sb to do sth: *The men did as their officer had commanded.* ○ *I command you to go!* (= said by an officer, or a King, Queen, etc) **2** [T] to control or be in charge of sb/sth: *to command a ship, regiment, army, etc* **3** [T] to deserve and get sth: *The old man commanded great respect.*
commanding *adj* **1** (used about a person who commands(2) sb/sth): *Who is your commanding officer?* **2** having or showing power or authority: *to speak in a commanding tone of voice* **3** strong: *The castle occupied a commanding position at the head of the valley.*
☆ **command²** /kə'mɑ:nd/ *noun* **1** [C] an order: *The captain's commands must be obeyed without question.* **2** [U] control over sb/sth: *Who is in command of the expedition?* ○ *to take command of a situation* **3** [sing] the state of being able to do or use sth: *She has a good command of French.*
(IDIOMS) **at/by sb's command** (*formal*) because you were ordered by sb: *At the command of their officer the troops opened fire.*
be at sb's command to be ready to obey sb: *I'm completely at your command.*
commandeer /ˌkɒmən'dɪə(r)/ *verb* [T] to take control or possession of sth for military use
commander /kə'mɑ:ndə(r); *US* -'mæn-/ *noun* [C] **1** a person who controls or is in charge of sb/sth **2** (*Brit*) an officer in the Navy
commandment (*also* **Commandment**) /kə'mɑ:ndmənt; *US* -'mænd-/ *noun* [C] (*formal*) one of the ten important laws that Christian people should obey
commando /kə'mɑ:ndəʊ; *US* -'mæn-/ *noun* [C] (*pl* **commandos** or **commandoes**) one of a group of soldiers who are trained to make quick attacks in enemy areas
commemorate /kə'meməreɪt/ *verb* [T] to keep a special event in people's memories; to

exist in order to make people remember a special event: *a statue commemorating all the soldiers who died in the last war* —**commemoration** /kə,memə'reɪʃn/ *noun* [C,U]: *The concerts were held in commemoration of the 200th anniversary of Mozart's death.*

commence /kə'mens/ *verb* [I,T] (*formal*) **commence sth/doing sth** to start or begin ☞ Look at the note at **begin**. —**commencement** *noun* [C,U]

commend /kə'mend/ *verb* [T] to say that sb/sth is very good: *Dean was commended for his excellent work.*

commendable /-əbl/ *adj* that you must praise: *She acted with commendable honesty and fairness.*

☆ **comment** /'kɒment/ *noun* [C,U] **comment (on sth)** something that you say or write that gives your opinion or feeling about sth: *The chancellor was not available for comment.* ○ *I have heard both favourable and unfavourable comments about the film.*

(IDIOM) **no comment** (used in reply to a question when you do not want to say anything at all): *'Mr President, how do you feel about these latest developments?' 'No comment.'*

comment *verb* [I,T] **comment (on sth)** to give your opinion or feeling about sth: *Several people commented on how lovely the garden looked.* ○ *Somebody commented that it didn't seem very fair.*

commentary /'kɒməntri; *US* -teri/ *noun* (*pl* **commentaries**) **1** [C,U] a spoken description on the radio or television of sth as it is happening: *the commentary on a football match* **2** [C] a written explanation of sth: *a translation of Shakespeare's plays with a commentary*

commentate /'kɒmənteɪt/ *verb* [I] to give a spoken description on the radio or television of sth as it is happening

commentator /'kɒmənteɪtə(r)/ *noun* [C] **1** a person who commentates on sth: *a sports commentator* **2** a person who gives his/her opinion about sth on the radio, on television or in a newspaper: *a political commentator*

commerce /'kɒmɜːs/ *noun* [U] the activities that are involved in buying and selling things: *the Minister for Industry and Commerce*

☆ **commercial** /kə'mɜːʃl/ *adj* **1** connected with buying and selling goods: *a specialist in commercial law* **2** making a profit: *Although it won a lot of awards, the film was not a commercial success.* —**commercially** /-ʃəli/: *The factory was closed down because it was no longer commercially viable.*

commercial *noun* [C] an advertisement on the radio or on television

commercialism /kə'mɜːʃəlɪzəm/ *noun* [U] the attitude that making a profit is more important than anything else

commercialize (*also* **commercialise**) /kə'mɜːʃəlaɪz/ *verb* [T] to try to make a profit out of sth, even if it means spoiling it: *Christmas has become very commercialized over recent years.*

commiserate /kə'mɪzəreɪt/ *verb* [I] **commiserate (with sb) (on/over sth)** (*formal*) to feel or show sympathy for sb who is very unhappy or in difficulty

commission /kə'mɪʃn/ *noun* **1** [C] an act of asking sb to do a piece of work for you: *He received a commission to write a play for the festival.* **2** often **Commission** [C, with sing or pl verb] an official group of people who are asked to find out about sth: *A Commission was appointed to investigate the causes of the accident.* **3** [C,U] money that you get for selling sth: *Agents get 10% commission on everything they sell* (= 10% of the value of the things they sell).

commission *verb* [T] to ask sb to do a piece of work: *to commission an architect to design a building*

commissioner /kə'mɪʃənə(r)/ *noun* [C] an official of high rank in an organization

☆ **commit** /kə'mɪt/ *verb* [T] (**committ**ing; **committed**) **1** to do sth bad or illegal: *to commit a crime* ○ *After years of mental illness Frank committed suicide.* **2** (*formal*) to send sb to a prison, mental hospital, etc: *He was committed to Broadmoor for five years.* **3** **commit sb/yourself (to sth/to doing sth)** to promise to do sth: *I can't commit myself to helping you tomorrow. I'm still not sure if I will be free.* **4** to decide to use sth for a particular purpose **5 commit yourself (on sth)** to say openly what you think or believe: *When asked for her opinion she refused to commit herself.* ☞ Look at **non-committal**.

commitment *noun* **1** [U] **commitment (to sth)** the state of giving a lot of your time and attention to sth because you believe it is right or important: *We are looking for a teacher with enthusiasm and commitment.* ○ *commitment to an ideal* **2** [C] something that you have promised to do; a responsibility: *Marriage is a great commitment.* ○ *We usually have family commitments on Sunday.* ○ *Japan has made a commitment to respect the new agreement.*

committed *adj* giving a lot of your time and attention to sth because you believe it is right or important: *a committed Christian*

☆ **committee** /kə'mɪti/ *noun* [C, with sing or pl verb] a group of people who have been chosen to discuss sth or decide on sth: *They have set up a committee to look into ways of reducing traffic in the city centre.* ○ *to be/sit on a committee* ○ *The planning committee meets/meet twice a week.*

commodity /kə'mɒdəti/ *noun* [C] (*pl* **commodities**) something that you buy or sell: *Salt was once a very valuable commodity.*

commodore /'kɒmədɔː(r)/ *noun* [C] an officer of middle rank in the Navy

☆ **common¹** /'kɒmən/ *adj* **1** happening or found often or in many places; usual: *Nowadays it is quite common for people to go abroad for their holidays.* ○ *The word is no longer in common use.* ○ *The daisy is a common wild flower.* **2 common (to sb/sth)** shared by or belonging to two or more people or groups, or by most or all people: *The Americans and the British share a common language.* ○ *This type of behaviour is common to most children of that age.* ○ *We have a common interest in gardening.* **3** (*only before* a noun) not special; ordinary: *The officers had much better living conditions*

iː	ɪ	e	æ	ɑː	ɒ	ɔː	ʊ	uː	ʌ
see	sit	ten	hat	arm	got	saw	put	too	cup

than the common soldiers. **4** (*informal*) having or showing a lack of education: *Don't speak like that. It's common!*
(IDIOM) **be common/public knowledge** ⇨ KNOWLEDGE

commonly *adv* often; usually: *These insects are commonly known as midges.*

,**common 'ground** *noun* [U] beliefs, interests, etc that two or more people or groups share: *They have very little common ground.*

,**common 'law** *noun* [U] laws in England that are based on decisions that judges have made, not laws that were made by Parliament

,**common-law 'wife**, ,**common-law 'husband** *noun* [C] a person who has been living with a person of the opposite sex for a long time but who is not married to him/her. A common-law wife/husband usually has the same rights as an official wife/husband.

the ,Common 'Market *noun* [sing] a name for the old European Economic Community (the EEC) ☛ This is now called the **European Community**.

'**common-room** *noun* [C] a room in a school, university, etc where students or teachers can go to relax when they are not in class

,**common 'sense** *noun* [U] the ability to make good sensible decisions because of your experience of life, not because of what you have learnt at school or from books: *Safety precautions are basically just common sense.*

common² /'kɒmən/ *noun* [C] an area of open land where the public is free to walk: *cricket on the village common*
(IDIOMS) **have sth in common (with sb/sth)** to share sth with sb/sth else: *They seem to be good friends although they have few interests in common.* ○ *to have a lot in common with sb*
in common with sb/sth like sb/sth: *This company, in common with many others, is losing a lot of money.*

commoner /'kɒmənə(r)/ *noun* [C] an ordinary person, ie not a member of a noble or royal family

commonplace /'kɒmənpleɪs/ *adj* not very exciting or unusual; ordinary: *Foreign travel has become commonplace in recent years.*

Commons /'kɒmənz/ *noun* [plural] **the Commons** (*Brit*) = THE HOUSE OF COMMONS ☛ Look at the note at **Parliament**.

Commonwealth /'kɒmənwelθ/ *noun* [sing] **the Commonwealth** the group of countries that once formed the British Empire and that try to work and to trade together in a friendly way

commotion /kə'məʊʃn/ *noun* [sing,U] great noise or excitement: *People looked out of their windows to see what all the commotion was about.*

communal /'kɒmjʊnl; kə'mju:nl/ *adj* shared by a group of people: *four bed-sits with a communal kitchen and bathroom*

commune /'kɒmju:n/ *noun* [C, with sing or pl verb] a group of people, not from the same family, who live together and share their property and responsibilities

☆ **communicate** /kə'mju:nɪkeɪt/ *verb* **1** [I,T] to make information or your opinions, feelings, etc known to sb: *Parents often have difficulty communicating with their teenage children* (= understanding them and being understood). ○ *They communicate by sign language.* ○ *to communicate news by satellite* **2** [I] **communicate (with sth)** to be joined or connected with sth: *two rooms with a communicating door*

☆ **communication** /kə,mju:nɪ'keɪʃn/ *noun* **1** [U] the act of communicating: *There is little real communication between father and daughter.* ○ *verbal/non-verbal communication* ○ *Radio is the only means of communication in remote areas.* **2** [C] (*formal*) a message: *a communication from our chairman* **3** **communications** [plural] the methods that are used for travelling to and from a place or for sending messages between places: *The telephone lines are down so communications are very difficult.*
(IDIOM) **be in communication with sb/sth** (*formal*) to be in regular contact with: *The astronauts are in direct communication with the control centre in Houston.*

communicative /kə'mju:nɪkətɪv; *US* -keɪtɪv/ *adj* willing to talk or give information: *Daphne seems shy and not very communicative.* ☛ The opposite is **uncommunicative**.

communion /kə'mju:niən/ *noun* **1 Communion** (*also* **Holy Communion**) [U] the ceremony in the Christian Church in which people share bread and wine as symbols of Christ's body and blood: *to take/go to Communion* **2** (*formal*) [U] the sharing of thoughts or feelings: *Modern man is no longer in communion with nature.*

communiqué /kə'mju:nɪkeɪ; *US* kə,mju:nə'keɪ/ *noun* [C] an official statement, especially from a government, a political group, etc

communism /'kɒmjʊnɪzəm/ *noun* [U] the political and economic system or theory in which the state owns and controls the means of production and in which everybody is supposed to be equal

communist /'kɒmjʊnɪst/ *noun* [C] a person who believes in or supports communism
—**communist** *adj*: *communist sympathies* ☛ When we are talking about a particular society or political party which is organized according to the principles of communism we often use a capital letter for **communism** and **communist**: *Russian Communism* ○ *He was a member of the Communist Party.*

☆ **community** /kə'mju:nəti/ *noun* (*pl* **communities**) **1 the community** [sing] the group of people who live in a particular place, area or country: *She was given an award for her work with young people in the community.* ○ *Recent increases in crime have disturbed the whole community.* **2** [C, with sing or pl verb] a group of people who have sth (eg nationality, interests, type of work, etc) in common: *the Asian community in Britain* ○ *the business community*

com'munity centre *noun* [C] a building where local people can take part in classes, sports, etc

commute /kə'mju:t/ *verb* [I] to travel a long distance from home to work every day: *A lot of people commute to London from nearby towns.*

—**commuter** noun [C]: *The trains are always full of commuters at this time of day.*

compact /kəmˈpækt/ adj small, neat and taking up little space: *a compact camera* ○ *The compact design of the iron makes it ideal for travel.*

compact disc /ˌkɒmpækt ˈdɪsk/ noun [C] (*abbr* **CD**) a small, round piece of hard plastic, like a record, on which sound is recorded or information stored. You play a compact disc on a special machine (**compact disc player**).

companion /kəmˈpæniən/ noun [C] a person or animal with whom you spend a lot of time or go somewhere: *They were constant companions at school.* ○ *a travelling companion* ○ *His dog is his only companion.*

companionship noun [U] friendship or company: *A lot of people get married for companionship.*

☆ **company** /ˈkʌmpəni/ noun (pl **companies**) **1** [C, with sing or pl verb] a business organization selling goods or services: *an engineering company* ○ *Is the telephone company here private or state-owned?* ○ *She applied to several companies for a job.* ○ *The company is/are planning to build a new factory in Derby.* ☛ In names company is written with a capital letter. The abbreviation is **Co**: *the Walt Disney Company* ○ *Milton & Co* **2** [U] being with a person: *I always enjoy her company because she always has amusing stories to tell.* ○ *She was very good company* (= pleasant to be with) *and I thoroughly enjoyed our evening together.* **3** [U] a visitor or visitors: *We were surprised when the doorbell rang because we weren't expecting company.* **4** [C, with sing or pl verb] a group of actors, singers, dancers, etc: *a ballet company* ○ *the Royal Shakespeare Company*

(IDIOMS) **keep sb company** to go or be with sb so that he/she is not alone: *She was nervous so I went with her to keep her company.*
part company ➔ PART²

comparable /ˈkɒmpərəbl/ adj **comparable (to/with sb/sth)** of a similar standard or size; that can be compared with sth: *A comparable flat in my country would be a lot cheaper.*

comparative /kəmˈpærətɪv/ adj **1** compared with sth else or with what is usual or normal: *He had problems with the written exam but passed the practical exam with comparative ease.* **2** involving comparing things of the same kind: *a comparative study of systems of government* **3** (*grammar*) (used about the form of an adjective or adverb) expressing a greater amount, quality, size, etc: *'Hotter' is the comparative form of 'hot'.*

comparative noun [C] (*grammar*) the form of an adjective or adverb that expresses a greater amount, quality, size, etc: *'Worse' is the comparative of 'bad'.*

comparatively adv as compared with sth else or with what is usual: *The disease is comparatively rare nowadays.* ○ *Most of the houses are old but this one was built comparatively recently.*

☆ **compare** /kəmˈpeə(r)/ verb **1** [T] **compare A and B; compare A with/to B** to consider people or things in order to find ways in which they are similar or different: *If you compare the old and the new models, you'll see the changes we've made.* ○ *When the police compared the two letters, they realized that they had been written by the same person.* ○ *Write an essay comparing Britain in the eighteenth century with Britain today.* **2** [T] **compare A to B** to say that things or people are similar in a way or ways: *When it was built, people compared the cathedral to a huge tent.* **3** [I] **compare with sb/sth** to be of the same quality as sb/sth: *Her last film was brilliant but this one simply doesn't compare.* ○ *There is nothing to compare with the taste of bread fresh from the oven.*

(IDIOM) **compare notes (with sb)** to discuss your opinions, ideas, experiences, etc with sb else: *At the beginning of term we met and compared notes about the holidays.*

compared adj **compared to/with** in comparison with; considered in relation to: *I'm quite a patient person, compared with him.* ○ *Compared to the place where I grew up, this town is exciting.*

☆ **comparison** /kəmˈpærɪsn/ noun [C,U] a act of comparing; a statement in which people or things are compared: *Put the new one and the old one side by side, for comparison.* ○ *A comparison of this year's figures with last year's shows that the economy is improving.* ○ *It's hard to make comparisons between Ian's painting and Sheila's because he's been learning so much longer.*

(IDIOMS) **by/in comparison (with sb/sth)** when compared: *He's quite tall, by comparison with some of the older boys.* ○ *In comparison with many other people, they're quite well-off.* ○ *When she told me about her problems I realized that mine were small by comparison.*
draw a comparison/a parallel ➔ DRAW²

compartment /kəmˈpɑːtmənt/ noun [C] **1** one of the separate sections into which some railway carriages are divided: *a first-class compartment* **2** one of the separate sections into which certain containers are divided: *The drugs were discovered in a secret compartment in his suitcase.* ○ *the glove compartment* (= the space where you can keep maps, etc in a car)

☆ **compass** /ˈkʌmpəs/ noun [C] **1** an instrument for finding direction, with a needle that always points north: *a ship's compass* ○ *They had to find their way back to the camp using a map and a compass.* **2 compasses** [plural] a V-shaped instrument that is used for drawing circles, etc: *a pair of compasses*

compassion /kəmˈpæʃn/ noun [U] **compassion (for sb)** sympathy or pity for sb who is suffering

compassionate /kəmˈpæʃənət/ adj having or showing sympathy or pity for sb who is suffering

compatible /kəmˈpætəbl/ adj **compatible (with sb/sth)** suitable to live together or to be used together: *As a couple, they are simply not compatible.* ○ *Is my computer compatible with yours?* ☛ The opposite is **incompatible**.
—**compatibility** /kəmˌpætəˈbɪləti/ noun [U]

compatriot /kəmˈpætriət; *US* kəmˈpeɪtriət/ noun [C] a person who comes from the same country as another

p	b	t	d	k	g	tʃ	dʒ	f	v	θ	ð
pen	bad	tea	did	cat	got	chin	June	fall	van	thin	then

compel /kəmˈpel/ verb [T] (compelling; compelled) (formal) to force sb to do sth: *I felt compelled to tell her what I really thought of her.*

compelling adj **1** very exciting; holding your attention: *a compelling story* **2** forcing sb to do sth; convincing: *I felt that there was no compelling reason to stay, so I left.* ☞ The noun is **compulsion**.

compensate /ˈkɒmpenseɪt/ verb **compensate (sb) for sth 1** [I,T] to pay sb money because you have injured him/her or lost or damaged his/her property: *To compensate for the loss of my luggage, the airline sent me a cheque.* **2** [I] to remove or reduce the bad effect of sth; to make up for sth: *His willingness to work hard compensates for his lack of skill.*

compensation /ˌkɒmpenˈseɪʃn/ noun **compensation (for sth) 1** [U] money that you pay to sb because you have injured him/her or lost or damaged his/her property: *She claimed compensation from the company for the injury she suffered while working there.* **2** [C,U] a fact or action that removes or reduces the bad effect of sth: *City life can be very tiring but there are compensations* (= good things about it). o *He took the children to the zoo as compensation for not taking them on holiday.*

compère /ˈkɒmpeə(r)/ noun [C] (*Brit*) a person who introduces the different performers in a show at the theatre or on television

compère verb [T] (*Brit*) to act as a compère

☆ **compete** /kəmˈpiːt/ verb [I] **compete (against/with sb) (for sth)** to try to win or achieve sth, or to try to be better than sb else: *The world's best athletes compete in the Olympic Games.* o *The teams are competing for a silver trophy.* o *As children, they always used to compete with each other.* o *They had to compete against several larger companies to get the contract.* o *We can't compete with overseas firms unless we improve the quality of our goods.*

competent /ˈkɒmpɪtənt/ adj **1** having the ability or skill needed for sth: *a highly competent player* o *She is competent at her job.* o *He is not competent to be a manager.* ☞ The opposite is **incompetent**. **2** satisfactory but not excellent: *a competent, but not particularly exciting, performance*

competence /ˈkɒmpɪtəns/ noun [U] having the ability or skill that is needed: *She quickly proved her competence in her new position.* ☞ The opposite is **incompetence**. —**competently** adv

☆ **competition** /ˌkɒmpəˈtɪʃn/ noun **1** [C] an organized event in which people try to win sth: *She entered a competition in the newspaper and won a car.* o *They're holding a competition to find the best name for the new magazine.* o *He came second in an international piano competition.* **2** [U] a situation where two or more people are trying to achieve the same thing or gain an advantage: *There was fierce competition among the players for places in the team.* o *He is in competition with three other people for promotion.* o *Competition from the supermarkets means that many small shops have had to close.* **3 the competition** [sing, with sing or pl verb] the other people, companies, etc who are trying to achieve the same as you: *If we are going to succeed, we must offer a better product than the competition.*

competitive /kəmˈpetətɪv/ adj **1** involving people competing against each other: *The travel industry is a highly competitive business.* o *competitive sports* **2** able to be as successful as or more successful than those competing: *They are trying to make the company competitive in the international market.* o *Our prices are highly competitive* (= as low as or lower than those of the others). **3** (used about people) eager to win or to be more successful than others: *She's a very competitive player.* —**competitively** adv

competitor /kəmˈpetɪtə(r)/ noun a person, company, product, etc that is competing with another or others: *All competitors must wear a number in the race.* o *Two local companies are our main competitors.*

compile /kəmˈpaɪl/ verb [T] to collect information and arrange it in a list, book, etc: *to compile a list of addresses*

compilation /ˌkɒmpɪˈleɪʃn/ noun **1** [U] the act of compiling: *The compilation of the encyclopedia took many years.* **2** [C] something that has been compiled: *The record is a compilation of the band's previous hits.*

complacent /kəmˈpleɪsnt/ adj feeling so satisfied with yourself or with the situation that you think (perhaps wrongly) that there is no need to worry: *He had won his matches so easily that he was in danger of becoming complacent.* —**complacency** /kəmˈpleɪsnsi/ noun [U]: *We have achieved a high standard but there is no cause for complacency. We can still improve.* —**complacently** adv: *We had complacently assumed that it was not our problem.*

☆ **complain** /kəmˈpleɪn/ verb **1** [I,T] **complain (about sth); complain (that...)** to say that you are not satisfied with or happy about sth: *I wish you wouldn't keep complaining.* o *People are always complaining about the weather.* o *We complained to the hotel manager that the room was too noisy.* ☞ Look at the notes at **grumble** and **protest**. **2** [I] **complain of sth** to say that you have a pain or illness: *He went to the doctor, complaining of chest pains.*

☆ **complaint** /kəmˈpleɪnt/ noun **complaint (about sth); complaint (that...) 1** [U] an act or acts of complaining: *I wrote a letter of complaint to the manager about the service I had received.* o *a cause for complaint* **2** [C] a statement that you are not satisfied with sth: *You should make a complaint to the company that made the machine.* **3** [C] an illness or disease: *a heart complaint* o *minor complaints*

complement /ˈkɒmplɪmənt/ noun **1** a thing that goes perfectly well with sth else: *A cream sauce is the perfect complement to this dessert.* **2** the total number that makes a group complete: *Without a full complement of players, the team will not be able to take part in the match.* **3** (*grammar*) a word or words, especially a noun or adjective, used after a verb such as 'be' or 'become' and describing the subject of that verb: *In 'He's friendly' and 'He's a fool', 'friendly' and 'fool' are complements.*

complement *verb* [T] to go together well with: *The colours of the furniture and the carpet complement each other.*

complementary /ˌkɒmplɪˈmentri/ *adj* going together well with sth; adding sth which the other thing does not have: *They work well together because their skills are complementary: he's practical and she's creative.*

☆ **complete¹** /kəmˈpliːt/ *adj* **1** having or including all parts; with nothing missing: *I gave a complete list of the stolen items to the police.* ○ *a complete set of Dickens' novels* ○ *The book explains the complete history of the place.* **2** (not before a noun) finished or ended: *The repair work should be complete by Friday.* **3** (only *before* a noun) as great as is possible; total; in every way: *the complete reorganization of the department* ○ *It was a complete waste of time.*

completely *adv* as much as is possible; totally; in every way: *The building was completely destroyed by fire.* ○ *We're trying a completely new method.* —**completeness** *noun* [U]

☆ **complete²** /kəmˈpliːt/ *verb* [T] **1** to make sth whole: *We need two more players to complete the team.* ○ *I finally managed to complete my collection.* **2** to finish sth; to bring sth to an end: *When the building has been completed, it will look impressive.* ○ *He completed his teacher training course in June 1991.* **3** to fill in sth (eg a form): *Please complete the following in capital letters.* ○ *Completed application forms should be received by December 9th.*

completion /kəmˈpliːʃn/ *noun* [U] the act of completing or the state of being complete: *The new motorway is due for completion within two years.*

☆ **complex¹** /ˈkɒmpleks; *US* kəmˈpleks/ *adj* made up of several connected parts and often difficult to understand; complicated: *a complex system of taxation* ○ *You can't expect to find a simple solution when the problem is so complex.*

complexity /kəmˈpleksəti/ *noun* (*pl* **complexities**) **1** [U] the state of being complex: *an issue of great complexity* **2** [C] one of the many details that make sth complicated: *I haven't time to explain the complexities of the chemical process now.*

complex² /ˈkɒmpleks/ *noun* [C] **1** a group or set of things, especially buildings, designed for a particular purpose: *a shopping complex* ○ *a sports complex* **2 a complex (about sth)** a mental problem that causes sb to worry or be upset about sth: *He's got a complex about his height.* ○ *an inferiority complex*

complexion /kəmˈplekʃn/ *noun* [C] **1** the natural colour and quality of the skin or the face: *a fair complexion* ○ *a healthy complexion* **2** [usually sing] the general nature or character of sth: *This news puts a completely different complexion on our situation.*

☆ **complicate** /ˈkɒmplɪkeɪt/ *verb* [T] to make sth difficult to understand: *Let's not complicate things by adding too many details.*

complicated *adj* difficult to understand; made up of many parts: *a novel with a very complicated plot* ○ *a complicated mathematical calculation* ○ *I can't tell you all the details now, it's too complicated.*

complication /ˌkɒmplɪˈkeɪʃn/ *noun* [C] **1** something that complicates sth: *Unless there are any unexpected complications, I'll be arriving next month.* ○ *The fact that she changed her mind was yet another complication.* **2** a new illness that you get when you are already ill

complicity /kəmˈplɪsəti/ *noun* [U] being involved, with sb else, in a crime

compliment /ˈkɒmplɪmənt/ *noun* **1** [C] **a compliment (on sth)** a statement or action that praises or expresses admiration for sb: *People have often paid her compliments on her piano playing.* **2 compliments** [plural] (*formal*) greetings or good wishes given in a message: *Tea and coffee are provided with the compliments of the hotel management* (= without charge).

compliment /ˈkɒmplɪment/ *verb* [T] **compliment sb (on sth)** to praise or express admiration for sb: *She complimented them on their smart appearance.*

complimentary /ˌkɒmplɪˈmentri/ *adj* **1** praising or expressing admiration for sb: *He made several complimentary remarks about her work.* **2** given free of charge: *a complimentary theatre ticket*

comply /kəmˈplaɪ/ *verb* [I] (*pres part* **complying**; *3rd pers sing pres* **complies**; *pt, pp* **complied**) **comply (with sth)** (*formal*) to obey an order or request: *All office buildings must comply with the fire and safety regulations.*

component /kəmˈpəʊnənt/ *noun* [C] one of the parts that together form sth, especially a machine: *car components* ○ *the components of a video recorder*

component *adj* being one of the parts that together form sth: *the component parts of an engine*

compose /kəmˈpəʊz/ *verb* **1** [I,T] to write music: *Mozart composed forty-one symphonies.* **2** [T] to produce a piece of writing, using careful thought: *I sat down and composed a letter of reply.* **3** [T] to be the parts that form sth: *the parties that compose the coalition government* **4** [T] **compose yourself/sth** to make yourself, your feelings, etc become calm and under control: *The news came as such a shock that it took me a while to compose myself.* ○ *She tried to compose her thoughts and answer calmly.*

composed *adj* **1 composed of sth** made up of sth; having as its parts: *The committee is composed of politicians from all parties.* **2** calm, in control of your feelings: *Although he felt very nervous, he managed to appear composed.*

composer /kəmˈpəʊzə(r)/ *noun* [C] a person who writes music professionally

composite /ˈkɒmpəzɪt/ *adj* consisting of different parts, substances or materials

composition /ˌkɒmpəˈzɪʃn/ *noun* **1** [C] a piece of music that has been written by sb: *'Finlandia' is probably Sibelius's best-known composition.* **2** [U] the act of composing a piece of music or writing **3** [U] the skill or technique of writing music: *She studied both musical theory and composition.* **4** [C] a short piece of writing done as part of an educational course or

iː	ɪ	e	æ	ɑː	ɒ	ɔː	ʊ	uː	ʌ
see	sit	ten	hat	arm	got	saw	put	too	cup

exam: *Write a composition of about 500 words on one of the following subjects.* **5** [U] the parts that form sth: *the chemical composition of a substance* o *the composition of the population*

compost /'kɒmpɒst/ *noun* [U] a mixture of decaying substances, such as plants and waste material, that is added to soil to help plants to grow

composure /kəm'pəʊʒə(r)/ *noun* [U] the state of being calm and having your feelings under control

compound¹ /'kɒmpaʊnd/ *noun* **1** something that consists of two or more things or substances combined: *a chemical compound* **2** (*grammar*) a word or phrase consisting of two or more parts that combine to make a single meaning: *'General election' and 'letterbox' are compounds.*

compound² /kəm'paʊnd/ *verb* [T] **1** to make sth (a problem, etc) worse **2** (usually passive) to form by combining two or more things

compound³ /'kɒmpaʊnd/ *noun* [C] an area of land with a group of buildings on it, surrounded by a wall or fence

comprehend /ˌkɒmprɪ'hend/ *verb* [T] (*formal*) to understand sth completely: *She's too young to comprehend what has happened.*

comprehensible /ˌkɒmprɪ'hensəbl/ *adj* easy to understand: *The book is written in clear, comprehensible language.* ☞ The opposite is **incomprehensible**.

comprehension /ˌkɒmprɪ'henʃn/ *noun* **1** [U] the ability to understand or the act of understanding: *How such a peculiar thing could happen is beyond my comprehension.* ☞ The opposite is **incomprehension**. **2** [C,U] an exercise that tests how well you understand spoken or written language: *a listening comprehension* o *The first part of the exam is reading comprehension.*

comprehensive /ˌkɒmprɪ'hensɪv/ *adj* **1** including everything or nearly everything that is connected with a particular subject: *a guide book giving comprehensive information on the area* o *The store offers a comprehensive range of kitchen equipment.* **2** (*Brit*) (used about education) educating pupils of all levels of ability in the same school: *a comprehensive education system*

comprehensively *adv* thoroughly; completely

compre'hensive school (*also* **comprehensive**) *noun* [C] (*Brit*) a secondary school in which pupils of all levels of ability are educated: *I went to the local comprehensive.*

compress /kəm'pres/ *verb* [T] **compress sth (into sth) 1** to press sth together so that it takes up less space **2** to express sth briefly or in a shorter form —**compression** /kəm'preʃn/ *noun* [U]

comprise /kəm'praɪz/ *verb* [T] **1** to consist of; to have as parts or members: *The set comprises a pen, pencil, ruler and rubber.* o *a house comprising three bedrooms, kitchen, bathroom and a living-room* **2** to be the parts or members that make up sth; to form: *Women comprise 62% of the staff.*

compromise /'kɒmprəmaɪz/ *noun* [C,U] a **compromise (between/on sth)** an agreement that is reached when each side allows the other side part of what it wanted: *Unless the union and the management can reach a compromise on pay, there will be a strike.* o *It's difficult to find a compromise between the protection of the countryside and the need for more housing.* o *'There can be no compromise on the subject of terrorism,' a government minister said.*

compromise *verb* **1** [I] **compromise (with sb) (on sth)** to reach an agreement by which each side gets sth it wants and allows the other side to have sth it wants **2** [T] **compromise yourself** to put yourself in a position in which other people can criticize you for not being honest: *He compromised himself by accepting money from them.* **3** [T] to do sth that is harmful to sth: *She refused to compromise her principles by signing the letter.*

compulsion /kəm'pʌlʃn/ *noun* **1** [U] forcing sb to do sth or being forced to do sth: *There is no compulsion to take part. You can decide yourself.* ☞ The verb is **compel**. **2** [C] a strong desire that you cannot control, often to do sth that you should not do

compulsive /kəm'pʌlsɪv/ *adj* **1** (used about a bad or harmful habit) caused by a strong desire that you cannot control: *compulsive eating* **2** (used about a person) having a bad habit that he/she cannot control: *a compulsive gambler* **3** so interesting or exciting that you cannot take your attention away from it: *This book makes compulsive reading.* —**compulsively** *adv*

compulsory /kəm'pʌlsəri/ *adj* that must be done, by law, rules, etc: *Maths and English are compulsory subjects on this course; Art and Music are optional.* o *It is compulsory to wear a hard hat on the building site.* ☞ Something that you do not have to do is **voluntary**.

☆ **computer** /kəm'pju:tə(r)/ *noun* [C] an electronic machine that can store and arrange information, make calculations and control other machinery: *The bills are all done by computer.* o *a computer program* o *a computer programmer* o *a home computer* o *a personal computer* o *computer software* o *computer games* o *These days the whole process is done by computer.* o *First of all, the details are fed into a computer.* ☞ picture on page A13.

computerize (*also* **computerise**) /-təraɪz/ *verb* [T] **1** to put computers in a place of work: *The whole factory has been computerized.* **2** to deal with sth by computer; to store information in a computer: *We have now computerized the library catalogue.* —**computerization** (*also* **computerisation**) /kəmˌpju:tərai'zeɪʃn; *US* -rɪ'z-/ *noun* [U]

computing *noun* [U] the skill of using computers: *She did a course in computing.*

comrade /'kɒmreɪd; *US* -ræd/ *noun* [C] **1** (used by members of a union or of a socialist party when they talk about or to each other): *Comrades, we will fight against injustice!* **2** (*formal*) a friend or companion, especially one with whom you share a difficult experience: *an old army comrade* —**comradeship**

/'kɒmreɪdʃɪp/ noun [U]: *He enjoys the comradeship of the army.*

con¹ /kɒn/ *verb* [T] (**con**ning; **con**ned) **con sb (into sth/out of sth)** (*informal*) to cheat sb, especially in order to get money: *He conned her into investing in a company that didn't really exist.*
▶ **con** *noun* [C] (*informal*) a trick, especially in order to cheat sb out of some money: *I didn't sign anything because I suspected that the whole scheme was a con.*

con² /kɒn/ *noun*
(IDIOM) **the pros and cons** ⇨ PRO

concave /'kɒŋkeɪv/ *adj* (used about a surface) curving inwards
☞ Look at **convex**.

conceal /kən'siːl/ *verb* [T] **conceal sth/sb (from sb/sth)** to hide sb/sth; to prevent sb/sth from being seen or discovered: *She tried to conceal her anger from her friend.* ○ *The film was taken with a concealed camera.* —**concealment** *noun* [U]: *the concealment of the facts of the case*

concede /kən'siːd/ *verb* [T] **1** to admit that sth is true, often unwillingly: *When it was clear that he would lose the election, he conceded defeat.* ○ *She conceded that the problem was mostly her fault.* **2 concede sth (to sb)** to allow sb to take sth, often unwillingly: *They lost the war and had to concede territory to their enemy.* ○ *Despite conceding two late goals, they still won.* ☞ The noun is **concession**.

conceit /kən'siːt/ *noun* [U] too much pride in yourself, too high an opinion of your abilities and importance
▶ **conceited** *adj* too proud of yourself, your abilities, your importance, etc: *He's so conceited – he thinks he's the best at everything!*

conceive /kən'siːv/ *verb* **1** [I,T] to become pregnant: *Tests showed that she was unable to conceive.* ○ *Their first child was conceived soon after they got married.* **2** [T] to form or think of sth (an idea, plan, etc); to imagine: *He conceived the idea for the novel during his journey through India.* ○ *I cannot conceive that she would lie to me.* **3** [I] **conceive (of) sb/sth (as sth)** to think of sb/sth in a particular way: *He started to conceive of the world as a dangerous place.* ☞ The noun is **conception**.

conceivable /-əbl/ *adj* possible to imagine or believe: *I made every conceivable effort to succeed.* ☞ The opposite is **inconceivable**. —**conceivably** /-əbli/ *adv*: *She might just conceivably be telling the truth.*

☆**concentrate** /'kɒnsntreɪt/ *verb* [I,T] **1 concentrate (sth) (on sth/doing sth)** to give all your attention or effort to sth: *How can you concentrate on your work with so much noise going on?* ○ *It is important to concentrate on the road when you are driving.* ○ *I tried to concentrate my thoughts on the problem.* **2** to come together or to bring people or things together in one place: *The general concentrated most of his tanks on the border.*

▶ **concentrated** *adj* **1** aimed at one particular point: *With another concentrated attack we should break through the enemy's defences.* **2** made stronger by the removal of some liquid: *This is concentrated orange juice. You have to add water before you drink it.*

concentration /ˌkɒnsn'treɪʃn/ *noun* **1** [U] **concentration (on sth)** the act of giving all your attention or effort to sth: *This type of work requires total concentration.* ○ *She lost her concentration when she heard a door bang.* **2** [C] **concentration (of sth)** a large amount of people or things in one place: *There are high concentrations of nitrates in the drinking water here.*

concen'tration camp *noun* [C] a prison (usually a number of buildings inside a high fence) where political prisoners are kept in very bad conditions: *Millions of Jews died in Nazi concentration camps.*

concentric /kən'sentrɪk/ *adj* (used about circles) having the same centre

☆**concept** /'kɒnsept/ *noun* [C] **concept (of sth/that...)** an idea; a basic principle: *The basic concepts of physics can be quite difficult to understand.* ○ *The concept that 'big is beautiful' is no longer as popular as it was.*

conception /kən'sepʃn/ *noun* [C,U] **1** the beginning of a new life inside a female person or animal: *an embryo 14 days after conception* ☞ The verb is **conceive**. **2** an idea or a plan: *We have no real conception of what people suffered during the war.*

☆**concern¹** /kən'sɜːn/ *verb* [T] **1** to affect or be of importance to sb: *The destruction of the world's forests concerns everybody in some way.* ○ *This does not concern you. Please go away.* ○ *The closure of the factory came as a shock to all those concerned.* ○ *It is important that no risks are taken where safety is concerned.* **2 concern yourself with sth** to give your attention to sth: *You needn't concern yourself with the hotel booking. The travel agent will take care of it.* **3** to worry sb: *What concerns the experts most is the increasing level of pollution in our cities.*

(IDIOMS) **as/so far as sb/sth is concerned** ⇨ FAR²

to be concerned in sth to have a connection with or be involved in sth: *She was concerned in a drugs case some years ago.*

to be concerned with sth to be about sth: *Tonight's programme is concerned with the effects of the law on ordinary people.*

▶ **concerned** *adj* **concerned (about/for sth)**; **concerned (that...)** worried or anxious: *If you are concerned about your baby's health you should consult a doctor immediately.* ☞ The opposite is **unconcerned**.

concerning *prep* about; on the subject of: *She refused to answer questions concerning her private life.*

concern² /kən'sɜːn/ *noun* **1** [U] **concern (for/about/over sb/sth)**; **concern (that...)** worry: *Following the accident there is growing concern over the safety of rail travel.* ○ *Don't worry. There is no cause for concern.* **2** [C,U] something that affects you or is of importance to you: *Edward's family problems are not my concern.* ○ *He showed great concern for the poor.* **3** [C] a company or business: *a large industrial concern*

(IDIOM) **a going concern** ⇨ GOING²

p	b	t	d	k	g	tʃ	dʒ	f	v	θ	ð
pen	bad	tea	did	cat	got	chin	June	fall	van	thin	then

concert /'kɒnsət/ *noun* [C] a performance of music: *a rock concert* ○ *The concert was held in the Albert Hall.* ○ *The orchestra is giving concerts in Liverpool, Glasgow and London.*

concerted /kən'sɜːtɪd/ *adj* done by a group of people working together: *We must all make a concerted effort.*

concertina /ˌkɒnsə'tiːnə/ *noun* [C] a musical instrument that you hold in your hands and play by pressing the ends together and pulling them apart, so that the material in the middle folds and unfolds ☛ A concertina is like a small **accordion**.

concerto /kən'tʃeətəʊ/ *noun* [C] (*pl* **concertos**) a piece of music for an orchestra with one instrument playing an important part (**solo**): *Tchaikovsky's piano concerto*

concession /kən'seʃn/ *noun* **1** [C,U] **concession (to sb/sth)** something that you agree to do or give up in order to end an argument: *Employers have been forced to make concessions to the union.* ☛ The verb is **concede**. **2** [C] a lower price for certain groups of people: *Concessions are available for students and pensioners.* **3** [C] a special right to do sth that is given or sold to sb/sth: *mining concessions*

concessionary /kən'seʃənəri; *US* -neri/ *adj* having a lower price for certain groups of people: *a concessionary fare*

conciliate /kən,sɪli'eɪt/ *verb* [I,T] to try to end a disagreement between two groups

conciliation /kən,sɪli'eɪʃn/ *noun* [U] the process of ending a disagreement: *All attempts at conciliation have failed and civil war seems inevitable.* —**conciliatory** /kən'sɪliətəri; *US* -tɔːri/ *adj*: *a conciliatory speech*

concise /kən'saɪs/ *adj* giving a lot of information in a few words; short: *He gave a clear and concise summary of what had happened.* —**concisely** *adv* —**conciseness** (*also* **concision** /kən'sɪʒn/) *noun* [U]

conclude /kən'kluːd/ *verb* **1** [I,T] (*formal*) to end or to bring sth to an end: *May I conclude by thanking our guest speaker.* ○ *The Prince concluded his tour with a visit to a charity concert.* **2** [T] **conclude sth from sth** to reach a belief or opinion as a result of thought or study: *From their studies the archaeologists concluded that the area was the site of an ancient temple.* **3** [T] **conclude sth (with sb)** to arrange or agree to sth formally: *to conclude a treaty, business deal, etc*

☆**conclusion** /kən'kluːʒn/ *noun* **1** [C, usually sing] the end: *The conclusion of the novel was quite unexpected.* ○ *to bring sth to a conclusion* ○ *The conclusion is just as important a part of your essay as the introduction.* **2** [C] **the conclusion (that...)** a belief or opinion that you reach after considering sth carefully: *We came to the conclusion that he was right.* ○ *What conclusions can you draw from her remarks?* ○ *The jury reached the conclusion that the men were guilty.* **3** [U] an act of arranging or agreeing to sth formally: *The summit ended with the conclusion of an arms-reduction treaty.*

(IDIOMS) **a foregone conclusion** ⇨ FOREGONE

in conclusion finally; lastly: *In conclusion, I would like to wish you continued success in the future.*

jump to conclusions ⇨ JUMP¹

conclusive /kən'kluːsɪv/ *adj* that shows sth is definitely true or real: *conclusive proof of sb's guilt* ☛ The opposite is **inconclusive**. —**conclusively** *adv*: *Tests can now prove conclusively who is the father of a child.*

concoct /kən'kɒkt/ *verb* [T] **1** to make sth by mixing different things together **2** to make or invent sth (an excuse, a story, etc) —**concoction** /kən'kɒkʃn/ *noun* [C,U]

concourse /'kɒŋkɔːs/ *noun* [C] a large hall or space inside a building such as a station or an airport

concrete¹ /'kɒŋkriːt/ *adj* **1** that can be touched, felt, etc; real: *a concrete object* **2** definite; particular: *Can you give me a concrete example of the behaviour you're complaining about?* —**concretely** *adv*

concrete² /'kɒŋkriːt/ *noun* [U] a hard substance made from cement mixed with sand, water, small stones (**gravel**), etc, that is used in building: *a modern office building of glass and concrete*

concrete *verb* [T] **concrete sth (over)** to cover sth with concrete

concur /kən'kɜː(r)/ *verb* [I] (**concurring**; concurred) (*formal*) **concur (with sb/sth) (in sth)** to agree

concurrent /kən'kʌrənt/ *adj* existing or happening at the same time as sth else —**concurrently** *adv*: *He will study French and Spanish concurrently.*

concuss /kən'kʌs/ *verb* [T] (often passive) to injure sb's brain by hitting his/her head: *to be badly concussed*

concussion /kən'kʌʃn/ *noun* [U] an injury to the brain that was caused by a blow to the head: *He was rushed to hospital suffering from concussion.*

☆**condemn** /kən'dem/ *verb* [T] **1** **condemn sb/sth (for/as sth)** to say strongly that you think sb/sth is very bad or wrong: *A government spokesman condemned the bombing as a cowardly act of terrorism.* **2** **condemn sth (as sth)** to say officially that sth is not good enough to use: *The building was condemned and had to be demolished.* **3** **condemn sb (to sth/to do sth)** to say what sb's punishment will be: *The murderer was condemned to death.* ○ (*figurative*) *Their poor education condemns them to a series of low-paid jobs.*

condemnation /ˌkɒndem'neɪʃn/ *noun* [C,U] the act of condemning sth; a statement that condemns: *The bombing of the airport brought condemnation from all around the world.*

condensation /ˌkɒnden'seɪʃn/ *noun* [U] small drops of liquid that are formed when warm air touches a cold surface: *On cold mornings the windows are covered in condensation.*

condense /kən'dens/ *verb* **1** [I,T] to change from gas to liquid; to make a gas change to liquid: *Steam condenses into water when it touches a cold surface.* ☛ Look at **evaporate**. **2** [I,T] to become or to make sth thicker: *condensed soup* **3** [T] **condense sth (into sth)** to

s	z	ʃ	ʒ	h	m	n	ŋ	l	r	j	w
so	zoo	she	vision	how	man	no	sing	leg	red	yes	wet

condense a piece of writing shorter: *We'll have to condense these three chapters into one.*

condescend /ˌkɒndɪˈsend/ *verb* [I] **1** to do sth that you believe is below your level of importance: *Celia only condescends to speak to me when she wants me to do something for her.* **2 condescend (to sb)** to behave towards sb in a way that shows that you think you are better or more important than him/her: *The teacher must be able to explain things at the right level for the children without condescending to them.* —**condescending** *adj*: *a condescending smile* —**condescendingly** *adv* —**condescension** /ˌkɒndɪˈsenʃn/ *noun* [U]

☆ **condition¹** /kənˈdɪʃn/ *noun* **1** [sing, U] the state that sb/sth is in: *The car is three years old but it is still in very good condition.* ○ *He looks really ill. He is certainly not in a condition to drive home.* **2** [C] something that must happen so that sth else can happen or be possible: *One of the conditions of the job is that you agree to work on Sundays.* ○ *We agreed to the conditions that the landlord laid down.* **3 conditions** [plural] a situation or circumstances: *The prisoners were kept in terrible conditions.* ○ *poor housing conditions* ○ *The weather conditions were very favourable for the expedition.* **4** [C] an illness: *to have a heart condition*
(IDIOMS) **on condition (that...)** only if: *I agreed to help on condition that I got half the profit.*
on no condition (*formal*) not at all; for no reason: *On no condition must the press find out about this.*
out of condition not very healthy; unfit: *I need to get more exercise. I'm really out of condition.*

condition² /kənˈdɪʃn/ *verb* [T] **1** to affect or control the way that sb/sth behaves: *Boys are conditioned to feel that they are stronger than girls.* ○ *to be conditioned by your environment* **2** to keep sth in a good condition: *a cream that moisturizes and conditions your skin*

conditioner /kənˈdɪʃənə(r)/ *noun* [C, U] a substance that keeps sth in a good condition: *hair conditioner*

☆ **conditional** /kənˈdɪʃənl/ *adj* **1 conditional (on/upon sth)** if sth is conditional on sth else, it can only happen if this other thing happens first; the one thing depends on the other: *My university place is conditional on my getting good marks in the exams.* **2** (*grammar*) (used about a phrase or sentence) expressing a condition: *A conditional clause usually begins with 'if' or 'unless'.* —**conditionally** /-ʃənəli/ *adv*

condolence /kənˈdəʊləns/ *noun* [C, usually pl, U] an expression of sympathy to sb whose relative or close friend has just died: *Please accept my condolences on your sister's death.*

condom /ˈkɒndəm/ (also *informal* **rubber**) *noun* [C] a rubber covering that a man wears over his penis during sexual intercourse to prevent the woman from becoming pregnant or as protection against disease

condominium /ˌkɒndəˈmɪniəm/ *noun* [C] (*US*) a flat or block of flats owned by the people who live in them

condone /kənˈdəʊn/ *verb* [T] to accept sth; not to consider sth to be wrong: *I can never condone violence – no matter what the circumstances are.*

conducive /kənˈdjuːsɪv; *US* -ˈduːs-/ *adj* **conducive (to sth)** helping or making sth likely to happen: *This hot weather is not conducive to hard work.*

conduct¹ /ˈkɒndʌkt/ *noun* [U] **1** a person's behaviour: *His conduct has always been of the highest possible standard.* ○ *a code of conduct* (= a set of rules for behaviour) **2 conduct of sth** the act of controlling or organizing sth: *She was criticized for her conduct of the bank's affairs.*

conduct² /kənˈdʌkt/ *verb* [T] **1** to lead or guide sb/sth: *a conducted tour of the cathedral* **2** to carry out or organize sth: *Tests are being conducted to find the cause of the accident.* **3** to stand in front of an orchestra and direct the musicians: *The orchestra was conducted by Karajan.* **4 conduct yourself well, badly, etc** (*formal*) to behave in a particular way **5** to allow heat or electricity to pass along or through sth: *Rubber does not conduct electricity.*

conductor /kənˈdʌktə(r)/ *noun* [C] **1** a person who stands in front of an orchestra and directs the musicians **2** (*Brit*) a person who collects the fares on a bus **3** (*US*) = GUARD²(3) **4** a substance that allows heat or electricity to pass through or along it: *Water is a good conductor.*

cone /kəʊn/ *noun* [C] **1** a solid shape that has a round base and gets narrower, making a point at the top ☛ picture at **cube**. The adjective is **conical**. **2** an object of this shape: *Orange cones marked off the area where the road-works were.* ○ *an ice-cream cone* **3** the hard fruit of a pine or a fir tree ☛ Look at **conifer**.

confectionery /kənˈfekʃənəri; *US* -ʃəneri/ *noun* [U] sweets, cakes, chocolates, etc

confederation /kənˌfedəˈreɪʃn/ *noun* [C, U] an organization of smaller groups which have joined together: *a confederation of independent republics* ○ *The Confederation of British Industry represents employers.*

confer /kənˈfɜː(r)/ *verb* (**conferring; conferred**) **1** [I] **confer (with sb) (on/about sth)** to discuss sth with sb before making a decision: *The President is conferring with his advisers.* **2** [T] **confer sth (on sb)** to give sb a special right or advantage: *Oxford University first conferred degrees on women in 1920.*

☆ **conference** /ˈkɒnfərəns/ *noun* [C] a meeting for discussion, often one held every year where representatives of a particular profession, political party, etc meet for several days to hear speeches and vote on the matters discussed: *The Conservative Party conference is held in the autumn.* ○ *an international conference on global warming* ○ *a press conference* (= when a politician, etc talks to reporters)

☆ **confess** /kənˈfes/ *verb* [I, T] **1 confess (to sth/to doing sth); confess (sth) (to sb)** to say that you have done sth bad or wrong: *The young woman confessed to the murder of her boyfriend/to murdering her boyfriend.* ○ *Frank confessed that he had stolen the car.* ○ *They confessed to their mother that they had spent all the money.* ○ *I must confess I didn't understand a*

iː	ɪ	e	æ	ɑː	ɒ	ɔː	ʊ	uː	ʌ
see	sit	ten	hat	arm	got	saw	put	too	cup

word of that talk! **2 confess (sth) (to sb)** to tell a priest or God what you have done that is bad or wrong: *to confess a sin*

confession /kənˈfeʃn/ *noun* [C,U] an act of confessing sth: *The young man made a full confession to the police.* ○ *She goes to confession (= with a priest) twice a year.*

confetti /kənˈfeti/ *noun* [U] small pieces of coloured paper that people throw at the bride and bridegroom after a wedding

confide /kənˈfaɪd/ *verb* **confide sth to sb** to tell sb sth that is secret: *She did not confide her love to anyone – not even to her best friend.* (PHRASAL VERB) **confide in sb** to talk to sb whom you trust about sth that is secret or private.

☆ **confidence** /ˈkɒnfɪdəns/ *noun* **1** [U] **confidence (in sb/sth)** trust or strong belief in sb/sth: *I have every confidence in Edith's ability to do the job.* ○ *They don't have much confidence in him.* ○ *The public is losing confidence in the government's ability to improve the economy.* **2** [U] the feeling that you are sure about your own abilities, opinion, etc: *I didn't have the confidence to tell her I thought she was wrong.* ○ *to be full of confidence* ○ *'Of course we will win,' the team captain said with confidence.* ☛ Look at **self-confidence**.
(IDIOMS) **in (strict) confidence** as a secret: *The information was given to me in the strictest confidence.*
take sb into your confidence to tell sb a secret

ˈconfidence trick *noun* [C] a way of getting money by cheating sb

☆ **confident** /ˈkɒnfɪdənt/ *adj* **confident (of sth/that...)** feeling or showing that you are sure about your own abilities, opinions, etc: *Kate feels confident of passing/that she can pass the exam.* ○ *to be confident of success* ○ *Donald has a very confident manner.* ☛ Look at **self-confident**. —**confidently** *adv*: *She stepped confidently onto the stage and began to sing.* ○ *We confidently expect an improvement in sales next year.*

confidential /ˌkɒnfɪˈdenʃl/ *adj* secret; not to be shown or told to other people: *The letter was marked 'private and confidential'.* —**confidentiality** /ˌkɒnfɪˌdenʃiˈæləti/ *noun* [U] —**confidentially** /-ʃəli/ *adv*: *We have been told confidentially that another hostage will be released soon.*

confine /kənˈfaɪn/ *verb* [T] **1 confine sb/sth (in/to sth)** to keep a person or animal in a particular place, usually a small place: *The prisoners are confined to their cells for long periods at a time.* **2 confine sb/sth/yourself to sth** to stay within the limits of sth: *Please confine your questions and comments to the topic we are discussing.*

confined *adj* (used about a space) very small: *Sailors on submarines must get used to living in confined spaces.*

confinement *noun* [U] being kept in a small space: *to be kept in solitary confinement*

confines /ˈkɒnfaɪnz/ *noun* [plural] (*formal*) the limits or outer edges of sth: *Patients are not allowed beyond the confines of the hospital grounds.*

☆ **confirm** /kənˈfɜːm/ *verb* [T] **1** to say or show that sth is true; to make sth definite: *Please confirm your telephone booking in writing.* ○ *Seeing the two of them together confirmed our suspicions.* ○ *Can you confirm that you will be able to attend?* **2** to accept sb as a full member of a Christian Church: *He was baptized as a baby and confirmed at the age of thirteen.*

confirmation /ˌkɒnfəˈmeɪʃn/ *noun* **1** [C,U] a statement that confirms sth: *We are waiting for confirmation of the report.* ○ *You will receive a written confirmation of your reservation.* **2** [C] a religious service at which a person is confirmed(2)

confirmed *adj* (only *before* a noun) fixed in a particular habit or way of life: *a confirmed bachelor*

confiscate /ˈkɒnfɪskeɪt/ *verb* [T] to take sth away from sb as a punishment: *Any cigarettes found in school will be confiscated.* —**confiscation** /ˌkɒnfɪˈskeɪʃn/ *noun* [C,U]

☆ **conflict** /ˈkɒnflɪkt/ *noun* [C,U] **1** a fight or an argument: *an armed conflict* ○ *The new laws have brought the Government into conflict with the unions.* **2** a difference between two or more ideas, wishes, etc: *When both my wife and father were taken ill, I had a serious conflict of loyalties.* ○ *a conflict of interests*

conflict /kənˈflɪkt/ *verb* [I] **A and B conflict; A conflicts with B** to disagree with or be different from sb/sth: *The statements of the two witnesses conflict.* ○ *John's statement conflicts with yours.* ○ *The two studies came up with conflicting results.*

conform /kənˈfɔːm/ *verb* [I] **conform (to sth)** **1** to obey a rule or law; to come up to a particular standard: *This building does not conform to fire regulations.* **2** to behave in the way that other people and society expect you to behave: *Children are under a lot of pressure to conform when they first start school.*

conformist /kənˈfɔːmɪst/ *noun* [C] a person who behaves in the way that people are expected to behave by society

conformity /kənˈfɔːməti/ *noun* [U] (*formal*) behaviour which conforms to rules and customs

confront /kənˈfrʌnt/ *verb* [T] **1 confront sth; confront sb with sb/sth** to think about, or to make sb think about, sth that is difficult or unpleasant: *to confront a problem, difficulty, etc* ○ *When the police confronted him with the evidence, he confessed.* **2** to stand in front of sb, eg because you want to fight him/her: *The unarmed demonstrators were confronted by a row of soldiers.*

confrontation /ˌkɒnfrʌnˈteɪʃn/ *noun* [C,U] a fight or an argument

☆ **confuse** /kənˈfjuːz/ *verb* [T] **1** (usually passive) to make sb unable to think clearly or to know what to do: *I'm a bit confused. Could you explain that again?* ○ *He confused everybody with his pages of facts and figures.* **2 confuse A and/with B** to mistake sb/sth for sb/sth else: *I often confuse Lee with his brother. They look very much alike.* ○ *Don't confuse 'comple-*

ment' with 'compliment'. **3** to make sth unclear: *The situation is confused by the fact that so many organizations are involved.*

confused *adj* **1** not able to think clearly: *When he regained consciousness he was dazed and confused.* **2** difficult to understand: *The article is very confused – I don't know what the main point is.* —**confusedly** /-ɪdli/ *adv*

confusing *adj* difficult to understand: *Her instructions were contradictory and confusing.* —**confusingly** *adv*

☆ **confusion** /kənˈfjuːʒn/ *noun* [U] **1** the state of not being able to think clearly or to know what to do: *He stared in confusion at the crowd of people in front of his house.* **2** a state of disorder: *In the panic and confusion two people were trampled to death.* ○ *Their unexpected visit threw all our plans into confusion.* **3** the act of mistaking sb/sth for sb/sth else: *To avoid confusion, all luggage should be labelled with your name and destination.* **4** the state of being uncertain or unclear: *There is still a great deal of confusion as to the true facts.*

congeal /kənˈdʒiːl/ *verb* [I,T] to become solid; to make a liquid solid: *congealed blood*

congenial /kənˈdʒiːniəl/ *adj* (*formal*) pleasant: *We spent an evening in congenial company.*

congenital /kənˈdʒenɪtl/ *adj* (used about a disease) beginning at and continuing since birth: *congenital brain damage*

congested /kənˈdʒestɪd/ *adj* so full of sth that nothing can move: *The streets of London are congested with traffic.*

congestion /kənˈdʒestʃən/ *noun* [U] the state of being very full of sth: *severe traffic congestion*

conglomerate /kənˈglɒmərət/ *noun* [C] a large firm made up of several different companies

conglomeration /kən.glɒməˈreɪʃn/ *noun* [C] a group of many different things that have been gathered together

☆ **congratulate** /kənˈgrætʃuleɪt/ *verb* [T] **congratulate sb (on sth)** to praise sb or tell sb that you are pleased about sth he/she has done: *I congratulated Sue on passing her driving test.* ○ *They sent a card to congratulate the couple on their engagement.*

☆ **congratulations** /kən.grætʃuˈleɪʃnz/ *noun* [plural] (used for praising sb or telling sb that you are pleased about sth he/she has done): *Congratulations on the birth of your baby boy!* ○ *Congratulations! Your painting has won first prize.*

congregate /ˈkɒŋgrɪgeɪt/ *verb* [I] to come together in a crowd

congregation /.kɒŋgrɪˈgeɪʃn/ *noun* [C, with sing or pl verb] a group of people who attend church

☆ **congress** /ˈkɒŋgres; *US* -grəs/ *noun* [C, with sing or pl verb] **1** a large formal meeting or series of meetings: *a medical congress* ○ *When is the Trades Union Congress held?* **2 Congress** the name in some countries (eg the USA) for the group of people who are elected to make the laws

☛ The US Congress is made up of the **Senate** and the **House of Representatives**.

congressional /kənˈgreʃənl/ *adj* connected with a congress or Congress: *a congressional committee*

conical /ˈkɒnɪkl/ *adj* having a round base and getting narrower towards a point at the top ☛ The noun is **cone**.

conifer /ˈkɒnɪfə(r); ˈkəʊn-/ *noun* [C] a tree with long, very thin leaves (**needles**) that stay green all through the year and that has hard brown fruit (**cones**) —**coniferous** /kəˈnɪfərəs; *US* kəʊˈn-/ *adj*

conjecture /kənˈdʒektʃə(r)/ *verb* [I,T] to guess about sth without real proof or evidence —**conjecture** *noun* [C,U]

conjugate /ˈkɒndʒʊgeɪt/ *verb* [T] to give the different forms of a verb —**conjugation** /.kɒndʒʊˈgeɪʃn/ *noun* [C,U]

conjunction /kənˈdʒʌŋkʃn/ *noun* [C] a word that is used for joining other words, phrases or sentences: *'And', 'but' and 'or' are conjunctions.*

(IDIOM) **in conjunction with sb/sth** together with sb/sth: *Various charities are working in conjunction with the United Nations to help the disaster victims.*

conjure /ˈkʌndʒə(r)/ *verb* [I] to do tricks by clever, quick hand movements, that appear to be magic

(PHRASAL VERBS) **conjure sth up** to cause a picture to appear in your mind: *Hawaiian music conjures up images of sunshine, flowers and sandy beaches.*

conjure sth up; conjure sth (up) from/out of sth to make sth appear quickly or suddenly

conjurer (*also* **conjuror**) /ˈkʌndʒərə(r)/ *noun* [C] a person who does clever tricks that appear to be magic ☛ Look at **magician**. —**conjuring** /ˈkʌndʒərɪŋ/ *noun* [U]: *to perform conjuring tricks*

conker /ˈkɒŋkə(r)/ (*informal*) (*Brit*) (*also* **horse chestnut**) *noun* [C] the seed of the horse chestnut tree, used in a popular children's game

☆ **connect** /kəˈnekt/ *verb* **1** [I,T] **connect (sth) (up) (to/with sth)** to be joined or linked to sth; to join or link sth to sth else: *The tunnels connect (up) ten metres further on.* ○ *This pipe connects with the main drain outside the house.* ○ *The printer is connected to the computer.* ○ *This motorway connects Oxford with Birmingham.* ○ *The plumber hasn't connected the shower up yet.* ☛ Look at **disconnect**. **2** [T] (usually passive) **connect sb/sth (with sb/sth)** to associate sb/sth with sb/sth; to consider sb/sth to be related to sb/sth else: *There was no evidence that she was connected with the crime.* ○ *Doctors believe that the increase in asthma is connected with pollution levels.* **3** [I] **connect (with sth)** (used about a bus, train, plane, etc) to arrive at a particular time so that passengers can change to another bus, train, plane, etc: *This train connects with the ferry to Le Havre.* **4** [T] **connect sb (with sb)** to link sb by telephone: *Hold the line, please. I'm just trying to connect you.*

☆ **connection** (*US* **connexion**) /kəˈnekʃn/ *noun* **1** [C,U] **connection between A and B; connection with/to sth** connecting or being

p	b	t	d	k	g	tʃ	dʒ	f	v	θ	ð
pen	bad	tea	did	cat	got	chin	June	fall	van	thin	then

connected: *There is a clear connection between crime and alcoholism.* ○ *Is there any connection between the two organizations?* ○ *What is your connection with the school? Do you work here?* **2** [C] a place where two wires, pipes, etc join together: *The radio doesn't work. There must be a loose connection somewhere.* **3** [C] a bus, train, plane, etc that leaves soon after another arrives: *Our bus was late so we missed our connection.* **4** [C, usually pl] a person that you know who is important or of high rank: *Chris got a good job because of his mother's connections.*
(IDIOMS) **in connection with sb/sth** (*formal*) about or concerning: *I am writing to you in connection with your application.*
in this/that connection (*formal*) about or concerning this/that

connive /kəˈnaɪv/ *verb* [I] **1 connive at sth** to do nothing to stop sth that is illegal or wrong **2 connive (with sb) (to do sth)** to work together with sb to do sth that is wrong

connoisseur /ˌkɒnəˈsɜː(r)/ *noun* [C] a person who knows a lot about art, good food, music, etc: *a connoisseur of modern art*

connotation /ˌkɒnəˈteɪʃn/ *noun* [C] an impression that a word gives in addition to its meaning: *'Spinster' means a single woman but it has negative connotations.*

☆ **conquer** /ˈkɒŋkə(r)/ *verb* [T] **1** to take control of an area by winning a war: *Napoleon's ambition was to conquer Europe.* ○ (*figurative*) *The young singer conquered the hearts of audiences all over the world.* **2** to defeat an enemy, an army, etc; to overcome sth: *The Spanish conquered the Incas.* ○ *She's trying to conquer her fear of flying.*
conqueror /ˈkɒŋkərə(r)/ *noun* [C] a person who has conquered(1) sth

conquest /ˈkɒŋkwest/ *noun* **1** [C,U] an act of conquering sth: *the Norman conquest* (= of England in 1066) ○ *the conquest of Mount Everest* **2** [C] an area of land that has been taken by war

conscience /ˈkɒnʃəns/ *noun* [C,U] your own feeling about whether what you are doing is right or wrong: *a clear/a guilty conscience*
(IDIOM) **have sth on your conscience** to feel guilty because of sth that you have done that was wrong

conscientious /ˌkɒnʃiˈenʃəs/ *adj* **1** (used about people) careful to do sth correctly and well: *He's a very conscientious worker.* **2** (used about actions) done with great care and attention: *conscientious work* —**conscientiously** *adv*

ˌconscientious obˈjector *noun* [C] a person who refuses to join the army, etc because he/she believes it is morally wrong to kill other people

☆ **conscious** /ˈkɒnʃəs/ *adj* **1** able to see, hear, feel, etc things; awake: *She was badly injured but conscious and able to tell the doctor what had happened.* ☛ The opposite is **unconscious**. **2 conscious of sth/that...** noticing or aware of sth: *He suddenly became conscious that someone was following him.* ○ *She didn't seem conscious of the danger.* **3** that you do on purpose or for a particular reason: *We made a conscious effort to treat both children fairly.* ☛ Look at **deliberate**. It has a similar meaning. The opposite is **unconscious**. **4** being particularly interested in or aware of sth: *Young people today are very fashion-conscious.* —**consciously** *adv*: *I have never consciously harmed another human being.*

☆ **consciousness** /ˈkɒnʃəsnɪs/ *noun* **1** [U] the state of being conscious(1); being able to see, hear, feel, etc things: *As he fell, he hit his head and lost consciousness.* ○ *She regained consciousness after two weeks in a coma.* **2** [U,sing] the state of being aware of sth: *There is growing consciousness of the need to save energy.*

conscript /kənˈskrɪpt/ *verb* [T] to make sb join the army, navy or air force: *When war broke out all the young men were conscripted.*

conscript /ˈkɒnskrɪpt/ *noun* [C] a person who has been conscripted

conscription /kənˈskrɪpʃn/ *noun* [U] the system of making sb join the army, etc

consecrate /ˈkɒnsɪkreɪt/ *verb* [T] to make a place or an object holy in a special ceremony: *The Bishop consecrated the new church.* —**consecration** /ˌkɒnsɪˈkreɪʃn/ *noun* [C,U]

consecutive /kənˈsekjʊtɪv/ *adj* coming or happening one after the other: *We have had three consecutive hot summers.* —**consecutively** *adv*

consensus /kənˈsensəs/ *noun* [sing,U] agreement among a group of people: *to reach a consensus after a long discussion* ○ *There is no consensus among experts about the causes of global warming.*

consent /kənˈsent/ *verb* [I] **consent (to sth)** to agree to sth; to allow sth to happen

consent *noun* [U] agreement; permission: *The child's parents had to give their consent to the operation.*

☆ **consequence** /ˈkɒnsɪkwəns; *US* -kwens/ *noun* **1** [C] something that follows as a result or effect of sth else: *The power station was shown to be dangerous and, as a consequence, was closed down.* ○ *The error had tragic consequences.* **2** [U] (*formal*) importance: *It is of no consequence.*

consequent /ˈkɒnsɪkwənt/ *adj* (*formal*) following as the result of sth else: *The lack of rain and consequent poor harvests have led to food shortages.* —**consequently** *adv*: *She didn't work hard enough, and consequently failed the exam.*

conservation /ˌkɒnsəˈveɪʃn/ *noun* [U] **1** not allowing sth to be wasted, damaged or destroyed: *the conservation of energy* **2** the protection of the natural world: *Conservation groups are protesting against the plan to build a road through the forest.* ☛ The verb is **conserve**.

conservationist /-ʃənɪst/ *noun* [C] a person who believes in conservation(2)

conservatism /kənˈsɜːvətɪzəm/ *noun* [U] **1** the dislike of new ideas and change **2** usually **Conservatism** the beliefs of the Conservative Party

☆ **conservative** /kənˈsɜːvətɪv/ *adj* **1** not liking change; traditional: *They have very conservat-*

s	z	ʃ	ʒ	h	m	n	ŋ	l	r	j	w
so	zoo	she	vision	how	man	no	sing	leg	red	yes	wet

ive tastes. This design is too modern for them. **2 Conservative** connected with the British Conservative Party: *Conservative voters* **3** (used about a guess, estimate, etc) cautious, not extreme; rather low: *At a conservative estimate I would say the damage will cost about £4 000 to repair.*

conservative *noun* [C] **1** a conservative(1) person **2** usually **Conservative** a member of the British Conservative Party —**conservatively** *adv*: *We have estimated the costs conservatively.*

Con'servative Party *noun* [C] one of the main political parties in Britain. The Conservative Party supports a free market and is opposed to the state controlling industry ☛ Look at **Labour Party** and **Liberal Democrats**.

conservatory /kənˈsɜːvətrɪ; *US* -tɔːrɪ/ *noun* [C] (*pl* **conservatories**) a room with a glass roof and walls often built against the outside wall of a house

conserve /kənˈsɜːv/ *verb* [T] to avoid wasting sth: *Higher charges will encourage people to conserve water.* ☛ The noun is **conservation**.

☆ **consider** /kənˈsɪdə(r)/ *verb* [T] **1 consider sb/sth (for/as sth); consider doing sth** to think about sb/sth, often before making a decision: *We must consider the matter carefully before we make our choice.* ○ *They are considering him for the part of Romeo.* ○ *She had never considered nursing as a career.* ○ *He is still considering what material to include in the book.* ○ *We're considering going to Spain for our holidays.* **2** to have sth as your opinion; to think about sb/sth in a particular way: *He considered that the risk was too great.* ○ *He considered the risk (to be) too great.* **3** to remember or pay attention to sth: *I can't just move abroad. I have to consider my family.* ○ *Be tactful. Consider how other people feel.*

☆ **considerable** /kənˈsɪdərəbl/ *adj* great in amount or size: *We had considerable difficulty in getting tickets for the flights we wanted.* ○ *A considerable number of people preferred the old building to the new one.* —**considerably** /-əblɪ/ *adv*: *This flat is considerably larger than our last one.*

considerate /kənˈsɪdərət/ *adj* careful not to upset people; thinking of others: *It was very considerate of you to offer to drive me home.* ☛ The opposite is **inconsiderate**.

☆ **consideration** /kən,sɪdəˈreɪʃn/ *noun* **1** [U] (*formal*) an act of thinking about sth carefully or for a long time: *I have given some consideration to the idea but I don't think it would work.* ○ *After careful consideration, we regret that we cannot offer you the position.* **2** [U] **consideration (for sb/sth)** the quality of thinking about other people's wishes and feelings: *You should keep your music turned down low out of consideration for your neighbours.* **3** [C] something that you think about when you are making a decision: *If he changes his job, the salary will be an important consideration.*

(IDIOM) **take sth into consideration** to think about sth when you are forming an opinion or making a decision

considering /kənˈsɪdərɪŋ/ *prep, conj* (used for introducing a surprising fact) when you think about or remember sth: *He coped with the long journey well, considering his age.* ○ *Considering you've only been studying for a year, you speak English very well.*

consign /kənˈsaɪn/ *verb* [T] (*formal*) **1** to put sb/sth in, or to send sb/sth to, a particular place **2** to send goods to sb

consignment *noun* **1** [U] sending sb/sth to a particular place **2** [C] goods that are being sent to sb/sth: *We are expecting a new consignment of bicycles very soon.*

☆ **consist** /kənˈsɪst/ *verb*
(PHRASAL VERBS) **consist in sth** to have sth as its main point or feature: *Her job consisted in welcoming the guests as they arrived.*
consist of sth to be made up of sth: *Pastry consists of flour, fat and water.* ○ *The band consists of a singer, two guitarists and a drummer.*

consistency /kənˈsɪstənsɪ/ *noun* (*pl* **consistencies**) **1** [U] the quality of being consistent (1); always having the same standard, opinions, etc: *Your work lacks consistency. Sometimes it's excellent but at other times it's full of mistakes.* ☛ The opposite is **inconsistency**. **2** [C,U] the degree of thickness or firmness that a liquid substance has: *The mixture should have a thick, sticky consistency.*

consistent /kənˈsɪstənt/ *adj* **1** always having the same opinions, standard, behaviour, etc; not changing: *You must be consistent. If you punish Jason, you must punish Paul for doing the same thing.* **2 consistent (with sth)** agreeing with or similar to sth: *I'm afraid your statement is not consistent with what the other witnesses said.* —**consistently** *adv*: *We must try to maintain a consistently high standard.*

consolation /,kɒnsəˈleɪʃn/ *noun* **1** [U] making sb feel better when they are sad: *It was some consolation to me to know that I wasn't the only one who had failed the exam.* **2** [C] a person or thing that consoles you: *Having his children near him was a great consolation when his wife died.*

console /kənˈsəʊl/ *verb* [T] to make sb happier when he/she is very sad or disappointed; to comfort sb

consolidate /kənˈsɒlɪdeɪt/ *verb* [I,T] to become or to make sth firmer or stronger: *We're going to consolidate what we've learnt so far by doing some revision exercises today.* —**consolidation** /kən,sɒlɪˈdeɪʃn/ *noun* [U]

consonant /ˈkɒnsənənt/ *noun* [C] **1** a sound that you make by partly stopping the air as it comes out through your mouth **2** a letter that represents this sound: *The letters 't', 'm', 's' and 'b' are all consonants.* ☛ Look at **vowel**.

consortium /kənˈsɔːtɪəm; *US* ˈsɔːrʃɪəm/ *noun* [C] (*pl* **consortiums** or **consortia** /-tɪə; *US* ʃɪə/) a group of companies that work closely together for a particular purpose

conspicuous /kənˈspɪkjʊəs/ *adj* easily seen or noticed: *As a tall, blond American he was very conspicuous in China.* ☛ The opposite is **inconspicuous**. —**conspicuously** *adv*: *She was conspicuously dressed in bright colours.*

conspiracy /kənˈspɪrəsɪ/ *noun* (*pl* **conspir-**

acies) 1 [U] planning sth, especially a crime, together with other people: *They were accused of conspiracy to murder.* **2** [C] a secret plan to do sth bad or illegal: *Investigators have uncovered a conspiracy to defraud the bank of thousands of pounds.*

conspire /kənˈspaɪə(r)/ *verb* [I] **1** to plan sth, especially a crime, together with other people: *A group of terrorists were conspiring to blow up the plane.* **2 conspire (against sb/sth)** to work together to produce a particular, usually bad, result for sb/sth: *When we both lost our jobs in the same week, we felt that everything was conspiring against us.*

conspirator /kənˈspɪrətə(r)/ *noun* [C] a person who conspires(1)

constable /ˈkʌnstəbl/; *US* ˈkɒn-/ *noun* [C] = POLICE CONSTABLE

constabulary /kənˈstæbjʊləri/; *US* -leri/ *noun* [C] (*pl* **constabularies**) the police force of a particular area: *the West Yorkshire Constabulary*

☆ **constant** /ˈkɒnstənt/ *adj* **1** happening or existing all the time or again and again: *The constant noise gave me a headache.* ○ *Don't lock this door. It's in constant use.* ○ *There were constant interruptions so we didn't get the work finished.* **2** that does not change: *You use less petrol if you drive at a constant speed.*

constantly *adv* always; again and again: *The situation is constantly changing.*

constellation /ˌkɒnstəˈleɪʃn/ *noun* [C] a number of stars that are considered as a group

consternation /ˌkɒnstəˈneɪʃn/ *noun* [U] surprise and worry or fear: *We stared at each other in consternation.*

constipated /ˈkɒnstɪpeɪtɪd/ *adj* not able to pass waste material easily from the bowels: *If you are constipated you should eat more fibre and fresh fruit.* —**constipation** /ˌkɒnstɪˈpeɪʃn/ *noun* [U]

constituency /kənˈstɪtjuənsi/ *noun* [C] (*pl* **constituencies**) a district which has its own Member of Parliament

constituent /kənˈstɪtjuənt/ *noun* [C] **1** a person who lives in the district for which a particular Member of Parliament is responsible **2** one of the parts of sth

constitute /ˈkɒnstɪtjuːt/ *verb* [T] (*formal*) (not in the continuous tenses) to make up or form sth: *Women constitute a high proportion of part-time workers.* ○ *The presence of the troops constitutes a threat to peace.*

constitution /ˌkɒnstɪˈtjuːʃn; *US* -ˈtuːʃn/ *noun* **1** [C] the laws or rules of a country or organization: *the United States constitution* **2** [C] (*old-fashioned*) the condition of your body; your health **3** [U] the way sth is put together

constitutional /ˌkɒnstɪˈtjuːʃənl; *US* -ˈtuː-/ *adj* connected with a constitution(1)

constrain /kənˈstreɪn/ *verb* [T] (*formal*) to set limits on sth, especially sb's freedom; to force sb to do sth

constraint /kənˈstreɪnt/ *noun* [C,U] a limit on sth, or on your freedom to do sth: *There are always some financial constraints on a project like this.* ○ *He signed the document under constraint* (= he was forced to do it).

constrict /kənˈstrɪkt/ *verb* [T] **1** to make sth tighter or narrower; to reduce sth **2** to limit a person's freedom to do sth

constriction /kənˈstrɪkʃn/ *noun* [C,U] a reduction in the space or the range of possibilities available

construct /kənˈstrʌkt/ *verb* [T] to build or make sth: *Early houses were constructed out of mud and sticks.* ☛ Construct is more formal than build.

☆ **construction** /kənˈstrʌkʃn/ *noun* **1** [U] the act or method of building or making sth: *A new bridge is now under construction.* ○ *He works in the construction industry.* **2** [C] something that has been built or made: *The new pyramid was a construction of glass and steel.* **3** [C] the way that words used together in a phrase or sentence: *a complex sentence construction* ○ *Which construction is more common – 'to dress' or 'to get dressed'?*

constructive /kənˈstrʌktɪv/ *adj* useful or helpful: *She made a number of constructive criticisms to help us to improve our work.* —**constructively** *adv*

consul /ˈkɒnsl/ *noun* [C] an official who works in a foreign city helping people from his/her country who are living or visiting there ☛ Look at **ambassador**.

consular /ˈkɒnsjələ(r)/; *US* -səl-/ *adj* connected with a consul

consulate /ˈkɒnsjələt/; *US* -səl-/ *noun* [C] the office of a consul

consult /kənˈsʌlt/ *verb* **1** [T] **consult sb/sth (about sth)** to ask sb or to look sth up in a book, etc to get information or advice: *You should consult a doctor if the symptoms get worse.* ○ *He consulted the map to find the shortest route.* **2** [I] **consult with sb** to discuss sth with sb

consultant /kənˈsʌltənt/ *noun* [C] **1** a person who gives advice to people on business, law, etc: *a firm of management consultants* **2** (*Brit*) a hospital doctor of high rank who is a specialist in a particular area of medicine

consultation /ˌkɒnslˈteɪʃn/ *noun* **1** [U] discussing sth or looking sth up in a book to get information or advice **2** [C,U] a meeting at which sth is discussed: *Diplomats met for consultations on the hostage crisis.* ○ *The measures were introduced without consultation.*

consume /kənˈsjuːm; *US* -ˈsuːm/ *verb* [T] (*formal*) **1** to use sth: *The United States imports 45% of the oil it consumes.* **2** to eat or drink sth **3** (used about fire) to destroy sth **4** (used about an emotion) to affect sb very strongly: *She was consumed by grief when her son was killed.*

consuming *adj* (only *before* a noun) that takes up a lot of your time and attention: *Sport is her consuming passion.*

☆ **consumer** /kənˈsjuːmə(r)/; *US* -suː-/ *noun* [C] a person who buys things or uses services: *Consumers should complain if they are not satisfied with the service they receive.* ○ *the rights of the consumer* ○ *Consumer spending has risen in the past few months.*

consummate /ˈkɒnsəmeɪt/ *verb* [T] (*formal*) **1** to make sth complete **2** to make a marriage legal or complete by having sexual intercourse

ɜː	ə	eɪ	əʊ	aɪ	aʊ	ɔɪ	ɪə	eə	ʊə
fur	ago	pay	home	five	now	join	near	hair	pure

containers

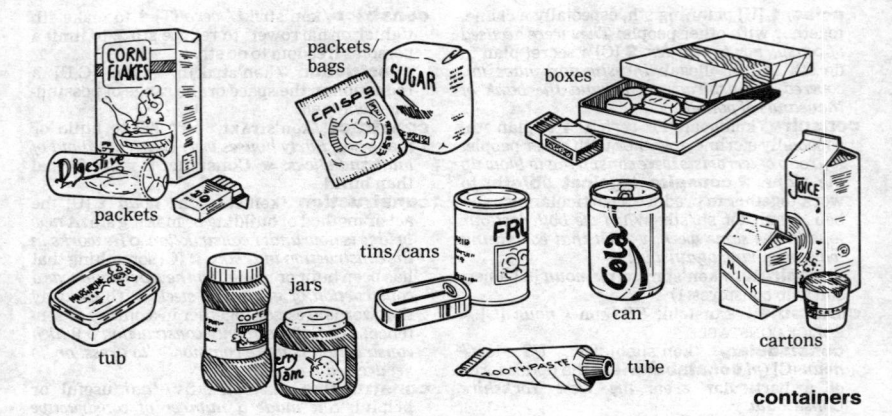

Labels: packets, packets/bags, boxes, tub, jars, tins/cans, can, tube, cartons

—**consummation** /ˌkɒnsə'meɪʃn/ noun [C,U]

consumption /kən'sʌmpʃn/ noun [U] **1** the act of using, eating, etc sth: *This fish is unfit for human consumption* (= for people to eat). **2** [U] meeting, talking to or writing to sb else: *We are in close contact with our office in New York.* o *I've lost contact with most of my old schoolfriends.* o *They are trying to make contact with the kidnappers.* o *Tom has not been in contact since he moved to Edinburgh.* o *Tom broke off contact with his family after a quarrel.* **3** [C] a person that you know who may be able to help you: *I have some useful business contacts in Berlin.*

☆ **contact** /'kɒntækt/ noun **1** [U] the state of touching sb/sth: *Don't let the wires come into contact with each other.* **2** [U] meeting, talking to or writing to sb else: *We are in close contact with our office in New York.* o *I've lost contact with most of my old schoolfriends.* o *They are trying to make contact with the kidnappers.* o *Tom has not been in contact since he moved to Edinburgh.* o *Tom broke off contact with his family after a quarrel.* **3** [C] a person that you know who may be able to help you: *I have some useful business contacts in Berlin.*

contact /'kɒntækt/ verb [T] to telephone, write to, etc sb: *Is there a phone number where I can contact you?*

'contact lens noun [C] a small piece of plastic that fits onto your eye to help you to see better ☛ picture at **glasses**.

contagious /kən'teɪdʒəs/ adj (used about a disease) that you can catch by touching sb/sth: *Smallpox is a contagious disease.* o *(figurative) contagious laughter* ☛ Look at **infectious**.

☆ **contain** /kən'teɪn/ verb [T] **1** to have sth inside (or as part of) itself: *Each box contains 24 tins.* o *petrol containing lead* **2** to keep sth within limits: *efforts to contain inflation* o *The children couldn't contain themselves – they burst out laughing.* o *She found it hard to contain her anger.* ☛ **Contain** or **include**? **Contain** is used when we are talking about objects which have other things inside them: *a jar containing olives* o *The parcel contained six books.* **Include** is used to show that several things are part of a whole or thought to belong to something: *The price of the holiday includes accommodation and evening meals but not lunch.* o *a team of seven people including a cameraman and a doctor*

☆ **container** /kən'teɪnə(r)/ noun [C] **1** a box, bottle, packet, etc in which sth is kept: *a plastic container* o *a watertight container* **2** a large metal box that is used for transporting goods by sea, road or rail: *a container lorry, ship, etc*

contaminate /kən'tæmɪneɪt/ verb [T] to add a substance which will make sth dirty, harmful or dangerous: *The town's drinking-water was contaminated with poisonous chemicals.* —**contamination** /kənˌtæmɪ'neɪʃn/ noun [U]: *There was widespread radioactive contamination of farmland after the accident at the nuclear power station.*

contemplate /'kɒntəmpleɪt/ verb [T] **1** to think about sth or the possibility of doing sth: *The idea was too awful to contemplate.* o *Before her illness she had never contemplated retiring.* **2** to look at sb/sth, often quietly or for a long time

contemplation /ˌkɒntəm'pleɪʃn/ noun [U] **1** looking at sth quietly **2** thinking deeply about sth

☆ **contemporary** /kən'temprərɪ; US -pərerɪ/ adj **1** belonging to the same time as sb/sth else: *Samuel Pepys' diary gives us a contemporary account of the Great Fire of London in 1666.* **2** of the present time; modern: *contemporary music, art, etc*

contemporary noun [C] (pl **contemporaries**) a person who lived or did sth at the same time as sb else: *Telemann, a contemporary of Bach*

contempt /kən'tempt/ noun [U] **contempt (for sb/sth)** the feeling that sb/sth does not deserve to be respected or is unimportant: *That country has shown contempt for human rights.*

contemptuous /kən'temptʃʊəs/ adj feeling or showing contempt for sb/sth

contend /kən'tend/ verb **1** [I] **contend with/against sb/sth; contend for sth** to struggle to overcome sth or to win sth: *She's had a lot of problems to contend with.* o *Two athletes are contending for first place.* **2** [T] (formal) to declare or argue that sth is true: *The young*

| p | b | t | d | k | g | tʃ | dʒ | f | v | θ | ð |
| pen | bad | tea | did | cat | got | chin | June | fall | van | thin | then |

man contended that he had never met the murdered girl.

contender noun [C] a person who takes part in a competition: *There were three contenders for the leadership.*

☆ **content¹** /kən'tent/ adj (not before a noun) **content (with sth); content to do sth** satisfied with what you have: *She is quite content to stay at home looking after her children.*

content noun [U] the state of being happy or satisfied: *His face was a picture of content.*

content verb [T] **content yourself with sth** to accept sth even though it was not exactly what you wanted: *The castle was closed, so we contented ourselves with a walk round the park.*

contented adj happy or satisfied: *The baby gave a contented chuckle.* —**contentedly** adv: *The cat purred contentedly.* —**contentment** noun [U]: *a sigh of contentment*

☆ **content²** /'kɒntent/ noun **1 contents** [plural] the thing or things that are inside sth: *Add the contents of this packet to a pint of cold milk and mix well.* o *The contents page tells you what is inside a book.* **2** [sing] the main subject, ideas, etc of a book, article, television programme, etc: *The content of the essay is good, but there are too many grammatical mistakes.* **3** [sing] the level or amount of a particular substance that sth contains: *Many processed foods have a high sugar content.*

contention /kən'tenʃn/ noun **1** [U] the situation of competing for sth: *Four players are still in contention for the cup.* **2** [U] arguing; disagreement **3** [C] your opinion; sth that you declare to be true: *The government's contention is that unemployment will start to fall next year.*

contentious /kən'tenʃəs/ adj likely to cause argument: *a contentious issue*

contest /kən'test/ verb [T] **1** to say that sth is wrong or that it was not done properly: *They contested the decision, saying that the judges had not been fair.* **2** to take part in a competition or try to win sth: *a hotly contested world-championship fight*

contest /'kɒntest/ noun [C] a competition to find out who is the best, strongest, most beautiful, etc: *a boxing contest* o *The by-election will be a contest between the two main parties.*

contestant /kən'testənt/ noun [C] a person who takes part in a contest: *Four contestants appear on the quiz show each week.*

context /'kɒntekst/ noun [C,U] **1** the words that come before or after a word, phrase, sentence, etc and that help you to understand its meaning: *You can often guess the meaning of a word from its context.* o *Taken out of context, his comment made no sense.* **2** the situation in which sth happens or that caused sth to happen: *The rise in nationalism must be seen in the context of changing attitudes in Europe.*

☆ **continent** /'kɒntɪnənt/ noun **1** [C] one of the seven main areas of land on the Earth: *Asia, Africa and Antarctica are continents.* **2 the Continent** [sing] (*Brit*) the main part of Europe, ie not the British Isles: *Hotels on the Continent are much cheaper than in Britain.*

continental /ˌkɒntɪ'nentl/ adj **1** connected with or typical of a continent: *Moscow has a* *continental climate: hot summers and cold winters.* **2** (*also* **Continental**) (*Brit*) connected with the main part of Europe: *continental holidays*

ˌcontinental 'breakfast noun [C] a breakfast of bread and jam with coffee ☛ Look at **English breakfast**.

contingency /kən'tɪndʒənsi/ noun [C] (pl **contingencies**) a possible future situation or event: *contingency plans*

contingent /kən'tɪndʒənt/ noun [C, with sing or pl verb] **1** a group of people from the same country, organization, etc who are attending an event: *the Irish contingent at the conference* **2** a group of armed forces forming part of a larger force

continual /kən'tɪnjuəl/ adj happening again and again: *His continual phone calls started to annoy her.* —**continually** adv: *She continually criticizes his behaviour.* ☛ **Continual** or **continuous?** We use **continuous** to describe an action or state that goes on without stopping: *There has been a continuous improvement in his work.* o *After climbing continuously for three hours we were exhausted.* **Continual** is used to describe something that happens repeatedly, especially something that annoys us: *They have had continual problems with the heating.*

continuation /kənˌtɪnju'eɪʃn/ noun **1** [sing,U] continuing to do sth without stopping; starting to do sth again after you have stopped **2** [sing] something that continues sth else or makes it longer: *a continuation of recent trends* o *The track was a continuation of the road.*

☆ **continue** /kən'tɪnju:/ verb [I,T] **continue (doing/to do sth); continue (with sth)** to go on, or to make sth go on, happening or existing: *If the pain continues, see your doctor.* o *They ignored me and continued their conversation.* o *He continued working/to work late into the night.* o *I shall continue with the lessons after the exam.* **2** [I,T] to begin to do or say sth again after you had stopped: *The meeting will continue after lunch.* o *I'm sorry I interrupted. Please continue.* o *The next day we continued our journey.* **3** [I,T] to go further or to make sth go further: *We continued along the path until we came to the river.* **4** [I] to remain in a particular situation or condition: *He will continue as headmaster until the end of term.*

continued adj going on without stopping: *There are reports of continued fighting near the border.*

continuity /ˌkɒntɪ'nju:əti; *US* -'nu:-/ noun [U] the state of continuing without interruption; linking one thing smoothly with the next: *The pupils will have the same teacher for two years to ensure continuity.*

☆ **continuous** /kən'tɪnjuəs/ adj happening or existing without stopping: *a period of continuous economic growth* o *a continuous process* o *There was a continuous line of cars stretching for miles.* —**continuously** adv: *It has rained continuously here for three days.* ☛ Look at the note at **continual**.

con'tinuous tense (*also* **progressive**

s	z	ʃ	ʒ	h	m	n	ŋ	l	r	j	w
so	zoo	she	vision	how	man	no	sing	leg	red	yes	wet

tense) *noun* [C] (*grammar*) the form of a verb such as 'I am waiting' or 'It was raining' which is made from a part of 'be' and a verb ending in '-ing' and is used to describe an action that continues for a period of time

contort /kən'tɔːt/ *verb* [I,T] to move or to make sth move into an unnatural shape: *His face contorted/was contorted with pain.* —**contortion** /kən'tɔːʃn/ *noun* [C]

contour /'kɒntʊə(r)/ *noun* [C] **1** the outline or shape of the outer surface of sth: *I could just make out the contours of the house in the dark.* **2** (*also* **contour line**) a line on a map joining places of equal height: *From the contour lines I could tell that there was a steep hill to climb.*

contraception /ˌkɒntrə'sepʃn/ *noun* [U] the means of preventing a woman from becoming pregnant: *Your doctor will be happy to advise you about contraception.* ○ *a reliable form of contraception*

contraceptive /ˌkɒntrə'septɪv/ *noun* [C] a pill or object that prevents a woman from becoming pregnant: *an oral contraceptive* ○ *a packet of contraceptives* —**contraceptive** *adj*: *a contraceptive pill*

☆ **contract¹** /'kɒntrækt/ *noun* [C] a written legal agreement: *They signed a three-year contract with a major record company.* ○ *The company has just won a contract to supply machinery to the government.* ○ *a temporary contract
contractual /kən'træktʃuəl/ *adj* connected with or included in a contract

contract² /kən'trækt/ *verb* **1** [I,T] to make a written legal agreement with sb to do sth or to have sb work for you: *His firm has been contracted to supply all the furniture for the new building.* **2** [T] to get an illness or disease: *She contracted pneumonia.*

contractor *noun* [C] a person or company that does work, especially building work, by contract: *a building contractor*

☆ **contract³** /kən'trækt/ *verb* [I,T] to become or to make sth smaller or shorter: *Metals contract as they cool.* ○ *'I'm' is the contracted form of 'I am.'* ☛ Look at **expand**. It is the opposite for the first example.
contraction /kən'trækʃn/ *noun* **1** [U] the process of getting smaller or of making sth smaller **2** [C] a contracted form of a word or words: *'Mustn't' is a contraction of 'must not.'* **3** [C] a strong tightening of muscles that happens to a woman as her baby is born

contradict /ˌkɒntrə'dɪkt/ *verb* **1** [I,T] to say that sth is wrong or untrue; to say the opposite of sth: *'We haven't got any tea.' 'Yes, we have,' she contradicted.* ○ *I didn't dare contradict him, but I think he was wrong.* **2** [T] (used about a statement, fact, etc) to be different from or opposite to sth: *These instructions seem to contradict previous ones.*
contradiction /ˌkɒntrə'dɪkʃn/ *noun* **1** [C] a statement or fact that is opposite to or different from another;: *There were a number of contradictions in what he told the police.* **2** [C,U] (a) **contradiction (between sth and sth)** the fact of two things being opposite to or not matching each other: *There is a contradiction between his public and private personalities.* ○ *This letter is in complete contradiction to their previous one.*
contradictory /ˌkɒntrə'dɪktəri/ *adj* being opposite to or not matching sth else: *Contradictory reports appeared in the newspapers.*

contraflow /'kɒntrəfləʊ/ *noun* [C] an arrangement where part of a wide road is closed, usually for repairs, and traffic going in both directions has to use one side of the road

contraption /kən'træpʃn/ *noun* [C] a strange or complicated piece of equipment

contrary¹ /'kɒntrəri; *US* -treri/ *adj* completely different; opposite: *I thought it was possible but she took the contrary view.*
contrary to *prep* completely different from; opposite to; against: *He's actually very nice, contrary to what people say about him.*

contrary² /'kɒntrəri; *US* -treri/ *noun*
(IDIOMS) **on the contrary** the opposite is true; certainly not: *'You look as if you're not enjoying yourself.' 'On the contrary, I'm having a great time'.*
to the contrary saying the opposite: *Unless I hear anything to the contrary, I shall assume that the arrangements haven't changed.*

☆ **contrast¹** /kən'trɑːst; *US* -'træst/ *verb* **1** [T] **contrast (A and/with B)** to compare people or things in order to show the differences between them: *It's interesting to contrast the various styles of architecture here.* ○ *The film contrasts his poor childhood with his later life as a millionaire.* **2** [I] **contrast with sb/sth** to be clearly different when compared: *The red cushions contrast dramatically with the black sofa.* ○ *This comment contrasts sharply with his previous remarks.*

☆ **contrast²** /'kɒntrɑːst; *US* -træst/ *noun* **contrast (to/with sb/sth); contrast (between A and B)** **1** [U] comparison between two people or things that shows the differences between them: *In contrast to previous years, we've had a very successful summer.* ○ *He was friendly and talkative; she, by contrast, said nothing.* **2** [C,U] a clear difference between two things or people that is seen when they are compared: *There is a tremendous contrast between the climate in the valley and the climate in the hills.* **3** [C] something that is clearly different from sth else when the two things are compared: *This house is quite a contrast to your old one!*

contravene /ˌkɒntrə'viːn/ *verb* [T] to break a law or a rule —**contravention** /ˌkɒntrə'venʃn/ *noun* [C,U]

☆ **contribute** /kən'trɪbjuːt/ *verb* **1** [I,T] to give a part of the total, together with others: *Would you like to contribute towards our collection for famine relief?* ○ *He didn't contribute anything to the conversation.* ○ *We contributed £5 each towards a retirement present for her.* **2** [I] to help to produce sth; to play a part in sth: *Every member of the team contributed to the victory.* **3** [I,T] to write articles for a magazine or newspaper
contributor *noun* [C] a person who contributes to sth

contribution /ˌkɒntrɪ'bjuːʃn/ *noun* [C,U] something that you give or do together with others; the act of giving your share: *All contri-*

iː	ɪ	e	æ	ɑː	ɒ	ɔː	ʊ	uː	ʌ
see	sit	ten	hat	arm	got	saw	put	too	cup

butions to the appeal will be gratefully received. o He made a significant contribution to the country's struggle for independence.

contributory /kənˈtrɪbjʊtəri; US -tɔːri/ adj helping to cause or produce sth: a contributory factor

contrive /kənˈtraɪv/ verb [T] **1** to plan or invent sth clever and/or dishonest **2** to manage to do or make sth, although there are difficulties
contrived adj clearly artificial or invented, not natural: The ending of the film seemed rather contrived.

☆ **control¹** /kənˈtrəʊl/ noun **1** [U] **control (of/over sb/sth)** power over sth; the ability to organize, direct or guide sb/sth: Rebels took control of the radio station. o He lost control of the car and crashed. o There's nothing I can do about the problem, it's outside my control. o I was late because of circumstances beyond my control. **2** [C,U] **(a) control (on/over sth)** a limit on sth; a way of keeping sb/sth within certain limits: price controls o crowd control **3** [C] one of the parts of a machine that is used for operating it: the controls of an aeroplane **4** [sing] the place from which sth is operated or where sth is checked: We went through passport control and then got onto the plane.
(IDIOMS) **be in control (of sth)** to be in command of sth; to have the power or ability to deal with sth: Who is in control of the project?
be/get out of control to be/become impossible to deal with or guide: The demonstration got out of control and fighting broke out.
under control being dealt with, directed or run successfully: It took several hours to bring the fire under control. o She finds it difficult to keep her feelings under control.

☆ **control²** /kənˈtrəʊl/ verb [T] (controll**ing**; controll**ed**) **1** to have power over sth or the ability to organize, direct or guide sth: One family controls the company. o Police struggled to control the crowd. o I couldn't control myself any longer and burst out laughing. **2** to keep sth within certain limits: measures to control price rises
controller noun [C] a person who directs sth: air traffic controllers

controversial /ˌkɒntrəˈvɜːʃl/ adj causing public discussion and disagreement: a controversial TV programme o a controversial new law

controversy /ˈkɒntrəvɜːsi; kənˈtrɒvəsi/ noun [C,U] (pl **controversies**) public discussion and disagreement about sth: The plans for changing the city centre caused a great deal of controversy.

conurbation /ˌkɒnɜːˈbeɪʃn/ noun [C] a group of towns that have grown and joined together

convalesce /ˌkɒnvəˈles/ verb [I] to rest and recover from an illness over a period of time
—**convalescence** /ˌkɒnvəˈlesns/ noun [sing,U] —**convalescent** /ˌkɒnvəˈlesnt/ adj

convene /kənˈviːn/ verb [I,T] to come together or to bring people together for a meeting, etc

convenience /kənˈviːniəns/ noun **1** [U] the quality of being suitable or practical for a particular purpose: a building designed for the convenience of disabled people o For convenience, you can pay for everything at once. **2** [C] something that is useful or suitable: houses with all modern conveniences **3** [C] (Brit) a public toilet: public conveniences ☛ Look at the note at **toilet**.

☆ **convenient** /kənˈviːniənt/ adj **1** suitable or practical for a particular purpose; not causing difficulty: I'm willing to meet you on any day that's convenient for you. o It isn't convenient to talk at the moment, I'm in the middle of a meeting. **2** close to sth; in a useful position: The hotel is convenient for the beach. ☛ The opposite is **inconvenient**. —**conveniently** adv: Conveniently, a bus was waiting when I got there. o She had conveniently forgotten that she owed me some money.

convent /ˈkɒnvənt; US -vent/ noun [C] a place where women (**nuns**) live in a religious community ☛ Look at **monastery**.

convention /kənˈvenʃn/ noun **1** [C] a large meeting or conference: the Democratic Party Convention **2** [C,U] a traditional way of behaving or of doing sth: A speech by the bride's father is one of the conventions of a wedding. o The film shows no respect for convention. **3** [C] a formal agreement, especially between nations: the Geneva Convention

conventional /kənˈvenʃənl/ adj following what is traditional or considered to be normal, sometimes too closely: conventional attitudes o The house was built with conventional materials but in a totally new style. o I quite like him but he's so conventional (= boring, because of this). ☛ The opposite is **unconventional**. —**conventionally** /-ʃənəli/ adv: He always dresses conventionally.

converge /kənˈvɜːdʒ/ verb [I] **converge (on sb/sth)** to move towards or meet at the same point from different directions: People from the surrounding areas converge on the village during the annual festival. o The paths converge at the bottom of the hill.

☆ **conversation** /ˌkɒnvəˈseɪʃn/ noun [C,U] informal talk: I had a long conversation with her about her plans for the future. o His job is his only topic of conversation. o They sat in the corner, deep in conversation. o She finds it difficult to make conversation (= to think of things to say).

converse /kənˈvɜːs/ verb [I] (formal) to talk informally; to have a conversation

conversion /kənˈvɜːʃn; US kənˈvɜːrʒn/ noun **(a) conversion (from sth) (into/to sth)** **1** [C,U] change from one form, system or use to another: a conversion table for miles and kilometres **2** [C,U] becoming a member of a new religion: conversion to Catholicism

convert¹ /kənˈvɜːt/ verb [I,T] **1 convert (sth) (from sth) (into/to sth)** to change from one form, system or use to another: a sofa that converts into a double bed o How do you convert pounds into kilos? o They're converting the house into four flats. **2 convert (sb) (from sth) (to sth)** to change to, or persuade sb to change to a new religion: As a young man he converted to Islam. o to convert people to Christianity

convert² /ˈkɒnvɜːt/ noun [C] **a convert (to**

ɜː	ə	eɪ	əʊ	aɪ	aʊ	ɔɪ	ɪə	eə	ʊə
fur	ago	pay	home	five	now	join	near	hair	pure

convertible /kən'vɜːtəbl/ *adj* able to be changed into another form: *a convertible sofa* (= one that unfolds to make a bed) ○ *convertible currencies* (= those that can be exchanged for other currencies)

convertible *noun* [C] a car with a roof that can be folded down or taken off

convex /'kɒnveks/ *adj* having a surface that curves outwards: *a convex lens* ☛ Look at **concave**.

convey /kən'veɪ/ *verb* [T] **1** (*formal*) to transport sb/sth from one place to another **2 convey sth (to sb)** to make ideas, thoughts, feelings, etc known to sb; to communicate sth: *The film conveys a lot of information but in an entertaining manner.* ○ *Please convey my sympathy to her at this sad time.*

con'veyor belt *noun* [C] a continuous moving belt that carries objects from one place to another, eg in a factory

convict /kən'vɪkt/ *verb* [T] **convict sb (of sth)** to declare in a court of law that sb is guilty of a crime: *He was convicted of armed robbery and sent to prison.* ○ *a convicted criminal* ☛ The opposite is **acquit**.

convict /'kɒnvɪkt/ (*formal*) *noun* [C] a person who has been found guilty of a crime and put in prison

conviction /kən'vɪkʃn/ *noun* **1** [C,U] an occasion when sb is found guilty of a crime in a court of law; the act of finding sb guilty in this way: *He has several previous convictions for burglary.* **2** [C] very strong opinion or belief: *religious convictions* **3** [U] being certain and able to convince others about what you are doing: *He played without conviction and lost easily.*

☆ **convince** /kən'vɪns/ *verb* [T] **1 convince sb (of sth/that...)** to succeed in making sb believe sth: *She convinced him of the need to go back.* ○ *I couldn't convince her that I was right.* **2 convince sb (to do sth)** to persuade sb to do sth: *The salesman convinced them to buy it.* ☛ Some people feel that this second use of 'convince' is incorrect.

convinced *adj* completely sure about sth: *He's convinced of his ability to win.* ○ *I'm convinced that she said it but she denies it.*

convincing *adj* **1** able to make sb believe sth: *Her explanation for her absence wasn't very convincing.* **2** (used about a victory) complete; clear: *a convincing win* —**convincingly** *adv*: *She argued convincingly that the law should be changed.* ○ *He won the race convincingly.*

convoy /'kɒnvɔɪ/ *noun* [C,U] a group of vehicles or ships travelling together: *a convoy of lorries* ○ *warships travelling in convoy*

convulse /kən'vʌls/ *verb* [I,T] to make sudden violent movements that you cannot control; to make sb move in this way

convulsion /kən'vʌlʃn/ *noun* [C, usually pl] a sudden violent movement of the body that you cannot control: *Children sometimes have convulsions when their temperature goes up.*

coo /kuː/ *verb* [I] **1** to make the sound that a dove or pigeon makes **2** to speak in a soft, gentle voice: *He went to the cot and cooed over the baby.*

☆ **cook** /kʊk/ *verb* **1** [I,T] to prepare food for eating by heating it: *My mother taught me how to cook.* ○ *The sauce should be cooked on low heat for twenty minutes.* ○ *He cooked us a meal.* **2** [I] (used about food) to be prepared for eating by being heated: *I could smell something cooking in the kitchen.*

☛ Food can be cooked in various ways: by **boiling** in a saucepan of hot water; by **frying** in a frying pan with hot oil or fat; or by **grilling** under a grill, which heats the food from above. We can **toast** bread under a grill or in a toaster to make it crisp and brown. Cakes and bread are **baked** in the oven, but we use the word **roast** for cooking meat or potatoes in the oven.

(PHRASAL VERB) **cook sth up** (*informal*) to invent sth that is not true: *She cooked up an excuse for not arriving on time.*

cook *noun* [C] a person who cooks: *My sister is an excellent cook.* ○ *He works as a cook in a hotel restaurant.*

cooking *noun* [U] **1** the preparation of food for eating: *Cooking is one of her hobbies.* ☛ A common way of talking about the activity of preparing food is **do the cooking**: *In our house, I do the cleaning and my husband does the cooking.* **2** food produced by cooking: *He missed his mother's cooking when he left home.*

'cookbook *noun* [C] = COOKERY BOOK

☆ **cooker** /'kʊkə(r)/ *noun* [C] a piece of kitchen equipment for cooking using gas or electricity, consisting of an oven, a flat top on which pans can be placed and often a grill

cookery /'kʊkəri/ *noun* [U] the skill or methods of cooking: *My new recipe book is called 'Chinese Cookery for Beginners'*

'cookery book (*also* **cookbook**) *noun* [C] a book of recipes and instructions for cooking

cookie (*also* **cooky**) /'kʊki/ *noun* [C] (*pl* **cookies**) (*US*) = BISCUIT

☆ **cool**[1] /kuːl/ *adj* **1** fairly cold; not hot or warm: *It was a cool evening so I put on a pullover.* ○ *This product should be stored in a cool place.* ○ *What I'd like is a nice cool drink.* ☛ Look at the note at **cold**. **2** calm; not excited or affected by strong emotions: *She always manages to remain cool under pressure.* **3** unfriendly; not showing interest: *When we first met, she was rather cool towards me, but later she became friendlier.*

cool *noun* [sing] **the cool** a cool temperature or place; the quality of being cool: *We sat in the cool of a café, out of the sun.*

(IDIOM) **keep/lose your cool** to remain

p	b	t	d	k	g	tʃ	dʒ	f	v	θ	ð
pen	bad	tea	did	cat	got	chin	June	fall	van	thin	then

calm/to stop being calm and become angry, nervous, etc

coolly /'ku:lli/ *adv* in a calm way; without showing much interest or excitement: *At first she was very angry; then she explained the problem coolly.* ○ *My offer was received rather coolly.*

coolness *noun* [U] the quality or state of being cool: *the coolness of the water* ○ *his coolness under stress* ○ *their coolness towards strangers*

☆ **cool²** /ku:l/ *verb* **1** [I,T] **cool (sth/sb) (down/off)** to lower the temperature of sth; to become cool(1): *Let the soup cool (down).* ○ *After the game we needed to cool off.* ○ *A nice cold drink will soon cool you down.* **2** [I] (used about feelings) to become less strong
(PHRASAL VERB) **cool (sb) down/off** to become or make sb calmer

cooling-'off period *noun* [C] a delay when sb is given time to think about sth

coop /ku:p/ *verb*
(PHRASAL VERB) **coop sb/sth up (in sth)** to keep sb/sth inside a small space: *The children were cooped up indoors all day because the weather was so bad.*

cooperate (*also* **co-operate**) /kəʊˈɒpəreɪt/ *verb* [I] **1** to work with sb else to achieve sth: *Our company is cooperating with a Danish firm on this project.* **2** to be helpful by doing what sb asks you to do: *If everyone cooperates by following the instructions, there will be no problem.* ○ *to cooperate with the police (eg by giving them information)*

cooperation (*also* **co-operation**) /kəʊˌɒpəˈreɪʃn/ *noun* [U] **1 cooperation (with sb)** working together with sb else to achieve sth: *international cooperation to protect the ozone layer* ○ *Schools are working in close cooperation with parents to improve standards.* **2** willingness to be helpful by doing what sb asks you to do: *The police asked the public for their cooperation in the investigation.*

cooperative (*also* **co-operative**) /kəʊˈɒpərətɪv/ *adj* **1** done by people working together: *a cooperative business venture* **2** helpful; doing what sb asks you to do: *My firm were very cooperative and allowed me to have time off.* ☛ The opposite is **uncooperative**.

cooperative *noun* [C] a business or organization that is owned and run by all of the people who work for it: *a workers' cooperative*

coordinate¹ (*also* **co-ordinate**) /kəʊˈɔ:dɪnət/ *noun* [C] one of the two sets of numbers and/or letters that are used for finding the position of a point on a map

coordinate² (*also* **co-ordinate**) /kəʊˈɔ:dɪneɪt/ *verb* [T] to organize different things or people so that they work together efficiently: *It is her job to coordinate the various departments.*

coordination /kəʊˌɔ:dɪˈneɪʃn/ *noun* [U] **1** the organization of different things or people so that they work together efficiently **2** the ability to control the movements of your body properly: *You need good coordination between eye and hand to play badminton well.*

coordinator *noun* [C] a person who is responsible for organizing different things or

people so that they work together efficiently: *a project coordinator*

cop¹ /kɒp/ *noun* [C] (*informal*) a policeman or policewoman

cop² /kɒp/ *verb* (**copp**ing; **copp**ed) (*informal*)
(PHRASAL VERB) **cop out (of sth)** to avoid sth that you should do, because you are afraid or lazy: *She was going to help me with the cooking but she copped out at the last minute.*

'cop-out *noun* [C] (*informal*) a way of avoiding sth that you should do: *I'm paying somebody to do the cooking for the party. It's a bit of a cop-out, I know.*

cope /kəʊp/ *verb* [I] **cope (with sb/sth)** to deal successfully with a difficult matter or situation: *She sometimes finds it difficult to cope with all the pressure at work.*

copious /'kəʊpiəs/ *adj* in large amounts; plentiful: *She made copious notes at the lecture.*
—**copiously** *adv*

copper¹ /'kɒpə(r)/ *noun* **1** [U] a common reddish-brown metal: *water pipes made of copper* ○ *copper wire* **2** [C] a coin of low value made of brown metal: *I only had a few coppers left.*

copper² /'kɒpə(r)/ *noun* [C] (*informal*) a policeman or policewoman

copse /kɒps/ *noun* [C] a small group of trees or bushes that are close together

copulate /'kɒpjuleɪt/ *verb* [I] (*formal*) (used especially about animals) to have sexual intercourse —**copulation** /ˌkɒpjuˈleɪʃn/ *noun* [U]

☆ **copy¹** /'kɒpi/ *noun* [C] (*pl* **copies**) **1** something that is made to look exactly like sth else: *I kept a copy of the letter I wrote.* ○ *The painting isn't an original, of course, it's only a copy.* ○ *the master copy* (= the original piece of paper from which copies are made) ○ *to make a copy of a computer file* ☛ Look at **photocopy**. **2** a book, newspaper, record, etc of which many have been printed or produced: *I managed to buy the last copy of the book left in the shop.*

☆ **copy²** /'kɒpi/ *verb* (*pres part* **copying**; *3rd pers sing pres* **copies**; *pt, pp* **copied**) **1** [T] **copy sth (down/out)** to write down sth exactly as it is written somewhere else: *The students copied what was written on the board.* ○ *I copied down the address on the brochure.* ○ *I copied out the letter more neatly.* **2** [T] to make a copy of a video, computer information, etc: *It is illegal to copy videos.* **3** [T] = PHOTOCOPY **4** [T] to do or try to do the same as sb else; to imitate: *She copies everything her friends do.* **5** [I] **copy (from sb)** to cheat by writing what sb else has written: *He was caught copying from his neighbour in the exam.*

copyright /'kɒpiraɪt/ *noun* [C,U] the legal right to be the only person who may print, copy, perform, etc a piece of original work, such as a book, a song or a computer program

coral /'kɒrəl; *US* 'kɔ:rəl/ *noun* [U] a hard red, pink or white substance formed from the bones of very small sea animals, often used for making jewellery: *a coral reef* (= a line of rock in the sea formed by coral) ○ *a coral necklace*

cord /kɔ:d/ *noun* **1** [C,U] (a piece of) strong, thick string **2** [C,U] (*especially US*) = FLEX¹ **3 cords** [plural] corduroy trousers

s	z	ʃ	ʒ	h	m	n	ŋ	l	r	j	w
so	**zoo**	**she**	**vision**	**how**	**man**	**no**	**sing**	**leg**	**red**	**yes**	**wet**

cordless /ˈkɔːdlɪs/ adj without a cord(2): *a cordless phone*

cordial /ˈkɔːdɪəl; US ˈkɔːrdʒəl/ adj friendly: *a cordial greeting* o *a cordial meeting* —**cordiality** /ˌkɔːdɪˈælətɪ; US ˌkɔːrdʒɪ-/ noun [U] —**cordially** /-dɪəlɪ; US -dʒəlɪ/ adv

cordon /ˈkɔːdn/ noun [C] a line or ring of police or soldiers that prevents people from entering or leaving an area

cordon verb
(PHRASAL VERB) **cordon sth off** to close an area by surrounding it with a ring of police or soldiers: *The street where the bomb was discovered was quickly cordoned off.*

corduroy /ˈkɔːdərɔɪ/ noun [U] a thick soft cotton cloth with raised lines on it, used for making clothes: *a corduroy jacket*

core /kɔː(r)/ noun **1** [C] the hard centre of certain fruits, containing seeds: *an apple core* **2** [sing] the central or most important part of sth: *the core curriculum* (= the subjects that all pupils have to study) o *the core vocabulary of a language* (= the most common and important words) **3** [C] the central part of a planet: *the earth's core*
(IDIOM) **to the core** completely; in every way: *The system is rotten to the core* (= bad in every part). o *The news shook him to the core* (= shocked him very much).

cork /kɔːk/ noun **1** [U] a light but tough substance which comes from the outside of a type of tree. It floats on water: *cork floor tiles* **2** [C] a round piece of cork that you push into the end of a bottle to close it, especially a bottle of wine

'corkscrew noun [C] a tool that you use for pulling corks out of bottles

☆ **corn¹** /kɔːn/ noun [U] **1** (*especially Brit*) a general word for grain crops such as wheat, or the seeds from these crops: *a field of corn* o *a cornfield* o *sacks of corn* **2** (*US*) = MAIZE

'cornflakes noun [plural] food made of small pieces of dried corn and eaten with milk for breakfast: *a bowl of cornflakes*

'cornflour noun [U] very fine flour often used for making puddings, sauces, etc

ˌcorn on the 'cob noun [U] the long round part of the maize plant with yellow grains on it that is cooked and eaten as a vegetable

corn² /kɔːn/ noun [C] a small, painful area of hard skin on the toe

☆ **corner¹** /ˈkɔːnə(r)/ noun [C] **1** a place where two lines, edges, surfaces or roads meet: *in a corner of the room* o *Write your address in the top right-hand corner.* o *The pub is on the corner of Wall Street and Long Road.* o *He went round the corner at top speed.* **2** a quiet or secret place or area: *a remote corner of Scotland* **3** a difficult situation which you cannot escape from: *to get yourself into a corner* **4** (*also* **'corner-kick**) (in football) a kick from the corner of a field

corn on the cob

(IDIOMS) **cut corners** to do sth quickly and not as well as you should

(just) round the corner very near: *There's a phone box just round the corner.*

☆ **corner²** /ˈkɔːnə(r)/ verb [T] **1** to get a person or an animal into a position from which it is difficult or impossible to escape: *He cornered me at the party and started telling me all his problems.* **2** to get control in some area of business so that there is no room for anybody else to have any success: *That company's really cornered the market in health foods.*

corny /ˈkɔːnɪ/ adj (**cornier, corniest**) (*informal*) too ordinary or familiar to be interesting or amusing: *a corny joke*

coronary /ˈkɒrənrɪ; US ˈkɔːrəneri/ adj connected with the heart

coronary noun [C] (*pl* **coronaries**) a type of heart attack in which the blood cannot flow to the heart because a tube (**artery**) is blocked. Coronaries can cause damage to the heart and death.

coronation /ˌkɒrəˈneɪʃn; US ˌkɔːr-/ noun [C] a ceremony at which a king or queen is crowned

coroner /ˈkɒrənə(r); US ˈkɔːr-/ noun [C] an official whose job is to find out the causes of death of people who have died in violent or unusual ways

corporal /ˈkɔːpərəl/ noun [C] a person of low rank in the army or air force

ˌcorporal 'punishment noun [U] the punishment of people by hitting them, especially the punishment of children by parents or teachers

corporate /ˈkɔːpərət/ adj of or shared by all the members of a group or organization: *corporate responsibility*

corporation /ˌkɔːpəˈreɪʃn/ noun [C, with sing or pl verb] **1** a large business company: *the Nikon Corporation* o *multinational corporations* o *the British Broadcasting Corporation* **2** a group of people elected to govern a particular town or city

corps /kɔː(r)/ noun [C, with sing or pl verb] (*pl* **corps** /kɔː(r)/) **1** a part of an army with special duties: *the medical corps* **2** a group of people involved in a special activity: *the diplomatic corps*

corpse /kɔːps/ noun [C] a dead body, especially of a person

☆ **correct¹** /kəˈrekt/ adj **1** with no mistakes; right or true: *Well done! All your answers were correct.* o *Have you got the correct time, please?* **2** (used about behaviour, manners, dress, etc) suitable according to normal customs and ideas: *What's the correct form of address for a vicar?* ☛ The opposite for 1 and 2 is **incorrect**.
—**correctly** adv —**correctness** noun [U]

☆ **correct²** /kəˈrekt/ verb [T] **1** to make a mistake, fault, etc right or better: *to correct a spelling mistake* o *to correct a test* (= mark the mistakes in it) **2** to point out the mistakes or faults of sb: *He's always correcting me when I'm talking to people.*

correction /kəˈrekʃn/ noun [C,U] (an act of) making sth right or changing sth: *Can you do your corrections to the essay, please?* o *Some parts of the report needed correction.*

corrective /kəˈrektɪv/ adj intended to put right sth that is wrong: *to take corrective action*

correlate /ˈkɒrəleɪt; US ˈkɔːr-/ verb [I,T] to have or to show a relationship or connection —**correlation** /ˌkɒrəˈleɪʃn; US ˌkɔːr-/ noun [C,U]: *a correlation between diet and intelligence*

correspond /ˌkɒrɪˈspɒnd; US ˌkɔːr-/ verb [I] **1 correspond (to sth)** to be similar or equal (to sth): *American High Schools correspond to British comprehensives.* **2 correspond (with sth)** to be the same as; to match: *Does the name on the envelope correspond with the name inside the letter?* **3 correspond (with sb)** to write letters to and receive them from sb: *They corresponded for a year before they got married.*

  corresponding adj (only before a noun) related or similar: *Sales are up 10% compared with the corresponding period last year.* —**correspondingly** adv

correspondence /ˌkɒrɪˈspɒndəns; US ˌkɔːr-/ noun **1** [U] the act of writing letters; the letters themselves: *There hasn't been any correspondence between them for years.* ○ *Please address all correspondence to the Arts Editor.* **2** [C,U] a close connection or relationship: *There is no correspondence between the two sets of figures.*

correspondent /ˌkɒrɪˈspɒndənt; US ˌkɔːr-/ noun [C] **1** a person who provides news or writes articles for a newspaper, etc, especially from abroad: *our Middle East correspondent, Andy Jenkins* **2** a person who writes letters

☆ **corridor** /ˈkɒrɪdɔː(r); US ˈkɔːr-/ noun [C] a long narrow passage in a building or train, with doors that open into rooms, etc: *to walk along a corridor*

corroborate /kəˈrɒbəreɪt/ verb [T] (*formal*) to support a statement, idea, etc by providing new evidence: *The witness corroborated Mr Patton's statement about the night of the murder.* —**corroboration** /kəˌrɒbəˈreɪʃn/ noun [U]

corrode /kəˈrəʊd/ verb [I,T] (used about metals) to become weak or to be destroyed by chemical action; to cause a metal to do this: *Parts of the car were corroded by rust.*

corrosion /kəˈrəʊʒn/ noun [U] the process of being destroyed by chemical action; the damage caused when sth is corroded —**corrosive** /kəˈrəʊsɪv/ adj

corrugated /ˈkɒrəgeɪtɪd/ adj (used about metal or cardboard) shaped into folds; not smooth and flat: *corrugated iron*

corrupt /kəˈrʌpt/ adj not honest, moral or legal: *corrupt business practices* ○ *corrupt officials who accept bribes*

corrupt verb [I,T] to cause sb/sth to become dishonest or to have lower moral standards: *Money corrupts.* ○ *Does television corrupt the minds of the young?*

corruption /kəˈrʌpʃn/ noun [U] **1** behaviour that is not honest or legal, especially by people in official positions: *There were accusations of corruption among senior police officers.* **2** the process of making sb/sth corrupt: *the corruption of an innocent young boy*

corset /ˈkɔːsɪt/ noun [C] a tight piece of clothing worn by some women close to their skin in order to make themselves look thinner

cosmetic /kɒzˈmetɪk/ noun [C] a substance that you put on your face or hair to make yourself look more attractive: *I only use cosmetics that are not tested on animals.*

cosmetic adj **1** used or done in order to improve your appearance: *cosmetic products* ○ *cosmetic surgery* **2** done in order to improve only the appearance of sth, without changing it in any other way: *changes in government policy which are purely cosmetic*

cosmic /ˈkɒzmɪk/ adj of the whole universe

cosmopolitan /ˌkɒzməˈpɒlɪtən/ adj **1** containing people from all over the world: *a cosmopolitan city* **2** having, or influenced by, wide experience of other countries and cultures: *the cosmopolitan atmosphere of the bars and cafés* ○ *a cosmopolitan and sophisticated young woman*

cosmos /ˈkɒzmɒs/ noun [sing] **the cosmos** the universe

☆ **cost¹** /kɒst; US kɔːst/ noun **1** [C,U] the money that you have to pay for sth: *The cost of petrol has gone up again.* ○ *the cost of living* (= the general level of prices for things that you need to live a normal life) ○ *The damage will have to be put right regardless of cost.* ☛ Look at the note at **price**. **2** [sing,U] what you have to give or lose in order to obtain sth else: *He achieved great success but only at the cost of a happy family life.* **3 costs** [plural] the cost of settling sth in a court of law; the amount of money that the losing side has to pay to the winning side: *a £250 fine and £100 costs*

(IDIOMS) **at all costs** using whatever means are necessary to achieve sth: *We must win at all costs.*

to your, etc cost as you, etc experienced it yourself: *Life can be lonely at university, as I found out to my cost.*

☆ **cost²** /kɒst; US kɔːst/ verb [T] (*pt, pp* **cost**) **1** to have the price of: *These apples cost 40p a pound.* ○ *How much does it cost?* ○ *It cost me £10 to go by train.* **2** to make you lose sth: *That one mistake cost him his job.* **3** to estimate the price to be asked for some goods, a service, etc: *Engineers costed the repairs at £2 million.* ☛ The past tense and past participle for this sense is **costed**.

co-star /ˈkəʊ stɑː(r)/ verb (co-sta**rr**ing; co-sta**rr**ed) **1** [T] (used of a film, play, etc) to have two or more famous actors as its stars: *a film co-starring Michael Caine and Sean Connery* **2** [I] (used of actors) to be one of two or more stars in a film, play, etc: *Michael Caine co-stars with Sean Connery in the film.*

co-star /ˈkəʊstɑː(r)/ noun [C] a famous actor or actress who has one of the most important parts in a film, play, etc in which another famous actor or actress also appears: *His co-star was Marilyn Monroe.*

costly /ˈkɒstli; US ˈkɔːst-/ adj (**costlier; costliest**) **1** costing a lot of money; expensive: *a costly repair bill* **2** involving great loss of time, effort, etc: *a costly mistake*

costume /ˈkɒstjuːm; US -tuːm/ noun [C,U] a set or style of clothes worn by people in a particular country or at a particular time: *She*

cosy *designs costumes for the theatre.* ○ *17th century costume* ○ *the Welsh national costume* ☞ Look at **swimming-costume**.

cosy /ˈkəʊzi/ *adj* (**cosier**; **cosiest**) (*US* **cozy**) warm and comfortable: *The room looked cosy and inviting in the firelight.*

cot /kɒt/ (*US* **crib**) *noun* [C] a bed for a baby or young child, with high sides to stop it from falling out

cottage /ˈkɒtɪdʒ/ *noun* [C] a small and usually old house, especially in the country: *a pretty village with little thatched cottages* ☞ picture on page A12.

cottage ˈcheese *noun* [U] a type of soft white cheese in small lumps

cottage ˈpie *noun* [C] = SHEPHERD'S PIE

☆ **cotton¹** /ˈkɒtn/ *noun* [U] **1** a natural cloth or thread; the tall tropical plant that produces it: *This shirt is 60% cotton and 40% polyester.* ○ *cottonfields in Mississippi* ○ *a reel of cotton* (= for sewing with) ☞ picture at **sew**. **2** (*US*) = COTTON WOOL

cotton ˈwool *noun* [U] soft, loose cotton in a mass, used for cleaning the skin

cotton² /ˈkɒtn/ *verb*
(PHRASAL VERB) **cotton on** (*informal*) to understand sth: *It took me ages to cotton on.*

couch¹ /kaʊtʃ/ *noun* [C] a long seat, often with a back and arms, for sitting or lying on: *They were sitting on the couch in the living-room.* ○ *a doctor's couch*

couch² /kaʊtʃ/ *verb* [T] (usually passive) (*formal*) to express a thought, idea, etc (in the way mentioned): *His reply was couched in very polite terms.*

☆ **cough** /kɒf; *US* kɔːf/ *verb* **1** [I] to send air out of your throat and mouth with a sudden loud noise, especially when you have a cold, have sth in your throat, etc: *I could hear him coughing all night.* ☞ picture at **sneeze**. **2** [T] **cough (sth) (up)** to send sth out of your throat and mouth with a sudden loud noise: *He was coughing blood.*
(PHRASAL VERB) **cough (sth) up** (*Brit informal*) to give money or information unwillingly: *Come on, cough up what you owe me!*

cough *noun* [C] **1** an act or the sound of coughing: *He gave a nervous cough before he started to speak.* **2** an illness or infection that makes you cough a lot: *She's had a cough for weeks.* ○ *cough medicine* ○ *coughs and colds*

☆ **could** /kəd/ *strong form* kʊd/ *modal verb* (*negative* **could not**; *short form* **couldn't** /ˈkʊdnt/) **1** (used as the past form of 'can' when you report what sb says): *She said that she couldn't come.* **2** (used for saying that sth is, will be, or was possible): *I could do it now if you like.* ○ *She could be famous one day.* ○ *Couldn't you come earlier?* (= I wish you could) ○ *He could have gone to university but he didn't want to.* ○ *I can't find my purse. I could have left it in the bank.* ○ *You could have said you were going to be late!* (= I wish that you had) ☞ If something was possible on one occasion in the past use **was/were able to**: *The firemen were able to rescue the children.* But in negative sentences **could not** can be used, too: *The firemen couldn't rescue the children.* **3** (used for saying that sb had the ability in the past to do sth): *I could run two miles without stopping when I was younger.* ○ *My mother could cook beautifully.* **4** (used for asking permission politely): *Could I possibly borrow your car?* **5** (used for asking sb politely to do sth for you): *Could you open the door? My hands are full.* **6 I could/ could have** I would like/have liked to: *I could scream, I'm so angry.* ○ *I was so angry I could have screamed.* **7** (used with the verbs 'feel', 'hear', 'see', 'smell', 'taste') ☞ These verbs are not used in the continuous tenses. If we want to talk about seeing, hearing, etc at a particular moment in the past, we use **could**: *We could hear the birds singing.* (NOT *We were hearing.*)

☆ **council** (*also* **Council**) /ˈkaʊnsl/ *noun* [C, with sing or pl verb] **1** a group of people who are elected to manage affairs for a town, city, country, etc: *The county council has/have decided to build a new road.* ○ *a council decision* ○ *Oxford City Council* ○ *a council house* (= one built and owned by a city or county council) **2** a group of people elected to give advice, manage affairs, etc for a particular organization or area of activity: *a student council* ○ *the Arts Council*

councillor /ˈkaʊnsələ(r)/ *noun* [C] a member of a council: *to elect new councillors*

counsel¹ /ˈkaʊnsl/ *verb* [T] (**counselling**; counselled; *US* counseling; counseled) **1** (*formal*) to advise or recommend: *Mr Dean's lawyers counselled him against making public statements.* **2** to give professional advice to sb with a problem

counselling (*US* **counseling**) /-səlɪŋ/ *noun* [U] professional advice given to people with problems: *Many students come to us for counselling.* ○ *psychiatric counselling*

counsellor (*US* **counselor**) /ˈkaʊnsələ(r)/ *noun* [C] a person whose job is to give advice: *a student counsellor*

counsel² /ˈkaʊnsl/ *noun* **1** [U] (*formal*) advice **2** [C] (*pl* **counsel**) a lawyer who speaks in a court of law: *the counsel for the defence/prosecution*

☆ **count¹** /kaʊnt/ *verb* **1** [I] to say numbers one after another in order: *Close your eyes and count (up) to 20.* ○ *to count from 0 to 100* **2** [T] **count sth (up)** to calculate the total number or amount of sth: *The teacher counted the children as they got on the bus.* **3** [I] **count (for sth)** to be important or valuable: *Your opinion really counts.* **4** [I] **count (as sth)** to be accepted: *'I won,' shouted Tom. 'But you cheated so it doesn't count,' replied Sarah.* ○ *Will my driving licence count as identification?* **5** [T] to consider to be: *You should count yourself lucky to have a good job.* **6** [T] to include sb/sth when you are calculating an amount or number: *The holiday costs about £1000, not counting the flights.*
(PHRASAL VERBS) **count against sb** to be considered as a disadvantage: *Do you think my age will count against me?*
count on sb/sth to expect sth with confidence; to rely on sb/sth: *In England you can't count on good weather in May.* ○ *Can I count on you to help me?*

p	b	t	d	k	g	tʃ	dʒ	f	v	θ	ð
pen	bad	tea	did	cat	got	chin	June	fall	van	thin	then

count sb/sth out 1 to count things slowly, one by one: *She carefully counted out £100 in five pound notes.* **2** (*informal*) not include sb/sth: *If you're going swimming, you can count me out!*

countable *adj* that can be counted ☞ The opposite is **uncountable**.

'countable noun (*also* **'count noun**) *noun* [C] (*grammar*) a noun that can be used in the plural, and with words like 'a', 'many' and 'few': *Countable nouns are marked [C] in this dictionary.*

'countdown *noun* [C] the act of saying numbers backwards to zero just before sth important happens: *the countdown to take-off*

count² /kaʊnt/ *noun* [C] **1** [usually sing] an act of counting or a number that you get after counting: *At the latest count, there were nearly 2 million unemployed.* **2** [usually pl] a point that is made in a discussion, argument, etc: *I proved her wrong on all counts.*
(IDIOM) **keep/lose count (of sth)** not know how many there are of sth: *I've lost count of the number of times he's told that joke!*

count³ (*also* **Count**) /kaʊnt/ *noun* [C] a title for a man of noble birth in some European countries

counter¹ /'kaʊntə(r)/ *noun* [C] **1** a long, flat surface or table in a shop, bank, etc, where customers are served **2** a small object (usually round and made of plastic) that is used in some games to show where a player is on the board

counter² /'kaʊntə(r)/ *adv* **counter to sth** in the opposite direction to sth: *Events seemed to be going counter to our expectations.*

counter³ /'kaʊntə(r)/ *verb* [I,T] to answer or react to sb/sth with a different opinion or a return attack: *He countered our criticism with a powerful defence of his actions.*

counteract /ˌkaʊntər'ækt/ *verb* [T] to reduce the effect of sth by acting against it: *measures to counteract traffic congestion*

counter-attack /'kaʊntərətæk/ *noun* [C] an attack made in reaction to an enemy's attack —**counter-attack** *verb* [I,T]

counterfeit /'kaʊntəfɪt/ *adj* not genuine, but copied so that it looks like the real thing: *counterfeit money*

counterfoil /'kaʊntəfɔɪl/ *noun* [C] the part of a cheque or receipt that you keep as a record

counterpart /'kaʊntəpɑːt/ *noun* [C] a person or thing that has a similar position or function to sb/sth else: *She's my counterpart in our New York office* (= she does the same job there that I do here).

counter-productive /ˌkaʊntə prə'dʌktɪv/ *adj* having the opposite effect to the one you want

countess /'kaʊntɪs/ *noun* [C] a woman who is married to a count or earl, or who has the same rank as one

countless /'kaʊntlɪs/ *adj* (only *before* a noun) very many: *I've tried to telephone him countless times.*

☆ **country** /'kʌntri/ *noun* (*pl* **countries**) **1** [C] an area of land with its own people, government, etc: *France, Spain and other European countries* ○ *There was snow over much of the country during the night.* ☞ **State** is used for talking about a country as an organized political community controlled by one government. It can also mean the government itself: *a politically independent state* ○ *the member states of the EC* ○ *You get a pension from the state when you retire.* ○ *state education*. **Land** is more formal or literary: *Explorers who set out to discover new lands.* **2 the country** [sing] the people who live in a country: *a survey to find out what the country really thinks* **3 the country** [sing] land which is away from towns and cities: *Do you live in the town or the country?* ○ *country life* ☞ The word **country** is used for emphasizing that an area of land is away from towns, etc: *city workers who like to get out into the country at weekends* The word **countryside** also refers to areas of land that are away from towns but it emphasizes the natural features such as hills, rivers, trees, etc that you find there: *beautiful countryside* ○ *the destruction of the countryside by new roads.* **Landscape** refers to everything you see when you look across an area of land either in the town or the country: *a dreary landscape of factories and chimneys* ○ *a landscape of forests and lakes* **4** [U] an area of land (especially considering its physical features): *We looked down over miles of open country.* ○ *hilly country*

country-and-'western *noun* [U] a type of popular music that comes from the southern and western USA

country 'house *noun* [C] a large house in the country, usually owned by an important family and often with a lot of land

countryman /'kʌntrimən/ *noun* [C] (*pl* **countrymen**; *feminine* **countrywoman** /'kʌntriwʊmən/; *pl* **countrywomen**) **1** a person from your own country **2** a person who lives in the country(3)

countryside /'kʌntrisaɪd/ *noun* [U,sing] **the countryside** land which is away from towns and cities, consisting of farms, woods, etc: *the French countryside* ○ *The countryside near York is very beautiful.* ☞ Look at the note at **country**.

county /'kaʊnti/ *noun* [C] (*pl* **counties**) an area in Britain, Ireland or the USA which has its own local government: *the county of Kent*

coup /kuː/ *noun* [C] (*pl* **coups** /kuːz/) **1** (*also* **coup d'état** /kuː deɪ'tɑː/ (*pl* **coups d'état** /kuː deɪ'tɑː/) a sudden and often violent change of government organized by a small group of people: *a coup to overthrow the President* ○ *an attempted coup* (= one which did not succeed) **2** a clever and successful thing to do: *Getting that promotion was a real coup.*

☆ **couple¹** /'kʌpl/ *noun* [C] two people who are married, living together, etc: *A very nice couple have moved in next door.* ○ *a married couple*
(IDIOM) **a couple of people/things 1** two people/things: *I need a couple of glasses.* **2** a few (not saying an exact number): *I last saw her a couple of months ago.*

couple² /'kʌpl/ *verb* [T] (usually passive) to join or link sb/sth to sb/sth else: *The fog, coupled with the amount of traffic on the roads, made driving very difficult.*

coupon /'kuːpɒn/ *noun* [C] **1** a small piece of

s	z	ʃ	ʒ	h	m	n	ŋ	l	r	j	w
so	zoo	she	vision	how	man	no	sing	leg	red	yes	wet

courage / **cover**

paper which you can use to buy goods at a lower price, or which you can collect and then exchange for goods: *a coupon worth £1 off your next purchase* **2** a small form in a newspaper or magazine which you fill in with your name and address and send off, in order to get information or to enter a competition: *To place your order, simply fill in the coupon at the bottom of this page.*

☆ **courage** /ˈkʌrɪdʒ/ *noun* [U] the ability to control fear in a situation that may be dangerous or unpleasant: *It took real courage to go back into the burning building.* ○ *She showed great courage all through her long illness.*
(IDIOM) **pluck up courage** ⇨ PLUCK
courageous /kəˈreɪdʒəs/ *adj* having or showing courage; brave —**courageously** *adv*
courgette /kɔːˈʒet/ (*especially US* **zucchini**) *noun* [C] a long vegetable with a thick green skin that is eaten cooked. A courgette is a small marrow.
courier /ˈkʊrɪə(r)/ *noun* [C] **1** a person whose job is to look after a group of tourists **2** a person whose job is to carry letters, important papers, etc, especially when they are urgent
☆ **course** /kɔːs/ *noun* **1** [C] one of the parts of a meal: *a three-course lunch* ○ *I had chicken for the main course.* **2** [C] **a course (in/on sth)** a complete series of lessons or studies: *I've enrolled on an English course.* ○ *I'm taking a course in self-defence.* ○ *At some universities the course lasts for four years.* **3** [C] an area where golf is played or where certain types of race take place: *a golf-course* ○ *a racecourse* (= where horse-races take place) ○ *Several of the horses didn't complete the course.* **4** [C] **a course (of sth)** a series of medical treatments: *The doctor put her on a course of tablets.* **5** [C,U] the route or direction that sth, especially an aeroplane, ship or river, takes: *We changed course and sailed towards land.* ○ *to be on/off course* (= going in the right/wrong direction) ○ *the course of the Rhine* ○ (*figurative*) *I'm on course* (= making the right amount of progress) *to finish this work by the end of the week.* **6** [sing] the development of sth over a period of time: *events that changed the course of history* ○ *In the normal course of events* (= the way things normally happen) *such problems do not arise.* **7** (*also* **course of action**) [C] a way of acting in or dealing with a particular situation: *In that situation resignation was the only course open to him.*
(IDIOMS) **in the course of sth** during sth: *He mentioned it in the course of conversation.*
in (the) course of time eventually; when enough time has passed: *I'm sure that all these problems will be sorted out in the course of time.*
in due course ⇨ DUE¹
a matter of course ⇨ MATTER¹
of course naturally; certainly: *Of course, having children has changed their lives a lot.* ○ *Of course it can be repaired but I think it will be too expensive to do it.* ○ *'Can I use your phone?' 'Of course you can.'* ○ *'You're not annoyed with me, are you?' 'Of course not.'*
☆ **court**¹ /kɔːt/ *noun* **1** [C,U] a place where trials take place in front of a judge or a jury, to decide whether a person has broken the law: *a magistrate's court* ○ *A man has been charged and will appear in court tomorrow.* **2 the court** [sing] the people in a court, especially those taking part in the trial: *Please tell the court exactly what you saw.* **3** *often* **Court** [C,U] the official home of a king or queen **4** [C,U] an area where certain ball games are played: *a tennis, squash, etc court* ○ *The players have been on court for nearly three hours.* ☛ picture at **tennis**.
(IDIOM) **take sb to court** to take legal action against sb in a court of law: *She took the company to court for breaking the contract.*
,**court of 'law** *noun* [C] = LAWCOURT
court² /kɔːt/ *verb* **1** [T] to try to gain sb's support by paying special attention to them: *Politicians from all parties will be courting voters this week.* **2** [T] to do sth that might lead to sth unpleasant: *Britain is courting ecological disaster if it continues to dump waste in the North Sea.* **3** [I] (used about two people) to spend time together in a relationship that may lead to marriage: *There were a lot of courting couples in the park.*
courtship /ˈkɔːtʃɪp/ *noun* [C,U] the period or situation of having a relationship that leads or may lead to marriage: *They got married after a brief courtship.*
courteous /ˈkɜːtɪəs/ *adj* polite and pleasant, showing respect for other people: *The assistant was courteous and helpful.* ☛ The opposite is **discourteous**. —**courteously** *adv*
courtesy /ˈkɜːtəsɪ/ *noun* (*pl* **courtesies**) **1** [U] polite and pleasant behaviour that shows respect for other people: *She didn't even have the courtesy to say that she was sorry.* **2** [C] (*formal*) a polite action or remark: *The two presidents exchanged courtesies before their meeting.*
(IDIOM) **(by) courtesy of sb** with the permission or because of the kindness of sb: *These pictures are being shown by courtesy of BBC TV.*
courtier /ˈkɔːtɪə(r)/ *noun* [C] (in the past) a companion of a king or queen at his/her court
court martial /ˌkɔːt ˈmɑːʃl/ *noun* [C] (*pl* **courts martial** *or* **court martials**) a military court that deals with matters of military law; a trial that takes place in such a court: *His case will be heard by a court martial.*
court-martial *verb* [T] (court-martial**l**ing; court-martial**l**ed; *US* court-martialing; court-martialed) to try sb in a military court
courtyard /ˈkɔːtjɑːd/ *noun* [C] an area of ground, without a roof, that has walls or buildings around it, eg in a castle, or between houses or flats
☆ **cousin** /ˈkʌzn/ (*also* **first 'cousin**) *noun* [C] the child of your aunt or uncle: *Have you met Lizzie? We're cousins.* ☛ The same word is used for both male and female cousins. A **second cousin** is the child of your cousin.
cove /kəʊv/ *noun* [C] a small bay on the coast: *a sandy cove*
☆ **cover**¹ /ˈkʌvə(r)/ *verb* [T] **1 cover sb/sth (up/over) (with sth)** to put sth on or in front of sth in order to hide or protect it: *Could you cover the food and put it in the fridge?* ○ *She couldn't look any more and covered her eyes.* ○

iː	ɪ	e	æ	ɑː	ɒ	ɔː	ʊ	uː	ʌ
see	sit	ten	hat	arm	got	saw	put	too	cup

She was asleep on the sofa so he covered her over with a blanket. ○ *I covered the floor with newspaper before I started painting.* **2** to be across or over the surface of sth: *Snow covered the ground.* **3 cover sb/sth in/with sth** to form a layer on sb/sth: *A car went through the puddle and covered me with mud.* **4** to fill or be spread over a certain area: *The smoke from the fire now covers about 15 000 square kilometres.* **5** to include or to deal with sth: *Part-time workers are not covered by the law.* ○ *The course covered both British and European history.* ○ *I think we've covered everything. Now, does anyone have a question?* **6** to travel a certain distance: *We covered about 500 kilometres that day.* **7** to be enough money for sth: *Will £20 cover your expenses?* **8** (used about the media) to report on or show sth: *All the papers covered the election in depth.* **9 cover sb/sth against/for sth** to protect sb/sth by insurance: *The insurance policy covers us for any damage to our property.* ○ *The policy even covers your garden furniture* (= it is insured).

(PHRASAL VERBS) **cover (sth) up** to prevent people hearing about a mistake or sth bad: *The police have been accused of trying to cover up the facts of the case.*

cover up for sb to hide a person's mistakes or crimes in order to protect him/her: *His wife covered up for him to the police.*

covered *adj* **1 covered in/with sth** having a layer or a large amount of sth on sb/sth: *The victim was lying on the floor, covered in blood.* ○ *The whole room was covered in dust.* **2** having a cover, especially a roof: *a covered shopping centre*

covering /ˈkʌvərɪŋ/ *noun* [C] something that covers the surface of sth: *A thick covering of snow lay on the ground.*

ˌcovering ˈletter *noun* [C] a letter that you send with a parcel, etc explaining it or giving more information about it

ˈcover-up *noun* [C] an act of preventing sth bad or dishonest from becoming known: *Several newspapers have claimed that there has been a government cover-up.*

☆ **cover²** /ˈkʌvə(r)/ *noun* **1** [C] something that is put on or over sth, especially in order to protect it: *a plastic cover for a computer* ○ *a duvet cover* **2** [C] the outside part of a book or magazine: *I can't remember the title of the book but I know it has a green cover.* ○ *I read the magazine from cover to cover* (= from beginning to end). **3 the covers** [plural] the blankets, sheets, etc that cover sb in bed: *She pulled the covers off him and said: 'Get up!'* **4** [U] **cover (against sth)** insurance against sth, so that if sth bad happens you get money or help in return: *The policy provides cover against theft.* **5** [U] shelter or protection from the weather, damage, etc: *When the storm started we took cover in a shop doorway.* ○ *The soldiers had no cover and were easy targets.* **6** [C, usually sing] **a cover (for sth)** something that hides the real nature of sth, especially sth illegal: *The whole company was just a cover for all kinds of criminal activities.*

(IDIOM) **under cover of sth** hidden by sth; not noticed because of sth: *They attacked under cover of darkness.*

coverage /ˈkʌvərɪdʒ/ *noun* [U] the act or amount of reporting on or showing an event in the media: *TV coverage of the Olympic Games was excellent.*

coveralls /ˈkʌvərɔːlz/ *noun* [plural] (*US*) = OVERALLS

covert /ˈkʌvət; *US* ˈkəʊvɜːrt/ *adj* done secretly, not openly: *a covert police operation* —**covertly** *adv*

covet /ˈkʌvɪt/ *verb* [T] to want very much to have sth (especially sth that belongs to sb else)

horn — cow — calf — bull

☆ **cow** /kaʊ/ *noun* [C] **1** a large female animal that is kept on farms to produce milk: *to milk a cow* ○ *a herd of cows* ☞ Cow is often used for both male and female members of the **cattle** family. The special word for a male is **bull**. A young cow is a **calf**. A number of cows together can be called **cattle**. Look at the note at **meat**. **2** the adult female of certain large animals, eg the elephant **3** (*slang*) an insulting word for a woman: *She's a real cow!*

coward /ˈkaʊəd/ *noun* [C] (used when disapproving) a person who has no courage and is afraid in dangerous or unpleasant situations: *I hate going to the dentist's because I'm a terrible coward.* ○ *I was too much of a coward to argue.*

cowardice /ˈkaʊədɪs/ *noun* [U] a lack of courage: *I was ashamed at the cowardice I showed in running away.* —**cowardly** *adj*

cowboy /ˈkaʊbɔɪ/ *noun* [C] **1** a man whose job is to look after cows (usually on a horse) in certain parts of the USA: *a cowboy film* **2** (*Brit informal*) a person in business who is not honest or who does work badly: *a cowboy builder*

cower /ˈkaʊə(r)/ *verb* [I] to move back or into a low position because of fear: *The dog cowered under the table.*

coy /kɔɪ/ *adj* **1** pretending to be shy or modest: *She lifted her head a little and gave him a coy smile.* **2** unwilling to say sth directly or to give information: *Don't be coy, tell me how much you earn.* —**coyly** *adv*

cozy (*US*) = COSY

crab /kræb/ *noun* [C] a sea animal with a flat body covered by a shell and five pairs of curved legs. The front two legs have long claws (**pincers**) on them. Crabs move sideways. ☞ picture at **shellfish**.

☆ **crack¹** /kræk/ *noun* [C] **1** a line on the surface of sth where it has broken, but not into separate pieces: *a pane of glass with a crack in it* ☞ picture at **chip**. **2** a narrow opening: *The wind blew through the cracks in the roof.* **3** a sudden loud, sharp sound: *There was a crack and he realized that he had broken his leg.* **4** an

amusing, often critical, remark; a joke: *She made a crack about his clothes.*
(IDIOMS) **the crack of dawn** very early in the morning
have a crack (at sth/at doing sth) (*informal*) to try to do sth: *I'm not sure how to play but I'll have a crack at it.*

crack *adj* (used especially about soldiers) very well-trained and skilful: *crack troops*

☆ **crack²** /kræk/ *verb* **1** [I,T] to break so that a line appears, but without breaking into pieces; to make sth do this: *Don't put boiling water into that glass, it'll crack.* o *You can crack this sort of glass but you can't break it.* o *Oh no, this glass is cracked.* ☛ picture at **chip**. **2** [T] to break sth open: *Crack two eggs into a bowl.* **3** [I,T] to make a sudden loud, sharp sound; to cause sth to make this sound: *The lion tamer cracked his whip.* **4** [T] to hit a part of your body against sth: *She stood up and cracked her head on the cupboard door.* **5** [I] to stop being able to deal with pressure and so lose control: *She cracked under the strain of all her problems.* **6** [T] (*informal*) to solve a problem: *I think I've cracked it!* **7** [T] to tell or make a joke
(IDIOM) **get cracking** to start doing sth immediately: *I have to finish this job today so I'd better get cracking.*
(PHRASAL VERBS) **crack down (on sb/sth)** (used about people in authority) to start dealing severely with bad or illegal behaviour: *The police have started to crack down on drug dealers.*
crack up (*informal*) to be unable to deal with pressure and so lose control and become mentally ill: *He cracked up when his wife left him.*

'**crack-down** *noun* [C] action to stop bad or illegal behaviour: *a police crack-down on street crime*

cracker /'krækə(r)/ *noun* [C] **1** a thin flat dry biscuit that is often eaten with cheese **2** (*also* **Christmas cracker**) a cardboard tube wrapped in coloured paper and containing a small present. Crackers are pulled apart by two people, each holding one end, at Christmas parties. They make a loud sharp noise as they break.

crackle /'krækl/ *verb* [I] to make a series of short, sharp sounds: *The radio started to crackle and then it stopped working.* —**crackle** *noun* [sing]: *the crackle of dry wood burning*

cradle /'kreɪdl/ *noun* [C] a small bed for a baby. Cradles can often be moved from side to side.

cradle *verb* [T] to hold sb/sth carefully and gently in your arms: *He cradled her head in his arms until the ambulance came.*

craft¹ /krɑːft; *US* kræft/ *noun* [C] **1** a job or activity for which you need skill with your hands: *an arts and crafts exhibition* o *the craft of basket making* o *craft, design and technology (CDT)* (= a subject at British secondary schools) ☛ Look at **handicraft**. **2** any job or activity for which you need skill: *He regards acting as a craft.*

craftsman /'krɑːftsmən/ *US* kræfts-/ *noun* [C] (*pl* **craftsmen**) a person who makes things skilfully, especially with the hands: *All the furniture we sell is individually made by craftsmen.*

craftsmanship *noun* [U] the skill used by sb to make sth of high quality with the hands

craft² /krɑːft; *US* kræft/ *noun* [C] (*pl* **craft**) a boat, aircraft or spaceship: *There were a few sailing craft on the lake.*

crafty /'krɑːfti; *US* 'kræfti/ *adj* (**craftier**; **craftiest**) clever at getting or achieving things by deceiving people or using indirect methods —**craftily** *adv*

crag /kræg/ *noun* [C] a steep, rough rock on a hill or mountain

cram /kræm/ *verb* (**cramm**ing; **cramm**ed) **1** [T] to push people or things into a small space: *I managed to cram all my clothes into the bag but I couldn't zip it up.* o *How many more people can they cram onto this train?* o *We only spent two days in Rome but we managed to cram a lot of sightseeing in.* **2** [I] to move, with a lot of other people, into a small space: *He only had a small car but they all managed to cram in.* **3** [I] to study very hard and learn a lot in a short time before an examination: *She's cramming for her exams.*

crammed *adj* very or too full: *That book is crammed with useful information.* o *Athens is crammed with tourists at that time of year.*

cramp /kræmp/ *noun* [U] a sudden pain that you get in a muscle, that makes it difficult to move: *One of the swimmers got cramp and we had to pull him out of the water.*

cramped /kræmpt/ *adj* not having enough space: *The flat was terribly cramped with so many of us living there.*

cranberry /'krænbəri; *US* -beri/ *noun* [C] (*pl* **cranberries**) a small red berry with a slightly sour taste

crane¹ /kreɪn/ *noun* [C] a large machine with a long metal arm that is used for moving or lifting heavy objects

crane² /kreɪn/ *verb* [I,T] to stretch your neck forward in order to see or hear sth: *We all craned forward to get a better view.*

crank /kræŋk/ *noun* [C] a person with strange ideas or who behaves in a strange way: *Lots of cranks phoned the police confessing to the murder.*

cranny /'kræni/ *noun* [C] (*pl* **crannies**) a small opening in a wall, a rock, etc
(IDIOM) **every nook and cranny** ⇨ **NOOK**

☆ **crash¹** /kræʃ/ *noun* [C] **1** a sudden loud noise made by sth breaking, hitting sth, etc: *I heard a crash and ran outside.* **2** an accident when a car or other vehicle hits sth and is damaged: *She was injured in a serious car crash.* o *a plane crash with no survivors* **3** an occasion when there is a failure in the business world: *the Stock Market crash of 1987*

crash *adj* done with a lot of effort in a short period of time: *She did a crash course in Spanish before going to work in Madrid.*

'**crash barrier** *noun* [C] a fence that keeps people or vehicles apart, eg when there are large crowds, or between the two sides of the road

'**crash-helmet** *noun* [C] a hard hat worn by

p	b	t	d	k	g	tʃ	dʒ	f	v	θ	ð
pen	**bad**	**tea**	**did**	**cat**	**got**	**chin**	**June**	**fall**	**van**	**thin**	**then**

motor cyclists, racing drivers, etc to protect their heads in an accident

☆**crash²** /kræʃ/ verb **1** [I] to fall or move suddenly, making a loud noise: *The tree crashed through the window.* ○ *The elephant went crashing through the jungle.* **2** [I,T] to have an accident in a vehicle; to cause a vehicle to have an accident: *He braked too late and crashed into the car in front.* ○ *He crashed his father's car.* **3** [I] to make a loud noise: *I could hear thunder crashing outside.* **4** [I] (used about a business or a financial organization) to fail suddenly **5** [I] (used about a computer) to stop working suddenly: *We lost the data when the computer crashed.*

crass /kræs/ adj **1** stupid, showing that you do not understand sth: *It was a crass comment to make when he knew how upset she was.* **2** extreme: *crass carelessness*

crate /kreɪt/ noun [C] a large box in which goods are transported or stored. Sometimes crates are divided into sections, for carrying bottles: *We had to pack everything into crates when we moved house.* ○ *a crate of beer*

crater /'kreɪtə(r)/ noun [C] **1** a large hole in the ground: *The bomb left a large crater.* ○ *craters on the moon* **2** the hole in the top of a volcano

cravat /krə'væt/ noun [C] a wide piece of cloth that men tie around their neck and wear inside the collar of their shirt

crave /kreɪv/ verb [I,T] **crave (for) sth** to want and need to have sth very much: *He craves attention from other people.*

craving noun [C] a strong desire for sth: *When she was pregnant she had cravings for all sorts of peculiar food.*

crawling

☆**crawl** /krɔːl/ verb [I] **1** to move slowly with the body on or close to the ground, or on the hands and knees: *An insect crawled across the floor.* ○ *Their baby has just started to crawl.* **2** (used about vehicles) to move very slowly: *The traffic crawls through the centre of town in the rush-hour.* **3** **crawl (to sb)** (*informal*) to be too polite or pleasant to sb in order to be liked or to gain sth: *He only got promoted because he crawled to the manager.*

(IDIOM) **crawling with sth** to be completely full of or covered with sb/sth that is moving and that is considered unpleasant: *The kitchen was crawling with insects.* ○ *The village is always crawling with tourists at this time of year.*

crawl noun [sing] **1** a very slow speed: *The traffic slowed to a crawl.* **2** often **the crawl** a style of swimming which you do on your front. When you do the crawl, you move first one arm and then the other over your head, turn your face to one side so that you can breathe and kick up and down with your legs.

crayon /'kreɪən/ noun [C,U] a soft, thick, coloured pencil sometimes made of wax, used for drawing or writing, especially by children —**crayon** verb [I,T]

craze /kreɪz/ noun [C] **a craze (for sth) 1** a strong interest in sth, that usually only lasts for a short time: *There was a craze for that kind of music years ago.* **2** something that a lot of people are very interested in: *Pocket TVs are the latest craze among teenagers.*

☆**crazy** /'kreɪzi/ adj (**crazier; craziest**) (*informal*) **1** very silly or foolish: *I think that that's a crazy idea.* ○ *You must be crazy to turn down such a wonderful offer.* **2** very angry: *She goes crazy when people criticize her.* **3** **crazy about sth** very interested in sth; liking sth very much: *He's always been crazy about horses.* **4** **crazy about sb** very much in love with sb **5** showing great excitement: *The fans went crazy when their team scored the first goal.* —**crazily** adv —**craziness** noun [U]

creak /kriːk/ verb [I] to make the noise of wood bending or of sth not moving smoothly: *The floorboards creaked when I walked across the room.* ○ *The lift creaked to a halt.* —**creak** noun [C] —**creaky** adj: *creaky stairs*

☆**cream¹** /kriːm/ noun **1** [U] the thick yellowish-white liquid that is the fatty part of milk and that rises to the top of it: *coffee with cream* ○ *strawberries and cream* ○ *whipped cream* (= cream that has been beaten) **2** [C,U] a substance that you rub into your skin to keep it soft or as a medical treatment **3** **the cream** [sing] the best part of sth or the best people in a group

cream adj having a yellowish-white colour

creamy adj (**creamier; creamiest**) **1** containing cream: *a creamy sauce* **2** thick, smooth and soft; looking or feeling like cream: *Beat the mixture until it is creamy and light.*

cream 'tea noun [C] (*Brit*) a meal taken in the afternoon consisting of tea with a special type of cake (**scone**) that is eaten with jam and cream

cream² /kriːm/ verb
(PHRASAL VERB) **cream sb/sth off** to take away the best people or part from sth for a particular purpose: *The big clubs cream off the country's best young players.*

crease /kriːs/ noun [C] **1** an untidy line on paper, material, a piece of clothing, etc that is caused by not treating it carefully: *Your shirt needs ironing, it's full of creases.* ○ *When I unrolled the poster, there was a crease in it.* **2** a neat line that is put on paper, material, a piece of clothing, etc intentionally: *He had a sharp crease in his trousers.*

crease verb [I,T] to get creases(1,2) ; to make sth get creases: *Hang up your jacket or it will crease.* ○ *I creased my skirt by sitting on the floor.*

☆**create** /kriː'eɪt/ verb [T] to cause sth new to happen or exist: *God created the world.* ○ *a plan to create new jobs in the area* ○ *All these changes will simply create confusion.* ○ *He created a bad impression at the interview.*

s	z	ʃ	ʒ	h	m	n	ŋ	l	r	j	w
so	zoo	she	vision	how	man	no	sing	leg	red	yes	wet

creation /kriˈeɪʃn/ noun **1** [U] the act of causing sth new to happen or exist: *the creation of new independent states* **2** usually **the Creation** [sing] the act of making the whole universe, as described in the Bible **3** [C] something that sb has made or produced, especially using skill or imagination: *This dish is a new creation, I didn't use a recipe.*

creative /kriˈeɪtɪv/ adj **1** using skill or imagination to make or do new things: *She's a fantastic designer – she's so creative.* o *We need some creative thinking to solve this problem.* **2** connected with producing new things, especially works of art: *His creative life went on until he was well over 80.* —**creatively** adv: *They haven't got a very big house but they use the space creatively.*

creativity /ˌkriːeɪˈtɪvəti/ noun [U] the ability to make or produce new things, especially using skill or imagination: *We want teaching that encourages children's creativity.*

creator /kriˈeɪtə(r)/ noun **1** a person who makes or produces sth new, especially using skill or imagination: *He was the creator of some of the best-known characters in literature.* **2 the Creator** [sing] God

☆ **creature** /ˈkriːtʃə(r)/ noun [C] a living thing such as an animal, a bird, a fish or an insect, but not a plant: *a living creature* o *a small black furry creature* o *creatures from other planets*

crèche /kreɪʃ; kreʃ/ noun [C] a place where small children are looked after while their parents are working

credentials /krɪˈdenʃlz/ noun [plural] **1** something that shows that a person is qualified or suitable for sth: *He has perfect credentials for the top job.* **2** a document that proves that sb is who he/she claims to be, or that he/she is qualified to do sth

credible /ˈkredəbl/ adj **1** that you can believe: *It's hardly credible that such a thing could happen without him knowing it.* ☛ The opposite is **incredible**. **2** that you can trust or take seriously: *We need to think of a credible alternative to nuclear energy.*

credibility /ˌkredəˈbɪləti/ noun [U] the quality of being able to be believed or trusted and taken seriously: *The Prime Minister had lost all credibility and had to resign.* —**credibly** /-əbli/ adv

credit[1] /ˈkredɪt/ noun **1** [U] the system of buying goods or services and not paying for them until later: *I bought the television on credit.* o *interest-free credit* (= payment over a period without any extra charges) o *Read the credit terms carefully before signing.* **2** [U] having money in an account at a bank: *No bank charges are made if your account remains in credit.* **3** [C] a payment made into an account at a bank ☛ Look at **debit**. **4** [C,U] a sum of money that a bank, etc lends: *The company was not able to get any further credit and went bankrupt.* **5** [U] praise for sth good that a person has done: *He got all the credit for the success of the project.* o *I can't take any credit; the others did all the work.* o *She didn't do very well but at least give her credit for trying.* **6 credits** [plural] the list of the names of the people who made a film or TV programme, shown at the beginning or end of the film **7** [sing] **a credit to sb/sth** a person or thing that gives honour: *She is a lovely girl and a credit to her school.* **8** [C] (*US*) a part of a course at a college or university, that a student has completed and that appears on his/her record

(IDIOMS) **do sb credit** to make sb deserve to be praised or respected: *His courage and optimism do him credit.*

(be) to sb's credit (used for showing that you approve of sth that sb has done, although you have criticized sth else): *The company, to its credit, apologized and refunded my money.*

have sth to your credit to have finished sth that is successful: *He has three best-selling novels to his credit.*

'credit card noun [C] a small plastic card that allows sb to get goods or services without using money. You usually receive a bill once a month for what you have bought: *Can I pay by credit card?* ☛ picture at **money**.

credit[2] /ˈkredɪt/ verb [T] **1 credit sb/sth with sth; credit sth to sb/sth** to accept or believe that sb/sth has a particular quality or is responsible for sth good or successful: *Of course I wouldn't do such a stupid thing – credit me with a bit more sense than that!* o *He credited his success to a lot of hard work.* **2** to record that money has been added to an account: *Has the cheque been credited to my account yet?* **3** (especially in negative sentences and questions) to believe: *I simply cannot credit that he has made the same mistake again!*

creditable /ˈkredɪtəbl/ adj deserving to be praised or respected (even if it is not excellent): *It was a creditable result considering that three players were injured.*

creditor /ˈkredɪtə(r)/ noun [C] a person or company to whom money is owed

creed /kriːd/ noun [C] a set of beliefs or principles (especially religious ones) that strongly influence sb's life

creek /kriːk/ noun [C] **1** (*Brit*) a narrow piece of water where the sea flows into the land **2** (*US*) a small river or stream

creep[1] /kriːp/ verb [I] (*pt, pp* **crept** /krept/) **1** to move very quietly and carefully, often with the body in a low position, so that nobody will notice you: *The cat crept silently towards the bird.* o *She crept into the room so as not to wake him up.* **2** to move forward slowly: *His latest record has crept up to number 10 in the charts.*

(PHRASAL VERB) **creep in** to begin to appear: *All sorts of changes are beginning to creep into the education system.*

creep[2] /kriːp/ noun [C] (*informal*) a person that you dislike because they try too hard to be liked by people in authority

(IDIOM) **give sb the creeps** (*informal*) to give sb an unpleasant feeling; to make sb feel frightened: *There's something about the way he laughs that gives me the creeps.*

creeper /ˈkriːpə(r)/ noun [C] a plant that grows up trees or walls or along the ground

creepy /ˈkriːpi/ adj (**creepier**; **creepiest**)

iː	ɪ	e	æ	ɑː	ɒ	ɔː	ʊ	uː	ʌ
see	sit	ten	hat	arm	got	saw	put	too	cup

(*informal*) that makes you feel rather nervous and frightened: *a creepy churchyard*

cremate /krɪˈmeɪt/ *verb* [T] to burn the body of a dead person as part of a funeral service

cremation /krɪˈmeɪʃn/ *noun* [C,U] an act of cremating a dead person ☛ Look at the note at **funeral**.

crematorium /ˌkreməˈtɔːriəm/ *noun* [C] (*pl* **crematoriums** or **crematoria** /-ˈtɔːriə/) (*US* **crematory** /ˈkreməˌtɔːri/ or /-ˌtəʊri/) a place where dead people are cremated

crept *pt*, *pp* of CREEP

crescendo /krɪˈʃendəʊ/ *noun* [C] (*pl* **crescendos**) a noise or piece of music that is very loud or that gets louder and louder

crescent /ˈkresnt/ *noun* [C] **1** the shape of the moon in its first and last stages; a curved shape that is pointed at both ends ☛ picture at **shape**. **2** a street or row of houses that is curved

cress /kres/ *noun* [U] a small plant with small green leaves that is eaten raw in salads

crest /krest/ *noun* [C] **1** a group of attractive feathers on the top of a bird's head **2** the top of a hill **3** the white part at the top of a wave

crestfallen /ˈkrestfɔːlən/ *adj* sad or disappointed

cretin /ˈkretɪn; *US* ˈkriːtn/ *noun* [C] (*slang*) a stupid person

crevasse /krɪˈvæs/ *noun* [C] a deep crack in thick ice

crevice /ˈkrevɪs/ *noun* [C] a narrow crack in a rock, wall, etc

☆ **crew** /kruː/ *noun* [C, with sing or pl verb] **1** all the people who work on a ship, aeroplane, etc: *The captain and his crew hope you had a pleasant flight* **2** a group of people who work together: *a camera crew* (= people who film things for television, etc)

ˈcrew cut *noun* [C] a very short hairstyle for men

ˈcrewman *noun* [C] a member of a crew(1): *Four crewmen were drowned.*

crib¹ /krɪb/ *noun* [C] (*especially US*) = COT

crib² /krɪb/ *verb* [I,T] (**cribbing**; **cribbed**) **crib (sth) (from/off sb)** to copy sb else's work and pretend it is your own: *She cribbed some of the answers off her friend.*

crick /krɪk/ *noun* [sing] a pain in your neck, back, etc that makes it difficult for you to move easily: *I've got a crick in my neck.* —**crick** *verb*: *I've cricked my neck.*

cricket¹ /ˈkrɪkɪt/ *noun* [U] a game that is played with a bat and ball on a large area of grass by two teams of eleven players (usually boys or men)

☛ In cricket the **bowler** bowls the ball to the **batsman** who tries to hit it with a **bat** and then score a **run** by running from one end of the pitch to the other.

cricketer *noun* [C] a person who plays cricket, especially as their job

cricket² /ˈkrɪkɪt/ *noun* [C] an insect that makes a loud noise by rubbing its wings together

☆ **crime** /kraɪm/ *noun* **1** [C] something which is against the law and which people are punished for, eg by being sent to prison: *to commit a crime* ○ *serious crimes such as murder and armed robbery* **2** [U] illegal behaviour in general: *There has been an increase in car crime recently.* ○ *to lead a life of crime* ○ *to fight crime* ○ *crime prevention measures* **3** usually **a crime** [sing] something that is morally wrong: *It is a crime to waste food when people are starving.*

criminal /ˈkrɪmɪnl/ *adj* **1** (only *before* a noun) connected with crime: *Deliberate damage to public property is a criminal offence.* ○ *criminal law* **2** morally wrong: *a criminal waste of taxpayers' money*

criminal *noun* [C] a person who has committed a crime

crimson /ˈkrɪmzn/ *adj, noun* [U] (of) a dark red colour ☛ Look at **maroon** and **scarlet**.

cringe /krɪndʒ/ *verb* [I] **1** to move away from sb/sth because you are frightened: *The dog cringed in terror when the man raised his arm.* **2** to feel embarrassed: *awful family photographs which make you cringe in embarrassment*

crinkle /ˈkrɪŋkl/ *verb* [I,T] **crinkle (sth) (up)** (to cause sth) to have thin folds or lines in it: *He crinkled the silver paper up into a ball.* —**crinkly** /ˈkrɪŋkli/ *adj*: *a type of soft crinkly material*

cripple /ˈkrɪpl/ *noun* [C] a person who cannot walk properly because his/her legs or back have been injured: *The accident left her a cripple at the age of 20.* ○ (*figurative*) *an emotional cripple* ☛ This is an old-fashioned word and the usual way of expressing the same meaning today is to say that somebody is **disabled** or that they have a **disability**.

cripple *verb* [T] **1** (usually passive) to cause sb to be a cripple: *He was crippled in a road accident.* **2** to damage sth badly: *The recession has crippled the motor industry.*

crippling *adj* that causes very great damage; that has a very harmful effect: *They had crippling debts and had to sell their house.*

crisis /ˈkraɪsɪs/ *noun* [C,U] (*pl* **crises** /ˈkraɪsiːz/) a time of great danger or difficulty; the moment when things change and either improve or get worse: *the international crisis caused by the invasion* ○ *Events reached a crisis during the summer of 1939.* ○ *a friend you can rely on in times of crisis*

crisp¹ /krɪsp/ *adj* **1** hard and dry: *Store the biscuits in a tin to keep them crisp.* **2** firm and fresh or new: *a crisp salad* ○ *a crisp apple* ○ *a crisp new £10 note* ○ *a crisp cotton dress* **3** (used about the air or weather) cold and dry: *a crisp winter morning* **4** (used about the way sb speaks) quick, clear but not very friendly: *a crisp reply*

crisply *adv* In a crisp¹(4) way: *'I disagree,' she said crisply.* —**crispy** *adj* (**crispier**; **crispiest**) (*informal*) = CRISP¹(1,2): *fish in crispy batter*

crisp² /krɪsp/ (*also* **poˌtato ˈcrisp**) (*US* **potato chip; chip**) *noun* [C] a very thin piece of potato that is fried in oil, dried and then sold in packets. Crisps usually have salt or another flavouring on them: *a packet of crisps* ☛ picture at **chip**.

criss-cross /ˈkrɪskrɒs; *US* -krɔːs/ *adj* (only

ɜː	ə	eɪ	əʊ	aɪ	aʊ	ɔɪ	ɪə	eə	ʊə
fur	ago	pay	home	five	now	join	near	hair	pure

before a noun) with many lines that cross over each other: *a criss-cross pattern* —**criss-cross** *verb* [I, T]: *the footpaths which criss-cross the countryside*

criterion /kraɪˈtɪərɪən/ *noun* [C] (*pl* **criteria** /-rɪə/) the standard that you use when you make a decision or form an opinion about sb/sth: *What is the criterion for deciding who gets a place on the course?*

critic /ˈkrɪtɪk/ *noun* [C] **1** a person who says what he/she thinks is bad or wrong with sb/sth: *He is a long-standing critic of the council's transport policy.* **2** a person whose job is to give his/her opinion about a play, film, book, work of art, etc: *a film critic* (= in a newspaper, etc).

☆ **critical** /ˈkrɪtɪkl/ *adj* **1 critical (of sb/sth)** saying what is wrong with sb/sth; disapproving: *The report was very critical of safety standards on the railways.* ○ *critical remarks* ☛ The opposite is **uncritical**. **2** (only *before* a noun) describing the good and bad points of a play, film, book, work of art, etc: *a critical guide to this month's new films* **3** dangerous or serious: *The patient is in a critical condition.* **4** very important; at a time when things can suddenly become better or worse: *The talks between the two leaders have reached a critical stage.* —**critically** /-ɪklɪ/ *adv*: *a critically ill patient* ○ *a critically important decision*

☆ **criticism** /ˈkrɪtɪsɪzəm/ *noun* **1** [C,U] (an expression of) what you think is bad about sb/sth: *The council has come in for severe criticism over the plans.* ○ *My main criticism is that it is too expensive.* **2** [U] the act of describing the good and bad points of a play, film, book, work of art, etc: *literary criticism*

☆ **criticize** (*also* **criticise**) /ˈkrɪtɪsaɪz/ *verb* [I,T] **criticize (sb/sth) (for sth)** to say what is bad or wrong with sb/sth: *The doctor was criticized for not sending the patient to hospital.* ○ *Stop criticizing!*

critique /krɪˈtiːk/ *noun* [C] a piece of writing that describes the good and bad points of sb/sth

croak /krəʊk/ *noun* [C] a deep low sound, like the noise that a frog makes
croak *verb* [I,T] to make a noise like a croak, eg because you have a cold and are losing your voice

crochet /ˈkrəʊʃeɪ; *US* krəʊˈʃeɪ/ *noun* [U] a way of making clothes, cloth, etc by using wool or cotton and one needle with a hook at one end —**crochet** *verb* [I,T] (*pt, pp* **crocheted** /-ʃeɪd/): *to crochet a shawl* ☛ Look at **knit**.

crockery /ˈkrɒkərɪ/ *noun* [U] cups, plates and dishes ☛ Look at **cutlery**.

crocodile /ˈkrɒkədaɪl/ *noun* [C] **1** a large, long animal with hard skin that lives in rivers in hot countries. A crocodile is a dangerous animal because it has a large mouth with a lot of sharp teeth in it. It is a reptile. ☛ Look at **alligator**. **2** (*Brit informal*) a line of children standing or walking in pairs

croissant /ˈkrwʌsɒŋ; *US* krʌˈsɒŋ/ *noun* [C] a type of light bread roll, shaped in a curve, that is eaten with butter at breakfast ☛ picture at **bread**.

crony /ˈkrəʊnɪ/ *noun* [C] (*pl* **cronies**) (*informal*) (often used in a critical way) a friend

crook /krʊk/ *noun* [C] **1** (*informal*) a dishonest person; a criminal **2** a bend or curve in sth: *the crook of your arm* (= the inside of your elbow)

crooked /ˈkrʊkɪd/ *adj* **1** not straight or even: *That picture is crooked. I'll straighten it up for you.* ○ *crooked teeth* **2** (*informal*) not honest: *a crooked accountant*

☆ **crop** /krɒp/ *noun* **1** [C] all the grain, fruit, vegetables, etc that grow or are collected at one time or place: *a crop of apples* ○ *Another year of crop failure would mean starvation for many people.* **2** [C, usually pl] plants that are grown on farms for food: *Rice and soya beans are the main crops here.* **3** [sing] a number of people or things which have appeared at the same time: *a crop of spots on his face*
crop *verb* (**cropping; cropped**) **1** [T] to cut sth very short: *cropped hair* **2** [I] to produce a crop(1)
(PHRASAL VERB) **crop up** to appear suddenly, when you are not expecting it: *Some problems have cropped up that we weren't expecting.*

cropper /ˈkrɒpə(r)/ *noun*
(IDIOM) **come a cropper** (*informal*) **1** to fall over **2** to fail; to have an accident

croquet /ˈkrəʊkeɪ; *US* krəʊˈkeɪ/ *noun* [U] a game that you play on grass. When you play croquet you use wooden sticks (**mallets**) to hit balls through metal arches (**hoops**).

☆ **cross¹** /krɒs; *US* krɔːs/ *noun* **1** [C] a mark that you make by drawing one line across another (eg +). The sign is used for showing the position of sth, for showing that sth is not correct, etc: *The cross on the map shows where our house is.* ○ *Incorrect answers were marked with a cross.* **2** (*also* **the Cross**) [sing] the two pieces of wood in the shape of a cross on which people were killed as a punishment in former times: *Christ's death on the cross* **3** [C] something in the shape of the cross¹(2) that is used as a symbol of the Christian religion: *She wore a gold cross round her neck.* ○ *The priest made the sign of the cross* (= by moving his right hand in front of his face and chest in the shape of a cross). ☛ Look at **crucifix**. **4** [C, usually sing] **a cross (between A and B)** something (especially a plant or an animal) that is a mixture of two different types of thing: *A fruit which is a cross between a peach and an apple.* **5** [C] (*formal*) something that makes you unhappy or worried or that makes your life more difficult: *We all have our own cross to bear.*

☆ **cross²** /krɒs; *US* krɔːs/ *verb* **1** [I,T] **cross (over) (from sth/to sth)** to go from one side of sth to the other: *to cross the road* ○ *You can't cross here, there's too much traffic.* ○ *Where did you cross the border?* **2** [I] (used about lines, roads, etc) to pass across each other: *The two roads cross just north of the village.* ○ (*figurative*) *Our letters crossed in the post.* **3** [T] to put sth across or over sth else: *to cross your arms* ☛ picture at **arm**. **4** [T] **cross yourself** to make the sign of a cross in front of your face and chest as a symbol of the Christian religion **5** [T] to refuse to do what sb wants you to do; to oppose sb: *He's an important man. It could be*

p	b	t	d	k	g	tʃ	dʒ	f	v	θ	ð
pen	bad	tea	did	cat	got	chin	June	fall	van	thin	then

dangerous to cross him. **6** [T] **cross sth with sth** to produce a new type of plant or animal by mixing two different types: *If you cross a horse with a donkey you get a mule.*
(IDIOMS) **cross my heart (and hope to die)** (*informal*) (used for emphasizing that what you are saying is true)
cross your fingers to hope that things will happen in the way that you want; to wish for good luck: *There's nothing more we can do now – just cross our fingers and hope for the best.*

☞ If a person says they are 'crossing their fingers' or 'keeping their fingers crossed' it doesn't mean that they are really doing this with their hands. It means that they are wishing somebody luck or hoping very much that something good will happen.

cross your mind (used about a thought, idea, etc) to come into your mind: *It never once crossed my mind that she was lying.*
(PHRASAL VERBS) **cross sth off (sth)** to remove sth from a list, etc by drawing a line through it: *Cross Dave's name off the guest list – he can't come.*
cross sth out to draw a line through sth that you have written because you have made a mistake, etc: *to cross out a spelling mistake*
cross³ /krɒs; *US* krɔːs/ *adj* **cross (with sb) (about sth)** (*informal*) angry or annoyed: *I was really cross with her for leaving me with all the work.* ○ *What are you so cross about?*
☞ **Cross** is less formal than **angry**. —**crossly** *adv*: *'Be quiet,' Dad said crossly.*
crossbar /'krɒsbɑː(r); *US* krɔːs-/ *noun* [C] **1** the piece of wood over the top of a goal in football, etc **2** the metal bar that joins the front and back of a bicycle
cross-country /ˌkrɒs'kʌntri; *US* ˌkrɔːs-/ *adj, adv* across fields, etc; not using main roads: *a cross-country run*
cross-examine /ˌkrɒsɪɡ'zæmɪn; *US* ˌkrɔːs-/ *verb* [T] to ask sb a lot of questions (eg in a court) in order to find out the truth about sth: *to cross-examine a witness in a court of law* —**cross-examination** /ˌkrɒsɪɡˌzæmɪ'neɪʃn; *US* ˌkrɔːs-/ *noun* [C,U]
cross-eyed /'krɒsaɪd; *US* 'krɔːs-/ *adj* having one or both your eyes looking towards your nose
crossing /'krɒsɪŋ; *US* 'krɔːs-/ *noun* [C] **1** a journey across water: *a rough sea crossing* **2** a place where roads or railway lines cross each other: *a level crossing* (= where a road crosses a railway line) **3** a place where you can cross over sth: *to cross the road at a pedestrian crossing* ○ *a border crossing*
cross-legged /ˌkrɒs'leɡd; *US* ˌkrɔːs-/ *adj, adv* sitting on the floor with your legs pulled up in front of you and with one leg or foot over the other: *to sit cross-legged*
cross-purposes /ˌkrɒs'pɜːpəsɪz; *US* ˌkrɔːs-/ *noun*
(IDIOM) **at cross-purposes** a state of confusion and misunderstanding between people who are talking about different things but think they are talking about the same thing: *I think we've been talking at cross-purposes. You mean next Saturday but I'm talking about this one.*
cross-reference /ˌkrɒs'refrəns; *US* ˌkrɔːs-/ *noun* [C] a note in a book, etc that tells you to look in another place in the book for more information
crossroads /'krɒsrəʊdz; *US* 'krɔːs-/ *noun* [C] (*pl* **crossroads**) a place where two or more roads cross each other: *When you come to the next crossroads turn right.*
cross-section /ˌkrɒs'sekʃn; *US* ˌkrɔːs-/ *noun* [C] **1** a picture of what the inside of sth would look like if you cut through it: *a diagram of a cross-section of the human brain* **2** a group of people that are typical of a larger group: *a representative cross-section of society*
crosswalk /'krɒswɔːk; *US* 'krɔːs-/ *noun* [C] (*US*) = PEDESTRIAN CROSSING

☆ **crossword** /'krɒswɜːd; *US* 'krɔːs-/ (*also* **'crossword puzzle**) *noun* [C] a word game with black and white squares where you write the words in the white squares, either across or down. The correct words are the answers to special questions (**clues**): *to do a crossword*
crotch /krɒtʃ/ (*also* **crutch**) *noun* [C] the place where a person's legs, or trouser legs, join at the top
crouch /kraʊtʃ/ *verb* [I] to bend down so that your body is close to the ground and lean forward slightly: *The cat crouched in front of the hole waiting for the mouse to appear.* ○ *He crouched down behind the sofa.* ☞ picture at **kneel**.
crow¹ /krəʊ/ *noun* [C] a large black bird that makes a loud noise
(IDIOM) **as the crow flies** (used for describing

s	z	ʃ	ʒ	h	m	n	ŋ	l	r	j	w
so	zoo	she	vision	how	man	no	sing	leg	red	yes	wet

distances) in a straight line: *It's a kilometre as the crow flies but three kilometres by road.*

crow² /krəʊ/ *verb* [I] **1** to make a loud noise, such as a male chicken, (**cock**) makes, eg early in the morning **2** (*informal*) to speak very proudly about sth; to boast

crowbar /'krəʊbɑː(r)/ *noun* [C] a long iron bar that is used for forcing sth open

☆ **crowd¹** /kraʊd/ *noun* **1** [C, with sing or pl verb] a large number of people in one place: *The crowd was/were extremely noisy.* ○ *A large crowd gathered to hear the President speak.* ○ *He pushed his way through the crowd.* ○ *There were crowds of people waiting outside the cinema.* **2 the crowd** [sing] most people: *to follow the crowd* (= to do what everybody else does) **3** [C, with sing or pl verb] (*informal*) a group of people who know each other: *John, Linda and Barry will be there – all the usual crowd.*

☆ **crowd²** /kraʊd/ *verb* **1** [I] **crowd around/ round (sb)** (used about a lot of people) to come together in one place: *Fans crowded round the singer hoping to get his autograph.* **2** [T] (used about a lot of people) to fill an area: *Groups of tourists crowded the main streets.*

(PHRASAL VERBS) **crowd into sth; crowd in** to go into a small place and make it very full: *Somehow we all crowded into their small living-room.*

crowd sb/sth into sth; crowd sb/sth in to put a lot of people into a small place: *Ten prisoners were crowded into one small cell.*

crowded *adj* full of people: *The town was crowded with Christmas shoppers.* ○ *a crowded bus*

crown¹ /kraʊn/ *noun* **1** [C] a round ornament made of gold and jewels, that a king or queen wears on the head on official occasions **2 the crown** [sing] the state as represented by a king or queen: *an area of land belonging to the Crown* **3** [sing] the top of your head or of a hat **4** [sing] the top of a hill

,crown 'prince (*feminine* ,crown prin'cess) *noun* [C] the person who has the right to become the next king or queen

crown² /kraʊn/ *verb* [T] **1** to put a crown on the head of a new king or queen in an official ceremony: *Elizabeth was crowned in 1952.* ○ (*figurative*) *the newly crowned British champion* **2 crown sth (with sth)** (*formal*) to cover the top of sth: *The mountain was crowned with snow.* **3** to be a good or successful end to sth: *years of hard work that were finally crowned with success*

(IDIOM) **to crown it all** to be the last in a number of lucky or unlucky events: *She failed her exam, her boyfriend left her and to crown it all her handbag was stolen.*

crowning *adj* (only *before* a noun) the best or most important: *Winning the World Championship was the crowning moment of her career.*

☆ **crucial** /'kruːʃl/ *adj* **crucial (to/for sth)** very important: *Early diagnosis of the illness is crucial for successful treatment.* —**crucially** /-ʃəli/ *adv: a crucially important decision, meeting, etc*

crucifix /'kruːsɪfɪks/ *noun* [C] a small model of a cross with a figure of Jesus on it

crucifixion /ˌkruːsɪ'fɪkʃn/ *noun* [C,U] the act of crucifying sb: *the Crucifixion of Christ*

crucify /'kruːsɪfaɪ/ *verb* [T] (*pres part* **crucifying**; *3rd pers sing pres* **crucifies**; *pt, pp* **crucified**) to kill sb by nailing or tying him/her to a cross

crude /kruːd/ *adj* **1** in its natural state: *crude oil* **2** done or made in a simple way; not skilful: *The method was crude but very effective.* **3** rude, talking or acting in a way that would offend many people: *He's always telling crude jokes.* —**crudely** *adv*

☆ **cruel** /kruːəl/ *adj* (**crueller**; **cruellest**) causing physical or mental pain or suffering to sb/sth; unkind: *I think it's cruel to keep animals in cages.* ○ *cruel words* ○ *Life can be cruel.* ○ *a cruel punishment* —**cruelly** /'kruːəli/ *adv*

☆ **cruelty** /'kruːəlti/ *noun* (*pl* **cruelties**) **1** [U] **cruelty (to sb/sth)** cruel behaviour: *cruelty to children* **2** [C, usually pl] a cruel act: *the cruelties of war*

cruise /kruːz/ *verb* [I] **1** to travel by boat, visiting a number of places, as a holiday: *to cruise around the Caribbean* **2** to travel by car, plane, etc staying at the same speed: *cruising at 70 miles an hour*

cruise *noun* [C] a holiday in which you travel on a ship and visit a number of different places: *After they retired they went on a world cruise.*

cruiser /'kruːzə(r)/ *noun* [C] **1** a large warship **2** (*also* **'cabin cruiser**) a motor boat which has room for people to sleep on it

crumb /krʌm/ *noun* [C] a very small piece of bread, cake or biscuit

crumble /'krʌmbl/ *verb* [I,T] **crumble (sth) (into/to sth); crumble (sth) (up)** (to cause sth) to break into very small pieces: *to crumble bread, biscuits, etc* ○ *The walls of the church are beginning to crumble.* ○ (*figurative*): *Support for the government is beginning to crumble.*

crummy /'krʌmi/ *adj* (**crummier**; **crummiest**) (*informal*) bad or unpleasant: *a crummy little backstreet hotel*

crumpet /'krʌmpɪt/ *noun* [C] (*Brit*) a flat round type of small cake with holes in the top that you eat hot with butter on it

crumple /'krʌmpl/ *verb* [I,T] **crumple (sth) (into sth); crumple (sth) (up)** (to cause sth) to be folded or pressed in an untidy or irregular way: *The front of the car crumpled when it hit the wall.* ○ *to crumple a piece of paper into a ball.*

crunch /krʌntʃ/ *verb* **1** [I,T] **crunch (sth)** to make a loud noise when you are eating sth hard: *to crunch an apple/a carrot* **2** (*also* **scrunch**) [I] to make a loud noise like the sound of sth being walked on and crushed: *We crunched through the snow.* ○ *The snow made a crunching noise under our feet.*

crunch *noun* [sing] an act or noise of crunching: *the crunch of their boots on the snow*

(IDIOM) **if/when it comes to the crunch; if/ when the crunch comes** if/when you are in a difficult situation and must make a difficult decision: *If it comes to the crunch, I'll stay and fight.*

crunchy *adj* (**crunchier**; **crunchiest**) hard and crisp, so that it makes a noise when you eat it or step on it: *a crunchy apple*

iː	ɪ	e	æ	ɑː	ɒ	ɔː	ʊ	uː	ʌ
see	sit	ten	hat	arm	got	saw	put	too	cup

crusade /kruːˈseɪd/ noun [C] **1 Crusade** one of the wars that European Christians fought with Muslims in the Middle Ages to win back land in the area that is now Israel **2** a fight for sth that you believe to be good or against sth that you believe to be bad: *a crusade against drugs*

cru'sader noun [C] a person who takes part in a crusade

crush¹ /krʌʃ/ verb [T] **1** to press sb/sth hard so that he/she/it is broken, damaged or injured: *Don't pack the cakes at the bottom of the box or they'll get crushed.* ○ *to be crushed to death* **2 crush sth (up)** to break sth hard into very small pieces or a powder: *First crush the garlic and fry in olive oil.* **3** to defeat sb/sth completely: *The army was sent in to crush the rebellion.*

(PHRASAL VERB) **crush (sb/sth) into, past, through, etc sth** (to cause sb/sth) to move into, past, through, etc a place by pushing or pressing: *Crowds of people crushed into the tiny church.*

crushing adj (only *before* a noun) that defeats sb/sth completely or upsets sb/sth a lot: *a crushing defeat* ○ *a crushing blow to the country's economy*

crush² /krʌʃ/ noun **1** [sing] a large group of people in a small space: *There was such a crush that I couldn't get near the bar.* **2** [C] **a crush (on sb)** (*informal*) a strong feeling of love and admiration for sb that does not usually last for a long time: *to have a crush on your teacher*

crust /krʌst/ noun [C,U] **1** the hard part on the outside of a loaf of bread, pie, etc: *I cut the crusts off the bread.* ☛ picture at **bread**. **2** [C] a hard layer on the outside of sth: *the Earth's crust*

crusty /ˈkrʌsti/ adj (**crustier; crustiest**) **1** having a hard crust(1): *crusty bread* **2** (*informal*) bad-tempered and impatient: *a crusty old professor*

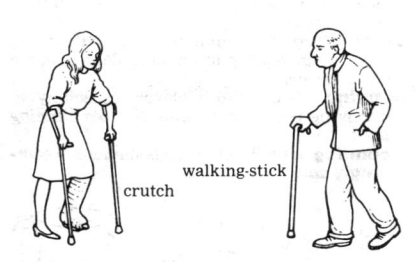

crutch /krʌtʃ/ noun [C] **1** a type of stick that you put under your arm to help you walk when you have hurt your leg or foot: *to be on crutches* (= to walk using crutches) **2** = CROTCH

crux /krʌks/ noun [sing] the most important or difficult part of a problem: *Now we come to the crux of the problem.*

☆ **cry¹** /kraɪ/ verb (*pres part* **crying**; *3rd pers sing pres* **cries**; *pt, pp* **cried**) **1** [I] to make a noise and produce tears in your eyes, eg because you are unhappy or have hurt yourself: *The baby never stops crying.* ○ *The child was crying for* (= because she wanted) *her mother.* ○ *to cry yourself to sleep* ○ *They were crying with cold and hunger.* **2** [I,T] **cry (out)** to shout or make a loud noise: *'Look,' he cried, 'There they are.'* ○ *to cry out in pain*

(PHRASAL VERB) **cry out for sth** to need sth very much: *London is crying out for a new transport system.*

☆ **cry²** /kraɪ/ noun (*pl* **cries**) **1** [C] a shout or loud noise: *the cries of the children in the playground* ○ *the cry of a seagull* ○ *a cry of pain, fear, joy, etc* **2** [sing] an act of crying¹(1): *After a good cry I felt much better.*

(IDIOM) **a far cry from sth/from doing sth** ⇨ **FAR¹**

crying /ˈkraɪɪŋ/ adj (only *before* a noun) very great (usually used when talking about a bad situation, etc): *There's a crying need for more doctors.* ○ *It's a crying shame that so many young people can't find jobs.*

crypt /krɪpt/ noun [C] a room that is under a church, where dead people are sometimes buried

cryptic /ˈkrɪptɪk/ adj having a hidden meaning that is not easy to understand; mysterious: *a cryptic message, remark, etc*

crystal /ˈkrɪstl/ noun **1** [U] a transparent rock or mineral **2** [U] very high-quality glass: *a crystal vase* **3** [C] a regular shape that some mineral substances form when they are solid: *salt crystals*

crystal 'ball noun [C] a glass ball in which some people believe you can see what is going to happen in the future

crystal 'clear adj very easy to understand: *The meaning is crystal clear.*

cub /kʌb/ noun [C] **1** a young fox, bear, lion, tiger or wolf **2 the Cubs** [plural] the part of the Boy Scout organization that is for younger boys

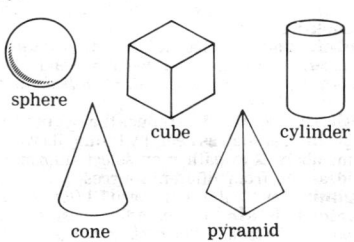

sphere

cube

cylinder

cone

pyramid

cube /kjuːb/ noun [C] **1** a solid shape that has six equal square sides **2** the number that you get if you multiply a number by itself twice: *the cube of 5 (5^3) is 125* (= 5x5x5).

cube verb [T] (usually passive) to multiply a number by itself twice: *Four cubed (4^3) is 64* (= 4 x 4 x 4).

cubic /ˈkjuːbɪk/ adj if a box is 2m long, 2m wide and 2m high, its volume is 8 cubic metres.

cubicle /ˈkjuːbɪkl/ noun [C] a small separate section of a larger room, eg for changing in at a swimming pool or trying on clothes in a shop

cuckoo /ˈkʊkuː/ noun [C] a bird which makes a

cucumber /ˈkjuːkʌmbə(r)/ noun [C,U] a long, thin vegetable with a dark green skin and a soft white inside that is often used in salads ☛ picture at **salad**.

cuddle /ˈkʌdl/ verb [I,T] to hold (sb/sth/each other) closely in your arms as a sign of love: *She cuddled her baby until he fell asleep.*
(PHRASAL VERB) **cuddle up (to/against sb/sth); cuddle up (together)** to move close to sb and sit or lie comfortably: *He cuddled up to his girlfriend on the sofa.* ○ *They cuddled up together for warmth.* —**cuddle** noun [C]: *He gave the child a cuddle and kissed her goodnight.*

cuddly /ˈkʌdli/ (**cuddlier**; **cuddliest**) adj soft and pleasant to hold close to you: *a cuddly toy*

cue[1] /kjuː/ noun [C] **1** a word or gesture that is the signal for sb else to say or do sth, especially in a play: *When Julia puts the tray on the table, that's your cue to come on stage.* **2** an example of how to behave: *I wasn't sure how to behave at a Japanese wedding, so I took my cue from my hosts.*
(IDIOM) **(right) on cue** at exactly the moment expected

cue[2] /kjuː/ noun [C] a long, thin wooden stick, used to hit the ball in games like snooker and billiards ☛ picture at **snooker**.

cuff[1] /kʌf/ noun [C] the end part of a sleeve, which often fastens at the wrist ☛ picture on page A10.
(IDIOM) **off the cuff** (used about a remark, etc) without previous thought or preparation: *I haven't got the figures here, but, off the cuff, I'd say the rise is about 10%.*

cuff[2] /kʌf/ verb [T] to hit sth (especially sb's head) lightly with your open hand

cuisine /kwɪˈziːn/ noun [U] a style of cooking: *Italian cuisine* ☛ A less formal word is **cooking**.

cul-de-sac /ˈkʌldəsæk/ noun [C] (pl **cul-de-sacs**) a street that is closed at one end

culinary /ˈkʌlɪnəri; *US* -neri/ adj connected with cooking

cull /kʌl/ verb [T] **1** to reduce the size of a group of animals such as deer, by killing its weakest members **2** to gather or select information, ideas, etc, from different sources

culminate /ˈkʌlmɪneɪt/ verb [I] (*formal*) **culminate in sth** to reach a final result or high point: *The team's efforts culminated in victory in the national championships.* —**culmination** /ˌkʌlmɪˈneɪʃn/ noun [sing]: *The joint space mission was the culmination of years of research.*

culottes /kjuːˈlɒts/ noun [plural] women's wide shorts that look like a skirt: *a pair of culottes*

culpable /ˈkʌlpəbl/ adj (*formal*) guilty; deserving blame

culprit /ˈkʌlprɪt/ noun [C] a person who has done sth wrong

cult /kʌlt/ noun [C] **1** a type of religion or religious group, especially one that is considered unusual **2** a person or thing that has become popular with a particular group of people: *His books have become a cult among young people.*

cultivate /ˈkʌltɪveɪt/ verb [T] **1** to prepare and use land for growing crops: *to cultivate the soil* **2** to grow crops: *Olives have been cultivated for centuries in Mediterranean countries.* **3** to try hard to develop sth: *He cultivated links with colleagues abroad.* **4** to try to form a friendship with sb who could be useful to you

cultivated adj well educated, with good manners —**cultivation** /ˌkʌltɪˈveɪʃn/ noun [U]

☆**cultural** /ˈkʌltʃərəl/ adj **1** connected with the customs, ideas, art, etc of a society: *cultural identities* ○ *The country's cultural diversity is a result of taking in immigrants from all over the world.* **2** connected with art, music, literature, etc: *The city has a rich cultural life, with many theatres, concert halls and art galleries.* —**culturally** /-rəli/ adv

☆**culture** /ˈkʌltʃə(r)/ noun **1** [C,U] the customs, ideas, civilization, etc of a particular society or group of people: *the language and culture of the Aztecs* ○ *The international conference aims to bring together people from many different cultures.* **2** [U] achievement in or understanding of art, literature, ideas, etc: *London has always been a centre of culture.* ○ *a man/woman of culture* **3** [U] the growing of plants or the keeping of certain types of animals

cultured adj well-educated, showing a good knowledge of the arts, etc: *a cultured manner, mind, person, etc*

ˈculture-shock noun [U] a feeling of confusion, etc that you may experience when you go to a country that is very different from your own

cum /kʌm/ prep (used for linking two nouns) also used as; as well as: *a bedroom-cum-study*

cumbersome /ˈkʌmbəsəm/ adj **1** heavy and difficult to carry, use, wear, etc **2** (used about a system, etc) slow; too complicated to be efficient: *Collection of the new tax proved cumbersome.*

cumulative /ˈkjuːmjʊlətɪv; *US* -leɪtɪv/ adj increasing steadily in amount, degree, etc: *a cumulative effect*

cunning /ˈkʌnɪŋ/ adj clever, especially at deceiving people: *a cunning liar* ○ *a cunning trick*
cunning noun [U] cunning behaviour —**cunningly** adv

handle
rim

cup and saucer   mug   jug

☆**cup**[1] /kʌp/ noun [C] **1** a small deep container with a round base and usually a handle, used for drinking liquids: *a cup and saucer* ○ *a teacup* ○ *a cup of coffee* **2** (in sport) a large metal

p	b	t	d	k	g	tʃ	dʒ	f	v	θ	ð
pen	bad	tea	did	cat	got	chin	June	fall	van	thin	then

cup given as a prize; the competition for such a cup: *Our team won the cup in the basketball tournament.* ○ *Is Scotland in the World Cup?* **3** an object shaped like a cup: *an egg-cup* (IDIOM) **(not) sb's cup of tea** not what sb likes or is interested in: *Horror films aren't my cup of tea.*

cup² /kʌp/ *verb* (**cup**ping; **cup**ped) [T] to form sth, especially your hands, into the shape of a cup; to hold sth with your hands shaped like a cup: *I cupped my hands to take a drink from the stream.* ○ *to cup your chin in your hands*

☆ **cupboard** /'kʌbəd/ *noun* [C] a piece of furniture, usually with shelves inside and a door or doors at the front, used for storing food, clothes, etc: *a kitchen cupboard* ○ *built-in cupboards*

curable /'kjʊərəbl/ *adj* that can be cured: *a curable disease* ☛ The opposite is **incurable**.

curate /'kjʊərət/ *noun* [C] a priest of the lowest rank in the Church of England, who helps the vicar of a church district (**parish**)

curator /kjʊə'reɪtə(r)/ *noun* [C] a person whose job is to look after the things that are kept in a museum, art gallery, etc

curb /kɜːb/ *noun* [C] **1 a curb (on sth)** something that controls or puts a limit on sth else: *a curb on local government spending* **2** (*especially US*) = KERB

curb *verb* [T] to control or set a limit on sth: *The law aims to curb pollution of rivers.*

curdle /'kɜːdl/ *verb* [I,T] to turn sour or to separate into different parts; to make something do this: *I've curdled the sauce.* ○ (*figurative*): *The scream made her blood curdle* (= made her very frightened). ☛ Look at **blood-curdling**.

☆ **cure¹** /kjʊə(r)/ *verb* [T] **1 cure sb (of sth)** to make sb healthy again: *The treatment cured him of cancer.* ○ *The doctors couldn't cure her.* **2** to make an illness, injury, etc end or disappear: *It is still not possible to cure the common cold.* ○ (*figurative*) *The plumber cured the problem with the central heating.* **3** to make certain types of food last longer by drying, smoking or salting them: *cured ham*

cure² /kjʊə(r)/ *noun* [C] **1** a medicine or treatment that can cure an illness, etc: *There is no known cure for AIDS.* **2** a return to good health; the process of being cured: *The new drug brought about a miraculous cure.*

curfew /'kɜːfjuː/ *noun* [C] a time after which people are not allowed to go outside their homes, eg during a war: *The government imposed a curfew.*

curiosity /ˌkjʊəri'ɒsəti/ *noun* [C,U] (*pl* **curiosities**) **1** [U] a desire to know or learn: *I was full of curiosity about their plans.* ○ *Out of curiosity, he opened her letter.* **2** [C] an unusual and interesting person or thing: *As the only girl who played football for the school team, she was quite a curiosity.*

☆ **curious** /'kjʊəriəs/ *adj* **1** eager to know or learn as much as you can: *He was curious to know how the machine worked.* ○ *Don't be so curious – it's got nothing to do with you.* **3** unusual or strange: *As I was walking home, a curious thing happened.* —**curiously** *adv*: *Curiously enough, we discovered that we had exactly the same name.*

curl¹ /kɜːl/ *noun* [C] **1** a piece of hair that curves round: *Her hair fell in curls round her face.* **2** a thing that has a curved round shape: *a curl of blue smoke*

curly *adj* (**curlier**; **curliest**) full of curls; shaped like a curl: *curly hair* ☛ picture at **hair**. The opposite is **straight**.

curl² /kɜːl/ *verb* [I,T] to form or to make sth form into a curl or curls: *Does your hair curl naturally?* ○ *The pages had curled with age.* ○ *He curled his lip and laughed scornfully.* **2** [I] to move round in a curve: *The snake curled around his arm.*

(PHRASAL VERB) **curl up** to pull your arms, legs and head close to your body: *I like to curl up on the couch and watch TV.* ○ *The animal curled up into a ball to protect itself.*

curler *noun* [C] a small plastic or metal tube that you wrap hair around in order to make it curly

currant /'kʌrənt/ *noun* [C] **1** a very small dried grape used to make cakes, etc **2** (often in compounds) one of several kinds of small soft fruit: *blackcurrants*

currency /'kʌrənsi/ *noun* (*pl* **currencies**) **1** [C,U] the system or type of money that a particular country uses: *The currency of Argentina is the austral.* ○ *foreign currency* ○ *a weak, strong, stable, etc currency* **2** [U] the state of being believed, accepted or used by many people: *The new ideas soon gained currency.*

☆ **current¹** /'kʌrənt/ *adj* **1** of the present time; happening now: *current fashions* ○ *current events* **2** generally accepted; in common use: *Is this word still current?*

currently *adv* at present: *He is currently working in Spain.*

current ac'count (*US* **checking account**) *noun* [C] a bank account from which you can take out money with a cheque book or cheque card

current af'fairs *noun* [plural] important political or social events that are happening at the present time

current² /'kʌrənt/ *noun* **1** [C] a continuous flowing movement of water, air, etc: *to swim against/with the current* ○ *You shouldn't swim in the river. There are dangerous currents.* ○ (*figurative*) *a current of anti-government feeling* **2** [U] the flow of electricity through a wire, etc: *Turn on the current.*

curriculum /kə'rɪkjʊləm/ *noun* [C] (*pl* **curriculums** or **curricula** /-lə/) all the subjects that are taught in a school, college or university; the contents of a particular course of study: *Latin is not on the curriculum at our school.* ○ *The curriculum for foreign languages emphasizes communication skills.*

curriculum vitae /kəˌrɪkjʊləm 'viːtaɪ/ (*abbr* **cv**) (*US also* **résumé** /ˌrezʊ'meɪ/) *noun* [sing] a short account of your education and work experience, often used when you are applying for a new job

curry /'kʌri/ *noun* [C,U] (*pl* **curries**) a hot-tasting dish of meat, vegetables, etc usually

served with rice: *some Indian vegetable curry* o *a hot/mild curry*
curried *adj* made into a curry: *curried chicken*
'curry powder *noun* [C] a fine mixture of strongly flavoured substances (**spices**) that is used to make curry

curse¹ /kɜːs/ *noun* [C] **1** a word used for expressing anger; a swear word **2** a word or words expressing the wish that sth terrible will happen to sb: *The witch put a curse on him.* o *The family seemed to be under a curse* (= lots of bad things happened to them). **3** something that causes great harm: *the curse of drug addiction*

curse² /kɜːs/ *verb* **1** [I,T] to swear at sb/sth; to use rude language to express your anger: *He dropped the box, cursed, and began to pick up the contents.* o *They cursed the traffic, realizing they would be late.* **2** [T] to use a curse¹(2) against sb/sth: *She cursed his family.*

cursor /'kɜːsə(r)/ *noun* [C] a small sign on a computer screen that you can move to indicate a particular position

cursory /'kɜːsəri/ *adj* quick and brief; done in a hurry: *a cursory glance*

curt /kɜːt/ *adj* short and not polite: *She gave him a curt reply and slammed the phone down.* — **curtly** *adv* **curtness** *noun* [U]

curtail /kɜːˈteɪl/ *verb* [T] to make sth shorter or smaller; to reduce — **curtailment** *noun* [C,U]

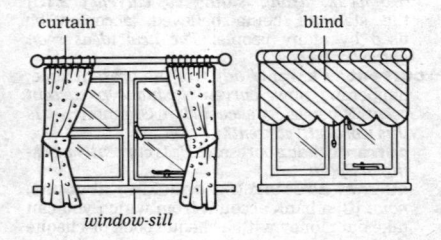

curtain   blind

window-sill

☆ **curtain** /'kɜːtn/ *noun* [C] **1** (*US also* **drape**) a piece of material that you can move sideways to cover a window, etc: *Could you draw the curtains, please?* o *lace curtains* o *The curtain goes up at 7pm* (= in a theatre, the play begins). **2** a thing that covers or hides sth: *a curtain of mist* (PHRASAL VERB) **curtain sth off** to divide a room, etc with a curtain: *The bed was curtained off from the rest of the room.*

curtsy (*also* **curtsey**) /'kɜːtsi/ *noun* [C] (*pl* **curtsies** *or* **curtseys**) a movement made by a woman as a sign of respect, done by bending the knees, with one foot behind the other

curtsy (*also* **curtsey**) *verb* (*pres part* **curtsying** *or* **curtseying**; *3rd pers sing pres* **curtsies** *or* **curtseys**; *pt, pp* **curtsied** *or* **curtseyed**) [I] to make a curtsy

☆ **curve** /kɜːv/ *noun* [C] a line that bends round: *a curve on a graph*

curve *verb* [I,T] to bend or to make sth bend in a curve: *The bay curved round to the south.* o *a curved line*

cushion /'kʊʃn/ *noun* [C] **1** a bag filled with soft material, eg feathers, which you put on a chair, etc to make it more comfortable: *She sat back in the armchair with a cushion behind her head.* ☛ A cushion on a bed is a **pillow**. **2** something that acts or is shaped like a cushion: *a cushion of air*

cushion *verb* [T] **1** to make a blow, etc less painful: *The snow cushioned his fall.* **2** to reduce the unpleasant effect of sth: *She spent her childhood on a farm, cushioned from the effects of the war.*

cushy /'kʊʃi/ *adj* (**cushier**; **cushiest**) (*informal*) too easy, requiring little effort (to a degree that seems unfair to others): *a cushy job*

custard /'kʌstəd/ *noun* [U] a sweet yellow sauce made from milk and cornflour and eaten hot or cold: *apple pie and custard*

custodian /kʌˈstəʊdiən/ *noun* [C] (*formal*) a person who looks after sth, especially a museum, library, etc

custody /'kʌstədi/ *noun* [U] **1** the legal right or duty to take care of sb/sth: *After the divorce, the mother was given custody of the children.* **2** the state of being guarded, or kept in prison temporarily, especially by the police: *The man was arrested and kept in custody until his trial.*

☆ **custom** /'kʌstəm/ *noun* **1** [C,U] a way of behaving which a particular group or society has had for a long time: *It's the custom in Britain for a bride to throw her bouquet to the wedding guests.* o *according to local custom* ☛ Look at the note at **habit**. **2** [C] something that a person regularly does: *They were walking through the park, as was their custom, when a large dog attacked them.* **3** [U] trade; the practice of people buying things regularly from a particular shop, etc: *The local shop lost a lot of custom when the new supermarket opened.*

customary /'kʌstəməri; *US* -meri/ *adj* according to custom; usual: *Is it customary to send cards at Christmas in your country?* — **customarily** /'kʌstəmərəli; *US* ˌkʌstəˈmerəli/ *adv*

☆ **customer** /'kʌstəmə(r)/ *noun* [C] **1** a person who buys goods or services: *a regular customer* o *The shop assistant was serving a customer.* **2** (*informal*) (after certain adjectives) a person: *a tough, awkward, odd, etc customer*

☆ **customs** (*also* **the Customs**) /'kʌstəmz/ *noun* [plural] the place at an airport, etc where government officials check your luggage to see whether you are bringing goods into the country illegally: *We went straight through customs with nothing to declare.* o *a customs officer*

☆ **cut¹** /kʌt/ *verb* (*pres part* **cutting**; *pt, pp* **cut**) **1** [I,T] to make an opening, wound or mark in sth using a sharp tool, eg a pair of scissors or a knife: *I cut my finger with a vegetable knife.* o *Be careful not to cut yourself on that broken glass!* o *This knife doesn't cut very well.* **2** [T] to remove sth or a part of sth, using a knife, etc: *She cut two slices of bread (from the loaf).* **3** [T] **cut sth (in/into sth)** to divide sth into pieces with a knife, etc: *She cut the cake into eight (pieces).* o *He cut the rope in two.* **4** [T] to make sth shorter by using scissors, etc: *I cut my own hair.* o *to have your hair cut* (= at the hairdressers). o *to cut the grass* **5** [T] to make or form sth by removing material with a sharp tool: *She cut a*

iː	ɪ	e	æ	ɑː	ɒ	ɔː	ʊ	uː	ʌ
see	sit	ten	hat	arm	got	saw	put	too	cup

hole in the card and pushed the string through. o *They cut a path through the jungle.* **6** [T] to reduce sth or make it shorter; to remove sth: *to cut taxes* o *Train services have been cut because of the strike.* o *Several violent scenes in the film were cut.*
(IDIOM) **cut sth/sb short** ⇨ SHORT²
(PHRASAL VERBS) **cut across sth** to go beyond the limits of: *The question of aid for the earthquake victims cuts across national boundaries.*
cut across, along, through, etc (sth) to go across, etc sth, in order to shorten your journey: *It's much quicker if we cut across the field.*
cut sth back; cut back (on sth) to reduce sth: *to cut back on public spending*
cut sth down 1 to make sth fall down by cutting it: *to cut down a tree* **2** to shorten sth: *I have to cut my essay down to 2 000 words.*
cut sth down; cut down (on sth) to reduce the quantity or amount of sth; to do sth less often: *You should cut down on fatty foods.*
cut in (on sb/sth); cut into sth to interrupt sb/sth: *to cut into a conversation*
cut sb off (often passive) to stop or interrupt sb's telephone conversation: *We were cut off before I could give her my message.*
cut sb/sth off (often passive) to stop the supply of sth to sb: *If you don't pay your gas bill they'll cut you off.* o *The electricity has been cut off.*
cut sth off to block a road, etc so that nothing can pass: *We must cut off all possible escape routes.*
cut sb/sth off (from sb/sth) (often passive) to prevent sb/sth from moving from a place or contacting people outside: *The farm was cut off from the village by heavy snow.*
cut sth open to open sth by cutting: *She fell and cut her head open.*
cut sth out 1 to remove sth or to form sth into a particular shape by cutting: *to cut out a dress from a piece of cloth* **2** to leave sth out: *Cut out the boring details!* **3** (*informal*) (often in orders) to stop saying or doing sth, usually sth annoying: *Cut that out and leave me alone!* **4** (*informal*) to stop doing or using sth: *You'll only lose weight if you cut out sweet things from your diet.*
cut sth out (of sth) to remove sth from sth larger by cutting: *He cut the job advertisement out of the newspaper.*
be cut out for sth; be cut out to be sth to have the qualities to be able to do sth; to be suitable for sth/sb: *You're not cut out to be a soldier.* o *David and Janet are cut out for each other.*
cut sth up to cut sth into small pieces with a knife, etc
'cut-back *noun* [C] a reduction in amount or number: *The management were forced to make cut-backs in staff.*
'cut-off *noun* [C] the level at which sth stops: *The cut-off date is 12 May. After that we'll end the offer.*
,cut-'price (*US* **cut-'rate**) *adj* sold at a reduced price; selling goods at low prices: *cut-price offers* o *a cut-price store*
☆ **cut²** /kʌt/ *noun* [C] **1** a wound or opening made with a knife, etc: *He had a deep cut on his forehead.* **2** an act of cutting: *to have a cut and* *blow-dry* (= at a hairdresser's) **3** **a cut (in sth)** a reduction in size, amount, etc: *a cut in government spending* o *a power cut* (= when the electric current is cut off temporarily) **4** a piece of meat from a particular part of an animal **5** (*informal*) a share, especially in profits

cute /kjuːt/ *adj* (*especially US*) attractive; pretty: *Your little girl is so cute!* o *a cute smile*

cutlery /'kʌtləri/ *noun* [U] the knives, forks and spoons that you use for eating food: *Where do you keep your cutlery?* ☛ Look at **crockery**.

cutlet /'kʌtlɪt/ *noun* [C] a small, thick piece of meat, eg lamb, often with bone in it, that is fried or grilled

cutter /'kʌtə(r)/ *noun* [C] (*also* **cutters** [plural]) a tool that you use for cutting through sth, eg metal: *a pair of wire-cutters*

cut-throat /'kʌtθrəʊt/ *adj* caring only about success and not worried about hurting anybody: *cut-throat business practices*

cutting¹ /'kʌtɪŋ/ *noun* [C] **1** (*US* **clipping**) a piece cut out from a newspaper, etc: *press cuttings* **2** a piece cut off from a plant that you use for growing a new plant

cutting² /'kʌtɪŋ/ *adj* **1** (used about sth you say) unkind; meant to hurt sb's feelings: *a cutting remark* **2** (of the wind, etc) cold, strong and unpleasant

cyanide /'saɪənaɪd/ *noun* [U] a poisonous chemical

☆ **cycle** /'saɪkl/ *noun* [C] **1** a series of events, etc that happen repeatedly in the same order: *the life cycle of a frog* **2** a bicycle or motor cycle: *a cycle shop*

cycle *verb* [I] to ride a bicycle: *He usually cycles to school.* ☛ **Go cycling** is a common way of talking about cycling for pleasure: *We like to go cycling at weekends.*

cyclist /'saɪklɪst/ *noun* [C] a person who rides a bicycle

cyclic /'saɪklɪk/ (*also* **cyclical** /'saɪklɪkl/) *adj* following a repeated pattern

cyclone /'saɪkləʊn/ *noun* [C] a violent wind that moves in a circle causing a storm ☛ Look at the note at **storm**.

cygnet /'sɪgnɪt/ *noun* [C] a young swan

cylinder /'sɪlɪndə(r)/ *noun* [C] **1** a shape or an object with circular ends and straight sides ☛ picture at **cube**. **2** a cylinder-shaped part of an engine, eg in a car: *a five-cylinder engine*

cylindrical /sɪ'lɪndrɪkl/ *adj* having the shape of a cylinder

cymbal /'sɪmbl/ *noun* [C, usually pl] one of a pair of round metal plates used as a musical instrument. Cymbals make a loud ringing sound when you strike them together or hit them with a stick.

cynic /'sɪnɪk/ *noun* [C] a person who believes that people only do things for selfish reasons: *Don't be such a cynic. He did it to help us, not for the money.* —**cynical** /'sɪnɪkl/ *adj*: *She takes a cynical view of politics.* o *a cynical remark* —**cynically** /-kli/ *adv* —**cynicism** /'sɪnɪsɪzəm/ *noun* [U]

Cyrillic /sɪ'rɪlɪk/ *adj* the Cyrillic alphabet is used in languages such as Russian

cyst /sɪst/ *noun* [C] a swelling filled with liquid in the body or under the skin

ɜː	ə	eɪ	əʊ	aɪ	aʊ	ɔɪ	ɪə	eə	ʊə
fur	ago	pay	home	five	now	join	near	hair	pure

Dd

D, d /diː/ *noun* [C] (*pl* **D's; d's**) the fourth letter of the English alphabet: *'David' begins with (a) 'D'.*

dab /dæb/ *verb* (**dab**bing; **dab**bed) [I,T] to touch sth lightly, usually several times: *He dabbed the cut with some cotton wool.*
(PHRASAL VERB) **dab sth on/off** to put sth on or to remove sth with a light stroke or strokes: *to dab some antiseptic on a wound*
dab *noun* [C] **1** a light touch: *She gave her eyes a dab with a handkerchief.* **2** a small quantity of sth that is put on a surface: *a dab of paint, perfume, etc*

dabble /ˈdæbl/ *verb* **1** [T] to put your hands, feet, etc in water and move them around: *We sat on the bank and dabbled our toes in the river.* **2** [I] to become involved in sth in a manner that is not very serious: *to dabble in politics*

☆ **dad** /dæd/ *noun* [C] (*informal*) father: *Is that your dad?* ○ *Come on, Dad!*

daddy /ˈdædi/ *noun* (*pl* **daddies**) (*informal*) (used by children) father: *I want my daddy!* ○ *Give daddy a kiss.*

daffodil /ˈdæfədɪl/ *noun* [C] a tall yellow flower that grows from a bulb in the spring

daft /dɑːft; *US* dæft/ *adj* (*informal*) silly; foolish: *Don't be daft.* ○ *a daft idea*

dagger /ˈdægə(r)/ *noun* [C] a type of knife with a point and two sharp edges used as a weapon, especially in former times: *He plunged a dagger into her heart.*

☆ **daily** /ˈdeɪli/ *adj, adv* done, made or happening every day: *Our airline flies to Japan daily.* ○ *a daily routine, delivery, newspaper, etc*
daily *noun* [C] (*pl* **dailies**) a newspaper that is published every day except Sunday

dainty /ˈdeɪnti/ *adj* (**daintier; daintiest**) small or delicate and pretty: *a dainty lace handkerchief* —**daintily** *adv*: *She walked daintily, with graceful little steps.*

dairy /ˈdeəri/ *noun* [C] (*pl* **dairies**) **1** a place on a farm where milk is kept and butter, cheese, etc are made **2** a shop which sells milk, butter, eggs, etc, or a company that supplies shops with these products
'dairy cattle *noun* [U] cows which are kept for their milk, not their meat
'dairy farm *noun* [C] a farm that produces mainly milk and milk products
'dairy products *noun* [plural] food made from milk, such as butter, cheese, etc

daisy /ˈdeɪzi/ *noun* [C] (*pl* **daisies**) a small white flower with a yellow centre, which usually grows wild on grass

dale /deɪl/ *noun* [C] a valley, especially in Northern England

dam /dæm/ *noun* [C] a wall built across a river to hold back the water and form a lake (**reservoir**) behind it —**dam** *verb* [T]

☆ **damage** /ˈdæmɪdʒ/ *noun* **1** [U] **damage (to sth)** harm or injury caused when sth is broken or spoiled: *The earthquake caused widespread damage* ○ *It will take weeks to repair the damage done by the vandals.* ○ *The arms scandal did considerable damage to relations between the two countries.* **2 damages** [plural] money that you can claim from sb if he/she damages sth of yours or hurts you
damage *verb* [T] to spoil or harm sth, eg by breaking it: *The roof was damaged by the storm.*
damaging *adj* having a bad or harmful effect

dame /deɪm/ *noun* [C] **1** (*US slang*) a woman **2 Dame** (*Brit*) a title given to a woman as an honour because of sth special that she has done: *Dame Agatha Christie*

damn¹ /dæm/ *verb* [T] **1** (*informal*) (used for expressing anger or annoyance): *Damn that stupid driver!* ○ *Damn! I've left my money behind.* **2** to describe sth as very bad: *The film was damned by all the critics.* **3** (used about God) to send sb to hell
the damned *noun* [plural] the people who suffer in hell: *The film was called 'The Journey of the Damned'.*
damning *adj* very unfavourable; extremely critical: *There was a damning article about the book in the newspaper.*

damn² /dæm/ *noun*
(IDIOM) **not care/give a damn (about sb/sth)** (*informal*) not care at all: *I don't give a damn what he thinks about me.*
damn *adj* (only *before* a noun) (*informal*) (used for expressing anger or annoyance): *Some damn fool has parked too close to me.*
damn *adv* (*informal*) (used for emphasizing that sth is good or bad) very: *Don't be so damn silly!* ○ *Read it! It's a damn good book.*

☆ **damp¹** /dæmp/ *adj* a little wet: *The grass is a bit damp. Sit on the rug.* ○ *The house had been empty and felt rather damp.*
damp *noun* [U] the state of being a little wet, especially in the air or in a house: *She hated the damp and the cold of the English climate.* ○ *We inspected the walls for signs of damp.* ☞ Look at the note at **wet**.

damp² /dæmp/ *verb* [T] **damp sth (down)** to make sth less strong or urgent: *He tried to damp down their expectations in case they failed.*

dampen /ˈdæmpən/ *verb* [T] **1 dampen sth (down)** to make sth less strong or urgent: *Even the awful weather did not dampen their*

p	b	t	d	k	g	tʃ	dʒ	f	v	θ	ð
pen	bad	tea	did	cat	got	chin	June	fall	van	thin	then

enthusiasm for the trip. **2** to make sth a little wet: *He dampened his hair to try to stop it sticking up.*

damson /'dæmzn/ *noun* [C] a small dark purple fruit; a type of plum

☆ **dance¹** /dɑːns; *US* dæns/ *noun* **1** [C] a series of steps and movements which you do to music: *What sort of dance is this? A waltz?* ○ *Would you like a dance?* **2** [C] a social meeting at which people dance with each other: *There's usually a dance at the end of term.* **3** [U] dancing as a form of art or entertainment: *She's very interested in modern dance.*

☆ **dance²** /dɑːns; *US* dæns/ *verb* **1** [I,T] to move around to the rhythm of music by making a series of steps: *Did you ever see Nureyev dance?* ○ *to dance the waltz* **2** [I] to move in a lively way, usually up and down: *She was dancing up and down with excitement.*

dancer *noun* [C] a person who dances, often as a job: *a ballet dancer* ○ *She's a good dancer.*

dancing *noun* [U] moving to music: *Will there be dancing at the party?* ○ *ballet-dancing* ☞ Look at **ballet**.

dandelion /'dændɪlaɪən/ *noun* [C] a small wild plant with a bright yellow flower

dandruff /'dændrʌf/ *noun* [U] small pieces of dead skin in the hair, that look like white dust

☆ **danger** /'deɪndʒə(r)/ *noun* **1** [U] the chance that sb/sth may be hurt, killed or damaged or that sth unpleasant may happen: *Danger! Steep hill!* ○ *As a fighter pilot, he had to face danger daily.* ○ *The men kept on running until they thought they were out of danger.* **2** [C] **a danger (to sb/sth)** a person or thing that can cause injury, pain or damage: *Drunk drivers are a danger to everyone on the road.*

☆ **dangerous** /'deɪndʒərəs/ *adj* likely to cause injury or damage: *a dangerous animal, road, illness, etc* ○ *The strong currents in the sea here are extremely dangerous for swimmers.*
—**dangerously** *adv*: *He was standing dangerously close to the cliff edge.*

dangle /'dæŋgl/ *verb* [I,T] to hang or swing freely; to hold sth so that it hangs in this way: *She sat on the fence with her legs dangling.* ○ *He dangled the keys in front of me. 'You can drive if you want,' he said.*

dank /dæŋk/ *adj* damp, cold and unpleasant: *a dank cave*

☆ **dare¹** /deə(r)/ *verb* (usually in negative sentences) to be brave enough to do sth: *I daren't ask her to lend me any more money.* ○ *We were so frightened that we didn't dare go into the room.* ○ *The government dared not increase taxes again that year.* ○ *If you dare say that again, I'll hit you!* ☞ The negative is **dare not** (usually **daren't** /deənt/) or **do not/does not** (= **don't/doesn't**) **dare**. In the past tense it is **did not (didn't) dare**, or (formal) **dared not**. **Dare** is usually followed by an infinitive without 'to': *Nobody dared (to) speak.*

(IDIOMS) **don't you dare** (used for telling sb very strongly not to do sth): *Don't you dare tell my parents about this.*

how dare you (used when you are angry about sth that sb has done): *How dare you speak to me like that!*

I dare say I suppose: *'I think you should accept the offer.' 'I dare say you're right.'*

☆ **dare²** /deə(r)/ *verb* [T] to try to persuade sb to do sth in order to prove how brave he/she is: *Can you jump off that wall? Go on, I dare you!* ○ *He dared his friend to put a worm on the teacher's desk.*

☆ **dare³** /deə(r)/ *noun* [C, usually sing] something you do because sb asks you to, to prove how brave you are: *'Why did you try to swim across the river?' 'It was a dare.'*

daredevil /'deədevl/ *noun* [C] a person who is willing to take risks, often foolishly

daring /'deərɪŋ/ *adj* willing to take risks or to do or say things which other people might not; brave; bold: *a daring attack*

☆ **dark¹** /dɑːk/ *noun* [sing] **the dark** the state of having no light: *He's afraid of the dark.* ○ *Why are you sitting alone in the dark?*

(IDIOMS) **before/after dark** before /after the sun goes down

(be/keep sb) in the dark (about sth) (be/keep sb) in a position of not knowing (about sth): *Don't keep me in the dark. Tell me!*

☆ **dark²** /dɑːk/ *adj* **1** with no light or very little light: *It was a dark night, with no moon.* **2** (used about a colour) nearer black than white; not light: *dark blue* **3** (used about a person) having brown or black skin or hair; not fair: *She was small and dark with brown eyes.* **4** (only *before* a noun) sad; without hope: *the dark days leading up to the start of the war* **5** (only *before* a noun) mysterious or slightly threatening: *He seemed friendly, but there was a dark side to his character.*

(IDIOM) **keep it/sth dark (from sb)** to keep sth secret

darkness *noun* [U] the state of being dark: *We sat in complete darkness, waiting for the lights to come back on.*

,dark 'glasses *noun* [plural] = SUNGLASSES

darken /'dɑːkən/ *verb* [I,T] to become or to make sth darker: *The sky suddenly darkened and it looked like rain.*

darling /'dɑːlɪŋ/ *noun* [C] a person or thing that you like or love: *Hello darling! How lovely to see you.* ○ *He's so kind. He's an absolute darling!*

darn /dɑːn/ *verb* [I,T] to mend a hole (in clothes) by sewing across it in one direction and then in the other

darts

dartboard — dart
bull's-eye

dart¹ /dɑːt/ *noun* **1** [C] an object like a small

arrow. It is thrown or shot as a weapon or in a game: *They first tranquillize the tiger with a special dart.* **2 darts** [U] a game in which you throw darts at a round board with numbers on it (**a dartboard**): *Darts is a popular game in English pubs.*

dart² /dɑːt/ *verb* [I,T] to move suddenly and quickly in a certain direction; to make sth move in this way: *A rabbit darted across the field.* ○ *She darted an angry glance at me* (= suddenly glanced angrily).

dash¹ /dæʃ/ *noun* **1** [sing] a sudden, quick forward movement: *We made a dash for the bus and just got on.* **2** [C, usually sing] a small amount of sth that you add to sth else: *a dash of lemon juice* **3** [C] a small horizontal line (—) used in writing, especially for adding extra information ☞ Look at **hyphen**.

dash² /dæʃ/ *verb* **1** [I] to go or run suddenly and quickly: *We all dashed for shelter when it started to rain* **2** [I,T] to hit sth with great force; to throw sth so that it hits sth else very hard: *The waves dashed against the harbour wall.* ○ *She dashed her racket to the ground.* ○ (*figurative*): *The accident dashed his hopes of becoming a pianist.*

(PHRASAL VERB) **dash sth off** to write or draw sth very quickly

dashboard /'dæʃbɔːd/ *noun* [C] the part in a car in front of the driver where most of the switches, etc are

☆ **data** /'deɪtə; 'dɑːtə; *US* 'dætə/ *noun* [U,plural] facts or information: *to gather data* ○ *The data is/are still being analysed.* ○ *How much data can we store on one disk?* (= on a computer). ☞ Data was originally the plural form of a Latin noun, but it is now often used as an uncountable noun: *The data we have is not very interesting.*

'database *noun* [C] a large amount of data that is stored in a computer and can easily be used, added to, etc

☆ **date¹** /deɪt/ *noun* **1** [C] a particular day of the month or of the year: *What's the date today?* ○ *What date is it today?* ○ *What's your date of birth?* **2** [sing] a particular time: *We can discuss this at a later date.* **3** [C] an appointment to meet sb, especially a boyfriend or girlfriend: *Shall we make a date to have lunch together?* ○ *I've got a date with Tom on Friday night.* **4** [C] (*especially US*) a boyfriend or girlfriend: *Who's your date – is it Sarah?*

(IDIOMS) **out of date 1** unfashionable; no longer useful: *out-of-date methods, machinery, etc* **2** no longer able to be used: *I must renew my passport. It's out of date.*

to date (*formal*) until now: *We've had very few complaints to date.*

up to date 1 modern: *The new kitchen will be right up to date, with all the latest gadgets.* **2** with all the latest information; having done everything that you should have done: *In this report we'll bring you up to date with the latest news from the area.* ○ *Are you up to date with your homework?*

☆ **date²** /deɪt/ *verb* **1** [T] to discover or guess how old sth is: *to date a skeleton, a rock, etc* **2** [T] to write the day's date on sth: *The letter is not dated so we can't tell when it was written.* **3** [I,T] to seem, or to make sb/sth seem, unfashionable: *We chose a simple style so that it wouldn't date as quickly.* **4** [I,T] (*especially US informal*) to meet a girlfriend or boyfriend regularly **5** [I] **date back to/from**... to have existed since...: *The house dates back to the seventeenth century.*

dated *adj* unfashionable: *This sort of jacket looks rather dated now.*

date³ /deɪt/ *noun* [C] a small, sweet, dark brown fruit that comes from a tree which grows in hot countries

☆ **daughter** /'dɔːtə(r)/ *noun* [C] a female child: *I have two sons and one daughter.* ○ *Janet's daughter is a doctor.*

daughter-in-law /'dɔːtərɪnlɔː/ *noun* [C] (*pl* **daughters-in-law**) the wife of your son

daunt /dɔːnt/ *verb* [T] (usually passive) to frighten or to worry sb by being too big or difficult: *I was rather daunted by the sudden responsibility.* —**daunting** *adj*: *A daunting journey lay ahead.*

dawdle /'dɔːdl/ *verb* [I] to be slow or to move slowly; to waste time: *Stop dawdling! We're waiting for you!*

dawn¹ /dɔːn/ *noun* **1** [C,U] the early morning, when light first appears in the sky: *a beautiful winter's dawn, still and cold* ○ *before/at dawn* **2** [sing] the beginning: *the dawn of civilization* (IDIOM) **the crack of dawn** ▷ CRACK¹

dawn² /dɔːn/ *verb* [I] **1** to begin to grow light, after the night: *The day dawned bright and cold.* ○ (*figurative*) *A new era of peace is dawning.* **2 dawn (on sb)** to become clear (to sb): *Suddenly it dawned on her. 'Of course!' she said. 'You're Mike's brother!'*

☆ **day** /deɪ/ *noun* **1** [C] a period of 24 hours, of which seven make up a week: *'What day is it today?' 'Tuesday.'* ○ *We went to Italy for ten days.* ○ *I saw that film a few days ago.* ○ *There's a meeting in two days' time.* ○ *The next day was Saturday.* ○ *the day before/the following day* ○ *New Year's Day* **2** [C,U] the time between sunrise and sunset: *The days were warm but the nights were freezing.* ○ *Have a good day! See you tonight.* ○ *It's been raining all day.* ☞ Look at **daily**. **3** [C] the hours of the day when you work: *She's expected to work a seven-hour day.* **4** [C] (*also* **days**) a particular period of time: *in Shakespeare's day* ○ *in the days of Shakespeare* ○ *In the old days, most houses had an outside toilet.*

(IDIOMS) **break of day** ▷ BREAK²

by day/night during the day/night: *These animals sleep by day and hunt by night.*

call it a day ▷ CALL²

the day after tomorrow not tomorrow, but the next day

the day before yesterday not yesterday, but the day before

day by day every day; as time passes: *Day by day, she was getting a little bit stronger.*

day in, day out every day, without any change: *He sits at his desk working, day in, day out.*

from day to day; from one day to the next within a short period of time: *Things change so*

iː	ɪ	e	æ	ɑː	ɒ	ɔː	ʊ	uː	ʌ
see	sit	ten	hat	arm	got	saw	put	too	cup

daylight

quickly that we never know what will happen from one day to the next.
make sb's day (*informal*) to make sb very happy
one day; some day at some time in the future: *Some day we'll go back and see all our old friends.*
the other day a few days ago; recently: *I bumped into him in town the other day.*
the present day ⇨ PRESENT¹
these days in the present age; nowadays: *More and more couples are getting divorced these days.*
'daybreak *noun* [U] the time in the early morning when light first appears: *at daybreak*
'day-dream *noun* [C] thoughts that are not connected with what you are doing; often pleasant scenes in your imagination: *The child stared out of the window, lost in a day-dream.*
—**' day-dream** *verb* [I]
day 'off *noun* [C] a day on which you do not go to work: *Wednesday's my day off next week.*
,day re'turn *noun* [C] (*Brit*) a train or bus ticket which is cheaper than normal. You have to go somewhere and come back on the same day.
'daytime *noun* [U] the time between sunrise and sunset: *These flowers open in the daytime and close up again at night.*
daylight /'deɪlaɪt/ *noun* [U] the light that there is during the day: *The colours look quite different in daylight.* ○ *daylight hours*
(IDIOM) **broad daylight** ⇨ BROAD
daze /deɪz/ *verb* [T] (usually passive) to make sb unable to think clearly
daze *noun*
(IDIOM) **in a daze** in a confused state
dazed /deɪzd/ *adj* confused; not showing normal reactions: *He had a dazed expression on his face.*
dazzle /'dæzl/ *verb* [T] (usually passive) **1** (used about a bright light) to make sb unable to see clearly: *She was dazzled by the other car's headlights.* **2** to impress sb very much: *He had been dazzled by her beauty.*
dazzling *adj* very bright or impressive: *a dazzling light* ○ *a dazzling performance*
deacon /'di:kən/ (*feminine* **deaconess**) *noun* [C] an official who has a rank below a priest, in some Christian churches
☆ **dead** /ded/ *adj* **1** no longer alive: *They rushed him to hospital, but he was dead on arrival.* ○ *There's a dead spider in the bath.* **2** (not before a noun) no longer able to feel anything (used about a part of the body): *My fingers had gone dead with the cold.* **3** (not before a noun) no longer working properly (used about a piece of equipment): *I picked up the telephone but the line was dead.* **4** (only *before* a noun) complete: *There was dead silence when she finished speaking.* **5** without movement, activity or interest: *This town is completely dead after 11 o'clock at night.* **6** no longer used; over and finished: *Latin is a dead language.* ○ *We've made our decision so the subject is now dead.*
(IDIOMS) **a dead end 1** a street that is only open at one end **2** a point, situation, etc from which you can make no further progress: *a*

deal

dead-end job (= one that offers no chance of promotion)
drop dead ⇨ DROP¹
dead *adv* completely, exactly or very: *The sign said 'Dead slow!'* ○ *He's dead keen to start work.*
the dead *noun* [plural] people who have died: *A church service was held in memory of the dead.*
(IDIOM) **in the/at dead of night** in the middle of the night, when it is very dark and quiet
,dead 'heat *noun* [C] the result in a race when two people finish at exactly the same time: *The race was a dead heat.*
,dead'pan *adj* without any expression on your face or in your voice: *He told the joke with a completely deadpan face.*
deaden /'dedn/ *verb* [T] to make sth less strong, painful, etc: *They gave her drugs to try and deaden the pain.*
deadline /'dedlaɪn/ *noun* [C] a time or date before which sth must be done: *A journalist is used to having to meet deadlines.*
deadlock /'dedlɒk/ *noun* [U] a situation in which an agreement between two sides cannot be reached
deadly /'dedli/ *adj* (**deadlier; deadliest**) **1** causing or likely to cause death: *a deadly poison* **2** very great: *They're deadly enemies.* **3** (*informal*) very boring
deadly *adv* extremely; very: *I'm not joking – I'm deadly serious!*
☆ **deaf** /def/ *adj* **1** unable to hear anything or unable to hear very well: *You'll have to speak louder. My father's a bit deaf.* **2** **deaf to sth** not wanting to listen to sth: *I've told her what I think but she's deaf to my advice.*
the deaf *noun* [plural] deaf people: *sign language for the deaf*
deafness *noun* [U] the state of being deaf
,deaf-and-'dumb *adj* unable to hear or speak
deafen /'defn/ *verb* [T] (usually passive) to make sb unable to hear by making a very loud noise: *We were deafened by the loud music and conversation was impossible.*
deafening *adj* very loud
☆ **deal¹** /di:l/ *noun*
(IDIOM) **a good/great deal (of sth)** a lot (of sth): *I've spent a great deal of time on this report.*
☆ **deal²** /di:l/ *verb* [I,T] (*pt, pp* **dealt** /delt/) **deal sth (out); deal sth (to sb)** to give cards to players in a game of cards: *Start by dealing seven cards to each player.*
(IDIOM) **deal sb/sth a blow; deal a blow to sb/sth 1** to hit sb/sth **2** to give sb a shock, etc: *This news dealt a terrible blow to my father.*
(PHRASAL VERBS) **deal in sth** to buy and sell sth; to trade in sth: *He deals in second-hand cars.*
deal sth out to give sth to a number of people: *The profits will be dealt out among us.*
deal with sb to behave towards sb; to handle sb: *He's a difficult man. Nobody quite knows how to deal with him.*
deal with sth 1 to act in a suitable way in order to solve a problem, complete a task, etc; to handle sth: *I'm not sure how to deal with the situation at work.* ○ *My secretary will deal with my correspondence while I'm away.* **2** to have

ɜ:	ə	eɪ	əʊ	aɪ	aʊ	ɔɪ	ɪə	eə	ʊə
fur	ago	pay	home	five	now	join	near	hair	pure

sth as its subject: *This chapter deals with letter-writing.*

☆ **deal³** /diːl/ *noun* [C] an agreement or arrangement, especially in business: *It was part of the deal that they would deliver by May.* ○ *We've done/made a deal with an Italian company.* ○ *a fair deal* ○ *a bad deal*

dealer /ˈdiːlə(r)/ *noun* [C] **1** a person whose business is buying and selling things: *a dealer in gold and silver* ○ *a drug dealer* **2** the person who gives the cards to the players in a game of cards

dealing /ˈdiːlɪŋ/ *noun* **1** [U] buying and selling: *drug dealing* **2 dealings** [plural] relations, especially in business: *We had some dealings with that firm several years ago.*

dealt *pt, pp* of DEAL²

dean /diːn/ *noun* [C] **1** a priest who is head of a large church or responsible for a number of small churches **2** an important official at some universities or colleges

☆ **dear** /dɪə(r)/ *adj* **1** (used at the beginning of a letter before the name or title of the person you are writing to): *Dear Sarah, ...* ○ *Dear Sir or Madam, ...* **2** (only *before* a noun) a word that is used with 'little' or 'old' to express your liking for sb/sth: *Dear old Jane! She always remembers to write at Christmas.* **3 dear (to sb)** loved by or important to sb: *She's one of my dearest friends.* ○ *It was a subject that was very dear to him.* **4** (*Brit*) expensive: *The coat was £100. It seemed rather dear.*

dear *adv* at a high price: *Always buy cheap and sell dear, if possible!*

dear *noun* [C] **1** a kind, gentle person: *She's a kind old lady – an absolute dear.* **2** (used for speaking to sb you know well or love): *Would you like a cup of tea, dear?*

dear *interj* (used for expressing disappointment, sadness, surprise, etc): *Oh dear! I've spilt the wine.* ○ *Dear me! Aren't you ready?*

dearly *adv* **1** very much: *He loves her dearly.* ○ *I'd dearly like to go there again.* **2** (*formal*) at great cost: *I've already paid dearly* (= suffered a lot) *for that mistake.*

dearth /dɜːθ/ *noun* [sing] a lack of sth; not enough of sth: *There's a dearth of young people in the village.*

☆ **death** /deθ/ *noun* **1** [C,U] the end of sb/sth's life; dying: *He continued to write until his death.* ○ *There were two deaths and many other people were injured.* ○ *Most people are afraid of death.* ○ *The police do not know the cause of death.* ○ *There was no food and people were starving to death.* **2** [U] the end (of sth): *the death of communism*

(IDIOMS) **put sb to death** (usually passive) to kill sb, usually as a punishment: *The general had ordered the prisoners to be put to death.*

sick to death of sb/sth ⇨ SICK
sudden death ⇨ SUDDEN

'death penalty *noun* [sing] the punishment of being killed

'death-toll *noun* [C] the number of people killed in a disaster, war, etc

deathly /ˈdeθli/ *adj, adv* like death: *There was a deathly silence.*

debase /dɪˈbeɪs/ *verb* [T] (usually passive) (*formal*) to reduce the quality or value of sth

debatable /dɪˈbeɪtəbl/ *adj* not certain; something that you could argue about

debate /dɪˈbeɪt/ *noun* **1** [C] a formal argument or discussion of a question at a public meeting or in Parliament. At the end there may be a vote: *a debate in Parliament on educational reform* **2** [C,U] a discussion; talk expressing different opinions: *There's been a lot of debate about the cause of acid rain.*

debate *verb* **1** [I,T] to discuss sth in a formal way or at a public debate **2** [T] to think about or discuss sth before deciding what to do: *They debated whether to go or not.*

debit /ˈdebɪt/ *noun* [C] a sum of money paid out of a bank account; a written note of this

debit *verb* [T] to take a sum of money out of a bank account, etc usually as a payment; to record this: *The bank hasn't debited my account with the money I paid for the car yet.*
☛ Look at **credit** and **direct debit**.

debris /ˈdeɪbriː; *US* dəˈbriː/ *noun* [U] pieces from sth that has crashed to the ground or been destroyed: *debris from the crashed plane*

☆ **debt** /det/ *noun* **1** [C] a sum of money that you owe sb: *She borrowed a lot of money and she's still paying off the debt.* ○ *the Third World debt crisis* **2** [U] the state of owing money: *After he lost his job, he got into debt.* **3** [C, usually sing] (*formal*) something that you owe sb, eg because they have helped or been kind to you: *In his speech he acknowledged his debt to his family and friends for their support.*

(IDIOMS) **be in/out of debt** to owe/not owe money

be in sb's debt (*formal*) to feel grateful to sb for sth that he/she has done for you

debtor /ˈdetə(r)/ *noun* [C] a person who owes money

début (*also* **debut**) /ˈdeɪbjuː; *US* dɪˈbjuː/ *noun* [C] a first appearance in public of an actor, etc: *She made her début in London in 1959.*

decade /ˈdekeɪd; dɪˈkeɪd/ *noun* [C] a period of ten years

decadence /ˈdekədəns/ *noun* [U] behaviour, attitudes, etc that show a fall in standards, especially moral ones —**decadent** /ˈdekədənt/ *adj*: *a decadent society*

decaffeinated /ˌdiːˈkæfɪneɪtɪd/ *adj* (used about coffee or tea) with most or all of the caffeine removed

decapitate /dɪˈkæpɪteɪt/ *verb* [T] (*formal*) to cut off a person's head

☆ **decay** /dɪˈkeɪ/ *verb* [I] **1** to become bad or fall apart: *The old farm buildings had been left to decay.* ○ *the decaying body of a dead sheep* ○ *Children's teeth will decay if they eat too many sweets.* **2** to become weaker or less efficient: *The Roman Empire had by then begun to decay.*

decay *noun* [U] the process of decaying, or the state reached after decaying: *It is better to prevent tooth decay than to treat it.* ○ *Many of the old houses had fallen into decay.* —**decayed** *adj*: *a decayed tooth*

decease /dɪˈsiːs/ *noun* [U] (*formal*) the death (of a person)

p	b	t	d	k	g	tʃ	dʒ	f	v	θ	ð
pen	bad	tea	did	cat	got	chin	June	fall	van	thin	then

deceased *adj* (*formal*) dead: *He inherited the house from his deceased parents.*

the deceased *noun* [sing] (*formal*) a person who has died, especially one who has died recently: *Many friends of the deceased were present at the funeral.*

deceit /dɪˈsiːt/ *noun* [U] dishonest behaviour; trying to make sb believe sth that is not true **deceitful** /dɪˈsiːtfl/ *adj* dishonest, and intending to make sb believe sth that is not true —**deceitfully** /-fəli/ *adv* —**deceitfulness** *noun* [U]

☆ **deceive** /dɪˈsiːv/ *verb* [T] **deceive sb/yourself (into doing sth)** to try to make sb believe sth that is not true: *He deceived his mother into believing that he had earned the money, not stolen it.* ○ *Her story didn't deceive me – I knew it was a lie.* ○ *You're deceiving yourself if you think there's an easy solution to the problem.* ☞ The noun is **deception** or **deceit**.

☆ **December** /dɪˈsembə(r)/ *noun* [C,U] (*abbr* **Dec**) the twelfth month of the year, coming before January ☞ For examples of the use of the months in sentences, look at **January**.

decency /ˈdiːsnsi/ *noun* [U] moral or correct behaviour: *She had the decency to admit that it was her fault.*

decent /ˈdiːsnt/ *adj* **1** satisfactory; of an acceptable standard: *All she wants is a decent job with decent wages.* **2** (used about people or behaviour) honest and respectable: *All decent people are appalled by such terrible crimes.* **3** not likely to embarrass or offend sb: *I can't come to the door, I'm not decent* (= I'm not dressed). ☞ The opposite is **indecent**. —**decently** *adv*

deception /dɪˈsepʃn/ *noun* [C,U] deceiving or being deceived; a trick: *He had obtained the secret papers by deception.*

deceptive /dɪˈseptɪv/ *adj* likely to give a false impression or to make sb believe sth that is not true: *The water is deceptive. It's much deeper than it looks.* —**deceptively** *adv*: *She made the task sound deceptively easy.*

decibel /ˈdesɪbel/ *noun* [C] a measurement of how loud a sound is

☆ **decide** /dɪˈsaɪd/ *verb* **1** [I,T] to think about two or more possibilities and choose one of them: *There are so many to choose from – I can't decide!* ○ *She decided against borrowing the money.* ○ *They decided on a name for the baby.* ○ *He decided that it was too late to go.* ○ *You'll have to decide what to do.* ○ *We've decided not to invite Isabel.* ○ *The date hasn't been decided yet.* **2** [T] to influence sth so that it produces a particular result: *Your votes will decide the winner.* **3** [T] to cause sb to make a decision: *What finally decided you to leave?* ☞ The noun is **decision**. The adjective is **decisive**.

decided *adj* clear; definite: *There has been a decided improvement in his work.* —**decidedly** *adv*: *The new office is decidedly better than the old one.*

deciduous /dɪˈsɪdjuəs; dɪˈsɪdʒuəs/ *adj* (used about a tree) of a type that loses its leaves every autumn ☞ Look at **evergreen**.

decimal /ˈdesɪml/ *adj* based on or counted in units of ten: *decimal currency*

decimal *noun* [C] part of a number, written after a dot (**decimal point**) and expressed in tenths, hundredths, etc: *Three quarters expressed as a decimal is 0·75.*

decipher /dɪˈsaɪfə(r)/ *verb* [T] to succeed in reading or understanding sth that is not clear: *It's impossible to decipher his handwriting.*

☆ **decision** /dɪˈsɪʒn/ *noun* **1** [C,U] **a decision (on/about sth); a decision (to do sth); a decision (that...)** a choice or judgement that you make after thinking about various possibilities: *'Have you made a decision yet?' 'No, I'm still thinking about it.'* ○ *I took the decision that I believed to be right.* ○ *I realize now that I made the wrong decision.* ○ *There were good reasons for his decision to leave.* ○ *Who made the decision that the school should be closed?* ○ *How you vote is a matter of personal decision.* **2** [U] being able to decide clearly and quickly

decisive /dɪˈsaɪsɪv/ *adj* **1** making sth certain or final: *the decisive battle of the war* **2** having the ability to make clear decisions quickly: *It's no good hesitating. Be decisive.* —**decisively** *adv* —**decisiveness** *noun* [U]

deck /dek/ *noun* [C] **1** one of the floors of a ship or bus: *The restaurant is on the upper deck.* **2** (*US*) = PACK¹(4) **3** a piece of equipment on which you can play records or tapes

(IDIOM) **on deck** on the floor of a ship which is in the open air: *I'm going out on deck for some fresh air.*

ˈdeck-chair *noun* [C] a chair that you use outside, especially on the beach. You can fold it up and carry it.

☆ **declaration** /ˌdekləˈreɪʃn/ *noun* **1** [C,U] a statement: *In his speech he made a strong declaration of support for the rebels.* ○ *Fighting has started without declaration of war.* **2** [C] a written statement giving information on goods or income on which you have to pay tax: *If you're sending a parcel abroad, you have to fill in a customs declaration.*

☆ **declare** /dɪˈkleə(r)/ *verb* [T] **1** to announce or to make sth known, especially in an official or forceful way: *to declare war on another country* ○ *The republic has declared its independence.* ○ *I declare that the winner of the award is Joan Taylor.* ○ *'I've had enough of this,' she declared and walked out of the room.* **2** to give information about goods or income on which you have to pay tax: *You must declare all your income on this form.*

decline¹ /dɪˈklaɪn/ *verb* **1** [I,T] (*formal*) to refuse, usually politely: *Thank you for the invitation but I'm afraid I have to decline.* ○ *The minister declined to make a statement.* **2** [I] to become weaker, smaller or less good: *declining profits* ○ *The standard of education has declined in this country.*

decline² /dɪˈklaɪn/ *noun* [C,U] **(a) decline (in sth)** a process or period of becoming weaker, smaller or less satisfactory: *a decline in sales* ○ *As an industrial power, the country is in decline.*

decode /ˌdiːˈkəʊd/ *verb* [T] to find the meaning of sth that is in code ☞ The opposite is **encode**.

decoder *noun* [C] a piece of equipment that allows you to receive satellite television channels for which you have to pay extra

s	z	ʃ	ʒ	h	m	n	ŋ	l	r	j	w
so	zoo	she	vision	how	man	no	sing	leg	red	yes	wet

decompose /ˌdiːkəmˈpəʊz/ verb [I,T] to decay or to make sth decay: *The body was so badly decomposed that it couldn't be identified.*

décor /ˈdeɪkɔː(r); US deɪˈkɔːr/ noun [U,sing] the furniture and decoration in a place

☆ **decorate** /ˈdekəreɪt/ verb **1** [T] **decorate sth (with sth)** to add sth in order to make a thing more attractive to look at: *Decorate the cake with cherries and nuts.* **2** [I,T] to put paint and/or wallpaper onto walls, ceilings and doors in a room or building: *I think it's about time we decorated the living-room.*

decoration /ˌdekəˈreɪʃn/ noun **1** [C,U] the decorating of a room or building with paint, wallpaper, etc; the wallpaper, curtains, etc that have been used in a room or building: *The house is in need of decoration.* ○ *The theatre has been renovated in the style of the original decoration.* **2** [C,U] something that is added to sth in order to make it look more attractive: *Christmas decorations*

decorative /ˈdekərətɪv; US ˈdekəreɪtɪv/ adj attractive to look at; added to sth to make it prettier: *The cloth had a decorative lace edge.*

decoy /ˈdiːkɔɪ/ noun [C] a person or object that is used to lead sb/sth in the wrong direction

☆ **decrease** /dɪˈkriːs/ verb [I,T] to become or to make sth smaller or less: *As the temperature decreases, the metal contracts.* ○ *Profits have decreased by 15%.* ○ *Decrease speed when you are approaching a road junction.* ☛ The opposite is **increase**.

decrease /ˈdiːkriːs/ noun [C,U] **(a) decrease (in sth)** a process of becoming or making sth smaller or less; a reduction: *a decrease in the number of students* ○ *a 10% decrease in sales*

decree /dɪˈkriː/ noun [C] an official order given by a government, a ruler, etc

decree verb [T] (*pt, pp* **decreed**) (used about a government, a ruler, etc) to give an official order

decrepit /dɪˈkrepɪt/ adj old and in very bad condition

dedicate /ˈdedɪkeɪt/ verb [T] **1** to give all your energy, time, efforts, etc to sth: *He dedicated his life to helping the poor.* **2 dedicate sth to sb** to say that sth is in honour of sb: *He dedicated the book he had written to his brother.*

dedicated adj giving a lot of your energy, time, efforts, etc to sth that you believe to be important: *dedicated nurses and doctors*

dedication /ˌdedɪˈkeɪʃn/ noun **1** [U] being willing to give your time and energy to sth: *I admire her dedication to her career.* **2** [C] a message at the beginning of a book or before a piece of music is played, saying that it is for a particular person

deduce /dɪˈdjuːs/ verb [T] to form an opinion using the facts that you already know: *From his name I deduced that he was Polish.* ☛ The noun is **deduction**.

deduct /dɪˈdʌkt/ verb [T] **deduct sth (from sth)** to take sth such as money or points away from a total amount: *Income tax is deducted from your salary.* ○ *Marks will be deducted for untidy work.*

deduction /dɪˈdʌkʃn/ noun [C,U] **1** something that you work out from facts that you already know; the skill of reasoning in this way: *It was a brilliant piece of deduction by the detective.* **2 deduction (from sth)** taking away an amount or number from a total; the amount or number taken away from the total: *What is your total income after deductions?* (= when tax, insurance, etc are taken away).

deed /diːd/ noun [C] (*formal*) something that you do; an action: *Deeds are more important than words.*

deem /diːm/ verb [T] (*formal*) to consider sth: *He did not even deem it necessary to apologize.*

☆ **deep¹** /diːp/ adj **1** going a long way down from top to bottom: *the deep end of a swimming-pool* ○ *to dig a deep hole* ○ *That's a deep cut — I think you'd better see a doctor.* ○ *a coat with deep pockets* ☛ The noun is **depth**. **2** going a long way from front to back: *deep shelves* **3** measuring a particular amount from top to bottom or from front to back: *The water is only a metre deep at this end of the pool.* ○ *shelves 40 centimetres deep* **4** (used about sounds) low: *a deep voice* **5** (used about colours) dark; strong: *a deep red* **6** strongly felt; serious: *Please accept my deepest sympathy on this sad occasion.* ○ *The country is in a deep recession and there is massive unemployment.* **7** (used about a breath) taking in or letting out a lot of air: *Take a few deep breaths.* **8** concentrating on or involved in sth: *She was deep in thought.* ○ *deep sleep* ○ *deep in conversation* **9** thorough, able to deal with the difficult parts of sth: *His books show a deep understanding of human nature.*

deepen /ˈdiːpən/ verb [I,T] to become or make sth deep or deeper: *The river deepens here.* ○ *This bad news deepened the atmosphere of depression.* —**deeply** adv: *a deeply unhappy person* ○ *to breathe deeply*

☆ **deep²** /diːp/ adv a long way down or inside sth: *The ship sank deep into the sea.* ○ *They talked deep into the night.*

(IDIOM) **deep down** in what you really think or feel: *I tried to appear optimistic but deep down I knew there was no hope.*

ˌdeep-ˈfreeze noun [C] = FREEZER

ˌdeep-ˈrooted (also **ˌdeep-ˈseated**) adj strongly felt or believed and therefore difficult to change: *deep-seated prejudices*

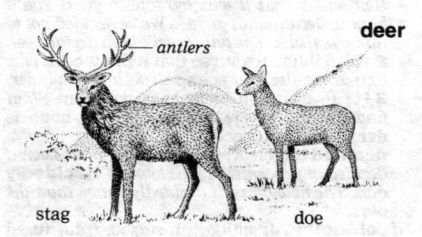

☆ **deer** /dɪə(r)/ noun [C] (*pl* **deer**) a large wild grass-eating animal. The male has horns shaped like branches (**antlers**).

☛ A male deer is called a **buck** or, especially if it has fully-grown antlers, a **stag**. The female is a **doe** and a young deer a **fawn**. **Venison** is the meat from deer.

deface /dɪˈfeɪs/ *verb* [T] to spoil the way sth looks by writing on or marking the surface of it: *Vandals defaced the statue with graffiti.*

default¹ /dɪˈfɔːlt/ *noun* [sing] (*computing*) a course of action taken by a computer when it is not given any other instruction
(IDIOM) **by default** because nothing happened, not because of successful effort: *They won by default, because the other team didn't turn up.*

default² /dɪˈfɔːlt/ *verb* [I] **1** not to do sth that you should do by law: *If you default on the credit payments* (= you don't pay them), *the car will be taken back.* **2** (*computing*) to take a particular course of action when no other command is given

☆ **defeat** /dɪˈfiːt/ *verb* [T] **1** to win a game, a fight, a vote, etc against sb: *The army defeated the rebels after three days of fighting.* ○ *In the last match France defeated Wales by ten points to six.* **2** to prevent sth from succeeding: *The local residents are determined to defeat the council's building plans.* **3** to be too difficult for sb to do or understand: *I've tried to work out what's wrong with the car but it defeats me.*

defeat *noun* **1** [C] an occasion when sb is defeated: *This season they have had two victories and three defeats.* **2** [U] defeating or being defeated: *She refused to admit defeat and kept on trying.*

defeatism /-ɪzəm/ *noun* [U] the attitude that you have when you expect sth to end unsuccessfully —**defeatist** /-ɪst/ *noun* [C]: *Don't be such a defeatist, we haven't lost yet!*

defecate /ˈdefəkeɪt/ *verb* [I] (*formal*) to pass waste materials from the bowels

defect¹ /ˈdiːfekt/ *noun* [C] something that is wrong with or missing from sb/sth: *a speech defect* ○ *defects in the education system* —**defective** /dɪˈfektɪv/ *adj*: *If you find any of our goods to be defective, please return them to the shop.*

defect² /dɪˈfekt/ *verb* [I] to leave your country, a political party, etc and go to or join an opposing one: *a spy who defected from the East* —**defection** *noun* [C,U]

☆ **defence** (*US* **defense**) /dɪˈfens/ *noun* **1** [U] **defence (against sth)** action to protect sb/sth from attack: *Would you fight in defence of your country?* **2** [C] **a defence (against sth)** something that protects sb/sth from sth or that is used for fighting against attack: *to build up a country's defences* ○ *the body's defences against disease* **3** [U] the military equipment, forces, etc for protecting a country: *the Defence Minister* ○ *Spending on defence can be cut if fewer weapons are needed.* **4** [C] something that you say or write to support sb/sth that is being attacked or accused: *In his speech, he made a strong defence of the party's policy.* ○ *I must say in her defence that I have always found her very reliable.* **5** [C] (in law) an argument in support of the accused person in a court of law: *His defence was that he was only carrying out orders.* **6 the defence** [sing, with sing or pl verb] (in law) the accused person in a court of law and the lawyer or lawyers who are acting for him/her: *The defence claims/claim that many of the witnesses were lying.* ○ *a witness giving evidence for the defence* **7** usually **the defence** [sing, with sing or pl verb] (in sport) action to prevent the other team scoring; the players who try to do this: *The defence was/were unable to stop Brown and he scored.* ○ *They put up no defence and were beaten by five points.*

defenceless *adj* unable to defend yourself against attack

☆ **defend** /dɪˈfend/ *verb* **1** [T] **defend sb/sth (against sb/sth)** to act, especially to fight, to protect sb/sth: *Would you be able to defend yourself if someone attacked you in the street?* **2** [T] **defend sb/sth (against sb/sth)** to say or write sth to support sb/sth: *The minister went on television to defend the government's policy.* **3** [T] (in law) to speak for sb who is accused of sth in a court of law **4** [I,T] to try to stop the other team or player scoring: *They defended well and managed to hold onto their lead.* **5** [T] to try to win a match so that you remain champion: *She successfully defended her title.*

defender *noun* [C] a person who defends sb/sth, especially in sport ☛ picture at **football**.

defendant /dɪˈfendənt/ *noun* [C] a person who is accused of sth in a court of law

defensive /dɪˈfensɪv/ *adj* **1** used or intended for protecting sb/sth from attack: *The troops took up a defensive position.* **2** showing that you feel that sb is accusing or criticizing you: *When I asked him about his new job, he became very defensive and tried to change the subject.*

defensive *noun*
(IDIOM) **on the defensive** ready to defend yourself against attack or criticism

defer /dɪˈfɜː(r)/ *verb* [T] (**deferring; deferred**) (*formal*) to leave sth until a later time; to postpone

deference /ˈdefərəns/ *noun* [U] polite behaviour that you show towards sb/sth, usually because you respect him/her
(IDIOM) **in deference to sb/sth** because you respect and do not wish to upset sb: *In deference to her father's wishes, she didn't mention the subject again.*

defiance /dɪˈfaɪəns/ *noun* [U] open refusal to obey: *As an act of defiance they continued to play their music loud.*
(IDIOM) **in defiance of sb/sth** openly refusing to obey sb/sth

defiant /dɪˈfaɪənt/ *adj* showing open refusal to obey —**defiantly** *adv*

deficiency /dɪˈfɪʃnsi/ *noun* (*pl* **deficiencies**) **1** [C,U] a condition of not having enough of sth; a lack: *a deficiency of vitamin C* **2** [C] something that is not good enough or that is wrong with sb/sth: *The problems were caused by deficiencies in the design.*

deficient /dɪˈfɪʃnt/ *adj* **1 deficient (in sth)** not having enough of sth: *food that is deficient in minerals* **2** not good enough or not complete

deficit /ˈdefɪsɪt/ *noun* [C] the amount by which

the money you receive is less than the money you have spent: *a trade deficit*

define /dɪˈfaɪn/ *verb* [T] **1** to say exactly what a word or idea means: *How would you define 'happiness'?* **2** to explain the exact nature of sth clearly: *Something is worrying me but I can't define exactly what it is.*

☆ **definite** /ˈdefmət/ *adj* **1** fixed and unlikely to change; certain: *I'll give you a definite decision in a couple of days.* **2** clear; easy to see or notice: *There has been a definite change in her attitude recently.*

definitely /ˈdefmətli/ *adv* certainly; without doubt: *I'll definitely consider your advice.* ○ *We definitely can't afford such a high price.*

definite 'article *noun* [C] the name used for the word 'the' ☞ Look at **indefinite article**.

definition /ˌdefɪˈnɪʃn/ *noun* [C,U] a statement of the exact meaning of a word or idea

definitive /dɪˈfɪnətɪv/ *adj* in a form that cannot be changed or that cannot be improved: *This is the definitive version.* ○ *the definitive performance of Hamlet* —**definitively** *adv*

deflate /dɪˈfleɪt/ *verb* [I,T] **1** to become or to make sth smaller by letting the air or gas out: *The balloon slowly deflated and began to come down.* ☞ The opposite is **inflate**. **2** [T] to make sb feel less confident, proud or excited

deflect /dɪˈflekt/ *verb* **1** [I,T] to change direction after hitting sb/sth; to make sth change direction in this way: *The ball was deflected off a defender and into the net.* **2** [T] to turn sb or sb's attention away from sth: *Nothing could deflect him from her aim.*

deflection /dɪˈflekʃn/ *noun* [C,U] a change of direction after hitting sb/sth

deforestation /ˌdiːˌfɒrɪˈsteɪʃn/ *noun* [U] cutting down trees over a large area: *Deforestation is a major cause of global warming.*

deform /dɪˈfɔːm/ *verb* [T] to change the shape of sth so that it is unnatural

deformed *adj* having an unnatural or ugly shape

deformity /dɪˈfɔːməti/ *noun* (*pl* **deformities**) [C,U] the state of being deformed; a part of the body that is deformed: *The drug caused women to give birth to babies with severe deformities.*

defraud /dɪˈfrɔːd/ *verb* [T] to get sth from sb by cheating

defrost /ˌdiːˈfrɒst/; *US* /ˌdiːˈfrɔːst/ *verb* **1** [T] to remove the ice from sth: *to defrost a fridge* (= by switching it off so that the ice melts) **2** [I,T] (used about frozen food) to return to a normal temperature; to make food do this: *Defrost the chicken thoroughly before cooking.*

deft /deft/ *adj* (used especially about movements) skilful and quick —**deftly** *adv*

defunct /dɪˈfʌŋkt/ *adj* no longer existing or in use

defuse /ˌdiːˈfjuːz/ *verb* [T] **1** to remove the part of a bomb that would make it explode: *Army experts defused the bomb safely.* **2** to make a situation calmer or less dangerous: *She defused the tension by changing the subject.*

defy /dɪˈfaɪ/ *verb* (*pp* **defying**; *3rd pers sing pres* **defies**; *pt, pp* **defied**) **1** to openly refuse to obey sb/sth: *She defied her parents and continued seeing him.* ☞ The adjective is **defiant** and the noun **defiance**. **2 defy sb to do sth** to tell sb to do sth that you believe to be impossible: *I defy you to prove me wrong.* **3** to make sth impossible or very difficult: *It's such a beautiful place that it defies description.*

degenerate /dɪˈdʒenəreɪt/ *verb* [I] to fall to a less satisfactory standard; to become worse: *It degenerated from a pleasant discussion into a nasty argument.* —**degeneration** /dɪˌdʒenəˈreɪʃn/ *noun* [U]

degrade /dɪˈɡreɪd/ *verb* [T] to make people respect sb less: *It's the sort of film that really degrades women.* —**degrading** *adj*: *Having to ask other people for money is degrading.*

degradation /ˌdeɡrəˈdeɪʃn/ *noun* [U] **1** degrading sb or being degraded: *the degradation of women* **2** causing the condition of sth to become worse: *environmental degradation*

☆ **degree** /dɪˈɡriː/ *noun* **1** [C] a measurement of temperature: *Water boils at 212 degrees Fahrenheit (212°F) or 100 degrees Celsius (100°C).* ○ *three degrees below zero/minus three degrees (-3°)* **2** [C] a measurement of angles: *a forty-five degree (45°) angle* ○ *An angle of 90 degrees is called a right angle.* **3** [C,U] (used about feelings or qualities) a certain amount or level: *There is always some degree of risk involved in mountaineering.* ○ *Our lives have changed to a considerable degree.* ○ *I sympathize with her to some degree.* **4** [C] a qualification gained by successfully completing a course at university or college: *She's got a degree in Philosophy.* ○ *He's at university, doing an Economics degree.*

☞ In Britain **degree** is the usual word for the qualification you get when you complete and pass a university course. You can study for a **diploma** at other types of college. The courses may be shorter and more practical than degree courses.

dehydrate /ˌdiːhaɪˈdreɪt/ *verb* **1** [T] (usually passive) to remove all the water from food so that it can be kept longer: *dehydrated vegetables* **2** [I,T] to lose or to take water from the body: *If you run for a long time in the heat, you start to dehydrate.* —**dehydration** /ˌdiːhaɪˈdreɪʃn/ *noun* [U]

deign /deɪn/ *verb* [T] to do sth in a way that shows people that you are really too important for it: *He didn't even deign to look up when I entered the room.*

deity /ˈdeɪəti/ *noun* [C] (*pl* **deities**) (*formal*) a god or goddess

dejected /dɪˈdʒektɪd/ *adj* very unhappy, especially because you are disappointed —**dejectedly** *adv* —**dejection** *noun* [U]

☆ **delay** /dɪˈleɪ/ *verb* **1** [T] to make sb/sth slow or late: *The plane was delayed for several hours because of bad weather.* **2** [I,T] **delay (doing sth)** to decide not to do sth until a later time: *I was forced to delay the trip until the following week.*

delay *noun* [C,U] a situation or period of time where you have to wait: *Delays are likely on the roads because of heavy traffic.* ○ *Because of an accident, all trains are subject to delay.*

delegate¹ /'delɪgət/ noun [C] a person who has been chosen to speak or take decisions for a group of people, especially at a meeting

delegate² /'delɪgeɪt/ verb [I,T] to give sb with a lower job or rank a particular task to carry out: *You can't do everything yourself. You must learn how to delegate.*

delegation /ˌdelɪ'geɪʃn/ noun **1** [U] giving sb with a lower job or rank a particular task to perform **2** [C, with sing or pl verb] a group of people who have been chosen to speak or take decisions for a larger group of people, especially at a meeting: *The British delegation walked out of the meeting in protest.*

delete /dɪ'liːt/ verb [T] to cross out or leave out part of sth that is written: *'I will/will not be able to attend the meeting. Delete as appropriate.'* (= on a form, cross out the words which do not apply to you).

deletion /dɪ'liːʃn/ noun **1** [U] the act of deleting **2** [C] part of sth written or printed (eg a word, a sentence, a paragraph, etc) that is deleted

☆ **deliberate¹** /dɪ'lɪbərət/ adj **1** done on purpose; planned: *Was it an accident or was it deliberate?* **2** done slowly and carefully, without hurrying: *She spoke in a calm, deliberate voice.*

deliberately adv **1** on purpose; intentionally: *I didn't break it deliberately, it was an accident.* **2** slowly and carefully, without hurrying

deliberate² /dɪ'lɪbəreɪt/ verb [I,T] (formal) to think about or discuss sth thoroughly before making a decision: *The judges deliberated for an hour before announcing the winner.*

deliberation /dɪˌlɪbə'reɪʃn/ noun **1** [C,U] discussion or thinking about sth: *After much deliberation I decided to reject the offer.* **2** [U] slowness and carefulness; lack of hurry: *He spoke with great deliberation.*

delicacy /'delɪkəsi/ noun (pl **delicacies**) **1** [U] lightness and gentleness; having a fine or detailed quality: *The pianist played the quiet song with great delicacy.* **2** [U] using or needing particular care or skill so as not to offend sb: *Be tactful! It's a matter of some delicacy.* **3** [C] a type of food that is considered particularly good: *Try this dish, it's a local delicacy.*

☆ **delicate** /'delɪkət/ adj **1** fine or thin; easy to damage or break: *delicate skin* ○ *delicate china teacups* ○ *the delicate mechanisms of a watch* **2** frequently ill or easily made ill: *He was a delicate child and often in hospital.* **3** (used about colours, flavours, etc) light and pleasant; not strong: *a delicate shade of pale blue* **4** requiring skilful treatment and care: *Repairing this is going to be a very delicate operation.*

delicately adv **1** lightly, gently or finely: *delicately painted vases* **2** with skilful and careful movement: *She stepped delicately over the broken glass.* **3** carefully so as not to offend sb: *I phrased my comments delicately so as not to upset her.*

delicatessen /ˌdelɪkə'tesn/ noun [C] a shop that sells special, unusual or foreign foods, especially cold cooked meat, cheeses, etc

☆ **delicious** /dɪ'lɪʃəs/ adj having a very pleasant taste or smell: *What are you cooking? It smells delicious.*

delight¹ /dɪ'laɪt/ noun **1** [U] great pleasure; joy: *She laughed with delight as she opened the present.* **2** [C] something that gives sb great pleasure: *The story is a delight to read.*
—**delightful** /-fl/ adj: *a delightful view* ○ *The people were delightful and I made a lot of friends.* —**delightfully** /-fəli/ adv

☆ **delight²** /dɪ'laɪt/ verb [T] to give sb great pleasure: *She delighted the audience by singing all her old songs.*
(PHRASAL VERB) **delight in sth/in doing sth** to get great pleasure from sth: *He delights in playing tricks on people.*

delighted adj **delighted (at/with sth); delighted (to do sth/that...)** extremely pleased: *'How do you feel about winning today?' 'Delighted.'* ○ *She was delighted at getting the job/that she got the job.* ○ *They're absolutely delighted with their baby.* ○ *'Would you like to come for dinner?' 'Thanks, I'd be delighted to.'*

delinquency /dɪ'lɪŋkwənsi/ noun [U] bad or criminal behaviour, usually among young people

delinquent /dɪ'lɪŋkwənt/ adj (usually used about a young person) behaving badly and often breaking the law: *delinquent children*
—**delinquent** noun [C]: *a juvenile delinquent*

delirious /dɪ'lɪriəs/ adj **1** speaking or thinking in a crazy way, often because of a fever **2** extremely happy —**deliriously** adv

☆ **deliver** /dɪ'lɪvə(r)/ verb **1** [I,T] to take sth (goods, letters, etc) to the place requested or to the address on it: *Your order will be delivered within five days.* **2** [T] to help a mother to give birth to her baby: *The doctor who delivered the baby said she was lucky to be alive.* **3** [T] to give sth (a speech, a warning, etc): *He delivered a long lecture to the staff about efficiency.* **4** [I] **deliver (on sth)** (informal) to do or give sth that you have promised: *He's made a lot of promises, but can he deliver?*
(IDIOM) **come up with/deliver the goods** ⇨ GOODS

delivery /dɪ'lɪvəri/ noun (pl **deliveries**) **1** [U] the act of taking sth (goods, letters, parcels, etc) to the place or person who has ordered it or whose address is on it: *Please allow 28 days for delivery.* ○ *a delivery van* **2** [C] an occasion when sth is delivered: *Are there any postal deliveries here on Sundays?* **3** [C] something (goods, letters, parcels, etc) that is delivered **4** [C] the process of giving birth to a baby: *an easy delivery*

delta /'deltə/ noun [C] an area of flat land shaped like a triangle where a river divides into smaller rivers flowing towards the sea

delude /dɪ'luːd/ verb [T] to make sb believe sth that is not true: *If he thinks he's going to get rich quickly, he's deluding himself.* ☞ The noun is **delusion**.

deluge /'deljuːdʒ/ noun [C] **1** a sudden very heavy fall of rain; a flood **2** a very large number of things that happen or arrive at the same time: *The programme was followed by a deluge of complaints from the public.*

deluge verb [T] (usually passive) to send or

s	z	ʃ	ʒ	h	m	n	ŋ	l	r	j	w
so	zoo	she	vision	how	man	no	sing	leg	red	yes	wet

give sb/sth a very large quantity of sth, all at the same time: *They were deluged with applications for the job.*

delusion /dɪˈluːʒn/ *noun* [C,U] a false belief: *He seems to be under the delusion that he's popular.* ☛ The verb is **delude**.

de luxe /dəˈlʌks; -ˈlʊks/ *adj* of extremely high quality and more expensive than usual: *a de luxe hotel*

delve /delv/ *verb* [I] **delve into sth** to search inside sth: *She delved into the bag and brought out a tiny box.* ○ (*figurative*) *We must delve further into the past to find the origins of the custom.*

☆ **demand¹** /dɪˈmɑːnd; *US* dɪˈmænd/ *noun* **1** [C] **a demand (for sth/that...)** a strong request or order that must be obeyed: *The demand for the kidnappers to release the hostage has not been met.* ○ *a demand for changes in the law* ○ *I was amazed by their demand that I should leave immediately.* **2** [U,sing] **demand (for sth/sb)** the desire or need for sth among a group of people: *We no longer stock that product because there is no demand for it.*

(IDIOMS) **in demand** wanted by a lot of people: *I'm in demand this weekend – I've had three invitations!*

make demands on sb to require a large amount of effort from sb: *Playing so many matches makes enormous demands on the players.*

on demand whenever you ask for it: *This treatment is available from your doctor on demand.*

☆ **demand²** /dɪˈmɑːnd; *US* dɪˈmænd/ *verb* [T] **1** to ask for sth in a way that shows you expect to get it: *I walked into the office and demanded to see the manager.* ○ *She demanded that I pay her immediately.* ○ *Your behaviour was disgraceful and I demand an apology.* **2** to ask a question in an aggressive way: *'Have you seen her?' he demanded.* **3** to require or need: *a sport that demands skill as well as strength*

demanding /dɪˈmɑːndɪŋ; *US* dɪˈmændɪŋ/ *adj* **1** (used about a job, task, etc) requiring a great deal of effort, care, skill, etc: *It will be a demanding schedule – I have to go to six cities in six days.* **2** (used about a person) constantly wanting attention or expecting very high standards of people: *a demanding child* ○ *a demanding boss*

demise /dɪˈmaɪz/ *noun* [sing] **1** (*formal*) the death of a person: *the King's demise* **2** the unsuccessful end of sth: *Poor business decisions led to the company's demise.*

☆ **democracy** /dɪˈmɒkrəsi/ *noun* (*pl* **democracies**) **1** [U] a system in which the government of a country is elected by all of the people **2** [C] a country that has this system: *How long has that country been a democracy?* **3** [U] the right of everyone in an organization, etc to vote on matters that affect them and to be treated equally: *There is a need for more democracy in the company.*

democrat /ˈdeməkræt/ *noun* [C] **1** a person who believes in and supports democracy **2 Democrat** a member or supporter of the Democratic Party of the USA ☛ Look at **Republican**.

☆ **democratic** /ˌdeməˈkrætɪk/ *adj* **1** based on the system of democracy: *democratic elections* ○ *a democratic government* **2** having or supporting equality for all members: *the democratic traditions of the party* ○ *a fully democratic society* —**democratically** /-klɪ/ *adv*: *a democratically elected government*

Demoˈcratic Party *noun* [sing] one of the two main political parties of the USA

demolish /dɪˈmɒlɪʃ/ *verb* [T] **1** to knock sth down (eg a building): *The old shops were demolished and a supermarket was built in their place.* **2** to destroy sth (an idea, a belief, etc): *She demolished his argument in one sentence.*

demolition /ˌdeməˈlɪʃn/ *noun* [C,U] the act of knocking down or destroying sth

demon /ˈdiːmən/ *noun* [C] an evil spirit: *He thinks he is possessed by demons.*

☆ **demonstrate** /ˈdemənstreɪt/ *verb* **1** [T] to show clearly that sth exists or is true; to prove: *Scientists demonstrated the presence of radioactivity in the soil.* ○ *The prison escape demonstrates the need for greater security.* **2** [T] to show and explain to sb how to do sth or how sth works: *The crew demonstrated the use of lifejackets just after take-off.* **3** [I] **demonstrate (against/for sb/sth)** to take part in a public protest or march in which a crowd of people express their opposition or support of sb/sth: *Enormous crowds have been demonstrating for human rights.*

☆ **demonstration** /ˌdemənˈstreɪʃn/ *noun* **1** [C,U] something that shows clearly that sth exists or is true: *This accident is a clear demonstration of the system's faults.* **2** [C,U] an act of showing or explaining to sb how to do sth or how sth works: *The salesman gave me a demonstration of what the computer could do.* **3** [C] **a demonstration (against/for sb/sth)** a public protest or march in which a crowd of people show how they oppose or support sb/sth: *Many thousands took part in demonstrations for greater political freedom.*

demonstrative /dɪˈmɒnstrətɪv/ *adj* (used about a person) showing feelings, especially affection, openly

demonstrator /ˈdemənstreɪtə(r)/ *noun* [C] a person who takes part in a public protest or march

demoralize (*also* **demoralise**) /dɪˈmɒrəlaɪz; *US* -ˈmɔːr-/ *verb* [T] to make sb lose confidence or the courage to continue doing sth: *Repeated defeats demoralized the team.* —**demoralization** (*also* **demoralisation**) /dɪˌmɒrəlaɪˈzeɪʃn; *US* -ˌmɔːrəlɪˈz-/ *noun* [U]

demure /dɪˈmjʊə(r)/ *adj* (used especially about a girl or young woman) shy, quiet and well behaved

den /den/ *noun* [C] **1** the hidden home of certain wild animals, eg lions **2** a secret meeting-place: *a den of thieves*

denial /dɪˈnaɪəl/ *noun* **1** [C] a statement that sth is not true: *The minister issued a denial that he was involved in the scandal.* **2** [C,U] **(a) denial (of sth)** refusing to allow sb to have or

iː	ɪ	e	æ	ɑː	ɒ	ɔː	ʊ	uː	ʌ
see	sit	ten	hat	arm	got	saw	put	too	cup

do sth: *a denial of personal freedom* ☞ The verb is **deny**.

denim /'denɪm/ *noun* **1** [U] a thick cotton material (often blue) that is used for making clothes, eg jeans **2 denims** [plural] trousers made of denim

denomination /dɪˌnɒmɪ'neɪʃn/ *noun* [C] a religious group that is part of a larger religious organization: *Anglicans, Methodists and members of other denominations attended the meeting.*

denote /dɪ'nəʊt/ *verb* [T] to indicate or be a sign of sth; to mean: *What does [U] denote in this dictionary?*

denounce /dɪ'naʊns/ *verb* [T] to say publicly that sth is wrong; to be very critical of a person in public: *Opposition MPs have denounced the government's decision.* o *The actor has been denounced as a bad influence on young people.* ☞ The noun is **denunciation**.

dense /dens/ *adj* **1** containing a lot of things or people close together: *dense forests* o *areas of dense population* **2** difficult to see through: *dense fog* **3** (*informal*) unintelligent; stupid
—**densely** *adv* densely populated

density /'densəti/ *noun* (*pl* **densities**) **1** [U] the number of things or people in a place in relation to its area: *the density of population* **2** [C,U] (*technical*) the relation of the weight of a substance to the space it occupies

dent /dent/ *noun* [C] a hollow place in the surface of sth hard, especially metal, that is the result of sth hitting or pressing against it: *This tin's got a dent in it.*

dent *verb* [T] to damage sth by hitting it and making a hollow place in it: *I hit a wall and dented the front of the car.*

dental /'dentl/ *adj* connected with teeth: *dental care*

☆**dentist** /'dentɪst/ (*also* **'dental surgeon**) *noun* [C] a person whose job is to look after people's teeth: *The dentist examined my teeth.* ☞ We refer to the dentist's surgery as 'the dentist's ': *I went to the dentist's to have a tooth out.*

dentures /'dentʃəz/ *noun* [plural] = FALSE TEETH

denunciation /dɪˌnʌnsɪ'eɪʃn/ *noun* [C,U] an expression of strong disapproval of sb/sth in public: *a strong denunciation of the invasion* ☞ The verb is **denounce**.

☆**deny** /dɪ'naɪ/ *verb* [T] (*pres part* **denying**; *3rd pers sing pres* **denies**; *pt, pp* **denied**) **1 deny sth/doing sth/that...** to state that sth is not true: *In court he denied all the charges.* o *When I challenged her, she denied telling lies/that she had told lies.* **2 deny sb sth; deny sth (to sb)** to refuse to allow sb to have sth: *She was denied permission to remain in the country.* ☞ The noun is **denial**.

deodorant /di:'əʊdərənt/ *noun* [C,U] a chemical substance that you put onto your body to destroy or prevent bad smells

depart /dɪ'pɑ:t/ *verb* [I] (*formal*) to leave a place, usually at the beginning of a journey: *Ferries depart for Spain twice a day.* o *The next train to the airport departs from platform 2.* ☞ Look at the note at **leave¹**.

☆**department** /dɪ'pɑ:tmənt/ *noun* [C] (*abbr* **Dept**) **1** = MINISTRY(1): *the Department of Health* **2** one of the sections into which an organization (eg a school or a business) is divided: *the Modern Languages department* o *The book department is on the second floor.* o *She works in the accounts department.*

departmental /ˌdi:pɑ:t'mentl/ *adj* concerning a department: *There is a departmental meeting once a month.*

de'partment store *noun* [C] a large shop that is divided into departments selling many different types of goods

☆**departure** /dɪ'pɑ:tʃə(r)/ *noun* [C,U] **1** leaving or going away from a place: *Arrivals and departures are shown on the board in the main hall of the station.* o *Passengers should check in at least one hour before departure.* **2** an action which is different from what is usual or expected: *a departure from normal practice*

☆**depend** /dɪ'pend/ *verb*
(IDIOM) **that depends; it (all) depends** (used alone or at the beginning of a sentence) it is not certain; it is influenced or decided by sth: '*Can you lend me some money?*' '*That depends. How much do you want?*' o *I don't know whether I'll see him. It all depends what time he gets here.*
(PHRASAL VERBS) **depend on sb/sth** to be sure that sb/sth will help you; to trust sb/sth to do sth: *If you ever need any help, you know you can depend on me.* o *You can't depend on the trains. They're always late.* o *I was depending on things going according to plan.* o *You can always depend on him to say what he thinks* (= you can be sure that he will say what he thinks).

depend on sb/sth (for sth) to need sb/sth to provide sth: *I depend on my parents for advice.* o *Our organization depends on donations from the public.*

depend on sth to be decided or influenced by sb/sth: *His whole future depends on these exams.* o *The starting salary will be between £11 000 and £12 000, depending on age and experience.*

dependable *adj* that can be trusted: *The bus service is usually very dependable.*

dependant (*especially US* **dependent**) /dɪ'pendənt/ *noun* [C] a person who depends on sb else for money, a home, food, etc: *Your insurance provides cover for you and all your dependants.*

dependence /dɪ'pendəns/ *noun* [U] **dependence on sb/sth** the state of needing sb/sth: *The country wants to reduce its dependence on imported oil.*

dependency /dɪ'pendənsi/ *noun* [U] the state of being dependent on sb/sth; the state of being unable to live without sth, especially a drug: *a drug dependency clinic*

dependent /dɪ'pendənt/ *adj* **1 dependent (on sb/sth)** needing sb/sth to support you: *The industry is heavily dependent on government funding.* o *dependent children* **2 dependent on sb/sth** influenced or decided by sth: *The price you pay is dependent on the number in your group.*

depict /dɪ'pɪkt/ *verb* [T] **1** to show sb/sth in a painting or drawing: *a painting depicting a*

deplete /dɪˈpliːt/ verb [T] to reduce the amount of sth: *We are depleting the world's natural resources.* —**depletion** /dɪˈpliːʃn/ noun [U]: *the depletion of the ozone layer*

deplore /dɪˈplɔː(r)/ verb [T] (*formal*) to feel or state that sth is morally bad: *I deplore such dishonest behaviour.*

deplorable /dɪˈplɔːrəbl/ adj morally bad and deserving disapproval —**deplorably** /-əbli/ adv

deploy /dɪˈplɔɪ/ verb [T] **1** to put soldiers or weapons in a position where they can be used **2** to arrange people or things so that they can be used efficiently —**deployment** noun [U]: *the deployment of troops*

deport /dɪˈpɔːt/ verb [T] to send a foreigner out of a country officially: *A number of illegal immigrants have been deported.* —**deportation** /ˌdiːpɔːˈteɪʃn/ noun [C,U]: *The illegal immigrants face deportation.*

depose /dɪˈpəʊz/ verb [T] to remove a ruler or leader from power: *There was a revolution and the dictator was deposed.*

deposit¹ /dɪˈpɒzɪt/ verb [T] **1** to put money into an account at a bank: *He deposited £20 a week into his savings account.* **2** to put sth valuable in an official place where it is safe until needed again: *Valuables can be deposited in the hotel safe.* **3** to pay a sum of money as the first payment for sth, with the rest of the money to be paid later: *You will have to deposit 10% of the cost when you book.* **4** to put sth down somewhere: *He deposited his bags on the floor and sat down.* **5** to leave sth lying on a surface, as the result of a natural or chemical process: *mud deposited by a flood*

deposit² /dɪˈpɒzɪt/ noun [C] **1** a sum of money paid into a bank account; the paying of a sum of money into a bank account **2 a deposit (on sth)** a sum of money which is the first payment for sth, with the rest of the money to be paid later: *Once you have paid a deposit, the booking will be confirmed.* **3 a deposit (on sth)** a sum of money that you pay when you rent sth and get back when you return it without damage: *Boats can be hired for £5 an hour, plus £20 deposit.* **4** a substance that has been left on a surface or has developed in the ground as the result of a natural or chemical process: *mineral deposits*

deˈposit account noun [C] a type of bank account where your money earns interest. You cannot take money out of a deposit account without arranging it first with the bank.

depot /ˈdepəʊ; *US* ˈdiːpəʊ/ noun [C] **1** a place where large numbers of vehicles (buses, lorries, etc) are kept when not in use **2** a place where military supplies are stored **3** (*US*) a bus or railway station

depreciate /dɪˈpriːʃieɪt/ verb [I] to lose value, especially as a result of use or age —**depreciation** /dɪˌpriːʃiˈeɪʃn/ noun [C,U]

depress /dɪˈpres/ verb [T] **1** to make sb unhappy: *The thought of going to work tomorrow really depresses me.* **2** (*formal*) to press sth down when operating sth: *To switch off the machine, depress the lever.* **3** (used especially in connection with business) to cause sth to become less successful or profitable: *The reduction in the number of tourists has depressed local trade.*

depressed adj very unhappy, often for a long period. If you are depressed you may be suffering from the medical condition of depression: *He's been very depressed since he lost his job.*

depressing adj making sb feel sad or without hope: *The outlook for the future of the company is very depressing.* —**depressingly** adv

depression /dɪˈpreʃn/ noun **1** [U] a feeling of unhappiness and hopelessness that lasts for a long time. Depression can be a medical condition and may have physical symptoms. **2** [C] a period when the economic situation is bad, with little business activity and many people without a job **3** [C] a hollow part in the surface of sth: *a depression in the ground*

deprive /dɪˈpraɪv/ verb [T] **deprive sb/sth of sth** to prevent sb/sth from having sth; to take away sth from sb: *to deprive people of their rights as citizens* ○ *The prisoners were deprived of food.*

deprived adj not having enough of the basic things in life, such as food, money, etc: *He came from a deprived background.* —**deprivation** /ˌdeprɪˈveɪʃn/ noun [C,U]

☆ **depth** /depθ/ noun **1** [C,U] the distance down from the top surface of sth; the measurement of how deep sth is: *What's the depth of the swimming-pool?* ○ *The hole should be 3cm in depth.* ☛ picture at **length**. **2** [C,U] the distance from the front to the back: *the depth of a shelf* ☛ picture at **length**. **3** [U] (used about emotions, knowledge, etc) the amount that a person has: *He tried to convince her of the depth of his feelings for her.*

(IDIOMS) **in depth** looking at all the details: *to discuss a problem in depth*

out of your depth 1 in water that is too deep for you to stand up in **2** in a situation that is too difficult for you: *When they start discussing politics I soon get out of my depth.*

deputation /ˌdepjuˈteɪʃn/ noun [C, with sing or pl verb] a group of people sent to sb to speak for others

deputize (*also* **deputise**) /ˈdepjutaɪz/ verb [I] **deputize (for sb)** to act for sb who is absent or unable to do sth

☆ **deputy** /ˈdepjuti/ noun [C] (*pl* **deputies**) the second most important person in a particular organization. A deputy does the work of his/her boss if the boss is absent: *the Deputy Manager* ○ *While I am away my deputy will take over.*

derail /dɪˈreɪl/ verb [T] to cause a train to come off a railway track

derailment noun [C,U] an occasion when this happens: *Due to a derailment, all trains have been cancelled this morning.*

deranged /dɪˈreɪndʒd/ adj thinking and behaving in a way that is not normal, especially because of mental illness

derby /ˈdɑːbi/ noun [C] (*pl* **derbies**) (*US*) = BOWLER

p	b	t	d	k	g	tʃ	dʒ	f	v	θ	ð
pen	**bad**	**tea**	**did**	**cat**	**got**	**chin**	**June**	**fall**	**van**	**thin**	**then**

derelict /ˈderəlɪkt/ adj no longer used and in bad condition: *a derelict house*

deride /dɪˈraɪd/ verb [T] to say that sb/sth is ridiculous; to laugh at sth in a cruel way —**derision** /dɪˈrɪʒn/ noun [U]: *Her comments were met with howls of derision.* —**derisive** /dɪˈraɪsɪv/ adj: *'What rubbish!' he said with a derisive laugh.*

derisory /dɪˈraɪsəri/ adj so small that it is ridiculous or does not deserve to be considered seriously: *He made a derisory offer, which I turned down immediately.*

derivation /ˌderɪˈveɪʃn/ noun [C,U] the origin from which a word or phrase has developed: *a word of Latin derivation*

derivative /dɪˈrɪvətɪv/ adj copied from sth or influenced by sth and therefore not new or original

derivative noun [C] a form of sth (especially a word) that has developed from the original form: *'Sadness' is a derivative of 'sad.'*

derive /dɪˈraɪv/ verb **1** [T] (*formal*) to get sth (especially a feeling or an advantage) from sth: *I derive great satisfaction from my work.* **2** [I,T] to come from sth; to have sth as its origin: *'Mutton' derives from the French word 'mouton'.* ○ *The town derives its name from the river on which it was built.*

derogatory /dɪˈrɒɡətri; *US* -tɔːri/ adj expressing a lack of respect for, or a low opinion of sth: *derogatory comments about the standard of my work*

descend /dɪˈsend/ verb [I,T] (*formal*) to go down to a lower place; to go down sth: *The plane started to descend and a few minutes later we landed.* ○ *She descended the stairs slowly.* ☞ The opposite is **ascend**.
(IDIOM) **be descended from sb** to have as a relative or relatives in the distant past: *He says he's descended from a Russian prince.*

descendant /-ənt/ noun [C] a person who is related to sb who lived a long time ago: *Her family are descendants of one of the first convicts who were sent to Australia.* ☞ Look at **ancestor**.

descent /dɪˈsent/ noun **1** [C] a movement down to a lower place: *The pilot informed us that we were about to begin our descent.* **2** [U] family origins, especially in connection with nationality: *He is of Italian descent.*

☆ **describe** /dɪˈskraɪb/ verb [T] **describe sb/sth (as sth)** to say what sb/sth is like, or what happened: *Can you describe the bag you lost?* ○ *It's impossible to describe how I felt.* ○ *She described what had happened to the reporter.* ○ *The thief was described as tall, thin, and aged about twenty.* ○ *Would you describe yourself as confident?*

☆ **description** /dɪˈskrɪpʃn/ noun **1** [C,U] a picture in words of sb/sth or an account of sth that happened; the ability to describe sb/sth: *The man gave the police a detailed description of the burglar.* ○ *Her description of the events that evening was most amusing.* **2** [C] a type or kind of sth: *It must be a tool of some description, but I don't know what it's for.*

descriptive /dɪˈskrɪptɪv/ adj **1** that describes sb/sth: *a piece of descriptive writing* **2** that describes sb/sth in a skilful and interesting way: *She gave a highly descriptive account of the journey.*

desert[1] /dɪˈzɜːt/ verb **1** [T] to leave sb/sth, usually for ever: *He deserted his wife and went to live with another woman.* ○ *Many people have deserted the countryside and moved to the towns.* **2** [I,T] (used especially about sb in the armed forces) to leave without permission: *He deserted because he didn't want to fight.*

deserted adj empty, because all the people have left: *a deserted house*

deserter noun [C] a person who leaves military duty without permission

desertion /dɪˈzɜːʃn/ noun [C,U] leaving sb/sth, especially your husband or wife, or leaving military duty without permission

☆ **desert**[2] /ˈdezət/ noun [C,U] a large area of land, usually covered with sand, that has very little water and very few plants: *the Gobi Desert*

ˌdesert ˈisland noun [C] an island, especially a tropical one, where nobody lives

☆ **deserve** /dɪˈzɜːv/ verb [T] (not used in the continuous tenses) to earn sth, especially a suitable reward or punishment, for sth that you have done: *We've done a lot of work and we deserve a break.* ○ *He deserves to be punished severely for such a crime.*

deservedly /dɪˈzɜːvɪdli/ adv as is deserved; rightly: *He deservedly won the Best Actor award.*

deserving /dɪˈzɜːvɪŋ/ adj that deserves help: *This charity is a most deserving cause.*

☆ **design** /dɪˈzaɪn/ noun **1** [C] a drawing that shows how sth should be made: *The architect showed us her design for the new theatre.* **2** [U] the way in which sth is planned and made or in which the parts of sth are arranged: *Design faults have been discovered in the car.* **3** [U] process and skill of making drawings that show how sth should be made: *to study industrial design* ○ *graphic design* **4** [C] a pattern of lines, shapes, etc that decorate sth: *a T-shirt with a geometric design on it*

design verb **1** [I,T] to plan and made a drawing of how sth will be made: *She designs the interiors of shops.* **2** [T] to invent, plan and develop sth for a particular purpose: *I designed a scheme for increasing profits.* ○ *The bridge wasn't designed for such heavy traffic.*

designate /ˈdezɪɡneɪt/ verb [T] (*formal*) **1** to give sth a name to show that it has a particular purpose: *This has been designated a conservation area.* **2** to choose sb for a particular job or task **3** to show or mark sth: *These arrows designate the emergency exits.*

designer /dɪˈzaɪnə(r)/ noun [C] a person whose job is to make drawings showing how sth will be made: *a fashion designer* ○ *designer jeans* (= made by a famous designer)

desirable /dɪˈzaɪərəbl/ adj **1** wanted, often by many people; worth having: *a desirable area* (= one that many people would like to live in) ○ *Experience is desirable but not essential for this job.* **2** sexually attractive

desire[1] /dɪˈzaɪə(r)/ noun [C,U] (a) **desire (for sth/to do sth) 1** the feeling of wanting sth very much; a strong wish: *the desire for a peace-*

ful solution to the crisis o *I have no desire to visit that place again.* **2** the wish for sexual relations with sb

desire² /dɪ'zaɪə(r)/ *verb* [T] **1** (*formal*) to want: *They have everything they could possibly desire.* **2** to find sb/sth sexually attractive

☆ **desk** /desk/ *noun* [C] **1** a type of table, often with drawers, that you sit at to write or work: *The pupils took their books out of their desks.* o *a computer that fits easily onto any desk* **2** a table or place in a building where a particular service is provided: *Brochures are available at the information desk.*

desolate /'desələt/ *adj* **1** (used about a place) sad, empty and depressing: *desolate wasteland* **2** (used about a person) lonely, very unhappy and without hope

 desolation /ˌdesə'leɪʃn/ *noun* [U] **1** the state of being empty because all the people have left: *All the factories closed, leaving the town a scene of desolation.* **2** the feeling of being lonely and without hope: *He felt utter desolation when his wife died.*

despair /dɪ'speə(r)/ *noun* [U] the state of having lost all hope: *I felt like giving up in despair.* o *Despair drove him to attempt suicide.*

 despair *verb* [I] **despair (of sb/sth)** to lose all hope and to feel that there will be no improvement: *Don't despair. Keep trying and I'm sure you'll get it right.* o *We began to despair of ever finding somewhere to live.* —**despairing** /dɪ'speərɪŋ/ *adj: a despairing cry*

despatch /dɪ'spætʃ/ = DISPATCH

☆ **desperate** /'despərət/ *adj* **1** out of control and willing to do anything to change the situation you are in because it is so terrible: *She became desperate when her money ran out.* o *I only took this job because I was desperate.* **2** done with little hope of success, as a last thing to try when everything else has failed: *I made a desperate attempt to persuade her to change her mind.* **3 desperate (for sth/to do sth)** wanting or needing sth very much: *Let's go into a café. I'm desperate for a drink.* **4** terrible, very serious: *There is a desperate shortage of skilled workers.* —**desperately** *adv: She was desperately* (= extremely) *unlucky not to win.*

 desperation /ˌdespə'reɪʃn/ *noun* [U] the feeling or state of being desperate: *She felt she wanted to scream in desperation.*

despicable /dɪ'spɪkəbl/ *adj* deserving to be hated: *a despicable liar* o *a despicable act of terrorism*

despise /dɪ'spaɪz/ *verb* [T] to hate sb/sth; to consider sb/sth worthless: *I despise him for lying about me to other people.*

despite /dɪ'spaɪt/ *prep* (used to show that sth happened although you would not expect it): *Despite having very little money, they enjoy life.* o *The scheme went ahead despite public opposition.*

despondent /dɪ'spɒndənt/ *adj* without hope; expecting no improvement —**despondency** /dɪ'spɒndənsɪ/ *noun* [U]

dessert /dɪ'zɜːt/ *noun* [C,U] something sweet that is eaten after the main part of a meal: *What would you like for dessert – ice-cream or fresh fruit?* ☛ Look at **pudding** and **sweet**.

dessertspoon *noun* [C] a spoon of medium size, used for eating dessert

destination /ˌdestɪ'neɪʃn/ *noun* [C] the place where sb/sth is going or being sent: *I finally reached my destination two hours late.*

destined /'destɪnd/ *adj* **1 destined for sth/to do sth** sure to or intended to be, have or do sth: *I think she is destined for success.* o *He was destined to become one of the country's leading politicians.* **2 destined for...** on a journey or moving towards a particular place: *I boarded a bus destined for New York.* o *They were destined for a new life in a new country.*

destiny /'destɪnɪ/ *noun* (*pl* **destinies**) **1** [U] a power that people believe influences their lives; fate **2** [C] the things that happen to you in your life, especially things that you do not control: *She felt that it was her destiny to be a great singer.* o *The destiny of the country lies in the hands of the people.*

destitute /'destɪtjuːt; *US* -tuːt/ *adj* not having the things that are necessary in life, such as money, food, a home, etc —**destitution** /ˌdestɪ'tjuːʃn; *US* -'tuːʃn/ *noun* [U]

☆ **destroy** /dɪ'strɔɪ/ *verb* [T] **1** to damage sth so badly that it can no longer be used or no longer exists: *The building was destroyed by fire.* o *The defeat destroyed his confidence.* **2** to kill an animal, especially because it is injured or dangerous: *The horse broke its leg and had to be destroyed.*

destroyer *noun* [C] **1** a person or thing that destroys sth **2** a small warship

☆ **destruction** /dɪ'strʌkʃn/ *noun* [U] destroying or being destroyed: *The war brought death and destruction to the city.* o *the destruction of the rainforests*

destructive /dɪ'strʌktɪv/ *adj* causing a lot of damage: *destructive weapons* o *the destructive effects of drink and drugs*

detach /dɪ'tætʃ/ *verb* [T] **detach sth (from sth)** to separate sth from sth it is attached to: *Detach the form at the bottom of the page and send it to this address...*

detached *adj* **1** not being or not feeling personally involved **2** (used about a house) not joined to any other house ☛ picture on page A12.

detachable /-əbl/ *adj* that can be separated from sth it is attached to

detachment /dɪ'tætʃmənt/ *noun* **1** [U] the fact or feeling of not being personally involved **2** [C] a group of soldiers who have been given a particular task away from the main group

☆ **detail¹** /'diːteɪl; *US* dɪ'teɪl/ *noun* [C,U] a small individual fact, point or piece of information: *Just give me the basic facts. Don't worry about the details.* o *On the application form you should give details of your education and experience.* o *For full details of the offer, contact your local travel agent.* o *The work involves close attention to detail.*

(IDIOMS) **go into detail(s)** to talk or write about the details of sth: *I can't go into detail now because it would take too long.*

in detail including the details; thoroughly: *We haven't discussed the matter in detail yet.*

detail² /'diːteɪl; *US* dɪ'teɪl/ *verb* [T] to give a

full list of sth; to describe sth fully: *He detailed all the equipment he needed for the job.*

detailed *adj* having many details or giving a lot of attention to details: *a detailed description of the accident*

detain /dɪ'teɪn/ *verb* [T] to stop sb from leaving a place; to delay sb: *A man has been detained by the police for questioning* (= kept at the police station). o *Don't let me detain you if you're busy.*
☛ The noun is **detention**.

detect /dɪ'tekt/ *verb* [T] to notice or discover sth that is difficult to see, feel, etc: *I detected a slight change in his attitude.* o *Traces of blood were detected on his clothes.* —**detection** /dɪ'tekʃn/ *noun* [U]: *The crime escaped detection for many years.*

detector *noun* [C] an instrument that is used for detecting sth: *a smoke detector*

☆ **detective** /dɪ'tektɪv/ *noun* [C] a person, especially a police officer, who tries to solve crimes and find the person who is guilty

de'tective story *noun* [C] a story about a crime in which sb tries to find out who the guilty person is

détente /ˌdeɪ'tɑːnt/ *noun* [U] (*formal*) a more friendly relationship between countries that had previously been very unfriendly towards each other

detention /dɪ'tenʃn/ *noun* [U] the act of stopping a person leaving a place, especially by keeping him/her in prison, often for political reasons ☛ The verb is **detain**.

deter /dɪ'tɜː(r)/ *verb* [T] (**deterring**; **deterred**) **deter sb (from doing sth)** to make sb decide not to do sth: *The council is trying to deter visitors from bringing their cars into the city centre.*

detergent /dɪ'tɜːdʒənt/ *noun* [C,U] a chemical liquid or powder that is used for cleaning things

deteriorate /dɪ'tɪərɪəreɪt/ *verb* [I] to become worse: *The political tension is deteriorating into civil war.* —**deterioration** /dɪˌtɪərɪə'reɪʃn/ *noun* [C,U]

determination /dɪˌtɜːmɪ'neɪʃn/ *noun* [U] **1** the quality of having firmly decided to succeed in doing sth, even if it is very difficult or people are against you: *her determination to win* o *You need great determination to succeed in business.* **2** the act of fixing or deciding sth: *the determination of future council policy*

determine /dɪ'tɜːmɪn/ *verb* [T] **1** to fix or decide sth: *The results of the tests will determine what treatment you need.* **2** to find sth out: *an attempt to determine the exact position of the enemy submarine* **3** (*formal*) to decide sth firmly: *He determined to give up smoking in the New Year.*

☆ **determined** /dɪ'tɜːmɪnd/ *adj* having firmly decided to succeed in doing sth, even if it is difficult or people are against you: *He is determined to leave school, even though his parents want him to stay.* o *I'm determined to enjoy myself tonight.*

determiner /dɪ'tɜːmɪnə(r)/ *noun* [C] (*grammar*) a word that comes before a noun to show how the noun is being used: *'Her', 'most' and 'those' are all determiners.*

deterrent /dɪ'terənt; *US* -'tɜː-/ *noun* [C] something that is intended to stop you doing sth: *Their punishment will be a deterrent to others.* o *the belief that nuclear weapons act as a deterrent* —**deterrent** *adj*

detest /dɪ'test/ *verb* [T] to hate or dislike sb/sth: *They absolutely detest each other.*

detonate /'detəneɪt/ *verb* [I,T] to explode or to make sth explode

detour /'diːtʊə(r); *US* dɪ'tʊər/ *noun* [C] **1** a longer route that you take from one place to another in order to avoid sth or in order to see or do sth: *Because of the accident we had to make a five-kilometre detour.* **2** (*US*) = DIVERSION

detract /dɪ'trækt/ *verb* [I] **detract from sth** to make sth seem less good or important: *These criticisms in no way detract from the team's achievements.*

detriment /'detrɪmənt/ *noun*
(IDIOM) **to the detriment of sb/sth** harming or damaging sb/sth: *Doctors claim that the changes will be to the detriment of patients.* —**detrimental** /ˌdetrɪ'mentl/ *adj*: *Too much alcohol is detrimental to your health.*

deuce /djuːs; *US* duːs/ *noun* [U] a score of 40 points to each player in a game of tennis

devalue /ˌdiː'væljuː/ *verb* [T] to reduce the value of the money of one country in relation to the value of the money of other countries: *The pound has been devalued against the deutschmark.* —**devaluation** /ˌdiːvæljʊ'eɪʃn/ *noun* [U]

devastate /'devəsteɪt/ *verb* [T] to destroy sth or damage it badly: *a land devastated by war*

devastated *adj* **1** completely destroyed **2** shocked or very upset: *The community was devastated by the killings.*

devastating /'devəsteɪtɪŋ/ *adj* **1** that destroys sth completely: *a devastating explosion* **2** that shocks or upsets sb very much: *The closure of the factory was a devastating blow to the workers.* —**devastatingly** *adv* —**devastation** /ˌdevə'steɪʃn/ *noun* [U]: *a scene of total devastation*

☆ **develop** /dɪ'veləp/ *verb* **1** [I,T] to grow slowly, increase, or change into sth else; to make sb/sth do this: *to develop from a child into an adult* o *Gradually their friendship developed into love.* o *a scheme to help pupils develop their natural talents* **2** [T] to begin to have sth: *to develop cancer* **3** [I] to begin to happen or be noticeable: *A fault developed when we'd only had the car a month.* o *Trouble is developing at the border.* **4** [T] to make pictures or negatives from a piece of film by using special chemicals: *to develop a film* **5** [T] to build houses, shops, factories, etc on a piece of land: *This site is being developed for offices.*

developed *adj* of a good level or standard: *a highly developed economy*

developer (*also* **property developer**) *noun* [C] a person or company that develops land

de'veloping country *noun* [C] a poor country that is trying to develop or improve its economy

☆ **development** /dɪ'veləpmənt/ *noun* **1** [U] developing or being developed: *the develop-*

ment of tourism in many Mediterranean resorts ○ the history of Japan's development from a feudal to an industrial society ○ Third World development (= the development of its economy) ○ a child's intellectual development **2** [C] a new event: *This week has seen a number of new developments in the Middle East crisis.* **3** [C,U] a new product or the act of making a new product: *a technological development* ○ *research and development* **4** [C] a piece of land on which houses, shops, factories, etc have been built: *a new housing development*

deviate /'di:vieɪt/ *verb* [I] to change the way you think or behave, or to start to behave in a way that is not acceptable to other people: *He never once deviated from his Christian principles.*
  deviation /ˌdi:vɪ'eɪʃn/ *noun* [C,U] a difference from what is usual or expected, or from what is approved of by society: *sexual deviation* ○ *a deviation from our usual way of doing things*

☆**device** /dɪ'vaɪs/ *noun* [C] **1** a tool or piece of equipment made for a particular purpose: *a security device which detects any movement or change in temperature* ○ *labour-saving devices such as washing-machines and vacuum cleaners* ☛ Look at the note at **tool**. **2** a trick or plan: *Critics dismissed the speech as a political device for winning support.*

☆**devil** /'devl/ *noun* [C] **1 the Devil** the most powerful evil being, according to the Christian religion ☛ Look at **Satan**. **2** an evil being or spirit **3** (*informal*) a word used when you are describing a person: *The poor devil died in hospital two days later.* ○ *You're a lucky devil!*
(IDIOM) **why, etc the devil** (used for expressing great surprise or annoyance about sth): *It's two o'clock in the morning. Where the devil have you been?*

devious /'di:viəs/ *adj* **1** clever but not honest or direct: *I wouldn't trust him – he can be very devious.* **2** (used about a route, path, etc) having many bends and curves; not straight

devise /dɪ'vaɪz/ *verb* [T] to invent a plan, system, etc: *They've devised a plan for keeping traffic out of the city centre.*

devoid /dɪ'vɔɪd/ *adj* (*formal*) **devoid of sth** not having a particular quality; without sth: *to be devoid of hope*

devolution /ˌdi:və'lu:ʃn; *US* ˌdev-/ *noun* [U] the transfer of power, especially from central to local government

devote /dɪ'vəʊt/ *verb* [T] **devote yourself/sth to sb/sth** to give a lot of time, energy, etc to sb/sth: *She gave up work to devote herself full-time to her music.* ○ *Schools should devote more time to science subjects.*
  devoted *adj* loving sb/sth very much: *Neil's absolutely devoted to his wife.*
  devotee /ˌdevə'ti:/ *noun* [C] a person who likes sb/sth very much: *Devotees of science fiction will enjoy this new film.*
  devotion /dɪ'vəʊʃn/ *noun* [U] **devotion (to sb/sth) 1** great love: *a mother's devotion to her children* **2** the act of giving a lot of your time, energy, etc to sb/sth: *devotion to duty* **3** great religious feeling

devour /dɪ'vaʊə(r)/ *verb* [T] to eat sth quickly and with enjoyment

devout /dɪ'vaʊt/ *adj* very religious: *a devout Muslim family* — **devoutly** *adv*

dew /dju:; *US* du:/ *noun* [U] small drops of water that form on plants, leaves, etc during the night

dexterity /dek'sterəti/ *noun* [U] skill at doing things, especially with your hands

diabetes /ˌdaɪə'bi:ti:z/ *noun* [U] a serious disease in which a person's body cannot control the level of sugar in the blood
  diabetic /ˌdaɪə'betɪk/ *adj* of or for diabetes or diabetics: *diabetic chocolate* (= safe for diabetics)
  diabetic *noun* [C] a person who suffers from diabetes

diagnose /'daɪəgnəʊz; *US* ˌdaɪəg'nəʊs/ *verb* [T] to find out what is wrong or what illness a person has: *His illness was diagnosed as bronchitis.*
  diagnosis /ˌdaɪəg'nəʊsɪs/ *noun* [C,U] (*pl* **diagnoses** /-'nəʊsi:z/) an act of diagnosing sth: *The doctor's diagnosis was proved right.* ○ *What's your diagnosis of the situation?*

diagonal /daɪ'ægənl/ *adj* **1** (used about a straight line) not vertical or horizontal; sloping ☛ picture at **vertical**. **2** going from one corner to the opposite corner of a square, rectangle, etc — **diagonally** /-nəli/ *adv*: *I was sitting diagonally opposite Diane at the table.*

diagram /'daɪəgræm/ *noun* [C] a simple picture that is used to explain how sth works or what sth looks like: *a diagram of the body's digestive system*

dial¹ /'daɪəl/ *verb* [I,T] (dialling; dialled; *US* dialing; dialed) to move the dial²(3) or push the buttons on a telephone in order to call a particular telephone number: *You can now dial direct to Singapore.* ○ *to dial the wrong number*
'dialling code *noun* [C] the numbers that you must dial for a particular area or country: *The dialling code for inner London is 0171.*
'dialling tone *noun* [C,U] the sound that you hear when you pick up a telephone before you begin to dial

dial² /'daɪəl/ *noun* [C] **1** the round part of a clock, watch or other piece of equipment that gives you information about the time or about a measurement. A dial has numbers and a hand or pointer on it: *a dial for showing air pressure* **2** the round part on a piece of equipment that you turn to change sth **3** the round part with holes in it on some telephones. You put your finger in one of the holes and turn the dial to call a number.

dialect /'daɪəlekt/ *noun* [C,U] a form of a language that is spoken in one part of a country: *a local dialect*

dialogue (*US* **dialog**) /'daɪəlɒg; *US* -lɔ:g/ *noun* [C,U] **1** (a) a conversation between people in a book, play, etc **2** (a) discussion between people who have different opinions: *a dialogue between the major political parties*

diameter /daɪ'æmɪtə(r)/ *noun* [C] a straight line that goes from one side to the other of a circle, passing through the centre ☛ Look at **radius**.

p	b	t	d	k	g	tʃ	dʒ	f	v	θ	ð
pen	bad	tea	did	cat	got	chin	June	fall	van	thin	then

☆**diamond** /ˈdaɪəmənd/ noun **1** [C,U] a hard, bright precious stone which is very expensive and is used for making jewellery and in industry. A diamond usually has no colour. **2** [C] a flat shape that has four sides of equal length and points at two ends ☛ picture at **shape**. **3 diamonds** [plural] the group (**suit**) of playing-cards with red shapes like diamonds(2) on them: *the seven of diamonds* ☛ picture at **card**. **4** [C] one of the cards from this suit: *If you haven't got a diamond, you can play a trump.*

ˌdiamond ˈwedding noun [C] the 60th anniversary of a wedding ☛ Look at **golden wedding** and **silver wedding**.

diaper /ˈdaɪəpə(r); *US* ˈdaɪpər/ noun [C] (*US*) = NAPPY

diaphragm /ˈdaɪəfræm/ noun [C] **1** the muscle between your lungs and your stomach that helps you to breathe **2** a thin piece of rubber that a woman puts inside her body before having sex to stop her having a baby

diarrhoea (*US* **diarrhea**) /ˌdaɪəˈrɪə/ noun [U] an illness that causes you to pass waste material (**faeces**) from your bowels very often and in a more liquid form than usual: *diarrhoea and vomiting*

☆**diary** /ˈdaɪəri/ noun [C] (*pl* **diaries**) **1** a book in which you write down your appointments, etc: *I'll just check in my diary to see if I'm free that weekend.* ☛ Look at the note at **calendar**. **2** a book in which you write down what happens to you each day: *Do you keep a diary?*

dice /daɪs/ noun [C] (*pl* **dice**) a small cube with a different number of spots (from one to six) on each side, used in certain games: *Throw the dice to see who goes first.*

dictate /dɪkˈteɪt; *US* ˈdɪkteɪt/ verb **1** [I,T] to say sth aloud so that sb else must write or type it: *to dictate a letter to a secretary* **2** [I,T] to tell or order sb to do sth: *Parents can't dictate to their children how they should run their lives.* **3** [I,T] to decide or influence sth: *an attempt by foreign banks to dictate the country's economic policy*

dictation /dɪkˈteɪʃn/ noun [C,U] spoken words that sb else must write or type: *We had a dictation in English today* (= a test in which we had to write down what the teacher said).

dictator /dɪkˈteɪtə(r); *US* ˈdɪkteɪtər/ noun [C] a ruler who has total power in a country, especially one who used force to gain power and who rules the country unfairly

dictatorship noun [C,U] government by a dictator; a country that is ruled by a dictator: *a military dictatorship*

☆**dictionary** /ˈdɪkʃənri; *US* -neri/ noun [C] (*pl* **dictionaries**) a book that lists the words of a language in alphabetical order and that tells you what they mean, in the same or another language: *to look up a word in a dictionary* ○ *a bilingual/monolingual dictionary* ○ *a French-English dictionary*

did *pt* of DO

didn't *short for* DID NOT

☆**die** /daɪ/ verb (*pres part* **dying**; *3rd pers sing pres* **dies**; *pt, pp* **died**) **1** [I] to stop living: *Thousands of people have died from this disease.* ○ *to die of hunger* ○ *to die of a heart attack* ○ *to die for what you believe in* ○ (*figurative*) *Our love will never die.* **2** [T] to have a particular kind of death: *to die a natural death*

(IDIOMS) **be dying for sth/to do sth** to want sth/to do sth very much: *I'm dying for a cup of coffee.*

die hard to change or disappear only slowly or with difficulty: *Old attitudes towards women die hard.*

(PHRASAL VERBS) **die away** to slowly become weaker before stopping or disappearing: *The sound of the engine died away as the car drove into the distance.*

die down to slowly become less strong: *Let's wait until the storm dies down before we go out.*

die out to disappear: *The use of horses on farms has almost died out in this country.*

diesel /ˈdiːzl/ noun **1** (*also* ˈ**diesel engine**) [C] an engine in buses, trains, and some cars that uses heavy oil **2** [U] the heavy oil that is used in these engines: *a taxi that runs on diesel* ☛ Look at **petrol**.

diet /ˈdaɪət/ noun **1** [C,U] the food that a person or animal usually eats: *The peasants live on a diet of rice and vegetables.* ○ *Poor diet is a cause of ill health.* **2** [C] certain foods that a person who is ill, or who wants to lose weight is allowed to eat: *a low-fat diet*

(IDIOM) **be/go on a diet** to eat only certain foods or a small amount of food because you want to lose weight: *I won't have a cake, thank you. I'm on a diet.*

diet *verb* [I] to be trying to lose weight by eating less food or only certain kinds of food: *You've lost some weight. Have you been dieting?*

☆**differ** /ˈdɪfə(r)/ verb [I] **1 differ** (**from sb/sth**) to be different: *How does this car differ from the more expensive model?* **2 differ** (**with sb**) (**about/on sth**) to have a different opinion: *I'm afraid I differ with you on that question.*

☆**difference** /ˈdɪfrəns/ noun **1** [C] **difference** (**between A and B**) the way that people or things are not the same or the way that sb/sth has changed: *the differences between men and women* **2** [C,U] **difference** (**in sth**) (**between A and B**) the amount by which people or things are not the same or by which sb/sth has changed: *There's an age difference of three years between the two children.* ○ *There's very little difference in price since last year.* ○ *We gave a 30% deposit and must pay the difference when the work is finished* (= the rest of the money). **3** [C] a disagreement that is not very serious: *All couples have their differences from time to time.*

(IDIOMS) **make a, some, etc difference (to sb/sth)** to have an effect (on sb/sth): *A week's holiday made a lot of difference to her health.*

make no difference (to sb/sth); not make any difference to not be important (to sb/sth): *It makes no difference to us if the baby is a girl or a boy.*

☆**different** /ˈdɪfrənt/ adj **1 different** (**from/to sb/sth**) not the same: *Cricket is quite different*

s	z	ʃ	ʒ	h	m	n	ŋ	l	r	j	w
so	zoo	she	vision	how	man	no	sing	leg	red	yes	wet

from baseball. ○ *The play was different to anything I had seen before.* ○ *The two houses are very different in style.* ☞ In US English **different than** is also used. **2** separate; individual: *This coat is available in three different colours.* —**differently** *adv*: *I think you'll feel differently about it tomorrow.*

differentiate /ˌdɪfəˈrenʃɪeɪt/ *verb* **1** [I,T] **differentiate between A and B; differentiate A (from B)** to see how things are different: *It is hard to differentiate between these two species of fungus.* **2** [T] **differentiate sth (from sth)** to make one thing different from another: *What differentiates him from previous prime ministers?* **3** [T] to treat one person or group differently from another: *We don't differentiate between the two groups – we treat everybody alike.*

☆ **difficult** /ˈdɪfɪkəlt/ *adj* **1** not easy to do or understand: *a difficult test* ○ *a difficult problem* ○ *a difficult language to learn* ○ *Dean found it difficult to pass the driving-test.* ○ *It was difficult for Dean to pass the driving-test.* ○ *I'm in a difficult situation. Whatever I do, somebody will be upset.* **2** (used about a person) not friendly, reasonable or helpful: *a difficult customer*

☆ **difficulty** /ˈdɪfɪkəltɪ/ *noun* (*pl* **difficulties**) **1** [U] **difficulty (in sth/in doing sth)** the state of being difficult or of not being able to do sth easily: *Gail had great difficulty in getting a visa to go to America.* ○ *We had no difficulty selling our car.* **2** [C, usually pl] something that is difficult to do or understand; a problem: *There will be some difficulties to start with but things should get easier later.* ○ *If you borrow too much money you may get into financial difficulties.*

diffident /ˈdɪfɪdənt/ *adj* not feeling or showing belief or confidence in your own strengths or abilities: *He has a very diffident manner.* —**diffidence** /-dəns/ *noun* [U]

☆ **dig** /dɪɡ/ *verb* (*pres part* **digging**; *pt, pp* **dug** /dʌɡ/) [I,T] to move earth and make a hole using your hands, a spade, a machine, etc: *The children are busy digging in the sand.* ○ *to dig a hole* ○ *to dig for gold*

(PHRASAL VERBS) **dig sth in; dig sth into sth** to push sth into sb/sth: *She dug her fingernails into my arm.*

dig sb/sth out (of sth) 1 to get sb/sth out of sth by digging: *Rescue workers dug the survivors out of the rubble.* **2** to get or find sb/sth by searching: *Bill went into the attic and dug out some old photos.*

dig sth up 1 to remove sth from the earth by digging: *to dig up potatoes* **2** to make a hole or take away soil by digging: *Workmen are digging up the road in front of our house.* **3** to find information by searching or studying: *Newspapers have dug up some embarrassing facts about his private life.*

dig *noun* **1** [C] a hard push: *to give sb a dig in the ribs* (= with your elbow, etc) **2** [C] something that you say to upset sb: *The others kept making digs at him because of the way he spoke.* **3 digs** [plural] (*Brit*) a room in a person's house that you rent and live in: *Some university students have flats, others live in digs.*

☆ **digest** /dɪˈdʒest; daɪ-/ *verb* [T] to change food in your stomach so that it can be used by the body **digestion** /dɪˈdʒestʃən; daɪ-/ *noun* [C,U] the process of digesting food —**digestive** /dɪˈdʒestɪv; daɪ-/ *adj*: *the digestive system*

digit /ˈdɪdʒɪt/ *noun* [C] any of the numbers from 0 to 9: *a six-digit telephone number*

digital /ˈdɪdʒɪtl/ *adj* a digital watch or clock shows the time by numbers alone and does not have hands or a dial ☞ picture at **clock**.

dignified /ˈdɪɡnɪfaɪd/ *adj* behaving in a calm, serious way that makes other people respect you: *dignified behaviour* ☞ The opposite is **undignified**.

dignity /ˈdɪɡnətɪ/ *noun* [U] **1** calm, serious behaviour that makes other people respect you: *to behave with dignity* ○ *He managed to keep his dignity, even in prison.* **2** the quality of being serious or formal: *the quiet dignity of the funeral service*

digress /daɪˈɡres/ *verb* [I] (*formal*) to stop talking or writing about the main subject under discussion and start talking or writing about another, possibly less important, one —**digression** /daɪˈɡreʃn/ *noun* [C,U]

dike ⇨ DYKE

dilapidated /dɪˈlæpɪdeɪtɪd/ *adj* (used about a building, furniture, etc) old and broken —**dilapidation** /dɪˌlæpɪˈdeɪʃn/ *noun* [U]

dilemma /dɪˈlemə/ *noun* [C] a situation in which you have to make a difficult choice between two or more things: *Doctors face the moral dilemma of when to keep patients alive artificially and when to let them die.*

dilute /daɪˈljuːt; -ˈluːt/ *verb* [T] **dilute sth (with sth)** to make a liquid weaker by adding water or another liquid ☞ Look at **concentrate**. —**dilute** *adj*

dim /dɪm/ *adj* (**dimmer**; **dimmest**) **1** not bright or easily seen; not clear: *The light was too dim to read by.* ○ *a dim shape in the distance* ○ *My memories of my grandmother are a bit dim.* **2** (*informal*) not very clever; stupid: *He's a bit dim.*

dim *verb* [I,T] (**dimming; dimmed**) to become or make sth dim(1): *to dim the lights* —**dimly** *adv*: *I dimly remember meeting him somewhere before.*

dime /daɪm/ *noun* [C] a coin used in the USA and Canada that is worth ten cents

dimension /dɪˈmenʃn/ *noun* **1** [C,U] a measurement of the length, width or height of sth **2 dimensions** [plural] the size of sth including its length, width and height: *to measure the dimensions of a room* ○ (*figurative*) *The full dimensions of this problem are only now being recognized.* **3** [C] something that affects the way you think about a problem or situation: *Global warming has added a new dimension to the problem of hunger in the world.*

-dimensional /-ʃənəl/ (in compounds) with the number of dimensions mentioned: *a three-dimensional object*

diminish /dɪˈmɪnɪʃ/ *verb* [I,T] (*formal*) to become or to make sth smaller or less important: *The bad news did nothing to diminish her enthusiasm for the plan.*

---

iː	ɪ	e	æ	ɑː	ɒ	ɔː	ʊ	uː	ʌ
see	sit	ten	hat	arm	got	saw	put	too	cup

diminutive /dɪˈmɪnjʊtɪv/ adj (formal) very small

dimple /ˈdɪmpl/ noun [C] a small round hollow area on your chin, cheek, etc which can often only be seen when you smile

din /dɪn/ noun [sing] a loud unpleasant noise that continues for some time: *Will you stop making such a din!*

dine /daɪn/ verb [I] (formal) to eat dinner: *We dined at an exclusive French restaurant.* o *We dined on fresh salmon.*
(PHRASAL VERB) **dine out** to eat in a restaurant

diner /ˈdaɪnə(r)/ noun [C] **1** a person who is eating at a restaurant **2** (*US*) a small restaurant beside a main road

'dining-room noun [C] a room where you eat meals

ding-dong /ˌdɪŋ ˈdɒŋ/ noun [U] the sound that a bell makes

dinghy /ˈdɪŋɡi/ noun [C] (*pl* **dinghies**) **1** a small sailing-boat ☞ Look at **yacht**. **2** a small open boat, often used to take people to or from a larger boat

dingy /ˈdɪndʒi/ adj (**dingier; dingiest**) dirty and not bright or cheerful: *a dark and dingy room*

dining → DINE

☆ **dinner** /ˈdɪnə(r)/ noun **1** [C,U] the main meal of the day, eaten either at midday or in the evening: *What time is dinner served?* o *That was a lovely dinner you cooked.* o *It's dinner time/time for dinner.* ☞ People from different parts of the country, different backgrounds, etc have different ways of talking about their meals. As a general rule, if dinner is eaten at midday the lighter meal eaten in the evening is then called **tea** or **supper**. **Supper** is eaten later in the evening than **tea**. **Tea** may also mean a drink with cake or biscuits in the late afternoon. If **dinner** is eaten in the evening, the lighter meal eaten at midday is then called **lunch**. **2** [C] a formal occasion in the evening during which a meal is served: *A dinner was given for the president.*

'dinner-jacket (*US* **tuxedo**) noun [C] a black or white jacket that a man wears on formal occasions. A dinner-jacket is usually worn with a bow-tie.

dinosaur /ˈdaɪnəsɔː(r)/ noun [C] a very large animal that disappeared from the earth (**became extinct**) before the appearance of Man

diocese /ˈdaɪəsɪs/ noun [C] an area containing a number of churches, for which a bishop is responsible

dip /dɪp/ verb (**dipping; dipped**) **1** [T] **dip sth (into sth); dip sth (in)** to put sth into liquid for a short time: *Julie dipped her toe into the pool to see how cold it was.* **2** [I,T] to go down; to lower sth: *The road suddenly dipped down to the river.* o *The driver dipped his headlights when a car came in the opposite direction.*
(PHRASAL VERB) **dip into sth 1** to take money out of sth: *Tim had to dip into his savings to pay for his new suit.* **2** to read parts, but not all, of sth: *I've only dipped into the book. I haven't read it all the way through.*

dip noun **1** [C] a drop; a downwards movement: *a dip in sales* **2** [C] (*informal*) a quick swim: *We went for a dip before breakfast.* **3** [C,U] a thick sauce that you eat by dipping pieces of vegetable, bread, etc into it **4** [C] an area of lower ground: *The cottage lay in a dip in the hills.*

diphtheria /dɪfˈθɪəriə/ noun [U] a serious disease of the throat that makes it difficult to breathe

diphthong /ˈdɪfθɒŋ; *US* -θɔːŋ/ noun [C] two vowel sounds pronounced together, making one sound: *The /aɪ/ sound in 'fine' is a diphthong.*

diploma /dɪˈpləʊmə/ noun [C] **1** a qualification that you receive when you complete a course of study, often at a college: *a diploma in hotel management* **2** the official piece of paper which shows that you have completed a course of study ☞ Look at the note at **degree**.

diplomacy /dɪˈpləʊməsi/ noun [U] **1** the management of the relations between countries **2** skill in dealing with people: *He handled the awkward situation with tact and diplomacy.*

diplomat /ˈdɪpləmæt/ noun [C] one of the officials who represent their country abroad: *a diplomat at the embassy in Rome*

diplomatic /ˌdɪpləˈmætɪk/ adj **1** connected with diplomacy(1): *The two countries will restore diplomatic relations and the embassies will be reopened.* **2** clever at dealing with people: *He searched for a diplomatic reply so as not to offend her.* —**diplomatically** /-kli/ adv

dire /ˈdaɪə(r)/ adj (formal) very bad or serious; terrible: *dire consequences* o *dire poverty*

☆ **direct¹** /dɪˈrekt; daɪ-/ adj **1** going from one place to another without turning or stopping; straight: *The most direct route is through the city centre.* o *a direct flight to Hong Kong* **2** with nobody/nothing in between; not involving anybody/anything else: *The Prime Minister is in direct contact with the President.* o *a direct attack on the capital* o *As a direct result of the new road, traffic jams in the centre have been reduced.* **3** saying what you mean; clear: *Politicians never give a direct answer to a direct question.* ☞ The opposite for senses 1, 2 and 3 is **indirect**. **4** (only *before* a noun) complete; exact: *What she did was in direct opposition to my orders.*

direct adv **1** not turning or stopping; straight: *This bus goes direct to London.* **2** not involving anybody/anything else: *I always deal direct with the manager.*

directly adv **1** exactly; in a direct way: *The bank is directly opposite the supermarket.* o *He refused to answer my question directly.* ☞ The opposite is **indirectly**. **2** immediately; very soon: *Wait where you are. I'll be back directly.*

directly conj as soon as: *I phoned him directly I heard the news.*

ɜː	ə	eɪ	əʊ	aɪ	aʊ	ɔɪ	ɪə	eə	ʊə
fur	ago	pay	home	five	now	join	near	hair	pure

di·rect 'debit noun [C,U] an order to your bank that allows sb else to take a particular amount of money out of your account on certain dates

di·rect 'object noun [C] a noun or phrase that is directly affected by the action of a verb: *In the sentence 'Anna bought a record', 'a record' is the direct object.* ☞ Look at **indirect object**.

direct 'speech noun [U] the actual words that a person said ☞ Look at **indirect speech**.

☆ **direct²** /dɪ'rekt; daɪ-/ verb [T] **1 direct sb (to...)** to tell or show sb how to get somewhere: *I was directed to an office at the end of the corridor.* ☞ Look at the note at **lead³**(1). **2** to manage or control sb/sth: *a policeman in the middle of the road, directing the traffic* o *to direct a play, film, etc* **3 direct sth to/towards sb/sth**; **direct sth at sb/sth** to turn or aim your attention or actions towards sb/sth: *In recent weeks the media's attention has been directed towards events abroad.* o *The advert is directed at young people.* **4** (*formal*) to tell or order sb to do sth: *Take the tablets as directed by your doctor.*

☆ **direction** /dɪ'rekʃn; daɪ-/ noun **1** [C] the path or line along which a person or thing is moving, looking or pointing: *When the path divided, they didn't know which direction to take.* o *A woman was seen running in the direction of the station.* o *The wind has changed direction.* o *People began arriving from all directions.* o *We met him coming in the opposite direction.* **2** [C, usually pl] information or instructions about how to do sth or how to get to a place **3** [U] management or control: *This department is under the direction of Mrs Walters.* o *the direction of a play, film, etc*

directive /dɪ'rektɪv/ noun [C] an official order to do sth: *an EC directive on safety at work*

☆ **director** /dɪ'rektə(r); daɪ-/ noun [C] **1** a person who manages or controls a company or organization: *the managing director of Rolls Royce* o *the director of studies of a language school* **2** a person who tells the actors, camera crew, etc, what to do in a film, play, etc

directory /dɪ'rektəri; daɪ-/ noun [C] (pl **directories**) an alphabetical list of names, addresses and telephone numbers

☆ **dirt** /dɜːt/ noun [U] **1** a substance that is not clean, such as dust or mud: *Wipe the dirt off your shoes before you come in.* **2** earth or soil: *a dirt track*

☆ **dirty¹** /'dɜːti/ adj (**dirtier**; **dirtiest**) **1** not clean: *Your hands are dirty. Go and wash them!* o *Lighting the fire can be a dirty job* (= it makes you dirty). **2** referring to sex in a way that may upset or offend people: *to tell a dirty joke* (IDIOM) **a dirty word** an idea or thing that you do not like or agree with

dirty² /'dɜːti/ verb [I,T] (*pres part* **dirtying**; *3rd pers sing pres* **dirties**; *pt, pp* **dirtied**) to become or to make sth dirty

disability /ˌdɪsə'bɪləti/ noun (pl **disabilities**) **1** [U] the state of being unable to use a part of your body properly: *physical/mental disability* **2** [C] something that makes you unable to use a part of your body properly: *Because of his disability, he needs constant care.*

disable /dɪs'eɪbl/ verb [T] (often passive) to make sb unable to use a part of his/her body properly: *Many soldiers were disabled in the war.* —**disabled** adj: *The car has been adapted for disabled drivers.*

the disabled noun [plural] people who are disabled: *The hotel has improved facilities for the disabled. There are new lifts and wheelchair ramps.*

☆ **disadvantage** /ˌdɪsəd'vɑːntɪdʒ; US -'væn-/ noun [C] **1** something that may make you less successful than other people: *Your qualifications are good. Your main disadvantage is your lack of experience.* **2** something that is not good or that causes problems: *The main disadvantage of the job is the long hours.* o *What are the advantages and disadvantages of nuclear power?*

(IDIOMS) **put sb/be at a disadvantage** to put sb/be in a situation where he/she/you may be less successful than other people: *The fact that you don't speak the language will put you at a disadvantage in France.*

to sb's disadvantage (*formal*) not good or helpful for sb: *The agreement will be to your disadvantage – don't accept it.*

disadvantaged adj in a bad social or economic situation; poor: *extra help for the most disadvantaged members of society*

☆ **disagree** /ˌdɪsə'griː/ verb [I] **1 disagree (with sb/sth) (about/on sth)** to have a different opinion from sb/sth; not agree: *Nigel often disagrees with his father about politics.* o *They strongly disagreed with the idea.* **2** to be different: *These two sets of statistics disagree.*

disagreement /ˌdɪsə'griːmənt/ noun **1** [U] **disagreement (about/on sth)** having a different opinion from sb or not agreeing with sb/sth: *There's great disagreement about what causes people to turn to crime.* **2** [C] an argument: *Mandy resigned after a disagreement with her boss.*

disagreeable /ˌdɪsə'griːəbl/ adj (*formal*) unpleasant —**disagreeably** /-əbli/ adv

disallow /ˌdɪsə'laʊ/ verb [T] to not allow or accept sth: *The goal was disallowed because the player was offside.*

☆ **disappear** /ˌdɪsə'pɪə(r)/ verb [I] **1** to become impossible to see; to go away: *He walked away and disappeared into a crowd of people.* o *My purse was here a moment ago and now it's disappeared.* **2** to go to a place where you cannot be found: *She disappeared five years ago and has never been heard of since.* **3** to stop existing: *Plant and animal species are disappearing at an alarming rate.* —**disappearance** /ˌdɪsə'pɪərəns/ noun [C,U]: *The mystery of her disappearance was never solved.*

☆ **disappoint** /ˌdɪsə'pɔɪnt/ verb [T] to make sb sad because what he/she had hoped for has not happened or because sb/sth is less good, interesting, etc than he/she had hoped: *I'm sorry to disappoint you but I'm afraid you haven't won the prize.*

disappointed adj **disappointed (about/at sth)**; **disappointed (in/with sb/sth)** sad because you/sb/sth did not succeed or because sth was not as good, interesting, etc as you had hoped: *They are very disappointed that they*

p	b	t	d	k	g	tʃ	dʒ	f	v	θ	ð
pen	bad	tea	did	cat	got	chin	June	fall	van	thin	then

can't stay longer. ○ *We were disappointed with our accommodation – we were expecting a luxury apartment.* ○ *Lucy was deeply disappointed at not being chosen for the team.* ○ *I'm disappointed in you. I thought you could do better.*

disappointing *adj* making you feel sad because sth was not as good, interesting, etc as you had hoped: *It has been a disappointing year for the company.* —**disappointingly** *adv*: *The amount of money they collected was disappointingly small.*

disappointment *noun* **1** [U] the state of being disappointed: *To his great disappointment he failed to get the job.* **2** [C] **a disappointment (to sb)** a person or thing that disappoints you: *Our holiday was a bit of a disappointment.*

☆ **disapprove** /ˌdɪsəˈpruːv/ *verb* [I] **disapprove (of sb/sth)** to think that sb/sth is bad, foolish, etc: *His parents strongly disapproved of him leaving college before he had finished his course.*

disapproval /-ˈpruːvl/ *noun* [U] a feeling that sth is bad or that sb is behaving badly: *to shake your head in disapproval* —**disapproving** *adj*: *After he had told the joke there was a disapproving silence.* —**disapprovingly** *adv*: *David frowned disapprovingly when I lit a cigarette.*

disarm /dɪsˈɑːm/ *verb* **1** [T] to take weapons away from sb: *The police caught and disarmed the terrorists.* **2** [I] (used about a country) to reduce the number of weapons it has **3** [T] to make sb feel less angry

disarmament /dɪsˈɑːməmənt/ *noun* [U] reducing the number of weapons that a country has: *nuclear disarmament*

disassociate = DISSOCIATE

☆ **disaster** /dɪˈzɑːstə(r)/; *US* -ˈzæs-/ *noun* **1** [C] an event that causes a lot of harm or damage: *earthquakes, floods and other natural disasters* **2** [C] a person or thing that is very bad, harmful or unsuccessful: *The school play was an absolute disaster. Everything went wrong.* **3** [U] failure; a terrible situation: *The drought brought disaster to the area.*

disastrous /dɪˈzɑːstrəs; *US* -ˈzæs-/ *adj* very bad, harmful or unsuccessful: *Our mistake had disastrous results.* —**disastrously** *adv*: *The plan went disastrously wrong.*

disband /dɪsˈbænd/ *verb* [I,T] to stop existing as a group; to break up

disbelieve /ˌdɪsbɪˈliːv/ *verb* [T] to think that sth is not true or that sb is not telling the truth: *I have no reason to disbelieve her.*

disbelief /ˌdɪsbɪˈliːf/ *noun* [U] not believing sb/sth: *'It can't be true!' he shouted in disbelief.*

disc (*especially US* **disk**) /dɪsk/ *noun* [C] **1** a round flat object **2** = RECORD¹(2) **3** one of the pieces of thin strong material (**cartilage**) between the bones in your back ☛ Look at **disk**, which is the usual spelling in words connected with computers such as **floppy disk** and **hard disk**.

'disc jockey *noun* [C] (*abbr* **DJ**) a person whose job is to play and introduce pop music on the radio or in a disco

discard /dɪsˈkɑːd/ *verb* [T] (*formal*) to throw sth away because it is not useful

discern /dɪˈsɜːn/ *verb* [T] to see or notice sth with difficulty: *I discerned a note of anger in his voice.*

discernible *adj* that can only be seen or noticed with difficulty: *The shape of a house was just discernible through the mist.*

discerning /dɪˈsɜːnɪŋ/ *adj* able to recognize the quality of sb/sth: *The discerning music lover will appreciate the excellence of this recording.*

discharge /dɪsˈtʃɑːdʒ/ *verb* [T] **1** to send sth out (a liquid, gas, etc): *Smoke and fumes are discharged from the factory and cause air pollution.* **2** to allow sb officially to leave; to send sb away: *to discharge sb from hospital, the army, etc* **3** to do or carry sth out (a duty, task, etc)

discharge /ˈdɪstʃɑːdʒ/ *noun* **1** [C,U] the action of sending sb/sth out or away: *The discharge of oil from the leaking tanker could not be prevented.* ○ *The wounded soldier was given a medical discharge.* **2** [C,U] a substance that has come out of somewhere: *yellowish discharge from a wound*

disciple /dɪˈsaɪpl/ *noun* [C] a person who follows a teacher, especially a religious one: *the twelve disciples of Jesus*

☆ **discipline** /ˈdɪsɪplɪn/ *noun* **1** [U] a way of training your mind and body so that you control your actions and obey rules: *military discipline* ○ *It takes a lot of self-discipline to train for three hours a day.* **2** [U] the result of such training: *A good teacher must be able to maintain discipline in the classroom.* **3** [C] a subject of study; a type of sporting event: *academic disciplines* ○ *Olympic disciplines*

discipline *verb* [T] **1** to train sb to obey and to behave in a controlled way: *You should discipline yourself to practise the piano every morning.* **2** to punish sb

disciplinary /ˈdɪsɪplɪnəri; *US* -neri/ *adj* connected with punishment for breaking rules

disclaim /dɪsˈkleɪm/ *verb* [T] to say that you do not have sth, especially responsibility or knowledge

disclose /dɪsˈkləʊz/ *verb* [T] (*formal*) to tell sth to sb or to make sth known publicly: *The newspapers did not disclose the victim's name.*

disclosure /dɪsˈkləʊʒə(r)/ *noun* [C,U] making sth known; the facts that are made known: *the disclosure of secret information* ○ *He resigned following disclosures about his private life.*

disco /ˈdɪskəʊ/ (also *formal* **discotheque** /ˈdɪskətek/) *noun* [C] (*pl* **discos**) a place where people dance to popular music on records, etc. Discos usually have loud music and bright coloured lights.

discolour (*US* **discolor**) /dɪsˈkʌlə(r)/ *verb* **1** [I] to change colour (often by the effect of light, age or dirt) **2** [T] to change or spoil the colour of sth

discomfort /dɪsˈkʌmfət/ *noun* **1** [U] a slight feeling of pain: *There may be some discomfort from the wound after the operation.* **2** [C] something that makes you feel uncomfortable or that causes a slight feeling of pain: *The beauty of the scenery made up for the discomforts of the journey.* **3** [U] a feeling of embarrassment

disconcert /ˌdɪskənˈsɜːt/ *verb* [T] (usually

passive) to make sb feel confused or worried: *She was disconcerted when everyone stopped talking and listened to her.* —**disconcerting** *adj* —**disconcertingly** *adv*

disconnect /ˌdɪskəˈnekt/ *verb* [T] to undo two things that are joined or connected together: *If you don't pay your gas bill your supply will be disconnected.*

discontent /ˌdɪskənˈtent/ (*also* **discontentment** /ˌdɪskənˈtentmənt/) *noun* [U] the state of being unhappy or not satisfied with sth

discontented *adj* unhappy or not satisfied

discontinue /ˌdɪskənˈtɪnjuː/ *verb* [T] (*formal*) to stop sth or stop producing sth

discord /ˈdɪskɔːd/ *noun* (*formal*) **1** [U] disagreement or argument **2** [C] two or more musical notes that do not sound pleasant when they are played together

discordant /dɪˈskɔːdənt/ *adj* not producing harmony; causing an unpleasant impression: *Her criticism was the only discordant note in the discussion.*

discotheque (*formal*) = DISCO

discount¹ /ˈdɪskaʊnt/ *noun* [C,U] a reduction in the price or cost of sth: *Staff get 20% discount on all goods.* ○ *Do you give a discount for cash?*

discount² /dɪsˈkaʊnt; *US* ˈdɪskaʊnt/ *verb* [T] to consider sth not true or not important: *I think we can discount that idea. It's just not practical.*

discourage /dɪˈskʌrɪdʒ/ *verb* [T] **1 discourage sb (from doing sth)** to make sb lose hope or feel less confident about sth: *Don't let these little problems discourage you.* **2 discourage sb from doing sth** to try to stop sb doing sth: *Consumers should be discouraged from throwing away glass and tins.* ☛ The opposite is **encourage**.

discouraged *adj* having lost hope; not feeling confident about sth: *After failing the exam again Paul felt very discouraged.*

discouragement *noun* [C,U] discouraging or being discouraged; something that discourages you: *High parking charges would be a discouragement to people taking their cars into the city centre.*

☆ **discover** /dɪsˈkʌvə(r)/ *verb* [T] **1** to find or learn sth that nobody knew or had found before: *Who discovered Australia?* ○ *Scientists are hoping to discover the cause of the epidemic.* **2** to find or learn sth new or unexpected or sth that you did not know before: *I think I've discovered why the computer won't print out.* ○ *We recently discovered that a famous writer used to live in this house.*

discoverer *noun* [C] a person who discovers sth

discovery /dɪsˈkʌvəri/ *noun* (*pl* **discoveries**) **1** [U] finding sth: *The discovery of X-rays changed the history of medicine.* ○ *The discovery of fingerprints in the car helped the police to find the thief.* **2** [C] something that has been discovered: *scientific discoveries*

discredit /dɪsˈkredɪt/ *verb* [T] to cause sb/sth to lose people's trust; to damage the reputation of sb/sth

discredit *noun* [U] loss of trust; damage to the reputation of sb/sth

discreet /dɪˈskriːt/ *adj* careful not to attract attention and so cause embarrassment or difficulty for sb: *She was too discreet to mention the argument in front of Neil.* —**discreetly** *adv* ☛ The noun is **discretion**. The opposite is **indiscreet**.

discrepancy /dɪˈskrepənsi/ *noun* [C,U] (*pl* **discrepancies**) a difference between two things that should be the same: *Something is wrong here. There is a discrepancy between these two sets of figures.*

discretion /dɪˈskreʃn/ *noun* [U] **1** care not to attract attention and so cause embarrassment or difficulty for sb: *This is confidential but I know I can rely on your discretion.* ☛ The adjective is **discreet**. **2** the freedom and ability to make decisions by yourself: *You must decide what is best. Use your discretion.*
(IDIOM) **at sb's discretion** depending on what sb thinks or decides: *Pay increases are awarded at the discretion of the director.*

discriminate /dɪˈskrɪmɪneɪt/ *verb* **1** [I] **discriminate (against sb)** to treat one person or group worse than others: *It is illegal to discriminate against any ethnic or religious group.* **2** [I,T] **discriminate (between A and B)** to see or make a difference between two people or things: *The immigration law discriminates between political and economic refugees.*

discrimination /dɪˌskrɪmɪˈneɪʃn/ *noun* [U] **1 discrimination (against sb)** treating one person or group worse than others: *sexual, racial, religious, etc discrimination* **2** the state of being able to judge what is good, true, etc

discus /ˈdɪskəs/ *noun* [C] a heavy round flat object that is thrown as a sport

☆ **discuss** /dɪˈskʌs/ *verb* [T] **discuss sth (with sb)** to talk or write about sth seriously or formally: *I must discuss the matter with my parents before I make a decision.* ○ *The article discusses the need for a change in the law.*

discussion /dɪˈskʌʃn/ *noun* [C,U] a time when you talk about sth: *After much discussion we all agreed to share the cost.* ○ *a long discussion on the meaning of life*
(IDIOM) **under discussion** being talked about: *Plans to reform the Health Service are under discussion in Parliament.*

disdain /dɪsˈdeɪn/ *noun* [U] the feeling that sb/sth is not good enough and does not deserve to be respected —**disdainful** /-fl/ *adj* —**disdainfully** /-fəli/ *adv*

☆ **disease** /dɪˈziːz/ *noun* [C,U] an illness of the body in humans, animals or plants: *an infectious disease* ○ *Many diseases can be prevented by vaccination.* ○ *Rats and flies spread disease.* —**diseased** *adj*: *His diseased kidney had to be removed.* ☛ **Illness** and **disease** can be used in a similar way. However, we use **disease** to describe a type of illness which has a name and is recognized by certain symptoms. Diseases may be caused by bacteria, viruses, etc, and you can often catch and pass them on to others. **Illness** is used to describe the general state of being ill and the time during which you are not well.

disembark /ˌdɪsɪmˈbɑːk/ *verb* [I] to get off a ship or an aeroplane: *All foot passengers should*

iː	ɪ	e	æ	ɑː	ɒ	ɔː	ʊ	uː	ʌ
see	sit	ten	hat	arm	got	saw	put	too	cup

disembark *from Deck B.* —**disembarkation** /ˌdɪsembɑːˈkeɪʃn/ *noun* [U]

disenchanted /ˌdɪsɪnˈtʃɑːntɪd; *US* -ˈtʃænt-/ *adj* having lost your good opinion of sb/sth —**disenchantment** *noun* [U]: *There is increasing disenchantment among voters with the government's policies.*

disentangle /ˌdɪsɪnˈtæŋgl/ *verb* [T] **1** to remove the knots from sth and make it straight: *to disentangle wool, rope, string, etc* **2** to free sb/sth that was stuck in or attached to sb/sth else: *I helped to disentangle the sheep from the bush.*

disfigure /dɪsˈfɪɡə(r); *US* dɪsˈfɪɡjər/ *verb* [T] to spoil the appearance of sb/sth

disgrace /dɪsˈɡreɪs/ *noun* **1** [U] the state of not being respected by other people, usually because you have behaved badly: *There is no disgrace in not having much money.* **2** [sing] **a disgrace (to sb/sth)** a person or thing that gives such a bad impression that other people feel ashamed: *The streets are covered in litter. It's a disgrace!*
(IDIOM) **(be) in disgrace (with sb)** (to be) in a position where other people do not respect you, usually because you have behaved badly
disgrace *verb* [T] **1** to cause disgrace to sb/yourself **2** to cause sb to lose his/her position of power: *the disgraced leader*

disgraceful /-fl/ *adj* very bad, making other people feel ashamed: *The football supporters' behaviour was absolutely disgraceful.* —**disgracefully** /-fəli/ *adv*

disgruntled /dɪsˈɡrʌntld/ *adj* rather angry; disappointed and annoyed

disguise /dɪsˈɡaɪz/ *verb* [T] **disguise sb/sth (as sb/sth)** to change the appearance, sound, etc of sb/sth so that people cannot recognize him/her/it: *They disguised themselves as fishermen and escaped in a boat.* ○ *to disguise your voice* ○ *(figurative) His smile disguised his anger.*

disguise *noun* [C,U] clothes or items such as false hair, glasses, etc, that you wear to change your appearance so that nobody recognizes you
(IDIOM) **in disguise** wearing or using a disguise

☆ **disgust** /dɪsˈɡʌst/ *noun* [U] a strong feeling of dislike or disapproval: *She looked round the filthy room with disgust.* ○ *The film was so bad that we walked out in disgust.*
disgust *verb* [T] to cause disgust: *Cruelty towards animals absolutely disgusts me.*
disgusted *adj* feeling disgust: *We were disgusted at the standard of service we received.*
disgusting *adj* causing disgust: *What a disgusting smell!* —**disgustingly** *adv*

☆ **dish**¹ /dɪʃ/ *noun* **1** [C] a shallow container for food. You can use a dish to cook sth in the oven, to serve food on the table or to eat from: *Is this dish ovenproof?* ☛ picture at **plate**. **2** [C] a type of food prepared in a particular way: *The main dish was curry. It was served with a selection of side dishes.* **3 the dishes** [plural] all the plates, cups, etc that you use during a meal: *I'll cook and you can wash the dishes.* **4** = SATELLITE DISH

'**dishwasher** *noun* [C] an electric machine that washes plates, cups, knives, forks, etc

dish² /dɪʃ/ *verb*
(PHRASAL VERBS) **dish sth out** (*informal*) to give away a lot of sth
dish sth up (*informal*) to serve food

disheartened /dɪsˈhɑːtnd/ *adj* sad or disappointed —**disheartening** /dɪsˈhɑːtnɪŋ/ *adj*

dishevelled (*US* **disheveled**) /dɪˈʃevld/ *adj* (used about a person's appearance) untidy

dishonest /dɪsˈɒnɪst/ *adj* not honest or truthful —**dishonestly** *adv* —**dishonesty** *noun* [U]

dishonour (*US* **dishonor**) /dɪsˈɒnə(r)/ *noun* [U,sing] (*formal*) the state of no longer being respected; shame
dishonour *verb* [T] (*formal*) to bring shame on sb/sth —**dishonourable** /-nərəbl/ *adj*

disillusion /ˌdɪsɪˈluːzn/ *verb* [T] to destroy sb's belief or good opinion of sb/sth
disillusioned *adj* disappointed because sb/sth is not as good as you first thought: *She's so disillusioned with nursing.*
disillusionment (*also* **disillusion**) *noun* [U] disappointment because sb/sth is not as good as you first thought

disinfect /ˌdɪsɪnˈfekt/ *verb* [T] to clean sth with a liquid that destroys bacteria: *to disinfect a toilet* ○ *to disinfect a wound*
disinfectant /ˌdɪsɪnˈfektənt/ *noun* [C,U] a substance that destroys bacteria and is used for cleaning: *wash the floor with disinfectant* —**disinfection** *noun* [U]

disintegrate /dɪsˈɪntɪɡreɪt/ *verb* [I] to break into many small pieces: *The spacecraft exploded and disintegrated.* —**disintegration** /dɪsˌɪntɪˈɡreɪʃn/ *noun* [U]: *the disintegration of the empire*

disinterested /dɪsˈɪntrəstɪd/ *adj* fair, not influenced by personal feelings: *disinterested advice* ☛ Look at **uninterested**. It has a different meaning.

disjointed /dɪsˈdʒɔɪntɪd/ *adj* (used especially about ideas, writing or speech) not clearly linked and therefore difficult to follow —**disjointedly** *adv*

disk /dɪsk/ *noun* [C] **1** (*US*) = DISC **2** (*computing*) a flat piece of plastic that stores information for use by a computer ☛ Look at **floppy disk** and **hard disk**.
'**disk drive** *noun* [C] a piece of electrical equipment that passes information to or from a computer disk ☛ picture on page A13.

diskette /dɪsˈket/ *noun* [C] = FLOPPY DISK

☆ **dislike** /dɪsˈlaɪk/ *verb* [T] to think that sb/sth is unpleasant: *I really dislike flying.* ○ *What is it that you dislike about living here?*
dislike *noun* [U,sing] **dislike (of/for sb/sth)** the feeling of not liking sb/sth: *She couldn't hide her dislike for him.* ○ *He seems to have a strong dislike of hard work.*
(IDIOMS) **likes and dislikes** ⇨ LIKES
take a dislike to sb/sth to start disliking sb/sth

dislocate /ˈdɪsləkeɪt; *US* ˈdɪsləʊkeɪt/ *verb* [T] to put sth (often a bone) out of its proper position: *He dislocated his shoulder during the*

3ː	ə	eɪ	əʊ	aɪ	aʊ	ɔɪ	ɪə	eə	ʊə
fur	ago	pay	home	five	now	join	near	hair	pure

game. —**dislocation** /ˌdɪsləˈkeɪʃn; US ˌdɪsləʊˈkeɪʃn/ noun [C,U]

dislodge /dɪsˈlɒdʒ/ verb [T] to make sb/sth move from a fixed position

disloyal /dɪsˈlɔɪəl/ adj doing or saying sth that is against sb/sth that you should support; not loyal: *It was disloyal of him to turn against his friends.* —**disloyalty** /-ˈlɔɪəlti/ noun [C,U] (pl **disloyalties**)

dismal /ˈdɪzməl/ adj **1** depressing; causing sadness: *dismal surroundings* o *a dismal failure* **2** (*informal*) of low quality; poor: *a dismal standard of work*

dismantle /dɪsˈmæntl/ verb [T] to take sth to pieces; to separate sth into the parts it is made from: *The photographer dismantled his equipment and packed it away.*

dismay /dɪsˈmeɪ/ noun [U] a strong feeling of worry and shock: *I realized to my dismay that I was going to miss the plane.* —**dismay** verb [T] (usually passive)

dismember /dɪsˈmembə(r)/ verb [T] to tear or cut a body apart

dismiss /dɪsˈmɪs/ verb [T] **1** to order an employee to leave his/her job: *He was dismissed for refusing to obey orders.* ☛ **Fire** and **sack** are less formal words for **dismiss**. **2** to allow sb to leave: *The lesson ended and the teacher dismissed the class.* **3** to remove sb/sth from your mind; to stop thinking about sb/sth completely: *She decided to dismiss her worries from her mind.* **4 dismiss sb/sth (as sth)** to say or think that sb/sth is not important or is not worth considering seriously: *He dismissed the idea as nonsense.*

dismissal /dɪsˈmɪsl/ noun **1** [C,U] ordering sb or being ordered to leave a job: *a case of unfair dismissal* **2** [U] refusing to consider sb/sth seriously: *She was hurt at their dismissal of her offer of help.*

dismissive adj saying or showing that you think that sb/sth is not important or is not worth considering seriously: *The boss was dismissive of all the efforts I had made.*

dismount /ˌdɪsˈmaʊnt/ verb [I] to get off sth that you ride (a horse, a bicycle, etc)

disobedient /ˌdɪsəˈbiːdiənt/ adj not willing to obey; refusing to do what you are told to do; not obedient —**disobedience** /-iəns/ noun [U]

disobey /ˌdɪsəˈbeɪ/ verb [I,T] to refuse to do what you are told to do; not to obey: *He was punished for disobeying orders.*

disorder /dɪsˈɔːdə(r)/ noun **1** [U] an untidy, confused or disorganized state: *His financial affairs are in complete disorder.* **2** [U] violent behaviour by a large number of people: *Disorder broke out on the streets of the capital.* **3** [C,U] an illness in which the mind or part of the body is not working properly: *a stomach disorder*

disordered adj untidy, confused or disorganized

disorderly adj **1** very untidy **2** (used about people or behaviour) out of control and violent; causing trouble in public: *They were arrested for being drunk and disorderly.*

disorganization (*also* **disorganisation**) /dɪsˌɔːgənaɪˈzeɪʃn; US -nɪˈz-/ noun [U] a lack of organization

disorganized (*also* **disorganised**) adj not organized; badly planned

disorientate /dɪsˈɔːriənteɪt/ (*especially US* **disorient** /dɪsˈɔːriənt/) verb [T] (usually passive) to make sb lose all sense of direction or become confused about where he/she is: *The road signs were very confusing and I soon became disorientated.* —**disorientation** /dɪsˌɔːriənˈteɪʃn/ noun [U]

disown /dɪsˈəʊn/ verb [T] to decide or say that you are no longer associated with sb/sth: *When he was arrested, his family disowned him.*

disparage /dɪˈspærɪdʒ/ verb [T] (*formal*) to talk about sb/sth in a critical way or to say that sb/sth is of little value or importance —**disparaging** adj: *disparaging remarks*

dispatch (*also* **despatch**) /dɪˈspætʃ/ verb [T] (*formal*) to send: *Your order will be dispatched from our warehouse within 7 days.*

dispel /dɪˈspel/ verb [T] (**dispel**ling; **dispel**led) to make sth disappear; to remove sth from sb's mind: *His reassuring words dispelled all her fears.*

dispensable /dɪˈspensəbl/ adj not necessary: *I suppose I'm dispensable. Anybody could do my job.* ☛ The opposite is **indispensable**.

dispense /dɪˈspens/ verb [T] **1** (*formal*) to give out: *a machine that dispenses hot and cold drinks* **2** to prepare and give out medicines in a chemist's shop: *a dispensing chemist*
(PHRASAL VERB) **dispense with sb/sth** to get rid of sb/sth that is not necessary: *They decided to dispense with luxuries and live a simple life.*

dispenser noun [C] a machine or container from which you can get sth: *a cash dispenser at a bank*

disperse /dɪˈspɜːs/ verb [I,T] to separate and go in different directions; to break sth up: *When the meeting was over, the group dispersed.* o *Police arrived and quickly dispersed the crowd.*

dispirited /dɪˈspɪrɪtɪd/ adj having lost confidence or hope; depressed

displace /dɪsˈpleɪs/ verb [T] **1** to force sb/sth to move from the usual or correct place **2** to remove and take the place of sb/sth: *She hoped to displace Seles as the top player in the world.*

☆ **display¹** /dɪˈspleɪ/ verb [T] **1** to put sth in a place where people will see it or where it will attract attention: *Posters for the concert were displayed throughout the city.* **2** to show sth (eg a feeling or personal quality): *She displayed no interest in the discussion.*

☆ **display²** /dɪˈspleɪ/ noun [C] **1** a public event in which sth is shown in action: *a firework display* **2** an arrangement of things for people to see: *The shops take a lot of trouble over their window displays at Christmas.* **3** behaviour that shows a particular feeling or quality: *a sudden display of aggression* **4** (*computing*) words, pictures, etc that can be seen on a computer screen
(IDIOM) **on display** in a place where people will see it and where it will attract attention: *Treasures from the sunken ship were put on display at the museum.*

p	b	t	d	k	g	tʃ	dʒ	f	v	θ	ð
pen	bad	tea	did	cat	got	chin	June	fall	van	thin	then

displease /dɪsˈpliːz/ verb [T] (formal) to annoy sb or to make sb angry or upset

displeasure /dɪsˈpleʒə(r)/ noun [U] (formal) the feeling of being annoyed or not satisfied: *I wrote to express my displeasure at not having been informed sooner.*

disposable /dɪˈspəʊzəbl/ adj intended to be thrown away after being used once or for a short time: *a disposable razor*

disposal /dɪˈspəʊzl/ noun [U] the act of getting rid of sth: *the disposal of dangerous chemical waste*
(IDIOM) **at sb's disposal** available for sb's use at any time: *They put their house at my disposal.*

dispose /dɪˈspəʊz/ verb
(PHRASAL VERB) **dispose of sb/sth** to throw away or sell sth; to get rid of sb/sth that you do not want

disproportionate /ˌdɪsprəˈpɔːʃənət/ adj larger or smaller than is acceptable or expected —**disproportionately** adv

disprove /ˌdɪsˈpruːv/ verb [T] to show or prove that sth is not true

☆ **dispute¹** /dɪˈspjuːt; ˈdɪspjuːt/ noun [C,U] disagreement or argument between people: *There was some dispute about whose fault it was.* ○ *a pay dispute*
(IDIOM) **in dispute** in a situation of arguing or being argued about: *He is in dispute with the tax office about how much he should pay.*

dispute² /dɪˈspjuːt/ verb [T] to argue about sth or to suggest that sth is not true: *The player disputed the referee's decision.*

disqualify /dɪsˈkwɒlɪfaɪ/ verb [T] (pres part **disqualifying**; 3rd pers sing pres **disqualifies**; pt, pp **disqualified**) **disqualify sb (from sth/from doing sth)** to officially forbid sb to do sth or to take part in sth, usually because he/she has broken a rule or law: *The team were disqualified for cheating.* —**disqualification** /dɪsˌkwɒlɪfɪˈkeɪʃn/ noun [C,U]

disregard /ˌdɪsrɪˈɡɑːd/ verb [T] to take no notice of sb/sth; to pay no attention to sb/sth: *These are the latest instructions. Please disregard any you received before.*
disregard noun [U,sing] **(a) disregard (for/of sb/sth)** lack of attention to, interest in or care for sb/sth: *He rushed into the burning building with complete disregard for his own safety.*

disrepair /ˌdɪsrɪˈpeə(r)/ noun [U] a bad condition, existing because repairs have not been made: *Over the years the building fell into a state of disrepair.*

disreputable /dɪsˈrepjʊtəbl/ adj not deserving to be trusted; having a bad reputation: *a disreputable area, full of criminal activity* ○ *disreputable business methods*

disrepute /ˌdɪsrɪˈpjuːt/ noun [U] the situation when people no longer respect sb/sth: *Such unfair decisions bring the legal system into disrepute.*

disrespect /ˌdɪsrɪˈspekt/ noun [U] behaviour or words that show that you do not respect sb/sth —**disrespectful** /-fl/ adj —**disrespectfully** /-fəli/ adv

disrupt /dɪsˈrʌpt/ verb [T] to disturb a process or system: *The strike severely disrupted flights to Spain.* —**disruption** /dɪsˈrʌpʃn/ noun [C,U] —**disruptive** /dɪsˈrʌptɪv/ adj: *A badly behaved child can have a disruptive influence on the rest of the class.*

dissatisfaction /ˌdɪˌsætɪsˈfækʃn/ noun [U] the feeling of not being satisfied or pleased: *There is some dissatisfaction among teachers with the plans for the new exam.*

dissatisfied /dɪˈsætɪsfaɪd/ adj **dissatisfied (with sb/sth)** not satisfied or pleased: *complaints from dissatisfied customers*

dissect /dɪˈsekt/ verb [T] to cut up a dead body, a plant, etc in order to examine its structure —**dissection** /dɪˈsekʃn/ noun [C,U]

dissent¹ /dɪˈsent/ noun [U] (formal) disagreement with official or generally agreed ideas or opinions: *There is some dissent within the Labour Party on these policies.*

dissent² /dɪˈsent/ verb [I] **dissent (from sth)** (formal) to have opinions that are different to those that are officially held
dissenting adj showing or feeling dissent

dissertation /ˌdɪsəˈteɪʃn/ noun [C] a long piece of writing on sth that you have studied, especially as part of a university degree ☞ Look at **thesis**.

disservice /dɪsˈsɜːvɪs/ noun [U,sing] **(a) disservice to sb/sth** an action that is unhelpful or has a negative effect

dissident /ˈdɪsɪdənt/ noun [C] a person who expresses disagreement with the actions or ideas of a government or organization —**dissidence** /ˈdɪsɪdəns/ noun [U]

dissimilar /dɪˈsɪmɪlə(r)/ adj **dissimilar (from/to sb/sth)** unlike; not similar; different

dissociate /dɪˈsəʊʃieɪt/ (also **disassociate** /ˌdɪsəˈsəʊʃieɪt/) verb [T] **dissociate sb/sth/yourself from sth** to say or believe that a thing or a person is not connected with another, or that you do not agree with sth: *She dissociated herself from the views of the extremists in her party.*

dissolve /dɪˈzɒlv/ verb [I,T] to become liquid or to make sth become liquid: *Sugar dissolves in water.* ○ *Dissolve two tablets in cold water.*

dissuade /dɪˈsweɪd/ verb [T] **dissuade sb (from doing sth)** to persuade sb not to do sth: *I tried to dissuade her from spending the money, but she insisted.*

☆ **distance¹** /ˈdɪstəns/ noun **1** [C,U] the amount of space between two places or points: *It's only a short distance from my home to work.* ○ *The map tells you the distances between the major cities.* ○ *We can walk home from here, it's no distance* (= it isn't far). ○ *The house is within walking distance of the shops.* **2** [sing] a point that is a long way from sb/sth: *At this distance I can't read the number on the bus.* ○ *From a distance the village looks quite attractive.*
(IDIOM) **in the distance** far away: *I could hear voices in the distance.*

distance² /ˈdɪstəns/ verb [T] **1** to make sb feel less friendly towards sb/sth: *Her wealth and success have distanced her from her old friends.* **2 distance yourself from sb/sth** to show that you are not involved or connected with *sb/sth*: *She was keen to distance herself from the views of her colleagues.*

☆ **distant** /ˈdɪstənt/ *adj* **1** a long way away in space or time: *travel to distant parts of the world* ○ *in the not-too-distant future* (= quite soon) **2** (used about a relative) not closely related: *a distant cousin* **3** not very friendly: *He has a rather distant manner and it's hard to get to know him well.* **4** seeming to be thinking about sth else: *She had a distant look in her eyes and clearly wasn't listening to me.*

distaste /dɪsˈteɪst/ *noun* [U,sing] **(a) distaste (for sb/sth)** dislike; the feeling that sb/sth is unpleasant or unacceptable: *She viewed business with distaste.* ○ *He seems to have a distaste for hard work.*

distasteful /dɪsˈteɪstfl/ *adj* causing the feeling of dislike; unpleasant or unacceptable

distil (*US* **distill**) /dɪˈstɪl/ *verb* [T] (distilling; distilled) to heat a liquid until it becomes steam and then collect the liquid that forms when the steam cools: *distilled water*

☆ **distinct** /dɪˈstɪŋkt/ *adj* **1** clear; easily seen, heard or understood: *There has been a distinct improvement in your work recently.* ○ *I had the distinct impression that she was lying.* **2 distinct (from sth)** clearly different: *Her books fall into two distinct groups: the novels and the travel stories.* ○ *This region, as distinct from other parts of the country, relies heavily on tourism.*

distinctly *adv* **1** clearly: *I distinctly heard her say that she would be here on time.* **2** very; particularly: *His behaviour has been distinctly odd recently.*

☆ **distinction** /dɪˈstɪŋkʃn/ *noun* [C,U] **1 (a) distinction (between A and B)** a clear or important difference between things or people: *We must make a distinction between classical and popular music here.* **2** the quality of being excellent; fame for what you have achieved: *a violinist of some distinction* ○ *She has the distinction of being the only player to win the championship five times.*

(IDIOM) **draw a distinction between sth and sth** ⇨ DRAW²

distinctive /dɪˈstɪŋktɪv/ *adj* clearly different from others and therefore easy to recognize: *the soldiers wearing their distinctive red berets* —**distinctively** *adv*

☆ **distinguish** /dɪˈstɪŋgwɪʃ/ *verb* **1** [I,T] **distinguish between A and B; distinguish A from B** to recognize the difference between things or people: *He doesn't seem able to distinguish between what's important and what isn't.* ○ *People who are colour-blind often can't distinguish red from green.* **2** [T] **distinguish A (from B)** to make sb/sth different from others; to show the difference between people or things: *distinguishing features* (= things by which sb/sth can be recognized) **3** [T] to see, hear or recognize with effort: *I listened carefully but they were too far away for me to distinguish what they were saying.* **4** [T] **distinguish yourself** to do sth which causes you to be noticed and admired: *She distinguished herself in the exams.*

distinguishable /dɪˈstɪŋgwɪʃəbl/ *adj* **1** possible to distinguish as different from sb/sth else: *The male bird is distinguishable from the female by the colour of its beak.* **2** possible to see, hear or recognize with effort: *The letter is so old that the signature is barely distinguishable.*

distinguished *adj* important and respected: *I am pleased to welcome our distinguished guests to the conference.*

distort /dɪˈstɔːt/ *verb* [T] **1** to change the shape or sound of sth so that it seems unnatural: *Her face was distorted with grief.* **2** to change sth and show it falsely: *Foreigners are often given a distorted view of this country.* —**distortion** /dɪˈstɔːʃn/ *noun* [C,U]

distract /dɪˈstrækt/ *verb* [T] to take sb's attention away from sth: *Could you stop talking please? You're distracting me from my work.*

distracted *adj* unable to concentrate because of being worried or thinking about sth else.

distraction /dɪˈstrækʃn/ *noun* [C,U] something that takes your attention away from what you were doing or thinking about: *I find it hard to work at home because there are so many distractions.*

distraught /dɪˈstrɔːt/ *adj* extremely sad and upset

distress¹ /dɪˈstres/ *noun* [U] **1** the state of being very upset or unhappy or of suffering great pain: *Their distress on hearing the bad news was obvious.* ○ *She was in such distress that I didn't want to leave her on her own.* **2** the state of being in great danger and needing immediate help: *The ship's captain radioed that it was in distress.*

distress² /dɪˈstres/ *verb* [T] (often passive) to make sb very upset or unhappy: *She was too distressed to talk.*

distressing *adj* causing sb to be very upset or unhappy

☆ **distribute** /dɪˈstrɪbjuːt/ *verb* [T] **1 distribute sth (to/among sb/sth)** to give things to a number of people; to divide sth up and give the parts to people or place them in various positions: *Protesters were distributing leaflets in the street.* ○ *Tickets will be distributed to all club members.* ○ *Make sure that the weight is evenly distributed.* **2 distribute sth (to sb/sth)** to transport and supply sth to various people or places: *They distributed emergency food supplies to the areas that were most in need.*

distribution /ˌdɪstrɪˈbjuːʃn/ *noun* **1** [sing,U] the act of giving sth: *the distribution of food parcels to the refugees* **2** [sing,U] the way sth is shared out; the pattern in which sth is found: *The uneven distribution of wealth causes many problems.* ○ *a map to show the distribution of rainfall in India* **3** [U] the transport and supply of goods, etc to various people or places: *The country produces enough food but distribution is a problem.*

distributor /dɪˈstrɪbjʊtə(r)/ *noun* [C] a person or company that transports and supplies goods to a number of shops and companies

☆ **district** /ˈdɪstrɪkt/ *noun* [C] **1** a part of a town or country that has a particular feature or is of a particular type: *railway services in rural districts* **2** an official division of a town or coun-

iː	ɪ	e	æ	ɑː	ɒ	ɔː	ʊ	uː	ʌ
see	sit	ten	hat	arm	got	saw	put	too	cup

try: *the district council* o *postal districts* ☛ A **district** may be part of a town or country, and it may have fixed boundaries: *the district controlled by a council*. A **region** is larger, usually part of a country only and may not have fixed boundaries: *the industrial regions of the country*. An **area** is the most general term and is used with the same meaning as both **district** and **region**: *the poorer areas of a town* o *an agricultural area of the country*. We use **part** more often when we are talking about a section of a town: *Which part of Paris do you live in?*

distrust /dɪs'trʌst/ *noun* [U,sing] **(a) distrust (of sb/sth)** the feeling that you cannot believe sb/sth; lack of trust —**distrust** *verb* [T]: *She distrusts him because he lied to her once before.*

☆ **disturb** /dɪ'stɜːb/ *verb* [T] **1** to interrupt and possibly annoy sb while he/she is doing sth or sleeping; to spoil a peaceful situation: *I'm sorry to disturb you but there's a phone call for you.* o *Keep the noise down! You'll disturb the neighbours.* o *Their sleep was disturbed by a loud crash.* **2** to cause sb to worry: *It disturbed her to think that he might be unhappy.* **3** to change sth from its normal position or condition: *I noticed a number of things had been disturbed and realized that there had been a burglary.*

disturbed *adj* having mental or emotional problems: *a school for disturbed young people*

disturbing *adj* causing sb to worry: *These disturbing developments suggest that war is a possibility.*

disturbance /dɪ'stɜːbəns/ *noun* **1** [C,U] an interruption; something that stops you concentrating, sleeping, etc **2** [C] an occasion when people behave violently or make a lot of noise in public: *Further disturbances have been reported in the capital city.*

disuse /dɪs'juːs/ *noun* [U] the state of not being used any more: *The farm buildings had fallen into disuse.*

disused /dɪs'juːzd/ *adj* not used any more: *a disused railway line*

ditch /dɪtʃ/ *noun* [C] a long narrow hole that has been dug into the ground, especially along the side of a road or field for water to flow through: *The car left the road and ended up in a ditch.*

ditch *verb* [T] (*informal*) to get rid of or leave sb/sth: *She ditched her old friends when she became famous.*

dither /'dɪðə(r)/ *verb* [I] to hesitate and be unable to decide sth: *Stop dithering and make up your mind!*

ditto /'dɪtəʊ/ *noun* [C] (represented by the mark (··) and used instead of repeating the thing written above it) the same

divan /dɪ'væn; *US* 'daɪvæn/ *noun* [C] a type of bed with only a base and a mattress, not with a frame

☆ **dive¹** /daɪv/ *verb* [I] (*pt* **dived**; *US also* **dove** /dəʊv/; *pp* **dived**) **1** to jump into water with your head first: *In Acapulco, men dive off the cliffs into the sea.* o *A passer-by dived in and saved the drowning man.* **2 dive (down) (for sth)** to go under water: *people diving for pearls* **3** to move downwards steeply and quickly through the air: *The engines failed and the plane dived.* **4** to move quickly in a particular direction, especially downwards: *He dived under the table and hid there.*

(PHRASAL VERB) **dive into sth/in** to put your hand quickly into sth in order to find or get sth: *She dived into her bag and brought out an old photograph.*

diver *noun* [C] a person whose job is going underwater using special equipment: *Police divers searching the lake found the body.*

diving *noun* [U] the activity or sport of diving into water or swimming under water: *The resort has facilities for sailing, water-skiing and diving.*

'diving-board *noun* [C] a board at the side of a swimming-pool from which people can dive into the water

dive² /daɪv/ *noun* [C] **1** the act of diving into the water **2** a quick movement in a particular direction, especially down or across: *Despite a desperate dive, the goalkeeper couldn't stop the ball.*

diverge /daɪ'vɜːdʒ/ *verb* [I] **diverge (from sth) 1** (used about roads, lines, etc) to separate and go in different directions: *The paths suddenly diverged and I didn't know which one to take.* **2** to be or become different (from each other): *Attitudes among teachers diverge on this question.*

diverse /daɪ'vɜːs/ *adj* very different from each other: *people with diverse social backgrounds*

diversify /daɪ'vɜːsɪfaɪ/ *verb* [I] (*pres part* **diversifying**; *3rd pers sing pres* **diversifies**; *pt, pp* **diversified**) **diversify (into sth)** (used about a business) to increase the range of activities, products, etc: *To remain successful in the future, the company will have to diversify.* —**diversification** /daɪˌvɜːsɪfɪ'keɪʃn/ *noun* [C,U]

diversion /daɪ'vɜːʃn/ *noun* **1** [C,U] the act of changing the direction or purpose of sth especially in order to solve or avoid a problem: *the diversion of a river to prevent flooding* o *the diversion of government funds to areas of greatest need* **2** [C] (*US* **detour**) a different route which traffic can take when a road is closed: *There are temporary traffic lights and diversions due to roadworks on the A161.* **3** [C] something that takes your attention away from sth: *Some prisoners created a diversion while others escaped.*

diversity /daɪ'vɜːsəti/ *noun* [U] the wide range or variety of sth: *a country of tremendous diversity, with landscape ranging from semi-desert to tropical*

divert /daɪ'vɜːt/ *verb* [T] **divert sb/sth (from sth) (to sth)** to change the direction or purpose of sb/sth, especially in order to avoid a problem: *During the road repairs, all traffic is being diverted.* o *Government money was diverted from defence to education and training.*

☆ **divide** /dɪ'vaɪd/ *verb* **1** [I,T] **divide (sth) (up) (into sth)** to separate into different parts: *The egg divides into two cells.* o *a book divided into ten sections* o *The house was divided into flats.* **2** [T] **divide sth (out/up) (between/among sb)** to separate sth into parts and give a share to each of a number of people: *The robbers di-*

vided the money among themselves. ○ When he died, his property was divided up among his children. **3** [T] **divide sth (between A and B)** to use different parts or amounts of sth for different purposes: *They divide their time between their two homes.* **4** [T] to separate two places by being a boundary or area between them: *The river divides the old part of the city from the new.* **5** [T] to cause people to disagree: *The question of immigration has divided the country.* **6** [T] **divide sth by sth** to calculate how many times a number will go into another number: *10 divided by 5 is 2.*

dividend /'dɪvɪdend/ *noun* [C] a part of a company's profits that is paid to the people who own shares in it

divine /dɪ'vaɪn/ *adj* connected with God or a god —**divinely** *adv*

divisible /dɪ'vɪzəbl/ *adj* that can be divided: *9 is divisible by 3.*

☆ **division** /dɪ'vɪʒn/ *noun* **1** [U] the dividing of sth into separate parts: *the division of Germany after the Second World War* **2** [U,sing] the sharing of sth: *a fair/unfair division of the profits* **3** [U] dividing one number by another: *the teaching of multiplication and division* **4** [C] a disagreement or difference in thought, way of life, etc: *deep divisions within the Labour Party* **5** [C] something that divides or separates: *There is no great division between being a child and being an adult.* **6** [C] a part or section of an organization: *the company's sales division* ○ *the First Division* (= of the football league)

divisive /dɪ'vaɪsɪv/ *adj* (*formal*) likely to cause disagreements or arguments between people: *a divisive policy*

☆ **divorce¹** /dɪ'vɔːs/ *noun* [C,U] the legal end of a marriage: *to get a divorce* ○ *One in three marriages ends in divorce.*

☆ **divorce²** /dɪ'vɔːs/ *verb* [T] **1** to legally end your marriage to sb: *She divorced him a year after their marriage.* ☛ It is more common to say **to get divorced** than **to divorce**: *My parents got divorced when I was three.* However when only one partner wants a divorce or when the reason for the divorce is given, we say **to divorce**: *She divorced her first husband for mental cruelty.* **2 divorce sb/sth from sth** to separate sb/sth from sth: *Sometimes these modern novels seem completely divorced from everyday life.* —**divorced** *adj*: *No I'm not married – I'm divorced.*

divorcee /dɪ,vɔː'siː/ *noun* [C] a person who is divorced

divulge /daɪ'vʌldʒ/ *verb* [T] (*formal*) to tell sth secret: *The phone companies refused to divulge details of their costs.*

dizzy /'dɪzi/ *adj* (**dizzier; dizziest**) feeling as if everything is spinning round and that you might fall: *to feel/get dizzy* —**dizziness** *noun* [U]: *He had been to the doctor complaining of headaches and dizziness.*

☆ **do¹** /duː/ *auxiliary verb* (*negative* **do not**, *short form* **don't** /dəʊnt/; *3rd pers sing pres* **does** /dʌz/; *strong form* /dʌz/; *negative* **does not**, *short form* **doesn't** /'dʌznt/; *pt* **did** /dɪd/; *negative* **did not**, *short form* **didn't** /'dɪdnt/) **1** (used with other verbs to form questions and negative sentences, also in short answers and question tags): *Do you know John?* ○ *He doesn't live in Oxford.* ○ *'Do you agree?' 'No, I don't/yes I do.'* ○ *She works in Paris, doesn't she?* ○ *He didn't say that, did he?* **2** (used for emphasizing the main verb): *'Why didn't you buy any milk?' 'I did buy some, It's in the fridge.'* **3** (used to avoid repeating the main verb): *He earns a lot more than I do.* ○ *She's feeling much better than she did last week.*

☆ **do²** /duː/ *verb* (*pres part* **doing**; *3rd pers sing pres* **does** /dʌz/; *pt* **did** /dɪd/; *pp* **done** /dʌn/) **1** [T] to perform an action: *What are you doing?* ○ *We didn't do much yesterday.* ○ *Please do as you're told.* ○ *It's not fair but what can we do about it* (= how can we change it)*?* ○ *What is the government doing about pollution?* ○ *What do you do* (= what is your job)*?* ○ *I don't know what I did with the keys* (= where I put them)*.* **2** [T] to carry out a particular activity: *Do* (= tidy) *your hair before you go out.* ○ *Has he done his homework?* ○ *Who does the cooking in your house?* ○ *Did you get your essay done* (= finished)*?* **3** [I] to make progress or develop: *'How's your daughter doing at school?' 'She's doing well* (= she is successful)*.'* **4** [T] to travel at a certain speed: *This car does 120 miles per hour.* **5** [T] to produce sth: *The photocopier does 60 copies a minute.* **6** [T] to study a subject: *I'm doing a course on hotel management.* **7** [T] to have a particular effect: *A holiday will do you good.* ○ *The storm did a lot of damage.* **8** [I,T] to be good enough: *I don't need much money – £10 will do.*

(IDIOMS) **be/have to do with sb/sth** to be connected with sb/sth: *Don't ask me about the accident. I had nothing to do with it.* ○ *'How much do you earn?' 'It's nothing to do with you.'*

could do with sth to want or need sth: *I could do with a holiday.*

how do you do? ⇨ HOW
make do with sth ⇨ MAKE¹

(PHRASAL VERBS) **do away with sth** to get rid of sth: *Most European countries have done away with their royal families.*

do sb out of sth to prevent sb having sth in an unfair way: *They've cheated me! They've done me out of £50!*

do sth up 1 to fasten a piece of clothing: *He can't do his shoelaces up yet.* **2** to repair a building and make it more modern: *They're doing up the old cottage.*

do without (sth) to manage without having sth: *If there isn't any coffee left, we'll just have to do without.*

do³ /duː/ *noun* [C] (*pl* **dos** or **do's** /duːz/) (*Brit informal*) a party or other social event: *We're having a bit of a do to celebrate Tim's birthday on Saturday.*

docile /'dəʊsaɪl/ ; *US* 'dɒsl/ *adj* (used about a person or animal) quiet and easy to control

dock¹ /dɒk/ **1** [C,U] an area of a port where ships stop to be loaded, unloaded, repaired, etc **2 docks** [plural] a group of docks with all the sheds, offices, etc that are around them: *He works down at the docks.*

dock *verb* [I,T] (used about a ship) to sail into a dock: *The ship had docked/was docked at Lisbon.*

p	b	t	d	k	g	tʃ	dʒ	f	v	θ	ð
pen	bad	tea	did	cat	got	chin	June	fall	van	thin	then

dock² /dɒk/ noun [C, usually sing] the place in a court of law where the person accused sits or stands

dock³ /dɒk/ verb [T] to take away part of sb's wages, especially as a punishment: *They've docked £20 off my wages because I was late.*

☆ **doctor** /'dɒktə(r)/ noun [C] (*abbr* **Dr**) **1** a person who has been trained in medical science and who treats people who are ill: *Our family doctor is Dr Young.* o *I've got a doctor's appointment at 10 o'clock.* o *What time is the doctor's surgery today?*

☞ We can say **go to the doctor** or **to the doctor's** (= the doctor's surgery). A doctor **sees** or **treats** his/her **patients**. He/she may **prescribe** treatment or **medicine**. This is written on a **prescription**.

2 a person who has got the highest degree from a university: *Doctor of Philosophy*

doctor verb [T] **1** to change sth that should not be changed in order to gain some advantage: *The results of the survey had been doctored.* **2** to add sth harmful to food or drink

doctorate /'dɒktərət/ noun [C] the highest university degree

doctrine /'dɒktrɪn/ noun [C,U] a belief or a set of beliefs that is taught by a church, political party, etc

☆ **document** /'dɒkjʊmənt/ noun [C] an official piece of writing which gives information, proof or evidence: *Her solicitor asked her to read and sign a number of documents.*

documentary /ˌdɒkjʊ'mentrɪ/ noun [C] (*pl* **documentaries**) a film or television or radio programme that gives facts or information about a particular subject: *a documentary on/about life in Northern Ireland*

doddle /'dɒdl/ noun [sing] (*Brit informal*) something that is very easy to do: *The work is an absolute doddle!*

dodge /dɒdʒ/ verb **1** [I,T] to move quickly in order to avoid sb/sth: *I managed to dodge the headmaster and slipped into the classroom.* **2** [T] to avoid doing or thinking about sth such as a duty, etc: *Don't try to dodge your responsibilities!*

dodge noun [C] **1** [usually sing] a quick movement to avoid sb/sth: *He made a sudden dodge to the right.* **2** (*informal*) a clever way of avoiding sth: *The man had been involved in a massive tax dodge.*

dodgy /'dɒdʒɪ/ adj (**dodgier**; **dodgiest**) (*especially Brit informal*) risky; not reliable or honest: *a dodgy business deal*

doe /dəʊ/ noun [C] a female deer or rabbit ☞ picture at **deer**.

does ⇒ DO¹,²

☆ **dog¹** /dɒg; *US* dɔ:g/ noun [C] **1** an animal that many people keep as a pet, or for working on farms, hunting, etc ☞ A dog can **bark**, **growl**, **whine** and **wag** its tail. **2** a male dog or fox: *If you're getting a puppy, bitches are gentler than dogs.*

'dog-collar noun [C] (*informal*) a white collar that is worn by priests in the Christian church

'dog-eared adj (used about a book or piece of paper) in bad condition and having the corners of the pages turned down because it has been used a lot

dog² /dɒg; *US* dɔ:g/ verb [T] (**dogging**; **dogged**) to follow closely: *A shadowy figure was dogging their every move.* o (*figurative*) *Bad luck and illness has dogged her career from the start.*

dogged /'dɒgɪd; *US* 'dɔ:gɪd/ adj refusing to give up even when sth is difficult: *I was impressed by his dogged determination to succeed.* —**doggedly** adv: *She doggedly refused all offers of help.*

dogma /'dɒgmə; *US* 'dɔ:gmə/ noun [C,U] a belief or set of beliefs that people are expected to accept as true without questioning

dogmatic /dɒg'mætɪk; *US* dɔ:g'mætɪk/ adj insisting that sth is true or right; not prepared to consider other opinions —**dogmatically** /-klɪ/ adv

dogsbody /'dɒgzbɒdɪ; *US* 'dɔ:g-/ noun [C] (*pl* **dogsbodies**) (*Brit informal*) a person who is made to do the boring or unpleasant jobs that no one else wants to do and who is treated as being less important than other people

doldrums /'dɒldrəmz/ noun [plural]
(IDIOM) **in the doldrums** (*informal*) **1** not active or busy: *Business has been in the doldrums but should improve later in the year.* **2** sad or depressed

dole¹ /dəʊl/ verb (*informal*)
(PHRASAL VERB) **dole sth out** to give sth, especially food, money, etc to a number of people, in small amounts

dole² /dəʊl/ noun [sing] **the dole** (*Brit informal*) money that the State gives every week to people who are unemployed: *He's been on the dole* (= receiving this money) *for six months.*

doleful /'dəʊlfl/ adj sad or depressed: *She looked at him with doleful eyes.* —**dolefully** /-fəlɪ/ adv

doll /dɒl; *US* dɔ:l/ noun [C] a child's toy that looks like a small person or a baby

☆ **dollar** /'dɒlə(r)/ noun [C] (*symbol* **$**) a unit of money in the US, Canada, Australia, etc ☞ There are 100 **cents** in a dollar. **2** [C] a note or coin that is worth one dollar **3** **the dollar** [sing] the value of the US dollar on international money markets

dollop /'dɒləp/ noun [C] (*informal*) a lump of sth soft, especially food

dolphin

dolphin /'dɒlfɪn/ noun [C] an intelligent animal that lives in the sea and looks like a large fish. Dolphins usually swim in large groups.

domain /dəʊ'meɪn/ noun [C] an area of knowledge or activity: *I'm afraid I don't know – that's really outside my domain.* o *This issue is now in the public domain* (= the public knows about it).

s	z	ʃ	ʒ	h	m	n	ŋ	l	r	j	w
so	zoo	she	vision	how	man	no	sing	leg	red	yes	wet

dome /dəʊm/ *noun* [C] a round roof on a building: *the dome of St Paul's in London*

☆**domestic** /də'mestɪk/ *adj* **1** connected with the home or family: *domestic responsibilities* ○ *domestic water, gas, etc supplies* **2** (used about a person) enjoying doing things in the home, such as cooking and housework **3** not international; of or inside a particular country: *domestic flights* (= within one country) **4** (used about animals) kept as pets or on farms; not wild: *domestic animals such as cats, dogs and horses*

domesticated /də'mestɪkeɪtɪd/ *adj* **1** (used about animals) used to living near people and being controlled by them **2** (used about people) able to do or good at housework, cooking, etc: *Men are expected to be much more domesticated nowadays.*

dominant /'dɒmɪnənt/ *adj* **1** the strongest or most important: *His mother was the dominant influence in his life.* **2** that you notice very easily: *The castle stands in a dominant position above the town.*

dominance /'dɒmɪnəns/ *noun* [U] control or power: *Japan's dominance of the car industry*

dominate /'dɒmɪneɪt/ *verb* **1** [I,T] to have strong control or influence; to be the most important person or thing in sth: *The Italian team dominated throughout the second half of the game.* ○ *She always tends to dominate the conversation at dinner parties.* **2** [T] (used about a building or place) to look down on or over: *The cathedral dominates the area for miles around.*

domination /ˌdɒmɪ'neɪʃn/ *noun* [U] strong control, power or influence

domineering /ˌdɒmɪ'nɪərɪŋ/ *adj* having a very strong character and wanting to control other people

dominion /də'mɪnɪən/ *noun* **1** [U] (*formal*) the power to rule and control: *to have dominion over an area* **2** [C] (*formal*) an area controlled by one government or ruler: *the Queen's dominions*

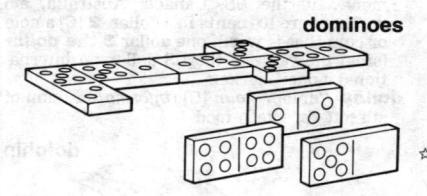

dominoes

domino /'dɒmɪnəʊ/ *noun* [C] (*pl* **dominoes**) one of a set of small flat pieces of wood or plastic that are used for playing a game (**dominoes**). Each domino has a different number of spots on one side of it.

donate /dəʊ'neɪt; *US* 'dəʊneɪt/ *verb* [T] to give money or goods to an organization, especially one for people or animals who need help: *She donated a large sum of money to Cancer Research.*

donation /dəʊ'neɪʃn/ *noun* [C] a gift of money or goods to an organization, especially one for people or animals who need help: *Would you like to make a small donation to the Red Cross?*

done¹ *pp* of DO²

done² /dʌn/ *adj* (not before a noun) **1** finished: *I've got to go out as soon as this job is done.* **2** (used about food) cooked enough: *The meat's ready but the vegetables still aren't done.*
(IDIOM) **over and done with** completely finished; in the past

done *interj* (used for saying that you accept an offer): *'I'll give you twenty pounds for it.' 'Done!'*

donkey

☆**donkey** /'dɒŋki/ *noun* [C] (*pl* **donkeys**) (*also* **ass**) an animal like a small horse, with long ears
(IDIOM) **donkey's years** (*Brit informal*) a very long time: *They've been going out together for donkey's years.*

donor /'dəʊnə(r)/ *noun* [C] **1** a person who gives blood or a part of his/her own body for medical use: *a blood donor* ○ *a kidney donor* **2** a person who gives money or goods to an organization that needs it, especially an organization for helping other people

don't ⇨ DO¹,²

doodle /'duːdl/ *verb* [I] to draw lines, patterns, etc without concentrating, especially when you are bored or thinking about sth else
—**doodle** *noun* [C]

doom /duːm/ *noun* [U] death or a terrible event in the future which you cannot avoid: *In the last scene of the film the villain plunges to his doom in the river.* ○ *a sense of doom* (= that something bad is going to happen)

doomed *adj* certain to fail or to suffer sth unpleasant: *The plan was doomed from the start.* ○ *a doomed love affair*

☆**door** /dɔː(r)/ *noun* [C] **1** a piece of wood, glass, etc that you open and close to get in or out of a room, building, car, etc: *to open/shut/close the door* ○ *Don't forget to lock the door when you leave the house.* ○ *Have you bolted the door?* ○ *Please don't slam the door.* ○ *I could hear someone knocking on the door.* ○ *the front/back door* ○ *the kitchen door* ○ *the fridge door* **2** the entrance to a building, room, car, etc: *I peeped through the door and saw her sitting there.*
(IDIOMS) **(from) door to door** (from) house to house: *The journey takes about five hours, door to door.* ○ *a door-to-door salesman* (= a person who visits people in their homes to try and sell them things)

next door (to sb/sth) in the next house, room, etc: *Do you know the people who live next*

iː	ɪ	e	æ	ɑː	ɒ	ɔː	ʊ	uː	ʌ
see	sit	ten	hat	arm	got	saw	put	too	cup

door? ○ *You'll find the bathroom next door to your bedroom.*
out of doors outside: *Shall we eat out of doors today?* ☛ The opposite is **indoors**.
'**doorbell** noun [C] a bell on the outside of a house which you ring when you want to go in
'**doormat** noun [C] a mat beside a door which you can wipe your shoes on to clean them before going inside
'**doorstep** noun [C] a step in front of a door, usually outside a building
(IDIOM) **on your doorstep** very near to you: *The sea was right on our doorstep.*
'**doorway** noun [C] an entrance into a building, room, etc: *She was standing in the doorway.*
dope /dəʊp/ noun (*informal*) **1** [U] a drug that is not legal, especially cannabis **2** [C] a stupid person: *What a dope!*
dope verb [T] to give a drug secretly to a person or animal, especially to make them sleep
dopey (*also* **dopy**) /'dəʊpi/ adj (**dopier**, **dopiest**) **1** sleepy and not able to think clearly, especially because of drugs, alcohol or lack of sleep **2** (*informal*) stupid; not very intelligent
dormant /'dɔːmənt/ adj not active for some time: *a dormant volcano*
dormitory /'dɔːmɪtri; *US* -tɔːri/ noun [C] (*pl* **dormitories**) **1** a large bedroom with a number of beds in it, especially in a school, etc **2** (*US*) a building at a college or university where students live
dosage /'dəʊsɪdʒ/ noun [C, usually sing] the amount of a medicine you should take over a period of time: *The recommended dosage is one tablet every four hours.*
dose /dəʊs/ noun [C] **1** an amount of medicine that you take at one time: *You should take a large dose of this cough medicine before going to bed.* **2** an amount of sth, especially sth unpleasant: *a dose of the flu* ○ *I can only stand my mother-in-law in small doses.*
dose verb [T] to give sb/yourself a medicine or drug
doss /dɒs/ verb
(PHRASAL VERB) **doss down** (*Brit slang*) to lie down to sleep, without a proper bed: *Do you mind if I doss down on your floor tonight?*
☆ **dot** /dɒt/ noun [C] **1** a small, round mark: *a white dress with black dots* ○ *The letters i and j have dots above them.* **2** something that looks like a dot: *He watched until the aeroplane was just a dot in the sky.*
(IDIOM) **on the dot** (*informal*) at exactly the right time or at exactly the time mentioned: *Lessons start at 9 o'clock on the dot.*
dot verb [T] (**dotting**; **dotted**) (usually passive) to mark with a dot
(IDIOMS) **be dotted about** to be scattered over an area: *There are little bars and restaurants dotted about all over the centre of town.*
be dotted with to have many things or people in or on it: *a hillside dotted with sheep and cows*
dotted 'line noun [C] a line of dots which show where sth is to be written on a form, etc ☛ picture at **line**.
dote /dəʊt/ verb [I] **dote on sb/sth** to have or show too much love for sb/sth and think they are perfect: *He's always doted on his eldest son.*
doting adj very or too loving: *doting parents*
☆ **double¹** /'dʌbl/ adj **1** twice as much or as many (as usual): *a double helping of ice-cream* **2** having two equal or similar parts: *Don't park on double yellow lines.* ○ *double doors* ○ *Does 'necessary' have a double 's'?* ○ *My phone number is two four double 0 four* (= 24004). **3** made for or used by two people or things: *a double garage*
,**double-'bass** (*also* **bass**) noun [C] the largest instrument of the violin family, that you play standing up
,**double 'bed** noun [C] a bed made for two people ☛ Look at **single** and **twin**.
,**double-'decker** noun [C] a bus with two floors
,**double 'Dutch** noun [U] talk or writing that you cannot understand at all
,**double 'figures** noun [U] a number that is more than 10: *Inflation is now in double figures.*
☆ **double²** /'dʌbl/ det twice as much or as many (as usual, as sb/sth, etc): *His income is double hers.* ○ *We'll need double the amount of wine.*
☆ **double³** /'dʌbl/ adv in twos or two parts: *When I saw her with her twin sister I thought I was seeing double.*
,**double-'breasted** adj (used about a coat or jacket) having the front parts cross over each other, with two rows of buttons
,**double-'check** verb [I,T] to check sth again, or with great care
,**double-'cross** verb [T] to cheat sb who believes that he/she can trust you
,**double-'glaze** verb [T] to put two layers of glass in a window, so that the building is kept warm or quiet —,**double-'glazing** noun [U]
☆ **double⁴** /'dʌbl/ noun **1** [U] twice the (usual) number or amount: *When you work overtime, you get paid double.* **2** [C] a person who looks very much like another: *I thought it was you I saw in Tesco's. You must have a double.* **3 doubles** [plural] (in some sports, eg tennis) with two pairs playing: *the Men's Doubles final* ☛ Look at **singles**(4).
☆ **double⁵** /'dʌbl/ verb [I,T] **1** to become or to make sth twice as much or as many: *The price of houses has almost doubled.* ○ *Think of a number and double it.* **2 double as sth** to have a second use or function: *The small room doubles as a study.*
(IDIOM) **double (sb) up** (to cause sb) to bend the body: *to be doubled up in pain, with laughter, etc*
doubly /'dʌbli/ adv **1** in two ways: *He was doubly blessed with both good looks and talent.* **2** more than usually: *I made doubly sure that the door was locked.*
☆ **doubt¹** /daʊt/ noun [C,U] (a feeling of) uncertainty: *If you have any doubts, feel free to ring me and discuss them.* ○ *You'll definitely pass. There's no doubt about it.* ○ *There was some doubt as to whether she was the right person for the job.*
(IDIOMS) **cast doubt on sth** ⇨ CAST²
give sb the benefit of the doubt ⇨ BENEFIT
in doubt not sure or definite

3ː	ə	eɪ	əʊ	aɪ	aʊ	ɔɪ	ɪə	eə	ʊə
fur	ago	pay	home	five	now	join	near	hair	pure

no doubt (used when you expect sth to happen but you are not sure that it will) probably: *No doubt she'll write when she has time.*

without (a) doubt definitely: *It was, without doubt, the coldest winter for many years.*

☆ **doubt²** /daʊt/ *verb* [T] to think sth unlikely or to feel uncertain (about sth): *She never doubted (= she was always sure) that he was telling the truth.* ○ *I doubt whether/if I'll have time to go to the shops today* (= I don't think I'll be able to go). ○ *He had never doubted her support.*

doubtful /'daʊtfl/ *adj* **1** unlikely or uncertain: *It's doubtful whether/if we'll finish in time for Christmas.* ○ *It was doubtful that he was still alive.* **2 doubtful (about sth/about doing sth)** (used about a person) not sure: *He still felt doubtful about his decision.* —**doubtfully** /-fəli/ *adv*: *'I suppose it'll be all right,' she said doubtfully.*

doubtless /'daʊtləs/ *adv* almost certainly: *Doubtless she'll have a good excuse for being late!*

dough /dəʊ/ *noun* [U] **1** a mixture of flour, water and sometimes fat and sugar. It is used for baking into bread, etc **2** (*informal*) money

'doughnut *noun* [C] a small cake in the shape of a ball or a ring, made from sweet dough cooked in fat ☛ picture at **bread**.

dour /dʊə(r)/ *adj* (used about a person's manner or expression) cold and unfriendly

douse (*also* **dowse**) /daʊs/ *verb* [T] **1** to cover sb/sth with liquid: *to douse yourself in perfume* (= wear too much of it) **2** to stop a fire, etc burning: *The firemen managed to douse the blaze.*

dove¹ /dʌv/ *noun* [C] a type of bird, similar to a pigeon, often used as a sign of peace

dove² /dəʊv/ (*US*) *pt of* DIVE¹

dowdy /'daʊdi/ *adj* (**dowdier**; **dowdiest**) (used about a person or the clothes he/she wears) dull and unfashionable

☆ **down¹** /daʊn/ *adv* **1** to or at a lower level or place; not up: *We sat and watched the sun go down.* ○ *Can you get that book down from the top shelf?* ○ *'Where's Mary?' 'She's down in the basement.'* **2** from a standing or vertical position to a sitting or horizontal one: *I think I'll sit/lie down.* **3** to or in the south: *We went down to Devon for our holiday.* **4** (used for showing that the level, amount, strength, etc of sth is less or lower): *Do you mind if I turn the heating down a bit?* **5** (written) on paper: *Put these dates down in your diary.* **6 down to sb/sth** even including: *Everybody was invited from the Director down to the tea ladies.*

(IDIOMS) **be down to sb** to be sb's responsibility: *When my father died it was down to me to look after the family's affairs.*

be down to sth to have only the amount mentioned left: *I can't lend you any money – I'm down to my last £5.*

be/go down with sth to be or become ill with sth: *Simon's gone down with flu.*

down and out having no money, job or home

down under (*informal*) (in) Australia: *He comes from down under.*

'down-and-out *noun* [C] a person who has not got money, a job or a home

down-to-'earth *adj* sensible and practical; not complicated or too clever

☆ **down²** /daʊn/ *prep* **1** along: *'Where's the nearest garage?' 'Go down this road and take the first turning on the right.'* **2** from the top towards the bottom of sth: *Her hair hung down her back.* ○ *The snow began to slide down the mountain.* **3** at or to a lower or further part of sth: *We sailed down the river towards the sea.*

down³ /daʊn/ *verb* [T] (*informal*) to finish a drink quickly: *He downed a pint of beer and left.*

down⁴ /daʊn/ *noun*
(IDIOM) **ups and downs** ⇨ UP

down⁵ /daʊn/ *adj* **1** sad: *You're looking a bit down today.* **2** lower than before: *Unemployment figures are down for the third month in succession.* **3** (used about computers) not working

down⁶ /daʊn/ *noun* [U] very soft feathers: *a duvet filled with down*

downcast /'daʊnkɑːst; *US* 'daʊnkæst/ *adj* **1** (used about a person) sad and without hope **2** (used about eyes) looking down

downfall /'daʊnfɔːl/ *noun* [sing] **1** a loss of power or success: *The government's downfall seemed inevitable.* **2** a thing that causes a loss of power or success

downgrade /'daʊngreɪd/ *verb* [T] to reduce sb/sth to a lower level or position of importance

downhearted /ˌdaʊn'hɑːtɪd/ *adj* sad or depressed

downhill /ˌdaʊn'hɪl/ *adj*, *adv* (going) down a slope; towards the bottom of a hill: *It's an easy walk. The road runs downhill most of the way.* ○ *Do you go downhill or cross-country skiing?*

(IDIOM) **go downhill** to get worse: *Their relationship has been going downhill for some time now.*

down-market /ˌdaʊn'mɑːkɪt/ *adj* cheap and of not very high quality

downpour /'daʊnpɔː(r)/ *noun* [C, usually sing] a heavy, sudden fall of rain

downright /'daʊnraɪt/ *adj* (only *before* a noun) (used about sth bad or unpleasant) complete: *The holiday was a downright disaster.*

downright *adv* completely or thoroughly: *That road is downright dangerous!*

downs /daʊnz/ *noun* [plural] an area of low, round hills, especially in the south of England: *the Sussex Downs*

Down's syndrome /'daʊnz sɪndrəʊm/ *noun* [U] a condition that a person is born with. People with this condition have a flat, wide face and lower than average intelligence.

☆ **downstairs** /ˌdaʊn'steəz/ *adv*, *adj* **1** down the stairs: *He fell downstairs and broke his arm.* **2** on or to the ground floor or a lower floor: *Dad's downstairs, in the kitchen.* ○ *a downstairs toilet* ☛ The opposite is **upstairs**.

downstream /ˌdaʊn'striːm/ *adv* in the direction in which a river flows: *We were rowing downstream, towards the sea.* ☛ The opposite is **upstream**.

downtrodden /'daʊntrɒdn/ *adj* (used about a person) made to suffer bad treatment or living conditions by people in power, but being too tired, poor, ill, etc to change things

p	b	t	d	k	g	tʃ	dʒ	f	v	θ	ð
pen	bad	tea	did	cat	got	chin	June	fall	van	thin	then

☆ **downward** /'daʊnwəd/ adj (only before a noun) towards the ground or a lower level: *a downward movement* ○ *There is still a downward trend in house prices.*

downwards (also **downward**) adv towards the ground or a lower level: *She laid the picture face downwards on the table.* ☛ The opposite is **upward(s)**.

dowry /'daʊəri/ noun [C] (pl **dowries**) an amount of money or property which, in some countries, a woman's family gives to the man she is marrying

dowse = DOUSE

doze /dəʊz/ verb [I] to sleep lightly and/or for a short time: *He was dozing in front of the television.*
(PHRASAL VERB) **doze off** to go to sleep, without meaning to: *I'm sorry – I must have dozed off for a minute.*

doze noun [C, usually sing] a light, short sleep

☆ **dozen** /'dʌzn/ noun [C] (pl **dozens** or **dozen**) twelve or a group of twelve: *A dozen eggs, please.* ○ *half a dozen* (= six) ○ *two dozen sheep*
(IDIOM) **dozens** (informal) very many: *I've tried phoning her dozens of times.*

dozy /'dəʊzi/ adj (**dozier**; **doziest**) **1** sleepy: *The wine had made her rather dozy.* **2** (*Brit informal*) stupid: *You dozy thing – look what you've done!*

drab /dræb/ adj (**drabber**; **drabbest**) dull and not interesting or attractive: *a drab grey office building*

draft[1] /drɑːft; *US* dræft/ noun **1** [C] a piece of writing, etc which will probably be changed and improved; not the final copy: *the first draft of a speech* **2** (*US*) = DRAUGHT

draft[2] /drɑːft; *US* dræft/ verb [T] **1** to make a first or early copy of a piece of writing: *I'll draft a letter and show it to you before I type it.* **2** (usually passive) (*US*) to order sb to join the armed forces: *He was drafted into the army.*

drafty (*US*) = DRAUGHTY

drag[1] /dræg/ noun **1** [sing] (*informal*) a person or thing that is boring or annoying: *'The car's broken down.' 'Oh no! What a drag!'* **2** [U] (*informal*) the wearing of women's clothes by a man, especially as part of a show, etc **3** [C] (*informal*) an act of breathing in cigarette smoke: *He took a long drag on his cigarette.*

☆ **drag**[2] /dræg/ verb (**dragg**ing; **dragg**ed) **1** [T] to pull sb/sth along with difficulty: *The box was so heavy we had to drag it along the floor.* **2** [T] to force or to make sb come or go somewhere: *She dragged the child up the steps by her arm.* ○ *Can I drag you away from the television for a moment?* **3** [I] **drag (on)** to be boring or to seem to last a long time: *The speeches dragged on for hours.*
(PHRASAL VERBS) **drag sth out** to make sth last longer than necessary: *Let's not drag this decision out – shall we go or not?*
drag sth out (of sb) to force or persuade sb to give you information that you want

dragon /'drægən/ noun [C] (in stories, etc) an imaginary animal with wings, which can breathe out fire

drain[1] /dreɪn/ noun [C] a pipe or hole that dirty water, etc goes down to be carried away: *The drain outside the kitchen is blocked.*
(IDIOMS) **a drain on sb/sth** something that uses up time, money, strength, etc: *The cost of travelling is a great drain on our budget.*
(**go**) **down the drain** (*informal*) (to be) wasted: *All that hard work has gone down the drain.*

'drainpipe noun [C] a pipe which goes down the side of a building, especially one that carries water from the roof into a drain

drain[2] /dreɪn/ verb **1** [I,T] to become dry as liquid flows away; to make sth dry in this way: *The whole area will have to be drained before it can be used for farming.* **2** [I,T] to flow away; to make a liquid flow: *The sink's blocked – the water won't drain away at all.* ○ *The plumber had to drain the water from the heating system.* **3** [T] to drink all the liquid (in a glass, etc): *He drained his glass in one gulp.* **4** [I] (used about a feeling) to become weaker and weaker until it disappears: *He felt all his anger begin to drain away.* **5** [T] **drain sb/sth (of sth)** to make sb/sth weaker, poorer, etc by slowly using all the strength, money, etc available

'draining-board (*US* **'drainboard**) noun [C] the place beside a kitchen sink where you put plates, cups, knives, etc to dry

drainage /'dreɪnɪdʒ/ noun [U] a system used for draining water, etc away from a place

drama /'drɑːmə/ noun **1** [C] a play for the theatre, radio or television: *a contemporary drama* **2** [U] plays as a form of writing; the performance of plays: *He wrote some drama, as well as poetry.* ○ *a drama student* **3** [C] an exciting event **4** [U] excitement: *Why is there so little drama in my life?* ○ *...and to add to all the drama, the lights went out!*

☆ **dramatic** /drə'mætɪk/ adj **1** noticeable or sudden: *a dramatic change* **2** exciting or impressive: *The opening scene of the film was extremely dramatic.* **3** (used about a person, a person's behaviour, etc) showing feelings, etc in a very obvious way because you want other people to notice you or pay attention to you: *Calm down. There's no need to be so dramatic about everything!* **4** connected with plays or the theatre: *Shakespeare's dramatic works*

dramatically /-kli/ adv in a dramatic way: *'I can't go on,' she said dramatically.*

dramatist /'dræmətɪst/ noun [C] a person who writes plays

dramatize (also **dramatise**) /'dræmətaɪz/ verb **1** [T] to make a book, an event, etc into a play: *The novel has been dramatized for television.* **2** [I,T] to make sth seem more exciting or important than it really is: *The newspaper was accused of dramatizing the situation.* —**dramatization** (also **dramatisation**) /ˌdræmətaɪ'zeɪʃn/ noun [C,U]

drank *pt* of DRINK

drape /dreɪp/ verb [T] **1 drape sth round/over sth** to put a piece of cloth, clothing, etc loosely on sth: *He quickly draped a towel round his waist.* **2 drape sth (in/with sth)** (usually passive) to cover sb/sth (with cloth, etc): *The furniture was draped in dustsheets.* —**drape** noun [C] (*US*) = CURTAIN

drastic /'dræstɪk/ adj **1** strong, effective and

s	z	ʃ	ʒ	h	m	n	ŋ	l	r	j	w
so	zoo	she	vision	how	man	no	sing	leg	red	yes	wet

usually quick: *The situation requires drastic action.* **2** very noticeable or serious: *There has been a drastic rise in crime in the area.* —**drastically** /-klɪ/ *adv*: *House prices have fallen drastically over the last two years.*

draught /drɑːft/ (*US* **draft** /dræft/) *noun* **1** [C] a current of air that comes into a room: *Can you shut the door? There's a draught in here.* **2 draughts** (*Brit*) (*US* **checkers**) [U] a game for two players that you play on a black and white board using round black and white pieces

draught *adj* (used about beer, etc) served from barrels, not bottles: *draught beer*

draughtsman /ˈdrɑːftsmən/ (*US* **draftsman** /ˈdræfts-/) *noun* [C] (*pl* **draughtsmen**; *US* **draftsmen** /-mən/) a person whose job is to make technical drawings

draughty /ˈdrɑːftɪ/ (*US* **drafty** /ˈdræftɪ/) *adj* (**draughtier**; **draughtiest**) having currents of air blowing through: *a large, draughty old house*

draw¹ /drɔː/ *noun* [C] a result of a game or competition in which both players or teams get the same score so that neither of them wins: *The match ended in a draw.*

☆ **draw²** /drɔː/ *verb* (*pt* **drew** /druː/; *pp* **drawn** /drɔːn/) **1** [I,T] to make a picture or diagram of sth with a pencil, pen, etc: *Shall I draw you a map of how to get there?* **2** [I] to move in the direction mentioned: *At last the train drew into/out of the station.* **3** [T] **draw sth out of/ from sth** to pull sth smoothly out of its present position: *She drew the letter out of her pocket and handed it to me.* **4** [T] to pull sb/sth gently into a new position: *He drew me by the hand into the room.* o *Why don't you draw your chairs up to the fire?* **5** [T] (used about horses, etc) to pull sth along: *The Queen's carriage was drawn by six horses.* **6** [T] to open or close curtains, etc: *It was getting dark so I switched on the lights and drew the curtains.* **7** [T] to pull a gun, sword or knife out of its holder, quickly and in order to attack sb: *The cowboy drew his gun.* **8** [T] **draw sth from sb/sth** to gain sth from sb/sth: *This information has been drawn from a number of sources.* **9** [T] **draw sth (from sth)** to learn sth from study, experience, etc: *Can we draw any conclusions from this survey?* **10** [T] **draw sth (from sb)** to produce a reaction or response to the thing mentioned: *The advertisement has drawn interest from people all over the country.* **11** [T] **draw sb (to sb/ sth)** to attract or interest sb: *She had always been drawn to older men.* o *The musicians drew quite a large crowd.* **12** [I,T] to finish a game, competition, etc with equal scores so that neither person or team wins: *The two teams drew.* o *The match was drawn.*

(IDIOMS) **bring sth/come/draw to an end** ⇨ END¹

draw sb's attention to sth to make sb aware of sth: *Can I draw your attention to point seven on the agenda?*

draw a blank to get no result or response: *Detectives investigating the case have drawn a blank so far.*

draw a comparison/a parallel to show how two things compare or are similar: *The programme drew an interesting comparison between education in Japan and Britain.*

draw a distinction between sth and sth to show how two things are different: *It's important to draw a distinction between the methods used now and those used previously.*

draw the line at sth to say 'no' to sth even though you are prepared to be helpful in other ways: *I do most of the cooking but I draw the line at washing up as well!*

draw lots to decide sth by chance: *They drew lots to see who should stay behind.*

(PHRASAL VERBS) **draw in 1** (used about the hours of daylight) to get shorter before the winter **2** (used about cars, buses, etc) to go to the side of the road and stop

draw out 1 (used about the hours of daylight) to get longer in the spring **2** (used about cars, buses, etc) to move out from the side of the road where they have stopped

draw sth out to take money out of a bank account: *How much money do I need to draw out?*

draw up (used about a car, etc) to drive up and stop in front of or near sth: *A police car drew up outside the building.*

draw sth up to prepare a document, list, etc and write it out: *Our solicitor is going to draw up the contract.*

drawback /ˈdrɔːbæk/ *noun* [C] a disadvantage or problem: *His lack of experience is a major drawback.*

☆ **drawer** /drɔː(r)/ *noun* [C] a container which forms part of a piece of furniture such as a desk, that you can pull out to put things in or take things out: *There's some paper in the top drawer of my desk.*

☆ **drawing** /ˈdrɔːɪŋ/ *noun* **1** [C] a picture made with a pencil, pen, etc **2** [U] the art of drawing pictures: *She's good at drawing and painting.*

ˈdrawing-pin (*US* **thumb-tack**) *noun* [C] a short pin with a flat top, used for fastening paper, etc to a board or wall ☞ picture at **pin**.

drawing-room /ˈdrɔːɪŋrʊm/ *noun* [C] a living-room, especially one used mainly for formal occasions

drawl /drɔːl/ *verb* [I,T] to speak slowly, making the vowel sounds very long —**drawl** *noun* [sing]: *a slow Kentucky drawl*

drawn¹ /drɔːn/ *adj* (used about a person or his/her face) looking tired, worried or ill: *He looked pale and drawn after the long journey.*

drawn² *pp* of DRAW²: *The match was drawn.* o *The curtains were drawn.*

dread /dred/ *noun* [U,sing] great fear: *He lived in dread of the same thing happening to him one day.* o *a secret dread of what might happen*

dread *verb* [T] to be very afraid of or worried about sth: *I'm dreading the exams.* o *She dreaded having to tell him what had happened.* o *I dread to think what my father will say.*

dreaded *adj* terrible; causing you to feel afraid or worried: *the most dreaded punishment of all*

dreadful /ˈdredfl/ *adj* very bad, unpleasant or poor in quality: *We had a dreadful journey – traffic jams all the way!* o *What a dreadful man!*

iː	ɪ	e	æ	ɑː	ɒ	ɔː	ʊ	uː	ʌ
see	sit	ten	hat	arm	got	saw	put	too	cup

o *I'm afraid there's been a dreadful* (= very serious) *mistake.* —**dreadfully** /-fəli/ *adv*

dreadlocks /'drɛdlɒks/ *noun* [plural] hair worn in long curled pieces, especially by some black people

☆ **dream¹** /driːm/ *noun* **1** [C] a series of events or pictures which happen in your mind while you are asleep: *I had a strange dream last night.* o *In my dream I was flying a helicopter...* ☛ Look at **nightmare. 2** [C] an event or situation that you want very much to happen, although it is not very likely that it will: *His dream was to give up his job and live in the country.* o *a dream house* (= one that you would like very much to own) **3** [sing] a state of mind in which you are not concentrating on what is happening around you: *You've been in a dream all morning!*

☆ **dream²** /driːm/ *verb* [I,T] (*pt, pp* **dreamed** /driːmd/ or **dreamt** /drɛmt/) **1** to see or experience pictures and events in your mind while you are asleep: *I dreamed about the house that I lived in as a child.* o *I woke up to find that I wasn't really rich. I had only dreamt it.* o *I dreamed that I was running but I couldn't get away.* **2** to imagine sth that you would like to happen: *I've always dreamt about winning lots of money.* o *I never dreamt that I would be so lucky!* ☛ Look at **daydream**.
(IDIOM) **I, etc would not dream of sth** I, etc would definitely not do sth, under any circumstances: *'Don't tell anybody.' 'Of course not. I wouldn't dream of it.'*
(PHRASAL VERB) **dream sth up** (*informal*) to think of sth such as a plan, etc especially sth unusual or slightly foolish: *Which of you dreamt up that idea?*

dreamer *noun* [C] a person who thinks a lot about ideas, plans, etc which may never happen instead of concentrating on what is really happening

dreamy /'driːmi/ *adj* (**dreamier; dreamiest**) (used about a person or his/her expression) having or showing thoughts that are far away from the real world: *a dreamy look, expression, etc* —**dreamily** /-ɪli/ *adv*

dreary /'drɪəri/ *adj* (**drearier; dreariest**) dull, boring or depressing: *What dreary weather! It's so grey.*

dredge /drɛdʒ/ *verb* [T] to clear the mud, etc from the bottom of a river or harbour using a special machine
(PHRASAL VERB) **dredge sth up** to mention again sth unpleasant from the past that it would be better to forget: *The newspaper had dredged up all sorts of embarrassing details about her private life.*

dregs /drɛgz/ *noun* [plural] **1** the unwanted liquid left at the bottom of sth, including any solid bits that have sunk down: *'Is there any wine left in that bottle?' 'Only the dregs.'* **2** the worst and most useless part of sth: *These people were regarded as the dregs of society.*

drench /drɛntʃ/ *verb* [T] (usually passive) to make sb/sth completely wet: *We got absolutely drenched in the storm.*

☆ **dress¹** /drɛs/ *noun* **1** [C] a piece of clothing worn by a girl or a woman. It covers the body from the shoulders to the knees or below and often covers the arms. **2** [U] clothes for either men or women: *formal/informal dress* o *evening dress*

☆ **dress²** /drɛs/ *verb* **1** [I,T] to put clothes on sb or yourself: *He dressed quickly and left the house with a minute to spare.* o *If you don't get dressed soon, we'll be late.* o *My husband dressed the children while I got breakfast ready.* o *Hurry up, Simon! Aren't you dressed yet?* ☛ It is more common to say **get dressed** than **dress**. **2** [I] to put or have clothes on, in the way or style mentioned: *to dress well, badly, etc* o *to be well-dressed, badly-dressed, etc* **3** [I] to put on formal clothes for the evening: *In the past wealthy families always dressed for dinner.* **4** [T] to clean and put a bandage, etc on a wound: *to dress a wound*
(IDIOM) **(be) dressed in sth** wearing sth: *The people at the funeral were all dressed in black.*
(PHRASAL VERB) **dress up 1** to put on special or unusual clothes for fun or for a play: *The children decided to dress up as pirates.* **2** to put on smart clothes, usually for a special occasion: *You don't need to dress up for the party.*

dresser /'drɛsə(r)/ *noun* [C] **1** (*especially Brit*) a piece of furniture with cupboards at the bottom and shelves above. It is used for holding dishes, cups, etc. **2** (*US*) a chest of drawers, usually with a mirror on top

dressing /'drɛsɪŋ/ *noun* **1** [C] a covering that you put on a wound to protect it and keep it clean **2** [C,U] a sauce for food, especially for salads **3** [U] the act or action of putting on clothes

'dressing-gown (*also* **bathrobe**; *US* **robe**) *noun* [C] a piece of clothing like a loose coat which you wear before or after a bath or over pyjamas, etc

'dressing-table *noun* [C] a piece of furniture in a bedroom. It has drawers and a mirror.

drew *pt* of DRAW²

dribble /'drɪbl/ *verb* **1** [I,T] (used about a liquid) to move downwards in a thin stream; to make a liquid move in this way: *The paint dribbled down the side of the pot.* **2** [I] to allow liquid (**saliva**) to run out of the mouth: *Small children often dribble.* **3** [I,T] (used in ball games) to make a ball move forward by using many short kicks or hits

dried *pt, pp* of DRY²

drier¹ *adj* ⇨ DRY¹

drier² *noun* [C] ⇨ DRY²

drift /drɪft/ *verb* [I] **1** to be carried or moved along by wind or water: *The boat drifted out to sea.* **2** (used about snow or sand) to be moved into piles by wind or water: *The snow drifted up to two metres deep in some places.* **3** to move slowly or without any particular purpose: *He drifted from room to room.* o *She drifted into acting almost by accident.* o *At one time they were close friends, but over the years they've drifted apart.*

drift *noun* **1** [C] a slow movement towards sth: *the country's drift into economic decline* **2** [sing] the general meaning of sth: *I couldn't understand every word but I got the drift of what he* was saying. **3** [C] a pile of snow or sand that was made by wind or water

drill[1] /drɪl/ *noun* [C] a tool or machine that is used for making holes in things: *a dentist's drill* ☞ picture at **tool**.
▶ **drill** *verb* [I,T] to make a hole in sth with a drill: *to drill a hole in sth* ○ *to drill for oil*

drill[2] /drɪl/ *noun* **1** [U] exercise in marching, etc that soldiers do **2** [C] something that you repeat many times in order to learn sth **3** [C,U] practice for what you should do in an emergency: *a fire-drill*
▶ **drill** *verb* [I,T] to teach sb by making him/her repeat sth many times

☆ **drink** /drɪŋk/ *verb* (*pt* **drank** /dræŋk/; *pp* **drunk** /drʌŋk/) **1** [I,T] to take liquid into your body through your mouth: *You've lost a lot of fluid. You must keep drinking.* ○ *We sat drinking coffee and chatting for hours.* **2** [I] to drink alcohol: *Don't drink and drive.*
(PHRASAL VERBS) **drink to sb/sth** to wish sb/sth good luck by raising your glass before you drink: *We all drank to the future of the bride and groom.* ☞ Look at **toast**[2].
drink (sth) up to finish drinking sth: *Drink up your tea – it's getting cold.*
▶ **drink** *noun* [C,U] **1** liquid for drinking: *Can I have a drink please?* ○ *a drink of milk* ○ *food and drink* **2** alcoholic drink: *the link between drink and crime* ○ *a strong drink*
▶ **drinker** *noun* [C] a person who drinks alcohol: *a heavy drinker*
▶ **drinking** *noun* [U] drinking alcohol: *Her drinking became a problem.*

'drinking-water *noun* [U] water that is safe to drink

drip /drɪp/ *verb* (**dripp**ing; **dripp**ed) **1** [I] (used about a liquid) to fall in small drops: *Water was dripping down through the roof.* **2** [I,T] to have drops of liquid falling: *The tap is dripping.* ○ *Her finger was dripping blood.*
▶ **drip** *noun* **1** [sing] the act or sound of water dripping: *the drip of a leaky tap* **2** [C] a drop of water that falls down from sb/sth **3** [C] a piece of medical equipment, like a tube, that is used for putting liquid food or medicine directly into a sick person's blood: *She's on a drip.*

☆ **drive**[1] /draɪv/ *verb* (*pt* **drove** /drəʊv/; *pp* **driven** /'drɪvn/) **1** [I,T] to control or operate a car, train, bus, etc: *Can you drive?* ○ *to drive a car, train, bus, lorry* etc **2** [I,T] to go or take sb somewhere in a car, etc: *I usually drive to work.* ○ *We drove Nancy to the airport.* **3** [T] to force people or animals to move in a particular direction: *The dogs drove the sheep into the field.* **4** [T] to force sth into a particular position by hitting it: *to drive a post into the ground* **5** [T] to cause sb to be in a particular state or to do a particular thing: *That noise is driving me mad.* ○ *to drive sb to despair* ○ *His loneliness drove him to commit suicide.* **6** [T] to make sb/sth work very hard: *You shouldn't drive yourself so hard.* **7** [T] to make a machine work, by giving it power: *What drives the wheels in this engine?*
(IDIOMS) **be driving at** (*informal*) to want to say sth; to mean: *I'm afraid I don't understand what you are driving at.*

drive sth home (to sb) to make sth clear so that people understand it
(PHRASAL VERBS) **drive off** (used about a car, driver, etc) to leave
drive sb/sth off to force sb/sth to go back or away: *The defenders drove off each attack.*

'drive-in *noun* [C] (*US*) a place where you can go to eat, watch a film, etc in your car

☆ **drive**[2] /draɪv/ *noun* **1** [C] a journey in a car: *The supermarket is only a five-minute drive away.* ○ *Let's go out for a drive.* **2** [C] a private road that leads to a house **3** [U] the energy and determination you need to succeed in doing sth **4** [C,U] a strong natural need or desire: *a strong sex-drive* **5** [C] a strong effort by a group of people in order to achieve sth: *a sales drive*

driven *pp* of DRIVE[1]

☆ **driver** /'draɪvə(r)/ *noun* [C] a person who drives a vehicle: *One passenger died in the accident but the driver was unhurt.*

☆ **driving**[1] /'draɪvɪŋ/ *noun* [U] the act of controlling a car, etc: *Driving in the fog is very frightening.* ○ *She was arrested for dangerous driving.*

'driving-licence (*US* **'driver's license**) *noun* [C] an official piece of paper that says you are allowed to drive a car, etc. You get this after you have passed a test (**the driving test**).

'driving school *noun* [C] an organization for teaching people to drive a car

driving[2] /'draɪvɪŋ/ *adj* very strong: *driving rain* ○ *Who's the driving force behind this plan?*

drizzle /'drɪzl/ *noun* [U] light rain that has many small drops: *A cloudy day with rain or drizzle is expected.* —**drizzle** *verb* [I] ☞ Look at the note at **weather**.

drone /drəʊn/ *verb* [I] to make a continuous low sound: *the sound of the tractors droning away in the fields*
(PHRASAL VERB) **drone on** to talk in a flat or boring voice
▶ **drone** *noun* [C, usually sing] a continuous low sound

drool /druːl/ *verb* [I] **1** to let liquid (**saliva**) come out from your mouth, usually at the sight or smell of sth good to eat **2 drool (over sb/sth)** to show in a foolish way how much you like or admire sb/sth: *teenagers drooling over photographs of their favourite pop stars*

droop /druːp/ *verb* [I] to bend or hang downwards, eg because of weakness or tiredness: *The flowers were drooping without water.* —**drooping** *adj*: *drooping shoulders* ○ *a drooping moustache*

☆ **drop**[1] /drɒp/ *verb* (**dropp**ing; **dropp**ed) **1** [T] to allow sth to fall: *The helicopters dropped food and medicine.* ○ *That vase was very expensive. Whatever you do don't drop it!* **2** [I] to fall: *The parachutist dropped safely to the ground.* **3** [I,T] to become weaker or lower; to make sth weaker or lower: *The temperature will drop to minus 3 overnight.* ○ *They ought to drop their prices.* ○ *to drop your voice* (= speak more quietly) **4** [T] **drop sb/sth (off)** to stop your car, etc so that sb can get out, or in order to take sth out: *Drop me off at the traffic-lights, please.* ○ *I'll drop the parcel at your house.* **5** [T] to no longer include sb/sth in sth: *Joe has been* *dropped from the team.* **6** [T] to stop doing sth: *I'm going to drop geography next term* (= stop studying it). ○ *Drop everything – I need your help right now!*

(IDIOMS) **drop dead** (*informal*) to die suddenly
drop sb a line to write a letter to sb: *Do drop me a line when you've time.*

(PHRASAL VERBS) **drop back; drop behind (sb)** to move into a position behind sb else, because you are moving more slowly: *Towards the end of the race she dropped behind the other runners.*

drop by/in; drop in on sb to visit sb informally or without having told them you were coming: *We were in the area so we thought we'd drop in and see you.*

drop off (*informal*) to fall into a light sleep: *I must have dropped off in front of the television.*

drop out (of sth) to leave or stop doing sth before you have finished: *His injury forced him to drop out of the competition.* ○ *to drop out of college*

'**drop-out** *noun* [C] **1** a person who leaves school, university, etc before finishing his/her studies **2** a person who does not accept the rules of society and who wants to live in a way that is different from one that most people consider is acceptable

☆ **drop²** /drɒp/ *noun* **1** [C] a small round mass of liquid: *I thought I felt a drop of rain.* **2 drops** [plural] liquid medicine that you put into your eyes, ears or nose **3** [C, usually sing] a small amount of liquid: *I'll just have a drop more wine.* **4** [sing] a vertical distance down from a place: *a sheer drop of 40 metres to the sea* **5** [sing] a smaller amount or level of sth: *The job is much more interesting but it will mean a drop in salary.*

droppings /'drɒpɪŋz/ *noun* [plural] waste material from the bodies of small animals or birds: *rabbit droppings*

drought /draʊt/ *noun* [C,U] a long period of weather which is too dry: *Drought has affected many countries in Africa.*

drove *pt* of DRIVE¹

☆ **drown** /draʊn/ *verb* **1** [I,T] to die in water because it is not possible to breathe; to make sb die in this way: *The girl fell into the river and drowned.* ○ *Twenty people were drowned in the floods.* **2** [T] (used about a sound) to be so loud that you cannot hear sb/sth else: *His answer was drowned by the music.*

drowsy /'draʊzi/ *adj* (**drowsier; drowsiest**) very sleepy: *The heat made me feel drowsy.* —**drowsily** /-əli/ *adv* —**drowsiness** *noun* [U]

drudgery /'drʌdʒəri/ *noun* [U] hard and uninteresting work

☆ **drug** /drʌg/ *noun* [C] **1** a chemical which is used as a medicine: *Some drugs can only be obtained with a prescription from a doctor.* **2** a chemical which people use to give them pleasant or exciting feelings. It is against the law in many countries to use drugs: *hard drugs such as heroin and cocaine*

drug *verb* [T] (**drug**ging; **drug**ged) **1** to give a person or animal a chemical to make them sleepy or unconscious: *The lion was drugged before the start of the journey.* **2** to put a drug into food or drink: *drugged food*

'**drug addict** *noun* [C] a person who cannot stop taking drugs

'**drug addiction** *noun* [U] the state of being a drug addict

druggist /'drʌgɪst/ *noun* [C] (*US*) = CHEMIST(1)

drugstore /'drʌgstɔː(r)/ *noun* [C] (*US*) a shop that sells medicine, soap, shampoo, film, etc as well as drinks and light meals

☆ **drum** /drʌm/ *noun* [C] **1** a round hollow musical instrument, with plastic or skin stretched across the ends. You play a drum by hitting it with your hands or with sticks: *She plays the drums in a band.* ☛ picture at **rock band**. **2** a round hollow container: *an oil drum*

drum *verb* (**drum**ming; **drum**med) **1** [I] to play a drum or drums **2** [I,T] to make a noise like a drum by hitting sth many times: *to drum your fingers on the table* (= because you are annoyed, impatient, etc)

(PHRASAL VERBS) **drum sth into sb** to make sb remember sth by repeating it many times: *Road safety should be drummed into children from an early age.*

drum sth up to try to get more of sth: *to drum up more custom*

drummer *noun* [C] a person who plays a drum or drums

drunk¹ *pp* of DRINK

☆ **drunk²** /drʌŋk/ *adj* (not before a noun) having drunk too much alcohol: *You're drunk!*

drunk *noun* [C] a person who is drunk

drunkard /-əd/ *noun* [C] a person who often gets drunk

drunken /'drʌŋkən/ *adj* (only *before* a noun) **1** having drunk too much alcohol: *drunken drivers* **2** showing the effects of too much alcohol: *drunken singing* —**drunkenly** *adv* —**drunkenness** *noun* [U]

☆ **dry¹** /draɪ/ *adj* (**drier; driest**) **1** without liquid in it or on it; not wet: *The washing isn't dry yet.* ○ *The paint is dry now.* ○ *Rub your hair dry with a towel.* ○ *In the hot weather the stream ran dry.* **2** having little or no rain: *a hot, dry summer* **3** (used about wine) not sweet: *Sweet or dry sherry?* **4** (used of a remark, etc) amusing, although it sounds serious: *a dry sense of humour* **5** dull or boring: *dry legal documents*

drily (*also* **dryly**) /'draɪli/ *adv* in a dry(4) way: *'I can hardly contain my excitement,' Peter said dryly* (= he was not excited at all). —**dryness** *noun* [U]

,**dry-'clean** *verb* [T] to clean clothes using special chemicals, without using water

,**dry-'cleaner's** (*also* **cleaner's**) *noun* [C] the shop where you take your clothes to be cleaned

,**dry 'land** *noun* [U] land, not the sea: *I was glad to be back on dry land again.*

☆ **dry²** /draɪ/ *verb* [I,T] (*pres part* **drying**; *3rd pers sing pres* **dries**; *pt, pp* **dried**) to become dry; to make sth dry: *Leave your swimsuit in the sun to dry.* ○ *to dry your hands on a towel*

(PHRASAL VERBS) **dry (sth) out** (to cause sth wet) to become very dry or too dry: *Don't allow the soil to dry out.*

dry up 1 (used about a river, etc) to have no more water in it **2** to stop being available:

Because of the recession a lot of building work has dried up. **3** to forget what you intended to say, eg because you are very nervous

dry (sth) up to dry plates, knives, forks, etc with a towel after they have been washed

dried adj (used about food) with all the liquid removed from it: *dried milk* o *dried fruit*

drier (also **dryer**) /'draɪə(r)/ noun [C] a machine that you use for drying sth: *a hairdrier* o *a tumble-drier*

dual /'djuːəl; *US* 'duːəl/ adj (only *before* a noun) having two parts; double: *the dual role of mother and working woman* o *to have dual nationality*

dual 'carriageway (*US* **divided highway**) noun [C] a road that has an area of grass or a fence down the middle to separate the traffic going in one direction from the traffic going in the other direction

dub /dʌb/ verb [T] (**dubb**ing; **dubb**ed) **1** to give sb/sth a new or amusing name (**a nickname**): *Margaret Thatcher was dubbed 'The Iron Lady'.* **2** to change the sound in a film so that what the actors said originally is spoken by actors using a different language: *I don't like foreign films when they're dubbed into English. I prefer subtitles.*

dubious /'djuːbɪəs; *US* 'duː-/ adj **1** not sure or certain (**about sth/about doing sth**) not sure or certain: *I'm very dubious about whether we're doing the right thing.* **2** that may not be honest or safe: *dubious financial dealings* —**dubiously** adv

duchess (also **Duchess**) /'dʌtʃɪs/ noun [C] **1** the wife of a duke **2** a woman who is of the same rank as a duke

☆**duck**[1] /dʌk/ noun (pl **duck** or **duck**s) **1** [C] a common bird that lives on or near water. Ducks have short legs, special (**webbed**) feet for swimming and a wide beak. They are kept on farms for their meat and eggs. **2** [C] a female duck

duck

☛ A male duck is called a **drake** and a young duck is a **duckling**. A duck **waddles** and **quacks**.

3 [U] the meat of a duck: *roast duck with orange sauce*

duck[2] /dʌk/ verb **1** [I,T] to move your head down quickly so that you are not seen or hit by sb/sth: *I saw the ball coming towards me and ducked.* **2** [I,T] (*informal*) **duck (out of) sth** to try to avoid sth difficult or unpleasant: *She tried to duck out of apologizing.* **3** [T] to push sb's head under water for a short time, especially when playing

duct /dʌkt/ noun [C] a tube that carries liquid, gas, etc: *They got into the building through the air-duct.* o *tear-ducts* (= in the eye)

dud /dʌd/ noun [C] (*informal*) a thing that is useless or that does not work properly

☆**due**[1] /djuː; *US* duː/ adj **1** (not before a noun) expected or planned to happen or arrive: *The conference is due to start in four weeks' time.* o *What time is the plane due?* **2** (not before a noun) having to be paid: *The rent is due on the fifteenth of each month.* **3** that is owed to you because it is your right to have it: *Make sure you claim all the benefits that are due to you.* **4 due to sb/sth** caused by or because of sb/sth: *His illness is probably due to stress.*
☛ Some careful speakers only use **due to** after the verb **to be**: *The strike was due to poor working conditions.* However, **due to** is often used in the same way as **owing to** and **because of**: *Due to/owing to/because of the bad weather many trains have been cancelled.* **5 due for sth** deserving or expecting to have sth: *I think that I'm due for a pay rise.* **6** (only *before* a noun) (*formal*) suitable or right: *After due consideration I have decided to accept your offer.*

(IDIOM) **in due course** at some time in the future, quite soon: *All applicants will be informed of our decision in due course.*

due[2] /djuː; *US* duː/ noun

(IDIOM) **give sb his/her due** to be fair to a person: *She doesn't work very quickly, but to give her her due, she is very accurate.*

due[3] /djuː; *US* duː/ adv (used before 'north', 'south', 'east' and 'west') exactly: *The aeroplane was flying due east.*

duel /'djuːəl; *US* 'duːəl/ noun [C] a formal type of fight with guns or swords which was used in the past to settle an argument between two men: *to challenge sb to a duel*

duet /dju:'et; *US* du:'et/ (also **duo**) noun [C] a piece of music for two people to sing or play

duffle-coat (also **duffel-coat**) /'dʌflkəʊt/ noun [C] a coat made of heavy woollen cloth with a hood. A duffle-coat has special long buttons (**toggles**).

dug pt, pp of DIG

☆**duke** /djuːk; *US* duːk/ (also **Duke**) noun [C] a nobleman of very high rank: *the Duke of York*
☛ Look at **duchess**.

☆**dull** /dʌl/ adj **1** not bright: *a dull and cloudy day* **2** not loud, sharp or strong: *Her head hit the floor with a dull thud.* o *a dull pain* **3** not interesting or exciting: *Life is never dull in the city.* —**dullness** noun [U]

dully /'dʌl-li/ adv **1** in a dull way **2** showing no interest: *Sheila didn't answer. She just stared dully at me.*

duly /'djuːli; *US* 'duːli/ adv (*formal*) in the correct or expected way: *We all duly assembled at 7.30 as agreed.*

☆**dumb** /dʌm/ adj **1** not able to speak: *to be deaf and dumb* o (*figurative*) *They were struck dumb with amazement.* **2** (*informal*) stupid: *What a dumb thing to do!*

dumbly adv without speaking: *Ken dumbly nodded agreement.*

dumbfounded /dʌm'faʊndɪd/ adj very surprised

dummy /'dʌmi/ noun [C] (pl **dummies**) **1** a model of the human body used for putting clothes on in a shop window or while you are making clothes: *a tailor's dummy* **2** a rubber object that you put in a baby's mouth to keep him/her quiet and happy **3** something that is

iː	ɪ	e	æ	ɑː	ɒ	ɔː	ʊ	uː	ʌ
see	sit	ten	hat	arm	got	saw	put	too	cup

made to look like sth else but that is not the real thing

dummy *adj* made to look like sth else but not the real thing: *dummy bullets*

dump /dʌmp/ *verb* [T] **1** to take sth that you do not want to a place, especially a place which is not suitable, and leave it there: *Nuclear waste should not be dumped in the sea.* ○ *piles of rubbish dumped by the side of the road* **2** to put something down quickly or in a careless way: *The children dumped their coats and bags in the hall and ran off to play.*

dump *noun* [C] **1** a place where rubbish or waste material from factories, etc is left: *the municipal rubbish dump* **2** (*informal*) a place that is very dirty, untidy or unpleasant: *The flat is cheap but it's a real dump.*

dumpling /'dʌmplɪŋ/ *noun* [C] a small ball of fat and flour (**dough**) that is cooked and usually eaten with meat

dumps /dʌmps/ *noun* [plural] (*informal*)
(IDIOM) **down in the dumps** unhappy or depressed

dune /dju:n; *US* du:n/ (*also* **sand-dune**) *noun* [C] a low hill of sand by the sea or in the desert ☛ picture at **beach**.

dung /dʌŋ/ *noun* [U] waste material from the bodies of large animals

dungarees /ˌdʌŋgə'ri:z/ *noun* [plural] a piece of clothing, similar to trousers, but covering your chest as well as your legs and with straps that go over the shoulders: *a pair of dungarees*

dungeon /'dʌndʒən/ *noun* [C] an underground prison, eg in a castle

duo /'dju:əʊ; *US* 'du:əʊ/ *noun* [C] **1** two people playing music or singing together **2** = DUET

dupe /dju:p; *US* du:p/ *verb* [T] (*informal*) to trick sb: *The woman was duped into carrying the drugs.*

duplicate¹ /'dju:plɪkət; *US* 'du:pləkət/ *adj* (only *before* a noun) exactly the same as sth else: *a duplicate key* (= a copy of another key)

duplicate *noun* [C] something that is exactly the same as sth else
(IDIOM) **in duplicate** with two copies (eg of an official piece of paper) that are exactly the same: *The contract must be in duplicate.*

duplicate² /'dju:plɪkeɪt; *US* 'du:pləkeɪt/ *verb* [T] **1** to make an exact copy of sth **2** to do sth that has already been done: *We don't want to duplicate the work of other departments.*
—**duplication** /ˌdju:plɪ'keɪʃn; *US* ˌdu:plə'keɪʃn/ *noun* [U]

durable /'djʊərəbl; *US* 'dʊərəbl/ *adj* that is able to last a long time: *a durable fabric*
—**durability** /ˌdjʊərə'bɪləti; *US* ˌdʊərə'bɪləti/ *noun* [U]

duration /dju'reɪʃn; *US* dʊ'reɪʃn/ *noun* [U] the time that sth lasts: *Please remain seated for the duration of the flight.*

duress /dju'res; *US* dʊ'res/ *noun* [U]
(IDIOM) **under duress** because of the threat of force being used; not willingly: *He signed the confession under duress.*

☆ **during** /'djʊərɪŋ; *US* 'dʊər-/ *prep* **1** for all of a period of time: *The audience must remain seated during the performance.* **2** on more than one occasion in a period of time: *During the summer holidays we went swimming every day.* **3** at some point in a period of time: *Grandpa was taken very ill during the night.* ☛ Notice that you use **during** to say when something happens and **for** to say how long something lasts: *I went shopping during my lunch break. I was out for about 25 minutes.*

dusk /dʌsk/ *noun* [U] the time in the evening when the sun has already gone down and it is nearly dark ☛ Look at **dawn**.

☆ **dust¹** /dʌst/ *noun* [U] a fine dry powder that is made of very small pieces of earth, dirt, etc: *There is dust everywhere in our house.* ○ *a thick layer of dust* ○ *chalk dust* ○ *The tractor came up the track in a cloud of dust.* ○ *a speck* (= small piece) *of dust*

'dustbin (*US* **garbage can**; **trash can**) *noun* [C] a large container for rubbish that you keep outside your house ☛ picture at **bin**.

'dustman /-mən/ (*pl* **dustmen** /-mən/) *noun* [C] a person whose job is to take away the rubbish that people put in their dustbins

'dustpan *noun* [C] a flat container with a handle into which you brush dust or dirt from the floor ☛ picture at **brush**.

☆ **dust²** /dʌst/ *verb* [I,T] to remove dust from furniture, etc with a cloth: *Let me dust those shelves before you put the books on them.* ☛ Look at the note at **clean²**.

duster *noun* [C] a soft cloth that you use for dusting furniture

dusty /'dʌsti/ *adj* (**dustier**; **dustiest**) having a lot of dust: *This shelf has got very dusty.*

Dutch *adj* from the Netherlands ☛ Look at Appendix 5.

dutiful /'dju:tɪfl; *US* 'du:-/ *adj* (*formal*) willing to respect and obey: *a dutiful daughter*

☆ **duty** /'dju:ti; *US* 'du:ti/ *noun* (*pl* **duties**) **1** [C,U] something that you have to do because people expect you to do it or because you think it is right: *A soldier must do his duty.* ○ *a sense of moral duty* ○ *It's your duty to look after your parents when they get older.* **2** [C,U] the tasks that you do when you are at work: *the duties of a policeman* ○ *to be on night duty* (= eg as a nurse) **3** [C] a tax that you pay, especially on goods that you bring into a country
(IDIOM) **on/off duty** (used about doctors, nurses, policemen, etc) to be working/not working: *The porter's on duty from 8 till 4.* ○ *What time does she go off duty?*

ˌduty-'free *adj, adv* (used about goods) that you can bring into a country without paying tax: *an airport duty-free shop* ○ *How much wine can you bring into Britain duty-free?*

duvet /'du:veɪ/ *noun* [C] a thick cover filled with feathers or another soft material that is placed on top of a bed instead of a sheet and blankets ☛ picture at **bed**. Look at **eiderdown** and **quilt**.

dwarf /dwɔ:f/ *noun* [C] (*pl* **dwarfs** or **dwarves** /dwɔ:vz/) **1** a person, animal or plant that is much smaller than the usual size **2** (in children's stories) a very small person, often with special powers: *Snow White and the Seven Dwarfs*

dwarf *verb* [T] (used about a large object) to make sth seem very small in comparison: *The*

dwell /dwel/ verb [I] (*pt, pp* **dwelt** /dwelt/ or **dwelled**) (*old-fashioned formal*) to live or stay in a place
(PHRASAL VERB) **dwell on/upon sth** to think, speak or write about sth for a long time: *I don't want to dwell on the past. Let's think about the future.*

dweller *noun* [C] (often in compounds) a person or animal that lives in the place mentioned: *city-dwellers*

dwelling *noun* [C] (*formal*) the place where a person lives; a house

dwindle /'dwɪndl/ *verb* [I] to become smaller or weaker: *Their savings dwindled away to nothing.*

dye¹ /daɪ/ *verb* [T] (*pres part* **dyeing**; *3rd pers sing pres* **dyes**; *pt, pp* **dyed**) to colour sth, especially by putting it into a liquid: *Does she dye her hair?* ○ *I'm going to dye this blouse black.*

dye² /daɪ/ *noun* [C,U] a substance, usually added to a liquid, that changes the colour of sth, eg cloth, hair

dying *pres part* of DIE

skyscraper dwarfs all the other buildings around.

dyke (*also* **dike**) /daɪk/ *noun* [C] **1** a wall made of earth, etc used for preventing a river or the sea from flooding **2** a channel used for taking water away from land

dynamic /daɪ'næmɪk/ *adj* **1** (used about a person) full of energy and ideas; active **2** (used about a force or power) that causes movement —**dynamism** /'daɪnəmɪzəm/ *noun* [U]

dynamite /'daɪnəmaɪt/ *noun* [U] **1** a type of explosive, used especially in mining **2** a thing or person that causes great excitement, shock, etc: *His news was dynamite.*

dynamo /'daɪnəməʊ/ *noun* [C] (*pl* **dynamos**) a device that changes a type of power such as steam or water into electricity

dynasty /'dɪnəstɪ; *US* 'daɪ-/ *noun* [C] (*pl* **dynasties**) a series of rulers who are from the same family: *the Ming dynasty*

dysentery /'dɪsəntrɪ; *US* -terɪ/ *noun* [U] a serious disease which causes a severe form of diarrhoea

dyslexia /dɪs'leksɪə; *US* dɪs'lekʃə/ *noun* [U] a problem in sb's brain that causes difficulties in reading and spelling —**dyslexic** /dɪs'leksɪk/ *noun* [C], *adj*

Ee

E, e /iː/ *noun* [C] (*pl* **E's; e's**) the fifth letter of the English alphabet: *'Egg' begins with (an) 'E'.*

☆ **each** /iːtʃ/ *det, pron* every one of two or more things or people in a group, when you think about them individually: *Each lesson lasts an hour.* ○ *Each of the lessons lasts an hour.* ○ *The lessons each last an hour.* ○ *He gave each child a present.* ○ *He gave each of the children a present.* ○ *He gave the children a present each.*

each other

He's looking at himself.

They're looking at **each other**.

each 'other (used for saying that sb feels, does or has the same thing as another person/other people in the group): *They loved each other very much.* ○ *We looked at each other.*

☆ **eager** /'iːgə(r)/ *adj* full of desire or interest: *He is eager to meet you.* ○ *eager for success* —**eagerly** *adv* —**eagerness** *noun* [U]

beak

eagle

eagle /'iːgl/ *noun* [C] a very large bird that can see very well. It eats small birds and animals.

☆ **ear¹** /ɪə(r)/ *noun* **1** [C] one of the two parts of the body of a person or animal that are used for hearing: *Elephants have large ears.* ○ *He pulled his hat down over his ears.* ○ *Whisper in my ear!* **2** [sing] **an ear (for sth)** an ability to recognize or appreciate sounds, especially in music or language: *an ear for music*
(IDIOMS) **play (sth) by ear** to play a piece of

p	b	t	d	k	g	tʃ	dʒ	f	v	θ	ð
pen	bad	tea	did	cat	got	chin	June	fall	van	thin	then

music, etc from memory and without using written notes

play it by ear (*informal*) to decide what to do as things happen, instead of planning in advance

prick up your ears ⇨ PRICK²

'earache *noun* [U] a pain in your ear: *I've got earache.* ☛ Look at the note at **ache**.

'eardrum *noun* [C] a thin piece of skin inside the ear that is tightly stretched and that allows you to hear sound

'earphones *noun* [plural] a piece of equipment that fits over the ears and is used for listening to music, the radio, etc

'earring *noun* [C] a piece of jewellery that is worn in or on the lower part of the ear: *Do these earrings clip on or are they for pierced ears?* ☛ picture at **jewellery**.

'earshot *noun* [U]

(IDIOM) **(be) out of/within earshot** where a person cannot/can hear: *Wait until he's out of earshot before you say anything about him.*

ear² /ɪə(r)/ *noun* [C] the top part of a plant that produces grain: *an ear of corn*

earl /ɜːl/ *noun* [C] a British nobleman of high rank ☛ A woman of the same rank is called a **countess**.

☆ **early** /'ɜːli/ (**earlier; earliest**) *adj, adv* **1** near the beginning of a period of time, a piece of work, a series, etc: *Come in the early afternoon.* ○ *I have to get up early on weekday mornings.* ○ *He died in his early twenties.* ○ *The project is still in its early stages.* ○ *The tunnel should be finished early next year.* **2** before the usual or expected time: *She arrived five minutes early for her interview.* ○ *Spring is early this year.*

(IDIOMS) **at the earliest** not before the date or time mentioned: *I can repair it by Friday at the earliest.*

the early hours very early in the morning, ie the hours after midnight

an early/a late night ⇨ NIGHT

early on soon after the beginning: *He achieved fame early on in his career.*

earmark /'ɪəmɑːk/ *verb* [T] **earmark sb/sth (for sth/sb)** to choose sb or keep sth for a particular job or purpose: *She was earmarked as a possible future director.*

☆ **earn** /ɜːn/ *verb* [T] **1** to get money by working: *How much does a dentist earn?* ○ *I earn £20 000 a year.* ○ *He earns his living as an artist.* ○ *How much interest will my savings earn* (= produce) *in the bank?* **2** to get sth that you deserve: *The team's victory today has earned them a place in the final.* ○ *You've earned a holiday.*

earnings *noun* [plural] the money that a person earns by working: *Average earnings have increased by 5%.*

earnest /'ɜːnɪst/ *adj* serious or determined: *He's such an earnest young man – he never makes a joke.* ○ *They were having a very earnest discussion.*

earnest *noun*

(IDIOM) **in earnest 1** serious and sincere about what you are going to do: *His mother was worried that he was in earnest about wanting to leave university.* **2** happening more seriously or with more force than before: *Work began in earnest on the project.*

earnestly *adv* in an earnest way

the earth

northern hemisphere

Arctic Circle
tropic of Cancer
axis
North Pole
line of longitude
equator
tropic of Capricorn
South Pole
line of latitude
Antarctic Circle

southern hemisphere

☆ **earth¹** /ɜːθ/ *noun* **1** (*also* **the earth; the Earth**) [sing] the world; the planet on which we live: *life on earth* ○ *The earth is protected by the ozone layer.* **2** [sing] the surface of the world; land: *The spaceship fell towards earth.* ○ *The earth shook.* **3** [U] soil (that plants grow in): *The earth is very fertile here.* ☛ Look at the note at **ground**.

(IDIOMS) **charge, cost, pay, etc (sb) the earth** (*informal*) to charge, etc a very large amount of money

how, why, where, who, etc on earth/in the world (*informal*) (used for emphasizing sth or expressing surprise): *Where on earth have you been?*

'earthworm *noun* [C] a common type of worm that lives in the soil

earth² /ɜːθ/ (*especially US* **ground**) *verb* [T] to make a piece of electrical equipment safer by connecting it to the ground with a wire: *Make sure the plug is earthed.*

earth *noun* [C, usually sing] (*especially Brit*) (*US* **ground**) a wire that makes a piece of electrical equipment safer by connecting it to the ground: *The green and yellow wire is the earth.*

earthly /'ɜːθli/ *adj* **1** connected with this world, not heaven: *The monks gave up all their earthly possessions.* **2** (often in questions or negatives) possible: *What earthly use is a gardening book to me? I haven't got a garden!*

☆ **earthquake** /'ɜːθkweɪk/ (*also informal* **quake**) *noun* [C] a sudden violent movement of the earth's surface: *Thousands of people were killed and many more left homeless by the earthquake.*

ease¹ /iːz/ *noun* [U] a lack of difficulty: *She answered the questions with ease.* ○ *The ease with which he won the match amazed the spectators.* ☛ Look at **easy**.

(IDIOM) **(be/feel) at (your) ease** to be/feel

s	z	ʃ	ʒ	h	m	n	ŋ	l	r	j	w
so	zoo	she	vision	how	man	no	sing	leg	red	yes	wet

comfortable, relaxed, etc: *They were all so kind and friendly that I felt completely at ease.*

ease² /iːz/ *verb* **1** [I,T] to become or make sth less painful or severe: *The pain should ease by this evening.* ○ *What can I take to ease this headache?* ○ *This money will ease their financial problems a little.* ○ *The tension has eased.* **2** [T] to cause sth to move slowly and gently: *He eased the key into the lock.*

(IDIOM) **ease sb's mind** to make sb feel less worried: *The doctor tried to ease her mind about her son's illness.*

(PHRASAL VERBS) **ease off** to become less severe: *Let's wait until the rain eases off.*

ease up to work less hard: *Ease up a bit or you'll make yourself ill!*

easel /ˈiːzl/ *noun* [C] a wooden frame that holds a blackboard or a picture that is being painted

☆ **east** /iːst/ *noun* [sing] (*abbr* **E**) **1** (*also* **the east**) one of the four main points of the compass; the direction you look towards in order to see the sun rise: *Which way is east?* ○ *a cold wind from the east* ○ *Which county is to the east of Oxfordshire?* ☞ picture at **north**. **2 the east; the East** the part of any country, city, etc that lies further to the east than the other parts: *Norwich is in the East of England.* **3 the East** the countries of Asia, eg China, Japan ☞ Look at **Far East** and **Middle East**.

east (*also* **East**) *adj* in or towards the east, or from the east: *the East Coast of America* ○ *an east wind* ○ *East London*

east *adv* to or towards the east: *They headed east.* ○ *We live east of the city.*

easterly /ˈiːstəli/ *adj* **1** to, towards or in the east: *They travelled in an easterly direction.* **2** (used about winds) coming from the east: *cold easterly winds*

eastward /ˈiːstwəd/ *adj* towards the east: *to travel in an eastward direction*

eastward (*also* **eastwards**) *adv* towards the east: *The Amazon flows eastwards.*

'eastbound *adj* travelling or leading towards the east: *The eastbound carriageway of the motorway is blocked.*

☆ **Easter** /ˈiːstə(r)/ *noun* [U] the Sunday in March or April when Christians celebrate Christ's return to life

'Easter egg *noun* [C] an egg, usually made of chocolate, that you give as a present at Easter

☆ **eastern** (*also* **Eastern**) /ˈiːstən/ *adj* **1** of, in or from the east of a place: *Eastern Scotland* ○ *the eastern shore of the lake* **2** from or connected with the countries of the East: *Eastern cookery* (= that comes from Asia).

☆ **easy¹** /ˈiːzi/ *adj* (**easier; easiest**) **1** not difficult: *an easy question* ○ *It isn't easy to explain the system.* ○ *The system isn't easy to explain.* **2** without any pain, trouble or worry: *an easy life* ○ *My mind's easier now.* ☞ Look at **ease**.

(IDIOMS) **free and easy** ⇒ **FREE¹**

I'm easy (*informal*) I don't mind; whichever you prefer: *'Would you like to go first or second?' 'I'm easy.'*

easily *adv* **1** without difficulty: *I can easily ring up and check the time.* **2** without doubt: *It's easily his best novel.* —**easiness** *noun* [U]

,easy 'chair *noun* [C] a large comfortable chair with arms

,easy'going *adj* (used about a person) calm, relaxed and not easily worried: *Her parents are very easygoing. They let her do what she wants.*

☆ **easy²** /ˈiːzi/ *adv* (**easier; easiest**)

(IDIOMS) **easier said than done** more difficult to do than to talk about: *'You should get her to help you.' 'That's easier said than done.'*

go easy (*informal*) to work less hard: *My doctor advised me to go easy until I'm fully recovered.*

go easy on/with sb/sth (*informal*) **1** to be gentle or less strict with sb: *Go easy on him; he's just a child.* **2** to avoid using too much of sth: *Go easy with the salt; it's bad for your heart.*

take it/things easy to relax and not work too hard or worry too much

☆ **eat** /iːt/ *verb* (*pt* **ate** /et/; *US* eɪt/; *pp* **eaten** /ˈiːtn/) **1** [I,T] to put food into your mouth, then chew and swallow it: *Have you eaten all the biscuits?* ○ *Eat your dinner up, Joe* (= Finish it all). ○ *She doesn't eat properly. No wonder she's so thin.* **2** [I] to have a meal: *What time shall we eat?*

(IDIOM) **have your cake and eat it** ⇒ **CAKE**

(PHRASAL VERBS) **eat sth away/eat away at sth** to damage or destroy sth gradually: *The sea had eaten away at the cliff.*

eat out to have a meal in a restaurant: *Would you like to eat out tonight?*

eater *noun* [C] a person who eats in a particular way: *My uncle's a big eater* (= he eats a lot).

eau-de-cologne /ˌəʊdəkəˈləʊn/ (*also* **cologne**) *noun* [U] a type of perfume that is not very strong

eaves /iːvz/ *noun* [plural] the edges of a roof that come out beyond the walls: *There's a bird's nest under the eaves.*

eavesdrop /ˈiːvzdrɒp/ *verb* [I] (**eavesdropping; eavesdropped**) to listen secretly to other people talking: *They caught her eavesdropping on their conversation.*

ebb /eb/ *verb* [I] **1** (used about the tides of the sea) to go out **2** (used about a feeling, etc) to become weaker: *The crowd's enthusiasm began to ebb.*

ebb *noun* [sing] **the ebb** the time when the tide is flowing away from the shore

(IDIOM) **the ebb and flow (of sth)** (used about a situation, noise, feeling, etc) a regular increase and decrease in the progress or strength of sth

ebony /ˈebəni/ *noun* [U] a hard black wood

eccentric /ɪkˈsentrɪk/ *adj* (used about people or their behaviour) strange or unusual: *People said he was mad but I think he was just slightly eccentric.*

eccentric *noun* [C] an eccentric person: *She is quite an eccentric.* —**eccentricity** /ˌeksenˈtrɪsəti/ *noun* [C,U] (*pl* **eccentricities**)

ecclesiastical /ɪˌkliːziˈæstɪkl/ *adj* connected with the Christian Church: *ecclesiastical law*

echo /ˈekəʊ/ *noun* [C] (*pl* **echoes**) a sound that is repeated as it is sent back off a surface such as the wall of a cave: *'Is anybody there?' she shouted. '...ere,' came back the echo.*

iː	ɪ	e	æ	ɑː	ɒ	ɔː	ʊ	uː	ʌ
see	sit	ten	hat	arm	got	saw	put	too	cup

echo verb **1** [I] (used about a sound) to be repeated; to come back as an echo: *Their footsteps echoed in the empty church.* **2** [T] **echo sth (back)** to repeat or send back a sound: *The tunnel echoed back their calls.* o *(figurative) The child echoed everything his mother said.* **3** [I] **echo (to/with sth)** (used about places) to be full of a particular sound: *The valley echoed with their laughter.*

éclair /ɪˈkleə(r)/ noun [C] a type of long thin cake, usually filled with cream and covered with chocolate

eclipse /ɪˈklɪps/ noun [C] **1** an occasion when the moon passes between the earth and the sun or the earth's shadow falls on the moon, cutting off all or some of the light: *a total/partial eclipse of the sun* **2** the loss of a person's importance, success, etc

eclipse verb [T] **1** (used about the moon, etc) to cause an eclipse of the sun, etc **2** (used about a person) to make another person seem less interesting, important, etc

ecology /iːˈkɒlədʒi/ noun [U] the relations between living things and their surroundings; the study of this subject —**ecological** /ˌiːkəˈlɒdʒɪkl/ adj: *an ecological disaster* o *The Green Party has tried to make people aware of ecological issues.* —**ecologically** adv

ecologist /iːˈkɒlədʒɪst/ noun [C] a expert in ecology

☆**economic** /ˌiːkəˈnɒmɪk; ˌekəˈnɒmɪk/ adj **1** (only *before* a noun) connected with the supply of money, trade, industry, etc: *the government's economic policy* o *The country faces growing economic problems.* **2** producing a profit: *The mine was closed because it was not economic.* ☛ Look at **economical**. It has a different meaning. —**economically** /-klɪ/ adv: *The country was economically very underdeveloped.*

economical /ˌiːkəˈnɒmɪkl; ˌekəˈnɒmɪkl/ adj costing less time, money, fuel, etc; using sth carefully: *an economical car to run* ☛ Look at **economic**. It has a different meaning. —**economically** /-klɪ/ adv: *The train service could be run more economically.*

economics /ˌiːkəˈnɒmɪks; ˌekəˈnɒmɪks/ noun [U] the study or principles of the way money, trade and industry are organized: *a degree in economics* o *the economics of a company*

economist /ɪˈkɒnəmɪst/ noun [C] an expert in economics

economize (also **economise**) /ɪˈkɒnəmaɪz/ verb [I] **economize (on sth)** to save money, time, resources, etc; to use less of sth

☆**economy** /ɪˈkɒnəmi/ noun (pl **economies**) **1** [C] (also **the economy**) the operation of a country's money supply, trade and industry: *The economy of the country is based on agriculture.* o *There are signs of improvement in the economy.* o *the economies of America and Japan* **2** [C,U] careful spending of money, time, resources, etc; trying to save, not waste sth: *Our department is making economies in the amount of paper it uses.* o *For reasons of economy, please turn off all unnecessary lights.* o *economy class* (= the cheapest class of air travel)

ecstasy /ˈekstəsi/ noun [C,U] (pl **ecstasies**) a feeling or state of great happiness: *to be in ecstasy* o *She went into ecstasies about the ring he had bought her.*

ecstatic /ɪkˈstætɪk/ adj extremely happy

ecu (also **ECU**) /ˈekjuː; ˈeɪkjuː/ noun [C] the unit of currency used for trade between member countries of the European Community ☛ Ecu is short for **European Currency Unit.**

ecumenical /ˌiːkjuːˈmenɪkl; ˌekjuː-/ adj connected with the idea of uniting all the different parts of the Christian Church

eczema /ˈeksɪmə; *US* ɪgˈziːmə/ noun [U] a disease which makes the skin red and itchy

eddy /ˈedi/ noun [C] (pl **eddies**) a circular movement of water, wind, dust, etc

☆**edge¹** /edʒ/ noun [C] **1** the place where sth, especially a surface, ends; the limit: *the edge of a table* o *The leaves were brown and curling at the edges.* o *I stood at the water's edge.* o *to fall off the edge of a cliff* **2** the sharp cutting part of a knife, etc

(IDIOMS) **an/the edge on/over sb/sth** a slight advantage over sb/sth: *She knew she had the edge over the other candidates.*

(be) on edge to be nervous, excited or quick to lose your temper: *I'm a bit on edge because I get my exam results today.* ☛ Look at **edgy**. It has a similar meaning.

edge² /edʒ/ verb **1** [T] (usually passive) **edge sth (with sth)** to arrange sth along the edge of sth else: *The cloth was edged with lace.* **2** [I,T] **edge (sth/your way) across, along, away, back, etc** to move slowly and carefully across, etc: *The burglar edged his way along the roof.* o *We edged closer to get a better view.* o *She edged her chair up to the window.*

edgeways /ˈedʒweɪz/ (also **edgewise** /ˈedʒwaɪz/) adv

(IDIOM) **get a word in edgeways** ⇨ WORD

edgy /ˈedʒi/ adj (informal) nervous, worried or quick to become upset: *You seem very edgy. What's bothering you?*

edible /ˈedɪbl/ adj good or safe to eat: *Are these mushrooms edible?* ☛ The opposite is **inedible**.

edifice /ˈedɪfɪs/ noun [C] (formal) a large impressive building

edit /ˈedɪt/ verb [T] **1** to prepare a piece of writing to be published, making sure that it is correct, the right length, etc **2** to prepare a film, television or radio programme by arranging filmed material in a particular order **3** to be in charge of a newspaper, magazine, etc

edition /ɪˈdɪʃn/ noun [C] **1** the form in which a book is published: *a paperback/hardback edition* **2** one of a series of television or radio programmes: *And now for this week's edition of 'Panorama'...* **3** the number of copies of a book, etc that are printed at the same time: *the morning edition of a newspaper*

☆**editor** /ˈedɪtə(r)/ noun [C] **1** a person whose job is to prepare a book, television or radio programme **2** the person who is in charge of a newspaper or part of a newspaper: *the financial editor* o *Who is the editor of 'The Times'?*

editorial /ˌedɪˈtɔːriəl/ noun [C] an article in a newspaper, usually written by the editor, giving an opinion on an important subject

ɜː	ə	eɪ	əʊ	aɪ	aʊ	ɔɪ	ɪə	eə	ʊə
fur	ago	pay	home	five	now	join	near	hair	pure

educate /'edʒukeɪt/ verb [T] to teach or train sb, especially in school: *Young people should be educated to care for their environment.* ○ *All their children were educated in public schools.*

educated /'edʒukeɪtɪd/ adj having learnt a lot of things to a high standard: *a highly educated woman*

☆ **education** /,edʒu'keɪʃn/ noun [C, usually sing, U] the teaching or training of people, especially in schools, etc to improve their knowledge and develop their skills: *primary, secondary, higher, adult education* ○ *She received an excellent education.*

educational /-ʃənl/ adj connected with or providing education: *an educational toy, visit, experience, etc*

eel /iːl/ noun [C] a long fish that looks like a snake

eerie (*also* **eery**) /'ɪəri/ adj strange and frightening —**eerily** adv —**eeriness** noun [U]

☆ **effect** /ɪ'fekt/ noun **1** [C,U] **(an) effect (on sb/sth)** a change that is caused by sth; a result: *the effects of acid rain on the lakes and forests* ○ *His words had a strong effect on me.* ○ *Her shouting had little or no effect on him.* ☞ Look at **after-effect** and **side-effect**. **2** [C,U] the impression that a speaker, book, film, etc gives: *How does the artist create the effect of moonlight?* ○ *He likes to say things just for effect* (= to impress people). **3 effects** (*formal*) your personal possessions

(IDIOMS) **come into effect** (used especially about laws or rules) to begin to be used; to come into operation

in effect 1 in fact; for all practical purposes: *Though they haven't made an official announcement, she is, in effect, the new director.* **2** (used about a rule, a law, etc) in operation; in use: *The new rules will be in effect from next season.*

take effect 1 (used about a drug, etc) to begin to work; to produce the desired result: *The anaesthetic took effect immediately.* **2** (used about a law, etc) to come into operation: *The cease-fire takes effect from midnight.*

to this/that effect with this/that meaning: *I told him to leave her alone, or words to that effect.*

effect verb [T] (*formal*) to cause sth to happen; to have sth as a result: *to effect a change* ☞ Look at **affect**. It has a different meaning.

☆ **effective** /ɪ'fektɪv/ adj **1** producing the result that you want: *Scientists are looking for an effective way to reduce energy consumption.* ○ *a medicine that is effective against the common cold* ☞ The opposite is **ineffective**. **2** making a pleasing impression: *That picture would look more effective on a dark background.* **3** real or actual, although perhaps not official: *The soldiers gained effective control of the town.*

effectively adv **1** in a effective way: *She dealt with the situation effectively.* **2** in effect; for practical purposes: *It meant that, effectively, they had lost.* —**effectiveness** noun [U]

effeminate /ɪ'femɪnət/ adj (used about a man or his behaviour) like a woman

☆ **efficient** /ɪ'fɪʃnt/ adj able to work well without making mistakes or wasting time and energy: *Our secretary is very efficient.* ○ *You must find a more efficient way of organizing your time.* ☞ The opposite is **inefficient**. —**efficiency** /ɪ'fɪʃnsi/ noun [U] —**efficiently** adv

☆ **effort** /'efət/ noun **1** [U] the use of strength or energy: *They have put a lot of effort into their garden this summer.* ○ *He made no effort to contact his parents.* **2** [C] something that is done with difficulty or the use of energy: *It was a real effort to stay awake in the lecture.*

effortless /'efətləs/ adj (apparently) needing little or no effort —**effortlessly** adv

egalitarian /ɪ,gælɪ'teəriən/ adj (used about a person, system, society, etc) following the principle that everyone should have equal rights

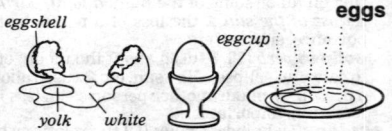

eggs

eggshell
eggcup
yolk   white
a boiled egg   a fried egg

☆ **egg¹** /eg/ noun **1** [C] an oval object with a hard shell that contains a young bird, reptile or insect ☞ A female bird **lays** her eggs and then **sits on** them until they **hatch**. **2** [C,U] an egg from a hen, etc, used as food: *Would you like bacon and eggs for breakfast?* ☞ Eggs may be **boiled**, **fried**, **poached** (cooked in water without their shells) or **scrambled**. **3** [C] the small seed in a female animal that can join with a male seed (**a sperm**) to make a baby

(IDIOM) **put all your eggs in one basket** to risk everything by depending completely on one thing, plan, etc

'eggcup noun [C] a small cup for holding a boiled egg

'eggplant noun [C,U] (*especially US*) = AUBERGINE

'eggshell noun [C,U] the hard outside part of an egg

egg² /eg/ verb
(PHRASAL VERB) **egg sb on (to do sth)** to encourage sb to do sth (bad or dangerous)

ego /'egəʊ; *US* 'iːgəʊ/ noun [C] (*pl* **egos**) the (good) opinion that you have of yourself: *It was a blow to her ego when she lost her job.*

egocentric /,egəʊ'sentrɪk; *US* ,iːg-/ adj interested only in yourself; selfish

egoism /'egəʊɪzəm; *US* 'iːg-/ noun [U] thinking about yourself too much; selfishness

egoist /-ɪst/ noun [C] a person who thinks about himself/herself too much; a selfish person —**egoistic** /,egəʊ'ɪstɪk; *US* ,iːg-/ adj

eh /eɪ/ *interj* (*informal*) **1** (used for asking sb to agree with you): *'Good party, eh?'* **2** (used for asking sb to repeat sth): *'Did you like the film?' 'Eh?' 'I asked if you liked the film!'*

eiderdown /'aɪdədaʊn/ noun [C] a covering for a bed filled with soft feathers (**down**), usually used on top of blankets ☞ Look at **duvet**.

☆ **eight** /eɪt/ *number* 8; one more than seven ☞ For examples of how to use numbers in sentences, look at **six**.

p	b	t	d	k	g	tʃ	dʒ	f	v	θ	ð
pen	bad	tea	did	cat	got	chin	June	fall	van	thin	then

eight- (in compounds) having eight of sth: *an eight-sided coin*

eighth /eɪtθ/ *pron, det, adv* 8th; next after seventh

eighth *noun* [C] the fraction ⅛; one of eight equal parts of sth ☛ Look at the examples at **sixth**.

☆ **eighteen** /ˌeɪˈtiːn/ *number* 18; one more than seventeen ☛ For examples of how to use numbers in sentences, look at **six**.

eighteenth /ˌeɪˈtiːnθ/ *pron, det, adv* 18th; next after seventeenth ☛ Look at the examples at **sixth**.

☆ **eighty** /ˈeɪti/ *number* 80; one more than seventy-nine ☛ For examples of how to use numbers in sentences, look at **sixty**.

eightieth /ˈeɪtiəθ/ *pron, det, adv* 80th; next after seventy-ninth ☛ Look at the examples at **sixth**.

☆ **either** /ˈaɪðə(r); ˈiːðər/ *det, pron* **1** one or the other of two; it does not matter which: *There's cake or ice-cream. You can have either.* ○ *You can ask either of us for advice.* ○ *Either of us is willing to help.* ☛ **Either** is used with a singular verb but in spoken informal English a plural verb can be used after **either of** and a plural noun: *Either of us are willing to help.* **2** both: *It is a pleasant road, with trees on either side.*

either *conj* **either... or...** (used when you are giving a choice, usually of two things): *You can have the car in either black or blue.* ○ *Either you leave or I do.* ○ *You can either write or phone.*

either *adv* **1** (used after two negative statements) also: *I don't like Pat and I don't like Nick much either.* ○ *'I can't remember his name.' 'I can't either.'* ☛ We can also say **neither can** I. **2** (used for emphasizing a negative statement): *The restaurant is quite good. And it's not expensive either.*

ejaculate /ɪˈdʒækjʊleɪt/ *verb* **1** [I] to send out liquid (**semen**) from the penis **2** [I,T] (*formal*) to say sth suddenly —**ejaculation** /ɪˌdʒækjʊˈleɪʃn/ *noun* [C,U]

eject /ɪˈdʒekt/ *verb* **1** [T] (often passive) to push or send sb/sth out of a place (usually with force): *The protesters were ejected from the building.* **2** [I] to make an emergency exit from an aeroplane

eke /iːk/ *verb*
(IDIOM) **eke out a living** to manage to live with very little money
(PHRASAL VERB) **eke sth out** to make a small amount of sth last longer

elaborate /ɪˈlæbərət/ *adj* very complicated; done or made very carefully: *elaborate plans*

elaborate /ɪˈlæbəreɪt/ *verb* [I] **elaborate (on sth)** (*formal*) to give details about sth

elapse /ɪˈlæps/ *verb* [I] (*formal*) (used about time) to pass

elastic /ɪˈlæstɪk/ *noun* [U] material with rubber in it which can stretch

elastic *adj* **1** (used about material, etc) able to return to its original size after being stretched **2** (*figurative*) able to be changed; not fixed: *Our rules are quite elastic.*

eˌlastic ˈband *noun* [C] = RUBBER BAND

elated /ɪˈleɪtɪd/ *adj* (*formal*) very happy and excited —**elation** /ɪˈleɪʃn/ *noun* [U]

☆ **elbow** /ˈelbəʊ/ *noun* [C] **1** the joint where the arm bends in the middle ☛ picture on page A8. **2** the part of the sleeve of a coat, jacket, etc that covers the elbow

elbow *verb* [T] to push with the elbows: *She elbowed me out of the way to get to the food first.*

ˈelbow-room *noun* [U] enough space to move freely

☆ **elder** /ˈeldə(r)/ *adj* (only *before* a noun) older (of two members of a family): *My elder daughter is at university now but the other one is still at school.*

elder *noun* **1** [sing] the older of two people: *Who is the elder of the two?* **2 my, etc elder** [sing] a person who is older than me, etc: *He is her elder by several years.* **3 elders** [plural] older people: *Do children still respect the opinions of their elders?*

elderly /ˈeldəli/ *adj* (used about a person) old ☛ This is a polite way of saying 'old'. You can use **the elderly** to refer to old people in general: *The elderly need special care in winter.*

☆ **eldest** /ˈeldɪst/ *adj, noun* [C] oldest (of three or more members of a family): *Their eldest child is a boy.* ○ *John's got 4 boys. The eldest has just gone to university.*

☆ **elect** /ɪˈlekt/ *verb* [T] **1 elect sb (to sth)**; **elect sb (as sth)** to choose a Member of Parliament, President, representative, etc by voting: *He was elected to Parliament in 1970.* ○ *The committee elected her as their representative.* **2 elect to do sth** (*formal*) to decide to do sth

☆ **election** /ɪˈlekʃn/ *noun* [C,U] (the time of) choosing a Member of Parliament, President, etc by voting: *In America, presidential elections are held every four years.* ○ *I will not be standing for election again.* ○ *election results*

☛ In Britain, **general elections** are held about every five years. Sometimes **by-elections** are held at other times. In each region (**constituency**) voters must choose one from a list of **candidates**.

elector /ɪˈlektə(r)/ *noun* [C] a person who has the right to vote in an election ☛ **Voter** is a more common word. —**electoral** /ɪˈlektərəl/ *adj*: *the electoral register/roll* (= the list of electors in an area)

electorate /ɪˈlektərət/ *noun* [C, with sing or pl verb] all the people who can vote in a region, country, etc

☆ **electric** /ɪˈlektrɪk/ *adj* **1** producing or using electricity: *an electric current* ○ *an electric kettle* **2** (*figurative*) very emotional: *The atmosphere in the room was electric.*

the eˌlectric ˈchair *noun* [sing] a chair used for putting criminals to death with a very strong electric current

eˌlectric ˈrazor = SHAVER

eˌlectric ˈshock (also **shock**) *noun* [C] the effect on the body when an electric current goes through it: *That light switch isn't safe. I got a shock when I touched it.*

☆ **electrical** /ɪˈlektrɪkl/ *adj* of or about electricity: *an electrical fault* ○ *an electrical appliance* (= a machine that uses electricity) ○ *an electrical engineer* (= a person who produces electrical systems and equipment)

s	z	ʃ	ʒ	h	m	n	ŋ	l	r	j	w
so	zoo	she	vision	how	man	no	sing	leg	red	yes	wet

☆ **electrician** /ɪˌlek'trɪʃn/ noun [C] a person whose job is to install and repair electrical systems and equipment

☆ **electricity** /ɪˌlek'trɪsəti/ noun [U] a type of energy that provides heat, light and power to work machines, etc: *Turn that light off. We don't want to waste electricity.*

☛ Electricity is usually **generated** in **power stations**. It may also be produced by **generators** or by **batteries** (eg in personal stereos).

electrify /ɪ'lektrɪfaɪ/ verb [T] (pres part **electrifying**; 3rd pers sing pres **electrifies**; pt, pp **electrified**) **1** to supply sth with electricity: *The railways are being electrified as quickly as possible.* **2** (figurative) to make sb excited

electrocute /ɪ'lektrəkju:t/ verb [T] (usually passive) to kill sb with an electric current that passes through the body: *Don't touch that wire! You'll electrocute yourself.* —**electrocution** /ɪˌlektrə'kju:ʃn/ noun [U]

electrode /ɪ'lektrəʊd/ noun [C] one of two points (**terminals**) where an electric current enters or leaves a battery, etc

☆ **electronic** /ɪˌlek'trɒnɪk/ adj using electronics: *electronic equipment* ○ *This dictionary is available in electronic form* (= on a computer disk). —**electronically** /-klɪ/ adv
electronic 'mail (*also* **email, e-mail**) noun [U] sending information using a computer

electronics /ɪˌlek'trɒnɪks/ noun [U] the technology of using silicon chips, etc to produce computers, radios, etc: *the electronics industry*

elegant /'elɪɡənt/ adj showing style or good design: *She looked very elegant in her new dress.* ○ *an elegant coat* —**elegance** /'elɪɡəns/ noun [U] —**elegantly** adv

☆ **element** /'elɪmənt/ noun **1** [C] one important part of sth: *Cost is an important element when we're thinking about holidays.* **2** [C, usually sing] **an element of sth** a small amount of sth: *There was an element of truth in what he said.* **3** [C] people of a certain type: *The criminal element at football matches causes a lot of trouble.* **4** [C] one of the basic substances eg water, oxygen, gold, etc **5** [C] the part of a kettle, an electric heater, etc that produces heat **7 the elements** [plural] (*formal*) (bad) weather: *exposed to the elements*
(IDIOM) **in/out of your element** in a situation where you feel comfortable/uncomfortable

☆ **elementary** /ˌelɪ'mentri/ adj **1** at or in the beginning stages: *an elementary course in English* ○ *a book for elementary students* **2** basic; not difficult: *elementary physics*
ele'mentary school noun [C] (US) a school for children aged six to eleven

☆ **elephant** /'elɪfənt/ noun [C] a very large grey animal with two long curved teeth (**tusks**) and a long nose (**a trunk**)

elevate /'elɪveɪt/ verb [T] (*formal*) to raise sb/sth to a higher place or position: *an elevated railway* ○ *He was elevated to the Board of Directors.*
elevating adj (*formal*) improving the mind; educating: *an elevating book*

elevation /ˌelɪ'veɪʃn/ noun **1** [C,U] (*formal*) elevating or being elevated **2** [C] the height of a place (above sea-level): *The city is at an elevation of 2 000 metres.*

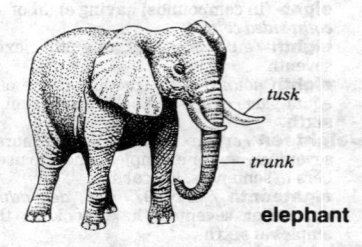

elevator /'elɪveɪtə(r)/ noun [C] (US) = LIFT

☆ **eleven** /ɪ'levn/ number 11, one more than ten
☛ For examples of how to use numbers in sentences, look at **six**.
eleventh /ɪ'levnθ/ pron, det, adv 11th, next after tenth ☛ Look at the examples at **sixth**.

elf /elf/ noun [C] (pl **elves** /elvz/) (in stories) a small creature with pointed ears who has magic powers

elicit /ɪ'lɪsɪt/ verb [T] **elicit sth (from sb)** (*formal*) to get information, facts, a reaction, etc from sb

eligible /'elɪdʒəbl/ adj **eligible (for sth/to do sth)** having the right qualifications for sth; suitable: *In Britain, you are eligible to vote when you are eighteen.* ○ *an eligible young man* (= a man who might be a suitable husband)

eliminate /ɪ'lɪmɪneɪt/ verb [T] **1** to remove sb/sth that is not wanted or needed: *We must try and eliminate wastage.* **2** (often passive) to stop sb going further in a competition, etc: *The school team was eliminated in the first round of the competition.* —**elimination** /ɪˌlɪmɪ'neɪʃn/ noun [U]

élite /eɪ'li:t/ noun [C, with sing or pl verb] a social group that is thought to be the best or most important because of its power, money, intelligence, etc: *the ruling élite* ○ *an intellectual élite* ○ *an élite group*
élitism /eɪ'li:tɪzəm/ noun [U] the belief that élites should be treated in a special way —**élitist** /-tɪst/ noun [C], adj

elk /elk/ (US **moose**) noun [C] a very large deer with large flat horns (**antlers**)

elm /elm/ (*also* **'elm tree**) noun [C] a tall tree with broad leaves

elocution /ˌelə'kju:ʃn/ noun [U] the art of speaking clearly (especially in public)

elongated /'i:lɒŋɡeɪtɪd; US ɪ'lɔ:ŋ-/ adj long and thin

elope /ɪ'ləʊp/ verb [I] **elope (with sb)** to run away secretly to get married: *She eloped with one of her students.*

eloquent /'eləkwənt/ adj (*formal*) able to speak well and influence other people —**eloquence** /'eləkwəns/ noun [U] —**eloquently** adv

☆ **else** /els/ adv (used after words formed with *any-, no-, some-* and after question words) **1** in addition: *What else would you like?* ○ *Does anybody else* (= any other person) *know about this?* **2** different: *There's nothing on the television. Let's find something else to do.* ○ *This isn't mine.*

i:	ɪ	e	æ	ɑ:	ɒ	ɔ:	ʊ	u:	ʌ
see	sit	ten	hat	arm	got	saw	put	too	cup

elsewhere / **emotion**

It must be somebody else's (= belong to another person). ○ You'll have to pay. Nobody else (= no other person) will. **3** apart from: Everybody else (= everybody apart from me) is allowed to stay up late.
(IDIOM) **or else** otherwise; if not: You'd better go to bed now or else you'll be tired in the morning. ○ He's either forgotten or else he's decided not to come.

☆ **elsewhere** /ˌels'weə(r); US -'hweər/ adv (formal) in or to another place: If she doesn't like it here, she can go elsewhere. ○ He's travelled a lot – in Europe and elsewhere.

elude /ɪ'luːd/ verb [T] (formal) **1** to escape (from sb/sth) (sometimes by using a trick) **2** to be difficult or impossible to remember: I remember his face but his name eludes me.

elusive /ɪ'luːsɪv/ adj not easy to find, catch or remember

elves pl of ELF

'em /əm/ pron (informal) = THEM

emaciated /ɪ'meɪʃɪeɪtɪd/ adj (used about a person) thin and weak because of illness, lack of food, etc —**emaciation** /ɪˌmeɪsɪ'eɪʃn/ noun [U]

email (also **e-mail**) /'iːmeɪl/ noun [U] = ELECTRONIC MAIL

emancipate /ɪ'mænsɪpeɪt/ verb [T] to give sb the same legal, social and political rights as other people —**emancipation** /ɪˌmænsɪ'peɪʃn/ noun [U]

embankment /ɪm'bæŋkmənt/ noun [C] a thick wall of earth, stone, etc that is built to stop a river overflowing or to carry a road or railway

embargo /ɪm'bɑːgəʊ/ noun [C] (pl **embargoes**) an official order to stop trade with another country: to impose an oil embargo ○ to lift/remove the embargo on the trade in oil

embark /ɪm'bɑːk/ verb [I] to get on a ship: Passengers with cars must embark first. ☛ The opposite is **disembark**.
(PHRASAL VERB) **embark on sth** (formal) to start sth (new): I'm embarking on a completely new career. —**embarkation** /ˌembɑː'keɪʃn/ noun [C,U]

☆ **embarrass** /ɪm'bærəs/ verb [T] to make sb feel ashamed or uncomfortable: She was very embarrassed when her child behaved badly in public. ○ He felt really embarrassed to be seen in odd socks. ○ The Minister's mistake embarrassed the government. —**embarrassing** adj —**embarrassingly** adv

embarrassment noun **1** [U] the feeling you have when you are embarrassed **2** [C] a person or thing that makes you embarrassed

☆ **embassy** /'embəsi/ noun [C] (pl **embassies**) (the official building of) a group of people (**diplomats**) headed by an ambassador, who are sent to live in a foreign country and represent their government there ☛ Look at **consulate**.

embed /ɪm'bed/ verb [T] (**embedding**; **embedded**) (usually passive) to fix sth firmly and deeply (in sth else): The axe was embedded in the piece of wood.

embezzle /ɪm'bezl/ verb [T] to steal money, etc that you are responsible for (eg in a firm or organization)

emblem /'embləm/ noun [C] an object or symbol that represents sth: The dove is the emblem of peace.

embody /ɪm'bɒdi/ verb [T] (pres part **embodying**; 3rd pers sing pres **embodies**; pp, pt **embodied**) (formal) **1** to be a very good example of sth: To me she embodies all the best qualities of a teacher. **2** to include or contain sth: This latest model embodies many new features.

embrace /ɪm'breɪs/ verb **1** [I,T] to take sb into your arms as a sign of love or affection **2** [T] (formal) to include: His report embraced all the main points. **3** [T] (formal) to accept sth eagerly: She embraced Christianity in her later years.

embrace noun [C] the act of embracing(1)

embroider /ɪm'brɔɪdə(r)/ verb **1** [I,T] to decorate cloth by sewing with small stitches: She embroidered flowers on the cushion in gold thread. **2** [T] to add untrue details to a story, etc to make it more interesting

embroidery /-dəri/ noun [U] decorative sewing with small stitches; something that has been embroidered(1)

embryo /'embriəʊ/ noun [C] (pl **embryos** /-əʊz/) an animal or a plant in the early stages of development before birth ☛ Look at **foetus**. —**embryonic** /ˌembrɪ'ɒnɪk/ adj

emerald /'emərəld/ noun [C] a bright green precious stone

emerald (also **emerald 'green**) adj bright green

emerge /ɪ'mɜːdʒ/ verb [I] **emerge (from sth)** **1** to appear or come from somewhere (unexpectedly): A man emerged from the shadows. ○ (figurative) to emerge strengthened from a difficult experience **2** to become known: During investigations it emerged that she was lying about her age. —**emergence** /-dʒəns/ noun [U] —**emergent** /-dʒənt/ adj

☆ **emergency** /ɪ'mɜːdʒənsi/ noun [C,U] (pl **emergencies**) a serious event that needs immediate action: In an emergency phone 999 for help. ○ The government has declared a state of emergency. ○ an emergency exit

e'mergency room noun [C] (US) = CASUALTY(3)

emigrate /'emɪgreɪt/ verb [I] to leave your own country to go and live in another: They emigrated to Australia twenty years ago.

emigrant /'emɪgrənt/ noun [C] a person who has gone to live in another country —**emigration** /ˌemɪ'greɪʃn/ noun [C,U] ☛ Look at **immigrant** and **immigration**.

eminent /'emɪnənt/ adj (formal) (used about a person) famous and important: an eminent scientist

eminently adv obviously; very: She is eminently suitable for the job.

emit /ɪ'mɪt/ verb [T] (**emitting**; **emitted**) (formal) to send out sth (a smell, a sound, smoke, heat, light, etc) —**emission** /ɪ'mɪʃn/ noun [C,U]: controls on sulphur dioxide emissions from power stations

☆ **emotion** /ɪ'məʊʃn/ noun **1** [C] a strong feeling such as love, anger, fear, jealousy, etc **2** [U]

3ː	ə	eɪ	əʊ	aɪ	aʊ	ɔɪ	ɪə	eə	ʊə
fur	ago	pay	home	five	now	join	near	hair	pure

emotive strength of feeling: *His voice was filled with emotion.*

emotional /-ʃənl/ *adj* **1** connected with the emotions: *emotional problems* **2** causing strong feelings: *He gave an emotional speech* **3** having strong emotions and showing them openly: *She always gets very emotional when I leave.* ○ *He's a very emotional sort of person* (= his moods change suddenly). —**emotionally** /-ʃənəli/ *adv*

emotive /ɪˈməʊtɪv/ *adj* causing strong emotions: *emotive language* ○ *an emotive issue*

empathy /ˈempəθi/ *noun* [U] the ability to imagine how another person is feeling and so understand his/her mood

emperor /ˈempərə(r)/ *(feminine* **empress**) *noun* [C] the ruler of an empire

☆**emphasis** /ˈemfəsɪs/ *noun* [C,U] *(pl* **emphases** /-əsiːz/) **1** the force that you give to a word or phrase when you are speaking to show that it is important **2 emphasis (on sth)** (giving) special importance or attention (to sth): *There's a lot of emphasis on science at our school.* ○ *We should really put a greater emphasis on getting our facts right.*

☆**emphasize** *(also* **emphasise**) /ˈemfəsaɪz/ *verb* [T] **emphasize (that...)** to put emphasis on sth; stress: *They emphasized that healthy eating is important.* ○ *They emphasized the importance of healthy eating.*

emphatic /ɪmˈfætɪk/ *adj* having or using emphasis: *an emphatic refusal* —**emphatically** /-klɪ/ *adv*

empire /ˈempaɪə(r)/ *noun* [C] **1** a group of countries that is governed by one country: *the Roman Empire* ☞ Look at **emperor** and **empress**. **2** a group of companies that is controlled by one parent company

empirical /ɪmˈpɪrɪkl/ *adj* (*formal*) based on observation and practical experience, not on theory: *empirical evidence*

☆**employ** /ɪmˈplɔɪ/ *verb* [T] **1 employ sb (in/on sth)**; **employ sb (as sth)** to pay sb to work for you: *He is employed in a chocolate factory.* ○ *She is employed as a lorry driver.* ○ *They employ 600 workers.* ☞ Look at **unemployed**. **2 employ sb/sth (in/on) sth** (*formal*) to use: *We must employ all our expertise in solving this problem.*

employee /ˌemplɔɪˈiː; ɪmˈplɔɪiː/ *noun* [C] a person who works for sb: *The factory has 500 employees.*

employer /ɪmˈplɔɪə(r)/ *noun* [C] a person or company that employs other people: *The car factory is a large employer in this town.*

employment /ɪmˈplɔɪmənt/ *noun* [U] **1** the state of having a paid job: *She is in/out of employment.* ○ *This bank can give employment to ten extra staff.* ○ *It is difficult to find employment in the north of the country.* ☞ Look at **unemployment** and at the note at **work¹**. **2** (*formal*) the use of sth: *the employment of force*

em'ployment agency *noun* [C] a business that helps people to find work

empower /ɪmˈpaʊə(r)/ *verb* [T] (usually passive) (*formal*) to give sb power or authority (to do sth)

empress /ˈemprɪs/ *noun* [C] **1** a woman who rules an empire **2** the wife or widow of an emperor

☆**empty¹** /ˈempti/ *adj* **1** having nothing or nobody inside it: *an empty box* ○ *The bus was half empty.* ○ *That house has been empty for months.* **2** without meaning or value: *It was an empty threat* (= it was not meant seriously). ○ *My life feels empty now the children have left home.* —**emptiness** /ˈemptinəs/ *noun* [U]

ˌempty-ˈhanded *adj* bringing or taking nothing: *She went out to buy a new dress but returned empty-handed.*

☆**empty²** /ˈempti/ *verb* (*pres part* **emptying**; *3rd pers sing pres* **empties**; *pt, pp* **emptied**) **1** [T] **empty sth (out)** to make sth empty: *'Where can I empty my cup?' 'Oh, empty it into the sink.'* ○ *Empty your pockets out, please.* **2** [T] **empty sth (out) (into/onto sth)** to take sth from a container and put it somewhere else: *Empty that milk into the sink. It's gone sour.* ○ *The boy emptied out all his toys onto the floor.* **3** [I] to become empty: *The cinema emptied very quickly once the film was finished.*

emulate /ˈemjuleɪt/ *verb* [T] (*formal*) to try to do sth as well as, or better than, sb ☞ A less formal word is **copy**.

☆**enable** /ɪˈneɪbl/ *verb* [T] **enable sb/sth to do sth** to make sb/sth able to do sth (by giving him/her/it power, authority, etc): *The new law has enabled more women to return to work.*

enamel /ɪˈnæml/ *noun* [U] **1** a hard, shiny substance used for protecting or decorating metal, etc: *enamel paint* **2** the hard white outer covering of a tooth

enchanted /ɪnˈtʃɑːntɪd; *US* -ˈtʃænt-/ *adj* **1** pleased or delighted: *The audience was enchanted by her singing.* **2** under a magic spell: *an enchanted forest*

enchanting /ɪnˈtʃɑːntɪŋ; *US* -ˈtʃænt-/ *adj* very nice or pleasant; delightful

encircle /ɪnˈsɜːkl/ *verb* [T] (*formal*) to make a circle round sth; to surround: *London is encircled by the M25 motorway.*

☆**enclose** /ɪnˈkləʊz/ *verb* [T] **1 enclose sth (in/with sth)** to surround sth with a wall, fence, etc: *The garden is enclosed by a high hedge.* ○ *He gets very nervous in enclosed spaces.* **2** to put sth in an envelope, parcel, etc: *Can I enclose a letter with this parcel?*

enclosure /ɪnˈkləʊʒə(r)/ *noun* [C] **1** a piece of land that is enclosed by a wall, fence, etc **2** something that is enclosed in an envelope, parcel, etc

encore /ˈɒŋkɔː(r)/ *interj* (called out by an audience that wants the performers in a play, concert, etc to perform sth extra)

encore *noun* [C] (a call for) an extra performance at the end of a play, concert, etc

encounter /ɪnˈkaʊntə(r)/ *verb* [T] **1** (*formal*) to meet sb unexpectedly **2** to experience sth (a danger, difficulty, etc): *I've never encountered any discrimination at work.* ☞ **Meet with** is used as a synonym for encounter in this sense.

encounter *noun* [C] an unexpected (often unpleasant) meeting

☆**encourage** /ɪnˈkʌrɪdʒ/ *verb* [T] **1 encourage sb/sth (in sth/to do sth)** to give hope, support or confidence to sb: *The teacher encour-*

p	b	t	d	k	g	tʃ	dʒ	f	v	θ	ð
pen	bad	tea	did	cat	got	chin	June	fall	van	thin	then

aged her students to ask questions. ○ *His friends encouraged him in his attempt to stop smoking.* ☛ The opposite is **discourage**. Note that we say **discourage sb from doing sth**: *The teacher discouraged her students from asking questions.* **2** to make sth happen more easily: *The government wants to encourage new businesses.* —**encouragement** *noun* [C,U] —**encouraging** *adj*

encroach /ɪnˈkrəʊtʃ/ *verb* [I] *(formal)* **encroach (on/upon sth)** to take away part of sth or use more of sth than is right: *I do hope that I am not encroaching too much upon your free time.*

encyclopedia *(also* **encyclopaedia)** /ɪnˌsaɪkləˈpiːdɪə/ *noun* [C] *(pl* **encyclopedias)** a book or set of books that gives information about very many subjects, arranged in alphabetical order (ie from A to Z)

☆ **end¹** /end/ *noun* [C] **1** the furthest or last part of sth; the place or time where sth stops: *the end of a road, room, line, piece of string, etc* ○ *Join the end of the queue.* ○ *My house is at the end of the street.* ○ *The man on the other end of the phone spoke so quietly that I didn't catch his name.* ○ *There are some seats at the far end of the room.* ○ *I'm going on holiday at the end of October.* ○ *He promised to give me an answer by the end of the week.* ○ *She couldn't wait to hear the end of the story.* ☛ Look at the noun **finish**. It is used to mean **end** only in connection with races and competitions **End** is sometimes used before another noun: *the end house* ○ *the end seat* **2** a little piece of sth that is left after the rest has been used: *a cigarette end* **3** *(formal)* an aim or purpose: *They were prepared to do anything to achieve their ends.*

(IDIOMS) **at an end** *(formal)* finished or used up: *Her career is at an end.*

at the end of your tether having no more patience or strength

at a loose end ⇨ LOOSE

at your wits' end ⇨ WIT

bring sth/come/draw to an end (to cause sth) to finish: *His stay in England was coming to an end and he was thinking about going home again.*

a dead end ⇨ DEAD

end to end in a line with the ends touching: *They put the tables end to end.*

get (hold of) the wrong end of the stick ⇨ WRONG¹

in the end at last; finally: *He wanted to get home early but in the end it was midnight before he left.*

make ends meet to have enough money for your needs: *It's hard for us to make ends meet.*

a means to an end ⇨ MEANS¹

no end of sth *(informal)* very many or much; a lot of sth: *She has given us no end of trouble.*

odds and ends ⇨ ODDS

on end (used about time) continuously: *He sits and reads for hours on end.*

put an end to sth to stop sth from happening any more

'end-product *noun* [C] the final product of a manufacturing process or an activity

☆ **end²** /end/ *verb* [I,T] **end (in/with sth)** (to cause sth) to finish: *The road ends here.* ○ *How does this story end?* ○ *The match ended in a draw.* ○ *Most adverbs in English end in -ly.* ○ *I think we'd better end this conversation now.*

(PHRASAL VERB) **end up (as sth)**; **end up (doing sth)** to find yourself in a place/situation that you did not intend or expect: *We got lost and ended up in the centre of town.* ○ *She had always wanted to be a writer but ended up as a teacher.* ○ *There was nothing to eat at home so we ended up going out for fish and chips.*

endanger /ɪnˈdeɪndʒə(r)/ *verb* [T] to cause danger to sb/sth: *Smoking endangers your health.*

endangered *adj* (used about animals, plants, etc) in danger of disappearing from the world **(becoming extinct)**: *The panda is an endangered species.*

endear /ɪnˈdɪə(r)/ *verb* [T] **endear sb/yourself to sb** *(formal)* to make sb/yourself liked by sb: *She managed to endear herself to everybody by her kindness.* —**endearing** *adj* —**endearingly** *adv*

endeavour *(US* **endeavor)** /ɪnˈdevə(r)/ *verb* [I] *(formal)* **endeavour (to do sth)** to try: *She endeavoured to make the best of a very difficult situation.* —**endeavour** *noun* [C,U] *(formal)*

☆ **ending** /ˈendɪŋ/ *noun* [C] **1** the end (of a story, play, film, etc): *That film made me cry but I was pleased that it had a happy ending.* **2** *(grammar)* the last part of a word, which can change: *When nouns end in -ch or -sh or -x, the plural ending is -es not -s.*

endive /ˈendaɪv/ *noun* [C,U] *(US)* = CHICORY

☆ **endless** /ˈendləs/ *adj* without end: *Our plane was delayed for hours and the wait seemed endless.* —**endlessly** *adv*

endorse /ɪnˈdɔːs/ *verb* [T] **1** to write your name on the back of a cheque **2** *(Brit)* to write a note in a driving-licence to say that the driver has broken the law **3** to give (official) support or agreement to a plan, statement, decision, etc —**endorsement** *noun* [C,U]

endure /ɪnˈdjʊə(r); *US* -ˈdʊər/ *verb* *(formal)* **1** [T] to suffer sth painful or uncomfortable: *She endured ten years of loneliness.* ☛ **Endure** is often used in the negative: *My parents can't endure pop music.* In this sense **can't bear** or **can't stand** are less formal. **2** [I] to last; continue

endurance /ɪnˈdjʊərəns; *US* -ˈdʊə-/ *noun* [U] the ability to endure(1): *You need endurance to play a four-hour match.*

☆ **enemy** /ˈenəmɪ/ *noun* *(pl* **enemies) 1** [C] a person who hates and tries to harm sb/sth: *It's strange that people who used to be friends can become bitter enemies.* ○ *He has made several enemies since his arrival in the school.* ☛ The noun is **enmity**. **2 the enemy** [with sing or pl verb] the army or country that your country is fighting against: *The enemy is/are attacking at daybreak.* ○ *enemy forces*

☆ **energetic** /ˌenəˈdʒetɪk/ *adj* full of or needing energy(1): *Jogging is a very energetic form of exercise.* —**energetically** /-klɪ/ *adv*

☆ **energy** /ˈenədʒɪ/ *noun* *(pl* **energies) 1** [U] the ability to be very active or do a lot of work without getting tired: *Children are usually full*

s	z	ʃ	ʒ	h	m	n	ŋ	l	r	j	w
so	zoo	she	vision	how	man	no	sing	leg	red	yes	wet

of energy. ○ *This flu has left me with no energy at all.* **2 energies** [plural] the effort and attention which you give to doing sth: *She devoted all her energies to helping the blind.* **3** [U] the power that comes from coal, electricity, gas, etc that is used for driving machines, etc: *nuclear energy*

enforce /ɪn'fɔːs/ *verb* [T] **1** to make sure that laws, etc are obeyed: *How will they enforce the new law?* **2** to force sth to be done or to happen: *Enforcing discipline by using threats is not often successful.* —**enforcement** *noun* [U]

engage /ɪn'geɪdʒ/ *verb* [T] **1** to occupy sb's thoughts, time, interest, etc: *You need to engage the students' attention right from the start.* **2** to give work to sb: *They engaged him as a cook.* **3** to make parts of a machine fit together: *Engage first gear, look in the mirror, lift your foot off the clutch and move off.*
(PHRASAL VERB) **engage in sth** to take part in sth: *I don't engage in that kind of gossip!*

☆ **engaged** /ɪn'geɪdʒd/ *adj* **1 engaged (to sb)** having agreed to get married: *We've just got engaged.* ○ *Susan is engaged to Jim.* **2** (*US* **busy**) (used about a telephone) in use: *That line/number is engaged.* ○ *the engaged tone* **3** (used about a toilet, etc) in use **4** (used about a person) busy or occupied with sth: *I'm afraid I can't come. I'm otherwise engaged.*

engagement /ɪn'geɪdʒmənt/ *noun* [C] **1** an agreement to get married; the time when you are engaged: *Their engagement was announced in the paper.* ○ *Their engagement only lasted for six months.* ○ *He broke off their engagement.* **2** an arrangement to go somewhere or do sth at a fixed time; an appointment: *a lunch engagement*

en'gagement ring *noun* [C] a ring, usually with precious stones in it, that a man gives to a woman on their engagement(1)

☆ **engine** /'endʒɪn/ *noun* [C] **1** the part of a machine that changes energy (from oil, electricity, etc) into movement: *This engine runs on diesel.* ○ *a car engine* ○ *a jet engine* ☛ Look at the note at **motor**. **2** (*also* **locomotive**) a machine that pulls a railway train

'engine-driver (*US* **engineer**) *noun* [C] a person whose job is to drive a railway engine

☆ **engineer¹** /ˌendʒɪ'nɪə(r)/ *noun* [C] **1** a person whose job is to design, build or repair engines, machines, roads, bridges, railways, mines, etc: *a civil, chemical, electrical, mechanical, etc engineer* **2** (*US*) = ENGINE-DRIVER

engineering /ˌendʒɪ'nɪərɪŋ/ *noun* [U] (the study of) the work that is done by an engineer: *mechanical engineering* ○ *a degree in engineering*

engineer² /ˌendʒɪ'nɪə(r)/ *verb* [T] (*formal*) to arrange for sth to happen by careful (secret) planning: *Her promotion was engineered by her father.*

☆ **English** /'ɪŋglɪʃ/ *noun* **1** [U] the language that is spoken in Britain and the USA and in some other countries: *Do you speak English?* ○ *I've been learning English for 5 years.* ○ *I don't know what 'cadeau' is in English.* **2 the English** [with pl verb] the people of England
English *adj* belonging to England, the English people, the English language, etc: *English history* ○ *the English countryside*

☛ Be careful. The people of Scotland (the Scots) and of Wales (the Welsh) are **British** not English. Look at the note at **United Kingdom**.

English 'breakfast *noun* [C] a breakfast that consists of cereals, cooked bacon and eggs, toast and marmalade and tea or coffee, etc ☛ Look at **continental breakfast**.

the English 'Channel (*also* **the Channel**) *noun* [sing] the sea between England and France

'Englishman /-mən/ *noun* [C] (*pl* **Englishmen**) **Englishwoman** *noun* [C] (*pl* **Englishwomen**) a person who comes from England or whose parents are English ☛ We normally say: *'I'm English'* not *'I'm an Englishman/-woman.'*

engrave /ɪn'greɪv/ *verb* [T] **engrave B on A/engrave A with B** to cut patterns or words on metal, stone, etc: *His name is engraved on the cup.* ○ *The cup is engraved with his name.*

engraving /ɪn'greɪvɪŋ/ *noun* [C] a picture that is printed from an engraved metal plate

engrossed /ɪn'grəʊst/ *adj* **engrossed (in sth)** very interested in sth so that you forget other things: *She was completely engrossed in the play on television.*

enhance /ɪn'hɑːns; *US* -'hæns/ *verb* [T] (*formal*) to improve sth or to make sth look better

enigma /ɪ'nɪgmə/ *noun* [C] (*pl* **enigmas**) a person, thing or situation that is difficult to understand —**enigmatic** /ˌenɪg'mætɪk/ *adj*

☆ **enjoy** /ɪn'dʒɔɪ/ *verb* [T] **1 enjoy sth/enjoy doing sth** to get pleasure from: *I really enjoyed that meal – thank you very much.* ○ *Do you enjoy your work?* ○ *He enjoys listening to music while he's driving.* **2 enjoy yourself** to be happy; to have a good time: *I enjoyed myself at Sue's party last night – did you?*

enjoyable /-əbl/ *adj* giving pleasure: *We spent an enjoyable few days in Scotland.*

enjoyment /ɪn'dʒɔɪmənt/ *noun* [C,U] pleasure or a thing which gives pleasure: *She gets a lot of enjoyment from travelling.* ○ *One of her main enjoyments is foreign travel.*

enlarge /ɪn'lɑːdʒ/ *verb* [I,T] (to cause sth) to become larger: *I'm going to have this photo enlarged.*
(PHRASAL VERB) **enlarge on sth** to say or write more about sth

enlargement *noun* [C,U] making sth larger or sth that has been made larger: *an enlargement of a photo*

enlighten /ɪn'laɪtn/ *verb* [T] to give sb more information about sth so that he/she knows the truth

enlist /ɪn'lɪst/ *verb* **1** [I,T] to join the army, navy or air force; to make sb a member of the army, etc: *They enlisted as soon as war was declared.* **2** [T] to get help, support, etc: *We need to enlist the support of everybody who works here.*

enmity /'enmətɪ/ *noun* [U] the feeling of hatred towards an enemy

enormity /ɪˈnɔːmətɪ/ *noun* [sing] (*formal*) the extent or seriousness of sth; how bad sth is

☆ **enormous** /ɪˈnɔːməs/ *adj* very large or very great: *an enormous building* ○ *enormous pleasure* ○ *There is an enormous amount of work involved in this.* —**enormously** *adv*

☆ **enough¹** /ɪˈnʌf/ *det, pron* **1** as much or as many of sth as necessary: *We've saved enough money to buy a computer.* ○ *Not everybody can have a book – there aren't enough.* ○ *Are there enough chairs?* ○ *If enough of you are interested, we'll arrange a trip to the theatre.* **2** as much or as many as you want: *I've had enough of living in a town* (= I don't want to live in a town any more). ○ *Don't give me any more work. I've got quite enough already.*

☆ **enough²** /ɪˈnʌf/ *adv* (used *after* verbs, adjectives and adverbs) **1** to the necessary degree; sufficiently: *You don't practise enough.* ○ *He's not old enough to travel alone.* ○ *Does she speak Italian well enough to get the job?* ☞ picture at **too**. **2** quite, but not very: *She plays well enough, for a beginner.*

(IDIOMS) **fair enough** ⇨ FAIR²

funnily, strangely, etc enough it is funny, etc that...: *Funnily enough, I thought exactly the same myself.*

sure enough ⇨ SURE

enquire, enquiry = INQUIRE, INQUIRY

enrage /ɪnˈreɪdʒ/ *verb* [T] to make sb very angry

enrich /ɪnˈrɪtʃ/ *verb* [T] **1** to make sb/sth rich or richer **2** to improve the quality, flavour, etc of sth: *These cornflakes are enriched with vitamins/are vitamin-enriched.*

enrol (*US* **enroll**) /ɪnˈrəʊl/ *verb* [I,T] (enrolling; enrolled) **enrol** (**sb**) (**in/as sth**) to become or to make sb a member of a club, school, etc: *I've enrolled in my local swimming class.* ○ *They enrolled 100 new students last year.* —**enrolment** (*US* **enrollment**) *noun* [U]: *Enrolment for the course will take place next week.*

en route /ˌɒn ˈruːt/ *adv* **en route (from...) (to...); en route (for...)** on the way: *The car broke down when we were en route for Dover.*

ensue /ɪnˈsjuː; -ˈsuː/ *verb* [I] (*formal*) to happen after (and often as a result of) sth else

en suite /ˌɒn ˈswiːt/ *adv* (used about rooms) forming one unit: *The bedroom has a bathroom en suite.*

☆ **ensure** (*US* **insure**) /ɪnˈʃɔː(r); *US* ɪnˈʃʊər/ *verb* [T] to make sth certain to happen: *Please ensure that the door is locked before you leave.*

entail /ɪnˈteɪl/ *verb* [T] (*formal*) to make sth necessary; to involve: *This is going to entail a lot of hard work.* ○ *The job sounds interesting but I'm not sure what it entails.*

entangled /ɪnˈtæŋɡld/ *adj* caught in sth else: *The bird was entangled in the net.* ○ (*figurative*) *I've got myself entangled in some financial problems.*

☆ **enter** /ˈentə(r)/ *verb* **1** [I,T] (*formal*) to come or go into a place: *Don't enter without knocking.* ○ *They all stood up when he entered the room.* ○ (*figurative*): *We have just entered a new phase in international relations.* ☞ Note that **enter** is used without a preposition. **Come into** and **go into** are much more common. ☞ Look at **entrance, entrant** and **entry. 2** [I,T] **enter (for) sth** to put your name on the list for an exam, race, competition, etc: *I entered that competition in the Sunday paper and I won £20!* **3** [T] **enter sth (in/into/on/onto sth)** to put names, numbers, details, etc in a list, book, computer, etc: *Please enter your name in the book.* ○ *I've entered all the data onto the computer.* **4** [T] to become a member of a school, a college, a profession, an institution, etc: *She entered politics in 1960.*

(PHRASAL VERBS) **enter into sth 1** to start to think or talk about sth: *I don't want to enter into details now.* **2** to be part of sth: *This is a business matter. Friendship doesn't enter into it.*

enter into sth (with sb) to begin sth: *The government has entered into negotiations with the unions.*

enterprise /ˈentəpraɪz/ *noun* **1** [C] something (eg a plan or a project) that is new and difficult: *It's a very exciting new enterprise.* **2** [U] the courage that you need to start such an enterprise: *We need men and women of enterprise and energy.* **3** [C,U] a business; the way business is organized: *a new industrial enterprise* ○ *This government supports private enterprise.*

enterprising *adj* having enterprise(2) ☞ The opposite is **unenterprising**.

☆ **entertain** /ˌentəˈteɪn/ *verb* **1** [T] to interest and amuse sb: *He entertained us with jokes all evening.* ○ *I find it very hard to keep my class entertained on a Friday afternoon.* **2** [I,T] to welcome sb as a guest; to give sb food and drink: *They entertain a lot./They do a lot of entertaining.*

entertainer *noun* [C] a person who entertains(1) as a job

entertaining *adj* interesting and amusing

☆ **entertainment** /ˌentəˈteɪnmənt/ *noun* [C,U] things to do that interest and amuse people: *There isn't much entertainment for young people in this town.* ○ *Entertainments Guide* (= a list in a newspaper of the cinema, theatre, concert, etc programmes)

enthral (*US* **enthrall**) /ɪnˈθrɔːl/ *verb* [T] (enthralling; enthralled) to hold sb's interest and attention completely: *He was enthralled by her story.* —**enthralling** *adj*

☆ **enthusiasm** /ɪnˈθjuːziæzəm; *US* -ˈθuː-/ *noun* [U] **enthusiasm (for/about sb/sth)** a strong feeling of eagerness or interest: *Jan showed great enthusiasm for the new project.* ○ *There wasn't much enthusiasm when I mentioned the trip to the museum.*

enthusiast /ɪnˈθjuːziæst; *US* -ˈθuː-/ a person who is very interested in an activity or subject: *She is a jazz enthusiast.*

enthusiastic /ɪnˌθjuːziˈæstɪk; *US* -θuː-/ *adj* full of enthusiasm —**enthusiastically** /-klɪ/ *adv*

entice /ɪnˈtaɪs/ *verb* [T] to persuade sb to do sth by offering something nice: *Advertisements try to entice people into buying more things than they need.* —**enticement** *noun* [C,U]

enticing *adj* attractive

☆ **entire** /ɪnˈtaɪə(r)/ *adj* (only *before* a noun) whole or complete: *Surely she didn't eat the entire cake herself?* ○ *We invited the entire vil-*

ɜː	ə	eɪ	əʊ	aɪ	aʊ	ɔɪ	ɪə	eə	ʊə
fur	ago	pay	home	five	now	join	near	hair	pure

lage to the party. ☛ **Entire** is stronger than **whole**.
   entirely *adv* completely: *I entirely agree with you.* —**entirety** /ɪnˈtaɪərəti/ *noun* [U]: *We must consider the problem in its entirety* (= as a whole).
entitle /ɪnˈtaɪtl/ *verb* [T] to give sb the right to have or do sth: *I think I'm entitled to a day's holiday – I've worked hard enough.*
   entitled *adj* (used about books, plays, etc) with the title: *Duncan's first book was entitled 'Aquarium'.*
entity /ˈentəti/ *noun* [C] (*pl* **entities**) something that exists separately from sth else: *The kindergarten and the school are in the same building but they're really separate entities.*
☆ **entrance** /ˈentrəns/ *noun* **1** [C] the door, gate or opening where you go into a place: *I'll meet you at the entrance to the theatre.* ☛ **Entry** is used in American English with the same meaning. **2** [C] **entrance (into/onto sth)** the act of coming or going in: *He made a dramatic entrance onto the stage.* ☛ **Entry** can be used with the same meaning. **3** [U] **entrance (to sth)** the right to enter a place: *They were refused entrance to the disco because they were wearing shorts.* ○ *an entrance fee* ☛ **Entry** is also possible. Look at **admission**, **admittance**. **4** [U] **entrance (into/to sth)** the right to join a club, institution, etc: *You don't need to take an entrance exam to get into university.* ☛ Look at **admission**.
entrant /ˈentrənt/ *noun* [C] a person who enters a profession, competition, examination, university, etc
entreat /ɪnˈtriːt/ *verb* [T] (*formal*) to ask sb, with great feeling, to do sth (that may be difficult)
entrust /ɪnˈtrʌst/ *verb* [T] **entrust A with B/entrust B to A** (*formal*) to make sb responsible for sth that is given to him/her: *I entrusted Rachel with the arrangements for the party./I entrusted the arrangements for the party to Rachel.*
☆ **entry** /ˈentri/ *noun* (*pl* **entries**) **1** [C] **entry (into sth)** the act of coming or going in; entering(1): *The thieves forced an entry into the building.* ☛ **Entrance** is also possible. **2** [U] **entry (to sth)** the right to enter a place: *The immigrants were refused entry at the airport.* ○ *The sign says 'No Entry'.* ○ *an entry visa* ☛ **Entrance** is also possible. Look at **admission** and **admittance**. **3** [C] (*US*) a door, gate, passage, etc where you enter a building, etc; an entrance hall ☛ **Entrance** is also possible in American English and is the only word used in British English. **4** [C] **entry (in sth)** one item that is written down in a list, diary, account book, dictionary, etc: *You'll find 'ice-skate' at the entry for 'ice'.* **5** [C] **entry (for sth)** a person or thing that is entered for a competition, etc: *There were fifty entries for the Eurovision song contest.* ○ *The winning entry is number 45!*
envelop /ɪnˈveləp/ *verb* [T] (*formal*) to cover or surround sb/sth completely (in sth): *The hills were enveloped in mist.*
☆ **envelope** /ˈenvələʊp; ˈɒn-/ *noun* [C] the paper cover for a letter ☛ After writing a letter you **address** the envelope, **seal** it and stick a stamp in the top right-hand corner. Sometimes when you answer an advertisement you are asked to send an **SAE**. This is a 'stamped addressed envelope', addressed to yourself.
enviable /ˈenviəbl/ *adj* (used about sth that sb else has and that you would like) attractive ☛ The opposite is **unenviable**.
envious /ˈenviəs/ *adj* **envious (of sb/sth)** feeling or showing envy, ie wanting sth that sb else has: *She was envious of her sister's success.* —**enviously** *adv*
☆ **environment** /ɪnˈvaɪərənmənt/ *noun* **1** [C,U] the conditions in which you live, work, etc: *A bad home environment can affect a child's progress at school.* **2** **the environment** [sing] the natural world, eg land, air, water, etc in which people, animals and plants live: *We need stronger laws to protect the environment.* —**environmental** /ɪnˌvaɪərənˈmentl/ *adj*: *environmental science*
   environmentalist /ɪnˌvaɪərənˈmentəlɪst/ *noun* [C] a person who wants to protect the environment —**environmentally** /ɪnˌvaɪərənˈmentəli/ *adv*: *These products are environmentally friendly.*
envisage /ɪnˈvɪzɪdʒ/ *verb* [T] (*formal*) to think of sth as being possible in the future; to imagine: *I don't envisage any problems with this.*
envoy /ˈenvɔɪ/ *noun* [C] a person who is sent by a government with a message to another country
☆ **envy** /ˈenvi/ *noun* [U] **envy (of sb)**; **envy (at/of sth)** the feeling that you have when sb else has sth that you want: *It was difficult for her to hide her envy of her friend's success.* ☛ Look at **enviable** and **envious**.
   (IDIOM) **the envy of sb** the thing that causes sb to feel envy: *The city's transport system is the envy of many of its European neighbours.*
   envy *verb* [T] (*pres part* **envying**; *3rd pers sing pres* **envies**; *pt, pp* **envied**) **envy (sb)(sth)** to want sth that sb else has; to feel envy: *I've always envied your good luck.* ○ *I don't envy you that job* (= I'm glad that I don't have it).
epic /ˈepɪk/ *noun* [C] a long book, poem, film, etc that describes exciting adventures: *The film 'Glory' is an American Civil War epic.*
   epic *adj* of or like an epic: *an epic struggle*
epidemic /ˌepɪˈdemɪk/ *noun* [C] a large number of cases of people or animals suffering from the same disease at the same time: *A flu epidemic broke out in February.*
epilepsy /ˈepɪlepsi/ *noun* [U] a disease of the brain that can cause a person to become unconscious (sometimes with violent uncontrolled movements)
   epileptic /ˌepɪˈleptɪk/ *adj* connected with or suffering from epilepsy: *an epileptic fit* ○ *She's epileptic.*
   epileptic *noun* [C] a person who suffers from epilepsy
epilogue /ˈepɪlɒg/ (*US* **epilog** /-lɔːg/) *noun* [C] a short passage that is added at the end of a book, play, etc and that comments on what has gone before ☛ Look at **prologue**.

p	b	t	d	k	g	tʃ	dʒ	f	v	θ	ð
pen	bad	tea	did	cat	got	chin	June	fall	van	thin	then

episode /ˈepɪsəʊd/ noun [C] **1** one separate event in sb's life, a novel, etc: *That's an episode in my life I'd rather forget.* **2** one part of a TV or radio drama that is broadcast in several parts (**a serial**): *Don't miss tomorrow's exciting episode.*

epitaph /ˈepɪtɑːf; US -tæf/ noun [C] words that are written or said about a dead person, especially words written on a gravestone

epitome /ɪˈpɪtəmɪ/ noun [sing] a perfect example of sth
▶ **epitomize** /ɪˈpɪtəmaɪz/ verb [T] to be typical of sth

epoch /ˈiːpɒk; US ˈepək/ noun [C] a period of time in history (that is important because of special events, features, etc)

☆ **equal** /ˈiːkwəl/ adj **1** the same in size, amount, value, number, status, etc: *They are equal in weight.* ○ *They are of equal weight.* ○ *Divide it into two equal parts.* ○ *Women are demanding equal pay for equal work.* ○ *We've appointed an Equal Opportunities Officer* (= a person who makes sure that people are treated equally). ☛ The opposite is **unequal**. **2 equal to sth** (*formal*) having the strength, ability etc to do sth: *I'm afraid Bob just isn't equal to the job.*
(IDIOM) **be on equal terms (with sb)** to have the same advantages and disadvantages as sb else

equal noun [C] a person who has the same ability, rights, etc as you do: *to treat sb as an equal*

equal verb [T] (equa**ll**ing; equa**ll**ed; *US* equal-ing; equaled) **1** (used about numbers, etc) to be the same as sth: *44 plus 17 equals 61 is written: 44 + 17 = 61.* **2 equal sb/sth (in sth)** to be as good as sb/sth: *He ran an excellent race, equalling the club record.* ○ *Nowhere quite equals France for food.*

equally /ˈiːkwəlɪ/ adv **1** to the same degree or extent: *They both worked equally hard.* **2** in equal parts: *His money was divided equally between his children.* **3** (used when you are comparing two ideas or commenting on what you have just said) at the same time; but/and also: *I do not think what he did was right. Equally, I can understand why he did it.*

☆ **equality** /ɪˈkwɒlətɪ/ noun [U] the situation in which everybody has the same rights and advantages; being equal: *Absolute equality is probably impossible to achieve.* ○ *racial equality* (= between people of different races) ○ *equality of opportunity* ☛ The opposite is **inequality**.

equalize (*also* **equalise**) /ˈiːkwəlaɪz/ verb [I] (*sport*) to reach the same number of points as your opponent: *Wales equalized in the 87th minute to make the score 2 all.*

equate /ɪˈkweɪt/ verb [T] **equate sth (with sth)** to consider one thing as being the same as sth else: *It is a mistake to equate wealth with happiness.*

equation /ɪˈkweɪʒn/ noun [C] (in mathematics) a statement that two quantities are equal: *2x + 5 = 11 is an equation.*

equator (*also* **Equator**) /ɪˈkweɪtə(r)/ noun [sing] the imaginary line around the earth at an equal distance from the North and South Poles: *north/south of the equator* ○ *on the equator* ☛ picture at **earth**.

equestrian /ɪˈkwestrɪən/ adj (*formal*) connected with horse-riding: *equestrian events at the Olympic Games*

equip /ɪˈkwɪp/ verb [T] (equi**pp**ing; equi**pp**ed)
equip sb/sth (with sth) 1 (usually passive) to supply sb/sth with what is needed (for a particular purpose): *We shall equip all schools with new computers in the next year.* ○ *The schools in France are much better equipped than ours.* ○ *The flat has a fully-equipped kitchen.* **2** to prepare sb for a particular task: *We were just not equipped to deal with the problem.*

☆ **equipment** /ɪˈkwɪpmənt/ noun [U] the things that are needed for carrying out a particular activity: *office equipment* ○ *sports equipment* ○ *Standard equipment in the car includes power steering and central door locking.* ☛ Note that **equipment** is uncountable. We have to say 'a piece of equipment' if we are talking about one item: *a very useful piece of kitchen equipment.*

equivalent /ɪˈkwɪvələnt/ adj **equivalent (to sth)** equal in value, amount, meaning, importance, etc: *The price of British cars is higher than that of equivalent French or German models.* ○ *Is the British House of Commons roughly equivalent to the American House of Representatives?* ○ *People in Britain smoked 94 billion cigarettes last year, equivalent to 1680 per person.*

equivalent noun [C] something that is equivalent: *There is no English equivalent to the French 'bon appetit'.*

er /ɜː(r)/ interj (used in writing to show that sb cannot decide what to say next): *Well, er, ladies and gentlemen, I, er, I'm very pleased to be here today.*

era /ˈɪərə/ noun [C] a period of time in history (that is special for some reason): *We are living in the era of the computer.* ○ *the Victorian era* (= the years when Victoria was queen)

eradicate /ɪˈrædɪkeɪt/ verb [T] (*formal*) to destroy sth completely —**eradication** /ɪˌrædɪˈkeɪʃn/ noun [U]

erase /ɪˈreɪz; *US* ɪˈreɪs/ verb [T] (*formal*) to remove sth (a pencil mark, a recording on tape, etc): (*figurative*) *He tried to erase the memory of those terrible years from his mind.* ☛ We usually say **rub out** a pencil mark. —**eraser** /ɪˈreɪzə(r); *US* -sər/ noun [C] (*especially US*) = RUBBER(2)

erect¹ /ɪˈrekt/ adj **1** standing straight up; upright: *He stood with his head erect.* **2** (used about the penis) stiff and upright because of sexual excitement

erect² /ɪˈrekt/ verb [T] (*formal*) to build sth or to put sth in an upright position: *to erect a statue* ○ *Huge TV screens were erected so that everybody could see what was going on.*

erection /ɪˈrekʃn/ noun **1** [U] (*formal*) the act of putting sth in an upright position or of building sth **2** [C] the hardening of the penis in sexual excitement: *to get/have an erection*

erode /ɪˈrəʊd/ verb [T] (usually passive) (used about the sea, the weather, etc) to destroy sth slowly: *The cliff has been eroded by the sea.* ○

s	z	ʃ	ʒ	h	m	n	ŋ	l	r	j	w
so	zoo	she	vision	how	man	no	sing	leg	red	yes	wet

(*figurative*) *Freedom of speech is being eroded.* —**erosion** /ɪˈrəʊʒn/ *noun* [U]: *the erosion of the coastline by the sea*

erotic /ɪˈrɒtɪk/ *adj* causing sexual excitement: *an erotic film, poem, etc*

err /ɜː(r); *US* eər/ *verb* [I] (*formal*) to be or do wrong; to make mistakes: *It is better to err on the side of caution* (= it is better to be too careful rather than not careful enough).

errand /ˈerənd/ *noun* [C] a short journey to take or get sth for sb, eg to buy sth from a shop

erratic /ɪˈrætɪk/ *adj* (used about a person's behaviour, or about the quality of sth) changing without reason; that you cannot rely on: *Jones is a talented player but he's very erratic* (= sometimes he plays well, sometimes badly). —**erratically** *adv*

☆ **error** /ˈerə(r)/ *noun* **1** [C] a mistake: *The telephone bill was far too high due to a computer error.* ○ *an error of judgement* ○ *to make an error* ☛ **Error** is more formal than **mistake**. There are some expressions, eg *error of judgement, human error* where only **error** can be used. **2** [U] the state of being wrong in behaviour or belief: *The letter was sent to you in error.* ○ *The accident was the result of human error.*
(IDIOM) **trial and error** ➪ TRIAL

erupt /ɪˈrʌpt/ *verb* [I] **1** (used about a volcano) to explode and throw out fire, rock that has melted (**lava**), etc **2** (used about violence, anger, etc) to start suddenly: *The demonstration erupted into violence.* **3** (used about people) to suddenly become very angry: *George erupted when he heard the news.* —**eruption** /ɪˈrʌpʃn/ *noun* [C,U]

escalate /ˈeskəleɪt/ *verb* [I,T] **1** (to cause sth) to become stronger or more serious: *The demonstrations are escalating into violent protest in all the major cities.* ○ *The terrorist attacks escalated tension in the capital.* **2** (to cause sth) to become greater or higher; to increase: *The cost of housing has escalated in recent years.* —**escalation** /ˌeskəˈleɪʃn/ *noun* [C,U]

escalator /ˈeskəleɪtə(r)/ *noun* [C] a moving staircase in a shop, etc

escapade /ˌeskəˈpeɪd/ *noun* [C] an exciting adventure that may be dangerous

☆ **escape¹** /ɪˈskeɪp/ *verb* **1** [I] **escape (from sb/sth)** to get away from a place where you do not want to be; to get free: *Two prisoners have escaped.* ○ *A lion escaped from its cage at Bristol Zoo last night.* **2** [I] (used about gases or liquids) to find a way out of a container, etc: *There's gas escaping somewhere.* **3** [I,T] to be safe from sth; to avoid sth: *The two men in the other car escaped unhurt in the accident.* ○ *David Smith escaped injury when his car skidded off the road.* ○ *to escape criticism* **4** [T] to be forgotten or not noticed by sb: *His name escapes me.* ○ *to escape sb's notice* (= not be noticed by sb)

escaped *adj* having escaped from a place: *The escaped prisoners have not been recaptured.*

☆ **escape²** /ɪˈskeɪp/ *noun* **1** [C,U] **escape (from sth)** the act of escaping(1,2,3): *Escape from Alcatraz prison was impossible.* ○ *There have been twelve escapes from the local prison this year.* ○ *She had a narrow escape when a lorry crashed into her car* (= she was nearly killed or seriously hurt). **2** [C] a means of escaping: *a fire-escape* **3** [U,sing] something that helps you forget your daily life: *For him, listening to music is a means of escape.* ○ *an escape from reality*

escort¹ /ˈeskɔːt/ *noun* [C] **1** [with sing or pl verb] a person or vehicle (or group of people and vehicles) that goes with and protects sb/sth, or that goes with sb/sth as an honour: *a police escort* ☛ Note the phrase **under escort**: *He arrived under military escort.* **2** (*formal*) a companion for a particular social event

escort² /ɪˈskɔːt/ *verb* [T] **1** to go with sb as an escort: *The President's car was escorted by several police cars.* **2** to take sb somewhere: *Philip escorted her to the door.*

Eskimo /ˈeskɪməʊ/ *noun* [C] (*pl* **Eskimo** or **Eskimos**) a member of a people who live in the Arctic regions of North America and Eastern Siberia ☛ Eskimos prefer to be called **Inuits** or **Innuits**.

especial /ɪˈspeʃl/ *adj* (only *before* a noun) (*formal*) not usual; special: *This will be of especial interest to you.*

☆ **especially** /ɪˈspeʃəli/ *adv* **1** to an unusual degree; in particular: *She loves animals, especially dogs.* ○ *The Irish, especially, are proud of their traditions.* ○ *The car is rather small especially if you have a large family.* ○ *He was very disappointed with his mark in the exam especially as he had worked so hard for it.* **2** for a particular purpose: *I made this especially for you.* ☛ **Specially** is also possible with this meaning. It is less formal. **3** very (much): *It's not an especially difficult exam.* ○ *'Do you like jazz?' 'Not especially.'*

espionage /ˈespiənɑːʒ/ *noun* [U] the system of finding out secret information about another country or organization ☛ Look at **spy**.

☆ **essay** /ˈeseɪ/ *noun* [C] a short piece of writing on one subject: *to write an essay on tourism*

essence /ˈesns/ *noun* **1** [sing] the basic or most important quality of sth: *The essence of the problem is that there is not enough money available.* **2** [C,U] a substance (usually a liquid) that is taken from a plant or food and that has a strong smell or taste of that plant or food: *vanilla essence*

☆ **essential** /ɪˈsenʃl/ *adj* absolutely necessary; that you must have or do: *Essential medical supplies will be delivered to the area by plane.* ○ *Maths is essential for a career in computers.* ○ *It is essential that all school-leavers should have a qualification.* ○ *It is essential to book in advance if you are travelling by coach.* ○ *Local clubs are an essential part of village life.*

essential *noun* [C, usually pl] something that is necessary or very important: *food, and other essentials such as clothing and heating*

essentially /ɪˈsenʃəli/ *adv* basically; really: *The problem is essentially one of money.*

☆ **establish** /ɪˈstæblɪʃ/ *verb* [T] **1** to start sth (especially an organization or institution): *The school was established in 1875.* **2** to make sth exist: *We must establish good relations with the local newspaper.* **3 establish sb/sth (as sth)** to place sb/sth in a position permanently: *She*

iː	ɪ	e	æ	ɑː	ɒ	ɔː	ʊ	uː	ʌ
see	sit	ten	hat	arm	got	saw	put	too	cup

has been trying to get established as a novelist for several years. ○ The festival has become established as one of the most popular events in the town. **4** to decide sth: *We need to establish our aims before we can go any further.* **5** to make certain of sth; to prove: *The police are not able to establish where he was at the time of the murder.*

☆ **establishment** /ɪˈstæblɪʃmənt/ *noun* **1** [U] the act of starting sth such as an organization or institution: *the establishment of a new government department* **2** [C] a shop or business **3 the Establishment** [sing] (*Brit*) the people in positions of power in a country, who usually do not support change

☆ **estate** /ɪˈsteɪt/ *noun* [C] **1** a large area of land in the country that is owned by one person or family: *He owns a large estate in Scotland.* **2** (*Brit*) an area of land that has a lot of buildings of the same type on it: *an industrial estate* (= where there are a lot of factories) ○ *a housing estate* **3** all the money and property that sb leaves when he/she dies

es'tate agent (*US* **Realtor**; **real estate agent**) *noun* [C] a person who buys and sells houses and land for other people

es'tate car (*US* **station-wagon**) *noun* [C] a car with a door at the back and a large area for luggage behind the back seat ☛ picture at **car**.

esteem /ɪˈstiːm/ *noun* [U] (*formal*) great respect; a good opinion of sb

esthetic (*US*) = AESTHETIC

☆ **estimate**[1] /ˈestɪmət/ *noun* [C] **1** a guess or judgement about the size, cost, etc of sth, before you have all the facts and figures: *Can you give me a rough estimate of how many people will be at the meeting?* **2** a written statement from a builder, etc giving a price for a particular job

☆ **estimate**[2] /ˈestɪmeɪt/ *verb* [T] to calculate the size, cost, etc of sth approximately, before you have all the facts and figures: *She estimated that the work would take three months.* ○ *The police estimated the crowd at 10 000.* ○ *Work on the new bridge will cost an estimated five million pounds.*

estimation /ˌestɪˈmeɪʃn/ *noun* [U] (*formal*) opinion or judgement

estranged /ɪˈstreɪndʒd/ *adj* **1** no longer living with your husband/wife: *He's estranged from his wife.* **2** no longer friendly towards sb who used to be close to you

estuary /ˈestʃʊəri; *US* -ʊeri/ *noun* [C] (*pl* **estuaries**) the wide part (**mouth**) of a river where it joins the sea

eternal /ɪˈtɜːnl/ *adj* **1** without beginning or end; lasting for ever: *eternal life* (= after death) **2** happening too often; seeming to last for ever: *I'm tired of these eternal arguments!* —**eternally** /-əli/ *adv*: *I'll be eternally grateful if you could help me.*

eternity /ɪˈtɜːnəti/ *noun* **1** [U] time that has no end; the state or time after death **2 an eternity** [sing] (*informal*) a period of time that seems endless: *It seemed like an eternity before the ambulance arrived.*

ethics /ˈeθɪks/ *noun* **1** [U] the study of what is right and wrong in human behaviour: *Ethics is a branch of philosophy.* **2** [plural] beliefs about what is morally right and wrong: *The medical profession has its own code of ethics.*

ethical /ˈeθɪkl/ *adj* **1** connected with ethics(2): *That is an ethical problem.* **2** morally correct: *She had not broken the law but her behaviour had not been ethical.* ☛ The opposite is **unethical**.

ethnic /ˈeθnɪk/ *adj* connected with or typical of a racial group or groups: *ethnic minorities* ○ *ethnic food, music, etc*

etiquette /ˈetɪket/ *noun* [U] the rules of polite and correct behaviour

etymology /ˌetɪˈmɒlədʒi/ *noun* (*pl* **etymologies**) **1** [U] the study of the origins and history of words and their meanings **2** [C] an explanation of the origin and history of a particular word

euphemism /ˈjuːfəmɪzəm/ *noun* [C,U] (using) a polite word or expression instead of a more direct one when you are talking about sth that is unpleasant or embarrassing: *'Pass water' is a euphemism for 'urinate'.*

euphoria /juːˈfɔːriə/ *noun* [U] (*formal*) a strong feeling of happiness

Eurocheque /ˈjʊərəʊtʃek/ *noun* [C] a cheque that can be used in many European countries

☆ **European** /ˌjʊərəˈpiːən/ *adj* of or from Europe: *European languages* ○ *the European Championship*

European *noun* [C] a person from a European country

Euroˌpean Comˈmunity *noun* [sing] (*abbr* **EC**) an economic and political association of certain European countries

euthanasia /ˌjuːθəˈneɪziə; *US* -ˈneɪʒə/ *noun* [U] the painless killing of sb who is very old or suffering from a disease that cannot be cured

evacuate /ɪˈvækjueɪt/ *verb* [T] to move people from a dangerous place to somewhere safer; to leave a place because it is dangerous: *During the war children were evacuated from London to the country.* ○ *The village had to be evacuated when the river burst its banks.* —**evacuation** /ɪˌvækjuˈeɪʃn/ *noun* [C,U]

evade /ɪˈveɪd/ *verb* [T] **1** to get out of the way of or to escape from sb/sth: *They managed to evade capture and escaped to France.* **2** to avoid doing sth: *He was accused of evading income tax.* ○ *I asked her directly, but she evaded the question.* ☛ The noun is **evasion**.

evaluate /ɪˈvæljueɪt/ *verb* [T] (*formal*) to study the facts and then give your opinion about the meaning of sth or about how good sth is: *We evaluated the situation very carefully before we made our decision.* —**evaluation** /ɪˌvæljuˈeɪʃn/ *noun* [C,U]

evangelical /ˌiːvænˈdʒelɪkl/ *adj* (of certain Protestant churches) believing that religious ceremony is not as important as faith in Jesus Christ and study of the Bible

evaporate /ɪˈvæpəreɪt/ *verb* [I] **1** (used about a liquid) to change into steam or a gas and disappear: *The water evaporated in the sunshine.* ☛ Look at **condense**. **2** (used about feelings) to disappear: *All her hopes evaporated when she heard the news.* —**evaporation** /ɪˌvæpəˈreɪʃn/ *noun* [U]

ɜː	ə	eɪ	əʊ	aɪ	aʊ	ɔɪ	ɪə	eə	ʊə
fur	ago	pay	home	five	now	join	near	hair	pure

evasion /ɪ'veɪʒn/ noun [C,U] an action, statement, etc that is used for avoiding sth unpleasant: *He has been sentenced to two years' imprisonment for tax evasion.* ☞ The verb is **evade**.

evasive /ɪ'veɪsɪv/ adj trying to avoid sth; not direct: *Ann gave an evasive answer.*

eve /iːv/ noun [C] the day or evening before a religious festival, important event, etc: *Christmas Eve*

☆ **even¹** /'iːvn/ adj **1** flat, level or smooth: *The game must be played on an even surface.* **2** not changing; regular: *This wine must be stored at an even temperature* **3** (used about a competition, etc) with one side being as good as the other: *The contest was very even until the last few minutes of the game.* ☞ The opposite for senses 1,2,3 is **uneven**. **4** (used about numbers) that can be divided by two: *4, 6, 8, 10, etc are even numbers.* ☞ The opposite is **odd**.
(IDIOMS) **be/get even (with sb)** to hurt or harm sb who has hurt or harmed you
break even to make neither a loss nor a profit
evenly adv in an even way: *The match was very evenly balanced.* o *Spread the cake mixture evenly in the dish.*

☆ **even²** /'iːvn/ adv **1** (used for emphasizing sth that is surprising): *It isn't very warm here even in summer.* o *Even the children helped in the garden.* o *He didn't even open the letter* (= so he certainly didn't read it). o *I have been so busy that I haven't even had time to read the newspaper.* o *I like her very much even though she can be very annoying.* ☞ Look at the note at **although**. **2** (used when you are comparing things, to make the comparison stronger): *You know even less about it than I do.* o *It is even more difficult than I expected.* o *We are even busier than yesterday.*
(IDIOMS) **even if** (used for saying that what follows 'if' makes no difference): *I wouldn't do it, even if you paid me a thousand pounds.*
even so (used for introducing a new idea, fact, etc that is surprising) in spite of that; nevertheless: *There are a lot of spelling mistakes; even so it's quite a good essay.*

☆ **evening** /'iːvnɪŋ/ noun [C,U] the part of the day between the afternoon and the time that you go to bed: *What are you doing this evening?* o *We were out yesterday evening.* o *I went to the cinema on Saturday evening.* o *Tom usually goes swimming on Wednesday evenings.* o *Most people watch television in the evening.* o *an evening class* (= a course of lessons for adults that takes place in the evening)
(IDIOM) **good evening** (used when you see sb for the first time in the evening) o Often we just say *Evening*: *'Good evening, Mrs Wilson.' 'Evening, Mr Mills.'*

☆ **event** /ɪ'vent/ noun [C] **1** something that happens, especially sth important or unusual: *an historic event* o *The events of the past few days have made things very difficult for the Government.* **2** one of the races, competitions, etc in a sports programme: *The next event is the 800 metres.*
(IDIOMS) **at all events/in any event** whatever happens: *I hope to see you soon, but in any event I'll phone you on Sunday.*
in the event of sth (formal) if sth happens: *In the event of fire, leave the building as quickly as possible.*

eventful /-fl/ adj full of interesting or important events ☞ The opposite is **uneventful**.

eventual /ɪ'ventʃuəl/ adj (only before a noun) happening as a result; happening at last: *It is impossible to say what the eventual cost will be.*

eventually /-tʃuəli/ adv in the end; at last: *He eventually managed to persuade his parents to let him buy a motor bike.*

☆ **ever** /'evə(r)/ adv **1** (used in questions and negative sentences, when you are comparing things, and in sentences with 'if') at any time: *Do you ever wish you were famous?* o *Nobody ever comes to see me.* o *She hardly ever* (= almost never) *goes out.* o *Today is hotter than ever.* o *This is the best meal I have ever had.* o *If you ever visit England, you must come and stay with us.* **2** (used in questions with verbs in the perfect tenses) at any time up to now: *Have you ever been to Spain?* ☞ Notice that when you answer a question like this, you do not use 'ever'. You say, 'Yes, I have' or 'No, I haven't' (or 'No, never'). **3** (used with a question that begins with 'when', 'where', 'who', 'how', etc, to show that you are surprised or shocked): *How ever did he get back so quickly?* o *What ever were you thinking about when you wrote this?* ☞ Look at **whatever, whenever, however,** etc. **4 ever-** (in compounds) always; continuously: *the ever-growing problem of pollution*
(IDIOMS) **(as) bad, good, etc as ever** (as) bad, good, etc as usual or as you expected: *In spite of his problems, Andrew is as cheerful as ever.*
ever after (used especially at the end of stories) from that moment on for always: *The prince married the princess and they lived happily ever after.*
ever since (...) all the time from (...) until now: *She has had a car ever since she was at university.*
ever so/ever such a (informal) (Brit) very: *He's ever so kind.* o *He's ever such a kind man.*
for ever ⇨ FOREVER(1)

evergreen /'evəɡriːn/ noun [C], adj (a tree, etc) with green leaves throughout the year ☞ Look at **deciduous**.

everlasting /ˌevə'lɑːstɪŋ; US -'læst-/ adj (formal) lasting for ever: *everlasting life*

☆ **every** /'evri/ det **1** (used with singular nouns) all the people or things in a group of three or more: *She knows every student in the school.* o *There are 200 students in the school, and she knows every one of them.* o *I've read every book in this house.* o *You were out every time I phoned.* **2** all that is possible: *You have every chance of success.* o *She had every reason to be angry.* **3** (used for saying how often sth happens): *We see each other every day.* o *Take the medicine every four hours* (= at 8, 12, 4, etc). o *The milkman comes every other day* (= on Monday, Wednesday, Friday, etc). o *One in every three marriages ends in divorce.*

everybody /'evribɒdi/ (also **everyone** /'evriwʌn/) pron every person; all people: *Is*

everybody here? o The police questioned everyone who was at the party. o I'm sure everybody else (= all the other people) will agree with me.
☛ **Everyone** is only used about people and is not followed by 'of'. **Every one** means 'each person or thing' and is often followed by 'of': *Every one of his records has been successful.* Look also at the note at **somebody**.

everyday /'evrɪdeɪ/ *adj* (only before a noun) normal and usual: *The computer is now part of everyday life.*

everyplace /'evrɪpleɪs/ *adv* (US) = EVERYWHERE

everything /'evriθɪŋ/ *pron* [with sing verb] **1** each thing; all things: *Sam lost everything in the fire.* o *Everything is very expensive in this shop.* o *We can leave everything else* (= all the other things) *at my parents' house.* **2** the most important thing: *Money isn't everything.*

everywhere /'evriweə(r); *US* -hweə(r)/ *adv* in or to every place: *I've looked everywhere, but I still can't find it.*

evict /ɪ'vɪkt/ *verb* [T] to force sb (officially) to leave the house or land where he/she is living: *They were evicted for not paying the rent.*
—**eviction** /ɪ'vɪkʃn/ *noun* [C,U]

☆ **evidence** /'evɪdəns/ *noun* [U] something that gives a reason for believing sth: *There was no evidence of a struggle in the room.* o *There was not enough evidence to prove him guilty.* o *Her statement to the police was used in evidence against him.* o *The witnesses to the accident will be asked to give evidence in court.* o *You have absolutely no evidence for what you're saying!*
☛ Note that **evidence** is uncountable. We use **piece** if we are talking about single items that are evidence: *One piece of evidence is not enough to prove somebody guilty.*
(IDIOM) **(to be) in evidence** to be seen; to be noticeable: *When we arrived there was no ambulance in evidence. It didn't arrive until ten minutes later.*

evident /'evɪdənt/ *adj* clear (to the eye or mind); obvious: *It was evident that the damage was very serious.*

evidently *adv* **1** it appears that: *Evidently he has decided to leave.* **2** it is obvious that: *She was evidently extremely shocked at the news.*

☆ **evil** /'iːvl/ *adj* very bad; causing trouble or harm: *Dr Jekyll and the evil Mr Hyde* o *In the play Richard is portrayed as an evil king.*
☛ Another word for **evil** is **wicked**. These are very strong words. Children are usually described as **naughty** or **mischievous**.

evil *noun* [C,U] (*formal*) something that is very bad; wickedness: *The play is about the good and evil in all of us.* o *Drugs and alcohol are two of the evils of modern society.*
(IDIOM) **the lesser of two evils** ⇨ LESSER

evoke /ɪ'vəʊk/ *verb* [T] (*formal*) to produce a memory, feeling, etc: *For me, that music always evokes long summer evenings.* o *Her article evoked a lot of interest.*

evolution /ˌiːvə'luːʃn; *US* ˌev-/ *noun* [U] **1** the development of living things over many thousands of years from simple early forms: *Darwin's theory of evolution* **2** the process of change and development: *Political evolution is a slow process.*

evolve /ɪ'vɒlv/ *verb* **1** [I] (used about living things) to develop from simple early forms **2** [I,T] (*formal*) to develop or to make sth develop: *His style of painting has evolved gradually over the past 20 years.* o *The twins have evolved a language of their own.*

ewe /juː/ *noun* [C] a female sheep ☛ Look at the note and picture at **sheep**.

☆ **exact**[1] /ɪg'zækt/ *adj* **1** (completely) correct; accurate: *He's in his mid-fifties. Well, 56 to be exact.* o *What is the exact time?* o *I can't tell you the exact number of people who are coming.* o *She's the exact opposite of her sister.* **2** able to work in a way that is completely accurate: *You need to be very exact when you calculate the costs.*

exactly *adv* **1** (used for emphasizing sth) just: *You've arrived at exactly the right moment.* o *I found exactly what I wanted.* **2** (used when you are asking for, or giving, completely correct information): *Where exactly are you going on holiday?* o *He took exactly one hour to finish.* **3** (used for agreeing with a statement) yes; you are right: *'But I don't think she's old enough to travel on her own.' 'Exactly.'*
(IDIOM) **not exactly** (*informal*) **1** not really; not at all: *He's not exactly the most careful driver I know.* **2** (used as an answer to say that sth is almost true): *'So you think I'm wrong?' 'No, not exactly, but ...'*

exactness *noun* [U] the quality of being exact

exact[2] /ɪg'zækt/ *verb* [T] (*formal*) to demand and get sth

exacting *adj* needing a lot of care and attention; difficult: *exacting work*

☆ **exaggerate** /ɪg'zædʒəreɪt/ *verb* [I,T] to make sth seem larger, better, worse, more than it really is: *Don't exaggerate. I was only two minutes late, not twenty.* o *The problems have been greatly exaggerated.*

exaggeration /ɪgˌzædʒə'reɪʃn/ *noun* [C,U] making sth seem bigger, etc than it really is; sth that does this: *It's rather an exaggeration to say that all the students are lazy.*

☆ **exam** /ɪg'zæm/ *noun* [C] (*informal*) examination(2): *an English exam* o *the exam results*

☆ **examination** /ɪgˌzæmɪ'neɪʃn/ *noun* **1** [C,U] the act of looking at sth carefully: *They made a thorough examination of the car before buying it.* o *On close examination, it was found that the passport was false.* o *a medical examination* **2** (also *informal* **exam**) [C] a written, spoken or practical test of what you know or can do: *I've got an examination in French next week.* o *to take/sit an examination* o *to pass/fail an examination* ☛ A **test** is less formal and usually shorter than an examination.

☆ **examine** /ɪg'zæmɪn/ *verb* [T] **1 examine sb/sth (for sth)** to look at sb/sth carefully in order to find out sth: *The detective examined the room for clues.* o *I'm going to have my teeth examined next week.* o *Please examine your change carefully before you leave the shop.* **2 examine sb (in/on sth)** (*formal*) to test what sb knows or can do: *You will be examined*

s	z	ʃ	ʒ	h	m	n	ŋ	l	r	j	w
so	zoo	she	vision	how	man	no	sing	leg	red	yes	wet

on everything that has been studied in the course.

examiner /ɪɡˈzæmɪnə(r)/ noun [C] a person who tests sb in an examination(2)

☆ **example** /ɪɡˈzɑːmpl; US -ˈzæmpl/ noun [C] **1** a thing that shows a general rule about what sth is like: *This dictionary gives many examples of how words are used in sentences.* ○ *I don't quite understand you. Can you give me an example of what you mean?* ○ *This is a typical example of a Victorian house.* **2** a person or thing or a type of behaviour that is good and should be copied: *Joe's bravery should be an example to us all.*
(IDIOMS) **follow sb's example/lead** ⇨ FOLLOW
for example (used for giving an illustration of what you are talking about): *In many countries, Italy, for example, family life is much more important than here.* ☛ The short form is eg.
set a good, bad, etc example (to sb) to behave in a way that should/should not be copied: *Parents should always take care when crossing roads in order to set their children a good example.*

exasperate /ɪɡˈzæspəreɪt/ verb [T] to make sb angry; to annoy: *She was exasperated by the lack of progress.* —**exasperating** adj: *I spent an exasperating morning trying to arrange our flights.* —**exasperation** /ɪɡˌzæspəˈreɪʃn/ noun [U]: *She finally threw the book across the room in exasperation.*

excavate /ˈekskəveɪt/ verb [I,T] **1** to dig a hole in the ground **2** to uncover objects or buildings from the past by digging in an area of land: *A Roman villa has been excavated in a valley near the village.* —**excavation** /ˌekskəˈveɪʃn/ noun [C,U]: *Excavations on the site have revealed several Roman buildings.*

exceed /ɪkˈsiːd/ verb [T] **1** to be greater than sth: *The price must not exceed £100.* **2** to go beyond what is allowed or necessary: *He was stopped by the police for exceeding the speed limit.* ☛ Look at **excess** and **excessive**.

exceedingly adv very: *an exceedingly difficult problem*

excel /ɪkˈsel/ verb [I] (**excelling; excelled**) (formal) **excel in/at sth** to be very good at sth

excellence /ˈeksələns/ noun [U] the quality of being very good: *The headteacher said that she wanted the school to be a centre of academic excellence.*

☆ **excellent** /ˈeksələnt/ adj very good; of high quality: *He speaks excellent French.* —**excellently** adv

☆ **except**¹ /ɪkˈsept/ prep **except (for) sb/sth; except (that...)** not including sb/sth; apart from the fact that: *The museum is open every day except Mondays.* ○ *Everyone except Tony is going on the trip.* ○ *I can answer all of the questions except for the last one.* ○ *It was a good hotel except that it was rather noisy.*

except² /ɪkˈsept/ verb [T] (often passive) **except sb/sth (from sth)** (formal) to leave sb/sth out; to not include sb/sth

excepting /ɪkˈseptɪŋ/ prep not including; except¹

☆ **exception** /ɪkˈsepʃn/ noun [C] a person or thing that is not included: *Most of his songs are awful but this one is an exception.* ○ *There's an exception to every rule.*
(IDIOMS) **to make an exception (of sb/sth)** to treat sb/sth differently: *We don't usually allow children under 14 but we'll make an exception in your case.*
with the exception of except for; apart from: *He has won every major tennis championship with the exception of Wimbledon.*
without exception in every case; including everybody/everything: *Everybody without exception must take the test.*

exceptional /ɪkˈsepʃənl/ adj very unusual; unusually good: *You will only be allowed to leave early in exceptional circumstances.* ○ *We have had a really exceptional summer.* —**exceptionally** /-ʃənəlɪ/ adv: *The past year has been exceptionally difficult for us.*

excerpt /ˈeksɜːpt/ noun [C] a short piece taken from a book, film, piece of music, etc

excess¹ /ɪkˈses/ noun [sing] more of sth than is needed or usual; too much of sth: *An excess of fat in your diet can lead to heart disease.*
(IDIOM) **in excess of** more than: *Her debts are in excess of £1 000.*

excess² /ˈekses/ adj (only before a noun) more than is usual or allowed; extra: *There are high charges for excess baggage on planes.*

excessive /ɪkˈsesɪv/ adj too much; too great: *I think £200 for a dress is excessive.* —**excessively** adv: *I think you are being excessively pessimistic about this.*

☆ **exchange**¹ /ɪksˈtʃeɪndʒ/ noun **1** [C,U] giving or receiving sth in return for sth else: *a useful exchange of information* ○ *We can offer free accommodation in exchange for some help in the house.* **2** [C] an (angry) conversation or argument **3** [U] the relation in value between kinds of money used in different countries: *What's the exchange rate/rate of exchange for dollars?* ○ *The exchange rate is one pound to three deutschmarks.* **4** [U] money that can be used to pay for goods or services from other countries: *Most of the country's foreign exchange comes from oil.* **5** [C] a visit by a group of students or teachers to another country and a return visit by a similar group from that country: *an exchange with a school in France* ○ *an exchange visit* **6** = TELEPHONE EXCHANGE ☛ Look at **Stock Exchange**.

☆ **exchange**² /ɪksˈtʃeɪndʒ/ verb [T] **exchange A for B; exchange sth (with sb)** to give or receive sth in return for sth else: *I would like to exchange this skirt for a bigger one.* ○ *Mary and Jane exchanged addresses with the boys.* ○ *They exchanged glances* (= they looked at each other).

excise /ˈeksaɪz/ noun [U] a government tax on certain goods that are produced or sold in a country, eg tobacco, alcohol, etc ☛ Look at **customs**.

excitable /ɪkˈsaɪtəbl/ adj easily excited

excite /ɪkˈsaɪt/ verb [T] **1** to cause strong feelings (eg of happiness or nervousness): *Don't excite the baby too much or we'll never get him off to sleep.* **2** to cause a reaction in sb: *The programme excited great interest.*

☆ **excited** /ɪkˈsaɪtɪd/ adj feeling very happy

iː	ɪ	e	æ	ɑː	ɒ	ɔː	ʊ	uː	ʌ
see	sit	ten	hat	arm	got	saw	put	too	cup

because you are looking forward to sth happening; not calm: *Are you getting excited about your holiday?* o *We're all very excited at the thought of moving into our new house.* —**excitedly** *adv*

☆ **excitement** /ɪk'saɪtmənt/ *noun* **1** [U] the state of being excited; a feeling of pleasure, especially because sth interesting is happening or will happen: *The children could not hide their excitement on Christmas Eve.* o *There was great excitement as the winner's name was announced.* o *The match was full of excitement until the very last minute.* **2** [C] something that makes you feel excited: *After all the excitements of the last few weeks, it's nice to relax at home for a while.*

☆ **exciting** /ɪk'saɪtɪŋ/ *adj* causing strong feelings of pleasure and interest: *That's very exciting news.* o *Berlin is one of the most exciting cities in Europe.* ☛ The opposite is **unexciting**.

exclaim /ɪk'skleɪm/ *verb* [I,T] to say sth suddenly because you are surprised, angry, etc: *'I just don't believe it!'* he exclaimed.

exclamation /ˌekskləˈmeɪʃn/ *noun* [C] a sound or word that expresses sudden pain, anger, surprise, etc: *'Ouch!' is an exclamation.*

excla'mation mark (*US* **excla'mation point**) *noun* [C] a mark (!) that is written after an exclamation

☆ **exclude** /ɪkˈskluːd/ *verb* [T] **1 exclude sb/sth (from sth)** to prevent sb/sth from getting in: *Women are excluded from the temple.* o *Try and exclude draughts from the room, and you will save money on your heating bills.* **2** to decide that sth is not true: *The police had excluded the possibility that the child had run away.* **3** to leave out; not include: *The price excludes all extras such as drinks or excursions.*

excluding *prep* not including: *Lunch costs £10 per person excluding drinks.*

exclusion /ɪkˈskluːʒn/ *noun* [U] keeping or leaving sb/sth out

exclusive /ɪkˈskluːsɪv/ *adj* **1** expensive and not welcoming people who are thought to be socially unsuitable: *an exclusive restaurant* o *a flat in an exclusive part of the city* **2** (only *before* a noun) for only one person, group, etc; not to be shared: *This car is for the Director's exclusive use.* o *Tonight we are showing an exclusive interview with the new leader of the Labour Party* (= on only one television or radio station). **3 exclusive of sb/sth** not including sb/sth; without: *Lunch costs £7 per person exclusive of drinks.*

exclusive *noun* [C] a newspaper story that is given to and published by only one newspaper

exclusively *adv* only; not involving anybody/anything else: *The swimming-pool is reserved exclusively for members of the club.*

excrement /ˈekskrɪmənt/ *noun* [U] (*formal*) the solid waste matter that is passed from the body through the bowels ☛ Look at **faeces**.

excrete /ɪkˈskriːt/ *verb* [T] (*formal*) to pass out waste matter from the body

excruciating /ɪkˈskruːʃɪeɪtɪŋ/ *adj* (used about pain, etc) very bad

excursion /ɪkˈskɜːʃn/; *US* -ˈskɜːrʒn/ *noun* [C] a short journey or trip (that a group of people make for pleasure): *to go on an excursion*
☛ Look at the note at **travel**.

☆ **excuse¹** /ɪkˈskjuːs/ *noun* [C] **excuse (for sth/for doing sth)** a reason (that may be true or untrue) that you give in order to explain your behaviour: *There's no excuse for rudeness.* o *He always finds a good excuse for not helping with the housework.*

☆ **excuse²** /ɪkˈskjuːz/ *verb* [T] **1 excuse sb/sth (for sth/for doing sth)** to forgive sb/sth: *Please excuse the interruption but I need to talk to you.* **2** to explain sb's bad behaviour and make it seem less bad: *Nothing can excuse such behaviour.* o *She excused herself for arriving late and sat down.* **3 excuse sb (from sth)** to free sb from a duty, responsibility, etc: *You can be excused from homework today because it's your birthday.*

☛ The expression **excuse me** is used when you interrupt somebody or when you want to start talking to somebody that you don't know: *Excuse me, can you tell me the way to the station?* In US English and sometimes in British English **excuse me** is used when you apologize for something: *Did I tread on your toe? Excuse me.*

excusable /ɪkˈskjuːzəbl/ *adj* that can be forgiven ☛ The opposite is **inexcusable**.

execute /ˈeksɪkjuːt/ *verb* [T] **1** to kill sb as an official punishment: *He was executed for murder.* **2** (*formal*) to perform a task, etc or to carry out a plan

execution /ˌeksɪˈkjuːʃn/ *noun* **1** [C,U] the act of killing sb as an official punishment **2** [U] (*formal*) carrying out a plan, order, etc

executioner /ˌeksɪˈkjuːʃənə(r)/ *noun* [C] a person whose job is to execute criminals

executive /ɪgˈzekjʊtɪv/ *adj* **1** (used in connection with people in business, government, etc) concerned with managing, carrying out decisions, plans, etc: *an executive director of the company* **2** (used about goods, buildings, etc) designed to be used by important business people: *an executive briefcase*

executive *noun* [C] **1** a person who has an important position in a business: *She's a senior executive in a computer company.* **2** The part of an organization which takes important decisions

exemplary /ɪgˈzemplərɪ/ *adj* very good; that can be an example to other people: *exemplary behaviour*

exemplify /ɪgˈzemplɪfaɪ/ *verb* (*pres part* **exemplifying**; *3rd pers sing pres* **exemplifies**; *pt, pp* **exemplified**) [T] to be a typical example of sth

exempt /ɪgˈzempt/ *adj* (not before a noun) **exempt (from sth)** free from having to do sth or pay sth: *Children under 16 are exempt from dental charges.*

exempt *verb* [T] **exempt sb/sth (from sth)** (*formal*) to say officially that sb does not have to do sth or pay sth —**exemption** /ɪgˈzempʃn/ *noun* [C,U]

☆ **exercise¹** /ˈeksəsaɪz/ *noun* **1** [U] use of the body in a way that will keep you healthy: *The*

ɜː	ə	eɪ	əʊ	aɪ	aʊ	ɔɪ	ɪə	eə	ʊə
fur	ago	pay	home	five	now	join	near	hair	pure

doctor advised him to take regular exercise. o *Swimming is a good form of exercise.* **2** [C] (often plural) a movement or activity that you do in order to keep healthy or to train sth: *I do keep-fit exercises every morning.* o *You need to do some exercises to improve your technique.* **3** [C] a piece of work that is intended to help you learn or practise sth: *an exercise on phrasal verbs* o *an exercise book* (= a notebook for writing in, usually in school) **4** [C] a series of actions that have a particular aim: *The project is an exercise in getting the best results at a low cost.* **5** [U] (*formal*) the use of sth (eg a power, right, etc) **6** [C] a series of activities by soldiers to practise fighting: *military exercises*

☆ **exercise²** /ˈeksəsaɪz/ *verb* **1** [I] to do some form of physical movement in order to stay fit and healthy: *It is important to exercise regularly.* **2** [T] to make use of sth (eg a power, right, etc): *You should exercise your right to vote.*

exert /ɪgˈzɜːt/ *verb* [T] **1** to make use of sth (eg influence, strength, etc): *Parents exert a powerful influence on their children's opinions.* **2** exert yourself to make an effort: *You won't make any progress if you don't exert yourself a bit more.*

exertion /ɪgˈzɜːʃn; *US* -ˈɜːrʒn/ *noun* [C,U] using your body in a way that takes a lot of effort; sth that you do that makes you tired: *I'm tired after the exertions of the past few days.* o *At his age physical exertion was dangerous.*

exhaust¹ /ɪgˈzɔːst/ *noun* **1** [C] a pipe (particularly at the back of a car) through which waste gas escapes from an engine or machine **2** [U] the waste gas that escapes from an engine or machine

☆ **exhaust²** /ɪgˈzɔːst/ *verb* [T] **1** to make sb very tired: *The long journey to work every morning exhausted him.* **2** to use sth up completely; to finish sth: *All the supplies of food have been exhausted.* **3** to say everything you can about a subject, etc: *Well, I think we've exhausted that topic.*

exhausted /ɪgˈzɔːstɪd/ *adj* very tired

exhausting /ɪgˈzɔːstɪŋ/ *adj* making sb very tired: *Teaching young children is exhausting work.*

exhaustion /ɪgˈzɔːstʃən/ *noun* [U] great tiredness

exhaustive /ɪgˈzɔːstɪv/ *adj* including everything possible: *This list is certainly not exhaustive.*

exhibit¹ /ɪgˈzɪbɪt/ *noun* [C] an object that is shown in a museum, etc

exhibit² /ɪgˈzɪbɪt/ *verb* [T] **1** to show sth to the public: *His paintings have been exhibited in the local art gallery.* **2** (*formal*) to show sth (eg a feeling or quality): *The refugees are exhibiting signs of exhaustion and stress*

exhibitor *noun* [C] a person who shows his/her work to the public

☆ **exhibition** /ˌeksɪˈbɪʃn/ *noun* **1** [C] a collection of objects that are shown to the public: *an exhibition of photographs* o *Have you seen the Picasso exhibition?* o *the National Exhibition Centre in Birmingham* ☛ Notice the expression **on exhibition**: *Her paintings will be on exhibition in London for the whole of April.* **2** [C] an occasion when a particular skill is shown to the public: *We saw an exhibition of Scottish dancing last night.* **3** [sing] (*formal*) the act of showing a quality, feeling, etc: *The game was a superb exhibition of football at its best.*

exhilarate /ɪgˈzɪləreɪt/ *verb* [T] (usually passive) to make sb feel very happy, excited, etc: *We felt exhilarated by our walk along the beach.*
— **exhilarating** *adj* — **exhilaration** /ɪgˌzɪləˈreɪʃn/ *noun* [U]

exile /ˈeksaɪl/ *noun* **1** [U] the state of being forced to live outside your own country (especially for political reasons): *He went into exile after the revolution of 1968.* o *They lived in exile in London for many years.* **2** [C] a person who is forced to live outside his/her own country (especially for political reasons): *Trotsky spent his last years as a political exile in Mexico.*
☛ Look at **refugee**.

exile *verb* [T] (usually passive) to send sb to live in another country (especially for political reasons): *After the revolution the king was exiled.*

☆ **exist** /ɪgˈzɪst/ *verb* [I] **1** to be real; to be found in the real world; to live: *Does God exist?* o *I don't think that word exists, does it?* o *Fish cannot exist out of water.* **2** **exist (on sth)** to manage to live: *I don't know how she exists on the wage she earns.*

existing /ɪgˈzɪstɪŋ/ *adj* (only *before* a noun) that is already there or being used; present: *Under the existing law you are not allowed to work in this country.*

☆ **existence** /-əns/ *noun* **1** [U] the state of existing: *This is the oldest human skeleton in existence.* o *The country of Yugoslavia came into existence in 1918.* **2** [sing] a way of living; life: *They lead a miserable existence in a tiny flat in London.*

☆ **exit** /ˈeksɪt; ˈegzɪt/ *noun* [C] **1** a door or way out of a public building: *an emergency exit* **2** the act of leaving sth: *When he saw her coming he made a quick exit.* o *an exit visa* (= one that allows you to leave a country) **3** a place where traffic can turn off a motorway, roundabout, etc: *At the roundabout take the third exit.*

exit *verb* [I] to go out or away

exonerate /ɪgˈzɒnəreɪt/ *verb* [T] (often passive) (*formal*) to free sb from blame, responsibility etc

exorbitant /ɪgˈzɔːbɪtənt/ *adj* (*formal*) (used about the cost of sth) much more expensive than it should be

exotic /ɪgˈzɒtɪk/ *adj* unusual or interesting because it comes from a different country or culture: *exotic plants, animals, etc*

☆ **expand** /ɪkˈspænd/ *verb* [I,T] to become bigger or to make sth bigger: *Metals expand when they are heated.* o *We hope to expand our business this year.* ☛ The opposite is **contract**.
(PHRASAL VERB) **expand on sth** to give more details of a story, plan, point of view, etc

expanse /ɪkˈspæns/ *noun* [C] a large open area (of land, sea, sky, etc)

☆ **expansion** /ɪkˈspænʃn/ *noun* [U] the action of expanding or the state of being expanded: *The*

p	b	t	d	k	g	tʃ	dʒ	f	v	θ	ð
pen	bad	tea	did	cat	got	chin	June	fall	van	thin	then

rapid expansion of the university has caused a lot of problems.

expansive /ɪk'spænsɪv/ adj (formal) (used about a person) willing to talk a lot; friendly

expatriate /,eks'pætrɪət; US -'peɪt-/ (also informal **expat**) noun [C] a person who lives outside his/her own country

☆ **expect** /ɪk'spekt/ verb [T] **1** to think or believe that sb/sth will come or that sth will happen: *She was expecting a letter from the bank this morning but it didn't come.* ○ *I expect that it will rain this afternoon.* ○ *He expected it to be hot in Washington and it was.* ○ *'I'm really disappointed - she forgot my birthday.' 'Well, what did you expect?'* (= it's not surprising) ○ *She's expecting a baby in the spring* (= she's pregnant). ☛ Look at the note at **wait¹**. **2 expect sth (from sb); expect sb to do sth** to hope that you will get sth from sb or that he/she will do what you want: *He expects a high standard of work from everyone.* ○ *Factory workers are often expected to work at nights.* **3** (not in the -ing forms) (Brit) (used when you think sth is probably true): *'Who's eaten all the biscuits?' 'Oh it was Tom, I expect.'* ○ *'Will you be able to help me later on?' 'I expect so.'*

expectancy /ɪk'spektənsɪ/ noun [U] the state of expecting sth to happen; hope: *a look, feeling, etc of expectancy* ☛ Look at **life expectancy**.

expectant /ɪk'spektənt/ adj expecting sth good; hopeful: *an expectant audience* ○ *expectant faces* —**expectantly** adv ☛ Expectant also means 'pregnant' or 'waiting for a baby': *Expectant mothers need a lot of rest.*

expectation /,ekspek'teɪʃn/ noun (formal) **1** [U] the belief that sth will happen: *There's no expectation of the weather getting better for some days yet.* **2** [C, usually pl] hope for the future: *They had great expectations for their daughter, but she didn't really live up to them.*
(IDIOMS) **against/contrary to (all) expectation(s)** quite different to what was expected: *Contrary to all expectations, Val won first prize.*
not come up to (sb's) expectations to be less good than expected: *I'm afraid the hotel did not come up to our expectations.*

expedient /ɪk'spiːdɪənt/ adj (formal) (used about an action) convenient or helpful for a purpose (but not always good or moral): *Before the election the government thought that it was expedient not to increase taxes.* —**expediency** /-ənsɪ/ noun [U]

expedition /,ekspɪ'dɪʃn/ noun [C] **1** a long journey for a special purpose: *a scientific expedition to Antarctica* **2** a short journey that you make for pleasure: *a shopping expedition*

expel /ɪk'spel/ verb [T] (expelling; expelled) **1** to force sb to leave a country, school, club, etc: *The government has expelled all foreign journalists.* ○ *The boy was expelled from school for smoking.* **2** to send sth out by force: *to expel air from the lungs* ☛ The noun is **expulsion**.

expend /ɪk'spend/ verb [T] (formal) to spend or use money, time, care, etc in doing sth: *I have expended a lot of time and energy on that project.*

expendable adj (formal) not thought of as important or worth saving: *In a war human life is expendable.*

expenditure /ɪk'spendɪtʃə(r)/ noun [U, sing] (formal) the act of spending or using money, etc; the amount of money, etc which is spent: *Government expenditure on education is very low.* ○ *an expenditure of £2 000*

☆ **expense** /ɪk'spens/ noun **1** [C,U] the cost of sth in time or money: *Running a car is a great expense.* ○ *Expense wasn't important when they were deciding where to go on holiday.* ☛ Note the expressions: **at great expense** (= at a high cost) and **at no expense** (= at no cost). **2 expenses** [plural] money that is spent for a particular purpose: *You can claim back your travelling expenses.*
(IDIOMS) **at sb's expense 1** with sb paying; at sb's cost: *My trip is at the company's expense.* **2** against sb, so that he/she looks silly: *They were always making jokes at Paul's expense.*
at the expense of sth harming or damaging sth: *He was a successful businessman, but it was at the expense of his family life.*

☆ **expensive** /ɪk'spensɪv/ adj costing a lot of money: *Houses are very expensive in this area.* ○ *It's too expensive.* ☛ The opposite is **inexpensive** or **cheap**. —**expensively** adv

☆ **experience** /ɪk'spɪərɪəns/ noun **1** [U] the things that you have done; the knowledge or skill that you get from seeing or doing sth: *We all learn by experience.* ○ *She has five years' teaching experience.* ○ *You need a lot of experience in this job.* ○ *I know from experience what will happen.* **2** [C] something that has happened to you (often something unusual or exciting): *She wrote a book about her experiences in Africa.* ○ *It's an experience not to be missed.*

experience verb [T] to have experience of sth; to feel: *It was the first time I'd ever experienced failure.* ○ *to experience pleasure, pain, difficulty, etc*

experienced adj having the knowledge or skill that is necessary for sth: *He's not a very experienced driver.* ☛ The opposite is **inexperienced**.

☆ **experiment** /ɪk'sperɪmənt/ noun [C,U] a scientific test or trial that is done in order to prove sth or to get new knowledge: *Researchers often perform experiments on animals.* ○ *It's difficult to do experiments into how people learn languages.* ○ *I'm going to try cycling to work - it's just an experiment.* ○ *We need to prove this theory by experiment.*

experiment verb [I] **experiment (on sth) (with sth)** to do an experiment or to test: *Is it really necessary to experiment on animals?* ○ *We're experimenting with a new timetable this month.*

experimental /ɪk,sperɪ'mentl/ adj connected with experiments or new ideas: *We're still at the experimental stage with the new product.* ○ *experimental schools* —**experimentally** /-təlɪ/ adv

☆ **expert** /'ekspɜːt/ noun [C] **an expert (at/in/on sth)** a person who has special knowledge or skill: *He's an expert on the history of rock music.* ○ *She's a computer expert.* ○ *Let me*

s	z	ʃ	ʒ	h	m	n	ŋ	l	r	j	w
so	zoo	she	vision	how	man	no	sing	leg	red	yes	wet

try – I'm an expert at parking cars in small spaces.

expert *adj* **expert (at/in/on sth)** with special knowledge or skill: *He's an expert cook.* ○ *I think we should get expert advice on the problem.* —**expertly** *adv*

expertise /ˌekspɜːˈtiːz/ *noun* [U] special knowledge or skill: *I was amazed at his expertise on the word processor.*

expire /ɪkˈspaɪə(r)/ *verb* [I] (*formal*) (used about sth that only lasts for a certain period of time) to come to the end of the time when you can use it: *My passport's expired. I'll have to get it renewed.* ☞ A less formal expression is **run out**.

expiry /ɪkˈspaɪərɪ/ *noun* [U] the end of a period when you can use sth: *The expiry date on this yoghurt was 20 November.*

☆ **explain** /ɪkˈspleɪn/ *verb* [I,T] **1** to make sth clear or easy to understand: *A dictionary explains the meaning of words.* ○ *She explained how I should fill in the form.* ○ *I don't understand this. Can you explain?* **2** to give a reason for sth: *'This work isn't very good.' 'I wasn't feeling very well.' 'Oh, that explains it then.'* ○ *That explains why she was looking so miserable.* ○ *The manager explained to the customers why the goods were late.*

☆ **explanation** /ˌekspləˈneɪʃn/ *noun* **1** [U] making sth clear or giving a reason for sth: *That idea needs some explanation.* **2** [C] something that makes a situation clear or understandable: *He could not give a satisfactory explanation for his behaviour.*

explanatory /ɪkˈsplænətrɪ; *US* -tɔːrɪ/ *adj* giving an explanation: *There are some explanatory notes at the back of the book.* ○ *Those instructions are self-explanatory* (= they don't need explaining).

explicable /ɪkˈsplɪkəbl; ˈeksplɪkəbl/ *adj* (*formal*) (usually used about people's behaviour) that can be explained ☞ The opposite is **inexplicable**.

explicit /ɪkˈsplɪsɪt/ *adj* **1** clear, not making anything difficult to understand: *I gave you explicit instructions not to touch anything.* ○ *She was quite explicit about her feelings on the subject.* **2** not hiding anything: *Some of the sex scenes in that TV play were very explicit.* —**explicitly** *adv*: *He was explicitly forbidden to stay out later than midnight.*

☆ **explode** /ɪkˈspləʊd/ *verb* [I,T] to burst with a loud noise: *The bomb exploded without warning.* ○ *The bomb was taken away and the army exploded it at a safe distance from the houses.* ○ (*figurative*) *My father exploded* (= became very angry) *when I told him how much the car would cost to repair.* ☞ The noun is **explosion**.

☆ **exploit¹** /ɪkˈsplɔɪt/ *verb* [T] **1** to use sth to treat sb unfairly or selfishly: *Third World countries are often exploited by the richer nations.* **2** to develop sth or make the best use of sth: *Solar energy is a source of power that needs to be exploited more fully.*

exploitation /ˌeksplɔɪˈteɪʃn/ *noun* [U] exploiting or being exploited: *They're only paying £3 an hour? That's exploitation!*

exploit² /ˈeksplɔɪt/ *noun* [C] a brave or adventurous action

☆ **explore** /ɪkˈsplɔː(r)/ *verb* [I,T] to travel around a place, etc in order to learn about it: *They went on an expedition to explore the River Amazon.* ○ *I've never been to Paris before – I'm going out to explore.* ○ (*figurative*) *We need to explore* (= look carefully at) *all the possibilities before we decide.*

exploration /ˌekspləˈreɪʃn/ *noun* [C,U] the act of exploring: *space exploration*

exploratory /ɪkˈsplɒrətrɪ; *US* -tɔːrɪ/ *adj* done in order to find sth out: *The doctors are doing some exploratory tests to try and find out what's wrong.*

explorer /ɪkˈsplɔːrə(r)/ *noun* [C] a person who travels round a place in order to find out about it

☆ **explosion** /ɪkˈspləʊʒn/ *noun* [C] the sudden and violent bursting and loud noise that happen when sth like a bomb explodes: *The explosion may have been caused by a gas leak.* ○ (*figurative*) *the population explosion* (= the sudden increase in the number of people in a country or in the world)

explosive /ɪkˈspləʊsɪv/ *adj* **1** capable of exploding and therefore dangerous: *Hydrogen is extremely explosive.* **2** causing strong feelings or having dangerous effects: *The situation is explosive. We must do all we can to calm people down.*

explosive *noun* [C] a substance that can explode: *Dynamite and TNT are powerful explosives.*

☆ **export¹** /ɪkˈspɔːt/ *verb* [I,T] to send goods, etc to another country, usually for sale: *India exports tea and cotton.*

exporter *noun* [C] a person, firm or country that exports goods: *Japan is the largest exporter of electronic goods.* ☞ The opposites are **import, importer**.

☆ **export²** /ˈekspɔːt/ *noun* **1** [U] sending goods to another country for sale: *Most of our goods are produced for export.* ○ *the export trade* **2** [C, usually pl] something that is sent to another country for sale: *What are the main exports of Brazil?* ☞ The opposite is **import**.

☆ **expose** /ɪkˈspəʊz/ *verb* [T] **1** to make it possible to see sth that is usually hidden: *He liked to wear his shirt open to expose his chest.* ○ *The rocks are exposed at low tide.* **2** to put sb/sth or yourself in a situation that could be difficult or dangerous: *Thousands of people were exposed to radiation when the nuclear reactor exploded.* **3** to make public the truth about a bad person or situation: *This is an injustice which needs to be exposed.* **4** (in photography) to allow light to reach the film by opening the shutter of the camera

exposed *adj* (used about a place) not protected from the wind and bad weather

exposure /ɪkˈspəʊʒə(r)/ *noun* **1** [U] being affected or influenced by sth: *Exposure to radiation is almost always harmful.* **2** [U] a harmful condition when a person becomes very cold because he/she has been outside in very bad weather: *The climbers all died of exposure.* **3** [C,U] the act of making sth public; the

iː	ɪ	e	æ	ɑː	ɒ	ɔː	ʊ	uː	ʌ
see	sit	ten	hat	arm	got	saw	put	too	cup

thing that is made public: *The minister resigned because of the exposures about his private life.* **4** [U] attention from newspapers, television, etc; publicity: *The President's visit has been given a lot of exposure in the media.* **5** [C] the amount of film that is exposed(4) when you take one photograph: *How many exposures are there on this film?* (= how many photographs can I take?)

☆ **express¹** /ɪk'spres/ *verb* [T] **1** to show sth such as a feeling or an opinion by words or actions: *I found it very hard to express what I felt about her.* **2 express yourself** to speak or write: *I don't think she expresses herself very well in that article.*

express² /ɪk'spres/ *adj* (only *before* a noun) **1** going or sent quickly: *an express letter* ∘ *an express coach* **2** (used about a wish, command, etc) clearly and openly stated: *It was her express wish that he should have the picture after her death.*

express *adv* by a special service that does sth faster than usual: *We'd better send the parcel express if we want it to get there on time.*

expressly *adv* **1** clearly; definitely: *I expressly told you not to eat in the classroom.* **2** for a special purpose; specially: *These scissors are expressly designed for left-handed people.*

ex'pressway *noun* [C] (*US*) = MOTORWAY

express³ /ɪk'spres/ (*also* **express train**) *noun* [C] a fast train that does not stop at all stations

☆ **expression** /ɪk'spreʃn/ *noun* **1** [C] a number of words that belong together: *You haven't quite got the right expression here.* ∘ *a slang expression* ∘ *'It isn't half hot' is quite a difficult expression for foreign students to understand.* **2** [C] the look on a person's face that shows what he/she is thinking or feeling: *He had a puzzled expression on his face.* **3** [C,U] putting feelings or thoughts into words or actions; an example of doing this: *Freedom of expression* (= freedom to say what you think) *is a basic human right.* ∘ *These flowers are an expression of our gratitude.* ∘ *She read the poem with great expression* (= showing feeling for the meaning of it).

expressive /ɪk'spresɪv/ *adj* showing feelings or thoughts: *That is a very expressive piece of music.* —**expressively** *adv*

expulsion /ɪk'spʌlʃn/ *noun* [C,U] making sb leave a place or an institution (when he/she does not want to go): *There have been three expulsions from school this year.* ☞ The verb is **expel**.

exquisite /'ekskwɪzɪt, ɪk'skwɪzɪt/ *adj* very beautiful and pleasing: *She has an exquisite face.* ∘ *I think that ring is exquisite.*

☆ **extend** /ɪk'stend/ *verb* **1** [T] to make sth longer or larger (in space or time): *They are planning to extend the motorway as far as Fishguard.* ∘ *Could you extend your visit for a few days?* ∘ *We're going to extend the sitting-room.* **2** [I] (usually used about space, land, time, etc) to continue or stretch: *How far does your garden extend?* ∘ *This project will extend well into next year.* **3** [T] to stretch out a part of the body: *She extended her hand to her new colleague.* **4** [T] (*formal*) to offer or give sth (such as an invitation or a welcome): *The whole town extended a warm welcome to the president.*

extension /ɪk'stenʃn/ *noun* [C] **1** a part which is added to a building: *They've just opened the hospital extension.* **2** an extra period of time that is given to you by an official: *I've applied for an extension to my work permit.* **3** a telephone that is connected to a central phone in a house or to a central point (**switchboard**) in a large office building: *What's your extension number?* ∘ *Can I have extension 4342, please?*

extensive /ɪk'stensɪv/ *adj* large in area or amount: *The house has extensive grounds.* ∘ *Most of the buildings suffered extensive damage.* —**extensively** *adv*

☆ **extent** /ɪk'stent/ *noun* [U] the length, area or size of sth: *From the roof we could see the full extent of the park.* ∘ *I was amazed at the extent of his knowledge.* ∘ *The full extent of the damage is not yet known.*

(IDIOMS) **to a certain/to some extent** (words used to show that sth is only partly true): *I agree with you to a certain extent but there are still a lot of points I disagree on.*

to what extent how far: *I'm not sure to what extent I believe her.*

exterior /ɪk'stɪəriə(r)/ *adj* on the outside: *the exterior walls of a house* ☞ The opposite is **interior**.

exterior *noun* [C] the appearance of sb/sth; the outside of sth: *The exterior of the house is fine but inside it isn't in very good condition.*

exterminate /ɪk'stɜːmɪneɪt/ *verb* [T] to kill a large group of people or animals —**extermination** /ɪkˌstɜːmɪ'neɪʃn/ *noun* [U]

☆ **external** /ɪk'stɜːnl/ *adj* **1** connected with the outside of sth: *The cream is for external use only* (= to be used on the skin). **2** coming from another place: *You will be tested by an external examiner.* ☞ The opposite is **internal**.

extinct /ɪk'stɪŋkt/ *adj* **1** (used about a type of animal, plant, etc) no longer existing: *Tigers are nearly extinct in the wild.* **2** (used about a volcano) no longer active —**extinction** /ɪk'stɪŋkʃn/ *noun* [U]: *The panda is in danger of extinction.*

extinguish /ɪk'stɪŋgwɪʃ/ *verb* [T] (*formal*) to cause sth to stop burning: *The fire was extinguished very quickly.* ∘ *The stewardess asked everybody to extinguish their cigarettes.* ☞ A less formal expression is **put out**. —**extinguisher** *noun* [C] = FIRE EXTINGUISHER

extort /ɪk'stɔːt/ *verb* [T] **extort sth (from sb)** to get sth by using threats, violence, etc —**extortion** /ɪk'stɔːʃn/ *noun* [U]

extortionate /ɪk'stɔːʃənət/ *adj* (used about demands, prices, etc) too great or high: *Three pounds for a cup of coffee? That's extortionate!*

☆ **extra** /'ekstrə/ *adj, adv* more than is usual: *I'll need some extra money for the holidays.* ∘ *The football match went into extra time.* ∘ *'What size is this pullover?' 'Extra large.'* ∘ *The meal costs £10 and wine is extra.* ∘ *They charge £1 extra if you want to reserve a seat.* ∘ *I tried to be extra nice to him yesterday because it was his birthday.*

extra noun [C] **1** something that is or costs extra: *The holiday costs £300. It seems a lot but there are no hidden extras.* **2** a person in a film, etc who has a small unimportant part, for example in a crowd

extract /ɪkˈstrækt/ verb [T] to take or get sth out (with force or difficulty): *I think this tooth will have to be extracted.* ○ *I wasn't able to extract an apology from her.*

extract /ˈekstrækt/ noun [C] a part of a book, piece of music, etc. An extract has often been specially chosen to show sth: *We're reading extracts from modern British novels this term.*

extraction /ɪkˈstrækʃn/ noun **1** [U] the act of taking or getting sth out **2** [C] the removal of a tooth **3** [U] (*formal*) family origin: *He's an American but he's of Italian extraction.*

extracurricular /ˌekstrəkəˈrɪkjələ(r)/ adj not part of the normal course of studies (**curriculum**) in a school or college: *The school offers many extracurricular activities such as sport, music, drama, etc.*

extradite /ˈekstrədaɪt/ verb [T] to send a person who may be guilty of a crime from the country in which he/she is living to the country which wants to try him/her for the crime: *The suspected terrorists were captured in Spain and extradited to France.* —**extradition** /ˌekstrəˈdɪʃn/ noun [C,U]

☆ **extraordinary** /ɪkˈstrɔːdnri/; *US* -dəneri/ adj **1** very unusual: *She had an extraordinary ability to learn new languages.* **2** very strange (and not what you would expect in a particular situation): *That was extraordinary behaviour for a teacher!* —**extraordinarily** /ɪkˈstrɔːdnrəli/; *US* -dənerəli/ adv: *He was an extraordinarily talented musician.*

extravagant /ɪkˈstrævəgənt/ adj **1** spending or costing too much money: *He's terribly extravagant – he never looks at the price of anything.* ○ *an extravagant present* **2** (used about ideas, behaviour, etc) not controlled, not realistic: *The advertisements made extravagant claims for the new medicine.* —**extravagance** /-gəns/ noun [C,U] —**extravagantly** adv

☆ **extreme** /ɪkˈstriːm/ adj **1** (only *before* a noun) as far away as possible; at the very beginning or at the very end: *Kerry is in the extreme West of Ireland.* **2** (only *before* a noun) the greatest or strongest possible: *You must take extreme care when driving at night.* **3** (used about a person and his/her political opinions) not usual or moderate: *She holds extreme views on immigration.* ○ *the extreme left/right* ☞ This word is used in a disapproving way.

extreme noun [C] something that is completely different from or opposite to sth else: *Alex used to be very shy but now she's gone to the opposite extreme.*

extremely adv very

extremity /ɪkˈstreməti/ noun [C] (pl **extremities**) the furthest point of sth

extremist noun [C] a person who has extreme(3) political opinions —**extremism** noun [U]

extricate /ˈekstrɪkeɪt/ verb [T] to free sb/sth/ yourself from a difficult situation or position: *I finally managed to extricate myself from the meeting by saying that I had a train to catch.*

extrovert /ˈekstrəvɜːt/ noun [C] a person who is lively and cheerful and who prefers being with other people to being alone ☞ The opposite is **introvert**.

exuberant /ɪgˈzjuːbərənt/; *US* -ˈzuː-/ adj (used about a person and his/her behaviour) full of energy and excitement —**exuberance** /-rəns/ noun [U]

☆ **eye**¹ /aɪ/ noun [C] **1** one of the two organs of the body that we use to see with: *She opened/closed her eyes.* ○ *He is blind in one eye.* ○ *She's got blue eyes.* ○ *an eye operation*

☞ If somebody hits you on the eye you might get a **black eye**. When you close both eyes very quickly and open them again you **blink**. To close one eye quickly and open it again is to **wink**.

2 the power of seeing: *He has sharp eyes* (= he can see very well). ○ *She has an eye for detail* (= she notices small details). **3** the part at one end of a needle that the thread passes through

(IDIOMS) **be up to your eyes in sth** (*informal*) to have more of sth than you can easily do or manage: *I can't come out with you tonight – I'm up to my eyes in work.*

cast an eye/your eye(s) over sb/sth ⇨ CAST²

catch sb's attention/eye ⇨ CATCH¹

in the eyes of sb/in sb's eyes in the opinion of sb: *She was still a child in her mother's eyes.*

keep an eye on sb/sth to make sure that sb/sth is safe; to look after sb/sth: *Please could you keep an eye on the house while we are away?*

keep an eye open/out (for sb/sth) to watch or look out for sb/sth: *I've lost my ring – could you keep an eye out for it?*

the naked eye ⇨ NAKED

see eye to eye with sb to agree with sb; to have the same opinion as sb: *We're good friends but we don't always see eye to eye on political matters.*

set eyes on sb/sth ⇨ SET²

turn a blind eye ⇨ BLIND

with your eyes open knowing what you are doing: *He married her with his eyes open so he can't complain now.*

'eyeball noun [C] the whole of the eye (including the part which is hidden inside the head)

'eyebrow (*also* **brow**) noun [C] the line of hair that is above your eye: *She doesn't pluck her eyebrows.* ☞ picture on page A8.

(IDIOM) **raise your eyebrows** ⇨ RAISE

'eyeglasses noun [plural] (*US*) = GLASSES

'eyelash (*also* **lash**) noun [C] one of the hairs that grow on the edges of your eyelids

'eye-level adj level with sb's eyes when he/ she is standing up: *an eye-level grill*

'eyelid (*also* **lid**) noun [C] the piece of skin that can move to close your eye

p	b	t	d	k	g	tʃ	dʒ	f	v	θ	ð
pen	bad	tea	did	cat	got	chin	June	fall	van	thin	then

(IDIOM) **not bat an eyelid** ⇨ BAT³
'**eye-opener** *noun* [C] something that makes you realize the truth about sth: *That television programme about the inner cities was a real eye-opener.*
'**eyesight** *noun* [U] the ability to see: *good/poor eyesight*

'**eyesore** *noun* [C] something that is ugly and unpleasant to look at: *All this litter in the streets is a real eyesore.*
'**eyewitness** *noun* [C] = WITNESS(1)
eye² /aɪ/ *verb* [T] (*pres part* **eyeing** or **eying**; *pt, pp* **eyed**) to look at sb/sth closely: *She eyed him with suspicion.*

Ff

F, f /ef/ *noun* [C] (*pl* **F's**; **f's**) the sixth letter of the English alphabet: *'Father' begins with (an) 'F'.*
fable /'feɪbl/ *noun* [C] a short story that teaches a lesson (**a moral**) and that often has animals as speaking characters: *Aesop's fables*
fabric /'fæbrɪk/ *noun* **1** [C,U] (a type of) cloth: *cotton fabrics* **2** [sing] the walls, floor, roof, etc (of a building): *The fabric of the church is in need of repair.* ○ (*figurative*) *The Industrial Revolution changed the fabric* (= the basic structure) *of society.*
fabulous /'fæbjʊləs/ *adj* **1** (*informal*) very good; excellent: *It was a fabulous concert.* **2** (used about beauty, wealth, etc) very great
façade (*also* **facade**) /fə'sɑːd/ *noun* [C] **1** the front wall of a large building that you see from the outside **2** something that gives you the wrong impression about a situation: *His good humour was just a façade.*
☆**face¹** /feɪs/ *noun* [C] **1** the front part of your head and the expression on it: *Go and wash your face.* ○ *She has a very pretty face.* ○ *He came in with a smile on his face.* ○ *the children's happy faces* **2** the front or one side of sth: *the north face of the mountain* ○ *He put the cards face up/down on the table.* ○ *a clock face*
(IDIOMS) **face to face (with sb/sth)** close to and looking at sb/sth: *She turned the corner and came face to face with the headmaster.*
keep a straight face ⇨ STRAIGHT¹
lose face ⇨ LOSE
make/pull faces/a face (at sb) to make an expression that shows that you dislike sb/sth: *When she saw what was for dinner she pulled a face.*
make/pull faces to make rude expressions with your face: *The children made faces behind the teacher's back.*
save face ⇨ SAVE
to sb's face openly and directly: *I wanted to say that I was sorry to her face, not on the phone.*
☛ The opposite is **behind sb's back**.
faceless *adj* without individual character: *faceless civil servants*
'**face-cloth** (*also* **face-flannel**; **flannel**) (*US* **wash-cloth**) *noun* [C] a small square towel that is used for washing the face, hands, etc

'**face-lift** *noun* [C] a medical operation that makes your face look younger
'**face-saving** *adj* done to stop yourself looking silly or losing other people's respect: *In his interview, the captain made face-saving excuses for his team's defeat.*
,**face 'value** *noun* [C,U] the cost or value that is shown on stamps, coins, etc
(IDIOM) **take sb/sth at (its, his, etc) face value** to accept sb/sth as it, he, etc appears to be: *Don't take his story at face value. There is something he hasn't told us yet.*
☆**face²** /feɪs/ *verb* [T] **1** to have or turn the face or front towards sb/sth: *The garden faces south.* ○ *Can you all face the front, please?* ○ *Turn round and face the camera.* **2** to have to deal with sth unpleasant; to deal with sb in a difficult situation: *They faced a lot of problems when they moved house.* ○ *I can't face another argument.* ○ *He couldn't face going to work yesterday – he felt too ill.* ○ *I didn't know how to face my mother after I'd crashed her car.* **3** to need attention from sb: *Several problems face the government.* ○ *There are several problems facing the government.* **4** (often passive) to force somebody to deal with a situation, etc: *We are faced with a difficult decision.*
(IDIOM) **let's face it** (*informal*) we must accept it as true: *Let's face it, your spelling is terrible.*
(PHRASAL VERB) **face up to sth** to accept a difficult or unpleasant situation and do sth about it: *She faced up to the fact that she had no money and went out and got a job.*
-faced (in compounds) with a particular type of face: *red-faced*
facet /'fæsɪt/ *noun* [C] **1** one part of sth: *There are many facets to this argument* (= points that must be considered). **2** one side of a precious stone
facetious /fə'siːʃəs/ *adj* trying to be amusing at an unsuitable time or about an unsuitable subject: *He kept making facetious remarks during the lecture.* —**facetiously** *adv*
facial /'feɪʃl/ *adj* of or for the face: *a facial expression*
facile /'fæsaɪl; *US* 'fæsl/ *adj* (used about a remark, argument, etc) not carefully thought out

s	z	ʃ	ʒ	h	m	n	ŋ	l	r	j	w
so	zoo	she	vision	how	man	no	sing	leg	red	yes	wet

facilitate /fəˈsɪlɪteɪt/ verb [T] (formal) to make sth possible or easier

☆ **facility** /fəˈsɪlətɪ/ noun (pl **facilities**) **1 facilities** [plural] a service, building, piece of equipment, etc that makes it possible to do sth: *Our town has excellent sports facilities* (eg a stadium, swimming-pool, etc). ○ *The room was nice but there were no cooking facilities.* **2** [C] an extra feature that a machine, etc may have: *This word processor has a facility for checking spelling.*

facsimile /fækˈsɪməlɪ/ noun [C,U] an exact copy of a picture, piece of writing, etc ☛ Look at **fax**.

☆ **fact** /fækt/ noun **1** [C] something that you know has happened or is true: *It is a scientific fact that light travels faster than sound.* ○ *We need to know all the facts before we can decide.* ○ *I know for a fact that Peter wasn't ill yesterday.* ○ *The fact that I am older than you makes no difference at all.* ○ *You must face facts and accept that he has gone.* **2** [U] true things; reality: *The film is based on fact.* ☛ The opposite is **fiction**.
(IDIOMS) **as a matter of fact** ⇨ MATTER¹
the fact (of the matter) is (that)... the truth is that...: *I would love a car, but the fact is that I just can't afford one.*
facts and figures (informal) detailed information: *Before we make a decision, we need some more facts and figures.*
the facts of life the details of sexual behaviour and how babies are born
hard facts ⇨ HARD¹
in (actual) fact 1 (used for emphasizing that sth is true) really; actually: *I thought the lecture would be boring but in actual fact it was rather interesting.* **2** (used for introducing more detailed information): *It was cold. In fact it was freezing.*

factor /ˈfæktə(r)/ noun [C] **1** one of the things that influences a decision, situation, etc: *economic factors* ○ *His unhappiness at home was a major factor in his decision to go abroad.* **2** (in mathematics) a whole number (except 1) by which a larger number can be divided: *2, 3, 4 and 6 are factors of 12.*

☆ **factory** /ˈfæktərɪ/ (pl **factories**) noun [C] a large building or group of buildings where goods are manufactured or put together in large quantities (by machine): *a car factory* ○ *factory workers*

factual /ˈfæktʃuəl/ adj based on or containing facts: *a factual account of the events* ☛ Look at **fictional**.

faculty /ˈfækltɪ/ noun [C] **1** one of the natural abilities of a person's body or mind: *the faculty of hearing, sight, etc* **2** (also **Faculty**) one department in a university, college, etc: *the Faculty of Law* ☛ **The Faculty** can also mean the teaching staff of a university or college department and is then used with either a singular or a plural verb: *The Faculty has/have been invited to the meeting.*

fad /fæd/ noun [C] (informal) a fashion, interest, etc that will probably not last long

☆ **fade** /feɪd/ verb **1** [I] to become lighter in colour or less strong or fresh: *Jeans fade when you wash them.* ○ *The sun was setting and the light was fading fast.* **2** [T] to make sth fade: *Look how the sun has faded these curtains.* **3** [I] **fade (away)** to disappear slowly (from sight, hearing, memory, etc): *The cheering of the crowd faded away.* ○ *The smile faded from his face.*

faeces (US **feces**) /ˈfiːsiːz/ noun [plural] (formal) solid waste matter that is passed from the body through the bowels ☛ **Faeces** is used mainly in a medical context. Look at **excrement**.

fag /fæg/ noun **1** [C] (Brit slang) a cigarette **2** [sing] (informal) a piece of work that you do not want to do: *I've got to wash the car. What a fag!*

Fahrenheit /ˈfærənhaɪt/ noun [U] (abbr **F**) the name of a scale which measures temperatures: *Water freezes at 32° Fahrenheit (32°F).* ☛ Look at **Celsius**.

☆ **fail** /feɪl/ verb **1** [I,T] to be unsuccessful in sth: *She failed her driving test.* ○ *I feel that I've failed – I'm 21 and I still haven't got a steady job.* ☛ Look at **pass** and **succeed**. **2** [T] (used about an examiner, etc) to decide that sb is unsuccessful in a test, examination, etc: *The examiners failed half of the candidates.* ☛ The opposite is **pass**. **3** [I] **fail to do sth** to not do sth: *Jimmy failed to arrive on time.* ○ *She never fails to do her homework.* **4** [I,T] to not be enough or not do what people are expecting or wanting: *If the crops fail, people will starve.* ○ *Words fail me!* (= I don't know how to express my feelings.) ○ *I think the government has failed us.* **5** [I] (used about health, eyesight, etc) to become weak: *His health is failing.* **6** [I] to stop working: *My brakes failed on the hill but I managed to stop the car.*

fail noun [C] a failure in an examination ☛ The opposite is a **pass**.
(IDIOM) **without fail** always, even if there are difficulties: *The postman always comes at 8 o'clock without fail.*

failing¹ /ˈfeɪlɪŋ/ noun [C] a weakness or fault: *She's not very patient – that's her only failing.*

failing² /ˈfeɪlɪŋ/ prep if sth is not possible: *Ask Jackie to go with you, or failing that, try Anne.*

☆ **failure** /ˈfeɪljə(r)/ noun **1** [U] lack of success: *All my efforts ended in failure.* **2** [C] a person or thing that is unsuccessful: *I was a failure as a mother.* ○ *His first attempt at ice-skating was a miserable failure.* **3** [C,U] **failure to do sth** not doing sth that people expect you to do: *I was very disappointed at his failure to come to the meeting.* **4** [C,U] an example of sth not working or functioning properly: *She died of heart failure.* ○ *There's been a failure in the power supply.*

☆ **faint** /feɪnt/ adj **1** (used about things that you can see, hear, feel, etc) not strong or clear: *a faint light in the distance* ○ *They heard a faint cry, then there was silence.* ○ *There is still a faint hope that they will find more people alive.* **2** (used about people) on the point of losing consciousness; very weak: *I feel faint – I'd better sit down.* **3** (used about actions, etc) done without much effort: *He made a faint protest.*
(IDIOM) **not have the faintest/foggiest (idea)** not to know at all: *I haven't the faintest idea where they've gone.*

iː	ɪ	e	æ	ɑː	ɒ	ɔː	ʊ	uː	ʌ
see	sit	ten	hat	arm	got	saw	put	too	cup

faint *verb* [I] to lose consciousness: *She fainted from shock and loss of blood.*

☆**fair¹** /feə(r)/ *adj* **1 fair (to/on sb)** treating each person or side equally, according to the law or the rules, etc: *That's not fair – he got the same number of mistakes as I did and he's got a better mark.* o *It wasn't fair on her to ask her to stay so late.* o *a fair trial* **2** right, according to what people generally accept as right: *That's a fair price for that house, I think.* o *I think it's fair to say that the number of homeless people is increasing.* ☛ The opposite for senses 1 and 2 is **unfair**. **3** quite good, large, etc: *They have a fair chance of success.* o *It is a fair-sized house.* **4** (used about the skin or hair) light in colour: *We think of Germans as having fair hair but a lot of them are dark.* **5** (used about the weather) good, without rain

(IDIOMS) **fair play** equal treatment of both/all sides according to the rules: *The referee is there to ensure fair play during the match.*

(**more than**) **your fair share of sth** (more than) the usual or expected amount of sth: *We've had more than our fair share of trouble this year.*

fairness *noun* [U] the state or quality of being fair

fair-'haired *adj* with light-coloured or blond hair

☆**fair²** /feə(r)/ *adv* in a fair way: *You must play fair in all team games.*

(IDIOM) **fair enough** (used for showing that you agree with what sb has suggested): *'I'd rather go on Sunday, if that's all right with you.' 'Fair enough, Sunday is fine.'*

fair³ /feə(r)/ *noun* [C] **1** (*also* **funfair**) a public entertainment which is held outside. At a fair you can ride on machines or try and win prizes at games. Fairs usually travel from town to town. **2** a large exhibition of commercial or industrial goods: *a trade fair* o *the Frankfurt book fair*

'**fairground** *noun* [C] a large outdoor area where fairs³(1) are held

☆**fairly** /'feəli/ *adv* **1** in a fair¹(1) way: *I felt that the teacher didn't treat us fairly.* ☛ The opposite is **unfairly**. **2** quite, not very: *He is fairly tall.* o *We must leave fairly soon.* ☛ Look at the note at **rather**.

fairy /'feəri/ *noun* [C] (*pl* **fairies**) (in stories) a small creature with magical powers

'**fairy story** (*also* '**fairy tale**) *noun* [C] a story that is about fairies, magic, etc: *Grimm's fairy tales*

☆**faith** /feɪθ/ *noun* **1** [U] **faith (in sb/sth)** strong belief in sb/ sth); trust: *I've got great faith in your ability to do the job* (= I'm sure that you can do it). o *I have lost faith in him.* **2** [U] strong religious belief: *I've lost my faith.* **3** [C] a religion: *the Christian faith*

(IDIOM) **in good faith** with honest reasons for doing sth: *I bought the car in good faith. I didn't know it was stolen.*

☆**faithful** /'feɪθfl/ *adj* **1** not changing; loyal: *Peter has been a faithful friend.* o *He was always faithful to his wife* (= he didn't have sexual relations with anyone else). ☛ The opposite is **unfaithful**. **2** true to the facts; accurate: *a faithful description* —**faithfully** /-fəli/ *adv* ☛ **Yours faithfully** is used to end formal letters. —**faithfulness** *noun* [U]

fake /feɪk/ *noun* [C] **1** a work of art, etc that seems to be real or genuine but is not: *That's not a real diamond necklace. It's just a fake!* **2** a person who pretends to be sb/sth else in order to deceive people

fake *adj* not real or genuine: *a fake passport*

fake *verb* [T] **1** to copy sth in order to deceive people: *He faked his father's signature.* **2** to pretend that you are feeling sth that you are not: *I faked surprise when he told me the news.*

falcon /'fɔːlkən; *US* 'fælkən/ *noun* [C] a small bird of the type that kills and eats other animals (**a bird of prey**). Falcons can be trained to hunt.

☆**fall¹** /fɔːl/ *verb* [I] (*pt* **fell** /fel/; *pp* **fallen** /'fɔːlən/) **1** to drop down towards the ground: *He fell off the ladder onto the grass.* o *Don't walk along that wall – you might fall.* o *Autumn came and the leaves started to fall.* o *The rain was falling steadily.* **2 fall (down/over)** to suddenly stop standing: *She slipped on the ice and fell.* o *The little boy fell over and hurt his knee.* **3** (*formal*) to come or happen: *Christmas Day falls on a Sunday this year.* o *In the word 'interesting' the stress falls on the first syllable.* **4** to hang down: *Her hair fell down over her shoulders.* **5** to become lower or less: *The temperature is falling.* o *The price of coffee has fallen again.* o *When he heard the bad news, his spirits fell* (= he felt sad). **6** to be killed (in battle): *Millions of soldiers fell in the Second World War.* **7** to be defeated: *The Government fell because of the scandal.* **8** to change into a different state; to become: *He fell asleep on the sofa.* o *They fell in love with each other in Spain.* o *I must get some new shoes – these ones are falling to pieces.* **9** to belong to a particular group, type, etc: *Animals fall into two groups, those with backbones and those without.*

(IDIOMS) **fall flat** ⇨ FLAT³

fall in love ⇨ LOVE¹

fall short (of sth) ⇨ SHORT²

(PHRASAL VERBS) **fall apart** to break (into pieces): *My car is falling apart.*

fall back on sb/sth to use sb/sth when you are in difficulty: *When the electricity was cut off we fell back on candles.*

fall for sb (*informal*) to fall in love with sb

fall for sth (*informal*) to be tricked into believing sth that is not true: *He makes excuses and she falls for them every time.*

fall out (with sb) to quarrel or fight (with sb)

fall through to fail or not happen: *Our trip to Japan has fallen through.*

'**fallout** *noun* [U] radioactive waste matter that is carried in the air after a nuclear explosion

☆**fall²** /fɔːl/ *noun* **1** [C] an act of falling(1, 2): *She*

fall had a nasty fall from her horse. **2** [C] **a fall (of sth)** the amount of sth that has fallen or the distance that sth has fallen: *We have had a heavy fall of snow.* o *a fall of four metres* **3** [C] a decrease (in value, quantity, etc): *There has been a sharp fall in the price of oil.* ☛ The opposite is **rise**. **4** [sing] **the fall of sth** a (political) defeat: *the fall of the Roman Empire* **5** [C, usually pl] a waterfall: *Niagara Falls*

fall[3] /fɔːl/ *noun* [C] (*US*) = AUTUMN: *I visited Europe in the fall of 1963.*

fallacy /'fæləsi/ *noun* (*pl* **fallacies**) [C,U] (*formal*) a false or mistaken belief or argument: *It's a fallacy to believe that money brings happiness* (= it's not true).

fallen *pp* of FALL[1]

fallible /'fæləbl/ *adj* able or likely to make mistakes: *Even our new computerized system is fallible.* ☛ The opposite is **infallible**.

☆ **false** /'fɒls; fɔːls/ *adj* **1** not true; incorrect: *Bucharest is the capital of Romania – true or false?* o *I think the information you have been given is false.* **2** not real; artificial: *false hair, eyelashes, etc* **3** based on wrong information or belief: *I got a completely false impression of him from our first meeting.* **4** made or done incorrectly in order to deceive people: *This suitcase has a false bottom.* o *a false name* **5** not faithful; not loyal: *a false friend*

(IDIOMS) **a false alarm** a warning about a danger that does not happen

on/under false pretences pretending to be or to have sth in order to deceive people: *She got into the club under false pretences – she isn't a member at all!*

false 'teeth (*also* **dentures**) *noun* [plural] teeth that are made of plastic, etc, worn by a person who has lost his/her natural teeth

falsify /'fɔːlsɪfaɪ/ *verb* [T] (*pres part* **falsifying**; *3rd pers sing pres* **falsifies**; *pt, pp* **falsified**) (*formal*) to change a document, information, etc in order to deceive other people

falter /'fɔːltə(r)/ *verb* [I] **1** to become weak or move in a weak, unsteady way: *As she began to speak her voice faltered.* o *The engine faltered and stopped.* **2** to lose confidence and hesitate: *Becker faltered and missed the ball.*

☆ **fame** /feɪm/ *noun* [U] being known or talked about by many people: *Pop stars achieve fame at a young age.*

famed *adj* well-known (for sth): *Welsh people are famed for their singing.* ☛ Look at **famous**, which is the more usual word.

☆ **familiar** /fə'mɪliə(r)/ *adj* **1** (not before a noun) **familiar with sth** having a good knowledge of sth: *People in Europe aren't very familiar with Chinese music.* **2 familiar (to sb)** well-known (to sb): *Chinese music isn't very familiar to people in Europe.* o *It was a relief to see a familiar face in the crowd.* ☛ The opposite for senses 1 and 2 is **unfamiliar**. **3** too friendly and informal: *I was annoyed by the waiter's familiar behaviour.*

familiarity /fə,mɪli'ærəti/ *noun* [U] **1** good knowledge of sth: *His familiarity with the area was an advantage.* **2** being too friendly and informal

familiarize (*also* **familiarise**) /fə'mɪliəraɪz/ *verb* [T] to inform sb/yourself about sth: *I want to familiarize myself with the plans before the meeting.*

☆ **family** /'fæməli/ *noun* (*pl* **families**) **1** [C, with sing or pl verb] a group of people who are related to each other ☛ Sometimes we use 'family' to mean 'parents and their children' (a **nuclear family**), sometimes we use it to include other relatives, eg grandparents, aunts, uncles, etc (an **extended family**). Family is used with a singular verb when we are talking about a family as a unit: *Almost every family in the village owns a television.* A plural verb is used when we are thinking about the members of a family as individuals: *My family are all very tall.* Family can be used before another noun to describe things that are suitable for or that can be used by all the family: *family entertainment* o *the family car.* **2** [C,U] children: *Do you have any family?* o *We are planning to start a family next year* (= to have our first baby). **3** [C] a group of animals, plants, etc that are related to each other: *Lions belong to the cat family.*

(IDIOM) **run in the family** to be found very often in a family: *Red hair runs in the family.*

'family name *noun* [C] the name that is shared by members of a family; surname ☛ Look at the note at **name**.

,family 'planning *noun* [U] controlling the number of children in a family by using birth control ☛ Look at **contraception**.

,family 'tree *noun* [C] a diagram that shows the relationships between different members of a family

famine /'fæmɪn/ *noun* [C,U] a lack of food in a large area that can cause the death of many people: *There is a severe famine in many parts of Africa.* o *The long drought was followed by famine.*

famished /'fæmɪʃt/ *adj* (not before a noun) (*informal*) very hungry: *When's lunch? I'm famished!*

☆ **famous** /'feɪməs/ *adj* **famous (for sth)** well-known to many people: *a famous singer* o *Glasgow is famous for its museums and art galleries.* ☛ Look at **infamous** and **notorious**, which mean 'famous for being bad'.

famously *adv* (*informal*) very well: *She's getting on famously in the new job.*

☆ **fan**[1] /fæn/ *noun* [C] something that is used for making a (cool) wind, eg an object made of paper, feathers, etc in the shape of half a circle or an (electric) machine with large blades that turn around very quickly

fan *verb* [T] (**fann**ing; **fann**ed) **1** to cool sb/sth by moving the air with a fan or sth like a fan: *She used a newspaper to fan her face.* **2** to make a fire burn more strongly: *The strong wind really fanned the flames.*

(PHRASAL VERB) **fan out** to spread out: *The police fanned out across the field.*

'fan belt *noun* [C] the belt that drives the fan to cool the engine of a car, etc

☆ **fan**[2] /fæn/ *noun* [C] somebody who admires and is very enthusiastic about a sport, a film star, a singer, etc: *football fans* o *He's a Van*

p	b	t	d	k	g	tʃ	dʒ	f	v	θ	ð
pen	bad	tea	did	cat	got	chin	June	fall	van	thin	then

fans

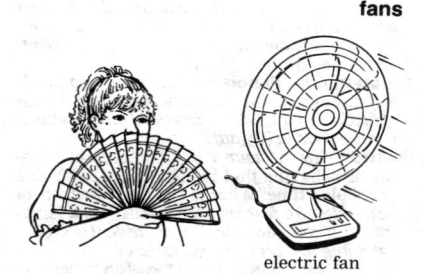

electric fan

Morrison fan. ○ *I'm not a great fan of modern jazz* (= I don't like it very much).

fanatic /fə'nætɪk/ *noun* [C] a person who is too enthusiastic about sth (especially about religion or politics): *a religious fanatic* ○ *She's a health-food fanatic.*

▶ **fanatic** (*also* **fanatical** /-kl/) *adj* feeling very strongly or being too enthusiastic about sth: *He's fanatical about keeping things tidy.* — **fanatically** /-klɪ/ *adv* — **fanaticism** /-tɪsɪzəm/ *noun* [C,U]

fancy¹ /'fænsɪ/ *noun*
(IDIOMS) **take sb's fancy** to attract or please sb: *If you see something that takes your fancy I'll buy it for you.*
take a fancy to sb/sth to start liking sb/sth: *I think that Alan's really taken a fancy to you.*

fancy² /'fænsɪ/ *adj* not simple or ordinary: *My father doesn't like fancy food.* ○ *I just want a pair of black shoes – nothing fancy.*

,fancy 'dress *noun* [U] special clothes that you wear to a party at which people dress up to look like a different person (eg from history or a story): *We've been invited to a fancy dress party – I'm going as Napoleon.* ○ *It was a Hallowe'en party and everyone went in fancy dress.*

fancy³ /'fænsɪ/ *verb* (*pres part* **fancying**; *3rd pers sing pres* **fancies**; *pt, pp* **fancied**) **1** [T] (*informal*) to like the idea of having or doing sth: *What do you fancy for supper?* ○ *I don't fancy going out in this rain.* **2** [T] (*Brit informal*) to be (sexually) attracted to sb: *Alan keeps looking at you. I think he fancies you.* **3** [I,T] (used for expressing surprise, shock, etc): *'They're getting married next week.' 'Well, fancy that!'* ○ *Fancy meeting you here!* **4** [T] (*formal*) to think or imagine sth: *He fancied that he heard footsteps behind him.*

fanfare /'fænfeə(r)/ *noun* [C] a short loud piece of music played on trumpets that is used for introducing sb/sth

fang /fæŋ/ *noun* [C] a long sharp tooth of a dog, poisonous snake, etc

fantasize (*also* **fantasise**) /'fæntəsaɪz/ *verb* [I,T] to imagine sth that you would like to happen: *He liked to fantasize that he had won a gold medal at the Olympics.*

fantastic /fæn'tæstɪk/ *adj* **1** (*informal*) very good; excellent: *She's a fantastic swimmer.* ○ *You passed your test. Fantastic!* **2** strange and difficult to believe: *a story full of fantastic creatures from other worlds* **3** (*informal*) very large or great: *A Rolls Royce costs a fantastic amount of money.* — **fantastically** /-klɪ/ *adv*

fantasy (*also* **phantasy**) /'fæntəsɪ/ *noun* [C,U] (*pl* **fantasies**) situations that are not true, that you just imagine: *They live in a world of fantasy.* ☛ Look at the note at **imagination**.

☆ **far¹** /fɑː(r)/ *adj* (**farther** /'fɑːðə(r)/ *or* **further** /'fɜːðə(r)/, **farthest** /'fɑːðɪst/ *or* **furthest** /'fɜːðɪst/) **1** distant; a long way away: *Let's walk – it's not far.* ○ (*formal*) *The explorers sailed to far countries.* **2** (only *before* a noun) more distant (used about one of two ends, sides, etc): *My friend lives at the far end of the street.* ○ *In the far north, days are short in winter.*
(IDIOM) **a far cry from sth/from doing sth** an experience that is very different from sth/doing sth
the Far 'East China, Japan and other countries in E and SE Asia

☆ **far²** /fɑː(r)/ *adv* (**farther** /'fɑːðə(r)/, *or* **further** /'fɜːðə(r)/, **farthest** /'fɑːðɪst/ *or* **furthest** /'fɜːðɪst/) **1** (at) a distance: *London's not far from here.* ○ *Do you live far from Oxford?* ○ *How far did we walk yesterday?* ○ *Call me if you need me; I won't be far away.* ☛ **Far** in this sense is usually used in negative sentences and questions. In positive sentences we say **a long way**: *It's a long way from here to the sea.* Some sentences have a negative meaning although they are positive in form. **Far** can be used in them: *Let's get a bus. It's much too far to walk.* **2** a long time: *This story began far back, in 1850.* ○ *We danced far into the night.* **3** (before comparative adjectives) very much: *She's far more intelligent than I thought.* ○ *It's far wetter in England than in Italy.*
(IDIOMS) **as far as** to the place mentioned but not further: *We walked as far as the river and then turned back.*
as/so far as 1 the same distance as (sb): *I can't swim as far as you.* **2** to the degree that: *As far as I know, she's not coming, but I may be wrong.*
as far as I can see (used for introducing your opinion): *As far as I can see, the accident was John's fault, not Ann's.*
as/so far as sb/sth is concerned on the subject of sb/sth; as sb/sth is affected or influenced by sth: *As far as school work is concerned, he's hopeless.* ○ *As far as I'm concerned* (= in my opinion), *this is the most important point.*
by far (used for emphasizing comparative or superlative words) by a large amount: *Jane is by far the best student in the class.*
far afield far away, especially from where you live or from where you are staying: *We decided to hire a car in order to explore further afield.*
far from doing sth instead of doing sth: *Far from enjoying the film, he fell asleep in the middle.*
far from sth/from doing sth almost the opposite of sth: *He's far from happy* (= he's sad).
far from it (*informal*) certainly not; just the

s	z	ʃ	ʒ	h	m	n	ŋ	l	r	j	w
so	zoo	she	vision	how	man	no	sing	leg	red	yes	wet

farce — 230 — **fastidious**

opposite: *'Did you enjoy your holiday?' 'No, far from it. It was awful.'*
few and far between ⇨ FEW¹
go too far to behave in a way that causes trouble or upsets other people: *He's always been naughty but this time he's gone too far.*
so far until now: *So far the weather has been good but it might change.*

ˈfar-away *adj* **1** distant: *He told us stories of far-away countries.* **2** (used about a look in a person's eyes) as if you are thinking of sth else: *She stared out of the window with a far-away look in her eyes.*

ˌfar-ˈfetched *adj* not easy to believe: *It's a good book but the story's too far-fetched.*

ˌfar-ˈreaching *adj* having, or going to have, a great influence on a lot of other things: *far-reaching changes*

ˌfar-ˈsighted *adj* **1** being able to see what will be necessary and making plans for it **2** (*US*) = LONG-SIGHTED

farce /fɑːs/ *noun* [C] **1** a funny play for the theatre full of ridiculous situations **2** something important or serious that is not organized well or treated with respect: *The interview was a farce. I knew that I'd got the job already.* —**farcical** /ˈfɑːsɪkl/ *adj*

☆ **fare**¹ /feə(r)/ *noun* [C] the amount of money you pay to travel by bus, train, taxi, etc: *What's the fare to Birmingham?* ○ *Train fares are going up next month.* ☞ Adults pay **full fare**, children pay **half fare**.

fare² /feə(r)/ *noun* [U] food, especially that served at a restaurant, pub or hotel

fare³ /feə(r)/ *verb* [I] (*formal*) to be successful/unsuccessful in a particular situation: *How did you fare in your examination?* (= did you do well or badly?)

farewell /ˌfeəˈwel/ *interj* (*old-fashioned*) goodbye — **farewell** *noun* [C]: *He said a sad farewell and left.* ○ *a farewell party*

☆ **farm**¹ /fɑːm/ *noun* [C] an area of land with fields and buildings that is used for growing crops and keeping animals: *In the summer holidays I often work on a farm.* ○ *farm buildings*

ˈfarmhouse (*also* **farm**) *noun* [C] the house on a farm where the farmer lives

ˈfarmyard *noun* [C] an outside area near a farmhouse surrounded by buildings or walls

☆ **farm**² /fɑːm/ *verb* [I,T] to use land for growing crops or keeping animals: *He's farming in Scotland.* ○ *She farms 200 acres.*

farmer *noun* [C] a person who owns or manages a farm

farming *noun* [U] managing a farm or working on it: *Farming is extremely hard work.*

☆ **farther** /ˈfɑːðə(r)/ *adj, adv* more distant in space or time; a greater distance: *Rome is farther from London than Paris is.* ○ *I can swim farther than you.*
☞ **Farther** is the comparative of **far**. Look at the note at **further**.

☆ **farthest** /ˈfɑːðɪst/ (*also* **furthest**) *adj, adv* most distant in space or time; the greatest distance: *the farthest corner of Europe* ○ *Who can swim farthest?* ☞ **Farthest** is the superlative of **far**.

☆ **fascinate** /ˈfæsɪneɪt/ *verb* [T] to attract or interest sb very much: *He fascinated the children with his magic tricks.* ○ *I was fascinated by that film.* —**fascinating** *adj* —**fascination** /ˌfæsɪˈneɪʃn/ *noun* [C,U]

fascism (*also* **Fascism**) /ˈfæʃɪzəm/ *noun* [U] an extreme right-wing political system: *the rise of fascism in the 1930s* —**fascist** (*also* **Fascist**) /ˈfæʃɪst/ *noun* [C], *adj*

☆ **fashion** /ˈfæʃn/ *noun* **1** [C,U] the style of dressing or behaving that is the most popular at a particular time: *What is the latest fashion in hairstyles?* ○ *a fashion show, model, etc* **2** [sing] the way you do sth: *Watch him. He's been behaving in a very strange fashion.*

(IDIOMS) **come into/be in fashion** to become or to be popular as a style: *Jeans are always in fashion.*

go/be out of fashion to become or to be unpopular as a style: *That colour is out of fashion this year.*

☆ **fashionable** /ˈfæʃnəbl/ *adj* following the latest popular style: *a fashionable woman, suit, restaurant, idea, etc* ☞ The opposite is **unfashionable** or **old-fashioned**. —**fashionably** /-əblɪ/ *adv*

☆ **fast**¹ /fɑːst; *US* fæst/ *adj* **1** able to move or act at great speed: *a fast car, train, worker, etc* ☞ Look at the note at **quick**. There is no noun formed from **fast**. Use **speed**: *The car was travelling very fast./The car was travelling at great speed.* **2** (used about a clock or watch) showing a time that is later than the real time: *I'm early – my watch must be fast.* ○ *The clock is five minutes fast.* ☞ The opposite is **slow**.
fast *adv* quickly: *Don't drive so fast.*

fast ˈfood *noun* [U] food like hamburgers and chips that can be cooked and eaten quickly in a restaurant or taken away from the restaurant: *a fast food restaurant*

fast² /fɑːst; *US* fæst/ *adj* **1** (only *after* a noun) firmly fixed: *Peter made the boat fast* (= he tied it to something) *before he got out.* **2** (used about colours) not likely to change when washed: *Colour-fast materials can be washed in hot water.*
fast *adv* firmly or deeply: *The children were fast asleep when we got home.* ○ *Our car was stuck fast in the mud.*

fast³ /fɑːst; *US* fæst/ *verb* [I] to eat no food for a certain time usually for religious reasons: *Muslims fast during Ramadan.* —**fast** *noun* [C]

☆ **fasten** /ˈfɑːsn; *US* ˈfæsn/ *verb* **1** [T] to fix, join or shut and lock sth firmly: *Please fasten your seat-belts.* ○ *Could you fasten this suitcase for me?* **2** [I] to become closed or fixed: *My blouse fastens at the back.* **3** [T] **fasten sth (on/to sth); fasten A and B (together)** to attach sth to sth, or two things together: *Fasten this badge on your jacket.* ○ *How can I fasten these pieces of wood together?* ○ (*figurative*) *His eyes were fastened on me all the time I was speaking.*

fastener /ˈfɑːsnə(r)/; *US* ˈfæs-/ (*also* **fastening** /ˈfɑːsnɪŋ/; *US* ˈfæs-/) *noun* [C] something that fastens things together: *trousers with a zip-fastener at the side*

fastidious /fəˈstɪdiəs; fæ-/ *adj* (used about people) difficult to please, wanting everything to be very clean and tidy

iː	ɪ	e	æ	ɑː	ɒ	ɔː	ʊ	uː	ʌ
see	sit	ten	hat	arm	got	saw	put	too	cup

☆**fat¹** /fæt/ adj (**fatter**; **fattest**) **1** (used about bodies) covered with too much flesh: *You'll get fat if you eat too much.* ☛ The opposite is **thin**. It is not very polite to describe a person as **fat**. Less direct words are **plump**, **stout** or **overweight**. **2** (used about a thing) thick or full: *a fat wallet, book, etc*

☆**fat²** /fæt/ noun **1** [U] the greasy substance under the skins of animals and people: *I don't like meat with too much fat on it.* ☛ The adjective is **fatty**. **2** [C,U] the substance we obtain from animals, plants or seeds and use for cooking: *Cook the onions in a little fat.* ○ *Vegetable fats are healthier than animal fats.*

☆**fatal** /'feɪtl/ adj **1** causing or ending in death: *It was a fatal accident – both drivers were killed.* **2** causing trouble or a bad result: *She made the fatal mistake of drinking too much at the party.* —**fatally** adv

fatality /fə'tæləti/ noun [C] (pl **fatalities**) a person's death caused by an accident or in war, etc: *There were no fatalities in the fire.*

fate /feɪt/ noun **1** [U] the power that some people believe controls everything that happens: *It was fate that brought them together again after twenty years.* **2** [C] your future or something that happens to you: *Both men suffered the same fate – they both lost their jobs.*

fateful /'feɪtfl/ adj having an important effect on the future: *a fateful decision*

☆**father** /'fɑːðə(r)/ noun [C] **1** a person's male parent: *John looks exactly like his father.* **2** a man who starts something important: *Shakespeare is the father of English drama.* **3 Father** the title of certain priests: *Father O'Reilly*

fatherhood noun [U] the state of being a father: *How are you enjoying fatherhood?*

fatherly adj like or typical of a father: *Would you like a piece of fatherly advice?*

Father 'Christmas (also **Santa Claus**) an old man with a red coat and a long white beard who, children believe, brings presents at Christmas

'father-in-law noun [C] (pl **fathers-in-law**) the father of your husband or wife

fathom /'fæðəm/ noun [C] a measure of the depth of water; 6 feet (1·8 metres)

fathom verb [T] (usually in the negative) to understand sth: *I can't fathom what he means.*

fatigue /fə'tiːg/ noun [U] **1** great tiredness **2** weakness in metals caused by a lot of use

fatten /'fætn/ verb [T] **fatten sb/sth (up)** to maker sb/sth fatter: *He's fattening the pigs up for market.*

fattening adj (used about food) that makes people fat: *You shouldn't eat too much chocolate. It's very fattening.*

fatty /'fæti/ adj (**fattier**; **fattiest**) (used about food) having a lot of fat in or on it

faucet /'fɔːsɪt/ noun [C] (US) = TAP¹

☆**fault** /fɔːlt/ noun **1** [C] something wrong or not perfect in a person's character or in a thing: *One of my faults is that I'm always late.* ○ *a fault in the electricity supply* ☛ Look at the note at **mistake**. **2** [U] responsibility for a mistake: *'We're going to be late.' 'Well, it's not my fault – I was ready on time.'* ○ *It will be your own fault if you don't pass your exams.*

(IDIOMS) **be at fault** be wrong or responsible for a mistake: *The other driver was at fault – he didn't stop at the traffic-lights.*

find fault ⇨ FIND¹

fault verb [T] to find a fault or mistake in sb/sth: *It was impossible to fault her English.*

faultless adj without any mistakes; perfect: *The pianist gave a faultless performance.*

faulty adj (used especially about electricity or machinery) not working properly: *a faulty switch*

fauna /'fɔːnə/ noun [U] all the animals of an area or a period of time: *the flora and fauna of South America* ☛ Look at **flora**.

faux pas /ˌfəʊ 'pɑː/ noun [C] (pl **faux pas** /ˌfəʊ 'pɑːz/) something you say or do that is embarrassing or offends people

☆**favour¹** (US **favor**) /'feɪvə(r)/ noun **1** [C] something that helps sb: *Would you do me a favour and post this letter for me?* ○ *Could I ask you a favour – could you baby-sit for us tonight?* **2** [U] liking or approval: *In the end the politician won the crowd's favour.*

(IDIOMS) **be in/out of favour (with sb)** to have/not have a person's approval: *I'm afraid I'm out of favour with my neighbour since our last argument.*

in favour of sb/sth in agreement with: *Are you in favour of private education?*

in sb's favour to the advantage of sb: *The committee decided in their favour.*

☆**favour²** (US **favor**) /'feɪvə(r)/ verb [T] **1** to support sb/sth; to prefer: *Which suggestion did they favour?* **2** to treat one person very well and so be unfair to others: *Parents must try not to favour one of their children.*

favourable (US **favorable**) /'feɪvərəbl/ adj **1** showing liking or approval: *Did you get a favourable report on your work?* ○ *He made a favourable impression on his bank manager.* **2** (often used about the weather) suitable or helpful: *Conditions are favourable for skiing today.* ☛ The opposite for both senses is **unfavourable**. —**favourably** (US **favorably**) /-əbli/ adv

☆**favourite¹** (US **favorite**) /'feɪvərɪt/ adj liked more than any other: *What is your favourite colour?* ○ *Who is your favourite singer?*

favourite² (US **favorite**) /'feɪvərɪt/ noun [C] **1** a person or thing that you like more than any others: *This restaurant is a great favourite of mine.* ○ *That sweater is my husband's favourite.* **2 the favourite** (especially in horse-racing) the horse that is expected to win

favouritism (US **favoritism**) /-ɪzəm/ noun [U] giving unfair advantages to the people that you like best

fawn¹ /fɔːn/ noun [C] a young deer ☛ Look at the note at **deer**.

fawn² /fɔːn/ adj, noun [U] (of a) light yellowish-brown colour: *a fawn coat* ○ *Fawn doesn't really suit you.*

fax /fæks/ noun **1** [C,U] a copy of a letter, etc which you can send by telephone lines using a special machine: *I need an answer today. Send them a fax!* ○ *They contacted us by fax.* **2** [C]

ɜː	ə	eɪ	əʊ	aɪ	aʊ	ɔɪ	ɪə	eə	ʊə
fur	ago	pay	home	five	now	join	near	hair	pure

(also **fax machine**) the machine that you use for sending faxes: *Have you got a fax?* o *What's your fax number?*

fax *verb* [T] **fax sth (to sb); fax sb (sth)** to send sb a fax: *We will fax our order to you tomorrow.* o *I've faxed her a copy of the letter.*

faze /feɪz/ *verb* [T] (*informal*) (*especially US*) to make sb anxious or nervous: *He doesn't get fazed by things going wrong.*

☆ **fear¹** /fɪə(r)/ *noun* [C,U] the feeling that you have when sth dangerous, painful or frightening might happen: *He was shaking with fear after the accident.* o *She showed no fear.* o *My fears for his safety were unnecessary.*
(IDIOM) **no fear** (used when answering a suggestion) certainly not

fearful /-fl/ *adj* **1 fearful (of sth/of doing sth); fearful (that)** anxious or afraid about sth: *You should never be fearful of starting something new.* ☛ Look at **frightened** and the note at **afraid**. These words are much more common. **2** terrible: *There's going to be a fearful storm tonight.* —**fearfully** /-fəlɪ/ *adv* —**fearfulness** *noun* [U]

fearless *adj* not afraid; brave —**fearlessly** *adv* —**fearlessness** *noun* [U]

☆ **fear²** /fɪə(r)/ *verb* **1** [I,T] to be afraid of sb/sth great or important: *We all fear illness and death.* o *We'll get there in time – never fear!* (= don't worry). **2** [T] to feel that something bad might happen: *The government fears that it will lose the next election.* ☛ Look at **afraid** and at the note at **frightened**.
(PHRASAL VERB) **fear for sb/sth** to be worried about sb/sth: *Parents often fear for the safety of their children.*

feasible /'fi:zəbl/ *adj* possible to do: *a feasible plan* —**feasibility** /ˌfi:zə'bɪlətɪ/ *noun* [U]

feast /fi:st/ *noun* [C] a large, special meal (sometimes to celebrate sth) —**feast** *verb* [I]

feat /fi:t/ *noun* [C] something you do that shows great strength, skill or courage: *That new bridge is a feat of engineering.*

☆ **feather** /'feðə(r)/ *noun* [C] one of the light, soft things that grow in a bird's skin and cover its body

☆ **feature** /'fi:tʃə(r)/ *noun* [C] **1** an important or noticeable part of sth: *Mountains and lakes are the main features of the landscape of Wales.* o *Noise is a feature of city life.* **2** a part of the face: *Her eyes are her best feature.* **3** an important newspaper or magazine article or television programme: *a front-page feature* **4** (*also* **feature film**) a full-length film with a story

feature *verb* **1** [T] to include sb/sth as an important part: *The film features many well-known actors.* **2** [I] **feature in sth** to have a part in sth: *Does marriage feature in your future plans?*

featureless *adj* uninteresting; with no features(1)

☆ **February** /'februərɪ; *US* -verɪ/ *noun* [C,U] (*abbr* **Feb**) the second month of the year, coming before March ☛ For examples of the use of the months in sentences, look at **January**.

feces (*US*) = FAECES

fed *pt, pp* of FEED¹

federal /'fedərəl/ *adj* **1** organized as a federation: *the Federal Republic of Germany* **2** relating to the central government of a federation: *That is a federal, not a state, law.*

federation /ˌfedə'reɪʃn/ *noun* [C] a political union of states for the control of foreign affairs, defence, etc by the central (federal) government but with local (state) government for areas such as education

fed up /ˌfed'ʌp/ *adj* (not before a noun) (*informal*) bored or unhappy; tired of sth: *What's the matter? You look really fed up.* o *I'm fed up with waiting for the phone to ring.*

☆ **fee** /fi:/ *noun* [C] **1** (usually plural) the money you pay for professional advice or service from private doctors, lawyers, schools and universities, etc: *We can't afford private school fees.* **2** the cost of an examination, club membership, entrance etc: *How much is the entrance fee?* ☛ Look at the note at **pay¹**.

feeble /'fi:bl/ *adj* **1** with no energy or power; weak: *a feeble old man* o *a feeble cry* **2** not able to convince sb: *a feeble argument*

☆ **feed¹** /fi:d/ *verb* (*pt, pp* **fed** /fed/) **1** [T] to give food to a person or an animal: *Don't forget to feed the dog.* o *I can't come yet. I haven't fed the baby.* o *I've cooked enough to feed us for weeks.* **2** [I] (used about animals or babies) to eat: *What do horses feed on in the winter?* **3** [T] **feed A (with B); feed B into A** to put sth into sth else: *Can you feed the computer with the necessary information?* o *Can you feed this information into the computer?*

feed² /fi:d/ *noun* **1** [C] a meal for an animal or a baby: *When's the baby's next feed due?* **2** [U] food for animals

feedback /'fi:dbæk/ *noun* [U] information about sth that you have done or made which tells you how good or successful it is: *We need some more feedback from the people who use our textbooks.*

☆ **feel¹** /fi:l/ *verb* (*pt, pp* **felt** /felt/) **1** [I] (usually with an adjective) to be in the state that is mentioned: *to feel cold, sick, tired, happy, etc* o *How are you feeling today?* o *You'll feel better in the morning.* **2** [I] **feel (to sb) (like sth/sb)** to give an impression of sth: *The hole in my tooth feels much bigger than it is.* o *My new coat feels like leather but it's not.* **3** [T] to learn about sth by touching it with your hands: *Feel this material. Is it silk or cotton?* o *I felt her forehead and knew that she had a temperature.* **4** [T] to be aware of sth: *I felt something crawling up my back.* o *I could feel myself dropping off to sleep.* **5** [T] to believe or think: *I felt (that) it was a mistake not to ask her advice.* **6** [T] to suffer from sth: *Do you feel the cold in winter?* o *She felt it badly when her mother died.* **7** [I] **feel (about) (for sb/sth)** to try to find something with your hands instead of your eyes: *She felt about in the dark for the light switch.* **8** [I] **feel (to sb) as if/as though** to have or give the impression that: *He felt as if he had been there before.* o *My head feels as though it will burst.* ☛ It is often used as the subject of **feel** in this sense: *It feels as if it is going to snow soon.*
(IDIOM) **feel like sth/doing sth** to want sth or to want to do sth: *Do you feel like going out?*

☆ **feel²** /fi:l/ *noun* [sing] **1 the feel** the im-

p	b	t	d	k	g	tʃ	dʒ	f	v	θ	ð
pen	bad	tea	did	cat	got	chin	June	fall	van	thin	then

pression something gives you when it is touched; the impression an experience gives you: *You can tell it's wool by the feel.* **2** an act of touching sth in order to learn about it: *Let me have a feel.*

feelers /ˈfiːlə(r)/ *noun* [plural] the long thin parts at the front of an insect's head that it uses to feel things with

☆ **feeling** /ˈfiːlɪŋ/ *noun* **1** [C] **a feeling (of sth)** something that you feel in your mind or body: *a feeling of hunger, happiness, fear, success, etc* **2 feelings** [plural] a person's emotions: *I don't want to hurt his feelings* (= make him unhappy). ○ *She's not very good at hiding her feelings.* **3** [U] the ability to feel in your body: *After the accident he lost all feeling in his legs.* **4** [sing] a belief or idea that you cannot explain exactly: *I had a feeling that something terrible would happen.* **5** [U] sympathy or understanding: *She hasn't much feeling for music.*
(IDIOMS) **bad/ill feeling** unhappy relations between people: *The decision caused a lot of bad feeling at the factory.*
have mixed feelings about sb/sth ⇒ MIXED

feet *pl* of FOOT¹

feline /ˈfiːlaɪn/ *adj* of or like a cat

fell¹ *pt* of FALL¹

fell² /fel/ *noun* [C] an area of mountain country: *the fells of the Lake District*

fell³ /fel/ *verb* [T] to cut down a tree

fellow¹ /ˈfeləʊ/ *noun* [C] **1** (*informal*) a man: *What's that fellow over there doing?* **2** a member of an academic society or sb who teaches at, and helps to govern, a college at some universities (eg Oxford and Cambridge)

fellow² /ˈfeləʊ/ *adj* (only *before* a noun) another or others like yourself in the same situation: *Her fellow students were all older than her.*

fellowship /ˈfeləʊʃɪp/ *noun* **1** [U] friendly relations with others **2** [C] a group or society **3** [C] the position of a college or university fellow

felt¹ *pt, pp* of FEEL¹

felt² /felt/ *noun* [U] a type of soft cloth made from wool, etc which has been pressed flat

ˌfelt-ˈpen (*also* ˌfelt-ˈtip, ˌfelt-tip ˈpen) *noun* [C] a type of pen with a tip made of felt

☆ **female** /ˈfiːmeɪl/ *adj* **1** of the sex that can give birth to young: *Please state sex: male or female* (eg on a form). **2** (used about plants and flowers) producing fruit
female *noun* [C] a female animal or plant: *Is your mouse a male or a female?* ☛ **Female** and **male** are used only to describe the sex of a creature. To describe the qualities we think of as typical of females and males, we use **feminine** and **masculine**.

☆ **feminine** /ˈfemənɪn/ *adj* (*abbr* **fem**) **1** of or like a woman: *My daughter always dresses like a boy. She hates looking feminine.* ☛ Look at **masculine** and the note at **female**. **2** (*grammar*) (in English) of the forms of words used to describe females: *'Lioness' is the feminine form of 'lion'.* **3** (*grammar*) (in certain languages) belonging to a certain grammatical class: *The German word 'Blume' is feminine.* ☛ Look at

masculine and neuter. —**femininity** /ˌfeməˈnɪnəti/ *noun* [U]

feminism /ˈfemɪnɪzəm/ *noun* [U] the belief that women should have the same rights and opportunities as men

feminist /ˈfemɪnɪst/ *noun* [C] a person who believes in and supports the aims of feminism

fen /fen/ *noun* [C] an area of low wet land

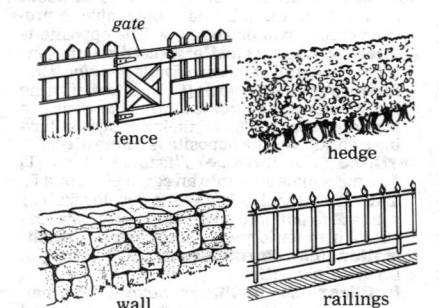

☆ **fence¹** /fens/ *noun* [C] a line of wooden or metal posts joined by wood, wire, metal, etc to divide land or to keep in animals: *a garden fence* ○ *an electric fence* ○ *a barbed-wire fence*
(IDIOM) **sit on the fence** ⇒ SIT
fence *verb* [T] to surround land with a fence
(PHRASAL VERBS) **fence sb/sth in** to surround sb/sth with a fence: *They fenced in their garden to make it more private.*
fence sth off to separate one area from another with a fence

fence² /fens/ *verb* [I] to fight with a long thin sword (a **foil**) as a sport
fencing *noun* [U] the sport of fighting with swords

fend /fend/ *verb*
(PHRASAL VERBS) **fend for yourself** to look after yourself: *It's time Ben left home and learned to fend for himself.*
fend sth/sb off to defend yourself from sth/sb: *He fended off the dog with his stick.* ○ *Politicians usually manage to fend off awkward questions.*

fender /ˈfendə(r)/ *noun* [C] **1** a low metal guard put in front of an open fire to stop coal or wood from falling out **2** (*US*) = WING(4)

ferment /fəˈment/ *verb* [I,T] to (make sth) change chemically: *The wine is starting to ferment.*
ferment /ˈfɜːment/ *noun* [U] a state of excitement and change: *Russia is in ferment and nobody's sure what will happen next.*

fern /fɜːn/ *noun* [C] a green plant with no flowers and a lot of long thin leaves

ferocious /fəˈrəʊʃəs/ *adj* very fierce and violent —**ferociously** *adv*

ferocity /fəˈrɒsəti/ *noun* [U] violent cruelty

ferret /ˈferɪt/ *noun* [C] a small fierce animal used for hunting rats and rabbits

☆ **ferry** /ˈferi/ *noun* [C] (*pl* **ferries**) a boat that transports people and goods on short journeys:

s	z	ʃ	ʒ	h	m	n	ŋ	l	r	j	w
so	zoo	she	vision	how	man	no	sing	leg	red	yes	wet

a car ferry o a cross-channel ferry o We used to cross the river by ferry but now there's a bridge.
ferry verb [T] (pres part **ferrying**; 3rd pers sing pres **ferries**; pt, pp **ferried**) to carry people or goods by boat, aeroplane, car, etc from one place to another: *Could you ferry us across to the island?* o *We share the job of ferrying the children to school.*

fertile /'fɜːtaɪl; US 'fɜːrtl/ adj **1** (used about land, plants, animals and people) able to produce crops, fruit or young ☛ The opposite is **infertile**. Look at **sterile**. **2** (used about a person's mind) full of ideas: *a fertile imagination*

fertility /fə'tɪləti/ noun [U] the state of being fertile: *Nowadays women can take drugs to increase their fertility* (= their chances of having a child). ☛ The opposite is **infertility**.

fertilize (also **fertilise**) /'fɜːtəlaɪz/ verb [T] **1** to put a male seed into an egg, a plant or a female animal so that it starts to develop fruit or young **2** to put natural or artificial substances on soil in order to make it more fertile —**fertilization** (also **fertilisation**) /ˌfɜːtəlaɪ'zeɪʃn; US -lɪ'z-/ noun [U]

fertilizer (also **fertiliser**) noun [C,U] a natural or chemical substance that is put on land to make plants grow better

fervent /'fɜːvənt/ adj showing strong feelings: *She's a fervent believer in women's rights.* —**fervently** adv

fervour (US **fervor**) /'fɜːvə(r)/ noun [U] strong feeling

fester /'festə(r)/ verb [I] **1** (used about a cut or wound) to become infected **2** (used about an unpleasant situation, feeling or thought) to become more unpleasant or painful

☆ **festival** /'festəvl/ noun [C] **1** a day or time when people celebrate sth (especially a religious event): *Christmas is an important Christian festival.* **2** a series of musical or dramatic performances often held regularly in one place: *the Cannes Film Festival* o *a jazz festival*

festive /'festɪv/ adj happy, because people are enjoying themselves: *the festive season* (= Christmas)

festivity /fe'stɪvəti/ noun (pl **festivities**) **1** [U] being happy and celebrating: *Birthdays are not always occasions for festivity.* **2 festivities** [plural] happy events when people celebrate sth: *The festivities went on until dawn.*

☆ **fetch** /fetʃ/ verb [T] **1** to go for and bring back sb/sth: *Shall I fetch you your coat?/Shall I fetch your coat for you?* o *I left my keys on the table; could you fetch them for me?* o *It's my turn to fetch the children from school.* **2** (used about goods) to be sold for the price mentioned: *'How much will your car fetch?' 'It should fetch about £900.'*

fête /feɪt/ noun [C] an outdoor event with competitions, entertainment and things to buy, often organized to make money for a particular purpose: *the church fête*

fetus (US) = FOETUS

feud /fjuːd/ noun [C] a long and serious quarrel between two people or groups —**feud** verb [I]

feudal /'fjuːdl/ adj relating to the system of feudalism

feudalism /'fjuːdəlɪzəm/ noun [U] the social system which existed in the Middle Ages in Europe, in which people worked and fought for a landowner and received land and protection from him

fever /'fiːvə(r)/ noun **1** [C,U] a condition of the body when it is too hot because of illness: *A high fever can be dangerous, especially in small children.* o *Aspirin can reduce fever.* ☛ When somebody's body is very hot we normally say they **have a temperature**. **2** [sing] (figurative) a state of nervous excitement

feverish /'fiːvərɪʃ/ adj **1** showing the signs of a fever **2** showing great excitement

feverishly adv very quickly and excitedly

☆ **few**¹ /fjuː/ det, adj, pron (used with a plural noun and a plural verb) not many: *Few people live to be 100.* o *There are fewer cars here today than yesterday.* o *The few people I have asked thought the same as I do.* o *Few of the players played really well.* o *Very few of the books were new.*

(IDIOM) **few and far between** not happening very often: *Our visits to the theatre are few and far between.*

☆ **few**² /fjuː/ **a few** det, pron (used with a plural noun and a plural verb) a small number of; some: *a few people* o *a few letters* o *Only a few of the people who applied were suitable.* o *She's written lots of books but I've only read a few (of them).* o *I knew a few* (= some) *of the people there.* ☛ Compare with: *I knew few of the people* (= not many).

(IDIOM) **a good few; quite a few** quite a lot: *It's been a good few years since I saw him last.*

☆ **fiancé** /fi'ɒnseɪ; US ˌfiːɑːn'seɪ/ noun [C] a man to whom a woman is engaged to be married: *This is my fiancé Dave. We got engaged a few weeks ago.*

☆ **fiancée** /fi'ɒnseɪ; US ˌfiːɑːn'seɪ/ noun [C] a woman to whom a man is engaged to be married: *Can I introduce you to my fiancée?*

fiasco /fi'æskəʊ/ noun [C] (pl **fiascos**; US also **fiascoes**) the ridiculous failure of an organized event: *Our last party was a complete fiasco.*

fib /fɪb/ noun [C] (informal) something you say that is not true; a small lie: *Please don't tell fibs.*

fib verb [I] (**fibbing**; **fibbed**) to say untrue things, to tell a fib ☛ Look at **lie**. Fib is used when the lie does not seem very important.

fibre (US **fiber**) /'faɪbə(r)/ noun **1** [C] one of the thin threads which form a natural or artificial substance: *a fibre of cotton* o *a muscle fibre* **2** [C,U] material or a substance made from fibres ☛ **Natural** fibres are, for example, cotton and wool. **Man-made** or **synthetic** fibres are nylon, polyester, etc. **3** [U] the parts of plants (used as food) that your body cannot digest and that are thought to be good for it: *Wholemeal bread is high in fibre.*

fibreglass /'faɪbəˌglɑːs/ (US **fiberglass** /'faɪbərˌglæs/) (also **glass fibre**) noun [U] a material made from plastic and glass fibres, used for making small boats, parts of cars, etc

fickle /'fɪkl/ adj always changing your mind or your feelings

☆ **fiction** /'fɪkʃn/ noun [U] stories, novels, etc which describe events and people that do not really exist: *I don't read much fiction.*

iː	ɪ	e	æ	ɑː	ɒ	ɔː	ʊ	uː	ʌ
see	sit	ten	hat	arm	got	saw	put	too	cup

fictitious 235 **figurative**

☛ Fiction is one type of **literature**. Look at **drama** and **poetry**. The opposite is **non-fiction**. Look at **fact**.

fictional /-ʃənl/ *adj* only existing in fiction: *The book gave a fictional account of a doctor's life.* ☛ Look at **factual**.

fictitious /fɪk'tɪʃəs/ *adj* invented; not real: *They used fictitious names in the newspaper article.*

fiddle¹ /'fɪdl/ *noun* [C] (*informal*) **1** a dishonest action, especially one that is connected with money: *a tax fiddle* **2** a violin or an instrument of the violin family

fiddle² /'fɪdl/ *verb* **1** [I] **fiddle (about/around) (with sth)** to play with sth carelessly, nervously or without thinking: *He sat nervously, fiddling with a paper-clip.* **2** [T] (*informal*) to change sth (business accounts, income tax forms, etc) to gain money: *She fiddled her expenses form.*

fiddly /'fɪdli/ *adj* (*informal*) difficult to do or manage with your hands (because small or complicated parts are involved)

fidelity /fɪ'delətɪ; *US* faɪ-/ *noun* [U] **1** (*formal*) the quality of being faithful ☛ The opposite is **infidelity**. A less formal word is **faithfulness**. **2** (used in connection with texts, translations, reproduction of music, etc) the quality of being accurate or close to the original ☛ Look at **hi-fi**.

fidget /'fɪdʒɪt/ *verb* [I] **fidget (about) (with sth)** to move about or play with sth in a restless way because you are nervous, bored, etc: *Stop fidgeting!* ○ *The children were fidgeting with their books while they waited for the bell to ring.* —**fidgety** *adj*

☆ **field¹** /fiːld/ *noun* [C] **1** an area of land on a farm, usually surrounded by fences or hedges and used for growing crops or keeping animals in: *a cornfield* ○ *a field of corn* **2** an area of land used for sports, games or some other activity: *a football field* ○ *the playing fields* (= the area of grass in a village or town or belonging to a school where people go to play games, sports, etc) ○ *an airfield* (= where aeroplanes land and take off) ○ *a battlefield* **3** an area of land where oil, coal or other minerals are found: *a coalfield* ○ *a North Sea oilfield* **4** an area of study or knowledge: *He's an expert in the field of economics.* ○ *That question is outside my field.* **5** an area affected by or included in sth: *a magnetic field* ○ *It's outside my field of vision* (= I can't see it).

'field-day *noun* [C] a day or time of great excitement: *The newspapers always have a field-day when there's a royal wedding.*

'field-event *noun* [C] an athletics event that is not running, eg jumping and throwing ☛ Look at **track events**.

'fieldwork *noun* [U] practical research work done outside the classroom, laboratory, etc

field² /fiːld/ *verb* **1** [I,T] (to be ready) to catch and throw back the ball (in cricket and baseball) ☛ When one team is **fielding**, the other is **batting**. **2** [T] to choose a team for a game of football, cricket, hockey, etc: *New Zealand is fielding an excellent team for the next match.*

fiend /fiːnd/ *noun* [C] **1** a devil or a very cruel person **2** (*informal*) a person who is unusually fond of or interested in one particular thing: *a fresh-air fiend*

fiendish /'fiːndɪʃ/ *adj* **1** very fierce or cruel **2** clever and complicated: *a fiendish plan* —**fiendishly** *adv* very, extremely: *fiendishly clever*

☆ **fierce** /fɪəs/ *adj* **1** angry and aggressive: *The house was guarded by fierce dogs.* **2** very strong: *fierce competition for jobs* ☛ The noun is **ferocity**. —**fiercely** *adv*

fiery /'faɪəri/ *adj* **1** looking like fire **2** (used about a person's character or temper) quick to become angry

☆ **fifteen** /ˌfɪf'tiːn/ *number* 15, one more than fourteen ☛ For examples of how to use numbers in sentences, look at **six**.

fifteenth /ˌfɪf'tiːnθ/ *pron, det, adv* 15th, next after fourteenth ☛ Look at the examples at **sixth**.

☆ **fifth** /fɪfθ/ *pron, det, adv* 5th, next after fourth ☛ Look at **five**.

fifth *noun* [C] the fraction ⅕; one of five equal parts of sth ☛ Look at the examples at **sixth**.

☆ **fifty** /'fɪfti/ *number* 50, one more than forty-nine ☛ For examples of how to use numbers in sentences, look at **sixty**.

fiftieth /'fɪftiəθ/ *pron, det, adv* 50th, next after forty-ninth ☛ Look at the examples at **sixth**.

ˌfifty-'fifty *adj, adv* (*informal*) equal or equally (between two people, groups, etc): *You've got a fifty-fifty chance of winning.* ○ *We'll divide the money fifty-fifty.*

fig /fɪg/ *noun* [C] (a type of tree with) a soft sweet fruit full of small seeds that grows in warm countries and is often eaten dried

☆ **fight¹** /faɪt/ *verb* (*pt, pp* **fought** /fɔːt/) **1** [I,T] **fight (against/with sb/sth) (about/over sth)** to use physical strength, guns, weapons etc against sb/sth: *Did he fight in the Gulf War?* ○ *What were the boys fighting each other about?* ○ *Have you been fighting with your sister again?* **2** [I,T] **fight (against sth)** to try very hard to stop or prevent sth: *to fight a fire, a decision, etc* ○ *to fight against crime, disease, etc* **3** [I] **fight (for sth/to do sth)** to try very hard to get or keep sth: *to fight for your rights* **4** [I] **fight (about/over sth)** to quarrel: *It's not worth fighting about money.*

(PHRASAL VERB) **fight back** to protect yourself by fighting with actions or with words: *If he hits you again, fight back!*

fighter *noun* [C] **1** a person who fights in war or in sport (especially a boxer) **2** (*also* **fighter plane**) a small fast aircraft used for shooting down enemy aircraft

fighting *noun* [U] an occasion when people fight: *There has been street fighting in many parts of London today.*

☆ **fight²** /faɪt/ *noun* [C] an act of fighting or a struggle: *Don't get into a fight at school, will you?* ○ *the government's fight against inflation* **2** [U] the desire to continue trying or struggling: *I've had some bad luck but I've still got plenty of fight in me.*

(IDIOM) **pick a fight** ⇨ PICK¹

figurative /'fɪgərətɪv/ *adj* (used about a word

ɜː	ə	eɪ	əʊ	aɪ	aʊ	ɔɪ	ɪə	eə	ʊə
fur	ago	pay	home	five	now	join	near	hair	pure

or an expression) not used with its exact meaning but used for giving an imaginative description or a special effect: *'He exploded at the news' is a figurative use of the verb 'to explode'.* ☛ The opposite is **literal**.
—**figuratively** *adv*

☆ **figure**[1] /'fɪgə(r); *US* 'fɪgjər/ *noun* [C] **1** a written sign for a number (0 to 9): *Write the numbers in figures, not words.* ○ *He has a five-figure income/an income in five figures* (= more than £10 000). ○ *Our pay rise is going to be in single figures* (= less than 10 per cent). ○ *double figures* (= more than 10) **2** an amount (in numbers) or a price: *The unemployment figures are lower this month.* ○ *What sort of figure are you thinking of for your house?* **3** a person (that you cannot see very clearly): *Two figures were coming towards us in the dark.* **4** a person (in a picture or photograph): *There were two figures on the right of the photo that I didn't recognize.* **5** the shape of the human body: *She's got a beautiful slim figure.* ○ *I'll lose my figure* (= I'll get fat) *if I eat too much chocolate.* ☛ Look at the note at **build**. **6** a well-known or important person: *an important political figure* **7** a diagram or illustration used in a book to explain sth: *Figure 3 shows the major cities of Italy.* **8 figures** arithmetic: *I'm not very good at figures.*
(IDIOMS) **facts and figures** ⇨ FACT
in round figures/numbers ⇨ ROUND[1]

figure of 'eight (*US* **figure eight**) *noun* [C] (*pl* **figures of eight**) something in the shape of an 8

figure of 'speech *noun* [C] (*pl* **figures of speech**) a word or expression used not with its original meaning but in an imaginative way to make a special effect ☛ Look at **figurative**.

figure[2] /'fɪgə(r); *US* 'fɪgjər/ *verb* **1** [I] **figure (in sth)** to be included in sth; to be an important part of sth: *Women don't figure much in his novels.* **2** [T] **figure (that)** (*especially US*) to think or guess sth: *I figured he was here because I saw his car outside.*
(IDIOM) **it/that figures** (*informal*) that is what I expected
(PHRASAL VERBS) **figure on sth/on doing sth** (*especially US*) to include sth in your plans: *I figure on arriving in New York on Wednesday.*
figure sb/sth out to find an answer to sth or to understand sb

☆ **file**[1] /faɪl/ *noun* [C] **1** a box or a cover that is used for keeping papers together and in order: *Students are given a file to keep their course notes in.* **2** a collection of papers or information kept in a file: *I can't remember what exactly I said in the letter. I'll need to look at the file.* **3** a collection of information or material on one subject that is stored in a computer or on a disk: *to open/close a file*
(IDIOMS) **on file** kept in a file: *We have all the information you need on file.*
the rank and file ⇨ RANK
file *verb* [T] **file sth (away)** to put in a file: *File these letters under 'Job Applications'.*

file[2] /faɪl/ *noun* [C] a metal tool with a rough surface used for making rough surfaces smooth: *a nail-file*

file *verb* [I,T] to use a file to cut sth or make sth smooth

file[3] /faɪl/ *noun*
(IDIOM) **in single file** in a line, one behind the other: *You'll have to go in single file – the path is very narrow.*

file verb [I] **file in, out, past, etc** to walk or march in a line

☆ **fill** /fɪl/ *verb* **1** [I,T] **fill (sth/sb) (with sth)** to make sth full or to become full: *Can you fill the kettle for me?* ○ *The news filled him with excitement.* ○ *The room filled with smoke within minutes.* **2** [T] to occupy a position or time: *I'm afraid that teaching post has just been filled* (= somebody has got the job).
(PHRASAL VERBS) **fill sth in** (*US also* **fill sth out**) to complete a form, etc by writing information on it: *Could you fill in the application form, please?*
fill (sth) up to become or to make sth completely full: *There weren't many people at first but then the room filled up.* ○ *Fill up the tank, please* (= with petrol).

'**filling station** (*US*) = PETROL STATION

fillet (*US* **filet**) /'fɪlɪt/ *noun* [C,U] (a piece of) meat or fish with the bones taken out

filling /'fɪlɪŋ/ *noun* **1** [C] the material that a dentist uses to fill a hole in a tooth: *a gold filling* **2** [C,U] food put inside a sandwich, pie, cake, etc to make it taste nice

☆ **film**[1] /fɪlm/ *noun* **1** (*US also* **movie**) [C] a story, play, etc shown in moving pictures at the cinema or on television: *There's a good film on at the cinema this week, do you fancy going?* ○ *the film industry* ○ *the film version of 'Hamlet'*

☛ Some types of film are **documentary, feature, horror films** and **westerns**.

2 [C,U] a roll of thin plastic that you use in a camera to take photographs: *A 35 millimetre film, please.* ○ *a black and white film* ○ *a colour film* ○ *Fast film is better in this light.*

☛ You **load** a film into a camera and **rewind** it when it is finished. When the film is **developed**, you can have **prints** made from the **negatives**. picture at **camera**.

3 [usually sing] a thin layer of a substance or material: *a film of oil*

'**film star** *noun* [C] a person who is a well-known actor or actress in films

☆ **film**[2] /fɪlm/ *verb* [I,T] to make a film of an event, story, etc with a camera: *They're filming in Oxford today.* ○ *A lot of westerns are filmed in Spain.*

filter /'fɪltə(r)/ *noun* [C] **1** an apparatus for holding back solid substances from a liquid or gas that passes through it: *a coffee filter* ○ *an oil filter* **2** a piece of coloured glass used with a camera to hold back some types of light

filter *verb* **1** [T] to pass a liquid through a filter: *Do you filter your water?* **2** [I] **filter in, out, through, etc** to move slowly: (*figurative*) *News of her illness filtered through to her friends.*

filth /fɪlθ/ *noun* [U] **1** disgusting dirt: *The room was covered in filth.* **2** extremely rude words,

p	b	t	d	k	g	tʃ	dʒ	f	v	θ	ð
pen	bad	tea	did	cat	got	chin	June	fall	van	thin	then

pictures, etc usually in books, magazines or films

filthy *adj* (**filthier; filthiest**) **1** very dirty: *They got absolutely filthy playing football in the rain.* **2** (used about language, books, films, etc) extremely rude and unpleasant

fin /fɪn/ *noun* [C] a part of a fish, shaped like a thin wing. Fish use fins for swimming.

☆ **final** /'faɪnl/ *adj* **1** (only *before* a noun) last (in a series): *This will be the final lesson of our course.* ○ *I don't want to miss the final episode of that serial.* **2** not to be changed: *The judge's decision is always final.*

(IDIOM) **the last/final straw** ⇨ STRAW

final *noun* [C] **1** (*also* **finals**) the last game or match in a series of competitions or sporting events: *I wonder who'll get through to the final at Wimbledon this year?* ○ *The finals of the swimming championship will be held in Cardiff.* ☛ Look at **semi-final**. **2 finals** the examinations you take in your last year at university: *I'm taking my finals in June.*

finalist /-nəlɪst/ *noun* [C] a person who is in the final of a competition ☛ Look at **semi-finalist**.

finalize (*also* **finalise**) *verb* [T] to make firm decisions about plans, dates, etc: *Have you finalized your holiday arrangements yet?*

finale /fɪ'nɑːli; *US* -'næli/ *noun* [C] the last part of a piece of music, an opera, show, etc

☆ **finally** /'faɪnəli/ *adv* **1** (used at the beginning of a sentence when you have a list of things to say, especially in a speech) as a last point: *Finally, I would like to say how much we have all enjoyed this evening.* **2** after a long time or delay: *It was getting dark when the plane finally took off.* **3** in a definite way so that sth cannot be changed: *We haven't finally decided yet – it depends on the cost.*

☆ **finance** /'faɪnæns; fɪ'næns/ *noun* **1** [U] the money you need to start or support a business, etc: *How will you raise the finance to start your own business?* **2** [U] the management of (public) money: *Who is the new Minister of Finance?* ○ *an expert in finance* **3 finances** [plural] the money a person, company, country, etc has to spend: *What are our finances like at the moment?* (= how much money have we got?)

finance *verb* [T] to provide the money to pay for sth: *Your trip will be financed by the company.*

financial /faɪ'nænʃl; fɪ'næ-/ *adj* connected with money: *The business got into financial difficulties.* ○ *New York and Tokyo are important financial centres.* —**financially** *adv* /-ʃəli/

finch /fɪntʃ/ *noun* [C] a small bird with a strong beak

☆ **find¹** /faɪnd/ *verb* [T] (*pt, pp* **found** /faʊnd/) **1** to get back sth that you have lost: *Did you find the pen you lost?* ○ *I can't find my new sweater anywhere.* **2** to discover sth or get sth that you want (after a search): *After six months she finally found a job.* ○ *Did you manage to find a good hotel?* ○ *Scientists haven't yet found a cure for colds.* ○ *They've found oil in the North Sea.* ○ *I hope you find an answer to your problem.* ☛ Notice the expressions **find the time, find the money**: *I never seem to find the time to write letters these days.* ○ *We'd like to go on holiday but we can't find the money.* **3** to discover sth by chance: *Tom found a £20 note in the park.* ○ *I've found a piece of glass in this milk.* ○ *We went into the house and found her lying on the floor.* **4** to think or to have an opinion about sth (because of your own experience): *I find that book very difficult to understand.* ○ *We didn't find the film at all funny.* ○ *How are you finding life as a student?* ☛ When we are expressing an opinion we say **I think that**... NOT **I find that**...

(IDIOMS) **find fault (with sb/sth)** to look for things that are wrong with sb/sth and complain about them

find your feet to become confident and independent in a new situation: *Don't worry if the job seems difficult at first – you will soon find your feet.*

(PHRASAL VERBS) **find (sth) out** to get some information by asking or studying: *Have you found out how much the tickets cost?*

find sb out to discover that sb has done sth wrong: *He used a false name for years before they found him out.*

finder *noun* [C] a person that finds sth: *The lucky finder of the buried treasure will win a holiday in Spain.*

finding *noun* [C] (usually plural) something that is discovered by research or investigation: *the findings of a survey, a report, a committee, etc*

find² /faɪnd/ *noun* [C] a thing or a person that is unusually good or valuable: *That new software is a real find.*

☆ **fine¹** /faɪn/ *adj* **1** (only *before* a noun) of very good quality, beautiful: *a fine piece of work* ○ *That's the finest painting I've ever seen by that artist.* **2** good enough: *'Do you want some more milk in your coffee?' 'No that's fine, thanks.'* ○ *Don't cook anything special – a sandwich will be fine.* ○ *The hotel rooms were fine but the food was awful.* **3** in good health, or happy and comfortable: *'How are you?' 'Fine thanks.'* ○ *'Do you want to change places?' 'No I'm fine here, thanks.'* ☛ We do not use meanings 2 and 3 in questions or in the negative form, so you CANNOT say 'Are you fine?' or 'This isn't fine'. **4** (used about weather) bright and sunny; not raining: *Let's hope it stays fine for our picnic tomorrow.* **5** thin: *That hairstyle's no good for me – my hair's too fine.* ○ *You must use a fine pencil for the diagrams.* ☛ The opposite is **thick**. **6** made of very small pieces, grains, etc: *Salt is finer than sugar.* ☛ The opposite is **coarse**. **7** difficult to see; very detailed: *The difference in meaning between those two words is very fine.* ○ *I couldn't understand the finer points of his argument.*

finely *adv* **1** into small pieces: *The onions must be finely chopped for this recipe.* **2** very delicately: *a finely tuned instrument*

☆ **fine²** /faɪn/ *noun* [C] a sum of money that you have to pay for breaking a law or rule: *a parking fine* ○ *You'll get a fine if you park your car there.* ○ *He'll either have to pay a heavy fine or go to prison.*

fine *verb* [T] **fine sb (for sth/for doing sth)**

s	z	ʃ	ʒ	h	m	n	ŋ	l	r	j	w
so	zoo	she	vision	how	man	no	sing	leg	red	yes	wet

to make sb pay a sum of money because he/she has broken a law or rule: *He was fined £50 for speeding.*

☆ **finger¹** /'fɪŋɡə(r)/ *noun* [C] one of the five parts at the end of each hand (or a glove): *little finger, ring finger, middle finger, forefinger (or index finger), thumb* ○ *Children learn to count on their fingers.* ☛ Sometimes we think of the thumb as one of the fingers, sometimes we contrast it: *Hold the pen between your thumb and finger.* The 'fingers' on our feet are called **toes**.
(IDIOM) **keep your fingers crossed** to hope that sb/sth will be successful or lucky: *I'll keep my fingers crossed for you in your exams.* ☛ Look also at **cross your fingers** at **cross²**.
snap your fingers ⇨ SNAP¹

'**finger-mark** *noun* [C] a mark on a wall, door, book, etc made by a dirty finger

'**fingernail** (*also* **nail**) *noun* [C] the hard parts on the ends of the fingers: *Your fingernails are filthy!* ○ *She always paints her fingernails bright red.*

'**fingerprint** *noun* [C] the mark made by the skin of a finger, used for identifying people: *The burglar left his fingerprints all over the house.* ○ *The police took the suspect's fingerprints.*

'**fingertip** *noun* [C] the end of a finger
(IDIOM) **have sth at your fingertips** to have sth ready for quick and easy use: *They asked some difficult questions but luckily I had all the facts at my fingertips.*

finger² /'fɪŋɡə(r)/ *verb* [T] to touch or feel sth with your fingers

☆ **finish¹** /'fɪnɪʃ/ *verb* **1** [I,T] **finish (sth/doing sth)** to come or bring sth to an end or to reach the end of sth: *What time does the film finish?* ○ *Haven't you finished yet? You've taken ages!* ○ *The US sprinters finished first, second and third* (eg in a race). ○ *Finish your work quickly!* ○ *Have you finished typing that letter?* **2** [T] **finish sth (off/up)** to eat, drink or use the last part of sth: *Finish up your milk, Tom!* **3** [T] **finish sth (off)** to complete the last details of sth or make sth perfect: *He's just adding the finishing touches to his painting.* ○ *He stayed up all night to finish off the article he was writing.*
(PHRASAL VERBS) **finish sb/sth off** (*informal*) to kill sb/sth: *The cat pounced and finished off the mouse.* ○ (*figurative*) *It was losing his job that really finished him off* (= depressed him).
finish with sb/sth 1 to stop needing or using sb/sth: *Don't go away. I haven't finished with you yet.* ○ *I'll borrow that book when you've finished with it.* **2** to end a relationship with sb: *Sally's not going out with David any more – she finished with him last month.*

finish² /'fɪnɪʃ/ *noun* [C] **1** (used especially about a race) the end: *The last race was a very close finish* (= the runners at the front were close together at the end). ☛ The opposite is **start**. **2** (used especially about wood and furniture) the feel or look that sth has when it has been polished, etc: *This table has a beautiful finish.*

☆ **finished** /'fɪnɪʃt/ *adj* **1** (not before a noun) **finished (with sb/sth)** having stopped doing sth, using sth or dealing with sb/sth: *'Are you using the computer?' 'Yes, I won't be finished with it for another hour or so.'* **2** (not before a noun) not able to continue: *The business is finished – there's no more money.* **3** made; completed: *the finished product, article, etc*

fiord (*also* **fjord**) /fɪ'ɔːd/ *noun* [C] a long narrow piece of sea between cliffs, especially in Norway

fir /fɜː(r)/ (*also* **'fir-tree**) *noun* [C] a straight tree that keeps its thin leaves (**needles**) in winter

'**fir-cone** *noun* [C] the fruit of the fir

☆ **fire¹** /'faɪə(r)/ *noun* **1** [U] hot bright flames produced by sth that is burning: *Many animals are afraid of fire.* **2** [C,U] burning that destroys and is out of control: *Firemen struggled for three hours to put out the fire.* ○ *It had been a dry summer so there were many forest fires.* ○ *You need to insure your house against fire.* ○ *The furniture caught fire within seconds* (= started burning). ○ *Did someone set fire to that pile of wood?* ○ *Help! The frying-pan's on fire!* **3** [C] burning wood or coal to warm people or cook food: *They lit a fire to keep warm.* ○ *It's cold – don't let the fire go out!* ○ *a camp fire* ○ *Many older houses have an open fire in the sitting-room.* **4** [C] an apparatus for heating a room, etc: *a gas fire* ○ *an electric fire* **5** [U] shooting from guns: *The soldiers were under fire from all sides.* ○ *I could hear gunfire in the distance.*
(IDIOM) **open fire** ⇨ OPEN²

'**fire-alarm** *noun* [C] a bell or other signal to warn people that there is a fire: *If the fire-alarm goes off, leave the building immediately.*

'**firearm** *noun* [C, usually pl] a gun that you can carry: *Most policemen don't carry firearms.*

'**fire brigade** (*US* '**fire-department**) *noun* [C, with sing or pl verb] an organization of people trained to put out (= stop) fires: *Dial 999 to call the fire brigade.*

'**fire-engine** *noun* [C] a special vehicle that carries equipment for fighting large fires

'**fire-escape** *noun* [C] a special staircase on the outside of a building that people can escape down if there is a fire

'**fire extinguisher** (*also* **extinguisher**) *noun* [C] a metal container with water or chemicals inside that you use for fighting small fires: *Shops and offices have fire extinguishers on every floor.*

'**fire-fighter** *noun* [C] a person whose job is to fight fires

'**firelight** *noun* [U] the light that comes from a fire in a fireplace: *It's quite romantic sitting here in the firelight.*

'**fireman** /-mən/ *noun* [C] (*pl* **firemen** /-mən/) a person whose job is to fight fires: *Firemen have to wear special uniforms.*

'**fireplace** *noun* [C] the open place in a room (at the bottom of a chimney) where you light a fire

'**fireside** *noun* [C, usually sing] the part of a room beside the fireplace: *Come and sit by the fireside.*

'**fire station** *noun* [C] a building where fire-engines are kept and firemen wait to be called

'**firewood** *noun* [U] wood used for burning on fires

fire² /'faɪə(r)/ *verb* **1** [I,T] **fire (sth) (at sb/**

iː	ɪ	e	æ	ɑː	ɒ	ɔː	ʊ	uː	ʌ
see	sit	ten	hat	arm	got	saw	put	too	cup

fireplace

ornaments, *mantelpiece*, *poker*, *grate*

sth); **fire (sth) into sth** to shoot with a gun or shoot bullets, etc from a gun: *'Fire!' shouted the officer.* ○ *Can you hear the guns firing?* ○ *He fired his gun at the ceiling.* ○ *They fired rubber bullets into the crowd.* **2** [T] (*informal*) to dismiss sb from a job: *He was fired for always being late.* **3** [T] **fire sth at sb** to ask questions, or make remarks, quickly and aggressively: *If you stop firing questions at me I might be able to answer!* **4** [T] **fire sb with sth** to produce a strong feeling in sb: *Her speech fired me with determination.*

-fired (in compounds) using the fuel mentioned: *gas-fired central heating*

'firing-squad *noun* [C] a group of soldiers who have been ordered to shoot and kill a prisoner

firework /'faɪəwɜːk/ *noun* [C] a small container with chemicals inside that burns or explodes with coloured lights and bangs, used for entertainment: *Be careful not to burn your fingers when you let off that firework.* ○ *a firework display/party* ☞ Firework is often used in the plural: *We went to watch the fireworks in Hyde Park.*

fireworks

☆ **firm¹** /fɜːm/ *noun* [C, with sing or pl verb] a business company: *Which firm do you work for?* ○ *My firm's moving to Manchester soon.*

☆ **firm²** /fɜːm/ *adj* **1** able to stay the same shape when pressed; quite hard: *a firm mattress* **2** strong or steady or not likely to change: *She kept a firm grip on her mother's hand.* ○ *Have you got a firm date for your holiday yet?* ○ *We've taken a firm decision – we're not going to change it now.* ○ *I've got a firm offer of a job in New York.* **3 firm (with sb)** insisting that people do what you want: *He's very firm with his children.*
—**firmly** *adv* —**firmness** *noun* [U]

☆ **first¹** /fɜːst/ *det* coming before all others; that has not happened before: *his first day at school* ○ *their first baby* ○ *the first half of the game* ○ *You've won first prize!* ○ *My first choice is blue, but I'll take green if there's no blue left.* ○ *first impressions* ○ *The first time she went skiing, she*

broke her leg. ○ *King Charles I* (= King Charles the First)

(IDIOMS) **at first glance/sight** when first seen or examined: *At first glance it looked like solid gold.*

first/last/next but one, two, etc: *I live in the first house but one* (= the second house) *on the right.* ○ *X is the last letter but two of the alphabet* (= the third letter from the end).

first/last thing ⇨ THING

firstly *adv* (used to introduce the first point in a list): *They were angry firstly because they had to pay extra, and secondly because no one had told them about it.*

,first-'aid *noun* [U] medical help that you give to sb who is hurt or ill before the doctor arrives

,first 'class *adj, adv* **1** excellent; of the best quality: *a first-class player* ○ *This book is really first class.* **2** giving or using the best and most expensive type of service: *Are the first-class carriages at the front or the back of the train?* ○ *He always travels first class.* ○ *Ten first-class stamps, please.* ○ *If you send the letter first class, it should arrive tomorrow.*

,first 'cousin = COUSIN

,first 'floor *noun* [C] **1** (*Brit*) the floor of a building above the one on street level (**the ground floor**): *I live in a flat on the first floor/a first-floor flat.* **2** (*US*) the floor of a building on street level

,first 'gear *noun* [C] the lowest gear on a car, bicycle, etc

'first name [C] the name that is given to a child when he/she is born: *'What's Mrs Brown's first name?' 'Alice, I think.'* ○ *Do you know him well enough to call him by his first name?* ☞ Look at the note at **name¹**.

the ,first 'person *noun* [sing] **1** (*grammar*) the words such as 'I', 'me', 'we', and the verb forms that go with them: *'I am' is the first person singular of the verb 'to be'.* **2** the style of telling a story as if it happened to you: *The author writes in the first person* (= he writes, 'I...').

,first-'rate *adj* excellent; of the best quality

☆ **first²** /fɜːst/ *adv* **1** before any others: *Sue arrived first at the party.* ○ *Our team came first in the race* (= we won). ○ *Do you want to go first or second?* **2** before doing anything else: *I'll come out later. I've got to finish my homework first.* **3** for the first time: *Where did you first meet your husband?* **4** at the beginning: *When I first started my job I hated it.* **5** (used for introducing the first thing in a list): *There are several people I would like to thank: First, my mother.*

(IDIOMS) **at first** at the beginning: *At first I thought he was joking, but then I realized he was serious.*

come first to be more important (to sb) than anything else: *Her family has always come first.*

first and foremost more than anything else; most importantly: *He worked in television but he was a stage actor first and foremost.*

first of all as the first thing (to be done or said): *In a moment I'll introduce our guest*

speaker, but first of all, let me thank you all for coming.
head first ⇨ HEAD

☆ **first³** /fɜːst/ *noun, pron* **1** [C] (*pl* **first**) **the first** the first person or thing, people or things: *Are we the first to arrive?* ○ *You are the first to hear the news.* ○ *They enjoyed the holiday – their first for ten years.* **2** [sing] an important event that is happening for the first time: *This operation is a first in medical history.* **3** [C] **a first (in sth)** (*Brit*) the highest grade of university degree

firsthand /ˌfɜːstˈhænd/ *adj, adv* (used about information, experience, a story, etc) heard, seen or learnt directly, not from other people: *He gave me a firsthand account of the accident* (= he had seen it). ○ *I've experienced the problem firsthand, so I know exactly how you feel.*

☆ **fish¹** /fɪʃ/ *noun* (*pl* **fish** or **fishes**) **1** [C] an animal that lives and breathes in water using its fins and tail for swimming: *How many fish have you caught?* ○ *I went diving on holiday – it was fantastic to see so many different fishes* (= types or species of fish). ☛ The plural form **fish** is more common. **Fishes** is used when we are talking about different types of fish. **2** [U] fish as food: *We're having fresh fish for supper.*

fishy *adj* (**fishier**; **fishiest**) **1** of or like a fish, especially in taste or smell: *a fishy smell* **2** (*informal*) seeming suspicious or untrue: *The police thought the man's story sounded extremely fishy.*

ˌfish and ˈchips *noun* [U] fried fish and potato chips often bought already cooked and taken away to eat

☛ We buy fish and chips at a **fish and chip shop**. The fish is covered with **batter** (a mixture of flour, egg and milk) and **deep-fried**. You find a fish and chip shop in most towns.

ˌfish ˈfinger (*US* **ˌfish ˈstick**) *noun* [C] a small oblong piece of fish covered in breadcrumbs: *a packet of fish fingers*

ˈfishmonger /-mʌŋɡə(r)/ *noun* [C] (*Brit*) a person whose job is to sell fish, or a shop that sells fish (= the fishmonger's): *I bought it at the fishmonger's.*

☆ **fish²** /fɪʃ/ *verb* [I] **1 fish (for sth)** to try to catch fish with rods, nets, etc: *He's fishing for trout.* ☛ When we are talking about spending time fishing we usually say **go fishing**: *They often go fishing at weekends.* **2 fish for sth** to search for sth in water or in a deep or hidden place: *She fished (around) for her keys in the bottom of her bag.*

(PHRASAL VERBS) **fish for sth** to try to get sth you want in an indirect way: *to fish for an invitation*

fish sth out (of sth) to take or pull sth out (of sth) especially after searching for it: *After the accident they fished the car out of the canal.* ○ *She fished a pair of socks out of the bottom of the cupboard.*

fisherman /ˈfɪʃəmən/ *noun* [C] (*pl* **fishermen** /ˈfɪʃəmən/) a person who catches fish especially as a job but also as a sport ☛ Look at **angler**.

fishing /ˈfɪʃɪŋ/ *noun* [U] catching fish as a job, sport or hobby: *Fishing is a major industry in Iceland.* ☛ The sport or hobby of fishing is also called **angling**.

ˈfishing-rod *noun* [C] a long thin stick with a line and a hook on it for catching fish

☆ **fist** /fɪst/ *noun* [C] a hand with the fingers closed together tightly: *She clenched her fists.*

☆ **fit¹** /fɪt/ *adj* (**fitter**; **fittest**) **1 fit for sb/sth**; **fit to do sth** good enough; suitable: *These houses are not fit (for people) to live in.* ○ *Do you think she is fit for the job?* **2 fit (for sth/to do sth)** in good physical health (especially because of exercise): *He keeps fit by jogging five miles a day.* ○ *I'm afraid you won't be fit enough for work for a long time yet.* ○ *She goes to keep-fit classes.* ☛ The opposite is **unfit**.

fitness *noun* [U] **1** the condition of being fit(2): *Fitness is important in most sports.* **2 fitness for sth/to do sth** the quality of being suitable: *The directors were not sure about his fitness for the job.*

☆ **fit²** /fɪt/ *verb* (**fitting**; **fitted**) **1** [I,T] to be the right size or shape for sb/sth: *These jeans don't fit.* ○ *This dress doesn't fit me any more.* ○ *This key doesn't fit the lock.* ○ *My car won't fit into your garage.* **2** [T] **fit sb/sth in/into/on/onto sth** to find enough space for sb/sth: *Can you fit one more person in the car?* ○ *I can't fit all these books onto the shelf.* **3** [T] to put or fix sth in the right place: *The builders are fitting new windows today.* ○ *I can't fit these pieces of the model together.* **4** [T] to be or make sb/sth right or suitable: *Her experience fits her for the job.* ○ *The punishment should fit the crime.*

(PHRASAL VERBS) **fit sb/sth in**; **fit sb/sth in/into sth** to find time to see sb or to do sth: *The doctor managed to fit me in this morning.* ○ *You're tired because you're trying to fit too much into one day.*

fit in (with sb/sth) to be able to live, work, etc in an easy and natural way (with sb/sth): *The new girl found it difficult to fit in (with the other children) at school.* ○ *I will happily change my plans to fit in with yours.*

fitted *adj* made or cut to fit a particular space and fixed there: *fitted cupboards* ○ *a fitted carpet* ○ *a fitted kitchen* (= one with fitted cupboards)

fit³ /fɪt/ *noun* [sing] (usually after an adjective) the way in which sth (eg a piece of clothing) fits: *a good, bad, tight, etc fit*

fit⁴ /fɪt/ *noun* [C] **1** a sudden loss of consciousness with movements that are not controlled and sometimes violent **2** a sudden (usually short) attack of illness: *a fit of coughing* **3** a sudden period of activity or violent feeling: *a fit of laughter, energy, etc* ○ *a fit of anger*

fitting¹ /ˈfɪtɪŋ/ *adj* (*formal*) right; suitable

fitting² /ˈfɪtɪŋ/ *noun* [C, usually pl] the things that are fixed in a building or on a piece of furniture but that can be changed or moved if necessary ☛ Look at **fixture**.

☆ **five** /faɪv/ *number* 5; one more than four ☛ For examples of how to use numbers in sentences, look at **six**.

five- (used in compounds) having five of the thing mentioned: *a five-day week* ○ *a five-hour flight*

fiver /ˈfaɪvə(r)/ *noun* [C] **1** (*Brit informal*) a

five pound note; £5: *Can you lend me a fiver?* **2** (*US informal*) a five dollar note; $5

☆ **fix**[1] /fɪks/ *verb* [T] **1** to put sth firmly in place so that it will not move: *Can you fix this new handle to the door?* ○ *He fixed the post firmly in the ground.* ○ (*figurative*) *I found it difficult to keep my mind fixed on what they were saying.* **2 fix sth (up)** to decide or arrange sth: *We need to fix the price.* ○ *Have you fixed (up) a date for the party?* **3** to repair: *The electrician's coming to fix the cooker.* **4** (usually passive) (*informal*) to arrange the result of sth in a way that is not honest or fair: *The race was fixed* (= the result was arranged before it happened). **5 fix sth (for sb)** (*especially US*) to prepare sth (especially food or drink) for sb: *Can I fix you a drink/a drink for you?*

(PHRASAL VERB) **fix sb up (with sth)** (*informal*) to arrange for sb to have sth: *I can fix you up with a job, a car, a place to stay, etc.*

fixed /fɪkst/ *adj* **1** already decided: *a fixed date, rent, price, etc* **2** not changing: *He has such fixed ideas that you can't discuss anything with him.* ○ *She looked at him with a fixed smile.*

(IDIOM) **(of) no fixed abode/address** (with) no permanent place to live: *Mr Smith, of no fixed abode, was found guilty of robbery.*

fix[2] /fɪks/ *noun* [C] **1** (usually sing) (*informal*) a difficult situation: *I was in a real fix – I'd locked the car keys inside the car.* **2** (*slang*) an injection of a drug such as heroin

fixation /fɪkˈseɪʃn/ *noun* [C] a feeling (about sb/sth) that is too strong and not normal

fixture /ˈfɪkstʃə(r)/ *noun* [C] **1** (usually pl) a piece of furniture or equipment that is fixed in a house or building and sold with it: *Does the price of the house include fixtures and fittings?* ☛ Look at **fitting**. **2** a sporting event arranged for a particular day: *a fixture list* ○ *We had to cancel our fixture last week.*

fizz /fɪz/ *verb* [I] to produce many small bubbles and/or make a hissing sound

fizz *noun* [U] the bubbles in a liquid and the sound they make: *This lemonade's lost its fizz.*

fizzy /ˈfɪzi/ *adj* (**fizzier; fizziest**) (used about a drink) containing many small bubbles ☛ Wine or mineral water is usually described as **sparkling**, not fizzy. The opposite of fizzy is **still**.

fizzle /ˈfɪzl/ *verb*

(PHRASAL VERB) **fizzle out** to end in a weak or disappointing way: *The game started well but it fizzled out in the second half.*

fjord = FIORD

flabbergasted /ˈflæbəɡɑːstɪd; *US* -ɡæst-/ *adj* (*informal*) extremely surprised

flabby /ˈflæbi/ *adj* (**flabbier; flabbiest**) **1** (used about a person) having too much soft loose flesh **2** (used about muscles, arms, legs, etc) too soft

☆ **flag**[1] /flæɡ/ *noun* [C] a piece of cloth with a pattern or picture on it, often attached to a pole (**flag-pole**) or rope and used as a symbol of a country, club, etc or as a signal: *The flag is flying for the Queen's birthday.* ○ *The train will leave when the guard waves his flag.*

flag[2] /flæɡ/ *verb* [I] (**flagging; flagged**) to become tired or less strong or active

flagrant /ˈfleɪɡrənt/ *adj* (only *before* a noun) easily seen to be bad and shocking

flail /fleɪl/ *verb* [I,T] to wave or swing about without control: *The insect's legs were flailing in the air.* ○ *The drowning child flailed his arms above his head.*

flair /fleə(r)/ *noun* **1 (a) flair for sth** [sing] a natural ability to do sth well: *She has a flair for languages* (= she's good at learning them). **2** [U] the quality of being interesting or having style: *That poster is designed with her usual flair.*

flake /fleɪk/ *noun* [C] a small thin piece of sth: *snowflakes* ○ *cornflakes* ○ *soap-flakes*

flake *verb* [I] **flake (off)** to come off in flakes: *My skin is very dry – it's beginning to flake (off).*

flamboyant /flæmˈbɔɪənt/ *adj* **1** (used about a person) acting in a loud, confident way **2** very easily noticed: *flamboyant colours* —**flamboyance** /-ˈbɔɪəns/ *noun* [U] —**flamboyantly** *adv*

☆ **flame** /fleɪm/ *noun* [C,U] an area of bright burning gas that comes from sth that is on fire: *The flame of the candle flickered by the open window.* ○ *The house was in flames when the fire-engine arrived.* ○ *The piece of paper burst into flame in the fire* (= suddenly began to burn strongly). ☛ picture at **candle**.

flaming /ˈfleɪmɪŋ/ *adj* (only *before* a noun) **1** burning brightly: *a flaming torch* **2** (used about colours, especially red) very bright: *flaming red hair* ○ *a flaming sunset* **3** (used about anger, an argument, etc) violent: *He was in a flaming temper.* **4** (*informal*) (used as a mild swear word): *I can't get in – I've lost the flaming key.*

flammable /ˈflæməbl/ *adj* able to burn easily ☛ The opposite is **non-flammable**. **Inflammable** has the same meaning as flammable and is more common.

flan /flæn/ *noun* [C,U] a round open pie that is filled with cheese, vegetables, fruit, etc ☛ Look at the note at **pie**

flank /flæŋk/ *noun* [C] the side of an animal or of an army ready for battle

flank *verb* [T] (usually passive) to be placed at the side or sides of: *The road was flanked by trees.*

flannel /ˈflænl/ *noun* **1** [U] a type of soft woollen cloth **2** [C] = FACE-CLOTH

flap[1] /flæp/ *noun* [C] a piece of material that is fixed to sth at one side only, often covering an opening: *a tent flap* ○ *a cat flap* (= in a door for a cat to get through)

(IDIOM) **be in/get into a flap** (*informal*) to be in/get into a state of worry or excitement

flap[2] /flæp/ *verb* (**flapping; flapped**) **1** [I,T] to move sth up and down or from side to side; to move in this way, especially in the wind: *The sails were flapping in the wind.* ○ *The bird flapped its wings and flew away.* **2** [I] (*informal*) to become worried or excited: *You don't need to flap – it's all organized!*

flare /fleə(r)/ *verb* [I] to burn with a sudden bright flame

(PHRASAL VERB) **flare up 1** (used about a fire) to suddenly burn more fiercely **2** (used about violence, anger, a person's temper, etc) to start suddenly or become worse

flare noun **1** [sing] a sudden bright light or flame **2** [C] a thing that produces a bright light or flame, used especially as a signal

flared /fleə(r)d/ adj (used about trousers and skirts) becoming wider towards the bottom

☆ **flash**[1] /flæʃ/ noun **1** [C] a sudden bright light that comes and goes quickly: *a flash of lightning* **2** [C] a sudden ability (to guess, understand or imagine sth): *With a flash of inspiration I saw what the answer must be.* **3** [C,U] a bright light that you use with a camera for taking photographs when the light is not good; the apparatus for producing this light: *The light's not very good. You'll need flash.* ○ *My new camera's got a built-in flash.* ☞ picture at **camera**.

'**flashlight** noun [C] (*US*) = TORCH

☆ **flash**[2] /flæʃ/ verb **1** [I,T] to produce a sudden bright light or to make sth produce it: *The disco lights were flashing on and off all night.* ○ *That lorry-driver's flashing his lights at us* (= in order to tell us sth). **2** [I] to move very fast: *I saw something flash past the window.* ○ *Thoughts kept flashing through my mind and I couldn't sleep.* **3** [T] to show sth quickly: *The detective flashed his card and went straight in.* **4** [T] to send a particular look towards sb (suddenly, and only for a moment): *He flashed a smile at her and drove away.* **5** [T] to send sth by radio, television, etc: *The news of the disaster was flashed across the world.*

(PHRASAL VERB) **flash back** (used about a person's thoughts) to return suddenly to a time in the past: *Something he said made my mind flash back to my childhood.*

'**flashback** noun [C,U] a part of a film, play, etc that shows sth that happened before the main story

flashy /'flæʃi/ adj (**flashier**; **flashiest**) attracting attention by being too bright and smart: *a flashy car a flashy clothes*

flask /flɑːsk/; *US* flæsk/ noun [C] **1** a bottle with a narrow neck that is used in a laboratory **2** a small flat bottle used for carrying alcoholic drink in a pocket **3** = VACUUM FLASK

flat[1] /flæt/ (*especially US* **apartment**) noun [C] a set of rooms that is used as a home (usually on one floor in a larger building): *Do you rent your flat or have you bought it?* ○ *That old house has been divided into luxury flats.* ☞ **Apartment** is much more common in American English. In British English we usually say a **flat**. But we do say apartment when talking about a flat we are renting for a holiday, etc rather than to live in: *We're renting an apartment in the South of France.* You **rent** a flat from a **landlord/landlady**. The landlord/lady **lets** the flat to you, the **tenant**. The money you have to pay is called **rent**. Your flat may be **furnished** or **unfurnished**. A tall modern building that contains many flats is a **block** of flats. A person who shares the flat with you is your **flatmate**.

☆ **flat**[2] /flæt/ adj (**flatter**; **flattest**) **1** smooth and level, with no parts that are raised above the rest: *The countryside in Essex is quite flat* (= there are not many hills). ○ *I need a flat surface to write this letter on.* ○ *a flat roof* **2** not high or deep: *You need flat shoes for walking.* ○ *a flat dish* (used about a tyre) without enough air in it: *This tyre looks flat – has it got a puncture?* ☞ picture at **puncture**. **4** without much interest or energy: *Things have been a bit flat since Alex left.* **5** (used about a drink) not fresh because it has lost its bubbles: *Open a new bottle. That lemonade has gone flat.* **6** (used about a battery) no longer producing electricity; not working: *We couldn't start the car because the battery was completely flat.* **7** (*symbol* b) (in music) half a tone lower than the stated note: *a symphony in B flat* ☞ Look at **sharp**(9). **8** (in music) lower than the correct note: *That last note was flat. Can you sing it again?* ☞ Look at **sharp**(10). **9** that will not change; firm (used about sth that you say or decide): *He answered our request with a flat 'No!'* **10** (used about the cost of sth) that is the same for everybody; that is fixed: *We charge a flat fee of £20, however long you stay.*

flatly adv **1** in a way that shows no interest **2** in a direct way; absolutely: *He flatly denied the allegations.*

flatten /'flætn/ verb [I,T] **flatten (sth) (out)** to become flat or to make sth flat: *The countryside flattens out as you get nearer the sea.* ○ *The storms have flattened crops all over the country.*

☆ **flat**[3] /flæt/ adv **1** in a level position: *She lay flat on her back in the sunshine.* ○ *He fell flat on his face in the mud.* **2** lower than the correct note: *You're singing flat.* ☞ Look at **sharp**(9). **3** (used for emphasizing how quickly sth is done) in exactly the time mentioned and no longer: *She can get up and out of the house in ten minutes flat.*

(IDIOMS) **fall flat** (used about a joke, a story, an event, etc) to fail to produce the effect that you wanted

flat out as fast as possible; without stopping: *He's been working flat out for two weeks and he needs a break.*

flat[4] /flæt/ noun **1** [C] (*symbol* b) (in music) a note which is half a tone lower than the note with the same letter ☞ Look at **sharp**. **2** [sing] **the flat (of sth)** the flat part or side of sth: *the flat of your hand* **3** [C] (*especially US*) a tyre on a car, etc that has no air in it

flatter /'flætə(r)/ verb [T] **1** to praise sb too much because you want to please him/her or because you want to get an advantage for yourself **2** (usually passive) to give pleasure or honour to sb: *I felt very flattered when they gave me the job.* **3 flatter yourself (that)** to choose to believe sth good about yourself although you may be wrong: *He flatters himself that he speaks fluent French.*

flattering /'flætərɪŋ/ adj making sb look or sound more attractive or important than he/she really is

flattery /'flætəri/ noun [U] praise that you do not really mean

flaunt /flɔːnt/ verb [T] to show sth that you are proud of so that other people will admire it

flautist /'flɔːtɪst/ (*US* **flutist**) noun [C] a person who plays the flute

iː	ɪ	e	æ	ɑː	ɒ	ɔː	ʊ	uː	ʌ
see	sit	ten	hat	arm	got	saw	put	too	cup

☆**flavour** (US **flavor**) /ˈfleɪvə(r)/ noun [C,U] **1** the taste and smell (of food): *Do you think a little salt would improve the flavour?* ○ *ten different flavours of yoghurt* ○ *yoghurt in ten different flavours* **2** the particular quality or character of sth

flavour (US **flavor**) verb [T] to give flavour to sth: *strawberry-flavoured milk shake* ○ *I flavoured the soup with lemon and parsley.*

flavouring (US **flavoring**) /ˈfleɪvərɪŋ/ noun [C,U] something that you add to food or drink to give it a particular taste

flaw /flɔː/ noun [C] **1** a mark or crack in an object that means that it is not perfect **2** a mistake in sth that makes it not satisfactory: *a flaw in an argument* **3** a bad quality in sb's character

flawed adj with a fault or weakness so that it is not perfect

flawless adj perfect

flea /fliː/ noun [C] a very small jumping insect without wings that lives on animals, eg cats and dogs. Fleas bite people and animals and make them scratch.

'flea market noun [C] a market, often in a street, that sells old and used goods

fleck /flek/ noun [C] a tiny mark on sth; a tiny piece of sth

flee /fliː/ verb [I,T] (pt, pp **fled** /fled/) to run away or escape from sth: *When the hunter fired his gun the tiger turned and fled.* ○ *The man whom the police want to interview has fled the country.*

fleet /fliːt/ noun [C, with sing or pl verb] **1** a group of ships or boats that are sailing together **2** a group of vehicles (especially taxis, buses or aircraft) that are travelling together or owned by one person

☆**flesh** /fleʃ/ noun [U] **1** the soft part of a human or animal body (between the bones and under the skin) ☛ Flesh that we eat is called **meat**. **2** the part of a fruit or vegetable that is soft and can be eaten

flew pt of FLY²

flex¹ /fleks/ (especially US **cord**) noun [C,U] (a piece of) electric wire inside a plastic tube, used for carrying electricity to electrical equipment

☛ At the end of a flex there is a **plug** which you fit in to a **power point**.

flex² /fleks/ verb [T] to bend or move a leg, arm, muscle, etc in order to exercise it

flexible /ˈfleksəbl/ adj **1** able to bend easily without breaking **2** that can change or be changed in order to suit different situations or conditions ☛ The opposite is **inflexible**. —**flexibility** noun [U]

flick /flɪk/ verb **1** [I,T] to move, or to make sth move, with a quick sudden movement: *The frog's tongue flicked out and caught the fly.* ○ *She flicked the switch and the light came on.* **2** [T] to hit sb/sth lightly and quickly

(PHRASAL VERBS) **flick sth away**; **flick sth off sth** to remove sth with a quick movement of your hand or finger

flick/flip through sth to turn over the pages of a book, magazine, etc quickly

flick noun [C] a quick sudden movement or light blow

flicker /ˈflɪkə(r)/ verb [I] **1** (used about a light or a flame) to burn or shine in a weak or unsteady way: *The candle flickered and went out.* **2** to move lightly and quickly up and down or backwards and forwards: *His eyelids flickered for a second and then he lay still.*

flicker noun [C, usually sing] **1** a flickering movement **2** a slight feeling of sth: *a flicker of hope*

flies /flaɪz/ noun [plural] = FLY³

☆**flight¹** /flaɪt/ noun **1** [C] a journey in an aeroplane, etc: *The captain and crew hope that you have enjoyed the flight.* ○ *to book a flight* ○ *a direct flight* ○ *a scheduled flight* ○ *a charter flight* ○ *a manned space flight to Mars* **2** [C] an aeroplane that takes you on a particular journey: *Flight number 340 from London to New York is boarding now* (= is ready for passengers to get on it). **3** [U] the action of flying: *It's unusual to see swans in flight* (= when they are flying). **4** [C] a number of stairs or steps leading up or down: *a flight of stairs*

flight² /flaɪt/ noun [C,U] the act of running away or escaping

(IDIOM) **put sb to flight** to make sb run away

flimsy /ˈflɪmzi/ adj (**flimsier**, **flimsiest**) **1** (used about material) light and thin **2** (used about an object) not strong; easily broken **3** weak; not convincing you that it is true: *He gave a flimsy excuse for his absence.*

flinch /flɪntʃ/ verb [I] **1** to make a slight movement backwards because of sth painful or frightening **2 flinch from sth/from doing sth** to avoid doing sth because it is unpleasant: *She didn't flinch from telling him the whole truth.*

fling¹ /flɪŋ/ verb [T] (pt, pp **flung** /flʌŋ/) to throw sb/sth suddenly or with great force: *He flung his book on the floor and rushed out.*

fling² /flɪŋ/ noun [C] a short period of fun and pleasure

flint /flɪnt/ noun **1** [U] very hard grey stone that produces small flames (**sparks**) when you strike it against steel **2** [C] a small piece of flint or metal that is used to produce sparks (for example in a cigarette lighter)

flip /flɪp/ verb (**flipping**; **flipped**) **1** [I,T] to turn with a quick movement: *She flipped the book open and started to read.* **2** [T] to throw sth into the air and make it turn over: *Let's flip a coin to see who starts.* **3** [I] (informal) to become very angry or excited

(PHRASAL VERB) **flick/flip through sth** ⇨ FLICK

flippant /ˈflɪpənt/ adj not serious or respectful enough about things that are important

flipper /ˈflɪpə(r)/ noun [C] **1** a flat limb that some sea animals use for swimming **2** a rubber shoe shaped like an animal's flipper that people wear so that they can swim better (especially under water): *a pair of flippers*

flipping /ˈflɪpɪŋ/ adj, adv (informal) (used as a mild way of swearing): *When's the flipping bus coming?*

flirt /flɜːt/ verb [I] **1** to behave in a way that suggests you find sb attractive and are trying to

flit attract him/her: *Who was that boy Irene was flirting with at the party?* **2 flirt with sth** to think about doing sth (but not very seriously)
flirt *noun* [C] a person who often flirts
flit /flɪt/ *verb* [I] (**flitting**; **flitted**) to fly or move quickly from one place to another

float/sink

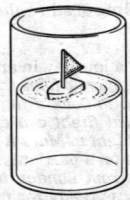

floating　　　sinking

☆ **float¹** /fləʊt/ *verb* [I] **1** to stay on the surface of a liquid and not sink; to move gently on the surface of a liquid: *Cork floats in water.* ○ *There was something floating near the bank of the river.* **2** to move slowly through the air: *A leaf floated gently down to the ground.*
floating *adj* not fixed; not living permanently in one place: *London's floating population* ○ *a floating voter* (= a person who does not always vote for the same political party)
float² /fləʊt/ *noun* [C] **1** a light floating object used for helping people learn to swim **2** a light floating object used on a fishing-line or net **3** a lorry or other vehicle that is decorated and used in a procession
flock /flɒk/ *noun* [C] **1** a group of sheep, goats or birds ☛ Look at **herd**. **2** a large number of people: *Flocks of tourists visit London every summer.*
flock *verb* [I] to gather or go somewhere in large numbers: *People are flocking to the exhibition in large numbers.*
flog /flɒg/ *verb* [T] (**flogging**; **flogged**) **1** (*informal*) to sell sth **2** to hit sb hard with a whip or stick as a punishment
flogging *noun* [C,U] hitting sb with a whip or stick as a punishment
☆ **flood¹** /flʌd/ *verb* [I,T] **1** to fill a place with water; to be filled or overflow with water: *The river burst its banks and flooded the village.* ○ *The river Trent floods almost every year.* **2** (used about a thought, feeling, etc) to fill sb's mind suddenly: *At the end of the day all his worries came flooding back.*
(PHRASAL VERB) **flood in** to arrive in large numbers: *Entries for the competition have been flooding in.*
☆ **flood²** /flʌd/ *noun* [C] **1** (*also* **floods** [plural]) a large amount of water (from a river, the sea, etc) that covers an area which should be dry: *Many people have been forced to leave their homes because of the floods.* **2** a large number or amount: *She received a flood of letters after the accident.* ○ *The little boy was in floods of tears* (= crying a great deal).
floodlight /'flʌdlaɪt/ *noun* [C] a powerful light that is used for lighting sports grounds, the outside of public buildings, etc ☛ picture at **football**.
floodlit /'flʌdlɪt/ *adj* lit by floodlights: *a floodlit hockey match*
☆ **floor¹** /flɔː(r)/ *noun* **1** [C, usually sing] the flat surface that you walk on indoors: *Don't come in – there's broken glass on the floor!* ○ *There aren't enough chairs so some people will have to sit on the floor.* ○ *to sweep the floor* ○ *a wooden floor* ☛ Look at the note at **ground**. **2** [C, usually sing] the ground or surface at the bottom of the sea, a forest, etc: *the ocean floor* **3** [C] a level in a building: *Which floor is the men's department on, please?* ☛ In Britain, the **ground floor** is the floor at street level, and the floor above is the **first floor**. In US English the **first floor** is the floor at street level.
'floorboard *noun* [C] one of the long wooden boards used to make a floor
floor² /flɔː(r)/ *verb* [T] to surprise or completely confuse sb with a question or a problem
flop /flɒp/ *verb* [I] (**flopping**; **flopped**) **1** to move or fall in a heavy or an awkward way: *I was so tired that all I could do was flop onto the sofa and watch TV.* **2** to hang down loosely: *I can't bear my hair flopping in my eyes.* **3** (used about a book, film, record, etc) to be unsuccessful with the public
flop *noun* [C] **1** [usually sing] a floppy movement **2** something that is not a success; a failure: *Her first novel was very successful but her second was a flop.*
floppy /'flɒpi/ *adj* (**floppier**; **floppiest**) soft, loose and hanging downwards; not stiff: *a floppy hat*
floppy 'disk (*also* **floppy**; **diskette**) *noun* [C] a square piece of plastic that can store information for a computer: *Don't forget to back up your files onto a floppy disk.* ☛ picture on page A13. Look at **hard disk**.
flora /'flɔːrə/ *noun* [plural] all the plants growing in a particular area: *He's studying the flora and fauna* (= the plants and animals) *of South America.* ☛ Look at **fauna**.
floral /'flɔːrəl/ *adj* decorated with a pattern of flowers, or made with flowers
florist /'flɒrɪst; *US* 'flɔːr-/ *noun* [C] a person who has a shop that sells flowers ☛ The shop itself is called **the florist's**: *I bought her a bunch of flowers at the florist's.*
flounder /'flaʊndə(r)/ *verb* [I] **1** to move with difficulty or to struggle (eg when you are trying not to sink in water) **2** to find it difficult to speak or act in a suitable way (usually in an awkward situation)
☆ **flour** /'flaʊə(r)/ *noun* [U] a fine powder made from wheat or other grain and used for making breads, cakes, biscuits, etc
flourish /'flʌrɪʃ/ *verb* **1** [I] to be strong and healthy; to develop in a successful way: *These plants flourish in a sunny position.* ○ *a flourishing new sports centre* **2** [T] to wave sth in the air so that people will notice it
flourish *noun* [C, usually sing] a movement that you make to attract attention
flout /flaʊt/ *verb* [T] to refuse to obey or accept

p	b	t	d	k	g	tʃ	dʒ	f	v	θ	ð
pen	bad	tea	did	cat	got	chin	June	fall	van	thin	then

sth: *to flout the rules of the organization* o *to flout sb's advice*

☆ **flow** /fləʊ/ *verb* [I] **1** to move in a smooth and continuous way (like water): *This river flows south into the English Channel.* o *a fast-flowing stream* o *It was three hours before the traffic began to flow normally after the accident.* o *People have been steadily flowing out of the country since the trouble began.* **2** (used about hair and clothes) to hang down in a loose way: *a long flowing dress.*

flow *noun* [sing] **1** a steady, continuous movement of sth/sb: *There's a steady flow of young people from the country to the towns.* **2** a supply of sth: *Press hard on the wound to stop the flow of blood.* o *a flow of information between the school and the parents*

☆ **flower** /ˈflaʊə(r)/ *noun* [C] **1** the beautiful coloured part of a plant or tree from which seeds or fruit grow

☛ A flower consists of several **petals**. It grows from a **bud** on the end of a **stem**.

2 a plant that is grown for its flowers; a flower and its stem: *She grows a lot of flowers but no vegetables.* o *a lovely bunch of flowers*

☛ We **pick** flowers and **arrange** them in a vase. Flowers that are given or carried on a special occasion are called a **bouquet**.

flower *verb* [I] to produce flowers: *This plant flowers in late summer.*

flowery *adj* **1** covered or decorated with flowers: *a flowery dress, hat, wallpaper, etc* ☛ picture at **pattern**. **2** (used about a style of speaking or writing) using long, difficult words

'flower-bed (*also* **bed**) *noun* [C] a piece of ground in a garden or park where flowers are grown

'flower-pot *noun* [C] a pot in which a plant can be grown ☛ picture at **pot**.

flown *pp* of FLY²

flu /fluː/ (*also formal* **influenza**) *noun* [U] an illness that is like a bad cold but more serious. You usually have a temperature and your arms and legs ache: *The whole family has got flu.* o *They're in bed with flu.* o *There's a lot of flu about* (= a lot of people have got it).

fluctuate /ˈflʌktʃʊeɪt/ *verb* [I] **fluctuate (between A and B)** (used about prices and numbers, or people's feelings) to change frequently from one thing to another: *The number of students fluctuates between 100 and 150.* o *Many people find that their moods fluctuate with the weather.* —**fluctuation** /ˌflʌktʃʊˈeɪʃn/ *noun* [C,U]

fluent /ˈfluːənt/ *adj* **1 fluent (in sth)** able to speak or write a language easily and accurately: *After a year in France she was fluent in French.* **2** (used about speech, reading or writing) expressed in a smooth and accurate way: *He speaks fluent German.* —**fluency** /ˈfluːənsɪ/ *noun* [U] —**fluently** *adv*

fluff /flʌf/ *noun* [U] **1** small pieces of waste material (from woollen clothes, etc) that form into balls and collect under furniture, in the corners of a room, etc or on people's clothes **2** the soft new fur on young animals or birds

fluffy *adj* (**fluffier; fluffiest**) very soft and light like fur: *a fluffy jumper*

fluid /ˈfluːɪd/ *noun* [C] a substance that can flow; a liquid: *The doctor told her to drink plenty of fluids.* o *body fluids* o *cleaning fluids*

fluid *adj* **1** able to flow like a liquid **2** (used about plans, etc) able or likely to be changed

ˌfluid ˈounce *noun* [C] (*abbr* **fl oz**) a measure of liquid; 0·0284 of a litre. There are 20 fluid ounces in a British pint and 16 fluid ounces in an American pint.

fluke /fluːk/ *noun* [C, usually sing] (*informal*) something good that happens by accident, not because you have been clever or skilful: *The result was not a fluke. The better team won.*

flung *pt*, *pp* of FLING¹

fluorescent /ˌflɔːˈresnt/ *adj* **1** shining with a particular kind of hard white light: *People often have fluorescent lighting in the kitchen.* **2** very bright; seeming to shine: *fluorescent pink socks*

fluoride /ˈflɔːraɪd; *US* ˈflʊər-/ *noun* [U] a chemical substance that can be added to water or toothpaste to help prevent tooth decay

flurry /ˈflʌrɪ/ *noun* [C] (*pl* **flurries**) **1** a small amount of wind, rain or snow that comes suddenly **2** a short sudden burst of activity or feelings: *a flurry of excitement.*

flush¹ /flʌʃ/ *verb* [I] (used about a person or his/her face) to go red: *Susan flushed and could not hide her embarrassment.*

flush *noun* [sing] a rush of blood to the face that makes it look red

flushed *adj* with a hot red face: *You look very flushed. Are you sure you're all right?*

flush² /flʌʃ/ *verb* **1** [T] to clean a toilet by pressing or pulling a handle that sends a stream of water into the toilet: *Please remember to flush the toilet.* **2** [I] (used about a toilet) to be cleaned with a stream of water: *The toilet won't flush.* **3** [T] **flush sth away, down, etc** to get rid of sth in a stream of water: *You can't flush tea-leaves down the sink – they'll block it.*

fluster /ˈflʌstə(r)/ *verb* [T] (usually passive) to make sb feel nervous and confused (because there is too much to do or not enough time): *Don't get flustered – there's plenty of time.*

flute   recorder

flute /fluːt/ *noun* [C] a musical instrument like a pipe that you hold sideways and play by blow-

flutter

ing over a hole at one side —**flutist** /ˈfluːtɪst/ noun [C] (US) = FLAUTIST

flutter /ˈflʌtə(r)/ verb **1** [I,T] to move up and down or from side to side quickly and lightly; to make sth move in this way: *The flags were fluttering in the wind.* ○ *The bird fluttered its wings and tried to fly.* **2** [I] to move lightly through the air: *The dead leaves fluttered to the ground.* **3** [I] when your heart or stomach flutters, you are feeling nervous and excited

flutter noun [C, usually sing] **1** a quick, light movement **2** a state of nervous excitement: *I always get in a flutter before I go on holiday.*

☆ **fly**[1] /flaɪ/ verb (pres part **flying**; 3rd pers sing pres **flies**; pt **flew** /fluː/; pp **flown** /fləʊn/) **1** [I] (used about a bird, insect, aeroplane, etc) to move through the air: *This bird has a broken wing and cannot fly.* ○ *I can hear a plane flying overhead.* **2** [I,T] to travel in or to carry sth in an aeroplane, etc: *My daughter is flying (out) to Singapore next week.* ○ *Supplies of food were flown (in) to the starving people.* **3** [I,T] (used about a pilot) to control an aeroplane, etc: *You have to have special training to fly a jumbo jet.* **4** [T] to travel over an area of land or sea by flying: *Concorde can fly the Atlantic in three hours.* **5** [I] to move quickly or suddenly: *It's late. I must fly.* ○ *A large stone came flying through the window.* **6** [I] (used about time) to pass quickly: *The weekend has just flown (by) and now it's Monday again.* **7** [I,T] to move about in the air; to make sth move about in the air: *The flags are flying.* ○ *Let's go and fly our kite!* ☞ The noun from fly is **flight**.
(IDIOMS) **as the crow flies** ⇒ CROW[1]
fly off the handle (*informal*) to become very angry
let fly (at sb/sth) 1 to shout angrily at sb: *My parents really let fly at me when I got home late.* **2** to attack sb in anger: *She let fly at him with her fists.*

☆ **fly**[2] /flaɪ/ noun [C] (pl **flies**) a small insect with two wings: *There were flies buzzing round the dead cow.* ☞ picture at **insect**.

fly[3] /flaɪ/ noun [C] (also **flies** [plural]) a flap of cloth that covers the zip or buttons on the front of a pair of trousers: *Henry, your flies are undone.*

flying /ˈflaɪɪŋ/ adj able to fly: *flying insects*
(IDIOMS) **with flying colours** with great success; very well: *Martin passed the exam with flying colours.*
get off to a flying start to begin sth well and so get some advantage

flying noun [U] travelling in an aeroplane, etc: *I don't like flying.*

ˌflying ˈvisit noun [C] a very quick visit: *I can't stop. This is just a flying visit.*

flyover /ˈflaɪəʊvə(r)/ (*Brit*) (*US* **overpass**) noun [C] a type of bridge that carries a road over another road

foal /fəʊl/ noun [C] a young horse ☞ Look at the note at **horse**.

foam /fəʊm/ noun [U] **1** a mass of small white bubbles that are formed when air and a liquid are mixed together: *white foam on the tops of the waves* **2** an artificial substance that looks like foam: *shaving foam* **3** (also ˌfoam ˈrub-*

foil

ber**) soft rubber or plastic that is used inside seats, cushions, etc

foam verb [I] to produce foam: *The dog was foaming at the mouth.*

fob /fɒb/ verb (fob**bing**; fob**bed**)
(PHRASAL VERB) **fob sb off (with sth); fob sth off on sb** to try to give sb something that is not suitable or that is not what he/she wants: *Don't try to fob me off with that old car – I want a new one.* ○ *Don't try and fob that old car off on me.*

focal point /ˈfəʊkl pɔɪnt/ noun [sing] the centre of interest or activity

focus /ˈfəʊkəs/ noun [C] (pl **focuses**) **1** the point at which rays of light meet or from which they appear to come **2** [usually sing] the centre of interest or attention; special attention that is given to sb/sth: *The school used to be the focus of village life.* ○ *Tonight our focus will be on modern jazz.*
(IDIOM) **in focus/out of focus** (used about a photograph or sth in a photograph) clear/not clear: *It's a shame. Tony's face is out of focus on this photo.*

focus verb (focus**ing**; focus**ed** or focus**sing**; focus**sed**) **focus (sth) (on sth) 1** [T] to direct rays of light onto one particular point **2** [I,T] to be or become able to see clearly; to adjust your eyes so that you can see clearly: *Gradually his eyes focussed.* ○ *She focussed her eyes on the page.* **3** [I,T] to adjust a camera so that the picture that you are taking will be clear: *I focussed on the person in the middle of the group.* **4** [I,T] to give all your attention to sth: *to focus on a problem* ○ *to focus attention on a problem*

fodder /ˈfɒdə(r)/ noun [U] food that is given to farm animals

foe /fəʊ/ noun [C] (*formal*) an enemy

foetus (*US* **fetus**) /ˈfiːtəs/ noun [C] (pl **foetuses**; **fetuses**) a young human or animal that is still developing in its mother's body ☞ An **embryo** is at an earlier stage of development.

☆ **fog** /fɒg; *US* fɔːg/ noun **1** [U] thick cloud that forms close to or just above the land or sea. Fog makes it difficult for us to see: *Patches of dense fog are making driving dangerous.* ○ *The fog had lifted/cleared by midday.*

☞ Fog is thicker than **mist**. **Haze** is caused by heat. **Smog** is caused by pollution. Look at the note at **weather**.

2 [C] a period of fog: *Bad fogs are common in November.*

foggy adj (**foggier**; **foggiest**) used to describe the weather when there is a fog: *a foggy morning*
(IDIOM) **not have the faintest/foggiest (idea)** ⇒ FAINT

foil[1] /fɔɪl/ noun [U] metal that has been rolled or beaten into very thin sheets, often used when you are wrapping or cooking food: *tin/aluminium foil*

foil[2] /fɔɪl/ verb [T] to prevent sb from succeeding or from carrying out his/her plans; to prevent a plan from succeeding: *The prisoners tried to escape but all their attempts were foiled.*

iː	ɪ	e	æ	ɑː	ɒ	ɔː	ʊ	uː	ʌ
see	sit	ten	hat	arm	got	saw	put	too	cup

foist /fɔɪst/ *verb*
(PHRASAL VERB) **foist sth on/upon sb** to force sb to accept sth that he/she does not want

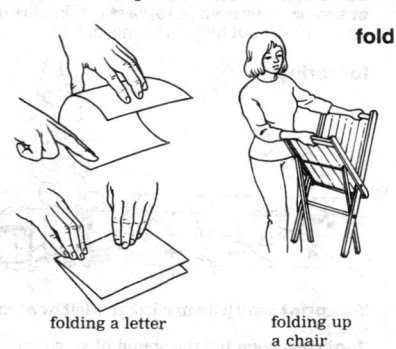

folding a letter   *folding up a chair*

☆ **fold** /fəʊld/ *verb* **1** [T] **fold sth (up)** to bend one part of sth over another part in order to make it smaller, tidier, etc: *He folded the letter into three before putting it into the envelope.* ○ *Fold up your clothes neatly, please.* ☞ The opposite is **unfold**. **2** [I] **fold (up)** to be able to be folded in order to be easier to carry or to store: *This garden table folds up flat.* ○ *a folding bed* **3** [I] **fold (up)** (used about a business, a play in the theatre, etc) to close because it is unsuccessful
(IDIOM) **cross/fold your arms** ➪ ARM¹
fold *noun* [C] **1** the mark or line where sth has been folded **2** a curved shape that is made by a piece of material, etc that has been folded: *the folds of a dress*

folder /ˈfəʊldə(r)/ *noun* [C] **1** a cardboard or plastic cover that is used for holding papers, etc **2** a collection of information or files on one subject that is stored in a computer or on a disk

foliage /ˈfəʊliɪdʒ/ *noun* [U] (*formal*) all the leaves of a tree or plant

folk /fəʊk/ *noun* **1** [plural] (*US* **folks**) (*informal*) people in general: *Some folk are never satisfied.* **2** [plural] a particular type of people: *Old folk often don't like change.* ○ *country folk* **3 folks** [plural] (*informal*) your parents or close relatives: *How are your folks?*
folk *adj* traditional in a community; of a traditional style: *Robin Hood is an English folk hero.* ○ *folk music* ○ *a folk song*

'folklore /ˈfəʊklɔː(r)/ *noun* [U] (the study of) traditional stories and beliefs

☆ **follow** /ˈfɒləʊ/ *verb* **1** [I,T] to come, go or happen after sb/sth: *You go first and I'll follow (on) later.* ○ *The dog followed her wherever she went.* ○ *The crash was followed by a scream and then there was silence.* ○ *The news will be followed by a programme on the situation in West Africa.* ○ *We had steak followed by fresh fruit.* **2** [T] to go after sb in order to catch him/her: *Go a bit slower! I think the police are following us!* **3** [T] to go along a road, etc; to go in the same direction as sth: *Follow this road for a mile and then turn right at the pub.* ○ *The road follows the river for a few miles.* **4** [T] to accept advice, instructions, an example, etc and do what you have been told or shown to do: *When lighting fireworks, it is important to follow the instructions carefully.* ○ *She always follows the latest fashions.* **5** [I,T] to understand the meaning of sth: *I'm sorry, I don't follow.* ○ *The children couldn't follow the plot of that film.* **6** [T] to watch or listen to sb/sth very carefully: *You'll have to follow what he says very carefully if you want to understand it.* **7** [T] to take an active interest in sth: *Have you been following the tennis championships?* **8** [I] **follow (on) (from sth)** to happen as a result of sth; to be the necessary result of sth: *It doesn't follow that old people can't lead active lives.* **9** [T] to happen in the planned or expected way: *The day's events followed the usual pattern.*
(IDIOMS) **as follows** (used for introducing a list): *The names of the successful candidates are as follows...*
follow sb's example/lead to do what sb else has done or decided to do
follow suit to do the same thing that sb else has just done
(PHRASAL VERBS) **follow sth through** to continue doing sth until it is finished
follow sth up 1 to take further action about sth: *You should follow up your letter with a phone call.* **2** to find out more about sth: *We need to follow up the story about the school.*
follower *noun* [C] a person who follows or supports a person, belief, etc
'follow-up *noun* [C] something that is done to continue sth: *As a follow-up to the television series, the BBC is publishing a book on the subject.*

following /ˈfɒləʊɪŋ/ *adj* **1** next (in time): *He was taken ill on Sunday and died the following week.* **2** (in a list) that I will mention now: *Please could you bring the following items to the meeting...* ☞ We can also use the **following** as a noun: *The following are the winners of the competition...*
following *noun* [sing] a group of people who support or admire sth: *Buddhism has quite a large following in Japan.*
following *prep* after; as a result of: *Following the riots many students have been arrested.*

folly /ˈfɒli/ *noun* [C,U] (*pl* **follies**) (*formal*) a foolish act: *It would be folly to ignore their warnings.*

☆ **fond** /fɒnd/ *adj* **1** (not before a noun) **fond of sb/sth; fond of doing sth** liking a person or a thing, or liking doing sth: *We're all very fond of Mrs Simpson.* ○ *He's a good cook. I'm especially fond of his chicken casserole.* ○ *I'm not very fond of staying up late.* **2** (only *before* a noun) kind and loving: *I have fond memories of both my aunts.* **3** (only *before* a noun) wished or hoped for but unlikely to come true: *She had a fond belief that David would come back.*
fondly *adv* **1** in a loving way **2** in a foolish way: *I fondly imagined that you liked me.*
fondness *noun* [U] a liking for sb/sth

fondle /ˈfɒndl/ *verb* [T] to touch or stroke sb/sth in a loving way

☆ **food** /fuːd/ *noun* **1** [U] something that people, animals or plants take into their bodies in

ɜː	ə	eɪ	əʊ	aɪ	aʊ	ɔɪ	ɪə	eə	ʊə
fur	ago	pay	home	five	now	join	near	hair	pure

order to keep them alive and healthy: *Plants get food from the soil.* ○ *There is a shortage of food in some areas.* **2** [C,U] a particular type of food that you eat: *baby food* ○ *We eat a lot of health foods.* ○ *food and drink*

'food poisoning *noun* [U] an illness that is caused by eating food that is bad

'food processor *noun* [C] an electric machine that can mix food and also cut or slice food into small pieces

'foodstuff *noun* [C, usually pl] a substance that is used as food: *There has been a sharp rise in the cost of basic foodstuffs.*

☆ **fool** /fu:l/ *noun* [C] a person who is silly or who acts in a silly way: *I felt such a fool when I realized my mistake.* ○ *She was fool enough to believe it when he said that he loved her.* ☛ Look at **April Fool**.

(IDIOM) **make a fool of sb/yourself** to make sb/yourself look foolish or silly

fool *verb* **1** [T] to trick sb: *Don't be fooled into believing everything that the salesman says.* **2** [I] to speak without being serious: *You didn't really believe me when I said I was going to America, did you? I was only fooling.*

(PHRASAL VERB) **fool about/around** to behave in a silly way: *Stop fooling around with that knife or someone will get hurt!*

foolhardy /'fu:lha:di/ *adj* taking unnecessary risks

☆ **foolish** /'fu:lɪʃ/ *adj* **1** silly; not sensible: *I was foolish enough to trust him.* **2** looking silly or feeling embarrassed: *He felt rather foolish when he couldn't start his motor cycle in front of his friends.* —**foolishly** *adv* —**foolishness** *noun* [U]

foolproof /'fu:lpru:f/ *adj* not capable of going wrong or being wrongly used: *Our security system is absolutely foolproof.*

☆ **foot**[1] /fʊt/ *noun* [C] (*pl* **feet** /fi:t/) **1** the lowest part of the leg, below the ankle, on which a person or animal stands: *She rose to her feet* (= she stood up). ○ *What size feet have you got?* ○ *big/small feet* ○ *wide/narrow feet* ○ *She sat by the fire and the dog sat at her feet.* ○ *a foot brake* (= one that is operated by your foot)

☛ When you walk somewhere you go **on foot**. The nails on your feet are called **toe-nails**. If you have no shoes or socks on you are **barefoot** or **in bare feet**.

2 the part of a sock, etc into which you put your foot **3** (*abbr* **ft**) a measure of length; 30·48 centimetres. There are 12 inches in a foot, and 3 feet in a yard: *'How tall are you?' 'Five foot two (inches).'* ○ *a six-foot high wall* ☛ The plural can be **feet** or **foot**. **4** [sing] the bottom of sth: *There's a note at the foot of the page.* ○ *sitting at the foot of the stairs* ☛ The opposite is **top**. **5** [sing] the end of a bed where the feet go ☛ The opposite is **head**.

(IDIOMS) **find your feet** ⇨ FIND
get/have cold feet ⇨ COLD[1]
put your foot down (*informal*) to say firmly that sth must (not) happen: *Susan put her foot down and said that the children could only watch an hour of television each evening.*

put your foot in it (*informal*) to say or do sth that upsets or embarrasses sb

set foot in/on sth ⇨ SET[2]

stand on your own (two) feet to take care of yourself without help; to be independent

footprints

'footprint *noun* [C] a mark that is left by a foot or a shoe

'footstep *noun* [C] the sound of sb walking; the mark that a person leaves when walking: *I heard his footsteps in the hall.*

'footwear *noun* [U] boots or shoes

foot[2] /fʊt/ *verb*

(IDIOM) **foot the bill (for sth)** to pay (for sth)

☆ **football** /'fʊtbɔ:l/ *noun* **1** (*also* **soccer**) [U] a game that is played by two teams of eleven players who try to kick a round ball into a goal: *a football pitch* ○ *a football match* ☛ The word **soccer** is used in newspapers and on television in Britain. In the US **soccer** is the usual word for this game since Americans use the word **football** to refer to **American Football**. **2** [C] the large round ball that is used in this game

footballer *noun* [C] a person who plays football, especially as a professional

'football pools (*also* **the pools**) *noun* [plural] a game in which people bet money on the results of football matches and can win large amounts

foothold /'fʊthəʊld/ *noun* [C] a place where you can safely put your foot when you are climbing: (*figurative*) *We need to get a foothold in the European market.*

footing /'fʊtɪŋ/ *noun* [sing] **1** being able to stand firmly on a surface: *He lost his footing on the wet floor and fell.* ○ (*figurative*) *The company is now on a firm footing and should soon show a profit.* **2** the level or position of sb/sth (in relation to sb/sth else): *to be on an equal footing with sb*

footnote /'fʊtnəʊt/ *noun* [C] an extra piece of information that is added at the bottom of a page in a book

footpath /'fʊtpɑ:θ/ *noun* [C] a path in the country for people to walk on: *a public footpath*

☆ **for**[1] /fə(r); strong form fɔ:(r)/ *prep* **1** (showing the person who will receive sth): *Here is a letter for you.* ○ *Save a piece of cake for Mary.* ○ *He made lunch for them.* ○ *She bought some sweets for the children.* **2** (showing purpose or use): *What's this gadget for?* ○ *Let's go for a walk.* ○ *Please get me a shampoo for dry hair.* ○ *Shall we have eggs for breakfast?* ○ *What did you do that for?* (= Why did you do that?) **3** (showing where sb/sth is going to): *Is this the train for*

p	b	t	d	k	g	tʃ	dʒ	f	v	θ	ð
pen	bad	tea	did	cat	got	chin	June	fall	van	thin	then

Football diagram labels: floodlight, stand, centre circle, referee, forwards (also strikers), linesman, sweeper, mid-field players, defenders, goal, goalkeeper, pitch, touch-line, penalty area, goal-line

football

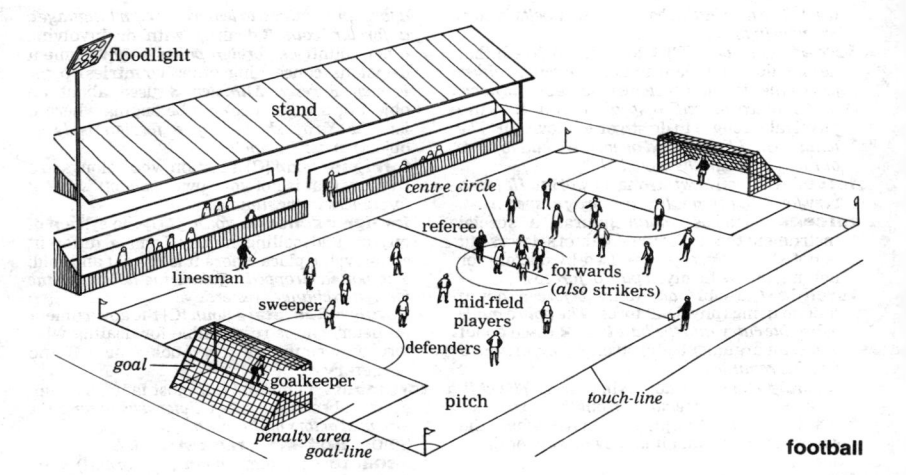

Glasgow? ○ *They set off for the shops.* **4** intended to be used by a particular group or in a particular way: *It's a book for children.* ○ *That chair is for visitors.* ○ *Is the flat for sale?* **5** in order to help sb/sth: *What can I do for you?* ○ *You should take some medicine for your cold.* ○ *Doctors are fighting for his life.* ○ *Take care of her for my sake.* **6** (showing the price of sth): *I bought this car for £2 000.* ○ *She gave me their old TV for nothing.* **7** (showing a reason): *He was sent to prison for robbery.* ○ *I couldn't speak for laughing.* **8** on the occasion of: *What did they give you for your birthday?* **9** in support of (sb/sth): *Three cheers for the winner!* ○ *Are you for or against shops opening on Sundays?* **10** as a representative of (sb/sth): *Who's the MP for Bradford?* ○ *She plays hockey for England.* **11** meaning or representing (sb/sth): *What's the 'C' for in 'BBC'?* ○ *What's the Russian for 'window'?* **12** (after a verb) in order to have or get sth: *She asked me for help.* **13** (after an adjective) when you consider what you could expect: *She's tall for her age.* ○ *It's quite warm for January.* **14** (after a comparative adjective) after sth: *We'll all feel better for a good night's sleep.* **15** (used when you give one thing and get sth else back): *I want to exchange this sweater for a larger one.* **16** (showing a length of time): *I'm going away for a few days.* ○ *They have left the town for good* (= they will not return). ○ *He was in prison for 20 years* (= he is not in prison now). ○ *He has been in prison for 20 years* (= he is still in prison). ☛ **Since** is used with a point in time for showing when something began: *He has been in prison since 1970.* **Ago** is also used for showing when something began: *He went to prison 20 years ago.* **17** (showing that sth has been arranged to happen at a particular time): *The appointment is for 10.30.* ○ *We've booked our holiday for the second week in July.* **18** (showing when sth happens): *I'm warning you for the last time.* ○ *I met him for the second time yesterday.* **19** (showing a distance): *He walked for ten miles.*

(IDIOMS) **for all** in spite of: *For all his money, he's a very lonely man.*

for ever ⇨ FOREVER(1)

for² /fə(r); strong form fɔː(r)/ conj (formal) because: *The children soon lost their way for they had never been in the forest alone before.*

☆**forbid** /fə'bɪd/ verb [T] (pres part **forbidding**; pt **forbade** /fə'bæd; US fə'beɪd/ or **forbad** /fə'bæd/; pp **forbidden** /fə'bɪdn/) **1** forbid sb to do sth to order sb not to do sth: *My parents forbade me to see Tim again.* **2** to not allow sth: *Smoking is forbidden inside the building.*

forbidding adj looking unfriendly or unattractive: *The coast near the village is rather grey and forbidding.*

☆**force¹** /fɔːs/ noun **1** [U] physical strength or power: *The force of the explosion knocked them to the ground.* ○ *The police used force to break up the demonstration.* **2** [U] power and influence: *His arguments lost some of their force when they were translated into French.* **3** [C] a person or thing that has power or influence: *Britain is no longer a major force in international affairs.* **4** [C,U] (*technical*) a power that can cause change or movement: *the force of gravity* **5** [C, usually sing] a measure of wind strength: *a force 9 gale* **6** [C] a group of people who are trained for a particular purpose: *a highly trained workforce* ○ *a UN peace-keeping force* ○ *the police force*

(IDIOMS) **bring sth/come into force** to start using a new law, etc; to start being used: *The government want to bring new anti-pollution legislation into force next year.*

in force 1 (used about people) in large numbers: *The police were present in force at the football match.* **2** (used about a law, rule, etc) being

s	z	ʃ	ʒ	h	m	n	ŋ	l	r	j	w
so	zoo	she	vision	how	man	no	sing	leg	red	yes	wet

used: *The new laws about rear seat-belts in cars are now in force.*

force² /fɔːs/ *verb* [T] **1** to make sb do sth that he/she does not want to do: *The bank robber forced the staff and customers to lie on the floor.* ○ *She forced herself to speak to him.* **2** to use physical strength to do sth or to move sth: *The window had been forced open.* ○ *We had to force our way through the crowd.*

forceful /ˈfɔːsfl/ *adj* strong; powerful: *He has a very forceful personality.* ○ *a forceful speech*

forceps /ˈfɔːseps/ *noun* [plural] a special instrument that looks like a pair of scissors but is not sharp. Forceps are used by doctors for holding things firmly: *a pair of forceps*

forcible /ˈfɔːsəbl/ *adj* (only *before* a noun) **1** done using (physical) force: *The police made a forcible entry into the building.* **2** (used about ideas, an argument, etc) strong; convincing: *a forcible reminder*

forcibly /ˈfɔːsɪbli/ *adv* using force: *The children were forcibly removed from their parents.*

ford /fɔːd/ *noun* [C] a place in a river where the water is shallow and it is easy to walk or drive across

fore /fɔː(r)/ *noun*
(IDIOM) **be/come to the fore** to be in or get into an important position so that you are noticed by people

forearm /ˈfɔːrɑːm/ *noun* [C] the lower part of your arm between your elbow and your wrist

foreboding /fɔːˈbəʊdɪŋ/ *noun* [U,sing] a strong feeling that danger or trouble is coming

☆ **forecast** /ˈfɔːkɑːst; *US* -kæst/ *verb* [T] (*pt*, *pp* **forecast** or **forecasted**) to say (with the help of information) what will probably happen in the future: *The Chancellor did not forecast the sudden rise in inflation.* ○ *Rain has been forecast for tomorrow.* —**forecast** *noun* [C]: *The weather forecast said it would be fine tomorrow.*

forecourt /ˈfɔːkɔːt/ *noun* [C] a large open area in front of a building such as a petrol station

forefinger /ˈfɔːfɪŋɡə(r)/ *noun* [C] the finger next to the thumb ☛ We also say **index finger**.

forefront /ˈfɔːfrʌnt/ *noun* [sing] the leading position; the position at the front: *Our department is right at the forefront of scientific research.*

forego = FORGO

foregone /ˈfɔːɡɒn; *US* -ɡɔːn/ *adj*
(IDIOM) **a foregone conclusion** a result that is or was certain to happen

foreground /ˈfɔːɡraʊnd/ *noun* [sing] **the foreground 1** the part of a view, picture, etc that appears closest to the person looking at it: *Notice the artist's use of colour in the foreground of the picture.* **2** a position where you will be noticed most: *He likes to be in the foreground at every meeting.* ☛ Look at **background**.

forehand /ˈfɔːhænd/ *noun* [C] a stroke in tennis, etc that is made with the inside of your hand facing forward ☛ Look at **backhand**.

☆ **forehead** /ˈfɒrɪd; ˈfɔːhed; *US* ˈfɔːrɪd/ (*also* **brow**) *noun* [C] the flat part of a person's face above the eyes and below the hair ☛ picture on page A8.

☆ **foreign** /ˈfɒrən; *US* ˈfɔːr-/ *adj* **1** belonging to or connected with a country that is not your own: *a foreign country* ○ *to learn a foreign language* ○ *a foreign coin* **2** dealing with or involving other countries: *foreign policy* (= government decisions concerning other countries) ○ *the French Foreign Minister* **3** (used about an object or a substance) not belonging where it is: *The X-ray showed up a foreign body* (= object) *in her stomach.*

foreigner *noun* [C] a person who belongs to a country that is not your own: *London is full of foreigners in the summer.*

foreign ex'change *noun* [C,U] the system of buying and selling money from a different country; the place where it is bought and sold: *The pound dropped against the dollar on the foreign exchanges yesterday.*

Foreign 'Secretary *noun* [C] the government minister who is responsible for dealing with foreign countries ☛ Look at **Home Secretary**.

foremost /ˈfɔːməʊst/ *adj* most famous or important; best: *Laurence Olivier was among the foremost actors of this century.*
(IDIOM) **first and foremost** ⇨ FIRST²

forename /ˈfɔːneɪm/ *noun* [C] (*formal*) your first name, that is given to you when you are born ☛ Look at the note at **name**.

forensic /fəˈrensɪk; *US* -zɪk/ *adj* connected with the law and finding out about a crime: *The police are carrying out forensic tests to try and find out the cause of death.* ○ *forensic medicine*

forerunner /ˈfɔːrʌnə(r)/ *noun* [C] a person or thing that is an early example or a sign of sth that appears or develops later

foresee /fɔːˈsiː/ *verb* [T] (*pt* **foresaw** /fɔːˈsɔː/; *pp* **foreseen** /fɔːˈsiːn/) to know or guess that sth is going to happen in the future: *Nobody could have foreseen the result of the election.* ☛ Look at **unforeseen**.

foreseeable /-əbl/ *adj* that can be expected: *These problems were foreseeable.* ○ *The weather won't change in the foreseeable future* (= as far ahead as we can see).

foresight /ˈfɔːsaɪt/ *noun* [U] the ability to see what will probably happen in the future (and to make wise plans): *My neighbour had the foresight to move house before the new motorway was built.* ☛ Look at **hindsight**.

foreskin /ˈfɔːskɪn/ *noun* [C] the loose piece of skin that covers the end of the penis

☆ **forest** /ˈfɒrɪst; *US* ˈfɔːr-/ *noun* [C,U] a large area of land that is covered with trees: *tropical rain forests* ○ *A large part of Canada is covered in forest.* ○ *a forest fire* ☛ A **forest** is larger than a **wood**. A **jungle** is a forest in a tropical part of the world.

forestry *noun* [U] the science of planting and taking care of trees in forests

forestall /fɔːˈstɔːl/ *verb* [T] to act before sb else in order to prevent him/her from doing sth; to prevent an action from taking place by doing sth that will stop it

foretell /fɔːˈtel/ *verb* [T] (*pt*, *pp* **foretold** /fɔːˈtəʊld/) (*formal*) to say what will happen in the future

forethought /ˈfɔːθɔːt/ *noun* [U] careful thought about, or preparation for, the future

foretold *pt*, *pp* of FORETELL

forever /fəˈrevə(r)/ adv 1 (also **for ever**) for all time; permanently: *I wish the holidays would last forever!* ○ *I realized that our relationship had finished forever.* ○ *My sister always takes forever* (= a very long time) *in the bathroom.* 2 (with verbs in the continuous forms) very often: *Our neighbours are forever having noisy parties.*

foreword /ˈfɔːwɜːd/ noun [C] a piece of writing at the beginning of a book that introduces the book and/or its author

forfeit /ˈfɔːfɪt/ verb [T] to lose sth or no longer have sth because you have done sth wrong or because you want to achieve an aim: *Because of his violent behaviour he forfeited the right to visit his children.*

forgave pt of FORGIVE

forge¹ /fɔːdʒ/ noun [C] a workshop where metals are heated and shaped, especially one where a person (**blacksmith**) works making and fitting shoes for horses

forge² /fɔːdʒ/ verb [T] 1 to make a copy of sth in order to deceive people: *to forge a signature* 2 to create a relationship with sb/sth: *Our school has forged links with a school in Romania.*

forgery /ˈfɔːdʒəri/ noun (pl **forgeries**) 1 [U] the crime of copying a document, signature, painting, etc in order to deceive people 2 [C] a document, signature, picture, etc that has been forged: *The painting that had been sold as a Rembrandt was discovered to be a forgery.*

forge³ /fɔːdʒ/ verb
(PHRASAL VERB) **forge ahead** to go forward very quickly; to move into the leading position: *The cleverest pupils should be allowed to forge ahead.*

☆ **forget** /fəˈɡet/ verb (pt **forgot** /fəˈɡɒt/; pp **forgotten** /fəˈɡɒtn/) 1 [I,T] **forget about sth** to fail to remember sth; to lose the memory of sth: *'Why didn't you come to the party?' 'Oh dear! I completely forgot about it!'* ○ *You never forget how to ride a bicycle.* ○ *I've forgotten what I was going to say.* ○ *I've forgotten the telephone number.* ○ *He forgot that he had invited her to the party.* ○ *I'll never forget meeting my husband for the first time.* 2 [I,T] to fail to remember to do sth: *Try not to forget about feeding the cat!* ○ *Don't forget to do your homework!* 3 [T] to fail to bring sth with you: *When my father got to the airport he realized he'd forgotten his passport.* ☛ When we are talking about *where* we have forgotten something we have to use the word **leave**. We CANNOT say: '*My father forgot his passport at home*'. We have to say: '*He left his passport at home*'. 4 [T] to stop thinking about sth: *Forget about your work and enjoy yourself!* ○ *'I'm sorry I shouted at you.' 'Forget it.'* (= don't worry about it) 5 [T] **forget yourself** to behave without proper control; to behave in a way that is not like the way you usually behave: *When he heard the news he completely forgot himself and kissed everybody in the room!*

forgetful /-fl/ adj often forgetting things: *My mother's nearly 80 and she's starting to get a bit forgetful.*

☆ **forgive** /fəˈɡɪv/ verb [T] (pt **forgave** /fəˈɡeɪv/; pp **forgiven** /fəˈɡɪvn/) 1 **forgive sb** (**sth/for sth/for doing sth**) to stop being angry towards sb or about sth: *I can't forgive his behaviour last night.* ○ *I can't forgive him for his behaviour last night.* ○ *I can't forgive him for his behaviour last night.* ○ *I can't forgive him for behaving like that last night.* 2 (used for apologizing politely): *Forgive me for asking, but where did you get that dress?*

forgivable /-əbl/ adj that can be forgiven ☛ The opposite is **unforgivable**.

forgiveness noun [U] the act of forgiving

forgiving adj ready and willing to forgive

forgo (also **forego**) /fɔːˈɡəʊ/ verb [T] (pt **forwent** /fɔːˈwent/; pp **forgone** /fɔːˈɡɒn; US -ˈɡɔːn/) to be willing not to have sth nice or sth that you have a right to: *We'll have to forgo a holiday this year if we want to buy a car.*

forgot pt of FORGET

forgotten pp of FORGET

☆ **fork** /fɔːk/ noun [C] 1 a small implement with a handle and two or more points (**prongs**). You use a fork for lifting food to your mouth when eating: *knives, forks and spoons* 2 a large tool with a handle and three or more points (**prongs**) that you use for digging the ground 3 a place where a road, river, etc divides into two parts; one of these parts: *After about two miles you'll come to a fork in the road. Take the right fork and keep going for another two miles.*

fork verb [I] 1 (used about a road, river, etc) to divide into two parts 2 to go along the left or right fork of a road: *Fork right up the hill.*
(PHRASAL VERB) **fork out** (*informal*) to pay: *I forked out over £20 for that book.*

forlorn /fəˈlɔːn/ adj lonely and unhappy; not cared for

☆ **form¹** /fɔːm/ noun 1 [C] a particular type of sth or way of doing sth: *Swimming is an excellent form of exercise.* ○ *We never eat meat in any form.* ○ *What form will the meeting take?* (= How will it be organized?) 2 [C,U] the shape of sb/sth: *The articles will be published in book form.* 3 [C] a piece of paper with questions on it and spaces where you give answers and personal information: *a booking form* ○ *an entry form for a competition* ○ *to fill in an application form* ☛ In American English we fill **out** a form. 4 [C] a class in a school: *the sixth form* 5 [C] (*grammar*) a way of spelling or changing a word in a sentence: *the irregular forms of the verbs* ○ *The plural form is 'mice'.* 6 [U] the strength or fitness of a sports player, team, etc: *to be in/out of form* ○ *to be on/off form* 7 [U] the record of how well sb/sth has done sth recently: *On present form the Italian team should win easily.*
(IDIOM) **true to form** ⇒ TRUE

☆ **form²** /fɔːm/ verb 1 [T] to make or organize sth: *They formed a group called 'Citizens for Nature'.* ○ *to form a government* ○ *In English we usually form the past tense by adding '-ed'.* 2 [T] to take the shape of sth: *A sofa bed is a sofa that you can pull out to form a bed.* 3 [T] to move into the shape or order mentioned: *The police formed a circle around the house.* 4 [T] to be the thing mentioned: *Seminars form the main part of the course* (= The main part of the course consists of seminars). 5 [I,T] to begin to exist or to make sth exist; to begin to have sth: *Buds form on trees in the early spring.* o *The rain had formed a huge puddle on the road.* o *We formed a very good impression of the school on our first visit.*

☆ **formal** /ˈfɔːml/ *adj* **1** (used about language or behaviour) used when you want to appear serious or official and when you are in a situation in which you do not know the other people very well: *'Yours faithfully' is a formal way of ending a letter.* o *She has a very formal manner–she doesn't seem to be able to relax.* o *a formal occasion* (= one where you must behave politely and wear the clothes that people think are suitable) ☛ In this dictionary some words and) phrases are marked *(formal)* or *(informal).* This will help you to choose the right word for a particular situation. Often there is an informal or neutral word with a similar meaning to a more formal one. **2** public and official: *I shall make a formal complaint to the hospital about the way I was treated.* **3** (only *before* a noun) obtained in a school or college: *You do not need any formal qualifications for this job but we would like you to have some experience.* —**formally** /-məli/ *adv*

formality /fɔːˈmæləti/ *noun (pl* **formalities)** **1** [C] an action that is necessary according to custom or law: *There are certain formalities to attend to before we can give you a visa.* ☛ If an action is *just a formality,* we mean that people think that it is necessary according to custom or law but that it has no real importance or effect otherwise. **2** [U] careful attention to rules of language and behaviour

format /ˈfɔːmæt/ *noun* [C] the shape of sth or the way it is arranged or produced: *It's the same book but in a different format.*

format *verb* [T] (format**t**ing; format**t**ed) to arrange sth in a particular format, usually for a computer: *to format a disk*

formation /fɔːˈmeɪʃn/ *noun* **1** [U] the making or developing of sth: *the formation of a new government* **2** [C,U] an arrangement or pattern (especially of soldiers, aeroplanes, ships, etc): *A number of planes flew over in formation.* **3** [C] a thing that is formed; the particular way in which it is formed: *rock formations* o *cloud formations*

formative /ˈfɔːmətɪv/ *adj* having an important and lasting influence (on sb's character and opinions): *A child's early years are thought to be the most formative ones.*

☆ **former¹** /ˈfɔːmə(r)/ *adj* (only *before* a noun) of an earlier time; previous: *Jimmy Carter, the former American President* o *Their new neighbour is a former teacher.* o *In former times people often had larger families.*

☆ **former²** /ˈfɔːmə(r)/ *adj, noun* the first (of two people or things just mentioned): *Of the two hospitals in the town–the General and the Royal–the former* (= the General) *has the better reputation.* ☛ The opposite is **the latter.**

☆ **formerly** /ˈfɔːməli/ *adv* in the past; previously: *the country of Myanmar (formerly Burma)* o *The hotel was formerly a castle.* ☛ **Used to** is a more common way of expressing the same meaning: *The hotel used to be a castle.*

formidable /ˈfɔːmɪdəbl/ *adj* **1** causing you to be rather frightened: *His mother is a rather formidable lady.* **2** difficult to deal with; needing a lot of effort: *Reforming the education system will be a formidable task.*

formula /ˈfɔːmjʊlə/ *noun* [C] (*pl* **formulas** or **formulae** /-mjuliː/) **1** a group of signs, letters or numbers used in science or mathematics to express a general law or fact: *The formula for carbon monoxide is CO.* o *What is the formula for converting miles to kilometres?* **2** a list of substances used for making sth; the instructions necessary for making sth: *The formula for the new vaccine has not yet been made public.* **3** a plan of how to get sth or how to do sth: *What is her formula for success?*

formulate /ˈfɔːmjʊleɪt/ *verb* [T] **1** to prepare and organize a plan or ideas for doing sth: *The Labour Party still has not formulated its policy on Northern Ireland.* **2** to express sth (clearly and exactly)

forsake /fəˈseɪk/ *verb* [T] (*pt* **forsook** /fəˈsʊk/; *pp* **forsaken** /fəˈseɪkən/) *(formal)* to leave a person or a place for ever (especially when you should stay)

fort /fɔːt/ *noun* [C] a strong building that is used for military defence

forth /fɔːθ/ *adv*
(IDIOMS) **and so forth** and other things like those just mentioned: *The sort of job that you'll be doing is taking messages, making tea and so forth.*

back and forth ⇒ BACK³

forthcoming /ˌfɔːθˈkʌmɪŋ/ *adj* **1** going to happen or appear in the near future: *Look in the local paper for a list of forthcoming events.* **2** (not before a noun) offered or given: *If no money is forthcoming we shall not be able to continue the project.* **3** (not before a noun) willing to be helpful, give information, etc: *Don't ask the lady in the post office – she's never very forthcoming.*

forthright /ˈfɔːθraɪt/ *adj* saying clearly and honestly what you think

forthwith /ˌfɔːθˈwɪθ; *US* -ˈwɪð/ *adv* (*formal*) immediately

fortieth ⇒ FORTY

fortify /ˈfɔːtɪfaɪ/ *verb* [T] (*pres part* **fortifying**; *3rd pers sing pres* **fortifies**; *pt, pp* **fortified**) to make a place stronger and ready for an attack: *to fortify a city*

fortification /ˌfɔːtɪfɪˈkeɪʃn/ *noun* [C, usually pl] walls, ditches, etc that are built to protect a place against attack

☆ **fortnight** /ˈfɔːtnaɪt/ *noun* [C, usually sing] (*Brit*) two weeks: *We're going on holiday for a fortnight.* o *a fortnight's holiday* o *School finishes in a fortnight/in a fortnight's time* (= two weeks from now).

fortnightly *adj, adv* (happening or appearing) once a fortnight: *This magazine is published fortnightly.*

fortress /ˈfɔːtrɪs/ *noun* [C] a castle or other large building that has been made strong so that it is not easy to attack

☆ **fortunate** /ˈfɔːtʃənət/ *adj* lucky: *You were fortunate to have such lovely weather for your holi-*

| p | b | t | d | k | g | tʃ | dʒ | f | v | θ | ð |
| pen | bad | tea | did | cat | got | chin | June | fall | van | thin | then |

day. ○ *It was fortunate that he was at home when you phoned.* ☛ The opposite is **unfortunate**.
fortunately *adv* by good luck; luckily: *Fortunately the traffic wasn't too bad so I managed to get to the meeting on time.* ○ *Jane arrived late but, fortunately for her, everybody was too busy to notice.*

☆**fortune** /'fɔːtʃuːn/ *noun* **1** [U] the power that affects what happens in a person's life; luck: *Fortune was not on our side that day* (= we were unlucky). **2** [C, usually pl] the things (both good and bad) that happen to a person, family, country, etc: *The country's fortunes depend on its industry being successful.* **3** [C] what is going to happen to a person in the future: *Show me your hand and I'll try to tell your fortune.* **4** [C] a very large amount of money: *I always spend a fortune on presents at Christmas.*
'fortune-teller *noun* [C] a person who tells people's fortunes(3)

☆**forty** /'fɔːti/ *number* 40, one more than thirty-nine ☛ For examples of how to use numbers in sentences, look at **sixty**.
fortieth /'fɔːtiəθ/ *pron, det, adv* 40th, next after thirty-ninth ☛ Look at the examples at **sixth**.

forum /'fɔːrəm/ *noun* [C] a place or meeting where people can exchange and discuss ideas

☆**forward¹** /'fɔːwəd/ *adv* **1** (*also* **forwards**) in the direction that is in front of you; towards the front, end or future: *Keep going forward and try not to look back.* ○ *We seem to be going backwards, not forwards.* **2** in the direction of progress; ahead: *The new form of treatment is a big step forward in the fight against AIDS.* ☛ Forward is used after many verbs, eg **bring, come, look, put**. For the meaning of the expressions look at the verb entries.
(IDIOMS) **backward(s) and forward(s)** ⇨ BACKWARD
put the clock/clocks forward/back ⇨ CLOCK¹
'forward-looking *adj* thinking about or planning for the future; having modern ideas

☆**forward²** /'fɔːwəd/ *adj* **1** (only *before* a noun) towards the front or future: *forward planning* **2** having developed earlier than is normal or expected; advanced: *Children who read before they are five are considered very forward.* ☛ The opposite is **backward**(2).

forward³ /'fɔːwəd/ *verb* [T] to send a letter, etc to a new address: *The post office is forwarding all our mail.*

☛ If you are writing to somebody who has moved house and you do not know their new address, write the old address and **please forward** on the envelope.

'forwarding address *noun* [C] a new address to which post should be sent
forward⁴ /'fɔːwəd/ *noun* [C] an attacking player in a sport such as football ☛ picture at **football**.
forwent *pt of* FORGO
fossil /'fɒsl/ *noun* [C] the remains, or a mark, of a prehistoric animal or plant that has been buried in rock for a very long time and that has become hard

foster /'fɒstə(r); *US* 'fɔː-/ *verb* [T] **1** to take a child who needs a home into your family and to care for him/her without becoming the legal parents: *to foster a homeless child*

☛ The people who do this are **foster-parents**. The child is a **foster-child**. Look at **adopt**.

2 to help or encourage the development of sth (especially feelings or ideas)
fought *pt, pp of* FIGHT
foul¹ /faʊl/ *adj* **1** disgusting and dirty (often with a bad smell or taste): *The air in the room was foul and she opened the windows wide.* **2** very bad or unpleasant: *It's been a foul weekend.* ○ *Careful what you say – he's got a foul temper* (= he becomes angry very easily). ○ *What's in this drink? It tastes foul.* **3** (used about weather) very bad; stormy: *The foul weather prevented our plane from taking off.* **4** (used about language) very rude; full of swearing
,foul 'play *noun* [U] **1** action that is against the rules of a sport **2** violent crime that leads to murder

foul² /faʊl/ *verb* [T] to make sth dirty (with rubbish, waste, etc): *Dogs must not foul the pavement.* (PHRASAL VERB) **foul sth up** to spoil sth: *The weather really fouled up our holiday.*

foul³ /faʊl/ *noun* [C] (*sport*) an action that is against the rules: *to commit a foul* ○ *He was sent off for a foul on the Juventus goalkeeper.*
foul *verb* [I,T] (*sport*) to be guilty of a foul (against another player): *Van Basten was fouled inside the area and the referee awarded a penalty.*

found¹ *pt, pp of* FIND
found² /faʊnd/ *verb* [T] **1** to start an organization, institution, etc especially by providing money: *Oxford has Britain's oldest public museum (founded 1683).* **2** to begin to build a town or establish a country: *Liberia was founded by freed American slaves.* **3** (usually passive) to base sth on sth: *The book was founded on real life.*

☆**foundation** /faʊn'deɪʃn/ *noun* **1** [U] the act of founding sth (a building, town, organization, etc) **2** [C] an organization that provides money for a special purpose, eg for research or to help people who have a particular problem: *The British Heart Foundation* (= researching the causes of heart disease) **3** [plural] **foundations** the parts of a building beneath the ground that form its base: *The builders have only just started to lay the foundations of the new school.* **4** [C,U] the idea, principle, or fact on which sth is based: *That rumour is completely without foundation* (= it is not true).
founder /'faʊndə(r)/ *noun* [C] a person who founds or establishes sth
founder-'member *noun* [C] one of the first members of a club, organization, etc
foundry /'faʊndri/ *noun* [C] (*pl* **foundries**) a place where metal or glass is melted and shaped into objects

☆**fountain** /'faʊntɪn; *US* -tn/ *noun* [C] an ornament (in a garden or in a square in a town) that shoots a stream of water into the air. The water that comes out is also called a fountain.
☛ picture on next page.

s	z	ʃ	ʒ	h	m	n	ŋ	l	r	j	w
so	zoo	she	vision	how	man	no	sing	leg	red	yes	wet

fountain

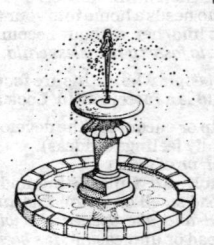

'fountain-pen *noun* [C] a type of pen that you fill with ink

☆ **four** /fɔː(r)/ *number* 4, one more than three ☛ For examples of how to use numbers in sentences, look at **six**.

(IDIOM) **on all fours** with your hands and knees on the ground; crawling: *The children went through the tunnel on all fours.*

four- (in compounds) having four of the thing mentioned: *four-legged animals*

fourth /fɔːθ/ *pron, det, adv* 4th, next after third ☛ For ¼ we use the word **quarter**: *a quarter of an hour* (= fifteen minutes). Look at the examples at **sixth**.

fourthly *adv* (used to introduce the fourth point in a list): *Fourthly (and this point is even more important than the other three), you must speak clearly.*

four-letter 'word *noun* [C] one of a type of word (often with four letters) that people think is very rude

four-wheel 'drive *adj* having an engine that turns all four wheels

☆ **fourteen** /ˌfɔːˈtiːn/ *number* 14, one more than thirteen ☛ For examples of how to use numbers in sentences, look at **six**.

fourteenth /ˌfɔːˈtiːnθ/ *pron, det, adv* 14th, next after thirteenth ☛ Look at the examples at **sixth**.

fowl /faʊl/ *noun* [C] (*pl* **fowl** or **fowls**) a bird, especially a hen that is kept on a farm

fox

☆ **fox** /fɒks/ *noun* [C] a wild animal with reddish fur that looks like a dog

☛ A fox is often described as **sly** or **cunning**. A female fox is a **vixen**, a young fox is a **cub**.

'fox-hunting *noun* [U] a sport in which a fox is hunted by people on horses with dogs (**foxhounds**)

foyer /ˈfɔɪeɪ; *US* ˈfɔɪər/ *noun* [C] an entrance hall in a cinema, theatre, hotel, etc where people can meet or wait

fraction /ˈfrækʃn/ *noun* [C] **1** a small part or amount: *For a fraction of a second I thought the car was going to crash.* **2** an exact part of a number: ½ *and* ¼ *are fractions.*

fractionally /-ʃənəlɪ/ *adv* to a very small degree; slightly: *Prost was fractionally faster than his nearest rival.*

fracture /ˈfræktʃə(r)/ *noun* [C] a break in sth hard, especially in a bone: *a fracture of the arm*

fracture *verb* [T] to break sth (especially a bone): *She fell and fractured her ankle.* ○ *a fractured ankle*

fragile /ˈfrædʒaɪl; *US* -dʒl/ *adj* easily damaged or broken: *This bowl is very fragile. Please handle it carefully.*

fragment /ˈfrægmənt/ *noun* [C] a small piece (that has broken off sth bigger): *The builders found fragments of Roman pottery on the site.* ○ (*figurative*) *I heard only a fragment of their conversation.*

fragment /frægˈment/ *verb* [I,T] (*formal*) to be broken into small pieces; to break sth into small pieces: *The country is becoming increasingly fragmented by civil war.*

fragrance /ˈfreɪɡrəns/ *noun* [C,U] a pleasant smell

fragrant *adj* having a pleasant smell

frail /freɪl/ *adj* not strong or healthy: *My aunt is still very frail after her accident.*

frailty /ˈfreɪltɪ/ *noun* [C,U] (*pl* **frailties**) moral or physical weakness

☆ **frame¹** /freɪm/ *noun* [C] **1** a border of wood or metal that goes around the outside of a door, picture, window, etc: *a window frame* **2** [usually pl] a structure made of plastic or metal that holds the lenses of a pair of glasses ☛ picture at **glasses**. **3** the basic structure of a piece of furniture, building, vehicle, etc onto which other pieces are added: *the frame of a bicycle* **4** [usually sing] the shape of a human or animal body: *He has a large frame but he is not fat.*

(IDIOM) **frame of mind** a particular state or condition of your feelings; mood: *I'm not in the right frame of mind for a party. I'd prefer to be on my own.*

frame² /freɪm/ *verb* [T] **1** to put a border around sth (especially a picture or photograph): *Let's have this photograph framed.* **2** (*formal*) to express sth in words, in a particular way: *The question was very carefully framed.* **3** (usually passive) to give false evidence against sb in order to make him/her seem guilty of a crime: *The man claimed that he had been framed by the police.*

☆ **framework** /ˈfreɪmwɜːk/ *noun* [C] **1** the basic structure of sth that gives it shape and strength: *A greenhouse is made of glass panels fixed in a metal framework.* **2** a system of rules or ideas which help you decide what to do: *The plan may be changed but it will provide a framework on which we can build.*

franc /fræŋk/ *noun* [C] the unit of money that is used in France, Belgium, Switzerland and several other countries

franchise /ˈfræntʃaɪz/ *noun* **1** [U] (*formal*) the right to vote in elections **2** [C] official permission to sell a company's goods or services

iː	ɪ	e	æ	ɑː	ɒ	ɔː	ʊ	uː	ʌ
see	sit	ten	hat	arm	got	saw	put	too	cup

in a particular area: *a franchise for a fast-food restaurant*

frank /fræŋk/ *adj* showing your thoughts and feelings openly; saying what you mean; honest: *To be perfectly frank with you, I don't think you'll pass your driving test.*
frankly *adv* **1** in a frank manner: *Please tell me frankly what you think about my idea.* **2** speaking openly and honestly: *Quite frankly, I'm not surprised at what has happened.* —**frankness** *noun* [U]: *She spoke with great frankness about her past life.*

frankfurter /'fræŋkfɜːtə(r)/ (*US* **wiener**) *noun* [C] a type of small smoked sausage

frantic /'fræntɪk/ *adj* **1** in a very emotional state because you are extremely worried or frightened: *The mother went frantic when she couldn't find her child.* ○ *frantic cries for help* **2** very busy or rushed; without organization: *a frantic search for the keys* —**frantically** /-kli/ *adv*: *They have been working frantically all week trying to get things ready in time.*

fraternal /frə'tɜːnl/ *adj* (*formal*) of or like brothers; friendly

fraternity /frə'tɜːnəti/ *noun* (*pl* **fraternities**) **1** [U] the feeling of friendship between people (like that between brothers) **2** [C] a group of people who share the same work or interests: *the medical fraternity*

fraud /frɔːd/ *noun* **1** [C,U] (an act of) deceiving or tricking sb in order to get money, etc in a way that is against the law: *The accountant was sent to prison for fraud.* ○ *Millions of pounds are lost every year in credit card frauds.* **2** [C] a person who deceives or tricks sb by pretending to be sb else
fraudulent /'frɔːdjulənt; *US* -dʒʊ-/ *adj* (*formal*) done in order to deceive sb; dishonest: *the fraudulent use of stolen cheques*

fraught /frɔːt/ *adj* **1** (not before a noun) filled with sth (unpleasant): *The situation was fraught with danger.* **2** (*informal*) (used about people) worried and nervous; (used about a situation) very busy so that people become nervous: *You look fraught – what's the matter?* ○ *Things are usually fraught at work on Monday mornings.*

fray /freɪ/ *verb* [I,T] (used about cloth, etc) to become worn so that some threads are loose; to cause cloth to do this: *This shirt is beginning to fray at the cuffs.* ○ *a frayed cuff* ○ (*figurative*): *Nerves began to fray towards the end of the match* (= the players started to get nervous).

freak /friːk/ *noun* [C] **1** a very strange or unusual event: *By some strange freak of nature we had snow in May.* ○ *a freak accident, storm, etc* **2** (*informal*) a person who has a very strong interest in sth: *a health freak* **3** a person or animal that is physically abnormal in some way; a person who behaves in a strange way: *Disabled people should never be treated as freaks.*

freckle /'frekl/ *noun* [C, usually pl] a small brown spot on a person's skin: *A lot of people with red hair have got freckles.* —**freckled** *adj*: *a freckled face*

☆ **free**[1] /friː/ *adj* **1** not in prison or in a cage, etc: *After twenty years in prison he was finally set free in 1989.* **2** **free (to do sth)** not controlled by the government, rules, etc: *There is free movement of people across the border.* ○ *a free press* ○ *You're free this afternoon to do exactly what you want.* **3** **free from/of sth** not having sth dangerous, unpleasant, etc: *How wonderful to go away for a month, free from all worries and responsibilities.* ○ *free from pain* **4** costing nothing: *Admission to the museum is free/free of charge.* ○ *a free sample* **5** not being used: *Do you have a single room free for Saturday night?* **6** without appointments; not busy: *I'm afraid Mr Spencer is not free this afternoon.* ○ *I don't get much free time.*
(IDIOMS) **free and easy** informal or relaxed: *The atmosphere in our office is very free and easy.*
get, have, etc a free hand to get, have, etc permission to make your own decisions about sth
of your own free will because you want to, not because sb forces you
free *adv* **1** in a free manner: *There is nowhere around here where dogs can run free.* **2** without cost or payment: *Children under five usually travel free on trains.*
free 'agent *noun* [C] a person who can do what he/she likes because he/she is not responsible to another person
free 'enterprise *noun* [U] the operation of trade and business without government control
'freehand *adj*, *adv* (done) by hand, without the help of an instrument, eg a ruler: *a freehand sketch*
free 'kick *noun* [C] (in football) a kick by a player of one team after a member of the other team has broken a rule
free-'range *adj* produced by hens that are allowed to move around freely: *free-range eggs*
free-'speech *noun* [U] the right to express any opinion in public

☆ **free**[2] /friː/ *verb* [T] **1** **free sb/sth (from sth)** to let sb/sth go; to set sb/sth free: *to free a prisoner* ○ *The protesters freed the animals from their cages.* **2** **free sb/sth of/from sth** to take away from sb sth that is unpleasant: *The medicine freed her from pain for a few hours.* **3** **free sb/sth (from sth)** to move sb/sth that is stuck or caught: *The emergency services took three hours to free the man from the wreckage of his car.* **4** **free sb/sth for sth** to make sth available so that it can be used; to put sb in a position in which he/she can do sth: *Cuts in defence spending would free money to spend on education.*

☆ **freedom** /'friːdəm/ *noun* **1** [U] the state of being free, ie of not being in prison or under the control of sb else: *The opposition leader was given his freedom after 25 years.* **2** [C,U] the right to do or say what you want: *You have the freedom to come and go as you please.* ○ *freedom of speech* ○ *the rights and freedoms of the individual* ☞ Look at **liberty**. **3 freedom from sth** the state of not having sth unpleasant: *freedom from fear, hunger, pain, etc*

Freefone /'friːfəʊn/ *noun* [U] (*Brit*) the system by which the person making a telephone call

ɜː	ə	eɪ	əʊ	aɪ	aʊ	ɔɪ	ɪə	eə	ʊə
fur	ago	pay	home	five	now	join	near	hair	pure

does not have to pay for the cost of the call ☞ Look at **Freepost**.

freelance /ˈfriːlɑːns; *US* -læns/ (*also* **freelancer**) *noun* [C] a person who works for several different employers and who is paid separately for each piece of work that he/she does —**freelance** *adj, adv: a freelance journalist* ○ *She works freelance.*

freely /ˈfriːli/ *adv* **1** in a way that is not controlled or limited: *He is the country's first freely elected president for 40 years.* ○ *There are no roadworks on the motorway and traffic is flowing freely.* ☞ Note that if you travel **free** it means that you do not have to pay anything. If you can travel **freely** it means that you can go wherever you like. **2** willingly, without hesitating: *I freely admit that I made a mistake.*

Freemason /ˈfriːmeɪsn/ (*also* **mason**) *noun* [C] a man who belongs to an international secret society whose members help each other and who recognize each other by secret signs

Freepost /ˈfriːpəʊst/ *noun* [U] (*Brit*) the system by which the person who sends a letter, etc does not pay for the cost of postage ☞ Look at **Freefone**.

freeway /ˈfriːweɪ/ *noun* [C] (*US*) = MOTORWAY

☆ **freeze** /friːz/ *verb* (*pt* **froze** /frəʊz/; *pp* **frozen** /ˈfrəʊzn/) **1** [I,T] to become hard (and often change into ice) because of extreme cold; to make sth do this: *Water freezes at 0° Celsius.* ○ *Leave the heating on when you're away or the pipes will freeze.* ○ *The ground was frozen solid for most of the winter.* ○ *I've picked ten pounds of raspberries and I'm going to freeze them.* ○ *Raspberries freeze well.* ○ *frozen peas* **2** [I] (used with 'it') to describe extremely cold weather, when water turns into ice: *I think it's going to freeze tonight.* **3** [I,T] (to cause a person) to be very cold or to die from cold: *The two men froze to death on the mountain.* ○ *Turn the heater up a bit – I'm frozen.* **4** [I] to stop suddenly or become still because you are frightened or shocked: *The terrible scream made her freeze with terror.* **5** [T] to keep wages, prices, fares, etc at a fixed level for a certain period of time: *Spending on defence has been frozen for one year.*

freeze *noun* [C] **1** a period of weather when the temperature stays below 0°C (freezing-point) **2** the fixing of wages, prices, fares, etc at a certain level for a certain period of time

freezing *adj* (*informal*) very cold (not necessarily below 0° Celsius): *Can we turn the central heating on? I'm freezing.* ○ *It's absolutely freezing outside.*

ˈfreezing-point (*also* **freezing**) *noun* [C,U] the temperature at which water, etc freezes: *Last night the temperature fell to six degrees below freezing.*

freezer /ˈfriːzə(r)/ (*also* ˌdeep-ˈfreeze) *noun* [C] a large box or cupboard in which you can store food for a long time at a temperature below 0°C (freezing-point) so that it stays frozen ☞ Look at **fridge**.

freight /freɪt/ *noun* [U] **1** the method of carrying goods from one place to another: *Your order will be sent by air freight.* **2** = GOODS(2): *a freight train*

freighter *noun* [C] a ship or aeroplane that carries only freight

ˈfreight car (*US*) = WAGON

French fry /ˌfrentʃ ˈfraɪ/ *noun* [C] (*pl* **French fries**) (*especially US*) = CHIP¹(3)

French window /ˌfrentʃ ˈwɪndəʊ/ (*US* ˌFrench ˈdoor) *noun* [C] one of a pair of glass doors that open onto a garden or balcony

frenzy /ˈfrenzi/ *noun* [sing,U] a state of great excitement; a period when a person cannot control his/her actions: *The speaker worked the crowd up into a frenzy.*

frenzied /ˈfrenzid/ *adj* wild and excited: *a frenzied attack*

frequency /ˈfriːkwənsi/ *noun* (*pl* **frequencies**) **1** [U] the rate at which sth happens (= the number of times sth happens in a particular period): *Fatal accidents have decreased in frequency in recent years* (= there are fewer of them). **2** [U] the fact that sth happens often: *The frequency of child deaths from cancer near the nuclear power station is being investigated.* **3** [C,U] the rate at which a sound wave or radio wave vibrates: *high-frequency/low-frequency sounds* ○ *Which frequency does the radio station broadcast on?*

☆ **frequent¹** /ˈfriːkwənt/ *adj* happening often: *There is a frequent bus service from the city centre to the airport.* ☞ The opposite is **infrequent**. —**frequently** *adv: Buses run frequently from the city centre to the airport.*

frequent² /frɪˈkwent/ *verb* [T] (*formal*) to go to a place often: *He spent most of his evenings in Paris frequenting bars and nightclubs.*

☆ **fresh** /freʃ/ *adj* **1** new or different: *They have decided to make a fresh start in a different town.* ○ *I'm sure he'll have some fresh ideas on the subject.* ○ *I'd like to put on some fresh clothes before we go out.* **2** not old (so there has been no time for any change): *There was fresh blood all over the walls.* ○ *Write a few notes while the lecture is still fresh in your mind.* **3** (used about food, flowers, etc) made or picked not too long ago: *fresh bread* ☞ The opposite for food is **stale**. **4** (used about food) not frozen or from a tin: *fresh fruit and vegetables* **5** (used about water) not salt; not sea water ☞ A fish that lives in such water is a **freshwater** fish. **6** (used about the air) clean and cool: *Open the window and let some fresh air in.* **7** (used about the weather) quite cold and windy **8** (used about colours, or a person's skin) bright or clear **9** not tired: *I'll think about the problem again in the morning when I'm fresh.* **10 fresh from/out of sth** having just finished sth: *Life isn't easy for a young teacher fresh from university.*

(IDIOM) **break fresh/new ground** ⇨ GROUND¹

freshly *adv* newly; recently: *freshly baked bread* —**freshness** *noun* [U]

freshen /ˈfreʃn/ *verb* **1** [T] **freshen sth (up)** to make sth cleaner or brighter: *Some new curtains and wallpaper would freshen up this room.* **2** [I] (used about the wind) to become stronger

(PHRASAL VERB) **freshen (yourself) up** to wash and make yourself clean and tidy

fresher /ˈfreʃə(r)/ *noun* [C] (*Brit informal*) a

p	b	t	d	k	g	tʃ	dʒ	f	v	θ	ð
pen	bad	tea	did	cat	got	chin	June	fall	van	thin	then

student who is in his/her first year at university, college, etc

freshman /ˈfreʃmən/ noun [C] (pl **freshmen** /-mən/) (US) a student who is in his/her first year at college, high school, university, etc

fret /fret/ verb [I] (**fret**ting; **fret**ted) **fret (about/at/over sth)** to be unhappy or worried about sth: *Don't fret. Everything will be all right.*

friction /ˈfrɪkʃn/ noun [U] **1** the rubbing of one surface or thing against another **2** disagreement between people or groups: *There is a lot of friction between the older and the younger members of staff.*

☆ **Friday** /ˈfraɪdɪ/ noun [C,U] (abbr **Fri**) the day of the week after Thursday and before Saturday ☞ For examples of the use of the days of the week in sentences, look at **Monday**.

☆ **fridge** /frɪdʒ/ noun (also formal **refrigerator**) (US **icebox**) noun [C] a metal container in which food, etc is kept cold (but not frozen) so that it stays fresh ☞ Look at **freezer**.

☆ **friend** /frend/ noun [C] **1** a person that you know and like (not a member of your family): *Trevor and I are old friends. We were at school together.* o *We're only inviting close friends and relatives to the funeral.* o *Do you know Helen Wilson? She's my best friend.* o *A friend of mine told me about this restaurant.* o *One of my friends told me about this restaurant.* ☞ Look at **boyfriend**, **girlfriend** and **penfriend**. **2 a friend of/to sth** a helper or supporter of sth: *the Friends of the Churchill Hospital*
(IDIOM) **be/make friends (with sb)** to be/become a friend (of sb): *Tony is rather shy and finds it hard to make friends.*

friendless adj without friends

☆ **friendly** /ˈfrendlɪ/ adj (**friendlier**; **friendliest**) **1** behaving in a kind and pleasant way; showing kindness and pleasantness: *Everyone here has been very friendly towards us.* o *a friendly smile* o *a small friendly hotel near the beach* **2 friendly with sb** being the friend of sb: *Nick's become quite friendly with the boy next door.* —**friendliness** noun [U]

friendly noun [C] a sports match that is not part of a serious competition

-friendly (in compounds) supporting or helping sb/sth: *Our computer is extremely user-friendly.*

☆ **friendship** /ˈfrendʃɪp/ noun **1** [U] the state of being friends: *Our relationship is based on friendship, not love.* **2** [C] a relationship between people who are friends: *The friendships that you make at school often last for life.*

fright /fraɪt/ noun [C,U] a sudden feeling of fear: *That loud bang gave me quite a fright.* o *The child cried out in fright.*

☆ **frighten** /ˈfraɪtn/ verb [T] to fill sb with fear: *Sorry, I didn't mean to frighten you.*
(PHRASAL VERB) **frighten sb/sth away/off** to cause a person or animal to go away by frightening him/her/it: *Walk quietly so that you don't frighten the birds away.*

frightened adj **1** full of fear or worry: *Frightened children were calling for their mothers.* o *He was frightened at the thought of being alone.* o *I was frightened that they would think that I was rude.* **2 frightened of sb/sth** fearing a particular person, thing or situation: *When I was young I was frightened of cats.* ☞ Look at the note at **afraid**.

frightening /ˈfraɪtnɪŋ/ adj causing fear: *It was a very frightening situation to be in.* o *It's frightening how quickly time passes.* o *It's frightening that time passes so quickly.*

frightful /ˈfraɪtfl/ adj **1** very bad or unpleasant: *The weather this summer has been frightful.* o *I felt frightful so I went home early.* **2** (informal) (used for emphasizing sth) very bad or great: *We're in a frightful rush.*

frightfully /-fəlɪ/ adv (informal) very: *I'm frightfully sorry.*

frigid /ˈfrɪdʒɪd/ adj (usually used about a woman) disliking sexual activity

frill /frɪl/ noun [C] **1** a special edge for a dress, shirt, etc which is made by forming many folds in a narrow piece of cloth **2** [usually pl] (figurative) something that is not necessary but is decorative or pleasant: *We just want a plain simple meal – no frills.*

frilly /ˈfrɪlɪ/ (**frillier**; **frilliest**) adj having many frills: *a frilly dress*

fringe /frɪndʒ/ noun [C] **1** (US **bangs** [plural]) the part of your hair that hangs, usually in a straight line, over your forehead: *Your hair looks better with a fringe.* ☞ picture at **hair**. **2** a decorative edge on a rug, etc or on clothes, that is made of loose or hanging threads **3** a place, part or position that is a long way from the centre or from what is usual: *the outer fringes of London* o *Some people on the fringes of the party are opposed to the policy on Europe.*

fringe verb
(IDIOM) **be fringed by/with sth** to have sth as a border: *The lake was fringed with pine trees.*

ˈfringe benefit noun [C] an extra benefit that is given to an employee in addition to his/her salary: *The fringe benefits of this job include a car and free health insurance.*

frisk /frɪsk/ verb **1** [T] to pass your hands over sb's body in order to search for hidden weapons, drugs, etc **2** [I] (used about an animal or child) to play and jump about in a lively and happy way

frisky adj (**friskier**; **friskiest**) lively and playful

fritter /ˈfrɪtə(r)/ verb
(PHRASAL VERB) **fritter sth away (on sth)** to waste time or money on things that are not important

frivolity /frɪˈvɒlətɪ/ noun [U] silly behaviour; not acting seriously

frivolous /ˈfrɪvələs/ adj not serious; silly: *This is a serious issue. Please don't make frivolous remarks.*

frizzy /ˈfrɪzɪ/ adj (used about hair) with a lot of very small curls

fro /frəʊ/ adv
(IDIOM) **to and fro** ⇨ TO³

frock /frɒk/ noun [C] (old-fashioned) a dress

frog /frɒg; US frɔːg/ noun [C] a small animal with smooth skin and long legs that are used for jumping. Frogs live in or near water: *the croaking of frogs* ☞ picture on next page.

s	z	ʃ	ʒ	h	m	n	ŋ	l	r	j	w
so	zoo	she	vision	how	man	no	sing	leg	red	yes	wet

frog   toad

¹frogman /-mən/ noun [C] (pl **frogmen** /-mən/) a swimmer who works underwater wearing special rubber clothes and using breathing equipment: *Police frogmen searched the river.*

☆ **from** /frəm; strong form frɒm/ prep **1** (showing the place where sb/sth starts or started): *Has the bus from London arrived?* ○ *She comes home from work at 7 o'clock.* ○ *Water was dripping from the tap.* ○ *A child fell from the seventh floor of a block of flats.* **2** (showing the time when sth starts or started): *Peter's on holiday from next Friday.* ○ *The supermarket is open from 8am till 8pm every day.* ○ *We lived in Wales from 1979 to 1986.* **3** (showing the person who sent, gave, said, etc sth): *Have you had a Christmas card from Roy?* ○ *I borrowed this jacket from my sister.* ○ *a phone call from my father* **4** (showing the origin of sb/sth): *'Where do you come from?' 'I'm from Australia.'* ○ *quotations from Shakespeare* ○ *There's a man from the bank to see you.* **5** (showing the material with which sth is made): *Paper is made from wood.* **6** (showing the distance between two places): *The house is five miles from Oxford.* **7** (showing the lower limit in a range of prices, figures, etc): *Our prices start from £2.50 a bottle.* ○ *Tickets cost from £3 to £11.* **8** (showing the state of sb/sth before a change): *The bus fare has gone up from 35p to 40p.* ○ *The article was translated from Russian into English.* ○ *Things have gone from bad to worse.* **9** (showing that sb/sth is taken away): *Children don't like being separated from their parents for a long period.* ○ *She borrowed the book from the library.* ○ *8 from 12 leaves 4.* **10** (showing sth that you want to avoid): *There was no shelter from the wind.* ○ *This game will stop you from getting bored.* **11** (showing the reason for sth): *People in the camps are suffering from hunger and cold.* **12** (showing the difference between two people, places or things): *Can you tell margarine from butter?* ○ *Is Portuguese very different from Spanish?* **13** (showing your position or point of view): *There is a wonderful view from the top of the tower.* ○ *From your point of view it would be better to fly to Birmingham rather than to London.* ○ *He always looks at things from his own point of view.*

(IDIOM) **from... on** starting at a particular time and continuing for ever: *She never spoke to him again from that day on.* ○ *From now on you must earn your own living.*

☆ **front** /frʌnt/ noun **1** [C, usually sing] the side or surface of sth that is most usually seen or that is most important: *a dress with buttons down the front* ○ *the front of a building* (= the front wall) ○ *a card with flowers on the front* **2** [C, usually sing] the most forward part of sth or the area that is just outside of or before sb/ sth: *Young children should not travel in the front of the car.* ○ *There is a small garden at the front of the house.* ☛ **On the front of** means 'on the front surface of sth': *The number is shown on the front of the bus.* **In front of** means 'further forward than another person or thing': *A car has stopped in front of the bus.* **At/In the front of** means 'in the most forward part inside sth': *The driver sits at the front of the bus.* Look at these sentences too: *The teacher usually stands in front of the class.* ○ *The noisy children were asked to sit at the front of the class* (= in the front seats). **3 the front** [sing] the line or area where fighting takes place in a war: *to be sent to the front* **4** [sing] a way of behaving that hides your true feelings: *His brave words were just a front. He was really feeling very nervous.* **5** [C] (*technical*) (used when talking about the weather) a line or area where warm air and cold air meet: *A cold front is moving in from the north.* **6** [C] a particular area of activity: *Things are difficult on the domestic front at the moment.*

(IDIOMS) **back to front** ⇨ BACK¹

in front ahead of or further forward than sb/ sth: *Some of the children ran on in front.* ○ *After three laps the Kenyan runner was in front.*

opposite   in front of

in front of 1 in a position further forward than but close to sb/sth: *The bus stops right in front of our house.* ○ *Don't stand in front of the television.* ○ *The book was open in front of her on the desk.* ☛ **In front of** does not mean the same as **opposite**. **2** in the presence of: *I couldn't talk about that in front of my parents.*

up front (*informal*) as payment before sth is

done: *I want half the money up front and half when the job is finished.*
front *adj* (only *before* a noun) of or at the front(1,2): *the front door, garden, room, etc* o *front teeth*
,front-'page *adj* interesting or important enough to appear on the front page of a newspaper: *front-page news*

frontal /'frʌntl/ *adj* (only *before* a noun) from the front: *a frontal attack*

☆ **frontier** /'frʌntɪə(r); *US* frʌn'tɪər/ *noun* **1** [C] **frontier (between A and B); frontier (with A)** the line where one country joins another; border: *We crossed the frontier between France and Italy.* o *France's frontier with Italy* ☛ Look at the note at **border**. **2 the frontiers** [plural] the border between what we know and what we do not know: *Scientific research is constantly pushing back the frontiers of our knowledge about the world.*

☆ **frost** /frɒst; *US* frɔːst/ *noun* **1** [C,U] the weather conditions when the temperature falls below freezing-point: *There was a hard frost last night.* o *ten degrees of frost* (= minus ten degrees Celsius) **2** [U] a very thin layer of little pieces of ice that is formed on surfaces when the temperature is below freezing-point: *The branches of the trees were white with frost.*
frost *verb* [T] (*especially US*) to decorate the top of a cake with a mixture containing sugar; to ice
(PHRASAL VERB) **frost over/up** to become covered with frost(2): *The window has frosted over/up.*

frosted *adj* (used about glass or a window) with a special surface so you cannot see through it

'frostbite *noun* [U] injury to the fingers, toes, etc that is caused by very low temperatures

frosting /'frɒstɪŋ; *US* 'frɔːstɪŋ/ *noun* [U] (*especially US*) = ICING

frosty /'frɒsti; *US* 'frɔːsti/ *adj* (**frostier; frostiest**) **1** very cold, with frost: *a cold and frosty morning* **2** cold and unfriendly: *a frosty welcome*

froth /frɒθ; *US* frɔːθ/ *noun* [U] a mass of small white bubbles on the top of a liquid, etc
froth *verb* [I] to have or produce froth: *The mad dog was frothing at the mouth.* —**frothy** *adj* (**frothier; frothiest**): *frothy beer*

frown /fraʊn/ *verb* [I] to bring your eyebrows together so that you make lines appear on your forehead. You frown when you are angry or worried: *'You're late', he said, frowning.*
(PHRASAL VERB) **frown on/upon sth** to think that sth is not good; to disapprove: *Smoking is very much frowned upon these days.*
frown *noun* [C] an act of frowning: *She read the letter quickly, a worried frown on her face.*

froze *pt* of FREEZE

frozen /'frəʊzn/ *pp* of FREEZE: *The pond is frozen. Let's go skating.* o *frozen vegetables* o *I'm frozen* (= very cold).

☆ **fruit** /fruːt/ *noun* **1** [C,U] the part of a plant or tree that contains seeds and that is used as food: *Try and eat more fresh fruit and vegetables.* o *Marmalade is made with citrus fruit* (= oranges, lemons, grapefruit, etc). o *Is a tomato a fruit or a vegetable?* o *fruit juice* ☛ When we say 'a fruit' we mean 'a type of fruit': *Most big supermarkets sell all sorts of tropical fruits.* When we are talking about one individual piece, eg a single apple, pear, banana, etc we must say 'a piece of fruit': *What would you like now? Cheese, or a piece of fruit?* It is more usual to use the uncountable form: *Would you like some fruit?* **2** [C] the part of a plant in which the seed is formed **3 the fruits** [plural] a good result or a reward for what you have done

fruitful /'fruːtfl/ *adj* producing good results; useful: *fruitful discussions*

fruition /fruː'ɪʃn/ *noun* [U] the time when a plan, etc starts to be successful: *After months of hard work, our efforts were coming to fruition.*

fruitless /'fruːtləs/ *adj* producing poor or no results; unsuccessful: *a fruitless search*

frustrate /frʌ'streɪt; *US* 'frʌstreɪt/ *verb* [T] **1** to prevent sb from doing sth or sth from happening: *The rescue work has been frustrated by bad weather conditions.* **2** to cause a person to feel angry or dissatisfied because things are not happening as he/she wants: *It's the lack of money that really frustrates him.*

frustrated *adj* angry or dissatisfied, eg because you cannot have or do what you want: *In the film she plays a bored, frustrated, middle-aged housewife.* o *He felt very frustrated at his lack of progress in learning Chinese.*

frustrating *adj* making you angry or dissatisfied: *I spent a frustrating morning at the Passport Office.*

frustration /frʌ'streɪʃn/ *noun* [C,U] a feeling of anger and dissatisfaction, or sth that causes it: *He felt anger and frustration at not being able to help the starving children.* o *Every job has its frustrations.*

☆ **fry** /fraɪ/ *verb* [I,T] (*pres part* **frying**; *3rd pers sing pres* **fries**; *pt, pp* **fried** /fraɪd/) to be cooked in hot fat or oil; to cook sth in this way: *to fry an egg* o *a fried egg* o *There was a smell of frying bacon in the kitchen.* ☛ Look at the note at **cook**.

'frying-pan (*US* **'fry-pan**) *noun* [C] a flat shallow pan with a long handle that is used for frying food ☛ picture at **pan**.

☆ **fuel** /'fjuːəl/ *noun* **1** [U] material that is burned to produce heat or power: *unleaded fuel* (= petrol without lead in it) o *What's the car's fuel consumption?* o *Our fuel bills are very high.* **2** [C] a type of fuel: *I think gas is the best fuel for central heating.*
fuel *verb* [T] (**fuelling; fuelled** ((*US* fueling; fueled) to provide fuel for sth: (*figurative*) *Her interest in the Spanish language was fuelled by a visit to Spain.*

fugitive /'fjuːdʒətɪv/ *noun* [C] a person who is running away from sth (eg from the police) ☛ Look at **refugee**.

fulfil (*US* **fulfill**) /fʊl'fɪl/ *verb* [T] (**fulfilling; fulfilled**) **1** to perform or carry out a duty, task, etc: *Germany now fulfils a most important role within the European Community.* **2** to make sth that you wish for, or have promised, happen: *He finally fulfilled his childhood dream of* *becoming a farmer.* ○ *to fulfil an ambition* ○ *The Government has not yet fulfilled its promises on education.* **3** to satisfy a need: *The local town can fulfil most of your shopping needs.* **4** to do or have what is necessary according to a contract, a rule, etc: *The conditions of entry to university in this country are quite difficult to fulfil.* **5 fulfil yourself** to develop your character and abilities fully: *She knew that she couldn't fulfil herself without first leaving home.*

fulfilled *adj* completely satisfied and happy

fulfilling *adj* making you feel happy and satisfied: *I found working abroad a very fulfilling experience.*

fulfilment (*US* **fulfillment**) *noun* [U] **1** the act of fulfilling or state of being fulfilled: *Moving into our own home was the fulfilment of a dream.* **2** the feeling of satisfaction that you have when you have done sth: *Some women find fulfilment in the home and in bringing up their children.*

☆ **full** /fʊl/ *adj* **1 full (of sb/sth)** holding or containing as much or as many as possible: *The bin needs emptying. It's full up.* ○ *a full bottle* ○ *I can't get anything else in my suitcase – it's full.* ○ *The bus was full so we had to wait for the next one.* ○ *'Is there any coffee left?' 'Yes, this jar's still half full.'* ○ (*figurative*) *The children are full of energy.* ○ (*figurative*) *We need a good night's sleep because we've got a full* (= busy) *day tomorrow.* **2** with a lot of people or things in it: *The room was full of people.* ○ *His work was full of mistakes.* ○ *The streets were full of litter.* **3 full (up)** having had enough to eat and drink: *No more, thank you. I'm full (up).* **4** (only before a noun) complete; not leaving anything out: *I should like a full report on the accident, please.* ○ *Full details of today's TV programmes are on page 20.* ○ *For the full story, please turn to page 14.* ○ *He took full responsibility for what had happened.* ○ *Please give your full address.* **5** (only before a noun) the highest or greatest possible: *She got full marks in her French exam.* ○ *The train was travelling at full speed when it hit the cow on the tracks.* **6 full of sb/sth/yourself** thinking or talking a lot about a subject or about yourself: *When she got back from holiday she was full of everything they had seen.* ○ *He's very full of himself* (= thinks that he is very important) *since he got that new job.* **7** round in shape: *a full figure* ○ *He's quite full in the face.* **8** (used about clothes) made with plenty of material: *a full skirt*

(IDIOMS) **have your hands full** ⇨ HAND¹

in full with nothing missing; completely: *Your money will be refunded in full* (= you will get all your money back). ○ *Please write your name in full.*

in full swing at the stage when there is a lot of activity: *When we arrived the party was already in full swing.*

in full view (of sb/sth) in a place where you can easily be seen: *In full view of the guards, he tried to escape over the prison wall.* ○ *in full view of the house*

to the full as much as possible: *to enjoy life to the full*

full *adv* directly; straight: *John hit him full in the face.*

,**full-'blown** *adj* fully developed: *to have full-blown AIDS*

,**full 'board** *noun* [U] (in a hotel, etc) with all your meals ☛ Look at **half board** and **bed and breakfast**.

,**full-'length** *adj* **1** (used about a picture, mirror, etc) showing a person from head to foot **2** (used about a dress, skirt, etc) reaching the ankles: *a full-length ball gown* **3** not shorter than normal: *a full-length film, book, etc*

,**full 'moon** *noun* [sing] the moon when it appears as a circle ☛ The opposite is a **new moon**.

,**full-'scale** *adj* **1** (used about a plan, drawing, etc) of the same size as the original object **2** using every means that is available: *The police have started a full-scale murder investigation.*

,**full 'stop** (*also* ,**full 'point**; *especially US* **period**) *noun* [C] a mark (.) that is used when you are writing to show the end of a sentence, etc

,**full-'time** *adj, adv* for a whole of the normal period of work: *He has a full-time job.* ○ *He works full-time.* ○ *We employ 800 full-time and 500 part-time staff.* ☛ Look at **part-time**.

☆ **fully** /'fʊli/ *adv* completely; to the highest possible degree: *John's never been fully accepted by the other members of staff.* ○ *I'm fully aware of the problem.* ○ *All our engineers are fully trained.* ○ *a fully automatic camera*

,**fully-'fledged** *adj* (*US also* **full-fledged**) completely trained or completely developed: *Computer science is now a fully-fledged academic subject.*

fumble /'fʌmbl/ *verb* [I] to use your hands in an awkward way, especially when you are looking for sth: *'It must be here somewhere', she said, fumbling in her pocket for her key.*

fume /fju:m/ *verb* [I] to feel or show anger: *They were nearly two hours late. By the time they arrived I was absolutely fuming.*

fumes /fju:mz/ *noun* [plural] smoke or gases that smell unpleasant and that can be harmful if you breathe them in: *Six people died in the fire when they were overcome by smoke and fumes.*

☆ **fun** /fʌn/ *noun* [U] pleasure and enjoyment; an activity or a person that gives you pleasure and enjoyment: *There isn't much fun in staying at home on your own.* ○ *Staying at home on your own isn't much fun.* ○ *We had a lot of fun at the party last night.* ○ *The party was great fun.* ○ *Have fun!* (= enjoy yourself!) ○ *Sailing can be quite good fun if you don't mind getting wet.* ○ *He was extremely clever but he was also great fun.* ☛ Be careful. **Funny** describes something that makes you laugh or that is strange. It is not the same as **fun**: *The party was fun* (= it was enjoyable). ○ *The film was funny* (= it made us laugh).

(IDIOMS) **(just) for fun/for the fun of it** (just) for amusement or pleasure; not seriously: *I don't need English for my work. I am just learning it for fun.*

(just) in fun as a joke: *It was said in fun. They didn't mean to upset you.*

p	b	t	d	k	g	tʃ	dʒ	f	v	θ	ð
pen	bad	tea	did	cat	got	chin	June	fall	van	thin	then

make fun of sb/sth to laugh at sb/sth in an unkind way; to make other people do this: *The older children are always making fun of him because of his accent.*
poke fun at sb/sth ⇨ POKE

'funfair *noun* [C] = FAIR³(1)

☆ **function** /'fʌŋkʃn/ *noun* [C] **1** the purpose or special duty of a person or thing: *One function of the school governors is to appoint new teachers.* ○ *The function of the heart is to pump blood through the body.* **2** an important social event, ceremony, etc: *The princess attends hundreds of official functions every year.*

function *verb* [I] to work; to be in action: *The doctor's new appointments system doesn't seem to be functioning very well.* ○ *Only one engine was still functioning.*

functional /-ʃənl/ *adj* **1** practical and useful rather than attractive: *cheap functional furniture* **2** working; being used: *The system is now fully functional.*

'function key *noun* [C] a key(3) on a computer which is used to carry out a particular operation

☆ **fund** /fʌnd/ *noun* **1** [C] a sum of money that is collected for a particular purpose: *They contributed £30 to the disaster relief fund.* **2 funds** [plural] money that is available and can be spent: *The government is making funds available to help pay for the storm damage.*

fund *verb* [T] to provide a project, etc with money: *The Channel Tunnel is not funded by government money.*

fundamental /ˌfʌndə'mentl/ *adj* important or basic; from which everything else develops: *There will be fundamental changes in the way the school is run.* ○ *There is a fundamental difference between your opinion and mine.* —**fundamentally** /-təli/ *adv*: *The government's policy has changed fundamentally.*

fundamentals *noun* [plural] basic facts or principles

☆ **funeral** /'fju:nərəl/ *noun* [C] a ceremony (usually in a church) for burying or burning a dead person: *The funeral will be held next week.* ○ *The mourners at the funeral were all in black.*

☛ The body of the dead person is carried in a **coffin**, on which there are often **wreaths** of flowers. The coffin is buried in a **grave** or is burned (**cremated**).

'funeral director *noun* [C] = UNDERTAKER

fungus /'fʌŋgəs/ *noun* [C,U] (*pl* **fungi** /-gaɪ, -dʒaɪ/ or **funguses**) a plant that is not green and that does not have leaves or flowers. One type has a thick stem and a big flat top, another type is like a powder. Fungi grow on other plants, decaying wood or food, etc: *There are many kinds of edible fungi. In Britain we usually only eat the mushroom.* ○ *The roses are covered in fungus.* ☛ Look at **mould** and **toadstool**.

funnel /'fʌnl/ *noun* [C] **1** an object that is wide at the top and narrow at the bottom, used for pouring liquid, powder, etc into a small opening **2** the metal chimney of a steam-engine, ship, etc

☆ **funny** /'fʌni/ *adj* (**funnier**; **funniest**) **1** that makes you smile or laugh: *She told us a funny story about taking a cow to church.* ○ *He's an extremely funny person* (= he can make people laugh). ○ *I didn't think it was very funny when somebody tipped a glass of wine down my dress.* **2** strange or unusual: *Oh dear, the engine is making a funny noise.* ○ *It's funny how English people never talk on trains.* ○ *What a funny little cottage!* ○ *It's funny that they didn't phone to let us know they couldn't come.* ○ *That's funny – he was here a moment ago and now he's gone.* ○ *Can I sit down for a minute? I feel a bit funny* (= a bit ill).

funnily /-ɪli/ *adv* **1** (used for expressing surprise at sth strange that has happened): *Funnily enough, my parents weren't at all cross about it.* **2** in a funny way: *She's breathing very funnily.*

☆ **fur** /fɜː(r)/ *noun* **1** [U] the soft thick hair that covers the bodies of some animals **2** [C,U] the skin and hair of an animal that is used for making clothes, etc; a piece of clothing that is made from this: *These boots are lined with fur.* ○ *a fur coat* ○ *Most of the women were dressed in furs.* —**furry** /'fɜːri/ *adj* (**furrier**; **furriest**): *a small furry animal*

furious /'fjʊəriəs/ *adj* **1 furious (with sb)/(at sth)** very angry: *He was furious with her.* ○ *He was furious at her behaviour.* ☛ The noun is **fury**. **2** very strong; violent: *A furious row has broken out over the closing of the school.* —**furiously** *adv*

furnace /'fɜːnɪs/ *noun* [C] a large enclosed fire that is used for heating water, melting metal, burning rubbish, etc

furnish /'fɜːnɪʃ/ *verb* [T] to put furniture in a room, house, etc: *The room was comfortably furnished.*

furnished *adj* having furniture: *She's renting a furnished room in Birmingham.* ☛ The opposite is **unfurnished**.

furnishings *noun* [plural] the furniture, carpets, curtains, etc in a room, house, etc

☆ **furniture** /'fɜːnɪtʃə(r)/ *noun* [U] the movable articles, eg tables, chairs, beds, etc in a room, house or office: *modern/antique/second-hand furniture* ☛ Be careful. 'Furniture' is an uncountable noun: *They only got married recently and they haven't got much furniture.* If we are talking about an individual item we must say 'a piece of furniture': *The only nice piece of furniture in the room was an antique desk.*

furrow /'fʌrəʊ/ *noun* [C] **1** a line in a field that is made by a plough **2** a line in a person's face, especially on the forehead

furry ⇨ FUR

☆ **further** /'fɜːðə(r)/ *adj* **1** more distant or far; farther: *Which is further – Glasgow or Edinburgh?* **2** more; additional: *Are there any further questions?* ○ *Please let us know if you require any further information.* ○ *I have nothing further to say on the subject.* ○ *The museum is closed until further notice* (= until another announcement is made).

further *adv* **1** at or to a greater distance in time or space; farther: *It's not safe to go any further.* ○ *The hospital is further down the road*

s	z	ʃ	ʒ	h	m	n	ŋ	l	r	j	w
so	zoo	she	vision	how	man	no	sing	leg	red	yes	wet

on the left. ○ I can't remember any further back than 1950. **2** more; to a greater degree: *Can I have time to consider the matter further?* ☞ **Further** and **farther** can both be used when you are talking about distance: *Bristol is further/farther from London than Oxford is.* ○ *I jumped further/farther than you did.* In other senses only **further** can be used: *We need a further week to finish the job.*
(IDIOM) **further afield** ⇨ FAR AFIELD

further verb [T] (*formal*) to help sth to be successful: *to further the cause of peace*

furthermore /ˌfɜːðəˈmɔː(r)/ adv in addition; also: *We are donating £6 million to the disaster fund. Furthermore, we shall send medical supplies immediately.*

ˌfurther eduˈcation noun [U] education for people who have left school (but not at a university) ☞ Look at **higher education**.

☆ **furthest** /ˈfɜːðɪst/ adj, adv = FARTHEST

furtive /ˈfɜːtɪv/ adj secret, acting as though you are trying to hide sth because you feel guilty: *a furtive glance at the letter* —**furtively** adv: *He crept furtively down the stairs and out of the front door.*

fury /ˈfjʊəri/ noun [U] very great anger: *She was speechless with fury.* ☞ The adjective is **furious**.

fuse¹ /fjuːz/ noun [C] **1** a (long) piece of rope, string, etc that is used for lighting a bomb, etc **2** a device that makes a bomb, etc explode at a particular time

fuse² /fjuːz/ verb [I,T] to join together: *Sadness and joy are fused in her poems.*

fuse³ /fjuːz/ noun [C] a small piece of wire in an electrical system, machine, etc that melts and breaks if there is too much power. This stops the flow of electricity and prevents fire or damage: *That plug needs a 15 amp fuse.* ○ *Do you know how to change a fuse?*

fuse verb [I,T] to stop working because a fuse³ has melted; to make a piece of electrical equipment do this: *The lights have fused.* ○ *I've fused the lights.*

fuselage /ˈfjuːzəlɑːʒ; *US* ˈfjuːsəlɑːʒ/ noun [C] the main part of an aeroplane (not the engines, wings or tail)

fusion /ˈfjuːʒn/ noun [C,U] the joining together of different things: *the fusion of two political systems* ○ *nuclear fusion* (= a method of releasing nuclear energy)

fuss /fʌs/ noun [sing,U] unnecessary nervous excitement or activity: *Now get on with your work without making a fuss.* ○ *What's all the fuss about?* **2** [sing] a time when people are angry: *There will be a dreadful fuss if my parents find out that I borrowed the car.*
(IDIOMS) **make, kick up, etc a fuss (about/over sth)** to complain strongly
make a fuss of/over sb/sth to pay a lot of attention to sb/sth

fuss verb [I] **1 fuss (about)** to be worried or excited about small things: *Stop fussing. We're not going to be late.* **2 fuss over sb/sth** to pay too much attention to sb/sth: *Stop fussing over all the details.*
(IDIOM) **not be fussed (about sb/sth)** (*informal*) not to care very much: *'Where do you want to go for lunch?' 'I'm not fussed.'*

fussy /ˈfʌsi/ adj (**fussier; fussiest**) **1** (used about people) giving too much attention to small details and therefore difficult to please: *He is very fussy about his food* (= there are many things which he does not eat). **2** having too much detail or decoration: *I don't like that pattern. It's too fussy.*

futile /ˈfjuːtaɪl; *US* -tl/ adj (used about an action) having no effect or result; useless: *They made a last futile attempt to make him change his mind.* —**futility** noun [U]: *the futility of war*

☆ **future** /ˈfjuːtʃə(r)/ noun **1** [sing] the time that will come after the present: *Who knows what will happen in the future?* ○ *in the near/distant future* (= soon/not soon) ○ *in the immediate future* (= very soon) **2** [C] what will happen to sb/sth in the time after the present: *Our children's futures depend on a good education.* ○ *The company's future does not look very hopeful.* ○ *The future of the local school is still undecided.* **3** [U] the possibility of being successful: *I could see no future in this country so I left to work abroad.* **4** [sing] (*also* **future tense**) (*grammar*) the tense of a verb that expresses what will happen after the present
(IDIOM) **in future** from now on: *Please try to be more careful in future.*

future adj (only *before* a noun) of or happening in the time after the present: *She met her future husband when she was still at school.* ○ *You can keep that book for future reference* (= to look at again later). ○ *What are your future plans?*

fuzzy /ˈfʌzi/ adj (**fuzzier; fuzziest**) not clear: *The photo was rather fuzzy but I could just make out my mother on it.*

Gg

G, g /dʒiː/ noun [C] (pl **G's; g's**) the seventh letter of the English alphabet: *'Girl' begins with (a) 'G'.*

gable /'ɡeɪbl/ noun [C] the pointed part at the top of an outside wall between two parts of a roof

gad /ɡæd/ verb (**gadd**ing; **gadd**ed)
(PHRASAL VERB) **gad about/around** (*informal*) to go around from one place to another in order to enjoy yourself

gadget /'ɡædʒɪt/ noun [C] (*informal*) a small tool or machine

Gaelic /'ɡeɪlɪk/ adj, noun [U] **1** (of) the Celtic language and culture of Ireland **2** / also 'ɡælɪk/ (of) the Celtic language and culture of Scotland

gag /ɡæɡ/ noun [C] **1** a piece of cloth, etc that is put in or over sb's mouth in order to stop him/her from talking **2** a joke or funny story

gag verb [T] (**gag**ging; **gag**ged) to put a gag in or over sb's mouth: (*figurative*) *The new laws are an attempt to gag the press.*

gage (*US*) = GAUGE

gaiety /'ɡeɪəti/ noun [U] a feeling of happiness and fun ☞ The adjective is **gay**.

gaily ⇨ GAY

☆ **gain¹** /ɡeɪn/ noun **1** [C,U] an increase in money; (a) profit or advantage: *Shares in the electricity companies have made big gains on the London stock market.* ○ *We didn't make any gain when we sold our house.* ○ *Everything he did was for personal gain.* **2** [C] an increase in size, amount or power: *a gain in weight of one kilo* ○ *The Liberal Democrat Party is expected to make gains at the next election.*

☆ **gain²** /ɡeɪn/ verb **1** [T] to get or win sth (especially sth that is wanted or needed): *They managed to gain access to secret information.* ○ *He has gained an international reputation as an artist.* ○ *You need to gain more experience before you take your driving test.* **2** [T] to get more of sth: *The train was gaining speed.* ○ *I've gained a lot of weight recently.* **3** [I] **gain by/from doing sth** to get an advantage from sth/from doing sth: *Many people will gain from the changes in the law.* ○ *I've got nothing to gain by staying in this job.* **4** [I,T] (used about a clock or watch) to go too fast and show the incorrect time: *My watch gains five minutes a day.* ○ When a clock gains we say it is **fast**. ☞ The opposite for 2, 3 and 4 is **lose**.
(IDIOM) **gain ground** to make progress; to become stronger or more popular: *The Green Party gained ground in the recent elections.*
(PHRASAL VERBS) **gain in sth** to get more of sth: *He's gained in confidence in the past year.*
gain on sb/sth to get closer to sb/sth that you are trying to catch

gait /ɡeɪt/ noun [sing] the way that sb walks

gala /'ɡɑːlə; *US* 'ɡeɪlə/ noun [C] a special social or sporting occasion: *a gala performance at the National Theatre* ○ *a swimming gala*

galaxy /'ɡæləksi/ noun [C] (pl **galaxies**) a large group of stars and planets in outer space

gale /ɡeɪl/ noun [C] a very strong wind: *It's blowing a gale outside.* ☞ Look at the note at **storm**.

gallant /'ɡælənt/ adj (*formal*) **1** brave: *a gallant soldier* **2** (used about men) polite to and showing special respect for women

gallantry /'ɡæləntri/ noun [C,U] (pl **gallantries**) **1** bravery, especially in a dangerous situation **2** polite behaviour towards women (by men)

gallery /'ɡæləri/ noun [C] (pl **galleries**) **1** a building or room where works of art are shown to the public: *an art gallery* **2** the highest level of seating in a theatre, etc **3** a raised area around the sides or at the back of a large hall. People can sit in the gallery and watch what is happening in the hall: *the public gallery*

gallon /'ɡælən/ noun [C] a measure of liquid; 4·5 litres. There are 8 pints in a gallon. ☞ An American gallon is the same as 3·8 litres.

gallop /'ɡæləp/ verb [I] (used about a horse or a rider) to go at the fastest speed, when the horse's four feet all leave the ground together

gallop noun [sing,C] the fastest speed of a horse, etc; a time when you ride at this speed: *They went for a gallop over the fields.*

gallows /'ɡæləʊz/ noun [C] (pl **gallows**) a wooden framework on which criminals used to be hanged

galore /ɡə'lɔː(r)/ adv (only *after* a noun) in large numbers: *There will be prizes galore at our children's party on Saturday.*

gamble /'ɡæmbl/ verb [I,T] to risk money on the result of a card-game, horse-race, etc: *He spent every evening gambling at poker.* ○ *She gambled £25 on the last race.*
(PHRASAL VERB) **gamble on sth/on doing sth** to act in the hope that sth will happen although it is possible that it will not: *I wouldn't gamble on the weather staying fine.*

gamble noun [C] something you do that is a risk (ie you might win sth but you might also lose): *Setting up this business was a bit of a gamble.*
(IDIOM) **take a gamble (on sth)** to take a chance (on sth or on sth happening) —**gambler** /'ɡæmblə(r)/ noun [C]: *He's always been a gambler.* —**gambling** /'ɡæmblɪŋ/ noun [U]:

ɜː	ə	eɪ	əʊ	aɪ	aʊ	ɔɪ	ɪə	eə	ʊə
fur	ago	pay	home	five	now	join	near	hair	pure

There has been a big increase in smoking, drinking and gambling among young people.

game¹ /geɪm/ *noun* **1** [C] a form of play or sport with rules; a time when you play it: *Let's have a game of chess.* o *a game of football, rugby, tennis, etc* o *'Monopoly' is still a very popular game.* o *Our next game is against the Oxford Tigers.* o *Tonight's game is between Holland and Italy.* o *What an exciting game!* o *The game ended in a draw.* **2** [C] a unit in a match of tennis, etc: *Becker won the first game of the second set.* **3 games** [plural] an (international) athletics or sports competition **4** [C] the set of equipment that you need in order to play a particular (indoor) game: *We usually buy a new board game at Christmas.* **5** [C, usually sing] (*informal*) a way of behaving according to a secret plan: *I wasn't sure what their game was but I didn't trust them.*

(IDIOM) **give the game away** to tell a person sth that you are trying to keep secret: *It was the expression on her face that gave the game away.*

game² /geɪm/ *adj* (used about a person) ready and willing to do sth new, unusual, difficult, etc: *I have never been sailing but I'm game to try.*

game³ /geɪm/ *noun* [U] wild animals or birds that are hunted for sport or food: *Shooting game is popular in Scotland.* o *big game* (= lions, tigers, etc that are hunted)

'gamekeeper *noun* [C] a person who looks after game³ on private land

gander /'gændə(r)/ *noun* [C] a male goose

gang /gæŋ/ *noun* [C, with sing or pl verb] **1** an organized group of criminals: *The police are looking for the gang that committed the robbery.* **2** a group of young people, especially young men, who sometimes cause trouble: *The phone box was vandalized by a gang of youths.* **3** a group of prisoners, building workers, etc who work together as a team **4** (*informal*) a group of (young) friends: *The whole gang is here tonight.*

gang *verb* (*informal*)
(PHRASAL VERB) **gang up on sb** to join together with other people in order to act against sb: *She felt that all her friends were ganging up on her.*

gangrene /'gæŋgriːn/ *noun* [U] the decay of a part of the body because the blood supply to it has been stopped

gangster /'gæŋstə(r)/ *noun* [C] a member of a gang of criminals

gangway /'gæŋweɪ/ *noun* [C] **1** a movable bridge that people use for getting on or off a ship **2** (*Brit*) a passage that you can walk along between two rows of seats

gaol, gaoler (*Brit*) = JAIL, JAILER

☆ **gap** /gæp/ *noun* [C] **a gap (in/between sth)** **1** an empty space in sth or between two things: *The sheep got out through a gap in the fence.* **2** an absence of sth; a space where sth should be: *There were several gaps in his history.* o *I think our new product should fill a gap in the market.* o *Her husband's death left a big gap in her life.* **3** a period of time that is not filled or when you are not doing what you normally do: *I returned to teaching after a gap of about five years.* o *a*

gap in the conversation **4** a difference between people or their ideas: *The gap between the rich and the poor is getting wider.* o *the generation gap* (= the difference in opinions between parents and their children)
(IDIOM) **bridge a/the gap** ⇒ BRIDGE¹

gape /geɪp/ *verb* [I] **1** to stare at sb/sth with your mouth open **2** to be or become wide open: *There was a gaping hole in the wall after the explosion.*

☆ **garage** /'gærɑːʒ; 'gærɪdʒ; *US* gə'rɑːʒ/ *noun* [C] **1** a building where cars, etc are kept: *The house has a double garage* (= with space for two cars). **2** a place where you can have your car serviced or repaired. It may also sell petrol, etc: *a garage mechanic* ☞ Look at **petrol station**.

garbage /'gɑːbɪdʒ/ *noun* [U] (*especially US*) = RUBBISH

'garbage can *noun* [C] (*US*) = DUSTBIN

garbled /'gɑːbld/ *adj* (used about a message, story, etc) difficult to understand; not clear

☆ **garden** /'gɑːdn/ *noun* [C] **1** (*US* **yard**) a piece of land (usually near a house) where flowers and vegetables are grown, usually with a piece of grass (**lawn**): *Let's have lunch in the garden.* o *the back/front garden* o *garden flowers* o *garden chairs* (= for using in the garden) ☞ Look at the note at **yard**. **2 gardens** [plural] a public park: *the Botanical Gardens*

garden *verb* [I] to work in a garden: *She's been gardening all afternoon.*

gardener /'gɑːdnə(r)/ *noun* [C] a person who works in a garden as a job or for pleasure: *They're keen gardeners.*

gardening /'gɑːdnɪŋ/ *noun* [U] looking after a garden: *I'm going to do some gardening this afternoon.* o *gardening gloves* (= used when you are working in a garden)

'garden centre *noun* [C] a place where plants, seeds, gardening equipment, etc are sold

'garden party *noun* [C] a formal social event that takes place outside (usually in a large garden) on a summer afternoon

gargle /'gɑːgl/ *verb* [I] to wash your throat with a liquid (which you do not swallow)

garish /'geərɪʃ/ *adj* too bright or highly decorated

garlic /'gɑːlɪk/ *noun* [U] a plant with a strong taste and smell that looks like a small onion and is used in cooking: *a clove of garlic* ☞ picture at **onion**.

garment /'gɑːmənt/ *noun* [C] (*formal*) one piece of clothing: *This garment must be dry-cleaned.*

garrison /'gærɪsn/ *noun* [C] a group of soldiers who are living in and guarding a town or building

☆ **gas** /gæs/ *noun* (*pl* **gases**; *US also* **gasses**) **1** [C,U] a substance that is like air (ie not solid or liquid): *Hydrogen and oxygen are gases.* **2** [U] a gas(1) or mixture of gases that is used for heating, cooking, etc: *Does your central heating run on gas or electricity?* o *a gas cooker* o *Turn the gas on the cooker up a bit!* **3** [U] a poisonous gas(1) that is used in war **4** [U] (*US*) = PETROL

p	b	t	d	k	g	tʃ	dʒ	f	v	θ	ð
pen	bad	tea	did	cat	got	chin	June	fall	van	thin	then

gas verb [T] (**gas**sing; **gas**sed) to poison or kill sb with gas

'gas chamber noun [C] a room that can be filled with poisonous gas in order to kill animals or people

,gas-'fired adj using gas as fuel: *gas-fired central heating*

'gas mask noun [C] an apparatus that you wear over your face to protect you against poisonous gas

'gas meter noun [C] an instrument that measures the amount of gas that you use

'gas station noun [C] (*US*) = PETROL STATION

gash /gæʃ/ noun [C] a long deep cut or wound: *He had a nasty gash in his arm.*

gash verb [T] to make a long deep cut or wound

gasoline (*also* **gasolene**) /'gæsəli:n/ noun [U] (*US*) = PETROL

gasp /gɑ:sp/ verb **1** [I] to breathe quickly and noisily (eg when you have been running fast): *At the end of the race some of the runners were gasping for breath.* **2** [I] **gasp (at sth)** to breathe in suddenly and noisily because you are surprised or in pain: *She gasped in surprise as she read the letter.* **3** [T] **gasp sth (out)** to say sth while you are finding it difficult to breathe: *'I can't go on,' he gasped, 'I've got to sit down.'*

gasp noun [C] a quick breath (when you are surprised, in pain, etc): *Suddenly she gave a gasp of surprise.*

gastronomic /ˌgæstrə'nɒmɪk/ adj connected with (good) food

☆ **gate** /geɪt/ noun [C] **1** a movable structure (like a door) that closes an opening in a wall, fence, hedge, etc: *Please keep the garden gate closed.* ☛ picture at **fence**. ☛ (*also* **gateway**) an opening in a wall, fence, hedge, etc that is closed by a gate(1): *Drive through the gates and you'll find the car park on the right.* **3** an entrance or exit at an airport: *Swissair Flight 139 to Geneva is now boarding at gate 16.*

'gatecrash verb [I,T] to go to a private party without being invited

'gatecrasher noun [C]

'gateway noun [C] **1** = GATE(2) **2** [sing] **gateway to sth** the place through which you must pass in order to get to somewhere else: *The port of Dover is England's gateway to Europe.* ○ (*figurative*) *A good education can be the gateway to success.*

gâteau /'gætəʊ; *US* gæ'təʊ/ noun [C] (*pl* **gâteaux** *or* **gâteaus**) a large cake that is usually decorated with cream, fruit, etc ☛ picture at **cake**.

☆ **gather** /'gæðə(r)/ verb **1** [I,T] **gather round (sb/sth); gather sb/sth round (sb/sth)** (used about people) to come together in a group; to make people come together: *A crowd soon gathered at the scene of the accident.* ○ *The children were gathered in a group around the teacher's desk.* **2** [T] **gather sth (together/up)** to bring many things together; to collect: *They gathered up all their picnic things and set off home.* ○ *They have gathered together a lot of information on the subject.* ○ *I need some time to gather my thoughts before I can give you an answer.* **3** [T] to collect plants, fruits, etc **4** [T] to understand or find out sth (from sb/sth): *I gather from your letter that you have several years' experience of this kind of work.* ○ *'She's been very ill recently.' 'So I gather.'* **5** [T] to pull material together into small folds and sew it: *a gathered skirt* **6** [I,T] to become greater or to make greater; to increase: *The train is gathering speed.* ○ *In the gathering darkness it was hard to see the ball.*

gathering noun [C] a time when people come together; a meeting: *a family gathering*

gaudy /'gɔ:di/ adj (**gaudier**; **gaudiest**) too bright or highly decorated

gauge (*US also* **gage**) /geɪdʒ/ noun [C] **1** an instrument for measuring the amount of sth: *a fuel gauge on a car* (= to show how much petrol is left) **2** the distance between the rails on a railway: *a narrow-gauge railway* **3** a fact that you can use to judge a situation, sb's feelings, etc

gauge verb [T] **1** to measure sth **2** to judge a situation, sb's feelings, etc: *It was difficult to gauge the mood of the audience.*

gaunt /gɔ:nt/ adj (used about a person) very thin because of hunger, illness, etc

gauze /gɔ:z/ noun [U] thin net-like material (often used for covering wounds)

gave *pt* of GIVE

gawp /gɔ:p/ verb [I] (*informal*) to look or stare (at sb/sth) in a stupid way (with your mouth open)

gay /geɪ/ adj **1** sexually attracted to people of the same sex; homosexual: *He told me he was gay.* ○ *the gay community of San Francisco* ☛ The noun is **gayness**. **2** (*old-fashioned*) happy and full of fun ☛ The noun is **gaiety**.

gaily /'geɪli/ adv in a gay(2) manner

gay noun [C] a person, especially a man, who is sexually attracted to people of the same sex; a homosexual: *a club for lesbians and gays*

gaze /geɪz/ verb [I] to look steadily for a long time: *She sat at the window gazing silently into space.*

gaze noun [sing] a long steady look: *She kept her gaze fixed on the man in the front row.*

gear /gɪə(r)/ noun **1** [C] a set of wheels that fit into another set in order to pass power from one part of a machine to another, eg from a car's engine to its wheels: *A car has four (or five) forward gears and a reverse.* **2** [U] a particular position of the gears (in a car, etc)

☛ A car can be **in** or **out of** gear. You use a **low** gear (**first** gear) when you first start moving and then **change** gear as you go faster. For the fastest speeds you use **top** gear.

3 [U] equipment or clothing that you need for a particular activity, etc: *camping gear* **4** [sing] (in compounds) an instrument or part of a machine that is used for a particular purpose: *the landing-gear of an aeroplane*

gear verb

(PHRASAL VERBS) **gear sth to/towards sth** (often passive) to make sth suitable for a particular purpose: *There is a special course geared towards the older learner.*

gear up (for sb/sth); gear sb/sth up (for sb/sth) to get ready or to make sb/sth ready: *I* was all geared up for the party but it was cancelled at the last minute.

'gearbox noun [C] the metal case that contains the gears(1) of a car, etc

'gear lever (US **'gearshift**) noun [C] a stick that is used for changing gear(2) (in a car, etc)

gee /dʒi:/ interj (US) (used for expressing surprise, pleasure, etc): Gee, I'm sorry. I didn't know you'd been ill.

geese pl of GOOSE

gel /dʒel/ noun [C,U] (often in compounds) a thick substance like jelly that is between a liquid and a solid: hair-gel

gelignite /'dʒelɪɡnaɪt/ noun [U] a substance that is used for making explosions

gem /dʒem/ noun [C] **1** a jewel or precious stone **2** a person or thing that has great value

Gemini /'dʒemɪnaɪ/ noun [C,U] the third sign of the Zodiac, the Twins; a person who was born under this sign ☞ picture at **zodiac**.

gender /'dʒendə(r)/ noun [C,U] **1** (formal) the classification of people into two sexes: male and female **2** (grammar) (in some languages) the classification of nouns, pronouns, etc into masculine, feminine and neuter; one of these divisions: There are three genders in German. ○ In French the adjective must agree with the noun in number and gender.

gene /dʒi:n/ noun [C] one of the parts of a cell of a living thing which decide its development. Genes are passed from parents to children. In human beings they decide, for example, the size of a child or the colour of his/her eyes.

☆ **general¹** /'dʒenrəl/ adj **1** affecting all or most people, places, things, etc: Fridges were once a luxury, but now they are in general use. ○ The bad weather has been fairly general (= it has affected most areas). ○ That is a matter of general interest. ○ The general feeling is that the situation is improving (= most people think so). ○ the general public (= most ordinary people) **2** (only before a noun) not limited to, or describing, one particular part; not detailed: Your general health is very good. ○ The introduction gives you a general idea of what the book is about. ○ Let's talk in general terms at first and then get down to details. **3** not limited to one subject or area of study; not specialized: Children need a good general education. ○ The quiz tests your general knowledge. ○ a general hospital **4** (often in compounds) with responsibility for the whole of an organization: The Secretary-General of the United Nations ○ a general manager

(IDIOM) **in general** in most cases; usually: In general, standards of hygiene are good.

,**general anaes'thetic** noun [C,U] a substance that is given to a patient in hospital before an operation so that he/she becomes unconscious and does not feel any pain ☞ Look at **local anaesthetic**.

General Certificate of Secondary Education = GCSE ☞ Look at the list of abbreviations.

,**general e'lection** noun [C] an election in which all the voters in a country choose their national parliament

,**general prac'titioner** noun [C] = GP ☞ Look at the list of abbreviations.

general² /'dʒenrəl/ noun [C] an army officer of very high rank: General Roberts

generalize (also **generalise**) /'dʒenrəlaɪz/ verb [I] **1** generalize (about sth) (from sth) to form an opinion using only a small amount of information: You can't generalize about English food from only two meals. **2** generalize (about sth) to make a general statement about sth and not look at the details: You're generalizing. Every case is different.

generalization (also **generalisation**) /,dʒenrəlaɪ'zeɪʃn; US -lɪ'z-/ noun **1** [U] the act of generalizing **2** [C] a general statement about sth that does not consider details

☆ **generally** /'dʒenrəli/ adv **1** usually: She generally cycles to work. **2** by most people: He is generally considered to be a good doctor. **3** in a general sense, without looking at the details: Generally speaking, houses in America are bigger than houses in this country.

generate /'dʒenəreɪt/ verb [T] **1** to produce power, heat, electricity, etc **2** to cause sth to exist: I think this new product will generate a lot of income for the company.

☆ **generation** /,dʒenə'reɪʃn/ noun **1** [U] the act of generating: the generation of electricity by water-power **2** [C] a single stage in a family history: This photograph shows three generations of my family (= children, parents and grandparents). **3** [C] all the people in a group or country who were born at about the same time: My grandmother's generation grew up without electricity or running water. ○ future generations ☞ Generation is used in the singular with either a singular or plural verb: The younger generation only seem/seems to be interested in money. **4** [C] a period of about 25 or 30 years (ie the time that a person takes to become an adult): A generation ago foreign travel was still only possible for a few people.

the gene'ration gap noun [sing] the difference in behaviour, and lack of understanding, between young people and older people

generator /'dʒenəreɪtə(r)/ noun [C] a machine that produces electricity

generosity /,dʒenə'rɒsəti/ noun [U] the quality of being generous

☆ **generous** /'dʒenərəs/ adj **1** willing to give more money, help, etc than is usual or necessary: It was very generous of your parents to lend us all that money. **2** larger than usual: You get very generous portions in that restaurant.
—**generously** adv: Please give generously.

genetics /dʒɪ'netɪks/ noun [U] the scientific study of the way that the development of living things is controlled by features that have been passed on from parents to children ☞ Look at **gene**.

genetic /dʒɪ'netɪk/ adj connected with genes or genetics: The disease is caused by a genetic defect. —**genetically** /-kli/ adv

ge,**netic engi'neering** noun [U] changes made by scientists in the genetic structure of plants and animals

genial /'dʒi:niəl/ adj (used about a person) pleasant and friendly

i:	ɪ	e	æ	ɑ:	ɒ	ɔ:	ʊ	u:	ʌ
see	sit	ten	hat	arm	got	saw	put	too	cup

genitals /'dʒenɪtlz/ *noun* [plural] (*formal*) the external sex organs —**genital** /'dʒenɪtl/ *adj*

genius /'dʒiːniəs/ *noun* (*pl* **geniuses**) **1** [U] very great and unusual ability: *Shakespeare's tragedies show true genius.* **2** [C] a person who has very great and unusual ability, especially in a particular subject: *Einstein was a mathematical genius.* **3** [sing] **a genius for (doing) sth** great natural ability for (doing) sth: *Our teacher had a genius for explaining difficult things in a simple way.*

genocide /'dʒenəsaɪd/ *noun* [U] the murder of a nation or race

gent /dʒent/ *noun* **1** [C] (*informal*) gentleman **2 a/the Gents** [sing] (*Brit informal*) a public toilet for men ☞ Look at the note at **toilet**.

genteel /dʒen'tiːl/ *adj* paying great (perhaps too much) attention to polite manners —**gentility** /dʒen'tɪləti/ *noun* [U]

☆ **gentle** /'dʒentl/ *adj* **1** (used about people) kind; calm; touching or treating people or things in a careful way so that they are not hurt: *He was a gentle, patient man who loved playing with his grandchildren.* ○ *'I'll try and be as gentle as I can', said the dentist.* **2** not rough or violent: *You should be able to take some gentle exercise next week.* ○ *It's just a gentle* (= not steep) *climb to the top of the hill.* —**gentleness** /'dʒentlnɪs/ *noun* [U] —**gently** /'dʒentli/ *adv*: *He touched her gently on the shoulder.* ○ *The beach slopes gently down to the sea.*

☆ **gentleman** /'dʒentlmən/ *noun* [C] (*pl* **gentlemen** /-mən/) **1** a man who is polite and who behaves well towards other people: *He is a real gentleman.* **2** (*formal*) (used when speaking to or about a man or men in a polite way): *Ladies and gentlemen!* (eg at the beginning of a speech) ○ *Mrs Flinn, there is a gentleman here to see you.* **3** a rich man with a high social position: *He likes to think of himself as a country gentleman.* ☞ For meanings 1, 2 and 3 we use **lady** when we are talking about a woman.

☆ **genuine** /'dʒenjuɪn/ *adj* **1** a person or thing that is genuine is exactly what he/she/it seems to be; real: *He thought that he had bought a genuine Rolex watch but it was a cheap fake.* ○ *There are only three genuine Scotsmen in the team.* **2** (used about a person or his/her feelings or behaviour) honest; real: *She seems genuine enough but can I trust her?* —**genuinely** *adv*: *I'm genuinely interested in a career in teaching.*

☆ **geography** /dʒɪ'ɒgrəfi/ *noun* [U] **1** the study of the countries of the world, of their natural and physical features and of the cities, industries, etc that have been made by man **2** the way in which the features of a particular country or place are arranged: *We're studying the geography of Japan.* —**geographer** /dʒɪ'ɒgrəfə(r)/ *noun* [C] a student of or expert in geography —**geographic** /,dʒɪə'græfɪk/ (*also* **geographical** /-ɪkl/) *adj* —**geographically** /-kli/ *adv*

geology /dʒɪ'ɒlədʒi/ *noun* [U] the study of rocks and soil, and of their development —**geological** /,dʒɪə'lɒdʒɪkl/ *adj*

geologist /dʒɪ'ɒlədʒɪst/ *noun* [C] a student of or expert in geology

geometry /dʒɪ'ɒmətri/ *noun* [U] the study in mathematics of lines, shapes, curves, etc

geometric /,dʒɪə'metrɪk/ (*also* **geometrical** /-ɪkl/) *adj* **1** of geometry **2** consisting of regular shapes and lines: *a geometric design/pattern* —**geometrically** /-kli/ *adv*

geriatrics /,dʒeri'ætrɪks/ *noun* [U] the medical treatment of very old people —**geriatric** *adj*: *a geriatric hospital*

germ /dʒɜːm/ *noun* **1** [C] a very small living thing that causes disease. Germs can only be seen with a microscope: *This disinfectant kills most germs.* ☞ Look at **bacteria** and **virus**. **2** [sing] **the germ of sth** the beginning of sth that may develop: *the germ of an idea*

German measles /,dʒɜːmən 'miːzlz/ (*also* **rubella**) *noun* [U] a mild disease that causes red spots all over the body. It may damage an unborn baby if the mother catches it.

germinate /'dʒɜːmɪneɪt/ *verb* [I,T] (used about a seed of a plant) to start growing; to cause a seed to do this —**germination** /,dʒɜːmɪ'neɪʃn/ *noun* [U]

gerund /'dʒerənd/ *noun* [C] (*grammar*) a noun, ending in -ing, that has been made from a verb: *In the sentence 'His hobby is collecting stamps', 'collecting' is a gerund.*

gesticulate /dʒe'stɪkjuleɪt/ *verb* [I] to make movements with your hands and arms in order to express sth

gesture /'dʒestʃə(r)/ *noun* [C] **1** a movement of the hand, head, etc that expresses sth: *The driver of the car in front made a rude gesture and drove off.* **2** something that you do that shows other people what you think or feel: *It would be a nice gesture to invite the neighbours in for a meal.*

gesture *verb* [I,T] to point at sth, to make a sign to sb: *She asked them if they were going and gestured towards the door.*

☆ **get** /get/ *verb* (*pres part* **getting**; *pt* **got** /gɒt/; *pp* **got**; *US* **gotten** /'gɒtn/) **1** [T] **have/has got** to have sth: *Have you got a bike?* **2** [I] to become: *It's getting dark.* ○ *She got angry.* **3** [T] to receive or obtain sth: *I got a letter from my sister.* ○ *What did you get for Christmas?* ○ *He went shopping and got a suit.* ○ *I got a shock when I saw the price.* ○ *She got a job in a travel agency.* ○ *You get a wonderful view from that window.* ○ *I'll do it if I get the time.* **4** [T] to fetch or collect sth: *Go and get me a pen, please.* ○ *I'll get the children from school today.* ○ *The police have got to* (= caught) *the gang who carried out the robbery.* **5** [T] to hear or understand sth: *I'm sorry, I didn't get that. Could you repeat it?* **6** [T] to catch a disease: *She got malaria in Africa.* **7** [T] to use a form of transport: *I didn't walk – I got the bus.* **8** [I] to move somewhere; to reach a place: *We got to Dover at about 10.* ☞ Look at **get in, on,** etc. **9** [T] to cause sth to be in a particular place: *We couldn't get the piano upstairs.* **10** [T] to prepare sth; to make sb/sth ready: *He got the breakfast.* **11** [I] (used with a past participle) to do sth that you are responsible for: *I'm just getting dressed.* ○ *They've got divorced.* **12** [I] to be in a certain

situation: *He's got into trouble with the police.* **13** [I] (used in a similar way to the passive) to have sth happen to you: *She got bitten by a dog.* **14** [T] to cause sb/sth to do sth or to happen: *I got him to agree to the plan.* o *I can't get the television to work.* o *She finally got the book finished.* ☛ Note that we also use **get** when we arrange for somebody else to do something: *You must get the car serviced every 10 000 miles* (= at a garage). **15** [I] to have the opportunity to do sth: *Did you get to see the Rembrandt exhibition?*
(IDIOM) **get somewhere/nowhere (with sb/sth)** to make progress: *I'm getting nowhere with my research.*

☛ For other idioms containing **get**, look at the noun and adjective entries, eg for **get rid of** look at **rid**.

(PHRASAL VERBS) **get about/around** to move or travel to and from many places: *Australia this week, Japan next week – you certainly get around!*

get about/around/round (used about news, a story, etc) to spread; to become known by many people

get sth across (to sb) to succeed in making people understand sth: *The party failed to get its policies across to the voters.*

get ahead to progress and be successful in sth, especially a career

get along ⇨ GET ON

get around 1 ⇨ GET ABOUT/AROUND **2** ⇨ GET ABOUT/AROUND/ROUND

get around sb ⇨ GET ROUND/AROUND SB

get around sth ⇨ GET ROUND/AROUND STH

get around to sth/doing sth ⇨ GET ROUND/AROUND TO STH/DOING STH

get at sb to say unkind or critical things to sb

get at sb/sth to succeed in reaching sb/sth: *The pen fell down between my desk and the wall and I couldn't get at it.*

get at sth (used only in the continuous tenses) to suggest sth indirectly; to mean sth but not to state it directly: *I'm not quite sure what you're getting at – am I doing something wrong?*

get away (from...) to succeed in leaving or escaping from sb or a place: *He kept talking to me and I couldn't get away from him.* o *The thieves got away in a stolen car.*

get away with sth/with doing sth to do sth bad and not be punished for it: *He lied but he got away with it.* o *I don't know how they get away with charging such high prices.*

get back to return to the place where you live or work: *When did you get back from Italy?*

get sth back to be given sth that you had lost or lent: *Can I borrow this book? You'll get it back next week, I promise.*

get back to sb to speak to, write to or phone sb later, especially in order to give an answer or deal with sth: *I'll get back to you when I've got some more information.*

get back to sth to return to doing sth or talking about sth: *I woke up early and couldn't get back to sleep.* o *Let's get back to the point you raised earlier.*

get behind (with sth) to fail to do or produce sth on time: *We got behind with our rent.*

get by (on sth) to manage, often with difficulty, to live, using a certain income: *It's very hard to get by on such a low income.*

get sb down to make sb miserable: *These cold winter days get me down.*

get sth down to make a note of sth; to write sth down: *Did you get the address for the competition down?*

get down to sth/doing sth to start doing or concentrating on sth: *I must get down to answering these letters.*

get in to reach a place: *What time does your train get in?*

get in; get into sth 1 to climb into a car: *We all got in and Tim drove off.* **2** to be elected to a political position: *Who do you think will get in at the next election?*

get sth in to manage to find an opportunity to say or do sth: *He talked all the time and I couldn't get a word in.*

get into sb (*informal*) (used about a feeling or attitude) to start affecting sb strongly, causing the person to behave in an unusual way: *I wonder what's got into him – he isn't usually unfriendly.*

get into sth to start a particular activity; to become involved in sth: *How did you first get into the music business?* o *She has got into the habit of turning up late.* o *We got into an argument about politics.*

get off (sth) 1 to leave a bus, train, bicycle, etc; to climb down from a horse **2** to leave work with permission at a particular time: *I might be able to get off early today.*

get sth off (sth) to remove sth from sth: *My foot was swollen and I couldn't get my shoe off.*

get off (with sth) to receive minor or no injuries when serious injury was possible: *She was lucky to get off with only a broken arm in such a bad accident.*

get (sb) off (with sth) to receive little or no punishment; to help sb to receive little or no punishment: *If you're lucky, you'll get off with a small fine.* o *Her lawyer told her that he was confident he would get her off.*

get off with sb (*Brit informal*) to start a sexual or romantic relationship with sb: *Ruth got off with Steve at the disco.*

get on 1 to progress or become successful in life, in a career, etc: *After leaving university she was determined to get on.* **2** to be getting old: *He's getting on – he's over 60, I'm sure.* **3** to be getting late: *Time's getting on – we don't want to be late.* ☛ Senses **2** and **3** are only used in the continuous tenses.

get on/along 1 to make progress: *How are you getting on in your course?* **2** to perform in a particular way or to have a good or bad experience in a particular situation: *How did you get on at your interview?*

get on/onto sth to climb onto a bus, train, bicycle, horse, etc: *I got on just as the train was about to leave.* o *I couldn't get onto the bus because it was full.*

get sth on to put on a piece of clothing: *Get your shoes on, we're going out now.*

p	b	t	d	k	g	tʃ	dʒ	f	v	θ	ð
pen	bad	tea	did	cat	got	chin	June	fall	van	thin	then

get on for (used only in the continuous tenses) to approach a certain time or age: *I'm not sure how old he is but he must be getting on for 50.*

get onto sb (about sth) to speak or write to sb about a particular matter

get on/along with sb; get on/along (together) to have a friendly relationship with sb: *Do you get on well with your colleagues?* ○ *We're not close friends but we get on together quite well.*

get on/along with sth to make progress with sth that you are doing: *How are you getting on with that essay?*

get on with sth to continue doing sth, especially after an interruption: *Stop talking and get on with your work!*

get out (used about a piece of information) to become known, having previously been secret

get sth out (of sth) to take sth from its container: *I got my keys out of my bag.*

get out (of sth) to leave or escape from a place: *My grandmother's very old and she doesn't get out of the house much.*

get out of sth/doing sth to avoid a duty or doing sth that you have said you will do: *I said I'd go to their party and I can't get out of it now.*

get sth out of sb to obtain sth from sb by force or persuasion: *His parents finally got the truth out of him.*

get sth out of sb/sth to gain sth from sb/sth: *I get a lot of pleasure out of music.*

get over sth 1 to overcome a problem: *We'll have to get over the problem of finding somewhere to live first.* **2** to recover from sth unpleasant, or from an illness: *He still hasn't got over his wife's death.* ○ *It took her a long time to get over her operation.* ○ *I can't get over how rude he was!* (= I still find it surprising)

get sth over with (*informal*) to do and complete sth unpleasant that has to be done: *I'll be glad to get my visit to the dentist's over with.*

get round ⇨ GET ABOUT/AROUND/ROUND

get round/around sb (*informal*) to persuade sb to do or agree with sth: *My father says I can't borrow his car but I think I can get round him.*

get round/around sth to find a way of avoiding or overcoming a problem

get round/around to sth/doing sth to find the time to do sth, after a delay: *I've been meaning to reply to that letter for ages but I haven't got round to it yet.*

get through sth to use or to complete a certain amount or number of sth: *I got through a lot of money at the weekend.* ○ *I got through an enormous amount of work today.*

get (sb) through (sth) to be successful in sth (often sth unpleasant); to help sb to be successful: *She got through her final exams easily.* ○ *It was a terrible time financially but I got through it and then things improved.* ○ *Her kindness got me through those awful days.*

get through (to sb) 1 to succeed in making a telephone connection with sb: *I couldn't get through to them because their phone was engaged all day.* **2** to succeed in making sb understand what you are saying: *They couldn't get through to him that he was completely wrong.*

get to sb (*informal*) to affect sb in a bad way: *Public criticism is beginning to get to the team manager.*

get together (with sb) to meet socially or in order to discuss or do sth: *We should get together one evening.* ○ *Let's get together and talk about it.*

get up to rise to a standing position; to stand up: *He got up to let an elderly woman sit down.*

get (sb) up to get out of bed or make sb get out of bed: *What time do you have to get up in the morning?* ○ *Could you get me up at 6 tomorrow?*

get up to sth 1 to reach a particular point or stage in sth: *We've got up to the last section of our grammar book.* **2** to do sth, especially sth bad: *I wonder what the children are getting up to?*

getaway /'ɡetəweɪ/ *noun* [C] an escape (after a crime): *to make a getaway* ○ *a getaway car*

get-together /'ɡet təɡeðə(r)/ *noun* [C] (*informal*) an informal social meeting or party: *We're having a little get-together on Saturday evening.*

ghastly /'ɡɑːstlɪ; *US* 'ɡæstlɪ/ *adj* (**ghastlier**; **ghastliest**) **1** causing fear and shock: *a ghastly accident* **2** (*informal*) very bad, ugly or unpleasant: *a ghastly mistake* ○ *I think these two colours look ghastly together.* **3** (used about a person) looking pale and ill: *You look ghastly. Do you want to lie down?*

ghetto /'ɡetəʊ/ *noun* [C] (*pl* **ghettoes**) a part of a town where many people of the same race, religion, etc live, often in poor conditions

ghost /ɡəʊst/ (*also* **spectre**; *US* **specter**) *noun* [C] the spirit of a dead person that is seen or heard by sb who is still living: *I don't believe in ghosts.* ○ *The tower is haunted by the ghost of Lady Anne.* ○ *a ghost story*

ghostly /'ɡəʊstlɪ/ *adj* (**ghostlier**; **ghostliest**) of or like a ghost: *ghostly noises*

'ghost town *noun* [C] a town whose inhabitants have all left

'ghost-writer *noun* [C] a person who writes a book, etc for a famous person (whose name appears as the author)

☆ **giant** /'dʒaɪənt/ *noun* [C] **1** (in children's stories) a person of human shape but enormous size and strength **2** something that is very large: *the multinational oil giants* (= very large companies)

giant (*also* **'giant-size**; **'giant-sized**) *adj* extremely large; enormous: *a giant new shopping-centre*

giddy /'ɡɪdɪ/ *adj* (**giddier**; **giddiest**) having the feeling that everything is going round and that you are going to fall: *I feel giddy. I must sit down.* —**giddily** /'ɡɪdɪlɪ/ *adv* —**giddiness** /'ɡɪdɪnɪs/ *noun* [U]

☆ **gift** /ɡɪft/ *noun* [C] **1** something that you give to a person; a present: *wedding gifts* ○ *He made a gift of £500 to charity.* ○ *Their teacher was presented with a gift of flowers and chocolates.* ○ *This week's magazine contains a free gift of some make-up.* ☞ Look at the note at **present**. **2 a gift (for sth/doing sth)** natural ability:

s	z	ʃ	ʒ	h	m	n	ŋ	l	r	j	w
so	zoo	she	vision	how	man	no	sing	leg	red	yes	wet

She has a gift for saying the right thing at the right time.

gifted /'gɪftɪd/ *adj* having natural ability or great intelligence: *an extremely gifted musician*

gig /gɪg/ *noun* [C] a performance by pop or jazz musicians

gigantic /dʒaɪ'gæntɪk/ *adj* extremely large

giggle /'gɪgl/ *verb* [I] to laugh in a silly way because you are amused or nervous

giggle *noun* [C] a laugh of this kind: *I've got the giggles* (= I can't stop laughing).

gilt /gɪlt/ *noun* [U] a thin covering of gold or sth that looks like gold

gimmick /'gɪmɪk/ *noun* [C] something unusual or amusing that is used to attract people's attention (usually so that they buy sth): *They're looking for a new gimmick to advertise the restaurant.*

gin /dʒɪn/ *noun* [C,U] a colourless alcoholic drink that is made from grain and a particular type of berry: *I'd like a gin and tonic, please.*

ginger /'dʒɪndʒə(r)/ *noun* [U] **1** the hot-tasting root of a plant (used in cooking): *ground ginger* **2** a reddish-orange colour

ginger *adj* **1** flavoured with ginger: *ginger biscuits* **2** of a ginger colour: *ginger hair*

ginger 'ale *noun* [U] a non-alcoholic drink that is flavoured with ginger, often mixed with alcoholic drinks ☛ **Ginger beer** is similar but has a little alcohol and is not mixed with other drinks.

gingerly /'dʒɪndʒəli/ *adv* very slowly and carefully so as not to cause harm, make a noise, etc

gipsy = GYPSY

giraffe /dʒɪ'rɑːf; *US* dʒə'ræf/ *noun* [C] (*pl* **giraffe** or **giraffes**) an African animal with a very long neck and legs and dark spots on its skin

girder /'gɜːdə(r)/ *noun* [C] a long iron or steel bar that is used in the construction of bridges, large buildings, etc

☆ **girl** /gɜːl/ *noun* [C] **1** a female child: *the little girl who lives next door* ∘ *There are more boys than girls in the class.* **2** a daughter: *They have two boys and a girl.* **3** a young woman: *He was eighteen before he became interested in girls.* ∘ *The girl at the cash desk was very helpful.* **4 the girls** [plural] female friends of any age: *a night out with the girls*

girlhood /'gɜːlhʊd/ *noun* [U] the time when sb is a girl

girlish *adj* of or like a girl

girlfriend *noun* [C] **1** a girl or woman with whom sb has a romantic and/or sexual relationship **2** (*US*) a girl or woman's female friend

Girl 'Guide (*also* **Guide**) (*US* **Girl 'Scout**) *noun* [C] a member of an organization for girls that encourages helpfulness and teaches practical skills ☛ Look at **Boy Scout**.

giro /'dʒaɪrəʊ/ *noun* (*pl* **giros**) (*Brit*) **1** [U] the system for transferring money from one bank, etc to another **2** [C] a cheque for money that is given by the government to people who are ill, unemployed, etc

gist /dʒɪst/ *noun* **the gist** [sing] the general meaning of sth rather than all the details: *I know a little Spanish so I was able to get the gist of what he said.*

☆ **give**¹ /gɪv/ *verb* (*pt* **gave** /geɪv/; *pp* **given** /'gɪvn/) **1** [T] **give sb sth; give sth to sb** to hand sth to sb as a present; to allow sb to have sth as a present: *My parents gave me a watch for my birthday.* ∘ *We don't usually give presents to all our nephews and nieces.* ∘ *She gave most of her money to cancer research.* **2** [T] **give sb sth; give sth to sb** to hand sth to sb so that he/she can look at it, use it or keep it for a time: *Could you give me that book over there, please?* ∘ *I gave my ticket to the lady at the check-in desk.* **3** [T] **give sb sth; give sth to sb** to provide sb with sth he/she wants, asks for or pays for: *He was thirsty so I gave him a drink.* ∘ *I hope the doctor will give me some new tablets.* ∘ *She gives Italian lessons to the people at work.* ∘ *He didn't give me the chance to reply.* ∘ *Could you give me some help with this essay?* **4** [T] **give sth to sb/sth** to spend time, etc on sb/sth: *I can only give you ten minutes.* ∘ *We'll have to give some more thought to the matter* (= think about it more). **5** [T] **give (sb) sth for sth** to pay: *How much would you give me for my old car?* **6** [T] **give sb sth** to cause sb/sth to have or feel sth: *The news about his father gave him a terrible shock.* ∘ *Hard work gives you an appetite.* ∘ *That noise is giving me a headache.* ∘ *She gave me the impression that she was thinking of leaving her job.* **7** [T] **give sb sth; give sb sth; give sth to sb/sth** to perform an action: *When the child saw the snow, he gave a shout of delight.* ∘ *to give a sigh* ∘ *to give a cry of pain* ∘ *She gave my hand a squeeze* (= she squeezed it). ∘ *They gave us a warm welcome.* ∘ *I asked a short question and he gave me a very long answer.* ∘ *She gave him a kiss.* **8** [T] to perform sth in public: *He gave a very interesting lecture on India.* ∘ *They're giving* (= having) *a party for their son's eighteenth birthday.* **9** [I] to bend or stretch under pressure: *The branch began to give under his weight.*

(IDIOMS) **not care/give a damn (about sb/ sth)** ⇒DAMN

give or take more or less the number mentioned: *It took us two hours to get here, give or take five minutes.*

give sb to believe/understand (that)... (often passive) to give sb the impression that sth is true: *He gave me to understand that I had got the job.*

☛ For other idioms containing **give**, look at the entries for the nouns, adjectives, etc, eg **give way** is at **way**.

(PHRASAL VERBS) **give sb away** (at a wedding in a church) to go with the bride into the church and officially give her to the bridegroom during the marriage ceremony: *Her father gave her away.*

give sth away to give sth, often sth that you no longer want, to sb without asking for or receiving money in return: *When she got older she gave all her toys away.* ∘ *We are giving a shirt away with every suit purchased.*

give sth/sb away to show or tell the truth about sth/sb which was secret: *He smiled politely and didn't give away his real feelings.*

iː	ɪ	e	æ	ɑː	ɒ	ɔː	ʊ	uː	ʌ
see	sit	ten	hat	arm	got	saw	put	too	cup

give sb sth back; give sth back (to sb) to return sth to the person from whom you took or borrowed it: *I lent him some books months ago and he still hasn't given them back to me.*

give sth in to hand sth to the authority collecting it: *I've got to give this essay in to my teacher by Friday.*

give in (to sb/sth) to stop fighting against sb/sth; to accept that you have been defeated

give sth off to send sth out (eg a smell, heat, etc) out into the air

give out (used about a machine) to stop working

give sth out to hand or pass sth to people: *Could you give out these books to the class, please?*

give up to stop trying to do sth; to accept that you cannot do sth: *They gave up once the other team had scored their third goal.* ○ *Don't give up now, you're improving all the time.* ○ *I give up. What's the answer?*

give sb up to stop expecting sb to arrive, succeed, improve or recover: *When he was four hours late, I gave him up.* ○ *Her work was so poor that all her teachers gave her up.* ○ *The doctors had given him up when he suddenly started to get better.*

give up sth to stop doing or having sth that you had done or had regularly before: *I've tried many times to give up smoking.* ○ *Don't give up hope. Things are bound to improve.*

give yourself/sb up (to sb) to go to the police when they are trying to catch you; to tell the police where sb is: *The suspected murderer gave himself up to the police.*

give sth up (to sb) to give sth to sb who needs or asks for it: *He gave up his seat on the bus to an elderly woman.*

give² /gɪv/ *noun* [U] the quality of being able to bend or stretch a little: *The leather has plenty of give in it.*

(IDIOM) **give and take** the willingness, within a relationship, to move towards another person's point of view because he/she is willing to move towards your point of view: *This dispute can only be settled if there is give and take on both sides.*

given /'gɪvn/ *adj* (only *before* a noun) already stated or fixed: *At a given time they all waved their flags and cheered.*

given *prep* taking sth into consideration: *Given that you had very little help, I think you did very well under the circumstances.*

'given name *noun* [C] (*especially US*) = CHRISTIAN NAME ☞ Look at the note at name.

glacial /'gleɪsɪəl/ *adj* **1** caused by ice or a glacier: *a glacial valley* **2** very cold; like ice: *glacial winds*

glacier /'glæsɪə(r)/ *noun* [C] a mass of ice that moves slowly down a valley

☆ **glad** /glæd/ *adj* (**gladder**; **gladdest**) **1** (not before a noun) **glad (about sth); glad (to do sth/that...)** happy; pleased: *Are you glad about your new job?* ○ *I'm glad to hear he's feeling better.* ○ *I'm glad (that) he's feeling better.* ○ *We'd be glad to see you if you're in the area.* ☞ You are usually **glad** or **pleased** about a particular event or situation. **Happy** is used for describing a state, condition of mind, etc and it *can* be used before the noun it describes: *This kind of music always makes me feel happy.* ○ *She's such a happy child – she's always laughing.* **2 glad (of sth)** grateful for sth: *If you are free, I'd be glad of some help.* **3** (only *before* a noun) bringing happiness: *I want to be the first to tell her the glad news.*

gladden /'glædn/ *verb* [T] to make sb glad or happy

gladly *adv* (usually used for politely agreeing to a request or accepting an invitation) happily; gratefully: *We will gladly help you if we can.* ○ *'Can you join us tonight?' 'Gladly.'* ○ *She gladly accepted the invitation to stay the night.* —**gladness** *noun* [U]

glade /gleɪd/ *noun* [C] (*formal*) an open space in a forest or wood where there are no trees ☞ **Clearing** is similar in meaning.

gladiator /'glædɪeɪtə(r)/ *noun* [C] (in ancient Rome) a man who fought against another man or a wild animal in a public show

glamour (*US also* **glamor**) /'glæmə(r)/ *noun* [U] the quality of seeming to be exciting or attractive: *Young people are often attracted by the glamour of city life.*

glamorize (*also* **glamorise**) /-məraɪz/ *verb* [T] to make sth appear more attractive or exciting that it really is: *Television tends to glamorize violence.*

glamorous /-mərəs/ *adj* attractive or full of glamour: *She didn't look very glamorous without her make-up.* ○ *a glamorous job* —**glamorously** *adv*

☆ **glance** /glɑːns; *US* glæns/ *verb* [I] to take a quick look: *She glanced round the room to see if they were there.* ○ *He glanced at her and smiled.* ○ *The receptionist glanced down the list of names.*

(PHRASAL VERB) **glance off (sth)** to hit sth at an angle and move off again in another direction: *The ball glanced off the goalpost and into the net.*

glance *noun* [C] a quick look: *I only had time for a glance at the newspaper.* ○ *They exchanged glances when no one was looking.* ○ *She stole a glance at her watch.*

(IDIOMS) **at a (single) glance** with one look: *I could tell at a glance that something was wrong.*

at first glance/sight ⇨ FIRST¹

gland /glænd/ *noun* [C] a small part (**an organ**) of the body that separates these substances from the blood that will be used by the body or removed from it: *sweat glands* ○ *the poison glands of a snake* ○ *swollen glands* (eg in your throat)

glare /gleə(r)/ *noun* **1** [U] strong light that hurts your eyes: *the glare of the sun on snow* ○ *the glare of a car's headlights* **2** [C] a (long) angry look

glare /gleə(r)/ *verb* [I] **1** to shine with strong light that hurts your eyes **2 glare (at sb/sth)** to stare at sb angrily: *They stood glaring at each other.*

glaring /'gleərɪŋ/ *adj* **1** (used about a light, etc) too strong and bright **2** angry: *glaring eyes* **3** great or very noticeable: *a glaring mistake*

☆ **glass** /glɑːs; *US* glæs/ *noun* **1** [U] a hard,

glasses

usually transparent, substance that windows, bottles, etc are made of: *He cut himself on broken glass.* ○ *a sheet/pane of glass* ○ *In case of emergency, break the glass and press the button.* ○ *a glass jar, dish, etc* **2** [C] a drinking container made of glass; the amount of liquid it contains: *a wineglass, champagne glass, brandy glass, etc* ○ *Could I have a glass of water, please?* **3 glassware** [U] a collection of objects made of glass

glassful /-fʊl/ *noun* [C] the amount of liquid that one glass(2) holds

glass 'fibre = FIBREGLASS

'glasshouse *noun* [C] a building with glass sides and roof for growing plants ☞ It is also called a **greenhouse**.

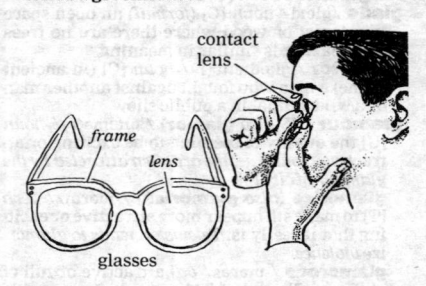

☆**glasses** /'glɑːsɪz; *US* 'glæsɪz/ (*also* **spectacles**, *informal* **specs**; *US also* **eyeglasses**) *noun* [plural] a pair of lenses in a frame that a person wears in front of his/her eyes (in order to be able to see better): *My sister has to wear glasses.* ○ *I've lost my glasses.* ○ *reading glasses* ○ *dark glasses/sunglasses* ○ *Where's my glasses case?* ☞ **Glasses** is more commonly used than **spectacles**. **Specs** is informal. **Glasses** is always plural so we cannot use it with the article *a*. We cannot say: *I need a new glasses.* We can say: *I need a new pair of glasses.*

glassy /'glɑːsɪ/ *adj* (**glassier**; **glassiest**) **1** looking like glass: *a glassy sea* **2** (used about the eyes) showing no interest or expression: *a glassy stare*

glaze /gleɪz/ *verb* [T] **1** to fit a sheet of glass into a window, etc ☞ Look at **double-glazing**. **2 glaze sth (with sth)** to cover a pot, brick, pie, etc with a shiny transparent substance (before it is put into an oven): *Glaze the pie with beaten egg.*

(PHRASAL VERB) **glaze over** (used about the eyes) to show no interest or expression

glaze *noun* [C,U] (a substance that gives) a shiny transparent surface on a pot, brick, pie, etc

glazed *adj* (used about the eyes, etc) showing no interest or expression

glazier /'gleɪzɪə(r); *US* -ʒər/ *noun* [C] a person whose job is to fit glass into windows, etc

gleam /gliːm/ *noun* **1** [C,sing] a soft light (that shines for a short time): *the first gleams of the morning sun* ○ *the gleam of moonlight on the water* **2** [sing] a brief or sudden show of a quality or emotion: *a gleam of hope, interest, etc*

gleam *verb* [I] **1** to shine softly: *The water of the lake gleamed in the moonlight.* **2 gleam with sth** (used about the face or eyes) to show a particular (happy) emotion: *Their eyes gleamed with pleasure.*

gleaming *adj* shining: *gleaming white teeth*

glee /gliː/ *noun* [U] a feeling of joy or happiness (at sth good that has happened to you or at sth bad that has happened to sb else): *The children laughed with glee at the clown's tricks.* ○ *She couldn't hide her glee when her rival came last in the race.* —**gleeful** /-fl/ *adj* —**gleefully** /-fəlɪ/ *adv*

glen /glen/ *noun* [C] a narrow mountain valley (in Scotland or Ireland)

glib /glɪb/ *adj* (**glibber**; **glibbest**) **1** (used about a person) speaking quickly and cleverly, in a way that will persuade people but that is not always truthful: *a glib salesman, politician, etc* **2** spoken quickly and without hesitation, but not always truthful: *a glib answer, excuse, etc* —**glibly** *adv* —**glibness** *noun* [U] ☞ Using the word *glib* shows that you have a low opinion of the person or thing you are describing.

glide /glaɪd/ *verb* [I] **1** to move smoothly without noise or effort: *The dancers glided across the floor.* ○ *The yachts went gliding past.* **2** to fly in a glider

glider /'glaɪdə(r)/ *noun* [C] a light aeroplane without an engine that flies using air currents

gliding *noun* [U] the sport of flying in gliders ☞ Look at **hang-gliding**.

glimmer /'glɪmə(r)/ *verb* [I] to give out a weak unsteady light

glimmer *noun* [C] **1** a weak unsteady light **2** a weak sign of sth: *a glimmer of hope*

glimpse /glɪmps/ *noun* [C] **a glimpse (at/of sth)** a quick incomplete view of sb/sth ☞ Most often used in the phrase **catch a glimpse of**: *I caught a glimpse of myself in the mirror as I walked past.*

glimpse *verb* [T] to get a quick look at sb/sth (often by chance): *I glimpsed Cathy in the crowd, but I don't think she saw me.*

glint /glɪnt/ *verb* [I] to give out small bright flashes of light: *She thought the diamond was lost until she saw something glinting on the carpet.* ○ (*figurative*) *His eyes glinted at the thought of all that money.* —**glint** *noun* [C]: *the glint of metal in the grass* ○ (*figurative*) *a glint of anger in his eyes*

glisten /'glɪsn/ *verb* [I] (used about wet surfaces) to shine: *Her eyes glistened with tears.* ○ *Tears glistened in her eyes.*

glitter /'glɪtə(r)/ *verb* [I] to give out many little flashes of light: *The stars glittered in the frosty sky.* —**glitter** *noun* [U]: *the glitter of jewellery* ○ (*figurative*) *the glitter of a career in show business*

glittering /'glɪtərɪŋ/ *adj* **1** shining brightly with many little flashes of light: *a glittering Christmas tree* **2** splendid or successful: *a glittering career, performance, etc*

gloat /gləʊt/ *verb* [I] **gloat (about/over sth)** to feel or express pleasure at sth good that has happened to you or at sth bad that has happened to sb else: *Don't gloat – you might be in* *the same position yourself some time.* —**gloatingly** *adv*

global /'gləʊbl/ *adj* **1** affecting the whole world: *the global effects of pollution* ○ *global warming* **2** affecting the whole of a group of facts, possibilities, etc: *We must take a global view of the problem.* —**globally** /-bəli/ *adv*

globe /gləʊb/ *noun* **1** [C] a model of the earth, in the shape of a ball, with the continents, etc painted on it **2 the globe** [sing] the earth: *to travel (all) over the globe* ○ *With the help of television, we can see things that are going on on the other side of the globe.*

globe 'artichoke *noun* [C] = ARTICHOKE

globe-trotter /'gləʊb trɒtə(r)/ *noun* [C] (*informal*) a person who travels to many countries

globule /'glɒbjuːl/ *noun* [C] a small drop or ball of a liquid or melted solid: *There were globules of fat in the soup.*

gloom /gluːm/ *noun* [U] **1** a feeling of sadness or hopelessness: *The news brought deep gloom to the village.* **2** (near) darkness: *It was hard to see anything in the gloom.*

gloomy /'gluːmɪ/ *adj* (**gloomier**; **gloomiest**) **1** dark (and depressing): *What a gloomy day!* ○ *This dark paint makes the room very gloomy.* **2** (making sb feel) sad or depressed: *For many young people leaving school, the prospects of finding work are gloomy.* ○ *Don't be so gloomy – cheer up!* —**gloomily** /-ɪlɪ/ *adv* —**gloominess** *noun* [U]

glorify /'glɔːrɪfaɪ/ *verb* (*pres part* **glorifying**; *3rd pers sing pres* **glorifies**; *pt, pp* **glorified**) [T] **1** (*formal*) to praise sb/sth highly **2** to make sb/sth appear better or more important than he/she/it really is: *His biography does not attempt to glorify his early career.*

glorified /'glɔːrɪfaɪd/ *adj* (only *before* a noun) described in a way that makes sb/sth seem better, bigger, more important, etc than he/she/it really is: *The 'holiday cottage' turned out to be a glorified barn.* ○ *An air hostess is really just a glorified waitress.*

glorious /'glɔːrɪəs/ *adj* **1** having or deserving fame or glory: *a glorious victory* **2** wonderful or splendid: *What glorious weather!* ○ *a glorious day, view, etc* —**gloriously** *adv*

☆**glory** /'glɔːrɪ/ *noun* [U] **1** fame or honour that is won by great achievements: *The winning team was welcomed home in a blaze of glory.* **2** great beauty: *Autumn is the best time to see the forest in all its glory.*

glory *verb* (*pres part* **glorying**; *3rd pers sing pres* **glories**; *pt, pp* **gloried**)
(PHRASAL VERB) **glory in sth** to take (too much) pleasure or pride in sth: *He gloried in his sporting successes.*

gloss /glɒs/ *noun* [U,sing] (a substance that gives) brightness or shine on a surface: *the gloss on wood, hair, silk, etc* ○ *gloss paint* ○ *gloss photographs* ☛ Look at **matt**.

gloss *verb*
(PHRASAL VERB) **gloss over sth** to avoid talking about a problem, mistake, etc in detail

glossy *adj* (**glossier**; **glossiest**) **1** smooth and shiny: *glossy hair* **2** (used about a magazine, etc) printed on good quality paper and having many colour photographs

glossary /'glɒsərɪ/ *noun* [C] (*pl* **glossaries**) a list of special or unusual words and their meanings (at the end of a book)

☆**glove** /glʌv/ *noun* [C] a piece of clothing that covers your hand (and has separate parts for the thumb and each finger): *I need a new pair of gloves for the winter.* ☛ Look at **mitten**.

☆**glow** /gləʊ/ *verb* [I] **1** to give out light and/or heat without smoke or flames: *A cigarette glowed in the dark.* **2 glow (with sth)** to be warm or red because of excitement, exercise, etc: *to glow with health, enthusiasm, pride, etc*

glow *noun* [sing] **1** a warm light: *the glow of the sky at sunset* **2** a feeling or look of warmth or satisfaction: *a rosy glow on the children's cheeks*

glowing *adj* giving high praise; favourable: *His teacher wrote a glowing report about his work.* —**glowingly** *adv*

glower /'glaʊə(r)/ *verb* [I] to look angrily (at sb/sth)

glucose /'gluːkəʊs/ *noun* [U] a type of sugar that is found in fruit

glue /gluː/ *noun* [U] a thick sticky liquid that is used for joining things together: *You can make glue from flour and water.* ○ *Stick the photo in with glue.*

glue *verb* [T] (*pres part* **gluing**) **glue A (to/ onto B)**; **glue A and B (together)** to join a thing or things together with glue: *Do you think you can glue the handle back onto the teapot?*
(IDIOM) **glued to sth** (*informal*) giving all your attention to sth and unwilling to leave it: *He just sits there every evening glued to the television.*

'glue-sniffing *noun* [U] breathing in the chemicals that are given off by glue to get the same effect as that produced by alcohol or drugs

glum /glʌm/ *adj* (**glummer**; **glummest**) (*informal*) sad or disappointed: *What are you looking so glum about?* —**glumly** *adv* —**glumness** *noun* [U]

glut /glʌt/ *noun* [C, usually sing] more of sth than is needed: *The glut of coffee has forced down the price.*

glutton /'glʌtn/ *noun* [C] **1** a person who eats too much **2 a glutton for sth** (*informal*) a person who is willing to have or do more of sth difficult, unpleasant, etc: *She's a glutton for hard work – she never stops.*

gluttony /-tənɪ/ *noun* [U] the habit of eating too much

gnarled /nɑːld/ *adj* rough and twisted, because of old age or hard work: *The old man had gnarled fingers.* ○ *a gnarled oak-tree*

gnash /næʃ/ *verb*
(IDIOM) **gnash your teeth** to make a noise with your teeth because of anger, pain, worry, etc

gnat /næt/ *noun* [C] a small insect like a mosquito, that stings

gnaw /nɔː/ *verb* [I,T] **gnaw (at) sth** to bite a bone, etc many times: *The dog lay on the carpet gnawing its bone.* ○ (*figurative*) *Fear of the future gnawed away at her all the time.*

gnome /nəʊm/ noun [C] (in children's stories, etc) a little old man with a beard and a pointed hat who lives under the ground: *a garden gnome* (= a model of a gnome that is used to decorate a garden)

☆ **go¹** /gəʊ/ verb [I] (pres part **going**; 3rd pers sing pres **goes**; pt **went** /went/; pp **gone** /gɒn/; US gɔːn/) **1** to move or travel from one place to another: *She always goes home by bus.* ○ *We're going to London tomorrow.* ○ *He went to the cinema yesterday.* ○ *We've still got fifty miles to go.* ○ *How fast does this car go?* ☛ **Been** is used as the past participle of **go** when somebody has travelled to a place and has returned. **Gone** means that somebody has travelled to a place but has not yet returned: *I've just been to Berlin. I got back this morning.* ○ *John's gone to Peru. He'll be back in two weeks.* **2** to travel to a place to take part in an activity or do sth: *Are you going to Dave's party?* ○ *Shall we go swimming this afternoon?* ○ *Let's go for a drive.* ○ *My aunt has gone on a cruise.* ○ *They've gone on holiday.* ○ *We went to watch the match.* ○ *I'll go and make the tea.* **3** to visit or attend a place regularly: *Does Simon go to school yet?* **4** to leave a place: *I have to go now. It's nearly 4 o'clock.* **5** to lead to or reach a place or time: *Where does this road go to?* ○ *This cut on my hand goes quite deep.* **6** to have as its usual place: *Where does this vase go?* **7** to fit into a space: *My clothes won't all go in one suitcase.* **8** to happen in a particular way; to develop: *How's the new job going?* ○ *My work's going well.* **9** to work correctly: *This clock doesn't go.* **10** to become; to reach a particular state: *Her hair is going grey.* ○ *He went blind when he was 20.* ○ *Everybody thought that we had gone mad.* ○ *The baby has gone to sleep.* **11** to remain in the state mentioned: *Many mistakes go unnoticed.* **12** to disappear: *Has your headache gone yet?* **13** to become worse or stop working correctly: *The brakes on the car have gone.* **14** to look or taste good with sth else: *Does this sweater go with my skirt?* **15** to have certain words or a certain tune: *How does that song go?* **16** to make a sound: *The bell went early today.* ○ *Cats go 'miaow'.* **17** (used about time) to pass: *The last hour went very slowly.* ○ *There's only one minute left to go.*

(IDIOMS) **as people, things, etc go** compared to the average person or thing: *As Chinese restaurants go, it wasn't bad.*

be going to do sth 1 (used for showing what you plan to do in the future): *We're going to sell our car.* **2** (used for saying that you are sure sth will happen): *It's going to rain soon.* ○ *Oh no! He's going to fall!*

go all out for sth; **go all out to do sth** to make a great effort to do sth

have a lot going for you to have many advantages

Here goes! (said just before you start to do sth difficult or exciting)

☛ For other idioms containing **go**, look at the entries for nouns, adjectives, etc, for example **go astray** is at **astray**.

(PHRASAL VERBS) **go about** ⇨ GO ROUND/AROUND/ABOUT

go about sth to continue to do what you usually do: *We went about our normal routine.*

go about sth/doing sth to start trying to do sth difficult: *I wouldn't have any idea how to go about building a house.*

go about with sb ⇨ GO ROUND/AROUND/ABOUT WITH SB

go against sb to be unfavourable to sb: *The referee's decision went against him.*

go against sb/sth to do sth that is opposed to sb/sth: *She went against her parents' wishes and married him.*

go against sth to be opposed or opposite to sth; not to be in agreement with sth: *It goes against my principles to use violence.*

go ahead to take place after being planned: *Although several members were missing, the meeting went ahead without them.*

go ahead (with sth) to begin to do sth that you have planned

go along to continue: *The course gets more difficult as you go along.*

go along with sb/sth to agree with sb/sth: *I'm happy to go along with whatever you suggest.*

go around ⇨ GO ROUND/AROUND/ABOUT

go around with sb ⇨ GO ROUND/AROUND/ABOUT WITH SB

go away 1 to leave the place where you live (eg for a holiday) for a period of time of at least one night: *We're going away this weekend and we'll be back on Sunday evening.* **2** to disappear: *I've tried to remove the stain in the carpet but it won't go away.*

go back (to...) to return (to a place): *It's a wonderful city and I'd like to go back there one day.*

go back (to sth) 1 to return to a previous matter or situation: *Let's go back to the subject we were discussing a few minutes ago.* **2** to have its origins in a previous period of time: *A lot of the buildings in the village go back to the fifteenth century.*

go back on sth to break a promise, an agreement, etc: *I promised to help them and I can't go back on it now.*

go back to sth/to doing sth to start doing again sth that you had stopped doing: *When the children got a bit older she went back to full-time work.*

go by 1 (used about time) to pass: *As time went by, her confidence grew.* **2** to pass a place: *She stood at the window watching people go by.*

go by sth 1 to obey, follow or be guided by sth: *You can't go by the railway timetables, the trains are very unreliable.* **2** to form an opinion according to a particular thing: *There are no clues so the police have nothing to go by.*

go down 1 (used about a ship, etc) to sink **2** (used about the sun) to disappear from the sky **3** to become lower in price, level, etc; to fall: *The price of these computers has gone down in the last two years.* ○ *The number of people out of work went down last month.*

go down (with sb) (used with adverbs, especially 'well' or 'badly' or in questions beginning with 'how') (used about sth that is said, a

| iː | ɪ | e | æ | ɑː | ɒ | ɔː | ʊ | uː | ʌ |
| see | sit | ten | hat | arm | got | saw | put | too | cup |

performance, etc) to be received by sb: *The film went down well with the critics.*
go down with sth to catch an illness; to become ill with sth: *Ten of our staff have gone down with flu.*
go for sb to attack sb
go for sb/sth to be true for a particular person or thing: *We've got financial problems but I suppose the same goes for a great many people.*
go in (used about the sun) to disappear behind a cloud
go in for sth 1 to enter or take part in an examination or competition **2** to start a career in sth: *He has decided to go in for journalism.*
go in for sth/doing sth to do or have sth as a hobby or interest: *He doesn't go in for sport much.*
go into sth 1 to start working in a certain type of job: *When she left school she went into nursing.* **2** to look at or describe sth in detail: *I haven't got time to go into all the details now.*
go off 1 to explode: *A bomb has gone off in the city centre.* **2** to make a sudden loud noise: *I woke up when my alarm clock went off.* **3** (used about lights, heating, etc) to stop working: *There was a power cut and all the lights went off.* **4** (used about food and drink) to become too old to eat or drink; to go bad **5** (used about an event) to take place or happen in a certain way: *I think their wedding went off very well.*
go off sb/sth to stop liking or being interested in sb/sth
go off with sth to take sth that belongs to sb else: *Who's gone off with my cup?*
go on 1 (used about lights, heating, etc) to start working: *I saw the lights go on in the house opposite.* **2** (used about time) to pass: *As time went on, she became more and more successful.* **3** (used especially in the continuous tenses) to happen or take place: *Can anybody tell me what's going on here?* **4** (used about a situation) to continue without changing: *This is a difficult period but it won't go on forever.* **5** to continue speaking after stopping briefly: *Go on. What happened next?* **6** (used as an order for encouraging sb to do sth): *Oh go on, let me borrow your car. I'll bring it back in an hour.*
go on sth to use sth as information so that you can understand a situation: *There were no witnesses to the crime, so the police had very little to go on.*
go on (about sb/sth) to talk about sb/sth for a long time in a boring or annoying way: *She went on and on about the people she works with.* o *I know I've made a mistake, there's no need to go on about it.*
go on (at sb) (about sth) to keep complaining about sth: *His parents are always going on at him to dress more smartly.*
go on (with sth) to continue doing sth, perhaps after a pause or break: *She ignored me and went on with her meal.*
go on doing sth to continue doing sth without stopping or changing: *We don't want to go on living here for the rest of our lives.*
go out 1 to leave the place where you live or work for a short time, returning on the same day: *Let's go out for a meal tonight* (= to a restaurant). o *I'm just going out for a walk, I won't be long.* **2** (used about the tide) to move away from the land: *The sea was a long way away because the tide had gone out.* **3** to stop being fashionable or in use: *That kind of music went out in the seventies.* o *Teaching methods like that went out years ago.* **4** to stop shining or burning: *Suddenly all the lights went out.*
go out with sb; go out (together) to spend time regularly with sb, having a romantic and/or sexual relationship: *He's going out with Jill Brown now.* o *They went out together for five years before they got married.*
go over sth to look at, think about or discuss sth carefully from beginning to end: *Go over your work before you hand it in.*
go round (used especially after 'enough') to be shared among all the people: *In this area, there aren't enough jobs to go round.*
go round/around/about 1 (used about a story, a belief, etc) to pass from person to person: *There's a rumour going round that he's going to resign.* **2** (used about an illness) to pass from person to person in a group or area: *There's a virus going round at work.*
go round (to...) to visit sb's home, usually a short distance away: *I'm going round to Jo's for dinner tonight.*
go round/around/about with sb to spend time and go to places regularly with sb: *Her parents don't like the people she has started going round with.*
go through to be completed successfully: *The deal went through as agreed.*
go through sth 1 to look in or at sth carefully, especially in order to find sth: *I went through all my pockets but I couldn't find my wallet.* **2** to look at, think about or discuss sth carefully from beginning to end: *Let's go through the arrangements for the trip again.* o *We'll start the lesson by going through your homework.* **3** to suffer an unpleasant experience: *I'd hate to go through such a terrible ordeal again.*
go through with sth to do sth unpleasant or difficult that you have decided, agreed or threatened to do: *Do you think she'll go through with her threat to leave him?*
go together (used about two or more things) **1** to belong to the same set or group **2** to look good together
go towards sth to be used as part of the payment for sth: *The money I was given for my birthday went towards my new bike.*
go under 1 to sink below the surface of water **2** (*informal*) (used about a company) to go out of business: *A lot of firms are going under in the recession.*
go up 1 to start burning suddenly and strongly: *The car crashed into a wall and went up in flames.* **2** to become higher in price, level, amount, etc; to rise: *Petrol has gone up again.* o *The birth rate has gone up by 10%.*
go with sth 1 to be included with sth; to happen as a result of sth: *Pressure goes with the job.* **2** to match or be suitable with sth: *What colour carpet would go with the walls?*
go without (sth) to manage without having

sth: *They went without sleep many nights when the baby was ill.*

'go-ahead *noun* [sing] permission to do sth: *We've been given the go-ahead for the new building.*

'go-ahead *adj* willing to try new ways of doing things

go² /gəʊ/ *noun* (*pl* **goes** /gəʊz/) **1** [C] a turn to play in a game, etc: *Whose go is it?* ○ *Hurry up – it's your go.* ☞ **Turn** has the same meaning. **2** [C] (*informal*) an occasion when you try to do sth: *Andrew passed his driving-test first go.* **3** [U] (*informal*) energy: *He's full of go.*

(IDIOMS) **be on the go** (*informal*) to be very active or busy: *I'm exhausted. I've been on the go all day.*

to have a go (at sth/doing sth) (*informal*) to try to do sth: *I'm not sure if I can fix it, but I'll have a go.*

goad /gəʊd/ *verb* [T] **to goad sb/sth (into sth/doing sth)** to cause sb to do sth by making him/her angry

☆ **goal** /gəʊl/ *noun* [C] **1** (in football, rugby, hockey, etc) the area between two posts into which the ball must be kicked, hit, etc for a point to be scored: *Who's in goal for Real Madrid?* ☞ picture at **football**. **2** a point that is scored when the ball goes into the goal: *Everton won by three goals to two.* ○ *to score a goal an own goal* (= when a player kicks, hits, etc the ball into his/her own goal) **3** your purpose or aim: *I've finally achieved my goal of visiting all the capital cities of Europe.*

goalless /'gəʊlɪs/ *adj* with no goal scored: *a goalless draw*

'goalkeeper (also *informal* **goalie** /'gəʊli/ or **keeper**) *noun* [C] the player who stands in front of the goal(1) and tries to stop the other team from scoring a goal(2): *The goalkeeper made a magnificent save.* ☞ picture at **football**.

'goalpost *noun* [C] one of the two posts that form the sides of a goal. They are joined together by a bar (**the crossbar**).

goat — horn
bell
kid   goat

goat /gəʊt/ *noun* [C] a small animal with horns which lives in mountainous areas or is kept on farms for its milk and meat

gobble /'gɒbl/ *verb* [I,T] (*informal*) **gobble sth (up/down)** to eat quickly and noisily: *He'd gobbled down all his food before I'd started mine.*

gobbledegook (also **gobbledygook**) /'gɒbldɪguːk/ *noun* [U] (*informal*) official language that is hard to understand

go-between /'gəʊ bɪtwiːn/ *noun* [C] a person who takes messages between two people or groups who do not or cannot meet: *In some countries, marriages are arranged by go-betweens.*

goblin /'gɒblɪn/ *noun* [C] (in stories) a small ugly creature who plays tricks on people

☆ **god** /gɒd/ *noun* **1** (*feminine* **goddess**) [C] a being or force who is worshipped by a group of people and who is believed to have the power to control nature and human affairs: *Mars was the Roman god of war and Venus was the goddess of love.* **2 God** [sing] (in Christianity, Islam and Judaism) the creator and ruler of all things: *Do you believe in God?* ○ *Muslims worship God in a mosque.* ○ *God the Father, God the Son and God the Holy Ghost* ☞ 'God' is used in a number of expressions. (Some people think that it is wrong to use God's name in this way.) *Oh my God!* expresses surprise or shock: *Oh my God! I've won £1000!* We use *thank God* when we are happy and relieved about something: *Thank God you've arrived – I was beginning to think you'd had an accident.* The expression *God forbid!* is used when we say that we don't want something to happen: *'I'm going to invite 50 people to the party'. 'God forbid!'* We use *'for God's sake'* when we are asking somebody to do something and want to sound more urgent or when we are angry with somebody: *For God's sake, shut up!*

'godchild, **'god-daughter**, **'godson** *noun* [C] a person for whom a godparent takes responsibility at a Christian baptism (or christening)

'godfather, **'godmother**, **'godparent** *noun* [C] a person who promises to take responsibility for a child (at his/her baptism or christening) and to make sure that he/she is educated as a Christian

goddess /'gɒdɪs/ *noun* [C] a female god

god-forsaken /'gɒd fəseɪkən/ *adj* (used about a place) depressing or having nothing of interest

godsend /'gɒdsend/ *noun* [C] something unexpected that is a great help to you because it comes just when it is needed: *The extra money was a real godsend just before Christmas.*

goggle /'gɒgl/ *verb* [I] to look at sb/sth with wide round eyes (in surprise)

goggles /'gɒglz/ *noun* [plural] special glasses that you wear to protect your eyes from water, wind, dust, etc ☞ Look at **mask**.

going¹ /'gəʊɪŋ/ *noun* **1** [sing] (*formal*) the act of leaving a place; departure: *We were all saddened by his going.* **2** [U] the rate or speed of travel, progress, etc: *Oxford to London in an hour? That's very good going.* ○ *Three children in four years? That's not bad going!* **3** [U] the condition of a path, the ground, etc: *The mud made the path very hard going.* ○ (*figurative*) *It'll be hard going if we need to finish this by Friday!* ○ (*figurative*) *I'm finding this novel very heavy going* (= difficult and not very interesting).

(IDIOM) **get out, go, leave, etc while the going is good** to leave a place or stop doing sth while it is still easy to do so

goings-'on *noun* [plural] (*informal*) unusual

p	b	t	d	k	g	tʃ	dʒ	f	v	θ	ð
pen	bad	tea	did	cat	got	chin	June	fall	van	thin	then

things that are happening: *The old lady was shocked by the goings-on in the house next door.*

going² /'gəʊɪŋ/ *adj* (IDIOMS) **a going concern** a successful business

the going rate (for sth) the usual cost (of sth): *The going rate for a cleaner is about £3 an hour.*

go-kart /'gəʊkɑːt/ *noun* [C] a very small racing car with no roof

☆ **gold** /gəʊld/ *noun* **1** [U] a precious yellow metal that is used for making coins, jewellery, etc: *Is your bracelet made of gold?* ○ *solid, pure, 22-carat, etc gold* ○ *What's the price of gold today?* ○ *a gold chain, ring, watch, etc* **2** [C] = GOLD MEDAL

(IDIOM) **(as) good as gold** very well-behaved: *The children were as good as gold while you were out.*

gold *adj* the colour of gold: *The invitation was written in gold letters.* ☞ Look at **golden**.

,**gold-'dust** *noun* [U] gold in the form of powder: *(figurative) Good English teachers are like gold-dust* (= very hard to find).

,**gold 'medal** (*also* **gold**) *noun* [C] the prize for first place in a sports competition: *How many gold medals did we win in the 1992 Olympics?* ☞ Look at **silver medal** and **bronze medal**.

,**gold 'medallist** *noun* [C] the winner of a gold medal

,**gold-mine** *noun* [C] a place where gold is mined

☆ **golden** /'gəʊldən/ *adj* made of gold or like gold: *a golden crown* ○ *golden hair* ○ *(figurative) a golden* (= excellent) *opportunity*

,**golden 'jubilee** *noun* [C] a 50th anniversary ☞ Look at **silver jubilee**.

,**golden 'wedding** *noun* [C] the 50th anniversary of a wedding ☞ Look at **diamond wedding** and **silver wedding**.

goldfish /'gəʊldfɪʃ/ *noun* [C] (*pl* **goldfish**) a small orange fish that is kept as a pet in a bowl or pond

☆ **golf** /gɒlf/ *noun* [U] a game that is played outdoors on a large area of grass (**a golf-course**) and in which you use a stick (**a golf club**) to hit a small hard ball (**a golf ball**) into a series of holes (usually 18): *to play a round of golf* ○ *a golf club* (= a club for golfers; the place where they meet and play golf)

golfer *noun* [C] a person who plays golf

golly /'gɒli/ *interj* (*informal*) (used for expressing surprise)

gone¹ *pp* of GO

gone² /gɒn; *US* gɔːn/ *adj* (not before a noun) not present any longer; completely used up: *He stood at the door for a moment, and then he was gone.* ○ *Can I have some more ice-cream please or is it all gone?* ☞ *Gone* meaning 'disappeared' or 'finished' is used with the verb *be*, as in the examples above. When we are thinking about where something has disappeared to, we use *have*: *Nobody knows where John has gone.*

gone³ /gɒn/ *prep* later than: *Hurry up! It's gone six already!* (= later than six o'clock)

gonna /'gɒnə/ (*informal*) a way of writing 'going to' to show that sb is speaking in an informal way or with a special accent ☞ Do not write 'gonna' yourself (unless you are copying somebody's accent) because it might be marked as a mistake. **Wanna** (= want to) and **gotta** (= got to) are similar.

goo /guː/ *noun* [U] (*informal*) a sticky wet substance

gooey /'guːi/ *adj* (**gooier**; **gooiest**) (*informal*) sticky: *gooey cakes*

☆ **good¹** /gʊd/ *adj* (**better** /'betə(r)/, **best** /best/) **1** of a high quality or standard: *a good book, film, concert, etc* ○ *The hotel was really good.* ○ *'Why don't you apply for the job?' 'I don't think my English is good enough.'* ○ *The car was in very good condition.* **2 good at sth; good with sb/sth** able to do sth or deal with sb/sth well; successful: *Jane's good at chemistry.* ○ *He's very good with children.* ○ enjoyable: *It's good to be home again.* ○ *good news, weather, etc* ○ *Have a good time!* **4** morally right or well behaved: *She was a very good person – she spent her whole life trying to help other people.* ○ *Were the children good while we were out?* **5 good (to sb)** kind; helpful: *They were good to me when I was ill.* ○ *It was good of you to come.* **6 good (for sb/sth)** having a positive effect on your health: *Green vegetables are very good for you.* **7** suitable or favourable: *This beach is very good for surfing.* ○ *I think Paul would be a good person for the job.* ○ *'When shall we meet?' 'Thursday would be a good day for me.'* **8** (only used before an adjective or noun) great in number, size, length, etc: *a good many people* (= a lot of people) ○ *Take a good* (= long and careful) *look at this photograph.* **9** (only *before* a noun) at least: *We waited for a good ten minutes.* ○ *It's a good three miles to the station.* **10** (used when you are pleased about sth): *'Tom's invited us to dinner next week.' 'Oh, good!'*

(IDIOMS) **a good/great many** ⇨ MANY

as good as almost: *She as good as said I was lying!* ○ *The project is as good as finished.*

in good faith ⇨ FAITH

good for you (*informal*) (used for congratulating sb): *Well done! Good for you!*

good gracious, good grief, good heavens, etc (used for expressing surprise) ☞ Look at the entries for **gracious**, etc

good morning/afternoon/evening/night (used for greeting sb) ☞ Look at the entries for **morning**, etc.

,**good-'humoured** *adj* pleasant and cheerful: *Although there were a lot of complaints, the manager remained polite and good-humoured.*

,**good 'looks** *noun* [plural] an attractive appearance (of a person)

,**good-'looking** *adj* (usually used about a person) attractive ☞ Look at the note at **beautiful**.

,**good-'natured** *adj* friendly or cheerful

,**good 'sense** *noun* [U] good judgement or intelligence: *He had the good sense to refuse the offer.*

,**good-'tempered** *adj* not easily made angry

good² /gʊd/ *noun* [U] **1** the quality of being morally right: *the difference between good and evil* ○ *I'm sure there's some good in everybody.* **2** something that will help sb/sth; advantage: *She did it for the good of her country.* ○ *I know*

s	z	ʃ	ʒ	h	m	n	ŋ	l	r	j	w
so	zoo	she	vision	how	man	no	sing	leg	red	yes	wet

you don't want to go into hospital, but it's for your own good. ○ *What's the good of learning French if you have no chance of using it?*
(IDIOMS) **be no good (doing sth)** to be of no use or value: *It's no good standing here in the cold. Let's go home.* ○ *This sweater isn't any good. It's too small.*
do you good to help or be useful to you: *It'll do you good to meet some new people.*
for good for ever: *I hope they've gone for good this time!*

☆ **goodbye** /ˌgʊdˈbaɪ; ˌgʊˈbaɪ/ interj (said when sb goes or you yourself go): *Goodbye! See you tomorrow!* ○ *We said goodbye to Steven at the airport.* ☛ **Cheerio**, **cheers** and **bye** are other words with the same meaning. *Goodbye* can also be used as a noun: *Their goodbye was very sad because they knew they wouldn't see each other again for years.*

Good Friday /ˌgʊd ˈfraɪdi/ noun [C] the Friday before Easter when Christians remember the death of Christ

goodies /ˈgʊdiz/ noun [plural] (*informal*) nice things to eat

goodness /ˈgʊdnɪs/ noun [U] **1** the quality of being good **2** the quality that helps sb/sth to grow: *Wholemeal bread has more goodness in it than white.*

☛ 'Goodness' is used in a number of expressions. We say *Goodness (me)!* to show that we are surprised. *Thank goodness* expresses happiness and relief: *Thank goodness it's stopped raining!* We say *For goodness' sake* when we are asking somebody to do something and want to sound more urgent or when we are angry with somebody: *For goodness' sake, hurry up!*

☆ **goods** /gʊdz/ noun [plural] **1** things that are for sale: *a wide range of consumer goods* ○ *electrical goods* ○ *stolen goods* **2** (*also* **freight**) things that are carried by train or lorry: *a goods train* ○ *a heavy goods vehicle* (= *HGV*) ☛ **Freight** (not **goods**) is always used in American English.
(IDIOM) **come up with/deliver the goods** (*informal*) to do what you have promised to do

goodwill /ˌgʊdˈwɪl/ noun [U] friendly, helpful feelings towards other people: *There is a new atmosphere of goodwill in international politics.*

goody-goody /ˈgʊdi ˌgʊdi/ noun [C] (*pl* **goody-goodies**) a person who always behaves well so that other people have a good opinion of him/her ☛ If you call somebody a goody-goody it usually means that you do not like him/her.

gooey ⇒ GOO

goof /guːf/ verb [I] (*informal*) (*especially US*) to make a silly mistake

goose /guːs/ noun (*pl* **geese** /giːs/) [C] a large white bird that is like a duck, but larger. Geese are kept on farms for their meat and eggs.

☛ A male goose is called a **gander** and a young goose is a **gosling**.

gooseberry /ˈgʊzbəri; *US* ˈguːsberi/ noun [C] (*pl* **gooseberries**) a small green fruit that is covered in small hairs and has a sour taste: *a gooseberry bush*
(IDIOM) **play gooseberry** to be present when two lovers want to be alone

goose-flesh /ˈguːs fleʃ/ noun [U] (*also* **'goose-pimples** noun [plural]) small points or lumps which appear on your skin because you are cold or frightened

gore¹ /gɔː(r)/ noun [U] the blood that comes from a cut or wound: *His new film is full of gore* (= there are many violent scenes in it). ☛ The adjective is **gory**.

gore² /gɔː(r)/ verb [T] to wound sb with a horn, etc: *She was gored by a bull.*

gorge¹ /gɔːdʒ/ noun [C] a narrow valley with steep sides and a stream or river running through it

gorge² /gɔːdʒ/ verb [I,T] **gorge (yourself) (on/with sth)** to eat a lot of food: *At Christmas people gorge themselves on rich food.*

gorgeous /ˈgɔːdʒəs/ adj (*informal*) very good; wonderful: *What gorgeous weather!* ○ *Thank you for my present – it's absolutely gorgeous!* —**gorgeously** adv

gorilla /gəˈrɪlə/ noun [C] a very large black African monkey that is the largest of the monkeys that are closely related to man (**apes**).

gory /ˈgɔːri/ adj (**gorier**; **goriest**) full of violence and blood: *a gory film* ○ (*figurative*) *He told me all the gory details about the divorce.*

gosh /gɒʃ/ interj (*informal*) (used for expressing surprise, shock, etc)

gosling /ˈgɒzlɪŋ/ noun [C] a young goose

gospel /ˈgɒspl/ noun **1 Gospel** [sing] one of the four books in the Bible that describe the life and teachings of Jesus Christ: *St Matthew's/Mark's/Luke's/John's Gospel* **2** [U] the truth: *You can't take what he says as gospel.* **3** [U] a style of religious music that is especially popular among black American Christians

gossip /ˈgɒsɪp/ noun **1** [U] informal talk about other people and their private lives: *Don't believe all the gossip you hear.* ○ *He loves spreading gossip about his neighbours.* **2** [C] a conversation (including gossip): *The two neighbours were having a gossip over the fence.* —**gossip** verb [I]: *I can't stand here gossiping all day.*

'gossip column noun [C] a part of a newspaper or magazine where you can read about the private lives of famous people

got *pt, pp* of GET
☛ Look at the note at **gotten**.

gotta /ˈgɒtə/ (*US*) a way of writing 'got to' or 'got a' to show that sb is speaking in an informal way or with a special accent ☛ Do not write 'gotta' yourself (unless you are copying somebody's accent) because it might be marked as a mistake. **Gonna** and **wanna** are similar: *I gotta go* (= I have got to go). ○ *Gotta* (= have you got a) *minute?*

gotten (*US*) *pp* of GET
☛ In most cases *gotten* is more commonly used in American English than *got*: *Has he gotten back yet?* ○ *I've gotten myself a new job.*

gouge /gaʊdʒ/ verb
(PHRASAL VERB) **gouge sth out** to take sth out

iː	ɪ	e	æ	ɑː	ɒ	ɔː	ʊ	uː	ʌ
see	sit	ten	hat	arm	got	saw	put	too	cup

gourmet with force (usually with a tool or with your fingers)

gourmet /'guəmeɪ/ *noun* [C] a person who enjoys food and wine and knows a lot about them: *a gourmet restaurant*

☆**govern** /'gʌvn/ *verb* **1** [I,T] to rule or control the public affairs of a country, city, etc: *Britain is governed by the Prime Minister and the Cabinet.* **2** [T] (often passive) to influence or control: *Our decision will be governed by the amount of money we have to spend.*

☆**government** /'gʌvənmənt/ *noun* **1** often **the Government** [C] the group of people who govern a country: *He has resigned from the Government.* ○ *After the Prime Minister's resignation a new government was formed.* ○ *The Government has been overthrown.* ○ *The foreign governments involved are meeting in Geneva.* ○ *government policy, money, ministers, etc* ☛ In the singular *government* may be followed by a singular or plural verb. We use a singular verb when we are thinking of the government as one single unit: *The Government welcomes the proposal.* We use a plural verb when we are thinking about all the individual members of the government: *The Government are still discussing the problem.* Different types of government are: *communist, conservative, democratic, liberal, reactionary, socialist,* etc. A country or state may also have a *military, provisional, central* or *federal, coalition,* etc government. Look at **local government** and **opposition**. **2** [U] the act or method of governing: *Six years of weak government had left the economy in ruins.*

(IDIOM) **in government** being the government: *The Labour Party was in government from 1964 to 1970.* —**governmental** /ˌgʌvn'mentl/ *adj: a governmental department* ○ *different governmental systems*

governor /'gʌvənə(r)/ *noun* [C] **1** a person who governs a province or state (especially in the USA): *the Governor of New York State* **2** the leader or member of a group of people who govern an organization: *the governor of the Bank of England* ○ *In many British schools the board of governors is responsible for appointing new teachers.*

gown /gaʊn/ *noun* [C] **1** a long woman's dress for a special occasion: *a ball-gown* **2** a loose piece of clothing that is worn by judges, lawyers, surgeons etc

grab /græb/ *verb* (grab**b**ing; grab**b**ed) **1** [I,T] to take sth suddenly or roughly: *Helen grabbed the toy car from her little brother.* ○ *Don't grab — there's plenty for everybody.* ○ (figurative): *He grabbed the opportunity of a free trip to America.* ○ (figurative): *I grabbed an hour's sleep on the train so I'm not too tired now.* ☛ Look at **snatch**. It is similar in meaning. **2** [I] **grab at sb/sth** to try to get or catch sb/sth: *Jonathan grabbed at the ball but missed.* —**grab** /græb/ *noun* [C]: *She made a grab for the boy but she couldn't stop him falling.*

grace /greɪs/ *noun* [U] **1** the ability to move in a smooth and attractive way: *to walk, dance, move, etc with grace* **2** extra time that is allowed for sth: *Payment is due today, but we have been given a week's grace* (= an extra week to pay). **3** a short prayer of thanks to God before or after a meal: *Father always says grace.* **4 His/Her/Your Grace** (used when speaking about, or to, a duke, duchess or archbishop)

(IDIOMS) **have the grace to do sth** to be polite enough to do sth: *At least she had the grace to apologize for what she did.*

with good grace willingly and cheerfully, not showing that you are disappointed: *He accepted the decision with good grace although it wasn't the one that he had been hoping for.*

graceful /'greɪsfl/ *adj* having grace and beauty: *a graceful dancer* ☛ Look at **gracious**. Its meaning is different. —**gracefully** /-fəli/ *adv*: *She accepted the decision gracefully* (= without showing her disappointment). —**gracefulness** *noun* [U]

graceless /'greɪsləs/ *adj* **1** without grace(1) or beauty **2** rude —**gracelessly** *adv*

gracious /'greɪʃəs/ *adj* **1** (used about a person or his/her behaviour) pleasant, kind or polite (to sb of a lower social position): *The Queen Mother gave a gracious smile as she drove past.* **2** (only *before* a noun) (*formal*) (used when speaking about royal people): *by gracious permission of Her Majesty* **3** (only *before* a noun) owned or enjoyed by rich people: *gracious living* ☛ Look at **graceful**. Its meaning is different.

(IDIOM) **good gracious!** (used for expressing surprise: *Good gracious! Is that the time?* —**graciously** *adv* —**graciousness** *noun* [U]

☆**grade**¹ /greɪd/ *noun* [C] **1** the quality or place in a series that sb/sth has: *Which grade of petrol do you need?* ○ *She has passed her violin exams at Grade 6.* ○ *We need to use high-grade materials for this job.* **2** a mark that is given for school work, etc or in an examination: *He got good/poor grades this term.* ○ *Only a small number of our pupils pass A level French with a grade A.* **3** (*US*) a class or classes in a school in which all the children are the same age: *My daughter is in the third grade.*

(IDIOM) **make the grade** (*informal*) to reach the expected standard; succeed

'**grade crossing** *noun* [C] (*US*) = LEVEL CROSSING

grade² /greɪd/ *verb* [T] (often passive) to divide things or people into groups, according to their quality or size: *I've graded their work from 1 to 10.* ○ *Students with 90% correct are graded A.* ○ *Eggs are graded by size.*

gradient /'greɪdiənt/ *noun* [C] the steepness of a slope: *The hill has a gradient of 1 in 4* (= 25%). ○ *a steep gradient*

☆**gradual** /'grædʒuəl/ *adj* happening slowly or over a long period of time; not sudden: *There has been a gradual increase in the number of people without jobs.* —**gradually** /-dʒuli/ *adv*: *After the storm things gradually got back to normal.*

graduate¹ /'grædʒuət/ *noun* [C] **1 a graduate (in sth)** a person who holds a (first) degree from a university, etc: *a law graduate/a graduate in law* ○ *a graduate student* (= a student who has already got a first degree and who is studying for a further (postgraduate) degree)

graduate 280 **grant**

☛ Look at **postgraduate, undergraduate** and **bachelor** and the note at **student**. **2** (US) a person who has completed a course at a school, college, etc: *a high-school graduate*

graduate² /'grædʒueɪt/ *verb* [I] **1 graduate (in sth) (from sth)** to get a (first) degree from a university, etc **2** (US) **graduate (in sth) (from sth)** to complete a course at a school, college, etc **3 graduate (from sth) to sth** to change (from sth) to sth more difficult, important, expensive, etc: *We've finally graduated from black and white to colour TV.*

graduation /ˌgrædʒu'eɪʃn/ *noun* **1** [U] graduating from a university, etc **2** [sing] a ceremony in which degree certificates are given to people who have graduated from a university, etc

graffiti /grə'fi:tɪ/ *noun* [U,plural] pictures or writing on a wall, etc in a public place that are rude, funny or political: *The wall was covered with graffiti.*

graft /grɑːft; US græft/ *noun* [C] **1** a piece of a living plant that is fixed inside another plant so that it will grow **2** a piece of living skin, bone, etc that is fixed onto a damaged part of a body in a medical operation: *a skin graft*

graft *verb* [T] **graft sth onto sth** to fix sth as a graft onto a plant, body, etc ☛ Look at **transplant**.

☆ **grain¹** /greɪn/ *noun* **1** [U] the seeds of wheat, rice, etc as a whole: *The USA is a major producer of grain.* ○ *grain exports* **2** [C] a single seed of wheat, rice, etc **3** [C] a very small piece of sth: *a grain of sand, salt, sugar, etc* ○ (*figurative*) *There isn't a grain of truth in what you say.*

grain² /greɪn/ *noun* [C] the natural pattern of lines that can be seen or felt in wood, rock, stone, etc: *to cut a piece of wood along/across the grain*

(IDIOM) **(be/go) against the grain** to be difficult to do because you do not really think that it is the right thing: *It goes against the grain to say I'm sorry when I'm not sorry at all.*

gram (*also* **gramme**) /græm/ *noun* [C] (*abbr* g) a measure of weight. There are 1 000 grams in a kilogram.

☆ **grammar** /'græmə(r)/ *noun* **1** [U] the rules of language, eg for forming words or joining words together in sentences: *Russian grammar can be difficult for foreign learners.* **2** [U] the way in which sb uses the rules of language: *You have a good vocabulary, but your grammar needs improvement.* **3** [C] a book that describes and explains the rules of grammar: *a French grammar*

'grammar school *noun* [C] (*Brit*) a type of secondary school that provides academic education

grammatical /grə'mætɪkl/ *adj* **1** connected with grammar: *the grammatical rules for forming plurals* **2** following the rules of grammar: *The sentence is not grammatical.* ☛ The opposite is **ungrammatical**. —**grammatically** /-klɪ/ *adv*

gramme /græm/ *noun* [C] = GRAM

gramophone /'græməfəʊn/ *noun* [C] (*Brit old-fashioned*) = RECORD-PLAYER: *a gramophone record*

gran /græn/ *noun* [C] (*Brit informal*) = GRANDMOTHER

☆ **grand¹** /grænd/ *adj* **1** looking splendid in size or appearance (also used in names): *Our house isn't very grand, but it has a big garden.* ○ *the Grand Canyon* ○ *the Grand Hotel* ☛ The noun is **grandeur**. **2** seeming to be important or thinking that you are important: *She thinks she's very grand because she drives a Porsche.* **3** (*informal*) very good or pleasant: *You've done a grand job!* —**grandly** *adv* —**grandness** *noun* [U]

ˌgrand pi'ano *noun* [C] a large flat piano (with horizontal strings)

ˌgrand 'slam *noun* [C] winning all the important matches or competitions in a particular sport, eg rugby or tennis

ˌgrand 'total *noun* [C] the amount that you get when you add several totals together

grand² /grænd/ *noun* [C] (*pl* **grand**) (*slang*) 1 000 pounds or dollars: *It'll cost you 50 grand!!*

☆ **grand-** /grænd/ (used before a noun to show a family relationship)

'grandchild, 'granddaughter, 'grandson *nouns* [C] the daughter or son of your child

'grandfather, 'grandmother, 'grandparent *nouns* [C] the father or mother of one of your parents

☛ If you need to distinguish between a grandparent on your mother's and your father's side you can say: *My maternal/paternal grandfather* or *my mother's/father's father*.

'grandfather clock *noun* [C] a clock that stands on the floor in a tall wooden case

grandad /'grændæd/ *noun* [C] (*Brit informal*) = GRANDFATHER

grandeur /'grændʒə(r)/ *noun* [U] (*formal*) **1** the quality of being large and impressive: *the grandeur of the Swiss alps* **2** the feeling of being important

grandiose /'grændɪəʊs/ *adj* bigger or more complicated than necessary: *Their grandiose scheme was completely impractical.* ☛ Using this word about something shows that you do not have a good opinion of it.

grandma /'grænmɑː/ *noun* [C] (*informal*) = GRANDMOTHER

grandpa /'grænpɑː/ *noun* [C] (*informal*) = GRANDFATHER

grandstand /'grændstænd/ *noun* [C] rows of seats (covered by a roof) from which you get a good view of a sports competition, etc

granite /'grænɪt/ *noun* [U] a hard grey rock

granny (*also* **grannie**) /'grænɪ/ *noun* [C] (*pl* **grannies**) (*informal*) = GRANDMOTHER

☆ **grant** /grɑːnt; US grænt/ *verb* [T] **1** (*formal*) to give sb what he/she has asked for: *A visa has been granted to one of our journalists.* ○ *He was granted permission to leave early.* **2** to agree (that sth is true): *I grant you that New York is an interesting place but I still wouldn't want to live there.*

(IDIOMS) **take sb/sth for granted** to show too little attention to sb/sth; not be grateful enough to a person or thing: *In developed countries we take running water for granted.* ○ *She*

p	b	t	d	k	g	tʃ	dʒ	f	v	θ	ð
pen	bad	tea	did	cat	got	chin	June	fall	van	thin	then

never says thank you – she just takes me for granted.

take sth for granted to accept sth as being true: *We can take it for granted that the new students will have at least an elementary knowledge of English.*

grant *noun* [C] money that is given (by the government, etc) for a particular purpose: *a student grant* (= to help pay for university education)

granted *adv* (used for saying that sth is true, before you make a comment about it): *'We've never had any problems before.' 'Granted, but this year there are 200 more people coming.'*

granule /'grænju:l/ *noun* [C] a small hard piece or grain of sth: *coffee granules*

☆ **grape** /greɪp/ *noun* [C] a green or purple berry that grows in bunches on a climbing plant (**a vine**) and that is used for making wine: *a bunch of grapes* ☛ Green grapes are usually called 'white' and purple grapes are usually called 'black'. Grapes that have been dried are called **raisins**, **currants** or **sultanas**.

the 'grapevine *noun* [sing] the way that news is passed from one person to another: *I heard on/through the grapevine that you are moving.*

grapefruit /'greɪpfru:t/ *noun* [C] (*pl* **grapefruit** or **grapefruits**) a large round yellow fruit with a thick skin that is like a big orange but with a sour taste

graph /grɑ:f; *US* græf/ *noun* [C] a mathematical diagram in which a line or a curve shows the relationship between two quantities, measurements, etc: *a graph showing/to show the number of cars sold each month* ○ *graph paper*

graphic /'græfɪk/ *adj* **1** (only *before* a noun) connected with drawings, letters, diagrams, etc: *graphic design* **2** (used about descriptions) clear and giving a lot of detail: *She described the accident in graphic detail.* —**graphically** /-kli/ *adv*

graphics *noun* [plural] the production of drawings, letters, diagrams, etc: *computer graphics*

grapple /'græpl/ *verb* [I] **grapple (with sb)** to get hold of sb and struggle or fight with him/her: *She grappled with the thief, but he got away.* ○ (*figurative*) *We have been grappling with this problem all day.*

☆ **grasp** /grɑ:sp; *US* græsp/ *verb* [T] **1** to take hold of sb/sth suddenly and firmly: *Lisa grasped the child firmly by the hand before crossing the road.* ○ (*figurative*) *to grasp an opportunity* **2** to understand sth: *I don't think you've grasped how serious the situation is.*

(PHRASAL VERB) **grasp at sth** to try to seize or grasp sth: *He grasped at the swinging rope, but missed.*

grasp *noun* [usually sing] **1** a firm hold or control over sb/sth: *a strong grasp* **2** the ability to get or achieve sth: *Finally their dream was within their grasp.* **3** understanding: *He has a good grasp of English grammar.*

grasping /'grɑ:spɪŋ; *US* 'græspɪŋ/ *adj* greedy for money, power, etc

☆ **grass** /grɑ:s; *US* græs/ *noun* **1** [U] the common green plant with thin leaves which covers fields and parts of gardens. Cows, sheep, horses, etc eat grass: *She lay on the grass and listened to the birds singing.* ○ *Don't walk on the grass.* ○ *I must cut the grass at the weekend.* ○ *a blade* (= one leaf) *of grass* ☛ An area of grass in a garden is called a **lawn**. **2** [C] one type of grass: *an arrangement of dried flowers and grasses*

grassy *adj* covered with grass

grass 'roots *noun* [plural] the ordinary people in an organization and not those who make decisions: *dissatisfaction with party policy at the grass roots*

grasshopper /'grɑ:shɒpə(r); *US* 'græs-/ *noun* [C] an insect that lives in long grass and that can jump high in the air

grate[1] /greɪt/ *noun* [C] the metal frame that holds the wood, coal, etc in a fireplace; the area surrounding it ☛ picture at **fireplace**.

grate[2] /greɪt/ *verb* **1** [T] to rub food into small pieces using a metal tool (**a grater**): *Grate the cheese and sprinkle it over the top of the dish.* **2** [I] to make a sharp unpleasant sound (when two surfaces rub against each other): *The hinges grated as the gate swung back.* **3** [I] **grate (on sb)** to annoy or irritate: *It's her voice that grates on me.*

grater *noun* [C] a kitchen utensil with a rough surface that is used for grating food

☆ **grateful** /'greɪtfl/ *adj* **grateful (to sb) (for sth)**; **grateful (that...)** feeling or showing thanks (to sb): *We are very grateful to you for all the help you have given us.* ○ *He was very grateful that you did as he asked.* ○ *I should be very grateful if you could send me a copy of your brochure.* ☛ The opposite is **ungrateful**. The noun is **gratitude**. —**gratefully** /-fəli/ *adv*

gratify /'grætɪfaɪ/ *verb* [T] (*pres part* **gratifying**; *3rd pers sing pres* **gratifies**; *pt, pp* **gratified**) (*formal*) (often passive) to give sb pleasure: *I was gratified to hear that you enjoyed my book.* —**gratifying** *adj*

grating /'greɪtɪŋ/ *noun* [C] a framework of metal bars that is fixed over a window or over a hole in the road, etc

gratitude /'grætɪtju:d; *US* -tu:d/ *noun* [U] **gratitude (to sb) (for sth)** the feeling of being grateful or thankful: *We should like to express our gratitude to David Stewart for all his help and advice.* ☛ The opposite is **ingratitude**.

grave[1] /greɪv/ *adj* (*formal*) **1** bad or serious: *These events could have grave consequences for us all.* **2** (used about people) sad or serious: *He was looking extremely grave.* ☛ The noun is **gravity**. **Serious** is much more common for both senses.

grave[2] /greɪv/ *noun* [C] the place where a dead body is buried: *The coffin was lowered into the grave.* ○ *I put some flowers on the grave.*

'gravestone *noun* [C] a stone over a grave that

shows the name, etc of the person who is buried there

'graveyard *noun* [C] an area of land (near a church) where dead people are buried ☛ Look at **cemetery** and **churchyard**.

gravel /'grævl/ *noun* [U] very small stones that are used for making roads, paths, etc

gravity¹ /'grævəti/ (*also* **gravitation**) *noun* [U] the natural force that makes things fall to the ground when you drop them: *the force of gravity*

gravity² /'grævəti/ *noun* [U] (*formal*) importance or seriousness: *Politicians are only now realizing the gravity of the situation.* ☛ **Seriousness** is more common. The adjective is **grave**.

gravy /'greɪvi/ *noun* [U] a thin sauce that is made from the juices that come out of meat while it is cooking. Gravy is served with meat, vegetables, etc. ☛ Look at **sauce**.

gray /greɪ/ *adj, noun* [C,U] (*especially US*) = GREY

graze¹ /greɪz/ *verb* [I] (used about cows, sheep, etc) to eat grass (that is growing in a field)

graze² /greɪz/ *verb* [T] **1** to injure your skin because you have scraped it against sth rough: *The child fell and grazed her knee.* **2** to pass sth and touch it lightly: *The car's tyre grazed the pavement.*

graze *noun* [C] the small wound where the skin has been grazed

grease /griːs/ *noun* [U] **1** a thick oily substance used, for example, in engines or on hair: *engine grease* ○ *grease marks* **2** animal fat that has been softened by cooking: *You'll need very hot water to get all the grease off those pans.*

grease *verb* [T] to put grease on or in sth: *Grease the tin thoroughly to stop the cake from sticking.*

greasy /'griːsi/ *adj* (**greasier**; **greasiest**) covered with or containing a lot of grease: *greasy fingers* ○ *greasy skin* ○ *greasy food*

☆**great** /greɪt/ *adj* **1** large in amount, degree, size, etc; a lot of: *We had great difficulty in solving the problem.* ○ *The party was a great success.* ○ *It gives me great pleasure to introduce tonight's guest.* ○ (*formal*) *The town was dominated by the great cathedral.* ☛ Look at the note at **big**. **2** particularly important; of unusually high quality: *Einstein was perhaps the greatest scientist of the century.* ○ *Alexander the Great* ○ *a great moment in history* **3** (*informal*) good; wonderful: *We had a great time in Paris.* ○ *It's great to see you again.* ☛ We sometimes use **great** in a sarcastic way, that is, when something is not good at all: *Oh great! I've spilled coffee all over my homework!* **4** (*informal*) (used to emphasize sth) very; very good: *There was a great big dog in the garden.* ○ *They were great friends.*

(IDIOMS) **go to great lengths** ⇒ LENGTH
a good/great deal ⇒ DEAL¹
a good/great many ⇒ MANY

great *noun* [C, usually pl] (*informal*) a person or thing of special ability or importance: *That film is one of the all-time greats.*

greatly *adv* very much: *She will be greatly missed by friends and family.* —**greatness** *noun* [U]

Great 'Britain (*also* **Britain**) (*abbr* **GB**) England, Wales and Scotland ☛ Look at the note at **United Kingdom**.

☆**great-** /greɪt/ (used before a noun to show a family relationship)

great-'grandchild, **great-'granddaughter**, **great-'grandson** *noun* [C] the daughter or son of your grandchild

great-'grandfather, **great-'grandmother**, **great-'grandparent** *noun* [C] the father or mother of one of your grandparents

☛ **Great-** can be added to other words for family members to show another generation: *your great-aunt* (= the aunt of your mother or father) ○ *your great-nephew* (= the son of your nephew or niece) ○ *your great-great-grandfather* (= the grandfather of one of your great-grandparents)

☆**greed** /griːd/ *noun* [U] **greed (for sth)** a strong desire for more food, money, power, etc than you really need

greedy *adj* (**greedier**; **greediest**) **greedy (for sth)** wanting more food, money, power, etc than you really need: *Don't be so greedy — you've had three pieces of cake already.* —**greedily** *adv* —**greediness** *noun* [U]

☆**green¹** /griːn/ *adj* **1** of the colour of grass or leaves: *dark/light/pale green* ○ *olive green* ○ *I love the spring when everything's green.* ○ *These bananas aren't ripe yet — they're still green.* **2** (*informal*) (used about a person) with little experience: *I'm not so green as to believe that!* **3** pale in the face (because you have had a shock or feel ill): *At the sight of all the blood he turned green and fainted.* **4** envious (wanting to have what sb else has got): *He was green with envy when he found out how much German teachers earn.* **5** connected with protecting the environment or the natural world: *the Green party* ○ *green products* (= that do not damage the environment)

(IDIOM) **give sb/get the green light** (*informal*) to give sb/get permission to do sth

greenish /'griːnɪʃ/ *adj* rather green

green 'belt *noun* [C,U] an area of land around a city where building is not allowed

green 'fingers *noun* [plural] (*informal*) the ability to make plants grow well

green 'pepper *noun* [C] ⇨ PEPPER(2)

☆**green²** /griːn/ *noun* **1** [C,U] the colour of grass and leaves: *They were dressed in green.* ○ *The room was decorated in greens and blues.* **2 greens** [plural] green vegetables, eg cabbage, that are usually eaten cooked **3** [C] (*Brit*) an area of grass in the centre of a village: *the village green* **4** [C] a flat area of very short grass used in games such as golf: *the green at the 18th hole* **5 Green** [C] a member of a green¹(5) political party

greengage /'griːngeɪdʒ/ *noun* [C] a small yellowish-green plum

greengrocer /'griːnˌgrəʊsə(r)/ *noun* [C] (*Brit*) a person who sells fruit and vegetables in a small shop (**a greengrocer's**): *I bought these strawberries at the greengrocer's.*

iː	ɪ	e	æ	ɑː	ɒ	ɔː	ʊ	uː	ʌ
see	sit	ten	hat	arm	got	saw	put	too	cup

greenhouse /'gri:nhaʊs/ noun [C] a building made of glass in which plants are grown

'greenhouse effect noun [sing] the warming of the earth's atmosphere as a result of pollution

☆ **greet** /gri:t/ verb [T] **1** to welcome sb when you meet him/her; to say hallo to sb: *He greeted me with a friendly smile.* ○ *(figurative) As we entered the house we were greeted by the smell of cooking.* **2 greet sth with sth** (usually passive) to receive sth in a particular way: *The news was greeted with a loud cheer.*

greeting noun [C] **1** the first words you say when you meet sb: *'Hello' and 'Hi' are informal greetings.* **2** [usually pl] a good wish: *a greetings card*

gregarious /grɪ'geərɪəs/ adj liking to be with other people

grenade /grə'neɪd/ noun [C] a small bomb that is thrown by hand or fired from a gun: *a hand-grenade*

grew pt of GROW

☆ **grey** (especially US **gray**) /greɪ/ adj **1** of the colour between black and white: *dark/light/pale grey* ○ *He was wearing a grey suit.* ○ *She looked grey with tiredness.* **2** with grey hair: *He's going grey.*

grey (especially US **gray**) noun [C,U] the colour between black and white

greyish (especially US **grayish**) adj rather grey

greyhound /'greɪhaʊnd/ noun [C] a large thin dog that can run very fast and that is used for racing: *greyhound racing*

☛ Greyhound racing (at a **stadium** or **track**) is very popular in Britain. People **bet** on which dog is going to win the race.

grid /grɪd/ noun [C] **1** a pattern of lines that cross each other to form squares **2** a system of squares that are drawn on a map so that the position of any place can be described or found: *a grid reference* **3** the system of electricity cables, etc taking power to all parts of a country: *the National Grid*

grief /gri:f/ noun [U] great sadness (especially because of the death of sb you love)
(IDIOM) **good grief** (*informal*) (used for expressing surprise or shock): *Good grief! Whatever happened to you?*

grievance /'gri:vns/ noun [C] **a grievance (against sb)** something that you think is unfair and that you want to complain or protest about: *The workers aired (= expressed) their grievances at the meeting.*

grieve /gri:v/ verb **1** [I] **grieve (for sb)** to feel great sadness (especially about the death of sb you love): *He is still grieving for his wife.* **2** [T] to cause unhappiness: *It grieves me to refuse.*

☆ **grill** /grɪl/ noun [C] **1** a part of a cooker where the food is cooked by heat from above: *Sprinkle with cheese and put under the grill to brown.* ☛ picture at **cooker**. **2** a framework of metal bars that you put food on to cook over a fire or on a barbecue

grill verb (especially US **broil**) [I,T] **1** to cook under a grill: *grilled steak* ☛ Look at the note at **cook**. **2** [T] (*informal*) to question sb for a long time: *When she got home her parents grilled her about where she had been.*

grille /grɪl/ noun [C] a framework of metal bars that is placed over a window, etc

grim /grɪm/ adj (**grimmer**; **grimmest**) **1** (used about a person) very serious; not smiling: *The fireman's face was grim when he came out of the burning house.* **2** (used about a situation, news, etc) unpleasant or worrying: *We face the grim prospect of even higher inflation.* ○ *The news is grim, I'm afraid.* **3** (used about a place) unpleasant to look at; not attractive: *They lived in a grim block of flats in South London.* **4** (*informal*) ill: *I was feeling grim yesterday but I managed to get to work.* —**grimly** adv

grimace /grɪ'meɪs; US 'grɪməs/ noun [C] an expression on your face that shows that you are angry or that sth is hurting you: *a grimace of pain*

grimace verb [I] to make a grimace: *She grimaced with pain.*

grime /graɪm/ noun [U] a thick layer of dirt

grimy adj (**grimier**; **grimiest**) very dirty

grin /grɪn/ verb [I] (**grinn**ing; **grinn**ed) to smile broadly (so that you show your teeth): *She grinned at me as she came into the room.* —**grin** noun [C]: *He came in with a big grin on his face and told us the good news.*

grind /graɪnd/ verb [T] (pt, pp **ground** /graʊnd/) **1** to crush sth into very small pieces or into a powder between two hard surfaces: *Wheat is ground into flour.* ○ *ground pepper* **2** to make sth sharp or smooth by rubbing it on a rough hard surface: *to grind a knife on a stone* **3** to press sth together or into sth firmly: *Some people grind their teeth while they're asleep.*
(IDIOM) **grind to a halt/standstill** to stop slowly: *(figurative) The talks ground to a halt yesterday.*

grinder /'graɪndə(r)/ noun [C] a machine for grinding: *a coffee-grinder*

grip /grɪp/ verb [T] (**gripp**ing; **gripp**ed) to take and keep hold of sb/sth firmly: *She gripped my arm in fear.* ○ *(figurative) The story really gripped my imagination.*

grip noun **1** [sing] **a grip (on sb/sth)** a firm hold (on sb/sth): *I relaxed my grip and he ran away.* ○ *You need tyres that give a good grip.* ○ *(figurative) The teacher kept a firm grip on the class.* **2** [C] (US) a bag that you use when you are travelling or for sports equipment
(IDIOMS) **come/get to grips with sth** to start dealing with a problem in an effective way: *The government is still trying to get to grips with inflation.*
get/keep/take a grip/hold on yourself (*informal*) to try to behave in a calmer or more sensible way

gripping adj exciting; holding your attention: *a gripping film*

grisly /'grɪzli/ adj (used for describing sth that is concerned with death) horrible; terrible: *The detective stared at the grisly remains of the bodies.* ☛ Look at **gruesome**. It is similar in meaning.

grit /grɪt/ noun [U] **1** small pieces of stone: *I've* got some grit/a piece of grit in my shoe. **2** (informal) courage; determination

grit verb [T] (gri**tt**ing; gri**tt**ed) to cover with grit: *The roads are gritted in icy weather.*

(IDIOM) **grit your teeth** to have courage or determination in a difficult situation: *If things get difficult, you'll have to grit your teeth and keep going.*

groan /grəʊn/ verb [I] to make a deep sad sound because you are in pain, or to show that you are unhappy or do not approve of sth: *He groaned with pain.* ○ *The children groaned when I told them we were going on a long walk.* ○ *The audience groaned at his terrible jokes.*

groan noun [C] the sound that you make when you groan

grocer /ˈgrəʊsə(r)/ noun [C] a person who sells food and other things for the home in a small shop ☞ Look at greengrocer.

groceries noun [plural] food such as flour, sugar, tea, coffee, etc that is sold by a grocer

groggy /ˈgrɒgi/ adj (**groggier**; **groggiest**) (informal) weak and unable to walk steadily because you feel ill, have not had enough sleep, etc

groin /grɔɪn/ noun [C] the place where the tops of the legs join the body

groom /gruːm/ noun [C] **1** a person who looks after horses **2** = BRIDEGROOM

groom verb [T] **1** to clean or look after a horse, etc by brushing, etc **2** (usually passive) to choose and prepare sb for a particular career or job: *He is clearly being groomed for the top job.*

groove /gruːv/ noun [C] a long deep line that is cut in the surface of sth: *the grooves on a record*

grope /grəʊp/ verb [I] **grope (about) (for/after sth)** to search for sth using your hands, as you do in the dark: *He groped for the light-switch.*

(PHRASAL VERB) **grope (your way) across, along, past, etc (sth)** to move across, along, past, etc sth by feeling the way with your hands: *Vic groped his way along the darkened landing and into his bedroom.*

gross /grəʊs/ adj **1** very impolite and unpleasant: *His behaviour was really gross.* **2** (formal) obvious or serious: *There is gross inequality between the rich and the poor.* **3** total: *gross income* (= before tax, etc is taken away) ☞ The opposite is net. **4** very fat and ugly

grossly adv very: *That is grossly unfair.*

grotesque /grəʊˈtesk/ adj strange or unnatural in a way that is funny or frightening

grotty /ˈgrɒti/ adj (**grottier**; **grottiest**) (informal) unpleasant; not nice: *She lives in a grotty bed-sitting room in London.*

☆ **ground¹** /graʊnd/ noun **1 the ground** [sing] the solid surface of the earth: *We sat on the ground to eat our picnic.* ○ *He slipped off the ladder and fell to the ground.* ○ *waste ground* (= that is not being used) ○ *ground level* **2** [U] an area or type of soil: *stony ground* ☞ The **Earth** is the name of the planet where we live. **Land** is the opposite of sea: *The sailors sighted land./ The astronauts returned to Earth.* **Land** is also something that you can buy or sell: *The price of land in Tokyo is extremely high.* When you are outside, the surface under your feet is called **the ground**. When you are inside it is called **the floor**: *Don't sit on the ground. You'll get wet.* ○ *Don't sit on the floor. I'll get another chair.* Plants grow in **earth** or **soil**. **3** [C] a piece of land that is used for a particular purpose: *a sports ground* ○ *a playground* **4 grounds** [plural] land or gardens surrounding a large building: *the grounds of Buckingham Palace* **5** [U] an area of interest, study, discussion, etc: *The lecture went over the same old ground/covered a lot of new ground.* **6** [C, usually pl] a reason for sth: *She retired on medical grounds.* ○ *grounds for divorce* **7** [C, usually sing] (*US*) = EARTH²

(IDIOMS) **above/below ground** above/below the surface of the earth

break fresh/new ground to make a discovery or introduce a new method or activity: *Scientists are breaking new ground in the field of genetic engineering.*

gain ground ⇨ GAIN²

get off the ground (used about a business, scheme, etc) to make a successful start

ˌground ˈfloor noun [C] the floor of a building that is at ground level: *a ground-floor flat* ☞ Look at the note at **floor**.

ground² /graʊnd/ verb [T] **1** to force an aeroplane, etc to stay on the ground: *to be grounded by fog* **2** = EARTH²

grounding noun [sing] knowledge of the basic facts or principles of a subject: *This book provides a good grounding in English grammar.*

ground³ pt, pp of GRIND: *ground rice*

ˌground ˈbeef noun [U] (*US*) = MINCE

groundless /ˈgraʊndləs/ adj without reason: *Our fears were groundless.* —**groundlessly** adv

groundwork /ˈgraʊndwɜːk/ noun [U] work that is done in preparation for further work or study

☆ **group** /gruːp/ noun [C] **1** [with sing or pl verb] a number of people or things that are together or that are connected: *Our discussion group is/are meeting this week.* ○ *A group of us are planning to meet for lunch.* ○ *Groups of people were standing around in the streets.* ○ *He is in the 40-50 age group.* ○ *Many young people start smoking because of pressure from their peer group* (= people of the same age). ○ *people of many different social groups* ○ *a pressure group* (= a political group that tries to influence the government) ○ *Which blood group* (eg A, O, etc) *do you belong to?* ○ *Divide the class into groups.* ○ *group work* ☞ **Group** can be used in the singular with either a singular or plural verb. If you are thinking of the members of the group individually, a plural verb is more common. **2** a number of people who play pop music together: *a pop group* ☞ Look at **band**.

group verb [I,T] to form or put into one or more groups: *Group these words according to their meaning.*

grouse /graʊs/ noun [C] (*pl* **grouse**) a fat brown bird that lives in hilly areas and that is shot for sport. Grouse can be eaten.

grovel /ˈgrɒvl/ verb [I] (**grovelling**; **grovelled**; *US* **groveling**; **groveled**) to act in a very humble way towards sb who is more important than you or who can give you sth that you want: *I had to grovel to the receptionist to get an appointment with the doctor.*

(PHRASAL VERB) **grovel about/around** to move around on your hands and knees (usually when you are looking for sth)

☆ **grow** /grəʊ/ *verb* (*pt* **grew** /gruː/; *pp* **grown** /grəʊn/) **1** [I] to increase in size or number; to develop into an adult form: *Goodness, haven't you grown!* ○ *a growing child* ○ *You must invest if you want your business to grow.* ○ *The population is growing too fast.* ○ *Plants grow from seeds.* ○ *Kittens soon grow into cats.* **2** [I] (used about plants) to be alive in a particular place: *Palm trees don't normally grow in Britain.* **3** [T] to cause or allow something to grow: *Mary wants to grow her hair long.* ○ *to grow a beard/moustache* ○ *My grandfather grows a lot of vegetables in his garden.* **4** [I] to become (gradually): *It began to grow dark.* ○ *to grow older, wiser, etc* ☞ Get is also possible and is less formal.

(PHRASAL VERBS) **grow into sth 1** to become (gradually): *She has grown into a very attractive child.* **2** to become big enough to fit clothes, etc: *The coat is too big for him, but he will soon grow into it.*

grow on sb to become more pleasing: *I didn't like it at first, but it's a taste that grows on you.*

grow out of sth to become too big or too old for sth: *She's grown out of that dress.*

grow up 1 to become mature or adult: *What do you want to be when you grow up?* (= what job do you want to do later?) ○ *Oh, grow up!* (= don't be silly!) **2** (used about a feeling, etc) to develop or become strong: *A close friendship has grown up between them.*

growing *adj* increasing: *a growing problem*

grown /grəʊn/ *adj* physically adult or mature: *a fully-grown elephant*

growth /grəʊθ/ *noun* **1** [U] growing or development: *A good diet is very important for children's growth.* ○ *a growth industry* (= one that is growing) **2** [U,sing] an increase (in sth): *population growth* ○ *There has been a sudden growth in the government's popularity.* **3** [C] an abnormal lump that grows in a person's or an animal's body

,**grown 'up** *adj* physically or mentally adult or mature: *What do you want to be when you're grown up?* ○ *She's very grown up for her age.* ○ *He must be at least 45 – he's got a grown-up daughter.*

grown-up /'grəʊnʌp/ *noun* [C] an adult person: *Don't use the cooker unless a grown-up is there to help you.*

growl /graʊl/ *verb* [I] (used about dogs and other animals) to make a low noise in the throat to show anger or to give a warning —**growl** *noun* [C]

grub /grʌb/ *noun* **1** [C] the first form that an insect takes (when it has just come out of the egg). Grubs look like short fat worms. **2** [U] (*informal*) food: *I'm starving – I need some grub.*

grubby /'grʌbi/ *adj* (**grubbier**; **grubbiest**) (*informal*) dirty

grudge /grʌdʒ/ *verb* [T] **grudge sth to sb** to be unwilling to give sth to sb: *I don't grudge him his success – he deserves it.* ☞ Look at begrudge.

grudge *noun* [C] **a grudge (against sb)** unfriendly feelings towards sb, because you are angry about what has happened in the past: *She still bears a grudge against me for what happened in Italy.*

grudging *adj* given or done unwillingly: *grudging thanks* —**grudgingly** *adv*

gruelling (*US* **grueling**) /'gruːəlɪŋ/ *adj* difficult and tiring: *We had a gruelling journey from Ostend to Warsaw.*

gruesome /'gruːsəm/ *adj* (used about sth concerned with death or injury) very unpleasant or shocking: *A gruesome sight awaited the policemen when they arrived at the accident.* ☞ Look at **grisly**. It is similar in meaning.

gruff /grʌf/ *adj* (used about a person or a voice) rough and unfriendly —**gruffly** *adv* —**gruffness** *noun* [U]

grumble /'grʌmbl/ *verb* [I] to complain or protest in a bad-tempered way; to keep saying that you do not like sth: *The students were always grumbling about the standard of the food.* ☞ People usually **grumble** (or **moan**) when something is not as good as they expect. If they want to take positive action they **complain** to somebody in authority.

grumble *noun* [C] a complaint: *I'm tired of listening to your grumbles.*

grumpy /'grʌmpi/ *adj* (**grumpier**; **grumpiest**) (*informal*) bad-tempered —**grumpily** /-ɪli/ *adv* —**grumpiness** *noun* [U]

grunt /grʌnt/ *verb* [I,T] to make a noise like a pig (a short low sound in the throat). People grunt when they do not like sth or are not interested and do not want to talk: *I tried to find out her opinion but she just grunted when I asked her.* —**grunt** *noun* [C]

☆ **guarantee** /ˌgærən'tiː/ *noun* [C,U] **1** a written promise by a company that it will repair or replace a product if it goes wrong in a certain period of time: *The watch comes with a year's guarantee.* ○ *It is still under guarantee.* ○ *The guarantee has expired.* **2** a promise that sth will be done or that sth will happen: *The refugees are demanding guarantees about their safety before they return home.*

guarantee /ˌgærən'tiː/ *verb* [T] **1** to give a guarantee on a product: *This washing-machine is guaranteed for three years.* **2** to promise that sth will be done or that sth is true: *They have guaranteed delivery within one week.* ○ *The food is guaranteed to be free of additives.* ○ *I can guarantee that you will have a good time.*

☆ **guard**[1] /gɑːd/ *verb* [T] **1** to keep sb/sth safe from other people; protect: *The building was guarded by men with dogs.* ○ *soldiers guarding the President* **2** to watch over sb and prevent him/her from escaping: *The prisoner was closely guarded on the way to court.*

(PHRASAL VERB) **guard against sth** to try to prevent sth or stop sth happening: *A good diet helps to guard against disease.*

guarded *adj* (used about a statement, an

answer, etc) not saying very much; careful —**guardedly** adv

guard² /gɑːd/ noun **1** [C] a person who guards sb/sth: *a border guard* ○ *a security guard* ☞ Look at **warder** and **bodyguard**. **2** [U] the state of being ready to prevent attack or danger: *Soldiers are keeping guard at the gate.* ○ *Who is on guard?* ○ *The prisoner arrived under armed guard.* ○ *a guard dog* **3** [sing, with sing or pl verb] a group of soldiers, policemen, etc who guard sb/sth: *the changing of the guard at Buckingham Palace* ○ *a guard of honour* (= for an important person) **4** (*US* **conductor**) [C] a person who is in charge of a train **5** [C] (often in compounds) something that covers sth dangerous or protects sth: *a fire-guard* ○ *a mud-guard* (= over the wheel of a bicycle)
(IDIOM) **off/on your guard** unprepared/prepared for an attack, surprise, mistake, etc: *The question caught me off my guard and I didn't know what to say.*

guardian /'gɑːdiən/ noun [C] **1** a person or institution that guards or protects sth: *The police are the guardians of law and order.* **2** a person who is responsible for a child whose parents are dead

guerrilla (also **guerilla**) /gə'rɪlə/ noun [C] a member of a small group of fighters (not an army) who make surprise attacks on the enemy: *guerrilla warfare*

guess /ges/ verb **1** [I,T] to give an answer or opinion about sth without being sure of all the facts: *Can you guess how much this cost?* ○ *to guess at sb's age* ○ *I'd guess that he's about 45.* **2** [T] to give the correct answer when you are not sure about it; to guess correctly: *He guessed the weight of the cake exactly.* ○ *'You've passed the test!' 'How did you guess?'* **3** [T] (*informal*) (*especially US*) (used when you think that sth is probably true) to suppose: *I guess you're tired after your long journey.* ○ *We ought to leave soon, I guess.*

guess noun [C] an attempt to give the right answer when you are not sure what it is: *If you don't know the answer, then have a guess!* ○ *My guess is that they've been delayed by the traffic.* ○ *Your guess is as good as mine* (= I don't know).
(IDIOM) **at a guess** making a guess: *I don't know how far it is, but at a guess I'd say about 50 miles.*

'guesswork noun [U] an act of guessing: *I arrived at the answer by pure guesswork.*

guest /gest/ noun [C] **1** a person that you invite to your home or to a party, etc: *We are having guests for the weekend.* ○ *wedding guests* ○ *an unexpected guest* ○ *an uninvited guest* **2** a person that you invite out and pay for at a restaurant, theatre, etc **3** a person who is staying at a hotel, etc: *This hotel has accommodation for 500 guests.* **4** a person who is invited to appear on a radio or television show: *tonight's mystery guest* ○ *a guest speaker*

'guest-house noun [C] a small hotel (sometimes in a private house)

guidance /'gaɪdns/ noun [U] help or advice: *We need expert guidance on this problem.*

guide¹ /gaɪd/ noun [C] **1** a person whose job is to show cities, towns, museums, etc to tourists: *a tour guide* **2** a person who shows the way to others where it is difficult or dangerous: *We found a guide who knew the mountains well.* **3** something that helps you plan what you are going to do: *As a rough guide, add three eggs per pound of flour.* **4** (also **guidebook**) a book for tourists, etc that gives information about interesting places, etc **5** a book that gives information about a subject: *a guide to French wines* **6 Guide** = GIRL GUIDE

'guideline noun [C, usually pl] advice on what to do about sth (that is given by sb in authority): *The government has issued new guidelines on food safety.*

guide² /gaɪd/ verb [T] **1** to help a person or a group of people to find the right way or direction to go: *He guided us through the busy streets to our hotel.* ○ *In earlier times sailors were guided by the stars.* **2** to have an influence on sb/sth: *I was guided by your advice.* ☞ Look at the note at **lead³**(1).

guided adj led by a guide: *a guided tour*

guillotine /'gɪləti:n/ noun [C] a machine with a heavy sharp blade that is dropped from a great height. The guillotine was used (especially in France) for executing criminals by cutting their heads off. —**guillotine** verb [T]

guilt /gɪlt/ noun [U] **1** the feeling that you have when you know that you have done sth wrong: *Now he was dead, she felt terrible guilt at the way she had behaved.* **2** the fact of having broken a law: *His guilt was not proved and so he went free.* ☞ The opposite is **innocence**. **3** blame or responsibility for doing sth wrong: *It's difficult to say whether the guilt lies with the parents or the children.*

guilty adj (**guiltier**; **guiltiest**) **1 guilty (of sth)** having broken a law; being responsible for doing sth wrong: *She pleaded guilty/not guilty to the crime.* ○ *to be guilty of murder* ☞ The opposite is **innocent**. **2** showing or feeling guilt(1): *I feel really guilty about not having written to you for so long.* ○ *a guilty conscience* —**guiltily** /-ɪli/ adv

guinea-pig /'gɪnɪpɪg/ noun [C] **1** a small furry animal with no tail that is often kept as a pet **2** a person who is used in an experiment

guitar /gɪ'tɑː(r)/ noun [C] a type of musical instrument with strings that you play with the fingers or with a piece of plastic (a **plectrum**): *an acoustic guitar* (= wooden, with a hollow body) ○ *an electric guitar* (= using electricity, with a solid plastic body) ☞ picture at **rock band**. Note that we say 'play **the** guitar'.

guitarist /gɪ'tɑːrɪst/ noun [C] a person who plays the guitar

gulf /gʌlf/ noun [C] **1** a part of the sea that is almost surrounded by land: *the Gulf of Mexico* **2** an important or serious difference between people or their opinions: *a wide gulf between people of different generations*

gull /gʌl/ (also **'seagull**) noun [C] a white or grey sea-bird with a loud cry

gullible /'gʌləbl/ adj (used about a person) easily tricked or deceived

gulp /gʌlp/ verb **1** [T] **gulp sth (down)** to eat or drink sth quickly **2** [I] to make a swallowing movement because you are afraid, surprised, etc

gulp noun [C] **1** the act of gulping **2** the amount that you can swallow when you gulp: *He took a gulp of coffee and rushed out.*

gum[1] /gʌm/ noun [C, usually pl] the hard pink part of the mouth that holds the teeth

☆ **gum**[2] /gʌm/ noun [U] **1** a substance that you use to stick things together (especially pieces of paper) **2** = CHEWING GUM ☛ Look at **bubble gum.**

gum verb (gumming; gummed) [T] **gum A to/onto B; gum A and B together** to stick sth with gum(1): *The labels were gummed onto the boxes.*

☆ **gun** /gʌn/ noun [C] a weapon that is used for shooting. A gun fires bullets from a metal tube (a **barrel**): *The robber held a gun to the bank manager's head.*

☛ Verbs often used with 'gun' are **load, unload, point, aim, fire.** Different types of gun include a **machine-gun, pistol, revolver, rifle, shotgun.**

gun verb [T] (gunning; gunned)
(PHRASAL VERB) **gun sb down** (*informal*) to shoot sb and kill or seriously injure him/her

'gunboat noun [C] a small warship that carries heavy guns

'gunfire noun [U] the act of firing a gun or several guns; the sound that it makes: *We were awakened by the sound of gunfire.*

'gunman /-mən/ noun [C] (*pl* **gunmen** /-mən/) a man who uses a gun to rob or kill people

'gunpoint noun
(IDIOM) **at gunpoint** threatening to shoot: *He held the hostages at gunpoint* (= he said that he would shoot them if they did not obey him).

'gunpowder noun [U] an explosive powder that is used in guns and fireworks

'gunshot noun [C] the firing of a gun or guns or the sound that it makes: *gunshot wounds*

gurgle /'gɜ:gl/ noun [C] a sound like water draining out of a bath

gurgle verb [I] to make a gurgle or gurgles: *The baby gurgled with pleasure.*

guru /'goru:; *US* gə'ru:/ noun [C] **1** a spiritual leader or teacher in the Hindu religion **2** somebody whose opinions you admire and respect, and whose ideas you follow

gush /gʌʃ/ verb [I] **1 gush (out) (from sth)** (used about a liquid) to flow out suddenly and in great quantities: *Blood gushed from the wound.* **2 gush over sb/sth** to express pleasure or admiration in an exaggerated way
—**gush** noun [C, usually sing]: *a sudden gush of water* —**gushing** adj: *a gushing stream* ○ *gushing praise* (= given in an exaggerated way)

gust /gʌst/ noun [C] a sudden rush of wind: *There will be gusts of wind of up to 80 miles per hour.*

gust verb [I] (used about the wind) to blow in gusts

gusto /'gʌstəʊ/ noun
(IDIOM) **with gusto** with great enthusiasm: *We all joined in the singing with gusto.*

gut /gʌt/ noun **1 guts** [plural] (*informal*) the organs inside your body (especially those in the lower part of the abdomen): *a pain in the guts* **2 guts** [plural] (*informal*) courage and determination: *It takes guts to admit that you are wrong.* **3** [C] the tube in the lower part of the body which food passes through ☛ Look at **intestine**, which is a more technical word.

gut verb (gutting; gutted) [T] **1** to remove the guts(1) from an animal, fish, etc **2** to destroy the inside of a building (in a fire): *The warehouse was gutted by fire.*

gut adj (only *before* a noun) based on emotion or feeling rather than on reason: *a gut feeling/reaction*

gutter /'gʌtə(r)/ noun [C] **1** a long metal or plastic pipe that is fixed under the edge of a roof to carry away rainwater. **2** a channel between the road and the pavement that carries away rainwater

guy /gaɪ/ noun [C] **1** (*informal*) a man or a boy: *He's a nice guy.* ☛ In American English *you guys* is used when speaking to both men and women: *What do you guys want to eat?* **2** (*Brit*) a figure of a man, made of straw and dressed in old clothes, that is burned on 5 November in memory of Guy Fawkes ☛ Look at **Bonfire Night.**

guzzle /'gʌzl/ verb [I,T] (*informal*) to eat or drink greedily

gym /dʒɪm/ noun (*informal*) **1** [C] = GYMNASIUM **2** [U] = GYMNASTICS: *gym-shoes* ○ *a gym class*

gymnasium /dʒɪm'neɪziəm/ (*also informal* **gym**) noun [C] (*pl* **gymnasiums** or **gymnasia** /-ziə/) a large room that contains equipment, eg bars, ropes, etc for doing physical exercises

gymnastics /dʒɪm'næstɪks/ (*also* **gym**) noun [U] physical exercises that are done indoors, often using special equipment such as bars and ropes

gymnast /'dʒɪmnæst/ noun [C] a person who is an expert at gymnastics

gynaecology (*US* **gynecology**) /ˌgaɪnə-ˈkɒlədʒi/ noun [U] the study and treatment of diseases and medical problems that only women have

gynaecologist (*US* **gynecologist**) noun [C] a doctor who has special training in gynaecology

gypsy (*also* **gipsy**) /'dʒɪpsi/ noun [C] (*pl* **gypsies**) (*also* **traveller**) a member of a race of people who spend their lives travelling around from place to place, living in caravans

---

3:	ə	eɪ	əʊ	aɪ	aʊ	ɔɪ	ɪə	eə	ʊə
fur	ago	pay	home	five	now	join	near	hair	pure

Hh

H, h /eɪtʃ/ *noun* [C] (*pl* **H's**; **h's**) the eighth letter of the English alphabet: *'Hat' begins with (an) 'H'*.

ha /hɑː/ *interj* **1** (used for showing that you are surprised or pleased) **2** (*also* **ha! ha!**) (used in written language to show that sb is laughing)

☆**habit** /'hæbɪt/ *noun* **1** [C] something that sb does very often (sometimes almost without thinking about it): *Biting your nails is a horrible habit.* ○ *He's got an annoying habit of coming round just as we're going out.* ☞ A **habit** is usually something that is done by one person. A **custom** is something that is done by a group, community or nation: *the custom of giving presents at Christmas.* **2** [U] doing sth regularly: *I think I only smoke out of habit now – I don't really enjoy it.*

(IDIOM) **be in/get into the habit of doing sth**; **make a habit of sth** to do sth regularly: *I've got into the habit of going for a jog every morning.* ○ *I don't make a habit of chatting to strange men at parties.*

habitable /'hæbɪtəbl/ *adj* (used about buildings) suitable to be lived in ☞ The opposite is **uninhabitable**.

habitat /'hæbɪtæt/ *noun* [C] the natural home of a plant or an animal

habitation /ˌhæbɪ'teɪʃn/ *noun* [U] (*formal*) living in a place: *These houses are not fit for human habitation.*

habitual /hə'bɪtʃuəl/ *adj* **1** doing sth very often: *a habitual liar* **2** which you always have or do; usual: *He had his habitual cigarette after lunch.* —**habitually** /-tʃuəli/ *adv*

hack¹ /hæk/ *verb* [I,T] to cut sth using rough strokes with a tool such as a large knife or an axe: *He hacked (away) at the branch of the tree until it fell.* ○ *The explorers hacked their way through the jungle.*

hack² /hæk/ *verb* [I,T] **hack (into) (sth)** (*informal*) to use a computer to look at (and change) information that is stored on another computer

hacker *noun* [C] (*informal*) **1** a person who hacks² **2** a person who spends a lot of time using computers

had¹ *pt, pp* of HAVE¹,²

had² /hæd/ *adj* (*informal*) tricked or deceived: *I've been had. This watch I bought doesn't go.*

haemophilia (*US* **hemophilia**) /ˌhiːmə'fɪliə/ *noun* [U] a disease that causes a person to bleed very heavily even from very small injuries because the blood does not thicken (**clot**) properly.

haemophiliac (*US* **hemophiliac**) /ˌhiːmə'fɪliæk/ *noun* [C] a person who suffers from haemophilia

haemorrhage (*US* **hemorrhage**) /'hemərɪdʒ/ *noun* [C,U] very heavy bleeding

haemorrhoids (*especially US* **hemorrhoids**) /'hemərɔɪdz/ (*also* **piles**) *noun* [plural] painful swellings in the veins near the anus

haggard /'hægəd/ *adj* (used about a person) looking tired or worried

haggle /'hægl/ *verb* [I] **haggle (with sb) (over/about sth)** to argue about the price of sth

hail¹ /heɪl/ *noun* [U] frozen rain that falls in small hard balls (**hailstones**) —**hail** *verb* [I]: *It is hailing.* ☞ Look at the note at **weather**.

hail² /heɪl/ *verb* [T] **1** to call or wave to sb/sth: *She raised her umbrella to hail the taxi.* **2 hail sb/sth as sth** to say in public that sth is very good: *The book was hailed as a masterpiece.*

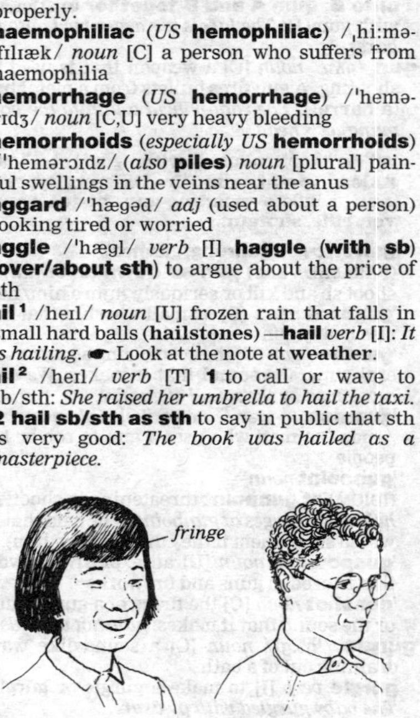

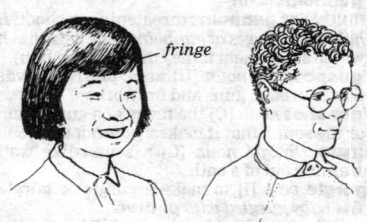

fringe

straight hair   curly hair

wavy hair   he's bald

☆**hair** /heə(r)/ *noun* **1** [C] one of the long thin things that grow on the skin of people and animals: *There's a hair in my soup.* ○ *The dog left hairs all over the furniture.* **2** [U] the mass of hairs on a person's head: *He has got short black hair.*

p	b	t	d	k	g	tʃ	dʒ	f	v	θ	ð
pen	bad	tea	did	cat	got	chin	June	fall	van	thin	then

☛ Some special words for the colour of hair are: **auburn, blond, fair, ginger** and **red**. In order to look after or style your hair you may **brush, comb, wash** (or **shampoo**) it and then **blow-dry** it. You may **part** it (or have **a parting**) in the middle or on one side. When you go to the **hairdresser's** you have your hair **cut, set** or **permed**.

(IDIOMS) **let your hair down** (*informal*) to relax and enjoy yourself (after being formal): *After the wedding ceremony you can let your hair down at the reception.*

split hairs ⇨ SPLIT

-haired (in compounds) having hair of the stated type: *a long-haired rabbit*

hairless *adj* without hair

hairy *adj* (**hairier; hairiest**) **1** having a lot of hair: *a hairy chest* **2** (*slang*) dangerous or worrying: *We had a hairy journey down the motorway in freezing fog.*

'hairbrush *noun* [C] a brush that you use on your hair ☛ picture at **brush**.

'haircut *noun* [C] **1** the cutting of your hair by a hairdresser, etc: *You need to have a haircut.* **2** the style in which your hair has been cut: *That haircut really suits you.*

'hairdresser *noun* [C] a person whose job is to cut and style people's hair: *I've made an appointment at the hairdresser's for 10 o'clock.*
☛ A **barber** is a hairdresser who only cuts men's hair.

'hair-drier (*also* **'hair-dryer**) *noun* [C] a machine that dries hair by blowing hot air through it

'hairpin *noun* [C] a U-shaped pin that is used for holding the hair in place

,hairpin 'bend (*US* **,hairpin 'curve; ,hairpin 'turn**) *noun* [C] a very sharp bend in a road on a steep hill

'hairstyle *noun* [C] the style in which your hair has been cut or arranged

hair-raising /'heə(r) reɪzɪŋ/ *adj* that makes you very frightened

☆ **half¹** /hɑːf; *US* hæf/ *noun* [C] (*pl* **halves** /hɑːvz; *US* hævz/) one of two equal parts of sth: *Two halves make a whole.* ∘ *The second half of the book is more exciting.* ∘ *Giggs scored in the first half* (= of a match). ☛ The verb is **halve**.

(IDIOMS) **break, cut, etc sth in half** to break, etc sth into two parts

go halves with sb to share the cost of sth with sb

☆ **half²** /hɑːf; *US* hæf/ *det, pron* forming one of two equal parts: *Half of this money is yours.* ∘ *He got half his aunt's money when she died.* ∘ *half a pint/a half-pint/half an hour* ∘ *Half the people in the office leave at 5.*

(IDIOM) **half past...** thirty minutes past an hour on the clock: *half past 6* (= 6.30)

,half 'board *noun* [U] (in a hotel, etc) breakfast and an evening meal ☛ Look at **full board** and **bed and breakfast**.

'half-brother, 'half-sister *nouns* [C] a brother or sister with whom you share one parent

,half-'price *adv* at half the usual price

,half-'term *noun* [C] a short holiday in the middle of a school term

,half-'time *noun* [sing] (in sport) the period of time between the two halves of a match

,half'way *adj, adv* at an equal distance between two places; in the middle of a period of time: *We live halfway between Oxford and Reading.* ∘ *They have a break halfway through the morning.*

☆ **half³** /hɑːf; *US* hæf/ *adv* to the extent of half; not completely: *half full* ∘ *The hotel was only half finished.* ∘ *I half thought he might come, but he didn't.* ∘ *He's half German.*

,half-'hearted *adj* without interest or enthusiasm —**,half-'heartedly** *adv*

☆ **hall** /hɔːl/ *noun* [C] **1** (*also* **'hallway**) to room or passage that is just inside the front entrance of a house or public building: *Leave your coat in the hall.* ∘ *There is a public telephone in the entrance hall of this building.* **2** a building or large room in which meetings, concerts, dances, etc can be held: *The end-of-year party will be held in the school hall.* ∘ *a concert hall*
☛ Look at **town hall**.

,hall of 'residence *noun* [C] (in colleges, universities, etc) a building where students live

☆ **hallo** (*also* **hello, hullo**) /hə'ləʊ/ *interj* (used for greeting sb, for attracting sb's attention or when you are using the telephone): *Hallo, how are you?* ∘ *Hallo, is anybody there?* ∘ *Hallo, this is Oxford 56767.*

☛ **Hallo** is the most common greeting in British English. **Hi** is used in US English. It is also used in British English but is quite informal.

Hallowe'en /,hæləʊ'iːn/ *noun* [sing] the night before All Saints' Day, 31 October

☛ By tradition Hallowe'en is the time when witches and ghosts are said to appear. Children now dress up as witches, etc and play tricks on people.

hallucination /hə,luːsɪ'neɪʃn/ *noun* [C,U] seeing sth that is not really there (because you are ill or have taken a drug)

halo /'heɪləʊ/ *noun* [C] (*pl* **halos** or **haloes**) the circle of light that is drawn around the head of a holy person in a painting

halt /hɔːlt/ *noun* [sing] a stop (that does not last very long): *Work came to a halt when the machine broke down.* ∘ *to bring sth to a halt*
(IDIOM) **grind to a halt/standstill** ⇨ GRIND

halt *verb* [I,T] to stop for a short time; to make sth stop

halve /hɑːv; *US* hæv/ *verb* [T] **1** to divide sth into two equal parts: *First halve the peach and then remove the stone.* **2** to make sth half as big as it was before: *We aim to halve the number of people on our waiting list in the next six months.*

ham /hæm/ *noun* [U] meat from a pig's back leg that has been smoked, etc to keep it fresh: *a slice of ham* ∘ *a ham sandwich* ☛ Look at **bacon** and **pork** and at the note at **meat**.

hamburger /'hæmbɜːgə(r)/ *noun* **1** (*also* **burger**) [C] minced meat that has been formed into a flat round shape. Hamburgers are often eaten in a bread roll. **2** [U] (*US*) = MINCE

hamlet /'hæmlɪt/ *noun* [C] a very small village

hammer¹ /'hæmə(r)/ *noun* [C] **1** a tool with a heavy metal head that is used for hitting nails,

s	z	ʃ	ʒ	h	m	n	ŋ	l	r	j	w
so	zoo	she	vision	how	man	no	sing	leg	red	yes	wet

hammer

etc ☛ picture at **tool**. **2 the hammer** a sports event in which a metal ball attached to a wire is thrown

hammer² /'hæmə(r)/ *verb* **1** [I,T] to hit with a hammer: *She hammered the nail into the wall.* **2** [I] to hit sth, making a loud noise: *He hammered on the door until somebody opened it.*
(IDIOMS) **hammer sth into sb** to force sb to remember sth by repeating it many times **hammer sth out 1** to hammer sth back into the shape that it should be **2** (*figurative*) to succeed in making a plan or agreement after a lot of difficulty: *Eventually a solution was hammered out.*

hammering /'hæmərɪŋ/ *noun* **1** [U] the noise that is made by sb using a hammer or by sb knocking sth many times **2** [C] (*informal*) a very bad defeat

hammock /'hæmək/ *noun* [C] a bed, made of canvas or strong net, which is hung up at both ends. Hammocks are used on board ships or in the garden.

hamper¹ /'hæmpə(r)/ *noun* [C] a large basket with a lid that is used for carrying food

hamper² /'hæmpə(r)/ *verb* [T] to make sth difficult: *The building work was hampered by bad weather.*

hamster /'hæmstə(r)/ *noun* [C] a small animal that is kept as a pet. Hamsters are like small rats but are fatter and do not have a tail. They store food in the sides of their mouths.

☆ **hand¹** /hænd/ *noun* **1** [C] the part of a person's arm below the wrist: *He took the child by the hand.* ○ *She lifted the pan out of the oven with her bare hands.* ○ *He held the bird gently in the palm of his hand.* **2 a hand** [sing] some help: *I'll give you a hand with the washing up.* **3** [C] the pointer on a clock or watch: *the hour/minute/second hand* ☛ picture at **clock**. **4** [C] a person who works with his/her hands: *All hands* (= all sailors) *on deck!* **5** [C] the set of playing-cards that sb has been given in a game of cards
(IDIOMS) **at first, second, etc hand** (used about information that you have received) from sb who was directly/not directly involved: *I have only heard about it at second hand* (= not from sb who was actually there). ☛ Look at **second-hand**.
(close/near) at hand (*formal*) near in space or time: *Help is close at hand.*
be an old hand (at sth) ⇨ OLD
by hand 1 done by a person and not by machine: *I had to do all the sewing by hand.* **2** not by post: *The letter was delivered by hand.*
change hands ⇨ CHANGE
get, have, etc a free hand ⇨ FREE¹
get, etc the upper hand ⇨ UPPER
give sb/get a big hand ⇨ BIG
hand in hand 1 holding each other's hands **2** (*figurative*) usually happening together; closely connected
hands off (sb/sth) (*informal*) (used for ordering sb not to touch sth or to leave sth alone)
hands up 1 (used in a classroom, etc for asking people to raise one hand and give an answer): *Hands up, who'd like to go on the trip this afternoon?* **2** (used by a person with a

hand

gun to tell other people to put their hands in the air)
have your hands full to be very busy so that you cannot do anything else
a helping hand ⇨ HELP¹
hold sb's hand to give help or comfort to sb in a difficult situation
hold hands (with sb) (used about two people) to hold each other's hands (because you like each other)
in hand 1 (used about money, etc) not yet used: *We still have about £50 in hand.* **2** being dealt with at the moment; under control: *Let's finish the job in hand first before we start something new.* ○ *The situation is in hand.* ☛ Look at **out of hand**.
in your/sb's hands in your/sb's possession, control or care: *The document is no longer in my hands.* ○ *The matter is in the hands of a solicitor.* ○ *She is in capable hands.*
off your hands not your responsibility any more: *Once the children are off our hands we want to go on a world cruise.*
on hand available to help or to be used: *There is a teacher on hand to help during your private study periods.*
on your hands being your responsibility: *We seem to have a problem on our hands.*
on the one hand... on the other (hand) (used for showing opposite points of view): *On the one hand, of course, cars are very useful. But on the other, they cause a huge amount of pollution.*
out of hand not under control: *Violence at football matches is getting out of hand.* ☛ Look at **in hand**.
out of your/sb's hands not in your/sb's control: *I can't help you, I'm afraid. The matter is out of my hands.*
shake sb's hand/shake hands (with sb)/shake sb by the hand ⇨ SHAKE
to hand near; within reach: *I'm afraid I haven't got my diary to hand.*
wash your hands of sb/sth ⇨ WASH¹
-handed (in compounds) having, using or made for the stated type of hand(s): *heavy-handed* ○ *right-handed* ○ *left-handed scissors*

handful /'hændfʊl/ *noun* **1** [C] **a handful (of sth)** as much or as many of sth as you can hold in one hand: *a handful of sand* **2** [sing] a small number (of sb/sth): *Only a handful of people came to the meeting.* **3 a handful** [sing] (*informal*) a person or an animal that is difficult to control: *The little girl is quite a handful.*

'handbag (*US* **purse**) *noun* [C] a small bag in which you carry money, keys, etc

'handbrake *noun* [C] a brake in a car, etc that is operated by hand and that is used when the car is not moving

'handcuffs *noun* [plural] a pair of metal rings that are joined together by a chain and put around the wrists of prisoners

'hand-luggage (*US* **'hand-baggage**) *noun* [U] a small bag, etc that you carry with you onto an aeroplane

'handmade *adj* made by hand, not by machine

,hand-'picked *adj* carefully chosen

i:	ɪ	e	æ	ɑ:	ɒ	ɔ:	ʊ	u:	ʌ
see	sit	ten	hat	arm	got	saw	put	too	cup

'handrail noun [C] a wooden or metal bar that you hold on to when going up or down stairs, or that stops you from falling from high places

'handset noun [C] **1** = RECEIVER(1) **2** = TELEPHONE(2)

'handshake noun [C] the act of shaking sb's right hand with your own as a greeting

,hands-'on adj learnt by you doing sth yourself, not watching sb else do it; practical: *She has hands-on computer experience.*

'handwriting noun [U] a person's style of writing by hand

'handwritten adj written by hand, not typed or printed

☆ **hand²** /hænd/ verb [T] to give or pass sth to sb: *Please hand me the scissors.* ○ *Please hand the scissors to me.* ○ *Could you hand round the biscuits, please?*

(PHRASAL VERBS) **hand sth down (to sb) 1** to pass customs, traditions, etc from older people to younger ones: *These stories have been handed down from generation to generation.* **2** to pass clothes, toys, etc from older children to younger ones in the family

hand sth in (to sb) to give sth to sb in authority: *I found a wallet and handed it in to the police.* ○ *She handed in her resignation.*

hand sth on (to sb) to send or give sth to another person: *When you have read the article, please hand it on to another student.*

hand sth out (to sb) to give sth to many people in a group: *Food was handed out to the starving people.*

hand sb over to sb (used at a meeting or on the television, radio, etc) to let another person speak: *I'm handing you over now to our foreign correspondent.*

hand sb/sth over (to sb) to give sb/sth (to sb): *People were tricked into handing over large sums of money.* ○ *The terrorist was handed over to the British police.*

handout /'hændaʊt/ noun [C] **1** food, money, etc given to people who need it badly **2** a printed sheet or leaflet that is given to a lot of people, to advertise sth or to explain sth in a lesson or lecture

handbook /'hændbʊk/ noun [C] a small book that gives useful information and advice about sth

handicap /'hændɪkæp/ noun [C] **1** something that makes doing sth more difficult; a disadvantage: *Not speaking French is going to be a bit of a handicap in my new job.* **2** something physical or mental that means you cannot lead a completely normal life: *The local services for people with a mental handicap have improved greatly.* **3** a disadvantage that is given to a strong competitor in a sports event, etc so that the other competitors have more chance

handicap verb (handicapping; handicapped) [T] (usually passive) to give or be a disadvantage to sb: *They were handicapped by their lack of education.*

handicapped adj having sth serious wrong with you (either physically or mentally) that means that you cannot lead a completely normal life: *a handicapped child* ○ *a club for the mentally handicapped* ○ *a special machine for the visually handicapped* ☛ Look at **disabled**.

handicraft /'hændɪkrɑːft; *US* -kræft/ noun **1** [C] an activity that needs skill with the hands as well as artistic ability, eg sewing **2 handicrafts** [plural] the objects that are produced by this activity

☆ **handkerchief** /'hæŋkətʃɪf; -tʃiːf/ noun (pl **handkerchiefs** or **handkerchieves** /-tʃiːvz/) a square piece of cloth or soft thin paper that you use for blowing your nose ☛ picture at **sneeze**. A handkerchief that is made of soft thin paper is also called a **paper handkerchief** or a **tissue**.

☆ **handle** /'hændl/ noun [C] a part of sth that is used for holding or opening it: *She turned the handle and opened the door.* ○ *the door handle* ○ *the handle of a frying-pan* ☛ picture at **pan**.

(IDIOM) **fly off the handle** ⇨ FLY²

handle verb [T] **1** to touch sth with, or hold sth in, your hand(s): *Wash your hands before you handle food.* ○ *Handle with care!* **2** to deal with or to control sb/sth: *This port handles 100 million tons of cargo each year.* ○ *I have a problem at work and I don't really know how to handle it.*

'handlebar noun [C, usually pl] the curved metal bar at the front of a bicycle that you hold when you are riding it ☛ picture at **bicycle**.

☆ **handsome** /'hænsəm/ adj **1** (used about a man) good-looking; attractive ☛ Look at the note at **beautiful**. **2** large or generous: *The company made a handsome profit.* —**handsomely** adv: *Her efforts were handsomely rewarded.*

handy /'hændi/ adj (**handier**; **handiest**) **1** useful; easy to use: *a handy tip* ○ *a handy gadget* **2** nearby or within easy reach of sth: *Always keep a first-aid kit handy.* ○ *The house is very handy for the shops.*

(IDIOM) **come in handy** to be useful at some time: *Don't throw that box away. It may come in handy.*

handyman /'hændimæn/ noun (pl **handymen** /-men/) a person who is clever at making or mending things

☆ **hang¹** /hæŋ/ verb (pt, pp **hung** /hʌŋ/) ☛ The past tense and past participle **hanged** is only used in sense 2. **1** [I,T] to fasten sth or be fastened at the top so that the lower part is free or loose: *Hang your coat on the hook.* ○ *I hung the washing on the line.* ○ *I left the washing hanging on the line all day.* ○ (figurative): *People were hanging out of windows to see the Queen go past.* **2** [T] to kill sb by putting a rope around their neck and allowing them to drop: *She hanged herself in a fit of depression.* ○ *He was hanged for murder.* **3** [I] **hang (above/over sb/sth)** to stay in the air (above/over sb/sth): *Smog hung in the air over the city.* ○ (figurative) *That essay I've got to write is hanging over me.*

(PHRASAL VERBS) **hang about/around** (informal) to stay in or near a place not doing very much: *I really hate hanging around in airports.*

hang on 1 to hold sth tightly: *Keep hanging on. We're very close to you now.* **2** to wait for a short time: *Hang on a minute. I'm nearly ready.*

o *The line is engaged. Would you like to hang on or call back later?*
hang on to sth 1 to hold sth tightly **2** (*informal*) to keep sth: *Let's hang on to the car for another year.*
hang sth out to put washing, etc on a clothesline so that it can dry
hang up (on sb) (*informal*) to end a telephone conversation by putting down the receiver ☛ Look at the note at **telephone**.
hanging *noun* [C,U] death by hanging: *Many members of the party would like to bring back hanging.*
hanger-on /ˌhæŋər'ɒn/ *noun* (*pl* **hangers-on** /ˌhæŋəz'ɒn/) a person who tries to be friendly with sb who is rich or important
'hang-glider *noun* [C] a type of large kite from which a person can hang and fly through the air
'hang-gliding *noun* [U] the sport of flying using a hang-glider
'hangman /-mən/ *noun* (*pl* **hangmen** /-mən/) a person who hangs criminals
'hang-up /'hæŋʌp/ *noun* [C] (*slang*) something that worries you a lot: *He has a real hang-up about his height.*

hang² /hæŋ/ *noun*
(IDIOM) **get the hang of sth** (*informal*) to learn how to use or do sth: *It took me a long time to get the hang of this new car.*

hangar /'hæŋə(r)/ *noun* [C] a big building where aeroplanes are kept

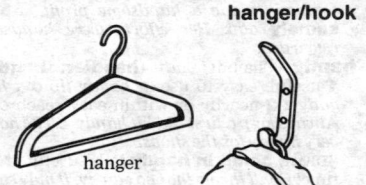

hanger/hook

hanger

hook

hanger /'hæŋə(r)/ (*also* **'clothes-hanger**; **'coat-hanger**) *noun* [C] a metal, plastic or wooden object with a hook that is used for hanging up clothes in a cupboard
hangover /'hæŋəʊvə(r)/ *noun* [C] a headache and a feeling of sickness that you wake up with if you have drunk too much alcohol the night before
hanker /'hæŋkə(r)/ *verb* [I] **hanker after/for sth** to want sth very much (often sth that you cannot easily have): *I've been hankering for a cigarette all morning.*
hanky (*also* **hankie**) /'hæŋki/ *noun* [C] (*pl* **hankies**) (*informal*) a handkerchief
haphazard /hæp'hæzəd/ *adj* without any order or organized plan: *Her system of filing seems to be completely haphazard.* —**haphazardly** *adv*
☆ **happen** /'hæpən/ *verb* [I] **1** (of an event or situation) to take place: *Can you describe to the police what happened after you left the party?* o *How did the accident happen?* ☛ **Happen** and **occur** are usually used with events that are not planned. **Occur** is more formal than **happen**. **Take place** suggests that an event is planned: *The wedding took place on Saturday June 13th.* **2 happen to sb/sth** to be what sb/sth experiences: *What do you think has happened to Julie? She should have been here an hour ago.* o *What will happen to the business when your father retires?* **3 happen to do sth** to do sth by chance: *I happened to meet him in London yesterday.* o *She happened to be in London yesterday, too.*
(IDIOMS) **as it happens/happened** (used when you are adding to what you have said) by chance; actually: *As it happens, I did remember to bring the book you wanted.*
it (just) so happens ⇨ SO¹
happening /'hæpənɪŋ/ *noun* [C, usually pl] a thing that happens; an event (that is usually strange or difficult to explain): *Strange happenings have been reported in that old hotel.*
☛ A **happening** is usually something that happens by chance. An **event** is usually something that is planned and suggests something special or important.
☆ **happy** /'hæpi/ *adj* (**happier; happiest**) **1** feeling, showing or giving pleasure or satisfaction: *a happy childhood* o *a happy family* o *a happy smile* o *The film is sad but it has a happy ending.* o *She doesn't feel happy about the salary she's been offered.* o *Are you happy in your work?* o *I'm not very happy with what you've done.* o *Congratulations! I'm very happy for you.* ☛ The opposite is **unhappy**. Look at the note at **glad**. **2** (not before a noun) **happy to do sth** willing; pleased: *I'll be happy to see you any day next week.* **3** Happy (used in greetings to wish sb an enjoyable time): *Happy Birthday!* o *Happy Christmas!* **4** (only *before* a noun) lucky; fortunate: *He's in the happy position of being able to retire at 50!* ☛ The opposite is **unhappy**.
(IDIOM) **many happy returns (of the day)** (used as a greeting to sb on his/her birthday)
happily *adv* **1** in a happy way: *They all lived happily ever after.* o *I would happily give up my job if I didn't need the money.* **2** it is lucky that; fortunately: *The police found my handbag and, happily, nothing had been stolen.* —**happiness** *noun* [U]: *Money can't buy happiness.*
ˌhappy-go-'lucky *adj* not worried about life and the future
harass /'hærəs; *US* hə'ræs/ *verb* [T] to annoy or put pressure on sb, especially continuously or on many different occasions: *The court ordered him to stop harassing his ex-wife.*
harassed *adj* tired and worried because you have too much to do: *Five children came in, followed by a harassed-looking mother.* —**harassment** *noun* [U]: *She accused her boss of sexual harassment.*
☆ **harbour** (*US* **harbor**) /'hɑːbə(r)/ *noun* [C] a place on the coast where ships can be tied up (**moored**) to shelter from the sea: *a busy little fishing harbour* o *The weather was too rough for the fishing boats to leave harbour yesterday.*
harbour (*US* **harbor**) *verb* [T] **1** to keep sth secret in your mind for a long time: *She harboured a deep dislike of him for years.* **2** to hide

or give shelter to sb/sth bad: *They were accused of harbouring terrorists.*

☆ **hard¹** /hɑːd/ *adj* **1** not soft to touch; not easy to break or bend; very firm: *The bed was so hard that I couldn't sleep.* ○ *Diamonds are the hardest known mineral.* **2 hard (for sb) (to do sth)** difficult to do or understand; not easy: *The first question in the exam was very hard.* ○ *This book is hard to understand./It is a hard book to understand.* ○ *It's hard to know why he made that decision.* ○ *It's hard for young people to find good jobs nowadays.* **3** needing or using a lot of effort: *It's a hard climb to the top of the hill.* ○ *Hard work is said to be good for you.* ○ *We had some long, hard talks before we came to an agreement.* ○ *He's a hard worker.* **4 hard (on sb)** (used about a person) not feeling or not showing kindness or pity; not gentle: *You have to be hard to succeed in business.* ○ *She used some very hard words to tell him what she thought of him.* ○ *He's much too hard on his children.* **5** (used about conditions) unpleasant or unhappy: *He had a hard time when his parents died.* **6** (used about the weather) very cold: *The forecast is for a hard winter.* ☞ The opposite is **mild**. **7** (used about water) containing particular minerals so that soap does not make many bubbles ☞ The opposite is **soft**.
(IDIOMS) **be hard on sb/sth 1** to hurt sb/sth or to make things difficult: *Managing with very little money can be hard on students.* **2** to be unfair to sb: *It's a bit hard on the people who haven't got a car.*

hard facts information that is true, not just people's opinions

hard luck ⇨ LUCK

a hard/rough time ⇨ TIME¹

hardness *noun* [U] being hard

'**hardback** *noun* [C] a book that has a hard stiff cover ☞ Note the phrase **in hardback**: *I'm afraid this book is only available in hardback.* Look at **paperback**.

'**hard core** *noun* [sing, with sing or pl verb] the members of a group who are the most active: *The hard core of the organization is/are meeting to discuss the matter.*

,**hard 'currency** *noun* [U] money belonging to a particular country that is easy to exchange

,**hard 'disk** *noun* [C] a piece of hard plastic used for storing information inside a computer. It can hold more information than a floppy disk.

,**hard 'drug** *noun* [C] a drug that is strong and dangerous because people may become dependent on (**addicted to**) it

,**hard-'headed** *adj* not influenced by feelings: *a hard-headed businessman*

,**hard-'hearted** *adj* not being kind to or thinking about other people

,**hard 'line** *noun* [sing] a way of thinking or a plan which will not be changed or influenced by anything: *The government has taken a very hard line on people who drink and drive.*

,**hard 'shoulder** *noun* [C] a narrow strip of road at the side of a motorway where cars are allowed to stop in an emergency

☆ **hard²** /hɑːd/ *adv* **1** with great effort, energy or attention: *He worked hard all his life.* ○ *You'll have to try a bit harder than that.* ○ *She looked hard at the man but she didn't recognize him.* **2** with great force; heavily: *It was snowing hard.* ○ *He hit her hard across the face.*
(IDIOMS) **be hard up** to have very little money: *We're too hard up to afford a holiday this year.*

die hard ⇨ DIE

hard done by not fairly treated: *He felt very hard done by when he wasn't chosen for the team.*

,**hard-'boiled** *adj* (used about an egg) boiled until it is hard inside

,**hard-'wearing** *adj* (used about materials, clothes, etc) strong and able to last for a long time

,**hard-'working** *adj* working with effort and energy: *a hard-working man*

harden /'hɑːdn/ *verb* **1** [I,T] to become or to make sth hard or less likely to change: *Allow the icing to harden before decorating the cake.* ○ *The firm has hardened its attitude on this question.* **2** [T] (usually passive) **harden sb (to sth)** to make sb less sensitive: *a hardened reporter* ○ *a hardened criminal* ☞ **Harden** is only used when hard means 'firm' or 'unkind': *The concrete will harden in 24 hours.* ○ *He hardened himself to the feelings of other people.* **Get harder** is used when hard has another meaning such as 'difficult': *Learning a foreign language gets harder as you get older.*

☆ **hardly** /'hɑːdli/ *adv* **1** only just; almost not; with difficulty: *Speak up – I can hardly hear you.* ○ *She'd hardly gone to sleep than it was time to get up again.* ○ *I can hardly wait for the holidays to begin.* ○ *It hardly matters whether you are there or not.* ○ *Winning this money could hardly have come at a better time.* ☞ Note that if 'hardly' is at the beginning of a sentence, the verb follows immediately: *Hardly had she gone to sleep than it was time to get up again.* **2** (used especially before 'any', 'ever', 'anybody', etc) almost none, never, nobody, etc: *There's hardly any* (= almost no) *coffee left.* ○ *We hardly ever* (= almost never) *go to the theatre nowadays.* ○ *Hardly anybody I knew was at the party.* **3** (used when you are saying that sth is not probable or that it is unreasonable): *He can hardly expect me to do all his washing for him!* ○ *She hasn't written for two years – she's hardly likely to write now* (= it's very improbable that she will write now).

hardship /'hɑːdʃɪp/ *noun* [C,U] difficulty or problems, eg because you do not have enough money; the situation in which these difficulties exist: *This new tax is going to cause a lot of hardship.* ○ *Not having a car is going to be a real hardship for us.*

☆ **hardware** /'hɑːdweə(r)/ *noun* [U] **1** tools and equipment that are used in the house and garden: *a hardware shop* **2** the machinery of a computer, not the programmes written for it ☞ Look at **software**. **3** heavy machinery or weapons

hardy /'hɑːdi/ *adj* (**hardier**; **hardiest**) (used about people, animals and plants) able to stand cold weather or difficult conditions

hare /heə(r)/ *noun* [C] an animal like a rabbit but bigger, faster and with longer ears and legs

s	z	ʃ		h	m	n	ŋ	l	r	j	w
so	zoo	she	vision	how	man	no	sing	leg	red	yes	wet

harem /ˈhɑːriːm; US ˈhærəm/ noun [C] a number of women living with one man, especially in Muslim societies. The part of the building the women live in is also called a harem.

☆ **harm** /hɑːm/ noun [U] hurt or damage: *Peter ate some of those berries but they didn't do him any harm.* ○ *The tax policy did the Labour party a lot of harm.*

(IDIOMS) **come to harm** to be hurt or damaged (usually with a negative): *Both the cars were badly damaged but none of the passengers came to any harm.*

out of harm's way in a safe place: *Put the medicine out of harm's way where the children can't reach it.*

there is no harm in doing sth; it does no harm (for sb) to do sth there's nothing wrong in doing sth (and something good may result): *I don't think I'll win the competition but there's no harm in trying, is there?*

harm verb [T] to cause injury or damage; hurt: *Too much sunshine can harm your skin.* ○ *It wouldn't harm him to work a bit harder!*

harmful /ˈhɑːmfl/ adj causing harm: *The new drug has no harmful side-effects.*

harmless adj **1** not able to cause harm; safe: *You needn't be frightened – these insects are completely harmless.* **2** not unpleasant or likely to upset people: *The children can watch that film – it's quite harmless.* —**harmlessly** adv

harmonica /hɑːˈmɒnɪkə/ noun [C] = MOUTH-ORGAN

harmonious /hɑːˈməʊniəs/ adj **1** without disagreement; peaceful: *Discussions between the two countries have been extremely harmonious.* **2** (used about musical notes) producing a pleasant sound when played together —**harmoniously** adv

harmonize (also **harmonise**) /ˈhɑːmənaɪz/ verb [I,T] to fit in well with other things or to make sth fit in: *That new house doesn't really harmonize with the older houses in the street.* —**harmonization** (also **harmonisation**) /ˌhɑːmənaɪˈzeɪʃn; US -nɪˈz-/ noun [U]

harmony /ˈhɑːməni/ noun (pl **harmonies**) **1** [U] a state of agreement (of feelings, interests, opinions, etc): *There is said to be a lack of harmony within the government.* **2** [C,U] the pleasant combination of different musical notes played or sung together: *They sang in harmony.* ○ *There are some beautiful harmonies in that music.*

harness /ˈhɑːnɪs/ noun [C] **1** a set of leather straps with which a horse is fastened to a cart, etc and controlled **2** a set of straps that fasten sth to a person's body or that stop a small child moving around too much: *a safety harness*

harness verb [T] **1** to put a harness on a horse or to attach a horse to a cart **2** to control sth so that you can use it to produce electricity

harp /hɑːp/ noun [C] a large musical instrument which has many strings stretching from the top to the bottom of a frame. You play the harp with your fingers.

harp verb
(PHRASAL VERB) **harp on (about) sth** to keep on talking or to talk too much about sth: *He's always harping on about his problems.*

harpist noun [C] a person who plays the harp

harpoon /hɑːˈpuːn/ noun [C] a long thin weapon with a sharp pointed end and a rope attached to it that is thrown or fired when hunting large sea animals

harrowing /ˈhærəʊɪŋ/ adj making people feel very sad or upset: *The programme showed harrowing scenes of life in the refugee camps.*

harsh /hɑːʃ/ adj **1** not thinking of people's feelings; severe or cruel: *a harsh punishment* ○ *The England team came in for some harsh criticism.* ○ *The judge had some harsh words for the journalist's behaviour.* **2** not pleasant to be in: *She grew up in the harsh environment of New York City.* **3** (used about light or sound or the way sth feels) unpleasantly bright, loud or rough: *a harsh light* —**harshly** adv —**harshness** noun

harvest /ˈhɑːvɪst/ noun **1** [C,U] the cutting and picking of crops when they are ripe; the time when this is done: *Farmers always need extra help with the harvest.* ○ *In our country harvest time is usually June.* **2** [C] the crops that have been gathered in; the amount or quality of them: *This year's wheat harvest was very poor.*

harvest verb [I,T] to cut, pick or gather a crop
☛ Look at **combine harvester**.

has ➔ HAVE[1,2]

has-been /ˈhæz biːn/ noun [C] (*informal*) a person or thing that is no longer as famous, successful or important as before

hash /hæʃ/ noun [U] a meal of meat cut into small pieces and fried with vegetables
(IDIOM) **make a hash of sth** (*informal*) to do sth badly: *I made a complete hash of the exam.*

hashish /ˈhæʃiːʃ/ (also **hash**) noun [U] a drug that is made from a part of the hemp plant and usually smoked or chewed for pleasure

hasn't short for HAS NOT

hassle /ˈhæsl/ noun [C,U] (*informal*) **1** a thing or situation that is difficult or that causes problems: *It's going to be a hassle having to change trains with all this luggage.* **2** an argument; trouble: *I've decided what to do – please don't give me any hassle about it.*

hassle verb [T] to bother or annoy sb by telling him/her to do sth: *I wish he'd stop hassling me about decorating the house.*

haste /heɪst/ noun [U] doing things too quickly: *In my haste to get to the airport on time I left my passport at home.*
(IDIOM) **in haste** quickly; in a hurry: *I am writing in haste to let you know that I will be arriving on Monday.*

hasten /ˈheɪsn/ verb (*formal*) **1** [T] to make sth happen or be done earlier or more quickly **2** [I] **hasten to do sth** to be quick to do or say sth: *She hastened to apologize.*

hasty /ˈheɪsti/ adj (**hastier**) **1 hasty (in doing sth/to do sth)** (used about a person) acting or deciding sth too quickly or without enough thought: *Don't be too hasty. This is an important decision.* **2** said or done too quickly: *He said a hasty 'goodbye' and left.* —**hastily** /-ɪli/ adv —**hastiness** noun [U]

☆ **hat** /hæt/ noun [C] a covering that you wear on

hats

beret
bowler hat
woolly hat
top hat — *brim*
cap

your head, usually when you are outside: *to wear a hat*
(IDIOM) **old hat** ⇨ OLD

'hat trick *noun* [C] (especially in sport) three successes, wins, goals, etc scored by the same person or team one after the other: *to score a hat trick*

hatch¹ /hætʃ/ *noun* [C] **1** an opening in the deck of a ship for loading and unloading cargo **2** an opening in a wall between two rooms, especially a kitchen and dining-room, which is used for passing food through **3** the door in an aeroplane or spaceship

hatch² /hætʃ/ *verb* **1** [I] **hatch (out)** (used about a baby bird, insect, fish, etc) to come out of an egg **2** [T] to make a baby bird, etc come out of an egg **3** [I] (used about an egg) to break open and allow the baby bird, etc inside to get out **4** [T] **hatch sth (out)** to think of a plan (usually to do sth bad): *He hatched out a plan to avoid paying any income tax.*

hatchback /'hætʃbæk/ *noun* [C] a car with a large door at the back that opens upwards ☛ picture at **car**.

hatchet /'hætʃɪt/ *noun* [C] a small axe

☆ **hate** /heɪt/ *verb* [T] **1** to have a very strong feeling of dislike for sb/sth): *She hated her stepmother as soon as she saw her.* ○ *I hate grapefruit.* ○ *I hate to see the countryside spoilt.* ○ *He hates driving at night.* ○ *I hate his/him having to work so hard.* ☛ Look at **detest** and **loathe**. They express an even stronger feeling. **2** (used as a polite way of apologizing for sth you are going to say) to be sorry: *I hate to bother you but did you pick up my keys by mistake?*

hate *noun* **1** [U] a very strong feeling of dislike ☛ Another word for hate is **hatred**. **2** [C] a thing that you especially dislike ☛ Often used with **pet** to mean something that you especially dislike: *Plastic flowers are one of my pet hates.*

hateful /'heɪtfl/ *adj* extremely unpleasant; horrible: *It was a hateful thing to say.*

hatred /'heɪtrɪd/ *noun* [U] **hatred (for/of sb/sth)** a very strong feeling of dislike ☛ Another word for hatred is **hate**.

haughty /'hɔːti/ *adj* (**haughtier**; **haughtiest**) proud, and thinking that you are better than other people: *She gave me a haughty look and walked away.* —**haughtily** /-ɪli/ *adv* —**haughtiness** *noun* [U]

haul /hɔːl/ *verb* [T] to pull or drag sth with great effort: *Try to haul yourself up using the rope.* ○ *A lorry hauled the car out of the mud.*

haul *noun* **1** [sing] the act of hauling **2** [sing] a distance to be travelled: *It seemed a long haul from the beach back to the hotel.* **3** [C, usually sing] an amount gained, especially of fish or in a net or stolen goods in a robbery

haulage /'hɔːlɪdʒ/ *noun* [U] the transport of goods by road, rail, etc; the money charged for this

haunt /hɔːnt/ *verb* [T] **1** (often passive) (used about a ghost of a dead person) to appear in a place regularly: *The ghost of a woman haunts the castle.* ○ *The house is said to be haunted.* **2** (used about sth unpleasant or sad) to be always in your mind: *His unhappy face has haunted me for years.*

haunt *noun* [C] a place that a person visits regularly: *This pub has always been a favourite haunt of mine.*

haunting *adj* having a quality that stays in your mind: *a haunting song*

☆ **have¹** /həv/; strong form hæv/ *auxiliary verb*

present tense	past tense
I **have** (I've)	I **had** (I'd)
you **have** (you've)	you **had** (you'd)
he/she/it **has** (he's/she's/it's)	he/she/it **had** (he'd/she'd/it'd)
we **have** (we've)	we **had** (we'd)
you **have** (you've)	you **had** (you'd)
they **have** (they've)	they **had** (they'd)
past participle	had
present participle	having
negative short forms	haven't, hasn't, hadn't

(used for forming perfect tenses): *I've seen this film before.* ○ *She's been in England for six months.* ○ *Ian hasn't written to me yet.* ○ *Have you been waiting long?* ○ *They had already told us the news.*

☆ **have²** /hæv/ *verb* (3rd pers sing pres **has**; pt, pp **had**) **1 have to** (*also* **have got to**) (used for saying that sb must do sth or that sth must happen): *I usually have to work on Saturday mornings.* ○ *Do you have to have a visa to go to America?* ○ *She's got to go to the bank this afternoon.* ○ *Oh good, I haven't got to get up early tomorrow!* ○ *We had to do lots of boring exercises.* **2** (*Brit also* **have got**) to own or possess: *I've got a new camera.* ○ *They haven't got a car.* ○ *The flat has two bedrooms.* ○ *He's got short dark hair.* ○ *Have you any brothers and sisters?* ○ *We had a lovely house when I was a child.* **3** (*also* **have got**) to be ill with sth: *She's got a bad cold.* ○ *to have flu, a headache, etc* ○ *to have Aids, cancer, etc* **4** (used with many nouns to talk about doing sth): *What time do you have break-*

fast? o *have a drink, a cigarette, a cup of coffee, a sandwich, etc* o *'Where's Jane?' 'She's having a shower.'* o *have an argument, talk, chat, etc* o *We're having a meeting next week.* **5** (used with many nouns to talk about experiencing sth): *Did you have a nice holiday?* o *have fun, a good time, etc* o *have problems, difficulties, etc* o *He's had a terrible shock.* o *have an accident, a heart attack, an operation, etc* **6** (also **have got**) (used with many abstract nouns): *I've got no patience with small children.* o *to have the time to do sth* o *have power, authority, etc* **7 have sth done** to arrange for sth to be done, usually for payment: *I have my hair cut every six weeks.* o *You should have your eyes tested.* **8 have sth done** (used when sth unpleasant happens to you): *She had her bag stolen on the underground.* o *Charles I had his head cut off.*
(IDIOM) **have had it** (used about things that are completely broken, or dead): *This television has had it. We'll have to buy a new one.*
(PHRASAL VERB) **have (got) sth on 1** to be wearing sth: *She's got a green jumper on.* o *What did the man have on?* **2** (*informal*) to have an arrangement to do sth: *I've got nothing on on Monday. Are you free then?* o *I've got a lot on this week* (= I'm very busy).

haven /ˈheɪvn/ *noun* [C] a place where people feel safe or where they can rest and be quiet ☛ A **tax haven** is a country where income tax is low.

havoc /ˈhævək/ *noun* [U] a state of confusion or disorder: *The rail strikes created havoc all over the country.*
(IDIOM) **play havoc with sth** to damage or upset sth: *The bad weather played havoc with our plans.*

hawk /hɔːk/ *noun* [C] **1** a type of bird that catches and eats small animals and birds. Hawks have very good eyesight. ☛ Hawks are a type of **bird of prey**. **2** (in politics) a person who supports strong action and the use of force rather than peaceful solutions

hay /heɪ/ *noun* [U] grass that has been cut and dried for use as animal food: *a bale of hay*

'hay fever *noun* [U] an illness like a bad cold, making a person sneeze a lot

☛ People get hay fever if they are **allergic** to the **pollen** of plants.

haywire /ˈheɪwaɪə(r)/ *adj*
(IDIOM) **be/go haywire** (*informal*) to be or become out of control; to be in a state of disorder

hazard /ˈhæzəd/ *noun* [C] a danger or risk: *Smoking is a serious health hazard.*
hazard *verb* [T] to make a guess or to suggest sth that you know may be wrong: *I don't know what he paid for the house but I could hazard a guess.*

hazardous /ˈhæzədəs/ *adj* dangerous; risky

haze /heɪz/ *noun* [C,U] a thin mist caused by heat, dust or smoke ☛ Look at the note at **fog**.

hazel /ˈheɪzl/ *noun* [C] a small tree or bush that produces nuts

hazel *adj* (used especially about eyes) light brown in colour

'hazelnut *noun* [C] a small nut that you can eat ☛ picture at **nut**.

hazy /ˈheɪzi/ *adj* (**hazier**; **haziest**) **1** not clear; misty: *The fields were hazy in the early morning sun.* o (*figurative*) *I have only a hazy memory of the holiday we spent in France.* **2** (used about a person) uncertain, not expressing things clearly: *She's a bit hazy about the details of the trip.*

☆ **he** /hiː/ *pron* (the subject of a verb) the male person or animal mentioned earlier: *I spoke to John before he left.* o *Look at that little boy – he's going to fall in!*

he *noun* [sing] a male animal: *Is your cat a he or a she?* ☛ **He**, **him** and **his** are often used to refer to a member of a group that includes both males and females: *A good teacher prepares his lessons well.* Many people think that this is not fair to women and the use of **he or she** , **him or her**, etc is becoming more common. In writing **he/she**, **s/he** or **(s)he** can be used: *If you are not sure, ask your doctor. He/she can give you further information.* o *When a baby cries, it means that s/he is tired, hungry or just unhappy.* In informal language **they**, **them** or **their** can be used: *Everybody knows what they want.* o *When somebody asks me a question I always try to give them a quick answer.* Or the sentence can be made plural: *A baby cries when he/she is tired* becomes: *Babies cry when they are tired.*

☆ **head¹** /hed/ *noun* [C] **1** the part of the body above the neck which has your eyes, nose, mouth and brain in it: *She turned her head to look at him.* o *He's in hospital with serious head injuries after the crash.*

☛ In Britain when you **nod** your head it means 'yes' or shows agreement. When you **shake** your head it means 'no' or shows disagreement.

2 a person's mind, brain or mental ability: *Use your head!* (= think!) o *A horrible thought entered my head...* o *He's got a good head for figures.* **3** the top, front or most important part or end: *to sit at the head of the table* o *Put your name at the head of the paper.* o *We were marching right at the head of the procession.* **4** something that is like a head in shape or position: *the head of a hammer* **5** the chief or most important person (in a family, company, country, etc): *the head of the family* o *The Queen is welcoming heads of state from all over the world.* o *the head waiter* o *I'm afraid I can't answer your question – I'll have to ask head office* (= the most important office) *in London.* **6** (also **head teacher**) the teacher in charge of a school; the headmaster or headmistress: *Who is going to be the new head?* **7 heads** the side of a coin with the head of a person on it: *Heads or tails? Heads I go first, tails you do.* **8 a head** [sing] the height or length of one head: *a head taller* **9 a head** [sing] (for) one person: *The set menu is £12 a head.* ☛ We also say **per head**.

(IDIOMS) **go to sb's head 1** to make sb drunk: *Wine always goes straight to my head.* **2** to make sb too proud: *If you keep telling him*

p	b	t	d	k	g	tʃ	dʒ	f	v	θ	ð
pen	bad	tea	did	cat	got	chin	June	fall	van	thin	then

how clever he is, it will go to his head!
head first 1 with your head before the rest of your body: *Don't go down the slide head first.* **2** too quickly or suddenly: *Don't rush head first into a decision.*
head over heels 1 turning the body over in a forward direction: *She did a head over heels on the mat.* **2** completely: *Jane's head over heels in love with her new boyfriend.*
hit the nail on the head ⇨ HIT¹
keep your head to stay calm
laugh, scream, etc your head off to laugh, scream, etc loudly
lose your head ⇨ LOSE
make head or tail of sth to understand sth: *I can't make head or tail of this exercise.*
off the top of your head ⇨ TOP¹
shake your head ⇨ SHAKE¹
'headache *noun* [C] **1** a pain in your head: *I've got a splitting (= very bad) headache.* ☛ Look at the note at **ache**. **2** a person or thing that causes worry or difficulty: *Paying the bills is a constant headache.*
'headlamp (*also* **'headlight**) *noun* [C] one of the two large bright lights at the front of a vehicle: *Switch your headlights on – it's getting dark.*
'headland *noun* [C] a narrow piece of land that sticks out into the sea
'headlong *adv, adj* **1** with your head before the rest of your body **2** too quickly; without enough thought: *He rushed headlong into buying the business.*
head'master, head'mistress *noun* [C] the man or woman who is in charge of a school
head-'on *adj, adv* with the front of one car, etc hitting the front of another: *There's been a head-on crash between two lorries on the A40.*
'headphones *noun* [plural] a pair of speakers that fit over each ear and are joined together with a band over the top of your head. Headphones are used for listening to radio messages, music, etc.
head'quarters *noun* [plural, with sing or pl verb] (*abbr* **HQ**) the central office, etc of an organization: *Where is/are the firm's headquarters?*
head 'start *noun* [sing] an advantage that you have from the beginning of a race or competition
'headstone *noun* [C] a large stone used to mark the head of a grave, usually with the dead person's name, etc on it
'headway *noun*
(IDIOM) **make headway** to go forward or make progress in a difficult situation: *It was impossible for the boat to make any headway against the wind.*
head² /hed/ *verb* **1** [T] to be in charge of or to lead sth: *Do you think that he has the experience necessary to head a government?* **2** [T] to be at the front of a line, top of a list, etc: *to head a procession* ○ *Two names headed the list of possible suspects.* **3** [T] (often passive) to give a title or some instructions at the top of a piece of writing: *The report was headed 'Private'.* **4** [I] to move in the direction mentioned: *The ship headed towards the harbour.* **5** [T] to hit the ball with your head in football: *He headed the ball into the net.*
(PHRASAL VERB) **head for** to move towards a place: *It's getting late – I think it's time to head for home.* ○ (*figurative*) *You're heading for trouble if you go on behaving like that.*

heading /'hedɪŋ/ *noun* [C] the words written as a title at the top of a page or a piece of writing
headline /'hedlaɪn/ *noun* **1** [C] the title of a newspaper article printed in large letters above the story **2 the headlines** [plural] the main items of news read on television or radio
headstrong /'hedstrɒŋ; *US* -strɔːŋ/ *adj* doing what you want, without listening to advice from other people
heal /hiːl/ *verb* [I,T] **heal (over/up)** to become healthy again; to make sth healthy again: *The cut will heal up in a few days if you keep it clean and dry.* ○ *It takes time to heal a broken leg.* ○ (*figurative*) *Nothing he said could heal the damage done to their relationship.*
☆ **health** /helθ/ *noun* [U] **1** the condition of a person's body or mind: *Fresh fruit and vegetables are good for your health.* ○ *in good /poor health* ○ *Cigarettes carry a government health warning.* ○ *health insurance* **2** the state of being well and free from illness: *Would you rather have health, wealth or beauty?*
'health centre *noun* [C] the central surgery and offices for a group of doctors, nurses, etc who work together

☛ Health Centres are not part of hospitals, they are where local doctors and nurses work.

'health food *noun* [C,U] natural food that many people think is especially good for your health because it has been made or grown without adding chemicals
'health service *noun* [C] the organization of the medical services of a country ☛ Look at **National Health Service**.
☆ **healthy** /'helθi/ *adj* (**healthier; healthiest**) **1** not often ill; strong and well: *a healthy child, animal, plant, etc* **2** showing good health (of body or mind): *healthy skin and hair* ○ *There was plenty of healthy competition between the brothers.* **3** helping to produce good health: *a healthy climate* ☛ The opposite for all senses is **unhealthy**. —**healthily** *adv*
heap /hiːp/ *noun* [C] **1** a large number or amount of sth which is piled up in an untidy way: *All his clothes are in a heap on the floor!* ○ *a rubbish heap* ☛ Look at the note at **pile**. **2 heaps** [plural] (*informal*) a large number or amount; plenty: *There's heaps of time before the train leaves.* ○ *There are heaps of places to go to.*
(IDIOM) **heaps better, more, older, etc** (*informal*) much better, etc
heap *verb* [T] **heap sth (up)** to put things in a pile: *I'm going to heap all the leaves up over there.* ○ *Add six heaped tablespoons of flour* (= in a recipe).
☆ **hear** /hɪə(r)/ *verb* (*pt, pp* **heard** /hɜːd/) **1** [I,T] (not in the *-ing* forms) to receive sounds with your ears: *Can you speak a little louder – I don't hear very well.* ○ *I'm sorry I'm late – I didn't hear my alarm clock this morning.* ☛ Compare

hear and **listen**. To **hear** is to receive a sound by chance or in a passive way with your ears; to **listen** is to make a conscious or active effort to hear something: *I always wake up when I hear the milkman come.* ○ *I love listening to music in the evening.* ○ *Listen! I've got something to tell you.* **2** [T] (not in the *-ing* forms) to be told or informed about sth: *I hear that you've been offered a job in Canada.* **3** [T] (used about a judge, a court, etc) to listen to the evidence in a trial in order to make a decision about it: *Your case will be heard this afternoon.*
(IDIOMS) **hear! hear!** (used for showing that you agree with what sb has just said, especially in a meeting)
won't/wouldn't hear of sth to refuse to allow sth: *I wanted to go to art school but my parents wouldn't hear of it.*
(PHRASAL VERBS) **hear from sb** to receive a letter, telephone call, etc from sb
hear of sb/sth (used especially in questions and negatives) to know or receive information about the existence of a person, place, thing, etc: *Have you heard of the Bermuda Triangle?*

hearing /'hɪərɪŋ/ noun **1** [U] the ability to hear: *Her hearing isn't very good so you need to speak louder.* **2** [U] the distance within which sb can hear: *I'd rather not talk about it within his hearing* (= when he's near enough to hear). **3** [C] a chance to give your opinion or explain your position: *If everybody comes to the meeting it will give all points of view a fair hearing.* **4** [C] a trial in a court of law: *Will the press be present at the hearing?*

hearsay /'hɪəseɪ/ noun [U] things you have heard another person or other people say, which may or may not be true

hearse /hɜːs/ noun [C] a large car used for carrying a dead body in a box (**coffin**) to the funeral

☆ **heart** /hɑːt/ noun **1** [C] the organ inside the chest that sends blood round the body: *When you exercise your heart beats faster.* ○ *heart disease* **2** [C] the centre of a person's feelings: *She has a kind heart* (= she is kind and gentle). ○ *In my heart I knew she was right.* **3** [sing] the most central part of sth; the middle: *Rare plants can be found in the heart of the forest.* ○ (*figurative*) *Let's get straight to the heart* (= to the most important part) *of the matter.* **4** [C] a symbol that is shaped like a heart, often red or pink and used to show love: *He sent her a card with a big red heart on it.* **5 hearts** [plural] the group (**suit**) of playing-cards with red shapes like hearts on them: *I know you've got the queen of hearts!* ☛ picture at **card**. **6** [C] one of the cards from this suit: *Play a heart, if you've got one.* **7** [U] complete interest or attention: *He's not working well because his heart isn't in the job.*
(IDIOMS) **after your own heart** (used about people) similar to yourself or of the type you like best
at heart really; in fact: *My father seems strict but he's a very kind man at heart.*
break sb's heart to make sb very sad
by heart by remembering exactly; from memory: *The teacher wanted us to learn the whole poem by heart.* ○ *Learning lists of words off by heart isn't a good way to increase your vocabulary.*
a change of heart ⇨ **CHANGE²**
cross my heart ⇨ **CROSS²**
your heart sinks you suddenly feel disappointed or depressed: *When I saw the queues of people in front of me my heart sank.*
lose heart ⇨ **LOSE**
not have the heart (to do sth) to be unable to do sth unkind: *I didn't have the heart to say no.*
take sth to heart to be greatly affected or upset by sth
young at heart ⇨ **YOUNG**

-hearted (in compounds) having the type of feelings or character mentioned: *kind-hearted*
heartless *adj* unkind; cruel: *heartless behaviour* —**heartlessly** *adv* —**heartlessness** *noun* [U]
'**heartache** *noun* [C,U] great sorrow or worry; emotional pain
'**heart attack** *noun* [C] a sudden serious illness when the heart stops working correctly, sometimes causing death: *She's had a heart attack.*
'**heartbeat** *noun* [C] the regular movement of the heart or the sound it makes
'**heartbreak** *noun* [U] very great unhappiness
'**heartbreaking** *adj* very sad
'**heartbroken** (also **broken-hearted**) *adj* extremely sad: *Mary was heartbroken at the news of her friend's death.*
'**heartfelt** *adj* deeply felt; sincere: *a heartfelt apology*
heartland /'hɑːtlænd/ *noun* [C] the most central or important part of a country, area, etc: *Germany's industrial heartland*
'**heart-rending** *adj* causing a strong feeling of pity: *The mother of the missing boy made a heart-rending appeal on television.*
,**heart-to-'heart** *noun* [C] a conversation in which you say openly what you really feel or think: *John's teacher had a heart-to-heart with him and found out what was worrying him.*

hearten /'hɑːtn/ *verb* [T] (usually passive) to encourage sb; to make sb feel more cheerful ☛ The opposite is **dishearten**.

hearth /hɑːθ/ *noun* [C] the floor of a fireplace or the area in front of it

hearty /'hɑːti/ *adj* (**heartier**; **heartiest**)
1 showing warm and friendly feelings: *They gave us a hearty welcome when we arrived.*
2 large: *a hearty breakfast* ○ *a hearty appetite*
heartily /'hɑːtɪli/ *adv* **1** in a loud cheerful way: *He joined in heartily with the singing.*
2 very much; completely: *I heartily dislike that sort of comment.* —**heartiness** *noun* [U]

☆ **heat¹** /hiːt/ *noun* **1** [U] the feeling of sth hot: *Too much heat from the sun is being trapped in the Earth's atmosphere.* ○ *This fire doesn't give out much heat.* **2** [sing] (often with *the*) hot weather: *I like the English climate because I can't stand the heat.* **3** [sing] a thing that produces heat: *Remove the pan from the heat* (= the cooker). **4** [U] a state or time of anger or excitement: *In the heat of the argument he said a lot of things he didn't mean.* **5** [C] one of the first parts of a race or competition. The winners of

the heats compete against other winners until the final result is decided: *He won his heat and went through to the final.*
(IDIOM) **be on heat** (used about some female animals) to be ready to mate because it is the right time of the year

'heatwave *noun* [C] a period of time when the weather is much hotter than usual

☆ **heat²** /hiːt/ *verb* [I,T] **heat (sth) (up)** to become or to make sth hot or warm: *Wait for the oven to heat up before you put the cake in.* ○ *Old houses are more difficult to heat than modern ones.* ○ *Is it a heated swimming-pool?* ○ *The meal is already cooked but it will need heating up.*

heated *adj* (used about a person or discussion) angry or excited —**heatedly** *adv*

heater *noun* [C] an apparatus used for heating water or the air in a room, car, etc: *an electric heater* ○ *a water-heater*

heating *noun* [U] a system for heating rooms and buildings: *Our heating goes off at 10pm and comes on again in the morning.* ☞ Look at **central heating**.

heath /hiːθ/ *noun* [C] an area of open land that is not used for farming and that is covered with rough plants and grass

heathen /'hiːðn/ *noun* [C] (*old-fashioned*) a person who does not belong to one of the major world religions

heather /'heðə(r)/ *noun* [U] a small tough plant that grows especially on hills and moors and has small purple, pink or white flowers

heave /hiːv/ *verb* **1** [I,T] to lift or pull sth heavy, using a lot of effort: *Take hold of this rope and heave!* ○ *We heaved the cupboard up the stairs.* **2** [T] to throw sth heavy: *He heaved a brick through the window.* **3** [I] to move up and down or in and out in a heavy but regular way: *His chest was heaving with the effort of carrying the cooker.*
(IDIOM) **heave a sigh** to give a big sigh: *He heaved a sigh of relief when he heard the good news.*

heave *noun* [C,U] a strong pull, push, throw, etc

☆ **heaven** /'hevn/ *noun* **1** [sing] the place where it is believed that God and the angels live and good people go when they die: *to go to/be in heaven* ☞ Look at **hell**. Heaven (often with a capital H) is used in a number of expressions to mean 'God'. For the meaning of *for Heaven's sake, Heaven forbid, etc* look at the entry for **God**. **2 the heavens** [plural] the sky: *The stars shone brightly in the heavens that night.*
(IDIOM) **(good) heavens!** (used to express surprise): *Good heavens! I didn't expect to see you!*

heavenly /'hevnli/ *adj* **1** (only *before* a noun) connected with heaven or the sky: *heavenly music* ○ *heavenly bodies* (= the sun, moon, stars, etc) **2** (*informal*) very pleasant; wonderful

☆ **heavy** /'hevi/ *adj* (**heavier; heaviest**) **1** weighing a lot, and difficult to lift or move: *This box is too heavy for me to carry.* **2** (used when asking or stating how much sb/sth weighs): *What's heavier – a ton of bricks or a ton of feathers?* **3** larger or stronger than usual: *heavy rain* ○ *heavy traffic* ○ *He felt a heavy blow on the back of his head.* ○ *a heavy smoker/drinker* (= a person who smokes/drinks a lot) ○ *The sound of his heavy* (= loud and deep) *breathing told her that he was asleep.* **4** (used about a material or substance) solid or thick: *a heavy soil* ○ *a heavy coat* **5** (used about food) difficult to digest (= difficult for the body to absorb): *He had a heavy meal and dropped off to sleep in the afternoon.* **6** full of hard work; (too) busy: *It's been a very heavy day.* ○ *The Queen had a heavy schedule of visits.* **7** serious, difficult or boring: *This book makes very heavy reading.* **8 heavy on sth** using large quantities of sth: *My car is rather heavy on petrol.*
(IDIOM) **make heavy weather of sth** to make sth seem more difficult than it really is
—**heavily** *adv* —**heaviness** *noun* [U]

,**heavy 'industry** *noun* [U] industry that produces materials such as steel or that makes large, heavy objects

heavy 'metal *noun* [U] a style of very loud rock music that is played on electric instruments

'heavyweight *noun* [C] a boxer weighing over 79.3 kilograms

heck /hek/ *interj, noun* [sing] (*informal*) (used to express or emphasize annoyance or surprise or to emphasize the amount or size of sth): *Oh heck! I've missed the train!* ○ *How the heck did you know where I was?* ○ *It's a heck of a long way to drive in one day.*

heckle /'hekl/ *verb* [I,T] to interrupt a speaker at a public meeting with difficult questions or rude remarks —**heckler** /'heklə(r)/ *noun* [C] —**heckling** /'heklɪŋ/ *noun* [U]

hectare /'hekteə(r)/ *noun* [C] (*abbr* **ha**) a measure of land; 10 000 square metres

hectic /'hektɪk/ *adj* very busy and full of a lot of things that you have to do quickly: *We had a hectic day at the office.* —**hectically** /-klɪ/ *adv*

he'd /hiːd/ *short for* HE HAD; HE WOULD

☆ **hedge** /hedʒ/ *noun* [C] a row of bushes planted close together at the edge of a garden or field ☞ picture at **fence**.

hedge *verb* **1** [T] to put a hedge round a field, garden, etc **2** [I] to avoid giving a direct answer to a question: *Stop hedging and tell us who you're meeting tonight!*
(IDIOM) **hedge your bets** to protect yourself against losing or making a mistake by supporting more than one person or opinion

'hedgerow *noun* [C] a row of bushes, etc forming a hedge especially along a country road or round a field

hedgehog /'hedʒhɒg; *US* -hɔːg/ *noun* [C] a small brown animal covered with stiff sharp needles (**prickles**)

heed /hiːd/ *verb* [T] (*formal*) to pay attention to advice, a warning, etc

heed *noun* (*formal*)
(IDIOM) **take heed (of sth)** to pay careful attention to what sb says: *You should take heed of your doctor's advice.*

☆ **heel** /hiːl/ *noun* [C] **1** the back part of the foot: *These shoes rub against my heels.* ☞ picture on page A8. **2** the part of a sock or stocking that covers your heel **3** the raised part of a shoe under the heel of your foot: *High heels* (= shoes

with high heels) *are not practical for long walks.* ☛ picture at **shoe**.
(IDIOM) **head over heels** ⇨ HEAD¹

heel *verb* [T] to repair the heel of a shoe

hefty /'heftɪ/ *adj* (**heftier; heftiest**) (*informal*) strong, heavy or big: *a hefty young man* o *He gave the door a hefty kick and it opened.* o *She's earning a hefty salary in London.*

☆ **height** /haɪt/ *noun* **1** [C,U] the measurement from the bottom to the top of a person or thing: *The nurse is going to check your height and weight.* o *She's of medium height.* o *We need a fence that's about two metres in height.* ☛ picture at **length**. Look at the note at **tall**. **2** [U] being tall: *He looks older than he is because of his height.* **3** [C,U] the distance that sth is above the ground or sea-level: *We are now flying at a height of 6 000 metres.* ☛ An aeroplane **gains** or **loses** height. **4** [C, usually pl] a high place or area: *I can't go up there. I'm afraid of heights.* **5** [U] the strongest or most important part of sth: *the height of summer* o *The tourist season is at its height in July and August.* o *She's always dressed in the height of fashion.*

heighten /'haɪtn/ *verb* [I,T] to become or to make sth greater or stronger: *I'm using yellow paint to heighten the sunny effect of the room.*

heir /eə(r)/ *noun* [C] the person with the legal right to receive (**inherit**) money, property or a title when the owner dies: *He's the heir to a large fortune.* o *Who is the heir to the throne?* (= Who will become king or queen?) *The queen had no sons so there wasn't an heir.* ☛ A female heir is often called an **heiress** especially when we are talking about somebody who has inherited a very large amount of money.

heirloom /'eəluːm/ *noun* [C] something valuable that has belonged to the same family for many years

held *pt, pp* of HOLD

☆ **helicopter** /'helɪkɒptə(r)/ (also *informal* **chopper**) *noun* [C] a small aircraft that can go straight up into the air. Helicopters fly with the help of large spinning blades.

☆ **hell** /hel/ *noun* **1** [sing] the place that some religions say bad people will go to when they die: *to go to/be in hell* ☛ Look at **heaven**. **2** [C,U] (*informal*) a situation or place that is very unpleasant, painful or miserable: *He went through hell when his wife left him.* **3** [U] (*informal*) (used as a swear-word to show anger or surprise or to make another expression stronger): *Oh hell, I've forgotten my money!* o *Go to hell!* (= go away!) o *Who the hell is that at the front door?*
(IDIOMS) **a/one hell of a...** (*informal*) (used to make an expression stronger or to mean 'very'): *He got into a hell of a fight* (= a terrible fight). o *She's a hell of a nice girl.*
give sb hell (*informal*) to speak to sb very angrily or to treat sb severely
like hell (*informal*) (used to make an expression stronger): *I'm working like hell* (= very hard) *at the moment.*

he'll /hiːl/ *short for* HE WILL

☆ **hello** = HALLO

helm /helm/ *noun* [C] the part of a boat or ship that is used to guide it

helmet /'helmɪt/ *noun* [C] a type of hard hat that you wear to protect your head: *a crash-helmet* o *a policeman's helmet*

☆ **help¹** /help/ *verb* **1** [I,T] to do sth for sb in order to be useful or to make a person's work easier: *Can I help?* o *Could you help me with the cooking?* o *I helped her to organize the party.* o *My son's helping in our shop at the moment.* o *to help sb off the train, out of a car, across the road, etc* (= to help sb move in the direction mentioned) **2** [I,T] to make sth better or easier: *If you apologize to him it might help* (= it might make the situation better). o *This medicine should help your headache.* **3** [T] **help yourself/sb (to sth)** to take or give sth (especially food and drink): *Help yourself to a drink!* o *Shall I help you to the vegetables?* o *'Can I borrow your pen?' 'Yes, help yourself.'* **4** [T] **help yourself to sth** to take sth without asking permission: *Don't just help yourself to my money!* **5** [I] (used to get sb's attention when you are in danger or difficulty): *Help! I'm going to fall!*
(IDIOMS) **can/can't/couldn't help sth** be able/not be able to stop or avoid doing sth: *It was so funny I couldn't help laughing.* o *I just couldn't help myself – I had to laugh.* o *He can't help being so small* (= it's not his fault). o *The accident couldn't be helped* (= it couldn't be avoided so we must accept that).
a helping hand some help: *My neighbour is always ready to give me a helping hand.*
(PHRASAL VERB) **help (sb) out** to help sb in a difficult situation or to give money to help sb: *My parents have promised to help us out with buying the car.*

helper *noun* [C] a person who helps (especially with work): *The teacher is always looking for extra helpers in the classroom.*

helping *noun* [C] the amount of food that sb serves: *A large helping of pudding, please!*

☆ **help²** /help/ *noun* **1** [U] the act of helping: *Do you need any help?* o *This map isn't much help.* o *I'll give you all the help I can.* **2** [sing] **a help (to sb)** a person or thing that helps: *Your directions were a great help – we found the place easily.*

helpful /-fl/ *adj* giving help: *helpful advice* o *Ask Mr Brown. He's always very helpful.* ☛ The opposite is **unhelpful**. —**helpfully** /-fəlɪ/ *adv* —**helpfulness** *noun* [U]

helpless *adj* needing help from other people: *a helpless baby* —**helplessly** *adv* —**helplessness** *noun* [U]

hem /hem/ *noun* [C] the edge of a piece of cloth (especially on a skirt, dress or trousers) that has been turned under and sewn down

hem *verb* [T] (**hemming; hemmed**) to sew a hem on sth
(PHRASAL VERB) **hem sb in** to surround sb and prevent him/her from moving away: *We were hemmed in by the crowd and could not leave.*

hemisphere /'hemɪsfɪə(r)/ *noun* [C] **1** the shape of half a ball; half a sphere **2** one half of the earth: *the northern/southern/eastern/western hemisphere* ☛ picture at **earth**.

hemophilia, hemophiliac (*US*) = HAEMOPHILIA, HAEMOPHILIAC

p	b	t	d	k	g	tʃ	dʒ	f	v	θ	ð
pen	bad	tea	did	cat	got	chin	June	fall	van	thin	then

hemorrhage (US) = HAEMORRHAGE
hemorrhoids (especially US) = HAEMORRHOIDS
hemp /hemp/ noun [U] a plant that is used for making rope and rough cloth and for producing the illegal drug cannabis

cock
hen
chick

☆ **hen** /hen/ noun [C] **1** a female bird that is often kept on farms for its eggs or its meat: *Our hens haven't laid many eggs this week.* o *the clucking of hens* ☛ Look at the note at **chicken**. **2** the female of any type of bird: *a hen pheasant* ☛ The male bird is a **cock**.

'henpecked adj (informal) used to describe a husband who always does what his wife tells him to do

hence /hens/ adv **1** (formal) from here or now: *a week hence* (= in a week's time) **2** for this reason: *I've got some news to tell you – hence the letter.* o *Microwaves have got cheaper and hence more people can afford them.*

henceforth /ˌhensˈfɔːθ/ (also **henceforward** /ˌhensˈfɔːwəd/) adv (formal) from now on; in future: *Henceforth all communication should be in writing.*

henchman /ˈhentʃmən/ noun [C] (pl **henchmen** /-mən/) a person who is employed by a political leader to protect him/her and who may do things that are illegal or violent: *the dictator and his henchmen*

henna /ˈhenə/ noun [U] a reddish-brown colour (**dye**) that is obtained from a type of plant. Henna is used to colour and decorate the hair, fingernails, etc

hepatitis /ˌhepəˈtaɪtɪs/ noun [U] a serious disease of the liver

☆ **her¹** /hɜː(r)/ pron (the object of a verb or preposition) a female person or animal that was mentioned earlier: *He told Sue that he loved her.* o *I've got a letter for your mother. Could you give it to her, please?* o (informal) *That must be her now.* ☛ Look at **she** and the note at **he**.

☆ **her²** /hɜː(r)/ det belonging to a female person or animal that was mentioned earlier: *That's her book. She left it there this morning.* o *Fiona has broken her leg.*

hers /hɜːz/ pron of or belonging to her: *I didn't have a swimsuit but Helen lent me hers.*

herald /ˈherəld/ noun [C] a person in former times who gave important messages from a ruler to the people

herald verb [T] to be a sign that sb/sth is coming: *The minister's speech heralded a change of policy.*

heraldry noun [U] the study of the history of old and important families and their special family symbols (**coats of arms**)

herb /hɜːb; US ɜːrb/ noun [C] a plant whose leaves, seeds, etc are used in medicine or for giving food more flavour: *Add some herbs, such as rosemary and thyme.* ☛ Look at **spice**.

herbal /ˈhɜːbl; US ˈɜːrbl/ adj made of or using herbs: *herbal tea* o *herbal medicine*

herd /hɜːd/ noun [C] a large number of animals that live and feed together: *a herd of cattle, deer, elephants, etc*

herd verb [T] to move people or animals forward as if they were in a herd: *The prisoners were herded onto the train.*

☆ **here** /hɪə(r)/ adv **1** (after a verb or a preposition) in, at or to the place where you are or which you are pointing to: *I live here.* o *Come (over) here.* o *The school is a mile from here.* o *Please sign here.* **2** (used for introducing or drawing attention to sb/sth): *Here is the nine o'clock news.* o *Here comes the bus.* o *Here we are* (= we've arrived). o *'Are the others coming?' 'Yes, here they are now.'* ☛ Note the word order in the last two examples. We say: *Here are the children* and: *Here they are.* Note also the expression: *Here you are* which is used when we are giving something to somebody: *Here you are – this is that book I was talking about.* **3** at this point: *Here the speaker stopped and looked around the room.* **4** (used for emphasizing a noun): *My friend here saw it happen.* o *I think you'll find this book here very useful.*

(IDIOMS) **here and there** in various places: *We could see small groups of people here and there along the beach.*

here goes (informal) (used before doing sth exciting, dangerous, etc): *I've never done a backward dive before, but here goes!*

here's to sb/sth (used for drinking to the health, success, etc of sb/sth): *Here's to your future happiness!*

neither here nor there not important: *My opinion is neither here nor there. If you like the dress then buy it.*

here interj (used for attracting sb's attention, when offering help or when giving sth to sb): *Here! Get down off that wall immediately!* o *Here, let me help!* o *Here, take this and buy yourself a bar of chocolate.*

hereabouts /ˌhɪərəˈbaʊts/ (US **hereabout**) adv (formal) around here

hereafter /ˌhɪərˈɑːftə(r); US -ˈæf-/ adv (formal) (used in legal documents, etc) from now on; in the future

herewith /ˌhɪəˈwɪð/ adv (formal) with this letter, etc: *Please fill in the form enclosed herewith.*

hereditary /hɪˈredɪtri; US -teri/ adj passed on from parent to child: *a hereditary disease* o *Do you think intelligence is hereditary?* o *a hereditary title* (eg that of a duke, that is passed from father to son) ☛ Look at **inherit**.

heredity /hɪˈredəti/ noun [U] the passing on of physical or mental features from parent to child ☛ Look at **inherit**.

s	z	ʃ	ʒ	h	m	n	ŋ	l	r	j	w
so	zoo	she	vision	how	man	no	sing	leg	red	yes	wet

heresy /ˈherəsɪ/ noun [C,U] (pl **heresies**) a (religious) opinion or belief that is against what is generally accepted to be true in the group you belong to

heretic /ˈherətɪk/ noun [C] a person who believes a heresy —**heretical** /hɪˈretɪkl/ adj

heritage /ˈherɪtɪdʒ/ noun [C, usually sing] the traditions, qualities and cultural achievements of a country that have existed for a long time and that have great importance for the country: *The countryside is part of our national heritage.* ○ *We must preserve our cultural heritage for future generations.*

hermit /ˈhɜːmɪt/ noun [C] a person who prefers to live alone, without contact with other people. In former times people became hermits for religious reasons.

hernia /ˈhɜːnɪə/ (*also* **rupture**) noun [C,U] the medical condition when an internal organ (eg the bowel) pushes through the wall of muscle which surrounds it

☆ **hero** /ˈhɪərəʊ/ noun [C] (pl **heroes**) **1** the most important male character in a book, play, film, etc ☛ Look at **villain**. **2** a person who has done sth brave or good and who is admired and remembered for it: *sporting heroes*

heroism /ˈherəʊɪzəm/ noun [U] great courage or bravery

heroic /hɪˈrəʊɪk/ adj (used about people or their actions) very brave: *a heroic effort* —**heroically** /-klɪ/ adv

heroin /ˈherəʊɪn/ noun [U] a drug (produced from morphine) that is used by doctors to stop pain. Some people take heroin for pleasure and then become addicted to it (= they cannot stop using it)

heroine /ˈherəʊɪn/ noun [C] **1** the most important female character in a book, play, film, etc **2** a woman who has done sth brave or good and who is admired and remembered for it

herring /ˈherɪŋ/ noun [C] (pl **herring** or **herrings**) a small silver fish that swims in large groups (**shoals**) in the sea and that is used for food ☛ Look at **kipper**.

(IDIOM) **a red herring** ⇨ RED¹

hers ⇨ HER²

☆ **herself** /hɜːˈself/ pron **1** (used as the object of a verb or preposition when the female person or animal who does an action is also affected by it): *She hurt herself quite badly when she fell down stairs.* ○ *Val bought herself a pie for lunch.* ○ *Irene looked at herself in the mirror.* **2** (used for emphasis): *She told me the news herself.* ○ *Has Rosemary done this herself?* (= or did sb else do it for her?) **3** in her normal state; healthy: *She's not feeling herself today* (= she's feeling ill).

(IDIOM) (**all**) **by herself 1** alone: *She lives by herself.* ☛ Look at the note at **alone**. **2** without help: *I don't think she needs any help – she can change a tyre by herself.*

he's short for HE IS, HE HAS

hesitant /ˈhezɪtənt/ adj **hesitant to do/about doing sth** slow to speak or act because you are not sure whether you should or not: *I'm very hesitant about criticizing him too much.* ○ *a hesitant manner* —**hesitancy** /-ənsɪ/ noun [U] —**hesitantly** adv

☆ **hesitate** /ˈhezɪteɪt/ verb [I] **1 hesitate (about/over sth)** to pause before you do sth or before you take a decision, usually because you are uncertain or worried: *He hesitated before going into the room.* ○ *She's still hesitating about whether to accept the job or not.* ○ *Alan replied without hesitating.* **2 hesitate (to do sth)** to be unwilling to do sth because you are not sure that it is right: *Don't hesitate to phone if you have any problems.*

hesitation /ˌhezɪˈteɪʃn/ noun [C,U] a time when you wait because you are not sure: *She agreed without a moment's hesitation.* ○ *He continued speaking after a slight hesitation.*

heterogeneous /ˌhetərəˈdʒiːnɪəs/ adj (*formal*) made up of different kinds of people or things: *the heterogeneous population of the USA* ☛ The opposite is **homogeneous**.

heterosexual /ˌhetərəˈsekʃuəl/ adj sexually attracted to a person of the other sex (= a man to a woman or a woman to a man) ☛ Look at **bisexual** and **homosexual**. —**heterosexual** noun [C]

het up /het ˈʌp/ adj (not before a noun) **het up (about/over sth)** (*informal*) worried or excited about sth: *What are you getting so het up about?*

hew /hjuː/ verb [I,T] (pt **hewed**; pp **hewed** or **hewn** /hjuːn/) (*formal*) to cut sth with an axe, sword, etc: *roughly hewn stone*

hexagon /ˈheksəɡən; US -ɡɒn/ noun [C] a shape with six sides —**hexagonal** /heksˈæɡənl/ adj

hey /heɪ/ interj (*informal*) what you shout when you want to attract sb's attention or to show that you are surprised or interested: *Hey, what are you doing here?* ○ *Hey, I like your new bike!*

heyday /ˈheɪdeɪ/ noun [sing] the period when sb/sth was most powerful, successful, rich, etc

hi /haɪ/ interj (*informal*) (used as a greeting when you meet sb) hallo

hibernate /ˈhaɪbəneɪt/ verb [I] (used about animals) to spend the winter in a state like deep sleep —**hibernation** /ˌhaɪbəˈneɪʃn/ noun [U]

hiccup (*also* **hiccough**) /ˈhɪkʌp/ noun **1** [C] a sudden stopping of the breath with a noise like a cough, usually caused by eating or drinking too quickly **2** (**the**) **hiccups** [plural] a series of hiccups: *Don't eat so fast or you'll get hiccups!* ○ *I had the hiccups.* **3** [C] a small problem or difficulty: *There's been a slight hiccup in our holiday arrangements but I've got it sorted out now.* —**hiccup** (*also* **hiccough**) verb [I]

☆ **hide**¹ /haɪd/ verb (pt **hid** /hɪd/; pp **hidden** /ˈhɪdn/) **1** [T] to put or keep sb/sth in a place where he/she/it cannot be seen: *Where shall I hide the money?* ○ *You couldn't see Bill in the photo – he was hidden behind John.* ○ *The trees hid the house from view.* **2** [I] to be or get in a place where you cannot be seen or found: *Quick, run and hide!* ○ *The child was hiding under the bed.* **3** [T] **hide sth (from sb)** to keep sth secret so that other people do not know about it: *She tried to hide her disappointment from them.*

hiding noun [U]

(IDIOM) **be in/go into hiding** to be in or go

iː	ɪ	e	æ	ɑː	ɒ	ɔː	ʊ	uː	ʌ
see	sit	ten	hat	arm	got	saw	put	too	cup

hide into a place where you cannot be found: *She escaped from prison and went into hiding.*

hide-and-seek /ˌhaɪdnˈsiːk/ *noun* [U] a children's game in which one person hides and the others try to find him/her

hide² /haɪd/ *noun* [C,U] the skin of an animal that will be used for making leather, etc

hideous /ˈhɪdiəs/ *adj* very ugly or unpleasant: *a hideous sight* ○ *a hideous crime* ○ (*informal*) *That new dress she's got is hideous.* —**hideously** *adv* **hideousness** *noun* [U]

hiding /ˈhaɪdɪŋ/ *noun* [C] (*informal*) a beating that is given as a punishment: *You deserve a good hiding for what you've done.*

hierarchy /ˈhaɪərɑːki/ *noun* [C] (*pl* **hierarchies**) a system or organization that has many grades or ranks from the lowest to the highest —**hierarchical** /ˌhaɪəˈrɑːkɪkl/ *adj*

hieroglyphics /ˌhaɪərəˈɡlɪfɪks/ *noun* [plural] the system of writing that was used in ancient Egypt in which a type of picture represents a word or sound

hi-fi /ˈhaɪfaɪ/ *adj* (*informal*) = HIGH FIDELITY: *a hi-fi set*

higgledy-piggledy /ˌhɪɡldiˈpɪɡldi/ *adv, adj* (*informal*) not in any order; mixed up together: *The books were piled up higgledy-piggledy on her desk.*

☆ **high¹** /haɪ/ *adj* **1** (used about things) measuring a great amount from the bottom to the top: *high cliffs* ○ *What's the highest mountain in the world?* ○ *high heels* (= on shoes) ○ *The garden wall was so high that we couldn't see over it.* ☞ Look at **height**, **low** and the note at **tall**. **2** having a particular height: *The hedge is one metre high.* ○ *knee-high boots* **3** at a level which is a long way from the ground, or from sea level: *Keep medicines on a high shelf where children cannot reach them.* ○ *The castle was built on high ground.* **4** above the usual or normal level or amount: *high prices* ○ *at high speed* ○ *a high level of unemployment* ○ *high-quality goods* ○ *He's got a high temperature.* ○ *Oranges are high in vitamin C.* **5** good or favourable: *Her work is of a very high standard.* ○ *He has a high opinion of you.* **6** having an important position or rank: *We shall have to refer the matter to a higher authority.* **7** morally good: *high ideals* **8** (used about a sound or voice) not deep or low: *She sang the high notes beautifully.* **9** **high (on sth)** (*informal*) under the influence of drugs, alcohol, etc **10** (not before a noun) (used about some kinds of food) beginning to go bad: *That cheese smells a bit high.* **11** (used about a gear in a car) that allows a faster speed

ˌhigh-ˈclass *adj* **1** of especially good quality: *a high-class restaurant* **2** (used about a person) having a high(6) position in society

ˌHigh ˈCourt *noun* [C] the most important court of law

ˌhigher eduˈcation *noun* [U] education at a university or polytechnic

ˌhigh fiˈdelity (*also* **ˈhi-fi**) *adj* (only *before* a noun) (used about electrical equipment for playing records, cassettes, CDs, etc) producing high-quality sound

ˈhigh-jump *noun* [sing] the sport in which people try to jump over a bar in order to find out who can jump the highest ☞ Look at **long-jump**.

ˈhighland /-lənd/ *adj* **1** in or connected with mountainous regions: *highland streams* ☞ Look at **lowland**. **2 the Highlands** [plural] the mountainous part of Scotland

ˌhigh-ˈlevel *adj* involving important people: *high-level talks*

ˌhigh-ˈpowered *adj* **1** (used about things) having great power: *a high-powered engine* **2** (used about people) important and successful: *high-powered executives*

ˌhigh ˈpressure *noun* [U] the condition of the atmosphere when the pressure of the air is above normal

ˈhigh school *noun* [C,U] (*especially US*) a secondary school

ˈhigh street *noun* [C] (often used in names) the main street of a town

ˌhigh-ˈtech *adj* (*informal*) **1** using a lot of modern equipment, especially computers **2** using designs or styles taken from industry, etc; very modern

ˌhigh ˈtide *noun* [C] the time when the sea comes closest to the shore

☆ **high²** /haɪ/ *adv* **1** at or to a high position or level: *The sun was high in the sky.* ○ *I can't jump any higher.* ○ *The plane flew high overhead.* ○ *You should aim high.* **2** (used about a sound) at a high level: *How high can you sing?*

(IDIOM) **high and low** everywhere: *We've searched high and low for the keys.*

☆ **high³** /haɪ/ *noun* [C] **1** a high level or point: *Profits reached an all-time high last year.* **2** an area of high atmospheric pressure: *A high over the Atlantic will move towards Britain in the next few days.* **3** (*slang*) a feeling of great pleasure or happiness that may be caused by a drug, alcohol, etc

(IDIOM) **on high** (*formal*) (in) a high place, the sky or heaven: *The order came from on high.* ○ *God on high*

highbrow /ˈhaɪbraʊ/ *noun* [C] a person who is interested in serious intellectual things —**highbrow** *adj*: *highbrow books*

highlight /ˈhaɪlaɪt/ *noun* **1** [C] the best or most interesting part of sth: *The highlights of the match will be shown on TV tonight.* **2 highlights** [plural] areas of lighter colour that are put in a person's hair

highlight *verb* [T] to give special attention to sth: *The report highlighted the need for improved safety at football grounds.*

☆ **highly** /ˈhaɪli/ *adv* **1** to a high degree; very: *The film was highly amusing.* ○ *The disease is highly contagious.* **2** (very) well or favourably: *I think highly of your work* (= I have a good opinion of it). ○ *a highly-paid job*

ˌhighly-ˈstrung *adj* (used about a person or animal) very nervous and excitable

Highness /ˈhaɪnɪs/ *noun* [C] (*pl* **Highnesses**) a title used when speaking about or to a member of a royal family: *Her Highness the Duchess of Kent* ○ *Their Royal Highnesses the Prince and Princess of Wales*

highway /ˈhaɪweɪ/ *noun* [C] (*especially US*) a main road (between towns) ☞ Look at the note at **road**.

ɜː	ə	eɪ	əʊ	aɪ	aʊ	ɔɪ	ɪə	eə	ʊə
fur	ago	pay	home	five	now	join	near	hair	pure

hijack /ˈhaɪdʒæk/ verb [T] to take control of a plane, etc by force, usually for political reasons: *The plane was hijacked on its flight to Sydney.*
   hijacker noun [C] a person who hijacks a plane, etc
   hijacking noun [C,U] an occasion when a plane, etc is hijacked: *Measures are being taken to prevent hijacking.*

hike /haɪk/ noun [C] a long walk in the country —**hike** verb [I] ☛ **Go hiking** is used when you are talking about spending time hiking: *They went hiking in Wales for their holiday.* —**hiker** noun [C]

hilarious /hɪˈleəriəs/ adj very funny —**hilariously** adv

hilarity /hɪˈlærəti/ noun [U] great amusement or loud laughter

☆ **hill** /hɪl/ noun [C] a high area of land that is not as high (or as rocky) as a mountain: *There was a wonderful view from the top of the hill.* ○ *Tim enjoys walking in the hills.* ○ *I had to push my bike up the hill – it was too steep to ride.* ☛ Note the words **uphill** and **downhill** (adj, adv): *an uphill climb* ○ *I like riding downhill on my bike.*
   hilly /ˈhɪli/ adj (**hillier**; **hilliest**) having many hills: *The country's very hilly around here.*
   'hillside noun [C] the sloping side of a hill: *a house built on the hillside*
   'hilltop noun [C] the top of a hill

hilt /hɪlt/ noun [C] the handle of a sword, etc
   (IDIOM) (**up**) **to the hilt** to a high degree or completely: *I'll support you to the hilt.*

☆ **him** /hɪm/ pron (the object of a verb or preposition) a male person or animal that was mentioned earlier: *Helen told Ian that she loved him.* ○ *I've got a letter for your father – can you give it to him, please?* ○ (informal) *That must be him now.* ☛ Look at the note at **he**.

☆ **himself** /hɪmˈself/ pron **1** (used as the object of a verb or preposition when the male person or animal who does an action is also affected by it): *He cut himself when he was shaving.* ○ *He's bought himself a new sweater.* ○ *John looked at himself in the mirror.* ☛ picture at **each other**. **2** (used for emphasis): *He told me the news himself.* ○ *The minister himself came to see the damage.* ○ *Did he write this himself?* (= or did sb else do it for him?) **3** in his normal state; healthy: *He's not feeling himself today* (= he's feeling ill).
   (IDIOM) (**all**) **by himself 1** alone: *He lives by himself.* ☛ Look at the note at **alone**. **2** without help: *He should be able to cook a meal by himself.*

hind /haɪnd/ adj (used about an animal's legs, etc) at the back ☛ We also say **back legs**. The legs at the front are **front legs** or **forelegs**.

hinder /ˈhɪndə(r)/ verb [T] to make it more difficult for sb/sth to do sth: *A lot of scientific work is hindered by lack of money.*

hindrance /ˈhɪndrəns/ noun [C] a person or thing that makes it difficult for you to do sth: *Mark wanted to help me but he was more of a hindrance than a help.*

hindsight /ˈhaɪndsaɪt/ noun [U] knowing afterwards why sth bad happened and how you could have stopped it happening: *It's very easy to criticize with the benefit of hindsight.* ☛ Look at **foresight**.

Hindu /ˌhɪnˈduː; *US* ˈhɪnduː/ noun [C] a person whose religion is Hinduism —**Hindu** adj: *Hindu beliefs*
   Hinduism /ˈhɪnduːɪzəm/ noun [U] the main religion of India. Hindus believe in many gods and that, after death, people will return to life in a different form

hinge¹ /hɪndʒ/ noun [C] a piece of metal that joins two sides of a box, door, etc together and allows it to be opened or closed

hinge² /hɪndʒ/ verb (PHRASAL VERB) **hinge on sth** to depend on sth: *The future of the project hinges on the meeting today.*

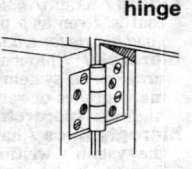

hint /hɪnt/ noun [C] **1** something that you suggest in an indirect way: *She kept looking at her watch as a hint that it was time to go.* **2** a small amount of sth: *There was a hint of sadness in his voice.* **3** a piece of advice or information: *The magazine had some helpful hints about how to make your own clothes.*
   hint verb [I,T] to suggest sth in an indirect way: *They only hinted at their great disappointment.* ○ *He hinted that he might be moving to Greece.*

hip¹ /hɪp/ noun [C] the part of the side of your body above your legs and below your waist: *He stood there angrily with his hands on his hips.* ○ *What do you measure round the hips?* ○ *She broke her hip* (= the bone inside her hip) *when she fell.* ☛ picture on page A8.

hip² /hɪp/ interj
   (IDIOM) **hip, hip, hurrah/hurray** (used when a group wants to show that it is pleased with sb or with sth that has happened): *'Three cheers for David. He's done a great job. Hip, hip...' 'Hurray!'*

hippie (also **hippy**) /ˈhɪpi/ noun [C] (pl **hippies**) a person who does not share the same ideas and values as most people in society. Hippies show that they are different by wearing long hair, colourful clothes, etc and sometimes by living in groups.

hippopotamus /ˌhɪpəˈpɒtəməs/ noun [C] (pl **hippopotamuses** /-məsɪz/ or **hippopotami** /-maɪ/) (also *informal* **hippo** /ˈhɪpəʊ/ (pl **hippos**)) a large African river animal with a large head and short legs and thick dark skin

☆ **hire** /ˈhaɪə(r)/ verb [T] **1** (*US* **rent**) **hire sth** (**from sb**) to have the use of sth for a short time by paying for it ☛ In British English, you **hire** something for a short time,: *We hired a car for the day.* ○ *I hired a suit for the wedding* but **rent** something if the period of time is longer: *rent a television, video, etc* ○ *rent a house, flat, holiday cottage, etc.* In American English **rent** is used in both situations. **2** to give sb a job for a short time: *We'll have to hire somebody to mend the roof.* ☛ In American English **hire** is also used for talking about permanent jobs: *We just hired a new secretary.* **3** (*US* **rent**) **hire sth** (**out**) (**to**

| p | b | t | d | k | g | tʃ | dʒ | f | v | θ | ð |
| pen | bad | tea | did | cat | got | chin | June | fall | van | thin | then |

sb) to allow sb to use sth for a short fixed period in exchange for money: *We hire (out) our vans by the day.* ☛ In British English, **rent** or **let** is used if the period of time is longer: *Mrs Higgs rents out rooms to students.* ○ *We let out our house while we were in France for a year.*

hire *noun* [U] (the cost of) hiring: *The hire of the hall is £3 an hour.* ○ *Car hire is expensive in this country.* ○ *Bicycles for hire!* ○ *a hire car*

ˌhire ˈpurchase *noun* [U] (Brit) (*abbr* **HP**) a way of buying goods. You do not pay the full price at once but make regular small payments (**instalments**) until the full amount is paid: *We're buying the video on hire purchase.*

☆ **his** /hɪz/ *det* belonging to a male person or animal that was mentioned earlier: *That's his book. He left it there this morning.* ○ *Matthew has hurt his shoulder.*

his /hɪz/ *pron* of or belonging to him: *This is my book so that one must be his.* ○ *Father has a lot of ties so I borrowed one of his.* ☛ Look at the note at **he**.

hiss /hɪs/ *verb* **1** [I,T] to make a sound like a very long 's' to show that you are angry or do not like sth: *The goose hissed at me.* ○ *The speech was hissed and booed.* **2** [T] to say sth in an angry hissing voice: *'Stay away from me!' she hissed.* —**hiss** *noun* [C]

historian /hɪˈstɔːrɪən/ *noun* [C] a person who studies history

historic /hɪˈstɒrɪk; *US* -ˈstɔːr-/ *adj* famous or important in history: *The opening of the Berlin Wall was a historic occasion.*

☆ **historical** /hɪˈstɒrɪkl; *US* -ˈstɔːr-/ *adj* **1** connected with history or the study of history: *There is very little historical evidence about the life of Christ.* ○ *This house has great historical interest.* **2** that really lived or happened: *Was Robin Hood really a historical figure?* ○ *historical events* —**historically** /-kli/ *adv*

☆ **history** /ˈhɪstri/ *noun* (*pl* **histories**) **1** [U] the study of past events and social, political and economic developments: *She has a degree in history.* ○ *History was my favourite subject at school.* ○ *a history teacher* **2** [U] events of the past (when you are thinking of them as a whole): *History often repeats itself.* ○ *an important moment in history* ☛ Look at **natural history**. **3** [C] a written description of past events: *a new history of Europe* **4** [C, usually sing] the series of events or facts that is connected with a person, place or thing: *There is a history of heart disease in our family.* ☛ **History** is something true that really happened. A **story** is a description of a series of events that may or may not have happened.

☆ **hit¹** /hɪt/ *verb* [T] (*pres part* **hitting**; *pt, pp* **hit**) **1** to touch sb/sth with a lot of force: *'Don't hit me',* she begged. ○ *The old man was hit by a car while he was crossing the road.* ○ *Someone hit her on the head and stole her handbag.* ○ *to hit a ball with a bat* ○ (*figurative*) *The smell of burning hit her as she entered the room.* ○ (*figurative*) *Things were going really well until we hit this problem.* ☛ **Strike** is a more formal word than **hit**. **Beat** means to hit many times: *He was badly beaten in the attack.* **2 hit sth (on/against sth)** to knock a part of your body, etc against sth: *Peter hit his head on the low beam.* **3** to have a bad effect upon sb/sth: *Inner city areas have been badly hit by unemployment.* ○ *Her father's death has hit her very hard.* **4** to find or reach sth: *If you follow this road you should hit the motorway in about ten minutes.* ○ *The price of oil hit a new high yesterday.*

(IDIOMS) **hit it off (with sb)** (*informal*) to like sb when you first meet him/her: *When I first met Tony's parents, we didn't really hit it off.*

hit the nail on the head to say sth that is exactly right

(PHRASAL VERBS) **hit back (at sb/sth)** to attack (with words) sb who has attacked you: *The Prime Minister hit back at his critics.*

hit out (at sb/sth) to attack sb/sth: *The man hit out at the policeman.* ○ *The newspapers hit out at the company for its poor safety record.*

ˌhit-and-ˈrun *adj* **1** (used about a car driver) causing an accident and not stopping to see if anybody is hurt **2** (used about a road accident) caused by a hit-and-run driver

ˌhit-or-ˈmiss (*also* ˌhit-and-ˈmiss) *adj* (*informal*) not well organized; careless: *She works in rather a hit-and-miss way, I'm afraid.*

☆ **hit²** /hɪt/ *noun* [C] **1** the act of hitting sth; a blow: *The ship took a direct hit and sank.* ○ *What a brilliant hit!* (eg in a game of cricket or baseball) ☛ Look at **miss**. **2** a person or thing that is very popular or successful: *He was quite a hit in America.* ○ *The record was a smash hit.*

(IDIOM) **make a hit (with sb)** (*informal*) to make a good impression on sb or to cause sb to like you

hitch¹ /hɪtʃ/ *verb* **1** [I,T] (*informal*) to get free rides in other people's cars as a way of travelling cheaply: *They hitched a lift in a lorry to London.* **2** [T] to fasten sth to sth else: *The horses were hitched to the fence.* ○ *to hitch a trailer to the back of a car*

ˈhitchhike *verb* [I] to travel by getting free rides in other people's cars: *He hitchhiked across Europe.*

ˈhitchhiker *noun* [C]

hitch² /hɪtʃ/ *noun* [C] a small problem or difficulty: *The wedding went off without a hitch.* ○ *a technical hitch*

hitherto /ˌhɪðəˈtuː/ *adv* (*formal*) until now

hive /haɪv/ *noun* [C] = BEEHIVE

hiya /ˈhaɪjə/ *interj* (*especially US informal*) (used as a greeting when you meet sb) hallo

h'm /hm/ *interj* (used when you are not sure or when you are thinking about sth)

hoard /hɔːd/ *noun* [C] a store of money, food, etc: *a hoard of treasure*

hoard *verb* [I,T] **hoard (sth) (up)** to collect and store large quantities of sth (often secretly)

hoarding /ˈhɔːdɪŋ/ (*US* **billboard**) *noun* [C] a large board in the street where advertisements are put

hoarse /hɔːs/ *adj* **1** (used about a voice) sounding rough and quiet, eg because you have a cold: *a hoarse whisper* **2** (used about people) with a hoarse voice: *The spectators shouted themselves hoarse.* —**hoarsely** *adv*

hoax /həʊks/ *noun* [C] a trick that is played on

s	z	ʃ	ʒ	h	m	n	ŋ	l	r	j	w
so	zoo	she	vision	how	man	no	sing	leg	red	yes	wet

sb: *The fire brigade answered the call, but found that it was a hoax.*

hob /hɒb/ *noun* [C] the flat surface on the top of a cooker that is used for boiling, frying, etc

hobble /'hɒbl/ *verb* [I] to walk with difficulty because your feet or legs are hurt: *He hobbled home on his twisted ankle.*

☆ **hobby** /'hɒbi/ *noun* [C] (*pl* **hobbies**) something that you do regularly for pleasure in your free time: *The children's hobbies are swimming and stamp-collecting.*

hockey /'hɒki/ *noun* [U] **1** a game that is played on a field (**a pitch**) by two teams of eleven players who try to hit a small hard ball into a goal with a curved wooden stick (**a hockey stick**) ☛ In the US hockey is usually called **field hockey** to distinguish it from **ice hockey**. **2** (*US*) = ICE HOCKEY

hoe /həʊ/ *noun* [C] a garden tool with a long handle that is used for turning the soil and for removing weeds

hog /hɒg; *US* hɔːg/ *noun* [C] (*US*) a male pig that is kept for its meat ☛ Look at the note at **pig**.

hog *verb* [T] (**hogging**; **hogged**) (*informal*) to take or keep too much or all of sth in a selfish way: *Don't hog the bathroom when everyone's getting ready to go out!* ○ *The red car was hogging the middle of the road so no one could overtake.*

Hogmanay /'hɒgməneɪ/ *noun* [C] the Scottish name for New Year's Eve (31 December) and the celebrations that take place then

hoist /hɔɪst/ *verb* [T] to raise or lift sth by using ropes, etc: *to hoist a flag, sail, etc*

☆ **hold¹** /həʊld/ *verb* (*pt, pp* **held** /held/) **1** [T] to take sb/sth and keep him/her/it in your hand, etc: *He held a gun in his hand.* ○ *The woman was holding a baby in her arms.* ○ *He manages to write by holding the pen between his teeth.* ○ *Hold my hand. This is a busy road.* **2** [T] to keep sth in a certain position: *Hold your head up straight.* ○ *Hold the camera still or you'll spoil the picture.* ○ *These two screws hold the shelf in place.* **3** [T] to keep a person in a position or place by force: *The terrorists are holding three men hostage.* ○ *A man is being held at the police station.* **4** [I,T] to contain or have space for a particular amount: *The car holds five people.* ○ *How much does this bottle hold?* **5** [T] to have sth (usually in an official way): *Does she hold a British passport?* ○ *She holds the world record in the 100 metres.* **6** [T] to have an opinion, etc: *They hold the view that we shouldn't spend any more money.* **7** [I] to remain the same: *I hope this weather holds till the weekend.* ○ *What I said still holds, nothing has changed.* **8** [T] to believe that sth is true about a person: *I hold the parents responsible for the child's behaviour.* **9** [T] to organize an event: *They're holding a party for his fortieth birthday.* ○ *The elections will be held in the autumn.* **10** [I,T] (when you are telephoning) to wait until the person you are calling is ready: *I'm afraid his phone is engaged. Will you hold the line?* **11** [T] to have a conversation: *It's impossible to hold a conversation with all this noise.*

(IDIOM) **Hold it!** Wait! Don't move!

☛ For other idioms containing **hold**, look at the entries for the nouns, adjectives, etc, eg **hold your own** is at **own**.

(PHRASAL VERBS) **hold sb/sth back 1** to prevent sb from making progress **2** to prevent sb/sth from moving forward: *The police tried to hold the crowd back.*

hold sth back not give information: *The police are sure that she is holding something back. She knows much more than she is saying.*

hold on 1 to wait: *Hold on. I'll be with you in a minute.* **2** to manage in a difficult or dangerous situation: *They managed to hold on until a rescue party arrived.*

hold on to sb/sth not let go of sb/sth: *The child held on to his mother; he didn't want her to go.*

hold on to sth not give or sell sth: *They've offered me a lot of money for this painting, but I'm going to hold on to it.*

hold out to last (in a difficult situation): *How long will our supply of water hold out?*

hold sth out to offer sth by moving it towards sb: *He held out a sweet and offered it to the girl.*

hold out for sth to continue to ask for sth

hold sb/sth up to make sb/sth late: *We were held up by the traffic.*

hold up sth to rob sth, using a gun, etc: *Masked men held up a bank in South London yesterday.*

¹**hold-up** *noun* [C] **1** a delay: *What's the hold-up?* **2** a robbery by people with guns

☆ **hold²** /həʊld/ *noun* [C,sing] the act or manner of holding sb/sth: *to have a firm hold on the rope* ○ *judo holds* ☛ 'Hold' is often used with the verbs **catch**, **get**, **grab**, **seize**, **take**, etc: *Catch hold of the other side of this sheet and help me to fold it, please.* ○ *I can touch it, but I can't quite get hold of it. It's too far away.* **2** [sing] **a hold (on/over sb/sth)** influence or control: *The new government has strengthened its hold on the country.* **3** [C] a place where a climber can put his/her hand or foot when climbing ☛ Look at **foothold**.

(IDIOM) **get hold of sb/sth 1** to find sth (that will be useful): *I must try and get hold of a good second-hand bicycle.* **2** to find sb or make contact with sb: *I've been trying to get hold of the complaints department all morning.*

hold³ /həʊld/ *noun* [C] the part of a ship or an aeroplane where goods are carried

holdall /'həʊldɔːl/ (*US* **carry-all**) *noun* [C] a large bag that is used for carrying clothes, etc when you are travelling

☆ **holder** /'həʊldə(r)/ *noun* [C] (often in compounds) **1** a person who has or holds sth: *a ticket-holder* ○ *the world record-holder in the 100 metres* ○ *holders of British passports* **2** something that contains or holds sth: *a plant pot holder*

☆ **hole** /həʊl/ *noun* **1** [C] an opening; a hollow or an empty space in sth solid: *The pavement is full of holes.* ○ *There are holes in my socks.* ○ *I've got a hole in my tooth.* ○ (*figurative*) *The repair of the roof has made a big hole in their savings.* **2** [C] the place where an animal lives in the ground or in a tree: *a rabbit hole* **3** [sing]

iː	ɪ	e	æ	ɑː	ɒ	ɔː	ʊ	uː	ʌ
see	sit	ten	hat	arm	got	saw	put	too	cup

(*informal*) a small dark and unpleasant room, flat, etc: *This place is a hole – you can't live here!* **4** [C] (in golf) the hole in the ground that you must hit the ball into. Each section of a golf-course is also called a hole: *an eighteen-hole golf-course* ○ *Barbara won the seventh hole.*

☆**holiday** /'hɒlədeɪ/ *noun* **1** [C] a day of rest when people do not go to work, school, etc: *Next Thursday is a holiday in some parts of Germany.* ○ *New Year's Day is a bank/public holiday in Britain.* ☛ **Holiday** in this sense is used in both British and American English. A day when you do not go to work is often also called **a day off**: *I'm having two days off next week when we move house.* **2** (*US* **vacation**) [C,U] a period of rest from work or school (often when you go and stay away from home): *We're going to Italy for our summer holidays this year.* ○ *Mr Philips isn't here this week. He's away on holiday.* ○ *I'm going to take a week's holiday in May and spend it at home.* ○ *the school, Christmas, Easter, summer, etc holidays* ☛ In British English **vacation** means the period of time when universities and courts of law are not working: *Maria wants to get a job in the long vacation.* **Leave** is time when you do not go to work for a special reason: *sick leave* ○ *maternity leave* (= when you are having a baby) ○ *unpaid leave.*

'holiday camp *noun* (*Brit*) [C] a place that provides accommodation and organized entertainment for people on holiday

'holiday-maker *noun* [C] a person who is away from home on holiday

holiness /'həʊlɪnɪs/ *noun* [U] the state of being holy

hollow /'hɒləʊ/ *adj* **1** with a hole or empty space inside: *a hollow tree* **2** (used about a sound) seeming to come from a hollow place: *hollow footsteps in the empty house*

hollow *noun* [C] an area that is lower than the surrounding land

hollow *verb*

(PHRASAL VERB) **hollow sth out** to take the inside part of sth out in order to make sth else: *They hollowed out a tree trunk to make a canoe.*

holly /'hɒli/ *noun* [U] a plant that has shiny dark-green leaves with prickles and red berries in the winter. It is often used as a Christmas decoration.

holocaust /'hɒləkɔːst/ *noun* [C] a situation where a great many things are destroyed and a great many people die: *a nuclear holocaust*

holster /'həʊlstə(r)/ *noun* [C] a leather case for a gun that is fixed to a belt or worn under the arm

☆**holy** /'həʊli/ *adj* (**holier; holiest**) **1** connected with God or with religion and therefore very special or sacred: *the Holy Bible* ○ *holy water* ○ *The Koran is the holy book of the Muslims.* **2** (used about a person) serving God; pure

Holy Com'munion *noun* [U] = COMMUNION(1)

the Holy 'Ghost (*also* **the Holy 'Spirit**) *noun* [sing] Christians believe God consists of three parts: God the Father, God the Son (Jesus Christ) and God the Holy Ghost

☆**home¹** /həʊm/ *noun* **1** [C,U] the place where you live (with your family) or where you feel that you belong: *She left home at the age of 21.* ○ *Children from broken homes* (= whose parents are divorced) *sometimes have learning difficulties.* ○ *That old house would make an ideal family home.* ○ *Stephen went abroad and made his home in Canada.* ○ *Now we've got this computer, we'd better find a home for it* (= somewhere to keep it). ☛ Look at the note at **house**. Be careful. The preposition *to* is not used before 'home': *It's time to go home.* ○ *She's usually tired when she gets home.* If you want to talk about somebody else's home you have to say: *at Jane and Andy's* or: *at Jane and Andy's place/house.* **2** [C] a place that provides care for a particular type of person or for animals: *a children's home* (= for children who have no parents to look after them) ○ *an old people's home* **3** [sing] the place where sth began: *Greece is said to be the home of democracy.*

(IDIOM) **at home 1** in your house, flat, etc: *Is anybody at home?* ○ *Tomorrow we're staying at home all day.* ☛ In US English **home** is often used without the preposition *at*: *Is anybody home?* **2** as if you were in your own home; comfortable: *Please make yourself at home.* ○ *They were warm and welcoming and I felt at home straight away.*

homeless *adj* having no home

the homeless *noun* [plural] people without a home —**homelessness** *noun* [U]

homeward /'həʊmwəd/ *adj* going towards home: *the homeward journey*

homewards /-wədz/ *adv* towards home

the ¸Home 'Counties *noun* [plural] the area of Britain around London

¸home-'grown *adj* (used about fruit and vegetables) grown in your own garden

'homeland *noun* [C] **1** the country where you were born or that your parents came from, or to which you feel you belong **2** [usually pl] one of the areas that are reserved for black people in the Republic of South Africa

¸home-'made *adj* made at home; not bought in a shop: *home-made cakes*

the 'Home Office *noun* [sing] the department of the British Government that is responsible for affairs inside the country, the police, prisons, etc. The Home Office also decides who can come and live in Britain.

¸Home 'Secretary *noun* [C] the British Government minister who is in charge of the Home Office

'homesick *adj* sad because you are away from home: *She was very homesick for Canada.*

'homesickness *noun* [U]

'homework *noun* [U] the work that teachers give to pupils to do away from school: *Have we got any homework?* ○ *We've got a translation to do for homework.* ○ (*figurative*) *The minister had not done his homework and there were several questions that he couldn't answer.* ☛ Look at the note at **housework**.

☆**home²** /həʊm/ *adj* (only *before* a noun) **1** connected with home: *home cooking* ○ *a happy home life* **2** connected with your own country, not with a foreign country: *The Home Secretary is responsible for home affairs.* ○ *goods for the home market* **3** (used in sport) connected with

ɜː	ə	eɪ	əʊ	aɪ	aʊ	ɔɪ	ɪə	eə	ʊə
fur	ago	pay	home	five	now	join	near	hair	pure

your own sports team or ground: *The home team has a lot of support.* ○ *a home game* ☛ The opposite is **away**.

☆ **home³** /həʊm/ *adv* at, in or to your home or home country: *We must be getting home soon.* ○ *She'll be flying home for Christmas.*
(IDIOMS) **bring sth home to sb** to make sb understand sth fully: *Looking at those pictures of hungry children really brought home to me how lucky we are.*
drive sth home (to sb) ➪ DRIVE¹

'**home-coming** *noun* [C,U] the arrival home (especially of sb who has been away for a long time)

homely /'həʊmli/ *adj* (**homelier**; **homeliest**) **1** plain and simple but also comfortable or welcoming: *a homely atmosphere* ○ *The farmer's wife was a large homely woman.* **2** (*US*) (used about a person) not very attractive

homicide /'hɒmɪsaɪd/ *noun* [U] the illegal killing of one person by another; murder —**homicidal** /ˌhɒmɪ'saɪdl/ *adj*

homoeopathy (*US* **homeopathy**) /ˌhəʊmi'ɒpəθi/ *noun* [U] the treatment of a disease by giving very small amounts of a drug that would cause the disease if given in large amounts

homoeopath (*US* **homeopath**) /ˌhəʊmiəpæθ/ *noun* [C] a person who treats sick people by using homoeopathy —**homoeopathic** (*US* **homeopathic**) /ˌhəʊmiə'pæθɪk/ *adj*: *homoeopathic medicine*

homogeneous /ˌhɒmə'dʒiːniəs/ *adj* made up of parts that are all of the same type ☛ The opposite is **heterogeneous**.

homonym /'hɒmənɪm/ *noun* [C] a word that is spelt and pronounced like another word but that has a different meaning

homosexual /ˌhɒmə'sekʃuəl/ *adj* sexually attracted to people of the same sex ☛ Look at **heterosexual**, **bisexual**, **gay** and **lesbian**.
homosexual *noun* [C] a homosexual person —**homosexuality** /ˌhɒməsekʃu'æləti/ *noun* [U]

☆ **honest** /'ɒnɪst/ *adj* **1** (used about a person) telling the truth; not deceiving people or stealing: *Just be honest—do you like this skirt or not?* ○ *We need somebody who's completely honest for this job.* **2** showing honest qualities: *an honest face* ○ *I'd like your honest opinion, please.* ☛ The opposite for both senses is **dishonest**.

honestly *adv* **1** in an honest way: *He tried to answer the lawyer's questions honestly.* **2** (used for emphasizing sth): *I honestly don't know where she has gone.* **3** (used for expressing disapproval): *Honestly! What a mess!*

☆ **honesty** /'ɒnəsti/ *noun* [U] the quality of being honest ☛ The opposite is **dishonesty**.

honey /'hʌni/ *noun* [U] the sweet sticky substance that is made by bees and that people eat: *Would you like honey on your bread?* ☛ **Honey** is also another word for **darling** (used especially in the US).

'**honeycomb** /'hʌnikəʊm/ *noun* [C,U] the wax structure with many six-sided holes that bees make for keeping their honey and eggs in

honeymoon /'hʌnimuːn/ *noun* [C] a holiday that is taken by a man and a woman who have just got married: *We went to Hawaii for our honeymoon.*

honk /hɒŋk/ *verb* [I,T] to sound the horn of a car; to make this sound

honorary /'ɒnərəri; *US* 'ɒnəreri/ *adj* **1** given as an honour (without the person needing the usual qualifications): *to be awarded an honorary degree* **2** often **Honorary** (*abbr* **Hon**) not getting any money for doing a job: *He is the Honorary President.*

☆ **honour¹** (*US* **honor**) /'ɒnə(r)/ *noun* **1** [sing] something that gives pride or pleasure: *It was a great honour to be asked to speak at the conference.* ○ *He did me the honour of mentioning my name in the introduction.* **2** [U] the respect from other people that a person, country, etc gets because of high standards of behaviour and moral character: *a man of honour* ○ *to fight for the honour of your country* ☛ Look at **dishonour**. **3** [C] something that is given to a person officially, to show great respect: *He has been given several honours for his work with handicapped children.* **4 Honours** [plural] a type of university degree that is higher than an ordinary degree
(IDIOMS) **in honour of sb/sth**; **in sb/sth's honour** out of respect for sb/sth: *A party was given in honour of the guests from Bonn.*

☆ **honour²** (*US* **honor**) /'ɒnə(r)/ *verb* [T] **1** honour sb/sth (with sth) to show great (public) respect for sb/sth or to give sb pride or pleasure: *I am very honoured by the confidence you have shown in me.* **2** to keep a promise to do sth

honourable (*US* **honorable**) /'ɒnərəbl/ *adj* **1** acting in a way that makes people respect you; having or showing honour: *The only honourable thing to do was to resign.* ○ *an honourable person* ☛ Look at **dishonourable**. **2 the Honourable** (*abbr* **Hon**) a title that is given to some high officials, to the children of some noblemen and to Members of Parliament when they are speaking to each other —**honourably** /-əbli/ *adv*

hood /hʊd/ *noun* [C] **1** the part of a coat, etc that you use to cover your head and neck in bad weather ☛ picture on page A11. **2** a soft cover for a car, or baby's pram that can be folded down in good weather **3** (*US*) = BONNET(1)

hoof /huːf/ *noun* [C] (*pl* **hoofs** or **hooves** /huːvz/) the hard part of the foot of horses and some other animals ☛ picture at **horse**.

hook¹ /hʊk/ *noun* [C] **1** a curved piece of metal, plastic, etc that is used for catching sth or hanging sth on: *a fish-hook* ○ *Put your coat on the hook over there.* ☛ picture at **hanger**. **2** (used in boxing) a blow or punch that is given with the elbow bent: *a right hook* (= with the right arm)
(IDIOM) **off the hook 1** (used about the telephone receiver) not in position, so that telephone calls cannot be received **2** (*informal*) out of a difficult situation: *My father paid the money I owed and got me off the hook.*

hook² /hʊk/ *verb* **1** [I,T] to fasten sth or to be fastened with a hook or sth like a hook **2** [T] to catch hold of sth with a hook or with sth shaped like a hook

(IDIOM) **be/get hooked (on sth)** (*slang*) **1** to like (doing) sth very much: *Brian is hooked on computer games.* **2** to be dependent on (**addicted to**) drugs, alcohol, etc: *to be hooked on gambling*
(PHRASAL VERB) **hook (sth) up (with sth)** to link one television station with another: *The BBC is hooked up with American television by satellite.*

hooked *adj* shaped like a hook: *a hooked nose*

hooligan /'hu:lɪgən/ *noun* [C] a young person who behaves in a violent and aggressive way in public places: *football hooligans* ☞ Look at **lout**. It is similar in meaning. —**hooliganism** /-ɪzəm/ *noun* [U]

hoop /hu:p/ *noun* [C] a large metal or plastic ring

hooray /hʊ'reɪ/ *interj* = HURRAY

hoot /hu:t/ *noun* **1** [C] the sound that is made by an owl, a ship's or car's horn, etc **2** [sing] (*informal*) something that is very funny: *That film is a real hoot!*

hoot *verb* [I,T] to sound the horn of a car or to make a loud noise: *The driver hooted at the dog but it wouldn't move.* ○ *They hooted with laughter at the suggestion.*

Hoover /'hu:və(r)/ *noun* [C] (*trade mark*) a vacuum cleaner (used to clean carpets by sucking up the dirt)
hoover *verb* [I,T] to clean a carpet, etc with a vacuum cleaner: *This carpet needs hoovering.* ○ *We'd better hoover up before our visitors arrive.*

hooves /hu:vz/ *pl* of HOOF

hop[1] /hɒp/ *verb* [I] (**hopping**; **hopped**) **1** (used about a person) to jump on one leg ☞ picture at **bounce**. **2** (used about an animal or bird) to jump with both or all feet together **3** (*informal*) to go somewhere quickly or for a short time: *Hop upstairs and get my glasses, would you?*
(IDIOM) **hop it!** (*slang*) Go away!
(PHRASAL VERBS) **hop in/into sth**; **hop out/out of sth** (*informal*) to get in or out of a car, etc (quickly): *Hop in! I'll give you a lift to town.*
hop on/onto sth; **hop off sth** to get onto/off a bus, etc (quickly)

hop *noun* [C] an act of hopping

hop[2] /hɒp/ *noun* **1** [C] a tall climbing plant with flowers **2 hops** [plural] the flowers of this plant that are used in making beer

☆ **hope** /həʊp/ *noun* **1** [C,U] **hope (of/for sth)**; **hope (of doing sth/that...)** the feeling of wanting sth to happen and thinking that it will: *She never gave up hope that a cure for the disease would be found.* ○ *What hope is there for the future?* ○ *There is no hope of finding anybody else alive.* ○ *David has high hopes of becoming an accountant.* **2** [C, usually sing] a person or thing that gives you hope: *Please can you help me? You're my last hope.*
(IDIOM) **in the hope of sth/that...** because you want sth to happen: *I came here in the hope that we could talk privately.*

hope *verb* [I,T] **hope (for sth); hope to do sth; hope (that) sth will happen** to want sth to happen or be true: *I hope that you feel better soon.* ○ *Hoping to hear from you soon* (= at the end of a letter). ○ *'Is it raining?' 'I hope not. I haven't got a coat with me.'* ○ *'Are you coming to London with us?' 'I'm not sure yet but I hope so.'* ○ *We're hoping for snow in January –we're going skiing.*

hopeful /'həʊpfl/ *adj* **1** thinking that sth that you want to happen will happen: *He's very hopeful about the success of the business.* ○ *The ministers seem hopeful that an agreement will be reached.* **2** making you think that sth good will happen: *a hopeful sign*

hopefully *adv* **1** in a hopeful way: *She smiled hopefully at me, waiting for my answer.* **2** I/We hope; if everything happens as planned: *Hopefully, we'll be finished by six o'clock.*

hopeless /'həʊpləs/ *adj* **1** giving no hope that sth will be successful or get better: *This is a hopeless situation. There is nothing we can do.* **2 hopeless (at sth)** (*informal*) (used about a person) often doing things wrongly; very bad at doing sth: *You're hopeless. You always forget my birthday.* ○ *I'm absolutely hopeless at tennis.* —**hopelessly** *adv*: *They were hopelessly lost.* —**hopelessness** *noun* [U]

horde /hɔːd/ *noun* [C] a very large number of people: *There were hordes of people shopping in town on Saturday.*

☆ **horizon** /hə'raɪzn/ *noun* [C] the line where the earth and sky appear to meet: *The ship appeared on/disappeared over the horizon.*

horizontal /ˌhɒrɪ'zɒntl; *US* ˌhɔːr-/ *adj* going from side to side, not up and down; flat or level: *The gymnasts were exercising on the horizontal bars.* ☞ picture at **vertical**. —**horizontally** /-təli/ *adv*

hormone /'hɔːməʊn/ *noun* [C] a substance in the body that influences growth and development

☆ **horn** /hɔːn/ *noun* [C] **1** one of the hard pointed things that cows, goats, etc have on their heads ☞ picture at **cow**. **2** the thing in a car, etc that gives a loud warning sound: *Don't sound your horn late at night.* ○ *a fog-horn* **3** one of the family of brass musical instruments that you play by blowing into them: *a French horn*

horoscope /'hɒrəskəʊp; *US* 'hɔːr-/ *noun* [C] (*also* **stars** [plural]) a statement about what is going to happen to a person in the future, based on the position of the stars and planets when he/she was born: *What does my horoscope for next week say?* ☞ Look at **astrology** and **zodiac**.

horrendous /hɒ'rendəs/ *adj* (*informal*) very bad or unpleasant: *The queues were absolutely horrendous.* —**horrendously** *adv*

horrible /'hɒrəbl; *US* 'hɔːr-/ *adj* **1** causing fear or shock: *a horrible murder* **2** (*informal*) very bad or unpleasant: *We had a horrible day in London.* ○ *This tastes horrible!* ○ *Don't be so horrible!* ○ *I've got a horrible feeling that I've forgotten something.* —**horribly** /-əblɪ/ *adv*

horrid /'hɒrɪd; *US* 'hɔːrɪd/ *adj* (*informal*) very unpleasant or unkind: *We had horrid weather in Italy.* ○ *I'm sorry that I was so horrid last night.*

horrific /hə'rɪfɪk/ *adj* **1** causing fear or shock: *a horrific road accident* **2** (*informal*) very bad or unpleasant: *We had a horrific journey –we were stuck in a traffic jam for two hours.* —**horrifically** /-klɪ/ *adv*: *horrifically expensive*

s	z	ʃ	ʒ	h	m	n	ŋ	l	r	j	w
so	zoo	she	vision	how	man	no	sing	leg	red	yes	wet

horrify /'hɒrɪfaɪ; US 'hɔːr-/ verb [T] (pres part **horrifying**; 3rd pers sing pres **horrifies**; pt, pp **horrified**) to shock sb greatly: *I was horrified by the conditions they were living in.* —**horrifying** adj

horror /'hɒrə(r); US 'hɔːr-/ noun **1** [U,sing] a feeling of great fear or shock: *They watched in horror as the building collapsed.* ○ *She has a horror of rats.* **2** [C] something that makes you feel frightened or shocked: *I'll never forget the horror of what I saw that day.* ○ *the horrors of war*

'horror film noun [C] a film that entertains people by showing frightening or shocking things

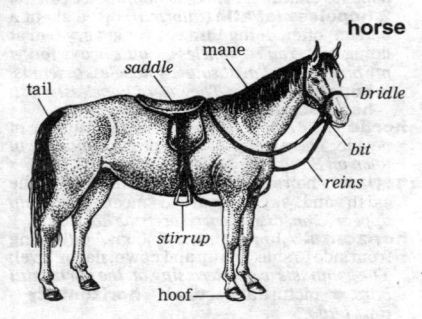

horse

tail, saddle, mane, bridle, bit, reins, stirrup, hoof

☆ **horse** /hɔːs/ noun [C] a large animal that is used for riding on or for pulling or carrying heavy loads

☛ A male horse is a **stallion**, a female horse is a **mare** and a young horse is a **foal**.

(IDIOM) **on horseback** sitting on a horse: *Policemen on horseback were controlling the crowds.* ☛ Police on horseback are also called **mounted police**.

'horseman /-mən/ noun [C] (pl **horsemen** /-mən/) a man who rides a horse (well): *an experienced horseman*

'horse-racing (also **racing**) noun [U] the sport in which a person (**jockey**) rides a horse in a race to win money

☛ Horse-racing takes place at a **racecourse**. People often **bet** on the results of **horse-races**.

'horseshoe (also **shoe**) noun [C] a U-shaped piece of metal that is fixed to the bottom of a horse's hoof. People believe that horseshoes bring good luck.

'horsewoman /-wʊmən/ noun [C] (pl **horsewomen** /-wɪmɪn/) a woman who rides a horse (well): *a good horsewoman*

horse chestnut /ˌhɔːs 'tʃesnʌt/ noun [C] **1** a large tree that has leaves divided into seven sections and pink or white flowers **2** (also *informal* **conker**) the nut from this tree

horsepower /'hɔːspaʊə(r)/ noun [C] (pl **horsepower**) (abbr **hp**) a measure of the power of an engine, etc: *a ten horsepower engine*

horticulture /'hɔːtɪkʌltʃə(r)/ noun [U] the study of how to grow flowers, fruit and vegetables —**horticultural** /ˌhɔːtɪ'kʌltʃərəl/ adj

hose /həʊz/ (also **'hose-pipe**) noun [C,U] a long rubber or plastic tube that is used for getting water from one place to another, in the garden or when there is a fire

hospice /'hɒspɪs/ noun [C] a special hospital where people who are dying are cared for

hospitable /hɒ'spɪtəbl; 'hɒspɪtəbl/ adj (used about a person) friendly and welcoming to visitors ☛ Look at **inhospitable**.

☆ **hospital** /'hɒspɪtl/ noun [C] a place where ill or injured people are treated: *He was rushed to hospital in an ambulance.* ○ *to be admitted to/discharged from hospital* ☛ Note the difference between: *My brother works in the local hospital* and: *He's very ill in hospital.* 'In hospital', 'to hospital' are special expressions that are used without 'a' or 'the': *All the people who were hurt in the accident have been taken to hospital.* A person who is being treated in a hospital by **doctors** and **nurses** is a **patient**. If you have an accident you are taken first to the **casualty** department (*US* **emergency room**).

hospitality /ˌhɒspɪ'tæləti/ noun [U] looking after guests and being friendly and welcoming towards them: *We're very grateful for your hospitality.*

☆ **host¹** /həʊst/ noun [C] **1** a person who receives and entertains visitors: *He acted as our host and showed us the city.* ○ *It's polite to write a thank-you letter to your host.* ○ *the host country for the next Olympic Games* ☛ Look at **hostess**. **2** a person who introduces a television or radio show and talks to visiting guests
host verb [T] to act as a host or hostess

host² /həʊst/ noun [C] a large number (of people or things): *I've got a whole host of things I want to discuss with him.*

☆ **hostage** /'hɒstɪdʒ/ noun [C] a person who is caught and kept prisoner by a person or group. The hostage may be killed or injured if that person or group does not get what it is asking for: *The hijackers released the women and children but kept the men as hostages.*
(IDIOM) **take/hold sb hostage** to catch/keep sb as a hostage

hostel /'hɒstl/ noun [C] a place (like a cheap hotel) where people can stay when they are living away from home: *a youth hostel* ○ *a hostel for the homeless* ○ *a student hostel*

hostess /'həʊstɪs/ noun [C] **1** a woman who receives and entertains visitors **2** a woman who introduces a television or radio show and talks to visiting guests **3** = AIR-HOSTESS

hostile /'hɒstaɪl; *US* -tl/ adj very unfriendly towards sb/sth; not having a good opinion of sb/sth: *a hostile crowd* ○ *They are very hostile to any change.*

hostility /hɒ'stɪləti/ noun **1** [U] being unfriendly towards sb/sth: *She didn't say anything but I could sense her hostility.* **2** [U] thinking that sth is bad: *They didn't try to hide their hostility to the government.* **3 hostilities** [plural] fighting in a war: *Negotiations have led to an end to hostilities.*

---

iː	ɪ	e	æ	ɑː	ɒ	ɔː	ʊ	uː	ʌ
see	sit	ten	hat	arm	got	saw	put	too	cup

☆**hot** /hɒt/ adj (**hotter; hottest**) **1** having (quite) a high degree of heat; not cold: *Can I open the window? I'm really hot.* ○ *Be careful. The plates are hot.* ○ *It's hot today, isn't it?* ○ *Do you like this hot weather?* ○ *a hot meal*

☛ You can describe the temperature of sth as **freezing** (cold), **cold**, **cool**, **tepid** (used about water), **warm**, **hot** or **boiling** (hot).

2 (used about food) causing a burning feeling in your mouth: *hot curry*
(IDIOM) **be hot at/on sth** to know a lot about sth: *Don't ask me. I'm not very hot on British history.*
hot verb (**hotting; hotted**)
(PHRASAL VERB) **hot up** (*informal*) to become more exciting, with more things happening, etc: *The election campaign has really hotted up in the past few days.*
hotly adv **1** angrily or with force: *They hotly denied the newspaper reports.* **2** closely: *The dog ran off, hotly pursued by its owner.*
hot-'air balloon noun [C] = BALLOON(2)
'hot dog noun [C] a hot sausage that is eaten in a soft bread roll
'hothouse noun [C] a heated building, made of glass, where plants are grown ☛ Look at **greenhouse**.
,hot-'water bottle noun [C] a rubber container that is filled with hot water and put in a bed to warm it
☆**hotel** /həʊˈtel/ noun [C] a place where you pay to stay (and perhaps have your meals) when you are on holiday or travelling: *We stayed in a really nice hotel in Devon.* ○ *I've booked a double room at the Grand Hotel.* ○ *a two-star hotel*

☛ You book a **double**, **single** or **twin-bedded** room at a hotel. When you arrive you **check in** or **register** and when you leave you **check out**. Look at the note at **inn**.

hotelier /həʊˈteliə(r); *US* ˌhəʊtelˈjeɪ/ noun [C] a person who owns or manages a hotel
hotline /ˈhɒtlaɪn/ noun [C] a direct telephone line
hound /haʊnd/ noun [C] a type of dog that is used for hunting or racing: *a foxhound*
hound verb [T] to follow and disturb sb: *The Royal Family are always being hounded by the press.*
☆**hour** /ˈaʊə(r)/ noun **1** [C] a period of 60 minutes: *He worked for three hours after supper.* ○ *The programme lasts about half an hour.* ○ *I've been waiting here for hours.* ○ *I'm going shopping now. I'll be back in about an hour.* ○ *a four-hour journey* **2 the hour** [sing] the time when a new hour starts (ie 1 o'clock, 2 o'clock, etc): *Trains to Reading leave at two minutes past the hour.* **3 hours** [plural] the period of time when sb is working or a shop, etc is open: *Office hours are usually from 9am to 5pm.* ○ *Visiting hours in the hospital are from 2 to 3pm.* ○ *The men are demanding shorter working hours.* **4** [C] a period of time: *I'm going shopping in my lunch hour.* ○ *The traffic is very bad in the rush hour.*

(IDIOMS) **at/till all hours** at/till any time: *She stays out till all hours* (= very late).
the early hours ⇨ EARLY
on the hour at exactly 1, 2, 3, etc o'clock: *The buses for London leave on the hour.*
hourly /ˈaʊəli/ adv every hour: *This medicine must be taken hourly.*
hourly adj **1** done or happening every hour: *an hourly news bulletin* **2** for an hour: *What is your hourly rate of pay?*
☆**house¹** /haʊs/ noun [C] (pl **houses** /ˈhaʊzɪz/) **1** a building that is made for one family to live in: *Is yours a four-bedroomed or a three-bedroomed house?* ☛ Look at **bungalow**, **cottage** and **flat**. Your **home** is the place where you live, even if it is not a house: *Let's go home to my flat.* Your home is also the place where you feel that you belong. A house is just a building: *We've only just moved into our new house and it doesn't feel like home yet.* You can **build**, **do up**, **redecorate** or **extend** a house. You may **rent** a house from somebody or **let** it out to somebody else. If you want to **move house** you go to an **estate agent**. **2** [usually sing] all the people who live in one house: *Don't shout. You'll wake the whole house up.* **3** a building that is used for a particular purpose: *a warehouse* ○ *a public house* **4 House** a group of people who meet to make a country's laws: *the House of Commons* ○ *the Houses of Parliament* ☛ Look at the note at **Parliament**. **5** [usually sing] the people at a theatre or cinema, or the area where they sit: *There was a full house for the play this evening.*
(IDIOMS) **move house** ⇨ MOVE²
on the house paid for by the pub, restaurant, etc that you are visiting; free: *Your first drink is on the house.*
'houseboat noun [C] a boat on a river, etc where sb lives and which usually stays in one place
'housebound adj unable to leave your house because you are old or ill
'housekeeper noun [C] a person who is paid to look after sb else's house and organize the work in it
'housekeeping noun [U] **1** managing and organizing the work in a house **2** the money that you need to manage a house
'houseman /-mən/ noun [C] (pl **housemen** /-mən/) (*US* **intern; interne**) a young doctor who lives and works at a hospital while he/she is completing his/her training ☛ Look at the note at **housewife**.
the ,House of 'Commons noun [sing] the group of people (**Members of Parliament**) who are elected to make new laws in Britain
the ,House of 'Lords noun [sing] the group of people (who are not elected) who meet to discuss the laws that have been suggested by the House of Commons
the ,House of ,Repre'sentatives noun [sing] the group of people who are elected to make new laws in the USA ☛ Look at **Congress** and **Senate**.
'house-proud adj paying great attention to the care, cleaning, etc of your house
,house-to-'house adj going to each house:

ɜː	ə	eɪ	əʊ	aɪ	aʊ	ɔɪ	ɪə	eə	ʊə
fur	ago	pay	home	five	now	join	near	hair	pure

The police are making house-to-house enquiries.

'house-warming *noun* [C] a party that you give when you have just moved into a new home

'housewife *noun* [C] (*pl* **housewives**) a woman who does not have a full-time job outside the home and who spends her time doing housework, cooking, looking after her family, etc ☞ A man who does this is called a **house husband**.

'housework *noun* [U] the work that is needed to keep a house clean and tidy ☞ Be careful. The word for work that is given to pupils by teachers to be done out of school hours is **homework**.

house² /haʊz/ *verb* [T] **1** to provide sb with a place to live: *The Council must house homeless families.* **2** to contain or keep sth: *Her office is housed in a separate building.*

☆ **household** /'haʊshəʊld/ *noun* [C] all the people who live in one house and the housework, money, organization, etc that is needed to look after them: *Almost all households have a television.* ○ *household expenses*

householder /-həʊldə(r)/ *noun* [C] a person who rents or owns a house

☆ **housing** /'haʊzɪŋ/ *noun* [U] houses, flats, etc for people to live in: *We need more housing that is suitable for elderly people.* ○ *the Council's housing department*

'housing estate *noun* [C] an area where a large number of houses are planned and built at the same time

hover /'hɒvə(r); *US* 'hʌvər/ *verb* [I] **1** (used about a bird, etc) to stay in the air in one place **2** (used about a person) to wait near sb/sth: *He hovered outside until he could see that she was free.*

'hovercraft *noun* [C] (*pl* **hovercraft**) a type of boat that moves over land or water on a cushion of air

☆ **how** /haʊ/ *adv* **1** (used in questions) in what way: *How do you spell your name?* ○ *Can you show me how to use this machine?* **2** (used when you are asking about sb's health): *'How is your mother?' 'She's much better, thank you.'* ☞ You use 'how' only when you are asking about a person's health. When you are asking about a person's character or appearance you say **what...like**?: *'What is your mother like?' 'Well, she's much taller than me and she's got dark hair.'* **3** (used when you are asking about a thing or a situation): *How was the weather?* ○ *How is your meal?* **4** (used in questions before an adjective or adverb when you are asking about the degree, amount, age, etc of sb/sth): *How old are you?* ○ *How much is that?* ○ *How long did it take to get here?* **5** (used for expressing surprise, shock, thanks, pleasure, etc): *How sweet of you to remember my birthday.* ○ *How could he have lied to me?*

(IDIOMS) **how/what about...?** ⇨ ABOUT²

how do you do? (*formal*) (used when meeting sb for the first time) ☞ Be careful. **How are you?** and **How do you do?** are answered quite differently: *'How do you do?'* is answered with the same words: *'How do you do?'* The answer to: *'How are you?'* depends on how you are feeling: *'I'm fine.'/'Very well.'/'Much better.'*

how *conj* the way in which: *I can't remember how to get there.*

☆ **however¹** /haʊ'evə(r)/ *adv* (before an adjective or adverb) to whatever degree: *He won't wear a hat however cold it is.* ○ *You can't catch her however fast you run.*

however *conj* in whatever way: *However I sat I couldn't get comfortable.* ○ *You can dress however you like.*

however *adv* (used in questions for expressing surprise) in what way; how: *However did you manage to find me here?* ○ *However could he afford a car like that?* ☞ When you use only **how** in a question like this there is not so much feeling of surprise.

☆ **however²** /haʊ'evə(r)/ *adv* (used for adding a comment on what you have just said) although sth is true: *Sales are poor this month. There may, however, be an increase before Christmas.*

howl /haʊl/ *noun* [C] a long loud cry made by a dog or a wolf: (*figurative*) *The Prime Minister's statement met with howls of protest.*

howl *verb* [I] to make a howl or say sth with a howl: *The wind howled around the house.*

hub /hʌb/ *noun* [C] the round central part of a wheel

huddle /'hʌdl/ *verb* [I] **1** to get close to other people because you are cold or frightened: *The campers huddled (together) around the fire.* **2 huddle (up)** to curl your body up and wrap your arms around yourself because you are cold or frightened: *She huddled up in her sleeping-bag and tried to get some sleep.*

huddle *noun* [C] a small group of people or things that are close together: *They all stood in a huddle, laughing and chatting.* —**huddled** *adj*: *We found the children lying huddled together on the ground.*

huff /hʌf/ *noun* [C, usually sing] a state of bad temper. You go off in a huff when you want to show people how angry you are.

hug /hʌg/ *verb* [T] (**hugging**; **hugged**) **1** to put your arms around sb to show that you love him/her: *There was a lot of hugging and kissing at the station before the French school party left.* **2** (used about a ship, car, etc) to keep close to sth: *to hug the coast*

hug *noun* [C] an act of hugging: *She gave the child a hug and he stopped crying.*

☆ **huge** /hju:dʒ/ *adj* very large: *There is a huge amount of work still to be done.* ○ *a huge building* —**hugely** *adv*: *The play was hugely successful.*

huh /hʌ/ *interj* (*informal*) (used for expressing anger, surprise, etc or for asking a question): *They've gone away, huh? They didn't tell me.*

hull /hʌl/ *noun* [C] the body of a ship

hullabaloo /ˌhʌləbə'lu:/ *noun* [C, usually sing] a lot of loud noise, eg people shouting

hullo = HALLO

hum /hʌm/ *verb* (**humming**; **hummed**) **1** [I] to make a continuous low noise like the noise bees make: (*figurative*) *The classroom was humming with activity.* **2** [I,T] to sing with your lips closed: *You can hum the tune if you don't know the words.*

hum *noun* [C, usually sing] a humming sound: *the hum of distant traffic*

☆ **human** /'hju:mən/ *adj* connected with people, not with animals or machines; typical of people: *the human body* ○ *The famine caused a terrible loss of human life.* ○ *A human skeleton was found by the building workers.* ○ *The disaster was caused by human error.* ○ *It's only human to be upset in a situation like that.*

human (*also* ˌhuman 'being) *noun* [C] a person; a man, woman or child —**humanly** *adv*: *They did all that was humanly possible to rescue him* (= everything that a human being could possibly do).

ˌhuman 'nature *noun* [U] feelings, behaviour, etc that are common to all people: *It's only human nature to want the best for yourself and your family.*

the ˌhuman 'race *noun* [sing] all the people in the world (when you are thinking of them as a group)

ˌhuman 'rights *noun* [plural] the basic freedoms that all people should have, eg the right to say what you think, travel freely, etc

humane /hju:'meɪn/ *adj* having or showing kindness or understanding especially to a person or animal that is suffering: *A civilized society treats mentally handicapped people in a humane way.* ☛ The opposite is **inhumane**. —**humanely** *adv*

humanitarian /hju:ˌmænɪ'teəriən/ *adj* concerned with trying to make people's lives better and reduce suffering

humanity /hju:'mænəti/ *noun* [U] **1** all the people in the world, thought of as a group; the human race: *crimes against humanity* **2** the quality of being kind and understanding: *The prisoners were treated with humanity.* ☛ The opposite is **inhumanity**.

humble /'hʌmbl/ *adj* **1** not thinking that you are better or more important than other people; not proud: *He became very rich and famous but he always remained a very humble man.* ☛ The noun is **humility**. **2** low in social status; unimportant: *She comes from a humble background.*

humble *verb* [T] to make sb/yourself humble: *a humbling experience* —**humbly** /'hʌmbli/ *adv*: *He apologized very humbly for his behaviour.*

humid /'hju:mɪd/ *adj* (used about the air or climate) containing a lot of water; damp: *Hong Kong is hot and humid in summer.* —**humidity** /hju:'mɪdəti/ *noun* [U]

humiliate /hju:'mɪlieɪt/ *verb* [T] to make sb feel ashamed: *Did you have to humiliate me in front of all those people?* —**humiliating** *adj*: *a humiliating defeat* —**humiliation** /hju:ˌmɪli'eɪʃn/ *noun* [C,U]

humility /hju:'mɪləti/ *noun* [U] the quality of being modest or humble, ie not thinking that you are better than other people

humorous /'hju:mərəs/ *adj* amusing or funny: *It's a very humorous book.* ○ *a humorous speaker* —**humorously** *adv*

☆ **humour** (*US* **humor**) /'hju:mə(r)/ *noun* [U] **1** the funny or amusing quality or qualities of sb/sth: *It's an awful situation but at least you can see the humour of it.* ○ *It is sometimes hard to understand the humour* (= the jokes) *of another country.* **2** being able to see when sth is funny and to laugh at things: *Rose has a good sense of humour.*

humour (*US* **humor**) *verb* [T] to keep sb happy by doing what he/she wants: *When she's in a mood like this it's best to humour her.*

-humoured (*US* **-humored**) (in compounds) having or showing a particular mood: *good-humoured*

humourless (*US* **humorless**) *adj* not able to see when things are funny

hump /hʌmp/ *noun* [C] a round lump, eg on the back of a camel ☛ picture at **camel**.

hunch¹ /hʌntʃ/ *noun* [C] (*informal*) a thought or an idea that is based on a feeling rather than on facts or information: *I'm not sure, but I've got a hunch that she's got a new job.*

hunch² /hʌntʃ/ *verb* [I,T] to bend your back and shoulders forward in a round shape: *They sat there hunched up with the cold.*

'hunchback *noun* [C] a person with a back that has a round lump (**hump**) on it

☆ **hundred** /'hʌndrəd/ *number* 100; one more than ninety-nine: *two hundred* ○ *There were a/one hundred people in the room.* ○ *She's a hundred today.* ☛ Note that when we are saying a number, eg 420, we put 'and' after the word **hundred**: *four hundred and twenty.* The plural **hundreds** is used when we mean 'many' or 'a lot': *The boat cost hundreds of pounds.* ○ *Hundreds of people were left without electricity after the storm.* Look at Appendix 2.

hundredth /'hʌndrədθ/ *pron, det, adv* 100th; next after ninety-ninth

hundredth *noun* [C] the fraction ¹⁄₁₀₀; one of a hundred equal parts of sth

'hundredweight *noun* [C] (*pl* **hundredweight**) (*abbr* **cwt**) a measure of weight; 50·8 kilograms. There are 112 pounds in a hundredweight. ☛ An American hundredweight is 100 pounds (45.4 kilograms).

hung *pt, pp* of HANG

☆ **hunger** /'hʌŋgə(r)/ *noun* [U] **1** the wish or need for food: *Hunger is one reason why babies cry.* **2** a lack of food: *In the Third World many people die of hunger each year.* ☛ Look at **thirst**. Be careful. You cannot say *I have hunger* in English. You must say: *I am hungry.*

hunger *verb* (*formal*)

(PHRASAL VERB) **hunger for/after sb/sth** to have a strong desire for sth

'hunger strike *noun* [C,U] a time when people (especially prisoners) refuse to eat because they are protesting about sth

☆ **hungry** /'hʌŋgri/ *adj* (**hungrier; hungriest**) wanting to eat: *I'm hungry. Let's eat soon.* ○ *There were hungry children begging for food in the streets.* ☛ Look at **thirsty**.

(IDIOM) **go hungry** not have any food: *I'd rather go hungry than eat that!* —**hungrily** /'hʌŋgrəli/ *adv*

hunk /hʌŋk/ *noun* [C] a large piece of sth: *a hunk of bread*

☆ **hunt**¹ /hʌnt/ *verb* [I,T] **1** to chase wild animals,

s	z	ʃ	ʒ	h	m	n	ŋ	l	r	j	w
so	zoo	she	vision	how	man	no	sing	leg	red	yes	wet

etc in order to catch or kill them either for sport or for food: *Owls hunt at night.* ○ *Are tigers still hunted in India?* ☛ We often use the expression **go hunting** when we are talking about spending time hunting. **2 hunt (for) (sb/sth)** to look or search for sb/sth: *I've hunted everywhere for my gloves but I can't find them.* ○ *The police are still hunting the murderer.*

hunter *noun* [C] a person or animal that hunts: (*figurative*) *a bargain-hunter*

hunting *noun* [U] the chasing and killing of wild animals ☛ Look at **shoot**.

☆ **hunt²** /hʌnt/ *noun* [C] **1** the act of hunting wild animals, etc: *a fox-hunt* **2** [usually sing] the act of searching or looking for sb/sth: *The police have launched a hunt for the missing child.*

hurdle /'hɜːdl/ *noun* **1** [C] a type of light fence that you jump over in a race **2 hurdles** [plural] a race over hurdles: *the 200 metres hurdles* **3** [C] a problem or difficulty that you must overcome

hurdle *verb* [I] to jump over a hurdle

hurl /hɜːl/ *verb* [T] to throw sth with force

☆ **hurray** (*also* **hooray**) /hʊ'reɪ/ (*also* **hurrah** /hʊ'rɑː/) *interj* (used for expressing great pleasure, approval, etc): *Hurray! We've won!* ○ *Hip, hip, hurray!*

hurricane /'hʌrɪkən; *US* -keɪn/ *noun* [C] a storm with very strong winds ☛ Look at the note at **storm**.

☆ **hurry¹** /'hʌri/ *noun* [U] a need or wish to do sth quickly: *Take your time. There's no hurry.* ○ *What's the hurry?*

(IDIOMS) **in a hurry 1** quickly: *She got up late and left in a hurry.* **2** wanting to do sth soon: *They are in a hurry to get the job done before the winter.*

in no hurry; not in any hurry 1 not needing or wishing to do sth quickly: *We weren't in any hurry so we stopped to admire the view.* **2** (*informal*) unwilling: *I am in no hurry to repeat that experience.*

hurry *verb* (*pres part* **hurrying**; *3rd pers sing pres* **hurries**; *pt, pp* **hurried**) **1** [I] to move or do sth quickly: *Don't hurry. There's plenty of time.* ○ *They hurried back home after school.* ○ *Several people hurried to help.* **2** [T] to cause sb/sth to do sth or to happen more quickly: *Don't hurry me. I'm going as fast as I can.* ○ *He was hurried into a decision.*

(PHRASAL VERB) **hurry up** (*informal*) to move or do sth more quickly: *Hurry up or we'll miss the train.*

hurried *adj* done (too) quickly: *a hurried meal* ☛ The opposite is **unhurried**. —**hurriedly** *adv*

☆ **hurt** /hɜːt/ *verb* (*pt, pp* **hurt**) **1** [T] to cause pain or injury: *Did he hurt himself?* ○ *I fell and hurt my arm.* ○ *No one was seriously hurt in the accident.* ○ (*figurative*) *The new tax will hurt families on low incomes.* ☛ Compare **hurt, injure** and **wound**. A person may be **wounded** with a knife, sword, gun, etc, usually as a result of fighting: *a wounded soldier.* People are usually **injured** in an accident: *Five people were killed in the crash and twelve others were injured.* **Hurt** and **injured** are similar in meaning but **hurt** is more often used when the damage is not very great: *I hurt my leg when I fell off my bike.* **2** [I] to produce a feeling of pain: *My leg hurts.* ○ *It hurts when I lift my leg.* ○ *These shoes hurt; they're too tight.* **3** [T] to make sb unhappy; to upset sb: *His unkind remarks hurt her deeply.*

(IDIOM) **it won't/wouldn't hurt (sb/sth) (to do sth)** (*informal*) it would be a good thing for sb/sth (to do): *It wouldn't hurt you to leave the car at home and walk.*

hurt *noun* [U] (*formal*) mental pain or suffering

hurt *adj* unhappy because sb has been unkind to you

hurtful /-fl/ *adj* unkind; upsetting: *Don't say such hurtful things to your father!*

hurtle /'hɜːtl/ *verb* [I] to move with great speed, perhaps causing danger: *Rocks hurtled down the mountainside.*

☆ **husband** /'hʌzbənd/ *noun* [C] a man that a woman is married to: *a good husband and father* ○ *Her ex-husband sees the children once a month.*

hush /hʌʃ/ *verb*

(PHRASAL VERB) **hush sth up** to stop people knowing about sth; to keep sth secret: *The police managed to hush up the whole affair.*

hush *noun* [sing] silence: *As he rose to speak a hush fell over the audience.*

hush-'hush *adj* (*informal*) very secret: *Her work is very hush-hush.*

husky¹ /'hʌski/ *adj* (**huskier**; **huskiest**) (used about a voice) sounding rough and quiet as if your throat were dry

husky² /'hʌski/ *noun* [C] (*pl* **huskies**) a strong dog with thick fur that is used in teams for pulling heavy loads over snow

hustle /'hʌsl/ *verb* [T] to push or move sb roughly: *The demonstrators were hustled into police vans.*

hut /hʌt/ *noun* [C] a small building with one room, usually made of wood or metal

hydrant /'haɪdrənt/ *noun* [C] a pipe in a street from which water can be taken for putting out fires, street-cleaning, etc

hydraulic /haɪ'drɔːlɪk/ *adj* worked by water or another liquid moving through pipes, etc: *hydraulic brakes*

hydroelectric /ˌhaɪdrəʊ'lektrɪk/ *adj* **1** using the power of water to produce electricity: *a hydroelectric dam* **2** (used about electricity) produced by the power of water: *hydroelectric power*

hydrogen /'haɪdrədʒən/ *noun* [U] (*symbol* **H**) a light colourless gas. Hydrogen and oxygen form water (H_2O).

hygiene /'haɪdʒiːn/ *noun* [U] (the rules of) keeping yourself and things around you clean, in order to prevent illness: *High standards of hygiene are essential when you are preparing food.* ○ *personal hygiene*

hygienic /haɪ'dʒiːnɪk; *US* ˌhaɪdʒɪ'enɪk; haɪ'dʒenɪk/ *adj* clean, without the germs that cause disease: *hygienic conditions* ☛ The opposite is **unhygienic**. —**hygienically** /-kli/ *adv*

---

iː	ɪ	e	æ	ɑː	ɒ	ɔː	ʊ	uː	ʌ
see	sit	ten	hat	arm	got	saw	put	too	cup

hymn /hɪm/ noun [C] a song of praise to God that Christians sing together in church, etc

hypermarket /'haɪpəmɑːkɪt/ noun [C] (Brit) a very large supermarket that is usually outside a town

hyphen /'haɪfn/ noun [C] the punctuation mark (-) used for joining two words together (eg *knock-out*, *red-hot*) or to show that a word has been divided and continues on the next line.

hyphenate /'haɪfəneɪt/ verb [T] to write with a hyphen: *Do you hyphenate 'girlfriend'?* —**hyphenation** /ˌhaɪfə'neɪʃn/ noun [U]

hypnosis /hɪp'nəʊsɪs/ noun [U] (the producing of) a state that is like deep sleep where sb's mind and actions can be controlled by another person: *She was questioned under hypnosis.* —**hypnotic** /hɪp'nɒtɪk/ adj: *The rhythmic dance had a hypnotic effect on the audience.*

hypnotism /'hɪpnətɪzəm/ noun [U] using hypnosis

hypnotist /'hɪpnətɪst/ noun [C] a person who uses hypnosis on other people

hypnotize (also **hypnotise**) /'hɪpnətaɪz/ verb [T] to use hypnosis on sb

hypochondriac /ˌhaɪpə'kɒndriæk/ noun [C] a person who is always worried about his/her health even when there is nothing wrong

hypocrisy /hɪ'pɒkrəsi/ noun [U] pretending to feel, believe, etc sth that is different from what you really feel, etc; saying one thing and doing another

hypocrite /'hɪpəkrɪt/ noun [C] a person who pretends to have feelings and opinions which he/she does not, in fact, have. Hypocrites say one thing and do another: *What a hypocrite!* —**hypocritical** /ˌhɪpə'krɪtɪkl/ adj —**hypocritically** /-kli/ adv

hypodermic /ˌhaɪpə'dɜːmɪk/ adj used for injecting drugs beneath the skin: *a hypodermic needle/syringe*

hypothesis /haɪ'pɒθəsɪs/ noun [C] (pl **hypotheses** /-siːz/) an idea that is suggested as the possible explanation for sth: *The hypothesis has been put forward that some chemicals used in food can affect children's behaviour.*

hypothetical /ˌhaɪpə'θetɪkl/ adj based on situations that have not yet happened, not on facts: *That's a hypothetical question because we don't know what the situation will be next year.* —**hypothetically** /-kli/ adv

hysteria /hɪ'stɪəriə/ noun [U] a state of excitement in which a person or a group of people cannot control their emotions, eg cannot stop laughing, crying, shouting, etc: *mass hysteria*

hysterical /hɪ'sterɪkl/ adj **1** caused by or suffering from hysteria: *hysterical laughter* ○ *She was hysterical with grief.* **2** (*informal*) very funny —**hysterically** /-kli/ adv

hysterics /hɪ'sterɪks/ noun [plural] **1** a state of hysteria: *She went into hysterics when they told her the news.* ○ (*informal*) *My father would have hysterics if he knew I was going out with you.* **2** (*informal*) uncontrolled laughter: *The audience was in hysterics.*

Ii

I, i¹ /aɪ/ noun [C] (pl **I's; i's**) the ninth letter of the English alphabet: *'Island' begins with (an) 'I'.*

☆ **I²** /aɪ/ pron (the subject of a verb) the person who is speaking or writing: *I phoned and said that I was busy.* ○ *I'm not going to fall, am I?* ○ *I'm taller than you, aren't I?* ○ *She and I are planning to go out later.*

☆ **ice¹** /aɪs/ noun **1** [U] water that has frozen solid: *Do you want ice in your orange juice?* ○ *I slipped on a patch of ice.* ○ *The ice on the lake isn't thick enough for skating.* ○ *The ice quickly melted in the sunshine.* ○ *black ice* (= ice on roads, that cannot be seen easily) **2** [C] an ice-cream: *Would you like an ice?*

iced /'aɪst/ adj (used about drinks) very cold

icy /'aɪsi/ adj (**icier; iciest**) **1** very cold: *an icy wind* **2** covered with ice: *icy roads*

iceberg noun [C] a very large block of ice that is floating in the sea: *The ship hit an iceberg and sank.*

(IDIOM) **the tip of the iceberg** ⇨ TIP¹

icebox noun [C] (US) = FRIDGE

ice-cold adj very cold: *ice-cold beer* ○ *Your hands are ice-cold.*

ice-cream noun **1** [U] a frozen sweet food that is made from cream (or other types of fat) **2** [C] a portion of ice-cream, usually in paper or a special container (**a cone**): *Four strawberry ice-creams, please.*

ice-cube noun [C] a small block of ice that you put in a drink to make it cold

ice hockey (US **hockey**) noun [U] a game that is played on ice by two teams who try to hit a small flat rubber object (**a puck**) into a goal with long wooden sticks

ice lolly noun [C] (pl **ice lollies**) (US **popsicle**) a piece of flavoured ice on a stick

ice-rink noun [C] = SKATING-RINK

ice-skate noun [C] = SKATE

ice-skate verb [I] = SKATE

ice-skating noun [U] = SKATING(1)

ice² /aɪs/ verb

(PHRASAL VERB) **ice (sth) over/up** to cover or

ɜː	ə	eɪ	əʊ	aɪ	aʊ	ɔɪ	ɪə	eə	ʊə
fur	ago	pay	home	five	now	join	near	hair	pure

become covered with ice: *The windscreen of the car had iced over in the night.*

ice³ /aɪs/ *verb* [T] to cover a cake with icing

icicle /'aɪsɪkl/ *noun* [C] a pointed piece of ice that is formed by water freezing as it falls or runs down from sth

icing /'aɪsɪŋ/ (*US* **frosting**) *noun* [U] a mixture of powdery sugar and egg-white or butter, flavouring, etc that is used for decorating cakes: *chocolate icing*

I'd /aɪd/ *short for* I HAD, I WOULD

☆**idea** /aɪ'dɪə/ *noun* **1** [C] a plan or suggestion: *That's a good idea.* ○ *He's got an idea for a new play.* ○ *I had the bright idea of getting Jane to help me with my homework.* ○ *Has anyone got any ideas of how to tackle this problem?* ○ *It was your idea to invite so many people to the party.* **2** [U,sing] a picture or thought in your mind: *Have you any idea how much this cost?* ○ *You have no idea* (= you can't imagine) *how difficult it was to find a time that suited everybody.* ○ *The programme gave a good idea of what life was like before the war.* **3** [C] an opinion or belief: *She has her own ideas about how to bring up children.* ○ *Hiding my handbag? If that's your idea of a joke, I don't think it's funny!* **4 the idea** [sing] the aim or purpose of sth: *The idea of the course is to teach the basics of car maintenance.*

(IDIOMS) **get the idea** to understand: *Right! I think I've got the idea now.*

get the idea that... to get the feeling or impression that...: *Where did you get the idea that I was paying for this meal?*

have an idea that... to have a feeling that...: *I'm not sure but I have an idea that they've gone on holiday.*

not have the faintest/foggiest (idea) ⇨ FAINT

☆**ideal** /aɪ'dɪəl/ *adj* the best possible; perfect: *In an ideal world there would be no poverty.*

ideal *noun* [C] **1** an idea or principle that seems perfect to you and that you want to achieve: *She finds it hard to live up to her parents' high ideals.* ○ *socialist ideals* **2** [usually sing] a perfect example of a person or thing: *My ideal would be to live in the country and have a flat in London.*

ideally *adv* **1** perfectly: *They are ideally suited to each other.* **2** in an ideal situation: *Ideally, no class should be larger than 25.*

idealism /aɪ'dɪəlɪzəm/ *noun* [U] the belief that people should have high ideals and live according to them, or that the world can be made perfect: *Young people are usually full of idealism.* ☛ Look at **realism**.

idealist /aɪ'dɪəlɪst/ *noun* [C] a person who has high ideals (but who is sometimes not very practical) —**idealistic** /ˌaɪdɪə'lɪstɪk/ *adj*

idealize (*also* **idealise**) /aɪ'dɪəlaɪz/ *verb* [T] to imagine or show sth as being better than it really is: *Old people often idealize their early life.*

identical /aɪ'dentɪkl/ *adj* **1 the identical** the same: *This is the identical room we stayed in last year.* **2 identical (to/with sb/sth)** exactly the same as: *I can't see any difference between these two pens – they look identical to me.* —**identically** /-kli/ *adv*

i,dentical 'twin *noun* [C, usually pl] Identical twins come from the same egg of the mother and so are of the same sex and look exactly alike.

☆**identify** /aɪ'dentɪfaɪ/ *verb* [T] (*pres part* **identifying**; *3rd pers sing pres* **identifies**; *pt, pp* **identified**) **1 identify sb/sth (as sb/sth)** to recognize or say who or what sb/sth is: *The police need someone to identify the body.* ○ *We must identify the cause of the problem before we look for solutions.* **2 identify sth with sth** to think or say that sth is the same as sth else: *You can't identify nationalism with fascism.*

(PHRASAL VERBS) **identify with sb** to feel that you understand and share what sb else is feeling: *I found it hard to identify with the woman in the film.*

identify (yourself) with sb/sth to be connected with sb/sth: *She became identified with the new political party.*

identification /aɪˌdentɪfɪ'keɪʃn/ *noun* [U] **1** the act of identifying or being identified: *The identification of the people killed in the explosion was very difficult.* ○ *children's identification with TV heroes* **2** (*abbr* **ID**) an official paper, etc that proves who you are: *Do you have any identification?*

☆**identity** /aɪ'dentəti/ *noun* [C,U] (*pl* **identities**) who or what a person or a thing is: *There are few clues to the identity of the killer.* ○ *The region has its own cultural identity and is demanding more independence.* ○ *The arrest was a case of mistaken identity* (= the wrong person was arrested by the police). ○ *Children of immigrants often suffer from a loss of identity* (= they are not sure which culture they belong to).

i'dentity card *noun* [C] a card that proves who you are

ideology /ˌaɪdi'ɒlədʒi/ *noun* [C,U] (*pl* **ideologies**) a set of ideas which form the basis for a political or economic system: *Marxist ideology* —**ideological** /ˌaɪdɪə'lɒdʒɪkl/ *adj*

idiom /'ɪdiəm/ *noun* [C] a expression with a meaning that you cannot guess from the meanings of the separate words: *The idiom 'bring sth home to sb' means 'make sb understand sth'.*

idiomatic /ˌɪdiə'mætɪk/ *adj* **1** containing an idiom or idioms: *an idiomatic expression* **2** using language in a way that sounds natural: *He speaks good idiomatic English.*

idiot /'ɪdiət/ *noun* [C] (*informal*) a stupid or foolish person: *I was an idiot to forget my passport.* —**idiotic** /ˌɪdi'ɒtɪk/ *adj* — **idiotically** /-kli/ *adv*

idle /'aɪdl/ *adj* **1** not doing anything; not being used: *She is always busy. She can't bear to be idle.* ○ *The factory stood idle while the machines were being repaired.* **2** not wanting to work hard; lazy: *He has the ability to succeed but he is just bone* (= very) *idle.* **3** (only *before* a noun) not to be taken seriously because it will not have any result: *an idle promise* —**idleness** *noun* [U] —**idly** /'aɪdli/ *adv*

idol /'aɪdl/ *noun* [C] **1** a statue that people worship as a god **2** a person (such as a film star pop musician) who is admired or loved: *When I was 14, Elvis Presley was my idol.*

idolize (*also* **idolise**) /'aɪdəlaɪz/ *verb* [T] to love or admire sb very much or too much: *He is an only child and his parents idolize him.*

idyllic /ɪ'dɪlɪk; *US* aɪ'd-/ *adj* very pleasant and peaceful: *We had an idyllic holiday in the West of Ireland.*

☆ **if** /ɪf/ *conj* **1** (used in sentences in which one thing happens or is true, depending on whether another thing happens or is true): *If you see him, give him this letter.* ○ *We won't go to the beach if it rains.* ○ *If I had more time, I would learn another language.* ○ *If I had known about the accident, I would have gone to see her in hospital.* ○ *I might see her tomorrow. If not, I'll see her at the weekend.* **2** (used after verbs such as 'ask', 'know', 'remember'): *They asked if we would like to go too.* ○ *I can't remember if I posted the letter or not.* ☛ Look at the note at **whether**. **3** (used when you are asking sb to do sth or suggesting sth politely): *If you could just come this way, sir.* ○ *If I might suggest something...*

(IDIOMS) **as if** ⇨ AS

even if ⇨ EVEN²

if I were you (used when you are giving sb advice): *If I were you, I'd leave now.*

if only (used for expressing a strong wish): *If only I could drive.* ○ *If only he'd write.*

igloo /'ɪɡluː/ *noun* [C] (*pl* **igloos**) a small house that is built from blocks of hard snow by people in the Arctic regions (**Eskimos**)

ignite /ɪɡ'naɪt/ *verb* [I,T] (*formal*) to start burning or to make sth start burning: *A spark from the engine ignited the petrol.*

ignition /ɪɡ'nɪʃn/ *noun* **1** [U] the process of igniting **2** [C] the electrical system that starts the engine of a car: *to turn the ignition on/off*

ignominious /ˌɪɡnə'mɪniəs/ *adj* (*formal*) making you feel ashamed: *The team suffered an ignominious defeat.* —**ignominiously** *adv*

ignorance /'ɪɡnərəns/ *noun* [U] lack of information or knowledge (about sth): *The workers were in complete ignorance of the management's plans.* ○ *The mistake was due to ignorance.*

ignorant /'ɪɡnərənt/ *adj* **1** not knowing about sth: *Many people are ignorant of their rights.* ○ *I'm very ignorant about modern technology, I'm afraid.* **2** (*informal*) rude or impolite (because you don't know how to behave): *That was a very ignorant remark!*

☆ **ignore** /ɪɡ'nɔː(r)/ *verb* [T] to pay no attention to sb/sth: *I said hello to Debby but she totally ignored me* (= acted as though she hadn't seen me). ○ *George ignored his doctor's advice about drinking and smoking less.* ☛ Be careful. **Ignore** and **be ignorant** are quite different in meaning.

☆ **ill¹** /ɪl/ *adj* **1** (*US* **sick**) (not before a noun) not in good health; not well: *I went to bed early because I felt ill but I felt even worse when I woke up.* ○ *I have been ill with flu.* ○ *My mother was taken ill suddenly last week.* ○ *My grandfather is seriously ill in hospital.* ☛ Look at the note at **sick**. **2** (only *before* a noun) bad or harmful: *There should be no ill will* (= bad feelings) between friends. ○ *I'm glad to say I suffered no ill effects from all that rich food.*

ill² /ɪl/ *adv* **1** (often in compounds) badly or wrongly: *You would be ill-advised to drive until you have fully recovered.* **2** only with difficulty; not easily: *They could ill afford the extra money for better heating.*

(IDIOMS) **augur well/ill for sb/sth** ⇨ AUGUR

bode well/ill (for sb/sth) ⇨ BODE

ill-'fated *adj* unlucky

ill-'treat *verb* [T] to treat sb/sth badly or unkindly: *This cat has been ill-treated.*

ill-'treatment *noun* [U]

I'll /aɪl/ *short for* I WILL, I SHALL

☆ **illegal** /ɪ'liːɡl/ *adj* not allowed by the law; not legal: *It is illegal to own a gun without a special licence.* —**illegally** /-ɡəli/ *adv*

illegible /ɪ'ledʒəbl/ *adj* difficult or impossible to read; not legible: *The doctor's handwriting is quite illegible.* —**illegibly** /-əbli/ *adv*

illegitimate /ˌɪlɪ'dʒɪtɪmət/ *adj* **1** (used about a child) born to parents who are not married to each other **2** not allowed by law; against the rules —**illegitimacy** /ˌɪlɪ'dʒɪtɪməsi/ *noun* [U]

illicit /ɪ'lɪsɪt/ *adj* (used about an activity or substance) not allowed by law or by the rules of society: *the illicit trade in ivory* ○ *They were having an illicit affair.* ☛ The usual opposite of illicit is **legal**.

illiterate /ɪ'lɪtərət/ *adj* **1** not able to read or write; not literate **2** showing that you have little education: *You must be illiterate if you've never heard of Sartre!* —**illiteracy** /ɪ'lɪtərəsi/ *noun* [U]: *adult illiteracy*

☆ **illness** /'ɪlnəs/ *noun* **1** [U] the state of being physically or mentally ill: *In case of illness you can cancel the holiday.* ○ *There is a history of mental illness in the family.* **2** [C] a type or period of physical or mental ill health: *Although it is serious, cancer is not always a fatal illness.* ○ *Father is just getting over his illness.* ☛ Look at the note at **disease**.

illogical /ɪ'lɒdʒɪkl/ *adj* not sensible or reasonable; not logical: *It seems illogical to me to pay somebody for doing work that you could do yourself.* —**illogicality** /ɪˌlɒdʒɪ'kæləti/ *noun* [C,U] (*pl* **illogicalities**) —**illogically** /-kli/ *adv*

illuminate /ɪ'luːmɪneɪt/ *verb* [T] (*formal*) **1** to give light to or to decorate sth with lights: *The palace was illuminated by spotlights.* ○ *an illuminated Christmas tree* **2** to explain sth or make sth clear

illuminating *adj* helping to explain sth or make sth clear: *an illuminating discussion*

illumination /ɪˌluːmɪ'neɪʃn/ *noun* **1** [U] the act of illuminating or state of being illuminated **2 illuminations** [plural] (*Brit*) bright colourful lights that are used for decorating a street, town, etc

illusion /ɪ'luːʒn/ *noun* **1** [C,U] a false idea, belief or impression: *I have no illusions about the situation – I know it's serious.* **2** [C] something that your eyes tell you is there or is true but in fact is not: *That line looks longer, but in fact they're the same length. It's an optical illusion.*

(IDIOM) **be under an/the illusion (that)** to

s	z	ʃ	ʒ	h	m	n	ŋ	l	r	j	w
so	zoo	she	vision	how	man	no	sing	leg	red	yes	wet

believe wrongly: *I think Peter's under the illusion that he will be the new director.*

☆ **illustrate** /'ɪləstreɪt/ *verb* [T] **1** to explain or make sth clear by using examples, pictures or diagrams: *These statistics illustrate the point that I was making very well.* **2** to add pictures, diagrams, etc to a book or magazine: *Most cookery books are illustrated.*

illustration /ˌɪləˈstreɪʃn/ *noun* **1** [C] an example that makes a point or an idea clear: *Can you give me an illustration of what you mean?* **2** [C] a drawing, diagram or picture in a book or magazine: *colour illustrations* **3** [U] the activity or art of illustrating

I'm /aɪm/ *short for* I AM

☆ **image** /'ɪmɪdʒ/ *noun* [C] **1** a mental picture or idea of sb/sth: *I have an image of my childhood as always sunny and happy.* **2** the general impression that a person or organization gives to the public: *Advertising has to create an attractive image for the product it is selling.* **3** a picture or description that appears in a book, film or painting: *horrific images of war* **4** a copy or reflection: *A perfect image of the building was reflected in the lake.* o *He's the image of his father* (= he looks exactly like him).

imagery /'ɪmɪdʒəri/ *noun* [U] the use of descriptions and comparisons in language in order to have a strong effect on people's imagination and emotions

imaginable /ɪˈmædʒɪnəbl/ *adj* (often *after* a noun) that you can think of: *His house was equipped with every luxury imaginable.*

☆ **imaginary** /ɪˈmædʒɪnəri; US -əneri/ *adj* existing only in the mind; not real: *Many children have imaginary friends.*

☆ **imagination** /ɪˌmædʒɪˈneɪʃn/ *noun* **1** [C,U] the ability to create mental pictures or new ideas: *He has a lively imagination.* o *You need a lot of imagination to see what the building will be like when it's finished.* o *She's very clever but she hasn't got much imagination.* ☛ Imagination is a creative quality that a person has. **Fantasy** consists of day-dreams about stories and situations that are not related to reality. **2** [C] the part of the mind that uses this ability: *If we really use our imaginations we should find a solution to this problem!*

imaginative /ɪˈmædʒɪnətɪv; US -əneɪtɪv/ *adj* having or showing imagination: *She's always full of imaginative ideas.* o *His writing is highly imaginative.* ☛ The opposite is **unimaginative**. —**imaginatively** *adv*

☆ **imagine** /ɪˈmædʒɪn/ *verb* [T] **1** to form a picture or idea of sth in the mind: *Imagine the seaside in summer.* o *Imagine that you're lying on a beach.* o *It's not easy to imagine your brother as a doctor.* o *I can't imagine myself cycling 20 miles a day.* o *I can imagine what you felt like.* **2** to see, hear or think sth that is not true or does not exist: *She's always imagining that she's ill but she's fine really.* **3** to think of sth as probable; to suppose: *I imagine he'll be coming by car.*

imbalance /ˌɪmˈbæləns/ *noun* [C] a difference or lack of equality: *an imbalance between our import and export trade*

imbecile /'ɪmbəsiːl; US -sl/ *noun* [C] a stupid person; a fool

imitate /'ɪmɪteɪt/ *verb* [T] **1** to copy the behaviour of sb/sth: *Small children learn by imitating their parents.* **2** to copy the speech or actions of sb/sth, often in order to be amusing: *She could imitate her mother perfectly.*

imitation /ˌɪmɪˈteɪʃn/ *noun* **1** [C] a copy (of a real thing): *Some artificial flowers are good imitations of real ones.* o *This suitcase is made of imitation leather* (= of material that is made to look like leather). ☛ Look at **genuine**. **2** [C] a copy (of a person's speech or behaviour): *That comedian does very good imitations of politicians.* **3** [U] the act of copying sth: *Good pronunciation of a language is best learnt by imitation.*

immaculate /ɪˈmækjʊlət/ *adj* **1** perfectly clean and tidy: *Her house is always immaculate.* o *immaculate white shirts* **2** without any mistakes; perfect: *His performance of 'Romeo' was immaculate.* —**immaculately** *adv*

immaterial /ˌɪməˈtɪəriəl/ *adj* **immaterial (to sb)** not important: *It's immaterial to me whether we go today or tomorrow.*

immature /ˌɪməˈtjʊə(r); US -tʊər/ *adj* **1** not fully grown or developed; not mature: *an immature body* **2** (used about a person) not behaving as sensibly as you would expect for a person of that age: *Some students are very immature when they go to university.*

☆ **immediate** /ɪˈmiːdiət/ *adj* **1** happening or done at once or without delay: *I'd like an immediate answer to my proposal.* o *The government responded with immediate action.* **2** (only *before* a noun) existing now and needing attention: *Tell me what your immediate needs are.* **3** (only *before* a noun) nearest in time, position or relationship: *They won't make any changes in the immediate future.* o *You can see the cathedral to your immediate right.* o *He has left most of his money to his immediate family* (= parents, children, brothers and sisters).

immediacy /-əsi/ *noun* [U] the close presence of sth that makes you notice it and become involved in it

immediately *adv* **1** at once; without delay: *Can you come home immediately after work?* o *I couldn't immediately see what he meant.* **2** directly; very closely: *He wasn't immediately involved in the crime.* **3** nearest in time or position: *Who's the girl immediately in front of Simon?* o *What did you do immediately after the war?*

immediately *conj* (*Brit*) as soon as: *I opened the letter immediately I got home.*

immense /ɪˈmens/ *adj* very large or great: *immense difficulties* o *She gets immense pleasure from her garden.*

immensely *adv* extremely; very much: *immensely enjoyable* o *'Did you enjoy the party?' 'Yes, immensely.'*

immensity /ɪˈmensəti/ *noun* [U] very large size or extent: *the immensity of the universe*

immerse /ɪˈmɜːs/ *verb* [T] **1 immerse yourself (in sth)** to involve yourself deeply in sth so that you give it all your attention: *Rachel's usually immersed in a book.* **2 immerse sth**

iː	ɪ	e	æ	ɑː	ɒ	ɔː	ʊ	uː	ʌ
see	sit	ten	hat	arm	got	saw	put	too	cup

(in sth) to put sth into a liquid so that it is covered: *Immerse the spaghetti in boiling water and cook for ten minutes.*

☆ **immigrant** /'ɪmɪgrənt/ *noun* [C] a person who has come into a foreign country to live there permanently: *Many immigrants to Britain have come from Asia.* ○ *The government plans to tighten controls to prevent illegal immigrants* (= people coming to live in the country without permission). ○ *London has a high immigrant population.*

☞ Great Britain has many immigrant communities which make it a **multicultural society**. Groups of immigrants or children of immigrants who share a common cultural tradition form an **ethnic minority**.

☆ **immigration** /,ɪmɪ'greɪʃn/ *noun* [U] **1** entering a country in order to live there permanently: *There are greater controls on immigration than there used to be.* ○ *the immigration office* **2** (*also* **immigration control**) the control point at an airport, port, etc where the passports and documents of people who want to come into a country are checked: *When you leave the plane you have to go through customs and immigration.*

☞ There is a verb 'immigrate' but it is very rarely used. We normally use the expression 'be an immigrant' or the verb 'emigrate' which is used in connection with the place that somebody has come from: *'Were you born here in Britain?' 'Yes I was, but my parents emigrated to Britain from Barbados.'* Look at **emigrate**, **emigrant** and **emigration**.

imminent /'ɪmɪnənt/ *adj* (usually used about sth unpleasant) almost certain to happen very soon: *Heavy rainfall in the south of England means that flooding is imminent.* —**imminently** *adv*

immobile /ɪ'məʊbaɪl; *US* -bl/ *adj* not moving or not able to move: *The hunter stood immobile until the lion had passed.*

immobility /,ɪmə'bɪləti/ *noun* [U] the state of being immobile

immobilize (*also* **immobilise**) /ɪ'məʊbəlaɪz/ *verb* [T] to prevent sb/sth from moving or working normally: *The railways have been completely immobilized by the strike.*

immoral /ɪ'mɒrəl; *US* ɪ'mɔːrəl/ *adj* wrong or wicked according to the accepted rules of behaviour; not moral: *I think experiments on animals are immoral.* —**immorality** /,ɪmə'rælətɪ/ *noun* [U] —**immorally** /-rəlɪ/ *adv*

immortal /ɪ'mɔːtl/ *adj* living or lasting for ever: *Nobody is immortal – we all have to die some time.* ○ (*figurative*) *Shakespeare's immortal plays* —**immortality** /,ɪmɔː'tælətɪ/ *noun* [U]

immortalize (*also* **immortalise**) /ɪ'mɔːtəlaɪz/ *verb* [T] to give lasting fame to sb/sth (especially in a book, film or painting): *He immortalized their relationship in a poem.*

immune /ɪ'mjuːn/ *adj* **1 immune (to sth)** protected against a certain disease or illness because you have a resistance to it: *You should be immune to measles if you've had it already.*

2 immune (to sth) not affected by sth: *You can say what you like – I'm immune to criticism!* **3 immune (from sth)** protected from a danger or punishment: *Young children are immune from prosecution.*

immunity /ɪ'mjuːnətɪ/ *noun* [U] the ability to avoid or be unaffected by disease, criticism, prosecution, etc: *In many countries people have no immunity to diseases like measles.* ○ *Ambassadors to other countries receive diplomatic immunity* (= protection from prosecution, etc).

immunize (*also* **immunise**) /'ɪmjʊnaɪz/ *verb* [T] to make sb immune to a disease, usually by giving an injection of a substance (**vaccine**): *Before visiting certain countries you will need to be immunized against cholera.* ☞ Look at **inoculate** and **vaccinate**. —**immunization** (*also* **immunisation**) /,ɪmjʊnaɪ'zeɪʃn; *US* -nɪ'z-/ *noun* [C,U]

imp /ɪmp/ *noun* [C] (in stories) a small creature like a little devil

☆ **impact** /'ɪmpækt/ *noun* **1** [C, usually sing] **an impact (on/upon sb/sth)** an effect or impression: *Her speech made a great impact on the audience.* **2** [U] the action or force of one object hitting another: *The impact of the crash threw the passengers out of their seats.* ○ *The bomb exploded on impact* (= when it hit something).

impair /ɪm'peə(r)/ *verb* [T] to damage or weaken sth: *Ear infections can result in impaired hearing.*

impale /ɪm'peɪl/ *verb* [T] **impale sb/sth (on sth)** to stick a sharp pointed object through sb/sth: *The boy fell out of the tree and was impaled on the railings.*

impart /ɪm'pɑːt/ *verb* [T] (*formal*) **1 impart sth (to sb)** to tell: *He rushed home eager to impart the good news.* **2 impart sth (to sth)** to give a certain quality to sth: *The low lighting imparted a romantic atmosphere to the room.*

impartial /ɪm'pɑːʃl/ *adj* fair or neutral; not preferring one to another: *The referee must be impartial.* —**impartiality** /,ɪm,pɑːʃɪ'ælətɪ/ *noun* [U] —**impartially** /-ʃəlɪ/ *adv*

impassable /ɪm'pɑːsəbl; *US* -'pæs-/ *adj* (used about a road, etc) impossible to travel on because it is blocked: *Flooding and fallen trees have made many roads impassable.*

impassive /ɪm'pæsɪv/ *adj* (used about a person) showing no emotion or reaction —**impassively** *adv*

☆ **impatient** /ɪm'peɪʃnt/ *adj* **1 impatient (at sth/with sb)** not able to wait for sb/sth calmly; easily annoyed by sth that seems slow; not patient: *Don't be so impatient – it's your turn next.* ○ *The passengers are getting impatient at the delay.* ○ *It's no good being impatient with small children.* **2 impatient (to do sth); impatient (for sth)** (not before a noun) wanting sth to happen soon: *By the time they are sixteen many young people are impatient to leave school.* ○ *At the end of winter we are often impatient for spring to arrive.* —**impatience** /ɪm'peɪʃns/ *noun* [U]: *He began to explain for the third time with growing impatience.* —**impatiently** *adv*

impeccable /ɪm'pekəbl/ *adj* perfect; without

any mistakes: *impeccable behaviour* o *His accent is impeccable.* —**impeccably** /-blɪ/ *adv*

impede /ɪmˈpiːd/ *verb* [T] (*formal*) to make it difficult for sb/sth to move or make progress: *The completion of the new motorway has been impeded by bad weather conditions.*

impediment /ɪmˈpedɪmənt/ *noun* [C] (*formal*) **1** something that makes it difficult for a person or thing to move or progress: *The high rate of tax will be a major impediment to new businesses.* **2** something that makes speaking difficult: *a speech impediment*

impending /ɪmˈpendɪŋ/ *adj* (only *before* a noun) (usually used about sth bad) that will happen soon: *There was a feeling of impending disaster in the air.*

impenetrable /ɪmˈpenɪtrəbl/ *adj* **1** impossible to enter or get through: *The jungle was impenetrable.* **2** impossible to understand: *an impenetrable mystery*

imperative /ɪmˈperətɪv/ *adj* very important or urgent: *It's imperative that you see a doctor immediately.*
imperative *noun* [C] (*grammar*) the form of the verb that is used for giving orders: *In 'Shut the door!' the verb is in the imperative.*

imperceptible /ˌɪmpəˈseptəbl/ *adj* too small to be seen or noticed; very slight: *The difference between the original painting and the copy was almost imperceptible.* ☞ The verb is **perceive**. —**imperceptibly** /-əblɪ/ *adv*: *Almost imperceptibly winter was turning into spring.*

imperfect /ɪmˈpɜːfɪkt/ *adj* **1** with mistakes or faults; not perfect: *This is a very imperfect system.* **2** (only *before* a noun) (*grammar*) used for expressing action in the past that is not completed: *In 'While I was having a bath', the verb is in the imperfect tense.* ☞ We can also use **imperfect** as a noun and say: *The verb is in the imperfect.* It is more usual to call this tense the **past continuous** or **past progressive**. —**imperfectly** *adv*

imperial /ɪmˈpɪəriəl/ *adj* **1** connected with an empire or its ruler: *the imperial palace* o *imperial power* **2** belonging to a system of weighing and measuring that was previously used for all goods in the United Kingdom and is still used for some ☞ Look at **metric** and at **inch**, **foot**, **yard**, **ounce**, **pound**, **pint** and **gallon**. The entries will tell you what these weights and measures are in metres, kilos and litres.

imperialism /ɪmˈpɪəriəlɪzəm/ *noun* [U] a political system in which a rich and powerful country controls other countries (**colonies**) which are not so rich and powerful as itself

imperialist /ɪmˈpɪəriəlɪst/ *noun* [C] a person who supports or believes in imperialism

impersonal /ɪmˈpɜːsənl/ *adj* **1** not showing friendly human feelings; cold in feeling or atmosphere: *A large organization can be very impersonal to work for.* o *The hotel room was very impersonal.* **2** not referring to any particular person: *Can we try to keep the discussion as impersonal as possible, please?*

impersonate /ɪmˈpɜːsəneɪt/ *verb* [T] to copy the actions and way of speaking of a person or to pretend to be a different person: *an actress who often impersonates the Queen* o *He was arrested for impersonating a policeman.* —**impersonation** /ɪmˌpɜːsəˈneɪʃn/ *noun* [C,U] —**impersonator** *noun* [C]

impertinent /ɪmˈpɜːtɪnənt/ *adj* rude; not showing respect: *I do apologize. It was impertinent of my daughter to speak to you like that.* ☞ The opposite is NOT **pertinent**. It is **polite** or **respectful**. —**impertinence** /-əns/ *noun* [U] —**impertinently** *adv*

imperturbable /ˌɪmpəˈtɜːbəbl/ *adj* (*formal*) not easily worried; calm ☞ The verb is **perturb**.

impervious /ɪmˈpɜːviəs/ *adj* **1** not allowing water, etc to pass through **2** not affected or influenced by sth: *impervious to criticism*

impetuous /ɪmˈpetʃuəs/ *adj* acting or done quickly and without thinking: *Her impetuous behaviour often got her into trouble.* ☞ A more common word is **impulsive**. —**impetuously** *adv*

impetus /ˈɪmpɪtəs/ *noun* [U,sing] something that encourages sth else to happen: *I need fresh impetus to start working on this essay again.*

impinge /ɪmˈpɪndʒ/ *verb* [I] **impinge on/upon sth** (*formal*) to have an effect on sth; to interfere with sth: *I'm not going to let my job impinge on my home life.*

implausible /ɪmˈplɔːzəbl/ *adj* not easy to believe: *an implausible excuse*

implement¹ /ˈɪmplɪmənt/ *noun* [C] a tool or instrument (especially for work outdoors): *farm implements* ☞ Look at the note at **tool**.

implement² /ˈɪmplɪment/ *verb* [T] to start using a plan, system, etc: *Some teachers are finding it difficult to implement the government's educational reforms.* —**implementation** /ˌɪmplɪmenˈteɪʃn/ *noun* [U]

implicate /ˈɪmplɪkeɪt/ *verb* [T] **implicate sb (in sth)** (*formal*) to show that sb is involved in sth unpleasant, especially a crime: *A well-known politician was implicated in the scandal.*

implication /ˌɪmplɪˈkeɪʃn/ *noun* **1** [C,U] something that is suggested but that is not said openly: *The implication of what she said was that we had made a bad mistake.* ☞ The verb is **imply**. **2** [C] the effect that sth will have on sth else in the future: *The new law will have serious implications for our work.*

implicit /ɪmˈplɪsɪt/ *adj* **1** not expressed directly but understood by the people involved: *We had an implicit agreement that we would support each other.* ☞ Look at **explicit**. **2** complete and asking no questions: *I have implicit faith in your ability to do the job.*
implicitly *adv* completely: *I trust you implicitly.*

implore /ɪmˈplɔː(r)/ *verb* [T] (*formal*) to ask sb for sth or to do sth. You implore sb when the situation is very serious and you feel desperate: *She implored him not to leave her alone.* o *'Don't leave me alone', she implored.* ☞ Look at **beg**. It is similar in meaning.

imply /ɪmˈplaɪ/ *verb* [T] (*pres part* **implying**; *3rd pers sing pres* **implies**; *pt, pp* **implied**) to suggest sth in an indirect way or without actually saying it: *He didn't say so – but he implied that I was lying.* ☞ The noun is **implication**.

impolite /ˌɪmpəˈlaɪt/ *adj* rude; not polite: *I*

think it was impolite of him to ask you to leave. —**impolitely** adv

☆ **import¹** /ɪmˈpɔːt/ verb [T] **import sth (from...)**; **import sth (into...)** to buy goods, etc from a foreign country and bring them into your own country: *This country has to import most of its raw materials.* ○ *imported goods* ○ *Britain imports wine from France, Italy, Spain, etc.* ○ *(figurative) We need to import some extra help from somewhere.* —**importer** noun [C]: *Is Britain the world's largest importer of tea?*
☛ The opposites are **export** and **exporter**.

☆ **import²** /ˈɪmpɔːt/ noun **1** [C, usually pl] goods bought from a foreign country for sale or use in your own country: *What are your country's major imports?* ☛ The opposite is **export**. **2** [U] (also **importation**) the action of importing goods: *The government is introducing new controls on the import of certain goods from abroad.*

☆ **important** /ɪmˈpɔːtnt/ adj **1** having great value or influence; very necessary: *an important meeting, decision, etc* ○ *Tomorrow will be the most important day of my life!* ○ *Is money important for happiness?* ○ *It's important not to be late.* ○ *It's important that people should learn at least one foreign language.* ○ *It's important for people to see the results of what they do.* ○ *It was important to me that you were there.* **2** (used about a person) having great influence or authority: *He was one of the most important writers of his time.* ○ *I soon got to know who was important in the company and who wasn't.* ☛ The opposite is **unimportant**.

importance /-tns/ noun [U] the state of being important; value: *The decision was of great importance to the future of the business.* —**importantly** adv

importation /ˌɪmpɔːˈteɪʃn/ noun [U] = IMPORT²(2)

impose /ɪmˈpəʊz/ verb **1** [T] to make sth be accepted because you are the person with power: *A new tax will be imposed on cigarettes.* ○ *The government should impose restrictions on the use of harmful chemicals.* ○ *Parents should try not to impose their own ideas on their children.* **2** [I] **impose (on/upon sb/sth)** to ask or expect sb to do sth that may cause extra work or trouble: *I hope I'm not imposing – but could you look after our cats while we're away?* ○ *I hate to impose on you but can you lend me some money?*

imposition /ˌɪmpəˈzɪʃn/ noun **1** [U] the action of imposing: *I'm against the imposition of unnecessary rules and regulations on people.* **2** [C] an unfair or unpleasant thing that sb has to accept; sth that causes extra work or trouble: *'Do stay for supper.' 'Are you sure it's not an imposition?'*

imposing /ɪmˈpəʊzɪŋ/ adj making an impression on people because it is big or important: *They lived in a large, imposing house near the park.*

☆ **impossible** /ɪmˈpɒsəbl/ adj **1** not able to be done or to happen; not possible: *It's impossible for me to be there before 12.* ○ *I find it almost impossible to get up in the morning!* ○ *That horse is impossible to control.* ○ *That's impossible!* (= I don't believe it!) **2** very difficult to deal with or to make better: *This is an impossible situation!* ○ *He's always been an impossible child.* —**impossibility** /ɪmˌpɒsəˈbɪləti/ noun [C,U] (pl **impossibilities**): *the impossibility of reaching an agreement* ○ *What you are suggesting is a complete impossibility.*

the impossible noun [sing] something that cannot be done: *Don't attempt the impossible!*

impossibly /-əbli/ adv extremely: *impossibly complicated*

impostor /ɪmˈpɒstə(r)/ noun [C] a person who pretends to be sb else in order to deceive other people

impotent /ˈɪmpətənt/ adj **1** without enough power or influence ☛ The opposite is **powerful**. **2** (used about men) not capable of having sexual intercourse —**impotence** /-əns/ noun [U]

impoverish /ɪmˈpɒvərɪʃ/ verb [T] (formal) to make sb/sth poor or poor in quality ☛ Look at **enrich**.

impracticable /ɪmˈpræktɪkəbl/ adj impossible to use or do in practice: *Your plan is completely impracticable.*

impractical /ɪmˈpræktɪkl/ adj **1** not sensible or reasonable; not practical: *an impractical suggestion* ○ *It would be impractical to take our bikes on the train.* **2** (used about a person) not good at doing ordinary everyday jobs: *He's clever but completely impractical.*

imprecise /ˌɪmprɪˈsaɪs/ adj not clear or exact; not precise: *imprecise instructions*

☆ **impress** /ɪmˈpres/ verb [T] **1 impress sb (with sth)** to make sb feel admiration and respect: *She's always trying to impress people with her new clothes.* ○ *It impressed me that he understood immediately what I meant.* **2** (formal) **impress sth on/upon sb** to make sth very clear to sb: *I wish you could impress on John that he must pass these exams.*

☆ **impression** /ɪmˈpreʃn/ noun [C] **1** the effect that a person or thing produces on sb else: *She gives the impression of being older than she really is.* ○ *I want to create an impression of light and space in the house.* ○ *Do you think I made a good impression on your parents?* **2** an opinion about sb/sth (that is sometimes unclear or wrong): *What's your impression of the new director?* ○ *I'm not sure but I have the impression that Jane's rather unhappy.* ○ *I was under the impression that you were married.* **3** an amusing imitation of the behaviour or speech of a well-known person: *My brother does some marvellous impressions of TV stars.* **4** a mark made by pressing an object hard into a surface

impressionable /ɪmˈpreʃənəbl/ adj easy to influence: *Sixteen is a very impressionable age.*

☆ **impressive** /ɪmˈpresɪv/ adj causing a feeling of admiration and respect because of importance, size, excellent quality, etc: *an impressive building, speech, etc* ○ *The way he handled the situation was most impressive.* ☛ The opposite is **unimpressive**.

imprint /ˈɪmprɪnt/ noun [C] the mark made by pressing an object on a surface: *the imprint of a foot in the sand*

s	z	ʃ	ʒ	h	m	n	ŋ	l	r	j	w
so	zoo	she	vision	how	man	no	sing	leg	red	yes	wet

imprison /ɪmˈprɪzn/ verb [T] (often passive) to put or keep in prison: *He was imprisoned for robbery with violence.*
imprisonment /-mənt/ noun [U] the state of being imprisoned: *She was sentenced to five years' imprisonment.* o *life imprisonment*

improbable /ɪmˈprɒbəbl/ adj not likely to be true or to happen; not probable: *an improbable explanation* o *an improbable result* o *It is highly improbable that she will arrive tonight.* ☛ Look at **unlikely**. —**improbability** /ɪmˌprɒbəˈbɪləti/ noun [U] —**improbably** /-əbli/ adv

impromptu /ɪmˈprɒmptju:; US -tu:/ adj, adv (done) without being prepared or organized: *an impromptu party*

improper /ɪmˈprɒpə(r)/ adj **1** rude or not suitable for the situation: *That was a very improper remark!* **2** illegal or not honest: *It seems that she had been involved in improper business deals.* **3** rude (in a sexual way): *He lost his job for making improper suggestions to several of the girls.* —**improperly** adv

impropriety /ˌɪmprəˈpraɪəti/ noun [C,U] (pl **improprieties**) (formal) the state of being improper; an improper act: *She was unaware of the impropriety of her remark.* o *We are certain there were no improprieties in the handling of the deal.*

☆ **improve** /ɪmˈpru:v/ verb [I,T] to become or to make sth better: *Your work has greatly improved.* o *I hope the weather will improve later on.* o *Your vocabulary is excellent but you could improve your pronunciation.*
(PHRASAL VERB) **improve on/upon sth** to produce sth that is better than sth else: *I think the film improved on the book* (= the film was better than the book). o *Nobody will be able to improve on that score* (= nobody will be able to make a higher score).
improvement noun [C,U] **improvement (on/in sth)** (a) change which makes the quality or condition of sb/sth better: *There's a considerable improvement in your mother's condition.* o *These marks are an improvement on your previous ones.* o *Housing and public transport are areas which need improvement.*

improvise /ˈɪmprəvaɪz; US ˌɪmprəˈvaɪz/ verb [I,T] **1** to make, do, or manage sth quickly or without preparation, using what you have: *If you're short of teachers today you'll just have to improvise* (= manage somehow with the people that you've got). **2** to play music, speak or act using your imagination instead of written or remembered material: *It was obvious that the actor had forgotten his lines and was trying to improvise.* o *a brilliant improvised speech*
improvisation /ˌɪmprəvaɪˈzeɪʃn; US ɪmˌprɒvəˈzeɪʃn/ noun [C,U] the act of improvising

impudent /ˈɪmpjʊdənt/ adj very rude; not respectful or polite
impudence /-əns/ noun [U] impudent behaviour or speech —**impudently** adv

impulse /ˈɪmpʌls/ noun [C] **1** a sudden desire to do sth without thinking about the results: *She felt a terrible impulse to rush out of the house and never come back.* **2** a single push or signal in a nerve, wire, etc that causes a reaction: *electrical impulses*
(IDIOM) **on impulse** without thinking or planning: *Sometimes it's fun to go away on impulse when the weather's nice.*

impulsive /ɪmˈpʌlsɪv/ adj likely to act suddenly and without thinking; done without careful thought: *an impulsive character* o *an impulsive remark* —**impulsively** adv —**impulsiveness** noun [U]

impure /ɪmˈpjʊə(r)/ adj **1** consisting of more than one substance (and therefore not of good quality); not pure: *impure metals* **2** (old-fashioned) (used about thoughts and actions connected with sex) not moral; bad

impurity /ɪmˈpjʊərəti/ noun (pl **impurities**) **1** [C, usually pl] a substance that is present in another substance, making it of poor quality: *People are being advised to boil their water because certain impurities have been found in it.* **2** [U] the state of being impure

☆ **in¹** /ɪn/ adv ☛ For special uses with many verbs, eg **give in**, look at the verb entries. **1** to a position within a particular area: *She opened the door and went in.* o *My suitcase is full. I can't get any more in.* o *When does the train get in?* (= to the station). **2** at home or at work: *She won't be in till late today.* **3** (used about the tides of the sea) at the highest point, when the water is closest to the land: *The tide's coming in.* **4** received by sb official: *Entries should be in by 20 March.*
(IDIOMS) **be in for sth** to be going to experience sth unpleasant: *He'll be in for a shock when he gets the bill.*
be/get in on sth to have a share in sth; to know about sth that is happening: *I'd like to be in on the new project.*
have (got) it in for sb (informal) to be unpleasant to sb because he/she has done sth to upset you

☆ **in²** /ɪn/ prep ☛ For special uses with many nouns, eg **in time**, look at the noun entries. **1** (showing place) within the area of sth; enclosed by sth: *a country in Africa* o *a town in France* o *an island in the Pacific* o *in a box* o *I read about it in the newspaper.* o *in bed* o *She put the keys in her pocket.* o *They were working in the garden.* o *His wife's in hospital.* **2** (showing time) during a period of time: *My birthday is in August.* o *He was born in 1980.* o *You could walk there in about an hour* (= it would take that long to walk there). **3** (showing time) after a period of time: *I'll be finished in ten minutes.* **4** contained in; forming the whole or part of sth: *There are 366 days in a leap year.* **5** (used for giving the rate of): *a new rate of tax of 50p in the pound* o *One family in ten owns a dishwasher.* **6** wearing sth: *They were all dressed in black for the funeral.* o *I've never seen you in a suit before.* **7** (used for saying how things are arranged): *We sat in a circle.* **8** (used for saying how sth is written or expressed): *Please write in pen.* o *They were talking in Italian.* **9** (used with feelings): *I watched in horror as the plane crashed to the ground.* **10** (showing the condition or state of sb/sth): *My parents are in poor health.* o *This room is in a mess!* o *Richard's in*

iː	ɪ	e	æ	ɑː	ɒ	ɔː	ʊ	uː	ʌ
see	sit	ten	hat	arm	got	saw	put	too	cup

love. **11** (showing sb's job or the activity sb is involved in): *He's got a good job in advertising.* o *All her family are in politics.* o *He's in the army.*

in³ /ɪn/ *noun*
(IDIOM) **the ins and outs (of sth)** the details and difficulties (involved in sth): *Will somebody explain the ins and outs of the situation to me?*

inability /ˌɪnəˈbɪlətɪ/ *noun* [U] **inability (to do sth)** lack of ability, power or skill: *He has a complete inability to listen to other people's opinions.* ☛ The adjective is **unable.**

inaccessible /ˌɪnækˈsesəbl/ *adj* very difficult or impossible to reach or contact: *That beach is inaccessible by car.* o *(figurative) His books are inaccessible to* (= cannot be understood by) *the average reader.* —**inaccessibility** /ˌɪnækˌsesəˈbɪlətɪ/ *noun* [U]

inaccurate /ɪnˈækjərət/ *adj* not correct; not accurate: *an inaccurate report, description, etc* —**inaccuracy** /ɪnˈækjərəsɪ/ *noun* (*pl* **inaccuracies**) **1** [U] being inaccurate: *The inaccuracy of the statistics was immediately obvious.* **2** [C] an inaccurate statement; a written or spoken mistake: *There are always some inaccuracies in newspaper reports.*

inaction /ɪnˈækʃn/ *noun* [U] doing nothing; lack of action: *The crisis was blamed on the government's earlier inaction.*

inactive /ɪnˈæktɪv/ *adj* doing nothing; not active: *The virus remains inactive in the body.* —**inactivity** /ˌɪnækˈtɪvətɪ/ *noun* [U]

inadequate /ɪnˈædɪkwət/ *adj* **1** not sufficient; not good enough: *the problem of inadequate housing* **2** (used about a person) not able to deal with a problem or situation, etc; not confident: *There was so much to learn in the new job that for a while I felt totally inadequate.* —**inadequacy** /ɪnˈædɪkwəsɪ/ *noun* [C,U] (*pl* **inadequacies**): *his inadequacy as a parent* o *The inadequacies of the health service are often blamed on the government.* —**inadequately** /ɪnˈædɪkwətlɪ/ *adv*

inadvertent /ˌɪnədˈvɜːtənt/ *adj* (used about actions) done without thinking, not on purpose; not intentional —**inadvertently** *adv*: *She had inadvertently left the letter where he could find it.*

inadvisable /ˌɪnədˈvaɪzəbl/ *adj* not sensible or wise: *It is inadvisable to go swimming when you have a cold.*

inane /ɪˈneɪn/ *adj* without any meaning; silly: *an inane remark* —**inanely** *adv*

inappropriate /ˌɪnəˈprəʊprɪət/ *adj* not suitable: *Isn't that dress rather inappropriate for the occasion?* ☛ Look at **unsuitable.**

inarticulate /ˌɪnɑːˈtɪkjʊlət/ *adj* **1** (used about a person) not able to express ideas and feelings clearly **2** (used about speech) not clear or well expressed —**inarticulately** *adv*

inasmuch as /ˌɪnəzˈmʌtʃ əz/ *conj* (*formal*) because of the fact that; to the extent that: *We felt sorry for the boys inasmuch as they had not realized that what they were doing was wrong.*

inattention /ˌɪnəˈtenʃn/ *noun* [U] lack of attention: *a moment of inattention*

inattentive /ˌɪnəˈtentɪv/ *adj* not paying attention; not attentive: *One inattentive student can disturb the whole class.*

inaudible /ɪnˈɔːdəbl/ *adj* not loud enough to be heard —**inaudibly** /ɪnˈɔːdəblɪ/ *adv*

inaugural /ɪˈnɔːgjʊrəl/ *adj* (only *before* a noun) (used about a speech or meeting that marks the beginning of a new organization, leadership, etc) first: *the President's inaugural speech*

inaugurate /ɪˈnɔːgjʊreɪt/ *verb* [T] **1** to introduce a new official, leader, etc at a special ceremony: *He will be inaugurated as President next month.* **2** to start, introduce or open sth new (often at a special ceremony) —**inauguration** /ɪˌnɔːgjʊˈreɪʃn/ *noun* [C,U]

incalculable /ɪnˈkælkjʊləbl/ *adj* very great; too great to calculate: *an incalculable risk* o *incalculable damage*

incapable /ɪnˈkeɪpəbl/ *adj* **1 incapable of sth/doing sth** not able to do sth; not capable of sth/doing sth: *She is incapable of hard work/working hard.* o *He's quite incapable of unkindness* (= too nice to be unkind). **2** not able to do, manage or organize anything well: *As a doctor, she's totally incapable.*

incapacitate /ˌɪnkəˈpæsɪteɪt/ *verb* [T] to make sb unable (to work, live normally, etc): *They were completely incapacitated by the heat in Spain.*

incarnation /ˌɪnkɑːˈneɪʃn/ *noun* [C] **1** (a person that is) a perfect example of a particular quality **2** a life on earth in a particular form

incendiary /ɪnˈsendɪərɪ; *US* -dɪerɪ/ *adj* that causes a fire: *an incendiary bomb*

incense /ˈɪnsens/ *noun* [U] a substance that produces a sweet smell when burnt, used especially in religious ceremonies

incentive /ɪnˈsentɪv/ *noun* [C,U] **incentive (to do sth)** something that encourages you (to do sth): *The company is offering cash incentives to staff to move to another area.* o *There's no incentive for young people to do well at school because there aren't any jobs when they leave.*

incessant /ɪnˈsesnt/ *adj* never stopping: *incessant rain, noise, etc* ☛ Look at **continual.** —**incessantly** *adv*

incest /ˈɪnsest/ *noun* [U] sexual intercourse between close members of a family, eg brother and sister

incestuous /ɪnˈsestjʊəs; *US* -tʃʊəs/ *adj* **1** involving incest: *an incestuous relationship* **2** (used about a group of people and their relationships with each other) too close; not open to anyone outside the group: *Life in a small community can be very incestuous.*

☆ **inch** /ɪntʃ/ *noun* [C] (*abbr* **in**) a measure of length; 2·54 centimetres. There are 12 inches in a foot: *He's 5 foot 10 inches tall.* o *Three inches of rain fell last night.*
(PHRASAL VERB) **inch forward, past, through, etc** to move slowly and carefully in the direction mentioned: *Inch the car forward till I tell you to stop.*

incidence /ˈɪnsɪdəns/ *noun* [sing] the number of times sth (usually sth unpleasant) happens; the rate of sth: *a high incidence of crime, disease, unemployment, etc.*

☆ **incident** /ˈɪnsɪdənt/ *noun* [C] (*formal*) **1** an

event (especially one that involves violence, danger, something strange, etc): *There were a number of unpleasant incidents after the football match.* o *Various strange incidents had made people suspicious.* o *The publishing of the book resulted in a diplomatic incident* (= a dangerous or unpleasant situation between countries). **2** something that happens that is not very important: *There was an amusing incident at work today.*

incidental /ˌɪnsɪ'dentl/ *adj* happening as part of sth more important; minor: *The incidental expenses of a holiday are often more than expected.* o *The book contains various themes that are incidental to the main plot.*

incidentally /-tli/ *adv* (used to introduce extra news, information, etc that the speaker has just thought of): *Incidentally, that new restaurant you told me about is excellent.* ☞ Another way of saying 'incidentally' is **by the way**.

incinerate /ɪn'sɪnəreɪt/ *verb* [T] (*formal*) to destroy sth completely by burning

incinerator /ɪn'sɪnəreɪtə(r)/ *noun* [C] a container or machine for burning rubbish, etc

incision /ɪn'sɪʒn/ *noun* [C,U] (*formal*) a cut carefully made into sth (especially into a person's body as part of a medical operation)

incite /ɪn'saɪt/ *verb* [T] **incite sb (to sth)** to encourage sb to do sth by making him/her very angry or excited: *He was accused of inciting the crowd to violence.* —**incitement** *noun* [C,U]: *He was guilty of incitement to violence.*

inclination /ˌɪnklɪ'neɪʃn/ *noun* [C,U] a feeling that makes sb want to behave in a particular way: *My inclination is to say 'no', but what do you think?*

incline /ɪn'klaɪn/ *verb* **1** [T] (*formal*) to bend (your head) forward: *They sat round the table, heads inclined, deep in discussion.* **2** [I] **incline towards sth** to lean or slope in the direction of sth: *The land inclines towards the shore.*

inclined /ɪn'klaɪnd/ *adj* **1 inclined to do sth** likely to do sth: *She's inclined to change her mind very easily.* **2 inclined (to do sth)** wanting to behave in a particular way: *I know Andrew well so I'm inclined to believe what he says.* **3 inclined to do sth** (used to make what is said sound less sure) holding a particular opinion: *I'm inclined to say 'yes', but I'll have to ask James first.* **4** having a natural ability in the subject mentioned: *to be musically inclined*

☆ **include** /ɪn'kluːd/ *verb* [T] **1** to have as one part; to contain (among other things): *The price of the holiday includes the flight, the hotel and car-hire.* o *The crew included one woman.* ☞ Look at **exclude** and at the note at **contain**. **2** to make sb/sth part (of another group, etc): *The children immediately included the new girl in their games.* o *Everyone was disappointed, myself included.*

including /ɪn'kluːdɪŋ/ *prep* having as a part: *It costs £17.99, including postage and packing.* —**inclusion** /ɪn'kluːʒn/ *noun* [U]: *The inclusion of all that violence in the film was unnecessary.*

inclusive /ɪn'kluːsɪv/ *adj* **1 inclusive (of sth)** (used about a price, charge, fee, etc) including or containing everything; including the thing mentioned: *Is that an inclusive price or are there some extras?* o *The rent is inclusive of electricity.* **2** (only *after* a noun) including the dates, numbers, etc mentioned: *You are booked at the hotel from Monday to Friday inclusive* (= including Monday and Friday). ☞ When talking about time **through** is often used in American English instead of **inclusive**: *We'll be away from Friday through Sunday.*

incognito /ˌɪnkɒɡ'niːtəʊ; *US* ɪn'kɒɡnətəʊ/ *adj, adv* hiding your real name and identity (especially if you are famous and do not want to be recognized): *to travel incognito*

incoherent /ˌɪnkəʊ'hɪərənt/ *adj* not clear or easy to understand; not expressing yourself clearly —**incoherence** /-əns/ *noun* [U] —**incoherently** *adv*

☆ **income** /'ɪnkʌm/ *noun* [C,U] the money you receive regularly as payment for your work or as interest on investments: *It's sometimes difficult for a family to live on one income.*

☞ We talk about a **monthly** or an **annual** income. An income may be **high** or **low**. Your **gross** income is the amount you earn before paying tax. Your **net** income is your income after tax. Look at the note at **pay**.

'income tax *noun* [U] the tax you pay on the money you earn

incoming /'ɪnkʌmɪŋ/ *adj* (only *before* a noun) **1** coming in or arriving: *incoming flights, passengers, etc* o *incoming telephone calls* **2** new; recently elected: *the incoming government*

incomparable /ɪn'kɒmprəbl/ *adj* so good or great that it does not have an equal: *incomparable beauty* ☞ The verb is **compare**.

incompatible /ˌɪnkəm'pætəbl/ *adj* **incompatible with sb/sth** not able to live or work happily with sb; not able to exist in harmony with sb/sth else: *Their marriage won't last, they're completely incompatible.* —**incompatibility** /ˌɪnkəmˌpætə'bɪləti/ *noun* [C,U] (*pl* **incompatibilities**)

incompetent /ɪn'kɒmpɪtənt/ *adj* lacking the necessary skill to do sth well: *He is completely incompetent at his job.* —**incompetence** /-əns/ *noun* [U] —**incompetently** *adv*

incomplete /ˌɪnkəm'pliːt/ *adj* having a part or parts missing; not total or complete: *The witness could only give an incomplete account of what had happened.* o *His happiness was incomplete without her.* o *Unfortunately the jigsaw puzzle was incomplete.* —**incompletely** *adv*

incomprehensible /ɪnˌkɒmprɪ'hensəbl/ *adj* impossible to understand: *an incomprehensible explanation* o *Her attitude is incomprehensible to the rest of the committee.*

inconceivable /ˌɪnkən'siːvəbl/ *adj* impossible or very difficult to believe or imagine

inconclusive /ˌɪnkən'kluːsɪv/ *adj* not leading to a definite decision or result: *an inconclusive discussion* o *inconclusive evidence* (= that doesn't prove anything) —**inconclusively** *adv*

incongruous /ɪn'kɒŋɡruəs/ *adj* strange; not

p	b	t	d	k	g	tʃ	dʒ	f	v	θ	ð
pen	bad	tea	did	cat	got	chin	June	fall	van	thin	then

in harmony; out of place: *He looked very incongruous in his T-shirt and jeans at the ball.* —**incongruity** /ˌɪŋkɒŋˈɡruːəti/ *noun* [U] —**incongruously** *adv*

inconsiderate /ˌɪŋkənˈsɪdərət/ *adj* (used about a person) not thinking or caring about the feelings, or needs of other people: *It was inconsiderate of you not to offer her a lift.* ☛ Another word for inconsiderate is **thoughtless**. —**inconsiderately** *adv* —**inconsiderateness** *noun* [U]

inconsistent /ˌɪnkənˈsɪstənt/ *adj* **1** (used about a person) likely to change (in attitude, behaviour, etc); not reliable: *She's so inconsistent – sometimes her work is good and sometimes it's really awful.* **2** inconsistent (**with** sth) not in agreement with sth: *These new facts are inconsistent with the earlier information.* —**inconsistency** /-ənsi/ *noun* [C,U] (*pl* **inconsistencies**) —**inconsistently** *adv*

inconspicuous /ˌɪŋkənˈspɪkjuəs/ *adj* not easily noticed: *inconspicuous colours such as grey and dark blue* ○ *I tried to make myself as inconspicuous as possible so that no one would ask me a question.* —**inconspicuously** *adv*

incontinent /ɪnˈkɒntɪnənt/ *adj* unable to control the passing of waste (urine and faeces) from the body —**incontinence** /-əns/ *noun* [U]

inconvenience /ˌɪŋkənˈviːniəns/ *noun* [C,U] (something that causes) difficulty or discomfort: *We apologize for any inconvenience caused by the delays.* —**inconvenience** *verb* [T]

inconvenient /ˌɪŋkənˈviːniənt/ *adj* causing difficulty or discomfort; not convenient: *It's a bit inconvenient at the moment – could you phone again later?* —**inconveniently** *adv*

incorporate /ɪnˈkɔːpəreɪt/ *verb* [T] **incorporate sth** (**in/into sth**) to make sth part of sth else or to have sth as a part; to include: *I'd like you to incorporate this information into your report.* ○ *The new car incorporates all the most modern safety features.*

incorporated /ɪnˈkɔːpəreɪtɪd/ *adj* (*abbr* **Inc**) (following the name of a company) formed into a legal organization (**corporation**)

incorrect /ˌɪŋkəˈrekt/ *adj* not right or true; not correct: *Incorrect answers should be marked with a cross.*

incorrectly *adv* wrongly: *The envelope was incorrectly addressed.*

incorrigible /ɪnˈkɒrɪdʒəbl; *US* -ˈkɔːr-/ *adj* (used about a person or behaviour) very bad; too bad to be corrected or improved: *an incorrigible liar*

☆ **increase¹** /ɪnˈkriːs/ *verb* [I,T] to become or to make sth larger in number or amount: *The number of people working from home will increase steadily during the next decade.* ○ *The rate of inflation has increased by 1% to 7%.* ○ *My employer would like me to increase my hours of work from 25 to 30.* ○ *She increased her speed to overtake the lorry.* ☛ The opposite is **decrease** or **reduce**.

increasingly /ɪnˈkriːsɪŋli/ *adv* more and more: *increasingly difficult, important, unhappy, etc*

☆ **increase²** /ˈɪŋkriːs/ *noun* [C,U] **increase (in sth)** a rise in the number, amount or level of sth: *a steady increase in the number of people taking holidays abroad* ○ *There has been a sharp increase of nearly 50% on last year's figures.* ○ *Doctors expect some further increase in the spread of the disease.* ○ *They are demanding a large wage increase in line with inflation.* ☛ The opposite is **decrease** or **reduction**. (IDIOM) **on the increase** becoming larger or more frequent; increasing: *Attacks by dogs on children are on the increase.*

incredible /ɪnˈkredəbl/ *adj* **1** amazing or fantastic; very great: *He earns an incredible salary.* **2** impossible or very difficult to believe: *I found his account of the event incredible.*

incredibly /ɪnˈkredəbli/ *adv* extremely: *We have had some incredibly strong winds recently.*

incriminate /ɪnˈkrɪmɪneɪt/ *verb* [T] to provide evidence that sb is guilty of a crime: *The police searched the house but found nothing to incriminate the man.*

incubate /ˈɪŋkjubeɪt/ *verb* [I,T] **1** (used about eggs) to keep or be kept warm until the young birds come out (**hatch**) **2** (used about an infectious disease, etc) to develop: *Some viruses take weeks to incubate.*

incubation /ˌɪnkjuˈbeɪʃn/ *noun* **1** [U] the process of incubating eggs **2** [C] (*also* **incuˈbation period**) the period between catching a disease and the time when signs of it (**symptoms**) appear

incubator /ˈɪŋkjubeɪtə(r)/ *noun* [C] **1** a heated apparatus used in hospitals for keeping small or weak babies alive **2** a similar apparatus for keeping eggs warm until they break open (**hatch**)

incur /ɪnˈkɜː(r)/ *verb* [T] (**incurred**; **incurring**) (*formal*) to cause or suffer sth unpleasant as a result of your own actions: *to incur debts/sb's anger, etc*

incurable /ɪnˈkjʊərəbl/ *adj* not able to be cured or changed: *an incurable disease* —**incurably** /-əbli/ *adv*: *incurably ill*

indebted /ɪnˈdetɪd/ *adj* **indebted to sb** (**for sth**) very grateful to sb: *I am deeply indebted to my family and friends for all their help and support.*

indecent /ɪnˈdiːsnt/ *adj* offending against accepted sexual, moral or social standards of behaviour; not decent —**indecency** /-nsi/ *noun* [C,U] (*pl* **indecencies**) —**indecently** *adv*

indecision /ˌɪndɪˈsɪʒn/ *noun* [U] being unable to decide: *This indecision about the future is really worrying me.*

indecisive /ˌɪndɪˈsaɪsɪv/ *adj* (used about a person) not able to make decisions —**indecisively** *adv*

☆ **indeed** /ɪnˈdiːd/ *adv* **1** (used for agreeing with sth that has just been said or for emphasis) really; certainly: *'Have you had a good holiday?' 'We have indeed.'* **2** (used for emphasizing a point that has just been made) in fact: *It's important that you come at once. Indeed, it's essential.* **3** (used for emphasis with 'very' plus an adjective or adverb): *Thank you very much indeed.* ○ *She's very happy indeed.* **4** (used for showing interest, surprise, anger, etc): *'They were talking about you last night.' 'Were they* *indeed!'* o *'Why did he go without us?' 'Why indeed?'*

indefensible /ˌɪndɪˈfensəbl/ *adj* (used about behaviour, etc) completely wrong; that cannot be defended or excused

indefinable /ˌɪndɪˈfaɪnəbl/ *adj* difficult or impossible to describe: *There was an indefinable atmosphere of hostility.* —**indefinably** /-əbli/ *adv*

indefinite /ɪnˈdefɪnət/ *adj* not fixed or clear; not definite: *Our plans are still rather indefinite.*
▸ **indefinitely** *adv* for an indefinite period of time (= you do not know how long it will last): *The meeting was postponed indefinitely.*

inˌdefinite ˈarticle *noun* [C] (*grammar*) the name used for the words *a* and *an* ☞ Look at definite article.

indelible /ɪnˈdeləbl/ *adj* that cannot be removed or washed out: *indelible ink* o *(figurative) an indelible impression* —**indelibly** /-əbli/ *adv*

indent /ɪnˈdent/ *verb* [I,T] to start a line of writing further from the left-hand side of the page than the other lines

☆ **independence** /ˌɪndɪˈpendəns/ *noun* [U] **independence (from sb/sth)** (used about a person, country, etc) the state of being free or not controlled by another person, country, etc: *In 1947 India achieved independence from Britain.* o *The old lady refused to go into a nursing home because she didn't want to lose her independence.* o *financial independence*

☞ On **Independence Day** (4 July) Americans celebrate the day in 1776 when America declared itself independent from Britain.

☆ **independent** /ˌɪndɪˈpendənt/ *adj* **1 independent (of sb/sth)** not dependent on or controlled by another person, country, etc: *Many former colonies are now independent nations.* o *to be independent of your parents* o *independent schools, television, etc* (= not dependent on the government for money) **2** not needing or wanting help: *My son likes travelling on his own – he's very independent for his age.* **3** not influenced by or connected with sb/sth: *Complaints against the police should be investigated by an independent body.* o *Two independent opinion polls have obtained similar results.* —**independently** *adv*: *Scientists working independently of each other have had very similar results in their experiments.*

indescribable /ˌɪndɪˈskraɪbəbl/ *adj* too good or bad to be described: *indescribable poverty, luxury, etc* —**indescribably** /-əbli/ *adv*

indestructible /ˌɪndɪˈstrʌktəbl/ *adj* that cannot be easily damaged or destroyed

☆ **index** /ˈɪndeks/ *noun* [C] **1** (*pl* **indexes**) an alphabetical list of names or subjects at the end of a book **2** (*pl* **indexes**) (*also* **card index**) an alphabetical list of names, books, subjects, etc written on a series of cards (**index cards**) **3** (*pl* **indexes** *or* **indices**) a way of showing how the price, value, rate, etc of sth has changed: *the cost-of-living index*

index *verb* [T] to make an index or include sth in an index

ˈindex finger *noun* [C] the finger next to your thumb that is used for pointing ☞ We also say **forefinger.**

☆ **Indian** /ˈɪndɪən/ *noun* [C], *adj* **1** (a person) from the Republic of India: *Indian food is hot and spicy.* **2** = NATIVE AMERICAN: *The Sioux were a famous Indian tribe.* ☞ Look also at **West Indian.**

☆ **indicate** /ˈɪndɪkeɪt/ *verb* **1** [T] to show or point to sth: *The receptionist indicated where I should sign.* o *(figurative) The report indicates a need for more spending on research.* **2** [T] to be or give a sign about sth: *If a horse has its ears forward, that indicates that it is happy.* **3** [T] to say sth briefly and in a general way: *The spokesman indicated that an agreement was likely soon.* **4** [I,T] to signal that your car, etc is going to turn: *Why didn't you indicate?* o *The lorry indicated left but turned right.*

indication /ˌɪndɪˈkeɪʃn/ *noun* [C,U] something that shows sth; a sign: *There was no indication of a struggle.* o *There is every indication that he will make a full recovery.*

indicative /ɪnˈdɪkətɪv/ *adj* (*formal*) being or giving a sign of sth: *Is the unusual weather indicative of fundamental climatic changes?*

indicator /ˈɪndɪkeɪtə(r)/ *noun* [C] **1** something that gives information or shows sth; a sign: *The indicator showed that we had plenty of petrol.* o *I've just seen my flight announced on the indicator board.* **2** the flashing light on a car, etc that shows that it is going to turn right or left

indices *pl* of INDEX

indictment /ɪnˈdaɪtmənt/ *noun* [C] **1** a written paper that officially accuses sb of a crime **2** (*figurative*) something that shows how bad sth is: *The fact that many children leave school with no qualifications is an indictment of our education system.*

indifference /ɪnˈdɪfrəns/ *noun* [U] a lack of interest or feeling (towards sb/sth): *He treated our suggestion with complete indifference.*

indifferent /ɪnˈdɪfrənt/ *adj* **1 indifferent (to sb/sth)** not interested in or caring about sb/sth: *How can you remain indifferent when children are suffering?* **2** of low quality: *The standard of football in the World Cup was rather indifferent.* —**indifferently** *adv*

indigenous /ɪnˈdɪdʒɪnəs/ *adj* (used about people, animals or plants) living or growing in the place where they are from originally

indigestible /ˌɪndɪˈdʒestəbl/ *adj* (used about food) difficult or impossible to eat and digest

indigestion /ˌɪndɪˈdʒestʃən/ *noun* [U] pain in the stomach that is caused by difficulty in digesting food: *Onions give me terrible indigestion.*

indignant /ɪnˈdɪgnənt/ *adj* shocked or angry (because sb has said or done sth that you do not like and do not agree with): *They were indignant that they had to pay more for worse services.* —**indignantly** *adv*

indignation /ˌɪndɪgˈneɪʃn/ *noun* [U] shock and anger: *The growing levels of unemployment have aroused public indignation.* o *to express indignation*

indirect /ˌɪndɪˈrekt; -daɪˈr-/ *adj* **1** not going in

iː	ɪ	e	æ	ɑː	ɒ	ɔː	ʊ	uː	ʌ
see	sit	ten	hat	arm	got	saw	put	too	cup

a straight line or using the shortest route; not direct: *We came the indirect route to avoid driving through London.* **2** not directly caused by or connected with sth: *an indirect result* **3** not mentioning sth openly: *She gave only an indirect answer to my question.* —**indirectly** *adv*
—**indirectness** *noun* [U]

indirect 'object *noun* [C] (*grammar*) an additional object¹(3) that is used after some verbs: *In the sentence, 'I wrote him a letter', 'him' is the indirect object.*

indirect 'speech (*also* **reported speech**) *noun* [U] (*grammar*) reporting what sb has said, not using the actual words ☞ *Tim's words were: 'I'll phone again later.'* In indirect speech this becomes: *Tim said that he would phone again later.*

indiscreet /ˌɪndɪˈskriːt/ *adj* not careful or polite in what you say or do —**indiscreetly** *adv*

indiscretion /ˌɪndɪˈskreʃn/ *noun* [C,U] behaviour that is indiscreet

indiscriminate /ˌɪndɪˈskrɪmɪnət/ *adj* not carefully chosen or done with careful thought: *the indiscriminate shooting of civilians*
—**indiscriminately** *adv*

indispensable /ˌɪndɪˈspensəbl/ *adj* very important, so that it is not possible to be without it; essential or necessary: *A car is indispensable nowadays if you live in the country.*

indisputable /ˌɪndɪˈspjuːtəbl/ *adj* definitely true; that cannot be proved wrong

indistinct /ˌɪndɪˈstɪŋkt/ *adj* not clear; not distinct: *indistinct figures, sounds, memories, etc*
—**indistinctly** *adv*

indistinguishable /ˌɪndɪˈstɪŋɡwɪʃəbl/ *adj* **indistinguishable (from sth)** appearing to be the same: *From a distance the two colours are indistinguishable.*

☆ **individual** /ˌɪndɪˈvɪdʒuəl/ *adj* **1** (only *before* a noun) single or particular: *Each individual animal is weighed and measured before being set free.* **2** for or from one person: *an individual portion of butter* (= for one person) o *Children need individual attention when they are learning to read.*

individual *noun* [C] **1** one (single) person: *Are the needs of society more important than the rights of the individual?* **2** (*informal*) a person of the type that is mentioned: *She's an awkward individual.*

individually /-dʒuəli/ *adv* separately; one by one: *The teacher talked to each member of the class individually.*

individuality /ˌɪndɪˌvɪdʒuˈæləti/ *noun* [U] the qualities that make sb/sth different from other people/things: *Young people often try to express their individuality by the way they dress.*

indivisible /ˌɪndɪˈvɪzəbl/ *adj* not able to be divided or split into smaller pieces

indoctrinate /ɪnˈdɒktrɪneɪt/ *verb* [T] to put ideas or beliefs into sb's mind so that they are accepted without criticism: *For 20 years the people have been indoctrinated by the government.* ☞ Using the word **indoctrinate** shows that you disapprove of what is happening.
—**indoctrination** /ɪnˌdɒktrɪˈneɪʃn/ *noun* [U]: *the indoctrination of political prisoners*

☆ **indoor** /ˈɪndɔː(r)/ *adj* (only *before* a noun) done or used inside a building: *indoor games* o *indoor shoes* o *an indoor swimming-pool*
☞ The opposite is **outdoor**.

☆ **indoors** /ˌɪnˈdɔːz/ *adv* in or into a building: *Let's go/stay indoors.* o *Oh dear. I've left my sunglasses indoors.* ☞ Look at **outdoors** and **out of doors**.

induce /ɪnˈdjuːs; *US* -ˈduːs/ *verb* [T] (*formal*) **1** to make or persuade sb to do sth: *Nothing could induce him to change his mind.* **2** to cause or produce

inducement *noun* [C,U] something that is offered to sb to make him/her do sth

indulge /ɪnˈdʌldʒ/ *verb* **1** [T] to allow sb to have or do whatever he/she wants: *You shouldn't indulge that child. It will make him very selfish.* **2** [I] **indulge (in sth)** to allow yourself to have or do sth for pleasure: *I'm going to indulge in a meal at that new French restaurant.* o *to indulge in self-pity*

indulgence /ɪnˈdʌlɡəns/ *noun* **1** [U] the state of having or doing whatever you want: *a life of indulgence* **2** [C] something that you have or do because it gives you pleasure: *A cigar after dinner is my only indulgence.*

indulgent /-ənt/ *adj* allowing sb to have or do whatever he/she wants: *indulgent parents*
—**indulgently** *adv*

☆ **industrial** /ɪnˈdʌstriəl/ *adj* **1** (only *before* a noun) connected with industry(1): *industrial development* o *industrial workers* o *coal for industrial purposes* **2** having a lot of factories, etc: *an industrial region, country, etc*

industrialist /-ɪst/ *noun* [C] a person who owns or manages a large industrial company

industrialize (*also* **industrialise**) /-aɪz/ *verb* [T] to develop industries in a country: *Japan was very rapidly industrialized in the late nineteenth century.* o *the industrialized nations of the world* —**industrialization** (*also* **industrialisation**) /ɪnˌdʌstriəlaɪˈzeɪʃn; *US* -lɪˈz-/ *noun* [U]

in‚dustrial 'action *noun* [U] the situation when a group of workers go on strike or refuse to work normally, eg because they want more money, shorter working hours, etc

industrious /ɪnˈdʌstriəs/ *adj* hard-working

☆ **industry** /ˈɪndəstri/ *noun* (*pl* **industries**) **1** [U] the work of making things in factories: *Is British industry being threatened by foreign imports?* o *heavy/light industry* **2** [C] all the people, buildings, etc that are involved in producing sth, providing a service, etc: *The new high-tech industries are replacing manufacturing industries in many areas.* o *the tourist, catering, entertainment, etc industry*

inedible /ɪnˈedɪbl/ *adj* (*formal*) not suitable to be eaten: *an inedible plant* o *The food in the canteen is absolutely inedible.*

ineffective /ˌɪnɪˈfektɪv/ *adj* not producing the effect or result that you want

inefficient /ˌɪnɪˈfɪʃnt/ *adj* not working or producing results in the best way, so that time and money is wasted: *an inefficient way of working* o *an inefficient use of space* o *Our heating system is very old and extremely inefficient.* o *The new manager is very nice but he's very inefficient.*

ɜː	ə	eɪ	əʊ	aɪ	aʊ	ɔɪ	ɪə	eə	ʊə
fur	ago	pay	home	five	now	join	near	hair	pure

ineligible 328 **infested**

—**inefficiency** /-nsɪ/ noun [U] —**inefficiently** adv

ineligible /ɪnˈelɪdʒəbl/ adj **ineligible (for sth/to do sth)** without the necessary qualifications to do or get sth: *She was ineligible for the job because she wasn't a German citizen.* o *ineligible to vote* —**ineligibility** /ˌɪnˌelɪdʒəˈbɪləti/ noun [U]

inept /ɪˈnept/ adj not able to do sth well: *She is totally inept at dealing with people.*

inequality /ˌɪnɪˈkwɒləti/ noun [C,U] (pl **inequalities**) (a) difference between groups in society because one has more money, advantages, etc than the other: *There will be problems as long as inequality between the races exists.*

inert /ɪˈnɜːt/ adj not able to move or act

inertia /ɪˈnɜːʃə/ noun [U] **1** a feeling of laziness, when you do not want to do anything **2** the physical force that tends to keep things in the position they are in or to keep them moving in the direction they are travelling: (figurative) *The inertia of the system makes change very difficult.*

inescapable /ˌɪnɪˈskeɪpəbl/ adj (formal) that cannot be avoided: *an inescapable conclusion*

inevitable /ɪnˈevɪtəbl/ adj that cannot be avoided or prevented from happening: *With more cars on the road, traffic jams are inevitable.* o *It was inevitable that she would find out the truth one day.* —**inevitability** /ɪnˌevɪtəˈbɪləti/ noun [U]

the inevitable noun [sing] something that cannot be avoided or stopped from happening —**inevitably** /-əblɪ/ adv: *Building new roads inevitably creates huge problems* (= they cannot be avoided).

inexcusable /ˌɪnɪkˈskjuːzəbl/ adj that cannot be allowed or forgiven: *Their behaviour was quite inexcusable.* o *inexcusable delays* ☛ Look at **unforgivable**.

inexhaustible /ˌɪnɪɡˈzɔːstəbl/ adj that cannot be finished or used up: *Our energy supplies are not inexhaustible.*

inexpensive /ˌɪnɪkˈspensɪv/ adj low in price; not expensive: *an inexpensive camping holiday* —**inexpensively** adv

inexperience /ˌɪnɪkˈspɪərɪəns/ noun [U] not knowing how to do sth because you have not done it before; lack of experience: *The mistakes were all due to inexperience.*

inexperienced adj not having the knowledge that you get from having done sth before; lacking in experience: *He's too young and inexperienced to be given such responsibility.*

inexplicable /ˌɪnɪkˈsplɪkəbl/ adj that cannot be explained: *Her sudden disappearance is quite inexplicable.* —**inexplicably** /-əblɪ/ adv

infallible /ɪnˈfæləbl/ adj **1** (used about a person) never making mistakes or being wrong: *Even the most careful typist is not infallible.* **2** always doing what you want it to do; never failing: *There is no infallible method of birth control.* —**infallibility** /ɪnˌfæləˈbɪləti/ noun [U]

infamous /ˈɪnfəməs/ adj **infamous (for sth)** famous for being bad: *an infamous dictator*

infancy /ˈɪnfənsɪ/ noun [U] the period when you are a baby or young child: (figurative) *Research in this field is still in its infancy.*

infant /ˈɪnfənt/ noun [C] a baby or very young child: *There is a high rate of infant mortality* (= many children die when they are still babies). o *Mrs Davies teaches infants* (= children aged between five and seven). o *2 adults, 2 children, 1 infant* (eg on an air ticket) ☛ **Baby**, **toddler** or **child** are more common in spoken or informal English.

'infant school noun [C] a school for children between the ages of five and seven

infantile /ˈɪnfəntaɪl/ adj of or like a baby or very young child: *infantile* (= very silly) *behaviour*

infantry /ˈɪnfəntrɪ/ noun [U, with sing or pl verb] soldiers who fight on foot: *The infantry was/were supported by heavy gunfire.*

infatuated /ɪnˈfætʃueɪtɪd/ adj having a strong but foolish feeling of love for sb/sth that usually does not last long: *The young girl was infatuated with one of her teachers.* —**infatuation** /ɪnˌfætʃuˈeɪʃn/ noun [C,U]

☆**infect** /ɪnˈfekt/ verb [T] (usually passive) to cause sb/sth to have a disease or illness or to become dirty or full of germs: *We must clean the wound before it becomes infected.* o *Many thousands of people have been infected with the virus.* o (figurative) *Paul's happiness infected the whole family.*

☆**infection** /ɪnˈfekʃn/ noun **1** [U] making sb ill: *A dirty water supply can be a source of infection.* o *There is a danger of infection.* **2** [C] a disease or illness that is caused by germs: *She is suffering from a chest infection.* o *an ear infection*

☛ Infections can be caused by **bacteria** or **viruses**. An informal word for these is **germs**.

☆**infectious** /ɪnˈfekʃəs/ adj (used about a disease, illness, etc) that can be easily passed on to another person: *Flu is very infectious.* o (figurative) *infectious laughter* ☛ Look at **contagious**.

infer /ɪnˈfɜː(r)/ verb [T] (inferring; inferred) **infer sth (from sth)** to reach a conclusion from the information you have: *I inferred from our conversation that he was unhappy with his job.*

inferior /ɪnˈfɪərɪə(r)/ adj **inferior (to sb/sth)** low or lower in social position, importance, quality, etc: *I felt very inferior when they started using long words that I didn't understand.* o *Cheaper goods are generally of inferior quality.* ☛ The opposite is **superior**.

inferior noun [C] a person who has a lower social position —**inferiority** /ɪnˌfɪərɪˈɒrətɪ; US -ˈɔːr-/ noun [U]

infe'riority complex noun [C] the state of feeling less important, clever, successful, etc than other people

infertile /ɪnˈfɜːtaɪl; US -tl/ adj **1** (used about land) not able to grow strong healthy plants **2** (used about a person or animal) not able to have a baby or young animal —**infertility** /ˌɪnfəˈtɪlətɪ/ noun [U]: *treatment for infertility*

infested /ɪnˈfestɪd/ adj **infested (with sth)** (used about a building) with large numbers of

p	b	t	d	k	g	tʃ	dʒ	f	v	θ	ð
pen	bad	tea	did	cat	got	chin	June	fall	van	thin	then

unpleasant animals or insects in it: *The warehouse was infested with rats.*

infiltrate /'ɪnfɪltreɪt/ *verb* [T] to enter an organization, etc secretly so that you can find out what it is doing: *The police managed to infiltrate the gang of terrorists.* —**infiltration** /ˌɪnfɪl'treɪʃn/ *noun* [C,U] —**infiltrator** /'ɪnfɪltreɪtə(r)/ *noun* [C]

infinite /'ɪnfɪnət/ *adj* **1** without end or limits: *Supplies of oil are not infinite.* **2** very great: *You need infinite patience for this job.*
infinitely *adv* very much: *Compact discs sound infinitely better than audio cassettes.*

infinitive /ɪn'fɪnətɪv/ *noun* [C] (*grammar*) the basic form of a verb ☞ In English the infinitive is sometimes used with and sometimes without *to*: *He can sing.* o *He wants to sing.*

infinity /ɪn'fɪnəti/ *noun* [U] **1** endless space or time **2** (in mathematics) the number that is larger than any other that you can think of

infirm /ɪn'fɜːm/ *adj* ill or weak, eg because of old age
infirmity /ɪn'fɜːməti/ *noun* [C,U] (*pl* **infirmities**) weakness or illness

infirmary /ɪn'fɜːməri/ *noun* [C] (*pl* **infirmaries**) a hospital (used mainly in names): *The Manchester Royal Infirmary*

inflamed /ɪn'fleɪmd/ *adj* (used about a part of the body) red and swollen because of some infection

inflammable /ɪn'flæməbl/ *adj* that burns easily: *Petrol is highly inflammable.* ☞ Look at **flammable**. It has the same meaning. The opposite is **non-flammable**.

inflammation /ˌɪnflə'meɪʃn/ *noun* [C,U] redness and swelling in a part of the body, because of infection

inflate /ɪn'fleɪt/ *verb* [I,T] (*formal*) to fill sth with air; to become filled with air ☞ The opposite is **deflate**.
inflatable /-əbl/ *adj* that can or must be filled with air: *an inflatable boat*

☆ **inflation** /ɪn'fleɪʃn/ *noun* [U] a general rise in prices: *High wage rises cause inflation.* o *the inflation rate/rate of inflation* o *Inflation now stands at 10%.* o *The government is taking measures to control inflation.* o *They've reduced inflation by 2%.*

inflection (*also* **inflexion**) /ɪn'flekʃn/ *noun* **1** [U] the act of changing the ending or form of a word to show its grammatical function **2** [C] something that is added to a word that changes its grammatical function, eg *-ed, -est* **3** [U] the rise and fall of your voice when you are talking ☞ Look at **intonation**.

inflexible /ɪn'fleksəbl/ *adj* not able to bend or be bent easily: (*figurative*) *He has a very inflexible attitude to change.* —**inflexibility** /ɪnˌfleksə'bɪləti/ *noun* [U] —**inflexibly** /-əbli/ *adv*

inflict /ɪn'flɪkt/ *verb* [T] **inflict sth** (**on sb**) to force sb to have sth unpleasant or unwanted: *Don't inflict your problems on me –I've got enough of my own.*

in-flight /ˌɪn'flaɪt/ *adj* happening or provided during a journey in a plane: *in-flight entertainment*

☆ **influence** /'ɪnfluəns/ *noun* **1** [U] **influence (on/over sb/sth)** the power to affect, change or control sb/sth: *I used my influence with the boss to get things changed.* o *The fact that he's rich and famous had no influence on our decision.* o *Nobody should drive while they are under the influence of alcohol.* **2** [C] **influence (on sb/sth)** a person or thing that affects or changes sb/sth: *His new girlfriend has been a good influence on him.*

influence *verb* [T] to have an effect or influence on sb/sth: *You must decide for yourself. Don't let anyone else influence you.* o *Her style of painting has been influenced by Japanese art.* ☞ **Affect** and **influence** are often very similar in meaning. **Affect** is usually used when the change is physical and **influence** is more often used to describe a change of feeling or attitude: *Drinking alcohol can affect your ability to drive.* o *The TV advertisements have influenced my attitude towards drinking and driving.*

influential /ˌɪnflu'enʃl/ *adj* having power or influence: *an influential politician* o *He was influential in getting the hostages set free.*

influenza /ˌɪnflu'enzə/ *noun* [U] (*formal*) = FLU

influx /'ɪnflʌks/ *noun* [C] a sudden arrival of people or things in large numbers: *the summer influx of visitors from abroad*

☆ **inform** /ɪn'fɔːm/ *verb* **1** [T] **inform sb (of/about sth)** to give sb information (about sth): *You should inform the police of the accident.* o *Do keep me informed of any changes.* **2** [I] **inform against/on sb** to give information, etc to the police, etc about what sb has done wrong: *The wife of the killer informed on her husband.*

informant /-ənt/ *noun* [C] a person who gives sb knowledge or information: *The journalist refused to name his informant.*

informed *adj* having knowledge or information about sth: *The radio keeps me well-informed about what is happening.* o *Consumers cannot make informed choices unless they are told all the facts.*

informer *noun* [C] a person who gives the police, etc information about what sb has done wrong

☆ **informal** /ɪn'fɔːml/ *adj* relaxed and friendly or suitable for a relaxed occasion; not formal: *I wear a suit to work but more informal clothes at the weekends.* o *Don't get dressed up for the party –it'll be very informal.* o *The two leaders had informal discussions before the conference began.* ☞ Some words and expressions in this dictionary are described as (*informal*). This means that you can use them when you are speaking to friends or people that you know well but that you should not use them in written work, official letters, etc. —**informality** /ˌɪnfɔː'mæləti/ *noun* [C,U] (*pl* **informalities**): *an atmosphere of informality* —**informally** /ɪn'fɔːməli/ *adv*: *I was told informally* (= unofficially) *that our plans had been accepted.*

☆ **information** /ˌɪnfə'meɪʃn/ *noun* [U] **information (on/about sb/sth)** knowledge or facts: *For further information please send for our fact sheet.* o *Can you give me some information about evening classes in Italian, please?* o *The*

s	z	ʃ	ʒ	h	m	n	ŋ	l	r	j	w
so	**zoo**	**she**	**vision**	**how**	**man**	**no**	**sing**	**leg**	**red**	**yes**	**wet**

information is fed into the computer and the results are printed out in the form of a graph. ☛ The word **information** is uncountable so you CANNOT say: *I need an information.* You can, however, talk about **a bit** or **piece of information**

information technology *noun* [U] the study or use of computer systems, etc for collecting, storing and sending out all kinds of information

informative /ɪnˈfɔːmətɪv/ *adj* giving useful knowledge or information ☛ The opposite is **uninformative**.

infrequent /ɪnˈfriːkwənt/ *adj* not happening often: *infrequent visits* —**infrequently** *adv*

infringe /ɪnˈfrɪndʒ/ *verb* (*formal*) **1** [T] to break a rule, law, agreement, etc **2** [I] **infringe on/upon sth** to reduce or limit sb's rights, freedom, etc —**infringement** /-mənt/ *noun* [C,U]

infuriate /ɪnˈfjʊərieɪt/ *verb* [T] to make sb very angry —**infuriating** *adj*: *an infuriating habit* —**infuriatingly** *adv*

ingenious /ɪnˈdʒiːniəs/ *adj* **1** (used about a person) clever at finding answers to problems or at thinking of new things **2** (used about a thing or an idea) cleverly made or thought out: *an ingenious plan for making lots of money* —**ingeniously** *adv* —**ingenuity** /ˌɪndʒɪˈnjuːəti; *US* -ˈnuː-/ *noun* [U]

ingrained /ɪnˈɡreɪnd/ *adj* deeply fixed; difficult to change

ingratiate /ɪnˈɡreɪʃieɪt/ *verb* [T] (*formal*) **ingratiate yourself (with sb)** to make yourself liked by doing or saying things that will please people: *He was always trying to ingratiate himself with his teachers.* —**ingratiating** *adj*: *an ingratiating smile* —**ingratiatingly** *adv*

ingratitude /ɪnˈɡrætɪtjuːd; *US* -tuːd/ *noun* [U] (*formal*) the state of not showing or feeling thanks for sth that has been done for you; a lack of gratitude ☛ A less formal word is **ungratefulness**.

ingredient /ɪnˈɡriːdiənt/ *noun* [C] one of the items of food you need to make sth to eat: (*figurative*) *The film has all the ingredients of success.*

☆ **inhabit** /ɪnˈhæbɪt/ *verb* [T] to live in a place: *Are the Aran Islands still inhabited?*
inhabitable *adj* that can be lived in: *The house was no longer inhabitable after the fire.* ☛ The opposite is **uninhabitable**.

inhabitant /-ənt/ *noun* [C] a person or animal that lives in a place: *How many inhabitants has Paris got?* ○ *The local inhabitants protested at the plans for a new motorway.*

inhale /ɪnˈheɪl/ *verb* [I,T] to breathe in: *Be careful not to inhale the fumes from the paint.*

inherit /ɪnˈherɪt/ *verb* [T] **inherit sth (from sb)** **1** to receive property, money, etc from sb who has died: *I inherited quite a lot of money from my mother. She left me £12 000 when she died.* **2** to receive a quality, disease, etc from your parents or family: *She has inherited her father's gift for languages.*

inheritance /-əns/ *noun* [C,U] the act of inheriting; what you inherit: *inheritance tax*

inhibit /ɪnˈhɪbɪt/ *verb* [T] to prevent sth or make sth happen more slowly: *a drug to inhibit the growth of tumours*
inhibited *adj* not able to express your feelings freely or naturally; not relaxed: *The young man felt shy and inhibited in the roomful of women.* ○ *inhibited about sex* ☛ The opposite is **uninhibited**. —**inhibition** /ˌɪnhɪˈbɪʃn; ˌɪnɪ-/ *noun* [C,U]: *She has no inhibitions about speaking in front of a large group of people.*

inhospitable /ˌɪnhɒˈspɪtəbl/ *adj* **1** (used about a person) not friendly or welcoming **2** (used about a place) not pleasant to live in: *the inhospitable Arctic regions*

inhuman /ɪnˈhjuːmən/ *adj* very cruel, not seeming to be human: *inhuman treatment*

inhumanity /ˌɪnhjuːˈmænəti/ *noun* [U] very cruel behaviour: *The twentieth century is full of examples of man's inhumanity to man.*

inhumane /ˌɪnhjuːˈmeɪn/ *adj* very cruel; not caring if people or animals suffer: *the inhumane conditions in which animals are kept on some large farms*

☆ **initial** /ɪˈnɪʃl/ *adj* (only *before* a noun) that is at the beginning; first: *My initial reaction was to refuse, but I later changed my mind.* ○ *the initial stages of our survey*

initial *noun* [C, usually pl] the first letter of a name: *Patricia Anne Morgan's initials are P. A. M.*

initial *verb* [T] (**initialling**; **initialled**; *US* **initialing**; **initialed**) to mark or sign sth with your initials

initially /-ʃəli/ *adv* at the beginning; at first: *I liked the job initially but it soon got quite boring.*

initiate /ɪˈnɪʃieɪt/ *verb* [T] **1** (*formal*) to start sth: *to initiate a programme of reform* **2 initiate sb (into sth)** to bring sb into a group by means of a special ceremony or by giving him/her special knowledge: *to initiate somebody into a secret society* —**initiation** /ɪˌnɪʃiˈeɪʃn/ *noun* [U]

☆ **initiative** /ɪˈnɪʃətɪv/ *noun* **1** [C] official action that is taken to solve a problem or improve a situation: *a new government initiative to help people start small businesses* **2 the initiative** [sing] the stronger position because you have done sth first; the advantage: *The enemy forces have lost the initiative.* **3** [U] the ability to see and do what needs to be done without help from others: *Don't keep asking me how to do it. Use your own initiative.*

(IDIOMS) **on your own initiative** without being told by sb else what to do

take the initiative to be first to do sth: *Let's take the initiative and start organizing things now.*

☆ **inject** /ɪnˈdʒekt/ *verb* [T] **1** to put a drug into sb/sth with a needle (**syringe**): *Something was injected into my arm and I soon fell asleep.* **2** to add sth: *They injected a lot of money into the business.* —**injection** /ɪnˈdʒekʃn/ *noun* [C,U]
injection (of sth) (into sb/sth): *The baby had her first injection yesterday.* ○ *a tetanus injection* ○ *fuel-injection*

injunction /ɪnˈdʒʌŋkʃn/ *noun* [C] an official order from a court of law to do/not do sth: *A*

iː	ɪ	e	æ	ɑː	ɒ	ɔː	ʊ	uː	ʌ
see	sit	ten	hat	arm	got	saw	put	too	cup

court injunction prevented the programme from being shown on TV.

☆ **injure** /'ɪndʒə(r)/ verb [T] to harm or hurt a person, animal or part of the body: *David was badly injured in the accident.* ○ *seriously injured* ○ *She fell and injured her back.* ☛ Look at the note at **hurt**.
injured adj physically or mentally hurt: *an injured leg* ○ *'Oh, don't be so nasty!' she said in an injured voice.*
the injured noun [plural] people who have been hurt: *The injured were rushed to hospital.*

☆ **injury** /'ɪndʒəri/ noun [C,U] (pl **injuries**) harm or hurt done to a person, animal or part of the body: *They escaped from the accident with only minor injuries.* ○ *Injury to the head can be extremely dangerous.* ○ (figurative) *injury to your pride, reputation, etc*

'**injury time** noun [U] time that is added to the end of a sports match when there has been time lost because of injuries to players

injustice /ɪn'dʒʌstɪs/ noun [C,U] **1** unfairness; a lack of justice: *People are protesting about the injustice of the new tax.* **2** an unjust action
(IDIOM) **do sb an injustice** to judge sb unfairly: *I'm afraid I've done you both an injustice.*

☆ **ink** /ɪŋk/ noun [C,U] a coloured liquid that is used for writing, drawing, etc: *Please write in ink, not pencil.*

inky /'ɪŋki/ adj made black with ink: *inky fingers*

inkling /'ɪŋklɪŋ/ noun [sing] a slight feeling (about sth): *I had an inkling that something was wrong.*

inland /'ɪnlənd/ adj in the middle of a country away from the coast or borders: *inland regions, away from the coast*
inland /,ɪn'lænd/ adv in or towards the middle of a country: *Goods are carried inland along narrow mountain roads.*

,**Inland** '**Revenue** noun [sing] (Brit) the government department that collects taxes

in-laws /'ɪn lɔːz/ noun [plural] (informal) your husband's or wife's mother and father or other relations: *My in-laws are coming to lunch on Sunday.*

inmate /'ɪnmeɪt/ noun [C] one of the people living in an institution such as a prison or mental hospital

inn /ɪn/ noun [C] (Brit) a small hotel or old pub in the country

☛ A **hotel** is a place where you can stay, and have your meals if you wish. A **pub** is a place where you go to drink alcohol or cold soft drinks. An **inn** is an old pub, usually in the country. Some pubs and inns serve food and some inns have rooms where you can stay.

innate /ɪ'neɪt/ adj being a natural quality of sb/sth: *innate ability*

☆ **inner** /'ɪnə(r)/ adj (only before a noun) **1** (of the) inside: *The inner ear is very delicate.* ☛ The opposite is **outer**. **2** (used about a feeling, etc) that you do not express or show to other people: *Everyone has inner doubts.*

innermost /-məʊst/ adj (only before a noun) **1** furthest from the outside **2** (used about a feeling, etc) most secret or private: *She never told anyone her innermost thoughts.*

,**inner** '**city** noun [C] the poor parts of a large city, near the centre, that often have a lot of social problems: *Inner-city schools often have difficulty in attracting good teachers.*

innings /'ɪnɪŋz/ noun [C] (pl **innings**) a period of time in a game of cricket when it is the turn of one player or team to hit the ball (**bat**)

☆ **innocent** /'ɪnəsnt/ adj **1 innocent (of sth)** not having done wrong; not guilty: *An innocent man was arrested by mistake.* ○ *to be innocent of a crime* **2** not causing harm or intended to upset sb: *He got very aggressive when I asked an innocent question about his past life.* **3** not knowing the bad things in life; believing everything you are told: *Twenty years ago I was still young and innocent.* ○ *She was so innocent as to believe that politicians never lie.* —**innocence** /-sns/ noun [U]: *The accused man protested his innocence throughout his trial.* ☛ The opposite is **guilt**. —**innocently** adv

innocuous /ɪ'nɒkjuəs/ adj (formal) not causing harm or intended to upset sb: *I made an innocuous remark about teachers and she got really angry.* —**innocuously** adv

innovate /'ɪnəveɪt/ verb [I] to introduce sth new; to change
innovation /,ɪnə'veɪʃn/ noun [C,U] something new that has been introduced: *technological innovations in industry*
innovator /'ɪnəveɪtə(r)/ noun [C] a person who introduces changes

Innuit (also **Inuit**) /'ɪnuːɪt; -njuː-/ noun [C] = ESKIMO

innumerable /ɪ'njuːmərəbl; US ɪ'nuː-/ adj too many to be counted

inoculate /ɪ'nɒkjuleɪt/ verb [T] **inoculate sb (with sth) (against sth)** to inject sb with a mild form of a disease. This protects him/her from getting the serious form: *The children have been inoculated against tetanus.* ☛ Look at **immunize** and **vaccinate**. —**inoculation** /ɪ,nɒkju'leɪʃn/ noun [C,U]

inoffensive /,ɪnə'fensɪv/ adj not upsetting or unpleasant

inordinate /ɪn'ɔːdɪnət/ adj (formal) much greater than usual or expected —**inordinately** adv

inorganic /,ɪnɔː'gænɪk/ adj not made of or coming from living things: *Rocks and metals are inorganic substances.*

input /'ɪnpʊt/ noun [C,U] **input (into/to sth)** what you add to sth to make it better; what you put into sth: *We need some input from teachers into this book.* ○ *The computer breakdown means we have lost the whole day's input.* ☛ Look at **output**.
input verb [T] (pres part **inputting**; pt, pp **input** or **inputted**) to put information into a computer

inquest /'ɪŋkwest/ noun [C] an official inquiry to find out about an unexplained death: *to hold an inquest*

☆ **inquire** (also **enquire**) /ɪn'kwaɪə(r)/ verb

(formal) [I,T] to ask for information about sth: *We must inquire whether it is possible to get a bus on a Sunday.* ○ *Could you inquire when the trains to Cork leave?* ○ *We need to inquire about hotels in Vienna.* ○ *'Do they take travellers' cheques here?' 'I don't know. I'll inquire.'*
(PHRASAL VERBS) **inquire after sb** to ask about sb's health

inquire into sth to study or investigate sth to find out all the facts: *The journalist inquired into the politician's financial affairs.*

inquirer /ɪnˈkwaɪərə(r)/ noun [C] a person who inquires

inquiring /ɪnˈkwaɪərɪŋ/ adj **1** interested in learning new things: *We should encourage children to have an inquiring mind.* **2** asking for information: *an inquiring look* —**inquiringly** adv

☆**inquiry** (also **enquiry**) /ɪnˈkwaɪəri; US ˈɪŋkwəri/ noun (pl **inquiries**) **1** [C] **inquiry (about/concerning sb/sth)** (formal) a question that you ask about sth: *I have made some inquiries into English language courses in Oxford.* **2** [U] the act of asking about sth: *After weeks of inquiry he finally found what he was looking for.* **3** [C] **inquiry (into sth)** an official investigation to find out the cause of sth: *After the accident there were many calls for an inquiry into safety procedures.*

inquisitive /ɪnˈkwɪzətɪv/ adj (formal) very interested in finding out about what other people are doing: *Don't be so inquisitive. It's none of your business.* —**inquisitively** adv —**inquisitiveness** noun [U]

insane /ɪnˈseɪn/ adj **1** mad or mentally ill **2** very foolish: *You must be insane to leave your job before you've found another one.* ☞ Look at the note at **mad**. —**insanely** adv: *insanely jealous* —**insanity** /ɪnˈsænəti/ noun [U]

insanitary /ɪnˈsænɪtri; US -teri/ adj (formal) likely to cause disease: *The restaurant was closed because of the insanitary conditions of the kitchen.*

insatiable /ɪnˈseɪʃəbl/ adj not able to be satisfied; very great: *an insatiable desire for knowledge* ○ *an insatiable appetite*

inscribe /ɪnˈskraɪb/ verb [T] (formal) **inscribe A (on/in B); inscribe B (with A)** to write or cut (**carve**) words on sth. You inscribe sth when you want it to be a permanent record: *The book was inscribed with the author's name.* ○ *The names of all the previous champions are inscribed on the cup.*

inscription /ɪnˈskrɪpʃn/ noun [C] words that are written or cut on sth: *There was a Latin inscription on the tombstone.*

☆**insect** /ˈɪnsekt/ noun [C] a small animal with six legs, two pairs of wings and a body which is divided into three parts: *Ants, flies, beetles, butterflies and mosquitoes are all insects.* ○ *an insect bite/sting* ☞ Some other small animals, eg spiders, are often also called insects although this is technically incorrect.

insecticide /ɪnˈsektɪsaɪd/ noun [C,U] a substance that is used for killing insects ☞ Look at **pesticide**.

insecure /ˌɪnsɪˈkjʊə(r)/ adj **1** not supported very well; not safe or secure: *Emily felt very insecure at the top of the ladder.* ○ *The future of the company looks very insecure.* **2 insecure (about sb/sth)** feeling anxious and not sure of yourself; not confident: *Some young people feel lost and insecure when they first leave home.* —**insecurely** adv —**insecurity** /ˌɪnsɪˈkjʊərəti/ noun [U]: *Their aggressive behaviour is really a sign of insecurity.*

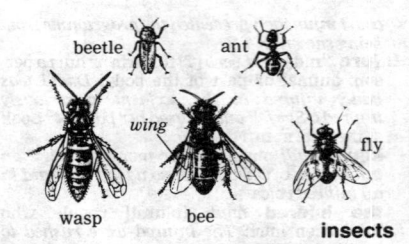

insensitive /ɪnˈsensətɪv/ adj **1** not knowing or caring how another person feels and whether you have hurt or upset him/her: *Some insensitive reporters tried to interview the families of the accident victims.* **2 insensitive (to sth)** not able to feel sth: *insensitive to pain, cold, etc* —**insensitively** adv —**insensitivity** /ɪnˌsensəˈtɪvəti/ noun [U]

inseparable /ɪnˈseprəbl/ adj not able to be separated from sb/sth: *inseparable friends*

insert /ɪnˈsɜːt/ verb [T] (formal) to put sth into sth or between two things: *Insert your money and then dial the number.* —**insertion** /ɪnˈsɜːʃn/ noun [C,U]

inshore /ˌɪnˈʃɔː(r)/ adj, adv in or towards the part of the sea that is close to the land: *inshore fishermen* ○ *Sharks don't often come inshore.*

☆**inside¹** /ɪnˈsaɪd/ noun **1** [C] the inner part or surface of sth: *The insides of the windows need a good clean.* ○ *The door was locked from the inside.* **2** [sing] (also **insides** /ɪnˈsaɪdz/ [plural]) (informal) the stomach: *I've got a pain in my insides.*

(IDIOM) **inside out**
1 with the inner surface on the outside: *You've got your jumper on inside out.*
2 very well, in great detail: *She knows these streets inside out.*

inside adj (only before a noun) **1** in or on the inner part or surface of sth: *the inside pocket of a jacket* ○ *the inside pages of a newspaper* **2** (used about information, etc) told secretly by sb who belongs to a group, organization, etc: *The robbers seemed to have had some inside information about the bank's security system.*

insider /ɪnˈsaɪdə(r)/ noun [C] a person who is a member of a group or an organization

ˌinside ˈlane noun [C] the part of a wide road or motorway where traffic moves more slowly

☆**inside²** /ɪnˈsaɪd/ (especially US **inside of**) prep

1 in or on the inner part or surface of sb/sth: *Is there anything inside the box?* ○ *It's safer to be inside the house in a thunderstorm.* **2** (*formal*) (used about time) in less than: *Your photos will be ready inside an hour.*

inside *adv* **1** in or to the inner part or surface of sth: *We'd better stay inside until the rain stops.* ○ *It's getting cold. Let's go inside.* ○ *Have a look inside and see what's in it.* **2** (*slang*) in prison

insight /'ɪnsaɪt/ *noun* [C,U] **insight (into sth)** (an example of) understanding the true nature of sb/sth: *The book gives a good insight into the lives of the poor.* ○ *You need insight into human nature for this job.*

insignificant /ˌɪnsɪg'nɪfɪkənt/ *adj* of little value or importance: *an insignificant detail* —**insignificance** /-kəns/ *noun* [U] —**insignificantly** *adv*

insincere /ˌɪnsɪn'sɪə(r)/ *adj* not meaning what you say; not truthful; not sincere: *His apology sounded insincere.* —**insincerely** *adv* —**insincerity** /ˌɪnsɪn'serəti/ *noun* [U]

insinuate /ɪn'sɪnjueɪt/ *verb* [T] to suggest sth unpleasant in an indirect way: *She seemed to be insinuating that our work was below standard.* —**insinuation** /ɪnˌsɪnju'eɪʃn/ *noun* [C,U]: *to make insinuations about sb's honesty*

insipid /ɪn'sɪpɪd/ *adj* without a strong taste, flavour or colour

☆**insist** /ɪn'sɪst/ *verb* **1** [I,T] **insist (on sth/on doing sth)** to say or demand that you must have or do sth or that sb else must do sth: *He always insists on the best.* ○ *My parents insist that I come home by taxi.* ○ *Dick insisted on coming too.* ○ *'Have another piece of cake.' 'Oh all right, if you insist.'* **2** [I,T] **insist (on sth)** to say firmly that sth is true (when sb does not believe you): *She insisted on her innocence.* ○ *James insisted that the accident wasn't his fault.*

insistent /-ənt/ *adj* saying or demanding that you must have or do sth or that sb else must do sth: *Grandma was most insistent that we should all be there.* ○ (*figurative*) *We could not ignore the insistent ringing of the telephone.* —**insistence** /-əns/ *noun* [U] —**insistently** *adv*

insolent /'ɪnsələnt/ *adj* (*formal*) rude or impolite: *The school cannot tolerate such insolent behaviour.* —**insolence** /-əns/ *noun* [U] —**insolently** *adv*

insoluble /ɪn'sɒljubl/ *adj* **1** impossible to dissolve in a liquid **2** not able to be explained or solved: *We faced almost insoluble problems.*

insomnia /ɪn'sɒmniə/ *noun* [U] if you suffer from insomnia you find it difficult to get to sleep and to sleep well

☆**inspect** /ɪn'spekt/ *verb* [T] **1 inspect sb/sth (for sth)** to look at sth closely or in great detail: *The detective inspected the room for fingerprints.* **2** to make an official visit to make sure that rules are being obeyed, work is being done properly, etc: *All food shops should be inspected regularly.* —**inspection** /ɪn'spekʃn/ *noun* [C,U]: *The fire prevention service carries out inspections of all public buildings.* ○ *On inspection, the passport turned out to be false.*

☆**inspector** /ɪn'spektə(r)/ *noun* [C] **1** an official who inspects(2) sth: *Keep your bus ticket. An inspector may ask to see it.* ○ *a health and safety inspector* **2** (*Brit*) a police officer of middle rank

inspiration /ˌɪnspə'reɪʃn/ *noun* **1** [C,U] **inspiration (to/for sb)**; **inspiration (to do sth)** (a person or thing that causes) a feeling of wanting and being able to do sth good, create a work of art, etc: *The beauty of the mountains was a great source of inspiration to the writer.* ○ *Her example has been an inspiration to many younger women.* **2** [C] (*informal*) a (sudden) good idea: *I've had an inspiration – why don't we all go?*

inspire /ɪn'spaɪə(r)/ *verb* [T] **1** to give sb a feeling of wanting and being able to do sth good, create a work of art, etc: *His novel was inspired by his relationship with his first wife.* **2 inspire sb (with sth); inspire sth (in sb)** to make sb feel, think, act sth: *The guide's nervous manner did not inspire much confidence in us.* ○ *to be inspired with enthusiasm*

inspired *adj* produced with the help of inspiration(1): *The pianist gave an inspired performance.* ○ *I didn't know the answer. It was just an inspired guess.* ☛ The opposite is **uninspired**. —**inspiring** /ɪn'spaɪərɪŋ/ *adj*: *I'm afraid it was not a very inspiring speech.* ☛ The opposite is **uninspiring**.

instability /ˌɪnstə'bɪləti/ *noun* [U] the state of being likely to change: *There are growing signs of political instability.* ☛ The adjective is **unstable**.

☆**install** (*US also* **instal**) /ɪn'stɔːl/ *verb* [T] **1** to put a piece of equipment, etc in place so that it is ready to be used: *We are waiting to have our new washing-machine installed.* **2** put sb/sth or yourself in a position or place: *He was installed as President yesterday.* ○ *She installed herself in a deck-chair for the afternoon.* —**installation** /ˌɪnstə'leɪʃn/ *noun* [C,U]

instalment (*US* **installment**) /ɪn'stɔːlmənt/ *noun* [C] **1** a single part of a book, television show, etc that is published or shown regularly over a period of time: *Don't miss next week's exciting instalment.* **2** one of the regular payments that you make for sth. People buy sth in instalments when they do not want to pay the whole amount at once

☆**instance** /'ɪnstəns/ *noun* [C] an example or case (of sth): *There have been several instances of racial attacks in the area.* ○ *In most instances the drug has no side-effects.*

(IDIOM) **for instance** for example: *There are several interesting places to visit around here – Dorchester, for instance.*

☆**instant¹** /'ɪnstənt/ *adj* **1** happening suddenly or at once; immediate: *The film was an instant success.* ○ *A new government cannot bring about instant change.* **2** (used about food) able to be prepared quickly and easily: *instant coffee*
instantly *adv* at once; immediately: *I asked him a question and he replied instantly.*

instant² /'ɪnstənt/ *noun* [usually sing] **1** a particular point in time: *At that instant I realized I had been tricked.* ○ *Stop doing that this instant!* (= now) **2** a very short period of time: *Alex thought for an instant and then agreed.*

instantaneous /ˌɪnstən'teɪniəs/ *adj* happen-

instead /ɪnˈsted/ adv in the place of sb/sth: *I couldn't go so my husband went instead.* ○ *There's nothing on at the cinema, let's go to the pub instead.*

instead of prep in the place of: *You should play football instead of just watching it on TV.* ○ *Could I come at 8.00 instead of 7.30?*

instigate /ˈɪnstɪɡeɪt/ verb [T] (formal) to make sth start to happen —**instigation** /ˌɪnstɪˈɡeɪʃn/ noun [U]

instil (US **instill**) /ɪnˈstɪl/ verb [T] (instilling; instilled) **instil sth (in/into sb)** to make sb think or feel sth: *Parents should try to instil a sense of responsibility into their children.*

instinct /ˈɪnstɪŋkt/ noun [C,U] the natural force that causes a person or animal to behave in a certain way without thinking or learning about it: *Birds learn to fly by instinct.* ○ *I didn't stop to think. I just acted on instinct.* —**instinctive** /ɪnˈstɪŋktɪv/ adj: *Your instinctive reaction is to run from danger.* —**instinctively** adv

institute¹ /ˈɪnstɪtjuːt; US -tuːt/ noun [C] (a building that contains) an academic society or organization: *the Institute of Science and Technology*

institute² /ˈɪnstɪtjuːt; US -tuːt/ verb [T] (formal) to set up or start a system, course of action, etc: *The government has instituted a new scheme for youth training.*

institution /ˌɪnstɪˈtjuːʃn; US -tuːʃn/ noun [C] **1** a large organization such as a bank, a university, etc: *the financial institutions in the City of London* **2** a building where certain people with special needs live and are looked after: *a mental institution* (= a hospital for the mentally ill) **3** a social custom or habit that has existed for a long time: *the institution of marriage*

institutional /-ʃənl/ adj connected with an institution(1,2,3): *The old lady is in need of institutional care.*

instruct /ɪnˈstrʌkt/ verb [T] **1 instruct sb (in sth)** (formal) to teach: *Children must be instructed in road safety before they are allowed to ride a bike on the road.* **2 instruct sb (to do sth)** to give an order to sb; to tell sb to do sth: *The soldiers were instructed to shoot above the heads of the crowd.*

instructor noun [C] a person who teaches (usually not in a school): *a driving instructor*

instruction /ɪnˈstrʌkʃn/ noun **1** [U] **instruction (in sth)** teaching or being taught: *The staff need instruction in the use of computers.* **2** [C] an order or direction that tells you what to do or how to do sth: *The guard was under strict instructions not to let anyone in or out.* ○ *The instruction you gave was confusing.* **3 instructions** [plural] information on how you should use sth, do sth, etc: *Read the instructions on the back of the packet carefully.* ○ *to follow the instructions*

instructive /ɪnˈstrʌktɪv/ adj giving useful information —**instructively** adv

instrument /ˈɪnstrəmənt/ noun [C] **1** a tool that is used for doing a particular job or task: *surgical instruments* ☞ Look at the note at **tool**. **2** something that is used for measuring speed, fuel levels, etc in a car, plane or ship: *the instrument panel of an aeroplane* **3** something that is used for playing music: *'What instrument do you play?' 'The violin.'*

☞ Musical instruments may be **stringed** (*violins, guitars, etc*), **brass** (*horns, trumpets, etc*) or **woodwind** (*flutes, clarinets, etc*). **Percussion** instruments include *drums* and *cymbals*.

instrumental /ˌɪnstrʊˈmentl/ adj **1** (not before a noun) **instrumental in doing sth** helping to make sth happen: *She was instrumental in getting him the job.* **2** for musical instruments without voices: *instrumental music*

insubordinate /ˌɪnsəˈbɔːdɪnət/ adj (formal) (used about a person or behaviour) not obedient; not easily controlled —**insubordination** /ˌɪnsəˌbɔːdɪˈneɪʃn/ noun [C,U]

insubstantial /ˌɪnsəbˈstænʃl/ adj not large, solid or strong; not substantial: *a hut built of insubstantial materials* ○ *an insubstantial meal*

insufferable /ɪnˈsʌfrəbl/ adj (used about a person or behaviour) extremely unpleasant or annoying —**insufferably** /-əblɪ/ adv

insufficient /ˌɪnsəˈfɪʃnt/ adj **insufficient (for sth/to do sth)** not enough; not sufficient: *The students complained that they were given insufficient time for the test.*

insular /ˈɪnsjələ(r); US -sələr/ adj not interested in, or able to accept new people or different ideas —**insularity** /ˌɪnsjʊˈlærətɪ; US -səˈl-/ noun [U]

insulate /ˈɪnsjʊleɪt; US -səl-/ verb [T] to protect or cover sth with a material that prevents electricity, heat or sound from passing through: *You can save a lot of money on heating if your house is well insulated.*

insulation /ˌɪnsjʊˈleɪʃn; US -səˈl-/ noun [U] **1** the material used for insulating sth **2** the process of insulating or the state of being insulated: *Foam rubber provides good insulation.*

insult /ɪnˈsʌlt/ verb [T] to speak or act rudely to sb: *I felt very insulted when I didn't even get an answer to my letter.*

insult /ˈɪnsʌlt/ noun [C] a rude remark or action: *The drivers were standing in the road yelling insults at each other.* ○ *Some television advertisements are an insult to people's intelligence.*

insulting adj rude: *A lot of women find his manner quite insulting.*

insuperable /ɪnˈsuːpərəbl; Brit also -ˈsjuː-/ adj (formal) (used about a problem, etc) impossible to solve or overcome

insurance /ɪnˈʃɔːrəns; US -ˈʃʊər-/ noun **1** [U] **insurance (against sth)** a contract in which, in return for regular payment, a company or the state agrees to pay a sum of money if sth (eg illness, death, loss of or damage to property) happens to sb: *Our roof was blown off in the storm but we claimed for it on the insurance.* ○

Builders should always have insurance against personal injury.

> ☞ We **take out** an **insurance policy**. An **insurance premium** is the regular amount you pay to the insurance company. We can take out **life, health, car, travel** and **household insurance**.

2 [U] the business of providing insurance contracts: *He works in insurance.* **3** [sing] **an insurance (against sth)** something you do to protect yourself (against sth unpleasant): *Many people take vitamin pills as an insurance against illness.*

☆ **insure** /ɪnˈʃɔː(r); *US* ɪnˈʃʊər/ *verb* [T] **1 insure sb/sth (against sth)** to take out or to provide insurance: *They insured the painting for £10 000 against damage or theft.* ○ *Are you insured against accident and medical expenses on your trip?* **2** (*US*) = ENSURE

insurmountable /ˌɪnsəˈmaʊntəbl/ *adj* (*formal*) (used about a problem, etc) impossible to solve or overcome

insurrection /ˌɪnsəˈrekʃn/ *noun* [C,U] violent action against the rulers of a country or the government

intact /ɪnˈtækt/ *adj* (not before a noun) complete; not damaged: *Very few of the buildings remained intact after the earthquake.*

intake /ˈɪnteɪk/ *noun* [C, usually sing] **1** (used about food, liquid, air, etc) the amount that sb/sth takes in or the process of taking it in: *If you're driving you should watch your alcohol intake carefully.* **2** the (number of) people who enter an organization or institution during a certain period

intangible /ɪnˈtændʒəbl/ *adj* (used about a quality or an idea) difficult to describe, understand or explain; not tangible

integral /ˈɪntɪgrəl/ *adj* essential (in order to make sth complete): *Spending a year in France is an integral part of the university course.*

☆ **integrate** /ˈɪntɪgreɪt/ *verb* **1** [I,T] **integrate (sb) (into sth/with sth)** to join in and become part of a group or community or to make sb do this: *The government has various schemes to help integrate immigrants into their local communities.* ☞ Look at **segregate**. **2** [T] **integrate sth (into sth); integrate A and B/integrate A with B** to join things so that they become one thing or fit together: *The two small schools were integrated to form one larger school.* —**integration** /ˌɪntɪˈgreɪʃn/ *noun* [U]: *racial integration* ☞ Look at **segregation**.

integrity /ɪnˈtegrəti/ *noun* [U] the quality of being honest; firmness of character and moral ideas: *He's a person of great integrity who will say exactly what he thinks.*

intellect /ˈɪntəlekt/ *noun* [C,U] the power of the mind to think and to learn

☆ **intellectual** /ˌɪntəˈlektʃuəl/ *adj* (only *before* a noun) using or able to use the power of the mind: *The boy's intellectual development was very advanced for his age.* ○ *intellectual people, interests, discussions, etc*

intellectual *noun* [C] a person who is interested in ideas, literature, art, etc: *The café was a well-known meeting place for artists and intellectuals.* —**intellectually** *adv*

☆ **intelligence** /ɪnˈtelɪdʒəns/ *noun* [U] **1** the ability to understand, learn and think: *Examinations are not necessarily the best way to measure intelligence.* ○ *a person of normal intelligence* ○ *an intelligence test* **2** important information about an enemy country: *The British intelligence service is called MI5.*

intelligent /-dʒənt/ *adj* having or showing intelligence; clever: *All their children are very intelligent.* ○ *an intelligent question* ☞ The opposite is **unintelligent**. —**intelligently** *adv*

intelligible /ɪnˈtelɪdʒəbl/ *adj* (used especially about speech or writing) possible or easy to understand ☞ The opposite is **unintelligible**.

☆ **intend** /ɪnˈtend/ *verb* [T] **1** to plan or mean to do sth: *I'm afraid I spent more money than I had intended.* ○ *I intended to telephone but I completely forgot.* ○ *They had intended staying in Wales for two weeks but the weather was so bad that they left after one.* ○ *I certainly don't intend to wait here all day!* ☞ The noun is **intention**. **2 intend sth for sb/sth; intend sb to do sth** to plan, mean or make sth for a particular person or purpose: *You shouldn't have read that letter – it wasn't intended for you.* ○ *This dictionary is intended for intermediate learners of English.* ○ *I didn't intend you to have all the work.*

☆ **intense** /ɪnˈtens/ *adj* very great, strong or serious: *intense heat* ○ *intense anger* ○ *an intense* (= very serious) *young man* —**intensely** *adv*: *They obviously dislike each other intensely.*

intensify /-sɪfaɪ/ *verb* (*pres part* **intensifying**; *3rd pers sing pres* **intensifies**; *pt, pp* **intensified**) [I,T] to become or to make sth greater or stronger: *The government has intensified its anti-smoking campaign.* —**intensity** /-səti/ *noun* [U]: *I wasn't prepared for the intensity of his reaction to the news.*

intensive /ɪnˈtensɪv/ *adj* concentrated on a particular activity or area within a limited amount of time: *an intensive investigation* ○ *The course only lasted a week but it was very intensive.* —**intensively** *adv*

in,tensive ˈcare *noun* [U] special care for patients who are very seriously ill or injured (or the department that gives this care): *I'm afraid your son's been seriously hurt and he's in intensive care.*

intent /ɪnˈtent/ *adj* **1** showing great attention: *He listened to the whole story with an intent expression on his face.* **2 intent on/upon sth/doing sth** determined to do sth or concentrating on sth: *He's always been intent on making a lot of money.* ○ *She was so intent upon her work that she didn't hear me come in.* —**intently** *adv*

☆ **intention** /ɪnˈtenʃn/ *noun* [C,U] what sb intends or means to do; a plan or purpose: *It's still not clear what his intentions are when he leaves university.* ○ *Our intention was to leave early in the morning.* ○ *I've got no intention of staying indoors on a nice sunny day like this.*

☆ **intentional** /ɪnˈtenʃənl/ *adj* done on purpose, not by chance: *I'm afraid what he told you was an intentional lie.* ○ *I'm sorry I took your jacket –*

ɜː	ə	eɪ	əʊ	aɪ	aʊ	ɔɪ	ɪə	eə	ʊə
fur	ago	pay	home	five	now	join	near	hair	pure

interact

it wasn't intentional! ☞ Look at **deliberate**. It is similar in meaning. —**intentionally** /-ʃənəli/ adv: *I can't believe the boys broke the window intentionally.*

interact /ˌɪntərˈækt/ verb [I] **1** (used about people) to communicate or mix in a way that has an influence or effect on sb else: *He is studying the way children interact with each other at different ages.* **2** (of two things) to have an effect on each other

interaction /-ˈækʃn/ noun [C,U] (an example of) co-operation or mixing: *An interaction of two chemicals produced the explosion.* ○ *There is a need for greater interaction among the different departments.*

interactive /-ˈæktɪv/ adj (technical) (used about computers) involving or allowing direct two-way communication between the computer and the person using it: *interactive computer games*

intercept /ˌɪntəˈsept/ verb [T] to stop or catch sb or sth that is moving from one place to another: *Detectives intercepted him at the airport.* —**interception** /ˌɪntəˈsepʃn/ noun [C,U]

interchangeable /ˌɪntəˈtʃeɪndʒəbl/ adj able to be used in place of each other without making any difference: *Are these two words interchangeable?* —**interchangeably** adv

intercom /ˈɪntəkɒm/ noun [C] a system of microphones and loudspeakers for communication between people in different parts of a factory, aeroplane, etc: *Please try to contact Mr. Pearson on/over the intercom.*

interconnect /ˌɪntəkəˈnekt/ verb [I] to be connected or linked —**interconnected** /-tɪd/ adj

intercontinental /ˌɪntəˌkɒntɪˈnentl/ adj between continents: *intercontinental flights*

intercourse /ˈɪntəkɔːs/ noun [U] = SEX(3)

interdependent /ˌɪntədɪˈpendənt/ adj depending on each other: *Exercise and good health are generally interdependent.* —**interdependence** /-əns/ noun [U]

☆ **interest¹** /ˈɪntrəst/ noun **1** [U,sing] **an interest (in sb/sth)** a desire to learn or hear more about sb/sth or to be involved with sb/sth: *She's begun to show a great interest in politics.* ○ *I wish he'd take more interest in his children.* ○ *Don't lose interest now!* **2** [C] something that you enjoy doing or learning about: *When applying for a job you often have to state your interests and hobbies.* **3** [U] the quality that makes sb curious or attracts sb's attention: *I thought this article might be of interest to you.* **4** [C] something that gives a benefit, profit or advantage to sb: *We have your interests at heart.* **5** [C] a legal right to share in a business, etc, especially in its profits: *When he retired he sold his interests in the company.* **6** [U] **interest (on sth)** the money that you earn from investments or that you pay for borrowing money: *If you invest your capital wisely it will earn a lot of interest.* ○ *We pay 10% interest on our mortgage at the moment.* ○ *The interest rate has never been so high/low.* ○ *Some companies offer interest-free loans.*

(IDIOMS) **in sb's interest(s)** to sb's advantage: *Using lead-free petrol is in the public interest.*

in the interest(s) of sth in order to achieve

or protect sth: *In the interest(s) of safety, please fasten your seat-belts.*

☆ **interest²** /ˈɪntrəst/ verb [T] **1** to make sb want to learn or hear more about sth or to become involved in sth: *The subject of the talk was one that interests me greatly.* **2** to make sb want to buy, have, do sth: *Can I interest you in our new brochure?*

interested /-tɪd/ adj **1** (not before a noun) **interested (in sth/sb)** wanting to know or hear about sth/sb; or to do or achieve sth: *They weren't interested in my news at all!* ○ *I was interested to hear that you've got a new job. Where is it?* ○ *Are young people nowadays more interested in success than they used to be?* (= in achieving success) ☞ The opposite is **uninterested**. **2** (only *before* a noun) involved in or affected by (a particular situation, etc): *I think they should have talked to the interested parties* (= people, groups, etc) *before they made that decision.* ☞ The opposite is **disinterested**.

interesting adj enjoyable and entertaining to do, think about, talk to, etc; holding your attention: *an interesting person, book, idea, job, etc* ○ *It's always interesting to hear about the customs and traditions of other societies.* ☞ The opposite is **uninteresting**. —**interestingly** adv

☆ **interfere** /ˌɪntəˈfɪə(r)/ verb [I] **1 interfere (in sth)** to try to take part in sb's affairs, etc when you and your help are not wanted: *You shouldn't interfere – let your children make their own decisions.* **2 interfere (with sb/sth)** to prevent sth or slow down the progress that sb/sth makes: *Every time the telephone rings it interferes with my work.* **3 interfere (with sth)** to touch or alter sth without permission: *Many people feel that scientists shouldn't interfere with nature.*

interference /ˌɪntəˈfɪərəns/ noun [U] **1 interference (in/with sth)** the act of interfering: *I left home because I couldn't stand my parents' interference in my affairs.* **2** noise that prevents the clear reception of radio, television or telephone signals (because of other signals or bad weather)

interfering adj involving yourself in other people's affairs when you are not wanted

interim /ˈɪntərɪm/ noun

(IDIOM) **in the interim** in the time between two things happening

interim adj (only *before* a noun) not final or lasting: *an interim arrangement* (= before sth definite can be decided)

☆ **interior** /ɪnˈtɪərɪə(r)/ noun **1** [C, usually sing] the inner part; inside: *I'd love to see the interior of the castle.* ○ *interior walls* (= ones that are in the inside of a building) ☞ The opposite is **exterior**. **2 the interior** [sing] the part of a country or continent that is not near the coast

interjection /ˌɪntəˈdʒekʃn/ noun [C] **1** (formal) something you say that interrupts sb else **2** (grammar) a word or phrase that is used as an expression of surprise, pain, pleasure, etc (eg *Oh!, Hurray!* or *Wow!*) ☞ Look at **exclamation**.

interlude /ˈɪntəluːd/ noun [C] a short period of time when an entertainment or activity stops

p	b	t	d	k	g	tʃ	dʒ	f	v	θ	ð
pen	bad	tea	did	cat	got	chin	June	fall	van	thin	then

for a break; an interval: *There will now be a 20-minute interlude.*

intermarry /ˌɪntəˈmærɪ/ *verb* (*pres part* **intermarrying**; *3rd pers sing pres* **intermarries**; *pt, pp* **intermarried**) [I] (used about people of different races, religions, etc) to marry each other

intermarriage /ˌɪntəˈmærɪdʒ/ *noun* [U] marriage between people of different races, religions, etc

intermediary /ˌɪntəˈmiːdɪərɪ; *US* -dɪerɪ/ *noun* [C] (*pl* **intermediaries**) a person who passes communications between two people or groups, usually in order to help them reach an agreement

☆**intermediate** /ˌɪntəˈmiːdɪət/ *adj* **1** coming between two people or things in position, level, etc **2** between two stages (elementary and advanced): *an intermediate student, class, course, book, level, etc*

interminable /ɪnˈtɜːmɪnəbl/ *adj* going on for a very long time or for too long —**interminably** /-əblɪ/ *adv*

intermission /ˌɪntəˈmɪʃn/ *noun* [C] (*especially US*) an interval in a film, play, etc

intermittent /ˌɪntəˈmɪtənt/ *adj* stopping for a while and then starting again: *There will be intermittent showers.* —**intermittently** *adv*

intern¹ /ɪnˈtɜːn/ *verb* [T] (*formal*) to keep sb in prison for political reasons, especially during a war —**internment** /ɪnˈtɜːnmənt/ *noun* [U]

intern² (*also* **interne**) /ˈɪntɜːn/ *noun* [C] (*US*) = HOUSEMAN

☆**internal** /ɪnˈtɜːnl/ *adj* **1** of or on the inside (of a place, person or object): *He was rushed to hospital with internal injuries.* **2** (used about political or economic affairs) inside a country; not abroad: *a country's internal affairs* **3** happening or existing inside a particular organization: *an internal examination* (= one arranged and marked inside a particular school or college) ☛ The opposite for all senses is **external**.

internally /-nəlɪ/ *adv* on the inside: *This medicine is not to be taken internally* (= not swallowed).

☆**international** /ˌɪntəˈnæʃnəl/ *adj* involving two or more countries: *an international agreement, flight, football match, etc* ○ *international trade, law, etc*

international *noun* [C] a sports match between teams from two different countries or a player in such a match —**internationally** /-nəlɪ/ *adv*

☆**interpret** /ɪnˈtɜːprɪt/ *verb* **1** [T] **interpret sth (as sth)** to explain or understand the meaning of sth: *I don't know how to interpret his behaviour.* ○ *How would you interpret this part of the poem?* **2** [I] to translate what sb is saying into another language: *He'll need somebody to interpret for him.*

interpretation /ɪnˌtɜːprɪˈteɪʃn/ *noun* [C,U] **1** an explanation or understanding of sth: *He's always putting a wrong interpretation on what I say* (= understanding it wrongly). ○ *What's your interpretation of these statistics?* **2** the way an actor or musician chooses to perform or understand a character or piece of music: *The actor's interpretation of Hamlet was severely criticized.*

interpreter *noun* [C] a person whose job is to translate what sb is saying immediately into another language: *The president spoke through an interpreter.* ☛ Look at **translator**.

interrelate /ˌɪntərɪˈleɪt/ *verb* [I,T] (usually passive) (*formal*) (used about two or more things) to connect or be connected very closely so that they have an effect on each other

interrelated *adj* connected with each other

interrogate /ɪnˈterəɡeɪt/ *verb* [T] **interrogate sb (about sth)** to ask sb questions in a thorough and sometimes aggressive way (in order to get information): *The prisoner was interrogated for six hours.*

interrogation /ɪnˌterəˈɡeɪʃn/ *noun* [C,U] the time when a person is interrogated: *The interrogations took place in a small underground room.* ○ *The prisoner was led away for interrogation.*

interrogator *noun* [C] a person who interrogates

interrogative /ˌɪntəˈrɒɡətɪv/ *adj* (*grammar*) having the form of a question: *We use 'any' in an interrogative or negative sentence.*

interrogative *noun* [C] (*grammar*) a word used for asking a question: *'Who', 'what' and 'where' are interrogatives.*

☆**interrupt** /ˌɪntəˈrʌpt/ *verb* **1** [I,T] **interrupt (sb/sth) (with sth)** to make sb stop speaking or doing sth by saying or doing sth yourself: *I'm sorry to interrupt but there's a phone call for you.* ○ *Stop interrupting me when I'm talking.* **2** [T] to stop sth or make a break in it: *The programme was interrupted by an important news flash.*

interruption /ˌɪntəˈrʌpʃn/ *noun* **1** [C] something that prevents an activity or situation continuing: *I've had so many interruptions this morning that I've done nothing!* **2** [U] the act of interrupting sb/sth: *I need one whole day without any interruption.*

intersect /ˌɪntəˈsekt/ *verb* **1** [I,T] (used about roads, lines, etc) to meet and go across each other **2** [T] (usually passive) to divide sth by going across it: *The fields were intersected by hedges and streams.*

intersection /ˌɪntəˈsekʃn/ *noun* [C] the place where two or more roads, lines, etc meet and cross each other: *a dangerous intersection*

intersperse /ˌɪntəˈspɜːs/ *verb* [T] (usually passive) to put things at various points in sth: *His speech was interspersed with jokes.*

☆**interval** /ˈɪntəvl/ *noun* [C] **1** a period of time between two events: *There was a long interval between sending the letter and getting a reply.* ○ *I hope we'll have a few sunny intervals between the showers!* **2** a short break between the parts of a play, film, concert, etc: *There will be two 15-minute intervals when the bar will be open.* ☛ Some words that have a similar meaning to interval are **intermission**, **break**, **recess** and **pause**. In British English we use **interval** for a break in a performance. The US word is **intermission**. A **break** is especially used in connection with periods of work or study eg **a lunch/tea-break** in an office, factory or

s	z	ʃ	ʒ	h	m	n	ŋ	l	r	j	w
so	zoo	she	vision	how	man	no	sing	leg	red	yes	wet

school: *The children play outside in the breaks at school.* ○ *You've worked so hard you've earned a break.* In US English a break at school is called **(a) recess**. In British English **recess** is a longer period of time when work or business stops, especially in Parliament or the lawcourts: *Parliament is in recess.* ○ *the summer recess* A **pause** is a short temporary stop in action or speech: *After a moment's pause, she answered.*
(IDIOM) **at intervals** with time or with spaces between: *I always write home at regular intervals.* ○ *The trees should be planted at two-metre intervals.*

intervene /ˌɪntəˈviːn/ *verb* [I] **1 intervene (in sth/between A and B)** to act in a way that prevents sth happening or influences the result of sth: *The police had to intervene between the two groups.* ○ *to intervene in a dispute* **2** to say sth that interrupts sb who is speaking: *'Wait a minute,' he intervened.* **3** (used about events, etc) to happen in the meantime or to delay sth: *If no further problems intervene we should be able to finish in time.* **4** (used about time) to come between: *During the months that intervened they wrote to each other nearly every day.*

intervening *adj* (only *before* a noun) coming or existing between (two events, dates, objects, etc): *the intervening years*

intervention /ˌɪntəˈvenʃn/ *noun* [C,U] an act of intervening, especially to prevent sth happening: *military intervention in the crisis*

☆ **interview** /ˈɪntəvjuː/ *noun* [C] **1** a meeting at which sb is asked questions to find out if he/she is suitable for a job: *Interviews will be held on June 10th.* ○ *You are invited to attend an interview for the position of assistant sales manager.* **2** a meeting at which a journalist asks sb questions in order to find out his/her opinion, etc (often shown on television or printed in a newspaper): *There was an interview with the Prime Minister on television last night.* ○ *an exclusive interview with a top television personality* ○ *The actress refused to give an interview.*

interview *verb* [T] **1 interview sb (for sth)** to ask sb questions in an interview (to find out if he/she is suitable for a job, etc): *How many applicants did you interview for the job?* **2 interview sb (about sth)** (used about a reporter, etc) to ask sb questions in an interview (to find out his/her opinions, etc)

interviewer /ˈɪntəvjuːə/ *noun* [C] a person who asks the questions in an interview

intestine /ɪnˈtestɪn/ *noun* [C, usually pl] the tube in your body that carries food from your stomach —**intestinal** /ɪnˈtestɪnl; ˌɪntesˈtaɪnl/ *adj*

intimate /ˈɪntɪmət/ *adj* **1** having a very close relationship: *They're intimate friends.* **2** private and personal: *They told each other their most intimate thoughts and secrets.* **3** (used about a place, atmosphere, etc) quiet and friendly: *I know an intimate little restaurant we could go to.* **4** very detailed: *He's lived here all his life and has an intimate knowledge of the area.*

intimacy /ˈɪntɪməsi/ *noun* [U] the state of being very close: *Their intimacy grew with the years.*

intimately *adv* in a close or personal way: *Do you know him intimately?*

intimidate /ɪnˈtɪmɪdeɪt/ *verb* [T] **intimidate sb (into sth/doing sth)** to frighten sb (often in order to make him/her do sth)

intimidating *adj* frightening (because of size or difficulty) —**intimidation** /ɪnˌtɪmɪˈdeɪʃn/ *noun* [U]: *The rebel troops controlled the area by intimidation.*

☆ **into** /ˈɪntə; *before vowels* ˈɪntu/ *prep* **1** moving to a position inside or in sth: *Come into the house.* ○ *I'm going into town.* **2** in the direction of sth: *Please speak into the microphone.* **3** to a point at which you hit sth: *I backed the car into a wall.* **4** (showing a change): *We're turning the spare room into a study.* ○ *She changed into her jeans.* ○ *The new rules will come into force next year.* **5** (used when you are dividing numbers): *4 into 10 won't go*
(IDIOM) **be into sth** to be very interested in sth (eg as a hobby): *I'm really into canoeing.*

intolerable /ɪnˈtɒlərəbl/ *adj* too bad or severe to stand or accept; not tolerable: *The living conditions were intolerable.* ○ *intolerable pain* ☞ The verb is **tolerate**. —**intolerably** /-əbli/ *adv*

intolerant /ɪnˈtɒlərənt/ *adj* **intolerant (of sb/sth)** not able to accept behaviour or opinions that are different from your own; not tolerant —**intolerance** /-əns/ *noun* [U] —**intolerantly** *adv*

intonation /ˌɪntəˈneɪʃn/ *noun* [C,U] the rise and fall of the level of your voice while you are speaking

intoxicated /ɪnˈtɒksɪkeɪtɪd/ *adj* (*formal*) **1** having had too much alcohol to drink; drunk **2** very excited: *She was intoxicated by her success.* —**intoxication** /ɪnˌtɒksɪˈkeɪʃn/ *noun* [U]

intransitive /ɪnˈtrænsətɪv/ *adj* (*grammar*) (used about a verb) used without an object ☞ Intransitive verbs are marked [I] in this dictionary. —**intransitively** *adv*

intrepid /ɪnˈtrepɪd/ *adj* (*formal*) (used about people and their actions) brave and without any fear

intricate /ˈɪntrɪkət/ *adj* having many small parts put together in a complicated way: *an intricate pattern* ○ *an intricate plot to the story*

intricacy /ˈɪntrɪkəsi/ *noun* **1 intricacies** [plural] the complicated details (of sth): *It's difficult to understand all the intricacies of the situation.* **2** [U] the quality of being intricate: *I was impressed by the intricacy of the design.* —**intricately** /-ətli/ *adv*

intrigue /ɪnˈtriːg/ *verb* [T] to make sb very interested or curious: *The idea intrigues me – tell me more!*

intrigue /ˈɪntriːg; ɪnˈtriːg/ *noun* [C,U] the making of a secret plan to do sth bad: *The book is about political intrigues against the government.*

intriguing *adj* very interesting; fascinating

intrinsic /ɪnˈtrɪnsɪk; -zɪk/ *adj* (only *before* a noun) (*formal*) (used about the value or quality of sth) belonging to sth as part of its nature;

iː	ɪ	e	æ	ɑː	ɒ	ɔː	ʊ	uː	ʌ
see	sit	ten	hat	arm	got	saw	put	too	cup

basic: *The object is of no intrinsic value* (= the material it is made of is not worth anything). —**intrinsically** /-klɪ/ *adv*

☆**introduce** /ˌɪntrə'djuːs; *US* -duːs/ *verb* [T] **1 introduce sb (to sb)** to tell two or more people who have not met before what each others' names are so that they can get to know each other: *'Who's that girl over there?' 'Come with me and I'll introduce you to her.'* **2 introduce yourself (to sb)** to tell sb what your name is so that you can get to know him/her: *He just walked over and introduced himself to me!* **3** to tell an audience the name of the person, who is going to speak, perform, entertain, etc: *May I introduce my guest on the show tonight...* **4** to announce and give details of a radio or television programme: *The programme was introduced by Charles Gordon.* **5 introduce sth (in/into sth)** to bring in, use, or take sth to a place for the first time: *The new law was introduced in 1991.* **6 introduce sb to sth** to make sb begin to learn about sth or do sth for the first time: *This pamphlet will introduce you to the basic aims of our society.*

☞ In Britain, when we introduce one person to another, there are a number of different ways of doing so, depending on the occasion (*informal*): *'John, meet Mary.'* o (*informal*) *'Mrs Smith, this is my daughter, Jane.'* o (*formal*) *'May I introduce you. Sir Godfrey, this is Mr Jones. Mr Jones, Sir Godfrey.'* An informal response to an introduction is *'Hello'* or *'Nice to meet you.'* A formal response is *'How do you do?'* The other person also replies: *'How do you do?'* When people are introduced they often shake hands.

☆**introduction** /ˌɪntrə'dʌkʃn/ *noun* **1** [U] bringing in or using of sth for the first time: *the introduction of computers into the classroom* **2** [sing] **introduction to sth** first experience of sth: *My first job – in a factory – was not a pleasant introduction to work.* **3** [C] the first part of a book or a talk which gives an explanation of the rest of it **4** [C] a book for people who are beginning to study a subject: *'An Introduction to English Grammar'* **5** [C] the act of telling two or more people each others' names for the first time: *I think I'll get my husband to make the introductions – he's better at remembering names!* o *Well, you don't need an introduction to each other, do you?* (= you already know each other)

introductory /ˌɪntrə'dʌktəri/ *adj* happening or said at the beginning in order to give a general idea of what will follow: *an introductory speech, chapter, remark,* etc

introvert /'ɪntrəvɜːt/ *noun* [C] a quiet, shy person who is concerned with his/her own thoughts or feelings ☞ The opposite is **extrovert**.

introverted /-tɪd/ *adj* quiet and shy

intrude /ɪn'truːd/ *verb* [I] **intrude on/upon sb/sth** to enter a place or situation without permission or when you are not wanted: *I'm sorry to intrude on your Sunday lunch but...* o *You're intruding – this is a private party.*

intruder *noun* [C] a person who enters a place without permission and often secretly

intrusion /ɪn'truːʒn/ *noun* [C,U] **intrusion (on/upon/into sth)** something that disturbs you or your life when you want to be private —**intrusive** /ɪn'truːsɪv/ *adj*

intuition /ˌɪntju'ɪʃn; *US* -tuː-/ *noun* [C,U] the feeling or understanding that makes you believe or know sth without any reason or proof: *She knew, by intuition, about his illness although he never mentioned it.* —**intuitive** /ɪn'tjuːɪtɪv; *US* -tuː-/ *adj* —**intuitively** *adv*

Inuit (*also* **Innuit**) /'ɪnuːɪt, -njuː-/ *noun* [C] = ESKIMO

inundate /'ɪnʌndeɪt/ *verb* [T] (usually passive) **1 inundate sb (with sth)** to send sb so many things that he/she can hardly deal with them all: *We were inundated with applications for the job.* **2** (*formal*) to cover with water; to flood: *After the heavy rains the fields were inundated.*

☆**invade** /ɪn'veɪd/ *verb* **1** [I,T] to enter a country with an army in order to attack, conquer it, etc: *They invaded the country with tanks and guns.* **2** [T] (usually passive) to enter in large numbers: *The town is invaded with tourists every summer.* **3** [T] to come in and disturb: *Everywhere you go new motorways invade the countryside.*

invader *noun* [C, usually pl] a person or thing that invades: *They forced back the invaders.* ☞ Look at **invasion**.

invalid[1] /'ɪnvəlɪd; 'ɪnvəliːd/ *noun* [C] a person who has been very ill for a long time and needs to be looked after by sb else: *He's been an invalid since the accident.*

invalid[2] /ɪn'vælɪd/ *adj* **1** not correct according to reason; not valid: *an invalid argument* **2** not able to be accepted by law; not valid: *I'm afraid your passport is invalid.*

invaluable /ɪn'væljuəbl/ *adj* very useful or valuable: *The mobile library is an invaluable service to many people.* ☞ Be careful. Invaluable is not the opposite of valuable. The opposite is **valueless** or **worthless**.

invariable /ɪn'veəriəbl/ *adj* not changing

invariably /ɪn'veəriəbli/ *adv* almost always: *She invariably arrives late.*

☆**invasion** /ɪn'veɪʒn/ *noun* [C,U] a time when the armed forces of one country enter another country in order to attack it: *Germany's invasion of Poland in 1939* o (*figurative*) *Such questions are an invasion of privacy.* ☞ The verb is **invade**.

☆**invent** /ɪn'vent/ *verb* [T] **1** to think of or make sth for the first time: *Laszlo Biro invented the ball-point pen.* o *When was the camera invented?* **2** to make up a story, excuse, etc that is not true: *He had invented the whole story.*

inventive /ɪn'ventɪv/ *adj* having clever and original ideas

inventor *noun* [C] a person who invents(1) sth for the first time

☆**invention** /ɪn'venʃn/ *noun* **1** [C] a thing that has been made or designed by sb for the first time: *The microwave oven is a very useful invention.* **2** [U] the act or process of making or designing sth for the first time: *Books had to be*

ɜː	ə	eɪ	əʊ	aɪ	aʊ	ɔɪ	ɪə	eə	ʊə
fur	ago	pay	home	five	now	join	near	hair	pure

written by hand before the invention of printing. **3** [U] telling a story or giving an excuse that is not true: *lies and invention*

inventory /ˈɪnvəntrɪ; US -tɔːrɪ/ *noun* [C] (*pl* **inventories**) a detailed list, eg of all the furniture in a house

invert /ɪnˈvɜːt/ *verb* [T] (*formal*) to put sth in the opposite order or position to the way it should be or usually is

in‚verted ˈcommas *noun* [plural] (*Brit*) = QUOTATION MARKS: *to put sth in inverted commas*

☆ **invest** /ɪnˈvest/ *verb* **1** [I,T] to put money in a bank, or use it to buy property or shares in a business, etc in the hope that you will make a profit: *We've invested in the Channel Tunnel project.* ○ *I've invested all my money in the bank.* ○ (*figurative*): *You have to invest a lot of time if you really want to learn a language well.* **2** [I] (*informal*) to buy sth (usually sth quite expensive): *Perhaps we should invest in some new garden chairs for the summer.*

investment *noun* **1** [U] **investment (in sth)** the act of putting money in a bank, property, business, etc: *The industry needs new capital investment.* ○ *investment in local industry* **2** [C] **investment (in sth)** an amount of money that has been put in a business, etc: *We got a good return on our original investment of £10 000.* ○ *Those shares were a good long-term investment.* **3** (*informal*) [C] a thing that you have bought: *This coat has been a good investment – I've worn it for three years.*

investor *noun* [C] a person who invests(1) in sth

☆ **investigate** /ɪnˈvestɪɡeɪt/ *verb* [I,T] to try to find out all the facts about sth: *A murder was reported and the police were sent to investigate.* ○ *A group of experts are investigating the cause of the crash.* —**investigation** /ɪnˌvestɪˈɡeɪʃn/ *noun* [C,U] **investigation (into sth)**: *The airlines are going to carry out a thorough investigation into security procedures at airports.* ○ *The matter is still under investigation.*

investigative /ɪnˈvestɪɡətɪv; US -ɡeɪtɪv/ *adj* trying to find out all the facts about sb/sth: *investigative journalism*

investigator /ɪnˈvestɪɡeɪtə(r)/ *noun* [C] a person who investigates sth

invigilate /ɪnˈvɪdʒɪleɪt/ *verb* [I,T] (*Brit*) to watch the people taking an examination to make sure that nobody is cheating —**invigilator** /ɪnˈvɪdʒɪleɪtə(r)/ *noun* [C]

invigorate /ɪnˈvɪɡəreɪt/ *verb* [I,T] to make sb feel fresher, more energetic, etc —**invigorating** *adj*: *an invigorating early-morning swim*

invincible /ɪnˈvɪnsəbl/ *adj* too strong or powerful to be defeated or beaten

invisible /ɪnˈvɪzəbl/ *adj* not able to be seen: *bacteria that are invisible to the naked eye* ○ *Frodo put on the magic ring and became invisible.* ○ (*figurative*) *Britain's invisible exports include tourism and insurance.* —**invisibility** /ɪnˌvɪzəˈbɪlətɪ/ *noun* [U] —**invisibly** *adv*

☆ **invite** /ɪnˈvaɪt/ *verb* [T] **invite sb (to/for sth)** to ask sb to come to (a party, etc): *We invited all the family to the wedding.* ○ *Shall we invite Louise and Pete for a meal next Saturday?* ○ (*figurative*) *Don't invite thieves by leaving your windows open.*

(PHRASAL VERBS) **invite sb back 1** to ask sb to return with you to your home: *Shall we invite the others back for coffee after the meeting?* **2** to ask sb to come to your home after you have been a guest at his/her home

invite sb in to ask sb to come into your home
invite sb over/round (*informal*) to ask sb to come to your home: *I've invited Trevor and his family round for tea on Sunday.* ☞ Note that **ask** can be used instead of **invite** in all senses.

invitation /ˌɪnvɪˈteɪʃn/ *noun* **1** [U] the act of being invited: *Entry is by invitation only.* ○ *a letter of invitation* **2** [C] **an invitation to sb/sth (to sth/to do sth)** a written or spoken request to go somewhere or do sth: *He has been sent an invitation to the opening ceremony.*

☞ You may **accept** an invitation or **turn it down**. (**Decline** is more formal.)

inviting /ɪnˈvaɪtɪŋ/ *adj* attractive and pleasant: *The log fire and smell of cooking were very inviting.*

invoice /ˈɪnvɔɪs/ *noun* [C] an official paper that lists goods or services that you have received and says how much you must pay for them

involuntary /ɪnˈvɒləntrɪ; US -terɪ/ *adj* done without wanting or meaning to: *She gave an involuntary gasp of pain as the doctor inserted the needle.* —**involuntarily** /ɪnˈvɒləntrəlɪ; US ɪnˌvɒlənˈterəlɪ/ *adv*

☆ **involve** /ɪnˈvɒlv/ *verb* [T] **1** to make necessary: *The job involves a lot of travelling.* **2** **involve sb/sth in (doing) sth** to cause sb/sth to take part in or be concerned with sth: *More than 100 people were involved in the project.* ○ *Please don't involve me in your family arguments.*

involved *adj* **1** difficult to understand; complicated: *The book has a very involved plot.* **2** **involved (in sth)** taking part in sth because you are very interested in it: *I'm very involved in local politics.* **3** **involved (with sb)** to be emotionally or sexually connected with sb: *She is involved with an older man.* —**involvement** *noun* [C,U]

inward /ˈɪnwəd/ *adj* inside your mind, not shown to other people: *my inward feelings*
☞ The opposite is **outward**.

inward (*also* **inwards**) *adv* towards the inside or centre: *Stand in a circle facing inwards.*
☞ The opposite is **outwards**.

inwardly *adv* secretly or privately: *He was inwardly relieved that they could not come.*

iodine /ˈaɪədiːn; US -daɪn/ *noun* [U] a dark-coloured substance that is found in sea water and used in photography and to clean wounds

irate /aɪˈreɪt/ *adj* (*formal*) very angry —**irately** *adv*

iris /ˈaɪərɪs/ *noun* [C] the coloured part of the eye

☆ **Irish** /ˈaɪərɪʃ/ *adj* of Ireland, its people, language, culture, etc: *Irish folk-music* ○ *Irish whiskey* ○ *the Irish Republic* (= Eire)

Irish *noun* **1 the Irish** [plural] the Irish people **2** [U] the original language of Ireland: *Few people speak Irish nowadays.*

ˈIrishman /-mən/ **ˈIrishwoman** /wʊmən/

---

p	b	t	d	k	ɡ	tʃ	dʒ	f	v	θ	ð
pen	bad	tea	did	cat	got	chin	June	fall	van	thin	then

noun [C] (pl **Irishmen** /-mən/, **Irishwomen** /-wɪmɪn/) a man or woman who comes from Ireland

☆ **iron**[1] /ˈaɪən; US ˈaɪərn/ noun [U] (symbol **Fe**) a common hard grey metal. Iron is used for making steel and is found in small quantities in food and in blood: *an iron bar* ○ *wrought-iron railings* ○ *The roof of the hut was made of corrugated iron.* ○ *a pot made of cast iron* ○ *iron ore* ○ *(figurative) The general has an iron* (= very strong) *will.*

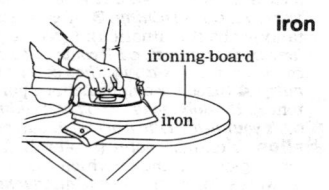

iron
ironing-board
iron

☆ **iron**[2] /ˈaɪən; US ˈaɪərn/ noun [C] an electrical instrument with a flat bottom that is heated and used to smooth clothes after you have washed and dried them: *Use a hot iron on cotton and a cool iron on polyester.* ○ *a steam iron*

iron verb [I,T] to use an iron to get the creases out of clothes: *Could you iron this dress for me?* ○ *That shirt needs ironing.* ☛ **Do the ironing** is often used instead of iron: *I usually do the ironing on Sunday.*

ironing noun [U] clothes, etc that need ironing or that have just been ironed: *a large pile of ironing*

ˈironing-board noun [C] a special table that is used for ironing clothes on

ironic /aɪˈrɒnɪk/ (also **ironical** /aɪˈrɒnɪkl/) adj **1** meaning the opposite of what you say: *'Oh, I'm so pleased,' she said in an ironic way.* ☛ Look at **sarcastic**. **2** (used about a situation) strange or amusing because it is unusual or unexpected: *It is ironic that the busiest people are often the most willing to help.* —**ironically** /-klɪ/ adv

irony /ˈaɪərəni/ noun (pl **ironies**) **1** [U] the way of speaking that shows you are joking or that you mean the opposite of what you say: *'The English are such good cooks,' he said with heavy irony.* **2** [C,U] the unusual or unexpected side of a situation, etc that seems strange or amusing: *The irony was that he was killed in a car accident soon after the end of the war.*

irradiate /ɪˈreɪdieɪt/ verb [T] to send rays of radioactivity through sth: *Irradiated food lasts longer, but some people think it is not safe.*

irrational /ɪˈræʃənl/ adj not based on reason or clear thought: *an irrational fear of spiders* —**irrationality** /ɪˌræʃəˈnæləti/ noun [U] **irrationally** /ɪˈræʃnəli/ adv

irreconcilable /ɪˈrekənsaɪləbl; ɪˌrekən-ˈsaɪləbl/ adj (formal) (used about people or their ideas and beliefs) so different that they cannot be made to agree —**irreconcilably** /-əbli/ adv

☆ **irregular** /ɪˈregjʊlə(r)/ adj **1** having parts or sides of different sizes or lengths; not even or regular: *an irregular shape* **2** happening at unequal intervals; not regular: *His visits became more and more irregular.* ○ *an irregular pulse* **3** not allowed according to the rules or social customs: *It is highly irregular for a doctor to give information about patients without their permission.* **4** not following the usual rules of grammar; not regular: *'Caught' is an irregular past tense form.* —**irregularity** /ɪˌregjʊˈlærəti/ noun [C,U] (pl **irregularities**) —**irregularly** adv

irrelevant /ɪˈreləvənt/ adj not connected with sth or important to it: *That's completely irrelevant to the subject under discussion.*

irrelevance /-əns/ noun [U] the state of being irrelevant

irrelevancy /-ənsi/ noun (pl **irrelevancies**) **1** [U] = IRRELEVANCE **2** [C] something that is irrelevant —**irrelevantly** adv

irreparable /ɪˈrepərəbl/ adj not able to be repaired or put right: *Irreparable damage has been done to the forests of Eastern Europe.* —**irreparably** adv

irreplaceable /ˌɪrɪˈpleɪsəbl/ adj (used about sth very valuable or special) not able to be replaced

irrepressible /ˌɪrɪˈpresəbl/ adj not able to be controlled; cheerful: *young people full of irrepressible good humour* —**irrepressibly** /-əbli/ adv

irresistible /ˌɪrɪˈzɪstəbl/ adj **1** very strong or powerful so that you cannot stop yourself doing or agreeing with sth: *Their arguments were irresistible – I had to agree.* ○ *an irresistible urge to laugh* **2** very attractive: *The swimming-pool is irresistible on a hot day like this.* ☛ The verb is **resist**. —**irresistibly** /-əbli/ adv

irrespective /ˌɪrɪˈspektɪv/ **irrespective of** prep not affected by: *Anybody can take part in the competition, irrespective of age.*

irresponsible /ˌɪrɪˈspɒnsəbl/ adj (used about a person of his/her actions) not thinking about the effect your actions will have; not responsible: *It is irresponsible to let small children go out alone when it's dark.* —**irresponsibility** /ˌɪrɪˌspɒnsəˈbɪləti/ noun [U] **irresponsibly** /-əbli/ adv

irreverent /ɪˈrevərənt/ adj not feeling or showing respect —**irreverence** /-əns/ noun [U] **irreverently** adv

irreversible /ˌɪrɪˈvɜːsəbl/ adj not able to be stopped or changed: *Once taken, the decision is irreversible.*

irrigate /ˈɪrɪgeɪt/ verb [T] to supply land and crops with water by means of pipes, channels, etc —**irrigation** /ˌɪrɪˈgeɪʃn/ noun [U]

irritable /ˈɪrɪtəbl/ adj easily made angry —**irritability** /ˌɪrɪtəˈbɪləti/ noun [U] —**irritably** /-əbli/ adv

irritate /ˈɪrɪteɪt/ verb [T] **1** to make sb angry; to annoy: *It really irritates me the way he keeps repeating himself.* **2** to cause a part of the body to be painful or sore: *Very bright sunlight can irritate your eyes.* —**irritation** /ˌɪrɪˈteɪʃn/ noun [C,U]

is ⇨ BE

☆ **Islam** /ɪzˈlɑːm; US ˈɪslɑːm/ noun [U] the religion of Muslim people. Islam teaches that there is only one God and that Muhammad is His Prophet. —**Islamic** /ɪzˈlæmɪk; US ɪsˈlɑːmɪk/ *adj*: *Islamic law*

☆ **island** /ˈaɪlənd/ *noun* [C] **1** a piece of land that is surrounded by water: *the tropical islands of the Caribbean* ○ *Robinson Crusoe spent many years living on a desert island.* **2** = TRAFFIC ISLAND

islander *noun* [C] a person who lives on a (small) island: *the Shetland Islanders*

isle /aɪl/ *noun* [C] an island: *the Isle of Wight* ○ *the British Isles* ☛ Isle is most commonly used in names.

isn't short for IS NOT: *It isn't far now.* ○ *This is enough, isn't it?*

isolate /ˈaɪsəleɪt/ *verb* [T] **isolate sb/sth (from sb/sth)** to put or keep sb/sth apart or separate from other people or things: *Some farms were isolated by the heavy snowfalls.* ○ *We need to isolate all the animals with the disease so that the others don't catch it*

isolated *adj* **1** not connected with others; separate: *Is this an isolated case or part of a general pattern?* **2** alone or apart from other people or things: *an isolated village deep in the countryside*

isolation /ˌaɪsəˈleɪʃn/ *noun* [U] away from other people or things; a feeling of being alone and lonely: *The millionaire lived in complete isolation from the outside world.*

(IDIOM) **in isolation (from sb/sth)** alone or separately: *Acting in isolation is not very effective. We must work together as a team.*

☆ **issue** /ˈɪʃuː; ˈɪsjuː/ *noun* **1** [C] a problem or subject for discussion: *I want to raise the issue of overtime pay at the meeting.* ○ *The government cannot avoid the issue of homelessness any longer.* **2** [C] one in a series of things that are published or produced: *Do you have last week's issue of this magazine?* ○ *There's usually a special issue of stamps for Christmas.* **3** [U] the act of publishing or giving sth to people: *the issue of blankets to the refugees*

(IDIOM) **make an issue (out) of sth** to give too much importance to a small problem: *OK, we disagree on this but let's not make an issue of it.*

issue *verb* **1** [T] to publish or give out sth for the public to use: *When was the new £5 note issued?* **2** [T] to give or supply sth to sb: *The new employees were issued with uniforms.* ○ *to issue a visa* **3** [I] (*formal*) to come or go out: *Strange sounds issued from the castle.*

☆ **it¹** /ɪt/ *pron* **1** (used as the subject or object of a verb, or after a preposition) an animal or thing mentioned earlier or that is being talked about now: *Look at that car. It's going much too fast.* ○ *The children went up to the dog and patted it.* ○ *This box is heavy. What's inside it?* ☛ It can also refer to a baby whose sex you do not know: *Is it a boy or a girl?* **2** (used for identifying a person): *It's your Mum on the phone.* ○ *'Who's that?' 'It's the postman.'* ○ *It's me!* ○ *It's him!*

(IDIOM) **that's it 1** (used for saying that you have had enough of a situation): *That's it. I'm leaving and I'm not coming back.* **2** that's right: *Just move it a little bit to the right – that's it, you've done it.*

its /ɪts/ *det* belonging to a thing, animal, etc:

The cat's had its dinner. ○ *The swimming club held its Annual General Meeting last night*

☆ **it²** /ɪt/ *pron* **1** (used in the position of the subject or object of a verb when the real subject or object is at the end of the sentence): *It's hard for them to talk about their problems.* ○ *I think it doesn't really matter what time we arrive.* **2** (used in the position of the subject of a verb when you are talking about time, the date, distance, the weather, etc): *It's nearly half past eight.* ○ *It's Tuesday today.* ○ *It's about 100 kilometres from London.* ○ *It was very cold at the weekend.* ○ *It's raining.* **3** (used when you are talking about a situation): *It gets very crowded here in the summer.* ○ *I'll come at 7 o'clock if it's convenient.* ○ *It's a pity they can't come to the party.* **4** (used for emphasizing a part of a sentence): *It's John who's good at cooking, not me.* ○ *It's your health I'm worried about, not the cost.*

italics /ɪˈtælɪks/ *noun* [U,plural] the type of writing or printing in which the letters slope forwards: *This sentence and all the example sentences in the dictionary are printed in italics.* —**italic** *adj*: *italic handwriting*

itch /ɪtʃ/ *noun* [C] the feeling on your skin that makes you want to rub or scratch it

itch *verb* [I] to have or cause an itch: *My nose is itching.* ○ *The spots itch terribly.*

itchy *adj* having or causing an itch —**itchiness** *noun* [U]

it'd /ˈɪtəd/ *short for* IT HAD, IT WOULD

☆ **item** /ˈaɪtəm/ *noun* [C] **1** one single thing on a list or in a collection: *Some items arrived too late to be included in the catalogue.* ○ *What is the first item on the agenda?* ○ *an item of clothing* **2** a single piece of news: *There was an interesting item about Spain in yesterday's news.*

itemize (*also* **itemise**) /ˈaɪtəmaɪz/ *verb* [T] to make a list of all the items(1) in sth: *an itemized bill*

itinerant /aɪˈtɪnərənt; ɪˈtɪnərənt/ *adj* (only *before* a noun) travelling from place to place: *an itinerant circus family*

itinerary /aɪˈtɪnərəri; ɪˈtɪnərəri; US* -reri/ *noun* [C] (*pl* **itineraries**) a plan of a journey, route, etc

it'll /ˈɪtl/ *short for* IT WILL

its ⇨ IT¹

it's /ɪts/ *short for* IT IS; IT HAS ☛ Be careful. **It's** is a short way of saying *it is* or *it has*. **Its** means 'belonging to it': *The bird has broken its wing.*

☆ **itself** /ɪtˈself/ *pron* **1** (used as the object of a verb or preposition when the animal or thing that does an action is also affected by it): *The cat was washing itself.* ○ *The company has got itself into financial difficulties.* **2** (used for emphasis): *The village itself is pretty but the surrounding countryside is rather dull.*

(IDIOM) **(all) by itself 1** without being controlled by a person; automatically: *The central heating comes on by itself before we get up.* **2** alone: *The house stood all by itself on the hillside.* ☛ Look at the note at **alone**.

I've /aɪv/ *short for* I HAVE

ivory /ˈaɪvəri/ *noun* [U] the hard white substance that an elephant's tusks are made of

ivy /ˈaɪvi/ *noun* [U] a climbing plant that has dark leaves with three or five points

iː	ɪ	e	æ	ɑː	ɒ	ɔː	ʊ	uː	ʌ
see	sit	ten	hat	arm	got	saw	put	too	cup

Jj

J, j /dʒeɪ/ noun [C] (pl **J's; j's**) the tenth letter of the English alphabet: *'Jam' begins with (a) 'J'*.

jab /dʒæb/ verb [I,T] **1 jab (at sb/sth) (with sth); jab sb/sth (with sth)** to push at sb/sth roughly, usually with sth sharp: *He kept jabbing at his potato with his fork.* o *She jabbed me in the ribs with her elbow.* **2 jab sth into sb/sth** to push sth roughly into sb/sth: *The robber jabbed a gun into my back and ordered me to move.*

jab noun [C] **1** a sudden rough push with sth sharp **2** (*informal*) a medical injection: *Have you had your typhoid jab yet?*

jack¹ /dʒæk/ noun [C] **1** a piece of equipment for lifting a car, etc off the ground, eg so that you can change its wheel **2** the card between the ten and the queen in a pack of cards: *the jack of hearts* ☛ Look at the note at **card**.

jack² /dʒæk/ verb
(PHRASAL VERBS) **jack sth in** (*slang*) to stop doing sth: *Jerry got fed up with his job and jacked it in.*
jack sth up to lift a car, etc using a jack

☆ **jacket** /'dʒækɪt/ noun [C] **1** a short coat with sleeves: *a tweed sports jacket* o *a formal dinner-jacket* ☛ Look at **life-jacket**. **2** a cover for a hot-water tank, etc that stops heat from being lost **3** (*US*) = SLEEVE(2)

jacket po'tato noun [C] a potato that is cooked in the oven in its skin

jackknife /'dʒæknaɪf/ noun [C] (pl **jackknives**) a large pocket-knife that folds in half when not in use

jackknife verb [I] (used about a lorry that is in two parts) to bend in the middle in an uncontrolled way

jackpot /'dʒækpɒt/ noun [C] the largest prize that you can win in a game

Jacuzzi /dʒə'ku:zi/ noun [C] (*trade mark*) a special bath with jets of water that make your body feel relaxed

jaded /'dʒeɪdɪd/ adj tired and overworked

jagged /'dʒægɪd/ adj rough and uneven with sharp points: *Be careful not to cut yourself, that metal has a jagged edge.* o *jagged rocks*

jaguar /'dʒægjuə(r)/ noun [C] a large spotted wild cat that comes from Central and South America

☆ **jail** /dʒeɪl/ noun [C,U] (a) prison: *She was sent to jail for ten years.*
jail verb [T] to put sb in prison: *She was jailed for ten years.*
jailer noun [C] a person whose job is to guard prisoners ☛ In British English **jail** and **jailer** can also be spelt **gaol** and **gaoler**.

☆ **jam¹** /dʒæm/ noun [U] a sweet substance that you spread on bread, made by boiling fruit and sugar together: *Let's have bread and jam for tea.* o *a jar of raspberry jam* o *a jam jar* (= a glass container for jam)

☛ Note that jam made from oranges or lemons is called **marmalade**.

jam² /dʒæm/ verb (**jamm**ing; **jamm**ed) **1** [T] **jam sb/sth in, under, between, etc sth** to push or force sb/sth into a place where there is not much room: *There were three of us jammed into a phone box.* o *She managed to jam everything into her suitcase.* **2** [I,T] **jam (sth) (up)** to fix sth or to be fixed in one position: *Something is jamming up the machine.* o *I can't open the door. The lock has jammed.* **3** [T] (usually passive) **jam sth (up)** to fill sth so that it is difficult to move: *All the roads were jammed with cars and people.* **4** [T] to send out signals in order to stop radio programmes, etc from being received or heard clearly
(PHRASAL VERB) **jam sth on** to push on a car's brakes, etc with force: *I jammed on the brakes as the child ran into the road.*

jam noun [C] **1** a lot of people or things that are crowded together making it difficult to move: *a traffic jam* **2** (*informal*) a difficult situation: *Oh dear. We're in a bit of a jam.*

jangle /'dʒæŋgl/ verb [I,T] to make a noise like metal striking against metal; to move sth so that it makes this noise: *The baby smiles if you jangle your keys.* —**jangle** noun [U]

janitor /'dʒænɪtə(r)/ noun [C] (*US*) = CARETAKER

☆ **January** /'dʒænjuəri; *US* -jueri/ noun [C,U] (pl **Januaries**) (abbr **Jan**) the first month of the year, coming before February: *We're going skiing in January.* o *We go skiing every year in January.* o *last/next January* o *the January before last* o *the January after next* o *Christine's birthday is (on) January 17* (we say 'January the seventeenth' or 'the seventeenth of January' or, in American English, 'January seventeenth'). o *The last two Januaries have been extremely cold.* o *January mornings can be very dark.*

☆ **jar¹** /dʒɑ:(r)/ noun [C] **1** a container with a lid, usually made of glass and used for keeping food, etc in: *a jam jar* o *a large storage jar for flour* o *I can't unscrew the lid of this jar.* ☛ picture at **container**. **2** the food that a jar contains: *a jar of honey*

jar² /dʒɑ:(r)/ verb (**jarr**ing; **jarr**ed) **1** [I] **jar (on sb/sth)** to have an unpleasant effect: *The dripping tap jarred on my nerves.* **2** [T] to hurt or damage sth as a result of a sharp knock: *He fell and jarred his back.*

jargon /'dʒɑ:gən/ noun [U] special or technical

ɜ:	ə	eɪ	əʊ	aɪ	aʊ	ɔɪ	ɪə	eə	ʊə
fur	ago	pay	home	five	now	join	near	hair	pure

jaundice /ˈdʒɔːndɪs/ noun [U] a disease that makes the skin and eyes yellow

javelin /ˈdʒævlɪn/ noun [C] a long pointed pole like a spear that is thrown in sports competitions

jaw /dʒɔː/ noun **1** [C] either of the bones in your face that contain the teeth: *the lower/upper jaw* ☞ picture on page A8. **2 jaws** [plural] the mouth (especially of an animal): *The lion was coming towards him with its jaws open.*

☆ **jazz** /dʒæz/ noun [U] a style of popular music with a strong rhythm, originally played by black Americans: *modern/traditional jazz* ○ *a jazz band*
jazz verb
(PHRASAL VERB) **jazz sth up** (*informal*) to make sth brighter, more interesting or lively

☆ **jealous** /ˈdʒeləs/ adj **1** feeling upset because you think that sb loves another person more than you: *Tim seems to be jealous whenever Sue speaks to another boy!* **2** feeling angry or sad because you want to be like sb else or because you want what sb else has: *He's always been jealous of his older brother.* ○ *I'm very jealous of your new car – how much did it cost?* —**jealously** adv —**jealousy** /ˈdʒeləsi/ noun [C,U] (*pl* **jealousies**)

☆ **jeans** /dʒiːnz/ noun [plural] trousers made of strong, usually blue, cotton cloth (**denim**): *These jeans are a bit too tight.* ○ *a pair of jeans*

Jeep /dʒiːp/ noun [C] (*trade mark*) a small, strong vehicle suitable for travelling over rough ground

jeer /dʒɪə(r)/ verb [I,T] **jeer (at sb/sth)** to laugh or shout rudely at sb/sth: *The spectators jeered the losing team.*
jeer noun [C] an unkind or rude remark or shout

jelly /ˈdʒeli/ noun (*pl* **jellies**) **1** [U,sing] a transparent soft solid substance that shakes when it is moved: *My legs felt like jelly before the exam* (= not steady because of fear, etc). **2** [C,U] a transparent, soft food made with gelatine that shakes when it is moved. Jelly usually has a fruit flavour and is eaten as a pudding. **3** [U] a type of jam made of fruit juice and sugar

jellyfish /ˈdʒelifɪʃ/ noun [C] (*pl* **jellyfish** or **jellyfishes**) a sea animal with a body that looks like colourless jelly. Jellyfish sometimes sting.

jeopardize (*also* **jeopardise**) /ˈdʒepədaɪz/ verb [T] to do sth that may damage sth or put it in a dangerous position

jeopardy /ˈdʒepədi/ noun
(IDIOM) **in jeopardy** in danger of losing, failing, being injured or damaged, etc

jerk /dʒɜːk/ noun [C] a sudden pull, push or other movement: *The car started with a jerk and we were off.*
jerk verb **1** [T] to pull sb/sth suddenly and quickly: *She jerked the door open.* **2** [I] to move with a jerk or a series of jerks: *The lorry jerked from one side to the other over the bumpy road.* —**jerky** adj —**jerkily** /-ɪli/ adv

jersey /ˈdʒɜːzi/ noun (*pl* **jerseys**) **1** [C] a piece of clothing made of knitted wool that you wear over a shirt or blouse ☞ Look at **jumper**, **pullover** and **sweater**. These words are more common than **jersey**. Look also at the note at **sweater**. **2** [U] a soft woollen material used for making clothes

Jesus /ˈdʒiːzəs/ = CHRIST

☆ **jet** /dʒet/ noun [C] **1** a fast modern aeroplane with a jet engine **2** a fast, thin stream of water, gas, etc coming out of a small hole

'jet engine noun [C] an engine that makes aeroplanes fly by pushing out a stream of hot air and gases at the back

'jet lag noun [U] the tired feeling that people often have after a long journey in an aeroplane to a place where the local time is different
'jet-lagged adj

the 'jet set noun [sing] the group of rich, successful and fashionable people (especially those who travel around the world a lot)

jet-black /ˌdʒet ˈblæk/ adj very dark black in colour

jetty /ˈdʒeti/ noun [C] (*pl* **jetties**) a stone wall or wooden platform built out into the sea or a river as a landing-place for boats

☆ **Jew** /dʒuː/ noun [C] a person whose family was originally from the ancient land of Israel or whose religion is Judaism —**Jewish** /ˈdʒuːɪʃ/ adj: *He's Jewish.* ○ *a Jewish synagogue*

☆ **jewel** /ˈdʒuːəl/ noun [C] a valuable stone (eg a diamond) or a necklace, ring, etc with such a stone in it

jeweller (*US* **jeweler**) noun [C] a person whose job is to buy, sell, make or repair jewellery and watches: *Take the watch to the jeweller's to see if he can mend it.*

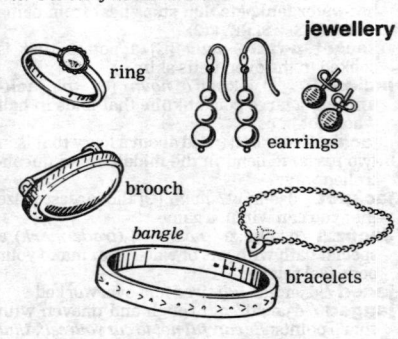

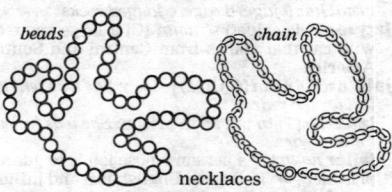

jewellery

- ring
- earrings
- brooch
- bangle
- bracelets
- beads
- chain
- necklaces

jewellery (*US* **jewelry**) /ˈdʒuːəlri/ noun [U] rings, necklaces, bracelets, etc that are

| p | b | t | d | k | g | tʃ | dʒ | f | v | θ | ð |
| pen | bad | tea | did | cat | got | chin | June | fall | van | thin | then |

jig /dʒɪg/ noun [C] a lively folk dance

jig verb [I] (**jigg**ing; **jigg**ed) **jig about/around** to move about in a way that shows that you are excited or impatient

jiggle /'dʒɪgl/ verb [T] (informal) to move sth quickly from side to side

jigsaw

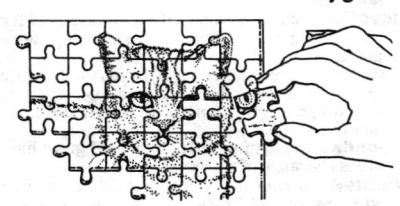

jigsaw /'dʒɪgsɔː/ (also **jigsaw puzzle**; **puzzle**) noun [C] a picture on cardboard or wood that is cut into small pieces. The pieces are then fitted together again as a game.

jingle /'dʒɪŋgl/ noun **1** [sing] a ringing sound like metal objects gently hitting each other: *the jingle of coins* **2** [C] a short simple tune or song, especially one that is used in an advertisement on television or radio

jingle verb **1** [I] to make a gentle ringing sound **2** [T] to move sth so that it makes a gentle ringing sound: *He jingled the coins in his pockets.*

jinx /dʒɪŋks/ noun [C, usually sing] bad luck; a person or thing that is thought to bring bad luck

jinx verb [T] (usually passive) (informal) to bring bad luck to (sb/sth)

jitters /'dʒɪtəz/ noun [plural] (informal) extremely nervous or anxious feelings: *Just thinking about the exam gives me the jitters!*

jittery /'dʒɪtəri/ adj (informal) nervous or anxious

☆ **job** /dʒɒb/ noun **1** [C] the work that you do regularly to earn money

☛ We **look for**, **apply for** or **find** a job. A job can be **well-paid/highly-paid** or **badly-paid/low-paid**. A job can be **full-time** or **part-time**, **permanent** or **temporary**. **Job sharing** is becoming popular with people who want to work part-time. Look at the note at **work**¹.

2 [C] a task or a piece of work that may be paid or unpaid: *I always have a lot of jobs to do in the house at weekends.* o *The garage has done a wonderful job on our car.* **3** [C, usually sing] a function or responsibility: *It's not his job to tell us what we can and can't do.*

(IDIOMS) **do the job/trick** (informal) to get the result that is wanted

a good job (informal) a good or lucky thing: *It's a good job you reminded me – I had completely forgotten!*

the job (informal) exactly what is needed: *This dress will be just the job for Helen's party.*

make a bad, good, etc job of sth to do sth badly, well, etc

make the best of a bad job ⇨ BEST³

out of a job without paid work ☛ A more formal word is **unemployed**.

jobless adj (used about large numbers of people) without paid work

the jobless noun [plural] the people who are without work —**joblessness** noun [U]

jockey /'dʒɒki/ noun [C] (pl **jockeys**) a person who rides in horse races, especially as a profession ☛ Look at **disc jockey**.

jodhpurs /'dʒɒdpəz/ noun [plural] special trousers that you wear for riding a horse

jog /dʒɒg/ verb (**jogg**ing; **jogg**ed) **1** [I] to run slowly, especially as a form of exercise ☛ We often say **go jogging** rather than jog: *I go jogging most evenings.* **2** [T] to push or knock sb/sth slightly: *He jogged my arm and I spilled the milk.*

(IDIOM) **jog sb's memory** to make sb remember sth: *I've got a photograph that will jog your memory.*

jog noun [sing] **1** a slow run as a form of exercise: *She goes for a jog before breakfast.* **2** a slight push or knock

jogger /'dʒɒgə(r)/ noun [C] a person who goes jogging for exercise

☆ **join** /dʒɔɪn/ verb **1** [I,T] **join (up) (with sb/sth)** to meet or unite (with sb/sth): *Do the two rivers join (up) at any point?* o *Where does this road join the motorway?* o *Would you like to join us for a drink?* **2** [T] to become a member of a club or organization: *James is going to join the army when he leaves school.* **3** [T] to take your place in sth or to take part in sth: *We'd better go and join the queue if we want to see the film.* **4** [T] **join A onto/to B**; **join A and B (together/up)** to fasten or connect one thing to another: *The Channel Tunnel will join Britain to Europe by road.* o *The two pieces of wood had been carefully joined together.* o *We've knocked down the wall and joined the two rooms into one.* **5** [I,T] **join (with) sb in doing sth/to do sth**; **join together in doing sth/to do sth** to take part with sb (in doing sth for sb else): *I know that everybody here joins me in wishing you the best of luck in your new job.* o *The whole school joined together to buy a present for the teacher who was leaving.*

(PHRASAL VERBS) **join in (sth/doing sth)** to take part in an activity: *Steve wouldn't join in when everybody else was playing football.*

join up to become a member of the army, navy or air force

join noun [C] a place where two things are fixed or joined together

☆ **joint**¹ /dʒɔɪnt/ noun [C] **1** a part of the body where two bones fit together and are able to bend **2** the place where two or more things are fastened or connected **3** a large piece of meat that you cook in the oven: *a joint of lamb*

☆ **joint**² /dʒɔɪnt/ adj (only before a noun) shared or owned by two or more people: *Have you and your husband got a joint account?* (= at a bank) o *a joint decision* o *The joint winners of the competition will each receive £500.* —**jointly** adv

☆ **joke** /dʒəʊk/ noun **1** [C] something said or done

to make you laugh, especially a funny story: *Have you heard the joke about the three men in a taxi?* o *a dirty joke* (= about sex) o *I'm sorry, I didn't get that joke. Can you explain it to me?* ☛ **A practical joke** is something you do, not just say. **2** [sing] a ridiculous person, thing or situation: *The salary he was offered was a joke!* (IDIOMS) **play a joke on sb** to trick sb in order to amuse yourself or other people
see the joke to understand what is funny about a joke or trick
take a joke to accept a trick or sth said about you in fun without getting angry
joke *verb* [I] to say things that are not meant to be serious: *I never joke about religion.*
(IDIOM) **you must be joking** (used to express great surprise) you cannot be serious

joker /'dʒəʊkə(r)/ *noun* [C] **1** a person who likes to make jokes or play tricks **2** an extra playing-card in a pack which can be used instead of any card in some games

jolly /'dʒɒli/ *adj* (**jollier; jolliest**) happy and cheerful
jolly *adv* (*Brit informal*) very: *It's a jolly good school.*
(IDIOM) **jolly well** (used for emphasizing what you are saying especially when you are angry) certainly: *I jolly well won't invite her again!*

jolt /dʒəʊlt/ *verb* **1** [T] to shake sth or make it move suddenly: *The crash jolted all the passengers forward.* **2** [I] to move in a jerky way: *The lorry jolted along the bumpy track.*
jolt *noun* [usually sing] **1** a sudden movement: *The train stopped with a jolt.* **2** a surprise or shock: *His sudden anger gave her quite a jolt.*

jostle /'dʒɒsl/ *verb* [I,T] to push against sb in a rough way (often in a crowd)

jot /dʒɒt/ *verb* (**jotting; jotted**)
(PHRASAL VERB) **jot sth down** to make a quick short note of sth: *Let me jot down your address.*

journal /'dʒɜːnl/ *noun* [C] **1** a magazine, especially one in which all the articles are about a particular subject: *a medical journal* **2** a written account of what you have done each day: *Have you read his journal of the years he spent in India?*

journalism /'dʒɜːnəlɪzəm/ *noun* [U] the profession of collecting, writing and publishing news in newspapers and magazines and on television and radio

☆**journalist** /'dʒɜːnəlɪst/ *noun* [C] a person whose job is to collect, write or publish news, in newspapers and magazines or on television and radio: *a job as a journalist on the local paper* ☛ Look at **reporter**.

☆**journey** /'dʒɜːni/ *noun* [C] (*pl* **journeys**) the act of travelling from one place to another: *Did you have a good journey?* o *a two-hour journey* o *a twenty-mile journey to work* o *We'll have to break the journey* (= stop for a rest). ☛ Look at the note at **travel**.

jovial /'dʒəʊviəl/ *adj* (used about a person) very cheerful and friendly

joy /dʒɔɪ/ *noun* **1** [U] a feeling of great happiness: *We'd like to wish you joy and success in your life together.* o *to dance, jump, shout, etc for joy* (= because you feel so happy) **2** [C] a person or thing that gives you great pleasure: *That class is a joy to teach.*

joyful /-fl/ *adj* very happy: *It was a joyful occasion.* —**joyfully** /-fəli/ *adv* —**joyfulness** *noun* [U]

joyless *adj* unhappy: *a joyless marriage*

joyride /'dʒɔɪraɪd/ *noun* [C] (*informal*) a drive or ride (usually in a stolen car) just for fun and excitement —**joyrider** *noun* [C] —**joyriding** *noun* [U]

joystick /'dʒɔɪstɪk/ *noun* [C] a handle used for controlling movement on a computer, aeroplane, etc

jubilant /'dʒuːbɪlənt/ *adj* (*formal*) extremely happy, especially because of a success: *The football fans were jubilant at their team's victory in the cup.*

jubilation /,dʒuːbɪ'leɪʃn/ *noun* [U] great happiness because of a success

jubilee /'dʒuːbɪliː/ *noun* [C] a day or period when people celebrate because it is a particular number of years after a special event: *It's the company's golden jubilee this year* (= it is fifty years since it was founded). ☛ There is also a **silver** jubilee (25 years) and a **diamond** jubilee (60 years). Look at **anniversary**.

Judaism /'dʒuːdeɪɪzəm; *US* -dɪɪzəm/ *noun* [U] the religion of the Jewish people

☆**judge¹** /dʒʌdʒ/ *noun* [C] **1** a person whose job is to apply the law and decide what punishment should be given to sb found guilty in a court of law: *The judge sentenced the man to three years in prison.* **2** a person who decides who has won a competition: *The judges included several well-known television personalities.* o *The judges' decision is final* (= it cannot be changed). **3** a person who has the ability or knowledge to give an opinion about sth: *You're a good judge of character – what do you think of him?*

☆**judge²** /dʒʌdʒ/ *verb* **1** [T] to decide the result or winner (in a competition): *The headmaster will judge the competition.* **2** [I,T] to form or give an opinion about sb/sth; to consider: *Judging from what he said, his work is going well.* o *Don't judge people by their appearance!* o *I would judge that this is not the right time to start a new business.* o *It's difficult to judge how long the project will take.* o *The party was judged a great success by everybody.* **3** [T] to be critical about sb; to decide whether he/she is good or bad: *Don't judge him too harshly – he's had a difficult time.* **4** [I,T] to act as a judge, in a court of law: *He said it was the hardest case he had ever had to judge.*

☆**judgement** (*also* **judgment**) /'dʒʌdʒmənt/ *noun* **1** [C] an opinion: *What, in your judgement, would be the best course of action?* **2** [C,U] an official decision made by a judge or a court of law: *The man collapsed when the judgment was read out in court.* **3** [U] the ability to form sensible opinions or to make wise decisions: *He always shows excellent judgement in his choice of staff.*

judicial /dʒuː'dɪʃl/ *adj* of a judge, a judgement or a court of law: *a judicial decision* o *judicial powers*

judicious /dʒuː'dɪʃəs/ *adj* (used about a de-

iː	ɪ	e	æ	ɑː	ɒ	ɔː	ʊ	uː	ʌ
see	sit	ten	hat	arm	got	saw	put	too	cup

judo /'dʒuːdəʊ/ noun [U] a sport from Asia in which two people try to throw each other to the ground. Judo is also a form of self-defence.

jug /dʒʌɡ/ (US **pitcher**) noun [C] a container with a handle used for holding or pouring liquids: *a milk jug* o *a jug of water* ☛ picture at **cup**.

juggle /'dʒʌɡl/ verb [I,T] **1 juggle (with sth)** to keep several objects in the air at the same time by throwing and catching them quickly: *He can dance, sing, juggle – whatever you like!* **2 juggle (with sth)** to keep changing the arrangement of sth in order to get a certain result: *I'll have to juggle my working days round so that I'm free on Mondays.*

juggler /'dʒʌɡlə(r)/ noun [C] a person who juggles to entertain people

☆ **juice** /dʒuːs/ noun [C,U] **1** the liquid that comes from fruit and vegetables: *lemon juice* o *I'll have an orange juice, please.* **2** the liquid that comes from a piece of meat when it is cooked **3** the liquid in the stomach or another part of the body that helps you to digest food

juicy /'dʒuːsi/ adj (**juicier; juiciest**) **1** containing a lot of juice: *juicy oranges* **2** (*informal*) interesting because it is connected with sth bad: *Tell me all the juicy details!*

jukebox /'dʒuːkbɒks/ noun [C] a machine in a café or bar, that plays records when a coin is put in

☆ **July** /dʒuː'laɪ/ noun [C,U] (pl **Julys**) (abbr **Jul**) the seventh month of the year, coming before August ☛ For examples of the use of the months in sentences, look at **January**.

jumble /'dʒʌmbl/ verb [T] (usually passive) **jumble sth (up)** to mix things up so that they are untidy or in the wrong place: *I must sort my clothes out – they're all jumbled up in the drawer.* o (*figurative*) *People from different stages of my life were all jumbled up together in my dream.*

jumble noun **1** [sing] an untidy group of things; a mess **2** [C] (*Brit*) a collection of old things for a jumble sale: *Have you got any jumble you don't want?*

'jumble sale (US **'rummage sale**) noun [C] a sale of old things that people do not want any more. Clubs, churches, schools and other organizations hold jumble sales to get money: *a jumble sale in the village hall in aid of the school*

jumbo /'dʒʌmbəʊ/ adj (*informal*) (only before a noun) very large

jumbo noun [C] (pl **jumbos**) (also ,**jumbo 'jet**) a very large jet aeroplane

☆ **jump¹** /dʒʌmp/ verb **1** [I] to move quickly off the ground by pushing yourself up with your legs and feet: *to jump into the air, over a stream, off the edge, onto a chair, etc* o *How high can you jump?* o *Jump up and down to keep warm.* ☛ picture at **bounce**. **2** [I] to move quickly and suddenly: *The telephone rang and she jumped up to answer it.* o *He jumped out of bed when he realized what time it was.* **3** [T] to get over sth by jumping: *The dog jumped the fence and ran off down the road.* **4** [I] to make a sudden movement because of surprise, fear or excitement: *'Oh, it's only you – you made me jump,' he said.* **5** [I] **jump (from sth) to sth**; **jump (by) (sth)** to increase suddenly by a very large amount: *His salary jumped from £15 000 to £25 000 last year.* o *Prices jumped (by) 50% in the summer.* **6** [I] **jump from sth to sth** to change suddenly from one subject to another: *The book kept jumping from the present to the past.*
(IDIOMS) **climb/jump on the bandwagon** ⇨ BANDWAGON

jump the queue to go to the front of a queue of people without waiting for your turn

jump to conclusions to decide that sth is true without thinking about it carefully enough

(PHRASAL VERB) **jump at sth** to accept an opportunity, offer, etc eagerly: *They asked me if I'd like to go on holiday with them and I jumped at it!*

☆ **jump²** /dʒʌmp/ noun [C] **1** an act of jumping: *With a huge jump the horse cleared the hedge.* ☛ Look at **high-jump** and **long-jump**. **2 a jump (in sth)** a sudden increase in amount, price or value **3** a thing to be jumped over: *The third jump consisted of a five-bar gate.*

jumpy adj (*informal*) nervous or anxious: *I always get a bit jumpy if I'm travelling by air.*

jumper /'dʒʌmpə(r)/ noun [C] **1** (*Brit*) a piece of clothing with sleeves, usually made of wool, that you wear on the top part of your body ☛ Look at the note at **sweater**. **2** a person or animal that jumps

junction /'dʒʌŋkʃn/ noun [C] a place where roads or railway lines meet or join: *Leave the motorway at junction 4 and follow the signs to Bath.*

☆ **June** /dʒuːn/ noun [C,U] (abbr **Jun**) the sixth month of the year, coming before July ☛ For examples of the use of the months in sentences, look at **January**.

jungle /'dʒʌŋɡl/ noun [C,U] a thick forest in a hot tropical country: *the jungles of Africa and South America*
☛ Look at the note at **forest**.

junior /'dʒuːniə(r)/ adj **1 junior (to sb)** having a low or lower position (than sb) in an organization, etc: *a junior officer* o *A lieutenant is junior to a captain in the army.* ☛ The opposite is **senior**. **2 Junior** (abbr **Jnr; Jr; Jun**) (*especially US*) (used after the name of a son who has the same first name as his father): *Sammy Davis, Junior* **3** (*Brit*) of or for children from the ages of about seven to eleven: *She's moving from the infant class to the junior class next term.*

junior noun **1** [C] a person who has a low position in an organization, etc **2** [sing] (with *his, her, your*, etc) a person who is younger than sb else by the number of years mentioned: *She's two years his junior/his junior by two years.*
☛ Look at **senior**. **3** [C] (*Brit*) a child who goes to junior school: *The juniors are having an outing to a museum today.*

'junior school noun [C] a school for children aged between seven and eleven

junk /dʒʌŋk/ noun [U] (*informal*) things that are old or useless or do not have much value:

There's an awful lot of junk up in the attic – we ought to clear it out.

'junk food noun [U] (informal) food that is not very good for you but that is ready to eat or easy to prepare: *junk food like crisps and sweets*

junta /'dʒʌntə; US 'hʊntə/ noun [C, with sing or pl verb] a group, especially of military officers, who rule a country by force

Jupiter /'dʒuːpɪtə(r)/ noun [sing] the planet that is fifth in order from the sun

jurisdiction /ˌdʒʊərɪs'dɪkʃn/ noun [U] legal power or authority; the area in which this power can be used: *That question is outside the jurisdiction of this council.*

juror /'dʒʊərə(r)/ noun [C] a member of a jury

☆ **jury** /'dʒʊəri/ noun [C, with sing or pl verb] (pl **juries**) **1** a group of twelve people in a court of law who listen to the facts about a crime and decide whether the accused person is guilty or not guilty: *Do/does the jury have to reach a unanimous decision?* ○ *The jury gave a verdict of not guilty.* **2** a group of people who decide who is the winner in a competition: *The jury is/are about to announce the winners.*

☆ **just¹** /dʒʌst/ adj fair and right; reasonable: *I don't think that was a very just decision.* ○ *a just punishment* ☛ The opposite is **unjust**.
justly adv fairly or correctly

☆ **just²** /dʒʌst/ adv **1** a very short time ago: *She's just been to the shops.* ○ *He'd just returned from France when I saw him.* **2 just (about to do sth); just (going to do sth)** at this/that moment; now or very soon: *We were just finishing supper when the telephone rang.* ○ *Wait a minute! I'm just coming.* ○ *I was just about to phone my mother when she arrived.* **3** exactly: *It's just eight o'clock.* ○ *That's just what I meant.* ○ *You're just as clever as he is.* **4** at exactly the same time (as); when: *Just as I was beginning to enjoy myself, John said it was time to go.* ○ *Just then the door opened.* **5** only: *She's just a child.* ○ *It's not just the money, it's the principle of the thing too.* ○ *It was worth it just to see her face as she opened the present.* ○ *Just a minute! I'm nearly ready.* **6** (often after *only*) almost not; hardly: *I could only just hear what she was saying.* **7** (often with the imperative) (used for getting attention or for emphasis): *Just let me speak for a moment, will you?* ○ *I just don't want to go to the party.* ○ *Just imagine how awful she must feel.* **8** really; absolutely: *The holiday was just wonderful.*

(IDIOMS) **all/just the same** ⇨ SAME²
it is just as well (that) it is a good thing: *It's just as well you remembered to bring your umbrella!* ☛ Look also at **(just) as well (to do sth)**at well.
just about almost; very nearly: *I've just about finished.*

just in case in order to be completely prepared or safe: *It might be hot in France – take your shorts just in case.*

just now at this exact moment or during this exact period: *I can't come with you just now – can you wait 20 minutes?* ○ *We haven't got very much money to spend just now.*

just so tidy and correct; exactly as it should be

☆ **justice** /'dʒʌstɪs/ noun **1** [U] fair behaviour or treatment: *a struggle for justice* **2** [U] the law and the way it is used: *a miscarriage of justice* (= a wrong legal decision) **3** [U] the quality of being fair or reasonable: *Everybody realized the justice of what he was saying.* **4** [C] (used as a title of a judge): *Mr Justice Smith* **5** [C] (*US*) a judge of a lawcourt

(IDIOMS) **do yourself justice** to do as well as you should do: *Because of his recent illness he wasn't able to do himself justice in the race.*

do justice to sb/sth; do sb/sth justice to treat sb/sth fairly or to show the real quality of sb/sth: *I don't like him, but to do him justice, he's a very clever man.* ○ *The photograph doesn't do you justice* (= make you look as nice as you are).

ˌJustice of the 'Peace (abbr **JP**) noun [C] a person who judges less serious cases in a lawcourt in Britain

☆ **justify** /'dʒʌstɪfaɪ/ verb [T] (pres part **justifying**; 3rd pers sing pres **justifies**; pt, pp **justified**) to give or be a good reason for sth: *Can you justify your decision?* ○ *Nothing can justify being unkind to children.*

justifiable /ˌdʒʌstɪ'faɪəbl; 'dʒʌstɪfaɪəbl/ adj possible to accept because there is a good reason for it: *His action was entirely justifiable.* ☛ The opposite is **unjustifiable**. —**justifiably** /-əbli/ adv: *She was justifiably angry and upset.*

justification /ˌdʒʌstɪfɪ'keɪʃn/ noun [C,U] **justification (for sth/doing sth)** (a) good reason

jut /dʒʌt/ verb (**jutting**; **jutted**)
(PHRASAL VERB) **jut out** to stand out from sth; to be out of line with the surroundings: *rocks that jut out into the sea*

juvenile /'dʒuːvənaɪl/ noun [C] (formal) a child or young person who is not yet adult
juvenile adj **1** (formal) of, for or involving young people who are not yet adults: *juvenile crime* **2** childish: *He's twenty but he has a rather juvenile manner.*

ˌjuvenile de'linquent noun [C] a young person who is guilty of committing a crime

juxtapose /ˌdʒʌkstə'pəʊz/ verb [T] (formal) to put two people, things, etc very close together, especially in order to show a contrast: *The artist achieves a special effect by juxtaposing light and dark.* —**juxtaposition** /ˌdʒʌkstəpə'zɪʃn/ noun [U]

p	b	t	d	k	g	tʃ	dʒ	f	v	θ	ð
pen	bad	tea	did	cat	got	chin	June	fall	van	thin	then

Kk

K, k /keɪ/ noun [C] (pl **K's**; **k's**) the eleventh letter of the English alphabet: *'Kate' begins with (a) 'K'*.

kaleidoscope /kəˈlaɪdəskəʊp/ noun [C] a toy that consists of a tube containing mirrors and small pieces of coloured glass. When you look into one end of the tube and turn it, you see changing patterns of colours.

kangaroo

pouch

kangaroo /ˌkæŋɡəˈruː/ noun [C] (pl **kangaroos**) an Australian animal that moves by jumping on its strong back legs and that carries its young in a pocket of skin (**a pouch**) on its stomach

karat (*US*) = CARAT

karate /kəˈrɑːtɪ/ noun [U] a style of fighting originally from Japan in which the hands and feet are used as weapons

kart /kɑːt/ noun [C] = GO-KART

kayak /ˈkaɪæk/ noun [C] a small narrow boat for one person, like a canoe

kebab /kɪˈbæb/ noun [C] small pieces of meat, vegetable, etc that are cooked (and served) on a stick (**a skewer**)

keel /kiːl/ noun [C] the wooden or metal bar at the bottom of a boat
keel *verb*
(PHRASAL VERB) **keel over** to fall over sideways: *Several people keeled over in the heat.*

☆ **keen** /kiːn/ adj **1** very interested in sth; wanting to do sth: *They are both keen gardeners.* ○ *I failed the first time but I'm keen to try again.* ○ *She was keen that we should all be there.* **2** (used about one of the senses, a feeling, etc) good or strong: *Foxes have a keen sense of smell.*
(IDIOM) **keen on sb/sth** very interested in or having a strong desire for sb/sth: *He's very keen on jazz.* ○ *Tracey seems very keen on a boy at college.* ○ *I'm not very keen on the idea of going camping.* —**keenly** *adv* —**keenness** *noun* [U]

☆ **keep¹** /kiːp/ verb (pt, pp **kept** /kept/) **1** [I] to continue to be in a particular state or position: *You must keep warm.* ○ *That child can't keep still.* ○ *Remember to keep left when you're driving in Britain.* **2** [T] to make sb/sth remain in a particular state, place or condition: *Please keep this door closed.* ○ *He kept his hands in his pockets.* ○ *It's hard to keep the children amused when they can't go outside.* ○ *I'm sorry to keep you waiting.* **3** [T] to continue to have sth, permanently or for a period of time: *You can keep that book – I don't need it any more.* ○ *Can I keep the car until next week?* ○ *Does the village shop keep batteries?* (= do they have them in stock) **4** [T] to have sth in a particular place: *Where do you keep the matches?* **5** [T] **keep doing sth** to continue doing sth; to do sth again and again: *Keep going until you get to the church and then turn left.* ○ *She keeps asking me silly questions.* **6** [T] to delay sb/sth; to prevent sb from leaving: *Where's the doctor? What's keeping him?* **7** [T] to support sb financially: *You can't keep a family on the money I earn.* **8** [T] to own and manage a shop or a restaurant: *Her father keeps a pub in Devon.* **9** [T] to have and look after animals: *They keep ducks on their farm.* **10** [T] to do what you promised or arranged: *Can you keep a promise?* ○ *She didn't keep her appointment at the dentist's.* ○ *to keep a secret* (= not tell it to anyone) **11** [T] to write down sth that you want to remember: *Keep a record of how much you spend.* **12** [I] (used about food) to stay fresh: *Drink up all the milk – it won't keep in this weather.*
(IDIOM) **keep it up** to continue doing sth as well as you are doing it now: *You've made very good progress this year. Keep it up!*

☞ For other expressions using **keep**, look at the entries for the nouns and adjectives, eg **keep count** is at **count**.

(PHRASAL VERBS) **keep at it/sth** to continue to work on/at sth: *Keep at it – we should be finished soon.*

keep away from sb/sth not go near sb/sth: *Keep away from the town centre this weekend.*

keep sb/sth back to prevent sb/sth from moving forwards: *The police tried to keep the crowd back.*

keep sth back (from sb) to refuse to tell sb sth: *I know he's keeping something back; he knows much more than he says.*

keep sth down to make sth remain at a low level, to stop sth increasing: *Keep your voice down.* ○ *The government is trying to keep prices down.*

keep sb from sth/from doing sth to prevent sb from doing sth: *His injury kept him from playing in the game yesterday.*

keep sth from sb to refuse to tell sb sth

s	z	ʃ	ʒ	h	m	n	ŋ	l	r	j	w
so	zoo	she	vision	how	man	no	sing	leg	red	yes	wet

keep off sth not approach or go on sth: *Keep off the grass!*
keep sth off (sb/sth) to stop sth touching or going on sb/sth
keep on (doing sth) to continue doing sth; to do sth again and again: *He keeps on interrupting me.*
keep on (at sb) (about sb/sth) to continue talking to sb in an annoying or complaining way: *Stop keeping on at me about my homework!*
keep out (of sth) not enter sth: *The sign said 'Danger – Keep out!'*
keep to sth not leave sth: *Keep to the path!* o *He didn't keep to the subject* (= he started talking about sth else).
keep sth up 1 to prevent sth from falling down **2** to cause sth to remain at a high level: *We want to keep up standards of education.* **3** to continue doing sth: *How long can the baby keep up that crying?*
keep up (with sb) to move at the same speed as sb: *Can't you walk a bit slower? I can't keep up.*
keep up (with sth) to know about what is happening: *You have to read the latest magazines if you want to keep up.*

keep² /kiːp/ *noun* [U] food and other things that you need for life: *Gary lives at home and gives his mother £25 a week for his keep.* o *to earn your keep*
(IDIOM) **for keeps** (*informal*) for always: *Take it. It's yours for keeps.*

keeper /'kiːpə(r)/ *noun* [C] **1** a person who guards or looks after sth: *a zoo-keeper* **2** (*informal*) = GOALKEEPER

keeping /'kiːpɪŋ/ *noun*
(IDIOM) **in/out of keeping (with sth) 1** that does/does not look right with sth: *That modern table is out of keeping with the style of the room.* **2** correct or expected according to a rule, belief, etc: *The Council's decision is in keeping with government policy.*

keg /keg/ *noun* [C] a small barrel

kennel /'kenl/ *noun* [C] a small house for a dog

kept *pt, pp* of KEEP¹

kerb (*especially US* **curb**) /kɜːb/ *noun* [C] the line of stones that form the edge of the pavement where it joins the road: *They stood on the kerb waiting to cross the road.*

kerosene (*also* **kerosine**) /'kerəsiːn/ *noun* [U] (*US*) = PARAFFIN

ketchup /'ketʃəp/ *noun* [U] a sauce made from tomatoes that is eaten cold with hot or cold food

kettles

☆ **kettle** /'ketl/ *noun* [C] a metal pot with a lid, handle and spout that is used for boiling water: *Shall I put the kettle on for a cup of tea?* o *The kettle's boiling.*

☆ **key¹** /kiː/ *noun* [C] **1** a metal object that is used for locking or unlocking a door, etc: *Have you seen my car keys anywhere?* o *We need a spare key to the front door.* o *a bunch of keys* **2** a set of musical notes that is based on one particular note: *The concerto is in the key of A minor.* **3** one of the parts of a piano, typewriter, etc that you press with your fingers to make it work **4** a set of answers to exercises or problems: *The key to the crossword will appear in next week's issue.* **5** a list of the symbols and signs used in a map or book, showing what they mean **6** [usually sing] something that helps you achieve or understand sth: *A good education is the key to success.* o *This letter holds the key to the mystery.*

'keyhole *noun* [C] the hole in a lock where you put the key

'key-ring *noun* [C] a ring on which you keep keys

key

lock   key-ring

key² /kiː/ (*also* **keyboard**) *verb* [T] **key sth (in)** to put information into a computer or give it an instruction by typing on the keyboard: *to key in some data* o *First, key in your password.*

key³ /kiː/ *adj* (only *before* a noun) very important: *Tourism is a key industry in Spain.*

keyboard /'kiːbɔːd/ *noun* [C] **1** the set of keys¹(3) on a piano, computer, etc ☞ picture on page A13. **2** [usually pl] an electrical musical instrument like a small piano ☞ picture at **rock band**. —**keyboard** *verb* [T] = KEY²

khaki /'kɑːki/ *adj, noun* [U] (of) a dull brownish-yellow colour: *The khaki uniforms of the desert soldiers.*

kibbutz /kɪ'bʊts/ *noun* (*pl* **kibbutzim** /kɪbʊ'tsiːm/) a farm or village in Israel where many people live and work together, sharing the work and the money that is earned

☆ **kick¹** /kɪk/ *verb* **1** [T] to hit or move sb/sth with your foot: *She was knocked to the ground and kicked in the stomach.* o *He kicked the ball over the top of the net.* **2** [I] to move your foot or feet: *You must kick harder if you want to swim faster.* o *The protesters were dragged kicking and screaming into the police vans.*
(IDIOM) **make, kick up, etc a fuss** ⇒ FUSS
(PHRASAL VERBS) **kick off** to start a game of football
kick sb out (of sth) (*informal*) to force sb to leave a place: *to be kicked out of university*
'kick-off *noun* [C] the start of a game of football: *The kick-off is at 2.30.*

☆ **kick²** /kɪk/ *noun* [C] **1** an act of kicking: *She gave the door a kick and it closed.* o *After one of*

iː	ɪ	e	æ	ɑː	ɒ	ɔː	ʊ	uː	ʌ
see	sit	ten	hat	arm	got	saw	put	too	cup

our players was tripped up, our team got a free kick. **2** [C] (*informal*) a feeling of great pleasure, excitement, etc: *He gets a real kick out of rock-climbing.* o *Some young people drive very fast just for kicks.*

☆ **kid¹** /kɪd/ *noun* [C] **1** (*informal*) a child or young person: *How are your kids?* **2 kid brother/sister** (*informal*) (*especially US*) younger brother/sister **3** a young goat ☞ picture at **goat**.

'kiddy (*also* **kiddie**) *noun* [C] (*pl* **kiddies**) (*informal*) a child

kid² /kɪd/ *verb* [I,T] (**kidd**ing; **kidd**ed) (*informal*) to trick or deceive sb/yourself; to make a joke about sth: *I didn't mean it. I was only kidding.* o *People were always kidding him about his funny name.* o *Don't kid yourself Martin, she doesn't really love you.*

kidnap /'kɪdnæp/ *verb* [T] (**kidnapp**ing; kid**napp**ed; *US* **kidnap**ing; **kidnap**ed) to take sb away by force and demand money for his/her safe return: *The child was kidnapped and £50 000 was demanded for her release.* ☞ Look at **hijack**.

kidnapper *noun* [C] a person who kidnaps sb
—**kidnapping** *noun* [C,U]: *The kidnapping took place just outside his home.*

kidney /'kɪdni/ *noun* [C] (*pl* **kidneys**) one of the two parts of the body that separate waste liquid from the blood: *My mother has had a kidney transplant.*

☆ **kill** /kɪl/ *verb* **1** [I,T] to make sb/sth die: *Smoking kills.* o *She was killed instantly in the crash.* ☞ **Murder** means to kill a person on purpose: *This was no accident. The old lady was murdered.* **Assassinate** means to kill for political reasons: *President Kennedy was assassinated.* **Slaughter** and **massacre** mean to kill a large number of people: *Hundreds of people were massacred when the army opened fire on the crowd.* **Slaughter** is also used of killing an animal for food. **2** [T] (*informal*) to cause sb pain; hurt: *My feet are killing me.* **3** [T] to cause sth to end or fail: *The minister's opposition killed the idea stone dead.*

(IDIOMS) **have an hour, etc to kill** to have some time when you have nothing to do, usually when you are waiting for sb/sth

kill time to do sth uninteresting or unimportant to pass the time

kill two birds with one stone to do one thing which will achieve two results

kill *noun* [sing] **1** the act of killing (an animal): *Lions often make a kill in the evening.* **2** an animal or animals that have been killed: *The eagle took the kill back to its young.*

killer *noun* [C] a person, animal or thing that kills: *a killer disease* o *He's a dangerous killer who may strike again.*

☆ **killing** /'kɪlɪŋ/ *noun* [C] act of killing a person on purpose; a murder: *There have been a number of brutal killings in the area recently.*

☆ **kilo** /'ki:ləʊ/ (*also* **kilogram**; **kilogramme** /'kɪləgræm/) *noun* [C] (*pl* **kilos**) (*abbr* **kg**) a measure of weight; 1 000 grams

☆ **kilometre** (*US* **kilometer**) /'kɪləmi:tə(r)/, kɪ'lɒmɪtə(r)/ *noun* [C] (*abbr* **km**) a measure of length; 1 000 metres

kilt /kɪlt/ *noun* [C] a skirt with many folds (**pleats**) that is worn by men as part of the national dress of Scotland ☞ picture at **bagpipes**.

kin /kɪn/ *noun* [plural] members of your family; relatives ☞ Kin is now a formal or old-fashioned word and is rarely used. **Next of kin** however, is still common. It means your closest relative who should be told first if you are injured or killed.

☆ **kind¹** /kaɪnd/ *noun* [C] a group whose members all have the same qualities: *The concert attracted people of all kinds.* o *The concert attracted all kinds of people.* o *Many kinds of plant and animal are being lost every year.* ☞ *Kinds of* may be followed by a singular noun or a plural noun: *There are so many kinds of camera/cameras on the market that it's hard to know which is best.* Sometimes you may hear people say something like: *Those kind/sort of dogs are really dangerous* but this is still thought by many people not to be correct English.

(IDIOMS) **a kind of** (*informal*) (used for describing sth in a way that is not very clear): *I had a kind of feeling that something would go wrong.* o *There's a funny kind of smell in here.*

kind of (*informal*) rather; a little bit: *I'm kind of worried about the interview.*

of a kind 1 very much the same: *The friends were two of a kind – very similar in so many ways.* **2** of poor quality: *The village has a bus service of a kind – two buses a week!*

☆ **kind²** /kaɪnd/ *adj* friendly and thoughtful about what other people want or need: *Would you be kind enough to give Sue a lift to the station?* o *It was kind of you to offer, but I don't need any help.* o *A present! How kind of you.* o *to be kind to children and animals* ☞ The opposite is **unkind**.

kindly *adv* **1** in a kind way: *The nurse smiled kindly.* **2** (used for asking sb to do sth) please: *Would you kindly wait a moment?* o *Kindly leave me alone!*

kindness *noun* **1** [U] the quality of being kind: *Be grateful. It was done out of kindness.* **2** [C] a kind act: *How can I repay your many kindnesses?*

,kind-'hearted *adj* having a kind nature

kindergarten /'kɪndəgɑːtn/ *noun* [C] a school for very young children, aged from about 3 to 5 ☞ Look at **nursery school**.

☆ **kindly¹** /'kaɪndli/ *adj* (**kindlier**; **kindliest**) kind and friendly: *a kindly face* o *kindly advice*
—**kindliness** *noun* [U]

kindly² ⇒ KIND²

☆ **king** /kɪŋ/ *noun* [C] **1** (the title of) a man who rules a country. A king is usually the son or close relative of the previous ruler: *The new king was crowned in Westminster Abbey.* o *King Edward VII* o *The king was deposed by a group of generals* o (*figurative*) *The lion is the king of the jungle.* ☞ Look at **queen**. **2** one of the four playing-cards in a pack with a picture of a king: *the king of spades* ☞ Look at the note at **card**.

'king-size (*also* **'king-sized**) *adj* very large: *a king-size bed*

ɜː	ə	eɪ	əʊ	aɪ	aʊ	ɔɪ	ɪə	eə	ʊə
fur	ago	pay	home	five	now	join	near	hair	pure

kingdom /ˈkɪŋdəm/ noun [C] **1** a country that is ruled by a king or queen: *the United Kingdom* **2** one of the parts of the natural world: *the animal kingdom*

kink /kɪŋk/ noun [C] a turn or bend in sth that should be straight: *There's a kink in the hosepipe so the water won't come out.*

kiosk /ˈkiːɒsk/ noun [C] **1** a small hut where newspapers, sweets, cigarettes, etc are sold **2** (*Brit*) a public telephone box

kip /kɪp/ noun [sing,U] (*Brit slang*) sleep: *It's time to have a kip.*
kip verb [I] (**kipp**ing; **kipp**ed) (*Brit*) to sleep: *You could kip on the sofa if you like.*

kipper /ˈkɪpə(r)/ noun [C] a type of fish that has been cut open, salted and hung in smoke

kiss /kɪs/ verb [I,T] to touch sb with your lips as a greeting or to show love or affection: *They sat in the back row of the cinema, kissing and cuddling.* o *He kissed her tenderly on the cheek.* o *They kissed each other goodbye.*
kiss noun [C] a touch with the lips: *Give Daddy a goodnight kiss.* o *a kiss on the lips*

kit /kɪt/ noun **1** [U] the clothes and other things that are needed eg by a soldier: *He packed all his kit into a rucksack and set off around Europe.* **2** [C,U] equipment that you need for a particular sport, activity, situation, etc: *a first-aid kit* o *a tool kit* o *sports kit* **3** [C] a set of parts that you buy and put together in order to make sth: *a kit for a model aeroplane*
kit verb (**kit**ting; **kit**ted)
(PHRASAL VERB) **kit sb out/up (with sth)** to give sb all the necessary clothes, equipment, tools, etc for sth: *Before you go skiing you must get kitted out with all the proper clothing.*

kitchen /ˈkɪtʃɪn/ noun [C] a room where food is prepared and cooked: *We usually eat in the kitchen.* o *a kitchen cupboard*

kite /kaɪt/ noun [C] a toy which is a light framework covered with paper or cloth. Kites are flown in the wind on the end of a long piece of string: *Several people were flying kites on the hill.*

kitten /ˈkɪtn/ noun [C] a young cat ☛ picture at **cat**.

kitty /ˈkɪti/ noun [C] (*pl* **kitties**) a sum of money that is collected from a group of people and used for a particular purpose: *All the students in the flat put £5 a week into the kitty.*

kiwi /ˈkiːwiː/ noun [C] **1** a New Zealand bird with a long beak and short wings that cannot fly **2** (*also* **kiwi fruit**) a fruit with brown skin that is green inside with black seeds

knack /næk/ noun [sing] the ability to do sth (difficult): *Knitting isn't difficult once you've got the knack of it.*

knead /niːd/ verb [T] to press and squeeze sth with your hands: *To make bread you mix flour and water into a dough and knead it for ten minutes.*

knee /niː/ noun [C] **1** the place where your leg bends in the middle: *Angie fell and grazed her knee.* o *Come and sit on my knee.* ☛ picture on page A8. **2** the part of a pair of trousers, etc that covers the knee: *There's a hole in the knee of those jeans.*

kneecap noun [C] the bone that covers the front of the knee

knee-'deep adj deep enough to reach the knees: *The water was knee-deep in places.*

kneeling   crouching

kneel /niːl/ verb [I] (*pt, pp* **knelt** /nelt/ or **kneeled**) **kneel (down)** to go down on one or both knees; to be in this position: *Kneel down while I comb your hair.* o *to kneel in prayer.*

knew *pt* of **KNOW**

knickers /ˈnɪkəz/ noun [plural] (*Brit*) a woman's or girl's underpants ☛ Note that you talk about a *pair of knickers*: *There's a clean pair of knickers in your drawer.*

knife /naɪf/ noun [C] (*pl* **knives** /naɪvz/) a sharp flat piece of metal (**a blade**) with a handle. A knife is used for cutting things or as a weapon: *The carving-knife is rather blunt.* o *Be careful. That bread-knife is very sharp.* o *Don't use your fingers. Use a knife and fork.* o *a pocket-knife*
knife verb [T] to injure sb with a knife: *The young man had been knifed in the chest.*

knight /naɪt/ noun [C] **1** a man who has been given a rank of honour and who can use *Sir* in front of his name **2** a soldier who fought on horseback in the Middle Ages
knighthood /-hʊd/ noun [C,U] the title or rank of a knight: *He was given a knighthood in last year's Honours List.*

knit /nɪt/ verb [I,T] (**knit**ting; **knit**ted) to make sth (eg an article of clothing) with wool using long needles or a special machine: *Grandma loves knitting.* o *I'm knitting a sweater for my nephew.*
-knit (in compounds) closely joined together: *a closely-knit village community*
knitting noun [U] the act of knitting or sth that is being knitted: *She put down her knitting and yawned.* o *I usually do some knitting while I'm watching TV.* o *a knitting machine*
'knitting needle noun [C] = NEEDLE(2)
'knitwear noun [U] articles of clothing that have been knitted: *the knitwear department*

knob /nɒb/ noun [C] **1** a round handle on a door, etc **2** a round button on a machine that controls a part of it **3** a (small) round lump: *Grease the pan with a knob of butter.*

knock¹ /nɒk/ noun [C] **1** a sharp blow and the sound it makes: *a nasty knock on the head* o *I*

p	b	t	d	k	g	tʃ	dʒ	f	v	θ	ð
pen	bad	tea	did	cat	got	chin	June	fall	van	thin	then

thought I heard a knock at the door. ○ *(figurative)* *She has suffered some hard knocks in her life.*

☆ **knock²** /nɒk/ *verb* **1** [T] to hit sb/sth with a sharp blow: *He knocked the vase onto the floor.* ○ *Be careful not to knock your head when you get up.* ○ *to knock sb unconscious* **2** [I] to make a noise by hitting sth: *Someone is knocking at the door.* **3** [T] *(informal)* to say bad or unfavourable things about sb/sth: *That newspaper is always knocking the government.*

(PHRASAL VERBS) **knock about/around** *(informal)* to be in a place: *I'm sure last week's newspaper is knocking around here somewhere.* ○ *I spent a few months knocking around Europe before I went to University.*

knock sb down to cause sb to fall to the ground/floor: *The old lady was knocked down by a cyclist.*

knock sth down to destroy a building, etc: *The old houses are to be knocked down to make way for blocks of flats.*

knock off (sth) *(informal)* to stop doing work, etc: *What time do you knock off?*

knock sth off 1 *(informal)* to reduce a price by a certain amount: *He agreed to knock £10 off the price.* **2** *(slang)* to steal sth

knock sb out 1 to hit sb so that he/she becomes unconscious or cannot get up again for a while: *The punch on the nose knocked him out.* **2** (used about a drug, alcohol, etc) to cause sb to sleep: *Three glasses of vodka knocked her out.*

knock sb out (of sth) to beat a person or team in a competition so that they do not play any more games in it: *Belgium was knocked out of the European Cup by France.*

knock sb/sth over to cause sb/sth to fall over: *Be careful not to knock over the drinks.*

'**knockout** *noun* [C] **1** a blow that causes sb to become unconscious or to be unable to get up again for a while **2** a competition in which the winner of each game goes on to the next part but the loser plays no more games

knocker /'nɒkə(r)/ *noun* [C] a piece of metal on the outside of a door that you knock to attract the attention of the people inside

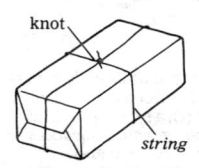

knot   bow
string   ribbon

knot¹ /nɒt/ *noun* [C] a place where two ends or pieces of rope, string, etc have been tied together firmly: *to tie/untie a knot* ○ *This knot is very tight – I can't undo it.*

knot *verb* [T] (knotting; knotted) to tie a knot in sth: *They knotted sheets together and climbed down them.*

knot² /nɒt/ *noun* [C] a measure of the speed of a ship or an aeroplane; 1 850 metres per hour

☆ **know** /nəʊ/ *verb* (*pt* **knew** /nju:; *US* nu:/; *pp* **known** /nəʊn/) (not in the continuous tenses) **1** [I,T] to have knowledge or information in your mind: *I don't know much about sport.* ○ *Do you know their telephone number?* ○ *'You've got a flat tyre.' 'I know.'* ○ *Did you know that Jonathan was a keen painter?* ○ *Do you know the whole poem by heart?* ○ *Knowing Barbara, she'll be out with her friends.* **2** [T] to have met or seen sb before: *We've known each other for years.* ☛ Notice the expression **get to know** sb: *Kevin's wife seems very interesting. I'd like to get to know her better.* **3** [T] to have seen, heard, etc sth: *I've known him go a whole day without eating.* ○ *It's been known to snow in June.* **4** [T] to be familiar with a place: *I don't know this part of London well.* **5** [T] (often passive) to give sth a particular name; to recognize sb/sth as sth: *Istanbul was previously known as Constantinople.* ○ *She's known as an excellent manager.* ○ *He knows a genuine antique when he sees one.* **6** [T] to speak or understand a language: *I don't know much Spanish.* **7** [T] to be able to do sth: *Do you know how to swim?* ☛ Be careful. You must use **how to**; you CANNOT say: *I know swim.* **8** [T] to have experience of sth: *They have known both wealth and poverty.* ○ *Many people in western countries don't know what it's like to be hungry.*

(IDIOMS) **God/goodness/Heaven knows 1** I don't know: *They've ordered a new car but goodness knows how they're going to pay for it.* **2** (used for emphasizing sth): *I hope I get an answer soon. Goodness knows, I've waited long enough.*

know better (than that/than to do sth) to have enough sense (not to do sth): *I thought you knew better than to go out in the rain with no coat on.*

know sb by sight to recognize sb without knowing him/her well

know sth inside out/like the back of your hand *(informal)* to be very familiar with: *I grew up here. I know these woods like the back of my hand.*

know what you are talking about *(informal)* to have knowledge of sth from your own experience

know what's what *(informal)* to have all the important information about sth

let sb know to tell sb; inform sb about sth: *Could you let me know when you've made up your mind?*

you know (used when the speaker is thinking of what to say next): *Well, you know, it's rather difficult to explain.*

(PHRASAL VERB) **know of sb/sth** to have information about or experience of sb/sth: *Do you know of any pubs around here that serve food?*

know *noun*

(IDIOM) **in the know** *(informal)* having information that other people do not: *People in the know say that the minister is going to resign.*

'**know-how** *noun* [U] *(informal)* knowledge of or skill in sth: *We are looking for someone with technical know-how in this field.*

s	z	ʃ	ʒ	h	m	n	ŋ	l	r	j	w
so	zoo	she	vision	how	man	no	sing	leg	red	yes	wet

knowing /'nəʊɪŋ/ adj showing that you know a lot about sth: *a knowing look*

knowingly adv **1** on purpose: *I've never knowingly lied to you.* **2** in a way that shows that you understand: *He smiled knowingly.*

☆ **knowledge** /'nɒlɪdʒ/ noun [U,sing] information or facts that you have in your mind about sth: *He has extensive knowledge of Ancient Egypt.* ○ *I have a working knowledge of French.* ○ *To my knowledge they are still living there.* ○ *She did it without my knowledge.*
(IDIOM) **be common/public knowledge** to be known by a lot of people

knowledgeable /-əbl/ adj having a lot of knowledge; well-informed: *She's very knowledgeable about history.* —**knowledgeably** /-əblɪ/ adv

knuckle /'nʌkl/ noun [C] the bones where the fingers join the rest of the hand ☞ picture on page A8.

koala /kəʊ'ɑːlə/ (also **koala bear**) noun [C] an Australian animal with thick grey fur that lives in trees and looks like a small bear

Koran /kə'rɑːn; US -'ræn/ noun [sing] **the Koran** the holy book of the Muslims

kosher /'kəʊʃə(r)/ adj (used about food) suitable to be eaten by religious Jews

Ll

L, l /el/ noun [C] (pl **L's; l's**) the twelfth letter of the English alphabet: *'Lake' begins with (an) 'L'.*

☆ **label** /'leɪbl/ noun [C] a piece of paper, etc on an object which gives information about it: *There is a list of all the ingredients on the label.* ○ (figurative) *She hated the label of 'housewife'.*

label verb [T] (labelling; labelled; *US* labeling; labeled) **1** to put a label or labels on sth: *All items of clothing should be clearly labelled with your name.* **2 label sb/sth (as) sth** to describe sb/sth as sth: *The press had labelled him an extremist.*

☆ **laboratory** /lə'bɒrətri; *US* 'læbrətɔːri/ noun [C] (pl **laboratories**) (also informal **lab**) a room or building that is used for scientific work or for teaching about science: *The blood samples were sent to the laboratory for analysis.* ○ *a physics laboratory* ☞ Look at **language laboratory**.

laborious /lə'bɔːriəs/ adj needing a lot of effort —**laboriously** adv

labour¹ (*US* **labor**) /'leɪbə(r)/ noun **1** [U] work, usually of a hard, physical kind: *manual labour* **2** [U] workers, when thought of as a group: *There is a shortage of skilled labour.* ○ *Most of the cotton plantations used slave labour.* ○ *Labour relations (= between workers and managers) have improved in recent years.* **3** [C,U] the process of giving birth: *She was in labour for ten hours.* ○ *She had a difficult labour.*

the 'Labour Party (also **Labour**) noun [sing, with sing or pl verb] one of the main political parties in Britain. The Labour Party supports the interests of working people: *Labour is/are in opposition.* ○ *The Labour Party lost the election in 1992.* ☞ Look at **Conservative Party** and **Liberal Democrats**.

'labour-saving adj reducing the amount of work needed to do sth: *labour-saving devices*

labour² (*US* **labor**) /'leɪbə(r)/ verb [I] **1** (formal) to work hard: *She laboured on her book for two years.* **2** to do sth with difficulty: *The old man laboured up the steep hill.*

laboured (*US* **labored**) adj done slowly or with difficulty: *laboured breathing*

labourer (*US* **laborer**) noun [C] a person whose job needs hard physical work: *Unskilled labourers are not usually well paid.* ○ *a farm labourer*

labyrinth /'læbərɪnθ/ noun [C] a complicated set of paths and passages, through which it is difficult to find your way: *a labyrinth of corridors* ☞ Look at **maze**.

lace

lace /leɪs/ noun **1** [U] cloth that is made of very fine threads in beautiful patterns: *lace curtains* ○ *a collar made of lace* **2** [C] a string that is used for tying a shoe, etc: *Do up your shoe-laces or you'll trip over them.* ☞ picture at **shoe**.

lace verb [I,T] **lace (sth) (up)** to fasten sth with a lace(2)

☆ **lack** /læk/ verb [T] to have too little or none of sth: *She seems to lack the will to succeed.*
(IDIOMS) **be lacking** to be needed: *Money is still lacking for the new hospital.*
be lacking in sth not have enough of sth: *He's certainly not lacking in intelligence.*

lack noun [U] an absence of sth that is needed: *A lack of food forced many people to leave their homes.*

iː	ɪ	e	æ	ɑː	ɒ	ɔː	ʊ	uː	ʌ
see	sit	ten	hat	arm	got	saw	put	too	cup

laconic /ləˈkɒnɪk/ *adj* (*formal*) using few words —**laconically** /-klɪ/ *adv*

lacquer /ˈlækə(r)/ *noun* [U] **1** a type of transparent paint that is put on wood, metal, etc in order to protect it and make it shiny **2** a liquid that is put on hair to keep the hairstyle in place

lacy /ˈleɪsɪ/ *adj* of or like lace

lad /læd/ *noun* [C] (*informal*) a boy or young man: *School has changed since I was a lad.*

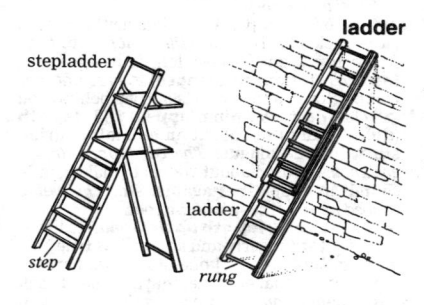

ladder

stepladder

ladder

step   rung

☆ **ladder** /ˈlædə(r)/ *noun* [C] **1** a piece of equipment that is used for climbing up sth. A ladder consists of two long pieces of metal, wood or rope with steps fixed between them: (*figurative*) *to climb the ladder of success* **2** (*US* **run**) a place in a stocking, etc where it has torn: *Oh no! I've got a ladder in my tights.*

laden /ˈleɪdn/ *adj* (not before a noun) having or carrying a lot of sth: *The travellers were laden down with luggage.* ○ (*figurative*) *to be laden with guilt*

Ladies /ˈleɪdɪz/ *noun* [sing] (*Brit*) a public toilet for women: *Is there a Ladies near here?* ☞ Look at **Gents** and at the note at **toilet**.

☆ **lady** /ˈleɪdɪ/ *noun* [C] (*pl* **ladies**) **1** a polite way of saying 'woman': *The old lady next door lives alone.* ○ *a lady doctor* ○ *The lady at reception told me to wait here.* **2** a woman who is polite and who behaves well to other people: *A real lady does not scream and shout.* ☞ Look at **gentleman**. **3** a woman who has a high social position: *The lords and ladies began arriving at the ball.* ☞ Look at **lord**. **4 Lady** a title that is used before the name of a woman who has a high social position: *Lady Randolph Churchill* ○ *Lady Phillipa Stewart* ☞ Look at **Lord**.
(IDIOM) **ladies and gentlemen** (used when you start making a speech to a large group of people)

ladylike *adj* having or showing suitable behaviour for a lady(2): *That's not a very ladylike way to sit.*

ladybird /ˈleɪdɪbɜːd/ (*US* **ladybug** /ˈleɪdɪbʌɡ/) *noun* [C] a small insect that is red or yellow with black spots

lag /læɡ/ *verb* [I] (**lagging**; **lagged**) **lag (behind) (sb/sth)** to go more slowly than sb/sth: *I'm always lagging behind when we go walking in the mountains.* ○ (*figurative*) *James has been ill and is lagging behind the others at school.*

lag (*also* **time-lag**) *noun* [C] a period of time between two events: *There will be a nine-month lag between the opening of the first part of the motorway and its completion.* ☞ Look at **jet lag**.

lager /ˈlɑːɡə(r)/ *noun* [C,U] (a glass or bottle of) a type of light beer: *Three pints of lager, please.*

lagoon /ləˈɡuːn/ *noun* [C] a salt-water lake

laid *pt, pp* of LAY¹

laid-back /ˌleɪd ˈbæk/ *adj* (*informal*) (used about a person) not worried; relaxed: *He's a really laid-back sort of person – he never gets worried about things going wrong.*

lain *pp* of LIE²

☆ **lake** /leɪk/ *noun* [C] a large area of water that is surrounded by land: *They've gone sailing on the lake.* ○ *Lake Constance* ○ *the Lake District* ☞ A **pond** is smaller than a lake.

☆ **lamb** /læm/ *noun* **1** [C] a young sheep ☞ Look at the note and picture at **sheep**. **2** [U] the flesh of a lamb when eaten as meat: *lamb chops* ☞ Look at the note at **meat**.

lame /leɪm/ *adj* **1** not able to walk properly because of an injury to the leg: *The horse is lame and cannot work.* ☞ **Lame** is not often used about a person. The verb and noun **limp** are more often used: *He's got a limp.* ○ *You're limping. Have you hurt your leg?* **2** (used about an excuse, argument, etc) not easily believed; weak

lament /ləˈment/ *verb* [I,T] (*formal*) to feel or express great sadness (about sth)

☆ **lamp** /læmp/ *noun* [C] a piece of equipment that uses electricity, gas or oil to produce light: *a street lamp* ○ *an oil lamp* ○ *a sunlamp* ○ *a table lamp* ☞ picture at **light**.

'lamppost *noun* [C] a tall pole in a public place with a street lamp on the top

'lampshade *noun* [C] a cover for a lamp that makes it look more attractive and makes the light softer ☞ picture at **light**.

☆ **land¹** /lænd/ *noun* **1** [U] the solid part of the surface of the earth (= not water): *After three months at sea she was glad to reach dry land.* ○ *Penguins can't move very fast on land.* ☞ Look at the note at **ground**. **2** [U] a piece of ground: *They have bought a plot of land and plan to build a house on it.* ○ *The moors are public land. You can walk where you like.* **3** [U] ground, soil or earth of a particular kind: *The land is rich and fertile.* ○ *barren land* **4** [C] (*formal*) a country: *She died far from her native land.* ☞ Look at the note at **country**.

'landslide *noun* [C] the sudden fall of earth, rocks, etc down the side of a mountain: (*figurative*) *a landslide* (= very great) *victory at the election*

☆ **land²** /lænd/ *verb* **1** [I,T] to go onto land or put sth onto land from a ship: *The troops landed on the beaches in Normandy.* ○ *The dockers refused to land the dangerous chemicals.* **2** [I,T] to come down from the air or bring sth down to the ground: *The bird landed on the roof.* ○ *He fell off the ladder and landed on his back.* ○ *The pilot landed the aeroplane safely.* ○ *He is due to land at 3 o'clock.* ☞ Look at **take off**. **3** [T] to get sth: *The company has just landed a big contract.*
(PHRASAL VERBS) **land up (in ...)** (*informal*) to

landing   356   **laser**

finish in a certain position or situation: *One of the balloons they released landed up in Spain.*

land sb with sb/sth (*informal*) to give sb a problem or sth difficult to do: *I've been landed with all the organization of the Youth Club disco.*

☆ **landing** /'lændɪŋ/ *noun* [C] **1** coming down onto the ground (in an aeroplane): *The plane made an emergency landing in a field.* o *a crash landing* o *a safe landing* ☛ Look at **take-off**. **2** the area at the top of a staircase or between one staircase and another

'landing-stage *noun* [C] a platform for people or things that are going onto or leaving a boat

landlady /'lændleɪdɪ/ *noun* [C] (*pl* **landladies**) **1** a woman who lets a house or room to people for money **2** a woman who owns or runs a pub, small hotel, etc

landlord /'lændlɔːd/ *noun* [C] **1** a person who lets a house or room to people for money **2** a person who owns or runs a pub, small hotel, etc

landmark /'lændmɑːk/ *noun* [C] **1** an object (often a building) that can be seen easily from a distance: *Big Ben is one of the landmarks on London's skyline.* **2** an important stage or change in the development of sth: *The Russian Revolution was a landmark in world history.*

☆ **landscape** /'lændskeɪp/ *noun* [C] **1** an area of country (when you are thinking about what it looks like): *Heather-covered hills dominate the Scottish landscape.* o *an urban landscape* ☛ Look at the note at **scenery**. **2** a picture that shows a view of the countryside: *one of Constable's landscapes*

☆ **lane** /leɪn/ *noun* [C] **1** a narrow road in the country: *We found a route through the lanes to avoid the traffic-jam on the main road.* **2** (often used in names) a narrow street between buildings: *Penny Lane* **3** a part of a wide road for one line of traffic: *You should look in your mirror and signal before you change lanes.* o *a four-lane motorway* o *Get into the inside lane. We leave the motorway soon.* **4** a route or path that is regularly used by ships or aeroplanes: *the busy shipping lanes of the English Channel* **5** a part of a sports track, swimming-pool, etc for one competitor in a race: *The British athlete is in lane two.*

☆ **language** /'læŋɡwɪdʒ/ *noun* **1** [U] the system of sounds and writing that human beings use to express their thoughts, ideas and feelings: *written language* o *the spoken language* o *the language development of young children* **2** [C,U] any system of signs, symbols, movements, etc that is used to express sth: *BASIC is a common computer language.* o *sign language* **3** [C] a form of language that is used by a particular group (usually in one country): *to learn to speak a foreign language* o *What is your first language?* o *Latin is a dead language.* **4** [U] words of a particular type or words that are used by a particular person or group: *bad* (= rude) *language* o *legal language* o *the language of Shakespeare*

'language laboratory *noun* [C] (*pl* **language laboratories**) a room that has special equipment, eg tape-recorders, to help you learn a foreign language

lanky /'læŋkɪ/ *adj* (used about a person) very tall and thin

lantern /'læntən/ *noun* [C] a type of light that can be carried. A lantern usually consists of a metal framework with glass sides and a lamp or candle inside.

lap¹ /læp/ *noun* [C] the flat area that is formed by the upper part of your legs when you are sitting down: *The child sat on his mother's lap and listened to the story.*

lap² /læp/ *noun* [C] **1** one journey around a race-track, etc: *There are three more laps to go in the race.* **2** one part of a long journey

lap *verb* [T] (**lapping; lapped**) to pass another competitor in a race who is one lap behind you

lap³ /læp/ *verb* (**lapping; lapped**) **1** [T] **lap sth (up)** (usually used about an animal) to drink sth using the tongue: *The cat lapped up the cream.* **2** [I] (used about water) to make gentle sounds as it splashes against sth: *The waves lapped against the side of the boat.*

(PHRASAL VERB) **lap sth up** (*informal*) to listen to or read sth eagerly and accept it as true

lapel /lə'pel/ *noun* [C] one of the two parts of the front of a coat or jacket that are folded back

lapse /læps/ *noun* [C] **1** a short time when you cannot remember sth or you are not thinking about what you are doing: *a lapse of memory* o *The crash was the result of a temporary lapse in concentration.* **2** a piece of bad behaviour that is unlike a person's usual behaviour **3** a period of time in which you do not do sth, go somewhere, etc: *She returned to work after a lapse of ten years bringing up her family.* ☛ Look at the verb **elapse**.

lapse *verb* [I] **1** to go into a particular state: *to lapse into silence, a coma, etc* **2** to be lost because it is not used, claimed or paid for: *My membership has lapsed because I forgot to renew it.*

larder /'lɑːdə(r)/ *noun* [C] a large cupboard or small room that is used for storing food.

☆ **large** /lɑːdʒ/ *adj* greater in size or amount than is usual: *Have you got this shirt in a large size?* o *Large amounts of money are spent on advertising.* o *There is a large increase in the numbers of young people going to college.* ☛ Look at the note at **big**.

(IDIOM) **by and large** mostly; in general: *By and large the school is very efficient.*

large *noun*

(IDIOM) **at large 1** (used about a criminal, animal, etc) free: *One of the escaped prisoners is still at large.* **2** as a whole; in general: *Society at large is becoming more concerned about the environment.*

largely *adv* mostly: *His success was largely due to hard work.*

'large-scale *adj* happening over a large area or affecting a lot of people

lark /lɑːk/ *noun* [C] a small brown bird that sings beautifully

laryngitis /ˌlærɪn'dʒaɪtɪs/ *noun* [U] a mild disease of the throat that makes it difficult to speak

laser /'leɪzə(r)/ *noun* [C] (a piece of equipment that produces) a very strong beam of light. Laser beams are used in weapons and medical

p	b	t	d	k	ɡ	tʃ	dʒ	f	v	θ	ð
pen	bad	tea	did	cat	got	chin	June	fall	van	thin	then

lash¹ /læʃ/ *noun* [C] **1** a blow that is given by a whip: *The prisoner was given twenty lashes.* **2** = EYELASH

lash² /læʃ/ *verb* **1** [I,T] to hit (as if) with a whip: *The rain lashed against the windows.* **2** [T] to move sth like a whip: *The tiger lashed its tail from side to side.* **3** [T] **lash A to B; lash A and B together** to tie two things together firmly with rope, etc: *The two boats were lashed together.*
(PHRASAL VERBS) **lash out (at/against sb/sth)** to suddenly attack sb/sth (with words or by hitting them): *When he came home drunk his wife lashed out at him.*
lash out (on sth) (*informal*) to spend a lot of money on sth: *We've decided to lash out on a foreign holiday next year.*

lass /læs/ (*also* **lassie** /'læsɪ/) *noun* [C] (*informal*) a girl or young woman ☞ Lass is most commonly used in Scotland and the North of England.

lasso /læ'su:; *US* 'læsəʊ/ *noun* [C] (*pl* **lassos** or **lassoes**) a long rope with a loop at one end that is used for catching cows and horses —**lasso** *verb* [T]

☆**last¹** /lɑ:st; *US* læst/ *det* **1** coming at the end; final: *December is the last month of the year.* ○ *Would the last person to leave please turn off the lights?* ○ *Our house is the last one in the row.* ○ *She lived alone for the last years of her life.* **2** (only *before* a noun) (used about a time, period, event, etc in the past that is nearest to the present): *I went shopping last Saturday.* ○ *We have been working on the book for the last six months.* ○ *The last time I saw her was in London.* ☞ **The latest** means 'most recent' or 'new'. **The last** means the one before the present one: *His last novel was a huge success, but the latest one is much less popular.* **3** (only *before* a noun) only remaining: *This is my last chance to take the exam.* ○ *Who's going to have the last cake?* **4** most unlikely; not suitable: *He's the last person to be trusted with money.* ○ *She's on a diet. Chocolates are the last thing she wants.*
(IDIOMS) **first/last/next but one, two, etc** ⇨ FIRST¹
first/last thing ⇨ THING
have, etc the last word 1 to make the final remark in a discussion or argument **2** to make the final decision about sth after a discussion
in the last resort; (as) a last resort when everything else has failed; the person or thing that helps when everything else has failed: *In the last resort we can always walk home.*
the last/final straw ⇨ STRAW
the last minute/moment the final minute/moment before sth happens: *We arrived at the last minute to catch the train.* ○ *a last-minute change of plan*
a week yesterday/last Monday, etc ⇨ WEEK

lastly *adv* finally; last of all: *Lastly, I would like to wish you all a Happy New Year.*

'last name *noun* [C] = SURNAME ☞ Look at the note at **name**.

☆**last²** /lɑ:st; *US* læst/ *adv* **1** at the end; after all the others: *The British athlete came in last.* ○ *Her name is last on the list.* **2** on the occasion in the past that is nearest to the present: *When did you last have your eyes checked?* ○ *When I saw her last she seemed very happy.*
(IDIOM) **last but not least** (used before the final item in a list) just as important as all the other items: *And last but not least, I'd like to thank you all very much.*

☆**last³** /lɑ:st; *US* læst/ *verb* [I,T] **1** to continue for a period of time: *Do you think this weather will last till the weekend?* ○ *The exam lasts three hours.* **2** to remain in a good condition: *It's only a cheap radio but it'll probably last a year or so.* **3** (used about the quantity, condition, etc of sth) to be good enough or sufficient for what sb needs: *The coffee won't last till next week.* ○ *This old coat will have to last another winter.* ○ *I can't afford a new one.* ○ *I've only got ten pounds to last me till Saturday.*

lasting *adj* continuing for a long time: *The children's faces left a lasting impression on me.*

last⁴ /lɑ:st; *US* læst/ *noun* [C] (*pl* **last**) **1** a person or thing that is last: *Alex was the last to arrive.* **2 the last (of sb/sth)** the only remaining part of sth: *We finished the last of the bread at breakfast so we'd better get some more.*
(IDIOM) **at (long) last** in the end; finally: *After months of separation they were together at last.*

latch /lætʃ/ *noun* [C] **1** a small metal bar that is used for fastening a door or a gate. You have to lift the latch in order to open the door. **2** a type of lock for a door that must be opened from the outside with a key
(IDIOM) **on the latch** (used about a door) closed but not locked

latch *verb*
(PHRASAL VERB) **latch on (to sth)** (*informal*) to understand: *It took them a while to latch on to what she was talking about.*

☆**late** /leɪt/ *adj, adv* **1** after the usual or expected time: *She was ten minutes late for school.* ○ *The ambulance arrived too late to save him.* ○ *to be late with the rent* ○ *It's never too late to learn.* ○ *to stay up late* ○ *The buses are running late today.* **2** near the end of a period of time: *The late nineteenth century was a time of great change.* ○ *in the late morning* ○ *His mother's in her late fifties* (= between 55 and 60). ○ *They are going on holiday in late May.* ○ *We got back home late in the evening.* **3 latest** very recent or new: *the latest fashions* ○ *the latest news* ○ *the terrorists' latest attack on the town* ☞ Look at the note at **last¹**. **4** (only *before* a noun) no longer alive; dead: *his late wife*
(IDIOM) **at the latest** no later than: *I need your report on my desk by Friday at the latest.*
an early/a late night ⇨ NIGHT
later on at a later time: *Later on you'll probably wish that you'd worked harder at school.* ○ *Bye – I'll see you a bit later on.*
sooner or later ⇨ SOON

latish /'leɪtɪʃ/ *adj, adv* rather late

'latecomer *noun* [C] a person who arrives late

☆**lately** /'leɪtli/ *adv* in the period of time up till now; recently: *What have you been doing lately?* ○ *Hasn't the weather been dreadful lately?*

---

s	z	ʃ	ʒ	h	m	n	ŋ	l	r	j	w
so	zoo	she	vision	how	man	no	sing	leg	red	yes	wet

latest /ˈleɪtɪst/ noun [U] (informal) the most recent (fashion, news, etc): *Have you heard the latest?* (= news) o *This is the latest in a series of attacks by the IRA.* o *They have the very latest in new machinery.*

lather /ˈlɑːðə(r); US ˈlæð-/ noun [U] white bubbles that you get when you mix soap with water

Latin /ˈlætɪn; US ˈlætn/ noun [U] the language that was used in ancient Rome

Latin adj **1** of or in Latin: *Latin poetry* **2** of the countries or people that use languages that developed from Latin, such as French, Italian, Spanish or Portuguese

Latin A'merican noun [C], adj (a person who comes) from Latin America (the parts of Central and South America where Spanish or Portuguese is spoken): *Latin American music*

latitude /ˈlætɪtjuːd; US -tuːd/ noun [U] (abbr **lat**) the distance of a place north or south of the equator ☞ picture at **earth**. Latitude is measured in **degrees**. Look at **longitude**

☆ **latter** /ˈlætə(r)/ adj (formal) (only before a noun) nearer to the end of a period of time; later: *Interest rates should fall in the latter half of the year.*

latter noun [sing], pron the second of two people or things that are mentioned: *The options were History and Geography. I chose the latter.* ☞ The first of two people or things that are mentioned is **the former**.

latterly adv (formal) lately; recently: *She has taught at the universities of London and Bristol and latterly at Durham.*

☆ **laugh** /lɑːf; US læf/ verb [I] to make the sounds that show you are happy or amused: *His jokes always make me laugh.* o *to laugh out loud* o *We laughed till we cried.*

(PHRASAL VERB) **laugh at sb/sth 1** to show, by laughing, that you think sb/sth is funny: *The children laughed at the clown.* **2** to show that you think sb is ridiculous: *Don't laugh at him. He can't help the way he speaks.*

laugh noun [C] **1** the sound or act of laughing: *Her jokes got a lot of laughs.* o *We all had a good laugh at what he'd written.* **2** (informal) a person or thing that is amusing: *Let's invite Tony. He's a good laugh.*

(IDIOM) **for a laugh** as a joke: *The boys put a spider in her bed for a laugh.*

laughable /-əbl/ adj (used about sth that is of poor quality) deserving to be laughed at; foolish or ridiculous

laughing /ˈlɑːfɪŋ; US ˈlæfɪŋ/ adj showing amusement or happiness by laughter: *laughing faces*

(IDIOM) **burst out laughing** to suddenly start to laugh loudly

'laughing-stock noun [C] a person or thing that other people laugh at or make fun of (in an unpleasant way)

☆ **laughter** /ˈlɑːftə(r); US ˈlæf-/ noun [U] the sound or act of laughing: *Everyone roared with laughter.*

launch¹ /lɔːntʃ/ verb [T] **1** to send a ship into the water or a rocket, etc into the sky **2** to start sth new or to show sth for the first time: *The enemy launched an attack at midnight.* o *to launch a new product onto the market*

launch noun [C, usually sing] the act of launching a ship, rocket, new product, etc: *The shuttle launch has been delayed by 24 hours.*

launch² /lɔːntʃ/ noun [C] a large motor boat

launderette /ˌlɔːndəˈret/ (also **laundrette** /lɔːnˈdret/) (US **laundromat** /ˈlɔːndrəmæt/) noun [C] a type of shop where you pay to wash and dry your clothes in washing-machines

laundry /ˈlɔːndri/ noun (pl **laundries**) **1** [U] clothes, etc that need washing or that are being washed: *a laundry basket* ☞ **Do the washing** is more common in spoken English than 'do the laundry.' **2** [C] a business where you send sheets, clothes, etc to be washed

lava /ˈlɑːvə/ noun [U] hot liquid rock that comes out of a volcano

☆ **lavatory** /ˈlævətri; US -tɔːri/ noun [C] (pl **lavatories**) **1** a large bowl, joined to a pipe and a drain, used for getting rid of waste that people pass from the body. Another word for 'toilet'. **2** a room that contains a toilet, wash-basin, etc: *Where's the ladies' lavatory, please?* ☞ Look at the note at **toilet**.

lavender /ˈlævəndə(r)/ noun [U] a garden plant with purple flowers that smells very pleasant

lavish /ˈlævɪʃ/ adj **1** giving or spending generously or in large quantities: *She was always very lavish with her presents.* **2** large in amount or number: *a lavish meal*

lavish verb

(PHRASAL VERB) **lavish sth on sb/sth** to give sth generously or in large quantities to sb: *He lavished expensive gifts on her.*

☆ **law** /lɔː/ noun **1** [C] an official rule of a country, etc that says what a person, company, etc may or may not do: *Parliament has recently passed a law about wearing seat-belts in the back of cars.* **2 the law** [U] all the laws in a country, etc: *Stealing is against the law.* o *to break the law* o *to obey the law* ☞ Look at **legal**. **3** [U] the law(2) as a subject of study or as a profession: *She is studying law.* o *My brother works for a law firm in Brighton.* ☞ Look at **legal**. **4** [C] (in science) a statement of what always happens in certain circumstances: *the laws of mathematics* o *the laws of gravity*

(IDIOM) **law and order** a situation in which the law is obeyed: *There has been a breakdown of law and order in this country over the past ten years.*

lawful /-fl/ adj allowed or recognized by law: *We shall use all lawful means to obtain our demands.* o *his lawful wife* ☞ Look at **legal**. The opposite is **unlawful**.

lawless adj (used about a person or his/her actions) breaking the law: *a gang of lawless hooligans* —**lawlessness** noun [U]

'law-abiding adj (used about a person) obeying the law: *We are all respectable law-abiding citizens.*

'lawbreaker noun [C] a person who does not obey the law; a criminal

'lawcourt (also **court of law**) noun [C] a place where a judge or jury decides legal matters (eg whether a person is innocent or guilty)

iː	ɪ	e	æ	ɑː	ɒ	ɔː	ʊ	uː	ʌ
see	sit	ten	hat	arm	got	saw	put	too	cup

lawn   359   **lead**

☞ A case is **tried** in a lawcourt. Look at **defence**, **prosecution** and **witness**.

'lawsuit *noun* [C] a legal argument in a court of law that is between two people or groups and not between the police and a criminal

lawn /lɔːn/ *noun* [C,U] an area of grass in a garden or park that is regularly cut: *I'm going to mow the lawn this afternoon.*

'lawnmower *noun* [C] a machine that is used for cutting the grass in a garden

,lawn 'tennis *noun* [U] = TENNIS

☆ **lawyer** /'lɔːjə(r)/ *noun* [C] a person who has studied law and whose job is to give advice on legal matters: *to consult a lawyer*

☞ A **solicitor** is a lawyer who gives legal advice, prepares legal documents, arranges the buying or selling of land, etc. A **barrister** is a lawyer who speaks for you in a court of law. The American term is **attorney**.

lax /læks/ *adj* not having high standards; not strict: *Their security checks are rather lax.*

☆ **lay¹** /leɪ/ *verb* [T] (*pt*, *pp* **laid** /leɪd/) **1** to put sb/sth carefully in a particular position or on a surface: *She laid a sheet over the dead body.* ○ *He laid the child gently down on his bed.* ○ *'Don't worry,' she said, laying her hand on my shoulder.* **2** to put sth in the correct position for a particular purpose: *They're laying new electricity cables in our street.* **3** to prepare sth for use: *The police have laid a trap for him; I think they'll catch him this time.* ○ *Can you lay the table please?* (= put the knives, forks, plates, etc on it). **4** to produce eggs: *Does a snake lay eggs?* **5** (used with some nouns to give a similar meaning to a verb): *They laid all the blame on him* (= they blamed him). ○ *lay emphasis on sth* (= emphasize it)

(PHRASAL VERBS) **lay sth down** to give sth as a rule: *It's all laid down in the rules of the club.*

lay off (sb) (*informal*) to stop annoying sb: *Can't you lay off me for a bit?*

lay sb off to stop giving work to sb: *They've laid off 500 workers at the car factory.*

lay sth on (*informal*) to provide sth: *They're laying on a trip to London for everybody.*

lay sth out 1 to spread out a group of things so that you can see them easily or so that they look nice: *All the food was laid out on a table in the garden.* **2** to arrange sth in a planned way: *The new shopping centre is very attractively laid out.*

lay² /leɪ/ *adj* (only *before* a noun) **1** a member of a church who is not a priest: *a lay preacher* **2** without special training in or knowledge of a particular subject

'layman /-mən/ *noun* [C] (*pl* **laymen** /-mən/) a person who does not have special training in or knowledge of a particular subject: *a medical reference book for the layman*

☆ **lay³** *pt* of LIE²

layabout /'leɪəbaʊt/ *noun* [C] (*Brit informal*) a person who is lazy and does not do much work

lay-by /'leɪbaɪ/ (*US* **rest stop**) *noun* [C] (*pl* **lay-bys**) an area at the side of a road where vehicles can park for a short time out of the way of the traffic

☆ **layer** /'leɪə(r)/ *noun* [C] a thickness or quantity of sth that is on sth else or between other things: *A thin layer of dust covered everything in the room.* ○ *The cake has a layer of jam in the middle.* ○ *It's very cold. You'll need several layers of clothing.* ○ *the top/bottom layer* ○ *the inner/outer layer*

layman ⇨ LAY²

laze /leɪz/ *verb* [I] **laze (about/around)** to do very little; to rest or relax: *We just lazed around all afternoon.*

☆ **lazy** /'leɪzi/ *adj* (**lazier; laziest**) **1** (used about a person) not wanting to work: *Don't be lazy. Come and give me a hand.* **2** moving slowly or without much energy: *a lazy smile* **3** making you feel that you do not want to do very much: *a lazy summer's afternoon* —**lazily** *adv* —**laziness** *noun* [U]

☆ **lead¹** /led/ *noun* **1** [U] (*symbol* **Pb**) a soft heavy grey metal. Lead is used in pipes, roofs, etc. **2** [C,U] the black substance inside a pencil that makes a mark when you write

☆ **lead²** /liːd/ *noun* **1** [sing] a position ahead of other people, organizations, etc: *Britain has taken the lead in developing computer software for that market.* **2 the lead** [sing] the first place or position: *The French athlete has gone into the lead.* ○ *Who is in the lead?* **3** [sing] the distance or amount by which sb/sth is in front of another person or thing: *The company has a lead of several years in the development of the new technology.* **4** [C] the main part or role in a play or show: *Who's playing the lead in the new film?* **5** [C] a piece of information that may help to give the answer to a problem: *The police are following all possible leads to track down the killer.* **6** [C] a long chain or piece of leather that is attached to the collar around a dog's neck and used for keeping the dog under control: *All dogs must be kept on a lead.* **7** [C] a piece of wire that is used for carrying electric current

(IDIOM) **follow sb's example/lead** ⇨ FOLLOW

'lead story *noun* [C] the most important piece of news in a newspaper or news broadcast

☆ **lead³** /liːd/ *verb* (*pt*, *pp* **led** /led/) **1** [T] to go with or in front of a person or animal to show the way or to make them go in the right direction: *The teacher led the children out of the hall and back to the classroom.* ○ *She led the horse into its stable.* ○ *The receptionist led the way to the boardroom.* ○ *to lead sb by the hand* ☞ You usually **guide** a tourist or somebody who needs special help: *to guide visitors around Oxford* ○ *He guided the blind woman to her seat.* If you **direct** somebody, you explain with words how to get somewhere: *Could you direct me to the nearest Post Office, please?* **2** [T] to influence what sb does or thinks: *He led me to believe he really meant what he said.* **3** [I] (used about a road or path) to go to a place: *I don't think this path leads anywhere.* **4** [I] **lead to sth** to have sth as a result: *Eating too much sugar can lead to all sorts of health problems.* **5** [T] to have a particular type of life: *They lead a very busy life.* ○ *to lead a life of crime* **6** [I,T] **lead (sb/sth) (in sth)** to be the best at sth or to be in first place: *Becker is leading by two sets to*

ɜː	ə	eɪ	əʊ	aɪ	aʊ	ɔɪ	ɪə	eə	ʊə
fur	ago	pay	home	five	now	join	near	hair	pure

love. ○ *Becker is leading Lendl by two sets to love.* **7** [I,T] to be in control or the leader of sth: *Who is going to lead the discussion?*
(PHRASAL VERB) **lead up to sth** to be an introduction to or cause of sth: *What were the events that led up to the First World War?*

☆ **leader** /ˈliːdə(r)/ *noun* [C] **1** a person who is the head of sth or in charge of sth: *Who is the leader of the Conservative Party?* ○ *a weak/strong leader* ○ *She is a natural leader* (= she knows how to tell other people what to do). **2** the person or team that is best or in first place: *The leader has just finished the third lap.* ○ (*figurative*) *The new brand of shampoo soon became a market leader.*

leadership *noun* **1** [U] the state of being a leader(1): *Who will take over the leadership?* **2** [U] the qualities that a leader(1) should have **3** [C, with sing or pl verb] a group of leaders(1): *Has/Have the leadership lost touch with ordinary people?*

leading /ˈliːdɪŋ/ *adj* **1** best or very important: *He's one of the leading experts in this field.* ○ *She played a leading role in getting the business started.* **2** in front or in first place: *Aldridge has been the leading goal scorer this season.*

☆ **leaf** /liːf/ *noun* [C] (*pl* **leaves** /liːvz/) one of the thin, flat parts of a plant or tree. Leaves are usually green and grow from a branch but different plants have different shaped leaves: *autumn leaves* ○ *The leaves rustled in the breeze.* ○ *tea leaves* ☛ picture at **tree**.

leaf *verb*
(PHRASAL VERB) **leaf through sth** to turn the pages of a book, etc quickly and without looking at them carefully

leafy *adj* (**leafier**; **leafiest**) **1** having many leaves: *cabbage, spinach, lettuce and other leafy vegetables* **2** (used about a place) having many trees and plants: *a pleasant leafy suburb*

☆ **leaflet** /ˈliːflɪt/ *noun* [C] a small printed piece of paper that advertises or gives information about sth. Leaflets are usually given free of charge: *I picked up a leaflet about bus services to Heathrow.*

league /liːɡ/ *noun* [C] **1** a group of sports clubs that compete with each other for a prize: *the football league* ○ *Which team is top of the league at the moment?* ☛ Look at **rugby league**. **2** a group of people, countries, etc that join together for a particular purpose: *the League of Nations* **3** (*informal*) a standard of quality or achievement: *He is so much better than the others. They're just not in the same league.*
(IDIOM) **in league (with sb)** having a secret agreement (with sb): *I don't trust them. I'm sure they're in league with each other.*

☆ **leak** /liːk/ *noun* [C] **1** a small hole or crack which liquid or gas can get through: *There's a leak in the pipe.* ○ *The roof has sprung a leak.* **2** the liquid or gas that gets through such a hole: *I can smell gas. Perhaps there's a leak.* **3** giving away information that should be kept secret

leak *verb* **1** [I,T] to allow liquid or gas to get through a hole or crack: *The boat was leaking badly.* **2** [I] (used about liquid or gas) to get out through a hole or crack: *Water is leaking in* above the window frame. **3** [T] **leak sth (to sb)** to give secret information: *The committee's findings were leaked to the press before the report was published.*
(PHRASAL VERB) **leak out** (used about secret information) to become known: *The government did not want the details to leak out.*

leakage /ˈliːkɪdʒ/ *noun* [C,U] an example of leaking; sth that has been leaked: *a leakage of dangerous chemicals*

leaky *adj* having a hole or holes through which liquid or gas can get in or out

lean¹ /liːn/ *adj* **1** (used about a person or animal) thin and in good health **2** (used about meat) having little or no fat **3** not producing much: *a lean harvest*

lean

leaning against a tree

leaning out of a window

☆ **lean²** /liːn/ *verb* (*pt, pp* **leant** /lent/ or **leaned** /liːnd/) **1** [I] to be in a position that is not straight or upright: *the Leaning Tower of Pisa* ○ *He leaned across the table to pick up the phone.* ○ *Don't lean out of the window when the train is moving.* ○ *to lean forwards, backwards, over to one side, etc* **2** [I] **lean against/on sth** to rest against sth so that it gives support: *She had to stop and lean on the gate.* ○ (*figurative*) *You can rely on me. I'll always be there for you to lean on.* **3** [T] to put sth against sth: *Please don't lean bicycles against this window.*

leap /liːp/ *verb* (*pt, pp* **leapt** /lept/ or **leaped** /liːpt/) [I] **1** to jump high or a long way: *The horse leapt over the wall.* ○ *The children leapt up and down with excitement.* **2** to move quickly: *I leapt upstairs when I heard the scream.*
(PHRASAL VERB) **leap at sth** to accept a chance or offer with enthusiasm: *She leapt at the chance to work in television.*

leap *noun* [C] **1** a big jump: *He took a flying leap at the wall but didn't get over it.* **2** a great change (for the better) or an increase in sth: *The development of penicillin was a great leap forward in the field of medicine.* ○ *a leap in the price of land*

ˈleap-frog *noun* [U] a children's game in which one person bends over and another person jumps over him/her

p	b	t	d	k	g	tʃ	dʒ	f	v	θ	ð
pen	bad	tea	did	cat	got	chin	June	fall	van	thin	then

'leap year *noun* [C] one year in every four, in which February has 29 days instead of 28

☆ **learn** /lɜːn/ *verb* (*pt, pp* **learnt** /lɜːnt/ or **learned** /lɜːnd/) **1** [I,T] **learn (sth) (from sb/sth)** to get knowledge, a skill, etc (from sb/sth): *I'm not very good at driving yet – I'm still learning.* ○ *Debby is learning to play the piano.* ○ *to learn a foreign language* ○ *Where did you learn how to swim?* ○ *I find it really difficult to learn lists by heart.* **2** [I] **learn (of/about) sth** to get some information about sth; to find out: *I was sorry to learn of your father's death.* **3** [T] to understand or realize: *We should have learned by now that we can't rely on her.*

learned /'lɜːnɪd/ *adj* **1** (used about a person) having a lot of knowledge from studying: *a learned scholar* **2** for learned people: *a learned journal*

learner *noun* [C] a person who is learning: *The 'L' plate on a car means the driver is a learner and hasn't passed the test yet.*

learning *noun* [U] knowledge that you get from studying: *men and women of learning*

lease /liːs/ *noun* [C] an official written agreement (**a contract**) in which land, a building, etc is let to sb else (**a tenant**) for a certain period of time in return for rent

☆ **least¹** /liːst/ *det, pron* (used as the superlative of *little*) smallest in size, amount, extent, etc: *He's got the least experience of all of us.* ○ *You've done the most work, and I'm afraid John has done the least.*

☆ **least²** /liːst/ *adv* to the smallest extent or degree; less than anybody/anything else: *He's the person who needs help least.* ○ *I bought the least expensive tickets.*

(IDIOMS) **at least 1** not less than, and probably more: *It'll cost at least £200.* **2** even if other things are wrong: *It may not be beautiful but at least it's cheap.* **3** (used for correcting sth that you have just said): *I saw him, at least I think I saw him.* **4** (used for saying that sth is the minimum you expect sb to do): *You could at least say you're sorry!*

least of all especially not: *Nobody should be worried, least of all you.*

not in the least not at all: *It doesn't matter in the least.*

last but not least ⇨ LAST²

☆ **leather** /'leðə(r)/ *noun* [U] the skin of animals which has been specially treated. Leather is used to make shoes, bags, coats, etc: *a leather jacket*

☆ **leave¹** /liːv/ *verb* (*pt, pp* **left** /left/) **1** [I,T] to go away from sb/sth: *When should we leave for the airport?* ○ *The train leaves Reading at just after ten.* ○ *He left his mother in tears.* ○ *Barry left his wife for another woman.* ☛ Notice that if you leave sb/sth it may be permanently or just for a short time: *He leaves home at 8.00 every morning.* ○ *He left home and went to live with his girlfriend.* **Depart** is a more formal word and is used about boats, trains, aeroplanes, etc: *The 6.15 train for Southampton departs from Platform 3.* **2** [T] to cause or allow sb/sth to stay in a particular place or condition: *Leave the door open, please.* ○ *Don't leave the iron on when you are not using it.* ○ *Don't leave your friend outside in the cold. Invite him in.* **3** [T] to forget to bring sth with you: *You go on. I've left my keys on the kitchen table.* ○ *I can't find my glasses. Where could I have left them?* **4** [T] to cause sth to remain as a result: *Don't put that cup on the table. It'll leave a mark.* **5** [T] not use sth: *Leave some cake for me, please.* ○ *Is there any bread left?* **6** [T] to put sth somewhere: *Val left a message on her answerphone.* ○ *I left him a note.* **7** [T] to wait until later to do sth: *Let's leave the washing-up till tomorrow.* **8** [T] to give sth to sb when you die: *In his will he left everything to his three sons.* **9** [T] to give the care of sb/sth to another person: *I'll leave it to you to organize all the food.* ○ *He left his assistant in charge when he went away on holiday.*

(IDIOMS) **leave sb/sth alone** not touch, bother or speak to sb/sth: *Leave other people's things alone!* ○ *She's very upset. Leave her alone for a few minutes.*

leave/let go (of sth) to stop touching or holding sth: *Let go of my arm or I'll scream.*

leave sb in the lurch to leave sb without help in a difficult situation

leave sth on one side ⇨ SIDE¹

(PHRASAL VERBS) **leave sb/sth behind** to forget to bring sth with you: *I left my gloves behind and now my hands are cold.*

leave sb/sth out (of sth) not include sb/sth: *This doesn't make sense. I think the typist has left out a line.*

☆ **leave²** /liːv/ *noun* [U] a period of time when you do not go to work: *Diplomats working abroad usually get a month's home leave each year.* ○ *annual leave* ○ *sick, maternity, etc leave* ○ *to be on leave* ☛ Look at the note at **holiday**.

leaves *pl* of LEAF

☆ **lecture** /'lektʃə(r)/ *noun* [C] **1 a lecture (on/about sth)** a talk or speech to a group of people on a particular subject: *He gave a very interesting lecture on the geology of the Pacific.* ○ *a course of lectures* **2** a serious talk to sb that explains what he/she has done wrong or how he/she should behave

lecture *verb* **1** [I] **lecture (on sth)** to give a lecture or lectures (on a particular subject) **2** [T] **lecture sb (about sth)** to talk seriously to sb about what he/she has done wrong or how he/she should behave: *The policeman lectured the boys about the dangers of playing ball games in the road.*

lecturer /'lektʃərə(r)/ *noun* [C] a person who gives lectures (especially one who teaches at a college or university)

led *pt, pp* of LEAD³

ledge /ledʒ/ *noun* [C] a narrow shelf underneath a window, or a narrow piece of rock that sticks out on the side of a cliff or mountain

leek /liːk/ *noun* [C] a long thin vegetable that is white at one end with thin green leaves. Leeks taste rather like onions. ☛ picture at **onion**.

☆ **left¹** *pt, pp* of LEAVE¹

left-'luggage office (*Brit*) (*US* **baggage room**) *noun* [C] the place at a railway station, etc where you can leave your luggage for a short time

'leftovers *noun* [plural] food that has not been eaten when a meal has finished

s	z	ʃ	ʒ	h	m	n	ŋ	l	r	j	w
so	zoo	she	vision	how	man	no	sing	leg	red	yes	wet

☆ **left²** /left/ *adj, adv* on or to the side (of your body) that is towards the west when you face north: *Turn left just past the Post Office.* ○ *I've hurt my left arm.* ○ *Can you write with your left hand?*

left *noun* **1** [U] the left side: *In Britain we drive on the left.* ○ *Take the first turning on the left.* **2 the Left** [with sing or pl verb] political parties or groups that support socialism: *The Left is losing popularity.*

ˌleft-ˈhand *adj* (only *before* a noun) of or on the left: *the left-hand side of the road.* ○ *a left-hand drive car* (= where the steering-wheel is on the left-hand side)

ˌleft-ˈhanded *adj* **1** (used about a person) using the left hand more easily than the right: *Are you left-handed?* **2** made for left-handed people to use: *left-handed scissors*

ˌleft ˈwing *noun* [sing, with sing or pl verb] the members of a political party, group, etc that want more social change than the others in their party: *the left wing of the Labour Party*
ˈleft-wing *adj: left-wing extremists* ○ *They're both very left-wing.*

☆ **leg** /leg/ *noun* [C] **1** the part of the body on which a person or animal stands or walks: *A spider has eight legs.* ○ *long/short legs* ○ *She sat down and crossed her legs.* ○ *Can you balance on one leg?* ○ *See if you can bend your leg at the knee.* ○ *(figurative) the leg of a table, chair, etc* **2** the part of a pair of trousers, shorts, etc that covers the leg **3** one part or section of a journey, competition, etc
(IDIOMS) **pull sb's leg** ⇨ PULL¹
stretch your legs ⇨ STRETCH

legacy /ˈlegəsi/ *noun* [C] (*pl* **legacies**) money or property that is given to you after sb dies, because he/she wanted you to have it

☆ **legal** /ˈliːgl/ *adj* **1** allowed by law: *It is not legal to own a gun without a licence.* ☞ The opposite is **illegal**. Look at **lawful** and **legitimate**. **2** (only *before* a noun) using or connected with the law: *legal advice* ○ *to take legal action against sb* ○ *the legal profession.* —**legally** /ˈliːgəli/ *adv: Schools are legally responsible for the safety of their pupils.*

legality /liːˈgæləti/ *noun* [U] the state of being legal: *The legality of the deal is not certain.*

legalize (*also* **legalise**) /ˈliːgəlaɪz/ *verb* [T] to make sth legal

legend /ˈledʒənd/ *noun* **1** [C] an old story that may or may not be true: *the legend of Robin Hood* **2** [U] such stories when they are grouped together: *According to legend, Robin Hood lived in Sherwood Forest.* **3** [C] a famous person or event

legendary /ˈledʒəndri/; *US* -deri/ *adj* **1** from a legend or legends: *the legendary heroes of Greek myths* **2** very famous: *Bjorn Borg, the legendary tennis star*

leggings /ˈlegɪŋz/ *noun* [plural] a piece of clothing, usually worn by women, that fits tightly over both legs and reaches from your waist to your ankles

legible /ˈledʒəbl/ *adj* (used about handwriting or things that are printed) clear enough to be read easily ☞ The opposite is **illegible**. —**legibility** /ˌledʒəˈbɪləti/ *noun* [U] —**legibly** /-əbli/ *adv*

legislate /ˈledʒɪsleɪt/ *verb* [I] **legislate (for/against sth)** to make a law or laws: *It is very difficult to legislate against racial discrimination.*

legislation /ˌledʒɪsˈleɪʃn/ *noun* [U] **1** the act of making laws **2** a group of laws: *The government is introducing new legislation to help small businesses.*

legitimate /lɪˈdʒɪtɪmət/ *adj* **1** having parents who are married to each other ☞ The opposite is **illegitimate**. **2** reasonable or acceptable: *Is government advertising a legitimate use of tax-payers' money?* **3** allowed by law: *Could he earn so much from legitimate business activities?* ☞ Look at **lawful** and **legal** —**legitimately** *adv.*

☆ **leisure** /ˈleʒə(r)/; *US* ˈliːʒər/ *noun* [U] the time when you do not have to work; spare time: *Shorter working hours mean that people have more leisure.* ○ *leisure activities*
(IDIOM) **at your leisure** when you have free time: *Look through the catalogue at your leisure and then order by telephone.*

leisurely *adj* without hurry: *a leisurely Sunday breakfast*

ˈleisure centre *noun* [C] a public building that has sports facilities and other activities for people to do in their free time

lemon /ˈlemən/ *noun* [C,U] a yellow fruit with sour juice that is used for giving flavour to food and drink: *a slice of lemon* ○ *Add the juice of 2 lemons.*

ˈlemon-squeezer *noun* [C] an instrument that is used for pressing the juice out of a lemon

lemonade /ˌleməˈneɪd/ *noun* [C,U] **1** a colourless sweet drink that is fizzy (= has many bubbles in it) **2** a drink that is made from fresh lemon juice, sugar and water

☆ **lend** /lend/ *verb* [T] (*pt, pp* **lent** /lent/) **1** to allow sb to use sth for a short time or to give sb money that must be paid back after a certain period of time: *Could you lend me £5 until Friday?* ○ *He lent me his car.* ○ *He lent his car to me.*

☞ If a bank, etc lends you money you must **pay it back/repay** it over a fixed period of time with extra payments (called **interest**). picture at **borrow**.

2 lend sth to sth (*formal*) to add or give: *to lend advice, support, etc* ○ *The flowers lent a touch of colour to the room.*

lender *noun* [C] a person or organization that lends sth

☆ **length** /leŋθ/ *noun* **1** [U] the distance or amount that sth measures from one end to the other; how long sth is: *to measure the length of a room* ○ *It took an hour to walk the length of Oxford Street.* ○ *The tiny insect is only one millimetre in length.* ○ *the length of a book, letter, etc* **2** [U] the amount of time that sth takes or lasts: *Many people complained about the length of time they had to wait.* **3** [C] the length(1) of a swimming-pool: *I can swim a length in twenty seconds.* **4** [C] a piece of sth (that is long and thin): *a length of material, rope, string, etc*

iː	ɪ	e	æ	ɑː	ɒ	ɔː	ʊ	uː	ʌ
see	sit	ten	hat	arm	got	saw	put	too	cup

lengthy   363   **let**

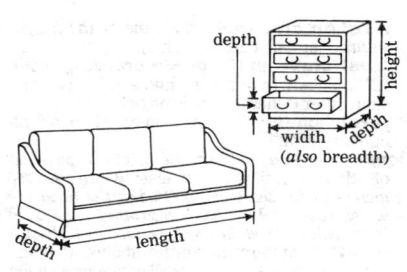

depth / *height* / *width* (*also* **breadth**) / *depth* / *length*

(IDIOMS) **at length** for a long time or in great detail: *We discussed the matter at great length.*
the length and breadth of sth to or in all parts of sth: *They travelled the length and breadth of India.*
go to great lengths to make more effort than usual in order to achieve sth
lengthen *verb* [I,T] to become longer or to make sth longer
lengthways (*also* **lengthwise**) *adv* in a direction along the length of sth: *Fold the paper lengthwise.*
lengthy /'leŋθi/ *adj* (**lengthier**; **lengthiest**) very long: *lengthy discussions* o *Recovery from the illness will be a lengthy process.*
lenient /'li:niənt/ *adj* (used about a punishment or person who punishes) not strict or severe —**lenience** /-əns/ (*also* **leniency** /-ənsi/) *noun* [U] —**leniently** *adv*
lens /lenz/ *noun* [C] (*pl* **lenses**) a piece of glass, etc that has one or more curved surfaces. Lenses are used in glasses, cameras, telescopes, microscopes, etc. ☛ picture at **glasses** and **camera**. You may wear **contact lenses** to help you see better. You may use a **zoom** or **telephoto lens** on your camera.
lent *pt, pp* of LEND
lentil /'lentl/ *noun* [C] the small orange or brown seed of a plant that is like a bean. Lentils are dried and then cooked and eaten: *lentil soup*
Leo /'li:əʊ/ *noun* [C,U] (*pl* **Leos**) the fifth sign of the zodiac, the Lion; a person who was born under this sign ☛ picture at **zodiac**.
leopard /'lepəd/ *noun* [C] a large wild animal of the cat family that has yellow fur with dark spots. Leopards live in Africa and Southern Asia. ☛ picture at **lion**. A female leopard is called a **leopardess** and a baby is called a **cub**.
leotard /'li:əta:d/ *noun* [C] a piece of clothing that fits close to the body and arms but does not cover the legs. Leotards are worn by dancers, people doing exercises, etc.
leper /'lepə(r)/ *noun* [C] a person who has leprosy
leprosy /'leprəsi/ *noun* [U] a serious infectious disease that affects the skin, nerves and flesh. Leprosy can cause fingers and toes to drop off.
lesbian /'lezbiən/ *noun* [C] a woman who is sexually attracted to other women —**lesbian** *adj*: *a lesbian relationship* —**lesbianism** *noun* [U] ☛ Look at **gay** and **homosexual**.
☆ **less**[1] /les/ *det, pron* (used with uncountable nouns) a smaller amount (of): *It took less time than I thought.* o *I'm too fat – I must try to eat less.* o *It's not far – it'll take less than an hour to get there.* ☛ Many people use **less** with plural nouns: *less cars*, but **fewer** is the form which is still considered to be correct: *fewer cars.*
☆ **less**[2] /les/ *adv* to a smaller extent; not so much (as): *He's less intelligent than his brother.* o *It rains less in London than in Manchester.* o *People work less well when they're tired.*
(IDIOMS) **less and less** becoming smaller and smaller in amount or degree: *I seem to have less and less time for the children.*
more or less ⇨ MORE[2]
less *prep* taking a certain number or amount away; minus: *You'll earn £10 an hour, less tax.*
lessen /'lesn/ *verb* [I,T] to become less; to make sth less: *This medicine will lessen the pain.*
lesser /'lesə(r)/ *adj, adv* (only *before* a noun) not as great/much as: *He is guilty and so, to a lesser extent, is his wife* o *a lesser-known artist*
(IDIOM) **the lesser of two evils** the better of two bad things
☆ **lesson** /'lesn/ *noun* [C] **1** a period of time when you learn or teach sth: *When does the next lesson start?* o *How many English lessons do you have a week?* o *She gives piano lessons.* o *I want to take extra lessons in English conversation.* o *a driving lesson* **2** something that you have learnt or that must be learnt: *I hope we can learn some lessons from this disaster.*
☆ **let**[1] /let/ *verb* [T] (*pres part* **letting**; *pt, pp* **let**) **1** to allow or permit sb/sth to do sth; to allow sth to happen: *My parents let me stay out till 11 o'clock.* o *How could you let her run away like that?* o *He wanted to go on a course but his boss wouldn't let him.* ☛ You cannot use **let** in the passive here. You must use **allow** or **permit** and **to**: *They let him take the exam again.* o *He was allowed to take the exam again.* Look at the note at **allow. 2** (used for offering help to sb): *Let me help you carry your bags.* o *Let us lend you the money for a new car.* **3** (used for making requests or giving instructions): *Don't help him. Let him do it himself.* o *If she refuses to come home with us now, let her walk home.* **4** to allow sb/sth to move in a particular direction: *She forgot to let the cat out this morning.* o *Open the windows and let some fresh air in.* o *They let him out of prison yesterday.* **5** (used for making suggestions about what you and other people can do): *'Let's go to the cinema tonight.' 'Yes, let's.'* ☛ The negative is **let's not** or (in British English only) **don't let's**: *Let's not/Don't let's go to that awful restaurant again.*
(IDIOMS) **let alone** and certainly not: *We haven't decided where we're going yet, let alone booked the tickets*
let sb/sth go; let go of sb/sth to stop holding sb/sth: *Let me go. You're hurting me!* o *I tried to take the book but he wouldn't let go of it.* o *Hold the rope and don't let go.*
let me see; let's see (used when you are thinking or trying to remember sth): *Where did I put the car keys? Let's see. I think I left them by the telephone.*
let us/let's say for example: *You could work*

3:	ə	eɪ	əʊ	aɪ	aʊ	ɔɪ	ɪə	eə	ʊə
fur	ago	pay	home	five	now	join	near	hair	pure

two mornings a week, let's say Tuesday and Friday.

let yourself go to allow yourself to behave as you wish, to feel free: *Just relax. Let yourself go!*

let yourself/sth go to allow yourself/sth to become untidy, dirty, etc: *She used to be so smart but after her husband died she just let herself go.*

(PHRASAL VERBS) **let sb down** not to do sth that you promised to do for sb; to disappoint sb

let on (about sth) (to sb) to tell sb a secret: *He didn't let on how much he'd paid for the vase.*

let sb off not to punish sb, or to give sb a lighter punishment than usual: *He expected to go to prison but they let him off with a fine.*

let sth out to tell people sth that was secret: *Who let the story about Princess Diana out?*

let sth out/down to make clothes larger/longer: *These trousers are too tight. I'll have to let them out.*

☆ **let²** /let/ *verb* [T] to offer a house, flat, etc for sb to live in, in exchange for rent: *She lets the cottage to holidaymakers in the summer.* ○ *There's a flat to let in our block.* ☛ Look at the note at **hire**.

lethal /'li:θl/ *adj* able to cause death or great damage —**lethally** /'li:θəli/ *adv*

lethargy /'leθədʒi/ *noun* [U] the feeling of being very tired and not having any energy —**lethargic** /lə'θɑ:dʒɪk/ *adj*

☆ **letter** /'letə(r)/ *noun* [C] **1** a written or printed sign that represents a sound in a language: *'Z' is the last letter of the English alphabet.*

☛ Letters may be written or printed as **capitals**, (also **upper case**), or **small** letters (also **lower case**): *Is 'east' written with a capital or a small 'e'?*

2 a written or printed message. A letter is usually put in an envelope and sent to sb by post: *I have written Denise a letter but I haven't sent it yet.* ○ *Have you had a letter from your son?* ○ *Letters are delivered by the postman.*

☛ When you have written a letter you put it in an **envelope**, **address** it, **put/stick a stamp** on it and then **post** (*US* **mail**) it. You may **forward** a letter to a person who has moved away.

'letter-box *noun* [C] **1** a hole in a door or wall through which letters, etc are delivered **2** (*US* **mailbox**) a box outside a house or building which letters can be left in when they are delivered **3** = POSTBOX

lettuce /'letɪs/ *noun* [C,U] a plant with large green leaves that are eaten raw in salads ☛ picture at **salad**.

leukaemia (*US* **leukemia**) /luː'kiːmɪə/ *noun* [U] a serious disease of the blood which often results in death

☆ **level¹** /'levl/ *adj* **1** with no part higher than any other; flat: *Make sure the shelves are level before you fix them in position.* ○ *Put the tent up on level ground.* ○ *a level teaspoon of sugar* **2** at the same height, standard or position: *The boy's head was level with his father's shoulder.* ○ *A red car drew level with mine at the traffic-lights* (= stopped next to mine).

'level 'crossing (*US* **grade crossing**) *noun* [C] a place where a road and a railway cross each other (where there is no bridge)

'level-'headed *adj* able to act calmly in a difficult situation

☆ **level²** /'levl/ *noun* [C] **1** the height or position of sth in relation to sth else: *We are at 500 metres above sea level.* ○ *During the flood the water reached knee-level.* ○ *ground level* ○ *an intermediate-level student* ○ *top-level discussions* **2** the amount, size or number of sth (compared to sth else): *a high level of unemployment* ○ *low levels of pollution* **3** a flat surface or layer: *a multi-level shopping centre*

level³ /'levl/ *verb* [T] (**levelling**; **levelled**; *US* **leveling**; **leveled**) to make sth flat, equal or level: *Lineker's goal levelled the score.* ○ *The ground needs levelling before we lay the patio.*

(PHRASAL VERBS) **level sth at sb/sth** to aim sth at sb/sth: *They levelled serious criticisms at the standard of teaching.*

level off/out to become flat, equal or level: *Share prices rose sharply yesterday but today they have levelled out* (= stayed at one level).

lever /'liːvə(r); *US* 'levər/ *noun* [C] **1** a bar or tool that is used to lift or open sth when you put pressure or force on one end **2** a handle that you pull or push in order to make a machine, etc work: *a gear-lever*

lever *verb* [T] to move or lift sth with a lever: *How did ancient man lever those huge lumps of stone into position?*

leverage /-ərɪdʒ/ *noun* [U] the force or pressure that is put on sth by a lever

levy /'levi/ *verb* [T] (*pt, pp* **levied**) **levy sth (on sb)** to officially demand and collect money, etc: *The new tax will be levied on all adults in the country.*

liability /ˌlaɪə'bɪləti/ *noun* (*pl* **liabilities**) **1** [U] **liability (for sth)** the state of being responsible (for sth): *The company cannot accept liability for damage to cars in this car park.* **2** [C] (*informal*) a person or thing that can cause a lot of problems, cost a lot of money, etc: *Our car's a real liability – it's always breaking down.*

liable /'laɪəbl/ *adj* (not before a noun) **1 liable to do sth** likely to do sth: *We're all liable to have accidents when we are very tired.* **2 liable to sth** likely to have or suffer from sth: *The area is liable to floods.* **3 liable (for sth)** responsible (in law) (for sth): *Is a wife liable for her husband's debts?*

liaise /li'eɪz/ *verb* [I] **liaise (with sb/sth)** (*informal*) to work closely with a person, group, etc and give him/her/it regular information about what you are doing

liaison /li'eɪzn; *US* 'liːəzɒn/ *noun* **1** [U] communication between two or more people or groups that work together **2** [C] a sexual relationship between two people who are not married to each other

liar /'laɪə(r)/ *noun* [C] a person who tells lies (= who says or writes things that are not true): *She called me a liar.* ☛ Look at the verb and noun **lie¹**.

libel /'laɪbl/ *noun* [C,U] something false that is

p	b	t	d	k	g	tʃ	dʒ	f	v	θ	ð
pen	bad	tea	did	cat	got	chin	June	fall	van	thin	then

written or printed about sb that would make other people think badly of him/her: *The singer is suing the newspaper for libel.* —**libel** *verb* [T] (**libel**ling; **libel**led; *US* libeling; libeled)

liberal /'lɪbərəl/ *adj* **1** willing to accept different opinions or kinds of behaviour; tolerant **2** generous (used to describe either the person who is giving or the amount that is given): *We were given liberal quantities of food and drink.*

liberal *noun* [C] a person who is liberal(1) in his/her way of thinking —**liberalism** /-ɪzəm/ *noun* [U]

liberally /-rəli/ *adv* freely or generously

the ˌLiberal ˈDemocrats *noun* [plural] a political party in Britain that represents moderate views

liberate /'lɪbəreɪt/ *verb* [T] **liberate sb/sth (from sth)** to set sb/sth free: *France was liberated in 1945.* ○ *to liberate people from poverty*

liberated *adj* not sharing traditional opinions or ways of behaving —**liberation** /ˌlɪbə'reɪʃn/ *noun* [U]: *The women's liberation movement wants equal rights for women.* ○ *an army of liberation*

liberator *noun* [C] a person who liberates

liberty /'lɪbəti/ *noun* [C,U] (*pl* **liberties**) the freedom to go where you want, do what you want, etc: *We must defend our civil liberties at all costs.* ○ *loss of liberty* (= being put in prison) (IDIOM) **at liberty (to do sth)** free or allowed to do sth: *You are at liberty to leave when you wish.* ○ *I am not at liberty to tell you how I got this information.*

Libra /'li:brə/ *noun* [C,U] the seventh sign of the zodiac, the Scales; a person who was born under this sign ☛ picture at **zodiac**.

☆ **library** /'laɪbrəri; *US* -breri/ *noun* [C] (*pl* **libraries**) **1** a room or building that contains a collection of books, etc that can be looked at or borrowed: *My library books are due back tomorrow.*

☛ Most towns and large villages in Britain have a **public library** where you can borrow books and read magazines and newspapers.

2 a private collection of books, etc

librarian /laɪ'breəriən/ *noun* [C] a person who works in or is in charge of a library

lice *pl* of LOUSE

☆ **licence** (*US* **license**) /'laɪsns/ *noun* **1** [C] an official paper that shows you are allowed to do or have sth: *a driving licence* ○ (*US*) *a driver's license* ○ *The shop has applied for a licence to sell alcoholic drinks.* **2** [U] (*formal*) freedom to do sth: *The soldiers were given licence to kill if they were attacked.*

ˈlicence plate (*US* **license plate**) *noun* [C] = NUMBER-PLATE

license (*US* **licence**) /'laɪsns/ *verb* [T] to give official permission for sth: *Is that gun licensed?*

licensee /ˌlaɪsən'si:/ *noun* [C] a person who has a licence to sell alcoholic drinks, etc

ˈlicensing laws *noun* [plural] (*Brit*) the laws that control where and when alcoholic drinks may be sold

lick /lɪk/ *verb* [T] to move your tongue across sth: *The child licked the spoon clean.* ○ *I licked the envelope and stuck it down.* —**lick** *noun* [C]: *Let me have a lick of your ice-cream.*

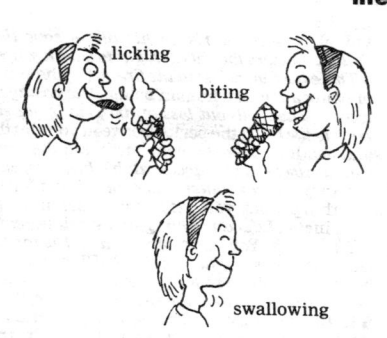

licorice = LIQUORICE

☆ **lid** /lɪd/ *noun* [C] **1** the top part of a box, pot, etc that can be lifted up or taken off ☛ picture at **pan**. Look at the note at **top**. **2** = EYELID

☆ **lie¹** /laɪ/ *verb* [I] (*pres part* **lying**; *pt, pp* **lied**) **lie (to sb) (about sth)** to say or write sth that you know is not true: *He lied about his age in order to join the army.* ○ (*figurative*) *The camera cannot lie.*

lie *noun* [C] a statement that you know is not true: *to tell a lie* ☛ *You tell a white lie in order not to hurt sb's feelings.* Look at **liar** and **fib**.

ˈlie-detector *noun* [C] a piece of equipment that can show if a person is lying or not

☆ **lie²** /laɪ/ *verb* [I] (*pres part* **lying**; *pt* **lay** /leɪ/; *pp* **lain** /leɪn/) **1** to be or put yourself in a flat or horizontal position (so that you are not standing or sitting): *He lay on the sofa and went to sleep.* ○ *to lie on your back/side/front* ○ *The book lay open in front of her.* ☛ Remember that **lie** cannot be used with an object. If you put an object in a flat position you **lay** it down. **2** to be or remain in a certain state or position: *Snow lay thick on the ground.* ○ *The hills lie to the north of the town.* ○ *The factory lay idle during the strike.* ○ *The final decision lies with the managing director.* ○ *They are young and their whole lives lie ahead of them.*

(PHRASAL VERBS) **lie about/around** to relax and do nothing: *We just lay around all day on Sunday.*

lie back to relax and do nothing while sb else works, etc

lie down (used about a person) to be or put yourself in a flat or horizontal position so that you can rest: *My head is spinning – I must lie down.* ☛ Note the related expression **have a lie-down**.

lie in (*informal*) to stay in bed later than usual ☛ Note the related expression **have a lie-in**.

lieutenant /lef'tenənt; *US* lu:'t-/ *noun* [C] a junior officer in the army or navy

☆ **life** /laɪf/ *noun* (*pl* **lives** /laɪvz/) **1** [U] the quality that people, animals or plants have when they are not dead: *Life on earth began in a very simple form.* ○ *Do you believe in life after death?* **2** [U] living things: *No life was found on the moon.* ○ *There was no sign of life in the deserted house.* ○ *plant life* **3** [C] the existence of an indi-

vidual person: *He risked his life to save the child.* ○ *Doctors fought all night to save her life.* ○ *Three lives were lost in the fire.* **4** [U] the state of being alive as a human being: *The hostages were rescued without loss of life.* ○ *to bring sb back to life* **5** [C] the period between your birth and death or between your birth and the present: *He worked as a doctor all his life.* ○ *I spent my early life in London.* ○ *to ruin sb's life* **6** [U] the things that you may experience during your life(5): *Life can be hard for a single parent.* ○ *That's life. You can't change it.* ○ *I want to travel and see something of life.* **7** [U] the period between the present and your death: *She was sent to prison for life.* ○ *life membership of a club* **8** [C,U] way of living: *They went to America to start a new life.* ○ *They lead a busy life.* ○ *married life* **9** [U] activity; liveliness: *Young children are full of life.* ○ *This town comes to life in the evenings.* **10** [C] the story of sb's life: *He's writing a life of John Lennon.*
(IDIOMS) **the facts of life** ⇨ FACT
lose your life ⇨ LOSE
take your (own) life to kill yourself
a walk of life ⇨ WALK²
a/sb's way of life ⇨ WAY¹
lifeless *adj* **1** dead **2** without life(9) or energy
ˌlife-and-ˈdeath (*also* ˌlife-or-ˈdeath) *adj* (*only before* a noun) very serious or dangerous: *a life-and-death struggle*
ˈlifebelt (*also* **lifebuoy** /ˈlaɪfbɔɪ/) *noun* [C] a ring that is made from light material which will float. A lifebelt is thrown to a person who has fallen into water to stop him/her from sinking.
ˈlifeboat *noun* [C] **1** a small boat that is carried on a large ship and that is used by people to escape from the ship if it is in danger of sinking **2** a special boat that is used for rescuing people who are in danger at sea
ˈlife cycle *noun* [C] the series of forms or stages of development that a plant, animal, etc goes through from the beginning of its life to the end
ˈlife ex‚pectancy *noun* [C,U] (*pl* **life expectancies**) the number of years that a person is likely to live
ˈlifeguard *noun* [C] a person at a beach or swimming-pool whose job is to rescue people who are in difficulties in the water
ˈlife-jacket *noun* [C] a plastic or rubber sleeveless jacket that can be filled with air. A life jacket is worn by sb to stop him/her from drowning in water.
ˈlifelike *adj* looking like the real person or thing: *The flowers are made of silk but they are very lifelike.*
ˈlifeline *noun* [C] a rope that you throw to sb who is in difficulties in water: (*figurative*) *For many old people their telephone is a lifeline.*
ˈlifelong *adj* (*only before* a noun) for all of your life: *a lifelong friend*
ˈlife-size(d) *adj* of the same size as the real person or thing: *a life-sized statue*
ˈlife-span *noun* [C] the length of time that sb/sth lives, works, lasts, etc

ˈlife story *noun* [C] (*pl* **life stories**) the story of sb's life
ˈlifestyle *noun* [C] the way that you live: *Getting married often means a sudden change in lifestyle.*
ˈlifetime *noun* [C] the period of time that sb is alive: *It's a chance of a lifetime. Don't miss it!*
☆ **lift** /lɪft/ *verb* **1** [T] **lift sb/sth (up)** to move sb/sth to a higher level or position: *He lifted the child up onto his shoulders so that she could see better.* ○ *Lift your arm very gently and see if it hurts.* ○ *It took two men to lift the grand piano.* **2** [T] to take hold of sb/sth and move him/her/it to a different position: *She lifted the suitcase down from the rack.* **3** [I] (used about clouds, fog, etc) to rise up or disappear: *The mist lifted towards the end of the morning.* **4** [T] **lift sth (from sb/sth)** (*informal*) to steal or copy sth: *Most of his essay was lifted straight from the textbook.* ☞ Look at **shoplift**. **5** [T] to end or remove a rule, law, etc: *The ban on public meetings has been lifted.*
(PHRASAL VERB) **lift off** (used about a rocket) to rise straight up from the ground
lift *noun* **1** [sing] lifting or being lifted **2** [C] (*US* **elevator**) a machine in a large building that is used for carrying people or goods from one floor to another: *It's on the third floor so we'd better take the lift.* **3** [C] = SKI-LIFT **4** [C] a free ride in a car, etc: *Can you give me a lift to the station, please?* ○ *I got a lift from a passing car.* **5** [sing] (*informal*) a feeling of happiness or excitement: *Her words of encouragement gave the whole team a lift.*
(IDIOM) **thumb a lift** ⇨ THUMB
ˈlift-off *noun* [C] the start of the flight of a rocket: *Only ten seconds to lift-off!*
ligament /ˈlɪgəmənt/ *noun* [C] a strong band in a person's or animal's body that holds the bones, etc together

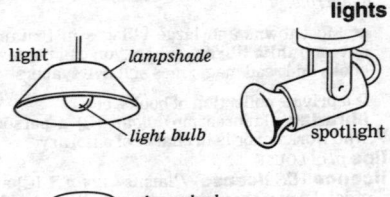

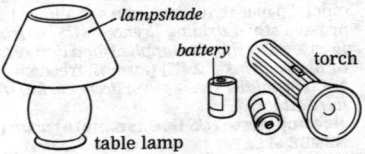

lights

light — lampshade
light bulb
spotlight

lampshade
battery
torch
table lamp

☆ **light¹** /laɪt/ *noun* **1** [U] the brightness that allows you to see things: *the light of the sun* ○ *The light was too bad for us to read by.* ○ *Strong light is bad for the eyes.*

☞ You may see things by **sunlight, moonlight, firelight, candlelight, lamplight,** etc

2 [C] something that produces light, eg an

| iː | ɪ | e | æ | ɑː | ɒ | ɔː | ʊ | uː | ʌ |
| see | sit | ten | hat | arm | got | saw | put | too | cup |

STUDY PAGES

USING THE WORDPOWER DICTIONARY
Dictionary quiz — A 2
Words that go together — A 4
Checking your work — A 6

VOCABULARY PAGES
Health and fitness — A 8
The Family — A 9
Clothes — A 10
Houses — A 12
Computers — A 13
Education — A 14
Government — A 16
The Environment — A 18
Keeping vocabulary records — A 20

STUDY NOTES
Word formation — A 22
List of prefixes and suffixes — A 24
Phrasal verbs — A 26
Punctuation — A 28
Letter-writing — A 30
American English — A 32

Dictionary quiz

This quiz shows how the **Wordpower Dictionary** can help you. You'll find the answers to all these questions in the dictionary.

> HOW CAN THE WORDPOWER DICTIONARY HELP ME?

1. What is **toffee** made of?
2. Who would wear a **nappy**?
3. What does a **teetotaller** not do?
4. What's the name of the part of a **telephone** that you pick up when you want to make a phone call?
5. What's the opposite of **honest**?
6. *I could see the **shade** of a man outside the window.*
   In this sentence the word **shade** is wrong. What's the correct word?
7. Which word in this sentence would you NOT use in an informal situation: *What time does the seminar commence?*
8. Is the word **meek** a noun, a verb or an adjective?
9. Is the word **luggage** countable or uncountable?
10. What's the past tense of **swear**?
11. How do you spell the plural of **factory**?
12. How do you spell the *-ing* form of the verb **travel**?

MEANINGS
The dictionary explains what words mean in language that is easy to understand, and the example sentences show you how to use the word correctly.

VOCABULARY
There are also notes (shown by the ☛ symbol) that give useful extra vocabulary associated with a word and explain the difference between words that people often confuse.

STYLE
The dictionary tells you if a word is formal or informal, and often suggests another word that you can use in most situations.

GRAMMAR
The dictionary tells you whether a word is a noun, verb, adjective, etc, and whether nouns are countable or uncountable. It also gives irregular forms (eg irregular past tenses of verbs).

SPELLING
You can use the dictionary to check how a word is spelled. It also tells you about small spelling changes in other forms of the word (eg irregular plurals).

13. Which letter is silent in the word **receipt**?

14. Where's the stress in the word **policeman**?

15. How many idioms are there that have the word **kill** in them?

16. How many phrasal verbs can you make with the word **burn**?

17. What two adjectives can you form from the word **cloud**?

18. How many compounds can you make from the word **lamp**?

19. What's the American English word for **handbag**?

20. How do Americans spell the word **centre**?

21. What do you call a person who comes from **Norway**?

22. What do the letters **GCSE** mean?

PRONUNCIATION
The dictionary gives the pronunciation of words, and at the bottom of each page there is a key that shows you how to read the phonetic spelling. Look also at the ' marks that show you where the main stress of the word is.

IDIOMS AND PHRASAL VERBS
These are given in two separate sections after the main meanings of the word. (Look also at the 'Phrasal verbs' page - page A26.)

WORDS FORMED FROM OTHER WORDS
Derivatives (**happily** and **happiness** are derivatives of **happy**) and compounds (**rainfall** is a compound, formed from the words **rain** and **fall**) are also given in two sections after the main meanings of the word.

AMERICAN ENGLISH
The dictionary tells you about words that are different in British and American English, and also gives American spelling. (There is more information about American English on page A32.)

EXTRA INFORMATION
At the back of the dictionary you will find: a list of expressions using numbers; a list of irregular verbs; a list of geographical names; a list of abbreviations.

Now turn the page upside down and check your answers.

Answers

1 sugar, butter and milk (or water) **2** a baby or very young child **3** drink alcohol **4** the receiver **5** dishonest **6** shadow **7** commence **8** an adjective **9** uncountable **10** swore **11** factories **12** travelling **13** the 'p' **14** po'liceman **15** three (have an hour, etc to kill; kill two birds with one stone) **16** four (burn (sth) down; burn sth out; burn sth up; burn up) **17** cloudless; cloudy **18** two (lamppost; lampshade) **19** purse **20** center **21** a Norwegian **22** General Certificate of Secondary Education

Words that go together

As well as explaining the meaning of a word, the Wordpower Dictionary also shows you how to use it correctly in a phrase or sentence.

THE EXAMPLE SENTENCES
Do we talk about **weak** cheese or **mild** cheese? Do you **say** a joke or **tell** a joke? (It's **mild** and **tell**.) If you look up a word in the dictionary, the example sentences show you which other words are often used with it:

cheque (*US* **check**) /tʃek/ *noun* [C,U] a piece of paper printed by a bank that you can fill in, sign and use to pay for things: *She wrote out a cheque for £20.* ○ *I went to the bank to cash a cheque.*

Write out and **cash** are verbs that are often used with the word **cheque**.

wind¹ /wɪnd/ *noun* 1 [C,U] (*also* **the wind**) air that is moving across the surface of the earth: *There was a strong wind blowing.* ○ *A gust of wind blew his hat off.* ○ *high winds* ○ *a cold north wind*

Strong, **high**, **cold** and **north** are adjectives that are often used with the word **wind**.

PRACTICE 1
Match a word in A with a word in B. Find the words in B in the dictionary and look at the example sentences.

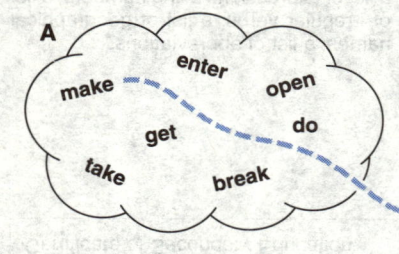

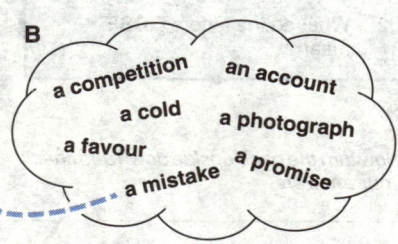

A: make, enter, open, get, do, take, break

B: a competition, an account, a cold, a photograph, a favour, a mistake, a promise

PRACTICE 2
What's the opposite of...

a) weak tea?   *strong tea*
b) sweet wine?   _____
c) dark skin?   _____
d) calm sea?   _____
e) a high salary?   _____
f) heavy traffic?   _____
g) a mild curry?   _____
h) an even number?   _____

PREPOSITIONS AND VERB PATTERNS
The dictionary also shows you which preposition to use after a noun, verb or adjective, and which construction to use after a verb:

married /'mærɪd/ *adj* **1 married (to sb)** having a husband or wife: *Shula's married to Mark.*

This shows that the preposition that goes with **married** is **to**.

enjoy /ɪn'dʒɔɪ/ *verb* [T] **1 enjoy sth/enjoy doing sth** to get pleasure from: *I really enjoyed that meal.* ○ *He enjoys listening to music.*

You can say that you **enjoy something** or that you **enjoy doing something**.

PRACTICE 3
Use the dictionary to complete these sentences with the right preposition.

a) Everybody laughed _ _ _ _ the joke.

b) We were very pleased _ _ _ _ the hotel.

c) She says she's found a solution _ _ _ _ the problem.

d) It took her a long time to recover _ _ _ _ the accident.

e) Do you believe _ _ _ _ life after death?

f) I apologized _ _ _ _ Sam _ _ _ _ breaking the chair.

g) She's very proud _ _ _ _ her new motor bike.

h) The house is quite close _ _ _ _ the shops.

PRACTICE 4
Complete these sentences with the correct form of the verb in brackets.

a) Haven't you finished _ _ _ _ _ _ _ _ _ (clean) your room yet?

b) He keeps _ _ _ _ _ _ _ _ _ (phone) me up.

c) I've persuaded Jan _ _ _ _ _ _ _ _ _ (come) to the party.

d) Try to avoid _ _ _ _ _ _ _ _ _ (make) mistakes.

e) You're not allowed _ _ _ _ _ _ _ _ _ (smoke) in here.

f) The bank has agreed _ _ _ _ _ _ _ _ (lend) me the money.

Answers
PRACTICE 1: make a mistake; enter a competition; open an account; do a favour; break a promise; get a cold; take a photograph.
PRACTICE 2: a) strong tea b) dry wine c) fair skin d) rough sea e) a low salary f) light traffic g) a hot curry h) an odd number.
PRACTICE 3: a) at b) with c) to d) from e) in f) to, for g) of h) to.
PRACTICE 4: a) cleaning b) phoning c) to come d) making e) to smoke f) to lend.

Checking your work

If you make a lot of mistakes in a letter, an essay or any other piece of written work, people will find it quite difficult to understand. You'll also lose a lot of marks in tests and exams! So it's important to check your work carefully when you've finished it and try to correct as many mistakes as you can. Your dictionary can help you with this.

Look at this piece of work that a student has written. There are a lot of mistakes in it. Check it carefully with the help of the dictionary, and correct the mistakes. Use the checklist on the next page, and tick the box ✓ when you've checked each point.

Last summer I went to Oxford to study english in a langage school. I was in Oxford during two months. I stayed with an english family, who dwell quite close to the city centre. Mrs Taylor works as a sollicitor, and her spouse has a good work in an insuranse company.

I enjoyed to be at the langage school. I meeted students of many different nationalitys — Japanesse, Italien, Portugal and Spain. The professors were very sympathetic and teached me a lot, but I didn't like making so many homeworks!

CHECKLIST

☐ 1 Have I used the right word?

The dictionary has notes that explain the difference between words that people often confuse, so check words like **work** and **sympathetic**, and any others that you're not sure about.

☐ 2 What about style?

Have you used any words that might be too formal or too informal in this situation? Check in the dictionary if you're not sure.

☐ 3 Have I used the right word combinations?

Is it '**make** homework' or '**do** homework'? If you're not sure about this sort of word combination, look up the main word (**homework**) in the dictionary and see which word is used with it in the example sentences.

☐ 4 What about prepositions?

Is it 'close **to**' or 'close **from**'? Everyone knows how easy it is to use the wrong preposition after a noun, verb or adjective – they always seem to be different in English! Check these carefully in the dictionary.

☐ 5 Have I used the correct verb patterns?

Is it 'enjoy **to do** something' or 'enjoy **doing** something'? The example sentences for **enjoy** will show you which construction to use. Make sure you've got things like this right.

☐ 6 What about spelling?

Be careful of words that are very similar to words in your language – often the spelling is different. Watch out for countries and nationalities – there's a list of these at the back of the dictionary. Check the spelling of plurals, past tenses, -*ing* forms and comparative and superlative adjectives.

☐ 7 Is the grammar all right?

Have you checked the nouns to see if they're countable or uncountable? Are the past tenses and past participles of irregular verbs right? The list of irregular verbs at the back of the dictionary will help you.

Now turn the page upside down and check your answers.

Answers

Last summer I went to Oxford to study English in a language school. I was in Oxford **for** two months. I stayed with an English family, who **live** quite close to the city centre. Mrs Taylor works as a solicitor, and her **husband** has a good **job** in an insurance company.

I enjoyed **being** at the language school. I **met** students of many different nationalities - Japanese, Italian, Portuguese and **Spanish**. The **teachers** were very **nice** and **taught** me a lot, but I didn't like **doing so much** homework!

Health and fitness

HEAD
- hair
- ear
- cheek
- jaw

FACE
- forehead
- eyebrow
- eyelash
- eye
- nose
- nostril
- mouth
- lips
- chin
- throat

HAND
- thumb
- fingernail
- wrist
- fingers
- knuckle
- palm

- neck
- shoulder
- armpit
- chest
- stomach
- back
- waist
- hip
- bottom
- thigh

ARM
- elbow

LEG
- calf
- knee
- shin

FOOT
- toenail
- big toe
- toes
- sole
- heel
- ankle

WAYS OF DESCRIBING YOUR BODY
fit/unfit
healthy/unhealthy
out of condition
in/out of shape
overweight/underweight

WAYS OF KEEPING FIT
do exercises
work out in a gym
do aerobics
go jogging/running/cycling
play tennis/badminton/squash

WAYS OF BECOMING HEALTHIER
go on a diet
lose/put on weight
give up smoking/drinking
cut down on sweet things
eat more fresh fruit

For more information about these expressions, look them up in the main part of the dictionary.

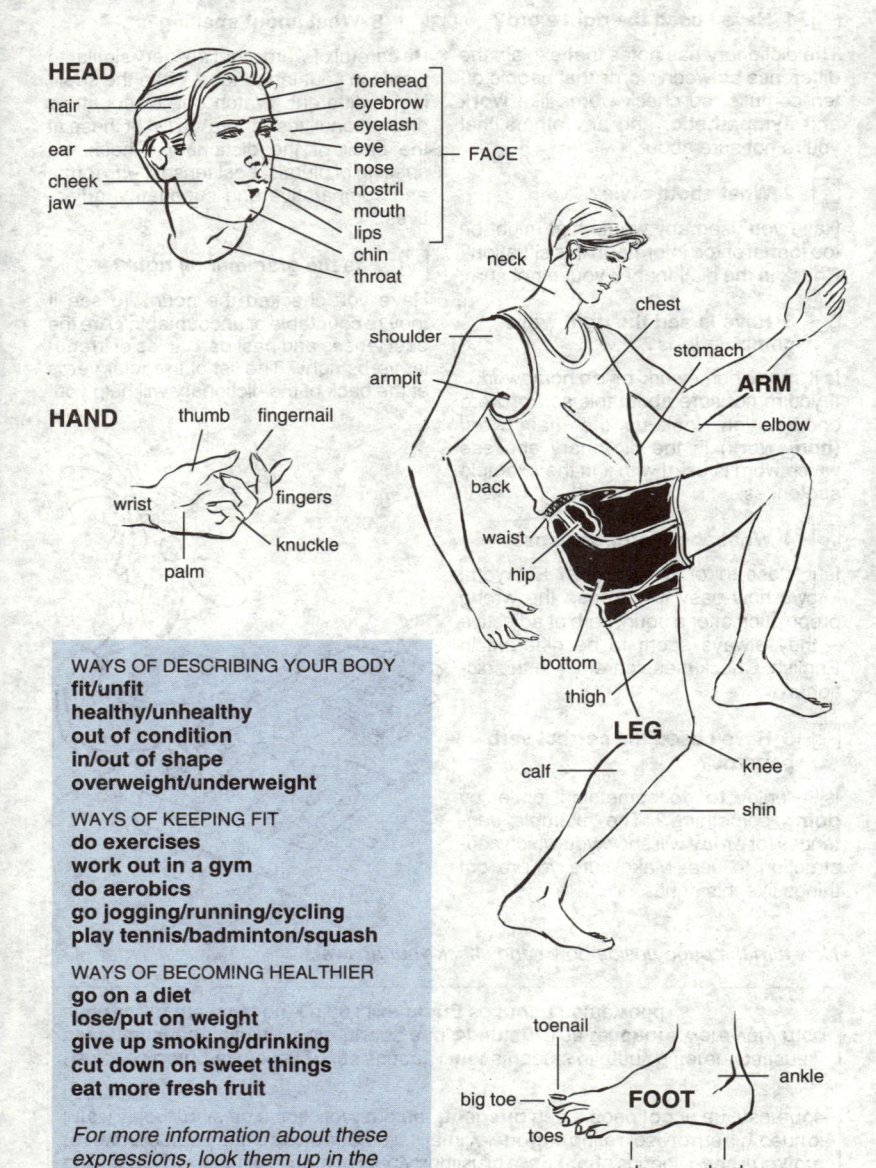

The Family

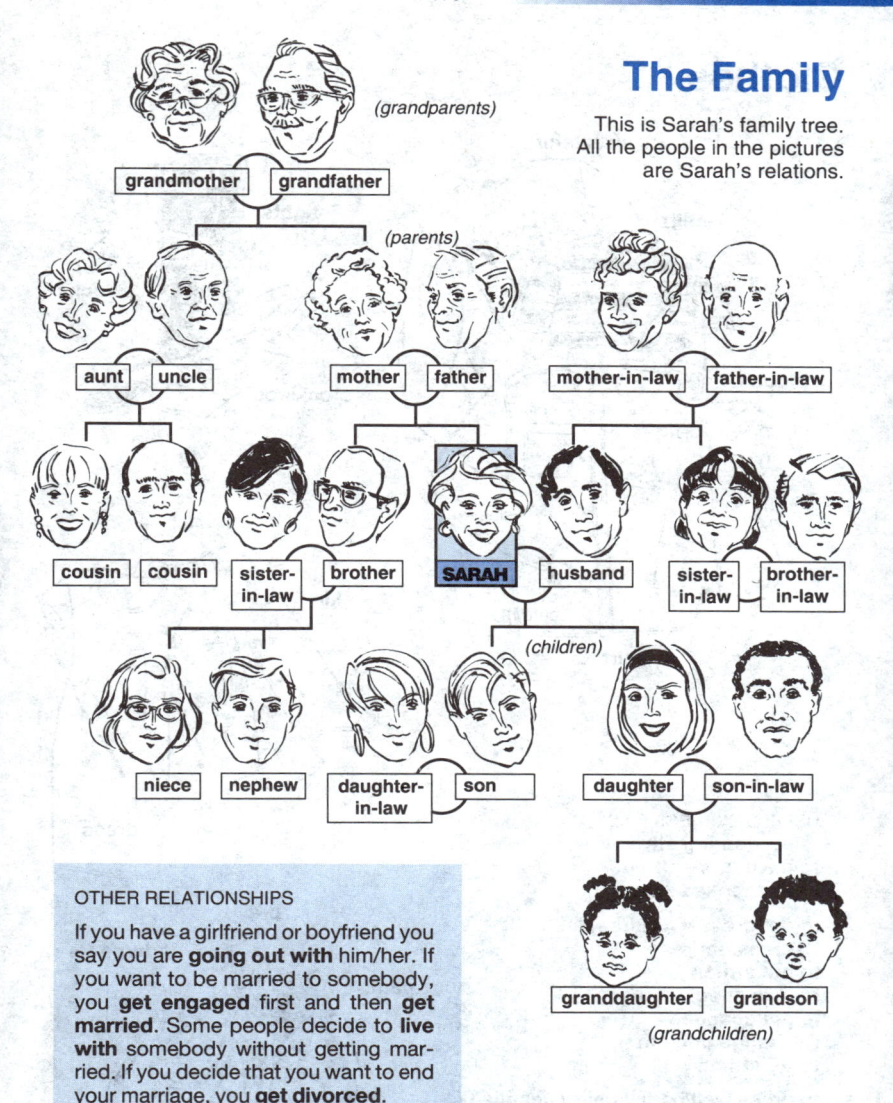

This is Sarah's family tree. All the people in the pictures are Sarah's relations.

(grandparents)
- grandmother
- grandfather

(parents)
- aunt
- uncle
- mother
- father
- mother-in-law
- father-in-law

- cousin
- cousin
- sister-in-law
- brother
- SARAH
- husband
- sister-in-law
- brother-in-law

(children)
- niece
- nephew
- daughter-in-law
- son
- daughter
- son-in-law

- granddaughter
- grandson

(grandchildren)

OTHER RELATIONSHIPS

If you have a girlfriend or boyfriend you say you are **going out with** him/her. If you want to be married to somebody, you **get engaged** first and then **get married**. Some people decide to **live with** somebody without getting married. If you decide that you want to end your marriage, you **get divorced**.

If your father dies, or if your parents get divorced, your mother may decide to marry again, and her new husband will be your **stepfather**. If your father remarries, his new wife will be your **stepmother**. If your stepfather or stepmother already has children from an earlier marriage, those children become your **stepsisters** and **stepbrothers,** and your mother's or father's **stepchildren**. If your mother and stepfather (or father and stepmother) then have children together, they are your **half-brothers** and **half-sisters**.

Clothes

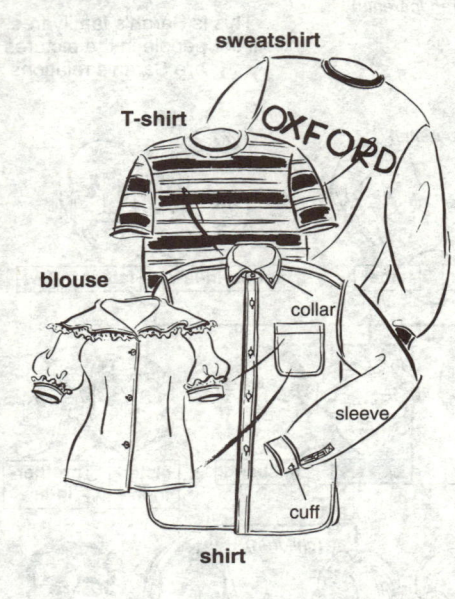

sweatshirt
T-shirt
OXFORD
blouse
collar
sleeve
cuff
shirt

tights
socks
stockings

skirt
dress

bra
underpants
pants
vest
slip
boxer shorts

USEFUL EXPRESSIONS
to be wearing sth
to have (got) sth on
to be dressed in sth

to get dressed/undressed
to dress/undress
to put sth on
to take sth off
to get changed
to change into sth
to try sth on

to dress well/badly/smartly/casually
to be well-dressed/elegant/scruffy
to dress up

Clothes can **fit** you or **suit** you.

For more information about how to use these expressions, look them up in the main part of the dictionary.

Clothes

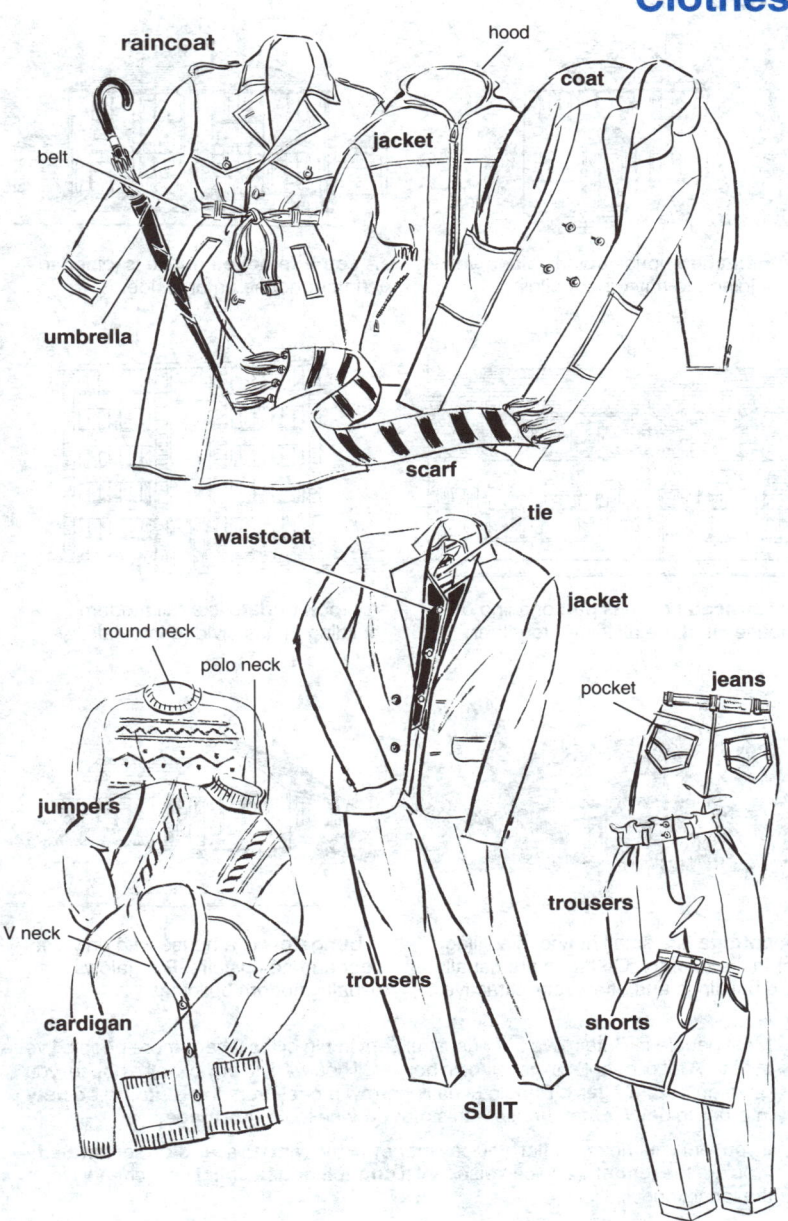

- raincoat
- belt
- umbrella
- hood
- jacket
- coat
- scarf
- round neck
- polo neck
- jumpers
- V neck
- cardigan
- waistcoat
- tie
- jacket
- trousers
- **SUIT**
- pocket
- jeans
- trousers
- shorts

Houses

A **detached** house stands alone and is not joined to any other building.

A **semi-detached** house is joined to another house on one side.

A **terraced** house is part of a line of houses that are all joined together.

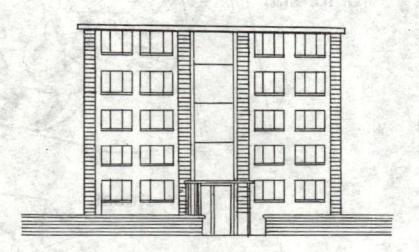

A **block of flats** is a tall modern building that is divided into flats.

A **cottage** is a small house in a village or in the country. Cottages are usually old buildings and often very attractive.

A **bungalow** is a house with only one floor and no upstairs. Bungalows are usually modern buildings.

Most people in Britain live in houses, except in big cities where more people live in flats. A lot of people own their own homes. If you want to buy or sell a house, you go to an **estate agent**. People usually borrow money from the **building society** in order to pay for their house – this money is called a **mortgage**.

If you rent your house or flat, you pay money (= the **rent**) to a **landlord** or **landlady** (you are the **tenant**). You can also rent a **council house** or **flat** very cheaply from the local council.

Computers

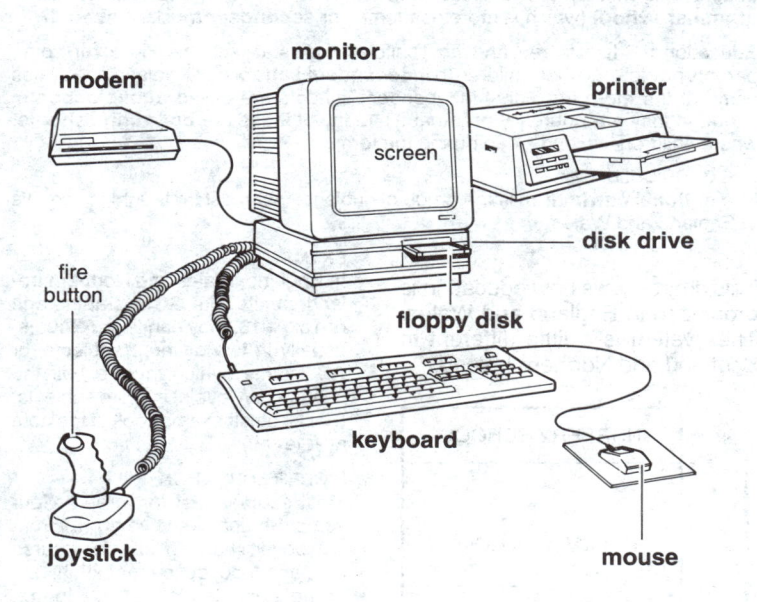

Labels on diagram: modem, monitor, screen, printer, disk drive, fire button, floppy disk, keyboard, joystick, mouse

Here are some of the special words that are used in computing. Many of them have a different meaning in ordinary English. For more information about these words, look them up in the main part of the dictionary.

The information that you put into a computer is called **data**. If you **enter** or **key in** data, the computer will **process** it. The list of instructions that the computer follows in order to process data is called a **program**.

If you want to store a program or data onto a disk or tape, you **save** it. You can organize the data by saving it into different **files** or **folders**. When you put the disk or tape back into the computer, you **load** it. You can **print out** information from a computer onto paper – this paper is then called a **printout**.

A **byte** is a unit of computer memory. It is usually made up of a series of eight smaller units called **bits**. One byte is just enough memory to store a single letter or figure.

Hardware means the computer and any equipment that is connected to it. The programs that are used in a computer are called **software**.

A person who writes computer programs is called a **programmer**.

Pictures on the computer are called **graphics**.

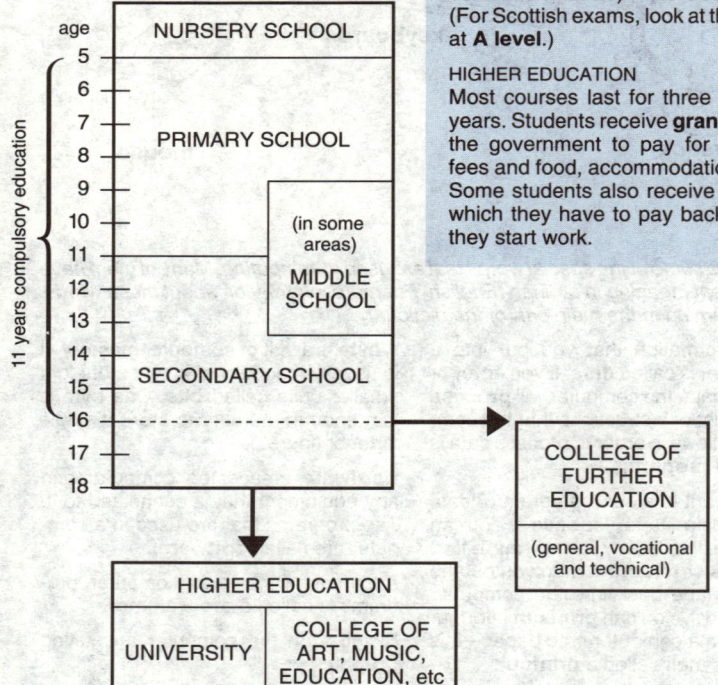

The British Education System

SECONDARY SCHOOLS
Most secondary schools are **comprehensive schools**, which offer a general education to children of all abilities. In some areas children are selected for either **grammar school** (which is more academic) or **secondary modern school**.

Education in Britain is free, and most children go to state schools. However, some parents pay to send their children to **independent schools**. In England and Wales some of the more traditional independent schools are called **public schools**, although they are not really public at all! Many of these are **boarding schools**, where children live and sleep during the term.

THE CURRICULUM
The **national curriculum** is the group of subjects that must be taught in schools in England and Wales.

This chart shows how education is organized in England and Wales. The system is a little different in Scotland and Northern Ireland.

EXAMS
In England, Wales and Northern Ireland, pupils take **GCSEs** at the age of 16. At 18, they can take **A levels**, usually in two or three subjects, or **AS** exams (which involve half the content of A levels) in more subjects. (For Scottish exams, look at the note at **A level**.)

HIGHER EDUCATION
Most courses last for three or four years. Students receive **grants** from the government to pay for course fees and food, accommodation, etc. Some students also receive **loans**, which they have to pay back when they start work.

age			
5	NURSERY SCHOOL		
6			
7	PRIMARY SCHOOL		
8			
9			
10		(in some areas)	
11			
12		MIDDLE SCHOOL	
13			
14	SECONDARY SCHOOL		
15			
16			→ COLLEGE OF FURTHER EDUCATION (general, vocational and technical)
17			
18			

11 years compulsory education

HIGHER EDUCATION: UNIVERSITY | COLLEGE OF ART, MUSIC, EDUCATION, etc

The American Education System

SCHOOLS
Most American children go to state schools, which are free. In the USA these are called **public schools**. (Don't confuse them with British public schools!) There are also some private schools, which are usually supported by religious organizations.

ASSESSMENT
There are no national exams, although some schools and states have their own exams. Generally examination is by **continuous assessment**, which means that teachers assess children throughout the year on how well they do in tests, classroom discussions and written and oral work. If students want to go on to higher education, some colleges and universities require them to take the **SAT** (Scholastic Aptitude Test).

This chart shows how education is generally organized in the USA, although in some states the system may be different.

GRADUATION
Students can **graduate** from high school if they have collected enough **units** (about 120 hours of classes in one subject). Most students collect units in basic subjects called **requirements** in their first years at high school, and then move on to specialist subjects called **electives** for the last two years.

HIGHER EDUCATION
Most college and university courses last for four years. Most universities are private, and students have to pay to go to both private and state universities. There are no final examinations, and students receive a **degree** if they have collected enough **credits** in a particular subject.

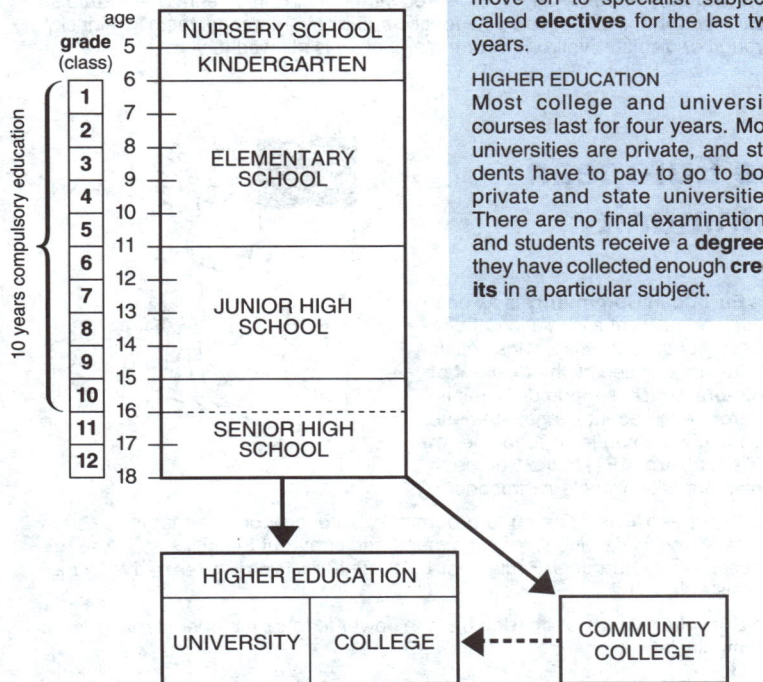

grade (class)	age	
	5	NURSERY SCHOOL
	6	KINDERGARTEN
1	7	
2	8	
3	9	ELEMENTARY SCHOOL
4	10	
5	11	
6	12	
7	13	JUNIOR HIGH SCHOOL
8	14	
9	15	
10	16	
11	17	SENIOR HIGH SCHOOL
12	18	

10 years compulsory education (grades 1–10)

HIGHER EDUCATION: UNIVERSITY | COLLEGE ◄------ COMMUNITY COLLEGE

British Government

PARLIAMENT
The British Parliament is made up of the **House of Commons** and the **House of Lords**. The House of Commons has 650 **Members of Parliament (MPs)**, who are elected directly by the people. The House of Lords has over 1 000 members, who are not elected, but are members of the nobility, bishops, judges, and people chosen by the Prime Minister.

GOVERNMENT
The **Prime Minister** chooses about 20 **ministers** to form a special advisory group called the **Cabinet.** Most cabinet ministers are heads of government departments. The **Chancellor of the Exchequer** is head of the finance department (the **Treasury**), and the **Foreign Secretary** is the minister in charge of foreign affairs.

ELECTIONS
About every five years there is a **general election**, when people in each area (**constituency**) vote for an MP to represent them in Parliament. There are also **local elections**, when people vote for **councillors** to represent them in their city, borough or district. Everyone over the age of 18 is allowed to vote.

The European Community

The **European Community** is an economic and political association of certain European countries. Most of its policies are decided by the **Council of Ministers**, which is made up of ministers from each country's government. Each country also elects a number of **MEPs** (or **Euro-MPs)** to the European Parliament, which meets in Strasbourg.

The **European Commission** is a permanent group of people that is based in Brussels, and whose job is to recommend and carry out EC policies. These are discussed in the European Parliament, but the final decision is taken by the Council of Ministers.

The **European Court of Justice** has the power to force member states to keep Community laws.

American Government

THE FEDERAL SYSTEM
The **American Constitution** divides power between the **federal government** and the governments of the individual states. Each state has its own laws and system of government. The federal government deals with national issues such as economic and foreign policy.

There are three branches of federal government: the executive branch (which is led by the **President**); the legislative branch (**Congress**, which is made up of the **Senate** and the **House of Representatives**); and the judicial branch (the **Supreme Court** and other federal courts). Laws are made by Congress, but the President can **veto** a law, and the Supreme Court can say that it is unconstitutional.

ELECTIONS
Each state is allowed to elect two **senators** to the Senate, and a number of **representatives** to the House of Representatives (the exact number depends on the size of its population). Elections for representatives are held every two years; one third of the senators are also elected every two years. The President is elected directly by the people, and **presidential elections** are held every four years.

The United Nations

Most countries in the world belong to the **United Nations** (the **UN**), an organization which was set up in 1945 to encourage international peace, security and cooperation. Its headquarters is in New York, and its chief administrator is called the **Secretary-General**.

Each country has a seat in the **General Assembly**, which meets to discuss world problems. The **UN Security Council** is a permanent group that tries to settle problems between nations peacefully. It may send the **UN Peace-keeping Force** to keep the peace in a particular area.

The UN also has specialized **agencies**, that deal with issues like food and agriculture, health, and education.

The Environment

GLOBAL WARMING

Scientists say the temperature of the earth could rise by 3°C over the next 50 years. This may cause **drought** in some parts of the world, and **floods** in others, as ice at the North and South Poles begins to melt and sea levels rise.

Global warming is caused by the **greenhouse effect**. Normally, heat from the sun warms the earth and then escapes back into space. But **carbon dioxide** and other gases in the atmosphere trap the sun's heat, and this is slowly making the earth warmer.

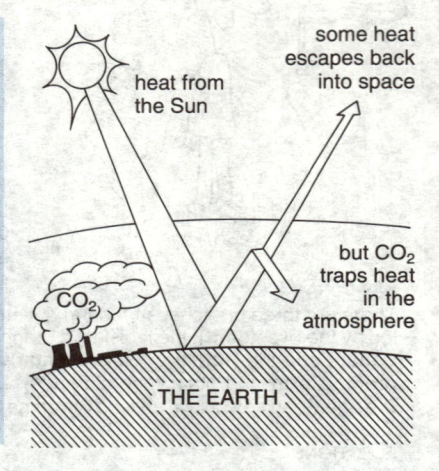

THE OZONE LAYER

The **ozone layer** is a layer of gas high above the surface of the earth that helps to protect it from the sun's **ultraviolet radiation**, which can damage our skins and cause **cancer**. Scientists have recently discovered holes in the ozone layer, caused by substances called **CFCs** (chlorofluorocarbons).

CFCs are used in refrigerators, **aerosol cans** and in the manufacture of some plastic products. Some companies now make aerosols that do not contain CFCs, and these are often marked **'ozone-friendly'**.

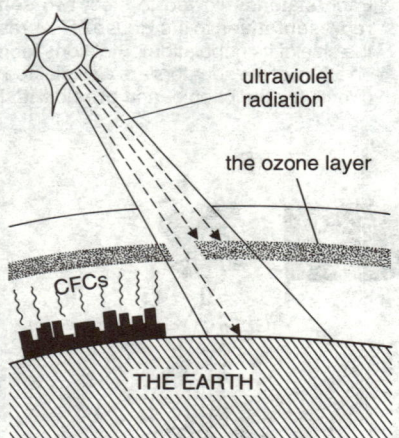

DEFORESTATION

Rainforests help to control global warming because they absorb carbon dioxide. In recent years, large areas have been destroyed, as the trees are cut down for wood or burned to clear the land for farming. The burning releases large amounts of carbon dioxide into the atmosphere.

Many rainforests grow on poor soils, and when they are cut down or burned, the soil is washed away in the tropical rains, so that the area may turn to **desert**. Many plant and animal species that live there could become **extinct**.

# The Environment

POLLUTION

Factories, power stations and motor vehicles pump large quantities of carbon dioxide and other waste gases into the air. This is a major cause of the greenhouse effect. A lot of petrol contains **lead**, which is very poisonous and can cause brain damage in children. Many people now prefer to use **unleaded petrol**.

Some poisonous gases dissolve in water in the atmosphere and then fall to the earth as **acid rain**. Acid rain damages trees and buildings, and can kill fish in lakes and rivers. Rivers can also be polluted by industrial waste from factories and chemical **fertilizers** and **pesticides** used by farmers.

ALTERNATIVE ENERGY

Most of the energy we use today comes from coal, oil and gas. But these will not last for ever, and burning them is slowly harming the atmosphere. We need to look for other ways of supplying energy.

Solar power is a way of using the sun's energy as heat or to make electricity. We can also use **wind-power** by building modern windmills that spin in the wind. There are several types of **water-power**: river water in mountainous areas can be used to generate **hydroelectric power**, and we can also create electricity from sea water flowing in and out with the tides.

RECYCLING

Recycling is the processing of used objects and materials so that they can be used again. About 60% of rubbish from homes and factories contain materials that could be **recycled**. Recycling saves energy and raw materials, and also reduces damage to the countryside.

Glass, paper and aluminium cans can all be recycled very easily. Many towns have **bottle banks** and **can banks** where people can leave their empty bottles and cans for recycling. A lot of paper bags, writing paper and greetings cards are now produced on **recycled paper**.

Keeping vocabulary records

It's important to organize your vocabulary learning by keeping a record of all the new words that you want to remember.

VOCABULARY NOTEBOOKS

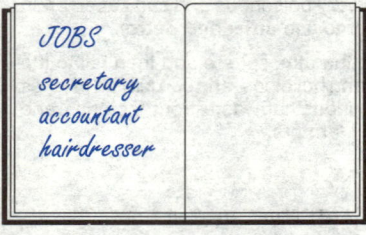

A

JOBS
secretary
accountant
hairdresser

B

H
honey
hairdresser
however

Many people like to buy a special notebook for vocabulary. You can divide your notebook into topic pages (as in picture A), or organize the pages alphabetically (as in picture B). Write in a few words when you first buy the book, and then keep adding more words as you meet them.

VOCABULARY CARDS

(front of card)

SHALLOW

(back of card)

not deep

EXAMPLE
The sea is very shallow here.

Another way of recording vocabulary is to write each new word on a card and keep all the cards in a box. Write the word on one side of the card, and the meaning and an example sentence on the other. Later you can test yourself: look at the word on the front of the card and try and remember what it means; or look at the information on the back of the card and see if you can remember the word!

RECORDING MEANINGS

There are several different ways of recording the meaning of a new word:

You can draw a picture

snake

You can explain the word in English

salary = the money you receive from your job

You can give the word in your own language

tired = cansado

Or you can show the word in an example sentence

Although it was raining, we decided to go for a walk.

PRACTICE 1
How would you record the meaning of these words? Choose the best way for each word.

banana   autumn   since   above   museum   rich

RECORDING OTHER INFORMATION
There may be other important things you want to remember about a new word. Find it in your dictionary and decide what you need to write down about it. Always try to write an example sentence, as this will help you remember how the word is used in English.

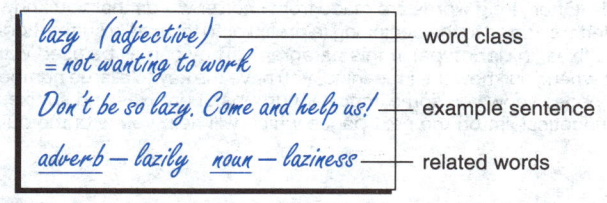

lazy (adjective) ——————— word class
= not wanting to work
Don't be so lazy. Come and help us! —— example sentence
adverb — lazily   noun — laziness —— related words

PRACTICE 2
Now write down the things you think are most important about these words. Use the dictionary to help you.

bleed   deaf   on the ball   fluent   swap

TABLES AND DIAGRAMS
It may sometimes be helpful to write down words in groups. Look at these two ways of recording groups of words:

a) WORD TABLES

SPORT	PERSON	PLACE
football	footballer	pitch
athletics	athlete	track
golf	golfer	course
tennis	tennis player	court

b) WORD DIAGRAMS

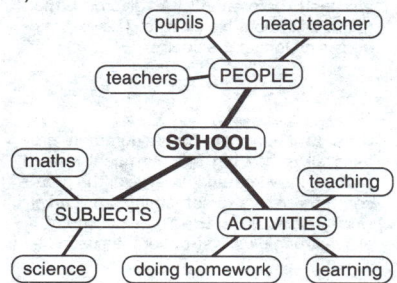

SCHOOL
- PEOPLE: pupils, head teacher, teachers
- SUBJECTS: maths, science
- ACTIVITIES: teaching, doing homework, learning

PRACTICE 3
a) Make a word table, using words for JOBS, PLACES OF WORK, and THINGS PEOPLE USE IN THEIR JOBS.

b) Draw a word diagram showing vocabulary connected with HOLIDAYS. You could divide the words into 'places to stay', 'ways of travelling' and 'activities'.

Word formation

When you find a new word in English, what do you do? Look it up in a **mono**lingual or a **bi**lingual dictionary? Ask a teach**er** or another stud**ent**? Try to **pre**dict the meaning from the rest of the sentence or the paragraph – the **con**text? There is another way to try to simpl**ify** difficult words. Often, long words are made from shorter words that you know, combined with a few letters added to the beginning (a prefix) or to the end (a suffix). Look at the prefixes and suffixes (in **dark** type) in this paragraph. They can all be used with many other words, so when you know their meaning, you have the key to a large number of new words. These pages show you some important groups of prefixes and suffixes. There is a longer alphabetical list on the next pages which will help you with the quiz questions.

Numbers Many common words have prefixes that tell us about numbers. A word that begins with **bi-** shows that there are two of something. A *bicycle* has two wheels (but a *tricycle* has three). Words for measurements are often made with the prefixes **cent-**, **kilo-**, etc. 100 *centimetres* = 1 metre, 1 *kilogram* = 1 000 grams, and so on.

1. How many sides has an **octagon**?
2. If 1991 was the **bicentenary** of Mozart's death, in which year did he die?
3. Which word is a **monosyllable**, 'but', 'although', or 'however'?
4. Does a **multi-storey car park** have more than one floor?

Time A number of prefixes are connected with time, for example **pre-** (before) and **ex-** (former). A *pre-arranged* meeting was arranged beforehand. A divorced man might talk about his *ex-wife*. The *ex-president* is no longer president.

5. If a house was built in the **postwar** period, was it built before or after the war?
6. Would a woman go to **ante-natal** classes before or after her baby was born?
7. If your teacher told you to **rewrite** your essay, why would you be angry?

Size and degree Some common prefixes tell us 'how big' or 'how much'. A word that begins with **maxi-** is large or the greatest; **mini-** refers to something small (*miniskirt; minibus*). **extra-** means 'more' – *extra-strong glue* is stronger than usual.

8. Which flies faster than the speed of sound, a **subsonic** plane or a **supersonic** plane?
9. Is a **micro-organism** a very large or very small creature?
10. How do you feel if you have **overeaten** – very full or still hungry?

Negative Many prefixes change the meaning of a word to its opposite or make it negative. A *non-smoker* does not smoke; the opposite of *happy* is *unhappy*. Besides **non-** and **un-** we also use **in-** (or before certain letters **im-**, **il-**, or **ir-**) in this way. It is important to learn which is the correct prefix to make the opposite of a word.

11. Which of the prefixes **un-, in-, im-, il-, ir-** would you use to make the opposites of these words?
    **correct   certain   possible
    regular   sure   legal   valid
    relevant   patient   legible**
    If you are not sure, use the list to help you.

Position These prefixes tell us where something is or happens. For example, **sub-** gives the idea of 'under': a *subway* goes under the road; we read the *subtitles* under the pictures of a foreign film.

12. Is an activity that is **extra-curricular** part of the curriculum of a school?
13. Is a flight from London to New York **transatlantic**?
14. in America, is an **Interstate** a road within one state or a road that links two or more states?

A **suffix** is added to the end of a word, and it often changes the function of the word. There is one suffix that you probably use very often: **-ly** to make an adjective into an adverb. (*He sings beautifully. The car was badly damaged.*) A suffix can also be added to a noun to make it into an adjective: you can change the noun *Japan* into an adjective describing the nationality of the people who live there by adding **-ese**: *Japanese*.

To make nouns that describe a **state**, an **action** or a **quality** you can add a suffix such as **-ation**. eg *inform + ation = information*; *examine + ation = examination*. There may be small changes in the spelling, eg the second 'e' is dropped in *examination*.

15. Use one of the suffixes **-ation, -ment, -ness** to make nouns from these verbs and adjectives:
develop kind arrange imagine happy organize
What happens to the spelling of 'happy'?

Other suffixes are used **to make nouns** that describe **people**, for example, **-er, -or, -ist, -ian, -ee, -ant, -ent**. They may be added to a verb to describe the person who does that action, eg *rider, sailor, typist,* or we can add them to nouns to describe someone who works on a particular subject (*artist, historian*).

16. Fill the gaps to make words that describe people and their jobs:
a--or   (works in a theatre)
b----er   (uses bricks and stone to make houses)
c------or   (stands in front of the orchestra)
e-----er   (goes out to discover new countries)

We can also make a noun or an adjective into a **verb** by adding a suffix such as **-ize, -en,** or **-ify**. If we make something wider, simpler or more modern, we *widen, simplify,* or *modernize* it.

17. Which verbs can you make from these words, using one of the suffixes **-ize, -en** and **-ify**?
magnet beauty sharp general loose pure
(You may need to change the spelling a little.)

Adjectives can be made with many different suffixes. Some very common ones are **-able** (or sometimes **-ible** or just **-ble**), which often means 'possible to' (*acceptable, avoidable*), **-y** and **-ful**, which often describe qualities: *cloudy, helpful, beautiful*. To show that something is missing, we can add **-less**: a situation where there is no hope is *hopeless*.

18. Solve the clues to find these adjectives: (They all end in one of the suffixes mentioned)
a) practical, that can be used a lot
b) having no friends
c) easy to see or notice
d) needing something to drink

Now turn the page upside down and check your answers:

1 eight 2 1791 3 but 4 yes 5 after 6 before 7 because you have to write it again 8 supersonic 9 very small 10 very full 11 incorrect uncertain impossible irregular unsure illegal invalid irrelevant impatient illegible 12 no 13 yes 14 a road that links two or more states 15 development kindness arrangement imagination happiness organization (the 'y' of 'happy' becomes an 'i') 16 actor builder conductor explorer 17 magnetize beautify sharpen generalize loosen purify 18 useful friendless noticeable thirsty

List of Prefixes and Suffixes

PREFIXES
a- not: *atypical*
Anglo- English: *Anglo-German relations*
ante- before: *antenatal* (= before birth)
anti- against: *anti-European, antisocial*
auto- self: *autobiography* (= the story of the writer's own life)
bi- two: *bicycle, bilingual* (= using two languages), *bimonthly* (= twice a month or every two months)
cent-, centi- hundred: *centenary* (= the hundredth anniversary), *centimetre* (= one hundredth of a metre)
circum- around: *circumnavigate* (= sail around)
co- with; together: *copilot, coexist, cooperation*
con- with; together: *context* (= the words or sentences that come before and after a particular word or sentence)
contra- against; opposite: *contradict* (= say the opposite), *contraflow* (= traffic travelling in the opposite direction to normal)
counter- against; opposite: *counter-revolution, counter-productive* (= producing the opposite of the desired effect)
de- taking sth away; the opposite: *defrost* (= removing the layers of ice from a fridge, etc), *decentralize*
deci- one tenth: *decilitre*
dis- reverse or opposite: *displease, disembark, discomfort*
Euro- European: *Euro-MP* (= member of the European Parliament)
ex- former: *ex-wife, ex-president*
extra- 1 very; more than usual: *extra-thin, extra-special* 2 outside; beyond: *extraordinary, extra-terrestrial* (= coming from somewhere beyond the earth)
fore- 1 before; in advance: *foretell* (= say what is going to happen), *foreword* (= at the beginning of a book) 2 front: *foreground* (= the front part of a picture), *forehead*
in- (il-, im-, ir-) not: *incorrect, invalid, illegal, illegible, immoral, impatient, impossible, irregular, irrelevant*
inter- between; from one to another: *international, interracial*
kilo- thousand: *kilogram, kilowatt*

maxi- most; very large: *maximum*
mega- million; very large: *megabyte, megastar* (= a very famous person)
micro- one millionth; very small: *microgram, micro-organism*
mid- in the middle of: *mid-afternoon, mid-air*
milli- thousandth: *milligram, millilitre*
mini- small: *miniskirt, minibus, miniseries*
mis- bad or wrong; not: *misunderstand, misbehave, miscalculate*
mono- one; single: *monolingual* (= using one language), *monorail*
multi- many: *multinational* (= involving many countries)
non- not: *nonsense, non-resident, non-smoker*
out- more; to a greater degree: *outdo, outrun* (= run faster or better than sb)
over- more than normal; too much: *overeat, oversleep* (= sleep too long), *overestimate* (= guess too high)
post- after: *postwar*
pre- before: *prepaid, preview*
pro- for; in favour of: *pro-European, pro-democracy*
quad- four: *quadruple* (= multiply by four), *quadruplet* (= one of four babies born at the same time)
re- again: *rewrite, rebuild*
semi- half: *semicircle, semi-detached* (= a house joined to the next at one side only)
sub- 1 below; less than: *subzero, subsonic* (= less than the speed of sound) 2 under: *subway, subtitles* (= translation under the pictures of a film)
super- extremely; more than: *superhuman* (= having greater power than humans normally have), *supersonic* (= faster than the speed of sound)
tele- far; over a long distance: *telecommunications, television, telephoto lens*
trans- across; through: *transatlantic, transcontinental*
tri- three: *triangle, tricolour* (= a flag with three colours)
ultra- extremely; beyond a certain limit: *ultra-modern, ultraviolet* (= light that is beyond what we can normally see)
un- not; opposite; taking sth away: *un-*

certain, uncomfortable, unsure, undo, undress
uni- one; single: *uniform* (= having the same form)

SUFFIXES
-able, -ible, -ble to make adjectives; possible to ~: *acceptable, noticeable, convertible, divisible* (= possible to divide), *irresistible* (= that you cannot resist)

-age to make nouns; a process or state: *shortage, storage*

-al to make adjectives; connected with: *experimental, accidental, environmental*

-ance, -ence, (-ancy, -ency) to make nouns; an action, process or state: *appearance, performance, elegance, importance, existence, intelligence, patience*

-ant, -ent to make nouns; a person who does sth: *assistant, immigrant, student*

-ation to make nouns; a state or action: *examination, imagination, organization*

-ble look at **-able**

-ee to make nouns; a person to whom sth is done: *employee* (= sb who is employed), *trainee* (= sb who is being trained)

-en to make verbs; to give sth a particular quality; to make sth more ~: *shorten, widen, blacken, sharpen, loosen*, (but note: *lengthen*)

-ence (-ency) look at **-ance**

-ent look at **-ant**

-er to make nouns; a person who does sth: *rider, painter, baker, builder; driver, teacher*

-ese to make adjectives; from a place: *Japanese, Chinese, Viennese*

-ess to make nouns; a woman who does sth as a job: *waitress, actress*

-ful to make adjectives; having a particular quality: *helpful, useful, thankful, beautiful*

-hood to make nouns; a state, often during a particular period of time: *childhood, motherhood*

-ian to make nouns; a person who does sth as a job or hobby: *historian, comedian, politician*

-ible look at **-able**

-ical to make adjectives from nouns ending in -y or -ics; connected with: *economical, mathematical, physical*

-ify to make verbs; to produce a state or quality: *beautify, simplify, purify*

-ise look at **-ize**

-ish to make adjectives; **1** describing nationality or language: *English, Swedish, Polish* **2** like sth: *babyish, foolish* **3** rather, quite: *longish* (= fairly long, but not very long), *youngish, brownish*

-ist to make nouns; **1** a person who has studied sth or does sth as a job: *artist, scientist, typist* **2** a person who believes in sth or belongs to a particular group: *capitalist, pacifist, feminist*

-ion to make nouns; a state or process: *action, connection, exhibition*

-ive to make adjectives; able to ~, having a particular quality: *attractive, effective*

-ize, -ise to make verbs; actions producing a particular state: *magnetize, standardize, modernize, generalize*

-less to make adjectives; not having sth: *hopeless, friendless*

-like to make adjectives; similar to: *childlike*

-ly to make adverbs; in a particular way: *badly, beautifully, completely*

-ment to make nouns; a state, action or quality: *development, arrangement, excitement, achievement*

-ness to make nouns; a state or quality: *kindness, sadness, happiness, weakness*

-ology to make nouns; the study of a subject: *biology, psychology, zoology*

-or to make nouns; a person who does sth, often as a job: *actor, conductor, sailor*

-ous to make adjectives; having a particular quality: *dangerous, religious, ambitious*

-ship to make nouns; showing status: *friendship, membership, citizenship*

-wards to make adverbs; in a particular direction: *backwards, upwards*

-wise to make adverbs; in a particular way: *clockwise*

-y to make adjectives; having the quality of the thing mentioned: *cloudy, rainy, fatty, thirsty, greeny* (= similar to green)

Phrasal verbs

Phrasal verbs are verbs that consist of two (or three) parts – an ordinary verb and another word (or words) like **in**, **for**, or **off**. They are very common in English. Here are some examples:

lie down   give up   look for   get on with

Some of them are easy to understand (you can guess the meaning of **lie down** if you know the words **lie** and **down**), but many phrasal verbs are more difficult because they have special meanings (you cannot guess that '**give up** smoking' means 'stop smoking' even if you know the words **give** and **up**).

If you want to find a phrasal verb in the dictionary, look under the first word (to find **give up**, look under **give**). The 'phrasal verbs' section comes after the ordinary meanings of the verb.

PRACTICE 1
Use the dictionary to complete these sentences with the correct word.

a) This meat smells horrible. It must have gone _ _ _ _ _.
   (over, off, past)
b) UK stands _ _ _ _ _ United Kingdom.
   (out, to, for)
c) I can't work _ _ _ _ _ how to use this video.
   (up, out, for)
d) Sue came _ _ _ _ _ the letter while she was tidying her room.
   (to, across, for)
e) I'm sure that story wasn't true. I think Pete made it _ _ _ _ _.
   (up, for, in)
f) She was offered a job in London, but she decided to turn it _ _ _ _ _.
   (over, up, down)
g) Oh no, I've run out _ _ _ _ _ milk. We'll have to buy some more.
   (for, of, with)
h) Can you write _ _ _ _ _ your address and telephone number, please?
   (down, up, in)

(*Answers:* a) off b) for c) out d) across e) up f) down g) of h) down)

THE FOUR TYPES

There are four main types of phrasal verbs:

> **TYPE 1 – phrasal verbs *without* an object**
>   The fire **went out**.
>   My car **broke down** on the motorway.
>
> In the dictionary these verbs are written like this:
>   **go out**
>   **break down**

TYPE 2 – phrasal verbs that can be separated by an object

a If the object is a noun, it can either go *after* both parts of the phrasal verb, or *between* them:

   She **tried on** the red dress.
   She **tried** the red dress **on**.

b If the object is a pronoun, it must go *between* the two parts of the phrasal verb:

   She **tried** it **on**. (NOT ~~She tried on it.~~)

In the dictionary this verb is written like this: **try sth on**. When you see **sth** or **sb** *between* the two parts of the phrasal verb, you know that they can be separated by an object.

TYPE 3 – phrasal verbs that cannot be separated by an object

The two parts of the phrasal verb must go together.

   John's **looking after** the children.
   (NOT ~~John's looking the children after.~~)

   John's **looking after** them.
   (NOT ~~John's looking them after.~~)

In the dictionary this verb is written like this: **look after sb**. When you see **sb** or **sth** *after* the two parts of the phrasal verb, you know that they *cannot* be separated by an object.

TYPE 4 – phrasal verbs with three parts

The three parts of the phrasal verb must go together:

   I can't **put up with** this noise any longer.

In the dictionary this verb is written like this: **put up with sb/sth**. Again, when you see **sb** or **sth** *after* the three parts of the phrasal verb, you know that they *cannot* be separated by an object.

PRACTICE 2
Complete these sentences by putting the word 'it' in the correct place. In each sentence you will have to leave one space empty.

a) You must be hot with your coat on. Why don't you take _ _ off _ _ ?
b) If you don't understand this word, look _ _ up _ _ in your dictionary.
c) He's had a big shock, and it will take him some time to get _ _ over _ _ .
d) I was going to do my homework last night, but I'm afraid I didn't get round _ _ to _ _ .
e) I thought you'd read the newspaper, so I threw _ _ away _ _ .
f) Jill can't come to the meeting tomorrow, so we'll have to put _ _ off _ _ till next week.

(*Answers:* a) take it off b) look it up c) get over it d) round to it e) threw it away f) put it off)

Punctuation

A **full stop (.)** (US **period**) is used at the end of a sentence, unless the sentence is a question or an exclamation:
We're leaving now. ○ *That's all.*
○ *Thank you.*
It is also often used after an abbreviation:
Acacia Ave. ○ *a.m.* ○ *Walton St.*

A **question mark (?)** is written at the end of a direct question:
'Who's that man?' Jenny asked.
but not after an indirect question:
Jenny asked who the man was.

An **exclamation mark (!)** (US **exclamation point**) is used at the end of a sentence which expresses surprise, enthusiasm, shock or horror:
What an amazing story! ○ *How well you look!* ○ *Oh no! The cat's been run over!*
or after an interjection or a word describing a loud sound:
Bye! ○ *Ow!* ○ *Crash!*

A **comma (,)** shows a slight pause in a sentence:
I ran all the way to the station, but I still missed the train. ○ *Although it was cold, the sun was shining.* ○ *He did, nevertheless, leave his phone number.* ○ *However, we may be wrong.*
It is also used before a quotation or direct speech:
Fiona said, 'I'll help you.' ○ *'I'll help you', said Fiona, 'but you'll have to wait till Monday.'*
Commas are also used between the items in a list, although they may be omitted before 'and':
It was a cold, rainy day. ○ *This shop sells records, tapes, and compact discs.*
In relative clauses, commas are used around a phrase which adds some new, but not essential information. Compare the two sentences:
The boy who had lots of sweets gave some to the boy who had none.
The boy, who had lots of sweets, was already eating.
We cannot understand the first sentence without the information introduced by 'who'. However, in the second sentence, the phrase 'who had lots of sweets', only adds extra information and is kept separate from the main part of the sentence by commas.

A **colon (:)** is used to introduce something, such as a long quotation or a list:
There is a choice of main course: roast beef, turkey or omelette.

A **semicolon (;)** is used to separate two contrasting parts of a sentence:
John wanted to go; I did not.
or to separate items in a list where commas have already been used:
The school uniform consists of navy skirt or trousers; grey, white or pale blue shirt; navy jumper or cardigan; grey, blue or white socks.

An **apostrophe (')** shows either that a letter is missing, in short forms such as *hasn't, don't, I'm, he's*
or that a person or thing belongs to somebody:
Peter's scarf ○ *Jane's mother* ○ *my friend's car*
With some names that end in 's', another 's' is not always added:
Jesus' name
Notice the position of the apostrophe with singular and plural nouns:
the girl's keys (= the keys belonging to the girl)
the girls' keys (= the keys belonging to the girls).

Quotation marks or **inverted commas** (' ' or " ") are used to show the words that somebody said :
'Come and see,' said Martin. ○ *'Oh, no!' said Martin. 'Come and see what's happened.'* ○ *Angela shouted, 'Over here!'*
or what somebody thought, when the thoughts are presented like speech:
'Will they get here on time?' she wondered.
They are also used around a title, for example of a book, play, film, etc:
'Pinocchio' was the first film I ever saw. ○ *'Have you read "Emma"?' he asked.*

A **hyphen (-)** is used to join two words which together form one idea:
the dining-room ○ *a ten-ton truck*
or sometimes to link a prefix to a word:
non-violent ○ *anti-British*
and in compound numbers:
thirty-four ○ *seventy-nine.*
You also write a hyphen at the end of a line if you have to divide a word and write part of it on the next line.

A **dash (–)** can be used to separate a phrase from the rest of a sentence. It can be used near the end of the sentence before a phrase which sums up the rest of the sentence:
The burglars had taken the furniture, the TV and stereo, the paintings – absolutely everything.
or you can put a dash at the beginning and the end of a phrase which adds extra information:
A few people – not more than ten – had already arrived.
A dash can also show that the speaker has been interrupted in the middle of a sentence:
'Have you seen –' 'Look out!' she screamed as the ball flew towards them.

Brackets () *(or especially in US English,* **parentheses***)* are also used to keep extra information separate from the rest of the sentence:
Two of the runners (Johns and Smith) finished the race in under an hour.
Numbers or letters used in sentences may also have a bracket after them or brackets around them:
The camera has three main advantages: 1) its compact size 2) its low price and 3) the quality of the photographs. ○ *What would you do if you won a lot of money? (a) save it (b) travel round the world (c) buy a new house (d) buy presents for your friends.*

Letter-writing

FORMAL LETTERS

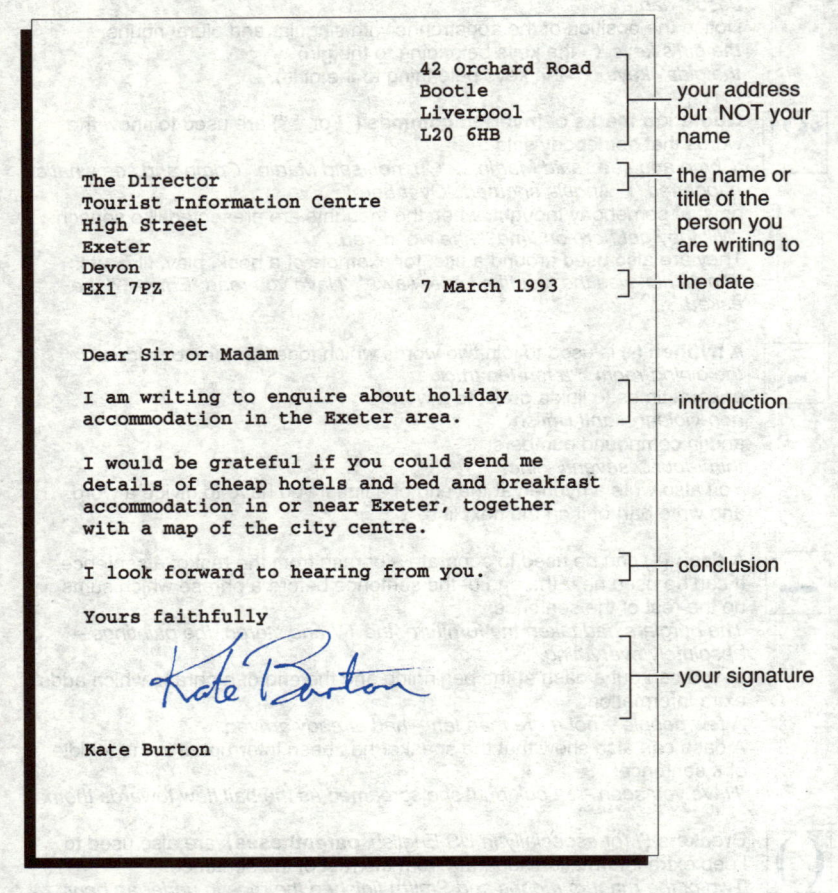

```
                                    42 Orchard Road        ┐
                                    Bootle                  │── your address
                                    Liverpool               │   but NOT your
                                    L20 6HB                ┘   name

The Director                                                ┐
Tourist Information Centre                                  │── the name or
High Street                                                 │   title of the
Exeter                                                      │   person you
Devon                                                       │   are writing to
EX1 7PZ                             7 March 1993           ┤── the date

Dear Sir or Madam

I am writing to enquire about holiday                      ┐── introduction
accommodation in the Exeter area.                          ┘

I would be grateful if you could send me
details of cheap hotels and bed and breakfast
accommodation in or near Exeter, together
with a map of the city centre.

I look forward to hearing from you.                        ┤── conclusion

Yours faithfully

         Kate Burton                                       ┤── your signature

Kate Burton
```

1. If you don't know the name of the person you're writing to, begin the letter with *Dear Sir or Madam* and finish with *Yours faithfully* (*Sincerely yours* or *Yours truly* in American English).

2. If you know the name of the person you're writing to, begin with *Dear Mr Roberts*, *Dear Ms Cooper*, *Dear Mrs Williams* or *Dear Miss Thomas*, and finish with *Yours sincerely* (*Sincerely yours* or *Yours truly* in American English).

3. The letter should be written in a formal style, so you should not use contractions – write *I am* and *do not*, NOT ~~I'm~~ and ~~don't~~.

INFORMAL LETTERS

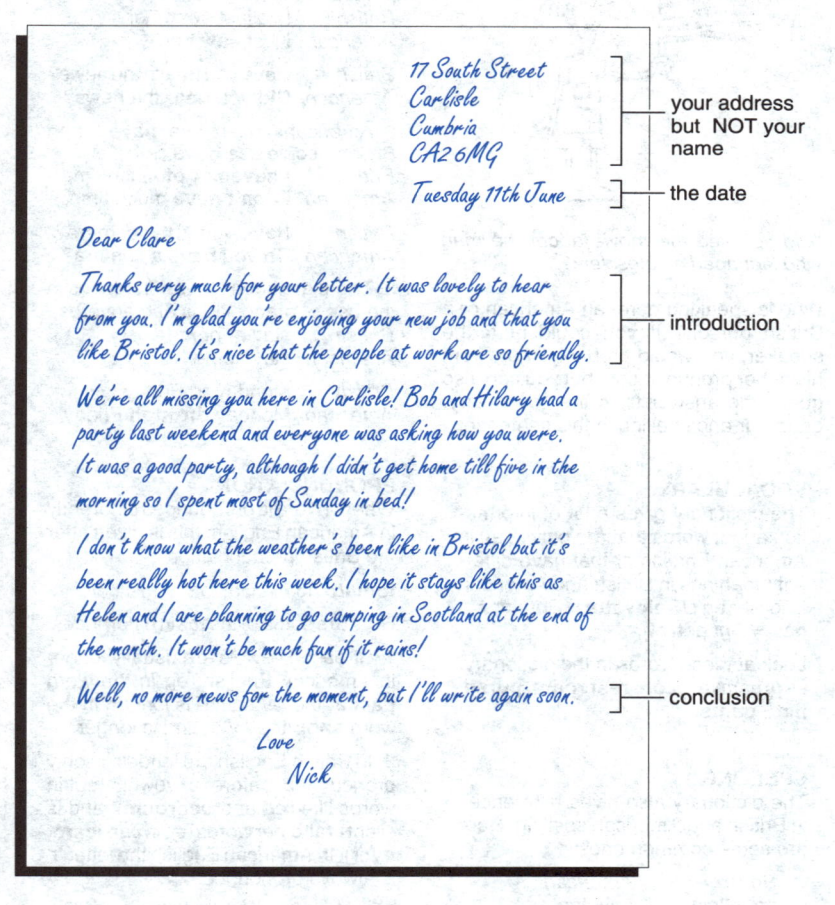

>   17 South Street
>   Carlisle
>   Cumbria
>   CA2 6MG — *your address but NOT your name*
>
>   Tuesday 11th June — *the date*
>
> Dear Clare
>
> Thanks very much for your letter. It was lovely to hear from you. I'm glad you're enjoying your new job and that you like Bristol. It's nice that the people at work are so friendly. — *introduction*
>
> We're all missing you here in Carlisle! Bob and Hilary had a party last weekend and everyone was asking how you were. It was a good party, although I didn't get home till five in the morning so I spent most of Sunday in bed!
>
> I don't know what the weather's been like in Bristol but it's been really hot here this week. I hope it stays like this as Helen and I are planning to go camping in Scotland at the end of the month. It won't be much fun if it rains!
>
> Well, no more news for the moment, but I'll write again soon. — *conclusion*
>
>   Love
>   Nick

1. If you know the person you're writing to very well, you can finish with *Love* or *Lots of love*. If you don't want to be quite so informal, you can finish with *Best wishes* or *With best wishes*.

2. The style of this letter is informal, so the writer uses lots of contractions – *it's, we're, didn't*, etc.

American English

"Did you see the movie about the man who kidnaped a salesclerk?"

Who is speaking here, an American or a British person? If you could hear the speaker, you would probably know from his or her pronunciation, but you can also guess the answer from the vocabulary, grammar and spelling in this sentence.

VOCABULARY
The dictionary gives a lot of information about words that are only used in American English or that have different meanings in British and American English (eg *US* **elevator** = *Brit* **lift**; *US* **gas** = *Brit* **petrol**).

Look at these words in the dictionary: **expressway, cab, rest room, purse, flat¹, pants**.

SPELLING
The dictionary also gives differences in British and American spelling. Here are some common ones:

	British	American
a	trave**ll**ed	trave**l**ed
	cance**ll**ing	cance**l**ing
b	met**re**	met**er**
	cent**re**	cent**er**
c	col**our**	col**or**
	hon**our**	hon**or**
d	defen**ce**	defen**se**
	licen**ce**	licen**se**
e	dialo**gue**	dialo**g**
	catalo**gue**	catalo**g**

GRAMMAR

1 Americans often use the simple past tense when British people use the present perfect:
British I**'ve** just **seen** her.
American I just **saw** her.

British **Have** you **heard** the news?
American **Did** you **hear** the news?

2 Americans often use **have** when British people use **have got**:
British I **haven't got** much time.
American I **don't have** much time.

British **Have** you **got** a camera?
American **Do** you **have** a camera?

3 There are often small differences in the use of prepositions and adverbs:
British stay **at** home
American stay home

British Monday **to** Friday
American Monday **through** Friday

PRONUNCIATION
When a word is pronounced differently in American English, this is given after the British pronunciation:

tomato /təˈmɑːtəʊ; *US* təˈmeɪtəʊ/

Here are some of the main differences:

1 Stressed vowels are usually longer in American English, eg in the word **packet** the /æ/ sound is longer; in the word **shop** the /ɒ/ sound is longer.

2 In British English the letter 'r' is only pronounced before a vowel, (eg in words like **red** and **bed<u>r</u>oom**), and is silent in all other words (eg in **car**, **learn**, **over**). In American English the letter 'r' is always pronounced.

3 In American English the letters 't' and 'd' have a very similar light /d/ sound when they come between two vowels, so that the words **writer** and **rider** sound almost the same; in British English the 't' is much stronger.

So who was speaking in that first sentence?

(Answer: an American)

of thought or action: *If this policy doesn't work, we'll have to take another line.* ○ *a line of argument* **10** [C] a company that provides transport by air, ship, etc: *an airline* **11** [sing] a type of goods in a shop, etc: *a new line in environment-friendly detergents* **12** [C] a route that people move along or send messages, goods, etc along: *lines of communication* ○ *Before you travel on the London Underground, check which line you need.* **13** [C] the place where an army is fighting: *a spy working behind enemy lines* (IDIOMS) **along/on the same, etc lines** in the way that is mentioned: *We both think along the same lines, so we work well together.*
draw the line at sth/doing sth ⇨ DRAW²
drop sb a line ⇨ DROP¹
hold the line to wait on the telephone, eg while sb finds the person you want to speak to: *The extension is engaged. Would you like to hold the line or call back later?*
in line for sth likely to get sth: *She's next in line for promotion.*
in line with sth similar to sth and fitting in with it
on line connected to a computer system
stand in/on line (*US*) to wait in a queue
toe the (party) line ⇨ TOE
line² /laɪn/ *verb* [T] **1** (often passive) to mark sth with lines¹(1): *lined paper* ○ *a face lined with age* **2** to make or form a line¹(2) along sth: *Crowds lined the streets to welcome the Prince.* ○ *a tree-lined avenue*
(PHRASAL VERBS) **line up (for sth)** (*US*) to form a line or queue (for sth)
line sth up (*informal*) to arrange or organize sth: *What have you got lined up for the weekend?*
line³ /laɪn/ *verb* [T] (often passive) to cover the inside surface of sth with a different material: *fur-lined boots*
lineman *noun* [C] (*US*) = LINESMAN
linen /ˈlɪnɪn/ *noun* [U] **1** a type of strong cloth that is made from a natural substance (**flax**) **2** sheets, tablecloths, etc (which often used to be made of linen): *bed linen*
liner¹ /ˈlaɪnə(r)/ *noun* [C] a large ship that carries people, over long distances
liner² /ˈlaɪnə(r)/ *noun* [C] something that is put inside sth else to keep it clean or protect it. A liner is usually thrown away after it has been used: *a dustbin liner*
linesman /ˈlaɪnzmən/ (*US* **lineman** /ˈlaɪnmən/) (*pl* **linesmen** /-mən/) *noun* [C] an official person in some games such as football or tennis. The linesman watches to see if a player breaks a rule or if the ball goes over the line¹(2). ☛ picture at **football**.
linger /ˈlɪŋɡə(r)/ *verb* [I] **1** to stay somewhere for a long time **2** to take a long time doing sth: *to linger over a meal*
lingerie /ˈlænʒəri:; *US* ˌlɑ:ndʒəˈreɪ/ *noun* [U] (used in shops, etc) women's underclothes
linguist /ˈlɪŋɡwɪst/ *noun* [C] a person who is good at learning foreign languages; a person who studies or teaches language(s)
linguistic /lɪŋˈɡwɪstɪk/ *adj* of language or linguistics
linguistics *noun* [U] the scientific study of language

lining /ˈlaɪnɪŋ/ *noun* [C,U] material that covers the inside surface of sth: *I've torn the lining of my coat.*
☆ **link** /lɪŋk/ *noun* [C] **1** one ring in a chain ☛ picture at **chain**. **2** a person or thing that connects two other people or things: *There is a strong link between smoking and heart disease.* ○ *Sporting links with South Africa were broken for many years.* ○ *a rail link*
link *verb* [T] **link A with B**; **link A and B** (**together**) to make or suggest a connection between two or more people or things: *The new tunnel will link Britain and France.* ○ *The police have evidence that links the priest with a terrorist organization.* ○ *to link arms*
(PHRASAL VERB) **link up (with sb/sth)** to join together (with sb/sth): *All our branches are linked up by computer.*
'link-up *noun* [C] the joining together or connection of two or more things
linoleum /lɪˈnəʊliəm/ (also *informal* **lino** /ˈlaɪnəʊ/) *noun* [U] a type of covering for floors

leopard
tiger
lion
lioness

☆ **lion** /ˈlaɪən/ *noun* [C] a large animal of the cat family that lives in Africa and parts of southern Asia. Male lions have a large amount of hair around their head and neck (**a mane**).

☛ A female lion is called a **lioness** and a young lion is called a **cub**. The noise a lion makes is a **roar**.

☆ **lip** /lɪp/ *noun* [C] **1** one of the two soft red parts above and below your mouth: *to kiss somebody on the lips* ☛ picture on page 8. You have a **top/upper** lip and a **bottom/lower** lip. **2** the edge of a cup or sth that is shaped like a cup
'lip-read *verb* [I,T] (*pt, pp* /-red/) to understand what sb is saying by looking at the movements of his/her lips
'lipstick *noun* [C,U] a substance that is used for giving colour to your lips: *to put on some lipstick* ○ *a new lipstick*
liqueur /lɪˈkjʊə(r); *US* -ˈkɜːr/ *noun* [U] a strong alcoholic (usually sweet) drink that is often drunk in small quantities after a meal
☆ **liquid** /ˈlɪkwɪd/ *noun* [C,U] a substance, eg water, that is not solid and that can flow or be poured

s	z	ʃ	ʒ	h	m	n	ŋ	l	r	j	w
so	zoo	she	vision	how	man	no	sing	leg	red	yes	wet

liquid *adj* in the form of a liquid: *The patient can only take liquid food.*

liquidate /'lɪkwɪdeɪt/ *verb* [T] **1** to close down a business because it has no money left **2** to kill sb —**liquidation** /ˌlɪkwɪ'deɪʃn/ *noun* [U]: *to go into liquidation* (= of a business) ○ *the liquidation of political opponents*

liquidize (*also* **liquidise**) /'lɪkwɪdaɪz/ *verb* [T] to cause sth to become liquid: *He liquidized the vegetables to make soup.*
 liquidizer (*also* **liquidiser**; **blender**) *noun* [C] an electric machine that is used for liquidizing food

liquor /'lɪkə(r)/ *noun* [U] (*US*) strong alcoholic drinks; spirits

liquorice (*also* **licorice**) /'lɪkərɪs/ *noun* [U] a black substance, made from a plant, that is used in sweets

lisp /lɪsp/ *noun* [C] an incorrect way of speaking in which 's' sounds like 'th': *He speaks with a slight lisp.* —**lisp** *verb* [I,T]

☆ **list** /lɪst/ *noun* [C] a series of names, figures, items, etc that are written or printed one after another: *Can you put butter on your shopping list?* ○ *a checklist of everything that needs to be done* ○ *an alphabetical list* ○ *Your name is third on the waiting-list.*
 list *verb* [T] to make a list of sth; to put or include sth on a list: *to list items in alphabetical order* ○ *Her name is not listed on police files.*

☆ **listen** /'lɪsn/ *verb* [I] **1 listen (to sb/sth)** to pay attention to sb/sth in order to hear him/her/it: *Now please listen carefully to what I have to say.* ○ *to listen to the radio, music, etc* ☛ Look at the note at **hear**. **2 listen to sb/sth** to take notice of or believe what sb says, etc: *I try to give them advice but they never listen to what I tell them.*
 (PHRASAL VERB) **listen (out) for sth** to wait to hear sth: *to listen (out) for a knock on the door*
 listen *noun* [sing] (*informal*) the act of listening: *Have a listen and see if you can hear anything.*

listener *noun* [C] a person who listens: *He is a good listener* (= he pays attention to you when you are speaking).

listless /'lɪstlɪs/ *adj* tired and without energy —**listlessly** *adv*

lit *pt, pp* of LIGHT²

liter (*US*) = LITRE

literacy /'lɪtərəsi/ *noun* [U] the ability to read and write ☛ Look at **illiteracy**.

literal /'lɪtərəl/ *adj* **1** (used about the meaning of a word or phrase) original or basic: *The word 'mad' isn't used very much in its literal sense any more.* ☛ Look at **figurative** and **metaphorical**. **2** (used about a translation, etc) translating each word separately without looking at the general meaning
 literally /'lɪtərəli/ *adv* **1** in a literal(2) way: *You can't translate this text literally.* **2** (*informal*) (used for emphasizing sth): *We were literally frozen to death* (= we were very cold).

literary /'lɪtərəri; *US* 'lɪtəreri/ *adj* of or concerned with literature: *literary criticism* ○ *a literary journal*

literate /'lɪtərət/ *adj* **1** able to read and write ☛ Look at **numerate**. **2** well-educated

☆ **literature** /'lɪtrətʃə(r); *US* -tʃʊər/ *noun* [U] **1** writing that is considered to be a work of art. Literature includes novels, plays and poetry: *French literature* **2** printed material on a particular subject: *Have you got any literature on opening a bank account in Britain?*

☆ **litre** (*US* **liter**) /'li:tə(r)/ *noun* [C] (*abbr* l) a measure of liquid: *ten litres of petrol* ○ *a litre bottle of wine*

litter /'lɪtə(r)/ *noun* **1** [U] pieces of paper, packets, etc that are left in a public place **2** [C] all the young animals that are born to one mother at the same time: *a litter of six puppies*
 litter *verb* [T] to make sth untidy with litter: *The streets were littered with rubbish.*

'litter-bin *noun* [C] a container to put litter in ☛ picture at **bin**.

'litter-lout (*US* **'litter-bug**) *noun* [C] a person who drops litter in a public place

☆ **little¹** /'lɪtl/ *adj* **1** not big; small: *There's a little hole in my sock.* ○ *the little hand of the clock* ○ *your little finger/toe* ☛ **Little** is often used with another adjective: *a little old lady* ○ *a dear little kitten* ○ *What a funny little shop!* ☛ Look at the note at **small**. **2** (used about distance or time) short: *Do you mind waiting a little while?* ○ *It's only a little further.* **3** young: *a little girl/boy* ○ *my little brother* **4** not important: *a little problem*

☆ **little²** /'lɪtl/ *det* (with uncountable [U] nouns) not much or not enough: *They have very little money.* ○ *There is little hope that she will recover.* ☛ Look at **less** and **least**.
 little *pron* (also as a noun after *the*) a small amount; not enough: *We studied Latin at school but I remember very little.* ○ *The little I know of him has given me a good impression.*
 little *adv* not much or not enough: *I slept very little last night.* ○ *a little-known author*
 (IDIOM) **little by little** slowly: *After the accident her strength returned little by little.*

☆ **little³** /'lɪtl/ **a little** *det* (with uncountable [U] nouns) a small amount of sth: *I like a little sugar in my tea.* ○ *Could I have a little help, please?*
 a little *pron* a small amount: *'Is there any butter left?' 'Yes, just a little.'*
 (IDIOM) **after/for a little** after/for a short distance or time: *You must rest for a little.*
 a little *adv* rather: *This skirt is a little too tight.*
 ☛ **A little bit** or **a bit** is often used instead of 'a little': *I was feeling a little bit tired so I decided not to go out.*

☆ **live¹** /laɪv/ *adj* **1** having life; not dead: *Have you ever touched a real live snake?* ☛ Look at **alive** and **living**. **2** (used about a bomb) that has not yet exploded **3** (used about a wire, etc) carrying electricity. If you touch sth that is live you will get an electric shock. **4** (used about a radio or TV programme) seen or heard as it is happening: *live coverage of the Wimbledon tennis tournament* **5** recorded from a concert, etc, ie not made in a studio: *a live recording of Bob Dylan's last concert*
 live *adv* broadcast at the same time as it is happening: *This programme is coming live from Wembley Stadium.* ○ *to go out live on TV*

☆ **live²** /lɪv/ *verb* **1** [I] to be or remain alive: *You*

livelihood

can't live without water. ○ *She hasn't got long to live.* ○ *to live to a great age* **2** [I] to have your home: *Where do you live?* ○ *He still lives with his parents.* **3** [I,T] to pass or spend your life in a certain way: *to live a quiet life* ○ *They have plenty of money and live well.* **4** [I] to be able to buy the things that you need: *Many families don't have enough to live.* **5** [I] to enjoy all the opportunities of life fully: *I want to live a bit before settling down and getting married.*
(PHRASAL VERBS) **live sth down** to make people forget sth bad or embarrassing that has happened to you: *They lost 10–nil? They'll never live it down!*

live on to continue to live: *After his retirement he lived on for another 25 years.* ○ (*figurative*) *Mozart is dead but his music lives on.*

live on sth 1 to have sth as your only food: *to live on bread and water* **2** to have sth as your income: *I don't know how they live on £8 000 a year!*

live together to live in the same house, etc as sb and have a sexual relationship with him/her

live up to sth to be as good as expected: *Children sometimes find it hard to live up to their parents' expectations.*

live with sb = LIVE TOGETHER

live with sth to accept sth unpleasant that you cannot change: *It can be hard to live with the fact that you are getting older.*

livelihood /ˈlaɪvlɪhʊd/ *noun* [C, usually sing] the way that you earn money: ○ *to lose your livelihood*

☆ **lively** /ˈlaɪvlɪ/ *adj* (**livelier; liveliest**) full of energy, interest, excitement, etc: *lively children* ○ *There was a lively debate on the route of the new motorway.* ○ *a lively imagination*

liven /ˈlaɪvn/ *verb*
(PHRASAL VERB) **liven (sb/sth) up** to become lively or to make sb/sth lively: *Once the band began to play the party livened up.*

liver /ˈlɪvə(r)/ *noun* **1** [C] the part of your body that cleans your blood **2** [U] the liver of an animal when it is cooked and eaten as food: *fried liver and onions*

'**liver sausage** (*US* **liverwurst** /ˈlɪvəwɜːst/) *noun* [U] a type of sausage that contains cooked liver and that is usually eaten cold with bread

lives *pl* of LIFE

livestock /ˈlaɪvstɒk/ *noun* [U] animals that are kept on a farm, eg cows, pigs, sheep, etc

living¹ /ˈlɪvɪŋ/ *adj* **1** alive now: *He has no living relatives.* **2** (used about a language, etc) still used ☞ The opposite for both meanings is **dead**.

☆ **living**² /ˈlɪvɪŋ/ *noun* **1** [C, usually sing] a means of earning money to buy the things you need: *What do you do for a living?* **2** [U] your way or quality of life: *The cost of living has risen in recent years.* ☞ Look at **standard of living**.

'**living-room** (*especially Brit* **sitting-room**) *noun* [C] the room in a house where people sit, relax, watch TV, etc together

lizard /ˈlɪzəd/ *noun* [C] a small reptile with four legs, rough skin and a long tail. A lizard has a long tongue that it uses for catching insects.

lizard

☆ **load**¹ /ləʊd/ *noun* [C] **1** something (heavy) that is being or is going to be carried **2** (often in compounds) the quantity of sth that can be carried: *a lorry-load of sand* ○ *bus-loads of tourists* **3 loads (of sth)** [plural] (*informal*) a lot (of sth): *There are loads of things to do in London in the evenings.*
(IDIOM) **a load of rubbish, etc** (*informal*) nonsense

☆ **load**² /ləʊd/ *verb* **1** [I,T] to put or have a load or large quantity of sth in or on sb/sth: *Have you finished loading yet?* ○ *Uncle Tim arrived loaded down with presents.* ○ *They loaded the plane with supplies for the refugees.* ○ *Load the washing into the machine and then add the powder.* **2** [I] to receive a load: *The ship is still loading* **3** [T] to put a program or disk into a computer: *First, switch on the machine and load the disk.* **4** [T] to put a film in a camera or a bullet in a gun

loaded *adj* **1** carrying a load **2** giving an advantage: *The system is loaded in their favour.*

☆ **loaf** /ləʊf/ *noun* [C] (*pl* **loaves** /ləʊvz/) bread shaped and baked in one piece: *a loaf of bread* ○ *Two sliced loaves, please.*

☆ **loan** /ləʊn/ *noun* **1** [C] money, etc that sb/sth lends you: *to take out a bank loan* ○ *to make a loan to sb* ○ *to pay off a loan* **2** [U] the act of lending sth or state of being lent: *The books are on loan from the library.*

loan *verb* [T] (*formal*) **loan sth (to sb)** to lend sth: *The painting is loaned from the Louvre for the period of the exhibition.* ☞ In American English **loan** is less formal and more common.

loathe /ləʊð/ *verb* [T] to feel strong hatred or dislike for sb/sth —**loathing** *noun* [U]

loathsome /-səm/ *adj* causing a strong feeling of dislike

loaves *pl* of LOAF

lob /lɒb/ *verb* [I,T] (**lobbing; lobbed**) (*sport*) to hit or throw a ball high into the air, so that it lands behind your opponent —**lob** *noun* [C]

lobby /ˈlɒbɪ/ *noun* (*pl* **lobbies**) **1** [C] the area that is just inside a large building. A lobby often has a reception desk and doors, stairs, lifts, etc that lead to other parts of the building: *a hotel lobby* **2** [C, with sing or pl verb] a group of people who try to persuade the government, etc to do or not to do sth: *the anti-abortion lobby*

lobby *verb* [I,T] (*pres part* **lobbying**; *3rd pers sing pres* **lobbies**; *pt, pp* **lobbied**) to try to persuade the government, etc that sth should or should not be done: *to lobby the Transport Minister for improved rail services*

lobe /ləʊb/ *noun* [C] the round soft part at the bottom of your ear

lobster /ˈlɒbstə(r)/ *noun* **1** [C] a large shell fish that has eight legs. A lobster is bluish-black but it turns red when it is cooked. ☞ picture at **shellfish**. **2** [U] a lobster when it is cooked and eaten as food

ɜː	ə	eɪ	əʊ	aɪ	aʊ	ɔɪ	ɪə	eə	ʊə
fur	ago	pay	home	five	now	join	near	hair	pure

☆ **local** /ˈləʊkl/ *adj* of a particular place (near you): *local newspapers* ○ *The local school is the centre of the community.*
local *noun* [C] **1** [usually pl] a person who lives in a particular place: *One of the locals agreed to be my guide.* **2** (*Brit informal*) a pub that is near your home where you often go to drink —**locally** *adv*: *I do most of my shopping locally.*

local anaes'thetic *noun* [C,U] medicine that is injected into one part of your body so that you do not feel pain there ☛ Look at **general anaesthetic**.

local au'thority *noun* [C, with sing or pl verb] (*pl* **local authorities**) the group of people who are responsible for local government in an area

'local call *noun* [C] a telephone call to sb who is not far away ☛ Look at **long-distance**.

local 'government *noun* [U] the government of a particular place by a group of people who are elected by the local residents

☛ The group of elected officials who are in charge of local government is called the **council**. The **local authority** consists of officials who are paid. These officials carry out the decisions that the council has made.

'local time *noun* [U] the time at a particular place in the world: *We arrive in Singapore at 2 o'clock in the afternoon, local time.*

localize (*also* **localise**) /ˈləʊkəlaɪz/ *verb* [T] to limit sth to a particular place or area: *localized pain*

locate /ləʊˈkeɪt; *US* ˈləʊkeɪt/ *verb* [T] **1** to find the exact position of sb/sth: *The damaged ship has been located and helicopters are arriving to rescue the crew.* **2** (often passive) to put, build, etc sth in a particular place: *The railway station is located to the west of the city.*

location /ləʊˈkeɪʃn/ *noun* [C] **1** a place or position: *Several locations have been suggested for the new housing estate.* **2** [U] finding where sb/sth is: *Police enquiries led to the location of the terrorists' hide-out.*
(IDIOM) **on location** (used about a film, television programme, etc) made in a suitable place (= not in a studio): *The series was filmed on location in Thailand.*

loch /lɒk/ *noun* [C] the Scottish word for a lake: *the Loch Ness monster*

☆ **lock¹** /lɒk/ *noun* [C] **1** something that is used for fastening a door, lid, etc so that you need a key to open it again: *to turn the key in the lock* ☛ picture at **key**. Look at **padlock**. **2** a part of a river or a canal where the level of water changes. Locks have gates at each end and are used to allow boats to move to a higher or lower part of the canal or river.

lock² /lɒk/ *verb* **1** [I,T] to close or fasten with a lock: *Have you locked the car?* ○ *The door won't lock.* ☛ Look at **unlock**. **2** [T] to put sb/sth inside sth that is locked: *Lock your passport in a safe place.* **3** [I,T] to fix sth or be fixed in one position: *The wheels locked and the car crashed into the wall.*
(PHRASAL VERBS) **lock sth away** to keep sth in a safe or secret place (that is locked)

lock sb in/out to lock a door so that a person cannot get in/out: *All the prisoners are locked in for the night.* ○ *to lock yourself out of your house*

lock (sth) up to lock all the doors, windows, etc of a building: *Make sure that you lock up before you leave.*

lock sb up to put sb in prison

locker /ˈlɒkə(r)/ *noun* [C] a small cupboard where personal things can be kept or left. Lockers are found in schools, sports centres, railway stations, etc.

locket /ˈlɒkɪt/ *noun* [C] a piece of jewellery that is worn around the neck on a chain. A locket is a small case that often contains a photograph.

locomotive /ˌləʊkəˈməʊtɪv/ *noun* [C] = ENGINE (2): *a steam locomotive*

locust /ˈləʊkəst/ *noun* [C] a flying insect from Africa and Asia that moves in very large groups, eating and destroying large quantities of plants

lodge¹ /lɒdʒ/ *noun* [C] **1** a small house at the gate of a large house **2** a house in the country that is used by hunters, sportsmen, etc: *a shooting lodge* **3** a room at the entrance to a college, block of flats, factory, etc

lodge² /lɒdʒ/ *verb* **1** [I] to live at sb's house in return for rent: *He lodged with a family for his first term at university.* **2** [I,T] to become firmly fixed or to make sth do this: *The bullet lodged in her shoulder.* ☛ Look at **dislodge**. **3** [T] (*formal*) to make an official statement complaining about sth: *to lodge a complaint*

lodger *noun* [C] a person who pays rent to live in a house as a member of the family

lodging /ˈlɒdʒɪŋ/ *noun* **1** [C,U] a place where you can stay: *Their nanny is paid £70 a week, plus board and lodging* (= her room and all meals are paid for). **2** **lodgings** [plural] a room or rooms in sb's house where you can stay in return for paying rent

loft /lɒft; *US* lɔːft/ *noun* [C] the room or space under the roof of a house or other building: *Our loft has been converted into a bedroom.* ☛ Look at **attic**.

log¹ /lɒg; *US* lɔːg/ *noun* [C] **1** the trunk or large branch of a tree that has been cut or has fallen down **2** a small piece of wood for a fire

log² /lɒg; *US* lɔːg/ (*also* **logbook**) *noun* [C] the official written record of a ship's or an aeroplane's journey: *to keep a log*

log *verb* [T] (**logging**; **logged**) to write sth in the log of a ship or aeroplane
(PHRASAL VERBS) **log in/on** to start using a computer that is part of a larger system

log off/out to finish using a computer that is part of a larger system

logarithm /ˈlɒgərɪðəm; *US* ˈlɔːg-/ (*also informal* **log**) *noun* [C] one of a series of numbers arranged in special charts (**tables**) that allow you to solve mathematical problems by adding or subtracting numbers instead of multiplying or dividing

loggerheads /ˈlɒgəhedz/ *noun*
(IDIOM) **at loggerheads (with sb)** strongly disagreeing (with sb)

logic /ˈlɒdʒɪk/ *noun* [U] **1** the science of using

p	b	t	d	k	g	tʃ	dʒ	f	v	θ	ð
pen	bad	tea	did	cat	got	chin	June	fall	van	thin	then

reason **2** the use of reason: *There is no logic in your argument.*

logical /ˈlɒdʒɪkl/ *adj* **1** according to the rules of logic; reasonable: *As I see it, there is only one logical conclusion.* **2** able to use logic: *a logical mind* ☛ The opposite is **illogical**. —**logically** /-klɪ/ *adv*

logo /ˈləʊgəʊ/ *noun* [C] a symbol or design that is used as an advertisement by a company or organization. A logo appears on the things the company owns and produces.

loiter /ˈlɔɪtə(r)/ *verb* [I] to stand somewhere or walk around without any real purpose

lollipop /ˈlɒlipɒp/ (also *informal* **lolly**) *noun* [C] a large sweet of boiled sugar on a stick ☛ Look at **ice lolly**.

lone /ləʊn/ *adj* (only *before* a noun) without any other people; alone: *a lone swimmer on the beach*

loner *noun* [C] (*informal*) a person who likes to be alone

☆ **lonely** /ˈləʊnlɪ/ *adj* (**lonelier**; **loneliest**) **1** unhappy because you are not with other people: *to feel sad and lonely* **2** (only *before* a noun) far from other people and places where people live: *a lonely house in the hills* ☛ Look at the note at **alone**. —**loneliness** *noun* [U]

lonesome /ˈləʊnsəm/ *adj* (US) lonely or making you feel lonely ☛ Look at the note at **alone**.

☆ **long¹** /lɒŋ/; *US* lɔːŋ/ *adj* (**longer** /-ŋgə(r)/, **longest** /-ŋgɪst/) measuring a great amount in distance or time: *She has lovely long hair.* ○ *We had to wait a long time.* ○ *a very long journey* ○ *War and Peace is a very long book.* ○ *a long dress* (= down to the floor) ☛ Look at **length**. **Long** is also used when you are asking for or giving information about how much something measures in length, distance or time: *How long is the film?* ○ *The insect was only 2 millimetres long.* ○ *a five-mile-long traffic jam* (IDIOMS) **at the longest** not longer than the stated time: *It will take a week at the longest.*

go a long way (used about money, food, etc) to be used for buying a lot of things, feeding a lot of people, etc: *to make a little money go a long way*

in the long run after a long time; in the end: *We ought to buy a new car – it'll be cheaper in the long run.*

in the long/short term ⇨ **TERM**

long-ˈdistance *adj*, *adv* (used about travel or communication) between places that are far from each other: *a long-distance lorry driver* ○ *to phone long-distance* ☛ Look at **local**.

ˈlong-jump *noun* [sing] the sport in which people try to jump as far as possible ☛ Look at **high-jump**.

ˈlong-life *adj* lasting for a long time: *a long-life battery* ○ *long-life milk*

ˈlong-range *adj* **1** of or for a long period of time starting from the present: *the long-range weather forecast* **2** that can go or be sent over long distances: *long-range nuclear missiles*

ˌlong-ˈsighted (*US* ˌfar-ˈsighted) *adj* able to see things clearly only when they are quite far away ☛ The opposite is **short-sighted** (*US* **near-sighted**).

ˌlong-ˈterm *adj* of or for a long period of time: *long-term planning*

ˈlong wave *noun* [U] (*abbr* **LW**) the system of broadcasting radio using sound waves of 1 000 metres or more ☛ Look at **short wave** and **medium wave**.

ˌlong-ˈwinded *adj* (used about sth that is written or spoken) boring because it is too long

☆ **long²** /lɒŋ/; *US* lɔːŋ/ *noun* [U] a long time: *They won't be gone for long.* ○ *It shouldn't take long.*

☆ **long³** /lɒŋ/; *US* lɔːŋ/ *adv* **1** for a long time: *She didn't stay long.* ○ *You shouldn't have to wait long.* ○ *I hope we don't have to wait much longer.* ☛ **Long** and **a long time** are both used as expressions of time. In positive sentences **a long time** is usually used: *They stood there for a long time.* **Long** is only used in positive sentences with another adverb, eg 'too', 'enough', 'ago', etc: *We lived here long ago.* ○ *I've put up with this noise long enough. I'm going to make a complaint.* Both **long** and **a long time** can be used in questions: *Were you away long/a long time?* In negative sentences there is sometimes a difference in meaning between **long** and **a long time**: *I haven't been here long* (= I arrived only a short time ago). ○ *I haven't been here for a long time* (= it is a long time since I was last here). **2** at a time that is distant from a particular point in time: *All that happened long ago.* ○ *We got married long before we moved here.* **3** for the whole of the time that is mentioned: *The baby cried all night long.*

(IDIOMS) **as/so long as** on condition that: *As long as no problems arise we should get the job finished by Friday.*

no/not any longer not any more: *They no longer live here.* ○ *They don't live here any longer.*

ˌlong-drawn-ˈout *adj* lasting longer than necessary: *long-drawn-out negotiations*

ˌlong-ˈlived *adj* living or lasting for a long time: *a long-lived dispute*

ˌlong-playing ˈrecord *noun* [C] (*abbr* **LP**) a record that plays for about 30 minutes on each side and turns 33⅓ times in a minute

ˌlong-ˈstanding *adj* that has lasted for a long time: *a long-standing arrangement*

ˌlong-ˈsuffering *adj* (used about a person) having a lot of troubles that he/she bears without complaining

long⁴ /lɒŋ/; *US* lɔːŋ/ *verb* [I] **long for sth**; **long (for sb) to do sth** to want sth very much: *He longed to hold her in his arms.*

longing /ˈlɒŋɪŋ/; *US* ˈlɔːŋɪŋ/ *noun* [C,U] a great desire (for sb/sth) —**longingly** *adv*: *She gazed longingly at the cakes in the shop window.*

longitude /ˈlɒŋgɪtjuːd/; *US* -tuːd/ *noun* [U] the distance of a place east or west of a line from the North Pole to the South Pole that passes through Greenwich in England. Longitude is measured in degrees. ☛ picture at **earth**. Look at **latitude**.

loo /luː/ *noun* [C] (*Brit informal*) toilet: *I need to go to the loo.* ☛ Look at the note at **toilet**.

☆ **look¹** /lʊk/ *verb* **1** [I,T] to turn your eyes in a particular direction (in order to pay attention to sb/sth): *Look carefully at the two pictures and try to spot the differences between them.* ○

s	z	ʃ	ʒ	h	m	n	ŋ	l	r	j	w
so	zoo	she	vision	how	man	no	sing	leg	red	yes	wet

She blushed and looked away. ○ *to look out of the window* ○ *Look who's come to see us.* ○ *Look where you are going!* ☞ You can **see** something without paying attention to it: *I saw a girl riding past on a horse.* If you **look at** something you pay attention to it with your eyes: *Look carefully. Can you see anything strange?* **2** [I] **look (like sb/sth) (to sb)**; **look (to sb) as if…/as though…** to seem or appear: *You look very smart in that shirt.* ○ *to look tired, ill, sad, well, happy, etc* ○ *The boy looks like his father.* ○ *The room looks (to me) as if it needs a coat of paint.* ○ *It looks like rain* (= as if it is going to rain). **3** [I] **look (for sb/sth)** to try to find (sb/sth): *We've been looking for you everywhere. Where have you been?* ○ *Have you found your watch? No, I'm still looking.* ○ *to look for work* **4** [I] to face a particular direction: *Our hotel room looks onto the sea.*
(IDIOMS) **look good** to seem to be encouraging: *This year's sales figures are looking good.*
look here 1 (used for protesting about sth): *Now look here! That's not fair!* **2** (used for asking sb to pay attention to sth): *Look here everyone. Let's form a committee to decide what to do next.*
(not) look yourself to (not) look as well or healthy as usual: *What's the matter? You're not looking yourself today.*
(PHRASAL VERBS) **look after sb/sth/yourself** to be responsible for or take care of sb/sth/yourself: *I want to go back to work if I can find somebody to look after the children.* ○ *The old lady's son looked after all her financial affairs.*
look ahead to think about or plan for the future: *Looking ahead a few years, there's going to be a shortage of skilled workers.*
look at sth 1 to examine sth (closely): *My tooth aches. I think a dentist should look at it.* **2** to think about or study sth: *The government is looking at ways of reducing the number of stray dogs.* **3** to read sth: *Could I look at the newspaper when you've finished with it.* **4** to consider sth: *Different races and nationalities look at life differently.*
look back (on sth) to think about sth in your past
look down on sb/sth (*informal*) to think that you are better than sb/sth: *Don't look down on them just because they haven't been as successful as you.*
look forward to sth/doing sth to wait with pleasure for sth to happen (because you expect to enjoy it): *The children are really looking forward to their holiday.* ○ *I'm looking forward to seeing you again.*
look into sth to study or investigate sth: *A committee was set up to look into the causes of the accident.*
look on to watch sth happening: *All we could do was look on as the house burned.*
look out to be careful or to pay attention to sth dangerous, etc: *Look out! There's a bike coming.*
look out (for sb/sth) to pay attention in order to see, find or be careful of sb/sth: *Look out for pickpockets!*

look round 1 to turn your head in order to see sb/sth **2** to look at many things (before buying sth): *She looked round but couldn't find anything she liked.*
look round sth to visit a place of interest, etc: *to look round the cathedral*
look through sth to read sth quickly
look to sb for sth; **look to sb to do sth** to expect sb to do or to provide sth: *He always looked to his father for advice.* ○ *You shouldn't look to the state to support you.*
look up 1 to raise your eyes: *She looked up and smiled.* **2** (*informal*) to improve: *Business is looking up.*
look sth up to search for information in a book: *to look up a word in a dictionary*
look up to sb to respect or admire sb
look *interj* (used for asking sb to listen to what you are saying): *Look, William, I know you are busy but could you give me a hand?*
-looking (used in compounds to form adjectives) having the stated appearance: *an odd-looking building* ○ *He's very good-looking.*

☆ **look²** /lʊk/ *noun* **1** [C] the act of looking: *Have a look at this article.* ○ *I knew something was wrong – everybody was giving me funny looks* (= looking at me strangely). **2** [C, usually sing] a search: *I've had a look but I can't find it.* **3** [C] the expression or appearance of sb/sth: *He had a worried look on his face.* **4** [C] a fashion or style: *The shop has a new look to appeal to younger customers.* **5 looks** [plural] a person's appearance: *He's lucky – he's got good looks and intelligence.*
(IDIOMS) **by/from the look of sb/sth** judging by the appearance: *It's going to be a fine day by the look of it.*
like the look/sound of sb/sth ➪ LIKE¹
look-in *noun*
(IDIOM) **(not) give sb/get/have a look-in** (*informal*) (not) give sb/have a chance to do sth: *The older children spend a lot of time on the computer so the younger ones don't get a look-in.*

lookout /ˈlʊkaʊt/ *noun* [C] a person who watches out for danger
(IDIOM) **be on the lookout for sb/sth**; **keep a lookout for sb/sth** = LOOK OUT FOR SB/STH

loom¹ /luːm/ *noun* [C] a machine that is used for making (**weaving**) cloth by passing pieces of thread across and under other pieces

loom² /luːm/ *verb* [I] to appear as a shape that is not clear and in a way that seems frightening: *The mountain loomed (up) in the distance.* ○ (*figurative*) *The threat of war loomed over the country.*

loony /ˈluːni/ *noun* [C], *adj* (*pl* **loonies**) (*slang*) (a person who is) crazy or mad

loop /luːp/ *noun* [C] a curved or circular shape, eg in a piece of rope or string
loop *verb* [T] **1** to make sth into a loop **2** to fasten or join sth with a loop

loophole /ˈluːphəʊl/ *noun* [C] a way of avoid-

iː	ɪ	e	æ	ɑː	ɒ	ɔː	ʊ	uː	ʌ
see	sit	ten	hat	arm	got	saw	put	too	cup

ing sth because the words of a rule or law are badly chosen: *a loophole in the tax law*

☆ **loose** /luːs/ *adj* **1** not tied up or shut in sth: *The dog broke loose and ran away.* o *She wore her long hair loose.* **2** not firmly fixed: *a loose tooth* **3** not contained in sth or joined together: *loose change in your trouser pocket* o *some loose sheets of paper* **4** not fitting closely; not tight: *These trousers don't fit. They're much too loose round the waist.*
(IDIOM) **at a loose end** having nothing to do and feeling bored
loosely *adv* in a loose way
loose-'leaf *adj* (used about a notebook, etc) with pages that can be removed or added: *a loose-leaf album*

loosen /'luːsn/ *verb* [I,T] to become or make sth loose or looser: *to loosen your tie*
(PHRASAL VERB) **loosen (sb/sth) up** to relax or make sb move more easily: *These exercises will help you to loosen up.*

loot /luːt/ *noun* [U] goods that have been stolen
loot *verb* [I,T] to steal things during a war or period of fighting: *Many shops were looted during the riot.*

lop /lɒp/ *verb* [T] (**lop**ping; **lop**ped) to cut branches, etc off a tree
(PHRASAL VERB) **lop sth off/away** to cut sth off/away

lopsided /ˌlɒpˈsaɪdɪd/ *adj* with one side lower or smaller, etc than the other: *a lopsided smile*

lord /lɔːd/ *noun* [C] **1** a man in a position of authority **2** **the Lord** God; Christ **3** a nobleman or a man who has been given the title 'Lord': *lords and ladies* **4** **the Lords** [with sing or pl verb] (*Brit*) (members of) the House of Lords: *The Lords has/have voted against the bill.* **5** (*Brit*) used as the title of some high officials or of men who have been made a lord(3): *the Lord Mayor of London* o *Lord Derby* **6** **My Lord** (used for addressing a judge, bishop, nobleman, etc)
(IDIOM) (**Good**) **Lord** (used for expressing surprise, worry, etc)
the Lord's Prayer *noun* [sing] a very important Christian prayer that was first taught by Christ to his followers (**disciples**)

lordship /'lɔːdʃɪp/ *noun* [C] (used when speaking to or about a judge, bishop, nobleman, etc): *Their lordships cannot be disturbed.*

☆ **lorry** /'lɒri; *US* 'lɔːri/ (*Brit*) *noun* [C] (*pl* **lorries**) (*especially US* **truck**) a large strong motor vehicle that is used for carrying goods, etc by road

☆ **lose** /luːz/ *verb* (*pt, pp* **lost** /lɒst; *US* lɔːst/) **1** [T] to be unable to find sth: *I've lost my purse. I can't find it anywhere.* **2** [T] to no longer have sb/sth: *She lost a leg in the accident.* o *He lost his wife last year* (= she died). o *to lose your job* **3** [T] to have less of sth: *to lose weight, interest, patience,* etc o *Small shops are losing business to the large supermarkets.* **4** [I,T] not to win; to be defeated: *The team lost by three goals to two.* o *to lose a court case* o *Cambridge lost to Oxford in the boat race.* o *to lose an argument* **5** [T] to waste time, a chance, etc: *Hurry up! There's no time to lose.* **6** [I,T] to become poorer (as a result of sth): *The company lost on the deal.* **7** [I,T] (used about a clock, watch, etc) to go too slowly: *My watch loses two minutes a day.* ☛ The opposite is **gain**. **8** [T] (*informal*) to cause sb not to understand sth: *You've totally lost me! Please explain again.*
(IDIOMS) **keep/lose your balance** ⇒ BALANCE²
keep/lose your cool ⇒ COOL¹
keep/lose count ⇒ COUNT²
keep/lose your temper ⇒ TEMPER¹
keep/lose track of sb/sth ⇒ TRACK
lose your bearings ⇒ BEARING
lose face to lose the respect of other people
lose your head to become confused or very excited
lose heart to believe that you will be unsuccessful
lose your life to be killed
lose your place to be unable to find the place in a book, etc where you stopped reading
lose sight of sb/sth 1 to no longer be able to see sb/sth **2** to forget sb/sth: *We mustn't lose sight of our original aim.*
lose your touch to lose a special skill or ability to do sth
lose touch (with sb/sth) to no longer have contact (with sb/sth): *I've lost touch with a lot of my old school friends.*
a losing battle a competition, struggle, etc in which it seems that you will be unsuccessful
win/lose the toss ⇒ TOSS
(PHRASAL VERB) **lose out (on sth)** (*informal*) to be at a disadvantage: *If a teacher pays too much attention to the bright students, the others lose out.*

loser *noun* [C] a person who is (often) defeated: *He is a bad loser. He always gets cross if I beat him.*

☆ **loss** /lɒs; *US* lɔːs/ *noun* **1** [U] no longer having sth or not having as much as before; the act of losing sth: *loss of blood, money,* etc o *The loss* (= death) *of his wife was very sad for him.* o *The plane crashed with great loss of life.* **2** [C] a disadvantage: *If she leaves, it will be a big loss to the school.* **3** [C] the amount of money which is

lost by a business: *The firm made a loss of £5 million.*
(IDIOM) **at a loss** not knowing what to do or say

lost¹ *pt, pp* of LOSE

☆ **lost²** /lɒst; *US* lɔːst/ *adj* **1** (used about a person or an animal) unable to find the way: *This isn't the right road – we're completely lost! o Don't get lost!* **2** difficult or impossible to find; missing: *The notice said, 'Lost: a black and white cat in North Street.'* **3 lost (without)** not able to work in an efficient way or to live happily: *I'm lost without my diary! o He would be lost without his old dog for company.* **4 lost on** not noticed or understood: *The humour of the situation was completely lost on Joe and he got quite angry.*
(IDIOMS) **get lost** (*slang*) go away: *'Get lost!' she said rudely and walked off.*

a lost cause an ambition or aim that cannot be achieved

lost 'property *noun* [U] things that people have lost or left in a public place and that are kept in a special office for the owners to collect

☆ **lot¹** /lɒt/ *noun* [sing] ☛ 'Lot' in this sense is always used in the phrases **the lot, all the lot, the whole lot.** It can be used with either a singular or plural verb. **1** the whole amount (of sth): *When we opened the bag of potatoes the whole lot was/were bad. o Just one more suitcase and that's the lot!* **2** a whole group (of people): *The manager has just sacked the lot of them!*

☆ **lot²** /lɒt/ *pron* **a lot; lots** (*informal*) a large amount or number: *'How many people are coming to the party?' 'I'm not sure but a lot!' o Have another piece of cake. There's lots left.*

a lot of (also *informal* **lots of**) *det* a large amount or number of (sb/sth): *There's been a lot of rain this year. o Lots of love, Billy.* (= an informal ending for a letter) o *There were a lot of people at the meeting.*

☆ **lot³** /lɒt/ *adv* (*informal*) **1 a lot; lots** (before adjectives and adverbs) very much: *It's a lot faster now that there's a motorway. o They see lots more of each other than before.* **2 a lot** very much or often: *Thanks a lot – that's very kind. o It generally rains a lot at this time of year.*

lot⁴ /lɒt/ *noun* **1** [C, with sing or pl verb] a group or set (of people or things of the same type): *This lot of clothes needs/need ironing – can you do it?* **2** [sing] the quality or state of a person's life; your fate: *Although things have not been easy for him, he's always been perfectly happy with his lot.* **3** [C] an object or group of objects that are for sale at an auction, (= a sale at which the object goes to the person who offers the highest price): *Lot 27: 6 chairs* **4** [C] (*US*) an area of land used for a particular purpose: *a parking lot* (= a car-park)
(IDIOM) **draw lots** ⇨ DRAW²

lotion /'ləʊʃn/ *noun* [C,U] liquid that you use on your hair or skin: *suntan lotion*

lottery /'lɒtəri/ *noun* [C] (*pl* **lotteries**) a way of raising money by selling tickets with numbers on them and giving prizes to the people who have bought certain numbers which are chosen by chance

☆ **loud** /laʊd/ *adj* **1** making a lot of noise; not quiet: *He's got such a loud laugh you can hear it next door! o Can you turn the television down, it's a bit loud.* ☛ **Loud** is usually used to describe the sound itself or the thing producing the sound: *a loud noise, a loud bang, loud music.* **Noisy** is used to describe a person, animal, place, event, etc that is very or too loud: *a noisy road, party, etc, noisy neighbours, children, etc.* **2** (used about clothes, colours, behaviour) too bright or noticeable: *Isn't that shirt a bit loud for a formal dinner?*

loud *adv* making a lot of noise: *Could you speak a bit louder – the people at the back can't hear.*
(IDIOM) **,out 'loud** so that people can hear it: *Shall I read this bit out loud to you?*

loudly *adv* in a loud way —**loudness** *noun* [U]

,loud'speaker *noun* [C] an apparatus for making sounds, voices, etc louder: *The winner of the competition was announced over the loudspeaker.* **2** (*also* **speaker**) the part of a radio, record-player, etc from which the sound comes out

lounge /laʊndʒ/ *noun* [C] **1** a room in a house or hotel where you can sit comfortably: *Let's go and have coffee in the lounge.* **2** a room at an airport where passengers wait: *the departure lounge*

lounge *verb* [I] **1** to sit or stand in a lazy way; to relax: *That looks a very comfortable sofa to lounge on.* **2 lounge about/around** to spend your time in a lazy way, not doing very much: *I wish Ann wouldn't lounge around in her room all day reading magazines.*

'lounge bar (also **sa'loon bar**) *noun* [C] a smart, comfortable bar in a pub or hotel (where the drinks are usually more expensive) ☛ Look at **public bar**.

louse /laʊs/ *noun* [C] (*pl* **lice** /laɪs/) a small insect that lives on the bodies of animals and people

lousy /'laʊzi/ *adj* (**lousier; lousiest**) (*informal*) very bad: *We had lousy weather on holiday. o You'll feel lousy tomorrow if you drink too much.*

lout /laʊt/ *noun* [C] a young man who behaves in a rude, rough or stupid way: *The train was full of louts returning from the football match.* ☛ Look at **hooligan**. It is similar in meaning. —**loutish** *adj*

lovable /'lʌvəbl/ *adj* easy to love because attractive and pleasant

☆ **love¹** /lʌv/ *noun* **1** [U] a very strong feeling of affection for sb/sth: *The deep love and understanding between them lasted throughout their lives. o It was love at first sight. o I don't think she's marrying him for love! o Love of one's country is perhaps less important to the young people of today.* ☛ The opposite is **hate** or **hatred**. **2** [U,sing] a strong feeling of interest in or enjoyment of sth: *a love of adventure* **3** [C] a thing in which you are very interested: *Computers are the love of his life at the moment.* **4** [C] a person who is loved: *Of course, my love.* ☛ Look at **darling**. **5** [C] (*Brit informal*) (a friendly way of speaking to sb (often sb you don't know) and used by women, or by men to women or children): *'Hello, love. What can I do for you?'* ☛ Often written **luv**. **6** [U] (used in tennis) a score of zero: *'15-love', called the umpire.* **7** [U] (*informal*) (a way of ending a letter to a friend or a member of your family): *Lots of love from us all, Denise.*

(IDIOMS) **be in love (with sb)** to have a strong feeling of affection and sexual attraction (for sb): *They're very much in love (with each other).*

fall in love (with sb) to start to feel a strong affection and attraction for sb: *They fell in love and were married within two months.*

give/send sb your love to give/send sb a friendly greeting: *I haven't seen Mary for ages – give her my love, will you?*

make love (to sb) to have sex

'love-affair *noun* [C] a (usually sexual) relationship between two people who love each other but are not married

'love-story *noun* [C] (*pl* **love-stories**) a story or novel that is mainly about love

☆ **love²** /lʌv/ *verb* [T] **1** to have a strong feeling of affection for sb/sth: *'Do you love him?' 'Yes, very much.'* ○ *It's wonderful to be loved.* **2** to like very much or to enjoy: *I love the summer!* ○ *My father loves to listen/listening to music.* ○ *'Would you like to come?' 'I'd love to.'* ○ *'What about a drink?' 'I'd love one.'* ○ *We'd love you to come and stay with us.* ○ *The cat loves you stroking her just here.*

☆ **lovely** /'lʌvli/ *adj* (**lovelier; loveliest**) **1** beautiful or attractive: *a lovely room* ○ *You look lovely with your hair short.* **2** very nice, enjoyable or pleasant: *We had a lovely holiday in Wales.* ○ *It's lovely to see you again.* —**loveliness** *noun* [U]

☆ **lover** /'lʌvə(r)/ *noun* [C] **1** a person who is having a sexual relationship outside marriage. ☛ Look at **mistress**. **2 lovers** [plural] (*old-fashioned*) two people who are in love or are having a sexual relationship without being married: *In the evening the park was full of young lovers walking hand in hand.* ○ *It wasn't long before they became lovers.* **3** a person who likes or enjoys the thing mentioned: *a music lover* ○ *an animal lover*

loving /'lʌvɪŋ/ *adj* feeling or showing love or care —**lovingly** *adv*

☆ **low¹** /ləʊ/ *adj* **1** not high: *The dog will be able to jump over that fence – it's much too low.* **2** close to the ground or to the bottom of sth: *Hang that picture a bit higher, it's much too low!* **3** below the usual or normal level or amount: *Temperatures were very low last winter.* ○ *The price of fruit is lower in the summer.* ○ *low wages* **4** below what is normal in quality, importance or development: *a low standard of living* ○ *low status* **5** (used about behaviour, etc) unpleasant; not respectable or honest: *That was a rather low trick to play on you!* **6** (used about a sound or voice) deep or soft and quiet: *I'll play the low notes and you play the high ones.* **7** not cheerful or bright: *He's been feeling rather low since his illness.* **8** (used about a gear in a car) that allows a slower speed: *You'll need to change into a low gear on this hill.*

(IDIOM) **high and low** ⇨ **HIGH²**

,lower 'case *adj, noun* [U] (in) small letters, not capitals: *A lower case R looks like this: r.* ☛ The opposite is **upper case**.

,lower-'class *adj* belonging to a low social class ☛ Look at **middle-class**, **upper-class**, and **working-class**.

,low-'key *adj* (used about the style of sth) quiet, without a lot of preparation or fuss: *The wedding will be very low-key. We're only inviting ten people.*

lowland /'ləʊlənd/ *noun* [C, usually pl] a flat area of land usually around sea level: *the lowlands near the coast* ○ *lowland areas*

,low 'tide *noun* [U] the time when the sea is at its lowest level: *At low tide you can walk out to the island.* ☛ The opposite is **high tide**.

☆ **low²** /ləʊ/ *adv* **1** in or to a low position, level, etc; near the ground or bottom; not high: *He reached down lower and lower – at last he had got it!* ○ *'Whereabouts is the pain? Here?' 'A bit lower down,'* she replied. **2** (in music) with deep notes: *Can you sing a bit lower?*

,low-'lying *adj* (used about land) near to sea-level; not high

,low-'paid *adj* not paying or earning much money: *low-paid workers*

low³ /ləʊ/ *noun* [C] a low point, level, figure, etc: *The pound has fallen to a new low against the dollar.*

low-down /'ləʊdaʊn/ *noun* [sing] (*informal*)

(IDIOM) **give sb/get the low-down (on sb/sth)** to tell sb/be told the true facts or secret information (about sb/sth): *Jeremy will give you the low-down on what went on at the meeting.*

☆ **lower¹** /'ləʊə(r)/ *adj* at the bottom of sth; being the bottom part of sth: *She bit her lower lip.* ○ *Write your notes in the lower left-hand corner.* ☛ The opposite is **upper**.

☆ **lower²** /'ləʊə(r)/ *verb* [T] **1** to move sb/sth down: *They lowered the boat into the water.* **2** to make sth less in amount or quality: *The virus lowers resistance to other diseases.* ☛ The opposite for 1 and 2 is **raise**.

☆ **loyal** /'lɔɪəl/ *adj* (used about a person) not changing in your friendship or beliefs; faithful: *a loyal friend* ○ *Will you remain loyal to the Conservatives at the next election?* ☛ The opposite is **disloyal**. —**loyally** /'lɔɪəli/ *adv*

loyalty /'lɔɪəlti/ *noun* (*pl* **loyalties**) **1** [U] the quality of being loyal: *A dog is capable of great loyalty to its master.* **2** [C] a feeling of friendship that makes you faithful towards sth/sb: *I know where my loyalties lie.*

lozenge /'lɒzɪndʒ/ *noun* [C] a sweet that you suck if you have a cough or sore throat

L-plate /'elpleɪt/ *noun* [C] a sign with a large red letter L (for 'learner') on it, that you fix to a car when you are learning to drive

lubricant /'luːbrɪkənt/ *noun* [C,U] a substance like oil used for making a machine, etc work smoothly

s	z	ʃ	ʒ	h	m	n	ŋ	l	r	j	w
so	zoo	she	vision	how	man	no	sing	leg	red	yes	wet

lubricate /ˈluːbrɪkeɪt/ verb [T] to put oil, etc onto or into sth so that it works smoothly —**lubrication** /ˌluːbrɪˈkeɪʃn/ noun [U]

lucid /ˈluːsɪd/ adj (formal) 1 (used about sth that is said or written) clear and easy to understand 2 (used about a person's mind) not confused; clear and normal —**lucidly** adv —**lucidity** /luːˈsɪdətɪ/ noun [U]

☆ **luck** /lʌk/ noun [U] 1 the fact of something happening by chance: *There's no skill in this game – it's all luck.* ○ *to have good, bad, etc luck* 2 success or good things that happen by chance: *We'd like to wish you lots of luck in your new career.* ○ *A four-leaved clover is supposed to bring you luck!*
(IDIOMS) **bad luck!**; **hard luck!** (used to express sympathy): *'Bad luck, darling. You can always try again.'*
be bad/hard luck (on sb) to be unlucky (for sb): *It was very hard luck on you that he changed his mind at the last minute.*
be in/out of luck to be lucky/unlucky: *I was in luck – the shop had the book I wanted.*
good luck (to sb) (used to wish that sb is successful): *Good luck! I'm sure you'll get the job.*
worse luck ⇨ WORSE

☆ **lucky** /ˈlʌkɪ/ adj (**luckier; luckiest**) 1 (used about a person) having good luck: *We were very lucky with the weather on holiday* (= it was fine). ○ *I'm very lucky to have such good friends.* 2 (used about a situation, event, etc) having a good result: *It's lucky you reminded me* (= or I would have forgotten). ○ *a lucky escape* 3 (used about a thing) bringing success or good luck: *a lucky number* ○ *It was not my lucky day* ☛ The opposite for all senses is **unlucky**.
luckily /ˈlʌkɪlɪ/ adv fortunately: *Luckily, I remembered to bring my umbrella.*

lucrative /ˈluːkrətɪv/ adj (formal) producing a lot of money

ludicrous /ˈluːdɪkrəs/ adj very silly; ridiculous: *What a ludicrous idea!* —**ludicrously** adv

lug /lʌg/ verb [T] (**lug**ging; **lug**ged) (informal) to carry or pull sth with great difficulty

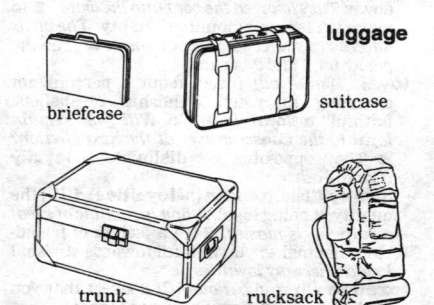

luggage
briefcase
suitcase
trunk
rucksack

☆ **luggage** /ˈlʌgɪdʒ/ (also **baggage**) noun [U] bags, suitcases, etc used for carrying a person's things on a journey: *'How much luggage are you taking with you?' 'Only one suitcase.'* ○ *We can fit one more piece of luggage in the boot!* ○ *All luggage should be checked in at the airport at least one hour before departure.*

☛ When flying you will be asked to pay for **excess luggage** if your suitcases weigh more than is allowed. You are only allowed one piece of **hand luggage** that you carry with you on the aeroplane.

'luggage rack noun [C] a shelf above the seats in a train or coach for putting your luggage on ☛ picture at **rack**.

lukewarm /ˌluːkˈwɔːm/ adj 1 (used about liquids) only slightly warm 2 **lukewarm (about sb/sth)** not showing much interest; not keen: *John's rather lukewarm about going to Iceland for a holiday.*

lull /lʌl/ verb [T] 1 to make sb/sth quiet or sleepy: *She sang a song to lull the children to sleep.* 2 to make sb/sth feel safe, especially by deceiving them: *Our first success lulled us into a false sense of security.*
lull noun [C, usually sing] a short period of quiet; a pause in activity: *When she entered the room there was a lull in the conversation.*

lullaby /ˈlʌləbaɪ/ noun [C] (pl **lullabies**) a gentle song that you sing to help a child to go to sleep

lumber¹ /ˈlʌmbə(r)/ noun [U] (especially US) = TIMBER(1)
lumber verb [T] **lumber sb (with sb/sth)** to give sb a responsibility or job that he/she does not want: *I've been lumbered with driving the children to school again.*

lumber² /ˈlʌmbə(r)/ verb [I] to move in a slow, heavy way: *He heaved himself out of bed and lumbered into the bathroom.*

luminous /ˈluːmɪnəs/ adj shining, especially in the dark: *a luminous watch*

☆ **lump¹** /lʌmp/ noun [C] 1 a piece of sth solid of any size or shape: *a lump of coal* ○ *The sauce was full of lumps.* 2 a hard swelling on or in the body: *You'll have a bit of a lump on your head where you banged it.*
lump verb [T] **lump sb/sth (together)** to put people or things together; to consider or treat them as being all alike
lumpy adj (**lumpier; lumpiest**) full of or covered with lumps

'lump sum noun [C] an amount of money paid all at once rather than in several smaller amounts: *You'll receive a lump sum when you retire as well as your pension.*

lump² /lʌmp/ verb
(IDIOM) **lump it** (informal) to accept sth unpleasant whether you want to or not: *'I don't like this sweater Mum.' 'Well you'll just have to lump it – it's the only one that's clean!'*

lunacy /ˈluːnəsɪ/ noun [U] very foolish behaviour: *It was lunacy to swim so far out to sea.*

lunar /ˈluːnə(r)/ adj connected with the moon: *lunar dust* ○ *a lunar spacecraft*

lunatic /ˈluːnətɪk/ noun [C] 1 (informal) a person who behaves in a very foolish way 2 (old-fashioned) a person who is mad
lunatic adj very foolish: *a lunatic idea* ☛ Look at the note at **mad**.

iː	ɪ	e	æ	ɑː	ɒ	ɔː	ʊ	uː	ʌ
see	sit	ten	hat	arm	got	saw	put	too	cup

'lunatic asylum *noun* [C] (*old-fashioned*) a place where mentally ill people were kept in the past

☆ **lunch** /lʌntʃ/ *noun* [C,U] a meal that you have in the middle of the day: *Hot and cold lunches are served between 12 and 2.* ○ *What would you like for lunch?*

> ☛ You might take a **packed lunch** or a **picnic lunch** if you're out for the day. If you're working you might have a **business lunch** or a **working lunch** (= working at the same time as having lunch). Look at the note at **dinner**.

lunch *verb* [I] to eat lunch: *Could you lunch with me one day next week?*

'lunch-time *noun* [C,U] the time around the middle of the day when lunch is eaten: *I'll meet you at lunch-time.*

luncheon /'lʌntʃən/ *noun* **1** [C] a formal meal eaten in the middle of the day: *The opening of the new shopping centre was followed by a luncheon in the town hall.* **2** [U] (*formal*) lunch

☆ **lung** /lʌŋ/ *noun* [C] one of the two parts of the body that are inside your chest and are used for breathing: *lung cancer*

lunge /lʌndʒ/ *noun* [C, usually sing] a sudden forward movement of the body, especially when trying to attack sb —**lunge** *verb* [I] *He lunged towards me with a knife.*

lurch¹ /lɜːtʃ/ *noun* [sing]
(IDIOM) **leave sb in the lurch** ⇨ LEAVE¹

lurch² /lɜːtʃ/ *noun* [C] a sudden movement to one side, especially when out of control: *The ship gave a tremendous lurch as it hit the iceberg.* —**lurch** *verb* [I]

lure /lʊə(r)/ *noun* [C] the power of attracting sb: *the lure of money, fame, adventure, etc*
lure *verb* [T] to attract or tempt sb/sth: *It's such a nice day – can I lure you away from your work?*

lurid /'lʊərɪd/ *adj* **1** shocking, especially because violent or unpleasant: *The newspaper was criticized for its lurid description of the disaster.* **2** having colours that are very or too bright: *a lurid dress in purple and orange* —**luridly** *adv*

lurk /lɜːk/ *verb* [I] to wait where you cannot be seen, especially when intending to do sth bad: *I thought I saw somebody lurking among the trees.*

luscious /'lʌʃəs/ *adj* (used about food) tasting very good

lush /lʌʃ/ *adj* (used about plants) growing very thickly and well

lust /lʌst/ *noun* **1** [U] strong sexual desire **2** [C,U] (a) very strong desire to possess or get sth: *a lust for power*
lust *verb* [I] **lust after/for sb/sth** to have a very strong desire for sb/sth: *to lust for power, success, fame, etc*

lustful /-fl/ *adj* full of (sexual) desire: *lustful thoughts* —**lustfully** /-fəlɪ/ *adv*

luxurious /lʌg'ʒʊərɪəs/ *adj* very comfortable; full of luxury: *a luxurious hotel* —**luxuriously** *adv*

☆ **luxury** /'lʌkʃərɪ/ *noun* (*pl* **luxuries**) **1** [U] great comfort and pleasure, often including the use and enjoyment of expensive and beautiful things: *They are said to be living in Barbados, in the greatest luxury.* ○ *to lead a life of luxury* ○ *a luxury hotel, car, yacht, etc* **2** [C] something that is enjoyable and expensive that you do not really need: *A holiday is a luxury we just can't afford this year.* ○ *luxury goods, such as wine and cigarettes* **3** [U,sing] a pleasure which you do not often have: *It was (an) absolute luxury to do nothing all weekend.*

lynch /lɪntʃ/ *verb* [T] (used about a crowd of people) to kill sb who is thought to be guilty of a crime, without a legal trial

lyric /'lɪrɪk/ *adj* (used about poetry) expressing personal feelings
lyrics *noun* [plural] the words of a song: *Who wrote the lyrics?*

lyrical /'lɪrɪkl/ *adj* like a song or a poem, expressing strong personal feelings

Mm

M, m /em/ *noun* [C] (*pl* **M's**; **m's**) the thirteenth letter of the English alphabet: *'Manchester' begins with (an) 'M'.*

ma'am /mæm; mɑːm/ *noun* [sing] (used when speaking to a woman, as a short form for 'madam') ☛ In British English **ma'am** is old-fashioned but it is often used in US English as a polite way of addressing a woman.

mac = MACKINTOSH

macabre /mə'kɑːbrə/ *adj* horrible and frightening because connected with death

macaroni /ˌmækə'rəʊnɪ/ *noun* [U] a type of Italian food made from dried flour and water (pasta) in the shape of hollow tubes

☆ **machine** /mə'ʃiːn/ *noun* [C] **1** (often in compounds) a piece of equipment with several moving parts, made to perform a particular task: *a washing-machine* ○ *Can you operate/work this machine?* ○ *One of the machines has broken down.* ☛ Look at the note at **tool**. **2** a system or organization carefully controlled and organized by a group of people: *It's hard to understand the workings of the party machine* (= a political party).

3ː	ə	eɪ	əʊ	aɪ	aʊ	ɔɪ	ɪə	eə	ʊə
fur	ago	pay	home	five	now	join	near	hair	pure

machinery /məˈʃiːnəri/ noun [U] machines in general or the moving parts of a machine: *There's an exhibition of the latest farm machinery.* o *the delicate machinery of a watch*

ma'chine-gun noun [C] a gun that fires bullets very quickly and continuously

macho /ˈmætʃəʊ/ adj (*informal*) (used about a man or his behaviour) very masculine in an aggressive way

mackintosh /ˈmækɪntɒʃ/ (*also* **mac**; **mack** /mæk/) noun [C] (*especially Brit*) a coat that is made to keep out the rain

☆ **mad** /mæd/ adj (**madder**; **maddest**) **1** with a sick mind; mentally ill: *In the past people who were considered mad were locked up in the most terrible conditions.* ☛ It is not usual nowadays to use **mad** or **insane** to describe a person who is not mentally normal. We would use the expression **mentally ill**. **2** very foolish; crazy: *My parents think I'm mad to leave school at 16.* **3 mad (at/with sb)** very angry: *His laziness drives me mad!* o *Don't get mad at him. He didn't mean to do it.* **4** not controlled; wild or very excited: *We're always in a mad rush to get ready in the morning.* o *The audience was cheering and clapping like mad* (= *very hard*). **5** (*informal*) **mad about/on sb/sth** extremely interested in sb/sth: *He's mad on computer games at the moment.* o *Steve's mad about Jane* (= he likes her very much).

madly adv **1** in a wild or crazy way: *Stop rushing about madly and sit down for a minute!* **2** extremely: *They're madly in love.*

madness noun [U] **1** the state of being mad(1) **2** foolish behaviour: *It would be madness to take a boat out in such rough weather.*

'madman /-mən/ **'madwoman** /-wʊmən/ noun [C] a person who is mad(1) or who behaves in a foolish way: *Stop behaving like a madman!* o *There's a madman trying to overtake a bus on the hill!*

madam /ˈmædəm/ noun [sing] **1** (*formal*) a polite way of speaking to a woman, especially to a customer in a shop: *Can I help you, madam?* ☛ Look at **ma'am** and **sir**. **2 Madam** used for beginning a formal letter to a woman when you do not know her name: *Dear Madam, I am writing in reply...*

madden /ˈmædn/ verb [T] to make sb very angry or annoyed —**maddening** /ˈmædnɪŋ/ adj: *She has some really maddening habits.* —**maddeningly** adv

made pt, pp of MAKE

☆ **magazine** /ˌmæɡəˈziːn; US ˈmæɡəziːn/ noun [C] (*also informal* **mag** /mæɡ/) a type of book with a paper cover which is published every week or month and contains articles, advertisements, photographs and stories by various writers: *a woman's, computer, gardening, etc magazine* o *a magazine article* o *How often does this magazine come out?*

maggot /ˈmæɡət/ noun [C] an insect that looks like a small worm. Maggots grow from the eggs of flies, which have been laid in meat, cheese, etc.

☆ **magic** /ˈmædʒɪk/ noun [U] **1** (in stories) a power that can make extraordinary or impossible things happen: *The witch had used her magic to turn the children into frogs.* ☛ Look at **black magic**. **2** the art of performing extraordinary tricks to entertain people **3** a special or fascinating quality or sth that has this quality: *I'll never forget the magic of that moment.* o *The whole holiday was magic from beginning to end.*

magic adj **1** used in or using magic: *a magic spell* **2** wonderful; excellent: *The way she sings is absolutely magic.*

magical /-kl/ adj **1** that seems to use magic or to produce it: *This is a magical box that makes things disappear.* **2** mysterious and exciting: *Father Christmas has a magical fascination for many children.* —**magically** /-klɪ/ adv

magician /məˈdʒɪʃn/ noun [C] **1** a person who performs magic tricks to entertain people ☛ Look at **conjuror**. **2** (in stories) a man who has magic power ☛ Look at **wizard**.

magistrate /ˈmædʒɪstreɪt/ noun [C] a judge in the lowest rank of lawcourt that deals especially with less serious crimes

magnanimous /mæɡˈnænɪməs/ adj generous (especially towards an enemy or a rival that you have beaten)

magnet /ˈmæɡnɪt/ noun [C] a piece of iron that can attract and pick up iron and steel

magnetic /mæɡˈnetɪk/ adj **1** having the ability of a magnet to attract iron and steel: *Let's see if this metal is magnetic or not.* **2** having a quality that strongly attracts people: *She was the most magnetic speaker I have ever listened to.*

magnetism /ˈmæɡnɪtɪzəm/ noun [U] **1** the power of magnets to attract **2** strong personal attraction: *His magnetism made him a powerful and dangerous political figure.*

magnetize (*also* **magnetise**) /ˈmæɡnətaɪz/ verb [T] **1** to make sth become magnetic **2** to attract sb strongly

magnetic 'tape noun [C,U] plastic tape covered with a magnetic substance and used for recording sound, films, etc

magnificent /mæɡˈnɪfɪsnt/ adj extremely good or beautiful; splendid: *What a magnificent castle!* —**magnificently** adv —**magnificence** /-sns/ noun [U]

magnify /ˈmæɡnɪfaɪ/ verb [T] (*pres part* **magnifying**; *3rd pers sing pres* **magnifies**; *pt, pp* **magnified**) **1** to make sth look bigger than it is: *to magnify sth under a microscope* **2** to make sth seem more important than it really is: *to magnify a problem* —**magnification** /ˌmæɡnɪfɪˈkeɪʃn/ noun [U]

'magnifying glass noun [C] a lens that is held in your hand, and used for making things look bigger than they are

magnitude /ˈmæɡnɪtjuːd; US -tuːd/ noun [U] the great size or importance of sth: *the magnitude of the problem*

mahogany /məˈhɒɡəni/ noun [U] hard red-

p	b	t	d	k	ɡ		tʃ	dʒ	f	v	θ	ð
pen	bad	tea	did	cat	got		chin	June	fall	van	thin	then

magnify

magnifying glass

dish-brown wood (from a tropical tree) that is used for making expensive furniture

maid /meɪd/ noun [C] a woman servant in a hotel or large house: *a chambermaid* o *a housemaid*

maiden /'meɪdn/ noun [C] (*old-fashioned*) a girl or unmarried woman

'**maiden name** noun [C] the surname that a woman had before she got married

maiden 'voyage noun [C] the first journey of a new ship

☆ **mail** /meɪl/ noun [U] **1** the system for collecting and delivering letters and parcels: *to send a parcel by airmail/surface mail* o *a mail van* **2** = POST³; *junk mail* (= letters, usually advertising sth, that are sent to people although they have not asked for them) ☛ Look at the note at **post**.
—**mail** verb [T] (*especially US*) = POST⁴

'**mailbox** noun [C] (*US*) **1** = LETTER-BOX(2) **2** = POSTBOX

'**mailing list** noun [C] a list of the names and addresses of people to whom advertising material or information is sent

'**mailman** /-mæn/ noun [C] (*pl* **mailmen** /-mən/) (*US*) = POSTMAN

'**mail order** noun [U] a method of shopping. You choose what you want from a special book (**a catalogue**) and the goods are then sent to you by post.

maim /meɪm/ verb [T] to hurt sb so badly that part of the body can no longer be used

☆ **main¹** /meɪn/ adj (only before a noun) most important; chief: *My main reason for wanting to learn English is to get a better job.* o *a busy main road* o *Do you eat your main meal at midday or in the evening?* o *Don't write everything down –just make a note of the main points.* o *He doesn't earn very much but he's happy. That's the main thing.*

(IDIOM) **in the main** generally; mostly: *We found English people very friendly in the main.*

mainly adv mostly: *The students here are mainly from Japan.*

'**main 'line** noun [C] the main railway line between two places: *a main-line station*

main² /meɪn/ noun [C] a large pipe or wire that carries water, gas or electricity to a building or that takes waste water away from it: *The water main has burst.* ☛ Often the form **mains** is used and this can take either a singular or plural verb: *Turn the water off at the mains.*

mainland /'meɪnlænd/ noun [sing] the main part of a country or continent, not including the islands around it: *They took the ferry back from Skye to the mainland.*

mainstay /'meɪnsteɪ/ noun [C] (*figurative*) a person or thing that helps sb/sth to work well or to be strong

mainstream /'meɪnstriːm/ noun [sing] the way that most people think or behave: *The Green Party is not in the mainstream of British politics.*

☆ **maintain** /meɪn'teɪn/ verb [T] **1** to continue to have or do sth; to keep sth at the same level or standard: *We need to maintain the quality of our goods but not increase the price.* o *to maintain law and order* o *to maintain a constant temperature* **2** to support sb by paying for the things he/she needs: *He has to maintain two children from his previous marriage* **3** to keep sth in good condition: *to maintain a road, building, machine, etc* **4** to say that sth is true: *In the Middle Ages people maintained that the Sun went round the Earth.*

maintenance /'meɪntənəns/ noun [U] **1** keeping sth in good condition: *This house needs a lot of maintenance.* o *car maintenance* **2** money that you pay to the people that you are legally responsible for, when you no longer live with them: *He has to pay maintenance to his ex-wife and children.*

maisonette (*also* **maisonnette**) /ˌmeɪzə'net/ noun [C] a flat on two floors that is part of a larger building

maize /meɪz/ (*US* **corn**) noun [U] a tall plant that produces yellow grains in a large mass (**a cob**) ☛ picture at **sweet corn**.

majestic /mə'dʒestɪk/ adj making a strong impression because it is dignified or beautiful: *a majestic mountain landscape* —**majestically** /-kli/ adv

majesty /'mædʒəsti/ noun (*pl* **majesties**) **1** [U] the quality of being grand or dignified like a king or queen: *the splendour and majesty of the palace and its gardens* **2 Majesty** [C] (used when speaking to or about a royal person): *Her Majesty the Queen*

☆ **major¹** /'meɪdʒə(r)/ adj (only before a noun) great in size, importance, seriousness, etc: *The patient needs major heart surgery.* o *a major road* o *There haven't been any major problems.* ☛ The opposite is **minor**.

major verb

(PHRASAL VERB) **major in sth** (*US*) to study sth as your main subject at college or university

major² /'meɪdʒə(r)/ noun [C] an officer of middle rank in the army

ˌ**major-'general** noun [C] an officer of high rank in the army

☆ **majority** /mə'dʒɒrəti; *US* -'dʒɔːr-/ noun (*pl* **majorities**) **1** [sing] the largest number or part of sth: *The majority of students in the class come from Japan.* ☛ Look at **minority**. **2** [C] **majority (over sb)** the difference in the number of votes in an election for the person/party who came first and the person/party who came second: *He was elected by a majority of over 5 000 votes.* ☛ If you have an **overall majority** you got more votes than all the other people/parties added together.

(IDIOM) **be in the/a majority** to form the lar-

s	z	ʃ	ʒ	h	m	n	ŋ	l	r	j	w
so	zoo	she	vision	how	man	no	sing	leg	red	yes	wet

gest number or part of sth: *The Labour Party is in the majority on the Council.*

☆ **make¹** /meɪk/ *verb* [T] (*pt, pp* **made** /meɪd/)
1 to produce sth or to cause sth to appear: *Can you make me a cup of tea, please?* ○ *They make VW cars in Wolfsburg.* ○ *made in Britain* (= on a label) ○ *What's that shirt made of?* (= what material) ○ *The coffee made a stain on the carpet.* **2** (used with nouns) to perform a certain action: *to make a mistake, a noise, a statement, a suggestion, etc* ○ *to make progress* ☞ Often there is a verb with a similar form, eg **decide/ make a decision**. If you use 'make' + noun, you can use an adjective with it: *He made the right decision.* ○ *They made a generous offer.* **3** to cause a particular action, feeling or situation: *The film made me cry.* ○ *That dress makes you look thin.* ○ *Flying makes him nervous.* ○ *Her remarks made the situation worse.* ○ *We can make this room into a bedroom.* **4** to force sb/sth to do sth: *They made him wait at the police station all day.* ☞ In the passive we must use **to**: *He was made to wait at the police station.* **5** (used with *clear, certain* and *sure*): *She made it clear that she didn't agree.* ○ *Make sure you lock the car.* ○ *I made certain I had enough money.* **6** (used with money, numbers and time): *He makes* (= earns) *£20 000 a year.* ○ *to make a lot of money* ○ *5 and 7 make 12.* ○ *'What do you make the answer?' '28'* ○ *'What's the time?' 'I make it 6.45.'* **7** to have the right qualities to be sth; to make sth perfect: *She'll make a good teacher.* ○ *The beautiful weather really made our holiday.* **8** to give sb a job or elect sb to a position: *She was made Minister of Health.* **9** to reach a place; to be able to go somewhere: *We should make Bristol by about 10.* ○ *I'm afraid I can't make the meeting next week.*

(IDIOMS) **make do with sth** to use sth that is not good enough because nothing better is available: *If we can't get limes, we'll have to make do with lemons.*

make it 1 to get to a place (in time); to go to a place you have been invited to: *The train leaves in 5 minutes. We'll never make it!* ○ *I'm afraid I can't make it to your party.* **2** to be successful: *She'll never make it as an actress.*

make the most of sth to get as much pleasure, profit, etc as possible from sth: *You won't get another chance – make the most of it!* ☞ For other expressions with **make**, look at the noun and adjective entries, eg for **make love** look at **love**.

(PHRASAL VERBS) **make for sb/sth** to move towards sb/sth

make for sth to help or allow sth to happen: *Arguing all the time doesn't make for a happy marriage.*

be made for sb/each other to be well suited to sb/each other: *Jim and Alice seem made for each other.*

make sb/sth into sb/sth to change sb/sth into sth: *She made her spare room into an office.*

make sth of sb/sth to understand sb/sth: *I don't know what to make of my boss* (= I can't understand him).

make off (*informal*) to leave or escape in a hurry

make off with sth (*informal*) to steal sth and leave quickly with it: *Someone's made off with my wallet!*

make sb/sth out 1 to understand sb/sth: *I just can't make him out.* ○ *Can you make this form out?* **2** to be able to see or hear sb/sth; to manage to read sth: *I could just make out her signature.*

make sth out to write or complete sth: *She made out a cheque for £100.*

make out that...; make yourself out to be sth to say that sth is true and try to make people believe it: *He made out that he was a millionaire.* ○ *She's not as clever as she makes herself out to be.*

make (sb) up to put powder, lipstick, etc on the face

make sth up 1 to form: *the different groups that make up our society* **2** to invent sth, often sth that is not true: *to make up an excuse* **3** to make a number or an amount complete: *We need one more person to make up our team.*

make up for sth to do sth that corrects a bad situation: *Her enthusiasm makes up for her lack of experience.*

make it up to sb (*informal*) to do sth that shows that you are sorry for what you have done to sb or that you are grateful for what they have done for you: *You've done me a big favour. How can I make it up to you?*

make (it) up (with sb) to become friends again after a quarrel: *Has she made it up with him yet?*

☆ **make²** /meɪk/ *noun* [C] the name of the company that produced sth: *'What make is your television?' 'It's a Sony.'*

make-believe /ˈmeɪk bɪliːv/ *noun* [U] pretending or imagining sth; the things that are imagined: *I don't believe his stories – they're all make-believe.*

☆ **maker** /ˈmeɪkə(r)/ *noun* [C] a person or company that makes sth: *a dressmaker*

makeshift /ˈmeɪkʃɪft/ *adj* used for a short time until there is sth better: *The refugees built makeshift shelters out of old cardboard boxes.*

make-up /ˈmeɪkʌp/ *noun* **1** [U] powder, cream, etc that you put on your face to make yourself more attractive. Actors use make-up to change their appearance when they are acting: *to put on/take off make-up* ○ *She wears a lot of make-up.* ☞ Look at **cosmetics**. The verb is **make up/make yourself up**. **2** [sing] a person's character: *He can't help his temper. It's part of his make-up.*

making /ˈmeɪkɪŋ/ *noun* [sing] the act of doing or producing sth: *breadmaking*

(IDIOMS) **be the making of sb** be the reason that sb is successful: *Rachel worked for a year before she went to university and it was the making of her.*

have the makings of sth to have the necessary qualities for sth: *The book has the makings of a good film.*

maladjusted /ˌmæləˈdʒʌstɪd/ *adj* (used about a person) not able to behave well with other people —**maladjustment** /ˌmæləˈdʒʌstmənt/ *noun* [U]

iː	ɪ	e	æ	ɑː	ɒ	ɔː	ʊ	uː	ʌ
see	sit	ten	hat	arm	got	saw	put	too	cup

malaria /mə'leərɪə/ noun [U] a serious disease that you may get when you have been bitten by a small flying insect (**a mosquito**) that lives in hot countries

☆ **male** /meɪl/ adj belonging to the sex that does not give birth to babies or lay eggs: *A male goat is called a billy.* ☛ Look at the note at **female**.
male noun [C] a male person or animal
male 'chauvinism noun [U] the belief that men are better than women —**male 'chauvinist** noun [C]

malice /'mælɪs/ noun [U] a wish to hurt other people —**malicious** /mə'lɪʃəs/ adj —**maliciously** adv

malignant /mə'lɪɡnənt/ adj (used to describe tumours in the body) likely to cause death if not controlled ☛ The opposite is **benign**.

mall /mæl; mɔːl/ noun [C] = SHOPPING MALL

mallet /'mælɪt/ noun [C] a heavy wooden hammer ☛ picture at **tool**.

malnutrition /ˌmælnjuː'trɪʃn; US -nuː-/ noun [U] bad health that is the result of not having enough food or enough of the right kind of food

malt /mɔːlt/ noun [U] grain that has been left in water for a long time and then dried. Malt is used for making beer and whisky

maltreat /ˌmæl'triːt/ verb [T] (formal) to treat a person or animal cruelly or unkindly —**maltreatment** noun [U]

mammal /'mæml/ noun [C] an animal of the type that gives birth to live animals and does not lay eggs. Mammals feed their babies on milk from their bodies: *Birds and fish are not mammals but whales and dolphins are.*

mammoth /'mæməθ/ adj very big

☆ **man¹** /mæn/ noun (pl **men** /men/) **1** [C] an adult male person: *a handsome man in his mid-twenties* ○ *men, women and children* **2** [C] a person of either sex, male or female: *All men are equal.* ○ *No man could survive long in such conditions.* **3** [sing] the human race; human beings: *Early man lived by hunting and gathering.* ○ *Why is man so destructive?* ☛ Some people do not like the way **man** is used in senses 2 and 3 (or the use of **mankind** to mean 'all men and women') because it seems that women are not included. They prefer to use **humanity, the human race,** or **people**. **4** [C] a husband, boyfriend or male lover: *to become man and wife* (= to get married) **5** [C, usually pl] a man of low rank in the army, etc who takes orders from an officer: *officers and men* **6** (informal) (used when you are talking to sb): *Hey, man, can you lend me a pound?*
(IDIOMS) **the man in the street** (Brit) an ordinary man or woman
the odd man/one out ⇨ ODD
-man (in compounds) **1** a person who lives in a particular place: *a Frenchman* ○ *a countryman* **2** a person who has a particular job: *a businessman* ○ *a fireman*

man² /mæn/ verb [T] (**man**ning; **man**ned) to operate sth or to provide people to operate sth: *to man a boat, gun, telephone, etc* ○ *When was the first manned space flight?*

☆ **manage** /'mænɪdʒ/ verb **1** [T] to be in charge or control of sth: *She manages a small advertising business.* **2** [I,T] (often with *can* or *could*) to be able to do sth or to deal with sth: *We are sorry we didn't manage to see you while we were in Scotland.* ○ *I can't manage this suitcase. It's too heavy.* ○ *However did you manage to find us here?* ○ *Paula can't manage next Tuesday* (= she can't come then) *so we'll meet another day.* **3** [I] **manage (on sth); manage (without sb/sth)** to have a reasonable way of life: *They live in the country and couldn't manage without a car.* ○ *It's hard for a family to manage on just one income.*

manageable adj not too big or too difficult to control or look after: *a garden of manageable size*

managing di'rector noun [C] a person who controls a business or company

☆ **management** /'mænɪdʒmənt/ noun **1** [U] the control or organization of sth: *Good management is the key to success in business.* ○ *management training* **2** [C] the people who control a business or company: *The hotel is now under new management.* ☛ In the singular, **management** can be used with a singular or plural verb: *The management is/are considering making some workers redundant.*

☆ **manager** /'mænɪdʒə(r)/ noun [C] **1** a man or woman who controls an organization or part of an organization: *Clive's the manager of a shoe shop.* ○ *a bank manager* ○ *a sales manager* ○ *an assistant manager* **2** a person who looks after the business affairs of a singer, actor, etc **3** a person who looks after a sports team: *the England team manager*

manageress /ˌmænɪdʒə'res/ noun [C] the woman who is in charge of a shop or restaurant

mandarin /'mændərɪn/ (also **mandarin orange**) noun [C] a type of small orange whose skin comes off easily

mandate /'mændeɪt/ noun [usually sing] the power that a group of people has to do sth as a result of winning an election: *The union leaders had a clear mandate from their members to call a strike.*

mane /meɪn/ noun [C] the long hair on the neck of a horse or male lion ☛ picture at **horse**.

maneuver (US) = MANOEUVRE

mangle /'mæŋɡl/ verb [T] to damage sth greatly so that it is difficult to see what it used to look like: *The motorway was covered with the mangled wreckage of cars and vans.* ☛ **Mangle** is most often used in the passive.

mango /'mæŋɡəʊ/ noun [C] (pl **mangoes** or **mangos**) a tropical fruit that has a yellowish red skin and is yellow inside

manhole /'mænhəʊl/ noun [C] a hole in the street with a lid over it through which sb can go to look at the pipes, wires, etc that are underground

manhood /'mænhʊd/ noun [U] the state of being a man rather than a boy: *to reach manhood*

mania /'meɪniə/ noun **1** [U] a serious mental illness that may cause a person to be very excited or violent **2** [C] (informal) a very great love (for sth): *She's got a mania for keeping things tidy.*

maniac /'meɪniæk/ noun [C] **1** a person who is

manicure /ˈmænɪkjʊə(r)/ noun [C,U] treatment to make your hands and fingernails look nice

manifest /ˈmænɪfest/ verb [T] (formal) **1** to show sth clearly **2 manifest itself/themselves** to appear: *Mental illness can manifest itself in many forms.*

manifestation /ˌmænɪfeˈsteɪʃn/ noun [C,U] (formal) a sign that sth is happening

manifesto /ˌmænɪˈfestəʊ/ noun [C] (pl **manifestos** or **manifestoes**) a written statement by a political party that explains what it hopes to do if it becomes the government in the future

manipulate /məˈnɪpjuleɪt/ verb [T] **1** to use or control sth with skill **2** to influence sb so that they do or think what you want: *Clever politicians know how to manipulate public opinion* —**manipulation** /məˌnɪpjʊˈleɪʃn/ noun [C,U]

mankind /ˌmænˈkaɪnd/ noun [U] all the people in the world: *A nuclear war would be a threat to all mankind.* ☛ Look at the note at **man**.

manly /ˈmænli/ adj typical of or suitable for a man: *a deep manly voice* —**manliness** noun [U]

man-made /ˌmæn ˈmeɪd/ adj made by people, not formed in a natural way; artificial: *man-made fabrics such as nylon and polyester* ☛ The opposite is **natural**.

☆ **manner** /ˈmænə(r)/ noun **1** [sing] the way that you do sth or that sth happens: *Stop arguing! Let's try to act in a civilized manner.* **2** [sing] the way that sb behaves towards other people: *Don't you think that David has got a very arrogant manner?* **3 manners** [plural] the way of behaving that is thought to be polite in your society or culture: *In some countries it is bad manners to show the soles of your feet.* o *Their children have beautiful table manners.*
(IDIOM) **all manner of...** every kind of...

mannerism /ˈmænərɪzəm/ noun [C] a way of speaking or a movement of part of the body that is typical for a particular person

manoeuvre (*US* **maneuver**) /məˈnuːvə(r)/ noun **1** [C] a movement that needs care or skill: *In the driving-test you must perform several manoeuvres such as reversing around a corner.* **2** [C] something clever that you do in order to win sth, trick sb, etc **3 manoeuvres** [plural] a way of training soldiers when large numbers of them practise fighting in battles: *large-scale military manoeuvres*

manoeuvre (*US* **maneuver**) verb [I,T] to move to a different position using skill: *The parking space wasn't very big but I managed to manoeuvre into it quite easily.*

manor /ˈmænə(r)/ (also **manor-house**) noun [C] a large house in the country that has land around it

☛ In the Middle Ages the family who lived in the manor-house owned all the surrounding land and villages. Look at **feudalism**.

manpower /ˈmænpaʊə(r)/ noun [U] the people that you need to do a particular job: *There is a shortage of skilled manpower in the computer industry.*

mansion /ˈmænʃn/ noun [C] a very large house

manslaughter /ˈmænslɔːtə(r)/ noun [U] the crime of killing sb without intending to do so ☛ Look at **murder**.

mantelpiece /ˈmæntlpiːs/ noun [C] a shelf that is above a fireplace ☛ picture at **fireplace**.

manual¹ /ˈmænjuəl/ adj using your hands; operated by hand: *Office work can sometimes be more tiring than manual work.* o *Does your car have a manual or an automatic gear-box?* o *a skilled manual worker*

manually /-juəli/ adv by hand, not automatically

manual² /ˈmænjuəl/ noun [C] a book that explains how to do or operate sth: *a training manual* o *Full instructions are given in the owner's manual.*

☆ **manufacture** /ˌmænjʊˈfæktʃə(r)/ verb [T] to make sth in large quantities using machines: *a local factory that manufactures high-quality furniture* o *manufacturing industries* —**manufacture** noun [U]: *The manufacture of chemical weapons should be illegal.*

manufacturer noun [C] a person or company that manufactures sth: *Faulty goods should be returned to the manufacturer.*

manure /məˈnjʊə(r)/ noun [U] the waste matter from animals that is put on the ground in order to make plants grow better ☛ Look at **fertilizer**.

manuscript /ˈmænjʊskrɪpt/ noun [C] **1** a very old book or document that was written by hand **2** a typed or hand-written copy of a book that has not yet been printed

Manx /mæŋks/ adj of the Isle of Man, its people or language

☆ **many** /ˈmeni/ det, pron (used with plural nouns or verbs) **1** a large number of people or things: *Many people do not get enough to eat.* o *There are too many mistakes in this essay.* o *Many of the people at the meeting left early.* o *Many of the mistakes were just careless.* **2** (used with 'how' to ask about the number of people or things): *How many children have you got?* o *How many mistakes did you make?* o *How many came to the meeting?* **3 many a** (used with a singular noun and verb) (formal) a large number of: *I've heard him say that many a time.*
(IDIOM) **a good/great many** very many

Maori /ˈmaʊri/ noun [C] a member of the race of people who were the original inhabitants of New Zealand —**Maori** adj

☆ **map** /mæp/ noun [C] a drawing or plan of (part of) the surface of the earth that shows countries, rivers, mountains, roads, etc: *a map of the world* o *a road map* o *a street map of Oxford* o *I can't find Cambridge on the map.* o *to read a map* o *My house is not easy to find so I'll draw you a map.* ☛ A book of maps is called an **atlas**.

map verb [T] (**mapp**ing; **mapp**ed) to make a map of a place

maple /ˈmeɪpl/ noun [C] a tree that has leaves

p	b	t	d	k	g	tʃ	dʒ	f	v	θ	ð
pen	bad	tea	did	cat	got	chin	June	fall	van	thin	then

with five points and that produces a very sweet liquid: *maple syrup*

marathon /'mærəθən; US -θɒn/ *noun* [C] a long-distance running race in which people run about 42 kilometres or 26 miles: *Have you ever run a marathon?* ○ *the London Marathon* ○ *(figurative) a marathon meeting* (= one that lasts a very long time)

marble /'mɑːbl/ *noun* **1** [U] a hard attractive stone that is used to make statues and parts of buildings: *a marble statue* ○ *This staircase is made of marble.* **2** [C] a small ball of coloured glass that children play with **3 marbles** [plural] the children's game that you play by rolling marbles along the ground trying to hit other marbles

☆ **March** /mɑːtʃ/ *noun* [C,U] (*abbr* **Mar**) the third month of the year, coming before April ☞ For examples of the use of the months in sentences, look at **January**.

☆ **march¹** /mɑːtʃ/ *verb* **1** [I] to walk with regular steps (like a soldier): *The President saluted as the troops marched past.* ○ *He marched in and demanded an explanation.* **2** [I] to walk in a large group to protest about sth: *The demonstrators marched through the centre of town.* **3** [T] to cause sb to walk or march somewhere: *The prisoner was marched away.*

march² /mɑːtʃ/ *noun* [C] **1** an act of marching: *The soldiers were tired after their long march.* **2** an organized walk by a large group of people who are protesting about sth: *a peace march* ☞ Look at **demonstration**.

mare /meə(r)/ *noun* [C] a female horse or donkey ☞ Look at the note at **horse**.

margarine /ˌmɑːdʒəˈriːn; *US* ˈmɑːdʒərɪn/ *noun* [U] a food that looks like butter, made of animal or vegetable fats. Margarine is used for spreading on bread and for cooking.

margin /'mɑːdʒɪn/ *noun* [C] **1** the empty space at the side of a page in a book, etc: *notes in the margin* ○ *a wide/narrow margin* **2** the amount of space, time, votes, etc by which you win sth: *He won the race by a comfortable margin.* **3** an amount of space, time, etc that is more than you need: *a safety margin* **4** the amount of profit that a company makes on sth

marginal /-nl/ *adj* small in size or importance: *The differences are marginal.*

marginally /-nəli/ *adv* a little; slightly: *In most cases costs will increase only marginally.*

marijuana (*also* **marihuana**) /ˌmærɪjʊˈɑːnə/ *noun* [U] an illegal drug that is smoked in cigarettes

marina /məˈriːnə/ *noun* [C] a small harbour for pleasure boats

marine¹ /məˈriːn/ *adj* **1** connected with the sea: *the study of marine life* **2** connected with ships or sailing: *marine insurance*

marine² /məˈriːn/ *noun* [C] a soldier who has been trained to fight on land or at sea

marital /'mærɪtl/ *adj* (only *before* a noun) connected with marriage: *marital problems*

ˌmarital ˈstatus *noun* [U] (*formal*) whether you are married, single, widowed or divorced

maritime /'mærɪtaɪm/ *adj* connected with the sea or ships

☆ **mark¹** /mɑːk/ *noun* [C] **1** a spot or line that spoils the appearance of sth: *There's a dirty mark on the front of your shirt.* ○ *If you put a hot cup down on the table it will leave a mark.* ☞ Look at **birthmark**. **2** something that shows who or what sb/sth is or that gives information about sb/sth: *Crusoe made a mark on a stick for each day that passed.* **3** a written or printed symbol that is a sign of sth: *a question, punctuation, exclamation, etc mark* **4** a sign of a quality or feeling: *They stood in silence for two minutes as a mark of respect.* **5** a number or letter you get for school work that tells you how good your work was: *She got very good marks in the exam.* ○ *The pass mark is 60 out of 100.* ○ *to get full marks* (= everything correct) **6** the level of sth: *The company's sales have now reached the million pound mark.*

(IDIOM) **on your marks, get set, go!** (used at the start of a sports race)

☆ **mark²** /mɑːk/ *verb* [T] **1** to put a sign on sth: *We marked the price on all items in the sale.* ○ *The route is marked with yellow arrows.* **2** to look at school, etc work that sb has done, show where there are mistakes and give it a number or letter to show how good it is: *Why did you mark that answer wrong?* ○ *He has 100 exam papers to mark before the weekend.* **3** to show where sth is or where sth happened: *Flowers mark the spot where he died.* **4** to celebrate sth: *The ceremony marked the fiftieth anniversary of the opening of the school.* **5** (in sport) to stay close to a player of the opposite team so that he/she cannot play easily

(PHRASAL VERB) **mark sth out** to draw lines to show the position of sth: *Spaces for each car were marked out in the car-park.*

marked /mɑːkt/ *adj* clear; noticeable: *There has been a marked increase in vandalism in recent years.*

marker *noun* [C] something that shows the position of sth: *A marker flag shows where the water is dangerous.*

marking *noun* [C, usually pl] patterns of colour on an animal or bird

mark³ /mɑːk/ *noun* [C] the unit of money in Germany

☆ **market¹** /'mɑːkɪt/ *noun* **1** [C] a place where people go to buy and sell things: *There is a market in the town every Wednesday.* ○ *an open-air/covered market* ○ *Wallingford is an old market town.* ○ *The farmers sell their sheep at the market in Hereford.* ☞ Look at **flea market, hypermarket** and **supermarket**. **2** [U,sing] the desire to buy a particular thing: *There's no market for very large cars when petrol is so expensive.* **3** [C] a country, area or group of people that may want to buy sth: *The company is hoping to expand into the European Market.* ○ *the overseas/overseas market* ☞ Look at **black market** and **stock market**.

(IDIOM) **on the market** for sale: *This is one of the best automatic cameras on the market.*

ˌmarket ˈgarden *noun* [C] a farm where vegetables and fruit are grown in large quantities

'market-place (*also* ˌmarket ˈsquare) *noun* [C] the place in a town where a market is or used to be held

s	z	ʃ	ʒ	h	m	n	ŋ	l	r	j	w
so	zoo	she	vision	how	man	no	sing	leg	red	yes	wet

market research noun [U] the study of what people want to buy and why

market² /ˈmɑːkɪt/ verb [T] to sell sth with the help of advertising

marketable adj able to be sold easily, because people want it

marketing noun [U] deciding how sth can be sold most easily, eg what price it should be or how it should be advertised: *Effective marketing will lead to increased sales.* ○ *the marketing department*

marksman /ˈmɑːksmən/ noun [C] (pl **marksmen** /-mən/) a person who can shoot very well with a gun

marmalade /ˈmɑːməleɪd/ noun [U] a type of jam that is made from oranges or lemons: *toast and marmalade for breakfast*

maroon /məˈruːn/ adj dark brownish-red in colour ☞ Look at **crimson** and **scarlet**.

marooned /məˈruːnd/ adj in a place that you cannot leave: *The sailors were marooned on a desert island.*

marquee /mɑːˈkiː/ noun [C] a very large tent that is used for parties, shows, etc

☆ **marriage** /ˈmærɪdʒ/ noun **1** [C,U] the state of being husband and wife: *They are getting divorced after five years of marriage.* ○ *a happy/an unhappy marriage* ○ *an arranged marriage* (= one where your partner is chosen for you by your parents) ○ *a mixed marriage* (= one between people of different races or religions) **2** [C] a wedding ceremony: *The marriage took place at a registry office in Birmingham.* ☞ Look at the note at **wedding**.

☆ **married** /ˈmærɪd/ adj **1 married (to sb)** having a husband or wife: *a married man/woman/couple* ○ *They've been married for nearly 50 years.* ○ *Shula's married to Mark.* ○ *They're getting married in June.* ☞ The opposite is **unmarried** or **single**. **2** (only before a noun) of marriage(1): *Married life seems to suit him.*

marrow¹ /ˈmærəʊ/ noun [U] = BONE MARROW

marrow² /ˈmærəʊ/ noun [C,U] a large vegetable with dark green skin that is white inside

☆ **marry** /ˈmæri/ verb (pres part **marrying**; 3rd pers sing pres **marries**; pt, pp **married**) **1** [I,T] to take sb as your husband or wife: *They married when they were very young.* ○ *When did Roger ask you to marry him?* ☞ **Get married** is more commonly used than **marry**: *When are Sue and Ian getting married?* ○ *They got married in 1982.* ○ *Many people live together without getting married.* ○ *Are you getting married in church or at the registry office?* **2** [T] to join two people together as husband and wife: *We asked the local vicar to marry us.* ☞ The noun is **marriage**.

Mars /mɑːz/ noun [sing] the planet that is fourth in order from the sun and second nearest to the earth ☞ Look at **Martian**.

marsh /mɑːʃ/ noun [C,U] an area of soft wet land —**marshy** adj

marshal /ˈmɑːʃl/ noun [C] **1** a person who helps to organize or control a large public event: *Marshals are directing traffic in the carpark.* **2** (US) an officer of high rank in the police or fire department or in a court of law

martial /ˈmɑːʃl/ adj (formal) connected with war

Martian /ˈmɑːʃn/ noun [C] (in stories) a creature that comes from the planet Mars

martyr /ˈmɑːtə(r)/ noun [C] **1** a person who is killed because of what he/she believes **2** a person who does not do or have what he/she wants in order to help other people or to be admired by them: *Don't be such a martyr! You don't have to do all the housework.* —**martyrdom** /ˈmɑːtədəm/ noun [U]

marvel /ˈmɑːvl/ noun [C] a person or thing that is wonderful or that makes you feel surprised: *the marvels of modern technology* ○ *It's a marvel that no one was killed in the accident.*

marvel verb [I] (**marvelling**; **marvelled**; US **marveling**; **marveled**) (formal) to be very surprised at how good, beautiful, etc sb/sth is: *We marvelled at how much they had been able to do in a short time.*

marvellous (US **marvelous**) /ˈmɑːvələs/ adj very good; wonderful: *Peter was marvellous while I was ill. He took care of everything.* ○ *It's marvellous to have such lovely weather.* —**marvellously** (US **marvelously**) adv

Marxism /ˈmɑːksɪzəm/ noun [U] the political and economic thought of Karl Marx, who said that important changes in history were caused by the struggle between social classes ☞ Look at **communism** and **socialism**.

Marxist /ˈmɑːksɪst/ noun [C] a person who believes in Marxism —**Marxist** adj: *Marxist ideology*

marzipan /ˈmɑːzɪpæn; ˌmɑːzɪˈpæn/ noun [U] a food that is made of sugar, egg and almonds. Marzipan is used to make sweets or to put on cakes.

mascara /mæˈskɑːrə; US -ˈskærə/ noun [U] a type of make-up that is used to make your eyelashes look darker and thicker

mascot /ˈmæskət; -skɒt/ noun [C] a person, animal or thing that is thought to bring good luck

masculine /ˈmæskjəlɪn/ adj with the qualities that people think are typical of men ☞ Look at **male** and **manly**, and at **feminine** and the note at **female**. In English grammar **masculine** words refer to male people or animals: *'He' is a masculine pronoun.* In some other languages all nouns are given a gender, either **masculine**, **feminine** or **neuter**. —**masculinity** /ˌmæskjʊˈlɪnəti/ noun [U]

mash /mæʃ/ verb [T] to mix or crush sth until is it soft: *mashed potatoes*

mask /mɑːsk; US mæsk/ noun [C] something that you wear that covers your face or part of your face. People wear masks in order to hide or protect their faces or to make themselves look different: *The bank robbers wore stocking masks.* ○ *The doctors and nurses had surgical masks on.* ○ *The children wore animal masks to the party.* ☞ Look at **gas mask** and **goggles**.

mask verb [T] **1** to cover or hide your face with a mask: *a masked gunman* **2** to hide your feelings: *He masked his anger with a smile.*

masochism /ˈmæsəkɪzəm/ noun [U] getting (sexual) pleasure from suffering or pain

iː	ɪ	e	æ	ɑː	ɒ	ɔː	ʊ	uː	ʌ
see	sit	ten	hat	arm	got	saw	put	too	cup

surgeon's mask

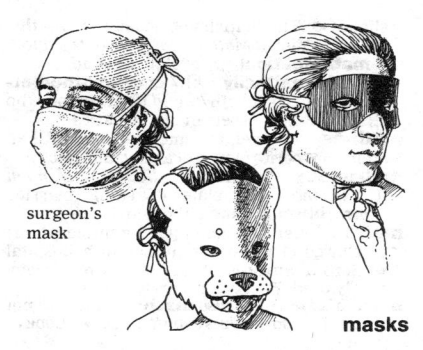

masks

☛ Look at **sadism**. —**masochist** /-kɪst/ *noun* [C] **masochistic** /ˌmæsəˈkɪstɪk/ *adj*

mason /ˈmeɪsn/ *noun* [C] **1** a person who makes things from stone **2** = FREEMASON

masonry /ˈmeɪsənri/ *noun* [U] the parts of a building that are made of stone: *The building is old and the masonry is crumbling.*

masquerade /ˌmɑːskəˈreɪd; *US* ˌmæsk-/ *verb* [I] to pretend to be sb/sth: *Two people, masquerading as doctors, knocked at the door and asked to see the child.*

Mass (*also* **mass**) /mæs/ *noun* [C,U] the ceremony in some Christian churches when people eat bread and drink wine in order to remember the last meal that Christ had before he died: *to go to Mass*

☆ **mass** /mæs/ *noun* **1** [C] a large amount or number of sth: *The garden was a mass of flowers.* ○ *a dense mass of smoke* ○ (*informal*) *There were masses of people at the market today.* **2** [U] (in physics) the amount of material that sth contains; weight **3 the masses** [plural] ordinary people when considered as a political group

mass *adj* (only *before* a noun) involving a large number of people: *a mass murderer* ○ *a mass meeting*

mass *verb* [I,T] to gather together in a mass: *The students massed in the square.*

mass 'media *noun* [plural] the means of communicating with large numbers of people, ie newspapers, television and radio

ˌmass-proˈduce *verb* [T] to make large numbers of similar things by machine in a factory ˌmass proˈduction *noun* [U]

massacre /ˈmæsəkə(r)/ *noun* [C] the killing of a large number of people or animals —**massacre** *verb* [T] ☛ Look at the note at **kill**.

massage /ˈmæsɑːʒ; *US* məˈsɑːʒ/ *noun* [C,U] rubbing or pressing sb's body in order to reduce pain or to help the person move more easily: *to give sb a massage* —**massage** *verb* [T]

massive /ˈmæsɪv/ *adj* very big: *a massive increase in prices*

mast /mɑːst; *US* mæst/ *noun* [C] **1** a tall wooden or metal pole for a flag, ship's sails, etc ☛ picture at **boat**. **2** a tall pole that is used for sending out radio or television broadcasts

master¹ /ˈmɑːstə(r); *US* ˈmæs-/ *noun* [C] **1** a man who has people or animals in his control: *The dog ran to his master.* ○ (*figurative*) *to be master of a difficult situation* ☛ Look at **mistress**. **2** a person who has great skill at doing sth: *a master builder* **3** a male teacher (usually in a private school): *the chemistry master* ☛ Look at **mistress** and **headmaster**. **4 Master** (sometimes used when speaking or writing to a boy who is too young to be called Mr): *Master James Wilson* **5** a film or tape from which copies can be made

Master's degree (*also* **Master's**) *noun* [C] a second or higher university degree. You usually get a Master's degree by studying for one or two years after your first degree: *Master of Arts (MA)* ○ *Master of Science (MSc)* ☛ Look at **Bachelor's degree**.

master² /ˈmɑːstə(r); *US* ˈmæs-/ *verb* [T] **1** to learn how to do sth well: *It takes a long time to master a foreign language.* **2** to control sth: *to master a situation*

mastermind /ˈmɑːstəmaɪnd; *US* ˈmæs-/ *noun* [C] a very clever person (who planned or organized sth) —**mastermind** *verb* [T]: *The police failed to catch the man who masterminded the whole operation.*

masterpiece /ˈmɑːstəpiːs; *US* ˈmæs-/ *noun* [C] a work of art, music, literature, etc that is of the highest quality: *Tolstoy's masterpiece, War and Peace*

mastery /ˈmɑːstəri/ *noun* [U] **1 mastery (of sth)** great skill at doing sth: *His mastery of the violin was quite exceptional for a child of his age.* **2 mastery (of/over sb/sth)** control over sb/sth: *The battle was fought for mastery of the seas.*

masturbate /ˈmæstəbeɪt/ *verb* [I] to make yourself feel sexually excited by handling and rubbing your sex organs —**masturbation** /ˌmæstəˈbeɪʃn/ *noun* [U]

mat¹ /mæt/ *noun* [C] **1** a piece of carpet or other thick material that you put on the floor: *a doormat* ○ *an exercise mat for gymnasts* ○ *a straw mat* ☛ Look at **rug**. **2** a small piece of material that you put under a hot dish, cup, glass, etc: *a table-mat* ○ *a beer mat*

mat² = MATT

☆ **match¹** /mætʃ/ *noun* [C] a short piece of wood with a tip that catches fire when it is rubbed against another surface: *to light/strike a match* ○ *a box of matches*

ˈ**matchbox** *noun* [C] a small box for matches
ˈ**matchstick** *noun* [C] the thin wooden part of a match

☆ **match²** /mætʃ/ *noun* **1** [C] an organized game or sports event: *a tennis, football, etc match* ○ *They beat us last time but we hope to win the return match.* ○ *Game, set and match to Becker!* **2** [sing] a person or thing that is as good as or better than sb/sth else: *Carol is no match for her mother when it comes to cooking* (= she doesn't cook as well as her mother). **3** [sing] **a match (for sb/sth)** something that looks good with sth else, eg because it has the same colour or pattern: *Those shoes aren't a very good match with your dress.* ○ (*figurative*) *Bill and Sue are a good match. They should be very happy together.*

ɜː	ə	eɪ	əʊ	aɪ	aʊ	ɔɪ	ɪə	eə	ʊə
fur	ago	pay	home	five	now	join	near	hair	pure

☆ **match³** /mætʃ/ *verb* **1** [I,T] to have the same colour or pattern as sth else, or to look nice with sth else: *That blouse doesn't match your skirt.* ○ *We've chosen the curtains but now we need a carpet to match.* **2** [T] to find sb/sth that is like or suitable for sb/sth else: *The agency tries to match single people with suitable partners.* **3** [T] to be as good as or better than sb/sth else: *The two teams are very evenly matched.* ○ *Taiwan produces the goods at a price that Europe cannot match.*
(PHRASAL VERBS) **match up** to be the same: *The statements of the two witnesses don't match up.*
match sth up (with sth) to fit or put sth together (with sth else): *What you have to do is match up each TV personality with his or her pet.*
match up to sb/sth to be as good as sb/sth: *The film didn't match up to my expectations* (= it wasn't as good as I thought it was going to be).

mate¹ /meɪt/ *noun* [C] **1** (*informal*) a friend or sb you live or work with: *He's an old mate of mine.* ○ *a flatmate* ○ *a classmate* **2** (*Brit slang*) (used when speaking to a man): *Hallo mate!* **3** one of a male and female pair of animals, birds, etc: *The female sits on the eggs while her mate hunts for food.* **4** an officer on a ship

mate² /meɪt/ *verb* **1** [I] (used about animals and birds) to have sex and produce young: *Pandas rarely mate in zoos.* **2** [T] to bring two animals together so that they can mate

mate³ /meɪt/ *noun* = CHECKMATE

☆ **material¹** /məˈtɪəriəl/ *noun* **1** [C,U] a substance that can be used for making or doing sth: *Many African countries export raw materials and import manufactured goods.* ○ *writing materials* (= pens, paper, ink) ○ *This new material is strong but it is also very light.* **2** [C,U] cloth (for making clothes, etc): *Is there enough material for a dress?* **3** [U] facts or information that you collect before you write a book, article, etc

material² /məˈtɪəriəl/ *adj* **1** connected with real or physical things rather than the spirit or emotions: *We should not value material comforts too highly.* ☛ Look at **spiritual**. **2** important: *material evidence* ☛ This word is not common but look at **immaterial**.

materialism /məˈtɪəriəlɪzəm/ *noun* [U] the belief that money and possessions are the most important things in life —**materialist** /məˈtɪəriəlɪst/ *noun* [C] —**materialistic** /məˌtɪəriəˈlɪstɪk/ *adj*

materialize (*also* **materialise**) /məˈtɪəriəlaɪz/ *verb* [I] to become real; to happen: *The pay rise that they had promised never materialized.*

maternal /məˈtɜːnl/ *adj* **1** of or like a mother: *maternal love* **2** related through your mother's side of the family: *your maternal grandfather* ☛ Look at **paternal**.

maternity /məˈtɜːnəti/ *adj* connected with women who are going to have or have just had a baby: *maternity clothes* ○ *the hospital's maternity ward*

☆ **mathematics** /ˌmæθəˈmætɪks/ *noun* [U] the science or study of numbers, quantities or shapes ☛ The British abbreviation is **maths**, the US is **math**: *Maths is my favourite subject.* —**mathematical** /ˌmæθəˈmætɪkl/ *adj* —**mathematically** /-klɪ/ *adv* —**mathematician** /ˌmæθəməˈtɪʃn/ *noun* [C] a person who studies or is an expert in mathematics

matinée /ˈmætɪneɪ; *US* ˌmætnˈeɪ/ *noun* [C] an afternoon performance of a play, film, etc

matrimony /ˈmætrɪməni; *US* -məʊni/ *noun* [U] (*formal*) the state of being married —**matrimonial** /ˌmætrɪˈməʊniəl/ *adj*

matron /ˈmeɪtrən/ *noun* [C] **1** a nurse who is in charge of the other nurses in a hospital ☛ **Senior nursing officer** is now more commonly used. **2** an older married woman

matt (*also* **mat**; *US also* **matte**) /mæt/ *adj* not shiny: *This paint gives a matt finish.* ☛ Look at **glossy**.

☆ **matter¹** /ˈmætə(r)/ *noun* **1** [C] a subject or situation that you must think about and give your attention to: *It's a personal matter and I don't want to discuss it with you.* ○ *They should try to settle matters between themselves before going to court.* ○ *to simplify/complicate matters* **2** [U] all physical substances; a substance of a particular kind: *waste matter* ○ *reading matter*
(IDIOMS) **as a matter of fact** to tell the truth; in reality: *I like him very much, as a matter of fact.*

for that matter in addition; as well: *Mick is really fed up with his course. I am too, for that matter.*

make matters/things worse ⇒ WORSE

(be) the matter (with sb/sth) to be the reason for unhappiness, pain, problems, etc: *She looks sad. What's the matter with her?* ○ *There seems to be something the matter with the car.* ○ *Eat that food! There's nothing the matter with it.*

a matter of course something that you do regularly; the usual practice: *Goods leaving the factory are checked as a matter of course.*

a matter of opinion a subject on which people do not agree: *'I think the government is doing a good job.' 'That's a matter of opinion.'*

a matter of sth/doing sth something that needs or requires sth: *Learning a language is largely a matter of practice.*

no matter who, what, where, etc whoever, whatever, wherever, etc: *They never listen no matter what you say.*

☆ **matter²** /ˈmætə(r)/ *verb* [I] to be important: *It doesn't really matter how much it costs.* ○ *Does it matter if we are a little bit late?* ○ *What matters most is giving the children a good start in life.* ○ *Some things matter more than others.*
☛ **Matter** is often used in negative sentences, questions and sentences containing *what, who, when, if,* etc. It is not used in the *-ing* forms.

mattress /ˈmætrɪs/ *noun* [C] a large soft thing that you lie on to sleep, usually put on a bed: *Don't worry about us – we can sleep on a mattress on the floor.* ☛ picture at **bed**.

mature¹ /məˈtjʊə(r); *US* -ˈtʊər/ *adj* **1** fully grown or fully developed: *a mature tree, bird, animal, etc* ☛ Look at **immature**. **2** behaving in a sensible adult way: *Is she mature enough*

for such responsibility? ☞ Look at **immature**.
—**maturity** /məˈtjʊərəti; US -ˈtʊə-/ *noun* [U]

mature² /məˈtjʊə(r); US -ˈtʊər/ *verb* [I] to become mature: *He matured a lot during his two years at college.*

maul /mɔːl/ *verb* [T] (usually used about a wild animal) to attack and injure sb

mauve /məʊv/ *adj, noun* [U] reddish purple

maxim /ˈmæksɪm/ *noun* [C] a few words that express a rule for good or sensible behaviour: *Their maxim is: 'If a job's worth doing, it's worth doing well.'*

maximize (*also* **maximise**) /ˈmæksɪmaɪz/ *verb* [T] to increase sth as much as possible: *to maximize profits* ☞ Look at **minimize**.

☆ **maximum** /ˈmæksɪməm/ *noun* [sing] (*abbr* **max**) the greatest amount or level of sth that is possible, allowed, recorded, etc: *The bus can carry a maximum of 40 people.* ○ *£500 is the maximum we can afford.* ○ *to set the dial to maximum* ☞ The opposite is **minimum**.
—**maximum** *adj* (only *before* a noun): *a maximum speed of 120 miles per hour* ○ *a maximum security prison*

☆ **May** /meɪ/ *noun* [C,U] the fifth month of the year, coming before June ☞ For examples of the use of the months in sentences, look at **January**.

'May Day *noun* [C] 1st May

☞ **May Day** is traditionally celebrated as a spring festival and in some countries it is also a day for socialist groups to hold meetings and demonstrations.

☆ **may** /meɪ/ *modal verb* (*negative* **may not**) **1** (used for saying that sth is possible): *'Where's Sue?' 'She may be in the garden.'* ○ *You may be right.* ○ *I may be going to China next year.* ○ *They may have forgotten the meeting.* ○ *He may have been driving too fast.* **2** (used as a polite way of asking for and giving permission): *May I use your phone?* ○ *You may only borrow books for two weeks.* **3** (used in the negative as a way of forbidding sb to do sth): *You may not take photographs in the museum.* **4** (used for contrasting two facts): *He may be very clever but he can't do anything practical.* **5** (*formal*) (used for expressing wishes and hopes): *May God be with you.*
(IDIOM) **may/might as well (do sth)** ⇒ WELL³

☆ **maybe** /ˈmeɪbi/ *adv* perhaps; possibly: *'Are you going to come?' 'Maybe.'* ○ *There were three, maybe four armed men.* ○ *Maybe I'll accept the invitation and maybe I won't.* ○ *Maybe we ought to try again.* ☞ Look at the note at **perhaps**.

mayn't /ˈmeɪənt/ *short for* MAY NOT

mayonnaise /ˌmeɪəˈneɪz; US ˈmeɪəneɪz/ *noun* [U] a thick yellow sauce made with eggs and oil and often eaten with salad

mayor /meə(r); US ˈmeɪər/ *noun* [C] a person who is elected to be the leader of the group of people (**a council**) who manage the affairs of a town or city

mayoress /meəˈres; US ˈmeɪərəs/ *noun* [C] **1** a mayor who is a woman **2** the wife of a mayor or a woman who helps the mayor with his official duties

maze /meɪz/ *noun* [C] a system of paths which is meant to confuse you so that it is difficult to find your way in or out: *We got lost in Hampton Court maze.* ○ (*figurative*) *a maze of winding streets*

☆ **me** /miː/ *pron* (used as an object or after the verb *be*) the person who is speaking or writing: *He telephoned me yesterday.* ○ *She wrote to me last week.* ○ *Could you pass me the salt?* ○ *'Somebody's spilt the wine.' 'I'm afraid it was me.'* ○ *'Who's this photograph of?' 'Me.'* ☞ **It is/was me** is much more common than **it is/was I**, although this can be used in formal speech or writing.

meadow /ˈmedəʊ/ *noun* [C] a field of grass

meagre (*US* **meager**) /ˈmiːgə(r)/ *adj* too small in amount: *a meagre salary* ○ *The food was good but the portions were meagre.*

☆ **meal** /miːl/ *noun* [C] a certain time when you eat or the food that is eaten at that time: *We're going out for a meal on Friday.* ○ *The pub round the corner serves hot and cold meals.* ○ *Do you have your main meal at lunchtime or in the evening?* ○ *a heavy/light meal*

☞ The main meals of the day are **breakfast, lunch** and **dinner**. **Tea** and **supper** are usually smaller meals (but look at the note at **dinner**). A very small meal is called a **snack**.

'mealtime *noun* [C] a time at which a meal is usually eaten

☆ **mean¹** /miːn/ *verb* [T] (*pt, pp* **meant** /ment/) **1** (not in the *-ing* forms) to express, show or have as a meaning: *What does this word mean?* ○ *The bell means that the lesson has ended.* ○ *'What does that symbol mean?' 'Environment-friendly.'* ○ *Does the name 'Charles Bell' mean anything to you?* **2** to want or intend to say sth; to refer to sb/sth: *I don't understand what you mean.* ○ *Well, she said 'yes' but I think she really meant 'no'.* ○ *What do you mean by 'a lot of money'?* ○ *I only meant that I couldn't come tomorrow – any other day would be fine.* ☞ Note that **mean** cannot be used with the meaning 'to have the opinion that'. We say: *I think that...* or *In my opinion...*: *I think that she'd be silly to buy that car.* **I mean** is often used in conversation when you want to explain something you have just said or to add more information: *What a terrible summer – I mean it's rained almost all the time.* ○ *I think the film will have started – I mean it's past 8 o'clock.* **I mean** is also used to correct something you have just said: *We went there on Tuesday, I mean Thursday.* **3** (not in the *-ing* forms) to be important to sb: *This job means a lot to me.* **4** (not in the *-ing* forms) to make sth likely; to cause: *The shortage of teachers means that classes are larger.* ○ *His new job means him travelling abroad.* **5** (not in the *-ing* forms) to be serious or sincere about sth: *He said he loved me but I don't think he meant it!* ○ *I'm never coming back – I mean it!* **6** to want or plan to do sth; to intend sth: *I'm sure she didn't mean to upset you.* ○ *She meant the card for both of us.* ○ *I didn't mean you to cook the whole meal!* **7** (usually passive) to intend or expect sb/sth to be or do sth: *It was only meant as a joke.* ○ *What's this picture meant to be?* ○ *You're meant*

s	z	ʃ	ʒ	h	m	n	ŋ	l	r	j	w
so	zoo	she	vision	how	man	no	sing	leg	red	yes	wet

to get to work at 9 o'clock. ○ *That restaurant is meant to be excellent* (= people say that it is).
(IDIOM) **mean well** to want to be kind and helpful but usually without success: *My mother means well but I wish she'd stop treating me like a child.*

☆**mean²** /miːn/ *adj* **1 mean (with sth)** not willing to give or use sth (especially money); not generous: *It's no good asking him for any money – he's much too mean.* ○ *Don't be mean with the cream.* **2 mean (to sb)** (used about people or their behaviour) unkind: *It was mean of him not to invite you too.* —**meanness** *noun* [U]

mean³ /miːn/ *adj* (only *before* a noun) average: *What is the mean annual temperature in California?*

meander /mɪˈændə(r)/ *verb* [I] **1** (used about a river, road, etc) to have a lot of curves and bends **2** (used about a person or animal) to walk or travel slowly or without any definite direction

☆**meaning** /ˈmiːnɪŋ/ *noun* **1** [C,U] what sth means or expresses; its sense or intention: *This word has two different meanings in English.* ○ *What do you think is the meaning of the last line of the poem?* **2** [U] purpose or importance: *With his child dead there seemed to be no meaning in life.*

meaningful /-fl/ *adj* **1** useful, important or interesting: *Most people need a meaningful relationship with another person.* **2** (used about a look, expression, etc) trying to express a certain feeling or idea: *They kept giving each other meaningful glances across the table.* —**meaningfully** /-fəli/ *adv*

meaningless *adj* without meaning, reason or sense: *The figures are meaningless if we have nothing to compare them with.*

☆**means¹** /miːnz/ *noun* [C] (*pl* **means**) a method of doing sth: *Have you any means of transport?* (= a car, bicycle, etc) ○ *Is there any means of contacting your husband?*
(IDIOMS) **a means to an end** a way of achieving sth where the thing or method you use is not as important as the result
by means of by using: *We got out of the hotel by means of the fire-escape.*
by no means; not by any means (used for emphasis) not at all: *I'm by no means sure that this is the right thing to do.*

means² /miːnz/ *noun* [plural] (*formal*) money or wealth

meant *pt, pp* of MEAN¹

meantime /ˈmiːntaɪm/ *noun*
(IDIOM) **in the meantime** in the time between two things happening: *The builders haven't finished so in the meantime we're living with my mother.*

☆**meanwhile** /ˈmiːnwaɪl/, *US* -hwaɪl/ *adv* during the same time or during the time between two things happening: *Peter was at home studying. Tony, meanwhile, was out with his friends.* ○ *The new computer will arrive next week. Meanwhile you'll have to manage without.*

measles /ˈmiːzlz/ *noun* [U] a common infectious disease, especially among children. You have a temperature and your skin is covered in small red spots ☛ **Measles** looks like a plural noun but it is used with a singular verb: *In many countries measles is a very dangerous disease.*

measly /ˈmiːzli/ *adj* (*informal*) much too small in size, amount or value: *a measly helping of ice-cream*

☆**measure¹** /ˈmeʒə(r)/ *verb* **1** [I,T] to find the size, weight, etc of sb/sth often by using an instrument such as a ruler: *to measure the height, width, length, depth, etc of sth* ○ *Could you measure the table to see if it will fit into our room?* ○ *Height is measured in metres and centimetres.* ○ *Britain now uses the metric system for measuring.* **2** [I] to be a certain height, width, length, etc: *The room measures five metres across.* ○ *The pool measures 25 metres by 5 metres.* **3** [T] to show or judge the size, amount, etc of sth: *A speedometer measures speed.* ○ (*figurative*) *How do you measure a person's success?*
(PHRASAL VERB) **measure up (to sth)** to be as good as you need to be or as sb expects you to be: *Did the holiday measure up to your expectations?*

measurement *noun* **1** [C] a size, amount, etc that is found by measuring: *What are the exact measurements of the room?* (= how wide, long, etc is it?) ○ *What's your waist measurement?* ○ *Let's start by taking your measurements* (= measuring the size of your chest, waist and other parts of the body). **2** [U] the act of measuring: *I'm not sure how accurate his measurement of the area was.*

'measuring-tape *noun* [C] = TAPE MEASURE

☆**measure²** /ˈmeʒə(r)/ *noun* **1** [sing] (*formal*) a certain amount or quantity; some but not much: *The play achieved a measure of success.* **2** [sing] a way of understanding or judging sth: *The school's popularity is a measure of the teachers' success.* **3** [C, usually pl] an action that is done for a special reason: *The government is taking new measures to reduce inflation.* ○ *As a temporary measure, the road will have to be closed.* ○ *emergency measures* ○ *New safety measures are to be introduced after a child was killed.* **4** [C] a way of describing the size, amount, etc of sth: *A metre is a measure of length.*

☆**meat** /miːt/ *noun* [U] the flesh of animals or birds that people eat: *She doesn't eat meat – she's a vegetarian.*

☛ Some types of meat have different names from the animals they come from. We get **pork**, **ham** or **bacon** from a pig, **beef** from a cow and **veal** from a calf. **Mutton** comes from a sheep but we get **lamb** from a lamb. For birds and fish there is not a different word. We often call beef, mutton and lamb **red meat**. The meat from birds is called **white meat**. We can **fry**, **grill**, **roast** or **stew** meat. We **carve** a **joint** of meat. Meat can be described as **tough** or **tender**, **lean** or **fatty**. Uncooked meat is **raw**.

Mecca /ˈmekə/ *noun* **1** the city in Saudi Arabia where Muhammad was born, which is the centre of Islam **2** [C, usually sing] **mecca** a place that many people wish to visit because of a particular interest: *Italy is a mecca for art-lovers.*

mechanic /mɪˈkænɪk/ *noun* [C] a person whose job is to repair and work with machines and tools: *a car mechanic*

☆ **mechanical** /mɪˈkænɪkl/ *adj* **1** connected with, worked by or produced by machines: *a mechanical pump* o *mechanical engineering* o *a mechanical mind* (= a mind that understands machines) **2** (used about a person's behaviour) done like a machine as if you are not thinking about what you are doing: *He played the piano in a dull and mechanical way.* —**mechanically** /-klɪ/ *adv*

mechanics /mɪˈkænɪks/ *noun* **1 the mechanics** [plural] the way in which sth works or is done: *Don't ask me – I don't understand the mechanics of the legal system.* **2** [U] the science of how machines work

mechanism /ˈmekənɪzəm/ *noun* [C] **1** a part of a piece of equipment or a machine that does a certain task: *Our car has an automatic locking mechanism.* **2** the way in which sth works or the process by which sth is done: *the mechanism of the heart* o *I'm afraid there is no mechanism for dealing with your complaint.*

mechanize (*also* **mechanise**) /ˈmekənaɪz/ *verb* [I,T] to use machines instead of people to do work: *We have mechanized the entire production process.* —**mechanization** (*also* **mechanisation**) /ˌmekənaɪˈzeɪʃn; *US* -nɪˈz-/ *noun* [U]: *Increased mechanization has led to unemployment.*

Med (*informal*) = MEDITERRANEAN

medal /ˈmedl/ *noun* [C] a flat piece of metal, usually with a design and words on it, which is given to sb for bravery or as a prize in a sporting event: *He was awarded a medal for bravery.* o *to win a gold/silver/bronze medal in the Olympics*

medallist (*US* **medalist**) /ˈmedəlɪst/ *noun* [C] a person who has won a medal, especially in sport: *an Olympic gold medallist*

medallion /mɪˈdælɪən/ *noun* [C] a small round piece of metal on a chain which is worn as jewellery around the neck

meddle /ˈmedl/ *verb* [I] **meddle (in/with sth)** to take too much interest (in sb's private affairs) or to handle sth that you should not: *She criticized her mother for meddling in her private life.* o *Somebody's been meddling with the papers on my desk.*

☆ **media** /ˈmiːdɪə/ *noun* [plural] **the media** television, radio and newspapers used as a means of communication: *The reports in the media have been greatly exaggerated.* ☛ Sometimes **media** is used with a singular verb, although it is a plural noun: *The media always take/takes a great interest in the Royal family.* Look at **mass media** and **the press**.

mediaeval = MEDIEVAL

mediate /ˈmiːdɪeɪt/ *verb* [I,T] to try to settle a disagreement between two or more people or groups: *As a supervisor she had to mediate between her colleagues and the management.* —**mediation** /ˌmiːdɪˈeɪʃn/ *noun* [U] —**mediator** *noun* [C]

☆ **medical** /ˈmedɪkl/ *adj* connected with medicine and the treatment or prevention of illness: *a medical school/student* o *Have you had any medical treatment during the last three years?* o *Some people take out an insurance that pays for private medical care.* o *medical research*

medical *noun* [C] an examination of your body by a doctor to check your state of health: *to have a medical*

medicated /ˈmedɪkeɪtɪd/ *adj* containing a substance like a medicine: *medicated shampoo*

medication /ˌmedɪˈkeɪʃn/ *noun* [C,U] (*especially US*) medicine that a doctor has given you: *I shall prescribe some medication for your heart problem.*

☆ **medicine** /ˈmedsn; *US* ˈmedɪsn/ *noun* **1** [U] the science of preventing and treating illness: *to study/practise medicine* **2** [C,U] pills, liquids, etc that you take in order to treat an illness: *Medicines should be kept out of the reach of children.* o *to take medicine* o *Did the doctor prescribe any medicine?* o *cough medicine*

medieval (*also* **mediaeval**) /ˌmedɪˈiːvl; *US* ˌmiːd- *also* mɪˈdiːvl/ *adj* of the Middle Ages in European history; ie between about 1100 and 1500 AD: *medieval art*

mediocre /ˌmiːdɪˈəʊkə(r); ˌmed-/ *adj* of not very high quality: *a mediocre performance* —**mediocrity** /ˌmiːdɪˈɒkrəti; ˌmed-/ *noun* [U]

meditate /ˈmedɪteɪt/ *verb* **1** [I,T] to think carefully and deeply (about sth): *I've been meditating on what you said last week.* **2** [I] to spend time thinking deeply in a special way so that you become calm and peaceful, often as part of religious training. —**meditation** /ˌmedɪˈteɪʃn/ *noun* [U]: *Meditation is practised by certain Eastern religions.*

the Mediterranean /ˌmedɪtəˈreɪnɪən/ (*also informal* **the Med**) *noun* [sing] the Mediterranean Sea or the countries around it —**Mediterranean** *adj*: *Mediterranean cookery*

☆ **medium¹** /ˈmiːdɪəm/ *noun* [C] **1** (*pl* usually **media**) a means you can use to express or communicate sth: *Many actors feel that the theatre is a more rewarding medium than the cinema.* o *He tried to keep the story out of the media* (= television, radio and newspapers). ☛ Look at **media** and **mass media**. **2** (*pl* **mediums**) a person who says that he/she can speak to and take messages from the spirits of dead people

☆ **medium²** /ˈmiːdɪəm/ *adj* of a size or amount that is neither very large nor very small; average: *She was of medium height and weight.* o *Would you like the small, medium or large packet?* o *a medium-sized dog*

ˈmedium wave *noun* [U] the system of broadcasting radio using sound waves between 100 and 1000 metres ☛ Look at **long wave** and **short wave**.

meek /miːk/ *adj* (used about people) quiet, and doing what other people say without asking questions or arguing: *She seems very meek but she can get very angry.* —**meekly** *adv* —**meekness** *noun* [U]

☆ **meet** /miːt/ *verb* (*pt, pp* **met** /met/) **1** [I,T] to come together by chance or because you have arranged it: *We happened to meet in the middle of Oxford Street!* o *Where did you first meet your*

ɜː	ə	eɪ	əʊ	aɪ	aʊ	ɔɪ	ɪə	eə	ʊə
fur	ago	pay	home	five	now	join	near	hair	pure

husband? ○ *What time shall we meet for lunch?* **2** [I] to be introduced to sb for the first time: *Have you two met before?* **3** [T] to go to a place and wait for sb/sth to arrive: *I'll come and meet you at the station.* ○ *A coach will meet your plane and take you to your destination.* **4** [I] (used about a group of people) to come together for a special purpose: *Representatives from both countries will meet for talks in London.* ○ *How often does the parish council meet?* **5** [T] to be enough for sth; to be able to deal with sth: *The money that I earn is enough to meet our basic needs.* ○ *I'm afraid this piece of work doesn't meet the requirements* (= it's not good enough). ○ *This year is going to be difficult but I'm sure that we can meet the challenge.* **6** [I,T] to touch, join or make contact with: *The rivers meet in Oxford.* ○ *Can you see where the road meets the motorway on the map?* ○ *His eyes met hers.*
(IDIOMS) **make ends meet** ⇨ END¹
there is more to sb/sth than meets the eye sb/sth is more interesting or complex than you might think at first: *Do you think there's more to their relationship than meets the eye?*
(PHRASAL VERBS) **meet up (with sb)** to meet sb, especially after first going in different directions or doing different things: *Let's both do our own shopping and meet up with each other for coffee.*
meet with sb (*US*) to meet sb, especially for discussion: *The President met with his advisers early this morning.*
meet with sth to get a certain answer, reaction or result: *I'm afraid the play did not meet with success.*

☆ **meeting** /'miːtɪŋ/ *noun* **1** [C] an organized occasion when a number of people come together in order to discuss or decide sth: *The next committee meeting will be held on 19 August.* ○ *What's on the agenda for the staff meeting?* ○ *to attend a meeting* ○ *a public meeting in the town hall*

☛ We **call**, **arrange** or **organize** a meeting. We can also **cancel** or **postpone** a meeting.

2 [sing] the people at a meeting: *The meeting was in favour of the new proposals.* **3** [C] the coming together of two or more people: *Christmas is a time of family meetings and reunions.* ○ *Can you remember your first meeting with your future husband?*

megaphone /'megəfəʊn/ *noun* [C] a piece of equipment that you speak through to make your voice sound louder, especially outside

melancholy /'melənkɒli/ *noun* [U] (*formal*) a feeling of sadness which lasts for a long time —**melancholy** *adj*

mellow /'meləʊ/ *adj* **1** (used about colours or sounds) soft, warm and pleasant **2** (used about people) wise, mature or relaxed because of age or experience —**mellow** *verb* [I,T]: *The colour of natural stone mellows with age.* ○ *Experience had mellowed her views about many things.*

melodrama /'melədrɑːmə/ *noun* [C,U] a type of play or novel in which a lot of exciting things happen and in which people's emotions are stronger than in real life

melodramatic /ˌmelədrə'mætɪk/ *adj* (used about a person's behaviour) making things seem more exciting and serious than they really are

melody /'melədi/ *noun* [C] (*pl* **melodies**) **1** a song or tune: *to play a melody* **2** the main tune in a piece of music that is in several parts: *The tenors have the melody here.*

melon /'melən/ *noun* [C,U] a large round fruit with a thick yellow or green skin and many seeds: *Would you like melon to start, or soup?*

☆ **melt** /melt/ *verb* **1** [I,T] to change from solid to liquid by means of heat: *When we got up in the morning the snow had melted.* ○ *First melt the butter in a saucepan.* **2** [I] (used about sb's feelings, etc) to become softer or less strong: *My heart melted when I saw the tiny puppy.*
(PHRASAL VERBS) **melt away** to disappear: *The crowd slowly melted away when the speaker had finished.*
melt sth down to heat a metal or glass object until it becomes soft

'melting-pot *noun* [C] a place where large numbers of people from different countries live together: *New York is a melting-pot of different nationalities.*

☆ **member** /'membə(r)/ *noun* [C] a person, animal or thing that belongs to a group, club, organization, etc: *All the members of the family were there.* ○ *If you would like to become a member of the club, please let us have your subscription as soon as possible.* ○ *a member of staff*

membership *noun* **1** [U] the state of being a member of a group, organization, etc: *To apply for membership, please fill in the enclosed form.* ○ *Annual membership costs £200.* **2** [C,U] the people who belong to a group, organization, etc: *Membership has fallen in the past year* (= the number of members). ☛ In the singular **membership** can be used with either a singular or a plural verb.

Member of 'Parliament (*also* **Member**) *noun* [C] (*abbr* **MP**) a person who has been elected to represent people in Parliament

membrane /'membreɪn/ *noun* [C] (*formal*) a thin skin which covers or connects parts of a person's or animal's body

memento /mɪ'mentəʊ/ *noun* [C] (*pl* **mementos** or **mementoes**) something that you keep to remind you of a person, a place or of sth that has happened

memo /'meməʊ/ *noun* [C] (*pl* **memos**) (*also formal* **memorandum**) a note sent from one person or office to another within an organization

memoirs /'memwɑːz/ *noun* [plural] a person's written account of his/her own life and experiences

memorable /'memərəbl/ *adj* worth remembering or easy to remember because it is special in some way: *The concert was a memorable experience.* —**memorably** *adv*

memorandum /ˌmemə'rændəm/ *noun* [C] (*pl* **memoranda** /-də/ or **memorandas**) (*formal*) = MEMO

memorial /mə'mɔːriəl/ *noun* [C] **memorial (to sb/sth)** something that is built or done to remind people of an event or a person: *a war* *memorial* (= a statue or cross) o *a memorial service*

memorize (*also* **memorise**) /'meməraɪz/ *verb* [T] to learn sth so that you can remember it exactly: *Actors have to memorize their lines.*

☆ **memory** /'meməri/ *noun* (*pl* **memories**) **1** [C] a person's ability to remember things: *a good/bad memory* o *A teacher needs to have a good memory for names.* **2** [C,U] the part of your mind in which you store things that you remember: *That day remained firmly in my memory for the rest of my life.* o *The appointment completely slipped my memory* (= I forgot it). o *He played the music from memory* (= without looking at notes or music). **3** [C] something that you remember: *That is one of my happiest memories.* o *I have no memories of that time at all.* o *childhood memories* **4** [C,U] the part of a computer where information is stored: *This computer has a 640k memory/640k of memory.*

(IDIOMS) **in memory of sb/to the memory of sb** in order to remind people of sb who has died: *A service was held in memory of the dead.*
refresh your/sb's memory ⇨ REFRESH

men *pl* of MAN

menace /'menəs/ *noun* **1** [C] a danger or threat: *The road is a menace to everyone's safety.* **2** [U] a quality, feeling, etc that is threatening or frightening: *He spoke with menace in his voice.*
menace *verb* [T] to be likely to hurt sb/sth; to threaten
menacing *adj* threatening or frightening

☆ **mend** /mend/ *verb* [T] to put sth that is broken or torn into a good condition again; to repair sth: *Can you mend the hole in this jumper for me?* o *This window needs mending – it won't shut properly.*
mend *noun*
(IDIOM) **be on the mend** (*informal*) to be getting better after an illness or injury; to be recovering: *She's been in bed for a week but she's on the mend now.*

menial /'mi:niəl/ *adj* (used about work) not skilled or important: *a menial job*

meningitis /,menɪn'dʒaɪtɪs/ *noun* [U] a serious illness which affects the brain and the spine

menopause /'menəpɔːz/ *noun* [sing] **the menopause** the time when a woman stops losing blood once a month (**menstruating**). This usually happens around the age of 50.

menstruate /'menstrueɪt/ *verb* [I] (*formal*) to lose blood from the uterus about once a month
☛ A less formal way of saying this is **to have periods**.
menstruation /,menstru'eɪʃn/ *noun* [U] the process or time of menstruating

☆ **mental** /'mentl/ *adj* (only *before* a noun) **1** of or in the mind: *It's fascinating to watch a child's mental development.* o *I've got a mental picture of the man but I can't remember his name.* **2** connected with illness of the mind: *a mental hospital* —**mentally** /'mentəli/ *adv*: *a home for mentally ill people*

mentality /men'tælətɪ/ *noun* [C] (*pl* **mentalities**) a type of mind or way of thinking: *I just can't understand his mentality!* o *the criminal mentality*

☆ **mention** /'menʃn/ *verb* [T] to say or write sth about sb/sth; to talk about sb/sth: *I wouldn't mention her exams to her – she's feeling nervous.* o *He mentioned (to me) that he might be late.* o *Did she mention what time the film starts?* o *Whenever I mention going out together she makes an excuse.* o *She mentioned Milton Keynes as a good place for shopping.*
(IDIOMS) **don't mention it** (used as a polite reply when sb thanks you for sth) I'm pleased to help; not at all: *'Thank you for all your help.' 'Don't mention it.'*
not to mention (used for emphasis) and also; as well as: *She's a housewife and a doctor, not to mention being a Conservative MP.*
mention *noun* [C,U] a brief remark about sb/sth: *It was odd that there wasn't even a mention of the riots in the newspaper.* o *I've heard no mention of a salary rise this year.*

☆ **menu** /'menju:/ *noun* [C] **1** a list of the food that you can choose at a restaurant: *Could we have/see the menu, please?* o *I hope there's some soup on the menu.* o *The menu here is always excellent* (= there's always a good choice of food). **2** a list of choices in a computer program which is shown on the screen

mercenary /'mɜːsɪnərɪ; *US* -nerɪ/ *adj* interested only in making money: *His motives are entirely mercenary.*
mercenary *noun* [C] (*pl* **mercenaries**) a person who fights for any group or country that will pay him/her

merchandise /'mɜːtʃəndaɪz/ *noun* [U] goods that are for sale

merchant /'mɜːtʃənt/ *noun* [C] a person whose job is to buy and sell goods, usually of one particular type, in large amounts: *a wine merchant*
,merchant 'navy *noun* [C, with sing or pl verb] all the ships and seamen of a country that are involved in carrying goods for trade

Mercury /'mɜːkjʊrɪ/ *noun* [sing] the planet that is nearest to the sun

mercury /'mɜːkjʊrɪ/ *noun* [U] (*symbol* **Hg**) a heavy silver-coloured metal that is usually in liquid form. Mercury is used in thermometers.

☆ **mercy** /'mɜːsɪ/ *noun* [U] kindness or forgiveness (that is shown to sb who has done sth wrong): *The prisoners begged for mercy from the king.* o *The rebels were shown no mercy. They were taken out and shot.*
(IDIOM) **at the mercy of sb/sth** having no power against sb/sth strong: *The climbers spent the night on the mountain at the mercy of the wind and rain.*
merciful /-fl/ *adj* feeling or showing mercy: *His death was a merciful release from pain.*
mercifully /-fəlɪ/ *adv* **1** in a merciful way **2** (*informal*) luckily: *It was bitterly cold but mercifully it was not raining.*
merciless *adj* showing no mercy —**mercilessly** *adv*

☆ **mere** /mɪə(r)/ *adj* (only *before* a noun) (used for emphasizing how small or unimportant sth is) nothing more than: *A mere ten per cent of young people in Britain go to university.*
(IDIOM) **the merest** even a small amount of

s	z	ʃ	ʒ	h	m	n	ŋ	l	r	j	w
so	zoo	she	vision	how	man	no	sing	leg	red	yes	wet

sth: *The merest smell of the fish market made her feel ill.*
merely *adv* only; just: *I don't want to place an order. I am merely making an enquiry.*
merge /mɜːdʒ/ *verb* **1** [I] **merge (with/into sth)**; **merge (together)** to become part of sth else: *Three small companies merged into one large one.* ○ *This stream merges with the Thames a few miles downstream.* ○ *Those colours seem to merge into each other.* **2** [T] to join things together so that they become one: *We have merged the two classes into one.*
merger /'mɜːdʒə(r)/ *noun* [C,U] the act of joining two or more companies together
meridian /məˈrɪdɪən/ *noun* [C] an imaginary line on the surface of the earth from the North Pole to the South Pole that passes through a particular place: *the Greenwich meridian* ☞ Look at **longitude**.
meringue /məˈræŋ/ *noun* **1** [U] a mixture of sugar and egg whites that is beaten together and cooked in the oven **2** [C] a small cake that is made of meringue
merit /'merɪt/ *noun* **1** [U] something that has merit is of high quality: *There is a lot of merit in her ideas.* ○ *a certificate of merit* ○ *a novel of great artistic merit* **2** [C, usually pl] an advantage or a good quality of sb/sth: *What are the merits of this new scheme?* ○ *Each case must be judged separately on its own merits* (= not according to general principles).
merit *verb* [T] (*formal*) to be good enough for sth; to deserve: *This suggestion merits further discussion.*
mermaid /'mɜːmeɪd/ *noun* [C] (in stories) a woman who has the tail of a fish instead of legs and who lives in the sea
merry /'meri/ *adj* (**merrier**; **merriest**) **1** happy and cheerful: *merry laughter* ○ *Merry Christmas!* **2** (*informal*) rather drunk —**merrily** /'merəli/ *adv*
merriment /'merɪmənt/ *noun* [U] (*formal*) laughter and enjoyment
'merry-go-round *noun* [C] = ROUNDABOUT²(2)
mesh /meʃ/ *noun* [C,U] material that is like a net (= made of plastic, wire or rope threads with holes in between): *a fence made of wire mesh*
mesmerize (*also* **mesmerise**) /'mezməraɪz/ *verb* [T] to hold sb's attention completely: *The audience seemed to be mesmerized by the speaker's voice.*
☆ **mess¹** /mes/ *noun* **1** [C, usually sing] the state of being dirty or untidy: *The kitchen's in a terrible mess!* **2** [sing] a person or thing that is dirty or untidy: *You look a mess! You can't go out like that!* ○ *My hair is a mess.* **3** [sing] the state of having problems or troubles: *The company is in a financial mess.* ○ *to make a mess of your life*
mess *verb* [T] (*informal*) (*US*) to make sth dirty or untidy: *Don't mess your hands.*
(PHRASAL VERBS) **mess about/around 1** to behave in a foolish way **2** to pass your time in a relaxed way without any real purpose: *We spent Sunday just messing around at home.*
mess sb about/around to treat sb in a way that is not fair or reasonable, eg by changing your plans without telling him/her: *The builders really messed us around. They never turned up when they promised to.*
mess about/around with sth to touch or use sth in a careless way: *It is dangerous to mess about with fireworks.*
mess sth up 1 to make sth dirty or untidy **2** to do sth badly or spoil sth: *I really messed up the last question in the exam.*
messy *adj* (**messier**; **messiest**) **1** dirty or untidy: *a messy room* **2** needing a lot of cleaning up: *Painting the ceiling is a messy job.* **3** having or causing problems or trouble: *a messy divorce*
mess² /mes/ *noun* [C] the room or building where soldiers eat together: *the officers' mess*
☆ **message** /'mesɪdʒ/ *noun* **1** [C] a written or spoken piece of information that is passed from one person to another: *Mr Thomas is not here at the moment. Can I take a message?* ○ *Could you give this message to the headmaster, please?* ○ *to get/receive a message from sb* **2** [sing] the main idea of a book, speech, etc: *It was a funny film but it also had a serious message.*
(IDIOM) **get the message** (*informal*) to understand what sb means even if it is not said directly: *He finally got the message and left Dick and Sarah alone together.*
messenger /'mesɪndʒə(r)/ *noun* [C] a person who carries a message
Messiah (*also* **messiah**) /mɪˈsaɪə/ *noun* [C] a person, eg Jesus Christ, who is expected to come and save the world
messy ⇨ MESS¹
met *pt* of MEET
☆ **metal** /'metl/ *noun* [C,U] a type of solid mineral substance, eg tin, iron, gold, steel, etc: *Aluminium is a non-magnetic metal.* ○ *to recycle scrap metal* ○ *a metal bar*
metallic /mɪˈtælɪk/ *adj* looking like metal or making a noise like one piece of metal hitting another: *a metallic blue car* ○ *harsh metallic sounds*
metamorphosis /ˌmetəˈmɔːfəsɪs/ *noun* [C] (*pl* **metamorphoses** /-əsiːz/) (*formal*) a complete change of form (as part of natural development): *the metamorphosis of a tadpole into a frog*
metaphor /'metəfə(r)/ *noun* [C,U] a way of describing sth by comparing it to sth else which has the same qualities (but without using the words 'as' or 'like'). For example, if you call sb a 'parrot' you are using a metaphor to say that the person just repeats things without thinking. —**metaphorical** /ˌmetəˈfɒrɪkl; *US* -ˈfɔːr-/ *adj*: *a metaphorical expression* —**metaphorically** /-klɪ/ *adv*
mete /miːt/ *verb*
(PHRASAL VERB) **mete sth out (to sb)** (*formal*) to give a punishment, reward, etc
meteor /'miːtɪə(r)/ *noun* [C] a small piece of rock, etc in space. When a meteor enters the earth's atmosphere it makes a bright line in the night sky.
meteoric /ˌmiːtɪˈɒrɪk; *US* -ˈɔːr-/ *adj* very fast or successful: *a meteoric rise to fame*
meteorology /ˌmiːtɪəˈrɒlədʒɪ/ *noun* [U] the

study of the weather and climate —**meteorological** /ˌmiːtɪərəˈlɒdʒɪkl; US ˌmiːtɪɔːr-/ adj: *the Meteorological Office*

meteorologist /ˌmiːtɪəˈrɒlədʒɪst/ noun [C] a person who studies the weather

meter¹ /ˈmiːtə(r)/ noun [C] a piece of equipment that measures the amount of gas, water, electricity, time, etc you have used: *The man has come to read the gas meter.* o *a parking-meter*

meter verb [T] to measure sth with a meter

meter² (*US*) = METRE

method /ˈmeθəd/ noun [C] a way of doing sth: *What method of payment do you prefer? Cash, cheque or credit card?* o *modern methods of teaching languages*

methodical /mɪˈθɒdɪkl/ adj having or using a well-organized and careful way of doing sth: *Paul is a very methodical worker.* —**methodically** /-klɪ/ adv

Methodist /ˈmeθədɪst/ noun [C], adj (a member) of a Protestant Church that was started by John Wesley in the 18th century

meticulous /mɪˈtɪkjʊləs/ adj giving or showing great attention to detail; very careful —**meticulously** adv

☆ **metre** (*US* **meter**) /ˈmiːtə(r)/ noun [C] (*abbr* **m**) a measure of length; 100 centimetres: *A metre is about 39 inches.* o *What's the record for the 100 metres?* (=the race)

metric /ˈmetrɪk/ adj using the system of measurement that is based on metres, grams, litres, etc (**the metric system**) ☞ Look at **imperial**.

metropolis /məˈtrɒpəlɪs/ noun [C] a very large city, usually the chief city of a country —**metropolitan** /ˌmetrəˈpɒlɪtən/ adj

miaow /miːˈaʊ/ noun [C] one of the sounds that a cat makes

miaow verb [I] to make the sound ☞ Look at **purr**.

mice pl of MOUSE

mickey /ˈmɪki/ noun

(IDIOM) **take the mickey (out of sb)** (*informal*) to make sb look silly by laughing at them: *Stop taking the mickey! You can't dance any better yourself.* ☞ Look at **tease**.

microchip /ˈmaɪkrəʊtʃɪp/ (also *informal* **chip**) noun [C] a very small piece of a special material (**silicon**) that is used inside a computer, etc to make it work

microcomputer /ˌmaɪkrəʊkəmˈpjuːtə(r)/ (also *informal* **micro**) noun [C] a small computer that is not part of a larger system

microcosm /ˈmaɪkrəʊkɒzəm/ noun [C] something that is a small example of sth larger: *Our little village is a microcosm of society as a whole.*

microfiche /ˈmaɪkrəʊfiːʃ/ noun [C,U] a piece of film on which information is stored in very small print

microphone /ˈmaɪkrəfəʊn/ (also *informal* **mike**) noun [C] a piece of electrical equipment that is used for making sounds louder or for recording them: *Speak into the microphone so that everyone can hear you.*

microscope /ˈmaɪkrəskəʊp/ noun [C] a piece of equipment that makes very small objects look large enough for you to be able to see them: *to examine sth under a microscope*

microscopic /ˌmaɪkrəˈskɒpɪk/ adj too small to be seen without a microscope

microwave /ˈmaɪkrəweɪv/ noun [C] **1** a short electric wave that is used for sending radio messages and for cooking food **2** (also **microwave oven**) a type of oven that cooks or heats food very quickly using microwaves

mid /mɪd/ adj (only *before* a noun) the middle of: *I'm away from mid June.* o *the mid 1950s*

mid- /mɪd/ (in compounds) in the middle of: *mid-morning coffee* o *a mid-air collision*

the Midwest noun [sing] the northern central part of the USA

☆ **midday** /ˌmɪdˈdeɪ/ noun [U] twelve o'clock in the middle of the day; noon: *We just have a light snack at midday.* ☞ Look at **midnight**.

☆ **middle** /ˈmɪdl/ noun **1 the middle** [sing] the part, point or position that is the same distance from the two ends of sth: *An unbroken white line in the middle of the road means you must not overtake.* o *Here's a photo of me with my two brothers. I'm the one in the middle.*

☞ **Centre** and **middle** are often very similar in meaning but centre is used when you mean to exact middle of something: *How do you find the centre of a circle?* o *There was a large table in the middle of the room.* When you are talking about a period of time only **middle** may be used: *The baby woke up in the middle of the night.* o *the middle of July* **2** [C] (*informal*) your waist: *I want to lose weight around my middle.*

middle adj (only *before* a noun) in the middle: *I wear my mother's ring on my middle finger.* o *There are three houses in a row and ours is the middle one.*

ˌmiddle ˈage noun [U] the time when you are about 40 to 60 years old: *in late middle age*

ˌmiddle-ˈaged adj of or in middle age: *middle-aged people*

the ˌMiddle ˈAges noun [plural] the period of European history from about AD1100 to AD1500

ˌmiddle ˈclass noun [C] the group of people in society who are between the working class and the upper class. Middle-class people include business people, managers, teachers, doctors, etc: *Most of the people who work here are middle class.* o *a comfortable middle-class lifestyle*

the ˌMiddle ˈEast noun [sing] the group of countries that are situated at the point where Europe, Africa and Asia meet

ˈmiddleman /-mæn/ noun [C] (pl **middlemen** /-men/) a person who buys sth from a producer or manufacturer and then sells it to sb else for more money

ˌmiddle ˈname noun [C] the second of two Christian or given names

ˈmiddle school noun [C] (*Brit*) a school for children aged between nine and thirteen

midge /mɪdʒ/ noun [C] a very small flying insect like a mosquito that can bite people ☞ Look at **gnat**.

midget /ˈmɪdʒɪt/ noun [C] a very small person

Midlands /ˈmɪdləndz/ noun [sing, with sing or pl verb] **the Midlands** the central part of England. The Midlands contains the industrial towns of Birmingham, Nottingham, Coventry, etc.

☆ **midnight** /'mɪdnaɪt/ *noun* [U] twelve o'clock at night: *They left the party at midnight.* ○ *The clock struck midnight.* ☛ Look at **midday**.

midriff /'mɪdrɪf/ *noun* [C] the part of your body between your chest and your waist

midst /mɪdst/ *noun* [U] (after a preposition) the middle part or position: *They realized with a shock that there was an enemy in their midst* (= among them).

midsummer /ˌmɪd'sʌmə(r)/ *noun* [U] the time around the middle of summer: *a beautiful midsummer/midsummer's evening*

midway /ˌmɪd'weɪ/ *adj, adv* **midway (between sth and sth)** in the middle or halfway (between sth and sth): *Our cottage is midway between Alston and Penrith.*

midweek /ˌmɪd'wiːk/ *noun* [U] the middle of the week (= Tuesday, Wednesday and Thursday) —**midweek** *adv*: *If you travel midweek it will be less crowded.*

midwife /'mɪdwaɪf/ *noun* [C] (*pl* **midwives** /-waɪvz/) a person who has been trained to help women give birth to babies

midwifery /'mɪdwɪfəri/; *US* -waɪf-/ *noun* [U] the work of a midwife

midwinter /ˌmɪd'wɪntə(r)/ *noun* [U] the time around the middle of winter

☆ **might¹** /maɪt/ *modal verb* (*negative* **might not**; *short form* **mightn't** /'maɪtnt/) **1** (used as the past form of 'may' when you report what sb has said): *He said he might be late* (= his words were, 'I may be late'). **2** (used for saying that sth is possible): *'Where's William?' 'He might be upstairs.'* ○ *We might be going to Spain on holiday this year.* ○ *She might not come if she's very busy.* ○ *If I'd have known the film was about Wales, I might have gone to see it* (= but I didn't know, so I didn't go). **3** (used in formal British English to ask for sth very politely): *I wonder if I might go home half an hour early today?* ○ *Might I say something?* **4** (used in formal British English to suggest sth politely): *Might I suggest that we discuss this in private?* ○ *If you need more information, you might try phoning our customer service department.*
(IDIOMS) **may/might as well (do sth)** ⇨ WELL³
you, etc might do sth (used when you are angry with sb) you should: *You might tell me if you're going to be late.* ○ *They might at least have phoned if they're not coming.*

I might have known (used for saying that you are not surprised that sth has happened): *I might have known he wouldn't help.*

might² /maɪt/ *noun* [U] (*formal*) great strength or power: *We pushed with all our might, but the rock did not move.*

mighty /'maɪti/ *adj* (**mightier; mightiest**) very strong or powerful

mighty *adv* (*US informal*) very: *That's mighty kind of you.*

migraine /'miːɡreɪn; *US* 'maɪɡreɪn/ *noun* [C,U] a very bad headache that makes you feel ill

migrate /maɪ'ɡreɪt; *US* 'maɪɡreɪt/ *verb* [I] **1** (used about animals and birds) to travel from one part of the world to another at the same time every year **2** to move from one place to go and live and work in another: *Many of the poorer people were forced to migrate to the cities to look for work.* ☛ Look at **emigrate**.

migrant /'maɪɡrənt/ *noun* [C] a person who goes from place to place in search of work: *migrant workers* —**migration** /maɪ'ɡreɪʃn/ *noun* [C,U]: *the annual migration to the south*

mike /maɪk/ *noun* [C] (*informal*) = MICROPHONE

milage = MILEAGE

☆ **mild** /maɪld/ *adj* **1** not hard, strong or severe: *a mild soap that is gentle to your skin* ○ *a mild winter* ○ *a mild punishment* **2** kind and gentle: *He's a very mild man – you never see him get angry.* **3** (used about food) not having a strong taste: *mild cheese*

mild (*also* **mild ale**) *noun* [U] (*Brit*) a type of beer that does not have a very strong flavour

mildly *adv* **1** in a mild way **2** not very; slightly: *I found the talk mildly interesting.* —**mildness** *noun* [U]

☆ **mile** /maɪl/ *noun* [C] **1** a measure of length; 1·6 kilometres. There are 1760 yards in a mile: *The nearest beach is seven miles away.* ○ *It's a seven-mile drive to the sea.* ○ *He ran the mile in less than four minutes.* ○ *My car does 35 miles to the gallon.* ○ *From the top of the hill you can see for miles and miles.* **2** (*also* **miles**) a lot: *to miss a target by a mile* ○ *I'm feeling miles better this morning.* **3 miles** a long way: *How much further is it? We've walked miles already.*

milestone *noun* [C] **1** a stone at the side of the road that shows how far it is to the next town **2** a very important event

mileage (*also* **milage**) /'maɪlɪdʒ/ *noun* **1** [C,U] the distance that has been travelled (measured in miles): *The car is five years old but it has a low mileage.* **2** [U] (*informal*) the amount of use or benefit you get from sth

militant /'mɪlɪtənt/ *adj* using or willing to use force or strong pressure to get what you want: *The workers were in a very militant mood.* —**militancy** /-ənsi/ *noun* [U]
militant *noun* [C] a militant person

☆ **military** /'mɪlɪtri; *US* -teri/ *adj* (only *before* a noun) of or for soldiers, the army, navy, etc: *Do you have military service in your country?* ○ *to take military action*

militia /mɪ'lɪʃə/ *noun* [C, with sing or pl verb] a group of people who are not regular soldiers but who have had military training

☆ **milk** /mɪlk/ *noun* [U] **1** a white liquid that is produced by women and animals to feed their babies. People drink cows', goats', etc milk and use it to make butter and cheese: *skimmed, powdered, long-life, low-fat, etc milk* ○ *Don't use that milk – it's gone sour.* ○ *I don't take milk in my coffee, thank you.* ○ *a bottle of milk* ○ *a milk bottle* **2** the juice of some plants or trees that looks like milk: *coconut milk*

milk *verb* **1** [I,T] to take milk from a cow, goat, etc **2** [T] (*figurative*) to get as much money, information, etc as you can from sb/sth: *The colonists milked the country of its natural resources.*

p	b	t	d	k	g	tʃ	dʒ	f	v	θ	ð
pen	bad	tea	did	cat	got	chin	June	fall	van	thin	then

milk 'chocolate noun [U] chocolate that is made with milk

'milkman /-mən/ noun [C] (pl **milkmen**) a person who delivers milk to your house

'milk shake noun [C,U] a drink made of milk, flavouring and sometimes ice-cream

milky /'mɪlki/ adj (**milkier; milkiest**) **1** made with milk: *a hot milky drink* **2** of a pale white colour

mill¹ /mɪl/ noun [C] **1** a building that contains a large machine that is used for grinding grain into flour: *a windmill* o *a water-mill* **2** a kitchen tool that is used for grinding sth into powder: *a pepper-mill* **3** a factory that is used for making certain kinds of material: *a paper-mill* o *a steel-mill*

mill² /mɪl/ verb [T] to grind sth in a mill
(PHRASAL VERB) **mill about/around** (*informal*) (used about a large number of people or animals) to move around in one place with no real purpose

millet /'mɪlɪt/ noun [U] grass-like plant whose seeds are used as food for people and birds

milligram (*also* **milligramme**) /'mɪlɪɡræm/ noun [C] (*abbr* **mg**) a measure of weight. There are 1 000 milligrams in a gram.

millilitre (*US* **milliliter**) /'mɪlɪliːtə(r)/ noun [C] (*abbr* **ml**) a measure of liquid. There are 1 000 millilitres in a litre.

millimetre (*US* **millimeter**) /'mɪlɪmiːtə(r)/ noun [C] (*abbr* **mm**) a measure of length. There are 1 000 millimetres in a metre.

millinery /'mɪlɪnəri; *US* 'mɪlɪneri/ noun [U] making or selling women's hats

million /'mɪljən/ number 1 000 000: *Nearly 60 million people live in Britain.* o *Millions are at risk from the disease.* o *'How much does it cost?' 'Half a million.'* ☛ For more information about numbers, look at Appendix 2 .

millionth det 1 000 000th: *the firm's millionth customer*

millionth noun [C] one of a million equal parts of sth: *a millionth of a second*

millionaire /ˌmɪljə'neə(r)/ noun [C] a person who has a million pounds, dollars, etc; a very rich person ☛ A female millionaire is a **millionairess**.

milometer (*also* **mileometer**) /maɪ'lɒmɪtə(r)/ (*US* **odometer**) noun [C] a piece of equipment that measures the distance you have travelled

mime /maɪm/ noun [C,U] acting or telling a story without speaking, by using your hands, body and the expressions on your face
mime verb [I,T] to act or express sth using mime

mimic /'mɪmɪk/ verb [T] (*pres part* **mimicking**; *pt, pp* **mimicked**) to copy sb's behaviour in an amusing way
mimic noun [C] a person who can mimic other people

mince /mɪns/ verb [T] to cut meat into very small pieces using a special machine: *a pound of minced beef*
mince (*Brit*) (*US* **hamburger**; **ground beef**) noun [U] meat that has been cut into very small pieces with a special machine

,mince 'pie noun [C] a small round cake with a mixture of dried fruit, sugar, etc (**mincemeat**) inside, traditionally eaten in Britain at Christmas time

mincemeat /'mɪnsmiːt/ noun [U] a mixture of dried fruit, nuts, sugar, etc

☆ **mind¹** /maɪnd/ noun [C,U] the part of your brain that thinks and remembers; your thoughts and intelligence: *He has a brilliant mind.* o *Not everybody has the right sort of mind for this work.*
(IDIOMS) **be out of your mind** (*informal*) to be crazy or mad: *He must be out of his mind to give up a good job like that.*
bear/keep sb/sth in mind to remember sb/sth: *We'll bear/keep your suggestion in mind for the future.*
change your mind ⇒ CHANGE¹
cross your mind ⇒ CROSS²
ease sb's mind ⇒ EASE¹
frame of mind ⇒ FRAME¹
have/keep an open mind ⇒ OPEN¹
keep your mind on sth to continue to pay attention to sth: *Stop talking and try to keep your mind on your work!*
make up your mind to decide: *I can't make up my mind which sweater to buy.*
on your mind worrying you: *Don't bother her with that. She's got enough on her mind already.*
put/set your/sb's mind at rest to make you/sb stop worrying: *The results of the blood test set his mind at rest.*
slip your mind ⇒ SLIP¹
state of mind ⇒ STATE¹
take your/sb's mind off sth to help you/sb not to think or worry about sth

☆ **mind²** /maɪnd/ verb **1** [I,T] (especially in questions, answers, and negative sentences) to feel annoyed, unhappy or uncomfortable: *'Do you mind if I smoke?' 'No, not at all.'* o *I'm sure Simon won't mind if you don't invite him.* o *We've got four children so I hope you won't mind about the mess!* o *I don't mind what you do – it's your decision.* o *Do you mind having to travel so far to work every day?* o *Are you sure your parents won't mind me coming?* o *'Would you like red or white wine?' 'I don't mind.'* (= I'm happy to have either) o *I wouldn't mind a holiday in the sun this year!* (= I would like it.) **2** [T] (used in a question as a polite way of asking sb to do sth) could you...?: *Would you mind closing the window for me?* o *Do you mind driving? I'm feeling rather tired.* **3** [T] (used as a command) be careful of/about...: *It's a very low doorway so mind your head.* o *Mind that step!* o *Mind you don't slip on the ice.*
(IDIOMS) **mind you** (used for attracting attention to a point you are making or for giving more information): *Paul seems very tired. Mind you, he has been working very hard recently.*
mind your own business to pay attention to your own affairs, not other people's: *Stop telling me what to do and mind your own business!*
never mind don't worry; it doesn't matter: *'I forgot to post your letter.' 'Never mind, I'll do it later.'* o *Never mind about the cost – just enjoy yourself!*

(PHRASAL VERB) **Mind out** (*informal*) Get out of the way!: *Mind out! There's a bicycle coming.*
minder *noun* [C] (especially in compounds) a person whose job is to look after sb/sth: *My son goes to a child-minder so that I can work part-time.*
-minded /'maɪndɪd/ *adj* **1** (in compounds) having the type of mind mentioned: *a strong-minded person* **2** (in compounds) interested in the thing mentioned: *money-minded*
mindless /'maɪndləs/ *adj* not having or not needing thought or intelligence: *mindless violence* ○ *mindless factory work*
☆ **mine¹** /maɪn/ *pron* of or belonging to me: *'Whose is this jacket?' 'It's mine.'* ○ *Don't take your car – you can come in mine.* ○ *May I introduce a friend of mine?* (= one of my friends) ☞ Look at **my**.
☆ **mine²** /maɪn/ *noun* [C] **1** a hole, or system of holes and passages, that people dig under the ground in order to obtain coal, tin, gold, etc: *a coal-mine* **2** a bomb that is hidden under the ground or under water
'minefield *noun* [C] **1** an area of land or sea where mines(2) have been hidden **2** a situation that is full of hidden dangers or difficulties
mine³ /maɪn/ *verb* **1** [I,T] to dig in the ground for coal, gold, etc; to get coal, etc by digging: *Diamonds are mined in South Africa.* ☞ Look at **mining**. **2** [T] to put hidden mines(2) in an area of land or sea
☆ **miner** /'maɪnə(r)/ *noun* [C] a person whose job is to work in a mine to get coal, etc
☆ **mineral** /'mɪnərəl/ *noun* [C] a natural substance such as coal, salt, oil, etc, especially one that is dug out of the ground for people to use: *a country rich in minerals*
'mineral water *noun* [U] water that comes directly from the ground, contains minerals and is thought to be good for your health
mingle /'mɪŋgl/ *verb* [I,T] to mix with another thing or with other people: *The colours slowly mingled together to make a muddy brown.* ○ *His excitement was mingled with fear.*
mini- /'mɪni/ (in compounds) very small: *a miniskirt* ○ *a minigolf*
miniature /'mɪnətʃə(r); *US* 'mɪniətʃuər/ *noun* [C] a small copy of sth which is much larger: *The children loved the miniature village with its tiny houses, church and farm.*
(IDIOM) **in miniature** in a very small form
minibus /'mɪnibʌs/ *noun* [C] (*especially Brit*) a small bus, usually for no more than 12 people
minimal /'mɪnɪməl/ *adj* very small in amount or level: *The project has had minimal support.*
minimize (*also* **minimise**) /'mɪnɪmaɪz/ *verb* [T] to make sth as small as possible (in amount or level): *We shall try to minimize the risks to the public.* ☞ The opposite is **maximize**.
☆ **minimum** /'mɪnɪməm/ *noun* [sing] the smallest amount or level that is possible or allowed: *I need a minimum of seven hours' sleep.* ○ *The minimum he will accept is £15 000 a year.* ○ *We will try and keep the cost of the tickets to a minimum.* ☞ The opposite is **maximum**.
minimum *adj* (only *before* a noun) the smallest possible or allowed: *What's the minimum age for leaving school in Britain?* ☞ The opposite is **maximum**.
mining /'maɪnɪŋ/ *noun* [U] (often in compounds) the process or industry of getting coal, metals, salt, etc out of the ground by digging: *tin-mining* ○ *a mining town*
☆ **minister** /'mɪnɪstə(r)/ *noun* [C] **1** (*US* **secretary**) a member of the government, often the head of a government department: *the Minister of Trade and Industry* ☞ Look at **Prime Minister** and **Cabinet Minister**. **2** a priest, especially in a Protestant church ☞ Look at **vicar**.
ministerial /ˌmɪnɪ'stɪəriəl/ *adj* of a government minister or department: *a ministerial decision*
☆ **ministry** /'mɪnɪstri/ *noun* (*pl* **ministries**) **1** (*also* **department**) [C] a division of the government responsible for a particular subject: *the Ministry of Defence* ☞ **Department** is the only word used in US English. **2 the ministry** [sing] the profession of being a priest (in Protestant Churches): *to enter the ministry* (= to become a priest)
mink /mɪŋk/ *noun* [C] a small wild animal whose fur is used for expensive coats: *a mink coat*
☆ **minor** /'maɪnə(r)/ *adj* **1** not very big, serious or important (when compared with others): *It's only a minor problem. Don't worry.* ○ *She's gone into hospital for a minor operation.* ☞ The opposite is **major**. **2** of one of the two types of key¹(2) in which music is usually written: *a symphony in F minor*
minor *noun* [C] a person who is not legally an adult

☞ In Britain you are a minor until you are eighteen.

☆ **minority** /maɪ'nɒrəti; *US* -'nɔːr-/ *noun* [C] (*pl* **minorities**) **1** [usually sing, with sing or pl verb] the smaller number or part of a group; less than half: *Most women continue to work when they are married. Only a minority stays/stay at home.* ○ *a minority interest* (= of only a small number of people) ☞ The opposite is **majority**. **2** a group of people who are of a different race or religion to most of the people in the community or country where they live: *Schools in Britain need to do more to help children of ethnic minorities.*
(IDIOM) **be in a/the minority** to be the smaller of two groups: *We take both boys and girls, but girls are in the minority.* ☞ Look at **in a/the majority**.
mint¹ /mɪnt/ *noun* **1** [U] a small plant (**a herb**) whose leaves are used for giving a flavour to food, drinks, toothpaste, etc: *lamb with mint sauce* ○ *mint chocolate* **2** [C] a sweet with a strong fresh flavour ☞ Another word is a **peppermint**.
minty /'mɪnti/ *adj* tasting of mint
mint² /mɪnt/ *noun* [sing] a place where coins and notes are made by the government —**mint** *verb* [T]
minus /'maɪnəs/ *prep* **1** less; subtract; take away: *Six minus two is four.* ☞ The opposite is **plus**. **2** (used about a number) below zero: *The*

iː	ɪ	e	æ	ɑː	ɒ	ɔː	ʊ	uː	ʌ
see	sit	ten	hat	arm	got	saw	put	too	cup

temperature will fall to minus 10. **3** (*informal*) without: *Are you minus your husband this evening?*

minus *adj* (used with grades given for school work) slightly lower than: *I got A minus (A-) for my essay.* ☛ Look at **plus**.

minus (*also* **'minus sign**) *noun* [C] the sign (-) which is used in mathematics to show that a number is below zero or that you should subtract the second number from the first

minuscule /'mɪnəskju:l/ *adj* very small; tiny

☆ **minute¹** /'mɪnɪt/ *noun* **1** [C] one of the 60 parts that make up one hour; 60 seconds: *It's five minutes to/past nine.* o *He telephoned ten minutes ago.* o *Hurry up! The plane leaves in twenty minutes!* o *The programme lasts for about fifty minutes.* **2** [sing] a very short time; a moment: *Wait a minute! You've forgotten your notes.* o *Have you got a minute to spare? I want to talk to you.* **3 the minutes** [plural] a written record of what is said and decided at a meeting: *to take the minutes* (= to write them down)

(IDIOMS) **(at) any minute/moment (now)** (*informal*) very soon: *The plane will be landing any minute now.*

in a minute very soon: *I think it's going to rain in a minute.*

just a minute (*informal*) (used for stopping a person, pausing to think, etc) to wait for a short time: *Just a minute. Is that your book or mine?*

the last minute/moment ⇨ LAST¹

the minute/moment (that) as soon as: *I'll tell him you rang the minute (that) he gets here.*

up to the minute (*informal*) recent; not old: *For up to the minute information on flight times, phone the following number...*

minute² /maɪ'nju:t; *US* -'nu:t/ *adj* (**minuter**; **minutest**) **1** very small; tiny: *I couldn't read his writing. It was minute!* **2** very exact or accurate: *She was able to describe the man in minute detail.*

miracle /'mɪrəkl/ *noun* [C] a wonderful and extraordinary event that is impossible to explain and that is thought to be caused by God or a god: *Christ performed many miracles, even bringing dead people back to life.* o *She's doing her best but nobody can work miracles!* o *It will be a miracle if he passes his driving test.*

miraculous /mɪ'rækjʊləs/ *adj* impossible to explain or understand; extraordinary —**miraculously** *adv*

mirage /'mɪrɑ:ʒ, mɪ'rɑ:ʒ/ *noun* [C] something that you think you see in very hot weather but which does not really exist, especially water in a desert

☆ **mirror** /'mɪrə(r)/ *noun* [C] a piece of special glass that you can look into in order to see yourself or what is behind you: *That dress looks lovely on you. Have a look in the mirror.* o *Use your rear mirror before you overtake.*

☛ A mirror **reflects** images. What you see in a mirror is a **reflection**.

mirror *verb* [T] to reflect sth as if in a mirror: *The trees were mirrored in the lake.*

mirth /mɜ:θ/ *noun* [U] (*formal*) amusement or laughter

misapprehension /ˌmɪsæprɪ'henʃn/ *noun*

(IDIOM) **to be under a/the misapprehension** (*formal*) to have a wrong idea or impression

misbehave /ˌmɪsbɪ'heɪv/ *verb* [I] to behave badly

misbehaviour (*US* **misbehavior**) /ˌmɪsbɪ'heɪvjə(r)/ *noun* [U] bad behaviour

miscalculate /ˌmɪs'kælkjʊleɪt/ *verb* [I,T] to make a mistake in calculating or estimating (a situation or an amount, distance, etc): *The driver miscalculated the speed at which the other car was travelling.* —**miscalculation** /ˌmɪskælkjʊ'leɪʃn/ *noun* [C,U]

miscarriage /'mɪskærɪdʒ/ *noun* [C,U] giving birth to a baby before it is ready to be born, with the result that it cannot live: *She's had several miscarriages.* ☛ Look at **abortion**.

miscarry /ˌmɪs'kæri/ *verb* [I] (*pres part* **miscarrying**; *3rd pers sing pres* **miscarries**; *pt, pp* **miscarried**) **1** to give birth to a baby before it is ready to be born, with the result that it cannot live **2** (used about a plan, idea, etc) to fail

miscellaneous /ˌmɪsə'leɪniəs/ *adj* of various, different types; mixed: *a box of miscellaneous items for sale*

mischief /'mɪstʃɪf/ *noun* [U] bad behaviour (usually of children) that is not very serious: *Why are the children so quiet? Are they up to mischief again?* o *You can go and see your friends but keep out of mischief this time.*

mischievous /'mɪstʃɪvəs/ *adj* (usually used about children) fond of having fun in a rather naughty way —**mischievously** *adv*

misconception /ˌmɪskən'sepʃn/ *noun* [C] a wrong idea or understanding of sth: *It is a popular misconception* (= many people wrongly believe) *that people need meat to be healthy.*

misconduct /ˌmɪs'kɒndʌkt/ *noun* [U] (*formal*) bad behaviour, especially by a professional person

misdemeanour (*US* **misdemeanor**) /ˌmɪsdɪ'mi:nə(r)/ *noun* [C] something slightly bad or wrong that a person does; a minor crime

miser /'maɪzə(r)/ *noun* [C] a person who loves having a lot of money but hates spending any

☆ **miserable** /'mɪzrəbl/ *adj* **1** very unhappy; sad: *Oh dear, you look miserable. What's wrong?* o *It's a miserable story. Are you sure you want to hear it?* **2** unpleasant (because difficult or uncomfortable): *It's miserable working in such an unfriendly atmosphere.* **3** too small or of bad quality: *I was offered a miserable salary so I didn't take the job.*

miserably /-əbli/ *adv* in a miserable way: *I stared miserably out of the window.* o *We failed miserably* (= in a disappointing way) *to achieve our aim.*

☆ **misery** /'mɪzəri/ *noun* [C,U] (*pl* **miseries**) great unhappiness or lack of comfort; suffering: *There was an expression of pain and misery on his face.* o *The period after the war was a time of economic and social misery.* o *the miseries of war*

misfire /ˌmɪs'faɪə(r)/ *verb* [I] to fail to have the right result or effect: *The plan misfired.*

misfit /'mɪsfɪt/ *noun* [C] a person who is or feels different from other people: *He's always lived*

ɜ:	ə	eɪ	əʊ	aɪ	aʊ	ɔɪ	ɪə	eə	ʊə
fur	ago	pay	home	five	now	join	near	hair	pure

misfortune in a town before so he seems a bit of a misfit in the village.

misfortune /ˌmɪsˈfɔːtʃuːn/ noun [C,U] (an event, accident, etc that brings) bad luck or disaster: *Various misfortunes had made her sad and bitter.* ○ *I hope I don't ever have the misfortune to meet him again.*

misgiving /ˌmɪsˈgɪvɪŋ/ noun [C,U] a feeling of doubt, worry or suspicion: *I had serious misgivings about leaving him on his own in that condition.*

misguided /ˌmɪsˈgaɪdɪd/ adj **1** (used about a person) acting in a way that is not sensible **2** (used about behaviour or opinions) based on wrong ideas or information

mishap /ˈmɪshæp/ noun [C,U] an unlucky accident or bad luck that does not have serious results: *to have a slight mishap*

misinform /ˌmɪsɪnˈfɔːm/ verb [T] to give sb the wrong information: *It seems that the public have been misinformed about the cause of the disease.*

misinterpret /ˌmɪsɪnˈtɜːprɪt/ verb [T] to understand sth wrongly

misinterpretation /ˌmɪsɪntɜːprɪˈteɪʃn/ noun [C,U] understanding sth in the wrong way: *Parts of the speech were open to misinterpretation* (= easy to misunderstand).

misjudge /ˌmɪsˈdʒʌdʒ/ verb [T] to form a wrong opinion of sb/sth or to estimate sth wrongly

misjudgement (also **misjudgment**) noun [C,U] (the forming of) a wrong opinion or idea

mislay /ˌmɪsˈleɪ/ verb [T] (pres part **mislaying**; 3rd pers sing pres **mislays**; pt, pp **mislaid** /-ˈleɪd/) to lose sth, usually for a short time because you cannot remember where you left it: *I'm afraid I've mislaid my car keys.*

mislead /ˌmɪsˈliːd/ verb [T] (pt, pp **misled** /-ˈled/) to make sb have the wrong idea or opinion: *Don't be misled by his smile – he's not very friendly really.*

misleading adj giving a wrong idea or impression: *a misleading advertisement*

mismanage /ˌmɪsˈmænɪdʒ/ verb [T] to manage or organize sth badly or without skill —**mismanagement** noun [U]

misplaced /ˌmɪsˈpleɪst/ adj given to sb/sth that does not deserve to have it: *misplaced loyalty*

misprint /ˈmɪsprɪnt/ noun [C] a mistake in printing

mispronounce /ˌmɪsprəˈnaʊns/ verb [T] to pronounce a word or letter wrongly: *Be careful not to mispronounce 'live' as 'leave'.* —**mispronunciation** /ˌmɪsprəˌnʌnsiˈeɪʃn/ noun [C,U]

misread /ˌmɪsˈriːd/ verb [T] (pt, pp **misread** /-ˈred/) to read or understand sth wrongly: *He misread my silence as a refusal.* ○ *I misread the bus timetable and missed the last bus home.*

misrepresent /ˌmɪsˌreprɪˈzent/ verb [T] (usually passive) to give a wrong description of sb/sth

misrepresentation /ˌmɪsˌreprɪzenˈteɪʃn/ noun [C,U] (a) wrong description: *That's a misrepresentation of what was actually said.*

☆ **Miss** /mɪs/ (used as a title before the name of a girl or unmarried woman): *'Is there a Miss Dean living here?' the postman asked.* ○ *'Dear Miss Harris,' the letter began.*

☆ **miss¹** /mɪs/ verb **1** [T] to not see, hear, understand, etc sb/sth: *The house is on the corner so you can't miss it.* ○ *There was so much noise that I missed a lot of what the speaker said.* ○ *They completely missed the point of what I was saying.* **2** [I,T] to not hit, catch, etc sth: *She tried hard to hit the ball but missed.* ○ *Drive more carefully. You only just missed that car.* **3** [T] to feel sad because sb is not with you any more, or because you have not got or cannot do sth that you once had or did: *I'll miss you terribly when you go away.* ○ *I don't miss teaching at all. I prefer my new job.* **4** [T] to arrive too late for sth or to fail to be at sth: *Hurry up or you'll miss the bus!* ○ *She'll be very cross if you miss her birthday party.* **5** [T] to notice that you have lost sb/sth: *When did you first miss your handbag?*

(PHRASAL VERBS) **miss sb/sth out** to not include sb/sth: *You've missed out several important points in your report.*

miss out (on sth) to lose a chance to gain sth/enjoy yourself, etc: *You'll miss out on all the fun if you stay at home.*

missing adj lost, or not in the right or usual place: *Some of my books are missing – have you seen them?* ○ *The roof has got some tiles missing.* ○ *The little girl has been missing from home for two days.* ○ *a missing person*

miss² /mɪs/ noun [C] a failure to hit, catch, etc sth that you are aiming at: *After several misses he finally managed to hit the target.*

(IDIOMS) **give sth a miss** (informal) to decide not to do sth, have sth, go to sth, etc: *I think I'll give the party a miss. I don't feel too well.*

a near miss ⇨ NEAR¹

missile /ˈmɪsaɪl; US ˈmɪsl/ noun [C] **1** a powerful exploding weapon that can be sent long distances through the air: *nuclear missiles* **2** an object or weapon that is fired from a gun or thrown: *Among the missiles thrown during the riot were broken bottles and stones.*

mission /ˈmɪʃn/ noun [C] **1** an important task or purpose that a person or group of people are sent somewhere to do: *Your mission is to send back information about the enemy's movements.* **2** a group of people who are sent abroad to perform a special task: *a British trade mission to China* **3** a special journey made by a space rocket or military aeroplane: *a mission to the moon* **4** a particular task or duty which you feel that you should do: *Her work with the poor was more than just a job – it was her mission in life.* **5** a place where the local people are taught about religion, given medical help, etc by people who are sent to do this (**missionaries**).

missionary /ˈmɪʃənri; US -neri/ noun [C] (pl **missionaries**) a person who is sent abroad to teach about the Christian religion

misspell /ˌmɪsˈspel/ verb [T] (pt, pp **misspelled** or **misspelt** /-ˈspelt/) to spell sth wrongly

misspent /ˌmɪsˈspent/ adj (of time or money) used in a foolish way; wasted

☆ **mist¹** /mɪst/ noun **1** [C,U] clouds made of small drops of water, close to the ground, which

p	b	t	d	k	g	tʃ	dʒ	f	v	θ	ð
pen	bad	tea	did	cat	got	chin	June	fall	van	thin	then

mist make it difficult to see very far; a thin fog: *Early morning mists often mean it will be sunny later on.* o *The fields were covered in mist.* ☛ Look at the notes at **fog** and **weather**. **2** [U] a very thin layer of tiny drops of water on a window, mirror, etc: *Is the mist on the inside or the outside of the windscreen?*

misty *adj* (**mistier**; **mistiest**) full of or covered with mist: *a misty day* ☛ Look at **foggy**.

mist² /mɪst/ *verb*
(PHRASAL VERB) **mist (sth) up** to cover or be covered with mist: *The back window's misted up again. Can you wipe it?*

☆ **mistake¹** /mɪˈsteɪk/ *noun* [C,U] something that you think or do that is wrong: *The teacher corrected the mistakes in my essay.* o *a spelling mistake* o *Waiter! I think you've made a mistake over the bill.* o *I think there must be some mistake. My name is Sedgley, not Selley.* o *It was a big mistake not to book our flight earlier.* o *We made the mistake of asking Paul to look after the house while we were away.*

(IDIOM) **by mistake** as a result of a mistake or carelessness: *The terrorists shot the wrong man by mistake.* ☛ **Error** is more formal than **mistake**: (*formal*) *Please accept my apologies. I opened your letter in error.* o (*informal*) *I'm sorry. I opened your letter by mistake.* **Fault** indicates who is to blame: *The accident wasn't my fault. The other driver pulled out in front of me.* **Fault** is also used to describe something that is wrong with, or not good about, a person or a thing: *a technical fault* o *Laziness is not one of her faults.*

☆ **mistake²** /mɪˈsteɪk/ *verb* [T] (*pt* **mistook** /mɪˈstʊk/; *pp* **mistaken** /mɪˈsteɪkən/) **1** to be wrong about sth: *to mistake sb's meaning* **2** to think (wrongly) that sb/sth is sb/sth else: *I'm sorry. I mistook you for a friend of mine.*

mistaken *adj* wrong; not correct: *I thought the film was a comedy but I must have been mistaken.* o *a case of mistaken identity* —**mistakenly** *adv*

mister /ˈmɪstə(r)/ ⇨ MR

mistletoe /ˈmɪsltəʊ/ *noun* [U] a plant with white berries and leaves that are green at all times of the year. Mistletoe grows on trees.

☛ Mistletoe is used as a decoration inside houses in Britain at Christmas time. There is a tradition of kissing people 'under the mistletoe'.

mistook *pt* of MISTAKE²

mistreat /ˌmɪsˈtriːt/ *verb* [T] to behave badly or cruelly towards a person or animal —**mistreatment** *noun* [U]

mistress /ˈmɪstrɪs/ *noun* [C] **1** a man's mistress is a woman who is having a (secret) sexual relationship with him ☛ Look at **lover**. **2** a female teacher (usually in a private school): *the chemistry mistress* ☛ Look at **master**. **3** a woman who has people or animals in her control ☛ Look at **master**.

mistrust /ˌmɪsˈtrʌst/ *verb* [T] to not believe sb/sth; to have no confidence in sb/sth; not to trust: *I always mistrust the information in newspapers.* —**mistrust** *noun* [U,sing]

misty ⇨ MIST

misunderstand /ˌmɪsʌndəˈstænd/ *verb* [T] (*pt, pp* **misunderstood** /-ˈstʊd/) to understand sb/sth wrongly: *Don't misunderstand me. I'm only trying to do what's best for you.* o *I misunderstood the instructions and answered three questions instead of four.*

misunderstanding *noun* [C,U] not understanding sb/sth properly; an example of this: *There must be some misunderstanding. I ordered spaghetti, not pizza.* o *It was all a misunderstanding but we've got it sorted out now.*

misuse /ˌmɪsˈjuːz/ *verb* [T] to use sth in the wrong way or for the wrong purpose: *These chemicals can be dangerous if misused.*

misuse /ˌmɪsˈjuːs/ *noun* [C,U] using sth in the wrong way or for the wrong purpose: *That project is a misuse of public money.*

mitigate /ˈmɪtɪgeɪt/ *verb* [T] (*formal*) to make sth less serious, painful, unpleasant, etc —**mitigating** *adj*: *Because of the mitigating circumstances* (= that made the crime seem less bad) *the judge gave her a lighter sentence.*

mitten /ˈmɪtn/ *noun* [C] a type of glove that has one part for the thumb and another part for the other four fingers: *a pair of mittens*

☆ **mix¹** /mɪks/ *verb* **1** [T] to put two or more substances together and shake or stir them until they form a new substance: *to mix oil and vinegar together to make a salad-dressing* o *Mix yellow and blue together to make green.* **2** [I] to join together to form a separate substance: *Oil and water don't mix.* **3** [T] to make sth (by mixing two or more substances together): *to mix cement* **4** [T] to do or have two or more things at the same time: *to mix business and pleasure* **5** [I] to be with and talk to other people: *He mixes with all types of people at work.* o *She is very shy and doesn't mix well.*

(IDIOM) **be/get mixed up in sth** (*informal*) to be/become involved in sth bad or unpleasant
(PHRASAL VERBS) **mix sth up** to put something in the wrong order: *He was so nervous that he dropped his speech and got the pages all mixed up.*

mix sb/sth up (with sb/sth) to confuse sb/sth with sb/sth else: *I think you've got us mixed up. I'm Jane and she's Sally.*

'mix-up *noun* [C] (*informal*) a mistake in the planning or organization of sth: *Because of a mix-up at the travel agent's we didn't get our tickets on time.*

mix² /mɪks/ *noun* **1** [C, usually sing] a group of different types of people or things: *We need a good racial mix in the police force.* **2** [C,U] a special powder that contains all the substances needed to make a cake, bread, etc. You add water or another liquid to this powder: *a packet of cake mix*

☆ **mixed** /mɪkst/ *adj* **1** made or consisting of different types of sth: *a mixed salad* o *The reaction to our suggestion has been very mixed.* **2** for both sexes, male and female: *a mixed school* ☛ The opposite is **single-sex**. Look also at **unisex**.

(IDIOM) **have mixed feelings (about sb/sth)** to have some good and some bad feelings about

mixer

sb/sth; not to be sure about what you think: *I have very mixed feelings about leaving school.*

mixed 'doubles *noun* [U] a game of tennis, etc in which there is a man and a woman on each side

mixed 'marriage *noun* [C] a marriage between people of different races or religions

mixed-'up *adj* (*informal*) confused or unsure about sth/yourself: *He has been very mixed-up since his parents' divorce.*

mixer /'mɪksə(r)/ *noun* [C] a machine that is used for mixing sth: *a food-mixer*

☆ **mixture** /'mɪkstʃə(r)/ *noun* **1** [C,U] something that is made by mixing together two or more substances: *cough mixture* ○ *Put the mixture into a baking dish and cook for half an hour.* **2** [sing] something that consists of several things that are different from one another: *I stood and stared with a mixture of amazement and horror.*

moan /məʊn/ *noun* [C] a low sound that you make if you are in pain or very sad

moan *verb* [I] **1** to make the sound of a moan: *to moan with pain* **2** (*informal*) to keep saying what is wrong about sth; to complain: *The English are always moaning about the weather.*

moat /məʊt/ *noun* [C] a deep ditch that was dug around a castle and filled with water in order to protect the castle

mob /mɒb/ *noun* [C, with sing or pl verb] a large crowd of people that may become violent or cause trouble: *The police used tear-gas to disperse the angry mob.*

mob *verb* [T] (**mo**bb**ing; mo**bb**ed**) to gather round sb, with a large crowd of people, because you are angry or are very interested in him/her: *The pop star was mobbed as he left the hotel.*

mobile /'məʊbaɪl; *US* -bl/ *adj* able to move or be moved easily: *My daughter is much more mobile now she has her own car.* ○ *a mobile phone* (= one that you can carry around with you) ☞ Look at **immobile**. —**mobility** /məʊ'bɪləti/ *noun* [U]

mobile 'home *noun* [C] a large caravan that sb lives in permanently (not just for holidays)

mobilize (*also* **mobilise**) /'məʊbɪlaɪz/ *verb* **1** [T] to organize sb/sth for a particular purpose: *They mobilized the local residents to oppose the new development.* **2** [I,T] to get ready for war

mock¹ /mɒk/ *verb* [I,T] (*formal*) to laugh at/sth in an unkind way or to make other people laugh at him/her ☞ **Laugh at** and **make fun of** are less formal and more common.

mock² /mɒk/ *adj* (only *before* a noun) not real or genuine: *We have mock* (= practice) *exams four months before the real ones.* ○ *The houses are built in a mock Georgian style.*

'mock-up *noun* [C] a model of sth that shows what the real thing looks like or how it will work

modal /'məʊdl/ (*also* **'modal verb**; **modal au'xiliary**) *noun* [C] a verb, eg 'might', 'can', 'must' that is used with another verb for expressing possibility, permission, necessity, etc

mode /məʊd/ *noun* (*formal*) a type of sth or way of doing sth: *a mode of transport* ○ *The mode of life in the village has not changed for 500 years.*

☆ **model¹** /'mɒdl/ *noun* [C] **1** a copy of sth that is usually smaller than the real thing: *a scale model of the railway station* ○ *a model aeroplane* **2** one of the machines, vehicles, etc that is made by a particular company: *The Ford Sierra has been a very popular model.* **3** a person or thing that is a good example to copy: *America's education system has been taken as a model by other countries.* **4** a person who is employed to wear clothes at a fashion show or for magazine photographs: *a male fashion model* **5** a person who is painted, drawn or photographed by an artist

☆ **model²** /'mɒdl/ *verb* (**modell**ing; **modell**ed; *US* **model**ing; **model**ed) **1** [T] to try to copy or be like sb/sth: *He modelled himself on his favourite teacher.* ○ *The house is modelled on the Palace of Versailles.* **2** [I,T] to wear and show clothes as a model¹(4): *to model swimsuits* **3** [I,T] to make a model¹(1) of sth

modelling (*US* **modeling**) *noun* [U] working as a model¹(4): *a career in modelling*

modem /'məʊdem/ *noun* [C] a piece of equipment that connects two or more computers together by means of a telephone line so that information can go from one to the other

☆ **moderate¹** /'mɒdərət/ *adj* **1** average or not very great in size, amount or degree: *a moderate speed* ○ *The change will affect thousands of people on moderate incomes.* **2** (used about a person's political opinions) not very different from those of most other people; not extreme: *to hold moderate views* ☞ Look at **extreme** and **radical**.

moderate /'mɒdərət/ *noun* [C] a person who has moderate political, etc opinions ☞ Look at **extremist**.

moderately *adv* not very; quite: *His career has been moderately successful.*

moderate² /'mɒdəreɪt/ *verb* [I,T] to become or to make sth less strong or extreme: *The stormy weather has moderated a little.*

moderation /ˌmɒdə'reɪʃn/ *noun* [U] the quality of being able to control your feelings or actions: *The people reacted violently but their leaders called for moderation.*

(IDIOM) **in moderation** within limits that are sensible: *Alcohol can harm unborn babies even if it's taken in moderation.*

☆ **modern** /'mɒdn/ *adj* **1** of the present or recent times: *Pollution is one of the major problems in the modern world.* ○ *Do you prefer modern or classical ballet?* ○ *Radar is very important in modern warfare.* ☞ Look at **ancient** and **traditional**. **2** with all the newest methods, equipment, buildings, etc: *It is one of the most modern hospitals in the country.* ☞ Look at **old-fashioned**.

modern 'language *noun* [C] a language that is spoken now

modernize (*also* **modernise**) /'mɒdənaɪz/ *verb* [I,T] to become or to make sth suitable for what is needed today: *The railway system is being modernized and high speed trains introduced.* —**modernization** (*also* **modernisa-**

iː	ɪ	e	æ	ɑː	ɒ	ɔː	ʊ	uː	ʌ
see	sit	ten	hat	arm	got	saw	put	too	cup

tion) /ˌmɒdənaɪˈzeɪʃn; US -nɪˈz-/ noun [U]: *The house is large but is in need of modernization.*

modest /ˈmɒdɪst/ adj **1** not having or expressing a high opinion of your own qualities or abilities: *She got the best results in the exam but she was too modest to tell anyone.* ☛ Look at **humble** and **proud**. **2** shy and easily embarrassed by anything that is connected with sex **3** not very large: *They live in a modest little house near the centre of town.* ○ *a modest increase in price* —**modestly** adv

modesty /ˈmɒdɪsti/ noun [U] the quality of being modest(1,2)

modify /ˈmɒdɪfaɪ/ verb [T] (pres part **modifying**; 3rd pers sing pres **modifies**; pt, pp **modified**) to change sth slightly: *We shall need to modify the existing plan.*

modification /ˌmɒdɪfɪˈkeɪʃn/ noun [C,U] a small change: *There have been some small modifications to our original design.*

module /ˈmɒdjuːl; US -dʒuːl/ noun [C] a unit that forms part of sth bigger: *The lunar module separated from the spacecraft to land on the moon.* ○ *You must complete three modules* (= courses that you study) *in your first year.*

mohair /ˈməʊheə(r)/ noun [U] very soft wool that comes from a type of goat

moist /mɔɪst/ adj slightly wet; damp: *Her eyes were moist with tears.* ○ *Keep the soil moist or the plant will die.* ☛ Look at the note at **wet**.

moisten /ˈmɔɪsn/ verb [I,T] to become or to make sth moist

moisture /ˈmɔɪstʃə(r)/ noun [U] water in small drops on a surface, in the air, etc

molar /ˈməʊlə(r)/ noun [C] one of the large teeth at the back of your mouth

mold (US) = MOULD¹,²

moldy (US) = MOULDY

mole¹ /məʊl/ noun [C] a small dark spot on a person's skin that never goes away ☛ Look at **freckle**.

mole² /məʊl/ noun [C] **1** a small animal with dark fur that lives underground and is almost blind **2** (informal) a person who works in one organization and gives secret information to another organization or country ☛ Look at **spy**.

'molehill noun [C] a small pile of earth that is made by a mole while it is digging underground

molecule /ˈmɒlɪkjuːl/ noun [C] the smallest unit into which a substance can be divided without changing its chemical nature. A molecule consists of one or more atoms.

molest /məˈlest/ verb [T] to seriously annoy sb or to attack sb in a sexual way

molt (US) = MOULT

molten /ˈməʊltən/ adj (used about metal or rock) made liquid by very great heat: *molten lava*

mom /mɒm/ noun [C] (US informal) = MUM

☆ **moment** /ˈməʊmənt/ noun **1** [C] a very short period of time: *Would you mind waiting for a moment?* ○ *He hesitated for a few moments and then knocked on the door.* **2** [sing] a particular point in time: *Just at that moment my mother arrived.* ○ *the moment of birth/death*

(IDIOMS) **(at) any minute/moment (now)** ⇨ MINUTE¹

at the moment now: *I'm afraid she's busy at the moment. Can I take a message?*

for the moment/present for a short time; for now: *I'm not very happy at work but I'll stay there for the moment.*

in a moment very soon: *Just wait here. I'll be back in a moment.*

the last minute/moment ⇨ LAST¹

the minute/moment (that) ⇨ MINUTE¹

momentary /ˈməʊməntri; US -teri/ adj lasting for a very short time: *a momentary lack of concentration*

momentarily /ˈməʊməntrəli; US ˌməʊmənˈterəli/ adv for a very short time

momentous /məˈmentəs; məʊˈm-/ adj very important: *There have been momentous changes in Eastern Europe in the last few years.*

momentum /məˈmentəm; məʊˈm-/ noun [U] strength or speed: *The ball gained momentum as it rolled downhill.* ○ *The environmental movement is gathering momentum.*

momma /ˈmɒmə/ (also **mommy** /ˈmɒmi/) noun [C] (US informal) = MUMMY¹

monarch /ˈmɒnək/ noun [C] a king or queen

monarchy /ˈmɒnəki/ noun (pl **monarchies**) **1** [sing,U] the system of government or rule by a monarch: *Should Britain abolish the monarchy?* **2** [C] a country that is governed by a monarch ☛ Look at **republic**.

monastery /ˈmɒnəstri; US -teri/ noun [C] (pl **monasteries**) a place where men (**monks**) live in a religious community ☛ Look at **convent**.

☆ **Monday** /ˈmʌndi/ noun [C,U] (abbr **Mon**) the day of the week after Sunday and before Tuesday: *I'm going to see her on Monday.* ○ *I'm going to see her Monday* (in American English and informal British English). ○ *We usually play badminton on Mondays/on a Monday.* ○ *They go to the youth club every Monday.* ○ *'What day is it today?' 'It's Monday.'* ○ *Monday morning/afternoon/evening/night* ○ *last/next Monday* ○ *the Monday before last* ○ *the Monday after next* ○ *a week on Monday/Monday week* (= not next Monday, but the Monday after that) ○ *The museum is open Monday to Friday, 10 till 4.30.* ○ *Did you see that article about Italy in Monday's paper?*

monetary /ˈmʌnɪtri; US -teri/ adj connected with money: *the government's monetary policy*

☆ **money** /ˈmʌni/ noun [U] the means of paying for sth or buying sth (= coins or notes): *How much money do you earn a week?* ○ *Young people spend a lot of money on clothes.* ○ *Our holiday cost an awful lot of money.* ○ *Don't change your money at the airport. They charge a lot there.* ○ *If we do the work ourselves we will save a lot of money.* ○ *to borrow/lend money* ○ *My father invested his money in stocks and shares.* ○ *Is this picture worth a lot of money?* ☛ Look also at **pocket money**.

(IDIOMS) **get your money's worth** to get full value for the money you have spent: *The meal was expensive but we got our money's worth because there were five courses.*

ɜː	ə	eɪ	əʊ	aɪ	aʊ	ɔɪ	ɪə	eə	ʊə
fur	ago	pay	home	five	now	join	near	hair	pure

money: cheque, credit card, cash, coin, note

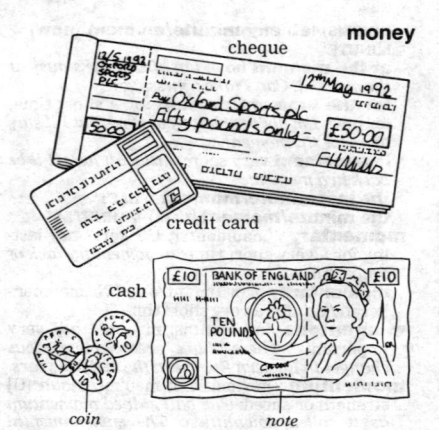

make money to earn money or to make a profit on a business

'money box noun [C] a box into which you put money that you want to save

mongrel /'mʌŋgrəl/ noun [C] a dog which has parents of different types (**breeds**)

monitor /'mɒnɪtə(r)/ noun [C] **1** a machine that shows information or pictures on a screen like a television ☛ picture on page A13. **2** a machine that records or checks sth: *A monitor checks the baby's heartbeat.* **3** a pupil who has a special job to do in the classroom

monitor verb [T] **1** to check, record or test sth regularly for a period of time: *Pollution levels in the lake are being monitored closely.* **2** to listen to and record foreign radio or television broadcasts

monk /mʌŋk/ noun [C] a man who has decided to leave the ordinary world and live a religious life in a community (**monastery**) ☛ Look at **nun**.

monkey

☆ **monkey** /'mʌŋki/ noun [C] (pl **monkeys**) a small, usually brown, animal with a long tail that lives in hot countries and can climb trees ☛ Look at **ape**. Chimpanzees and gorillas are apes, although people often call them monkeys.

mono /'mɒnəʊ/ adj (used about recorded music, etc, or a system for playing it) having the sound directed through one channel only ☛ Look at **stereo**. —**mono** noun [U]: *The concert was recorded in mono.*

monolingual /ˌmɒnə'lɪŋgwəl/ adj using only one language: *This is a monolingual dictionary.* ☛ Look at **bilingual**.

monologue (*US also* **monolog**) /'mɒnəlɒg; *US* -lɔːg/ noun [C] a long speech by one person, eg in a play

monopolize (*also* **monopolise**) /mə'nɒpəlaɪz/ verb [T] to control sth so that other people cannot have or use it: *She completely monopolized the conversation. I couldn't get a word in.*

monopoly /mə'nɒpəli/ noun [C] (pl **monopolies**) **1** the control of an industry or service by one company: *British Telecom had a monopoly on supplying telephone lines to people's houses.* **2** a company or organization that controls an industry: *British Rail was a state monopoly.*

monorail /'mɒnəʊreɪl/ noun [C] a railway in which the train runs on a single track

monosyllable /'mɒnəsɪləbl/ noun [C] a short word, such as 'leg', that has only one syllable

monotonous /mə'nɒtənəs/ adj boring and uninteresting because it does not change: *monotonous work* o *a monotonous voice* —**monotonously** adv

monotony /mə'nɒtəni/ noun [U] the state of being boring and uninteresting: *The monotony of the speaker's voice made us all feel sleepy.*

monsoon /ˌmɒn'suːn/ noun [C] the season of heavy rain in Southern Asia, or the wind which brings the rain

monster /'mɒnstə(r)/ noun [C] (in stories) a type of animal that is large, ugly and frightening: *Did you see the Loch Ness monster?* o *a story of dragons, serpents and other monsters* o (figurative) *The murderer was described as a dangerous monster.*

monstrous /'mɒnstrəs/ adj **1** very bad or unfair: *a monstrous crime* o *It's monstrous that she earns less than he does for the same job!* **2** very large (and often ugly or frightening): *a monstrous block of flats* o *a monstrous creature from the sea*

monstrosity /mɒn'strɒsəti/ noun [C] (pl **monstrosities**) something that is ugly (and usually very large): *That new building on the High Street is a monstrosity.*

☆ **month** /mʌnθ/ noun [C] **1** (*also* ,**calendar 'month**) one of the twelve periods of time into which the year is divided, eg January: *They are starting work next month.* o *We went on holiday last month.* o *The rent is £300 a month.* o *'When are the exams?' 'Later in the month.'* o *at the beginning/end of the month* **2** (*also* ,**calendar 'month**) the period of time from a certain date in one month to the same date in the next, eg 13 May to 13 June **3** a period of about four weeks: *'How long will you be away?' 'For about a month.'* o *a three-month course* o *The window cleaner will come again in a month/in a month's time.* o *I've got two children – the baby is six months old and I've also got a toddler of eighteen months.*

p	b	t	d	k	g	tʃ	dʒ	f	v	θ	ð
pen	bad	tea	did	cat	got	chin	June	fall	van	thin	then

monthly *adj, adv* (happening or produced) once a month or every month: *a monthly meeting* ○ *a monthly magazine* ○ *Are you paid weekly or monthly?*

monthly *noun* [C] (*pl* **monthlies**) a magazine that is published once a month

monument /'mɒnjʊmənt/ *noun* [C] **1** a building or statue that is built to remind people of a famous person or event **2** an old building or other place that is of historical importance: *Stonehenge is a famous ancient monument.*

monumental /ˌmɒnjʊ'mentl/ *adj* **1** (used about a building) very large and impressive **2** very great: *a monumental success*

moo /muː/ *noun* [C] the sound that a cow makes —**moo** *verb* [I]

☆ **mood** /muːd/ *noun* **1** [C,U] the way that you feel at a particular time, ie if you are happy, sad, etc: *Leave Dad alone for a while. He's in a very bad mood.* ○ *You're in a good mood today!* ○ *a sudden change of mood* ○ *Turn that music down a bit – I'm not in the mood for it.* **2** [C] a time when you are angry or bad-tempered: *Debby's in one of her moods again.* **3** [sing] the way that a group of people feel about sth: *The mood of the crowd changed and some stones were thrown.*

moody *adj* (**moodier; moodiest**) **1** having moods(1) that change often **2** bad-tempered or unhappy —**moodily** /-ɪli/ *adv* **moodiness** *noun* [U]

☆ **moon** /muːn/ *noun* **1 the moon** [sing] the object that shines in the sky at night and that moves round the earth once every 28 days: *The moon's very bright tonight.* ○ *When was the first landing on the moon?* ☛ You may see a **new moon**, a **full moon** or a **crescent moon**. **2** [C] an object like the moon that moves around another planet: *How many moons does Neptune have?*

(IDIOMS) **once in a blue moon** ⇨ ONCE

over the moon (*informal*) very pleased or happy

'moonlight *noun* [U] light that comes from the moon: *The lake looked beautiful in the moonlight.*

'moonlit *adj* having light from the moon: *a moonlit evening*

moor¹ /mɔː(r)/ *US* mʊər/ (*also* **moorland** /-lənd/) *noun* [C,U] a wild open area of high land that is covered with grass and other low plants

moor² /mɔː(r)/ *US* mʊər/ *verb* [I,T] to fasten a boat to the land or to an object in the water, with a rope or chain

mooring *noun* [C] a place where a boat is moored

moose /muːs/ *noun* [C] (*pl* **moose**) a type of large deer that comes from North America ☛ In northern Europe the same animal is called an **elk**.

mop /mɒp/ *noun* [C] a tool that is used for washing floors. A mop has a long handle and a bunch of thick strings or a sponge at the end.

mop *verb* [T] (**mop**ping; **mop**ped) **1** to clean sth with a mop **2** to remove liquid from sth using a dry cloth: *to mop your forehead with a handkerchief*

(PHRASAL VERB) **mop sth up** to clean unwanted liquid with a mop or dry cloth: *Mop up that tea you've spilt or it'll leave a stain!*

mope /məʊp/ *verb* [I] to feel unhappy and not try to do anything to make yourself feel better: *Moping in your room won't make the situation any better.*

moped /'məʊped/ *noun* [C] a type of small, not very powerful, motor cycle with pedals ☛ picture at **motor bike**.

☆ **moral¹** /'mɒrəl/ *US* mɔːrəl/ *adj* **1** concerned with what you believe is the right way to behave: *Some people refuse to eat meat on moral grounds* (= because they believe it to be wrong). ○ *Is the high divorce rate the result of declining moral standards?* ○ *the moral dilemma of whether or not abortion should be allowed* ○ *The state has a moral obligation to house homeless people.* **2** having high standards of behaviour: *She has always led a very moral life.* ☛ The opposite is **immoral**.

morally /-rəli/ *adv* **1** in a way that is good or right: *to behave morally* **2** connected with standards of what is right or wrong: *to be morally responsible for sb* (eg because it is your duty to look after them) ○ *What he did wasn't illegal but it was morally wrong.*

ˌmoral sup'port *noun* [U] help or encouragement that you give to sb (by being with him/her or saying that you agree with him/her): *I went to the dentist's with him just to give him some moral support.*

☆ **moral²** /'mɒrəl/ *US* mɔːrəl/ *noun* **1** [C] a lesson in the right way to behave that can be learnt from a story or from sth that happens: *The moral of the play is that friendship is more important than money.* **2 morals** [plural] standards or principles of good behaviour

morale /mə'rɑːl/ *US* -'ræl/ *noun* [U] the way that a group of people feel at a particular time: *The team's morale was high before the match* (= they were confident that they would win). ○ *Low pay in recent years has led to low morale.*

☆ **morality** /mə'rælətɪ/ *noun* [U] whether sth is right or wrong: *There was a lively debate about the morality of abortion.* ☛ The opposite is **immorality**.

moralize (*also* **moralise**) /'mɒrəlaɪz/ *US* mɔːr-/ *verb* [I] **moralize** (**about/on sth**) to talk or write about what is the right or wrong way to behave

morbid /'mɔːbɪd/ *adj* having or showing great interest in unpleasant things, eg disease and death

☆ **more¹** /mɔː(r)/ *det, pron* a larger number of people/things or larger amount of sth; sth in addition to what you already have: *There were more people than I expected.* ○ *I've bought some more plants for the garden.* ○ *We had more time than we thought.* ○ *There's room for three more people.* ○ *I couldn't eat any more.* ○ *Tell me more about your job.* ○ *I've found some more of those magazines you wanted.*

(IDIOM) **more and more** an increasing amount or number: *There are more and more cars on the road.*

☆ **more²** /mɔː(r)/ *adv* **1** (used to form the comparative of adjectives and adverbs with two or

s	z	ʃ	ʒ	h	m	n	ŋ	l	r	j	w
so	zoo	she	vision	how	man	no	sing	leg	red	yes	wet

more syllables): *He was more frightened than I was.* **2** *Please write more carefully.* **2** to a greater extent: *I like him more than his wife.* o *This one costs more.*

(IDIOMS) **not any/no more** not any longer: *She doesn't live here any more.*

more or less approximately; almost: *We are more or less the same age.*

what's more (used for adding another fact): *The hotel was awful and what's more it was miles from the hotel.*

☆ **moreover** /mɔːˈrəʊvə(r)/ *adv* (*formal*) (used, especially in writing, when you are giving some extra information that supports what you are saying) in addition; also: *This firm did the work very well. Moreover, the cost was not too high.*

morgue /mɔːg/ *noun* [C] a building where dead bodies are kept until they are buried or burned ☛ Look at **mortuary**.

☆ **morning** /ˈmɔːnɪŋ/ *noun* [C,U] **1** the early part of the day between the time when the sun rises and midday: *Pat's going to London tomorrow morning.* o *Pat stayed with us on Sunday night and went to London the next/the following morning.* o *I've been studying hard all morning.* o *Dave makes breakfast every morning.* o *She only works in the mornings. She's free in the afternoons.* o *morning coffee* o *the morning paper* **2** the part of the night that is after midnight: *I was woken by a strange noise in the the early hours of the morning.*

(IDIOMS) **good morning** (used when you see sb for the first time in the morning) ☛ Often we just say **Morning**: *'Good morning, Mrs Stevenson.' 'Morning, Mr Johnson.'*

in the morning 1 during the morning of the next day; tomorrow morning: *I'll try to speak to her about it in the morning.* **2** not in the afternoon or evening: *The time of death was about 10.30 in the morning.*

☛ When you use the adjectives *early* or *late* before 'morning', 'afternoon' or 'evening' you must use the preposition **in**: *The accident happened in the early morning.* o *We arrived in the late afternoon.* With other adjectives, use **on**: *School starts on Monday morning.* o *They set out on a cold, windy afternoon.* o *The accident happened on the following evening.* No preposition is used before *this, tomorrow, yesterday*: *Let's go swimming this morning.* o *I'll phone Liz tomorrow evening.* o *We went to the zoo yesterday afternoon.*

moron /ˈmɔːrɒn/ *noun* [C] (*informal*) a very foolish or stupid person —**moronic** /məˈrɒnɪk/ *adj*

morose /məˈrəʊs/ *adj* bad-tempered, and not saying much to other people

morphine /ˈmɔːfiːn/ *noun* [U] a drug made from opium that is used for reducing pain

morsel /ˈmɔːsl/ *noun* [C] a very small piece

mortal /ˈmɔːtl/ *adj* **1** not living forever: *We are all mortal.* ☛ The opposite is **immortal**. **2** that will result in death: *a mortal wound* ☛ Look at **fatal**, which is more common. **3** very great or extreme: *They were in mortal fear of the enemy.*

mortal *noun* [C] a human being

mortally /-təli/ *adv* **1** in a way that will result in death: *to be mortally wounded* **2** very; extremely

mortality /mɔːˈtæləti/ *noun* [U] **1** the fact that nobody can live forever **2** the number of deaths in a certain period of time or in a certain place: *Infant mortality is high in the region.*

mortar¹ /ˈmɔːtə(r)/ *noun* [U] a mixture of cement, sand and water that you put between bricks when you are building sth

mortar² /ˈmɔːtə(r)/ *noun* [C] a type of heavy gun

mortgage /ˈmɔːgɪdʒ/ *noun* [C] money that you borrow in order to buy a house: *We took out a £40 000 mortgage.* o *mortgage repayments*

☛ You usually borrow money from a **bank** or a **building society**, who decide what **rate** of **interest** you must pay on the **loan**.

mortician /mɔːˈtɪʃn/ *noun* [C] (*US*) = UNDERTAKER

mortuary /ˈmɔːtʃəri; *US* mɔːtʃʊeri/ *noun* [C] (*pl* **mortuaries**) a place in a hospital, etc where dead bodies are kept before they are buried or burned ☛ Look at **morgue**.

mosaic /məʊˈzeɪɪk/ *noun* [C,U] a picture or pattern that is made by placing together small coloured stones, pieces of glass, etc

Moslem = MUSLIM

mosque /mɒsk/ *noun* [C] a building where Muslims worship

☆ **mosquito** /məsˈkiːtəʊ; *Brit also* mɒs-/ *noun* [C] (*pl* **mosquitoes**) a small flying insect found in hot countries. Mosquitoes bite people and animals in order to suck their blood and some types of mosquito spread a very serious disease (**malaria**).

moss /mɒs; *US* mɔːs/ *noun* [C,U] a small green plant, with no flowers, that grows in a flat mass in damp places, especially on rocks or trees

☆ **most¹** /məʊst/ *det, pron* (used as the superlative of *many, much*) **1** greatest in number or amount: *Who picked the most apples?* o *The children had the most fun.* o *We all worked hard but I did the most.* **2** nearly all of a group of people or things: *Most families in this country have a television.* o *I like most Italian food.* ☛ When **most** is followed by a noun which has **the, this, my,** etc before it, we must use **most of**: *Most of the people I invited were able to come.* o *It rained most of the time we were in Ireland.*

(IDIOMS) **at (the) most** not more than a certain number, and probably less: *There were 20 people there, at the most.*

make the most of sth ⇨ MAKE¹

mostly *adv* **1** almost all: *The people at work are mostly very nice.* **2** usually: *We mostly go shopping in Oxford, not Reading.*

☆ **most²** /məʊst/ *adv* **1** (used to form the superlative of adjectives and adverbs that have two or more syllables): *It's the most beautiful house I've ever seen.* o *I think this machine works the most efficiently.* **2** more than anybody/anything else: *What do you miss most when you're abroad?* **3** (*formal*) very: *We heard a most interesting talk about Japan.*

motel /məʊˈtel/ *noun* [C] a hotel for people who

iː	ɪ	e	æ	ɑː	ɒ	ɔː	ʊ	uː	ʌ
see	sit	ten	hat	arm	got	saw	put	too	cup

moth /mɒθ; *US* mɔːθ/ *noun* [C] an insect like a butterfly that usually flies at night. Moths do not have such bright colours as butterflies. ☛ picture at **butterfly**.

'mothball *noun* [C] a small ball made of a chemical substance that protects clothes in cupboards from moths

☆ **mother** /'mʌðə(r)/ *noun* [C] the female parent of a person or animal: *an expectant mother* ○ *an unmarried mother* ○ *a foster mother* ○ *Working mothers need good child-care arrangements.* ○ *a mother cow and her calf* ☛ Look at **mum, mummy** and **stepmother**.

mother *verb* [T] to care for sb as a mother does: *He looked so young and helpless. All the women in the office tried to mother him.*

motherhood /-hʊd/ *noun* [U] the state of being a mother

motherless *adj* having no mother

motherly *adj* of a mother or like a mother: *She's a motherly sort of person.*

'mother country *noun* [C] (*formal*) the country where a person was born or grew up

'mother-in-law *noun* [C] (*pl* **mothers-in-law**) the mother of your husband or wife

'mother tongue *noun* [C] the first language that you learned to speak as a child

motif /məʊ'tiːf/ *noun* [C] a picture or pattern on sth: *The blouse has a butterfly motif on each sleeve.*

motion /'məʊʃn/ *noun* **1** [U] movement or a way of moving: *The swaying motion of the ship made us all feel sick.* ○ *Pull the lever to set the machine in motion.* ☛ Look at **slow motion**. **2** [C] a suggestion that you discuss and vote at a meeting: *The motion was carried/rejected by a majority of eight votes.*

motion *verb* [T] to make a movement that tells sb what to do: *The manager motioned me to sit down.*

motionless *adj* not moving

motivate /'məʊtɪveɪt/ *verb* [T] **1** to cause sb to act in a particular way: *Her reaction was motivated by fear.* ○ *The attack was politically motivated.* **2** to make sb want to do sth (by making it interesting): *Our new teacher certainly knows how to motivate his classes.* —**motivated** *adj*: *highly motivated students*

motivation /ˌməʊtɪ'veɪʃn/ *noun* [C,U] the need or reason for doing sth; a feeling of interest in doing sth: *I'm suffering from a lack of motivation. My new job is really boring.*

motive /'məʊtɪv/ *noun* [C,U] a reason for doing sth: *Nobody seemed to have a motive for the murder.*

☆ **motor** /'məʊtə(r)/ *noun* [C] a machine that changes power into movement: *The washing-machine doesn't work. I think something is wrong with the motor.* ○ *to start/turn off a motor* ☛ **Engine**, not **motor**, is usually used in connection with cars and motor cycles, but sometimes **motor** is also used. Cars are, in fact, sometimes called **motor cars**. **Engines** generally use petrol and **motors** use electricity.

motor *adj* (only *before* a noun) connected with vehicles that have an engine or a motor: *a motor boat* ○ *motor racing* ○ *a motor mechanic*

motoring /'məʊtərɪŋ/ *noun* [U] driving in a car: *to commit a motoring offence* ○ *a motoring holiday*

motorist /'məʊtərɪst/ *noun* [C] a person who drives a car ☛ Look at **pedestrian**.

motorized (*also* **motorised**) /'məʊtəraɪzd/ *adj* having an engine: *motorized transport*

scooter

moped

motor bike

'motor bike (*also* **'motor cycle**) *noun* [C] (*informal*) a large bicycle with an engine

'motor boat *noun* [C] a small fast boat that has an engine ☛ picture at **boat**.

'motor car *noun* [C] (*Brit formal*) = CAR(1)

'motor cycle *noun* [C] = MOTOR BIKE

'motor cyclist *noun* [C] a person who rides a motor cycle

motorway (*US* **expressway; freeway**) *noun* [C] a wide road that is specially built for fast traffic: *to join/leave a motorway* ○ *a motorway service station*

☛ A motorway has two or three **lanes** on each **carriageway**. On the left of each carriageway there is a **hard shoulder**. Look at the note at **road**.

motto /'mɒtəʊ/ *noun* [C] (*pl* **mottoes**) a short sentence that expresses a rule for a person's or an organization's behaviour: *My motto is: 'It could be worse'.* ○ *Everton Football Club's motto means: 'Nothing but the best'.*

mould¹ (*US* **mold**) /məʊld/ *noun* **1** [C] a hollow container that you use for making sth into a particular shape. You put a liquid substance into a mould and wait for it to become solid (**set**) in the shape of the mould. **2** [sing] a particular type (of person): *She doesn't fit into the usual mould of sales directors.*

mould *verb* [T] to make sth into a particular shape or form

mould² (*US* **mold**) /məʊld/ *noun* [U] a soft green substance (a type of fungus) that grows in warm, damp places or on food that has been kept too long —**mouldy** (*US* **moldy**) *adj*: *The cheese had gone mouldy.*

moult (*US* **molt**) /məʊlt/ *verb* [I] (used about an animal or bird) to lose hair or feathers

mound /maʊnd/ *noun* [C] **1** a large pile of earth; a small hill **2** a pile or heap of things: *I've got a mound of papers to work through.*

mount¹ /maʊnt/ *noun* [C] (*abbr* **Mt**) (used in names) a mountain: *Mt Everest*

☆ **mount²** /maʊnt/ *verb* **1** [T] (*formal*) to go to the top of sth: *to mount the stairs* ○ *He mounted the platform and began to speak.* **2** [I,T] to get on a horse or bicycle ☞ The opposite is **dismount**. **3** [I] to increase in level or amount: *The tension mounted as the end of the match approached.* **4** [T] to fix sth on or in sth else: *The gas boiler was mounted on the wall.* **5** [T] to organize sth: *to mount an exhibition* ○ *to mount an attack* (PHRASAL VERB) **mount up (to sth)** to increase (often more than you want): *When you're buying food for six people the cost soon mounts up.*

mounted *adj* riding a horse: *mounted police*

mounting *adj* increasing: *mounting unemployment*

☆ **mountain** /'maʊntɪn; *US* -ntn/ *noun* [C] **1** a very high hill: *Which is the highest mountain in the world?* ○ *Have you ever climbed a mountain?* ○ *a steep mountain road* ○ *a range of mountains* **2** a large amount of sth: *There is a mountain of unanswered letters on her desk.*

mountaineer /ˌmaʊntɪ'nɪə(r); *US* -ntn'ɪər/ *noun* [C] a person who climbs mountains

mountaineering /ˌmaʊntɪ'nɪərɪŋ; *US* -ntn'ɪə-/ *noun* [U] the sport of climbing mountains

mountainous /'maʊntɪnəs; *US* -ntnəs/ *adj* **1** having many mountains: *mountainous countryside* **2** very large: *The mountainous waves made sailing impossible.*

'mountainside *noun* [C] one of the steep sides of a mountain

mourn /mɔːn/ *verb* [I,T] **mourn (for/over sb/sth)** to feel great sadness, especially because sb has died: *She is still mourning for her child.*

mourner *noun* [C] a person who goes to a funeral as a friend or relative of the person who has died

mournful /-fl/ *adj* sad: *a mournful song* —**mournfully** /-fəli/ *adv*

mourning *noun* [U] a time when people feel or show great sadness because sb has died: *He wore a black armband to show he was in mourning.*

☆ **mouse** /maʊs/ *noun* [C] (*pl* **mice** /maɪs/) **1** a small furry animal with a long tail: *The cat has caught a mouse.* ○ *a field-mouse* ☞ Mice, like **rats**, **hamsters**, etc are members of the **rodent** family. **2** a piece of equipment, attached to a computer, for entering commands without using the keyboard ☞ picture on page A13. The mouse controls the **cursor** when you **click** on it.

mousse /muːs/ *noun* [C,U] a type of food that is made by beating together cream and eggs with either sth sweet (eg chocolate) or sth savoury (eg fish): *a chocolate mousse* ○ *salmon mousse*

moustache/beard

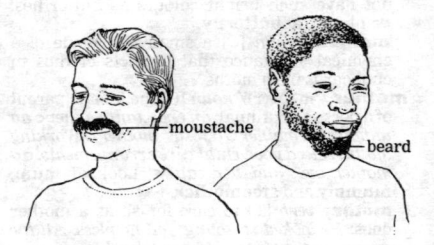

☆ **moustache** /mə'stɑːʃ/ (*US* **mustache** /'mʌstæʃ/) *noun* [C] hair that grows on the top lip, between the mouth and the nose: *Has he got a moustache?*

☆ **mouth¹** /maʊθ/ *noun* [C] (*pl* **mouths** /maʊðz/) **1** the part of your face that you use for eating and speaking: *Don't speak with your mouth full.* ○ *Open your mouth, please!* ○ *You can close your mouth now.* ○ *Keep your mouth closed when you're eating.* ○ (*figurative*) *They have a low income and five mouths to feed.* **2** the place where a river enters the sea

-mouthed /maʊðd/ (in compounds) **1** having a particular type of mouth: *We stared open-mouthed in surprise.* **2** having a particular way of speaking: *He's loud-mouthed and ill-mannered.*

mouthful /-fʊl/ *noun* **1** [C] the amount of food or drink that you can put in your mouth at one time **2** [sing] a word or phrase that is long or difficult to say

'mouth-organ (*also* **harmonica**) *noun* [C] a small musical instrument that you play by moving it across your lips while you are blowing

'mouthpiece *noun* [C] **1** the part of a telephone, musical instrument, etc that you put in or near your mouth **2** a person, newspaper, etc that a particular group uses to express its opinions: *Pravda was the mouthpiece of the Soviet government.*

'mouthwash *noun* [U] liquid that you use for cleaning your mouth and making it smell nice

'mouthwatering *adj* (used about food) that looks or smells very good

mouth² /maʊð/ *verb* [I,T] to move your mouth as if you were speaking but without making any sound

movable /'muːvəbl/ *adj* that can be moved ☞ Look at **portable**.

☆ **move¹** /muːv/ *noun* [C] **1** a change of place or position: *She sat watching every move I made.* ○ *One false move and I'll shoot!* **2** a change in the place where you live or work: *a move to a bigger house* ○ *I've been in the job for six years and feel it's time for a move.* **3** action that you take because you want to achieve a particular result: *Moves are being made to secure the release of the hostages.* ○ *Both sides want to negotiate but neither is prepared to make the first move.* ○ *Asking him to help me was a good*

p	b	t	d	k	g	tʃ	dʒ	f	v	θ	ð
pen	bad	tea	did	cat	got	chin	June	fall	van	thin	then

move 409 **muddle**

move. **4** a change in the position of a piece in a game like chess
(IDIOM) **get a move on** (*informal*) to hurry: *I'm late. I'll have to get a move on.*

☆ **move²** /muːv/ *verb* **1** [I,T] to change position or to put sth in a different position: *Don't move – there's a bee on your arm.* ○ *Please move your car. It's blocking the drive.* ○ *I thought I heard something moving in the bushes over there.* ○ *They are moving the patient to another hospital.* **2** [I] to go and live in another house, etc: *Our neighbours have sold their house and are moving next week.* **3** [I] to change or make progress: *When the new team of builders arrived things started moving very quickly.* **4** [T] to cause sb to have strong feelings (often of sadness): *The reports about the starving children moved many people to tears.* **5** [I] to take action: *Unless we move quickly lives will be lost.* **6** [I,T] to change the position of a piece in a game like chess
(IDIOMS) **get moving** to go, leave or do sth quickly
get sth moving to cause sth to make progress
move house to move your furniture, etc to another home
(PHRASAL VERBS) **move across/along/down/over/up** to move further in a particular direction in order to make space for sb/sth else: *The conductor asked the passengers to move down the bus.*
move in to start living in a new house
move off (used about a vehicle) to start a journey; to leave: *Maria waved from the window as the train moved off.*
move out to stop living in a house

moving *adj* **1** (only *before* a noun) that moves: *a moving staircase* ○ *It's a computerized machine with few moving parts.* **2** causing strong feelings: *The film is a moving story about a young boy's fight against cancer.*

☆ **movement** /ˈmuːvmənt/ *noun* **1** [C,U] an action that involves changing position or place or using the body in some way: *The dancer's movements were smooth and beautifully controlled.* ○ *The man lay still in the long grass, knowing that any movement would be seen by the police.* ○ *the slow movement of the clouds across the sky* **2** [C, usually sing] **a movement (away from/towards sth)** a general change in the way people think or behave: *There's a slight movement away from the materialism of the 1980s.* **3 movements** [plural] a person's actions or plans during a period of time: *Detectives have been watching the man's movements for several days.* **4** [C] a group of people who have the same aims or ideas (and who want to persuade other people that they are right): *I support the Animal Rights movement.* **5** [C] one of the main parts of a long piece of music: *a symphony in four movements*

movie /ˈmuːvi/ *noun* (*especially US*) **1** [C] = FILM¹(1): *Would you like to see a movie?* ○ *a science fiction movie* ○ *a movie director* **2 the movies** [plural] = CINEMA: *Let's go to the movies.*

mow /məʊ/ *verb* [I,T] (*pt* **mowed**; *pp* **mown** /məʊn/ or **mowed**) to cut grass using a machine or an instrument: *You need to mow the lawn at least once a week.*
mower *noun* [C] a machine for cutting grass or crops: *a lawnmower* ○ *an electric mower*

☆ **Mr** /ˈmɪstə(r)/ (used as a title before the name of a man): *Mr (John) Brown*

☆ **Mrs** /ˈmɪsɪz/ (used as a title before the name of a married woman): *Mrs (Jane) Brown*

☆ **Ms** /məz; mɪz/ (used as a title before the name of a woman, either married or unmarried): *Ms (Joan) Smith* ☛ Some women prefer the title **Ms** to **Mrs** or **Miss**. We can also use it when we do not know whether or not a woman is married.

☆ **much¹** /mʌtʃ/ *det, pron* (used with uncountable nouns, mainly in negative sentences and questions, or after *as, how, so, too*) a large amount of sth: *I haven't got much money.* ○ *Did you have much difficulty finding the house?* ○ *You've given me too much food.* ○ *How much time have you got?* ○ (*formal*) *I have much pleasure in introducing our speaker.* ○ *I didn't write much.* ○ *Did she say much?* ○ *How much do you want?* ○ *Eat as much as you can.* ○ *'Is there any post?' 'Not much.'* ☛ In statements we usually use **a lot of**, not **much** (which is extremely formal): *I've got a lot of experience.*
(IDIOMS) **not much of a...** not very good: *She's not much of a cook.*
not up to much ⇨ UP

☆ **much²** /mʌtʃ/ *adv* **1** to a great extent or degree: *I don't like her very much.* ○ *We are very much looking forward to meeting you.* ○ *Do you go to the cinema much?* (= very often) ○ *Their house is much nicer than ours.* ○ *You ate much more than me.* **2** (with past participles used as adjectives) to a great extent or degree: *a much-needed rest* ○ *She was much loved by all her friends.* ☛ Compare: *She was* **very** *popular*.
(IDIOMS) **much the same** very similar: *Polish food is much the same as German.*
not much good (at sth) not very good: *I'm not much good at singing.*

muck¹ /mʌk/ *noun* [U] (*informal*) **1** dirt **2** the waste from farm animals, used to make the land more fertile ☛ A more common word is **manure**.

muck² /mʌk/ *verb*
(PHRASAL VERBS) **muck about/around** (*informal*) to behave in a silly way or to waste time: *Stop mucking around and come and help me!*
muck sth up (*informal*) to do sth badly; to spoil sth: *I was so nervous that I completely mucked up my interview.*

mucus /ˈmjuːkəs/ *noun* [U] (*formal*) a sticky substance that is produced in some parts of the body, especially the nose

☆ **mud** /mʌd/ *noun* [U] soft, wet earth: *He came home from the football match covered in mud.*
muddy *adj* (**muddier**; **muddiest**) full of or covered in mud: *Take those muddy boots off at the door!* ○ *It's very muddy down by the river.*
'mudguard *noun* [C] a metal or plastic cover over the wheel of a bicycle, etc which stops mud and water from splashing up

muddle /ˈmʌdl/ *verb* [T] **1 muddle sth (up)** to put things in the wrong place or order or to

s	z	ʃ	ʒ	h	m	n	ŋ	l	r	j	w
so	zoo	she	vision	how	man	no	sing	leg	red	yes	wet

muesli — **murder**

make them untidy: *Try not to get those papers muddled up – I've got them all in the right order.* **2 muddle sb (up)** to confuse sb: *Stop muddling me up! I can only answer one question at a time.*

muddle *noun* [C,U] a state of disorder or confusion, in a place or in the mind: *Your room's in a terrible muddle.* ○ *I don't know who's responsible for all the muddle there's been.* ○ *I'm in a complete muddle! Is it Thursday or Friday?*

muddled *adj* not clear; confused: *He gave me a rather muddled explanation.*

muesli /'mju:zli/ *noun* [U] food made of grains, nuts, dried fruit, etc that you eat with milk for breakfast

muffle /'mʌfl/ *verb* [T] to make a sound quieter and more difficult to hear: *He put his hand over her mouth to muffle her cries.*

muffled *adj* (used about sounds) difficult to hear; quiet or not clear: *I could hear muffled voices outside but I couldn't tell what they were saying.*

muffled up *adj* wrapped up in warm clothes
muffler (*US*) = SILENCER

mug¹ /mʌg/ *noun* [C] a deep cup with straight sides, used without a saucer; the contents of a mug: *Would you prefer a cup or a mug?* ○ *a mug of coffee* ☞ picture at **cup**.

mug² /mʌg/ *verb* [T] (**mugging**; **mugged**) to attack and rob sb in the street

mugger *noun* [C] a person who attacks sb in this way

mugging *noun* [C,U] an occasion when a person is mugged

mug³ /mʌg/ *noun* [C] (*informal*) a stupid person who is easy to trick or deceive

muggy /'mʌgi/ *adj* (used about the weather) too warm and damp

mule /mju:l/ *noun* [C] an animal that has a horse and a donkey as its parents: *to be as stubborn as a mule*

☞ We say that a mule is a **cross** between a horse and a donkey.

mull /mʌl/ *verb*
(PHRASAL VERB) **mull sth over** to think about sth carefully and for a long time: *Don't ask me for a decision right now. I'll have to mull it over.*

multilateral /ˌmʌltɪˈlætərəl/ *adj* involving more than two groups of people, countries, etc: *a multilateral agreement* ☞ Look at **unilateral**.

multinational /ˌmʌltɪˈnæʃnəl/ *adj* involving many countries

multinational *noun* [C] a company that has offices or factories in many countries

multiple /'mʌltɪpl/ *adj* involving many people or having many parts, types, etc: *a multiple crash on the motorway* ○ *to receive multiple injuries*

multiple *noun* [C] a number that contains another number an exact number of times: *12, 18 and 24 are multiples of 6.*

multiple-'choice *adj* (used about examination questions) showing several different answers from which you have to choose the right one

multiple scle'rosis *noun* [U] (*abbr* **MS**) a serious disease which slowly causes you to lose control of your body and of the ability to move

multiplication /ˌmʌltɪplɪˈkeɪʃn/ *noun* [U] the process of multiplying a number: *The children will be tested on addition, subtraction and multiplication and division.*

☆ **multiply** /'mʌltɪplaɪ/ *verb* (*pres part* **multiplying**; *3rd pers sing pres* **multiplies**; *pt, pp* **multiplied**) **1** [I,T] **multiply A by B; multiply A and B (together)** to increase a number by the number of times mentioned: *to learn to multiply and divide* ○ *2 multiplied by 4 makes 8* (2 × 4 = 8) ○ *What do you get if you multiply 13 and 11?* ○ *Multiply the two numbers together and you should get the answer.* **2** [I,T] to become bigger or greater; to make sth bigger or greater; to increase: *Our profits have multiplied over the last two years.* ○ *Using this method, you can multiply your profit in a very short time.* **3** [I] (used especially about animals) to increase in number by producing large numbers of young

multitude /'mʌltɪtju:d; *US* -tu:d/ *noun* [C] (*formal*) a very large number of people or things: *a multitude of difficulties*

mum /mʌm/ (*US* **mom** /mɒm/) *noun* [C] (*informal*) mother: *Is that your mum?* ○ *What's for tea, Mum?* ☞ Look at **mummy**.

mumble /'mʌmbl/ *verb* [I,T] to speak quietly without opening your mouth properly, so that people cannot really hear the words: *I can't hear if you mumble – speak up!* ○ *Last night you kept mumbling something about a car crash in your sleep.* ☞ Look at **mutter**.

☆ **mummy¹** /'mʌmi/ *noun* [C] (*pl* **mummies**) (*US* **mommy** /*US* 'mɒmi/) (*informal*) (used by or to children) mother: *Here comes your mummy now.*

mummy² /'mʌmi/ *noun* [C] (*pl* **mummies**) a dead body of a person or animal which has been preserved by rubbing it with special oils and wrapping it in cloth: *an Egyptian mummy*

mumps /mʌmps/ *noun* [U] an infectious disease, especially of children. Mumps causes the neck and lower face to swell: *to have/catch (the) mumps* ○ *Mumps usually lasts for about one week.*

munch /mʌntʃ/ *verb* [I,T] to eat steadily. You usually munch sth hard, that makes a noise as you chew it: *He sat there munching an apple and didn't say a word.*

mundane /mʌnˈdeɪn/ *adj* ordinary; not interesting or exciting: *a mundane life, job, conversation, etc*

municipal /mju:ˈnɪsɪpl/ *adj* connected with a town or city that has its own local government: *municipal buildings* (= the town hall, public library, etc)

munitions /mju:ˈnɪʃnz/ *noun* [plural] military supplies, especially bombs and guns

mural /'mjʊərəl/ *noun* [C] a large picture which is painted on a wall

☆ **murder** /'mɜːdə(r)/ *noun* **1** [C,U] the crime of killing a person illegally and on purpose: *It is thought that both murders were committed by the same person.* ○ *He was sentenced to life imprisonment for murder.* ○ *the murder victim* ○ *the murder weapon* **2** [U] (*informal*) a very dif-

murky   411   **mutiny**

ficult or unpleasant experience: *It's murder trying to work when it's as hot as this.*

murder *verb* [T] to kill a person illegally and on purpose: *It seems that she was murdered with a knife.* ☛ Look at the note at **kill**.

murderer /'mɜːdərə(r)/ (*feminine* **murderess** /'mɜːdərɪs/) *noun* [C] a person who has murdered sb

murderous /'mɜːdərəs/ *adj* likely to murder or capable of murder

murky /'mɜːki/ *adj* (**murkier; murkiest**) dark and unpleasant or dirty: *The water in the river looked very murky.*

murmur /'mɜːmə(r)/ *noun* **1** [C] the sound of words that are spoken quietly: *A murmur of disagreement ran round the room.* **2** [sing] a low, gentle, continuous sound that is often not very clear: *the murmur of the wind in the trees*

murmur *verb* [I,T] to say sth in a low quiet voice: *'I love you,' he murmured.* ○ *Samantha murmured an answer.*

☆ **muscle** /'mʌsl/ *noun* [C,U] a piece of flesh inside the body which you can tighten or relax to produce movement: *Don't carry such heavy weights or you'll pull* (= damage) *a muscle.* ○ *Riding a bicycle is good for developing the leg muscles.* ○ *The heart is made of muscle.*

muscular /'mʌskjʊlə(r)/ *adj* **1** connected with muscles: *muscular pain* **2** having large strong muscles: *a muscular body*

☆ **museum** /mju:'zɪəm/ *noun* [C] a building where collections of valuable and interesting objects are kept and shown to the public: *Have you been to the Science Museum in London?* ○ *There's an exhibition of dinosaurs at the Natural History Museum.*

mushroom /'mʌʃrʊm; -ruːm/ *noun* [C] a type of plant (**a fungus**) which grows very quickly, has a flat rounded top on a short stem and can be eaten as a vegetable: *mushrooms with garlic* ○ *mushroom soup* ☛ A mushroom is a type of **fungus**. Some, but not all, **fungi** can be eaten. **Toadstool** is another name for some types of poisonous fungi.

☆ **music** /'mjuːzɪk/ *noun* [U] **1** an arrangement of sounds in patterns to be sung or played on instruments: *What sort of music do you like?* ○ *classical, folk, pop, rock, etc music* ○ *Who composed this piece of music?* ○ *That poem has been set to music.* ○ *a music lover* ○ *a music lesson* **2** the written signs that represent the sounds of music: *Can you read music?* ○ *I've forgotten my music – can I share yours?*

☆ **musical** /'mjuːzɪkl/ *adj* **1** connected with music: *musical instruments* (= the piano, the violin, the trumpet, etc) ○ *Would you like our programme of this month's musical events?* **2** interested in or good at music: *He's very musical.* ○ *a musical child* **3** pleasant to listen to because it is like music: *a musical voice*

musical *noun* [C] a play or film which has singing and dancing in it: *'Cats' is one of the most successful musicals ever produced.*

☆ **musician** /mju:'zɪʃn/ *noun* [C] **1** a person whose job is to play a musical instrument: *The band consists of ten musicians.* **2** a person who is good at writing or playing music: *At ten he was already a fine musician.*

☆ **Muslim** /'mʊzlɪm; *US* 'mʌzləm/ (*also* **Moslem** /'mɒzləm/) *noun* [C] a person whose religion is Islam —**Muslim** (*also* **Moslem**) *adj*: *Muslim traditions, beliefs, etc*

mussel /'mʌsl/ *noun* [C] a type of sea animal that lives inside a black shell and can be eaten ☛ picture at **shellfish**.

☆ **must** /məst; *strong form* mʌst/ *modal verb* (*negative* **must not**; *short form* **mustn't** /'mʌsnt/) **1** (used for saying that it is necessary that sth happens): *I must remember to go to the bank today.* ○ *Cars mustn't park in front of the entrance.* ○ *You mustn't take photographs in here. It's forbidden.* ○ *'Must we finish this exercise today?' 'Yes, you must.'* ☛ The negative for the last example is *'No, you don't have to'.* **2** (used for giving sb advice): *You really must see that film. It's wonderful.* **3** (used for saying that you are sure that sth is true): *Have something to eat. You must be hungry.* ○ *There's a lot of noise from next door. They must be having a party.* ○ *I can't find my cheque book. I must have left it at home.* ○ *It must have been a great shock when your mother died.* ○ *That car that passed us must have been doing 100 miles an hour.*

must *noun* [C] a thing that is absolutely necessary, or that must be seen, done, etc: *This book is a must for all science-fiction fans.*

mustache (*US*) = MOUSTACHE

mustard /'mʌstəd/ *noun* [U] a yellow or brown sauce which is made from the seeds of the mustard plant. The sauce has a very strong taste and is eaten in very small amounts, usually with meat.

musty /'mʌsti/ *adj* having an unpleasant stale or damp smell: *The rooms in the old house were dark and musty.*

mutant /'mjuːtənt/ *noun* [C] a living thing that is different from other living things of the same type because of a change in its basic (**genetic**) structure

mutation /mju:'teɪʃn/ *noun* [C,U] a change in the basic structure of a developing or living thing; an example of such a change: *mutations caused by radiation*

muted /'mjuːtɪd/ *adj* **1** (used about colours or sounds) not bright or loud; soft **2** (used about a feeling or reaction) not strong or not openly expressed: *muted criticism* ○ *a muted response*

mutilate /'mjuːtɪleɪt/ *verb* [T] (usually passive) to damage sb's body very badly, often by cutting off parts: *The body was too badly mutilated to be identified.* —**mutilation** /ˌmjuːtɪ'leɪʃn/ *noun* [C,U]

mutiny /'mjuːtɪni/ *noun* [C,U] (*pl* **mutinies**) an act that involves a group of people, especially sailors or soldiers, refusing to obey the person who is in command: *There'll be a mutiny if conditions don't improve.*

mutiny *verb* [I] (*pres part* **mutinying**; *3rd pers*

ɜː	ə	eɪ	əʊ	aɪ	aʊ	ɔɪ	ɪə	eə	ʊə
fur	ago	pay	home	five	now	join	near	hair	pure

sing pres **mutinies**; *pt, pp* **mutinied**) **mutiny (against sb/sth)** to refuse to obey your leader or to accept sth

mutter /ˈmʌtə(r)/ *verb* [I,T] to speak in a low, quiet and sometimes rather angry voice that is difficult to hear: *He muttered something about being late for an appointment and left the room.*

mutton /ˈmʌtn/ *noun* [U] the meat from an adult sheep: *a leg/shoulder of mutton* ☛ Look at the note at **meat**.

mutual /ˈmjuːtʃuəl/ *adj* **1** (used about a feeling or an action) felt or done by both or all the people involved: *We have a mutual agreement* (= we both agree) *to help each other out when necessary.* ○ *I just can't stand her and I'm sure the feeling is mutual* (= she doesn't like me either). **2** shared by two or more people: *We get on very well together because we have so many mutual interests.* ○ *It seems that Jane is a mutual friend of ours.* —**mutually** /-əli/ *adv*: *The statements of the two witnesses were mutually exclusive* (= they could not both be true).

muzzle /ˈmʌzl/ *noun* [C] **1** the nose and mouth of an animal (eg a dog or fox) **2** a cover made of leather or wire that is put over an animal's nose and mouth so that it cannot bite **3** the open end of a gun where the bullets come out

☆ **my** /maɪ/ *det* **1** of or belonging to me: *This is my husband, Jim.* ○ *It's my turn, not yours!* ○ *My favourite colour is blue.* **2** (used before a noun or adjective as a way of talking to sb): *My dear Anne, ...* ○ *Goodbye, my darling.* **3** (used in exclamations): *My goodness! Look at the time.*

☆ **myself** /maɪˈself/ *pron* **1** (used as the object of a verb or preposition when the person who does an action is also affected by it): *I saw myself in the mirror.* ○ *I felt rather pleased with myself.* **2** (used for emphasis): *I'll speak to her myself.* ○ *I myself don't agree.* ○ *I'll do it myself* (= if you don't want to do it for me).
(IDIOM) **(all) by myself 1** alone: *I live by myself.* ☛ Look at the note at **alone**. **2** without help: *I painted the house all by myself.*

☆ **mysterious** /mɪˈstɪəriəs/ *adj* **1** that you do not know about or cannot explain; strange: *Several people reported seeing mysterious lights in the sky.* **2** (used about a person) keeping sth secret or refusing to explain sth: *They're being very mysterious about where they're going this evening.* —**mysteriously** *adv*

☆ **mystery** /ˈmɪstəri/ *noun* (*pl* **mysteries**) **1** [C] a thing that you cannot understand or explain: *The cause of the accident is a complete mystery.* ○ *Detectives are still trying to solve the mystery of his disappearance.* ○ *It's a mystery to me what my daughter sees in her boyfriend.* ○ *It's one of the great mysteries of the natural world.* ○ *a mystery guest, tour, etc* (= one that you don't know anything about) **2** [U] the quality of being strange and secret and full of things that are difficult to explain: *novels full of mystery and suspense* ○ *a mystery story*

mystic /ˈmɪstɪk/ *noun* [C] a person who spends his/her life developing the spirit and communicating with God or a god

mystical /ˈmɪstɪkl/ (*also* **mystic** /ˈmɪstɪk/) *adj* of the spirit; involving hidden meaning, powers and feelings that are outside our normal everyday experience: *a mystical experience*

mysticism /ˈmɪstɪsɪzəm/ *noun* [U] the belief that you can reach complete truth and knowledge of God or gods by prayer, thought and development of the spirit

mystify /ˈmɪstɪfaɪ/ *verb* [T] (*pres part* **mystifying**; *3rd pers sing pres* **mystifies**; *pt, pp* **mystified**) to make sb puzzled or confused: *I was mystified by the strange note. What did it mean?*

myth /mɪθ/ *noun* [C] **1** a very old story, especially one about gods and heroes. Myths often explain natural or historical events. **2** an idea, belief or story which is untrue or impossible: *The idea that money makes you happy is a complete myth.*

mythical /ˈmɪθɪkl/ *adj* **1** existing only in myths(1): *mythical heroes* **2** not real; existing only in the imagination

mythology /mɪˈθɒlədʒi/ *noun* [U] very old stories and the beliefs contained in them: *Greek and Roman mythology*

Nn

N, n /en/ *noun* [C] (*pl* **N's** *or* **n's**) the fourteenth letter of the English alphabet: *'Nicolas' begins with (an) 'N'.*

nag /næg/ *verb* (**nagging**; **nagged**) **1** [I,T] **nag (at) sb** to talk to sb continuously in a complaining or critical way: *Stop nagging! I'll do it as soon as I can.* ○ *My parents are always nagging me about working harder.* **2** [T] to worry or hurt sb continuously: *a nagging doubt in my mind* ○ *a nagging headache*

☆ **nail** /neɪl/ *noun* [C] **1** a small thin piece of metal with a point at one end. It is used for holding pieces of wood together, hanging pictures on, etc: *We'll need some small nails, a hammer and some string.* ○ *to hammer in a nail* ☛ picture at **tool**. **2** the thin hard layer that covers the ends of your fingers and toes: *fingernails* ○ *toenails* ○ *I still bite my nails sometimes when I'm nervous.* ☛ picture on page A8.
(IDIOM) **hit the nail on the head** ⇒ HIT¹

p	b	t	d	k	g	tʃ	dʒ	f	v	θ	ð
pen	bad	tea	did	cat	got	chin	June	fall	van	thin	then

nail *verb* [T] to fasten sth with a nail or nails: *Do you think we should nail these pieces together or use glue?*
(PHRASAL VERB) **nail sb down (to sth)** to make a person say clearly what he/she wants or intends to do: *She says she'll visit us in the summer but I can't nail her down to a definite date.*

'nail-brush *noun* [C] a small brush for cleaning your fingernails ☛ picture at **brush**.

'nail-file *noun* [C] a small metal tool with a rough surface that you use for shaping your nails

'nail-scissors *noun* [plural] small scissors for cutting your nails: *a pair of nail-scissors* o *Have you got any nail-scissors?*

'nail-varnish (*Brit*) (*US* **'nail polish**) *noun* [U] a liquid that people paint on their nails to give them colour or to make them shine

naive (*also* **naïve**) /naɪˈiːv/ *adj* without enough experience of the world and too ready to believe what other people say: *I was too naive to really understand what was going on.* o *a naive remark* —**naively** (*also* **naïvely**) *adv*: *She naively accepted the first price he offered.* —**naivety** (*also* **naïvety** /naɪˈiːvəti/) *noun* [U]: *He showed complete naivety in financial matters.*

☆ **naked** /ˈneɪkɪd/ *adj* **1** without any clothes on: *He came to the door naked except for a towel.* ☛ Look at **bare** and **nude**. **2** (only *before* a noun) not covered (used about sth that is usually covered): *a naked flame* **3** (only *before* a noun) openly shown or expressed; easy to see and often shocking: *naked aggression*
(IDIOM) **the naked eye** the eye without the help of a microscope or telescope: *Bacteria are too small to be seen with the naked eye.*

☆ **name¹** /neɪm/ *noun* **1** [C] a word or words by which a person, animal, place or thing is known: *What's your name, please?* o *Do you know the name of this flower?* o *Has your house got a name or a number?* **2** [sing] an opinion that people have of a person or thing; reputation: *That area of London has rather a bad name.* o *The company needs to build up a good name for itself.* **3** [C] a famous person: *All the big names in show business were invited to the party.*
(IDIOMS) **by name** using the name of sb/sth: *It's a big school but the headmaster knows all the children by name.*
in the name of sth because you believe in sth; for the sake of: *They acted in the name of democracy.*
in the name of sb representing a certain group of people: *Could you write a letter in the name of all the young people in the village?*
make a name for yourself; make your name to become well known and respected: *It's not easy to make your name as a writer.*

'namesake *noun* [C] a person who has the same name as another

☛ Your **first name** (*US* often **given name**) is the name your parents choose for you when you are born. It is very common in Christian countries to call this your **Christian name**. It can also be called your **forename**, although this is more formal and may be found on forms, documents, etc. **Surname** is the word usually used for your **family name** which you are born with. When a woman marries she may change her surname to be the same as her husband's. Her surname before marriage is then called her **maiden name**.

☆ **name²** /neɪm/ *verb* [T] **1 name sb/sth (after sb)** to give sb/sth a name: *The boy was named James after his grandfather.* o *Columbia was named after Christopher Columbus.* ☛ Be careful. When you are talking about being known by a particular name **be called** is used: *The baby is called Dan and his brother is Joe.* **2** to say what the name of sb/sth is: *The journalist refused to name the person who had given her the information.* o *Can you name all the planets in order?* **3** to state a date, price, etc: *Have Alex and Julie named a date for their wedding?*

nameless /ˈneɪmləs/ *adj* **1** without a name or with a name that you do not know or want to say: *the nameless slaves who built the pyramids* **2** not easily described or explained, eg because it is so terrible: *the nameless horrors of war*

namely /ˈneɪmli/ *adv* (used for giving more detail about what you are saying) that is to say: *There is only one person who can overrule the death sentence, namely the President.*

nanny /ˈnæni/ *noun* [C] (*pl* **nannies**) (*Brit*) a woman whose job is looking after young children. A nanny usually works at or lives in the child's home.

nap /næp/ *noun* [C] a short sleep that you have during the day
nap *verb* [I] (**napp**ing; **napp**ed) to have a short sleep

nape /neɪp/ *noun* [sing] the back part of the neck

napkin /ˈnæpkɪn/ *noun* [C] a piece of cloth or paper that you use when you are eating to protect your clothes or for wiping your hands and mouth: *a paper napkin* ☛ Look at **serviette**.

nappy /ˈnæpi/ *noun* [C] (*pl* **nappies**) (*US* **diaper**) a piece of soft thick cloth or paper that a baby or very young child wears around its bottom and between its legs: *Does her nappy need changing?* o *disposable nappies* (= that you throw away when they have been used)

narcotic /nɑːˈkɒtɪk/ *noun* [C] a drug that makes you feel sleepy or stops you feeling pain. Some people take narcotics for pleasure and then cannot stop taking them (= they become addicted). —**narcotic** *adj*

narrate /nəˈreɪt; *US* ˈnæreɪt/ *verb* [T] (*formal*) to tell a story

narration /nəˈreɪʃn/ *noun* [C,U] telling a story; the story that you tell

narrative /ˈnærətɪv/ *noun* [C] (*formal*) a story or an account

narrator *noun* [C] the person who tells a story

s	z	ʃ	ʒ	h	m	n	ŋ	l	r	j	w
so	zoo	she	vision	how	man	no	sing	leg	red	yes	wet

or explains what is happening in a play, film, etc

narrow /'nærəʊ/ adj **1** having only a short distance from side to side: *The bridge is too narrow for two cars to pass.* ☛ The opposite is **wide** or **broad**. **2** not large: *a narrow circle of friends* **3** by a small amount: *That was a very narrow escape. You were lucky.* ○ *a narrow defeat/victory*

narrow verb [I,T] to become narrow or to make sth narrow: *The road narrows in 50 metres.*

(PHRASAL VERB) **narrow sth down** to make a list of things smaller: *We had a huge list of places we wanted to go to on holiday but we've managed to narrow it down to three.*

narrowly adv only by a small amount: *The driver swerved and narrowly missed hitting the boy.* —**narrowness** noun [U]

narrow-'minded /-'maɪndɪd/ adj not willing to accept new ideas or the opinions of other people if they are not the same as your own

nasal /'neɪzl/ adj connected with the nose

☆**nasty** /'nɑːsti; US 'næ-/ adj (**nastier**; **nastiest**) **1** ugly or unpleasant: *What's that nasty smell in this cupboard?* ○ *The new furniture looked cheap and nasty.* **2** angry or aggressive: *When she was asked to leave she got really nasty.* ○ *Luke has a really nasty temper.* **3** unkind: *That was a nasty thing to say to your brother.* **4** very bad: *a nasty accident* ○ *a nasty cut on the arm* —**nastily** adv —**nastiness** noun [U]

☆**nation** /'neɪʃn/ noun [C] a country or all the people in a country: *The President is going to speak to the nation on television.* ○ *a summit of the leaders of seven nations*

nation'wide adj, adv over the whole of a country: *The police launched a nationwide hunt for the killer.*

☆**national** /'næʃnəl/ adj concerning all of a nation or country; typical of a particular nation: *Here is today's national and international news.* ○ *a national newspaper* ○ *a young Swede dressed in his national costume* ○ *a national holiday* ☛ Look at **international** and **local**.

national noun [C] (formal) a person who comes from a particular country: *There are many Algerian nationals working in France.* —**nationally** adv: *to advertise sth nationally*

,**national 'anthem** noun [C] the official song of a country that is played at public events

National 'Health Service noun [sing] (abbr **NHS**) (Brit) the system that provides free or cheap medical care for everybody in Britain and that is paid for by taxes: *Can you get glasses on the NHS?*

,**National In'surance** noun [U] (abbr **NI**) (Brit) the system by which employers and employees pay money to the government so that the government can help people who are ill, unemployed, retired, etc: *National Insurance contributions*

,**national 'park** noun [C] a large area of beautiful land that is protected by the government so that the public can enjoy it

,**national 'service** noun [U] the period of time that a young person must spend in the army, navy, etc of his/her country: *to do national service*

☆**nationalism** /'næʃnəlɪzəm/ noun [U] **1** the strong feeling of love or pride that you feel for your own country. Nationalism often makes people think that their own country is better than others. **2** the desire of a group of people to form an independent country: *Nationalism is quite strong in Scotland.*

nationalist /'næʃnəlɪst/ noun [C] a person who wants a particular group of people to be able to form an independent country: *a Welsh nationalist*

nationalistic /,næʃnə'lɪstɪk/ adj having or showing strong feelings of love or pride in your own country ☛ **Nationalistic** is usually used in a critical way, meaning that a person's feelings of pride are too strong.

☆**nationality** /,næʃə'næləti/ noun [C,U] (pl **nationalities**) being a member of a particular nation or country: *Stuart lives in America but he still has British nationality.* ○ *students of many nationalities* ○ *to have dual nationality* (= of two countries) ○ *Am I eligible to take out British nationality?*

nationalize (also **nationalise**) /'næʃnəlaɪz/ verb [T] to put a company or organization under the control of the state: *The railways were nationalized after the war.* ☛ Look at **privatize**. —**nationalization** (also **nationalisation**) /,næʃnəlaɪ'zeɪʃn; US -lɪ'z-/ noun [U]

☆**native** /'neɪtɪv/ noun [C] **1** a person who was born in a particular place: *She lives in Oxford but she's a native of York.* **2** (usually used by white people about non-white people) a person who lives in a particular place: *When European explorers first arrived in South America they were given a warm welcome by the natives.* ☛ This sense of **native** is used by people who feel that they are better than the local people and it is becoming rare. **3** an animal or plant that lives or grows naturally in a particular place: *The koala is a native of Australia.*

native adj **1** (only before a noun) connected with the place where you were born: *Tadeusz's native land is Poland but he left in 1938.* **2** (used about an animal or plant) living or growing naturally in a particular place: *There are many grey squirrels in England but they are not a native species.*

,**Native A'merican** (also **American Indian**; **Indian**) adj, noun [C] (of) a member of the race of people who were the original inhabitants of America

,**native 'speaker** noun [C] a person who learnt a particular language as a very young child: *Are you a native speaker of Dutch?*

natter /'nætə(r)/ verb [I] (Brit informal) to talk a lot about things that are not very important ☛ Look at **chat**. —**natter** noun [sing]: *to have a natter*

☆**natural** /'nætʃrəl/ adj **1** connected with things that were not made by people: *natural disasters such as earthquakes and floods* ○ *I prefer to see animals in their natural surroundings rather than in zoos.* ○ *Britain's natural resources include coal, oil and gas.* ☛ If somebody dies of **natural causes** they die because they were ill or old, not because they were killed in an accident. **2** usual or normal; what you would expect: *It's natural to feel nervous before an interview.* ○ *It's only natural for people to be nervous.* ☛ The opposite is **unnatural**. **3** that you had from birth or that was easy for you to learn: *a natural gift for languages* ○ *natural charm*

,**natural 'history** *noun* [U] the study of plants and animals

naturalist /'nætʃrəlɪst/ *noun* [C] a person who studies plants and animals

naturalize (*also* **naturalise**) /'nætʃrəlaɪz/ *verb* [T] (usually passive) to make sb a citizen of a country where he/she was not born: *Lee was born in Hong Kong but was naturalized after living in Britain for five years.* —**naturalization** (*also* **naturalisation**) /,nætʃrəlaɪ'zeɪʃn; *US* -lɪ'z-/ *noun* [U]

naturally /'nætʃrəli/ *adv* **1** in a natural(3) way: *Vera is naturally a very cheerful person.* ○ *Working with computers comes naturally to Nick.* **2** of course; as you would expect: *The team was naturally upset about its defeat.* **3** in a way that is normal: *You look very stiff and tense. Try to stand naturally.* ○ *Don't try and impress people. Just act naturally.* **4** in a way that is not made or done by people: *naturally wavy hair*

☆ **nature** /'neɪtʃə(r)/ *noun* **1** [U] all the things in the world that were not made or caused by people: *the forces of nature* (eg volcanoes, hurricanes, etc) ○ *If we destroy too many forests we may upset the balance of nature.* ○ *the wonders of nature* ○ *On holiday we like to get away from civilization and back to nature.* **2** [C,U] the qualities or features of a person or thing: *He's basically honest by nature.* ○ *Our new cat has a very nice nature.* ○ *The nature of my work is secret and I cannot discuss it.* ○ *It's human nature never to be completely satisfied.* **3** [sing] the type or sort of sth: *I'm not very interested in things of that nature.*

(IDIOM) **second nature** ⇨ SECOND[1]

-natured (in compounds) having a particular quality or feature: *good-natured*

naughty /'nɔːti/ *adj* (**naughtier**; **naughtiest**) (used when you are talking to or about a child) not doing what an adult says; badly-behaved; causing trouble: *She's one of the naughtiest children in the class.* ○ *It was very naughty of you not to tell me where you were going.* —**naughtily** *adv* **naughtiness** *noun* [U]

nausea /'nɔːsɪə; *US* 'nɔːʒə/ *noun* [U] the feeling that you are going to vomit (= bring up food from your stomach): *A wave of nausea came over him at the sight of all the blood.* ☛ Look at **sick**(2).

nauseate /'nɔːsɪeɪt; *US* 'nɔːz-/ *verb* [T] to cause sb to feel nausea or strong dislike —**nauseating** *adj*

nautical /'nɔːtɪkl/ *adj* connected with ships, sailors or sailing

naval /'neɪvl/ *adj* connected with the navy: *a naval battle*

navel /'neɪvl/ *noun* [C] the small hollow in the middle of your stomach ☛ Look at **umbilical cord**.

navigable /'nævɪɡəbl/ *adj* that boats can sail along: *a navigable river*

navigate /'nævɪɡeɪt/ *verb* **1** [I] to use a map, etc to find out which way a car, ship, plane, etc should go: *Early explorers used the stars to navigate.* ○ *If you drive, I'll navigate.* **2** [T] to move or guide a ship, etc in a particular direction; to find a way through a difficult place: *We managed to navigate the yacht through the rocks.* ○ *Nobody had navigated the Amazon until then.* —**navigation** /,nævɪ'ɡeɪʃn/ *noun* [U] —**navigator** *noun* [C] a person who navigates

☆ **navy** /'neɪvi/ *noun* [C] (*pl* **navies**) **1 the Navy** the organization that controls the warships of a country and the people that work on them: *to join the Navy* ☛ When it is used in the singular **Navy** can take either a singular or a plural verb: *The Navy is/are introducing a new warship this year.* Look at **army**, **air force** and **merchant navy**. **2** a group of warships belonging to a country: *Does Switzerland have a navy?*

,**navy 'blue** (*also* **navy**) *adj*, *noun* [U] dark blue

☆ **near**[1] /nɪə(r)/ *adj* **1** not far in time or distance (from sb/sth): *Let's walk to the library. It's quite near.* ○ *We're hoping to move to Wales in the near future.* ○ *Where's the nearest Post Office?* ○ *The day of the interview was getting nearer.* ☛ **Close** and **near** are often the same in meaning but in some phrases only one of them may be used: *a close friend* ○ *the near future* ○ *a close contest.* Look at the note at **next**. **2** closely related to you: *My nearest relative who's still alive is my great-aunt.*

(IDIOMS) **or near(est) offer**; **ono** (used when you are selling sth) or an amount that is less than but near the amount that you have asked for: *Motor cycle for sale. £750 ono.*

a near miss a situation where sth nearly hits you or where sth bad nearly happens: *The bullet flew past his ear. It was a very near miss.*

,**near-'sighted** *adj* (*US*) = SHORT-SIGHTED

☆ **near**[2] /nɪə(r)/ *adv*, *prep* not far in time or distance; close to: *It's a little village near Cardiff.* ○ *I don't want to sit near the window.* ○ *I'd like to live near my parents, if possible.* ○ *Her birthday is very near Christmas.* ○ *I wasn't sitting near enough to see.* ○ *They live quite near.*

(IDIOM) **nowhere near** far from: *We've sold nowhere near enough tickets to make a profit.*

'**nearby** *adj* (only *before* a noun) not far away in distance: *We went out to a nearby restaurant.* ☛ Notice that **nearby** is only used before the noun. **Near** cannot be used before a noun in this way: *We went out to a restaurant near our house.* ○ *The restaurant is quite near.*

near'by *adv* not far away in distance: *A new restaurant has opened nearby.*

near[3] /nɪə(r)/ *verb* [I,T] to get closer to sth in time or distance: *The day was nearing when we would have to decide.* ○ *The job is nearing completion.*

☆ **nearly** /'nɪəli/ *adv* almost; not completely or exactly: *It's nearly five years since I've seen him.* ○ *It's nearly time to go.* ○ *Linda was so badly hurt she nearly died.* ○ *It's not far now. We're*

ɜː	ə	eɪ	əʊ	aɪ	aʊ	ɔɪ	ɪə	eə	ʊə
fur	ago	pay	home	five	now	join	near	hair	pure

nearly there. ○ *I've nearly finished.* ○ *He earns nearly £20 000 a year.*
(IDIOM) **not nearly** far from: *It's not nearly as warm as it was yesterday.*

☆ **neat** /niːt/ *adj* **1** arranged or done carefully or tidily: *Please keep your room neat and tidy.* ○ *neat rows of figures* **2** (used about a person) liking things to be done or arranged carefully or tidily **3** (US) good; nice: *That's a really neat car!* **4** (US **straight**) (used about alcoholic drinks) on its own, without ice, water or any other liquid: *a neat whisky* —**neatly** *adv* —**neatness** *noun* [U]

☆ **necessarily** /ˌnesəˈserəli/ *adv* in all cases; always: *Shouting is not necessarily the best way to make yourself understood.*

☆ **necessary** /ˈnesəsəri; *US* -seri/ *adj* needed in order to get sth or to do sth: *A good diet is necessary for a healthy life.* ○ *Don't spend more than £20 unless it's absolutely necessary.* ○ *It's not necessary for you all to come.*

necessitate /nɪˈsesɪteɪt/ *verb* [T] (*formal*) to make sth necessary

☆ **necessity** /nɪˈsesəti/ *noun* (*pl* **necessities**) **1** [U] **necessity (for sth/to do sth)** being necessary; need: *Is there any necessity for change?* ○ *There's no necessity to write every single name down.* **2** [C] something that you must have: *Clean water is an absolute necessity.* ○ *Food, clothing and shelter are all necessities of life.*

☆ **neck** /nek/ *noun* [C] **1** the part of the body that joins your head to your shoulders: *She wrapped a scarf around her neck.* ○ *I've got a stiff neck.* ○ *Giraffes have long necks.* **2** the part of a piece of clothing that goes round your neck: *a polo-neck sweater* ○ *a V-neck sweater* ☞ picture on page A11. **3** the narrow part of sth that looks like a neck: *the neck of a bottle*
(IDIOMS) **neck and neck (with sb/sth)** equal or level: *At the half-way point the two cars were neck and neck.*

up to your neck in sth very deeply involved in sth: *We're up to our necks in work at the moment.*

necklace /ˈnekləs/ *noun* [C] a piece of jewellery that you wear around your neck ☞ picture at **jewellery**.

'necktie *noun* [C] (*US*) = TIE¹(1)

née /neɪ/ *adj* (used before the surname that a woman had before she got married): *Christine Cowley, née Morgan* ☞ Look at **maiden name**.

☆ **need¹** /niːd/ *verb* [T] (not usually used in the continuous forms) **1** to require sth; to think that sth is necessary: *All living things need water.* ○ *I need a new film for my camera.* ○ *Does Bob need any help?* ○ *We've got enough coffee. We don't need any more.* ○ *Can I borrow your dictionary or do you need it?* ○ *She needs three volunteers to bring the food.* ○ *This jumper needs washing/to be washed.* ○ *He needed his eyes tested/testing.* **2** to have to; to be obliged to: *Do we need to buy the tickets in advance?* ○ *I need to ask some advice.* ○ *You didn't need to bring any food but it was very kind of you.* ☞ Note that the question form of the main verb **need** is **do I need?**, etc and the past tense is **needed** (question form **did you need?**, etc; negative **didn't need**).

☆ **need²** /niːd/ *verb* ☞ present tense **need** in all persons; negative **need not** (**needn't**), question form **need I?**, etc (not used in the continuous forms; used mainly in questions or negative sentences or with words like *hardly*, *only*, *never*) to have to; to be obliged to: *Need we pay the whole amount now?* ○ *You needn't come to the meeting if you're too busy.* ○ *I'll help you any time. You only need ask.* ○ *I hardly need remind you that this is very serious.* ☞ **Need not have** or **needn't have** and the past participle means that you did something but it was not necessary: *We needn't have packed our thick clothes. The weather was really warm.* ○ *He needn't have gone to the hospital* (= he went but it wasn't necessary). Compare this with the past tense of the main verb which usually means that the action did not take place: *He didn't need to go to the hospital* (= he didn't go because it wasn't necessary).

☆ **need³** /niːd/ *noun* **1** [U,sing] a situation in which sth is wanted or required: *We are all in need of a rest.* ○ *There is a growing need for low-cost housing in the London area.* ○ *There's no need for you to come if you don't want to.* ○ *Is there any need for all that noise?* ○ *Do phone me if you feel the need to talk to someone.* **2 needs** [plural] the things that you must have: *He doesn't earn enough to pay for his basic needs.* ○ *Parents must consider their children's emotional as well as their physical needs.* **3** [U] the state of not having enough money: *a campaign to help families in need*

needless *adj* that is not necessary: *We had gone through a lot of needless worry. He was safe at home.* ☞ Look at **unnecessary**. —**needlessly** *adv*

☆ **needle** /ˈniːdl/ *noun* [C] **1** a small thin piece of metal with a point at one end and a hole (**an eye**) at the other that is used for sewing: *to thread a needle with cotton* ☞ picture at **sew**. **2** (also **knitting needle**) a long thin piece of metal, plastic or wood with a point at one end that is used for knitting ☞ picture at **knit**. **3** the thin hollow part of a syringe that is used for injecting liquids into your body. **4** something that looks like a needle: *a pine needle* ○ *the needle of a compass*
(IDIOM) **pins and needles** ⇨ PIN¹

'needlework *noun* [U] work that you do by hand using a needle(1). Needlework includes sewing and embroidery.

needy /ˈniːdi/ *adj* (**needier**; **neediest**) not having enough money etc; poor

☆ **negative** /ˈnegətɪv/ *adj* **1** (used about a word, phrase or sentence) saying or meaning 'no' or 'not': *a negative sentence* ○ *'Don't you like England?' is a negative question.* ☞ Look at **affirmative**. **2** only thinking about the bad qualities of sb/sth: *I'm feeling very negative about my job – in fact I'm thinking about moving.* ☞ The opposite is **positive**. **3** (used about a medical or scientific test) showing that sth has not happened or has not been found: *The results of the pregnancy test were negative.* ☞ The opposite is **positive**. **4** (used about a

p	b	t	d	k	g	tʃ	dʒ	f	v	θ	ð
pen	bad	tea	did	cat	got	chin	June	fall	van	thin	then

number) less than zero ☛ The opposite is **positive**.

negative *noun* [C] **1** a word, phrase or sentence that says or means 'no' or 'not': *Carol answered in the negative* (= she said no). o *'Never', 'neither' and 'nobody' are all negatives.* **2** a piece of film from which we can make a photograph. The light areas of a negative are dark on the final photograph and the dark areas are light: *If you give me the negative, I can have another print made.*

☆ **neglect** /nɪ'glekt/ *verb* [T] to give too little or no attention or care to sb/sth: *Try hard not to neglect your health even when you are studying for your exams.*

neglect *noun* [U] giving too little care to sb/sth; the state of being neglected: *The house was empty and in a state of total neglect.*

neglected *adj* having or showing a lack of care and attention: *Neglected children often get into trouble.*

negligence /'neglɪdʒəns/ *noun* [U] not being careful enough; lack of care: *The accident was a result of human negligence.*

negligent /'neglɪdʒənt/ *adj* not giving enough care or attention to sth (that you are responsible for) —**negligently** *adv*

negligible /'neglɪdʒəbl/ *adj* not important because it is too small

negotiable /nɪ'gəʊʃɪəbl/ *adj* that can be decided or changed by discussion: *The price is not negotiable* (= it can't be changed).

☆ **negotiate** /nɪ'gəʊʃɪeɪt/ *verb* **1** [I] to talk to sb in order to decide or agree about sth: *The unions are still negotiating with management about this year's pay claim.* **2** [T] **negotiate sth (with sb)** to decide or agree sth by talking about it: *to negotiate an agreement* **3** [T] to get over, past or along sth difficult: *The canoeists had to negotiate several rapids on the river.*

negotiator *noun* [C] a person who negotiates(1, 2)

☆ **negotiation** /nɪ,gəʊʃɪ'eɪʃn/ *noun* [C,U] discussions at which people try to decide or agree sth: *The salary is a matter for negotiation.* o *The negotiations were extremely difficult.* o *to enter into/break off negotiations*

Negro /'ni:grəʊ/ *noun* [C] (*pl* **Negroes**) a black person ☛ Many people now find this word offensive.

neigh /neɪ/ *noun* [C] the long high sound that a horse makes —**neigh** *verb* [I]

☆ **neighbour** (*US* **neighbor**) /'neɪbə(r)/ *noun* [C] **1** a person who lives near you: *Don't make too much noise or you'll wake the neighbours.* o *our next-door neighbours* **2** a person or thing that is near or next to another: *Britain's nearest neighbour is France.* o *Try not to look at what your neighbour is writing.*

neighbourhood (*US* **neighborhood**) /'neɪbəhʊd/ *noun* [C] a particular part of a town and the people who live there: *We've just moved into the neighbourhood and don't know our way around yet.* o *a friendly neighbourhood*

neighbouring (*US* **neighboring**) /'neɪbərɪŋ/ *adj* (only *before* a noun) near or next to: *Farmers from neighbouring villages come into town each week for the market.*

neighbourly (*US* **neighborly**) *adj* friendly and helpful

☆ **neither** /'naɪðə(r); 'ni:ðə(r)/ *det, pron* (used about two people or things) not one and not the other: *Neither team played very well.* o *Neither of the teams played very well.* o *'Would you like a sandwich? Or a piece of cake?' 'Neither, thank you. I'm not hungry.'* o *There were two candidates for the job but neither of them was very good.* ☛ Notice that **neither** is followed by a singular noun and verb: *Neither day was suitable.* The noun or pronoun that follows **neither of** is in the plural but the verb may be singular or plural: (*formal*) *Neither of the days is suitable.* o (*informal*) *Neither of the days are suitable.*

neither *adv* **1** also not; not either: *I don't eat meat and neither does Tom.* o *Stella didn't attend the meeting and neither did Jane.* o *'I haven't seen that film.' 'Neither have I.'* ☛ In this sense **nor** can be used in the same way: *'I haven't seen that film.' 'Nor have I.'* Notice that when you use **not... either** the order of words is different: *I don't eat meat and Tom doesn't either.* o *'I haven't seen that film.' 'I haven't either.'* **2 neither... nor** not... and not: *Neither Tom nor I eat meat.* ☛ **Neither... nor** can be used with a singular or a plural verb: (*formal*) *Neither Stella nor Jane was at the meeting.* o (*informal*) *Neither Stella nor Jane were at the meeting.*

neon /'ni:ɒn/ *noun* [U] (*symbol* **Ne**) a type of gas that is used for making bright lights and signs: *the neon lights of the city*

☆ **nephew** /'nevju:; 'nefju:/ *noun* [C] the son of your brother or sister, or the son of your husband's or wife's brother or sister ☛ Look at **niece**.

Neptune /'neptju:n; *US* -tu:n/ *noun* [sing] the planet that is eighth in order from the sun

☆ **nerve** /nɜ:v/ *noun* **1** [C] one of the long thin threads in your body that carry feelings or other messages to and from your brain **2 nerves** [plural] the ability to stay calm and not get worried: *You need strong nerves for this job.* **3 nerves** [plural] the state of being very nervous or worried: *Breathing deeply should help to calm your nerves.* **4** [U] the courage that you need to do sth difficult or dangerous: *Racing drivers need a lot of nerve.* o *He didn't have the nerve to ask Mandy to go out with him.* o *She climbed to the highest diving-board but lost her nerve and couldn't jump.* **5** [U] the rudeness that is needed to do sth: *He had the nerve to ask me to lend him money, and he still owes me £20.*

(IDIOM) **get on sb's nerves** (*informal*) to annoy sb or make sb angry: *Turn that music down – it's getting on my nerves.*

'nerve-racking *adj* making you very nervous or worried: *Waiting for exam results can be very nerve-racking.*

☆ **nervous** /'nɜ:vəs/ *adj* **1** connected with the nerves of the body: *a nervous disorder* **2** worried or afraid: *I'm a bit nervous about travelling on my own.* o *I always get nervous just before a match.* o *nervous laughter* o *She was nervous of giving the wrong answer.*

s	z	ʃ	ʒ	h	m	n	ŋ	l	r	j	w
so	zoo	she	vision	how	man	no	sing	leg	red	yes	wet

nest 418 **new**

—**nervously** adv: *He sat there, biting his fingers nervously.* —**nervousness** noun [U]

nervous 'breakdown (*also* **breakdown**) noun [C] a time when sb is so depressed that he/she cannot continue living and working normally: *to have a nervous breakdown*

'nervous system noun [C] your brain and all the nerves in your body

☆ **nest** /nest/ noun [C] **1** a round hollow structure that a bird builds to lay its eggs in ☞ picture at **bird**. **2** the home of certain animals or insects: *a wasps' nest*
nest verb [I] to use or build a nest

nestle /'nesl/ verb [I,T] to move yourself or a part of your body into a comfortable position, against a person or sth soft: *The child nestled up against his mother and fell asleep.* ○ *The baby nestled her head on her mother's shoulder.* ○ (*figurative*) *Ulfa is a typical German village nestling in a beautiful river valley.*

☆ **net¹** /net/ noun **1** [U] material that is made of long pieces of string, thread, etc that are tied together, with spaces between them: *net curtains* (= very thin curtains that are used to stop people from seeing into a room) **2** [C] a piece of net that is used for a particular purpose: *a tennis net* (= in the centre of the court) ○ *a fishing net* ○ *a hair-net* ☞ picture at **tennis**. Look at **safety net**.
net verb [T] (**netting**; **netted**) to catch sth with a net; to kick a ball into a net

'netball noun [U] a game similar to basketball that is played by two teams of seven players. Each team tries to score goals by throwing a ball through a round net at the top of a pole. Netball is usually played by women.

☆ **net²** (*also* **nett**) /net/ adj **net (of sth)** from which nothing more needs to be taken away: *What is your net income?* (= after tax, etc has been paid) ○ *The net weight of the jam is 350g* (= not including the jar). ○ *net profit* ☞ The opposite is **gross**.
net verb [T] (**netting**; **netted**) to gain sth as a profit: *The sale of land netted £2 million.*

netting /'netɪŋ/ noun [U] material that is made of long pieces of string, thread, wire, etc that are tied together with spaces between them: *a fence made of wire-netting*

nettle /'netl/ noun [C] a wild plant with hairy leaves. Some nettles sting and make your skin red and painful if you touch them: *stinging nettles*

☆ **network** /'netwɜːk/ noun [C] **1** a complicated system of roads, railway lines, etc: *The underground railway network covers all areas of the capital.* **2** a group of people or companies, etc that work together closely: *We have a network of agents who sell our goods all over the country.* **3** a group of television or radio companies that broadcasts the same programmes in different parts of a country

neurosis /njʊəˈrəʊsɪs; *US* nʊ-/ noun [C] (*pl* **neuroses** /-ˈəʊsiːz/) a mental illness that causes strong feelings of fear and worry

neurotic /njʊəˈrɒtɪk; *US* nʊ-/ adj **1** suffering from neurosis **2** worried about things in a way that is not normal

neuter /'njuːtə(r); *US* 'nuː-/ adj (used about a word) not masculine or feminine according to the rules of grammar
neuter verb [T] to remove the sexual parts of an animal ☞ Look at **castrate**.

neutral /'njuːtrəl; *US* 'nuː-/ adj **1** not supporting or belonging to either side in an argument, war, etc: *Switzerland remained neutral during the war.* ○ *The two sides agreed to meet on neutral ground.* **2** having or showing no strong qualities, feelings or colour: *a blouse of a neutral colour that will go with anything*
neutral noun [U] the position that the gears of a car, etc are in when no power is sent from the engine to the wheels: *Make sure the car is in neutral before you turn on the engine.*

neutrality /njuːˈtræləti; *US* nuː-/ noun [U] the state of being neutral(1)

neutralize (*also* **neutralise**) verb [T] to take away the effect of sth

☆ **never** /'nevə(r)/ adv **1** at no time; not ever: *I never start work before 9 o'clock.* ○ *I've never been to Portugal.* ○ *After that he never saw his father again.* ○ *We shall never go back to that hotel.* ○ *You should never leave valuables in your car.* ○ *He never ever eats meat.* ○ (*formal*) *Never before has such a high standard been achieved.* **2** (used for emphasizing a negative statement): *I never realized she was so unhappy.* ○ *Roy never so much as looked at us* (= he didn't even look at us).
(IDIOM) **never mind** ⇨ MIND²

☆ **nevertheless** /ˌnevəðəˈles/ adv in spite of that: *It was a cold, rainy day. Nevertheless, more people came than we had expected.* ○ *She knew that the accident wasn't her fault. She still felt guilty, nevertheless.*

☆ **new** /njuː;; *US* nuː-/ adj **1** that has recently been built, made, invented, etc: *The Prince of Wales is coming to open the new hospital.* ○ *There have been record sales of new cars this month.* ○ *Have you seen Tom Cruise's new film?* ○ *a new method of treating mental illness* ○ *Paula came to show us her new baby.* **2** different; other; changed from what was before: *Our new house is much bigger than the old one.* ○ *I've just started reading a new book.* ○ *to make new friends* ○ *The star of the film is a housewife who dreams of a new life in Greece.* **3 new (to sb)** that has not been seen, learnt, etc before: *This type of machine is new to me.* ○ *to learn a new language* ○ *We've only just arrived here so the area is still new to us.* **4 new (to sth)** having just started being or doing sth: *We are new to the area.* ○ *a new parent* ○ *She's new to the job and needs a lot of help.* ○ *a new member of the club*
(IDIOM) **break fresh/new ground** ⇨ GROUND¹

new- (in compounds) recently: *a newborn baby*

newness noun [U] the state of being new

'newcomer noun [C] a person who has just arrived in a place

'newfangled adj new or modern in a way that the speaker dislikes or refuses to accept: *I don't need all these newfangled gadgets in the kitchen.*

new 'moon noun [sing] the moon when it appears as a thin line ☞ Look at **full moon**.

iː	ɪ	e	æ	ɑː	ɒ	ɔː	ʊ	uː	ʌ
see	sit	ten	hat	arm	got	saw	put	too	cup

'new town *noun* [C] (*Brit*) a town that is planned and built all at one time

new 'year *noun* [sing] the first few days of January: *Happy New Year!* ○ *We will get in touch in the new year.*

New Year's 'Day *noun* [U] 1 January

New Year's 'Eve *noun* [U] 31 December

newly /'nju:li/ *adv* (usually before a past participle) recently: *the newly appointed Minister of Health*

'newly-wed *noun* [C, usually pl] a person who has recently got married

☆ **news** /nju:z/ *noun* **1** [U] information about sth that has happened recently: *Have you heard the latest news? Mary and Joe are getting married!* ○ *She writes each Christmas telling us all her news.* ○ *Have you had any news from Malcolm recently?* ○ *That's news to me* (= I didn't know that). ○ *News is coming in of a plane crash in Thailand.* ○ *There will be a further news bulletin at 1 o'clock.* ○ *Our town has been in the news a lot recently* (= a lot has been written in newspapers, etc). ☛ **News** is an uncountable noun. If we are talking about an individual item we must say 'a piece of news': *We had a piece of good news yesterday.* **2 the news** [sing] a regular broadcast of the latest news on the radio and TV: *We always watch the nine o'clock news on television.* ○ *I heard on the news that there's been a plane crash in Thailand.* ○ *the local/national news*

(IDIOM) **break the news (to sb)** to be the first to tell sb about sth important that has happened

'newsagent (*US* **'newsdealer**) *noun* [C] a shopkeeper who sells newspapers, magazines, sweets, cigarettes, etc: *I must pop round to the newsagent's* (= the shop) *for my paper.*

'newscaster (*also* **'newsreader**) *noun* [C] a person who reads the news on the radio or on TV

'newsletter *noun* [C] a printed report about a club or organization that is sent regularly to members and other people who may be interested

'news-stand *noun* [C] (*US*) = BOOKSTALL

☆ **newspaper** /'nju:speɪpə(r); *US* 'nu:z-/ *noun* **1** (*also* **paper**) [C] large folded pieces of paper printed with news, advertisements and articles on various subjects. Newspapers are printed and sold either daily or weekly: *a daily/weekly/Sunday paper* ○ *a national/local newspaper* ○ *a morning/evening paper* ○ *a newspaper article* ○ *a newspaper headline* **2** (*also* **paper**) [C] an organization that produces a newspaper: *Which paper is he from?* **3** [U] the paper on which newspapers are printed: *We wrapped the plates in newspaper so they would not get damaged in the move.*

☛ **Journalists** and **reporters** collect news for newspapers. The **editor** decides what is printed. **Quality** newspapers deal with the news in a serious way. **Tabloids** are popular papers and are smaller in size with many more pictures.

☆ **next¹** /nekst/ *adj* **1** (usually with *the*) coming immediately after sth in order, space or time; closest: *The next bus leaves in twenty minutes.* ○ *She went into hospital on a Sunday and the next day she died.* ○ *Before we all go we'd better set a date for the next meeting.* ○ *the next name on the list* ○ *I must get this finished today because I will be on holiday for the next two weeks.* ○ *How far is it to the next service station?* ○ *Go to the Post Office and take the next turning on the left.* ○ *I felt dizzy and the next thing I knew I was lying on the ground.* ☛ Compare **nearest** and **next**. **The next** means 'the following' in a series of events or places: *When is your next appointment?* ○ *Turn left at the next traffic lights.* (**The**) **nearest** means 'the closest' in time or place: *Where's the nearest supermarket?* **2** (used without *the* before days of the week, months, seasons, years, etc) the one immediately following the present one: *See you again next Monday.* ○ *Let's go camping next weekend.* ○ *We are going to Greece next spring.* ○ *Rachel hopes to get a job abroad next year.*

(IDIOM) **first/last/next but one, two etc** ⇨ FIRST¹

the next *noun* [sing] the person or thing that is next(1): *If we miss this train we'll have to wait two hours for the next.*

,next'door *adj, adv* in or into the next house or building: *our next-door neighbours* ○ *Who lives next door?* ○ *The school is next door to an old people's home.* ○ *I'm going next door to borrow some eggs.*

,next of 'kin *noun* [plural,U] your closest living relative or relatives ☛ **Next of kin** is used to mean both a single relative and a group of relatives: *My husband is my next of kin.* ○ *Her next of kin have been informed of her death.*

next to *prep* **1** at the side of sb/sth; beside: *He sat down next to Pam.* ○ *There's a public telephone next to the pub.* **2** in a position after sth: *Next to Paris I think my favourite city is Madrid.*

(IDIOM) **next to nothing** almost nothing: *We took £50 but we've got next to nothing left.*

☆ **next²** /nekst/ *adv* after this or that; then: *I wonder what will happen next.* ○ *I know Joe arrived first, but who came next?* ○ *It was ten years until I next saw her.*

,next-'best *adj* not the best, but good enough if you cannot have the best

nib /nɪb/ *noun* [C] the metal point of a pen where the ink comes out

nibble /'nɪbl/ *verb* [I,T] to eat sth by taking small bites —**nibble** *noun* [C]

☆ **nice** /naɪs/ *adj* **1** pleasant; good: *The weather was quite nice yesterday.* ○ *Have a nice day!* ○ *You look very nice today.* ○ *I'm not eating this – it doesn't taste very nice.* **2** kind; friendly: *What a nice girl!* ○ *Try and be nice to Julie. She's not feeling very well.*

(IDIOM) **nice and ...** (*informal*) (used for saying that you like sth): *It's nice and warm by the fire.*

nicely *adv* **1** in a pleasant way: *You can have a biscuit if you ask nicely.* **2** (*informal*) very well: *This flat will suit us nicely.* —**niceness** *noun* [U]

niche /niːtʃ; niːʃ/ *noun* [C] **1** a hollow place in a wall, often with a shelf **2** a job, position, etc that is suitable for you: *to find your niche in life*

nick¹ /nɪk/ *noun* [C] a small cut in sth

(IDIOMS) **in good, bad, etc nick** (*Brit slang*) in a good, bad, etc state or condition

in the nick of time only just in time: *The ambulance arrived in the nick of time.*

nick *verb* [T] to make a nick or small cut in sb/sth

nick² /nɪk/ *noun* **the nick** [sing] (*Brit slang*) prison

nick *verb* [T] (*Brit slang*) **1 nick sb (for sth)** to arrest sb **2 nick sth (from sb/sth)** to steal sth

nickel /'nɪkl/ *noun* **1** [U] (*symbol* Ni) a hard silver-white metal that is often mixed with other metals **2** [C] an American or Canadian coin that is worth five cents

nickname /'nɪkneɪm/ *noun* [C] an informal name that is used instead of your own name, usually by your family or friends

nicotine /'nɪkəti:n/ *noun* [U] the poisonous chemical substance in tobacco

☆**niece** /ni:s/ *noun* [C] the daughter of your brother or sister; the daughter of your husband's or wife's brother or sister ☛ Look at **nephew**.

nigger /'nɪgə(r)/ *noun* [C] an extremely offensive word for a black person

niggle /'nɪgl/ *verb* **1** [I] to pay too much attention to things that are not very important: *It's not worth niggling over a few pence.* **2** [T] to annoy or worry sb: *His untidy habits really niggled her.*

niggling /'nɪglɪŋ/ *adj* not very serious (but that does not go away): *I've still got niggling doubts about whether we've done the right thing.*

☆**night** /naɪt/ *noun* [C,U] **1** the part of the day when it is dark and when most people sleep: *The nights are short in the summer.* o *a dark night* o *We will be away for a few nights.* o *Did you sleep well last night?* o *a sleepless night* o *The baby cried all night long.* o *It's a long way home. Why don't you stay the night?* o *Owls come out at night.* **2** the time between late afternoon and when you go to bed: *Let's go out on Saturday night.* o *He doesn't get home until 8 o'clock at night.* o *I tried to phone Nigel last night but he was out.* ☛ Note the use of different prepositions with **night**. At is most common: *I'm not allowed out after 11 o'clock at night.* By is used about something that you usually do in the daytime: *They slept by day and travelled by night.* In/during the night is usually used for the night that has just passed: *I woke up twice in the night.* On is used when you are talking about one particular night: *On the night of Saturday 30 June.* Tonight means the night or evening that will come next: *Where are you staying tonight?*

(IDIOMS) **an early/a late night** an evening when you go to bed earlier/later than usual

a night out an evening that you spend away from home enjoying yourself

in the/at dead of night ⇨ **DEAD**

good night (said late in the evening, before you go home or before you go to sleep)

nightly *adj, adv* (done or happening) every night: *You can see the play nightly, except Sundays, at the Abbey Theatre.*

'nightclub *noun* [C] a place where you can go to eat, drink, dance, etc until late at night

'nightdress (*also* **'nightgown**, *informal* **nighty**; **nightie** (*pl* **nighties**)) *noun* [C] a loose dress that a girl or woman wears in bed

'night-life *noun* [U] the entertainment that is available at night in a particular place: *It's a small town with very little night-life.*

'night school *noun* [C] a place where adults can go to classes in the evening

'night-time *noun* [U] the time when it is dark: *Many women are afraid to go out at night-time.*

,night-'watchman *noun* [C] (*pl* **night-watchmen**) a person who guards a building at night

nightingale /'naɪtɪŋgeɪl; *US* -tng-/ *noun* [C] a small brown bird that sings very beautifully

nightmare /'naɪtmeə(r)/ *noun* [C] **1** a dream that is frightening: *I had a terrible nightmare last night.* **2** something that is very unpleasant or frightening: *Travelling in the rush-hour can be a real nightmare.*

☆**nil** /nɪl/ *noun* [U] nothing (used especially about the score in a game): *We won by one goal to nil.* ☛ Look at the note at **zero**.

nimble /'nɪmbl/ *adj* able to move quickly and lightly: *For a large person she's very nimble on her feet.* —**nimbly** /'nɪmbli/ *adv*

☆**nine** /naɪn/ *number* 9; one more than eight ☛ For examples of how to use numbers in sentences, look at **six**.

(IDIOM) **nine to five** the hours that you work in most offices: *a nine-to-five job*

ninth /naɪnθ/ *pron, det, adv* 9th; next after eighth

ninth *pron, noun* [C] the fraction ⅑; one of nine equal parts of sth ☛ Look at the examples at **sixth**.

☆**nineteen** /,naɪn'ti:n/ *number* 19; one more than eighteen ☛ For examples of how to use numbers in sentences, look at **six**.

nineteenth /,naɪn'ti:nθ/ *pron, det, adv* 19th; next after eighteenth ☛ Look at the examples at **sixth**.

☆**ninety** /'naɪnti/ *number* 90; one more than 89 ☛ For examples of how to use numbers in sentences, look at **sixty**.

ninetieth /'naɪntiəθ/ *pron, det, adv* 90th; next after 89th ☛ Look at the examples at **sixth**.

nip /nɪp/ *verb* (**nipping**; **nipped**) **1** [I,T] to bite or pinch sb/sth lightly: *The dog nipped him on the ankle.* **2** [I] (*informal*) to move quickly; to hurry: *She nipped round to the shops for some bread and milk.*

nipple /'nɪpl/ *noun* [C] **1** the dark hard part in the centre of a woman's breast from which a baby drinks milk **2** the similar part on a man's chest

nit /nɪt/ *noun* [C] **1** the egg of a small insect that lives in the hair of people or animals **2** (*informal*) (*especially Brit*) a silly person

'nit-picking *adj, noun* [U] paying too much attention to small, unimportant details

nitrogen /'naɪtrədʒən/ *noun* [U] (*symbol* **N**) a gas that has no colour, taste or smell. Nitrogen forms about 80% of the air around the earth.

p	b	t	d	k	g	tʃ	dʒ	f	v	θ	ð
pen	bad	tea	did	cat	got	chin	June	fall	van	thin	then

nitty-gritty /ˌnɪtɪˈgrɪtɪ/ noun [sing] **the nitty-gritty** (informal) the most important facts, not the small or unimportant details

☆ **no** /nəʊ/ det **1** not any; not a: *I have no time to talk now.* ○ *No two days are the same.* ○ *No visitors may enter without a ticket.* ○ *He's no friend of mine.* ○ *There are no jobs for school-leavers in the town.* ○ *No news is good news.* **2** (used for saying that sth is not allowed): *No smoking.* ○ *No flash photography.* ○ *No parking.*

no interj **1** (used for giving a negative reply or statement): *'Are you ready?' 'No, I'm not.'* ○ *'Would you like something to eat?' 'No, thank you. I'm not hungry.'* ○ *'Can I borrow the car?' 'No, you can't.'* ○ *It's about 70 – no, I'm wrong – 80 kilometres from London.* ○ *No! Don't touch it. It's very hot.* ☛ You can also use **no** when you want to agree with a negative statement: *'This programme's not very good.' 'No, you're right. It isn't.'* **2** (used for expressing surprise or shock): *'Mike's had an accident.' 'Oh, no!'*

no adv not any: *Alice is feeling no better this morning.* ○ *Applications must be returned no later than 31 July.*

'no man's land noun [U] land between two armies in a war, between two frontiers, etc

'no one pron = NOBODY

nobility /nəʊˈbɪlətɪ/ noun **1** [U] the quality of being noble **2 the nobility** [sing, with sing or pl verb] the group of people who belong to the highest social class

noble /ˈnəʊbl/ adj **1** honest; brave; that other people should admire: *They made a noble effort in the face of many difficulties.* **2** belonging to the highest social class, with a title: *a noble family*
noble noun [C] (in former times) a person who belonged to the highest social class ☛ Look at **peer**. —**nobly** /ˈnəʊblɪ/ adv: *He nobly sacrificed his own happiness for that of his family.*

☆ **nobody** /ˈnəʊbədɪ/ (also **no one** /ˈnəʊwʌn/) pron no person; not anybody: *He screamed but nobody came to help him.* ○ *No one else was around.* ○ *There was nobody at home.* ☛ **None of**, not **nobody**, must be used before nouns like *the, his, her, those,* etc or before a pronoun: *Nobody remembered my birthday.* ○ *None of my friends remembered my birthday.* ○ *I've asked all my classmates but nobody is free.* ○ *None of them are free.*
nobody noun [C] (pl **nobodies**) a person who is not very important: *Do you want to be a nobody all your life?*

nocturnal /nɒkˈtɜːnl/ adj **1** happening in the night: *a nocturnal adventure* **2** (used about animals and birds) awake and active at night: *Owls are nocturnal birds.*

☆ **nod** /nɒd/ verb (**nodd**ing; **nodd**ed) [I,T] to move your head down and then up again quickly as a way of saying 'yes' or as a greeting or a sign: *'Would you like to come too?' he asked. She nodded and slowly got up.* ○ *Everybody at the meeting nodded in agreement.* ○ *Nod your head if you understand what I'm saying and shake it if you don't.* ○ *We nodded to each other across the room.* ○ *'Somebody will have to do it,' she said, nodding in my direction.* —**nod** noun [C]: *Give him a nod to show that you recognize him.*

☆ **noise** /nɔɪz/ noun [C,U] something that you hear; a sound, especially one that is loud, unpleasant or unwanted: *Did you hear a noise downstairs?* ○ *Try not to make a noise if you come home late.* ○ *What an awful noise!* ○ *Why is the engine making so much noise?*
noiseless adj making no sound —**noiselessly** adv

☆ **noisy** /ˈnɔɪzɪ/ adj (**noisier; noisiest**) making a lot of or too much noise; full of noise: *The clock was so noisy that it kept me awake.* ○ *Are small boys noisier than girls?* ○ *We live on a very noisy road.* ☛ Look at the note at **loud**. —**noisily** /-ɪlɪ/ adv

nomad /ˈnəʊmæd/ noun [C] a member of a tribe that travels around to find grass for its animals instead of living in one place —**nomadic** /nəʊˈmædɪk/ adj

nominal /ˈnɒmɪnl/ adj **1** being sth in name only but not in reality: *the nominal leader of the country* (= sb else is really in control) **2** (used about a price, sum of money, etc) very small; less than is normal: *Because we were friends he only charged me a nominal fee.*

nominate /ˈnɒmɪneɪt/ verb [T] **1 nominate sb/sth (for/as sth)** to suggest that sb/sth should be considered for an official position: *I would like to nominate Don Jones as chairman.* ○ *The novel has been nominated for the Booker prize.* **2 nominate sb (to/as sth) (to do sth)** to choose sb/sth for a position: *You may nominate a representative to speak for you.*

nomination /ˌnɒmɪˈneɪʃn/ noun [C,U] a formal suggestion that sb should be considered for an official position; the appointment of sb to such a position: *The closing date for nominations is September 8th.* ○ *The film has received 10 Oscar nominations.* ○ *His nomination as leader of the party was announced this morning.*

nominee /ˌnɒmɪˈniː/ noun [C] a person who is suggested or chosen for a position

non-aligned /ˌnɒn əˈlaɪnd/ adj (used about a country) not supporting any major country or group of countries

nonchalant /ˈnɒnʃələnt/ adj not feeling or showing interest or excitement; seeming calm —**nonchalance** /-ləns/ noun [U] —**nonchalantly** adv

noncommittal /ˌnɒnkəˈmɪtl/ adj not saying or showing exactly what you think, or what you are going to do

nonconformist /ˌnɒnkənˈfɔːmɪst/ noun [C] a person who behaves or thinks differently from most other people in society —**nonconformist** adj

nondescript /ˈnɒndɪskrɪpt/ adj not very interesting; dull

☆ **none** /nʌn/ pron not any, not one (of a group of three or more): *'Could you pass me the wine, please?' 'I'm afraid there's none left.'* ○ *They gave me a lot of information but none of it was very helpful.* ○ *I've got four brothers but none of them live/lives nearby.* ○ *'Have you brought any books to read?' 'No, none.'* ○ *I went to several shops but none had what I was looking for.* ☛ When we use **none of** with a plural noun, the verb can be singular, which is formal, or

s	z	ʃ	ʒ	h	m	n	ŋ	l	r	j	w
so	zoo	she	vision	how	man	no	sing	leg	red	yes	wet

plural, which is informal: *None of the trains is/are going to London.* When we are talking about two people or things we use **neither** not **none**: *Neither of my brothers lives nearby.* Note the difference between **none** and **no**: *I told him that I had no money left.* ○ *When he asked me how much money I had left, I told him that I had none.*
(IDIOM) **none the worse** ⇨ WORSE

none *adv* (with *the* and a comparative adjective) not at all: *We talked for a long time but I'm still none the wiser* (= I don't know any more than before).

nonetheless /ˌnʌnðəˈles/ (*also* **none the less**) *adv* anyway; in spite of what has just been said: *It won't be easy but they're going to try nonetheless.* ☛ **Nevertheless** has the same meaning.

non-existent /ˌnɒnɪɡˈzɪstənt/ *adj* not existing or not available: *In some areas public transport is completely non-existent.*

non-fiction /ˌnɒnˈfɪkʃn/ *noun* [U] writing that is about real people, events and facts

nonplussed /ˌnɒnˈplʌst/ *adj* very surprised or confused

☆ **nonsense** /ˈnɒnsns; *US* -sens/ *noun* [U] **1** something that sb says or writes that is not true or is just silly: *What you're saying is nonsense.* ○ *My father thinks people talk a lot of nonsense about health foods and fitness.* ○ *'I'm hopeless at sport,' said Tim. 'Nonsense!' said his mother, 'You're very good.'* ○ *I think that newspaper article is absolute nonsense.* **2** foolish or bad behaviour: *The headmaster doesn't allow any nonsense.*

nonsensical /nɒnˈsensɪkl/ *adj* not intelligent or sensible; stupid: *That was a completely nonsensical thing to say.*

non-smoker /ˌnɒnˈsməʊkə(r)/ *noun* [C] a person who does not smoke —**non-ˈsmoking** *adj*: *Would you like a seat in the smoking or the non-smoking part of the plane?*

non-starter /ˌnɒnˈstɑːtə(r)/ *noun* [C] a person, plan or idea that has no chance of success

non-stick /ˌnɒnˈstɪk/ *adj* (used about a pan, etc) covered with a substance that prevents food from sticking to it

non-stop /ˌnɒnˈstɒp/ *adj, adv* without a stop or a break: *a non-stop flight to Bombay* ○ *The 9.30 train goes non-stop to Manchester.* ○ *He talked non-stop for two hours about his holiday.*

non-violence /ˌnɒnˈvaɪələns/ *noun* [U] the refusal to use force to bring about political or social change —**non-violent** /-lənt/ *adj*

noodle /ˈnuːdl/ *noun* [C, usually pl] long thin pieces of pasta (= food made of flour, egg and water) that are cooked in boiling water or used in soups

nook /nʊk/ *noun* [C] a small quiet place or corner (in a house, garden, etc)
(IDIOM) **every nook and cranny** every part of a place

☆ **noon** /nuːn/ *noun* [U] 12 o'clock in the middle of the day; midday: *At noon the sun is at its highest point in the sky.* ○ *They arrived around noon and stayed all afternoon.*

noose /nuːs/ *noun* [C] **1** a circle that is tied in the end of a rope and that can be made tighter or looser **2** a circle like this in a rope that is used for hanging a person

☆ **nor** /nɔː(r)/ *conj, adv* **1** (used after *neither* or *not*) and not: *I received neither a telephone call nor a letter during the whole six months.* ○ (*formal*) *Not a building nor a tree was left standing.* **2** (used after a negative statement to add some further information) also not: *The sun hardly shone at all during the first week. Nor during the second, for that matter.* **3** (used before a positive verb to agree with sth negative that has just been said) also not; neither: *'I don't like football.' 'Nor do I.'* ○ *'I couldn't afford to stay there.' 'Nor could I.'* ○ *'We haven't been to America.' 'Nor have we.'*

norm /nɔːm/ *noun* [C] (often with *the*) a pattern of behaviour that is normal or expected: *Is it the norm in your country for children to leave home before they marry?*

☆ **normal** /ˈnɔːml/ *adj* **1** usual, ordinary or what you expect: *I'll pick you up at the normal time.* ○ *If you need to see a doctor outside normal surgery hours, ring the following number.* ○ *I just want to lead a normal life again.* ○ *We're just a normal respectable family.* ○ *It's quite normal to feel angry in a situation like this.* ○ *The amount of traffic was described as normal for a holiday weekend.* ○ *Under normal circumstances the meeting would only have lasted an hour.* **2** (used about a person or animal) formed or developed in the usual way: *The child was completely normal at birth.* ☛ Look at **abnormal**.

normal *noun* [U] the usual or average state, level, standard, etc: *Your temperature is slightly above normal.* ○ *I hope the situation will soon return to normal.* ○ *Things are back to normal at work now.*

normality /nɔːˈmæləti/ (*US* **normalcy** /ˈnɔːmlsi/) *noun* [U] the state of being normal

normalize (*also* **normalise**) /ˈnɔːməlaɪz/ *verb* [I,T] (*formal*) to become or make sth normal, good or friendly again

normally /ˈnɔːməli/ *adv* **1** usually: *I normally leave the house at 8 o'clock.* ○ *We don't normally have people round to dinner.* ○ *Normally he gets the bus.* **2** in a usual or an ordinary way: *The man wasn't behaving normally.*

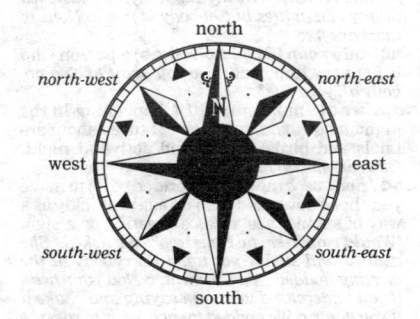

☆ **north** /nɔːθ/ *noun* [sing] (*abbr* **N**) **1** (*also* **the north**) one of the four main points of the compass; the direction that is on your left when you face the sunrise: *cold winds from the north* o *Which way is north?* **2 the north; the North** the part of any country, city, etc that lies further towards the north than other parts: *Leeds is in the North of England.* o *I live in the north of London.*

north (*also* **North**) *adj* in or towards the north, or from the north: *The new offices will be in North Oxford.* o *The north wing of the castle was destroyed in a fire.* o *a cold north wind*

north *adv* to or towards the north: *We got onto the motorway going north instead of south.* o *The house faces north.* o *Is Leeds north of Manchester?*

northerly /'nɔ:ðəli/ *adj* **1** to, towards or in the north: *Keep going in a northerly direction.* **2** (used about a wind) coming from the north

northward /'nɔ:θwəd/ *adj* towards the north: *in a northward direction*

northwards (*also* **northwards**) *adv* towards the north: *Continue northwards out of the city for about five miles.*

'northbound *adj* travelling or leading towards the north: *the northbound carriageway of the motorway*

ˌnorth-'east *noun* [sing] (*abbr* **NE**) **1** (*also* **the north-east**) the direction or point of the compass that is between north and east **2 the north-east; the North-East** a region that is towards the north-east: *the North-East of France*

ˌnorth-'east *adj, adv* in, from or to the north-east of a place or country: *the north-east coast of England* o *If you look north-east you can see the sea.*

ˌnorth-'easterly *adj* **1** towards the north-east: *in a north-easterly direction* **2** (used about a wind) coming from the north-east

ˌnorth-'eastern /-'i:stən/ *adj* in or from the north-east of a place or country: *north-eastern Africa*

ˌnorth-'eastward /-'i:stwəd/ (*also* **ˌnorth-'eastwards**) *adv* towards the north-east: *Follow the A619 north-eastward.*

the ˌNorth 'Pole *noun* [sing] the point on the earth's surface which is furthest north ☛ picture at **earth**.

ˌnorth-'west *noun* [sing] (*abbr* **NW**) **1** (*also* **the north-west**) the direction or point of the compass that is between north and west **2 the north-west; the North-West** a region that is towards the north-west: *the North-West of France*

ˌnorth-'west *adj, adv* in, from or to the north-west of a place or country: *the north-west coast of Scotland* o *If you look north-west you can see the sea.*

ˌnorth-'westerly *adj* **1** towards the north-west: *in a north-westerly direction* **2** (used about a wind) coming from the north-west

ˌnorth-'western /-'westən/ *adj* in or from the north-west of a place or country: *north-western Australia*

ˌnorth-'westward /-'westwəd/ (*also* **ˌnorth-'westwards**) *adv* towards the north-west: *Follow the A40 north-westward.*

☆ **northern** (*also* **Northern**) /'nɔ:ðən/ *adj* of, in or from the north of a place: *She has a northern accent.* o *in northern Australia* o *the northern hemisphere*

northerner (*also* **Northerner**) /'nɔ:ðənə(r)/ *noun* [C] a person who was born in or who lives in the northern part of a country

northernmost /-məʊst/ *adj* furthest north

☆ **nose**¹ /nəʊz/ *noun* [C] **1** the part of the face, above the mouth, that is used for breathing and smelling: *a broken nose* o *He received a nasty blow on the nose.* o *This medicine should stop your nose running.* o *Breathe in through your nose and out through your mouth.* o *Picking your nose is not a nice habit.* ☛ The adjective is **nasal. 2** the front part of sth, especially an aeroplane: *The nose of the plane was badly damaged.*

(IDIOMS) **blow your nose** ⇨ BLOW¹

look down your nose at sb/sth to think that you are better than sb; to think that sth is of poor quality

poke/stick your nose into sth to interfere in sth when you should not: *He's always poking his nose into other people's business!*

turn your nose up at sth to refuse sth because you do not think it is good or do not like it

-nosed (in compounds) having a nose of the type mentioned: *red-nosed* o *runny-nosed*

'nosebleed *noun* [C] a time when a lot of blood comes from your nose

'nosedive *verb* [I] to make a fast drop downwards towards the ground: *All of a sudden the plane nosedived.* —**'nosedive** *noun* [C]

nose² /nəʊz/ *verb* [I] to go forward slowly and carefully: *The bus nosed out into the line of traffic.*

(PHRASAL VERB) **nose about/around** (*informal*) to look around a private place trying to find sth interesting

nosey (*also* **nosy**) /'nəʊzi/ *adj* (**nosier; nosiest**) too interested in other people's affairs

nostalgia /nɒ'stældʒə/ *noun* [U] a feeling of affection, mixed with sadness, for things that are in the past —**nostalgic** /nɒ'stældʒɪk/ *adj* —**nostalgically** /-kli/ *adv*

nostril /'nɒstrəl/ *noun* [C] one of the two openings at the end of the nose ☛ picture on page A8.

☆ **not** /nɒt/ *adv* **1** (used to form the negative with verbs like *be, can, do, have, must, will,* etc and often shortened to *n't* in speech and informal writing): *It's not/It isn't raining now.* o *He's not coming/He isn't coming.* o *I'm not coming.* o *I cannot/can't see from here.* o *You shouldn't have said that.* o *He didn't invite me.* o *Don't you like spaghetti?* o *I hope she will not/won't be late.* o *You're German, aren't you?* **2** (used to give the following word or phrase a negative meaning or to reply in the negative): *He told me not to telephone.* o *I remember her but not her sister.* o *Not everybody was able to come.* o *Not all of the houses are as nice as this one.* o *'Whose turn is it to do the shopping?' 'Not mine.'* o *'Do you see each other a lot?' 'No, not often.'* o *'Are you coming to play tennis?' 'Not now.'* **3** (used after *be afraid, believe, expect, hope, suppose,* etc, to give a negative reply): *'Do you think*

ɜː	ə	eɪ	əʊ	aɪ	aʊ	ɔɪ	ɪə	eə	ʊə
fur	ago	pay	home	five	now	join	near	hair	pure

they'll get married?' 'I hope not.' (= I hope that they will not.) ○ 'You can't drive all that way alone.' 'I suppose not.' ○ 'Did you see her?' 'I'm afraid not.' **4** (used with *or* to give a negative possibility): *Shall we tell her or not?* ○ *I don't know if he's telling the truth or not.* **5** (used for saying that sth is not possible or that you do not want to do sth): *'Can I borrow £20?' 'Certainly not!'* ○ *'Are you coming to the theatre with us?' 'I'd rather not, if you don't mind.'* **6** (used for showing that you mean the opposite of the word or phrase that follows): *It's not easy* (= it's difficult).

(IDIOMS) **not at all 1** (a way of saying 'no' or 'not'): *'Do you mind if I come too?' 'Not at all.'* ○ *The instructions are not at all clear.* **2** (a way of replying when sb has thanked you): *'Thanks for the present.' 'Not at all, don't mention it.'*

not only... (but) also (used for emphasizing the fact that there is something more): *They not only have two houses in London, they also have one in France.*

notable /'nəʊtəbl/ *adj* deserving to be noticed; interesting or important: *The area is notable for its scenery and wildlife.*

notably /'nəʊtəbli/ *adv* (used for giving an especially important example of what you are talking about): *Many countries, notably Denmark, have refused to sign the agreement.*

notch /nɒtʃ/ *noun* [C] **1** a cut in an edge or surface in the shape of a V **2** a level on a scale of quality: *This meal is certainly a notch above the last one we had here.*

notch *verb*
(PHRASAL VERB) **notch sth up** to score or achieve sth: *Lewis notched up his best ever time in the 100 metres.*

☆ **note¹** /nəʊt/ *noun* **1** [C] a short letter: *This is just a note to thank you for having us all to stay.* **2** [C] some words that you write down quickly to help you remember sth: *I'd better make a note of your name and address.* ○ *Keep a note of who has paid and who hasn't.* ○ *The lecturer advised the students to take* (= write down) *notes while he was speaking.* **3** [C] a short explanation or extra piece of information that is given at the back of a book, etc or at the bottom or side of a page: *an edition of Shakespeare with student's notes* ○ *See note 5, page 340.* ☛ Look at **footnote**. **4** [C] (*also* **'banknote**; *US* **bill**) a piece of paper money: *I'd like the money in £10 notes, please.* ☛ picture at **money**. **5** [C] a single musical sound made by a voice or an instrument: *I can only remember the first few notes of the song.* ○ *high/low notes* **6** [C] a written sign that represents a musical sound **7** [sing] (something that suggests) a certain quality or feeling: *There was a note of embarrassment in her voice.* ○ *The meeting ended on a rather unpleasant note.*

(IDIOM) **compare notes (with sb)** ⇨ COMPARE

'notebook *noun* [C] a small book in which you write things that you want to remember

'notepad *noun* [C] some sheets of paper in a block that are used for writing notes(2) on: *I always keep a notepad by the telephone.*

'notepaper *noun* [U] paper that you write letters on: *a sheet of notepaper*

☆ **note²** /nəʊt/ *verb* [T] **1** to notice or be aware of sth: *He noted a slight change in her attitude towards him.* ○ *Note the fine detail in the painting.* **2** to mention sth: *I'd like to note that the project has so far been extremely successful.*
(PHRASAL VERB) **note sth down** to write sth down so that you remember it: *The policeman noted down the girl's description of the man.*

noted *adj* **noted (for/as sth)** (*formal*) well-known; famous: *The hotel is noted for its food.*

'noteworthy *adj* deserving to be noticed; interesting or important

☆ **nothing** /'nʌθɪŋ/ *pron* not anything; no thing: *There's nothing in this suitcase.* ○ *Nothing exciting ever happens to me.* ○ *There's nothing to do here.* ○ *There was nothing else to say.* ○ *'What's the matter?' 'Oh, nothing.'* ○ *'Thank you so much for all your help.' 'It was nothing.'* (= nothing of any importance) ☛ Look at the note at **zero**.

(IDIOMS) **be/have nothing to do with sb/sth** to have no connection with sb/sth: *That question has nothing to do with what we're discussing.* ○ *Put my diary down – it's nothing to do with you* (= you do not have the right to look at it).

come to nothing ⇨ COME

for nothing 1 for no good reason or with no good result: *His hard work was all for nothing.* **2** for no payment; free: *Children under four are allowed in for nothing.*

nothing but only: *He was wearing nothing but a pair of swimming trunks.*

(there's) nothing to it (it's) very easy: *You'll soon learn – there's nothing to it really.*

there is/was nothing for it (but to do sth) there is/was no other action possible: *There was nothing for it but to resign.*

☆ **notice** /'nəʊtɪs/ *noun* **1** [C] a written statement giving information or news that is put where everybody can read it: *There's a notice on the board saying that the meeting has been cancelled.* **2** [U] a warning that sth is going to happen: *I can't produce a meal at such short notice!* ○ *I wish you had given me more notice that you were going on holiday.* ○ *The swimming pool is closed until further notice* (= until we are told that it will open again). ○ *We've been given a month's notice to leave the flat* (= we have been told we must leave in a month). ○ *My boss has given me a month's notice* (= told me to leave my job in a month). ○ *She handed in her notice last week* (= a letter saying that she is going to leave her job).

(IDIOMS) **come to sb's notice** (*formal*) be seen or heard by sb: *It has come to my notice that you have missed a lot of classes.*

take notice (of sth) to act in a way that shows that you know sth is important: *The protests are finally making the government take notice.*

take no notice/not take any notice (of sb/sth) to pay no attention (to sb/sth): *Take no notice of what he said – he was just being silly.* ○ *Some people don't take any notice of speed limits.* ☛ If you **don't notice** something, eg a speed limit, it means that you don't see it at all.

p	b	t	d	k	g	tʃ	dʒ	f	v	θ	ð
pen	bad	tea	did	cat	got	chin	June	fall	van	thin	then

However if you **don't take any notice** of it, it means that you see it but you choose to ignore it.

notice verb [I,T] to see and be aware of sth: *'What kind of car was the man driving?' 'I'm afraid I didn't notice.'* o *Did you notice her eyes? They were the most brilliant blue.* o *I noticed (that) he was carrying a black briefcase.* o *Did you notice which direction she went in?* o *We didn't notice him leave/him leaving.*

noticeable /-əbl/ *adj* easy to see or notice: *The scar from the accident was hardly noticeable.* o *a noticeable difference* —**noticeably** /-əblɪ/ *adv*

'notice-board (*US* **'bulletin board**) *noun* [C] a board on a wall for putting notices(1) on

notify /'nəʊtɪfaɪ/ *verb* [T] (*pres part* **notifying**; *3rd pers sing pres* **notifies**; *pt*, *pp* **notified**) **notify sb (of sth)** to inform sb (about sth) officially: *The police should be notified of the theft.* o *You must notify your landlady that you intend to leave.* —**notification** /ˌnəʊtɪfɪ'keɪʃn/ *noun* [C,U]

notion /'nəʊʃn/ *noun* [C] something that you have in your mind; an idea: *I had a vague notion that I had seen her before.* o *You seem to have no notion of how difficult it is going to be.*

notional /-ʃənl/ *adj* existing only in the mind; based on a guess not a real figure: *The figures I gave you were only notional.*

notoriety /ˌnəʊtə'raɪətɪ/ *noun* [U] the state of being famous for sth bad

notorious /nəʊ'tɔːrɪəs/ *adj* **notorious (for/as sth)** well-known for sth bad: *a notorious drug dealer* o *This road is notorious for the number of accidents on it.* —**notoriously** *adv*: *The British are notoriously bad at learning languages.*

notwithstanding /ˌnɒtwɪθ'stændɪŋ/ *prep* (*formal*) without being affected by; in spite of: *The plane landed on time, notwithstanding the terrible weather conditions.*

notwithstanding *adv* (*formal*) anyway; in spite of this: *He was advised against the deal, but went ahead notwithstanding.*

nought /nɔːt/ *noun* [C] the figure 0: *We say 0·1 'nought point one'.*
(IDIOM) **noughts and crosses** a game for two players that is played with a pencil and paper. Each person tries to win by writing three 0s or three Xs in a line.

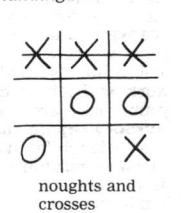

noughts and crosses

☆**noun** /naʊn/ *noun* [C] (*grammar*) a word that is the name of a person, place, thing or idea: *'Jane', 'London', 'table' and 'happiness' are all nouns.* ☛ Look at **countable** and **uncountable**.

nourish /'nʌrɪʃ/ *verb* [T] **1** to give a person or animal the right kind of food so that they can grow and be healthy **2** (*formal*) to allow a feeling or belief to grow stronger

nourishment *noun* [U] food that you need to stay healthy

☆**novel**[1] /'nɒvl/ *noun* [C] a book that tells a story about people and events that are not real: *the novels of Charles Dickens* o *a romantic novel*

novelist /'nɒvəlɪst/ *noun* [C] a person who writes novels

novel[2] /'nɒvl/ *adj* new and different: *That's a novel idea! Let's try it.*

novelty /'nɒvltɪ/ *noun* (*pl* **novelties**) **1** [U] the quality of being new and different: *The novelty of her new job soon wore off.* **2** [C] something new and unusual: *It was quite a novelty not to have to get up at 7 o'clock.* **3** [C] a small, cheap object that is sold as a toy or souvenir

☆**November** /nəʊ'vembə(r)/ *noun* [C,U] (*abbr* **Nov**) the eleventh month of the year, coming before December ☛ For examples of the use of the months in sentences, look at **January**.

novice /'nɒvɪs/ *noun* [C] a person who is new and without experience in a certain job, situation, etc; a beginner

☆**now** /naʊ/ *adv* **1** (at) the present time: *We can't go for a walk now – it's pouring with rain.* o *Where are you living now?* o *It's too late now to do anything about it.* o *From now on the nights will be getting longer.* o *I've been living with my parents until now.* o *Up till now we haven't been able to afford a house of our own.* o *He will be on his way home by now.* o *You must go to the doctor right now.* **2** because of what has happened: *I've lost my pen. Now I'll have to buy a new one.* **3** (used to introduce a new subject or to emphasize a request, command, etc, or while pausing to think): *Now this is how it all began.* o *Now listen to what he's saying.* o *Be quiet, now!* o *Now, let me think.* ☛ **Now then** is also used: *Now then, are there any questions?* o *Now then, what was I saying?*

(IDIOMS) **(every) now and again/then** occasionally: *We see each other now and then, but not very often.*

just now ⇨ JUST[2]

now *conj* **now (that)**... because of the fact that: *Now (that) the children have left home we can move to a smaller house.*

☆**nowadays** /'naʊədeɪz/ *adv* at the present time (when compared with the past): *I don't go to London much nowadays* (= but I did in the past).

☆**nowhere** /'nəʊweə(r); *US* -hweər/ *adv* not anywhere; (in or to) no place: *I'm afraid there's nowhere to stay in this village.* o *There's nowhere interesting to go round here.* o *It's so hot I'm getting nowhere with this work* (= making no progress). o *'Don't leave the car there!' 'There's nowhere else to park it.'*
(IDIOM) **nowhere near** ⇨ NEAR[2]

noxious /'nɒkʃəs/ *adj* (*formal*) harmful or poisonous: *noxious gases*

nozzle /'nɒzl/ *noun* [C] a narrow tube that is put on the end of a pipe, etc to control the liquid or gas coming out

nuance /'njuːɑːns; *US* 'nuː-/ *noun* [C] a very small difference in meaning, feeling, sound, etc

☆**nuclear** /'njuːklɪə(r); *US* 'nuː-/ *adj* **1** connected with the nucleus of an atom: *nuclear physics* **2** connected with the energy that is produced when the nucleus of an atom is split: *nuclear*

s	z	ʃ	ʒ	h	m	n	ŋ	l	r	j	w
so	zoo	she	vision	how	man	no	sing	leg	red	yes	wet

nucleus

energy ○ *a nuclear-power station* ○ *nuclear weapons* ☞ Look at **atomic**.

,nuclear dis'armament *noun* [U] stopping the use and development of nuclear weapons

,nuclear-'free *adj* not having or allowing nuclear weapons or nuclear energy: *This town has been declared a nuclear-free zone.*

,nuclear 'reactor (*also* **reactor**) *noun* [C] a very large machine that produces nuclear energy

nucleus /'nju:klɪəs; *US* 'nu:-/ *noun* [C] (*pl* **nuclei** /-klɪaɪ/) **1** the central part of an atom **2** the central or most important part of sth

nude /nju:d; *US* nu:d/ *adj* not wearing any clothes ☞ Look at **bare** and **naked**.

nude *noun* [C] a picture or photograph of a person who is not wearing clothes

(IDIOM) **in the nude** not wearing any clothes

nudist /-ɪst/ *noun* [C] a person who likes to be nude, often in groups with other people: *a nudist beach*

nudity /'nju:dətɪ; *US* 'nu:-/ *noun* [U] the state of being nude

nudge /nʌdʒ/ *verb* [T] to touch or push sb/sth with your elbow —**nudge** *noun* [C]: *to give sb a nudge*

☆ **nuisance** /'nju:sns; *US* 'nu:-/ *noun* [C] a person, thing or situation that annoys you or causes you trouble: *My pen's run out. What a nuisance!* ○ *I'm sorry to be a nuisance, but could you change my appointment to next Thursday?*

null /nʌl/ *adj*

(IDIOM) **null and void** (*formal*) not valid in law

numb /nʌm/ *adj* not able to feel anything; not able to move: *My fingers were numb with cold.* ○ *I'll give you an injection and the tooth will go completely numb.* ○ *He was numb with fear.*

numb *verb* [T] to make sb/sth numb: *The whole family was numbed and shocked by the news.* —**numbness** *noun* [U]: *The numbness should wear off after a few hours.*

☆ **number** /'nʌmbə(r)/ *noun* **1** [C] a word or symbol that indicates a quantity: *Choose a number between ten and twenty.* ○ *2 is an even number and 3 is an odd number.* ○ *Thirteen is considered to be an unlucky number.* ○ *a three-figure number* (= more than 99 and less than 1 000) ○ *high/low numbers* ○ *cardinal/ordinal numbers* **2** [C] a group of numbers that is used to identify sb/sth: *What is the number of your car?* ○ *a telephone number* **3** [C,U] a quantity or amount: *a large number of visitors* ○ *Pupils in the school have doubled in number in recent years.* ○ *a number of questions* (= several) ○ *We must reduce the number of accidents in the home.*

☞ When **number** has an adjective before it, it is always followed by a plural verb: *A small number of pupils study Latin.* **4** [C] (*abbr* **No**; **no**) (used before a number to show the position of sth in a series): *We live in Croft Road, at number 25.* ○ *room no 347* ○ *No 10 (Downing Street) is the official home of the British Prime Minister.* **5** [C] a copy of a magazine, newspaper, etc: *Back numbers of 'New Scientist' are available from the publishers.* **6** [C] (*informal*) a song or dance

(IDIOMS) **any number of** very many: *There are any number of language schools in Oxford.*

in round figures/numbers ⇨ ROUND¹

opposite number ⇨ OPPOSITE

number *verb* **1** [T] to give a number to sth: *It's a country lane and the houses are not numbered.* **2** [I] (used for expressing how many people or things there are): *Our forces number 40 000.*

'number-plate (*US* **license plate**) *noun* [C] the sign on the front and back of a vehicle that gives its registration number

numeral /'nju:mərəl; *US* 'nu:-/ *noun* [C] a sign or symbol that represents a quantity: *Roman numerals*

numerate /'nju:mərət; *US* 'nu:-/ *adj* having a good basic knowledge of mathematics ☞ Look at **literate**.

numerical /nju:'merɪkl; *US* nu:-/ *adj* of or shown by numbers: *to put sth in numerical order*

numerous /'nju:mərəs; *US* 'nu:-/ *adj* (*formal*) very many; existing in large quantities

nun /nʌn/ *noun* [C] a woman who has left the ordinary world and has gone to live in a religious community (**convent**) ☞ Look at **monk**.

☆ **nurse¹** /nɜ:s/ *noun* [C] a person whose job is to look after sick or injured people: *a trained nurse* ○ *a male nurse* ○ *Nurse Mills*

☞ A **community** or **district** nurse visits sick people in their homes to give them the care that they need. A **health visitor** is a nurse who gives help and advice to parents of babies and young children.

nurse² /nɜ:s/ *verb* [T] **1** to take care of sb who is sick or injured: *She nursed her mother until she died in 1969.* **2** to hold sb/sth in a loving way: *He nursed the child in his arms.* **3** (*formal*) to think a lot about sth: *Dan had long nursed the hope that Paula would marry him.*

nursing *noun* [U] the job of being a nurse: *She has decided to go into nursing.*

'nursing-home *noun* [C] a small private hospital, often for old people

☆ **nursery** /'nɜ:sərɪ/ *noun* [C] (*pl* **nurseries**) **1** a place where small children and babies are looked after so that their parents can go to work ☞ Look at **crèche**. **2** a place where young plants are grown and sold

'nursery rhyme *noun* [C] a traditional poem or song for children

'nursery school *noun* [C] a school for children aged from three to five ☞ Look at **kindergarten**.

☆ **nut** /nʌt/ *noun* [C] **1** a dry fruit that consists of a hard shell with a seed (**kernel**) inside. Many types of nut may be eaten: *chopped hazelnuts and almonds* **2** a six-sided piece of metal with a round hole in the middle through which you screw a long round piece of metal (**bolt**). Nuts and bolts are used for fixing things together: *Tighten the nut with a spanner.* **3** (*Brit slang*) the head **4** (*also* **nutter**) (*slang*) a mad or foolish person

(IDIOM) **do your nut** (*Brit slang*) to be very angry

---

iː	ɪ	e	æ	ɑː	ɒ	ɔː	ʊ	uː	ʌ
see	sit	ten	hat	arm	got	saw	put	too	cup

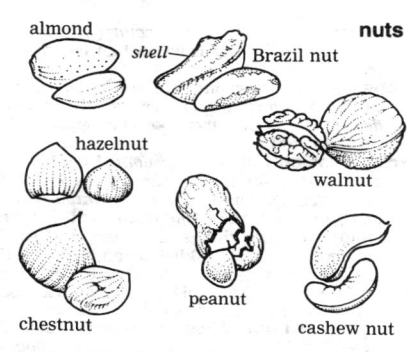

nuts: almond, shell, Brazil nut, hazelnut, walnut, chestnut, peanut, cashew nut

nutty adj (**nuttier**; **nuttiest**) **1** containing or tasting of nuts **2** (slang) mad or foolish

'nutcrackers noun [plural] a tool that you use for breaking open the shell of a nut

'nutshell /-ʃel/ noun
(IDIOM) **in a nutshell** using few words: *That, in a nutshell, is the answer to your question.*

nutmeg /'nʌtmeg/ noun [C,U] a type of spice, used for giving flavour to food

nutrition /nju:'trɪʃn; US nu:-/ noun [U] the food that you eat and the way that it affects your health: *Good nutrition is essential for children's growth.*

nutritious /nju:'trɪʃəs; US nu:-/ adj (used about a food) very good for you

nuzzle /'nʌzl/ verb [T] to press or rub sb/sth gently with the nose

nylon /'naɪlɒn/ noun [U] a very strong man-made material that is used for making clothes, rope, brushes, etc: *The blouse is 50% nylon.*

Oo

O, o /əʊ/ noun [C] (pl **O's**; **o's**) **1** the fifteenth letter of the English alphabet: *'Orange' begins with (an) 'O'.* **2** (used when you are speaking) zero: *My number is five O nine double four (= 50944).* ☛ Look at the note at **zero**.

O, Oh /əʊ/ interj (used for expressing surprise, fear, pain, sudden pleasure, etc): *Oh, thank you! What a lovely present!* o *Oh, that hurt.*

oak /əʊk/ noun **1** (also **'oak-tree**) [C] a type of large tree with hard wood that is common in many northern parts of the world **2** [U] the wood from the oak tree: *a solid oak table*

☛ The fruit of the oak is an **acorn**.

oar /ɔ:(r)/ noun [C] a long pole that is flat at one end and that is used for moving a small boat through water (**rowing**) ☛ Look at **paddle**.

oasis /əʊ'eɪsɪs/ noun [C] (pl **oases** /-si:z/) a place in the desert where there is water and where plants grow

oath /əʊθ/ noun [C] **1** a formal promise: *They have to swear an oath of loyalty.* **2** a word or words that are very impolite and that you use when you are really angry ☛ **Swear-word** is more common nowadays.
(IDIOM) **be on/under oath** to have made a formal promise to tell the truth in a court of law

oats /əʊts/ noun [plural] a type of grain that is used as food for people and animals: *porridge oats*

☆ **obedient** /ə'bi:diənt/ adj doing what you are told to do: *He was an obedient child and never caused any problems.* ☛ The opposite is **dis**-obedient. —**obedience** /-əns/ noun [U]: *unquestioning obedience* —**obediently** adv

☆ **obey** /ə'beɪ/ verb [I,T] to do what you are told to do: *Soldiers are trained to obey orders.* ☛ The opposite is **disobey**.

obituary /ə'bɪtʃʊəri; US -tʃueri/ noun [C] (pl **obituaries**) an article about a person's life that is printed in a newspaper soon after he/she has died

☆ **object¹** /'ɒbdʒɪkt/ noun [C] **1** a thing that can be seen and touched: *The shelves were filled with objects of all shapes and sizes.* **2 the object of sth** a person or thing that causes a feeling, interest, thought, etc **3** an aim or purpose: *Making money is his sole object in life.* **4** (grammar) the noun or phrase describing the person or thing that is affected by the action of a verb ☛ In the sentences: *I sent a letter to Moira* o *I sent Moira a letter* 'a letter' is the **direct** object of the verb and 'Moira' is the **indirect** object.
(IDIOM) **money, etc no object** money, etc is not important or is no problem: *They always buy the best. Money is no object.*

☆ **object²** /əb'dʒekt/ verb **1** [I] **object (to sb/sth)** to not like or to be against sb/sth: *Many people object to the new tax.* **2** [T] to say that you do not like sth or to say that sth is wrong: *'I think that's unfair,' he objected.*

objector noun [C] a person who objects to sth

☆ **objection** /əb'dʒekʃn/ noun [C,U] a statement or feeling that you do not like or are against sb/sth: *We listed our objections to the proposed new road and sent them to the council.* o *My parents have no objection to our marriage.*

ɜː	ə	eɪ	əʊ	aɪ	aʊ	ɔɪ	ɪə	eə	ʊə
fur	ago	pay	home	five	now	join	near	hair	pure

objectionable /əbˈdʒekʃənəbl/ *adj* very unpleasant

objective¹ /əbˈdʒektɪv/ *adj* not influenced by your own personal feelings (= based only on facts): *Please try and give an objective report of what happened.* ○ *It's hard to be objective about your own strengths and weaknesses.* ☛ The opposite is **subjective**. —**objectively** *adv*: *He is too upset to see things objectively.* —**objectivity** /ˌɒbdʒekˈtɪvəti/ *noun* [U]

objective² /əbˈdʒektɪv/ *noun* [C] your aim or purpose: *Our objective is to finish by the end of the year.* ○ *to achieve your objective*

obligation /ˌɒblɪˈɡeɪʃn/ *noun* **1** [C] something that you must do because it is your duty or because you promised to do it: *We have a moral obligation to help people who are in need.* **2** [U] having to do sth because it is is your duty: *Unfortunately the shop is under no obligation to give you your money back* (= they do not have to give you your money back).

obligatory /əˈblɪɡətri; *US* -tɔːri/ *adj* (*formal*) that you must do: *It is obligatory to get insurance before you drive a car.*

☆ **oblige** /əˈblaɪdʒ/ *verb* **1** [T] (usually passive) to force sb to do sth: *You are not obliged to answer these questions but it would be a great help if you did.* **2** [I,T] (*formal*) to do what sb asks; to be helpful: *The service there is excellent. They are always happy to oblige.*

obliged *adj* grateful: *Thanks for your help. I'm much obliged to you.*

obliging *adj* friendly and helpful

obliterate /əˈblɪtəreɪt/ *verb* [T] (*formal*) to destroy or ruin sth completely

oblivion /əˈblɪviən/ *noun* [U] **1** the state of having forgotten sth or of not being aware of sth: *I was in a state of complete oblivion.* **2** the state of being forgotten: *His work faded into oblivion after his death.*

oblivious /əˈblɪviəs/ *adj* not noticing or being aware of sth: *The baby slept, oblivious to all that was going on around him.*

oblong /ˈɒblɒŋ; *US* -lɔːŋ/ *adj, noun* [C] (of) a shape with two long sides and two short sides and four angles of 90° (**right angles**) ☛ Look at **rectangle**.

obnoxious /əbˈnɒkʃəs/ *adj* very unpleasant

oboe /ˈəʊbəʊ/ *noun* [C] a musical instrument that is made of wood. You play an oboe by blowing through it.

obscene /əbˈsiːn/ *adj* (used about words, thoughts, books, pictures, etc) shocking or disgusting (usually because of the way they talk about or show sex): *an obscene book* ○ (*figurative*) *It's obscene to spend so much on food when millions are starving.*

obscenity /əbˈsenəti/ *noun* (*pl* **obscenities**) **1** [U] the state of being obscene **2** [C] an obscene word or act

obscure /əbˈskjʊə(r)/ *adj* **1** not easy to see or understand: *The reasoning behind his comments was a bit obscure.* **2** not well-known: *an obscure Spanish poet*

obscure *verb* [T] to make sth difficult to see or understand: *Our view was obscured by a high fence.* —**obscurity** /əbˈskjʊərəti/ *noun* [U]: *The artist died penniless and in obscurity.*

observance /əbˈzɜːvəns/ *noun* [U] (*formal*) obeying or following a law, custom, ceremony, etc

observant /əbˈzɜːvənt/ *adj* quick at noticing things: *An observant witness gave the police a description of the men.* ☛ The opposite is **unobservant**.

☆ **observation** /ˌɒbzəˈveɪʃn/ *noun* **1** [U] the act of watching sb/sth carefully or the state of being watched carefully: *the observation of animals in their natural surroundings* **2** [U] the ability to notice things: *Scientists need good powers of observation.* **3** [C] something that you say or write; a remark: *to make an observation about the weather* ☛ Look at **remark** and **comment**. These words are more common.

(IDIOM) **be under observation** to be watched carefully: *The police are keeping the house under observation.*

observatory /əbˈzɜːvətri; *US* -tɔːri/ *noun* [C] (*pl* **observatories**) a building from which scientists can look at the stars, the moon, etc with telescopes

☆ **observe** /əbˈzɜːv/ *verb* [T] **1** to notice sb/sth or watch sb/sth carefully: *A man and a woman were observed leaving by the back door.* ○ *We observed the birds throughout the breeding season.* **2** (*formal*) to say or remark: *'We're late,' she observed.* **3** (*formal*) to obey a law, rule, etc: *to observe the speed limit*

observer *noun* [C] **1** a person who watches sb/sth: *Political observers have been predicting trouble for some time.* **2** a person who attends a meeting, lesson, etc to watch and listen but who does not say anything

obsess /əbˈses/ *verb* [T] (usually passive) to fill sb's mind all the time: *He became obsessed with getting his revenge.* ○ *Alison is obsessed with an older man.*

obsession /əbˈseʃn/ *noun* **1** [U] the state of being obsessed **2** [C] a person or thing that obsesses you: *Football is an obsession to some people.*

obsessive /əbˈsesɪv/ *adj* having or showing a way of thinking or behaving that you cannot stop: *He's obsessive about not being late.* ○ *obsessive cleanliness*

obsolete /ˈɒbsəliːt/ *adj* no longer used because it is out of date

obstacle /ˈɒbstəkl/ *noun* [C] something that makes it difficult for you to go somewhere or do sth: *Not speaking a foreign language was a major obstacle to her career.*

obstetrician /ˌɒbstəˈtrɪʃn/ *noun* [C] a doctor who looks after women who are pregnant

obstinate /ˈɒbstənət/ *adj* not willing to change your mind if you have decided sth: *an obstinate refusal to apologize* ☛ The word **obstinate** is usually used in a critical way. Look at **stubborn**, which has the same meaning. —**obstinacy** /ˈɒbstənəsi/ *noun* [U] —**obstinately** *adv*

obstruct /əbˈstrʌkt/ *verb* [T] to stop sb/sth from happening or moving: *Could you move on, please? You're obstructing the traffic if you park there.*

obstruction /əbˈstrʌkʃn/ *noun* **1** [U] stopping sth from happening or making progress **2** [C] a

p	b	t	d	k	g	tʃ	dʒ	f	v	θ	ð
pen	bad	tea	did	cat	got	chin	June	fall	van	thin	then

thing that stops sb/sth from moving: *This car is causing an obstruction.*
obstructive /əbˈstrʌktɪv/ *adj* trying to stop sth from happening
☆ **obtain** /əbˈteɪn/ *verb* [T] (*formal*) to get sth: *This book can now be obtained in paperback.*
obtainable *adj* that can be obtained: *That make of vacuum cleaner is no longer obtainable.* ☛ The opposite is **unobtainable**.
☆ **obvious** /ˈɒbvɪəs/ *adj* easily seen or understood; clear: *It was obvious that he was unwell.* ○ *His disappointment was obvious to everyone.* ○ *an obvious lie*
obviously *adv* as can easily be seen or understood; clearly: *There has obviously been a mistake.* ○ *Obviously we don't want to spend too much money if we can avoid it.*
☆ **occasion** /əˈkeɪʒn/ *noun* **1** [C] a particular time when sth happens: *I have met Bill on two occasions.* **2** [sing] **occasion (for sth)** the suitable or right time (for sth): *I shall tell her what I think if the occasion arises.* ☛ You use **occasion** when you mean the time is right or suitable for something: *I saw them at the funeral, but it was not a suitable occasion for discussing holiday plans.* You use **opportunity** or **chance** when you mean that it is possible to do something: *I was only in Paris for one day and I didn't get the opportunity/chance to visit the Louvre.* **3** [C] a special event, ceremony, etc: *Their wedding was a memorable occasion.* ○ *an official, special, great, etc occasion* (IDIOM) **on occasion(s)** sometimes
☆ **occasional** /əˈkeɪʒənl/ *adj* done or happening from time to time but not very often: *I rarely drink alcohol – just the occasional glass of wine.* —**occasionally** /-nəli/ *adv*: *We see each other occasionally.*
occult /ɒˈkʌlt; *US* əˈkʌlt/ *adj* connected with magic or supernatural powers
the occult *noun* [sing] magic or occult powers, ceremonies, etc
occupant /ˈɒkjʊpənt/ *noun* [C] (*formal*) a person who lives in or uses a room, house, etc
☆ **occupation** /ˌɒkjʊˈpeɪʃn/ *noun* **1** [U] living in a room, house, etc: *The new houses are now ready for occupation.* **2** [C] your job or sth that you do in your free time: *Please state your occupation on the form.* ○ *Fishing is his favourite occupation.* ☛ Look at the note at **work¹**. **3** [U] the control of a country by the army of another country
occupational /-ʃənl/ *adj* connected with your work: *Accidents are an occupational risk on building sites.*
occupier /ˈɒkjʊpaɪə(r)/ *noun* [C] a person who lives in or uses a house, piece of land, etc
☆ **occupy** /ˈɒkjʊpaɪ/ *verb* [T] (*pres part* **occupying**; *3rd pers sing pres* **occupies**; *pt, pp* **occupied**) **1** to live in or use a house, piece of land, etc: *The house next door has not been occupied for some months.* **2** to take control of a building, country, etc by force: *The rebel forces have occupied the television station.* **3** to fill a space or period of time: *The large table occupied most of the room.* **4 occupy sb/yourself (in doing sth/with sth)** to keep sb/yourself busy: *How does he occupy himself now that he's retired?*

occupied *adj* **1** being used: *Is this seat occupied?* **2** busy: *Looking after the children keeps me fully occupied.* **3** (used about a country or a piece of land) under the control of another country
☆ **occur** /əˈkɜː(r)/ *verb* [I] (**occurring**; **occurred**) **1** (*formal*) to happen: *The accident occurred late last night.* ☛ Look at the note at **happen**. **2** to be or exist: *Child abuse occurs in all classes of society.* **3 occur to sb** to come into sb's mind: *It never occurred to John that his wife might be unhappy.*
occurrence /əˈkʌrəns/ *noun* [C] something that happens: *Car theft is now a very common occurrence.*
☆ **ocean** /ˈəʊʃn/ *noun* **1** [sing] the mass of salt water that covers most of the surface of the earth: *the ocean floor* ○ *an ocean-going yacht* **2** [C] **Ocean** one of the five main areas into which the sea is divided: *the Atlantic Ocean*
☆ **o'clock** /əˈklɒk/ *adv* (used after the numbers one to twelve for saying what the time is): *Lunch is at twelve o'clock.* ☛ Be careful. **o'clock** can only be used with full hours: *We arranged to meet at 5 o'clock. It's 5.30 already and he's still not here.*
octagon /ˈɒktəgən; *US* -gɒn/ *noun* [C] a shape that has eight straight sides —**octagonal** /ɒkˈtægənl/ *adj*
octave /ˈɒktɪv/ *noun* [C] the set of eight musical notes that western music is based on
☆ **October** /ɒkˈtəʊbə(r)/ *noun* [C,U] (*abbr* **Oct**) the tenth month of the year, coming before November ☛ For examples of the use of the months in sentences, look at **January**.
octopus /ˈɒktəpəs/ *noun* [C] (*pl* **octopuses**) a sea animal with a soft body and eight long arms (**tentacles**)
☆ **odd** /ɒd/ *adj* **1** strange; unusual: *There's something odd about him.* ○ *It's a bit odd that she didn't phone to say she couldn't come.* **2** (used about a number) that cannot be divided by two: *One, three, five and seven are all odd numbers.* ☛ The opposite is **even**. **3** being one of a pair, from which the other is missing: *You're wearing odd socks.* **4** that remains after other similar things have been used: *He made the bookshelves out of a few odd bits of wood.* **5** (usually used after a number) a little more than: *'How old do you think he is?' 'Well, he must be 30 odd, I suppose.'* **6** not regular or fixed: *I do my exercises at odd moments during the day.*
(IDIOM) **the odd man/one out** one that is different from all the others or that is left behind when all the others are in groups: *Her brothers and sisters were much older than she was. She was always the odd one out.* ○ *'Carrot', 'lettuce', 'tomato' – which is the odd one out?*
oddly *adv* in a strange way: *He's behaving very oddly.* —**oddness** *noun* [U]
ˌodd ˈjobs *noun* [plural] small jobs of various kinds
oddity /ˈɒdɪti/ *noun* (*pl* **oddities**) **1** [U] the quality of being strange or unusual **2** [C] a person or thing that is unusual
oddment /ˈɒdmənt/ *noun* [C, usually pl] something that remains after the rest has been used

s	z	ʃ	ʒ	h	m	n	ŋ	l	r	j	w
so	zoo	she	vision	how	man	no	sing	leg	red	yes	wet

odds /ɒdz/ noun [plural] the chance or probability that sth will or will not happen: *The odds on him surviving are very slim.* ○ *The odds are against you.* ○ *The odds on that horse winning are seven to one* (= if you bet one pound and the horse wins, you will win seven pounds).
(IDIOMS) **against (all) the odds** happening although it seemed impossible; in spite of problems or disadvantages: *Graham passed his exam against all the odds.*
odds and ends (*Brit informal*) small things of little value or importance

odometer /ɒˈdɒmɪtə(r); əʊˈ-/ noun [C] (*US*) = MILOMETER

odour (*US* **odor**) /ˈəʊdə(r)/ noun [C] (*formal*) a smell (often an unpleasant one)
odourless adj without a smell

☆ **of** /əv; strong form ɒv/ prep **1** belonging to, relating to, or part of sth: *the roof of the house* ○ *the result of the exam* ○ *the back of the book* ○ *the leader of the party* **2** relating to a person: *a friend of mine* (= one of my friends) ○ *the poems of Milton* ○ *That was nice of her* (= she was nice to do that). **3** (used for saying what sb/sth is or what a thing contains or consists of): *a woman of intelligence* ○ *the city of Paris* ○ *a glass of milk* ○ *a crowd of people* ○ *It's made of silver.* ○ *a feeling of anger* **4** showing sth: *a map of York* **5** (showing that sb/sth is part of a larger group): *some of the people* ○ *three of the houses* **6** (with measurements and expressions of time and age): *five miles north of Leeds* ○ *a litre of milk* ○ *the fourth of July* ○ *a girl of 12* **7** (with some adjectives): *I'm proud of you.* ○ *She's jealous of her.* **8** (with some verbs): *This perfume smells of roses.* ○ *Think of a number.* ○ *It reminds me of you.* **9** (used after a noun which is connected with a verb. The noun after 'of' can be either the subject or the object): *the arrival of the president* (= he arrives) ○ *the murder of the president* (= he is murdered)

☆ **off**[1] /ɒf; *US* ɔːf/ adv, prep ☞ For special uses with many verbs, eg **go off**, look at the verb entries. **1** down or away from a place: *He fell off the ladder.* ○ *We got off the bus.* ○ *I shouted to him but he just walked off.* ○ *I must be off. It's getting late.* ○ *When are you off to Spain?* ○ (*figurative*) *We've got off the subject.* **2** (used with verbs that mean 'remove'): *She took her coat off.* ○ *He shook the rain off his umbrella.* ○ *Don't leave the top off the toothpaste.* **3** at a distance from sth: *The Isle of Wight is just off the south coast of England.* ○ *Christmas is still a long way off* (= it is a long time till then). **4** joined to and leading from: *The bathroom is off the main bedroom.* **5** (used about a machine, a light, etc) not working or being used: *Please make sure the lights are off.* **6** not present at work, school, etc: *She's off work with a cold.* **7** when you do not work: *I'm having a day off next week.* **8** no longer happening: *The meeting next Monday is off.* **9** cheaper; costing a certain amount less: *cars with £400 off* ○ *£400 off the price of a car* **10** not eating or using sth: *The baby's off his food.*
(IDIOMS) **off and on**; **on and off** sometimes, but not all the time

well/badly off having/not having a lot of money

off[2] /ɒf; *US* ɔːf/ adj (not before a noun) **1** no longer fresh (used about food or drink): *The milk's off.* **2** (*informal*) unfriendly: *My neighbour was rather off with me today. I wonder if I've upset her.*

'off chance noun [sing] a slight possibility: *She popped round on the off chance of finding him at home.*

offal /ˈɒfl; *US* ˈɔːfl/ noun [U] the heart, liver, kidneys, etc of an animal, used as food

off-day /ˈɒfdeɪ; *US* ˈɔːf-/ noun [C] (*informal*) a day when things go badly or you do not work well

☆ **offence** (*US* **offense**) /əˈfens/ noun **1** [C] **offence (against sth)** (*formal*) a crime; breaking the law: *to commit an offence* ○ *The new law makes it a criminal offence to drink alcohol in public places.* ○ *a minor/serious offence* ○ *She pleaded guilty to five driving offences.* **2** [U] **offence (to sb/sth)** annoyance, anger or sadness or sth that causes these feelings: *I didn't mean to cause you any offence.*
(IDIOM) **take offence (at sth)** to feel upset or hurt: *Be careful what you say – she takes offence rather easily.*

☆ **offend** /əˈfend/ verb **1** [T] (often passive) to hurt sb's feelings; to upset sb: *I hope they won't be offended if I don't come.* ○ *He felt offended that she hadn't written for so long.* **2** [I] **offend (against sb/sth)** (*formal*) to be wrong or act wrongly according to law, usual behaviour, certain beliefs, etc: *The prisoner had offended* (= committed a crime) *again within days of his release from jail.* ○ *Parts of the book offended against their religious beliefs.*

offender noun [C] **1** (*formal*) a person who commits a crime: *Young offenders should not be sent to adult prisons.* ○ *a first offender* **2** a person or thing that causes harm or trouble: *When it comes to polluting the North Sea, Britain is the worst offender.*

offensive /əˈfensɪv/ adj **1** unpleasant; insulting: *an offensive remark* ○ *offensive behaviour* ☞ Look at **inoffensive**. **2** (*formal*) used for or connected with attacking: *offensive weapons* ☞ The opposite is **defensive**.
offensive noun [C] an attack
(IDIOM) **take the offensive** to be the first to attack
offensively adv unpleasantly; rudely: *He was offensively outspoken in his remarks.*

☆ **offer** /ˈɒfə(r); *US* ˈɔːf-/ verb **1** [T] **offer sth (to sb)** to ask if sb would like sth or to give sb the opportunity to have sth: *He offered his seat on the bus to an old lady.* ○ *I've been offered a job in London.* ○ *She offered me a cigarette.* **2** [I,T] to say or show that you are willing to do sth: *I don't want to do it but I suppose I'll have to offer.* ○ *My brother's offered to help me paint the house.* **3** [T] to give or provide sth: *The brochure offers very little information about the surrounding area.* ○ *The job offers plenty of opportunity for travel.* **4** [T] to say that you will pay a certain amount: *He offered (me) £2 000 for the car and I accepted.*
offer noun [C] **1** a statement offering to do sth

iː	ɪ	e	æ	ɑː	ɒ	ɔː	ʊ	uː	ʌ
see	sit	ten	hat	arm	got	saw	put	too	cup

or give sth to sb: *She accepted my offer of help.* o *Thank you for your kind offer.* ☛ We can **make, accept, refuse** or **withdraw** an offer. **2** a low price for sth in a shop, or sth extra that you get when buying sth: *'Amazing offers,' the advertisement said, 'Buy now!'* o *See below for details of our special holiday offer.* **3** an amount of money that you say you will give for sth: *They've made an offer for the house.* o *We've turned down (= refused) an offer of £90 000.* (IDIOMS) **on offer 1** for sale or available: *The college has a wide range of courses on offer.* **2** for sale at a lower price than usual for a certain time: *This wine is on offer until next week.* **or nearest offer** ⇨ NEAR¹

offering /'ɒfərɪŋ; US 'ɔːf-/ noun [C] something that is given or produced: *He gave me a bottle of wine as a peace offering.* o *The latest offering from the Oxford Youth Theatre is 'Macbeth'.*

offhand /ˌɒf'hænd; US ˌɔːf-/ adj (used about behaviour) not friendly or polite

offhand adv without having time to think; immediately: *I can't tell you what it's worth offhand.*

offhandedly adv in an unfriendly way or in a way that shows that you are not interested: *'Oh really?' she said offhandedly, looking at her watch.*

☆ **office** /'ɒfɪs; US 'ɔːf-/ noun **1** [C] a room or building where written work is done, especially work connected with a business: *I usually get to the office at about 9 o'clock.* o *The firm's head office is in Glasgow.* o *office furniture, equipment, etc* o *Please phone again during office hours.* ☛ In America doctors and dentists have **offices**. In Britain they have **surgeries**. **2 Office** [sing] (often in compounds) a government department, including the people who work there and the work they do: *the Foreign Office* **3** [C] (often in compounds) a room or building that is used for a particular purpose, especially for providing a service: *the tax office* ☛ Look at **booking-office**, **box office** and **post office**. **4** [U] an official position, often as part of a government or other organization: *The chairman holds office for one year.* o *The Conservative party has been in office for over fourteen years.*

☆ **officer** /'ɒfɪsə(r); US 'ɔːf-/ noun [C] **1** a person who gives orders to others in the army, navy, etc: *an army, a naval, an air-force officer* **2** (often in compounds) a person with a position of authority or responsibility in the government or other organization: *a prison officer* **3** = POLICE OFFICER: *Excuse me, officer, is this the way to Victoria Station?* ☛ Look at the note on **official**.

☆ **official** /ə'fɪʃl/ adj **1** accepted and approved by the government or some other authority: *the official unemployment figures* o *The scheme has not yet received official approval.* **2** connected with a position of authority: *official duties* o *Her official title is now 'The Princess Royal'.* **3** known publicly: *Their engagement is not yet official.* o *The official reason for his resignation (= but perhaps not the real reason) was that he wanted to spend more time with his family.* ☛ The opposite is **unofficial**.

official noun [C] a person who has a position of authority: *The reception was attended by MPs and high-ranking officials.* o *a council official* ☛ An **office worker** is a person who works in an office, at a desk. An **official** is a person who has a position of responsibility in an organization, often the government: *senior government officials.* An **officer** is either a person who gives orders to others in the army, navy, etc or a policeman or -woman. However the word is sometimes used like **official**: *She's an executive officer in the Civil Service.*

officialdom /-dəm/ noun [U] officials as a group

officially /ə'fɪʃəli/ adv **1** as announced publicly but perhaps not strictly true: *Officially we don't accept children under 6, but we'll make an exception in this case.* **2** in an official way: *The new school was officially opened last week.*

officious /ə'fɪʃəs/ adj too ready to tell other people what to do

offing /'ɒfɪŋ; US 'ɔːf-/ noun (IDIOM) **in the offing** likely to appear or happen soon: *Do you think there's a romance in the offing? Jane and Trevor seem to be getting on very well.*

off-licence /'ɒflaɪsns/ noun [C] (*Brit*) (*US* **'package store**) a shop which sells beer, wine, spirits, etc

offload /ˌɒf'ləʊd; US ˌɔːf-/ verb [T] **offload sb/ sth on/onto sb** (*informal*) to give sb/sth that you do not want to sb else

off-peak /ˌɒf'piːk; US ˌɔːf-/ adj available or used at a less popular or busy time: *an off-peak train ticket*

off-putting /ˌɒf'pʊtɪŋ; US ˌɔːf-/ adj unpleasant or unattractive: *I must say that I find her manner rather off-putting.*

offset /'ɒfset; US 'ɔːf-/ verb [T] (**offsetting**; *pt, pp* **offset**) to make the effect of sth less strong or noticeable; to balance: *The disadvantages of the scheme are more than offset by the advantages.*

offshore /ˌɒf'ʃɔː(r); US ˌɔːf-/ adj in the sea not far from the land: *an offshore island*

offside¹ /ˌɒf'saɪd/ adj, adv (used about a player in football, etc) in a position that is not allowed by the rules of the game: *the offside rule* o *The Liverpool player seemed to be offside but the goal was allowed.*

offside² /ˌɒf'saɪd; US ˌɔːf-/ adj (*Brit*) (used about a car, etc) on the right side when you are driving: *The front offside tyre is punctured.*

offspring /'ɒfsprɪŋ; US 'ɔːf-/ noun [C] (*pl* **offspring**) (*formal*) a child or children; the young of an animal: *Parents can pass many diseases on to their offspring.*

off-white /ˌɒf'waɪt; US ˌɔːf'hwaɪt/ adj not pure white

☆ **often** /'ɒfn; 'ɒftən; US 'ɔːfn/ adv **1** many times; frequently: *We often go swimming at the weekend.* o *I've often seen him on the train.* o *I'm sorry I didn't write very often.* o *How often should you go to the dentist?* o *Write as often as you can.* **2** in many cases: *Women often go back to work after they have had a baby.*

ɜː	ə	eɪ	əʊ	aɪ	aʊ	ɔɪ	ɪə	eə	ʊə
fur	ago	pay	home	five	now	join	near	hair	pure

(IDIOMS) **more often than not** usually: *More often than not the buses are late in the morning.*
every so often occasionally; from time to time

ogre /'əʊgə(r)/ *noun* [C] **1** (in children's stories) a cruel and frightening giant **2** a person who is unpleasant and frightening

☆ **oh** /əʊ/ *interj* **1** (used for introducing a reply or remark, for attracting sb's attention or when pausing to think): *'What time should we leave?' 'Oh, early, I think.'* ○ *'I'm a teacher.' 'Oh? Where?'* ○ *Oh, Simon, take this letter to the post, would you?* ○ *'What time do you think it is?' 'Oh... about 3.30.'* **2** (used for expressing surprise, fear, etc): *'Oh no!' she cried as she began to read the letter.*

☆ **oil** /ɔɪl/ *noun* [U] **1** a thick liquid that comes from under the ground and is used as a fuel or to make machines work smoothly: *Britain obtains oil from the North Sea.* ○ *Your bicycle chain needs a little oil.* ○ *Crude oil* (= the raw material) *is transported by tanker to the refinery.* **2** a thick liquid that comes from animals or plants and is used in cooking: *cooking, vegetable, olive, etc oil*
oil *verb* [T] to put oil on or into sth, to make it work smoothly
oily /'ɔɪli/ *adj* (**oilier; oiliest**) covered with oil or like oil

'oilfield *noun* [C] an area where oil is found under the ground or the sea
'oil-painting *noun* [C] a painting that has been done using paint made with oil
'oil-slick *noun* [C] an area of oil that floats on the sea, usually when a ship carrying oil has leaked
'oil well (*also* **well**) *noun* [C] a hole that is made deep in the ground or under the sea in order to obtain oil

ointment /'ɔɪntmənt/ *noun* [C,U] a smooth substance that you put on sore skin or on an injury to help it to heal: *The doctor gave me an ointment to rub in twice a day.*

☆ **okay** (*also* **OK**) /,əʊ'keɪ/ *adj, adv* (*informal*) all right; good or well enough: *'Did you have a nice day?' 'Well, it was OK, I suppose.'* ○ *'How's your mother now?' 'Okay.'* ○ *If it's okay with you, I'll come at about 7.*
okay (*also* **OK**) *interj* yes; all right: *'Would you like to come to the cinema?' 'Okay.'*
okay (*also* **OK**) *noun* [sing] agreement or permission: *My parents have given me the OK to stay out late.*

☆ **old** /əʊld/ *adj* **1** (used about people, animals, etc) having lived a long time; not young: *My mother wasn't very old when she died.* ○ *He's only 50 but he looks older.* ○ *to get, grow, become old* **2** having existed for a long time; not modern: *a beautiful old stone house* ○ *old ideas, traditions, etc* **3** having been used a lot; not new: *My younger brother gets all my old clothes.* ○ *I'm going to exchange my old car for a new one.* ○ *Oh no, not that old joke again!* **4** (only before a noun) former; previous: *I earn more now than I did in my old job.* **5** (used with a period of time or with *how*) of a particular age: *Our car is only a year old.* ○ *My best friend and I have known each other since we were five years old.* ○ *They have a two-year-old* (= a child who is two years old). ○ *How old are you?* ○ *Are you older or younger than your sister?* ☛ Look at the note at **age**[1]. ☛ **Older** and **oldest** are the usual comparative and superlative forms of **old**: *My father's older than my mother.* ○ *That's the oldest story in the world!* **Elder** and **eldest** can be used when comparing the ages of people, especially members of a family. However they cannot be used with *than*. The adjectives are only used *before* the noun. **6** (only *before* a noun) known for a long time (but maybe not old in years): *She's a very old friend of mine. We knew each other at school.* **7** (only *before* a noun) (*informal*) (used for expressing friendship and affection): *Good old Tom has solved the problem!* **8** (only *before* a noun) (*informal*) (used for emphasizing that sth is not important): *'What time shall I come?' 'Oh, any old time - it doesn't matter.'*
(IDIOMS) **be an old hand (at sth)** to be good at sth because you have done it often before
old hat (*informal*) not new; old-fashioned
the old *noun* [plural] old people
,old 'age *noun* [U] the part of your life when you are old: *He's enjoying life in his old age.* ☛ Look at **youth**.
,old-age 'pension *noun* [U] money paid by the state to people above a certain age
,old-age 'pensioner (*also* **pensioner**) *noun* [C] (*abbr* **OAP**) a person who gets the old-age pension ☛ Nowadays the expression **senior citizen** is more acceptable.
,old-'fashioned *adj* **1** not modern; not commonly worn, used, etc now: *a long old-fashioned skirt* **2** (used about people) believing in old ideas, customs, etc: *My parents are rather old-fashioned about some things.*
the ,Old 'Testament *noun* [sing] the first part of the Bible, that tells the history of the Jewish people.

olive /'ɒlɪv/ *noun* [C] a small green or black fruit with a bitter taste, used for food and oil
olive (*also* **olive-green**) *adj* of a colour between yellow and green
,olive 'oil *noun* [U] oil obtained from olives and used in cooking or on salads

Olympic /ə'lɪmpɪk/ *adj* connected with the Olympic Games: *Who holds the Olympic record for the 1500 metres?*
the O,lympic 'Games (*also* **the Olympics**) *noun* [plural] the international sports competitions which are organized every four years in a different country: *to win a medal at/in the Olympics*

ombudsman /'ɒmbʊdzmən; -mæn/ *noun* [C] (*pl* **ombudsmen** /-mən/) a government official who reports on complaints made by ordinary people against public authorities

omelette (*also* **omelet**) /'ɒmlɪt/ *noun* [C] eggs, mixed and beaten and fried: *A plain omelette and a salad, please.* ○ *a mushroom omelette*

omen /'əʊmən/ *noun* [C] a sign of sth that will happen in the future: *a good/bad omen*

ominous /'ɒmɪnəs/ *adj* suggesting that sth bad is going to happen: *Those black clouds look ominous.*

p	b	t	d	k	g	tʃ	dʒ	f	v	θ	ð
pen	bad	tea	did	cat	got	chin	June	fall	van	thin	then

omission /əˈmɪʃn/ noun **1** [C] something that has not been included: *There were several omissions on the list of names.* **2** [U] the act of not including sb/sth: *The film was criticized for its omission of certain important details.*

omit /əˈmɪt/ verb [T] (omi**tt**ing; omi**tt**ed) **1** to not include sth: *Several verses of the song can be omitted.* **2** (formal) to not do sth: *He omitted to mention the man's name.*

☆ **on** /ɒn/ adv, prep ☞ For special uses with many verbs and nouns, eg **get on**, **on holiday**, see the verb and noun entries. **1** supported by a surface: *The plates are on the table.* ○ *We sat on the floor.* ○ *Make sure you put the lid on.* **2** touching or forming part of sth: *There's a mark on your skirt.* ○ *paintings on the wall* ○ *Write it down on a piece of paper.* **3** in an area of land; near the sea, a river, etc: *on the farm* ○ *We live on a large housing estate.* ○ *a house on the river Thames* **4** (showing direction): *on the right/left* **5** (used with means of transport): *on the bus, train, plane* ○ *'I got the bus.' 'Where did you get on?'* ○ *We came on foot* (= walking). ○ *on a bicycle* ☞ Note that we say **in** a car. **6** (with expressions of time): *on August 19th* ○ *on Monday* ○ *on Christmas Day* ○ *What are you doing on your birthday?* **7** immediately; soon after: *He telephoned her on his return from New York.* ○ *She began to weep on hearing the news.* **8** (showing that sth continues): *The man shouted at us but we walked on.* ○ *The war went on for five years.* **9** about sth: *We've got a test on irregular verbs tomorrow.* ○ *a talk on Japan* **10** working; being used: *All the lights were on.* ○ *Switch the television on.* **11** happening: *What's on at the cinema?* ○ *We haven't got anything on this weekend.* **12** using sth; by means of sth: *I spoke to her on the phone.* ○ *There's a good film on the television tonight.* **13** wearing sth: *What did she have on?* **14** having sth with you: *I've got no money on me.* **15** using drugs or medicine: *I've been on antibiotics for two weeks.* **16** receiving a certain amount of money: *I can't support a family on the salary I earn.* **17** (showing the way sth is spent): *He spends a lot on clothes.* ○ *Don't waste your time on that.* **18** paid for by sb: *The drinks are on me!*

(IDIOMS) **from now/then on** starting from this/that time and continuing: *From then on he never smoked another cigarette.*

not on not acceptable: *No, you can't stay out that late. It's just not on.*

off and on; on and off → OFF¹

on and on without stopping: *He just went on and on about his work.*

on at sb talking in a complaining way: *She's always on at me to mend the roof.*

☆ **once** /wʌns/ adv **1** one time only; on one occasion: *I've only been to France once.* ○ *once a week, month, year, etc* ○ *I have the car serviced once every six months.* **2** at some time in the past; formerly: *This house was once the village school.*

(IDIOMS) **all at once** all at the same time or suddenly: *People began talking all at once.* ○ *All at once she got up and left the room.*

at once 1 immediately; now: *Come here at once!* ○ *I'll telephone at once, before I forget.* **2** at the same time: *You can't all go on the slide at once! Take it in turns.*

just this once on this occasion only: *'Have a glass of wine.' 'Oh, all right. Just this once.'*

once again/more again, as before: *Spring will soon be here once again.*

once and for all now and for the last time: *You've got to make a decision once and for all.*

once in a blue moon (informal) very rarely; almost never: *We live in Glasgow, so I only go to London once in a blue moon.*

once in a while occasionally but not often

once more one more time: *Let's listen to that cassette once more, shall we?*

once upon a time (used at the beginning of a children's story) a long time ago; in the past: *Once upon a time there was a beautiful princess...*

once conj as soon as; when: *Once you've practised a bit you'll find that it's quite easy.* ○ *Once the meal was finished, the discussions began.*

oncoming /ˈɒnkʌmɪŋ/ adj (only before a noun) coming towards you: *oncoming traffic*

☆ **one¹** /wʌn/ pron, det, noun [C] **1** the number 1: *There's only one biscuit left.* ○ *The journey takes one hour.* ○ *If you take one from ten it leaves nine.* ☞ Look at **first**. **2** (used for emphasizing sth) only: *She's the one person I trust.* **3** (used when you are talking about a time in the past or future without actually saying which one) a certain: *He came to see me one evening last week.* ○ *We must go and visit them one day.* **4** (formal) (used in front of sb's name to show that you do not know the person) a certain: *I believe that one Mary Smith is the lady you need to see.* **5** (used with *the other*, *another* or *other(s)*) to make a contrast): *The twins are so alike that it's hard to tell one from the other.* **6** the same: *We can't all get in the one car.*

(IDIOMS) **(all) in one** all together or combined: *It's a bag and a raincoat all in one.*

one after another/the other first one, then the next, etc: *One after another the winners went up to get their prizes.*

one by one individually or separately: *I'd like to see the three boys one by one.*

one or two a few: *I've borrowed one or two new books from the library.* ○ *Just take one or two – not too many.*

,**one-'off** noun [C], adj (informal) (a thing) that is available or happens only once: *You'll never get a flight at that price again. It was a one-off.* ○ *a one-off opportunity*

,**one-'sided** adj **1** involving one person more than the other: *Her feelings for him seem to be rather one-sided* (= he doesn't feel the same). **2** unfair; seeing only one side (of an argument, etc): *I think you're being very one-sided. Think of my point of view.*

,**one-to-'one** adj, adv between only two people: *one-to-one English lessons* (= one teacher to one student)

,**one-'way** adv, adj **1** (used about roads) that you can only drive along in one direction: *a one-way street* **2** (used about a ticket) that you can use to travel somewhere but not back again: *I'd like to buy a one-way ticket to the Caribbean!*

s	z	ʃ	ʒ	h	m	n	ŋ	l	r	j	w
so	zoo	she	vision	how	man	no	sing	leg	red	yes	wet

☆ **one²** /wʌn/ *pron* **1** (used instead of repeating a noun): *I think I'll have an apple. Would you like one?* **2 one of** one member (of a certain group): *One of the plates is broken.* ○ *He's staying with one of his friends.* ○ *One of the children is crying.* ☛ **One of** is always followed by a plural noun. The verb is singular because the subject is **one**: *One of our assistants is ill.* ○ *One of the buses was late.*

‚one a'nother *pron* each other: *We exchanged news with one another.* ○ *You should listen to one another a bit more.*

☆ **one³** /wʌn/ *noun* [C] **1** (used after *this, that, which* or after an adjective which cannot stand alone): *'Which dress do you like?' 'This one.'* ○ *'Can I borrow some books of yours?' 'Yes. Which ones?'* ○ *'This coat's a bit small. You need a bigger one.'* ○ *That idea is a very good one.* **2** (used before a group of words that show which person or thing you are talking about): *My house is the one after the post office.* ○ *The girl he's going out with is the one with the red hair.* ○ *If you find some questions difficult, leave out the ones you don't understand.* **3** someone: *She's not one to get upset easily.*

☆ **one⁴** /wʌn/ *pron* (*formal*) (used for referring to people in general, including the speaker or writer): *One should try not to get annoyed.* ○ *Plenty of exercise makes one fit.* ○ *Fresh fruit is good for one.* ☛ It is very formal to use **one** in this way. In everyday English it is more common to use **you**. Note that the possessive form is **one's**: *One must be sure of one's facts before criticizing other people.* **One's** is also the short form of 'one is' or 'one has'.

☆ **oneself** /wʌn'self/ *pron* **1** (used for referring to people in general when **one** is the subject of the sentence): *One can teach oneself to play the piano but it is easier to have lessons.* **2** (used for emphasizing **one**): *One could easily arrange it all oneself.*
(IDIOM) **(all) by oneself 1** alone **2** without help

ongoing /'ɒŋgəʊɪŋ/ *adj* (only *before* a noun) continuing to exist now: *It's an ongoing problem.* ○ *an ongoing relationship*

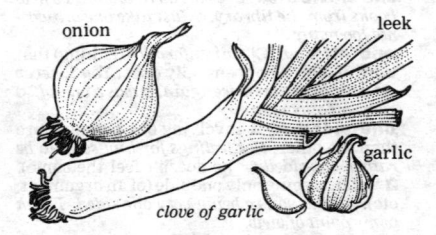

☆ **onion** /'ʌnɪən/ *noun* [C,U] a small white vegetable with many layers and a brown skin. Onions have a strong smell and taste, and are often used in cooking: *a pound of onions* ○ *onion soup*

on-line /‚ɒn'laɪn/ *adj* (*technical*) connected to and controlled by a computer: *an on-line ticket booking system*

onlooker /'ɒnlʊkə(r)/ *noun* [C] a person who watches sth happening without taking part in it: *The police were questioning several onlookers about the incident.*

☆ **only¹** /'əʊnli/ *adj* (only *before* a noun) **1** with no others existing or present: *I was the only woman in the bar.* ○ *This is the only dress we have in your size.* **2** the most suitable or the best: *It's so cold that the only thing to do is to sit by the fire.*

‚only 'child *noun* [C] a child who has no brothers or sisters

☆ **only²** /'əʊnli/ *adv* and no one or nothing else; no more than: *She only likes pop music.* ○ *I've only asked a few friends to the party.* ○ *It was only a little spider.* ○ *It's only one o'clock. There's plenty of time.* ☛ In written English **only** is usually placed before the word it refers to. In spoken English we can use stress to show which word it refers to and so **only** can have different positions: *I only kissed 'Jane* (= I kissed Jane and no one else). ○ *I only 'kissed Jane* (= I kissed Jane but I didn't do anything else).
(IDIOMS) **if only** ⇒ IF

not only... but also both... and: *He not only did the shopping but he also cooked the meal.*

only just 1 not long ago: *I've only just started the job.* **2** almost not; hardly: *We only just had enough money to pay for the meal.*

☆ **only³** /'əʊnli/ *conj* (*informal*) except that; but: *The film was very good, only it was a bit too long.*

onset /'ɒnset/ *noun* [sing] the beginning (often of sth unpleasant): *the onset of winter*

onslaught /'ɒnslɔːt/ *noun* [C] **onslaught (on sb/sth)** a fierce attack: *an onslaught on government policy*

☆ **onto** (*also* **on to**) /'ɒntə; *before vowels* 'ɒntu:/ *prep* to a position on sth: *The cat jumped onto the sofa.* ○ *The bottle fell onto the floor.*
(IDIOMS) **be onto sb** (*informal*) **1** to have found out about sth illegal that sb is doing: *The police were onto the car thieves.* **2** to talk to sb in order to pass on information or persuade him/her to do sth: *I've been onto the children to tidy their room.*

be onto sth to have some information, etc that could lead to an important discovery

onward /'ɒnwəd/ (*also* **onwards** /'ɒnwədz/) *adv* **1** and after: *From September onwards it usually begins to get colder.* **2** forward or towards progress: *The road stretched onwards into the distance.*

ooze /uːz/ *verb* [I,T] to flow slowly out or to allow sth to flow slowly out: *Blood was oozing from a cut on his head.* ○ *The toast was oozing with butter.* ○ (*figurative*) *She was oozing confidence* (= she was very confident).

op /ɒp/ *noun* [C] (*informal*) = OPERATION(3)

opaque /əʊ'peɪk/ *adj* **1** that you cannot see through; not transparent: *opaque glass in the door* **2** (*formal*) difficult to understand; not clear

☆ **open¹** /'əʊpən/ *adj* **1** not closed: *Don't leave the door open.* ○ *an open window* ○ *I can't get this bottle of wine open.* ○ *She stared at me with her eyes wide open.* ○ *The diary was lying open on*

iː	ɪ	e	æ	ɑː	ɒ	ɔː	ʊ	uː	ʌ
see	sit	ten	hat	arm	got	saw	put	too	cup

her desk. ○ *The curtains were open so that we could see into the room.* **2** honest and willing to talk: *Jane will tell you exactly what happened at the meeting – she's a very open person.* **3** not hidden or secret: *He looked at him with open dislike.* **4** with its doors unlocked so that customers can enter: *The bank isn't open till 9.30.* **5** (used about a new building, public area, etc) ready to be used for the first time: *The new shopping centre will soon be open.* **6 open (to sb/sth)** (used about a road, a course of action, etc) possible to use, do, etc: *After the heavy snow many minor roads were not open to traffic.* **7** (used about clothes) with the buttons not fastened: *His shirt was open at the neck.* **8** (only *before* a noun) with few buildings, villages, etc near (used about an area of land): *open country* **9** (only *before* a noun) at a distance from the land (used about an area of sea): *Once we were out in the open sea, the wind got stronger.* **10** (only *before* a noun) not covered: *an open fire* **11 open (to sb/sth)** that anyone can enter, visit, etc: *The competition is open to everyone.* ○ *The gardens are open to the public in the summer.* **12** not finally decided; still being considered: *Let's leave the details open.*
(IDIOMS) **have/keep an open mind (about/on sth)** to be willing to listen to or consider new ideas and suggestions
in the open air outside: *Somehow, food eaten in the open air tastes much better.*
keep an eye open/out (for sb/sth) ⇨ EYE¹
open to sth willing to receive sth: *I'm always open to suggestions.*
with your eyes open ⇨ EYE¹
with open arms in a friendly way that shows that you are pleased to see sb or have sth
the open *noun* [sing] outside or in open country: *After working in an office I like to be out in the open at weekends.*
(IDIOM) **bring sth out into the open; come out into the open** to make sth known publicly; to be known publicly: *I'm glad our secret has come out into the open at last.*
openly *adv* not secretly; honestly: *I think you should discuss your feelings openly with each other.*
openness *noun* [U] the quality of being honest and willing to talk: *I was surprised by her openness about her relationship with James.*
ˌopen-ˈair *adj* outside; not indoor: *an open-air swimming-pool*
ˈopen day *noun* [C] a day when the public can visit a place that is usually closed to them
ˌopen-ˈminded *adj* willing to consider new ideas and opinions
ˌopen-ˈplan *adj* (used about a large indoor area) not divided into separate rooms: *an open-plan office*
the ˌOpen Uniˈversity *noun* [sing] (*Brit*) a university whose students study mainly at home. Their work is sent to them by post and there are special television and radio programmes for them.
☆ **open²** /ˈəʊpən/ *verb* **1** [I,T] to become open or to make sth open: *This window won't open – it's stuck.* ○ *Do you mind if I open this window?* ○ *When I opened my eyes, she was gone.* **2** [I,T]

open (sth) (out) to fold out, back, etc: *The book opened at the very page I needed.* ○ *Open your hand – what have you got inside?* ○ *She opened the curtains and looked out.* **3** [I,T] (used about a shop, office, etc) to be unlocked so that business, work, etc can start; to unlock sth: *The shop hasn't opened yet.* ○ *They open the museum an hour later on Sundays.* **4** [T] to say officially that a new building, etc is ready for use: *The Mayor will open the college next week.* **5** [I,T] to start: *The play opens in London next month.* ○ *The chairman opened the meeting by welcoming everybody.* ○ *I'd like to open a bank account.* **6** [T] to make a road, etc available for use again: *Snow-ploughs have opened many major roads.*
(IDIOM) **open fire (at/on sb/sth)** to start shooting: *He ordered his men to open fire.*
(PHRASAL VERBS) **open into/onto sth** to lead straight to sth: *This door opens onto the garden.*
open out to become wider: *The road opened out and we were able to overtake the tractor.*
open (sth) up 1 to become available or to make sth available: *When I left school all sorts of opportunities opened up for me.* ○ *Parts of the desert may soon be opened up for farming.* **2** to open a door: *'Open up,' shouted the police to the man inside.*
opener /ˈəʊpnə(r)/ *noun* [C] (in compounds) a thing that takes the lid, etc off sth: *a tin-opener*
☆ **opening** /ˈəʊpnɪŋ/ *noun* **1** [sing] beginning: *The book is famous for its dramatic opening.* **2** [C] a hole; a way in or out: *We were able to get through an opening in the hedge.* **3** [C] an opportunity: *There are many new openings for trade with Eastern Europe.* **4** [C] a job which is available: *We have an opening for a sales manager at the moment.* **5** [C] a ceremony when a public building, etc is ready for use: *the opening of the new theatre*
opening *adj* (only *before* a noun) first: *the opening chapter of a book* ○ *His opening remarks were rather tactless.*
☆ **opera** /ˈɒprə/ *noun* **1** [C] a play in which the actors (**opera singers**) sing the words to music: *an opera by Wagner* ○ *a comic opera* **2** [U] works of this kind: *Do you like opera?* ○ *grand* (= serious) *opera* ○ *light* (= not serious) *opera* ☞ Look at **soap opera**.
operatic /ˌɒpəˈrætɪk/ *adj* connected with opera: *operatic music*
ˈopera-house *noun* [C] a theatre where operas are performed
☆ **operate** /ˈɒpəreɪt/ *verb* **1** [I,T] to do business; to manage or direct sth: *The firm operates from its central office in Bristol.* ○ *Many companies operate mail order services nowadays.* **2** [I] to act or to have an effect: *Several factors were operating to our advantage.* **3** [I,T] to work, or to make sth work: *I don't understand how this machine operates.* ○ *These switches here operate the central heating.* **4** [I] **operate (on sb/sth) (for sth)** to cut open a patient's body in order to deal with a part that is damaged, diseased, etc: *The surgeon is going to operate on her in the morning.* ○ *He was operated on for appendicitis.*
ˈoperating system *noun* [C] a computer pro-

ɜː	ə	eɪ	əʊ	aɪ	aʊ	ɔɪ	ɪə	eə	ʊə
fur	ago	pay	home	five	now	join	near	hair	pure

'operating theatre (*also* **theatre**) *noun* [C] a room in a hospital where operations(3) are performed

☆ **operation** /ˌɒpəˈreɪʃn/ *noun* **1** [C] an activity, often highly organized, that involves many people, actions, days, etc: *A rescue operation was mounted to find the missing children.* ○ *military operations* ○ *Building the garden shed was quite a tricky operation.* **2** [C] a business company: *a huge international operation* **3** [C] (*also informal* **op**) **operation (on sb) (for sth); operation (to do sth)** cutting open a patient's body in order to deal with a part inside: *The surgeon performed an operation on her for a kidney problem.* ○ *He had an operation to remove some damaged lung tissue.* **4** [U] the way in which sth works; working: *The operation of these machines is quite simple.*

(IDIOM) **be in operation; come into operation** to start working or having an effect: *The new tax system will come into operation in the spring.*

operational /ˌɒpəˈreɪʃənl/ *adj* **1** connected with an operation(1,4) **2** ready for use: *The new factory is now fully operational.*

operative /ˈɒpərətɪv; *US* -reɪt-/ *adj* (*formal*) working, able to be used; in use: *The new law will be operative from 1 May.*

☆ **operator** /ˈɒpəreɪtə(r)/ *noun* [C] **1** a person whose job is to connect telephone calls, for the public or in a particular building: *Dial 100 for the operator.* ○ *a switchboard operator* **2** a person whose job is to work a particular machine or piece of equipment: *a computer operator* **3** a person or company that does certain types of business: *a tour operator*

☆ **opinion** /əˈpɪnɪən/ *noun* **1** [C] **opinion (of sb/ sth); opinion (on/about sth)** what you think about sb/sth: *She asked me for my opinion of her new hairstyle and I told her.* ○ *He has very strong opinions on almost everything.* **2** [U] what people in general think about sth: *Public opinion is in favour of a change in the law.*

(IDIOMS) **be of the opinion that...** (*formal*) to think or believe that...: *In this case we are of the opinion that you took the right decision.*

have a good, bad, high, low, etc opinion of sb/sth to think that sb/sth is good, bad, etc

in my, your, etc opinion I, you, etc think that...: *In my opinion, you're making a terrible mistake.*

a matter of opinion ⇒ MATTER¹

o'pinion poll *noun* [C] = POLL¹(1)

opium /ˈəʊpɪəm/ *noun* [U] a drug that is made from the seeds of the poppy flower

☆ **opponent** /əˈpəʊnənt/ *noun* [C] **1** (in sport or games) a person who plays against sb **2 an opponent (of sth)** a person who disagrees with sb's actions, plans or beliefs and tries to stop or change them

☆ **opportunity** /ˌɒpəˈtjuːnətɪ; *US* -ˈtuːn-/ *noun* [C,U] (*pl* **opportunities**) a chance to do sth that you would like to do; a situation or a time in which it is possible to do sth that you would like to do: *There will be plenty of opportunity for asking questions later.* ○ *I should have gone abroad when I was young – it was a missed opportunity.* ○ *an equal opportunity employer* (= an employer who employs people regardless of sex, colour, etc) ☞ Look at the note at **occasion**.

(IDIOM) **take the opportunity to do sth/of doing sth** to make use of a chance that you have to do sth: *When we were finally alone, I took the opportunity to ask him a few personal questions.*

☆ **oppose** /əˈpəʊz/ *verb* [T] to disagree with sb's beliefs, actions or plans and to try to change or stop them: *They opposed the plan to build new houses in the village.*

opposed *adj* **opposed to sth** disagreeing with a plan, action, etc; believing that sth is morally wrong: *I'm not opposed to the idea but I need more details.* ○ *She has always been opposed to experiments on animals.*

(IDIOM) **as opposed to** (used to emphasize the difference between two things) in contrast with: *Your work will be judged by quality, as opposed to quantity.*

☆ **opposite** /ˈɒpəzɪt/ *adj, adv* **1** in a position directly on the other side of sb/sth; facing: *The two cathedrals are on opposite sides of the river.* ○ *The two families sat at opposite ends of the room to each other.* ○ *You sit there and I'll sit opposite.* ☞ picture at **front**. Sometimes **opposite** is used after the noun: *Write your answer in the space opposite.* **2** as different as possible: *I can't walk with you because I'm going in the opposite direction.* ○ *the opposite sex* (= men for women, women for men)

opposite *prep* directly on the other side of a space between sth and sth else; facing sb/sth: *I always buy my paper from the shop opposite our flat.*

opposite *noun* [C] the word, thing or person that is as different as possible from sb/sth: *'Hot' is the opposite of 'cold'.* ○ *She's very friendly whereas her brother is the complete opposite.*

ˌ**opposite 'number** *noun* [C] a person who does the same job or has the same position in a different company, organization, team, etc: *He played better than his opposite number in the other team.*

☆ **opposition** /ˌɒpəˈzɪʃn/ *noun* [U] **1 opposition (to sb/sth)** the feeling of disagreeing with sth and the action of trying to change it: *Despite strong opposition from local people, the city centre was completely rebuilt.* ○ *to express your opposition to sth* **2 the opposition** [sing] the person or team who plays against sb in sport or games: *Their manager has told them not to underestimate the opposition.* **3 the Opposition** [sing] the politicians or the political parties that are in Parliament but not in the government: *the leader of the Opposition* ○ *Opposition MPs* ☞ In numbers 2 and 3, **opposition** can be used with either a singular or a plural verb.

oppress /əˈpres/ *verb* [T] (usually passive) to rule sb (especially a nation or a part of society) in a way that allows the people no freedom; to control sb in an unjust way, using force

oppressed *adj* unfairly ruled or treated; not free: *an oppressed minority*

oppression /əˈpreʃn/ *noun* [U] the system or act of oppressing; the state of being oppressed: *a struggle against oppression*

oppressive /əˈpresɪv/ *adj* **1** allowing no freedom; controlling by force; unjust: *The military government announced oppressive new laws.* **2** (used especially about heat or the atmosphere) causing you to feel very uncomfortable

oppressor *noun* [C] a person who oppresses

opt /ɒpt/ *verb* [T] **opt to do sth** to choose or decide to do sth after thinking about it
(PHRASAL VERBS) **opt for sb/sth** to choose sth after you have decided that you do not want the other possibilities
opt out (of sth) to choose not to take part in sth; to decide to stop being involved in sth: *Schools and hospitals can now opt out of local government control and manage their own finances.*

optical /ˈɒptɪkl/ *adj* connected with the sense of sight: *optical instruments*

optical iˈlusion *noun* [C] something that tricks the eye and makes you believe sth is there or is true when it is not

optician /ɒpˈtɪʃn/ *noun* [C] a person who is qualified to test eyes, sell glasses, etc: *to go to the optician's* (= the shop)

optimism /ˈɒptɪmɪzəm/ *noun* [U] the feeling that the future or sth in the future will be good or successful: *There is considerable optimism that the economy will improve.* ☛ The opposite is **pessimism**.

optimist /-mɪst/ *noun* [C] a person who is always hopeful that things will be good or successful in the future ☛ The opposite is **pessimist**.

optimistic /ˌɒptɪˈmɪstɪk/ *adj* hoping or believing that what happens in the future will be good or successful: *I've applied for the job but I'm not very optimistic about my chances of getting it.* ☛ The opposite is **pessimistic**.
—**optimistically** /-klɪ/ *adv*

☆ **option** /ˈɒpʃn/ *noun* **1** [U,sing] the freedom to choose; choice: *If you're late again, you will give us no option but to dismiss you.* **2** [C] a thing that you choose or can choose; choice: *She looked carefully at all the options before deciding on a career.*

optional /-ʃənl/ *adj* that you can choose or not choose: *an optional subject at school* o *an optional extra* (= sth that you can have as an extra thing but must pay for) ☛ The opposite is **compulsory**.

☆ **or** /ɔː(r)/ *conj* **1** (used before another possibility or the last of a series of possibilities): *Would you like to sit here or next to the window?* o *Are you interested or not?* o *For the main course, you can have lamb, beef or fish.* ☛ Look at **either...or**. **2** if not; otherwise: *Don't drive so fast or you'll have an accident!* o *She must have loved him or she wouldn't have married him.* ☛ **Or else** and **otherwise** can be used with this meaning. **3** (after a negative) and neither; and not: *She hasn't phoned or written to me for weeks.* o *I've never been to Italy or Spain.* ☛ Look at **neither...nor**. **4** (used before a word or phrase that explains or comments on what has been said before): *20% of the population, or one in five* o *Oxford and Cambridge Universities, or 'Oxbridge' as they are sometimes known*
(IDIOMS) **or else** ⇨ ELSE(4)

or so about: *I should think the repairs will cost you £100 or so.*

or sb/sth/somewhere (*informal*) (used for showing that you are not sure, cannot remember or do not know which person, thing or place): *She's a computer programmer or something.* o *The film was set in Sweden or somewhere.* ☛ Another phrase that shows that you are not sure is **...or other**: *He muttered something or other about having no time and disappeared.*

☆ **oral** /ˈɔːrəl/ *adj* **1** spoken, not written: *an oral test* **2** concerning or using the mouth: *oral hygiene*

oral *noun* [C] a spoken examination: *I've got my German oral next week.*

orally *adv* **1** using speech, not writing: *Orally her English is good.* **2** through the mouth and swallowed

☆ **orange** /ˈɒrɪndʒ/; *US* /ˈɔːr-/ *noun* **1** [C] a round fruit with a thick skin, that is divided into sections (**segments**) inside, and is a colour between red and yellow: *orange juice* **2** [U] the colour of this fruit, between red and yellow **3** [U] a drink made from oranges or with the taste of oranges; a glass of this drink: *vodka and orange* o *freshly squeezed orange*

orange *adj* having the colour orange: *orange paint*

orange ˈsquash *noun* [C,U] (*Brit*) a drink made by adding water to an orange-flavoured liquid

orator /ˈɒrətə(r)/; *US* /ˈɔːr-/ *noun* [C] (*formal*) a person who is good at making public speeches

orbit /ˈɔːbɪt/ *noun* [C,U] the path taken by sth (a planet, a moon, a spacecraft, etc) going round sth else in space: *to put a satellite into orbit*

orbit *verb* [I,T] to move round sth (the moon, the sun, a planet etc) in orbit

orchard /ˈɔːtʃəd/ *noun* [C] a piece of land in which fruit trees are grown: *a cherry orchard*

☆ **orchestra** /ˈɔːkɪstrə/ *noun* [C] a large group of musicians who play many different musical instruments together: *a symphony orchestra*

☛ An orchestra usually plays classical music. Pop music, jazz, etc are played by a **group** or **band**.

orchestral /ɔːˈkestrəl/ *adj* played by or written for an orchestra

orchid /ˈɔːkɪd/ *noun* [C] a plant that has flowers of unusual shapes and bright colours

ordeal /ɔːˈdiːl; ˈɔːdiːl/ *noun* [C] a very unpleasant experience: *The woman who was attacked last night is in hospital recovering from her ordeal.*

☆ **order¹** /ˈɔːdə(r)/ *noun* **1** [C,U] the way in which people or things are arranged in relation to each other: *a list of names in alphabetical order* o *a list of dates in chronological order* **2** [U] an organized state, when everything is in its right place: *I really must put my notes in*

order, because I can never find what I'm looking for. **3** [U] the situation in which laws, rules, authority, etc are obeyed: *Following last week's riots, order has now been restored.* ☞ Look at **disorder**. **4** [C] an instruction or demand that sb must do sth, given by sb who has power over that person: *In the army, you have to obey orders at all times.* **5** [C] a request asking for sth to be made, supplied or delivered: *The company has just received a major export order.* **6** [C] a request for food, drink, etc in a hotel, restaurant, etc: *Can I take your order now, sir?*
(IDIOMS) **in order to do sth** with the purpose or intention of doing sth; so that sth can be done: *In order to obtain a passport, you need a birth certificate and two photographs.* ○ *We left early in order to avoid the traffic.*
in/into reverse order ⇒ REVERSE¹
in working order (used about machines, etc) working properly, not broken: *It's an old fridge but it's in perfect working order.*
law and order ⇒ LAW
out of order 1 (used about a machine, etc) not working properly or not working at all **2** (*informal*) (used about a person's behaviour) unacceptable, because it is rude, etc: *That comment was completely out of order!*

'order-form *noun* [C] a form that is filled in by sb ordering goods

☆ **order²** /'ɔːdə(r)/ *verb* **1** [T] **order sb (to do sth)** to tell sb to do sth in a strong way which does not permit him/her to refuse, and without saying 'please': *I'm not asking you to do your homework, I'm ordering you!* ○ *The police ordered the demonstrators to stop.* **2** [T] to ask for sth to be made, supplied or delivered: *The shop didn't have the book I wanted so I ordered it.* ○ *We've ordered some new chairs for the living-room.* **3** [I,T] to ask for food, drink, etc in a restaurant, hotel, etc: *Are you ready to order yet, madam?*
(PHRASAL VERB) **order sb about/around** to keep telling sb what to do and how to do it: *Stop ordering me about! You're not my father.*

orderly¹ /'ɔːdəli/ *adj* **1** well-arranged; well-organized; tidy: *an orderly office* ○ *an orderly life* **2** well-behaved; peaceful: *The teacher told the pupils to form an orderly queue.*

orderly² /'ɔːdəli/ *noun* (*pl* **orderlies**) a hospital assistant who has not had special training

ordinal /'ɔːdɪnl; *US* -dənl/ (*also* **ordinal 'number**) *noun* [C] a number that shows the order or position in a series: *'First', 'second', and 'third' are ordinals.*

☆ **ordinary** /'ɔːdənri; *US* 'ɔːrdəneri/ *adj* normal; not special or unusual or different from others: *It's interesting to see how ordinary people live in other countries.* ○ *They live in an ordinary sort of house.* ☞ The opposite is **extraordinary**.
(IDIOM) **out of the ordinary** unusual; different from normal

ordinarily /'ɔːdənrəli; *US* ˌɔːrdn'erəli/ *adv* usually; generally: *Ordinarily, I don't work as late as this.*

ore /ɔː(r)/ *noun* [C,U] rock or earth from which metal can be obtained

☆ **organ¹** /'ɔːgən/ *noun* [C] a part of the body that has a particular function: *vital organs* (= those such as the heart which help to keep you alive) ○ *sexual organs*

☆ **organ²** /'ɔːgən/ *noun* [C] a large musical instrument of the piano family, with pipes through which air is forced. Organs are often found in churches: *a church organ* ○ *organ music* ☞ Note that you play **the** organ: *When did you learn to play the organ?*
organist *noun* [C] a person who plays the organ

organic /ɔː'gænɪk/ *adj* **1** produced by or existing in living things: *You need to add a lot of organic matter to the soil.* ☞ The opposite is **inorganic**. **2** (used about food or agricultural methods) produced by or using natural materials, not chemicals: *organic vegetables* ○ *organic farming*

organism /'ɔːgənɪzəm/ *noun* [C] an animal or plant, especially one that is so small that you can only see it with a special instrument (microscope)

☆ **organization** (*also* **organisation**) /ˌɔːgənaɪ'zeɪʃn; *US* -nɪ'z-/ *noun* **1** [C] an organized group of people who do sth together: *She works for a voluntary organization helping homeless people.* **2** [U] the activity of organizing or arranging: *An enormous amount of organization went into the festival.* **3** [U] the way in which sth is organized: *The students all complained about the poor organization of their course.* —**organizational** (*also* **organisational**) /-ʃənl/ *adj*: *The job requires a high level of organizational ability.*

☆ **organize** (*also* **organise**) /'ɔːgənaɪz/ *verb* **1** [T] to plan or arrange an event, an activity, etc: *The school organizes trips to various places of interest.* **2** [I,T] to put things into order; to arrange into a system or logical order: *Can you decide what needs doing? I'm hopeless at organizing.*
organized (*also* **organised**) *adj* **1** planned or arranged: *My department is badly organized.* ○ *organized crime* **2** having a good system; working well: *I wish I was as organized as you are!* —**organizer** (*also* **organiser**) *noun* [C]: *The organizers of the concert said that it had been a great success.*

orgasm /'ɔːgæzəm/ *noun* [C,U] the point of greatest sexual pleasure: *to have an orgasm*

orgy /'ɔːdʒi/ *noun* [C] (*pl* **orgies**) **1** a wild party, involving a lot of sex and/or alcohol or drugs **2 an orgy (of sth)** a period of doing sth in an uncontrolled way: *an orgy of violence*

orient /'ɔːrɪənt/ *noun* [sing] **the Orient** (*formal*) the countries of the East or the Far East (China, Japan, etc)

oriental /ˌɔːri'entl/ *adj* coming from or belonging to the East or Far East: *oriental languages*

orientate /'ɔːrɪenteɪt/ *verb* [T] **orientate yourself** to find out where you are; to become familiar with a place: *When I came out of the station I couldn't orientate myself at first.*

orientated /'ɔːrɪenteɪtɪd/ (*also* **oriented** /'ɔːrɪentɪd/) *adj* aimed or directed at a particular type of person or thing: *Our products are male-orientated.* ○ *She's very career-orientated.*

orienteering /ˌɔːrɪən'tɪərɪŋ/ *noun* [U] a sport

in which you find your way across country on foot, using a map and compass

☆ **origin** /ˈɒrɪdʒɪn/ *noun* [C,U] **1** the time when or place where sth first comes into existence; the reason why sth starts: *Could you explain to me the origins of this tradition?* ○ *Many English words are of Latin origin.* **2** the family, race, class, etc that a person comes from: *people of African origin* ○ *working-class origins*

☆ **original** /əˈrɪdʒənl/ *adj* **1** first; earliest (before changes or developments): *The original meaning of this word is different from the meaning it has nowadays.* **2** new and interesting; different from others of its type: *There are no original ideas in his work.* **3** made or created first, before copies: *'Is that the original painting?' 'No, it's a copy.'*

original *noun* [C] **the original** the first one made or created; not a copy: *Could you make a photocopy and give the original back to me?*

originality /əˌrɪdʒəˈnæləti/ *noun* [U] the quality of being new and interesting

originally /-nəli/ *adv* **1** in the beginning; in the first form (before changes or developments): *I'm from London originally, but I left there when I was very young.* **2** in a way or style that is unlike others: *She has a talent for expressing simple ideas originally.*

originate /əˈrɪdʒɪneɪt/ *verb* (*formal*) **1** [I] to start or be caused to start: *This game originated in the nineteenth century.* **2** [T] to start or create first: *I wonder who originated the custom of sending birthday cards.*

ornament /ˈɔːnəmənt/ *noun* [C] an object that you have because it is attractive, not because it is useful. Ornaments are used to decorate rooms, etc. ☞ picture at **fireplace**.

ornamental /ˌɔːnəˈmentl/ *adj* made or put somewhere in order to look attractive, not for any practical use

ornate /ɔːˈneɪt/ *adj* having a lot of decoration: *an ornate building*

ornithology /ˌɔːnɪˈθɒlədʒi/ *noun* [U] the study of birds

ornithologist /ˌɔːnɪˈθɒlədʒɪst/ *noun* [C] a person who studies birds

orphan /ˈɔːfn/ *noun* [C] a child whose parents are dead

orphan *verb* [T] (usually passive) to cause a child to become an orphan: *She was orphaned when she was three and went to live with her grandparents.*

orphanage /ˈɔːfənɪdʒ/ *noun* [C] an institution where orphans live and are looked after

orthodox /ˈɔːθədɒks/ *adj* **1** generally believed, done or accepted: *orthodox opinions* ○ *orthodox methods* ☞ The opposite is **unorthodox**. **2** practising the old, traditional beliefs, ceremonies, etc of certain religions: *an orthodox Jew* ○ *the Greek Orthodox Church*

ostentatious /ˌɒstenˈteɪʃəs/ *adj* showing wealth, importance, etc very openly in order to attract attention and impress other people
—**ostentatiously** *adv*

ostracize (*also* **ostracise**) /ˈɒstrəsaɪz/ *verb* [T] (*formal*) (used about a group of people) to refuse to talk to or be with sb because he/she has done sth that you do not like: *When she left her husband, his family ostracized her.*

ostrich /ˈɒstrɪtʃ/ *noun* [C] a very large African bird with a long neck and long legs, which can run very fast but which cannot fly

☆ **other** /ˈʌðə(r)/ *det, pron* **1** in addition to or different from the one or ones that have already been mentioned or understood: *I hadn't got any other plans that evening so I accepted their invitation.* ○ *How many other students are there in your class?* ○ *If you're busy now, I'll come back some other time.* ○ *I like this jumper but I'm not keen on the colour. Have you got any others?* ○ *Some of my friends went to university, others didn't.* ○ *She doesn't care what other people think.* ☞ **Other** cannot be used after 'an'. Look at **another**. **2** (after *the* or a possessive with a singular noun) second of two: *I can only find one sock. Have you seen the other one?* ○ *My glasses broke, but fortunately I had my other pair with me.* **3** (after *the* or a possessive with a plural noun) the rest of a group or number of people or things: *Their youngest son still lives with them but their other children have left home.* ○ *I'll have to wear this shirt because all my others are dirty.*

(IDIOMS) **every other** ⇨ EVERY

in other words saying sth in a different way

one after another/the other ⇨ ONE¹

the other day, morning, week, etc recently, not long ago: *An old friend rang me the other day.*

sb/sth/somewhere or other ⇨ OR

other than *prep* **1** (usually after a negative) apart from; except (for): *The plane was a bit late but other than that the journey was fine.* **2** different(ly) from; not: *I've never seen her other than very smartly dressed.*

☆ **otherwise** /ˈʌðəwaɪz/ *adv* **1** in all other ways; apart from that: *I'm a bit tired but otherwise I feel fine.* **2** in a different or another way: *I'm afraid I can't see you next weekend, I'm otherwise engaged* (= I will be busy doing sth else). **3** of a different type: *I have no opinion, good or otherwise, on this subject.*

otherwise *conj* (used for stating what would happen if you do not do sth or if sth does not happen) if not: *You have to press the red button, otherwise it won't work.*

otter /ˈɒtə(r)/ *noun* [C] a river animal with brown fur that eats fish

ouch /aʊtʃ/ *interj* (used when reacting to a sudden feeling of pain): *Ouch! You're hurting me.*

☆ **ought to** /ˈɔːt tə; before vowels and in final position ˈɔːt tuː/ *modal verb* (*negative* **ought not to**; *short form* **oughtn't to** /ˈɔːtnt tə/ *before vowels and in final position* /ˈɔːtnt tuː/) **1** (used for asking for and giving advice about what to do): *What ought I to say to him?* ○ *You ought to read this book. It's really interesting.* ○ *You ought to have come to the meeting. It was very useful.* ○ *He asked if he ought to put the car in the garage.* **2** (used for telling sb what his/her duty is): *You ought to visit your parents more often.* ○ *She oughtn't to make private phone calls in work time.* ○ *I ought to have helped. I'm sorry.* ○ *He oughtn't to have been driving so fast.* **3** (used for saying that you

ɜː	ə	eɪ	əʊ	aɪ	aʊ	ɔɪ	ɪə	eə	ʊə
fur	ago	pay	home	five	now	join	near	hair	

expect sth is true, or that you expect sth to happen/to have happened): *She ought to pass her test.* ○ *They ought to be here by now. They left at six.* ○ *I bought six loaves of bread. That ought to have been enough.*

ounce /aʊns/ *noun* **1** [C] (*abbr* **oz**) a measure of weight; 28·35 grams. There are 16 ounces in a pound: *For this recipe you need four ounces of flour, six ounces of butter…* **2** [sing] **an ounce of sth** a very small amount of sth: *He hasn't got an ounce of imagination.*

☆ **our** /ɑ:(r); 'aʊə(r)/ *det* belonging to or connected with us: *Our house is at the bottom of the road.* ○ *Our teacher is excellent.* ○ *This is our first visit to Britain.*

ours /ɑ:z; 'aʊəz/ *pron* the one or ones belonging to, connected with or done by us: *Your hi-fi system is exactly the same as ours.* ○ *Their garden is quite nice but I prefer ours.*

☆ **ourselves** /ɑ:'selvz; aʊə'selvz/ *pron* **1** (used as the object of a verb or preposition when 'we' do an action and are also affected by it): *We should be angry with ourselves for making such a stupid mistake.* ○ *They asked us to wait so we sat down and made ourselves comfortable.* **2** (used for emphasis): *We haven't got children ourselves, but many of our friends have.* ○ *Do you think we should paint the flat ourselves?* (= or should we ask sb else to do it for us?)
(IDIOM) (**all**) **by ourselves 1** without help from anyone else: *We managed to move all our furniture into the new flat by ourselves.* **2** not with anyone else; alone: *Now that we're by ourselves, could I ask you a personal question?* ☞ Look at the note at **alone**.

☆ **out** /aʊt/ *adj, adv* ☞ For special uses with many verbs, eg **try sb/sth out**, look at the verb entries. **1** (used for showing movement away from a place): *He opened the box and took a gun out.* ○ *I threw out that old shirt of yours.* ○ *Her ears stick out.* ○ *He opened the window and put his head out.* **2** not at home or in your place of work: *I was out when she called.* ○ *They took me out for a meal when I was in Bristol.* **3** outside a house, building, etc: *You should be out in the fresh air.* **4** (used for showing that sth is no longer hidden): *Oh look! The sun's out.* **5** not in fashion: *Short skirts are completely out.* **6** (used about a light or a fire) not on; not burning: *The lights are out. They must be in bed.* **7** (used when you are calculating sth) making or containing a mistake: *This bill's out by five pounds.* **8** not possible or acceptable: *I'm afraid Friday is out. I've got a meeting that day.* **9** in a loud voice; clearly: *She cried out in pain.* **10** (used about the tide) away from the shore: *Don't swim when the tide is going out.*
(IDIOMS) **be out for sth**; **be out to do sth** to try hard to get or do sth

out-and-out *adj* complete: *It was out-and-out war between us.*

ˌout'loud *adv* = ALOUD

☆ **out of** /'aʊt əv/ *prep* **1** (used with verbs expressing movement away from the inside of sth): *She took her purse out of her bag.* ○ *to get out of bed* **2** away from, or no longer in, a place or situation: *He's out of the country on business.* ○ *The doctors say she's out of danger.* **3** at a distance from a place: *We live a long way out of London.* **4** (used for saying what you use to make sth): *You could make a table out of this wood.* **5** from among a number: *Nine out of ten people prefer this model.* **6** (used for saying that you no longer have sth): *We're out of milk.* ○ *I'm out of breath.* ○ *out of work* **7** (used for saying which feeling causes you to do sth): *I only helped them out of pity.* **8** from: *I copied the recipe out of a book.* ○ *I prefer to drink tea out of a cup, not a mug.* **9** (used for saying that sth is not as it should be): *The telephone's out of order.*
(IDIOMS) **be/feel out of it** to be/feel lonely and unhappy because you are not included in sth: *I didn't speak the language and I felt rather out of it at the meeting.*

out of bounds ⇒ BOUNDS

outback /'aʊtbæk/ *noun* [sing] the part of a country (especially Australia) which is a long way from where most people live

outboard motor /ˌaʊtbɔːd 'məʊtə(r)/ *noun* [C] an engine that can be attached to a boat

outbreak /'aʊtbreɪk/ *noun* [C] the sudden beginning or appearance of sth unpleasant (especially disease or violence): *an outbreak of cholera* ○ *outbreaks of fighting*

outburst /'aʊtbɜːst/ *noun* [C] a sudden expression of a strong feeling, especially anger: *an angry outburst*

outcast /'aʊtkɑːst; *US* -kæst/ *noun* [C] a person who is no longer accepted by society or by a group of people: *a social outcast*

outclass /ˌaʊt'klɑːs; *US* -'klæs/ *verb* [T] to be much better than sb/sth, especially in a game or competition

outcome /'aʊtkʌm/ *noun* [C, usually sing] how an event, action or situation ends; the result of sth: *We shall inform you of the outcome of the interview within a week.*

outcry /'aʊtkraɪ/ *noun* [C, usually sing] (*pl* **outcries**) a strong protest by a large number of people because they disagree with sth: *The public outcry forced the government to change its mind.*

outdated /ˌaʊt'deɪtɪd/ *adj* not useful or common any more; old-fashioned: *A lot of the computer equipment is getting outdated.*

outdo /ˌaʊt'duː/ *verb* [T] (*pres part* **outdoing**; *3rd pers sing pres* **outdoes** /-'dʌz/; *pt* **outdid** /-'dɪd/; *pp* **outdone** /-'dʌn/) to do sth better than another person; to be more successful than sb else: *He doesn't want to be outdone by his brother.*

☆ **outdoor** /'aʊtdɔː(r)/ *adj* happening, done, or used in the open air (not in a building): *an outdoor job* ○ *outdoor furniture* ☞ The opposite is **indoor**.

outdoors /ˌaʊt'dɔːz/ *adv* in the open air; outside a building: *It's a very warm evening so why don't we sit outdoors?* ☞ The opposite is **indoors**.

☆ **outer** /'aʊtə(r)/ *adj* **1** on the outside: *the outer layer of skin* **2** far from the inside or the centre: *the outer suburbs of a city* ☞ The opposite is **inner**.

outermost /'aʊtəməʊst/ *adj* furthest from the inside or centre; most distant: *the out-*

outfit

ermost planet in the solar system ☛ The opposite is **innermost**.

,outer 'space *noun* [U] = SPACE(2)

outfit /'aʊtfɪt/ *noun* [C] **1** a set of clothes that are worn together **2** (*informal*) an organization, a company, etc: *He works for a computer outfit I've never heard of.*

outgoing /'aʊtgəʊɪŋ/ *adj* **1** friendly and interested in other people and new experiences **2** leaving a job or a place: *The outgoing headmaster made a short speech.* ○ *Put all the outgoing mail in a pile on that table.* ☛ The opposite is **incoming**.

outgoings /'aʊtgəʊɪŋz/ *noun* [plural] the amounts of money that you spend: *Last month my outgoings were greater than my income.*

outgrow /,aʊt'grəʊ/ *verb* [T] (*pt* **outgrew** /-'gru:/; *pp* **outgrown** /-'grəʊn/) to become too old or too big for sth (especially clothes): *Children outgrow their shoes so quickly.*

outing /'aʊtɪŋ/ *noun* [C] a short trip for pleasure: *to go on an outing to the zoo*

outlandish /aʊt'lændɪʃ/ *adj* very strange or unusual: *outlandish clothes*

outlast /,aʊt'lɑ:st; *US* -'læst/ *verb* [T] to last or live longer than sb/sth

outlaw /'aʊtlɔ:/ *noun* [C] (*old-fashioned*) a criminal who is living outside society and trying to avoid being captured: *The film is about a band of outlaws in the Wild West.*

outlaw *verb* [T] to make sth illegal

outlay /'aʊtleɪ/ *noun* [C, usually sing] money that is spent, especially in order to start a business or a project

outlet /'aʊtlet/ *noun* [C] a hole through which a gas or liquid can escape: (*figurative*) *Gary found an outlet for his energy in playing football.*

☆ **outline** /'aʊtlaɪn/ *noun* [C] **1** a line that shows the shape or outside edge of sb/sth: *She could see the outline of a person through the mist.* **2** the most important facts or ideas about sth: *a brief outline of Indian history*

outline *verb* [T] to give the most important facts or ideas about sth

outlive /,aʊt'lɪv/ *verb* [T] to live or exist longer than sb/sth: *He outlived his wife by nearly twenty years.*

☆ **outlook** /'aʊtlʊk/ *noun* [C] **1** your attitude to or feeling about life: *an optimistic outlook on life* **2** outlook (**for sth**) what will probably happen: *The outlook for the economy is not good.*

outlying /'aʊtlaɪɪŋ/ *adj* (only *before* a noun) far from the centre of a town or city: *The bus service to the outlying villages is very poor.*

outmoded /,aʊt'məʊdɪd/ *adj* (only *before* a noun) no longer common or fashionable

outnumber /,aʊt'nʌmbə(r)/ *verb* [T] (often passive) to be greater in number than sb/sth: *The enemy troops outnumbered us by three to one.* ○ *We were completely outnumbered.*

out-patient /'aʊtpeɪʃnt/ *noun* [C] a person who goes to see a doctor in hospital but who does not stay there overnight

☆ **output** /'aʊtpʊt/ *noun* [sing] **1** the amount that a person or machine produces: *Output has

outskirts

increased in the past year. **2** the information that is given by a computer ☛ Look at **input**.

outrage /'aʊtreɪdʒ/ *noun* **1** [C] something that is very bad or wrong and that causes you to feel great anger: *It's an outrage that such poverty should exist in the 20th century.* **2** [U] great anger: *a feeling of outrage*

outrage *verb* [T] (often passive) to make sb feel very angry or upset: *His parents were outraged when he dyed his hair green.*

outrageous /aʊt'reɪdʒəs/ *adj* **1** making you very angry: *I refuse to pay such outrageous prices.* **2** very strange or unusual; shocking —**outrageously** *adv*

outright /'aʊtraɪt/ *adv* **1** without hiding anything; openly: *She told them outright what she thought about it.* **2** immediately or completely: *to be killed outright* ○ *They were able to buy the house outright.*

outright *adj* (only *before* a noun) complete and clear, without any doubt: *Lester was the outright winner.*

outset /'aʊtset/ *noun*
(IDIOM) **at/from the outset (of sth)** at/from the beginning (of sth): *There have been difficulties with this firm right from the outset.*

☆ **outside¹** /,aʊt'saɪd/ *noun* **1** [C, usually sing] the outer side or surface of sth: *There is a list of all the ingredients on the outside of the packet.* ○ *to paint the outside of a house* **2** [sing] the area that is near or round a building, etc: *We've only seen the church from the outside.*
(IDIOM) **at the outside** at the most: *It will cost £200 at the outside.*

outside /'aʊtsaɪd/ *adj* **1** of or on the outer side or surface of sth: *the outside walls of a building* **2** not part of the main building: *Many cottages still have outside toilets.* **3** not connected with or belonging to a particular group or organization: *We can't do all the work by ourselves. We'll need outside help.* **4** (used about a chance, possibility, etc) very small
(IDIOM) **the outside world** ➔ WORLD

,outside 'broadcast *noun* [C] a television or radio programme that was not made in a studio

,outside 'lane *noun* [C] the part of a wide road or motorway that is for the fastest cars

☆ **outside²** /,aʊt'saɪd/ *prep* **1** in, at or to a place that is not in but close to a building, etc: *Leave your muddy boots outside the door.* **2** (*US* also **outside of**) not in: *You may do as you wish outside office hours.* ○ *a small village just outside Southampton*

outside *adv* **1** in or to a place that is not in a room: *Please wait outside for a few minutes.* **2** in or to a place that is not in a building: *Let's eat outside. The weather is lovely.* ○ *Go outside and see if it's raining.* ☛ Look at **outdoors** and **out of doors** (at the entry for **door**).

outsider /,aʊt'saɪdə(r)/ *noun* [C] **1** a person who is not accepted as a member of a particular group **2** a person or animal in a race or competition that is not expected to win

outsize /'aʊtsaɪz/ *adj* (often used about clothes) larger than usual

outskirts /'aʊtskɜ:ts/ *noun* [plural] **the out-**

s	z	ʃ	ʒ	h	m	n	ŋ	l	r	j	w
so	zoo	she	vision	how	man	no	sing	leg	red	yes	wet

outspoken skirts the parts of a town or city that are farthest from the centre

outspoken /ˌaʊtˈspəʊkən/ *adj* saying exactly what you think or feel: *Linda is very outspoken in her criticism.* —**outspokenness** *noun* [U]

☆ **outstanding** /ˌaʊtˈstændɪŋ/ *adj* **1** very good indeed; excellent: *The results in the exams were quite outstanding.* **2** not yet paid or done: *Some of the work is still outstanding.*

outstandingly *adv* very well: *Huw played outstandingly.*

outstretched /ˌaʊtˈstretʃt/ *adj* spread out as far as possible: *outstretched arms*

outward /ˈaʊtwəd/ *adj* (only *before* a noun) **1** (used about a journey) going away from the place that you will return to later ☞ The opposite is **return**. **2** of or on the outside: *Her outward good humour hid her inner sadness.*

outwardly *adv* on the outside or surface: *He remained outwardly calm so as not to frighten the children.*

outwards /-wədz/ (*especially US* **outward**) *adv* towards the outside or away from the place where you are: *This door opens outwards.*

outweigh /ˌaʊtˈweɪ/ *verb* [T] to be more important than sth: *The advantages outweigh the disadvantages.*

outwit /ˌaʊtˈwɪt/ *verb* [T] (**outwitting**; **outwitted**) to defeat or get an advantage over sb by being cleverer than him/her

oval /ˈəʊvl/ *adj, noun* [C] shaped like an egg; a shape like that of an egg: *an oval mirror* ☞ picture at **shape**.

ovary /ˈəʊvəri/ *noun* [C] (*pl* **ovaries**) one of the two parts of the female body that produce eggs

ovation /əʊˈveɪʃn/ *noun* [C] a long period of clapping and applause: *The dancers were given a standing ovation* (= people stood up and clapped).

☆ **oven** /ˈʌvn/ *noun* [C] the part of a cooker that has a door. You put things inside an oven to cook them: *Cook in a hot oven for 50 minutes.* ○ *a microwave oven* ☞ *You* **roast** *or* **bake** *food in an oven.* picture at **cooker**.

☆ **over** /ˈəʊvə(r)/ *adv, prep* ☞ For special uses with many verbs, eg **get over sth**, look at the verb entries. **1** directly above sth, but not touching: *There's a painting over the bookcase.* ○ *We jumped when the plane flew over.* **2** on, and partly or completely covering or touching: *There's a cover over the chair.* ○ *She hung her coat over the back of the chair.* **3** down or sideways from an upright position: *He leaned over to speak to the woman next to him.* ○ *I fell over in the street this morning.* **4** across to the other side of sth: *The dog is jumping over the fence.* ○ *a bridge over the river* **5** on or to the other side: *She lives over the road.* ○ *Turn the patient over.* **6** (used for expressing distance): *He's over in America at the moment.* ○ *Sit down over there.* **7** not used: *There are a lot of cakes left over from the party.* **8** above or more than a number, price, etc: *She lived in Athens for over ten years.* ○ *suitable for children aged 10 and over* **9** (used with *all*) in every part or place: *There was blood all over the place.* ○ *I can't find my glasses. I've looked all over for them.* **10** (used for saying that sth is repeated): *You'll have to start all over again* (= from the beginning). ○ *She kept saying the same thing over and over again.* **11** about; on the subject of: *We quarrelled over our money.* **12** during: *We met over the Christmas holiday.*

over *adj* finished: *The exams are all over now.*

over- (used to form verbs, nouns, adjectives and adverbs) too; too much: *They're overexcited.* ○ *I'm overworked.* ○ *He overeats.*

overall¹ /ˌəʊvərˈɔːl/ *adj* (only *before* a noun) including everything: *The overall cost of the work will be about £200.*

overall *adv* **1** including everything: *What does the garden measure overall?* **2** speaking generally about sth: *Overall, I can say that we are pleased with the year's work.*

a painting **above**/ **over** a bookcase

a house **above** a village

a cover **over** an armchair

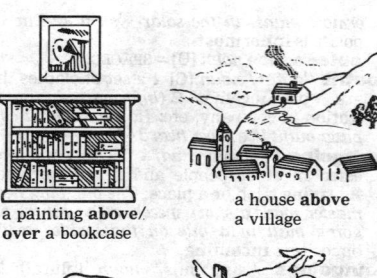

jumping **over** a fence

over/above

aprons

overall

overalls

overall² /ˈəʊvərɔːl/ *noun* **1** [C] a piece of clothing that is like a coat and that you wear over your clothes to keep them clean when you are working **2 overalls** (*US* **coveralls**) [plural] a piece of clothing that covers your legs and

iː	ɪ	e	æ	ɑː	ɒ	ɔː	ʊ	uː	ʌ
see	sit	ten	hat	arm	got	saw	put	too	cup

overawe

body (and sometimes your arms) and that you wear over your clothes to keep them clean when you are working

overawe /ˌəʊvərˈɔː/ verb [T] (usually passive) to cause sb to admire sb/sth and feel a little afraid: *They were rather overawed by the atmosphere in the hall.*

overbalance /ˌəʊvəˈbæləns/ verb [I] to fall over or nearly fall over because you cannot stand steadily

overboard /ˈəʊvəbɔːd/ adv over the side of a boat or ship into the water: *Man overboard!* ○ *She fell overboard and drowned.*
(IDIOM) **go overboard (about sb/sth)** to be too excited about sb/sth

overcast /ˌəʊvəˈkɑːst; US -ˈkæst/ adj (used about the sky) covered with cloud

overcharge /ˌəʊvəˈtʃɑːdʒ/ verb [I,T] to ask sb to pay too much money: *The man in the post office overcharged me by 50p.*

overcoat /ˈəʊvəkəʊt/ noun [C] a long thick coat that you wear in cold weather

☆**overcome** /ˌəʊvəˈkʌm/ verb [T] (pt **overcame** /-ˈkeɪm/; pp **overcome**) **1** to control or succeed in defeating sb/sth: *She tried hard to overcome her fear of flying.* **2** (usually passive) to cause sb to become weak or ill or to lose control: *He was overcome with emotion and had to leave the room.* ○ *to be overcome by smoke*

overcrowded /ˌəʊvəˈkraʊdɪd/ adj (used about a place) with too many people: *The trains are overcrowded on Friday evenings.*

overdo /ˌəʊvəˈduː/ verb [T] (pt **overdid** /-ˈdɪd/; pp **overdone** /-ˈdʌn/) **1** to use or show too much of sth: *He overdid the pepper in the stew.* ○ *You look nice but you overdid the make-up a bit.* **2** to cook sth too long: *The meat was overdone.*
(IDIOM) **overdo it/things** to work, etc too hard: *Exercise is fine but don't overdo it.*

overdose /ˈəʊvədəʊs/ noun [C] an amount of a drug or medicine that is too large and so is not safe: *Hugh killed himself by taking an overdose.*

overdraft /ˈəʊvədrɑːft; US -dræft/ noun [C] an amount of money that you have spent or want to spend that is greater than the amount you have in your bank account: *We took out an overdraft to pay for the holiday.* ○ *to pay off an overdraft*

overdrawn /ˌəʊvəˈdrɔːn/ adj having spent more money than you have in your bank account: *Darren is £500 overdrawn.*

overdue /ˌəʊvəˈdjuː; US -ˈduː/ adj late in arriving, happening, being paid, returned, etc: *Their train is ten minutes overdue.* ○ *Change is long overdue* (= it should have happened before now).

overestimate /ˌəʊvərˈestɪmeɪt/ verb [T] to think that sb/sth is bigger, better, more expensive, etc than he/she/it really is: *I overestimated how much we could paint in a day.*
☛ The opposite is **underestimate**.

overflow /ˌəʊvəˈfləʊ/ verb [I,T] to have liquid pouring over the edge; to pour over the edge of sth: *The tap was left on and the bath overflowed.* ○ *After the heavy rains the river overflowed its banks.*

overgrown /ˌəʊvəˈgrəʊn/ adj covered with

'Oh no! The bath's overflowing!'

overflow

plants that have not been looked after and that have grown too big: *The garden is neglected and overgrown.*

overhang /ˌəʊvəˈhæŋ/ verb [I,T] (pt, pp **overhung**) to stick out from or hang over sth: *I hit my head on an overhanging branch and fell off my bike.*

overhaul /ˌəʊvəˈhɔːl/ verb [T] to look at sth carefully and change or repair it if necessary: *to overhaul an engine* —**overhaul** /ˈəʊvəhɔːl/ noun [C]: *a complete overhaul of the social security system*

overhead /ˈəʊvəhed/ adj above your head: *overhead electricity cables* —**overhead** /ˌəʊvəˈhed/ adv: *A helicopter flew overhead.*

overheads /ˈəʊvəhedz/ noun [plural] money that a company must spend on things like salaries, heat, light, rent, etc

overhear /ˌəʊvəˈhɪə(r)/ verb [T] (pt, pp **overheard** /-ˈhɜːd/) to hear what sb is saying when he/she is speaking to sb else and not to you

overjoyed /ˌəʊvəˈdʒɔɪd/ adj (not before a noun) **overjoyed (at sth/to do sth)** very happy: *We were overjoyed at the news.*

overland /ˈəʊvəlænd/ adj not by sea or by air: *an overland journey* —**overland** adv: *We travelled overland from Paris to China.*

overlap /ˌəʊvəˈlæp/ verb [I,T] (overla**pp**ing; overla**pp**ed) **1** when two things overlap, part of one covers part of the other: *Make sure that the two pieces of material overlap.* **2** to be partly the same as sth: *Our jobs overlap to some extent.* —**overlap** /ˈəʊvəlæp/ noun [C]: *There will be a period of overlap between the new teacher arriving and the old one going.*

overlapping tiles

overleaf /ˌəʊvəˈliːf/ adv on the other side of the page: *Full details are given overleaf.*

overload /ˌəʊvəˈləʊd/ verb [T] **1** (often passive) to put too many people or things into or onto sth: *an overloaded vehicle* ○ (figurative) *to be overloaded with work* **2** to put too much electricity through sth: *If you use too many electrical appliances at one time you may overload the system.*

☆**overlook** /ˌəʊvəˈlʊk/ verb [T] **1** to have a view

ɜː	ə	eɪ	əʊ	aɪ	aʊ	ɔɪ	ɪə	eə	ʊə
fur	ago	pay	home	five	now	join	near	hair	pure

over sth: *The sitting-room overlooks the river.* **2** to fail to see, take notice of or remember sth: *to overlook a spelling mistake* o *The local people felt that their opinions had been completely overlooked.* **3** to take no action about sth that sb has done wrong: *I will overlook your behaviour this time but don't let it happen again.*

overnight /ˌəʊvə'naɪt/ *adj, adv* **1** for or during the night: *an overnight bag* o *Why don't you stay overnight?* **2** (happening) very suddenly: *an overnight success* o *She became a star overnight.*

overpass /'əʊvəpɑːs; *US* -pæs/ *noun* [C] (*US*) = FLYOVER

overpower /ˌəʊvə'paʊə(r)/ *verb* [T] to be too strong for sb; to defeat sb because you are stronger than him/her: *The police overpowered the burglars.* o *The fireman was overpowered by the heat and smoke.*

overpowering /ˌəʊvə'paʊərɪŋ/ *adj* very strong: *an overpowering smell*

overrate /ˌəʊvə'reɪt/ *verb* [T] (often passive) to have too high an opinion of sb/sth: *I think that the play is greatly overrated.* ☛ The opposite is **underrate**.

override /ˌəʊvə'raɪd/ *verb* [T] (*pt* **overrode** /-'rəʊd/; *pp* **overridden** /-'rɪdn/) **1** (used about sb/sth with authority) to pay no attention to a person's decisions or actions: *They overrode my protest and continued with the meeting.* **2** to be more important than sth

overriding /ˌəʊvə'raɪdɪŋ/ *adj* (only *before* a noun) more important than anything else

overrule /ˌəʊvə'ruːl/ *verb* [T] (used about sb/sth with authority) to decide that another person's decisions or actions are not valid: *The Home Secretary has the power to overrule the council's decision.*

overrun /ˌəʊvə'rʌn/ *verb* (*pt* **overran** /-'ræn/; *pp* **overrun** /-'rʌn/) **1** [T] (often passive) to spread all over an area in great numbers: *The city was overrun by rats.* **2** [I,T] to continue later than the expected time: *The meeting overran by 30 minutes.*

☆ **overseas** /ˌəʊvə'siːz/ *adj* (only *before* a noun) in, to or from another country (that you have to cross the sea to get to): *There are many overseas students studying in Britain.*

overseas *adv* in or to another country: *Frank has gone to live overseas.* o *People overseas will be able to vote in the election.*

oversee /ˌəʊvə'siː/ *verb* [T] (*pt* **oversaw** /-'sɔː/; *pp* **overseen** /-'siːn/) to watch sth to make sure that it is done properly

overshadow /ˌəʊvə'ʃædəʊ/ *verb* [T] **1** to cause sth to be less happy: *The Christmas celebrations were overshadowed by her illness.* **2** to cause sb/sth to seem less important or successful: *Colin always seemed to be overshadowed by his sister.*

oversight /'əʊvəsaɪt/ *noun* [C,U] something that you do not notice or do (that you should have noticed or done): *Through an oversight Len's name did not appear on the list.*

oversimplify /ˌəʊvə'sɪmplɪfaɪ/ *verb* [I,T] (*pres part* **oversimplifying**; *3rd pers sing pres* **oversimplifies**; *pt, pp* **oversimplified**) to explain sth in such a simple way that its real meaning is lost

oversleep /ˌəʊvə'sliːp/ *verb* [I] (*pt, pp* **overslept** /-'slept/) to sleep longer than you should have done

☆ **overtake** /ˌəʊvə'teɪk/ *verb* [I,T] (*pt* **overtook** /-'tʊk/; *pp* **overtaken** /-'teɪkən/) to go past another person, car, etc because you are moving faster: *The continuous white line in the middle of the road means you must not overtake.* o *I overtook a lorry.* o *He overtook me on the bend.*

overthrow /ˌəʊvə'θrəʊ/ *verb* [T] (*pt* **overthrew** /-'θruː/; *pp* **overthrown** /-'θrəʊn/) to remove a leader or government from power, by using force: *The dictator was overthrown in a military coup.* —**overthrow** /'əʊvəθrəʊ/ *noun* [sing]: *the overthrow of the French monarchy in 1789*

overtime /'əʊvətaɪm/ *noun* [U] time that you spend at work after your usual working hours: *Betty did ten hours overtime last week.* o *Do you get paid overtime?* —**overtime** *adv*: *I have been working overtime for weeks.*

overtone /'əʊvətəʊn/ *noun* [C, usually pl] something that is suggested but not expressed openly: *It's a funny play but it has serious overtones.*

overture /'əʊvətjʊə(r)/ *noun* **1** [C, usually pl] (*formal*) an act of being friendly towards sb (perhaps because you want sth): *It's time to make some peace overtures to the boss.* **2** [C] a piece of music that is the introduction to an opera, ballet, etc

overturn /ˌəʊvə'tɜːn/ *verb* [I,T] to turn over so that the top is at the bottom: *The car overturned but the driver escaped unhurt.* o (*figurative*) *to overturn a decision* (= to change it)

overweight /ˌəʊvə'weɪt/ *adj* too heavy or fat: *You're a bit overweight. Perhaps you should go on a diet?* ☛ Look at the note at **fat**.

overwhelm /ˌəʊvə'welm; *US* -'hwelm/ *verb* [T] (usually passive) **1** to cause sb to feel a very strong emotion: *The new world champion was overwhelmed by all the publicity.* **2** to defeat sb/sth because you have more people

overwhelming *adj* very great or strong: *Anna had an overwhelming desire to return home.* —**overwhelmingly** *adv*: *The meeting voted overwhelmingly against the plan.*

overwork /ˌəʊvə'wɜːk/ *verb* [I,T] to work too hard or to make sb work too hard: *They are overworked and underpaid.* —**overwork** /'əʊvəwɜːk/ *noun* [U]

☆ **owe** /əʊ/ *verb* [T] **1 owe sth (to sb) (for sth); owe sb sth for sb** to have to pay money to sb for sth that they have done or given: *We owe the bank £5 000.* o *We owe £5 000 to the bank.* o *I still owe you for that bread you bought me yesterday.* o (*figurative*) *Claudia owes me an explanation.* **2** to feel grateful to sb for sth: *I owe you a lot for all you did for me when I was young.* **3 owe sth (to sb/sth)** to have sth (for the reason given): *Britain owed her strength in the 19th century to her naval power.*

owing /'əʊɪŋ/ *adj* (not before a noun) not yet paid: *How much is still owing to you?*

owing to *prep* because of: *The match was cancelled owing to the bad weather.*

p	b	t	d	k	g	tʃ	dʒ	f	v	θ	ð
pen	bad	tea	did	cat	got	chin	June	fall	van	thin	then

owl /aʊl/ *noun* [C] a bird that flies at night and that catches and eats small animals. Owls are used as a symbol of wisdom.

☆**own¹** /əʊn/ *det, pron* **1** (used to emphasize that sth belongs to a particular person): *I saw him do it with my own eyes.* ○ *Use your own pen. I need mine.* ○ *This is his own house.* ○ *This house is his own.* ○ *Rachel would like her own room* (= she doesn't want to share one). ☞ **Own** cannot be used after *a* or *the*. You CANNOT say: *I would like an own car.* Say: *I would like my own car* or *I would like a car of my own.* **2** (used to show that sth is done or made without help from another person): *The children are old enough to get their own breakfast.* ○ *They grow all their own vegetables.*
(IDIOMS) **come into your own** to have your real value recognized: *The car phone really comes into its own when you break down on a country road.*
hold your own (against sb/sth) to be as strong, good, etc as sb/sth else
of your, etc own belonging to you and not to anyone else: *Kate has always wanted a pony of her own.*
(all) on your, etc own 1 alone: *John lives all on his own.* ☞ Look at the note at **alone**. **2** without help: *I managed to repair the car all on my own.*

get/have your own back (on sb) (*informal*) to hurt or do harm to sb who has hurt or done harm to you

☆**own²** /əʊn/ *verb* [T] to have sth belonging to you; possess: *We don't own the video. We just rent it.* ○ *Who is this land owned by?*
(PHRASAL VERB) **own up (to sth)** (*informal*) to tell sb that you have done sth wrong: *None of the children owned up to breaking the window.* ☞ Look at **confess**. It is more formal.

☆**owner** /'əʊnə(r)/ *noun* [C] a person who owns sth: *a dog owner*
ownership *noun* [U] the state of owning sth

ox /ɒks/ *noun* [C] (*pl* **oxen** /'ɒksn/) a male cow that has been castrated. Oxen are sometimes used for pulling or carrying heavy loads. ☞ Look at **bull**.

☆**oxygen** /'ɒksɪdʒən/ *noun* [U] (*symbol* **O**) a gas that you cannot see, taste or smell. Plants and animals cannot live and fire cannot burn without oxygen.

oyster /'ɔɪstə(r)/ *noun* [C] a shellfish that is eaten as food. Some oysters produce pearls. ☞ picture at **shellfish**.

ozone /'əʊzəʊn/ *noun* [U] a form of oxygen
ozone-'friendly *adj* (used about household products, etc) not containing chemicals that could damage the ozone layer: *Most aerosol sprays are now ozone-friendly.*
'ozone layer *noun* [sing] the layer of ozone high above the surface of the earth that helps to protect us from the dangerous rays of the sun: *a hole in the ozone layer*

Pp

P, p /piː/ *noun* [C] (*pl* **P's; p's**) the sixteenth letter of the English alphabet: *'Pencil' begins with (a) 'P'.*

☆**pace¹** /peɪs/ *noun* **1** [C] the distance that you move when you take one step: *Take two paces forward and then stop.* **2** [sing] the speed at which you do sth or at which sth happens: *Run at a steady pace and you won't get tired so quickly.* ○ *I can't stand the pace of life in London.*
(IDIOMS) **keep pace (with sb/sth)** to move or do sth at the same speed as sb/sth else; to change as quickly as sth else is changing: *Wages are not keeping pace with inflation.*
set the pace to move or do sth at the speed that others must follow
'pacemaker *noun* [C] **1** a person who sets the pace that others must follow **2** a machine that helps to make a person's heart beat regularly or more strongly
pace² /peɪs/ *verb* [I,T] to walk with slow regular steps: *Fran paced nervously up and down the room, waiting for news.*

pacifism /'pæsɪfɪzəm/ *noun* [U] the belief that all wars are wrong and that you should not fight in them
pacifist /-ɪst/ *noun* [C] a person who believes in pacifism
pacify /'pæsɪfaɪ/ *verb* [T] (*pres part* **pacifying**; *3rd pers sing pres* **pacifies**; *pt, pp* **pacified**) to cause sb who is angry or upset to be calm or quiet

☆**pack¹** /pæk/ *noun* [C] **1** a number of things that are wrapped or tied together and that you carry on your back or that are carried by an animal: *a packhorse* ☞ Look at **backpack**. **2** a packet or group of things that are sold together: *The pack contains a pencil, 10 envelopes and 20 sheets of writing-paper.* ○ (*figurative*) *Everything she told me was a pack of lies.* **3** [with sing or pl verb] a group of animals that

s	z	ʃ	ʒ	h	m	n	ŋ	l	r	j	w
so	zoo	she	vision	how	man	no	sing	leg	red	yes	wet

hunt together: *a pack of wolves* **4** (*US* **deck**) a complete set of playing-cards ☞ Look at the note at **card**.

☆ **pack²** /pæk/ *verb* **1** [I,T] to put your things into a suitcase, etc before you go away or on holiday: *I'll have to pack my suitcase in the morning.* ○ *Have you packed yet?* ○ *Have you packed your toothbrush?* ☞ Note the expression **do your packing**: *I'll do my packing in the morning.* **2** [I,T] to put things into boxes, in a factory or when you move house ☞ The opposite for 1 and 2 is **unpack**. **3** [T] (often passive) to fill or crowd: *The train was absolutely packed. We couldn't get a seat.* ○ *an action-packed film*

(PHRASAL VERBS) **pack sth in** (*informal*) to stop doing sth: *I've packed in my job. I'm leaving next month.*

pack sth in; pack sth in/into sth to do a lot in a short time: *They packed an awful lot into their three days in Rome.*

pack sth out to fill sth with people: *The cinemas are packed out every night.*

pack up (*informal*) **1** to finish working or doing sth: *There was nothing else to do so we packed up and went home.* **2** (used about a machine, engine, etc) to stop working

packed 'lunch *noun* [C] sandwiches, etc that you take with you to work or school

☆ **package** /'pækɪdʒ/ *noun* [C] **1** something, or a number of things, wrapped up in paper: *It was a strangely shaped package and no one could guess what was inside.* ☞ Look at the note at **parcel**. **2** (*US*) = PACKET **3** a number of things that must be bought or accepted together: *a word-processing package* ○ *The strike will go on until the firm offers a better pay and conditions package.*

package *verb* [T] to put sth into a packet, box, etc before it is sold or sent somewhere: *Goods that are attractively packaged sell more quickly.*

packaging *noun* [U] all the materials that are used to wrap sth before it is sold or sent somewhere: *Chocolates sometimes have four or five layers of packaging.*

'package holiday *noun* [C] a holiday that is organized by a travel agent who arranges your travel and accommodation for you

'package store *noun* [C] (*US*) = OFF-LICENCE

☆ **packet** /'pækɪt/ (*US* **package**) *noun* [C] a box, bag, etc in which things are packed to be sold in a shop: *a packet of sweets, cigarettes, biscuits, etc* ○ *a cigarette packet* ☞ Look at the note at **parcel**. picture at **container**.

packing /'pækɪŋ/ *noun* [U] **1** putting things into a box or suitcase: *I haven't done any packing yet and we're going away this evening.* **2** soft material that you use when you are packing to stop things from being damaged or broken: *Add 95p to the price for postage and packing.*

'packing-case *noun* [C] a wooden box that you put things in before they are transported or stored

pact /pækt/ *noun* [C] a formal agreement between two people, groups or countries

☆ **pad¹** /pæd/ *noun* [C] **1** a thick piece of soft material, used for cleaning or protecting sth: *Footballers wear shin pads to protect their legs.* ○ *a jacket with shoulder pads* ○ *Press the cotton-wool pad onto the wound to stop the bleeding.* **2** a number of pieces of paper that are fastened together at one end: *a writing pad* **3** the place from which helicopters and space rockets take off: *a launch pad* **4** the soft part on the bottom of the foot of some animals, eg dogs, cats, etc

pad² /pæd/ *verb* [T] (**pad**ding; **pad**ded) (usually passive) to fill or cover sth with soft material in order to protect it, make it larger or more comfortable, etc: *a padded bra* ○ *Violent prisoners are put in padded cells so they do not hurt themselves.*

(PHRASAL VERB) **pad sth out** to make a book, speech, etc longer by adding things that are not necessary

padding *noun* [U] material that you use to pad² sth

pad³ /pæd/ *verb* [I] (**pad**ding; **pad**ded) **pad about, along, around,** etc to walk rather quickly and quietly

paddle¹ /'pædl/ *noun* [C] a short pole that is wide at one or both ends and that you use for moving a small boat through water ☞ Look at **oar**.

paddle *verb* [I,T] to move a small boat through water using a paddle ☞ Look at **row**.

paddle² /'pædl/ *verb* [I] to walk with bare feet in shallow water

paddock /'pædək/ *noun* [C] a small field where horses are kept

padlock /'pædlɒk/ *noun* [C] a type of lock that is used for fastening gates, bicycles, etc ☞ picture at **chain**.

padlock *verb* [T] to fasten sth with a padlock

paediatrician (*US* **pediatrician**) /ˌpiːdɪə-ˈtrɪʃn/ *noun* [C] a doctor who specializes in looking after sick children

pagan /'peɪgən/ *adj* having religious beliefs that do not belong to any of the main religions: *Hallowe'en is an ancient pagan festival.*

☆ **page¹** /peɪdʒ/ *noun* [C] (*abbr* **p**) **1** one side of a piece of paper: *The letter was three pages long.* ○ *Start each answer on a new page.* ○ *to turn over the page* ○ *Full flight details are given on page 63.* ○ *the front page of a newspaper* ○ *the sports page* **2** one piece of paper in a book, etc: *One page had been torn from her diary.*

page² /peɪdʒ/ *verb* [T] to call sb's name over a loudspeaker in a place where there are a lot of people, so that you can give him/her a message

pageant /'pædʒənt/ *noun* [C] **1** a type of outdoor public entertainment at which there is a procession of people, often dressed up in historical costume **2** any colourful ceremony

pageantry /'pædʒəntri/ *noun* [U] the feeling and appearance of a grand ceremony when people are dressed in fine colourful clothes: *The pageantry of the Changing of the Guard is very popular with tourists.*

paid *pt, pp* of PAY²

pail /peɪl/ *noun* [C] a bucket

☆ **pain** /peɪn/ *noun* **1** [C,U] the unpleasant feeling that you have when a part of your body has been hurt or when you are ill: *to be in great pain* ○ *I've got a terrible pain in my back.* ○ *to scream with pain* ○ *chest pains* ○ *After I took the tablets the pain wore off.* ○ *The tablets relieved*

iː	ɪ	e	æ	ɑː	ɒ	ɔː	ʊ	uː	ʌ
see	sit	ten	hat	arm	got	saw	put	too	cup

the pain. ☛ Look at **ache**. Notice that we usually say: *I've got a headache, etc* instead of using an expression with 'pain'. **2** [U] unhappiness that you feel because sth bad has happened or because sb has been unkind: *It took me years to get over the pain of my mother's death.* **3** [C] (*informal*) a person, thing or situation that causes you to be angry or annoyed: *Having to clean the ice off the windscreen every morning is a real pain.*

pain *verb* [T] to cause sb to feel unhappy or upset

pained *adj* showing that you are unhappy or upset: *a pained expression*

painful /-fl/ *adj* that causes pain: *A wasp sting can be very painful.* ○ *The breakup of their marriage was very painful for the children.* —**painfully** /-fəli/ *adv*: *Progress is still painfully slow.*

painless *adj* that does not cause pain: *The animals' death is quick and painless.* —**painlessly** *adv*

'painkiller *noun* [C] medicine that is used for reducing or removing pain

pains /peɪnz/ *noun*
(IDIOMS) **be at (great) pains to do sth** to make a special effort to do sth: *He was at pains to hide his true feelings.*
take great pains (with/over/to do sth) to take great care with sth or to make a special effort to do sth: *She always takes great pains with her writing.*

painstaking /ˈpeɪnzteɪkɪŋ/ *adj* very careful: *The painstaking search of the wreckage gave us clues as to the cause of the crash.* —**painstakingly** *adv*

☆ **paint¹** /peɪnt/ *noun* **1** [U] a liquid that you put onto a surface with a brush in order to give it colour or to protect it: *The door will need two more coats of paint.* ○ *Wet paint!* ○ *spray paint* ○ *The paint was peeling off the walls.* **2** [U] coloured liquid that you can use to make a picture: *red paint* ○ *oil paint* **3 paints** [plural] a collection of tubes, blocks, etc of paint that an artist uses

'paintbox *noun* [C] a box that contains blocks of paint of many colours

'paintbrush *noun* [C] a brush that you use for painting with ☛ picture at **brush**.

'paintwork *noun* [U] a surface that has been painted

☆ **paint²** /peɪnt/ *verb* [I,T] **1** to put paint onto sth: *The bathroom needs painting.* ○ *Wear old clothes when you're painting.* ○ *The walls were painted pink.* **2** to make a picture of sb/sth using paints: *Vicky paints well.* ○ *to paint a self-portrait*

☆ **painter** /ˈpeɪntə(r)/ *noun* [C] **1** a person whose job is to paint buildings, walls, etc **2** a person who paints pictures ☛ Look at **artist**.

☆ **painting** /ˈpeɪntɪŋ/ *noun* **1** [U] the act of painting pictures or buildings **2** [C] a picture that sb has painted: *a famous painting by Van Gogh* ☛ Look at **drawing**.

☆ **pair** /peə(r)/ *noun* **1** [C] two things that are almost the same and that are used together: *a pair of shoes* ○ *a pair of gloves* **2** [C] a thing that consists of two parts that are joined together: *a pair of scissors* ○ *a pair of glasses* ○ *two pairs of trousers* **3** [C, with sing or pl verb] two people or animals that are closely connected with each other: *The pair from Didcot won all their matches easily.* ○ *A pair of blackbirds are nesting in the apple tree.* ☛ Look at **couple**.
(IDIOM) **in pairs** two at a time: *These earrings are only sold in pairs.*

pair *verb*
(PHRASAL VERBS) **pair (sb/sth) off (with sb)** to form a pair or pairs: *Stop trying to pair me off with your brother – I'm not interested.*
pair up (with sb) to join together with another person or group.

pajamas /pəˈdʒæməz/ (*US*) *noun* [plural] = PYJAMAS

pal /pæl/ *noun* [C] (*informal*) a friend

☆ **palace** /ˈpælɪs/ *noun* [C] a large house that is or was the home of a king or queen

palate /ˈpælət/ *noun* [C] the top part of the inside of your mouth

☆ **pale** /peɪl/ *adj* **1** (used about a person or his/her face, etc) having less colour than usual; rather white: *Are you OK? You look a bit pale.* ☛ The noun is **pallor**. Look at **pallid**. **2** not bright or strong in colour: *pale yellow*

pall /pɔːl/ *verb* [I] to become uninteresting or annoying

pallid /ˈpælɪd/ *adj* (used about a person or his/her face, etc) pale or rather white because he/she is ill or frightened

pallor /ˈpælə(r)/ *noun* [U] the state of being pale or rather white because you are ill or frightened

palm¹ /pɑːm/ *noun* [C] the flat part of the front of your hand: *Dora held the bird in the palm of her hand.* ☛ picture on page A8.

palm *verb*
(PHRASAL VERBS) **palm sb off (with sth)** (*informal*) to persuade sb to accept sth that is not true or that is of poor quality: *He tried to palm me off with some story about the train being late.*
palm sb/sth off (on sb) to get rid of sb/sth that you do not want by giving it to sb else

palm-trees

palm² /pɑːm/ (*also* **'palm-tree**) *noun* [C] a type of tree that grows in hot countries. Palms have no branches and a mass of large leaves at the top: *a date/coconut palm*

paltry /ˈpɔːltri/ *adj* very small and so not worth very much

pamper /ˈpæmpə(r)/ *verb* [T] to treat sb very or too kindly

pamphlet /ˈpæmflɪt/ *noun* [C] a thin book with

a paper cover that gives you information about sth

pans

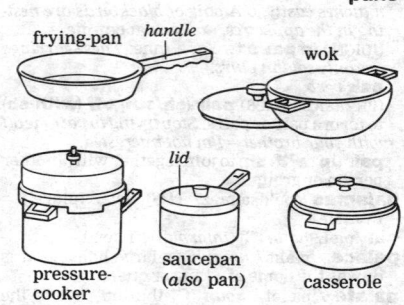

frying-pan, handle, wok, lid, pressure-cooker, saucepan (also pan), casserole

☆ **pan** /pæn/ noun [C] a metal container that is used for cooking: *Cook the spaghetti in a large pan of boiling salted water.* ○ *a frying-pan* ○ *All the pots and pans are kept in that cupboard.*

pancake /'pænkeɪk/ noun [C] a type of very thin round cake that is made by frying a mixture of flour, milk and eggs (**batter**)

'**Pancake Day** (*also* **Shrove Tuesday**) a Tuesday in February when people traditionally eat pancakes. Pancake Day is the day before the period of Lent begins.

panda /'pændə/ noun [C] a large black and white animal that looks like a bear and that comes from China. Pandas are very rare nowadays.

pandemonium /,pændɪ'məʊniəm/ noun [U] a state of great noise and confusion

pander /'pændə(r)/ verb
(PHRASAL VERB) **pander to sb/sth** to do or say what sb wants even if it is wrong or unpleasant

pane /peɪn/ noun [C] a piece of glass in a window, etc: *a pane of glass* ○ *the window-pane*

panel /'pænl/ noun **1** [C, with sing or pl verb] a group of people who are chosen to discuss sth, decide sth, answer questions, etc: *All the candidates were interviewed by a panel of four.* ○ *a panel of experts* ○ *a panel game on TV* ○ *What do/does the panel think about the changes in the education system?* **2** [C] a piece of wood, metal or glass that forms part of a door, wall, etc or that is fixed to it: *They smashed the glass panel in the front door.* **3** [C] a surface that contains the equipment for controlling a car, machine, etc: *the instrument panel*

panellist (*US* **panelist**) /'pænəlɪst/ noun [C] a member of a panel(1)

pang /pæŋ/ noun [C, usually pl] a sudden strong feeling (of pain, hunger, guilt, etc)

☆ **panic** /'pænɪk/ noun [C,U] a sudden feeling of fear that makes you do things without thinking carefully about them: *The rumours of war spread panic on the stock market.* ○ *to be in a state of panic* ○ *There was a mad panic when the alarm went off.*

panic *verb* [I] (panic**k**ing; panic**k**ed) to have a sudden feeling of fear that makes you act without thinking carefully: *Stay calm and don't panic.*

'**panic-stricken** adj very frightened

panorama /,pænə'rɑːmə; *US* -'ræmə/ noun [C] a view over a wide area of land —**panoramic** /,pænə'ræmɪk/ adj: *a panoramic view from the top of the hill*

pant /pænt/ verb [I] to take short quick breaths, eg after running or because it is very hot
pant noun [C] a short quick breath

panther /'pænθə(r)/ noun [C] a large wild cat (usually black)

panties /'pæntɪz/ noun [plural] (*informal*) a small piece of clothing that women and girls wear under their other clothes (from their waists to the top of their legs) ☛ Look at **pants** and **knickers**.

pantihose (*also* **pantyhose**) /'pæntɪhəʊz/ noun [plural] (*US*) = TIGHTS

pantomime /'pæntəmaɪm/ noun [C] a type of play for children that is usually performed just after Christmas. Pantomimes are based on traditional children's stories. They are funny and have singing and dancing in them.

pantry /'pæntrɪ/ noun [C] (*pl* **pantries**) a small room where food is kept ☛ Look at **larder**.

☆ **pants** /pænts/ noun [plural] **1** (*Brit*) = UNDERPANTS **2** (*US*) = TROUSERS

☆ **paper** /'peɪpə(r)/ noun **1** [U] a material that consists of thin sheets that you use for wrapping things in, writing or drawing on, etc: *a blank piece/sheet of paper* ○ *wallpaper* ○ *Scrap paper can be recycled.* ○ *a brown paper bag* ○ *a paper handkerchief* ☛ Types of paper include **filter, tissue, toilet** and **writing-paper**. **2** [C] = NEWSPAPER: *Where's today's paper?* ○ *a daily paper* ○ *a national/local paper* ☛ You buy a paper at a **paper shop** or **newsagent's**. **3 papers** [plural] pieces of paper that have information written on them. Papers are usually important: *If you don't have all your papers with you, you won't be allowed to cross the border.* ○ *The document you want is somewhere in the pile of papers on her desk.* **4** [C] an examination in which you have to write answers to a number of questions: *We have to take three papers in history.* **5** [C] a piece of writing on a particular subject that is written for or read to specialists
(IDIOM) **on paper 1** in writing: *I've had nothing on paper to say that I've been accepted.* **2** from what appearances show; in theory: *The scheme sounds fine on paper, but would it work in practice?*

'**paperback** noun [C,U] a book that has a paper cover: *The novel is available in paperback.* ○ *a cheap paperback*

'**paper-boy, 'paper-girl** noun [C] a boy or girl who delivers newspapers to people's houses

'**paper-clip** noun [C] a piece of wire or plastic that is used for holding pieces of paper together

'**paperwork** noun [U] the written work that you do in an office, including writing letters and reports, filling in forms, etc

par /pɑː(r)/ noun
(IDIOMS) **below par** (*informal*) not as good or as well as usual

on a par with sb/sth of an equal level, standard, etc to sb/sth else

parable /'pærəbl/ noun [C] a short story (especially in the Bible) that teaches a lesson

parachute /'pærəʃu:t/ noun [C] a piece of strong cloth that is folded and fastened with thin ropes to a person's body. A parachute lets the person fall to the ground slowly when they jump from an aeroplane: *a parachute jump* —**parachute** verb [I]

parade /pə'reɪd/ noun [C] an occasion when a group of people stand or walk in a procession so that people can look at them: *There used to be a military parade in Red Square on 1 May.* o *a fashion parade*

paradise /'pærədaɪs/ noun **1 Paradise** [sing] (without *a* or *the*) the place where some people think good people go after they die; heaven **2** [C] a perfect place: *This beach is a paradise for wind-surfers.*

paradox /'pærədɒks/ noun [C] **1** a statement that seems to be impossible but that is or may be true: *'A deafening silence' is a paradox.* **2** a situation that has two or more qualities that you would not expect to find together: *It's a paradox that some countries produce too much food while in other countries people are starving.* —**paradoxical** /,pærə'dɒksɪkl/ adj

paraffin /'pærəfɪn/ (*US* **kerosene**) noun [U] (*Brit*) a type of oil that is used in heaters, lamps, etc

☆ **paragraph** /'pærəgrɑ:f; *US* -græf/ noun [C] a part of a piece of writing that consists of one or more sentences. A paragraph always starts on a new line.

parallel /'pærəlel/ adj, adv **1** (used about two lines, etc) with the same distance between them for all their length: *parallel lines* o *The railway runs parallel to the road.* **2** similar: *The two brothers followed parallel careers in different companies.*

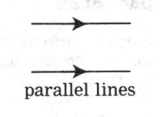

parallel noun **1** [C] (*also* **parallel 'line**) a line, etc that is parallel to another **2** [C,U] a person, thing or situation that is similar to sb/sth else: *Japan's economic success is without parallel in the post-war period.* **3** [C] an act of comparing sb/sth with sb/sth else: *He drew a parallel between Margaret Thatcher and Winston Churchill.*

paralyse (*US* **paralyze**) /'pærəlaɪz/ verb [T] **1** to make a person unable to move his/her body or a part of it: *Miriam is paralysed from the waist down.* **2** to make sb/sth unable to work in a normal way: *The railway system was completely paralysed by the strike.*

paralysis /pə'ræləsɪs/ noun [U] **1** the state of being unable to move your body or a part of it **2** being unable to work in the normal way: *There has been complete paralysis of the railway system.*

paramedic /,pærə'medɪk/ noun [C] a person who has had special training in caring for people who are ill or hurt, but who is not a doctor or nurse

paramilitary /,pærə'mɪlɪtri; *US* -teri/ adj organized in the same way as, but not belonging to, an official army

paramount /'pærəmaʊnt/ adj (*formal*) most important

paranoia /,pærə'nɔɪə/ noun [U] a type of mental illness in which sb wrongly believes that other people are trying to hurt him/her

paranoid /'pærənɔɪd/ adj wrongly believing that other people are trying to hurt you

paraphernalia /,pærəfə'neɪlɪə/ noun [U] a large number of different objects that you need for a particular purpose

paraphrase /'pærəfreɪz/ verb [T] to express sth again using different words so that it is easier to understand —**paraphrase** noun [C]

parasite /'pærəsaɪt/ noun [C] a plant or an animal that lives in or on another plant or animal and gets its food from it

paratroops /'pærətru:ps/ noun [plural] soldiers who are trained to drop from an aeroplane by parachute

☆ **parcel** /'pɑ:sl/ (*US also* **package**) noun [C] something that is wrapped in paper and sent by post, or carried: *to wrap/unwrap a parcel* ☛ A **parcel** (US **package**) is something that is wrapped up and sent by post, etc. A **package** is similar to a parcel but it is usually given by hand. A package may have an unusual shape. A **packet** (US **pack**) is one item or a number of things in a special box, bag, etc to be sold in a shop. A **pack** is a number of things that are not the same that are sold together: *The pack contains needles, a reel of white cotton and a pair of scissors.* **Packaging** is the material, box, bag, etc that something is put in before it is sold.

parcel verb (parcelling; parcelled; *US* parceling; parceled)
(PHRASAL VERB) **parcel sth up** to wrap sth up into a parcel

parch /pɑ:tʃ/ verb [T] (usually passive) to make sb/sth very hot, dry or thirsty: *Can I have a drink? I'm parched!*

☆ **pardon**¹ /'pɑ:dn/ noun [C,U] an act of forgiving sb. If a prisoner receives a pardon, he/she is released from prison. ☛ **I beg your pardon** is a formal way of saying 'sorry': *Oh, I do beg your pardon. I had no idea this was your seat.* It can also be used when you want to ask somebody to repeat what they have said because you did not understand.

pardon² /'pɑ:dn/ verb [T] **pardon sb (for sth/ for doing sth)** to forgive sb or to say that sb will not be punished

pardon (*also* **pardon 'me**) interj (used for asking sb to repeat what he/she has just said because you did not hear or understand it, and also for saying that you are sorry for sth that you have done)

pardonable /ˈpɑːdnəbl/ *adj* that can be forgiven or excused

☆ **parent** /ˈpeərənt/ *noun* [C] a mother or father: *Most parents try to bring up their children to be polite.*

☛ A **single parent** is a mother or father who is bringing up their child or children alone, without the other parent. A **foster parent** is a person who looks after a child who is not legally their own.

parental /pəˈrentl/ *adj* (only *before* a noun) of a parent or parents: *parental support*

parenthood /ˈpeərənthʊd/ *noun* [U] the state of being a parent: *the joys and sorrows of parenthood*

parentheses /pəˈrenθəsiːz/ *noun* [plural] (*especially US*) = BRACKETS (BRACKET 1)

parenthesis /pəˈrenθəsɪs/ *noun* (IDIOM) **in parenthesis** as an extra comment or piece of information

parish /ˈpærɪʃ/ *noun* [C] **1** an area or district which has its own church and priest: *the vicar of a country parish* ○ *the parish church* **2** a small area which has its own local government

parishioner /pəˈrɪʃənə(r)/ *noun* [C] a person who lives in a parish(1), especially one who goes to church there

ˌparish ˈcouncil *noun* [C, with sing or pl verb] a division of local government which looks after the interests of a very small area, especially a village ☛ Look at **local government** and **local authority**.

☆ **park¹** /pɑːk/ *noun* [C] **1** an open area with grass and trees, usually in a town, where anybody can go to walk, play, etc: *a walk in the park* ○ *the park gates* ○ *Hyde Park* **2** (*Brit*) the land that surrounds and belongs to a large country house **3** (in compounds) a large area of land that is open to the public and is used for special purposes: *Windsor Safari Park* ○ *a national park* ○ *a theme park* **4** (*US*) a sports ground or field

☆ **park²** /pɑːk/ *verb* [I,T] to stop and leave a car, lorry, etc somewhere for a time: *You can't park in the centre of town.* ○ *Somebody's parked their car in front of my garage.*

parka /ˈpɑːkə/ *noun* [C] a warm jacket or coat with a hood

parking /ˈpɑːkɪŋ/ *noun* [U] leaving a car, lorry, etc somewhere for a time; an area where you can do this: *The sign said 'No Parking'.* ○ *There is parking for employees behind the office buildings.* ○ *These parking spaces are reserved for residents.*

ˈparking-lot *noun* [C] (*US*) = CAR PARK

ˈparking-meter *noun* [C] a metal post that you put coins into to pay for parking a car in the space beside it

ˈparking-ticket *noun* [C] a piece of paper that orders you to pay money (**a fine**) for parking your car where it is not allowed

☆ **parliament** /ˈpɑːləmənt/ *noun* [C] **1** the group of people who discuss and make the laws of a country: *The German parliament is called the 'Bundestag'.* ☛ When **parliament** is singular it can be used with either a singular or plural verb. **2 Parliament** [sing] the group of people in the United Kingdom who discuss and make the laws: *the Houses of Parliament* (= the buildings where Parliament meets) ○ *a Member of Parliament (MP)*

☛ The UK Parliament consists of **The House of Commons** and **The House of Lords**. The House of Commons consists of Members of Parliament, who have been elected to represent areas of the country (called **constituencies**). The House of Lords consists of members of the nobility, bishops and other people who have been appointed, not elected.

parliamentary /ˌpɑːləˈmentrɪ/ *adj* (only *before* a noun) connected with parliament: *parliamentary debates*

parody /ˈpærədɪ/ *noun* (*pl* **parodies**) **1** [C,U] (a piece of) writing, speech or music that copies a writer's or musician's style: *His first novel, 'Snow White', is a parody of a traditional fairy story.* **2** [C] a very bad example or copy (of sth)

parody *verb* [T] (*pres part* **parodying**; *3rd pers sing pres* **parodies**; *pt, pp* **parodied**) to make a parody of sb/sth

parole /pəˈrəʊl/ *noun* [U] allowing a prisoner to go free before the end of his/her term in prison on condition that he/she continues to behave well: *She's hoping to get parole.* ○ *He's going to be released on parole.*

parrot /ˈpærət/ *noun* [C] a type of tropical bird with a curved beak and usually with very bright feathers. Parrots that are kept as pets often copy what people say.

ˈparrot-fashion *adv* without thinking about or understanding the meaning of sth: *to learn sth parrot-fashion*

parsley /ˈpɑːslɪ/ *noun* [U] a plant (**herb**) with small curly leaves that are used for flavouring or decorating food

parsnip /ˈpɑːsnɪp/ *noun* [C] a cream-coloured vegetable, shaped like a carrot, that grows under the ground

☆ **part¹** /pɑːt/ *noun* **1** [C] (often without *a/an*) **part (of sth)** one of the pieces, areas, periods, divisions, etc of sth; some, but not all: *Which part of Spain do you come from?* ○ *This part of the church has been rebuilt.* ○ *I enjoyed some parts of the film.* ○ *A large part of my job involves dealing with the public.* ○ *Part of the problem is lack of information.* ○ *a part of the body.* ○ *Getting up in the morning is always the hardest part of the day.* **2** [C] one of the essential pieces that make up a machine: *We always take a box of spare parts for the car with us when we go abroad.* **3** [C] an amount or quantity (of a liquid or substance): *Use one part of lemonade to three parts of beer.* **4** [C] a role or character in a play, film, etc: *He played the part of Macbeth.* ○ *a small part in the school play* **5** [C,U] **part (in sth)** a person's share in an activity, event, etc: *Did you have any part in the decision?*

(IDIOMS) **the best/better part of sth** most of sth; more than half of sth, often a period of

iː	ɪ	e	æ	ɑː	ɒ	ɔː	ʊ	uː	ʌ
see	sit	ten	hat	arm	got	saw	put	too	cup

time: *They've lived here for the best part of forty years.*
for the most part usually or mostly: *The countryside is, for the most part, flat and uninteresting.*
for my, your, etc part as far as it concerns me, you, etc: *I, for my part, am willing to go.*
in part not completely; to some extent: *The accident was, in part at least, the fault of the driver.*
on the part of sb/on sb's part made, done or felt by sb: *I'm sorry. It was a mistake on my part.* ○ *There is concern on the part of the teachers that class size will increase.*
play a part (in sth) to have a share in sth or to have an effect on sth
take part (in sth) to join with other people in an activity: *He was unable to take part in the race because of his recent accident.* ○ *Everybody took part in the discussion.*
part *adv* not completely one thing and not completely another: *A mule is part donkey and part horse.*
partly *adv* to some extent; not completely: *She was only partly responsible for the mistake.* ○ *I love Italy. Partly because of the weather, but mostly because of the people.*
,part-ex'change *noun* [U] a way of buying sth in which you give a used article as part of the payment for a more expensive one
,part of 'speech *noun* [C] (*grammar*) one of the groups that words are divided into, eg noun, verb, adjective, etc
,part-'time *adj, adv* for only a part of the working day or week: *She's got a part-time job.* ○ *I work part-time, about 20 hours a week.* ☛ Look at **full-time**.
part² /pɑːt/ *verb* **1** [I,T] **part (from sb); part sb (from sb)** to leave or go away from sb; to separate people or things: *We exchanged telephone numbers when we parted.* ○ *She parted from her husband several years ago.* ○ *He hates being parted from his children for long.* **2** [I,T] to divide or separate: *The curtains parted and a face looked out.* **3** [T] to separate the hair on the head with a comb so as to make a clear line: *Don't part your hair in the middle. It looks awful.* ☛ Look at **parting**.
(IDIOM) **part company (with sb/sth)** to go different ways or to separate after being together
(PHRASAL VERB) **part with sth** to give or sell sth to sb else: *When we went to live in Italy, we had to part with our horses and dogs.*
partial /ˈpɑːʃl/ *adj* **1** not complete: *The outing was only a partial success.* **2 partial to sb/sth** (*old-fashioned*) liking sth very much: *He's very partial to a glass of wine.*
partiality /ˌpɑːʃɪˈæləti/ *noun* [U] acting unfairly towards one person or side: *The referee was accused of partiality towards the home team.* ☛ Look at **impartial**.
partially /ˈpɑːʃəli/ *adv* partly; not completely: *The road was partially blocked by a fallen tree.*
participate /pɑːˈtɪsɪpeɪt/ *verb* [I] **participate (in sth)** to share or join (in an activity); to take part: *Students are encouraged to participate in sporting activities.*

participant /pɑːˈtɪsɪpənt/ *noun* [C] a person who takes part in an activity, etc —**participation** /pɑːˌtɪsɪˈpeɪʃn/ *noun* [U]
participle /ˈpɑːtɪsɪpl/ *noun* [C] (*grammar*) a word that is formed from a verb and that ends in *-ing* (*present participle*) or *-ed, -en*, etc (*past participle*). Participles are used to form tenses of the verb, or as adjectives: *'Hurrying' and 'hurried' are the present and past participles of 'hurry'.*
particle /ˈpɑːtɪkl/ *noun* [C] **1** a very small piece; a bit: *Particles of the substance were examined under a microscope.* **2** (*grammar*) a minor word that is not as important as a noun, verb or adjective: *In the phrasal verb 'break down', 'down' is an adverbial particle.*
☆ **particular** /pəˈtɪkjʊlə(r)/ *adj* **1** (only *before* a noun) (used to make it clear that you are talking about one person, thing, time, etc and not about others): *At that particular time I was working in London. It wasn't until later that I moved to Bristol.* ○ *One particular school, which I won't name, is having a lot of problems.* **2** (only *before* a noun) special or extra; more than usual: *Are you going to Dublin for any particular reason?* ○ *This article is of particular interest to you.* **3** connected with one person or thing and not with others: *Everybody has their own particular problems.* **4** (not before a noun) **particular (about/over sth)** difficult to please: *Some people are extremely particular about the wine they drink.* ☛ Look at **fussy**.
(IDIOM) **in particular 1** especially: *Is there anything in particular you'd like to do this weekend?* **2** (used for giving more detail about sth that you have said): *You must be careful about what you eat. In particular, avoid anything fatty.*
particularly *adv* especially: *I'm particularly interested in European history.* ○ *The meal was excellent, particularly the dessert.*
particulars *noun* [plural] (*formal*) details; facts: *The police took down all the particulars about the missing child.*
parting /ˈpɑːtɪŋ/ *noun* **1** [C,U] saying goodbye to, or being separated from, another person (usually for quite a long time): *the sadness of parting* **2** [C] the line on your head where you divide your hair and comb it in different directions: *a side parting* ☛ picture at **plait**.
partition /pɑːˈtɪʃn/ *noun* **1** [C] something that divides a room, etc into two parts, especially a thin or temporary wall in a house **2** [U] the division of a country into two or more countries: *the partition of Germany after the war* —**partition** *verb* [T]
☆ **partner** /ˈpɑːtnə(r)/ *noun* [C] **1** the person that you are married to or have a sexual relationship with **2** a person that you are dancing with or playing a game with **3** one of the people who own a business: *a partner in a private medical practice* ○ *business partners* ○ *a junior/senior partner* **4** a country or organization that has an agreement with another: *Britain's EC partners*
partner *verb* [T] to be sb's partner in a dance, game, etc: *Husbands were not allowed to partner their wives.*

partnership /-ʃɪp/ noun 1 [U] the state of being a partner or partners, especially in business: *Mary went into partnership with her sister and opened a toy shop in York.* 2 [C] an arrangement or business with two or more partners: *'Does your husband own the firm?' 'Well, it's a partnership.'* ○ *Their partnership has been extremely successful.*

☆ **party** /'pɑːti/ noun [C] (pl **parties**) 1 a social occasion to which people are invited in order to eat, drink and enjoy themselves: *to have a party* ○ *to go to a party* ○ *a birthday party* ○ *When they moved into the new house they had a house-warming party.* ○ *a garden party* ○ *a farewell party* ○ *a dinner party* 2 (also **Party**) a group of people who have the same political aims and ideas and who are trying to win elections to parliament, etc: *Which party are you going to vote for in the next election?* ○ *a member of the Labour Party* ○ *the Conservative Party conference* ○ *the party leader* ○ *party policy on defence* ○ *a left-wing/right-wing/centre party* ○ *the party in power* (= in government)

☞ The two main political parties in Great Britain are the **Conservative** (or **Tory**) Party (right-wing) and the **Labour** Party (left-wing). There is also a centre party called the **Liberal Democrats** and some other smaller parties. In the United States the main political parties are the **Republicans** and the **Democrats**.

3 (often in compounds) a group of people who are working, travelling, etc together: *A search party has set out to try and find the missing child.* ○ *a party of tourists* 4 (*formal*) a person or group of people forming one side of a legal agreement or argument: *the guilty party* ☞ Look at **third party**.

☆ **pass¹** /pɑːs; *US* pæs/ noun [C] 1 the act of kicking, hitting or throwing the ball to sb on your own team in various sports 2 a successful result in an examination: *Grades A, B and C are passes. D and E are fails.* 3 an official piece of paper that gives you permission to enter or leave a building, travel on a bus or train, etc: *Visitors to the research centre must obtain a pass from the reception desk.* ○ *to show a pass* ○ *a bus pass* 4 a road or way over or through mountains: *The pass was blocked by heavy falls of snow.*

☆ **pass²** /pɑːs; *US* pæs/ verb 1 [I,T] to move forward or to the other side of sb/sth; to leave sth behind or on one side as you go past: *The street was crowded and the two buses couldn't pass.* ○ *They passed a police checkpoint.* ○ *Do we pass a post-box on the way to the station?* ○ (*figurative*) *The number of children at the school has passed 500.* ☞ The past tense of **pass** is **passed**. It sounds like **past** which is an adjective and a preposition: *The summer months passed slowly.* ○ *The past week was very hot.* ○ *Our house is just past the church.* 2 [I] **pass along, down, etc (sth)** to go or move in the direction mentioned: *Which towns do we pass through on the way to Bath?* ○ *You pass over a bridge and then the pub is on the right.* 3 [T] **pass sth (to sb)** to pick sth up and give it to sb; to hand sth: *Could you pass (me) the salt, please?* ○ *He passed the bottle to his father.* 4 [T] **pass sth across, around, through, etc sth** to put or move sth in the direction mentioned: *We'll have to pass the wire through the window.* 5 [I,T] **pass (sth) (to sb)** to kick, hit or throw the ball to sb on your own team in various sports 6 [I] (used about time) to go by: *At least a year has passed since I last saw them.* ○ *The time passed very quickly.* 7 [T] to spend time: *I'll have to think of something to do to pass the time in hospital.* 8 [I,T] to achieve the necessary standard in an examination, test, etc: *Good luck in the exam! I'm sure you'll pass.* 9 [T] to test sb/sth and say that they are good enough: *The examiner passed most of the candidates.* 10 [T] to officially approve a law, proposal, etc: *One of the functions of Parliament is to pass new laws.* 11 [T] **pass sth (on sb/sth)** to give an opinion, judgement, etc: *The judge passed sentence on the young man* (= said what his punishment would be). 12 [I] to be allowed or accepted: *The headmaster won't let that sort of behaviour pass.* ○ *I didn't like what they were saying but I let it pass without comment.*

(IDIOMS) **pass the buck (to sb)** to give the responsibility or the blame for sth to sb else

pass water (*formal*) to urinate

(PHRASAL VERBS) **pass away** a way of saying 'die': *The old man passed away in his sleep.*

pass by (sb/sth) to go past: *I pass by your house on the way to work.*

pass sth down to give sth (to people who live after you have died): *The family home has been passed down from one generation to the next.*

pass sb/sth off (as sb/sth) to say that a person or a thing is sth that he/she/it is not: *He managed to pass the work off as his own.*

pass sth on (to sb) to give sth (to sb else) especially after you have been given it or used it yourself: *Could you pass the message on to Mr Roberts?*

pass out to become unconscious; to faint

passer-by /ˌpɑːsə'baɪ; *US* ˌpæsər-/ noun [C] (pl **passers-by** /ˌpɑːsəz'baɪ/) a person who is walking past sb/sth (by chance): *None of the passers-by had seen how the accident happened.*

passable /'pɑːsəbl; *US* 'pæs-/ adj 1 good enough but not very good: *My French is not brilliant but it's passable.* 2 (not before a noun) (used about roads, rivers, etc) possible to use or cross; not completely blocked ☞ The opposite is **impassable**.

☆ **passage** /'pæsɪdʒ/ noun 1 [C] (also **'passage-way**) a long, narrow way through sth, especially one in a building that leads to other rooms; a corridor: *We had to go down a dark passage to reach the bathroom.* 2 [C] a tube in your body which air, liquid, etc can pass through: *the nasal passages* 3 [C] a short part of a book, a speech or a piece of music: *The students were given a passage from the novel to study in detail.* 4 [U] the movement or progress of sb/sth from one place or stage to another: *We watched the ants' slow passage across the road.* 5 [C] a route by sea or a journey by ship: *You are advised to book your passage well in advance.* 6 [U] (used about time) the passing:

p	b	t	d	k	g	tʃ	dʒ	f	v	θ	ð
pen	bad	tea	did	cat	got	chin	June	fall	van	thin	then

With the passage of time these rocks will be broken into stones.

☆ **passenger** /ˈpæsɪndʒə(r)/ *noun* [C] a person who is travelling in a car, bus, train, plane, etc but who is not driving it or working on it: *Passengers are asked to remain seated until the plane has come to a complete standstill.* o *the passenger seat of a car*

passing /ˈpɑːsɪŋ; *US* ˈpæs-/ *adj* lasting for only a short time; brief: *No, I wasn't serious about going to Italy. It was only a passing thought.*

passing *noun* [U] the process of going by: *the passing of time*

(IDIOM) **in passing** done or said quickly, while you are thinking or talking about sth else: *He mentioned the house in passing but he didn't give any details.*

passion /ˈpæʃn/ *noun* **1** [U] very strong sexual love or attraction: *They loved each other but there was no passion in their relationship.* **2** [C,U] (a) very strong feeling, especially of love, hate or anger: *He was a violent man, controlled by his passions.* o *She argued her case with passion.* **3** [sing] **a passion for sth** a very strong liking for or interest in sth: *He has a passion for chocolate.*

passionate /ˈpæʃənət/ *adj* showing or caused by very strong, sometimes sexual feelings: *a passionate believer in democracy* o *a passionate speech* o *a passionate relationship* o *a passionate kiss* —**passionately** *adv*

passive /ˈpæsɪv/ *adj* **1** showing no reaction, feeling or interest; not active: *Television encourages people to be passive.* o *passive smoking* (= breathing in smoke from other people's cigarettes) **2** (used about the form of a verb or a sentence when the subject of the sentence is affected by the action of the verb): *In the sentence 'He was bitten by a dog', the verb is passive.* ☛ You can also say: 'The verb is in the passive'. Look at **active**. —**passively** *adv*

☆ **passport** /ˈpɑːspɔːt; *US* ˈpæs-/ *noun* [C] **1** an official document that identifies you and that you have to show when you enter or leave a country: *Do you have to show your passport at the check-in desk?*

☛ You **apply for** or **renew** your passport at the **passport office**. This office **issues** new passports.

2 a passport to sth a thing that makes it possible to achieve sth: *a passport to success*

password /ˈpɑːswɜːd; *US* ˈpæs-/ *noun* [C] **1** a secret word or phrase that you need to know in order to be allowed into a place **2** a secret word that you must type in order to use a computer system: *Please enter your password.*

☆ **past¹** /pɑːst; *US* pæst/ *adj* **1** already gone; belonging to a time before the present: *in past years, centuries, etc* o *I'd rather forget some of my past mistakes.* **2** (only *before* a noun) just finished; last: *He's had to work very hard during the past year.* o *The past few weeks have been very difficult.* **3** (not *before* a noun) over; finished; no longer existing: *Suddenly his childhood was past and he was a young man.*

past *noun* **1 the past** [sing] the time before the present; the things that happened in that time: *The story was set in the distant past.* o *We spent the evening talking about the past.* **2** [C] a person's life before now: *May I ask you a few questions about your past?* o *I think his past has been rather unhappy.* **3** [sing] (also **past tense**) a form of a verb used to describe actions in the past: *The past tense of the verb 'come' is 'came'.*

‚past ˈperfect (*also* **pluperfect**) *noun* [sing] (*grammar*) the tense of a verb that describes an action that was finished before another event happened: *In the sentence 'After they had finished the meal, they went for a walk', 'had finished' is in the past perfect.*

☆ **past²** /pɑːst; *US* pæst/ *prep* **1** (used when telling the time) after; later than: *It's ten (minutes) past three.* o *It's a quarter past seven.* **2** older than: *She's past 40.* **3** from one side to the other of sb/sth; further than or on the other side of sb/sth: *He walked straight past me.* o *Go past the pub and our house is the second on the right.* o *The phone-box is just past the village shop.* **4** beyond the limits or age when you can do sth: *I'm so tired that I'm past caring what we eat.* o *She was past the age when she could have children.*

(IDIOMS) **not put it past sb (to do sth)** ⇨ PUT

past it (*informal*) too old: *I don't think I'll go skiing this year. I'm afraid I'm past it.*

past *adv* by; from one side of sb/sth to another: *The bus went straight past without stopping.* o *He waved as he drove past.*

pasta /ˈpæstə; *US* ˈpɑːstə/ *noun* [U] a type of food made from a mixture of flour, eggs and water which is cut into various shapes and cooked: *Macaroni is a type of pasta.*

paste¹ /peɪst/ *noun* **1** [C,U] a soft, wet mixture, usually made of a powder and a liquid and sometimes used for sticking things: *wallpaper paste* o *Mix the flour and milk into a paste.* **2** [U] (usually in compounds) a soft mixture of food that you can spread onto bread, etc: *fish paste* o *chicken paste*

paste² /peɪst/ *verb* [T] to stick sth to sth else using glue or paste: *He pasted the picture into his book.*

pastel /ˈpæstl; *US* pæˈstel/ *adj* (used about colours) pale; not strong

pasteurized (*also* **pasteurised**) /ˈpɑːstʃəraɪzd; *US* ˈpæs-/ *adj* (used about milk or cream) free from bacteria because it has been heated

pastime /ˈpɑːstaɪm; *US* ˈpæs-/ *noun* [C] something that you enjoy doing when you are not working: *What are your favourite pastimes?* ☛ Look at **hobby**.

pastoral /ˈpɑːstərəl; *US* ˈpæs-/ *adj* **1** giving advice on personal rather than religious or educational matters: *Each child will have a tutor who is responsible for pastoral care.* **2** connected with the countryside and country life

pastry /ˈpeɪstri/ *noun* (*pl* **pastries**) **1** [U] a mixture of flour, fat and water that is used for making pies, etc and is baked in an oven **2** [C] a small cake made with pastry: *Danish pastries*

pasture /ˈpɑːstʃə(r); *US* ˈpæs-/ *noun* [C,U] a

s	z	ʃ	ʒ	h	m	n	ŋ	l	r	j	w
so	zoo	she	vision	how	man	no	sing	leg	red	yes	wet

field or land covered with grass, where cattle can feed

pasty /'pæstɪ/ noun [C] (pl **pasties**) a small pie containing meat and/or vegetables: *Cornish pasties*

pat¹ /pæt/ verb [T] (**patting; patted**) to hit sb/sth very gently with a flat hand or with sth flat: *'Good dog,' she said, patting him.*

pat noun [C] a gentle tap with a flat hand or with sth flat: *'Well done,' said the teacher, giving the child a pat on the head.*
(IDIOM) **a pat on the back** congratulations for sth good that a person has done

pat² /pæt/ adv at once; without hesitation: *The answer came back pat.*

pat adj (only *before* a noun) too quick (used about an answer, comment, etc)

patch¹ /pætʃ/ noun [C] **1** a piece of material that you use to mend a hole in clothes, etc: *an old pair of jeans with patches on both knees* ○ *to sew a patch on* **2** a small piece of material that you wear over one eye: *an eye patch* **3 a patch (of sth)** a part of a surface that is different in some way from the area around it: *Drive carefully. There are patches of ice on the roads.* ○ *a damp patch on the ceiling* **4** a small piece of land: *a vegetable patch*
(IDIOMS) **a bad patch** a difficult or unhappy period of time
not a patch on sb/sth (informal) not nearly as good as sb/sth: *The new singer isn't a patch on the old one.*

patch² /pætʃ/ verb [T] to put a piece of material over a hole in clothes, etc or to mend sth by doing this: *to patch a hole in sth* ○ *to patch an old pair of trousers*
(PHRASAL VERB) **patch sth up 1** to mend sth quickly or not very carefully: *The car had been patched up after an accident.* **2** to settle a quarrel: *It's time the boys patched up their differences and made friends.*

patchwork /'pætʃwɜːk/ noun **1** [U] a type of sewing in which small pieces of cloth of different colours and patterns are sewn together **2** [sing] a thing that is made of many different pieces or parts: *a patchwork of fields*

patchy /'pætʃɪ/ adj (**patchier; patchiest**) **1** not all the same or not complete: *His work is patchy* (= some, but not all, of it is good). ○ *I've only got some rather patchy* (= not complete) *information on the subject.* **2** in small quantities, not everywhere: *patchy fog*

pâté /'pæteɪ; *US* pɑː'teɪ/ noun [U] food that is made by mixing up meat, fish or vegetables into a smooth, thick form that you can spread on bread, etc: *liver pâté*

patent¹ /'peɪtnt; *US* 'pætnt/ adj (formal) clear; obvious: *a patent lie*
patently adv clearly: *She was patently very upset.* ○ *He was patently honest.*

patent² /'pætnt; 'peɪtnt; *US* 'pætnt/ noun [C] an official licence from the government that gives one person or company the right to make or sell a certain product and prevents others from copying it: *a patent on a new invention*
patent verb [T] to obtain a patent² for sth

patent leather /'peɪtnt 'leðə(r); *US* 'pætnt/ noun [U] a type of leather with a hard, shiny surface

paternal /pə'tɜːnl/ adj (only *before* a noun) **1** of a father: *the importance of paternal interest and support* **2** related through the father's side of the family: *my paternal grandparents* ☞ Look at **maternal**.

paternity /pə'tɜːnətɪ/ noun [U] the state of being a father

☆ **path** /pɑːθ; *US* pæθ/ noun [C] (pl **paths** /pɑːðz; *US* pæðz/) **1** a way across a piece of land that is made by or used by people walking: *The path follows the coastline for several hundred miles.* ○ *the garden path* ○ *Keep to the path or you may get lost.* ○ *Where does this path lead?* ○ (figurative) *We're on the path to victory!* ☞ **Pathway** is similar in meaning: *There was a narrow pathway leading down the cliff.* Look at **footpath**. **2** the line along which sb/sth moves: *the flight path of an aeroplane* ○ *The locusts moved across the country eating everything in their path.*

pathetic /pə'θetɪk/ adj **1** causing you to feel pity or sadness: *the pathetic cries of the hungry children* **2** (informal) very bad, weak or useless: *What a pathetic performance! The team deserved to lose.* —**pathetically** /-klɪ/ adv

pathological /ˌpæθə'lɒdʒɪkl/ adj **1** connected with pathology **2** (informal) caused by feelings that you cannot control; not reasonable: *He's a pathological liar.* ○ *a pathological fear of water* —**pathologically** /-klɪ/ adv

pathology /pə'θɒlədʒɪ/ noun [U] the scientific study of the diseases of the body

pathologist /pə'θɒlədʒɪst/ noun [C] a person who is an expert in pathology, especially one who tries to find out why a person has died

☆ **patience** /'peɪʃns/ noun [U] **1 patience (with sb/sth)** the quality of being able to remain calm and not get angry, especially when there is a difficulty or you have to wait a long time: *I'm sorry – I've got no patience with people who don't even try.* ○ *to lose patience with sb* ○ *After three hours of delay our patience was wearing thin.* ☞ The opposite is **impatience**. **2** (*US* **solitaire**) a card-game for one player

☆ **patient¹** /'peɪʃnt/ adj able to remain calm and not get angry, especially when there is a difficulty or you are waiting for sth: *It's hard to be patient with a screaming child.* ○ *It won't be long now. Just sit there and be patient.* ☞ The opposite is **impatient**. —**patiently** adv: *to wait patiently*

☆ **patient²** /'peɪʃnt/ noun [C] a person who is receiving medical treatment: *a hospital patient* ○ *a specialist who treats patients with heart problems* ○ *a private patient* (= one who pays for his/her treatment)

patio /'pætɪəʊ/ noun [C] (pl **patios** /-əʊz/) an area next to a house where people can sit, eat, etc outdoors ☞ Look at **verandah** and **terrace**.

patriot /'pætrɪət; *US* 'peɪt-/ noun [C] a person who loves his/her country

patriotism /-ɪzəm/ noun [U] love of your country

patriotic /ˌpætrɪ'ɒtɪk; *US* ˌpeɪt-/ adj having or showing a love for your country —**patriotically** /-klɪ/ adv

patrol /pəˈtrəʊl/ verb [I,T] (patrolling; patrolled) to go round a town, building, etc to make sure that there is no trouble and that nothing is wrong: *Guards patrol the grounds at regular intervals.*

patrol noun [C] **1** the act of patrolling: *The army makes hourly patrols of the area.* **2** a person or group of people that patrols sth: *a police patrol*

(IDIOM) **on patrol** patrolling sth

patron /ˈpeɪtrən/ noun [C] **1** a person who gives money to artists, musicians, etc or who supports a good cause: *a patron of the arts* ○ *The princess is a patron of the 'Save the Children' fund.* **2** a person who goes to a shop, theatre, restaurant, etc: *This car-park is for patrons only.*

ˌpatron ˈsaint noun [C] a saint who is believed to give help and protection to a particular place or to people doing a particular activity: *St David is the patron saint of Wales.*

patronize (*also* **patronise**) /ˈpætrənaɪz; US ˈpeɪt-/ verb [T] **1** to treat sb in a friendly way but as if you were better than him/her **2** to go to a shop, theatre, restaurant, etc

patronizing (*also* **patronising**) adj treating sb in a friendly way but as if you were better than him/her: *I really hate that patronizing smile of hers.* —**patronizingly** (*also* **patronisingly**) adv

patter /ˈpætə(r)/ noun [sing] the sound of many quick light steps or knocks on sth: *the patter of the children's feet on the stairs* —**patter** verb [I] *The rain pattered on the windowpane.*

patterns

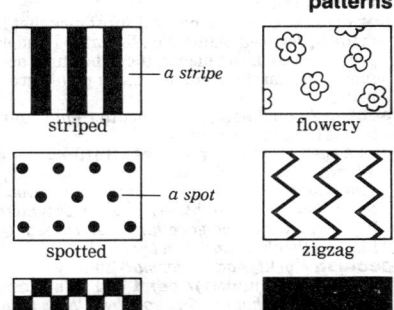

- striped — *a stripe*
- flowery
- spotted — *a spot*
- zigzag
- checked
- plain

☆**pattern** /ˈpætn/ noun [C] **1** an arrangement of lines, shapes, colours, etc. Patterns are often used to decorate clothes, wallpapers, carpets, etc: *Our new china has a flower pattern on it.* ○ *a geometric pattern* **2** the way in which sth happens, develops, is arranged, etc: *Her periods of mental illness all followed the same pattern.* ○ *patterns of behaviour* ○ *The second half of the match followed a similar pattern to the first.* **3** something that helps you to make sth, eg a piece of clothing, by showing the shape it should be: *a paper pattern*

patterned adj having a pattern(1): *patterned curtains*

☆**pause** /pɔːz/ noun [C] a short stop in sth: *He continued playing for twenty minutes without a pause.* ○ *a pause in the conversation* ☛ Look at the note at **interval**.

pause verb [I] **pause (for sth)** to stop for a short time: *to pause for breath*

pave /peɪv/ verb [T] (often passive) to cover an area of ground with flat stones

ˈpaving stone noun [C] a flat piece of stone that is used for covering the ground

pavement /ˈpeɪvmənt/ noun [C] (*US* **sidewalk**) the path at the side of the road that is for people to walk on: *Children should ride on the pavement, not on the road.*

pavilion /pəˈvɪliən/ noun [C] (*Brit*) a building at a sports ground where players can change their clothes

☆**paw** /pɔː/ noun [C] the foot of animals such as dogs, cats, bears, etc ☛ Look at **hoof**. picture at **cat**. Paws have sharp **claws** and soft **pads** underneath.

paw verb [I,T] **paw (at) sth** (used about an animal) to touch sb/sth with a paw or foot

pawn¹ /pɔːn/ noun [C] **1** one of the eight pieces in the game of chess that are of least value and importance ☛ picture at **chess**. **2** a person who is used or controlled by another person

pawn² /pɔːn/ verb [T] to give sth of value to a pawnbroker in return for money. If you cannot pay back the money after a certain period, the pawnbroker can keep or sell the thing that you gave him/her.

ˈpawnbroker noun [C] a person who lends money to people when they leave sth of value with him/her

☆**pay¹** /peɪ/ noun [U] money that you get regularly for work that you have done: *It's a dirty job but the pay is good.* ○ *a pay increase* ☛ **Pay** is the general word for money that you get regularly for work that you have done. **Wages** are paid weekly or daily in cash. A **salary** is paid monthly, directly into a bank account. You pay a **fee** for professional services, eg to a doctor, lawyer, etc. **Payment** is money for work that you do once or not regularly.

☆**pay²** /peɪ/ verb (*pt, pp* **paid**) **1** [I,T] **pay (sb) (for sth); pay sth (to sb) (for sth)** to give sb money for sth: *She is very well paid.* ○ *Do you want to pay by cheque or by credit card?* ○ *The work's finished but we haven't paid the builders yet.* ○ *to be paid by the hour* ○ *We paid the dealer £3 000 for the car.* **2** [T] **pay sth (to sb)** to give the money that you owe for sth: *Have you paid the gas bill?* **3** [I,T] to make a profit; to be worth doing: *The factory closed down because the owners couldn't make it pay.* ○ *It would pay you to get professional advice before making a decision.* **4** [I,T] **pay (for sth)** to suffer because of sth

(IDIOMS) **pay attention (to sb/sth)** to listen carefully to or to take notice of sb/sth

pay sb a compliment; pay a compliment to sb to say that you like sth about sb; to praise sb

ɜː	ə	eɪ	əʊ	aɪ	aʊ	ɔɪ	ɪə	eə	ʊə
fur	ago	pay	home	five	now	join	near	hair	pure

pay your respects (to sb) (*formal*) to visit sb as a sign of respect
pay tribute to sb/sth to praise and show your respect for sb/sth
put paid to sth to destroy or finish sth: *The bad weather put paid to our idea of a picnic.*
(PHRASAL VERBS) **pay sb back sth; pay sth back** to give money back to sb that you borrowed from him/her: *Can you lend me £5? I'll pay you back/I'll pay it back to you on Friday.*
pay sb back (for sth) to do sth unpleasant to sb who did sth unpleasant to you: *What a mean trick! I'll pay you back one day.*
pay off (*informal*) to be successful: *All their hard work has paid off! The house is finished at last.*
pay sth off to pay all the money that you owe for sth: *to pay off a debt*
pay up (*informal*) to pay the money that you owe: *If you don't pay up, we'll take you to court.*
payable /ˈpeɪəbl/ *adj* that should or must be paid: *This bill is payable immediately.* ○ *Make the cheque payable to Diane Weller.*
payee /peɪˈiː/ *noun* [C] a person that you must pay money to
paid-up *adj* having paid all the money that you owe, eg to become a member of sth: *He's a fully paid-up member of Friends of the Earth.*
☆ **payment** /ˈpeɪmənt/ *noun* **payment (for sth)** **1** [U] paying or being paid: *You get a 5% discount for prompt payment.* ○ *payment of a bill* ○ *I did the work last month but I haven't had any payment yet.* ☞ Look at the note at **pay¹**. **2** [C] an amount of money that you must pay: *They asked for a payment of £100 as a deposit.*
pea /piː/ *noun* [C] a small round green seed that is eaten as a vegetable. A number of peas grow together in a pod.
☆ **peace** /piːs/ *noun* [U] **1** the state of not being at war or of not having fighting, disorder, etc: *forty years of peace in Europe* ○ *a peace treaty* ○ *Peace has returned to the streets of Los Angeles.* **2** the state of being calm or quiet: *He longed to escape from the city to the peace of the countryside.* ○ *I'm tired – can't you just leave me in peace?* ○ *The noise of lawn-mowers disturbed the peace of the afternoon.*
peacetime *noun* [U] a period when a country is not at war
☆ **peaceful** /ˈpiːsfl/ *adj* **1** not wanting or involving war, fighting or disorder: *a peaceful demonstration* ○ *Nuclear power can be used for peaceful or military purposes.* ○ *a peaceful solution to the conflict* **2** calm and quiet: *a peaceful village near Oxford* —**peacefully** /-fəli/ *adv* —**peacefulness** *noun* [U]
peach /piːtʃ/ *noun* [C] a soft round fruit with orange-red skin. A peach is soft inside and has a large stone in its centre: *tinned peaches*
peacock /ˈpiːkɒk/ *noun* [C] a large bird with beautiful long blue and green tail feathers that it can lift up and spread out like a fan
peak¹ /piːk/ *noun* [C] **1** the pointed top of a mountain: *snow-covered peaks in the distance* **2** the pointed front part of a hat that is above your eyes **3** the highest level, value, rate, etc: *In the early evening demand for electricity is at*

peacock

its peak. ○ *a man at the peak of his career* ○ *Summer is the peak period for most hotels.* ☞ Look at **off-peak**.
peak² /piːk/ *verb* [I] to reach the highest level, value, rate, etc: *Sales usually peak just before Christmas.*
peal /piːl/ *noun* [C] the loud ringing of a bell or of a set of bells that all have different notes: (*figurative*) *peals of laughter*
peanut /ˈpiːnʌt/ (*also* **ground-nut**) *noun* [C] a nut that grows in a shell under the ground: *roasted and salted peanuts* ☞ picture at **nut**.
pear /peə(r)/ *noun* [C] a fruit that has a yellow or green skin and is white inside. Pears are thinner at the top (ie where they join onto the tree) than at the bottom.
☆ **pearl** /pɜːl/ *noun* [C] a small, hard, round, white object that grows inside the shell of an oyster (a type of shellfish). Pearls are used to make jewellery: *a pearl necklace*
peasant /ˈpeznt/ *noun* [C] a person who owns or rents a small piece of land on which he/she grows food and keeps animals in order to feed his/her family
peat /piːt/ *noun* [U] a natural substance that is made of decayed plants. Peat is formed underground in cool, wet places. It can be burnt as a fuel or put on the garden to make plants grow better.
pebble /ˈpebl/ *noun* [C] a smooth round stone that is found in or near water
peck /pek/ *verb* [I,T] **peck (at sth)** (used about a bird) to eat or bite sth with the beak: *The sparrows were pecking around for food.* ○ *Don't touch the bird – it might peck you.* —**peck** *noun* [C]: (*figurative*) *She gave him a quick peck* (= kiss) *on the cheek and then left.*
peckish /ˈpekɪʃ/ *adj* (*informal*) hungry
peculiar /pɪˈkjuːliə(r)/ *adj* **1** odd or strange: *'Moira left without saying goodbye.' 'How peculiar!'* ○ *There's a very peculiar smell in here.* **2** only belonging to a particular person or found in a particular place: *a fruit peculiar to South East Asia*
peculiarity /pɪˌkjuːliˈærəti/ *noun* (*pl* **peculiarities**) **1** [U] the quality of being strange or odd **2** [C] something that is strange or odd: *One of his peculiarities is that he never wears socks.* **3** [C] sth that only belongs to or is only found in sb/sth
peculiarly *adv* **1** in a peculiar(1) way: *Luke is behaving very peculiarly.* **2** especially; very: *The noise of chalk on a blackboard can be peculiarly annoying.* **3** in a way that is especially typical of sb/sth: *They demonstrated the pecu-*

| p | b | t | d | k | g | tʃ | dʒ | f | v | θ | ð |
| pen | bad | tea | did | cat | got | chin | June | fall | van | thin | then |

pedagogical 457 **penalize**

liarly English refusal to take anything seriously.

pedagogical /ˌpedəˈgɒdʒɪkl/ *adj* connected with ways and methods of teaching

pedal /ˈpedl/ *noun* [C] the part of a bicycle or other machine that you push with your foot in order to make it move or work ☛ picture at **bicycle**.
▶ **pedal** *verb* [I,T] (pedalling; pedalled; *US* pedaling; pedaled) to push the pedals of a bicycle: *She had to pedal hard to get up the hill.*

pedantic /prˈdæntɪk/ *adj* too worried about rules or details —**pedantically** /-klɪ/ *adv*

pedestal /ˈpedɪstl/ *noun* [C] the base on which a column, statue, etc stands

pedestrian /prˈdestriən/ *noun* [C] a person who is walking in the street (not travelling in a vehicle): *a subway for pedestrians to cross the busy junction* ☛ Look at **motorist**.
▶ **pedestrian** *adj* **1** of or for pedestrians: *a pedestrian bridge* **2** ordinary; not interesting; dull

peˌdestrian ˈcrossing (*US* **crosswalk**) *noun* [C] a place for pedestrians to cross the road ☛ Look at **zebra crossing**.

peˌdestrian ˈprecinct *noun* [C] a part of a town where there are many shops and where cars are not allowed

pediatrician (*US*) = PAEDIATRICIAN

pedigree /ˈpedɪgriː/ *noun* [C] **1** the parents, grandparents and other previous family members of an animal. The names of the ancestors are recorded on a document which is also called a 'pedigree'. **2** a person's background
▶ **pedigree** *adj* of high quality because the parents, grandparents, etc are all of the same breed and specially chosen

pee /piː/ *verb* [I] (*informal*) to send out waste water from your body; urinate —**pee** *noun* [sing] (*informal*): *I'm going to have a pee.*

peek /piːk/ *verb* [I] (*informal*) **peek (at sth)** to look at sth quickly or secretly: *No peeking at the presents before Christmas Day.* —**peek** *noun* [sing]: *to have a quick peek at the answers*

peel /piːl/ *verb* **1** [T] to take the skin off a fruit or vegetable: *Could you peel the potatoes, please?* **2** [I] to come off in one piece or in small pieces: *Soak the envelope in water and the stamp will peel off easily.* ○ *My nose got sunburnt and now it is peeling* (= the skin is coming off). ○ *The paint is starting to peel off.*
▶ **peel** *noun* [U] the skin of a fruit or vegetable: *lemon peel* ☛ Look at **rind**.

peep¹ /piːp/ *verb* [I] **1 peep (at sth)** to look at sth quickly and secretly: *to peep through a keyhole* **2** (used about part of sth) to appear: *The moon is peeping out from behind the clouds.*
▶ **peep** *noun* [sing] a quick or secret look: *Have a peep in the bedroom and see if the baby is asleep.*

peep² /piːp/ *noun* **1** [sing] the weak high sound that is made, for example, by a young bird: *There hasn't been a peep out of the children for hours.* **2** [C] **peep ˈpeep** the sound that a car's horn makes —**peep** *verb* [I]

peer¹ /pɪə(r)/ *noun* [C] **1** a person who is of the same age or rank: *Peer pressure is a great influence on the way people behave.* **2** (*Brit*) (*feminine* **peeress**) a person of noble rank
▶ **peerage** /ˈpɪərɪdʒ/ *noun* **1** [with sing or pl verb] all the peers(2) in a country **2** [C] the rank of a peer: *an hereditary peerage*

ˈpeer group *noun* [C] a group of people who are of the same age and rank

peer² /pɪə(r)/ *verb* [I] **peer (at sb/sth)** to look closely or carefully at sb/sth, eg because you cannot see very well: *I peered outside but it was too dark to see much.* ○ *I had to peer very hard at the handwriting to make out what it said.*

peeved /piːvd/ *adj* (*informal*) rather angry; annoyed

peevish /ˈpiːvɪʃ/ *adj* easily annoyed by things that are not important —**peevishly** *adv*

peg¹ /peg/ *noun* [C] **1** a piece of wood, metal, etc on a wall or door that you hang your coat, etc on: *Your coat is hanging on the peg in the hall.* **2** (*also* **tent-peg**) a piece of metal that you hammer into the ground to keep one of the ropes of a tent in place **3** (*also* **clothes-peg**) (*US* **clothes-pin**) a type of small wooden or plastic object used for fastening clothes to a clothes line

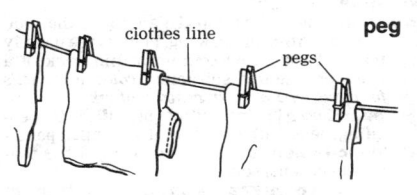

clothes line   peg
pegs

peg² /peg/ *verb* [T] (**pegg**ing; **pegg**ed) **1** to fix sth with a peg: *He pegged the washing out on the line.* **2** to fix or keep sth at a certain level: *Wage increases were pegged at 7%.*

pelican /ˈpelɪkən/ *noun* [C] a large water-bird that lives in warm countries. A pelican has a large beak that it uses for catching and holding fish.

pellet /ˈpelɪt/ *noun* [C] a small hard ball that is made from paper, mud, metal, etc: *shotgun pellets*

pelt /pelt/ *verb* **1** [T] to attack sb/sth by throwing things: *The speaker was pelted with tomatoes.* **2** [I] **pelt (down)** (used about rain) to fall very heavily **3** [I] to run very fast

pelvis /ˈpelvɪs/ *noun* [C] (*pl* **pelvises**) the set of wide bones at the bottom of your back, to which your leg bones are joined —**pelvic** /ˈpelvɪk/ *adj*

☆ **pen¹** /pen/ *noun* [C] an instrument that you use for writing in ink: *a fountain pen* ○ *a ball-point pen* ○ *a felt-tip pen*

ˈpen-friend (*especially US* **pen-pal**) *noun* [C] a person that you become friendly with by exchanging letters

pen² /pen/ *noun* [C] a small piece of ground with a fence around it that is used for keeping animals in

penal /ˈpiːnl/ *adj* (only *before* a noun) connected with punishment by law

penalize (*also* **penalise**) /ˈpiːnəlaɪz/ *verb* [T] **1** to punish sb for breaking a law or rule: *Players must be penalized if they behave badly.* ○ *Motorists who drink and drive should be heavily penalized.* **2** to cause sb to suffer a dis-

s	z	ʃ	ʒ	h	m	n	ŋ	l	r	j	w
so	zoo	she	vision	how	man	no	sing	leg	red	yes	wet

advantage: *Children should not be penalized because their parents cannot afford to pay.*

penalty /'penltɪ/ *noun* [C] (*pl* **penalties**) **1** a punishment for breaking a law or rule: *We need stiffer penalties for people who drop litter.* o *the death penalty* o *No parking. Penalty £25.* **2** a disadvantage or sth unpleasant that happens as the result of sth: *I didn't work hard enough and I paid the penalty. I failed all my exams.* **3** (in sport) a punishment for one team and an advantage for the other team because a rule has been broken: *The goalkeeper was fouled and the referee awarded a penalty.* ☛ In football, a penalty is a free shot at goal: *If the match ends in a draw, the result will be decided by a penalty shoot-out.*

'penalty area *noun* [C] the marked area in front of the goal in football ☛ picture at football.

penance /'penəns/ *noun* [C,U] a punishment that you give yourself to show you are sorry for doing sth wrong

☆ **pence** *pl* of PENNY

☆ **pencil** /'pensl/ *noun* [C,U] an object that you use for writing or drawing. Pencils are usually made of wood and contain a thin stick of a black or coloured substance: *coloured pencils for children* o *Write in pencil, not ink.*

pencil *verb* [T] (**pencilling**; **pencilled**; *US* **penciling**; **penciled**) to write or draw with a pencil

'pencil-case *noun* [C] a small bag or box that you keep pens, pencils, etc in

'pencil-sharpener *noun* [C] an instrument that you use for making pencils sharp

pendant /'pendənt/ *noun* [C] an ornament that you wear on a chain around your neck

pending /'pendɪŋ/ *adj* (*formal*) waiting to be done or decided: *The judge's decision is still pending.*

pending *prep* (*formal*) until: *He took over the leadership pending the elections.*

pendulum /'pendjʊləm; *US* -dʒʊləm/ *noun* [C] a string or stick with a heavy weight at the bottom. Some large clocks are worked by a swinging pendulum.

penetrate /'penɪtreɪt/ *verb* [I,T] **1** to make or force a way into or through sth: *The nail hadn't penetrated the skin.* o *The car's headlamps could not penetrate the thick fog.* o (*figurative*) *We've penetrated the Spanish market.* **2** to be understood: *I've tried to explain what is going to happen, but I'm not sure if it's penetrated.*

penetrating *adj* **1** showing the ability to think and understand quickly and well: *a penetrating question* **2** (used about a voice or sound) loud and carrying for a long way: *a penetrating scream*

penetration /,penɪ'treɪʃn/ *noun* [U] **1** the act of penetrating **2** the ability to think and understand quickly and well

penguin /'peŋgwɪn/ *noun* [C] a quite large black and white sea-bird that lives in the Antarctic. Penguins cannot fly.

penicillin /,penɪ'sɪlɪn/ *noun* [U] a substance that is used as a medicine for preventing and treating diseases caused by bacteria. Penicillin is a type of antibiotic.

peninsula /pə'nɪnsjʊlə; *US* -nsələ/ *noun* [C] an

penguin

area of land that is almost surrounded by water: *the Iberian peninsula* (= Spain and Portugal)

penis /'piːnɪs/ *noun* [C] the male sex organ that is used for passing waste water and having sex

penitent /'penɪtənt/ *adj* (*formal*) sorry for having done sth wrong

penitentiary /,penɪ'tenʃərɪ/ *noun* [C] (*pl* **penitentiaries**) (*US*) a prison

penknife /'pennaɪf/ *noun* [C] (*pl* **penknives**) (*also* **pocket knife**) a small knife with one or more blades that fold down into the handle

penknife

blade

penniless /'penɪlɪs/ *adj* having no money; poor

☆ **penny** /'penɪ/ *noun* [C] (*pl* **pence** /pens/, **pennies**) **1** (*abbr* **p**) a small brown British coin. There are a hundred pence in a pound: *Petrol costs 53p a litre.* o *a fifty pence coin* ☛ You use the plural form **pennies** when you are talking about penny coins: *She put five pennies in the slot.* You use **pence** or **p** when you are talking about an amount of money. **P** is more informal than pence. **2** (*US informal*) a cent

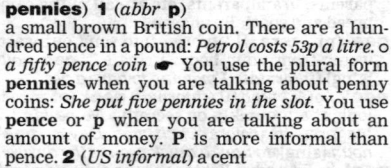

☆ **pension** /'penʃn/ *noun* [C] money that is paid regularly to sb who has stopped working (**retired**) because of old age. Pensions are also paid to people who are widowed or who cannot work because they are ill: *to live on a pension*

☛ Almost all men over 65 and women over 60 in Britain receive a pension from the government. This is called a **state pension**. Many people also get a **company pension** from their former employer.

pensioner /'penʃənə(r)/ *noun* [C] = OLD-AGE PENSIONER

pentagon /'pentəgən; *US* -gɒn/ *noun* [C] a shape that has five straight sides

pentathlon /pen'tæθlən; -lɒn/ *noun* [C] a sports competition in which each person has to take part in five different events

penthouse /'penthaʊs/ *noun* [C] an expensive flat at the top of a tall building

pent up /,pent'ʌp/ *adj* (used about feelings) that you do not express: *pent up anger and frustration*

penultimate /pen'ʌltɪmət/ *adj* (in a series)

the one before the last one: *'Y' is the penultimate letter of the alphabet.*
☆ **people** /'piːpl/ *noun* **1** [plural] more than one person: *How many people are coming to the party?* ○ *Young people often rebel against their parents.* ○ *What will people say if you go out looking like that?* ○ *He meets a lot of famous people in his job.* ☛ Be careful. **People** is almost always used instead of the plural form **persons**. **Persons** is very formal and is usually used in legal language, etc: *Persons under the age of eighteen are not permitted to buy alcohol.* **Folk** is an informal word for people. It is often used when you are talking about older people or people who live in the country: *The old folk have seen many changes in the village over the years.* **2** [C] (*pl* **peoples**) a nation, race, etc: *The Japanese are a hard-working people.* ○ *the French-speaking peoples of the world* **3** [plural] the inhabitants of a particular place: *the people of London* **4 the people** [plural] the ordinary citizens of a country, ie not those of high social rank: *a man of the people*

pepper /'pepə(r)/ *noun* **1** [U] a powder with a hot taste that is used for flavouring food: *salt and pepper* **2** [C] a hollow green, red or yellow vegetable: *stuffed green peppers*

pepper *verb* [T] **1** to put pepper(1) on sth **2 pepper sb/sth with sth** to hit sb/sth many times with sth: *The wall had been peppered with bullets.*

peppermint /'pepəmɪnt/ *noun* **1** [U] a natural substance with a strong flavour that is used in sweets and medicines **2** [C] (*also* **mint**) a sweet with a peppermint flavour

pep talk /'pep tɔːk/ *noun* [C] (*informal*) a speech that is given to encourage people to or to make them work harder

☆ **per** /pə(r); strong form pɜː(r)/ *prep* for each: *The speed limit is 30 miles per hour.* ○ *To hire a boat costs £5 per hour.*

perceive /pə'siːv/ *verb* [T] (*formal*) **1** to notice or realize sth: *Scientists failed to perceive how dangerous the levels of pollutants had become.* **2** to see or think of sth in a particular way: *I perceived his comments as a criticism.* ☛ The noun is **perception**.

☆ **per cent** (*US* **percent**) /pə'sent/ *adj, adv* (*symbol* **%**) in or of each hundred: *There is a ten per cent service charge.* ○ *a two per cent fall in the price of oil*

per cent (*US* **percent**) *noun* [C, with sing or pl verb] (*pl* **per cent**) (*symbol* **%**) one part in every hundred: *Nearly ten per cent of all children attend private schools.* ○ *90% of the population owns a television.* ○ *The price of bread has gone up by 50 per cent in two years.*

percentage /pə'sentɪdʒ/ *noun* [C, with sing or pl verb] a part of an amount, expressed as a number of hundredths of that amount: *'What percentage of people voted Labour in 1992?' 'About 30 per cent.'* ○ *Please express your answer as a percentage.*

perceptible /pə'septəbl/ *adj* (*formal*) that can be seen or felt: *a barely perceptible change in colour* ☛ The opposite is **imperceptible**. —**perceptibly** /-əblɪ/ *adv*

perception /pə'sepʃn/ *noun* **1** [U] the ability to notice or understand sth **2** [C] a particular way of looking at or understanding sth; an opinion: *What is your perception of the situation?* ☛ The verb is **perceive**.

perceptive /pə'septɪv/ *adj* (*formal*) quick to notice or understand things —**perceptively** *adv*

perch /pɜːtʃ/ *noun* [C] a branch (or a bar in a cage) where a bird sits

perch *verb* **1** [I] (used about a bird) to rest from flying on a branch, etc **2** [I,T] to sit, or be put, on the edge of sth: *The house was perched on the edge of a cliff.*

percussion /pə'kʌʃn/ *noun* [sing] **the percussion** [with sing or pl verb] the section of an orchestra that consists of the drums and other instruments that you play by hitting them

perennial /pə'renɪəl/ *adj* that happens often or that lasts for a long time: *the perennial problem of poverty in Britain*

☆ **perfect¹** /'pɜːfɪkt/ *adj* **1** as good as can be; without fault: *The car is two years old but it is still in perfect condition.* ○ *Nobody is perfect!* ○ *These shoes are a perfect fit.* ○ *What perfect weather!* ○ *a perfect piece of work* **2 perfect (for sb/sth)** very suitable or right: *Ken would be perfect for the job.* ○ *Wales is the perfect place for a family holiday.* ○ *the perfect solution to a problem* **3** (used to describe the tense of a verb that is formed with *has/have/had* and the past participle) **4** (only *before* a noun) complete; total: *What he was saying made perfect sense to me.* ○ *a perfect stranger*

the perfect *noun* [sing] the perfect tense: *the present/past perfect*

perfectly *adv* **1** in a perfect way: *He played the piece of music perfectly.* **2** very; completely: *Laura understood perfectly what I meant.*

perfect² /pə'fekt/ *verb* [T] to make sth perfect: *Hugh is spending a year in France to perfect his French.*

perfection /pə'fekʃn/ *noun* [U] the state of being perfect or without fault: *Perfection is impossible to achieve.* ○ *The steak was cooked to perfection.*

perfectionist /-ʃənɪst/ *noun* [C] a person who always does things as well as he/she possibly can and who expects others to do the same

perforate /'pɜːfəreɪt/ *verb* [T] to make a hole or holes in sth: *Tear along the perforated line.*

perforation /ˌpɜːfə'reɪʃn/ *noun* **1** [U] making a hole in sth **2** [C] a series of small holes in paper, etc that make it easy for you to tear

☆ **perform** /pə'fɔːm/ *verb* **1** [T] (*formal*) to do a piece of work or sth that you have been ordered to do: *Doctors performed an emergency operation.* ○ *to perform a task* **2** [I,T] to take part in a play, to sing, dance, etc in front of an audience: *She is currently performing at the London Palladium.* ○ *Children performed local dances for the Prince.* ○ *This play has never been performed previously.* **3** [I] (used about a machine, etc) to work: *The car performs badly in cold weather.*

performer *noun* [C] a person who performs(2) in front of an audience

☆ **performance** /pə'fɔːməns/ noun **1** [sing] (formal) doing sth: *the performance of your duties* **2** [C] sth that you perform(2) in front of an audience: *a live performance by the band 'Nirvana'* ○ *The Royal Shakespeare Company is putting on a performance of 'King Lear'.* **3** [C] the way in which you do sth, especially how successful you are: *The company's performance was disappointing last year.* ○ *Germany's fine performance in the World Cup* **4** [U] (used about a machine, etc) the ability to work well: *This car has a high performance engine.*

☆ **perfume** /'pɜːfjuːm; US also pər'fjuːm/ noun [C,U] **1** a pleasant smell **2** (Brit also **scent**) a liquid with a sweet smell that you put on your body to make yourself smell nice: *French perfume*

☆ **perhaps** /pə'hæps; præps/ adv (used when you are not sure about sth) maybe; possibly: *Perhaps he isn't coming.* ○ *She was, perhaps, one of the most famous writers of the time.* ○ '*Are you sure that you're doing the right thing?' 'No, perhaps not.'* ○ *If Barnes had played, they might have won. Or perhaps not.* ☛ **Perhaps** and **maybe** are similar in meaning. They are often used to make what you are saying sound more polite: *Perhaps I could borrow your book, if you're not using it?* ○ *Maybe I'd better explain...*

peril /'perəl/ noun (formal) **1** [U] great danger **2** [C] sth that is very dangerous: *the perils of the sea*

perilous /'perələs/ adj (formal) dangerous ☛ **Danger** and **dangerous** are more common.

perimeter /pə'rɪmɪtə(r)/ noun [C] the outside edge or boundary of an area of land: *the perimeter fence of the army camp*

☆ **period** /'pɪəriəd/ noun [C] **1** a length of time: *The weather tomorrow will be cloudy with sunny periods.* ○ *The scheme will be introduced for a six-month trial period.* ○ *Her son is going through a difficult period at the moment.* ○ *The play is set in the Tudor period in England.* ○ *period costume* (= costume of a particular period) **2** a lesson in school: *We have five periods of English a week.* **3** the monthly loss of blood from a woman's body: *period pains* ○ *My period started this morning.* **4** (especially US) = FULL STOP

periodic /ˌpɪəri'ɒdɪk/ (also **periodical** /-kl/) adj happening fairly regularly —**periodically** /-klɪ/ adv: *All machines need to be checked periodically.*

periodical /ˌpɪəri'ɒdɪkl/ noun [C] (formal) a magazine that is produced at regular intervals

perish /'perɪʃ/ verb [I] (formal) to die or be destroyed: *Thousands perished in the war.*

perishable adj (used about food) that will go bad quickly

perjure /'pɜːdʒə(r)/ verb [T] **perjure yourself** to tell lies in a court of law

perjury /'pɜːdʒəri/ noun [U] (formal) telling a lie (in a court of law)

perk¹ /pɜːk/ verb
(PHRASAL VERBS) **perk up** to become more cheerful or lively
perk sb/sth up to make sb/sth more cheerful or lively

perk² /pɜːk/ noun [C] (informal) something extra that you get from your employer in addition to your salary: *Travelling abroad is one of the perks of the job.*

perm /pɜːm/ noun [C] (informal) = PERMANENT WAVE —**perm** verb [T]: *She has had her hair permed.*

permanence /'pɜːmənəns/ noun [U] the state of lasting or remaining for a very long time or for ever

☆ **permanent** /'pɜːmənənt/ adj lasting for a long time or for ever; that will not change: *The accident left him with a permanent scar.* ○ *Are you looking for a permanent or a temporary job?* —**permanently** adv: *Has she left permanently?*
ˌpermanent 'wave (also informal **perm**) noun [C] (formal) the treatment of hair with special chemicals in order to make it curly or wavy

permissible /pə'mɪsəbl/ adj (formal) that is allowed (by the rules): *They have been exposed to radiation above the permissible level.*

☆ **permission** /pə'mɪʃn/ noun [U] the act of allowing sb to do sth: *I'm afraid you can't leave without permission.* ○ *Children under 18 need their parents' permission to attend.* ○ *to ask permission for sth* ○ *to give permission for sth* ○ *The refugees have been refused permission to stay in this country.* ☛ Be careful. **Permission** is uncountable. A piece of paper that says that you are allowed to do something is a **permit**.

permissive /pə'mɪsɪv/ adj having, allowing or showing a lot of freedom, especially in sexual matters: *the permissive society of the 1960s*

☆ **permit** /pə'mɪt/ verb (formal) (**permitting**; **permitted**) **1** [T] to allow sth: *Food and drink are not permitted in this building.* ○ *You are not permitted to smoke in the hospital.* ○ *His visa does not permit him to work.* ☛ Look at the note at **allow**. **2** [I,T] to make possible: *Let's have a picnic at the weekend, weather permitting.*

permit /'pɜːmɪt/ noun [C] an official paper that says you are allowed to do sth: *a work permit*

perpendicular /ˌpɜːpən'dɪkjʊlə(r)/ adj **1** at an angle of 90° to sth ☛ Look at **horizontal** and **vertical**. **2** pointing straight up; upright

perpetual /pə'petʃuəl/ adj not stopping or changing: *They lived in perpetual fear of losing their jobs.* ○ *the perpetual roar of traffic*

perpetually /-tʃuəli/ adv always: *People are perpetually complaining about the hospital food.*

perpetuate /pə'petʃueɪt/ verb [T] (formal) to cause sth to continue

perplexed /pə'plekst/ adj not understanding sth; confused

persecute /'pɜːsɪkjuːt/ verb [T] to cause sb to suffer, especially because of what he/she believes —**persecution** /ˌpɜːsɪ'kjuːʃn/ noun [C,U]: *the persecution of minorities* —**persecutor** /'pɜːsɪkjuːtə(r)/ noun [C]

persevere /ˌpɜːsɪ'vɪə(r)/ verb [I] **persevere (at/in/with sth)** to continue trying or having sth that is difficult: *The treatment is painful but I'm going to persevere with it.* —**perseverance** /ˌpɜːsɪ'vɪərəns/ noun [U]: *It takes a lot of perseverance to become a champion at any sport.*

p	b	t	d	k	g	tʃ	dʒ	f	v	θ	ð
pen	bad	tea	did	cat	got	chin	June	fall	van	thin	then

persist /pəˈsɪst/ verb [I] **1 persist (in sth/in doing sth)** to continue doing sth even though other people say that you are wrong or that you cannot do it: *If you persist in making so much noise, I shall call the police.* o *She persists in her belief that he did not kill himself.* **2** to continue to exist: *If your symptoms persist you should consult your doctor.*

persistence /-əns/ noun [U] **1** the state of continuing to do sth even though people say that you are wrong or that you cannot do it: *Finally her persistence was rewarded and she got what she wanted.* **2** the state of continuing to exist: *the persistence of unemployment at high levels*

persistent /-ənt/ adj **1** continuing to do sth even though people say that you are wrong or that you cannot do it: *Some salesmen can be very persistent.* **2** lasting for a long time or happening often: *a persistent cough* o *persistent rain* —**persistently** adv

☆ **person** /ˈpɜːsn/ noun [C] (pl **people** or **persons**) ☞ Look at the note at **people**. **1** a man or woman: *I would like to speak to the person in charge.* **2** one of the three types of pronoun in grammar. *I/we* are the first person, *you* is the second person and *he/she/it/they* are the third person.
(IDIOM) **in person** seeing or speaking to sb face to face, (not speaking on the telephone or writing a letter) *I went to apologize to her in person.*

☆ **personal** /ˈpɜːsənl/ adj **1** (only *before* a noun) of or belonging to a particular person: *Judges should not let their personal feelings influence their decisions.* o *The car is for your personal use only.* **2** of or concerning your feelings, health, relations with other people, etc: *I should like to speak to you in private. I have something personal to discuss.* o *The letter was marked 'personal' so I did not open it.* **3** (only *before* a noun) done or made by a particular person: *The Prime Minister made a personal visit to the victims in hospital.* **4** speaking about sb's appearance or character in an unpleasant or unfriendly way: *It started as a general discussion but then people started making personal remarks and an argument began.* **5** (only *before* a noun) connected with the body: *personal hygiene*

personally /-ənəli/ adv **1** in person, not with sb else acting for you: *I should like to deal with this matter personally.* **2** (used for expressing your own opinions): *Personally, I think that nurses deserve more money.* **3** as a person: *I wasn't talking about you personally – I meant all teachers.* o *The ship's captain was held personally responsible for the accident.*

,personal 'pronoun noun [C] (*grammar*) any of the pronouns *I, me, she, her, he, him, we, us, you, they, them*, etc

personality /,pɜːsəˈnæləti/ noun (pl **personalities**) **1** [C] the qualities and features of a person: *Joe has a very forceful personality.* **2** [C,U] the quality of having a strong, interesting and attractive character; a person who has this quality: *A good entertainer needs a lot of personality.* o *I think you'll like Judy – she's quite a personality.* **3** [C] a famous person (especially in sport, on television, etc): *a television personality*

personalize (also **personalise**) /ˈpɜːsənəlaɪz/ verb [T] to mark sth with your initials, etc to show that it belongs to you: *a car with a personalized number-plate*

personify /pəˈsɒnɪfaɪ/ verb [T] (*pres part* **personifying**; *3rd pers sing pres* **personifies**; *pt, pp* **personified**) **1** to be an example in human form of a particular quality **2** to describe sth as if it were a person, eg in a poem

personnel /,pɜːsəˈnel/ noun **1** [plural] the people who work for a large organization: *The army cannot afford to lose qualified personnel.* **2** [U, with sing or pl verb] (*also* **person'nel department**) the department of a large organization that looks after the people who work there

perspective /pəˈspektɪv/ noun **1** [U] the art of drawing on a flat surface so that some objects appear to be farther away than others: *the laws of perspective* o *in/out of perspective* **2** [C,U] the way that you think about sth; your point of view: *If you go away for a few days you will see everything in a new perspective.*

perspire /pəˈspaɪə(r)/ verb [I] (*formal*) to lose liquid through your skin ☞ **Sweat** is more informal.

perspiration /,pɜːspəˈreɪʃn/ noun [U] **1** the act of perspiring **2** the liquid that you lose through your skin: *a drop of perspiration*

☆ **persuade** /pəˈsweɪd/ verb [T] **1 persuade sb (to do sth); persuade sb (into/out of sth)** to cause sb to do sth by giving him/her good reasons: *It was difficult to persuade Louise to change her mind.* o *We eventually persuaded Tim into coming with us.* ☞ Look at **dissuade**. **2 persuade sb (of sth)** (*formal*) to cause sb to believe sth: *The jury was persuaded of her innocence.* ☞ Look at **convince**.

persuasion /pəˈsweɪʒn/ noun **1** [U] persuading or being persuaded: *It took a lot of persuasion to get Alan to agree.* o *I suggested going to the beach and the others didn't need much persuasion.* **2** [C] (*formal*) a religious or political belief: *The school is open to people of all persuasions.*

persuasive /pəˈsweɪsɪv/ adj able to make sb do or believe sth: *The arguments were very persuasive.* —**persuasively** adv **persuasiveness** noun [U]

pertinent /ˈpɜːtɪnənt; *US* -tənənt/ adj directly connected with sth: *to ask a pertinent question*

perturb /pəˈtɜːb/ verb [T] (often passive) (*formal*) to make sb worried or upset

pervade /pəˈveɪd/ verb [T] to spread to all parts of sth: *The smell from the factory pervaded the whole town.*

pervasive /pəˈveɪsɪv/ adj that is present in all parts of sth: *a pervasive mood of pessimism*

perverse /pəˈvɜːs/ adj (*formal*) having or showing behaviour that is not reasonable or that upsets other people: *Derek gets perverse pleasure from shocking his parents.* —**perversely** adv —**perversity** noun [U]

perversion /pəˈvɜːʃn; *US* -ʒn/ noun [C,U] **1** the changing of sth from right to wrong or

s	z	ʃ	ʒ	h	m	n	ŋ	l	r	j	w
so	zoo	she	vision	how	man	no	sing	leg	red	yes	wet

good to bad: *That statement is a perversion of the truth.* **2** sexual behaviour that is unnatural or not acceptable

pervert /pə'vɜːt/ *verb* [T] **1** to change sth so that it becomes bad or is used wrongly: *to pervert scientific knowledge for military purposes* **2** to cause sb to think or behave in a way that is not right or natural: *Children should be protected from influences that may pervert them.*

pervert /'pɜːvɜːt/ *noun* [C] a person whose sexual behaviour is not natural or normal

pessimism /'pesɪmɪzəm/ *noun* [U] the state of expecting or believing that bad things will happen

pessimist /-ɪst/ *noun* [C] a person who always thinks that is going to happen will be bad —**pessimistic** /,pesɪ'mɪstɪk/ *adj* **pessimistically** /-kli/ *adv* ☛ Look at optimism, optimist, and optimistic.

pest /pest/ *noun* [C] **1** an insect or animal that destroys plants, food, etc: *pest control* **2** (*informal*) a person or thing that annoys you

pester /'pestə(r)/ *verb* [T] to annoy or bother sb, eg by asking him/her sth many times: *to pester sb for money*

pesticide /'pestɪsaɪd/ *noun* [C,U] a chemical substance that is used for killing animals or insects that eat food crops ☛ Look at **insecticide**.

☆ **pet** /pet/ *noun* [C] **1** an animal that you keep in your home for company or for pleasure: *a pet guinea pig* ○ *to keep a pet* **2** a person who is treated as a favourite: *teacher's pet*

pet *verb* (**petting**; **petted**) **1** [T] to treat an animal with affection, eg by stroking it **2** [I] (*informal*) (used about two people) to kiss and touch in a sexual way

pet 'subject *noun* [C] a subject that you are very interested in or that you feel very strongly about

petal /'petl/ *noun* [C] one of the thin soft coloured parts of a flower

peter /'piːtə(r)/ *verb*
(PHRASAL VERB) **peter out** to finish or come to an end gradually: *The flow of water slowed down and finally petered out.*

petition /pə'tɪʃn/ *noun* [C] a written document, signed by many people, that asks a government, etc to do sth: *More than 50 000 people signed the petition protesting about the new road.*

petrified /'petrɪfaɪd/ *adj* very frightened

☆ **petrol** /'petrəl/ (*US* **gas**; **gasoline**) *noun* [U] the liquid that is used as fuel for motor vehicles such as cars and aeroplanes: *a petrol pump* ○ *to fill up with petrol*

'petrol station (*also* **filling station**; **service station**; *US* **gas station**) *noun* [C] a place where you can buy petrol and other things for your car

petroleum /pə'trəʊliəm/ *noun* [U] oil that is found under the surface of the earth and that is used for making petrol and other types of chemical substances

petticoat /'petɪkəʊt/ *noun* [C] a thin piece of women's clothing that is worn under a dress or a skirt

petty /'peti/ *adj* **1** small or not important: *He didn't want to get involved with the petty details.* ○ *petty crime* **2** unkind or unpleasant (for a reason that does not seem very important): *He's tried so hard that it would be petty to criticize him now.*

pew /pjuː/ *noun* [C] one of the long seats in a church

phantasy *noun* [C] (*pl* **phantasies**) = FANTASY

phantom /'fæntəm/ *noun* [C] **1** something with the shape of a dead person that seems to appear on earth and behave as if it was alive ☛ Ghost is a more common word. **2** something that you think exists, but that is not real

pharmaceutical /,fɑːmə'sjuːtɪkl/; *US* -'suː-/ *adj* connected with the production of medicines

pharmacist /'fɑːməsɪst/ *noun* [C] = CHEMIST(1)

pharmacy /'fɑːməsi/ *noun* (*pl* **pharmacies**) **1** [U] (the study of) the preparation of medicines **2** [C] a place where medicines are prepared and given out or sold

☛ A shop that sells medicine is also called a **chemist's (shop)** in British English or a **drugstore** in American English.

☆ **phase** /feɪz/ *noun* [C] a period in the development of sth: *the final phase of the hospital building programme* ○ *to enter a new phase* ○ *Julie went through a difficult phase when she started school.*

phase *verb*
(PHRASAL VERBS) **phase sth in** to introduce sth slowly or over a period of time: *The metric system was phased in over several years.*

phase sth out to take away or remove sth slowly or over a period of time: *The older machines are gradually being phased out and replaced by new ones.*

pheasant /'feznt/ *noun* [C] (*pl* **pheasants** or **pheasant**) a type of bird with a long tail. The males have brightly coloured feathers. Pheasants are often shot for sport and are eaten as food.

phenomenal /fə'nɒmɪnl/ *adj* unusual because it is so good or so great: *phenomenal success* —**phenomenally** /-nəli/ *adv*

phenomenon /fə'nɒmɪnən; *US* -nɒn/ *noun* [C] (*pl* **phenomena** /-mə/) something that happens or exists (often sth unusual): *Acid rain is not a natural phenomenon. It is caused by pollution.*

phew /fjuː/ (*also* **whew**) *interj* (used to show the sound which expresses tiredness, surprise, relief, shock, etc): *Phew, it's hot in here!*

philosopher /fɪ'lɒsəfə(r)/ *noun* [C] a person who has developed a set of ideas and beliefs about the meaning of life

☆ **philosophy** /fɪ'lɒsəfi/ *noun* (*pl* **philosophies**) **1** [U] the study of ideas and beliefs about the meaning of life **2** [C] a belief or set of beliefs that tries to explain the meaning of life or give rules about how to behave: *the philosophy of Nietzsche* ○ *Her philosophy is 'If a job's worth doing, it's worth doing well'.*

philosophical /,fɪlə'sɒfɪkl/ (*also* **philosophic**) *adj* **1** of or concerning philosophy: *a philosophical debate* **2** philosophical (about

iː	ɪ	e	æ	ɑː	ɒ	ɔː	ʊ	uː	ʌ
see	sit	ten	hat	arm	got	saw	put	too	cup

phlegm 463 **pick**

sth) having or showing a calm, quiet attitude when you are in danger, suffering or disappointed: *He was quite philosophical about failing the exam and says he will try again next year.* —**philosophically** /-klɪ/ *adv*

phlegm /flem/ *noun* [U] the thick yellow substance that is produced in your nose and your throat when you have a cold

phlegmatic /fleg'mætɪk/ *adj (formal)* not easily excited or upset; calm

phobia /'fəʊbɪə/ *noun* [C] a very strong fear or dislike that you cannot explain

☆ **phone** /fəʊn/ *noun (informal)* **1** [U] = TELEPHONE(1): *a phone call* ○ *You can book the tickets by phone.* **2** [C] = TELEPHONE(2): *The phone is ringing – could you answer it?*
(IDIOM) **on the phone/telephone 1** using the telephone: *'Where's Ian?' 'He's on the phone.'* **2** having a telephone in your home: *I'll have to write to her because she's not on the phone.*

phone *verb* [I,T] = TELEPHONE: *Did anybody phone while I was out?* ○ *Could you phone the restaurant and book a table?*

'**phone book** *noun* [C] = TELEPHONE DIRECTORY

'**phone box** *noun* [C] = TELEPHONE BOX

'**phone call** *noun* [C] = TELEPHONE CALL

'**phonecard** *noun* [C] a small plastic card that you can use to pay for calls in a public telephone box ☛ picture at **telephone**.

'**phone-in** (*US* **call-in**) *noun* [C] a radio or television programme during which you can ask a question or give your opinion by telephone

'**phone number** *noun* [C] = TELEPHONE NUMBER

phonetic /fə'netɪk/ *adj* **1** connected with the sounds of human speech **2** using a system for writing a language that has a different sign for each sound: *the phonetic alphabet* —**phonetically** /-klɪ/ *adv*

phonetics *noun* [U] the study of the sounds of human speech

phoney (*also* **phony**) /'fəʊnɪ/ *adj* not real; false

phoney (*also* **phony**) /'fəʊnɪ/ *noun* [C] (*pl* **phoneys**) a person who is not what he/she pretends to be —**phoniness** *noun* [U]

☆ **photo** /'fəʊtəʊ/ *noun* (*pl* **photos** /-təʊz/) (*informal*) = PHOTOGRAPH

photocopy /'fəʊtəʊkɒpɪ/ *noun* [C] (*pl* **photocopies**) a copy of a piece of paper, page in a book, etc that is made by a special machine (a **photocopier**) that can photograph sth quickly

photocopy *verb* [I,T] (*pres part* **photocopying**; *3rd pers sing pres* **photocopies**; *pt, pp* **photocopied**) to make a photocopy of sth

photocopier *noun* [C] a machine that makes photocopies

☆ **photograph** /'fəʊtəgrɑːf; *US* -græf/ (*also informal* **photo**) *noun* [C] a picture that is taken with a camera: *to take a photo* ○ *a colour photograph* ○ *She looks younger in real life than she did in the photograph.* ○ *This photo is a bit out of focus.* ○ *to have a photo enlarged* ☛ Look at **negative** and **slide**.

photograph *verb* [T] to take a photograph of sb/sth

photographer /fə'tɒgrəfə(r)/ *noun* [C] a person who takes photographs ☛ Look at **cameraman**.

photographic /ˌfəʊtə'græfɪk/ *adj* connected with photographs or photography: *photographic equipment*

photography /fə'tɒgrəfɪ/ *noun* [U] the skill or process of taking photographs: *wildlife photography*

phrasal verb /'freɪzl vɜːb/ *noun* [C] a verb that is combined with an adverb or a preposition to give a new meaning, such as 'look after' or 'put sb off'

☆ **phrase** /freɪz/ *noun* [C] a group of words that are used together. A phrase does not contain a full verb: *'First of all' and 'a bar of chocolate' are phrases.*

phrase *verb* [T] to express sth in a particular way: *The statement was phrased so that it would offend no one.*

'**phrase book** *noun* [C] a book that gives common words and phrases in a foreign language. People use phrase books when they travel abroad to a country whose language they do not know.

☆ **physical** /'fɪzɪkl/ *adj* **1** of or for your body: *physical exercise* ○ *Parents must consider their children's physical and emotional needs.* **2** connected with real things that you can touch, or with the laws of nature: *physical geography* ○ *It is a physical impossibility to be in two places at once.* **3** connected with physics —**physically** /-klɪ/ *adv*: *to be physically fit* ○ *It will be physically impossible to get to London before ten.*

physician /fɪ'zɪʃn/ *noun* [C] a doctor, especially one who treats diseases with medicine (= not a surgeon)

physicist /'fɪzɪsɪst/ *noun* [C] a person who studies physics

☆ **physics** /'fɪzɪks/ *noun* [U] the scientific study of natural forces such as light, sound, heat, electricity, pressure, etc

physiotherapy /ˌfɪzɪəʊ'θerəpɪ/ *noun* [U] the treatment of disease or injury by exercise, massage, heat, etc

physiotherapist /-pɪst/ *noun* [C] a person who is trained to use physiotherapy

physique /fɪ'ziːk/ *noun* [C] the size and shape of a person's body: *a strong muscular physique*

☆ **piano** /pɪ'ænəʊ/ *noun* [C] (*pl* **pianos** /-nəʊz/) (*also formal* **pianoforte** /pɪˌænəʊ'fɔːtɪ; *US* pɪˈænəfɔːrt/) a large musical instrument that you play by pressing down black and white bars (**keys**). This causes small hammers to hit strings inside the instrument: *an upright piano* ○ *a grand piano* ☛ Note that, as with all musical instruments, we play **the** piano.

pianist /'pɪənɪst/ *noun* [C] a person who plays the piano

☆ **pick**[1] /pɪk/ *verb* [T] **1** to choose sb/sth from a group of people or things: *She picked her words carefully so as not to upset anybody.* ○ *to be picked to play for the team* ○ *We picked a good day to go to the beach.* **2** to take a flower, fruit or vegetable from the place where it is growing: *I've picked you a bunch of flowers.* ○ *Don't pick wild flowers.* ○ *to go fruit-picking* **3** to

ɜː	ə	eɪ	əʊ	aɪ	aʊ	ɔɪ	ɪə	eə	ʊə
fur	ago	pay	home	five	now	join	near	hair	pure

remove a small piece or pieces of sth with your fingers: *Don't pick your nose!* **4** to take sth off sth: *Don't pick all the nuts off the top of the cake.* ○ *She picked a hair off her jacket.* **5** to open a lock without a key, eg with a piece of wire
(IDIOMS) **have a bone to pick with sb** ⇨ BONE
pick a fight (with sb) to start a fight with sb deliberately
pick sb's pocket to steal money, etc from sb's pocket or bag
(PHRASAL VERBS) **pick on sb** to behave unfairly or unkindly towards sb
pick sb/sth out to choose or recognize sb/sth from a number of people or things: *I immediately picked Jean out in the photo.*
pick up to become better; to improve
pick sb up 1 to collect sb, in a car, etc: *We've ordered a taxi to pick us up at ten.* **2** (*informal*) to start talking to sb you do not know and try to start a sexual relationship with him/her **3** (used about the police) to stop sb and question them: *The drug dealers were picked up in Dover.*
pick sb/sth up 1 to take hold of and lift sb/sth: *The phone stopped ringing just as I picked up the receiver.* ○ *Lucy picked up the child and gave him a cuddle.* ○ *Pick those things up off the floor!* **2** to hear or see sb/sth by means of a radio, television, etc: *In the north of France you can pick up English television programmes.*
pick sth up 1 to learn sth without formal lessons: *Joe picked up a lot of Italian by playing with the local children.* **2** to get or find sth: *You can pick up a lot of information about local history by talking to the older residents.* **3** to go and get sth; to collect sth: *We must pick up the tickets half an hour before the show begins.*

'pickpocket /ˈpɪkpɒkɪt/ *noun* [C] a person who steals things from other people's pockets or bags in public places

pick² /pɪk/ *noun* [sing] **1** the one that you choose; your choice: *You can have whichever cake you like. Take your pick.* **2** the best of a group: *You can see the pick of the new films at this year's festival.*

pick³ /pɪk/ *noun* [C] (*also* **pickaxe**; *US* **pickax** /ˈpɪkæks/) a tool that consists of a curved iron bar with sharp points at both ends, fixed onto a wooden handle. Picks are used for breaking stones or hard ground.

picket /ˈpɪkɪt/ *noun* [C] a worker or group of workers who stand outside a place of work during a strike and try to persuade other people not to go in —**picket** *verb* [I,T]

pickle /ˈpɪkl/ *noun* [C,U] food such as fruit and vegetables that is put in vinegar or salt water so that it can be kept for a long time: *a supper of cold meat and pickles* —**pickle** *verb* [T]: *pickled onions*

picky /ˈpɪki/ *adj* (**pickier**; **pickiest**) (*informal*) (*especially US*) difficult to please ☛ Look at **fussy**.

☆ **picnic** /ˈpɪknɪk/ *noun* [C] **1** a meal that you eat outdoors (in the country or on a beach, etc): *a picnic lunch* ○ *We had a picnic on the beach.* **2** a trip that you make for pleasure during which you eat a picnic: *It's a lovely day – let's go for a picnic.* —**picnic** *verb* [I] (*pres part* **picnicking**; *pt, pp* **picnicked**)

pictorial /pɪkˈtɔːriəl/ *adj* expressed in pictures

☆ **picture** /ˈpɪktʃə(r)/ *noun* **1** [C] a painting, drawing or photograph: *Many of Turner's pictures are of the sea.* ○ *to draw/paint a picture* ○ *Look at the picture on page 96 and describe what you see.* ○ *Come and have your picture* (= photograph) *taken.* **2** [C] an idea or memory of sth in your mind: *Dickens' novels give a good picture of what life was like in Victorian England.* **3** [C] the quality of what you see on a television: *I'm sorry, the television's quite old and the picture isn't very good.* **4** [C] (*Brit*) a film (in a cinema) **5 the pictures** [plural] (*Brit*) the cinema: *We're going to the pictures this evening.*
picture *verb* [T] **1** to imagine sth in your mind: *Kevin used to be so wild. I can't picture him as a father.* **2** to make a picture of sb/sth: *The happy couple, pictured above, left for a honeymoon in Bali.*

picturesque /ˌpɪktʃəˈresk/ *adj* (usually used about a place) attractive and interesting: *a picturesque fishing village*

☆ **pie** /paɪ/ *noun* [C,U] a type of food. A pastry case is filled with fruit, vegetables or meat and then baked: *apple pie and custard* ☛ Look at **shepherd's pie** and **mince pie**. In Britain a **pie** usually has pastry underneath and on top of the filling. (An American pie may only have pastry underneath). A **tart** or **flan** only has pastry under the filling and is usually sweet. A **quiche** is a type of flan with a savoury filling.

☆ **piece¹** /piːs/ *noun* [C] **1** an amount or example of sth: *a piece of paper* ○ *a lovely piece of furniture* ○ *Would you like another piece of cake?* ○ *a very good piece of work* ○ *a piece of advice* ○ *a very interesting piece of information* **2** one of the parts that sth is made of: *She took the model to pieces and started again.* ○ *We need a new three-piece suite* (= a sofa and two chairs). **3** one of the parts into which sth breaks: *The plate fell to the floor and smashed to pieces.* ☛ **Bit** and **piece** are very similar in meaning but **bit** is more informal. **4** one of the small objects that you use when you are playing indoor board games: *chess pieces* **5** a coin: *Does the machine accept fifty-pence pieces?* **6** an article in a newspaper or magazine **7** a single work of art, music, etc: *He played a piece by Chopin.*
(IDIOMS) **bits and pieces** ⇨ BIT¹
go to pieces to be unable to control yourself: *When his wife died he seemed to go to pieces.*
a piece of cake (*informal*) something that is very easy

piece² /piːs/ *verb*
(PHRASAL VERB) **piece sth together 1** to put sth together from several pieces **2** to discover the truth about sth from different pieces of information

piecemeal /ˈpiːsmiːl/ *adj, adv* done or happening a little at a time

pier /pɪə(r)/ *noun* [C] a large wooden or metal structure that is built out into the sea. Boats can stop at piers so that people can get on or off and goods can be loaded or unloaded.

☛ A **pier** in a seaside holiday town is a similar structure which is used as a place of entertainment, with a theatre, amusements, etc.

pierce /pɪəs/ verb [T] **1** to make a hole in sth with a sharp point: *Colin has had one ear pierced.* ○ *The sharp thorns pierced the ball.* **2** (used about light or a sound) to be seen or heard suddenly: *A scream pierced the air.*

piercing adj **1** (used about the wind, pain, a loud noise, etc) strong and unpleasant **2** (used about eyes or a look) seeming to know what you are thinking

piety /ˈpaɪəti/ noun [U] strong religious belief
☛ The adjective is **pious**.

☆ **pig** /pɪg/ noun [C] **1** a fat animal with short legs and a curly tail that is kept on farms for its meat (**pork**)

☛ A male pig is a **boar**, a female pig is a **sow** and a young pig is a **piglet**. When they make a noise, pigs **grunt**. Look at the note at **meat**.

2 (*informal*) an unpleasant person or one who eats too much

pig verb [T] (pigging; pigged) **pig yourself** to eat or drink too much

'piggyback noun [C] the way of carrying sb in which he/she rides on your back with his/her arms round your neck and knees round your waist: *to give sb a piggyback*

'piggy bank noun [C] a small box, often shaped like a pig, that children use for saving money in

pig'headed adj (*informal*) unwilling to change your mind or say that you are wrong
☛ Look at **stubborn** and **obstinate**. They are more formal.

'pigsty /-staɪ/ (*also* **sty**; *US* **'pigpen**) noun [C] (*pl* **pigsties**) a small building where pigs are kept: (*figurative*) *Tidy up your bedroom – it's a pigsty!*

pigeon /ˈpɪdʒɪn/ noun [C] a fat grey bird that often lives in towns

'pigeon-hole noun [C] one of a set of small open boxes that are used for putting papers or letters in

piglet /ˈpɪglɪt/ noun [C] a young pig

pigment /ˈpɪgmənt/ noun [C,U] a substance that gives colour to things: *The colour of your skin depends on the amount of pigment in it.*

pigtail /ˈpɪgteɪl/ noun [C] a piece of hair that has been divided into three and twisted together (**plaited**)

☆ **pile¹** /paɪl/ noun [C] **1** a number of things lying on top of one another, or an amount of sth that is in a large mass: *He always left his books in a neat pile.* ○ *A large pile of sand blocked the pavement.* ☛ A **pile** may be tidy or untidy. A **heap** is untidy. **2** (often plural) (*informal*) a lot of sth: *I've got piles of work to do this evening.*
☛ **Loads of** is also common.

pile² /paɪl/ verb [T] **1 pile sth (up)** to put things one on top of the other to form a pile: *Pile them on top of each other.* **2 pile A on(to) B; pile B with A** to put a lot of sth on sth: *She piled the papers on the desk.* ○ *The desk was piled with papers.*
(PHRASAL VERBS) **pile into sth/out of sth** (*informal*) to go in or out of sth in a disorganized way: *All the children tried to pile into the bus at the same time.*

pile up 1 to increase in quantity: *The problems really piled up while I was away.* **2** to put sth in a pile: *They piled up the logs at the side of the house.* **3** (used about several cars, etc) to crash into each other

'pile-up noun [C] a crash that involves several cars, etc

piles /paɪlz/ noun [plural] = HAEMORRHOIDS

pilgrim /ˈpɪlgrɪm/ noun [C] a person who travels to a holy place for religious reasons: *Many pilgrims visit Mecca every year.*

pilgrimage /-ɪdʒ/ noun [C,U] a journey that is made by a pilgrim: *to make a pilgrimage to Lourdes*

pill /pɪl/ noun **1** [C] a small round piece of medicine that you swallow: *Take one pill, three times a day after meals.* ○ *a sleeping pill* ☛ Look at **tablet**. **2 the pill** (*also* **the Pill**) [sing] a pill that some women take regularly so that they do not become pregnant: *She is on the pill.*

pillar /ˈpɪlə(r)/ noun [C] **1** a column of stone, wood or metal that is used for supporting part of a building **2** an important and active member of sth: *a pillar of the local golf club*

'pillar-box noun [C] (*Brit*) a tall round red box in a public place into which you can post letters, which are then collected by a postman
☛ Look at **postbox**.

pillion /ˈpɪliən/ noun [C] a seat for a passenger behind the driver on a motor cycle

☆ **pillow** /ˈpɪləʊ/ noun [C] a large cushion that you put under your head when you are in bed
☛ picture at **bed**. You use a **pillow** in bed. In other places, eg on a chair, you use a **cushion**.

'pillowcase (*also* **'pillowslip**) noun [C] a cover for a pillow

☆ **pilot** /ˈpaɪlət/ noun [C] **1** a person who flies an aircraft: *Philip is an airline pilot.* **2** a person with special knowledge of a difficult area of water, who guides ships through it

pilot adj (only *before* a noun) done as an experiment or to test sth: *The pilot scheme will run for six months and then we will judge how successful it has been.*

pilot verb [T] **1** to guide or help sb/sth (through sth) **2** to act as the pilot of a vehicle

pimp /pɪmp/ noun [C] a man who controls prostitutes, finds customers for them and takes part of the money they earn

pimple /ˈpɪmpl/ noun [C] a small red spot on your skin

pins

pin

drawing-pin

safety pin

☆ **pin¹** /pɪn/ noun [C] **1** a short thin piece of metal with a round head at one end and a sharp point at the other. Pins are used for fastening together pieces of cloth, paper, etc. ☛ Look at **drawing-pin** and **safety pin**. **2** a small piece of wood or metal that is used for a particular purpose: *a hairpin*

'pinpoint *verb* [T] **1** to find the exact position of sth: *to pinpoint a place on the map* **2** to describe or explain exactly what sth is: *Once the cause of the failure has been pinpointed, we can decide what to do about it.*

,pins and 'needles *noun* [plural] (*informal*) the little pains that you get in a part of your body after it has been in one position for too long and when the blood is returning to it: *I've got pins and needles in my hand.*

pin² /pɪn/ *verb* [T] (pi**nn**ing; pi**nn**ed) **pin sth to/on sth**; **pin sth together** to fasten sth with a pin or pins: *Could you pin this notice on the board, please?* ○ *The dress is just pinned together. I've not sewn it yet.* ○ (*figurative*) *The policeman held him with his arms pinned to his sides.* ○ (*figurative*) *All our hopes are pinned on him.*

(PHRASAL VERBS) **pin sb/sth against/under sth** to keep sb/sth in one position so that it is impossible to move: *He was pinned under the fallen tree.* ○ *to be pinned against a wall*

pin sb down 1 to cause sb to be unable to move **2** to make sb decide sth or say exactly what he/she is going to do: *Can you pin her down and find out what time she will be coming?*

pin sth down to describe or explain exactly what sth is

'pin-up *noun* [C] (*informal*) a picture of an attractive person, in a magazine or pinned on a wall

pinafore /'pɪnəfɔː(r)/ *noun* [C] a piece of clothing for the front part of your body that you wear to keep your other clothes clean when you are cooking or doing dirty jobs ☛ Look at **apron**.

pincer /'pɪnsə(r)/ *noun* **1** [C] one of the two front claws of some shellfish that are used for catching and eating food **2 pincers** [plural] a tool that is used for holding things, pulling nails out of wood, etc

pinch /pɪntʃ/ *verb* [T] **1** to squeeze a piece of sb's skin tightly between your thumb and first finger: *The lesson was so boring I had to pinch myself to stay awake.* ○ *Paul pinched his brother and made him cry.* **2** (*informal*) to steal: *Someone's pinched my umbrella.*

pinch *noun* [C] **1** an act of pinching(1): *She gave him a little pinch on the arm.* **2** the amount of sth that you can pick up with your thumb and first finger: *a pinch of salt*

(IDIOMS) **at a pinch** if necessary but with some difficulty: *We really need three but we could manage with two at a pinch.*

take sth with a pinch of salt to believe that sth is probably not true or completely accurate

pinched *adj* (used about sb's face) thin and pale because of illness, cold, etc

pine¹ /paɪn/ *noun* **1** [C] (*also* **'pine tree**) a tall tree that has thin sharp leaves (**needles**) and woody fruit (**pine cones**): *a Swedish pine forest* ☛ Trees, like the pine, that do not lose their leaves in winter are called **evergreen**. **2** [U] the wood from pine trees (which is often used for making furniture): *a pine table*

pine² /paɪn/ *verb* [I] to be very unhappy because sb has died or gone away or because you cannot have sth that you want: *I hope you haven't been pining for me while I've been away.*

pineapple /'paɪnæpl/ *noun* [C,U] a large juicy fruit that is yellow inside and has a thick brown skin with sharp points. Pineapples grow in hot countries: *pineapple juice*

ping /pɪŋ/ *noun* [C] the short high noise that is made by a small bell or by a metal object hitting against sth hard —**ping** *verb* [I]: *The microwave oven will ping when the food is ready.*

ping-pong /'pɪŋpɒŋ/ *noun* [U] (*informal*) = TABLE TENNIS

☆ **pink** /pɪŋk/ *adj* pale red in colour: *Baby girls are often dressed in pink clothes.*

pink *noun* [U] a pink colour: *The bedroom was decorated in pink.*

pinkish *adj* rather pink

pinnacle /'pɪnəkl/ *noun* [C] **1** a pointed stone ornament on the top of a church or castle **2** a high rock on a mountain **3** the highest point of sth: *Mary is at the pinnacle of her career.*

☆ **pint** /paɪnt/ *noun* [C] **1** (*abbr* **pt**) a measure of liquid; 0·57 of a litre. There are 8 pints in a gallon: *a pint of milk* ☛ An American pint is 0·47 of a litre. **2** (*informal*) a pint of beer: *Let's have a pint at the pub.*

pioneer /,paɪə'nɪə(r)/ *noun* [C] **1** a person who is one of the first to go and live in a particular area: *the pioneers of the American West* **2** a person who is one of the first to do somewhere or do sth: *Yuri Gagarin was one of the pioneers of space exploration.*

pioneer *verb* [I,T] to be one of the first people or organizations to go somewhere, do sth or develop sth: *The hospital is famous for its pioneering work in heart surgery.*

pious /'paɪəs/ *adj* having or showing a deep belief in and love of religion —**piously** *adv* ☛ The noun is **piety**.

pip¹ /pɪp/ *noun* [C] the small seed of an apple, a lemon, or orange

pip² /pɪp/ *verb* (pi**pp**ing; pi**pp**ed)

(IDIOM) **pip sb at the post** to defeat sb at the last moment or by a small amount

☆ **pipe¹** /paɪp/ *noun* [C] **1** a hollow tube that carries gas or liquid: *The burglar climbed up a drainpipe and got in through an open window.* ○ *a gas-pipe* ○ *The hot-water pipe has burst.* **2** a small tube with a bowl at one end that is used for smoking tobacco: *Does Don smoke a pipe?* **3** a simple musical instrument that consists of a tube with holes. You blow into it to play it. **4 pipes** [plural] = BAGPIPES

'pipeline *noun* [C] a line of pipes¹(1) that are used for carrying liquid or gas: *The oil pipeline stretches from Iraq to the Turkish coast.*

(IDIOM) **in the pipeline** being planned or prepared

pipe² /paɪp/ *verb* **1** [T] to carry liquid or gas in pipes(1): *Water is piped to all the houses in the village.* ○ (*figurative*) *Many supermarkets have piped music playing all the time.* **2** [I,T] to play music on a pipe(3)

iː	ɪ	e	æ	ɑː	ɒ	ɔː	ʊ	uː	ʌ
see	sit	ten	hat	arm	got	saw	put	too	cup

piper /ˈpaɪpə(r)/ noun [C] a person who plays a pipe(3) or the bagpipes

pirate /ˈpaɪərət/ noun [C] **1** a sailor who attacks and robs ships at sea **2** a person who copies books, video tapes, computer programs, etc in order to sell them illegally
  piracy /ˈpaɪərəsi/ noun [U] **1** robbery by pirates **2** illegal copying of books, video tapes, etc
  pirate verb [T] to copy a book, video tape, etc in order to sell it

Pisces /ˈpaɪsiːz/ noun [C,U] the twelfth sign of the zodiac, the Fishes; a person who was born under this sign ☞ picture at **zodiac**.

pistol /ˈpɪstl/ noun [C] a small gun that you hold in one hand: *She aimed the pistol and fired.* ○ *a water-pistol* ☞ Look at the note at **gun**.

piston /ˈpɪstən/ noun [C] a piece of metal in an engine, etc that fits tightly inside a tube. The piston is moved up and down inside the tube and itself causes other parts of the engine to move.

pit[1] /pɪt/ noun [C] **1** a large hole that is made in the ground: *a gravel-pit* **2** = COALMINE: *to work down the pit* **3 the pits** [plural] the place near a race-track where cars stop for fuel, new tyres, etc during a race
  (IDIOM) **be the pits** (*informal*) (*especially US*) to be very bad: *The food in that restaurant is the pits!*

pit[2] /pɪt/ verb [T] (**pitting**; **pitted**) to make shallow holes in the surface of sth: *The front of the building was pitted with bullet marks.*
  (PHRASAL VERB) **pit sb/sth against sb/sth** to test sb/sth against sb/sth else in a fight or competition: *The two strongest teams were pitted against each other in the final.*

pitch[1] /pɪtʃ/ verb **1** [T] to set sth at a particular level: *The talk was pitched at people with far more experience than me.* ○ *a high-pitched voice* **2** [I,T] (to cause sb/sth) to fall over: *His bike hit a stone and he was pitched forwards over the handlebars.* **3** [I] (used about a ship or an aeroplane) to move up and down or from side to side **4** [T] to put up a tent or tents: *They pitched camp in the valley.* **5** [T] to throw sth (often a ball)
  (PHRASAL VERB) **pitch in** (*informal*) to join in and work together with other people: *Everybody has to pitch in when we're on holiday.*

pitch[2] /pɪtʃ/ noun **1** [C] a special area of ground where you play certain sports: *a cricket, football, hockey, etc pitch* ○ *on/off the pitch* ○ *The fans invaded the pitch when the match ended.* ☞ picture at **football**. Look at **court**. **2** [sing] the level of sth: *The children's excitement almost reached fever pitch.* **3** [U] the degree of highness or lowness of a musical note or a voice **4** [U] the movement of a ship or an aeroplane up or down or from side to side

pitch-black /ˌpɪtʃ ˈblæk/ (*also* **pitch-dark**) adj completely dark; with no light at all

pitcher /ˈpɪtʃə(r)/ noun [C] a large container for holding and pouring liquids ☞ In US English this is the usual word for **jug**.

piteous /ˈpɪtiəs/ adj (*formal*) that makes you feel pity or sadness —**piteously** adv

pitfall /ˈpɪtfɔːl/ noun [C] an unexpected danger; a mistake that you might easily make

pith /pɪθ/ noun [U] the white substance inside the skin of an orange, etc

pithy /ˈpɪθi/ adj expressed in a clear, direct way: *a pithy comment*

pitiful /ˈpɪtɪfl/ adj causing you to feel pity or sadness: *the pitiful groans of the wounded soldiers* ☞ Look at **pathetic**. —**pitifully** /-fəli/ adv: *The children were pitifully thin.*

pitiless /ˈpɪtɪləs/ adj having or showing no pity for other people's suffering —**pitilessly** adv

☆ **pity** /ˈpɪti/ noun **1** [U] a feeling of sadness that you have for sb/sth that is suffering or in trouble: *The dog was in such a terrible state that we took it home with us out of pity.* ○ *He showed no pity at the way they had been treated.* ○ *All I feel for her now is pity – I'm not angry any more.* **2** [sing] something that makes you feel a little sad or disappointed: *'You're too late. Emily left five minutes ago.' 'Oh, what a pity!'* ○ *Isn't it a pity that Jane couldn't come after all?* ○ *It would be a pity not to use the car now that we've got it.* ○ *'There's a street map in the car.' 'It's a pity you didn't think of it before.'*
  (IDIOM) **take pity on sb** to help sb who is suffering or in trouble because you feel sorry for him/her
  pity verb [T] (*pres part* **pitying**; *3rd pers sing pres* **pities**; *pt, pp* **pitied**) to feel pity or sadness for sb who is suffering or in trouble: *It is not enough to pity these people; we must try to help them.* ○ *I pity the person who has to clean his room!*

pitying adj showing pity: *a pitying look*

pivot /ˈpɪvət/ noun [C] the central point on which sth balances or turns
  pivot verb [I] to balance or turn on a central point

pixie (*also* **pixy**) /ˈpɪksi/ noun [C] (*pl* **pixies**) (in children's stories) a small person (a kind of fairy) who has magic powers

pizza /ˈpiːtsə/ noun [C,U] a round flat piece of dough (like bread) that is covered with tomatoes, cheese, onions, etc and cooked in an oven

placard /ˈplækɑːd/ noun [C] a large notice that is fixed onto a wall or carried (in a demonstration, etc)

placate /pləˈkeɪt; *US* ˈpleɪkeɪt/ verb [T] to make sb feel less angry

☆ **place**[1] /pleɪs/ noun [C] **1** a particular position or area: *No one can be in two places at once.* ○ *This is a good place for a picnic.* ○ *The wall was damaged in several places.* ○ *to mark your place in a book* (= where you have read to) ○ *Do you think that lamp is in the right place?* **2** a building, village, town, country, etc: *What is your place of birth?* ○ *Vienna is a very beautiful place.* ○ *a popular meeting-place for young people* **3** a seat or position for sb/sth: *They went into the classroom and sat down in their places.* ○ *Go on ahead and save me a place in the queue.* ○ *to lay six places for dinner* ☞ A **place** [C] is a seat or position for sb/sth: *If you arrive first, can you keep a place for me?* A place where you can park your car is also called a **space** [C]. You use **space** [U] and **room** [U] when you are talking

ɜː	ə	eɪ	əʊ	aɪ	aʊ	ɔɪ	ɪə	eə	ʊə
fur	ago	pay	home	five	now	join	near	hair	pure

about area in general: *This piano takes up a lot of space/room.* o *There is enough space/room for three people in the back of the car.* **4** your rank or position in society; your role: *I feel it is not my place to criticize my boss.* **5** an opportunity to study at a college, play for a team, etc: *Douglas has got a place to study law at Hull.* o *Lucy is now sure of a place in the England team.* **6** the usual or proper position or occasion for sth: *The room was tidy. Everything had been put away in its place.* o *I saw him at the funeral but it was not the place to discuss business.* **7** the position of a number after the decimal point: *Your answer should be correct to three decimal places.* **8** the position that you have at the end of a race, competition, etc: *Clare finished in second place.* **9** (*informal*) the house, etc where you live: *Why not stay the night at our place?*

(IDIOMS) **change/swap places (with sb)** to take sb's seat, position, etc and let him/her have yours: *Let's change places so that you can look out of the window.*

fall, fit, slot, etc into place (used about sth that is complicated or difficult to understand) to become organized or clear in your mind: *Pete spent two hours working on the timetable before it all fell into place.*

in the first, second, etc place (used when you are explaining or giving reasons for sth) firstly, secondly, etc

in my, your, etc place in my, your, etc situation or position: *If I were in your place I would wait a year before getting married.*

in place of sb/sth; in sb/sth's place instead of sb/sth: *The professor was too ill to travel but she sent one of her colleagues in her place.*

put yourself in sb else's/sb's place to imagine that you are sb else: *Put yourself in Steve's place and you will realize how worried he must be.*

out of place 1 not in the correct or usual place **2** not suitable for a particular situation: *I felt very out of place among all those clever people.*

take place to happen: *The ceremony took place in glorious sunshine.*

'place-name *noun* [C] the name of a city, town, hill, etc

☆ **place²** /pleɪs/ *verb* [T] **1** to put sth in a particular position or in its usual or proper position: *Dominic placed the cup on the table.* o *The chairs had all been placed in neat rows.* o *to place an advertisement in a newspaper* o (*figurative*) *We placed out trust in you and you failed us.* o (*figurative*) *The blame for the disaster was placed firmly on the company.* **2** to put sb in a particular position or situation: *His behaviour placed me in a difficult situation.* o *to place sb in charge* o *Jane was placed third.* **3** to remember who sb is or where you have seen them before **4** to give an order for sth to a person or company: *We placed an order for 150 T-shirts with a company in York.*

placid /'plæsɪd/ *adj* calm or not easily excited —**placidly** *adv*

plague /pleɪɡ/ *noun* **1** [C,U] a disease that spreads quickly and kills many people **2** [C] a large number of unpleasant animals or insects that come into an area at one time: *a plague of ants*

plague *verb* [T] to cause sb/sth trouble or discomfort: *The project was plagued by a series of disasters.*

plaice /pleɪs/ *noun* [C,U] (*pl* **plaice**) a type of flat sea-fish, eaten as food

☆ **plain¹** /pleɪn/ *adj* **1** (only *before* a noun) all one colour; without a pattern, etc: *Shall we have a plain or patterned carpet?* ← picture at **pattern**. **2** simple in style: *The rooms are quite plain, but very comfortable.* o *My father likes plain English cooking.* o *Do you prefer plain* (= dark and strong) *or milk chocolate?* **3** easy to see, hear or understand; clear: *It was plain that he didn't want to talk about it.* o *She made it plain that she didn't want to see me again.* o *His instructions were very plain.* **4** (used about people, thoughts, actions, etc) saying what you think; direct and honest: *I'll be plain with you. I don't like the idea.* **5** (used especially about a woman or girl) not beautiful: *She's a rather plain child.*

plain *adv* (*especially US*) completely: *That is plain wrong.*

plainly *adv* clearly: *Smoke was plainly visible nearly twenty miles away.* o *He was plainly very upset.*

,plain 'clothes *noun* [plural] (used in connection with the police) ordinary clothes; not uniform: *The detectives were in plain clothes.* o *a plain-clothes detective*

,plain 'flour *noun* [U] flour that does not contain a powder (**baking powder**) which makes cakes, etc rise ← Look at **self-raising flour.**

plain² /pleɪn/ *noun* [C] a large area of flat land with few trees: *the great plains of the American Midwest*

plain³ /pleɪn/ *noun* [C] a simple stitch used in knitting: *knit two plain, one purl*

plaintiff /'pleɪntɪf/ *noun* [C] (*formal*) a person who starts a legal action against sb in a court of law ← Look at **defendant.**

plaintive /'pleɪntɪv/ *adj* sounding sad —**plaintively** *adv*

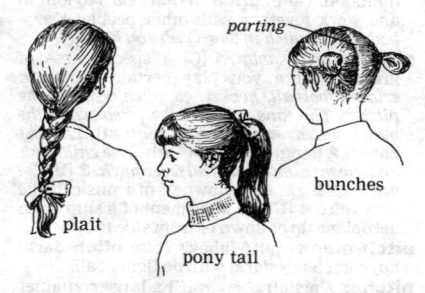

plait /plæt/ (*US* **braid**) *verb* [T] to twist three or more long thin pieces of hair, rope, etc over and under each other to make one thick piece

plait *noun* [C] a long piece of hair, rope, etc

p	b	t	d	k	ɡ	tʃ	dʒ	f	v	θ	ð
pen	bad	tea	did	cat	got	chin	June	fall	van	thin	then

that has been plaited: *to wear your hair in a plait/in plaits*

☆ **plan** /plæn/ *noun* [C] **1** an idea or arrangement for doing or achieving sth in the future: *Have you got any plans for the weekend?* ○ *We usually make our holiday plans in January.* ○ *The firm has no plans to employ more people.* ○ *The best plan is to ask him to meet us on Monday.* **2** a list, drawing or diagram that shows how sth is to be organized: *Before you start writing an essay, it's a good idea to make a brief plan.* **3** a map showing how a particular place is arranged: *a plan of the Safari Park* ○ *a street plan of Berlin* **4** a drawing that shows a building, part of a building, machine, road, etc as seen from different positions: *We're getting an architect to draw up some plans for a new kitchen extension.* ○ *You can study the plans for the motorway at the Town Hall.*

(IDIOM) **go according to plan** to happen as planned

plan *verb* (**plan**ning; **plan**ned) **1** [I,T] to decide, organize or prepare for sth: *to plan for the future* ○ *You need to plan your work more carefully.* **2** [I,T] **plan (on sth)** to intend doing sth: *I'm planning on having a holiday in July.* ○ *We're planning to arrive at about 4 o'clock.* **3** [T] to make a plan of or for sth; to design sth: *You need an expert to help you plan the garden.* ○ *The new shopping centre seems to be very badly planned.*

planning *noun* [U] making plans or arrangements: *The project requires careful planning.* ○ *Family planning* (= using contraception) *enables people to control the number of children they have.*

☆ **plane¹** /pleɪn/ *noun* [C] = AEROPLANE: *We boarded the plane in Geneva.* ○ *a plane ticket* ○ *Has her plane landed yet?* ○ *a Pan Am plane* ○ *a plane crash*

plane² /pleɪn/ *noun* [C] (*technical*) a flat surface

plane³ /pleɪn/ *noun* [C] a tool used for making the surface of wood smooth by taking very thin pieces off it —**plane** *verb* [T]

☆ **planet** /ˈplænɪt/ *noun* [C] a large body in space (like a star) that moves around the sun or another star: *the natural resources of our planet* (= of the Earth) ○ *The planets of our solar system are Mercury, Venus, Earth, Mars, Jupiter, Saturn, Uranus, Neptune and Pluto.*

planetarium /ˌplænɪˈteərɪəm/ *noun* [C] (*pl* **planetariums** or **planetaria** /-ɪə/) a building that contains an apparatus for showing the positions and movements of the planets and stars

plank /plæŋk/ *noun* [C] a long flat piece of wood (that is used for making floors, etc)

☆ **plant¹** /plɑːnt; *US* plænt/ *noun* **1** [C] a living thing that grows in earth and has a stem, leaves and roots: *a tomato plant* ○ *a house plant* (= one that grows in a pot inside a house) ○ *to water the plants* **2** [C] a building where an industrial process takes place; a large factory

☆ **plant²** /plɑːnt; *US* plænt/ *verb* [T] **1** to put plants, seeds, etc in the ground to grow: *Bulbs should be planted in the autumn.* **2 plant sth (with sth)** to cover or supply a garden, area of land, etc with plants: *It takes a lot of hard work to plan and plant a new garden.* ○ *The field's been planted with wheat this year.* **3** to put sb/sth firmly in a certain position: *He planted himself in the best seat.* **4 plant sth (on sb)** to hide sth somewhere for a secret and usually criminal purpose (sometimes in order to make sb seem guilty of a crime): *The police think that terrorists may have planted the bomb.* ○ *The women claimed that the drugs had been planted on them.*

plantation /plænˈteɪʃn; plɑːn-/ *noun* [C] **1** a large area of land, especially in a tropical country, where tea, cotton, tobacco, etc are grown **2** an area of land planted with trees: *plantations of fir and pine*

plaque¹ /plɑːk; *US* plæk/ *noun* [C] a flat piece of stone or metal that is fixed on a wall as a way of remembering a famous person or past event: *a memorial plaque*

plaque² /plɑːk; *US* plæk/ *noun* [U] a harmful substance that forms on teeth

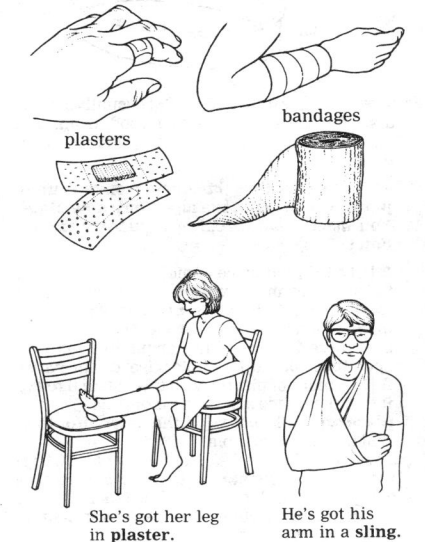

plasters

bandages

She's got her leg in **plaster**.

He's got his arm in a **sling**.

plaster /ˈplɑːstə(r); *US* ˈplæs-/ *noun* **1** [U] a soft mixture of sand, water, etc that becomes hard when it is dry. Plaster is put on walls and ceilings to form a smooth surface. **2** [C] a small piece of sticky material that is used to cover a cut, etc on the body: *a waterproof plaster* ☛ Another word for a plaster is a **sticking plaster**. **3** [U] a white substance that becomes hard when dry and is used for putting round broken bones, etc until they mend: *When Alan broke his leg it was in plaster for six weeks.*

plaster *verb* [T] **1** to cover a wall, etc with plaster(1) **2** to cover sth thickly with sth; to put things onto a surface: *The car was plastered with mud.* ○ *She had plastered her room with*

s	z	ʃ	ʒ	h	m	n	ŋ	l	r	j	w
so	zoo	she	vision	how	man	no	sing	leg	red	yes	wet

posters. ○ She had plastered pictures of the singer all over her room.

☆ **plastic** /'plæstɪk/ noun [C,U] a light, artificial material which does not break easily and is used for making many different sorts of objects: *A lot of kitchen utensils are made of plastic.* ○ *Plastics and other synthetic materials are commonly used today.*

plastic adj (used about goods) made of plastic: *plastic cups and spoons* ○ *a plastic bag*

,plastic 'surgery noun [U] doing a surgical operation to repair or replace damaged skin or to improve the appearance of a person's face or body: *Several of the fire victims needed plastic surgery.*

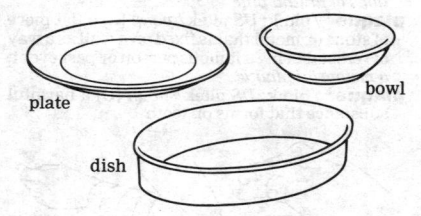

plate

bowl

dish

☆ **plate** /pleɪt/ noun **1** [C] a flat, usually round, dish for eating or serving food from: *Put the cake on a plate.* ○ *a plastic plate* ○ *a paper plate*

☞ You eat your main course from a **dinner plate**. You may put bread, etc on a **side plate**. You usually eat cereal or a pudding from a **bowl**.

2 [C] a thin flat piece of metal or glass **3** [C] a flat piece of metal with sth written on it: *I couldn't read the car's number-plate.* **4** [U] metal that has a thin covering of gold or silver: *gold plate* **5** [C] a picture or photograph in a book that takes up a whole page: *colour plates* **6** [C] a piece of plastic with false teeth fixed to it that fits inside a person's mouth

plateful /-fʊl/ noun [C] the amount of food that a plate(1) can hold

plateau /'plætəʊ; *US* plæ'təʊ/ noun [C] (pl **plateaus** or **plateaux** /-təʊz/) **1** a large area of high, flat land **2** a state where there is little development or change: *House prices seem to have reached a plateau.*

☆ **platform** /'plætfɔːm/ noun [C] **1** a raised floor in a public place, where people stand to make speeches or to perform **2** a flat raised surface, especially the area beside the track at a railway station where passengers get on and off trains: *Which platform does the train to York leave from?* **3** the ideas and aims of a political party, especially as expressed before an election

platinum /'plætɪnəm/ noun [U] a valuable greyish-white metal that is often used for making jewellery: *a platinum ring*

platonic /plə'tɒnɪk/ adj (used about a relationship between two people) not sexual

platoon /plə'tuːn/ noun [C] a small group of soldiers

plausible /'plɔːzəbl/ adj sounding as if it is true; reasonable: *a plausible excuse* ☞ The opposite is **implausible**.

☆ **play¹** /pleɪ/ *verb* **1** [I] to do sth to enjoy yourself; to have fun: *They've been playing on the beach all day.* ○ *He's playing with his new toy.* ○ *Jane's found a new friend to play with.* **2** [I,T] to take part in a sport, game or match: *'What about a game of chess?' 'I'm afraid I don't know how to play.'* ○ *Who's playing in the World Cup tonight?* ○ *I play football on Saturdays.* **3** [I,T] **play (sth) (with/against sb); play sb (at sth)** to compete against sb in a game or sport: *I usually play against Bob.* ○ *The school plays rugby against other schools nearby.* ○ *She played him at cards and won!* **4** [T] **play sth (on sb)** to do sth which may surprise or annoy sb for your own amusement: *School children often play tricks on their teachers.* **5** [I,T] to make music with a musical instrument: *My son's learning the piano. He plays very well.* ○ *She played a few notes of the tune on the violin.* ○ *Could you play that piece of music again?* ☞ We always use the definite article **the** before the names of musical instruments: *to play the piano* ○ *to learn the trumpet, etc.* **6** [T] to turn on a record, tape, etc so that it produces sound: *Shall I play the tape for you again?* **7** [I] (*formal*) to move quickly and lightly: *A smile played on her lips.*

(PHRASAL VERBS) **play at sth/being sth** to do sth with little interest or effort: *He's only playing at studying. He'd prefer to get a job now.* ○ *Whatever is that driver playing at?* (= doing)

play sth back (to sb) to turn on a tape or a film after recording the material on it: *We made a video of the occasion and played it back to all the guests before they left.*

play sth down to make sth seem less important than it really is: *to play down a crisis*

play A off against B to make people compete or argue with each other, especially for your own advantage: *I think she enjoys playing one boyfriend off against the other.*

play (sb) up to cause sb trouble or pain: *The car always plays up in wet weather.*

'**play-off** noun [C] a match between two teams or players who have equal scores, to decide the winner

☆ **play²** /pleɪ/ noun [U] **1** activity done for enjoyment only, especially by children: *Young children learn through play.* ○ *Everybody needs a balance of work and play.* **2** the playing of a game or sport; the way it is played: *Bad weather stopped play yesterday.* ○ *rough play* ☞ We **play** tennis, football, etc but we CANNOT say **a play** of tennis. We have **a game** of tennis.

(IDIOM) **fair play** ⇨ FAIR¹

'**playboy** noun [C] a rich man who spends his time enjoying himself and spending money

'**playground** noun [C] a public area of land where children can play: *the school playground*

'**plaything** noun [C] (*formal*) a toy

'**playtime** noun [C,U] a period of time when children at school can go outside to play

☆ **play³** /pleɪ/ noun [C] a story which is written to be performed by actors in the theatre, on tele-

iː	ɪ	e	æ	ɑː	ɒ	ɔː	ʊ	uː	ʌ
see	sit	ten	hat	arm	got	saw	put	too	cup

vision or radio: *Would you like to see/go to a play while you're in London?* o *a radio play* o *The children always put on a school play at Christmas.* o *the opening night of the play*

☛ Actors and actresses **rehearse** a play. A theatre company, drama group, etc **produces** a play. A play is usually acted on a **stage**.

play *verb* [I,T] to act a part in a play: *Simon is going to play Romeo.*

☛ **Play a part, role**, etc is often used in a figurative way: *Britain has played an active part in the recent discussions.* o *John played a key role in organizing the protest.*

playwright /'pleɪraɪt/ *noun* [C] a person who writes plays

☆ **player** /'pleɪə(r)/ *noun* [C] **1** a person who plays a game: *a game for two players* o *She's an excellent tennis player.* **2** a person who plays a musical instrument: *a piano player* **3** (*old-fashioned*) an actor

playful /'pleɪfl/ *adj* **1** done or said in fun; not serious: *a playful remark* **2** full of fun; lively: *a playful puppy*

playing-card /'pleɪɪŋ kɑːd/ *noun* [C] = CARD(4)

playing-field /'pleɪɪŋ fiːld/ *noun* [C] a large field used for sports such as cricket and football

plea /pliː/ *noun* [C] **1** a strong request; an appeal: *a last plea for mercy* **2** a statement made by sb in a court of law in which he/she claims to be guilty or not guilty of a certain crime: *a plea of guilty/not guilty*

plead /pliːd/ *verb* (*pt, pp* **pleaded**; *US* **pled** /pled/) **1** [I] **plead (with sb) (for sth)** to ask sb for sth in a very strong and serious way: *She pleaded with him not to leave her.* o *The hostages' families pleaded for their release.* **2** [T] to give sth as an excuse or explanation for sth: *He pleaded family problems as the reason for his lack of concentration.* **3** [I,T] **plead (for/against sb)** (*formal*) (used especially about a lawyer in a court of law) to support sb's case: *He needs the very best lawyer to plead for him.* **4** [T] (*formal*) (used about sb accused of a crime in a court of law) to say that you are guilty or not guilty: *The defendant pleaded not guilty to the charge of theft.*

☆ **pleasant** /'pleznt/ *adj* nice, enjoyable or friendly: *The weather was very pleasant.* o *What a pleasant surprise!* o *It must be pleasant to live in such a peaceful place.* o *He's a very pleasant young man.* o *My father's never very pleasant to my boyfriends.* ☛ The opposite is **unpleasant.** —**pleasantly** *adv*

☆ **please** /pliːz/ *verb* **1** [I,T] to make sb happy; to satisfy: *The shop assistant was a bit too eager to please.* o *I'll put on my best clothes to please my mother.* o *That teacher's very difficult to please.* **2** [I] (not used as the main verb in a sentence; used after words like *as, what, whatever, anything*, etc) to want; to choose: *You can't always do exactly as you please.* o *She has so much money she can buy anything she pleases.*

please *interj* (used as a polite way of making a request, an inquiry or giving an order): *Come in, please.* o *Is this the right road for Brighton, please?* o *Please don't spend too much money.* o *Sit down, please.* o *Two cups of coffee, please.*

☛ We do not use **please** in English when we are giving something to somebody.

(IDIOM) **yes, please** (used when you are accepting sth politely): *'Sugar?' 'Yes, please.'*

pleased *adj* (not before a noun) **pleased (with sb/sth); pleased to do sth** happy or satisfied: *John seems very pleased with his new car.* o *My parents aren't at all pleased with me at the moment.* o *We were very pleased to hear your wonderful news.* o *I'm pleased that you've decided to stay another week.* ☛ Look at the note at **glad**. The opposite is **displeased**.

pleasing *adj* giving pleasure: *The results are very pleasing, I must say.* ☛ The opposite is **displeasing**.

☆ **pleasure** /'pleʒə(r)/ *noun* **1** [U] the feeling of being happy or satisfied: *Parents get a lot of pleasure out of watching their children grow up.* o *He stood back and looked at his work with obvious pleasure.* o *It gives me great pleasure to introduce our next speaker.* **2** [U] enjoyment (rather than work): *Are you in Paris on business, or is it for pleasure?* **3** [C] an event or activity, that you enjoy or that makes you happy: *It's been a pleasure to work with you.* o *This car is a pleasure to drive.* o *'Thanks for your help.' 'It's a pleasure.'*

(IDIOMS) **take (no) pleasure in sth/doing sth** to enjoy/not enjoy (doing) sth

with pleasure (used as a polite way of saying that you are happy to accept or agree to sth): *'Could you give me a lift into town?' 'Yes, with pleasure.'*

pleasurable /'pleʒərəbl/ *adj* (*formal*) enjoyable: *a pleasurable experience*

pleat /pliːt/ *noun* [C] a fold that is sewn or pressed into a piece of cloth: *a skirt with pleats at the front*

pled (*US*) *pt, pp* of PLEAD

pledge /pledʒ/ *noun* [C] a promise or agreement: *The government made a pledge to bring down interest rates.*

pledge *verb* [T] **pledge (sth) (to sb/sth)** to promise to give or do sth: *They pledged their support to us.* o *The Government has pledged £250 000 to help the victims of the crash.* o *The President pledged to find a peaceful solution.* o *The management pledged that an agreement would be reached.*

plentiful /'plentɪfl/ *adj* available in large amounts or numbers: *Fruit is plentiful at this time of year.* ☛ Look at **scarce**.

☆ **plenty** /'plentɪ/ *pron* as much or as many as you need; a lot: *'Shall I get some more coffee?' 'No, we've still got plenty.'* o *Make sure you take plenty of warm clothes with you.* o *There's still plenty of time to get there.* o *Have you brought plenty to drink?*

plenty *adv* **1** (before *more*) a lot: *There's plenty more ice-cream.* **2** (with *big, long, tall*, etc followed by *enough*): *'This shirt's too small.' 'Well, it looks plenty big enough to me.'*

pliable /'plaɪəbl/ (*also* **pliant** /'plaɪənt/) *adj* **1** easy to bend or shape: *Plastic is more pliable* than wood. **2** (used about a person or a person's mind) easy to influence

pliers /'plaɪəz/ *noun* [plural] a tool that is used for holding things tightly, pulling nails out of wood, cutting wire, etc: *Have you got the/some pliers?* ○ *a pair of pliers* ☞ picture at **tool**.

plight /plaɪt/ *noun* [sing] (*formal*) a bad or difficult state or situation: *to be in an awful plight*

plimsoll /'plɪmsəl/ *noun* [C] (*Brit*) (*US* **sneaker**) a light shoe made of canvas that is especially used for sports, etc: *a pair of plimsolls* ☞ Look at **trainer**.

plod /plɒd/ *verb* [I] (plodding; plodded) **plod (along/on) 1** to walk slowly and in a heavy or tired way: *We plodded on through the rain for nearly an hour.* **2** to do sth or to work slowly and with difficulty: *I just plod on with the work day after day and never seem to get anywhere.*

plonk¹ /plɒŋk/ *noun* [sing] (*informal*) a sound of sth dropping heavily: *The tin fell onto the floor with a plonk.* —**plonk** *adv*: *The lamp fell plonk onto the floor.*

plonk *verb* [T] **plonk sth (down)** (*informal*) to put sth down or to drop sth heavily: *He plonked his suitcase down on my foot.*

plonk² /plɒŋk/ *noun* [U] (*informal*) (*Brit*) cheap wine: *Let's open a bottle of plonk!*

plop /plɒp/ *noun* (usually sing) a sound like that of a smooth object dropping into water: *With a tiny plop the ring disappeared into the water.*

plop *verb* [I] (plopping; plopped) to fall with a plop: *The fish plopped back into the water.*

☆ **plot¹** /plɒt/ *noun* [C] **1** a secret plan made by several people, to do sth that is wrong: *a plot to kill the Pope* **2** the events in a story, film, etc and how they develop: *The play had a very strong plot but the acting was terrible.* ○ *I can't follow the plot of this novel.*

plot *verb* [I,T] to make a secret plan to do sth: *They were accused of plotting against the government.* ○ *The terrorists had been plotting this campaign for years.*

plot² /plɒt/ *noun* [C] a small piece of land, used for a special purpose: *a vegetable plot* ○ *They're selling two plots of land for development.*

plot *verb* [T] (plotting; plotted) to mark sth on a map, diagram, graph, etc: *to plot the ship's course on the map* ○ *to plot the figures on a graph*

plough (*US* **plow**) /plaʊ/ *noun* [C] a large tool which is used on a farm and is pulled by a tractor or by an animal. A plough turns the soil over and is used especially before seeds are planted: *a snowplough* (= a tool like a plough that is used for clearing snow from roads)

plough (*US* **plow**) *verb* [I,T] to break up and turn over the soil, with a plough: *to plough the fields* ○ (*figurative*) *The book was long and boring but I managed to plough through it* (= read it with difficulty).

ploy /plɔɪ/ *noun* [C] something that you say or do in order to get what you want or to persuade sb to do sth: *He realized that her kindness had been a ploy to get him to stay.*

pluck /plʌk/ *verb* **1** [T] to pull sth in order to pick or remove it: *He plucked the letter from my hands.* ○ *to pluck your eyebrows* (= to pull out the hairs you do not want) **2** [I,T] **pluck (at sth)** to pull sth, often in order to get attention: *The little girl plucked at her mother's skirt.* **3** [T] to pull the feathers out of a chicken, etc in order to prepare it for cooking **4** [T] to pull the strings of a musical instrument and let them go again, in order to make music

(IDIOM) **pluck up courage** to try to be brave enough to do sth

pluck *noun* [U] (*informal*) courage

plucky *adj* (**pluckier**; **pluckiest**) brave

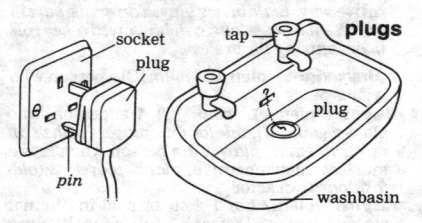

plug /plʌɡ/ *noun* [C] **1** a plastic or rubber object with two or three metal pins, which connects the wire on a piece of electrical equipment to a point in the wall where there is electricity (**a socket**): *Everybody should learn how to change a plug* (= to put on a new one). **2** (*informal*) = SOCKET: *I'll get the electrician to fit a plug beside the bed.* **3** a piece of rubber, metal or plastic that fits tightly into a hole (eg in a bath, basin, etc) **4** a favourable reference to a book, record, etc made in public in order to make people buy the thing mentioned

plug *verb* [T] (plugging; plugged) **1** to fill or block a hole with sth: *He managed to plug the leak in the pipe with a piece of plastic.* **2** (*informal*) to praise a book, record, etc in public in order to make people buy the thing mentioned: *They're really plugging that song on the radio at the moment.*

(PHRASAL VERB) **plug sth in** to connect sth to the electricity supply with a plug(1): *The video isn't plugged in.* ☞ The opposite is **unplug**.

'plug-hole *noun* [C] (*Brit*) a hole in a bath, sink, etc into which you put a plug(3)

plum /plʌm/ *noun* [C] a soft, round fruit with red or yellow skin and a stone in the middle

plumber /'plʌmə(r)/ *noun* [C] a person whose job is to put in and repair water-pipes, baths, sinks, etc

plumbing /'plʌmɪŋ/ *noun* [U] **1** all the pipes, water tanks, etc in a building: *The plumbing in this house is very old and noisy.* **2** the work of a person who puts in and repairs the water-pipes, tanks, etc

plume /plu:m/ *noun* [C] **1** a large and often bright feather **2** something worn in the hair or on a hat, made from feathers or long, thin pieces of material **3** a quantity of smoke that rises in the air

plump¹ /plʌmp/ *adj* (used about a person or an animal) rather fat (but looking nice): *the baby's plump cheeks* ○ *a nice, plump chicken*

plump² /plʌmp/ *verb*

(PHRASAL VERBS) **plump (oneself/sb/sth)**

down to sit down or to put sth down heavily: *She plumped herself down by the fire.*

plump for sb/sth to choose or decide to have: *I think I'll plump for the roast chicken, after all.*

plunder /'plʌndə(r)/ *verb* [I,T] to steal things from a place, especially during war or fighting: *They captured the city, killing and plundering as they advanced.*

plunder *noun* [U] **1** the act of stealing from people or places **2** the goods that are stolen: *to escape with the plunder*

plunge /plʌndʒ/ *verb* **1** [I] **plunge (into sth)** to go, jump, dive, fall, etc suddenly and with force into sth: *He turned and plunged into the crowd.* ○ *A woman plunged to her death from the cliffs at Beachy Head yesterday.* **2** [T] **plunge sth in/into sth** to push sth suddenly and with force into sth: *He plunged the knife into the woman's arm and ran off.* **3** [T] to cause sb/sth to be in the state mentioned: *The country has been plunged into chaos by the first snow of the winter.* **4** [I] **plunge into sth** to suddenly start or become involved in sth: *She plunged into the life of the village with enthusiasm.* **5** [I] to move suddenly downwards; to decrease: *The horse tripped and plunged to the ground.* ○ *The value of the pound plunged overnight.*

plunge *noun* [C] a sudden forward or downward movement, a dive, fall or decrease: *a plunge into cold water* ○ *the plunge in house prices*

(IDIOM) **take the plunge** to decide to do sth difficult after thinking about it for quite a long time

pluperfect /ˌpluːˈpɜːfɪkt/ *noun* [sing] (*grammar*) = PAST PERFECT

☆ **plural** /'plʊərəl/ *noun* [C] (*grammar*) the form of a noun, verb, etc which refers to more than one person or thing: *The plural of 'man' is 'men'.* ○ *The verb should be in the plural.*

plural *adj* (*grammar*) referring to more than one person or thing: *A plural noun must be followed by a plural verb.* ☞ Look at **singular**.

☆ **plus** /plʌs/ *prep* **1** and; added to: *Two plus two is four (2 + 2 = 4).* ☞ Look at **minus**. **2** as well as: *I've got an essay to write this evening plus some reading to do.*

plus *adj* (only *after* a noun) **1** or more: *He gets a salary of £30 000 plus.* **2** (used for marking work done by students) slightly above: *I got a B plus (written 'B+') for my homework.* ☞ Look at **minus**.

plus *noun* [C] **1** the sign (+): *He mistook a plus for a minus.* **2** an advantage: *The job involves a lot of travel, which is a definite plus.* ☞ Look at **minus**.

plush /plʌʃ/ *adj* smart and expensive: *a plush hotel*

Pluto /'pluːtəʊ/ *noun* [sing] the planet that is furthest from the sun

plutonium /pluːˈtəʊniəm/ *noun* [U] a radioactive substance used especially as a fuel in nuclear power stations

ply /plaɪ/ *verb* (*pres part* **plying**; *3rd pers sing pres* **plies**; *pt, pp* **plied** /plaɪd/) [I,T] (used about ships, boats, buses, etc) to travel regularly on a certain route: *ships that ply the Atlantic*

(PHRASAL VERB) **ply sb with sth** to keep giving sb food and drink, or asking sb questions: *He plied her with one glass of wine after another.*

plywood /'plaɪwʊd/ *noun* [U] board made by sticking thin layers of wood on top of each other

pneumonia /njuːˈməʊniə; *US* nuː-/ *noun* [U] a serious illness of the lungs which makes breathing difficult

poach[1] /pəʊtʃ/ *verb* [T] **1** to cook an egg without its shell in boiling water: *poached eggs* **2** to cook food (especially fish) in water or milk that is boiling gently

poach[2] /pəʊtʃ/ *verb* **1** [I,T] to catch or shoot birds, animals or fish on sb else's land without permission **2** [T] to take an idea from sb else and use it in an unfair way **3** [T] to take members of staff from another company

poacher *noun* [C] a person who catches birds, animals or fish on sb else's land without permission

☆ **pocket** /'pɒkɪt/ *noun* [C] **1** a small bag that is sewn inside or on sth you wear and is used for carrying things in: *He always walks with his hands in his trouser pockets.* ○ *a pocket dictionary, calculator, etc* (= one small enough to fit in your pocket) ☞ picture on page A11. **2** a bag or flap that is fixed to the inside of a car-door, suitcase, etc and used for putting things in: *There are safety instructions in the pocket of the seat in front of you.* **3** a small area or group of sth: *pockets of unemployment* ○ *a pocket of warm air*

(IDIOM) **pick sb's pocket** ⇨ PICK[1]

pocket *verb* [T] **1** to put sth in your pocket: *He took the letter and pocketed it quickly.* **2** to steal sth or to keep money for yourself

pocketful /-fʊl/ *noun* [C] the amount that a pocket holds

'pocketbook *noun* [C] **1** a small book or notebook **2** (*US*) = WALLET

'pocket knife *noun* [C] (*pl* **pocket knives**) = PENKNIFE

'pocket money *noun* [U] an amount of money that parents give a child, usually every week

pod /pɒd/ *noun* [C] the long, green part of some plants, such as peas and beans, that holds the seeds

podium /'pəʊdiəm/ *noun* [C] a small platform for a speaker, a performer, etc to stand on

☆ **poem** /'pəʊɪm/ *noun* [C] a piece of writing, often arranged in short lines which rhyme. Poems try to express thoughts and feelings with the help of sound and rhythm: *a Wordsworth poem* ○ *to write a poem*

☆ **poet** /'pəʊɪt/ *noun* [C] a person who writes poems ☞ There is a word **poetess** for a woman poet but it is rarely used nowadays.

poetic /pəʊˈetɪk/ (*also* **poetical** /-kl/) *adj* **1** beautiful and full of imagination **2** of or like poets and poetry: *poetic language* —**poetically** /-klɪ/ *adv*

☆ **poetry** /'pəʊɪtri/ *noun* [U] poems, thought of as a group or a form of literature: *Shakespeare's poetry and plays* ○ *poetry and prose*

poignant /'pɔɪnjənt/ *adj* causing sadness or pity: *a poignant memory*

poignancy /-jənsi/ *noun* [U] (*formal*) the

s	z	ʃ	ʒ	h	m	n	ŋ	l	r	j	w
so	zoo	she	vision	how	man	no	sing	leg	red	yes	wet

state or quality of being poignant —**poignantly** /-jəntlı/ adv

☆ **point¹** /pɔɪnt/ noun [C,sing] **1** [C] something that you say as part of a discussion; a particular fact, idea or opinion: *During the meeting she made some interesting points.* ○ *I see your point but I don't agree with you.* ☛ We **bring up, raise, make, argue, emphasize** and **illustrate** a point. **2** [C] an important idea or thought that needs to be considered: *'Supposing it rains – where shall we have the barbecue?' 'That's a point!'* **3 the point** [sing] the most important part of what is being said; the main piece of information: *The point is that we can't go on holiday until the car's been repaired.* ○ *She always talks and talks and takes ages to get to the point.* **4** [C] a detail, single item, quality of sb/sth: *What would you say are your strong and your weak points?* (= good and bad qualities) **5** [sing] the meaning, reason, purpose, etc of sth: *What's the point of telephoning her again?* ○ *There's no point in telling my parents all my problems.* **6** [C] (often in compounds) a particular place or position: *We should be reaching the point where the road joins the motorway.* ○ *The library is a good starting-point for that sort of information.* ○ *He aimed the gun at a point just above the man's head.* **7** [C] any of the 32 marks on a compass that show direction, especially North, South, East and West **8** [C] the thin sharp end of sth: *the point of a pin, needle, pencil,* etc **9 points** [plural] (*Brit*) a set of rails where a railway line divides into two tracks. Points can be moved to allow a train to use either track. **10** [C] a small round dot used when writing parts of numbers **11** [C] a particular time or moment; a stage of progress, development, etc: *At one point I thought I was going to laugh.* ○ *He has reached the high point of his career.* ○ *the boiling/freezing point of water* **12** [C] a single mark in some games, sports, etc that you add to others to get the score: *to score a point* ○ *After the first round of the competition Mrs Wilson had scored 32 points.* ○ *Agassi has two match points.* **13** [C] a unit of measurement for certain things: *The value of the dollar has fallen by a few points.*

(IDIOMS) **beside the point** not connected with the subject you are discussing

have your, etc **points** to have some good qualities

if/when it comes to the point if or when the moment to act or decide comes: *If it comes to the point I will have to tell him what I really think.*

make a point of doing sth to be especially careful to do sth: *I'll make a point of inviting them to our next party.*

on the point of doing sth just going to do sth: *I was on the point of going out when the bell rang.*

point of view a way of looking at a situation; an opinion: *You must try to understand other people's points of view.* ○ *From my point of view it would be better to wait a little longer.* ☛ Do not confuse **from my point of view** with **in my opinion**. The first means 'from my position in life' ie as a woman, child, teacher, etc. The second means 'I think': *From an advertiser's point of view, television is a wonderful medium.* ○ *In my opinion people watch too much television.*

prove your/the case/point ⇨ PROVE
a sore point ⇨ SORE
stretch a point ⇨ STRETCH
sb's strong point ⇨ STRONG
take sb's point to understand and accept what sb is saying: *I tried to explain what I meant but I don't think he took my point.*
to the point connected with what is being discussed: *His speech was short and to the point.*
up to a point partly: *I agree with you up to a point.*

☆ **point²** /pɔɪnt/ verb **1** [I] **point (at/to sb/sth)** to show where sth is or to draw attention to sth using your finger, a stick, etc: *'I'll have that one,' she said, pointing to a big chocolate cake.* **2** [T] **point sth (at/towards sb/sth)** to aim sth in the direction of sb/sth: *The farmer pointed his gun at the rabbit and fired.* **3** [I] to face in a particular direction or to show that sth is in a particular direction: *Go down this road and you'll see the sign pointing towards the motorway.* **4** [I] **point to sth** to show that sth is likely to exist, happen, be true, etc: *Research points to a connection between smoking and cancer.*

(PHRASAL VERB) **point sth out (to sb)** to direct attention to sth; to make sth clear to sb: *The guide pointed out all the places of interest to us on the way.* ○ *I'd like to point out that we haven't got much time left to decide the matter.*

pointed adj **1** having a point at one end: *a pointed nose* **2** done or spoken in a way that makes it clear that you are being critical: *She made a pointed comment about people who are always late.* —**pointedly** adv

point-blank /ˌpɔɪnt ˈblæŋk/ adj, adv **1** (used about sth that is said) in a way that is very direct and often rather rude; not allowing any discussion: *He told her point-blank to get out of the house.* **2** (used about a shot) from a very close position: *The shot was fired at point-blank range.*

pointer /ˈpɔɪntə(r)/ noun [C] **1** a piece of helpful advice or information: *Could you give me some pointers on how best to tackle the problem?* **2** a stick or rod which is used to point to things on a map, etc.

pointless /ˈpɔɪntlɪs/ adj without any use or purpose: *It's pointless to try and make him agree.* ○ *My whole life seemed pointless after my husband died.* —**pointlessly** adv **pointlessness** noun [U]

poise /pɔɪz/ noun [U] a calm, confident way of behaving: *The job requires poise and an ability to deal with people.*

poised adj **1** not moving but ready to move: *'Shall I call the doctor or not?' he asked, his hand poised above the telephone.* **2 poised (to do sth)** ready to act; about to do sth: *The government is poised to take action if the crisis continues.* **3** calm and confident

☆ **poison** /ˈpɔɪzn/ noun [C,U] a substance that kills or harms you if you eat or drink it: *The label on the bottle said, 'Poison. Not to be taken internally.'* ○ *rat poison* ○ *poison gas*

poison verb [T] **1** to give poison to sb/sth; to kill, harm or damage sb/sth with poison: *The police confirmed that the murder victim had been poisoned.* **2** to put poison in sth: *The cup of coffee had been poisoned.* **3** to spoil or ruin sth: *The quarrel had poisoned their relationship.*

poisoned adj **1** containing poison: *a poisoned drink* **2** damaged by dangerous substances: *our poisoned water*

poisoner /ˈpɔɪzənə(r)/ noun [C] a person who uses poison to murder sb

poisoning /ˈpɔɪzənɪŋ/ noun [U] the giving or taking of poison or a dangerous substance: *His death was the result of poisoning.* ○ *food poisoning* (= illness as a result of eating bad food)

poisonous /ˈpɔɪzənəs/ adj **1** causing death or illness if you eat or drink it: *a poisonous plant* **2** (used about animals, etc) producing and using poison to attack its enemies: *poisonous snakes, insects, etc* **3** very unpleasant: *She wrote him a poisonous letter criticizing his behaviour.*

poke /pəʊk/ verb [T] **1** to push sb/sth with a finger, stick or other long, thin object: *He poked the insect with his finger to see if it was alive.* **2 poke sth into, through, out of, down, etc** to push sth quickly into sth or in a certain direction: *'Hello Jane,' she called, poking her head out of the window.* ○ *He poked the stick down the hole to see how deep it was.*
(IDIOMS) **poke fun at sb/sth** to make jokes about sb/sth, often in an unkind way
poke/stick your nose into sth ⇨ NOSE¹
(PHRASAL VERBS) **poke about/around** (*informal*) to try to find sth by looking behind, under, etc things: *I noticed that somebody had been poking about in my desk.*
poke out of/through sth; poke out/through/up to appear in a certain place in a sudden or surprising way: *A rabbit's head poked up in the middle of the field and then disappeared.*

poke noun [C] a sharp push: *I gave him a poke in the side to wake him up.*

poker¹ /ˈpəʊkə(r)/ noun [C] a metal stick for moving the coal or wood in a fire ☛ picture at **fireplace**.

poker² /ˈpəʊkə(r)/ noun [U] a type of card game usually played to win money: *a game of poker*

poky /ˈpəʊki/ adj (**pokier; pokiest**) (*informal*) (used about a house, room, etc) too small: *It's a nice house but the bedrooms are a bit poky.*

polar /ˈpəʊlə(r)/ adj (only *before* a noun) of or near the North or South Pole: *the polar regions*

polar bear noun [C] a large white bear that lives in the area near the North Pole

☆ **pole¹** /pəʊl/ noun [C] either of the two points at the exact top and bottom of the earth: *the North/South Pole* ☛ picture at **earth**.

pole² /pəʊl/ noun [C] a long, thin piece of wood or metal, used especially to hold sth up: *a flagpole* ○ *a tent pole*

the ˈpole-vault noun [C] the sport of jumping over a high bar with the help of a long pole

☆ **police** /pəˈliːs/ noun [plural] the official organization whose job is to make sure that people obey the law, and to prevent and solve crime, etc: *Dial 999 if you need to call the police.* ○ *Have the police been informed of the incident?* ○ *a police car* ○ *a police report* ○ *There were over 100 police on duty* (= members of the police). ☛ **Police** is a plural noun, always used with a plural verb. You cannot say 'a police' meaning one man or woman. When we are talking about the organization, we always use **the**: *The police are investigating the murder.*

police verb [T] to keep control in a place by using the police or a similar official group: *The cost of policing football games is extremely high.*

poˌlice ˈconstable (*also* **constable**) noun [C] (*abbr* **PC**) a policeman or policewoman of the lowest rank

poˈlice force noun [C] (the organization of) all the police officers in a country or area: *We don't have a national police force in Britain.* ○ *the Thames Valley Police Force*

poˈliceman /-mən/ noun [C] (*pl* **policemen** /-mən/) a man who is a member of the police

poˈlice officer (*also* **officer**) noun [C] a policeman or policewoman: *a plain-clothes police officer* (= one who is not wearing uniform) ☛ Look at **detective**.

poˈlice station noun [C] an office of a local police force

poˈlicewoman noun [C] (*pl* **-women**) a woman who is a member of the police

☆ **policy¹** /ˈpɒləsi/ noun [C,U] (*pl* **policies**) **policy** (**on sth**) a plan of action or statement of aims and ideas, especially that of a government, company or other organization: *Labour has a new set of policies on health and education.* ○ *It is company policy not to allow smoking in meetings.* ☛ Look at the note at **politics**.

policy² /ˈpɒləsi/ noun [C] (*pl* **policies**) a document that shows an agreement that you have made with an insurance company: *an insurance policy*

polio /ˈpəʊliəʊ/ (*also formal* **poliomyelitis** /ˌpəʊliəʊˌmaɪəˈlaɪtɪs/) noun [U] a serious disease which can cause you to lose the power in certain muscles

polish /ˈpɒlɪʃ/ verb [T] to make sth shine by rubbing it and often by putting a special cream or liquid on it: *Don't forget to polish your shoes!*
(PHRASAL VERB) **polish sth off** (*informal*) to finish sth quickly: *I'm just going to polish off one or two jobs and then I'll join you.*

polish noun **1** [U] a cream, liquid, wax, etc that you put on sth to clean it and make it shine: *a tin of shoe polish* **2** [sing] an act of polishing: *I'll give the glasses a quick polish before the guests arrive.*

polished adj **1** shiny because of polishing: *polished wood floors* **2** (used about a performance, etc) of a high standard: *a polished performance of Mozart's 'Magic Flute'*

☆ **polite** /pəˈlaɪt/ adj having or showing good manners, eg that you are helpful and thoughtful towards other people and do not say or do things that might upset them; not rude: *The assistants in that shop are always very helpful and polite.* ○ *It's polite to say thank you.* ○ *He gave me a polite smile.* ☛ The opposite is **impolite**. —**politely** adv —**politeness** noun [U]

☆ **political** /pəˈlɪtɪkl/ adj **1** connected with polit-

ɜː	ə	eɪ	əʊ	aɪ	aʊ	ɔɪ	ɪə	eə	ʊə
fur	ago	pay	home	five	now	join	near	hair	pure

ics and government: *The two main political parties are Conservative and Labour.* ○ *She has very strong political opinions.* ○ *a political prisoner* (= one who has been put in prison for criticizing the government) ○ *Michael White, political correspondent of the 'Guardian'* **2** (used about people) interested or active in politics: *I'm afraid I'm not very political.*

politically /-klɪ/ *adv* with regard to politics: *Politically he's fairly right wing.*

po,litical a'sylum *noun* [U] protection given by a state to a person who has left his/her own country for political reasons: *to seek political asylum*

☆ **politician** /ˌpɒlɪˈtɪʃn/ *noun* [C] a person whose job is in politics, especially one who is a member of parliament or of the government: *a Conservative politician* ○ *Politicians of all parties supported the war.*

☆ **politics** /ˈpɒlətɪks/ *noun* **1** [U, with sing or pl verb] the work and ideas that are connected with governing a country, a town, etc: *Are you interested in politics?* ○ *My son wants to go into politics* (= become a politician). ○ *local politics* ○ *Politics has/have never been of great interest to me.* **2** [plural] a person's political opinions and beliefs: *What are your politics?* ☛ A government's **policy** (= plan of action or aim) will depend on its **politics** (= its ideas and beliefs). **3** [U] the scientific study of government: *She studied Politics, Philosophy and Economics at university.*

poll¹ /pəʊl/ *noun* [C] **1** (*also* **opinion poll**) a way of finding out public opinion by asking a number of people their views on sth: *The Conservatives had a five point lead over Labour in the latest poll.* **2** (giving votes at) a political election: *The result of the poll is still uncertain.* ○ *There was a heavy poll at the local elections* (= a large number of people voted).

'poll tax *noun* [sing] a tax to pay for local services. Every adult in a particular area must pay at the same rate.

poll² /pəʊl/ *verb* [T] **1** to ask sb his/her opinion on a subject: *Of those polled, only 20 per cent were in favour of changing the law.* **2** to receive a certain number of votes in an election: *The Liberal Democrat candidate polled over 3000 votes.*

polling *noun* [U] voting in an election: *Polling takes place today in the Henley by-election.*

'polling-day *noun* [C] the day when people vote in an election

pollen /ˈpɒlən/ *noun* [U] a fine, usually yellow, powder which is formed in flowers. It makes other flowers of the same type produce seeds when it is carried to them by the wind, insects, etc.

☆ **pollute** /pəˈluːt/ *verb* [T] to make air, rivers, etc dirty and dangerous: *Almost all of Britain's beaches are polluted.*

pollutant /-ənt/ *noun* [C] a substance that pollutes air, water, etc

pollution /pəˈluːʃn/ *noun* [U] **1** the act of polluting: *Major steps are being taken to control the pollution of beaches.* **2** substances that pollute: *Five years after the disaster the pollution on the coast of Alaska has still not been cleared.*

polo /ˈpəʊləʊ/ *noun* [U] a game for two teams of horses and riders. The players try to score goals by hitting a ball with long wooden hammers.

polo neck /ˈpəʊləʊ nek/ *noun* [C] a high collar (on a sweater, etc) that is rolled over and that covers most of your neck: *I'd like a jumper with a polo neck.* ☛ picture on page A11. The sweater itself can also be called a **polo neck**.

poly /ˈpɒli/ *noun* [C] (*pl* **polys**) (*informal*) = POLYTECHNIC

polyester /ˌpɒliˈestə(r)/; *US* ˈpɒliestər/ *noun* [U] a type of man-made material that is used for making clothes, etc: *The sheets are half cotton and half polyester.*

polystyrene /ˌpɒliˈstaɪriːn/ *noun* [U] a light firm plastic substance that is used for stopping heat from escaping or for packing things so that they do not get broken

polytechnic /ˌpɒliˈteknɪk/ (*also informal* **poly**) *noun* [C] (formerly in Britain) a college for students who are 18 or over, offering more practical courses than those at traditional universities. Since 1992 polytechnics have had university status.

polythene /ˈpɒliθiːn/ *noun* [U] a type of very thin plastic material often used to make bags for food or to keep things dry

polyunsaturated /ˌpɒliʌnˈsætʃəreɪtɪd/ *adj* (used about fats and oils) having the type of chemical structure that is thought to be good for your health: *polyunsaturated margarine*

pomp /pɒmp/ *noun* [U] the splendid nature of a public ceremony: *the pomp of the royal tour of Australia*

pompous /ˈpɒmpəs/ *adj* feeling or showing that you think you are more important than other people, eg by using long and important-sounding words ☛ This word is used in a critical way.

pond /pɒnd/ *noun* [C] an area of water that is smaller than a lake ☛ A **lake** is usually big enough to sail on: *a boating lake*. A **pond** may be big enough for animals to drink from or may be a very small area of water in a garden: *We have a fish pond in our garden.* A **pool** is a much smaller area of water: *When the tide went out, pools of water were left among the rocks.*

ponder /ˈpɒndə(r)/ *verb* [I,T] **ponder** (**on**/**over sth**) to think about sth carefully or for a long time

pong /pɒŋ/ *noun* [C] (*Brit informal*) a strong unpleasant smell —**pong** (*Brit informal*) *verb* [I]

pony /ˈpəʊni/ *noun* [C] (*pl* **ponies**) a type of small horse

'pony-tail *noun* [C] long hair that is tied at the back of the head and that hangs down like the tail of a horse ☛ picture at plait.

'pony-trekking *noun* [U] riding horses for pleasure in the country (often for several days, as a holiday)

poodle /ˈpuːdl/ *noun* [C] a type of dog with thick curly hair that is often cut into a special pattern

pooh /puː/ *interj* (*informal*) (used when you smell sth unpleasant)

☆ **pool¹** /puːl/ *noun* [C] **1** a small shallow area of

pool water: *The heavy rain left pools of water on the pavement.* o *rock pools* ☛ Look at **puddle** and at the note at **pond**. **2** a small area of any liquid or of light: *They found her lying in a pool of blood.* o *a pool of light* **3** = SWIMMING-POOL: *a heated indoor pool* o *He swam ten lengths of the pool.*

pool² /puːl/ *noun* **1** [C] a quantity of money, goods, workers, etc that is shared between a group of people: *There is a pool of cars that anyone in the company can use.* **2** [U] an indoor game that is played on a table with 16 coloured and numbered balls. Two players try to hit these balls into holes in the table (**pockets**) with long thin sticks (**cues**). ☛ Look at **billiards** and **snooker**. **3 the pools** [plural] = FOOTBALL POOLS

pool *verb* [T] to collect money, ideas, etc from a number of people and share them: *If we pool our ideas we should come up with a good plan.*

☆ **poor** /pɔː(r); *US* pʊər/ *adj* **1** having very little money and a very low standard of living: *The family was too poor to buy proper food.* o *We have a duty to help poorer countries.* ☛ The opposite is **rich**. **2** of low quality or in a bad condition: *Paul is in very poor health.* o *a poor harvest* o *The industry has a poor safety record.* o *Attendance at the meeting was poor* (= not as many people came as had been expected). **3** (used when you are showing that you feel sorry for somebody): *That poor child has lost both her parents.* o *Poor Don! He's very upset!*

the poor *noun* [plural] people who have little money ☛ Note that we use **the poor** in the plural. It always means 'poor people' and CANNOT mean 'the poor person'.

poorly¹ /ˈpɔːli; *US* ˈpʊərli/ *adv* not well; badly: *a poorly-paid job* o *The science lab is very poorly equipped.*

poorly² /ˈpɔːli; *US* ˈpʊərli/ *adj* (*informal*) not well; ill: *I'm feeling a bit poorly.*

pop¹ /pɒp/ *noun* **1** [C] a short sharp sound like a small explosion: *There was a loud pop as the champagne cork came out of the bottle.* **2** [U] (*informal*) a sweet drink with bubbles in it that does not contain alcohol. —**pop** *adv*: *The balloon went pop.*

pop² /pɒp/ *verb* (**popping**; **popped**) [I,T] (to cause sth) to make a short sharp sound like a small explosion: *The balloon popped.* o *He popped the balloon.*

(PHRASAL VERBS) **pop across**, **down**, **out**, **etc** to come or go somewhere quickly or suddenly: *I'm just popping out to the shops.*

pop sth across, **in**, **into**, **etc sth** to put or take sth somewhere quickly or suddenly: *He popped his head round the door and said goodbye.*

pop in to make a quick visit: *Why don't you pop in for a cup of tea?*

pop out to come out (of sth) suddenly or quickly: (*figurative*) *Her eyes nearly popped out of her head in surprise.*

pop up (*informal*) to appear or happen when you are not expecting it

popcorn /ˈpɒpkɔːn/ *noun* [U] a type of corn (**maize**) that is heated until it bursts and becomes light and fluffy

☆ **pop³** /pɒp/ *noun* [U] (*informal*) modern music that is most popular among young people: *I like pop and jazz.* o *pop music* o *a pop group* ☛ Look at **jazz**, **rock** and **classical**.

pop⁴ /pɒp/ *noun* [C] (*US informal*) father

☆ **pope** /pəʊp/ *noun* [C] the head of the Roman Catholic Church: *Pope John Paul*

popper /ˈpɒpə(r)/ (*Brit*) (*also* **press-stud**) *noun* [C] two round pieces of metal or plastic that you press together in order to fasten a piece of clothing ☛ picture at **zip**.

poppy /ˈpɒpi/ *noun* [C] (*pl* **poppies**) a bright red wild flower that has small black seeds: *a roll with poppy seeds on top*

popsicle /ˈpɒpsɪkl/ *noun* [C] (*US*) = ICE LOLLY

☆ **popular** /ˈpɒpjələ(r)/ *adj* **1** liked by many people or by most people in a group: *Discos are popular with young people.* o *Spain is a popular holiday destination.* o *He's always been very popular with his pupils.* ☛ The opposite is **unpopular**. **2** for ordinary people (= not for specialists or people with a high level of education): *The popular newspapers seem more interested in scandal than news.* **3** (only *before* a noun) of or for a lot of people: *The programme is being repeated by popular demand.*

popularity /ˌpɒpjuˈlærəti/ *noun* [U] the quality or state of being liked by many people: *The Green Party has been gaining in popularity recently.* o *to lose popularity*

popularize (*also* **popularise**) /ˈpɒpjələraɪz/ *verb* [T] to make sth popular with, or known to, a lot of people: *The film did a lot to popularize her novels.*

popularly *adv* by many people; generally: *The Conservatives are popularly known as Tories.*

populate /ˈpɒpjuleɪt/ *verb* [T] (usually passive) to fill a particular area with people: *Parts of Wales are very thinly populated.* o *Britain as a whole is very densely populated.*

☆ **population** /ˌpɒpjuˈleɪʃn/ *noun* **1** [C,U] a number of people who live in a particular place: *What is the population of your country?* o *an increase/a fall in population* **2** [C] all the people who live in a particular area: *The report examines the effects of the changes on the local population.* o *The local population is/are very much against the changes.* **3** [C] all the people or animals of a particular type that live in an area: *The prison population has greatly increased in recent years.* o *the black population of South Africa* o *the civilian population* (= the people who are not soldiers) o *the penguin population of the island* ☛ In senses 2 and 3, **population** is sometimes used in the singular with a plural verb when you are thinking about the individual people who form the population.

porcelain /ˈpɔːsəlɪn/ *noun* [U] a hard white substance that is made by baking clay in an oven. Porcelain is used for making expensive cups, plates, etc.

porch /pɔːtʃ/ *noun* [C] **1** a covered area at the entrance to a house or church **2** (*US*) = VERANDA

pore¹ /pɔː(r)/ *noun* [C] one of the small holes in your skin through which sweat can pass

pore² /pɔː(r)/ *verb*

(PHRASAL VERB) **pore over sth** to study or read sth very carefully

pork /pɔːk/ *noun* [U] meat from a pig: *roast pork* ○ *pork sausages* ☛ Look at **bacon** and **ham** and at the note at **meat**.

pornography /pɔːˈnɒɡrəfi/ (*also informal* **porn** /pɔːn/) *noun* [U] books, magazines, films, etc that describe or show sexual acts in order to cause sexual excitement —**pornographic** /ˌpɔːnəˈɡræfɪk/ *adj*: *pornographic films*

porous /ˈpɔːrəs/ *adj* allowing liquid or air to pass through slowly: *Sand is a porous material.*

porpoise /ˈpɔːpəs/ *noun* [C] a sea animal that looks like a large fish. It is very similar to a dolphin and also lives in groups.

porridge /ˈpɒrɪdʒ; *US* ˈpɔːr-/ *noun* [U] a food that is made from oats mixed with milk or water and usually eaten for breakfast

☆ **port**[1] /pɔːt/ *noun* **1** [C,U] an area where ships load and unload goods and passengers: *a fishing port* ○ *The fleet spent two days in port.* ○ *The damaged ship reached port safely.* **2** [C] a town or city that has a harbour: *Hull is a major port.*

port[2] /pɔːt/ *noun* [U] the side of a ship that is on the left when you are facing towards the front of the ship ☛ The opposite is **starboard**.

port[3] /pɔːt/ *noun* [U] a strong sweet red wine that is often drunk after a meal

portable /ˈpɔːtəbl/ *adj* that can be moved or carried easily: *a portable television set*

porter /ˈpɔːtə(r)/ *noun* [C] **1** a person whose job is to carry suitcases, etc at a railway station, airport, etc **2** a person whose job is to be in charge of the entrance of a hotel or other large building: *a hotel porter*

porthole /ˈpɔːthəʊl/ *noun* [C] a small round window in a ship or an aeroplane

portion /ˈpɔːʃn/ *noun* [C] **1** a part or share of sth: *What portion of your salary goes on tax?* ○ *We must both accept a portion of the blame.* **2** an amount of food for one person (especially in a restaurant): *Could we have two extra portions of chips, please?* ☛ Look at **helping**.

portrait /ˈpɔːtreɪt/ *noun* [C] **1** a picture, painting or photograph of a person: *to paint sb's portrait* **2** a description of sb/sth in words

portray /pɔːˈtreɪ/ *verb* [T] **1** to make a picture, painting or photograph of sb: *The writer was portrayed sitting at his desk.* **2** to describe sb/sth in words; to show sb/sth in a particular way: *Dickens portrayed life in 19th century England.* ○ *In many of his novels life is portrayed as being hard and brutal.* **3** to act the part of sb in a play or film: *It's hard for a young actress to portray a very old woman.* —**portrayal** /pɔːˈtreɪəl/ *noun* [C]: *He won an award for his portrayal of King Lear.*

pose /pəʊz/ *verb* **1** [I] to sit or stand in a particular position for a painting, photograph, etc: *After the wedding we all posed for photographs.* **2** [I] to behave in a way that makes other people notice you: *They hardly swam at all. They just sat posing at the side of the pool.* **3** [I] **pose as sb/sth** to pretend to be sb/sth: *The robbers got into the house by posing as telephone engineers.* **4** [T] to set, cause or create sth: *The rise in the cost of living is posing problems for many families.* ○ *to pose a question*

pose *noun* [C] **1** a position in which you pose, eg for a painting or photograph **2** a way of behaving that is intended to trick people or to make people notice you

posh /pɒʃ/ *adj* (*informal*) **1** fashionable and expensive: *We went for a meal in a really posh hotel.* **2** (used about people) belonging to or typical of a high social class: *He's got a really posh accent.*

☆ **position** /pəˈzɪʃn/ *noun* **1** [C,U] the place where sb/sth is or should be: *The enemy's position was marked on the map.* ○ *That plant's in the wrong position. It doesn't like too much sun.* ○ *All the dancers were in position waiting for the music to begin.* **2** [C,U] the way in which sb/sth sits, stands or is placed: *I've got a stiff neck. I must have been sitting in an awkward position.* ○ *Turn the switch to the off position.* ○ *He woke in pain every time he changed position.* **3** [C] **a position (on sth)** what you think about sth; your opinion: *What is your government's position on South Africa?* **4** [C, usually sing] a state or situation: *What would you do if you were in my position?* ○ *I'm in a very difficult position.* ○ *I'm sorry, I'm not in a position to help you financially.* **5** [C,U] your place or rank in society, in a group, or in a race or competition: *Max finished the race in second position.* **6** [C] a job: *There have been over a hundred applications for the position of Sales Manager.* **7** [C] the part you play in a team game: *'What position do you play?' 'I'm the goalkeeper.'*

position *verb* [T] to put sb/sth in a particular place or position: *Mary positioned herself near the door so she could get out quickly.*

☆ **positive** /ˈpɒzətɪv/ *adj* **1 positive (about sth/that**...) certain; sure: *Are you positive that this is the woman you saw?* **2** clear; definite: *There is no positive evidence that he is guilty.* ○ *We must take positive action to stop the situation getting worse.* **3** helpful or encouraging: *The teacher tried to make positive suggestions.* ○ *Their reaction to my idea was generally positive.* **4** hopeful or confident: *I feel very positive about our team's chances this season.* ○ *Positive thinking will help you to succeed.* **5** (used about a medical or scientific test) showing that sth has happened or is present: *The result of the pregnancy test was positive.* **6** (used about a number) more than zero ☛ In senses 3-6 the opposite is **negative**.

positively *adv* **1** (*informal*) really; extremely: *Mother was positively furious when I told her.* **2** quite certainly or firmly: *I was positively convinced that I was doing the right thing.*

☆ **possess** /pəˈzes/ *verb* [T] **1** (*formal*) to have or own: *They lost everything they possessed in the fire.* ○ *It is illegal to possess a gun without a licence.* **2** to influence sb or to make sb do sth: *Whatever possessed you to say a thing like that!*

possessor *noun* [C] a person who has or owns sth

☆ **possession** /pəˈzeʃn/ *noun* **1** [U] the state of having or owning sth: *Enemy forces took possession of the hill.* ○ *He was arrested for pos-*

session of an illegal weapon. **2** [C, usually pl] something that you have or own: *Bob packed all his possessions into a suitcase and left without a word.* ○ *to insure your possessions*
(IDIOM) **in possession (of sth)** having or owning sth: *Two youths were caught in possession of stolen goods.*

possessive /pə'zesɪv/ *adj* **1** not wanting to share sb/sth: *Dan is so possessive with his toys – he won't let anyone else play with them.* **2** (used in grammar to describe words that show who or what a person or thing belongs to): *'My', 'your', 'his' are possessive adjectives.* ○ *'Mine', 'yours', 'his' are possessive pronouns.*

☆ **possibility** /,pɒsə'bɪləti/ *noun* (*pl* **possibilities**) **1** [U] **possibility (of sth/of doing sth)**; **possibility (that…)** the situation when sth might happen or be true; the state of being possible: *Is there any possibility that I can see you this weekend?* ○ *What's the possibility of the weather getting better before the weekend?* ○ *There's not much possibility of the letter reaching you before Saturday.* **2** [C] something that might happen or be true; sth that is possible: *There is a strong possibility that the fire was started deliberately.* ○ *One possibility would be for you to go by train and for me to come later by car.*

☆ **possible** /'pɒsəbl/ *adj* **1** that can happen or be done: *I'll phone you back as soon as possible.* ○ *It is now possible to phone America direct.* ○ *Could you give me your answer today, if possible?* ○ *The doctors did everything possible to save his life.* ○ *You were warned of all the possible dangers.* ☞ Look at **impossible**. **2** that may be true or suitable: *There are several possible explanations for her strange behaviour.* ○ *There are four possible candidates for the job.* ☞ Look at **probable**.

possibly /-əbli/ *adv* **1** perhaps: *'Will you be free on Sunday?' 'Possibly.'* ○ *Edward phoned to say he would possibly be late home.* **2** (used for emphasizing sth) according to what is possible: *I will leave as soon as I possibly can.*

☆ **post¹** /pəʊst/ *noun* [C] an upright piece of metal or wood that is put in the ground to mark a position or to support sth: *The wooden gate post is rotten.* ○ *a goal post* ○ *Can you see a signpost anywhere?*
(IDIOM) **pip sb at the post** ⇨ PIP²

☆ **post²** /pəʊst/ *noun* [C] **1** a job: *the best candidate for the post* ○ *The post was advertised in the local newspaper.* **2** a place where sb is on duty or is guarding sth: *The soldiers had to remain at their posts all night.*
post *verb* [T] **1** to send sb to go and work somewhere: *After two years in London, Rosa was posted to the Tokyo office.* **2** to put sb on guard or on duty in a particular place: *Policemen were posted at the front door of the building.*
posting /-ɪŋ/ *noun* [C] a job in another country that you are sent to do by your employer

☆ **post³** /pəʊst/ (*especially US* **mail**) *noun* **1** [U] the system or organization for collecting and delivering letters, parcels, etc: *The document is too valuable to send by post.* ○ *Your cheque is in the post.* **2** [sing,U] letters, parcels, etc that are collected or delivered: *Has the post come yet this morning?* ○ *There wasn't any post for you.* ○ *I'll stop now or I'll miss the post* (= collection). ○ *to open the post*
(IDIOM) **by return (of post)** ⇨ RETURN²

'**postbox** (*also* **letter-box**) (*US* **mailbox**) *noun* [C] a box in a public place where you put letters, etc that you want to send ☞ Look at **pillar-box**.

'**postcard** *noun* [C] a card that you write a message on and send to sb. Postcards often have a picture on one side and are usually sent without an envelope.

'**postcode** (*also* **postal code**) (*US* **Zip code**) *noun* [C] a group of letters and/or numbers that you put at the end of an address. The postcode helps the Post Office to sort letters by machine.

'**postman** *noun* [C] (*pl* **postmen**) (*US* **mailman**) a person whose job is to collect and deliver letters, parcels, etc

'**postmark** *noun* [C] an official mark over a stamp on a letter, parcel, etc that says when and where it was posted

'**post office** *noun* [C] **1** a building or part of a shop where you can buy stamps, post parcels, etc **2 the Post Office** the national organization that is responsible for collecting and delivering letters, parcels, etc

'**post-office box** *noun* [C] (*abbr* **PO box**) a place in a post office where letters, parcels, etc are kept until they are collected by the person they were sent to

☆ **post⁴** /pəʊst/ (*also especially US* **mail**) *verb* [T] to send a letter, parcel, etc to sb by putting it in a post-box or taking it to a post office: *This letter was posted in Edinburgh yesterday.*

☞ **Post** (noun and verb) is more commonly used in British English and **mail** in American English. However, British English uses the noun **mail** quite often. The official name of the Post Office organization is the **Royal Mail**. Note too, the expressions **airmail** and **surface mail**. When we order goods in a letter, we use a **mail-order** service.

☆ **postage** /'pəʊstɪdʒ/ *noun* [U] the amount that you must pay to send a letter, parcel, etc: *The cost of postage and packing is £2.*

'**postage stamp** *noun* [C] = STAMP¹

☆ **postal** /'pəʊstl/ *adj* connected with the collecting and delivering of letters, parcels, etc: *postal charges*

'**postal code** *noun* [C] = POSTCODE

'**postal order** *noun* [C] a piece of paper that you can buy at a post office that represents a certain amount of money. A postal order is a safe way of sending money by post.

☆ **poster** /'pəʊstə(r)/ *noun* [C] a large printed picture or a notice in a public place, often used to advertise sth

posterity /pɒ'sterəti/ *noun* [U] the future and the people who will be alive then: *We should look after our environment for the sake of posterity.*

postgraduate /,pəʊst'grædʒuət/ *noun* [C] a person who is doing further studies at a university after taking his/her first degree ☞ Look at **graduate** and **undergraduate**.

ɜː	ə	eɪ	əʊ	aɪ	aʊ	ɔɪ	ɪə	eə	ʊə
fur	ago	pay	home	five	now	join	near	hair	pure

posthumous /'pɒstjʊməs; US 'pɒstʃəməs/ adj given or happening after sb has died: *a posthumous medal for bravery* —**posthumously** adv: *Her last novel was published posthumously.*

post-mortem /ˌpəʊst 'mɔːtəm/ noun [C] a medical examination of a dead body to find out how the person died

postpone /pə'spəʊn/ verb [T] to arrange that sth will happen at a later time than the time you had planned; to delay: *The wedding was postponed until August because the bride's mother was ill.* ○ *Because of illness, the concert is postponed until further notice* (= no date for it can be given now). ☞ Look at **cancel**. —**postponement** noun [C,U]

postscript /'pəʊsskrɪpt/ noun [C] (abbr **PS**) a short message that you add to the end of a letter after you have signed your name: *PS, I love you.*

posture /'pɒstʃə(r)/ noun **1** [U] the way that a person sits, stands, walks, etc: *Poor posture can lead to backache.* **2** [C] a position that your body is in: *an upright posture*

postwar /ˌpəʊst'wɔː(r)/ adj existing or happening in the period after the end of a war: *postwar reconstruction*

teapot coffee-pot

a pot/tin of paint

flowerpots

☆ **pot¹** /pɒt/ noun [C] **1** a round container that is used for cooking food: *pots and pans* **2** a container that you use for a particular purpose: *That plant needs a larger pot.* ○ *a flowerpot* ○ *a teapot* ○ *a pot of paint* **3** the amount that a pot contains: *We drank two pots of tea.*

'pot plant noun [C] a plant that you keep indoors

pot² /pɒt/ verb [T] (**potting**; **potted**) to put a plant into a flowerpot

☆ **potato** /pə'teɪtəʊ/ noun [C,U] (pl **potatoes**) a round vegetable with a brown, yellow or red skin. Potatoes are white or yellow inside. They grow under the ground on the roots of the potato plant: *mashed potato* ○ *potatoes baked in their jackets* ○ *roast potatoes* (= cooked in fat in the oven) ○ *Linda peeled the potatoes for supper.*

potato 'crisp (US **po'tato chip**) noun [C] = CRISP²

potent /'pəʊtnt/ adj strong or powerful: *This cider is very potent.* —**potency** /-nsɪ/ noun [U]

☆ **potential** /pə'tenʃl/ adj (only before a noun) that may possibly become sth, happen, be used, etc: *Wind power is a potential source of energy.* ○ *potential customers*

potential noun [U] the qualities or abilities that sb/sth has but that may not be fully developed yet: *That boy has great potential as a pianist.* ○ *to realize your full potential* —**potentially** /-ʃəlɪ/ adv: *That machine is in bad condition and is potentially very dangerous.*

pothole /'pɒthəʊl/ noun [C] **1** a deep hole in rock that was made by water. Potholes often lead to underground caves. **2** a hole in the surface of a road, etc

'potholing noun [U] going down inside potholes and underground caves as a sport

potter¹ /'pɒtə(r)/ (US **putter** /'pʌtər/) verb [I] **potter (about/around)** to spend your time doing small jobs in an unhurried way: *Grandpa spends most of the day pottering in the garden.*

potter² /'pɒtə(r)/ noun [C] a person who makes pots, dishes, etc (**pottery**) from baked clay

pottery /'pɒtərɪ/ noun (pl **potteries**) **1** [U] pots, dishes, etc that are made from baked clay **2** [U] the activity of making pottery **3** [C] a place where pottery is made

potty¹ /'pɒtɪ/ adj (**pottier**; **pottiest**) (Brit informal) **1** mad or foolish **2 potty about sb/sth** liking sb/sth very much

potty² /'pɒtɪ/ noun [C] (pl **potties**) (informal) a pot that children sit on when they are too small to use a toilet

pouch /paʊtʃ/ noun [C] **1** a small leather bag **2** a pocket of skin in which some animals, eg kangaroos, carry their babies ☞ picture at **kangaroo**.

poultry /'pəʊltrɪ/ noun **1** [plural] birds, eg hens, ducks, geese, turkeys, etc that are kept for their eggs or their meat: *to keep poultry* **2** [U] the meat from these birds ☞ Look at the note at **meat**.

pounce /paʊns/ verb [I] **pounce (on sb/sth)** to jump or land on sb/sth suddenly in order to attack: *The cat sat motionless, waiting to pounce on the mouse.* ○ (figurative) *He was quick to pounce on any mistakes I made.*

☆ **pound¹** /paʊnd/ noun **1** [C] (also **pound 'sterling**) (symbol **£**) the unit of money in Britain; one hundred pence (100p): *Melissa earns £16 000 a year.* ○ *a ten-pound note* ○ *Grandpa sent me a cheque for £25.* ○ *a pound coin* ○ *How many pesetas will I get for a pound?* **2** [sing] **the pound** the value of the British pound on international money markets: *The pound has fallen against the dollar.* ○ *The pound used to be worth 13 deutschmarks.* ○ *How many pesetas are there to the pound?* **3** [C] (abbr **lb**) a measure of weight; 0·454 of a kilogram. There are 16 ounces in a pound: *The carrots cost 30p a pound.* ○ *The baby weighed six pounds at birth.* ○ *Half a pound of mushrooms, please.*

pound² /paʊnd/ verb **1** [T] to beat sth with a heavy tool to make it soft or like powder **2** [I] **pound (away) (at/against/on sth)** to hit or beat sth many times: *Great waves pounded against the rocks.* ○ *to pound on a door* ○ (figurative) *My heart was pounding with excitement.* **3** [I] **pound along, down, up, etc** to move quickly and with heavy steps in a particular

p	b	t	d	k	g	tʃ	dʒ	f	v	θ	ð
pen	bad	tea	did	cat	got	chin	June	fall	van	thin	then

direction: *Jason went pounding up the stairs three at a time.*

☆ **pour** /pɔː(r)/ *verb* **1** [I] (used about a liquid) to flow out of or into sth, quickly and steadily, and in large quantities: *Water poured through the hole in the sea-wall.* ○ *Tears were pouring down her cheeks.* ○ *There was blood pouring out of the wound.* ○ *(figurative) People were pouring out of the station.* **2** [T] to make sth flow steadily out of or into a container: *I spilled some of the oil when I tried to pour it back into the bottle.* ○ *Pour the sugar into a bowl.* **3** [T] **pour sth (for sb)** to serve drinks to sb: *Have you poured out the tea?* ○ *Pour me another glass of wine, would you?* **4** [I] to rain heavily: *The rain poured down all day long.* ○ *I'm not going out. It's pouring.*

(PHRASAL VERB) **pour sth out** to speak freely about what you think or feel about sth that has happened to you: *to pour out all your troubles*

pout /paʊt/ *verb* [I] to push your lips, or your bottom lip, forward to show that you are not pleased about sth —**pout** *noun* [C]

☆ **poverty** /'pɒvəti/ *noun* [U] the state of having very little money; the state of being poor: *There are millions of people in this country who are living in poverty.*

'**poverty-stricken** *adj* very poor

☆ **powder** /'paʊdə(r)/ *noun* **1** [C,U] a dry substance that is in the form of very small particles or grains: *This new washing-powder doesn't get the clothes very clean.* ○ *baking-powder* **2** [U] powder that you use on your skin: *face-powder* ○ *talcum powder*

powder *verb* [T] to put powder(2) on sb/sth: *to powder a baby after a bath*

powdered *adj* (used about a substance that is usually liquid) dried in the form of a powder: *powdered milk*

☆ **power** /'paʊə(r)/ *noun* **1** [U] the ability to do sth: *The minister promised to do everything in her power to make sure the hostages were not harmed.* ○ *He has great powers of observation.* **2** [U] force or strength: *The ship was helpless against the power of the storm.* **3** [U] control or influence over other people: *When did this government come to power?* ○ *the power of the trade unions* ○ *He sacrificed everything for power and money.* ○ *to have sb in your power* **4** [C] the right or authority to do sth: *Do the police have the power to stop cars without good reason?* **5** [C] a person, organization or country that controls or influences others: *Britain is no longer a world power.* **6** [U] energy that is used for making machines work, giving light, heat, etc: *nuclear power* ○ *the power supply* ○ *This car has power steering.*

powered *adj* driven by or having a particular type of energy: *a nuclear-powered submarine* ○ *a high-powered engine*

'**power cut** *noun* [C] a time when the supply of electricity is cut off

'**power point** *noun* [C] = SOCKET(1)

'**power station** *noun* [C] a place where electricity is made (**generated**)

☆ **powerful** /'paʊəfl/ *adj* **1** very strong in a physical way: *That car has a very powerful engine.* ○ *Adrian is a powerful swimmer.* **2** having a strong effect: *The Prime Minister made a powerful speech.* **3** having a lot of influence over other people: *There was a meeting of some of the most powerful people in the country.* —**powerfully** /-fəli/ *adv*

powerless /'paʊələs/ *adj* **1** without strength or influence **2** not able to do sth: *I stood and watched him struggle, powerless to help.*

practicable /'præktɪkəbl/ *adj* that can be done successfully: *The scheme is just not practicable. It is too complicated and too expensive.* ☞ The opposite is **impracticable**.

☆ **practical** /'præktɪkl/ *adj* **1** concerned with actually doing sth rather than ideas or theory: *A degree in agriculture is not very useful without practical experience of working on a farm.* ☞ Look at **theoretical**. **2** very suitable for a particular purpose; useful: *Plastic tablecloths are practical but they're not very elegant.* **3** (used about people) making sensible decisions and good at dealing with problems: *We must be practical. It's no good buying a house we cannot afford.* **4** that is likely to succeed: *Your plan just isn't practical.* ☞ The opposite in senses 2, 3, 4 is **impractical**. **5** clever at doing things with your hands: *A dentist has to have good practical skills.*

practical *noun* [C] *(informal)* a lesson or examination where you do or make sth rather than just writing

practicality /ˌpræktɪ'kæləti/ *noun* [U] the state of being sensible or possible: *I am not convinced of the practicality of the scheme.*

practically /-kli/ *adv* **1** almost; nearly: *The city centre is practically deserted on Sundays.* ○ *He practically begged me not to go.* **2** in a practical way

ˌ**practical 'joke** *noun* [C] a trick that you play on sb (that involves doing sth that will make him/her look silly)

☆ **practice** /'præktɪs/ *noun* **1** [U] the actual doing of sth rather than ideas or theory: *Your suggestion sounds fine in theory, but would it work in practice?* ○ *I can't wait to put what I've learnt into practice.* **2** [C,U] (a period of) doing sth many times so that you become good at it: *You need plenty of practice when you're learning to drive.* ○ *His accent should improve with practice.* ○ *The team met for a practice twice a week.* **3** [C,U] *(formal)* the usual way of doing sth; sth that is done regularly: *It is standard practice not to pay bills until the end of the month.* ○ *The practice of banks closing at 3.30 is very annoying.* **4** [U] the work of a doctor or lawyer: *Dr Roberts doesn't work in a hospital. He's in general practice* (= he's a family doctor). **5** [C] the business of a doctor or lawyer: *There are two practices in our local health centre.*

(IDIOM) **in/out of practice** having spent/not having spent a lot of time practising sth recently: *I'm not playing very well at the moment. I'm really out of practice.*

☆ **practise** (*US* **practice**) /'præktɪs/ *verb* **1** [I,T] to do sth many times so that you become very good at it: *If you want to play a musical instrument well, you must practise every day.* ○ *They practised the dance until it was perfect.* ○ *You need to practise saying 'th' in front of a mirror.*

practitioner — **précis**

2 [T] to do sth or take part in sth regularly or openly: *For many years people were not allowed to practise their religion.* **3** [I,T] to work as a doctor or lawyer: *She's practising as a doctor in Leeds.*

practised (*US* **practiced**) *adj* very good at sth, because you have had a lot of practice

practitioner /præk'tɪʃənə(r)/ *noun* [C] (*formal*) a person who works as a doctor or lawyer ☛ Look at **general practitioner**.

pragmatic /præg'mætɪk/ *adj* dealing with problems in a practical way rather than by following theory or principles

prairie /'preəri/ *noun* [C] a very large area of flat land covered in grass with few trees (especially in North America)

☆ **praise¹** /preɪz/ *verb* [T] **praise sb/sth (for sth)** to say that sb/sth is good and should be admired: *Her new novel has been highly praised.* ○ *The Prime Minister praised the efforts of the rescue services.* ○ *The fireman was praised for his courage.*

☆ **praise²** /preɪz/ *noun* [U] what you say when you are expressing admiration for sb/sth: *His new play has received a lot of praise.* ○ *Children respond better to praise than to criticism.*

'praiseworthy /-wɜːði/ *adj* deserving praise

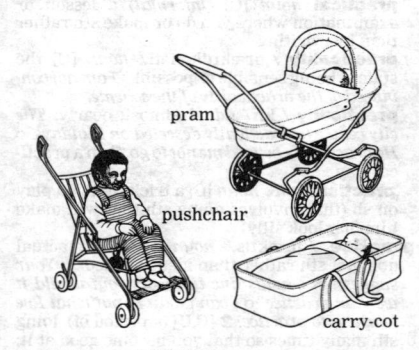

pram

pushchair

carry-cot

pram /præm/ (*US* **'baby carriage**) *noun* [C] a small carriage for a baby to go out in. A pram has four wheels, a hood and a handle to push it with.

prance /prɑːns; *US* præns/ *verb* [I] to move about with quick steps, as if you were jumping or dancing, often because you feel proud or pleased with yourself

prat /præt/ *noun* [C] (*slang*) a stupid person: *What a prat!*

prawn /prɔːn/ *noun* [C] a small sea animal with a shell. Prawns can be eaten as food; they turn pink when you cook them. ☛ picture at **shellfish**. Look at **scampi** and **shrimp**.

☆ **pray** /preɪ/ *verb* [I,T] **pray (to sb) (for sb/sth)** to speak to God or a god in order to give thanks or to ask for sth: *Let us pray.* ○ *They knelt down and prayed for peace.* ○ *to pray to Allah* ○ *They prayed that the war would end soon.*

☆ **prayer** /preə(r)/ *noun* **1** [C] the words that you use when you speak to God or a god: *to say your prayers* ○ *The vicar said a prayer for all the people who were ill.* ○ *a prayer book* (= a book containing the prayers regularly used in a religious service) **2** [U] the act of praying: *to kneel in prayer*

preach /priːtʃ/ *verb* **1** [I,T] to give a talk (**a sermon**) on a religious subject: *Who's preaching in church today?* ○ *The vicar preached a sermon on the meaning of love.* ○ *Jesus preached that we should love our neighbours as ourselves.* ○ (*figurative*) *Stop preaching at me! You're no better than I am.* **2** [T] to say that sth is good and to persuade others to accept it: *I always preach caution in situations like this.*

preacher *noun* [C] a person who gives religious talks (**sermons**), eg in a church

precarious /prɪ'keəriəs/ *adj* not safe or certain; dangerous: *Working on the roof of that building looks very precarious.* —**precariously** *adv*: *They lived precariously on his part-time earnings.*

precaution /prɪ'kɔːʃn/ *noun* [C] something that you do in order to avoid danger or problems: *We took the precaution of locking our valuables in the hotel safe.* ○ *precautions against fire* —**precautionary** /prɪ'kɔːʃənəri; *US* -neri/ *adj*: *I'm going to photocopy all these documents as a precautionary measure.*

precede /prɪ'siːd/ *verb* [I,T] (*formal*) to come or go before sb/sth: *The Queen was preceded by soldiers on horseback.* ○ *The results of the experiment are given in the table on the preceding page.*

precedence /'presɪdəns/ *noun* [U] **precedence (over sb/sth)** the right that sb/sth has to come before sb/sth else because of greater importance: *In business, making a profit seems to take precedence over everything else.*

precedent /'presɪdənt/ *noun* [C,U] something that is considered as an example or rule for what happens later: *We don't want to set a precedent by allowing one person to come in late or they'll all want to do it.* ○ *The princess was not allowed to break with precedent and marry a divorced man.* ☛ Look at **unprecedented**.

precinct /'priːsɪŋkt/ *noun* **1** [C] (*Brit*) a special area of shops in a town where cars are not allowed: *a shopping precinct* **2** [C] (*US*) a part of a town that has its own police and fire services **3 precincts** [plural] the area near or around a building, etc: *Security guards patrol the hospital and its precincts.*

☆ **precious** /'preʃəs/ *adj* **1** of great value (usually because it is rare or scarce): *Gold and silver are precious metals.* ○ *In overcrowded Hong Kong, every small piece of land is precious.* **2** loved very much: *My mother's old ring is one of my most precious possessions.* ○ *Her husband was very precious to her.*

precious 'stone *noun* [C] a stone which is very rare and valuable and often often used in jewellery: *diamonds, rubies and other precious stones*

precipice /'presɪpɪs/ *noun* [C] a very steep slope on the side of a mountain: (*figurative*) *The British economy is on the edge of a precipice.*

précis /'preɪsiː; *US* preɪ'siː/ *noun* [C,U] (*pl* **précis**) a shortened form of a speech or written

iː	ɪ	e	æ	ɑː	ɒ	ɔː	ʊ	uː	ʌ
see	sit	ten	hat	arm	got	saw	put	too	cup

text that contains only the most important points ☛ Look at **summary**.

☆ **precise** /prɪ'saɪs/ adj **1** clear and accurate: *Try to be precise in your measurements.* ○ *I gave them precise instructions how to get here.* ○ *The answer was 10, or 9·98 to be precise.* ○ *She couldn't be very precise about what her attacker was wearing.* **2** (only *before* a noun) exact; particular: *I'm sorry. I can't come just at this precise moment.* **3** (used about a person) taking care to get small details right: *He's very precise.* ☛ In senses 1 and 3 the opposite is **imprecise**.
precisely adv **1** clearly or exactly: *The time is 10.03 precisely.* ○ *That's precisely what I mean.* ○ *I mean precisely what I say.* **2** (used before 'because' to emphasize that the reason you are giving is different from the reason that people might expect): *'But he was so friendly.' 'I didn't trust him precisely because he was so friendly.'* **3** (used for agreeing with a statement) yes, that is right: *'So, if we don't book now, we probably won't get a flight?' 'Precisely.'*

precision /prɪ'sɪʒn/ (*also* **preciseness**) noun [U] the quality of being clear or exact: *The plans were drawn with great precision.*

precocious /prɪ'kəʊʃəs/ adj **1** (used about children) acting in a way that makes them seem older than they really are ☛ This word is often used in a critical way. **2** developed very early: *a precocious talent for playing the piano*

preconceived /ˌpriːkən'siːvd/ adj (used about an idea or opinion) formed before you have knowledge or experience: *When I visited Russia last year I soon forgot all my preconceived ideas about the country.*

preconception /ˌpriːkən'sepʃn/ noun [C] an idea or opinion that you have formed about sb/sth before you have enough knowledge or experience

predator /'predətə(r)/ noun [C] an animal that kills and eats other animals

predecessor /'priːdɪsesə(r); *US* 'predə-/ noun [C] **1** the person who was formerly in the job or position that sb else is in now: *The new head teacher is much better than her predecessor.* **2** something that is no longer used and has been replaced by sth else: *Our latest car is more reliable than most of its predecessors.* ☛ Look at **successor**.

predicament /prɪ'dɪkəmənt/ noun [C] a difficult situation

predicative /prɪ'dɪkətɪv; *US* 'predɪkeɪtɪv/ adj (used about an adjective) not used before a noun; coming after a verb such as 'be', 'become', 'get', 'seem', 'look': *You cannot say 'an asleep child' because 'asleep' is a predicative adjective.* —**predicatively** adv: *'Asleep' can only be used predicatively.*

☆ **predict** /prɪ'dɪkt/ verb [T] to say that sth will happen (often because you have special knowledge): *to predict the results of the election* ○ *Scientists still cannot predict when earthquakes will happen.* ○ *Mrs Jones predicted that all the students would pass the exam, and they did.*

predictable /-əbl/ adj **1** that was or could be expected **2** (used about a person) always behaving in the way that is expected: *I knew you were going to say that – you're so pre-* *dictable.* ☛ The opposite is **unpredictable**.
—**predictably** adv: *Predictably, all the applause came from the politician's own supporters.*

prediction /prɪ'dɪkʃn/ noun [C,U] saying what will happen; what sb thinks will happen: *Prediction of the result is extremely difficult.* ○ *The Institute's prediction of economic chaos has been proved correct.*

predominant /prɪ'dɒmɪnənt/ adj most noticeable, powerful or important: *The predominant colour was yellow.*

predominance /-əns/ [sing,U] the state of being most important or greatest in number: *There is a predominance of Japanese tourists in Hawaii.*

predominantly adv mostly; mainly: *The population of the island is predominantly Spanish.*

predominate /prɪ'dɒmɪneɪt/ verb [I] **predominate** (**over sb/sth**) (*formal*) to be most important or greatest in number: *In the colder regions, pine trees predominate.*

preface /'prefɪs/ noun [C] a written introduction to a book that explains what it is about or why it was written

prefect /'priːfekt/ noun [C] (*Brit*) an older pupil in a school who has special duties and responsibilities. Prefects often help to make sure that the younger pupils behave properly.

☆ **prefer** /prɪ'fɜː(r)/ verb [T] (preferring; preferred) **prefer sth** (**to sth**) to choose sth rather than sth else; to like sth better: *Would you prefer tea or coffee?* ○ *I prefer skating to skiing.* ○ *You go to the cinema if you want. I'd prefer to stay in tonight.* ○ *Marianne prefers not to walk home on her own at night.* ☛ Notice the different ways that **prefer** can be used: *Helen prefers going by train to flying.* ○ *Helen prefers to go by train rather than to fly.* ○ *My parents would prefer me to study law at university.* ○ *My parents would prefer it if I studied law at university.* ○ *My parents would prefer that I studied law at university.* The last two sentences are more formal. Note that **prefer** is generally rather formal. Instead of: *Would you prefer tea or coffee?* we can say: *Would you rather have tea or coffee?* Instead of: *I prefer skating to skiing* we can say: *I like skating better than skiing.*

preferable /'prefrəbl/ adj **preferable** (**to sth/to doing sth**) better or more suitable: *Going anywhere is preferable to staying at home for the weekend.* ○ *Cold drinks are preferable in hot weather.*

preferably /'prefrəbli/ adv more suitably; better: *Come round on Sunday morning but preferably not before ten!*

☆ **preference** /'prefrəns/ noun **1** [sing,U] **preference** (**for sth**) a liking for sth rather than for sth else: *What you wear is entirely a matter of personal preference.* ○ *We have both red and white wine. Do you have a preference for one or the other?* **2** [U] **preference** (**to/towards sb**) special treatment that you give to one person or group rather than to others: *When allocating accommodation, we will give preference to families with young children.* ○ *Please list your*

3:	ə	eɪ	əʊ	aɪ	aʊ	ɔɪ	ɪə	eə	ʊə
fur	ago	pay	home	five	now	join	near	hair	pure

choices in order of preference (= put the thing you want most first on the list, and so on).

preferential /ˌprefəˈrenʃl/ adj giving or showing preference(2): *I don't see why he should get preferential treatment – I've worked here just as long!*

prefix /ˈpriːfɪks/ noun [C] a word or group of letters that you put at the beginning of a word to change its meaning: *The prefix 'im-' means 'not', eg 'impossible'.* ☞ Look at **suffix**.

☆ **pregnant** /ˈpregnənt/ adj (used about a woman or female animal) having a baby developing in her body: *Liz is five months pregnant.* ☞ It is more common and less formal to say: *She's expecting a baby* or: *She's going to have a baby.*

pregnancy /-nənsi/ noun (pl **pregnancies**) **1** [U] the state of being pregnant: *You should try to rest during pregnancy.* o *a pregnancy test* **2** [C] the period of time when a woman or female animal is pregnant: *to have a difficult pregnancy*

prehistoric /ˌpriːhɪˈstɒrɪk; *US* -ˈstɔːrɪk/ adj of the time before history was written down: *prehistoric cave paintings*

☆ **prejudice** /ˈpredʒʊdɪs/ noun [C,U] a strong feeling of like or dislike towards sb/sth that is not based on reason or experience: *racial prejudice* o *He has a prejudice against women doctors.*

prejudice verb [T] **1 prejudice sb (against/in favour of sb/sth)** to influence sb; to cause sb to have a prejudice: *The newspaper stories had prejudiced the jury against him.* **2** to hurt or weaken sth: *Your appearance may prejudice your chances of getting the job.*

prejudiced adj having or showing prejudice: *You can't rely on his opinion – he's prejudiced.*

preliminary /prɪˈlɪmɪnəri; *US* -neri/ adj coming before sth else that is more important: *After a few preliminary remarks the discussions began.*

preliminary noun [C] a thing that you do before sth more important: *Once the preliminaries are over, we can get down to business.*

prelude /ˈpreljuːd/ noun [C] **1** something that comes before sth else or that forms an introduction to sth: *The build-up of troops seemed to be a prelude to war.* **2** a piece of music that forms the first part of a longer piece

premature /ˈpremətjʊə(r); *US* ˌpriːməˈtʊər/ adj **1** coming or happening before the proper or expected time: *Premature babies* (= babies who are born before the expected time) *need special care.* **2** acting or happening too soon: *I think our decision was premature. We should have thought about it for longer.* —**prematurely** adv: *The shock caused her to go prematurely grey.*

premeditated /ˌpriːˈmedɪteɪtɪd/ adj planned in advance: *Was the attack premeditated?*

premier /ˈpremɪə(r); *US* ˈpriːmɪər/ adj (only *before* a noun) most important; best: *the premier division of the football league*

premier noun [C] the leader of the government of a country

première /ˈpremɪeə(r); *US* prɪˈmɪər/ noun [C] the first performance of a play, film, etc

premises /ˈpremɪsɪz/ noun [plural] (*formal*) a building and the land that surrounds it: *The company is moving to larger premises.* o *Smoking is not allowed on the premises.*

premium /ˈpriːmɪəm/ noun [C] **1** an amount of money that you pay regularly to a company for insurance: *monthly premiums of £25* **2** an extra payment: *You must pay a premium for express delivery.*

premonition /ˌpreməˈnɪʃn; priː-/ noun [C] a feeling that sth unpleasant is going to happen

preoccupation /priˌɒkjʊˈpeɪʃn/ noun **1** [U] **preoccupation (with sth)** the state of thinking or being worried about sth all the time **2** [C] a thing that you think or worry about all the time: *The family's main preoccupation at that time was finding somewhere to live.*

preoccupy /priˈɒkjʊpaɪ/ verb [T] (pres part **preoccupying**; 3rd pers sing pres **preoccupies**; pt, pp **preoccupied**) to fill sb's mind so that he/she does not think about anything else

preoccupied adj not paying attention to sb/sth because you are thinking or worrying about sb/sth else

☆ **preparation** /ˌprepəˈreɪʃn/ noun **1** [U] the act of getting sb/sth ready: *Hygiene is essential during the preparation of food.* o *exam preparation* **2** [C, usually pl] **preparation (for sth/to do sth)** something that you do to get ready for sth: *The wedding preparations are almost complete.*

(IDIOM) **in preparation (for sth)** in order to get ready for sth: *Get a good night's sleep in preparation for the journey.*

preparatory /prɪˈpærətri; *US* -tɔːri/ adj done in order to get ready for sth: *a preparatory course in English for students who wish to study at a British university*

pre'paratory school (also *informal* **'prep school**) noun [C] **1** (*Brit*) a private school for pupils aged between seven and thirteen. **2** (*US*) a private school that prepares students for college or university

☆ **prepare** /prɪˈpeə(r)/ verb [I,T] **prepare (sb/ sth) (for sb/sth)** to get ready or to make sb/sth ready: *Bob helped me prepare for the party.* o *I didn't leave myself enough time to prepare for the exam.* o *to prepare a meal* o *The spokesman read out a prepared statement but refused to answer any questions.* o *I'm afraid you're going to have to prepare yourself for a shock.*

(IDIOMS) **be prepared for sth** to be ready for sth difficult or unpleasant

be prepared to do sth to be willing to do sth: *I am not prepared to stay here and be insulted.*

preposition /ˌprepəˈzɪʃn/ noun [C] a word or phrase that is used before a noun or pronoun to show place, time, direction, etc: *'In', 'for', 'to', 'out of', 'on behalf of'* are all prepositions.

preposterous /prɪˈpɒstərəs/ adj silly; ridiculous; not to be taken seriously

prerequisite /ˌpriːˈrekwɪzɪt/ noun [C] **prerequisite (for/of sth)** something that is necessary for sth to happen or exist: *Is a good education a prerequisite of success?*

prerogative /prɪˈrɒgətɪv/ noun [C] a special right that sb/sth has: *It is the Prime Minister's prerogative to fix the date of the general election.*

p	b	t	d	k	g	tʃ	dʒ	f	v	θ	ð
pen	bad	tea	did	cat	got	chin	June	fall	van	thin	then

prescribe /prɪˈskraɪb/ verb [T] **1** to say what medicine or treatment you should have; to order medicine on a special form (**prescription**): *Can you prescribe something for my cough please, doctor?* **2** (*formal*) (used about a person or an organization with authority) to say that sth must be done: *The law prescribes that the document must be signed in the presence of two witnesses.*

prescription /prɪˈskrɪpʃn/ noun **1** [C,U] a form on which a doctor has written the name of the medicine that you need. You take your prescription to a chemist's and get the medicine there: *a prescription for sleeping-pills* ○ *Some medicines are only available on prescription* (= with a prescription from a doctor). **2** [U] the act of prescribing sth

☆ **presence** /ˈprezns/ noun **1** [U] being in a place or with sb: *He apologized to her in the presence of the whole family.* ○ *to request sb's presence at a meeting* ☛ The opposite is **absence**. **2** [sing] a number of soldiers or policemen who are in a place for a special reason: *There was a huge police presence at the demonstration.*

☆ **present¹** /ˈpreznt/ adj **1** (not before a noun) being in a particular place: *There were 200 people present at the meeting.* ☛ The opposite is **absent**. **2** (only *before* a noun) existing or happening now: *We hope to overcome our present difficulties very soon.*
(IDIOM) **the present day** modern times: *In some countries traditional methods of farming have survived to the present day.* ○ *present-day attitudes to women*
present noun [sing] **1 the present** the time now: *We live in the present but we must learn from the past.* **2 the present** = PRESENT TENSE
(IDIOMS) **at present** now: *I'm rather busy at present. Can I call you back later?*
for the moment/present ⇨ MOMENT
present 'participle noun [C] the form of the verb that ends in -*ing*: '*Going*', '*walking*' and '*trying*' are all present participles.
present 'tense noun [C] the tense of the verb that you use when you are talking about what is happening or what exists now

☆ **present²** /ˈpreznt/ noun [C] something that you give to sb or receive from sb; a gift: *The tie was a present from my sister.* ○ *a birthday, wedding, Christmas, etc present* ○ *I must buy a present for my friend.* ☛ **Gift** is more formal and is often used in shops, catalogues, etc.

☆ **present³** /prɪˈzent/ verb [T] **1 present sb with sth; present sth (to sb)** to give sth to sb, eg at a formal ceremony: *All the dancers were presented with flowers.* ○ *Flowers were presented to all the dancers.* ○ *The duchess presented a silver cup to the winner.* **2 present sb (to sb)** to introduce sb to a person of higher social rank: *to be presented to the Queen* **3** to give or show sth: *Good teachers try to present their material in an interesting way.* ○ *to present a report to the board of directors* **4** to cause or provide sth: *Learning English presented no problem to him.* ○ *The course aims to present each participant with new challenges.* **5** to show a play, etc to the public: *The Theatre Royal is presenting a new production of 'Ghosts'.* **6** to introduce a television or radio programme or the people who appear on it

presenter noun [C] a person who introduces a television or radio programme

presentable /prɪˈzentəbl/ adj quite good, and suitable to be seen in public: *I'm going to wear this dress to the party – it's still quite presentable.*

presentation /ˌpreznˈteɪʃn; *US* ˌpriːzen-/ noun **1** [U] presenting sth or being presented: *the presentation of new material in a textbook* **2** [U] the appearance of sth or the impression that it makes on other people: *Untidy presentation of your work may lose you marks.* **3** [C] a formal ceremony at which a prize, etc is given to sb **4** [C] (*formal*) a talk that gives information on a particular subject

presently /ˈprezntli/ adv **1** soon: *I'll be finished presently.* **2** after a short time: *Presently I heard the car door shut.* **3** (*especially US*) now: *The management are presently discussing the matter with the unions.* ☛ Notice that when **presently** means 'soon' it usually comes at the end of the sentence and when it means 'after a short time' it usually comes at the beginning of the sentence. When **presently** means 'now' it goes with the verb.

☆ **preservation** /ˌprezəˈveɪʃn/ noun [U] keeping sth in the same or in good condition: *the preservation of law and order* ○ *The society is working for the preservation of wildlife.*

preservative /prɪˈzɜːvətɪv/ noun [C,U] a substance that is used for keeping food, etc in good condition

☆ **preserve** /prɪˈzɜːv/ verb [T] to keep sth safe or in good condition: *They've managed to preserve most of the wall-paintings in the caves.* ○ *You can preserve fruit by making it into jam.* ○ *Efforts to preserve peace have failed.*

preside /prɪˈzaɪd/ verb [I] to be in charge of a discussion, meeting, etc
(PHRASAL VERB) **preside over sth** to be in control of or responsible for sth: *Our present director has presided over a period of expansion.*

presidency /ˈprezɪdənsi/ noun (*pl* **presidencies**) **1 the presidency** [sing] the position of being president: *to be nominated for the presidency* **2** [C] the period of time that sb is president

☆ **president** /ˈprezɪdənt/ noun [C] **1** (*also* **President**) the leader of the country and head of the government in many countries that do not have a king or queen. A president is usually chosen in an election: *President Mitterrand of France.* ○ *the vice-president* **2** the person with the highest position in some organizations

presidential /ˌprezɪˈdenʃl/ adj connected with a president

☆ **press¹** /pres/ noun **1** [sing] often **the press** [with sing or pl verb] newspapers, and the journalists who work for them. The news departments of television and radio are also part of the press: *The minister refused to speak to the press.* ○ *the local/national press* ○ *a press pho-*

s	z	ʃ	ʒ	h	m	n	ŋ	l	r	j	w
so	zoo	she	vision	how	man	no	sing	leg	red	yes	wet

press | 486 | **pretty**

tographer ○ *The press support/supports government policy.*

☞ If a person gets **a good press** it means that he/she is praised by the press. The opposite is **a bad press**.

2 [U] the act of printing books, newspapers, etc: *All details were correct at the time of going to press.* **3** = PRINTING-PRESS **4** [C] an act of pushing sth firmly: *With a press of a button you can call up all the information you need.* ○ *This shirt needs a press* (= with an iron).

press conference *noun* [C] a meeting when a famous or important person answers questions from newspaper and television journalists: *to hold a press conference*

☆ **press**² /pres/ *verb* **1** [I,T] to push firmly: *Just press that button and the door will open.* ○ *Don't press too hard on the brakes.* ○ *The child pressed her nose against the window.* **2** [T] to put weight onto sth, eg in order to get juice out of it: *to press grapes* ○ *to press wild flowers between the pages of a book* **3** [T] to make a piece of clothing smooth and smart by using an iron **4** [T] to hold sb/sth firmly as a sign of love, etc: *She pressed his hand to her heart.* **5** [I,T] **press (sb) (for sth)** to try to get sth or to make sb do sth: *I pressed them to stay for supper.* ○ *to press sb for an answer* ○ *The opposition is pressing for a public inquiry into the accident.* **6** [T] to try to get sth accepted: *I don't want to press the point, but you do owe me £200.*

(IDIOM) **be pressed for sth** to not have enough of sth: *I must hurry. I'm really pressed for time.*

(PHRASAL VERBS) **press across, against, around, etc (sth)** (used about people) to move in a particular direction by pushing: *The crowd pressed against the wall of policemen.*

press ahead/forward/on (with sth) to continue doing sth even though it is difficult or hard work: *They pressed on with the building work in spite of the bad weather.*

pressing *adj* that you must do or deal with immediately: *I can't stop now. I have a pressing engagement.*

press-stud /'prestʌd/ *noun* [C] = POPPER

'press-up (*US* **'push-up**) *noun* [C] a type of exercise in which you lie on your front on the floor and push your body up with your arms

☆ **pressure** *noun* **1** [U] the force that is produced when you press on or against sth: *Apply pressure to the cut and it will stop bleeding.* ○ *The pressure of the water caused the dam to crack.* ○ (*figurative*) *His illness was caused by pressure of work.* **2** [C,U] the force that a gas or liquid has when it presses against sth: *high/low blood pressure* ○ *You should check your tyre pressures regularly.* ○ *Low air pressure often brings rain.* **3** [C,U] a situation that causes you to be worried or unhappy: *financial pressures* ○ *They moved to the country to escape the pressures of city life.*

(IDIOMS) **put pressure on sb (to do sth)** to persuade or force sb to do sth: *The press are putting pressure on the minister to resign.*

under pressure 1 (used about liquid or gas) having great force: *Water is forced out through the hose under pressure.* **2** being forced to do sth: *The workers were under pressure to get the job finished as quickly as possible.* ○ *Anna was under pressure from her parents to leave school and get a job.* —**pressure** *verb* [T] = PRESSURIZE

'pressure-cooker *noun* [C] a large pan with a lid in which you can cook things quickly using steam under high pressure ☞ picture at **pan**.

'pressure group *noun* [C, with sing or pl verb] a group of people who are trying to influence what a government or other organization does: *Transport 2000 is a pressure group that is campaigning for better public transport.*

pressurize (*also* **pressurise**) /'preʃəraɪz/ (*also* **pressure** /'preʃə(r)/) *verb* [T] **pressurize sb into sth/into doing sth** to use force or influence to make sb do sth: *Some workers were pressurized into taking early retirement.*

pressurized (*also* **pressurised**) *adj* (used about air in an aeroplane, etc) kept at the pressure at which people can breathe

prestige /pre'stiːʒ/ *noun* [U] the respect and admiration that people feel for a person because he/she has a high social position or has been very successful: *Nursing isn't a very high-prestige job but it gives you a lot of satisfaction.*

prestigious /pre'stɪdʒəs/ *adj* respected or admired; bringing prestige: *Eton is one of Britain's most prestigious schools.*

presumably /prɪ'zjuːməblɪ; *US* -'zuː-/ *adv* I imagine; I suppose: *Presumably this rain means the match will be cancelled?*

presume /prɪ'zjuːm; *US* -'zuːm/ *verb* [T] to think that sth is true even if you do not know for sure; to suppose: *The house looks empty so I presume they are away on holiday.* ○ *The soldiers were missing, presumed dead.*

presumption /prɪ'zʌmpʃn/ *noun* [C] something that you presume or suppose to be true

presumptuous /prɪ'zʌmptʃʊəs/ *adj* doing sth that you have no right or authority to do: *It was very presumptuous of him to say that I would help without asking me first.*

pretence (*US* **pretense**) /prɪ'tens/ *noun* [U,sing] an action that makes people believe sth that is not true: *Why make any pretence? You don't like it, so say so!* ○ *to make a pretence of being ill*

(IDIOM) **on/under false pretences** ⇨ FALSE

☆ **pretend** /prɪ'tend/ *verb* [I,T] to appear to do or be sth, in order to trick or deceive sb: *Frances walked past pretending (that) she hadn't seen me.* ○ *Paul's not really asleep. He's just pretending.* ○ *The children are pretending to be space explorers.*

pretentious /prɪ'tenʃəs/ *adj* trying to appear more serious or important than you really are: *a pretentious modern film* ☞ The opposite is **unpretentious**.

pretext /'priːtekst/ *noun* [C] a reason that you give for doing sth that is not the real reason: *Clive left on the pretext of having an appointment at the dentist's.*

☆ **pretty**¹ /'prɪtɪ/ *adj* (**prettier; prettiest**) pleasant to look at; attractive: *Rachel looks really pretty in that dress, doesn't she?* ○ *What a pretty*

iː	ɪ	e	æ	ɑː	ɒ	ɔː	ʊ	uː	ʌ
see	sit	ten	hat	arm	got	saw	put	too	cup

garden! ○ *very pretty material with yellow and blue flowers on it* ☞ When we are talking about people, we use **pretty** to describe girls and women. To describe men we use **good-looking** or **handsome**. Look at the note at **beautiful**.
—**prettily** *adv*: *to smile prettily* —**prettiness** *noun* [U]

☆ **pretty**² /ˈprɪti/ *adv (informal)* quite; rather: *It's pretty cold outside.* ○ *I'm pretty certain that Alex will agree.* ☞ Look at the note at **rather**.
(IDIOM) **pretty much/nearly/well** almost: *I won't be long. I've pretty well finished.*

prevail /prɪˈveɪl/ *verb* [I] **1** to exist or be common: *In some remote areas a lot of superstition still prevails.* **2** *(formal)* to win or gain control: *In the end justice prevailed and the men were set free.*

prevailing *adj* (only before a noun) **1** most common or general: *the prevailing climate of opinion* **2** (used about the wind) most common in a particular area: *The prevailing wind is from the south-west.*

prevalent /ˈprevələnt/ *adj (formal)* common in a particular place at a particular time: *The prevalent atmosphere was one of fear.*

☆ **prevent** /prɪˈvent/ *verb* [T] **prevent sb/sth (from) (doing sth)** to stop sth happening or to stop sb doing sth: *Everyone hopes the negotiations will prevent a war.* ○ *I don't think that we can prevent them finding out about this.* ○ *Her parents tried to prevent her from going to live with her boyfriend.* ☞ **Prevent** is more formal than **stop**.

preventable *adj* that can be prevented: *Many accidents are preventable.*

☆ **prevention** /prɪˈvenʃn/ *noun* [U] the act of preventing sth: *The NSPCC is the National Society for the Prevention of Cruelty to Children.*

preventive /prɪˈventɪv/ *(also* **preventative** /prɪˈventətɪv/) *adj* intended to stop or prevent sth (especially crime or disease) from happening: *preventive measures to reduce crime* ○ *preventive medicine*

preview /ˈpriːvjuː/ *noun* [C] a chance to see a play, film, etc before it is shown to the general public

☆ **previous** /ˈpriːviəs/ *adj* coming or happening before or earlier: *Do you have previous experience of this type of work?* ○ *Giles has two children from his previous marriage.* ○ *The previous owners of our house moved to Liverpool.* —**previously** *adv*: *Before I moved to France I had previously worked in Italy and Spain.*

prey /preɪ/ *noun* an animal or bird that is killed and eaten by another animal or bird: *Antelope and zebra are prey for lions.* ○ *The eagle is a bird of prey* (= it kills and eats other birds or small animals).
prey *verb*
(IDIOM) **prey on sb's mind** to cause sb to worry or think about sth: *The thought that he was responsible for the accident preyed on the train-driver's mind.*
(PHRASAL VERB) **prey on sth** (used about an animal or bird) to kill and eat other animals or birds: *Cats prey on rats and mice.*

☆ **price** /praɪs/ *noun* [C] the amount of money that you must pay in order to buy sth: *What's the price of petrol now?* ○ *to charge high/low prices* ○ *We can't afford to buy the car at that price.* ○ *She offered me a fair price for the car.* ○ *(figurative) Is pollution the price we have to pay for progress?* ☞ A **charge** is the amount of money that you must pay for using something: *Is there a charge for parking here?* ○ *admission charges*. You use **cost** when you are talking about paying for services or about prices in general without mentioning an actual sum of money: *The cost of electricity is going up.* ○ *the cost of living*. The **price** of something is the amount of money that you must pay in order to buy it. A shop may **raise/increase**, **reduce/bring down** or **freeze** its prices. The prices **rise/go up** or **fall/go down**.
(IDIOMS) **at any price** even if the cost is very high or if it will have unpleasant results: *Richard was determined to succeed at any price.*
not at any price in no circumstances; never
price *verb* [T] **1** to fix the price of sth: *The books were priced between £5 and £10.* **2** to mark the price on goods in a shop

priceless *adj* of very great value: *priceless jewels and antiques* ☞ Look at **worthless**, **valuable** and **invaluable**.

pricey *(also* **pricy**) /ˈpraɪsi/ *adj* (**pricier**; **priciest**) *(Brit informal)* expensive

'price-list *noun* [C] a list of the prices of the goods that are on sale

prick¹ /prɪk/ *noun* [C] the sharp pain that you feel when sth pricks you: *the sharp prick of a needle*

prick² /prɪk/ *verb* [T] to make a small hole in sth or to cause sb pain with a sharp point: *You should prick the sausage skins before you cook them.* ○ *Ouch! I pricked myself on that needle.*
(IDIOM) **prick up your ears** (used about an animal) to raise the ears in order to listen carefully to sth: *(figurative) He pricked up his ears when he heard Mandy's name.*

prickle /ˈprɪkl/ *noun* [C] one of the sharp points on some plants and animals: *Hedgehogs are covered in prickles.*
prickle *verb* [I] to have a feeling of pricking: *His skin prickled with fear.*

prickly /ˈprɪkli/ *adj* **1** covered with prickles: *a prickly bush* **2** *(informal)* (used about a person) easily made angry

pricy = PRICEY

☆ **pride** /praɪd/ *noun* **1** [U] **pride (in sb/sth)** the feeling of pleasure that you have when you (or people who are close to you) do sth good or own sth good: *Her parents watched with pride as Mary went up to collect her prize.* ○ *to feel pride in your achievement* ☞ The adjective is **proud**. **2** [sing] **the pride of sth** a person or thing that is very important or of great value to sb: *The new stadium was the pride of the whole town.* **3** [U] the feeling that you are better than other people: *the sin of pride* **4** [U] the sense of your own worth or value; self-respect: *You'll hurt his pride if you refuse to accept the present.*
(IDIOMS) **take (a) pride in sb/sth** to feel pleased and proud about sth good that sb has done: *The manager took great pride in his team's success.*

ɜː	ə	eɪ	əʊ	aɪ	aʊ	ɔɪ	ɪə	eə	ʊə
fur	ago	pay	home	five	now	join	near	hair	pure

take pride in sth/in doing sth to do sth very well or carefully: *I wish you'd take more pride in your work.*
pride *verb*
(PHRASAL VERB) **pride yourself on sth/on doing sth** to feel pleased about sth good or clever that you can do: *Henry prides himself on his ability to cook.*

☆ **priest** /priːst/ *noun* [C] **1** a person (usually a man) who performs religious ceremonies in the Christian Church ☛ **Priest** is a general word and is used in all churches but especially in the Roman Catholic Church. A priest in the Anglican Church is also called a **vicar** or a **clergyman**. A priest in other Protestant churches is also called a **minister**. **2** a person who performs religious ceremonies in some other religions ☛ For sense 2 there is a feminine form **priestess**.

prim /prɪm/ *adj* (used about a person) always behaving very correctly and easily shocked by anything that is rude —**primly** *adv*

☆ **primary¹** /ˈpraɪməri; *US* -meri/ *adj* most important; main: *Smoking is one of the primary causes of lung cancer.* ○ *A high standard of service should be of primary importance.*

primarily /ˈpraɪmərəli; *US* praɪˈmerəli/ *adv* more than anything else; mainly: *The course will be aimed primarily at people who have no previous experience.*

primary 'colour *noun* [C] any of the colours red, yellow or blue. You can make any other colour by mixing primary colours in different ways.

primary edu'cation *noun* [U] the education of children in their first years at school

'primary school *noun* [C] (*Brit*) a school for children aged five to eleven

primary² /ˈpraɪməri; *US* -meri/ (*also* **primary e'lection**) *noun* [C] (*pl* **primaries**) (*US*) an election in which a political party chooses the person who will be its candidate in a later important election, eg for president

prime¹ /praɪm/ *adj* (*only before a noun*) **1** most important; main: *The prime cause of the company's failure was high interest rates.* **2** of very good quality; best: *prime pieces of beef* **3** having all the typical qualities: *That's a prime example of what I was talking about.*

prime 'minister *noun* [C] the leader of the government in Britain and some other countries

prime² /praɪm/ *noun* [sing] the time when sb is strongest, most beautiful, most successful, etc: *Becker is past his prime as a tennis player.* ○ *to be in the prime of life*

prime³ /praɪm/ *verb* [T] to give sb information in order to prepare him/her for sth: *The minister had been well primed with all the facts before the interview.*

primitive /ˈprɪmɪtɪv/ *adj* **1** (*only before a noun*) connected with a very early stage of development (particularly of human life): *Primitive man lived in caves and hunted wild animals.* **2** very simple; not developed: *The washing facilities in the camp were very primitive.* ○ *a primitive shelter made out of bits of wood and cloth*

primrose /ˈprɪmrəʊz/ *noun* [C] a common yellow spring flower

☆ **prince** /prɪns/ *noun* [C] **1** a son or other close male relative of the king or queen: *In Britain the eldest son of the king or queen has the title 'Prince of Wales'.* **2** the male ruler of a small country

princess /ˌprɪnˈses/ *noun* [C] **1** a daughter or other close female relative of a king or queen: *Princess Margaret is the Queen's sister.* **2** the wife of a prince: *Princess Diana*

☆ **principal** /ˈprɪnsəpl/ *adj* (*only before a noun*) most important; main: *The principal aim of the talks is to reduce the numbers of weapons.* ○ *the principal characters in a play*

principal *noun* [C] the head of some schools, colleges, etc

principally /-pli/ *adv* mainly; mostly: *Our products are designed principally for the European market.*

☆ **principle** /ˈprɪnsəpl/ *noun* **1** [C] a basic general rule or truth about sth: *We believe in the principle of equal opportunity for everyone.* ○ *The course teaches the basic principles of car maintenance.* **2** [C,U] a rule for good behaviour, based on what each person believes is right: *She refuses to wear fur. It's a matter of principle with her.* ○ *a person of high moral principles* **3** [sing] a law of science: *The system works on the principle that heat rises.*

(IDIOMS) **in principle** in general, but possibly not in detail: *His proposal sounds fine in principle, but there are a few points I'm not happy about.*

on principle because of your moral beliefs or principles(2): *Tessa refuses to eat meat on principle.*

☆ **print¹** /prɪnt/ *noun* **1** [U] the letters, words, etc in a book, newspaper, etc: *The print is too small for me to read without my glasses.* **2** [C] a mark that is made by sth pressing onto sth else: *The police are searching the room for fingerprints.* ○ *footprints in the snow* **3** [C] a picture that was made by printing **4** [C] a photograph (when it has been printed from a negative): *24 colour prints for only £4.99!*

(IDIOM) **out of print** (used about a book, etc) that is not available from the publisher; not being printed any more: *I'm sorry, the book you ordered is out of print.*

☆ **print²** /prɪnt/ *verb* **1** [T] to put words, pictures, etc onto paper by using a metal or wood surface covered with ink: *How much did it cost to print the posters?* **2** [I,T] to make a book, newspaper, etc in this way: *50 000 copies of the textbook were printed.* **3** [T] to include sth in a book, newspaper, etc: *The newspaper should not have printed the photograph of the princess in her bikini.* **4** [I,T] to write with letters that are not joined together: *Children learn to print when they first go to school.* **5** [T] to put a pattern onto cloth, paper, etc: *printed cotton, wallpaper, etc* **6** [T] to make a photograph from a piece of negative film

(PHRASAL VERB) **print (sth) out** to print information from a computer onto paper: *I'll just print out this file.* ○ *The computer's printing out the results now.*

p	b	t	d	k	g	tʃ	dʒ	f	v	θ	ð
pen	bad	tea	did	cat	got	chin	June	fall	van	thin	then

printer *noun* [C] **1** a person or company that prints books, newspapers, etc **2** a machine that prints out information from a computer onto paper: *a laser printer* ☞ picture on page A13. —**printing** *noun* [U]: *the invention of printing by Gutenberg*

'printing-press (*also* **press**) *noun* [C] a machine that is used for printing books, newspapers, etc

printout /'prɪntaʊt/ *noun* [C,U] information from a computer that is printed onto paper

prior /'praɪə(r)/ *adj* (only *before* a noun) coming before or earlier: *Miss Parker was unable to attend because of a prior engagement.*

prior to *prep* (*formal*) before: *Passengers are asked to report to the check-in desk prior to departure.*

☆ **priority** /praɪ'ɒrəti; *US* -'ɔːr-/ *noun* (*pl* **priorities**) **1** [U] **priority (over sb/sth)** the state of being more important than sb/sth else or coming before sb/sth else: *Families with small children will be given priority.* ○ *Emergency cases take priority over other patients in hospital.* ○ *On roundabouts in Britain traffic coming from the right has priority.* **2** [C] something that is most important or that you must do before anything else: *Our top priority is to get food and water to the refugee camps.* ○ *You must decide what your priorities are.*

prise /praɪz/ (*especially US* **prize**, **pry**) *verb* [T] to use force to open sth, remove a lid, etc: *He prised the door open with an iron bar.*

☆ **prison** /'prɪzn/ (*also* **jail**) *noun* [C,U] a building where criminals are kept as a punishment: *She was sent to a maximum-security prison.* ○ *The terrorists were sent to prison for twenty-five years.* ○ *to escape from prison* ○ *He will be released from prison next month.* ○ *a prison warder* ☞ You talk about **prison** (no 'the') when you are talking about somebody going or being there as a prisoner: *He's in prison.* You talk about **the prison** if you are talking about people going there for a different reason: *The minister visited the prison and said that conditions were poor.* You also use *a* or *the* when more information is given: *a high-security prison.* Look at **imprison** and **jail**.

☆ **prisoner** *noun* [C] a person who is being kept in a prison: *In many prisons, there are three prisoners in a cell.* ○ *a political prisoner*

,prisoner of 'war *noun* [C] a soldier, etc who is caught by the enemy during a war and who is kept in a prison until the end of the war

privacy /'prɪvəsi; 'praɪv-/ *noun* [U] the state of being alone or away from other people who may disturb you: *There is not much privacy in large hospital wards.*

☆ **private** /'praɪvət/ *adj* **1** belonging to one particular person or group and not to be used by others: *This is private property. You may not park here.* **2** secret; not to be shared by other people: *a private letter* **3** with no one else present: *I would like a private interview with the personnel manager.* **4** not connected with work or business: *He never discusses his private life with his colleagues at work.* **5** owned, done or organized by a person or company, and not by the government: *a private hospital* (= you must pay to go there). ○ *a private school* ○ *The Channel Tunnel is being paid for by private enterprise, not by public money.* ○ *a private detective* (= one who is not in the police) ☞ Look at **public**.

(IDIOM) **in private** with no one else present: *May I speak to you in private?*

private *noun* [C] a soldier of the lowest rank

privately *adv* not in public: *She said she agreed but privately she had her doubts.*

privatize (*also* **privatise**) /'praɪvətaɪz/ *verb* [T] to change the ownership of an organization from the government to a private company: *The water industry has been privatized.* ☞ The opposite is **nationalize**. —**privatization** (*also* **privatisation**) /,praɪvətaɪ'zeɪʃn; *US* -tɪ'z-/ *noun* [U]

☆ **privilege** /'prɪvəlɪdʒ/ *noun* **1** [C,U] a special right or advantage that only one person or group has: *Prisoners who behave well enjoy special privileges.* ○ *the wealth and privilege of the upper classes* **2** [C] a special advantage or opportunity that gives you great pleasure: *It was a great privilege to hear her sing in Milan.*

privileged *adj* having an advantage or opportunity that most people do not have: *I feel very privileged to be playing for the England team.*

☆ **prize¹** /praɪz/ *noun* [C] something of value that is given to sb who is successful in a race, competition, game, etc: *She won first prize in the competition.* ○ *He was awarded second prize for his painting.* ○ *a prize-winning novel*

prize *adj* (only *before* a noun) winning, or good enough to win, a prize: *a prize flower display*

prize *verb* [T] to consider sth to be very valuable: *This picture is one of my most prized possessions.*

prize² *verb* [T] (*especially US*) = PRISE

pro¹ /prəʊ/ *noun*

(IDIOM) **the pros and cons** the reasons for and against doing sth: *We should consider all the pros and cons before reaching a decision.*

pro² /prəʊ/ *noun* [C] (*pl* **pros**) (*informal*) a person who is a professional(2,3): *a golf pro*

probability /,prɒbə'bɪləti/ *noun* (*pl* **probabilities**) **1** [U] the state of being probable or likely: *At that time there seemed little probability of success.* **2** [C] something that is probable or likely: *There is a high probability that mistakes will be made.*

☆ **probable** /'prɒbəbl/ *adj* that you expect to happen or to be true; likely: *I suppose it's possible that they might still come but it doesn't seem very probable.* ☞ The opposite is **improbable**.

probable *noun* [C] a person or thing that is likely to be chosen for sth or to win sth: *a probable for the next Olympic team*

probably /-əbli/ *adv* almost certainly: *I will phone next week, probably on Wednesday.* ○ *'Are you coming to London with us?' 'Probably not.'* ☞ Notice that **probable** and **likely** mean the same but are used differently: *It's probable that he will be late.* ○ *He is likely to be late.*

probation /prə'beɪʃn; *US* prəʊ-/ *noun* [U] **1** the system of keeping an official check on a person who has broken the law instead of sending him/her to prison: *The prisoner was released on probation.* **2** a period of time at the start of a new job when you are tested to see if you are really suitable: *a three-month probation period*

pro'bation officer *noun* [C] a person who keeps an official check on people who are on probation(1)

probe /prəʊb/ *noun* [C] **1** a long thin tool that you use for examining sth that is difficult to reach, especially a part of the body **2** asking questions, collecting facts, etc in order to find out all the information about sth: *a police probe into illegal financial dealing*

probe *verb* **1** [T] to examine sth carefully with a probe(1) or sth like it **2** [I,T] **probe (into sth)** to try to find out all the facts about sth —**probing** *adj*: *to ask probing questions*

☆ **problem** /'prɒbləm/ *noun* [C] **1** a difficult situation that you must deal with: *Unemployment causes a lot of social problems.* ○ *The problem of racial discrimination is very difficult to solve.* ○ *I'm facing a lot of problems at work at the moment.* ○ *to have financial problems* ○ *There's a problem with the washing-machine. It won't work.* ○ *'Can you fix this for me?' 'No problem.'* ○ *It's a problem finding a good plumber these days.* **2** a question that you must solve by thinking about it: *Vicky had ten problems to do for homework.*

☆ **procedure** /prə'siːdʒə(r)/ *noun* [C,U] the action that you must take in order to do sth in the usual or correct way: *If you want to make a complaint, please follow the correct procedure.*

☆ **proceed** /prə'siːd; prəʊ-/ *verb* [I] **1** to go on to do sth else: *After getting an estimate we can decide whether or not to proceed with the work.* ○ *Once he had calmed down he proceeded to tell us what had happened.* **2** (*formal*) to continue: *The building work was proceeding according to schedule.*

proceedings /prə'siːdɪŋz/ *noun* [plural] **1 proceedings (against sb/for sth)** legal action: *to start divorce proceedings* **2** events that happen, especially at a formal meeting, ceremony, etc: *The proceedings of the council were interrupted by the demonstrators.*

proceeds /'prəʊsiːdz/ *noun* [plural] **proceeds (of/from sth)** money that you get when you sell sth, or for sth that you have organized: *The proceeds from the sale will go to charity.*

☆ **process** /'prəʊses; *US* 'prɒses/ *noun* [C] **1** a series of actions that you do for a particular purpose: *the process of producing steel* ○ *Foreigners wishing to work in Britain have to go through the complicated process of getting a work permit.* **2** a series of changes that happen naturally: *Trees go though the process of growing and losing leaves every year.*

(IDIOMS) **in the process** while you are doing sth else: *We washed the dog yesterday – and we all got very wet in the process.*

in the process of sth/doing sth in the middle of doing sth: *They are in the process of moving house.*

process *verb* [T] **1** to change a raw material, eg with chemicals, before it is sold or used: *Cheese is processed so that it lasts longer.* ○ *to process a film* (= to develop it so that you can print photographs from it) **2** to deal with information, eg on a computer: *When we have collected all the data the computer will process it for us.* ○ *It will take about ten days to process your application.*

processor *noun* [C] a machine that processes food or information: *a food processor* ○ *a word processor*

procession /prə'seʃn/ *noun* [C,U] a number of people, vehicles, etc that move slowly in a line, eg as part of a ceremony: *to walk in procession* ○ *a funeral procession*

proclaim /prə'kleɪm/ *verb* [T] (*formal*) to make sth known officially or publicly: *The day of the royal wedding was proclaimed a national holiday.* ○ *to proclaim a state of emergency* —**proclamation** /ˌprɒklə'meɪʃn/ *noun* [C,U]: *to make a proclamation of war*

procure /prə'kjʊə(r)/ *verb* [T] **procure sth (for sb)** (*formal*) to obtain or get sth

prod /prɒd/ *verb* [I,T] (**prodding; prodded**) to push or press sb/sth with your finger or other pointed object: (*figurative*) *Ruth works quite hard but she does need prodding occasionally.* —**prod** *noun* [C]: *to give the fire a prod with a stick* —**prodding** *noun* [U] (*figurative*): *Harold needs a lot of prodding before he will go and see a doctor.*

prodigious /prə'dɪdʒəs/ *adj* very great: *He seemed to have a prodigious amount of energy.*

prodigy /'prɒdɪdʒi/ *noun* [C] (*pl* **prodigies**) a person (especially a child) who is unusually good at sth: *Mozart was a child prodigy.* ☞ Look at **genius**.

☆ **produce** /prə'djuːs; *US* -'duːs/ *verb* [T] **1** to make or grow sth: *VW cars are produced in Wolfsburg.* ○ *East Anglia produced much of the country's wheat.* ○ *The children have produced some beautiful pictures for the exhibition.* ○ *The burning of coal produces carbon dioxide.* **2** to cause sth to happen: *Her remarks produced roars of laughter.* **3** to give birth to a young animal: *Our cat's just produced six kittens!* **4** to show sth so that sb else can look at or examine it: *The inspector got on the bus and asked all the passengers to produce their tickets.* ○ *to produce evidence in court* **5** to organize a play, film, etc so that it can be shown to the public: *She is producing 'Romeo and Juliet' at the local theatre.*

produce /'prɒdjuːs; *US* -duːs/ *noun* [U] food, etc that is grown on a farm and sold: *fresh farm produce* ☞ Look at the note at **production**.

producer /prə'djuːsə(r); *US* -'duː-/ *noun* [C] **1** a person, company or country that makes or grows sth: *Brazil is a major producer of coffee.* **2** a person who deals with the business side of organizing a play, film, etc

☆ **product** /'prɒdʌkt/ *noun* [C] **1** something that is made in a factory or that is formed naturally: *Coal was once a major product of South Wales.* ○ *waste products* ○ *We have to find the right product for the market.* ○ *The finished product should look very much like this design.* ☞ Look at the note at **production**. **2 product of sth** the result of sth: *The industry's problems are the product of government policy.* **3** the amount that you get if you multiply one number by another: *The product of three and five is fifteen.*

☆ **production** /prə'dʌkʃn/ *noun* **1** [U] the act of

iː	ɪ	e	æ	ɑː	ɒ	ɔː	ʊ	uː	ʌ
see	sit	ten	hat	arm	got	saw	put	too	cup

making or growing sth: *This farm specializes in the production of organic vegetables.* o *mass production* o *The price increases were the result of rising production costs.* **2** [U] the amount of sth that is made or grown: *Saudi Arabia is increasing its production of oil.* **3** [C] a play, film, etc ☛ Notice that **produce** means food, etc that comes from a farm and a **product** is something that was made in a factory. A **production** is a play, film, etc: *The label on the bottle says 'Produce of Italy'.* o *The company's main products are plastic toys.* o *the Bolshoi Ballet's production of Swan Lake*

(IDIOMS) **in production** being made: *The new car is now in production.*

on production of sth when you show sth: *You can get a ten per cent discount on production of your membership card.*

productive /prəˈdʌktɪv/ *adj* **1** that can make or grow sth well or in large quantities: *The company wants to sell off its less productive factories.* o *productive land* **2** useful (because results come from it): *a productive discussion* ☛ The opposite is **unproductive**.

productivity /ˌprɒdʌkˈtɪvəti/ *noun* [U] the state of being productive(1) or the amount that sb/sth produces(1): *More efficient methods will lead to greater productivity.*

profess /prəˈfes/ *verb* [T] **1** (*formal*) to say that sth is true (even if it is not): *Marianne professed to know nothing at all about it, but I did not believe her.* **2** to say openly that you think or believe sth: *He professed his hatred of war.*

☆ **profession** /prəˈfeʃn/ *noun* [C] **1** a job that requires a lot of training and that is respected by other people: *the medical, legal, teaching, etc profession* ☛ Look at the note at **work¹**. **2 the profession** [with sing or pl verb] all the people who work in a particular profession: *The legal profession is/are trying to resist the reforms.*

(IDIOM) **by profession** as your profession or job: *Graham is an accountant by profession.*

☆ **professional** /prəˈfeʃənl/ *adj* **1** (only *before* a noun) of or concerning sb who has a profession: *The flat would be ideal for a professional couple.* o *Get professional advice from your lawyer before you take any action.* **2** doing sth in a way that shows skill, training or care: *The police are trained to deal with every situation in a calm and professional manner.* o *Her application was neatly typed and looked very professional.* ☛ The opposite is **unprofessional**. **3** doing a sport, etc as a job or for money: *After his success at the Olympic Games he turned professional.* **4** (used about a sport, etc) done by people who are paid: *professional football* ☛ The opposite for 3 and 4 is **amateur**.

professional *noun* [C] **1** a person who works in a profession(1) **2** (also *informal* **pro**) a person who plays or teaches a sport, etc for money **3** (also *informal* **pro**) a person who does his/her work with skill and care

professionalism /-ʃənəlɪzəm/ *noun* [U] the quality of showing great skill or care when you are doing a job: *Although they were students, they performed with great professionalism.*

professionally /-ʃənəli/ *adv* **1** in a professional(1,2) way **2** for money, by a professional person: *Rob plays the saxophone professionally.* o *to have your photograph taken professionally*

☆ **professor** /prəˈfesə(r)/ *noun* [C] (*abbr* **Prof**) **1** a university teacher of the highest rank: *Professor Brown* o *Professor Anthony Clare* o *She's professor of English at Bristol University.* **2** (*US*) a teacher at a college or university

proficient /prəˈfɪʃnt/ *adj* **proficient (in/at sth/doing sth)** able to do a particular thing well; skilled: *We are looking for someone who is proficient in French.*

proficiency /-nsi/ *noun* [U] **proficiency (in sth/doing sth)** the ability to do sth well; skill: *a cycling proficiency test* o *a certificate of proficiency in English*

profile /ˈprəʊfaɪl/ *noun* [C] **1** a person's face or head seen from the side, not the front **2** a short description of sb's life, character, etc

(IDIOM) **a high/low profile** a way of behaving that does/does not attract other people's attention: *I don't know much about the subject – I'm going to keep a low profile at the meeting tomorrow.*

☆ **profit¹** /ˈprɒfɪt/ *noun* [C,U] the money that you make when you sell sth for more than it cost you: *Did you make a profit on your house when you sold it?* o *an annual profit of £25 000* o *I'm hoping to sell my shares at a profit.* o *We won't make much profit in the first year.* ☛ Look at **loss**.

profit² /ˈprɒfɪt/ *verb*

(PHRASAL VERB) **profit from sth** (*formal*) to get some advantage from sth: *Who will profit most from the tax reforms?*

profitable /ˈprɒfɪtəbl/ *adj* **1** that makes a profit: *a profitable business* **2** helpful or useful: *We had a very profitable discussion yesterday.*

profitability /ˌprɒfɪtəˈbɪləti/ *noun* [U] the state of being profitable(1)

profitably /-əbli/ *adv* in a profitable(1,2) way: *to invest money profitably* o *to spend your time profitably*

profound /prəˈfaʊnd/ *adj* **1** great; that you feel very strongly: *The experience had a profound influence on her.* **2** serious; showing knowledge or thought: *She's always making profound statements about the meaning of life.*

profoundly *adv* very; extremely: *I was profoundly relieved to hear the news.*

profuse /prəˈfjuːs/ *adj* (*formal*) produced in great quantity: *profuse apologies* —**profusely** *adv*: *She apologized profusely for being late.* o *The blood was flowing profusely.*

program /ˈprəʊgræm; *US* -grəm/ *noun* [C] **1** a set of instructions that you give to a computer so that it will carry out a particular task: *to write a program* o *to load a program into the computer* ☛ When we are talking about computers both the US and the British spelling is **program**. For every other meaning the British spelling is **programme** and the US spelling is **program**. **2** (*US*) = PROGRAMME

program *verb* [T] (**programming**; **programmed**; *US also* **programing**; **programed**) to give a set of instructions to a computer

programmer (*US also* **programer**) *noun* [C]

ɜː	ə	eɪ	əʊ	aɪ	aʊ	ɔɪ	ɪə	eə	ʊə
fur	ago	pay	home	five	now	join	near	hair	pure

a person whose job is to write programs for a computer: *a computer programmer*

☆ **programme** (*US* **program**) /ˈprəʊgræm; *US* -grəm/ *noun* [C] **1** a show or other item that is broadcast on the radio or television: *a TV/ radio programme* ○ *Do you want to watch the programme on Italian cookery at 8 o'clock?* ○ *We've just missed an interesting programme on California.* **2** a plan of things to do; a scheme: *What's (on) your programme today?* (= what are you going to do today?) ○ *The leaflet outlines the government's programme of educational reforms.* **3** a little book or piece of paper which you get at a play, concert, etc that gives you information about what you are going to see

programme (*US* **program**) *verb* [T] (programmed; programming; *US also* programing; programed) to make sb/sth work or act automatically in a particular way: *The lights are programmed to come on as soon as it gets dark.*

☆ **progress** /ˈprəʊgres; *US* ˈprɒg-/ *noun* [U] **1** movement forwards or towards achieving sth: *The heavy traffic meant that we made very slow progress.* ○ *Anna's making steady progress at school.* ○ *The talks have made very little progress towards solving the problem.* ○ *a progress report* **2** change or improvement in society: *scientific progress* ○ *People who oppose new roads are accused of holding back progress.*
(IDIOM) **in progress** happening: *Silence! Examination in progress.*

progress /prəˈgres/ *verb* [I] **1** to become better; to develop (well): *Medical knowledge has progressed rapidly in the last twenty years.* **2** to move forward; to continue: *I got more and more tired as the evening progressed.*

progression /prəˈgreʃn/ *noun* [C,U] **progression (from sth) (to sth)** movement forward or a development from one stage to another: *There seems to be no logical progression in your thoughts in this essay.*

progressive /prəˈgresɪv/ *adj* **1** using or agreeing with modern methods and ideas: *a progressive school* **2** happening or developing steadily: *a progressive reduction in the number of staff*

progressively *adv* steadily; a little at a time: *The situation became progressively worse.*

progressive ˈtense *noun* [sing] = CONTINUOUS TENSE

prohibit /prəˈhɪbɪt; *US* prəʊ-/ *verb* [T] (*formal*) **prohibit sb/sth (from doing sth)** to say that sth is not allowed by law; to forbid: *English law prohibits children under 16 from buying cigarettes.* ○ *That sign means that smoking is prohibited.*

prohibition /ˌprəʊhɪˈbɪʃn; *US* ˌprəʊəˈbɪʃn/ *noun* **1** [C] (*formal*) a law or rule that forbids sth **2** [U] the forbidding of sth: *the prohibition of corporal punishment in schools*

prohibitive /prəˈhɪbətɪv; *US* prəʊ-/ *adj* (used about a price etc) so high that people cannot afford it: *It's a lovely shop but the prices are prohibitive.* —**prohibitively** *adv*: *prohibitively expensive*

☆ **project¹** /ˈprɒdʒekt/ *noun* [C] **1** a piece of work, often involving many people, that is planned and organized carefully; a plan for some work: *The new television series was an extremely expensive project.* ○ *a major project to reduce pollution in our rivers* ○ *the Channel Tunnel project* ○ *His latest project is making a pond in the garden.* **2** a piece of school work in which the student has to collect information about a certain subject and then write about it: *The whole class is doing a project on rainforests.*

project² /prəˈdʒekt/ *verb* **1** [T] (usually passive) to plan: *the Queen's projected tour of Canada* **2** [T] (usually passive) to estimate or calculate: *a projected increase of 10%* **3** [T] **project sth (on/onto sth)** to make sth (light, a shadow, a picture from a film, etc) fall on a surface: *Coloured lights were projected onto the dance floor.* **4** [T] to show or represent sb/sth/ yourself in a certain way: *The government is trying to project a more caring image.* **5** [I] (*formal*) to stick out: *The balcony projects one metre out from the wall.*

projection /prəˈdʒekʃn/ *noun* **1** [C] a guess about a future amount, situation, etc based on the information you have at present: *sales projections for the next five years* **2** [U] the act of making light, a picture from a film, etc fall on a surface: *film projection*

projector /prəˈdʒektə(r)/ *noun* [C] an apparatus that projects pictures or films onto a screen or wall: *a film projector* ○ *a slide projector* ○ *an overhead projector*

proliferate /prəˈlɪfəreɪt; *US* prəʊ-/ *verb* [I] (*formal*) to increase quickly in number —**proliferation** /prəˌlɪfəˈreɪʃn; *US* prəʊ-/ *noun* [U]

prolific /prəˈlɪfɪk/ *adj* (used especially about a writer, artist, etc) producing a lot: *a prolific writer of short stories*

prologue (*US* **prolog**) /ˈprəʊlɒg; *US* -lɔːg/ *noun* [C] a piece of writing or a speech that introduces the rest of a play, poem, etc ☞ Look at **epilogue**.

prolong /prəˈlɒŋ; *US* -ˈlɔːŋ/ *verb* [T] to make sth last longer: *Careful treatment will prolong the life of the furniture.*

prolonged *adj* continuing for a long time: *There was a prolonged silence before anybody spoke.*

prom /prɒm/ *noun* [C] **1** = PROMENADE **2** (*US*) a formal dance that is held by a high school class at the end of a school year

promenade /ˌprɒməˈnɑːd; *US* -ˈneɪd/ *noun* [C] a wide path or pavement where people walk beside the sea in a seaside town

prominent /ˈprɒmɪnənt/ *adj* **1** important or famous: *a prominent political figure* ○ *The new party hopes to play a prominent role in political life.* **2** noticeable; easy to see: *The church is the most prominent feature of the village.*

prominence /-əns/ *noun* [U] the state of being important or easily noticed: *The newspaper gave the affair great prominence.*
—**prominently** *adv*: *Display your ticket prominently at the front of your car.*

promiscuous /prəˈmɪskjʊəs/ *adj* having sexual relations with many people
promiscuity /ˌprɒmɪˈskjuːəti/ *noun* [U] promiscuous behaviour

☆ **promise¹** /ˈprɒmɪs/ *noun* **1** [C] a written or

| p | b | t | d | k | g | tʃ | dʒ | f | v | θ | ð |
| pen | bad | tea | did | cat | got | chin | June | fall | van | thin | then |

spoken statement or agreement that you will or will not do sth: *He made a promise not to tell anyone what he had seen.* o *Her parents kept their promise to buy her a dog for her birthday.* o *You should not break a promise* (= you should do what you have said you will do). o *They both gave me a promise of their complete support.* **2** [U] signs that you will be able to do sth well or be successful: *He showed great promise as a musician.*

☆ **promise²** /'prɒmɪs/ *verb* **1** [I,T] to say definitely that you will or will not do sth: *I'll try to be back at 6 o'clock but I can't promise.* o *'I'll pay you back tomorrow,' his friend promised.* o *She promised that she would write every week.* o *She promised not to forget to write.* o *Tom promised me that he'd never be late again.* o *The finance minister has promised to bring down the rate of inflation by the end of the year.* **2** [T] **promise sth (to sb)** to say definitely that you will give sth to sb: *My father has promised me a new bicycle.* o *Can you promise your support?* **3** [T] to show signs of sth, so that you expect it to happen: *It promises to be a lovely day.*

promising *adj* showing signs of being very good or successful: *a promising writer*

promote /prə'məʊt/ *verb* [T] **1** (often passive) to give sb a higher position, more important job, etc: *He's been promoted from assistant manager to manager.* **2** to encourage sth; to help sth to happen or develop: *The meetings of the leaders have helped to promote good relations between the two countries.* **3** to advertise sth (in order to increase its sales or popularity): *In order to sell a new product you need to promote it in the right way.*

promoter *noun* [C] a person who organizes or provides the money for an event

☆ **promotion** /prə'məʊʃn/ *noun* **1** [C,U] (the giving or receiving of) a higher position or more important job: *The new job is a promotion for her.* o *The job offers a good salary and excellent chances of promotion.* o *the team's promotion from Division 2 to Division 1* **2** [U] making sth successful or popular: *We need to work on the promotion of health, not the treatment of disease.* **3** [C,U] things that you do in order to advertise a product: *It's all part of a special promotion of the new book.* o *Millions of pounds were spent on advertising and promotion.*

☆ **prompt¹** /prɒmpt/ *adj* **1** quick; done without delay: *I received a prompt reply from the solicitor.* o *We need a prompt decision on this matter.* **2 prompt (in doing sth/to do sth)** (used about a person) quick; acting without delay: *We are always prompt in paying our bills.* o *She was prompt to point out my mistake.*

prompt *adv* exactly: *I'll pick you up at 7 o'clock prompt.*

promptly *adv* **1** immediately; without delay: *I invited her to dinner and she promptly accepted.* **2** punctually; at the time that you have arranged: *We arrived promptly at 12 o'clock.*

prompt² /prɒmpt/ *verb* **1** [T] to cause sth; to make sb decide to do sth: *Whatever prompted that remark?* o *What prompted you to give up your job?* **2** [I,T] to help sb to continue speaking or to remind an actor of his/her words: *'And can you tell the court what happened next?' the lawyer prompted.* o *The speaker had to be prompted several times.* o *We need somebody to prompt at the performance tonight.*

prompting *noun* [C,U] an act of persuading or reminding sb to do sth: *He apologized without any prompting.*

prone /prəʊn/ *adj* (not before a noun) **prone to sth/to do sth** likely to suffer from sth or to do sth: *Young people are especially prone to this disease.* o *This area is very prone to fog in winter.* o *to be accident-prone* (= to have a lot of accidents) o *He's rather prone to criticize people without thinking first.*

pronoun /'prəʊnaʊn/ *noun* [C] (*grammar*) a word that is used in place of a noun or a phrase that contains a noun: *'He', 'it', 'hers', 'me', 'them' are all pronouns.*

☆ **pronounce** /prə'naʊns/ *verb* **1** [T] to make the sound of a word or letter: *You don't pronounce the 'b' at the end of 'comb'.* o *How do you pronounce your surname?* **2** [T] (*formal*) to say in a formal or official way that sb/sth is in a particular state: *The doctors pronounced him fit.* **3** [I,T] **pronounce (on sth)** (*formal*) to give your opinion on sth, especially formally: *I can't pronounce on the quality of a wine.* o *The play was pronounced 'brilliant' by all the critics.*

pronounced *adj* very noticeable: *His English is excellent although he speaks with a pronounced French accent.*

☆ **pronunciation** /prə,nʌnsɪ'eɪʃn/ *noun* **1** [C,U] the way in which a language or a word is pronounced: *The dictionary gives two different pronunciations for this word.* o *American pronunciation* **2** [U] a person's way of speaking a language: *His grammar is good but his pronunciation is awful!*

☆ **proof¹** /pruːf/ *noun* [U] a fact or piece of information which shows that sth is true: *'We need some proof of your identity,' the shop assistant said.* o *What proof have we got that what he is saying is true?* ☞ The verb is **prove**.

proof² /pruːf/ *adj* (in compounds) able to protect from or to be protected against the thing mentioned: *a soundproof room* o *bulletproof glass*

prop¹ *noun* [C] a stick or other object that you use to support sth

prop *verb* [T] (**prop**ping; **prop**ped) **1** to support sth or keep sth in position: *I'll use this book to prop the window open* **2** to lean sth against sth else: *He propped his bicycle against the wall.*

(PHRASAL VERBS) **prop sb/sth up** to put an object under or behind sb/sth in order to give support

prop sth up to support sth that would otherwise fail

prop² /prɒp/ *noun* [C, usually pl] a piece of furniture or another object that is used in a play, film, etc

propaganda /ˌprɒpə'gændə/ *noun* [U] information and ideas that are made public by a government or large organization, in order to influence people or persuade them about

s	z	ʃ	ʒ	h	m	n	ŋ	l	r	j	w
so	zoo	she	vision	how	man	no	sing	leg	red	yes	wet

sth: *political propaganda* o *anti-German propaganda*

propel /prə'pel/ *verb* [T] (propel**l**ing; propel**l**ed) to move, drive or push sb/sth forward

propeller *noun* [C] a device with several blades, which turns round very fast in order to make a ship or a plane move

☆ **proper** /'prɒpə(r)/ *adj* **1** (only *before* a noun) real or genuine: *I've been to stay with my mother but I haven't had a proper holiday this year.* o *We haven't got any proper friends around here.* o *I didn't see much of the flat yesterday. I'm going to go today and have a proper look.* **2** (only *before* a noun) right, suitable or correct: *That's not the proper way to eat spaghetti!* o *If you're going skiing you must have the proper clothes.* o *I've got to get these pieces of paper in the proper order.* **3** (*formal*) accepted as socially correct: *I think it would be only proper for you to apologize.* ☞ The opposite for 3 is **improper**. **4** (only *after* a noun) real or main: *We travelled through miles of suburbs before we got to the city proper.*

properly *adv* **1** correctly; in an acceptable way: *The teacher said I hadn't done my homework properly.* o *These shoes don't fit properly.* **2** in a way that is socially correct; politely ☞ The opposite for 2 is **improperly**.

'**proper name** (*also* '**proper noun**) *noun* [C] (*grammar*) a word which is the name of a particular person or place and begins with a capital letter: *'Mary', 'Rome' and 'the Houses of Parliament' are all proper names.*

☆ **property** /'prɒpəti/ *noun* (*pl* **properties**) **1** [U] something that belongs to sb; all the things that belong to sb: *'Is this your property?' the policeman asked, pointing to a small brown suitcase.* o *The sack contained stolen property.* o *private/public property* o *When she died she left her entire property to a cousin in America.* ☞ Look at **lost property**. **2** [C] (*formal*) a building and the land around it: *'What sort of property are you hoping to buy?' asked the estate agent.* **3** [U] land and buildings: *to invest your money in property* **4** [C] a special quality that a substance, etc has: *Some plants have healing properties.*

prophecy /'prɒfəsi/ *noun* [C] (*pl* **prophecies**) a statement about what is going to happen in the future: *His prophecy that there would be a disaster has come true.*

prophesy /'prɒfəsaɪ/ *verb* [T] (*pres part* **prophesying**; *3rd pers sing pres* **prophesies**; *pt, pp* **prophesied**) to say what you think will happen in the future: *to prophesy disaster* o *to prophesy that there will be a war*

prophet /'prɒfɪt/ *noun* **1** (*also* **Prophet**) a person who is chosen by God to give his message to people: *the Prophet Muhammad* o *the prophets of the Old Testament* **2** a person who tells or claims to tell what will happen in the future — **prophetic** /prə'fetɪk/ *adj*

☆ **proportion** /prə'pɔːʃn/ *noun* **1** [C] a part or share of a whole: *A large proportion of the earth's surface is covered by sea.* **2** [C] **proportion (of sth to sth)** the relationship between the size or amount of two things: *I was not impressed by the proportion of teachers to students* (= there were not enough teachers for the number of students). **3 proportions** [plural] the size and shape of sth: *He stood and gazed at the magnificent proportions of the cathedral.* o *Political unrest is reaching alarming proportions.*

(IDIOMS) **in proportion** in the correct relation to other things: *to draw sth in proportion* (= so that the parts are balanced as they are in reality) o *She's so upset that she can't see the problem in proportion any more* (= it seems more important than it really is).

in proportion to sth 1 by the same amount or number as sth else: *Salaries have not risen in proportion to inflation.* **2** compared with: *In proportion to the number of students as a whole, there are very few women.*

out of proportion (to sth) 1 too big, small, etc in relation to other things **2** too great, serious, important, etc in relation to sth: *His reaction was completely out of proportion to the situation.* o *Haven't you got this matter rather out of proportion?* (= you think it's more important than it really is).

proportional /prə'pɔːʃənl/ *adj* directly linked in size, amount, etc: *The cost will be proportional to the amount used.*

pro,portional represen'tation *noun* [U] a system in which all political parties have a number of representatives in parliament in proportion to the number of votes they receive in an election

☆ **proposal** /prə'pəʊzl/ *noun* [C] **1** a plan that is suggested; a scheme: *a new proposal for raising money* o *The recent proposal has been rejected.* o *May I put forward a proposal that the canteen should serve more salads?* **2** an offer of marriage

☆ **propose** /prə'pəʊz/ *verb* **1** [T] to suggest sth as a possible plan or action: *I propose a day in the country and lunch at a pub. What do you think?* o *Our neighbours proposed that we should go on holiday together.* o *John Carter proposed the motion* (= the idea to be discussed) *at last night's student debate.* **2** [T] to intend; to have as a plan: *It seems they propose to build a motorway behind our house.* **3** [I,T] **propose (to sb)** to ask sb to marry you: *We've been going out for a long time but he still hasn't proposed.* o *to propose marriage* **4** [T] **propose sb for/as sth** to suggest sb for an official position: *I'd like to propose Denise Roberts for/as Chair.*

proposition /,prɒpə'zɪʃn/ *noun* [C] **1** an idea or opinion that sb expresses about sth: *That's a very interesting proposition. But can you prove it?* **2** an arrangement or offer, especially in business; a suggestion: *He made me a proposition to buy my share of the company.* o *A month's holiday in Spain is an attractive proposition.* **3** a problem or task that you must deal with: *Getting the work finished on time is going to be quite a difficult proposition.*

proprietor /prə'praɪətə(r)/ (*feminine* **proprietress** /prə'praɪətrɪs/) *noun* [C] the owner, especially of a hotel, business, newspaper etc

prose /prəʊz/ *noun* [U] written or spoken lan-

iː	ɪ	e	æ	ɑː	ɒ	ɔː	ʊ	uː	ʌ
see	sit	ten	hat	arm	got	saw	put	too	cup

guage that is not in verse: *to write in prose* o *a prose writer* ☞ Look at **poetry**.

prosecute /'prɒsɪkjuːt/ *verb* [I,T] **prosecute sb (for sth)** to accuse sb of a crime and to try to prove it in a court of law: *Which of the barristers is prosecuting?* o *He was prosecuted for theft.* ☞ Look at **defend**.

prosecution /ˌprɒsɪ'kjuːʃn/ *noun* **1** [C,U] (an example of) accusing sb of a crime and trying to prove it in a court of law: *to bring a prosecution against sb for a driving offence* o *the Director of Public Prosecutions* o *Failure to pay your parking fine will result in prosecution.* **2** [sing, with sing or pl verb] a person or group of people who try to prove in a court of law that sb is guilty of a crime: *a witness for the prosecution* o *The prosecution claim/claims that Lloyd was driving at 100 miles per hour.* ☞ Look at **defence**.

prospect /'prɒspekt/ *noun* **1** [C,U] **prospect (of sth/of doing sth)** the chance or hope that sth will happen: *There's little prospect of better weather before next week.* o *Prospects for peace do not look good.* **2** [C,U] an idea of what may or will happen: *'We'll have to manage without central heating this winter.' 'What an awful prospect.'* **3 prospects** [plural] chances of being successful: *The job offers a good salary and excellent prospects.*

prospective /prə'spektɪv/ *adj* likely to be or to happen; possible: *prospective changes in the law* o *a prospective buyer for the car*

prospectus /prə'spektəs/ *noun* [C] a small book which gives details about a school, college, new business, etc

prosper /'prɒspə(r)/ *verb* [I] to be successful, especially financially

prosperity /prɒ'sperəti/ *noun* [U] the state of being successful, especially financially: *Tourism has brought prosperity to many parts of Spain.* o *economic prosperity*

prosperous /'prɒspərəs/ *adj* rich and successful: *the prosperous countries of Western Europe*

prostitute /'prɒstɪtjuːt; *US* -tuːt/ (also old-fashioned **whore**) *noun* [C] a person, especially a woman, who earns money by having sex with people

prostitution /ˌprɒstɪ'tjuːʃn; *US* -'tuːʃn/ *noun* [U] working as a prostitute

prostrate /'prɒstreɪt/ *adj* lying flat on the ground, facing downwards

☆ **protect** /prə'tekt/ *verb* [T] **protect sb/sth (against/from sth)** to keep sb/sth safe; to defend sb/sth: *It was interesting to watch the bird trying to protect its young.* o *Wear something to protect your head against the sun.* o *Politicians always try to protect themselves against criticism.* o *Parents try to protect their children from danger as far as possible.* o *Bats are a protected species* (= they must not be killed).

☆ **protection** /prə'tekʃn/ *noun* [U] **protection (against sth)** (a way of) keeping sb/sth safe so that he/she/it is not harmed or damaged: *the protection of the environment* o *Vaccination against measles gives you protection against the disease.* o *the Royal Society for the Protection of Birds* o *After the attack he was given police protection.*

protective /prə'tektɪv/ *adj* **1** that prevents sb/sth from being damaged or harmed: *In certain jobs workers need to wear protective clothing.* **2 protective (towards sb)** wanting to protect sb and keep him/her safe: *He's been very protective towards his wife since she became ill.*

protector /prə'tektə(r)/ *noun* [C] a person who protects

protein /'prəʊtiːn/ *noun* [C,U] a substance found in food such as meat, fish and beans. It is important for helping people and animals to grow and be healthy.

☆ **protest¹** /'prəʊtest/ *noun* [C,U] the showing of disagreement; a statement or action that shows that you do not like or agree with sth: *The union organized a protest against the redundancies.* o *The centre has been closed after protests from local residents.* o *We've received thousands of letters of protest.* o *He resigned in protest against the decision.* o *a protest march* (IDIOM) **under protest** not happily or willingly: *Fiona agreed to pay in the end but only under protest.*

☆ **protest²** /prə'test/ *verb* **1** [I,T] **protest (about/against/at sth)** to say or show that you do not like or agree with sth: *The prisoner was brought, protesting, into the court room.* o *Students have been protesting against the government's decision.* o *The children protested loudly at being taken home early.* o *Many of the holiday-makers protested about the lack of information at the airport.* ☞ In American English **protest** is used without a preposition: *They protested the government's handling of the situation.* **2** [T] to say sth firmly: *He protested a total lack of knowledge of the affair.* o *He protested that he hadn't been in the country when the robbery took place.* o *'That's simply not true,' she protested.* ☞ **Protest** is stronger and usually used about more serious things than **complain**. You **protest** about something that you feel is not right or fair, you **complain** about the quality of something or about a less serious action: *to protest about the new tax* o *to complain about the weather.*

protester *noun* [C] a person who protests: *Protesters blocked the road as the minister's car drove up.*

☆ **Protestant** /'prɒtɪstənt/ *noun* [C] a member of the Christian church that separated from the Catholic church in the 16th century: *to be a Protestant* —**Protestant** *adj*: *The majority of the population is Protestant.* o *a Protestant church* o *a Protestant area of Belfast* ☞ Look at **Roman Catholic.**

prototype /'prəʊtətaɪp/ *noun* [C] the first model or design of sth from which other forms will be copied or developed

protrude /prə'truːd; *US* prəʊ-/ *verb* [I] to stick out from a surface: *protruding teeth*

☆ **proud** /praʊd/ *adj* **1 proud (of sb/sth); proud (to do sth/that**...) feeling pleased and satisfied about sth that you own or have done, or are connected with: *a proud father of twins* o *They are very proud of their new house.* o *I feel*

3ː	ə	eɪ	əʊ	aɪ	aʊ	ɔɪ	ɪə	eə	ʊə
fur	ago	pay	home	five	now	join	near	hair	pure

very proud to be part of such a successful organization. o You should feel very proud that you have been chosen. **2** not wanting help from other people: *He was too proud to ask for help.* **3** feeling that you are better than other people: *Now she's at university she'll be much too proud to talk to us!* ☛ The noun is **pride**. —**proudly** *adv*: *'I did all the work myself,' he said proudly.*

☆ **prove** /pruːv/ *verb* (*pp* **proved**; *US* **proven**) **1** [T] **prove sth (to sb)** to show that sth is true: *It will be difficult to prove that she was lying.* o *to prove sb's innocence to the court* ☛ The noun is **proof**. **2** [I,T] to be found to be sth: *The job proved more difficult than we'd expected.* o *He was proved innocent.* o *Lisa proved herself to be just as strong as the men.*

(IDIOM) **prove your/the case/point** to show that what you say is true: *No one will believe you unless you have evidence to prove your case.*

proven /ˈpruːvn/ *adj* that has been shown to be true: *a proven fact*

proverb /ˈprɒvɜːb/ *noun* [C] a short well-known sentence or phrase that gives advice or a general truth about life: *'A stitch in time saves nine,' is a proverb.*

☆ **provide** /prəˈvaɪd/ *verb* [T] **provide sb (with sth); provide sth (for sb)** to give or supply sth to sb: *This book will provide you with all the information you need.* o *We are able to provide accommodation for two students.* o *The course lasts all day and lunch will be provided.*

(PHRASAL VERBS) **provide for sb** to give sb all that he/she needs to live: *Robin has four children to provide for.*

provide for sth to make arrangements to deal with sth that might happen in the future: *We did not provide for such a large increase in prices.*

☆ **provided** /prəˈvaɪdɪd/ (*also* **provided that**; **providing**; **providing that**) *conj* only if: *She agreed to go and work abroad provided that her family could go with her.*

☆ **province** /ˈprɒvɪns/ *noun* **1** [C] one of the main parts into which some countries are divided for the purposes of government: *Canada has ten provinces.* ☛ Look at **county** and **state**. **2 the provinces** [plural] the part of a country that is not the capital city

provincial /prəˈvɪnʃl/ *adj* **1** (only *before* a noun) of a province or the provinces: *the provincial government* o *a provincial town* **2** (used about a person or his/her ideas) typical of the provinces; not modern or fashionable: *provincial attitudes*

☆ **provision** /prəˈvɪʒn/ *noun* **1** [U] the act of giving or supplying sth to sb: *The council is responsible for the provision of education and social services.* **2** [U] **provision for/against sth** arrangements that you make to deal with sth that might happen in the future: *She made provision for the children in the event of her death.* **3 provisions** [plural] (*formal*) supplies of food and drink

provisional /prəˈvɪʒənl/ *adj* only for the present time, that may be changed: *The provisional date for the next meeting is 18 November.* o *a provisional driving-licence* (= that you use when you are learning to drive) —**provisionally** /-nəli/ *adv*: *The meeting has been provisionally arranged for 18 November.*

provocation /ˌprɒvəˈkeɪʃn/ *noun* **1** [U] the act of trying to make sb angry: *You should never hit children, even under extreme provocation.* **2** [C] something that sb does to make you angry: *It was a provocation to call him a liar.*

provocative /prəˈvɒkətɪv/ *adj* **1** intending to cause anger or argument: *He made a provocative remark about a woman's place being in the home.* **2** intending to cause sexual excitement

provoke /prəˈvəʊk/ *verb* [T] **1** to make a person or an animal angry by annoying them: *The cat will scratch if you provoke it.* o *Stop trying to provoke me!* **2** to cause a feeling or reaction: *Edwina's remarks provoked a storm of controversy.*

prow /praʊ/ *noun* [C] the front part of a ship or boat ☛ The back of a ship is the **stern**.

prowess /ˈpraʊɪs/ *noun* [U] (*formal*) skill at doing sth

prowl /praʊl/ *verb* [I,T] **prowl (about/around)** (used about an animal that is hunting or a person who is waiting for a chance to steal sth, etc) to move quietly so that you are not seen or heard: *I could hear someone prowling around outside so I called the police.* ☛ A person or animal that is prowling is **on the prowl**. —**prowler** *noun* [C]: *The police arrested a prowler outside the hospital.*

proximity /prɒkˈsɪməti/ *noun* [U] (*formal*) the state of being near to sth: *One advantage is the town's proximity to London.*

proxy /ˈprɒksi/ *noun* [U] the right that you give to sb to act for you: *to vote by proxy*

prude /pruːd/ *noun* [C] a person who does not like to see or hear anything connected with sex —**prudish** /ˈpruːdɪʃ/ *adj*

prudent /ˈpruːdnt/ *adj* having or showing careful thought; wise and sensible: *It would be prudent to find out more before you decide.* ☛ The opposite is **imprudent**. —**prudence** *noun* [U] —**prudently** *adv*

prune¹ /pruːn/ *noun* [C] a dried plum

prune² /pruːn/ *verb* [T] to cut branches or parts of branches off a tree or bush in order to make it a better shape

pry /praɪ/ *verb* (*pres part* **prying**; *3rd pers sing pres* **pries**; *pt, pp* **pried**) **1** [I] **pry (into sth)** to try to find out about other people's private affairs: *I don't want to pry – but is everything all right?* **2** [T] (*especially US*) = PRISE

pseudonym /ˈsjuːdənɪm/; *US* /ˈsuːdənɪm/ *noun* [C] a name used by an author, etc that is not his/her real name: *to write under a pseudonym*

psych /saɪk/ *verb*

(PHRASAL VERB) **psych yourself up** (*informal*) to prepare yourself in your mind for sth difficult, eg by telling yourself that you will be successful

psychiatry /saɪˈkaɪətri/; *US* sɪ-/ *noun* [U] the study and treatment of mental illness ☛ Look at **psychology**.

psychiatric /ˌsaɪkiˈætrɪk/ *adj* connected with psychiatry: *a psychiatric hospital*

psychiatrist /-ɪst/ *noun* [C] a doctor who is trained to treat people with mental illness

p	b	t	d	k	g	tʃ	dʒ	f	v	θ	ð
pen	bad	tea	did	cat	got	chin	June	fall	van	thin	then

psychic /ˈsaɪkɪk/ *adj* (used about a person or his/her mind) having unusual powers, eg knowing what sb else is thinking or being able to see into the future

psychoanalysis /ˌsaɪkəʊəˈnæləsɪs/ *noun* [U] a way of treating sb with a mental illness by asking about his/her past life and dreams in order to find out what is making him/her ill

psychoanalyst /ˌsaɪkəʊˈænəlɪst/ *noun* [C] a person who uses psychoanalysis to treat people

psychoanalyse (*US* **-lyze**) /ˌsaɪkəʊˈænəlaɪz/ *verb* [T] to treat sb with a mental illness using psychoanalysis

psychology /saɪˈkɒlədʒi/ *noun* **1** [U] the study of the mind and the way that people behave: *child psychology* ☛ Look at **psychiatry**. **2** [sing] the type of mind that a person or group of people has: *If we understood the psychology of the killer we would have a better chance of catching him.*

psychological /ˌsaɪkəˈlɒdʒɪkl/ *adj* **1** connected with the mind or the way that it works: *Has her ordeal caused her long-term psychological damage?* **2** connected with psychology: *psychological tests* —**psychologically** /-kli/ *adv*: *Psychologically it was a bad time to be starting a new job.*

psychologist /-ɪst/ *noun* [C] a person who is trained in psychology

psychopath /ˈsaɪkəʊpæθ/ *noun* [C] a person who has a serious mental illness and who may hurt or kill other people

psychotherapy /ˌsaɪkəʊˈθerəpi/ *noun* [U] the treatment of people with mental illness by psychological methods rather than with drugs

☆ **pub** /pʌb/ (also *formal* **public house**) *noun* [C] (*Brit*) a place where people go to have a drink and meet their friends. Pubs can serve alcoholic drinks and they also often serve food: *He's gone down to the pub.* ○ *We're having a pub lunch.*

☛ In a pub you order your own drinks at the **bar**. There are often two parts of a pub: the **public bar** and the **saloon** or **lounge bar**. Look at the note at **inn**.

puberty /ˈpjuːbəti/ *noun* [U] the time when a child's body is changing and becoming physically like that of an adult: *to reach puberty*

pubic /ˈpjuːbɪk/ *adj* of the area around the sexual organs: *pubic hair*

☆ **public** /ˈpʌblɪk/ *adj* **1** of or concerning all the people in a country or area: *The rubbish tip is a danger to public health.* ○ *How much public support is there for the government's policy?* ○ *to increase public awareness* ○ *The public announcement urged people to use water carefully.* **2** provided for the use of people in general; not private: *a public library* ○ *a public telephone* ○ *public spending* (= money that the government spends on education, health care, etc) **3** known by many people: *We're going to make the news public soon.* ☛ Compare **keep sth secret**.

(IDIOM) **be common/public knowledge** ⇨ KNOWLEDGE

public *noun* [sing, with sing or pl verb] **1 the public** people in general: *Is Buckingham Palace open to the public?* ○ *The police have asked for help from members of the public.* ○ *The public is/are generally in favour of the new law.* **2** a group of people who are all interested in sth or who have sth in common: *the travelling public*

(IDIOM) **in public** when other people are present: *This is the first time that Jane has spoken about her experience in public.* —**publicly** /-kli/ *adv*: *The company refused to admit publicly that it had acted wrongly.*

public 'bar *noun* [C] one of the rooms in a pub, where the furniture is less comfortable and the drinks are cheaper than in other bars ☛ Look at **lounge bar** and **saloon bar**.

public 'company (*also* **public limited 'company**) *noun* [C] (*abbr* **PLC**; **plc**) a large company that sells shares(2) in itself to the public

public con'venience *noun* [C] (*Brit*) a toilet in a public place that anyone can use ☛ Look at the note at **toilet**.

public 'house *noun* [C] (*formal*) = PUB

public o'pinion *noun* [U] what people in general think about sth: *Public opinion was in favour of the war.*

public re'lations *noun* (*abbr* **PR**) **1** [plural] the state of the relationship between an organization and the public: *Giving money to local charities is good for public relations.* **2** [U] the job of making a company, organization, etc popular with the public

public 'school *noun* [C] **1** (*Brit*) a private school for children aged between 13 and 18. Parents must pay to send their children to one of these schools. Many of the children at public schools live (**board**) there during term-time. **2** (*US*) a local school that any child can go to, that provides free education

public-'spirited *adj* willing to help other people and the public in general

public 'transport *noun* [U] (the system of) buses, trains, etc that run according to a timetable and that anybody can use: *to travel by public transport*

publican /ˈpʌblɪkən/ *noun* [C] a person who owns or manages a pub

☆ **publication** /ˌpʌblɪˈkeɪʃn/ *noun* **1** [U] the act of printing a book, magazine, etc and making it available to the public: *His latest book has just been accepted for publication.* **2** [C] a book, magazine, etc that has been published **3** [U] the act of making sth known to the public: *the publication of exam results*

publicity /pʌbˈlɪsəti/ *noun* [U] **1** notice or attention from the newspapers, television, etc: *to seek/avoid publicity* **2** giving information about sth in order to attract people's attention; advertising: *There has been a lot of publicity for Dustin Hoffman's latest film.* ○ *a publicity campaign*

publicize (*also* **publicise**) /ˈpʌblɪsaɪz/ *verb* [T] to attract people's attention to sth or to give people information about sth: *The event has been well publicized and should attract a lot of people.*

☆ **publish** /ˈpʌblɪʃ/ *verb* **1** [I,T] to prepare and

print a book, magazine, etc and make it available to the public: *This dictionary was published by Oxford University Press.* **2** [T] (used about a writer, etc) to have your work put in a book, magazine, etc: *Dr Fraser has published several articles on the subject.* **3** [T] to make sth known to the public: *Large companies must publish their accounts every year.*

publisher *noun* [C] a person or company that publishes books, magazines, etc

publishing *noun* [U] the business of preparing books, magazines, etc to be printed and sold

☆ **pudding** /ˈpʊdɪŋ/ *noun* [C,U] **1** (*Brit*) the sweet part (**course**) of a meal that is eaten at the end of it: *What's for pudding today?* ☛ **Dessert** is more formal. **2** (*Brit*) sweet food that is made from bread, flour or rice with fat, eggs, milk, etc and cooked in the oven or over water: *rice pudding* ○ *Christmas pudding*

puddle /ˈpʌdl/ *noun* [C] a small amount of water (especially rain) that has gathered on the ground ☛ Look at **pool**.

puff¹ /pʌf/ *noun* [C] **1** a small amount of air, smoke, wind, etc that is blown or sent out: *a puff of smoke* **2** one breath that you take when you are smoking a cigarette or pipe: *to take a puff on a cigarette*

puffy *adj* (used about a part of a person's body) looking soft and swollen: *Your eyes look a bit puffy. Have you been crying?*

puff² /pʌf/ *verb* **1** [I,T] to cause air, smoke, wind, etc) to blow or come out in puffs: *Smoke was puffing out of the chimney.* ○ *Stop puffing smoke in my face.* **2** [I,T] to smoke a cigarette, pipe etc: *to puff away at a cigarette* ○ *He sat puffing his pipe.* **3** [I] to breathe loudly or quickly, eg when you are running: *He was puffing hard as he ran up the hill.*
(PHRASAL VERBS) **puff along, in, out, up,** etc to move in a particular direction with loud breaths or small clouds of smoke: *to puff up the stairs* ○ *The train puffed into the station.*

puff sth out/up to cause sth to become larger by filling it with air

puffed (*also* **puffed out**) *adj* finding it difficult to breathe, eg because you have been running: *She was puffed out after running to catch the bus.*

puffin /ˈpʌfɪn/ *noun* [C] a N Atlantic sea-bird with a large brightly-coloured beak

puke /pjuːk/ *verb* [I,T] (*slang*) to be sick; to vomit —**puke** *noun* [U]

☆ **pull¹** /pʊl/ *verb* **1** [I,T] to use force to move or try to move sb/sth towards yourself: *Ian pulled at the rope to make sure that it was secure.* ○ *to pull sb's hair* ○ *to pull a door open* ○ *You push and I'll pull.* ○ *to pull the trigger of a gun* ○ *I felt someone pull at my sleeve and turned round.* ○ *They managed to pull the child out of the water just in time.* **2** [T] to move sth in the direction that is described: *She pulled her sweater on/ She pulled on her sweater.* ○ *He pulled up his trousers/He pulled his trousers up.* ○ *Pull your chair a bit nearer to the table.* ○ *to pull the curtains* (= across the windows) **3** [T] to move sth behind you in the direction that you are moving: *The train is pulling six coaches.* ○ *That cart is too heavy for one horse to pull.* **4** [T] to damage a muscle, etc by using too much force
(IDIOMS) **make/pull faces/a face** ⇒ FACE

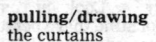

pull sb's leg (*informal*) to make fun of sb by trying to make him/her believe sth that is not true

pull strings to use your influence to gain an advantage

pull your weight to do your fair share of the work

(PHRASAL VERBS) **pull (sth) away** to move your body or part of it away with force: *She pulled away as he tried to kiss her.*

pull sth down to destroy a building: *The old cinema has been pulled down.*

pull in (to sth); pull into sth 1 (used about a train) to enter a station **2** (used about a car, etc) to move to the side of the road in order to stop

pull sth off (*informal*) to succeed in sth: *to pull off a business deal*

pull out (used about a car, etc) to move away from the side of the road: *I braked as a car suddenly pulled out in front of me.*

pull out (of sth) (used about a train) to leave a station

pull (sb/sth) out (of sth) (to cause sb/sth) to leave sth: *The Americans have pulled their forces out of the island.* ○ *We've pulled out of the deal.*

pull sth out to take sth out of a place suddenly or with force: *She walked into the bank and pulled out a gun.*

pull yourself together to control your feelings and behave in a calm way: *Pull yourself together and stop crying.*

pull up (to cause a car, etc) to stop: *to pull up at traffic-lights*

pull² /pʊl/ *noun* **1** [C] **a pull (at/on sth)** an act of pulling: *The diver gave a pull on the rope to show she wanted to go back up to the surface.* ○ *He took a long pull on his cigarette.* **2** [sing] a hard climb that takes a lot of effort: *It was a hard pull to the top of the hill.*

pulley /ˈpʊli/ *noun* [C] (*pl* **pulleys**) a piece of equipment, consisting of a wheel and a rope, that is used for lifting heavy things

pullover /ˈpʊləʊvə(r)/ noun [C] a piece of clothing that is usually made of wool and that covers the top part of your body and your arms. You put on a pullover by pulling it over your head. ☞ Look at the note at **sweater**.

pulp /pʌlp/ noun **1** [U] the soft inner part of some fruits or vegetables **2** [U] a soft substance made from wood that is used for making paper **3** [sing,U] a soft substance that you make by pressing and mixing sth for a long time: *Crush the strawberries to a pulp.*

pulpit /ˈpʊlpɪt/ noun [C] a raised wooden or stone platform in a church where the priest stands when he/she is speaking to the people there

pulsate /pʌlˈseɪt; US ˈpʌlseɪt/ verb [I] to move or shake with strong regular movements: *a pulsating rhythm*

pulse /pʌls/ noun [C, usually sing] the regular beating in your body as blood is pumped through it by your heart. You can feel your pulse at your wrist, neck, etc: *Your pulse rate increases after exercise.* ○ *to have a strong/weak pulse* ○ *to feel/take sb's pulse* (= to count how many times it beats in one minute)
▶ **pulse** verb [I] **pulse (through sth)** to move with strong regular movements

pulses /ˈpʌlsɪz/ noun [C,plural] the seeds of some plants, eg peas, beans, etc that are cooked and eaten as food: *Some pulses such as lentils and soya beans are very rich in protein.*

☆ **pump** /pʌmp/ noun [C] a machine that is used for forcing a gas or liquid in a particular direction: *Have you got a bicycle pump? My tyre's flat.* ○ *a petrol pump*
▶ **pump** verb [I,T] to force a gas or liquid to go in a particular direction: *Your heart pumps blood around your body.*
(PHRASAL VERB) **pump sth up** to fill sth with air, eg by using a pump: *to pump up a car tyre*

pumpkin /ˈpʌmpkɪn/ noun [C,U] a very large round fruit with thick orange-coloured skin that is cooked and eaten like a vegetable: *pumpkin pie* ○ *The children made a lantern out of a pumpkin.*

pun /pʌn/ noun [C] **pun (on sth)** an amusing use of a word that can have two meanings or of different words that sound the same: *'A Major success' and other puns on the Prime Minister's name were in all the papers.*

punch¹ /pʌntʃ/ verb [T] to hit sb/sth hard with your closed hand (**fist**): *Annie punched him hard in the stomach and ran away.*
▶ **punch** noun [C] a hard blow with your closed hand (**fist**)
'punch-line noun [C] the last and most important words of a joke or story
'punch-up noun [C] (*Brit informal*) a fight in which people punch or hit each other

punch² /pʌntʃ/ noun [U] a drink made from wine, fruit juice, sugar, etc

punch³ /pʌntʃ/ noun [C] a machine or tool that you use for making holes in sth: *a ticket punch*
▶ **punch** verb [T] to make a hole in sth with a punch: *He punched a hole in the ticket.* ○ *He punched the ticket.*

☆ **punctual** /ˈpʌŋktʃʊəl/ adj doing sth or happening at the right time; not late: *It is important to be punctual for your classes.* ☞ We often say the train, etc was **on time** rather than punctual. ▶ **punctuality** /ˌpʌŋktʃʊˈælɪti/ noun [U]: *The punctuality of British Rail services has improved.* ▶ **punctually** adv: *to pay your bills punctually*

punctuate /ˈpʌŋktʃʊeɪt/ verb **1** [I,T] to use punctuation marks when you are writing **2** [T] **punctuate sth (with sth)** to interrupt sth many times: *Her speech was punctuated with bursts of applause.*

punctuation /ˌpʌŋktʃʊˈeɪʃn/ noun [U] the use of punctuation marks when you are writing
punctu'ation mark noun [C] one of the signs that you use when you are writing in order to divide the words into sentences, show that sb is speaking, etc: *Punctuation marks include full stops, commas, question marks and speech marks.*

puncture

'Oh no! I've got a puncture!'

puncture /ˈpʌŋktʃə(r)/ noun [C] **1** a bicycle or car tyre that has a hole in it: *Oh, no! My tyre's flat. I must have a puncture.* **2** a small hole in a bicycle or car tyre: *If you put the tyre in water you should be able to see where the puncture is.*
▶ **puncture** verb [T] to make a small hole in sth with sth sharp: *That stone must have punctured the tyre.*

pungent /ˈpʌndʒənt/ adj (used about a smell) very strong

☆ **punish** /ˈpʌnɪʃ/ verb [T] **punish sb (for sth) (by/with sth)** to cause sb to suffer because he/she has done sth wrong: *They have broken the law and they deserve to be punished.* ○ *The children were severely punished for telling lies.* ○ *Minor offenders should be punished by being made to work for the community.* ○ *Dangerous driving should be punished with imprisonment.*

punishable adj **punishable (by sth)** (used about a crime, etc) that you can be punished for doing: *a punishable offence* ○ *In some countries drug-smuggling is punishable by death.*

punishing adj that makes you very tired or weak: *The Prime Minister had a punishing schedule, visiting five countries in five days.*

punishment noun **1** [U] the act of punishing or the state of being punished: *Do you have capital punishment?* (= punishment by death) *in your country?* **2** [C] a way in which sb is punished: *Ideally, the punishment should fit the crime.*

punitive /ˈpjuːnətɪv/ adj (*formal*) **1** intended as a punishment: *a punitive expedition against the rebels* **2** very hard or severe: *punitive taxation*

punk /pʌŋk/ *noun* **1** [U] a type of rock music that was popular in Britain in the late 1970s and early 1980s. Punk music often protests strongly about the way that society is organized. **2** [C] a person who likes punk music and often has brightly-coloured hair and unusual clothes: *punks wearing torn jeans and safety pins in their ears*

puny /'pjuːni/ *adj* (**punier; puniest**) small and weak

pup /pʌp/ *noun* [C] **1** = PUPPY **2** the young of some animals, eg seals

☆ **pupil**[1] /'pjuːpl/ *noun* [C] **1** a child in school: *There are 28 pupils in the class.* **2** a person who is being taught ☛ Look at **student**.

pupil[2] /'pjuːpl/ *noun* [C] the round black hole in the middle of the eye

puppet /'pʌpɪt/ *noun* [C] **1** a model of a person or animal that you can move by pulling the strings which are attached to it or by putting your hand inside it and moving your fingers **2** a person or organization that is controlled by sb else

puppy /'pʌpi/ *noun* [C] (*pl* **puppies**) (*also* **pup**/) a young dog

☆ **purchase**[1] /'pɜːtʃəs/ *noun* (*formal*) **1** [U] the act of buying sth: *to take out a loan for the purchase of a car* ○ *Please state the date and place of purchase.* **2** [C] something that you buy: *to make a purchase*

☆ **purchase**[2] /'pɜːtʃəs/ *verb* [T] (*formal*) to buy sth: *Many employees have the opportunity to purchase shares in the company they work for.*

purchaser *noun* [C] (*formal*) a person who buys sth: *The purchaser of the house agrees to pay a deposit of 10%* ☛ The opposite is **vendor**.

☆ **pure** /pjʊə(r)/ *adj* **1** not mixed with anything else: *a pure silk blouse* ○ *She was dressed in pure white.* ○ *Declan is of pure Irish descent.* **2** not containing any harmful substances: *the pure mountain air* **3** not doing or knowing anything evil or anything that is connected with sex: *a young girl still pure in mind and body* ☛ The opposite for 2 and 3 is **impure**. **4** (only *before* a noun) (*informal*) complete: *We met by pure chance.* ○ *a pure waste of time* **5** (used about a sound) clear **6** (only *before* a noun) (used about an area of learning) concerned only with theory rather than practical uses: *pure mathematics* ☛ The opposite for 6 is **applied**.

purely *adv* only or completely: *It's not purely a question of money.*

purée /'pjʊəreɪ; *US* pjʊə'reɪ/ *noun* [C,U] a food that you make by cooking a fruit or vegetable and then pressing and mixing it until it is smooth and liquid: *apple purée*

purge /pɜːdʒ/ *verb* [T] to remove people that you do not want from a political party or other organization

purge *noun* [C] an action to remove people that you do not want from a political party or other organization: *Stalin's purges*

purify /'pjʊərɪfaɪ/ *verb* [T] (*pres part* **purifying**; *3rd pers sing pres* **purifies**; *pt, pp* **purified**) to remove dirty or harmful substances from sth: *purified water*

puritan /'pjʊərɪtən/ *noun* [C] a person who thinks that it is wrong to enjoy yourself —**puritan** (*also* **puritanical** /ˌpjʊərɪ'tænɪkl/) *adj*: *a puritan attitude to life*

purity /'pjʊərəti/ *noun* [U] the state of being pure: *to test the purity of the air* ☛ Look at **impurity**.

purl /pɜːl/ *noun* [U] a simple stitch used in knitting: *knit two plain, one purl*

☆ **purple** /'pɜːpl/ *adj* of a reddish-blue colour: *the purple robes of the King*

purple *noun* [U] a reddish-blue colour

☆ **purpose** /'pɜːpəs/ *noun* **1** [C] the reason for doing or making sth: *The main purpose of this meeting is to decide what we should do about the problem of noise.* ○ *You may only use the telephone for business purposes.* **2** [U] (*formal*) having an aim or plan and acting according to it: *A good leader inspires people with a sense of purpose.*

(IDIOMS) **on purpose** not by accident; with a particular intention: *'You've torn a page out of my book!' 'I'm sorry, I didn't do it on purpose.'* ○ *I came a bit early on purpose, to see if I could help you.*

serve your/the purpose ⇨ SERVE

purposeful /-fl/ *adj* having a definite aim or plan: *Graham strode off down the street looking purposeful.* —**purposefully** /-fəli/ *adv*

purposely *adv* with a particular intention: *I purposely waited till everyone had gone so that I could speak to you in private.*

purr /pɜː(r)/ *verb* [I] (used about a cat) to make a continuous low sound that shows pleasure

☆ **purse**[1] /pɜːs/ *noun* [C] **1** a small bag that you keep money in ☛ Look at **wallet**. **2** (*US*) HANDBAG

purse[2] /pɜːs/ *verb* [T] to press your lips together to show that you do not like sth

purser /'pɜːsə(r)/ *noun* [C] the person on a ship who looks after the accounts and who deals with passengers' problems

☆ **pursue** /pə'sjuː; *US* -'suː/ *verb* [T] (*formal*) **1** to follow sb/sth in order to catch him/her/it: *The robber ran off pursued by two policemen.* ○ (*figurative*) *The goal that he is pursuing is completely unrealistic.* ☛ **Pursue** is more formal than **chase**. **2** to continue with sth; to find out more about sth: *to pursue a career in banking* ○ *She didn't seem to want to pursue the discussion so I changed the subject.*

pursuer *noun* [C] a person who pursues(1) sb/sth

pursuit /pə'sjuːt; *US* -'suːt/ *noun* **1** [U] the act of pursuing sb/sth: *the pursuit of pleasure* **2** [C] something that you spend your time doing, either for work or for pleasure: *outdoor pursuits* ○ *leisure pursuits*

(IDIOM) **in pursuit (of sb/sth)** trying to catch or get sb/sth: *a dog in pursuit of a cat* ○ *He neglected his family in pursuit of his own personal ambitions.*

pus /pʌs/ *noun* [U] a thick yellowish liquid that may form in a part of your body that has been hurt

☆ **push**[1] /pʊʃ/ *verb* **1** [I,T] to use force to move or try to move sb/sth forward or away from you: *You push and I'll pull.* ○ *You can pull a rope but you can't push it!* ○ *Christine pushed him into the water.* ○ *to push sb in a wheelchair* ○ *to push*

p	b	t	d	k	g	tʃ	dʒ	f	v	θ	ð
pen	bad	tea	did	cat	got	chin	June	fall	van	thin	then

push

pushing somebody into the water

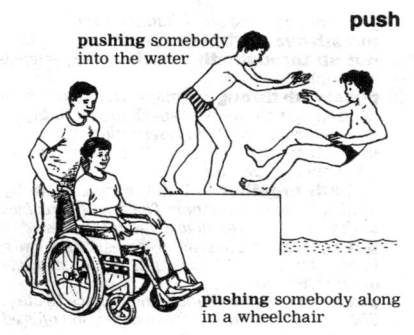

pushing somebody along in a wheelchair

a pram ○ *She pushed the door shut with her foot.* **2** [I,T] to move forward by pushing sb/sth: *John pushed his way through the crowd.* ○ *to push past sb* **3** [I,T] to press or use force, eg with your finger, to move sth: *Push the red button if you want the bus to stop.* **4** [T] (*informal*) to try to make sb do sth, eg by asking or telling him/her many times: *Ella will not work hard unless you push her.* ○ *to push sb for an answer* **5** [T] (*informal*) to try to make sth seem attractive, eg so that people will buy it: *They are launching a major publicity campaign to push their new product.*
(IDIOM) **be pushed for sth** (*informal*) to not have enough of sth: *Hurry up. We're really pushed for time.*
(PHRASAL VERBS) **push ahead (with sth)** to continue with sth

push for sth to try hard to get sth: *The Opposition are pushing for greater freedom of information.*

push in to join a queue in front of other people who were there before you

pusher *noun* [C] a person who sells illegal drugs

'push-button *adj* (only *before* a noun) (used about a machine, etc) that you work by pushing a button: *a radio with push-button tuning*
'pushchair (*Brit also* **buggy**) *noun* [C] a chair on wheels that you use for pushing a young child in. You can fold up a pushchair when you are not using it. ☛ picture at **pram**.
'pushover *noun* [C] (*informal*) **1** something that is easy to do or win: *With four of their players injured, the game won't be a pushover for Liverpool.* **2** a person who is easy to persuade or convince
'push-up *noun* [C] (*US*) = PRESS-UP
☆ **push²** /pʊʃ/ *noun* [C] an act of pushing: *Paul gave the door a push and it opened.* ○ *Can you help me give the car a push to get it started?* ○ *The car windows opened at the push of a button.*
(IDIOMS) **at a push** (*informal*) if it is necessary (but only with difficulty): *We can get ten people round the table at a push.*

give sb the push to end a relationship with sb or to dismiss sb from a job

pushy /'pʊʃi/ *adj* (**pushier**; **pushiest**) (*informal*) (used about a person) behaving in a forceful way in order to gain an advantage or to make people notice you: *You need to be pushy to be successful in show business.*
puss /pʊs/ *noun* [C] (used when you are speaking to or calling a cat)
pussy /'pʊsi/ *noun* [C] (*pl* **pussies**) (*informal*) a cat
☆ **put** /pʊt/ *verb* [T] (*pres part* **putting**; *pt, pp* **put**)
1 to move sb/sth so that it is in a particular place or position: *She put the book on the table.* ○ *I put the knife back in the drawer.* ○ *Did you put sugar in my tea?* ○ *When do you put the children to bed?* **2** to fix sth to or in sth else: *Can you put* (= sew) *a button on this shirt?* ○ *We're going to put a new window in this room.* **3** to make sb feel or experience sth: *This sort of weather always puts me in a bad mood.* ○ *Your decision puts me in a difficult position.* **4** to say or express sth: *I don't know exactly how to put this, but...* **5** to ask sb a question, make a suggestion, etc: *I'd like to put a question to the minister.* ○ *Can I put a suggestion to you?* **6** to write sth: *12.30 on Friday? I'll put it in my diary.* ○ *What did you put for question 2?*
(IDIOMS) **not put it past sb (to do sth)** (used with *would*) to think sb is capable of doing sth bad: *I wouldn't put it past him to do a thing like that.*

put it to sb that... (*formal*) to suggest to sb that sth is true: *I put it to you that this man is innocent.*

put together (used after a noun or nouns referring to a group of people or things combined: *You got more presents than the rest of the family put together.*

☛ For other idioms containing **put**, look at the entries for the nouns, adjectives, etc, eg **put an end to sth** is at **end**.

(PHRASAL VERBS) **put sth across/over** to say sth clearly, so that people can understand it: *He didn't put his ideas across very well at the meeting.*

put sth aside to save sth, especially money, to use later

put sb away (*informal*) to send sb to prison
put sth away to put sth where you usually keep it, eg in a cupboard
put sth back 1 to return sth to its place: *to put books back on the shelf* **2** to change the time shown on a clock, etc to an earlier time: *We have to put the clocks back tonight.* ☛ The opposite is **put sth forward**. **3** to change sth to a later time or date; to postpone: *I'll have to put back my dental appointment till next week.*
put sth by to save money to use later: *Her grandparents had put some money by for her wedding.*
put sb down (*informal*) to say things to make sb seem stupid or foolish: *He's always putting his wife down.*
put sth down 1 to place sth, eg on the floor, a table, etc: *The policeman persuaded him to put the gun down.* **2** (used about a government, an army or the police) to stop sth by force: *to put down a rebellion* **3** to kill an animal because it is old, sick or dangerous: *The dog was put down because it attacked a child.*
put sth down to sth to believe that sth is

caused by sth: *The education minister puts the children's reading problems down to bad teaching.*

put yourself/sb forward to suggest that you or a particular person should be considered for a job, etc: *His name was put forward for the position of chairman.*

put sth forward 1 to change the time shown on a clock, etc to a later time: *We put the clocks forward in spring.* ☛ The opposite is **put sth back. 2** to suggest sth: *The minister put forward a plan to help the homeless.*

put sth in 1 to include a piece of information, etc in sth that you write: *In your letter, you forgot to put in the time your plane would arrive.* **2** to ask for sth in an official manner: *to put in a demand for a wage increase*

put sth in; put sth into sth/into doing sth to spend time, etc on sth: *She puts all her time and energy into her business.*

put sb off 1 to make sb dislike a person: *I'm sure he's a very nice person but his accent puts me off.* **2** to say to a person that you can no longer do what you had agreed: *They were coming to stay last weekend but I had to put them off at the last moment.*

put sb off (sth/doing sth) ‡ to cause sb to dislike sth/doing sth: *My first visit to Liverpool put me off the place.* ○ *The accident put me off driving for a long time.* **2** to make sb unable to concentrate: *Don't stare at me – you're putting me off!*

put sth off to turn or switch a light off: *She put off the light and went to sleep.*

put sth off; put off doing sth to move sth to a later time; to delay doing sth: *'I've got an appointment.' 'Can't you put it off?'* ○ *She put off writing her essay until the last minute.*

put sth on 1 to pretend to be feeling sth; to pretend to have sth: *He's not angry with you really: he's just putting it on.* ○ *She put on a Scottish accent.* **2** to place clothes on your body: *Put on your coat!* ○ *I'll have to put my glasses on.* **3** to make a piece of electrical equipment, etc start working, usually by pressing a switch: *It's too early to put the lights on yet.* **4** to make sth (eg a record, a tape, etc) begin to play: *Let's put some music on.* **5** to become fatter or heavier (by the amount mentioned): *I put on weight very easily.* ○ *She's put on several pounds since I last saw her.*

put sth on sth to add an amount of money, etc to the cost or value of sth: *The government want to put 50p on the price of a packet of cigarettes.*

put sb out 1 to give sb trouble or extra work: *He put his hosts out by arriving very late.* **2** to make sb upset or angry: *I was quite put out by their selfish behaviour.*

put sth out 1 to make sth stop burning: *to put out a fire* **2** to switch sth off: *They put out the lights and locked the door.* **3** to give or tell the public sth, often by using the television, radio or newspapers: *The police put out a warning about the escaped prisoner.*

put yourself out (*informal*) to do sth for sb, even though it brings you trouble or extra work: *'I'll give you a lift home.' 'I don't want you to put yourself out. I'll take a taxi.'*

put sth over ➔ PUT STH ACROSS

put sb through sth to make sb experience sth unpleasant

put sb/sth through to make a telephone connection that allows sb to speak to sb: *Could you put me through to flight reservations, please?*

put sth to sb to suggest sth to sb; to ask sb sth: *I put the question to her.*

put sth together to build or repair sth by joining its parts together: *The furniture comes with instructions on how to put it together.*

put up sth to offer or give resistance in a fight, etc: *The old lady put up a struggle against her attacker.*

put sb up to give sb food and a place to stay: *She had missed the last train home, so I offered to put her up for the night.*

put sth up 1 to raise or hold sth up: *Put your hand up if you know the answer.* **2** to build sth: *to put up a fence* **3** to fix sth to a wall, etc so that everyone can see it: *to put up a notice* **4** to increase sth: *Some shops put up their prices just before Christmas.*

put up with sb/sth to suffer sb/sth unpleasant and not complain about it: *I don't know how they put up with this noise.*

putt /pʌt/ verb [I,T] (used in golf) to hit the ball gently when it is near the hole

putter /ˈpʌtər/ verb [I] (*US*) = POTTER¹

putty /ˈpʌti/ noun [U] a substance that is used for fixing glass into windows. Putty is soft when you use it but it turns hard later.

puzzle /ˈpʌzl/ noun [C] **1** [usually sing] something that is difficult to understand or explain; a mystery: *The reasons for his action have remained a puzzle to historians.* **2** a game or toy that tests your knowledge, skill, intelligence, etc: *to do a crossword puzzle* ○ *The solution to the puzzle is on page 27.* ○ *a jigsaw puzzle*

puzzle verb **1** [T] to cause sb to think hard about sth he/she cannot understand or explain: *The appearance of strange circles in fields of corn has puzzled all the experts.* **2** [I]

puzzle over sth to think hard about sth in order to understand or explain it: *to puzzle over a mathematical problem*

(PHRASAL VERB) **puzzle sth out** to find the answer to sth by thinking hard: *The letter was in Italian and it took us an hour to puzzle out what it said.*

puzzled /ˈpʌzld/ adj not able to understand or explain sth: *a puzzled expression*

☆ **pyjamas** /pəˈdʒɑːməz/ (*US* **pajamas** /pəˈdʒæməz/) noun [plural] loose trousers and a loose jacket or top that you wear in bed ☛ Notice that you use **pyjama** (without an 's') before another noun: *pyjama trousers*

pylon /ˈpaɪlən; *US* ˈpaɪlɑn/ noun [C] a tall metal tower that carries heavy electricity wires

pyramid /ˈpɪrəmɪd/ noun [C] a shape with a flat base and three or four triangular sides ☛ picture at **cube.**

python /ˈpaɪθn; *US* ˈpaɪθɒn/ noun [C] a large snake that kills animals by squeezing them very hard

iː	ɪ	e	æ	ɑː	ɒ	ɔː	ʊ	uː	ʌ
see	sit	ten	hat	arm	got	saw	put	too	cup

Qq

Q, q /kjuː/ noun [C] (pl **Q's**; **q's** /kjuːz/) the seventeenth letter of the English alphabet: *'Queen' begins with (a) 'Q'.*

quack /kwæk/ noun [C] the sound that a duck makes —**quack** verb [I]

quadrangle /ˈkwɒdræŋgl/ (also *informal* **quad**) noun [C] a square open area with buildings round it, in a school, college, etc

quadruple /ˈkwɒdrupl; *US* kwɒˈdruːpl/ verb [I,T] to multiply or be multiplied by four: *Profits have quadrupled in the past ten years.*

quaint /kweɪnt/ adj attractive or unusual because it seems to belong to the past: *The village has quaint narrow streets leading down to the sea.*

quake /kweɪk/ verb [I] to shake: *to quake with fear, cold, etc* —**quake** noun [C] (*informal*) = EARTHQUAKE

☆**qualification** /ˌkwɒlɪfɪˈkeɪʃn/ noun **1** [C] an examination that you have passed or a course of study that you have completed: *a teaching qualification* ○ *Please list your qualifications on your CV.* ○ *40 per cent of children left school at 16 with no formal qualifications.* **2** [C] a skill or quality that you need to do a particular job: *Is there a height qualification for the police force?* **3** [C,U] something that limits or weakens the meaning of a general statement: *I can recommend him for the job without qualification.* ○ *She accepted the proposal with only a few qualifications.*

☆**qualify** /ˈkwɒlɪfaɪ/ verb (*pres part* **qualifying**; *3rd pers sing pres* **qualifies**; *pt, pp* **qualified**) **1** [I] to pass the examination that is necessary to do a particular job; to have the qualities that are necessary for sth: *It takes five years to qualify as a vet.* ○ *A cup of coffee and a sandwich doesn't really qualify as a meal.* **2** [T] to give sb the right to do a particular job: *This exam will qualify me to teach music.* **3** [I] to be successful in one part of a competition and to go on to the next part: *Our team has qualified for the final.* **4** [I,T] to have or give sb the right to have or do sth: *How many years must you work to qualify for a pension?* ○ *Residence in this country does not qualify you to vote.* **5** [T] to limit or weaken the meaning of a general statement: *I must qualify what I said earlier – it wasn't quite true.*

qualified adj **1** having passed an examination or completed a course of study: *Edward is well qualified for this job.* ○ *a fully qualified doctor* **2** having the skill, knowledge or quality that you need to do sth: *I don't feel qualified to comment – I know nothing about the subject.* **3** not complete; limited: *My boss gave only qualified approval to the plan.* ☛ The opposite is **unqualified**.

☆**quality** /ˈkwɒləti/ noun (pl **qualities**) **1** [U] how good or bad sth is: *This paper isn't very good quality.* ○ *These photos are of poor quality.* ○ *a high-quality magazine* ○ *the quality of life in our cities* **2** [U] a high standard or level: *We aim to provide quality at a reasonable price.* ○ *'The Times' is a quality newspaper.* **3** [C] something that is typical of a person or thing: *Vicky has all the qualities of a good manager.* ○ *One quality of oil is that it floats on water.*

qualm /kwɑːm/ noun [C, usually pl] a feeling of doubt or worry about whether what you are doing is right: *I don't have any qualms about asking them to lend us some money.*

quandary /ˈkwɒndəri/ noun [C] (pl **quandaries**) a state of not being able to decide what to do; a difficult situation: *to be in a quandary*

☆**quantity** /ˈkwɒntəti/ noun (pl **quantities**) **1** [U] the measurement of sth by stating how much of it there is: *Don't write too much in your essay – quality is more important than quantity.* **2** [C,U] a number or an amount: *Add a small quantity of salt.* ○ *It's cheaper to buy goods in quantity* (= in large amounts). ○ *It's cheaper to buy goods in large quantities.*

(IDIOM) **an unknown quantity** ⇨ UNKNOWN

quarantine /ˈkwɒrəntiːn/ noun [U] a period of time when a person or animal that has or may have an infectious disease must be kept away from other people or animals: *All dogs brought into Britain must be kept in quarantine for six months.*

☆**quarrel** /ˈkwɒrəl; *US* ˈkwɔːrəl/ noun [C] **1** an angry argument or disagreement: *We're always having quarrels about who should do the washing-up.* ☛ Look at **argument** and **fight**. **2 quarrel with sb/sth** a reason for complaining about or disagreeing with sb/sth: *I have no quarrel with what has just been said.*

quarrel verb [I] (quarrelling; quarrelled; *US* quarreling; quarreled) **1 quarrel (with sb) (about/over sth)** to have an angry argument or disagreement: *The children are always quarrelling!* ○ *I don't want to quarrel with you about it.* ☛ Look at **argue** and **fight**. **2 quarrel with sth** to disagree with sth: *I wouldn't quarrel with Moira's description of what happened.*

quarry[1] /ˈkwɒri; *US* ˈkwɔːri/ noun [C] (pl **quarries**) a place where sand, stone, etc is dug out of the ground ☛ Look at **mine**.

quarry verb [T] (*pres part* **quarrying**; *3rd pers sing pres* **quarries**; *pt, pp* **quarried**) to dig, stone, sand, etc out of the ground: *to quarry for marble*

quarry[2] /ˈkwɒri; *US* ˈkwɔːri/ noun [sing] a person or animal that is being hunted

quart /kwɔːt/ noun [C] (*abbr* **qt**) a measure of

3ː	ə	eɪ	əʊ	aɪ	aʊ	ɔɪ	ɪə	eə	ʊə
fur	ago	pay	home	five	now	join	near	hair	pure

quarter /'kwɔːtə(r)/ noun **1** [C] one of four equal parts into which sth is divided: *The programme lasts for three quarters of an hour.* ○ *a mile and a quarter* ○ *to cut an apple into quarters* **2** [sing] fifteen minutes before or after every hour: *I'll meet you at (a) quarter past six.* ○ *It's (a) quarter to three.* ☛ In American English you say '(a) quarter **after**' and '(a) quarter **of**': *I'll meet you at a quarter after six.* ○ *It's a quarter of three.* **3** [C] a period of three months: *You get a gas bill every quarter.* **4** [C] four ounces of sth; ¼ of a pound: *A quarter of mushrooms, please.* **5** [C] a part of a town, especially a part where a particular group of people live: *the Chinese quarter of the city* **6** [C] a person or group of people who may give help or information or who have certain opinions: *Jim's parents haven't got much money so he can't expect any help from that quarter.* ○ *Racist attitudes still exist in some quarters.* **7** [C] (in America or Canada) a coin that is worth 25 cents (¼ dollar) **8 quarters** [plural] a place that is provided for a person (especially a soldier) to live in: *married quarters* (= for soldiers and their families)
(IDIOM) **at close quarters** ➪ CLOSE¹

quarter-'final noun [C] one of the four matches between the eight remaining players or teams in a competition. The players that win in the quarter-finals go on to the semi-finals.

quarterly /'kwɔːtəli/ adj, adv (produced or happening) once every three months: *a quarterly magazine* ○ *The committee meets quarterly.*

quartet /kwɔː'tet/ noun [C] **1** four people who sing or play music together **2** a piece of music for four people to sing or play together

quartz /kwɔːts/ noun [U] a type of hard rock that is used in making very accurate clocks or watches

quash /kwɒʃ/ verb [T] (*formal*) **1** to declare that an official decision, judgment, etc is no longer true or legal: *The appeal court quashed the verdict of the lower court.* **2** to stop or defeat sth by force: *to quash a rebellion*

quay /kiː/ noun [C] a stone or metal platform in a harbour where boats are loaded and unloaded

'quayside noun [sing] the area of land that is near a quay

☆**queen** /kwiːn/ noun [C] **1** (*also* **Queen**) the female ruler of a country: *Queen Victoria reigned for more than fifty years.* ○ *to crown a new queen* ○ *Should the Queen abdicate in favour of her son?* ☛ Queen Elizabeth II is pronounced 'Queen Elizabeth **the Second**'. Look at **king** and **princess**. **2** (*also* **Queen**) the wife of a king **3** the largest and most important female in a group of insects: *the queen bee* **4** one of the four playing-cards in a pack with a picture of a queen: *the queen of hearts* ☛ Look at the note at **card**.

queen 'mother noun [C] the mother of a king or queen

queer /kwɪə(r)/ adj **1** strange; odd: *His behaviour seemed rather queer.* ○ *The meat has a queer smell.* **2** (*slang*) homosexual ☛ Look at **gay**. **Queer** is often used in an offensive way, but some homosexuals use it about themselves.

queer noun [C] (*slang*) a homosexual man

quell /kwel/ verb [T] to put an end to sth: *to quell a rebellion* ○ *to quell sb's fears*

quench /kwentʃ/ verb [T] to satisfy your feeling of thirst by drinking: *to quench your thirst*

query /'kwɪəri/ noun [C] (pl **queries**) a question: *Does anyone have any queries?*

query verb [T] (*pres part* **querying**; *3rd pers sing pres* **queries**; *pt, pp* **queried**) to ask a question about sth: *We queried the bill but were told it was correct.*

quest /kwest/ noun [C] (*formal*) a long search for sth that is difficult to find: *the quest for eternal youth*

☆**question¹** /'kwestʃən/ noun **1** [C] a sentence or phrase that asks for an answer: *Are there any questions on what I've just said?* ○ *Put up your hand if you want to ask a question.* ○ *In the examination, you must answer five questions in one hour.* ○ *What's the answer to Question 5?* **2** [C] a problem or difficulty that needs to be discussed or dealt with: *His resignation raises the question of who will take over from him.* ○ *It's not difficult. It's just a question of finding the time to do it.* ○ *We all agree that more money should be spent on education. The question is where that money is going to come from.* **3** [U] doubt or uncertainty: *There is no question about Brenda's enthusiasm for the job.* ○ *His honesty is beyond question.*
(IDIOMS) **in question** that is being considered or talked about: *The lawyer asked where she was on the night in question.*

no question of no possibility of: *I'm afraid there is no question of any new jobs here at present.*

out of the question impossible: *A new car is out of the question. It's just too expensive.*

'question mark noun [C] the sign (?) that you use when you write a question.

'question tag (*also* **tag**) noun [C] a short phrase at the end of a sentence that changes it into a question: *In the sentence 'It's very expensive, isn't it?', the use of the question tag means that the speaker is asking the listener to agree.*

☆**question²** /'kwestʃən/ verb [T] **1** to ask sb a question or questions: *The police questioned him for several hours.* ○ *The interviewers questioned me on my past experience.* **2** to express or feel doubt about sth: *She told me she was from the council so I didn't question her right to be there.* ○ *to question sb's sincerity*

questionable adj **1** that is not certain: *It's questionable whether we'll be able to finish in time.* **2** that may not be true, suitable or honest: *A lot of money has been spent on very questionable projects.* ○ *questionable motives*

questionnaire /ˌkwestʃə'neə(r)/ noun [C] a list of questions that are answered by many people A questionnaire is used to collect information about a particular subject: *to complete/fill in a questionnaire*

p	b	t	d	k	g	tʃ	dʒ	f	v	θ	ð
pen	bad	tea	did	cat	got	chin	June	fall	van	thin	then

☆ **queue** /kju:/ (US **line**) noun [C] a line of people, cars, etc that are waiting for sth or to do sth: *We had to wait in a queue for hours to get tickets.* ○ *to join the end of a queue*
(IDIOM) **jump the queue** ⇨ JUMP¹
queue verb [I] **queue (up) (for sth)** to form a line when you are waiting for sth: *to queue for a bus* ○ *They're queueing up to see the film.*

quiche /ki:ʃ/ noun [C,U] a pie without a top that is filled with a mixture of eggs and milk with cheese, ham, etc and cooked in the oven. You can eat quiche hot or cold. ☞ Look at the note at **pie**.

☆ **quick** /kwɪk/ adj **1** doing sth at great speed or in a short time: *It's quicker to travel by train.* ○ *Nick is a quick worker.* ○ *She was quick to point out all the mistakes I had made.* ○ *Run and get your coat and be quick about it.* **2** done in a short time: *May I make a quick telephone call?*
☞ **Fast** is more often used for describing a person or thing that moves or can move at great speed: *a fast horse, car, runner, etc.* **Quick** is more often used for describing sth that is done in a short time: *a quick decision, breakfast, visit, etc.*
(IDIOM) **quick/slow on the uptake** ⇨ UPTAKE
quick adv (informal) quickly: *to get rich quick*
quickly adv at speed or in a short time: *Tom quickly undressed and got into bed.* ○ *The cooker's on fire! Do something quickly!* ○ *I'd like you to get here as quickly as possible.*

quid /kwɪd/ noun [C] (pl **quid**) (Brit informal) a pound (in money); £1: *It costs a quid.* ○ *The tickets are five quid each.*

☆ **quiet¹** /'kwaɪət/ adj **1** with very little or no noise: *Be quiet!* ○ *His voice was quiet but firm.* ○ *Please keep the children quiet when I'm on the phone.* ○ *Go into the library if you want to work. It's much quieter in there.* ☞ The opposite is **loud**. **2** without many people or much activity; without anything very exciting happening: *London is very quiet on Sundays.* ○ *'Have you been busy?' 'No, we've had a very quiet day today.'* ○ *a quiet country village* ○ *a quiet life* **3** (used about a person) not saying very much; not attracting other people's attention: *You're very quiet today. Is anything wrong?*
(IDIOM) **keep quiet about sth; keep sth quiet** to say nothing about sth: *Would you keep quiet about me leaving until I've told the boss?*
quietly adv in a quiet way: *Try and shut the door quietly!* ○ *'She was my best friend,' Rose said quietly.* ○ *He quietly got up and left the room.* —**quietness** noun [U]

quiet² /'kwaɪət/ noun [U] the state of being quiet: *the peace and quiet of the countryside*
(IDIOM) **on the quiet** secretly: *She's given up smoking but she still has an occasional cigarette on the quiet.*

quieten /'kwaɪətn/ verb [T] to make sb/sth quiet
(PHRASAL VERB) **quieten (sb/sth) down** to become quiet or to make sb/sth quiet: *When you've quietened down, I'll tell you what happened.*

quilt /kwɪlt/ noun [C] a cover for a bed that has a thick warm material, eg feathers, inside it ☞ Look at **duvet**.

quintet /kwɪn'tet/ noun [C] **1** a group of five people who sing or play music together **2** a piece of music for five people to sing or play together

quirk /kwɜ:k/ noun [C] **1** a strange habit or type of behaviour **2** a strange happening: *By a quirk of fate they met again several years later.*
quirky adj (used about a person's behaviour) unusual

quit /kwɪt/ verb (pres part **quitting**; pt, pp **quit**)
1 [I,T] (often used in newspapers, etc) to leave a job, etc or to go away from a place: *Tennis star says, 'I felt the time had come to quit.'* ○ *Thousands of people have decided to quit Hong Kong for good.* **2** [T] (informal) to stop doing sth: *to quit smoking* **3** [I,T] (computing) to close a computer program

☆ **quite** /kwaɪt/ adv **1** not very; to a certain degree; rather: *The film was quite good.* ○ *Beth plays the piano quite well but she needs more practice.* ○ *My husband quite enjoys cooking.* ○ *They had to wait quite a long time.* ○ *It's quite cold today.* ○ *We still meet up quite often.*
☞ Look at the note at **rather**. **2** (used for emphasizing sth) completely; very: *Are you quite sure you don't mind?* ○ *Life in Japan is quite different from here.* ○ *I quite agree – you're quite right.* ○ *To my surprise, the room was quite empty.* ○ *The party was quite awful.* **3** (used for showing that you agree with or understand sth): *'I feel that we shouldn't spend more than £20.' 'Quite.'*
(IDIOMS) **not quite** (used for showing that there is nearly enough of sth, or that it is nearly suitable): *There's not quite enough bread for breakfast.* ○ *These shoes don't quite fit.*
quite a (used for showing that sth is unusual): *It's quite a climb to the top of the hill.* ○ *That's quite a problem.*
quite a few; quite a lot (of) not a lot, but a certain amount of sb/sth: *We've received quite a few enquiries.* ○ *They've worked hard but there's still quite a lot left to do.*

quits /kwɪts/ adj
(IDIOM) **be quits (with sb)** if two people are quits, it means that neither of them owes the other any money: *You give me £2 and then we're quits.*

quiver /'kwɪvə(r)/ verb [I] to tremble or shake: *to quiver with rage, excitement, fear, etc*

quiz /kwɪz/ noun [C] (pl **quizzes**) a game or competition in which you must answer questions: *a quiz programme on TV* ○ *a general knowledge quiz*

quizzical /'kwɪzɪkl/ adj (used about a look, smile, etc) seeming to ask a question —**quizzically** /-klɪ/ adv

quorum /'kwɔ:rəm/ noun [sing] the minimum number of people that must be at a meeting before it can make decisions

quota /'kwəʊtə/ noun [C] the number or amount of sth that is allowed or that you must do: *There is a quota on the number of cars that can be imported each year.* ○ *We have a fixed quota of work to get through each day.*

quotation /kwəʊˈteɪʃn/ (also *informal* **quote**) noun [C] **1** a group of words from a book, speech, play, etc, that you repeat exactly: *That's a quotation from a poem by Keats.* ○ *Please include quotations from the text to support your argument.* **2** the amount that sb thinks a piece of work will probably cost: *You should get a quotation from three builders.* ☛ Look at **estimate**.

quoˈtation marks (also *informal* **quotes**; *Brit also* **inverted commas**) noun [plural] the signs ('...') or ("...") that you use at the beginning and end of words that were spoken or that are being quoted.

☆ **quote** /kwəʊt/ verb **1** [I,T] **quote (sth) (from sb/sth)** to repeat exactly sth that sb else has said or written before: *The interviewer quoted a statement that the minister had made several years earlier.* ○ *to quote from the Bible* ○ *She was quoted as saying that she disagreed with the decision.* ○ *The minister asked the newspaper not to quote him.* **2** [T] to give sth as an example to support what you are saying: *She quoted several reasons why she was unhappy about the decision.* **3** [T] to say what the cost of a piece of work, etc will probably be: *The catering company quoted us £4.50 a head for a buffet lunch.*

Rr

R, r /ɑː(r)/ noun [C] (*pl* **R's; r's**) the eighteenth letter of the English alphabet: *'Rabbit' begins with an 'R'.*

rabbi /ˈræbaɪ/ noun [C] (*pl* **rabbis**) a Jewish religious leader and teacher of Jewish law

☆ **rabbit** /ˈræbɪt/ noun [C] a small animal with long ears: *a wild rabbit* ○ *a tame rabbit* (= one that you keep as a pet) ○ *a rabbit-hutch* (= a cage for rabbits) ☛ The children's word for rabbit is **bunny**.

rabble /ˈræbl/ noun [C] a noisy uncontrolled crowd of people

rabies /ˈreɪbiːz/ noun [U] a serious, usually fatal, disease that can be given to humans by the bite of an animal that has the disease

☆ **race¹** /reɪs/ noun **1** [C] **race (against/with sb/sth)** a competition between people, animals, cars, etc to see which is the fastest: *to run/win/lose a race* ○ *to come first, second, last, etc in a race* ○ *a five kilometre race* ○ *a horse-race* ○ *What a close race!* ○ *Let's have a race to the end of the road.* ○ (*figurative*) *the race to find a cure for AIDS* **2 the races** [plural] (*Brit*) an occasion when a number of horse-races are held in one place: *We're going to the races for the day.* (IDIOM) **rat race** ⇒ RAT

ˈracecourse (*US* **ˈracetrack**) noun [C] a place where horse-races are held

ˈracehorse noun [C] a horse that is trained to run in horse-races

☛ In Britain going to horse-races and greyhound races is very popular. People often **bet** with a **bookie** on the result of a race.

☆ **race²** /reɪs/ verb **1** [I,T] **race (against/with/ sb/sth)** to have a competition with sb/sth to find out who is the fastest: *I'll race you home.* ○ *In the 5 000 metres he'll be racing against some of the finest runners in the country.* **2** [I,T] to go very fast or to move sb/sth very fast: *We raced to catch the bus.* ○ *The child had to be raced to hospital.* **3** [T] to cause an animal or a car, etc to take part in a race

racing noun [U] **1** = HORSE-RACING **2** the sport of taking part in races: *motor racing* ○ *a racing car* ○ *powerboat racing*

☆ **race³** /reɪs/ noun **1** [C,U] one of the groups into which people can be divided according to the colour of their skin, their hair type, the shape of their face, etc: *the different races of South Africa* ○ *a child of mixed race* ○ *People should not be discriminated against on grounds of race, religion or sex.* ☛ Look at **human race**. **2** [C] a group of people who have the same language, customs, history, etc: *the Spanish race*

ˌrace reˈlations noun [plural] the relations between people of different races who live in the same town, area, etc: *Community leaders are working to improve race relations.*

racial /ˈreɪʃl/ *adj* connected with people's race; happening between people of different races: *racial tension* ○ *racial discrimination* —**racially** /-ʃəli/ *adv: a racially mixed school*

racism /ˈreɪsɪzəm/ noun [U] the belief that some races are better than others and people of other races are not as good as people of your own race; ways of treating people that show this belief: *to take measures to combat racism* —**racist** /ˈreɪsɪst/ noun [C], *adj: He's a racist.* ○ *a racist remark*

rack¹ /ræk/ noun [C] (often in compounds) a sort of shelf, made of bars, that you can put things in or on: *Put your coat in the luggage rack.* ○ *We need a roof-rack on the car for all this luggage.*

rack² /ræk/ verb (IDIOM) **rack your brains** to try hard to think

racks

wine rack

roof-rack

luggage rack

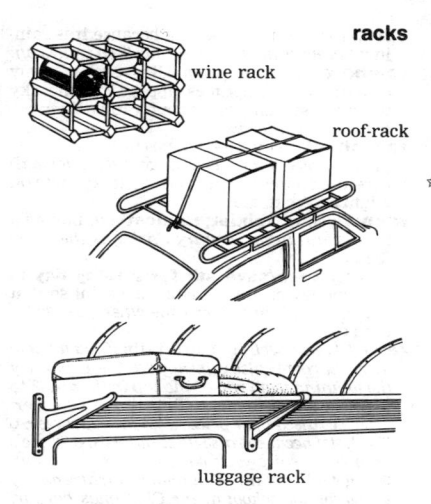

of sth or remember sth: *Steve racked his brains trying to remember where they'd met before.*

rack³ /ræk/ *noun*
(IDIOM) **go to rack and ruin** to be in or get into a bad state because of lack of care

racket¹ (*also* **racquet**) /'rækɪt/ *noun* [C] a piece of sports equipment that you use to hit the ball with in the games of tennis, badminton and squash ☛ picture at **tennis**. Rackets are different from **bats** because they have **strings**. Look also at **club²**(2) and **stick¹**(3).

racket² /'rækɪt/ *noun* (*informal*) **1** [sing] a loud noise: *Stop making that terrible racket!* **2** [C] an illegal way of making money: *a drugs racket*

radar /'reɪdɑː(r)/ *noun* [U] the system for finding out the position of sth that you cannot see, with the help of radio waves

radiant /'reɪdiənt/ *adj* **1** sending out light or heat: *radiant energy* **2** showing great happiness: *a radiant smile*

radiate /'reɪdieɪt/ *verb* **1** [T] to send out heat or light: (*figurative*) *to radiate health* **2** [I] **radiate from sth** to go out in all directions from a central point: *Narrow streets radiate from the harbour.*

radiation /ˌreɪdi'eɪʃn/ *noun* [U] powerful and very dangerous rays that are sent out from certain substances. You cannot see or feel radiation but it can cause serious illness or death: *High levels of radiation have been recorded near the power station.* ○ *to be exposed to radiation* ☛ Look at **radioactive**.

radiator /'reɪdieɪtə(r)/ *noun* [C] **1** a piece of equipment that is used for heating a room. Radiators are made of metal and filled with hot water. They are usually part of a central heating system: *Turn the radiator down a bit!* **2** a piece of equipment that is used for keeping an engine cool

radical /'rædɪkl/ *adj* **1** (used about changes in sth) very great: *The tax system needs radical reform.* ○ *radical change* **2** wanting great social or political change: *The students' demands were too radical to be accepted.* ○ *to hold radical views* ☛ Look at **moderate**.
radical *noun* [C] a person who wants great social or political change —**radically** /-klɪ/ *adv*: *The First World War radically altered the political map of Europe.*

☆ **radio** /'reɪdiəʊ/ *noun* (*pl* **radios**) **1** [U] the process of sending or receiving messages through the air by electrical signals: *The yachtsman was in contact with the coast by radio.* ○ *a radio signal* **2** [C] (*also old-fashioned* **wireless**) a piece of equipment that is used for receiving and/or sending radio messages or broadcasts (on a ship, aeroplane, etc or in the house): *a ship's radio* ○ *a portable radio* ○ *A radio cassette player was stolen from the car.* ☛ You may **put**, **switch** or **turn** a radio **on** or **off**. You may also **turn** it **up** or **down** to make it louder or quieter. **3** often **the radio** [U,sing] the broadcasting of programmes for people to listen to on their radios: *I always listen to the radio in the car.* ○ *I heard an interesting report on the radio this morning.* ○ *a radio station, programme, etc* ○ *national/local radio*
radio *verb* [I,T] (*pt, pp* **radioed**) to send a message by radio: *to radio for help*

radioactive /ˌreɪdiəʊ'æktɪv/ *adj* sending out powerful and very dangerous rays that are produced when atoms are broken up. These rays cannot be seen or felt but can cause serious illness or death: *the problem of the disposal of radioactive waste from power stations* ☛ Look at **radiation**.

radioactivity /ˌreɪdiəʊæk'tɪvəti/ *noun* [U] **1** the state of being radioactive **2** the energy that is produced by radioactive substances

radiographer /ˌreɪdi'ɒgrəfə(r)/ *noun* [C] a person who is trained to take X-rays for medical purposes

radish /'rædɪʃ/ *noun* [C] a small red or white vegetable with a strong taste that you eat raw. A radish is the root of a radish plant.

radius /'reɪdiəs/ *noun* [C] (*pl* **radii** /-diaɪ/) **1** the distance from the centre of a circle to the outside edge ☛ Look at **diameter**. **2** a circular area that is measured from a point in its centre: *The wreckage of the plane was scattered over a radius of several miles.*

raffle /'ræfl/ *noun* [C] a way of making money for a good cause by selling tickets with numbers on them. Later some numbers are chosen and the tickets with these numbers on them win prizes.

raft /rɑːft; *US* ræft/ *noun* [C] a type of simple flat boat that you make by tying pieces of wood together

rafter /'rɑːftə(r); *US* 'ræf-/ *noun* [C] one of the long pieces of wood that support a roof

rag /ræg/ *noun* **1** [C,U] a small piece of old cloth that you use for cleaning **2 rags** [plural] clothes that are very old and torn: *to be dressed in rags*

rage /reɪdʒ/ *noun* [C,U] great anger: *He was trembling with rage.* ○ *to fly into a rage*
rage *verb* [I] **1** to show great anger about sth **2** (used about a battle, disease, storm, etc) to

ɜː	ə	eɪ	əʊ	aɪ	aʊ	ɔɪ	ɪə	eə	ʊə
fur	ago	pay	home	five	now	join	near	hair	pure

continue with great force: *The battle raged for several days.*

raging *adj* (only *before* a noun) very strong: *a raging headache*

ragged /'rægɪd/ *adj* **1** (used about clothes) old and torn **2** not straight; untidy: *a ragged edge*

raid /reɪd/ *noun* [C] **raid (on sth) 1** A surprise attack on an enemy: *an air raid* **2** an attack in order to steal sth: *a bank raid* **3** a surprise visit by the police: *Police found 2 kilos of cocaine during a raid on a London hotel last night.*

raid *verb* [T] to make a raid on a place: *Police raided the club looking for guns.*

☆ **rail** /reɪl/ *noun* **1** [C] a bar fixed to a wall, which you can hang things on: *a towel rail* ○ *a curtain rail* **2** [C] a bar, usually of metal or wood, which protects people from falling (on stairs, from a building, etc): *Hold on to the handrail – these steps are very slippery.* **3** [C, usually pl] the tracks that trains run on **4** [U] the railway system; trains as a means of transport: *British Rail* ○ *I much prefer travelling by rail to flying.* ○ *There's going to be a new rail link between Paddington and Liverpool Street stations.*

'railcard *noun* [C] a special card that allows you to buy train tickets more cheaply if you are an old person, student, etc

railing /'reɪlɪŋ/ *noun* [C, usually pl] a fence (around a park, garden, etc) that is made of metal bars: *The boys climbed over the railings and got into the zoo without paying.* ☞ picture at **fence**.

☆ **railway** /'reɪlweɪ/ (*US* **railroad**) *noun* [C] **1** the metal lines on which trains run between one place and another: *In Canada there is a railway which goes right across the Rocky Mountains.* **2** (*also* **railways**) the system that organizes travel by train: *He works on the railways.* ○ *a railway engine*

'railway line *noun* [C] the track for trains to run on; the route by train between two places: *the railway line between London and Bristol*

'railway station *noun* [C] = STATION(1)

☆ **rain¹** /reɪn/ *noun* **1** [U] the water that falls from the sky: *The grass is so green in England because we get so much rain.* ○ *Take your umbrella, it looks like rain.* ○ *It's pouring with rain* (= the rain is very heavy). ☞ Look at **shower**(3) and **acid rain** and at the note at **weather**. **2 rains** [plural] (in tropical countries) the time of the year when there is a lot of rain: *When the rains come in July, the people move their houses to higher ground.*

(IDIOM) (**as**) **right as rain** ⇨ RIGHT²(6)

'raincoat *noun* [C] a special coat which you wear when it is raining

'raindrop *noun* [C] a single drop of rain

'rainfall *noun* [U] the total amount of rain that falls in a particular place during a month, year, etc: *The annual rainfall in Cairo is less than 3 cm.*

'rain forest *noun* [C] a forest in a tropical part of the world

☆ **rain²** /reɪn/ *verb* [I] (used with *it*) to fall as rain: *Oh no! It's raining again!* ○ *Is it raining hard?* ○ *We'll go out when it stops raining.*

(PHRASAL VERB) **rain** (**sth**) **off** (usually passive) to stop sth happening because it is raining: *I'm sorry but the picnic has been rained off.*

rainbow /'reɪnbəʊ/ *noun* [C] an arch of many colours that sometimes appears in the sky when the sun shines through rain: *all the colours of the rainbow*

'rain check /'reɪn tʃek/ *noun* (*US*)
(IDIOM) **take a rain check on sth** (*informal*) to refuse an invitation or offer but say that you might accept it later

rainy /'reɪni/ (**rainier**; **rainiest**) *adj* having a lot of rain: *In my country Spring is the rainy season.*
(IDIOM) **keep/save sth for a rainy day** to save money or sth valuable or useful so that you can use it at a later time when you really need to

☆ **raise¹** /reɪz/ *verb* [T] **1** to lift sth: *If you want to leave the room raise your hand.* ○ *The captain of the winning team raised the cup in the air.* **2** to increase sth or to make sth better or stronger: *They've raised their prices a lot since last year.* ○ *The hotel needs to raise its standards.* ○ *There's no need to raise your voice* (= speak angrily). **3** to get sth; obtain: *We managed to raise nearly £1 000 for the school at the Christmas bazaar.* **4** to look after a child until he/she is grown up: *You can't raise a family on what I earn.* **5** to make a plant or animal grow so that you can use it: *In New Zealand sheep are raised for meat and wool.* **6** to introduce a subject that needs to be talked about: *I would like to raise the subject of money.* ○ *This raises the question of why nothing was done before.* **7** to cause sth or make sth happen: *The neighbours raised the alarm when they saw smoke coming out of the window.*

(IDIOM) **raise your eyebrows** to show that you are surprised or that you do not approve of sth

raise² /reɪz/ *noun* [C] (*US*) = RISE¹(2)

raisin /'reɪzn/ *noun* [C] a dried grape, used in cakes, etc ☞ Look at **sultana**.

rake /reɪk/ *noun* [C] a garden tool with a long handle, used for collecting leaves or making the earth smooth

rake *verb* [T] to use a rake on sth: *to rake up the leaves*
(PHRASAL VERB) **rake sth up** to start talking about sth that it would be better to forget: *Don't rake up all those old stories again.*

rally¹ /'ræli/ *noun* [C] (*pl* **rallies**) **1** a race for cars or motor bikes **2** a meeting of people for a political reason: *20 000 people attended the peace rally in Trafalgar Square.* **3** the series of strokes in a game of tennis before a point is won

rally² /'ræli/ *verb* (*pres part* **rallying**; *3rd pers sing pres* **rallies**; *pt, pp* **rallied**) **1** [I] to get stronger: *The pound has rallied against the mark.* **2** [I,T] to come together or to bring people together: *Mr de Klerk has rallied the party behind him.*
(PHRASAL VERB) **rally round** to come together to help sb: *When I was in trouble my family rallied round.*

ram¹ /ræm/ *noun* [C] a male sheep ☞ Look at the note and picture at **sheep**.

ram² /ræm/ *verb* [T] (**ram**ming; **ram**med) to

p	b	t	d	k	g	tʃ	dʒ	f	v	θ	ð
pen	bad	tea	did	cat	got	chin	June	fall	van	thin	then

crash into sth or push sth with great force: *The battleship rammed the submarine.*

ramble /'ræmbl/ *verb* [I] **1** to walk in the countryside **2 ramble (on) (about sth)** to talk for a long time in a confused way

ramble *noun* [C] an organized walk in the country, usually for a group of people

rambling *adj* **1** (used about sth written) not saying things in a clear way; confused **2** (used about a building) spreading in many directions

ramp /ræmp/ *noun* [C] a sloping path which we can use instead of steps to get from one place to another higher or lower place: *We drove the car up the ramp and onto the ship.*

rampage /ræm'peɪdʒ/ *verb* [I] to rush from one place to another, breaking things and attacking people: *The football fans rampaged through the town.*

rampage /'ræmpeɪdʒ/ *noun*
(IDIOM) **be/go on the rampage** to rush around breaking things and attacking people

rampant /'ræmpənt/ *adj* very common and very difficult to control: *Car theft is rampant in this town.*

ramshackle /'ræmʃækl/ *adj* (used about a building or a car, etc) old and needing repair

ran *pt* of RUN¹

ranch /rɑːntʃ; *US* ræntʃ/ *noun* [C] a large farm in the US or Canada, usually where cows or horses are kept

random /'rændəm/ *adj* chosen by chance: *a random number, selected by a computer* ○ *For the opinion poll they interviewed a random selection of people in the street.*
(IDIOM) **at random** not in any special order or for any special reason: *He ran through the town shooting people at random.* ○ *The competitors were chosen at random from the audience.* —**randomly** *adv*

randy /'rændi/ *adj* (*informal*) sexually excited

rang *pt* of RING²

☆ **range¹** /reɪndʒ/ *noun* **1** [C] different things that belong to the same group: *The course will cover a whole range of topics.* ○ *This shop has a very small range of clothes.* **2** [C] the amount between certain limits: *There's a very wide range of ability in the class.* ○ *That car is outside my price range.* ○ *What's the salary range for this job?* ○ *I don't think this game is suitable for all age ranges.* **3** [C] a line of mountains or hills **4** [U] the distance that it is possible for sb or sth to travel, see or hear, etc: *Keep out of range of the guns.* ○ *The gunman shot the policeman at close range.* ○ *They can pick up signals at a range of 400 metres.*

range² /reɪndʒ/ *verb* **1** [I] **range between A and B; range from A to B** to stretch from one thing to another, within certain limits: *The ages of the students range from 15 to 50.* **2** [T] (usually passive) to arrange things or people in a line **3** [I] (used about sth that is written or spoken) dealing with a large number of subjects: *The discussion ranged widely but we didn't come to any conclusions.*

☆ **rank** /ræŋk/ *noun* **1** [C,U] the level of importance that sb has in an organization, particularly the army, or in society: *General is one of the highest ranks in the army.* ○ *She's much higher in rank than I am.* ○ *As a writer, he's absolutely first rank.* **2** [C] a group or line of things or people, especially soldiers: *a taxi rank* **3 ranks** [plural] the ordinary soldiers in the army; the members of any large group: *the ranks of the unemployed*
(IDIOM) **the rank and file** the ordinary members of an organization

rank *verb* [I,T] to have or to give a place in an order of importance: *She's ranked as one of the world's top players.* ○ *I think Tokyo ranks as one of the world's most expensive cities.* ○ *a high-ranking police officer*

ransom /'rænsəm/ *noun* [C,U] the money that you must pay to free sb who has been captured by terrorists or criminals: *The kidnappers demanded a ransom of £500 000 for the boy's release.*
(IDIOM) **hold sb to ransom** to capture sb and say that you will not free them until you have received some money ☞ Look at **hostage**.

rap /ræp/ *noun* **1** [C] a knock, on a door or window, etc, which is quick and quite loud **2** [C,U] a style or piece of rock music with a strong beat, in which the words of a song are spoken, not sung

rap *verb* (**rapping**; **rapped**) **1** [I,T] to hit sth quickly and lightly, making a noise **2** [T] (*informal*) to criticize sb strongly: *Minister raps police over rise in crime.* **3** [I] to speak the words of a song (a **rap**) that has music with a very strong beat

rape /reɪp/ *verb* [T] to force a person to have sex when he/she does not want to

rape *noun* [C,U] **1** the act of forcing sb to have sex: *to commit rape* **2** destroying sth beautiful: *Industry has been responsible for the rape of the countryside.*

rapist /'reɪpɪst/ *noun* [C] a person who is guilty of rape

☆ **rapid** /'ræpɪd/ *adj* happening very quickly or moving with great speed: *She made rapid progress and was soon the best in the class.* ○ *After leaving hospital he made a rapid recovery and was soon back at work.* —**rapidity** /rə'pɪdəti/ *noun* [U] (*formal*): *The rapidity of change has astonished most people.* —**rapidly** *adv*

rapids /'ræpɪdz/ *noun* [plural] the part of a river where the water flows very fast over rocks

rapture /'ræptʃə(r)/ *noun* [U] a feeling of great joy or happiness
(IDIOM) **go into raptures (about/over sb/sth)** to show that you think that sb/sth is very good: *I didn't like the film much but my boyfriend went into raptures about it.*

☆ **rare¹** /reə(r)/ *adj* not found or seen very often: *a rare bird, flower, etc* ○ *It's very rare to have hot weather like this in April.*

rarely *adv* not happening often: *The Queen is rarely seen at football matches.*

rare² /reə(r)/ *adj* (used about meat) not cooked for very long: *a rare steak*

raring /'reərɪŋ/ *adj* **raring to do sth** wanting to start doing sth very much: *They were raring to try out the new computer.* ○ *When can we start* *work on the new project? We're all raring to go* (= very eager to start).

rarity /ˈreərəti/ *noun* (*pl* **rarities**) **1** [U] being unusual or difficult to find: *The rarity of this stamp increases its value a lot.* **2** [C] a thing or a person that is not found very often: *Women lorry drivers are still quite a rarity.*

rascal /ˈrɑːskl; US ˈræskl/ *noun* [C] a dishonest person or a child who does naughty things ☞ When you call a person a rascal, it usually means that you are not seriously angry with them.

rash¹ /ræʃ/ *noun* [C, usually sing] **1** an area of small red spots that appear on your skin when you are ill or have been stung by an insect, plant, etc: *He came out in a rash where the plant had touched him.* **2** a series of unpleasant events of the same kind happening close together: *There has been a rash of attacks on old people this month.*

rash² /ræʃ/ *adj* **1** doing things that might be dangerous without thinking about it: *You were very rash to give up your job before you had found another one.* **2** done without much thought: *a rash decision* o *a rash promise* (= one which you cannot keep easily) —**rashly** *adv*

rasher /ˈræʃə(r)/ *noun* [C] a slice of bacon

raspberry /ˈrɑːzbri; US ˈræzberi/ *noun* [C] (*pl* **raspberries**) **1** a small, soft, red fruit which grows on bushes: *raspberry jam* **2** a rude sound that you make with your mouth to show sb that you think they are stupid: *to blow a raspberry at sb*

☆ **rat** /ræt/ *noun* [C] an animal like a large mouse ☞ Rats belong to the family of animals that are called **rodents**. If you call a person a **rat** it means that you have a very low opinion of them.

(IDIOM) **rat race** the way of life in which everyone is rushing to be better or more successful than everyone else

☆ **rate¹** /reɪt/ *noun* [C] **1** a measurement of one amount or of how fast or how often sth is happening in relation to another amount: *The birth rate is falling.* o *a rise in the annual rate of inflation from 6 to 7%* o *The population increased at the rate of less than 0.5% a year.* o *an exchange rate of one pound to ten francs* **2** the amount that sth costs or that sb is paid: *The higher rate of income tax is 40%.* o *The basic rate of pay is £10 an hour.* ☞ Look at **first-rate** and **second-rate**.

(IDIOMS) **at any rate 1** (used when you are giving more exact information about sth): *He said that they would be here by ten. At any rate, I think that's what he said.* **2** whatever else might happen: *Well, that's one good piece of news at any rate.*

the going rate (for sth) ⇨ GOING²

rate² /reɪt/ *verb* [T] **1** to say how good you think sb/sth is: *She's rated among the best tennis players of all time.* **2** to deserve or to get sth: *The accident wasn't very serious – it didn't rate a mention in the local newspaper.*

☆ **rather** /ˈrɑːðə(r); US ˈræ-/ *adv* quite; to some extent: *It was a rather nice present.* o *It was a rather a nice present.* o *No, I didn't fail the exam, in fact I did rather well.* o *I'm afraid I owe her rather a lot of money.* o *He spoke rather too quickly for me to understand.* o *It's rather a pity that you can't come tomorrow.* o *I was rather hoping that you'd be free on Friday.* ☞ **Fairly**, **quite**, **rather** and **pretty** can all mean 'not very', or 'moderately'. **Fairly** is the weakest. **Rather** and **pretty** (informal) are the strongest. **Fairly** is mostly used with words that are positive: *This room was fairly tidy.* **Rather** is used when you are criticizing sth: *This room's rather untidy.* If you use **rather** with a positive word, it sounds as if you are surprised or pleased: *The new teacher is rather nice. I'm surprised – he didn't look very friendly.*

(IDIOMS) **or rather** a way of correcting sth you have said, or making it more exact: *She lives in London, or rather she lives in a suburb of London.*

rather than in the place of; instead of: *I think I'll just have a sandwich rather than a full meal.*

would rather... (than) would prefer to: *'How old are you?' 'I'd rather not say.'* o *Would you rather eat at home tonight or go to a restaurant?*

rating /ˈreɪtɪŋ/ *noun* [C] **1** a measurement of how popular or how good sth is: *The government's popularity rating has fallen sharply.* **2** usually **the ratings** a measurement of the number of people who have watched a TV programme, etc: *Soap operas are always high in the ratings.*

ratio /ˈreɪʃiəʊ/ *noun* [C] the relation between two numbers which shows how much bigger one quantity is than another: *The ratio of boys to girls in this class is three to one* (= there are three times as many boys as girls).

ration /ˈræʃn/ *noun* [C] the amount of food, petrol, etc that you get when there is not enough for everybody to get as much as they want: *During the war our bread ration was three loaves a week.*

ration *verb* [T] to give people only a small amount of sth, not as much as they want: *In the desert water is strictly rationed.* —**rationing** *noun* [U]: *In the oil crisis of 1973 the government introduced petrol rationing.*

rational /ˈræʃnəl/ *adj* **1** (used about a person) able to use thought to make decisions, not just feelings: *We're both rational human beings – let's sit down and talk about the problem.* ☞ The opposite is **irrational**. **2** based on reason; sensible or logical: *There must be a rational explanation for why he's behaving like this.* —**rationally** *adv*

rationalize (*also* **rationalise**) /ˈræʃnəlaɪz/ *verb* [I,T] **1** to find reasons that explain why you have done sth (perhaps because you do not like the real reason): *She rationalized her decision to buy the car by saying that it would save money on bus fares.* **2** [T] to make a business, etc better organized —**rationalization** (*also* **rationalisation**) /ˌræʃnəlaɪˈzeɪʃn; US -lɪˈz-/ *noun* [C,U]

rattle¹ /ˈrætl/ *verb* **1** [I,T] to make a noise like things hitting each other or to shake sth so that it makes this noise: *The windows were rattling all night in the wind.* o *He rattled the money in the tin.* **2** [T] (*informal*) to make sb unsure and

afraid: *The news of his arrival really rattled her.*
(PHRASAL VERB) **rattle off** to say a list of things you have learned very quickly: *She rattled off the names of every player in the team.*

rattle² /'rætl/ *noun* **1** [C,sing] a noise made by things hitting each other: *There's a funny rattle coming from the back of the car.* **2** [C] a toy that a baby can shake to make a noise

raucous /'rɔːkəs/ *adj* (used about people's voices) loud and rough: *The raucous laughter of the men in the bar could be heard across the road.*

ravage /'rævɪdʒ/ *verb* [T] to damage sth very badly: *The forests were ravaged by the winter storms.*

rave /reɪv/ *verb* [I] **1 rave (about sb/sth)** (*informal*) to praise sb/sth very much: *Everyone's raving about her latest record!* **2** to speak angrily or wildly

raving *adj* (*informal*) acting in a wild, uncontrolled way: *I think you're all raving mad!*

rave re'view *noun* [C] an article in a newspaper, that praises a book, film, record, etc very much

raven /'reɪvn/ *noun* [C] a large black bird, like a crow, that has a harsh voice

ravenous /'rævənəs/ *adj* very hungry: *After spending the whole day walking we were ravenous.* —**ravenously** *adv*

ravine /rə'viːn/ *noun* [C] a narrow deep valley with steep sides

☆ **raw** /rɔː/ *adj* **1** not cooked: *The Japanese eat raw fish.* ○ *Raw vegetables are good for your teeth.* **2** used about an injury where the skin has been rubbed away: *There's a nasty raw place on my heel where my shoes have rubbed.* **3** in the natural state: *raw sugar* ○ *raw materials* (= that are used to make things with, in factories, etc)

☆ **ray** /reɪ/ *noun* [C] a line of light, heat or energy: *A single ray of light came through a hole in the roof.* ○ *the rays of the sun* ☛ Look at **X-ray**.
(IDIOM) **a ray of hope** a small chance that things will get better

☆ **razor** /'reɪzə(r)/ *noun* [C] a sharp instrument which people use to cut off the hair from their skin (= to **shave**): *an electric razor*

'razor-blade *noun* [C] the thin sharp piece of metal that you put in a razor

☆ **reach** /riːtʃ/ *verb* **1** [T] to arrive at a place or condition: *The letter will reach you on Wednesday.* ○ *We won't reach Dover before 12.* ○ *Tell me when you have reached the end of the book.* ○ *Anyone who has reached the age of 60 knows something about the world.* ○ *Sometimes the temperature reaches 45°C.* ○ *We finally reached an agreement after hours of discussion.* ○ *Have you reached a decision yet?* **2** [I,T] **reach (out) (for sb/sth)** to stretch out your arm to try and touch sth or get sth: *The child reached for her mother.* ○ *The monkey reached out its hand for the banana.* ○ *She reached into her bag for her purse.* **3** [I,T] to be able to touch sth: *Can you get me that book off the top shelf? I can't reach.* ○ *He couldn't reach the light switch.* ○ *I need a longer ladder. This one won't reach.* **4** [T] to

contact sb: *You can reach me at this number.* ○ *She can't be reached until Monday morning.*

reach *noun* [U] the distance that you can stretch
(IDIOMS) **beyond/out of (sb's) reach 1** outside the distance that you can stretch your arm: *Keep this medicine out of reach of children.* **2** not able to be got or done by sb: *A job like that is completely beyond his reach.*
within (sb's) reach 1 inside the distance that you can stretch your arm: *The boat's almost within reach. I can nearly touch it now.* ○ *Always keep a glass of water within reach.* **2** able to be got or done by sb: *Becker led by five games to two – victory was almost within reach!*
within (easy) reach of sth not far from: *The school is within easy reach of the house.*

☆ **react** /rɪ'ækt/ *verb* [I] **1 react (to sb/sth)** to do or say sth because of sth that has happened or been said: *If she's rude I won't react. I don't want an argument.* ○ *He wasn't sure how to react to the news.* **2 react (against sb/sth)** to behave or talk in a way that shows that you do not like the influence of sb/sth (eg authority, your family, etc): *She reacted against the strict way she had been brought up.*

☆ **reaction** /rɪ'ækʃn/ *noun* **1** [C,U] **(a) reaction (to sb/sth)** sth that you do or say because of sth that has happened or been said: *Could we have your reaction to the latest news, Minister?* ○ *a hostile reaction* ○ *I shook him to try and wake him up but there was no reaction.* **2** [C,U] **(a) reaction (against sb/sth)** behaviour that shows that you do not like the influence of sb/sth (eg authority, your family, etc): *Her strange clothes are a reaction against the conservative way she was brought up.* **3** [C, usually pl] the physical ability to act quickly when sth happens: *If the other driver's reactions hadn't been so good, there would have been an accident.*

reactionary /rɪ'ækʃənri; *US* -əneri/ *adj* trying to prevent (political) progress or change

reactionary *noun* [C] (*pl* **reactionaries**) a person who tries to prevent (political) progress or change: *The reactionaries in the party want to bring back hanging.*

reactor /rɪ'æktə(r)/ *noun* [C] = NUCLEAR REACTOR

☆ **read** /riːd/ *verb* (*pt, pp* **read** /red/) **1** [I,T] to look at words and understand them: *In their first years at school, children learn to read and write.* ○ *Don't interrupt me, I'm reading.* ○ *Have you read any good books lately?* ○ *I read an interesting article about Japan recently.* ○ *I read in the paper that they've found a cure for migraine.* **2** [I,T] **read (sb) (sth); read sth (to sb)** to say written words to sb: *My father used to read me stories when I was a child.* ○ *Read that sentence to me again, I didn't understand it.* ○ *I hate reading out loud.* **3** [T] to be able to see and understand sth: *I can't read the clock – I haven't got my glasses on.* ○ (*figurative*) *She doesn't know what you're thinking. She can't read your mind.* **4** [I] to show sth; to have sth written on it: *The sign read 'Keep Left'.* ○ *What does the thermometer read?*
(PHRASAL VERBS) **read on** to continue read-

ing; to read the next part(s) of sth: *If you read on, you'll find that the story gets exciting.*

read sth into sth to think that there is meaning in sth that it may not really have: *Don't read too much into the letter. They're only asking you for an interview, not offering you the job.*

read sth out to read sth to other people

read /ri:d/ *noun* [sing] (*informal*) a period or an act of reading: *I had a quick read of the newspaper during breakfast.* ☛ A writer or book that is interesting is **a good read**.

readable /'ri:dəbl/ *adj* **1** able to be read: *machine-readable data* ☛ Look at **legible**. **2** easy or pleasant to read

☆ **reader** /'ri:də(r)/ *noun* [C] **1** a person who reads sth (a particular newspaper, magazine, type of book, etc) **2** (with an adjective) a person who reads (in a particular way): *a fast/slow reader* **3** a book for practising reading

readership *noun* [sing] the number of people who regularly read a particular newspaper, magazine, etc

☆ **reading** /'ri:dɪŋ/ *noun* [U] **1** what you do when you are reading: *I haven't had time to do much reading lately.* ○ *On the form she described her interests as reading and tennis.* ○ *This report makes interesting reading* (= reading it is an interesting thing to do). **2** the figure or measurement that is shown on an instrument: *a reading of 20°*

readjust /ˌri:ə'dʒʌst/ *verb* **1** [I,T] **readjust (to sth)** to get used to being in a situation again that you have been in before: *After her divorce, it took her a long time to readjust to being single again.* **2** [T] to change the position or organization of sth again in order to make it correct

readjustment *noun* [C,U] the act of readjusting(1,2)

☆ **ready** /'redɪ/ *adj* **ready (for sb/sth); ready (to do sth)** prepared and able to be used or to do sth: *Dinner will be ready in ten minutes.* ○ *The car will be ready for you to collect on Friday.* ○ *He isn't ready for his driving test, he hasn't had enough lessons.* ○ *I can't talk now, I'm getting ready to go out.* **2 ready to do sth** willing to do sth: *You know me – I'm always ready to help.* **3** in a place which makes it possible for you to use or reach it easily and quickly: *Have your money ready before you get on the bus.*

readily /-ɪlɪ/ *adv* **1** easily, without difficulty: *Most vegetables are readily available at this time of year.* **2** without hesitating: *He readily admitted that he was wrong.*

readiness /'redɪnɪs/ *noun* [U] **1** the state of being ready or prepared **2** willingness: *The bank have indicated their readiness to lend him the money.*

ready *adv* (before a past participle) already; previously: *ready-cooked food*

ˌready-'made *adj* already prepared and ready for use, not made especially for you: *You can buy ready-made reading glasses now.* ○ (*figurative*) *He always has a ready-made answer to every question.*

☆ **real** /rɪəl/ *adj* **1** actually existing, not imagined: *The film is based on real life.* ○ *This isn't a real word, I made it up.* **2** actually true, not what may appear to be true: *The name he gave to the police wasn't his real name.* ○ *She said she had missed the bus, but that's not the real reason why she was late.* **3** natural, not imitation or artificial: *This shirt is real silk.* **4** (used when you are making what you say stronger, usually when you are saying how bad sth is) big; complete: *The meal I cooked was a real disaster.* ○ *Money is a real problem for us at the moment.*

(IDIOM) **the real thing 1** something genuine, not an imitation: *This painting is just a copy. The real thing is in a gallery.* **2** the truest and best example of sth: *She's had boyfriends before but this time she says it's the real thing* (= real love).

real *adv* (*US informal*) very; really: *It was real kind of you to help me.*

ˈreal estate *noun* [U] property that cannot be moved, such as land and buildings

ˈreal estate agent *noun* [C] (*US*) = ESTATE AGENT

realism /'rɪəlɪzəm/ *noun* [U] **1** behaviour that shows that you accept the facts of a situation and are not too influenced by your feelings **2** (in art, literature, etc) showing things as they really are

realist *noun* [C] a person who accepts the facts of life and situations, and who thinks and behaves according to them: *I'm a realist, I don't expect the impossible.*

realistic /ˌrɪə'lɪstɪk/ *adj* **1** accepting the facts of a situation (not believing or making yourself believe that they are different): *Be realistic! You're not going to get a job like that without qualifications.* ○ *a realistic price* **2** showing things as they really are: *a realistic description of the lives of ordinary people in London* **3** not real but appearing to be real: *The monsters in the film were very realistic.* ☛ The opposite for 1, 2 and 3 is **unrealistic**. —**realistically** /-klɪ/ *adv*: *Think about your future realistically.*

☆ **reality** /rɪ'ælətɪ/ *noun* (*pl* **realities**) **1** [U] the way life really is, not the way it may appear to be or what you would like it to be: *It's been a lovely holiday but now it's back to reality.* **2** [C] the way sth really is when you experience it: *We had hoped that things would get easy but the reality was very different.* ○ *The realities of living in a foreign country were too much for Susie and she went home.* **3** [C] something that really exists, not sth that is imagined: *Death is a reality that everyone has to face eventually.*

(IDIOM) **in reality** in fact, really (not the way sth appears or has been described): *People say this is an exciting city but in reality it's rather boring.*

☆ **realize** (*also* **realise**) /'rɪəlaɪz/ *verb* [T] **1** to know and understand that sth is true or that sth has happened: *I'm sorry I mentioned the subject, I didn't realize how much it upset you.* ○ *Do you realize how much work I've done today?* **2** to become aware of sth or that sth has happened, usually some time later: *When I got home, I realized that I had left my keys at the office.* ○ *I'm beginning to realize that this job isn't as easy as I thought it was.* **3** to make sth

p	b	t	d	k	g	tʃ	dʒ	f	v	θ	ð
pen	bad	tea	did	cat	got	chin	June	fall	van	thin	then

(an ambition, hope, etc) become reality: *She finally realized her ambition to see the Taj Mahal.*

realization (*also* **realisation**) /ˌrɪəlaɪˈzeɪʃn; *US* -lɪˈz-/ *noun* [U] the act of realizing sth: *He was suddenly hit by the realization that he might die.* ○ *Becoming Managing Director was the realization of all her dreams.*

☆**really** /ˈrɪəli/ *adv* **1** actually; in fact; truly: *I couldn't believe it was really happening.* ○ *He said that he was sorry but I don't think he really meant it.* ○ *She wasn't really angry, she was only pretending.* ○ *Is it really true?* **2** very; very much: *I'm really tired.* ○ *He really enjoys his job.* ○ *Are you really sure?* ○ *I really tried but I couldn't do it.* **3** (used as a question for expressing surprise, interest, doubt, etc): *'She's left her husband.' 'Really? When did that happen?'* ○ *'He's a very happy person.' 'Really? I've never seen him smile.'* **4** (used in questions when you are expecting sb to answer 'No'): *You don't really expect me to believe that, do you?*

realm /relm/ *noun* [C] (*formal*) a country that has a king or queen

Realtor /ˈrɪəltə(r)/ *noun* [C] (*US*) (*trade mark*) = ESTATE AGENT

reap /riːp/ *verb* [T] to cut and collect a crop (corn, wheat, etc): (*figurative*) *Work hard now and you'll reap the benefits later on.*

reappear /ˌriːəˈpɪə(r)/ *verb* [I] to appear again or be seen again: *If any signs of the illness reappear, see your doctor immediately.* —**reappearance** /-rəns/ *noun* [C,U]

reappraisal /ˌriːəˈpreɪzl/ *noun* [C,U] the examination of sth (a situation, way of doing sth, etc) in order to decide whether any changes are necessary

☆**rear¹** /rɪə(r)/ *noun* [sing] **1 the rear** the back part: *Smoking is only permitted at the rear of the bus.* ○ *I only saw him from the rear* (= from behind). **2** the part of your body that you sit on; bottom

(IDIOM) **bring up the rear** to be the last one in a race, parade, etc: *At the moment the British runner is bringing up the rear.*

rear *adj* (used especially about parts of a car) placed at the back: *the rear window* ○ *rear lights*

rear² /rɪə(r)/ *verb* **1** [T] to care for and educate children: *This generation of children will be reared without fear of war.* **2** [T] to look after animals on a farm, etc: *They rear ducks in their garden.* **3** [I] **rear (up)** (used about horses) to stand on the back legs

rearrange /ˌriːəˈreɪndʒ/ *verb* [T] **1** to change a plan, appointment, etc that has been fixed: *The match has been rearranged for next Wednesday.* **2** to change the way that sth is organized or arranged: *We've rearranged the living-room to make more space.*

☆**reason¹** /ˈriːzn/ *noun* **1** [C,U] **reason (for sth/for doing sth); reason (why... /that...)** the cause of sth; sth that explains why sth happens or exists: *What's your reason for being so late?* ○ *Is there any reason why you couldn't tell me this before?* ○ *The reason that I'm phoning you is to ask a favour.* ○ *For some reason or another they can't give us an answer until next week* (= I don't know what the reason is). ○ *She left the job for personal reasons.* **2** [C,U] **reason (for sth) (to do sth)** something that shows that it is right or logical to do sth: *I think we have reason for complaint.* ○ *There is a reason for doing things this way – it's cheaper.* ○ *I chose this colour for a reason* (= the reason was important). ○ *He had no reason to be rude to me, I hadn't been rude to him.* ○ *You have every reason* (= you are completely right) *to be angry, considering how badly you've been treated.* ○ *I have reason to believe that you've been lying.* **3** [U] the ability to think and to make sensible decisions: *I tried to persuade him not to drive but he just wouldn't listen to reason.*

(IDIOMS) **make sb see reason** to persuade sb not to continue acting in a stupid or extreme way: *They were determined to have a fight and nobody could make them see reason.*

(do anything) in/within reason if it is not too extreme or completely unacceptable: *I'll pay anything within reason for a ticket.*

reason² /ˈriːzn/ *verb* [T] to form a judgement or opinion, after thinking about sth in a logical way

(PHRASAL VERB) **reason with sb** to talk to sb in order to persuade him/her to behave or think in a more reasonable or less extreme way: *The police tried to reason with the gunman but he refused to give them his gun.*

reasoning *noun* [U] **reasoning (behind sth)** the process of thinking and making a judgement or decision: *What's the reasoning behind his sudden decision to leave?*

☆**reasonable** /ˈriːznəbl/ *adj* **1** (used about people) willing to listen to other people's opinions; not asking too much; fair: *You're not being reasonable – I can't change all my plans for you.* ○ *I tried to be reasonable even though I was very angry.* **2** (used about actions, decisions, etc) resulting from good reasons; logical: *That seems a reasonable decision in the circumstances* **3** (used about opinions or about what you expect people to do) not expecting too much; fair: *I think it's reasonable to expect people to keep their promises.* **4** (used about a price) not too high; not higher than it should be: *It was a lovely meal and the bill was very reasonable.* ○ *'How much do you want for the car?' 'About £1 000.' 'Well, that seems a reasonable price.'* ☛ The opposite for 1, 2, 3 and 4 is **unreasonable**. **5** quite good; not bad: *Her work is of a reasonable standard.* **6** (used about amounts or numbers) not very large: *They've got a reasonable amount of money but they certainly aren't rich.*

reasonably /-əbli/ *adv* **1** fairly or quite (but not very): *The weather was reasonably good but not brilliant.* **2** in a reasonable way: *If you think about my suggestion reasonably, you'll realize that I'm right.*

reassure /ˌriːəˈʃɔː(r); *US* -ˈʃʊər/ *verb* [T] to say or do sth in order to make sb feel less frightened, worried or nervous: *I keep trying to reassure my parents that there are no problems at school, but they just don't believe me.*

reassurance /-rəns/ *noun* **1** [U] the act of reassuring or being reassured: *I don't think*

s	z	ʃ	ʒ	h	m	n	ŋ	l	r	j	w
so	zoo	she	vision	how	man	no	sing	leg	red	yes	wet

there's anything wrong with you but go to another doctor for reassurance, if you like. ○ I need some reassurance that I'm doing things the right way. **2** [C] something that reassures: *The people in the village are asking for reassurances that the water is fit to drink.*

reassuring *adj* causing sb to feel less worried, frightened or nervous —**reassuringly** *adv*

rebate /ˈriːbeɪt/ *noun* [C] a sum of money that is given back to you (by sb official) because you have paid too much: *a tax rebate*

☆ **rebel** /ˈrebl/ *noun* [C] **1** a person who fights against or refuses to co-operate with authority, society, an order, a law, etc: *At school he had a reputation as a rebel.* **2** a person who fights against his/her country's government because he/she wants things to change: *During the revolution, the rebels took control of the capital.*

rebel /rɪˈbel/ (rebelling; rebelled) *verb* [I] **rebel (against sb/sth) 1** to fight against authority, society, an order, a law, etc: *She rebelled against her parents by marrying a man she knew they didn't approve of.* **2** to fight against the government in order to bring change

rebellion /rɪˈbeliən/ *noun* [C,U] fighting against authority or the government: *The rebellion ended in failure when all the leaders were shot.* ○ *Voting against the leader of the party was an act of open rebellion.*

rebellious /rɪˈbeliəs/ *adj* not doing what authority, society, etc wants you to do: *Why do little children have to turn into rebellious teenagers?*

rebound /rɪˈbaʊnd/ *verb* [I] to hit sth and then go in a different direction: *The ball rebounded off a defender and went into the goal.*

rebuff /rɪˈbʌf/ *noun* [C] an unkind refusal of an offer, etc —**rebuff** *verb* [T]

rebuild /ˌriːˈbɪld/ *verb* [T] (*pt, pp* **rebuilt** /ˌriːˈbɪlt/) to build again: *Following the storm, a great many houses will have to be rebuilt.* ○ (*figurative*) *She's trying to rebuild her life now that her husband is dead.*

rebuke /rɪˈbjuːk/ *verb* [T] (*formal*) to speak angrily to sb because he/she has done sth wrong —**rebuke** *noun* [C]

recall /rɪˈkɔːl/ *verb* [T] to remember sth (a fact, event, action, etc) from the past: *I don't recall exactly when I first met her.* ○ *She couldn't recall meeting him before.*

recapitulate /ˌriːkəˈpɪtʃuleɪt/ (*informal*) (*also* **recap** /ˈriːkæp/) *verb* [I,T] to repeat or look again at the main points of sth to make sure that they have been understood: *Let's quickly recap what we've done in today's lesson, before we finish.*

recapture /ˌriːˈkæptʃə(r)/ *verb* [I,T] **1** to capture again a person or animal that has escaped **2** to create or experience again a feeling or period from the past: *The film brilliantly recaptures the lives of ordinary people in the 1930s.*

recede /rɪˈsiːd/ *verb* [I] **1** to move away or seem to move away and begin to disappear: *The coast began to recede into the distance.* ☞ If a person's **hairline is receding** or if a person **is receding**, he is losing his hair from the front of the head. **2** (used about a hope, a fear, a chance, etc) to become smaller or less strong: *The threat of war is receding because negotiations between the two countries have started.*

☆ **receipt** /rɪˈsiːt/ *noun* **1** [C] a piece of paper that is given to show that you have paid for sth: *Keep the receipt in case you want to exchange the pullover.* ○ *Could I have a receipt, please?* **2** [U] **receipt (of sth)** (*formal*) the act of receiving: *Payment must be made within seven days of receipt of the goods.*

☆ **receive** /rɪˈsiːv/ *verb* [T] **1 receive sth (from sb/sth)** to get or take sth that sb sends or gives to you: *Have you received the parcel I sent you?* ○ *I received a letter from an old friend last week.* **2** (often passive) to react to sth (news, ideas, work, etc) in a particular way: *My suggestions at the meeting were received in silence.*

receiver /rɪˈsiːvə(r)/ (*also* **handset**) *noun* [C] **1** the part of a telephone that is used for listening and speaking ☞ To answer or make a telephone call you **pick up** or **lift** the receiver. To end a telephone call you **put down** or **replace** the receiver or you **hang up**. picture at **telephone**. **2** a radio or television set

☆ **recent** /ˈriːsnt/ *adj* having happened, been done or produced a short time ago: *In recent years there have been many changes.* ○ *Does this brochure include all the most recent information?* ○ *This is a recent photograph of my daughter.*

recently *adv* **1** a short time ago: *I don't know her very well, I only met her recently.* ○ *She worked here until quite recently.* **2** during a period between not long ago and now: *Have you seen Paul recently?* ○ *She's been feeling ill recently.* ☞ **Recently** can refer to both a point in time and a period of time. If it refers to a point in time, use the past simple tense: *He died recently.* If it refers to a period, use the present perfect or present perfect continuous tense: *I haven't done anything interesting recently.* ○ *She's been working hard recently.* **Lately** can only refer to a period of time. Use only present perfect or present perfect continuous tense: *I've seen a lot of films lately.* ○ *I've been spending too much money lately.*

receptacle /rɪˈseptəkl/ *noun* [C] (*formal*) a container that is used for putting or keeping things in

☆ **reception** /rɪˈsepʃn/ *noun* **1** [U] the place in a hotel or office building where you go to say that you have arrived, to make enquiries, appointments, etc: *Leave your key at reception if you go out, please.* ○ *All visitors must report to reception.* **2** [C] a formal party to celebrate sth (especially a wedding) or to welcome an important person: *Their wedding reception was held at a local hotel.* ○ *There will be an official reception at the Embassy for the visiting Ambassador.* **3** [sing] the way people react to sth: *The play got a mixed reception* (= some people liked it, some people didn't). ○ *The President received a warm reception during his visit to China* (= people showed that they liked him). **4** [U] the quality of radio or television signals: *TV reception is very poor where we live.*

receptionist *noun* [C] a person who works in a hotel, office, etc answering the phone, deal-

iː	ɪ	e	æ	ɑː	ɒ	ɔː	ʊ	uː	ʌ
see	sit	ten	hat	arm	got	saw	put	too	cup

ing with guests, customers, visitors, etc: *a hotel receptionist*

receptive /rɪ'septɪv/ *adj* **receptive (to sth)** willing to listen to new ideas, suggestions, etc

recess /rɪ'ses; *US* 'ri:ses/ *noun* **1** [C,U] a period when Parliament, etc is on holiday **2** [U] (*US*) a short period of free time between classes at school ☛ Look at the note at **interval**.

recession /rɪ'seʃn/ *noun* [C,U] a period when the business and industry of a country is not successful: *The country is now in recession.* o *How long will the recession last?*

☆ **recipe** /'resəpi/ *noun* [C] **1 a recipe (for sth)** the instructions for cooking or preparing sth to eat. A recipe tells you what to use (**the ingredients**) and what to do. **2 a recipe for sth** the way to get or produce sth: *What's the recipe for a happy marriage?*

recipient /rɪ'sɪpiənt/ *noun* [C] a person who receives sth

reciprocal /rɪ'sɪprəkl/ *adj* both given and received: *The arrangement is reciprocal. They help us and we help them.*

recital /rɪ'saɪtl/ *noun* [C] a public performance of music or poetry, by one person or a small group: *a piano recital* ☛ Look at **concert**.

recite /rɪ'saɪt/ *verb* [I,T] to say aloud a piece of writing (especially a poem) or a list from memory: *He can recite the names and dates of all the kings and queens of England.*

reckless /'rekləs/ *adj* not thinking about whether what you are doing is dangerous or might have bad results: *reckless driving* —**recklessly** *adv*

reckon /'rekən/ *verb* [T] **1** to believe or consider; to have the opinion: *This is generally reckoned to be the nicest area in the city.* **2** (*informal*) to think or suppose: *She's very late now. I reckon she isn't coming.* **3** to calculate approximately or guess: *I reckon the journey will take about half an hour.* **4** to expect to do sth: *We reckon to sell about twenty of these suits a week.*

(PHRASAL VERBS) **reckon on sb/sth** to expect sth to happen and therefore to base a plan or action on it: *I didn't book in advance because I wasn't reckoning on tickets being so scarce.*

reckon with sb/sth to expect sth; to think about sth as a possible problem: *When they decided to buy a bigger house, they didn't reckon with the enormous cost involved.*

reclaim /rɪ'kleɪm/ *verb* [T] **1 reclaim sth (from sb/sth)** to get back sth that you have lost or put in a place where it is kept for you to collect: *Reclaim your luggage after you have been through passport control.* **2** to get back useful materials from waste products: *The aluminium used in cans can be reclaimed and recycled.* **3** to make land suitable for use: *The Dutch have reclaimed huge areas of land from the North Sea.*

recline /rɪ'klaɪn/ *verb* [I] to lie back or down in order to be more comfortable: *If you wish to recline, press the button on the side of your seat.*

reclining *adj* lying back; able to be adjusted so that you can lie back: *The car has reclining seats at the front.*

recognition /ˌrekəg'nɪʃn/ *noun* [U] the act of recognizing sth or of showing or receiving respect: *He showed no sign of recognition when he passed me in the street.* o *She has received public recognition for her services to charity.*

☆ **recognize** (*also* **recognise**) /'rekəgnaɪz/ *verb* [T] **1 recognize sb/sth (by/from sth)** to know again sb/sth that you have seen or heard before: *I recognized him but I couldn't remember his name.* o *This district has changed so much since I was last here that I hardly recognize it now.* **2** to accept or admit that sth is true: *I recognize that some of my ideas are unrealistic.* **3** to accept sth officially (usually done by institutions or governments): *My qualifications are not recognized in other countries.* **4** to show that you think sth that sb has done is good: *The company gave her a special present to recognize her long years of service.*

recognizable (*also* **recognisable**) /'rekəgnaɪzəbl; ˌrekəg'naɪzəbl/ *adj* able to be recognized —**recognizably** (*also* **recognisably**) /-əbli/ *adv*

recoil /rɪ'kɔɪl/ *verb* [I] to react to sb/sth with a feeling of fear, horror, etc: *to recoil from the sight of blood*

recollect /ˌrekə'lekt/ *verb* [I,T] to remember sth from the past: *I don't recollect exactly when it happened.*

recollection /ˌrekə'lekʃn/ *noun* **1** [U] **recollection (of sb/sth)** the ability to remember: *I have no recollection of promising to lend you money.* **2** [C, usually pl] something that you remember: *I have only vague recollections of the town where I spent my early years.*

☆ **recommend** /ˌrekə'mend/ *verb* [T] **1** to say that sb/sth is good and that it would be liked or useful: *Which film would you recommend?* o *Could you recommend me a good hotel in Paris?* o *We hope that you'll recommend this restaurant to all your friends.* o *The head of her department recommended her for promotion.* o *Doctors don't always recommend drugs as the best treatment for every illness.* **2** to strongly suggest sth; to tell sb what you strongly believe he/she should do: *My doctor has recommended a long period of rest.* o *I don't recommend you to park there because it's against the law.* o *I recommend that you get some legal advice.* o *I wouldn't recommend (your) travelling on your own. It could be dangerous.*

recommendation /ˌrekəmen'deɪʃn/ *noun* **1** [C,U] saying that sth is good and will be liked or useful: *I visited Seville on a friend's recommendation and I really enjoyed it.* **2** [C] a statement about what should be done in a particular situation: *After the train crash, a committee of enquiry made several recommendations on how safety could be improved.*

recompense /'rekəmpens/ *verb* [T] (*formal*) to give money, etc to sb for special efforts or work or because you are responsible for a loss he/she has suffered: *The airline has agreed to recompense us for the damage to our luggage.* —**recompense** *noun* [sing,U] (*formal*): *Please accept this cheque in recompense for our poor service.*

reconcile /ˈrekənsaɪl/ *verb* [T] **1** (often passive) **reconcile sb (with sb)** to cause people to become friendly with or close to each other again: *After years of not speaking to each other, she and her parents were eventually reconciled.* **2 reconcile sth (with sth)** to find a way to make two things (ideas, situations, statements, etc) be possible together, when in fact they seem to oppose each other: *She finds it difficult to reconcile her career ambitions with her responsibilities to her children.* **3 reconcile yourself to sth** to accept an unpleasant situation because there is nothing you can do to change it

reconciliation /ˌrekənˌsɪliˈeɪʃn/ *noun* [C,U] becoming friendly or close again (after an argument, etc): *to bring about a reconciliation between the two sides*

reconnaissance /rɪˈkɒnɪsns/ *noun* [C,U] the study of a place or area for military reasons

reconsider /ˌriːkənˈsɪdə(r)/ *verb* [I,T] to think again about sth (a decision, situation, etc): *Public protests have forced the government to reconsider their policy.*

reconstruct /ˌriːkənˈstrʌkt/ *verb* [T] **1** to build again sth that has been destroyed or damaged: *The cathedral was reconstructed after the fire.* **2** to get a full description or picture of sth using the facts that are known: *The police are trying to reconstruct the victim's movements on the day of the murder.* —**reconstruction** /-ˈstrʌkʃn/ *noun* [C,U]: *Reconstruction of the city after the earthquake took years.* ○ *a reconstruction of the crime using actors*

☆ **record¹** /ˈrekɔːd; *US* ˈrekərd/ *noun* [C] **1 record (of sth)** a written account of what has happened, been done, etc: *The teachers keep records of the children's progress.* ○ *medical records* **2** (*also* **disc**) a thin, round piece of plastic which can store music and other sounds so that you can play it when you want: *to put on/play/listen to some records* ○ *a record collection* **3** the best performance or the highest or lowest level, etc ever reached in sth, especially in sport: *Who holds the world record for high jump?* ○ *to set a new record* ○ *to break a record* ○ *We've had so little rain this year – I'm sure it must be a record* (= the lowest amount ever). ○ *He did it in record time* (= very fast). ○ *record sales* **4** [sing] the facts, events, etc that are known (and sometimes written down) about sb/sth: *The police said that the man had a criminal record* (= he had been found guilty of crimes in the past). ○ *This airline has a bad safety record.*

(IDIOM) **put/set the record straight** to correct a misunderstanding by telling sb the true facts

'record-breaking *adj* (only *before* a noun) the best, fastest, highest, etc ever: *We did the journey in record-breaking time.*

'record-player (*Brit also* **gramophone**) *noun* [C] a machine that you use for playing records

☆ **record²** /rɪˈkɔːd/ *verb* **1** [T] to write sth down, put it into a computer, film it, etc so that it can be used later and will not be forgotten: *Their childhood is recorded in diaries and photographs of those years.* **2** [I,T] to put music, a film, a programme, etc onto a cassette or record so that it can be listened to or watched again later: *Quiet, please! We're recording.* ○ *The band has recently recorded a new album.* ○ *There's a concert I would like to record from the radio this evening.*

recorder /rɪˈkɔːdə(r)/ *noun* [C] **1** a machine for recording sound or pictures or both: *a tape recorder* ○ *a video recorder* **2** a type of musical instrument that is often played by children. You play it by blowing through it and covering the holes in it with your fingers. ☞ picture at flute.

recording /rɪˈkɔːdɪŋ/ *noun* **1** [C] sound or pictures that have been put onto a cassette, record or film: *the Berlin Philharmonic's recording of Mahler's Sixth symphony* **2** [U] the process of making cassettes, records or films: *a recording studio*

recount /rɪˈkaʊnt/ *verb* [T] (*formal*) to tell a story or describe an event: *He recounted the story to us in vivid detail.*

recourse /rɪˈkɔːs/ *noun*
(IDIOM) **have recourse to sb/sth** (*formal*) to turn to sb/sth for help

☆ **recover** /rɪˈkʌvə(r)/ *verb* **1** [I] **recover (from sth)** to become well again after you have been ill: *It took him two months to recover from the operation.* **2** [I] **recover (from sth)** to get back to normal again after a bad experience, etc: *It took her a long time to recover from her father's death.* **3** [T] **recover sth (from sb/sth)** to find or get back sth that has been lost or stolen: *Police recovered the stolen goods from a warehouse in South London.* **4** [T] to get back a state of health, an ability to do sth, etc: *He needs daily exercise if he's going to recover the use of his legs.* ○ *She recovered consciousness in the ambulance.*

☆ **recovery** /rɪˈkʌvəri/ *noun* **1** [sing,U] **recovery (from sth)** a return to good health after an illness or to a normal state after a difficult period of time: *to make a good, quick, slow, etc recovery* ○ *Nobody is optimistic about the prospects of economic recovery this year.* **2** [U] **recovery (of sth/sb)** getting sth back: *He offered a reward for the recovery of the paintings.*

recreation /ˌrekriˈeɪʃn/ *noun* [C,U] enjoying yourself and relaxing when you are not working; a way of doing this: *What do you do for recreation?* ○ *His only recreation is watching TV.*

recruit /rɪˈkruːt/ *noun* [C] a person who has just joined the army or another organization; a new member

recruit *verb* [I,T] to get sb to join sth, to work as sth or to help with sth: *to recruit young people to the teaching profession*

recruitment *noun* [U] the process of getting people to join sth or work as sth: *Many companies are having problems with recruitment.*

rectangle /ˈrektæŋgl/ *noun* [C] a shape with four straight sides and four angles of 90 degrees (**right angles**). Two of the sides are usually longer than the other two. ☞ picture at **shape**. —**rectangular** *adj* /rekˈtæŋgjʊlə(r)/

p	b	t	d	k	g	tʃ	dʒ	f	v	θ	ð
pen	bad	tea	did	cat	got	chin	June	fall	van	thin	then

rectify /'rektɪfaɪ/ verb [T] (pres part **rectifying**; 3rd pers sing pres **rectifies**; pt, pp **rectified**) (formal) to change sth so that it is right: *All these errors will need to be rectified.*

rector /'rektə(r)/ noun [C] (in the Church of England) a priest in charge of a certain area (**a parish**) ☛ Look at **vicar**.

recuperate /rɪ'ku:pəreɪt/ verb [I] to get well again after an illness or injury —**recuperation** noun [U]

recur /rɪ'kɜ:(r)/ verb [I] (recur**ring**; recur**red**) to happen again or many times: *a recurring problem* ○ *It was a theme that recurred in many of her books.* —**recurrence** /rɪ'kʌrəns/ noun [C,U] —**recurrent** /-ənt/ adj

recycle /ˌri:'saɪkl/ verb [T] **1** to process used objects and materials so that they can be used again: *recycled paper* ○ *Aluminium cans can be recycled.* ○ *We take our empty bottles to the bottle bank for recycling.* **2** to keep used objects and materials and use them again: *Don't throw away your plastic carrier bags – recycle them!* —**recyclable** adj that can be recycled: *Most plastics are recyclable.*

☆ **red**[1] /red/ adj (**redder**; **reddest**) **1** of the colour of blood: *red wine* ○ *The berries on that bush turn bright red in October.* ☛ We use **crimson**, **maroon** and **scarlet** to describe different shades of red. **2** (used about a person's face) a darker colour than usual because of anger, sadness, shame, etc: *He went bright red when she spoke to him.* ○ *to turn/be/go red in the face* **3** (used about a person's hair or an animal's fur) of a colour between red, orange and brown: *She's got red hair and freckles.*
(IDIOM) **a red herring** an idea or subject which takes people's attention away from what is really important

'**redbrick** adj (Brit) (of British universities) started in the late 19th or early 20th century

,**red 'card** noun [C] (in football, etc) a card that is shown to a player who is being sent off the field ☛ Look at **yellow card**.

,**red 'carpet** noun [sing] a piece of red carpet that is put out to receive an important visitor; a special welcome for an important visitor

,**red'currant** noun [C] a small red berry that you can eat: *redcurrant jelly*

'**redhead** noun [C] a person, especially a woman, who has red hair

,**red-'hot** adj (used about a metal) so hot that it turns red

,**Red 'Indian** noun [C] a North American Indian ☛ It is offensive to call somebody a Red Indian nowadays. Use **Native American**.

,**red 'tape** noun [U] official rules that seem unnecessary and often cause delay and difficulty in achieving sth

,**red 'wine** noun [U] wine that is made from black grapes ☛ Look at **white wine** and **rosé**.

☆ **red**[2] /red/ noun [C,U] the colour of blood: *She was dressed in red* (= in red clothes).
(IDIOM) **be in the red** (informal) to have spent more money than you have in the bank, etc

redden /'redn/ verb [I,T] to become red or to make sth red: *She reddened with embarrassment.* ☛ Go **red** or **blush** are more common.

reddish /'redɪʃ/ adj slightly red

redeem /rɪ'di:m/ verb [T] **1** to prevent sth from being completely bad: *The redeeming feature of the job is the good salary.* **2 redeem yourself** to save yourself from blame: *It was all his fault. There's nothing he can say to redeem himself.* **3** to get sth back by paying the amount needed

redemption /rɪ'dempʃn/ noun [U] (formal) being saved or redeemed
(IDIOM) **beyond redemption** not able to be saved

redevelop /ˌri:dɪ'veləp/ verb [T] to build or arrange an area, a town, a building, etc in a different and more modern way: *They're redeveloping the city centre.*
redevelopment noun [U] new building work: *There's a lot of redevelopment going on around us at the moment.*

red-handed /ˌred'hændɪd/ adj
(IDIOM) **to catch sb red-handed** ⇨ CATCH[1]

redistribute /ˌri:dɪ'strɪbju:t/ verb [T] to share sth among people, groups, etc in a different way —**redistribution** /ˌri:dɪstrɪ'bju:ʃn/ noun [U]

☆ **reduce** /rɪ'dju:s; US -'du:s/ verb [T] **1** to make sth less: *The sign said 'Reduce speed now'.* ○ *Doctors have advised us to reduce the amount of fat in our diets.* ☛ The opposite is **increase**. **2 reduce sb/sth (from sth) to sth** (often passive) to make sb/sth be in the (usually bad) state mentioned: *One of the older boys reduced the little child to tears.* ○ *They were reduced from wealth to poverty almost overnight.*

☆ **reduction** /rɪ'dʌkʃn/ noun **1** [U] making sth less or becoming less; an example of this happening: *a reduction in the numbers of people unemployed* ○ *a reduction in the rate of inflation* **2** [C] the amount by which sth is made smaller, especially in price: *There were huge price reductions during the sale.*

redundant /rɪ'dʌndənt/ adj **1** (used about employees) no longer needed for a job and therefore out of work: *When the factory closed 800 people were made redundant.* **2** not necessary or wanted
redundancy /-ənsi/ noun (pl **redundancies**) **1** [C, usually pl] a case of having lost your job because there is no work for you: *Due to economic pressure the firm were forced to announce fifty redundancies.* **2** [U] the state of having lost your job because there is no work: *Computers have caused some redundancy but have also created jobs.* ○ *redundancy pay*

reed /ri:d/ noun [C,U] a tall plant, like grass, that grows in or near water

reef /ri:f/ noun [C] a long line of rocks, sand, etc just below or above the surface of the sea: *a coral reef*

reek /ri:k/ noun [sing] a strong bad smell
reek verb [I] to smell strongly of sth unpleasant: *His breath reeked of alcohol.*

reel[1] /ri:l/ noun [C] a round object that cotton, wire, film for cameras, a fishing-line, etc is wound around: *a cotton reel*
reel verb [T] **reel sth in/out** to wind sth on or off a reel or to pull it towards you using a reel: *to reel out the hosepipe* ○ *to reel in a fish*
(PHRASAL VERB) **reel sth off** to say or repeat

s	z	ʃ	ʒ	h	m	n	ŋ	l	r	j	w
so	zoo	she	vision	how	man	no	sing	leg	red	yes	wet

sth from memory quickly and without effort: *She reeled off a list of all the people she'd invited to the party.*

reel² /riːl/ *verb* [I] **1** to move in an unsteady way: *They reeled home from the pub soon after midnight.* **2** (used about the mind) to be unclear or confused: *His mind was reeling at the shock.*

refectory /rɪˈfektrɪ/ *noun* [C] (*pl* **refectories**) a large dining-room in a college, school, etc

☆ **refer** /rɪˈfɜː(r)/ *verb* (referring; referred) **1** [I] **refer to sb/sth** to mention or talk about sb/sth: *When he said 'some students', do you think he was referring to us?* ○ *Many people still refer to Germany as West Germany.* **2** [I] **refer to sb/sth** to be used to describe sb/sth: *The term 'adolescent' refers to young people between the ages of 12 and 17.* **3** [I] to be connected with or important for: *The figures in brackets refer to holidays in July.* **4** [I] **refer to sb/sth** to go to sb/sth or to look at sth for information: *If you don't understand a word you may refer to your dictionaries.* **5** [T] **refer sb/sth to sb/sth** to send or direct sb/sth to sb/sth for help or to be dealt with: *The doctor has referred me to a specialist.* ○ *The dispute was referred to the United Nations.*

referee /ˌrefəˈriː/ *noun* [C] (also *informal* **ref**) the person in football, boxing, etc who controls the match and prevents the rules from being broken ☞ picture at **football**. Look at **umpire**.

referee *verb* [I,T] to act as a referee: *Who refereed the match?*

☆ **reference** /ˈrefərəns/ *noun* **1** [C,U] **reference (to sb/sth)** a statement that mentions sb/sth; the act of mentioning sb/sth: *The article made a direct reference to a certain member of the royal family.* ○ *Don't make any reference to his behaviour last night.* **2** [C] a note, especially in a book, etc, that tells you where certain information has been or can be found. **3** [C] a statement or letter describing a person's character and ability. When you are applying for a job, you give names as references: *My former employer provided me with a very good reference.* ○ *May I give your name as a reference?* **4** [C] (*abbr* **ref**) (used on business letters, etc) a special number that identifies a letter, etc: *Please quote our reference when replying.*

(IDIOM) **with reference to sb/sth** (*formal*) about or concerning sb/sth: *I am writing with reference to your letter of 10 April...*

'reference book *noun* [C] a book that is used for obtaining information, not for reading right through

referendum /ˌrefəˈrendəm/ *noun* [C] (*pl* **referendums** or **referenda** /-də/) an occasion when all the people of a country are able to vote on a particular political question

refill /ˌriːˈfɪl/ *verb* [T] to fill sth again: *Can I refill your glass?*

refill /ˈriːfɪl/ *noun* [C] (*informal*) the container which holds the amount that is needed to refill sth: *a refill for a pen*

refine /rɪˈfaɪn/ *verb* [T] **1** to make a substance pure and free from other substances: *to refine sugar, oil, etc* **2** to improve sth by changing little details: *to refine a theory*

refined *adj* **1** (used about a person) having extremely good manners **2** that has been improved or made pure: *refined sugar* ☞ The opposite for 1 and 2 is **unrefined**.

refinery /-nərɪ/ *noun* [C] (*pl* **refineries**) a factory where a certain substance is refined: *an oil refinery*

refinement /rɪˈfaɪnmənt/ *noun* **1** [C] (often plural) a small change that improves sth: *The new model has electric windows and other refinements.* **2** [U] good manners, polite behaviour, etc: *a person of great refinement*

☆ **reflect** /rɪˈflekt/ *verb* **1** [T] to show or express sth: *The increase in wages will be reflected in prices soon.* **2** [T] to send back light, heat or sound: *Silver paper behind a radiator helps to reflect heat into the room.* **3** [T] **reflect sb/sth (in sth)** (used about a mirror, water, etc) to send back an image of sb/sth: *She caught sight of herself reflected in the shop window.* **4** [I,T] **reflect (on/upon sth)** to think, especially deeply: *I really need some time to reflect on what you've said.*

(PHRASAL VERB) **reflect (well, badly, etc) on sb/sth** to give a particular impression of sb/sth: *It reflects badly on the whole school if some of the pupils misbehave in public.*

☆ **reflection** (*also* **reflexion**) /rɪˈflekʃn/ *noun* **1** [C] a thing that shows or expresses sth: *His success is a reflection of all the hard work he puts into his job.* **2** [sing] **reflection on/upon sb/sth** a thing that causes a bad impression of sb/sth: *Parents often feel that their children's behaviour is a reflection on themselves.* **3** [C] an image that you see in a mirror or in water **4** [U] (*technical*) the process of sending light, heat or sound back from a surface **5** [C,U] thinking deeply about sth: *A moment's reflection will show you that you are wrong.*

(IDIOM) **on reflection** after thinking again: *I think, on reflection, that we were wrong.*

reflective /rɪˈflektɪv/ *adj* **1** (used about a person, mood, etc) thoughtful: *a reflective expression* **2** (used about a surface) reflecting light: *Wear reflective strips when you're cycling at night.*

reflector /rɪˈflektə(r)/ *noun* [C] a thing that reflects light, heat or sound

reflex /ˈriːfleks/ *noun* **1** [C] (*also* **'reflex action**) a sudden movement or action that you make automatically: *'I'm going to tap your knee to test your reflexes,' said the doctor.* **2** **reflexes** [plural] the ability to act quickly when necessary: *A good tennis player needs to have excellent reflexes.*

reflexion (*Brit*) = REFLECTION

reflexive /rɪˈfleksɪv/ *adj*, *noun* [C] (*grammar*) (a word or verb form) showing that the action of a sentence is done to the subject of the sentence: *In the sentence 'He cut himself', 'himself' is a reflexive pronoun.*

☆ **reform** /rɪˈfɔːm/ *verb* **1** [T] to change sth in order to make it better: *to reform the examination system* **2** [I,T] to behave better or fit into society better; to make sb do this: *He's done wrong in the past but he has made serious*

iː	ɪ	e	æ	ɑː	ɒ	ɔː	ʊ	uː	ʌ
see	sit	ten	hat	arm	got	saw	put	too	cup

efforts to reform. ○ Our prisons aim to reform criminals, not simply to punish them.

reform noun [C,U] (a) change in sth in order to make it better: *a major reform to the system* ○ *political reform in Eastern Europe*

reformer noun [C] a person who tries to change society and make it better

refrain¹ /rɪˈfreɪn/ verb [I] **refrain (from sth)** (formal) to stop yourself doing sth; not do sth: *Please refrain from smoking in the hospital.*

refrain² /rɪˈfreɪn/ noun [C] a part of a song which is repeated, especially at the end of each verse

refresh /rɪˈfreʃ/ verb [T] to make sb/sth feel fresh, strong or full of energy again: *He looked refreshed after a good night's sleep.*
(IDIOM) **refresh your/sb's memory (about sb/sth)** to remind yourself/sb about sth: *Could you refresh my memory about what we said on this point last week?*

refreshing adj **1** interesting, different and enjoyable: *It's refreshing to meet somebody who is so enthusiastic.* **2** making you feel fresh and strong again: *a refreshing swim*

refreshment /rɪˈfreʃmənt/ noun **1 refreshments** [plural] light food and drinks that are available at a cinema, theatre or other public event: *Refreshments will be sold during the interval.* **2** [U] being refreshed, or the food and drink that makes you feel refreshed: *There will be two stops for refreshment on the coach journey.* ○ *Can I offer you some refreshment?*

refrigerate /rɪˈfrɪdʒəreɪt/ verb [T] to put food, etc in a fridge in order to keep it fresh —**refrigerator** /rɪˈfrɪdʒəreɪtə(r)/ noun [C] (formal) = FRIDGE

refuge /ˈrefjuːdʒ/ noun [C,U] **refuge (from sb/sth)** a place that is safe; the protection that this place gives you against sth unpleasant: *a refuge from the heat of the sun* ○ *They took refuge in foreign embassies.*

☆ **refugee** /ˌrefjuˈdʒiː; US ˈrefjʊdʒiː/ noun [C] a person who has been forced to leave his/her country for political or religious reasons, because there is a war, not enough food, etc: *political refugees* ○ *a refugee camp*

refund /rɪˈfʌnd; ˈriːfʌnd/ verb [T] to pay back money: *Your travelling expenses will be refunded.*

refund /ˈriːfʌnd/ noun [C] a sum of money that is returned to you, for example if you take goods back to a shop

refundable adj that will be paid back: *The deposit is not refundable.*

☆ **refusal** /rɪˈfjuːzl/ noun **1** [U] not wanting or not being able to do sth or to accept sth: *Refusal to pay the new tax may result in imprisonment.* **2** [C] a statement or act that shows you will not do or accept sth: *The employers warned that a refusal to return to work would result in people losing their jobs.* ○ *So far we've had ten replies to the invitation: eight acceptances and two refusals.*

☆ **refuse¹** /rɪˈfjuːz/ verb [I,T] to say or show that you do not want to do, give, accept, etc sth: *I asked her to come but she refused.* ○ *He refused to listen to what I was saying.* ○ *My application for a grant has been refused.* ○ *We offered her a lift but she refused it.*

refuse² /ˈrefjuːs/ noun [U] (formal) things that you throw away; rubbish: *household refuse* ○ *the refuse collection* (= when dustbins are emptied)

regain /rɪˈɡeɪn/ verb [T] to get sth back that you have lost: *to regain your freedom* ○ *to regain consciousness*

regal /ˈriːɡl/ adj very splendid; like or suitable for a king or queen

☆ **regard¹** /rɪˈɡɑːd/ verb [T] **1 regard sb/sth (as sth); regard sb/sth (with sth)** to think of sb/sth (in the way mentioned): *I regard him as my best friend.* ○ *Do you regard this issue as important?* ○ *Her work is highly regarded* (= people have a high opinion of it). ○ *In some villages newcomers are regarded with suspicion.* **2** (formal) to look steadily at sb/sth: *She regarded herself thoughtfully in the mirror.*
(IDIOM) **as regards sb/sth** (formal) about or concerning sb/sth: *What are your views as regards this proposal?*

regarding prep (formal) about or concerning: *Please write if you require further information regarding this matter.*

regard² /rɪˈɡɑːd/ noun **1** [U] **regard (for sb/sth)** a feeling of admiration for sb/sth: respect: *She obviously has great regard for your ability.* **2** [U] **regard to/for sb/sth** care or consideration for sb/sth: *He shows little regard for other people's feelings.* **3 regards** [plural] (used especially at the end of a letter) kind thoughts and greetings: *Please give my regards to your parents.*
(IDIOM) **in/with regard to sb/sth; in this/that/one regard** (formal) about or concerning this or that: *With regard to the details – these will be finalized later.* ○ *It has been a successful year financially, so in this regard we have been fortunate.*

regardless adv paying no attention to sb/sth: *I suggested she should stop but she carried on regardless.*

regardless of prep paying no attention to sb/sth: *Everybody will receive the same, regardless of how long they've worked here.*

regatta /rɪˈɡætə/ noun [C] an event at which there are boat races

reggae /ˈreɡeɪ/ noun [U] a type of West Indian popular music with a strong rhythm

☆ **regime** /reɪˈʒiːm; ˈreɪʒiːm/ noun [C] a method or system of government: *a military regime*

regiment /ˈredʒɪmənt/ [C, with sing or pl verb] a group of soldiers in the army, under the command of a colonel —**regimental** /ˌredʒɪˈmentl/ adj

regimented /ˈredʒɪmentɪd/ adj (formal) (too) strictly controlled: *University life is much less regimented than life at school.*

☆ **region** /ˈriːdʒən/ noun [C] **1** a part of the country or the world; a large area of land: *desert, tropical, polar, etc regions* ○ *This region of France is very mountainous.* ○ *She is responsible for the organization in the London region.* ☛ Look at the note at **district**. **2** an area of your body: *He's been having pains in the region of his heart.*

ɜː	ə	eɪ	əʊ	aɪ	aʊ	ɔɪ	ɪə	eə	ʊə
fur	ago	pay	home	five	now	join	near	hair	pure

(IDIOM) **in the region of sth** about or approximately: *It must have cost somewhere in the region of £1 000.*
▶ **regional** /-nl/ *adj* connected with a particular region: *regional accents*

☆ **register¹** /'redʒɪstə(r)/ *noun* [C] an official list of names, etc or a book that contains such a list: *The teacher calls the register first thing in the morning.* ○ *the electoral register* (= of people who are able to vote in an election)
▶ **'register office** *noun* [C] ⇨ REGISTRY OFFICE

☆ **register²** /'redʒɪstə(r)/ *verb* **1** [I,T] to put a name on an official list: *I'd like to register for the course in June.* ○ *You should register with a doctor while you're living in England.* ○ *All births, deaths and marriages must be registered.* **2** [I,T] to show on a measuring instrument: *The thermometer registered 32°C.* **3** [T] to show feelings, opinions, etc: *Her face registered intense dislike.* **4** [T] to send a letter or parcel by special (**registered**) post: *Parcels containing valuable goods should be registered.*
▶ **registered 'post** *noun* [U] a postal service that you pay extra for. If your letter or parcel is lost the post office will make some payment to you.

registrar /,redʒɪ'strɑː(r); 'redʒɪstrɑː(r)/ *noun* [C] **1** a person whose job is to keep official lists, especially of births, marriages and deaths **2** a person who is responsible for admissions, examinations, etc at a college or university

registration /,redʒɪ'streɪʃn/ *noun* [U] the act of putting sth or sb's name on an official list: *Registration for evening classes will take place on 8 September.*
▶ **regi'stration number** *noun* [C] the numbers and letters on the front and back of a car, etc that are used to identify it

registry /'redʒɪstri/ *noun* [C] (*pl* **registries**) a place where official lists are kept: *the church registry*
▶ **'registry office** (*also* **register office**) *noun* [C] an office where a marriage can take place and where births, marriages and deaths are officially recorded ☞ Look at the note at **wedding**.

☆ **regret¹** /rɪ'gret/ *noun* [C,U] a feeling of sadness about sth that cannot now be changed: *Do you have any regrets that you didn't go to university?* ○ *I accepted his decision to leave with great regret.*
▶ **regretful** /-fl/ *adj* feeling or expressing sadness —**regretfully** /-fəli/ *adv*

☆ **regret²** /rɪ'gret/ *verb* [T] (**regretting**; **regretted**) **1** to feel sorry or sad about sth; to wish that you had not done sth: *I hope you won't regret your decision later.* ○ *I soon regretted having been so rude.* ○ *Do you regret what you said to him?* ○ *Everyone regretted his leaving the school.* **2** (*formal*) (used as a way of saying that you are sorry for sth): *I regret to inform you that your application has been unsuccessful.*
▶ **regrettable** /-əbl/ *adj* that you should feel sorry or sad about
▶ **regrettably** /-əbli/ *adv* **1** in a way that makes you feel sad or sorry **2** it is to be regretted that: *Regrettably, most hotels are not well-equipped for disabled people.*

☆ **regular** /'regjələ(r)/ *adj* **1** having the same amount of space or time between each thing or part: *regular breathing* ○ *Nurses checked her blood pressure at regular intervals.* **2** happening at the same time each day, week, etc (as a result of an arrangement or a plan): *We have regular meetings every Thursday.* **3** going somewhere or doing sth often: *a regular customer* ○ *We're regular visitors to Britain.* **4** normal or usual: *Who is your regular dentist?* **5** evenly shaped: *regular teeth* ○ *a regular geometric pattern* **6** (*grammar*) (used about a noun, verb, etc) having the usual or expected plural, verb form, etc: *'Walk' is a regular verb.*
☞ Look at **irregular**.
▶ **regular** *noun* [C] **1** (*informal*) a person who goes to a particular shop, pub, etc very often **2** a permanent member of the army, navy, etc
▶ **regularity** /,regjʊ'lærəti/ *noun* [U] the state of being regular
▶ **regularly** *adv* **1** at regular times or in a regular way: *to have a car serviced regularly* **2** often: *Mr Davis regularly takes part in competitions but this is the first one that he has won.*

regulate /'regjʊleɪt/ *verb* [T] **1** to control sth by using laws: *a strict law to regulate carbon dioxide emissions from factories* **2** to control a machine, piece of equipment, etc: *Special valves in the radiator allow you to regulate the temperature in each room.*

☆ **regulation** /,regjʊ'leɪʃn/ *noun* **1** [U] control of sth: *state regulation of agriculture* **2** [C, usually pl] a law or rule that controls how sth is done: *to observe/obey the safety regulations* ○ *It is against the fire regulations to smoke on underground trains.* ○ *The plans must comply with the new EC regulations.* ○ *to enforce a regulation*

rehabilitate /,riːə'bɪlɪteɪt/ *verb* [T] to help sb to live a normal life again after an illness, being in prison, etc —**rehabilitation** /,riːə,bɪlɪ'teɪʃn/ *noun* [U]

rehearse /rɪ'hɜːs/ *verb* [I,T] to practise a play, dance, piece of music, etc before you perform it to other people

rehearsal /-sl/ *noun* [C,U] the time when you practise a play, dance, piece of music, etc before you perform it to other people: *a dress rehearsal* (= when all the actors wear their stage clothes)

reign /reɪn/ *noun* [C] the period of time that a king or queen rules a country: *the long reign of Queen Victoria*
▶ **reign** *verb* [I] **1 reign** (**over sb/sth**) (used about a king or queen) to rule a country: (*figurative*) *the reigning world champion* **2** to be present as the most important feature of a particular situation: *Chaos reigned after the first snow of the winter.*

reimburse /,riːɪm'bɜːs/ *verb* [T] (*formal*) to pay money back to sb: *The company will reimburse you in full for your travelling expenses.* ○ *Your expenses will be reimbursed in full.*

rein /reɪn/ *noun* [C, usually pl] a long thin piece of leather that you use for controlling a horse. Reins are joined to a bridle which fits over a horses's head. ☞ picture at **horse**.

p	b	t	d	k	g	tʃ	dʒ	f	v	θ	ð
pen	bad	tea	did	cat	got	chin	June	fall	van	thin	then

reindeer /'reɪndɪə(r)/ *noun* [C] (*pl* **reindeer**) a type of large deer that lives in Arctic regions

☛ According to tradition, reindeer pull Santa Claus's sledge at Christmas when he brings presents to children.

reinforce /ˌriːɪn'fɔːs/ *verb* [T] to make sth stronger: *Concrete can be reinforced by putting steel bars inside it.* o *evidence to reinforce her argument*
  reinforcement *noun* **1** [U] the act of supporting or strengthening sth: *The sea wall is weak in places and needs reinforcement.* **2 reinforcements** [plural] extra people who are sent to make an army, navy, etc stronger

reinstate /ˌriːɪn'steɪt/ *verb* [T] to put sb back into his/her previous job or position —**reinstatement** *noun* [U]

☆ **reject** /rɪ'dʒekt/ *verb* [T] to refuse to accept sb/sth: *The plan was rejected as being impractical.* o *I've rejected all the candidates for the job except one.*
  reject /'riːdʒekt/ *noun* [C] a person or thing that is not accepted because he/she/it is not good enough: *Rejects are sold at half price.* —**rejection** /rɪ'dʒekʃn/ *noun* [C,U]: *Penny got a rejection from Leeds University.* o *There has been total rejection of the new policy.*

rejoice /rɪ'dʒɔɪs/ *verb* [I] **rejoice (at/over sth)** (*formal*) to feel or show great happiness: *The people rejoiced at the news of the victory.* —**rejoicing** *noun* [U]

rejuvenate /rɪ'dʒuːvəneɪt/ *verb* [T] (often passive) to cause sb/sth to feel or look younger —**rejuvenation** /rɪˌdʒuːvə'neɪʃn/ *noun* [U]

relapse /rɪ'læps/ *verb* [I] to become worse again after an improvement: *to relapse into bad habits* —**relapse** *noun* [C]: *The patient had a relapse and then died.*

☆ **relate** /rɪ'leɪt/ *verb* **1** [T] **relate sth to/with sth** to show a connection between two or more things: *The report relates heart disease to high levels of stress.* **2** [T] **relate sth (to sb)** (*formal*) to tell a story to sb
  (PHRASAL VERB) **relate to sb/sth 1** to be concerned with; to have sth to do with: *That question is very interesting but it doesn't really relate to the subject that we're discussing.* **2** to be able to understand how sb feels: *Some teenagers find it hard to relate to their parents.*
  related *adj* **related (to sb/sth) 1** connected with sb/sth: *The rise in the cost of living is directly related to the price of oil.* **2** of the same family: *We are related by marriage.* o *to be closely/distantly related*

☆ **relation** /rɪ'leɪʃn/ *noun* **1** [U] **relation (between sth and sth)**; **relation (to sth)** the connection between two or more things: *There seems to be no relation between the cost of the houses and their size.* o *The film bore no relation to the book* (= it was very different). **2** [C] a member of your family: *a close/distant relation*
  ☛ Note the expressions: '*What relation are you to each other?*' and '*Are you any relation to each other?*' **3 relations** [plural] the way that people, groups, countries, etc feel about or behave towards each other: *The police officer stressed that good relations with the community were essential.* o *to break off diplomatic relations*
  (IDIOM) **in/with relation to sb/sth 1** concerning sb/sth: *Many questions were asked, particularly in relation to the cost of the new buildings.* **2** compared with: *Prices are low in relation to those in other parts of Europe.*

☆ **relationship** /rɪ'leɪʃnʃɪp/ *noun* [C] **1** the way that people, groups, countries, etc feel about or behave towards each other: *The police have a poor relationship with the local people.* o *The relationship between the parents and the school has improved greatly.* **2** a friendship or love affair: *to have a relationship with sb* o *The film describes the relationship between a young man and an older woman.* o *a close relationship* **3** a family connection: '*What is your relationship to Bruce?*' '*He is married to my cousin.*' **4** the connection between two or more things: *Is there a relationship between violence on TV and the increase in crime?*

☆ **relative¹** /'relətɪv/ *noun* [C] a member of your family: *a close/distant relative*

☆ **relative²** /'relətɪv/ *adj* **1** when compared to sb/sth else: *They live in relative luxury.* o *We're in a period of relative calm after the winds of the past few days.* o *It's hard to assess the relative importance of the two jobs.* **2** (*grammar*) referring to an earlier noun, phrase or sentence: *In the phrase 'the lady who lives next door', 'who' is a relative pronoun.*
  relatively *adv* to a certain degree; quite: *Spanish is a relatively easy language.* o *It's a small house but the garden is relatively large.*

☆ **relax** /rɪ'læks/ *verb* **1** [I,T] to make or become less worried or tense; to spend time not doing very much: *This holiday will give you a chance to relax.* o *A hot bath will relax you after a hard day's work.* o *They spent the evening relaxing in front of the television.* **2** [I,T] to make or become less stiff or tight: *You should be able to feel all your muscles relaxing.* **3** [T] to make rules or laws less strict: *The regulations on importing animals have been relaxed.*
  relaxation /ˌriːlæk'seɪʃn/ *noun* **1** [U] the act of relaxing(1,2,3): *the relaxation of a rule* **2** [C,U] sth that you do in order to rest or relax (1): *Everyone needs time for rest and relaxation.* o *He paints as a relaxation.*
  relaxed *adj* not worried or tense: *The relaxed atmosphere made everyone feel at ease.*
  relaxing *adj* pleasant, helping you to rest and become less worried: *a quiet relaxing holiday*

relay¹ /'riːleɪ/ (*also* **relay race**) *noun* [C] a race in which each member of a team runs, swims, etc one part of the race: *the 4 x 100m relay*
  (IDIOM) **in relays** with one group of people replacing another when the first group has completed a period of work: *The men worked in relays throughout the night to get the building finished.*

relay² /'riːleɪ; rɪ'leɪ/ *verb* [T] (*pt, pp* **relayed**) **1** to receive and send on a signal or message **2** (*Brit*) to broadcast a radio or television programme

☆ **release** /rɪ'liːs/ *verb* [T] **1** to allow sb/sth to be free: *The hostages will be released before Christ-*

mas. ○ *He's been released from prison.* ○ *The driver of the wrecked car had to be released by firemen.* ○ *(figurative) His firm released him for two months so he could take part in the Olympic Games.* **2** to stop holding sth: *She released his hand and walked off.* **3** to move sth from a fixed position: *He released the handbrake and drove off.* **4** to allow sth to be known by the public: *The identity of the victim has not been released.* **5** to make a film, record, etc available so the public can see or hear it: *Their new single is due to be released next week.* **6** to let substances escape into the air, sea, etc: *The new power station would release 230 000 tons of carbon dioxide into the atmosphere every year.*

release *noun* **1** [C,U] **release (from sth)** the act of freeing or the state of being freed: *The release of the hostages took place this morning.* ○ *I had a great feeling of release when my exams were finished.* **2** [C] a book, film, record, piece of news, etc that has been made available to the public: *a press release* ○ *The band played their latest release.*

(IDIOM) **on (general) release** being shown or available to the public: *Batman flies into action in a new video out on release this month.*

relegate /ˈrelɪgeɪt/ *verb* [T] to put sb/sth into a lower rank or position: *West Ham was relegated to the Second Division* (= in football). —**relegation** /ˌrelɪˈgeɪʃn/ *noun* [U]

relent /rɪˈlent/ *verb* [I] to become less strict or hard, eg by allowing sth that you had previously forbidden: *Her parents finally relented and allowed her to go.*

relentless *adj* not stopping or changing: *the relentless fight against crime* —**relentlessly** *adv*: *The sun beat down relentlessly.*

☆ **relevant** /ˈreləvənt/ *adj* **relevant (to sb/sth) 1** connected with what is happening or being talked about: *Please enclose all the relevant documents with your visa application.* ○ *Much of what was said was not directly relevant to my case.* **2** important and useful: *Many people feel that poetry is no longer relevant in today's world.* ☛ The opposite is **irrelevant**. —**relevance** /-əns/ *noun* [U]: *I honestly can't see the relevance of what he said.* ○ *Does the Bible have any relevance for life today?*

☆ **reliable** /rɪˈlaɪəbl/ *adj* that you can trust: *Japanese cars are usually very reliable.* ○ *I'm surprised she didn't phone back – she's usually very reliable.* ○ *reliable information* ○ *Is he a reliable witness?* ☛ The opposite is **unreliable**. Look at the verb **rely**. —**reliability** /rɪˌlaɪəˈbɪləti/ *noun* [U]: *These cars have a good reputation for reliability.* —**reliably** /-əbli/ *adv*: *It has been reliably estimated that £10 million will be needed to complete the project.*

reliance /rɪˈlaɪəns/ *noun* [U] **1 reliance on sb/sth** being able to trust sb/sth: *Don't place too much reliance on her promises.* **2** not being able to live or work without sb/sth; being dependent on sb/sth: *the country's reliance on imported oil*

reliant /-ənt/ *adj* **reliant on sb/sth** (not before a noun) not being able to live or work without sb/sth: *They are totally reliant on the state for financial support.* ☛ Look at **self-reliant**.

relic /ˈrelɪk/ *noun* [C] something from the past that still exists today

☆ **relief** /rɪˈliːf/ *noun* **1** [U,sing] **relief (from sth)** the feeling that you have when sth unpleasant stops or becomes less strong: *The drugs brought him some relief from the pain.* ○ *What a relief! That awful noise has stopped.* ○ *It was a great relief to know they were safe.* ○ *to breathe a sigh of relief* ○ *To my relief, he didn't argue with my suggestion at all.* **2** [U] money or food that is given to help people who are in trouble: *disaster relief for the flood victims* **3** [U] a reduction in the amount of tax you have to pay

☆ **relieve** /rɪˈliːv/ *verb* [T] to make an unpleasant feeling or situation better: *This injection should relieve the pain.* ○ *Four new prisons are being built to relieve overcrowding.*

(PHRASAL VERB) **relieve sb of sth** to take sth away from sb

relieved *adj* pleased because your fear or worry has been taken away: *I was very relieved to hear that you weren't seriously hurt.*

☆ **religion** /rɪˈlɪdʒən/ *noun* **1** [U] the belief in a god or gods who made the world and who can control what happens in it: *I never discuss politics or religion with them.* **2** [C] one of the systems of worship that is based on this belief: *the Christian, Hindu, Muslim, etc religion*

☆ **religious** /rɪˈlɪdʒəs/ *adj* **1** connected with religion: *religious faith* **2** having a strong belief in a religion: *I'm not very religious, I'm afraid, but I do go to church at Christmas.*

religiously *adv* **1** in a religious way **2** regularly: *They clean their teeth religiously, every night and every morning.*

relinquish /rɪˈlɪŋkwɪʃ/ *verb* [T] (*formal*) to stop having or doing sth ☛ **Give up** is more common.

relish /ˈrelɪʃ/ *verb* [T] to enjoy sth or to look forward to sth very much

relive /ˌriːˈlɪv/ *verb* [T] to remember sth and imagine that it is happening again

reluctant /rɪˈlʌktənt/ *adj* **reluctant (to do sth)** not willing and so rather slow to agree to do sth: *I was rather reluctant to lend him the car because he's such a fast driver.* —**reluctance** /-əns/ *noun* [U]: *Tony left with obvious reluctance* (= it was clear that he didn't want to go). —**reluctantly** *adv*

☆ **rely** /rɪˈlaɪ/ *verb* [I] (*pres part* **relying**; *3rd pers sing pres* **relies**; *pt, pp* **relied**) **rely on/upon sb/sth (to do sth) 1** to need sb/sth and not be able to live or work properly without them: *The old lady had to rely on other people to do her shopping for her.* ○ *Many students do not like having to rely on their parents for money.* **2** to trust sb/sth to work or behave well: *You can't rely on the weather in Britain.* ○ *Can I rely on you to keep a secret?* ☛ The noun is **reliance** and the adjective is **reliable**.

☆ **remain** /rɪˈmeɪn/ *verb* [I] **1** to be left after other people or things have gone: *Today only a few stones remain of the castle.* **2** to remain behind after class ○ *They spent the two remaining days of their holidays buying presents to take home.* ○ *Tottenham scored with five minutes of the*

i:	ɪ	e	æ	ɑ:	ɒ	ɔ:	ʊ	u:	ʌ
see	sit	ten	hat	arm	got	saw	put	too	cup

match remaining. **2** to stay or continue in the same place or condition: *They remained silent throughout the trial.* ○ *They're divorced but they remain friends.* ○ *Josef went to live in America but his family remained behind in Europe.* ○ (*figurative*) *Although he seems very pleasant, the fact remains that I don't trust him.*

remainder /rɪ'meɪndə(r)/ *noun* [sing, with sing or pl verb] the people, things, etc that are left after the others have gone away or been dealt with; the rest: *There are seats for twenty people – the remainder must stand.* ○ *They couldn't decide what to do for the remainder of the afternoon.*

remains /rɪ'meɪnz/ *noun* [plural] **1** what is left behind after other parts have been used or taken away: *The builders found the remains of a Roman mosaic floor.* **2** (*formal*) a dead body (sometimes one that has been found somewhere a long time after death): *Human remains were discovered in the wood.*

remand /rɪ'mɑːnd/; *US* -'mænd/ *verb* [T] to order sb to come back to court at a later date: *to remand sb in custody*

remand *noun* [U] the time before a prisoner's trial takes place: *a remand prisoner*

(IDIOM) **on remand** (used about a prisoner) waiting for the trial to take place

☆ **remark** /rɪ'mɑːk/ *verb* [I,T] **remark (on/upon sb/sth)** to say or write sth; to comment: *'What a strange film,' he remarked.* ○ *Millie remarked that she had found the film very interesting.* ○ *A lot of people have remarked on the similarity between them.*

remark *noun* [C] something that you say or write; a comment: *a few personal remarks at the end of the letter* ○ *to make a rude remark*

remarkable /-əbl/ *adj* unusual or noticeable: *She certainly is a remarkable woman.* ○ *That is a remarkable achievement for someone so young.* —**remarkably** /-əbli/ *adv*

remedy /'remədi/ *noun* [C] (*pl* **remedies**) **remedy (for sth) 1** something that makes you better when you are ill or in pain: *Hot lemon with honey is a good remedy for colds.* **2** a way of solving a problem: *There is no easy remedy for unemployment.*

remedial /rɪ'miːdiəl/ *adj* **1** used to improve sth (eg sb's health or a difficult situation) **2** helping people who are slow at learning sth: *remedial English classes*

remedy *verb* [T] (*pres part* **remedying**; *3rd pers sing pres* **remedies**; *pt, pp* **remedied**) to change or improve sth that is wrong or bad: *to remedy an injustice*

☆ **remember** /rɪ'membə(r)/ *verb* **1** [I,T] to have sth in your mind or to bring sth back into your mind: *When did we go to Spain? I just don't remember.* ○ *I'm sorry. I don't remember your name.* ○ *Do you remember the night we first met?* ○ *Remember that we're having visitors tonight.* ○ *I know her face but I can't remember what she's called.* ○ *Can you remember when we bought the stereo?* ☛ If you remember **to do** something, you don't forget to do it: *I remembered to buy the coffee.* ○ *Remember to turn the lights off before you leave.* If you remember **doing** something, you have a picture or memory in your mind of doing it: *Polly remembers seeing her keys on the table yesterday.* **2** [T] to give money, etc to sb/sth: *to remember sb in your will*

(PHRASAL VERB) **remember sb to sb** to pass greetings from one person to another: *Please remember me to your wife.* ☛ Look at the note at **remind**.

remembrance /rɪ'membrəns/ *noun* [U] (*formal*) the act of remembering and showing respect for sb who is dead: *a service in remembrance of those killed in the war*

☆ **remind** /rɪ'maɪnd/ *verb* [T] **1** to say sth to help sb remember sth: *'It's Christmas in two weeks!' 'Oh don't remind me, I haven't bought any presents yet.'* ○ *She reminded him of his dentist's appointment at two o'clock.* ○ *He reminded the children to wash their hands.* ○ *The doctor reminded me that I should see her again in two months.* **2 remind sb of sb/sth** to cause sb to remember sb/sth: *This song reminds me of Paris.* ○ *You remind me of your father.* ☛ You **remember** something by yourself. If somebody or something **reminds** you of something he/she/it causes you to remember it: *Lucy remembered to say thank you after the party.* ○ *Mother reminded Lucy to say thank you after the party.*

reminder *noun* [C] sth that makes you remember sth: *We received a reminder that we hadn't paid the electricity bill.* ○ *Eddie kept the ring as a reminder of happier days.*

reminisce /ˌremɪ'nɪs/ *verb* [I] **reminisce (about sb/sth)** to talk about (pleasant) things that happened in the past

reminiscent /ˌremɪ'nɪsnt/ *adj* (not before a noun) that makes you remember sb/sth; like: *I think that painting is very reminiscent of one by Monet.*

remnant /'remnənt/ *noun* [C] a piece of sth that remains after the rest has gone

remorse /rɪ'mɔːs/ *noun* [U] a feeling of sadness because you have done sth wrong: *She was filled with remorse for what she had done.* ☛ Look at **guilt**.

remorseful /-fl/ *adj* feeling remorse

remorseless *adj* **1** showing no pity **2** not stopping or becoming less strong —**remorselessly** *adv*

remote /rɪ'məʊt/ *adj* **1** far away from where other people live: *a cottage in a remote area of Scotland* ○ (*figurative*) *The film star's life-style was very remote from that of most ordinary people.* **2** far away in time: *the remote past/future* **3** not very great: *I haven't the remotest idea who could have done such a thing.* ○ *a remote possibility* **4** not very friendly: *He seemed rather remote.*

remotely *adv* (used in negative sentences) to a very small degree; at all: *I'm not remotely interested in your problems.* —**remoteness** *noun* [U]

re‚mote con'trol *noun* [U] a system for controlling sth from a distance: *You can change channels on the television by remote control.*

☆ **remove** /rɪ'muːv/ *verb* [T] (*formal*) **1 remove sb/sth (from sth)** to take sb/sth off or away: *Please remove your shoes before entering the* *temple.* ○ *This washing-powder will remove most stains.* ○ *to remove doubts, fears, problems, etc* ○ *I would like you to remove my name from your mailing list.* ☛ **Take off, out, etc** is less formal. **2 remove sb (from sth)** to make sb leave his/her job or position: *The person responsible for the error has been removed from his post.*

removal /-vl/ *noun* **1** [U] taking sb/sth away: *I demanded the removal of my name from the list.* **2** [C,U] an act of moving from one house, etc to another: *The company has agreed to pay all our removal expenses.* ○ *a removal van*

removed *adj* (not before a noun) far or different from sth: *Hospitals today are far removed from what they were fifty years ago.*

remover *noun* [C,U] a substance that cleans off paint, stains, etc: *a stain remover*

render /'rendə(r)/ *verb* [T] (*formal*) **1** to give help, etc to sb: *to render sb a service* **2** to cause sb/sth to be in a certain condition: *She was rendered speechless by the attack.*

rendezvous /'rɒndɪvu:/ *noun* [C] (*pl* **rendezvous** /-z/) **1 rendezvous (with sb)** a meeting that you have arranged with sb **2** a place where people often meet

renew /rɪ'nju:; *US* -'nu:/ *verb* [T] **1** to give new strength or energy: *After a break he set to work with renewed enthusiasm.* **2** to start sth again: *renewed outbreaks of violence* ○ *to renew a friendship* **3** to make sth valid for a further period of time: *to renew a contract*

renewable /-əbl/ *adj* that can be continued or renewed for another period of time: *The contract is for two years but it is renewable.* —**renewal** /-'nju:əl; *US* -'nu:əl/ *noun* [C,U]

renounce /rɪ'naʊns/ *verb* [T] (*formal*) to say formally that you no longer have a right to sth or that you no longer want to be connected with sth: *When he married a divorced woman he renounced his right to be king.* ☛ The noun is **renunciation**.

renovate /'renəveɪt/ *verb* [T] to repair an old building and put it back into good condition —**renovation** /,renə'veɪʃn/ *noun* [C,U]: *The house is in need of complete renovation.*

☆ **rent** /rent/ *noun* [C,U] money that you pay regularly for the use of land, a house or a building: *a high/low rent* ○ *How much rent do you pay?*

rent *verb* [T] **1** to pay money for the use of land, a building, a machine, etc: *Do you own or rent your television?* ○ *to rent a holiday cottage* ☛ Look at the note at **hire**(1). **2** (*US*) = HIRE(1) **3 rent sth (out) (to sb)** to allow sb to use land, a building, a machine, etc for money: *We could rent out the small bedroom to a student.* ☛ Look at **hire**(3). **4** (*US*) = HIRE(3)

rental /'rentl/ *noun* [C,U] money that you pay when you rent a telephone, television, etc

renunciation /rɪ,nʌnsɪ'eɪʃn/ *noun* [U] (*formal*) saying that you no longer want sth or believe in sth: *the renunciation of chemical weapons* ☛ The verb is **renounce**.

reorganize (*also* **reorganise**) /,ri:'ɔ:gənaɪz/ *verb* [I,T] to organize sth again or in a new way so that it works better —**reorganization** (*also* **reorganisation**) /,ri:,ɔ:gənaɪ'zeɪʃn; *US* -nɪ'z-/ *noun* [C,U]

rep /rep/ (*informal*) (*also formal* **representative**) *noun* [C] a person whose job is to travel round a particular area and visit companies, etc, to sell the products of the firm for which he/she works: *a sales rep*

☆ **repair** /rɪ'peə(r)/ *verb* [T] to put sth old or damaged back into good condition: *How much will it cost to repair the car?* ○ (*figurative*) *It's difficult to see how their marriage can be repaired.* ☛ Look at **irreparable**.

repair *noun* [C,U] something that you do to mend sth that is damaged: *The bridge is under repair.* ○ *The swimming-pool is closed for repairs to the roof.* ○ *to be damaged beyond repair*

(IDIOM) **in good, bad, etc repair** in a good, bad, etc condition

repatriate /,ri:'pætrieɪt; *US* -'peɪt-/ *verb* [T] to send sb back to his/her own country —**repatriation** /,ri:,pætri'eɪʃn/ *noun* [C,U]

repay /rɪ'peɪ/ *verb* [T] (*pt, pp* **repaid** /rɪ'peɪd/) **1 repay sth (to sb)** to pay back money that you owe to sb: *to repay a debt* **2 repay sb (for sth)** to give sth to sb in return for help, kindness, etc: *How can I ever repay you for all you have done for me?*

repayable /-əbl/ *adj* that you can or must pay back: *The loan is repayable over three years.*

repayment *noun* **1** [U] paying sth back: *the repayment of a loan* **2** [C] money that you must pay back to sb/sth regularly: *monthly mortgage repayments*

repeal /rɪ'pi:l/ *verb* [T] (in a parliament) to make a law no longer valid

☆ **repeat** /rɪ'pi:t/ *verb* **1** [I,T] to say, write or do sth more than once: *Don't repeat the same mistake again.* ○ *Could you repeat what you said? I didn't quite catch it.* ○ *'I really don't want to do it,' he repeated.* ○ *The essay is quite good, but you repeat yourself several times* (= you say the same thing more than once). ○ *History often seems to repeat itself.* **2** [T] to say or write sth that sb else has said or written or that you have learnt: *Repeat each sentence after me.* ○ *Please don't repeat what you've heard here.* ☛ The noun is **repetition**.

repeat *noun* [C] something that is done, shown, given, etc again, especially a programme on television

repeated *adj* (only *before* a noun) done or happening many times: *There have been repeated accidents on this stretch of road.*

repeatedly *adv* many times; often

repel /rɪ'pel/ *verb* [T] (**repelling**; **repelled**) **1** to send or push sb/sth back or away: *The army repelled the enemy attack.* **2** to cause sb to feel strong dislike or disgust: *The dirt and smell repelled her.* ☛ The noun is **repulsion**.

repellent /-ənt/ *adj* causing a strong feeling of dislike or disgust

repellent *noun* [C,U] a chemical substance that is used to keep insects, etc away: *a mosquito repellent*

repent /rɪ'pent/ *verb* [I,T] **repent (of sth)** (*formal*) to be sorry about sth bad that you

p	b	t	d	k	g	tʃ	dʒ	f	v	θ	ð
pen	bad	tea	did	cat	got	chin	June	fall	van	thin	then

have done: *to repent of your sins* —**repentance** /-əns/ *noun* [U] —**repentant** /-ənt/ *adj*

repercussion /ˌriːpəˈkʌʃn/ *noun* [C, usually pl] the unpleasant effect or result of sth you do: *His resignation will have serious repercussions.*

repertoire /ˈrepətwɑː(r)/ *noun* [C] all the plays or music that an actor or a musician knows and can perform

repetition /ˌrepəˈtɪʃn/ *noun* [C,U] doing sth again; sth that you do or that happens again: *We don't want any repetition of what happened on Friday.* ○ *We're trying to avoid a repetition of what happened on Friday.* ☛ The verb is **repeat**.

repetitive /rɪˈpetətɪv/ (*also* **repetitious** /ˌrepɪˈtɪʃəs/) *adj* not interesting because the same thing is repeated many times: *repetitive factory work*

☆ **replace** /rɪˈpleɪs/ *verb* [T] **1** to put sth back in the right place: *Please replace the books on the shelves when you have finished with them.* ☛ **Put back** is more common and less formal. **2** to take the place of sb/sth: *Margaret Thatcher was replaced as Prime Minister by John Major.* **3 replace sb/sth (with sb/sth)** to exchange sb/sth for sb/sth that is better or newer: *We will replace any goods that are damaged.*

replaceable /-əbl/ *adj* that can be replaced ☛ The opposite is **irreplaceable**.

replacement *noun* **1** [U] exchanging sb/sth for sb/sth that is better or newer: *The carpets are in need of replacement.* **2** [C] a person or thing that will take the place of sb/sth: *Mary is leaving next month so we must advertise for a replacement for her.*

replay /ˌriːˈpleɪ/ *verb* [T] **1** to play a sports match, etc again **2** to play again sth that you have recorded

replay /ˈriːpleɪ/ *noun* [C] **1** a sports match that is played again **2** something on the television, on a film or a cassette tape that you watch or listen to again: *Now let's see an action replay of that tremendous goal!*

replica /ˈreplɪkə/ *noun* [C] an exact copy of sth

☆ **reply** /rɪˈplaɪ/ *verb* [I,T] (*pres part* **replying**; *3rd pers sing pres* **replies**; *pt, pp* **replied**) to give an answer: *I wrote to Sue but she hasn't replied.* ○ *'Yes, I will,' she replied.* ○ *I asked Matthew how he had got on at the interview but he replied that it was none of my business.* ○ *to reply to a question* ☛ Look at the note at **answer**.

reply *noun* [C,U] (*pl* **replies**) (an) answer: *Adrian nodded in reply to my question.* ○ *How many replies did you get to your advertisement?*

☆ **report**¹ /rɪˈpɔːt/ *verb* **1** [I,T] **report (on sb/sth)(to sb/sth); report sth (to sb)** to say or write what you have seen, heard, done, etc: *All accidents must be reported to the police.* ○ *Several people reported having seen the boy.* ○ *Several people reported that they had seen the boy.* **2** [I,T] (in a newspaper or on the television or radio) to write or speak about sth that has happened: *Kate reported on the events in China for the BBC.* ○ *The strike was not reported in the newspapers.* **3** [T] **report sb (to sb) (for sth)** to tell a person in authority about sth wrong that sb has done: *She was reported to the head teacher for smoking.* **4** [I] **report (to sb/sth) for sth** to tell sb that you have arrived: *On your arrival, please report to the reception desk.*

reporter *noun* [C] a person who writes about the news in a newspaper or speaks about it on the television or radio ☛ Look at **journalist**.

reˌported ˈspeech *noun* [U] = INDIRECT SPEECH

☆ **report**² /rɪˈpɔːt/ *noun* [C] **1** a written or spoken description of what you have seen, heard, done, etc: *a report of a bomb attack in Northern Ireland* ○ *newspaper reports* ○ *an annual report on the company's finances* ○ *a firsthand report* (= from the person who saw what happened) **2** a written statement about the work of a school pupil: *a school report*

☆ **represent** /ˌreprɪˈzent/ *verb* [T] **1** to be a picture, sign, example, etc of sb/sth: *The yellow lines on the map represent minor roads.* ○ *an abstract painting that represents pain* ○ *Each phonetic symbol represents one sound.* ○ *Some people think that having to carry an identity card represents a loss of freedom.* **2** to describe sb/sth in a particular way: *In the book Susan is represented as a very ordinary person.* **3** to be equal to: *A pay-rise of 5% represents a drop in income if you take inflation into account.* **4** to act or speak in the place of sb else; to be the representative of a group or country: *You will need a lawyer to represent you in court.* ○ *The British Ambassador represented the Prime Minister at the funeral.*

representation /ˌreprɪzenˈteɪʃn/ *noun* **1** [U] representing or being represented: *Minority groups are demanding more representation in Parliament.* ☛ Look at **proportional representation**. **2** [C] (*formal*) a picture, sign, etc of sb/sth

☆ **representative** /ˌreprɪˈzentətɪv/ *adj* **representative (of sb/sth)** typical of a larger group to which it belongs: *Tonight's audience is not representative of national opinion.* ☛ The opposite is **unrepresentative**.

representative *noun* [C] **1** a person who has been chosen to act or speak for sb else or for a group **2** (*formal*) = REP

repress /rɪˈpres/ *verb* [T] **1** to control an emotion or to try to prevent it from being shown or felt **2** to prevent an action or a protest

repressed *adj* **1** (used about an emotion) that you do not show **2** (used about a person) not showing natural, especially sexual, feelings —**repression** /rɪˈpreʃn/ *noun* [U]: *Religion is still alive in Eastern Europe after forty years of repression.*

repressive /rɪˈpresɪv/ *adj* allowing little freedom: *a repressive government*

reprieve /rɪˈpriːv/ *verb* [T] to stop or delay the punishment of a prisoner who has been condemned to death —**reprieve** *noun* [C]: *to grant sb a last-minute reprieve*

reprimand /ˈreprɪmɑːnd; *US* -mænd/ *verb* [T] **reprimand sb (for sth)** to tell sb officially that he/she has done sth wrong —**reprimand** *noun* [C]: *a severe reprimand*

reprisal /rɪˈpraɪzl/ *noun* [C,U] punishment, especially by military force, for harm that one group of people does to another: *The army carried out reprisals on the village that had sheltered the rebels.* o *Civilian targets were bombed in reprisal.*

reproach /rɪ'prəʊtʃ/ *verb* [T] **reproach sb (for/with sth)** to tell sb that he/she has done sth wrong (or not done sth that he/she ought to have done); to blame: *You've nothing to reproach yourself for. It wasn't your fault.*

reproach *noun* [C,U] blame or criticism; a comment, etc that shows that you do not approve of sth: *His behaviour is beyond reproach* (= cannot be criticized). o *Alison felt his reproaches were unjustified.* —**reproachful** /-fl/ *adj*: *a reproachful look* —**reproachfully** /-fəli/ *adv*

☆ **reproduce** /ˌriːprə'djuːs/ *US* -'duːs/ *verb* **1** [T] to produce a copy of sth: *It is very hard to reproduce a natural environment in the laboratory.* **2** [I,T] (used about people, animals and plants) to produce young: *Fish reproduce by laying eggs.*

reproduction /ˌriːprə'dʌkʃn/ *noun* **1** [U] the act or process of reproducing or being reproduced: *The sound reproduction on a compact disc is better than on a cassette.* o *sexual reproduction* **2** [C] a copy of a painting, etc: *That painting is a reproduction, not an original.*

reproductive /ˌriːprə'dʌktɪv/ *adj* connected with the production of young animals, plants, etc: *the male reproductive organs*

reproof /rɪ'pruːf/ *noun* [C,U] (*formal*) something that you say to tell sb that you do not approve of what he/she has done

reptile /'reptaɪl; *US* -tl/ *noun* [C] an animal, such as a snake or a crocodile, that has a scaly skin, is cold-blooded and lays eggs

☆ **republic** /rɪ'pʌblɪk/ *noun* [C] a country that has an elected government and an elected leader (**president**): *the Republic of Ireland*

republican /rɪ'pʌblɪkən/ *adj* connected with or supporting a republic

republican *noun* [C] **1** a person who supports the system of republican government **2 Republican** a member of the Republican Party (one of the two main political parties in the US) ☛ *The other main party is the Democratic Party, whose members are called* **Democrats**.

repudiate /rɪ'pjuːdɪeɪt/ *verb* [T] to say that you will not accept sth

repulsion /rɪ'pʌlʃn/ *noun* [U] a strong feeling of dislike; disgust

repulsive /rɪ'pʌlsɪv/ *adj* that causes a strong feeling of dislike; disgusting

reputable /'repjʊtəbl/ *adj* that is known to be good: *Make sure that your boiler is fitted by a reputable engineer.* ☛ Look at **disreputable**.

☆ **reputation** /ˌrepjʊ'teɪʃn/ *noun* [C] **reputation (for sth)** the opinion that people in general have about what sb/sth is like: *to have a good/bad reputation* o *The restaurant has a reputation for serving some of the finest food in the country.* o *an international reputation* o *She began to make her reputation as a novelist in the 1960s.*

reputed /rɪ'pjuːt/ *adj* generally said to be sth, although it is not certain: *He's reputed to earn more than £100 000 a year.* —**reputedly** *adv*

☆ **request** /rɪ'kwest/ *noun* [C] **request (for sth/ that...)** an act of asking for sth: *a request for help* o *to make an official request* o *to grant/turn down a request*

(IDIOMS) **at sb's request/at the request of sb** because sb asked for it: *Aid was sent to the earthquake victims at the request of the Iranian government.*

on request if you ask: *Single rooms are available on request.*

request *verb* [T] **request sth (from/of sb)** (*formal*) to ask for sth: *Passengers are requested not to smoke on this bus.* o *to request a loan from the bank* ☛ Request *is more formal than* ask.

☆ **require** /rɪ'kwaɪə(r)/ *verb* [T] **1** to need: *Do you require any assistance?* o *a situation that requires tact and diplomacy* ☛ Require *is more formal than* need. **2** (often passive) to demand or order sth: *Passengers are required by law to wear seat-belts.*

requirement *noun* [C] something that you need or that is demanded: *They grow enough vegetables for their own requirements.* o *university entrance requirements*

☆ **rescue** /'reskjuː/ *verb* [T] **rescue sb/sth (from sb/sth)** to save sb/sth from a situation that is dangerous or unpleasant: *to rescue sb from drowning* o *You rescued me from an embarrassing situation.*

rescue *noun* [C,U] an act of rescuing or the state of being rescued: *Ten fishermen were saved in a daring sea rescue off the Welsh coast.*

(IDIOM) **come/go to the/sb's rescue** to try to help or rescue sb: *She was attacked in the street and no one came to her rescue.*

rescuer *noun* [C] a person who rescues sb/sth

☆ **research** /rɪ'sɜːtʃ; *US* 'riːsɜːtʃ/ *noun* [U] (*also* **researches** [plural]) **research (into/on sth)** a detailed and careful study of sth to find out more information about it: *Bob is doing research into the practical applications of solar power.* o *scientific, medical, historical, etc research* o *Market research has shown that many people now prefer lager to beer.*

research /rɪ'sɜːtʃ/ *verb* [I,T] to study sth carefully and in detail: *Scientists are still researching the possible causes of childhood cancer in the area.*

researcher *noun* [C] a person who carries out research

resemble /rɪ'zembl/ *verb* [T] to be or look like sb/sth else: *Laura resembles her brother.* —**resemblance** /rɪ'zembləns/ *noun* [C,U] **resemblance (between A and B)**: *a family resemblance* o *The film bore no resemblance to the novel.*

resent /rɪ'zent/ *verb* [T] to feel angry about sth because you think it is unfair: *Louise bitterly resented being treated differently from the men.* —**resentful** /-fl/ *adj*: *William felt very resentful at being unfairly criticized.* —**resentment** *noun* [sing,U]: *Do you feel any resentment towards her new husband?*

reservation /ˌrezə'veɪʃn/ *noun* **1** [C] a seat, table, room, etc that you have booked: *I made a reservation for a table for two in the name of Morgan.* **2** [C,U] a feeling of doubt about sth (such as a plan or an idea): *I would recommend*

---

iː	ɪ	e	æ	ɑː	ɒ	ɔː	ʊ	uː	ʌ
see	sit	ten	hat	arm	got	saw	put	too	cup

Irene for the job without reservation. ○ *I don't share your reservations about the flat – I think it's fine.*

☆ **reserve¹** /rɪˈzɜːv/ *verb* [T] **reserve sth (for sb/sth) 1** to keep sth for a special reason or to use at a later time: *The car-park is reserved for hotel patrons only.* **2** to book a seat, table, room, etc: *to reserve theatre tickets*

reserve² /rɪˈzɜːv/ *noun* **1** [C, usually pl] something that you keep for a special reason or to use at a later date: *The US have huge oil reserves.* **2** [C] (in sport) a person who will play in a game if one of the usual members of the team cannot play **3** [C] an area of land where the plants, animals, etc are protected by law: *a nature reserve* **4** [U] the quality of being shy or keeping your feelings hidden: *It took a long time to break down her reserve and get her to relax.*

(IDIOM) **in reserve** that you keep and do not use unless you need to: *Keep some money in reserve for emergencies.*

reserved /rɪˈzɜːvd/ *adj* shy and keeping your feelings hidden: *Fred is very reserved until you get to know him well.*

reservoir /ˈrezəvwɑː(r)/ *noun* [C] a large lake where water to be used in a town or city is stored

reside /rɪˈzaɪd/ *verb* [I] (*formal*) **reside (in/at…)** to have your home in or at

residence /ˈrezɪdəns/ *noun* **1** [C] (*formal*) the place where sb (famous or important) lives: *The Prime Minister's official residence is 10 Downing Street.* **2** [U] the state of having your home in a particular place: *The family applied to take up permanent residence in the United States.* ○ *a hall of residence for college students*

☆ **resident** /ˈrezɪdənt/ *noun* [C] **1** a person who lives in a place: *Local residents have complained of the smell from the factory.* **2** a person who is staying in a hotel: *The hotel bar is open to non-residents.*

resident *adj* living in a place: *If you are resident abroad, you lose your right to vote.*

residential /ˌrezɪˈdenʃl/ *adj* **1** (used about a place or an area) that has houses rather than offices, large shops or factories: *residential suburbs* **2** where you live or stay: *This home provides residential care for the elderly.* ○ *a residential course*

residue /ˈrezɪdjuː; *US* -duː/ *noun* [C, usually sing] what remains of sth after the main part is taken or used

☆ **resign** /rɪˈzaɪn/ *verb* **1** [I,T] **resign (from sth)** to leave your job or position: *She's threatening to resign if she doesn't get a pay increase.* ○ *He's resigned as chairman of the committee.* ○ *I wonder why she resigned her job?* **2** [T] **resign yourself to sth/doing sth** to accept sth that is unpleasant but that cannot be changed: *Larry resigned himself to the fact that she was not coming back to him.*

resigned *adj* accepting sth that is unpleasant but that cannot be changed: *a resigned sigh*

(IDIOM) **be, etc resigned to sth/doing sth** to accept sth that is unpleasant but that cannot be changed: *Ben was resigned to the fact that he would never be a rock star.*

☆ **resignation** /ˌrezɪgˈneɪʃn/ *noun* **1** [C,U] **resignation (from sth)** a letter or statement that says you want to leave your job or position: *to hand in your resignation* ○ *He has threatened resignation many times in the past.* ○ *a letter of resignation* **2** [U] the state of accepting sth unpleasant that you cannot change

resilient /rɪˈzɪliənt/ *adj* strong enough to recover quickly from damage, illness, a shock, change, etc —**resilience** /-əns/ *noun* [U]

☆ **resist** /rɪˈzɪst/ *verb* **1** [I,T] to try to stop sth happening or to stop sb from doing sth; to fight against sb/sth: *The trade unions are resisting the introduction of new technology.* ○ *If the enemy attacks, we shall not resist.* ○ *to resist arrest* **2** [T] to stop yourself from having or doing sth that you want to have or do: *The cakes looked so delicious that I couldn't resist them.* ○ *I couldn't resist opening my present.*

☆ **resistance** /rɪˈzɪstəns/ *noun* [U] **1 resistance (to sb/sth)** trying to stop sth from happening or to stop sb from doing sth; fighting against sb/sth: *The government troops overcame the resistance of the rebel army.* ○ *There is strong resistance to the plan for a new motorway in the area.* **2 resistance (to sth)** the power in a person's body not to be affected by disease: *People with AIDS have very little resistance to infection.*

resistant /rɪˈzɪstənt/ *adj* **resistant (to sth) 1** not wanting sth and trying to prevent it happening: *resistant to change* **2** not harmed by sth: *This watch is water-resistant.*

resolute /ˈrezəluːt/ *adj* (used about a person or his/her actions) firm and determined; not willing to change because other people want you to: *a resolute refusal to make any concessions* ☛ **Determined** is more common. —**resolutely** *adv*: *They are resolutely opposed to any change.*

resolution /ˌrezəˈluːʃn/ *noun* **1** [U] the quality of being firm and determined **2** [C] a firm decision to do or not to do sth: *Rose made a New Year's resolution to give up smoking.* **3** [C] a formal decision that is taken after a vote by a group of people: *The UN resolution condemned the invasion.*

resolve /rɪˈzɒlv/ *verb* (*formal*) **1** [T] to find a solution to a problem: *Most of the difficulties have been resolved.* **2** [I,T] to decide sth and be determined not to change your mind: *Ray resolved never to let the same thing happen again.*

resort¹ /rɪˈzɔːt/ *verb* **resort to sth** to do or use sth bad or unpleasant because you feel you have no choice: *People who owe huge amounts of money have had to resort to selling their houses.*

resort² /rɪˈzɔːt/ *noun*

(IDIOM) **in the last resort; (as) a last resort** ⇒ LAST¹

resort³ /rɪˈzɔːt/ *noun* [C] a place where a lot of people go on holiday: *a seaside resort, such as Blackpool or Brighton*

resounding /rɪˈzaʊndɪŋ/ *adj* (only *before* a noun) **1** very loud: *resounding cheers* **2** (used about a success, etc) very great: *a resounding victory*

☆ **resource** /rɪˈsɔːs; -ˈzɔːs/ /*US* ˈriːsɔːrs/ *noun*

ɜː	ə	eɪ	əʊ	aɪ	aʊ	ɔɪ	ɪə	eə	ʊə
fur	ago	pay	home	five	now	join	near	hair	pure

[C, usually pl] something that a person, country, etc has or can use: *Russia is rich in natural resources such as oil and minerals.* ○ *The video is an excellent resource for teachers.*

resourceful /-fl/ *adj* good at finding ways of doing things

☆ **respect¹** /rɪˈspekt/ *noun* **1** [U] **respect (for sb/sth)** the feeling that you have when you admire or have a very high opinion of sb/sth: *They stood in silence for one minute as a mark of respect for the dead.* ○ *to win/lose sb's respect* ☛ Look at **self-respect**. **2** [U] **respect (for sb/sth)** the quality of being polite to sb: *We should all treat older people with more respect.* ☛ The opposite is **disrespect**. **3** [U] **respect (for sb/sth)** care for or attention to sb/sth: *The secret police show little respect for human rights.* ○ *Electricity is dangerous and should be treated with respect.* **4** [C] a detail or point: *In what respects do you think things have changed in the last ten years?* ○ *Her performance was brilliant in every respect.*

(IDIOMS) **with respect to sth** (*formal*) about or concerning: *I am writing with respect to your recent enquiry.*

pay your respects ⇨ PAY²

☆ **respect²** /rɪˈspekt/ *verb* [T] **1 respect sb/sth** (for sth) to admire or have a high opinion of sb/sth: *I respect him for his honesty.* **2** to show care for or pay attention to sb/sth: *We should respect other people's cultures and values.* ○ *to respect sb's wishes* (= do what they want)

respectable /rɪˈspektəbl/ *adj* **1** considered by society to be good, proper or correct: *a respectable middle-class family* ○ *Wear something respectable to the party!* **2** quite good or large: *a respectable salary* —**respectability** /rɪˌspektəˈbɪləti/ *noun* [U]

respectful /rɪˈspektfl/ *adj* **respectful (to/towards sb)** showing respect(2) or politeness towards sb/sth: *The crowd listened in respectful silence.* ☛ The opposite is **disrespectful**. —**respectfully** /-fəli/ *adv*

respective /rɪˈspektɪv/ *adj* (only *before* a noun) belonging separately to each of the people who have been mentioned: *After lunch we all got on with our respective jobs.*

respectively *adv* in the same order that sb/sth was mentioned: *German and Italian courses are held in Munich and Rome respectively.*

respiration /ˌrespəˈreɪʃn/ *noun* [U] (*formal*) the act of breathing

respite /ˈrespaɪt/ *noun* [sing,U] **respite (from sth)** a short period of rest from sth that is difficult or unpleasant: *There was a brief respite from the fighting.*

☆ **respond** /rɪˈspɒnd/ *verb* [I] **1 respond (to sb/sth) (with/by sth)** (*formal*) to say or do sth as an answer or reaction to sth: *I wrote to them last week but they haven't responded.* ○ *He responded to my question with a nod.* ○ *The government has responded to criticism by giving an extra £5 million to the National Health Service.* ☛ **Respond** is more formal than **answer** or **reply**. **2 respond (to sb/sth)** to have or show a good or quick reaction to sb/sth: *The patient did not respond well to the new treatment.*

☆ **response** /rɪˈspɒns/ *noun* [C,U] **response (to sb/sth)** an answer or reaction to sb/sth: *I've sent out 20 letters of enquiry but I've had no responses yet.* ○ *The government acted in response to economic pressure.* ○ *He knocked on the door but there was no response.* ○ *Meryl Streep's new film has received a very favourable response.*

☆ **responsibility** /rɪˌspɒnsəˈbɪləti/ *noun* (*pl* **responsibilities**) **1** [U] **responsibility (for sb/sth)** the state of being responsible; having to take decisions about sth so that you are blamed if sth goes wrong: *The new job means taking on more responsibility.* ○ *I refuse to take responsibility if anything goes wrong.* ○ *The IRA has admitted responsibility for planting the bomb.* ○ *a minister with special responsibility for women's affairs* **2** [U] the quality of being sensible: *I wish that you would show a little more responsibility.* **3** [C] a job or duty that you must do: *It is John's responsibility to make sure the orders are sent out on time.* ○ *I feel that I have a responsibility to help them – after all, they did help me.* ○ *the responsibilities of parenthood* ○ *The children are my responsibility* (= I am responsible for them).

☆ **responsible** /rɪˈspɒnsəbl/ *adj* **1** (not before a noun) **responsible (for sb/sth)**; **responsible (for doing sth)** having the job or duty of doing or looking after sb/sth (so that you are blamed if sth goes wrong): *The school is responsible for the safety of the children between 9 am and 3 pm.* ○ *The manager is responsible for making sure the shop is run properly.* **2** (not before a noun) **responsible (for sth)** being the cause of or to blame for sth: *Who was responsible for the accident?* **3** (not before a noun) **responsible (to sb/sth)** having to report to sb/sth with authority or in a higher position about what you have been doing: *Members of Parliament are responsible to the electors.* **4** (used about a person) that you can trust to behave well and sensibly: *All children must be accompanied by a responsible adult.* ☛ The opposite is **irresponsible**. **5** (used about a job) that is important and that should be done by a person who can be trusted

responsibly /-əbli/ *adv* in a responsible(4) way: *Please behave responsibly while I am out.*

responsive /rɪˈspɒnsɪv/ *adj* paying attention to sb/sth and reacting in a suitable or positive way: *By being responsive to changes in the market, the company has had great success.*

☆ **rest¹** /rest/ *verb* **1** [I] to relax, sleep or do nothing after a period of activity or because of illness: *We've been walking for hours. Let's rest here for a while.* ○ *The nurse said we couldn't visit him because he was resting.* **2** [T] to allow sb/sth to rest(1): *Your knee will get better as long as you rest it as much as you can.* **3** [I,T] **rest (sth) on/against sth** to place sth in a position where it is supported by sth else; to be in such a position: *She rested her head on his shoulder and went to sleep.* **4** [I] not be talked about any longer: *He didn't want to answer any more questions so I let the subject rest.*

(PHRASAL VERB) **rest on sb/sth** to depend or

be based on sth: *The whole theory rests on a very simple idea.*

☆ **rest²** *noun* [C,U] a period or the action of relaxing, sleeping or doing nothing: *I can't walk any further! I need a rest.* ○ *Try not to worry now. Get some rest and think about it again tomorrow.* ○ *Yes, okay, you're right and I'm wrong. Now give it a rest!* (= Stop talking about it)
(IDIOMS) **at rest** not moving: *Do not open the door until the vehicle is at rest.*
come to rest to stop moving: *The car crashed through a wall and came to rest in a field.*
put/set your/sb's mind at rest ⇨ MIND¹

restful /-fl/ *adj* giving a relaxed, peaceful feeling: *I find this piece of music very restful.*

'**rest room** *noun* [C] (*US*) a public toilet in a hotel, shop, restaurant, etc ← Look at the note at **toilet**.

☆ **rest³** *noun* **the rest (of sth) 1** [sing] the part that is left: *We had lunch and spent the rest of the day on the beach.* ○ *If you don't want the rest, I'll eat it.* ○ *She takes no interest in what happens in the rest of the world.* **2** [plural] the ones that are left; the others: *One of the questions was difficult but the rest were quite easy.* ○ *They were the first people to arrive. The rest came later.* ○ *The rest of our bags are still in the car.*

☆ **restaurant** /'restrɒnt; *US* -tərənt/ *noun* [C] a place where you can buy and eat a meal: *a Chinese restaurant* ○ *We went out to a restaurant to celebrate my birthday.* ○ *She's taken a job as a waitress in a local restaurant.* ← Look at **café** and **take-away**.

restless /'restlɪs/ *adj* **1** unable to relax or be still because you are bored, nervous or impatient: *The children always get restless on long journeys.* **2** (of a period of time) without sleep or rest: *a restless night* —**restlessly** *adv*

restoration /ˌrestə'reɪʃn/ *noun* **1** [C,U] the act of returning sth to its original condition: *the restoration of the cathedral* ○ *The house is advertised as 'in need of restoration'.* ○ *Restorations are being carried out at the castle.* **2** [C,U] the act of bringing sth back into use or existence: *a gradual restoration of democracy to the country* **3** [U] the act of returning sth to its original owner: *the restoration of territory captured during the war*

☆ **restore** /rɪ'stɔː(r)/ *verb* [T] **restore sb/sth (to sb/sth) 1** (*formal*) to give sth that was lost or stolen back to sb **2** to put sb/sth back into a previous condition or position: *In the recent elections, the former president was restored to power.* **3** to bring sth back into existence or use: *Following the riots, law and order have been restored.* ○ *Winning their last two games has restored the team's confidence.* **4** to put sth (a building, a painting, a piece of furniture, etc) back into a condition that is as close as possible to its original condition: *The castle has been restored and is open to the public.*

restrain /rɪ'streɪn/ *verb* [T] **restrain sb/sth (from sth/from doing sth)** to keep sb or sth under control; to prevent sb or sth from doing sth: *Can't you restrain your dog?* ○ *I had to restrain myself from saying something rude.*

restrained *adj* not showing strong feelings; calm

restraint /rɪ'streɪnt/ *noun* **1** [U] the quality of behaving in a calm or moderate way: *It took a lot of restraint on my part not to hit him.* **2** [C] **restraint (on sb/sth)** a limit or control on sth: *Are there any restraints on what the newspapers are allowed to publish?* ○ *a head restraint* (= a part of a car seat that stops your head being hurt in an accident)

restrict /rɪ'strɪkt/ *verb* [T] **1** to limit the number, amount, size, freedom, etc of sb/sth: *I'm trying to restrict myself to two cups of coffee a day.* ○ *Having small children tends to restrict your freedom.* ○ *There is a plan to restrict the use of cars in the city centre.* **2** to make sb/yourself concentrate on a particular thing or things and not on others: *I suggest that you restrict yourself to dealing with the most urgent matters.*

restricted *adj* controlled or limited in some way: *Entry to the club is restricted to members only.* ○ *There is only restricted parking available.*

restriction /rɪ'strɪkʃn/ *noun* **restriction (on sth) 1** [U] the act of limiting the freedom of sb/sth: *This ticket permits you to travel anywhere, without restriction.* **2** [C] something (sometimes a rule or law) that limits the number, amount, size, freedom, etc of sb/sth: *parking restrictions in the city centre* ○ *The government has imposed restrictions on the number of immigrants permitted to settle in this country.*

restrictive /rɪ'strɪktɪv/ *adj* limiting; preventing people from doing what they want

☆ **result** /rɪ'zʌlt/ *noun* **1** [C,U] **result (of sth)** something that happens because of sth else; the final situation at the end of a series of actions: *The result of our argument was that we never spoke to each other again.* ○ *The traffic was very heavy and as a result I arrived late.* ○ *This wasn't really the result that I was expecting.* **2** [C,U] a good effect of an action: *He has tried very hard to find a job, but with no result.* ○ *The treatment is beginning to show results.* **3** [C] the score or final position at the end of a game, competition or election: *Do you know today's football results?* ○ *The results of this week's competition will be published next week.* ○ *The result of the by-election was a win for the Liberal Democrats.* **4** [C] the mark or grade given for an examination or test: *exam results* **5** [C] something that is discovered by a medical test: *I'm still waiting for the result of my X-ray.*

result /rɪ'zʌlt/ *verb* [I] **result (from sth)** to happen or exist because of sth: *Ninety per cent of the deaths resulted from injuries to the head.*
(PHRASAL VERB) **result in sth** to cause sth to happen or exist; to produce as an effect: *There has been an accident on the motorway, resulting in long delays.*

resume /rɪ'zjuːm; *US* -'zuːm/ *verb* [I,T] to begin again or continue after a pause or interruption: *Normal service will resume as soon as possible.* *We apologize for the delay.* ○ *After the birth of the baby, she resumed her career.*

résumé /ˌrezju'meɪ/ *noun* [C] (*US*) = CURRICULUM VITAE

resumption /rɪ'zʌmpʃn/ *noun* [sing,U]

s	z	ʃ	ʒ	h	m	n	ŋ	l	r	j	w
so	zoo	she	vision	how	man	no	sing	leg	red	yes	wet

(*formal*) the act of beginning again or continuing after a pause or interruption: *a resumption of diplomatic relations between the two countries* ○ *At the resumption of trade on the Stock Exchange this morning, the dollar fell slightly.*

resurrect /ˌrezəˈrekt/ *verb* [T] to bring sth that has not been used or has not existed for a long time back into use or existence: *From time to time they resurrect old black and white programmes and show them again on television.*

resurrection /ˌrezəˈrekʃn/ *noun* **1** [U] the act of resurrecting sth: *There will be no resurrection of previous policies.* **2** [sing] (in the Christian religion) the return of all dead people to life at the end of the world **3 the Resurrection** [sing] (in the Christian religion) the return to life of Jesus Christ

resuscitate /rɪˈsʌsɪteɪt/ *verb* [T] to bring sb who has stopped breathing back to life: *Unfortunately, all efforts to resuscitate the patient failed.* —**resuscitation** /rɪˌsʌsɪˈteɪʃn/ *noun* [U]

retail /ˈriːteɪl/ *noun* [U] the selling of goods to the public in shops, etc (for personal use, not to be sold again): *the recommended retail price* ☞ Look at **wholesale**.

retailer *noun* [C] a person or company who sells goods in a shop

retain /rɪˈteɪn/ *verb* [T] (*formal*) to keep or continue to have; not to lose: *Despite all her problems, she has managed to retain a sense of humour.* ○ *If you wish to leave the stadium and return later, please retain your ticket.* ○ *The village has retained much of its original character.* ○ *These cups retain the heat.* ☞ The noun is **retention**.

retaliate /rɪˈtælieɪt/ *verb* [I] **retaliate (against sb/sth)** to react to sth unpleasant that sb does to you by doing sth unpleasant in return: *They have announced that they will retaliate against anyone who attacks their country.*

retaliation /rɪˌtæliˈeɪʃn/ *noun* [U] **retaliation (against sb/sth); retaliation (for sth)** the act of retaliating: *The IRA said that the shooting was in retaliation for recent attacks on nationalists.*

retarded /rɪˈtɑːdɪd/ *adj* (used about people) less advanced mentally than other people of the same age

retention /rɪˈtenʃn/ *noun* [U] the act of keeping sth or of being kept: *Many experts are against the retention of this type of exam.*

rethink /ˌriːˈθɪŋk/ *verb* [I,T] (*pt, pp* **rethought** /-ˈθɔːt/) to think about sth again because you probably need to change it: *The government has been forced to rethink its economic policy.*

☆ **retire** /rɪˈtaɪə(r)/ *verb* [I] **1 retire (from sth)** to leave your job and stop working usually because you have reached a certain age: *She's worried that she won't have enough money to live on when she retires.* ○ *Bjorn Borg retired from professional tennis when he was still a young man.* **2** (*formal*) to leave and go to a quiet or private place: *We were a bit tired, so we retired to our hotel room after dinner.*

retired *adj* having stopped work permanently, usually because of having reached a certain age: *a retired teacher* ○ *He's been very unhappy since he's been retired.*

☆ **retirement** /rɪˈtaɪəmənt/ *noun* **1** [C,U] the act of stopping or being forced to stop working permanently, usually because of reaching a certain age: *What's the age of retirement/retirement age in this country?* ○ *There have been a number of retirements in our department this year.* ○ *She has decided to take early retirement.* ○ *The former world champion has announced his retirement* (= that he is not going to play, etc again). **2** [sing,U] the situation or period after retiring from work: *We all wish you a long and happy retirement.*

☞ A **pension** is the income received by somebody who has retired. It comes from the State, the employer or both. A **pensioner** or an **old age pensioner** is a person who has retired because of age.

retiring /rɪˈtaɪərɪŋ/ *adj* (of a person) shy or quiet

retort /rɪˈtɔːt/ *verb* [I] to reply quickly to what sb says, in an angry or amusing way: *'Who asked you for your opinion?' she retorted.* ○ *He retorted that there was no such thing as an honest politician.*

retort *noun* [C] an angry answer

retrace /riːˈtreɪs/ *verb* [T] to repeat a past journey, series of events, etc: *I retraced my steps* (= I went back the way I had come) *in an attempt to find my wallet.*

retract /rɪˈtrækt/ *verb* [I,T] (*formal*) to say that sth you have said before is not true or not valid: *When he appeared in court, he retracted the confession he had made to the police.*

retreat /rɪˈtriːt/ *verb* [I] **1** (of an army, etc) to move backwards in order to leave a battle or in order not to become involved in a battle: *The troops were heavily outnumbered and so they were forced to retreat.* ○ *The order was given to retreat.* ☞ Look at **advance**. **2** to move backwards; to go to a safe or private place: *A neighbour tried to get into the burning house but he was forced to retreat by the intense heat.* ○ (*figurative*) *She seems to retreat into a world of her own sometimes.*

retreat *noun* **1** [C,U] the act of retreating: *The invading forces are now in retreat.* ○ *the Minister's retreat from his original opinion* ○ *Psychiatrists say that her behaviour is really a retreat into childhood.* **2** [C] a private place where you can go when you want to be quiet or to rest

retribution /ˌretrɪˈbjuːʃn/ *noun* [U] **retribution (for sth)** (*formal*) punishment for a crime: *Public opinion is demanding retribution for the recent acts of terrorism.*

retrieve /rɪˈtriːv/ *verb* [T] **1 retrieve sth (from sb/sth)** to get sth back from the place where it was left or lost: *The river police retrieved the body from the Thames near Goring.* **2** (*computing*) to find information that has been stored: *The computer can retrieve all the data about a particular customer.* **3** to make sth (a situation, a mistake, etc) better; to put sth right: *The team was losing two nil at half-time but they managed to retrieve the situation* in the second half. —**retrieval** /-vl/ noun [U]: *Retrieval of the bodies from the wreckage of the plane took several hours.*

retrospect /'retrəspekt/ noun
(IDIOM) **in retrospect** thinking about sth that happened in the past (and often seeing it differently from the way you saw it at the time): *In retrospect, I can see what a stupid mistake it was.*

retrospective /,retrə'spektɪv/ adj **1** looking again at the past: *a retrospective analysis of historical events* **2** (used about laws, decisions, payments, etc) applying to the past as well as to the present and future: *Is this new tax law retrospective?* —**retrospectively** adv

☆ **return¹** /rɪ'tɜːn/ verb **1** [I] **return (to...); return (from...)** to come or go back to a place: *I leave on the 10th and return on the 25th.* ○ *I shall be returning to this country in six months.* ○ *When did you return from Italy?* ○ *He left his home town when he was 18 and never returned.* **2** [I] **return (to sth)** to start doing a previous activity or talking about a previous subject again: *The strike is over and they will be returning to work on Monday.* ○ *We'll return to this subject in next week's lesson.* **3** [I] **return (to sth/to doing sth)** to come or go back to a previous situation or condition: *It is hoped that train services will return to normal soon.* **4** [I] to come back; to happen again: *If the pain returns, make another appointment to see me.* ○ *I expect that the cold weather will return soon.* **5** [T] **return sth (to sb/sth)** to give, send, put or take sth back: *I've stopped lending him things because he never returns them.* ○ *Application forms must be returned by 14 March.* **6** [T] to react to sth that somebody does, says or feels by doing, saying, or feeling sth similar: *I've phoned them several times and left messages but they haven't returned any of my calls.* ○ *We'll be happy to return your hospitality if you ever come to our country.* **7** [T] (in sport) to hit or throw the ball back: *He hit the ball so hard that I couldn't return it.*

returnable /-əbl/ adj that can or must be given or taken back: *a non-returnable deposit.*

☆ **return²** /rɪ'tɜːn/ noun **1** [sing] **a return (to/from...)** the act of coming or going back to a place, a previous activity, a previous situation or a previous condition: *I'll contact you on my return* (= when I come back). ○ *Our return flight is at 3 o'clock in the morning.* ○ *He has recently made a return to form* (= started playing well again). **2** [U] the act of giving, sending, putting or taking sth back: *I demand the return of my passport immediately.* **3** [C] (in sport) the act of hitting or throwing the ball back: *She hit a brilliant return.* **4** [C,U] (*also* **returns** [plural]) the profit from a business or an investment: *They're not expecting any return on their new restaurant for at least a year.* ○ *This account offers high returns on all investments.* **5** [C] (*Brit*) (*also* **return 'ticket**; *US* **round trip**; **round trip ticket**) a ticket to travel to a place and back again: *A day return to Oxford, please.* ○ *I asked for a return but I was given a single by mistake.*
(IDIOMS) **by return (of post)** (*Brit*) immediately; by next post: *Please enclose a stamped addressed envelope and we will send you a receipt by return.*

in return (for sth) as payment or in exchange (for sth); as a reaction to sth: *Please accept this present in return for all your help.*

many happy returns ➔ HAPPY

re,turn 'fare noun [C] (*Brit*) the price of a ticket to travel to a place and back again: *Is the return fare cheaper than two singles?*

reunion /,riː'juːnɪən/ noun **1** [C] a party or occasion when friends or colleagues meet again after they have not seen each other for a long time: *The college holds an annual reunion for former students.* ○ *a family reunion* **2** [C,U] the act of coming together again after a separation: *The released hostages had an emotional reunion with their families at the airport.*

reunite /,riːjuː'naɪt/ verb [I,T] **reunite (sb/sth)(with sb/sth)** to come together again; to cause sb/sth to come together again: *The separate regions of the country reunited a few years ago.* ○ *The missing child was found by the police and reunited with his parents.* ○ *The new leader's first task will be to reunite the party.*

rev /rev/ noun [C, usually pl] (*informal*) = REVOLUTION(3): *4 000 revs per minute*

rev verb (rev**v**ing; rev**v**ed) **1** [I] **rev (up)** (used about an engine) to turn (quickly); to increase the speed of turning: *I was woken up by the sound of a car revving up outside.* **2** [T] **rev sth (up)** to increase the speed of an engine (usually before driving the car): *Rev the engine for a while before you drive off.*

☆ **reveal** /rɪ'viːl/ verb [T] **1 reveal sth (to sb)** to make sth known that was previously secret or unknown: *She revealed that she had serious money problems.* ○ *He refused to reveal any names to the police.* **2** to allow sth to be seen that was previously hidden: *Close inspection of the photograph revealed the identity of the gunman.* ○ *In a moment, the curtains will open to reveal tonight's star prize.*

revealing adj **1** allowing sth (facts previously unknown, secrets, etc) to be known: *This book provides a revealing insight into the world of politics.* **2** allowing sth to be seen that is usually hidden: *a very revealing swimsuit*

revel /'revl/ verb [I] (revelling; revelled; *US* reveling; reveled)
(PHRASAL VERB) **revel in sth/in doing sth** to enjoy sth very much: *He likes being famous and revels in the attention he gets.*

revelation /,revə'leɪʃn/ noun **1** [C] something that is made known, that was previously secret or unknown (especially sth surprising): *This magazine is full of revelations about the private lives of famous people.* **2** [sing] a thing or a person that surprises you and causes you to change your attitude to sb/sth: *It's a horrible house from the outside but the inside is a revelation.*

revenge /rɪ'vendʒ/ noun [U] something that you do to punish sb who has hurt you, made you suffer, etc: *He made a fool of me and now I want revenge.* ○ *The attack was an act of revenge.*
(IDIOMS) **get/have/take your revenge (on**

ɜː	ə	eɪ	əʊ	aɪ	aʊ	ɔɪ	ɪə	eə	ʊə
fur	ago	pay	home	five	now	join	near	hair	pure

revenue — **revive**

sb) (for sth); **take revenge (on sb) (for sth)** to punish sb in return for sth bad that he/she has done to you: *He wants to take revenge on the judge who sent him to prison.*

out of/in revenge (for sth) as a way of punishing sb in return for sth bad he/she has done to you: *The shooting was in revenge for an attack by the nationalists.*

revenge *verb* [T] **revenge yourself on sb** to punish sb who has done sth bad to you by doing sth bad in return: *She revenged herself on her enemy.*

revenue /ˈrevənjuː; *US* -ənuː/ *noun* [U,plural] income received by a government, company, etc: *Revenue from income tax rose last year.* ○ *Oil revenues are a vital part of the country's economy.*

reverence /ˈrevərəns/ *noun* [U] a feeling of great respect: *The royal family are often treated with reverence.*

Reverend /ˈrevərənd/ *adj* **the Reverend** (*abbr* **Rev**) the title of a Christian priest: *the Reverend Charles Gray*

reverent /ˈrevərənt/ *adj* showing respect: *a reverent silence in memory of the dead*

reversal /rɪˈvɜːsl/ *noun* [C,U] the act of changing sth to the opposite; an occasion when sth changes to the opposite of what is usual or expected: *The government insists that there will be no reversal of policy.* ○ *The decision taken yesterday was a complete reversal of last week's decision.* ○ *a reversal of roles* (= when each person does what the other person was doing)

☆ **reverse¹** /rɪˈvɜːs/ *adj* opposite to what is expected or has just been described: *In Germany the reverse situation is true.*

(IDIOM) **in/into reverse order** starting with the last one and going backwards to the first one: *The results will be announced in reverse order.*

☆ **reverse²** /rɪˈvɜːs/ *noun* **1** [sing] the reverse (of sth) the complete opposite of the previous statement or of what is expected: *Of course I don't dislike you – quite the reverse* (= I like you very much). ○ *This should be a relaxing holiday but it's just the reverse.* **2** [U] (*also* ˌreverse ˈgear**) the control in a car, etc that allows it to move backwards: *Leave the car in reverse while it's parked on this hill.* ○ *Where's reverse in this car?*

(IDIOM) **in/into reverse** in the opposite order, starting at the end and going backwards to the beginning; in the opposite way to the previous direction

☆ **reverse³** /rɪˈvɜːs/ *verb* **1** [T] to put sth in the opposite position: *Writing is reversed in a mirror.* **2** [I,T] to go backwards in a car, etc; to make a car go backwards: *It will probably be easier to reverse into that parking space.* ○ *He reversed his brand new car into a wall.* **3** [T] to change sth to the opposite: *Today's results have reversed the order of the top two teams.* ○ *It's too late to reverse your decision now, you've already signed the contract.* **4** [T] to exchange the positions or functions of two things or people: *My husband and I have reversed roles – he stays at home now and I go to work.*

(IDIOM) **reverse (the) charges** to make a telephone call that will be paid for by the person who receives it: *Phone us when you get there, and reverse the charges.* ○ *Could I make a reverse charge call to London, please?* ☞ The US expression is to **call collect.**

reversible /-əbl/ *adj* (used about clothes) that can be worn with either side on the outside: *a reversible coat*

revert /rɪˈvɜːt/ *verb* [I] **revert (to sth)** to return to a previous state or to sth that you did previously: *Hong Kong will revert to Chinese rule in 1997.* ○ *The land will soon revert to jungle if it is not farmed.*

☆ **review** /rɪˈvjuː/ *noun* **1** [C,U] the act of examining or considering sth again in order to decide whether changes are necessary: *There will be a review of your contract after the first six months.* ○ *The system is in need of review.* **2** [C] the act of looking back at sth in order to check, remember, or be clear about sth: *a review of the major events of the year* **3** [C] a newspaper or magazine article, or an item on television or radio, in which sb gives an opinion on a new book, film, play, etc: *The film got bad reviews.* ○ *a book review*

review *verb* [T] **1** to examine or consider again in order to decide whether changes are necessary: *Your salary will be reviewed after one year.* **2** to look at or think about sth again to make sure that you understand so it: *Let's review what we've done in this lesson so far.* **3** to write an article or to talk on television or radio, giving an opinion on a new book, film, play, etc: *In today's edition our film critic reviews the latest films.*

reviewer *noun* [C] a person who writes reviews of books, films, etc

☆ **revise** /rɪˈvaɪz/ *verb* [T] **1** to make changes to sth in order to correct or improve it: *The book has been revised for this new edition.* ○ *I revised my opinion of him when I found out that he had lied.* **2** [I,T] **revise (for sth)** to read or study again sth that you have learnt, especially when preparing for an exam: *I can't come out tonight. I'm revising for my exam.* ○ *None of the things I had revised came up in the exam.*

revision /rɪˈvɪʒn/ *noun* **1** [C,U] the act of changing sth in order to correct or improve it: *It has been suggested that the whole system is in need of revision.* **2** [U] the work of reading or studying again sth you have learnt, especially when preparing for an exam: *I've done a lot of revision for History.*

revival /rɪˈvaɪvl/ *noun* **1** [C,U] the act of becoming or making sth strong or popular again: *economic revival* ○ *a revival of interest in traditional farming methods* **2** [C] a new performance of a play that has not been performed for some time: *a revival of the musical 'Kiss me Kate'*

revive /rɪˈvaɪv/ *verb* [I,T] **1** to become or make sb/sth strong or healthy again; to come or to bring sb back to life or consciousness: *Hopes have revived for an early end to the fighting.* ○ *I'm terribly tired but I'm sure a cup of coffee will revive me.* ○ *Attempts were made to revive him but he was already dead.* **2** to become or make sth popular again; to begin to do or use sth

p	b	t	d	k	g	tʃ	dʒ	f	v	θ	ð
pen	bad	tea	did	cat	got	chin	June	fall	van	thin	then

revolt again: *Public interest in rugby has revived now that the national team is doing well.* o *to revive an old custom*

revolt /rɪ'vəʊlt/ *verb* **1** [I] **revolt (against sb/sth)** to protest in a group (often violently) against the person or people in power: *A group of generals have revolted against the government.* **2** [T] to make sb feel disgusted or ill: *Some of her opinions revolt me.* o *The sight and the smell revolted him.* ☞ The noun for this meaning is **revulsion**.

revolt *noun* [C,U] the act of revolting(1): *The revolt was quickly put down by the army.* o *What started as a small protest has turned into widespread revolt.*

revolting /rɪ'vəʊltɪŋ/ *adj* extremely unpleasant; disgusting: *a revolting smell of fish* o *What a revolting colour!*

☆ **revolution** /ˌrevə'luːʃn/ *noun* **1** [C,U] changing or trying to change the political system by violent action, etc: *the French Revolution of 1789* o *Student leaders are calling for revolution.* **2** [C] **a revolution (in sth)** a complete change in methods, opinions, etc, often as a result of progress: *a revolution in the treatment of diseases such as cancer* o *the Industrial Revolution* **3** [C,U] (also *informal* **rev**) a movement around sth; one complete turn around a central point (eg in a car engine): *400 revolutions per minute*

revolutionary /-ʃənəri; *US* -neri/ *adj* **1** connected with or supporting political revolution: *Revolutionary forces have attacked the president's palace.* o *the revolutionary leaders* **2** producing great changes; very new and different: *a revolutionary new scheme to ban cars from the city centre*

revolutionary *noun* [C] (*pl* **revolutionaries**) a person who takes part in and supports a revolution

revolutionize (also **revolutionise**) /-ʃənaɪz/ *verb* [T] to change sth completely: *a discovery that could revolutionize the treatment of mental illness*

revolve /rɪ'vɒlv/ *verb* [I] to move in a circle around a central point; to go round: *The earth revolves around the sun.* o *This little wheel should revolve when you switch the engine on.*
(PHRASAL VERB) **revolve around sb/sth** to have sth as the most important part: *Her life revolves around the family.*

revolving *adj* designed to work by going round: *revolving doors*

revolver /rɪ'vɒlvə(r)/ *noun* [C] a type of small gun with a container for bullets that goes round

revulsion /rɪ'vʌlʃn/ *noun* [U] a feeling of disgust (because sth is extremely unpleasant)

☆ **reward** /rɪ'wɔːd/ *noun* **1** [C,U] something that is given in return for work, effort, etc: *She feels that she has done a lot of work for little or no reward.* o *Being a parent is often hard work but it has its rewards.* **2** [C] an amount of money that is given in exchange for helping the police, returning sth that was lost, etc: *Police are offering a reward for information leading to a conviction.*

reward *verb* [T] **reward sb (for sth/for doing sth)** to give a reward to sb: *Eventually her efforts were rewarded and she got a job.* o *His parents bought him a bicycle to reward him for passing the exams.*

rewarding *adj* giving satisfaction: *She finds her work with handicapped children very rewarding.*

rewind /ˌriː'waɪnd/ *verb* [T] (*pt, pp* **rewound**) to make a tape go backwards: *Please rewind the tape at the end of the film.*

rewrite /ˌriː'raɪt/ *verb* [T] (*pt* **rewrote** /-'rəʊt/; *pp* **rewritten** /-'rɪtn/) to write sth again in a different or better way

rhetoric /'retərɪk/ *noun* [U] a way of speaking or writing that is intended to impress or influence people —**rhetorical** /rɪ'tɒrɪkl; *US* -'tɔːr-/ *adj* —**rhetorically** /-klɪ/ *adv*

rhe,torical 'question *noun* [C] a question that is not really a question because it does not expect an answer

rheumatism /'ruːmətɪzəm/ *noun* [U] an illness that causes pain in muscles and joints

rhino /'raɪnəʊ/ *noun* [C] (*pl* **rhinos**) (*informal*) = RHINOCEROS

rhinoceros /raɪ'nɒsərəs/ *noun* [C] (*pl* **rhinoceros** or **rhinoceroses**) a large animal from Africa or Asia, with a thick skin and either one or two horns on its nose

rhubarb /'ruːbɑːb/ *noun* [U] a plant with long red stems and very large leaves. The stems can be cooked and eaten as fruit.

rhyme /raɪm/ *noun* **1** [U] the technique of using words that have the same sound as each other especially at the ends of lines: *All of his poetry was written in rhyme.* **2** [C] a word that has the same sound as another: *Can you think of a rhyme for 'peace'?* **3** [C] a short piece of writing, or something spoken, in which the words at the end of each line sound the same as the words at the end of previous lines ☞ Look at **nursery rhyme**.

rhyme *verb* **1** [I] to have the same sound as another word; to consist of lines that end with words that sound the same: *'Tough' rhymes with 'stuff'.* o *'Book' and 'look' rhyme.* o *He thinks that all poetry should rhyme.* **2** [T] to put together words that have the same sound: *You can't rhyme 'face' with 'stays'.*

☆ **rhythm** /'rɪðəm/ *noun* [C,U] a regular repeated pattern of sound or movement: *the rhythms of Latin America* o *I'm not keen on the tune but I love the rhythm.* o *He's a terrible dancer because he has no sense of rhythm.*

rhythmic /'rɪðmɪk/ (also **rhythmical** /'rɪðmɪkl/) *adj* having rhythm: *the rhythmic qualities of African music* —**rhythmically** /-klɪ/ *adv*

rib /rɪb/ *noun* [C] one of the curved bones that go round the chest: *He's so thin that you can see his ribs.*

ribbon /'rɪbən/ *noun* [C,U] **1** a long, thin piece of cotton, nylon, etc that is used for tying or decorating sth ☞ picture at **knot**. **2** a long, thin piece of material that contains ink and is used in a typewriter

☆ **rice** /raɪs/ *noun* [U] the grain from a plant grown in hot, wet countries, that we cook and eat: *Rice or potatoes?* o *brown rice* o *boiled rice* o

s	z	ʃ	ʒ	h	m	n	ŋ	l	r	j	w
so	zoo	she	vision	how	man	no	sing	leg	red	yes	wet

rice pudding (= made by cooking rice in milk and sugar)

☆ **rich** /rɪtʃ/ *adj* **1** having a lot of money or property; not poor: *a rich family.* ☞ Look at **wealthy**. **2** (not before a noun) **rich in sth** containing a lot of sth: *Oranges are very rich in vitamin C.* **3** able to produce sth in large amounts: *rich soil* **4** (used about food) containing a lot of fat, oil, sugar, cream, etc: *a rich sauce* ○ *a rich chocolate cake* **5** (used about colours, sounds or smells) strong and deep: *a rich purple*

the rich *noun* [plural] rich people: *The rich are getting richer and the poor are getting poorer.*

richly *adv* **1** extremely well: *She was richly rewarded for her hard work.* **2** fully: *His promotion was richly deserved.* —**richness** *noun* [U]

riches /'rɪtʃɪz/ *noun* [plural] (*formal*) a lot of money or property; wealth: *Despite all his riches, he was a deeply unhappy man.*

rickety /'rɪkəti/ *adj* likely to fall or break; not strongly made: *a rickety old fence*

ricochet /'rɪkəʃeɪ; *US* ˌrɪkə'ʃeɪ/ *verb* [I] (*pt, pp* **ricocheted; ricochetted** /-ʃeɪd/) **ricochet (off sth)** (used about a bullet, etc) to fly away from a surface after hitting it

☆ **rid** /rɪd/ *verb* [T] (*pres part* **ridding**; *pt, pp* **rid**) **rid sb/sth of sb/sth** (*formal*) to make sb/sth free from sb/sth that is unpleasant or unwanted: *They have managed to rid the world of smallpox.* ○ *He was unable to rid himself of his fears and suspicions.*

(IDIOM) **be/get rid of sb/sth** to be/become free of sb/sth or to remove sb/sth: *I didn't enjoy having my family to stay. In fact I was glad to get rid of them.* ○ *I can't get rid of this mark on the carpet.* ○ *Let's get rid of that old chair and buy a new one.*

riddance /'rɪdns/ *noun*

(IDIOM) **good riddance (to sb/sth)** (*informal*) (used for expressing pleasure or relief that sb/sth that you do not like has gone)

ridden[1] /'rɪdn/ *pp* of RIDE[2]

ridden[2] /'rɪdn/ *adj* (usually in compounds) full of: *She was ridden with guilt.* ○ *She was guilt-ridden.*

riddle /'rɪdl/ *noun* [C] **1** a type of question that you ask people for fun that has a clever or amusing answer **2** a person, thing or event that you cannot understand

riddled /'rɪdəld/ *adj* **riddled with** full of: *The car was riddled with bullet holes.* ○ *This essay is riddled with mistakes.*

☆ **ride**[1] /raɪd/ *noun* [C] a journey on a horse or bicycle, or in a car, bus, etc: *They went for a ride in the woods.* ○ *It's only a short bus ride into Oxford.* ○ *Would you like to have a ride in my new car?*

(IDIOM) **take sb for a ride** (*informal*) to cheat or deceive sb

☆ **ride**[2] /raɪd/ *verb* (*pt* **rode** /rəʊd/; *pp* **ridden** /'rɪdn/) **1** [I,T] to sit on a horse and be carried along, controlling its movements: *I'm learning to ride at the moment.* ○ *We rode through the woods and over the moor.* ○ *Which horse is Cauthen riding in the next race?* ☞ **Go riding** is a common way of talking about riding for pleasure: *She goes riding every weekend.* **2** [I,T] to sit on a bicycle, etc and be carried along, controlling its movements: *On Sunday thousands of cyclists rode from London to Oxford to raise money for charity.* ○ *She jumped onto her motor bike and rode off.* ○ *Can John ride a bicycle yet?* **3** [I] to travel as a passenger in a bus, car, etc: *Smokers are asked to ride at the back of the coach.*

rider *noun* [C] a person who rides a horse, bicycle, etc

riding /'raɪdɪŋ/ *noun* [U] the sport or hobby of riding a horse: *riding-boots* ○ *a riding-school*

ridge /rɪdʒ/ *noun* [C] **1** a long, narrow piece of high land along the top of hills or mountains: *We walked along the ridge looking down at the view.* **2** a line where two sloping surfaces meet

ridicule /'rɪdɪkjuːl/ *noun* [U] unkind laughter or behaviour that is meant to make sb/sth appear silly

ridicule *verb* [T] to laugh at sb/sth in an unkind way: *The idea was ridiculed by everybody present.*

☆ **ridiculous** /rɪ'dɪkjʊləs/ *adj* very silly; foolish: *That's a ridiculous suggestion!* ○ *It's ridiculous to drive so fast along these lanes.* ○ *They're asking a ridiculous* (= very high) *price for that house.* —**ridiculously** *adv*: *She's paid a ridiculously low salary for the work she does.*

riding ⇒ RIDE

rife /raɪf/ *adj* (not before a noun) (*formal*) (used especially about bad things) very common: *The use of drugs was rife among certain groups of students.*

rifle[1] /'raɪfl/ *noun* [C] a long gun that you hold against your shoulder to shoot with ☞ We **load**, **aim** and **fire** a rifle.

rifle[2] /'raɪfl/ *verb* [I,T] to search sth usually in order to steal from it: *I caught him rifling through the papers on my desk.*

rift /rɪft/ *noun* [C] **1** a serious disagreement between friends, groups, etc: *a growing rift between the brothers* **2** a crack or split in sth

rig[1] /rɪɡ/ *verb* [T] (**rigging**; **rigged**)

(PHRASAL VERB) **rig sth up** to make sth quickly, using any materials you can find: *We tried to rig up a shelter, using our rugs and coats.*

rig *noun* [C] (usually in compounds) a large platform, with special equipment for a certain purpose: *an oil rig*

rigging *noun* [U] the ropes, etc that support a ship's sails

rig[2] /rɪɡ/ *verb* [T] (**rigging**; **rigged**) to arrange or control an event, etc in an unfair way, in order to get the result you want: *They claimed that the competition had been rigged.*

☆ **right**[1] /raɪt/ *adj* on or of the side of the body that faces east when a person is facing north; not left: *Do you write with your right hand or your left?* ○ *Your seats are on the right side of the theatre.*

right *adv* to the right side; not left: *Turn right at the traffic lights.*

right *noun* **1** [U] the right side or direction; not left: *We live in the first house on the right.* ○ *If you look slightly to the right you will see Windsor Castle in the distance.* **2** **the Right** [sing,

'right-hand adj (only before a noun) of or on the right of sb/sth: The post-box is on the right-hand side of the road. ○ a sharp right-hand bend

right-'handed adj using the right hand more than the left for writing, etc

right-hand 'man noun [C] (pl **right-hand men**) the person you rely on most to help and support you in your work

right 'wing noun [sing] the people in a political party who support more conservative ideas: He is on the right wing of the Labour party.

right-'wing adj supporting conservative ideas rather than socialist ones: a right-wing government ☞ The opposite is **left-wing**.

☆ **right²** /raɪt/ adj **1** correct; true: I'm afraid that's not the right answer. ○ Have you got the right time? ○ You're quite right – the film does start at 7 o'clock. ○ You were right about the weather – it did rain. **2** best; most suitable: I don't think this is the right colour for the walls. ○ I hope I've made the right decision. ○ We wouldn't have missed the boat if we'd left at the right time. ○ You have to know the right people if you want to join that golf club. **3** normal; satisfactory: Her voice didn't sound quite right on the phone. **4** (used about behaviour, actions, etc) good; fair or what the law allows: It's not right to pay people so badly. ○ It was right of her to give you the news at once. ○ It's never right to steal. **5** (Brit informal) (used for emphasizing sth bad) real or complete: I'll look a right idiot in that hat!

(IDIOMS) **all right** ⇨ ALL¹

get on the right/wrong side of sb ⇨ SIDE¹

on the right/wrong track ⇨ TRACK

right (you are)! (informal) yes, I will; yes, I agree: 'See you later.' 'Right you are!'

(as) right as rain healthy or working properly

rightly adv correctly or fairly: As you rightly said, it's time to decide what we want. ○ He's been sacked and quite rightly, I believe. —**rightness** noun [U]: She's always convinced of the rightness of her own opinions.

'right angle noun [C] an angle of 90°: A square has four right angles. ☞ picture at **angle**.

☆ **right³** /raɪt/ adv **1** correctly; in a satisfactory way: Have I spelt your name right? ○ Nothing seems to be going right for me at the moment. **2** (used for preparing for sth that is about to happen) get ready; listen: Have you got your seatbelts on? Right, off we go. **3** exactly: The train was right on time. **4** all the way: Did you watch the film right to the end? **5** immediately: He left right after dinner. ○ Wait here a minute – I'll be right back. **6** (used in some titles): the Right Honourable James Smith, Foreign Secretary ○ the Right Reverend Richard Pearson, Bishop of Gloucester

(IDIOMS) **right/straight away** ⇨ AWAY

right now at this moment; exactly now: We can't discuss this right now.

serve sb right ⇨ SERVE

☆ **right⁴** /raɪt/ noun **1** [U] what is morally good and fair: Children learn about right and wrong at a very early age. ○ Does right always win in the end? **2** [C] a thing that you are allowed to do according to the law: In Britain everybody has the right to vote at 18. ○ Freedom of speech is one of the basic human rights. ○ civil rights (= the rights each person has to political and religious freedom, etc) **3** [U] **right to sth/to do sth** a moral authority to do sth: You have no right to tell me what to do.

(IDIOMS) **be in the right** to be doing what is correct and fair: You don't need to apologize. You were in the right and he was in the wrong.

by rights according to what is fair or correct: By rights, half the profit should be mine.

in your own right because of what you are yourself and not because of other people: She's a very wealthy lady in her own right (= not only because she has married somebody who is rich).

within your rights (to do sth) acting in a reasonable or legal way: You are quite within your rights to demand to see your lawyer.

right of 'way noun **1** [U] (used in road traffic) the right'(2) to continue while other traffic must stop **2** [C] a path across private land that the public may use: Is there a right of way across this field?

right⁵ /raɪt/ verb [T] **1** to return to a normal position: The boat tipped over and then righted itself again. **2** to correct sth ☞ This verb is almost always used in this sense with the noun **wrong**: There are many wrongs that need to be righted. You do not 'right' a mistake, you **correct** it.

righteous /'raɪtʃəs/ adj (formal) morally good or fair ☞ Look at **self-righteous**.

rightful /'raɪtfl/ adj (only before a noun) (formal) fair, proper or legal: You have a rightful claim to your father's property. —**rightfully** /-fəli/ adv

rigid /'rɪdʒɪd/ adj **1** not able or willing to change or be changed; strict: Some students complained about the rigid rules and regulations at the school. **2** stiff, not easy to bend: For air travel a rigid suitcase is better than a soft bag. ○ She was rigid with fear. —**rigidity** /rɪ'dʒɪdəti/ noun [U]

rigidly verb stiffly, strictly or without any possibility of change: You don't have to keep rigidly to what I've written – use your imagination.

rigour (US) (also **rigor**) /'rɪgə(r)/ noun (formal) **1** [U] the quality of being strict or severe: the rigour of the law **2** [C, usually pl] severe conditions; difficulties: the rigours of a hard climate

rigorous /'rɪgərəs/ adj thorough and careful: Very rigorous tests have been carried out on the drinking water. —**rigorously** adv —**rigorousness** noun [U]

rim /rɪm/ noun [C] an edge at the top or outside of sth that is round: the rim of a cup ○ spectacles with silver rims

rind /raɪnd/ noun [C,U] the thick hard skin on the outside of some fruits and some types of cheese, bacon, etc ☞ **Rind** is hard and is not usually removed with the fingers. We say the **rind** or **peel** of a lemon but only the **peel** of an orange. A fruit with a thinner or softer covering has a **skin**. So bananas, apples, pears, etc all have **skins**.

☆ **ring**¹ /rɪŋ/ noun [C] **1** a piece of jewellery, a round piece of metal, often of silver or gold, that you wear on your finger: *a wedding ring* ○ *an engagement ring* ○ *a gold, diamond, etc ring* ☞ picture at **jewellery**. **2** (usually in compounds) a round object of any material with a hole in the middle: *a key-ring* (= for holding keys) ☞ picture at **key**. **3** a circle: *Stand in a ring and hold hands*. **4** the space with seats all around it where a performance, match, etc takes place: *a circus ring* ○ *a boxing ring* **5** one of the round parts on the top of an electric or gas cooker, on which you can put pans: *an electric cooker with an oven, a grill and four rings* ☞ picture at **cooker**. **6** a number of people involved together in sth that is secret or not legal: *a drugs ring*

ring verb (*pt, pp* **ringed**) [T] **1** to draw a circle around sth: *Ring the correct answer with your pencil*. **2** to surround sb/sth: *The whole area was ringed with police*.

'ringleader noun [C] a person who leads a group of people who are doing sth wrong or causing trouble: *Who is the ringleader of the group?*

'ring road noun [C] (*Brit*) a road that is built all around a town so that traffic does not have to go into the town centre

☆ **ring**² /rɪŋ/ verb (*pt* **rang** /ræŋ/; *pp* **rung** /rʌŋ/) **1** [I,T] (*especially US* **call**) **ring (sb/sth) (up)** to telephone (sb/sth): *What time will you ring me tomorrow?* ○ *I rang up yesterday and booked the hotel*. ○ *Ring the station and ask what time the next train leaves*. **2** [I,T] to make a sound like a bell or to cause sth to make this sound: *Is that the phone ringing?* ○ *We rang the door bell again and again but nobody answered*. **3** [I] **ring (for sb/sth)** to ring a bell in order to call sb, ask for sth, etc: *'Did you ring, sir?' asked the stewardess*. **4** [I] to have a certain effect when you hear it: *Her words didn't ring true* (= you felt that you could not believe what she said). **5** [I] **ring (with sth)** to be filled with loud sounds: *When I left the disco my head was ringing with the noise*.

(IDIOM) **ring a bell** to sound familiar or to remind you, not very clearly, of sth: *'Do you know Jane Sykes?' 'Well, her name rings a bell.'*

(PHRASAL VERBS) **ring (sb) back** to phone sb again: *'I'm afraid Mary isn't in.' 'Oh well, I'll ring back later.'* ○ *I can't talk now – can I ring you back?*

ring off to end a telephone conversation: *I'd better ring off – supper's ready*.

ring out to sound loudly and clearly: *A pistol shot rang out*.

ring noun **1** [C] the sound made by a bell: *a ring at the door* **2** [sing] **a ring of sth** a feeling or quality of a particular kind: *What the man said had a ring of truth about it* (= sounded true).

(IDIOM) **give sb a ring** to telephone sb: *I'll give you a ring in the morning*.

rink /rɪŋk/ noun [C] = SKATING-RINK

rinse /rɪns/ verb [T] to wash sth in water in order to remove soap or dirt, etc: *Rinse your hair thoroughly after each shampoo*. ○ *I should rinse the apples before you eat them*.

rinse noun **1** [C] an act of rinsing: *Give the bath a good rinse after using it*. **2** [C,U] a liquid used for colouring the hair

☆ **riot** /'raɪət/ noun [C] fighting and noisy violent behaviour by a crowd of people: *Further riots have broken out in Manchester*. ○ *Police have been brought in to deal with the riots*.

(IDIOM) **run riot** to behave in a wild way, without any control: *At the end of the football match, the crowd ran riot*. ○ (*figurative*) *You really let your imagination run riot when you painted that picture*.

riot verb [I] to take part in a riot: *There is a danger that the prisoners will riot if conditions don't improve*.

rioter noun [C] a person who takes part in a riot

riotous /-əs/ adj **1** (*formal*) wild or violent; lacking in control: *The crowd was becoming increasingly riotous*. **2** wild and full of fun: *a riotous party*

rip /rɪp/ verb (**ripp**ing; **ripp**ed) **1** [I,T] to tear quickly and sharply: *Oh no! The hem of my dress has ripped!* ○ *He ripped the letter in two and threw it in the bin*. ○ *The blast of the bomb ripped the house apart*. **2** [T] to pull sth quickly and violently: *He ripped the poster from the wall*. ○ *The roof was ripped off in the gale*. **3** to move very quickly: *The house was badly damaged when fire ripped through the roof and first floor*.

(PHRASAL VERBS) **rip sb off** (*informal*) to cheat sb by asking too much money for sth

rip sth up to tear sth into small pieces

rip noun [C] a long tear or cut (in material, etc)

'rip-off noun [C] (*informal*) an act of charging too much money for sth: *A pound for a cup of coffee is a rip-off!*

☆ **ripe** /raɪp/ adj **1** (used about fruit, grain, etc) ready to be picked and eaten **2 ripe (for sth)** ready for sth or in a suitable state for sth: *The country was ripe for a change of leader*.

ripen /'raɪpən/ verb [I,T] to make sth ripe or to become ripe

ripple /'rɪpl/ noun [C] **1** a very small wave or movement on the surface of water: *The breeze sent tiny ripples across the lake*. **2** a gentle sound: *A ripple of laughter ran round the room*.

ripple verb [I,T] to move gently: *The branches of the trees rippled in the wind*. ○ *The wind rippled the surface of the sea*.

☆ **rise**¹ /raɪz/ noun **1** [C] an increase: *There has been a rise in the number of people out of work*. ○ *a sharp price rise* ☞ Look at **drop** and **fall**. **2** [C] (*US* **raise**) an increase in wages, salary, etc: *I'm hoping to get a rise next April*. ○ *a 10% pay rise* **3** [sing] the process of becoming more powerful or important: *His rise in the world of politics was remarkable*.

(IDIOM) **give rise to sth** to cause sth: *The news gave rise to considerable anxiety among many people*.

☆ **rise**² /raɪz/ verb [I] (*pt* **rose** /rəʊz/; *pp* **risen** /'rɪzn/) **1** to move upwards, to become higher or to increase: *Smoke was rising from the chim-*

ney. ○ *Cycling became harder as the road began to rise.* ○ *Her voice rose in anger* (= became louder). ○ *Do you think inflation will continue to rise?* ○ *The temperature has risen to nearly forty degrees.* ☛ Look at **fall**. **2** to stand up: *The audience rose and applauded the singers.* **3** to get out of bed: *They rose at dawn in order to be in London by eight.* ☛ In this sense **get up** is more common. **4** (used about the sun, moon, etc) to appear above the horizon: *The sun rises in the east and sets in the west.* **5** to show (as sth tall above the surroundings): *A range of mountains rose in the distance.* **6** to come from: *Shouts of protest rose from the crowd.* **7 rise (up) (against sb/sth)** to start opposing or fighting people in authority: *The people were afraid to rise up against the dictator.* **8** to move to a higher position (in rank, society, career, etc): *He rose rapidly within the company.*
(IDIOM) **rise to the occasion, challenge, task, etc** to deal with or cope with sth successfully: *Do you think she will rise to the demands of the job?*

rising *noun* [C] fighting by a number of people (against people in authority) ☛ Look also at **uprising**.

rising *adj* **1** sloping upwards: *The new offices are being built on rising ground outside the town.* **2** increasing: *the rising cost of living* **3** becoming well-known or popular: *a rising young rock star*

☆ **risk** /rɪsk/ *noun* **1** [C,U] **risk (of sth/that...)** a possibility (of sth dangerous or unpleasant happening): *The risks involved in the enterprise were considerable.* ○ *Do you think there's any risk of rain?* **2** [sing] a dangerous or silly thing to do: *It was an unnecessary risk to overtake that lorry there.* **3** [sing] a person or thing that might cause danger: *If he knows your real name he's a security risk.*
(IDIOMS) **at your own risk** having the responsibility for whatever may happen: *This building is in a dangerous condition – enter at your own risk.*
at risk in danger: *Small children are most at risk from the disease.*
at the risk of (doing sth) with the possibility of (sth unpleasant): *At the risk of interfering, may I offer you some advice?*
run the risk (of doing sth) to do sth knowing that the result might be bad or unpleasant; to risk: *If we don't leave early we run the risk of missing the plane.*
take a risk/risks to do sth that you know might fail or be dangerous, etc: *You shouldn't take risks when driving.* ○ *He's very young but I'm prepared to take a risk and give him a job.*

risk *verb* [T] **1** to take the chance of sth unpleasant happening: *If you don't work hard now you risk failing your exams.* **2** to put sth or yourself in a dangerous position: *The man had risked his life to save the little boy.*

risky *adj* (**riskier; riskiest**) dangerous: *It's risky to drive fast when the roads are icy.*

ritual /'rɪtʃuəl/ *noun* [C,U] an action, ceremony or process which is usually repeated in the same pattern: *English people often go through the ritual of talking about the weather when they meet.*

ritual *adj* done according to a particular pattern or tradition —**ritually** *adv*

☆ **rival** /'raɪvl/ *noun* [C] a person or thing that is competing with another: *They're business rivals.* ○ *It seems that we're rivals for the sales manager's job.* ○ *A rival shop has set up in the same street.*

rival *verb* [T] (rivalling; rivalled; *US* rivaling; rivaled) **rival sb/sth (for/in sth)** to be as good as sb/sth: *This novel doesn't rival his earlier writing.* ○ *Nothing rivals skiing for sheer excitement.*

rivalry /'raɪvlri/ *noun* [C,U] (*pl* **rivalries**) competition between people, groups, etc: *There was a lot of rivalry between the sisters.*

☆ **river** /'rɪvə(r)/ *noun* [C] a large natural stream of water that flows across country: *the River Thames* ○ *a picnic on the bank of the river* ☛ A river **flows** into the sea. Where it joins the sea is the river **mouth**. A boat sails **on** the river. We walk, sail, etc **up** or **down river**.

'riverside *noun* [sing] the land beside the banks of a river: *People were strolling along the riverside.* ○ *a riverside hotel*

rivet¹ /'rɪvɪt/ *noun* [C] a metal pin for fastening two pieces of metal together

rivet² /'rɪvɪt/ *verb* [T] (usually passive) to interest sb greatly: *I was riveted by her story.*

riveting *adj* extremely interesting: *His speech was absolutely riveting.*

roach /rəʊtʃ/ *noun* [C] (*US*) = COCKROACH

☆ **road** /rəʊd/ *noun* **1** [C] a way between places, with a hard surface which cars, buses, etc can drive along: *Is this the right road to Beckley?* ○ *Take the London road and turn right at the first roundabout.* ○ *Turn left off the main* (= big, important) *road.* ○ *major/minor roads* ○ *If you get onto the ring road you'll avoid the town centre.* ○ *road signs* ○ *a road junction* ☛ **Roads** (*US* **highways**) connect towns and villages: *a road-map of England.* A road in a town, city or village that has buildings at the side is often called a **street**. **Street** is not used for roads outside towns: *a street-map of London.* However streets in towns may have the word **Road** as part of their names: *Bayswater Road, London.* **Motorways** (*US* **freeways/expressways**) are roads with two **carriageways**, each with two or three **lanes**, that are built for traffic covering long distances, avoiding towns. **A-roads** are big important roads that link towns. **B-roads** are smaller country roads. **M** on a map stands for **motorway**. **2 Road** (*abbr* **Rd**) [sing] (used in names of roads, especially in towns): *60 Marylebone Road, London*
(IDIOMS) **by road** in a car, bus, etc: *It's going to be a terrible journey by road – let's take the train.*
on the road travelling: *We were on the road for 14 hours.*

'roadblock *noun* [C] a barrier put across the road by the police or army to stop traffic

'roadside *noun* [C, usually sing] the edge of a road: *We had to stop at the roadside and wait for the engine to cool.* ○ *a roadside café*

'road tax *noun* [C,U] the tax which the owner

of a car, etc must pay to be allowed to drive it on public roads

the 'roadway noun [C] (formal) the part of the road used by cars, etc; not the side of the road

'roadworks noun [plural] work that involves repairing or building roads: *The sign said 'Slow down. Roadworks ahead.'*

'roadworthy adj in good enough condition to be driven on the road

roam /rəʊm/ verb [I,T] to walk or travel with no particular plan or aim: *The police said that several groups of youths roamed Oxford city centre late last Saturday night.*

roar /rɔː(r)/ noun [C] a loud, deep sound like that made by a lion: *the roar of heavy traffic on the motorway* ○ *roars of laughter*

roar verb **1** [I] to make a loud, deep sound: *The river roared past, taking trees and rocks with it.* ○ *She roared with laughter at the joke.* **2** [I] to shout very loudly: *I often hear the teacher roaring at the children.* **3** [I] to make the sound that is typical of a lion: *The lion opened its huge mouth and roared.* **4** [T] **roar sth (out)** to express sth very loudly: *The audience roared its approval.*

(PHRASAL VERB) **roar along, down, past, etc** to move in the direction mentioned, making a loud, deep sound: *A motorbike roared past us.*

roaring /ˈrɔːrɪŋ/ adj **1** making a very loud noise: *the roaring waves* **2** (used about a fire) burning very well **3** very great: *a roaring success*

roast /rəʊst/ verb **1** [I,T] to cook or be cooked in an oven or over a fire: *a smell of roasting meat* ○ *to roast a chicken* ☞ Look at the note at **cook**. **2** [T] to heat and dry sth: *roasted peanuts*

roast adj (only before a noun) cooked by roasting: *roast beef and roast potatoes*

roast noun **1** [C,U] a piece of meat that has been roasted **2** [C] (especially US) an outdoor meal at which food is roasted ☞ Look at **barbecue**.

☆ **rob** /rɒb/ verb [T] (**robbing**; **robbed**) **rob sb/sth (of sth) 1** to take sth (money, property, etc) from a person or place illegally: *to rob a bank* ○ *Several people on the train were robbed of their money and jewellery.* ☞ Look at the note at **steal**. **2** to take sth away from sb/sth that they should have: *His illness robbed him of the chance to play for his country.*

robber noun [C] a person who steals from a bank, etc ☞ Look at the note at **thief**.

robbery /ˈrɒbəri/ noun [C,U] (pl **robberies**) the crime of stealing from a bank, etc: *They were accused of robbery with violence.* ○ *There's been a robbery. They've taken half a million pounds.*

robe /rəʊb/ noun [C] **1** a long, loose piece of clothing **2** (US) = DRESSING GOWN

robin /ˈrɒbɪn/ noun [C] a small brown bird with a bright red breast

robot /ˈrəʊbɒt/ noun [C] a machine that can move and that can be made to do some of the work that a person does. Some robots are made to look like people.

robust /rəʊˈbʌst/ adj strong and healthy: *a robust child*

☆ **rock¹** /rɒk/ noun **1** [U] the hard, stony part of the earth: *layers of rock formed over millions of years* **2** [C] a large piece or area of this that sticks out of the sea or the ground: *The ship hit the rocks and started to sink.* **3** [C] a large, separate stone: *The beach was covered with rocks that had broken away from the cliffs.* **4** [C] (US) a small piece of stone that can be picked up: *The boy threw a rock at the dog.* **5** [U] (Brit) a type of hard sweet made in long, round sticks

(IDIOM) **on the rocks 1** (used about drinks) served with ice but no water: *whisky on the rocks* **2** (used about a marriage, business, etc) having problems and likely to fail

rocky adj (**rockier**; **rockiest**) full of rocks or not level and smooth: *a rocky road* ○ *a rocky coastline*

,rock-'bottom noun [U] the lowest point: *They say that house-prices have reached rock-bottom and will soon start to rise again.* ○ *a rock-bottom price*

'rock-climbing noun [U] the sport of climbing rocks and mountains with ropes, etc

rock² /rɒk/ verb **1** [I,T] to move backwards and forwards or from side to side; to make sb/sth do this: *fishing-boats rocking gently on the waves* ○ *The baby won't go to sleep unless you rock her pram for a while.* **2** [T] to shake sth violently: *The city was rocked by a bomb blast.* **3** [T] to cause shock to sb/sth: *The country was rocked by the news of the riots.*

rock band

keyboard

drums

bass guitar

electric guitar

rock³ /rɒk/ (also **'rock music**) noun [U] a type of pop music with a very strong beat, played on electric guitars, etc: *I prefer jazz to rock.* ○ *a rock singer* ○ *a rock band*

,rock and 'roll (also **rock 'n' roll**) noun [U] a type of music with a strong beat that was most popular in the 1950s: *Elvis Presley was the king of rock and roll.*

rocket /ˈrɒkɪt/ noun [C] **1** a vehicle shaped like a tube, that is used for travel into space: *a space rocket* ○ *to launch a rocket* **2** an object of a similar shape that is used as a weapon and that carries a bomb **3** a firework that shoots high into the air when you light it, and then explodes

rocket verb [I] to increase or rise very quickly

rod /rɒd/ *noun* [C] (often in compounds) a thin straight piece of wood or metal: *a fishing-rod*

rode *pt* of RIDE²

rodent /'rəʊdnt/ *noun* [C] a type of small animal (such as a rat, a rabbit, a mouse, etc) which have strong sharp front teeth

rodeo /'rəʊdiəʊ; rəʊ'deɪəʊ/ *noun* [C] (*pl* **rodeos**) a contest or performance in which people show their skill in riding wild horses, catching cows, etc

roe /rəʊ/ *noun* [U] the eggs or male seed of a fish, which can be eaten as food

rogue /rəʊg/ *noun* [C] (*old-fashioned*) a person who is not honest or reliable

☆ **role** /rəʊl/ *noun* [C] **1** a person's part in a play, film, etc: *Many actresses have played the role of Cleopatra.* o *a leading role in the film* **2** the position and importance of sb/sth: *During her colleague's illness, she took on the role of supervisor.* o *Parents play a vital role in their children's education.*

'role-play *noun* [C,U] an activity, used especially in teaching, in which a person acts a part

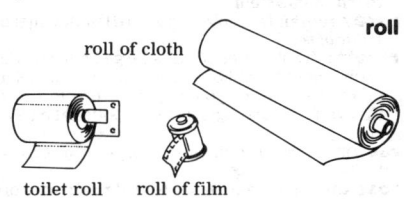

roll of cloth

toilet roll   roll of film

roll

☆ **roll¹** /rəʊl/ *noun* [C] **1** something made into the shape of a tube by winding it around itself: *a roll of film* **2** a very small loaf of bread for one person: *a roll and butter for breakfast* o *a ham roll* (= a roll filled with ham) ☛ picture at **bread**. **3** an official list of names: *There are two hundred children on the school roll.* o *the electoral roll* (= the list of people who can vote in an election) **4** a long, low sound: *a roll of drums* o *the roll of thunder* **5** a movement from side to side: *the roll of a ship*

roll² /rəʊl/ *verb* **1** [I,T] to move by turning over and over; to make sth move in this way: *The apples fell out of the bag and rolled everywhere.* o *We couldn't stop the ball rolling into the river.* o *He tried to roll the rock up the hill.* **2** [I] to move smoothly (on wheels or as if on wheels): *The car began to roll back down the hill.* o *Tears were rolling down her cheeks.* o *Big black clouds came rolling across the sky.* **3** [I,T] to turn over or upwards; to make sb/sth do this: *She rolled over and looked up at him.* o *We rolled the mattress onto its other side.* **4** [I,T] **roll (sth) (up)** to make sth into the shape of a ball or tube; to be made into this shape: *He was rolling himself a cigarette.* o *The insect rolled up when I touched it.* ☛ The opposite is **unroll**. **5** [T] to make sth become flat by moving sth heavy over it: *Roll out the pastry* (= using a rolling-pin). **6** [I] to rock or swing from side to side: *The ship was beginning to roll in the storm.* o *She was rolling about with laughter.*

(IDIOM) **be rolling in money/in it** (*slang*) to have a lot of money

(PHRASAL VERBS) **roll in** (*informal*) to arrive in large numbers or quantities: *Offers of help have been rolling in.*

roll up (*informal*) (used about a person or a vehicle) to arrive (often late)

'rolling-pin *noun* [C] a piece of wood, etc in the shape of a tube, that you use for making pastry flat and thin before cooking

roller /'rəʊlə(r)/ *noun* [C] **1** a long object in the shape of a tube, which is usually part of a machine or a piece of equipment and can have various uses: *The tins are then crushed between two rollers.* o *a roller-blind* (= a type of window blind on a roller) **2** [usually pl] small plastic tubes that women wind their hair round to make it curl

'roller-coaster *noun* [C] a type of railway with open carriages, sharp bends and very steep slopes. People go on roller-coasters for fun at fairs, etc.

'roller-skate (*also* **skate**) *noun* [C] a type of shoe with small wheels on the bottom. It allows you to move quickly over a smooth surface: *a pair of roller skates* ☛ picture at **skate**.

'roller-skate *verb* [I] —**'roller-skating** *noun* [U]

Roman /'rəʊmən/ *adj* connected with ancient Rome: *the remains of a Roman villa* o *Roman coins*

Roman *noun* [C] a citizen of Rome

the ,Roman 'alphabet *noun* [sing] the letters A to Z, used especially in West European languages

,Roman 'Catholic (*also* **Catholic**) *noun* [C], *adj* (a member) of the Christian Church which has the Pope as its head: *She's (a) Roman Catholic.* ☛ Look at **Protestant**.

,Roman Ca'tholicism (*also* **Catholicism**) *noun* [U] the beliefs of the Roman Catholic Church

,Roman 'numerals *noun* [plural] the letters used by the ancient Romans as numbers

☛ Roman numerals, eg IV=4 and X=10, are still used sometimes. For example they may be found numbering the pages and chapters of books or on some clocks.

romance /rəʊ'mæns/ *noun* **1** [C] a love affair: *The film was about a teenage romance.* **2** [U] a feeling or atmosphere of love or of sth new, special and exciting: *The stars were out, the night was warm and romance was in the air.* **3** [C] a novel about a love affair: *She writes historical romances.*

☆ **romantic** /rəʊ'mæntɪk/ *adj* **1** having or showing ideas about life and love that are emotional rather than real or practical: *He has a romantic idea that he'd like to live on a farm in Scotland.* **2** involving a love affair; describing situations involving love: *Reports of a romantic relationship between the two film stars have been strongly denied.* o *a romantic novel* **3** having a quality that strongly affects your emotions or makes you think about love; showing feelings of love: *a romantic candle-lit dinner* o *He isn't very romantic – he never says he loves me.*

ɜː	ə	eɪ	əʊ	aɪ	aʊ	ɔɪ	ɪə	eə	ʊə
fur	ago	pay	home	five	now	join	near	hair	pure

romantic *noun* [C] a person who has ideas that are not based on real life or that are not very practical —**romantically** /-kli/ *adv*

romanticize (*also* **romanticise**) /rəʊˈmæntɪsaɪz/ *verb* [I,T] to make sth seem more interesting, exciting, etc than it really is

romp /rɒmp/ *verb* [I] (used about children and animals) to play in a noisy way with a lot of running, jumping, etc —**romp** *noun* [C]

☆ **roof** /ruːf/ *noun* [C] (*pl* **roofs**) **1** the part of a building, vehicle, etc which covers the top of it: *the roof of the school* ○ *a flat roof* ○ *The coach had windows in the roof which allowed some air in.* ○ *The library and the sports hall are under one roof* (= in the same building). ○ *We can store a lot of things in the roof* (= in the space directly under the roof of a house). **2** the highest part of sth: *The roof of the cave had collapsed.*

'roof-rack *noun* [C] a structure that you fix to the roof of a car and use for carrying luggage or other large objects ☞ picture at **rack**.

'rooftop *noun* [C, usually *pl*] the outside of the roofs of buildings: *From the tower we looked down over the rooftops of Florence.*

☆ **room** /ruːm; rʊm/ *noun* **1** [C] a part of a house or building that is separated from the rest by its own walls, floor and ceiling: *The house has three rooms downstairs and four bedrooms.* ○ *a sitting-room* ○ *a dining-room* ○ *a spare room* (= for guests) ○ *There is a common room where students can meet and watch television.* ○ *to book a room at a hotel* ○ *a single/double room* **2** [U] **room (for sb/sth)**; **room (to do sth)** space; enough space: *There isn't room for any more furniture in here.* ○ *The table takes up too much room.* ○ *They're pulling down those old factories to make room for new development.* ○ *There were so many people that there wasn't any room to move.* **3** [U] **room (for sth)** the opportunity or need for sth: *There's room for improvement in your work* (= it could be much better). ☞ Look at the note at **place¹**.

roomful /-fʊl/ *noun* [C] the amount or number that a room can contain: *There was a roomful of reporters waiting to interview him.*

roomy *adj* (**roomier**; **roomiest**) having plenty of space: *a roomy house, car, etc*

'room-mate *noun* [C] a person that you share a room with in a flat, etc

roost /ruːst/ *noun* [C] a place where birds rest or sleep

rooster /ˈruːstə(r)/ *noun* [C] (*US*) = COCK¹(1)

☆ **root¹** /ruːt/ *noun* **1** [C] the part of a plant that grows under the ground and takes in water and food from the soil **2** [C] the part of a hair or tooth that is under the skin and that attaches it to the rest of the body **3 roots** [plural] the place where you feel that you belong, because you grew up there, live there or your relatives once lived there **4** [C] the cause or source of sth: *Let's try and get to the root of the problem.* ☞ Look at **square root**.

root² /ruːt/ *verb*
(PHRASAL VERBS) **root about/around (for sth)** to search through things, especially in an untidy or careless way: *What are you rooting around in my desk for?*
root for sb/sth to give support to sb who is in a competition, etc: *Good luck in the match – we'll all be rooting for you.*
root sb/sth out to find and destroy sth bad completely

☆ **rope** /rəʊp/ *noun* [C,U] very thick, strong cord, that is used for tying or lifting heavy things, climbing up, etc: *We need some rope to tie up the boat with.* ○ *a skipping rope* (= one that children use to jump over)

rope *verb* [T] to tie sb/sth with a rope: *The climbers were roped together when they crossed the glacier.*
(PHRASAL VERBS) **rope sb in (to do sth)** (*informal*) to persuade sb to help in some activity: *I've been roped in to help at the school play.*
rope sth off to put ropes round or across an area in order to keep people out of it

'rope-ladder *noun* [C] a ladder made of two long ropes and steps of rope, wood or metal

rosary /ˈrəʊzəri/ *noun* [C] (*pl* **rosaries**) a string of beads used for counting prayers

rose¹ *pt* of RISE²

☆ **rose²** /rəʊz/ *noun* [C] a flower with a sweet smell, that grows on a bush and usually has thorns on its stem

rosé /ˈrəʊzeɪ; *US* rəʊˈzeɪ/ *noun* [U] pink wine: *a bottle of rosé*

rosette /rəʊˈzet/ *noun* [C] a large badge made from coloured ribbons. You may get one as a prize in a show or you may wear one to show that you support a sports team, political party, etc.

roster /ˈrɒstə(r)/ *noun* [C] (*especially US*) = ROTA

rostrum /ˈrɒstrəm/ *noun* [C] (*pl* **rostrums** or **rostra** /ˈrɒstrə/) a platform that sb stands on to make a public speech, etc

rosy /ˈrəʊzi/ *adj* (**rosier**; **rosiest**) **1** deep pink in colour and (used about a person) healthy-looking: *rosy cheeks* **2** (used about a situation) full of good possibilities: *The future was looking rosy.*

rot /rɒt/ *verb* (**rotting**; **rotted**) **1** [I] to go bad (as part of a natural process); to decay: *Wood will rot in damp conditions.* **2** [T] to make sth go bad or decay: *Too many sweets will rot your teeth!*

rot *noun* [U] **1** the condition of being bad or rotten: *The floorboards have got rot in them.* **2** (*old-fashioned informal*) nonsense: *Don't talk rot!*

rota /ˈrəʊtə/ *noun* [C] (*pl* **rotas**) (*US also* **roster**) a list of people who share a certain job or task and the times that they are each going to do it: *I have a rota with some other mothers for taking the children to school.*

rotary /ˈrəʊtəri/ *adj* moving in circles round a central point

rotate /rəʊˈteɪt/ *verb* [I,T] **1** to turn in circles round a central point; to make sth do this: *The earth rotates around the sun.* ○ *You can see the parts that rotate the hands of the clock.* **2** to happen in turn or in a particular order; to make sth do this: *The position of president is rotated among all the member countries.*

rotation /rəʊˈteɪʃn/ *noun* **1** [U] movement in circles: *the earth's rotation* **2** [C] one complete turn around sth: *one rotation every 24 hours*

rotor /ˈrəʊtə(r)/ *noun* [C] a part of a machine

p	b	t	d	k	g	tʃ	dʒ	f	v	θ	ð
pen	bad	tea	did	cat	got	chin	June	fall	van	thin	then

that turns round, especially the blades on top of a helicopter

rotten /ˈrɒtn/ adj **1** (used about food and other substances) old and not fresh enough or good enough to use: *rotten vegetables* ○ *Some of the stairs were rotten and not safe.* **2** (*informal*) very bad: *We had rotten weather all week.* **3** (*informal*) unfair, unkind or unpleasant: *That was a rotten thing to say to you!* **4** (*informal*) (used for emphasizing that you are angry): *He spent all weekend working on his rotten car!*

rottweiler /ˈrɒtvaɪlə(r)/ noun [C] a large, often fierce, black and brown dog

rouge /ruːʒ/ noun [U] a red powder or cream used for giving more colour to the cheeks

☆ **rough¹** /rʌf/ adj **1** not smooth or level: *It's not easy to walk over such rough ground.* ○ *Her hands were rough with too much work.* **2** moving or behaving with too much force and not enough care; not gentle or calm: *There was rather a rough game of football going on.* ○ *The ferry was cancelled because the sea was so rough* (= because of a storm). ○ *I wouldn't walk alone in that part of London at night. It's very rough* (= there is a lot of crime or violence). **3** made or done quickly or without much care; approximately correct: *a rough estimate of what the work would cost* ○ *Can you give me a rough idea of what time you'll be arriving?* **4** (*informal*) rather ill; unwell: *You look a bit rough – are you feeling all right?*

(IDIOMS) **be rough (on sb)** be unpleasant or unlucky (for sb)

a hard/rough 'time ⇒ TIME¹

roughly adv **1** in a violent way; not gently: *He grabbed her roughly by her arm.* **2** not exactly; approximately: *It took roughly three hours, I suppose.*

roughness noun [U] the quality or state of being rough: *The roughness of the material irritated my skin.*

rough² /rʌf/ adv in a rough way: *One of the boys was told off for playing rough.*

(IDIOM) **sleep rough** ⇒ SLEEP²(3)

rough³ /rʌf/ noun

(IDIOMS) **in rough** in an early form, not finished properly: *Write out your essay in rough first.*

take the rough with the smooth to accept difficult or unpleasant things as well as pleasant things

rough⁴ /rʌf/ verb

(IDIOM) **rough it** to live without the usual comforts of life: *The boys love roughing it when they go camping in the summer.*

roughage /ˈrʌfɪdʒ/ noun [U] the types or parts of food which help you to digest other foods

roughen /ˈrʌfn/ verb [T] to make sth rough: *Her skin was roughened by the wind and cold.*

roulette /ruːˈlet/ noun [U] a game in which a ball is dropped onto a moving wheel that has holes with numbers on it. The players bet on which number hole the ball will be in when the wheel stops.

☆ **round¹** /raʊnd/ adj having the shape of a circle or a ball: *a round table* ○ *People used to think the earth was flat, not round.* ○ *He had a fat, round face and fair hair.*

(IDIOM) **in round figures/numbers** given to the nearest 10, 100, 1 000, etc; not given in exact figures or numbers

‚round 'trip noun [C] **1** a journey to one or more places and back again, often by a different route **2** (*US*) = RETURN²(5): *a round-trip ticket*

☆ **round²** /raʊnd/ adv ☛ For special uses with many verbs, eg **come, get, go,** etc see the verb entries **1** in a circle or curve to face another way or the opposite way: *She moved her chair round so that she could see out of the window.* ○ *Don't look round but the teacher's just come in.* **2** in a full circle: *The wheels spun round and round but the car wouldn't move.* **3** measuring or marking a circle or the edge of sth: *You can't get in because there's a fence all round.* **4** from one place, person, etc to another: *Pass the photographs round for everyone to see.* ○ *I've been rushing round all day.* **5** to a particular place, especially where sb lives: *I'll pop round to see you at about 8 o'clock.*

(IDIOMS) **round about** in the area near a place: *We've been to most of the pubs round about.*

the other way round in the opposite way or order: *I'm not going to go to Paris then Brussels – I'll do it the other way round.* ☛ **Around** has the same meaning as **round** and is more common in American English.

☆ **round³** /raʊnd/ prep **1** (used about movement) in a circle round a fixed point: *Chichester sailed round the world in a yacht.* **2** to or on the other side of sth: *There's a post-box just round the corner.* ○ (*figurative*) *It wasn't easy to see a way round the problem* (= a way of solving it). **3** on all sides of sth; surrounding sth: *He had a bandage right round his head.* ○ *We sat round the table, talking late into the night.* **4** in the area near a place: *Do you live round here?* **5** in or to many parts of sth: *Let me show you round the house.* ○ *We drove round France, stopping here and there.* **6 round about sth** approximately: *We hope to arrive round about 6.* ☛ **Around** has the same meaning as **round** and is more common in American English.

☆ **round⁴** /raʊnd/ noun [C] **1** a number or set of events, etc: *a further round of talks with other European countries* **2** a regular series of visits, etc, often as part of a job: *The postman's round takes him about three hours.* **3** a number of drinks (one for all the people in a group): *I'll buy the first round.* ○ *It's my round* (=it's my turn to buy the drinks). **4** one part of a game or competition: *the third round of the boxing match* ○ *The winners of the first round will go on to the second stage of the competition.* **5** (in golf) one game: *to play a round of golf* **6** a bullet or a number of bullets, fired from a gun: *He fired several rounds at us.*

round⁵ /raʊnd/ verb [T] to go round sth: *The police car rounded the corner at high speed.*

(PHRASAL VERBS) **round sth off** to end or complete sth in a satisfactory way: *We rounded off the meal with coffee and chocolates.*

round sb/sth up to gather sb/sth in one place: *The teacher rounded up the children.*

s	z	ʃ	ʒ	h	m	n	ŋ	l	r	j	w
so	zoo	she	vision	how	man	no	sing	leg	red	yes	wet

round sth up/down to increase/decrease a number, price, etc to the nearest whole number: *Please round the price up to the nearest penny.*

roundabout¹ /ˈraʊndəbaʊt/ *adj* longer than necessary, or usual; not direct: *We got lost and came by rather a roundabout route.*

roundabout² /ˈraʊndəbaʊt/ *noun* [C] **1** a circular area where several roads meet. You drive round it until you come to the exit you want: *Give way to traffic that is already on the roundabout.* **2** (*also* **merry-go-round**; *US* **carousel**) a big round platform at a fair, etc that turns round and round mechanically. It has model animals, etc on it for children to ride on: *to have a ride on a roundabout* **3** a round platform in a playground. Children sit or stand on it and sb pushes it round.

rounders /ˈraʊndəz/ *noun* [U] (*Brit*) a game for two teams played with a bat and ball. Players have to hit the ball and then run round the outside of four posts arranged in a square.

rouse /raʊz/ *verb* [T] **1** (*formal*) to make sb wake up: *She was sleeping so soundly that I couldn't rouse her.* **2** to make sb very angry, excited, interested, etc: *He can get very angry when he's roused.*

rousing *adj* exciting and powerful: *a rousing speech*

rout /raʊt/ *noun* [C] a complete defeat, ending in disorder

rout *verb* [T] to defeat sb completely

☆ **route** /ruːt; *US* raʊt/ *noun* [C] **1** a way from one place to another: *We took the fastest and most direct route to the coast.* ○ *I got a leaflet about the bus routes from the information office.* ○ *Thousands of people were waiting beside the route that the President's car would take.* **2** a way of achieving sth: *Hard work is the only route to success.*

☆ **routine** /ruːˈtiːn/ *noun* **1** [C,U] the fixed and usual way of doing things: *If you work out a routine you will get things done more quickly.* ○ *Children like routine. They like to know what to expect.* **2** [U] tasks that have to be done again and again and so are boring: *I gave up the job because I couldn't stand the routine.*

routine *adj* **1** normal and regular; not unusual or special: *The police would like to ask you some routine questions.* **2** boring; not exciting: *It's a very routine job, really.*

routinely *adv* very often; regularly; as part of a routine: *The machines are routinely checked every two months.*

☆ **row¹** /rəʊ/ *noun* [C] **1** a line of people or things: *a row of books* ○ *The children were all standing in a row at the front of the class.* **2** a line of seats in a theatre, cinema, etc: *Our seats were in the back row.* ○ *a front-row seat*
(IDIOM) **in a row** one after another; without a break: *It rained solidly for four days in a row.*

row² /rəʊ/ *verb* **1** [I,T] to move a boat through the water using oars: *We often go rowing on the Thames.* ○ *He rowed the boat slowly down the river.* **2** [T] to carry sb/sth in a boat that you row: *Could you row us over to the island?*

row *noun* [sing] a trip in a boat that you row: *We went for a row on the river.*

ˈrowing-boat (*US* **ˈrow-boat**) *noun* [C] a small boat that you move through the water using oars

row³ /raʊ/ *noun* **1** [C] a noisy argument between two or more people: *Lucy has had a row with her boyfriend.* **2** [C] a public argument especially among politicians: *There have been new developments in the row about the future of the National Health Service.* **3** [sing] a loud noise: *What a row! Could you be a bit quieter?*

row *verb* [I] to quarrel noisily: *My husband and I are always rowing about money!*

rowdy /ˈraʊdi/ *adj* (**rowdier**; **rowdiest**) noisy and uncontrolled: *rowdy behaviour among a group of football fans* —**rowdily** *adv* —**rowdiness** *noun* [U]

☆ **royal** /ˈrɔɪəl/ *adj* **1** connected with a king, queen or a member of their family: *the royal family* ○ *the royal visit to New Zealand* **2** (used in the names of organizations supported by a member of the royal family: *the Royal Society for the Protection of Birds*

royal *noun* [C] (*informal*) a member of the royal family

ˌroyal ˈblue *adj* deep bright blue in colour

ˌRoyal ˈHighness *noun* [C] (used when you are speaking to or about a member of the royal family): *their Royal Highnesses, the King and Queen of Spain*

royalty /ˈrɔɪəlti/ *noun* (*pl* **royalties**) **1** [U] members of the royal family **2** [C] an amount of money that is paid to the person who wrote a book, piece of music, etc every time his/her work is sold or performed

☆ **rub** /rʌb/ *verb* (**rubbing**; **rubbed**) **1** [I,T] to move your hand, a cloth, etc backwards and forwards on the surface of sth while pressing firmly: *Ralph rubbed his hands together to keep them warm.* ○ *Rub hard and the mark should come out.* ○ *The cat rubbed against my leg.* ○ *The cat rubbed its head against my leg.* ○ *He rubbed his face with his hand.* ○ *He rubbed his hand across his face.* ○ *He rubbed the sweat off his face with his hand.* **2** [T] to put a cream, liquid, etc onto a surface by rubbing(1): *Apply a little of the lotion and rub it into the skin.* **3** [I] **rub (on/against sth)** to press on/against sth (often causing pain or damage): *These new shoes are rubbing my heels.*

(PHRASAL VERBS) **rub off (on/onto sb)** (used about a good quality) to be transferred from one person to another: *Let's hope some of her enthusiasm rubs off onto her brother.*

rub sth out to remove the marks made by a pencil, chalk, etc using a rubber, cloth, etc: *That answer is wrong. Rub it out.*

rub *noun* [C] an act of rubbing(1): *Give your shoes a rub before you go out.*

☆ **rubber** /ˈrʌbə(r)/ *noun* **1** [U] a strong substance that is made chemically or from the juice of a tropical tree. Rubber is elastic (= it can stretch and then return to its original shape) and it is also waterproof: *Car tyres are made of rubber.* ○ *foam rubber* ○ *rubber gloves for washing up* **2** [C] (*especially US* **eraser**) a small piece of rubber that you use for remov-

iː	ɪ	e	æ	ɑː	ɒ	ɔː	ʊ	uː	ʌ
see	sit	ten	hat	arm	got	saw	put	too	cup

ing pencil marks from paper **3** [C] (*informal*) = CONDOM

rubbery /'rʌbəri/ *adj* like rubber

,rubber 'band (*also* **elastic band**) *noun* [C] a thin circular piece of rubber that is used for holding things together: *Her hair was tied back with a rubber band.*

,rubber 'stamp *noun* [C] a piece of equipment with rubber letters on it that you use for printing a name, date, etc on a document

,rubber-'stamp *verb* [T] (usually used about sb with authority) to agree to sth without thinking about it carefully

☆ **rubbish** /'rʌbɪʃ/ (*US* **garbage**; **trash**) *noun* [U] **1** things that you do not want any more; waste material: *The dustmen collect the rubbish every Monday.* ○ *a rubbish bin* ○ *It's only rubbish – throw it away.* ☛ picture at **bin**. **2** something that you think is bad, silly or wrong: *Don't talk such rubbish.*

rubble /'rʌbl/ *noun* [U] pieces of broken brick, stone, etc, especially from a damaged building

rubella /ru:'belə/ *noun* [U] = GERMAN MEASLES

ruby /'ru:bi/ *noun* [C] (*pl* **rubies**) a type of precious stone that is red

rucksack /'rʌksæk/ (*US also* **backpack**) *noun* [C] a bag that you use for carrying things on your back. You often use a rucksack when you are walking, camping, etc. ☛ picture at **luggage**.

rudder /'rʌdə(r)/ *noun* [C] a piece of wood or metal that is used for controlling the direction of a boat or an aeroplane

☆ **rude** /ru:d/ *adj* **1** not polite: *It's rude to interrupt when people are speaking.* ○ *He's often rude to his mother.* ○ *I think it was rude of them not to phone and say that they weren't coming.* ☛ Look at **impolite**. **2** connected with sex, using the toilet, etc: *a rude joke* ○ *a rude word* **3** sudden and unpleasant: *If you're expecting any help from him, you're in for a rude shock.*
—**rudely** *adv* —**rudeness** *noun* [U]

rudimentary /,ru:dɪ'mentri/ *adj* basic or very simple

ruffle /'rʌfl/ *verb* [T] **1** to make sth untidy or no longer smooth: *The bird ruffled up its feathers.* ○ *to ruffle sb's hair* **2** (often passive) to make sb annoyed or confused

rug /rʌg/ *noun* [C] **1** a piece of thick material that covers a small part of a floor ☛ Look at **carpet**. **2** a type of blanket that you put over your legs or around your shoulders

rugby /'rʌgbi/ (*also* **rugby 'football**) *noun* [U] a form of football that is played by two teams of 13 or 15 players with an oval ball that can be carried or kicked

☛ In Britain Rugby **League** is a professional game with 13 players in a team, Rugby **Union** is an amateur game with 15 players.

rugged /'rʌgɪd/ *adj* **1** (used about land) rough and rocky with few plants: *a rugged coastline* **2** (used about a man) looking strong

☆ **ruin** /'ru:ɪn/ *noun* **1** [U] a state of destruction, when sth is completely spoilt: *The city was in a state of ruin.* **2** [U] the cause or state of having lost all your money, hope of being successful, etc: *Many small companies are facing financial ruin.* **3** [C] a building, town, etc that has been badly damaged or destroyed; the parts of a building, town, etc that are left when it has been almost completely destroyed: *The old house is now a ruin.* ○ *We went to look at the ruins of the castle.* ○ *the ruins of the ancient city of Pompeii*

(IDIOMS) **go to rack and ruin** ⇒ RACK³

in ruin(s) badly damaged or destroyed: *After the accident her life seemed to be in ruins.* ○ *The city of Berlin was in ruins at the end of the war.*

ruin *verb* [T] **1** to damage sth badly, to destroy: *a ruined building* ○ *The crops were ruined by the late frost.* **2** to spoil sth so that it is no longer good: *Much of the coast has been ruined by tourism.* ○ *My dress was ruined when I spilled wine over it.* **3** to cause sb to lose all his/her money, hope of being successful, etc: *The cost of the court case nearly ruined them.*

ruinous /'ru:ɪnəs/ *adj* costing much more money than you can afford to spend

☆ **rule** /ru:l/ *noun* **1** [C] an official statement that tells you what you can or cannot do, say, etc: *to obey/break a rule* ○ *Do you know the rules of chess?* ○ *It's against the rules to smoke in this area.* ○ *rules and regulations* ☛ A **law** is stronger. You can be officially punished if you break it. **2** [C] (in a language) a description of what is usual or correct: *What is the rule for forming the past tense?* **3** [sing] what is usual: *Large families are the exception rather than the rule nowadays.* **4** [U] government; control: *Indonesia was formerly under Dutch rule.* ○ *the rule of law*

(IDIOMS) **as a (general) rule** (*formal*) usually: *Women, as a rule, live longer than men.*

bend the rules ⇒ BEND¹

work to rule a form of industrial protest in which you follow the rules of your employment very closely so that your work takes longer than usual

rule *verb* [I,T] **1 rule (over sb/sth)** to have the power over a country, etc: *Britain once ruled over a vast empire.* ○ *The Congress Party ruled India for almost 40 years.* ○ (*figurative*) *His whole life was ruled by his ambition to become Prime Minister.* **2** to make an official decision: *The judge ruled that the police officers had not acted unlawfully.*

(PHRASAL VERB) **rule sb/sth out** to say that sb/sth is not thought to be possible: *The government has ruled out further increases in train fares next year.*

☆ **ruler** /'ru:lə(r)/ *noun* [C] **1** a person who rules a country, etc **2** a straight piece of wood, plastic, etc marked with inches or centimetres, that you use for measuring sth or for drawing straight lines

ruling¹ /'ru:lɪŋ/ *adj* (only *before* a noun) with the most power in an organization, country, etc: *the ruling Nationalist Party in South Africa*

ruling² /'ru:lɪŋ/ *noun* [C] an official decision: *a ruling of the European Court of Justice*

rum /rʌm/ *noun* [U] a strong alcoholic drink that is made from the juice of the sugar cane plant

rumble /'rʌmbl/ *verb* [I] to make a deep heavy sound: *Thunder was rumbling in the distance.* ○

ɜː	ə	eɪ	əʊ	aɪ	aʊ	ɔɪ	ɪə	eə	ʊə
fur	ago	pay	home	five	now	join	near	hair	pure

I was so hungry that my stomach was rumbling. —**rumble** noun [sing]: *the distant rumble of thunder*

rummage /ˈrʌmɪdʒ/ verb [I] to move things and make them untidy while you are looking for sth: *Nina rummaged through the drawer looking for the tin-opener.*

☆ **rumour** (*US* **rumor**) /ˈruːmə(r)/ noun [C,U] (a piece of) news or information that many people are talking about but that is possibly not true: *There's a rumour going round that the firm is going to close.* ○ *Rumour has it* (= people are saying) *that Len has resigned.* ○ *to confirm/deny a rumour* (= to say that it is true/not true)

rumoured (*US* **rumored**) adj said in an unofficial way (but perhaps not true): *It is rumoured that they are getting divorced.* ○ *They are rumoured to be getting divorced.*

rump /rʌmp/ noun [C] the back end of an animal: *rump steak* (= meat from the rump)

☆ **run¹** /rʌn/ verb [I,T] (*pres part* **running**; *pt* **ran** /ræn/; *pp* **run**) **1** [I,T] to move using your legs, going faster than when you walk: *I had to run to catch the bus.* ○ *The children came running to meet us.* ○ *She's running in the 100 metres* (= in a race). ○ *I ran nearly ten kilometres this morning.* **2** [I,T] to move, or move sth, quickly in a particular direction: *The car ran downhill and crashed into a wall.* ○ *She ran her finger down the list of passengers.* **3** [I] to go in a particular direction: *The road runs along the side of a lake.* **4** [I] (used about water, a liquid, or a river, etc) to flow: *When it's really cold, my nose runs.* ○ *I can hear a tap running somewhere* (= the water from a tap). **5** [T] to start water flowing, eg in a bath: *She's running the children's bath.* **6** [I] (used about the colour in material, etc) to spread (eg when the material is washed): *Don't put that red shirt in the washing-machine. It might run.* **7** [I] (used about buses, trains, etc) to travel at regular times: *All the trains are running late this morning.* **8** [I] (used about a machine, an organization, a system, etc) to work or function: *The engine is running very smoothly now.* **9** [T] to start a machine, etc and make it work: *Run the engine for a few minutes before you start.* ○ *We're running a new computer program today.* **10** [T] to organize or be in charge of sth: *They run a restaurant in Bath.* **11** [T] to use and pay for sth: *It costs a lot to run a car.* **12** [I] to be one of the people to be chosen (**a candidate**) in an election: *He's running for president.* **13** [I] to continue for a time: *The play ran for nearly two years in a London theatre.* **14** [T] to publish sth in a newspaper or magazine: *'The Independent' is running a series of articles on pollution.*

(IDIOMS) **be running at** to be at a certain level: *The interest rate is now running at 10%.*
up and running ⇨ UP

☛ For other idioms containing **run**, look at the entries for the nouns, adjectives, etc, eg **run in the family** is at **family**.

(PHRASAL VERBS) **run across sb/sth** to meet or find sb/sth by chance

run away to escape from somewhere: *He's run away from school.*
run sb/sth down to criticize sb/sth: *He's always running his children down.*
run into sb to meet sb by chance
run into sth to have difficulties or a problem: *If you run into any problems, just let me know.*
run (sth) into sb/sth to hit sb/sth with a car, etc: *He ran his car into a brick wall.*
run sth off to copy sth, using a machine: *Could you run me off ten copies please?*
run off with sth to take or steal sth: *Who's run off with my pen?*
run out (of sth) to finish your supply of sth; to come to an end: *We've run out of coffee.* ○ *Time is running out.*
run sb over to hit sb with a car, etc: *The child was run over as he was crossing the road.*
run through sth to discuss or read sth quickly: *She ran through the names on the list.*

'runaway adj **1** out of control: *a runaway train* **2** happening very easily: *His first novel was a runaway success.*

,run-'down adj **1** in bad condition: *a run-down block of flats* **2** not healthy: *You're looking very run-down.*

'run-up noun [sing] the period of time before a certain event: *the run-up to the election*

☆ **run²** /rʌn/ noun **1** [C] an act of running on foot: *Kate goes for a three-mile run every morning.* ○ *a cross-country run* **2** [C] a journey by car, train, etc: *We went for a very pleasant run through the Cotswolds.* **3** [C] a continuous series of performances of a play, film, etc: *Agatha Christie's 'Mousetrap' has had a run of more than twenty years.* **4** [sing] a series of similar events or sth that continues for a very long time: *We've had a run of bad luck recently.* **5** [sing] **a run on sth** a sudden great demand for sth: *There's always a run on ice-cream in the warmer weather.* **6** [C] a point in the games of baseball and cricket **7** (*US*) = LADDER(2)

(IDIOMS) **the ordinary, average, etc run of sth** the ordinary, average, etc type of sth
in the long run ⇨ LONG¹(2)
on the run hiding or trying to escape from sb/sth: *The escaped prisoner is still on the run.*

rung¹ /rʌŋ/ noun [C] one of the bars that form the steps of a ladder ☛ picture at **ladder**.

rung² *pp* of RING²

☆ **runner** /ˈrʌnə(r)/ noun [C] **1** a person or animal that runs, especially in a race: *a long-distance runner* **2** a person who takes guns, drugs, etc illegally from one country to another

runner-up /ˌrʌnərˈʌp/ noun [C] (*pl* **runners-up** /ˌrʌnəzˈʌp/) the person or team that finished second in a race or competition

☆ **running** /ˈrʌnɪŋ/ noun [U] **1** the act or sport of running: *Ian goes running every morning.* ○ *running shoes* **2** the management of a business or other organization: *She's not involved in the day-to-day running of the office.* ○ *the running costs of a car* (= petrol, insurance, repairs, etc)

(IDIOM) **in/out of the running (for sth)** (*informal*) having/not having a good chance of getting or winning sth

p	b	t	d	k	g	tʃ	dʒ	f	v	θ	ð
pen	**bad**	**tea**	**did**	**cat**	**got**	**chin**	**June**	**fall**	**van**	**thin**	**then**

running *adj* **1** (only *before* a noun) not stopping; continuous: *a running battle between two rival gangs* **2** (used after a number and a noun) one after another, without a break: *Our school has won the competition for four years running.* **3** (only *before* a noun) flowing or available from a tap (used about water): *There is no running water in many villages in India.*

,running 'commentary *noun* [C] a spoken description of sth while it is happening

runny /'rʌni/ *adj* (**runnier; runniest**) (*informal*) **1** containing more liquid than is usual or than you expected: *runny jam* **2** (used about your eyes or nose) producing too much liquid: *Their children always seem to have runny noses.*

runway /'rʌnweɪ/ *noun* [C] a long piece of ground with a hard surface where aircraft take off and land

rupture /'rʌptʃə(r)/ *noun* [C,U] **1** a sudden breaking or tearing **2** = HERNIA

rupture *verb* [I,T] to break or tear

rural /'ruərəl/ *adj* connected with the country, not the town: *We spent our holiday exploring rural France.* ○ *a museum of rural life* ○ *They said that the new road would spoil the rural character of the area.* ☛ The opposite is **urban**.

ruse /ruːz/ *noun* [C] a trick or clever plan

☆**rush¹** /rʌʃ/ *verb* **1** [I] to go or come very quickly: *Don't rush – take your time.* ○ *The children rushed out of school.* ○ *I rushed back home when I got the news.* ○ *Don't rush off – I want to talk to you.* **2** [I] **rush to do sth** to do sth without delay: *The public rushed to buy shares in the new company.* **3** [T] to take sb/sth to a place very quickly: *He suffered a heart attack and was rushed to hospital.* **4** [I,T] **rush (sb) (into sth/into doing sth)** to do sth in a hurry or without enough thought; to make sb act in this way: *I'm afraid that we rushed into buying the house – it was a mistake.* ○ *Don't rush your food – there's plenty of time.* ○ *Don't let yourself be rushed into marriage.*

☆**rush²** /rʌʃ/ *noun* **1** [sing] a sudden quick movement: *At the end of the match there was a rush for the exits.* **2** [sing,U] (a need for) hurry: *I can't stop now. I'm in a terrible rush.* ○ *Don't hurry your meal. There's no rush.* **3** [sing] a time when many people try to get sth: *There's been a rush to buy petrol before the price goes up.* **4** [sing] a time when there is a lot of activity and people are very busy: *There is always a rush in the shops before Christmas.*

'rush hour *noun* [C] the time each day when the traffic is busy because people are travelling to or from work: *rush-hour traffic*

rush³ /rʌʃ/ *noun* [C] a type of tall grass that grows near water. Rushes can be dried and then used for making chair-seats, baskets, etc.

☆**rust** /rʌst/ *noun* [U] a reddish-brown substance that forms on the surface of iron, etc, caused by the action of air and water

rust *verb* [I,T] to (cause sth to) be attacked by rust: *Some parts of the car had rusted quite badly.* ○ *The sea air had rusted the car quite badly.*

rusty *adj* (**rustier; rustiest**) **1** covered with rust: *rusty tins* **2** (used about a skill) of poor quality because you have not used it for a long time: *I'm afraid my French is rather rusty.*

rustic /'rʌstɪk/ *adj* typical of the country (and therefore simple and unspoilt): *The whole area is full of rustic charm.* ○ *The rooms are decorated in a rustic style.* ☛ Look at **rural** and **urban**.

rustle /'rʌsl/ *verb* [I,T] to make a sound like dry leaves moving together; to cause sth to make this sound: *There was a rustling noise in the bushes.* ○ *Somebody behind me was rustling his newspaper all through the concert.*
 (PHRASAL VERB) **rustle sb/sth up** (*informal*) to find sb or prepare sth in a short time: *to rustle up a quick snack*

rustle *noun* [sing] the sound that dry leaves, etc make when they move

rut /rʌt/ *noun* [C] a deep track that a wheel makes in soft ground
 (IDIOM) **be in a rut** to have a boring way of life that is difficult to change

ruthless /'ruːθləs/ *adj* showing no pity or sympathy towards other people; thinking first about yourself and what you want: *You have to be ruthless to succeed in politics.* —**ruthlessly** *adv* —**ruthlessness** *noun* [U]

rye /raɪ/ *noun* [U] a plant that is grown in colder countries for its grain, which is used to make flour and also whisky

s	z	ʃ	ʒ	h	m	n	ŋ	l	r	j	w
so	zoo	she	vision	how	man	no	sing	leg	red	yes	wet

Ss

S, s /es/ noun [C] (pl **S's; s's**) the nineteenth letter of the English alphabet: *'School' begins with (an) 'S'*.

sabbath /'sæbəθ/ noun [sing] (also **the Sabbath**) the day of the week for rest and worship in certain religions (Sunday for Christians, Saturday for Jews)

sabotage /'sæbətɑːʒ/ noun [U] damage that is done on purpose and secretly in order to prevent an enemy or competitor being successful, eg by destroying machinery, roads, bridges, etc or by spoiling plans: *There has been an explosion at the oil refinery, and sabotage is suspected.*

sabotage verb [T] to destroy or damage sth by using sabotage: *There are rumours that the plane which crashed has been sabotaged.*

saccharin /'sækərɪn/ noun [U] a very sweet substance that can be used instead of sugar

sachet /'sæʃeɪ; US sæ'ʃeɪ/ noun [C] a small (often plastic) packet that contains a small amount of a product: *a sachet of shampoo*

sack¹ /sæk/ noun [C] a large bag made from rough heavy material, paper or plastic, used for carrying or storing things (eg vegetables, flour, coal, etc): *sacks of flour* ○ *We threw away several sacks of rubbish when we moved house.*

sack² /sæk/ verb [T] (*Brit*) to say that sb can no longer work for you (because of bad work, bad behaviour, etc): *Her boss has threatened to sack her if she's late again.*

☞ We can also say **give sb the sack**. The person gets the sack: *Tony's work wasn't good enough and he was given the sack.* ○ *Tony got the sack for poor work.*

sacred /'seɪkrɪd/ adj **1** connected with God, a god or religion; having a special religious meaning: *sacred music* (= music played in religious services) ○ *The Koran is the sacred book of Muslims.* **2** too important and special to be changed or harmed: *a sacred tradition*

sacrifice /'sækrɪfaɪs/ noun **1** [U] the act of offering sth, eg an animal that has been killed, to a god **2** [C] the thing that has been offered in this way: *They killed a lamb as a sacrifice.* **3** [C,U] the act of giving up sth that is important or valuable in order to achieve sth; the thing that you give up in this way: *If we're going to have a holiday this year, we'll have to make some sacrifices.* ○ *He was willing to make any sacrifice in order to succeed.*

sacrifice verb **1** [I,T] to offer sth to a god, often by killing it **2** [T] to give up sth important or valuable in order to achieve sth: *to sacrifice your life for your country* ○ *She is not willing to sacrifice her career in order to have children.*

sacrilege /'sækrɪlɪdʒ/ noun [U] treating sth that is considered holy or very special without the respect that it deserves

☆ **sad** /sæd/ adj (**sadder; saddest**) **1** unhappy or causing unhappiness: *I was sad to hear of the death of your father.* ○ *I'm very sad that you don't trust me.* ○ *That's one of the saddest stories I've ever heard!* **2** bad or unsatisfactory: *It's a sad state of affairs when your best friend doesn't trust you.*

sadden /'sædn/ verb [T] to cause sb to feel sad: *The news of your father's death saddened me greatly.*

sadly adv **1** in a way that shows unhappiness: *He spoke sadly about the death of his father.* **2** unfortunately: *I'd love to come to your party but sadly I'm busy that night.* **3** in a way that is wrong: *If you think that I've forgotten what you did, you're sadly mistaken.*

sadness noun [C,U] the feeling of being sad or a thing that causes unhappiness

saddle /'sædl/ noun [C] **1** a seat, usually made of leather, that you put on a horse so that you can ride it ☞ picture at **horse**. **2** a seat on a bicycle or motor cycle ☞ picture at **bicycle**.

saddle verb [I,T] to put a saddle on a horse, etc (PHRASAL VERB) **saddle sb with sth** to give sb a responsibility or task that he/she does not want: *I've been saddled with organizing the office party.*

sadism /'seɪdɪzəm/ noun [U] getting enjoyment or sexual pleasure from being cruel or causing pain

sadist /'seɪdɪst/ noun [C] a person who gets enjoyment or sexual pleasure from being cruel or causing pain

sadistic /sə'dɪstɪk/ adj showing or involving sadism — **sadistically** /-klɪ/ adv

safari /sə'fɑːrɪ/ noun [C,U] (pl **safaris**) a trip, especially in Africa, for hunting or looking at wild animals

☆ **safe¹** /seɪf/ adj **1 safe (from sb/sth)** free from danger; not able to be hurt: *You shouldn't walk home alone at night. You won't be safe.* ○ *Do you think my car will be safe in this street?* ○ *Keep the papers where they will be safe from fire.* **2** not causing danger, harm or risk: *Don't sit on that chair, it isn't safe.* ○ *I left my suitcase in a safe place and went for a cup of coffee.* ○ *Is this drug safe for children?* ○ *He hid from the police until it was safe to come out.* ○ *She's a very safe driver.* ○ *I thought it would be a safe investment but I lost everything.* ○ *Is it safe to drink the water here?* ○ *I think it's safe to say that the situation is unlikely to change for some time.* **3** not hurt or damaged: *After the accident he checked that all the passengers were safe.*

iː	ɪ	e	æ	ɑː	ɒ	ɔː	ʊ	uː	ʌ
see	sit	ten	hat	arm	got	saw	put	too	cup

safe   547   **sale**

(IDIOMS) **on the safe side** not taking risks; being very careful: *I think this is enough money to pay for the meal, but I'll take a bit more to be on the safe side.*

safe and sound not hurt or damaged: *The missing child was found safe and sound by the police.* —**safely** *adv*: *I rang my parents to tell them I had arrived safely.*

safe² /seɪf/ *noun* [C] a strong metal box or cupboard with a special lock that is used for keeping money, jewellery, documents, etc in

safeguard /'seɪfgɑːd/ *noun* [C] **a safeguard (against sb/sth)** something that protects against possible dangers: *Make a copy of all your computer disks as a safeguard against accidents.*

safeguard *verb* [T] **safeguard sb/sth (against sb/sth)** to keep sth safe; to protect: *When parents get divorced the children's rights must be safeguarded.*

☆ **safety** /'seɪfti/ *noun* [U] the state of being safe; not being dangerous or in danger: *In the interests of safety, smoking is forbidden.* ○ *road safety* (= the prevention of road accidents) ○ *She has been missing for several days and police now fear for her safety.* ○ *After Chernobyl people questioned the safety of nuclear energy.* ○ *New safety measures have been introduced on trains.*

'safety-belt *noun* [C] = SEAT-BELT

'safety net *noun* [C] **1** a net that is placed to catch sb who is performing high above the ground if he/she falls **2** something that will help you (usually with money) in a difficult situation

'safety pin *noun* [C] a metal pin that is used for fastening things together. The pin is bent round and the point goes under a cover so that it cannot be dangerous. ☛ picture at **pin**.

'safety-valve *noun* [C] a device in a machine that allows steam, gas, etc to escape if the pressure becomes too great

sag /sæg/ *verb* [I] (sa**gg**ing; sa**gg**ed) to hang loosely or to sink down, especially in the middle: *The skin on your face starts to sag as you get older.*

saga /'sɑːgə/ *noun* [C] a very long story; a long series of events

Sagittarius /ˌsædʒɪ'teəriəs/ *noun* [C,U] the ninth sign of the zodiac, the Archer; a person who was born under this sign ☛ picture at **zodiac**.

said *pt, pp* of SAY

sail¹ /seɪl/ *noun* **1** [C] a large piece of strong material that is fixed onto a ship or boat. The wind blows against the sail and drives the ship along. ☛ picture at **boat**. **2** [sing] a trip on water in a ship or boat with a sail: *Would you like to go for a sail in my boat?*
(IDIOM) **set sail** ⇨ SET²

'sailboard *noun* [C] = WINDSURFER

☆ **sail²** /seɪl/ *verb* **1** [I] to travel on water in a ship or boat of any type; to move on water: *On the cruise we sailed all along the coast of Norway.* ○ *I stood at the window and watched the ships sailing by.* **2** [I,T] to travel in and control a boat with sails, especially as a sport: *My father is teaching me to sail.* ○ *I've never sailed this kind of yacht before.* ☛ When you are talking about spending time sailing a boat, the form **go sailing** is very common: *We often go sailing at weekends.* **3** [I] to begin a journey on water: *When does the ship sail?* ○ *We sail for Santander at six o'clock tomorrow morning.* **4** [I] to move somewhere quickly in a smooth or proud way: *The ball sailed over the fence and into the neighbour's garden.* ○ *Mary sailed into the room and sat down at the head of the table.*

(IDIOM) **sail through (sth)** to get through a test or exam easily: *He was a clever boy and sailed through all his exams.*

sailing /'seɪlɪŋ/ *noun* **1** [U] the sport of being in, and controlling, small boats with sails: *They do a lot of sailing.* **2** [C] a journey made by a ship or boat carrying passengers from one place to another: *Could you tell me the times of sailings to Ostend?*

'sailing-boat *noun* [C] a boat that uses a sail or sails

☆ **sailor** /'seɪlə(r)/ *noun* [C] a member of the crew of a ship (usually not an officer): *soldiers, sailors and airmen*
(IDIOM) **a good/bad sailor** a person who is not often/often sick when travelling on a boat

☆ **saint** /seɪnt; snt/ *noun* [C] **1** a very good or holy person who is given special respect after death by the Christian church ☛ When it is used as a title *saint* is written with a capital letter: *Saint Patrick*. In the names of places, churches, etc the short form **St** is usually used: *St Andrew's Church*. Before names **saint** is pronounced /snt/. Look at **patron saint**. **2** a very good, kind person

☆ **sake** /seɪk/ *noun* [C]
(IDIOMS) **for Christ's, God's, goodness', Heaven's, etc sake** (used as part of a question or order, to make it stronger or to show that you are angry): *Why have you taken so long, for God's sake?* ○ *For Christ's sake, don't be so stupid!* ○ *For goodness' sake, hurry up!* ☛ **For Christ's sake** and **for God's sake** are stronger and may offend some people.

for the sake of sb/sth; for sb's/sth's sake in order to help sb/sth: *Don't go to any trouble for my sake.* ○ *They only stayed together for the sake of their children/for their children's sake.*

for the sake of sth/of doing sth in order to get or keep sth; for the purpose of sth: *It's not worth complaining for the sake of a few pence.* ○ *You're just arguing for the sake of arguing* (= because you like arguing).

☆ **salad** /'sæləd/ *noun* [C,U] a mixture of vegetables, usually uncooked, that you often eat together with other foods: *All main courses are served with chips or salad.* ○ *I had chicken salad* (= chicken with salad) *for lunch.* ○ *I don't feel like a heavy meal, I think I'll have a salad.* ☛ picture on next page.

☆ **salary** /'sæləri/ *noun* [C] (*pl* **salaries**) the money that a person receives (usually every month) for the work he/she has done: *My salary is paid directly into my bank account.* ○ *a high/low salary* ○ *an increase in salary of £500* ☛ Look at the note at **pay¹**.

☆ **sale** /seɪl/ *noun* **1** [C,U] the act of selling or being sold; the exchange of an item for money; the occasion when sth is sold: *The sale of al-*

ɜː	ə	eɪ	əʊ	aɪ	aʊ	ɔɪ	ɪə	eə	ʊə
fur	ago	pay	home	five	now	join	near	hair	pure

salad, lettuce, cucumber, tomato

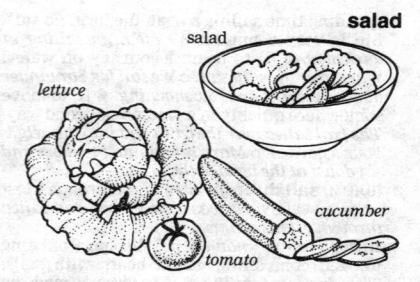

cohol to anyone under the age of 18 is forbidden. ○ *Business is bad. I haven't made a sale all week.* ○ *a sale of used toys* **2 sales** [plural] the amount sold: *Sales of personal computers have increased rapidly.* **3** [C] a time when shops sell things at prices that are lower than usual: *Sale! All this week! Everything at half price.* ○ *I got these trousers cheap in a sale.* ○ *I got several bargains in the sales* (= the period when many shops reduce their prices).

(IDIOMS) **for sale** offered for sb to buy: *This painting is not for sale.*

on sale 1 available for sb to buy, especially in shops: *This week's edition is on sale now at your local newsagents.* **2** (*US*) offered at a lower price than usual

'salesclerk (*also* **clerk**) *noun* [C] (*US*) = SHOP ASSISTANT

'sales department *noun* [C] the section of a company that is responsible for selling the products

'salesman /-mən/ **'saleswoman, 'salesperson** *noun* [C] a person whose job is selling things to people

saliva /sə'laɪvə/ *noun* [U] the liquid that is produced in the mouth

salmon /'sæmən/ *noun* [C,U] (*pl* **salmon**) a large fish with silver skin and pink flesh: *smoked salmon*

salmonella /ˌsælmə'nelə/ *noun* [U] a type of bacteria that causes food poisoning

salon /'sælɒn; *US* sə'lɒn/ *noun* [C] a shop where a hairdresser works or where you can have beauty treatment, etc: *a hairdressing salon* ○ *a beauty salon*

saloon /sə'lu:n/ *noun* [C] **1** (*US* **sedan**) a car with a fixed roof and a separate area (**boot**) for luggage **2** (*US old-fashioned*) a place where you can buy drinks; a bar

sa'loon bar *noun* [C] = LOUNGE BAR

☆ **salt** /sɔ:lt/ *noun* [U] a common white substance that is found in sea water and the earth, that is used especially for flavouring and preserving food: *Season with salt and pepper.* ○ *Pass the salt, please.* ○ *Add a pinch* (= a small amount) *of salt.*

(IDIOM) **take sth with a pinch of salt** ⇒ PINCH

salt *verb* [T] to put salt on or in sth: *salted peanuts*

salt *adj* having the taste of or containing salt: *salt water*

salty *adj* (**saltier**; **saltiest**) having the taste of, or containing, salt: *I didn't like the meat, it was too salty.*

'salt-water *adj* living in the sea: *a salt-water fish* ☛ Fish in rivers are **freshwater** fish.

salute /sə'lu:t/ *noun* [C] **1** a sign that a soldier, etc makes to show respect, by raising his/her hand to the forehead: *to give a salute* **2** an action that shows respect for sb: *The next programme is a salute to one of the world's greatest film stars.*

salute *verb* [I,T] to show respect with a salute(1,2): *The soldiers saluted as they marched past the general.* ○ *The soldiers saluted the general.* ○ *This is the day on which we salute those who died in the war.*

salvage /'sælvɪdʒ/ *noun* [U] the act of removing things from a damaged ship, building, etc; the things that are removed: *a salvage operation*

salvage *verb* [T] to rescue sth from a damaged building or ship; to rescue sth from a disaster: *They salvaged as much as they could from the house after the fire.* ○ (*figurative*) *The team has only 20 minutes left in which to salvage something from the game.*

salvation /sæl'veɪʃn/ *noun* **1** [U,sing] a thing or a person that saves sb/sth from danger or a difficult situation **2** [U] (in the Christian religion) the state of being saved from evil

☆ **same¹** /seɪm/ *adj* **1 the same ... (as sb/sth/that...)**, not different, not another or other; exactly the one or ones that you have mentioned before: *My brother and I had the same teacher at school.* ○ *She comes from the same town as me.* ○ *I'm going to wear the same clothes as I wore yesterday.* ○ *Are you the same person that I spoke to on the phone yesterday?* **2 the same ... (as sb/sth/that...)** exactly like the one already mentioned: *I wouldn't buy the same car again* (= the same model of car). ○ *You don't read the same newspaper as me, do you?* ○ *I had the same experience as you some time ago.* ○ *I've had the same experience that you've had.* ☛ We cannot say **a same ...** To express this idea we use **the same sort of**: *I'd like the same sort of job as my father.*

(IDIOMS) **at the same time 1** together; at one time: *I can't think about more than one thing at the same time.* **2** on the other hand; however: *It's a very good idea but at the same time it's rather risky.*

on the same wavelength able to understand sb because you have similar ideas and opinions

the same *adv* in the same way; not differently: *We treat all the children in the class the same.*

☆ **same²** /seɪm/ *pron* **the same (as sb/sth/...)** the same thing, person, situation, etc: *Is there another word that means the same as this?* ○ *Look at what I'm doing and then do the same.* ○ *Things will never be the same again now that my father has died.*

(IDIOMS) **all/just the same** nevertheless; in spite of this/that; anyway: *I understand what you're saying. All the same, I don't agree with*

p	b	t	d	k	g	tʃ	dʒ	f	v	θ	ð
pen	bad	tea	did	cat	got	chin	June	fall	van	thin	then

you. ○ *I don't need to borrow any money but thanks all the same for offering.*
much the same ⇨ MUCH²
(the) same again (a request to be served or given the same drink as before): *'What would you like to drink?' 'Same again, please.'*
same here (*informal*) the same thing is also true for me: *'I'm bored.' 'Same here.'*
(the) same to you (used as an answer when sb says sth rude to you or wishes you sth): *'You idiot!' 'Same to you!'* ○ *'Have a good weekend.' 'The same to you.'*

sample /ˈsɑːmpl; *US* ˈsæmpl/ *noun* [C] **1** a small quantity of sth that is typical of the rest of it: *She sent a sample of her work in an attempt to get a job.* ○ *a blood sample* **2** a small number of people who are asked questions in order to find out information about a larger group **3** a small amount of a product, that is given free to the public in order to show what it is like: *a free sample of a chocolate bar*

sample *verb* [T] to taste or use a small amount of sth (in order to find out what it is like or to decide whether you like it or not): *You are welcome to sample any of our wines before making a purchase.*

sanatorium /ˌsænəˈtɔːrɪəm/ *noun* [C] (*pl* **sanatoriums** or **sanatoria**) (*US* **sanitarium** /ˌsænəˈteərɪəm/) a type of hospital where patients who need a long period of treatment for an illness can stay

sanction /ˈsæŋkʃn/ *noun* **1** [U] official permission to do sth **2** [C] a punishment for breaking a rule or law: *Many people feel that the death penalty is the best sanction against murder.* **3** [C, usually pl] an action, especially the stopping of trade, that is taken by other countries against a country that has broken an international law: *The United Nations imposed economic sanctions on South Africa.* ○ *The sanctions on South Africa have been lifted.*

sanction *verb* [T] to give official permission for sth

sanctuary /ˈsæŋktʃʊərɪ; *US* -ʊerɪ/ *noun* (*pl* **sanctuaries**) **1** [C] a place where birds or animals are protected from hunters and other dangers: *a wildlife sanctuary* **2** [C,U] a place where sb can be safe from enemies, the police, etc

☆ **sand** /sænd/ *noun* **1** [U] a powder consisting of very small grains of rock, found in deserts and on beaches: *You need sand to make concrete.* ○ *It was so hot that I couldn't walk on the sand without shoes.* ○ *When we go on holiday all we want is sun, sea and sand.* **2 the sands** [plural] a large area of sand

sandy *adj* (**sandier**; **sandiest**) covered with sand or with a lot of sand in it: *miles of sandy beach* ○ *sandy soil*

'sandcastle *noun* [C] a pile of sand that looks like a castle, made by children playing on a beach

'sand-dune *noun* [C] = DUNE

'sandpaper *noun* [U] strong paper with sand on it that is used for rubbing surfaces in order to make them smoother

sandal /ˈsændl/ *noun* [C] a type of light, open shoe with straps that people wear when the weather is warm ☞ picture at **shoe**.

☆ **sandwich** /ˈsænwɪdʒ; *US* -wɪtʃ/ *noun* [C] two slices of bread with food between them: *a ham sandwich* ○ *It's going to be a long journey so let's take some sandwiches.* ○ *What's in that sandwich?*

sandwich *verb* [T] **sandwich sb/sth (between sb/sth)** to place sb/sth in a very narrow space between two other things or people: *I had a most uncomfortable flight, sandwiched between two very large people.*

sane /seɪn/ *adj* **1** (used about a person) mentally normal; not mad: *With a job like mine, it's incredible that I'm still sane!* **2** (used about a person or an idea, a decision, etc) sensible; showing good judgement: *I had to accept the offer. It was the only sane thing to do.*
☞ The opposite is **insane**. The noun is **sanity**.

sang *pt* of SING

sanitarium (*US*) = SANATORIUM

sanitary /ˈsænɪtrɪ; *US* -terɪ/ *adj* for or connected with the protection of health, eg how human waste is removed: *Sanitary conditions in the refugee camps were terrible.* ☞ Look at **insanitary**.

'sanitary towel *noun* [C] a thick pad that women use to soak up blood during their period(3)

sanitation /ˌsænɪˈteɪʃn/ *noun* [U] a system for protecting public health, especially by removing waste

sanity /ˈsænətɪ/ *noun* [U] **1** the state of being sane(1); the ability to think and behave in a normal way **2** the quality of being sane(2); sensible or normal thought or behaviour: *I tried to introduce some sanity into the discussion but nobody was willing to listen.* ☞ The opposite is **insanity**.

sank *pt* of SINK
Santa Claus /ˈsæntə klɔːz/ = FATHER CHRISTMAS

sap¹ /sæp/ *noun* [U] the liquid in a plant or tree
sap² /sæp/ *verb* [T] (**sapping**; **sapped**) to make sth weak or to destroy it

sapling /ˈsæplɪŋ/ *noun* [C] a young tree
sapphire /ˈsæfaɪə(r)/ *noun* [C,U] a bright blue precious stone

sarcasm /ˈsɑːkæzəm/ *noun* [U] the use of words or expressions to mean the opposite of what they actually say. People use sarcasm in order to criticize other people or to make them look silly: *'No, you didn't take long to get ready. Only two hours,' she said with heavy sarcasm.*
— **sarcastic** /sɑːˈkæstɪk/ *adj*: *a sarcastic sense of humour* ○ *a sarcastic comment* — **sarcastically** /-klɪ/ *adv*

sardine /sɑːˈdiːn/ *noun* [C] a type of very small fish: *a tin of sardines*

sari /ˈsɑːrɪ/ *noun* [C] a dress worn by Indian women that consists of a long piece of material that is wrapped around the body

sash /sæʃ/ *noun* [C] a long piece of material that is worn round the waist or over the shoulder, often as part of a uniform, etc

sat *pt*, *pp* of SIT
Satan /ˈseɪtn/ a name for the Devil
satchel /ˈsætʃəl/ *noun* [C] a bag, often carried

s	z	ʃ	ʒ	h	m	n	ŋ	l	r	j	w
so	zoo	she	vision	how	man	no	sing	leg	red	yes	wet

over the shoulder, used by schoolchildren for taking books to and from school

☆ **satellite** /'sætəlaɪt/ noun [C] **1** a natural object in space that goes round a bigger object, usually a planet **2** a man-made object that has been sent into space and that moves around a planet for a particular purpose: *satellite pictures of today's weather*

'satellite television (*also* **'satellite TV**) *noun* [U] television programmes that are broadcast by means of a satellite ☛ In order to receive satellite TV you need a satellite **dish**.

satin /'sætɪn; *US* 'sætn/ *noun* [U] a type of cloth that is smooth and shiny

satire /'sætaɪə(r)/ *noun* **1** [U] the use of humour to attack a person, an idea or behaviour that you think is bad or foolish **2** [C] **satire** (**on sb/sth**) a piece of writing or a play, film, etc that uses satire: *a satire on university life*

satirical /sə'tɪrɪkl/ *adj* using satire: *a satirical magazine* —**satirically** /-kli/ *adv*

☆ **satisfaction** /ˌsætɪs'fækʃn/ *noun* **1** [U] the feeling of pleasure that you have when you have done, got or achieved what you wanted: *Gwen stood back and looked at her work with a sense of satisfaction.* ○ *We finally made a decision that was to everyone's satisfaction* (= that everyone was pleased with). ☛ The opposite is **dissatisfaction**. **2** [C] something that gives you a feeling of pleasure: *It was a great satisfaction to me to know that I had done the job well.*

☆ **satisfactory** /ˌsætɪs'fæktəri/ *adj* **1** good enough (but not very good): *This piece of work is not satisfactory. Please do it again.* **2** giving satisfaction; suiting a particular purpose: *It will be much more satisfactory if we all travel together.* ☛ The opposite is **unsatisfactory**. —**satisfactorily** /-tərəli/ *adv*: *Work is progressing satisfactorily.*

☆ **satisfy** /'sætɪsfaɪ/ *verb* [T] (*pres part* **satisfying**; *3rd pers sing pres* **satisfies**; *pt, pp* **satisfied**) **1** to make sb pleased by doing or giving him/her what he/she wants: *No matter how hard I try, my piano teacher is never satisfied.* ○ *Nothing satisfies him – he's always complaining.* **2** to have or do what is necessary for sth: *She satisfied all the entrance requirements for university.* ○ *I had a quick look inside the parcel just to satisfy my curiosity.* **3 satisfy sb (that...)** to show or prove to sb that sth is true or has been done: *Once the police were satisfied that they were telling the truth, they were allowed to go.* ○ *She checked the room once again to satisfy herself that everything was ready.*

satisfied *adj* **satisfied (with sb/sth)** pleased because you have had or done what you wanted: *a satisfied smile* ○ *a satisfied customer* ○ *I hope you're satisfied with what you've done!* ☛ The opposite is **dissatisfied**.

satisfying *adj* pleasing, giving satisfaction: *It was a very satisfying feeling knowing that we'd finished the job on time.*

satsuma /sæt'suːmə/ *noun* [C] a type of small orange with a loose skin

saturate /'sætʃəreɪt/ *verb* [T] **1** to make sth very wet: *Her clothes were completely saturated.* **2** to fill sth completely: *The market is saturated with cheap imports.* —**saturation** /ˌsætʃə'reɪʃn/ *noun* [U]: *The market for cars has reached saturation point* (= there can be no more increases in sales).

☆ **Saturday** /'sætədi/ *noun* [C,U] (*abbr* **Sat**) the day of the week after Friday and before Sunday ☛ For examples of the use of the days of the week in sentences, look at **Monday**.

Saturn /'sætən/ *noun* [sing] the planet that is sixth in order from the sun and that has rings around it

☆ **sauce** /sɔːs/ *noun* [C,U] a thick liquid (that can be hot or cold) that you eat on or with other food: *The chicken was served in a delicious sauce.* ○ *tomato sauce* ○ *In Britain we often eat mint sauce with lamb.* ☛ **Gravy** is a type of thin sauce that is made from meat juices and eaten hot with meat.

saucepan /'sɔːspən; *US* -pæn/ *noun* [C] a round metal pot that is used for cooking things on top of a stove. A saucepan usually has a lid and one or more handles. ☛ picture at **pan**.

☆ **saucer** /'sɔːsə(r)/ *noun* [C] a small round plate that you put under a cup: *a cup and saucer*

sauna /'sɔːnə/ *noun* [C] **1** a type of bath where you sit in a room that is very hot and full of steam: *to have a sauna* **2** a room or building where there is a sauna: *The apartment block has a swimming-pool and sauna.*

saunter /'sɔːntə(r)/ *verb* [I] to walk without hurrying

☆ **sausage** /'sɒsɪdʒ; *US* 'sɔːs-/ *noun* [C,U] a mixture of chopped meat, spices, etc that is made into a long thin shape. Some sausage is eaten cold in slices, other types are cooked and then served whole: *garlic sausage* ○ *liver sausage* ○ *We had sausages and chips for lunch.*

ˌsausage 'roll *noun* [C] a piece of sausage meat that is covered in pastry

savage /'sævɪdʒ/ *adj* very cruel or fierce: *a savage attack by a big dog* ○ *The book has received some savage criticism.*

savage *verb* [T] to attack sb/sth fiercely —**savagely** *adv* —**savagery** /'sævɪdʒri/ *noun* [U]: *The savagery of the punishment disgusted them.*

☆ **save** /seɪv/ *verb* **1** [T] **save sb/sth (from sth/ from doing sth)** to make or keep sb/sth safe from changes, loss, death, etc: *to save sb's life* ○ *to save sb from drowning* ○ *a campaign to save the whale* ○ *We are trying to save the school from closure.* **2** [I,T] **save (sth) (up) (for sth)** to keep or not spend money, etc so that you can use it later: *Carol is saving up for a holiday in Greece.* ○ *We try and save £50 a month.* **3** [T] to keep sth for future use: *I'll be home late so please save me some dinner.* ○ *Save that box. It might come in useful.* ○ *If you get there first, please save me a seat.* **4** [T] to store information in a computer by giving it a special instruction: *Don't forget to save the file before you close it.* **5** [I,T] to prevent the spending or waste of time or money: *You can save on petrol by getting a smaller car.* ○ *This car will save you a lot on petrol.* **6** [T] to make sth unnecessary; to make it unnecessary for sb to use sth, spend sth, etc: *You could save yourself a lot of time and effort if you organized*

iː	ɪ	e	æ	ɑː	ɒ	ɔː	ʊ	uː	ʌ
see	sit	ten	hat	arm	got	saw	put	too	cup

your work better. ○ *Can you lend me your bike? It'll save me having to walk.* **7** [T] to stop a goal being scored in football, etc
(IDIOMS) **keep/save sth for a rainy day** ⇨ RAINY

save face to prevent yourself losing the respect of other people: *The remarks he made were an attempt to save face in a difficult situation.*

save *noun* [C] (in football, etc) an act of preventing a goal from being scored: *The goalkeeper made a great save.*

saver *noun* [C] a person who saves money for future use: *The rise in interest rates is good news for savers.*

☆ **saving** /'seɪvɪŋ/ *noun* **1** [C] an amount of time, money, etc that you do not have to use or spend: *The sale price represents a saving of 25%.* **2 savings** [plural] money that you have saved for future use: *All our savings are in the building society.*

saviour (*US* **savior**) /'seɪvɪə(r)/ *noun* [C] a person who rescues or saves sb/sth from danger, loss, death, etc ☛ In Christianity Jesus Christ is the **Saviour**.

savoury (*US* **savory**) /'seɪvəri/ *adj* (used about food) having a salty or spicy taste; not sweet

saw¹ *pt* of SEE

saw² /sɔː/ *noun* [C] a tool that is used for cutting wood, etc. A saw has a long metal blade with sharp teeth on it: *an electric chainsaw* ☛ picture at **tool**.

saw *verb* [I,T] (*pt* **sawed**; *pp* **sawn** /sɔːn/) to cut sth with a saw: *to saw through the trunk of a tree* ○ *Paula sawed the branch off the tree.* ○ *He sawed the log up into small pieces.* ☛ The US past participle is **sawed**.

'sawdust *noun* [U] very small pieces of wood that fall like powder when you are sawing

sax /sæks/ *noun* [C] (*informal*) = SAXOPHONE

saxophone /'sæksəfəʊn/ (also *informal* **sax**) *noun* [C] a metal musical instrument that you play by blowing into it. Saxophones are usually used for playing jazz.

☆ **say¹** /seɪ/ *verb* (3rd pers sing pres **says** /sez/; *pt, pp* **said** /sed/) **1** [T] **say sth (to sb)** to speak words: '*Please come back,*' *she said.* ○ *The teacher said we should hand in our essays on Friday.* ○ *to say goodbye* ○ *to say your prayers* ○ *He said to his mother that he would phone back later.* ○ *They just sat there without saying anything.* ○ '*This isn't going to be easy,' she said to herself* (= she thought). ☛ **Say** or **tell**? **Say** is often used with the actual words that were spoken or before **that** in indirect speech: '*I'll catch the 9 o'clock train,' he said.* ○ *He said that he would catch the 9 o'clock train.* Notice that you say sth **to** sb: *He said to me that he would catch the 9 o'clock train.* **Tell** is always followed by a noun or pronoun, showing who you were speaking to: *He told me that he would catch the 9 o'clock train.* **Tell**, not **say**, can also be used when you are talking about giving orders or advice: *I told them to hurry up.* ○ *She's always telling me what I ought to do.* **2** [T] (used about a book, notice, etc) to give information: *What time does it say on that clock?* ○ *The map says the hotel is just past the railway bridge.* **3** [I,T] to express a thought, feeling, answer, opinion, etc: '*What time is she coming?' 'I don't know – she didn't say.'* ○ *I should like to say how happy I am to be here today.* ○ *He is said to be very rich* (= people say that he is very rich). ○ *What is the artist trying to say in this painting?* ○ *His angry look said everything about the way he felt.* ○ *Well, what do you say? Do you think it's a good idea?* **4** [T] to suppose sth: *We will need, say, £5 000 for a new car.* ○ *Say you don't get a place at university, what will you do then?*
(IDIOMS) **go without saying** to be clear, so that you do not need to say it: *It goes without saying that the children will be well looked after at all times.*

that is to say... which means...: *We're leaving on Friday, that's to say in a week's time.*

say² /seɪ/ *noun* (sing,U) **say (in sth)** the power or right to decide sth: *I'd like to have some say in the arrangements for the party.*
(IDIOM) **have your say** to express your opinion: *Thank you for your comments. Now let somebody else have their say.*

saying /'seɪɪŋ/ *noun* [C] a well-known phrase that gives advice about sth: '*A stitch in time saves nine' is an old saying.* ☛ Look at **proverb**.

scab /skæb/ *noun* [C,U] a mass of dried blood that forms over a part of the body where the skin has been cut or broken ☛ Look at **scar**.

scaffold /'skæfəʊld/ *noun* [C] a platform on which criminals were killed, eg by hanging

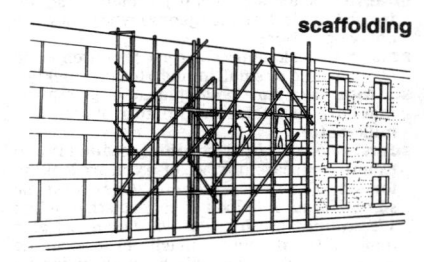

scaffolding /'skæfəʊldɪŋ/ *noun* [U] long metal poles and wooden boards that form a structure which is put next to a building so that builders, painters, etc can stand and work on it

scald /skɔːld/ *verb* [T] to burn sb/sth with very hot liquid

scald *noun* [C] a burn that was caused by very hot liquid — **scalding** *adj*: *scalding hot water*

☆ **scale¹** /skeɪl/ *noun* **1** [C] a series of marks on a tool or piece of equipment that you use for measuring sth: *The ruler has one scale in centimetres and one scale in inches.* **2** [C] a series of numbers amounts, etc that are used for measuring or fixing the level of sth: *The earthquake measured 6.5 on the Richter scale.* o *the new pay scale for nurses* **3** [C] the relationship between the actual size of sth and its size on a map or plan: *The map has a scale of one centimetre to the kilometre.* o *a scale of 1: 50 000* o *We need a map with a larger scale.* o *a scale model* o *The plan of the building is not drawn to scale* (= the parts of the drawing do not have the same relationship to each other as the parts of the actual building do). **4** [C,U] the size or extent of sth when compared to other things: *We shall be making the product on a large scale next year.* o *I think we have only just realized the scale of the problem* (= how serious it is). **5** [C] a series of musical notes which go up or down in a fixed order. People play or sing scales to practise their musical technique: *the scale of C major*

scale² /skeɪl/ *noun* [C] one of the small flat pieces of hard material that cover the body of some fish and animals: *the scales of a snake*

scale³ /skeɪl/ *verb* [T] to climb up a high wall, steep cliff, etc

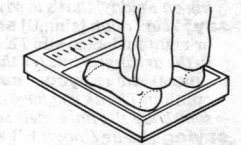

kitchen scales   bathroom scales

scales /skeɪlz/ *noun* [plural] a piece of equipment that is used for weighing sb/sth: *I weighed it on the kitchen scales.*

scalp /skælp/ *noun* [C] the skin on the top of your head that is under your hair

scalpel /'skælpəl/ *noun* [C] a small knife that is used by doctors (**surgeons**) when they are doing operations

scamper /'skæmpə(r)/ *verb* [I] (often used about a child or small animal) to run quickly

scampi /'skæmpi/ *noun* [plural] large prawns that have been fried in a mixture of flour and milk (**batter**)

scan /skæn/ *verb* [T] (sca**nn**ing; sca**nn**ed) **1** to examine sth carefully because you are looking for sth: *The sailors scanned the horizon for signs of land.* **2** to look at or read sth quickly: *Vic scanned the list until he found his own name.* **3** (used about a machine) to examine what is inside a person's body or inside an object such as a suitcase: *Machines scan all the luggage for bombs and guns.*

scan *noun* [C] an act of scanning: *The scan showed the baby was in the normal position.*

scanner *noun* [C] a machine that scans(3)

scandal /'skændl/ *noun* **1** [C,U] an action or a situation or behaviour that shocks people; the public feeling that is caused by such behaviour: *There has been another major financial scandal involving a bank in London.* o *There was no suggestion of scandal in his private life.* o *The poor state of school buildings is a real scandal.* **2** [U] talk about sth bad or wrong that sb has or may have done: *to spread scandal about sb*

scandalize (*also* **scandalise**) /'skændəlaɪz/ *verb* [T] to cause sb to feel shocked by doing sth that he/she thinks is bad or wrong

scandalous /'skændələs/ *adj* very shocking or wrong: *It is scandalous that so much money is wasted.*

Scandinavia /ˌskændɪ'neɪviə/ *noun* [U] the group of countries in northern Europe that consists of Denmark, Norway and Sweden. Sometimes Finland and Iceland are also said to be part of Scandinavia. —**Scandinavian** *adj*

scant /skænt/ *adj* (only *before* a noun) not very much; not as much as necessary: *They paid scant attention to my advice.*

scanty /'skænti/ *adj* (**scantier**; **scantiest**) too small in size or quality: *We didn't learn much from the scanty information they gave us.* —**scantily** *adv*: *She was scantily dressed in a short night-gown.*

scapegoat /'skeɪpɡəʊt/ *noun* [C] a person who is blamed for sth that sb else has done

scar /skɑː(r)/ *noun* [C] a mark on the skin that is caused by a cut or wound that has now healed: *The operation didn't leave a very big scar.* o (*figurative*) *The city centre still bears the scars of the recent fighting.* ☛ Look at **scab**.

scar *verb* [I,T] (sca**rr**ing; sca**rr**ed) to leave a scar on sb/sth: *William's face was scarred for life in the accident.*

☆ **scarce** /skeəs/ *adj* not existing in large quantities; hard to find: *Food for birds and animals is scarce in the winter.* ☛ The opposite is **plentiful**. —**scarcity** /'skeəsəti/ *noun* [C,U] (*pl* **scarcities**): *There will be food scarcities in most regions.* o *The scarcity of building land has forced the price up.*

scarcely /'skeəsli/ *adv* **1** only just; almost not: *Scarcely had I sat down, when the phone rang.* o *There was scarcely a car in sight.* o *She's not a friend of mine. I scarcely know her.* ☛ Look at **hardly**. **2** surely not: *You can scarcely expect me to believe that after all you said before.*

☆ **scare** /skeə(r)/ *verb* [T] to make a person or an animal frightened: *The sudden noise scared us all.*

(PHRASAL VERB) **scare sb/sth away/off** to make a person or animal leave or stay away by frightening them: *Don't make any noise or you'll scare the birds away.*

scare *noun* [C] **1** a feeling of being frightened: *It wasn't a serious heart attack but it gave him a scare.* **2** a situation where many people are afraid or worried about sth: *Last night there was a bomb scare at Victoria Station.*

scared /skeəd/ **scared (of sb/sth); scared (of doing sth/to do sth)** frightened: *Are you scared of the dark?* o *She's scared of walking home alone.* o *Everyone was too scared to move.*

scary /'skeəri/ *adj* (**scarier**; **scariest**) (*informal*) rather frightening: *a scary ghost story* o *It was a bit scary driving in the mountains at night.*

'scarecrow *noun* [C] a model of a person that is dressed in old clothes and put in a field to frighten away the birds

scarf /skɑ:f/ noun [C] (pl **scarfs** /skɑ:fs/ or **scarves** /skɑ:vz/) **1** a long thin piece of cloth, usually made of wool, that you wear around your neck to keep warm: *He wrapped a scarf around his neck and set off.* ☞ picture on page A11. **2** a square piece of cloth that (usually) women wear around their neck or shoulders or over their heads to keep warm or for decoration: *She tied a scarf around her neck and set off.*

scarlet /'skɑ:lət/ adj, noun [U] (of) a bright red colour ☞ Look at **crimson** and **maroon**.

scathing /'skeɪðɪŋ/ adj expressing a very strong negative opinion about sb/sth; very critical: *a scathing attack on the new leader* ○ *scathing criticism*

scatter /'skætə(r)/ verb **1** [I] (used about a group of people or animals) to move away quickly in different directions: *The deer scattered when they heard us approaching.* **2** [T] to drop or throw things in different directions over a wide area: *The wind scattered the papers all over the room.*

scattered adj spread over a large area or at intervals: *There will be sunny intervals with scattered showers today.*

scavenge /'skævɪndʒ/ verb [I,T] to look for food, etc among waste and rubbish

scavenger noun [C] a person or animal that scavenges

scenario /sɪ'nɑ:rɪəʊ; *US* -'nær-/ noun [C] (pl **scenarios**) **1** a description of what happens in a play or film **2** one way that things may happen in the future: *The doctor described a scenario in which the disease spread rapidly across the whole country.*

☆ **scene** /si:n/ noun **1** [C] the place where sth happened: *the scene of a crime, accident, etc* **2** [C] an occasion when sb expresses great anger or another strong emotion in public: *There was quite a scene when she refused to pay the bill.* ○ *There were emotional scenes at the dock side as the boat pulled away.* **3** [C] one part of a book, play, film, etc in which the events happen in one place: *The first scene of 'Hamlet' takes place on the castle walls.* **4** [C,U] what you see around you in a particular place: *Constable painted many scenes of rural life.* ○ *Her new job was no better, but at least it would be a change of scene.* **5 the scene** [sing] the way of life or present situation in a particular area of activity: *The political scene in Eastern Europe is very confused.* ○ *the fashion scene*

☆ **scenery** /'si:nərɪ/ noun [U] **1** the natural features that you see around you in the country: *The scenery is superb in the mountains.* **2** the furniture, painted cloth, boards, etc that is used on the stage in a theatre: *The scenery is changed during the interval.* ☞ We say that an area of the country has beautiful **scenery** when it is attractive to look at. The **landscape** of a particular area is the way the natural features of it are arranged: *Trees and hedges are a typical feature of the British landscape.* You have a **view** of something when you look out of a window or down from a tower: *There was a marvellous view of the sea from our hotel room.*

scenic /'si:nɪk/ adj having beautiful scenery: *a scenic route through the country lanes*

scent /sent/ noun **1** [C,U] a pleasant smell: *This flower has no scent.* **2** [U] (*especially Brit*) = PERFUME(2): *a bottle of scent* **3** [C,U] the smell that an animal leaves behind and that some other animals may follow —**scented** adj

sceptic (*US* **skeptic**) /'skeptɪk/ noun [C] a person who doubts that sth is true, right, etc

sceptical (*US* **skeptical**) /-kl/ adj **sceptical (of/about sth)** doubting that sth is true, right, etc: *Many doctors are sceptical about the value of alternative medicine.*

scepticism (*US* **skepticism**) /'skeptɪsɪzəm/ noun [U] a general feeling of doubt about sth; a feeling that you are unwilling to believe sth: *They listened with scepticism to the President's promises of reform.*

schedule /'ʃedju:l; *US* 'skedʒʊl/ noun **1** [C,U] a plan of things that will happen or of work that must be done: *Max has a busy schedule for the next few days.* ○ *to be ahead of/behind schedule* (= to have done more/less than was planned) ○ *to be on schedule* (= to have done the amount that was planned) **2** (*US*) = TIMETABLE

schedule verb [T] **schedule sth (for sth)** to arrange for sth to happen or be done at a particular time: *We've scheduled the meeting for Monday morning.* ○ *The train was scheduled to arrive at 10.07.* ○ *Is it a scheduled flight?* (= on the regular timetable)

☆ **scheme** /ski:m/ noun [C] **1** an official plan or system for doing or organizing sth: *a new scheme to provide houses in the area* ○ *Are you paying into a private pension scheme?* **2** a clever plan to do sth: *He's thought of a new scheme for making money fast.* ☞ Look at **colour scheme**.

scheme verb [I,T] to make a secret or dishonest plan

schizophrenia /ˌskɪtsəʊ'fri:nɪə/ noun [U] a serious mental illness in which a person confuses the real world and the world of the imagination and often behaves in strange and unexpected ways

schizophrenic /ˌskɪtsəʊ'frenɪk/ adj, noun [C] (of) a person who is suffering from schizophrenia

scholar /'skɒlə(r)/ noun [C] **1** a person who studies and has a deep knowledge of a particular subject: *a leading Shakespeare scholar* **2** a person who has passed an exam or won a competition and has been given some money (**a scholarship**) to help pay for his/her studies: *a British Council scholar* ☞ Look at **student**.

scholarship /'skɒləʃɪp/ noun **1** [C] an amount of money that is given to a person who has passed an exam or won a competition, in order to help pay for his/her studies: *to win a scholarship to Yale* **2** [U] serious study; the work of scholars

☆ **school** /sku:l/ noun **1** [C] the place where children go to be educated: *Paul goes to the local school.* ○ *They're building a new school in our area.* ○ *Do you have to wear school uniform?* ○ *We go on the school bus.* ○ *Every school has several computers.* **2** [U] the time you spend at a

s	z	ʃ	ʒ	h	m	n	ŋ	l	r	j	w
so	zoo	she	vision	how	man	no	sing	leg	red	yes	wet

school; the process of being educated in a school: *Children start school at 5 in Britain and can leave school at 16.* ○ *School starts at 9 o'clock and finishes at about 3.30.* ○ *After school we usually have homework to do.* ○ *Because of the snow there will be no school today.* ☛ You talk about **school** (no 'the') when you are talking about going there for the usual reason (that is, as a pupil or teacher): *Where do your children go to school?* ○ *I enjoyed being at school.* ○ *Do you walk to school?* You talk about **the school** if you are talking about going there for a different reason (for example, as a parent): *I have to go to the school on Thursday to talk to John's teacher.* You must also use **a** or **the** when more information about the school is given: *Pat goes to the local school.* ○ *She teaches at a school in Leeds.* **3** [sing, with sing or pl verb] all the pupils and teachers in a school: *The whole school cheered the winner.* **4** [C] a place where you go to learn a particular subject: *a driving school* ○ *a language school* **5** [C] *(US)* a college or university **6** [C] a department of a university that teaches a particular subject: *the school of geography at Leeds University* **7** [C] a group of writers, painters, etc who have the same ideas or style: *the Flemish school of painting*
(IDIOM) **a school of thought** the ideas or opinions that one group of people share: *There are various schools of thought on this matter.*

schooling *noun* [U] the time that you spend at school; your education: *Irene's schooling was interrupted because she was ill so often.*

'school age *noun* [U] the age when a child must go to school, eg in Britain, between 5 and 16

'schoolboy, 'schoolgirl, 'schoolchild *noun* [C] a boy/girl/child who goes to school

'school-days *noun* [plural] the period of your life when you go to school

,school-'leaver *noun* [C] a person who has just left school

'schoolmaster (*feminine* **'schoolmistress**) *noun* [C] a teacher, especially one at a private school

'schoolteacher *noun* [C] a person who teaches in a school

☆ **science** /'saɪəns/ *noun* **1** [U] the study of and knowledge about the physical world and natural laws: *science and technology* ○ *Modern science has discovered a lot about the origin of life.* ○ *Fewer young people are studying science at university.* ○ *a science teacher* (= one who teaches biology, chemistry or physics) **2** [C,U] one of the subjects into which science can be divided: *Biology, chemistry and physics are all sciences.* ○ *Is mathematics a science?* ☛ The study of people and society is called **social science**.

scientist /'saɪəntɪst/ *noun* [C] a person who studies or teaches science, especially biology, chemistry or physics

,science 'fiction *noun* [U] books, films, etc about events that take place in the future, especially connected with travel in space

☆ **scientific** /,saɪən'tɪfɪk/ *adj* **1** connected with science: *We need more funding for scientific research.* **2** using the methods that are used in science(1) (= observing facts and testing ideas with experiments): *a scientific study of the way people use language* —**scientifically** /-klɪ/ *adv*: *It will be hard to prove the idea scientifically* (= using the methods of science).

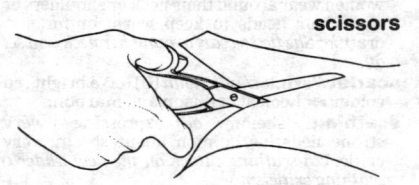

scissors

☆ **scissors** /'sɪzəz/ *noun* [plural] a tool for cutting things that consists of two flat sharp blades that are joined together ☛ **Scissors** is a plural noun: *These scissors are blunt.* We CANNOT say 'a scissors': we must use the word **pair**: *I need a new pair of scissors.*

scoff /skɒf; *US* skɔːf/ *verb* [I] **scoff (at sb/sth)** to speak about sb/sth without respect

scold /skəʊld/ *verb* [I,T] **scold sb (for sth/for doing sth)** to speak angrily to sb because he/she has done something bad or wrong: *The teacher scolded her for being late.* ☛ **Tell off** is more common.

scone /skɒn; skəʊn/ *noun* [C] a small plain cake made from fat and flour. You often put butter and jam on scones.

scoop /skuːp/ *noun* [C] **1** a tool like a spoon used for picking up ice-cream, flour, grain, etc **2** the amount that one scoop contains: *apple pie served with a scoop of ice-cream* **3** an exciting piece of news that is reported by one newspaper, TV or radio station before it is reported anywhere else

scoop *verb* [T] **scoop sth (out/up)** to make a hole in sth or to take sth out by using a scoop(1) or sth similar: *Scoop out the middle of the pineapple.*

scooter /'skuːtə(r)/ *noun* [C] **1** a light motor cycle with a small engine ☛ picture at **motor bike. 2** a child's toy with two wheels that you stand on and move by pushing one foot against the ground

scope /skəʊp/ *noun* **1** [U] **scope (for sth/to do sth)** the chance or opportunity to do sth: *The job offers plenty of scope for creativity.* **2** [sing] the range of subjects that are being discussed or considered: *The government was unwilling to extend the scope of the inquiry.* ○ *It is not within the scope of this book to discuss these matters in detail.*

scorch /skɔːtʃ/ *verb* [T] to burn sth slightly so that its colour changes but it is not destroyed: *I scorched my blouse when I was ironing it.* ○ *the scorched landscape of the Arizona desert*

scorching *adj* very hot: *It was absolutely scorching on Tuesday.*

☆ **score¹** /skɔː(r)/ *noun* **1** [C] the number of points, goals, etc that sb/sth gets in a game, competition, examination, etc: *What was the final score?* ○ *The score is 3-2 to Oxford.* ○ *Graf won the match with a score of 6-4, 6-1.* ○ *The top*

score in the test was 80%. **2 scores** [plural] very many: *Scores of people have written to offer their support.* **3** [C] the written form of a piece of music
(IDIOM) **on that score** about that: *Len will be well looked after. Don't worry on that score.*

'scoreboard *noun* [C] a large board that shows the score during a game, competition, etc

☆ **score²** /skɔː(r)/ *verb* [I,T] to get points, goals, etc in a game, competition, examination, etc: *The team still hadn't scored by half-time.* ○ *Louise scored the highest marks in the exam.* ○ *Senna scored an easy victory in the new Honda.* ○ *England scored three goals against France.*

scorn /skɔːn/ *noun* [U] **scorn (for sb/sth)** the strong feeling that you have when you do not respect sb/sth: *She looked at him with scorn and contempt.*

scorn *verb* [T] **1** to feel or show scorn for sb/sth: *The President scorned his critics.* **2** to refuse to accept help or advice, especially because you are too proud: *The old lady scorned all offers of help.*

scornful /-fl/ *adj* feeling or showing scorn: *a scornful look, smile, etc* —**scornfully** /-fəlɪ/ *adv*

Scorpio /'skɔːpɪəʊ/ *noun* [C,U] (*pl* **Scorpios**) the eighth sign of the zodiac, the Scorpion; a person who was born under this sign ☞ picture at **zodiac**.

scorpion /'skɔːpɪən/ *noun* [C] a creature which looks like a large insect and lives in warm climates. A scorpion has a long tail with a poisonous sting in it.

☆ **Scot** /skɒt/ *noun* [C] a person who comes from Scotland

Scotch /skɒtʃ/ *noun* **1** [U] a strong alcoholic drink (**whisky**) that is made in Scotland **2** [C] a glass of Scotch: *Two Scotches, please.* ☞ Look at the note at **Scottish**.

☆ **Scots** /skɒts/ *adj* of or connected with people from Scotland ☞ Look at the note at **Scottish**.

'Scotsman /-mən/ **Scotswoman** /-wʊmən/ *noun* [C] a man or woman who comes from Scotland

☆ **Scottish** /'skɒtɪʃ/ *adj* of or connected with Scotland, its people, culture, etc ☞ Scots is usually only used about the people of Scotland: *a Scots piper.* Scottish is used about Scotland and about both people and things that come from Scotland: *Scottish law, dancing, lochs, etc.* ○ *She speaks with a strong Scottish accent.* ○ *the Scottish Highlands.* Scotch is used for whisky and some kinds of food. You should not use it for Scottish people.

scoundrel /'skaʊndrəl/ *noun* [C] (*old-fashioned*) a man who behaves very badly towards other people, especially by being dishonest

scour¹ /'skaʊə(r)/ *verb* [T] to clean sth by rubbing it hard with sth rough: *to scour dirty pots and pans*

scour² /'skaʊə(r)/ *verb* [T] to search a place very carefully because you are looking for sb/sth: *Helen scoured the shops for a suitable dress.*

scourge /skɜːdʒ/ *noun* [C] a person or thing that causes a lot of trouble or suffering: *the scourge of unemployment*

scout /skaʊt/ *noun* [C] **1** a soldier who is sent on in front of the rest of the group to find out where the enemy is or which is the best route to take **2 Scout** (*also* **Boy 'Scout**) a member of an organization that teaches boys how to look after themselves and encourages them to help others. Scouts do sport, learn useful skills, go camping, etc. ☞ Look at **Girl Guide**.

scowl /skaʊl/ *noun* [C] a look on your face that shows you are angry or in a bad mood ☞ Look at **frown**. —**scowl** *verb* [I]

scrabble /'skræbl/ *verb* [I] to move your fingers around, trying to find sth or get hold of sth: *She scrabbled about in her purse for some coins.*

scramble /'skræmbl/ *verb* [I] **1** to climb quickly up or over sth using your hands to help you: *to scramble up a steep hill, over a wall, etc* **2** to move or do something quickly because you are in a hurry: *She scrambled into some clean clothes.* **3 scramble (for sth)** to struggle to get sth which a lot of people want: *Everyone was scrambling to get the best bargains.*

scramble *noun* [sing] an act of scrambling: *There was a real scramble as everyone rushed for the best seats.*

scrambled 'egg *noun* [U] eggs that are mixed together with milk and then cooked in a pan

scrap¹ /skræp/ *noun* **1** [C] a small piece or amount of sth: *a scrap of paper* ○ *scraps of food* ○ (*figurative*) *There is not a scrap of truth in what she told me.* **2** [U] something that you do not want any more but that is made of material that can be used again: *The old car was sold for scrap* (= so the metal could be used again). ○ *scrap paper*

scrap *verb* [T] (**scrapping**; **scrapped**) to get rid of sth that you do not want any more: *the government's decision to scrap nuclear weapons* ○ *I think we should scrap that idea.*

scrappy *adj* (**scrappier; scrappiest**) not neat or well-organized: *a scrappy letter*

'scrapbook *noun* [C] a large book with blank pages that you can stick pictures, newspaper articles, etc in

'scrap heap *noun* [C] a large pile of rubbish
(IDIOM) **on the scrap heap** not wanted any more: *Many of the unemployed feel that they are on the scrap heap.*

scrap² /skræp/ *noun* [C] (*informal*) a fight or quarrel which is not very serious

scrape¹ /skreɪp/ *verb* **1** [T] **scrape sth (down/out/off)** to make sth clean or smooth by moving a sharp edge across it firmly: *to scrape a pan clean* **2** [T] to remove sth by moving a sharp edge across a surface: *Scrape all the mud off your boots before you come in.* **3** [T] **scrape sth (against/along/on sth)** to damage or hurt sth by rubbing it against sth rough or hard: *Mark fell and scraped his knee.* ○ *Jenny scraped the car against the gatepost.* **4** [I,T] **scrape (sth) against/along/on sth** rub (sth) against sth and make a sharp unpleasant noise: *The branches scraped against the window.*

(PHRASAL VERBS) **scrape through sth** to succeed with difficulty in doing sth: *to scrape through an exam* (= just manage to pass it)

ɜː	ə	eɪ	əʊ	aɪ	aʊ	ɔɪ	ɪə	eə	ʊə
fur	ago	pay	home	five	now	join	near	hair	pure

scrape sth together/up to get or collect sth together with difficulty: *We just managed to scrape enough money together for a week's holiday.*

scrape² /skreɪp/ *noun* [C] **1** an act of scraping or the sound of sth scraping on/against sth: *the scrape of a spoon on a metal pan* **2** (*informal*) a difficult situation that was caused by your own foolish behaviour: *The children are always getting into scrapes.*

scrappy ⇨ SCRAP¹

☆ **scratch¹** /skrætʃ/ *verb* **1** [I,T] to make a mark on a surface or a small wound on a person's skin with sth sharp: *The cat will scratch if you annoy it.* ○ *I've scratched myself quite badly on the rose bush.* ○ *The table was badly scratched.* **2** [T] to put sth somewhere or to take it away by scratching: *He scratched his name on the top of his desk.* ○ *I tried to scratch the paint off the table.* **3** [I,T] to rub a part of the body, often to stop it itching: *I put some lotion on his skin to try and stop him scratching.* ○ *Could you scratch my back for me?* ○ *She sat and thought about the problem, scratching her head occasionally.*

scratch² /skrætʃ/ *noun* **1** [C] a cut, mark or sound that was made by sb/sth scratching sb/sth else: *There's a scratch on the car door.* ○ *They survived the accident without even a scratch.* **2** [sing] an act of scratching(3): *The dog had a good scratch.*

(IDIOMS) **from scratch** from the very beginning: *I'm learning Spanish from scratch.*

(be/come) up to scratch (*informal*) to be/ become good enough: *Karen's singing isn't really up to scratch.*

scrawl /skrɔːl/ *verb* [I,T] to write in an untidy and careless way —**scrawl** *noun* [sing]: *Her signature was just a scrawl.* ☞ Look at **scribble**.

☆ **scream** /skriːm/ *verb* [I,T] **scream (sth) (out) (at sb)** to cry out loudly in a high voice because you are afraid, excited, angry, in pain, etc: *She saw a rat hiding in the corner of the room and screamed.* ○ *'Don't touch that,' he screamed.* ○ *She screamed at the children to stop.* ○ *The horse screamed with pain.* ○ *He clung to the edge of the cliff, screaming for help.* ☞ Look at **shout**.

scream *noun* **1** [C] a loud cry in a high voice: *a scream of pain* **2** [sing] (*informal*) a person or thing that is very funny: *She's a real scream.*

screech /skriːtʃ/ *verb* [I,T] to make an unpleasant loud high sound: *The car's brakes screeched as it came to a halt.* ○ *'Get out of here,' she screeched at him.* ☞ Look at **shriek**.

screech *noun* [sing] an unpleasant high sound: *the screech of brakes*

☆ **screen** /skriːn/ *noun* **1** [C] a flat vertical surface that is used for dividing a room or keeping sb/sth out of sight: *There was only a screen between the two desks.* ○ *The house was hidden by a screen of tall trees.* **2** [C] the blank surface on which films are shown **3** [C] the glass surface of a television or computer where the picture or information appears ☞ picture on page A13. **4 the screen** [sing] cinema films: *a star of stage and screen* (= a famous actor who appears in both plays and films)

screen *verb* [T] **1 screen sb/sth (off) (from sb/sth)** to hide or protect sb/sth from sb/sth: *The bed was screened off while the doctor examined him.* ○ *to screen your eyes from the sun* **2 screen sb (for sth)** to examine or test sb to find out if he/she has a particular disease or if he/she is suitable for a particular job: *All women over 50 should be screened for breast cancer.* ○ *The Ministry of Defence screens all job applicants.* **3** to show sth on TV or in a cinema: *The programme was too violent to be screened before 9 o'clock.*

screw /skruː/ *noun* [C] a small piece of metal with a sharp end and a round head used for fixing two things, eg pieces of wood, together. A screw is like a nail but you fix it into sth by turning it round with a special tool (**a screwdriver**). ☞ picture at **tool**.

screw *verb* **1** [T] to fasten sth with a screw or screws: *The bookcase is screwed to the wall.* **2** [I,T] to fasten sth, or to be fastened, by turning: *The legs screw into holes in the underside of the seat.* ○ *Make sure that you screw the top of the jar on tightly.*

(PHRASAL VERB) **screw sth up 1** to make paper, cloth, etc into a tight ball: *Joanne screwed up the letter and threw it in the bin.* **2** to change the expression on your face by nearly closing your eyes, in pain or because the light is strong **3** (*slang*) to ruin sth or cause sth to fail: *You'd better not screw up this deal.*

'screwdriver *noun* [C] a tool that you use for turning screws ☞ picture at **tool**.

scribble /'skrɪbl/ *verb* [I,T] **1** to write sth quickly and carelessly: *to scribble a note down on a pad* ☞ Look at **scrawl**. **2** to make marks with a pen or pencil that are not letters or pictures: *The children had scribbled all over the walls.*

scribble *noun* [C,U] something that has been scribbled

script /skrɪpt/ *noun* **1** [C] the written form of a play, film, speech, etc **2** [C,U] a system of writing: *Arabic, Cyrillic, Roman, etc script*

scripture /'skrɪptʃə(r)/ *noun* [U] (*also* **the scriptures** [plural]) the holy books of religion, such as the Bible

scroll /skrəʊl/ *noun* [C] a long roll of paper with writing on it

scroll *verb* [I,T] to move text up or down on a computer screen until you find the part you want

scrounge /'skraʊndʒ/ *verb* [I,T] **scrounge (sth) (from/off sb)** (*informal*) to get sth by asking another person to give it to you instead of making an effort to get it for yourself: *Lucy is always scrounging money off her friends.*

scrub¹ /skrʌb/ *noun* [U] small trees and bushes that grow in an area that has poor soil or low rainfall

scrub² /skrʌb/ *verb* (**scrubbing**; **scrubbed**) [I,T] **scrub (sth) (down/out)** to clean sth with soap and water by rubbing it hard, often with a brush: *to scrub down the floor/walls*

(PHRASAL VERB) **scrub sth off** to remove sth by scrubbing: *to scrub the dirt off the walls*

scrub *noun* [sing] an act of scrubbing: *This floor needs a good scrub.*

scruff /skrʌf/ *noun*

(IDIOM) **by the scruff of the/your neck** by the back of the/your neck: *She picked up the puppy by the scruff of the neck.*

scruffy /'skrʌfɪ/ *adj* (**scruffier**; **scruffiest**) dirty and untidy: *He always looks so scruffy.* ○ *scruffy jeans*

scrum /skrʌm/ *noun* [C] the part of a game of rugby when several players put their heads down in a circle and push against each other in order to try to get the ball

scruples /'skru:plz/ *noun* [plural] moral beliefs which stop you from doing sth that you think is wrong: *Haven't you any scruples?* ○ *I've got no scruples about asking them for money* (= I don't think it's wrong).

scrupulous /'skru:pjʊləs/ *adj* **1** very careful or paying great attention to detail: *a scrupulous investigation into the causes of the disaster* **2** careful to do what is right or honest: *Even the most scrupulous businessman might have been tempted.* ☞ The opposite is **unscrupulous**.
—**scrupulously** *adv*: *scrupulously clean, honest, etc*

scrutinize (*also* **scrutinise**) /'skru:tɪnaɪz; *US* -tənaɪz/ *verb* [T] to look at or examine sth carefully

scrutiny /'skru:tɪnɪ; *US* skru:tənɪ/ *noun* [U] a careful examination or observation of sb/sth: *The police kept all the suspects under close scrutiny.*

scuba-diving /'sku:bə daɪvɪŋ/ *noun* [U] swimming underwater using special equipment for breathing

scuff /skʌf/ *verb* [T] to make a mark on your shoes or with your shoes, eg by kicking sth or by dragging your feet along the ground

scuffle /'skʌfl/ *noun* [C] a fight in which people try to push each other roughly: *There were scuffles between police and demonstrators.*

sculptor /'skʌlptə(r)/ *noun* [C] a person who makes figures or objects from stone, wood, etc

sculpture /'skʌlptʃə(r)/ *noun* **1** [U] the art of making figures or objects from stone, wood, clay, etc **2** [C,U] a work or works of art that were made in this way: *'The King and Queen' is a sculpture by Henry Moore.*

scum /skʌm/ *noun* [U] a covering of a dirty or unpleasant substance on the surface of a liquid

scurry /'skʌrɪ/ *verb* [I] (*pres part* **scurrying**; *3rd pers sing pres* **scurries**; *pt, pp* **scurried**) to run quickly with short steps; to hurry

scuttle /'skʌtl/ *verb* [I] to run quickly with short steps; to hurry

scythe /saɪð/ *noun* [C] a tool with a long handle and a long curved blade. You use a scythe to cut long grass, corn etc.

☆ **sea** /si:/ *noun* [U] **1** often **the sea** the salt water that covers large parts of the surface of the earth: *Do you live by the sea?* ○ *The sea is quite calm/rough today.* ○ *The Thames flows into the sea at Gravesend.* ○ *There were several people swimming in the sea.* ○ *We finally sighted land after we had been at sea for several days.* **2** [C] often **Sea** a particular large area of salt water. A Sea may be part of the ocean or may be surrounded by land: *the Mediterranean Sea* ○ *the Black Sea* **3** [sing] (*also* **seas** [plural]) the state or movement of the waves of the sea: *The captain said that we would not sail in heavy seas* (= when the waves are very big). **4** [sing] a large amount of sth: *The square was just a sea of people.*
(IDIOM) **at sea 1** sailing in a ship: *They spent about three weeks at sea.* **2** not understanding or not knowing what to do: *When I first started this job I was completely at sea.*

'sea bed *noun* [C] the floor of the sea

'seafood *noun* [U] fish and shellfish from the sea that can be eaten as food

'seagull *noun* [C] = GULL

'sea level *noun* [sing] the level of the sea when it is halfway between high tide and low tide (used for measuring the height of things on land): *50 metres above/below sea level*

'sea lion *noun* [C] a type of large seal

'seaman /-mən/ *noun* [C] (*pl* **seamen** /-mən/) a sailor

'sea shell *noun* [C] the empty shell of a small animal that lives in the sea

'seashore *noun* [U] the part of the land that is next to the sea

'seasick *adj* feeling ill because of the movement of a boat or ship: *to feel/get seasick*

'seaside *noun* [sing] often **the seaside** an area on the coast, especially one where people go on holiday: *It's a lovely day. Let's go to the seaside.* ○ *a seaside hotel*

'seaweed *noun* [U] a plant that grows in the sea

seal¹ /si:l/ *noun* [C] a grey animal with short fur that lives in and near the sea and that eats fish. Seals have no legs and swim with the help of short flat limbs (**flippers**).

seal² /si:l/ *noun* [C] **1** a piece of wax, etc that you put on an important piece of paper or letter to show that it is genuine and that it has not been opened **2** a small piece of paper, metal, plastic, etc on a packet, bottle, etc that you must break before you can open it **3** something that stops air or liquid from getting in or out of something: *The seal has worn and oil is escaping.* ○ *the rubber seal in the lid of a jar*

seal *verb* [T] **1 seal sth (up/down)** to close or fasten a parcel, envelope, etc: *The parcel was sealed with tape.* ○ *to seal (down) an envelope* **2 seal sth (up)** to fill a hole or cover sth so that air or liquid does not get in or out **3** to show formally that you have agreed sth: *to seal an agreement*
(PHRASAL VERB) **seal sth off** to stop any person or thing from entering or leaving an area or building: *The building was sealed off by the police.*

seam /si:m/ *noun* [C] **1** the line where two pieces of cloth are sewn together **2** a layer of coal under the ground

seance (*also* **séance**) /'seɪɑ:ns/ *noun* [C] a meeting at which people try to talk to the spirits of dead people

☆ **search** /sɜ:tʃ/ *verb* [I,T] **search (sb/sth) (for sb/sth)**; **search (through sth)(for sth)** to examine sb/sth carefully because you are looking for something; to look for sth that is missing: *to search sb for drugs* ○ *The police searched the area for clues.* ○ *They are still searching for*

the missing child. ○ *She searched through the papers on the desk, looking for the letter.*
search *noun* [C] an act of searching: *the search for the missing boy*
(IDIOM) **in search of sb/sth** looking for sb/sth: *The early explorers went in search of gold.*
searching *adj* (used about a look, question, etc) trying to find out the truth: *The customs officers asked a lot of searching questions about our trip.*
'search-party *noun* [C] a group of people who look for sb who is lost or missing: *to send out a search-party*
'search warrant *noun* [C] an official piece of paper that gives the police the right to search a building, etc
☆ **season¹** /'si:zn/ *noun* [C] **1** one of the four periods into which the year is divided (spring, summer, autumn and winter) **2** the period of the year when sth is common or popular or when sth usually happens or is done: *The football season is from August to May.* ○ *the dry/rainy season* ○ *the height of the holiday season*
(IDIOMS) **in season 1** (used about fresh foods) available in large quantities: *Tomatoes are cheapest when they are in season.* **2** (used about a female animal) ready to mate
out of season 1 (used about fresh foods) not available in large quantities **2** (of a holiday destination) at the time of year when it is least popular with tourists: *It's much cheaper to go to Spain out of season.*
'season ticket *noun* [C] a ticket that allows you to make a particular journey by bus, train, etc as often as you like for a fixed period of time.
season² /'si:zn/ *verb* [T] to add salt, pepper, spices, etc to food in order to make it taste better
seasonal /'si:zənl/ *adj* happening or existing at a particular time of the year: *There are a lot of seasonal jobs in the summer.*
seasoned /'si:znd/ *adj* having a lot of experience of sth: *a seasoned traveller*
seasoning /'si:zənɪŋ/ *noun* [C,U] salt, pepper, spices, etc that you add to food to make it taste better
☆ **seat¹** /si:t/ *noun* [C] **1** something that you sit on: *Please take a seat* (= please sit down). ○ *the back seat of a car* ○ *The seats for the ballet cost £30 each.* **2** the part of a chair, etc that you sit on **3** the part of a piece of clothing that covers your bottom **4** a place on a council or in a parliament that you win in an election: *The Conservatives have a majority of 21 seats.* ○ *to win/lose a seat*
'seat-belt (also **'safety-belt**) *noun* [C] a belt that you wear in a car or an aeroplane to protect you from injury if there is an accident
seat² /si:t/ *verb* [T] **1** (often passive) (*formal*) to sit down: *Please be seated.* **2** to have seats or chairs for a particular number of people: *The hall can seat about 500 people.*
seating *noun* [U] the seats or chairs in a place or the way that they are arranged: *The seating will need to be changed.* ○ *a seating plan*
sec /sek/ *noun* [C] (*Brit informal*) = SECOND³(2)
secluded /sɪ'klu:dɪd/ *adj* far away from other people, roads, etc; very quiet: *secluded beaches* ○ *a secluded garden* —**seclusion** /sɪ'klu:ʒn/ *noun* [U]

☆ **second¹** /'sekənd/ *pron, det, adv* 2nd; next after first: *We are going on holiday in the second week in July.* ○ *Birmingham is the second largest city in Britain.* ○ *She poured herself a second glass of wine.* ○ *Our team finished second.* ○ *I came second in the competition.*
secondly *adv* (used when you are giving your second reason or opinion) also: *Firstly, I think it's too expensive and secondly, we don't really need it.*
,second-'best *adj* not quite the best but the next one after the best: *the second-best time in the 100 metres race*
,second-'best *noun* [U] something that is not as good as the best, or not as good as you would like: *I'm not prepared to accept second-best.*
,second 'class *noun* [U] **1** ordinary accommodation in a train, boat, aeroplane, etc: *You can never get a seat in the second class.* **2** the type of postage that is cheaper but that takes longer than first class
,second-'class *adj* **1** used about ordinary accommodation in a train, aeroplane, etc: *a second-class ticket* ○ *a second-class compartment* **2** (used about a university degree) of the level that is next after first-class: *a second-class honours degree in geography* **3** of little importance: *Old people should not be treated as second-class citizens.*
,second-'class *adv* using second-class accommodation or postage: *to travel second-class* ○ *to send a letter second-class*
,second 'cousin *noun* [C] the child of your mother's or father's cousin
,second 'floor *noun* [C] the floor in a building that is next above the first floor, (= two floors above the ground): *I live on the second floor.* ○ *a second-floor flat* ☛ In American English the second floor is next above the ground.
,second-'hand *adj, adv* **1** already used or owned by sb else: *a second-hand car* ○ *I bought this camera second-hand.* **2** (used about news or information) that you heard from sb else, (= that you did not see or experience yourself)
,second 'language *noun* [C] a language that is not your native language but which you learn because it is used, often for official purposes, in your country: *French is the second language of several countries in Africa.*
,second 'nature (to sb) *noun* [U] something that has become a habit or that you can do easily because you have done it so many times: *With practice, typing becomes second nature.*
,second-'rate *adj* of poor quality: *a second-rate poet*
,second 'thoughts *noun* [plural] a change of mind or opinion about sth; doubts that you have when you are not sure if you have made the right decision: *On second thoughts, let's go today, not tomorrow.* ○ *I'm having second thoughts about accepting their offer.*
☆ **second²** /'sekənd/ *noun, pron* **1 the second** [sing] a person or thing that comes next after the first: *Queen Elizabeth the Second* ○ *the second of January* ○ *January the second* ○ *Terry*

was the second to arrive. **2** [C] **second (in sth)** a second-class university degree: *to get an upper/lower second in physics* **3** [U] the second gear of a car, etc: *Don't try to start the car in second.* **4** [C, usually pl] something that has a small fault and that is sold cheaply: *The clothes are all seconds.*

☆ **second³** /'sekənd/ *noun* [C] **1** one of the 60 parts into which a minute is divided **2** (also *informal* **sec**) a short time: *Wait a second, please.*

'**second hand** *noun* [C] the hand on some clocks and watches that records seconds

second⁴ /'sekənd/ *verb* [T] to support sb's proposal or idea at a meeting so that it can then be discussed and voted on

second⁵ /sɪ'kɒnd/ *verb* [T] **second sb (from sth)(to sth)** to move sb from his/her job for a fixed period of time to do another job: *Our teacher has been seconded to another school for a year.* —**secondment** *noun* [C,U]: *to be on secondment*

☆ **secondary** /'sekəndri; *US* -deri/ *adj* **1** of less importance than sth else: *Other people's opinions are secondary, it's my opinion that counts.* **2** caused by or developing from sth else: *She developed a secondary infection following a bad cold.*

'**secondary school** *noun* [C] (*Brit*) a school for children aged from eleven to eighteen

secrecy /'si:krəsi/ *noun* [U] the state of being or keeping sth secret: *The negotiations took place in the strictest secrecy.* ○ *I must stress the importance of secrecy in this matter.*

☆ **secret** /'si:krɪt/ *adj* **1 secret (from sb)** that is not or must not be known by other people: *The file was marked 'Top Secret'.* ○ *a secret address* ○ *secret talks between the government and the ANC* ○ *a secret love affair* **2** doing sth that you do not tell anyone else about: *a secret drinker* ○ *She's got a secret admirer.*

secret *noun* **1** [C] something that is not or must not be known by other people: *to keep a secret* ○ *to tell sb a secret* ○ *I can't tell you where we're going – it's a secret.* ○ *It's no secret that they don't like each other* (= everybody knows). **2** [sing] the only way or the best way of doing or achieving sth: *What is the secret of your success* (= how did you become so successful)*?*

(IDIOM) **in secret** without other people knowing: *to meet in secret*

secretly *adv* without other people knowing: *The government secretly agreed to pay the kidnappers.* ○ *The couple were secretly engaged for years.*

,**secret 'agent** (*also* **agent**) *noun* [C] a person who tries to find out secret information especially about the government of another country ☞ Look at **spy**.

,**secret 'service** *noun* [C] the government department that tries to find out secret information about other countries and governments

☆ **secretary** /'sekrətri; *US* -rəteri/ *noun* [C] (*pl* **secretaries**) **1** a person who works in an office. A secretary types letters, answers the telephone, makes appointments, etc: *the director's personal secretary* **2** a person who does similar work for a club or other organization: *The secretary must take the minutes of the meetings.* **3** (*US*) = MINISTER

secretarial /,sekrə'teəriəl/ *adj* connected with the work that a secretary(1) does: *secretarial skills*

,**Secretary of 'State** *noun* [C] the head of one of the main government departments: *the Secretary of State for Defence*

secrete /sɪ'kri:t/ *verb* [T] **1** (used about a part of a plant, animal or person) to produce a liquid: *a hormone secreted by the female of the species* **2** (*formal*) to hide sth in a secret place

secretion /sɪ'kri:ʃn/ *noun* (*formal*) **1** [C] a liquid that is produced by a plant or an animal **2** [U] producing this liquid

secretive /'si:krətɪv/ *adj* liking to keep things secret from other people: *Wendy is very secretive about her private life.* —**secretively** *adv* —**secretiveness** *noun* [U]

sect /sekt/ *noun* [C] a group of people who have a particular set of religious or political beliefs. A sect has often broken away from a larger group.

sectarian /sek'teəriən/ *adj* connected with one particular sect or the differences between sects: *sectarian violence*

☆ **section** /'sekʃn/ *noun* [C] **1** one of the parts into which something can be or has been divided: *The final section of the road will be open in June.* ○ *the string section of an orchestra* ○ *the financial section of a newspaper* ○ *The library has an excellent reference section.* **2** a view or drawing of sth as if it was cut from the top to the bottom and seen from the side

sector /'sektə(r)/ *noun* [C] **1** a part of the business activity of a country: *The manufacturing sector has declined in recent years.* ○ *the public/private sector* **2** a part of an area or of a large group of people: *the Christian sector of the city* ○ *All sectors of the community should be consulted before a decision is made.*

secular /'sekjələ(r)/ *adj* not concerned with religion or the church

☆ **secure** /sɪ'kjʊə(r)/ *adj* **1** free from worry or doubt, confident: *to feel secure about the future* ○ *Children need to feel secure.* ○ *to be financially secure* ☞ The opposite is **insecure**. **2** not likely to be lost; safe: *Business is good so his job is secure.* ○ *a secure investment* **3** not likely to fall or be broken; firmly fixed: *That ladder doesn't look very secure.* **4 secure (against/from sth)** well locked or protected: *Make sure the house is secure before you go to bed.* ○ *a country with secure borders*

secure *verb* [T] **1** to fix or lock sth firmly: *The load was secured with ropes.* ○ *Secure the rope to a tree or a rock.* **2 secure sth (against/from sth)** to make sth safe: *The sea wall needs strengthening to secure the town against flooding.* —**securely** *adv*: *All doors and windows must be securely fastened.*

☆ **security** /sɪ'kjʊərəti/ *noun* (*pl* **securities**) **1** [U] the state of feeling safe and being free from worry: *Children need the security of a stable home environment.* ○ *financial security* (= having enough money for your present and future needs) ☞ The opposite is **insecurity**.

ɜː	ə	eɪ	əʊ	aɪ	aʊ	ɔɪ	ɪə	eə	ʊə
fur	ago	pay	home	five	now	join	near	hair	pure

2 [U] things that you do to protect sb/sth from thieves, attack, war, etc: *Security was tightened at the airport before the president arrived.* o *a maximum security prison* (= for dangerous criminals) o *the security forces* (= military police, soldiers, etc) **3** [C,U] something of value that you use when you borrow money. If you cannot pay the money back then you lose the thing you gave as security: *You may need to use your house as security for the loan.*

sedan /sɪ'dæn/ *noun* [C] (*US*) = SALOON(1)

sedate¹ /sɪ'deɪt/ *adj* quiet, calm and well-behaved

sedate² /sɪ'deɪt/ *verb* [T] to give sb a drug or medicine to make him/her calm or sleepy —**sedation** /sɪ'deɪʃn/ *noun* [U]: *The doctor put her under sedation.*

sedative /'sedətɪv/ *noun* [C] a drug or medicine that makes you calm or sleepy ☞ Look at **tranquillizer**.

sedentary /'sedntri; *US* -teri/ *adj* spending a lot of time sitting down: *a sedentary life-style*

sediment /'sedɪmənt/ *noun* [C,U] a solid substance that forms at the bottom of a liquid

seduce /sɪ'dju:s; *US* -'du:s/ *verb* [T] **1** to persuade sb to do sth they would not usually agree to do: *shops attempting to seduce customers into parting with their money* **2** to persuade sb to have sex with you, especially sb young and without much experience

seducer *noun* [C] a person who seduces(2) sb —**seduction** /sɪ'dʌkʃn/ *noun* [C,U]

seductive /sɪ'dʌktɪv/ *adj* **1** sexually attractive, especially referring to a woman: *a seductive smile* **2** very attractive or appealing: *a novel set in the seductive atmosphere of 19th century Florence* o *a seductive argument/opinion* (= one which you are tempted to agree with)

☆ **see** /si:/ *verb* (*pt* **saw** /sɔ:/; *pp* **seen** /si:n/) **1** [I,T] to become aware of sth, using your eyes: *It was so dark that we couldn't see.* o *I can't see the number of that bus without my glasses.* o *I've just seen a rat!* o *He looked for her but couldn't see her in the crowd.* ☞ Look at the note at **look¹**. **2** [T] to look at or watch a film, play, television programme, etc: *Did you see that programme on Dickens on television last night?* o *Have you seen Spielberg's latest film?* **3** [T] to get information: *Go and see if the postman has been yet.* o *I saw in the paper that they're building a new theatre.* **4** [T] to meet or visit sb: *I saw Alan at the weekend; we had dinner together.* o *You should see a doctor about that cough.* o *I'm seeing a lot of Paul these days* (= meeting him often). **5** [T] to go with or accompany sb: *He asked me if he could see me home, but I said no.* **6** [T] to understand sth; to realize sth: *Do you see what I mean?* o *Everybody laughed, but I couldn't see the joke.* o *She doesn't see the point in spending so much money on a car.* o *I thought he was a gentleman, but now I see I'm wrong.* o *'You have to press the return key first.' 'Oh, I see.'* **7** [T] to imagine: *I can't see her changing her mind now.* **8** [T] to do what is necessary in a situation; to make sure that sb does sth: *I'll see that he gets the letter.* o *Please see that the children clean their teeth.* **9** [T] to be the time when an event happens: *Last year saw huge changes in the education system.*

(IDIOMS) **as far as I can see** ⇨ FAR²

I'll see I'll think about what you have asked me and give you my decision later: *'Can we go swimming today, Dad?' 'I'll see.'* ☞ Also used with **we**: *We'll see.*

let me see; let's see ⇨ LET¹

see if… to try: *I'll see if I can find time to do it.*

see you around (used for saying goodbye to sb you have made no arrangement to see again)

see you (later) (used for saying goodbye to sb you expect to see soon or later that day)

you see (used for giving a reason): *She's very unhappy. He was her first real boyfriend, you see.*

(PHRASAL VERBS) **see about sth/doing sth** to deal with sth: *I've got to go to the bank to see about my traveller's cheques.*

see sb off to go with sb to the railway station, the airport, etc in order to say goodbye to him/her

see through sb/sth to be able to see that sb/sth is not what he/she/it appears: *The police immediately saw through his story.*

see to sb/sth to do what is necessary in a situation; to deal with sth: *Can you see to the sandwiches for the meeting, please?*

☆ **seed** /si:d/ *noun* **1** [C,U] the small hard part of a plant from which a new plant of the same kind can grow: *a packet of sunflower seeds* o *Grass seed should be sown in the spring.* **2** [C] a player in a sports competition, especially in tennis, who is expected to finish in a high position at the end of the competition: *Courier was the top seed.*

seed *verb* [T] (in a sports competition, especially tennis) to arrange the matches for a good player so that he/she has a better chance of winning; to give a good player a number saying which position you expect him/her to finish in: *Capriati was seeded second at Wimbledon.*

seedless *adj* having no seeds: *seedless grapes*

seedling /'si:dlɪŋ/ *noun* [C] a very young plant that has grown from a seed

seedy /'si:di/ *adj* (**seedier; seediest**) looking untidy, dirty, or in bad condition; not respectable: *a seedy nightclub, hotel, etc*

seeing /'si:ɪŋ/ (*also* **seeing that; seeing as**) *conj* (*informal*) because: *Seeing as we're going the same way, I'll give you a lift.*

☆ **seek** /si:k/ *verb* [T] (*pt, pp* **sought** /sɔ:t/) **1** to try to find or get sth: *Dick went to London to seek his fortune.* o *Politicians are still seeking a peaceful solution.* **2 seek sth (from sb)** to ask sb for sth: *You should seek advice from a solicitor about what to do next.* o *to seek help* **3 seek (to do sth)** to try to do sth: *They are still seeking to find a peaceful solution to the conflict.*

☆ **seem** /si:m/ *verb* [I] **seem (to sb) (to be) sth; seem like sth** (not in the continuous tenses) to give the impression of being or doing sth; to appear: *Emma seems like a very nice girl.* o *Emma seems to be a very nice girl.* o *It seems to me that we have no choice.* o *Keith seems very in-*

terested in a career in farming. ○ *It doesn't seem as if/though they will find a solution to the problem.*

seeming *adj* (only *before* a noun) appearing to be sth: *Despite her seeming enthusiasm, Sandra didn't really help much.* —**seemingly** *adv*: *a seemingly endless list of complaints*

seen *pp* of SEE¹

seep /siːp/ *verb* [I] (used about a liquid) to flow very slowly through sth: *Water started seeping in through small cracks.*

see-saw /'siːsɔː/ *noun* [C] an outdoor toy for children that consists of a long piece of wood, etc that is balanced in the middle. One child sits on each end of the see-saw and one goes up while the other is down.

seethe /siːð/ *verb* [I] **1** to be very angry: *I was absolutely seething.* **2** to be very crowded: *The streets were seething with people.* ○ *a seething mass of people* (= a lot of people crowded together)

segment /'segmənt/ *noun* [C] **1** a section or part of sth: *a segment of a circle* ○ *a segment of the population* **2** one of the parts into which an orange can be divided

segregate /'segrɪgeɪt/ *verb* [T] **segregate sb/sth (from sb/sth)** to separate one group of people or things from the rest: *The two groups of football fans were segregated to avoid trouble.* ☛ Look at **integrate**. —**segregation** /ˌsegrɪ'geɪʃn/ *noun* [U]: *racial segregation* (= separating people of different races)

☆ **seize** /siːz/ *verb* [T] **1** to take hold of sth suddenly and firmly: *The thief seized her handbag and ran off with it.* ○ *to seize sb by the arm* ○ (*figurative*) *Mark was seized by a strong desire to laugh.* **2** to take control or possession of sb/sth: *The police seized 50 kilos of illegal drugs.* ○ *to seize power* ○ *Rebel forces seized the radio station early this morning.*

(PHRASAL VERBS) **seize (on/upon) sth** to recognize an opportunity and to use it eagerly: *The Opposition seized upon any opportunity to embarrass the Government.*

seize up (used about a machine) to stop working because it is too hot, does not have enough oil, etc

seizure /'siːʒə(r)/ *noun* [U] seizing or being seized: *the seizure of 30 kilos of heroin by French police*

☆ **seldom** /'seldəm/ *adv* not often: *There is seldom snow in Athens.* ○ *We very seldom go to the theatre.*

select /sɪ'lekt/ *verb* [T] to choose sb/sth from a number of similar things: *You may select whatever you want from the prizes on display.* ○ *The best candidates will be selected for interview.* ☛ **Select** is more formal than **choose** and suggests that a great deal of care is taken when making the decision.

select *adj* **1** carefully chosen: *a select audience of academics* **2** consisting of or available to only a small group of special people: *A university education is no longer the privilege of a select few.* ○ *a select neighbourhood* (= one where the houses are very expensive)

☆ **selection** /sɪ'lekʃn/ *noun* **1** [U] choosing or being chosen: *All candidates must go through a rigorous selection procedure.* ○ *the selection of the England cricket team* **2** [C] a number of people or things that have been chosen: *a selection of hits from the fifties and sixties* **3** [C] a collection of goods in a shop that are for sale: *This shop has a very good selection of toys.*

selective /sɪ'lektɪv/ *adj* **1** careful when choosing: *She's very selective about who she invites to her parties.* **2** of or concerning only some people or things; not general: *By using selective breeding* (= by allowing only some animals to breed) *the quality of the herd has increased greatly over the years.* —**selectively** *adv*

self /self/ *(pl **selves** /selvz/) noun* [C] a person's own nature or qualities: *It's good to see you back to your old self again* (= said to sb who has been ill, sad, worried, etc). ○ *Her spiteful remark revealed her true self.*

self-assured /ˌself ə'ʃɔːd; *US* -'ʃʊərd/ *adj* = ASSURED —**self-assurance** /-ə'ʃɔːrəns; *US* -ʃʊər-/ *noun* [U] = ASSURANCE(1)

self-catering /ˌself 'keɪtərɪŋ/ *adj* (used about a holiday or accommodation) where meals are not provided for you but you cook them yourself

self-centred (*US* **self-centered**) /ˌself 'sentə(r)d/ *adj* thinking only about yourself and not about other people ☛ Look at **selfish**.

self-confessed /ˌself kən'fest/ *adj* admitting that you are sth or do sth that most people consider to be bad: *a self-confessed drug-user*

self-confident /ˌself 'kɒnfɪdənt/ *adj* feeling sure about your own value and abilities —**self-confidence** /-dəns/ *noun* [U]: *Many women lack the self-confidence to apply for senior jobs.*

self-conscious /ˌself 'kɒnʃəs/ *adj* too worried about what other people think about you: *Men are often very self-conscious about losing their hair.* —**self-consciously** *adv* —**self-consciousness** *noun* [U]

self-contained /ˌself kən'teɪnd/ *adj* (used about a flat, etc) having its own private entrance, kitchen, bathroom, etc

self-control /ˌself kən'trəʊl/ *noun* [U] the ability to control your emotions and appear calm even when you are angry, afraid, excited, etc: *to lose/keep your self-control*

self-defence /ˌself dɪ'fens/ *noun* [U] the use of force to protect yourself or your property: *Lee is learning karate for self-defence.* ○ *to shoot sb in self-defence* (= because they are about to attack you)

self-employed /ˌself ɪm'plɔɪd/ *adj* working for yourself and earning money from your own business

self-evident /ˌself 'evɪdənt/ *adj* that does not need proving or explaining; clear

self-explanatory /ˌself ɪk'splænətri; *US* -tɔːri/ *adj* that does not need explaining; clear: *a self-explanatory diagram* ○ *The book's title is self-explanatory.*

self-indulgent /ˌself ɪn'dʌldʒənt/ *adj* allowing yourself to have or do things you enjoy (sometimes when it would be better to control yourself): *a self-indulgent morning spent relaxing in the bath* —**self-indulgence** /-dʒəns/ *noun* [C,U]

s	z	ʃ	ʒ	h	m	n	ŋ	l	r	j	w
so	zoo	she	vision	how	man	no	sing	leg	red	yes	wet

self-interest /ˌself 'ɪntrɪst/ noun [U] concern for what is best for yourself rather than for other people

☆ **selfish** /'selfɪʃ/ adj thinking only about your own needs or wishes and not about other people's needs or wishes: *a selfish attitude* ○ *I'm sick of your selfish behaviour!* ☞ The opposite is unselfish. —**selfishly** adv —**selfishness** noun [U]

selfless /'selflɪs/ adj (formal) thinking about other people's needs or wishes rather than your own: *his years of selfless devotion to his sick wife*

self-made /ˌself 'meɪd/ adj having become rich or successful by your own efforts: *a self-made millionaire*

self-pity /ˌself 'pɪti/ noun [U] the state of thinking too much about your own problems or troubles and feeling how unlucky you are

self-portrait /ˌself 'pɔːtreɪt, -trɪt/ noun [C] a picture that you drew or painted of yourself

self-raising flour /ˌself reɪzɪŋ 'flaʊə(r)/ (*US* **self-rising flour** /-'raɪzɪŋ/) noun [U] flour that contains a substance that makes it rise up during cooking (used for cakes, etc) ☞ Look at **plain flour**.

self-reliant /ˌself rɪ'laɪənt/ adj not depending on help from sb/sth else

self-respect /ˌself rɪ'spekt/ noun [U] the feeling of pride in yourself: *Old people need to keep their dignity and self-respect.* —**self-respecting** adj (in negative sentences): *No self-respecting Elvis Presley fan should be without this book* (= nobody who is proud to be a fan of Elvis Presley).

self-righteous /ˌself 'raɪtʃəs/ adj believing that you are always right and other people are wrong; thinking that you are better than other people —**self-righteously** adv: *'I have never been in debt,' she said self-righteously.* —**self-righteousness** noun [U]

self-sacrifice /ˌself 'sækrɪfaɪs/ noun [U] not having or doing what you want, in order to help others: *Rebuilding the country after the war demanded hard work and self-sacrifice.*

self-service /ˌself'sɜːvɪs/ adj in a self-service shop or restaurant, you serve yourself and then pay at a special desk (**cash desk**)

self-sufficient /ˌselfsə'fɪʃənt/ adj able to produce or provide everything that is needed without help from or having to buy from others

☆ **sell** /sel/ verb (pt, pp **sold** /səʊld/) **1** [I,T] **sell (sb) (sth)**; **sell (sth) (to sb)** to give sth to sb who pays for it and is then the owner of it: *We are going to sell our car.* ○ *I sold my guitar for £200.* ○ *Would you sell me your ticket?* ○ *I was too late, the car had already been sold.* ○ *I offered them a lot of money but they wouldn't sell.* ○ *He sold his business at an enormous profit.* **2** [T] to offer for sale: *Excuse me, do you sell stamps?* **3** [I] **sell (for/at sth)** to be sold or available for sale at a particular price: *These watches sell at £1 000 each in the shops but you can have this one for £500.* **4** [I] to be sold to or bought by many people; to attract buyers: *Her books sell well abroad.* **5** [T] to be sold in a particular quantity: *This newspaper sells over a million copies a day.* **6** [T] to cause people to want to buy sth; to help sth to attract buyers: *They rely on advertising to sell their products.* ☞ The noun for 1-6 is sale. **7** [T] **sell sth to sb** to persuade sb to accept sth: *to sell an idea to sb* ○ *She's completely sold on the idea of moving to France* (= she thinks it's a very good idea and wants to do it).

(IDIOM) **be sold out** (used about a concert, an event, etc) to have had all the tickets bought so that no more are available: *The concert was sold out weeks ago.*

(PHRASAL VERBS) **sell sth off** to sell sth that is not wanted or is not popular with buyers, often at a low price, in order to get rid of it: *The shops sell their winter clothes off in the spring.*

sell out to be sold completely so that no more are available for sale: *By the time I got to the shop, all the newspapers had sold out.*

sell out (of sth) to sell all of sth so that no more are available to be bought: *I'm afraid we've sold out of the book but we could order a copy for you.*

sell up to sell everything you own, especially your house, your business, etc (in order to start a new life, move to another country, retire, etc): *When his wife died he sold up and moved to the coast.*

'**sell-by date** noun [C] the date after which an item of food or drink should not be offered for sale

seller /'selə(r)/ noun [C] **1** (often in compounds) a person or business that sells: *a bookseller* **2** something that is sold (especially in the amount described): *This magazine is a big seller in the 25-40 age group.* ☞ Look at **best seller**.

Sellotape /'seləʊteɪp/ noun [U] (*Brit trade mark*) a type of clear tape that is sold in rolls and used for sticking things

sellotape verb [T] to put or hold sth together with Sellotape; to attach by using Sellotape

selves pl of SELF

semblance /'sembləns/ noun [sing,U] (*formal*) (**a**) **semblance of sth** the appearance of being sth or of having a certain quality: *After the war, life is now returning to some semblance of normality.*

semen /'siːmen/ noun [U] the liquid containing sperm that is produced by the male sex organs

semi /'semi/ noun [C] (pl **semis** /'semiz/) (*Brit informal*) a semi-detached house

semicircle /'semisɜːkl/ noun [C] one half of a circle; something that is arranged in this shape: *I want you all to sit in a semicircle.*

semicolon /ˌsemi'kəʊlən; *US* 'semɪk-/ noun [C] a mark (;) used in writing or printing for separating parts of a sentence or items in a list

semi-detached /ˌsemɪdɪ'tætʃt/ adj (used about a house) joined to another house with a shared wall on one side forming a pair of houses ☞ picture on page A12.

semifinal /ˌsemi'faɪnl/ noun [C] one of the two matches after which the winners play in the final

semifinalist /-'faɪnəlɪst/ noun [C] a player or team that plays in a semifinal

seminar /'semɪnɑː(r)/ noun [C] **1** a class at a

iː	ɪ	e	æ	ɑː	ɒ	ɔː	ʊ	uː	ʌ
see	sit	ten	hat	arm	got	saw	put	too	cup

university, college, etc in which a small group of students discuss or study a subject with a teacher **2** a short business conference in which working methods, etc are taught or discussed: *a seminar on becoming self-employed*

Senate /'senɪt/ *noun* [C, with sing or pl verb] often **the Senate** the upper body of government in some countries, eg the USA: *the Senate Foreign Affairs Committee* ☛ Look at **Congress** and **House of Representatives**.

senator /'senətə(r)/ *noun* [C] often **Senator** (*abbr* **Sen**) a member of a Senate: *Senator McCarthy*

☆ **send** /send/ *verb* [T] (*pt, pp* **sent** /sent/) **1 send sth/sb (to sb/sth); send (sb) sth** to cause sth/sb to go or be taken somewhere without going there yourself: *to send a letter/parcel* ○ *to send a message to sb* ○ *Don't forget to send me a postcard.* ○ *If you are not satisfied with these goods, send them back within 7 days.* ○ *We sent out the invitations two months before the wedding.* ○ *She sent the children to bed early.* ○ *My company is sending me on a training course next month.* ○ *I asked someone the way to the airport but he sent me in the wrong direction.* ○ *to send sb to prison* ○ *Her parents sent her to a private school when she was 11.* **2** to cause sb/sth to move in a particular direction, often quickly or as a reaction that cannot be prevented: *I accidentally pushed the table and sent all the drinks flying.* ○ *This year's poor harvest has sent food prices up.* **3** cause sb/sth to have a particular feeling or to enter a particular state: *The movement of the train sent me to sleep.*

(IDIOM) **give/send sb your love** ⇨ LOVE(1)

(PHRASAL VERBS) **send for sb/sth** to ask for sb to come to you; to ask for sth to be brought or sent to you by telephone, message, letter, etc: *I sent for the manager so that I could make a complaint.* ○ *Quick! Send for an ambulance!*

send sth in to send sth to a place where it will be officially dealt with: *I sent my application in three weeks ago but I still haven't had a reply.*

send off (for sth) to write to sb and ask for sth to be sent to you: *Let's send off for some holiday brochures.*

send sb off (*Brit*) (used about a referee in a sports match) to order a player who has broken a rule to leave the game and not to return: *Two players were sent off for fighting.*

send sth off to post sth: *I'll send the information off today.*

send sb/sth up (*Brit informal*) to make sb/sth look ridiculous or foolish especially by imitating him/her in a way that is intended to be amusing

senile /'siːnaɪl/ *adj* confused, unable to remember things or to look after yourself properly (because of old age) —**senility** /sɪ'nɪləti/ *noun* [U]

☆ **senior** /'siːniə(r)/ *adj* **senior (to sb) 1** having a high or higher rank in a company, organization, etc: *a senior managerial position* ○ *He's senior to me.* ○ *a meeting of senior government ministers* **2** older: *This common room is for the use of senior pupils only.* **3** often **Senior** (*abbr*

Sen) (used to show that a person is the parent of sb with the same name): *John Brown Senior*
☛ Look at **junior**.

senior *noun* [C] **1** somebody who is older or of higher rank (than one or more other people): *My oldest sister is ten years my senior.* **2** an older pupil at a school **3** (*US*) a student in the final year of school, college or university

seniority /ˌsiːni'ɒrəti; *US* -'ɔːr-/ *noun* [U] the rank or importance that a person has in a company, organization, etc in relation to others: *The names are listed below in order of seniority.*

ˌsenior ˈcitizen *noun* [C] = OLD-AGE PENSIONER

sensation /sen'seɪʃn/ *noun* **1** [C] a feeling that is caused by sth affecting the body or part of the body: *a pleasant/unpleasant sensation* ○ *I felt a burning sensation on my skin.* **2** [U] the ability to feel when touching or being touched: *For some time after the accident he had no sensation in his legs.* **3** [C] a feeling or impression in the mind or body that is not caused by anything definite and may be false: *I had the peculiar sensation that I was floating in the air.* **4** [C] a feeling of great excitement, surprise or interest among a group of people or people in general; something that causes this: *The young American caused a sensation by beating the top seed.* ○ *The show got wonderful reviews and was an overnight sensation* (= became famous and popular immediately).

sensational /-ʃənl/ *adj* **1** causing, or trying to cause, a feeling of great excitement, surprise or interest among people: *sensational events* ○ *the most sensational murder trial this century* ○ *This magazine specializes in sensational stories about the rich and famous.* **2** (*informal*) extremely good; beautiful; very exciting: *You look sensational!* —**sensationally** *adv*

☆ **sense** /sens/ *noun* **1** [C] one of the five natural physical powers that make it possible for a person or animal to get information about the world around: *I've got a cold and I've lost my sense of smell.* **2** [U,sing] the ability to understand or appreciate sth; the ability to recognize what sth is: *She seems to have lost all sense of reality.* ○ *I like him – he's got a great sense of humour.* ○ *I'm always getting lost. I've got absolutely no sense of direction.* **3** [U,sing] a natural ability to do or produce sth well: *Good business sense made her a millionaire.* ○ *He's got absolutely no dress sense* (= he dresses very badly). **4** [U,sing] a feeling or consciousness of sth: *I felt a tremendous sense of relief when the exams were finally over.* ○ *She only visits her family out of a sense of duty.* **5** [U] the ability to think or act in a reasonable or sensible way; practical intelligence: *At least he had enough sense to stop when he realized he was making a mistake.* ○ *I think there's a lot of sense in what you're saying.* ○ *They buy the most ridiculous things. They've got more money than sense.*
☛ Look at **common sense**. **6** [U] good reason; use or point: *There's no sense in going any further – we're obviously lost.* ○ *What's the sense in making things more difficult for yourself?* **7** [C] (used about a word, phrase, etc) a meaning or possible meaning: *This word has two*

senses. ○ *This is an epic film in every sense of the word.*
(IDIOMS) **in a sense** in one particular way but not in other ways; partly: *In a sense you're right, but there's more to the matter than that.*

make sense 1 to be possible to understand; to have a clear meaning: *What does this sentence mean? It doesn't make sense to me.* **2** (used about an action) to be sensible or logical: *I think it would make sense to wait for a while before making a decision.*

make sense of sth to manage to understand sth that is not clear or is difficult to understand: *I can't make sense of these instructions.*

talk sense ⇨ TALK¹(6)

sense *verb* [T] to realize or become aware of sth; to get the feeling that sth is the case: *I sensed that something was wrong.*

senseless /'senslɪs/ *adj* **1** having no meaning or purpose: *The police described the murder as 'a senseless act of violence'.* **2** unconscious

☆ **sensible** /'sensəbl/ *adj* having or showing the ability to think or act in a reasonable way; having or showing good judgement: *a sensible man* ○ *a sensible decision* ○ *Stop joking and give me a sensible answer.* ○ *I think it would be sensible to leave early, in case there's a lot of traffic.* —**sensibly** /-əblɪ/ *adv: Let's sit down and discuss the matter sensibly.* ☛ Compare **sensible** and **sensitive**. Sensible is connected with common sense, reasonable action and good judgement. Sensitive is connected with feelings and emotions and with the five senses.

☆ **sensitive** /'sensətɪv/ *adj* **1** easily hurt or damaged; painful, especially if touched: *a new cream for sensitive skin* **2** sensitive (about/to sth) easily upset, offended or annoyed, perhaps because of having strong feelings about a particular matter: *Don't be so sensitive! I was only joking.* ○ *She's still a bit sensitive about her divorce.* ○ *He's very sensitive to criticism.* **3 sensitive (to sth)** showing that you are aware of and understand people's feelings, problems, etc: *It wasn't exactly sensitive of you to keep mentioning her boyfriend. You know they've just split up.* ○ *to be sensitive to sb's feelings/wishes* ☛ The opposite for senses 2 and 3 is **insensitive**. **4** (used about a scientific instrument, a piece of equipment, etc) able to measure very small changes **5** (used about a subject, a situation, etc) needing to be dealt with carefully because it is likely to cause anger or trouble: *Religion is often a sensitive subject.* ○ *This is a sensitive period in the negotiations between the two countries.* —**sensitively** *adv: The investigation will need to be handled sensitively.*

sensitivity /ˌsensə'tɪvətɪ/ *noun* [U] the quality of being sensitive: *I think your comments showed a complete lack of sensitivity.*

sensual /'sensjuəl/ *adj* connected with physical or sexual pleasure: *the sensual rhythms of Latin music* ○ *a life devoted to sensual pleasure and luxury* —**sensuality** /ˌsensju'ælətɪ/ *noun* [U]

sensuous /'sensjuəs/ *adj* giving pleasure to or affecting the mind or body through the senses:

the sensuous feel of pure silk —**sensuously** *adv* —**sensuousness** *noun* [U]

sent *pt, pp* of SEND

☆ **sentence** /'sentəns/ *noun* **1** [C] (*grammar*) a group of words containing a subject and a verb, that expresses a statement, a question, etc. When a sentence is written it begins with a capital letter and ends with a full stop: *a grammatically correct sentence* ○ *You don't need to write a long letter. A couple of sentences will be enough.* **2** [C,U] the punishment given by a judge to sb who has been found guilty of a crime: *20 years in prison was a very harsh sentence.* ○ *He is serving his sentence in a maximum security prison.* ○ *the death sentence*

sentence *verb* [T] **sentence sb (to sth)** (used about a judge) to tell sb who has been found guilty of a crime what the punishment will be: *The judge sentenced her to three months in prison for shoplifting.* ○ *He was sentenced to life imprisonment for murder.*

sentiment /'sentɪmənt/ *noun* **1** [C,U] (often plural) an attitude or opinion that is often caused or influenced by emotion: *His comments expressed my sentiments exactly.* ○ *Nationalist sentiment is quite strong throughout the country.* **2** [U] gentle feelings such as sympathy, love, happy memories, etc that influence action or behaviour (sometimes in situations where this is not suitable): *There's no room for sentiment in business.*

sentimental /ˌsentɪ'mentl/ *adj* **1** caused by or connected with gentle feelings such as sympathy, love, happy memories, etc: *The jewellery had great sentimental value to me.* **2** having or showing these gentle emotions, sometimes in a silly way: *How can you be sentimental about an old car!* ○ *a sentimental love song* —**sentimentality** /ˌsentɪmen'tælətɪ/ *noun* [U] —**sentimentally** /-təlɪ/ *adv*

sentry /'sentrɪ/ *noun* [C] (*pl* **sentries**) a soldier who stands outside a building and guards it

separable /'sepərəbl/ *adj* able to be separated ☛ The opposite is **inseparable**.

☆ **separate¹** /'seprət/ *adj* **1 separate (from sth/sb)** apart; not joined or together: *You should always keep your cash and credit cards separate.* **2** different: *A lot of married couples have separate bank accounts.* ○ *We stayed in separate rooms in the same hotel.*

separately *adv* apart; not together; at different times or in different places: *Shall we pay separately or all together?* ○ *Let's deal with each matter separately.*

☆ **separate²** /'sepəreɪt/ *verb* **1** [I,T] **separate (sb/sth) (from sb/sth)** to stop being together; to cause people or things to stop being together; to divide people or things: *I think we should separate into two groups.* ○ *The friends separated at the airport.* ○ *I got separated from my friends in the crowd.* ○ *Separate the egg yolk from the white.* **2** [T] **separate sb/sth (from sb/sth)** to keep people or things apart, or to be between people or things with the result that they are apart: *I always try to separate business from pleasure.* ○ *When the players started fighting, the referee moved in to separate them.* ○ *The*

p	b	t	d	k	g	tʃ	dʒ	f	v	θ	ð
pen	bad	tea	did	cat	got	chin	June	fall	van	thin	then

two sides of the city are separated by the river. ○ Often the language barrier separates different parts of a community. **3** [I] (used about a married couple, etc) to stop living together: *His parents separated when he was still a baby.*

separated *adj* (used about a married couple) not living together any more but not divorced: *My wife and I are separated.*

☆ **separation** /ˌsepəˈreɪʃn/ *noun* [C,U] **1** the act of separating or being separated; a situation or period of being apart: *Separation from family and friends made me very lonely.* **2** a legal agreement where a married couple live apart (but do not get a divorce): *a trial separation*

☆ **September** /sepˈtembə(r)/ *noun* [C,U] (*abbr* **Sept**) the ninth month of the year; coming before October ☛ For examples of the use of the months in sentences, look at **January**.

septic /ˈseptɪk/ *adj* infected with poisonous bacteria: *The wound went septic.*

sequel /ˈsiːkwəl/ *noun* [C] **1** a book, film, etc that continues the story of the previous one **2** something that happens after, or is the result of, a previous event

sequence /ˈsiːkwəns/ *noun* **1** [C] a number of things (actions, events, etc) that happen or come one after another: *the sequence of events leading to war* ○ *Complete the following sequence: 1, 4, 8, 12, …* **2** [U] the order in which a number of things happen or are arranged: *The photographs are in sequence.*

serene /sɪˈriːn/ *adj* calm and peaceful: *a serene smile* —**serenely** *adv* —**serenity** /sɪˈrenəti/ *noun* [U]

sergeant /ˈsɑːdʒənt/ *noun* [C] (*abbr* **Sergt**, **Sgt**) **1** an officer of low rank in the army or air force **2** an officer in the police with a rank below that of inspector

serial /ˈsɪəriəl/ *noun* [C] a single story in a magazine or on television or radio that is told in a number of parts over a period of time: *the first part of a six-part drama serial* ☛ Look at the note at **series**.

serialize (*also* **serialise**) /-riəlaɪz/ *verb* [T] to broadcast a story or publish a book in the form of a serial

ˈserial number *noun* [C] the number marked on sth to identify it and to distinguish it from other things of the same type: *the serial numbers of travellers' cheques*

☆ **series** /ˈsɪəriːz/ *noun* [C] (*pl* **series**) **1** a number of things that come one after another and are of the same type or connected: *a series of events* ○ *The orchestra is visiting Britain for a series of concerts next month.* ○ *There has been a series of burglaries in this district recently.* **2** a number of programmes on radio or television which have the same main characters and each tell a complete story ☛ Compare **series** and **serial**. In a **series** each part is a different, complete story involving the same main characters. In a **serial** the same story continues in each part.

☆ **serious** /ˈsɪəriəs/ *adj* **1** (used about problems, situations, etc) bad; important; causing worry: *a serious accident* ○ *a serious illness* ○ *Pollution is a very serious problem.* ○ *serious crime* **2** needing to be treated as important, not just for fun: *Don't laugh, it's a serious matter.* ○ *a serious discussion* ○ *She's had a number of boyfriends but only one serious relationship.* **3** (used about a person) not joking; thoughtful: *Are you serious about starting your own business?* (= are you really going to do it) *?* ○ *He's terribly serious. I don't think I've ever seen him laugh.* ○ *You're looking very serious. Was it bad news?*

seriousness *noun* [U] the quality of being serious: *It would be unwise to underestimate the seriousness of this situation.*

seriously /ˈsɪəriəsli/ *adv* **1** in a serious way: *Three people were seriously injured in the accident.* ○ *My mother is seriously ill.* ○ *It's time you started to think seriously about the future.* **2** (used for indicating that you are not joking or that you really mean what you are saying): *Seriously, I do appreciate all your help.* ○ *Seriously, you've got nothing to worry about.* **3** (used for expressing surprise at what someone has said and asking whether it is really true): *'I'm 40 today.' 'Seriously? You look a lot younger.'*

(IDIOM) **take sb/sth seriously** to treat sb or sth as important: *He's such a fool that nobody takes him seriously.* ○ *You take everything too seriously! Relax and enjoy yourself.*

sermon /ˈsɜːmən/ *noun* [C] a speech on a religious or moral matter that is given as part of a service in church

serrated /sɪˈreɪtɪd; *US* ˈsereɪtɪd/ *adj* having a row of points in V-shapes along the edge: *a knife with a serrated edge*

☆ **servant** /ˈsɜːvənt/ *noun* [C] a person who is paid to work in sb's house, doing work such as cooking, cleaning, etc ☛ Look at **civil servant**.

☆ **serve** /sɜːv/ *verb* **1** [I,T] to work for a country, a company, an organization, the army, etc; to be useful to sb: *The role of the police is to serve the community.* ○ *She has served on a number of committees.* ○ *During the war, he served in the Army.* ○ *During his long political career he served under three different Prime Ministers.* **2** [T] to give food or drink to sb during a meal; to take an order and then bring food or drink to sb (in a restaurant, bar, etc): *Breakfast is served from 7.30 to 9.00 am.* ○ *We waited for half an hour until a waiter finally served us.* **3** [I,T] (in a shop) to take a customer's order; to give help, sell goods, etc: *Excuse me madam. Are you being served?* **4** [T] to provide sb (especially the public) with sth necessary or useful in daily life: *The town is served by three hospitals.* **5** [I,T] **serve (sb) (as sth)** to be good enough for or suitable for a particular purpose; to perform a particular function: *The smallest bedroom serves as my office.* ○ *His pathetic excuses only served to make me even angrier.* **6** [T] to spend a period of time in prison as punishment: *He is currently serving a ten-year sentence for fraud.* **7** [T] (used about an amount of food) to be enough for a certain number of people: *According to the recipe, this dish serves four.* **8** [I,T] (in tennis and similar sports) to start play by hitting the ball

(IDIOMS) **serve your/the purpose** to have or

s	z	ʃ	ʒ	h	m	n	ŋ	l	r	j	w
so	**zoo**	**she**	**vision**	**how**	**man**	**no**	**sing**	**leg**	**red**	**yes**	**wet**

be what you need: *It's an old car but it will serve our purpose for a few months.*
serve sb right (used when sth unpleasant happens to sb and you have no sympathy) to be deserved by sb: *'I feel sick.' 'It serves you right for eating so much.'*

☆ **service** /'sɜːvɪs/ *noun* **1** [U] working for a country, a company, an organization, the army, etc: *The minister was thanked for his years of service to the party.* ○ *Military service is no longer compulsory.* ○ *He left the police force after thirty years' service.* **2** [C] a system or organization that provides the public with sth necessary or useful in daily life; the job that an organization does: *the train/bus service* ○ *the postal service* ○ *The airline is starting a new international service.* ○ *We offer a number of financial services.* **3** [C, usually sing] one of certain government departments or public institutions: *the National Health Service* ☞ Look at **Civil Service**. **4 the services** [plural] the armed forces; the army, navy or air force **5** [U] the work or the quality of work done by sb when serving a customer: *I enjoyed the meal but the service was terrible.* ○ *We offer after-sales service on all our photocopiers.* ○ *Is service included in the bill?* **6** [C, usually pl] work done for sb; help given to sb: *He was given an award for his services to the film industry.* **7** [C,U] the examination (and, if necessary, repair) of a car, machine, etc to make sure that it is working properly: *We take our car for a service every six months.* **8** [C] a religious ceremony, usually including prayers, singing, etc: *a funeral service* **9** [C] (in tennis and similar sports) the act of hitting the ball at the start of play; a player's turn to serve: *She's not a bad player but her service is weak.* **10 services** [C] (usually with a plural verb) (*pl* **services**) a place at the side of a motorway where there is a petrol station, a shop, toilets, a restaurant, etc: *It's five miles to the next services.*

service *verb* [T] to examine and, if necessary, repair a car, machine, etc: *All cars should be serviced at regular intervals.*

'service charge *noun* [C] the amount of money that is added to a restaurant bill for the service given by the waiters and waitresses

'service station *noun* [C] = PETROL STATION

serviette /ˌsɜːvɪ'et/ *noun* [C] a square of cloth or paper that you use when you are eating to keep your clothes clean and to wipe your mouth or hands

session /'seʃn/ *noun* [C] **1** a meeting or series of meetings of an official body (a court, a parliament, etc) **2** a period of doing a particular activity: *The whole tape was recorded in one session.* ○ *She has a session on a sunbed every week.*
(IDIOM) **in session** (used about an official body) holding a meeting; doing its official work; not on holiday: *Silence! This court is now in session.*

☆ **set¹** /set/ *noun* **1** [C] a number of things that belong together: *a set of kitchen knives* ○ *In the first set of questions, you have to fill in the gap.* ○ *a set of instructions* **2** [C] a piece of equipment for receiving television or radio: *a television set* **3** [C] the scenery for a play or film on the stage or in the studio: *a musical with spectacular sets* **4** [C] (in tennis) a group of games forming part of a match: *game, set and match*

☆ **set²** /set/ *verb* (*pres part* **setting**; *pt, pp* **set**) **1** [T] to put sb/sth in a particular position; to place sth somewhere: *He set a large bowl of soup in front of me.* ○ *The hotel is set in beautiful grounds.* **2** [T] (often passive) to place the action of a book, play, film, etc in a particular time, situation, etc: *The film is set in 16th-century Spain.* **3** [T] to cause a particular state or event; to start sth happening: *The new government set the prisoners free.* ○ *The rioters set a number of cars on fire.* ○ *Her comment set him thinking.* **4** [T] to prepare or arrange sth for a particular purpose: *I set my alarm for 6.30.* ○ *to set the table* (= put the plates, knives, forks, etc on it) ○ *Did you set the video to record that film?* **5** [T] to fix or establish sth: *Try to set a good example to the younger children.* ○ *Can we set a limit of £100 for the cost of materials?* ○ *They haven't set the date of the next meeting yet.* ○ *He has set a new world record.* **6** [T] to give sb a piece of work: *We've been set a lot of homework this weekend.* **7** [I] to become firm or hard: *Put the jelly in the fridge for two hours to set.* **8** [T] to fix a precious stone, etc in a piece of jewellery: *The brooch had three diamonds set in gold.* **9** [T] to arrange sb's hair while it is wet so that it becomes curly, wavy, etc: *She went to the hairdresser's to have her hair set.* **10** [T] to write music to go with words: *She writes the words of the song and Harry sets them to music.* **11** [T] to put a broken bone in a position (and often to fix it in plaster) so that it can heal: *The doctor set her broken leg.* **12** [I] (used about the sun, etc) to go down below the horizon ☞ The opposite is **rise**.
(IDIOMS) **put/set your/sb's mind at rest** ⇒ MIND¹

set eyes on sb/sth to see sb/sth: *He loved the house the moment he set eyes on it.*

set foot (in/on sth) to visit, enter or arrive at/in a place: *No woman has ever set foot in the temple.*

set sail to begin a journey by sea: *Columbus set sail for India.*

(PHRASAL VERBS) **set sb/sth back** to delay sb/sth: *The bad weather has set our plans back six weeks.*

set in to arrive and remain for a period of time: *I'm afraid that the bad weather has set in.*

set off to leave on a journey: *We set off at 3 o'clock this morning.*

set sth off to do sth which starts a reaction: *When this door is opened, it sets off an alarm.*

set out to leave on a journey: *They set out at dawn.*

set out to do sth to decide to achieve sth: *She set out to become Britain's first woman Prime Minister*

set (sth) up to start; to establish a business: *The company has set up a new branch in Wales.* ○ *After she qualified as a doctor, she set up in practice in Yorkshire.*

set³ /set/ *adj* **1** placed in a particular position: *Our house is set back quite a long way from the*

road. ○ deep-set eyes **2** fixed and not changing; firm: *There are no set hours in my job.* ○ *He's getting more and more set in his ways as he gets older* (= with fixed habits and routines which he is unwilling to change). **3 set (for sth); set (to do sth)** ready, prepared or likely to do sth: *Okay, I'm all set – let's go!* ○ *I was all set to leave when the phone rang.* ○ *The England team look set for victory.*
(IDIOMS) **be set against sth/against doing sth** to be opposed to sth: *She's set against moving house.*
be set on sth/on doing sth to be determined to do sth: *She's set on a career in acting.* ○ *My heart was set on that house* (= I really wanted it).
,set'book *noun* [C] a book that must be studied in a course for an exam

set-back /'setbæk/ *noun* [C] a difficulty or problem that stops you progressing as fast as you would like

settee /se'tiː/ *noun* [C] a long soft seat with a back and arms that more than one person can sit on

☆ **setting** /'setɪŋ/ *noun* [C] **1** surroundings; the place where sth happens: *The hotel is in a beautiful setting, close to the sea.* ○ *They decided that the village church would be the perfect setting for their wedding.* **2** one of the positions of the controls of a machine: *Cook it in the oven at a moderate setting.*

☆ **settle** /'setl/ *verb* **1** [I] to go and live permanently in a new country, an area, a town, etc: *A great many immigrants have settled in this country.* **2** [T] to reach an agreement about sth; to end an argument; to find a solution to a disagreement: *They settled the dispute without going to court.* **3** [T] to decide or arrange sth finally (eg a plan, an action, etc): *Everything's settled. We leave on the nine o'clock flight on Friday.* **4** [I,T] to get into or put sb into a comfortable position: *I settled in front of the television for the evening.* ○ *She settled herself beside him on the sofa.* **5** [I,T] to become or to make sb/sth calm or relaxed: *The baby wouldn't settle.* ○ *Have a drink. It might settle your stomach.* **6** [T] to pay sth (a bill, a debt, etc): *to settle a bill* ○ *The insurance company settled the claim very quickly.* **7** [I] to come to rest after falling on sth; to land: *A flock of birds settled on the roof.* ○ *The snow didn't settle* (= remain on the ground) *for long.* **8** [I] (used about a liquid) to become clear or still
(PHRASAL VERBS) **settle down 1** to get into a comfortable position, sitting or lying: *I made a cup of tea and settled down with the newspapers.* **2** to start having a quieter way of life, especially by staying in the same place or getting married, etc: *She had a number of jobs abroad before she eventually settled down.* **3** to become calm and quiet: *Settle down! It's time to start the lesson.*
settle down to sth to start concentrating on sth: *Before you settle down to your work, could I ask you something?*
settle for sth to accept sth that is not as good as you hoped it would be: *You'll have to settle for something cheaper.*

settle in/into sth to get used to or start feeling comfortable in a new home, job, etc: *How are the children settling in at their new school?*
settle on sth to choose sth after considering many different things; to decide on sth
settle up (with sb) to pay money that you owe sb

settled /'setld/ *adj* **1** not changing or not likely to change: *More settled weather is forecast for the next few days.* **2** comfortable; feeling that you belong in a home, a job, a way of life, etc): *We feel very settled here.*

☆ **settlement** /'setlmənt/ *noun* **1** [C,U] (an) agreement, usually official, that ends an argument; the act of reaching this kind of agreement: *The strike lasted for several weeks until a settlement was reached.* **2** [C] a place that a group of people have built and live in, where few or no people lived before: *a settlement in the jungle*

settler /'setlə(r)/ *noun* [C] a person who goes to live permanently in a new country, particularly an undeveloped one or one with a small population: *the first settlers in Australia*

☆ **seven** /'sevn/ *number* 7; one more than 6
☞ For examples of how to use numbers in sentences, look at **six**.
seven- (in compounds) having seven of the thing mentioned: *a seven-sided coin*
seventh *pron, det, adv* 7th; next after sixth
seventh *noun* [C] the fraction ⅐; one of seven equal parts of sth ☞ Look at the examples at **sixth**.

☆ **seventeen** /,sevn'tiːn/ *number* 17; one more than sixteen ☞ For examples of how to use numbers in sentences, look at **six**.
seventeenth /,sevn'tiːnθ/ *pron, det, adv* 17th; next after sixteenth ☞ Look at the examples at **sixth**.

☆ **seventy** /'sevnti/ *number* 70; one more than sixty-nine ☞ For examples of how to use numbers in sentences, look at **sixty**.
seventieth /'sevntiəθ/ *pron, det, adv* 70th; next after sixty-ninth ☞ Look at the examples at **sixth**.

sever /'sevə(r)/ *verb* [T] **1** to break, separate or divide by cutting: *The builders accidentally severed a water pipe.* **2** to end sth (a relationship, etc): *He has severed all links with his former friends.*

☆ **several** /'sevrəl/ *pron, det* more than two but not very many; some: *It took her several days to recover from the shock.* ○ *There were lots of applications for the job – several of them from very well-qualified people.* ○ *I've asked him several times for the money.*

☆ **severe** /sɪ'vɪə(r)/ *adj* **1** not kind or gentle: *Such terrible crimes deserve the severest punishment.* ○ *a severe teacher* ○ *a severe expression* ○ *I think your criticism of her work was too severe.* **2** very bad; causing unpleasant results or feelings: *The company is in severe financial difficulty.* ○ *a severe cold, headache, illness, pain, etc* ○ *a severe winter* (= a very cold one) —**severely** *adv*: *The roof was severely damaged in the storm.* ○ *The report severely criticizes the Minister.* —**severity** /sɪ'verəti/ *noun* [U]: *I don't think you realize the severity of the problem.*

ɜː	ə	eɪ	əʊ	aɪ	aʊ	ɔɪ	ɪə	eə	ʊə
fur	ago	pay	home	five	now	join	near	hair	pure

sew /səʊ/ *verb* (*pt* **sewed**; *pp* **sewn** /səʊn/ or **sewed**) [I,T] to join pieces of cloth, or to join sth to cloth, using a needle and thread and forming stitches: *I can't sew.* ○ *to sew a new button on a shirt* (PHRASAL VERB) **sew sth up 1** to join two things by sewing; to repair sth by sewing two things together: *to sew up a hole* ○ *The surgeon sewed up the wound.* **2** to arrange or organize sth so that it is certain to happen or be successful: *I think we've got the deal sewn up.*

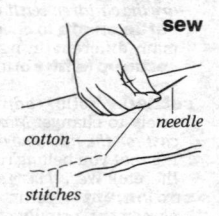

sewing *noun* [U] **1** using a needle and thread to make or repair things: *Do you like sewing?* **2** something that is being sewn: *Have you seen my sewing?*

'sewing-machine *noun* [C] a machine that is used for sewing

sewage /'suːɪdʒ; *Brit also* 'sjuː-/ *noun* [U] the waste material from people's bodies that is carried away from their homes in water in large underground pipes (**sewers**)

sewer /'suːə(r); *Brit also* 'sjuː-/ *noun* [C] an underground pipe that carries waste to a place where it can be treated

sewn *pp* of SEW

☆ **sex** /seks/ *noun* **1** [U] the state of being either male or female: *Applications are welcome from anyone, regardless of sex or race.* ○ *Do you mind what sex your baby is?* **2** [C] one of the two groups consisting of all male people or all female people: *the male/female sex* ○ *He's always found it difficult to get on with the opposite sex* (= women). **3** (also *formal* **intercourse**; **sexual intercourse**) [U] the physical act in which the sexual organs of two people touch and which can result in a woman having a baby: *to have sex with somebody* ○ *It's against their religion to have sex before marriage.* **4** [U] activities or matters connected with this act: *There's too much sex and violence on TV.*

sexy *adj* (**sexier**; **sexiest**) (*informal*) sexually attractive: *a sexy man* ○ *a sexy dress* ☛ Look at **sexual**.

sexism /'seksɪzəm/ *noun* [U] treating a person unfairly, or thinking that they are inferior, because of their sex, eg thinking that only men can do certain jobs, such as being an engineer

sexist /'seksɪst/ *adj* connected with or showing sexism: *a sexist attitude to women* ○ *sexist jokes*

☆ **sexual** /'sekʃuəl/ *adj* connected with sex: *sexual problems* ○ *the sexual organs* ○ *a campaign for sexual equality* (= a campaign to get fair and equal treatment for both men and women)

sexuality /,sekʃu'æləti/ *noun* [U] the nature of sb's sexual activities or desires: *He found it difficult to come to terms with his sexuality.* —**sexually** /-əli/ *adv*: *to be sexually attracted to sb*

sexual 'intercourse *noun* [U] (*formal*) = SEX(3)

sh /ʃ/ *exclamation* be quiet!: *Sh! People are trying to sleep in here.*

shabby /'ʃæbi/ *adj* (**shabbier**; **shabbiest**) **1** in bad condition because of having been used or worn too much: *a shabby suit* **2** (used about people) dressed in an untidy way; wearing clothes that are in bad condition: *a shabby little man* **3** (used about the way that sb is treated) unfair; not generous —**shabbily** *adv*: *shabbily dressed* ○ *shabbily treated*

shack /ʃæk/ *noun* [C] a small, roughly built shed or hut

shade/shadow

a shadow   They're sitting in the shade.

☆ **shade** /ʃeɪd/ *noun* **1** [U] an area that is out of direct sunlight and is darker and cooler than areas in the sun: *It was so hot that I had to go and sit in the shade.* ☛ **Shade** [U] is an area or part of a place that is protected from the heat of the sun. **A shadow** [C] is a dark shape made by light shining on a person or object. **Shadow** [U] is an area of darkness in which it is difficult to distinguish things easily. **2** [C] something that keeps out light or makes it less bright: *a lampshade* **3 shades** [plural] (*informal*) (*especially US*) = SUN-GLASSES **4** [C] **a shade (of sth)** a type of a particular colour: *a shade of green* ○ *I'd prefer a darker shade if you have one.* ○ *a pale shade of grey* **5** [C] a small difference or variation in the form or nature of sth: *a word with various shades of meaning* **6** [sing] a little bit: *I feel a shade more optimistic now.*

shade *verb* [T] to protect sth from direct light; to give shade to sth: *The sun was so bright that I had to shade my eyes.*

shading *noun* [U] the use of or the result of using pencil, etc in part of a picture to create an effect of darkness

☆ **shadow** /'ʃædəʊ/ *noun* **1** [C] a dark shape on a surface that is caused by sth being between light and that surface: *The dog was chasing its own shadow.* ○ *The shadows lengthened as the sun went down.* ○ (*figurative*) *He has always lived in the shadow of his older brother.* ○ (*figurative*) *News of the tragedy cast a shadow over the day.* **2** [U] an area that is dark because sth prevents direct light from reaching it: *His face was in shadow.* ☛ Look at the note at **shade**. **3** a very small amount: *There isn't a shadow of doubt that he's lying.*

p	b	t	d	k	g	tʃ	dʒ	f	v	θ	ð
pen	bad	tea	did	cat	got	chin	June	fall	van	thin	then

shadow *verb* [T] to follow and watch the actions of sb, often secretly: *The police shadowed the suspect for three days.*

Shadow *adj* (in British politics) belonging to the opposition party, with special responsibility for a particular subject, eg education or defence. Shadow ministers would probably become government ministers if their party won the next election: *the Shadow Cabinet*

shadowy *adj* **1** having many shadows; dark: *a shadowy forest* **2** difficult to see or identify clearly: *a shadowy figure coming towards me* **3** mysterious; difficult to know much about: *the shadowy world of the secret police*

shady /ˈʃeɪdɪ/ *adj* (**shadier**; **shadiest**) **1** giving shade; giving shelter from the sun: *We ate our picnic in a shady spot.* **2** (*informal*) not completely honest or legal: *She's made a lot of money from some rather shady deals.*

shaft /ʃɑːft; *US* ʃæft/ *noun* [C] **1** a long, narrow hole in which sth can go up and down or enter or leave: *a lift shaft* o *a mine shaft* **2** a bar that connects parts of a machine so that power can pass between them

shaggy /ˈʃægɪ/ *adj* (**shaggier**; **shaggiest**) **1** (used about hair, material, etc) long, thick and untidy **2** covered with long, thick, untidy hair: *a shaggy dog*

☆ **shake**¹ /ʃeɪk/ *verb* (*pt* **shook** /ʃʊk/; *pp* **shaken** /ˈʃeɪkən/) **1** [I,T] to move from side to side or up and down with short, quick movements: *I was so nervous that I was shaking.* o *The whole building shakes when big lorries go past.* o (*figurative*) *His voice shook with emotion as he described the tragedy.* o *Shake the bottle before taking the medicine.* o *She shook him to wake him up.* **2** [T] to disturb or upset sb/sth: *The scandal has shaken the whole country.* **3** [T] to cause sth to be less certain; to cause doubt about sth: *Nothing seems to shake her belief that she was right.*

shaking hands

(IDIOMS) **shake sb's hand/shake hands (with sb)/shake sb by the hand** to take sb's hand and move it up and down (as a greeting, to show that you have agreed on sth, etc)

shake your head to move your head from side to side, as a way of expressing that you mean 'No'

(PHRASAL VERB) **shake sb/sth off** to escape from sb/sth; to remove by shaking: *I don't seem to be able to shake off this cold.* o *Shake the crumbs off the tablecloth.*

'shake-up *noun* [C] a complete change in the structure or organization of sth: *a massive shake-up in the government*

shake² /ʃeɪk/ *noun* [C] the act of shaking or being shaken physically: *a shake of the head* o *You'll have to give the bottle a few shakes.*

shaky /ˈʃeɪkɪ/ *adj* (**shakier**; **shakiest**) **1** shaking or feeling weak because you are frightened or ill **2** not firm; weak or not very good: *The table's a bit shaky so don't put anything heavy on it.* o *They've had a shaky start to the season and have lost most of their games.* —**shakily** /-ɪlɪ/ *adv*

☆ **shall** /ʃəl/; strong form ʃæl/ *modal verb* (*negative* **shall not**; *short form* **shan't** /ʃɑːnt/) **1** (used with 'I' and 'we' in future tenses, instead of 'will'): *I shall be very happy to see him again.* o *We shan't be arriving until ten o'clock.* o *At the end of this year, I shall have been working here for five years.* **2** (used for asking for information or advice): *What time shall I come?* o *Where shall we go for our holiday?* **3** (used for offering to do sth): *Shall I help you carry that box?* o *Shall we drive you home?* **4 shall we** (used for suggesting that you do sth with the person or people that you are talking to): *Shall we go out for a meal this evening?* **5** (*formal*) (used for saying that sth must happen or that sb must/must not do sth): *In the rules it says that a player shall be sent off for using bad language.* o *If you really want a pony, you shall have one.*

☆ **shallow** /ˈʃæləʊ/ *adj* **1** not deep; with not much distance between top and bottom: *The sea is very shallow here.* o *Put in a shallow dish and bake for 20 minutes.* **2** not having or showing serious or deep thought: *rather a shallow young man* —**shallowness** *noun* [U]

☆ **shame** /ʃeɪm/ *noun* **1** [U] the guilty feeling that you have when you think that you have done sth morally wrong, sth that causes other people to have a bad opinion of you, or sth extremely embarrassing: *She was filled with shame at the thought of how she had lied to her mother.* ☛ The adjective that describes this feeling is **ashamed**. **2** [U] the ability to have this feeling: *He doesn't care how he behaves in public. He's got no shame!* **3** [U] loss of respect from others; loss of honour: *the shame of defeat* o *His actions have brought shame on his whole family.* **4 a shame** [sing] a fact or situation that makes you feel disappointed: *It's a shame you can't come. I was looking forward to seeing you.* o *'I failed my exam.' 'Oh, what a shame!'* o *What a shame you have to leave so soon.*

shame *verb* [T] to make sb feel ashamed

shameful *adj* which sb should be ashamed of: *a shameful waste of public money* —**shamefully** *adv: I think you have behaved shamefully.*

shameless *adj* not having or showing the feeling of shame that people would expect you to have in a particular situation: *a shameless display of greed and bad manners* —**shamelessly** *adv*

shampoo /ʃæmˈpuː/ *noun* (*pl* **shampoos**) **1** [C,U] a liquid that you use for washing your hair: *a shampoo for greasy hair* **2** [C] the act of washing sth with shampoo

shampoo *verb* [T] (*pres part* **shampooing**;

shamrock

3rd pers sing pres **shampoos**; pt, pp **shampooed**) to wash with shampoo

shamrock /'ʃæmrɒk/ noun [C,U] a plant with three leaves on each stem, which is the national symbol of Ireland

shandy /'ʃændi/ noun [C,U] (pl **shandies**) a drink that is a mixture of beer and lemonade

shan't short for SHALL NOT

shanty town /'ʃænti taʊn/ noun [C] a town or part of a town where poor people live in bad conditions in badly built huts, etc

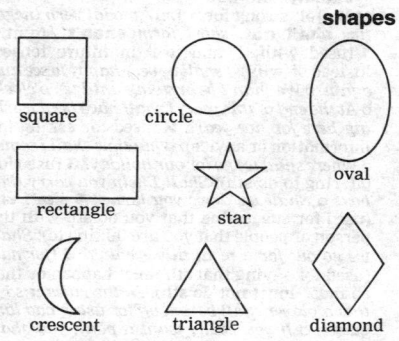

shapes

- square
- circle
- oval
- rectangle
- star
- crescent
- triangle
- diamond

☆ **shape¹** /ʃeɪp/ noun **1** [C,U] the physical outline or outer form of sth: *a round/square/oblong shape* ○ *an ashtray in the shape of a hand* ○ *clothes to fit women of all shapes and sizes* **2** [C] something that has a particular outline or outer form: *Squares, circles and triangles are all different shapes.* **3** [U] the condition of sb or sth; the good or bad state of sb or sth: *The economy has been in bad shape for some time.* ○ *She was in such bad shape (= so ill) that she had to be taken to hospital.* **4** [sing] **the shape (of sth)** the organization, form or structure of sth: *Recent developments have changed the shape of the company.*

(IDIOMS) **in shape** healthy and physically fit: *Regular exercise will keep your body in shape.*

out of shape 1 not in the usual or correct shape: *My sweater's gone out of shape now that I've washed it.* **2** not physically fit: *You're out of shape. You should get more exercise.*

take shape to start to develop well: *Plans to expand the company are beginning to take shape.*

shapeless adj not having a definite or attractive shape: *a shapeless dress*

☆ **shape²** /ʃeɪp/ verb [T] **1 shape sth (into sth)** to make sth into a particular form: *Shape the mixture into small balls.* **2** to influence the way in which sth develops; to cause sth to have a particular form or nature: *His political ideas were shaped by his upbringing.*

-shaped (in compounds) having a certain shape; having the shape of the thing mentioned: *an L-shaped room*

☆ **share¹** /ʃeə(r)/ noun **1** [sing] **share (of sth)** a part or amount of sth that has been divided between several people: *We each pay a share of the household bills.* ○ *I'm willing to take my share of the blame.* **2** [C, usually pl] **shares (in sth)** one of the equal parts into which the ownership of a company is divided. Shares in a company can be bought and sold.

(IDIOM) **have, etc (more than) your fair share of sth** ⇨ FAIR¹(6)

share verb **1** [T] **share sth (out)** to divide sth and give shares to others: *We shared the pizza between the four of us.* **2** [I,T] **share (sth) (with sb)** to have, use, do or pay sth together with another person or other people; to have sth that sb else also has: *I share a flat with four other people.* ○ *There's only one room available so we'll have to share.* ○ *We share the same interests.* **3** [T] **share sth (with sb)** to tell sb about sth; to allow sb to know sth: *Sometimes it helps to share your problems.*

'shareholder noun [C] an owner of shares in a company

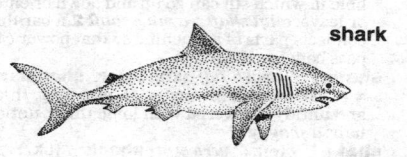

shark

shark /ʃɑːk/ noun [C,U] a large, often dangerous, sea-fish that has many sharp teeth

☆ **sharp** /ʃɑːp/ adj **1** having a fine edge or point; that can cut or make a hole in sth easily: *a sharp knife* ○ *sharp teeth* ☛ The opposite is **blunt**. **2** (used about a change of direction) very great and sudden: *a sharp rise/fall in inflation* ○ *a sharp bend* (= on a road) **3** clear; allowing details to be seen clearly: *the sharp outline of the hills* ○ *a sharp contrast between the lives of the rich and the poor* **4** able to think, act, understand, see or hear quickly: *a sharp mind* ○ *sharp eyesight* **5** (used about actions or movements) quick and sudden: *One short sharp blow was enough to end the fight.* **6** (used about words, remarks, etc) intended to upset or be critical: *During the debate there was a sharp exchange of views between the two parties.* **7** (used about pain) very strong and sudden: *a sharp pain in the chest* ☛ The opposite is **dull**. **8** (used about sth that affects the senses) not mild or gentle, often causing an unpleasant feeling: *a sharp taste* ○ *a sharp wind* **9** (symbol ♯) (in music) half a tone higher than the stated note: *in the key of C sharp minor* ☛ Look at **flat²**(7). **10** (in music) higher than the correct note: *That last note was sharp. Can you sing it again?* ☛ Look at **flat²**(8).

sharp noun [C] (symbol ♯) (in music) a note that is half a tone higher than the note with the same letter ☛ Look at **flat**.

sharp adv **1** (used about a time) exactly, punctually: *Be here at three o'clock sharp.* **2** in a sharp(2) way: *Go to the traffic lights and turn sharp right.* **3** (in music) slightly higher than the correct note ☛ Look at **flat**.

sharpen /'ʃɑːpən/ verb [I,T] to become, or to

iː	ɪ	e	æ	ɑː	ɒ	ɔː	ʊ	uː	ʌ
see	sit	ten	hat	arm	got	saw	put	too	cup

shatter — shell

make sth, sharp or sharper: *to sharpen a knife* o *The campaign sharpened public awareness of the problem.*

sharpener /'ʃɑːpnə(r)/ *noun* [C] an object or tool that is used for making sth sharp

sharply *adv* in a sharp way: *The road bends sharply to the left.* o *'Mind your own business!' she said sharply.* o *Share prices fell sharply this morning.* —**sharpness** *noun* [U]

shatter /'ʃætə(r)/ *verb* **1** [I,T] (of glass, etc) to break into very small pieces: *I dropped the glass and it shattered on the floor.* o *The force of the explosion shattered the windows.* **2** [T] to destroy completely: *Her hopes were shattered by the news.*

shattered *adj* **1** very upset because of sth shocking that has happened **2** (*informal*) very tired: *I'm absolutely shattered.*

☆ **shave** /ʃeɪv/ *verb* [I,T] **shave (sth) (off)** to remove hair from the face or another part of the body with a razor: *He's too young to shave.* o *I was shaving when the doorbell rang.* o *I cut myself shaving this morning.* o *When did you shave off your moustache?*
(PHRASAL VERB) **shave sth off (sth)** to cut very thin pieces from a surface (in order to make it smooth or to make it fit sth): *We'll have to shave a bit off the door to make it close properly.*

shave *noun* [C, usually sing] the act of shaving: *to have a shave*
(IDIOM) **a close shave/thing** ⇨ CLOSE¹

shaven /'ʃeɪvn/ *adj* having been shaved: *clean-shaven* (= not having a beard or moustache)

shaver (*also* **electric razor**) *noun* [C] an electric tool that is used for shaving hair

shawl /ʃɔːl/ *noun* [C] a large piece of cloth, made of wool, etc that is worn by a woman round the shoulders or head or that is wrapped round a baby

☆ **she** /ʃiː/ *pron* (the subject of a verb) the female person or animal who has already been mentioned: *'What does your sister do?' 'She's a dentist.'* o *I asked her a question but she didn't answer.*

shear /ʃɪə(r)/ *verb* [T] (*pt* **sheared**; *pp* **sheared** *or* **shorn**) to cut the wool off a sheep

shears /ʃɪəz/ *noun* [plural] a tool that is like a very large pair of scissors and that is used for cutting things in the garden

sheath /ʃiːθ/ *noun* [C] (*pl* **sheaths** /ʃiːðz/) the cover for a knife or other sharp weapon

shed¹ /ʃed/ *noun* [C] a small building that is used for keeping things or animals in: *a garden shed* o *a bicycle shed*

shed² /ʃed/ *verb* [T] (*pres part* **shedding**; *pt, pp* **shed**) **1** to lose sth because it falls off: *This snake sheds its skin every year.* o *Autumn is coming and the trees are beginning to shed their leaves.* o *A lorry has shed its load.* **2** to get rid of or remove sth that is not wanted: *She was forced to shed some of her responsibilities through illness.* o *Firms in the area have shed thousands of jobs in the past year.*
(IDIOMS) **shed blood** to kill or injure people: *Much blood was shed during the war.*

shed light on sth to make sth clear and easy to understand

shed tears (*formal*) to cry: *It was a sad occasion and many tears were shed.*

she'd /ʃiːd/ *short for* SHE HAD, SHE WOULD

sheep

— horn
fleece
ram
lamb
ewe

☆ **sheep** /ʃiːp/ *noun* [C] (*pl* **sheep**) an animal with a coat of wool that is kept on farms and used for its wool or meat

☛ A male sheep is a **ram**, a female sheep is a **ewe** and a young sheep is a **lamb**. When sheep make a noise they **bleat**. This is written as **baa**. The meat from sheep is called **mutton**. Look at the note at **meat**.

'sheepdog *noun* [C] a dog that has been trained to control sheep

'sheepskin *noun* [U] the skin of a sheep, including the wool, from which coats, etc are made

sheepish /'ʃiːpɪʃ/ *adj* feeling rather ashamed or embarrassed because you have done sth silly: *a sheepish grin* —**sheepishly** *adv*

sheer /ʃɪə(r)/ *adj* **1** (only *before* a noun) complete, absolute; involving nothing else except: *It's sheer stupidity to drink and drive.* o *It was sheer luck that I happened to be in the right place at the right time.* o *Her success is due to sheer hard work.* **2** very steep; almost vertical: *Don't walk near the edge. It's a sheer drop to the sea.*

☆ **sheet** /ʃiːt/ *noun* [C] **1** a large piece of material used on a bed. Sheets are used in pairs and you sleep between the top and bottom sheet. ☛ picture at **bed**. **2** a piece of paper (usually of a particular size) that is used for writing, printing, etc on: *a sheet of notepaper* o *a sheet of A4* o *Write each answer on a separate sheet.* ☛ Look at **balance sheet**. **3** a flat, thin piece of any material, especially glass or metal

sheikh (*also* **sheik**) /ʃeɪk/; *US* ʃiːk/ *noun* [C] an Arab ruler

☆ **shelf** /ʃelf/ *noun* [C] (*pl* **shelves** /ʃelvz/) a long flat piece of wood, glass, etc that is fixed to a wall or in a cupboard, used for standing things on: *I put up a shelf in the kitchen.* o *a bookshelf*

☆ **shell** /ʃel/ *noun* [C,U] **1** a hard covering that protects eggs, nuts and some animals: *a collection of sea-shells* o *an empty shell* o *a piece of eggshell* **2** the walls of a building that is not finished or that has been seriously damaged by fire, etc **3** a metal container filled with explosives that is fired by a large gun

shell *verb* [T] **1** to take the shell(1) off sth that can be eaten: *to shell peas* **2** to fire shells(3)

ɜː	ə	eɪ	əʊ	aɪ	aʊ	ɔɪ	ɪə	eə	ʊə
fur	ago	pay	home	five	now	join	near	hair	pure

shellfish

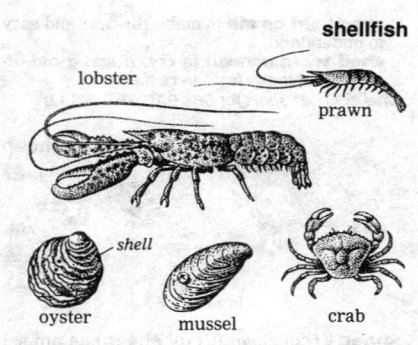

lobster, prawn, shell, oyster, mussel, crab

shellfish noun (pl **shellfish**) **1** [C] a type of animal that lives in water and has a shell **2** [U] these animals used as food: *I love shellfish.*

she'll /ʃiːl/ short for SHE WILL

☆ **shelter** /ˈʃeltə(r)/ noun **1** [U] **shelter (from sth)** protection from danger or bad weather: *to give somebody food and shelter* ○ *I took shelter under his umbrella.* **2** [C] a small building that gives protection or cover, eg from bad weather or attack: *a bus shelter* ○ *an air-raid shelter*

shelter verb **1** [I] **shelter (from sth)** to find protection or shelter: *Let's shelter from the rain under that tree.* ○ *There are 100 refugees sheltering in foreign embassies.* **2** [T] **shelter sb/sth (from sb/sth)** to protect sb/sth; to give sb/sth shelter: *The trees shelter the house from the wind.* ○ *The embassy is now sheltering nearly 100 refugees.*

sheltered adj **1** (used about a place) protected from bad weather: *The campers found a sheltered spot for their tent.* **2** protected from unpleasant things in your life: *a sheltered childhood in the country*

shelve¹ /ʃelv/ verb [T] to decide not to continue with a plan, etc: *Plans for a new motorway have been shelved.*

shelve² /ʃelv/ verb [I] (used about land) to slope in one direction: *The beach shelves down to the sea.*

shelves /ʃelvz/ pl of SHELF

shelving /ˈʃelvɪŋ/ noun [U] a set of shelves

shepherd /ˈʃepəd/ noun [C] a person who looks after sheep

shepherd verb [T] to guide and look after people so that they do not get lost: *She shepherded the children onto the train.*

shepherd's 'pie (also **cottage pie**) noun [C] a type of meal made from meat covered with a layer of mashed potato

sheriff /ˈʃerɪf/ noun [C] an officer of the law in an American county

sherry /ˈʃeri/ noun [C,U] (pl **sherries**) a type of strong Spanish wine; a glass of this wine: *sweet/dry sherry* ○ *Would you like a sherry?*

she's /ʃiːz/ short for SHE IS, SHE HAS

shield /ʃiːld/ noun [C] **1** a large piece of metal or wood that soldiers used to carry to protect themselves. Now certain policemen carry shields: *riot shields* **2** a person or thing that is used for protection: *The metal door acted as a shield against the explosion.* **3** an object or drawing in the shape of a shield, sometimes used as a school or team badge or as a prize in a sports competition

shield verb [T] **shield sb/sth (against/from sb/sth)** to protect sb/sth from danger or damage: *I shielded my eyes from the bright light with my hand.*

shift¹ /ʃɪft/ verb **1** [T] to move sb/sth from one position to another: *She shifted the furniture around.* **2** [I] to change position or direction: *The captain waited for the wind to shift.*

'shift-key noun [C] the part of a typewriter that you press in order to type capital letters

shift² /ʃɪft/ noun [C] **1 a shift (in sth)** a change in the position or nature of sth: *There has been a shift in public opinion away from war.* ○ *a shift in policy/a policy shift* **2** (in a factory, etc) a division of the working day; the group who work this period: *an eight-hour shift* ○ *Firemen do shift work.* ○ *the day/night shift*

shifty /ˈʃɪfti/ adj (**shiftier; shiftiest**) (used about a person or his/her appearance) giving the impression that you cannot trust him/her: *shifty eyes*

shilling /ˈʃɪlɪŋ/ noun [C] a British coin that is no longer in use and that was worth 5p

shimmer /ˈʃɪmə(r)/ verb [I] to shine with a soft light that seems to be moving: *The tears shimmered in her eyes.* ○ *moonlight shimmering on the sea*

shin /ʃɪn/ noun [C] the front part of your leg above your ankle and below your knee ☞ picture on page A8.

'shin-pad noun [C] a thick piece of material used to protect the shin when playing football, etc

☆ **shine** /ʃaɪn/ verb (pt, pp **shone** /ʃɒn; US ʃəʊn/) **1** [I] to give out or to reflect light: *moonlight shining on the sea* ○ *The sea shone in the light of the moon.* ○ (figurative) *The child's eyes shone with happiness.* **2** [T] to point the light of a torch, etc at sb/sth: *The policeman shone a torch on the stranger's face.* **3** [I] **shine (at/in sth)** to do a school subject, a sport, etc very well: *She has always shone at languages.*

shine noun [sing] **1** brightness, caused by light reflecting, because sth has been polished: *There's a lovely shine on that table.* **2** the act of polishing sth so that it shines: *He gave his shoes a shine.*

shiny adj (**shinier; shiniest**) bright; reflecting light: *The shampoo leaves your hair soft and shiny.* ○ *a shiny new car*

shingle /ˈʃɪŋgl/ noun [U] small pieces of stone lying in a mass on a beach

☆ **ship¹** /ʃɪp/ noun [C] a large boat used for carrying passengers or cargo by sea: *to travel by ship* ○ *to launch a ship* ○ *The captain went on board ship.* ○ *The ship sails at noon.* ○ *The ship sank.* ☞ picture at boat. A **boat** is smaller than a ship. A **liner** is used to carry people for long journeys and a **ferry** is used for short journeys. We use **vessel** in formal English for ship.

'shipbuilding noun [U] the building of ships

p	b	t	d	k	g	tʃ	dʒ	f	v	θ	ð
pen	bad	tea	did	cat	got	chin	June	fall	van	thin	then

ship 573 **shoot**

'shipwreck noun [C,U] an accident at sea in which a ship is destroyed by a storm, rocks, etc
☛ A person or a ship that has suffered such an accident has been **shipwrecked**.

'shipyard noun [C] a place where ships are repaired or built

ship² /ʃɪp/ verb [T] (ship**p**ing; ship**p**ed) to send or carry by ship: *All their furniture was shipped to Australia when they emigrated.*

shipment /'ʃɪpmənt/ noun **1** [C] a quantity of goods sent by ship: *a shipment of grain* **2** [U] the transport of goods by ship: *cargo ready for shipment*

shipping /'ʃɪpɪŋ/ noun [U] **1** ships considered as a group or as traffic: *'Attention all shipping' is part of a warning given on the radio about bad weather.* **2** the transport of goods by ship

shirk /ʃɜːk/ verb [I,T] to avoid doing sth that is difficult or unpleasant: *to shirk your responsibilities*

☆ **shirt** /ʃɜːt/ noun [C] a piece of clothing made of cotton, etc, worn (especially by men) on the upper part of the body: *He wears a shirt and tie for work.*

☛ A shirt usually has a **collar** at the neck, long or short **sleeves**, and **buttons** down the front.

shiver /'ʃɪvə(r)/ verb [I] to shake slightly, especially because you are cold or frightened: *shivering with cold/fright*

shiver noun [C] an act of shivering: *The thought sent a shiver down my spine.*

shoal /ʃəʊl/ noun [C] a large group of fish that feed and swim together

☆ **shock¹** /ʃɒk/ noun **1** [C,U] the feeling that is caused by sth unpleasant happening suddenly; the situation that causes this feeling: *The sudden noise gave him a shock.* ○ *The bad news came as a shock to her?* ○ *I'm still suffering from shock at the news.* **2** [C] = ELECTRIC SHOCK: *Don't touch that wire – you'll get a shock.* **3** [C] a violent blow or shaking (from a crash, explosion, etc): *the shock of the earthquake* **4** [U] (in medicine) a condition of extreme weakness caused by damage to the body: *He was in/went into shock after the accident.*

shock² /ʃɒk/ verb [T] **1** to cause an unpleasant feeling of surprise in sb: *We were shocked by his death.* ○ *The staff were shocked at the news that the firm was going to close.* **2** to make sb feel disgust and anger: *The pictures of the starving children shocked the world.*

shocking adj **1** making you feel worried, upset or angry: *a shocking accident* ○ *shocking behaviour* **2** (*informal*) very bad: *The weather has been absolutely shocking.*

shod pt, pp of SHOE

shoddy /'ʃɒdi/ adj (**shoddier**; **shoddiest**) made carelessly or with poor quality materials: *shoddy goods* ○ (*figurative*) *He received shoddy treatment* (= he was treated badly).
—**shoddily** adv

☆ **shoe** /ʃuː/ noun [C] **1** a type of covering for the foot, usually made of leather or plastic: *a pair of shoes* ○ *running shoes* ○ *What size are your shoes?* ○ *I tried on a nice pair of shoes but they didn't fit.* ○ *Wait for me – I've just got to do my shoes up.* **2** = HORSESHOE

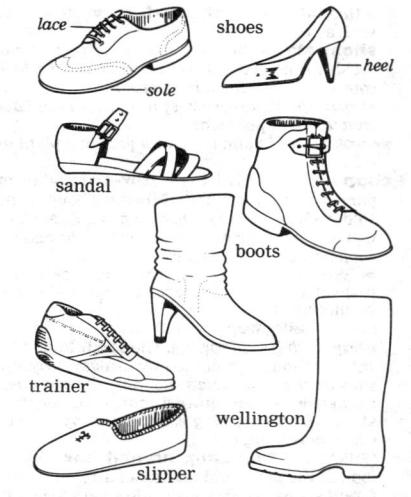

shoe verb [T] (*pt, pp* **shod** /ʃɒd/) to fit a shoe (on a horse)

'shoelace (*especially US* **shoestring**) noun [C] a long piece of cord used to fasten a shoe: *to tie/untie a shoelace*

'shoestring noun [C] (*especially US*) = SHOELACE
(IDIOM) **on a shoestring** using very little money: *My mother brought up five children on a shoestring.*

shone pt, pp of SHINE

shoo /ʃuː/ interj (usually said to animals or small children) Go away!

shoo verb (*pt, pp* **shooed**)
(PHRASAL VERB) **shoo sb/sth away, off, out, etc** to make sb/sth go away by saying 'shoo' and waving your hands: *I shooed the birds away from the seeds.*

shook pt of SHAKE

☆ **shoot¹** /ʃuːt/ verb (*pt, pp* **shot** /ʃɒt/) **1** [I,T] **shoot (sth) (at sb/sth)** to fire a gun, etc: *Don't shoot!* ○ *She shot an arrow at the target, but missed it.* **2** [T] to injure or kill sb/sth with a gun: *The policeman was shot in the arm.* ○ *The soldier was shot dead.* **3** [I,T] to hunt and kill birds and animals with a gun as a sport: *He goes shooting at the weekends.* **4** [I,T] to move quickly and suddenly in one direction; to make sth move in this way: *The car shot past me at 100 miles per hour.* ○ *She shot her boyfriend an angry look* (= looked at him very quickly and angrily). **5** [I] **shoot (down, up, etc sth)** (of pain) to go very suddenly along part of your body: *The pain shot up my leg.* **6** [I] **shoot (at sth)** (in football, etc) to try to kick or hit the ball into the goal: *He shot at goal but missed.* **7** [I,T] to make a film or photograph of sth: *They shot the scene ten times.*

s	z	ʃ	ʒ	h	m	n	ŋ	l	r	j	w
so	zoo	she	vision	how	man	no	sing	leg	red	yes	wet

(PHRASAL VERBS) **shoot sb down** to kill sb with a gun

shoot sth down to make an aeroplane, etc crash to the ground by shooting it: *The helicopter was shot down by a missile.*

shoot up to increase very quickly: *Prices have shot up in the past year.*

shoot² /ʃuːt/ *noun* [C] a new part of a plant or tree

☆ **shop** /ʃɒp/ *noun* [C] **1** (*US* **store**) a building or part of a building where things are bought and sold: *a shoe shop* ○ *a corner shop* (= a local shop, usually at the corner of a street) ○ *When do the shops open?* ○ *a butcher's, baker's, etc shop* ☛ We usually say **at the butcher's**, etc instead of 'at the butcher's shop', etc. **2** = WORKSHOP(1)

(IDIOM) **talk shop** ⇨ TALK¹

shop *verb* [I] (sho**pp**ing; sho**pp**ed) to go to a shop or shops in order to buy things: *I prefer to shop on my own.* ○ *He's shopping for some new clothes.* ☛ **Go shopping** is more common than **shop**: *We go shopping every Saturday.* ○ *to go Christmas shopping*

(PHRASAL VERB) **shop around (for sth)** to look at the price and quality of an item in different shops before you decide where to buy it: *If you want a bargain you'd better shop around.*

shopper *noun* [C] a person who is shopping

shopping *noun* [U] **1** the food, clothing, etc that you have bought in a shop: *Can you help me to put away the shopping?* **2** the activity of shopping: *She did the shopping.* ○ *a shopping basket*

'**shop assistant** (*US* '**salesclerk**; **clerk**) *noun* [C] a person who works in a shop

,**shop-'floor** *noun* [sing] (the workers in) an area of a factory where things are made

'**shopkeeper** (*US* '**storekeeper**) *noun* [C] a person who owns or manages a small shop

'**shoplift** *verb* [I,T] to steal sth from a shop while pretending to be a customer

'**shoplifter** *noun* [C]: *Shoplifters will be prosecuted.* ☛ Look at the note at **thief**. —'**shoplifting** *noun* [U]: *He was arrested for shoplifting.*

'**shopping centre** *noun* [C] a place where there are many shops, either outside or in a covered building

'**shopping mall** (*also* **mall**) *noun* [C] (*US*) a covered area or building where there are many shops

☆ **shore** /ʃɔː(r)/ *noun* [C,U] the land along the edge of a sea or lake: *The swimmer kept close to the shore.* ○ *The sailors went on shore* (= on land). ☛ **Ashore** is also possible for 'on shore'.

shorn *pp* of SHEAR

☆ **short¹** /ʃɔːt/ *adj* **1** not measuring much from one end to the other: *a short line* ○ *a short distance* ○ *This essay is rather short.* ○ *short hair* ☛ The opposite is **long**. **2** less than the average height: *The opposite is* **tall**. **3** not lasting a long time: *a short visit* ○ *She left a short time ago.* ○ *to have a short memory* (= to only remember things that have happened recently) **4 short (of sth)** not having enough of what is needed: *Because of illness, the team is two players short.* ○ *Good secretaries are in short supply* (= there are not enough of them). ○ *We're a bit short of money at the moment.* **5 short for sth** used as a shorter way of saying sth: *'Bill' is short for 'William'.*

(IDIOMS) **for short** as a short form: *She's called 'Diana', or 'Di' for short.*

in the long/short term ⇨ TERM

in short in a few words; briefly: *Einstein had one of the greatest minds the world has ever known: in short, he was a genius.*

,**short 'circuit** (*also informal* **short**) *noun* [C] a bad electrical connection that causes a machine to stop working properly

,**short-'circuit** *verb* [I,T] to have a short circuit or to cause a machine to have one: *The lights short-circuited.*

'**shortcoming** *noun* [C, usually pl] a fault or weakness: *As a leader, she had many shortcomings.*

short 'cut *noun* [C] a quicker, easier or more direct way to get somewhere or to do sth: *He took a short cut to school through the park.*

'**shorthand** *noun* [U] a method of writing quickly that uses signs or short forms of words: *to write in shorthand* ○ *a shorthand typist*

'**short list** *noun* [C] a list of the best people for a job, etc chosen from a larger number of people

,**short-'lived** /ˌʃɔːtˈlɪvd/; *US* /ˈlaɪvd/ *adj* lasting only for a short time

,**short-'sighted** (*US* ,**near-'sighted**) *adj* **1** only able to see things clearly when they are close ☛ The opposite is **long-sighted**. **2** not considering what will probably happen in the future: *a short-sighted attitude*

,**short-'staffed** *adj* (used of an office, a shop, etc) not having enough staff

,**short-'story** *noun* [C] a piece of writing that is shorter than a novel: *a collection of short stories by Thomas Hardy*

,**short-'term** *adj* lasting for a short period of time from the present: *short-term plans*

'**short wave** *noun* [U] (*abbr* **SW**) the system of broadcasting radio using sound waves of less than 100 metres

short² /ʃɔːt/ *adv* suddenly: *She stopped short when she saw the accident.*

(IDIOMS) **cut sth/sb short** to interrupt: *I tried to explain but he cut me short.*

fall short (of sth) not to be enough; not to reach sth: *The pay rise fell short of the workers' demands.*

go short (of sth) to be without enough (of sth): *He made sure his family never went short of food.*

run short (of sth) to have used up most of sth so there is not much left: *We're running short of coffee.*

short of sth except for: *He's tried to make money by every means, short of stealing it.*

stop short of sth/doing sth ⇨ STOP¹

short³ /ʃɔːt/ *noun* [C] **1** (*informal*) = SHORT CIRCUIT **2** a small drink of strong alcohol

shortage /ˈʃɔːtɪdʒ/ *noun* [C] a situation where there is not enough of sth: *a food, housing, water, etc shortage* ○ *a shortage of physics teachers*

iː	ɪ	e	æ	ɑː	ɒ	ɔː	ʊ	uː	ʌ
see	sit	ten	hat	arm	got	saw	put	too	cup

shortbread /'ʃɔːtbred/ noun [U] a sweet biscuit made with sugar, flour and butter

shorten /'ʃɔːtn/ verb [I,T] to become shorter or to make sth shorter: *I'll have to shorten these trousers – they're much too long.*

shortly /'ʃɔːtli/ adv **1** soon; in a short time: *The manager will see you shortly.* **2** in an impatient, impolite way: *She spoke rather shortly to the customer.*

☆ **shorts** /ʃɔːts/ noun [plural] **1** a type of short trousers ending above the knee that you wear in hot weather, while playing sports, etc ☛ picture on page A11. **2** (*US*) men's underpants ☛ Notice that, because **shorts** is a plural word, we cannot say, for example, 'a new short'. The following are possible: *I need to get some new shorts.* ○ *I need to get a new pair of shorts.*

☆ **shot¹** /ʃɒt/ noun [C] **1** an act of firing a gun, etc, or the noise that this makes: *to take a shot at the target* ○ *The policeman fired a warning shot into the air.* **2 a shot (at sth/at doing sth)** (*informal*) an attempt to do sth: *Let me have a shot at it* (= let me try to do it). **3** (in sport) an act of kicking or hitting a ball: *to have a shot at goal* **4** a photograph or a picture in a film: *I got some good shots of the runners as they crossed the line.* **5** an injection of a drug: *a shot of penicillin* **6** often **the shot** a heavy metal ball that is thrown as a sport: *to put* (= throw) *the shot*

'shotgun noun [C] a gun used for shooting small animals and birds that fires small metal balls

shot² *pt, pp of* SHOOT¹

☆ **should** /ʃəd; strong form ʃʊd/ modal verb (negative **should not**; short form **shouldn't** /'ʃʊdnt/) **1** (used for saying that it is right for sb to do sth, or for sth to happen): *The police should do something about it.* ○ *Children shouldn't be left on their own.* **2** (used for giving or asking advice): *You should try that new restaurant.* ○ *He really shouldn't work so hard.* ○ *Should I try again?* **3** (used with 'have' to say that sb did the wrong thing): *I'm tired. I shouldn't have gone to bed so late/I should have gone to bed earlier.* **4** (used for saying that you expect sth is true or will happen): *It's 4.30. They should be in New York by now.* ○ *He should have arrived by now.* **5** (*formal*) (used with 'I/we' instead of 'would' in 'if' sentences): *I should be most grateful if you could send me…* **6** (used after 'if' and 'in case' when you think that sth is not likely to happen): *If you should decide to accept, please phone us.* ○ *Should you decide to accept…* **7** (used as the past tense of 'shall' when we report what sb says): *He asked me if he should come today* (= Shall I come today?). **8** (*formal*) (used after 'so that', 'in order that'): *In order that there should be no delay, we took action immediately.* **9** (used after certain verbs, eg when sth is arranged or suggested): *We arranged that they should book the hotel.* ○ *I suggested that he should cancel the meeting.* **10** (used after certain adjectives): *It's shocking that something like this should happen.* ○ *It's strange that you should mention that…* ○ *Is it important that we should all go?*

(IDIOMS) **I should…** (used when you are giving advice): *I should get to bed early if I were you.*

I should think my opinion is: *This picture is worth a lot of money, I should think.*

☆ **shoulder** /'ʃəʊldə(r)/ noun **1** [C] the part of the body between the neck and the top of the arm: *He hurt his shoulder.* ○ *to shrug your shoulders* (= to raise your shoulders, especially as a way of showing that you do not know an answer or that you are not interested) ☛ picture on page A8. **2** [C] a part of a dress, coat, etc that covers this part of the body **3 shoulders** [plural] the part of your body between your two shoulders: *He carried his little girl on his shoulders.*

(IDIOM) **have a chip on your shoulder** ⇨ CHIP¹

shoulder verb [T] **1** to accept the responsibility for sth: *She shouldered all the blame for the accident.* **2** to push sb/sth with your shoulder: *He shouldered everybody aside and disappeared out of the door.*

'shoulder-bag noun [C] a type of bag that you carry over one shoulder with a long strap

'shoulder-blade noun [C] either of the two large flat bones on each side of your back, below your shoulders

☆ **shout** /ʃaʊt/ noun [C] a loud call or cry: *She gave a warning shout.*

shout verb **1** [I] **shout (at/to sb); shout (out)** to speak or cry out in a very loud voice: *There's no need to shout – I can hear you.* ○ *The teacher shouted angrily at the boys.* ○ *to shout out in pain, excitement, etc* **2** [T] **shout sth (at/to sb); shout sth out** to say sth in a loud voice: *'Look out,' she shouted.* ○ *The captain shouted out instructions to his team.*

(PHRASAL VERB) **shout sb down** to prevent sb from being heard by shouting at them (often in a public meeting): *to shout a speaker down*

shove /ʃʌv/ verb [I,T] to push with a sudden, rough movement: *They pushed and shoved to the front of the queue.* ○ *The policeman shoved the thief through the door.* ○ (*informal*) *'What should I do with this box?' 'Oh, just shove it over here.'*

shove noun [C, usually sing] a sudden, rough push: *to give sb/sth a shove*

shovel /'ʃʌvl/ noun [C] a tool, like a spade, used for moving earth, snow, sand, etc

shovel verb [I,T] (shovelling; shovelled; *US* shoveling; shoveled) to move sth with a shovel

☆ **show¹** /ʃəʊ/ noun **1** [C] a type of entertainment that has singing, dancing, acting, etc in the theatre or on television, etc: *a comedy show on TV* ○ *We've booked tickets to see a show in London.* **2** [C] a collection of things for people to look at, often in a special large building: *a dog show* ○ *the motor show* (= where new makes of car are displayed) **3** [C,U] the outward expression of an emotion that is not what you really feel or that does not have much meaning: *Although she hated him, she put on a show of politeness.* ○ *His bravery is all show* (= he is not as brave as he pretends to be). **4** [sing] a sign of sth: *The parade of weapons was a show of strength by the government.*

(IDIOMS) **for show** intended to impress people;

ɜː	ə	eɪ	əʊ	aɪ	aʊ	ɔɪ	ɪə	eə	ʊə
fur	ago	pay	home	five	now	join	near	hair	pure

show

not to be used: *Those books are only for show – nobody ever reads them.*
on show put in a place where people can see it: *The collection is on show at the British Museum.*
'show business (also *informal* **showbiz** /'ʃəʊbɪz/) *noun* [U] the business of entertaining people, in the theatre, in films, on television, etc
'showdown *noun* [C] a final argument at the end of a long disagreement: *I think it's time for a showdown.*
'showjumping *noun* [U] a competition in which people ride horses over a series of fences (jumps)
'showroom *noun* [C] a type of shop where goods such as cars and electrical items are displayed

☆ **show²** /ʃəʊ/ *verb* (*pt* **showed**; *pp* **shown** /ʃəʊn/ or **showed**) **1** [T] **show sb/sth (to sb)** to make it possible for other people to see sb/sth: *I showed the letter to him.* ○ *I showed him the letter.* ○ *She showed me what she had bought.* ○ *They're showing his latest film at our local cinema.* **2** [T] to lead or guide sb to a place: *Shall I show you to your room?* ○ *A guide showed us round the museum.* **3** [T] to help sb to do sth by doing it yourself; to explain sth: *Can you show me how to put the disk in the computer?* **4** [T] to make sth clear; to give information about sth: *Research shows that most people get too little exercise.* ○ *The picture showed the effects of the storm.* **5** [I] to be able to be seen; to appear: *Her anger showed in her eyes.* ○ *I've got a hole in my sock but it doesn't show.* **6** [T] to allow sth to be seen: *These brown trousers don't show the dirt.* **7** [T] to have a particular quality: *She was showing signs of stress.* **8** [T] to cause people to notice a particular quality: *She was the only one who ever showed him any kindness.* ○ *She didn't want to show what she was really thinking.*

(PHRASAL VERBS) **show (sth) off** (*informal*) to try to impress people by showing them how clever you are or by showing them sth that you are proud of: *John drove his new car very fast in order to show off.* ○ *She wanted to show off her new bike.*

show up (*informal*) to arrive, especially when sb is expecting you: *I thought you'd never show up.*
show (sth) up to allow sth to be seen: *The sunlight shows up those dirty marks on the window.*
show sb up (*informal*) to make someone feel ashamed or embarrassed by behaving badly: *He showed her up by shouting at the waiter.*

showing *noun* **1** [C] an act of showing a film, etc: *The second showing of the film begins at 8 o'clock.* **2** [sing] how sb/sth behaves; how successful sb/sth is: *On its present showing, the party should win the election.*
'show-off *noun* a person who tries to impress others by showing them how clever he/she is: *She's such a show-off.* ☛ This word is used when we are criticizing somebody.

☆ **shower** /'ʃaʊə(r)/ *noun* [C] **1** a way of washing the body by standing under running water: *He had a shower after the tennis match.* **2** the apparatus used for washing yourself in this way; the small room or part of a bathroom where it is fixed: *The shower doesn't work.* ○ *She's in the shower.* ○ *I'd like a room with a shower, please.* **3** a short period of rain or snow **4** a lot of very small objects that fall together: *a shower of dust*
shower *verb* **1** [T] **shower sb with sth** to cause a great number of very small objects to fall on sb/sth: *to be showered with leaves, dust, water* ○ (*figurative*) *He was showered with praise for his excellent work.* **2** [I] to have a shower(1)

shown *pp* of SHOW²
shrank *pt* of SHRINK
shrapnel /'ʃræpnəl/ *noun* [U] small pieces of metal that are thrown in various directions from an exploding bomb or shell(3)
shred /ʃred/ *noun* **1** [C] a small thin piece of material that has been cut or torn off: *He tore the letter to shreds.* **2** **a shred of sth** [sing] (in negative sentences) a very small amount of sth: *There wasn't a shred of truth in her story.*
shred *verb* [T] (**shred**ding; **shred**ded) to tear or cut sth into shreds: *shredded cabbage*
shrewd /ʃruːd/ *adj* able to make good decisions because you understand a situation well: *a shrewd thinker* ○ *a shrewd decision* —**shrewdly** *adv*
shriek /ʃriːk/ *verb* **1** [I] to give a sudden scream in a high voice: *She shrieked in fright.* ○ *The children were shrieking with laughter.* **2** [T] to scream in a high voice: *'Stop it!' he shrieked.* —**shriek** *noun* [C]: *She gave a loud shriek of pain.*
shrill /ʃrɪl/ *adj* (used about a sound) high and unpleasant: *a shrill cry*
shrimp /ʃrɪmp/ *noun* [C] a small sea creature with a shell that turns pink when you cook it. Shrimps are smaller than prawns.
shrine /ʃraɪn/ *noun* [C] a place that is holy for members of a religion, because it is associated with a special person or thing

shrink

'Oh no! My T-shirt has shrunk!'

shrink /ʃrɪŋk/ *verb* (*pt* **shrank** /ʃræŋk/ or **shrunk** /ʃrʌŋk/; *pp* **shrunk**) [I,T] to become smaller, often after being washed; to make sth smaller: *Oh no! My T-shirt's shrunk!* ○ *I've*

p	b	t	d	k	g	tʃ	dʒ	f	v	θ	ð
pen	bad	tea	did	cat	got	chin	June	fall	van	thin	then

shrunk my T-shirt. The water must have been too hot. ○ *Television has shrunk the world.* ○ *The rate of inflation has shrunk to 4%.*
(PHRASAL VERB) **shrink from sth/doing sth** to be unwilling to do sth because you find it unpleasant

shrivel /'ʃrɪvl/ *verb* [I,T] (shrivelling; shrivelled; *US* shriveling; shriveled) **shrivel (sth) (up)** to dry up and become smaller and wrinkled, usually in hot or dry conditions; to make sth do this

shroud /ʃraʊd/ *noun* [C] a cloth or sheet used to wrap a dead body before it is buried

shroud *verb* [T] (usually passive) to cover or hide sth with sth: *The tops of the mountains were shrouded in mist.* ○ *His past is shrouded in mystery.*

Shrove Tuesday /ˌʃrəʊv 'tjuːzdɪ; *US* 'tuːz-/ *noun* [C] the day before the beginning of a period called Lent when some Christians do not eat certain foods, etc

☞ In some countries the period before Shrove Tuesday is celebrated as **carnival**. In Britain many people eat **pancakes** on this day.

shrub /ʃrʌb/ *noun* [C] a small bush
shrubbery /'ʃrʌbəri/ *noun* [C] (*pl* **shrubberies**) an area planted with shrubs

shrug /ʃrʌg/ *verb* [I,T] (shrugging; shrugged) to raise your shoulders as a way of showing that you do not know or do not care about sth: *'Who knows?' he said and shrugged.* ○ *'It doesn't matter to me,' he said, shrugging his shoulders.*
(PHRASAL VERB) **shrug sth off** to treat sth as if it is not important to you

shrug *noun* [C, usually sing] a movement of shrugging the shoulders: *He answered his mother with a shrug.*

shrunk, shrunken ⇨ SHRINK

shudder /'ʃʌdə(r)/ *verb* [I] to shake with fear, etc: *Just to think about the accident makes me shudder.* ○ *I shudder to think how much this meal is going to cost.* —**shudder** *noun* [C]

shuffle /'ʃʌfl/ *verb* **1** [I] to walk by sliding your feet along instead of lifting them from the ground: *The child shuffled past, wearing her mother's shoes.* **2** [I,T] to move your body or feet around because you are uncomfortable or nervous: *The audience were so bored that they began to shuffle in their seats.* **3** [I,T] to mix a pack of playing-cards before a game: *It's your turn to shuffle.* ○ *He shuffled the cards carefully.*

shuffle *noun* [C, usually sing] **1** a shuffling way of walking **2** an act of shuffling cards

shun /ʃʌn/ *verb* [T] (shunning; shunned) to avoid sth/sb; to keep away from sth/sb: *The film star shunned publicity.* ○ *The tennis tournament has been shunned by all the world's leading players.*

shunt /ʃʌnt/ *verb* [T] **1** to move a railway train from one track to another **2** to move a person from one place to another: *He was shunted around from one hospital to another.*

☆ **shut** /ʃʌt/ *verb* [I,T] (*pres part* **shutting**; *pt, pp* **shut**) **1** [T] to change the position of sth so that it covers a hole, etc; to fold sth together; to close: *Could you shut the door, please?* ○ *I can't shut my suitcase.* ○ *Shut your books, please.* ○ *He* *shut his eyes and tried to go to sleep.* **2** [I] to move or be moved into a closed position: *This window won't shut properly.* **3** [I,T] (used about a shop, restaurant, etc) to stop being open; to close sth (a shop, restaurant, etc): *What time do the shops shut on Saturday?* ○ *I shut the shop early and went home.* **4** [T] to prevent sb/sth from leaving or moving; to trap sth: *She shut herself in her room and refused to come out.* ○ *Tony shut his fingers in the door of the car.*

(PHRASAL VERBS) **shut sb/sth away** to keep sb/sth in a place where people cannot find or see him/her/it

shut (sth) down (used about a factory, etc) to be closed for a long time or for ever; to close sth (a factory, etc) for a long time or for ever: *Financial problems forced the business to shut down.* ○ *They have shut down the factory for reasons of safety.*

shut sb/sth off (from sth) to keep sb/sth apart from sth: *He shuts himself off from the rest of the world.*

shut sb/sth out to keep sb/sth out: *He tried to shut out all thoughts of the accident.*

shut (sb) up (*informal*) **1** to stop talking; to be quiet: *I wish you'd shut up!* **2** to make sb stop talking: *Nothing can shut him up once he's started.*

shut sb/sth up (in sth) to put sb/sth somewhere and stop them leaving: *He was shut up in prison for nearly ten years.* ☞ Look at the note at **close**.

shut *adj* (not before a noun) **1** in a closed position: *Make sure the door is shut properly before you leave.* ☞ Remember that we can use **closed** before a noun: *a closed door*, but not **shut**. **2** not open to the public: *The restaurant was shut so we went to one round the corner.*

shut up! *interj* (*informal*) a way of telling sb (rather rudely) that you want them to be quiet: *Shut up! Can't you see I'm working?*

shutter /'ʃʌtə(r)/ *noun* [C] **1** a wooden or metal cover that is fixed outside a window and that can be open or shut. A shop's shutter usually slides down from the top of the shop window. **2** the part at the front of a camera that opens for a very short time to let light in so that a photograph can be taken

shuttle /'ʃʌtl/ *noun* [C] an aeroplane or bus that travels regularly between two places: *I'm catching the seven o'clock shuttle to Glasgow.*
'**shuttle service** *noun* [C] a regular air, bus or train service between two places

shuttlecock /'ʃʌtlkɒk/ *noun* [C] the small light object that is hit over a net in the sport of badminton

☆ **shy** /ʃaɪ/ *adj* (shyer; shyest) nervous and uncomfortable with other people. Shy people do not usually say very much to people they do not know: *She's very shy with strangers.* ○ *a shy smile*

shy *verb* (*pres part* **shying**; *3rd pers sing pres* **shies**; *pt, pp* **shied**) [I] (used about a horse) to move back or sideways suddenly in fear
(PHRASAL VERB) **shy away from sth/from doing sth** to avoid doing sth because you are afraid: *He shied away from telling her the truth.*

s	z	ʃ	ʒ	h	m	n	ŋ	l	r	j	w
so	zoo	she	vision	how	man	no	sing	leg	red	yes	wet

shyly *adv* in a shy way: *The girl walked shyly into the room.* —**shyness** *noun* [U]: *He didn't overcome his shyness till he had left school.*

sibling /ˈsɪblɪŋ/ *noun* [C] (*formal*) a brother or a sister. *Jealousy between siblings is very common.* ☞ In ordinary language we use **brother(s) and sister(s)**: *Have you got any brothers and sisters?*

☆ **sick** /sɪk/ *adj* **1** not well; ill: *a sick child* ○ *She's been off work sick for the past week.* ☞ In British English **to be sick** usually means 'to bring up food from the stomach'. We do not usually say that somebody **is sick**, to mean 'ill'. We *can* use **sick** before a noun: *a sick child* ○ *his sick mother.* We also talk of people who are ill as **the sick**. In American English **be sick** can be used to mean 'be ill': *She's been sick for several weeks now.* **2** feeling ill in your stomach so that any food in it may be thrown up through your mouth: *I feel sick – I think it was that fish I ate.* **3 sick of sb/sth** feeling bored or annoyed because you have had too much of a person or thing: *I'm sick of my job.* ○ *I'm sick of tidying up your mess!* **4 sick (at/about sth)** very annoyed or disgusted by sth: *He felt sick at the sight of so much waste.* **5** (*informal*) cruel or in bad taste: *a sick joke about blind people*
(IDIOMS) **be sick** to throw up food from the stomach; vomit: *How many times have you been sick?*

make sb sick to make sb very angry: *Oh, stop complaining. You make me sick!*

sick to death of sb/sth feeling tired of or annoyed by sb/sth: *I'm sick to death of his grumbling.*

sick *noun* **1** [U] (*informal*) vomit: *There was sick all over the car seat.* **2 the sick** [plural] people who are ill

-sick (in compounds) feeling sick(2) as a result of travelling: *I get carsick on long journeys.* ○ *to be seasick*

ˈsick-leave *noun* [U] a period spent away from work, etc because of illness

sicken /ˈsɪkən/ *verb* [T] to make sb feel disgusted: *Even the smell of the place sickens me.*

sickening *adj* disgusting; very unpleasant: *It was a sickening sight.*

sickly /ˈsɪkli/ *adj* (**sicklier; sickliest**) **1** (used about a person) weak, unhealthy and often ill: *a sickly child* **2** unpleasant; causing a feeling of sickness(2): *the sickly smell of rotten fruit*

sickness /ˈsɪknɪs/ *noun* **1** [U] the state of being ill: *A lot of workers are absent because of sickness.* **2** [U] a feeling in your stomach that may make you throw up food through your mouth: *sickness and diarrhoea* **3** [C,U] a particular type of illness: *seasickness pills*

☆ **side¹** /saɪd/ *noun* [C] **1** any of the flat outer surfaces of an object: *A cube has six sides.* ○ *this side up* (= an instruction on a parcel, etc that tells you which way to store it) **2** [C] any of the flat outer surfaces of an object except the top or the bottom: *A box has a top, a bottom and four sides.* **3** any of the surfaces of sth except the top, bottom, front or back: *I went round to the side of the building.* ○ *The side of the car was damaged.* **4** the edge or boundary of sth; the area near this: *A triangle has three sides.* ○ *She sat at the side of his bed/at his bedside.* ○ *He waited at the side of the road.* **5** either of the two flat surfaces of sth thin: *Write on both sides of the paper.* **6** the right or the left part of your body, especially from under your arm to the top of your leg: *She lay on her side.* ○ *The soldier stood with his hands by his sides.* **7** either of the two parts of a place or object, separated by a real or an imaginary line or boundary: *We drive on the left side of the road in Britain.* ○ *He was sitting at the far side of the room.* ○ *I live on the other side of the city.* ○ *on the other side of the wall* ○ (*figurative*) *She has a generous side to her nature.* **8** either of two teams or groups of people who fight or play against each other: *The two sides agreed to stop fighting.* ○ *the winning/losing side* ○ *Whose side are you on?* (= Who do you support?) **9** the position, opinion or attitude of a person or group of people that is different from that held by another person or group of people: *Do you believe his side of the story?* **10** your mother's or your father's family: *There is no history of illness on his mother's side.*
(IDIOMS) **get on the right/wrong side of sb** to please/annoy sb: *He tried to get on the right side of his new boss.*

on/from all sides; on/from every side in/from all directions; generally: *The army was attacked from every side.* ○ *There was agreement on all sides.*

on the big, small, high, etc side (*informal*) slightly too big, small, high, etc

on the safe side ➔ SAFE¹(4)

put sth on/to one side; leave sth on one side to leave or keep sth so that you can use it or deal with it later: *You should put some money to one side for the future.* ○ *I'll put this problem on one side until later.*

side by side next to each other; close together: *They walked side by side.*

take sides (with sb) to show that you support one person rather than another: *Parents should never take sides when their children are quarrelling.*

-sided (in compounds) having a certain number or type of sides: *a six-sided coin*

ˈside-effect *noun* [C] the unpleasant effect that sth may have in addition to the effects it is supposed to have: *Unpleasant side-effects of the drug may be headaches or sickness.*

ˈsidelong *adj* directed from the side; sideways: *a sidelong glance*

ˈside-road *noun* [C] a road which leads from a main road and which is less important or busy

ˈside-street *noun* [C] a narrow or less important street that usually joins a main street

ˈsidetrack *verb* [T] to make sb forget what he/she is supposed to be doing or talking about and start doing or talking about sth less important

ˈsidewalk *noun* [C] (*US*) = PAVEMENT

ˈsideways *adj, adv* **1** to, towards or from one side: *He jumped sideways to avoid being hit.* ○ *a sideways glance* **2** with one of the sides at the top: *We'll have to turn the sofa sideways to get it through the door.*

side² /saɪd/ *verb*

iː	ɪ	e	æ	ɑː	ɒ	ɔː	ʊ	uː	ʌ
see	sit	ten	hat	arm	got	saw	put	too	cup

(PHRASAL VERB) **side with sb (against sb)** to support sb in an argument: *She always sides with her son against her husband.*

sideboard /'saɪdbɔːd/ *noun* **1** [C] a type of low cupboard about as high as a table, that is used for storing plates, etc in a dining-room **2 sideboards** (*US* **sideburns**) [plural] hair that grows down a man's face in front of and below his ears

sideline /'saɪdlaɪn/ *noun* **1** [C] something that you do in addition to your regular job, usually to earn extra money: *He's an engineer, but he repairs cars as a sideline.* **2 sidelines** [plural] the lines that mark the two long sides of a football pitch or tennis court; the area behind this: *The team's manager was giving orders from the sidelines.*

siding /'saɪdɪŋ/ *noun* [C] a short track at the side of a main railway line

sidle /'saɪdl/ *verb* [I] **sidle up/over (to sb/sth)** to move towards sb/sth in a nervous way, as if you do not want anybody to notice you

siege /siːdʒ/ *noun* [C,U] **1** the situation in which an army surrounds a town in order to capture it. When there is a siege nobody is allowed into or out of the town: *the siege of Troy* **2** a situation in which a building containing a criminal is surrounded by police for a long period of time: *The house was under siege for several hours, until the man released the prisoners.*

siesta /sɪ'estə/ *noun* [C] a short sleep or rest that people take after lunch, especially in hot countries: *to have/take a siesta*

sieve /sɪv/ *noun* [C] a type of kitchen tool that has a metal or plastic net, used for separating solids from liquids or very small pieces of food from large pieces —**sieve** *verb* [T]: *Sieve the flour before adding it to the mixture.*

sift /sɪft/ *verb* **1** [T] to pass a fine substance through a sieve: *to sift flour, sugar* **2** [I,T] **sift (through) sth** (*figurative*) to examine sth very carefully: *It took weeks to sift through all the evidence.*

☆**sigh** /saɪ/ *verb* **1** [I] to let out a long, deep breath that shows you are tired, sad, relieved, etc: *She sighed with disappointment at the news.* **2** [I] to make a sound like sighing: *The wind sighed in the trees.* **3** [T] to say sth with a sigh: '*I'm so tired,' he sighed.*

sigh *noun* [C] the act or sound of sighing: '*Well, that's over,' she said, with a sigh of relief.*

☆**sight¹** /saɪt/ *noun* **1** [U] the ability to see: *He lost his sight in the war* (= he became blind). ○ *My grandmother has very poor sight.* **2** [sing] **sight of sb/sth** the act of seeing sb/sth: *We flew over Paris and had our first sight of the Eiffel Tower.* ○ *Throw that dress out. I can't stand the sight of it any more.* **3** [U] a position where sb/sth can be seen: *They waited until the plane was within sight* (= until they could see it) *and then fired.* ○ *She didn't let the child out of her sight.* ○ '*Get out of my sight!' he shouted, angrily* (= go away!). **4** [C] something that you see: *It was good to be back home, amid all the familiar sights and sounds.* **5 sights** [plural] places of interest that are often visited by tourists: *When you come to New York I'll show you the sights.* **6 a sight** [sing] (*informal*) a person or thing that looks untidy or that makes you laugh: *Look at that girl with green hair. What a sight!* **7** [C, usually pl] a part of a weapon that you look through in order to aim it: *the sights of a gun*

(IDIOMS) **at first glance/sight** ⇨ FIRST¹

at/on sight as soon as sb/sth is seen: *The soldiers were ordered to shoot the enemy on sight.*

catch sight/a glimpse of sb/sth ⇨ CATCH¹(9)

in sight likely to happen or come soon: *A peace settlement is in sight.*

know sb by sight ⇨ KNOW(9)

lose sight of sb/sth ⇨ LOSE(9)

-sighted (in compounds) having a certain type of eyesight: *I'm short-sighted.*

'sightseeing *noun* [U] visiting the sights of a city, etc as a tourist: *We did some sightseeing in Rome.*

'sightseer *noun* [C] a person who does this ☛ Look at **tourist**.

sight² /saɪt/ *verb* [T] to see sb/sth, especially after looking out for him/her/it: *After many weeks at sea, they sighted land.* ○ *The wanted man has been sighted in Spain.*

sighting *noun* [C] an occasion when sb/sth is seen: *the first sighting of a new star*

☆**sign¹** /saɪn/ *noun* [C] **1** a type of shape, mark or symbol that has a particular meaning: *In mathematics, a cross is a plus sign.* **2** a board, notice, etc that gives you a piece of information, an instruction or a warning: *What does that sign say?* ○ *a road sign* ○ *Follow the signs to Banbury.* **3** a movement that you make with your head, hands or arms that has a particular meaning: *I made a sign for him to follow me.* **4 sign (of sth)** something that shows that sb/sth is present or exists or may happen: *The patient was showing some signs of improvement.* ○ *There are some signs that things are getting better.* ○ *As we drove into the village there wasn't a sign of life anywhere* (= we couldn't see anyone). **5** (*also* **sign of the 'zodiac**) one of the twelve divisions or symbols of the zodiac: *I'm a Leo. What sign are you?*

'sign language *noun* [U] a language used especially by deaf and dumb people using signs instead of spoken words

'signpost *noun* [C] a sign at the side of a road that gives information about directions and distances to towns

☆**sign²** /saɪn/ *verb* [I,T] to write your name on a letter, document, etc to show that you have written it or that you agree with what it says. When you sign your name you always write it in the same way: '*Could you sign here, please?'* ○ *I forgot to sign the cheque.* ○ *The two presidents signed the treaty.*

(PHRASAL VERBS) **sign in/out** to write your name to show that you have arrived at or left a hotel, club, etc

sign sb up to get sb to sign a contract to work for you: *Real Madrid have signed up two new players.*

sign up (for sth) to agree formally to do sth: *I've signed up for evening classes.*

☆**signal** /'sɪɡnəl/ *noun* [C] **1** a sign, action or

ɜː	ə	eɪ	əʊ	aɪ	aʊ	ɔɪ	ɪə	eə	ʊə
fur	ago	pay	home	five	now	join	near	hair	pure

signatory / **similar**

sound that sends a particular message: *The army waited for the signal to attack.* ○ *The flag went down as a signal for the race to begin.* **2** a set of lights used to give information to train drivers **3** a series of radio waves, etc that are sent out or received: *a signal from a satellite*
signal *verb* [I,T] (signalling; signalled; *US* signaling; signaled) to make a signal; to send a particular message using a signal: *She was signalling wildly that something was wrong.* ○ *He signalled his disapproval by leaving the room.* ○ *The policeman signalled to the driver to stop.*

signatory /'sɪgnətrɪ; *US* -tɔːrɪ/ *noun* [C] (*pl* **signatories**) **signatory (to sth)** any of the people or countries that sign an agreement, etc

☆ **signature** /'sɪgnətʃə(r)/ *noun* [C] a person's name, written by himself/herself and always written in the same way: *I couldn't read his signature.*

significance /sɪg'nɪfɪkəns/ *noun* [U] the importance or meaning of sth: *Few people realized the significance of the discovery.*

☆ **significant** /sɪg'nɪfɪkənt/ *adj* **1** important: *Police said that the time of the murder was extremely significant.* **2** so large that you notice it: *There has been a significant increase in the number of crimes reported this year.* **3** having a particular meaning: *She gave me a significant smile.*

significantly *adv* **1** in a noticeable way: *Attitudes have changed significantly since the 1960s.* **2** in a way that shows a particular meaning: *He thanked almost everybody but, significantly, he did not mention Terry.*

signify /'sɪgnɪfaɪ/ *verb* [T] (*pres part* **signifying**; *3rd pers sing pres* **signifies**; *pt, pp* **signified**) (*formal*) **1** to be a sign of sth; to mean: *What do those lights signify?* **2** to express or indicate sth: *They signified their agreement by raising their hands.*

Sikh /siːk/ *noun* [C] a member of one of the religions of India (**Sikhism**) that developed from Hinduism but teaches that there is only one god —**Sikhism** /'siːkɪzm/ *noun* [U]

☆ **silence** /'saɪləns/ *noun* [C,U] **1** [U] complete quietness; no sound: *A loud crash broke the silence.* ○ *There must be silence during examinations.* **2** [C] a period when nobody speaks or makes a noise: *There was a silence immediately after the explosion.* ○ *My question was met with an awkward silence.* **3** [U] not making any comments on sth: *I can't understand his silence on the matter*
(IDIOM) **in silence** without talking or making a noise
silence *verb* [T] to make sb/sth be silent or quiet: *He silenced the crowd by raising his hand.*

silencer /'saɪlənsə(r)/ (*US* **muffler**) *noun* [C] **1** the part of a car which reduces the noise made by an exhaust pipe **2** the part of a gun that reduces the noise when it is fired

☆ **silent** /'saɪlənt/ *adj* **1** making no noise; very quiet: *The house was empty and silent.* **2** not speaking; not using spoken words: *The policeman told her she had the right to remain silent.* ○ *a silent prayer* (= one that is not said out loud) ○ *So far he has remained silent on his future plans.* **3** (of a letter) not pronounced: *The 'b' in 'comb' is silent.* —**silently** *adv*

silhouette /ˌsɪluː'et/ *noun* [C] the dark outline or black shape of sth seen against a light background
silhouetted *adj* seen as a silhouette: *the spire of the cathedral, silhouetted against a bright blue sky*

silicon chip /ˌsɪlɪkən 'tʃɪp/ *noun* [C] a piece of a chemical element (silicon) that is used in computers, etc

silk /sɪlk/ *noun* [U] the soft smooth cloth that is made from threads produced by an insect (**the silkworm**): *a silk shirt*

silky /'sɪlkɪ/ *adj* (**silkier; silkiest**) smooth, soft and shiny; like silk: *silky hair*

sill /sɪl/ *noun* [C] a long thin piece of wood or stone that is at the bottom of a window, either inside or outside: *a window-sill*

☆ **silly** /'sɪlɪ/ *adj* (**sillier; silliest**) **1** not showing thought or understanding; foolish: *a silly mistake* ○ *What a silly thing to say!* ○ *Don't be so silly!* **2** appearing ridiculous, so that people will laugh: *I'm not wearing that hat – I'd look silly in it.* —**silliness** *noun* [U]

silt /sɪlt/ *noun* [U] sand, soil or mud that is carried along by a river and then left somewhere when the river flows more slowly

☆ **silver** /'sɪlvə(r)/ *noun* [U] **1** a valuable grey-white metal that is used for making jewellery, ornaments, coins, etc: *a silver spoon* ○ *That's a nice ring. Is it silver?* **2** coins made from silver or sth that looks like silver: *Could you change £10 of silver for a £10 note please?* **3** objects that are made of silver, eg knives, forks, spoons, dishes: *The thieves stole some jewellery and some valuable silver.*
silver *adj* having the colour of silver: *a silver sports car*

silvery /'sɪlvərɪ/ *adj* having the appearance or colour of silver: *an old lady with silvery hair* ○ *silvery light over the lake*

ˌsilver 'jubilee *noun* [C] the 25th anniversary of an important event

ˌsilver 'medal *noun* [C] a small flat round piece of silver that is given to the person or team that comes second in a sports competition: *to win a silver medal at the Olympic Games* ☛ Look at **gold medal** and **bronze medal**.

ˌsilver 'medallist *noun* [C] a person who wins a silver medal

ˌsilver 'wedding *noun* [C] the 25th anniversary of a wedding ☛ Look at **golden wedding**.

☆ **similar** /'sɪmələ(r)/ *adj* **similar (to sb/sth)** the same in a way or in some ways but not completely the same: *All the books he writes are very similar.* ○ *Your handwriting is very similar to mine.*

similarly *adv* also; in a similar way: *The plural of 'shelf' is 'shelves'. Similarly, the plural of 'wolf' is 'wolves'.*

similarity /ˌsɪmə'lærətɪ/ *noun* (*pl* **similarities**) **1** [U] the quality of being similar: *I noticed the similarity in the way the two sisters thought and spoke.* **2** [C] a way in which people or things are similar: *Although there are some*

p	b	t	d	k	g	tʃ	dʒ	f	v	θ	ð
pen	bad	tea	did	cat	got	chin	June	fall	van	thin	then

similarities between the two towns, there are a lot of differences too.

simmer /'sɪmə(r)/ verb [I,T] to cook gently in a liquid that is just below boiling point: *Let the vegetables simmer for a few more minutes.* o *Simmer the soup for 30 minutes.*

☆ **simple** /'sɪmpl/ adj **1** easy to understand, do or use; not difficult or complicated: *This dictionary is written in simple English.* o *a simple task* o *I can't just leave the job. It's not as simple as that.* **2** without decoration or unnecessary extra things; plain: *a simple black dress* o *The food is simple but perfectly cooked.* **3** (used about a person or a way of life) natural and uncomplicated: *a simple life in the country* **4** unintelligent; slow to understand **5** (used for saying that the thing you are talking about is the only thing that is important or true): *I'm not going to buy it for the simple reason that I haven't got enough money.*

simply /'sɪmpli/ adv **1** in a way that makes sth easy to understand: *Could you explain it more simply?* **2** in a plain way; without decoration or unnecessary extra things: *They live simply, with very few luxuries.* **3** (used for emphasis) absolutely; completely: *What a simply marvellous idea!* **4** only; just: *There's no need to get angry. The whole problem is simply a misunderstanding.*

simplicity /sɪm'plɪsəti/ noun [U] **1** the quality of being uncomplicated and easy to understand, do or use: *We all admired the simplicity of the plan.* **2** the quality of having no decoration or unnecessary extra things; plainness: *I like the simplicity of her paintings.*

simplify /'sɪmplɪfaɪ/ verb [T] (pres part **simplifying**; 3rd pers sing pres **simplifies**; pt, pp **simplified**) to make sth easier to do or understand; to make sth less complicated: *The process of applying for visas has been simplified.* —**simplification** /ˌsɪmplɪfɪ'keɪʃn/ noun [C,U]

simplistic /sɪm'plɪstɪk/ adj making sth that is complicated seem simpler than it really is

simulate /'sɪmjuleɪt/ verb [T] to create the effect or appearance of sth else: *The astronauts trained in a machine that simulates conditions in space.*

simulation /ˌsɪmju'leɪʃn/ noun [C,U] the act of simulating or a simulated form of a real situation, event, etc: *a computer simulation of a nuclear attack*

simultaneous /ˌsɪml'teɪniəs; US ˌsaɪm-/ adj happening at exactly the same time: *There were simultaneous demonstrations in London, Paris and Bonn.* —**simultaneously** adv

sin /sɪn/ noun [C,U] an act or way of behaving that breaks a religious law: *He believes it is a sin for two people to live together without being married.* o *They confess their sins to the priest every week.*

sin verb [I] (**sinning**; **sinned**) to do sth that breaks a religious law

sinful /-fl/ adj breaking a religious law; immoral

sinner /'sɪnə(r)/ noun [C] a person who sins

☆ **since** /sɪns/ prep from a particular time in the past until a later time in the past or until now: *It was the first time they'd won since 1974.* o *I haven't seen him since last Tuesday.* o *Where have you been? I've been waiting for you since 5.30.* o *She has had a number of jobs since leaving university.* ☞ We use both **since** and **for** to talk about how long something has been happening. We use **since** when we are talking about the *beginning* of the period of time, and **for** when we are talking about the *length* of the period of time: *I've known her since 1983.* o *I've known her for ten years.*

since conj **1** from the time when sth happened until a later time in the past or until now: *He hasn't written to us since he arrived in Britain.* o *I've been working in a bank ever since I left school.* o *It was strange to see my old house again because I hadn't been there since I was a child.* **2** because; as: *Since they've obviously forgotten to phone me, I'll have to phone them.*

since adv **1** from a particular time in the past until a later time in the past or until now: *He had come to see us a few weeks earlier but he hadn't been back since.* o *We went out for dinner together about six months ago but I haven't seen her since.* o *My parents bought this house in 1975 and we've been living here ever since.* **2** at a time after a particular time in the past: *We were divorced two years ago and she has since married someone else.* o *He had left school at the age of 16 and had since got a job in a hotel.*

☆ **sincere** /sɪn'sɪə(r)/ adj **1** (used about a person) really meaning or believing what you say; honest; not pretending: *Do you think she was being sincere when she said she admired me?* **2** (used about sth that a person says or feels) true; that is really meant: *Please accept our sincere apologies.* ☞ The opposite is **insincere**. —**sincerely** adv: *I am sincerely grateful to you for all your help.* o *Yours sincerely, ...* (at the end of a formal letter)

sincerity /sɪn'serəti/ noun [U] the quality of being sincere; honesty: *Nobody doubts the sincerity of her political views.* ☞ The opposite is **insincerity**.

☆ **sing** /sɪŋ/ verb [I,T] (pt **sang** /sæŋ/; pp **sung** /sʌŋ/) to make musical sounds with the voice: *He always sings when he's in the bath.* o *The birds were singing outside my window.* o *She sang all her most popular songs at the concert.*

singer noun [C] a person who sings, especially in public

singing noun [U] the act of singing: *singing lessons*

singe /sɪndʒ/ verb [I,T] (pres part **singeing**) to burn or to make sth burn slightly on the edge or tip: *He leaned over the candle and accidentally singed his eyebrows.*

☆ **single** /'sɪŋgl/ adj **1** (only before a noun) only one: *He gave her a single red rose.* o *I managed to finish the whole job in a single afternoon.* **2** (only before a noun) (used for emphasis when you are thinking about the individual things which together form a group): *You answered every single question correctly. Well done!* **3** not married: *Are you married or single?* o *a single woman* **4** (only before a noun) for the use of only one person: *I'd like to book a single room, please.* o *a single bed* ☞ Look at **double**.

s	z	ʃ	ʒ	h	m	n	ŋ	l	r	j	w
so	zoo	she	vision	how	man	no	sing	leg	red	yes	wet

5 (*also* **one-way**) (only *before* a noun) only to a place, not to a place and back from it (used about a ticket or the cost of a ticket for a journey): *How much is the single fare to Rome, please?* ☛ Look at **return**.
(IDIOM) **in single file** ⇨ FILE³

single *noun* **1** [C] a ticket for a journey to a place only, not to a place and back from it: *Two singles to Hull, please.* ☛ Look at **return²**(5). **2** [C] a bedroom for one person only in a hotel, etc: *The hotel has 25 bedrooms: 10 singles and 15 doubles.* **3** [C] a small record that has only one song on each side: *Seal's new single* ☛ Look at **LP** and **album**. **4 singles** [plural] a game of tennis, etc in which one player plays against one other player: *the final of the women's singles.* ☛ Look at **doubles**.

single *verb*
(PHRASAL VERB) **single sb/sth out (for sth)** to give special attention or treatment to one person or thing from a group: *He singled Sue Taylor out for praise.*

singly /'sɪŋglɪ/ *adv* one by one; individually: *You can buy the tapes either singly or in packs of three.*

,single-'handed *adj, adv* done by one person, done without help from anybody else: *a single-handed yacht race*

,single-'minded *adj* having one clear aim or purpose: *I admired her single-minded determination to win.*

,single 'parent *noun* [C] a parent who looks after his/her child or children alone: *a single-parent family*

singular /'sɪŋgjʊlə(r)/ *adj* **1** (*grammar*) in the form that is used for talking about one person or thing only: *'Table' is a singular noun; 'tables' is a plural noun.* **2** (*formal*) unusual: *a person of singular intelligence*

singular *noun* [sing] (*grammar*) the singular form: *The word 'clothes' has no singular.* ○ *What's the singular of 'people'?*

singularly *adv* (*formal*) unusually; particularly: *The government has been singularly unsuccessful in its policy against terrorism.*

sinister /'sɪnɪstə(r)/ *adj* making you feel that sth bad will happen; frightening: *a sinister atmosphere* ○ *There's something sinister about him. He frightens me.*

sink¹ /sɪŋk/ *verb* (*pt* **sank** /sæŋk/; *pp* **sunk** /sʌŋk/) **1** [I,T] to go down or make sth go down under the surface or to the bottom of water, etc: *If you throw a stone into water, it sinks.* ○ *The boat sank to the bottom of the sea.* ○ *Three ships were sunk by enemy planes.* ○ *My feet sank into the mud.* ☛ picture at **float**. **2** [I] to get lower; to fall to a lower position or level: *After a few days the flood water began to sink.* ○ *We watched the sun sink slowly below the horizon.* **3** [I] (used about a person) to move or fall to a lower position, usually because you are tired or weak: *I came home very tired and sank into a chair.* **4** [I] to decrease in value, number, amount, strength, etc: *The share price has sunk from over £2 to 65p.*
(IDIOM) **your heart sinks** ⇨ HEART
(PHRASAL VERB) **sink in/sink into sth**
1 (used about a liquid) to go into sth solid; to be absorbed: *Quick! Clean up that wine before it sinks into the carpet.* **2** (used about information, an event, an experience, etc) to be completely understood; to become clear in the mind: *It took a long time for the terrible news to sink in.*

sink² /sɪŋk/ *noun* [C] a basin in a kitchen that is connected to the water supply with pipes and taps and used for washing dishes, vegetables, etc

sinus /'saɪnəs/ *noun* [C] (often plural) one of the spaces in the bones of the face that are connected to the nose: *I've got a terrible cold and all my sinuses are blocked.* ○ *a sinus infection*

sip /sɪp/ *verb* [I,T] (**sipp**ing; **sipp**ed) to drink, taking only a very small amount of liquid into your mouth at a time: *We sat in the sun, sipping lemonade.* —**sip** *noun* [C]: *a sip of water*

siphon /'saɪfn/ *verb* [T] **siphon sth into/out of sth; siphon sth off/out** to remove a liquid from a container (or to transfer it from one container to another) through a tube

☆ **sir** /sɜː(r)/ *noun* [C] **1** (used as a formal or very polite way of speaking to a man, especially one of higher rank in the armed forces, or a male customer in a restaurant or shop): *You should always address a superior officer as 'sir'.* ○ *I'm afraid we haven't got your size, sir.* ☛ Look at **madam** and **miss**. **2 Sir, Sirs** (used at the beginning of a formal letter to a male person or male people): *Dear Sir...* ○ *Dear Sirs...* ☛ Look at **madam**. **3 Sir** /sə(r)/ the title that is used in front of the name of a man who has received one of the highest British honours: *Sir Laurence Olivier*

siren /'saɪərən/ *noun* [C] a machine that makes a long, loud sound in order to warn people about sth, eg on an ambulance, fire-engine or police car: *an air-raid siren*

☆ **sister** /'sɪstə(r)/ *noun* [C] **1** a girl or woman who has the same parents as another person: *I've got one brother and two sisters.* ○ *We're sisters.* ☛ Look at **half-sister** and **stepsister**. In English there is no common word that means 'both brothers and sisters': *Have you got any brothers and sisters?* The word **sibling** is very formal. **2** often **Sister** a senior hospital nurse **3 Sister** a member of certain female religious groups; a nun **4** a company, organization or ship, etc that belongs to the same group: *We have a sister company in Japan.* ○ *a sister ship*

sisterly *adj* of or like a sister: *sisterly love*

'sister-in-law *noun* [C] (*pl* **sisters-in-law**) **1** the sister of your husband or wife **2** the wife of your brother

☆ **sit** /sɪt/ *verb* (*pres part* **sitting**; *pt, pp* **sat** /sæt/) **1** [I] to be in a position on a chair, etc in which the upper part of your body is upright and your weight is supported at the bottom of your back: *We sat in the garden all afternoon.* ○ *She was sitting on the sofa, talking to her mother.* **2** [I] **sit (down)** to lower the body into the position of sitting: *Come and sit next to me. I want to talk to you.* **3** [T] **sit sb (down)** to put sb into a sitting position; make sb sit down: *He picked up his daughter and sat her down on a chair.* ○ *She sat me down and offered me a cup of tea.* **4** [I] to be in a particular place or position: *The letter sat*

i:	ɪ	e	æ	ɑ:	ɒ	ɔ:	ʊ	u:	ʌ
see	sit	ten	hat	arm	got	saw	put	too	cup

on the table for several days before anybody opened it. **5** [T] (*Brit*) to take an examination: *If I fail, will I be able to sit the exam again?* **6** [I] (*formal*) (used about an official group of people) to have a meeting or series of meetings: *Parliament was still sitting at 3 am.*

(IDIOM) **sit on the fence** to be unwilling to decide between two things

(PHRASAL VERBS) **sit around** (*informal*) to sit and do nothing active for a period of time: *people sitting around chatting*

sit back to relax and not take an active part in what other people are doing: *Sit back and take it easy while I make dinner.*

sit sth out to stay in a difficult or unpleasant situation until the end, without taking any action

sit through sth to stay in your seat until sth has finished (especially if it is boring): *I don't think I can sit through another two hours of this film.*

sit up 1 to move into a sitting position when you have been lying down or leaning back: *Sit up straight or you'll hurt your back!* **2** to not go to bed although it is very late: *We sat up all night talking.*

'**sitting-room** *noun* [C] (*especially Brit*) = LIVING-ROOM

☆ **site** /saɪt/ *noun* [C] **1** a piece of land that is used or will be used for building on or for another special purpose: *a building site* (= a place where a building is being constructed) o *The company is looking for a site for its new offices.* o *a caravan site* **2** a place where sth happened or existed in the past: *the site of a famous battle between the English and the Scots*

site *verb* [T] to put or build sth in a particular place: *The new sports centre is to be sited in Church Street.*

sitting /'sɪtɪŋ/ *noun* [C] **1** a period of time during which a meal is served to a number of people, when it is not possible to serve everybody at the same time: *Dinner will be in two sittings.* **2** a period during which an official group of people meets and does its work

situated /'sɪtjʊeɪtɪd/ *adj* (*formal*) in a particular place or position: *The hotel is conveniently situated close to the beach.*

☆ **situation** /ˌsɪtʃʊ'eɪʃn/ *noun* [C] **1** the things that are happening in a particular place or at a particular time: *The situation in the north of the country is extremely serious.* o *Tim is in a difficult situation at the moment.* o *the economic situation* **2** the position of a building, town, etc in relation to the area around it: *The house is in a beautiful situation on the edge of a lake.* **3** (*formal*) a job: *Situations Vacant* (= the part of a newspaper where jobs are advertised)

☆ **six** /sɪks/ *number* 6; one more than five: *The answers are on page six.* o *She invited twenty people, but only six came.* o *Six (of the pupils) are absent today.* o *There are six of us for dinner tonight.* o *They have six cats.* o *My son is six (years old) next month.* o *She lives at 6 Elm Drive.* o *a birthday card with a big six on it*

six- (in compounds) having six of the thing mentioned: *a six-day week*

sixth /sɪksθ/ *pron, det, adv* 6th; next after fifth: *I've had five cups of tea already, so this is my sixth.* o *This is the sixth time I've tried to phone him.* o *Mahler's Sixth Symphony* o *George VI* (= George the Sixth) ☛ For more information about numbers in dates, measurements, prices, etc, look at Appendix 2.

sixth *noun* [C] the fraction ⅙; one of six equal parts of sth

'**sixth form** *noun* [C, usually sing, with sing or pl verb] (*Brit*) the classes of pupils in the final year(s) of secondary school, usually from the age of 16 to 18 and often studying for A level examinations

'**sixth-former** *noun* [C] a pupil in the sixth form

☆ **sixteen** /sɪks'tiːn/ *number* 16; one more than fifteen ☛ For examples of how to use numbers in sentences, look at **six**.

sixteenth /sɪks'tiːnθ/ *pron, det, adv* 16th; next after fifteenth ☛ Look at the examples at **sixth**.

☆ **sixty** /'sɪksti/ *number* **1** 60; one more than fifty-nine: *Sixty people went to the meeting.* o *There are sixty pages in the book.* o *He retired at sixty/when he was sixty.* **2 the sixties** [plural] the numbers, years or temperatures between 60 and 69: *I don't know the exact number of members, but it's in the sixties.* o *The most famous pop group of the sixties was The Beatles.* o *The temperature tomorrow will be in the high sixties.*

(IDIOM) **in your sixties** between the age of 60 and 69: *I'm not sure how old she is but I should think she's in her sixties.* o *in your early/mid/late sixties*

sixtieth /'sɪkstiəθ/ *pron, det, adv* 60th; next after fifty-ninth ☛ Look at the examples at **sixth**. ☛ For more information about numbers in dates, measurements, prices, etc, look at Appendix 2.

☆ **size** /saɪz/ *noun* **1** [U] the amount by which sth is big or small: *I was surprised at the size of the hotel. It was enormous!* o *The British 5p piece is about the same size as the old sixpence.* o *The planet Uranus is about four times the size of Earth.* ☛ When we ask about the size of something, we usually say, 'How big…?': *How big is your house?* We say, 'What size…?' when we ask about the size of something that is produced in a number of fixed measurements: *What size shoes do you take?* **2** [C] one of a number of fixed measurements in which sth is made: *Have you got this dress in a bigger size?* o *What size pizza would you like? Medium or large?*

size *verb*

(PHRASAL VERB) **size sb/sth up** to think carefully about sb/sth in order to form an opinion: *She looked at the man in the white suit for a long time, trying to size him up.*

sizeable (*also* **sizable**) /-əbl/ *adj* quite large: *a sizeable flat* o *a sizeable sum of money*

-sized (*also* **-size**) (in compounds) of the size that is mentioned: *a medium-sized flat*

sizzle /'sɪzl/ *verb* [I] to make the sound of food frying in hot fat: *I could hear the bacon sizzling in the kitchen.*

skate /skeɪt/ *noun* [C] **1** (*also* **ice-skate**) a

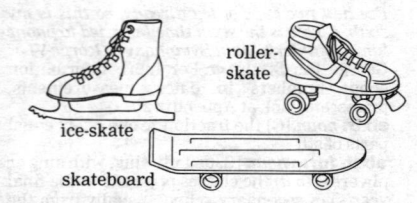

[Illustrations: ice-skate, roller-skate, skateboard; downhill skiing showing binding, boot, ski, pole; cross-country skiing]

boot with a thick metal blade on the bottom that is used for skating **2** = ROLLER-SKATE

skate verb [I] **1** (also **ice-skate**) to move over ice on skates: *Can you skate?* ○ *They skated across the frozen lake.* ☞ **Go skating** is a common way of talking about skating for pleasure: *We go skating every weekend.* **2** = ROLLER-SKATE

skater noun [C] a person who skates

skating noun **1** (also **ice-skating**) [U] the activity or sport of moving over ice on skates **2** = ROLLER-SKATING

'skateboard noun [C] a narrow board with wheels attached to it that you can stand on and ride —**'skateboarding** noun [U]

'skating-rink (also **ice-rink**; **rink**) noun [C] a large area of ice, or a building containing a large area of ice, that is used for skating on

skeleton /'skelɪtn/ noun [C] the structure formed by all the bones in a human or animal body: *a dinosaur skeleton in the Natural History Museum* ○ *the human skeleton*

skeleton adj (used about an organization, a service, etc) having the smallest number of people that is necessary for it to operate: *On Sundays, the office is kept open by a skeleton staff.*

skeptic (*US*) = SCEPTIC

sketch /sketʃ/ noun [C] **1** a simple, quick drawing without many details: *He drew a rough sketch of the new building on the back of an envelope.* **2** a short description without any details: *a sketch of life in Paris in the 1920s* **3** a short comedy scene, usually part of a television or radio programme

sketch verb [I,T] to draw a sketch: *I sat on the grass and sketched the castle.*

sketchy adj (**sketchier**; **sketchiest**) not having many or enough details: *He only gave me a sketchy account of the accident.*

ski /skiː/ noun [C] one of a pair of long, flat, narrow pieces of wood, metal or plastic that are fastened to boots and used for moving over snow: *a pair of skis*

ski verb [I] (pres part **skiing**; pt, pp **skied**) to move over snow on skis: *When did you learn to ski?* ☞ **Go skiing** is a common way of talking about skiing for pleasure: *They go skiing in France every year.*

ski adj connected with skiing: *a ski resort, instructor, etc*

skier /'skiːə(r)/ noun [C] a person who skis: *a good skier*

skiing noun [U] the activity of moving on skis; the sport of racing on skis

skid /skɪd/ verb [I] (**skidd**ing; **skidd**ed) (used about a vehicle) to be out of control and move or slide sideways on the road: *I skidded on a patch of ice.* —**skid** noun [C]: *The car went into a skid and came off the road.*

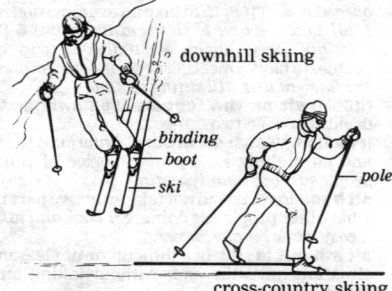

☆ **skilful** (*US* **skillful**) /'skɪlfl/ adj **1** (used about a person) very good at doing sth: *a skilful painter, politician, etc* ○ *He's very skilful with his hands.* **2** done very well: *skilful guitar playing* —**skilfully** /-fəlɪ/ adv: *The play was skilfully directed by a young student.*

☆ **skill** /skɪl/ noun **1** [U] the ability to do sth well, especially because of training, practice, etc: *It takes great skill to make such beautiful jewellery.* ○ *This is an easy game to play. No skill is required.* **2** [C] an ability that is required in order to do a job, an activity, etc well: *The course will help you to develop your reading and listening skills.* ○ *management skills* ○ *Typing is a skill I have never mastered.*

skilled adj **1** (used about a person) having skill; skilful: *a skilled worker* **2** (used about work, a job etc) requiring skill or skills; done by people who have been trained: *a highly skilled job* ○ *Skilled work is difficult to find in this area.* ☞ The opposite is **unskilled**.

skim /skɪm/ verb (**skimm**ing; **skimm**ed) **1** [T] to remove sth from the surface of a liquid: *to skim the cream off the milk* **2** [I,T] to move quickly over a surface, near it but without touching it, or without touching it very often: *The plane flew very low, skimming the tops of the buildings* ○ *I watched a big bird skim across the water.* **3** [I,T] **skim (through/over) sth** to read sth quickly in order to get the main idea, without paying attention to the details and without reading every word: *I usually just skim through the newspaper in the morning.*

,skimmed 'milk noun [U] milk from which the cream has been removed

skimp /skɪmp/ verb [I,T] **skimp (on sth)** to use or provide less of sth than is necessary: *I don't think we should skimp on books. The students must have one each.*

skimpy adj (**skimpier**; **skimpiest**) using or having less than is necessary: *a skimpy meal* ○ *a skimpy swimsuit* (= not covering much of the body)

☆ **skin** /skɪn/ noun [C,U] **1** the natural outer covering of a human or animal body: *to have fair, dark, sensitive, etc skin* ○ *skin cancer* **2** (often in compounds) the skin of an animal

p	b	t	d	k	g	tʃ	dʒ	f	v	θ	ð
pen	bad	tea	did	cat	got	chin	June	fall	van	thin	then

that has been removed from its body and that is often used for making things: *a sheepskin jacket* **3** the natural outer covering of some fruits or vegetables; the outer covering of a sausage: *a banana skin* ☛ Look at the note at **rind**. **4** the thin solid surface that can form on a liquid: *Drink your hot chocolate before it gets a skin on it.*

(IDIOMS) **by the skin of your teeth** (*informal*) (used about a successful action) only just; with very little time, space etc to spare: *I ran into the airport and caught the plane by the skin of my teeth.*

have a thick skin ⇨ THICK

skin *verb* [T] (**skinn**ing; **skinn**ed) to remove the skin from sth

skinny *adj* (**skinnier**; **skinniest**) (*informal*) (used about a person) too thin ☛ Look at the note at **thin**.

'skinhead *noun* [C] a young person with shaved or extremely short hair. Skinheads are often associated with violent behaviour.

,skin 'tight *adj* (used about a piece of clothing) fitting very tightly and showing the shape of the body

skip¹ /skɪp/ *verb* (**skipp**ing; **skipp**ed) **1** [I] to move along quickly and lightly in a way that is similar to dancing, with little jumps and steps, from one foot to the other: *A little girl came skipping along the road.* **2** [I] to jump over a rope that you or two other people hold at each end, turning it round and round over the head and under the feet **3** [T] to not go to sth that you should go to; to not have sth that you should have: *I skipped my French class today and went swimming.* ○ *I got up rather late, so I skipped breakfast.* **4** [T] (used about part of a book, story, etc) to miss sth out; to not read or talk about sth and move to the next part: *I think I'll skip the next chapter. It looks really boring.*

skip *noun* [C] a skipping movement

'skipping-rope *noun* [C] a rope, often with handles at each end, that is used for skipping

skip² /skɪp/ *noun* [C] a very large, open metal container for rubbish, often used during building work

skipper /'skɪpə(r)/ *noun* [C] (*informal*) the captain of a boat or ship, or of a sports team

skirmish /'skɜːmɪʃ/ *noun* [C] a small fight or battle

☆ **skirt** /skɜːt/ *noun* [C] a piece of clothing that is worn by women and girls and that hangs down from the waist: *a short skirt* ☛ Look at **culottes**.

skirt *verb* [I,T] to go around the edge of sth
(PHRASAL VERB) **skirt round sth** to avoid talking about sth directly: *The manager skirted round the subject of our pay increase.*

skittle /'skɪtl/ *noun* **1** [C] a wooden object in the shape of a bottle that is used as one of the targets in the game of skittles **2 skittles** [U] a game in which players try to knock down as many skittles as possible by throwing or rolling a ball at them

skive /skaɪv/ *verb* [I] (*Brit slang*) **skive (off)** to avoid work, especially by staying away from the place of work or leaving it without permission when you should be working: *I don't think he was ill – he was skiving.*

skulk /skʌlk/ *verb* [I] to stay somewhere quietly and secretly, hoping that nobody will notice you, usually because you are planning to do sth bad: *a strange man skulking behind a tree*

skull /skʌl/ *noun* [C] the bone structure of a human or animal head: *a fractured skull*

☆ **sky** /skaɪ/ *noun* [C,U] (*pl* **skies**) the space that you can see when you look up from the earth, and where you can see the sun, moon and stars: *a clear blue sky* ○ *I saw a bit of blue sky between the clouds.* ☛ We usually talk about **the sky**: *I saw a plane high up in the sky.* ○ *The sky's gone very dark. I think it's going to rain.* However, when **sky** follows an adjective, we usually use **a/an**: *a cloudless sky* or sometimes the plural form **skies**: *cloudless skies*

,sky-'high *adj, adv* very high

'skyline *noun* [C] the shape that is made by tall buildings, etc against the sky: *the Manhattan skyline*

'skyscraper *noun* [C] a very tall building

slab /slæb/ *noun* [C] a thick, flat piece of sth: *huge concrete slabs*

slack /slæk/ *adj* **1** loose; not tightly stretched: *Leave the rope slack.* **2** (used about a period of business) not busy; not having many customers or much activity: *Trade is very slack here in winter.* **3** not carefully or properly done: *Slack security made terrorist attacks possible.* **4** (used about a person) not doing your work carefully or properly: *You've been rather slack about your homework lately.*

slacken /'slækən/ *verb* [I,T] **1** to become or make sth less tight: *The rope slackened and he pulled his hand free.* ○ *After a while she slackened her grip on my arm.* **2 slacken (sth) (off)** to become or make sth slower or less active: *Industrial production has slackened off in recent months.* ○ *His pace slackened towards the end of the race.*

slacks /slæks/ *noun* [plural] trousers (especially not very formal ones): *a pair of slacks*

slag heap /'slæg hiːp/ *noun* [C] a hill made of the waste material that remains when metal has been removed from rock

slain *pp* of SLAY

slalom /'slɑːləm/ *noun* [C] a race (in skiing, canoeing, etc) along a course on which competitors have to move from side to side between poles

slam /slæm/ *verb* (**slamm**ing; **slamm**ed) **1** [I,T] to shut or make sth shut very loudly and with great force: *I heard the front door slam.* ○ *She slammed her book shut and rushed out of the room.* **2** [T] to put sth somewhere very quickly and with great force: *He slammed my letter on the table and stormed out.* ☛ Look at **grand slam**.

slander /'slɑːndə(r); *US* 'slæn-/ *noun* [C,U] an untrue spoken statement about sb that is intended to damage the good opinion that other people have of him/her; the crime of making this kind of statement: *If you repeat that in public I shall take legal action for slander.* —**slander** *verb* [T]

s	z	ʃ	ʒ	h	m	n	ŋ	l	r	j	w
so	zoo	she	vision	how	man	no	sing	leg	red	yes	wet

slang /slæŋ/ noun [U] very informal words and expressions that are more common in spoken language. Slang is sometimes used only by a particular group of people (eg schoolchildren, soldiers) and often stays in fashion for a short time. Some slang is not polite: *'The nick' is slang for 'the police station'.*

slant /slɑːnt/ *US* slænt/ verb **1** [I,T] to lean or make sth lean in a particular direction; to be not straight: *My handwriting slants backwards.* **2** [T] (usually passive) to describe information, events, etc in a way that supports a particular group or opinion: *All the political articles in that newspaper are slanted towards the government.*

slant noun **1** [sing] a position that leans in a particular direction **2** [C] a way of thinking about sth, especially one that supports a particular group or opinion: *There is a left-wing slant to all his writing.*

slanting adj leaning in a particular direction; not straight

slap /slæp/ verb [T] (**slapp**ing; **slapp**ed) **1** to hit sb/sth with the inside of your hand: *She slapped him across the face.* ○ *to slap sb on the back* (= to congratulate him/her) **2** to put sth onto a surface quickly and carelessly: *to slap some paint onto a wall* —**slap** noun [C]: *I gave him a slap across the face.*

slap (also **slap-'bang**) adv (*informal*) **1** directly and with great force: *I hurried round the corner and walked slap into someone coming the other way.* **2** exactly; right: *The phone rang slap-bang in the middle of my favourite programme.*

slapdash /'slæpdæʃ/ adj careless, or done quickly and carelessly: *slapdash building methods*

slapstick /'slæpstɪk/ noun [U] a type of comedy that is based on simple jokes, eg people falling over or hitting each other

slap-up /'slæpʌp/ adj (*Brit informal*) (used about a meal) very large and very good

slash /slæʃ/ verb **1** [I,T] to make a long cut in sth with a violent action: *Several cars have had their tyres slashed in that car park.* **2** [T] to reduce an amount of money, etc very much: *The price of coffee has been slashed by about 20%.*

slat /slæt/ noun [C] one of the long narrow pieces of wood, metal or plastic in a cupboard door, venetian blind, etc

slate /sleɪt/ noun **1** [U] a type of dark grey rock that can easily be split into thin flat pieces **2** [C] one of the thin flat pieces of slate that are used for covering roofs

slaughter /'slɔːtə(r)/ verb [T] **1** to kill an animal, usually for food **2** to kill a large number of people at one time, especially in a cruel way or when they cannot defend themselves: *Men, women and children were slaughtered and whole villages destroyed.* ☞ Look at the note at **kill**. —**slaughter** noun [U]: *the slaughter of innocent people during the war*

'slaughterhouse (also **abattoir**) noun [C] the place where animals are killed for food

☆ **slave** /sleɪv/ noun [C] a person who is owned by another person and has to work for that person

slave verb [I] **slave** (**away**) to work very hard

slavery /'sleɪvəri/ noun [U] **1** the system of having slaves: *the abolition of slavery in America* **2** the situation of being a slave: *The two boys were captured and sold into slavery.*

slay /sleɪ/ verb [T] (*pt* **slew** /sluː/; *pp* **slain** /sleɪn/) to kill violently; to murder: *Many young soldiers were slain in the battle.* ☞ **Slay** is very old-fashioned in British English but is more common in American English.

sleazy /'sliːzi/ adj (**sleazier; sleaziest**) (often used about a place) dirty, in poor condition and having an immoral or criminal atmosphere: *a sleazy nightclub*

sledge

sledge /sledʒ/ (*US also* **sled** /sled/) noun [C] a vehicle without wheels that is used for travelling on snow. You can slide down a hill on a small sledge. Large sledges are often pulled by dogs. ☞ Look at **sleigh** and **toboggan**.

sledge verb [I] to go down hills on a sledge

sleek /sliːk/ adj **1** (used about hair or fur) smooth and shiny because it is healthy **2** (used about a vehicle) having an elegant, smooth shape: *a sleek new sports car*

☆ **sleep¹** /sliːp/ noun **1** [U] the natural condition of rest when your eyes are closed and your mind and body are not active or conscious: *Most people need about eight hours' sleep every night.* ○ *I didn't get much sleep last night.* ○ *Do you ever talk in your sleep?* **2** [sing] a period of sleep: *You'll feel better after a good night's sleep.*
(IDIOMS) **get to sleep** to succeed in sleeping: *I couldn't get to sleep last night.*

go to sleep 1 to start sleeping; to enter the state of sleep: *He got into bed and soon went to sleep.* ○ *Go to sleep. Everything will seem better in the morning.* **2** (used about an arm, leg, etc) to lose the sense of feeling in it

put (an animal) to sleep to kill an animal that is ill or injured because you want to stop it suffering

sleepless adj (used about a period, usually the night) without sleep —**sleeplessness** noun [U] ☞ Look at **insomnia**.

'sleepwalk verb [I] to walk around while you are asleep

☆ **sleep²** /sliːp/ verb (*pt, pp* **slept** /slept/) **1** [I] to be in a state of sleep for a period of time: *Did you sleep well last night?* ○ *I only slept for a couple of hours last night.* ☞ We use **to sleep** for talking about sleeping in general, but we use **to be asleep** to talk about being in the state of sleep when something else happens: *I was asleep when the telephone rang.* We use **to go to**

iː	ɪ	e	æ	ɑː	ɒ	ɔː	ʊ	uː	ʌ
see	sit	ten	hat	arm	got	saw	put	too	cup

sleep to talk about starting to sleep. (NOT: *I slept at ten o'clock last night* but: *I went to sleep at ten o'clock last night.*) **2** [T] (used about a place) to have enough beds for a particular number of people: *an apartment that sleeps four people*
(IDIOM) **sleep rough** to sleep outside, usually because you have no home
(PHRASAL VERBS) **sleep in** to sleep until later than usual in the morning because you do not have to get up
sleep together; sleep with sb to have sex with sb (usually when you are not married to or living with that person): *Do you think she's slept with him?*

'sleeping-bag *noun* [C] a large soft bag that you use for sleeping in when you go camping, etc

'sleeping-pill *noun* [C] a pill that helps you to sleep

sleeper /'sli:pə(r)/ *noun* [C] **1** (with an adjective) a person who sleeps in a particular way. If you are a light sleeper you wake up easily: *a light/heavy sleeper* **2** a bed on a train; a train with beds: *I've booked a sleeper on the night train.* ○ *The midnight train to Edinburgh? Yes, that's a sleeper.*

sleepy /'sli:pi/ *adj* (**sleepier**; **sleepiest**) **1** tired and ready to go to sleep: *These pills might make you feel a bit sleepy.* **2** (used about a place) very quiet and not having much activity: *a sleepy little village* —**sleepily** /-ɪli/ *adv*

sleet /sli:t/ *noun* [U] a mixture of rain and snow ☛ Look at the note at **weather**.

☆**sleeve** /sli:v/ *noun* [C] **1** one of the two parts of a piece of clothing that cover the arms or part of the arms: *a blouse with long sleeves* ☛ picture on page A10. **2** (US **jacket**) a record cover
-sleeved (in compounds) with sleeves of a particular kind: *a short-sleeved shirt*
sleeveless *adj* without sleeves

sleigh /sleɪ/ *noun* [C] a vehicle that is used for travelling on snow and that is usually pulled by horses ☛ Look at **sledge**.

slender /'slendə(r)/ *adj* **1** (used about a person or part of sb's body) thin in an attractive way: *long slender fingers* **2** smaller in amount or size than you would like: *My chances of winning are very slender.*

slept *pt, pp* of SLEEP

slew *pt* of SLAY

☆**slice** /slaɪs/ *noun* [C] **1** a flat piece of food that is cut from a larger piece: *a thick/thin slice of bread* ☛ picture at **bread**. **2** a part of sth: *The directors had taken a large slice of the profits.*
slice *verb* **1** [T] to cut into slices: *Peel and slice the apples.* ○ *thinly sliced ham* **2** [I,T] to cut through or into sth: *He sliced through the rope with a knife.*

slick¹ /slɪk/ *adj* **1** done smoothly and well, and seeming to be done without any effort: *The actors gave a slick, highly professional performance.* **2** clever at persuading people but perhaps not completely honest: *slick advertising*

slick² /slɪk/ *noun* [C] = OIL-SLICK

☆**slide¹** /slaɪd/ *verb* (*pt, pp* **slid** /slɪd/) **1** [I,T] to move or make sth move smoothly along a surface: *She fell over and slid along the ice.* ○ *A large drop of rain slid down the window.* ○ *'Here you are,' he said, sliding the keys across the table.* ○ *a sliding door* (= one that you open by sliding it to one side) **2** [I,T] to move or make sth move quietly without being noticed: *I slid out of the room when nobody was looking.* ○ *She slid her hand into her pocket and took out a gun.* **3** [I] (used about prices, values, etc) to go down slowly and continuously: *The pound is sliding against the dollar.*

☆**slide²** /slaɪd/ *noun* [C] **1** a small piece of photographic film in a plastic or cardboard frame

☛ If you shine light through a slide using a **projector** you can make the photograph appear on a **screen**.

2 a small piece of glass that you put sth on when you want to examine it under a microscope **3** a long piece of metal, etc that children use for sliding down, (eg in a playground) **4** a continuous slow movement down (eg of prices, values, levels, etc): *a slide in the value of the pound*

☆**slight** /slaɪt/ *adj* **1** very small; not important or serious: *I've got a slight problem, but it's nothing to get worried about.* ○ *a slight change, difference, increase, improvement, etc* ○ *I haven't the slightest idea* (= no idea at all) *what you're talking about.* **2** (used about a person's body) thin and delicate: *his slight figure*
(IDIOM) **not in the slightest** not at all: *'Are you angry with me?' 'Not in the slightest.'*
slightly *adv* a little: *I'm slightly older than her.*

slim /slɪm/ *adj* (**slimmer**; **slimmest**) **1** thin in an attractive way: *a tall, slim woman* ☛ Look at the note at **thin**. **2** not as big as you would like: *Her chances of success are very slim.*
slim *verb* [I] (**slimm**ing; **slimm**ed) to become or try to become thinner and lighter by eating less food, taking exercise, etc: *'Another piece of cake?' 'No thanks. I'm slimming.'* ☛ Look at **diet**.

slime /slaɪm/ *noun* [U] a thick unpleasant sticky liquid: *The pond was covered with slime and had a horrible smell.*

slimy /'slaɪmi/ *adj* (**slimier**; **slimiest**) **1** covered with slime **2** (used about a person) very friendly, but in a way that you do not trust or like

sling¹ /slɪŋ/ *noun* [C] a piece of cloth that you put under your arm and tie around your neck to support a broken arm, wrist, etc ☛ picture at **plaster**.

sling² /slɪŋ/ *verb* [T] (*pt, pp* **slung**) **1** to put or throw sth somewhere in a rough or careless way: *Don't just sling your clothes on the floor!* **2** to put sth into a position where it hangs loosely: *She was carrying her bag slung over her shoulder.*

slink /slɪŋk/ *verb* [I] (*pt, pp* **slunk**) to move somewhere slowly and quietly because you do not want anyone to look at you, often when you feel guilty, embarrassed or ashamed

☆**slip¹** /slɪp/ *verb* (**slipp**ing; **slipp**ed) **1** [I] **slip (on sth)** to slide accidentally, lose your balance and fall or nearly fall: *Don't slip on that floor. I've just washed it.* ○ *His foot slipped on the*

ɜː	ə	eɪ	əʊ	aɪ	aʊ	ɔɪ	ɪə	eə	ʊə
fur	ago	pay	home	five	now	join	near	hair	pure

step and he fell down. **2** [I] to slide accidentally out of the correct position or out of sb's hand: *This hat's too big. It keeps slipping down over my eyes.* ○ *The glass slipped out of my hand and smashed on the floor.* ○ *(figurative) I didn't intend to tell them. It just slipped out.* **3** [I] to move or go somewhere quietly, quickly, and often without being noticed: *While everyone was dancing we slipped away and went home.* **4** [T] **slip sth (to sb); slip (sb) sth** to put sth somewhere or give sth quietly and often without being noticed: *She picked up the money and slipped it into her pocket.* **5** [I,T] **slip into/out of sth; slip sth on/off** to put on or take off a piece of clothing quickly and easily: *I'm just going to slip into something cooler.* ○ *I slipped off my shoes.* **6** [I] to fall a little (in value, level, etc): *Sales have been slipping slightly over the last few months.*

(IDIOMS) **let sth slip** to tell a secret, some information, etc without intending to: *He let slip that he had been in prison.*

slip your mind to be forgotten: *I'm sorry, the meeting completely slipped my mind.*

(PHRASAL VERB) **slip up** (*informal*) to make a mistake: *I'm afraid somebody must have slipped up. Your name isn't on the list.*

,slipped 'disc *noun* [C] one of the discs of the spine (in a person's back) that has moved out of its correct position, causing pain

'slip-road *noun* [C] a road that leads onto or off a motorway

slip² /slɪp/ *noun* [C] **1** an act of slipping(1): *Be careful when you go up onto the roof. One slip and you could fall off.* **2** a small mistake: *to make a slip* **3** a small piece of paper: *I made a note of her name on a slip of paper.* **4** a piece of clothing with no sleeves that is worn by a woman under a dress or skirt

(IDIOM) **give sb the slip** (*informal*) to escape from sb who is following or chasing you

slipper /'slɪpə(r)/ *noun* [C] a light soft shoe that is worn in the house: *a pair of slippers* ☛ picture at **shoe**.

slippery /'slɪpəri/ *adj* (used about a surface or an object) difficult to move over or hold because it is smooth, wet, greasy, etc: *a slippery floor* ○ *The fish was cold and slippery.*

slit /slɪt/ *noun* [C] a long narrow cut or opening: *We could see into the room through a slit in the curtains.*

slit *verb* [T] (**slitting**; *pt, pp* **slit**) to make a long narrow cut in sth: *She slit the envelope open with a knife.* ○ *He slit his wrists in a suicide attempt.*

slither /'slɪðə(r)/ *verb* [I] to slide along in an unsteady or twisting way: *I slithered along the pavement in the snow and ice.* ○ *I saw a snake slithering down a rock.*

slob /slɒb/ *noun* [C] (*informal*) (used as an insult) a very lazy or untidy person

slog /slɒg/ *verb* [I] (**slogging**; **slogged**) **1 slog (away) at sth** (*informal*) to work hard for a long period at sth difficult or boring: *I've been slogging away at this homework for hours.* **2 slog down, up, along, etc** to walk or move in a certain direction with a lot of effort: *Part of their training involves slogging up and down hills with packs on their backs.*

slog *noun* [sing] a period of long, hard, boring work or a long, tiring journey

slogan /'sləʊgən/ *noun* [C] a short phrase that is easy to remember and that is used in politics or advertising: *Anti-government slogans had been painted all over the walls.* ○ *'Faster than light' is the advertising slogan for the new car.*

slop /slɒp/ *verb* (**slopping**; **slopped**) **1** [I] (used about a liquid) to spill over the edge of its container: *He filled his glass too full and beer slopped onto the table.* **2** [T] to cause a liquid to do this

☆ **slope** /sləʊp/ *noun* **1** [C] a piece of land that goes up or down: *We walked down a slope and came to the river.* ○ *a steep/gentle slope* ○ *ski slopes* **2** [sing] the amount that a surface is not level; the fact of not being level: *a slope of 20 degrees* ○ *The slope of the pitch makes it quite difficult to play on.*

slope *verb* [I] to not be level or upright; to have a slope(2): *The road slopes down to the river.* ○ *a sloping roof*

sloppy /'slɒpi/ *adj* (**sloppier**; **sloppiest**) **1** (used about a piece of work, etc) not done carefully, tidily or thoroughly **2** (used about a person) careless or untidy: *a sloppy worker* **3** showing emotions in a silly way; sentimental: *I can't stand sloppy love songs.*

slosh /slɒʃ/ *verb* (*informal*) **1** [I] (used about a liquid) to move around noisily inside a container: *The water sloshed around in the bucket.* **2** [T] to put liquid somewhere in a careless and untidy way: *Careful! You're sloshing water all over the floor!*

sloshed *adj* (*slang*) drunk: *She won't remember what she said. She was completely sloshed.*

slot /slɒt/ *noun* [C] **1** a long straight narrow opening in a machine, etc: *Put your money into the slot and take the ticket.* ☛ picture at **telephone**. **2** a place in a timetable, system, organization, etc: *Oxford students have been given a new half-hour slot on our local radio station.*

slot *verb* [I,T] (**slotting**; **slotted**) to fit into a particular space: *These two metal bits slot in here.*

'slot-machine *noun* [C] a machine that sells drinks, cigarettes, etc or on which you can play games. You work it by putting money into a slot.

slouch /slaʊtʃ/ *verb* [I] to sit, stand or walk in a lazy way, with your head and shoulders hanging down

slovenly /'slʌvnli/ *adj* lazy, careless and untidy

☆ **slow¹** /sləʊ/ *adj* **1** moving, doing sth or happening without much speed; not fast: *The traffic is always very slow in the city centre.* ○ *Haven't you finished your homework yet? You're being very slow.* ○ *a slow improvement in his condition* **2 slow to do sth; slow (in/about) doing sth** not doing sth immediately: *Jane was slow to react to the news.* ○ *They've been rather slow in replying to my letter!* **3** not busy, lively or exciting: *Business is very slow at the moment.* **4** not quick to learn or understand: *I'm afraid I don't understand what you mean. I*

p	b	t	d	k	g	tʃ	dʒ	f	v	θ	ð
pen	**bad**	**tea**	**did**	**cat**	**got**	**chin**	**June**	**fall**	**van**	**thin**	**then**

must be a bit slow. o *a slow learner* **5** showing a time that is earlier than the real time: *That clock is five minutes slow* (= it says it is 8.55 when the correct time is 9.00).
(IDIOM) **quick/slow on the uptake** → UPTAKE

slowly *adv* at a slow speed; not quickly: *He walked slowly along the street.* —**slowness** *noun* [U]

slow 'motion *noun* [U] (in a film or on television) a method of making action appear much slower than in real life: *They showed the winning goal again, this time in slow motion.*

slow² /sləʊ/ *adv* at a slow speed; slowly ☞ It is possible to use **slow** as an adverb, but **slowly** is much more common. However, **slow** is often used in compounds: *slow-moving traffic*. The comparative forms **slower** and **more slowly** are both common: *Could you drive a bit slower/more slowly, please?*

☆ **slow³** /sləʊ/ *verb* [I,T] to start to move, do sth or happen at a slower speed; to cause sth to do this: *Jane ran along the path for a few minutes and then slowed to a walk.*
(PHRASAL VERB) **slow (sb/sth) down/up** to start to move, do sth or happen at a slower speed; to cause sth to do this: *Can't you slow down a bit? You're driving much too fast.* o *These problems have slowed up the whole process.*

sludge /slʌdʒ/ *noun* [U] thick, soft mud

slug /slʌg/ *noun* [C] a small animal like a snail without a shell. Slugs have long slimy bodies, move slowly along the ground and eat plants. ☞ picture at snail.

sluggish /'slʌgɪʃ/ *adj* slow-moving; not lively: *This hot weather is making me feel very sluggish.* o *sluggish economic growth*

slum /slʌm/ *noun* [C] (*also* **the slums** [plural]) an area of a city where living conditions are extremely bad, and where the buildings are dirty and have not been repaired for a long time

slumber /'slʌmbə(r)/ *verb* [I] (*old-fashioned*) to be asleep; to sleep peacefully
slumber *noun* [C] (*old-fashioned*) sleep: *The princess fell into a deep slumber.*

slump /slʌmp/ *verb* [I] **1** to fall or sit down suddenly when your body feels heavy and weak, usually because you are tired or ill: *Her face went very white, and then suddenly she slumped over the table.* **2** (used about trade, prices, the value of sth, etc) to fall suddenly and by a large amount: *Shares in BP slumped 33p to 181p yesterday.*
slump *noun* [C] **1** a sudden large fall in trade, the value of sth, etc: *a slump in house prices* **2** a period when a country's economy is doing very badly and there is a lot of unemployment

slung *pt, pp* of SLING
slunk *pt, pp* of SLINK

slur /slɜː(r)/ *verb* [T] (**slurring**; **slurred**) to speak words in a way that is not clear, often because you are drunk
slur *noun* [C] **a slur (on sb/sth)** a false statement or an insult that could damage sb's reputation: *The suggestion that our teachers are racist is a slur on the good name of the school.*

slurp /slɜːp/ *verb* [I,T] (*informal*) to drink noisily: *I hate the way he slurps when he drinks his tea.*

slush /slʌʃ/ *noun* [U] snow that has partly melted and that is often watery and dirty
slushy *adj* (**slushier**; **slushiest**) **1** covered in melting snow: *slushy roads* **2** romantic or sentimental in a silly way: *a slushy love song*

slut /slʌt/ *noun* [C] a sexually immoral woman; a very lazy and untidy woman ☞ This word is used as a very strong insult.

sly /slaɪ/ *adj* **1** (used about a person) good at deceiving people or doing things in secret **2** (used about an action) suggesting that you know sth secret: *a sly smile* —**slyly** *adv*

smack¹ /smæk/ *verb* [T] to hit sb/sth with the inside of your hand: *I never smack my children.*
smack *noun* [C] an act of smacking

smack² /smæk/ *verb*
(PHRASAL VERB) **smack of sth** to make you think that sb/sth has an unpleasant attitude or quality: *Her remarks about your new car smacked of jealousy.*

☆ **small** /smɔːl/ *adj* **1** not large in size, number, amount, etc: *a small car, flat, town, etc* o *a small group of people* o *a small amount of money* **2** young: *He has a wife and three small children.* o *When I was small we lived in a big old house.* **3** not important or serious; slight: *Don't worry. It's only a small problem.* ☞ **Small** is the most usual opposite of **big** or **large**. **Little** is often used with another adjective to express an emotion, as well as the idea of smallness: *a horrible little man* o *a lovely little girl* o *a nice little house*. The comparative and superlative forms **smaller** and **smallest** are common, and **small** is often used with words like 'rather', 'quite' and 'very': *My flat is smaller than yours.* o *The village is quite small.* o *a very small car.* **Little** is not often used with these words and does not usually have a comparative or superlative form.
small *adv* in a small size: *She's painted the picture far too small.*

'small ads *noun* [plural] (*Brit informal*) = CLASSIFIED ADVERTISEMENTS

small 'change *noun* [U] coins that have a low value

'small hours *noun* [plural] the early morning hours soon after midnight: *We sat up into the small hours discussing the problem.*

small 'print *noun* [U] a part or parts of a legal contract, document, etc that contain important details that you might not notice: *Make sure you read the small print before you sign anything.*

small-'scale *adj* (used about an organization or activity) not large; limited in what it does: *a small-scale business*

'small talk *noun* [U] polite conversation, eg at a party, about unimportant things at social events

smallpox /'smɔːlpɒks/ *noun* [U] a serious infectious disease that causes a high fever and leaves marks on the skin. In the past many people died from smallpox.

☆ **smart¹** /smɑːt/ *adj* **1** (used about a person) clean, tidy and well-dressed; wearing formal or fairly formal clothes: *You look smart. Are you going somewhere special?* **2** (used about a piece of clothing, etc) clean, tidy and new-looking: *a smart suit* **3** fashionable and usually expensive: *a smart restaurant* **4** (*especially US*) clever; able to think quickly: *He's not smart enough to be a politician.* **5** (used about a movement or action) quick: *The race began at a smart speed.*

smarten /'smɑ:tn/ *verb*
(PHRASAL VERB) **smarten (yourself/sb/sth) up** to make yourself, sb or sth look smarter
smartly *adv* in a smart way: *She's always smartly dressed.*

smart² /smɑ:t/ *verb* [I] to feel a stinging pain in your body: *The smoke made her eyes smart.* o (*figurative*) *He was still smarting from her insult.*

smash /smæʃ/ *verb* **1** [I,T] **smash sth (up); smash sth open** to break violently into many pieces: *The glass smashed into a thousand pieces.* o *The police had to smash the door open.* **2** [T] **smash sth (up)** to crash sth (a car, etc), usually causing a lot of damage: *I smashed up my father's car.* **3** **smash (sth) against, into, through,** etc [I,T] to move with great force in a particular direction: *The car smashed into a tree.* o *He smashed his hand through the window.* **4** [T] (in tennis) to hit a ball that is high in the air down and over the net, making it travel very fast

smash *noun* **1** [sing] an act or the noise of sth breaking violently: *I heard the smash of breaking glass.* **2** [C] (*also* **'smash-up**) a car crash **3** [C] (in tennis) a way of hitting a ball that is high in the air down and over the net, making it travel very fast **4** [C] (*also* **smash 'hit**) (*informal*) a song, play, film, etc that is very successful

smashing *adj* (*Brit informal*) extremely good; wonderful: *We had a smashing time at the party.*

smear /smɪə(r)/ *verb* [T] **smear sth on/over sth/sb; smear sth/sb with sth** to spread a sticky substance across sth/sb: *The child had smeared chocolate over his clothes.* o *Her face was smeared with grease.*

smear *noun* [C] **1** a mark made by smearing: *a smear of paint on her dress* **2** something untrue that is said in a newspaper, etc about an important person: *a smear against the prime minister*

☆**smell¹** /smel/ *noun* **1** [U] the ability to smell: *Dogs have a very good sense of smell.* **2** [C] the impression that you get of sth by using your nose; the thing that is smelled: *What's that smell?* o *There's a smell of gas.* o *a strong smell* **3** [usually sing] an act of smelling: *Have a smell of this milk; is it all right?*
smelly *adj* (**smellier; smelliest**) (*informal*) having a bad smell: *smelly feet*

☆**smell²** /smel/ *verb* (*pt, pp* **smelt** /smelt/ or **smelled**) **1** [T] to notice, identify or examine sb/sth by using your nose: *He could smell something burning.* o *Can you smell gas?* **2** [I] to be able to smell: *I can't smell properly because I've got a cold.* **3** [I] **smell (of sth)** to have a particular smell: *Dinner smells good!* o *This per-* *fume smells of roses.* **4** [I] to have a bad smell: *Your feet smell.* ☞ We do not use **smell** or other verbs of the senses (eg **taste, see, hear**) with the continuous tense. Instead we often use **can**, eg: *I can smell smoke.*

☆**smile** /smaɪl/ *noun* [C] an expression on your face in which the corners of your mouth turn up, showing happiness, pleasure, etc: *to have a smile on your face* o *'It's nice to see you,' he said with a smile.*
smile *verb* **1** [I] **smile (at sb/sth)** to have or give a smile: *She smiled at the camera.* o *He was smiling with happiness.* **2** [T] to express sth by means of a smile: *I smiled a greeting to them.*

smirk /smɜ:k/ *noun* [C] a silly or unpleasant smile which you have when you are pleased with yourself or think you are very clever
—**smirk** *verb* [I]

smock /smɒk/ *noun* [C] a type of long loose shirt that was once worn by farmers but is now usually worn by women who are expecting a baby

smog /smɒg/ *noun* [U] a mixture of fog and smoke, caused by pollution, that is in the air over some industrial cities

☆**smoke¹** /sməʊk/ *noun* **1** [U] the gas that you can see in the air when something is burning: *Thick smoke poured from the chimney.* o *a room full of cigarette smoke* **2** [C, usually sing] (*informal*) an act of smoking a cigarette, etc: *He went outside for a quick smoke.*

☆**smoke²** /sməʊk/ *verb* **1** [I,T] to breathe in smoke through a cigarette, etc and let it out again; to have the habit of smoking cigarettes, etc: *Do you mind if I smoke?* o *I used to smoke 20 cigarettes a day.* **2** [I] to give out smoke: *The factory chimneys were smoking.*
smoked *adj* (used of certain types of food) preserved and given a special taste by being hung in smoke: *smoked salmon*
smoker *noun* [C] a person who smokes cigarettes, etc: *She's a chain smoker* (= she finishes one cigarette and then immediately lights another). ☞ The opposite is **non-smoker**.
smoking *noun* [U] the act or habit of smoking cigarettes, etc: *My doctor has advised me to give up smoking.*
smoky *adj* (**smokier; smokiest**) **1** full of smoke; producing a lot of smoke: *a smoky room* o *a smoky fire* **2** with the smell, taste or appearance of smoke: *This cheese has a smoky flavour.*

smolder (*US*) = SMOULDER

☆**smooth** /smu:ð/ *adj* **1** having a flat surface with no lumps or holes: *smooth skin* o *a smooth piece of wood* **2** (of a liquid mixture) without lumps: *Stir the sauce until it is smooth.* **3** (of a journey in a car, etc) with an even, comfortable movement: *You get a very smooth ride in this car.* **4** without difficulties: *The transition from the old method to the new has been very smooth.* **5** too pleasant or polite to be trusted ☞ We use this word in a critical way, usually about a man.

(IDIOM) **take the rough with the smooth** ⇨ ROUGH³

smoothly *adv* without any difficulty: *My work*

iː	ɪ	e	æ	ɑː	ɒ	ɔː	ʊ	uː	ʌ
see	sit	ten	hat	arm	got	saw	put	too	cup

has been going quite smoothly. —**smoothness** *noun* [U]

smooth² /smuːð/ *verb* [T] **smooth sth (away, back, down, out, etc)** to move your hands in the direction mentioned over the surface of sth to make it smooth: *She smoothed her hair away from her face.* ○ *I smoothed the tablecloth out.*

smother /'smʌðə(r)/ *verb* [T] **1** to kill sb by not allowing him/her to breathe: *She was smothered with a pillow.* **2** to cover sth (with too much of a substance): *He smothered his cake with cream.* **3** to stop sth burning by covering it: *to smother the flames with a blanket* **4** to hide a feeling, etc: *She managed to smother a yawn.*

smoulder (*US* **smolder**) /'sməʊldə(r)/ *verb* [I] to burn slowly without a flame: *a cigarette smouldering in the ashtray.* ○ (*figurative*) *Her eyes were smouldering with rage.*

smudge /smʌdʒ/ *noun* [C] a dirty or untidy mark: *The child's homework was covered in smudges of ink.*

smudge *verb* **1** [T] to make sth dirty or untidy by touching it: *Leave your painting to dry or you'll smudge it.* **2** [I] to become untidy, without a clean line around it: *Her lipstick smudged when she kissed him.*

smug /smʌɡ/ *adj* (**smugger**; **smuggest**) too pleased with yourself: *Don't look so smug.* ☛ We use this word in a critical way. —**smugly** *adv* —**smugness** *noun* [U]

smuggle /'smʌɡl/ *verb* [T] to take things into or out of a country in a way which is against the law; to take a person into or out of a place in secret: *The drugs had been smuggled through customs.* ○ *The refugees were smuggled across the border.* —**smuggler** /'smʌɡlə(r)/ *noun* [C]: *a drug smuggler* —**smuggling** /'smʌɡlɪŋ/ *noun* [U]

☆ **snack** /snæk/ *noun* [C] a small meal, eg a sandwich, that you eat quickly between main meals: *I had a snack on the train.*

snack *verb* [I] (*informal*) to eat a snack instead of a meal or between meals: *I snacked on a chocolate bar instead of having lunch.*

'snack bar *noun* [C] a type of small café where you can buy a snack

snag¹ /snæɡ/ *noun* [C] a small difficulty or disadvantage that is often unexpected or hidden: *His offer is very generous – are you sure there isn't a snag?*

snag² /snæɡ/ *verb* [T] (**snagging**; **snagged**) to catch a piece of clothing, etc on sth sharp and tear it

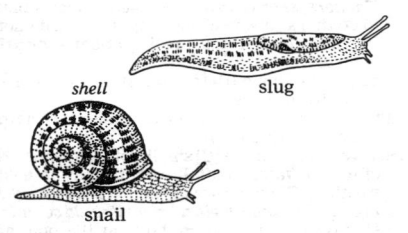

shell   slug

snail

snail /sneɪl/ *noun* [C] a type of animal with a soft body without legs that is covered by a shell. Snails move very slowly.

☆ **snake** /sneɪk/ *noun* [C] a type of long thin animal without legs that slides along the ground by moving its body from side to side: *a poisonous snake* ○ *a snake-bite*

snake *verb* [I] (*also* **snake its way**) to move like a snake: *The road snakes its way through mountain villages.*

☆ **snap¹** /snæp/ *verb* (**snapping**; **snapped**) **1** [I,T] to break suddenly with a sharp noise: *The branch snapped.* ○ *The weight of the snow snapped the branch in two.* ○ (*figurative*) *Suddenly something just snapped and I lost my temper with him.* **2** [I,T] to close quickly with a sharp noise: *The lid of the box snapped shut.* **3** [I,T] to speak or say sth in a quick angry way: *Why do you always snap at me?* **4** [I,T] to try to bite sb/sth: *The dog snapped at the child's hand.* **5** [T] (*informal*) to take a quick photograph of sb/sth
(IDIOM) **snap your fingers** to make a sharp noise by moving your middle finger quickly against your thumb, especially when you want to attract sb's attention
(PHRASAL VERB) **snap sth up** to buy or take sth quickly, especially because it is very cheap

snap² /snæp/ *noun* **1** [C] an act or the sound of snapping: *The piece of wood broke with a snap.* **2** [C] (*also* **'snapshot**) a photograph that is taken quickly and informally: *I showed them some holiday snaps.* **3** [U] (*Brit*) a type of cardgame where players call out 'Snap' when two cards that are the same are put down by different players

snap *adj* (*informal*) done quickly and suddenly, often without much careful thought: *a snap decision*

snap *interj* (*Brit*) said when two similar things appear together: *We've got the same skirt on. Snap!*

snare /sneə(r)/ *noun* [C] a trap used to catch birds or small animals —**snare** *verb* [T]

snarl /snɑːl/ *verb* [I,T] (used about an animal) to make an angry sound while showing the teeth: *The dog snarled at the stranger.* ○ (*figurative*) *'Get out of here!' he snarled.* —**snarl** *noun* [C, usually sing]

snatch¹ /snætʃ/ *verb* **1** [I,T] to (try to) take or pull sth/sb away quickly: *It's rude to snatch.* ○ *He snatched the gun from her hand.* ○ *My bag was snatched* (= stolen). ○ (*figurative*) *The team snatched a 2-1 victory.* ☛ Look at **grab**. It is similar in meaning. **2** [T] to take or get sth quickly when you have just enough time to do so: *I managed to snatch some sleep on the train.*
(PHRASAL VERB) **snatch at sth** to (try to) take hold of sth eagerly: *to snatch at somebody's hand* ○ (*figurative*) *He snatched at the opportunity to travel abroad.*

snatch *noun* **1** [sing] an act of snatching(1) at sth: *I made a snatch at the ball.* **2** [C, usually pl] a short part or period of something: *I heard snatches of conversation from the next room.*

sneak /sniːk/ *verb* **1** [I] **sneak into, out of, past, etc sth**; **sneak in, out, away, etc** to go very quietly in the direction mentioned, so that no one can see or hear you: *Instead of*

ɜː	ə	eɪ	əʊ	aɪ	aʊ	ɔɪ	ɪə	eə	ʊə
fur	ago	pay	home	five	now	join	near	hair	pure

working, he sneaked out to play football. ○ *The prisoner sneaked past the guards.* **2** [T] (*informal*) to take sth secretly or without permission: *She sneaked a chocolate when no one was looking.*
(PHRASAL VERB) **sneak up** (**on sb/sth**) to approach sb very quietly, especially so that you can surprise him/her

sneak *noun* [C] (*informal*) a person who tells an official or a person in authority about the bad things sb has done ☛ This word is used in a critical way.

sneaking *adj* (of feelings, etc) not expressed; secret: *I've a sneaking suspicion that he's lying.*

sneaker /'sni:kə(r)/ *noun* [C] (*US*) = PLIMSOLL, TRAINER: *a pair of sneakers*

sneer /snɪə(r)/ *verb* [I] **1** to smile unpleasantly with one side of your mouth raised to show that you dislike sb/sth **2 sneer** (**at sb/sth**) to behave or speak as if sth is not good enough for you: *She sneered at his attempts to speak French.*

sneer *noun* [C] an unpleasant smile or remark

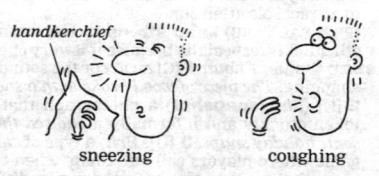

handkerchief

sneezing   coughing

☆ **sneeze** /sni:z/ *noun* [C] a sudden burst of air coming out through your nose and mouth that happens, for example, when you have a cold: *He gave a loud sneeze.*
sneeze *verb* [I] to give a sneeze: *Dust makes me sneeze.*

snide /snaɪd/ *adj* (of an expression or remark) critical in an unpleasant way

sniff /snɪf/ *verb* **1** [I] to breathe air in through the nose in a way that makes a sound, especially because you have a cold or you are crying: *Stop sniffing and blow your nose.* **2** [I,T] **sniff** (**at**) **sth** to smell sth by sniffing: *'I can smell gas,' he said, sniffing the air.* ○ *The dog sniffed at the bone.*
sniff *noun* [C] an act or the sound of sniffing

sniffle /'snɪfl/ *verb* [I] to sniff continuously, especially because you have a cold or you are crying

snigger /'snɪɡə(r)/ *verb* [I] **snigger** (**at sb/sth**) to laugh quietly to yourself in an unpleasant way: *They sniggered at his old clothes.*
—**snigger** *noun* [C]

snip¹ /snɪp/ *verb* [I,T] (**snipping**; **snipped**) to cut using scissors, with a short quick action

snip² /snɪp/ *noun* [C] **1** a small cut **2** (*Brit informal*) something that is surprisingly cheap: *It's a snip at only £25!*

snippet /'snɪpɪt/ *noun* [C] a small piece of sth, especially information or news

snivel /'snɪvl/ *verb* [I] (**snivelling**; **snivelled**; *US* sniveling; sniveled) to keep crying in a way that is annoying

snob /snɒb/ *noun* [C] a person who thinks he/she is better than sb of a lower social class and who admires people who have a high social position: *Don't be such a snob!*

snobbery /'snɒbəri/ *noun* [U] behaviour or attitudes that are typical of a snob

snobbish *adj* of or like a snob: *She had a snobbish attitude towards her husband's family.*
—**snobbishly** *adv* —**snobbishness** *noun* [U]

snog /snɒɡ/ *verb* [I] (**snogging**; **snogged**) (*Brit informal*) (used about a couple) to keep kissing each other for a period of time: *A teenage couple were snogging in the corner.* —**snog** *noun* [sing]

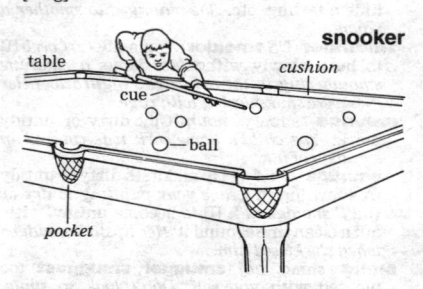

snooker

table, *cushion*, *cue*, *ball*, *pocket*

snooker /'snu:kə(r)/ *noun* [U] a game in which two players try to hit a number of coloured balls into pockets at the edges of a large table using a long stick (**cue**): *to play snooker* ☛ Look at **billiards**.

snoop /snu:p/ *verb* [I] to look around secretly and without permission in order to find out information, etc: *If I catch you snooping around here again, I'll call the police!*

snooty /'snu:ti/ *adj* (**snootier**; **snootiest**) (*informal*) acting in a rude way because you think you are better than other people

snooze /snu:z/ *verb* [I] (*informal*) to have a short sleep, especially during the day —**snooze** *noun* [C, usually sing]: *I had a bit of a snooze on the train.* ☛ Look at **nap**.

snore /snɔ:(r)/ *verb* [I] to breathe noisily through your nose and mouth while you are asleep: *She heard her father snoring in the next room.* —**snore** *noun* [C]

snorkel /'snɔ:kl/ *noun* [C] a short tube that a swimmer who is just below the surface of the water can use to breathe through

snort /snɔ:t/ *verb* [I] **1** (used about animals) to make a noise by blowing air through the nose: *The horse snorted in fear.* **2** (used about people) to do this as a way of showing that you do not like sth, or that you are impatient —**snort** *noun* [C]

snot /snɒt/ *noun* [U] (*informal*) the liquid produced by the nose

snout /snaʊt/ *noun* [C] the long nose of certain animals: *a pig's snout*

☆ **snow¹** /snəʊ/ *noun* [U] small, soft, white pieces of frozen water that fall from the sky in cold weather: *Three inches of snow fell during the night.* ○ *The snow melted before it could settle* (= stay on the ground). ☛ Look at the note at **weather**.

p	b	t	d	k	g	tʃ	dʒ	f	v	θ	ð
pen	bad	tea	did	cat	got	chin	June	fall	van	thin	then

'snowball noun [C] a lump of snow that is pressed into the shape of a ball and used by children for playing

'snowball verb [I] to quickly grow bigger and bigger or more and more important: *Business has just snowballed so that we can hardly keep up with demand.*

'snowdrift noun [C] a deep pile of snow that has been made by the wind

'snowdrop noun [C] a type of small white flower that appears at the end of winter

'snowfall noun **1** [C] the snow that falls on one occasion: *heavy snowfalls* **2** [U] the amount of snow that falls in a particular place: *What is the average snowfall in Scotland?*

'snowflake noun [C] one of the small, soft, white pieces of frozen water that fall together as snow

'snowman /-mæn/ noun [C] (pl **snowmen**) /-men/ the figure of a person made out of snow, usually by children

'snowplough (*US* **snowplow**) noun [C] a type of vehicle that is used to clear snow away from roads or railways

☆ **snow²** /snəʊ/ verb [I] (used of snow) to fall from the sky: *It snowed all night.*

snowed 'in adj not able to leave home or travel because the snow is too deep

snowed 'under adj with more work, etc than you can deal with

snowy adj (**snowier**; **snowiest**) with a lot of snow: *snowy weather* o *a snowy scene*

snub /snʌb/ verb (**snubbing**; **snubbed**) [T] to treat sb rudely, eg by refusing to look at or speak to him/her: *She snubbed them by not inviting them to the party.* —**snub** noun [C]: *When they weren't invited to the party, they felt it was a snub.*

snuff /snʌf/ noun [U] tobacco which people breathe up into the nose in the form of a powder: *to take a pinch of snuff*

snuffle /'snʌfl/ verb [I] (used of people and animals) to make a noise through your nose: *The dog snuffled around the lamp-post.*

snug /snʌg/ adj (**snugger**; **snuggest**) warm and comfortable: *a snug little room* o *The children were snug in bed.*

snugly adv **1** warmly and comfortably: *The baby was wrapped snugly in a blanket.* **2** tidily and tightly: *The present fitted snugly into the box.*

snuggle /'snʌgl/ verb [I] **snuggle (up to sb)**; **snuggle (up/down)** to get into a position that makes you feel safe, warm and comfortable, usually next to another person: *She snuggled up to her mother.* o *I snuggled down under the blanket to get warm.*

☆ **so¹** /səʊ/ adv **1** (used to emphasize an adjective or adverb, especially when there is a particular result) to the extent (that); to a great degree: *She's so ill (that) she can't get out of bed.* o *He was driving so fast that he couldn't stop.* o *I haven't enjoyed myself so much for years.* o *So many people came to the concert that some couldn't get in.* ☛ Look at the note at **such**. **2** (used in negative sentences for comparing people or things): *She's not so clever as we thought.* **3** very: *You've been so kind. How can I thank you?* **4** (used in place of something that has been said already, to avoid repeating it): *Are you coming by plane? If so,* (= if you are coming by plane) *I can meet you at the airport.* o *'I failed, didn't I?' 'I'm afraid so, Susan.'* ☛ In formal language, you can refer to actions that somebody has mentioned using **do** with **so**: *He asked me to write to him and I did so* (I wrote to him). **5** (not with verbs in the negative) also, too: *He's a teacher and so is his wife.* o *I've been to New York.' 'So have I.'* o *I like singing and so does Helen.* ☛ For negative sentences, look at **neither**. **6** (used to show that you agree that sth is true, especially when you are surprised): *'It's getting late.' 'So it is. We'd better go.'* **7** (*formal*) (used when you are showing sb sth) in this way: *Raise your right hand, so.*

(IDIOMS) **and so on (and so forth)** (used at the end of a list to show that it continues in the same way): *They sell pens, pencils, paper and so on.*

I told you so (used to tell sb that he/she should have listened to your advice): *'I missed the bus.' 'I told you so. I said you needed to leave earlier.'*

it (just) so happens (used to introduce a surprising fact) by chance: *It just so happened that we were going the same way, so he gave me a lift.*

just so ⇨ JUST²

or so (used to show that a number, time, etc is not exact): *A hundred or so people came to the meeting.*

so as to do sth with the intention of doing sth; in order to do sth: *We went early so as to get good seats.*

so much for (used for expressing that sth is finished or not helpful): *So much for that diet! I didn't lose any weight at all.*

that is so (*formal*) that is true: *'Mr Jones, you were in Lincoln on May 14. Is that so?' 'That is so.'*

'so-and-so noun [C] (pl **so-and-so's**) (*informal*) **1** a person who is not named: *Imagine a Mrs So-and-so telephones. What would you say?* **2** a person that you do not like: *He's a bad-tempered old so-and-so.*

,so-'called adj (used to show that the words you describe sb/sth with are not correct): *Her so-called friends only wanted her money* (= they are not really her friends).

☆ **so²** /səʊ/ conj **1** with the result that; therefore: *She felt very tired so she went to bed early.* **2** **so (that)** with the purpose that; in order that: *She wore dark glasses so that nobody would recognize her.* **3** (used to show how one part of a story follows another): *So that's how I first met your mother.*

(IDIOM) **so what?** (*informal*) (showing that you think sth is not important) Why should I care?: *'It's late.' 'So what? We don't have to go to school tomorrow.'*

soak /səʊk/ verb **1** [I,T] to become or make sth completely wet: *Leave the dishes to soak for a while.* o *I'm going to soak these trousers in hot water to get the stain out.* **2** [I] **soak into/through sth**; **soak in** (used about a liquid) to pass into or through sth: *Blood had soaked through the bandage.*

---

s	z	ʃ	ʒ	h	m	n	ŋ	l	r	j	w
so	zoo	she	vision	how	man	no	sing	leg	red	yes	wet

soap

(PHRASAL VERB) **soak sth up** to draw sth in (especially a liquid): *I soaked the water up with a cloth.* ○ (*figurative*) *She loves to lie on a beach, soaking up the sunshine.*

soaked /səʊkt/ *adj* (not before a noun) extremely wet: *I got soaked waiting for my bus in the rain.*

soaking /ˈsəʊkɪŋ/ (*also* ˌsoaking ˈwet) *adj* extremely wet

☆ **soap** /səʊp/ *noun* [U] a substance that you use for washing and cleaning: *He washed his hands with soap.* ○ *a bar of soap* ○ *soap powder* (= for washing clothes)

soapy *adj* full of soap: *Wash in plenty of warm soapy water.*

ˈ**soap opera** (*also informal* **soap**) *noun* [C] a story about the lives and problems of a group of people which continues every day or several times a week on television or radio: *'Coronation Street' is our longest running soap opera.*

soar /sɔː(r)/ *verb* [I] **1** to fly high in the air: *There were sea birds soaring overhead.* **2** to rise very fast: *The plane soared into the air.* ○ (*figurative*) *Prices are soaring because of inflation.*

sob /sɒb/ *verb* [I] (**sobbing**; **sobbed**) to cry loudly while taking in sudden, sharp breaths; to speak while you are crying: *The child was sobbing because he'd lost his toy.*

sob *noun* [C] an act or the sound of sobbing

sober /ˈsəʊbə(r)/ *adj* **1** (of a person) not affected by alcohol **2** (of a person or attitude) serious or thoughtful: *a sober expression* ○ *a sober reminder of just how dangerous drugs can be* **3** (of a colour) not bright or likely to be noticed: *a sober grey suit*

sober *verb*

(PHRASAL VERB) **sober (sb) up** to become, or to make sb, sober(1): *I need a cup of black coffee to sober me up.*

sobering *adj* making you feel serious

soccer /ˈsɒkə(r)/ *noun* [U] = FOOTBALL(1)

sociable /ˈsəʊʃəbl/ *adj* enjoying the company of other people, friendly

☆ **social** /ˈsəʊʃl/ *adj* **1** concerning the relations between people or groups of people; relating to the organization of society: *The 1980s were a period of social change.* ○ *social problems* **2** concerning the rank of people in society: *We share the same social background.* ○ *social class* **3** to do with meeting people and enjoying yourself: *a social club* ○ *She has a busy social life.* **4** (used about animals) living and looking for food together: *Lions are social animals.* —**socially** /-ʃəli/ *adv*: *We work together but I don't know him socially.*

ˌsocial ˈscience *noun* [C,U] the study of people in society, including economics, politics and sociology

ˌsocial seˈcurity (*US* ˈwelfare) *noun* [U] money paid regularly by the government to people who are poor, old, ill, or who have no job

ˌsocial ˈservices *noun* [plural] a group of services organized by local government to help people who have social problems (eg with housing, child care, etc)

ˈsocial work *noun* [U] work that involves giving help to people with problems because they are poor, ill, etc

ˈsocial worker *noun* [C] a person whose job is to do social work

☆ **socialism** /ˈsəʊʃəlɪzəm/ *noun* [U] the political theory and practice that is based on the belief that all people are equal and that wealth should be equally divided

socialist /ˈsəʊʃəlɪst/ *noun* [C] a person who believes in socialism; a member of a socialist party —**socialist** *adj*

☆ **society** /səˈsaɪəti/ *noun* (*pl* **societies**) **1** [C,U] the people in a country or area, thought of as a group, who have shared customs and laws: *a civilized society* ○ *in Western society* ○ *The aim is to create a classless society in Britain.* ○ *Society's attitude to women has changed considerably this century.* **2** [C] an organization of people who share a particular interest or purpose; a club: *a drama society* ○ *The Royal Society for the Prevention of Cruelty to Animals*

sociology /ˌsəʊsiˈɒlədʒi/ *noun* [U] the study of human society and social behaviour —**sociological** /ˌsəʊsiəˈlɒdʒɪkl/ *adj*

sociologist /ˌsəʊsiˈɒlədʒɪst/ *noun* [C] a student of or an expert in sociology

☆ **sock** /sɒk/ *noun* [C] a piece of clothing that you wear on your foot and lower leg, inside your shoe: *a pair of socks*

(IDIOM) **pull your socks up** (*Brit informal*) (to try) to work harder, do better, etc than before

socket /ˈsɒkɪt/ *noun* [C] **1** (*also* **power point**, *informal* **plug**) a place in a wall where an electrical appliance can be connected to the electricity supply ☞ *picture at* **plug**. **2** a hollow place where sth fits: *your eye socket*

soda /ˈsəʊdə/ (*also* **soda water**) *noun* [C,U] water that has bubbles in it and is used for mixing with other drinks: *a whisky and soda*

sofa /ˈsəʊfə/ *noun* [C] a comfortable seat with a back and arms. It is long enough for two or more people to sit on: *a sofa-bed* (= a sofa that you can pull out to make a bed)

☆ **soft** /sɒft; *US* sɔːft/ *adj* **1** not hard or firm: *a soft bed* ○ *The ground is very soft after all that rain.* **2** smooth and nice to touch; not rough: *soft skin, hands, etc* ○ *a soft towel* **3** (used about sounds, voices, words, etc) quiet or gentle; not loud or angry: *She spoke in a soft whisper.* **4** (used about light, colours etc) gentle and pleasant; not bright: *The room was decorated in soft pinks and greens.* **5** (used about people and animals) (too) kind and gentle: not hard or strict: *A good manager can't afford to be too soft.* **6** (used about illegal drugs) less dangerous and serious than the type of illegal drugs which can kill people: *soft drugs such as marijuana*

(IDIOM) **have a soft spot for sb/sth** (*informal*) to be especially fond of sb/sth: *I've got rather a soft spot for my old teacher.*

softly *adv* gently or quietly: *'Don't wake the children,' she whispered softly.*

softness *noun* [U] the quality of being soft

ˌsoft ˈdrink *noun* [C] a cold drink that contains no alcohol

ˌsoft-ˈhearted *adj* kind and able to sym-

i:	ɪ	e	æ	ɑ:	ɒ	ɔ:	ʊ	u:	ʌ
see	sit	ten	hat	arm	got	saw	put	too	cup

pathize with other people's feelings ☛ The opposite is **hard-hearted**.

ˌsoft 'option *noun* [C] the easier thing to do of two or more possibilities, but not always the best one: *The government has taken the soft option of agreeing to their demands.*

ˌsoft-'spoken *adj* having a gentle, quiet voice: *He was a kind, soft-spoken man.*

soften /'sɒfn/ *US* 'sɔ:fn/ *verb* **1** [I,T] to become softer or gentler; to make sb/sth softer or gentler: *First soften the butter in a bowl.* o *The teacher's expression softened as I explained why I was late.* **2** [T] to make sth seem less severe: *to try to soften the effect of bad news*

software /'sɒftweə(r)/ *noun* [U] programs that you use to operate a computer: *There's a lot of new educational software available now.* ☛ Look at **hardware**.

soggy /'sɒgi/ *adj* (**soggier; soggiest**) very wet; having too much liquid in it

☆**soil** /sɔɪl/ *noun* **1** [C,U] the substance that plants, trees, etc grow in; earth: *poor soil* ☛ Look at the note at **ground¹**. **2** [U] the land that is part of a country: *to set foot on British soil* (= to arrive in Britain)

soil *verb* [T] (*formal*) to make sth dirty

solace /'sɒlɪs/ *noun* [C,U] (something that gives you) comfort or relief when you are sad

solar /'səʊlə(r)/ *adj* **1** of or relating to the sun: *solar energy* **2** using the sun's energy: *solar heating*

the 'solar system *noun* [sing] the sun and the planets that move around it

sold *pt, pp* of SELL

☆**soldier** /'səʊldʒə(r)/ *noun* [C] a member of an army: *The soldiers marched past.*

☆**sole¹** /səʊl/ *adj* (only *before* a noun) **1** only; single: *His sole interest is football.* **2** belonging to one person only; not shared: *Do you have sole responsibility for the accounts?*

solely /'səʊlli/ *adv* only: *I agreed to come solely on account of your mother.*

sole² /səʊl/ *noun* [C] **1** the flat part of your foot that you walk on ☛ picture on page A8. **2** the part of a shoe or sock that covers the bottom surface of your foot: *These shoes have leather soles and man-made uppers.* ☛ picture at **shoe**.

sole³ /səʊl/ *noun* [C,U] (*pl* **sole**) a small flat sea fish that can be eaten as food

solemn /'sɒləm/ *adj* **1** very serious: *Her solemn face told them that the news was bad.* **2** sincere; done or said in a formal way: *to make a solemn promise* o *a solemn warning* —**solemnity** /sə'lemnəti/ *noun* [U]

solemnly *adv* in a serious or sincere way: *'I have something very important to tell you,' she began solemnly.*

solicit /sə'lɪsɪt/ *verb* **1** [T] (*formal*) to ask sb for money, help, support, etc: *They tried to solicit support for the proposal.* **2** [I,T] to approach sb, especially in a public place, and offer sex in return for money

solicitor /sə'lɪsɪtə(r)/ *noun* [C] (*Brit*) a person whose job is to give legal advice, prepare legal documents and speak in the lower courts ☛ Look at the note at **lawyer**.

☆**solid** /'sɒlɪd/ *adj* **1** hard and firm; not in the form of liquid or gas: *It was so cold that the village pond had frozen solid.* o *Our central heating runs on solid fuel* (= coal, wood, etc, not gas or electricity). **2** having no holes or spaces inside; not hollow: *a solid mass of rock* o *The briefcase was packed solid with £50 notes.* **3** (only *before* a noun) made of the same substance inside and outside: *a solid gold chain* **4** strong, firm and therefore reliable: *a solid little car* **5** reliable; of sufficient quality and amount: *The police cannot make an arrest without solid evidence.* **6** without a break or pause: *I was so tired that I slept for twelve solid hours/ twelve hours solid.*

solid *noun* [C] **1** a substance or object that is hard; not a liquid or gas: *Liquids become solids when frozen.* **2** an object that has length, width and height, not a flat object: *A cube is a solid.*

solidity /sə'lɪdəti/ *noun* [U] the quality or state of being solid

solidly *adv* **1** strongly: *a solidly built house* **2** continuously: *It rained solidly all day.*

solidarity /ˌsɒlɪ'dærəti/ *noun* [U] the support of one group of people for another, because they agree with their aims: *Many local people expressed solidarity with the strikers.*

solidify /sə'lɪdɪfaɪ/ *verb* [I] (*pres part* **solidifying**; *3rd pers sing pres* **solidifies**; *pt, pp* **solidified**) to become hard or solid

solitaire /ˌsɒlɪ'teə(r); *US* 'sɒlɪteə(r)/ *noun* [U] *US* = PATIENCE (2)

solitary /'sɒlɪtri; *US* -teri/ *adj* **1** living alone, without other people: *She lives a solitary life in a remote part of Scotland.* **2** done alone: *Writing novels is a solitary occupation.* **3** (only *before* a noun) one on its own with no others around: *a solitary figure walking up the hillside* **4** (only *before* a noun) only one; single: *I can't think of a solitary example* (= not even one).

ˌsolitary con'finement *noun* [U] a punishment in which a person in prison is kept completely alone

solitude /'sɒlɪtju:d; *US* -tu:d/ *noun* [U] the state of being alone: *to live in solitude*

solo /'səʊləʊ/ *noun* [C] (*pl* **solos**) a piece of music for only one person to play or sing: *a piano solo* o *to sing/play a solo* ☛ Look at **duet**.

solo *adj, adv* (done) alone; by yourself: *a solo flight* o *to fly solo*

soloist *noun* [C] a person who plays or sings a piece of music alone

soluble /'sɒljʊbl/ *adj* **1** that will dissolve in liquid: *These tablets are soluble in water.* **2** that has an answer ☛ The opposite is **insoluble**.

☆**solution** /sə'lu:ʃn/ *noun* **1** [C] **a solution (to sth)** a way of solving a problem, dealing with a difficult situation, etc: *a solution to the conflict in the Middle East* **2** [C] **solution (to sth)** the answer (to a puzzle, etc): *The solution to the competition will be published next week.* **3** [C,U] (a) liquid in which sth solid has been dissolved

☆**solve** /sɒlv/ *verb* [T] to find an answer to or a way of dealing with a problem, question, difficulty, etc: *The government is trying to solve the problem of inflation.* o *The police have not managed to solve the crime.* o *to solve a puzzle, mystery, etc* ☛ The noun is **solution**.

ɜ:	ə	eɪ	əʊ	aɪ	aʊ	ɔɪ	ɪə	eə	ʊə
fur	ago	pay	home	five	now	join	near	hair	pure

solvent /'sɒlvənt/ noun [C,U] a liquid that can dissolve another substance

sombre (US **somber**) /'sɒmbə(r)/ adj **1** dark and dull: *sombre colours* **2** sad and serious: *a sombre mood* —**sombrely** adv

☆ **some** /səm; strong form sʌm/ det, pron **1** a certain amount or number: *We need some butter and some potatoes.* ○ *I don't need any more money – I've still got some.* ☛ In negative sentences and in questions we use **any** instead of **some**: *Do we need any butter?* ○ *I need some more money. I haven't got any.* But look at **2** for examples of questions where **some** is used. **2** (used in questions when you expect or want the answer 'yes'): *Would you like some more cake?* ○ *Can I take some of this paper?* **3** (used when you are referring to certain members of a group or certain types of a thing and not all of them): *Some pupils enjoy this kind of work, some don't.* ○ *Some of his books are very exciting.* **4** (*also* **some...or other**) (used for talking about a person or thing whose name you do not know): *There's some woman at the door.* ○ *I read about it in some newspaper or other.*

☆ **somebody** /'sʌmbədɪ/ (*also* **someone** /'sʌmwʌn/) pron a person (not known or not mentioned by name): *How are you? Somebody said that you'd been ill.* ○ *She's getting married to someone she met at work.* ○ *There's somebody at the door.* ○ *I think you should talk to someone else* (= another person) *about this problem.* ☛ **Somebody**, **anybody** and **everybody** are used with a singular verb but are often followed by a plural pronoun (except in formal language): *Somebody is coming.* ○ *Somebody has left their coat behind.* ○ *Has everybody got something to eat?* ○ *I'll see everybody concerned and tell them the news.* The difference between **somebody** and **anybody** is the same as the difference between **some** and **any**. Look at the note at **some**.

someday /'sʌmdeɪ/ adv (*also* **some day**) at some time in the future: *I hope you'll come and visit me someday.*

☆ **somehow** /'sʌmhaʊ/ adv **1** in a way that is not known or certain: *The car's broken down but I'll get to work somehow.* ○ *Somehow we had got completely lost.* **2** for a reason you do not know or understand: *I somehow get the feeling that I've been here before.*

☆ **someone** /'sʌmwʌn/ pron = SOMEBODY

someplace /'sʌmpleɪs/ adv (US) = SOMEWHERE

somersault /'sʌməsɔːlt/ noun [C] a movement in which you roll right over with your feet going over your head: *to do a forward/backward somersault.*

☆ **something** /'sʌmθɪŋ/ pron **1** a thing that is not known or not named: *I've got something in my eye.* ○ *Wait a minute – I've forgotten something.* ○ *Would you like something else* (= another thing) *to drink?* ☛ The difference between **something** and **anything** is the same as the difference between **some** and **any**. Look at the note at **some**. **2** a thing that is helpful, useful or worth considering: *There's something in what your mother says.*

(IDIOMS) **or something** (*informal*) (used for showing that you are not sure about what you have just said): *'What's his job?' 'I think he's a plumber, or something'.*

something like similar to: *A loganberry is something like a raspberry.*

something to do with connected or concerned with: *The programme's something to do with the environment.*

sometime /'sʌmtaɪm/ adv (*also* **some time**) at a time that you do not know exactly or have not yet decided: *I'll phone you sometime this evening.* ○ *I must go and see her sometime.*

☆ **sometimes** /'sʌmtaɪmz/ adv on some occasions; now and then: *Sometimes I drive to work and sometimes I go by bus.* ○ *I sometimes watch television in the evenings.*

☆ **somewhat** /'sʌmwɒt; US -hwɒt/ adv rather: *We missed the train, which was somewhat unfortunate.* ○ *Somewhat to my surprise he apologized.*

☆ **somewhere** /'sʌmweə(r); US -hweər/ (US *also* **someplace**) adv **1** at, in, or to a place that you do not know or name exactly: *I've seen your glasses somewhere downstairs.* ○ *'Have they gone to France?' 'No, I think they've gone somewhere else* (= to another place) *this year.'* ☛ The difference between **somewhere** and **anywhere** is the same as the difference between **some** and **any**. Look at the note at **some**. **2** (used when you do not know the exact time, number, etc): *Your ideal weight should probably be somewhere around 9 stone.*

☆ **son** /sʌn/ noun [C] a male child ☛ Look at **daughter**.

'son-in-law noun [C] (*pl* **sons-in-law**) your daughter's husband

sonata /sə'nɑːtə/ noun [C] a piece of music written for the piano, or another instrument with a piano accompanying it

☆ **song** /sɒŋ; US sɔːŋ/ noun **1** [C] a piece of music with words that you sing: *a folk song* **2** [U] the act of singing: *to burst into song* **3** [C,U] the musical sounds that a bird makes: *birdsong*

'songwriter noun [C] a person whose job is to write songs

sonic /'sɒnɪk/ adj connected with sound-waves

☆ **soon** /suːn/ adv **1** not long after the present time or the time mentioned: *It will soon be dark.* ○ *He left soon after me.* ○ *We should arrive at your house soon after twelve.* **2** early; quickly: *Don't leave so soon. Stay for tea.* ○ *How soon can you get here?*

(IDIOMS) **as soon as** at the moment (that); when: *Phone me as soon as you hear some news.* ○ *I'd like your reply as soon as possible* (= at the earliest possible moment).

no sooner...than immediately when or after: *No sooner had I shut the door than I realized I'd left my keys inside.*

sooner or later at some time in the future; one day: *I suppose I'll hear from her sooner or later.*

soot /sʊt/ noun [U] black powder that comes from burning things and collects in chimneys

soothe /suːð/ verb [T] **1** to make sb calmer or less upset; to comfort sb: *to soothe a crying child* **2** to make aches or pains less severe: *The doctor gave me some skin cream to soothe the irrita-*

p	b	t	d	k	g	tʃ	dʒ	f	v	θ	ð
pen	bad	tea	did	cat	got	chin	June	fall	van	thin	then

tion. —**soothing** adj: soothing music o a soothing massage —**soothingly** adv

sophisticated /sə'fɪstɪkeɪtɪd/ adj **1** having or showing a lot of experience of the world and social situations; knowing about things such as fashion, new ideas, etc: She's a very sophisticated young woman. **2** able to understand difficult or complicated things: Voters are much more sophisticated these days. **3** (used about machines, systems, etc) advanced and complicated: sophisticated computer equipment ☞ The opposite is **unsophisticated**. —**sophistication** /sə,fɪstɪ'keɪʃn/ noun [U]

soppy /'sɒpi/ adj (**soppier; soppiest**) (informal) full of unnecessary emotion; silly: a soppy romantic film

soprano /sə'prɑːnəʊ; US -'præn-/ noun [C] (pl **sopranos** /-nəʊz/) the highest singing voice; a woman, girl, or boy with this voice

sordid /'sɔːdɪd/ adj **1** unpleasant; not honest or moral: We discovered the truth about his sordid past. **2** dirty and depressing: a sordid backstreet

☆ **sore** /sɔː(r)/ adj aching or painful: to have a sore throat o I feel all right after the operation but my stomach is still very sore.
(IDIOM) **a sore point** a subject that is likely to make sb upset or angry when mentioned
sore noun [C] a painful place on the body where the skin or flesh is infected
sorely adv (formal) very greatly; severely: You'll be sorely missed when you leave. —**soreness** noun [U]: You might get some soreness of the skin.

sorrow /'sɒrəʊ/ noun (formal) **1** [U] great sadness: I'd like to express my sorrow at the death of your father. **2** [C] an event, etc that causes great sadness: His decision to leave home was a great sorrow to his parents. —**sorrowful** adj —**sorrowfully** adv

☆ **sorry** /'sɒri/ adj (**sorrier; sorriest**) **1** (not before a noun) **sorry (for/about sth); sorry (to do sth/that...)** (used for apologizing for sth that you have done): I'm sorry I've kept you all waiting. o I'm awfully sorry for spilling that wine. o I'm sorry to be so late. o I'm so sorry that I've disturbed your meal. I'll phone again later. **2** (not before a noun) **sorry (to do sth/that...); sorry (for/about sth)** sad or disappointed: I was sorry to miss you on Saturday. o I was sorry not to get the job. o 'Simon's mother died last week.' 'Oh, I am sorry.' **3** (used for politely saying 'no' to sth, disagreeing with sth or introducing bad news): 'Would you like to come to supper on Friday?' 'I'm sorry, I'm busy that evening.' o I'm sorry, I don't agree with you. I think we should accept the offer. o I'm sorry to tell you that your application has been unsuccessful. **4** (only before a noun) very bad: The house was in a sorry state when we first moved in.
(IDIOM) **be/feel sorry for sb** to feel sympathy or pity for sb: I feel very sorry for the families of the victims. o Stop feeling sorry for yourself!

sorry interj **1** (used for apologizing, making excuses, etc): Sorry, I didn't see you standing behind me. o Sorry I'm late – the bus didn't come on time. **2** (used for asking sb to repeat sth you have not heard properly): 'My name's Maggie Wiseman' 'Sorry? Maggie who?' **3** (used for correcting yourself when you have said sth wrong): Take the second turning, sorry, the third turning on the right.

☆ **sort¹** /sɔːt/ noun **1** [C] a type or kind: What sort of music do you like? o That's the sort of car I'd like to have. o different sorts of people o She's got all sorts of problems at the moment. **2** [sing] a type of character; a person: You can ask him for help – he's a good sort.
(IDIOMS) **a sort of sth** (informal) a type of sth; sth similar to sth: Can you hear a sort of ticking noise?
sort of (informal) rather; in a way: I feel sort of sick. o I'd sort of like to go, but I'm not sure.

☆ **sort²** /sɔːt/ verb [T] **1** to put things into different groups or places so that they are properly organized: I'm just sorting these papers into the correct files. o The computer will sort the words into alphabetical order. **2** (informal) to find an answer to a problem or difficult situation: I'll have more time when I've got things sorted at home.
(PHRASAL VERBS) **sort sth out 1** to tidy or organize sth: The toy cupboard needs sorting out. **2** to find an answer to a problem: I haven't found a flat yet but I hope to sort something out soon.
sort through sth to go through a number of things, in order to tidy them or find sth that you are looking for

so-so /,səʊ'səʊ/ adj, adv (informal) all right but not particularly good/well: 'How are you?' 'So-so.'

soufflé /'suːfleɪ; US suː'fleɪ/ noun [C,U] a type of food made mainly from egg whites, flour and milk, beaten together and baked: a cheese soufflé

sought pt, pp of SEEK

sought-after /'sɔːt ɑːftə(r)/ adj that people want very much, because it is of high quality or rare

☆ **soul** /səʊl/ noun **1** [C] the part of a person that is believed to continue to exist after the body is dead: Christians believe that your soul goes to heaven when you die. **2** [sing] the part of a thing or a place that shows its true nature: You will find the real soul of France in the countryside. **3** [C,U] deep feeling and thought: The music was performed perfectly but it lacked soul. **4** [C] (used with adjectives expressing affection or pity) person: She's a kind old soul. **5** [sing] (in negative statements) a person: There wasn't a soul in sight (= there was nobody). **6** [U] (also **soul music**) a type of popular Black American music: a soul singer

soulful /-fl/ adj having or showing deep feeling: a soulful expression

soulless /'səʊlɪs/ adj without feeling, warmth or interest: soulless industrial towns

☆ **sound¹** /saʊnd/ verb **1** [I] to give a particular impression when heard or heard about; to seem: That sounds like a child crying. o She sounded upset and angry on the phone. o The rain sounds heavy. o You sound like my mother! o He sounds a very nice person from his letter. o Does she sound like the right person for the job?

s	z	ʃ	ʒ	h	m	n	ŋ	l	r	j	w
so	zoo	she	vision	how	man	no	sing	leg	red	yes	wet

○ *It doesn't sound as if he's very reliable.* **2** [T] to cause sth to make a sound: *to sound the horn of your car*
(PHRASAL VERB) **sound sb out** to ask sb questions in order to find out what he/she thinks or intends: *Do you mind if I sound you out about these new proposals?*

☆ **sound²** /saʊnd/ *noun* **1** [C] something that you hear or that can be heard: *the sound of voices* ○ *She opened the door without a sound.* **2** [U] what you hear; impressions received by hearing: *Light travels faster than sound.* ○ *sound waves* **3 the sound** [sing] the volume on a television, radio, etc: *Can you turn the sound up/down?*
(IDIOM) **the sound of sth** the impression that you have of sth when you hear or read about it: *She must be an interesting person, by the sound of it.*

'sound effect *noun* [C, usually pl] sounds other than speech or music that are used in a play, film or computer game to create the required effect

'soundproof *adj* made so that no sound can get in or out

'soundtrack *noun* [C] the recorded sound and music from a film or computer game

☆ **sound³** /saʊnd/ *adj* **1** healthy and strong; in good condition: *a sound state of health* ○ *The structure of the bridge is basically sound.* **2** sensible; that you can rely on: *sound advice*
(IDIOM) **safe and sound** ➪ SAFE¹
sound *adv*
(IDIOM) **be sound asleep** to be deeply asleep
soundly *adv* thoroughly or deeply: *Our team was soundly beaten this afternoon.* ○ *The children were sleeping soundly.* — **soundness** *noun* [U]

☆ **soup** /suːp/ *noun* [U] liquid food made by cooking meat, vegetables, etc in water: *chicken soup* ○ *a tin of soup*

☆ **sour** /saʊə(r)/ *adj* **1** having a sharp taste like that of a lemon: *We had pork with a sweet and sour sauce.* **2** (used especially about milk) tasting or smelling unpleasant because it is no longer fresh **3** having or showing a bad temper; unpleasant: *a sour expression*
(IDIOMS) **go/turn sour** to become unpleasant or unsatisfactory: *Their relationship turned sour after a few months.*
sour 'grapes pretending to dislike or not to want sth when you secretly want it but cannot have it: *She said she didn't want to come to the party anyway, but I think that was just sour grapes.*
sourly *adv* in a sour(3) way — **sourness** *noun* [U]

☆ **source** /sɔːs/ *noun* [C] **1** a place, person or thing where sth comes or starts from or where sth is obtained: *Britain's oil reserves are an important source of income.* ○ *the source of the Nile* (= the place where the river starts) **2** a person, book, etc that supplies information: *Police have refused to reveal the source of their information.*

☆ **south** /saʊθ/ *noun* [sing] (*abbr* **S**) **1** (*also* **the south**) one of the four main points of the compass; the direction that is on your right when you face the sunrise: *warm winds from the south* ○ *Which way is south?* ☞ picture at **north**. **2 the south; the South** the part of any country, city, etc that lies further towards the south than other parts: *Winchester is in the South of England.*

south (*also* **South**) *adj* in or towards the south, or from the south: *the south coast of Cornwall* ○ *The new offices will be in South Oxford.* ○ *a south wind*

south *adv* to or towards the south: *If you keep going south, you will soon join the motorway.* ○ *We live just south of Birmingham.* ○ *The house faces south.*

southerly /ˈsʌðəli/ *adj* **1** to, towards or in the south: *Keep going in a southerly direction.* **2** (used about winds) coming from the south: *a southerly wind*

southward /ˈsaʊθwəd/ *adj* towards the south: *in a southward direction*

southward /ˈsaʊθwəd/ (*also* **southwards**) *adv* towards the south: *We're flying southward at the moment.*

'southbound *adj* travelling or leading towards the south: *the southbound carriageway of the M1*

south-'east *noun* [sing] (*abbr* **SE**) **1** (*also* **the south-east**) the direction or point of the compass that is between south and east ☞ picture at **north**. **2** (*also* **the south-east; the South-East**) a region that is towards the south-east: *the South-East of England*

south-'east *adj, adv* in, from or to the south-east of a place or country: *the coast of south-east Spain* ○ *Continue south-east for about ten miles.*

south-'easterly *adj* **1** towards the south-east: *in a south-easterly direction* **2** (used about a wind) coming from the south-east

south-'eastern /-ˈiːstən/ *adj* in or from the south-east of a place or country: *the south-eastern states of the USA*

south-'eastward /-ˈiːstwəd/ (*also* **south-'eastwards**) *adv* towards the south-east: *Follow the A423 south-eastward.*

the ˌSouth 'Pole *noun* [sing] the point on the surface of the Earth which is furthest south ☞ picture at **earth**.

south-'west *noun* [sing] (*abbr* **SW**) **1** (*also* **the south-west**) the direction or point of the compass that is between south and west ☞ picture at **north**. **2** (*also* **the south-west; the South-West**) a region that is towards the south-west: *Devon is in the South-West.*

south-'west *adj, adv* in, from or to the south-west of a place or country: *the south-west coast of France* ○ *If you look south-west you can see the sea.*

south-'westerly *adj* **1** towards the south-west: *in a south-westerly direction* **2** (used about a wind) coming from the south-west

south-'western /-ˈwestən/ *adj* in or from the south-west of a place or country: *south-western Italy*

south-'westward /-ˈwestwəd/ (*also* **south-'westwards**) *adv* towards the south-west: *Follow the B409 south-westward.*

☆ **southern** (*also* **Southern**) /ˈsʌðən/ *adj* of, in

iː	ɪ	e	æ	ɑː	ɒ	ɔː	ʊ	uː	ʌ
see	sit	ten	hat	arm	got	saw	put	too	cup

or from the south of a place: *Greece is in southern Europe.* ○ *the Southern hemisphere*

southerner *noun* [C] a person who was born in or lives in the southern part of a country

souvenir /ˌsuːvəˈnɪə(r)/ *US* ˈsuːvənɪər/ *noun* [C] something that you buy and keep to remind you of somewhere you have been on holiday or of a special event

sovereign /ˈsɒvrɪn/ *noun* [C] a king or queen

sovereign *adj* **1** (used about a country) not controlled by any other country; independent **2** (used about power) without limit; highest

sovereignty /ˈsɒvrənti/ *noun* [U] the power that a country has to control its own government

sow¹ /saʊ/ *noun* [C] an adult female pig ☞ Look at the note at **pig**.

sow² /səʊ/ *verb* [T] (*pt* **sowed**; *pp* **sown** /səʊn/ or **sowed**) **sow A (in B); sow B (with A)** to plant seeds in the ground: *to sow seeds in pots* ○ *to sow a field with wheat*

soya bean /ˈsɔɪə biːn/ (*US* **soy bean** /ˈsɔɪ biːn/) *noun* [C] a type of bean that can be cooked and eaten or used to make flour, oil and a sort of milk

ˌsoya ˈsauce (*also* ˌsoy ˈsauce) *noun* [U] a dark brown sauce that is made from soya beans and that you add to food to make it taste better

spa /spɑː/ *noun* [C] (*pl* **spas**) a place where mineral water comes out of the ground and where people go to drink this water because it is considered to be healthy

☆ **space** /speɪs/ *noun* **1** [C,U] an area that is empty or not used: *Is there enough space for me to park the car there?* ○ *a parking space* ○ *We're a bit short of space.* ○ *There's a space here for you to write your name.* ○ *wide open spaces* (= empty areas of countryside) ☞ Look at **room** and the note at **place¹**. **2** [U] (*also* ˌouter ˈspace) the vast area which surrounds the planet Earth and the other planets and stars: *Yuri Gagarin was the first man to go into space.* ○ *space travel* **3** [C, usually sing] a period of time: *Mandy had been ill three times in the space of four months.*

space *verb* [T] **space sth (out)** to arrange things so that there are spaces between them

ˈspacecraft *noun* [C] (*pl* **spacecraft**) a vehicle that travels in space

ˈspaceman, **ˈspacewoman** *noun* [C] a person who travels in space

ˈspaceship *noun* [C] a vehicle in which people can travel in space

spacious /ˈspeɪʃəs/ *adj* having a lot of space or room; large in size —**spaciousness** *noun* [U]

☆ **spade¹** /speɪd/ *noun* [C] a tool that you use for digging. A spade has a long wooden handle and a flat piece of metal (**a blade**) at one end. ☞ Look at **shovel**.

spade² /speɪd/ *noun* **1 spades** [plural] the group (**suit**) of playing-cards with pointed black leaves on them: *the king of spades* ☞ picture and note at **card**. **2** [C] one of the cards from this suit: *Have you got a spade?*

spaghetti /spəˈɡeti/ *noun* [U] a type of Italian food (**pasta**) made from flour and water that looks like long strings: *I'll cook some spaghetti.*

span /spæn/ *noun* [C] **1** the length of sth from one end to the other: *the wing-span of a bird* **2** the length of time that sth lasts or continues: *Young children have a short attention span.*

span *verb* [T] (**spanning; spanned**) **1** to form a bridge over sth: *The road is spanned by a railway bridge.* **2** to last or continue for a particular period of time: *Her career in politics spanned more than fifty years.*

spank /spæŋk/ *verb* [T] to hit a child on its bottom with an open hand as a punishment

spanner /ˈspænə(r)/ (*US* **wrench**) *noun* [C] a metal tool with an end shaped so that it can be used for turning nuts ☞ picture at **tool**.

☆ **spare¹** /speə(r)/ *adj* **1** not needed now but kept because it may be needed in the future: *The spare tyre is kept in the boot.* ○ *a spare room* **2** not used for work: *What do you do in your spare time?* **3** not being used; free: *There were no seats spare so we had to stand.*

spare *noun* [C] an extra thing of the same kind that you can use: *The fuse has blown. Where do you keep your spares?*

ˌspare ˈpart *noun* [C] a part for a machine, engine, etc that you can use to replace an old part which is damaged or broken

☆ **spare²** /speə(r)/ *verb* [T] **1** to be able to give sb/sth to sb: *Can you spare any money?* ○ *I am very grateful for you sparing the time to see me.* **2** to not hurt or damage sb/sth: *to spare sb's life* **3** to use as little as possible of sth: *No expense was spared at the wedding.* **4** to stop sb from having an unpleasant experience: *I told him what happened but spared him all the details.*

(IDIOM) **to spare** more than is needed: *There's no time to spare. We must leave straight away.*

sparing /ˈspeərɪŋ/ *adj* (*formal*) using only a little of sth; careful: *Try to be sparing with the salt.* —**sparingly** *adv*: *to use sth sparingly*

spark /spɑːk/ *noun* [C] **1** a small bright piece of burning material **2** a flash of light that is caused by electricity: (*figurative*) *a spark of anger*

spark *verb*

(PHRASAL VERB) **spark sth off** (*informal*) to cause sth: *Eric's comments sparked off a tremendous argument.*

ˈspark-plug (*also* **ˈsparking-plug**) *noun* [C] the small piece of equipment that produces sparks in an engine

sparkle /ˈspɑːkl/ *verb* [I] to shine with many small points of light: *The river sparkled in the sunlight.* ○ (*figurative*) *Trudy's eyes sparkled with excitement.* —**sparkle** *noun* [C,U]

sparkling /ˈspɑːklɪŋ/ *adj* **1** that sparkles: *sparkling blue eyes* **2** (used about wine) with bubbles in it: *sparkling white wine* **3** full of life; appearing interesting and intelligent: *a sparkling, witty speech*

sparrow /ˈspærəʊ/ *noun* [C] a small brown bird that is very common

sparse /spɑːs/ *adj* small in quantity or amount: *a sparse crowd* —**sparsely** *adv*: *a sparsely populated area* —**sparseness** *noun* [U]

spartan /ˈspɑːtn/ *adj* (*formal*) very simple and not comfortable: *spartan living conditions*

spasm /ˈspæzəm/ *noun* [C,U] a sudden tighten-

ɜː	ə	eɪ	əʊ	aɪ	aʊ	ɔɪ	ɪə	eə	ʊə
fur	ago	pay	home	five	now	join	near	hair	pure

spastic ing of a muscle that you cannot control: *painful muscular spasms in the leg*

spastic /'spæstɪk/ *adj, noun* [C] (of) a person who is suffering from a disease of the brain (**cerebral palsy**) and who cannot control his/her movements properly

spat *pt, pp* of SPIT

spate /speɪt/ *noun* [sing] a sudden large number or amount of sth: *a spate of burglaries in the area*

spatial /'speɪʃl/ *adj (formal)* connected with the size or position of sth

spatter /'spætə(r)/ *verb* [T] to cover sb/sth with small drops of liquid: *to spatter sb with water* ○ *to spatter water on sb*

☆ **speak** /spiːk/ *verb* (*pt* **spoke** /spəʊk/; *pp* **spoken** /'spəʊkən/) **1 speak (to sb) (about sb/sth)** [I] to talk or say things: *I'd like to speak to the manager, please.* ○ *Could you speak more slowly?* ○ *I was so angry I could hardly speak.*
☛ **Speak** and **talk** have almost the same meaning, although **speak** is slightly more formal. In addition, **talk** is more likely to be used about a conversation, while **speak** is often used when only one person is saying something: *Speaking personally, I'm all in favour of the idea.* ○ *We talked all night.* ○ *I must speak to Ben's parents about his bad behaviour.* **2** [T] to know and be able to use a language: *Does anyone here speak German?* ○ *a French-speaking guide* **3** [I] **speak (on/about sth)** to make a speech to a group of people: *Professor Hurst has been invited to speak on American foreign policy.* **4** [I] **speak (to sb)** *(informal)* (usually in negative sentences) to be friendly with sb: *They had an argument and now they're not speaking to each other.*
(IDIOMS) **be on speaking terms (with sb)** to be friendly with sb (after an argument): *Thankfully they are back on speaking terms again.*

so to speak (used when you are describing sth in an unusual way or in a way which is not strictly true): *She turned green, so to speak, after watching a television programme about the environment.*

speak for itself to be very clear so that no other explanation is needed: *The statistics speak for themselves.*

speak your mind to say exactly what you think, even though you might offend sb
(PHRASAL VERBS) **speak for sb** to express the thoughts or opinions of sb else: *I cannot speak for my colleagues.*

speak out (against sth) to say clearly and publicly that you think sth is bad or wrong

speak up to speak louder

speaker *noun* [C] **1** a person who makes a speech to a group of people: *Tonight's speaker is a well-known writer and journalist.* **2** (*informal*) = LOUDSPEAKER(2) **3** a person who speaks a particular language: *a Russian speaker*

spear /spɪə(r)/ *noun* [C] a long pole with a sharp point at one end, used for hunting or fighting

'spearhead *noun* [C, usually sing] a person or group that begins or leads an attack, etc

'spearhead *verb* [T] to lead an attack: *The RSPCA is spearheading the campaign.*

spearmint /'spɪəmɪnt/ *noun* [U] a type of leaf with a fresh taste that is used in sweets, etc: *spearmint chewing gum* ☛ Look at **peppermint**.

☆ **special** /'speʃl/ *adj* **1** not usual or ordinary; important for some particular reason: *He shouldn't get special treatment just because he is famous.* ○ *a special occasion* ○ *Are you doing anything special tonight?* **2** (only *before* a noun) for a particular purpose: *The little boy goes to a special school for the deaf.* ○ *There's a special tool for doing that.*

special *noun* [C] something that is not of the usual or ordinary type: *the all-night election special on TV*

specialist /-ʃəlɪst/ *noun* [C] a person with special or deep knowledge of a particular subject: *She's a specialist in diseases of cattle.* ○ *to give specialist advice*

specially /-ʃəli/ (*also* **especially**) *adv* **1** for a particular purpose or reason: *I made this specially for you.* **2** particularly; very; more than usual: *The hotel was clean but the food was not specially good.* ○ *It's not an especially difficult exam.*

speciality /ˌspeʃɪ'æləti/ *noun* [C] (*pl* **specialities**) (*US* **specialty** /'speʃəlti/ *pl* **specialties**) **1** an area of study or a subject that you know a lot about **2** something made by a person, place, business, etc that is very good and that they are known for: *The cheese is a speciality of the region.*

specialize (*also* **specialise**) /'speʃəlaɪz/ *verb* [I] **specialize (in sth)** to give most of your attention to one subject, type of product, etc: *This shop specializes in clothes for taller men.* ○ *a lawyer who specializes in divorce cases* —**specialization** (*also* **specialisation**) /ˌspeʃəlaɪ'zeɪʃn; *US* -lɪ'z-/ *noun* [U]

specialized (*also* **specialised**) *adj* **1** to be used for a particular purpose: *a specialized system* **2** having or needing deep or special knowledge of a particular subject: *We have specialized staff to help you with any problems.*

specialty (*US*) = SPECIALITY

☆ **species** /'spiːʃiːz/ *noun* [C] (*pl* **species**) a group of plants or animals that are very similar to each other and that can breed together: *an endangered species*

☆ **specific** /spə'sɪfɪk/ *adj* **1** detailed or exact: *You must give the class specific instructions on what they have to do.* **2** particular; not general: *Everyone has been given a specific job to do.* —**specifically** /-kli/ *adv*: *specifically for television* ○ *I specifically asked you not to do that.*

specification /ˌspesɪfɪ'keɪʃn/ *noun* [C,U] detailed information about how sth has been or must be built or made: *The kitchen was designed to our own specification.*

specify /'spesɪfaɪ/ *verb* [T] (*pres part* **specifying**; *3rd pers sing pres* **specifies**; *pt, pp* **specified**) to say or name sth clearly or in detail: *Please specify any dates that you are not available.* ○ *The regulations specify the maximum number of people allowed in.*

p	b	t	d	k	g	tʃ	dʒ	f	v	θ	ð
pen	bad	tea	did	cat	got	chin	June	fall	van	thin	then

specimen /'spesɪmən/ noun [C] **1** an example of a particular type of thing, often studied by experts or scientists: *There is a fine specimen of that type of tree in the Botanical Gardens.* **2** a small amount of sth that is tested for medical or scientific purposes: *Specimens of the patient's blood were tested in the hospital laboratory.*

speck /spek/ noun [C] a very small spot or mark: *a speck of dust* ○ *The car was just a tiny speck on the horizon.*

specs /speks/ noun [plural] (*informal*) = GLASSES

spectacle /'spektəkl/ noun [C] something that is grand, interesting or unusual to look at: *The London Marathon is a popular sporting spectacle.*

spectacles /'spektəklz/ noun [plural] = GLASSES

spectacular /spek'tækjʊlə(r)/ adj very grand, interesting or attractive: *The view from the top of the hill is quite spectacular.* ○ *a spectacular display of fireworks* —**spectacularly** adv

☆ **spectator** /spek'teɪtə(r); US 'spekteɪtər/ noun [C] a person who watches a show, game, sport, etc

spectre (*US* **specter**) /'spektə(r)/ noun [C] **1** = GHOST **2** an idea that frightens you because of sth bad that might happen in the future: *the spectre of unemployment*

spectrum /'spektrəm/ noun [C, usually sing] (*pl* **spectra** /'spektrə/) **1** the set of seven colours into which white light can be separated: *You can see the colours of the spectrum in a rainbow.* **2** a full or wide range of sth: *speakers representing the whole spectrum of political opinions*

speculate /'spekjʊleɪt/ verb **1** [I,T] **speculate (about/on sth)** to think about sth without having all the facts or information: *to speculate about the result of the next election* **2** [I] to buy and sell with the aim of making money but with the risk of losing it: *to speculate on the stock market* —**speculator** noun [C]

speculation /ˌspekjʊ'leɪʃn/ noun [C,U] an act of speculating(1,2): *There was a lot of speculation about the date of the election.* ○ *He bought some shares as a speculation.*

sped pt, pp of SPEED

☆ **speech** /spiːtʃ/ noun **1** [U] the act of speaking or the state of being able to speak: *to lose the power of speech* ○ *freedom of speech* (= to speak your opinions openly) **2** [U] the particular way of speaking of a person or group of people: *She's doing a study of children's speech.* **3** [C] a formal talk that you give to a group of people: *The Chancellor is going to make a speech to city businessmen.* ○ *an after-dinner speech* **4** [C] a group of words that one person must say in a play: *the King's speech in Act II*

speechless adj not able to speak, eg because you are shocked, very angry, etc

☆ **speed** /spiːd/ noun **1** [U] fast movement: *to gather/pick up speed* ○ *With a final burst of speed, Christie won the race.* **2** [C,U] the rate at which sb/sth moves or travels: *The car was travelling at a speed of 40 miles an hour.* ○ *to travel at top speed*

speed verb [I] (*pt, pp* **sped** /sped/) **1** to go or move very quickly: *He sped round the corner on his bicycle.* ○ *The holiday seemed to speed by.* **2** (only used in the continuous tenses) to drive a car, etc faster than the legal speed limit: *The police said she had been speeding.*
(PHRASAL VERB) **speed (sth) up** (*pt, pp* **speeded**) (to cause sth) to go faster: *Plans to speed up production in the factory.* ○ *The traffic speeded up once it reached the motorway.*

speeding noun [U] the act of driving a car, etc faster than the legal speed limit

speedy adj (**speedier; speediest**) fast; quick: *to make a speedy recovery from an illness* —**speedily** adv —**speediness** noun [U]

'speedboat noun [C] a small fast boat with an engine

'speed limit noun [C, usually sing] the highest speed that you may drive without breaking the law on a particular piece of road

'speedway noun [U] the sport of racing on motor bikes

speedometer /spiː'dɒmɪtə(r)/ noun [C] a piece of equipment in a car, etc that tells you how fast you are travelling

☆ **spell**¹ /spel/ verb (*pt, pp* **spelled** /speld/ or **spelt** /spelt/) **1** [I,T] to write or say the letters of a word in the correct order: *I find that children today just can't spell.* ○ *How do you spell your surname?* ○ *His name is spelt P-H-I-L-I-P.* **2** [T] (used about a set of letters) to form a particular word: *A-I-S-L-E spells aisle.* **3** [T] to mean; to have sth as a result: *Another poor harvest would spell disaster for the region.*
(PHRASAL VERB) **spell sth out 1** to write or say the letters of a word or name in the correct order **2** to explain sth in detail or in a very clear way

spelling noun **1** [C,U] the way that a word is spelt: *'Center' is the American spelling of 'centre'.* **2** [U] the act of spelling or the state of being able to spell: *Roger is very poor at spelling.*

spell² /spel/ noun [C] a short period of time: *a spell of cold weather*

spell³ /spel/ noun [C] **1** [usually sing] (in stories, etc) a state or condition that was caused by magic: *The witch put a spell on the prince.* ○ (*figurative*) *He's completely under her spell.* **2** a set of words that are believed to have magic power

spelt pt, pp of SPELL¹

☆ **spend** /spend/ verb (*pt, pp* **spent** /spent/) **1** [I,T] **spend (sth) (on sth)** to give or pay money for sth: *How much do you spend on food each week?* ○ *You shouldn't go on spending like that.* **2** [T] to pass time: *I spent a whole evening writing letters.* ○ *I'm spending the weekend at my parents' house.* ○ *He spent two years in Rome.*

spending /'spendɪŋ/ noun [U] the giving of large amounts of money by an organization to pay for services such as education: *The government wants to increase spending on health care.*

sperm /spɜːm/ noun **1** [C] a very small cell that is produced by a male animal and that can join

s	z	ʃ	ʒ	h	m	n	ŋ	l	r	j	w
so	zoo	she	vision	how	man	no	sing	leg	red	yes	wet

with a female egg to create a new life **2** [U] the liquid that contains sperms

sphere /sfɪə(r)/ noun [C] **1** any round object shaped like a ball ☛ picture at **cube**. **2** an area of interest or activity: *Many countries are having difficulties in the economic sphere.* —**spherical** /'sferɪkl/ adj

spice /spaɪs/ noun **1** [C,U] a substance (especially a powder) that is made from part of a plant and used to give flavour to food: *I use a lot of herbs and spices in my cooking.* o *Pepper and paprika are two common spices.* **2** [U] excitement and interest: *to add spice to a situation*

spice verb [T] **spice sth (with sth) 1** to add spice to food **2** to add excitement to sth

spicy adj (**spicier**; **spiciest**) containing spice: *Indonesian food is rather spicy.*

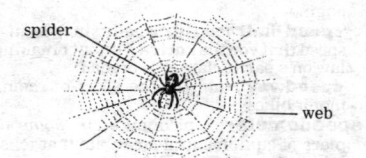

spider

web

spider /'spaɪdə(r)/ noun [C] a type of small animal (like an insect) with eight legs. Spiders make (**spin**) special nets (**webs**) to catch insects for food.

spike /spaɪk/ noun [C] a piece of metal, wood, etc that has a sharp point at one end: *metal railings with spikes on the top*

spill

He's **spilled** his milk.

☆ **spill** /spɪl/ verb [I,T] (pt, pp **spilt** /spɪlt/ or **spilled**) (to cause a liquid) to pour out from sth by accident: *I've spilt some wine on the carpet.* o (*figurative*) *There were so many people that the party spilled over into the garden.*

(IDIOM) **spill the beans** (*informal*) to tell a person sth when you are supposed to be keeping it secret

☆ **spin** /spɪn/ verb (**spinning**; pt, pp **spun** /spʌn/) **1** [I,T] **spin (sth) (round)** (to cause sth) to turn round quickly: *Mary spun round when she heard someone call her name.* o *to spin a coin* o (*figurative*) *After three glasses of whisky my head was spinning.* **2** [I,T] to make thread from a mass of wool, cotton, etc **3** [T] = SPIN-DRY

(PHRASAL VERB) **spin sth out** to make sth last as long as possible: *I managed to spin the discussion out until lunchtime.*

spin noun [U] an act of spinning(1): *to put some spin on a ball* (= in sports like cricket, tennis, etc)

spin-'dry (*also* **spin**) verb [T] to remove water from clothes by spinning(1) them round very fast in a special machine (**a spin-drier**)

'spin-off noun [C] a useful result that you did not expect

spinach /'spɪnɪdʒ; US -ɪtʃ/ noun [U] a plant with large green leaves that can be cooked and eaten as a vegetable

spinal /'spaɪnl/ adj connected with the bones of the back (**the spine**)

spine /spaɪn/ noun [C] **1** the bones of the back of a person or animal; the backbone **2** one of the sharp points on some plants and animals ☛ Look at **prickle**. **3** the narrow part of a book that you can see when it is on a shelf

spineless adj weak and easily frightened

spinster /'spɪnstə(r)/ noun [C] (*old-fashioned*) a woman who has never been married ☛ **Bachelor** can be used about a man of any age but you usually use **spinster** when you are talking about an older woman.

spiral /'spaɪərəl/ noun [C] a long curve that moves upwards going round and round a central point —**spiral** adj: *a spiral staircase*

spiral verb [I] (**spiralling**; **spiralled**; US **spiraling**; **spiraled**) to move upwards or downwards in a spiral, especially very quickly: *Food prices are spiralling up.*

spire /'spaɪə(r)/ noun [C] a tall pointed tower on the top of a church, etc

☆ **spirit** /'spɪrɪt/ noun **1** [sing] the part of a person that is not physical; your thoughts and feelings, not your body: *On the lonely island I saw another world, another life, the life of the spirit.* **2** [C] the part of a person that many people believe still exists after his/her body is dead: *the spirits of the dead* **3** [C] a ghost or being that exists but that does not have a body: *the Holy Spirit* **4** [U] energy, strength of mind or liveliness: *The constant setbacks finally broke his spirit.* **5** [C] the mood or attitude of mind of sb/sth: *the spirit of goodwill at Christmas* o *to be in high/low spirits* (= in a happy/sad mood) o *Everyone entered into the spirit of the party* (= joined in with enthusiasm). o *the 16th-century spirit of exploration* **6** [U] the real and intended meaning of a rule, agreement, etc: *Judges should consider the spirit as well as the letter of the law.* **7 spirits** [plural] strong alcoholic drinks, eg whisky: *I never drink spirits.*

spirit verb

(PHRASAL VERB) **spirit sb/sth away/off** to take sb/sth away secretly

spirited /'spɪrɪtɪd/ adj lively, energetic or having strength of mind: *The Prime Minister gave a spirited defence of his policies.* o *a spirited debate*

-spirited (in compounds) having a particular mood or attitude of mind: *a group of high-spirited teenagers*

spiritual /'spɪrɪtʃuəl/ adj **1** concerning your deep thoughts, feelings or emotions: *to fulfil your spiritual needs* ☛ Look at **material**. **2** concerning the Church or religion: *Tibet's*

| i: | ɪ | e | æ | ɑ: | ɒ | ɔ: | ʊ | u: | ʌ |
| see | sit | ten | hat | arm | got | saw | put | too | cup |

exiled spiritual leader, the Dalai Lama —**spiritually** /-tʃʊli/ adv

spiritualism /'spɪrɪtʃʊəlɪzəm/ noun [U] the belief that you can get messages from the spirits(2) of people who are dead

spiritualist /-ɪst/ noun [C] a person who believes in or who is involved with spiritualism

☆ **spit** /spɪt/ verb [I,T] (**spitt**ing; pt, pp **spat** /spæt/ **spit (sth) (out)** to send liquid, food, etc out from your mouth: No spitting allowed! ○ He took one sip of the wine and spat it out. ☛ In US English the past tense and past participle can also be **spit**.

spit noun [U] (informal) the liquid in your mouth ☛ Look at **saliva**.

☆ **spite** /spaɪt/ noun [U] the desire to hurt or annoy sb: He stole her letters out of spite.

in spite of prep used for introducing sth that may be unexpected or surprising: The match was played in spite of the awful weather. ○ In spite of all her hard work, Sue failed her exam.

spite verb [T] to try to hurt or annoy sb: I think he only said it to spite me.

spiteful /-fl/ adj feeling or showing spite(1); unkind: He's been saying spiteful things about his ex-girlfriend. —**spitefully** /-fəli/ adv

☆ **splash** /splæʃ/ verb [I,T] (to cause a liquid) to fly about in drops and make sb/sth wet: The children were splashing each other with water. ○ They were splashing around in the pool. ○ Be careful not to splash paint onto the floor.

(PHRASAL VERB) **splash out (on sth)** (informal) to spend money on sth that is an expensive luxury or that you do not really need

splash noun [C] **1** an act or sound of splashing: Paul jumped into the pool with a big splash. **2** a mark or spot that was made by sth splashing: splashes of oil on the cooker **3** a bright area of colour: Flowers add a splash of colour to a room.

splatter /'splætə(r)/ verb [I,T] (used about a liquid) to splash and make sb/sth wet or dirty; to make a liquid do this: The paint was splattered all over the floor.

splay /spleɪ/ verb [I,T] (to cause sth) to become spread out or become wider at one end: splayed fingers

☆ **splendid** /'splendɪd/ adj **1** very good; excellent: What a splendid idea! **2** of fine or grand appearance: the splendid royal palace —**splendidly** adv

splendour (US **splendor**) /'splendə(r)/ noun [U] beauty that is grand and that impresses people: the splendour of the Swiss Alps

splint /splɪnt/ noun [C] a piece of wood or metal that is used to keep a broken bone in the right position

splinter /'splɪntə(r)/ noun [C] a small thin sharp piece of wood, metal or glass that has broken off a larger piece: I've got a splinter in my finger.

splinter verb [I,T] to break into small thin sharp pieces

☆ **split** /splɪt/ verb (pres part **splitt**ing; pt, pp **split**) **1** [I,T] **split (sth) (up) (into sth)** to break into two or more parts, usually from end to end, making a long line: My jeans have split (open). **2** [I,T] **split (sb) (up) (into sth)** (to cause people) to divide into different groups: Let's split into two groups. ○ The children have been split into five groups according to their ability. **3** [T] to divide or share sth: We split the cost of the meal between the six of us.

(IDIOMS) **split the difference** to agree on an amount or figure that is halfway between the two amounts or figures already mentioned

split hairs to try to find small differences between things that are almost the same ☛ Usually used in a critical way.

(PHRASAL VERB) **split up (with sb)** to end a marriage or relationship: He's split up with his girlfriend.

split noun [C] **1** a division in a group: Disagreement about European policy led to a split within the Conservative party. **2** a long cut or hole in sth

,split 'second noun [C] a very short period of time: It only took me a split second to decide.

splutter /'splʌtə(r)/ verb **1** [I,T] to speak with difficulty eg because you are very angry or excited: 'How dare you!' she spluttered indignantly. **2** [I] to make a series of sounds like a person spitting or coughing: He fell into the pool and came up coughing and spluttering. —**splutter** noun [C]

☆ **spoil** /spɔɪl/ verb (pt) (pp **spoilt** /spɔɪlt/ or **spoiled** /spɔɪld/) **1** [T] to make sth useless or unsuccessful, or not as good as before: The new office block will spoil the view. ○ Our holiday was spoilt by bad weather. ○ Eating between meals will spoil your appetite. **2** [T] to do too much for sb, especially a child, so that you have a bad effect on his/her character: a spoilt child **3** [T] to treat sb/yourself very well for a certain period of time in order to make this person/yourself happy: Why not spoil yourself with one of our new range of beauty products? (= in an advertisement)

spoils noun [plural] things that have been stolen, or taken in a war or battle

'spoilsport noun [C] a person who tries to stop other people enjoying themselves

spoke[1] /spəʊk/ noun [C] one of the thin pieces of metal that connect the centre of a wheel (**the hub**) to the outside edge (**the rim**) ☛ picture at **bicycle**.

spoke[2] pt of SPEAK

spoken pp of SPEAK

☆ **spokesman** /'spəʊksmən/ noun [C] (pl **spokesmen** /-mən/) a person who is chosen to speak for a group or organization ☛ A woman is called a **spokeswoman**. **Spokesperson** is now often preferred because it can be used for a man or a woman.

sponge /spʌndʒ/ noun [C,U] **1** a piece of rubber or plastic (or of a natural substance also called 'sponge'). Sponges have many small holes, soak up water and are used for cleaning things or for washing yourself. **2** [C,U] = SPONGE CAKE

sponge verb [T] to clean sth with a wet sponge or cloth

(PHRASAL VERB) **sponge on/off sb** (informal) to get money, food, etc from sb without doing or giving anything in return: It's about time you stopped sponging off your parents!

ɜː	ə	eɪ	əʊ	aɪ	aʊ	ɔɪ	ɪə	eə	ʊə
fur	ago	pay	home	five	now	join	near	hair	pure

'sponge bag noun [C] (*Brit*) a bag in which you put soap, toothpaste, etc when you are travelling

'sponge cake (*also* **sponge**) noun [C,U] a light cake made with eggs, flour and sugar, and sometimes fat

☆ **sponsor** /'spɒnsə(r)/ noun [C] **1** a person or an organization that helps to pay for a special sports event, etc (usually so that it can advertise its products) **2** a person who agrees to pay money to a charity if sb else completes a particular activity: *I need sponsors for a bike ride to Brighton in aid of Cancer Research.*

sponsor verb [T] to be a sponsor(1,2) for sb/sth: *A large cigarette company is sponsoring the next football tournament.* o *a sponsored walk to raise money for handicapped children* —**sponsorship** noun [U]: *Many theatres depend on industry for sponsorship.*

spontaneous /spɒn'teɪniəs/ adj done or happening naturally; not planned: *a spontaneous burst of applause* —**spontaneously** adv **spontaneity** /ˌspɒntə'neɪəti/ noun [U]

spooky /'spu:ki/ adj (**spookier**; **spookiest**) (*informal*) frightening: *It's spooky in the house alone at nights.*

spool /spu:l/ noun [C] a round object which thread, film, wire, etc are wound around when you buy them ☛ Look at **reel**.

☆ **spoon** /spu:n/ noun [C] **1** an object with a round end and a long handle that you use for eating, stirring or serving food: *Give each person a knife, fork and spoon.* o *a wooden spoon for cooking* **2** (*also* **'spoonful**) the amount that one spoon can hold: *Two spoons of sugar in my coffee, please.* o *Add a teaspoonful of salt.*

spoon verb [T] to lift or serve sth with a spoon

sporadic /spə'rædɪk/ adj not done or happening regularly: *There have been sporadic outbursts of gunfire during the night.* —**sporadically** /-kli/ adv

☆ **sport** /spɔ:t/ noun **1** [U] a physical game or activity that you do for exercise or because you enjoy it: *John did a lot of sport when he was at school.* o *amateur/professional sport* o *And now with the news, sport and weather here's Mark Foster* (= on the radio or on television). **2** [C] a particular game or type of sport: *Which sports do you like playing?* o *the sports page of a newspaper* o *winter sports* (= skiing, skating, etc) **3** [C] (*informal*) a person who does not get angry or upset if he/she loses a game or if sb plays a joke on him/her ☛ Look at **spoilsport**.

sporting adj connected with sport: *a sporting achievement*

'sports car noun [C] a low, fast car often with a roof that you can open

'sportsman /-mən/ noun [C] (*pl* **sportsmen** /-mən/) a man who plays sports: *a keen sportsman*

sportsmanlike adj behaving well and fairly when you are playing sport

sportsmanship noun [U] the quality of being sportsmanlike

'sportswoman /-wʊmən/ noun [C] (*pl* **sportswomen** /-wɪmɪn/) a woman who plays sports

☆ **spot¹** /spɒt/ noun [C] **1** a small round mark of a different colour on sth: *Leopards have dark spots.* o *a blue skirt with red spots on it* ☛ picture at **pattern**. **2** a small dirty mark on sth: *You've got a spot of gravy on your shirt.* **3** a small red mark on your skin, sometimes caused by a disease: *Many teenagers get spots on their face.* **4** a particular place or area: *a nice spot for a picnic* **5** = SPOTLIGHT(1) **6** [usually sing] **a spot of sth** (*informal*) a small amount of sth: *Can you help me? I'm having a spot of trouble.*

(IDIOMS) **have a soft spot for sb/sth** ⇨ SOFT

on the spot 1 immediately: *Paul was caught stealing money and was dismissed on the spot.* **2** at the place where sth happened or where sb/sth is needed: *The fire brigade were on the spot within five minutes.*

put sb on the spot to make sb answer a difficult question or make a difficult decision without having much time to think

spotted adj marked or covered with spots(1): *a spotted blouse* ☛ picture at **pattern**.

spotless adj having no spots(2) or marks; very clean: *Her house is always spotless.*

spotty adj (**spottier**; **spottiest**) having spots (3) on your skin: *a spotty young man*

'spot check noun [C] a test on one of a group of people or things which is not planned or expected

spot'on adj (*informal*) exactly right: *Your estimate was spot on.*

spot² /spɒt/ verb [T] (**spotting**; **spotted**) to see or notice sb/sth: *I've spotted a couple of spelling mistakes.*

spotlight /'spɒtlaɪt/ noun **1** [C] (*also* **spot**) a lamp that can send a strong beam of light onto a small area. Spotlights are often used in theatres. ☛ picture at **light**. **2** **the spotlight** [sing] the centre of public attention or interest: *to be in the spotlight*

spouse /spaʊz; *US* spaʊs/ noun [C] your husband or wife ☛ Spouse is a formal or official word, used on forms, documents, etc.

spout /spaʊt/ noun [C] a tube or pipe through which liquid comes out: *the spout of a teapot*

spout verb [I,T] **1** (used about a liquid) to come out from sth with force; to make a liquid do this: *Water spouted out from the broken pipe.* **2** (*informal*) to say sth, using a lot of words, in a way that is not interesting: *She was spouting poetry at me.*

sprain /spreɪn/ verb [T] to injure part of your body by bending or turning it suddenly: *to sprain your ankle* —**sprain** noun [C]: *Your wrist isn't broken. It's just a bad sprain.*

sprang *pt* of SPRING³

sprawl /sprɔ:l/ verb [I] **1** to sit or lie with your arms and legs spread out in an untidy way: *People lay sprawled out in the sun.* **2** to cover a large area of land (in an unplanned way): *The city sprawls along the coast.* —**sprawling** adj: *the sprawling city suburbs*

spray /spreɪ/ noun **1** [U] liquid in very small drops that is blown through the air: *clouds of spray from the waves* **2** [C,U] liquid in a special container (**aerosol**) that is forced out under pressure when you push a button: *hair spray*

spray verb [I,T] (used about a liquid) to be sent

spray

aerosol

spraying

out in very small drops with great force; to send a liquid out in this way: *The water sprayed out from the hole in the pipe.* ○ *Somebody's sprayed paint on my door!* ○ *Somebody's sprayed my door with paint.*

☆ **spread** /spred/ *verb* (*pt, pp* **spread**) **1** [T] **spread sth (out) (on/over sth)** to open sth so that you can see all of it: *Spread out the map on the table so we can all see it!* **2** [T] **spread A on B; spread B with A** to cover a surface with a soft substance: *to spread jam on bread* ○ *to spread bread with jam* **3** [I,T] to affect a larger area or a bigger group of people; to make sth do this: *Fear spread through the village.* ○ *Rats and flies spread disease.* **4** [I] to continue for a great distance: *The swamp spreads for several miles along the coast.* **5** [T] **spread sth (over sth)** to divide sth so that it continues for a longer period of time: *You can spread your repayments over a period of three years.*
(PHRASAL VERB) **spread (sb/yourself) out** to move away from the others in a group of people: *The police spread out to search the whole area.*

spread *noun* **1** [U] the act of spreading sth or being spread: *Dirty drinking water encourages the spread of disease.* **2** [C,U] soft food that you eat on bread: *Don't eat butter. Use a low-fat spread.* **3** [C] a newspaper or magazine article that covers one or more pages: *a double-page spread*

spreadsheet /ˈspredʃiːt/ *noun* [C] a computer program for working with rows of numbers, used especially for doing accounts

spree /spriː/ *noun* [C] (*informal*) a time when you go out and enjoy yourself

sprig /sprɪg/ *noun* [C] a small piece of a plant with leaves on it

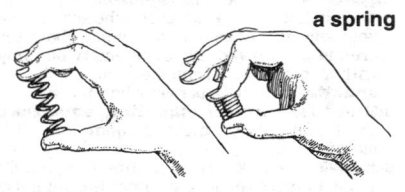

a spring

☆ **spring¹** /sprɪŋ/ *noun* [C] **1** a place where water comes up naturally from under the ground: *a hot spring* **2** a long piece of thin metal or wire that is bent round and round. After you push or pull a spring it goes back to its original shape and size: *the springs of a bed* **3** an act of springing³(1) or jumping up: *With one spring the cat landed on the table.*

springy *adj* able to go back to its original shape or size after being pushed, pulled, etc: *soft springy grass*

ˈspringboard *noun* [C] a low board that you jump on before diving into water, jumping over sth, etc. It helps you jump higher.

☆ **spring²** /sprɪŋ/ *noun* [C,U] the season of the year which follows winter and comes before summer. In spring the weather gets warmer and plants begin to grow: *Daffodils bloom in the spring.* ○ *There's a feeling of spring in the air.*

ˌspring-ˈclean *verb* [T] to clean a house thoroughly

ˈspringtime *noun* [U] the period of spring

☆ **spring³** /sprɪŋ/ *verb* (*pt* **sprang** /spræŋ/; *pp* **sprung** /sprʌŋ/) [I] **1** to jump or move quickly: *When the alarm went off, Ray sprang out of bed.* ○ *to spring to your feet* ○ (*figurative*) *Everyone sprang to her defence when the boss started criticizing her.* **2** to happen suddenly or when not expected: *The door sprang open and Bella walked in.* **3 spring from sth** to be the result of: *Her behaviour springs from fear.*
(PHRASAL VERBS) **spring sth on sb** (*informal*) to tell sb sth that is a surprise or not expected: *I hate to spring this on you, but can you get me those figures by tomorrow?*

spring up to appear or develop quickly or suddenly: *Video rental shops are springing up everywhere.*

sprinkle /ˈsprɪŋkl/ *verb* [T] **sprinkle A (on/onto/over B); sprinkle B (with A)** to throw drops of water or small pieces of sth over a surface: *to sprinkle sugar on a cake* ○ *to sprinkle a cake with sugar*

sprinkler /ˈsprɪŋklə(r)/ *noun* [C] a piece of equipment that sends out water in small drops. Sprinklers are used in gardens and for putting out fires in buildings.

sprint /sprɪnt/ *verb* [I,T] to run a short distance as fast as you can

sprint *noun* [C] a short run or a short fast race

sprout /spraʊt/ *verb* [I,T] (used about a plant) to begin to grow or to produce new leaves: *The seeds are sprouting.*

sprout *noun* [C] **1** a new part that has grown on a plant **2** = BRUSSELS SPROUT

spruce /spruːs/ *verb*
(PHRASAL VERB) **spruce (sb/yourself) up** to make sb/yourself clean and tidy

sprung *pp* of SPRING³

spud /spʌd/ *noun* [C] (*informal*) a potato

spun *pp* of SPIN

spur /spɜː(r)/ *noun* [C] **1** a sharp piece of metal that a rider wears on the back of his/her boots to help control a horse and to make it go faster **2** something that encourages you or that makes sth happen more quickly
(IDIOM) **on the spur of the moment** without planning; suddenly: *I decided to go on the spur of the moment.*

spur *verb* [T] (**spurring**; **spurred**) **1** to make a horse go faster by using spurs **2 spur sb/sth (on/onto sth)** to encourage sb or make sb work harder or do sth more quickly: *The general spurred his men on to a fresh attack.*

spurn /spɜːn/ *verb* [T] (*formal*) to refuse sth

s	z	ʃ	ʒ	h	m	n	ŋ	l	r	j	w
so	zoo	she	vision	how	man	no	sing	leg	red	yes	wet

that sb has offered to you: *to spurn an offer of friendship*

spurt /spɜːt/ *verb* **1** [I,T] (used about a liquid) to come out with great force; to make a liquid do this: *Blood spurted from the wound.* **2** [I] to increase your speed or effort

spurt *noun* [C] **1** when a liquid comes out in a spurt, it comes out suddenly and with great force **2** a sudden increase in speed or effort: *She put on a spurt to catch up with the other runners.*

spy /spaɪ/ *noun* [C] (*pl* **spies**) a person who tries to get secret information about another country, person or organization

spy *verb* (*pres part* **spying**; *3rd pers sing pres* **spies**; *pt, pp* **spied**) **1** [I] **spy (on sb/sth)** to try to get (secret) information about sb/sth ☞ Look at **espionage**. **2** [T] (*formal*) to see: *They spied a horseman in the distance.*

squabble /'skwɒbl/ *verb* [I] to quarrel or argue in a noisy way about sth that is not very important —**squabble** *noun* [C]

squad /skwɒd/ *noun* [C, with sing or pl verb] a group of people who work as a team: *the police drugs squad*

squadron /'skwɒdrən/ *noun* [C, with sing or pl verb] a group of soldiers, military ships or aeroplanes, etc

squalid /'skwɒlɪd/ *adj* very dirty, untidy and unpleasant: *squalid housing conditions*

squall /skwɔːl/ *noun* [C] a sudden storm with strong winds

squalor /'skwɒlə(r)/ *noun* [U] the state of being very dirty, untidy or unpleasant: *to live in squalor*

squander /'skwɒndə(r)/ *verb* [T] to waste time, money, etc: *Karen squandered everything she earned on clothes and records.*

☆ **square¹** /skweə(r)/ *adj* **1** having four straight sides of the same length: *a square tablecloth* **2** shaped like a square: *a square face* ○ *square shoulders* **3** not owing any money: *Here is the £10 I owe you. Now we're all square.* **4** having equal points (in a game, etc): *The teams were square at half-time.* **5** (used for talking about the area of sth): *If a room is 5 metres long and 4 metres wide, its area is 20 square metres.* **6** (used about sth that is square(1) in shape) having sides of a particular length: *The picture is twenty centimetres square* (= each side is twenty centimetres long).

(IDIOM) **a square meal** a good meal that makes you feel full

square (*also* **squarely**) *adv* directly: *to look sb square in the eye* ○ *I think the blame falls squarely on her.*

,square 'root *noun* [C] a number that produces another particular number when it is multiplied by itself: *The square root of four is two.* ☞ Look at **square²(3)**.

☆ **square²** /skweə(r)/ *noun* [C] **1** a shape that has four sides of the same length and four angles of 90 degrees (**right angles**): *There are 64 squares on a chess board.* ☞ picture at **shape**. **2** (*also* **Square**) an open space in a town or city that has buildings all around it: *The American Embassy is in Grosvenor Square.* ○ *the market square* **3** the number that you get when you multiply another number by itself: *Four is the square of two.* ☞ Look at **square root**.

square³ /skweə(r)/ *verb* [I,T] **square (sth) with sth** to agree, or make sth agree, with sth else: *Your conclusion doesn't really square with the facts.*

(PHRASAL VERB) **square up (with sb)** to pay sb the money that you owe him/her

squash¹ /skwɒʃ/ *verb* **1** [T] to damage sth by pressing it hard so that it becomes flat: *My hat got squashed when somebody sat on it.* ○ (*figurative*) *to squash a suggestion* **2** [I,T] to go into a place, or move sb/sth to a place, where there is not much space: *We all squashed into the back of the car.*

squash² /skwɒʃ/ *noun* **1** [C, usually sing] a lot of people in a small space: *We can get ten people around the table, but it's a bit of a squash.* **2** [C,U] (*Brit*) a drink that is made from fruit juice and sugar. You add water to squash before you drink it: *orange squash*

squash

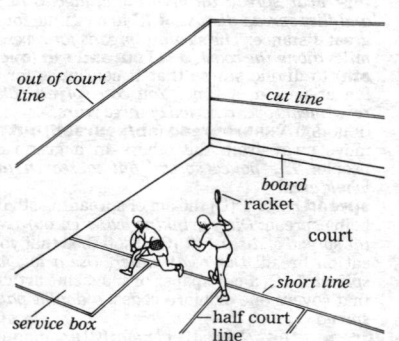

squash³ /skwɒʃ/ *noun* [U] a game for two people, played in a special room (**court**). You play squash by hitting a small rubber ball with a racket against any one of the walls of the room: *Let's have a game of squash.*

squat¹ /skwɒt/ *verb* [I] (**squatting**; **squatted**) **1** to sit down with your feet on the ground and your legs bent and your bottom just above the ground **2** to go and live in an empty building without permission from the owner

squatter *noun* [C] a person who squats(2)

squat² /skwɒt/ *adj* (**squatter**; **squattest**) short and fat or thick: *a squat and ugly building*

squawk /skwɔːk/ *verb* [I] (used especially about a bird) to make a loud unpleasant noise —**squawk** *noun* [C]

squeak /skwiːk/ *noun* [C] a short high noise that is not very loud: *the squeak of a mouse* ○ *a little squeak of surprise* —**squeak** *verb* [I,T] —**squeaky** *adj* (**squeakier**; **squeakiest**): *a squeaky floor-board* ○ *a squeaky voice*

squeal /skwiːl/ *verb* [I,T] to make a loud high noise that is a sign of pain, fear or enjoyment:

i:	ɪ	e	æ	ɑː	ɒ	ɔː	ʊ	uː	ʌ
see	sit	ten	hat	arm	got	saw	put	too	cup

The baby squealed in delight at the new toy. —**squeal** *noun* [C]: *The car stopped, with a squeal of tyres.* ☛ A **squeal** is louder and longer than a **squeak** but it is not as loud as a **scream**.

squeamish /ˈskwiːmɪʃ/ *adj* (used about a person) easily upset by sth unpleasant, eg the sight of blood

☆**squeeze** /skwiːz/ *verb* 1 [T] **squeeze sth (out)**; **squeeze sth (from/out of sth)** to press sth hard for a particular purpose: *She squeezed his hand as a sign of affection.* o *to squeeze a tube of toothpaste* o *to squeeze an orange/lemon* (= to get the juice) o *to squeeze a cloth dry*

squeezing

2 [I,T] **squeeze (sb/sth) into, through, etc sth**; **squeeze (sb/sth) through, in, past, etc** to go or move sth into, through, etc a place where there is not much space: *Excuse me, please. Can I squeeze past?* o *We can squeeze another person into the back of the car.* o *(figurative) Do you think you can squeeze in another appointment this afternoon?*

squeeze *noun* 1 [C] an act of squeezing(1) sb/sth, eg as a sign of love or affection: *to give someone a squeeze* ☛ Look at **hug**. 2 [C] the amount of liquid that you get from squeezing an orange, lemon, etc: *a squeeze of lemon* 3 [sing] a situation where there is not much space: *It was a tight squeeze to get everybody in the car.* 4 [C, usually sing] a difficult situation in which there is not enough money, time, etc: *a government squeeze on spending*

squelch /skweltʃ/ *verb* [I] to make the sound your feet make when you are walking in deep wet mud

squiggle /ˈskwɪɡl/ *noun* [C] (*informal*) a short curly line, eg in sb's handwriting

squint /skwɪnt/ *verb* [I] 1 to have eyes that do not move together properly and appear to look in different directions at the same time 2 to look at sth with your eyes almost closed: *to squint in bright sunlight*

squint *noun* [C] the condition in which your eyes do not move together properly: *to have a squint*

squire /ˈskwaɪə(r)/ *noun* [C] (in the past) a man who owned land in a country area

squirm /skwɜːm/ *verb* [I] to move your body in a way which shows you are uncomfortable, ashamed or embarrassed

squirrel /ˈskwɪrəl; *US* ˈskwɜːrəl/ *noun* [C] a small red or grey animal with a long thick tail that lives in trees and eats nuts

squirt /skwɜːt/ *verb* [I,T] (used about a liquid) to be forced out from sth in a thin fast stream; to make a liquid move in this way; to hit sb/sth with a liquid in this way: *I squeezed the bottle and oil squirted out.* o *He squirted water at me from a water-pistol.* o *He squirted me with water.*

stab /stæb/ *verb* [T] (**stabb**ing; **stabb**ed) to push a knife or other pointed object into sb/sth: *The man had been stabbed in the back.*

stab *noun* [C] 1 an injury that was caused by a knife, etc: *a stab in the back* o *a stab wound* 2 a sudden sharp pain: *a stab of pain* o *(figurative) a stab of guilt*

(IDIOM) **have a stab at sth/doing sth** (*informal*) to try to do sth: *I'll have a stab at painting your portrait.*

stabbing *adj* (used about a pain) sudden and strong

stabbing *noun* [C] an occasion when sb stabs sb else: *Following last night's stabbing, police are looking for a tall blond man.*

☆**stable¹** /ˈsteɪbl/ *adj* not likely to move, change or end: *This ladder doesn't seem very stable.* o *The patient is in a stable condition.* o *a stable relationship* ☛ The opposite is **unstable**.

stability /stəˈbɪləti/ *noun* [U] the state or quality of being stable: *After so much change we now need a period of stability.*

stabilize (*also* **stabilise**) /ˈsteɪbəlaɪz/ *verb* [I,T] to become or to make sth stable ☛ The opposite is **destabilize**.

stable² /ˈsteɪbl/ *noun* [C] a building where horses are kept

stack /stæk/ *noun* [C] 1 a tidy pile of sth: *a stack of plates, books, etc* 2 (often plural) (*informal*) a lot of: *I've still got stacks of work to do.*

stack *verb* [T] **stack sth (up)** to put sth into a pile: *Could you stack those chairs for me?*

stacked /stækt/ *adj* full of; covered in: *The floor was stacked with books.*

☆**stadium** /ˈsteɪdiəm/ *noun* [C] (*pl* **stadiums** or **stadia** /-diə/) a large sports ground with rows of seats around it: *a football stadium* o *the Olympic stadium in Barcelona*

☆**staff** /stɑːf; *US* stæf/ *noun* [C, usually sing,U] the group of people who work for a particular organization: *The hotel staff were very helpful.* o *Two members of staff will accompany the students on the school trip.* o *Our London office has a staff of 28.* o *All staff must attend the meeting on Friday.* o *a staffroom* (= in a school) ☛ **Staff** is usually only used in the singular and is usually used with a plural verb: *The staff all speak good English.* We say **a member of staff** (NOT **a staff**) to talk about one person who works for an organization. —**staff** *verb* [T] (usually passive): *The school is staffed by highly qualified teachers.*

stag /stæɡ/ *noun* [C] an adult male deer ☛ picture at **deer**.

'stag-night (*also* **'stag-party**) *noun* [C] a party for men only that is given for a man just before his wedding day

☆**stage¹** /steɪdʒ/ *noun* [C] one part of the progress or development of sth: *The first stage of the course lasts for three weeks.* o *I suggest we do the journey in two stages.* o *the early stages of the match* o *At this stage it's too early to say what will happen.*

☆**stage²** /steɪdʒ/ *noun* 1 [C] a raised floor in a theatre or concert hall, etc on which actors, musicians, etc perform: *to go on stage* 2 **the stage** [sing] the world of theatre; the profession of acting: *After starring in several films he has decided to return to the stage.*

ɜː	ə	eɪ	əʊ	aɪ	aʊ	ɔɪ	ɪə	eə	ʊə
fur	ago	pay	home	five	now	join	near	hair	pure

stage verb [T] **1** to organize a performance of a play, concert, etc for the public **2** to organize an event: *They have decided to stage a 24-hour strike.*

stage-'manager noun [C] the person who is responsible for the stage and scenery during a theatre performance

stagger /'stægə(r)/ verb [I] to walk in an unsteady way, as if you could fall at any moment, eg because you are ill, drunk or carrying sth heavy

staggered adj **1** very surprised: *I was absolutely staggered when I heard the news.* **2** (used about a set of times, payments, etc) arranged so that they do not all happen at the same time: *staggered working hours* (= when people start and finish work at different times)

staggering adj that you find difficult to believe: *a staggering £2 billion profit* —**staggeringly** adv

stagnant /'stægnənt/ adj **1** (used about water) not flowing and therefore dirty and having an unpleasant smell **2** (used about business, etc) not active; not developing: *a stagnant economy*

stagnate /stæg'neɪt; *US* 'stægneɪt/ verb [I] to be inactive; not to develop or change: *a stagnating economy* —**stagnation** /stæg'neɪʃn/ noun [U]

staid /steɪd/ adj (used about a person) serious, old-fashioned and rather boring

☆ **stain** /steɪn/ verb [I,T] to leave a coloured mark that is difficult to remove: *Don't spill any of that red wine. It'll stain the carpet.* —**stain** noun [C]: *The blood had left a stain on his shirt.*

stained 'glass noun [U] pieces of coloured glass that are used in church windows, etc: *a stained-glass window*

stainless 'steel noun [U] steel that does not stain or rust: *a stainless steel pan*

☆ **stair** /steə(r)/ noun **1 stairs** [plural] a series of steps inside a building that lead from one level to another: *The lift wasn't working so I had to use the stairs* o *at the bottom/top of the stairs* o *two flights* (= sets) *of stairs* o *I heard somebody coming down the stairs.* o *She ran up the stairs.* ☛ Look at **downstairs** and **upstairs**. **2** [C] one of the steps in this series: *She sat down on the bottom stair to read the letter.*

'staircase (also **'stairway**) noun [C] a set of stairs with rails on each side that you can hold on to ☛ Look at **escalator**. Compare **stair** and **step**. Stairs or flights of stairs are usually inside buildings. Steps are usually outside buildings and made of stone or concrete.

☆ **stake¹** /steɪk/ noun **1 stakes** [plural] the things that you might win or lose in a game or in a particular situation: *We play cards for money, but never for very high stakes.* **2** [C] a part of a company, etc that you own, usually because you have invested money in it: *Foreign investors now have a 20% stake in the company.*

(IDIOM) **at stake** in danger of being lost; at risk: *He thought very carefully about the decision because he knew his future was at stake.*

stake verb [T] **stake sth (on sth)** to put your future, etc in danger by doing sth, because you hope that it will bring you a good result: *He is staking his political reputation on this issue.*

(IDIOM) **stake a/your claim (to sth)** to say that you have a right to have sth: *Both companies have staked their claim to the same piece of land.*

stake² /steɪk/ noun [C] a wooden or metal pole with a point at one end that you push into the ground, eg to support a young tree

☆ **stale** /steɪl/ adj **1** (used about food or air) old and not fresh any more: *The bread had gone stale.* o *stale cigarette smoke* **2** not interesting or exciting any more: *She says her marriage has gone stale.*

stalemate /'steɪlmeɪt/ noun [sing,U] a situation in an argument in which neither side can win or make any progress

stalk¹ /stɔːk/ noun [C] one of the long thin parts of a plant which the flowers, leaves or fruit grow on

stalk² /stɔːk/ verb **1** [T] to follow an animal quietly, closely and secretly in order to catch or kill it: *a lion stalking its prey* **2** [I] to walk stiffly in an angry or arrogant way: *He got up and stalked angrily out of the room.*

stall¹ /stɔːl/ noun **1** [C] a small shop with an open front or a table with things for sale in a market, street, railway station, etc: *a stall in the market* o *a bookstall on Victoria Station* **2 stalls** [plural] the level of seats nearest the front in a theatre or cinema

stall² /stɔːl/ verb [I,T] **1** (used about a vehicle) to stop suddenly because the engine fails; to make a vehicle do this accidentally: *A bus had stalled in the middle of the road.* o *I kept stalling the car.* **2** to avoid doing sth or to try to stop sth happening until a later time: *I've asked them several times for the money but they keep stalling.*

stallion /'stæliən/ noun [C] an adult male horse, especially one that is kept for breeding ☛ Look at the note at **horse**.

stalwart /'stɔːlwət/ adj loyal and hard-working: *a stalwart member of the Labour Party*

stamina /'stæmɪnə/ noun [U] the ability to do sth that requires a lot of physical or mental effort for a long time: *You need a lot of stamina to run long distances.*

stammer /'stæmə(r)/ verb **1** [I] to speak with difficulty and sudden pauses, repeating the same sounds or words again and again, because you have a speech problem or because you are nervous **2** [T] to say sth in this way: *He stammered an apology and left quickly.* —**stammer** noun [sing]: *to have a stammer*

☆ **stamp¹** /stæmp/ noun **1** (also **postage stamp**) a small piece of paper that you stick onto a letter or parcel to show that you have paid for it to be posted: *three 26p stamps*

☛ In the British postal system, there are two types of stamp for posting letters, etc to other parts of Britain, **first-class** stamps and **second-class** stamps. Letters with first-class stamps are more expensive and arrive more quickly.

2 a small object that prints some words, a design, the date, etc when you press it onto a

p	b	t	d	k	g	tʃ	dʒ	f	v	θ	ð
pen	bad	tea	did	cat	got	chin	June	fall	van	thin	then

surface: *a date stamp* **3** the mark made by a stamp(2): *a stamp in my passport* **4 the stamp of sth** [usually sing] something that shows a particular quality or that sth was done by a particular person: *Her novels bear the stamp of genius.*

'**stamp album** *noun* [C] a book in which you put stamps that you have collected

'**stamp-collecting** *noun* [U] the hobby of collecting stamps

stamp² /stæmp/ *verb* **1** [I,T] **stamp (on sth)** to put your foot down very heavily on the ground or on sth else: *He stamped on the spider and squashed it.* ○ *It was so cold that I had to stamp my feet to keep warm.* **2** [I] to walk with loud heavy steps usually because you are angry: *She stamped around the room, shouting angrily.* **3** [T] **stamp A (on B); stamp B (with A)** to print some words, a design, the date, etc by pressing a small object (**a stamp**) onto a surface: *to stamp a passport* ○ *The date is stamped on the receipt.*

(PHRASAL VERB) **stamp sth out** to put an end to sth completely: *The police are trying to stamp out this kind of crime.*

stamped *adj* with a stamp(1) on it: *Please enclose a stamped addressed envelope with your application.*

stampede /stæmˈpiːd/ *verb* [T] (used about a group of animals or people) to rush in a particular direction in a wild and uncontrolled way

stance /stæns; stɑːns/ *noun* [C, usually sing] **1** the position in which somebody stands (especially in sport when you are preparing to hit the ball) **2 stance (on sth)** an attitude (especially moral or political) towards sth: *the Prime Minister's stance on foreign affairs*

☆ **stand¹** /stænd/ *verb* [I,T] (*pt, pp* **stood** /stʊd/) **1** [I] to be on your feet; to be upright: *He was standing near the window.* **2** [I] **stand (up)** to rise to your feet from another position: *He stood up when I entered the room.* **3** [T] to put sb/sth in a particular place or position: *She stood her wet umbrella in the corner of the office.* **4** [I] to be or to remain in a particular position or situation: *The castle stands on a hill.* ○ *The house has stood empty for ten years.* ○ *He was very critical of the law as it stands* (= as it is now). **5** [I] (used about an offer, a decision, etc) to be or to remain unchanged: *Does your decision still stand?* **6** [I] to be of a particular height, level, amount, etc: *The world record stands at 6·59 metres.* **7** [I] to have an opinion or view (about sth): *I don't know where I stand on abortion.* **8** [I] to be in a situation where you are likely to do sth: *If he has to sell the company, he stands to lose a lot of money.* **9** [I] to be a candidate in an election: *She's standing for the European Parliament.* **10** [T] (in negative sentences and questions, with *can/could*) to be able to bear sb/sth: *I can't stand that woman – she's so rude.* **11** [T] to buy a meal or drink for sb: *He stood me lunch.*

(PHRASAL VERBS) **stand aside** to move to one side: *People stood aside to let the police pass.*

stand back to move back: *The policeman told everybody to stand back.*

stand by 1 to be present, but do nothing in a situation: *How can you stand by and let them treat their animals like that?* **2** to be ready to act: *The police are standing by in case there's trouble.*

stand for sth 1 to be a short form of sth: *What does BBC stand for?* **2** to support sth (eg an idea or opinion): *I hate everything that the party stands for.*

stand in (for sb) to take sb's place for a short time: *Mr Jones is standing in for Miss Evans this week.*

stand out to be easily seen or noticed

stand sb up (*informal*) not keep an appointment with sb: *She never came! I'd been stood up.*

stand up for sb/sth to say or do sth which shows that you support sb/sth: *I admire him. He really stands up for his rights.*

stand up to sb/sth to defend yourself against sb who is stronger or more powerful

'**stand-by** *noun* [C] (*pl* **stand-bys**) a person or thing that is ready to be used if necessary: *I've got a word processor now, but I still keep my old typewriter as a stand-by.* ○ *a stand-by ticket* (= a cheap ticket, eg for a flight, that you can get at the last moment if a seat is free)

(IDIOM) **on stand-by** ready; waiting to do sth: *When fighting began, the hospitals were put on stand-by.*

☆ **stand²** /stænd/ *noun* [C] **1** a table or small shop in the street or in a large public building from which you can buy things or get information: *a news-stand* ○ *a company stand at a trade fair* **2** a piece of furniture that you can put things on or in: *a music stand* **3** a large building at a sports ground that is open at the front and where people sit or stand in rows to watch the sport ☞ picture at **football**.

(IDIOMS) **make a stand (against sb/sth)** to defend yourself, your opinion, etc strongly against sb/sth

take a stand (on sth) to say publicly what you think and intend to do about sth

☆ **standard** /ˈstændəd/ *noun* [C] **1** a level of quality: *We complained about the low standard of service in the hotel.* ○ *the high standard of teaching* ○ *We need to improve educational standards in this country.* ○ *This work is not up to your usual standard.* **2** a level of quality that you compare sth else with: *By European standards this is a very expensive city.* ○ *He is a brilliant player by any standard.* **3** [usually pl] a level of behaviour that is morally acceptable: *Many people are worried about falling standards in modern society.*

standard *adj* **1** of the normal type; without anything special or extra: *This is the standard model of the car. The de luxe version costs more.* **2** part of the normal situation; not unusual in any way: *It is standard practice to ask students to fill in this form when they arrive.* **3** (used about language) that people generally accept as normal and correct: *standard English* **4** (used about a book, etc) that people most often read when they are studying a particular subject: *the standard work on the legal system*

,**standard of 'living** *noun* [C] the level of wealth and comfort that a person, group or country has in everyday life: *There is a higher*

s	z	ʃ	ʒ	h	m	n	ŋ	l	r	j	w
so	zoo	she	vision	how	man	no	sing	leg	red	yes	wet

standard of living in the north than in the south. ☛ An expression with a similar meaning is **living standards**. This is used in the plural: *Living standards have improved.*

standardize (*also* **standardise**) /'stændədaɪz/ *verb* [T] to make things that are different the same: *The EC intends to standardize public holidays in Europe.* —**standardization** /ˌstændədaɪ'zeɪʃn/ (*also* **standardisation**) *noun* [U]

standing /'stændɪŋ/ *noun* [U] **1** the opinion that other people (in public life) have of you: *The consequences for Britain's international standing could be extremely serious.* **2** the amount of time during which sth has continued to exist: *a problem of many years' standing*

standing *adj* continuing to exist; permanent: *I have a standing invitation to go and stay with them whenever I like.*

standing 'order *noun* [C] an instruction to your bank to make a regular payment to sb from your account

standpoint /'stændpɔɪnt/ *noun* [C] a particular way of thinking about sth: *The television programme looked at the problems of education from the standpoint of the teacher.*

standstill /'stændstɪl/ *noun* [sing] a situation of no movement, progress or activity: *The traffic came to a complete standstill.*
(IDIOM) **grind to a halt/standstill** ⇨ GRIND

stank *pt* of STINK

staple¹ /'steɪpl/ *noun* [C] a small thin piece of bent wire that you push through pieces of paper in order to fasten them together using a special tool (**stapler**) —**staple** *verb* [T]: *Staple the letter to the application form.* —**stapler** /'steɪplə(r)/ *noun* [C]

staple² /'steɪpl/ *adj* (used especially about food) forming the main part of what people eat: *a staple diet of rice and fish*

☆ **star** /stɑː(r)/ *noun* **1** [C] a large ball of burning gas in outer space that you see as a small point of light in the sky at night: *It was a clear night and the stars were shining brightly.* **2** [C] a shape with a number of points sticking out in a regular pattern: *The children decorated the classroom with paper stars.* ☛ picture at **shape**. **3** [C] a printed shape of this type that is used for indicating a level of quality: *a five-star hotel* **4** [C] a famous person in acting, music or sport: *a film star* **5 stars** [plural] = HOROSCOPE: *Your stars say you're going to be very lucky this month.*

star *verb* (**starring**; **starred**) **1** [I] **star** (**in sth**) to be one of the main actors in a play, film, etc: *Michelle Pfeiffer is to star in an exciting new adventure film.* **2** [T] to have sb as a star: *The film stars Jane Fonda as a teacher in Mexico.*

stardom /'stɑːdəm/ *noun* [U] the position of being a famous person in acting, music or sport

starry (**starrier**; **starriest**) *adj* full of stars: *a starry night*

'starlight *noun* [U] the light that is given out by stars

starboard /'stɑːbəd/ *noun* [U] the side of a ship that is on the right when you are facing towards the front of it ☛ The opposite is **port**.

starch /stɑːtʃ/ *noun* [C,U] **1** a white substance with no taste in foods such as potatoes, rice and bread **2** a substance that is used for making cloth stiff

starched *adj* made stiff with starch: *a starched shirt collar*

☆ **stare** /steə(r)/ *verb* [I] **stare (at sb/sth)** to look at sb or sth continuously for a long time because you are interested, surprised, etc: *Everybody stared at his hat.* ○ *'I'm going to get married,' he said. I stared at him in disbelief.* ○ *He didn't reply, he just stared into the distance.*

stark /stɑːk/ *adj* **1** very bare and plain and therefore not attractive: *a stark landscape* **2** clearly unpleasant: *the stark realities of a life of poverty* **3** very clear: *In stark contrast to the old buildings in the area are five enormous new tower blocks.*

stark *adv* completely: *stark naked*

starry ⇨ STAR

☆ **start¹** /stɑːt/ *verb* **1** [I,T] **start (sth/to do sth/doing sth)** to begin doing sth: *Turn over your exam papers and start now.* ○ *We'll have to start* (= leave) *early if we want to be in Dover by 10.* ○ *Prices start at £5.* ○ *After waiting for an hour, the customers started to complain.* ○ *She started playing the piano when she was six.* ○ *What time do you have to start work in the morning?* **2** [I,T] to begin to happen or to make sth begin to happen: *What time does the concert start?* ○ *I'd like to start the meeting now.* ○ *The fight started when the boys were leaving the disco.* ○ *The police think a young woman may have started the fire.* ☛ Look at the note at **begin**. **3** [I,T] **start (sth) (up)** to create a company, an organization, etc; to be created: *They've decided to start their own business.* ○ *There are a lot of new companies starting up in that area now.* **4** [I,T] **start (sth) (up)** (used about an engine, a car, etc) to begin to work; to make an engine, a car, etc begin to work: *The car won't start.* ○ *We heard an engine starting up in the street.* ○ *He got onto his motor bike, started the engine and rode away.* **5** [I] to make a sudden, quick movement because you are surprised or afraid: *A loud noise outside made me start.*

(IDIOMS) **to start (off) with 1** in the beginning; at first: *To start with everything was fine but then there were problems.* **2** (used for giving your first reason for sth): *'Why are you so angry?' 'Well, to start off with you're late, and secondly you've lied to me.'*

set/start the ball rolling ⇨ BALL

(PHRASAL VERBS) **start off** to begin in a particular way: *I'd like to start off by welcoming you all to Oxford.*

start on sth to begin doing sth that needs to be done: *Haven't you started on the washing-up yet?*

start out to begin your life, career, etc in a particular way: *She started out as a teacher in Glasgow.*

start over (US) to begin again: *I've made a lot of mistakes – I'd better start over.*

'starting-point *noun* [C] **1** an idea or topic that you use to begin a discussion with **2** the

iː	ɪ	e	æ	ɑː	ɒ	ɔː	ʊ	uː	ʌ
see	sit	ten	hat	arm	got	saw	put	too	cup

start 611 **stature**

place where you begin a journey: *This town is a good starting-point for a tour of the area.*

☆ **start²** /sta:t/ *noun* **1** [C, usually sing] the beginning or first part of sth: *The chairman made a short speech at the start of the meeting.* ○ *I told you it was a bad idea from the start.* **2** [C, usually sing] an act of starting: *We've got a lot of work to do today, so let's make a start.* ○ *a fresh start in life* **3 the start** [sing] the place where a race starts: *The athletes are now lining up at the start.* **4** [C, usually sing] an advantage that you give to a weaker person at the beginning of a race, game, etc **5** [C, usually sing] a sudden quick movement that your body makes because you are surprised or afraid
(IDIOMS) **for a start** (used for giving your first reason for sth): *'Why can't we go on holiday?' 'Well, for a start we can't afford it...'*

get off to a good, bad, etc start to start well, badly, etc: *My day got off to a good start – I was told I'd got a pay rise.*

starter /'sta:tə(r)/ *noun* [C] a small amount of food that you eat as the first part of a meal

startle /'sta:tl/ *verb* [T] to make sb/sth suddenly surprised or frightened —**startled** *adj*: *He had a startled look on his face.* —**startling** /'sta:tlɪŋ/ *adj*: *I've got some startling news for you!*

☆ **starve** /sta:v/ *verb* [I,T] to suffer very badly or die from hunger; to make sb/sth suffer or die in this way: *Millions of people are starving in the poorer countries of the world.* ○ *That winter many animals starved to death.* ○ *You must eat more – you're starving yourself.*
(IDIOMS) **be starved of sth** to suffer because you are not getting enough of sth that you need: *The children had been starved of love for years.*

be starving (*informal*) to be extremely hungry: *When will dinner be ready? I'm starving!*

starvation /sta:'veɪʃn/ *noun* [U] suffering or death because there is not enough food: *to die of starvation*

☆ **state¹** /steɪt/ *noun* **1** [C] the condition that sb/sth is in at a particular time: *the state of the economy* ○ *a state of shock* ○ *The house is in a terrible state.* **2** [C] (*also* **State**) a country with its own government: *Pakistan has been an independent state since 1947.* ☛ Look at the note at **country**. **3** [C] (*also* **State**) a part of a country that has its own government: *California is one of the biggest states in the US.* **4** [U] especially **the State** the government of a country: *the relationship between the Church and the State* ○ *State schools* ○ *heads of State* (= government leaders) **5 the States** [plural] (*informal*) the United States of America: *We lived in the States for about five years.* **6** [U] very formal events and behaviour connected with governments and the leaders of countries: *The Queen is going on a state visit to China.* ○ *The President was driven in state through the streets.*
(IDIOMS) **in/into a state** (*informal*) very nervous or upset: *Now don't get into a state! I'm sure everything will be all right.*

state of affairs a situation: *This state of affairs must not be allowed to continue.*

state of mind mental condition: *She's in a very strange state of mind.*

☆ **state²** /steɪt/ *verb* [T] to say or write sth, often formally: *Your letter states that you sent the goods on 31 March, but we have never received them.* ○ *As I stated earlier, I do not believe that this information is accurate.*

statement *noun* [C] **1** something that you say or write, often formally: *The Prime Minister will make a statement about the defence cuts today.* ○ *After the accident I had to go to the police station to make a statement.* **2** = BANK STATEMENT

stately /'steɪtli/ *adj* (**statelier**; **stateliest**) formal and dignified: *a stately old building*

stately 'home *noun* [C] (*Brit*) a large old house that has historical interest and can be visited by the public

statesman /'steɪtsmən/ *noun* [C] (*pl* **statesmen** /-mən/) an important and experienced politician who has earned public respect

static /'stætɪk/ *adj* not moving or changing: *House prices are static.*

static (*also* **static elec'tricity**) *noun* [U] **1** electricity that collects on a surface **2** sudden loud noises on a radio or television, caused by electricity in the atmosphere

☆ **station** /'steɪʃn/ *noun* [C] **1** (*also* **railway station**) a building on a railway line where trains stop so that passengers can get on an off: *I got to the station two minutes before my train left.* ○ *Which station are you getting off at?* **2** a building from which buses or coaches begin and end journeys: *The coach leaves Victoria Coach Station at 9.30 am.* **3** a building where a particular service or activity is based: *a fire station* (= where the fire brigade is based) ○ *a petrol station* ○ *a police station* ○ *a power station* **4** a company that broadcasts programmes on a particular frequency on the radio or on television: *a local radio station* ☛ Look at **channel**.

station *verb* [T] (often passive) to send soldiers, etc to a particular place: *During his time in the army, he was stationed in Germany.* ○ *Guards stationed themselves at every entrance to the building.*

'station-wagon *noun* [C] (*US*) = ESTATE CAR

stationary /'steɪʃənri; *US* -neri/ *adj* not moving: *He crashed into the back of a stationary vehicle.*

☆ **stationery** /'steɪʃənri; *US* -neri/ *noun* [U] equipment for writing, eg pens, pencils, paper, envelopes

stationer *noun* [C] a person that sells stationery ☛ The shop is called a **stationer's**.

☆ **statistics** /stə'tɪstɪks/ *noun* **1** [plural] numbers that have been collected in order to provide information about sth: *Statistics indicate that 90% of homes in this country have a television.* ○ *crime statistics* **2** [U] the science of collecting and analysing these numbers —**statistical** /stə'tɪstɪkl/ *adj*: *statistical information, evidence, etc* —**statistically** /-kli/ *adv*

☆ **statue** /'stætʃu:/ *noun* [C] the figure of a person or animal, that is made of stone or metal and usually put in a public place: *the Statue of Liberty in New York*

stature /'stætʃə(r)/ *noun* [U] (*formal*) **1** the height of a person: *He's quite small in stature.*

ɜ:	ə	eɪ	əʊ	aɪ	aʊ	ɔɪ	ɪə	eə	ʊə
fur	ago	pay	home	five	now	join	near	hair	pure

2 the importance that sb has because people have a high opinion of his/her skill or achievement: *Her research has given her considerable stature in the scientific world.*

☆ **status** /ˈsteɪtəs/ *noun* **1** [sing] your social or professional position in relation to other people: *Teachers don't have a very high status in this country.* **2** [U] a high social position: *The new job gave him much more status.* **3** [U] your legal position: *Please indicate your name, age and marital status* (= whether you are married or single).

ˈstatus symbol *noun* [C] something that a person owns that shows that he/she has a high position in society

status quo /ˌsteɪtəs ˈkwəʊ/ *noun* [sing] **the status quo** the situation that exists at a particular time

statute /ˈstætʃuːt/ *noun* [C] (*formal*) a rule or law

statutory /ˈstætʃʊtri; *US* -tɔːri/ *adj* (*formal*) decided by law: *a statutory right*

staunch /stɔːntʃ/ *adj* believing in sth or supporting sb/sth very strongly; loyal: *a staunch supporter of the Liberal Democrats*

stave /steɪv/ *verb*
(PHRASAL VERB) **stave sth off** to stop sth unpleasant from happening now, although it may happen at a later time: *to stave off a financial crisis*

☆ **stay** /steɪ/ *verb* [I] **1** to continue to be somewhere and not go away: *Patrick stayed in bed until 11 o'clock.* ○ *I can't stay long.* ○ *Stay on this road until you get to Wells.* **2** to continue to be in a particular state or situation without change: *I can't stay awake any longer.* ☛ **Remain** and **stay** are similar in meaning but **remain** is more formal. **3** to be somewhere as a visitor or guest: *We stayed with friends in France.* ○ *to stay at a hotel* ○ *Can you stay for lunch?* ○ *Why don't you stay the night?*
(IDIOM) **stay put** (*informal*) to remain in one place: *We like this flat so we'll probably stay put for a few years.*
(PHRASAL VERBS) **stay behind** to remain in a place after other people have gone
stay in to remain at home: *I'm going to stay in and watch TV.*
stay on (at ...) to remain at a place of work or study longer than necessary or normal: *I've decided to stay on at school to do A levels.*
stay out to remain out, especially late at night
stay up not go to bed: *I'm going to stay up to watch the film on BBC 1.*
stay *noun* [C] a period of time that you stay(3) somewhere: *Did you enjoy your stay in Crete?*

☆ **steady** /ˈstedi/ *adj* (**steadier**; **steadiest**) **1** not moving or shaking: *You need a steady hand to take good photographs.* ☛ The opposite is **unsteady**. **2** developing or happening at a regular rate: *a steady increase in exports* **3** staying the same; not changing: *If you drive at a steady 50 miles an hour, you will use less petrol.* —**steadily** /ˈstedɪli/ *adv*: *Unemployment has risen steadily since April 1991.*

steady *verb* [I,T] (*pres part* **steadying**; *3rd pers sing pres* **steadies**; *pt, pp* **steadied**) to make sth steady or to become steady: *She thought she was going to fall, so she put out a hand to steady herself.*

☆ **steak** /steɪk/ *noun* [C,U] a thick flat piece of meat or fish: *a piece of steak* ○ *a salmon steak* ☛ Look at **chop**².

☆ **steal** /stiːl/ *verb* (*pt* **stole** /stəʊl/; *pp* **stolen** /ˈstəʊlən/) **1** [I,T] **steal (sth) (from sb/sth)** to take sth that belongs to another person secretly and without permission: *The terrorists were driving a stolen car.* ☛ You steal things, but you **rob** people (of things): *My camera has been stolen!* ○ *I've been robbed!* ○ *They robbed me of all my money!* Look also at the note at **thief**. **2** [I] **steal away, in, out,** etc to move somewhere secretly and quietly

stealth /stelθ/ *noun* [U] (*formal*) behaviour that is secret or quiet: *The terrorists operate by stealth.* —**stealthy** *adj* (**stealthier**; **stealthiest**): *to make a stealthy approach* —**stealthily** *adv*

☆ **steam** /stiːm/ *noun* [U] **1** the hot gas that water changes into when it boils: *Steam was rising from the coffee.* **2** the power that can be produced from steam: *a steam engine*
(IDIOMS) **let off steam** (*informal*) to release energy or express strong feeling by behaving in a noisy or uncontrolled way
run out of steam (*informal*) to have no more energy

steam *verb* **1** [I] to send out steam: *steaming hot soup* **2** [T] to cook sth in steam: *steamed vegetables*
(IDIOM) **be/get steamed up** (*informal*) to be/ become very angry or worried about sth
(PHRASAL VERB) **steam (sth) up** to cover sth or become covered with steam: *My glasses have steamed up.*

steamer *noun* [C] a ship that is driven by steam

ˈsteamroller *noun* [C] a big heavy vehicle that is used for making the surface of a road flat

☆ **steel** /stiːl/ *noun* [U] a very strong metal that is made from iron mixed with carbon. Steel is used for making knives, tools, machines, etc.

steel *verb* [T] **steel yourself** to prepare yourself for sth difficult or unpleasant: *Steel yourself for a shock.*

ˈsteelworks *noun* [C, with sing or pl verb] (*pl* **steelworks**) a factory where steel is made

☆ **steep** /stiːp/ *adj* **1** (used about a hill, mountain, street, etc) rising or falling quickly: *I don't think I can cycle up that hill. It's too steep.* **2** (used about an increase in sth) very big **3** (*informal*) too expensive —**steeply** *adv*: *House prices have risen steeply this year.* —**steepness** *noun* [U]

steeped /stiːpt/ *adj* having a lot of; full of: *The city of Oxford is steeped in history.*

steeple /ˈstiːpl/ *noun* [C] a church tower that has a pointed top (**spire**)

☆ **steer** /stɪə(r)/ *verb* [I,T] to control the direction that a vehicle is going in, by using a wheel, etc: *Can you push the car while I steer?* ○ *to steer a boat, ship, bicycle, motor bike,* etc ○ (*figurative*) *She tried to steer the conversation away from the subject of money.* ☛ **Steer** means to control the direction of a vehicle. If you **ride** a bicycle/

motor bike or **sail** a boat you steer it and you are also in control of everything else.

steering /'stɪərɪŋ/ *noun* [U] the mechanical parts that control the direction that a vehicle is going in

'steering-wheel (*also* **wheel**) *noun* [C] the wheel in a car, etc that you use for steering

☆ **stem¹** /stem/ *noun* [C] **1** one of the long thin parts of a plant which the leaves or flowers grow on **2** the main part of a word onto which other parts are added: *'Writ-' is the stem of the words 'write', 'writing', 'written' and 'writer'.*

stem *verb* (**stemm**ing; **stemm**ed)
(PHRASAL VERB) **stem from sth** to be caused by sth; to have sth as an origin: *His interest in Egypt stems from the time he spent there when he was a child.*

stem² /stem/ *verb* [T] (**stemm**ing; **stemm**ed) to stop sth that is increasing or spreading: *Leaders of the party are trying to stem the tide of anti-government feeling.*

stench /stentʃ/ *noun* [C, usually sing] (*formal*) a very unpleasant smell

☆ **step¹** /step/ *verb* [I] (**stepp**ing; **stepp**ed) to lift one foot and put it down in a different place when you are walking: *Be careful! Don't step in the mud.* ○ *to step forward/back* ○ *Ouch! You stepped on my foot!*

(PHRASAL VERBS) **step down** to give up a position of authority: *Anne is stepping down as chairperson at the end of the year.*

step in to become involved in a difficult situation, usually in order to help

step sth up to increase sth: *The Army has decided to step up its security arrangements.*

'stepping-stone *noun* [C] one of a line of flat stones that you can step on in order to cross a river, etc

☆ **step²** /step/ *noun* [C] **1** the act of lifting one foot and putting it down in a different place: *Nick took two steps forwards and then stopped.* ○ *I heard steps outside the window.* **2** one action in a series of actions that you take in order to achieve sth: *the first step towards peace* **3** one of the surfaces on which you put your foot when you are going up or down stairs, a ladder, etc: *the top/bottom step* ○ *a flight* (= a set) *of steps* ☛ Look at the note at **stair**.

(IDIOMS) **in/out of step (with sb/sth)** moving/not moving your feet at the same time as other people when you are marching, dancing, etc

step by step (used for talking about a series of actions) moving slowly and gradually from one action or stage to the next: *clear step-by-step instructions*

take steps to do sth to take action in order the achieve sth: *to take steps to reduce unemployment*

watch your step 1 to be careful about where you are walking **2** to be careful about how you behave

'stepladder *noun* [C] a short ladder with two parts that can stand on its own. You can fold it up when you are not using it. ☛ picture at **ladder**.

step- /step/ (in compounds) related through one parent

'stepbrother, 'stepsister *noun* [C] the child of your stepmother or stepfather from an earlier marriage

'stepchild *noun* [C] (*pl* **stepchildren**) the child of your husband or wife from an earlier marriage

'stepfather *noun* [C] the man who has married your mother after the death or divorce of your father

'stepmother *noun* [C] the woman who has married your father after the death or divorce of your mother

'stepson, 'stepdaughter *noun* [C] the child of your husband or wife from an earlier marriage

☆ **stereo** /'sterɪəʊ/ *noun* **1** [U] the system for playing recorded music, speech etc in which the sound is directed through two channels: *This programme is in stereo.* **2** [C] (*also* **'stereo system**) a piece of equipment for playing recorded music, etc that has two speakers: *a car stereo* ○ *a personal stereo* —**stereo** *adj*: *a stereo television*

stereotype /'sterɪətaɪp/ *noun* [C] a fixed idea about a type of person or thing, which is often not true in reality: *the stereotype of the London businessman as a man with a black hat and umbrella*

stereotype *verb* [T] to have or show a fixed idea about a type of person or thing: *In advertisements, women are often stereotyped as housewives.*

sterile /'steraɪl; *US* 'sterəl/ *adj* **1** not able to produce young animals or babies **2** completely clean and free from bacteria: *All equipment used during a medical operation must be sterile.* **3** with no interest or life: *a sterile discussion* —**sterility** /stə'rɪlətɪ/ *noun* [U]

sterilize (*also* **sterilise**) *verb* [T] **1** to make sb/sth completely clean and free from bacteria **2** (usually passive) to carry out an operation on a person or an animal so that they cannot have babies —**sterilization** (*also* **sterilisation**) /ˌsterəlaɪ'zeɪʃn; *US* -lɪ'z-/ *noun* [U]

sterling /'stɜːlɪŋ/ *noun* [U] the system of money that is used in Britain: *the pound sterling*

sterling *adj* of very high quality: *sterling work*

stern¹ /stɜːn/ *adj* very serious and severe; not smiling: *a stern expression* ○ *a stern warning* —**sternly** *adv*

stern² /stɜːn/ *noun* [C] the back end of a ship or boat ☛ Look at **bow³**.

stethoscope /'steθəskəʊp/ *noun* [C] the piece of equipment that a doctor uses for listening to your breathing and heart

stew /stjuː; *US* stuː/ *noun* [C,U] a type of food that you make by cooking meat and/or vegetables in liquid for a long time

stew *verb* [I,T] to cook sth slowly in liquid: *stewed apple*

steward /'stjʊəd; *US* 'stuːərd/ *noun* [C] **1** a man who looks after the passengers on an aeroplane, a ship, a train, etc **2** a person who helps to organize a large public event, eg a race

stewardess /ˌstjʊə'des; *US* 'stuːərdəs/ *noun* [C] a woman who looks after the passengers on an aeroplane, a ship, a train, etc

s	z	ʃ	ʒ	h	m	n	ŋ	l	r	j	w
so	zoo	she	vision	how	man	no	sing	leg	red	yes	wet

☆ **stick¹** /stɪk/ noun [C] **1** a small thin piece of wood from a tree **2** = WALKING-STICK **3** (in some sports) a long thin piece of wood that you use for hitting the ball: *a hockey stick* ☛ Look at **bat²**, **club²**(2) and **racket¹**. **4** a long thin piece of sth: *a stick of celery*
(IDIOM) **get (hold of) the wrong end of the stick** ⇨ WRONG¹

☆ **stick²** /stɪk/ verb (pt, pp **stuck** /stʌk/) **1** [I,T] **stick (sth) in/into (sth)** to push a pointed object into sth; to be pushed into sth: *Stick a fork into the meat to see if it's ready.* ○ *I can't move. There's a piece of wire sticking in my leg.* **2** [I,T] to attach sth to sth else or to become attached to sth else by using glue, etc: *to stick a stamp on an envelope* ○ *Jam sticks to your fingers.* **3** [I] **stick (in sth)** (used about sth that can usually be moved) to become fixed in one position so that it cannot be moved: *The car was stuck in the mud.* **4** [T] (*informal*) to put sth somewhere: *Can you stick these plates on the table?* **5** [T] (*informal*) (often in negative sentences and questions) to stay in a difficult or unpleasant situation: *I can't stick this job much longer.*
(IDIOM) **poke/stick your nose into sth** ⇨ NOSE¹
(PHRASAL VERBS) **stick around** (*informal*) to stay or wait somewhere
stick at sth (*informal*) to continue working at sth even when it is difficult
stick by sb (*informal*) to continue to give sb help and support even in difficult times
stick out (*informal*) to be very noticeable: *The new office block really sticks out from the older buildings around it.*
stick (sth) out to be further out than sth else or to push sth further out than sth else: *The boy's head was sticking out of the window.* ○ *Don't stick your tongue out.*
stick it/sth out (*informal*) to stay in a difficult or unpleasant situation until the end
stick to sth (*informal*) to continue with sth and not change to anything else: *I'm sticking to orange juice tonight because I'm driving.*
stick together (*informal*) (used about a group of people) to stay friendly and loyal to each other
stick up to point upwards: *You look funny. Your hair's sticking up!*
stick up for sb/yourself/sth (*informal*) to support or defend sb/yourself/sth: *Don't worry. I'll stick up for you if there's any trouble.*

sticker /'stɪkə(r)/ noun [C] a piece of paper with writing or a picture on one side that you can stick onto a car window, book, file, etc

☆ **sticky** /'stɪki/ adj (**stickier**; **stickiest**) **1** (used for describing a substance that can stick to sth else, or sth that is covered with this kind of substance): *These sweets are very sticky.* ○ *I've got sticky fingers from eating that ice-cream.* ○ *sticky tape* **2** (*informal*) (used about a situation) difficult or unpleasant

☆ **stiff** /stɪf/ adj **1** (used about material, paper, etc) quite hard and not easy to bend: *My new shoes feel rather stiff.* **2** (used about a handle, door, etc) not easy to turn or move: *This door's very stiff. Can you open it for me?* **3** (used about parts of the body) not easy to move: *My arm feels really stiff after playing tennis yesterday.* **4** (used about a liquid) very thick; almost solid: *Beat the egg whites until they are stiff.* **5** difficult or strong: *a stiff exam* ○ *stiff opposition to the plan* **6** (used about sb's behaviour) not relaxed or friendly; formal: *She's often a bit stiff with strangers.* **7** (used about an alcoholic drink) strong: *a stiff whisky*
stiff adv (*informal*) extremely: *to be bored, frozen, scared, etc stiff*
stiffly adv in a stiff(6) way: *He smiled stiffly.*
—**stiffness** noun [U]

stiffen /'stɪfn/ verb **1** [I] (used about a person) to suddenly become very still, usually because you are afraid or angry: *Alison stiffened as she heard a noise outside the door.* **2** [I,T] to become stiff; to make sth stiff: *a stiffened shirt collar*

stifle /'staɪfl/ verb **1** [I,T] to be or to make sb unable to breathe easily: *Richard was almost stifled by the smoke.* **2** [T] to stop sth from happening, developing or continuing: *Her strict education had stifled her natural creativity.* ○ *to stifle a yawn* —**stifling** /'staɪflɪŋ/ adj: *The heat was stifling.*

stigma /'stɪgmə/ noun [C,U] a bad reputation that sth has because a lot of people have a fixed idea that it is wrong, often unfairly: *There is still a lot of stigma attached to being unemployed.*

☆ **still¹** /stɪl/ adv **1** (used for talking about sth that started at an earlier time) continuing until now or until the time you are talking about: *Do you still live in London?* ○ *It's still raining.* ○ *In 1984 Rob was still a student.* **2** in addition; more: *There are still ten days to go until my holiday.* **3** (used for making a comparative adjective stronger): *It was very cold yesterday, but today it's colder still.* **4** (used for talking about an action or opinion that you do not expect, because sth else makes it surprising) even so: *He had a bad headache but he still went to the disco.*

☆ **still²** /stɪl/ adj, adv **1** without moving: *Stand still! I want to take a photograph!* **2** quiet or calm: *The water was perfectly still.* **3** (used about a drink) not containing gas: *still orange* ☛ Look at **fizzy** and **sparkling**.

still noun [C] a single photograph that is taken from a cinema film

stillness noun [U] the quality of being still: *the stillness of the air on a cold winter's night*

'stillborn adj (used about a baby) dead when it is born

stilt /stɪlt/ noun [C] **1** one of two long pieces of wood, with places to rest your feet on, on which you can walk above the ground: *a pair of stilts* **2** one of a set of poles that support a building above the ground or water

stilted /'stɪltɪd/ adj (used about a way of speaking or writing) unnatural and very formal

stimulant /'stɪmjʊlənt/ noun [C] a drug or medicine that makes you feel more active: *Caffeine is a mild stimulant.*

stimulate /'stɪmjʊleɪt/ verb [T] **1** to make sth active or more active: *Exercise stimulates the blood circulation.* ○ *The government has decided to cut taxes in order to stimulate the*

iː	ɪ	e	æ	ɑː	ɒ	ɔː	ʊ	uː	ʌ
see	sit	ten	hat	arm	got	saw	put	too	cup

economy. **2** to make sb feel interested and excited about sth: *The teaching he gets doesn't really stimulate him.*
stimulating *adj* interesting and exciting: *a stimulating discussion* —**stimulation** /ˌstɪmjʊˈleɪʃn/ *noun* [U]

stimulus /ˈstɪmjʊləs/ *noun* [C,U] (*pl* **stimuli** /-laɪ/) something that causes activity, development or interest: *The Spanish Civil War was a great stimulus for Picasso's art.*

☆ **sting¹** /stɪŋ/ *verb* [I,T] (*pt, pp* **stung** /stʌŋ/) **1** (used about an insect, plant, etc) to make sb/ sth feel a sudden pain by pushing sth sharp into their skin and injecting poison into them: *Ow! I've been stung by a bee! o Be careful. Those plants sting.* **2** to make sb/sth feel a sudden, sharp pain: *Soap stings if it gets in your eyes.* **3** to make sb feel very hurt and upset because of sth you say: *Kate was stung by her father's words.*

☆ **sting²** /stɪŋ/ *noun* [C] **1** the sharp pointed part of some insects and animals that is used for pushing into the skin of a person or another animal and injecting poison **2** the pain that you feel when an animal or insect pushes its sting into you: *a wasp sting on the leg* **3** a sharp pain that feels like a sting: *the sting of soap in your eyes*

stink /stɪŋk/ *verb* [I] (*pt* **stank** /stæŋk/ or **stunk** /stʌŋk/; *pp* **stunk**) (*informal*) **1** to have a very strong and unpleasant smell: *to stink of fish* **2** to seem to be very bad, unpleasant or dishonest: *The whole business stinks of corruption.*

stink *noun* [C] (*informal*) a very unpleasant smell

stint /stɪnt/ *noun* [C] a fixed period of time that you spend doing sth

stipulate /ˈstɪpjʊleɪt/ *verb* [T] (*formal*) to say exactly and officially what must be done: *The law stipulates that all schools must be inspected every three years.* —**stipulation** /ˌstɪpjʊˈleɪʃn/ *noun* [C,U] (*formal*): *One of the stipulations is that all team members must be British nationals.*

☆ **stir** /stɜː(r)/ *verb* (**stirring**; **stirred**) **1** [T] to move a liquid, etc round and round, using a spoon, etc: *She stirred her coffee with a teaspoon.* **2** [I,T] to move or make sb/sth move gently: *The boy stirred in his sleep. o A sudden wind stirred the leaves.* **3** [T] to make sb feel a strong emotion: *The story stirred Carol's imagination. o a stirring speech*
(PHRASAL VERB) **stir sth up** to cause a strong feeling in other people: *The manager accused him of stirring up trouble.*

stir /stɜː(r)/ *noun* **1** [C] the action of stirring: *Give the soup a stir.* **2** [sing] general excitement or shock: *Short skirts caused quite a stir when they first appeared in the 1960s.*

stirrup /ˈstɪrəp/ *noun* [C] one of the two metal objects that you put your feet in when you are riding a horse ☞ picture at **horse**.

☆ **stitch** /stɪtʃ/ *noun* [C] **1** one of the small lines of thread that you can see on a piece of material after it has been sewn ☞ picture at **sew**. **2** one of the small pieces of thread that a doctor uses to sew your skin together if you cut yourself very badly, or after an operation **3** one of the small circles of wool that you put round a needle when you are knitting ☞ picture at **knit**. **4** [usually sing] a sudden pain that you get in the side of your body, eg after you have been running
(IDIOM) **in stitches** (*informal*) laughing so much that you cannot stop

stitch *verb* [I,T] to sew: *This handle of this bag needs stitching.*

☆ **stock¹** /stɒk/ *noun* **1** [C,U] the supply of things that a shop, etc has for sale: *The new shop has a large stock of records, tapes and CDs. o We'll have to order extra stock if we sell a lot more this week.* **2** [C] a supply or store of sth that is ready to be used: *Food stocks in the village were very low.* **3** [C,U] a share in the capital of a company; money that you lend to a company: *to invest in stocks and shares* **4** [C,U] a liquid that you use to make soups, sauces, etc. It is made by boiling meat, bones, vegetables, etc in water.
(IDIOMS) **in/out of stock** in/not in the supply of things that a shop, etc has for sale
take stock (of sth) to think about sth very carefully before deciding what to do next: *Let's see how things go for a week or so and then take stock of the situation.*

stock *adj* (only *before* a noun) (used for describing sth that sb says) used so often that it does not have much meaning: *the usual stock answers*

ˈ**stockbroker** (*also* **broker**) *noun* [C] a person whose job it is to buy and sell stocks(3) and shares(2) for other people

ˈ**stock exchange** *noun* [C] **1** a place where stocks(3) and shares(2) are bought and sold: *the London Stock Exchange* **2** (*also* ˈ**stock market**) the business or activity of buying and selling stocks and shares

ˈ**stocktaking** *noun* [U] the activity of counting the total supply of things that a shop or business has at a particular time

stock² /stɒk/ *verb* [T] **1** (usually used about a shop) to have a supply of sth: *They stock food from all over the world.* **2** to provide sth with a supply of sth: *a well stocked bookshop*
(PHRASAL VERB) **stock up (on/with sth)** to collect a large supply of sth for future use: *to stock up with food for the winter*

stockist *noun* [C] a shop that sells goods made by a particular company

stocking /ˈstɒkɪŋ/ *noun* [C] one of a pair of thin pieces of clothing that fit tightly over a woman's foot and leg: *a pair of stockings* ☞ Look at **tights**.

stocky /ˈstɒki/ *adj* (used about a person's body) short but strong and heavy

stoic /ˈstəʊɪk/ (*also* **stoical** /-kl/) *adj* (*formal*) suffering pain or difficulty without complaining —**stoically** /-kli/ *adv* —**stoicism** /ˈstəʊɪsɪzəm/ *noun* [U]

stole *pt* of **STEAL**

stolen *pp* of **STEAL**

stolid /ˈstɒlɪd/ *adj* (used about a person) showing very little emotion or excitement

☆ **stomach** /ˈstʌmək/ (*also informal* **tummy**) *noun* [C] **1** the part of your body where food is

ɜː	ə	eɪ	əʊ	aɪ	aʊ	ɔɪ	ɪə	eə	ʊə
fur	ago	pay	home	five	now	join	near	hair	pure

digested after you have eaten it **2** the front part of your body below your chest and above your legs: *a fat stomach* ○ *She turned over onto her stomach.* ☛ picture on page A8.

stomach *verb* [T] (*informal*) (usually in negative sentences and questions) to be able to watch, listen to, accept, etc sth that you think is unpleasant: *I can't stomach too much violence in films.*

'stomach-ache *noun* [C,U] a pain in your stomach: *I've got terrible stomach-ache.* ☛ Look at the note at **ache**.

stomp /stɒmp/ *verb* [I] (*informal*) to walk with heavy steps

☆ **stone** /stəʊn/ *noun* **1** [U] a hard solid substance that is found in the ground: *The house was built of grey stone.* ○ *a stone wall* **2** [C] a small piece of rock: *The boy picked up a stone and threw it into the river.* **3** [C] = PRECIOUS STONE **4** [C] the hard seed inside some fruits, eg peaches, plums, cherries and olives **5** [C] (*pl* **stone**) a measure of weight; 6·35 kilograms. There are 14 pounds in a stone.

stone *verb* [T] to throw stones at sb/sth, eg as a punishment: *The two women were stoned to death.*

stoned *adj* (*slang*) under the influence of drugs or very drunk

'stonework *noun* [U] the parts of a building that are made of stone

stony /'stəʊni/ *adj* (**stonier**; **stoniest**) **1** (used about the ground) having a lot of stones in it, or covered with stones **2** not friendly: *There was a stony silence as he walked into the room.*

stood *pt, pp* of STAND¹

stool /stuːl/ *noun* [C] a seat that does not have a back or arms: *a piano stool*

stoop /stuːp/ *verb* [I] to bend your head and shoulders forwards and downwards: *Cathy had to stoop to get through the low doorway.*

(PHRASAL VERB) **stoop to sth/to doing sth** to do sth bad or wrong (that you would normally not do): *I would never stoop to cheating.* —**stoop** *noun* [sing]: *to walk with a stoop*

☆ **stop¹** /stɒp/ *verb* (**stopping**; **stopped**) **1** [I] to finish moving, happening or operating: *He walked along the road for a bit, and then stopped.* ○ *Does this train stop at Oxford?* ○ *I think the rain has stopped.* ○ *Oh no! My watch has stopped.* **2** [T] to make sb/sth finish moving, happening or operating: *I stopped someone in the street to ask the way to the station.* ○ *Can you stop the car, please?* **3** [T] to end or finish an activity: *Stop making that terrible noise!* ○ *We stopped work for half an hour to have a cup of coffee.* ○ *It's stopped raining now.* ☛ If you **stop to do** something, you stop in order to do it: *On the way home I stopped to buy a newspaper.* If you **stop doing** something you do not do it any more: *Stop talking and listen to me!* **4** [T] **stop sb/sth (from) doing sth** to make sb/sth end or finish an activity; prevent sb/sth from doing sth: *Can't you stop the car making that noise?* ○ *Nothing will stop me from loving you.* **5** [T] to prevent money from being paid: *The bank stopped the cheque because there was no money in his account.*

(IDIOMS) **stop at nothing** to do anything to get what you want, even if it is wrong or dangerous

stop short of sth/doing sth to almost do sth, but then decide not to do it at the last minute: *They were very rude but they stopped short of calling her a liar.*

(PHRASAL VERB) **stop off (at/in...)** to stop during a journey to do sth: *We stopped off in Paris to see some friends before coming home.*

stoppage /'stɒpɪdʒ/ *noun* [C] the act of refusing to work because of a disagreement with your employers; a strike

'stopgap *noun* [C] a person or a thing that does a job for a short time until sb/sth can be found

'stopover *noun* [C] a short stop in a journey: *a stopover in Singapore on the way to Australia*

'stopwatch *noun* [C] a watch which can be started and stopped by pressing a button, so that you can measure exactly how long sth takes

☆ **stop²** /stɒp/ *noun* [C] **1** an act of stopping or state of being stopped: *Our first stop will be in Edinburgh.* ○ *The lift came to a stop on the third floor.* **2** the place where a bus, train, etc stops so that people can get on and off: *a bus-stop*

(IDIOM) **put a stop to sth** to prevent sth bad or unpleasant from continuing

stopper /'stɒpə(r)/ *noun* [C] an object that you put into the top of a bottle in order to close it. A stopper can be made of glass, plastic or cork.

☆ **storage** /'stɔːrɪdʒ/ *noun* [U] the keeping of things until they are needed; the place where they are kept: *This room is being used for storage at the moment.* ○ *storage space* ○ *to keep meat in cold storage*

☆ **store** /stɔː(r)/ *noun* **1** [C] a large shop: *Harrods is a large department store.* ○ *a furniture store* ☛ Look at **chain store**. **2** [C] = SHOP(1) **3** [C,U] a supply of sth that you keep for future use; the place where it is kept: *a good store of food for the winter* ○ *We'll have to put our furniture into store while we're in Australia.*

(IDIOMS) **in store (for sb/sth)** going to happen in the future: *There's a surprise in store for you when you get home!*

set... store by sth to think that sth has a particular amount of importance or value: *Nigel sets great store by his mother's opinion.*

store *verb* [T] to keep sth or a supply of sth for future use: *to store information on a computer* ○ *The rice is stored in a large building near the village.*

'storekeeper *noun* [C] (*US*) = SHOPKEEPER

'storeroom *noun* [C] a room where things are kept until they are needed

storey /'stɔːri/ (*US* **story**) *noun* [C] (*pl* **storeys**; *US* **stories**) one floor or level of a building: *The building will be five storeys high.* ○ *a two-storey house* ○ *a multi-storey car park*

stork /stɔːk/ *noun* [C] a large white bird with a long beak, neck and legs. Storks often make their nests on the top of a building.

☆ **storm** /stɔːm/ *noun* [C] very bad weather, with heavy rain, strong winds, etc: *Look at those black clouds. I think there's going to be a storm.* ○ *a thunderstorm, snowstorm, etc* ○ (*figurative*)

p	b	t	d	k	g	tʃ	dʒ	f	v	θ	ð
pen	bad	tea	did	cat	got	chin	June	fall	van	thin	then

The introduction of the new tax caused a storm of protest. ☛ **Storm** is the general word for very bad weather. A very strong wind is a **gale**. A very bad snowstorm is a **blizzard**. A storm with a very strong circular wind is called a **cyclone, hurricane, tornado** or **whirlwind**.

storm *verb* **1** [I,T] to enter or leave somewhere in a very angry and noisy way **2** [T] to attack a building, town, etc suddenly and violently in order to take control of it: *to storm a castle*

stormy *adj* (**stormier; stormiest**) **1** (used for talking about very bad weather, with strong winds, heavy rain, etc): *a stormy night* **2** involving a lot of angry argument and strong feeling: *a stormy debate in Parliament* ○ *a stormy relationship*

☆ **story¹** /ˈstɔːri/ *noun* [C] (*pl* **stories**) **1** a description of people and events that are not real: *He always reads the children a bedtime story.* ○ *a detective, fairy, ghost, love, etc story* ○ *She told us a story about an old woman who lived in a shoe.* **2** a description of true events that happened in the past: *the story of the Russian Revolution* ○ *his life story* **3** an article or report in a newspaper or magazine: *The plane crash was the front-page story in most newspapers.*

story² (*US*) = STOREY

stout /staʊt/ *adj* **1** (used about a person) rather fat **2** strong and thick: *stout walking boots*

stove /stəʊv/ *noun* [C] **1** the top part of a cooker that is fitted with gas or electric rings: *He put a pan of water to boil on the stove.* **2** a type of heater. A stove is a closed metal box in which you burn wood, coal, etc: *a wood-burning stove*

stow /stəʊ/ *verb* [T] **stow sth (away)** to put sth away in a particular place until it is needed

ˈstowaway *noun* [C] a person who hides in a ship or aeroplane so that he/she can travel without paying

straddle /ˈstrædl/ *verb* [T] **1** (used about a person) to sit or stand with your legs on each side of sth: *to straddle a chair* **2** (used about a building, bridge, etc) to be on both sides of sth: *The village straddles the border between the two states.*

straggle /ˈstrægl/ *verb* [I] **1** to grow or cover sth in an untidy or irregular way: *a straggling moustache* **2** to walk, etc more slowly than the rest of the group: *The children straggled along behind their parents.*

straggler /ˈstræglə(r)/ *noun* [C] a person who straggles(2)

straggly /ˈstrægli/ *adj* untidy: *long straggly hair*

☆ **straight¹** /streɪt/ *adj* **1** not bent or curved: *a straight line* ○ *straight hair* (= not curly) ○ *Keep your back straight!* ☛ picture at **hair** and **line**. **2** (not before a noun) in a level or upright position: *That picture isn't straight.* **3** honest, truthful and direct: *Politicians never give straight answers.* ○ *Are you being straight with me?* **4** (*US*) = NEAT(4)

(IDIOMS) **get sth straight** to make sure that you understand sth completely: *Let's get this straight. You're sure that you've never seen this man before?*

keep a straight face to stop yourself from smiling or laughing

put/set the record straight ⇒ RECORD¹

straighten /ˈstreɪtn/ *verb* [I,T] **straighten (sth) (up/out)** to become straight or to make sth straight: *The road straightens out at the bottom of the hill.* ○ *to straighten your tie*

(PHRASAL VERBS) **straighten sth out** to remove the confusion or difficulties from a situation

straighten up to stand up straight and tall

☆ **straight²** /streɪt/ *adv* **1** in a straight line: *Go straight on for about two miles until you come to some traffic lights.* ○ *He was looking straight ahead.* ○ *to sit up straight* (= with a straight back) **2** without stopping; directly: *I took the children straight home after school.* ○ *to walk straight past sb/sth*

(IDIOMS) **go straight** to become honest after being a criminal

right/straight away ⇒ AWAY

straight out in an honest and direct way: *I told Tom straight out that I didn't want to see him any more.*

straightforward /ˌstreɪtˈfɔːwəd/ *adj* **1** easy to do or understand; simple: *straightforward instructions* **2** honest and open: *a straightforward person*

☆ **strain¹** /streɪn/ *noun* **1** [C,U] the condition of being pulled or stretched too tightly: *The rope finally broke under the strain.* ○ (*figurative*) *The war has put a great strain on the country's economy.* **2** [C,U] a state of worry and tension: *to be under a lot of strain at work* ○ *Mum's illness has put a strain on the whole family.* **3** [C] something that makes you feel worried and tense: *I always find exams a terrible strain.* **4** [C,U] an injury to part of your body that is caused by using it too much: *a back strain*

strain² /streɪn/ *verb* **1** [I,T] to make a great effort to do sth: *I had to strain my ears to catch what they were saying.* **2** [T] to injure a part of your body by using it too much: *Don't read in the dark. You'll strain your eyes.* ○ *to strain a muscle* **3** [T] to put a lot of pressure on sth: *Money problems have strained their relationship.* **4** [T] to separate a solid and a liquid by pouring them into a special container with small holes in it: *This tea hasn't been strained* (= it's full of tea-leaves).

strained *adj* **1** not natural or friendly: *Relations between the two countries are strained.* **2** worried and tense: *Martin looked tired and strained.*

strait /streɪt/ *noun* [C, usually pl] a narrow piece of sea that joins two larger seas: *the straits of Gibraltar*

strait-jacket /ˈstreɪtdʒækɪt/ *noun* [C] a type of strong jacket that is used to stop mental patients, etc from moving their arms, so that they cannot hurt themselves or other people

strand /strænd/ *noun* [C] **1** a single piece of cotton, wool, hair, etc **2** one part of a story, situation or idea: *At the end of the film all the different strands of the story are brought together.*

stranded /ˈstrændɪd/ adj left in a place that you cannot get away from, eg because you have no money or transport

☆ **strange** /streɪndʒ/ adj **1** unusual or unexpected: *A very strange thing happened to me on the way home.* ○ *a strange noise* ○ *She usually wears jeans. It's really strange to see her in a skirt.* **2** that you have not seen, visited, met, etc before: *a strange town* ○ *My mother told me not to talk to strange men.* ☛ We do not use **strange** to talk about a person or thing that comes from a different country. Look at **foreign**. —**strangely** adv: *The streets were strangely quiet.* ○ *Tim's behaving very strangely at the moment.* —**strangeness** noun [U]

☆ **stranger** /ˈstreɪndʒə(r)/ noun [C] **1** a person that you do not know: *I had to ask a complete stranger to help me with my suitcase.* ☛ We do not use **stranger** to talk about a person who comes from a different country. Look at **foreigner**. **2** a person who is in a place that he/she does not know: *I'm a stranger to this part of the country.*

strangle /ˈstræŋgl/ verb [T] **1** to kill sb by squeezing his/her neck or throat with your hands, a rope, etc **2** to prevent sth from developing

☆ **strap** /stræp/ noun [C] a long narrow piece of leather, cloth, plastic, etc that you use for carrying sth or for keeping sth in position: *a watch-strap* ○ *a dress with thin shoulder-straps* ☛ picture at **clock**.

strap verb [T] to keep sb/sth in position by using a strap or straps: *The racing driver was securely strapped into the car.*

strategic /strəˈtiːdʒɪk/ (also **strategical**) adj **1** helping you to achieve a plan; giving you an advantage **2** connected with a country's plans to achieve success in a war or in its defence system: *strategic planning* **3** (used about bombs and other weapons) intended to hit places of military or economic importance in an enemy country —**strategically** /-klɪ/ adv: *The island is strategically important.*

strategy /ˈstrætədʒi/ noun (pl **strategies**) **1** [C] a plan that you use in order to achieve sth: *a strategy to reduce inflation* **2** [U] the act of planning how to do or achieve sth: *military strategy*

☆ **straw** /strɔː/ noun **1** [U] the long stems of plants (eg wheat) that are dried and then used for animals to sleep on or for making baskets, mats, etc: *a straw hat* **2** [C] one piece of straw **3** [C] a long plastic or paper tube that you can use for drinking through

(IDIOM) **the last/final straw** an extra problem that is added to a difficult or unpleasant situation, and which makes you think you cannot tolerate the situation any longer

strawberry /ˈstrɔːbəri; US -beri/ noun [C] (pl **strawberries**) a soft red fruit with small yellow seeds in it: *strawberries and cream* ○ *strawberry jam*

stray /streɪ/ verb [I] **1** to go away from the place where you should be for no particular reason: *The sheep had strayed onto the road.* **2** not keeping to the subject you should be thinking about or discussing: *My thoughts strayed for a few moments.*

stray adj (only before a noun) lost from home: *a stray dog*

stray noun [C] an animal that is lost from home

streak /striːk/ noun [C] **1 streak (of sth)** a thin line or mark: *The cat had brown fur with streaks of white in it.* **2** a part of a person's character that sometimes shows in the way he/she behaves: *a selfish streak* **3** a continuous period of good or bad luck in a game of sport: *a winning/losing streak*

streak verb [I] (informal) to run fast

streaked adj **streaked (with sth)** having streaks(1) of sth: *black hair streaked with grey*

☆ **stream** /striːm/ noun [C] **1** a small river **2** the constant movement of a liquid or gas: *a stream of blood* **3** a constant movement of people or things: *a stream of traffic* **4** a large number of things which happen one after another: *a stream of letters, telephone calls, questions, etc* **5** a group of schoolchildren who are in the same class because they have similar abilities

stream verb **1** [I] (used about a liquid, gas or light) to flow in large amounts: *Tears were streaming down his face.* ○ *Sunlight was streaming in through the windows.* **2** [I] (used about people or things) to move somewhere in a continuous flow: *People were streaming out of the station.* **3** [T] (usually passive) to put schoolchildren into groups of similar ability

streamer noun [C] a long piece of coloured paper that you use for decorating a room before a party, etc

streamline /ˈstriːmlaɪn/ verb [T] **1** to give a vehicle, etc a long smooth shape so that it will move easily through air or water **2** to make an organization, process, etc work better by making it simpler and more efficient: *The company has decided to streamline its production processes.*

☆ **street** /striːt/ noun [C] **1** a road in a town, village or city that has shops, houses, etc on one or both sides: *to walk along/down the street* ○ *to cross the street* ○ *I met Karen in the street this morning.* ○ *a narrow street* ○ *a street map* ☛ Look at the note at **road**. **2 Street** (abbr **St**) [sing] (used in names of streets): *64 High Street* ○ *to go shopping in Oxford Street*

(IDIOMS) **the man in the street** ➔ MAN¹

streets ahead (of sb/sth) (informal) much better than sb/sth

(right) up your street (informal) (used about an activity, subject, etc) exactly right for you because you know a lot about it, like it very much, etc

'streetcar noun [C] (US) = TRAM

☆ **strength** /streŋθ/ noun **1** [U] the quality of being physically strong; the amount of this quality that you have: *a woman of great physical strength* ○ *He pulled with all his strength but the rock would not move.* **2** [U] the ability of an object to hold heavy weights or not to break or be damaged easily: *All our suitcases are tested for strength before they leave the factory.* **3** [U] the quality of being powerful: *Germany's economic strength* **4** [U] how strong a feeling or

i:	ɪ	e	æ	ɑ:	ɒ	ɔ:	ʊ	u:	ʌ
see	sit	ten	hat	arm	got	saw	put	too	cup

opinion is: *There is great strength of feeling against nuclear weapons in this country.* **5** [C,U] the good qualities and abilities of a person or thing: *His greatest strength is his ability to communicate with people.* o *the strengths and weaknesses of a plan*
(IDIOMS) **at full strength** (used about a group) having the number of people it needs or usually has
below strength (used about a group) not having the number of people it needs or usually has
on the strength of as a result of information, advice, etc: *She was given the job on the strength of your recommendation.*
strengthen /ˈstreŋθn/ *verb* [I,T] to become stronger or to make sth stronger: *exercises to strengthen your muscles* o *Support for the President seems to be strengthening.*
strenuous /ˈstrenjuəs/ *adj* needing or using a lot of effort or energy: *a strenuous effort to improve her English* —**strenuously** *adv*
☆ **stress** /stres/ *noun* **1** [C,U] a state of worry and tension that is caused by difficulties in your life, having too much work, etc: *He's been under a lot of stress since his wife went into hospital.* o *The doctor told her that she was suffering from stress.* o *the stresses and strains of life in a big city* **2** [U] **stress (on sth)** the special force or emphasis that you give to sth because you think it is important: *There should be more stress on learning foreign languages in schools.* **3** [U] the force or emphasis that you put on a word or part of a word when you say it: *In the word 'dictionary' the stress is on the first syllable, 'dic'.* **4** [C,U] **stress (on sth)** a physical force that may cause sth to bend or break
stress *verb* [T] to give sth special force or emphasis because you think it is important: *The minister stressed the need for a peaceful solution.*
stressful /-fl/ *adj* causing stress(1): *a stressful job*
☆ **stretch¹** /stretʃ/ *verb* **1** [I,T] to pull sth so that it becomes longer or wider; to become longer or wider in this way: *The artist stretched the canvas tightly over the frame.* o *My T-shirt stretched when I washed it.* **2** [I,T] to push out your arms, legs, etc as far as possible: *He got out of bed and stretched before going into the bathroom.* o *She stretched out her arm to take the book.* **3** [I] (used about a piece of land or water, etc) to cover a large area: *The long white beaches stretch for miles along the coast.*
(IDIOMS) **stretch your legs** to go for a walk after sitting down for a long time
stretch a point to agree to sth that you do not normally allow
(PHRASAL VERB) **stretch (yourself) out** to relax by lying down with all your body flat: *to stretch out in front of the fire*
stretch² /stretʃ/ *noun* **1** [C] **stretch (of sth)** an area of land or water: *a beautiful stretch of countryside* **2** [C, usually sing] the act of stretching(2): *Stand up, everybody, and have a good stretch.*
(IDIOM) **at a stretch** without stopping: *six hours at a stretch*

stretcher /ˈstretʃə(r)/ *noun* [C] a piece of cloth supported by two poles that is used for carrying a person who has been injured in an accident, etc
☆ **strict** /strikt/ *adj* **1** not allowing people to break rules or behave badly: *Tom's always very strict with his children.* o *a strict teacher* o *I went to a very strict school.* **2** that must be obeyed completely: *I gave her strict instructions to be home before 9.* **3** exactly correct; precise: *a strict interpretation of the law*
strictly *adv* in a strict way: *Smoking is strictly forbidden.*
(IDIOM) **strictly speaking** to be exactly correct or precise: *Strictly speaking, the tomato is not a vegetable. It's a fruit.*
stride /straɪd/ *verb* [I] (*pt* **strode** /strəʊd/; *pp* **stridden** /ˈstrɪdn/) to walk with long steps, often because you are feeling very confident or determined: *He strode up to the house and knocked on the door.*
stride *noun* [C] a long step
(IDIOMS) **get into your stride** to start to do sth confidently and well after an uncertain beginning
make great strides to make very quick progress
take sth in your stride to deal with a new or difficult situation easily and without worrying
strident /ˈstraɪdnt/ *adj* (used about a voice or a sound) loud and unpleasant
strife /straɪf/ *noun* [U] (*formal*) trouble or fighting between people or groups
☆ **strike¹** /straɪk/ *noun* [C] **1** a period of time when people refuse to go to work, usually because they want more money or better working conditions: *a one-day strike* o *to go on strike for better working conditions* o *The workers have been on strike for two weeks now.* o *to take strike action* **2** a sudden military attack, especially by aircraft
☆ **strike²** /straɪk/ *verb* (*pt, pp* **struck** /strʌk/) **1** [T] to hit: *The stone struck me on my face.* o *to strike sb with your hand* o *The boat struck a rock and began to sink.* ☞ In these three examples it is more common to use the word **hit**: *The stone hit me on my face* but if you are talking about lightning you must use **strike**: *The building had been struck by lightning.* **2** [I,T] to attack sb/sth suddenly: *The enemy aircraft struck just after 2 am.* o *The earthquake struck Armenia in 1988.* **3** [T] **strike sb (as sth)** to give sb a particular impression, often a strong one: *Does anything here strike you as unusual?* **4** [T] (used about a thought or an idea) to come suddenly into sb's mind: *It suddenly struck me that she would be the ideal person for the job.* **5** [T] to produce fire: *to strike a match* **6** [I,T] (used about a clock) to ring a bell so that people know what time it is: *The church clock struck three.* **7** [T] to discover gold, oil, etc **8** [I] to go on strike¹(1): *The workers voted to strike for more money.*
(IDIOMS) **strike a balance (between A and B)** to find a middle way between two extremes
strike a bargain (with sb) to make an agreement with sb
strike a chord (with sb) to say or do sth that

makes other people feel sympathy, excitement, etc

within striking-distance near enough to be reached or attacked easily

(PHRASAL VERBS) **strike back** to attack sb/sth that has attacked you: *The President threatened to strike back if the army attacked the capital.*

strike up sth (with sb) to start a conversation or friendship with sb

striker /ˈstraɪkə(r)/ *noun* [C] **1** a person who is on strike¹(1) **2** (in football) an attacking player ☛ picture at **football**.

striking /ˈstraɪkɪŋ/ *adj* very noticeable; making a strong impression: *There was a striking similarity between the two men.* —**strikingly** *adv*: *strikingly attractive*

☆ **string¹** /strɪŋ/ *noun* **1** [C,U] the thin cord that you use for tying things, etc; a piece of this: *I need some string to tie round this parcel.* o *a ball of string* o *a balloon on the end of a string* ☛ picture at **knot**. **2** [C] a piece of thin wire, etc on a musical instrument: *A guitar has six strings.* **3 the strings** [plural] the musical instruments in an orchestra, etc that have strings(2) **4** [C] **a string of sth** a line of things that are joined together on the same piece of thread: *a string of beads* **5** [C] **a string of sth** a series of people, things or events that follow one after another: *a string of visitors* o *a string of complaints*

(IDIOMS) **(with) no strings attached; without strings** with no special conditions: *We will send you a free copy of the magazine, with no strings attached.*

pull strings ⇨ PULL¹

string² /strɪŋ/ *verb* [T] (*pt, pp* **strung** /strʌŋ/) **string sth (up)** to hang up a line of things with a piece of string, etc: *Coloured lights were strung up along the front of the hotel.*

(PHRASAL VERBS) **string sb/sth out** to make people or things form a line with spaces between each person or thing

string sth together to put words or phrases together to make a sentence, speech, etc

stringent /ˈstrɪndʒənt/ *adj* (used about a law, rule, etc) very severe and strict

☆ **strip** /strɪp/ *noun* [C] a long narrow piece of sth: *a strip of paper* o *a strip of water*

strip *verb* (**stripp**ing; **stripp**ed) **1** [I,T] **strip (sth) (off)** to take off your clothes; to take off sb else's clothes: *The doctor asked him to strip.* o *I was stripped and searched at the airport by two customs officers.* **2** [T] **strip sb/sth (of sth)** to take sth away from sb/sth: *They stripped the house of all its furniture.* o *The President has been stripped of most of her power.* **3** [T] **strip sth (off)** to remove sth that is covering a surface: *to strip the paint off a door*

stripper *noun* [C] a person whose job is to take off his/her clothes in order to entertain people

ˈstrip cartoon *noun* [C] (*Brit*) = COMIC STRIP

ˈstriptease *noun* [C,U] entertainment in which sb takes off his/her clothes, usually to music

☆ **stripe** /straɪp/ *noun* [C] a long narrow band of colour: *Zebras have black and white stripes.*

striped /straɪpt/ *adj* having stripes: *a red-and-white striped dress* ☛ picture at **pattern**.

strive /straɪv/ *verb* [I] (*pt* **strove** /strəʊv/; **striven** /ˈstrɪvn/) (*formal*) **strive (for sth)** to try very hard to do or get sth: *The company always strives to satisfy its customers.*

strode *pt* of STRIDE

stroke¹ /strəʊk/ *verb* [T] to move your hand gently over sb/sth: *She stroked his hair affectionately.* o *to stroke a dog*

☆ **stroke²** /strəʊk/ *noun* **1** [C] one of the movements that you make when you are writing or painting: *a brush stroke* **2** [C] one of the movements that you make when you are swimming, rowing, playing tennis, etc: *a forehand stroke* (= in tennis) **3** [C,U] one of the styles of swimming: *backstroke* ☛ Look at **crawl**. **4** [C] a sudden illness which attacks the brain and can leave a person unable to move part of their body, speak clearly, etc: *to have a stroke* **5** [sing] **a stroke of sth** something that happens unexpectedly: *a stroke of luck*

(IDIOMS) **at a/one stroke** with a single action: *You can't change people's opinions at a stroke.*

not do a stroke (of work) not do any work at all

stroll /strəʊl/ *noun* [C] a slow walk for pleasure: *to go for a stroll along the beach* —**stroll** *verb* [I]

☆ **strong** /strɒŋ/; *US* strɔːŋ/ *adj* **1** (used about a person) physically powerful; able to lift or carry heavy things: *I need someone strong to help me move this bookcase.* o *to have strong arms, muscles, etc* **2** (used about an object) able to hold heavy weights; not easily broken or damaged: *That chair isn't strong enough for you to stand on.* o *a pair of strong walking boots* **3** intense; felt deeply: *There was strong opposition to the idea.* o *strong support for the government's plan* o *He has strong views on the subject* (= he will not change them easily). o *strong feelings* **4** powerful and likely to succeed: *She's a strong candidate for the job.* **5** (used about a smell, taste, etc) powerful and intense: *a strong smell of garlic* o *strong tea* o *a strong drink* (= with a lot of alcohol in it) **6** powerful and moving quickly: *strong winds* ☛ In 1-6, the related noun is **strength**. **7** (used after a noun) having a particular number of people: *The army was 50 000 strong.*

(IDIOMS) **going strong** (*informal*) continuing, even after a long time: *The company was formed in 1851 and is still going strong.*

sb's strong point something that a person is good at: *Maths is not my strong point.*

strongly *adv* very much; to a great degree: *The directors are strongly opposed to the idea.* o *to feel very strongly about sth*

ˌstrong-ˈminded *adj* having firm ideas or beliefs

stroppy /ˈstrɒpi/ *adj* (**stroppier**; **stroppiest**) (*Brit slang*) (used about a person) bad-tempered; not helpful

strove *pt* of STRIVE

struck *pt, pp* of STRIKE

☆ **structure** /ˈstrʌktʃə(r)/ *noun* **1** [C,U] the way that the parts of sth are put together or organized: *the structure of the brain* o *the political and social structure of a country* **2** [C] a building or sth that has been built or made from a

p	b	t	d	k	g	tʃ	dʒ	f	v	θ	ð
pen	bad	tea	did	cat	got	chin	June	fall	van	thin	then

number of parts: *The old office had been replaced by a modern glass structure.*

structure *verb* [T] to arrange sth in an organized way: *a carefully structured English course* —**structural** /'strʌktʃərəl/ *adj*: *Several windows were broken in the explosion but there was no structural damage* (= no damage to the walls, floors, etc).

☆ **struggle** /'strʌgl/ *verb* [I] **1** to try very hard to do sth although it is difficult: *We struggled along the road with our heavy suitcases.* ○ *Maria was struggling with her English homework.* **2** to make violent movements when you are trying to escape from sb/sth: *He shouted and struggled but he couldn't get free.*

(PHRASAL VERB) **struggle on** to continue to do sth although it is difficult: *I felt terrible but managed to struggle on to the end of the day.*

struggle *noun* [C] **1** a fight: *All countries should join together in the struggle against terrorism.* **2** [usually sing] a great effort: *After a long struggle she finally managed to complete the course.*

strum /strʌm/ *verb* [I,T] (**strumm**ing; strumm**ed**) to play a guitar by moving your hand up and down over the strings

strung *pt, pp* of STRING²

strut /strʌt/ *verb* [I] (**strutt**ing; strutt**ed**) to walk in a proud way

stub /stʌb/ *noun* [C] a short piece of a cigarette or pencil that remains after the rest of it has been used

stubble /'stʌbl/ *noun* [U] **1** the short stems that are left in a field after corn, wheat, etc has been cut **2** the short hairs that grow on a man's face when he has not shaved for some time

stubborn /'stʌbən/ *adj* not wanting to do what other people want you to do; refusing to change your plans or decisions: *She's too stubborn to apologize.* ○ *a stubborn refusal* —**stubbornly** *adv* —**stubbornness** *noun* [U]

stuck¹ *pt, pp* of STICK²

stuck² /stʌk/ *adj* **1** not able to move: *This drawer's stuck. I can't open it at all.* **2** not able to continue with an exercise, etc because it is too difficult: *If you get stuck, ask your teacher for help.*

stud¹ /stʌd/ *noun* [C] **1** a small round earring that you wear through a hole in your ear **2** a small round piece of metal on the surface of sth: *a black leather jacket with studs all over it* ○ *the studs on the bottom of football boots*

studded *adj* **studded with sth** covered or decorated with studs or other small objects: *The crown is studded with diamonds.*

stud² /stʌd/ *noun* **1** [C,U] a number of horses or other animals that are kept for breeding young animals (of high quality): *to keep a stallion at stud* (= available for breeding) **2** (*also* **'stud-farm**) [C] a place where such horses are kept

☆ **student** /'stju:dnt; *US* 'stu:-/ *noun* [C] a person who is studying at a college or university: *Julia is a medical student at Bristol university.* ○ *a full-time/part-time student* ○ *a student teacher* (= a person who is learning to be a teacher) ☛ Look at **graduate** and **undergraduate**.

studied /'stʌdid/ *adj* (*formal*) carefully planned or done, especially when you are trying to give a particular impression

☆ **studio** /'stju:diəʊ; *US* 'stu:-/ *noun* [C] (*pl* **studios**) **1** a room where an artist or photographer works **2** a room or building where radio or television programmes are made **3** a room or building where cinema films or records are made: *a recording studio*

studious /'stju:diəs; *US* 'stu:-/ *adj* (used about a person) spending a lot of time studying

studiously *adv* with great care: *It was a question that I had studiously avoided.*

☆ **study¹** /'stʌdi/ *noun* (*pl* **studies**) **1** [U] the act of learning about sth: *One hour every afternoon is left free for quiet study.* **2** [plural] the subjects that you study: *the School of Oriental and African Studies at London University* **3** [C] scientific research into a particular subject and a book or article that a person writes after studying it: *a scientific study of the causes of heart disease in Britain* **4** [C] a room in a house where you go to read, write or study

☆ **study²** /'stʌdi/ *verb* (*pres part* **studying**; *3rd pers sing pres* **studies**; *pt, pp* **studied**) **1** [I,T] to spend time learning about sth: *Leslie has been studying hard for his exams.* ○ *to study French at university* **2** [T] to look at sth very carefully: *to study a map*

☆ **stuff¹** /stʌf/ *noun* [U] (*informal*) a substance, thing or group of things (used instead of the name of the thing that you are talking about): *What's that green stuff at the bottom of the bottle?* ○ *I bought some computer paper but when I got it home I found it was the wrong stuff.* ○ *The shop was burgled and a lot of stuff was stolen.* ○ *The hotel was great – there was a swimming pool and a games room and stuff.*

stuff² /stʌf/ *verb* **1** [T] **stuff sth (with sth)** to fill sth with sth: *The pillow was stuffed with feathers.* **2** [T] **stuff sth into sth** (*informal*) to put sth into sth quickly or carelessly: *He quickly stuffed a few clothes into a suitcase.* **3** [I,T] **stuff (yourself) (with sth)** to eat a lot: *The children have been stuffing themselves with sweets and chocolate all afternoon.* **4** [T] **stuff sth (with sth)** to put a mixture of small pieces of food (**stuffing**) into a chicken, vegetable, etc before you cook it: *stuffed vine leaves* **5** [T] to fill the body of a dead bird or animal with special material so that it continues to look as if it is alive

(IDIOM) **get stuffed** (*slang*) (a rude expression used when you are angry with sb): *He offered to drive me home but I told him to get stuffed.*

stuffing *noun* [U] **1** a mixture of small pieces of food that you put inside a chicken, vegetable, etc before you cook it **2** the material that you put inside cushions, soft toys, etc

stuffy /'stʌfi/ *adj* (**stuffier**; **stuffiest**) **1** (used of a room, etc) having air that is not fresh **2** (*informal*) (used of a person, of behaviour, etc) formal and old-fashioned

stumble /'stʌmbl/ *verb* [I] **1** to hit your foot against sth when you are walking or running and almost fall over: *I stumbled as I was getting out of the boat.* **2** to make a mistake when you are speaking, playing music, etc: *The news-*

ʃ	z	ʃ	ʒ	h	m	n	ŋ	l	r	j	w
so	zoo	she	vision	how	man	no	sing	leg	red	yes	wet

reader stumbled over the name of the Russian tennis player.
(PHRASAL VERB) **stumble across/on sb/sth** to meet or find sb/sth by chance

'stumbling-block noun [C] something that causes trouble or a difficulty, so that you cannot get what you want

stump¹ /stʌmp/ noun [C] the part that is left after sth has been cut down, broken off, etc: *a tree stump*

stump² /stʌmp/ verb **1** [I] to walk with slow heavy steps **2** [T] (*informal*) to cause sb to be unable to answer a question or find a solution for a problem: *I was completely stumped by question 14.*

stun /stʌn/ verb [T] (**stun**ning; **stun**ned) **1** to make a person or animal unconscious or confused by hitting him/her/it on the head **2** to make a person very surprised by giving him/her some unexpected news: *His sudden death stunned his friends and colleagues.* —**stunned** *adj*: *There was a stunned silence after Margaret announced her resignation.*

stunning *adj* (*informal*) very attractive or impressive: *a stunning woman ○ a stunning new novel by the author of...*

stung *pt, pp* OF STING¹

stunk *pp* OF STINK

stunt¹ /stʌnt/ noun [C] **1** something that you do to get people's attention: *a publicity stunt* **2** a very difficult or dangerous thing that sb does to entertain people: *His latest stunt was walking on a tightrope over Niagara Falls.*

'stunt man, 'stunt woman noun [C] a person who does a stunt(2) in a film in the place of an actor or actress

stunt² /stʌnt/ verb [T] to stop sb/sth growing or developing properly: *A poor diet can stunt a child's growth.*

stupendous /stjuːˈpendəs/; *US* stuː-/ *adj* very large, grand or impressive: *a stupendous achievement*

☆ **stupid** /ˈstjuːpɪd/; *US* ˈstuː-/ *adj* **1** not clever or intelligent; foolish: *Don't be so stupid, of course I'll help you! ○ It was stupid of her to trust him. ○ He was stupid to trust her.* **2** (only before a noun) (*informal*) a word that shows that you do not like sb/sth: *I'm tired of hearing about his stupid car.* —**stupidity** /stjuːˈpɪdəti/; *US* stuː-/ noun [U] —**stupidly** *adv*

stupor /ˈstjuːpə(r)/; *US* ˈstuː-/ noun [sing,U] the state of being nearly unconscious or being unable to think properly: *a drunken stupor*

sturdy /ˈstɜːdi/ *adj* (**sturdier**; **sturdiest**) strong and healthy; that will not break easily: *a sturdy child ○ sturdy shoes* —**sturdily** *adv*
sturdiness noun [U]

stutter /ˈstʌtə(r)/ verb [I,T] to have difficulty when you speak, so that you keep repeating the first sound of a word —**stutter** noun [C]: *to have a stutter*

sty (*also* **stye**) /staɪ/ noun [C] (*pl* **sties** or **styes**) **1** a large and painful spot on the eyelid **2** = PIGSTY

☆ **style** /staɪl/ noun **1** [C,U] the way that sth is done, built, etc: *a new style of architecture ○ a cathedral in Gothic style ○ The Japanese adopted an American-style education system.* **2** [C,U] the way that sb usually writes, behaves, etc: *Chekhov's style is very clear and simple. ○ I'm afraid going to nightclubs isn't my style.* **3** [U] the state of being of very good quality in appearance or behaviour: *a dress with style ○ They don't have many parties but when they do, they do it in style.* **4** [C,U] the fashion, shape or design of sth: *We stock all the latest styles. ○ a hairstyle ○ Swedish-style pine furniture*

stylish *adj* fashionable and attractive

suave /swɑːv/ *adj* (usually used about a man) very polite, charming, and well behaved (sometimes too much so)

subconscious /ˌsʌbˈkɒnʃəs/ (*also* **unconscious**) noun [sing] **the subconscious** the hidden part of your mind that can affect the way that you behave, even though you do not know it exists —**subconscious** *adj*: *the subconscious mind* —**subconsciously** *adv*

subdivide /ˌsʌbdɪˈvaɪd/ verb [I,T] to divide or be divided into smaller parts —**subdivision** /ˌsʌbdɪˈvɪʒn/ noun [C,U]

subdue /səbˈdjuː/; *US* -ˈduː/ verb [T] to defeat or bring sb/sth under control: *to subdue a rebel army ○ She tried hard to subdue her emotions.*

subdued /səbˈdjuːd/; *US* -ˈduːd/ *adj* **1** not very loud or bright: *subdued lighting* **2** (used about a person) sad or quiet

☆ **subject¹** /ˈsʌbdʒɪkt/ noun [C] **1** a person or thing that is being considered, shown or talked about: *the subject of an essay ○ What are your views on this subject? ○ to change the subject* (= start talking about sth else) *○ I've tried several times to bring up the subject of money.* **2** an area of knowledge that you study at school, university, etc: *She's studying three subjects at A-level, English French and German* **3** (*grammar*) the person or thing that performs the action described by the verb in a sentence: *In the sentence 'The cat sat on the mat', 'the cat' is the subject.* **4** a person from a particular country; a citizen: *a British subject*

'subject-matter noun [U] the idea, problem, etc that a book, film, play, etc is about

subject² /səbˈdʒekt/ verb
(PHRASAL VERB) **subject sb/sth to sth** to cause sb/sth to experience sth unpleasant

subject³ /ˈsʌbdʒɪkt/ *adj* (not before a noun) **1** controlled by or having to obey sb/sth: *Everyone is subject to the law.* **2** often experiencing or suffering from sth unpleasant: *The area is subject to regular flooding.* **3** **subject to sth** depending on sth as a condition: *The plan for new housing is still subject to approval by the minister.*

subjective /səbˈdʒektɪv/ *adj* influenced by your own feelings and opinions instead of by facts alone: *I don't agree — but maybe I'm just being subjective.* ☛ The opposite is **objective**.
—**subjectively** *adv*

subjunctive /səbˈdʒʌŋktɪv/ noun [sing] the form of a verb that expresses doubt, possibility, a wish, etc in certain languages —**subjunctive** *adj*

sublime /səˈblaɪm/ *adj* wonderful; having a quality that makes you admire it very much
—**sublimely** *adv*

submarine /ˌsʌbməˈriːn; *US* ˈsʌbməriːn/ *noun* [C] a type of boat that can travel under the water as well as on the surface

submerge /səbˈmɜːdʒ/ *verb* [I,T] to go or make sth go under water: *The whale spouted out a jet of water before submerging.* ○ *The fields were submerged by the floods.*

submerged *adj* under water: *submerged rocks just below the surface*

submission /səbˈmɪʃn/ *noun* **1** [U] the state of accepting sb else's power or control **2** [C,U] the act of sending a plan or statement to an official organization so that it can be discussed; the plan or statement that you send: *The council requires submission of plans for the new buildings by the end of the year.*

submissive /səbˈmɪsɪv/ *adj* willing to obey other people

submit /səbˈmɪt/ *verb* (submitting; submitted) **1** [I] **submit (to sb/sth)** to accept sb/sth's power or control: *After a bitter struggle the rebels were forced to submit.* **2** [T] **submit sth (to sb/sth)** to give or propose sth to sb/sth so that it can be discussed or considered: *Applications must be submitted by 31 March.*

subnormal /ˌsʌbˈnɔːml/ *adj* having a very low level of intelligence: *a school for educationally subnormal children*

subordinate /səˈbɔːdɪnət; *US* -dənət/ *adj* less important than sth else

subordinate *noun* [C] a person who is of lower rank or position

subordinate /səˈbɔːdɪneɪt; *US* -dəneɪt/ *verb* [T] **subordinate sth (to sth)** to treat sth as less important than sth else

su‚bordinate ˈclause *noun* [C] (*grammar*) a phrase with a verb that usually begins with a conjunction and that adds information to the main part of the sentence: *In the sentence 'We left early because it was raining', 'because it was raining' is the subordinate clause.*

subscribe /səbˈskraɪb/ *verb* [I] **1 subscribe (to sth)** to pay for a newspaper or magazine to be sent to you regularly: *Do you subscribe to 'Private Eye'?* **2 subscribe to sth** to agree with an idea, belief, etc: *I don't subscribe to the view that all war is wrong.*

subscriber *noun* [C] **1** a person who pays to receive a newspaper or magazine regularly **2** a person who uses a particular service: *a telephone subscriber* **3** a person who has a particular opinion: *I'm not a subscriber to the view that all war is wrong.*

subscription /səbˈskrɪpʃn/ *noun* [C] an amount of money that you pay to receive a newspaper or magazine regularly or to belong to a particular society or organization

subsequent /ˈsʌbsɪkwənt/ *adj* (only *before* a noun) (*formal*) coming after or later: *I thought that was the end of the matter but subsequent events proved me wrong.*

subsequently *adv* afterwards: *The Queen visited the new museum and subsequently attended a banquet in the Town Hall.*

subservient /səbˈsɜːviənt/ *adj* **1** (*formal*) too ready to obey other people **2** considered to be less important than sb/sth else —**subservience** /-əns/ *noun* [U]

subside /səbˈsaɪd/ *verb* [I] **1** (used about land, a building, etc) to sink down **2** to become less strong: *The storm seems to be subsiding.*

subsidence /səbˈsaɪdns/ *noun* [U] the sinking of land, buildings, etc

subsidiary /səbˈsɪdiəri; *US* -dieri/ *adj* connected to but less important than sth else: *You must study two subsidiary subjects as well as your main subject.*

subsidiary *noun* [C] (*pl* **subsidiaries**) a business company that belongs to a larger and more important company

☆ **subsidy** /ˈsʌbsɪdi/ *noun* [C,U] (*pl* **subsidies**) money that the government, etc pays to help an organization or to help keep the cost of sth low: *The price of bread was kept low by subsidy.*

subsidize (*also* **subsidise**) /ˈsʌbsɪdaɪz/ *verb* [T] (of a government, etc) to pay money in order to keep prices or the cost of a service low: *Public transport should be subsidized.*

subsist /səbˈsɪst/ *verb* [I] (*formal*) to manage to live with very little food or money —**subsistence** /-təns/ *noun* [U]: *to live at subsistence level*

☆ **substance** /ˈsʌbstəns/ *noun* **1** [C] a solid or liquid material: *poisonous substances* ○ *The cloth is coated in a new waterproof substance.* **2** [U] the most important points or ideas of sth: *Don't repeat everything. Just tell me the substance of what they said.* **3** [U] importance, value or truth: *There's little substance to the film but it's very entertaining.*

substandard /ˌsʌbˈstændəd/ *adj* of poor quality; not as good as usual or as it should be

☆ **substantial** /səbˈstænʃl/ *adj* **1** large in amount: *The storms caused substantial damage.* ○ *a substantial sum of money* **2** large or strong: *The furniture was cheap and not very substantial.*

substantially /-ʃəli/ *adv* **1** by a large amount: *House prices have fallen substantially.* **2** generally; in most points: *The landscape of Wales has remained substantially the same for centuries.*

substitute /ˈsʌbstɪtjuːt; *US* -tuːt/ *noun* [C] **substitute (for sb/sth)** a person or thing that takes the place of sb/sth else: *One player was injured so the substitute was sent on to play.*

substitute *verb* **1** [T] **substitute sb/sth (for sb/sth)** to put a person or thing in the place of sb/sth else: *You can substitute margarine for butter.* **2** [I] **substitute (for sb/sth)** to be used instead of sb/sth —**substitution** /ˌsʌbstɪˈtjuːʃn; *US* -ˈtuːʃn/ *noun* [C,U]

subtitle /ˈsʌbtaɪtl/ *noun* [C, usually pl] the words at the bottom of the picture on television or at the cinema. The subtitles translate the words of a foreign film or programme or show the words that are spoken, to help deaf people.

subtle /ˈsʌtl/ *adj* **1** not very noticeable; not very strong or bright: *subtle colours* ○ *I noticed a subtle difference in her.* **2** very clever, eg at deceiving or persuading people: *Advertisements persuade us to buy things in very subtle ways.* —**subtlety** /ˈsʌtlti/ *noun* [C,U] (*pl* **subtleties**) —**subtly** /ˈsʌtli/ *adv*

☆ **subtract** /səbˈtrækt/ *verb* [T] **subtract sth (from sth)** to take one number or quantity

ɜː	ə	eɪ	əʊ	aɪ	aʊ	ɔɪ	ɪə	eə	ʊə
fur	ago	pay	home	five	now	join	near	hair	pure

away from another: *If you subtract five from nine you get four.* —**subtraction** /səb'trækʃn/ *noun* [C,U]

☆ **suburb** /'sʌbɜːb/ *noun* [C] an area where people live that is outside the central part of a town or city: *Most people live in the suburbs and work in the centre of town.* ○ *an industrial suburb* —**suburban** /sə'bɜːbən/ *adj*: *suburban life* ☛ People often think of life in the suburbs as dull, so **suburban** sometimes means 'dull and uninteresting'.

suburbia /sə'bɜːbɪə/ *noun* [U] the suburbs of towns and cities

subversive /səb'vɜːsɪv/ *adj* trying to weaken or destroy a government, religion, etc or to challenge accepted ideas

subversive *noun* [C] a person who is subversive

subvert /sʌb'vɜːt/ *verb* [T] to try to weaken or destroy a government, religion, etc, or to challenge accepted ideas —**subversion** /səb'vɜːʃn; *US* -'vɜːrʒn/ *noun* [U]

subway /'sʌbweɪ/ *noun* [C] **1** a passage under a busy road or railway that is for people who are walking (**pedestrians**) **2** (*US*) = UNDERGROUND

☆ **succeed** /sək'siːd/ *verb* **1** [I] **succeed (in sth/in doing sth)** to manage to achieve what you want; to do well: *Our plan succeeded.* ○ *If you keep on trying you will succeed in the end.* ○ *A good education will help you succeed in life.* ○ *to succeed in passing an exam* ☛ Look at **fail**. **2** [I,T] to have a job or important position after sb else; doing well: *John Major succeeded Margaret Thatcher as Prime Minister in 1990.*

☆ **success** /sək'ses/ *noun* **1** [U] achieving what you want; doing well: *Hard work is the key to success.* ○ *Her attempts to get a job for the summer have not met with much success* (= she hasn't managed to do it). **2** [C] something that achieves what it wants to, or becomes very popular: *You must try to make a success of your marriage.* ○ *The film 'Batman' was a huge success.* ☛ Look at **failure**.

successful /-fl/ *adj* having achieved what was wanted; having become popular: *a successful attempt to climb Mount Everest* ○ *a successful actor* —**successfully** /-fəli/ *adv*

succession /sək'seʃn/ *noun* **1** [C] a number of people or things that follow one after another: *We've had a succession of hot dry summers.* **2** [U] the right to have an important position after sb else: *Prince William is second in succession to the throne.*

(IDIOM) **in succession** following one after another: *There have been three deaths in the family in quick succession.*

☆ **successor** /sək'sesə(r)/ *noun* [C] a person who has a job or important position after sb else ☛ Look at **predecessor**.

succinct /sək'sɪŋkt/ *adj* said clearly, in a few words —**succinctly** *adv*

succulent /'sʌkjʊlənt/ *adj* (used about food) very good to eat because it is not dry

succumb /sə'kʌm/ *verb* [I] **succumb (to sth)** (*formal*) to stop fighting against sth: *He succumbed to temptation and took another cake.* ○ *to succumb to an illness* (= to die)

☆ **such** /sʌtʃ/ *det* **1** (used for referring to sb/sth that you are talking about or that you mentioned earlier) of this or that type: *'Can I speak to Mr Wallis?' 'I'm sorry, there's no such person here.'* ○ *I don't believe in ghosts. There's no such thing.* **2** (used for emphasizing the degree of sth): *It was such a boring film that I fell asleep.* ○ *Let's have lunch in the garden. It's such a lovely day.* ○ *It seems such a long time since we last met.* ☛ You use **such** before a noun or before a noun that has an adjective in front of it: *Tommy is such a darling!* ○ *Susan is such a good athlete.* You use **so** before an adjective that is used without a noun: *Don't be so silly.* ○ *It was so cold we stayed at home.* Compare: *It was such a cold night that we stayed at home.* **3** (used for talking about the result of sth): *The statement was worded in such a way that it did not upset anyone.*

such *pron* (used for referring to sb/sth that you are talking about or that you mentioned earlier) this or that type of person or thing: *The economic situation is such that we all have less money to spend.*

(IDIOMS) **as such 1** in the exact meaning of the word: *I don't believe in God as such, but I do believe in the power of good.* **2** without anything else; alone: *Poverty as such does not mean unhappiness but it can make life very uncomfortable.*

such as for example: *Fatty foods such as chips are bad for you.*

suck /sʌk/ *verb* **1** [I,T] to pull a liquid into your mouth, by making your lips into a round shape and pulling your cheeks in: *to suck milk up through a straw* ☛ picture at **blow**. **2** [T] to pull sth in a particular direction, using force: *Vacuum cleaners suck up the dirt.* **3** [I,T] to have sth in your mouth and keep touching it with your lips and tongue: *All my children sucked their thumbs.*

sucker /'sʌkə(r)/ *noun* [C] **1** (*informal*) a person who believes everything that you tell him/her and who is easy to cheat **2** a part of some plants, animals or insects that is used for helping them stick onto a surface

suction /'sʌkʃn/ *noun* [U] **1** the act of removing air from a space so that another substance is pulled in: *A vacuum cleaner works by suction.* **2** the act of making two surfaces stick together by removing the air between them: *The hook is attached to the wall by a suction pad.*

☆ **sudden** /'sʌdn/ *adj* done or happening quickly, or when you do not expect it: *a sudden decision* ○ *a sudden loud noise*

(IDIOMS) **all of a sudden** suddenly; unexpectedly: *All of a sudden the lights went out.*

sudden death a way of deciding who wins a game where the score is equal by playing one more point or game: *a sudden-death play-off* —**suddenly** *adv*: *Suddenly, everybody started shouting.* —**suddenness** *noun* [U]

suds /sʌdz/ *noun* [plural] the bubbles that you get when you mix soap and water

☆ **sue** /suː; *Brit also* sjuː/ *verb* [I,T] **sue (sb) (for sth)** to go to a court of law and ask for money from sb because he/she has done sth bad to you, or said sth bad about you

p	b	t	d	k	g	tʃ	dʒ	f	v	θ	ð
pen	bad	tea	did	cat	got	chin	June	fall	van	thin	then

suede /sweɪd/ noun [U] a type of soft leather which does not have a smooth surface and feels rather like cloth

suet /'suːɪt; Brit also 'sjuːɪt/ noun [U] a type of hard animal fat that is used in cooking

☆ **suffer** /'sʌfə(r)/ verb 1 [I,T] to experience sth unpleasant, eg pain, sadness, difficulty, etc: *Mary often suffers from severe headaches.* ○ *Our troops suffered heavy losses.* ○ *In a recession it's the poor who suffer most.* 2 [I] to become worse in quality: *If you have problems at home your work will suffer.* —**sufferer** /'sʌfərə(r)/ noun [C]: *cancer sufferers* —**suffering** /'sʌfərɪŋ/ noun [C,U]: *The famine caused great hardship and suffering.*

☆ **sufficient** /sə'fɪʃnt/ adj (formal) as much as is necessary; enough: *We have sufficient oil reserves to last for three months.* ☞ The opposite is **insufficient**. —**sufficiently** adv

suffix /'sʌfɪks/ noun [C] a letter or group of letters that you add at the end of a word, and that change its meaning or the way it is used: *To form the noun from the adjective 'sad', add the suffix 'ness'.* ☞ Look at **prefix**.

suffocate /'sʌfəkeɪt/ verb [I,T] to die because there is no air to breathe; to kill sb in this way —**suffocating** adj: *The heat is suffocating.* —**suffocation** /ˌsʌfə'keɪʃn/ noun [U]

☆ **sugar** /'ʃʊɡə(r)/ noun 1 [U] a sweet substance that you get from certain plants: *Do you take sugar in tea?* 2 [C] one spoonful or lump of sugar (in a cup of tea, coffee, etc): *Two sugars, please.*

sugary /'ʃʊɡəri/ adj very sweet

☆ **suggest** /sə'dʒest; US səg'dʒ-/ verb [T] 1 **suggest sth (to sb)** to propose a plan or idea for sb to discuss or consider: *Can anybody suggest ways of raising more money?* ○ *Tony suggested going out for a walk.* ○ *Tony suggested that we go out for a walk.* ○ *Tony suggested a walk.* ○ *How do you suggest we get out of this mess?* 2 to say that a person or thing is suitable, especially a person or thing that you know more about from your own experience: *Can you suggest someone for the job?* ○ *Ann suggested Egypt as a good place for a winter holiday.* 3 to say or show sth in an indirect way: *Are you suggesting the accident was my fault?* ○ *Forecasts suggest that inflation will fall by the end of next year.*

suggestive /-ɪv/ adj 1 making you think of sth: *music that was suggestive of Asia* 2 making you think about sex: *a suggestive dance* —**suggestively** adv

☆ **suggestion** /sə'dʒestʃən; US səg'dʒ-/ noun 1 [C] a plan or idea that sb proposes or suggests: *May I make a suggestion?* 2 [U] putting an idea into a person's mind; giving advice about what to do: *I came here at my friend's suggestion.* 3 [sing] a small amount or sign of sth: *He spoke with a suggestion of a Scottish accent.*

☆ **suicide** /'suːɪsaɪd; Brit also 'sjuːɪ-/ noun 1 [U] the act of killing yourself: *Ben has tried to commit suicide several times.* 2 [C] an example of this: *There have been nine suicides from this bridge this year.*

suicidal /ˌsuːɪ'saɪdl; Brit also 'sjuːɪ-/ adj 1 (used about a person) wanting to kill himself/herself: *to feel suicidal* 2 that will probably result in your being killed: *a suicidal risk*

☆ **suit**[1] /suːt; Brit also sjuːt/ noun [C] 1 a set of clothes that are made of the same material and that are rather formal. A man's suit usually consists of a jacket and trousers, and a woman's suit of a jacket and skirt. 2 an article of clothing or set of clothes that you wear for a particular activity: *a spacesuit* ○ *a tracksuit* ○ *a suit of armour* 3 one of the four sets of thirteen playing-cards (= hearts, clubs, diamonds and spades) ☞ Look at the note at **card**.
(IDIOM) **follow suit** ⇨ FOLLOW

☆ **suit**[2] /suːt; Brit also sjuːt/ verb 1 [T] to look attractive on sb: *That dress really suits you.* 2 [I,T] to be convenient or suitable for sb/sth: *Would Thursday at 9.30 suit you?* ○ *Living in the country wouldn't suit me at all.*

suited adj **suited (for/to sb/sth)** suitable or right for sb/sth: *She and her husband are very well suited.*

☆ **suitable** /'suːtəbl; Brit also 'sjuːt-/ adj **suitable (for sb/sth)** right or convenient for sb/sth: *The film isn't suitable for children.* ○ *Is this a suitable time to have a word with you?* ☞ The opposite is **unsuitable**. —**suitability** /ˌsuːtə'bɪləti; Brit also 'sjuːt-/ noun [U] —**suitably** /-əbli/ adv: *to be suitably dressed for the party*

☆ **suitcase** /'suːtkeɪs; Brit also 'sjuːt-/ (also **case**) noun [C] a flat box with a handle that you use for carrying your clothes, etc in when you are travelling ☞ picture at **luggage**.

suite /swiːt/ noun [C] 1 a set of two or more pieces of furniture of the same style or covered in the same material: *a three-piece suite* (= a sofa and two armchairs) 2 a set of rooms in a hotel (= a bedroom, sitting-room and bathroom)

suitor /'suːtə(r); Brit also 'sjuː-/ noun [C] (old-fashioned) a man who wants to marry a particular woman

sulfur (US) = SULPHUR

sulk /sʌlk/ verb [I] to be very quiet or bad-tempered because you are angry with sb about sth —**sulky** adj —**sulkily** /-ɪli/ adv

sullen /'sʌlən/ adj looking bad-tempered and not speaking to people: *a sullen face, expression, etc* —**sullenly** adv

sulphur (US **sulfur**) /'sʌlfə(r)/ noun [U] (symbol **S**) a yellow substance with a strong unpleasant smell

sultan (also **Sultan**) /'sʌltən/ noun [C] the ruler in some Muslim countries: *the Sultan of Brunei*

sultana /sʌl'tɑːnə; US -ænə/ noun [C] a dried grape with no seeds in it that is used in cooking ☞ Look at **raisin**.

sultry /'sʌltri/ adj 1 (used about the weather) hot and damp 2 (used about a woman) very sexually attractive

☆ **sum** /sʌm/ noun [C] 1 when children do sums they add or subtract, multiply or divide numbers: *I've got some sums to do for homework.* 2 an amount of money: *The industry has spent huge sums of money modernizing its equipment.* 3 [usually sing] the amount that you get when

s	z	ʃ	ʒ	h	m	n	ŋ	l	r	j	w
so	zoo	she	vision	how	man	no	sing	leg	red	yes	wet

you add two or more numbers together: *The sum of two and five is seven.*
sum *verb* (su**mm**ing; su**mm**ed)
(PHRASAL VERBS) **sum (sth) up** to describe in a few words the main ideas of what sb has said or written: *to sum up the main points of an argument*
sum sb/sth up to form an opinion about sb/sth: *He summed the situation up immediately.*
,**summing-'up** *noun* [C] (*pl* **summings-up**) a speech in which a judge sums up what has been said in a court of law before a decision (**verdict**) is reached

☆ **summary**¹ /'sʌmərɪ/ *noun* [C] (*pl* **summaries**) a short description of the main ideas or events of sth: *A brief summary of the experiment is given at the beginning of the report.* o *a news summary* —**summarize** (*also* **summarise**) /'sʌməraɪz/ *verb: Could you summarize the story so far?*

summary² /'sʌmərɪ/ *adj* (*formal*) done quickly and without taking time to think about whether it is the right thing to do: *summary arrests and executions*

☆ **summer** /'sʌmə(r)/ *noun* [C,U] the second season of the year, after spring and before autumn. Summer is the warmest season of the year: *Are you going away this summer?* o *a summer's day* o *the summer holidays* —**summery** /'sʌmərɪ/ *adj: summery weather* o *a summery dress*

'**summer-house** *noun* [C] a small building in a park or garden where you can sit and relax in good weather

'**summertime** *noun* [U] the season of summer: *It's busy here in the summertime.*

☆ **summit** /'sʌmɪt/ *noun* [C] **1** the top of a mountain **2** an important meeting between the leaders of two or more countries: *the EC summit in Madrid*

summon /'sʌmən/ *verb* [T] **1** (*formal*) to order a person to come to a place: *The boys were summoned to the headmaster's office.* **2 summon sth (up)** to find strength, courage or some other quality that you need even though it is difficult for you to do so: *She couldn't summon up the courage to leave him.*

summons /'sʌmənz/ *noun* [C] (*pl* **summonses**) an order to go somewhere, especially to a court of law

☆ **sun** /sʌn/ *noun* **1 the sun** [sing] the star that shines in the sky during the day and that gives the earth heat and light: *The sun rises in the east and sets in the west.* o *the rays of the sun* **2 the sun** [sing,U] light and heat from the sun: *Don't sit in the sun too long.* o *Too much sun can be harmful.*
(IDIOM) **catch the sun** ⇨ CATCH¹
sun *verb* [T] (su**nn**ing; su**nn**ed) **sun yourself** sit or lie in the sun(2) in order to enjoy the heat
sunny *adj* (**sunnier**; **sunniest**) having a lot of light from the sun: *a sunny garden* o *a sunny day*

'**sunbathe** *verb* [I] to take off most of your clothes and sit or lie in the sun in order to make your skin go brown

'**sunbeam** *noun* [C] a line (**ray**) of sunlight
'**sunburn** *noun* [U] red painful skin which you get after sitting or lying too long in strong sunlight

'**sunburned**, '**sunburnt** *adj* suffering from sunburn

sundial /'sʌndaɪəl/ *noun* [C] a piece of equipment that uses shadow to show what the time is

'**sunflower** *noun* [C] a tall plant that has a very large yellow flower with a black centre. The seeds of the plant are used to make cooking oil and margarine.

'**sun-glasses** (*also* ,**dark 'glasses**) (*also informal* **shades**) *noun* [plural] glasses that have dark glass in them to protect your eyes from bright sunlight

'**sunlight** *noun* [U] the light from the sun
'**sunlit** *adj* having bright light from the sun: *a sunlit terrace*

'**sunrise** *noun* [U] the time when the sun comes up and the day begins: *to get up at sunrise* ☛ Look at **dawn**.

'**sunset** *noun* [C,U] the time when the sun goes down and night begins: *The park closes at sunset.* o *a beautiful sunset*

'**sunshine** *noun* [U] heat and light from the sun: *warm spring sunshine*

'**sunstroke** *noun* [U] an illness that is caused by spending too much time in strong sunlight

'**suntan** (*also* **tan**) *noun* [C] when you have a suntan, your skin is brown because you have spent time in the sun: *to have a suntan* o *suntan oil*

'**suntanned** *adj: suntanned bodies on the beaches*

sundae /'sʌndeɪ; *US* -di:/ *noun* [C] a type of food that consists of ice-cream with fruit, nuts, etc on the top

☆ **Sunday** /'sʌndɪ/ *noun* [C,U] (*abbr* **Sun**) the first day of the week, coming before Monday ☛ For examples of the use of the days of the week in sentences, look at **Monday**.

sundry /'sʌndrɪ/ *adj* (only *before* a noun) of various kinds: *a shop selling toys, games and sundry gift items*
(IDIOM) **all and sundry** (*informal*) everyone

sung *pp* of SING
sunk *pp* of SINK¹

sunken /'sʌŋkən/ *adj* **1** below the water: *a sunken ship* **2** (used about cheeks or eyes) curving inwards and making you look ill **3** at a lower level than the surrounding area: *a luxury bathroom with a sunken bath*

☆ **super** /'su:pə(r); *Brit also* 'sju:-/ *adj* (*informal*) **1** very good; wonderful: *We had a super time.* o *You've done a super job.* **2** bigger or better than other things which are similar: *a new super computer*

superb /su:'pɜ:b; *Brit also* sju:-/ *adj* very good, excellent —**superbly** *adv*

supercilious /,su:pə'sɪlɪəs; *Brit also* ,sju:-/ *adj* showing that you think that you are better than other people: *a supercilious smile* —**superciliously** *adv*

superficial /,su:pə'fɪʃl; *Brit also* ,sju:-/ *adj* **1** (used about people) not caring about serious or important things: *He's a very superficial sort of person.* **2** only on the surface, not deep: *Don't worry. It's only a superficial wound.* **3** not deep,

i:	ɪ	e	æ	ɑ:	ɒ	ɔ:	ʊ	u:	ʌ
see	sit	ten	hat	arm	got	saw	put	too	cup

complete or thorough: *a superficial knowledge of the subject* —**superficiality** /ˌsuːpəˌfɪʃɪˈælətɪ; *Brit also* ˌsjuː-/ *noun* [U] —**superficially** /-ʃəlɪ/ *adv*

superfluous /suːˈpɜːfluəs; *Brit also* sjuː-/ *adj* more than is wanted; not needed: *Any further explanation is superfluous.*

superhuman /ˌsuːpəˈhjuːmən; *Brit also* ˌsjuː-/ *adj* greater than is usual for human beings: *superhuman strength*

superimpose /ˌsuːpərɪmˈpəʊz; *Brit also* ˌsjuː-/ *verb* [T] **superimpose sth (on sth)** to put sth on top of sth else so that what is underneath can still be seen

superintendent /ˌsuːpərɪnˈtendənt; *Brit also* ˌsjuː-/ *noun* [C] **1** a police officer of high rank: *Detective Superintendent Ron Marsh* **2** a person who looks after a building, etc

☆ **superior** /suːˈpɪərɪə(r); *Brit also* sjuː-/ *adj* **1** better than usual or than sb/sth else: *He is clearly superior to all the other candidates.* ☛ The opposite is **inferior**. **2** higher in rank: *a superior officer* **3** thinking that you are better than other people: *There's no need to be so superior.*

superior *noun* [C] a person of higher rank or position —**superiority** /suːˌpɪərɪˈɒrətɪ; *Brit also* sjuː-/ *noun* [U]: *the superiority of the new method*

superlative /suːˈpɜːlətɪv; *Brit also* sjuː-/ *noun* [C] the form of an adjective or adverb that expresses its highest degree: *'Most beautiful', 'best' and 'fastest' are all superlatives.*

☆ **supermarket** /ˈsuːpəmɑːkɪt; *Brit also* ˈsjuː-/ *noun* [C] a large shop that sells food, drink, things for cleaning your house, etc. You choose what you want from the shelves in a supermarket and pay for everything when you leave.

supernatural /ˌsuːpəˈnætʃrəl; *Brit also* ˌsjuː-/ *adj* that cannot be explained by the laws of science: *a creature with supernatural powers*

the supernatural *noun* [sing] things that are supernatural: *I don't believe in the supernatural.*

supersede /ˌsuːpəˈsiːd; *Brit also* ˌsjuː-/ *verb* [T] to take the place of sb/sth which was present or used before and which has become old-fashioned: *Records have been almost completely superseded by CDs and cassettes.*

supersonic /ˌsuːpəˈsɒnɪk; *Brit also* ˌsjuː-/ *adj* faster than the speed of sound

superstar /ˈsuːpəstɑː(r); *Brit also* ˈsjuː-/ *noun* [C] (*informal*) a singer, film star, etc who is very famous and popular

superstition /ˌsuːpəˈstɪʃn; *Brit also* ˌsjuː-/ *noun* [C,U] a belief that cannot be explained by reason or science: *the superstition that black cats are lucky* —**superstitious** /-ˈstɪʃəs/ *adj*: *I never do anything important on Friday the 13th – I'm superstitious.*

superstore /ˈsuːpəstɔː(r); *Brit also* ˈsjuː-/ *noun* [C] a very large shop that sells food or a wide variety of one type of goods: *a giant superstore on the edge of town*

☆ **supervise** /ˈsuːpəvaɪz; *Brit also* ˈsjuː-/ *verb* [I,T] to watch sb/sth to make sure that work, etc is being done properly and that people are behaving correctly: *Your job is to supervise the building work.* —**supervision** /ˌsuːpəˈvɪʒn; *Brit also* ˌsjuː-/ *noun* [U]: *Children should not play here without supervision.*

supervisor *noun* [C] a person who supervises

☆ **supper** /ˈsʌpə(r)/ *noun* [C,U] the last meal of the day, either a cooked meal in the evening or a small meal that you eat quite late, not long before you go to bed ☛ Look at the note at **dinner**.

supple /ˈsʌpl/ *adj* that bends or moves easily; not stiff —**suppleness** *noun* [U]

supplement /ˈsʌplɪmənt/ *noun* [C] **a supplement (to sth)** something that is added to sth else: *There is a £10 supplement for a single room.* ⚬ *a Sunday newspaper with a colour supplement* (= a free magazine with colour pictures)

supplement /ˈsʌplɪmənt/ *verb* [T] **supplement sth (with sth)** to add sth to sth else: *to supplement your diet with vitamins*

supplementary /ˌsʌplɪˈmentrɪ; *US* -terɪ/ *adj* added to sth else; extra: *supplementary exercises at the back of the book*

☆ **supply** /səˈplaɪ/ *verb* [T] (*pres part* **supplying**; *3rd pers sing pres* **supplies**; *pt, pp* **supplied**) **supply sth (to sb); supply sb (with sth)** to give or provide sth: *The farmer supplies eggs to the surrounding villages.* ⚬ *He supplies the surrounding villages with eggs.*

supplier /səˈplaɪə(r)/ *noun* [C] a person or company that supplies sth

supply *noun* (*pl* **supplies**) **1** [C] something that is supplied: *The water supply was contaminated.* **2** [C,U] a store or amount of sth: *Supplies of food were dropped by helicopter.* ⚬ *In many parts of the country water is in short supply* (= there is not much of it).

☆ **support** /səˈpɔːt/ *verb* [T] **1** to carry the weight of sb/sth: *Large columns support the roof.* **2** to agree with the aims of sb/sth and to give him/her/it help, money, etc: *I'll support you as much as I can.* ⚬ *Which political party do you support?* **3** to have a particular sports team as your favourite: *Which football team do you support?* **4** to show that sth is true or correct: *What evidence do you have to support what you say?* **5** to give or provide sb with the money he/she needs for food, clothes, etc: *Jim has to support two children from his previous marriage.*

support *noun* **1** [U] **support (for sth)** help that you give to a person or thing (often sth that is encouraging in a difficult situation): *public support for the campaign* ⚬ *The theatre closed because of lack of support.* ⚬ *Thank you for your support at this difficult time.* **2** [C,U] something that carries the weight of sb/sth: *a roof support* **3** [U] money to buy food, clothes, etc: *She has no job, no home and no means of support.*

(IDIOM) **in support of sb/sth** supporting or agreeing with sb/sth: *Steve spoke in support of the proposal.*

supporter *noun* [C] a person who supports a political party, sports team, etc: *football supporters*

supportive /səˈpɔːtɪv/ *adj* giving help or sympathy

☆ **suppose** /səˈpəʊz/ *verb* [T] **1** to think, believe

ɜː	ə	eɪ	əʊ	aɪ	aʊ	ɔɪ	ɪə	eə	ʊə
fur	ago	pay	home	five	now	join	near	hair	pure

supposition

or consider that sth is probable: *I suppose he seems unfriendly because he is shy.* ○ *What do you suppose could have happened?* ○ *I don't suppose that they're coming now.* **2** to pretend that sth will happen or is true: *Suppose you won a million pounds. What would you do?*
(IDIOMS) **I suppose 1** (used to show that you are not certain about sth): *I suppose it's all right, but I'm not sure.* ○ *It's about ten years old, I suppose.* **2** (used when you agree with sth, but are not very happy about it): *'Can we give Andy a lift?' 'Yes, I suppose so, if we must.'*

be supposed to do sth 1 to be expected to do sth or to have to do sth: *The train was supposed to arrive ten minutes ago.* ○ *This is secret and I'm not supposed to talk about it.* **2** (*informal*) to be considered or thought to be sth: *I haven't seen it, but it's supposed to be a good play.* ○ *This is supposed to be the oldest pub in London.*

supposedly /səˈpəʊzɪdli/ *adv* as people believe or suppose: *Supposedly, this is the place where St George fought the dragon.*

supposing *conj* if sth happens or is true: *Supposing the plan goes wrong, what will we do then?*

supposition /ˌsʌpəˈzɪʃn/ *noun* [C,U] an idea that a person thinks is true but which has not been proved

suppress /səˈpres/ *verb* [T] **1** to stop sth by using force: *The army suppressed the rebellion.* **2** to stop sth from being seen or known: *to suppress the truth* **3** to stop yourself from expressing your feelings, etc: *to suppress a yawn* ○ *suppressed anger* —**suppression** /səˈpreʃn/ *noun* [U]

☆ **supreme** /suːˈpriːm; *Brit also* sjuː-/ *adj* **1** highest in rank or position: *a supreme ruler* **2** greatest or most important: *a moment of supreme joy*

supremacy /suːˈpreməsi; *Brit also* sjuː-/ *noun* [U] **supremacy (over sb/sth)** the state of being most powerful: *the military supremacy of the United States*

supremely /suːˈpriːmli; *Brit also* sjuː-/ *adv* very: *to be supremely happy*

surcharge /ˈsɜːtʃɑːdʒ/ *noun* [C] an extra amount of money that you have to pay for sth: *a surcharge for excess baggage*

☆ **sure** /ʃɔː(r); *US* ʃʊər/ *adj* **1** (not before a noun) having no doubt about sth; certain: *You must be sure of your facts before you make an accusation.* ○ *I'm not sure what to do next.* ○ *Craig was sure that he'd made the right decision.* ○ *I think I had my bag when I got off the bus but I'm not sure.* ☛ **Sure** and **certain** are very similar in meaning. **Sure**, however, cannot be used in the phrase 'It is ... that ...' **Certain** can: *It is certain that there will be an election next year.* With **sure** we must say: *There is sure to be an election next year.* **2** (not before a noun) **sure of sth** certain to get sth: *If you go and see them you can be sure of a warm welcome.* **3 sure to do sth** certain to happen or do sth: *If you work hard you are sure to pass the exam.* **4** that you can trust: *A noise like that is a sure sign of engine trouble.*
(IDIOMS) **Be sure to do sth** Don't forget to do sth: *Be sure to write and tell me what happens.*

make sure 1 to find out whether sth is in a certain state or has been done: *I must go back and make sure I closed the window.* **2** to take the action that is necessary to make sth happen: *Make sure you are back home by 11 o'clock.*

sure of yourself confident about your opinions, or about what you can do

sure (thing) (*US informal*) yes: *'Can I borrow this book?' 'Sure thing.'*

sure *adv*
(IDIOM) **sure enough** as was expected: *I expected him to be early and sure enough he arrived five minutes before the others.*

☆ **surely** /ˈʃɔːli; *US* ˈʃʊərli/ *adv* **1** without doubt: *This will surely cause problems.* **2** (used for expressing surprise at sb else's opinions, plans, actions, etc): *Surely you're not going to walk home in this rain?* ○ *'Tom's looking for another job.' 'Surely not.'* **3** (*US informal*) yes; of course

surf /sɜːf/ *noun* [U] the white part on the top of waves in the sea

surf *verb* [I] to stand or lie on a special board (a **surfboard**) and ride on a wave towards the shore

surfer *noun* [C] a person who surfs

☆ **surface** /ˈsɜːfɪs/ *noun* **1** [C] the outside part of sth: *the earth's surface* ○ *a new cleaning product for all your kitchen surfaces* **2** [C, usually sing] the top part of an area of water: *The submarine slowly rose to the surface.* **3** [sing] the qualities of sb/sth that you see or notice, that are not hidden: *Everybody seems very friendly but there are a lot of tensions beneath the surface.*

surface *verb* **1** [T] to cover the surface(2) of sth: *to surface a road with tarmac* **2** [I] to come to the surface of a liquid: *The submarine surfaced quickly.* **3** [I] (*informal*) to appear again: *All the old arguments surfaced again in the discussion.*

'surface mail *noun* [U] letters, parcels, etc that go by road, rail or sea, not by air ☛ Look at **airmail**.

surfeit /ˈsɜːfɪt/ *noun* [sing] (*formal*) **a surfeit (of sth)** too much of sth

surge /sɜːdʒ/ *verb* [I] to move forwards with great strength: *The crowd surged forward.*

surge *noun* [C, usually sing] **a surge (of/in sth) 1** a forward movement of a large mass: *a surge forward* ○ (*figurative*) *a surge (= an increase) in the demand for electricity* **2** a sudden strong feeling: *a surge of pity*

surgeon /ˈsɜːdʒən/ *noun* [C] a doctor who performs medical operations (**surgery**): *a brain surgeon*

☆ **surgery** /ˈsɜːdʒəri/ *noun* (*pl* **surgeries**) **1** [U] medical treatment in which your body is cut open so that part of it can be removed or repaired: *to undergo emergency surgery* ☛ Look at **plastic surgery**. **2** [C,U] the place or time when a doctor or dentist sees patients: *Her surgery is in Mill Lane.* ○ *Surgery hours are from 9.00 to 11.30 in the morning.*

surgical /ˈsɜːdʒɪkl/ *adj* used in surgery(1) or connected with surgery: *surgical instruments* —**surgically** /-kli/ *adv*

surly /ˈsɜːli/ *adj* (**surlier**; **surliest**) unfriendly and rude: *a surly expression*

p	b	t	d	k	g	tʃ	dʒ	f	v	θ	ð
pen	bad	tea	did	cat	got	chin	June	fall	van	thin	then

surmount /sə'maʊnt/ *verb* [T] to overcome a problem or difficulty ☞ Look at **insurmountable**.

☆ **surname** /'sɜ:neɪm/ (*also* **last name**) *noun* [C] the name that you share with other people in your family. Your surname is usually your last name: *'What's your surname?' 'Jones.'* ☞ Look at the note at **name**.

surpass /sə'pɑ:s; *US* -'pæs/ *verb* [T] (*formal*) do sth better than sb/sth else or better than expected

surplus /'sɜ:pləs/ *noun* [C,U] an amount that is extra or more than you need: *the food surplus in Western Europe* —**surplus** *adj*

☆ **surprise** /sə'praɪz/ *noun* **1** [U] the feeling that you have when sth happens that you do not expect: *They looked up in surprise when she walked in.* ○ *To my surprise the boss agreed.* **2** [C] something that you did not expect: *What a pleasant surprise to see you again!* ○ *a surprise visit, attack, etc* ○ *'What's my present?' 'It's a surprise.'*
(IDIOM) **take sb by surprise** to happen or be done to sb when sb is not expecting it: *His remarks took me by surprise.*

surprise *verb* [T] **1** to cause sb to feel surprise: *It wouldn't surprise me if you get the job.* **2** to attack or find sb suddenly and unexpectedly: *We surprised the burglars just as they were leaving our house.*

surprised *adj* feeling or showing surprise: *I was very surprised to see Carol there. I thought she was still abroad.*

surprising *adj* that causes surprise: *It's surprising how many adults can't read or write.* —**surprisingly** *adv*

surreal /sə'rɪəl/ (*also* **surrealistic** /sə,rɪə-'lɪstɪk/) *adj* very strange, like a dream

surrender /sə'rendə(r)/ *verb* **1** [I,T] **surrender (to sb)** to stop fighting and admit that you have lost **2** [T] **surrender sth/sb (to sb)** (*formal*) to give sb/sth to sb else: *The police ordered them to surrender their weapons.* —**surrender** *noun* [C,U]

surreptitious /,sʌrəp'tɪʃəs/ *adj* done secretly —**surreptitiously** *adv*

surrogate /'sʌrəgeɪt/ *noun* [C], *adj* (a person or thing) that takes the place of sb/sth else: *a surrogate mother* (= a woman who has a baby and gives it to another woman who cannot have children)

☆ **surround** /sə'raʊnd/ *verb* [T] **surround sb/sth (by/with sth)** to be or go all around sb/sth: *The garden is surrounded by a high wall.* ○ *Troops have surrounded the parliament building.* ○ (*figurative*) *He is surrounded by friends.*

surrounding *adj* (only *before* a noun) that is near or around sth: *Oxford and the surrounding villages*

surroundings *noun* [plural] everything that is near or around you; the place where you live: *to live in pleasant surroundings* ○ *animals living in their natural surroundings* (= not in zoos) ☞ Look at **environment**.

surveillance /sɜ:'veɪləns/ *noun* [U] a careful watch on sb who may have done sth wrong: *The suspect was under police surveillance.*

☆ **survey** /sə'veɪ/ *verb* [T] **1** to look at the whole of sth from a distance: *We stood at the top of the hill and surveyed the countryside.* ○ (*figurative*) *Her new book surveys the problems of the Third World in the 1990s.* **2** to carefully measure and make a map of an area of land **3** to examine a building carefully in order to find out if it is in good condition

survey /'sɜ:veɪ/ *noun* [C] **1** a study of sth: *Surveys have shown that more and more people are getting into debt.* **2** an act of examining an area of land and making a map of it **3** an act of examining a building in order to find out if it is in good condition

☆ **survival** /sə'vaɪvl/ *noun* **1** [U] the state of continuing to live or exist: *the struggle for survival* **2** [C] a person or thing that has continued to exist from an earlier time: *The festival is a survival from pre-Christian times.*

☆ **survive** /sə'vaɪv/ *verb* [I,T] to continue to live or exist, in or after a difficult or dangerous situation: *More than a hundred people were killed in the crash and only five passengers survived.* ○ *to survive a plane crash* ○ *The old man survived all his children* (= lived longer than them). ○ (*figurative*) *She's managed to survive two divorces* (= to deal with them well and to continue with her life). —**survivor** *noun* [C]: *There were five survivors of the crash.*

susceptible /sə'septəbl/ *adj* (not before a noun) **susceptible to sth** easily influenced, damaged or affected by sb/sth: *The young are susceptible to advertising.* ○ *The plant is highly susceptible to frost.*

☆ **suspect** /sə'spekt/ *verb* [T] **1** to believe that sth may happen or be true: *The situation is worse than we first suspected.* ○ *Nobody suspected that she was thinking of leaving.* **2** to have doubts about whether you can trust sb or believe sth: *I rather suspect his motives for offering to help.* **3 suspect sb (of sth)** to believe that sb is guilty of sth: *I suspect Laura of taking the money.* ○ *She strongly suspected that he was lying.* ☞ Look at **suspicion**.

suspect /'sʌspekt/ *noun* [C] a person who is thought to be guilty of a crime

suspect /'sʌspekt/ *adj* possibly not true or to be trusted: *to have suspect motives* ○ *a suspect parcel* (= one possibly containing a bomb)

suspend /sə'spend/ *verb* [T] **1 suspend sth (from sth)** to hang sth: *to suspend sth from the ceiling* **2** to stop or delay sth for a time: *Some rail services were suspended during the strike.* ○ *The young man was given a suspended sentence* (= he will not go to prison unless he commits another crime). **3 suspend sb (from sth)** to send sb away from his/her school, job, position, etc for a period of time, usually as a punishment for doing sth bad: *to be suspended from school* ☞ The noun is **suspension**.

suspender /sə'spendə(r)/ *noun* **1** [C, usually pl] (*Brit*) a short piece of elastic that women use to hold up a stocking by its top **2 suspenders** [plural] (*US*) = BRACES

suspense /sə'spens/ *noun* [U] the feeling that you have when you are waiting for news or for sth exciting or important to happen: *Don't keep us in suspense. Tell us what happened.*

suspension /sə'spenʃn/ *noun* [U] **1** delaying

s	z	ʃ	ʒ	h	m	n	ŋ	l	r	j	w
so	zoo	she	vision	how	man	no	sing	leg	red	yes	wet

sth for a period of time: *the suspension of the train service* **2** not being allowed to do your job for a period of time, usually as a punishment: *suspension on full pay* **3** the parts that are attached to the wheels of a car, etc that make it more comfortable to ride in

☆ **suspicion** /səˈspɪʃn/ *noun* **1** [C,U] a feeling or belief that sth is wrong or that sb has done sth wrong: *He always treats new situations with suspicion.* ○ *She was arrested on suspicion of murder.* **2** [C] a feeling that sth may happen or be true: *We have a suspicion that they are not happy together.*
(IDIOM) **under suspicion** (used about a person) believed to have done sth wrong

☆ **suspicious** /səˈspɪʃəs/ *adj* **1** that makes you feel or believe that sth is wrong or that sb has done sth wrong: *The old man died in suspicious circumstances.* ○ *It's very suspicious that she was not at home on the evening of the murder.* ○ *a suspicious-looking person* **2** **suspicious (of/about sb/sth)** not trusting sb/sth: *His strange behaviour made the police suspicious.* —**suspiciously** *adv*: *The house was suspiciously quiet* (= as if something was wrong). ○ *to behave suspiciously*

sustain /səˈsteɪn/ *verb* [T] **1** to keep sb/sth alive or healthy: *Oxygen sustains life.* ○ *His belief in God sustained him through his long illness.* **2** to cause sth to continue for a long period of time: *It's hard to sustain interest for such a long time.* **3** (*formal*) to suffer an injury, etc: *The victim sustained multiple bruises.*

swagger /ˈswægə(r)/ *verb* [I] to walk with a swinging movement that shows that you are too confident or proud of yourself —**swagger** *noun* [sing]

☆ **swallow** /ˈswɒləʊ/ *verb* **1** [T] to make food, drink, etc pass from your mouth down your throat: *It's easier to swallow pills if you take them with water.* ○ (*figurative*) *The rent swallows up most of our monthly income.* ☛ picture at **lick**. **2** [I] to make a movement in your throat, often because you are afraid or surprised, etc: *She swallowed hard and tried to speak, but nothing came out.* **3** [T] to accept or believe sth, often too easily: *You shouldn't swallow everything they tell you!* **4** [T] to accept an insult, etc without protest: *I find her criticisms very hard to swallow.* —**swallow** *noun* [C]

swam *pt* of SWIM

swamp¹ /swɒmp/ *noun* [C,U] (an area of) soft wet land

swamp² /swɒmp/ *verb* [T] **1** to cover or fill sth with water: *The fishing-boat was swamped by enormous waves.* **2** (usually passive) **swamp sb/sth (with sth)** to give sb so much of sth that they cannot deal with it: *We've been swamped with applications for the job.*

swan /swɒn/ *noun* [C] a large, usually white, bird with a very long neck that lives on lakes and rivers

swap (*also* **swop**) /swɒp/ *verb* [I,T] (**swapping**; **swapped**) (*informal*) to give sth for sth else; to exchange: *When we finish these books shall we swap* (= you have my book and I'll have yours)*?* ○ *Would you swap jobs with me?* ○ *I'd swap my job for hers any day.*
(IDIOM) **change/swap places (with sb)** ⇒ PLACE¹

swap *noun* [C] an act of exchanging: *Let's do a swap.*

swarm /swɔːm/ *noun* [C] **1** a large group of insects, especially bees, moving around together **2** a large number of people together

swarm *verb* [I] to fly or move in large numbers: *When the gates opened the fans swarmed into the stadium.*
(PHRASAL VERB) **swarm with sb/sth** to be too crowded or full: *London is swarming with tourists at the moment.*

swat /swɒt/ *verb* [T] (**swatting**; **swatted**) to hit sth, especially an insect, with sth flat

sway /sweɪ/ *verb* **1** [I,T] to move or swing slowly from side to side **2** [T] to influence: *Many people were swayed by his convincing arguments.*

☆ **swear** /sweə(r)/ *verb* (*pt* **swore** /swɔː(r)/; *pp* **sworn** /swɔːn/) **1** [I] **swear (at sb/sth)** to use rude or bad language: *He hit his thumb with the hammer and swore loudly.* ○ *There's no point in swearing at the car just because it won't start!* ☛ Look at **curse**. **2** [I,T] to make a serious promise: *When you give evidence in court you have to swear to tell the truth.* ○ *Will you swear not to tell anyone?* ○ *I could have sworn* (= I'm quite sure) *I heard a knock at the door.*
(PHRASAL VERBS) **swear by sb/sth** to believe completely in the value of sth

swear sb in (usually passive) to make sb declare that he/she will accept the responsibility of a new position: *The President will be sworn in next week.*

ˈ**swear-word** *noun* [C] a word that is considered rude or bad and that may offend people

☆ **sweat** /swet/ *noun* [U] the liquid that comes out of your skin when you are hot, ill or afraid: *He stopped digging and wiped the sweat from his forehead.* ☛ Look at **perspiration**.

sweat *verb* [I] **1** to produce sweat through your skin **2** **sweat (over sth)** to work hard: *I've been sweating over that problem all day.*

sweaty *adj* (**sweatier**; **sweatiest**) **1** wet with sweat: *I was hot and sweaty after the match and needed a shower.* **2** causing you to sweat: *a hot, sweaty day*

☆ **sweater** /ˈswetə(r)/ *noun* [C] a warm piece of clothing with long sleeves, often made of wool, which you put over your head ☛ **Sweater**, **jumper**, **pullover** and **jersey** are all words for the same piece of clothing. They are often made from wool or a similar material. A **sweatshirt** is usually made from cotton and may be worn informally on its own or for sport. A **cardigan** fastens with buttons down the front.

sweatshirt /'swetʃɜːt/ noun [C] a sweater made from thick cotton or a mixture of cotton and another material ☛ picture on page A10. Look at the note at **sweater**.

swede /swiːd/ noun [C,U] a large, round, yellow vegetable that grows under the ground

☆ **sweep¹** /swiːp/ verb (pt, pp **swept** /swept/) **1** [I,T] to clean by moving dust, dirt, etc away with a brush: *Could you sweep under the table too?* ○ *Take your shoes off! I've just swept the floor.* ○ *I'm going to sweep the leaves off the path.* ☛ Look at the note at **clean²**. **2** [T] to push, move or remove sb/sth quickly and smoothly: *He swept the money into his pocket and went out.* ○ *The huge waves swept her overboard.* **3** [I,T] to move quickly and smoothly over the area or in the direction mentioned: *Fire swept through the building.* ○ *The epidemic swept the country within weeks.* **4** [I] to move in a proud or impressive way: *Five big black Mercedes swept past us.* ○ *She swept angrily out of the room.*
(PHRASAL VERB) **sweep (sth) up** to remove dirt, dust, leaves, etc using a brush

sweep² /swiːp/ noun [C] **1** a long, curving shape or movement: *a bay with a broad sweep of golden sand* **2** [usually sing] an act of sweeping: *I'd better give the floor a sweep.* **3** = CHIMNEY-SWEEP
(IDIOM) **a clean sweep** ⇨ CLEAN¹

sweeper /'swiːpə(r)/ noun [C] **1** a person or thing that sweeps¹(1): *road-sweepers* ○ *a carpet-sweeper* **2** (in football) the defending player who plays behind the other defending players and who can come forward to attack ☛ picture at **football**.

sweeping /'swiːpɪŋ/ adj **1** (used about statements, etc) too general and perhaps not accurate **2** having a great and important effect: *sweeping reforms*

☆ **sweet¹** /swiːt/ adj **1** tasting of or like sugar; not sour: *Children usually like sweet things.* ○ *This cake's too sweet.* ☛ Look at **savoury**. **2** attractive; lovely: *What a sweet little cottage!* ○ *Isn't that little girl sweet?* **3** (used about a person) kind and thoughtful: *It's very sweet of you to remember my birthday!* **4** (used about a smell or a sound) pleasant: *The garden was full of the sweet smells of summer.* ○ *the sweet sound of children singing*
(IDIOM) **have a sweet tooth** to like eating sweet things

sweetly adv in an attractive, kind or pleasant way: *She smiled sweetly.* ○ *sweetly-scented flowers* —**sweetness** noun [U]

'sweet corn noun [U] yellow grains of maize that taste sweet and are eaten as a vegetable

'sweetheart noun [C] (old-fashioned) a boyfriend or girlfriend: *They were childhood sweethearts.*

☆ **sweet²** /swiːt/ noun **1** [C, usually pl] (US **candy**) a small piece of boiled sugar, chocolate, etc, often sold in a packet: *He was sucking a sweet.* ○ *a sweetshop* **2** [C,U] sweet food often served at the end of a meal: *As a sweet you can have ice-cream or chocolate mousse.* ○ *I won't have any sweet, thank you.* ☛ Look at **pudding** and **dessert**.

sweeten /'swiːtn/ verb [T] to make sth sweet by adding sugar, honey, etc

sweetener /'swiːtnə(r)/ noun [C,U] a substance used instead of sugar for sweetening food or drink: *artificial sweeteners*

☆ **swell** /swel/ verb (pt **swelled** /sweld/; pp **swollen** /'swəʊlən/ or **swelled**) **1** [I,T] **swell (up)** to become or to make sth bigger, fuller or thicker: *After the fall her ankle began to swell up.* ○ *His eyes swelled with tears.* ○ *Heavy rain had swollen the rivers.* **2** [I,T] to increase: *The crowd swelled to 600 by the end of the evening.* **3** [I] (formal) (used about feelings or sound) to become stronger or louder suddenly: *Hatred swelled inside him.*

swell noun [sing] the slow movement up and down of the surface of the sea

☆ **swelling** /'swelɪŋ/ noun **1** [C] a place on the body that is bigger or fatter than usual because of an injury or illness: *a swelling on my knee* **2** [U] the condition of being swollen: *The disease often causes swelling of the ankles and knees.*

swelter /'sweltə(r)/ verb [I] (informal) to be much too hot: *It was sweltering in London today.*

swept pt, pp of SWEEP¹

swerve /swɜːv/ verb [I] to change direction suddenly: *The car swerved to avoid the child.* —**swerve** noun [C]

swift /swɪft/ adj quick or fast; happening without delay: *a swift runner* ○ *a swift reaction* —**swiftly** adv

swig /swɪɡ/ verb [I,T] (**swigging**; **swigged**) (informal) to take a drink, especially of alcohol, quickly and in large amounts: *He swigged the whisky down and poured another glass.* —**swig** noun [C]

swill /swɪl/ verb [T] **swill sth (out/down)** to wash sth by pouring large amounts of water, etc into, over or through it

☆ **swim** /swɪm/ verb (pres part **swimming**; pt **swam** /swæm/; pp **swum** /swʌm/) **1** [I] to move your body through water: *How far can you swim?* ○ *Hundreds of tiny fish swam past.*
☛ **Go swimming** is a common way of talking about swimming for pleasure: *We go swimming every Saturday.* ○ *They went swimming before breakfast.* We can also say **go for a swim** when we are talking about one particular occasion: *I went for a swim this morning.* **2** [T] to cover or cross a distance, etc by swimming: *I swam 25 lengths of the pool.* **3** [I] to seem to be moving or turning: *The floor began to swim before my eyes and I fainted.* **4** [I] (used about your head) to feel unclear or confused: *My head was swimming with so much new information.* —**swim** noun [sing]: *Would you like to have a swim?* —**swimmer** noun [C]: *a strong swimmer*

'swimming-bath noun [C] (also **swimming-baths** [plural]) a public swimming-pool, usually indoors

'swimming-pool (also **pool**) noun [C] a pool

ɜː	ə	eɪ	əʊ	aɪ	aʊ	ɔɪ	ɪə	eə	ʊə
fur	ago	pay	home	five	now	join	near	hair	pure

that is built especially for people to swim in: *an indoor/outdoor/open-air swimming-pool*
'swimming-trunks *noun* [plural] a piece of clothing like shorts that a man wears to go swimming: *a pair of swimming-trunks*
'swimsuit (*also* **swimming-costume**) *noun* [C] a piece of clothing that a woman wears to go swimming ☛ Look at **bikini**.
swindle /ˈswɪndl/ *verb* [T] **swindle sb/sth (out of sth)** to cheat sb (in order to get money, etc): *He swindled his sister out of her inheritance.* —**swindle** *noun* [C]: *a tax swindle*
swindler /ˈswɪndlə(r)/ *noun* [C] a person who swindles
swine /swaɪn/ *noun* **1** [plural] (*old-fashioned*) pigs **2** [C] (*informal*) a very unpleasant person: *Her husband's an absolute swine.*
☆ **swing¹** /swɪŋ/ *verb* (*pt, pp* **swung** /swʌŋ/)
1 [I,T] to move backwards and forwards or from side to side, while hanging from sth; to make sb/sth move in this way: *The rope was swinging from a branch.* ○ *She sat on the wall, swinging her legs.* **2** [I,T] to move in a curve or to make sb/sth move in this way: *The window swung open and a head peeped out.* ○ *He swung the child up onto his shoulders.* **3** [I] to turn quickly: *She swung round when she heard the door open.* ○ (*figurative*) *His moods swing from one extreme to the other.* **4** [I,T] **swing (at sb/sth)** to try to hit sb/sth: *He swung violently at the other man but missed.*
☆ **swing²** /swɪŋ/ *noun* **1** [sing] a swinging movement or action: *He took a swing at the ball.* **2** [C] a seat that you can swing backwards and forwards on, eg in a children's playground **3** [C] a change (in public opinion, etc): *Opinion polls indicate a significant swing towards the right.*
(IDIOM) **in full swing** ⇨ FULL
swipe /swaɪp/ *verb* **1** [I,T] **swipe (at) sb/sth** (*informal*) to (try to) hit sb/sth in an uncontrolled way: *He swiped at the wasp with a newspaper but missed.* ○ *She swiped the ball into the neighbours' garden.* **2** [T] (*informal*) to steal sth
swipe *noun* [C] a careless blow
swirl /swɜːl/ *verb* [I,T] to move round and round quickly; to make sth do this: *Her long skirt swirled round her legs as she danced.* —**swirl** *noun* [C]
☆ **switch** /swɪtʃ/ *noun* [C] **1** a small button or sth similar that you press up or down in order to turn on electricity: *the light switch* **2** a sudden change: *a switch in policy*
switch *verb* **1** [I,T] **switch (sth) (over) (to sth)** to change or be changed from one thing to another: *We've switched from reading 'The Times' to 'The Independent' now.* ○ *The match has been switched from Saturday to Sunday.* **2** [I,T] **switch (sth) (with sb/sth); switch (sth) (over/round)** to exchange positions, activities, etc: *This week you can have the car and I'll go on the bus, and next week we'll switch over.* ○ *Someone switched the signs round and everyone went the wrong way.*
(PHRASAL VERB) **switch (sth) off/on** to press a switch in order to connect/disconnect electric power: *Don't forget to switch off the cooker.*

switchboard /ˈswɪtʃbɔːd/ *noun* [C] the place in a large office, etc where all the telephone calls are connected
swivel /ˈswɪvl/ *verb* [I,T] (**swivelling**; swivelled; *US* **swiveling**; swiveled) **swivel (sth) (round)** to turn around a central point; to make sth do this: *She swivelled round to face me.* ○ *He swivelled his chair towards the door.*
swollen¹ *pp* of SWELL
swollen² /ˈswəʊlən/ *adj* thicker or wider than usual: *Her leg was badly swollen after the accident.*
swoop /swuːp/ *verb* [I] to fly or move down suddenly: *The bird swooped down on its prey.*
swoop *noun* [C] **swoop (on sb/sth)** a swooping movement or a sudden attack: *The troops made a swoop on the capital last night.*
swop = SWAP
☆ **sword** /sɔːd/ *noun* [C] a weapon with a handle and a long thin metal blade
swore *pt* of SWEAR
sworn *pp* of SWEAR
swot /swɒt/ *verb* [I,T] (**swotting**; **swotted**) **swot (up) (for/on sth); swot sth up** (*informal*) to study sth very hard, especially to prepare for an exam: *She's swotting for her A levels.*
swot *noun* [C] (*informal*) a person who studies too hard
swum *pp* of SWIM
swung *pt, pp* of SWING
syllable /ˈsɪləbl/ *noun* [C] a word or part of a word which contains one vowel sound: '*Mat*' has one syllable and '*mattress*' has two syllables.
syllabus /ˈsɪləbəs/ *noun* [C] (*pl* **syllabuses**) a list of subjects, etc that are included in a course of study: *Does the syllabus cover modern literature?*
☆ **symbol** /ˈsɪmbl/ *noun* [C] **1 a symbol (of sth)** a sign, object, etc which represents an idea or an aspect of life: *The cross is the symbol of Christianity.* ○ *Some people think a fast car is a symbol of power and strength.* **2 symbol (for sth)** a letter, number or sign that has a particular meaning: *O is the symbol for oxygen.*
symbolic /sɪmˈbɒlɪk/ (*also* **symbolical** /-kl/) *adj* used or seen as a symbol: *The violent sea is symbolic of the character's emotions.* —**symbolically** /-klɪ/ *adv*
symbolism /ˈsɪmbəlɪzəm/ *noun* [U] the use of symbols to represent things, especially in art and literature
symbolize (*also* **symbolise**) /ˈsɪmbəlaɪz/ *verb* [T] to be a symbol of sth: *The deepest notes in music often symbolize danger or despair.*
symmetry /ˈsɪmətrɪ/ *noun* [U] the state of having two halves that match each other exactly in size, shape, etc
symmetric /sɪˈmetrɪk/ **symmetrical** /-rɪkl/ *adj* having two halves that are exactly the same in size and shape —**symmetrically** /-klɪ/ *adv*
☆ **sympathetic** /ˌsɪmpəˈθetɪk/ *adj* **1** showing that you understand other people's feelings, especially their problems: *When Sandra was ill, everyone was very sympathetic.* ○ *I felt very sympathetic towards him.* ○ *He gave me a sympath-*

p	b	t	d	k	g	tʃ	dʒ	f	v	θ	ð
pen	bad	tea	did	cat	got	chin	June	fall	van	thin	then

etic smile. ☛ In English, **sympathetic** does not mean 'friendly and pleasant'. If you want to express this meaning, you say a person is **nice**: *I met Alex's sister yesterday. She's very nice.* **2 sympathetic (to sb/sth)** being in agreement with or willing to support sb/sth: *I explained our ideas but she wasn't sympathetic to them.* ☛ The opposite is **unsympathetic**. —**sympathetically** /-klɪ/ *adv*

☆ **sympathy** /ˈsɪmpəθɪ/ *noun* (*pl* **sympathies**) **1** [U] **sympathy (for/towards sb)** an understanding of other people's feelings, especially their problems: *Everyone feels great sympathy for the victims of the attack.* ○ *I don't expect any sympathy from you.* ○ *When his wife died he received dozens of letters of sympathy.* **2** [plural] feelings of support or agreement: *Some members of the party have nationalist sympathies.* (IDIOM) **in sympathy (with sb/sth)** in agreement, showing that you support or approve of sb/sth: *He is not in sympathy with all the ideas of the party.*

sympathize (*also* **sympathise**) /ˈsɪmpəθaɪz/ *verb* [I] **sympathize (with sb/sth) 1** to understand and share sb's feelings: *I sympathize with her, but I don't know what I can do to help.* **2** to be in agreement with sb/sth: *I find it difficult to sympathize with his opinions.*

sympathizer *noun* [C] a person who agrees with and supports an idea or aim: *a Communist sympathizer*

symphony /ˈsɪmfənɪ/ *noun* [C] (*pl* **symphonies**) a long piece of music written for a large orchestra

☆ **symptom** /ˈsɪmptəm/ *noun* [C] **1** a change in your body that is a sign of illness: *What are the symptoms of flu?* **2** a sign (that sth bad is happening or exists): *The riots are a symptom of a deeper problem.* —**symptomatic** /ˌsɪmptəˈmætɪk/ *adj*

synagogue /ˈsɪnəgɒg/ *noun* [C] a building where Jewish people go to pray or to study their religion

synchronize (*also* **synchronise**) /ˈsɪŋkrənaɪz/ *verb* [T] to make sth happen or work at the same time or speed

syndicate /ˈsɪndɪkət/ *noun* [C] a group of people or business companies that join together for a common purpose

syndrome /ˈsɪndrəʊm/ *noun* [C] **1** a group of signs or changes in the body that are typical of an illness: *Down's syndrome* ○ *Acquired Immune Deficiency Syndrome (AIDS)* **2** a group of events, actions attitudes, etc that are typical of a particular state or condition

synonym /ˈsɪnənɪm/ *noun* [C] a word or phrase that has the same meaning as another word or phrase in the same language: *'Big' and 'large' are synonyms.* —**synonymous** /sɪˈnɒnɪməs/ *adj* **synonymous (with sth)** (*figurative*): *Wealth is not always synonymous with happiness.*

syntax /ˈsɪntæks/ *noun* [U] the system of rules for the structure of a sentence

synthesizer (*also* **synthesiser**) /ˈsɪnθəsaɪzə(r)/ *noun* [C] an electronic musical instrument that can produce a wide range of different sounds

synthetic /sɪnˈθetɪk/ *adj* made by a chemical process; not natural —**synthetically** /-klɪ/ *adv*

syphilis /ˈsɪfɪlɪs/ *noun* [U] a serious disease that passes from one person to another by sexual contact

syringe /sɪˈrɪndʒ/ *noun* [C] an instrument that consists of a tube and a needle. It is used for taking a small amount of blood out of the body or for giving injections.

syrup /ˈsɪrəp/ *noun* [U] **1** thick sweet liquid made by boiling sugar with water or fruit juice: *peaches in syrup* **2** thick liquid food made from sugar that you buy in a tin

☆ **system** /ˈsɪstəm/ *noun* **1** [C] a set of ideas or rules for organizing sth: *We have a new computerized system in the library.* ○ *the metric system* ○ *The government is planning to reform the education system.* **2** [C] a group of things or parts that work together: *a central heating system* **3** [C] the body of a person or animal; parts of the body that work together: *We must get him to hospital before the poison gets into his system.* ○ *the central nervous system* **4** (**the system**) [sing] the traditional methods and rules of a society (IDIOM) **get sth out of your system** (*informal*) to free yourself of a strong feeling

systematic /ˌsɪstəˈmætɪk/ *adj* done using a fixed plan or method: *a systematic search* —**systematically** /-klɪ/ *adv*

s	z	ʃ	ʒ	h	m	n	ŋ	l	r	j	w
so	zoo	she	vision	how	man	no	sing	leg	red	yes	wet

Tt

T, t /tiː/ noun [C] (pl **T's; t's**) the twentieth letter of the English alphabet: *'Table' begins with (a) 'T'.*

'T-junction noun [C] a place where two roads join to form the shape of a T

'T-shirt (also **teeshirt**) noun [C] a shirt with short sleeves and without buttons or a collar

ta /tɑː/ interj (Brit informal) thank you

tab /tæb/ noun [C] **1** a small piece of cloth, metal or paper that is fixed to sth to help you open, hold or identify it: *You open the tin by pulling the metal tab.* **2** (US) a bill: *I'll pick up the tab* (= I'll pay the bill).
(IDIOM) **keep a tab/tabs on sb/sth** (informal) to watch sb/sth carefully; to check sth

tabby /'tæbi/ noun [C] (pl **tabbies**) a cat with grey or brown fur and dark stripes

☆ **table** /'teɪbl/ noun [C] **1** a piece of furniture with a flat top on one or more legs: *a dining-table* o *a bedside-table* o *a kitchen table* o *a coffee-table* o *Could you lay the table for lunch?* (= put the knives, forks, plates, etc on it) o *Don't read the newspaper at the table* (= during the meal). ☛ We put things **on the table** but we sit **at the table** (= around the table). **2** a list of facts or figures, usually arranged in rows down a page: *a table of contents* o *Table 3 shows the results.*

'tablecloth noun [C] a piece of cloth that you put over a table, especially when having a meal

'table manners noun [plural] the way you behave while you are eating

'tablespoon noun [C] **1** a large spoon used for serving or measuring food **2** (also **'tablespoonful**) the amount that a tablespoon holds: *Add two tablespoons of sugar.*

'table tennis (also informal **ping-pong**) noun [U] a game with rules like tennis in which you hit a light plastic ball across a table with a small round bat

tablet /'tæblɪt/ noun [C] a small amount of medicine in solid form, that you swallow: *Take two tablets every four hours.*

tabloid /'tæblɔɪd/ noun [C] a newspaper with small pages, a lot of pictures and short simple articles

taboo /tə'buː; US tæ'buː/ noun [C] (pl **taboos**) a religious or social custom that forbids certain actions or words —**taboo** adj: *a taboo subject*

tacit /'tæsɪt/ adj (formal) understood but not actually said: *They haven't replied. I think that's a tacit admission that they were wrong.* —**tacitly** adv

tack /tæk/ noun **1** [C] a small nail with a broad head **2** [U,sing] a way of achieving sth: *If people won't listen we'll have to try a different tack.*

tack verb [T] **1** to fasten sth with tacks(1) **2** to sew with loose stitches
(PHRASAL VERB) **tack sth on (to sth)** to put sth extra on the end of sth: *Restaurants sometimes tack extra charges on to the bill.*

☆ **tackle** /'tækl/ verb [T] **1** to deal boldly with sth difficult: *The government must tackle the problem of rising unemployment.* o *Firemen were brought in to tackle the blaze.* **2** [I,T] (used in football, etc) to try to take the ball from sb in the other team **3** [T] (used in rugby, etc) to stop another player by pulling him down **4** [T] **tackle sb about/over sth** to speak to sb about a difficult subject: *Somebody should tackle Simon about the amount he drinks.*

tackle noun **1** [C] the act of tackling(2, 3): *a skilful tackle by Walker* **2** [U] the equipment you use in a sport: *fishing tackle*

tacky /'tæki/ adj (**tackier; tackiest**) (informal) **1** cheap and of poor quality: *tacky souvenirs* **2** (used about paint, glue, etc) not quite dry; sticky

tact /tækt/ noun [U] the ability to deal with people without offending or upsetting them: *He had the tact not to mention my divorce.*

tactful /-fl/ adj careful not to say or do things that could offend people: *Talking about his ex-wife like that wasn't very tactful!* —**tactfully** /-fəli/ adv —**tactless** adj: *It was rather tactless of you to ask him how old he was.* o *a tactless suggestion* —**tactlessly** adv

☆ **tactic** /'tæktɪk/ noun **1** [C, usually pl] a way of achieving sth: *We must decide what our tactics are going to be at the next meeting.* o *I don't think this tactic will work.* **2 tactics** [U, with sing or pl verb] the skilful arrangement and use of military forces in order to win a battle

tactical /-kl/ adj **1** connected with tactics(2): *a tactical error* **2** designed to bring a future advantage: *a tactical decision* —**tactically** /-kli/ adv

tadpole /'tædpəʊl/ noun [C] a young form of a frog, when it has a large black head and a long tail

tag /tæg/ noun [C] **1** a small piece of card, material, etc fastened to sth to give information about it; a label: *a name tag* o *How much is this dress? There isn't a price tag on it.* **2** = QUESTION TAG

tag verb [T] (**tagging; tagged**) to fasten a tag to sth
(PHRASAL VERB) **tag along** to follow or go with sb: *The little boy tagged along with the older children when they went to the playground.*

☆ **tail** /teɪl/ noun **1** [C] the long thin part at the

iː	ɪ	e	æ	ɑː	ɒ	ɔː	ʊ	uː	ʌ
see	sit	ten	hat	arm	got	saw	put	too	cup

end of the body of an animal, bird, fish, etc: *The dog barked and wagged its tail.* ☛ picture at **cat**. **2** [C] a thing like an animal's tail in its shape or position: *the tail of an aeroplane* **3 tails** [plural] a man's coat, short at the front but with a long, divided piece at the back. It is worn on very formal occasions, such as weddings. **4 tails** [plural] the side of a coin that does not have the head of a person on it: *'We'll toss a coin to decide,' said my father. 'Heads or tails?'* ☛ Look at **heads**.
(IDIOM) **make head or tail of sth** ⇨ HEAD¹
tail *verb* [T] to follow sb closely, especially to watch where he/she goes, etc
(PHRASAL VERB) **tail off** to become less, smaller, quieter, etc: *His voice tailed off into a whisper.*

tailor /ˈteɪlə(r)/ *noun* [C] a person whose job is to make clothes, especially for men
tailor *verb* [T] (usually passive) **1** to make clothes: *a well-tailored coat* **2** to make or design sth for a special purpose: *We specialize in holidays tailored to meet your individual needs.*
ˌtailor-ˈmade *adj* very suitable; perfect: *I knew the house was tailor-made for me as soon as I saw it.*

taint /teɪnt/ *noun* [sing] (*formal*) a sign of some bad quality or that sth is no longer fresh, pure, etc: *the taint of corruption.*
taint *verb* [T] (usually passive) to have a bad effect on sth; to spoil sth: *Her reputation was tainted by the scandal.*

☆ **take** /teɪk/ *verb* [T] (*pt* **took** /tʊk/; *pp* **taken** /ˈteɪkən/) **1** to carry sb/sth or to go with sb from one place to another: *Take your coat with you – it's cold.* ○ *Could you take this letter home to your parents?* ○ *The ambulance took him to hospital.* ○ *I'm taking the children swimming this afternoon.* ☛ picture at **bring**. **2** to put your hand round sth and hold it (and move it towards you): *She held out the keys, and I took them.* ○ *He took a sweater out of the drawer.* ○ *She took my hand/me by the hand.* **3** to remove sth without permission: *Who's taken my pen?* **4** to accept or receive sth: *Will you take £2 000 for the car?* ○ *Do you take traveller's cheques?* ○ *I'm not taking the blame for the accident.* ○ *She's not going to take the job.* **5** to need or require sth: *It takes about an hour to drive to Oxford from here.* ○ *I took three years to learn to drive.* ○ *It took a lot of courage to say that.* **6** to have enough space for sth: *How many passengers can this bus take?* **7** to use a form of transport; to go by a particular road: *I always take the train to York.* ○ *Which road do you take to Hove?* **8** to swallow sth: *Take two tablets four times a day.* **9** to write or record sth: *She took notes during the lecture.* **10** to measure sth: *I took his temperature and it was nearly 40.* **11** (used with nouns to say that sb is performing an action): *Take a look at this article* (= look at it). ○ *We have to take a decision* (= decide). **12** to photograph sth: *I took some nice photos of the wedding.* **13** to have a particular feeling or opinion: *He takes great pleasure in his grandchildren.* ○ *I wish you would take things more seriously.* **14** to understand sth in a particular way: *She took what he said as a compliment.* **15** to be able to bear sth: *I find his criticism a bit hard to take.* **16** to capture a place by force: *The Allies took the enemy's capital last night.* **17** to give lessons to sb: *Who takes you for History?* (= who is your teacher) **18** to have a certain size of shoes or clothes: *What size shoes do you take?*
(IDIOMS) **I take it (that...)** I suppose: *I take it that you're not coming?*
take it from me believe me: *Take it from me, she's going to resign.*
take a lot out of sb to make sb very tired
take a lot of/some doing to require a lot of work or effort

☛ For other idioms containing **take**, look at the entries for the nouns, adjectives, etc, eg **take place** is at **place¹**.

(PHRASAL VERBS) **take sb aback** to surprise or shock sb
take after sb to look or behave like an older member of your family
take sth apart to separate sth into the different parts it is made of
take sth away to cause a feeling, etc to disappear: *These aspirins will take the pain away.*
take sb/sth away (from sb) to remove sb/sth: *She took the scissors away from the child.*
take sth back 1 to return sth to the place that you got it from **2** to admit that sth you said was wrong
take sth down 1 to remove a structure by separating it into the pieces it is made of: *They took the fence down and put up a wall.* **2** to write down sth that is said
take sb in to deceive sb: *I was completely taken in by her story.*
take sth in to understand what you see, hear or read: *There was too much in the museum to take in at one go.*
take off 1 (used about an aeroplane, etc) to leave the ground and start flying **2** to become successful or popular
take sb off to copy the way sb speaks or behaves
take sth off 1 to remove sth, especially clothes: *Come in and take your coat off.* **2** to have the period of time mentioned as a holiday: *I'm going to take a week off.*
take sb on to start to employ sb: *The firm is taking on new staff.*
take sth on to accept or decide to do sth: *He's taken on a lot of extra work.*
take sb out to go out with sb (for a social occasion): *I'm taking Sarah out for a meal tonight.*
take sth out to remove a part of the body: *He's having two teeth taken out.*
take sth out (of sth) to remove sth: *He took a notebook out of his pocket.* ○ *I'd like to take £50 out* (= of a bank account).
take it out on sb to behave badly towards sb because you are angry or upset about sth, even though it is not this person's fault: *I know you don't feel well but don't take it out on me!*
take (sth) over to get control of sth or responsibility for sth: *The firm is being taken*

3:	ə	eɪ	əʊ	aɪ	aʊ	ɔɪ	ɪə	eə	ʊə
fur	ago	pay	home	five	now	join	near	hair	pure

over by a large company. ○ *Who's going to take over as assistant when Tim leaves?*

take to sb/sth to feel a liking for sb/sth: *I took to his parents immediately.*

take to sth/doing sth to begin doing sth regularly: *We've taken to getting up very late on Sundays.*

take up sth to use or fill an amount of time or space: *All her time is taken up looking after the new baby.*

take sth up to start doing sth regularly (eg as a hobby): *I've taken up yoga recently.*

take sb up on sth 1 to say that you disagree with sth that sb has just said, and ask him/her to explain it: *I must take you up on that last point.* **2** to accept an offer, etc that sb has made: *'Come and stay with us any time.' 'We'll take you up on that!'*

take sth up with sb to ask or complain about sth: *I'll take the matter up with my MP.*

be taken with sb/sth to find sb/sth attractive or interesting

'**take-away** *noun* [C] **1** a restaurant that sells food that you can eat somewhere else: *There's an Indian take-away in the village.* **2** the food that such a restaurant sells: *Let's get a take-away.*

'**take-off** *noun* [C,U] the time when an aeroplane leaves the ground: *The plane crashed on take-off.*

'**take-over** *noun* [C] the act of taking control of sth: *the take-over of a company* ○ *a military take-over* (= in a country)

takings /'teɪkɪŋz/ *noun* [plural] the amount of money that a shop, theatre, etc gets from selling goods, tickets, etc

talcum powder /'tælkəm paʊdə(r)/ (*also* **talc** /tælk/) *noun* [U] a soft powder which smells nice. People put it on their skin after a bath.

tale /teɪl/ *noun* [C] **1** a story about events that are not real: *fairy tales* **2** a report or description of sb/sth that is not necessarily true: *I've heard a lot of tales about the people who live in that house.*

☆**talent** /'tælənt/ *noun* [C,U] **talent (for sth)** a natural skill or ability: *She has a talent for painting.* ○ *His work shows great talent.* —**talented** *adj: a talented musician*

☆**talk¹** /tɔːk/ *verb* **1** [I] **talk (to/with sb); talk (about/of sth)** to say things; to speak: *I could hear them talking downstairs.* ○ *Can I talk to you for a minute?* ○ *Anne is not an easy person to talk to.* ○ *We need to talk about the plans for the weekend.* ○ *I didn't understand what she was talking about.* ○ *He's been talking of going to Australia for some time now.* ○ *Their little boy is just learning to talk.* ☞ Look at the note at **speak**. **2** [I] to discuss people's personal affairs: *His strange life-style started the local people talking.* **3** [T] to discuss sth: *Could we talk business after dinner?* **4** [I] **talk on/about sth** to give a lecture or speech to a group of people about a certain subject: *Mrs Phipps will be talking about Byzantine Art.* **5** [I] to give information: *'He hasn't talked yet', said the detective, 'but he will.'*

(IDIOMS) **know what you are talking about** ⇨ KNOW

talk sense to say things that are correct and sensible

talk shop to talk about work with colleagues outside working hours

(PHRASAL VERBS) **talk down to sb** to talk to sb as if he/she is less clever, important, etc than you

talk sb into/out of doing sth to persuade sb to do/not to do sth: *I didn't really want to go with them, but they talked me into it.*

talkative /'tɔːkətɪv/ *adj* liking or tending to talk a lot

☆**talk²** /tɔːk/ *noun* **1** [C] a conversation or discussion: *Tim and I had a long talk about the problem.* **2 talks** [plural] formal discussions: *The Foreign Ministers of the two countries will meet for talks next week.* **3** [U] talking, especially without action, results or the right information: *'Alan says they're going to get married.' 'Don't believe it! It's only talk.'* **4** [C] a lecture or speech: *He's giving a talk on 'Our changing world'.*

☆**tall** /tɔːl/ *adj* **1** (used about people or things) of more than average height; not short: *a tall young man* ○ *a tall tree, tower, chimney, etc* ○ *Nick is taller than his brother.* **2** (used about people) of a particular height: *Claire is five feet tall.* ○ *How tall are you?* ☞ **Tall** and **high** have similar meanings. We use **tall** to describe the height of people (*He is six foot three inches tall.*), of trees (*A tall oak tree stood in the garden.*) and also sometimes to talk about narrow objects (*the tall skyscrapers of Manhattan*).

tambourine /ˌtæmbə'riːn/ *noun* [C] a small round musical instrument with a skin like a drum and metal discs round the edge. You can hit it or shake it.

☆**tame** /teɪm/ *adj* **1** (used about animals or birds) not wild or afraid of people: *The birds are so tame they will eat from your hand.* **2** boring; not interesting or exciting: *After the big city, you must find village life very tame.*

tame *verb* [T] to bring sth wild under your control

tamper /'tæmpə(r)/ *verb* [I] **tamper with sth** to use, touch, change, etc sth when you should not: *Don't eat the sweets if the packaging has been tampered with.*

tampon /'tæmpɒn/ *noun* [C] a tightly-rolled piece of cotton-wool that a woman puts inside her body to collect blood during her period(3)

tan /tæn/ *noun* **1** [C] = SUN-TAN **2** [U] a colour between yellow and brown: *Have you got this handbag in tan?*

tan *adj* of this colour: *tan shoes*

tan *verb* [I,T] (**tanning; tanned**) to become or to let sth become brown with the effect of sunshine: *Do you tan easily?* ○ *I'm trying to tan my legs.* —**tanned** *adj: You're looking very tanned – have you been on holiday?*

tandem /'tændəm/ *noun* [C] a bicycle with seats for two people, one behind the other

tangent /'tændʒənt/ *noun* [C] a straight line that touches a curve but does not cross it

(IDIOM) **go/fly off at a tangent** to change suddenly from one subject, action, etc to another

p	b	t	d	k	g	tʃ	dʒ	f	v	θ	ð
pen	bad	tea	did	cat	got	chin	June	fall	van	thin	then

tangerine /ˌtændʒəˈriːn; US ˈtændʒəriːn/ noun [C] a fruit like a small sweet orange with a skin that is easy to take off

tangible /ˈtændʒəbl/ adj clear and definite: *There are tangible benefits in the new system.*

tangle /ˈtæŋgl/ noun [C] a confused mass, especially of threads, hair, branches, etc that cannot easily be separated from each other: *My hair's full of tangles.* o *This string's in a tangle.* —**tangled** adj: *The wool was all tangled up.*

☆ **tank** /tæŋk/ noun [C] **1** a container for holding liquids or gas: *How many litres does the petrol tank hold?* o *a water tank* **2** a large, heavy military vehicle covered with steel and armed with guns, that moves on special wheels: *Hundreds of tanks have crossed the desert ready to attack.*

tanker noun [C] **1** a ship for carrying petrol, etc in large amounts: *an oil tanker* **2** (*US* **ˈtank truck**) a heavy road vehicle with a big round tank for carrying large amounts of oil, milk, etc

tantalizing (*also* **tantalising**) /ˈtæntəlaɪzɪŋ/ adj (used about sth that you cannot have) attractive or tempting: *A tantalizing smell of cooking was coming from the kitchen.* —**tantalizingly** (*also* **tantalisingly**) adv: *tantalizingly close*

tantrum /ˈtæntrəm/ noun [C] a sudden burst of anger, especially in a child

☆ **tap¹** /tæp/ (*US* **faucet**) noun [C] a type of handle that you turn to let water, gas, etc out of a pipe or container: *Turn the hot tap on.* o *Don't leave the taps running!* (= turn them off) ☛ picture at **plug**.

tap verb [T] (**tapp**ing; **tapp**ed) **1** to make use of sth from a supply or reserve: *to tap the skills of young people* **2** to fit a piece of equipment to sb's telephone wires so that you can listen to telephone conversations on that line

ˈtap water noun [U] water that comes out of taps, not water sold in bottles

☆ **tap²** /tæp/ verb (**tapp**ing; **tapp**ed) [I,T] **tap (at/on sth); tap sb/sth (on/with sth)** to touch or hit sb/sth quickly and gently: *Their feet were tapping in time to the music.* o *They won't hear if you only tap on the door – knock harder!* o *She tapped me on the shoulder and said, 'Excuse me, I think you dropped this notebook.'*

tap noun [C] a quick gentle blow or the sound it makes: *a tap on the shoulder*

ˈtap-dance noun [C], verb [I] (to do) a dance in which you tap the rhythm with your feet, wearing special shoes

☆ **tape** /teɪp/ noun **1** [U] magnetic material used for recording sound, pictures or information: *I've got the whole concert on tape* (= recorded). **2** [C] a cassette with magnetic material wound round it, which is used for recording or playing music, videos, etc: *a blank tape* o *I've got a new tape of Bryan Adams. Shall I put it on?* o *We've made a tape* (= video tape) *of the children playing in the garden.* o *to rewind a tape* **3** [C,U] a narrow piece of cloth used for tying or labelling things or in sewing, etc: *We have to sew name tapes into school clothes.* **4** [C] a piece of material stretched across a race track to mark where the race finishes **5** [U] sticky paper used for wrapping parcels, covering electric wires, etc: *sticky tape* o *insulating tape*

tape verb [T] **1** to record sound, music, television programmes, etc using a cassette: *There's a film on TV tonight that I'd like to tape.* **2 tape sth (up)** to fasten sth with sticky tape

ˈtape deck noun [C] the part of a hi-fi system on which you play tapes

ˈtape-measure (*also* **ˈmeasuring tape**) noun [C] a long thin piece of plastic or cloth with centimetres or inches marked on it. It is used for measuring things.

ˈtape-recorder noun [C] a machine that is used for recording or playing back music or other sounds

ˈtape-recording noun [C]: *We made a tape-recording of our voices.*

tapestry /ˈtæpəstri/ noun [C,U] (pl **tapestries**) a piece of heavy cloth with pictures or designs sewn on it in coloured thread

tar /tɑː(r)/ noun [U] **1** a thick black sticky liquid that becomes hard when it is cold. It is used for making roads, etc. **2** a similar substance formed by burning tobacco: *low-tar cigarettes*

☆ **target** /ˈtɑːgɪt/ noun [C] **1** a person or thing that you aim at when shooting or attacking: *Attacks have been launched on military targets such as airfields.* o *The bomb missed its target and fell into the sea.* o *The politician was a likely target for terrorist attacks.* **2** an object, often a round board with circles on, that you aim at in shooting practice: *I hit the target twice but missed it once.* **3** a person or thing that people blame, criticize, laugh at, etc: *The education system has been the target of heavy criticism.* **4** a result that you are aiming at: *Our target is to raise £10 000 for 'Save the Children'.* o *So far we're right on target* (= making the progress we expected).

target verb [T] (usually passive) **target sth (at/on sb/sth)** to aim sth at: *They targeted the product at teenagers.*

tariff /ˈtærɪf/ noun [C] **1** a tax that has to be paid on goods brought into a country **2** a list of prices

Tarmac /ˈtɑːmæk/ noun (*trade mark*) **1** [U] a material used for making the surfaces of roads **2 tarmac** [sing] an area covered with a Tarmac surface: *The plane waited for two hours on the tarmac.*

tarnish /ˈtɑːnɪʃ/ verb **1** [I,T] (used about a mirror, metal, etc) to become less bright; to make less bright **2** [T] (used about a reputation) to spoil: *His reputation was tarnished by the scandal.*

tarpaulin /tɑːˈpɔːlɪn/ noun [C] a large piece of strong, waterproof material that is used for covering things

tart¹ /tɑːt/ noun [C,U] an open pie with a sweet filling such as fruit or jam ☛ Look at the note at **pie**.

tart² /tɑːt/ noun [C] (*informal*) a woman or girl who accepts money in return for sex ☛ A more formal word is **prostitute**.

tartan /ˈtɑːtn/ noun [C,U] **1** a traditional Scottish pattern with coloured squares and stripes

s	z	ʃ	ʒ	h	m	n	ŋ	l	r	j	w
so	zoo	she	vision	how	man	no	sing	leg	red	yes	wet

that cross each other **2** material made from wool with this pattern on it: *a tartan skirt*

☆ **task** /tɑːsk/ *US* tæsk/ *noun* [C] a piece of work that has to be done, especially an unpleasant or difficult one: *Your first task will be to type these letters.* ○ *I found learning Arabic an almost impossible task.* ○ *You have three minutes to complete the three tasks.* ○ *They gave me the task of organizing the school trip.*

☆ **taste**[1] /teɪst/ *noun* **1** [U] the ability to recognize the flavour of food or drink: *Taste is one of the five senses.* **2** [sing] the flavour of food or drink: *I don't like the taste of this coffee.* **3** [C, usually sing] **a taste (of sth)** a small amount of sth to eat or drink: *Have a taste of this cheese to see if you like it.* ○ (*figurative*) *I had my first taste* (= experience) *of Italy when I was about fifteen.* **4** [sing] **a taste (for sth)** a liking for sth: *She has developed a taste for modern art.* **5** [U] the ability to make good choices about whether things are suitable, of good quality, etc: *He has excellent taste in music.*
(IDIOM) **(be) in bad taste** (used about sb's behaviour) (to be) unsuitable and unpleasant: *Some of his comments were in very bad taste.*
tasteful /-fl/ *adj* attractive and well-chosen: *The furniture was very tasteful.* —**tastefully** /-fəli/ *adv*
tasteless *adj* **1** unattractive; not well-chosen: *She was wearing a lot of rather tasteless jewellery.* **2** likely to offend sb: *His joke about the funeral was particularly tasteless.* **3** having little or no flavour: *We had some tasteless cheese sandwiches for lunch.*
tasty *adj* (**tastier**; **tastiest**) having a good, strong flavour: *spaghetti with a tasty mushroom sauce*

☆ **taste**[2] /teɪst/ *verb* **1** [T] to be aware of or recognize the flavour of food or drink: *Can you taste the garlic in this soup?* **2** [T] to try a small amount of food and drink; to test: *Can I taste a piece of that cheese to see what it's like?* **3** [I] **taste (of sth)** to have a particular flavour: *The pudding tasted of oranges.* ○ *to taste sour, sweet, delicious, etc*

tatters /'tætəz/ *noun*
(IDIOM) **in tatters** badly torn or damaged: *Her dress was in tatters.* ○ (*figurative*) *After the divorce my life seemed to be in tatters.*

tattered /'tætəd/ *adj* old and torn: *a tattered coat*

tattoo /tə'tuː; *US* tæ'tuː/ *noun* [C] (*pl* **tattoos**) a picture or pattern on sb's body that is made by pricking his/her skin with a needle and filling the holes with coloured liquid
tattoo *verb* [T] to make a tattoo on sb's body: *She had the word 'love' tattooed on her left hand.*

tatty /'tæti/ *adj* (**tattier**; **tattiest**) (*informal*) in bad condition: *tatty old clothes*

taught *pt, pp* of TEACH

taunt /tɔːnt/ *verb* [T] to try to make sb angry or unhappy by saying unpleasant or cruel things: *They taunted him with the words 'You're scared!'* —**taunt** *noun* [C]

Taurus /'tɔːrəs/ *noun* [C,U] the second sign of the zodiac, the Bull; a person who was born under this sign ☞ picture at **zodiac**.

taut /tɔːt/ *adj* (used about rope, wire, etc) stretched very tight; not loose

tavern /'tævən/ *noun* [C] (*old-fashioned*) a pub

☆ **tax** /tæks/ *noun* [C,U] the money that you have to pay to the government so that it can provide public services: *income tax* ○ *You do not have to pay tax on books in this country.* ○ *tax cuts*
tax *verb* [T] (often passive) **1** to take tax from a sum of money or from the price of goods and services: *Income is taxed at a rate of 25p in the pound.* ○ *Alcohol, cigarettes and petrol are heavily taxed.* **2** to make a person or an organization pay tax: *Husbands and wives are taxed separately in Britain.*
taxable *adj* on which you have to pay tax: *taxable income*
taxation /tæk'seɪʃn/ *noun* [U] **1** the system by which a government takes money from people so that it can pay for public services: *direct/indirect taxation* **2** the amount of money that people have to pay in tax: *to increase/reduce taxation* ○ *high/low taxation*
tax-'free *adj* on which you do not have to pay tax ☞ Look at **duty-free**.

☆ **taxi**[1] /'tæksi/ (*also* **'taxi-cab**; *especially US* **cab**) *noun* [C] a car with a driver, whose job is to take you somewhere in exchange for money: *Shall we go by bus or take a taxi?* ○ *I'll phone for a taxi to take us to the airport.*

☞ The amount of money that you have to pay (your **fare**) is shown on a **meter**. People often give the taxi-driver a **tip** (= a small extra sum of money that is not included in the fare).

'taxi rank (*US* **'cab stand**) *noun* [C] a place where taxis park while they are waiting to be hired

taxi[2] /'tæksi/ *verb* [I] (used about an aircraft) to move slowly along the ground before or after flying

taxing /'tæksɪŋ/ *adj* difficult; needing a lot of effort: *a taxing problem*

☆ **tea** /tiː/ *noun* **1** [U] a hot brown drink that you make by pouring boiling water onto the dried leaves of a bush grown in hot countries such as India and China: *a cup/pot of tea* ○ *I'll make some tea.* ○ *weak/strong tea* ☞ We usually say '**have** a cup of tea', and *not* '**drink** a cup of tea ': *I had three cups of tea this morning.* **2** [U] the dried leaves that are used for making tea: *A packet of Earl Grey tea, please.* **3** [C] a cup of tea: *Two teas and one coffee, please.* **4** [U] a drink that you make by pouring hot water onto the leaves of other plants: *herb tea* **5** [C,U] (*especially Brit*) a small afternoon meal of cakes, biscuits etc and a cup of tea: *The hotel serves afternoon teas.*

iː	ɪ	e	æ	ɑː	ɒ	ɔː	ʊ	uː	ʌ
see	sit	ten	hat	arm	got	saw	put	too	cup

☛ Some people call their main evening meal **tea**. This is usually eaten at 5 or 6 o'clock. **Supper** and **dinner** are later meals.

(IDIOM) **(not) sb's cup of tea** ⇨ CUP¹

'tea bag noun [C] a small paper bag with tea leaves in it, that you use for making tea

'tea cloth noun [C] (Brit) = TEA TOWEL

'teacup noun [C] a cup that you drink tea from

'tea leaf noun [C, usually pl] one of the small leaves that are left in a cup or pot after you have drunk the tea

'teapot noun [C] a container that you use for making tea in and for pouring tea into cups. It has a lid, a handle and a small thin tube (**a spout**) that the tea is poured out of. ☛ picture at **pot**.

'teashop (also **'tearoom**) noun [C] a small restaurant which serves tea, coffee, etc, also cakes and light meals

'teaspoon noun [C] **1** a small spoon that is used for stirring tea, etc **2** (also **teaspoonful** /-fʊl/) the amount that a teaspoon can hold

'teatime noun [C] the time in the afternoon when people usually have tea: *We'll expect to arrive at about teatime.*

'tea towel (also **tea cloth**) noun [C] a small towel that is used for drying plates, knives, forks, etc

☆ **teach** /tiːtʃ/ verb (pt, pp **taught** /tɔːt/) **1** [I,T] to give sb lessons or instructions so that he/she knows how to do sth: *Jeremy is teaching us how to use the computer.* ○ *My mother taught me to play the piano.* ○ *He teaches English to foreign students.* **2** [T] to make sb believe sth or behave in a certain way: *The story teaches us that history often repeats itself.* ○ *My parents taught me always to tell the truth.*

teaching noun **1** [U] the work or profession of a teacher: *My son went into teaching and my daughter became a doctor.* ○ *part-time teaching* ○ *teaching methods* **2** [C, usually pl] ideas and beliefs that are taught by sb/sth: *the teachings of Gandhi*

☆ **teacher** /ˈtiːtʃə(r)/ noun [C] a person whose job is to teach, especially in a school or college: *He's a teacher at a primary school.* ○ *a French teacher*

☆ **team** /tiːm/ noun [C] **1** a group of people who play a sport or game together against another group: *a football team* ☛ *Are you in the team?* **2** a group of people who work together: *a team of medical workers* ☛ When **team** is used in the singular, it can be followed by either a singular or a plural verb: *The team play/plays two matches every week.*

(PHRASAL VERB) **team up (with sb)** to join sb in order to do sth together

'teamwork noun [U] the ability of people to work together: *Good teamwork between nurses and doctors is very important.*

☆ **tear¹** /tɪə(r)/ noun [C, usually pl] a drop of water that comes from your eye when you are crying, etc: *She wiped away her tears.* ○ *I was in tears* (= crying) *at the end of the film.* ○ *The little girl burst into tears* (= suddenly started to cry).

tearful /-fl/ adj crying or nearly crying

'tear-gas noun [U] a type of gas that makes people's eyes fill with tears. It is used by the police, etc to control large groups of people.

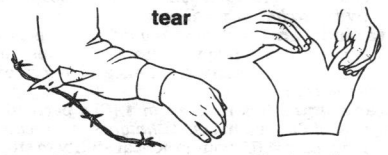

tear

'Oh no! I've **torn** my shirt!'   She **tore** the letter in half.

☆ **tear²** /teə(r)/ verb (pt **tore** /tɔː(r)/; pp **torn** /tɔːn/) **1** [T] to pull paper, cloth, etc so that it comes apart, goes into pieces or gets a hole in it: *I tore my shirt on that nail.* ○ *Tear the paper along the dotted line.* ○ *She tore the letter in half.* ○ *I tore a page out of my notebook.* **2** [I] to become torn: *This material doesn't tear easily.* **3** [T] to remove sth by pulling it violently and quickly: *Paul tore the poster down from the wall.* **4** [I] to move very quickly in a particular direction: *An ambulance went tearing past.*

(IDIOM) **wear and tear** ⇨ WEAR²

(PHRASAL VERBS) **tear sth apart 1** to pull sth violently into pieces: *The bird was torn apart by the two dogs.* **2** to destroy sth completely: *The country has been torn apart by the war.*

tear yourself away (from sb/sth) to make yourself leave sb/sth or stop doing sth: *Tim can't tear himself away from that computer game.*

be torn between A and B to find it difficult to choose between two things or people

tear sth down (used about a building or monument) to bring it to the ground: *They tore down the old houses and built a shopping centre.*

tear sth up to pull sth (usually sth made of paper) into pieces: *'I hate this photograph,' she said, tearing it up.*

tear noun [C] a hole in paper, cloth, etc that is caused by tearing

tease /tiːz/ verb [I,T] to say unkind or personal things to or about sb because you think it is funny: *Don't pay any attention to those boys. They're only teasing.* ○ *They teased her about being fat.*

☆ **technical** /ˈteknɪkl/ adj **1** involving detailed knowledge of the machines, materials, systems, etc that are used in industry or science: *They haven't got the technical knowledge to develop nuclear weapons.* **2** (used about sb's practical ability in a particular activity): *The pianist performed with great technical skill but without much feeling.* **3** (only *before* a noun) relating to a particular subject: *the technical terms connected with computers*

technicality /ˌteknɪˈkæləti/ noun [C] (pl **technicalities**) one of the details of a particular subject or activity

technically /-kli/ adv **1** following a very exact interpretation of facts or laws: *Technically, you should pay by May 1st, but it doesn't matter if it's a few days late.* **2** in a way that in-

technician /tek'nɪʃn/ noun [C] a person whose work involves practical skills, especially in industry or science: *a laboratory technician*

☆ **technique** /tek'ni:k/ noun **1** [C] a particular way of doing sth: *new techniques for teaching languages* **2** [U] your practical ability in sth

☆ **technology** /tek'nɒlədʒɪ/ noun (pl **technologies**) **1** [U] the study and use of science for practical purposes in industry, etc **2** [C,U] the scientific knowledge that is needed for a particular industry, etc: *developments in computer technology* —**technological** /,teknə'lɒdʒɪkl/ adj: *technological developments*

technologist /tek'nɒlədʒɪst/ noun [C] a person who is an expert in technology

teddy /'tedɪ/ (also **'teddy bear**) noun [C] (pl **teddies**) a toy for children that looks like a bear

tedious /'ti:dɪəs/ adj boring and lasting for a long time: *a tedious train journey*

teem /ti:m/ verb [I] **teem with sth** (used about a place) having a lot of people or things moving about in it: *The streets were teeming with people.*

☆ **teenager** /'ti:neɪdʒə(r)/ noun [C] a person who is between 13 and 19 years old: *Her music is very popular with teenagers.*

teenage /'ti:neɪdʒ/ adj (only *before* a noun) **1** between 13 and 19 years old: *teenage children* **2** typical of or suitable for people between 13 and 19 years old: *teenage fashion*

teens /ti:nz/ noun [plural] the period of a person's life between the ages of 13 and 19: *to be in your late/early teens*

teeshirt = T-SHIRT

teeth pl of TOOTH

teethe /ti:ð/ verb [I] (usually in the -*ing* forms) (used about a baby) to start growing its first teeth

'teething troubles (also **'teething problems**) noun [plural] the problems that can develop when a person, system, etc is new

teetotal /ti:'təʊtl/; *US* 'ti:təʊtl/ adj (used about a person) never drinking alcohol

teetotaller (*US* **teetotaler**) /-tlə(r)/ noun [C] a person who never drinks alcohol

telecommunications /,telɪkə,mju:nɪ'keɪʃnz/ noun [plural] the process of communicating over long distances by using electronic equipment, eg by radio, television or telephone

telegram /'telɪgræm/ noun [C] a message that you can send very quickly to sb over a long distance. The message is sent for you by a telephone company, etc and delivered on a printed form

☛ Within the UK telegrams are now called **telemessages**.

telegraph /'telɪgrɑ:f; *US* -græf/ noun [U] a system of sending messages by using radio or electrical signals

'telegraph pole noun [C] a tall wooden pole that is used for supporting telephone wires

telepathy /tɪ'lepəθɪ/ noun [U] the communication of thoughts between people's minds without speaking, etc

telephone

☆ **telephone** /'telɪfəʊn/ (also *informal* **phone**) noun **1** [U] an electrical system for talking to sb in another house, town, country, etc by speaking into a special piece of equipment: *Can I contact you by telephone?* ○ *to make a telephone call* ○ *What's your telephone number?*

☛ When you make a telephone call you first **pick up the receiver** and **dial** the number. The telephone **rings** and the person at the other end **answers** it. If he/she is already using the telephone, it is **engaged** (*US* **busy**). When you finish speaking you **put down** the receiver and **ring off**.

2 [C] (also **handset**) the piece of equipment that you use when you talk to sb by telephone: *Could I use your telephone?* ○ *a portable telephone* (= one that you can carry around) ○ *a public telephone*

(IDIOM) **on the phone/telephone** ⇨ PHONE

telephone (*also* **phone**) verb [I,T] to use a telephone in order to speak to sb: *Sarah telephoned. She's going to be late.*

telephonist /tɪ'lefənɪst/ noun [C] a person whose job is to answer the telephone and make telephone connections in an office or telephone exchange

'telephone box (*also* **'phone box**; **'callbox**) noun [C] a small covered place in a street, etc that contains a telephone for public use

'telephone directory (also *informal* **'phone book**) noun [C] a book that gives a list of the names, addresses and telephone numbers of the people in a particular area

'telephone exchange (*also* **exchange**) noun [C] a place belonging to the telephone company where telephone lines are connected so that people can speak to each other

'telephone number (also *informal* **'phone number**) noun [C] the number that you dial when you speak to sb on the telephone

p	b	t	d	k	g	tʃ	dʒ	f	v	θ	ð
pen	bad	tea	did	cat	got	chin	June	fall	van	thin	then

☞ The number that you dial before the telephone number if you are telephoning a different area or country is called the **code**: *'What's the code for Spain?' '0034.'*

telescope /'telɪskəʊp/ *noun* [C] an instrument in the shape of a tube with special glass inside it. You look through it to make distant things appear bigger and nearer. ☞ picture at binoculars. Look at microscope.

teletext /'telɪtekst/ *noun* [U] a service that provides news and other information in written form on television

☆**television** /'telɪvɪʒn/ (*also* **TV**; *Brit informal* **telly**) *noun* **1** [C] (*also* **television set**) a piece of electrical equipment in the shape of a box. It has a glass screen which shows programmes with moving pictures and sounds: *to turn the television on/off* **2** [U] the electrical system and business of sending out programmes so that people can watch them on their television sets: *Television and radio have helped people to learn more about the world they live in.* ○ *cable/satellite television* ○ *She works in television.* **3** [U] the programmes that are shown on a television set: *Paul's watching television.*
(IDIOM) **on television** being shown by television: *What's on television tonight?*

televise /'telɪvaɪz/ *verb* [T] to show sth on television: *a televised concert*

telex /'teleks/ *noun* **1** [U] a system of sending written messages using special machines. The message is typed on a machine in one place, and then sent by telephone to a machine in another place, which immediately prints it out. **2** [C] a machine for sending out such messages; a message that is sent or received by telex ☞ Look at fax.

☆**tell** /tel/ *verb* (*pt, pp* **told** /təʊld/) **1** [T] **tell sb (sth)**; **tell sth (to sb)** to give information to sb by speaking or writing: *She told me her address but I've forgotten it.* ○ *He wrote to tell me that his mother had died.* ○ *Tell us about your holiday.* ○ *Tell me what you did yesterday.* ○ *to tell the truth/a lie* ○ *to tell a story* ○ *Excuse me, could you tell me where the station is?* ☞ Look at the note at **say**. **2** [T] **tell sb (to do sth)** to order or advise sb to do sth: *The policewoman told us to get out of the car.* ○ *Dad told me not to worry about my exams.* ○ *Please tell me what to do.* ○ *You'll be all right if you do as you're told.* **3** [I,T] to know, see or judge (sth) correctly: *'What do you think Jenny will do next?' 'It's hard to tell.'* ○ *I could tell that he had enjoyed the evening.* ○ *I can't tell which coat is mine. They look exactly the same.* **4** [T] (used about a thing) to give information to sb: *This book will tell you all you need to know.* **5** [I] **tell (on sb/sth)** to have a noticeable effect: *Your age is beginning to tell!*
(IDIOMS) **all told** with everybody or everything counted and included: *The holiday cost over £1 000, all told.*

I told you (so) (*informal*) I warned you that this would happen

tell A and B apart ⇨ APART

tell the time to read the time from a clock or watch

(PHRASAL VERB) **tell sb off (for sth/for doing sth)** to speak to sb angrily because he/she has done sth wrong

telling *adj* **1** having a great effect: *a telling argument* **2** showing your real feelings or thoughts: *a telling remark*

'tell-tale *adj* giving information about sth secret or private: *the tell-tale signs of worry on his face*

telly /'telɪ/ *noun* [C,U] (*pl* **tellies**) (*Brit informal*) = TELEVISION

temp /temp/ *noun* [C] (*informal*) a temporary employee, especially a secretary, who works somewhere for a short period of time when sb else is ill or on holiday

☆**temper** /'tempə(r)/ *noun* **1** [C,U] If you have a temper you are often angry and impatient, and you cannot control your behaviour: *Be careful of Paul. He's got quite a temper!* ○ *You must learn to control your temper.* **2** [C] the way you are feeling at a particular time: *Leave her alone. She's in a bad temper* (= feeling angry). ○ *I went for a long walk and came back in a better temper.*
(IDIOMS) **in a temper** feeling very angry and not controlling your behaviour
keep/lose your temper to stay calm/to become angry ☞ Look at **bad-tempered**.

temperament /'temprəmənt/ *noun* [C,U] a person's character, especially as it affects the way he/she behaves and feels: *to have a calm temperament*

temperamental /,temprə'mentl/ *adj* often and suddenly changing the way you behave

temperate /'tempərət/ *adj* (used about a climate) not very hot and not very cold

☆**temperature** /'temprətʃə(r); US 'tempərtʃʊər/ *noun* **1** [C,U] how hot or cold sth is: *Heat the oven to a temperature of 200°C.* ○ *Temperatures in some parts of Britain will fall below freezing tomorrow.* ○ *a high/low temperature* **2** [C] how hot or cold a person's body is
(IDIOMS) **have a temperature** to have a temperature of the body that is higher than normal (when you are ill)
take sb's temperature to measure the temperature of sb's body with a special instrument (**thermometer**)

temple¹ /'templ/ *noun* [C] a building where people pray to and worship a god or gods: *a Buddhist temple*

temple² /'templ/ *noun* [C] one of the flat parts on each side of your forehead

tempo /'tempəʊ/ *noun* (*pl* **tempos** /'tempəʊz/) **1** [sing,U] the speed of an activity or event **2** [C,U] (*technical*) the speed of a piece of music

☆**temporary** /'temprərɪ; US -pərerɪ/ *adj* lasting for a short time; not permanent: *a temporary job* ○ *This arrangement is only temporary.*
—**temporarily** /'temprərəlɪ; US ,tempə'rerəlɪ/ *adv*

☆**tempt** /tempt/ *verb* [T] to try to persuade or attract sb to do sth, especially sth that is wrong or silly: *His dream of riches had tempted him into a life of crime.* ○ *She was tempted to stay in bed all morning.* ○ *I'm very tempted by the idea of working in another country.*

s	z	ʃ	ʒ	h	m	n	ŋ	l	r	j	w
so	zoo	she	vision	how	man	no	sing	leg	red	yes	wet

tempting *adj* attractive: *a tempting offer* ○ *That chocolate cake looks very tempting!*

temptation /temp'teɪʃn/ *noun* **1** [U] a feeling that you want to do sth, although you know that it is wrong or silly: *I resisted the temptation to have another glass of wine.* **2** [C] a thing that attracts you to do sth wrong or silly: *All that money is certainly a big temptation.*

☆ **ten** /ten/ *number* 10; one more than nine ☛ For examples of how to use numbers in sentences, look at **six**.

tenth /tenθ/ *pron, det, adv* 10th; next after ninth

tenth *noun* [C] the fraction ¹⁄₁₀; one of ten equal parts ☛ Look at the examples at **sixth**.

tenacious /tɪ'neɪʃəs/ *adj* very determined about sth; not likely to give up or accept defeat: *a tenacious defender of human rights* —**tenacity** /tɪ'næsəti/ *noun* [U]

☆ **tenant** /'tenənt/ *noun* [C] a person who pays money (**rent**) to the owner of a room, flat, building or piece of land so that he/she can live in it or use it: *The previous tenants of the flat were university students.* ☛ The owner is called a **landlord** or **landlady**.

tenancy /-ənsi/ (*pl* **tenancies**) *noun* [C,U] the use of a room, flat, building or piece of land, for which you pay rent to the owner: *a six-month tenancy* ○ *a tenancy agreement*

☆ **tend¹** /tend/ *verb* [I] **1** to often or normally do or be sth: *Women tend to live longer than men.* ○ *There tends to be a lot of heavy traffic on that road.* ○ *My brother tends to talk a lot when he's nervous.* **2** (used for giving your opinion in a polite way): *I tend to think that we shouldn't interfere.*

tendency /'tendənsi/ *noun* [C] (*pl* **tendencies**) something that a person or thing does; a way of behaving: *He has a tendency to be late for appointments.* ○ *The dog began to show vicious tendencies.* ○ *She seems to have a tendency towards depression.* ○ *There's a growing tendency for people to travel to work by bicycle.*

tend² /tend/ *verb* [T] (*formal*) to look after sb/sth: *He tended the child day and night throughout his illness.*

tender¹ /'tendə(r)/ *adj* **1** kind and loving: *She whispered a few tender words in his ear.* **2** (used about meat) soft and easy to cut or bite; not tough **3** (used about a part of the body) painful when you touch it **4** young and without much experience of life: *She went to live in London at the tender age of 15.* —**tenderly** *adv* —**tenderness** *noun* [U]

tender² /'tendə(r)/ *verb* [I,T] (*formal*) to offer or give sth formally: *After the scandal the Foreign Minister was forced to tender his resignation.* ○ *Five different companies tendered for the building contract* (= stated a price for doing the work).

tender (*also* **bid**) *noun* [C] (*technical*) a formal offer to supply goods or do work at a certain price.

tendon /'tendən/ *noun* [C] a strong cord in your body that joins a muscle to a bone

tenement /'tenəmənt/ *noun* [C] a large building that is divided into small flats, especially in a poor area of a city

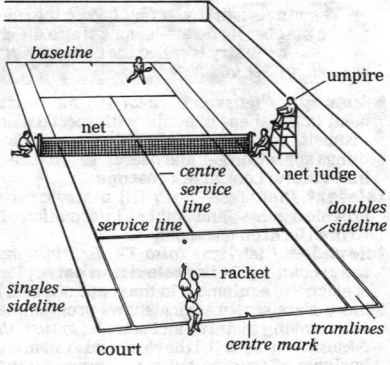

☆ **tennis** /'tenɪs/ (*also* **lawn tennis**) *noun* [U] a game for two or four players who hit a ball to each other over nets with rackets: *Let's play tennis.* ○ *to have a game of tennis* ○ *a tennis match*

☛ In tennis you can play **singles** (a game between two people) or **doubles** (a game between two teams of two people).

tenor /'tenə(r)/ *noun* [C] **1** the highest normal singing voice for a man; a man with this voice: *a lovely tenor voice* ○ *Pavarotti is a famous Italian tenor.* **2** a musical instrument with the same range as a tenor voice: *a tenor saxophone*

tenpin bowling /,tenpɪn 'bəʊlɪŋ/ *noun* [U] a game in which you roll a heavy ball towards ten objects (**tenpins**) and try to knock them down

☆ **tense¹** /tens/ *adj* **1** (used about a person) not able to relax because you are worried or nervous: *She looked pale and tense.* **2** (used about a person's body) having stiff muscles because you are not relaxed **3** (used about an atmosphere or situation) making people feel worried and not relaxed: *Reporters described the atmosphere in the capital as 'very tense'.*

tense *verb* [I,T] to become tense or to make your body tense

☆ **tense²** /tens/ *noun* [C,U] (*grammar*) a form of a verb that shows whether sth happens in the past, present or future

☆ **tension** /'tenʃn/ *noun* **1** [C,U] the condition of not being able to relax that is caused by worry or nervousness: *I could hear the tension in her voice as she spoke.* **2** [C,U] a condition of bad feeling and lack of trust between people, countries, etc: *There are signs of growing tensions between the two countries.* **3** [U] (used about a rope, wire, etc) how tightly it is stretched

☆ **tent** /tent/ *noun* [C] a shelter made of nylon or canvas that is held up by poles and ropes. You use a tent to sleep in when you go camping.

tentative /'tentətɪv/ *adj* **1** (used about plans, etc) uncertain; not definite: *I've made a tentative arrangement to meet Paul for lunch next week, but it's not definite yet.* **2** (used about a

i:	ɪ	e	æ	ɑ:	ɒ	ɔ:	ʊ	u:	ʌ
see	sit	ten	hat	arm	got	saw	put	too	cup

tenterhooks /ˈtentəhʊks/ noun [plural] (IDIOM) **(be) on tenterhooks** to be in a very nervous or excited state because you are waiting to find out what is going to happen

tenth ⇨ TEN

tenuous /ˈtenjuəs/ adj (used about a connection or an idea) very small and weak and possibly not really existing: *My father says we are related to the Churchill family, but actually the link is extremely tenuous.*

tenure /ˈtenjuə(r); US -jər/ noun [U] a legal right to live in a place, hold a job, use land, etc for a certain time

tepid /ˈtepɪd/ adj (used about liquids) only slightly warm

☆ **term** /tɜːm/ noun **1** [C] a word or group of words, especially one that is used in connection with a particular subject: *What exactly do you mean by the term 'racist'?* o *a technical term* **2 terms** [plural] **in ... terms; in terms of ...** (used for indicating which particular way you are thinking about sth or from which point of view): *The flat would be ideal in terms of size, but it is very expensive.* o *We must think about this in political terms.* o *Let's talk in terms of opening a new office in June* (=let's think about doing this). **3 terms** [plural] the conditions of an agreement: *Under the terms of the contract you must give a week's notice.* o *peace terms* **4** [C,U] a period of time into which a school or university year is divided: *the autumn/spring/summer term* **5** [C] a period of time for which sth lasts: *The US President is now in his second term of office.*

(IDIOMS) **be on equal terms (with sb)** ⇨ EQUAL

be on good, friendly etc terms (with sb) to have a friendly relationship with sb

come to terms with sth to accept sth unpleasant or difficult

in the long/short term over a long/short period of time in the future: *We're aiming at a tax rate of 20% in the long term.*

term verb [T] to describe sb/sth by using a particular word or expression: *the period of history that is often termed the 'Dark Ages'*

terminal¹ /ˈtɜːmɪnl/ adj (used about an illness) slowly causing death: *terminal cancer* —**terminally** /-nəli/ adv: *a terminally ill patient*

☆ **terminal²** /ˈtɜːmɪnl/ noun **1** [C] a large railway station, bus station or building at an airport where journeys begin and end: *the bus terminal* o *British Airways flights depart from Terminal 1 at Heathrow.* **2** a piece of computer equipment (usually a keyboard and screen) that you use for getting information from a central computer or for putting information into it

terminate /ˈtɜːmɪneɪt/ verb [I,T] (formal) to end or to make sth end: *to terminate a contract* —**termination** (formal) noun [U]

terminology /ˌtɜːmɪˈnɒlədʒi/ noun [C,U] (pl **terminologies**) the special words and expressions that are used in a particular profession, subject or activity: *computer terminology*

terminus /ˈtɜːmɪnəs/ noun [C] (pl **termini** /-nəsɪz/) the last stop or station at the end of a bus route or railway line

terrace /ˈterəs/ noun [C] **1** a flat area of stone next to a restaurant or large house where people can have meals, sit in the sun, etc: *lunch on the terrace* ☛ Look at **patio**. **2** a line of similar houses that are all joined together **3** [usually pl] one of a series of steps that are cut into the side of a hill so that crops can be grown there **4** [plural] the wide steps that people stand on to watch a football match

terraced /ˈterəst/ adj **1** (Brit) (used about a house) forming part of a line of similar houses that are all joined together ☛ picture on page A12. **2** (used about a hill) having steps cut out of it so that crops can be grown there

terrain /təˈreɪn/ noun [U] a type of land: *rough terrain*

☆ **terrible** /ˈterəbl/ adj **1** very unpleasant or serious: *a terrible accident* o *What a terrible thing to do!* **2** ill or very upset: *I feel terrible. I think I'm going to be sick.* o *He felt terrible when he realized what he had done.* **3** very bad; of poor quality: *The hotel was terrible.* **4** (only before a noun) great: *It was a terrible shame that you couldn't come.*

terribly /-əbli/ adv **1** very: *I'm terribly sorry.* **2** very badly: *I played terribly.*

terrier /ˈteriə(r)/ noun [C] a type of small dog

terrific /təˈrɪfɪk/ adj **1** (informal) extremely nice or good; excellent: *You're doing a terrific job!* **2** (only before a noun) very great: *The food was terrific value.*

terrifically /-kli/ adv (informal) extremely: *terrifically expensive*

terrify /ˈterɪfaɪ/ verb [T] (pres part **terrifying**; 3rd pers sing pres **terrifies**; pt, pp **terrified**) to frighten sb very much

terrified adj **terrified (of sb/sth)** very afraid: *to be terrified of spiders* o *a terrified face*

☆ **territory** /ˈterətri; US -tɔːri/ noun (pl **territories**) **1** [C,U] an area of land that belongs to one country or ruler: *former French territories in Africa* o *to fly over enemy territory* **2** [C,U] an area that an animal has as its own

territorial /ˌterəˈtɔːriəl/ adj (only before a noun) connected with the land or area of sea that belongs to a country or ruler: *territorial waters*

☆ **terror** /ˈterə(r)/ noun **1** [U] very great fear: *He screamed in terror as the rats came towards him.* **2** [C] a person or thing that makes you feel afraid: *the terrors of the night* **3** [U] violent action (eg bombing, killing) for political purposes: *a terror campaign*

terrorize (also **terrorise**) /ˈterəraɪz/ verb [T] to make sb feel frightened by using or threatening to use violence against him/her

☆ **terrorism** /ˈterərɪzəm/ noun [U] the use of violent action (eg bombing, killing) for political purposes: *an act of terrorism*

terrorist /ˈterərɪst/ noun [C] a person who is involved in terrorism —**terrorist** adj

terse /tɜːs/ adj said in few words and in a not very friendly way: *a terse reply*

ɜː	ə	eɪ	əʊ	aɪ	aʊ	ɔɪ	ɪə	eə	ʊə
fur	ago	pay	home	five	now	join	near	hair	pure

tertiary /ˈtɜːʃəri; US -ʃieri/ adj (used about education) after primary and secondary: *a tertiary college*

☆ **test¹** /test/ noun [C] **1** a short examination to measure sb's knowledge or skill in sth: *a spelling test* ☛ When you **take** a test you can either **pass** it (which is good) or **fail** it (which is bad). **2** a short medical examination of a part of your body: *an eye test* **3** an experiment to find out whether sth works or to find out more information about it: *Tests show that the new drug is safe and effective.* **4** a situation or event that shows how good, strong, effective, etc sb/sth is: *The local elections will be a good test of the government's popularity.*

☆ **test²** /test/ verb [T] **1 test sb/sth (for sth); test sth (on sb/sth)** to try, use or examine sth carefully to find out if it is working properly or what it is like: *These cars have all been tested for safety.* ○ *Do you think drugs should be tested on animals?* **2** to examine a part of the body to find out if it is healthy: *to have your eyes tested* **3 test sb (on sth)** to examine sb's knowledge or skill in sth

'test-tube noun [C] a thin glass tube that is used in chemical experiments

'test-tube baby noun [C] a baby that develops from an egg which has been taken out of the mother's body. The egg is fertilized and then put back inside to develop normally.

testament /ˈtestəmənt/ noun [C, usually sing] (*formal*) **a testament (to sth)** something that shows that sth else exists or is true: *Puttnam's new film is a testament to his talent and experience.*

testicle /ˈtestɪkl/ noun [C] one of the two male sex organs that produce sperm

testify /ˈtestɪfaɪ/ verb (*pres part* **testifying**; *3rd pers sing pres* **testifies**; *pt, pp* **testified**) [I,T] to make a formal statement that sth is true, especially as a witness in a court of law

testimony /ˈtestɪməni/; US -məʊni/ noun (*pl* **testimonies**) **1** [C,U] a formal statement that sth is true, especially one that is made in a court of law **2** [U,sing] (*formal*) something that shows that sth else exists or is true: *The design was testimony to her architectural skill.*

tetanus /ˈtetənəs/ noun [U] a serious disease that makes your muscles, especially the muscles of your face, become stiff. It is caused by bacteria entering the body when a cut becomes infected.

tether /ˈteðə(r)/ verb [T] to tie an animal to sth with a rope, etc —**tether** noun [C]
(IDIOM) **at the end of your tether** ⇒ END¹

☆ **text** /tekst/ noun **1** [U] the main written part of a book, newspaper, etc (not the pictures, notes, index, etc) **2** [C] the written form of a speech, interview, article, etc: *The newspaper printed the complete text of the interview.* **3** [C] a book or a short piece of writing that people study as part of a literature and language course: *a set text* (= one that has to be studied for an examination)

textbook /ˈtekstbʊk/ noun [C] a book that teaches a particular subject and that is used especially in schools

textile /ˈtekstaɪl/ noun [C] (in industry) a material that is made by weaving or knitting: *cotton textiles*

texture /ˈtekstʃə(r)/ noun [C,U] the way that sth feels when you touch it: *material with a silky texture*

☆ **than** /ðən; strong form ðæn/ conj, prep **1** (used when you are comparing two things): *He's taller than me.* ○ *He's taller than I am.* ○ *London is more expensive than Madrid.* ○ *You speak French much better than she does.* **2** (used with 'more' and 'less' before numbers, expressions of time, distance, etc): *He earns more than £20 000 a year.* **3** (used after 'would rather' to say that you prefer one thing to another): *I'd rather go to France than to Italy.*

☆ **thank** /θæŋk/ verb [T] **thank sb (for sth/for doing sth)** to tell sb that you are grateful: *I'm writing to thank you for the present you sent me.* ○ *I'll go and thank him for offering to help.* ☛ **Thank you** and **thanks** are both used for telling somebody that you are grateful for something. **Thanks** is more informal: *Thank you very much for your letter.* ○ *'How are you, Rachel?' 'Much better, thanks.'* You can also use **thank you** and **thanks** to accept something that somebody has offered to you: *'Have a piece of cake.' 'Thank you. That would be nice.'* When you want to refuse something you can say **no, thank you** or **no, thanks**: *'Would you like some more tea?' 'No, thanks.'*
(IDIOM) **thank God/goodness/heavens** (used for expressing relief): *Thank goodness it's stopped raining.*

thankful /-fl/ adj (not before a noun) pleased and grateful: *We were thankful when the winter was over that year.*

thankfully /-fəli/ adv **1** in a pleased or thankful way **2** fortunately: *Thankfully, no one was injured.*

thankless adj involving hard work that other people do not notice or thank you for: *Being a housewife can sometimes be a thankless task.*

thanks noun [plural] words which show that you are grateful: *I'd like to express my thanks to all of you for coming here today.*
(IDIOMS) **thanks to sb/sth** because of sb/sth: *We're late, thanks to you!*
a vote of thanks ⇒ VOTE

Thanksgiving (Day) noun [U] a public holiday in the USA and in Canada

☛ Thanksgiving Day is on the fourth Tuesday in November in the USA and on the second Monday in October in Canada. It was originally a day when people thanked God for the harvest.

'thank-you noun [C] an expression of thanks: *Let's have a big thank-you to everybody who worked so hard.*

☆ **that¹** /ðæt/ det, pron (pl **those** /ðəʊz/) **1** (used for describing a person or thing, especially when it is not near the person speaking): *I like that house over there.* ○ *What's that in the road?* ○ *'Could you pass me the book?' 'This one?' 'No, that one over there.'* **2** (used for talking about a person or thing already known or mentioned): *That was the year we went to Spain wasn't it?* ○

p	b	t	d	k	g	tʃ	dʒ	f	v	θ	ð
pen	bad	tea	did	cat	got	chin	June	fall	van	thin	then

Can you give me back that money I lent you last week? (IDIOMS) **that is (to say)** (used when you are giving more information about sb/sth): *I'm on holiday next week. That's to say, from Tuesday.* **that's that** there is nothing more to say or do: *I'm not going and that's that.*

☆ **that²** /ðət; strong form ðæt/ *pron* (used for introducing a relative clause) the person or thing already mentioned: *I'm reading the book that won the Booker prize.* ○ *The people that live next door are French.* ☞ When **that** is the object of the verb in the relative clause, it is often left out: *I want to see the doctor (that) I saw last week.* ○ *I wore the dress (that) I bought in Paris.*

☆ **that³** /ðət; strong form ðæt/ *conj* (used after certain verbs, nouns and adjectives to introduce a new part of the sentence): *She told me that she was leaving.* ○ *I hope that you feel better soon.* ○ *I'm certain that he will come.* ○ *It's funny that you should say that.* ☞ **That** is often left out in this type of sentence: *I thought (that) you would like it.*

☆ **that⁴** /ðæt/ *adv* (used with adjectives, adverbs) to that degree or extent: *30 miles? I can't walk that far.* ○ *She can't play the piano that well.*

thatched /θætʃt/ *adj* (used about a building) having a roof made of straw: *a thatched cottage*

thaw /θɔː/ *verb* [I,T] **thaw (sth) (out)** to become or to make sth become soft or liquid again after freezing: *Is the snow thawing?* ○ *It's starting to thaw* (= the weather is getting warmer). ○ *Always thaw chicken thoroughly before you cook it.* ☞ Look at **melt**. —**thaw** *noun* [C, usually sing]

☆ **the** /ðə; ði; strong form ðiː/ *definite article* **1** (used for talking about a person or thing that is already known or that has already been mentioned): *I took the children to the dentist.* ○ *We met the man who bought your house.* ○ *The milk is in the fridge.* **2** (used when there is only one or only one group): *The sun is very strong today.* ○ *Who won the World Cup?* **3** (used with numbers and dates): *This is the third piece of cake I've had.* ○ *Friday the thirteenth* ○ *I grew up in the sixties.* **4** (used with adjectives to name a group of people): *the French* ○ *the poor* **5** (used with a singular noun when you are talking generally about sth): *The dolphin is an intelligent animal.* **6** (with units of measurement, meaning 'every'): *The car does forty miles to the gallon.* **7** (with musical instruments): *Do you play the piano?* **8** most well-known or important: *You don't mean you met the Tom Cruise?* ☞ 'The' is pronounced /ðiː/ in this sense. **9 the... the...** (used for saying that two things change to the same extent): *The more you eat, the fatter you get.*

☆ **theatre** /ˈθɪətə(r)/ (*US* **theater** /ˈθiːətər/) *noun* **1** [C] a building where you go to see plays, musicals, etc: *the Royal Shakespeare Theatre* ○ *I'm going to the theatre this evening* (= to see a play). **2** [U] plays in general; drama: *to study modern British theatre* **3** [sing,U] the work of acting in or producing plays: *He's worked in the theatre for thirty years.* **4** [C] = OPERATING THEATRE

theatrical /θiˈætrɪkl/ *adj* **1** (only *before* a noun) connected with the theatre **2** (used about behaviour) unnatural and dramatic because you want people to notice it: *a theatrical gesture*

theft /θeft/ *noun* [C,U] the crime of taking sth that belongs to another person secretly and without permission: *There have been a lot of thefts in this area recently.* ○ *The woman was arrested for theft.* ☞ Look at the note at **thief**.

☆ **their** /ðeə(r)/ *det* belonging to them: *What colour is their car?* ○ *The children picked up their books and walked to the door.*

theirs /ðeəz/ *pron* of or belonging to them: *Our flat isn't as big as theirs.*

☆ **them** /ðəm; strong form ðem/ *pron* (the object of a verb or preposition) **1** the people, animals or things mentioned earlier: *I'll phone them now.* ○ *'I've got the keys here.' 'Oh good. Give them to me.'* ○ *We have students from several countries but most of them are Italian.* ○ *'Did you post those letters?' 'Oh dear, I forgot about them.'* **2** (*informal*) him or her: *If anyone phones, tell them I'm busy.*

theme /θiːm/ *noun* [C] **1** a subject of a talk or piece of writing: *The theme of today's discussion will be 'Our changing cities'.* **2** an idea that is developed or repeated in the work of a writer or artist: *The themes of heaven and hell were very common in paintings of this period.*

'**theme park** *noun* [C] a park with a lot of things to do, see, ride on, etc, which are all based on a single idea

☆ **themselves** /ðəmˈselvz/ *pron* **1** (used as the object of a verb or preposition when the people or animals who do an action are affected by it): *Helen and Sarah seem to be enjoying themselves.* ○ *People often talk to themselves when they are worried.* **2** (used for emphasis): *They themselves say that the situation cannot continue.* ○ *Did they paint the house themselves?* (= or did sb else do it for them?)

(IDIOM) **(all) by themselves 1** alone: *The boys are too young to go to the shops by themselves.* ☞ Look at the note at **alone**. **2** without help: *The children cooked the dinner all by themselves.*

☆ **then** /ðen/ *adv* **1** (at) that time: *In 1970? I was at university then.* ○ *I'm afraid I'll be on holiday then.* ○ *I haven't seen him since then.* ○ *I'm going tomorrow. Can you wait until then?* **2** next; after that: *We're going to France for a week and then down to Spain.* ○ *There was silence for a minute. Then he replied.* **3** in that case; therefore: *'I don't feel at all well.' 'Then why don't you go to the doctor?'* **4** (used for emphasis after words like *now, okay, right*, etc): *Now then, are we all ready to go?* ○ *Right then, I'll see you tomorrow.*

(IDIOM) **(but) then (again)** (used for introducing a new and different piece of information): *The weather forecast says it'll rain but then again it's often wrong.*

thence /ðens/ *adv* (*old-fashioned formal*) from there: *They travelled by coach to Dover and thence by boat to France.*

theology /θiˈɒlədʒi/ *noun* [U] the study of reli-

s	z	ʃ	ʒ	h	m	n	ŋ	l	r	j	w
so	zoo	she	vision	how	man	no	sing	leg	red	yes	wet

gion —**theological** /ˌθɪəˈlɒdʒɪkl/ adj: *a theological college*

theoretical /ˌθɪəˈretɪkl/ adj **1** based on ideas and principles, not on practical experience: *A lot of university courses are still too theoretical these days.* **2** based on ideas about sth which may not be true in reality: *a theoretical possibility* (= which will probably never happen) —**theoretically** /-kli/ adv: *Theoretically, we could still win, but I don't think we will.*

☆**theory** /ˈθɪəri/ noun (pl **theories**) **1** [C] an idea or set of ideas that try to explain sth: *the theory about how life on earth began* **2** [U] the general ideal or principles of a particular subject: *political theory*
(IDIOM) **in theory** as a general idea which may not be true in reality: *Your plan sounds fine in theory, but I don't know if it'll work in practice.*

therapeutic /ˌθerəˈpjuːtɪk/ adj **1** helping you to relax and feel better: *I find listening to music very therapeutic.* **2** helping you to recover from an illness: *therapeutic drugs*

therapy /ˈθerəpi/ noun [U] treatment to help or cure a mental or physical illness, usually without drugs or operations: *speech therapy* —**therapist** /ˈθerəpɪst/ noun [C]: *a speech therapist*

☆**there¹** /ðeə(r)/ adv **1** in, at or to that place: *Could you put the table there, please?* ○ *I like Oxford. My husband and I met there.* ○ *Have you been to Bath? We're going there next week.* ○ *Have you looked under there?* **2** at that point (in a conversation, story, etc): *Could I interrupt you there for a minute?* **3** available: *Her parents are always there if she needs help.*
(IDIOMS) **there and then; then and there** immediately; at that time and place
there you are 1 (used when you give sth to sb): *There you are. I've bought you a newspaper.* **2** (used when you are explaining sth to sb): *There you are – just press the switch and it starts.* **3** (used for saying that you are not surprised): *'He's left his wife.' 'There you are, I knew he would.'*

☆**there²** /ðə(r); strong form ðeə(r)/ pron **1** (used as the subject of 'be', 'seem', 'appear', etc to say that sth exists): *Is there a god?* ○ *There's a man at the door.* ○ *There wasn't much to eat.* ○ *There's somebody singing outside.* ○ *There seems to be a mistake here.* **2** (used for calling attention to sth): *Oh look, there's Kate!*

thereabouts /ˈðeərəbaʊts/ (US **thereabout** /ˈðeərəbaʊt/) adv (usually after *or*) **1** somewhere near a number, time or place: *There are 100 students, or thereabouts.* **2**: *She lives in Oxford, or thereabouts.*

thereafter /ˌðeərˈɑːftə(r); US -ˈæf-/ adv (formal) after that: *You will receive £1 000 in May, and £650 per month thereafter.*

thereby /ˌðeəˈbaɪ/ adv (formal) in that way: *We started our journey early, thereby avoiding most of the traffic.*

☆**therefore** /ˈðeəfɔː(r)/ adv for that reason: *The new trains have more powerful engines and are therefore faster.*

therein /ˌðeərˈɪn/ adv (formal) because of sth that has just been mentioned: *The school is too big. Therein lies the problem.*

thereupon /ˌðeərəˈpɒn/ adv (formal) immediately after that and often as the result of sth: *The minister refused to help her. Ms Short thereupon went to the Prime Minister.*

thermal /ˈθɜːml/ adj **1** of heat: *thermal energy* **2** (used about clothes) made to keep you warm in cold weather: *thermal underwear*

☆**thermometer** /θəˈmɒmɪtə(r)/ noun [C] an instrument for measuring the temperature of sb's body or of a room (= how hot or cold it is)

Thermos /ˈθɜːməs/ noun [C] (pl **Thermoses**) (also **'Thermos flask**) (US **'Thermos bottle**) (trade mark) = VACUUM FLASK

thermostat /ˈθɜːməstæt/ noun [C] a device that controls the level of heat in a house or machine by switching it on and off as necessary

thesaurus /θɪˈsɔːrəs/ noun [C] (pl **thesauruses**) a book that contains lists of words and phrases with similar meanings

these ⇒ THIS

thesis /ˈθiːsɪs/ noun [C] (pl **theses** /ˈθiːsiːz/) **1** a long piece of writing on a particular subject that you do as part of a university degree **2** a statement of an idea or theory

☆**they** /ðeɪ/ pron (the subject of a verb) **1** the people, animals or things that have been mentioned: *We've got two children. They're both boys.* ○ *'Have you seen my keys?' 'Yes, they're on the table.'* **2** people in general or people whose identity is not known or stated: *They say it's going to be a hard winter.* **3** (used informally instead of *he* or *she*): *Somebody phoned for you but they didn't leave their name.*

they'd /ðeɪd/ short for THEY HAD, THEY WOULD
they'll /ðeɪl/ short for THEY WILL
they're /ðeə(r)/ short for THEY ARE
they've /ðeɪv/ short for THEY HAVE

☆**thick¹** /θɪk/ adj **1** (used about sth solid) having a large distance between its opposite sides; not thin: *a thick black line* ○ *These walls are very thick.* **2** (used for saying what the distance is between the two opposite sides of something): *The ice was six inches thick.* **3** having a lot of things close together: *a thick forest* ○ *thick hair* **4** (used about a liquid) stiff; that doesn't flow easily: *thick cream* ○ *This paint is too thick.* ☛ The opposite for 1 to 4 is **thin**. **5** (used about fog, smoke, etc) difficult to see through **6** (used about sb's accent) very strong **7** (informal) (used about a person) stupid; not intelligent
(IDIOM) **have a thick skin** to be not easily upset or worried by what people say about you
—**thick** adv: *snow lying thick on the ground*

thicken /ˈθɪkən/ verb [I,T] to become thicker or to make sth thicker: *Tonight the cloud will thicken and more rain will move in from the south-west.* ○ *Add flour to thicken the sauce.*
—**thickly** adv: *Spread the butter thickly.* ○ *a thickly wooded area*

thickness noun [U] the quality of being thick or how thick sth is: *The children were amazed at the thickness of the castle walls.*

thick-'skinned adj not easily worried or upset by what other people say about you: *Politicians have to be thick-skinned.*

thick² /θɪk/ noun

iː	ɪ	e	æ	ɑː	ɒ	ɔː	ʊ	uː	ʌ
see	sit	ten	hat	arm	got	saw	put	too	cup

(IDIOMS) **in the thick of sth** in the most active or crowded part of sth; very involved in sth: *She always likes to be in the thick of things.*
through thick and thin through difficult times and situations

thief /θi:f/ *noun* [C] (*pl* **thieves** /θi:vz/) a person who steals things from another person
☞ A **thief** is a general word for a person who steals things, usually secretly and without violence. The name of the crime is **theft**. A **robber** steals from a bank, shop, etc and often uses violence or threats. A **burglar** steals things by breaking into a house, shop, etc, usually at night, and a **shoplifter** goes into a shop when it is open and takes things without paying. Look also at the note at **steal**.

thigh /θaɪ/ *noun* [C] the top part of the leg, above the knee ☞ picture on page A8.

thimble /'θɪmbl/ *noun* [C] a small object made of metal or plastic that you wear on the end of your finger to protect it when you are sewing

☆ **thin** /θɪn/ *adj* (**thinner**; **thinnest**) **1** (used about sth solid) having a small distance between the opposite sides; not thick: *a thin brown book* o *a thin cotton shirt* o *a thin slice of meat* **2** having very little flesh on the body; not fat: *You need to eat more. You're too thin!*
☞ **Thin**, **skinny**, **slim** and **underweight** all have a similar meaning. **Thin** is the most general word for describing people who have very little flesh on their bodies. **Slim** is used to describe people who are thin in an attractive way: *You're so slim! How do you do it?* If you say sb is **skinny**, you mean that he/she is too thin and not attractive. **Underweight** is a much more formal word, and is often used for describing people who are too thin in a medical sense: *The doctor says I'm underweight.* **3** (used about a liquid) that flows easily; not stiff or thick: *a thin sauce* **4** (used about mist, smoke, etc) not difficult to see through **5** having only a few people or things with a lot of space between them: *The population is rather thin in this part of the country.*
(IDIOMS) **through thick and thin** ⇨ THICK²
vanish, etc into thin air to disappear completely
wear thin ⇨ WEAR¹

thin *adv* thinly: *I don't like bread that's cut too thin.*

thin *verb* [I,T] (**thin**ning; **thin**ned) **thin** (**sth**) (**out**) to become thinner or fewer in number; to make sth thinner: *The fog was beginning to thin.* o *The trees thin out towards the edge of the forest.* o *Thin the sauce by adding milk.*
—**thinly** *adv*: *thinly sliced bread* o *thinly populated areas*

☆ **thing** /θɪŋ/ *noun* **1** [C] an object that is not named: *What's that red thing on the table?* o *A pen is a thing you use for writing with.* o *I need to get a few things at the shops.* **2** [C] a quality or state: *There's no such thing as evil* (= it doesn't exist). o *The best thing about my job is the way it changes all the time.* **3** [C] an action, event or statement: *When I get home the first thing I do is have a cup of tea.* o *A strange thing happened to me yesterday.* o *What a nice thing to say!* **4** [C] a fact, subject, etc: *He told me a few*

things that I didn't know before. **5 things** [plural] your clothes or personal possessions: *I'll just go and pack my things.* **6 things** [plural] the circumstances or conditions of your life: *Things seem to be going very well for me at the moment.* **7** [C] (used for expressing your feelings about a person or animal): *Look how thin that cat is! Poor little thing!* **8 the thing** [sing] what is very suitable or popular: *A week in our hotel is just the thing for tired business people.*
(IDIOMS) **a close shave/thing** ⇨ CLOSE¹
be a good thing (that) be lucky that: *It's a good thing you remembered your umbrella.*
first/last thing as early/late as possible: *I'll telephone her first thing tomorrow morning.* o *I saw him last thing on Friday evening.*
for one thing (used for introducing a reason for something): *I think we should go by train. For one thing it's cheaper.*
have a thing about sb/sth (*informal*) to have strong feelings about sb/sth
make matters/things worse ⇨ WORSE
take it/things easy ⇨ EASY²

☆ **think¹** /θɪŋk/ *verb* (*pt, pp* **thought** /θɔ:t/) **1** [I] **think (about sth)** to use your mind to consider sth or to form connected ideas: *Think before you speak.* o *He had to think hard* (= a lot) *about the question.* **2** [T] to consider or believe; to have as an opinion: *'Do you think it's going to snow?' 'No, I don't think so.'* o *'Sue's coming tomorrow, isn't she?' 'Yes, I think so.'* o *I think that they've moved to York but I'm not sure.* o *What did you think of the film?* o *I don't think they are very good musicians.* **3** [I] **think of/about doing sth** to intend or plan to do sth: *We're thinking of moving house.* **4** [I] **think about/of sb** to consider the feelings of sb else: *She never thinks about anyone but herself.* **5** [T] (used in negative sentences after *can* or *could*) to remember or understand sth: *I couldn't think what he meant.* **6** [T] to expect sth: *The job took longer than we thought.*
(IDIOMS) **think better of (doing) sth** to decide not to do sth; to change your mind
think highly, a lot, not much, etc of sb/sth to have a good, poor, etc opinion of sb/sth
think the world of sb to love and admire sb very much
(PHRASAL VERBS) **think of sth** to create an idea in your imagination: *Who first thought of the plan?*
think sth out to consider carefully all the details of a plan, idea, etc: *a well-thought-out scheme*
think sth over to consider sth carefully: *I'll think your offer over and let you know tomorrow.*
think sth up to create sth in your mind; to invent: *to think up a new advertising slogan*

☆ **think²** /θɪŋk/ *noun* [sing] an act of thinking: *I'm not sure. I'll have to have a think about it.*

thinker /'θɪŋkə(r)/ *noun* [C] a person who thinks about serious and important subjects

thinking /'θɪŋkɪŋ/ *adj* intelligent and using your mind to think about important subjects: *a newspaper for thinking people*

thinking *noun* [U] **1** the act of using your

3:	ə	eɪ	əʊ	aɪ	aʊ	ɔɪ	ɪə	eə	ʊə
fur	ago	pay	home	five	now	join	near	hair	pure

third /θɜːd/ *pron, det, adv* 3rd; next after second ☞ Look at the examples at **sixth**.

third *noun* [C] **1** the fraction ⅓; one of three equal parts of sth **2** (*Brit*) a grade in final university exams, below first and second class degrees

thirdly *adv* (used to introduce the third point in a list): *We have made savings in three areas: firstly, defence, secondly, education and thirdly, health.*

third 'party *noun* [C] a person who is not one of the two main people or groups involved in sth

the ,Third 'World *noun* [sing] the poorer countries of Asia, Africa and South America

☆ **thirst** /θɜːst/ *noun* **1** [U,sing] the feeling that you have when you want or need to drink: *Cold tea really quenches your thirst.* ○ *to die of thirst* **2** [sing] **a thirst for sth** a strong desire for sth

thirsty *adj* (**thirstier**; **thirstiest**) wanting or needing a drink: *I'm thirsty. Can I have a drink of water, please?* —**thirstily** /-ɪlɪ/ *adv*

☆ **thirteen** /ˌθɜːˈtiːn/ *number* 13; one more than twelve ☞ For examples of how to use numbers in sentences, look at **six**.

thirteenth /ˌθɜːˈtiːnθ/ *pron, det, adv* 13th; next after twelfth ☞ Look at the examples at **sixth**.

☆ **thirty** /ˈθɜːtɪ/ *number* 30; one more than twenty-nine ☞ For examples of how to use numbers in sentences, look at **sixty**.

thirtieth /ˈθɜːtɪəθ/ *pron, det, adv* 30th; next after twenty-ninth ☞ Look at the examples at **sixth**.

☆ **this** /ðɪs/ *det, pron* (*pl* **these** /ðiːz/) **1** (used for talking about sb/sth that is close to you in time or space): *Have a look at this photo.* ○ *These boots are really comfortable. My old ones weren't.* ○ *Is this the book you asked for?* ○ *These are the letters to be filed, not those over there.* **2** (used for talking about sth that was mentioned or talked about before): *Where did you hear about this?* **3** (used for introducing sb or showing sb sth): *Charles, this is my wife, Claudia, and these are our children, David and Vicky.* **4** (used with days of the week or periods of time) of today or the present week, year, etc: *Are you busy this afternoon?* ○ *this Friday* (= the Friday of this week) **5** (*informal*) (used when you are telling a story) a certain: *Then this woman said...*

(IDIOM) **this and that; this, that and the other** various things: *We chatted about this and that.*

this *adv* (used when you are describing sth) so; as much as this: *The road is not usually this busy.*

thistle /ˈθɪsl/ *noun* [C] a wild plant with purple flowers and sharp points (**prickles**) on its leaves ☞ The thistle is the national emblem of Scotland.

thorn /θɔːn/ *noun* [C] one of the hard sharp points on the stem of some plants and bushes, eg on rose bushes

thorny *adj* **1** having thorns **2** (used about a problem, etc) difficult

☆ **thorough** /ˈθʌrə/; *US* ˈθɜːroʊ/ *adj* **1** careful and complete: *The police made a thorough search of the house.* **2** doing things in a very careful way, making sure that you look at every detail: *Pam is slow but she is very thorough.*

thoroughly *adv* **1** in a thorough way: *to study a subject thoroughly* **2** completely; very; very much: *We thoroughly enjoyed our holiday.* —**thoroughness** *noun* [U]

those *pl* of **THAT**¹

☆ **though** /ðəʊ/ *conj* **1** in spite of the fact that; although: *Though he had very little money, Alex always managed to dress smartly.* ○ *She still loved him even though he had treated her so badly.* **2** but: *I'll come as soon as I can, though I can't promise to be on time.*

(IDIOMS) **as if/though** ⇒ **AS**

as though ⇒ **AS**

though *adv* (*informal*) however: *I quite like him. I don't like his wife, though.* ☞ Look at the note at **although**.

thought¹ *pt, pp* of **THINK**¹

☆ **thought**² /θɔːt/ *noun* **1** [C,U] the act of thinking: *Irene sat, lost in thought, looking at the old photographs.* **2** [U] particular ideas or a particular way of thinking: *a change in medical thought on the subject* **3** [sing] an act of being kind or caring about sb/sth: *They sent me flowers. What a kind thought!* **4** [C] an idea or opinion: *What are your thoughts on this subject?* ○ *The thought of living alone filled her with fear.* ☞ Look at **second thoughts**.

(IDIOM) **a school of thought** ⇒ **SCHOOL**

thoughtful /-fl/ *adj* **1** thinking deeply: *a thoughtful expression* **2** thinking about what other people want or need: *It was very thoughtful of you to send her some flowers.* —**thoughtfully** /-fəlɪ/ *adv* —**thoughtfulness** *noun* [U]

thoughtless *adj* not thinking about what other people want or need or what the result of your actions will be —**thoughtlessly** *adv* —**thoughtlessness** *noun* [U]

☆ **thousand** /ˈθaʊznd/ *number* 1 000; one more than nine hundred and ninety-nine ☞ Notice that you use **thousand** in the singular when you are talking about a number. You use **thousands** when you mean 'a lot': *She earns eighteen thousand pounds a year.* ○ *Thousands of people attended the meeting.* For more information about numbers, look at Appendix 2.

thousandth /ˈθaʊznθ/ *det* 1 000th; next after nine hundred and ninety-ninth

thousandth *noun* [C] the fraction ¹⁄₁₀₀₀; one of a thousand equal parts of sth

thrash /θræʃ/ *verb* **1** [T] to hit sb/sth many times with a stick, whip, etc **2** [I] **thrash (about/around)** to move your arms, legs, etc in an uncontrolled way, eg because you are in pain **3** [T] to defeat sb easily in a game, competition, etc

(PHRASAL VERB) **thrash sth out** to talk about sth until you reach an agreement

thrashing *noun* [C] an act of thrashing(1,3) sb/sth

☆ **thread** /θred/ *noun* **1** [C,U] a long thin piece of cotton, etc that you use for sewing, etc: *a needle*

p	b	t	d	k	g	tʃ	dʒ	f	v	θ	ð
pen	bad	tea	did	cat	got	chin	June	fall	van	thin	then

and thread **2** [C] the connection between ideas, the parts of a story, etc: *I've lost the thread of this argument.*

thread verb [T] **1** to put thread through the hole in a needle: *to thread a needle* **2** to link things together by putting them onto a string, etc **3** to pass sth narrow through a space and into a particular position: *He threaded the belt through the loops on the trousers.*
(IDIOM) **thread your way through sth** to pass through sth with difficulty, moving around things or people that are in your way

'threadbare /'θredbeə(r)/ *adj* (used about material or clothes) old and very thin

☆**threat** /θret/ *noun* **1** [C,U] a warning that sb may hurt, kill or punish you if you do not do what he/she wants: *Under threat of death he did as they asked.* ○ *to carry out a threat* **2** [C, usually sing] a person or thing that may damage sth or hurt sb; something that indicates future danger: *a threat to national security*

☆**threaten** /'θretn/ *verb* **1** [T] **threaten sb (with sth); threaten (to do sth)** to warn that you may hurt, kill or punish sb if he/she does not do what you want: *to threaten sb with a knife* ○ *She was threatened with dismissal.* ○ *The man threatened to kill her if she didn't tell him where the money was.* **2** [I,T] to seem likely to do sth unpleasant: *The oil slick is threatening the coastline with pollution.* —**threatening** *adj* —**threateningly** *adv*

☆**three** /θri:/ *number* 3; one more than two ☛ Look at **third**. For examples of how to use numbers in sentences, look at **six**.

three- (in compounds) having three of the thing mentioned: *a three-bedded room*

,three-di'mensional, 3-D /,θri:'di:/ *adj* having length, width and height: *a three-dimensional model*

threshold /'θreʃhəʊld/ *noun* [C] **1** the bottom part of a doorway; the entrance to a building: *She stood on the threshold* (= in the entrance). **2** the time when you are just about to start sth or find sth: *on the threshold of a scientific breakthrough*

threw *pt* of THROW¹

thrift /θrɪft/ *noun* [U] the quality of being careful not to spend too much money —**thrifty** *adj* (**thriftier; thriftiest**)

thrill /θrɪl/ *noun* [C] a sudden strong feeling of pleasure or excitement

thrill *verb* [T] to make sb feel a thrill: *His singing thrilled the audience.* —**thrilled** *adj*: *He was absolutely thrilled with my present.*

thriller *noun* [C] a play, film, book, etc with a very exciting story, often about a crime

thrilling *adj* very exciting

thrive /θraɪv/ *verb* [I] (*pt* **thrived** or **throve**; *pp* **thrived**) to grow or develop well —**thriving** *adj*: *a thriving industry*

☆**throat** /θrəʊt/ *noun* [C] **1** the front part of your neck: *The attacker grabbed the man by the throat.* ☛ picture on page A8. **2** the back part of your mouth and the passage down your neck through which air and food pass: *She got a piece of bread stuck in her throat.* ○ *I've got a terrible sore throat.*

throb /θrɒb/ *verb* [I] (**throbbing; throbbed**) to make strong regular movements or noises; to beat strongly: *His heart was throbbing.* ○ *Her finger throbbed with pain.* —**throb** *noun* [C]: *the throb of the ship's engines*

throne /θrəʊn/ *noun* **1** [C] the special chair where a king or queen sits **2 the throne** [sing] the position of being king or queen: *The Queen came to the throne in 1952.*

throng /θrɒŋ; *US* θrɔːŋ/ *noun* [C] a large crowd of people

throng *verb* [I,T] (used about a crowd of people) to move into or fill a particular place: *Crowds thronged to the palace gates.*

throttle /'θrɒtl/ *verb* [T] to hold sb tightly by the throat and stop him/her breathing

☆**through** (*US also* **thru**) /θruː/ *prep* **1** from one end or side of sth to the other: *We drove through the centre of London.* ○ *She could see the outline of a tree through the mist.* ○ *to look through a telescope* ○ *James cut through the rope.* ○ *to push through a crowd of people* **2** from the beginning to the end of sth: *Food supplies will not last through the winter.* ○ *We're halfway through the book.* **3** (*US*) until, and including: *They are staying Monday through Friday.* **4** because of; with the help of: *Errors were made through bad organization.* ○ *David got the job through his uncle.*

through (*US also* **thru**) *adv* **1** from one end or side to the other: *The gate was opened and they ran through.* ☛ On a **through train** you can reach your destination without changing trains. A road with a sign **No through road** is open at only one end. **2** from the beginning to the end of sth: *He read the letter through and handed it back.* **3** (*Brit*) connected by telephone: *Can you put me through to extension 5678, please?*
(PHRASAL VERB) **be through (with sb/sth)** to have finished with sth

☆**throughout** /θruː'aʊt/ *adv, prep* **1** in every part: *The house is beautifully decorated throughout.* **2** from the beginning to the end of sth: *We didn't enjoy the holiday because it rained throughout.* ○ *The match can be watched live on television throughout the world.* ○ *Food was scarce throughout the war.*

throve *pt* of THRIVE

☆**throw¹** /θrəʊ/ *verb* (*pt* **threw** /θruː/; *pp* **thrown** /θrəʊn/) **1** [I,T] to send sth through the air by pushing it out of your hand: *How far can you throw?* ○ *Throw the ball to Wayne.* ○ *Throw Wayne the ball.* ○ *Don't throw stones at people.* **2** [T] to put sth somewhere quickly or carelessly: *He threw his bag down in a corner.* **3** [T] to move your body or part of it quickly or suddenly: *Jenny threw herself onto the bed and sobbed.* ○ *Lee threw back his head and roared with laughter.* **4** [T] to cause sb to fall down: *The bus braked and we were thrown to the floor.* **5** [T] (*informal*) to make sb feel upset, confused or surprised: *The question threw me and I didn't know what to reply.* **6** [T] to put sb in a particular (usually unpleasant) situation: *Many people were thrown out of work in the recession.* **7** [T] to send light or shade onto sth: *The house threw a shadow across the lawn.*
(PHRASAL VERBS) **throw sth away 1** to get rid

s	z	ʃ	ʒ	h	m	n	ŋ	l	r	j	w
so	zoo	she	vision	how	man	no	sing	leg	red	yes	wet

of sth that you do not want, eg by putting it in a dustbin: *That's rubbish. You can throw it away.* **2** to waste or not use sth useful: *to throw away a good opportunity*

throw sth in (*informal*) to include sth else without increasing the price

throw sb out to force sb to leave

throw sth out 1 to refuse to accept sb's idea or suggestion **2** = THROW STH AWAY

throw up (*informal*) to send out the food in your stomach through your mouth; to be sick

throw sth up 1 to give up your job, position, studies, etc **2** to produce or show sth: *Our research has thrown up some interesting facts.*

throw² /θrəʊ/ *noun* [C] **1** an act of throwing **2** the distance that sb throws sth: *a record throw of 75 metres*

thru (*US*) = THROUGH

thrust /θrʌst/ *verb* [I,T] (*pt, pp* **thrust**) **1** to push sb/sth/yourself suddenly and with force: *The man thrust her out of the way and ran off.* **2** to make a sudden forward movement with a knife, etc

(PHRASAL VERB) **thrust sb/sth upon sb** to force sb to accept sb/sth

thrust *noun* **1** [C] a strong push **2** [U] the main part or ideas of sth: *The main thrust of our research is to find ways of preventing cancer.*

thud /θʌd/ *noun* [C] the low sound that is made when sth heavy falls down —**thud** *verb* [I] (**thud**ding; **thud**ded): *A snowball thudded against the window.*

thug /θʌɡ/ *noun* [C] a violent person who may harm other people

☆ **thumb** /θʌm/ *noun* [C] **1** the short thick finger at the side of each hand ☛ picture on page A8. **2** the part of a glove, etc that covers your thumb

thumb *verb* [I,T] **thumb (through) sth** to turn the pages of a book, etc quickly

(IDIOM) **thumb a lift** to hold out your thumb to cars going past, to ask sb to give you a free ride ☛ Look at **hitchhike**.

'thumb-tack (*US*) = DRAWING-PIN

thump /θʌmp/ *verb* **1** [T] to hit sb/sth with sth heavy, usually your fist **2** [I] to make a loud sound by hitting or beating heavily: *His heart was thumping with excitement.*

thump *noun* [C] an act or the sound of thumping

thunder /ˈθʌndə(r)/ *noun* [U] the loud noise that comes after lightning when there is a storm

thunder *verb* **1** [I] (used with *it*) to make the sound of thunder: *The rain poured down and it started to thunder.* **2** [I,T] to make a loud noise like thunder: *Traffic thundered across the bridge.*

'thunderstorm *noun* [C] a storm with thunder and lightning

☆ **Thursday** /ˈθɜːzdɪ/ *noun* [C,U] (*abbr* **Thur**; **Thurs**) the day of the week after Wednesday and before Friday ☛ For examples of the use of the days of the week, look at **Monday**.

☆ **thus** /ðʌs/ *adv* (*formal*) **1** like this; in this way: *Thus began the series of incidents which changed her life.* **2** because of or as a result of this: *I had been driving very carefully. I was thus very surprised when the police stopped me.*

thwart /θwɔːt/ *verb* [T] to stop sb doing what he/she planned to do; to prevent sth happening

tick /tɪk/ *noun* [C] **1** the regular short sound that a watch or clock makes when it is working **2** (*informal*) a moment: *Hang on a tick, please.* **3** (*US* **check**) a mark (✓) that shows sth is correct or has been done: *Put a tick after each correct answer.*

tick

tick

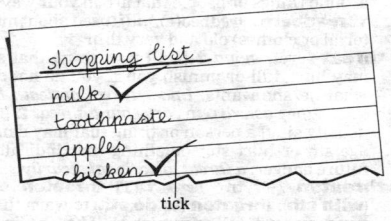

tick *verb* **1** [I] (used about a clock or watch) to make regular short sounds: *I could hear the clock ticking all night.* **2** [T] **tick sth (off)** to mark sth with a tick: *Tick off each job on the list when you've finished it.*

(PHRASAL VERBS) **tick away/by** (used about time) to pass: *The minutes ticked by but there was still no sign of Zoe.*

tick over (*informal*) to continue at a slow rate: *Just keep things ticking over while I'm on holiday.*

☆ **ticket** /ˈtɪkɪt/ *noun* [C] **1** a piece of paper or card that shows you have paid for a journey, or to enter a place of entertainment, etc: *a single/return ticket* ○ *two tickets for the concert* ☛ Look at **season ticket**. **2** a piece of paper or card that shows the price, size, etc of sth that is for sale **3** an official piece of paper that you get when you have parked in the wrong place, driven too fast, etc

tickle /ˈtɪkl/ *verb* **1** [T] to touch sb lightly with your fingers or with sth soft so that he/she laughs: *She tickled the baby's toes.* **2** [I,T] to feel or to cause the sensation of sth touching you lightly: *My nose tickles/is tickling.* ○ *The woollen scarf tickled her neck.* **3** [T] (*informal*) to amuse sb —**tickle** *noun* [C]: *I've got a tickle in my throat.*

ticklish /ˈtɪklɪʃ/ *adj* if a person is ticklish, he/she laughs a lot when sb tickles him/her

tidal /ˈtaɪdl/ *adj* connected with the tides in the sea

tidal 'wave *noun* [C] a very large wave in the sea, often caused by earthquakes

☆ **tide** /taɪd/ *noun* [C,U] the regular change in the level of the sea. At high tide the sea is closer to the shore, at low tide it is farther away: *The tide is coming in/going out.* ○ (*figurative*) *The tide* (= of public opinion) *seems to have turned in the government's favour.*

tide *verb*

(PHRASAL VERB) **tide sb over** to give sb sth to help him/her through a difficult time

☆ **tidy** /ˈtaɪdɪ/ *adj* (**tidier**; **tidiest**) **1** arranged in

iː	ɪ	e	æ	ɑː	ɒ	ɔː	ʊ	uː	ʌ
see	sit	ten	hat	arm	got	saw	put	too	cup

good order; neat: *If you keep your room tidy it is easier to find things.* **2** (used about a person) liking to keep things neat and in good order: *Mark is a very tidy boy.*

tidy *verb* [I,T] (*pres part* **tidying**; *3rd pers sing pres* **tidies**; *pt, pp* **tidied**) **tidy (sb/sth/ yourself) (up)** to make sb/sth/yourself tidy: *We must tidy this room up before the visitors arrive.*

(PHRASAL VERB) **tidy sth away** to put sth into the drawer, cupboard, etc where it is kept —**tidily** *adv* **tidiness** *noun* [U]

☆ **tie¹** /taɪ/ *noun* [C] **1** (*US* **necktie**) a long thin piece of cloth that you wear round your neck with a shirt ☛ Look at **bow-tie**. **2** [usually pl] something that connects you with a particular group of people: *Our school has ties with another school in America.* ○ *family ties* **3** something that limits your freedom: *He never married because he didn't want any ties.* **4** a game or competition in which two or more teams or players get the same score: *There was a tie for first place.*

☆ **tie²** /taɪ/ *verb* (*pres part* **tying**; *3rd pers sing pres* **ties**; *pt, pp* **tied**) **1** [T] to fasten sb/sth or fix sb/sth in position with rope, string, etc: *The prisoner was tied to a chair.* ○ *Kay tied her hair back with a ribbon.* ○ *to tie sth in a knot* ○ *to tie your shoe-laces* **2** [I] **tie (with sb) (for sth)** to have the same score as another player or team in a game or competition: *England tied with Italy for third place.*

(PHRASAL VERBS) **tie sb/yourself down** to limit your freedom: *Having young children really ties you down.*

tie in (with sth) to agree with other facts or information that you have

tie sb/sth up 1 to fix sb/sth in position with rope, string, etc: *The dog was tied up in the back garden.* **2** (usually passive) to occupy or keep sb busy: *Mr Jones is tied up in a meeting.*

tier /tɪə(r)/ *noun* [C] one of a number of levels: *a stadium with many tiers of seats*

tiger /'taɪɡə(r)/ *noun* [C] a large wild cat that has yellow fur with black stripes. Tigers live in Asia. ☛ picture at **lion**. A female tiger is called a **tigress** and a baby is called a **cub**.

☆ **tight** /taɪt/ *adj* **1** firm and difficult to move: *a tight knot* ○ *Keep a tight hold on this rope.* **2** fitting very closely: *These shoes hurt. They're too tight.* ☛ The opposite is **loose**. **3** (in compounds) not allowing sth to get in or out: *an airtight tin* **4** not having much spare time or space: *My schedule this week is very tight.* **5** stretched or pulled hard: *When you're towing another car, keep the rope between the two cars tight.* **6** controlled very strictly: *Security is very tight at Heathrow Airport.*

tight *adv* firmly; closely: *Hold tight please* (= on a bus). ☛ **Tightly**, not **tight**, is used before a past participle: *The van was packed tight with boxes.* ○ *The van was tightly packed with boxes.*

tighten /'taɪtn/ *verb* [I,T] **tighten (sth) (up)** to become tighter; to make sth tighter: *His grip on her arm tightened.* ○ *He tightened the screws as far as they would go.*

(PHRASAL VERB) **tighten up (on sth)** to cause sth to become stricter: *to tighten up the law on the sale of alcohol to children*

tightly *adv* firmly; closely: *Screw the lid on tightly.* ○ *She kept her eyes tightly closed.* —**tightness** *noun* [U]

tightrope /'taɪtrəʊp/ *noun* [C] a rope stretched high above the ground on which people walk, eg in a circus

☆ **tights** /taɪts/ (*US* **pantihose; pantyhose**) *noun* [plural] a piece of thin clothing, usually worn by women, that fits tightly from the waist over the legs and feet: *a pair of tights* ☛ Look at **stocking**.

☆ **tile** /taɪl/ *noun* [C] one of the flat, square objects that are arranged in rows to cover roofs, floors, bathroom walls, etc: *The wind had blown several tiles off the roof.* ○ *carpet tiles* —**tile** *verb*: *a tiled bathroom*

till¹ ⇨ UNTIL

till² /tɪl/ *noun* [C] the drawer or box where money is kept in a shop, etc

tilt /tɪlt/ *verb* [I,T] to have one end or side higher than the other; to put sth in this position: *The front seats of the car tilt forward.* ○ *She tilted her head to one side.* —**tilt** *noun* [sing]

timber /'tɪmbə(r)/ *noun* **1** [U] (especially *US* **lumber**) wood that is going to be used for building **2** [C] a large piece of wood: *a ship's timbers*

☆ **time¹** /taɪm/ *noun* **1** [C] a particular point in the day or night: *What's the time?* ○ *Can Mark tell the time yet?* ○ *Can you tell me the times of trains to Bristol, please?* ○ *It's time to go home.* ○ *By the time I get home, Alex will have cooked the dinner.* **2** [U] the passing of minutes, hours, days, etc: *As time passed and there was still no news, we got more worried.* **3** [C,U] an amount of minutes, hours, days, etc: *You're wasting time – get on with your work!* ○ *I'll go by car to save time.* ○ *free time* ○ *We haven't got time to stop now.* ○ *I've been waiting a long time.* **4** [C] a period in the past: *Did you enjoy your time in Spain?* ○ *In Shakespeare's times, few people could read.* **5** [C,U] an occasion when sth happens: *I phoned them three times.* ○ *I'll do it better next time.* ○ *Last time I saw him, he looked ill.* **6** [sing] a system for measuring time in a particular part of the world: *Central European Time* ○ *We arrive in Atlanta at eleven, local time.* **7** [C,U] the number of minutes, etc, taken to complete sth, especially a race: *What was his time in the hundred metres?*

(IDIOMS) **all the time** during the time that sb was doing sth or that sth was happening: *I searched everywhere for my keys and they were in the door all the time.*

at the same time ⇨ SAME¹

at a time on each occasion: *The lift can hold six people at a time.*

at one time in the past; previously

at the time at a particular moment or period in the past: *I agreed at the time but later changed my mind.*

at times sometimes: *At times I wish we'd never had children.*

beat time (to sth) ⇨ BEAT¹

before your time before you were born

behind the times not modern or fashionable

ɜː	ə	eɪ	əʊ	aɪ	aʊ	ɔɪ	ɪə	eə	ʊə
fur	ago	pay	home	five	now	join	near	hair	pure

for the time being just for the present; not for long

from time to time sometimes; not often

have a good, great, etc time to enjoy yourself: *We had a wonderful time at the party.*

have a hard/rough time to have problems or difficulties

have no time for sb/sth to not like sb/sth: *I have no time for people who aren't prepared to work.*

in good time early; at the right time: *We arrived in good time.*

in the nick of time ⇨ NICK¹

in time (for sth/to do sth) not late; at the right time: *Don't worry. We'll get to the station in time for your train.*

kill time ⇨ KILL

once upon a time ⇨ ONCE

on time not late or early

take your time to do sth without hurrying

tell the time ⇨ TELL

time after time; time and (time) again again and again; many times

'time-consuming *adj* that takes or needs a lot of time

'time-lag *noun* [C] = LAG

'time-limit *noun* [C] a time during which sth must be done

'timetable *noun* [C] a list that shows the times when sth happens

time² /taɪm/ *verb* [T] **1** to choose or arrange the time that sth happens: *They timed their journey to avoid the rush-hour.* **2** to measure how long sth takes

timer *noun* [C] a person or machine that measures time

timing *noun* [U] **1** the act of choosing or arranging when sth will happen: *The timing of the meeting is not convenient for many people.* **2** your skill at choosing or arranging the best time for sth

timeless /'taɪmlɪs/ *adj (formal)* that does not seem to be changed by time

timely /'taɪmli/ *adj* happening at just the right time: *The accident was a timely reminder of the dangers involved.*

times /taɪmz/ *prep* (used when you are multiplying one figure by another): *Three times four is twelve.*

times *noun* [plural] (used for comparing things): *Tea is three times as/more expensive in Spain than in England* (= if it costs £1 in England it costs £3 in Spain).

timid /'tɪmɪd/ *adj* easily frightened; shy —**timidity** /tɪ'mɪdəti/ *noun* [U] —**timidly** *adv*

☆ **tin** /tɪn/ *noun* **1** [U] a soft whitish metal that is often mixed with other metals **2** [C] a closed container in which food is stored and sold, made of tin: *a tin of peas* ☛ picture at **container**. **3** [C] a metal container for food, etc, with a lid: *a biscuit tin*

tinned *adj* (used about food) that is in a tin(2) so that you can keep it for a long time: *tinned peaches*

'tin-opener *noun* [C] a tool that you use for opening a tin(2)

tinge /tɪndʒ/ *noun* [usually sing] a small amount of a colour or a feeling: *a tinge of sadness* —**tinged** *adj*: *Her joy at leaving was tinged with regret.*

tingle /'tɪŋgl/ *verb* [I] to have a slight stinging or prickling feeling in the skin: *His cheeks tingled as he came in from the cold.* —**tingle** *noun* [usually sing]: *a tingle of excitement*

tinker /'tɪŋkə(r)/ *verb* [I] to try to repair or improve sth without having the proper skill or knowledge: *He's been tinkering with the car all afternoon but it still won't start.*

tinkle /'tɪŋkl/ *verb* [I] to make a light, ringing sound, like that of a small bell —**tinkle** *noun* [C, usually sing]

tinsel /'tɪnsl/ *noun* [U] strings covered with little pieces of shiny paper, used as a Christmas decoration

tint /tɪnt/ *noun* [C] a type or shade of a colour: *cream paint with a pinkish tint*

tint *verb* [T] to add a little colour to sth: *tinted glass* ○ *She had her hair tinted.*

☆ **tiny** /'taɪni/ *adj* (**tinier; tiniest**) very small: *the baby's tiny fingers*

☆ **tip¹** /tɪp/ *noun* [C] the thin or pointed end of sth: *the tips of your toes, fingers, etc* ○ *the southernmost tip of South America*

(IDIOMS) **(have sth) on the tip of your tongue** to be about to remember or say sth that you have forgotten for the moment: *Their name is on the tip of my tongue. It'll come back to me in a moment.*

the tip of the iceberg a small part of a problem that is much larger

☆ **tip²** /tɪp/ *verb* [I,T] (**tipping; tipped**) **1 tip (sth) (up)** to move so that one side is higher than the other; to make sth move in this way: *When I stood up, the bench tipped up and the person on the other end fell off.* **2 tip (sth) (over)** to fall or turn over; to make sth turn over: *The tractor turned the corner too fast and the trailer tipped over.* ○ *The baby leaned out of his pushchair and tipped it over.* **3** to empty or pour sth out of a container: *Tip the dirty water down the drain.* ○ *The child tipped all the toys onto the floor.*

tip *noun* [C] **1** a place where you can take rubbish: *We took the broken furniture to the tip.* **2** *(informal)* a place that is very dirty or untidy

☆ **tip³** /tɪp/ *verb* (**tipping; tipped**) to give a small amount of money (in addition to the normal charge) to a waiter, taxi-driver, etc to thank him/her —**tip** *noun* [C]: *Service wasn't included so we left a tip for the waitress.*

tip⁴ /tɪp/ *verb* [T] (**tipping; tipped**) **tip sb/sth (as sth/to do sth)** to think that sb/sth is likely to do sth: *This horse is tipped to win the race.* ○ *He is widely tipped as the next Prime Minister.*

tip *noun* [C] a piece of useful advice

tip⁵ /tɪp/ *verb* (**tipping; tipped**)

(PHRASAL VERB) **tip sb off** to give sb secret information: *The police had been tipped off and were waiting when the burglars broke in.* —**'tip-off** *noun* [C]: *Acting on a tip-off the police searched the flat for drugs.*

tiptoe /'tɪptəʊ/ *noun*

(IDIOM) **on tiptoe** standing or walking on the ends of your toes with your heels off the ground

tiptoe *verb* [I] to walk quietly and carefully on tiptoe

p	b	t	d	k	g	tʃ	dʒ	f	v	θ	ð
pen	bad	tea	did	cat	got	chin	June	fall	van	thin	then

☆ **tire**¹ /'taɪə(r)/ verb **1** [I,T] to feel that you need to rest or sleep; to make sb feel like this: *However hard he works, he never seems to tire.* o *The long walk tired us all out.* **2** [I] **tire of sth/of doing sth** to become bored or not interested in sth/doing sth: *I never tire of this view.*

tired /'taɪəd/ adj feeling that you need to rest or sleep: *She was tired after a hard day's work.* (IDIOMS) **be tired of sb/sth/doing sth** to be impatient with or annoyed by sb/sth/doing sth: *I'm tired of this game. Let's play something else.* o *I'm tired of listening to the same thing again and again.*

tired out very tired

tiredness noun [U] the state of being tired

tireless adj not stopping for rest

tiresome /'taɪəsəm/ adj (formal) that makes you a little angry or bored

tiring /'taɪərɪŋ/ adj making you tired: *a long and tiring journey*

tire² (US) = TYRE

tissue /'tɪʃu:/ noun **1** [C,U] the material that the bodies of animals and plants are made of: *brain tissue* o *Radiation can destroy the body's tissues.* **2** [C] a thin piece of soft paper that you use as a handkerchief and throw away after you have used it: *a box of tissues* **3** [U] (also **tissue-paper**) thin soft paper that you use for wrapping things that may break

tit¹ /tɪt/ noun
(IDIOM) **tit for tat** something unpleasant that you do to sb because he/she has done sth to you

tit² /tɪt/ noun [C] (slang) a woman's breast

titbit /'tɪtbɪt/ (US **tidbit**) noun [C] **1** a small but very nice piece of food **2** an interesting piece of information

☆ **title** /'taɪtl/ noun [C] **1** the name of a book, play, film, picture, etc **2** a word that shows a person's rank or profession: *'Lord', 'Doctor', 'Reverend', 'Mrs' and 'General' are all titles.* **3** the position of champion in a sport: *Sue is playing this match to defend her title* (= to stay champion).

titled /'taɪtld/ adj having a noble rank, eg 'Duke'

'title-holder noun [C] the champion in a sport: *the current 400-metres title-holder*

'title role noun [C] the part in a play or film that is used as the title of it

titter /'tɪtə(r)/ noun [C] a short silly or nervous laugh —**titter** verb: *The speaker dropped his notes and the audience tittered.*

☆ **to**¹ /tə; before vowels tʊ; tu:; strong form tu:/ prep **1** in the direction of; as far as: *She's going to London.* o *Turn to the left.* o *This road goes to Dover.* o *Pisa is to the west of Florence.* o *He has gone to school.* **2** (used before the person or thing that receives, sees, etc sth): *Give that to me.* o *You must be kind to animals.* **3** (nearly) touching sth: *He put his hands to his ears.* o *They sat back to back.* **4** (used about time) before: *It's two minutes to three.* **5** (used before the upper limit of a range): *from Monday to Friday* o *from beginning to end* o *Hypermarkets sell everything from matches to washing machines.* **6** (used for expressing a reaction to sth): *To my surprise, I saw two strangers coming out of my house.* **7** as far as sb is concerned; in sb's opinion: *To me, it was the wrong decision.* **8** (used when comparing things): *I prefer Italy to Spain.* **9** (used for expressing quantity) for each unit of money, measurement, etc: *It's 2.67 Swiss francs to the pound at the moment.*

☆ **to**² /tə; before vowels tʊ; tu:; strong form tu:/ (used with verbs to form the infinitive): *I want to go home now.* o *Don't forget to write.* o *She's learning English in order to get a better job.* o *Do you know which button to press?* o *I didn't know what to do.* o *He asked me to go but I didn't want to.*

to³ /tu:/ adv (used about a door) in or into a closed position: *Push the door to.*
(IDIOM) **to and fro** backwards and forwards

toad /təʊd/ noun [C] a small cold-blooded animal that looks similar to a frog but that is bigger, has a rough skin and lives mainly on land ☞ picture at **frog**.

toadstool /'təʊdstu:l/ noun [C] a type of poisonous fungus that looks like a mushroom

☆ **toast**¹ /təʊst/ noun [U] a thin piece of bread that is heated to make it brown: *toast and marmalade* o *fried egg on toast* —**toast** verb [I,T]

toaster noun [C] an electrical machine for making toast

toast² /təʊst/ verb [T] to hold up your glass and wish sb success, happiness, etc before you drink: *Everyone stood up and toasted the bride and groom.* —**toast** noun [C]: *a toast to the Queen*

☆ **tobacco** /tə'bækəʊ/ noun [U] the substance that people smoke in cigarettes and pipes (the dried leaves of the tobacco plant)

tobacconist /tə'bækənɪst/ noun [C] a person who sells cigarettes, tobacco, etc ☞ Note that **the tobacconist** is the person who runs the shop and **the tobacconist's** is the shop.

toboggan /tə'bɒgən/ noun [C] a type of flat board, often with metal strips underneath, that people use for travelling downhill on snow for fun ☞ A **toboggan** is a small **sledge**.

☆ **today** /tə'deɪ/ noun [U], adv **1** (on) this day: *Today is Monday.* o *What shall we do today?* o *School ends a week today* (= on this day next week). o *Where is today's paper?* **2** (in) the present age: *Young people have more freedom today than in the past.* o *Today's computers are much smaller than the early models.*

toddle /'tɒdl/ verb [I] to walk with short unsteady steps, like a young child

toddler /'tɒdlə(r)/ noun [C] a child who has only just learnt to walk

☆ **toe** /təʊ/ noun [C] **1** one of the five small parts like fingers at the end of each foot **2** the part of a sock, shoe, etc that covers your toes
toe verb (pres part **toeing**; pt, pp **toed**)
(IDIOM) **toe the (party) line** to obey the orders of your group, party, etc

'toenail noun [C] one of the hard pieces that cover the end of your toes

toffee /'tɒfi; US 'tɔ:fi/ noun [C,U] a hard sticky sweet that is made by cooking sugar and butter together with milk or water

☆ **together** /tə'geðə(r)/ adv **1** with each other; in or into the same place as or near to sb/sth else: *Can we have lunch together?* o *They*

s	z	ʃ	ʒ	h	m	n	ŋ	l	r	j	w
so	zoo	she	vision	how	man	no	sing	leg	red	yes	wet

walked home together. ○ *I'll get all my things together tonight because I want to leave early.* ○ *Stand with your feet together.* **2** so that two or more things are mixed with, joined to or added to each other: *Mix the butter and sugar together.* ○ *Tie the two ends together.* ○ *Add these numbers together to find the total.* **3** at the same time: *Don't all talk together.*

(IDIOMS) **get your act together** ⇨ ACT²

together with in addition to; as well as: *I enclose my order together with a cheque for £15.*

together *adj* (*informal*) (used about a person) organized, capable

togetherness *noun* [U] a feeling of friendship

toil /tɔɪl/ *verb* [I] (*formal*) to work very hard or for a long time at sth —**toil** *noun* [U] (*formal*)

☆ **toilet** /'tɔɪlɪt/ *noun* [C] a large bowl with a seat, attached to a drain, that you use when you need to get rid of waste material or water from your body; the room containing this: *I'm going to the toilet.* ○ *Could I use your toilet, please?* ○ *to flush the toilet* ☞ People usually refer to the **toilet** (or, informally, the **loo**) in their houses. **Lavatory** and **WC** are formal and becoming less common. In public places the toilets are called **Public Conveniences** or the **Ladies**/**Gents**. In American English people talk about the **bathroom** in their houses and the **washroom** or **rest room** in public places.

toiletries /'tɔɪlɪtriz/ *noun* [plural] things such as soap, toothpaste, etc that you use when you are getting washed, doing your hair, etc

'**toilet paper** *noun* [U] paper that you use to clean your body after going to the toilet

'**toilet roll** *noun* [C] a long piece of toilet-paper rolled round a tube ☞ picture at **roll**.

token /'təʊkən/ *noun* [C] **1** something that represents or is a sign of sth else: *Please accept this gift as a token of our gratitude.* **2** a piece of metal, plastic, etc that you use for a particular purpose, often instead of a coin **3** a piece of paper or card that you can use to buy sth of a certain value in a particular shop. Tokens are often given as presents: *a gift token* ☞ Look at **voucher**.

token *adj* (only *before* a noun) **1** small, but done or given as a sign that sth larger or more serious could follow: *a token payment* **2** done, chosen, etc to give the impression that you are interested in sth when you do not intend it sincerely: *There is a token woman on the board.* ○ *The troops put up only token resistance.*

told *pt, pp* of TELL

tolerate /'tɒləreɪt/ *verb* [T] **1** to allow or accept sth that you do not like or agree with: *In a democracy we must tolerate opinions that are different from our own.* **2** to accept or stand sb/sth unpleasant without complaining: *The noise was more than she could tolerate.*

tolerable /'tɒlərəbl/ *adj* of a level that you can tolerate: *Drugs can reduce the pain to a tolerable level.*

tolerance /'tɒlərəns/ *noun* [U] the ability or willingness to allow or accept sth that is unpleasant or that you do not like or agree with: *religious tolerance* ☞ The opposite is **intolerance**.

tolerant /-rənt/ *adj* **tolerant (of/towards sb/sth)** having or showing tolerance ☞ The opposite is **intolerant**. —**toleration** /ˌtɒləˈreɪʃn/ *noun* [U] = TOLERANCE

toll /təʊl/ *noun* [C] **1** money that you pay to use a road, bridge, etc **2** [usually sing] the amount of damage done or the number of people who were killed or injured by sth: *The death-toll from the earthquake was 35.*

(IDIOM) **take a heavy toll/take its toll (of sth)** to cause loss, damage, suffering, etc

tom /tɒm/ *noun* [C] = TOM-CAT

☆ **tomato** /təˈmɑːtəʊ; *US* təˈmeɪtəʊ/ *noun* [C] (*pl* **tomatoes**) a soft red fruit that is often eaten raw in salads or cooked as a vegetable: *tomato juice* ☞ picture at **salad**.

tomb /tuːm/ *noun* [C] a place where a body is buried, often one with a large decorated stone above it

'**tombstone** *noun* [C] a stone over a grave that shows the name of the person who is buried there

tomboy /'tɒmbɔɪ/ *noun* [C] a young girl who likes to play rough games

tom-cat /'tɒmkæt/ (*also* **tom**) *noun* [C] a male cat

☆ **tomorrow** /təˈmɒrəʊ/ *noun* [U], *adv* **1** (on) the day after today: *Today is Friday so tomorrow is Saturday.* ○ *The advertisement will appear in tomorrow's papers.* ○ *See you tomorrow.* ○ *I'm going to bed. I've got to get up early tomorrow morning.* ○ *Tomorrow night's concert has been cancelled.* ○ *a week tomorrow* (= a week from tomorrow) ☞ Look at the note at **morning**. **2** the future: *The schoolchildren of today are tomorrow's workers.*

(IDIOM) **the day after tomorrow** ⇨ DAY

☆ **ton** /tʌn/ *noun* **1** [C] a measure of weight; 2 240 pounds ☞ Do not confuse **ton** and **tonne**. A ton is the same as 1·016 tonnes. An American ton is 2 000 pounds or 0·907 of a tonne. **2 tons** [plural] (*informal*) a lot: *tons of homework*

☆ **tone¹** /təʊn/ *noun* **1** [C,U] the quality of a sound, especially of the human voice: *'Do you know each other?' she asked in a casual tone of voice.* ○ *His tone changed. He was angry now.* **2** [sing] the general quality or style of sb/sth: *The tone of the meeting was optimistic.* **3** [C] one of the shades of a colour: *warm tones of red and orange* **4** [C] a sound that you hear on the telephone: *the dialling tone*

ˌtone-'deaf *adj* not able to sing or hear the difference between notes in music

tone² /təʊn/ *verb*

(PHRASAL VERB) **tone sth down** to change sth that you have said, written, etc, to make it seem less strong

tongs /tɒŋz/ *noun* [plural] a tool that looks like a pair of scissors but that you use for holding or picking things up

☆ **tongue** /tʌŋ/ *noun* **1** [C] the soft part inside your mouth that you can move. You use your tongue for speaking, tasting things, etc. **2** [C,U] the tongue of an animal, eg a cow, which can be eaten: *ham and tongue salad* **3** [C] (*formal*) a language: *your mother tongue* (= the language you learned as a child)

(IDIOMS) **on the tip of your tongue** ⇨ TIP¹
put/stick your tongue out to put your

tongue outside your mouth, for the doctor to examine or to be rude to sb
(**with**) **tongue in cheek** done or said as a joke; not meant seriously

'tongue-tied *adj* not saying anything because you are shy or nervous

'tongue-twister *noun* [C] a phrase or sentence that is difficult to say correctly when you are speaking quickly

tonic /'tɒnɪk/ *noun* [C,U] something that makes you feel stronger, healthier, happier, etc: *A relaxing holiday is a wonderful tonic.*

'tonic water (*also* **tonic**) *noun* [U] a type of water with bubbles in it and a rather bitter taste that is often added to alcoholic drinks: *Gin and tonic, please.*

☆ **tonight** /tə'naɪt/ *noun* [U], *adv* (on) the evening or night of today: *Tonight is the last night of our holiday.* ○ *tonight's weather forecast* ○ *What's on TV tonight?* ○ *We are staying with friends tonight and travelling home tomorrow.*

☆ **tonne** /tʌn/ *noun* [C] a measure of weight; 1 000 kilograms ☞ Look at **ton**.

tonsil /'tɒnsl/ *noun* [C] one of the two soft lumps in your throat on each side of the back of your tongue

tonsillitis /,tɒnsɪ'laɪtɪs/ *noun* [U] an illness in which the tonsils become very sore

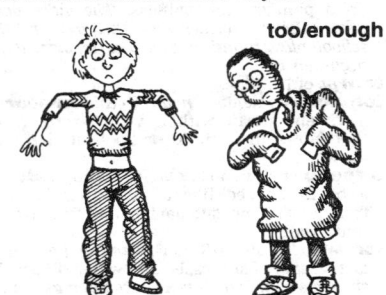

too/enough

Tom's jumper is **not** big **enough**.

Kevin's jumper is **too** big.

☆ **too** /tu:/ *adv* **1** in addition; also: *Red is my favourite colour but I like blue, too.* ○ *Phil thinks you're right and I do too.* ☞ Notice that you say 'There were lions and tigers at the zoo. There were elephants, **too**' but 'There were no zebras and there were no giraffes, **either**.' Look at the note at **also**. **2** (used for expressing surprise or disappointment): *Her purse was stolen. And on her birthday too.* **3** (used before adjectives and adverbs) more than is good, allowed, possible, etc: *These boots are too small.* ○ *It's too cold to go out without a coat.* ○ *It's too long a journey for you to make alone.* ☞ Notice that you cannot say 'It's a too long journey'. **4** (usually used in negative sentences) very: *The weather is not too bad today.*

took *pt* of TAKE

☆ **tool** /tu:l/ *noun* [C] a piece of equipment that you use to help you do a particular type of job: *Hammers, screwdrivers and saws are all car-*

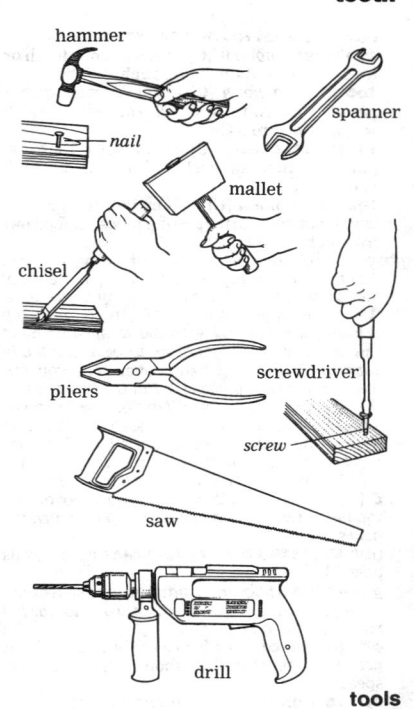

penter's tools. ○ *garden tools* ○ *A word-processor is an indispensable tool for a journalist.* ☞ A tool is usually something you can hold in your hand, eg a spanner or hammer. An **implement** is often used outside, eg for farming or gardening. A **machine** has moving parts and works by electricity, with an engine, etc. An **instrument** is often used for technical or delicate work: *a dentist's instruments* ○ *precision instruments.* A **device** is a more general word for a piece of equipment that you consider to be useful: *The machine has a safety device which switches the power off if there is a fault.*

toot /tu:t/ *noun* [C] the short sound that a whistle, horn, etc makes —**toot** *verb* [I,T]: *Michael tooted the horn as he drove away.*

☆ **tooth** /tu:θ/ *noun* [C] (*pl* **teeth** /ti:θ/) **1** one of the hard white parts in your mouth that you use for biting: *to have a tooth out* ○ *The old man took out his false teeth.* ○ *wisdom teeth*

> ☞ You **brush**/**clean** your teeth to remove bits of food. If a tooth is **decayed**, the dentist may **fill** it or **extract** it/**take** it **out**. If you have had all your teeth out, you can have **false teeth** or **dentures**.

2 one of the long pointed parts of a comb, saw, etc

(IDIOMS) **by the skin of your teeth** ⇨ SKIN
grit your teeth ⇨ GRIT

ɜː	ə	eɪ	əʊ	aɪ	aʊ	ɔɪ	ɪə	eə	ʊə
fur	ago	pay	home	five	now	join	near	hair	pure

have a sweet tooth ➪ SWEET¹

'toothache noun [C,U] a pain in your tooth or teeth ☞ Look at the note at **ache**.

'toothbrush noun [C] a small brush with a handle that you use for cleaning your teeth ☞ picture at **brush**.

'toothpaste noun [U] a substance that you put on your toothbrush and use for cleaning your teeth

'toothpick noun [C] a short pointed piece of wood that you use for getting pieces of food out from between your teeth

☆ **top¹** /tɒp/ noun **1** [C] the highest part of sth: *The flat is at the top of the building.* ○ *the top of the stairs* ○ *Start reading at the top of the page.* **2** [C] the upper surface of sth: *a desk top* **3** [sing] **the top (of sth)** the highest or most important rank or position: *to be at the top of your profession* **4** [C] the cover that you put onto sth in order to close it: *Put the tops back on the felt-tip pens or they will dry out.* ☞ A **top** or a **cap** is often small and round. You take it off by turning or screwing: *a bottle top* ○ *Unscrew cap to open.* A **lid** may be larger. You can lift it off: *a saucepan lid* ○ *Put the lid back on the box.* **5** [C] a piece of clothing that you wear on the top part of your body: *I need a top to match my new skirt.*

(IDIOMS) **at the top of your voice** as loudly as possible

get on top of sb *(informal)* to make sb feel sad or depressed: *I've got so much work to do. It's really getting on top of me.*

off the top of your head *(informal)* without preparing or thinking about sth before you speak

on top 1 on or onto the highest point: *There's a pile of books on the desk. Please put this one on top.* **2** stronger or better: *Throughout the match Liverpool were on top.*

on top of sb/sth 1 on or onto sb/sth else: *Several demonstrators stood on top of the tank, waving flags and shouting.* **2** in addition to sb/sth else: *On top of all our other problems the car's broken down.* **3** *(informal)* very close to sb/sth: *modern houses built on top of each other*

over the top *(informal) (especially Brit)* stronger or more extreme than necessary

top adj highest in position, rank or degree: *one of Britain's top businessmen* ○ *at top speed* ○ *the top floor of the building*

topless adj, adv not covering the breasts; with the breasts not covered: *a topless swimsuit* ○ *to sunbathe topless*

,**top 'hat** noun [C] the tall black or grey hat that a man wears on formal occasions ☞ picture at **hat**.

,**top-'heavy** adj heavier at the top than the bottom and likely to fall over

'topmost /-məʊst/ adj (only *before* a noun) highest: *the topmost branches of the tree*

,**top 'secret** adj that must be kept very secret

top² /tɒp/ verb [T] (**top**ping; **top**ped) **1** to be or form a top for sth: *cauliflower topped with cheese sauce* **2** to be higher or greater than sth: *Inflation has topped the 10% mark.*

(PHRASAL VERB) **top (sth) up** to fill sth that is partly empty: *We topped up our glasses.*

topping noun [C,U] something such as cream or a sauce that is put on the top of food to decorate it or make it taste nicer

top³ /tɒp/ noun [C] a child's toy that spins round quickly, balancing on a point

☆ **topic** /'tɒpɪk/ noun [C] a subject that you talk, write or learn about

topical /-kl/ adj connected with sth that is happening now; that people are interested in now

topple /'tɒpl/ verb **1** [I] **topple (over)** to become unsteady and fall over: *Don't add another book to the pile or it will topple over.* **2** [T] to cause a government or leader of a country to lose power: *A coup by the army has toppled the country's president.*

☆ **torch** /tɔːtʃ/ noun [C] **1** (*US* **flashlight**) a small electric light that you carry in your hand. A torch runs on batteries: *Shine the torch under the sofa and see if you can find my ring.* ☞ picture at **light**. **2** a long piece of wood with burning material at the end that you carry to give light

tore pt of TEAR²

torment /'tɔːment/ noun [C, usually pl,U] great pain in your mind or body; sth that causes this pain: *to be in torment*

torment /tɔː'ment/ verb [T] to cause sb great pain or unhappiness: *The older boys were always tormenting Richard in the school playground.* ○ *She was tormented by nightmares.*

torn pp of TEAR²

tornado /tɔː'neɪdəʊ/ noun [C] (*pl* **tornadoes**) a violent storm with a very strong wind that blows in a circle ☞ Look at the note at **storm**.

torpedo /tɔː'piːdəʊ/ noun [C] (*pl* **torpedoes**) a bomb, shaped like a tube, that is fired from a ship or submarine and can travel underwater

torrent /'tɒrənt; *US* 'tɔːr-/ noun [C] a strong fast stream of sth, especially water: *When the snow melts, this little river becomes a torrent.* ○ *(figurative) She poured out a torrent of abuse at him.*

torrential /tə'renʃl/ adj (used about rain) very heavy

torso /'tɔːsəʊ/ noun [C] (*pl* **torsos**) the main part of the body, not the head, arms and legs

tortoise /'tɔːtəs/ (*US* **turtle**) noun [C] a small animal with a hard shell that moves very slowly. A tortoise can pull its head and legs into its shell to protect them.

tortuous /'tɔːtʃuəs/ adj **1** complicated, not clear and simple: *a tortuous explanation* **2** (used about a road, etc) with many bends

torture /'tɔːtʃə(r)/ noun [C,U] the act of causing very great pain to a person, as a punishment or to make him/her give some information: *The rebel army has been accused of rape, torture and murder.* —**torture** verb [T]: *Most of the prisoners were tortured into making a confession.* ○ *(figurative) She was tortured by the thought that the accident was her fault.*

torturer /'tɔːtʃərə(r)/ noun [C] a person who tortures other people

p	b	t	d	k	g	tʃ	dʒ	f	v	θ	ð
pen	bad	tea	did	cat	got	chin	June	fall	van	thin	then

Tory /ˈtɔːri/ noun [C] (pl **Tories**) adj a member or supporter of the British Conservative Party; connected with this party: *the Tory Party conference* ☛ Look at the note at **party**.

toss /tɒs; US tɔːs/ verb **1** [T] to throw sth carelessly, not using all your strength: *Bob opened the letter and tossed the envelope into the paper bin.* **2** [T] to move your head back quickly: *I asked her to stay but she just tossed her head and walked away.* **3** [I,T] to keep moving up and down or from side to side; to make sb/sth do this: *He lay tossing and turning in bed, unable to sleep.* ○ *The rough seas tossed the ship about.* **4** [I,T] **toss (up) (for sth)** to throw a coin into the air in order to decide sth. The person who guesses correctly which side of the coin will face upwards when it lands has the right to choose. ☛ Look at **heads** and **tails**. These are the names of the two sides of a coin and we say 'heads' or 'tails' when we are guessing which side will face upwards: *Let's toss to see who does the washing-up.* ○ *to toss a coin* ○ *There's only one cake left. I'll toss you for it.*

toss noun [C] an act of tossing: *an angry toss of the head*

(IDIOM) **win/lose the toss** to guess correctly/incorrectly which side of a coin will face upwards when it lands: *Miss Graf won the toss and chose to serve first.*

tot¹ /tɒt/ noun [C] **1** a small child **2** a small glass of a strong alcoholic drink

tot² /tɒt/ verb (totting; totted)
(PHRASAL VERB) **tot (sth) up** (informal) to add up numbers

☆**total** /ˈtəʊtl/ adj counting everything; complete: *What was the total number of people killed?* ○ *a total failure* ○ *They ate in total silence.*

total noun [C] the number that you get when you add two or more numbers or amounts together

(IDIOM) **in total** when you add two or more numbers or amounts together: *The appeal raised £4 million in total.*

total verb [T] (totalling; totalled; US also totaling; totaled) to add up to a certain amount or number; to make a total of: *His debts totalled more than £10 000.*

totally /ˈtəʊtəli/ adv completely: *I totally agree with you.*

totter /ˈtɒtə(r)/ verb [I] to stand or move in an unsteady way as if you are going to fall

☆**touch¹** /tʌtʃ/ verb **1** [I,T] (used about two or more things, surfaces, etc) to be or go so close together that there is no space between them: *They were sitting so close that their heads touched.* ○ *This bicycle is too big. My feet don't touch the ground.* **2** [T] to put a part of your body, usually your hand or fingers onto sb/sth: *Don't touch!* ○ *He touched her gently on the cheek.* ○ *The police asked us not to touch anything.* ○ (figurative) *June never touches alcohol* (= she never drinks it). **3** [T] to make sb feel sadness, sympathy, thanks, etc: *a sad story that touched our hearts* ☛ Look at **touched**. **4** [T] (in negative sentences.) to be as good as sb/sth: *He's a much better player than all the others. No one else can touch him.*

(IDIOM) **touch wood** an expression that people use (often while touching a piece of wood) to prevent bad luck: *I've been driving here for 20 years and I haven't had an accident yet – touch wood!*

(PHRASAL VERBS) **touch down** (used about an aeroplane) to land

touch on/upon sth to talk or write about sth for only a short time

☆**touch²** /tʌtʃ/ noun **1** [C, usually sing] an act of touching(2) sb/sth: *I felt the touch of her hand on my arm.* **2** [U] one of the five senses: the ability to feel: *The sense of touch is very important to blind people.* **3** [U] the way sth feels when you touch it: *Marble is cold to the touch.* **4** [C] a small detail: *The flowers on our table were a nice touch.* **5** [sing] **a touch (of sth)** a small amount of sth: *He's not very ill. It's just a touch of flu.*

(IDIOMS) **in/out of touch (with sb)** being/not being in contact with sb by speaking or writing to him/her: *During the year she was abroad, they kept in touch by letter.*

in/out of touch with sth having/not having recent information about sth: *We're out of touch with what's going on.*

lose touch ⇨ LOSE

lose your touch ⇨ LOSE

touched /tʌtʃt/ adj (not before a noun) made to feel sadness, sympathy, thanks, etc: *We were very touched by your kind offer.*

touching /ˈtʌtʃɪŋ/ adj that makes you feel sadness, sympathy, thanks, etc: *Romeo and Juliet is a touching story of young love.*

touchy /ˈtʌtʃi/ adj **1** easily upset or made angry: *Don't ask about her first marriage. She's very touchy about it.* **2** (used about a subject, situation, etc) that may easily upset people or make them angry

☆**tough** /tʌf/ adj **1** not easily broken or cut; very strong: *tough boots* ○ *tough plastic* **2** not easily weakened by pain or difficulty; very strong: *You need to be tough to go climbing in winter.* **3** difficult to cut and eat: *This meat is tough.* **4** strict; firm: *The government is introducing tough new laws about drinking and driving.* **5** difficult: *It will be a tough decision to make.* ○ *He's had a very tough time recently.* **6** **tough (on sb)** (informal) unfortunate; bad luck: *That's tough!* ○ *It's tough that she was ill just before she went on holiday.*

toughen /ˈtʌfn/ verb [I,T] **toughen (sb/sth) up** to become tough; to make sb/sth tough
—**toughness** noun [U]

☆**tour** /tʊə(r)/ noun **1** [C] a journey that you make for pleasure during which you visit many places: *a ten-day coach tour of Scotland* **2** [C] a short visit around a city, famous building, etc: *a guided tour round St Paul's Cathedral* ☛ Look at the note at **travel**. **3** [C,U] a series of visits that you make to play sports matches, give concerts, etc: *Phil Collins is on tour in America.*

tour verb [I,T] to go on a journey during which you visit many places: *We spent three weeks touring in southern Spain.* ○ *We toured southern Spain for three weeks.*

tourism /ˈtʊərɪzəm/ noun [U] the business of

s	z	ʃ	ʒ	h	m	n	ŋ	l	r	j	w
so	zoo	she	vision	how	man	no	sing	leg	red	yes	wet

tournament providing and arranging holidays and services for people who are visiting a place: *The Spanish economy is no longer so dependent on tourism.*

tourist /'tʊərɪst/ *noun* [C] a person who visits a place for pleasure: *a foreign tourist* ○ *the Tourist Information Office*

tournament /'tɔ:nəmənt; *US* 'tɜ:rn-/ *noun* [C] a competition in which many players or teams play games against each other

tow /təʊ/ *verb* [T] to pull a car, etc along by a rope or chain
  tow *noun* [sing,U] an act of towing sth: *Can you give me a tow?* ○ *a car on tow*
  (IDIOM) **in tow** (*informal*) following behind: *He arrived with his wife and five children in tow.*

☆**towards** /tə'wɔ:dz; *US* tɔ:rdz/ (*also* **toward** /tə'wɔ:d; *US* tɔ:rd/) *prep* **1** in the direction of sb/sth: *I saw Ken walking towards the station.* ○ *She had her back towards me.* ○ *a first step towards world peace* **2** (used when you are talking about your feelings about sb/sth) in relation to: *Pat felt very protective towards her younger brother.* ○ *What is your attitude towards private education?* **3** as part of the payment for sth: *The money will go towards the cost of a new minibus.* **4** near a time or date: *It gets cool towards evening.*

☆**towel** /'taʊəl/ *noun* [C] a piece of cloth or paper that you use for drying sb/sth/yourself: *a bath towel* ○ *paper towels* ☛ Look at **sanitary towel** and **tea towel**.

☆**tower** /'taʊə(r)/ *noun* [C] a tall narrow building or part of a building such as a church or castle: *the Eiffel Tower* ○ *a church tower*
  'tower block *noun* [C] (*Brit*) a very tall block of flats or offices

☆**town** /taʊn/ *noun* **1** [C] a place with many streets and buildings. A town is larger than a village but smaller than a city: *Romsey is a small market town.* **2** [sing] all the people who live in a town: *The whole town was on the streets, waving flags and shouting.* **3** [U] the main part of a town, where the shops, etc are: *I've got to go into town this afternoon.*
  (IDIOM) **go to town (on sth)** (*informal*) to spend a lot of time or money on sth
  ,town **'council** *noun* [C] (*Brit*) a group of people who are responsible for the local government of a town
  ,town **'hall** *noun* [C] a large building that contains the local government offices and often a large room for public meetings, concerts, etc

township /'taʊnʃɪp/ *noun* [C] (in South Africa) a town or part of a town where non-white people live

toxic /'tɒksɪk/ *adj* poisonous: *Toxic chemicals had leaked into the water.*

☆**toy**¹ /tɔɪ/ *noun* [C] an object for a child to play with: *Here are some toys to keep the children amused.* ○ *toy cars* ○ *a toy soldier* ○ *a toy farm* ○ *a toyshop*

☆**toy**² /tɔɪ/ *verb*
  (PHRASAL VERB) **toy with sth 1** to think about doing sth, perhaps not very seriously: *She's toying with the idea of going abroad for a year.* **2** to move sth about without thinking about what you are doing: *He toyed with his food but hardly ate any of it.*

☆**trace**¹ /treɪs/ *noun* **1** [C,U] a mark or sign that shows that sb/sth existed or happened: *traces of a bronze age village* ○ *The man disappeared without trace.* **2** [C] a very small amount of sth: *Traces of blood were found under her finger-nails.*

☆**trace**² /treɪs/ *verb* [T] **1** to find out where sb/sth is by following marks, signs or other information: *The wanted man was traced to an address in Amsterdam.* **2** to find out or describe the development of sth: *She traced her family tree back to the 16th century.* **3** to make a copy of sth by placing a piece of transparent paper over it and drawing over the lines

☆**track** /træk/ *noun* [C] **1** (usually plural) a line or series of marks that are left behind by a car, person, animal, etc: *The hunter followed the tracks of a deer.* ○ *tyre tracks* ☛ Look at **footprint**. **2** a path or rough road: *The road became just a muddy track.* **3** the two metal rails on which a train runs: *The train stopped because there was a tree across the track.* **4** a special path, often in a circle, for racing: *a running track* **5** one song or piece of music on a cassette, CD or record
  (IDIOMS) **keep/lose track of sb/sth** to know/not know what is happening somewhere or to sb/sth: *As a journalist, he has to keep track of events all over the Middle East.*
  off the beaten track ⇨ BEAT¹
  on the right/wrong track having the right/wrong sort of idea about sth: *That's not the answer but you're on the right track.*
  track *verb* [T] **track sb/sth (to sth)** to follow tracks or signs in order to find sb/sth: *to track enemy planes on a radar screen*
  (PHRASAL VERB) **track sb/sth down** to find sb/sth after searching for him/her/it
  'track events *noun* [plural] athletic events that involve running ☛ Look at **field events**.
  'track record *noun* [C] what a person or organization has achieved that other people know about
  'track suit *noun* [C] a suit that consists of loose trousers and a jacket or sweater. You wear a track suit for sports practice or when you are relaxing at home.

☆**tractor** /'træktə(r)/ *noun* [C] a large vehicle that is used on farms for pulling heavy pieces of machinery

☆**trade**¹ /treɪd/ *noun* **1** [U] the buying or selling of goods or services: *an international trade agreement* ○ *Trade is not very good* (= not many goods are sold) *at this time of year.* **2** [C] **trade (in sth)** a particular type of business: *Many seaside resorts depend on the tourist trade.* ○ *We do quite a good trade in second-hand books.* **3** [C,U] a job for which you need special skill, especially with your hands: *Jeff is a plumber by trade.* ○ *to learn a trade* ☛ Look at the note at **work**.
  'trade mark *noun* [C] a special mark or name that a company can put on its products and that cannot be used by any other company
  'tradesman /-zmən/ *noun* [C] (*pl* **tradesmen**

iː	ɪ	e	æ	ɑː	ɒ	ɔː	ʊ	uː	ʌ
see	sit	ten	hat	arm	got	saw	put	too	cup

trade

(/-mən/) a person who delivers goods to people's homes or who has a shop

,trade 'union (*also* **,trades 'union; union**) *noun* [C] an organization for people who all do the same type of work. Trade unions try to get better pay and working conditions for their members.

☆ **trade²** /treɪd/ *verb* **1** [I] **trade (in sth) (with sb)** to buy or sell goods or services: *The shop was losing money and ceased trading last week.* ○ *More and more countries are trading with China.* ○ *to trade in arms* **2** [T] **trade sth for sth** to exchange sth for sth else: *The explorer traded his watch for food.*
(PHRASAL VERB) **trade sth in (for sth)** to give sth old in part payment for sth new or newer

trader *noun* [C] a person who buys and sells things, especially in a market

☆ **tradition** /trəˈdɪʃn/ *noun* [C,U] a custom or belief that has continued from the past to the present: *It's a tradition to play tricks on people on 1 April.* ○ *Vienna has a great musical tradition.* ○ *By tradition, the bride's family pays the costs of the wedding.* —**traditional** /-ʃənl/ *adj*: *It is traditional to eat turkey at Christmas.* —**traditionally** /-ʃənəli/ *adv*

☆ **traffic** /ˈtræfɪk/ *noun* [U] **1** the cars, etc that are on a road: *heavy/light traffic* ○ *The traffic is at a standstill.* **2** the movement of ships, aeroplanes, etc: *Cross-channel traffic was affected by a strike at the French ports.* ○ *air traffic controllers* **3 traffic (in sth)** the illegal buying and selling of sth: *the traffic in arms*

traffic *verb* [I] (*pres part* **trafficking**; *pt, pp* **trafficked**) **traffic (in sth)** to buy and sell sth illegally: *drug trafficking*

'traffic island (*also* **island**) *noun* [C] a raised area in the middle of the road, where you can stand when you are crossing

'traffic jam *noun* [C] a long line of cars, etc that cannot move or that can only move very slowly

'traffic-light *noun* [C, usually pl] a sign with three coloured lights (red, amber and green) that is used for controlling the traffic at a road junction: *When the traffic-lights are red you must stop.*

'traffic warden *noun* [C] a person who checks whether cars are parked in the wrong place or for longer than is allowed

☆ **tragedy** /ˈtrædʒədi/ *noun* (*pl* **tragedies**) **1** [C,U] an event or situation that causes great sadness: *A trip to Brighton ended in tragedy for a local couple when they were involved in a car crash on the M23.* ○ *It's a tragedy that so many children leave school without any qualifications.* **2** [C] a serious play that has a sad ending: *'King Lear' is a tragedy.* ☛ Look at **comedy**.

tragic /ˈtrædʒɪk/ *adj* **1** that causes great sadness: *It's tragic that he died so young.* ○ *a tragic accident* **2** (only *before* a noun) with a sad ending or in the style of tragedy: *a tragic novel* —**tragically** /-kli/ *adv*

☆ **trail** /treɪl/ *noun* [C] **1** a series of marks in a long line that a person or thing leaves behind: *a trail of muddy footprints* ○ *The storm left behind a trail of destruction.* **2** a path through the country: *a nature trail through the woods* **3** the tracks or smell that you follow when you are hunting sb/sth: *The dogs ran off on the trail of the fox.* ○ (*figurative*) *The burglar got away in a stolen car with the police on his trail.*

trail *verb* **1** [I,T] to be pulled or dragged along behind you; to make sth do this: *Her long hair trailed behind her in the wind.* ○ *Joe sat in the boat trailing a stick in the water.* **2** [I] **trail along behind (sb/sth)** to move or walk slowly behind sb/sth else, usually because you are tired **3** [I,T] to have a lower score than the other player or team during a game or competition: *At half-time Everton were trailing by two goals to three.* **4** [I] (used about plants) to grow over a surface: *ivy trailing over the wall* ○ (*figurative*) *wires from the stereo trailing across the floor*

trailer /ˈtreɪlə(r)/ *noun* [C] **1** a vehicle with no engine that is pulled by a car, lorry, etc **2** (*US*) = CARAVAN(1) **3** a series of short pieces taken from a cinema film and used to advertise it

☆ **train¹** /treɪn/ *noun* [C] **1** a number of carriages or wagons that are pulled by an engine along a railway line: *a passenger/goods/freight train* ○ *a fast/slow train* ○ *an express/a stopping train* ○ *to catch/get/take a train* ○ *the 12 o'clock train to Bristol* ○ *to get on/off a train* ○ *Hurry up or we'll miss the train.* ○ *You have to change trains at Reading.* ○ *The train pulled into/out of the station.* ☛ Note that we travel **by** train. We can also say **on** the train **2** (usually sing) a series of thoughts or events that are connected: *A knock at the door interrupted my train of thought.*

☆ **train²** /treɪn/ *verb* **1** [T] **train sb (as sth/to do sth)** to teach a person to do sth which is difficult or which needs practice: *The organization trains guide dogs for the blind.* ○ *There is a shortage of trained teachers.* **2 train (as sth) (to do sth)** [I] to learn how to do a job: *She's training as an engineer.* ○ *He's training to be a doctor.* **3** [I,T] to prepare for a race or match by exercising; to help a person or an animal to do this: *I'm training for the London Marathon.* ○ *to train racehorses* **4** [T] to point a gun, camera, etc at sb/sth

trainee /ˌtreɪˈniː/ *noun* [C] a person who is being trained(1): *a trainee manager*

trainer *noun* [C] **1** a person who trains(3) animals or sportsmen and –women **2** (*US* **sneaker**) [usually pl] a type of soft shoe that you wear for running ☛ picture at **shoe**.

training *noun* [U] the preparation for a sport or job: *staff training* ○ *to be in training for the Olympics*

trait /treɪt/ *noun* [C] a quality; part of sb's character

traitor /ˈtreɪtə(r)/ *noun* [C] a person who is not loyal to his/her country, friends, etc and harms them ☛ Look at **betray** and at **treason**.

tram /træm/ *noun* (*US* **streetcar**) *noun* [C] a type of bus that works by electricity and that runs on special rails in the road

tramp¹ /træmp/ *noun* [C] a person who has no home or job and who moves from place to place

tramp² /træmp/ *verb* [I,T] to walk with slow heavy steps

ɜː	ə	eɪ	əʊ	aɪ	aʊ	ɔɪ	ɪə	eə	ʊə
fur	ago	pay	home	five	now	join	near	hair	pure

tramp noun [sing] the sound of people walking with heavy steps

trample /'træmpl/ verb [I,T] **trample sth/sb (down)**; **trample on sb/sth** to walk on sb/sth and damage or hurt him/her/it: *The cows trampled the corn.* ○ *The child was trampled to death by the crowd.* ○ *The boys trampled on the flower-beds.*

trampoline /'træmpəli:n/ noun [C] a piece of equipment for jumping up and down on, made of a piece of strong material fixed to a metal frame by springs

trance /trɑ:ns; *US* træns/ noun [C] a condition of the mind in which you do not notice what is going on around you or in which you move and speak as if you were being controlled by another person or force

tranquil /'træŋkwɪl/ adj (formal) calm and quiet

tranquillizer (also **tranquilliser**; *US* also **tranquilizer**) noun [C] a drug that is used for making people sleepy or calmer

transaction /træn'zækʃn/ noun [C] a piece of business: *financial transactions*

transatlantic /ˌtrænzət'læntɪk/ adj to or from the other side of the Atlantic; across the Atlantic: *a transatlantic flight*

transcend /træn'send/ verb [T] (formal) to be greater or more important than sb/sth; to go beyond the limits of sth: *Environmental issues transcend national boundaries.*

transcript /'trænskrɪpt/ noun [C] a written copy of what sb said

☆ **transfer¹** /træns'fɜ:(r)/ verb (**transferring**; **transferred**) **1** [I,T] **transfer (sb/sth) (from...) (to...)** to move, or to make sb/sth move, from one place to another: *He has been transferred to our Tokyo branch.* ○ *I want to transfer £1 000 from my deposit to my current account* (= in a bank). ○ *Transfer the data onto floppy disk.* **2** [T] to change the ownership of sth from one person to another —**transferable** /-'fɜ:rəbl/ adj: *This ticket is not transferable.*

☆ **transfer²** /'trænsfɜ:(r)/ noun **1** [C,U] moving or being moved from one place, job or state to another: *Paul is not happy here and has asked for a transfer.* ○ *the transfer of power from a military to a civilian government* **2** [U] changing to a different vehicle, route, etc during a journey **3** [C] (*US*) a ticket that allows you to travel on two or more buses, etc during one journey **4** [C] (*especially Brit*) a piece of paper with a picture or writing on it that you can stick onto another surface by pressing or heating it

☆ **transform** /træns'fɔ:m/ verb [T] **transform sb/sth (from sth) (into sth)** to change sth completely: *The arrival of electricity transformed people's lives.* —**transformation** /ˌtrænsfə'meɪʃn/ noun [C,U]

transfusion /træns'fju:ʒn/ noun [C] the act of putting one person's blood into another person's body: *a blood transfusion*

transistor /træn'zɪstə(r); -'sɪst-/ noun [C] **1** a small piece of electrical equipment that is used in radios and televisions **2** (also ˌ**transistor** ˈ**radio**) a small radio that you can carry easily

transit /'trænzɪt; -sɪt/ noun [U] the act of moving or being taken from one place to another: *The goods had been damaged in transit.*

transition /træn'zɪʃn/ noun [C,U] **transition (from sth) (to sth)** a change from one state or form to another: *the transition from childhood to adolescence* —**transitional** /-ʃənl/ adj: *We're still in a transitional stage.*

transitive /'trænsətɪv/ adj (grammar) (used about a verb) that has a direct object: *In this dictionary transitive verbs are marked* '[T]'. The opposite is **intransitive**.

☆ **translate** /trænz'leɪt/ verb [I,T] **translate (sth) (from sth) (into sth)** to change sth spoken or written from one language to another: *This book has been translated from Czech into English.* ☞ Look at **interpret**. —**translation** /-'leɪʃn/ noun [C,U]: *a word-for-word translation* ○ *an error in translation*

translator noun [C] a person who translates sth that has been written ☞ Look at **interpreter**.

transmission /trænz'mɪʃn/ noun **1** [U] sending out or passing on: *the transmission of television pictures by satellite* ○ *the transmission of disease* **2** [C] a TV or radio programme **3** [C,U] the set of parts of a car, etc that take power from the engine to the wheels

☆ **transmit** /trænz'mɪt/ verb [T] (**transmitting**; **transmitted**) **1** to send out television or radio programmes, electronic signals, etc: *The match was transmitted live all over the world.* **2** to send or pass sth from one person or place to another: *a sexually transmitted disease*

transmitter noun [C] a piece of equipment that sends out television or radio programmes, electronic signals, etc

☆ **transparent** /træns'pærənt/ adj that you can see through: *Glass is transparent.*

transparency /-rənsi/ noun [C] (pl **transparencies**) a type of photograph that is printed on transparent plastic, or a piece of plastic on which you can write or draw. You look at a transparency by putting it in a special machine (**projector**) and shining light through it: *a transparency for the overhead projector* ☞ Look at **slide**.

transplant /træns'plɑ:nt; *US* -'plænt/ verb [T] **1** to take a plant out of the soil and plant it in another place **2** to take out an organ or other part of sb's body and put it into another person's body

transplant /'trænsplɑ:nt; *US* -plænt/ noun [C] an operation in which an organ, etc is transplanted: *a heart transplant*

☆ **transport¹** /træn'spɔ:t/ verb [T] to move sb/sth from one place to another in a vehicle

☆ **transport²** /'trænspɔ:t/ noun (*especially US* **transportation**) noun [U] **1** moving sb/sth from one place to another by vehicle: *road, rail, sea, etc transport* **2** vehicles that you travel in: *Do you have your own transport?* (eg a car) ○ *I travel to school by public transport.*

transvestite /trænz'vestaɪt/ noun [C] a person who likes to wear the clothes of sb of the opposite sex

☆ **trap** /træp/ noun [C] **1** a piece of equipment that you use for catching animals: *a mousetrap*

| p | b | t | d | k | g | tʃ | dʒ | f | v | θ | ð |
| pen | bad | tea | did | cat | got | chin | June | fall | van | thin | then |

○ *The rabbit's leg was caught in the trap.* ○ *(figurative) He thought of marriage as a trap.* **2** something that tricks or deceives you: *He fell into the trap of thinking she would always be there.*

trap *verb* [T] (**trap**ping; **trap**ped) **1** to catch an animal, etc in a trap **2** to keep sb in a place from which he/she cannot move or escape: *The door closed behind them and they were trapped.* ○ *Many people are trapped in low-paid jobs.* **3** to catch and keep or store sth: *Special glass panels trap heat from the sun.* **4 trap sb (into sth/into doing sth)** to make sb do sth by tricking or deceiving him/her

ˌtrap'door *noun* [C] a door in a floor or ceiling

trapeze /trəˈpiːz; *US* træ-/ *noun* [C] a bar hanging from two ropes high above the ground, used as a swing by gymnasts and acrobats

trappings /ˈtræpɪŋz/ *noun* [plural] clothes, possessions, etc which are signs of a particular rank or position: *a large car, expensive clothes and all the other trappings of success*

trash /træʃ/ *noun* [U] (*US*) = RUBBISH

trashy *adj* of poor quality: *trashy novels*

'trash can *noun* [C] (*US*) = DUSTBIN

trauma /ˈtrɔːmə; *US* ˈtraʊmə/ *noun* [C,U] (an event that causes) a state of great unhappiness or shock ☞ Look at **stress**. —**traumatic** /trɔːˈmætɪk; *US* traʊ-/ *adj*: *Getting divorced can be a traumatic experience.*

☆ **travel** /ˈtrævl/ *verb* (**travell**ing; **travell**ed; *US* **travel**ing; **travel**ed) **1** [I] to make a journey: *Charles travels a lot on business.* ○ *to travel by sea/air* ○ *They travelled overland from Turkey.* ○ *travelling expenses* ○ *(figurative) News travels fast in the village.* **2** [T] to make a journey of a particular distance: *They travelled 60 kilometres to come and see us.*

travel *noun* **1** [U] the act of travelling: *Air travel has made the world seem a smaller place.* ○ *a travel book* **2 travels** [plural] journeys, especially to places that are far away: *You must have seen lots of interesting places on your travels.* ☞ **Travel** is an uncountable word and you can only use it to talk about the general activity of moving from place to place: *Foreign travel is very popular these days.* When you talk about going from one particular place to another, you use **journey**. A journey can be long: *the journey across Canada* or short, but repeated: *the journey to work.* A **tour** is a journey or walk during which you visit several places. You may go on a tour round a country, city, place of interest, etc: *a three-week tour around Italy* ○ *a guided tour of the castle.* You often use **trip** when you are thinking about the whole visit (including your stay in a place and the journeys there and back): *They're just back from a trip to Japan. They had a wonderful time.* (but: '*How was your journey?' 'Awful – the plane was delayed!'*) A trip may be short: *a day trip*, or longer: *a trip round the world*, and can be for business or pleasure: *How about a trip to the seaside this weekend?* ○ *He's on a trip to New York to meet a client.* An **excursion** is an organized trip that you go on with a group of people: *The holiday includes a full-day excursion by coach to the Lake District.*

traveller (*US* **traveler**) /ˈtrævlə(r)/ *noun* [C] **1** a person who is travelling or who often travels **2** (*Brit*) = GYPSY

'travel agency *noun* [C] (*pl* **travel agencies**) a company that makes travel arrangements for people (booking tickets, making hotel reservations, etc)

'travel agent *noun* [C] a person who works in a travel agency

'traveller's cheque (*US* **'traveler's check**) *noun* [C] a cheque that you can change into foreign money when you are travelling abroad: *to cash a traveller's cheque*

ˌtravelling 'salesman *noun* [C] a person who visits shops, offices, etc trying to sell the products of one company

☆ **tray** /treɪ/ *noun* [C] **1** a flat piece of wood, plastic, metal, etc with raised edges that you use for carrying food, drink, etc on: *When she was ill in bed, he took her meals to her on a tray.* **2** a shallow container in which you put papers, etc on a desk

treacherous /ˈtretʃərəs/ *adj* **1** that you cannot trust **2** full of hidden danger: *The roads are treacherous this morning. There are icy patches.*

treachery /ˈtretʃəri/ *noun* [U] the act of causing harm to sb/sth that trusts you

treacle /ˈtriːkl/ *noun* [U] a thick, dark, sticky liquid that is made from sugar ☞ Look at **syrup**.

tread /tred/ *verb* (*pt* **trod** /trɒd/; *pp* **trodden** /ˈtrɒdn/) **1** [I] to step or put your foot down: *Don't tread in the puddle!* ○ *He trod on my toe and didn't even say sorry!* ○ *(figurative) We must tread carefully or we'll offend him.* **2** [T] **tread sth (in/down/out)** to press sth with your foot: *The cake crumbs had been trodden into the carpet.* ○ *She planted the seeds and trod the earth down.* **3** [T] to walk on sth: *He walked down the path he had trodden so many times before.*

tread *noun* **1** [sing] the sound you make when you are walking: *the heavy tread of soldiers' boots* **2** [C,U] the raised pattern on the outside surface of a tyre

treason /ˈtriːzn/ *noun* [U] the act of causing harm to your country, eg by helping its enemies

☆ **treasure** /ˈtreʒə(r)/ *noun* **1** [C,U] a collection of very valuable objects, eg made of gold, silver, etc: *to find buried treasure* **2** [C] something that is very valuable: *the nation's art treasures*

treasure *verb* [T] to consider sb/sth to be very special or valuable: *I will treasure those memories forever.*

'treasure hunt *noun* [C] a game in which people try to find sth by following special signs (**clues**)

treasurer /ˈtreʒərə(r)/ *noun* [C] the person who looks after the money that belongs to a club, organization, etc

treasury /ˈtreʒəri/ *noun* [sing, with sing or pl verb] **the Treasury** the government department that controls public money

☆ **treat** /triːt/ *verb* [T] **1** to act or behave towards sb/sth in a particular way: *Teenagers hate being treated like children.* ○ *You should treat older people with respect.* ○ *to treat sb badly, fairly, etc* **2 treat sth as sth** to consider sth in

s	z	ʃ	ʒ	h	m	n	ŋ	l	r	j	w
so	zoo	she	vision	how	man	no	sing	leg	red	yes	wet

a particular way: *The bomb scare was not taken seriously. It was treated as a hoax.* **3** to deal with or discuss: *This book treats the subject in great detail.* **4 treat sb (for sth)** to use medicine or medical care to try to make a sick or injured person well again: *a new drug to treat cancer* ○ *The boy was treated for burns at the hospital.* **5 treat sth (with sth)** to put a substance onto sth in order to protect it from damage: *Most vegetables are treated with insecticide.* **6 treat sb/yourself (to sth)** to give sb/yourself sth that is very special or enjoyable: *Clare treated the children to an ice-cream* (= she paid for them).
▸ **treat** *noun* [C] something that is very special or enjoyable: *I've brought some cream cakes as a treat for tea.* ○ *It's a real treat for me to stay in bed late.*
(IDIOM) **trick or treat** ⇨ TRICK

☆**treatment** /'tri:tmənt/ *noun* **1** [U] the way that you behave towards sb or deal with sth: *The treatment of the prisoners of war was very harsh.* **2** [C,U] the use of medicine or medical care to try to make a sick or injured person well again: *a new treatment for cancer* ○ *In Britain medical treatment is provided free on the NHS.*

☆**treaty** /'tri:ti/ *noun* [C] (*pl* **treaties**) a written agreement between two or more countries: *to sign a peace treaty*

treble¹ /'trebl/ *verb* [I,T] to become or to make sth three times bigger: *Prices have trebled in the past ten years.* —**treble** *det*: *This figure is treble the number five years ago.*

treble² /'trebl/ *noun* [C] **1** a high singing voice, especially that of a young boy **2** a boy who has a high singing voice

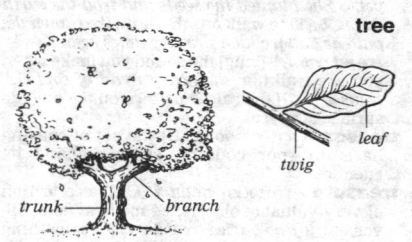

tree

leaf
twig
trunk *branch*

☆**tree** /tri:/ *noun* [C] a tall plant with a thick wooden stem from which branches grow: *an oak tree* ○ *The house was surrounded by tall trees.* ○ *to climb a tree* ○ *to plant/cut down a tree*

☛ The stem of a tree is called a **trunk**. The outer surface of this is **bark**. The **branches** grow out from the trunk. A tree may have **leaves** or **needles**. Look at **Christmas tree** and **family tree**.

trek /trek/ *noun* [C] a long hard journey, often on foot —**trek** *verb* [I] (**trekking**; **trekked**)

☆**tremble** /'trembl/ *verb* [I] to shake, eg because you are cold, frightened, weak, etc: *She was pale and trembling with shock.* ○ *His hand was trembling as he picked up his pen to sign.* ○ *Sue's voice trembled with excitement.* —**tremble** *noun* [C]: *There was tremble in his voice as he told them the sad news.*

tremendous /trɪ'mendəs/ *adj* **1** very large or great: *a tremendous amount of work* ○ *a tremendous difference* ○ *a tremendous explosion* **2** (*informal*) very good: *You were tremendous.*
tremendously *adv* very; very much: *tremendously exciting* ○ *Prices vary tremendously from one shop to another.*

tremor /'tremə(r)/ *noun* [C] a slight shaking or trembling: *a tremor in his voice* ○ *an earth tremor* (= a small earthquake)

trench /trentʃ/ *noun* [C] a long narrow hole in the ground for water to flow along or for soldiers to hide in

☆**trend** /trend/ *noun* [C] a general movement or direction: *The current trend is towards smaller families.* ○ *There is a trend for people to retire earlier.* ○ *He always followed the latest trends in fashion.*
(IDIOM) **set a/the trend** to start a new style or fashion

trendy *adj* (**trendier**; **trendiest**) (*informal*) fashionable

trespass /'trespəs/ *verb* [I] to go onto sb's land without permission —**trespasser** *noun* [C]: *Trespassers will be prosecuted.*

☆**trial** /'traɪəl/ *noun* **1** [C,U] the process in a court of law where a judge, etc listens to evidence and decides if sb is guilty of a crime or not: *a fair trial* ○ *He was on trial for murder.* ○ *trial by jury* **2** [C,U] an act of testing sb/sth: *New drugs must go through extensive trials.* ○ *a trial period of three months* ○ *We've got the car on trial for a week.*
(IDIOM) **trial and error** trying different ways of doing sth until you find the best one

,**trial 'run** *noun* [C] an occasion when you practise doing sth in order to make sure you can do it correctly later on

☆**triangle** /'traɪæŋgl/ *noun* [C] **1** a shape that has three straight sides and three angles: *a right-angled triangle* ☛ picture at **shape**. **2** a metal musical instrument in the shape of a triangle that you play by hitting it with a metal stick

triangular /traɪ'æŋgjʊlə(r)/ *adj* shaped like a triangle

☆**tribe** /traɪb/ *noun* [C] a group of people that have the same language and customs and that are ruled by a chief or chiefs: *the Zulu tribes of South Africa* —**tribal** /'traɪbl/ *adj*: *tribal dances*

tribunal /traɪ'bju:nl/ *noun* [C] a court or group of officials who have the authority to decide who is right in particular types of dispute: *an industrial tribunal*

tributary /'trɪbjʊtri; *US*-teri/ *noun* [C] (*pl* **tributaries**) a river or stream that flows into a larger river

tribute /'trɪbju:t/ *noun* **1** [C,U] something that you say or do to show that you respect or admire sb/sth: *A special concert was held as a tribute to the composer on his 80th birthday.* **2** [sing] **a tribute (to sth)** a sign of how good sb/sth is: *The success of the festival is a tribute to the organizers.*
(IDIOM) **pay tribute to sb/sth** ⇨ PAY²

i:	ɪ	e	æ	ɑ:	ɒ	ɔ:	ʊ	u:	ʌ
see	sit	ten	hat	arm	got	saw	put	too	cup

☆ **trick** /trɪk/ noun [C] **1** something that you do to deceive sb, in order to make him/her look stupid or to cheat him/her: *The children played a trick on the teacher.* o *The thieves got into the house by a trick.* **2** a clever or the best way of doing sth: *I can't get the top off this jar. Is there a trick to it?* **3** an act that uses special skills to make people believe sth which is not true: *The magician performed a trick in which he made a rabbit disappear.*
(IDIOMS) **do the job/trick** ⇨ JOB
trick or treat (*especially US*) a tradition in which children dressed as witches, etc go to people's houses at Hallowe'en. The children may do sth bad to you if you do not give them sweets, money, etc.

trick verb [T] to deceive sb in order to make him/her do or believe sth: *He tricked me into lending him money.* o *Stella was tricked out of her share of the money.*

trickery /-əri/ noun [U] the use of a trick(1) in order to deceive sb

trickle /'trɪkl/ verb [I] (used about a liquid) to flow in a thin stream: *Tears trickled down his cheek.* o (*figurative*): *At first no one came, but then people began to trickle in.* —**trickle** noun [C, usually sing]: *The stream was only a trickle.* o (*figurative*) *The flood of refugees had been reduced to a trickle.*

tricky adj (**trickier**; **trickiest**) difficult to do or deal with: *a tricky situation*

tricycle /'traɪsɪkl/ (*also informal* **trike**) noun [C] a bicycle that has one wheel at the front and two at the back

trifle /'traɪfl/ noun **1** [C] something that is of little value or importance **2** [C,U] a type of cold dessert made from cake with fruit in jelly covered with custard and cream
(IDIOM) **a trifle** rather: *It's a trifle odd that they didn't phone.*

trigger /'trɪɡə(r)/ noun [C] the piece of metal that you press to fire a gun: *to pull the trigger*
trigger verb [T] **trigger sth (off)** to cause sth to start or happen: *The smoke from her cigarette triggered off the fire-alarm.*

trike /traɪk/ noun [C] (*informal*) = TRICYCLE

trillion /'trɪliən/ number one million million ☛ For more information about numbers, look at Appendix 2.

trilogy /'trɪlədʒi/ noun [C] (*pl* **trilogies**) a group of three books, plays, etc that form one set

trim¹ /trɪm/ adj **1** in good order; tidy **2** not fat: *a trim figure*

trim² /trɪm/ verb [T] (**trim**ming; **trim**med)
1 to cut sth so that it is neat and tidy: *to trim a beard* **2 trim sth (off sth/off)** to cut sth off because you do not need it: *Trim the fat off the meat.* **3 trim sth (with sth)** to decorate the edge of sth with sth: *a skirt trimmed with lace*
trim noun [C, usually sing] an act of cutting sth in order to make it neat and tidy: *My hair needs a trim.*

trimming noun **1** [C,U] material that you use for decorating the edge of sth **2 trimmings** [plural] extra things which you add to sth to improve its appearance, taste, etc: *turkey with all the trimmings*

trinity /'trɪnəti/ noun [sing] **the Trinity** (in the Christian religion) the three forms of God: the Father, Jesus the Son and the Holy Spirit

trio /'triːəʊ/ noun (*pl* **trios**) **1** [C, with sing or pl verb] a group of three people who play music or sing together **2** [C] a piece of music for three people to play or sing

☆ **trip** /trɪp/ verb (**trip**ping; **trip**ped) **1** [I] **trip (over/up)** to knock your foot against sth when you are walking and fall or nearly fall over: *Don't leave your bag on the floor. Someone might trip over it.* o *She caught her foot in the root of a tree and tripped up.* **2** [T] **trip sb (up)** to cause sb to fall or nearly fall over: *Lee stuck out his foot and tripped John up.*
(PHRASAL VERB) **trip (sb) up** to make a mistake; to make sb say sth that he/she did not want to say: *The journalist asked a difficult question to try to trip the Minister up.*
trip noun [C] a journey during which you visit a place and return: *a trip to the mountains* o *a business trip to Brussels* ☛ Look at the note at **travel**. —**tripper** noun [C]: *Brighton was full of day trippers from London.*

triple /'trɪpl/ adj **1** made up of three parts: *the triple jump* **2** happening three times or containing three times as much as usual: *a triple world champion* (= one who has won three times) o *a triple whisky*
triple verb [I,T] to make sth, or to become, three times greater

triplet /'trɪplət/ noun [C] one of three children or animals that are born to one mother at the same time ☛ Look at **twin**.

tripod /'traɪpɒd/ noun [C] a piece of equipment with three legs that you use for putting a camera, etc on

☆ **triumph** /'traɪʌmf/ noun [C,U] success, especially in a competition or battle; the feeling of joy that you have because of this: *The soldiers returned home in triumph.* o *The fans gave a shout of triumph.* o *Putting a man on the moon was one of the triumphs of the twentieth century.*
triumph verb [I] **triumph (over sb/sth)** to achieve success; to defeat sb/sth: *Hull triumphed over Stoke in the championship.* o *Although he was blind, he triumphed over his disability to become an MP.*

triumphant /traɪ'ʌmfnt/ adj feeling or showing great happiness because you have won or succeeded at sth: *a triumphant cheer* —**triumphantly** adv

trivial /'trɪviəl/ adj of little importance —**triviality** /ˌtrɪvi'æləti/ noun [C,U] (*pl* **trivialities**)
trivialize (*also* **trivialise**) /'trɪviəlaɪz/ verb [T] to make sth seem unimportant

trod *pt* of TREAD

trodden *pp* of TREAD

trolley /'trɒli/ noun [C] (*pl* **trolleys**) a cart on wheels that you use for carrying things: *a supermarket trolley*

trombone /trɒm'bəʊn/ noun [C] a large brass musical instrument that you play by blowing into it and moving a long tube backwards and forwards

☆ **troop** /truːp/ noun **1** [C] a large group of people or animals **2 troops** [plural] soldiers
troop verb [I] to move in a large group: *When*

3:	ə	eɪ	əʊ	aɪ	aʊ	ɔɪ	ɪə	eə	ʊə
fur	ago	pay	home	five	now	join	near	hair	pure

trolleys

supermarket trolley

luggage trolley

the bell rang everyone trooped from one classroom to another.

trophy /'trəʊfɪ/ *noun* [C] (*pl* **trophies**) a silver cup, etc that you get for winning a competition or race

☆ **tropic** /'trɒpɪk/ *noun* **1** [C, usually sing] one of the two lines of latitude that are 23° 27' north and south of the equator: *the tropic of Cancer* ○ *the tropic of Capricorn* ☛ picture at **earth**. **2 the tropics** [plural] the part of the world that is between these two lines, where the climate is hot —**tropical** /-kl/ *adj*: *tropical fruit* ○ *tropical rainforest*

trot /trɒt/ *verb* (**trotting**; **trotted**) [I] (used about a horse) to move fairly quickly, lifting the feet quite high off the ground: (*figurative*) *The child trotted along behind his father.*

(PHRASAL VERB) **trot sth out** (*informal*) to repeat an old idea rather than thinking of sth new to say: *to trot out the same old story*

trot *noun* [sing] the speed that a horse goes when it is trotting; a ride at this speed

(IDIOM) **on the trot** (*informal*) one after another; without a break: *We worked for six hours on the trot.*

☆ **trouble** /'trʌbl/ *noun* **1** [C,U] (a situation that causes) problems, difficulty, worry, etc: *If I don't get home by 11 o'clock I'll be in trouble.* ○ *I'm having trouble getting the car started.* ○ *financial troubles* ○ *It's a very good school. The only trouble is it's rather a long way away.* **2** [sing,U] extra work or effort: *Let's eat out tonight. It will save you the trouble of cooking.* ○ *Why don't you stay the night with us. It's no trouble.* ○ *I'm sorry to put you to so much trouble.* **3** [C,U] a situation where people are fighting or arguing with each other: *There's often trouble in town on Saturday night after the pubs have closed.* **4** [U] illness or pain: *I've got back trouble again.*

(IDIOMS) **ask for trouble** ⇒ ASK

get into trouble to get into a situation which is dangerous or in which you may be punished

go to a lot of trouble (to do sth) to put a lot of work or effort into sth: *They went to a lot of trouble to make us feel welcome.*

take trouble over sth/with sth/to do sth/doing sth to do sth with care

take the trouble to do sth to do sth even though it means extra work or effort: *He took the trouble to write and thank everyone for his presents.*

trouble *verb* [T] **1** to cause sb worry, problems, etc **2 trouble sb for sth** (*formal*) (used when you are politely asking sb for sth or to do sth): *I'm sorry to trouble you, but would you mind answering a few questions?* ○ *Could I trouble you for some change?*

troublesome /-səm/ *adj* that causes trouble(1)

'**troublemaker** *noun* [C] a person who often causes trouble(1,3)

trough /trɒf; *US* trɔːf/ *noun* [C] **1** a long narrow container from which farm animals eat or drink **2** a low area or point, between two higher areas: *a trough of low pressure*

☆ **trousers** /'traʊzəz/ (*US* **pants**) *noun* [plural] a piece of clothing that covers both legs and reaches from your waist to your ankles ☛ Note that, because **trousers** is a plural word, we cannot say, for example, 'a new trouser'. The following are possible: *I need some new trousers.* ○ *I need a new pair of trousers.* Before another noun the form **trouser** is used: *a trouser leg.*

trout /traʊt/ *noun* [C,U] (*pl* **trout**) a type of fish that lives in rivers and that is eaten as food

truant /'truːənt/ *noun* [C] a pupil who stays away from school without permission

(IDIOM) **play truant** to stay away from school without permission —**truancy** /-ənsɪ/ *noun* [U]: *Truancy is on the increase in some schools.*

truce /truːs/ *noun* [C] an agreement to stop fighting for a period of time ☛ Look at **cease-fire**.

☆ **truck** /trʌk/ *noun* [C] **1** (*especially US*) = LORRY **2** (*Brit*) an open railway wagon that is used for carrying goods **3** (in compounds) a large heavy vehicle, used for a particular purpose: *a fork-lift truck*

trudge /trʌdʒ/ *verb* [I] to walk with slow, heavy steps, eg because you are very tired

☆ **true** /truː/ *adj* **1** that really happened: *The novel was based on a true story.* **2** right or correct; agreeing with fact: *Is it true that Adam is leaving?* ○ *I didn't think the film was at all true to life* (= it didn't show life as it really is). ○ *Read the statements and decide if they are true or false.* **3** real or genuine: *How do you know when you have found true love?* ○ *the true value of the house* **4 true (to sth)** behaving as expected or as promised: *to be true to your word* (= to do what you promised) ☛ The noun is **truth**.

(IDIOMS) **come true** to happen in the way you hoped or dreamed: *My dream has come true!*

true to form typical; as usual: *True to form, Carol started organizing everything straight away.*

truly /'truːlɪ/ *adv* **1** really: *We are truly grateful to you for your help.* ○ *'I'm sorry, truly I am,' he whispered.* **2** completely: *With her passport in her hand she at last felt truly American.* **3** expressing the truth: *I cannot truly say that I was surprised at the news.* ☛ **Yours truly** is often used at the end of a formal letter.

(IDIOM) **well and truly** ⇒ WELL³

trump /trʌmp/ *noun* [C] (in some card games) a card of the suit that has a higher value than the other three suits during a particular game: *Spades are trumps.*

'**trump-card** *noun* [C] a special advantage that you keep secret until the last moment

trumpet /'trʌmpɪt/ *noun* [C] a brass musical instrument that you play by blowing into it.

p	b	t	d	k	g	tʃ	dʒ	f	v	θ	ð
pen	bad	tea	did	cat	got	chin	June	fall	van	thin	then

There are three buttons on it which you can press to make different notes.

truncheon /'trʌntʃən/ (*also* **baton**) *noun* [C] a short thick stick that a police officer carries as a weapon

trundle /'trʌndl/ *verb* **1** [I] to move slowly: *A lorry trundled down the hill.* **2** [T] to push or pull sth along slowly on wheels

☆ **trunk** /trʌŋk/ *noun* **1** [C] the thick main stem of a tree ☞ picture at **tree**. **2** [C] the main part of your body (= not including your head, arms and legs) **3** [C] a large box, like a large suitcase, that you use for storing or transporting things ☞ picture at **luggage**. **4** [C] an elephant's long nose ☞ picture at **elephant**. **5 trunks** [plural] short trousers that men or boys wear when they go swimming **6** [C] (*US*) = BOOT(2)

☆ **trust¹** /trʌst/ *noun* **1** [U] **trust (in sb/sth)** the feeling that you have when you know that you can rely on sb/sth to do what he/she/it is supposed to do: *Our marriage is based on love and trust.* ○ *I put my trust in him, but he failed me.* **2** [U] responsibility: *As a teacher you are in a position of trust.* **3** [C,U] an arrangement by which a person or organization looks after money and property for sb else: *The money was put into a trust for the children.*

(IDIOM) **on trust** without having proof; without checking: *I can't prove it. You must take it on trust.*

trustworthy *adj* that you can trust

☆ **trust²** /trʌst/ *verb* [T] to believe that you can rely on sb/sth to do what he/she/it is supposed to do; to believe that sb/sth will not harm you: *He said the car was safe but I just don't trust him.* ○ *Can I trust you to behave sensibly while I am out?* ○ *You can't trust her with money.* ○ *She is not to be trusted with money.* ○ *I don't trust that dog. It looks dangerous.*

(IDIOM) **Trust sb (to do sth)** It is typical of sb to do sth: *Trust Alice to be late. She's never on time!*

trusting *adj* having or showing trust

trustee /trʌ'sti:/ *noun* [C] a person who looks after money or property for sb else

☆ **truth** /tru:θ/ *noun* (*pl* **truths** /tru:ðz/) **1** [U] the state or quality of being true: *There's a lot of truth in what she says.* **2** [sing] what is true: *Please tell me the truth.* ○ *the whole truth* **3** [C] a fact or idea that is true: *scientific truths*

truthful /-fl/ *adj* **1** true or correct: *a truthful account* **2** (used about a person) who tells the truth; honest —**truthfully** /-fəli/ *adv*

☆ **try¹** /traɪ/ *verb* (*pres part* **trying**; *3rd pers sing pres* **tries**; *pt, pp* **tried**) **1** [I] to make an effort to do sth: *I tried to phone you but I couldn't get through.* ○ *She was trying hard not to laugh.* ○ *to try your best/hardest* ○ *I'm sure you can do it if you try.* ☞ **Try and** is more informal than **try to**. It cannot be used in the past tense: *I'll try to get there on time.* (*informal*): *I'll try and get there on time.* ○ *I tried to get there on time, but I was too late.* **2** [T] to do, or use or test sth in order to see how good or successful it is: *'I've tried everything but I can't get the baby to sleep.' 'Have you tried taking her out in the pram?'* ○ *Have you ever tried raw fish?* ○ *We tried the door but it was locked.* ○ *He tried several bookshops but none of them stocked the books he wanted.* **3** [T] to examine sb in a court of law in order to decide if he/she is guilty of a crime or not: *He was tried for murder.*

(PHRASAL VERBS) **try sth on** to put on a piece of clothing to see if it fits you properly: *Can I try these jeans on, please?*

try sb/sth out to test sb/sth by using him/her/it

trying *adj* that makes you tired or angry: *a trying journey*

☆ **try²** /traɪ/ *noun* [C] (*pl* **tries**) an occasion when you make an effort to do sth; an attempt: *I don't know if I can move it by myself, but I'll give it a try.*

T-shirt ⇒ T

tub /tʌb/ *noun* [C] **1** a large round container with a flat bottom and no lid: *On the terrace there were several tubs with flowers in them.* **2** a small plastic container with a lid that is used for holding food: *a tub of margarine, ice-cream, etc* ☞ picture at **container**.

tuba /'tju:bə; *US* 'tu:-/ *noun* [C] a large brass musical instrument that makes a low sound

☆ **tube** /tju:b; *US* tu:b/ *noun* **1** [C] a long hollow pipe made of glass, metal, rubber, etc: *Blood flowed along the tube into the bottle.* ○ *the inner tube of a bicycle tyre* ○ *a laboratory test-tube* **2** [C] a long thin soft container with a cap at one end made of plastic or metal. Tubes are used for holding soft substances such as toothpaste and you squeeze them to get the substance out. ☞ picture at **container**. **3** (*Brit informal*) = UNDERGROUND

tubing *noun* [U] a long piece of metal, rubber, etc in the shape of a tube

tuberculosis /tju:,bɜ:kjʊ'ləʊsɪs; *US* tu:-/ *noun* [U] (*abbr* **TB**) a serious disease that especially affects the lungs

tuck /tʌk/ *verb* [T] **1** to put or fold the ends or edges of sth into or round sth else so that it looks tidy: *Tuck your shirt in – it looks untidy like that.* ○ *He tucked the blanket round the old man's knees.* **2** to put sth away tidily or in a safe or hidden place: *He tucked his wallet away in his inside pocket.* ○ *The letter was tucked behind a pile of books.*

(PHRASAL VERBS) **tuck sth away** (*informal*) **1** to store sth: *They've got a lot of money tucked away.* **2** to hide sth: *Their house is tucked away behind the church.*

tuck into sth; tuck in (*informal*) (*especially Brit*) to eat with pleasure

☆ **Tuesday** /'tju:zdɪ; *US* 'tu:-/ *noun* [C,U] (*abbr* **Tue; Tues**) the day of the week after Monday and before Wednesday ☞ For examples of the use of the days of the week in sentences, look at **Monday**.

tuft /tʌft/ *noun* [C] a small bunch of hair, grass, etc

tug /tʌg/ *verb* [I,T] (**tugging; tugged**) to pull sth hard and quickly

tug *noun* [C] **1** a sudden hard pull: *She gave the rope a tug.* **2** (*also* **tug-boat**) a small strong boat that is used for pulling larger ships into a harbour

tuition /tju:'ɪʃn; *US* tu:-/ *noun* [U] (*formal*)

teaching, especially to a small group of people: *private tuition in Italian* ○ *tuition fees*

tulip /'tju:lɪp/ *US* 'tu:-/ *noun* [C] a brightly-coloured flower, shaped like a small cup, that grows from a bulb in the spring

tumble /'tʌmbl/ *verb* [I] **1** to fall suddenly in a heavy way, without control: *He tripped and tumbled all the way down the steps.* **2** (used about prices, etc) to become lower: *Hotel prices have tumbled.* **3** to move in a particular direction in an untidy way: *I got undressed and tumbled into bed.* ○ *She opened her suitcase and all her things tumbled out of it.*
(PHRASAL VERB) **tumble down** to fall down; to collapse: *The walls of the old house were tumbling down.*

tumble *noun* [C] a sudden fall

'tumble-drier (*also* **tumble-dryer**) *noun* [C] a machine that dries clothes by moving them about in hot air

tumbler /'tʌmblə(r)/ *noun* [C] a drinking-glass with straight sides that has no handle or stem

tummy /'tʌmi/ *noun* [C] (*pl* **tummies**) (*informal*) = STOMACH (*informal*): *I've got (a) tummy-ache.*

tumour (*US* **tumor**) /'tju:mə(r); *US* 'tu:-/ *noun* [C] a mass of diseased cells that are growing abnormally in the body: *a brain tumour*

tumultuous /tju:'mʌltʃuəs/ *adj* very noisy, because people are excited: *a tumultuous welcome*

tuna /'tju:nə; *US* 'tu:nə/ *noun* (*pl* **tuna**) **1** [C] a large sea-fish **2** [U] (*also* **tuna-fish**) the flesh of the fish, which is often sold in tins

☆ **tune** /tju:n; *US* tu:n/ *noun* [C,U] a series of musical notes that are arranged in a pleasant pattern: *The children played us a tune on their recorders.* ○ *I can't remember the tune of that song.* ○ *a signature tune* (= one that is always played at the beginning of a TV or radio performance) ○ *Some people complain that modern music has no tune to it.*
(IDIOMS) **change your tune** → CHANGE¹

in/out of tune 1 at/not at the correct musical level (**pitch**): *You're singing out of tune.* **2** in/not in agreement with sb/sth: *The President doesn't seem to be in tune with what ordinary people are thinking.*

tune *verb* [T] **1** to adjust a musical instrument so that it is at the correct musical level (**pitch**) **2** to adjust an engine so that it runs well
(IDIOM) **tuned (in) to sth** listening to a particular radio station: *Stay tuned to this station for the latest news.*
(PHRASAL VERBS) **tune in (to sth)** to move the controls of a radio or television so that you can listen to or watch a particular station
tune up to adjust a group of musical instruments so that they play together in tune

tuneful /-fl/ *adj* (used about music) pleasant to listen to

tunic /'tju:nɪk; *US* 'tu:-/ *noun* [C] **1** the jacket that is part of the uniform of a policeman, soldier, etc **2** a piece of loose clothing without sleeves that is like a dress

☆ **tunnel** /'tʌnl/ *noun* [C] a passage under the ground or sea, river, etc: *The train disappeared into a tunnel.* ○ *the Channel Tunnel*

tunnel *verb* [I,T] (tunnelling; tunnelled; *US* tunneling; tunneled) to dig a tunnel

turban /'tɜ:bən/ *noun* [C] a covering for the head worn by Muslim and Sikh men. A turban is made by wrapping a long piece of cloth around the head.

turbulent /'tɜ:bjʊlənt/ *adj* **1** in a state of disorder and confusion when things are changing fast **2** (used about water or air) moving in a violent way

turf /tɜ:f/ *noun* [U] short thick grass and the layer of soil underneath it

turf *verb* [T] to cover ground with turf
(PHRASAL VERB) **turf sb out (of sth)** (*Brit informal*) to force sb/sth to leave a place

turkey /'tɜ:ki/ *noun* [C,U] (*pl* **turkeys**) a large bird that is kept on farms. Turkeys are usually eaten at Christmas in Britain and at Thanksgiving in the US.

turmoil /'tɜ:mɔɪl/ *noun* [C, usually sing,U] a state of great excitement, noise or confusion

☆ **turn¹** /tɜ:n/ *verb* [I,T] **1** [I] to move or go round a fixed point: *The wheels turned faster and faster.* **2** [T] to hold and move sth round a central point; to make sth go round: *She turned the handle on the door.* ○ *Turn the steering wheel to the right.* **3** [I] to change your position so that you are facing in a different direction: *He turned round when he heard my voice.* **4** [T] to change the position of sth: *I turned the box upside down.* ○ *He turned the page and started the next chapter.* **5** [I,T] to change direction when you are moving: *Go straight on and turn left at the church.* ○ *The car turned the corner.* ○ *He turned the lorry into the yard.* **6** [I,T] (to cause) to become: *He turned very red when I asked him about the money.* ○ *The fairy waved her wand and the prince turned into a frog.* ○ *She turned him into a frog.*

☞ For expressions with **turn**, look at the noun and adjective entries, eg for **turn a blind eye**, look at **blind**.

(PHRASAL VERBS) **turn away** to stop looking at sb/sth: *She turned away in horror at the sight of the blood.*
turn sb away to refuse to allow a person to go into a place
turn back to go back in the same direction as you came
turn sb/sth down to refuse an offer, etc or the person who makes it: *Why did you turn that job down?* ○ *He asked her to marry him, but she turned him down.*
turn sth down to reduce the sound or heat that sth produces: *Turn the television down!*
turn off (sth) to leave one road and go on another: *We turn off the motorway at junction 10.*
turn sth off to move the switch, etc on a piece of machinery, etc to stop it working: *He turned the TV off.*
turn sth on to move the switch, etc on a piece of machinery, etc to start it working: *Turn the lights on!*
turn out (for sth) to be present or appear for sth: *Thousands of people turned out to welcome the team home.*

i:	ɪ	e	æ	ɑ:	ɒ	ɔ:	ʊ	u:	ʌ
see	sit	ten	hat	arm	got	saw	put	too	cup

turn out (to be sth) to be sth in the end: *The weather turned out fine.* ○ *The house that they had promised us turned out to be a tiny flat.*
turn sth out to move the switch, etc on a light so that it is no longer shining: *Turn the lights out before you go to bed.*
turn to sb to go to sb to get help
turn to sth to find a page in a book: *Turn to page 45.*
turn up 1 to arrive: *What time did they finally turn up?* **2** to be found: *I lost my glasses a week ago and they haven't turned up yet.*
turn sth up to increase the sound or heat that sth produces: *Turn the heating up – it's freezing!*
'turn-off *noun* [C] the point where a road leads away from a larger or more important one: *This is the turn-off for York.*
'turnout *noun* [C, usually sing] the number of people who go to the meeting, match, etc
'turnover *noun* [sing] **1** the amount of business that a company does in a particular period of time **2** the rate at which workers leave a company and are replaced by new ones: *a high turnover of staff*
'turnstile *noun* [C] a gate that goes round and that allows one person at a time to enter a place
☆ **turn²** /tɜːn/ *noun* [C] **1** an act of turning sb/sth round: *Give the screw another couple of turns to make sure it is really tight.* **2** a change of direction: *to make a left/right turn* ○ *a U-turn* (= when you turn round and go back in the opposite direction) **3** a bend or corner in a road, river, etc: *Take the next turn on the left.* **4** [usually sing] the time when you must or may do sth: *Please wait in the queue until it is your turn.* **5** a change: *The patient's condition has taken a turn for the worse.*
(IDIOMS) **do sb a good/bad turn** to do sth helpful/unhelpful for sb
in turn one after the other: *I spoke to each of the children in turn.*
take turns (at sth) to do sth one after the other: *You can't both play on the computer at the same time. You'll have to take turns.*
wait your turn ⇒ WAIT¹
☆ **turning** /'tɜːnɪŋ/ *noun* [C] a place where one road joins or leads off from another: *Take the third turning on the right.*
'turning-point *noun* [C] a time when an important change happens
turnip /'tɜːnɪp/ *noun* [C,U] a round white vegetable that grows under the ground
turpentine /'tɜːpəntaɪn/ *noun* [U] a clear liquid with a strong smell that you use for removing paint or for making paint thinner
turquoise /'tɜːkwɔɪz/ *adj, noun* [U] (of) a greenish-blue colour
turret /'tʌrɪt/ *noun* [C] a small tower on the top of another tower
turtle /'tɜːtl/ *noun* [C] **1** a reptile with a soft body and a thick shell that lives in the sea **2** (*US*) = TORTOISE
tusk /tʌsk/ *noun* [C] one of the two very long pointed teeth of an elephant, etc ☞ picture at **elephant**. Elephants' tusks are made of **ivory**.
tussle /'tʌsl/ *noun* [C] (*informal*) a rough fight, eg between two or more people who want to have the same thing
tut /tʌt/ (*also* **tut-'tut**) *interj* the way of writing the sound that people make when they think that sth is bad, foolish, etc
tutor /'tjuːtə(r); *US* 'tuː-/ *noun* [C] **1** a private teacher who teaches one person or a very small group **2** (*Brit*) a teacher who is responsible for a small group of pupils at school, or students at college or university. A tutor advises students on their work or helps them if they have problems in their private life. Sometimes tutors teach small groups.
tutorial /tjuː'tɔːrɪəl; *US* tuː-/ *noun* [C] a lesson given by a tutor(2) to a student or a small group of students
tuxedo /tʌk'siːdəʊ/ *noun* [C] (*pl* **tuxedos** /-dəʊz/) (*also informal* **tux**) (*US*) = DINNER-JACKET
twang /twæŋ/ *noun* [C] the sound that you make when you pull a tight string or wire and then let it go —**twang** *verb* [I,T]
tweed /twiːd/ *noun* [U] thick woollen cloth with a rough surface
tweezers /'twiːzəz/ *noun* [plural] a small tool consisting of two pieces of metal that are joined at one end. You use tweezers for picking up or pulling out very small things: *a pair of tweezers*
☆ **twelve** /twelv/ *number* 12; one more than eleven ☞ Look at **dozen**. For examples of how to use numbers in sentences, look at **six**.
twelfth /twelfθ/ *pron, det, adv* 12th; next after eleventh ☞ Look at the examples at **sixth**.
☆ **twenty** /'twentɪ/ *number* 20; one more than nineteen ☞ For examples of how to use numbers in sentences, look at **sixty**.
twentieth /'twentɪəθ/ *pron, det, adv* 20th; next after nineteenth ☞ Look at the examples at **sixth**.
☆ **twice** /twaɪs/ *adv* two times: *I've been to Egypt twice – once last year and once in 1984.* ○ *The film will be shown twice daily.* ○ *Take the medicine twice a day.* ○ *Prices have risen twice as fast in this country as in Japan.*
twiddle /'twɪdl/ *verb* [I,T] to keep turning or moving sth with your fingers
twig /twɪg/ *noun* [C] a small thin branch on a tree or bush ☞ picture at **tree**.
twilight /'twaɪlaɪt/ *noun* [U] the time after the sun has set and before it gets completely dark
☆ **twin** /twɪn/ *noun* [C] **1** one of two children or animals that are born to the same mother at the same time: *They're very alike. Are they twins?* ○ *a twin brother/sister* ○ *identical twins* **2** one of a pair of things that are the same or very similar: *twin beds* (= two single beds in a room for two people) ○ *a twin-bedded room*
twin *verb* [T] (**twinn**ing; **twinn**ed) to join two towns in different countries together in a special relationship: *Oxford is twinned with Bonn.*
twin 'town *noun* [C] one of two towns in different countries that have a special relationship: *Grenoble is Oxford's twin town.*
twinge /twɪndʒ/ *noun* [C] **a twinge (of sth) 1** a sudden thought or feeling: *a twinge of fear* **2** a sudden short pain
twinkle /'twɪŋkl/ *verb* [I] **1** to shine with a

light that seems to be moving: *Stars twinkled in the night sky.* **2** (used about your eyes) to look bright because you are happy —**twinkle** noun [sing]: *From the twinkle in her eyes we knew she was joking.*

twirl /twɜːl/ verb **1** [I] to spin or turn around, eg when you are dancing **2** [T] to twist or turn sth

☆ **twist¹** /twɪst/ verb **1** [I,T] to turn yourself or a part of your body: *She twisted round to see where the noise was coming from.* ○ *He kept twisting his head from side to side.* **2** [I,T] to turn or make sth turn into a shape or position that is not normal: *The metal twisted into strange shapes.* ○ *He twisted his knee while he was playing squash.* **3** [T] to turn sth in a particular direction: *Twist the dial as far as it will go.* ○ *Most containers have twist-off caps.* **4** [I] (used about a road, etc) to change direction often: *a narrow twisting lane* **5** [T] to wind sth round and round an object: *I twisted the bandage round her knee.* **6** [T] to change the meaning of what sb said: *Journalists often twist your words.*
(IDIOM) **twist sb's arm** (*informal*) to force or persuade sb to do sth

twist² /twɪst/ noun [C] **1** an act of twisting sth: *She killed the chicken with one twist of its neck.* **2** a place where sth has become twisted: *Straighten out the wire so that there are no twists in it.* **3** a place where a road, river, etc bends or changes direction: *the twists and turns of the river* **4** a change or development (especially one that you do not expect): *an unexpected twist at the end of the book*

twit /twɪt/ noun [C] (*Brit informal*) a stupid person

twitch /twɪtʃ/ verb [I,T] to make a sudden movement; to cause sth to make a sudden movement: *The rabbit twitched and then lay still.* ○ *Can you twitch your ears?* —**twitch** noun [C]

twitter /'twɪtə(r)/ verb [I] (used about birds) to make a series of short high sounds

☆ **two** /tuː/ number 2; one more than one ☛ Look at **second**. For examples of how to use numbers in sentences, look at **six**.
(IDIOM) **in two** in or into two pieces: *The plate fell on the floor and broke in two.*

two- (in compounds) having two of the thing mentioned: *a two-week holiday*

tycoon /taɪˈkuːn/ noun [C] (*informal*) a person who is very successful in business and who is rich and powerful

☆ **type¹** /taɪp/ noun [C] **1 a type (of sth)** a group of people or things that share certain qualities and that are part of a larger group; a kind or sort: *Which type of paint should you use on metal?* ○ *Spaniels are a type of dog.* ○ *There are several different types of apartment to choose from.* ○ *That's just the type of situation that you should avoid.* ○ *You meet all types of people in this job.* ○ *the first building of its type in the world* **2** a person of a particular kind: *He's the careful type.* ☛ If you say somebody is not **your type** you mean that they are not the sort of person that you would be friendly with. Look at **typical**.

☆ **type²** /taɪp/ verb [I,T] to write sth using a typewriter, word processor, etc: *Can you type?* ○ *to type a letter*

type noun [U] the letters that you use when you are typing or printing: *The type is too small to read.*

typing noun [U] **1** the act of typing: *typing skills* **2** work that has been or must be typed: *There is still a lot of typing to be done.*

typist /'taɪpɪst/ noun [C] a person who types, especially as a job

'typewriter noun [C] a machine that you use for writing in print

'typewritten adj written using a typewriter or word processor

typhoid /'taɪfɔɪd/ noun [U] a serious disease that can cause death. People get typhoid from bad food or water.

typhoon /taɪˈfuːn/ noun [C] a violent tropical storm with very strong winds ☛ Look at the note at **storm**.

☆ **typical** /'tɪpɪkl/ adj **typical (of sb/sth)** having or showing the usual qualities of a particular person, thing or type: *a typical Italian village* ○ *There's no such thing as a typical American* (= they are all different). ○ *It was absolutely typical of him not to reply to my letter.*

typically adv **1** in a typical case: *Typically it is the girls who offer to help, not the boys.* **2** in a typical manner: *typically British*

typify /'tɪpɪfaɪ/ verb [T] (*pres part* **typifying**; *3rd pers sing pres* **typifies**; *pt, pp* **typified**) to be a typical mark or example of sb/sth: *The film typified the Hollywood westerns of that time.*

☆ **typist** ➔ TYPE²

tyranny /'tɪrəni/ noun [U] the cruel and unjust use of power by a person or small group to govern a country or state —**tyrannical** /tɪˈrænɪkl/ adj: *a tyrannical ruler*

tyrannize (*also* **tyrannise**) /'tɪrənaɪz/ verb [I,T] to use power over other people in a cruel and unjust way

tyrant /'taɪərənt/ noun [C] a cruel ruler who has complete power over the people in his/her country ☛ Look at **dictator**.

☆ **tyre** (*US* **tire**) /'taɪə(r)/ noun [C] the thick rubber ring that fits around the outside of a wheel: *a flat tyre* ○ *Remember to check your tyre pressure.* ☛ picture at **puncture**.

p	b	t	d	k	g	tʃ	dʒ	f	v	θ	ð
pen	bad	tea	did	cat	got	chin	June	fall	van	thin	then

Uu

U, u /juː/ noun [C] (pl **U's; u's** /juːz/) the twenty-first letter of the English alphabet: *'Ulcer' begins with (a) 'U'.*

udder /ˈʌdə(r)/ noun [C] the part of a female cow, goat, etc that hangs like a bag between its legs and produces milk

ugh /ɜː/ interj (used in writing to express the sound that you make when you think sth is very unpleasant)

☆ **ugly** /ˈʌgli/ adj (**uglier; ugliest**) **1** unpleasant to look at or listen to; unattractive: *an ugly scar on her face* ○ *an ugly modern office-block* **2** (used about a situation) dangerous or threatening: *The situation became ugly when people started throwing stones.* —**ugliness** noun [U]

ulcer /ˈʌlsə(r)/ noun [C] a painful area on your skin or inside your body. Ulcers may produce a poisonous substance and sometimes bleed: *a mouth ulcer* ○ *a stomach ulcer*

ulterior /ʌlˈtɪərɪə(r)/ adj (formal) that you keep hidden or secret: *Why is he suddenly being so nice to me? He must have an ulterior motive.*

ultimate /ˈʌltɪmət/ adj (only before a noun) **1** being or happening at the end; last or final: *Our ultimate goal is complete independence.* **2** the greatest, best or worst: *For me the ultimate luxury is to stay in bed till ten o'clock on a Sunday.*

ultimate noun [sing] **the ultimate (in sth)** (informal) the greatest or best: *This new car is the ultimate in comfort.*

ultimately adv **1** in the end: *Whatever decision we ultimately take will be in the best interests of the school.* **2** at the most basic level: *Ultimately, this discussion is not about quality but about money.*

ultimatum /ˌʌltɪˈmeɪtəm/ noun [C] (pl **ultimatums**) a warning to a person or country that, if they do not do what you ask, you will use force or take action against them

ultra- /ˈʌltrə/ (in compounds) extremely: *ultra-modern*

ultraviolet /ˌʌltrəˈvaɪələt/ adj of a type of light that causes your skin to turn darker and that can be dangerous in large amounts

umbilical cord /ˌʌmˌbɪlɪkl ˈkɔːd/ noun [C] the tube that connects a baby to its mother before it is born

☆ **umbrella** /ʌmˈbrelə/ noun [C] an object that you carry to keep you dry when it is raining. An umbrella consists of a piece of cloth on a frame and a long handle. You can fold an umbrella up when you are not using it: *to put an umbrella up/down*

umpire /ˈʌmpaɪə(r)/ noun [C] a person who watches a game such as tennis or cricket to make sure that the players obey the rules ☛ picture at **tennis**. Look at **referee**. —**umpire** verb [I,T]

umpteen /ˈʌmptiːn/ pron, det (informal) very many; a lot: *I've told you umpteen times to phone me if you're going to be late.* —**umpteenth** /ˈʌmptiːnθ/ pron, det: *For the umpteenth time – phone if you're going to be late!*

☆ **unable** /ʌnˈeɪbl/ adj (not before a noun) **unable to do sth** not having the time, knowledge, skill, etc to do sth; not able to do sth: *Thank you for the invitation. I regret that I shall be unable to attend.* ☛ The noun is **inability**.

unacceptable /ˌʌnəkˈseptəbl/ adj that you cannot accept or allow —**unacceptably** /-blɪ/ adv

unaccompanied /ˌʌnəˈkʌmpənɪd/ adj alone, without sb/sth else going too: *unaccompanied children*

unaffected /ˌʌnəˈfektɪd/ adj **1** not changed by sth: *Our department will be unaffected by the decision.* **2** natural in the way you behave

unaided /ʌnˈeɪdɪd/ adv without any help

unanimous /juːˈnænɪməs/ adj **1** (used about a group of people) all agreeing about sth: *The members of the jury were unanimous in their decision.* **2** (used about a decision, etc) agreed by everybody —**unanimously** adv

unarmed /ʌnˈɑːmd/ adj having no guns, knives, etc; not armed

unashamed /ˌʌnəˈʃeɪmd/ adj feeling or showing no guilt —**unashamedly** adv: *The film was unashamedly sentimental.*

unassuming /ˌʌnəˈsjuːmɪŋ/; US /ˌʌnəˈsuː-/ adj not wishing to be noticed by other people

unattached /ˌʌnəˈtætʃt/ adj **1** not connected to sb/sth else: *This group is unattached to any political party.* **2** not married; without a regular partner

unattended /ˌʌnəˈtendɪd/ adj not watched or looked after: *Young children should not be left unattended.*

unauthorized /ʌnˈɔːθəraɪzd/ adj done without permission

unavoidable /ˌʌnəˈvɔɪdəbl/ adj that cannot be avoided or prevented —**unavoidably** /-əblɪ/ adv: *We were unavoidably delayed.*

unaware /ˌʌnəˈweə(r)/ adj (not before a noun) **unaware (of sb/sth)** not knowing about or not noticing sb/sth: *She seemed unaware of all the trouble she had caused.*

unawares /-ˈweəz/ adv by surprise; without expecting sth or being prepared for it: *I was taken completely unawares by his suggestion.*

unbalanced /ʌnˈbælənst/ adj **1** (used about a person) rather mad **2** not fair to all ideas or sides of an argument: *an unbalanced newspaper report*

s	z	ʃ	ʒ	h	m	n	ŋ	l	r	j	w
so	zoo	she	vision	how	man	no	sing	leg	red	yes	wet

unbearable /ʌnˈbeərəbl/ adj too unpleasant, painful, etc for you to accept —**unbearably** /-əblɪ/ adv: It was unbearably hot.

unbeatable /ˌʌnˈbiːtəbl/ adj that cannot be defeated or improved on: A few years ago Steffi Graf seemed unbeatable. ○ We offer you quality at unbeatable prices.

unbeaten /ˌʌnˈbiːtn/ adj that has not been beaten or improved on: Her world record remains unbeaten.

unbelievable /ˌʌnbɪˈliːvəbl/ adj very surprising; difficult to believe ☞ Look at **incredible**. —**unbelievably** adj: unbelievably bad

unborn /ˌʌnˈbɔːn/ adj not yet born: Smoking can damage the unborn child.

unbroken /ˌʌnˈbrəʊkən/ adj **1** continuous; not interrupted: a period of unbroken silence **2** that has not been beaten: His record for the 1500 metres remains unbroken.

uncalled-for /ʌnˈkɔːld fɔː(r)/ adj not necessary or right: That comment was quite uncalled-for.

uncanny /ʌnˈkænɪ/ adj strange and mysterious; that you cannot easily explain

☆ **uncertain** /ʌnˈsɜːtn/ adj **1 uncertain (about/of sth)** not sure; not able to decide: She was still uncertain of his true feelings for her. ○ Chris seemed uncertain about what to do next. **2** not known exactly or not decided: He's lost his job and his future seems very uncertain. —**uncertainly** adv: Kate stood uncertainly, waiting for someone to speak to her.

uncertainty /ʌnˈsɜːtntɪ/ noun [C,U] (pl **uncertainties**) the state of being uncertain: Today's decision will put an end to all the uncertainty.

unchanged /ʌnˈtʃeɪndʒd/ adj staying the same; not changed: The town has remained almost unchanged since the eighteenth century.

uncharacteristic /ˌʌnkærəktəˈrɪstɪk/ adj not typical or usual —**uncharacteristically** adv

☆ **uncle** /ˈʌŋkl/ noun [C] **1** the brother of your father or mother: Uncle Steven **2** the husband of your aunt ☞ Some children use 'Uncle' before the first name of an adult that they know well but who is not related to them. Look at **aunt**.

☆ **uncomfortable** /ʌnˈkʌmftəbl/ adj **1** not pleasant to wear, sit in, lie on, etc: The chairs are hard and very uncomfortable. **2** not able to sit, lie etc in a position that is pleasant: I was very uncomfortable for most of the journey. **3** feeling or causing worry or embarrassment: I felt very uncomfortable when they started arguing in front of me. —**uncomfortably** /-əblɪ/ adv

uncommon /ʌnˈkɒmən/ adj unusual: Red squirrels are uncommon in England.

uncompromising /ʌnˈkɒmprəmaɪzɪŋ/ adj not willing to discuss sth or change a decision

unconcerned /ˌʌnkənˈsɜːnd/ adj not interested in sth or not worried about it

unconditional /ˌʌnkənˈdɪʃənl/ adj without limits or conditions: an unconditional surrender —**unconditionally** /-ʃənəlɪ/ adv

☆ **unconscious** /ʌnˈkɒnʃəs/ adj **1** in a state that is like sleep. You may be unconscious after an accident if you hit your head: He was found lying unconscious on the kitchen floor. **2 unconscious of sb/sth** not knowing or aware of sb/sth: He seemed unconscious of everything that was going on around him. **3** done, spoken, etc without you thinking about it or being aware of it: The article was full of unconscious humour. —**the unconscious** noun [sing] = SUBCONSCIOUS —**unconsciously** adv

unconsciousness noun [U] the state of being unconscious

uncontrollable /ˌʌnkənˈtrəʊləbl/ adj that you cannot control: an uncontrollable urge to giggle —**uncontrollably** adv

uncountable /ˌʌnˈkaʊntəbl/ adj (grammar) an uncountable noun cannot be counted and so does not have a plural. In this dictionary uncountable nouns are marked '[U]'.

uncover /ʌnˈkʌvə(r)/ verb [T] **1** to remove the cover from sth **2** to find out or discover sth

undecided /ˌʌndɪˈsaɪdɪd/ adj **1** not having made a decision: I'm still undecided about whether to take the job or not. **2** without any result or decision; not decided: The future of our jobs is still undecided.

undeniable /ˌʌndɪˈnaɪəbl/ adj clear, true or certain: The charm of the city is undeniable. —**undeniably** /-əblɪ/ adv

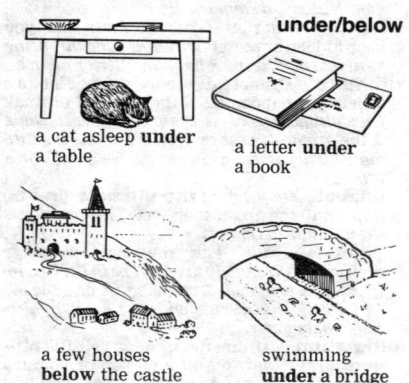

under/below

a cat asleep **under** a table

a letter **under** a book

a few houses **below** the castle

swimming **under** a bridge

☆ **under** /ˈʌndə(r)/ prep **1** in or to a position that is below or beneath sth: Put the suitcase under the bed. ○ to hide under the table ○ The dog crawled under the gate and ran into the road. ☞ Compare **under**, **below**, **beneath** and **underneath**. You use **under** to say that one thing is directly under another thing. There may be a space between the two things: The cat is asleep under the table or one thing may be touching or covered by the other thing: I think your letter is under that book. You can use **below** to say that one thing is in a lower position than another thing when they are both in the same building, on the same hill, on the same part of the body, etc: They live on the floor below us. ○ We could see a few houses below the castle. ○ It hurts here – just below the knee. You

iː	ɪ	e	æ	ɑː	ɒ	ɔː	ʊ	uː	ʌ
see	sit	ten	hat	arm	got	saw	put	too	cup

use **under** (not **below**) to talk about movement from one side of something to the other side: *We swam under the bridge.* You can use **beneath** to say that one thing is directly under another thing, but **under** is more common. **Beneath** is rather a literary word. You can use **underneath** in place of **under** when you want to emphasize that something is being covered or hidden by another thing: *Have you looked underneath the sofa as well as behind it?* **2** below the surface of sth; covered by sth: *Most of an iceberg is under the water.* o *Are you wearing a vest under your shirt?* **3** younger than: *Nobody under eighteen is allowed to buy alcohol.* **4** less than: *People earning under £10 000 a year will pay no extra tax.* **5** working for or in the control of sb: *This hotel is under new management.* **6** ruled or governed by sb/sth: *The country is now under martial law.* o *the Soviet Union under Gorbachev* **7** according to a law, agreement, system, etc: *Under English law you are innocent until you are proved guilty.* **8** in a particular state or condition: *under the influence of alcohol* o *a building under construction* o *I was under the impression that Bill was not very happy here.* **9** using a particular name: *to travel under a false name* **10** found in a particular part of a book, list, etc: *You'll find some information on Budapest under 'Hungary'.*
under *adv* **1** under water: *How long can you stay under for?* **2** less; younger: *The prices quoted are for children aged 12 and under.*

under- /'ʌndə(r)/ (in compounds) **1** lower in rank or position: *the minister's under-secretary* **2** not enough: *underdeveloped countries*

underclothes /'ʌndəkləʊðz/ *noun* [plural] = UNDERWEAR

undercover /ˌʌndə'kʌvə(r)/ *adj* working or happening secretly: *an undercover agent* (= a spy)

undercut /ˌʌndə'kʌt/ *verb* [T] (*pres part* **undercutting**; *pt, pp* **undercut**) to sell at a lower price than other shops, etc: *Supermarkets can undercut smaller shops.*

underdog /'ʌndədɒg/ *US* -dɔːg/ *noun* [C] a person who is in a weak position

underestimate /ˌʌndər'estɪmeɪt/ *verb* [T] **1** to guess that the amount, etc of sth will be less than it really is: *We underestimated the amount of food we would need.* **2** to think that sb/sth is not as strong, etc as he/she/it really is: *Don't underestimate your opponent. He's a really good player.* —**underestimate** /-mət/ *noun* [C]

underfoot /ˌʌndə'fʊt/ *adv* under your feet; where you are walking: *It's very wet underfoot.*

undergo /ˌʌndə'gəʊ/ *verb* [T] (*pt* **underwent** /-'went/; *pp* **undergone** /-'gɒn/; *US* -'gɔːn/) to have a difficult or unpleasant experience: *She underwent a five-hour operation at Harefield Hospital.*

undergraduate /ˌʌndə'grædʒuət/ *noun* [C] a university or college student who has not yet taken his/her first degree ☞ Look at **graduate** and **postgraduate**.

☆ **underground** /'ʌndəgraʊnd/ *adj* **1** under the surface of the ground: *an underground car park* **2** secret or illegal: *an underground radio station that supports the rebels*

under'ground *adv* **1** under the surface of the ground: *The cables all run underground.* **2** into a secret place: *She went underground to escape from the police.*

'underground (*US* **subway**) *noun* [sing] an underground railway system: *We travel to work by underground.* o *an underground station* ☞ In London the underground railway is called **the underground** or **the tube**.

undergrowth /'ʌndəgrəʊθ/ *noun* [U] bushes and plants that grow around and under trees

underhand /ˌʌndə'hænd/ *adj* secret or not honest

☆ **underline** /ˌʌndə'laɪn/ *verb* [T] **1** to draw a line under a word, etc **2** to show clearly or to emphasize sth: *This accident underlines the need for greater care.*

underlying /ˌʌndə'laɪɪŋ/ *adj* important but hidden: *the underlying causes of the disaster*

undermine /ˌʌndə'maɪn/ *verb* [T] to make sth weaker: *The public's confidence in the quality of our drinking water has been undermined.*

☆ **underneath** /ˌʌndə'niːθ/ *prep, adv* under or below: *The coin rolled underneath the chair.* o *a flat with a shop underneath* o *What does a Scotsman wear underneath his kilt?* o *This sweater's not very warm but I've got a T-shirt on underneath.*

the underneath *noun* [sing] the bottom or lowest part of something: *There is a lot of rust on the underneath of the car.*

underpants /'ʌndəpænts/ (*Brit* **pants**) *noun* [plural] a piece of clothing that men or boys wear under their trousers

underpass /'ʌndəpɑːs; *US* -pæs/ *noun* [C] a road or path that goes under another road, railway, etc

underpay /ˌʌndə'peɪ/ *verb* [T] (*pt, pp* **underpaid**) to pay a person too little: *Teachers in this country are underpaid.*

underprivileged /ˌʌndə'prɪvəlɪdʒd/ *adj* having less money, rights, opportunities, etc than other people in society

underrate /ˌʌndə'reɪt/ *verb* [T] to think that sb/sth is less clever, important, good, etc than he/she/it really is

undershirt *noun* [C] (*US*) = VEST

☆ **understand** /ˌʌndə'stænd/ *verb* (*pt, pp* **understood** /-'stʊd/) **1** [I,T] to get the meaning of sb/sth: *I'm not sure that I really understand.* o *I didn't understand the instructions.* o *Please speak more slowly. I can't understand you.* o *He can understand Italian but he can't speak it.* o *Can Italians and Spaniards understand each other?* **2** [T] to know how or why sth happens: *I can't understand why the engine won't start.* **3** [T] to know why sb behaves in a particular way and to feel sympathy: *It's easy to understand why she felt so angry.* o *His parents don't understand him.* **4** [T] (*formal*) to have heard or been told sth: *I understand that you have decided to leave.* **5** [T] to judge a situation, etc: *As far as I understand it, the changes won't affect us.*

(IDIOMS) **give sb to believe/understand (that)** ⇒ GIVE¹

ɜː	ə	eɪ	əʊ	aɪ	aʊ	ɔɪ	ɪə	eə	ʊə
fur	ago	pay	home	five	now	join	near	hair	pure

make yourself understood to make your meaning clear: *I can just about make myself understood in Russian.*

understandable /-əbl/ *adj* that you can understand —**understandably** /-əblɪ/ *adv*: *She was understandably angry at the decision.*

☆ **understanding** /ˌʌndəˈstændɪŋ/ *noun* **1** [U] the ability to think or learn about sth: *The book is beyond the understanding of most ten-year-olds.* **2** [U,sing] knowledge of a subject, how sth works, etc: *A basic understanding of physics is necessary for this course.* **3** [U,sing] the ability to feel sympathy and trust for sb: *understanding between nations* **4** [U] the way in which you think sth is meant: *My understanding of the arrangement is that he will only phone if there is a problem.* **5** [C, usually sing] an informal agreement: *We came to an understanding about the money I owed him.*
(IDIOM) **on the understanding that...** only if...; because it was agreed that...: *We let them stay in our house on the understanding that it was only for a short period.*

understanding *adj* kind; showing sympathy towards sb

understate /ˌʌndəˈsteɪt/ *verb* [T] to say that sth is smaller or less important than it really is —**understatement** *noun* [C]: *'Is she pleased?' 'That's an understatement. She's delighted.'*

understudy /ˈʌndəstʌdɪ/ *noun* [C] (*pl* **understudies**) an actor who learns the role of another actor and replaces him/her if he/she is ill

undertake /ˌʌndəˈteɪk/ *verb* [T] (*pt* **undertook** /-ˈtʊk/; *pp* **undertaken** /-ˈteɪkən/) **1** to agree or promise to do sth: *The firm undertook to deliver the machines by Friday.* **2** to carry out: *The zoo is undertaking a major programme of modernization.*

undertaking /ˌʌndəˈteɪkɪŋ/ *noun* [C, usually sing] **1** a piece of work or business: *a risky undertaking* **2 undertaking (that.../to do sth)** a formal or legal promise (to do sth): (*formal*) *He gave an undertaking that he would not leave the country.*

undertaker /ˈʌndəteɪkə(r)/ (*also* **funeral director**; *US also* **mortician**) *noun* [C] a person whose job is to prepare bodies to be buried and to arrange funerals

undertone /ˈʌndətəʊn/ *noun* [C] **1** a feeling or attitude that is not directly expressed **2** a low, quiet voice

undervalue /ˌʌndəˈvæljuː/ *verb* [T] to place too low a value on sb/sth

underwater /ˌʌndəˈwɔːtə(r)/ *adj, adv* existing, happening or used below the surface of water: *underwater exploration* ○ *an underwater camera* ○ *Can you swim underwater?*

☆ **underwear** /ˈʌndəweə(r)/ *noun* [U] clothing that is worn next to the skin under other clothes ☞ **Underclothes** has the same meaning and is a plural noun.

underweight /ˌʌndəˈweɪt/ *adj* weighing less than is normal or correct ☞ Look at the note at **thin**.

underworld /ˈʌndəwɜːld/ *noun* [sing] **the underworld** people who are involved in crime

undesirable /ˌʌndɪˈzaɪərəbl/ *adj* unwanted or unpleasant; likely to cause problems

undid *pt* of UNDO

undignified /ʌnˈdɪɡnɪfaɪd/ *adj* clumsy, embarrassing or unsuitable: *Everyone rushed for the food in a most undignified way!*

undivided /ˌʌndɪˈvaɪdɪd/ *adj*
(IDIOMS) **give sb your undivided attention (to sb/sth)** to concentrate fully on sth
get/have sb's undivided attention to receive sb's full attention

☆ **undo** /ʌnˈduː/ *verb* [T] (*3rd pers sing pres* **undoes**; *pt* **undid**; *pp* **undone**) **1** to open sth that was tied or fastened: *He undid his shoelaces and took off his shoes.* ○ *to undo a knot* **2** to destroy the effect of sth that has already happened: *The damage cannot be undone.*

undone *adj* **1** open; not fastened or tied: *My zip was undone.* **2** not done: *I left the housework undone.*

undoubted /ʌnˈdaʊtɪd/ *adj* definite; accepted as being true —**undoubtedly** *adv*

☆ **undress** /ʌnˈdres/ *verb* **1** [I] to take off your clothes: *I undressed and the doctor examined me.* ☞ **Get undressed** is more commonly used than **undress**: *He got undressed and had a shower.* **2** [T] to take off sb's clothes: *She undressed the child and put her into bed.*

undressed *adj* wearing no or few clothes

undue /ʌnˈdjuː; *US* -ˈduː/ *adj* more than is necessary or reasonable —**unduly** *adv*: *She didn't seem unduly worried by their unexpected arrival.*

unearth /ʌnˈɜːθ/ *verb* [T] to dig sth up out of the ground; to discover sth that was hidden: *Archaeologists have unearthed a Roman villa.* ○ (*figurative*) *A journalist unearthed the true facts of the case.*

unearthly /ʌnˈɜːθlɪ/ *adj* **1** strange or frightening **2** (used about a time) very early or very late: *I can't get up at such an unearthly hour as 5 am!*

uneasy /ʌnˈiːzɪ/ *adj* **1** worried; not feeling relaxed or comfortable **2** not settled; unlikely to last: *an uneasy compromise*

unease /ʌnˈiːz/ (*also* **uneasiness**) *noun* [U] an anxious or uncomfortable feeling —**uneasily** /ʌnˈiːzɪlɪ/ *adv*

uneconomic /ˌʌnˌiːkəˈnɒmɪk; *US* ˌʌnˌek-/ *adj* (used about a company, etc) not making or likely to make a profit

uneconomical /ˌʌnˌiːkəˈnɒmɪkl; *US* ˌʌnˌek-/ *adj* wasting money, time, materials, etc —**uneconomically** /-klɪ/ *adv*

☆ **unemployed** /ˌʌnɪmˈplɔɪd/ *adj* not having a job; out of work: *She lost her job six months ago and has been unemployed ever since.*

the unemployed *noun* [plural] the people who do not have a job: *What does the government do to help the unemployed?*

☆ **unemployment** /ˌʌnɪmˈplɔɪmənt/ *noun* [U] **1** the situation of being unemployed: *If the factory closes, many people face unemployment.* **2** the number of people who are unemployed: *The economy is doing very badly and unemployment is rising.* ○ *unemployment benefit* (= money given by the state) ☞ Look at **dole**.

p	b	t	d	k	g	tʃ	dʒ	f	v	θ	ð
pen	bad	tea	did	cat	got	chin	June	fall	van	thin	then

unending /ʌnˈendɪŋ/ adj having or seeming to have no end

unequal /ˌʌnˈiːkwəl/ adj **1** different in size, amount, level, etc **2** not fair or balanced: *It was an unequal contest because he's a far better player than me.* —**unequally** /-kwəlɪ/ adv

uneven /ˌʌnˈiːvn/ adj **1** not completely smooth, level or regular: *The sign was painted in rather uneven letters.* **2** not always of the same level or quality —**unevenly** adv: *The country's wealth is unevenly distributed.*

☆ **unexpected** /ˌʌnɪkˈspektɪd/ adj not expected and therefore causing surprise: *His death was quite unexpected.* —**unexpectedly** adv: *I got there late because I was unexpectedly delayed.*

☆ **unfair** /ˌʌnˈfeə(r)/ adj **1 unfair (on/to sb)** not dealing with people as they deserve; not treating each person equally: *It was unfair to blame her for something that was not her fault.* ○ *This law is unfair to women.* **2** not following the rules and therefore giving an advantage to one person, team, etc: *unfair play* —**unfairly** adv —**unfairness** noun [U]

unfaithful /ˌʌnˈfeɪθfl/ adj **unfaithful (to sb/sth)** having a sexual relationship with sb who is not your husband, wife or partner: *She discovered that her husband was being unfaithful to her.* ○ *Have you ever been unfaithful to your husband?*

unfamiliar /ˌʌnfəˈmɪlɪə(r)/ adj **1 unfamiliar (to sb)** not well-known to you: *an unfamiliar part of town* **2 unfamiliar (with sth)** not having knowledge or experience of sth

unfashionable /ˌʌnˈfæʃnəbl/ adj not popular: *unfashionable ideas* ➡ Look at **old-fashioned**.

unfit /ˌʌnˈfɪt/ adj **1 unfit (for sth/to do sth)** unsuitable or not good enough for sth: *If goods are unfit for use, you should take them back to the shop.* **2** not in good physical health (especially because you do not get enough exercise): *The doctor said I was overweight and unfit.*

unfold /ʌnˈfəʊld/ verb [I,T] **1** to open out and become flat; to open out sth that was folded: *The sofa unfolds into a spare bed.* ○ *I unfolded the letter and read it.* **2** to become known, or to allow sth to become known a little at a time: *As the story unfolded, more and more surprising things were revealed.*

unforeseen /ˌʌnfɔːˈsiːn/ adj not expected: *an unforeseen problem*

unforgettable /ˌʌnfəˈgetəbl/ adj making such a strong impression that you cannot forget it

☆ **unfortunate** /ʌnˈfɔːtʃənət/ adj **1** unlucky: *The unfortunate people who lived near the river lost their homes in the flood.* **2** that you regret: *I would like to apologize for this unfortunate mistake.*

unfortunately adv unluckily; it is a pity that...: *I'd like to help you but unfortunately there's nothing I can do.*

unfounded /ʌnˈfaʊndɪd/ adj not based on or supported by facts: *He said that the rumour was completely unfounded.*

unfriendly /ˌʌnˈfrendlɪ/ adj unpleasant or impolite to sb; not friendly

ungainly /ʌnˈgeɪnlɪ/ adj moving in a way that lacks grace

ungrateful /ʌnˈgreɪtfl/ adj not feeling or showing thanks (to sb) —**ungratefully** /-fəlɪ/ adv

unguarded /ˌʌnˈgɑːdɪd/ adj **1** not protected or guarded **2** careless; saying more than you wanted to: *He admitted the truth in an unguarded moment.*

☆ **unhappy** /ʌnˈhæpɪ/ adj (**unhappier**; **unhappiest**) **1 unhappy (about sth)** sad or miserable; not happy: *She's terribly unhappy about losing her job.* ○ *a very unhappy childhood* **2 unhappy (about/at sth)** not satisfied or pleased; worried: *I'm unhappy about the work you did for me. Can you do it again?*

unhappily /-ɪlɪ/ adv **1** sadly **2** unfortunately: *Unhappily, we are unable to help.* —**unhappiness** noun [U]

unhealthy /ʌnˈhelθɪ/ adj (**unhealthier**; **unhealthiest**) **1** not having or showing good health: *He looks pale and unhealthy.* **2** likely to cause illness or poor health: *unhealthy conditions* **3** not natural: *an unhealthy interest in torture*

unheard /ˌʌnˈhɜːd/ adj not listened to or given attention: *My suggestions went unheard.*

unheard-of /ʌnˈhɜːd ɒv/ adj not known; never having happened before: *Years ago it was unheard-of for women to do jobs like that.*

unicorn /ˈjuːnɪkɔːn/ noun [C] an imaginary animal that looks like a white horse and has one horn growing out of its forehead

unidentified /ˌʌnaɪˈdentɪfaɪd/ adj whose identity is not known: *An unidentified body has been found in the river.*

uniform[1] /ˈjuːnɪfɔːm/ adj not varying; the same in all cases or at all times —**uniformity** /ˌjuːnɪˈfɔːmətɪ/ noun [U]: *Tests are standardized to ensure uniformity.*

☆ **uniform**[2] /ˈjuːnɪfɔːm/ noun [C,U] the set of clothes worn at work by the members of certain organizations or groups and by some schoolchildren: *Did you have to wear a uniform when you were at school?* ○ *I didn't know he was a policeman because he wasn't in uniform.* —**uniformed** adj: *uniformed policemen*

unify /ˈjuːnɪfaɪ/ verb [T] (*pres part* **unifying**; *3rd pers sing pres* **unifies**; *pt, pp* **unified**) to join or link separate parts together to make one unit, or to make them similar to each other —**unification** /ˌjuːnɪfɪˈkeɪʃn/ noun [U]: *the unification of Germany*

unilateral /ˌjuːnɪˈlætrəl/ adj done or made by one of the sides involved without the agreement of the other side or sides: *a unilateral declaration of independence* —**unilaterally** /-rəlɪ/ adv: *The decision was taken unilaterally.*

uninhabitable /ˌʌnɪnˈhæbɪtəbl/ adj not possible to live in

uninhibited /ˌʌnɪnˈhɪbɪtɪd/ adj behaving in a free and natural way, showing what you feel without worrying what other people think of you

unintelligible /ˌʌnɪnˈtelɪdʒəbl/ adj impossible to understand

uninterested /ʌnˈɪntrəstɪd/ adj **uninter-**

s	z	ʃ	ʒ	h	m	n	ŋ	l	r	j	w
so	zoo	she	vision	how	man	no	sing	leg	red	yes	wet

ested (in sb/sth) having or showing no interest in sb/sth: *She seemed uninterested in anything I had to say.*

☆ **union** /'juːnɪən/ *noun* **1** [U,sing] the act of joining or the situation of being joined: *the union of the separate groups into one organization* **2** [C] a group of states or countries that have been joined together to form one country: *the Soviet Union* **3** [C] = TRADE UNION **4** [C] an organization for a particular group of people: *the Athletics Union*

the ˌUnion 'Jack *noun* [C] the national flag of the United Kingdom, with red and white crosses on a dark blue background

☆ **unique** /juː'niːk/ *adj* **1** unlike anything else; being the only one of its type: *Shakespeare made a unique contribution to the world of literature.* **2 unique to sb/sth** connected with only one place, person or thing: *This dance is unique to this region.* **3** (*informal*) very unusual: *There's nothing unique about that sort of crime.*

unisex /'juːnɪseks/ *adj* designed for and used by both sexes: *unisex fashions*

unison /'juːnɪsn; -ˈjuːnɪzn/ *noun*
(IDIOM) **in unison** saying, singing or doing the same thing at the same time as sb else: *'No, thank you,' they said in unison.* ○ *The chorus should be sung in unison.*

☆ **unit** /'juːnɪt/ *noun* [C] **1** a single thing which is complete in itself, although it can be part of sth larger: *The book is divided into ten units.* **2** a fixed amount or number used as a standard of measurement: *a unit of currency* **3** a group of people who perform a certain special function in a large organization: *the intensive care unit of a hospital* **4** a small machine that performs a particular task or that is part of a larger machine: *The heart of a computer is the central processing unit.* **5** a piece of furniture that fits with other pieces of furniture and has a particular use: *matching kitchen units*

☆ **unite** /juː'naɪt/ *verb* **1** [I,T] to join together and act in agreement; to make this happen: *Unless we unite, our enemies will defeat us.* ○ *The leader united the party behind him.* **2** [I] **unite (in sth/in doing sth)** to join together for a particular purpose: *We should all unite in seeking a solution to this terrible problem.*

united *adj* joined together by a common feeling or aim: *Throughout the crisis, the whole country remained united.*

the Uˌnited 'Kingdom *noun* (*abbr* **UK**) England, Scotland, Wales and Northern Ireland

☛ The **UK** includes England, Scotland, Wales and Northern Ireland, but *not* the Republic of Ireland (Eire), which is a separate country. **Great Britain** is England, Scotland and Wales only. **The British Isles** include England, Scotland, Wales, Northern Ireland and the Republic of Ireland.

the Uˌnited 'Nations *noun* [with sing or pl verb] (*abbr* **UN**) the organization formed to encourage peace in the world and to deal with problems between nations

the Uˌnited 'States (of A'merica) *noun* [with sing or pl verb] (*abbr* **US**; **USA**) a large country in North America made up of 50 states and the District of Columbia

☆ **unity** /'juːnəti/ *noun* [U] the situation in which people are united or in agreement

☆ **universal** /ˌjuːnɪ'vɜːsl/ *adj* connected with, done by or affecting everybody in the world or everybody in a particular group: *The environment is a universal issue.* ○ *There was universal agreement that it was a splendid wedding.*
—**universally** /-səli/ *adv*

☆ **universe** /'juːnɪvɜːs/ *noun* [sing] **the universe** everything that exists, including the planets, stars, space, etc

☆ **university** /ˌjuːnɪ'vɜːsəti/ *noun* [C] (*pl* **universities**) the highest level of educational institution, in which students study for degrees and in which academic research is done: *Which university did you go to?* ○ *a university lecturer* ○ *He studied at Hull University; the University of Hull.* ☛ We use the expressions **at university** and **go to university** without *a* or *the* when we mean that somebody attends the university as a student: *He's hoping to go to university next year* but not if somebody goes there for any other reason: *I'm going to a conference at the university in July.* Look at **polytechnic** and **redbrick**.

☆ **unkind** /ˌʌn'kaɪnd/ *adj* not friendly or thoughtful; cruel: *That was an unkind thing to say.*
—**unkindly** *adv* —**unkindness** *noun* [C,U]

☆ **unknown** /ˌʌn'nəʊn/ *adj* **1 unknown (to sb)** not known (by sb): *She left the job for unknown reasons.* ○ *Unknown to the boss, she went home early.* **2** not famous or familiar to other people: *an unknown actress*

(IDIOM) **an unknown quantity** a person or thing that you know very little about

unknown *noun* **1** usually **the unknown** [sing] a place or thing that you know nothing about: *a fear of the unknown* **2** [C] a person who is not well known: *A complete unknown won the tournament.*

unleaded /ˌʌn'ledɪd/ *adj* not containing lead: *unleaded petrol*

☆ **unless** /ən'les/ *conj* if... not; except if: *Unless something unexpected happens, I'll see you next week.* ○ *I was told that unless my work improved, I would lose the job.* ○ *'Would you like a cup of coffee?' 'Not unless you've already made some.'* ○ *Unless anyone has anything else to say, the meeting is closed.* ○ *Don't switch that on unless I'm here.* ○ *That's what I've decided to do – unless there are any objections?*

☆ **unlike** /ˌʌn'laɪk/ *adj* not like; different from: *She's unlike anyone else I've ever met.* ○ *My new job is completely unlike my previous one.* ○ *The film is not unlike several others I've seen.*

unlike *prep* **1** in contrast to; differing from: *Unlike all the others, I wasn't very keen on the idea.* ○ *He's extremely ambitious, unlike me.* ○ *This is an exciting place to live, unlike my home town.* **2** not typical of; unusual for: *It's unlike him to be so rude, he's usually very polite.*

☆ **unlikely** /ʌn'laɪkli/ *adj* (**unlikelier**; **unlikeliest**) **1** not likely to happen; not expected; not probable: *He is seriously ill and unlikely to recover.* ○ *I suppose she might win but I think it's*

iː	ɪ	e	æ	ɑː	ɒ	ɔː	ʊ	uː	ʌ
see	sit	ten	hat	arm	got	saw	put	too	cup

very unlikely. o *It's unlikely that I'll have any free time next week.* **2** difficult to believe: *an unlikely excuse*

unlimited /ˌʌn'lɪmɪtɪd/ *adj* without limit; as much or as great as you want

☆ **unload** /ˌʌn'ləʊd/ *verb* **1** [I,T] **unload (sth) (from sth)** to take things that have been transported off or out of a vehicle: *to unload goods* o *I unloaded the car when I got home from the shops.* **2** [I,T] (used about a vehicle) to have the things removed that have been transported: *Parking here is restricted to vehicles that are loading or unloading.* **3** [T] **unload sb/sth (on/onto sb)** (*informal*) to get rid of sth you do not want or to pass it to sb else

☆ **unlock** /ˌʌn'lɒk/ *verb* [T] to open the lock on sth using a key

☆ **unlucky** /ˌʌn'lʌki/ *adj* (**unluckier; unluckiest**) having or causing bad luck; not lucky: *They were unlucky to lose because they played so well.* o *Thirteen is often thought to be an unlucky number.*
unluckily *adv* as a result of bad luck; unfortunately: *Unluckily, I arrived just too late to meet them.*

unmarried /ˌʌn'mærɪd/ *adj* not married; single: *unmarried mothers*

unmistakable /ˌʌnmɪ'steɪkəbl/ *adj* that cannot be mistaken for anything else —**unmistakably** *adv*

unmoved /ˌʌn'muːvd/ *adj* not affected emotionally; feeling no sympathy, pity, sadness etc

unnatural /ˌʌn'nætʃrəl/ *adj* different from what is normal or expected; not natural: *This hot dry weather is unnatural for April.* —**unnaturally** /-rəli/ *adv*: *unnaturally quiet* o *Not unnaturally, she was delighted by the news.*

☆ **unnecessary** /ˌʌn'nesəsri; *US* -seri/ *adj* not necessary; more than is needed or acceptable: *It was unnecessary to ask because I already knew the answer.* o *unnecessary expense* —**unnecessarily** /ˌʌn'nesəsərəli; *US* ˌʌnˌnesə'serəli/ *adv*: *unnecessarily rude*

unnoticed /ˌʌn'nəʊtɪst/ *adj* not noticed or seen: *All your hard work has not gone unnoticed.*

unobtrusive /ˌʌnəb'truːsɪv/ *adj* avoiding being noticed; not attracting attention

unofficial /ˌʌnə'fɪʃl/ *adj* not accepted or approved by a person or people in authority; not known publicly: *an unofficial strike* o *The news of the royal divorce is still unofficial.* —**unofficially** /-ʃəli/ *adv*

unorthodox /ˌʌn'ɔːθədɒks/ *adj* different from what is generally accepted, usual or traditional: *Some of his methods are rather unorthodox.*

unpack /ˌʌn'pæk/ *verb* [I,T] to take out the things that were in a bag, suitcase, etc: *When we arrived at the hotel we unpacked and went to the beach.* o *to unpack a suitcase*

unpaid /ˌʌn'peɪd/ *adj* **1** not yet paid: *an unpaid bill* **2** not receiving money for work done: *an unpaid assistant* **3** (used about work) done without payment: *unpaid overtime*

☆ **unpleasant** /ˌʌn'pleznt/ *adj* **1** causing you to have a bad feeling; not pleasant: *This news has come as an unpleasant surprise.* **2** unfriendly; impolite: *There's no need to get unpleasant, we can discuss this in a friendly way.* —**unpleasantly** *adv*

unplug /ˌʌn'plʌg/ *verb* [T] (**unplugging; unplugged**) to disconnect a piece of electrical equipment by removing the plug from the socket: *Could you unplug the cassette recorder and bring it here, please?*

☆ **unpopular** /ˌʌn'pɒpjʊlə(r)/ *adj* **unpopular (with sb)** not popular; not liked by many people —**unpopularity** /ˌʌnˌpɒpjʊ'lærəti/ *noun* [U]: *What is the reason for her unpopularity?*

unprecedented /ˌʌn'presɪdentɪd/ *adj* never having happened or existed before

unprovoked /ˌʌnprə'vəʊkt/ *adj* not caused by an earlier action: *an unprovoked attack*

unqualified /ˌʌn'kwɒlɪfaɪd/ *adj* **1** not having the qualifications or knowledge for sth: *Being unqualified, she found her job opportunities were limited.* o *I'm unqualified to offer an opinion on this matter.* **2** complete; absolute: *an unqualified success*

unquestionable /ˌʌn'kwestʃənəbl/ *adj* certain; that cannot be doubted —**unquestionably** /-əbli/ *adv*: *She is unquestionably the most famous opera singer in the world.*

unravel /ˌʌn'rævl/ *verb* (**unravelling; unravelled;** *US* **unraveling; unraveled**) [I,T] **1** (used about threads which are knitted or woven) to come undone: *The knitting I was doing started to unravel.* **2** (used about a complicated story, etc) to become or to make sth become clear: *Eventually the mystery unravelled and the truth came out.*

unreal /ˌʌn'rɪəl/ *adj* very strange and seeming to be imagined

unreasonable /ˌʌn'riːznəbl/ *adj* **1** not willing to listen to other people; acting without good reasons: *I think she is being totally unreasonable.* **2** too great, expecting too much: *He makes unreasonable demands on his staff.* —**unreasonably** /-əbli/ *adv*

unrelenting /ˌʌnrɪ'lentɪŋ/ *adj* continuously strong, not becoming weaker or stopping: *unrelenting hard work*

unreserved /ˌʌnrɪ'zɜːvd/ *adj* without limit; complete: *The government's action received the unreserved support of all parties.* —**unreservedly** /ˌʌnrɪ'zɜːvɪdli/ *adv*: *We apologize unreservedly for our mistake and will refund your money.*

unrest /ˌʌn'rest/ *noun* [U] a situation in which people are angry or dissatisfied and likely to protest or fight: *social unrest*

unrivalled (*US* **unrivaled**) /ˌʌn'raɪvld/ *adj* better than any other of the same type; having no rival: *He had an unrivalled knowledge of Greek theology.*

unroll /ˌʌn'rəʊl/ *verb* [I,T] to open from a rolled position: *He unrolled the poster and stuck it on the wall.*

unruly /ˌʌn'ruːli/ *adj* difficult to control; without discipline: *an unruly crowd* —**unruliness** *noun* [U]

unsavoury (*US* **unsavory**) /ˌʌn'seɪvəri/ *adj*

ɜː	ə	eɪ	əʊ	aɪ	aʊ	ɔɪ	ɪə	eə	ʊə
fur	ago	pay	home	five	now	join	near	hair	pure

unpleasant; that you do not trust: *a rather unsavoury individual*

unscathed /ˌʌnˈskeɪðd/ *adj* not hurt, without injury: *He came out of the fight unscathed.*

unscrew /ˌʌnˈskruː/ *verb* [T] **1** to remove the screws from sth **2** to open or undo sth by turning it: *Could you unscrew the top of this bottle for me?*

unscrupulous /ʌnˈskruːpjʊləs/ *adj* willing to be dishonest, cruel or unfair in order to get what you want

unsightly /ʌnˈsaɪtli/ *adj* very unpleasant to look at; ugly: *an unsightly new building*

unskilled /ˌʌnˈskɪld/ *adj* not having or requiring special skill or training: *an unskilled job*

unsolicited /ˌʌnsəˈlɪsɪtɪd/ *adj* not asked for: *unsolicited praise*

unsound /ˌʌnˈsaʊnd/ **1** in poor condition; weak: *The building is structurally unsound.* **2** based on wrong ideas and therefore mistaken

unstable /ˌʌnˈsteɪbl/ *adj* **1** likely to fall down or move; not firmly fixed **2** likely to change or fail: *a period of unstable government* **3** (used about a person's moods or behaviour) likely to change suddenly or frequently: *She has such an unstable personality that you never know what she's going to do next.*

unstuck /ˌʌnˈstʌk/ *adj* no longer stuck together or glued down: *The label on the parcel came unstuck.*
(IDIOM) **come unstuck** to fail badly; to be unsuccessful

unsure /ʌnˈʃʊə(r); *US* -ˈʃʊər/ *adj* **1 unsure of yourself** not feeling confident about yourself: *He's young and still quite unsure of himself.* **2 unsure (about/of sth)** not certain; having doubts: *I didn't argue because I was unsure of the facts.*

unsuspecting /ˌʌnsəˈspektɪŋ/ *adj* not aware of danger: *He came up quietly behind his unsuspecting victim.*

untangle /ʌnˈtæŋgl/ *verb* [T] to separate threads which have become tied together in a confused way: *The wires got mixed up and it took me ages to untangle them.*

unthinkable /ʌnˈθɪŋkəbl/ *adj* (used of an event, etc) impossible to imagine or consider, especially because it is too painful or difficult

unthinking /ˌʌnˈθɪŋkɪŋ/ *adj* done, said, etc without thinking carefully —**unthinkingly** *adv*

☆ **untidy** /ʌnˈtaɪdi/ *adj* (**untidier**; **untidiest**) **1** not neat or well arranged: *an untidy bedroom* ○ *untidy hair* **2** (used about a person) not keeping things neat or in good order: *My flatmate is so untidy!* —**untidily** /-ɪli/ *adv* —**untidiness** *noun* [U]

untie /ʌnˈtaɪ/ *verb* [T] (*pres part* **untying**; *3rd pers sing pres* **unties**; *pt, pp* **untied**) to undo a knot; to free sb by undoing a rope, etc: *I can't get this knot untied.*

☆ **until** /ənˈtɪl/ (*also* **till** /tɪl/) *conj* up to the time when: *She waited until he had finished.* ○ *Most men work until they're 65.* ○ *We won't leave until the police get here* (= we won't leave before they come).

until (*also* **till**) *prep* up to the time or the event mentioned: *The restaurant is open until midnight.* ○ *Until that moment she had been happy.* ○ *We can't leave until 10 o'clock* (= we can leave at 10 but not before). ☛ We can use **until** in both formal and informal English. **Till** is more common in informal English and is not usually used at the beginning of a sentence. Make sure that you only use **till/until** to talk about a time. We use **as far as** to talk about distance: *I walked as far as the shops.* We use **up to** to talk about a number: *You can take up to 20 kilos of luggage.*

untold /ˌʌnˈtəʊld/ *adj* very great; so big, etc that you cannot count it: *untold suffering* ○ *untold wealth*

untoward /ˌʌntəˈwɔːd; *US* ʌnˈtɔːrd/ *adj* (*formal*) (used about an event, etc) unexpected and unpleasant

untruth /ʌnˈtruːθ/ *noun* [C] (*pl* **untruths** /-ˈtruːðz/) (*formal*) something that is not true; a lie: *to tell an untruth* —**untruthful** /ʌnˈtruːθfl/ *adj*: *I don't like being untruthful.*

unused[1] /ˌʌnˈjuːzd/ *adj* that has not been used: *an unused stamp*

unused[2] /ʌnˈjuːst/ *adj* (not before a noun) not having any experience of sth; not accustomed to sth: *She was unused to such a lot of attention.*

☆ **unusual** /ʌnˈjuːʒl/ *adj* **1** not expected or usual: *It's unusual for Joe to be late.* **2** interesting because it is different: *What an unusual hat!*

unusually /-ʒəli/ *adv* **1** more than is common; extremely: *an unusually hot summer* **2** in a way that is not normal or typical of sb/sth: *Unusually for her, she forgot his birthday.*

unveil /ˌʌnˈveɪl/ *verb* [T] to remove a type of cloth or curtain in order to show a new painting, etc to the public: *Princess Diana unveiled a plaque and opened the new leisure centre.*

unwanted /ˌʌnˈwɒntɪd/ *adj* not wanted: *an unwanted pregnancy* ○ *a cream to remove unwanted hair*

unwarranted /ʌnˈwɒrəntɪd; *US* -ˈwɔːr-/ *adj* that is not deserved or for which there is no good reason

unwell /ʌnˈwel/ *adj* (not before a noun) ill; sick: *She's feeling rather unwell.* ☛ Look at the note at **sick**.

unwieldy /ʌnˈwiːldi/ *adj* difficult to move or carry because it is too big, heavy, etc: *an unwieldy parcel*

unwind /ˌʌnˈwaɪnd/ *verb* (*pt, pp* **unwound** /-ˈwaʊnd/) **1** [I,T] (used of sth that is wound round sth else) to become undone or to be pulled out: *The bandage had unwound.* **2** [I] (*informal*) to relax, especially after working hard: *After a hard day at the office, it takes me a couple of hours to unwind.*

unwitting /ʌnˈwɪtɪŋ/ *adj* not realizing sth; not intending to do sth: *an unwitting accomplice to the crime* —**unwittingly** *adv*: *The bank may have unwittingly broken the law.*

☆ **up** /ʌp/ *prep, adv* ☛ For special uses with many verbs eg **pick sth up**, look at the verb entries. **1** to a high or higher level or position: *The monkey climbed up the tree.* ○ *I carried her suitcase up to the third floor.* ○ *Put your hand up if you know the answer.* ○ *I walked up the hill.* **2** into an upright position: *Stand up, please.* ○

upbringing

Is he up yet? (= out of bed) o *I had to get up early.* **3** (used for showing that an action continues until it is completed): *Eat up, everybody, I want you to finish everything on the table.* **4** (used with verbs of closing): *Do up your coat. It's cold.* o *She tied the parcel up with string.* **5** very close to a person or thing: *She ran up to her mother and kissed her.* **6** (used about a period of time) finished: *Stop writing. Your time's up.* **7** further along: *I live just up the road.* **8** in a particular direction, usually north: *We're going up to York tomorrow.* **9** into pieces: *We chopped the old table up and used it for firewood.* **10** (used for showing that sth is increasing): *Prices have gone up.* o *Turn the volume up.* **11** (used about computers) working; in operation: *Are the computers back up yet?*
(IDIOMS) **up and running** (used about sth new) working well: *The new system is already up and running.*
be up to sb to be sb's responsibility: *I can't take the decision. It's not up to me.*
not up to much (*informal*) not very good: *The programme wasn't up to much.*
up and down backwards and forwards, or so as to rise and fall: *He was running up and down the road screaming with pain.*
up to sth 1 as much/many as: *We're expecting up to 100 people at the meeting.* **2** as far as now: *Up to now, things have been easy.* **3** capable of sth: *I don't feel up to cooking this evening. I'm too tired.* **4** doing sth secret and perhaps forbidden: *What are the children up to? Go and see.*
what's up? (*informal*) what's the matter?
ups *noun*
(IDIOM) **ups and downs** both good and bad luck: *Our marriage is happy but we've had our ups and downs.*

upbringing /'ʌpbrɪŋɪŋ/ *noun* [sing] the way a child is treated and taught how to behave by his/her parents: *a religious upbringing*

update /ˌʌp'deɪt/ *verb* [T] **1** to make sth more modern **2** to put the latest information into sth; to give sb the latest information: *Our database of addresses is updated regularly.* o *Shall I update you on what happened at the meeting?*
—**update** /'ʌpdeɪt/ *noun* [C]: *an update on a news story* (= the latest information)

upgrade /ˌʌp'greɪd/ *verb* [T] to change sth so that it is of a higher standard

upheaval /ʌp'hiːvl/ *noun* [C,U] a sudden big change, especially one that causes a lot of trouble

uphill /ˌʌp'hɪl/ *adj, adv* **1** going up a slope, towards the top of a hill: *a long walk uphill* ☞ The opposite is **downhill**. **2** needing a lot of effort: *It was an uphill struggle to find a job.*

uphold /ˌʌp'həʊld/ *verb* [T] (*pt, pp* **upheld** /-'held/) to support sth (a decision, etc) especially when other people are against it: *We must uphold the court's decision.*

upholstered /ʌp'həʊlstəd/ *adj* (used about a chair, etc) fitted with a layer of soft material and covered with cloth

upholstery /ʌp'həʊlstəri/ *noun* [U] the thick soft materials used to cover chairs, car seats, etc

upkeep /'ʌpkiːp/ *noun* [U] the cost or process of keeping sth in a good condition: *The landlord pays for the upkeep of the building.*

upland /'ʌplənd/ *adj* situated on a hill or mountain: *an upland area*

upland *noun* [C, usually pl] high areas of land

uplifting /ˌʌp'lɪftɪŋ/ *adj* producing a feeling of hope and happiness: *an uplifting speech*

upon /ə'pɒn/ *prep* (*formal*) = ON

☆ **upper** /'ʌpə(r)/ *adj* in a higher position than sth else; situated above sth: *the upper floors of a building* o *the upper lip*
(IDIOM) **get, etc the upper hand** to get into a stronger position than another person; to gain control over sb

ˌ**upper 'case** *noun* [U] letters that are written or printed in a large form; capital letters: *'BBC' is written in upper case.* ☞ The opposite is **lower case**.

ˌ**upper 'class** *adj, noun* [C, with sing or pl verb] (of) the social class that is above the middle class; people with a lot of money and land and sometimes special titles

uppermost /'ʌpəməʊst/ *adj* in the highest or most important position: *Concern for her family was uppermost in her mind.*

☆ **upright** /'ʌpraɪt/ *adj* **1** with a straight back; standing vertically: *Please put the back of your seat in an upright position.* o *an upright piano* **2** honest and responsible: *an upright citizen*
(IDIOM) **bolt upright** ⇨ BOLT

upright *adv* with a straight back; into a vertical position: *to stand upright*

uprising /'ʌpraɪzɪŋ/ *noun* [C] a situation in which a group of people start to fight against the people in power in their country: *an armed uprising*

uproar /'ʌprɔː(r)/ *noun* [sing,U] a loud noise of excitement, confusion, anger, etc; an angry discussion about sth: *The meeting ended in uproar.*

uproarious /ʌp'rɔːriəs/ *adj* very noisy: *uproarious laughter*

uproot /ˌʌp'ruːt/ *verb* [T] to tear up a plant by the roots: *Strong winds had uprooted the tree.* o (*figurative*) *Many people have to uproot themselves when they change jobs* (= leave the place where they have lived for a long time).

☆ **upset** /ˌʌp'set/ *verb* [T] (*pres part* **upsetting**; *pt, pp* **upset**) **1** to make sb worry or feel unhappy: *The pictures of starving children upset her.* o *I was quite upset at losing my purse.* **2** to make sth go wrong: *to upset someone's plans* **3** to knock sth over: *I upset a bottle of wine all over the tablecloth.* **4** to make sb ill in the stomach: *Rich food usually upsets me.*

upset /'ʌpset/ *noun* **1** [C,U] the act of upsetting(1,2) or being upset: *I've had quite a few upsets recently.* **2** [C] a slight illness in your stomach: *a stomach upset*

upset /ˌʌp'set/ *adj* **1** worried and unhappy: *She was looking very upset about something.* **2** slightly ill: *I've got an upset stomach.*

☞ Note that the adjective is pronounced /'ʌpset/ when it comes before a noun and /ˌʌp'set/ in other positions in the sentence.

upshot /'ʌpʃɒt/ *noun* [sing] **the upshot (of**

upside down /ˌʌpsaɪd ˈdaʊn/ *adv* **1** with the top part turned to the bottom: *You're holding the picture upside down.* o *She was hanging upside down.* **2** (*informal*) in or into a very untidy state: *He turned the house upside down looking for his keys.*

upstairs /ˌʌpˈsteəz/ *adv* to or on the upper floor of a building: *to go upstairs* o *She's sleeping upstairs.* —**upstairs** *adj*: *an upstairs window*

upstairs *noun* [sing] (*informal*) **the upstairs** the upper floor of a house: *We're going to paint the upstairs.*

upstream /ˌʌpˈstriːm/ *adv* moving against the direction that a river flows: *He swam slowly upstream.*

upstream *adj* (not before a noun) situated nearer to the place that a river flows from

upsurge /ˈʌpsɜːdʒ/ *noun* (U, usually sing) a sudden increase of sth: *an upsurge in violent crime*

uptake /ˈʌpteɪk/ *noun*
(IDIOM) **quick/slow on the uptake** quick/slow to understand the meaning of sth: *I gave him a hint but he's slow on the uptake.*

uptight /ˌʌpˈtaɪt/ *adj* (*informal*) **1** nervous: *He gets uptight before an exam.* **2** angry: *Don't get so uptight – it's only a game.*

up-to-date /ˌʌptəˈdeɪt/ *adj* **1** modern: *up-to-date fashions* **2** having the most recent information: *an up-to-date dictionary*

up-to-the-minute /ˌʌptəðəˈmɪnɪt/ *adj* having the most recent information possible: *an up-to-the-minute news report*

upturn /ˈʌptɜːn/ *noun* [C] an improvement or gain in sth: *an upturn in support for the government*

upturned /ˌʌpˈtɜːnd/ *adj* **1** pointing upwards: *an upturned nose* **2** turned upside down: *an upturned boat*

upward /ˈʌpwəd/ *adj* moving or directed towards a higher place: *an upward glance* o *an upward trend in exports* (= an increase)

upward (*also* **upwards** /-wədz/) *adv* moving towards, or in the direction of, a higher place: *I looked upwards.*

upwards of *prep* more than (the number mentioned): *They've invited upwards of a hundred guests.*

uranium /jʊˈreɪniəm/ *noun* [U] (*symbol* **U**) a radioactive metal that can be used to produce nuclear energy

Uranus /ˈjʊərənəs; jʊˈreɪnəs/ *noun* [sing] the planet that is seventh in order from the sun

urban /ˈɜːbən/ *adj* of a town or city: *urban development*

urge /ɜːdʒ/ *verb* [T] **1** to try hard to persuade sb to do sth: *I urged him to fight the decision.* **2** to advise strongly, especially that sth is necessary: *Drivers are urged to take care on icy roads.* **3** to force or drive sb/sth in a certain direction: *He urged his horse over the fence.*
(PHRASAL VERB) **urge sb on** to encourage sb: *The captain urged his team on.*

urge *noun* [C] a strong need or desire: *sexual urges*

urgent /ˈɜːdʒənt/ *adj* needing immediate attention: *an urgent message* o *It's not urgent; I'll tell you about it later.* —**urgency** /-dʒənsi/ *noun* [U]: *a matter of the greatest urgency* —**urgently** *adv*: *I must see you urgently.*

urine /ˈjʊərɪn/ *noun* [U] the yellow liquid that is passed from your body when you go to the toilet

urinate /ˈjʊərɪneɪt/ *verb* [I] (*formal*) to pass urine from the body

urn /ɜːn/ *noun* [C] **1** a type of vase, especially one in which the ashes of a dead person are kept **2** a large metal container used for making a large quantity of tea or coffee and for keeping it hot

us /əs; *strong form* ʌs/ *pron* (used as the object of a verb, or after *be*) me and another person or other people; me and you: *Come with us.* o *Leave us alone.* o *Will you write to us?* o *Hello, it's us again!*

usage /ˈjuːsɪdʒ; ˈjuːzɪdʒ/ *noun* **1** [U] the way that sth is used; the amount that sth is used: *With normal usage, the machine should last for years.* **2** [C,U] the way that words are normally used in a language: *a guide to English grammar and usage*

use¹ /juːz/ *verb* [T] (*pres part* **using**; *pt, pp* **used** /juːzd/) **1** when you use sth, you do sth with it for a purpose: *Could I use your phone?* o *We used the money to buy a house.* o *The building was used as a shelter for homeless people.* o *A gun is used for shooting with.* o *Use your imagination!* o *That's a word I never use.* **2** to need or to take sth: *Don't use all the milk.* **3** to treat sb/sth in a selfish or unkind way: *He just used me to get what he wanted and then forgot about me.*
(PHRASAL VERB) **use sth up** to use sth until no more is left

usable /ˈjuːzəbl/ *adj* that can be used

use² /juːs/ *noun* **1** [U] using or being used: *The use of computers is now widespread.* o *She kept the money for use in an emergency.* **2** [C,U] the purpose for which sth is used: *This machine has many uses.* **3** [U] the ability or permission to use sth: *He lost the use of his hand after the accident.* o *She offered them the use of her car.* **4** [U] the advantage of sth; how useful sth is: *It's no use studying for an exam at the last minute.* o *What's the use of trying?*
(IDIOMS) **come into/go out of use** to start/stop being used
make use of sth/sb to use sth in a way that will give you an advantage

used¹ /juːzd/ *adj* that has had an owner before: *a garage selling used cars* ☛ Another word with the same meaning is **second-hand**.

used² /juːst/ *adj* **used to sth/to doing sth** familiar with; accustomed to: *He's used to the heat.* o *I'll never get used to getting up at five.*

used to /ˈjuːstə; *before a vowel and in final po-*

---

iː	ɪ	e	æ	ɑː	ɒ	ɔː	ʊ	uː	ʌ
see	sit	ten	hat	arm	got	saw	put	too	cup

sition /'ju:stu:/ *modal verb* (for talking about sth that happened often or continuously in the past or about a situation which existed in the past): *She used to live with her parents* (= but she doesn't now). o *You used to live in Glasgow, didn't you?* o *Did you use to smoke?* o *I used not to like him.* o *He didn't use to speak to me.* ☛ **1** We usually use **did** to form negatives and questions with **used to**: *I didn't use to like jazz.* o *Did she use to be in your class?* The following negative and question forms of **used to** are more formal and not often used: *He used not to drive a car.* o *Used they to work here?* **2** Be careful not to confuse **used to** + infinitive, which only refers to the past, with **to be used to (doing) sth**, which can refer to the past, present or future. Compare: *I used to live on my own* (= but now I don't). o *I'm used to living on my own* (= I am accustomed to it).

☆ **useful** /'ju:sfl/ *adj* having some practical use; helpful: *a useful tool* o *useful advice*
(IDIOM) **come in useful** to be of practical help, especially in a situation where there is no other help available —**usefully** /-fəlɪ/: *Make sure your time is spent usefully.* —**usefulness** /-fəlnɪs/ *noun* [U]

☆ **useless** /'ju:slɪs/ *adj* **1** that does not work well, or is of no use: *This new machine is useless.* o *It's useless complaining/to complain; you won't get your money back.* **2** (*informal*) (of a person) weak or not successful at sth: *I'm useless at sport.* —**uselessly** *adv* —**uselessness** *noun* [U]

☆ **user** /'ju:zə(r)/ *noun* [C] (often in compounds) a person that uses a service, machine, place, etc: *users of public transport*
user-friendly /ˌju:zə'frendlɪ/ *adj* (used of computers, books, machines, etc) easy or not too complicated to use

usher /'ʌʃə(r)/ *noun* [C] a person who shows people to their seats in a cinema, church, etc
usher *verb* [T] to lead sb carefully in the direction mentioned: *I was ushered to my seat.*
(PHRASAL VERB) **usher sth in** to mark the beginning of sth: *The agreement ushered in a new period of peace for the two countries.*

usherette /ˌʌʃə'ret/ *noun* [C] a woman who shows people to their seats in a cinema or theatre

☆ **usual** /'ju:ʒl/ *adj* happening or used most often: *It's usual for her to work at weekends.* o *He got home later than usual.* o *I sat in my usual seat.*
(IDIOM) **as usual** in the way that has often happened before: *Here's Derek, late as usual!*
usually /'ju:ʒəlɪ/ *adv* in the way that is usual; most often: *She's usually home by six.* o *Usually, we go out on Saturdays.*

utensil /ju:'tensl/ *noun* [C] a type of tool or object used in the home: *cooking utensils*

uterus /'ju:tərəs/ *noun* [C] (*pl* **uteruses** or, in scientific use, **uteri** /-raɪ/) (*formal*) the part of a woman's body where a baby grows ☛ A less formal word is **womb**.

utility /ju:'tɪlətɪ/ *noun* (*pl* **utilities**) **1** [U] (*formal*) the usefulness (of a machine, etc) **2** [C] a useful public service such as the supplying of water or gas
u'tility room *noun* [C] a small room in a house, often next to the kitchen, where people sometimes keep a washing-machine, etc

utilize (*also* **utilise**) /'ju:təlaɪz/ *verb* [T] (*formal*) to make use of sth: *to utilize natural resources*

utmost /'ʌtməʊst/ *adj* (only *before* a noun) (*formal*) greatest: *a message of the utmost importance*
utmost *noun* [sing] the greatest extent, amount, degree, etc that is possible: *I did my utmost to help.*

Utopia /ju:'təʊpɪə/ *noun* [C,U] an imaginary society or place where everything is perfect —**Utopian** /-pɪən/ *adj*

utter¹ /'ʌtə(r)/ *adj* (only *before* a noun) complete; total: *That's utter nonsense!* o *He felt an utter fool.* —**utterly** *adv*: *It's utterly impossible.*

utter² /'ʌtə(r)/ *verb* [T] to speak or make a sound with your mouth: *She left without uttering a word.*
utterance /'ʌtərəns/ *noun* [C] (*formal*) something that is said

U-turn /'ju:tɜ:n/ *noun* [C] **1** a type of movement where a car, etc turns round so that it goes back in the direction it came **2** a sudden change from one plan to a completely different one

Vv

V, v /viː/ noun [C] (pl **V's; v's**) **1** the twenty-second letter of the English alphabet: *'Van' begins with (a) 'V'.* **2** the shape of a V: *The birds were flying in a V.*

vacancy /'veɪkənsɪ/ noun [C] (pl **vacancies**) **1** a room in a hotel, etc that is not being used: *The sign outside the hotel said 'No Vacancies'.* **2** a job that has not been filled: *We have a vacancy for a secretary in our office.*

☆**vacant** /'veɪkənt/ adj **1** (of a house, room, seat, etc) not being used **2** (of a job, etc) not filled: *the 'Situations Vacant' page* (= the page of a newspaper where jobs are advertised) **3** showing no sign of intelligence or understanding: *a vacant expression* —**vacantly** adv: *She stared vacantly out of the window.*

vacation /vəˈkeɪʃn; US veɪ-/ noun **1** [C,U] (US) (a) holiday: *The boss is on vacation.* ☞ Look at the note at **holiday**. **2** [C] any of the holiday periods when a university is closed: *the Easter vacation*

vaccinate /'væksɪneɪt/ verb [T] to give an injection to prevent a person or an animal from getting a disease: *Were you vaccinated against measles as a child?* —**vaccination** /ˌvæksɪˈneɪʃn/ noun [C,U]

vaccine /'væksiːn; US vækˈsiːn/ noun [C] a substance that is given to people in an injection in order to protect them against a disease

vacuum /'vækjuəm/ noun [C] **1** a space that contains no substance and no air or gas: *(figurative) a vacuum in her life* (= a feeling of emptiness) **2** (informal) = VACUUM CLEANER

vacuum verb [I,T] to clean sth using a vacuum cleaner

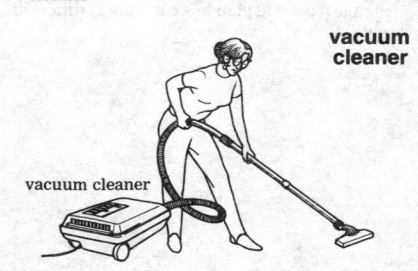

vacuum cleaner

'vacuum cleaner noun [C] an electric machine that cleans carpets, etc by sucking up dirt

'vacuum flask (*US* **'vacuum bottle**) (*also* **flask; Thermos**, trade mark)) a type of container used for keeping a liquid hot or cold

vagina /vəˈdʒaɪnə/ noun [C] the passage in the body of a woman or female animal that connects the outer sex organs to the part where a baby grows (**womb**)

vague /veɪɡ/ adj **1** not clear or definite: *vague memories of my childhood home* **2** (used about a person) not thinking or understanding clearly: *She looked vague when I tried to explain.* **3** not clearly seen: *a vague shape in the distance* **vaguely** adv **1** in a way that is not clear; slightly: *Her name is vaguely familiar.* **2** without thinking about what is happening: *He smiled vaguely and walked away.* —**vagueness** noun [U]

☆**vain** /veɪn/ adj **1** (used about a person) too proud of your appearance, of what you can do, etc ☞ The noun is **vanity**. **2** useless; without any hope of success: *a vain attempt*
(IDIOM) **in vain** without success: *The firemen tried in vain to put out the fire.* —**vainly** adv

vale /veɪl/ noun [C] a valley: *the Vale of York* ☞ We use this word in place names and in poetry.

valentine /'væləntaɪn/ noun [C] **1** (*also* **'valentine card**) a card that you send, usually secretly, to someone you love or like in a romantic way ☞ It is traditional to send these cards on **St Valentine's Day** (14 February). **2** the person you send this card to: *Be my valentine* (= written on a valentine card).

valiant /'væliənt/ adj (formal) very brave —**valiantly** adv

☆**valid** /'vælɪd/ adj **1** that can be used or accepted legally at a certain time: *This passport is valid for one year only.* **2** acceptable in a court of law: *a valid contract* **3** (used about a reason, etc) strong enough to convince sb; acceptable: *I could raise no valid objections to the plan.* ☞ The opposite is **invalid**. —**validity** /vəˈlɪdətɪ/ noun [U]: *the validity of an argument o the validity of a law*

☆**valley** /'vælɪ/ noun [C] the flat land that lies between two lines of mountains or hills and which often has a river flowing through it

valour (*US* **valor**) /'vælə(r)/ noun [U] great bravery, especially in war: *the soldiers' valour in battle* ☞ This word is used in old, formal or poetic writing.

☆**valuable** /'væljuəbl/ adj **1** worth a lot of money: *Is this ring valuable?* **2** very useful: *a valuable piece of information* ☞ The opposite is **valueless** or **worthless**, not **invaluable**.

valuables noun [plural] the small things that you own that are worth a lot of money, such as jewellery, etc: *Please put your valuables in the hotel safe.*

valuation /ˌvæljuˈeɪʃn/ noun [C,U] the act of estimating how much sth is worth

☆**value** /'væljuː/ noun **1** [U] the usefulness or

p	b	t	d	k	g	tʃ	dʒ	f	v	θ	ð
pen	bad	tea	did	cat	got	chin	June	fall	van	thin	then

valve 681 **vegetable**

importance of sth: *the value of education* o *of great/little value* **2** [C,U] the amount of money that sth is worth: *The thieves stole goods with a total value of £10 000.* o *IBM shares have increased in value this month.* o *to go up/down in value* ☛ Look at **face value**. **3** [U] the worth of sth compared with its price: *The hotel was good value at £20 a night.* **4 values** [plural] a set of beliefs about the way people should behave; moral principles: *the traditional values of Western society*

value *verb* [T] (*pres part* **valuing**) **1 value sth (at sth)** to decide the amount of money that sth is worth: *The house was valued at £70 000.* **2** to think sb/sth is very important and worth a lot: *Laura has always valued her independence.*

valueless *adj* without value or use; worthless ☛ Look at **invaluable**.

value 'added tax *noun* [U] (*abbr* **VAT**) a tax on the increase in value of sth at each stage of its production

valve /vælv/ *noun* [C] a mechanical device which controls the flow of air, liquid or gas in a pipe or tube: *a radiator valve* o *the valve on a bicycle tyre*

vampire /'væmpaɪə(r)/ *noun* [C] (in horror stories) a dead person who comes out of his/her grave at night and sucks the blood of living people

☆ **van** /væn/ *noun* [C] a road vehicle that is used for transporting things ☛ picture at **lorry**. A van is smaller than a **lorry** and is always covered.

vandal /'vændl/ *noun* [C] a person who damages property (eg telephone boxes, cars, shop-windows) intentionally and for no purpose —**vandalism** /-dəlɪzəm/ *noun* [U]: *The police are worried about the recent increase in vandalism.*

vandalize (*also* **vandalise**) /'vændəlaɪz/ *verb* [T] (usually passive) to damage property intentionally and for no purpose

vanilla /və'nɪlə/ *noun* [U] a substance from a plant that is used for giving flavour to sweet food: *Strawberry, chocolate or vanilla ice-cream?*

☆ **vanish** /'vænɪʃ/ *verb* [I] **1** to disappear suddenly and completely: *When he turned round, the two men had vanished.* o *His fear vanished when he heard his sister's voice outside the door.* **2** (used about types of things) to disappear little by little over a period of time: *This species of plant is vanishing from the British countryside.*

vanity /'vænəti/ *noun* [U] the quality of being too proud of your appearance or abilities ☛ The adjective is **vain**.

vapour (*US* **vapor**) /'veɪpə(r)/ *noun* [C,U] a substance made of very small drops of liquid which hang together in the air like a cloud or mist: *water vapour*

variable /'veəriəbl/ *adj* not staying the same; changeable —**variability** /ˌveəriə'bɪləti/ *noun* [U]

variant *noun* [C] a different form of sth

☆ **variation** /ˌveəri'eɪʃn/ *noun* **1** [C,U] **variation (in sth)** a difference in quality or quantity between a number of things: *There was a lot of variation in the examination results* (= the results were very different from each other). o *There may be a slight variation in price from shop to shop.* **2** [C] **variation (on/of sth)** something that is almost the same as another thing but has some small differences: *All Spielberg's films are just variations on a basic theme.*

varied /'veərid/ *adj* having many different kinds of things or activities: *The restaurant has a varied menu of meat, fish and vegetables.* o *The work of an English teacher is interesting and varied.*

☆ **variety** /və'raɪəti/ *noun* (*pl* **varieties**) **1** [U] the quality of not being the same: *There's so much variety in my new job. I do something different every day!* **2** [C] **a variety (of sth)** a number of different kinds of things: *You can take evening classes in a variety of subjects including photography, Spanish and computing.* **3** [C] **a variety (of sth)** a type of sth: *a new variety of apple called 'Perfection'*

☆ **various** /'veəriəs/ *adj* (used for describing things that are different from each other) more than one; several: *Our shop sells hats in various shapes, colours and sizes.* o *I decided to leave London for various reasons.*

varnish /'vɑːnɪʃ/ *noun* [U] a clear liquid that you paint onto wood or other hard surfaces to protect them and make them shine ☛ Look at **nail varnish**. —**varnish** *verb* [T]

☆ **vary** /'veəri/ *verb* (*pres part* **varying**; *3rd pers sing pres* **varies**; *pt, pp* **varied**) **1** [I] (used about a number of things) to be different from each other: *The hotel bedrooms vary in size from medium to very large.* **2** [I] to become different; to change: *The price of the holiday varies from £500 to £1 200, depending on the time of year.* **3** [T] to make sth different by changing it often in some way: *I try to vary my work as much as possible so I don't get bored.*

☆ **vase** /vɑːz; *US* veɪs; veɪz/ *noun* [C] a glass or china container used for holding cut flowers

vasectomy /və'sektəmi/ *noun* [C] (*pl* **vasectomies**) a small medical operation that prevents a man from having children, by cutting the tube that carries sperm

☆ **vast** /vɑːst; *US* væst/ *adj* extremely big: *a vast sum of money* o *a vast country* —**vastly** *adv*: *a vastly improved traffic system*

vault¹ /vɔːlt/ *noun* [C] **1** a strong underground room in a bank, etc that is used for keeping money and other valuable things safe **2** a room under a church where dead people are buried **3** a high roof or ceiling in a church, etc, made from a number of arches joined together at the top

vault² /vɔːlt/ *verb* [I,T] **vault (over sth)** to jump over or onto sth in one movement, using your hands or a pole to help you: *The boy vaulted over the wall.* o *to pole-vault*

veal /viːl/ *noun* [U] the meat from a young cow (**calf**) ☛ Look at the note at **meat**.

veer /vɪə(r)/ *verb* [I] (used about vehicles) to change direction suddenly: *The car veered across the road and hit a tree.*

vegan *noun* [C] a person who does not eat any animal products ☛ Look at **vegetarian**.

☆ **vegetable** /'vedʒtəbl/ *noun* [C] a plant which

s	z	ʃ	ʒ	h	m	n	ŋ	l	r	j	w
so	zoo	she	vision	how	man	no	sing	leg	red	yes	wet

vegetarian /ˌvedʒɪˈteərɪən/ *noun* [C] a person who does not eat meat or fish

vegetation /ˌvedʒɪˈteɪʃn/ *noun* [U] (*formal*) plant life in general; all the plants that are found in a particular place: *tropical vegetation*

vehement /ˈviːəmənt/ *adj* showing strong (often negative) feeling: *a vehement attack on the government*

☆ **vehicle** /ˈvɪəkl; *US* ˈviːhɪkl/ *noun* [C] (*formal*) **1** something which transports people or things from place to place, especially on land, eg cars, bicycles, lorries, buses: *a motor vehicle* **2** something which is used for communicating particular ideas or opinions: *This newspaper has become a vehicle for Conservative opinion.*

veil /veɪl/ *noun* [C] a piece of thin material for covering the head and face of a woman

vein /veɪn/ *noun* **1** [C] one of the tubes which carry blood from all parts of the body to the heart ☞ Look at **artery**. **2** [sing,U] a particular style or quality: *After a humorous beginning, the programme continued in a more serious vein.*

Velcro /ˈvelkrəʊ/ *noun* [U] (*trade mark*) a material for fastening parts of clothes together. Velcro is made of nylon and is used in small strips, one rough and one smooth, that stick together.

velocity /vɪˈlɒsəti/ *noun* [U] (*technical*) the speed at which sth moves

velvet /ˈvelvɪt/ *noun* [U] a kind of material made of cotton, silk or nylon with a soft thick surface on one side only

vendetta /venˈdetə/ *noun* [C] a serious argument or quarrel which lasts for a long time (especially between an individual and an organization or between families)

vendor *noun* [C] (*formal*) a person who sells sth ☞ Look at **purchaser**.

veneer /vəˈnɪə(r)/ *noun* [C,U] **1** a thin layer of wood or plastic which you stick onto sth made of cheaper material to give it a better appearance **2 a veneer (of sth)** (*formal*) a part of sb's behaviour or of a situation which hides what it is really like: *a thin veneer of politeness*

venetian blind /vəˌniːʃn ˈblaɪnd/ *noun* [C] a covering for a window that is made of horizontal strips of plastic. You can alter the position of the strips in order to let more or less light into the room.

vengeance /ˈvendʒəns/ *noun* (*formal*) [U] the act of hurting sb because he/she has hurt you in some way that you think is unjust: *The man wanted vengeance for the death of his wife.* ☞ Look at **revenge**.

(IDIOM) **with a vengeance** with more force and determination than before or than you expected: *After a week of good weather winter returned with a vengeance today.*

venison /ˈvenɪzn/ *noun* [U] the meat from a deer ☞ Look at the note at **meat**.

venom /ˈvenəm/ *noun* [U] **1** extreme anger or hatred that you show when you speak **2** the poisonous fluid that snakes, etc inject into you when they bite you —**venomous** /ˈvenəməs/ *adj*

vent /vent/ *noun* [C] a hole in the wall of a room or machine which allows air to come in, and smoke, steam or smells to go out: *an air vent*

ventilate /ˈventɪleɪt; *US* -təleɪt/ *verb* [T] to allow air to move freely in and out of a room or building: *The office is badly ventilated.* —**ventilation** /ˌventɪˈleɪʃn; *US* -təˈleɪʃn/ *noun* [U]: *There was no ventilation in the room except for one tiny window.*

venture /ˈventʃə(r)/ *noun* [C] a project which is new and often risky, because you cannot be sure that it will succeed: *I wish you luck in your new business venture.*

venture *verb* [I] to do sth or go somewhere new and risky, when you are not sure what will happen: *The company has decided to venture into computer production as well as design.* ○ *He ventured out into the storm in a thick coat, hat and scarf.*

venue /ˈvenjuː/ *noun* [C] the place where a concert, sports match, conference, etc happens: *a change of venue*

Venus /ˈviːnəs/ *noun* [sing] the planet that is second in order from the sun and nearest to the earth

veranda (*also* **verandah**) /vəˈrændə/ (*US also* **porch**) *noun* [C] a platform attached to the side of a house, with a roof and floor but no outside wall: *to sit on the veranda* ☞ Look at **balcony**, **patio** and **terrace**.

☆ **verb** /vɜːb/ *noun* [C] a word or group of words that is used to indicate an action or state, eg *bring, happen, be*

verbal /ˈvɜːbl/ *adj* (*formal*) **1** spoken, not written: *a verbal warning* **2** of words, or the use of words: *verbal skill* —**verbally** /ˈvɜːbəli/ *adv*

☆ **verdict** /ˈvɜːdɪkt/ *noun* [C] **1** the decision in a court of law about whether a person is guilty or not guilty, or about the facts of a case¹(5): *The jury gave a verdict of 'not guilty'.* **2** your opinion or decision about sth, which you tell to other people: *The general verdict was that the restaurant was too expensive.*

verge /vɜːdʒ/ *noun* [C] the narrow piece of land at the side of a road, that is usually covered in grass: *a grass verge*

(IDIOM) **on the verge of sth/doing sth** very near to doing sth, or to sth happening: *on the verge of an exciting new discovery* ○ *on the verge of discovering a cure for AIDS*

verge *verb*

(PHRASAL VERB) **verge on sth** to be almost the same as sth; to be close to sth: *What they are doing verges on the illegal.*

verify /ˈverɪfaɪ/ *verb* [T] (*pres part* **verifying**; *3rd pers sing pres* **verifies**; *pt, pp* **verified**) (*formal*) to check or state that sth is true: *to verify a statement* —**verification** /ˌverɪfɪˈkeɪʃn/ *noun* [C,U]

vermin /ˈvɜːmɪn/ *noun* [plural] small wild animals (eg rats) that carry disease and destroy plants and food

versatile /ˈvɜːsətaɪl; *US* -tl/ *adj* **1** (used about an object) having many different uses: *a versatile tool that drills, cuts or polishes* **2** (used about a person) having many different skills or abilities: *She's so versatile! She can dance, sing, act and play the guitar!*

☆ **verse** /vɜːs/ *noun* **1** [U] writing arranged in lines which have a definite rhythm and which often rhyme at the end: *He wrote his Valentine's message in verse.* **2** [C] a group of lines which form one part of a song or poem: *This song has five verses.*

☆ **version** /'vɜːʃn/ *noun* [C] **1** a thing which is based on sth else but which has some details that are different: *the five-door version of the Ford Escort* ○ *the film version of 'Romeo and Juliet'* **2** a person's description of sth that has happened: *The two drivers gave very different versions of the accident.*

versus /'vɜːsəs/ *prep* **1** (*abbr* **v**, **vs**) (used in sport for showing that two teams or people are playing against each other): *England versus Argentina* **2** (used for showing that two ideas or things are in opposition to each other, especially when you are trying to choose one of them): *It's a question of quality versus price.*

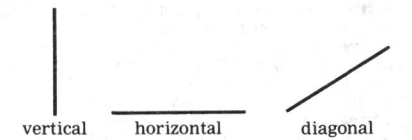

vertical	horizontal	diagonal

☆ **vertical** /'vɜːtɪkl/ *adj* going straight up at an angle of 90° from the ground: *a vertical line* ○ *The cliff was almost vertical.* —**vertically** /-klɪ/ *adv*

☆ **very**¹ /'veri/ *adv* (used with an adjective or adverb to make it stronger): *very small* ○ *very slowly* ○ *very much* ○ *'Are you hungry?' 'Not very.'* ☛ We use **very** with superlative adjectives: *very best, youngest, etc* but with comparative adjectives we use **much** or **very much**: *much/very much better; much/very much younger*

(IDIOM) **very well** (used for showing that you agree to do sth): *Very well, Mrs Dawson, we'll replace your shoes with a new pair.*

very² /'veri/ *adj* (used with a noun for emphasis): *We climbed to the very top of the mountain* (= right to the top). ○ *You're the very person I wanted to talk to* (= exactly the right person).

vessel /'vesl/ *noun* [C] **1** (*formal*) a ship or large boat **2** (*old-fashioned*) a container for liquids, eg a bottle, cup or bowl

☆ **vest** /vest/ *noun* [C] **1** (*US* **undershirt**) a piece of clothing that you wear under your other clothes, on the top part of your body **2** (*US*) = WAISTCOAT

vested interest /ˌvestɪd 'ɪntrəst/ *noun* [C] a strong and often secret reason for doing sth that will bring you an advantage of some kind (eg more money or power)

vestige /'vestɪdʒ/ *noun* [C] a small part of sth that remains after the rest of it has gone; trace: *the last vestige of the old system*

☆ **vet**¹ /vet/ (also *formal* **veterinary surgeon**) *noun* [C] a person whose job is to give medical help to sick or injured animals; a doctor for animals: *We took the cat to the vet/to the vet's.*

vet² /vet/ *verb* [T] (**vetting**; **vetted**) to examine sb/sth carefully before deciding whether to accept him/her/it or not: *All new employees at the Ministry of Defence are carefully vetted* (= somebody examines the details of their past lives).

veteran /'vetərən/ *noun* [C] **1** a person who has served in the army, navy or air force, especially during a war **2** a person who has very long experience of a particular job or activity

veteran 'car *noun* [C] a car that was made before 1916 ☛ Look at **vintage**.

veterinary /'vetrɪnri; *US* 'vetərɪneri/ *adj* connected with the medical treatment of sick or injured animals: *a veterinary surgeon* ☛ Look at **vet**.

veto /'viːtəʊ/ *verb* [T] (*pres part* **vetoing**; *3rd pers sing pres* **vetoes**; *pt, pp* **vetoed**) to refuse to give official permission for an action or plan, when other people have agreed to it: *The Prime Minister vetoed the proposal to reduce taxation.*

veto *noun* (*pl* **vetoes**) **1** [C,U] the official power to refuse permission for an action or plan: *Britain used its veto to block the UN resolution.* ○ *the right of veto* **2** [C] the act of vetoing on a particular occasion: *the Government's veto of the European Parliament's proposal*

vexed /vekst/ *adj* causing difficulty, worry, and a lot of discussion: *the vexed question of our growing prison population*

via /'vaɪə/ *prep* **1** going through a place: *We flew from London to Sydney via Bangkok.* **2** by means of; using: *These pictures come to you via our satellite link.*

viable /'vaɪəbl/ *adj* that will be successful: *I'm afraid your idea is just not commercially viable.* —**viability** /ˌvaɪə'bɪləti/ *noun* [U]

viaduct /'vaɪədʌkt/ *noun* [C] a long, high bridge which carries a railway or road across a valley

vibrant /'vaɪbrənt/ *adj* **1** full of life and energy; exciting: *a vibrant city, atmosphere, personality, etc* **2** (used about colours) bright and strong

vibrate /vaɪ'breɪt; *US* 'vaɪbreɪt/ *verb* [I] to move continuously and very quickly from side to side: *When a guitar string vibrates it makes a sound.* —**vibration** /vaɪ'breɪʃn/ *noun* [C,U]: *Even at full speed the engine causes very little vibration.*

vicar /'vɪkə(r)/ *noun* [C] a priest of the Church of England. A vicar looks after a church and the people in the surrounding area (**parish**)

vicarage /'vɪkərɪdʒ/ *noun* [C] the house where a vicar lives

vice¹ /vaɪs/ *noun* **1** [U] evil or immoral actions: *The authorities are trying to stamp out vice and corruption.* **2** [C] a moral weakness or bad habit: *Greed and envy are terrible vices.* ○ *My only vice is eating too much chocolate.* ☛ Look at **virtue**.

vice² (*US* **vise**) /vaɪs/ *noun* [C] a tool that you use to hold a piece of wood, metal, etc firmly while you are working on it

vice- /vaɪs/ (in compounds) next in importance

ɜː	ə	eɪ	əʊ	aɪ	aʊ	ɔɪ	ɪə	eə	ʊə
fur	ago	pay	home	five	now	join	near	hair	pure

to the rank mentioned: *Vice-President* o *the vice-captain*

vice versa /ˌvaɪsɪ'vɜːsə/ *adv* in the opposite way to what has just been said: *We can go on the bus and walk back or vice versa* (= or walk there and come back on the bus).

vicinity /vɪ'sɪnəti/ *noun*
(IDIOM) **in the vicinity (of sth)** (*formal*) in the surrounding area: *There's no bank in the immediate vicinity.*

vicious /'vɪʃəs/ *adj* **1** cruel; done in order to hurt sb/sth: *a vicious attack* **2** (used about an animal) dangerous —**viciously** *adv*
(IDIOM) **a vicious circle** a situation in which one problem leads to another and the new problem makes the first problem worse

☆ **victim** /'vɪktɪm/ *noun* [C] a person or animal that is injured, killed or hurt by sb/sth: *a murder victim* o *The children are often the innocent victims of a divorce.*

victimize (*also* **victimise**) /'vɪktɪmaɪz/ *verb* [T] to punish or make sb suffer unfairly —**victimization** (*also* **victimisation**) /ˌvɪktɪmaɪ'zeɪʃn; *US* -mɪ'z-/ *noun* [U]

victor /'vɪktə(r)/ *noun* [C] (*formal*) the person who wins a game, competition, battle, etc

Victorian /vɪk'tɔːriən/ *adj* **1** connected with the time of Queen Victoria (1837-1901): *Victorian houses* **2** having the qualities of middle-class people during this time (= believing in hard work, religion, strict discipline and moral behaviour)
Victorian *noun* [C] a person who lived during this time

☆ **victory** /'vɪktəri/ *noun* [C,U] (*pl* **victories**) success in winning a battle, game, competition, etc: *Hannibal's victory over the Roman army* o *The Liberal Democrats won a decisive victory in the by-election.* o *Becker led his team to victory in the Davis Cup.* —**victorious** /vɪk'tɔːriəs/ *adj*: *the victorious team* (= the one that won)

☆ **video** /'vɪdiəʊ/ *noun* (*pl* **videos**) **1** the system of recording moving pictures and sound by using a camera, and showing them by using a recorder and a television: *We recorded the wedding on video.* o *The film is coming out on video in May.* **2** [C] a tape or cassette on which you record moving pictures and sound or on which a film or television programme has been recorded: *Would you like to see the video we made on holiday?* o *a video rental shop* **3** [C] = VIDEO CASSETTE RECORDER

video *verb* [T] (*3rd pers sing pres* **videos**; *pres part* **videoing**; *pt, pp* **videoed**) to record moving pictures and sound or a film or television programme onto a video(2): *We hired a camera to video the school play.* o *I'm going out tonight, so I'll have to video that programme I wanted to watch.*

ˌ**video caˈssette reˈcorder** (*also* ˈ**video recorder**; **video**) (*abbr* **VCR**) a machine that is connected to a television on which you can record or play back moving pictures and sound or a film or television programme

ˈ**videotape** *noun* [C,U] tape used for recording moving pictures and sound

ˈ**videotape** *verb* [T] = VIDEO

☆ **view**[1] /vjuː/ *noun* **1** [U] the ability to be seen from a particular place: *The garden was hidden from view behind a high wall.* o *to come into/disappear from view* **2** [C] what you can see from a particular place. A view usually means sth pleasant to look at, eg beautiful natural scenery: *There are breathtaking views from the top of the mountain.* o *a room with a sea view* ☛ Look at the note at **scenery**. **3** [sing] the ability to see sth from a particular place: *A large lorry was blocking her view of the road.* **4** [C] **a view (about/on sth)** an opinion or idea about sth: *He expressed the view that standards were falling.* o *In my view, she has done nothing wrong.* o *The poet was jailed for his political views.* o *strong views on the subject*
(IDIOMS) **have, etc sth in view** (*formal*) to have sth as a plan or idea in your mind
in full view ⇨ FULL
in view of sth because of sth; as a result of sth: *In view of her apology we decided to take no further action.*
a point of view ⇨ POINT
with a view to doing sth (*formal*) with the aim or intention of doing sth

ˈ**viewpoint** *noun* [C] = POINT OF VIEW

☆ **view**[2] /vjuː/ *verb* [T] (*formal*) **1 view sth (as sth)** to consider or think about sth: *She viewed holidays as a waste of time.* o *He views these changes with suspicion.* **2** to watch or look at sth: *Viewed from this angle, the building looks much taller than it really is.*

viewer /'vjuːə(r)/ *noun* [C] a person who watches television

vigil /'vɪdʒɪl/ *noun* [C,U] a period when you stay awake all night for a special purpose: *a candle-lit vigil for peace* o *All night she kept vigil over the sick child.*

vigilant /'vɪdʒɪlənt/ *adj* (*formal*) careful and looking out for danger —**vigilance** /-əns/ *noun* [U]

vigilante /ˌvɪdʒɪ'lænti/ *noun* [C] a member of an unofficial organization (not the police) that tries to prevent crime in a particular area

vigour (*US* **vigor**) /'vɪgə(r)/ *noun* [U] strength or energy: *After the break we started work again with renewed vigour.*

vigorous /'vɪgərəs/ *adj* strong or energetic: *vigorous exercise* —**vigorously** *adv*: *Campaigners have protested vigorously about the plans to close the local railway line.*

vile /vaɪl/ *adj* very bad or unpleasant: *She's in a vile mood.* o *a vile smell*

villa /'vɪlə/ *noun* [C] a pleasant house with a garden, usually in a warm country. A villa is often used as a holiday house.

☆ **village** /'vɪlɪdʒ/ *noun* **1** [C] a group of houses with other buildings, eg a church, shop, school, etc, in a country area. A village is smaller than a town: *a small fishing village* o *the village pub* **2** [sing, with sing or pl verb] all the people who live in a village: *All the village is/are taking part in the carnival.*

villager /'vɪlɪdʒə(r)/ *noun* [C] a person who lives in a village

villain /'vɪlən/ *noun* [C] **1** an evil person, especially in a book or play: *In the play 'Othello', Iago is the villain.* ☛ Look at **hero**. **2** (*in-*

p	b	t	d	k	g	tʃ	dʒ	f	v	θ	ð
pen	bad	tea	did	cat	got	chin	June	fall	van	thin	then

vindictive /vɪnˈdɪktɪv/ *adj* being particularly unpleasant to sb; trying to hurt sb more than he/she deserves

vine /vaɪn/ *noun* [C] the climbing plant that grapes grow on

vinegar /ˈvɪnɪɡə(r)/ *noun* [U] a liquid with a strong sharp taste that is made from wine, etc. Vinegar is often mixed with oil and put onto salads.

vineyard /ˈvɪnjəd/ *noun* [C] a piece of land where vines are grown

vintage /ˈvɪntɪdʒ/ *noun* [C] the wine that was made in a particular year: *1979 was an excellent vintage.*

vintage *adj* **1** (used about wine) that was produced in a particular year and district: *a bottle of vintage champagne* **2** (used about a car) made between 1917 and 1930 ☞ Look at **veteran car. 3** of very high quality: *a vintage performance by Dustin Hoffman*

vinyl /ˈvaɪnl/ *noun* [C,U] a type of strong plastic that is used for making raincoats, records, floor coverings, etc

viola /viˈəʊlə/ *noun* [C] a musical instrument with strings that looks like a violin but is slightly larger ☞ Note that we play **the viola.**

violate /ˈvaɪəleɪt/ *verb* [T] **1** to break sth (eg a rule or agreement): *to violate a peace treaty* **2** to disturb sth, not to respect sth: *to violate sb's privacy, rights, etc* —**violation** /ˌvaɪəˈleɪʃn/ *noun* [C,U]: *violation of human rights*

☆**violent** /ˈvaɪələnt/ *adj* **1** using physical strength, often in an uncontrolled way, to hurt or kill sb; caused by this behaviour: *a violent man, who abused his children* ○ *The demonstration started peacefully but later turned violent.* ○ *a violent death* **2** very strong; uncontrolled: *He has a violent temper.* ○ *a violent storm*

violence /-əns/ *noun* [U] **1** violent behaviour: *They threatened to use violence if we didn't give them the money.* ○ *Is there too much violence on TV?* ○ *an act of violence* **2** great force or energy —**violently** *adv*

violet /ˈvaɪələt/ *noun* **1** [C] a small plant that grows wild or in gardens and has purple or white flowers and a pleasant smell **2** [U] a bluish purple colour —**violet** *adj*

☆**violin** /ˌvaɪəˈlɪn/ *noun* [C] a musical instrument with strings, that you hold under your chin and play with a bow ☞ Note that we play **the violin.**

virgin /ˈvɜːdʒɪn/ *noun* [C] a person, especially a girl or woman, who has never had sexual intercourse

virgin *adj* that has not yet been used, touched, damaged, etc: *virgin forest*

virginity /vəˈdʒɪnəti/ *noun* [U] the state of being a virgin: *to keep/lose your virginity*

Virgo /ˈvɜːɡəʊ/ *noun* (*pl* **Virgos**) [C,U] the sixth sign of the zodiac, the Virgin; a person who was born under this sign ☞ picture at **zodiac.**

virile /ˈvaɪraɪl/; *US* /ˈvɪrəl/ *adj* (used about a man) strong and having great sexual energy

virility /vɪˈrɪləti/ *noun* [U] the sexual power of men

virtual /ˈvɜːtʃuəl/ *adj* (only *before* a noun) being almost or nearly sth: *Her disability has made her a virtual prisoner in her own home.* —**virtually** /-tʃuəli/ *adv*: *The building is virtually finished.*

☆**virtue** /ˈvɜːtʃuː/ *noun* **1** [U] behaviour which shows high moral standards; goodness: *to lead a life of virtue* **2** [C] a good quality or habit: *Patience is a great virtue.* ☞ Look at **vice**[1]. **3** [C,U] **the virtue (of sth/of being/doing sth)** an advantage or a useful quality of sth: *This new material has the virtue of being strong as well as very light.*

(IDIOM) **by virtue of** (*formal*) because of

virtuous /ˈvɜːtʃuəs/ *adj* behaving in a moral or good way

virtuoso /ˌvɜːtʃuˈəʊzəʊ/ *noun* (*pl* **virtuosos** or **virtuosi**) a person who is unusually good at sth (often singing or playing a musical instrument)

virulent /ˈvɪrʊlənt/ *adj* **1** (used about a poison or a disease) very strong and dangerous: *a particularly virulent form of influenza* **2** (*formal*) very strong and full of anger: *a virulent attack on the leader*

☆**virus** /ˈvaɪərəs/ *noun* [C] (*pl* **viruses**) **1** a living thing, too small to be seen without a microscope, that causes disease in people, animals and plants: *HIV, the virus that is thought to cause AIDS* ☞ Look at **bacteria** and **germ. 2** (*computing*) instructions that are put into a computer program in order to cause errors and destroy information

visa /ˈviːzə/ *noun* [C] an official mark in your passport that shows you are allowed to enter, leave or travel through a country: *She applied for an extension when her visa expired.* ○ *a tourist visa*

viscount /ˈvaɪkaʊnt/ *noun* [C] a member of the British aristocracy who is higher in rank than a baron but lower than an earl

vise (*US*) = **VICE**[2]

☆**visible** /ˈvɪzəbl/ *adj* that can be seen or noticed: *The church tower was visible from the other side of the valley.* ○ *a visible improvement* ☞ The opposite is **invisible.**

visibility /ˌvɪzəˈbɪləti/ *noun* [U] the distance that you can see in particular light or weather conditions: *In the fog visibility was down to 50 metres.* ○ *poor/good visibility*

visibly /-əbli/ *adv* noticeably or clearly: *Tom was visibly upset.*

☆**vision** /ˈvɪʒn/ *noun* **1** [U] the ability to see; sight: *to have good, poor, normal, perfect, etc vision* **2** [U] the ability to make great plans for the future: *a statesman of great vision* **3** [C] a picture in your imagination: *They have a vision of a world without weapons.* ○ *I had visions of being left behind, but in fact the others had waited for me.* **4** [C] a dreamlike state often connected with a religious experience: *God appeared to Paul in a vision.* **5** [U] the picture on a television or cinema screen: *a temporary loss of vision*

☆**visit** /ˈvɪzɪt/ *verb* [I,T] to come or go to see a person or place and to spend a short time there: *I don't live here. I'm just visiting.* ○ *We often visit relatives at the weekend.* ○ *She's going to visit*

her son in hospital. o *When you go to London you must visit Madame Tussaud's.*
visit *noun* [C] a short stay with sb or in a particular place: *The Prime Minister is on an official visit to Germany.* o *We had a visit from Richard on Sunday.* o *They paid us a flying visit* (= a very short one).

☆ **visitor** /'vɪzɪtə(r)/ *noun* [C] a person who visits sb/sth: *We're not free on Sunday. We're having visitors.* o *visitors to London from overseas*

visor /'vaɪzə(r)/ *noun* [C] **1** the part of a hard hat (**a helmet**) that you can pull down to protect your eyes or face **2** a piece of plastic, cloth, etc on a cap or in a car, which keeps the sun out of your eyes

☆ **visual** /'vɪʒuəl/ *adj* connected with seeing: *the visual arts* (= painting, sculpture, cinema, etc)
visualize (*also* **visualise**) /-aɪz/ *verb* [T] to imagine or have a picture in your mind of sb/sth: *It's hard to visualize what this place looked like before the factory was built.* o *I can't visualize Liz as a mother.* —**visually** /'vɪʒuəli/ *adv*: *to be visually handicapped* (= to be partly or completely blind)
,**visual 'aid** *noun* [C] a picture, film, map, etc that helps a pupil to learn sth
,**visual dis'play unit** *noun* [C] (*abbr* **VDU**) a screen on which you can see information from a computer

☆ **vital** /'vaɪtl/ *adj* **1** very important or necessary; essential: *Practice is vital if you want to speak a language well.* o *vital information* **2** full of energy; lively —**vitally** /'vaɪtəli/ *adv*: *vitally important*
vitality /vaɪ'tæləti/ *noun* [U] the state of being lively or full of energy

☆ **vitamin** /'vɪtəmɪn; *US* 'vaɪt-/ *noun* [C] one of several substances that are found in certain types of food and that are very important for growth and good health: *Oranges are rich in vitamin C.* o *a vitamin deficiency*

vivacious /vɪ'veɪʃəs/ *adj* (used about a person, usually a woman) full of energy; lively and cheerful

vivid /'vɪvɪd/ *adj* **1** (used about light or a colour) strong and bright: *the vivid reds and yellows of the flowers* **2** having or producing a strong, clear picture in your mind: *a vivid description of his time in the army* o *a vivid dream* —**vividly** *adv*

vivisection /,vɪvɪ'sekʃn/ *noun* [U] doing scientific experiments on live animals

vixen /'vɪksn/ *noun* [C] a female fox

☆ **vocabulary** /və'kæbjələri; *US* -leri/ *noun* (*pl* **vocabularies**) **1** [sing] all the words in a language: *New words are always coming into the vocabulary.* **2** [C,U] all the words that sb knows or that are used in a particular book, subject, etc: *He has an amazing vocabulary for a five-year-old.* o *There are many ways to increase your English vocabulary.*

vocal /'vəʊkl/ *adj* **1** connected with the voice: *vocal music* **2** expressing your ideas or opinions loudly or freely: *a small but vocal group of protesters*
vocalist /'vəʊkəlɪst/ *noun* [C] a singer, especially in a pop or jazz group

vocation /vəʊ'keɪʃn/ *noun* [C,U] the feeling that you are especially suited for a particular kind of work, often one which involves helping other people; the ability to do this kind of work: *Peter followed his vocation to become a priest.* o *She has no vocation for teaching.*
vocational /-ʃənl/ *adj* connected with the skills or qualifications that you need to do a particular job: *vocational training*

vodka /'vɒdkə/ *noun* [U] a strong clear alcoholic drink originally from Russia

☆ **voice** /vɔɪs/ *noun* **1** [C] the sounds that you make when you speak or sing; the ability to make these sounds: *I heard voices near the house and went out to see who it was.* o *She has a beautiful voice* (= she can sing beautifully). o *He had a bad cold and lost his voice.* o *to speak in a loud, soft, low, hoarse, etc voice* o *Shh! Keep your voice down!* o *to raise/lower your voice* o *Alan is 13 and his voice is beginning to break* (= to become deep and low like a man's). **2** [U,sing] **voice (in sth)** (the right to express) your ideas or opinions: *The workers want more voice in the running of the company.* **3** [sing] (*grammar*) the form of a verb that shows whether a sentence is active or passive: *'Keats wrote this poem' is in the active voice.* o *'This poem was written by Keats' is in the passive voice.*
(IDIOM) **at the top of your voice** ⇨ TOP¹
voice *verb* [T] to express your opinions or feelings: *The party voiced its objections to the leader's plans.*

void /vɔɪd/ *noun* [C, usually sing] (*formal*) an empty space: (*figurative*): *Her death left a void in their lives.*
void *adj* (*formal*) empty; without sth
(IDIOM) **null and void** ⇨ NULL

volatile /'vɒlətaɪl; *US* -tl/ *adj* **1** (used about a liquid) that can easily change into a gas **2** that can change suddenly: *The situation in the Middle East is still very volatile.* o *a volatile personality*

☆ **volcano** /vɒl'keɪməʊ/ *noun* [C] (*pl* **volcanoes**) a mountain with a hole (**crater**) at the top through which steam, hot rocks (**lava**), fire, etc sometimes come out: *an active/dormant/extinct volcano* o *When did the volcano last erupt?* —**volcanic** /vɒl'kænɪk/ *adj*

☆ **volley** /'vɒli/ *noun* [C] (*pl* **volleys**) **1** a number of stones, bullets, etc that are thrown, shot, etc at the same time: *The soldiers fired a volley over the heads of the crowd.* o (*figurative*) *a volley of abuse* **2** (in tennis, etc) a stroke in which you hit the ball before it touches the ground
volley *verb* [I,T] (in tennis) to hit the ball before it touches the ground
'**volleyball** *noun* [U] a game in which two teams try to hit a ball over a high net with their hands and not let it touch the ground

☆ **volt** /vəʊlt/ *noun* [C] (*abbr* **v**) a unit for measuring electrical force
voltage /'vəʊltɪdʒ/ *noun* [C,U] the electrical force that is measured in volts: *Danger! High voltage.* o *The voltage in Europe is 240 volts, but in the United States it is 110 volts.*

☆ **volume** /'vɒljuːm; *US* -jəm/ *noun* **1** [C] a book, especially one of a set or series: *The library has over 10 000 volumes.* o *The dictionary comes in three volumes.* **2** [C,U] the amount of space that

iː	ɪ	e	æ	ɑː	ɒ	ɔː	ʊ	uː	ʌ
see	sit	ten	hat	arm	got	saw	put	too	cup

sth contains or occupies: *What is the volume of this sphere?* o *A kilo of feathers is greater in volume than a kilo of gold.* ☛ Look at **area**. **3** [U] the quantity or amount of sth: *the volume of traffic on the roads* **4** [U] the strength or degree of sound that sth makes: *to turn the volume on a radio up/down*

☆**voluntary** /'vɒləntrɪ; *US* -terɪ/ *adj* **1** done or given willingly, not because you have to do it: *Overtime is voluntary where I work and I seldom do any.* o *Parents often make voluntary contributions to the school funds.* ☛ Something that you must do is **compulsory**. **2** done or working without payment: *voluntary work at the local hospital* o *Voluntary organizations are sending workers to help the refugees.* —**voluntarily** /'vɒləntrəlɪ; *US* ˌvɒlən'terəlɪ/ *adv*: *She left the job voluntarily, she wasn't sacked.*

☆**volunteer** /ˌvɒlən'tɪə(r)/ *noun* [C] **1** a person who offers or agrees to do sth without being forced or paid to do it **2** a person who joins the armed forces without being ordered to

volunteer *verb* **1** [I,T] **volunteer (sth); volunteer (to do sth)** to offer sth or to do sth which you do not have to do or for which you will not be paid: *They volunteered their services free.* o *She frequently volunteers for extra work because she really likes her job.* o *One of my friends volunteered to take us all in his car.* **2** [I] **volunteer (for sth)** to join the armed forces without being ordered **3** [T] to give information, etc or make a comment or suggestion without being asked to: *I volunteered a few helpful suggestions.*

vomit /'vɒmɪt/ *verb* [I,T] to bring food, etc up from the stomach and out of the mouth: *How many times did the patient vomit this morning?* ☛ In everyday English we say **be sick**: *I ate too much last night and I was sick.* —**vomit** *noun* [U]: *the smell of vomit*

☆**vote** /vəʊt/ *noun* **1** [C] a method of deciding sth by asking people to express their choice and finding out what the majority want: *The democratic way to decide this would be to take a vote.* o *Let's have a vote. All those in favour, raise your hands.* **2** [C] **a vote (for/against sb/sth)** an expression of your choice in an election, etc, which you show by raising your hand or writing on a piece of paper: *The votes are still being counted.* o *The Tory candidate got nearly 20 000 votes.* **3 the vote** [sing] the votes given or received by a certain group in an election: *The Conservatives were elected with 42% of the vote.* **4 the vote** [sing] the legal right to vote in political elections: *In some countries, women don't have the vote.*

(IDIOM) **a vote of thanks** a short speech to thank sb, usually a guest at a meeting, dinner, etc: *The club secretary proposed a vote of thanks to the guest speaker.*

vote *verb* **1** [I,T] **vote (for/against sb/sth); vote (on sth)** to show a choice of opinion with a vote: *Who did you vote for in the last general election?* o *Very few MPs voted against the new law.* o *Now that we've heard everybody's opinion, I think it's time we voted on it.* o *They voted to change the rules of the club.* o *I voted Liberal Democrat.* **2** [T] to choose sb for a particular position or honour: *He was voted best actor.* **3** [T] (*informal*) to decide and state that sth is/was good or bad: *We all voted the trip a success.*

voter *noun* [C] a person who votes or has the right to vote in a political election

vouch /vaʊtʃ/ *verb* [I] **vouch (for sb/sth)** to state that a person is honest or good or that sth is true or genuine; to guarantee

voucher /'vaʊtʃə(r)/ *noun* [C] (*Brit*) a piece of paper that you can exchange for some goods or services: *luncheon vouchers* (= ones given by some employers and which can be exchanged at certain restaurants for food)

vow /vaʊ/ *noun* [C] a formal promise (especially in a religious ceremony): *marriage vows* o *a vow of silence*

vow *verb* [T] to make a serious promise: *We vowed never to discuss the subject again.*

☆**vowel** /'vaʊəl/ *noun* [C] a sound that you make with your lips and teeth open; the sounds represented in English by the letters 'a', 'e', 'i', 'o' or 'u' ☛ Look at **consonant**.

voyage /'vɔɪdʒ/ *noun* [C] a long journey by sea or in space: *Magellan's voyages of discovery* o *a spacecraft on a voyage to Jupiter*

voyager /'vɔɪdʒə(r)/ *noun* [C] a person who makes a voyage

vulgar /'vʌlgə(r)/ *adj* **1** not having or showing good taste¹(5) or good manners; not educated: *He said my accent sounded vulgar.* **2** rude or likely to offend people: *a vulgar joke* o *a vulgar gesture* —**vulgarity** /vʌl'gærətɪ/ *noun* [C,U] (*pl* **vulgarities**)

vulnerable /'vʌlnərəbl/ *adj* **vulnerable (to sth/sb)** easy to attack, hurt or defeat; open to danger: *Poor organization left the troops vulnerable to enemy attack.* o *She felt lonely and vulnerable, living on her own in the big city.* ☛ The opposite is **invulnerable**. —**vulnerability** /ˌvʌlnərə'bɪlətɪ/ *noun* [U]: *This attack draws attention to the vulnerability of old people living alone.*

vulture /'vʌltʃə(r)/ *noun* [C] a large bird that has no feathers on its head or neck and that eats the flesh of dead animals

Ww

W, w /ˈdʌblju:/ *noun* [C] (*pl* **W's**; **w's**) the twenty-third letter of the English alphabet: *'Water' begins with (a) 'W'.*

wacky /ˈwækɪ/ *adj* (**wackier**; **wackiest**) (*informal*) exciting, new and rather crazy: *a wacky comedian*

wad /wɒd/ *noun* [C] **1** a lump or ball of soft material that is used for blocking sth, keeping sth in place, etc: *The nurse used a wad of cotton wool to stop the bleeding.* **2** a large number of papers or banknotes in a pile or rolled together

waddle /ˈwɒdl/ *verb* [I] to walk with short steps, leaning to one side then the other, like a duck: *A small, fat person waddled past.*

wade /weɪd/ *verb* [I] to walk with difficulty through fairly deep water, mud, etc: (*figurative*) *She had to wade through three thick books before she could write the essay.*

wafer /ˈweɪfə(r)/ *noun* [C] a very thin, crisp biscuit

waffle¹ /ˈwɒfl/ *noun* [C] a small, crisp cake, made of flour, eggs and milk, that has a pattern of squares on it and is often eaten warm with a sweet sauce (**syrup**)

waffle² /ˈwɒfl/ *verb* [I] (*Brit informal*) to talk or write for much longer than necessary without saying anything important: *Don't waffle, get to the point.* —**waffle** *noun* [U]: *The last two paragraphs of your essay are just waffle.*

waft /wɒft; *US* wæft/ *verb* [I,T] to move lightly through the air; to make sth move in this way: *The smell of her perfume wafted through the room.*

wag /wæg/ *verb* [I,T] (**wagging**; **wagged**) to shake up and down or move from side to side: *The dog is wagging his tail.*

☆ **wage¹** /weɪdʒ/ *noun* **1** [sing] the amount of money paid for a week's work: *What's the average wage in this country?* **2** [plural] the pay you receive: *Our wages are paid every Thursday.* ☛ Wage in the singular is mainly used to talk about the amount of money paid or when the word is combined with another, for example 'wage packet', 'wage rise', etc. Wages in the plural means the money itself: *I have to pay the rent out of my wages.* Look at the note at **pay¹**.

wage² /weɪdʒ/ *verb* [T] **wage sth (against/on sb/sth)** to begin and continue sth, especially a war: *to wage war* ○ *The police are waging a campaign against illegal drugs.*

waggle /ˈwægl/ *verb* [I,T] (*informal*) to move up and down or from side to side with quick, short movements; to make sth move in this way: *Can you waggle your ears?*

wagon (*also* **waggon**) /ˈwægən/ *noun* [C] **1** a vehicle with four wheels that is pulled by horses, etc and used for transporting things **2** (*US* **freight car**) an open railway truck used for transporting goods: *coal transported in goods wagons*

waif /weɪf/ *noun* [C] a child or animal who has nowhere to live and is not looked after

wail /weɪl/ *verb* **1** [I,T] to cry or complain in a loud, high voice: *the sound of children wailing* ○ *'Won't somebody help me?', she wailed.* **2** [I] to make a sound like this: *sirens wailing in the streets outside*

wail *noun* [C] a loud cry of pain or sadness; a sound similar to this: *the wails of a child* ○ *the wail of sirens*

☆ **waist** /weɪst/ *noun* [C, usually sing] **1** the part around the middle of the body between the stomach and the hips (and often narrower than them): *What's your waist measurement?* ○ *a 26-inch waist* ○ *She put her arms around his waist.* ☛ picture on page A8. **2** the part of a piece of clothing that goes round the waist

ˈwaistline *noun* [C, usually sing] **1** the measurement or size of the body around the waist: *a slim waistline* **2** the part of a piece of clothing that fits around or close to the waist: *a dress with a high waistline*

waistcoat /ˈweɪskəʊt; *US* ˈweskət/ (*US* **vest**) *noun* [C] a piece of clothing with buttons down the front and no sleeves that is often worn under a jacket as part of a man's suit ☛ picture on page A11.

☆ **wait¹** /weɪt/ *verb* [I] **1 wait (for sb/sth) (to do sth)** to remain in a particular place, and not do anything until sb/sth arrives or until sth happens: *Wait here. I'll be back in a few minutes.* ○ *Have you been waiting long?* ○ *If I'm a bit late, can you wait for me?* ○ *I wrote to them a few weeks ago and I'm still waiting for a reply.* ○ *I'm waiting to see the doctor.* ○ *He's waiting for them to tell him whether he got the job or not.* ○ *I can't wait* (= I am very keen) *to find out what happens at the end.* ☛ Compare **wait** and **expect**: *I was expecting him to be there at 7.30 but at 8 I was still waiting.* ○ *I'm waiting for the exam results but I'm not expecting to pass.* If you **wait**, you pass the time often doing little else, until sth happens: *I waited outside the theatre until they arrived.* If you **expect** sth, you believe that sth will happen: *I'm expecting a reply from them soon, because it's a month since I wrote.* **2** to be left or delayed until a later time; not to be done or dealt with immediately: *Is this matter urgent or can it wait?*

(IDIOMS) **keep sb waiting** to make sb wait: *I'm sorry if I've kept you waiting.*

wait and see to wait and find out what will happen (perhaps before deciding to do sth)

p	b	t	d	k	g	tʃ	dʒ	f	v	θ	ð
pen	bad	tea	did	cat	got	chin	June	fall	van	thin	then

wait your turn to wait until the time when you are allowed to do sth

(PHRASAL VERBS) **wait about/around** to stay in a place doing nothing because sb or sth is late

wait behind to stay in a place after others have left it

wait in to stay at home because you are expecting sb to come or sth to happen: *I waited in all evening but she didn't phone.*

wait on sb to bring food, drink etc to sb, usually in a restaurant

wait up (for sb) not go to bed because you are waiting for sb to come home: *I won't be back until very late, so don't wait up.*

'waiting-list noun [C] a list of people who are waiting for sth that will be available in the future: *to put sb's name on the waiting-list*

'waiting-room noun [C] a room at a doctor's surgery, railway station, etc where people can sit and wait

☆ **wait²** /weɪt/ noun [C, usually sing] **a wait (for sth/sb)** a period of time when you wait: *a short/long wait*

☆ **waiter** /'weɪtə(r)/ (feminine **waitress**) noun [C] a person whose job is to take orders from customers and bring food and drink to them in a restaurant, hotel dining-room, etc

waive /weɪv/ verb [T] (formal) to state that a rule, etc need not be obeyed; to give up a right to sth: *The management waived the no-smoking rule in the office for the annual party.* ○ *She signed a contract in which she waived all rights to her husband's money.*

☆ **wake¹** /weɪk/ verb (pt **woke** /wəʊk/; pp **woken** /'wəʊkən/) **1** [I] **wake (up)** to stop being asleep: *I woke early in the morning and got straight out of bed.* ○ *Wake up! It's nearly 8 o'clock!* **2** [T] **wake sb (up)** to make sb stop sleeping: *Could you wake me up at 7.30 tomorrow morning, please?* **3** [T] **wake sb/sth up** to make sb/sth become more lively or active: *She always has some coffee to wake her up when she gets to work.*

(PHRASAL VERB) **wake up to sth** to become aware of sth: *By the time he had woken up to the danger, it was too late.*

waken /'weɪkən/ verb [I,T] (formal) to wake up or to make sb/sth wake up: *She wakened from a deep sleep.* ○ *Shh. You'll waken the baby!*

wake² /weɪk/ noun [C] the track that a moving ship leaves behind on the surface of the water

(IDIOM) **in the wake of sth** following or happening after sth, often as a result of it: *The floods brought a great deal of suffering in their wake.*

☆ **walk¹** /wɔːk/ verb **1** [I] to move along on foot at a fairly slow speed: *Our little girl is just learning to walk.* ○ *The dog walked in and lay down.* ○ *'How did you get here? By bus?' 'No, I walked.'* ○ *The children ran ahead as we walked to the beach.* ○ *He walked with a limp.* ○ *Are the shops within walking distance?* (= are they close enough to walk to?) **2** [I] to move in this way for exercise or pleasure ☞ **Go walking** is a common way of talking about taking long walks for pleasure: *I often go walking in the Alps in the summer.* Look at the note at **walk²**. **3** [T] to walk with sb/sth; to guide or help sb to walk: *I'll walk you home if you don't want to go on your own.* ○ *The park was full of people walking their dogs.* **4** [T] to go along or through sth on foot: *He walked the streets all night.*

(PHRASAL VERBS) **walk off with sth 1** to win sth easily: *She walked off with all the prizes.* **2** to take sth; to take sth that does not belong to you by mistake: *When I got home I realized that I had walked off with her pen.*

walk out (of sth) to leave suddenly and angrily: *She walked out of the meeting in disgust.*

walk out on sb (informal) to leave sb for ever: *He walked out on his wife and children after 15 years of marriage.*

walk over sb (informal) **1** to defeat sb completely: *He played brilliantly and walked all over his opponent.* **2** to deal with sb as if he/she is not important: *I don't know why she lets her husband walk over her like that.*

walk up (to sb/sth) to approach (sb/sth): *He walked up to her and asked her if she wanted to dance.*

walker noun [C] a person who walks: *a fast walker* ○ *This area is very popular with walkers.*

'walking-stick (also **stick**) noun [C] a stick that you use to lean on if you have difficulty walking ☞ picture at **crutch**.

'Walkman noun [C] (pl **Walkmans**) (trade mark) a small cassette player with earphones that you can carry round with you

'walk-over noun [C] an easy win

☆ **walk²** /wɔːk/ noun **1** [C] a trip on foot for pleasure, exercise, etc: *We went for a walk in the country.* ○ *I'm just going to take the dog for a walk.* ☞ We use **go for a walk** when we are talking about a short walk that we take for pleasure. When we mean a long walk, of perhaps a day or more and for which you need special boots, etc, we use **go walking**. **2** [sing] the time taken to go somewhere on foot; the distance to a place on foot: *The hotel is five minutes' walk from the station.* **3** [sing] a way or style of walking: *He has a funny walk.* **4** [sing] the speed of walking: *She slowed to a walk.* **5** [C] a route for walking for pleasure: *From here there's a lovely walk through the woods.*

(IDIOM) **a walk of life** position in society: *She has friends from many different walks of life.*

walkie-talkie /ˌwɔːkɪ'tɔːkɪ/ noun [C] (informal) a small radio that you can carry with you and use to talk and listen to sb: *The policeman called for help on his walkie-talkie.*

☆ **wall** /wɔːl/ noun [C] **1** a solid, upright structure made of stone, brick, etc that is built round an area of land to protect it or to show a boundary: *There is a high wall all around the prison.* ☞ picture at **fence**. **2** one of the sides of a room or building joining the ceiling and the floor: *You could hear the people in the next room talking because the wall was so thin.* ○ *He put the poster up on the wall.*

(IDIOM) **up the wall** extremely angry: *She went up the wall when I turned up an hour late.*

walled adj surrounded by a wall: *an ancient walled city*

'wallpaper noun [U] paper with a pattern on it

that you stick to the walls of a room —**wallpaper** verb [T]: *We spent the weekend wallpapering the bedroom.*

wall-to-wall adj, adv (used especially about a carpet) covering the whole floor of a room

☆ **wallet** /'wɒlɪt/ (*US* **billfold**; **pocket-book**) noun [C] a small, flat, folding case in which you keep banknotes, credit cards, etc ☞ Look at **purse**.

wallop /'wɒləp/ verb [T] (*informal*) to hit sb/sth very hard

wallow /'wɒləʊ/ verb [I] **wallow (in sth) 1** to lie and roll around in water, etc: *I spent an hour wallowing in a hot bath.* **2** to take great pleasure in sth (a feeling, situation, etc): *He seems to wallow in self-pity.*

wally /'wɒlɪ/ noun [C] (*pl* **wallies**) (*Brit informal*) a silly person; a fool

walnut /'wɔːlnʌt/ noun [C] a nut that you can eat, with a hard brown shell that is in two halves ☞ picture at **nut**.

walrus /'wɔːlrəs/ noun [C] a large animal that lives in the sea in Arctic regions. It is similar to a seal but has two long teeth (**tusks**) coming out of its face.

waltz /wɔːls; *US* wɔːlts/ noun [C] a dance that you do with a partner, to music which has a rhythm of three beats; the music for this dance: *a Strauss waltz*

waltz verb [I] **1** to dance a waltz: *They waltzed around the floor.* **2** (*informal*) to move easily, carelessly or confidently: *You can't just waltz in and expect your meal to be ready for you.*

wan /wɒn/ adj very pale and looking ill or tired

wand /wɒnd/ noun [C] a thin stick that magicians, etc hold when they are doing magic: *I wish I could wave a magic wand and make everything better.*

☆ **wander** /'wɒndə(r)/ verb **1** [I,T] to move slowly around a place or to go from place to place with no particular purpose: *We spent a pleasant day wandering around the town.* ○ *He was found in a confused state, wandering the streets.* **2** [I] **wander (away/off); wander (from/off sth)** to leave a place or the path that you were on: *We must stay together while visiting the town so I don't want anybody to wander off.* ○ (*figurative*) *I seem to have wandered off the subject – what was I talking about?* **3** [I] (used about sb's mind, thoughts, etc) to stop concentrating; to be unable to stay on one subject: *The lecture was so boring that my attention began to wander.* ○ *The old man's mind is wandering. He doesn't know where he is any more.*

wane /weɪn/ verb [I] **1** (used about the moon) to appear to become smaller **2** to become less powerful, less important, smaller or weaker: *Britain's influence on world events has been waning for years.*

wangle /'wæŋgl/ verb [T] (*informal*) to get sth by finding a way of persuading or tricking sb: *Somehow he wangled a day off to meet me.*

wanna /'wɒnə/ a way of writing 'want to' or 'want a' to show that sb is speaking in an informal way or with a special accent: *I wanna go home now.* ☞ Look at the note at **gonna**.

☆ **want¹** /wɒnt; *US* wɔːnt/ verb [T] **1** to desire; to wish for: *He wants a new bike.* ○ *Do you want anything else?* ○ *What do they want for breakfast?* ○ *Is there anything you want to watch on television?* ○ *I don't want to discuss it now.* ○ *I want you to phone me when you get there.* ○ *The boss wants this letter typed.* ○ *I don't want Emma going out on her own at night.* ○ *They want Stevens as captain.* ☞ **Want** and **would like** are similar in meaning, but 'would like' is more polite: *'I want a drink!' screamed the child.* ○ *'Would you like some more tea, Mrs Jones?'* **2** to need or require sth: *The button on my shirt wants sewing on.* ○ *The house wants a new coat of paint.* **3** (*informal*) (used as a warning, as advice, etc) should or ought to: *He wants to be more careful about what he tells people.* ○ *If you're bored, you want to go out more often.* **4** (usually passive) to need sb to be in a particular place or for a particular reason: *Mrs Lewis, you are wanted on the phone.* ○ *She is wanted by the police* (= the police are looking for her because she is suspected of committing a crime).

☆ **want²** /wɒnt; *US* wɔːnt/ noun **1** [C] desire or need for sth; sth you desire or need: *All our wants were satisfied.* **2** [U,sing] **want of sth** a lack of sth: *Want of a proper water supply has resulted in disease and death.* ○ *I took the job for want of a better offer.*

wanton /'wɒntən; *US* 'wɔːn-/ adj (used about an action) done in order to hurt sb or damage sth for no good reason

☆ **war** /wɔː(r)/ noun **1** [U] a state of fighting between different countries or groups within countries, using armies and weapons: *war and peace* ○ *The Prime Minister announced that the country was at war.* ○ *to declare war* (= announce that a war has started) ○ *When war broke out, thousands of men volunteered for the army.* ○ *civil war* (= fighting between different groups in one country) **2** [C] a period of military fighting: *the Second World War* ○ *He was killed in the war.* ○ *to fight a war* **3** [C,U] a struggle; very strong competition between groups of people: *a price war among oil companies* **4** [sing] **a war (against sb/sth)** efforts to end sth: *the war against organized crime*

warfare /'wɔːfeə(r)/ noun [U] methods of fighting a war; types of war: *guerrilla warfare* ○ *nuclear warfare*

warlike /'wɔːlaɪk/ adj liking to fight or good at fighting: *a warlike nation*

'warpath noun
(IDIOM) **(be/go) on the warpath** (*informal*) to be very angry and ready to quarrel or fight

'warship noun a ship for use in war

'wartime noun [U] a period of time during which there is a war: *wartime Britain*

warble /'wɔːbl/ verb [I] (used usually about a bird) to sing gently, varying the notes up and down

☆ **ward** /wɔːd/ noun [C] **1** a separate part or room in a hospital often for a particular group of patients: *the children's ward* **2** one of the sections into which a town is divided for elections **3** a child who is under the protection of a court of law; a child whose parents are dead and who is cared for by another adult (**guardian**)

ward verb

iː	ɪ	e	æ	ɑː	ɒ	ɔː	ʊ	uː	ʌ
see	sit	ten	hat	arm	got	saw	put	too	cup

(PHRASAL VERB) **ward sb/sth off** to keep away sb/sth that is dangerous or unpleasant: *They lit a fire to ward off wild animals.*

warden /'wɔ:dn/ *noun* [C] **1** a person whose job is to check that rules are obeyed or to look after the people in a particular place: *a traffic warden* (= a person who checks that cars are not parked in the wrong place) o *the warden of a youth hostel* **2** (*US*) the governor of a prison

warder /'wɔ:də(r)/ *noun* [C] (*Brit*) a prison guard

wardrobe /'wɔ:drəʊb/ *noun* [C] **1** a large cupboard in which you can hang your clothes **2** a person's collection of clothes: *I need a whole new wardrobe.*

ware /weə(r)/ *noun* **1** [U] (in compounds) made from a particular type of material or suitable for a particular use: *a hardware shop* (= one that sells tools, household equipment, etc) o *an earthenware pot* **2 wares** [plural] (*old-fashioned*) goods offered for sale

warehouse /'weəhaʊs/ *noun* [C] a building where large quantities of goods are stored before being sent to shops

warfare ⇨ WAR

warily, wariness ⇨ WARY

☆ **warm¹** /wɔ:m/ *adj* **1** having a temperature that is fairly high, between cool and hot: *Are you warm enough or would you like me to put the heating on?* o *It's quite warm in the sunshine.* o *I jumped up and down to keep my feet warm.* ☛ Look at the note at **hot**(1). **2** (used about clothing) preventing you from getting cold: *Take plenty of warm clothes.* **3** friendly; kind and pleasant; sincere: *I was given a very warm welcome.* **4** creating a pleasant, comfortable feeling: *warm colours* —**warmly** *adv*: *warmly dressed* o *She thanked him warmly for his help.*

warmth /wɔ:mθ/ *noun* [U] **1** a fairly high temperature or effect created by this, especially when it is pleasant: *She felt the warmth of the sun on her face.* **2** friendliness or kindness: *I was touched by the warmth of their welcome.*

warm-'hearted *adj* kind and friendly

☆ **warm²** /wɔ:m/ *verb* [I,T] **warm (sb/sth) (up)** to become or to make sb/sth become warm or warmer: *It was cold earlier but it's beginning to warm up now.* o *I sat in front of the fire to warm up.* o *There's some meat left over from lunch, so we can warm it up* (= heat it again) *tonight.*
(PHRASAL VERBS) **warm to/towards sb** to begin to like sb
warm to sth to become more interested in sth
warm up to prepare for sth by practising gently: *The team warmed up before the match.*

warm³ /wɔ:m/ *noun* [sing] **the warm** a warm place or atmosphere: *It's awfully cold out here – I want to go back into the warm.*

☆ **warn** /wɔ:n/ *verb* [T] **1 warn sb (of sth); warn sb about/against sb/sth; warn sb against doing sth** to tell sb to be careful or aware of sth, often unpleasant or dangerous, that exists or might happen: *When I saw the car coming I tried to warn him, but it was too late.* o *The government is warning (the public) of possible terrorist attacks.* o *The radio warned people about delays on the roads this morning.* o *They put up a red flag to warn you against swimming in the sea here.* o *She warned me that he was not an easy man to work for.* **2** to advise sb (not) to do sth: *I warned you not to trust him.*

warning *noun* [C,U] something that tells you to be careful or tells you about sth before it happens: *There was a warning on the gate: 'Beware of the dog'.* o *Your employers can't dismiss you without warning.* o *He gave me no warning of his arrival.*

warp /wɔ:p/ *verb* [I,T] to become bent and out of shape (because of heat or damp); to make sth become like this: (*figurative*) *His view of life had been warped by his unhappy experiences.* —**warped** *adj*: *the killer's warped* (= abnormal) *mind*

warrant /'wɒrənt; *US* 'wɔ:r-/ *noun* [C] a written statement that gives sb the authority to do sth: *a search warrant* (= a document that allows the police to search a house)

warrant *verb* [T] (*formal*) to make sth seem right or necessary; to deserve: *I don't think her behaviour warrants such criticism.*

warranty /'wɒrənti; *US* 'wɔ:r-/ *noun* [C,U] (*pl* **warranties**) a written statement that you get when you buy sth, which promises to repair or replace it if it is broken or does not work ☛ Look at **guarantee**.

warrior /'wɒrɪə(r)/; *US* 'wɔ:r-/ *noun* [C] (*old-fashioned formal*) a person who fights in battle; a soldier

wart /wɔ:t/ *noun* [C] a small hard dry lump that sometimes grows on the face or body

wary /'weərɪ/ *adj* (**warier; wariest**) **wary (of sb/sth)** careful because you are uncertain or afraid of sth: *He was wary of accepting the suggestion in case it meant more work for him.* —**warily** /-rəlɪ/ *adv*

was ⇨ BE

☆ **wash¹** /wɒʃ; *US* wɔ:ʃ/ *verb* **1** [I,T] to clean sb/sth/yourself with water and often soap: *You'll have to wash this jumper by hand.* o *Wash and dress quickly or you'll be late!* (= wash yourself). o *I'll wash, you dry* (= wash the dishes). ☛ Look at the note at **clean²**. **2** [I] (used about water) to flow in the direction mentioned: *I let the waves wash over my feet.* **3** [T] to carry sth by the movement of water: *The current washed the ball out to sea.* **4** [I] to be able to be washed without being damaged: *Does this material wash well, or does the colour come out?*
(IDIOM) **wash your hands of sb/sth** to refuse to be responsible for sb/sth any longer
(PHRASAL VERBS) **wash sb/sth away** (used about water) to carry sb/sth away: *The floods had washed away the path.*
wash (sth) off to make (sth) disappear from sth by washing: *Go and wash that make-up off!*
wash out to be removed from a material by washing: *These grease marks won't wash out.*
wash sth out to wash sth or the inside of sth in order to remove dirt: *I'll just wash out these jeans so that they're ready for tomorrow.*
wash (sth) up 1 (*Brit*) to wash the plates, knives, forks, etc after a meal: *Whose turn is it to wash up?* o *Don't forget to wash the saucepans up.* **2** (*US*) to wash your face and hands: *Go and*

wash up quickly and put on some clean clothes. **3** (often passive) (used about water) to carry sth to land and leave it there: *Police found the girl's body washed up on the beach.*

washable /-əbl/ *adj* that can be washed without being damaged

'wash-basin (*also* **basin**) *noun* [C] a large bowl for water that has taps and is fixed to a wall, in a bathroom, etc ☞ picture at **plug**. Look at **sink**.

'wash-cloth *noun* [C] (*US*) = FACE-CLOTH

,washed 'out *adj* tired and pale: *They arrived looking washed out after their long journey.*

'washout *noun* [C] (*informal*) a person or thing that is a complete failure

'washroom *noun* [C] (*US*) a room with a toilet ☞ Look at the note at **toilet**.

☆ **wash²** /wɒʃ/ *noun* **1** [C, usually sing] an act of cleaning or being cleaned with water: *I'd better go and have a wash before dinner.* **2** [sing] the waves caused by the movement of a ship through water

(IDIOM) **in the wash** being washed: *'Where's my red T-shirt?' 'It's in the wash.'*

☆ **washing** /'wɒʃɪŋ/; *US* wɔː-/ *noun* [U] **1** clothes that need to be washed or are being washed: *Could you put the washing in the machine?* ○ *a pile of dirty washing* **2** the act of cleaning clothes, etc with water: *I usually do the washing on Mondays.*

'washing-machine *noun* [C] an electric machine for washing clothes

'washing-powder *noun* [U] soap in the form of powder for washing clothes

,washing-'up *noun* [U] the work of washing the plates, knives, forks, etc after a meal: *I'll do the washing-up.* ○ *washing-up liquid*

wasn't *short for* WAS NOT

wasp /wɒsp/ *noun* [C] a black and yellow flying insect that can sting ☞ picture at **insect**.

wastage /'weɪstɪdʒ/ *noun* [U] (*formal*) using too much of sth; the amount that is lost

☆ **waste¹** /weɪst/ *verb* [T] **1 waste sth (on sb/sth)** to use or spend sth in a careless way or for sth that is not necessary: *She wastes a lot of money on cigarettes.* ○ *He wasted his time at university because he didn't work hard.* **2** (usually passive) to be too good, intelligent, etc for sb/sth: *Expensive wine is wasted on me. I don't know anything about it.*

wasted *adj* not necessary or successful: *a wasted journey*

☆ **waste²** /weɪst/ *noun* **1** [sing,U] an action that involves not using sth carefully or using sth in an unnecessary way: *If he gives up acting it will be a waste of great talent.* ○ *The seminar was a waste of time – I'd heard it all before.* **2** [U] material, food, etc that is not needed and is therefore thrown away: *nuclear waste* ○ *A lot of household waste can be recycled and reused.* ☞ Look at **rubbish**. **3 wastes** [plural] (*formal*) large areas of land that are not lived in and not cultivated: *the wastes of the Sahara desert*

(IDIOM) **go to waste** to be unused, thrown away and wasted: *I can't bear to see good food going to waste!*

wasteful /-fl/ *adj* using more of sth than necessary; causing waste: *a costly and wasteful advertising campaign*

waste³ /weɪst/ *adj* (*only before* a noun) **1** (used about land) not used or not suitable for use; not looked after: *There's an area of waste ground outside the town where people dump their rubbish.* **2** no longer useful; to be thrown away: *waste material*

,waste 'paper *noun* [U] paper that is not wanted and is to be thrown away

,waste-'paper basket (*US* **'waste-basket**; **'waste-bin**) *noun* [C] a basket or other container in which you put paper, etc which is to be thrown away ☞ picture at **bin**.

☆ **watch¹** /wɒtʃ/ *noun* [C] a small instrument that shows you what time it is. You wear it on a strap on your wrist: *a gold watch* ○ *a digital watch* ○ *to wind up/set your watch* ○ *My watch is a bit fast/slow* (= shows a time that is later/earlier than the correct time). ☞ picture at **clock**.

☆ **watch²** /wɒtʃ/ *verb* **1** [I,T] to look carefully at sb/sth: *'Would you like to play too?' 'No thanks. I'll just watch.'* ○ *I watched in horror as the car swerved and crashed.* ○ *I'm watching to see how you do it.* ○ *We watch television most evenings.* ○ *Watch what she does next.* ○ *We went to watch John rowing.* ○ *I watched him open the door and walk away.* ○ *Detectives are watching the suspect day and night.* **2** [I,T], **watch (for sth)** to pay very careful attention to a situation; to observe: *Doctors are watching for further signs of the disease.* **3** [T] to be careful about sb/sth in order to do the right thing or keep control: *You'd better watch what you say to her. She gets upset very easily.*

(IDIOM) **watch your step** ⇒ STEP

(PHRASAL VERBS) **watch out** to be careful because of possible danger or trouble: *Watch out! There's a car coming.* ○ *If you don't watch out you'll lose your job.*

watch out for sb/sth to look carefully and be ready for sb/sth: *Watch out for snakes if you walk through the fields.*

watch over sb/sth to look after or protect sb/sth: *For two weeks she watched over the sick child.*

watch³ /wɒtʃ/ *noun* [sing] a person or group of people whose job is to guard and protect a place or a person: *The police put a watch on the suspect's house.*

(IDIOMS) **keep a close watch on sb/sth** ⇒ CLOSE³

keep watch to guard or to look out for danger

watchful /-fl/ *adj* careful to notice things

'watchdog *noun* [C] a person or group whose job is to protect people's rights, especially in relation to large companies: *OFTEL, the telecommunications watchdog*

☆ **water¹** /'wɔːtə(r)/ *noun* **1** [U] the clear liquid that falls as rain and is in rivers, seas and lakes: *a glass of water* ○ *The bath water's too hot.* ○ *All the rooms have hot and cold running water.* ○ *The pipe burst and water poured out everywhere.* ○ *drinking water* ○ *tap water* ○ *mineral water*

p	b	t	d	k	g	tʃ	dʒ	f	v	θ	ð
pen	bad	tea	did	cat	got	chin	June	fall	van	thin	then

☛ When water is **heated** to 100° Celsius, it **boils** and becomes **steam**. When steam touches a cold surface, it **condenses** and becomes water again. When water is **cooled** below 0° Celsius, it **freezes** and becomes ice. If the temperature increases, the ice **melts**. When talking about **icy** weather becoming warmer, we say it **thaws**. Frozen food **thaws** or **defrosts** when we take it out of the freezer.

2 [U,plural] a large amount of water, especially the water in a lake, river or sea: *Don't go too near the edge or you'll fall in the water!* ○ *the clear blue waters of the Mediterranean* **3 waters** [plural] the sea near a particular country: *The ship was still in British waters.*
(IDIOMS) **pass water** ⇨ PASS²
under water 1 in and covered by water: *to swim under water* **2** covered by floods: *After the heavy rain several fields were under water.*

'**water-colour** *noun* **1 water-colours** [plural] paints that are mixed with water, not oil **2** [C] a picture that has been painted with water-colours

'**watercress** *noun* [U] a type of plant with bunches of green leaves which have a strong taste and are often eaten in salads

'**waterfall** *noun* [C] a stream of water that falls down from a cliff, rock, etc

'**waterlogged** /-lɒgd; *US* -lɔ:gd/ *adj* **1** very wet: *Our boots sank into the waterlogged ground.* **2** (used about a boat) full of water and likely to sink

'**water melon** *noun* [C] a large, round fruit with a thick, green skin. It is pink or red inside with a lot of black seeds.

'**waterproof** *adj* that does not let water go through: *a waterproof anorak*

'**watershed** *noun* [C] an event or point which is important because it marks the beginning of sth new

'**water-ski** *verb* [I] to move across the surface of water standing on narrow boards (**water-skis**) and being pulled by a boat

'**watertight** *adj* **1** made so that water cannot get in or out **2** (used about an excuse, an agreement, an argument, etc) impossible to prove wrong; without any faults: *His alibi for the night of the murder was absolutely watertight.*

'**waterway** *noun* [C] a canal, river, etc along which boats or ships can travel

water² /'wɔ:tə(r)/ *verb* **1** [T] to give water to plants **2** [I] (used about the eyes or mouth) to fill with water: *The smoke in the room made my eyes water.* ○ *The food smelled so delicious that it made my mouth water.*
(PHRASAL VERB) **water sth down 1** to add water to a liquid in order to make it weaker **2** to change a statement, report, etc so that it is weaker

'**watering-can** /'wɔ:tərɪŋkæn/ *noun* [C] a container with a long pipe on one side which is used for watering plants

watery /'wɔ:təri/ *adj* **1** (used especially about food or drink) containing too much water; thin and weak **2** weak and pale: *watery sunshine*

watt /wɒt/ *noun* [C] a unit of electrical power: *a 60-watt light-bulb*

☆ **wave¹** /weɪv/ *verb* **1** [I,T] **wave (your hand) (at/to sb)** to move your hand from side to side in the air, usually to attract sb's attention or as you meet or leave sb: *She waved to me as the train left the station.* ○ *Who are you waving at?* **2** [T] **wave sth (at sb)**; **wave sth (about)** to hold sth in the air and move it from side to side: *The crowd were waving flags as the Queen came out.* ○ *She was talking excitedly and waving her arms about.* **3** [T] **wave sth (to sb)** to give a greeting (to sb) by waving your hand: *Wave goodbye to Granny, Tim.* **4** [I] to move gently up and down or from side to side: *The branches of the trees waved gently in the breeze.*
(PHRASAL VERBS) **wave sth aside** to decide not to pay attention to a comment, etc because you think it is not important

wave sb/sth away, on, etc to move your hand in a particular direction to show sb/sth which way to go: *There was a policeman in the middle of the road, waving us on.*

☆ **wave²** /weɪv/ *noun* [C] **1** a raised line of water moving on the surface of water, especially the sea: *boats bobbing about on the waves* ○ *A huge wave swept me off my feet.* ○ *We watched the waves roll in and break on the shore.* ○ (*figurative*) *a wave of tourists* ☛ picture at **beach**. **2** a sudden increase or spread of a feeling or type of behaviour: *There has been a wave of sympathy for the refugees.* ○ *A wave of strikes has hit the industry.* ☛ Look at **heatwave**. **3** a form in which some types of energy move, shaped like a wave on the sea: *sound waves* ○ *shock waves from the earthquake* **4** a gentle curve in hair: *Are your waves natural?* ☛ Look at **perm**. **5** a movement of sth, especially your hand, from side to side in the air: *With a wave of his hand, he said goodbye and left.*

wavy *adj* having curves: *wavy hair* ○ *a wavy line* ☛ picture at **hair** and **line**.

waveband /'weɪvbænd/ (*also* **band**) *noun* [C] a set of radio waves of similar length

wavelength /'weɪvleŋθ/ *noun* [C] **1** the distance between two sound waves **2** the length of wave on which a radio station broadcasts its programmes
(IDIOM) **on the same wavelength** ⇨ SAME¹

waver /'weɪvə(r)/ *verb* [I] **1** to become weak or uncertain: *He never wavered in his support for her.* **2 waver (between sth and sth)** to hesitate, especially when making a decision or choice **3** to move in an unsteady way: *His hand wavered as he reached for the gun.*

wax /wæks/ *noun* [U] **1** a substance made from fat or oil that melts easily and is used for making candles, polish, etc **2** a yellow substance like wax that is found in your ears

'**waxwork** *noun* [C] **1** a model of sb/sth, especially of a famous person, made of wax **2 waxworks** [with sing or pl verb] a place where wax models of famous people are shown to the public

☆ **way¹** /weɪ/ *noun* **1** [C] a path or road along which you can walk or travel: *the way in/out* ☛ Look at **highway**, **motorway** and **railway**. **2** [sing] the route along which you move or

The painting is the wrong way up.

would move if there were space: *There were some cows in the lane, blocking our way.* ○ *Get out of my way!* **3** [C, usually sing] the route you take to reach somewhere: *Can you tell me the way to James Street?* ○ *She lost her way and had to turn back.* ○ *We stopped on the way to Leeds for a meal.* ○ *Can I drive you home? It's on my way.* **4** [sing] a direction or position: *Look this way!* ○ *That painting is the wrong way up* (= with the wrong edge at the top). ○ *Are you sure these two words are the right way round?* (= in the right order?) ○ *Shouldn't you be wearing that hat the other way round?* (= facing in the other direction) ○ *He thought I was older than my sister but in fact it's the other way round* (= the opposite of what he thought). ☛ Look at **back to front**. **5** [sing] a distance in space or time: *It's a long way from London to Edinburgh.* ○ *Christmas is still a long way off.* **6** [C] a method, style or manner of doing sth; a habit: *What is the best way to learn a language?* ○ *I've discovered a brilliant way of losing weight!* ○ *There are various ways in which we can help.* ○ *They'll have to find the money one way or another.* ○ *He always does things his way.* ○ *She smiled in a friendly way.* ○ *As you get older, it becomes more difficult to change your ways.* **7** [C] a particular point or part of sth: *In some ways the meeting was very useful.* ○ *In a way, I rather like him.* ○ *Can I help you in any way?*

(IDIOMS) **be set in your ways** to be unable to change your habits, attitudes, etc

by the way (used for adding sth to the conversation) on a new subject: *Oh, by the way, I saw Mary in town yesterday.*

get/have your own way to get or do what you want, although others may want sth else

give way to break or fall down: *The branch of the tree suddenly gave way and came crashing down.*

give way (to sb/sth) 1 to stop or to allow sb/sth to go first: *Give way to traffic coming from the right.* **2** to allow sb to have what he/she wants although you did not at first agree with it: *We shall not give way to the terrorists' demands.*

go out of your way (to do sth) to make a special effort to do sth

in a big/small way (used for expressing the size or importance of an activity): *'Have you done any acting before?' 'Yes, but in a very small way.'* (= not very much)

in the way 1 blocking the road or path: *I can't get past. There's a big lorry in the way.* **2** not needed or wanted: *I felt rather in the way at my daughter's party.*

no way (*informal*) definitely not: *'Can we swim in the sea?' 'No way! Not in April!'*

under way having started and making progress: *Discussions between the two sides are now under way.*

a/sb's way of life the behaviour and customs that are typical of a person or group of people

way² /weɪ/ *adv* (*informal*) very far: *I finally found his name way down at the bottom of the list.*

☆ **we** /wiː/ *pron* (the subject of a verb; used for talking about the speaker and one or more other people): *We're going to the theatre.* ○ *We are both very pleased with the house.* ○ *We all left together.*

☆ **weak** /wiːk/ *adj* **1** (used about the body) having little strength or energy; not strong: *The child was weak with hunger.* ○ *Her legs felt weak.* ○ (*figurative*) *a weak economy* **2** likely to break: *That bridge is too weak to take heavy traffic.* **3** (used about a person's character) easy to influence; not firm: *He is too weak to be a good leader.* **4** (used about an argument, excuse, etc) that does not convince you or seem right; not strong: *She made some weak excuse about washing her hair tonight.* **5** not easy to see or hear; not definite or strong: *I heard a weak voice whispering for help.* ○ *She gave a weak smile.* **6** (used about liquids) containing a lot of water, not strong in taste: *weak tea* **7 weak (at/in/on sth)** not able to achieve a high standard in sth: *He's weak at Maths.* ○ *His maths is weak.*

weaken /ˈwiːkən/ *verb* [I,T] **1** to become less strong; to make sb/sth less strong: *The illness had left her weakened.* ○ *The building had been weakened by the earthquake.* **2** to become less certain about sth: *Their mother was weakening. 'Oh all right,' she said, 'You can go.'*
—**weakly** *adv*: *The little kitten struggled weakly to its feet.*

weakness *noun* **1** [U] the state of being weak: *They were relying on the enemy's weakness in the air.* **2** [C] a fault or lack of strength, especially in a person's character: *It's important to know your own strengths and weaknesses.* **3** [C, usually sing] **a weakness for sth/sb** a special and often foolish liking for sth/sb: *I have a weakness for chocolate.*

ˈweak form *noun* [C] a way of pronouncing a word when it is not emphasized

☆ **wealth** /welθ/ *noun* **1** [U] (owning) a lot of money, property, etc: *They were a family of enormous wealth.* **2** [sing] **a wealth of sth** a large number or amount of sth: *He has a wealth of experience in this area.*

wealthy *adj* (**wealthier**; **wealthiest**) having a lot of money, etc; rich

wean /wiːn/ *verb* [T] to start feeding a baby or young animal with other food as well as its mother's milk

☆ **weapon** /ˈwepən/ *noun* [C] an object which is used for fighting or for killing people, such as a gun, sword, bomb, etc

☆ **wear¹** /weə(r)/ *verb* (*pt* **wore** /wɔː(r)/; *pp* **worn** /wɔːn/) **1** [T] to have clothes, jewellery,

iː	ɪ	e	æ	ɑː	ɒ	ɔː	ʊ	uː	ʌ
see	sit	ten	hat	arm	got	saw	put	too	cup

wear etc on your body: *He was wearing a suit and tie.* o *I wear glasses for reading.* o *Would you like to wear my necklace?* o *to wear your hair short* **2** [T] to have a certain look on your face: *He was wearing an expression of delight.* **3** [I] to become thinner or damaged because of being used or rubbed a lot **4** [T] to make a hole, path, etc in sth by rubbing, walking, etc: *Put some slippers on or you'll wear a hole in your socks!* **5** [I] to last for a long time without becoming thinner or damaged: *This material wears well.* (IDIOM) **wear thin** to have less effect because of being used too much: *We've heard that story so often that it's beginning to wear thin.*
(PHRASAL VERBS) **wear (sth) away** to damage sth or to make it disappear over a period of time, by using, touching, etc it a lot; to disappear or become damaged in this way: *The writing on the floor of the church had worn away over the years.* o *The sea had worn the bottom of the cliffs away.*
wear (sth) down to become or to make sth smaller or shorter
wear sb/sth down to make sb/sth weaker by attacking, persuading, etc: *They wore him down with constant arguments until he changed his mind.*
wear off to become less strong or to disappear completely: *The effects of the drug wore off after a few hours.*
wear on (used about time) to pass slowly: *They got to know each other better as the summer wore on.*
wear (sth) out to become too thin or damaged to use any more; to cause sth to do this: *Children's shoes wear out very quickly.* o *You've worn out two pairs of jeans in the last six months!*
wear sb out to make sb very tired: *She wore herself out walking home with the heavy bags.* ☛ Look at **worn out**.

wear² /weə(r)/ *noun* [U] **1** wearing or being worn; use as clothing: *You'll need jeans and jumpers for everyday wear.* **2** (usually in compounds) things that you wear; clothes: *menswear* o *underwear* **3** long use which damages the quality or appearance of sth
(IDIOMS) **wear and tear** the damage caused by ordinary use
the worse for wear ⇨ WORSE

weary /'wɪəri/ *adj* (**wearier; weariest**) tired: *He gave a weary smile.* —**wearily** /'wɪərəli/ *adv* —**weariness** *noun* [U]

☆**weather¹** /'weðə(r)/ *noun* [U] the climate at a certain place and time, how much wind, rain, sunshine, etc there is and how hot or cold it is: *What was the weather like on holiday?* o *We'll go to the seaside if the weather stays fine.* o *They say that the weather won't change for the next few days.*
(IDIOMS) **make heavy weather of sth** ⇨ HEAVY
under the weather (*informal*) not very well
'weather-beaten *adj* made rough and often darker by the sun and wind: *the fishermen's weather-beaten faces*
'weather forecast *noun* [C] a description of the weather that is expected for the next day or few days ☛ **Rain** is drops of water that fall from the clouds. **Snow** is frozen rain. It is soft and white and often settles on the ground. **Sleet** is rain that is not completely frozen. **Hail** is rain frozen so hard that it feels and sounds like small stones falling. When it is only raining very slightly it is **drizzling**. When it is raining very hard it is **pouring**. **Fog** is like a cloud at ground level. It makes it difficult to see very far ahead. **Mist** is a very thin type of fog. Look also at **storm**.

weather² /'weðə(r)/ *verb* **1** [T] (used about a ship or a person) to pass safely through a storm or a difficult time **2** [I,T] to change in appearance (because of the effect of the sun, air or wind)

weave /wi:v/ *verb* [I,T] (*pt* **wove** /wəʊv/ or in sense 2 **weaved**; *pp* **woven** /'wəʊvn/ or in sense 2 **weaved**) **1** to make cloth, etc by passing threads under and over a set of threads that is fixed to a framework (**loom**): *woven cloth* **2** to change direction often when you are moving so that you are not stopped by anything: *He weaved in and out through the traffic.*

web /web/ *noun* [C] a type of fine net that a spider makes in order to catch small insects: *A spider spins webs.* ☛ picture at **spider**. Look at **cobweb**.

we'd /wi:d/ *short for* WE HAD, WE WOULD

☆**wedding** /'wedɪŋ/ *noun* [C] a marriage ceremony and often the meal or party that follows it (**the reception**): *I've been invited to his sister's wedding.* o *a wedding dress, guest, present, etc* o *a wedding ring* (= one that is placed on the third finger of the left hand during a marriage ceremony and worn to show that a person is married) o *a wedding anniversary*

☛ Look at **golden** and **silver wedding**. **Marriage** is the word for the state of being married to somebody. It can also be used for the ceremony, with the same meaning as **wedding**. The man who is getting married is the **bridegroom**, the woman is the **bride**. Other important people at the ceremony are the **best man** and the **bridesmaids**. A wedding can take place in church (a **church wedding**) or in a **registry office**.

wedge /wedʒ/ *noun* [C] a piece of wood, etc with one thick and one narrow end that you can push into a space, in order, for example, to keep things apart: *The door was kept open with a wedge.*

wedge *verb* [T] **1** to force sth apart or to prevent sth from moving by using a wedge: *to wedge a door open* **2** to force sth/sb to fit into a space: *The cupboard was wedged between the table and the door.*

☆**Wednesday** /'wenzdɪ/ *noun* [C,U] (*abbr* **Wed**) the day of the week after Tuesday and before Thursday ☛ For examples of the use of the days of the week in sentences, look at **Monday**.

wee¹ /wi:/ *adj* little, small: *a wee boy* o *I'm a wee bit tired.* ☛ This word is used especially by Scottish people.

wee² /wi:/ *noun* [C,U] (*informal*) (used by young children or when you are talking to

3:	ə	eɪ	əʊ	aɪ	aʊ	ɔɪ	ɪə	eə	ʊə
fur	ago	pay	home	five	now	join	near	hair	pure

weed /wiːd/ noun **1** [C] a wild plant that is not wanted in a garden because it prevents other plants from growing properly: *Our garden is full of weeds.* **2** [U] a mass of tiny green plants that floats on the surface of a pond or river **3** [C] (*informal*) a thin, weak person or sb who has a weak character: *You're not going out with that weed, are you?*
weed verb [I,T] to remove weeds from a piece of ground, etc
(PHRASAL VERB) **weed sth/sb out** to remove the things or people that you do not think are good enough: *He weeded out all the letters with spelling mistakes in them.*
weedy adj (**weedier**; **weediest**) (*informal*) thin and weak in appearance; of weak character: *a small weedy man*
☆ **week** /wiːk/ noun [C] **1** a period of seven days (usually beginning on Sunday and ending on Saturday or beginning on Monday and ending on Sunday): *We arrived last week.* ○ *Can I see you this week? No? How about next week?* ○ *He left two weeks ago.* ○ *I haven't seen her for a week.* ○ *I play tennis twice a week.* ○ *They'll be back in a week/in a week's time.* ○ *I was on holiday the week before last.* ○ *My course ends the week after next.* ☛ A period of two weeks is usually called a **fortnight**. **2** the part of the week when people go to work, etc, usually from Monday to Friday: *She works hard during the week so that she can enjoy herself at the weekend.* ○ *I work a 40-hour week.*
(IDIOMS) **today, tomorrow, Monday, etc week** seven days after today, tomorrow, Monday, etc
week in, week out every week without a rest or change
a week yesterday, last Monday, etc seven days before yesterday, Monday, etc: *They got married a week last Saturday.*
weekly adj, adv happening or appearing once a week or every week: *We are paid weekly.* ○ *a weekly report*
weekly noun [C] (pl **weeklies**) a newspaper or magazine that is published every week
'weekday /-deɪ/ noun [C] any day except Sunday (and usually Saturday): *I only work on weekdays.*
,week'end (*US* **'weekend**) noun [C] Saturday and Sunday: *What are you doing at the weekend?* ☛ In American English we say '**on the weekend**'
weep /wiːp/ verb [I,T] (pt, pp **wept** /wept/) (*formal*) to let tears fall because of strong emotion; to cry: *She wept at the news of his death.* ○ *to weep for joy* ○ *to weep tears of pity*
☆ **weigh** /weɪ/ verb **1** [T] to measure how heavy sth is, especially by using a machine (**scales**): *I weigh myself every day.* ○ *Can you weigh this parcel for me, please?* **2** [T] to have or show a certain weight: *I weigh 56 kilos.* **3** [T] **weigh sth (up)** to consider sth carefully: *You need to weigh up your chances of success.* **4** [T] **weigh sth (against sb/sth)** to consider whether one thing is better, more important, etc than another: *We shall weigh the advantages of the plan against the risks.* **5** [I] **weigh against (sb/sth)** to be considered important when sb/sth is being judged: *She didn't get the job because her lack of experience weighed against her.*
(PHRASAL VERBS) **weigh sb down** to make sb feel worried and sad: *weighed down by cares and responsibilities*
weigh sb/sth down to make it difficult for sb/sth to move (by being heavy): *I was weighed down by heavy shopping.*
weigh on sb/sth to make sb worry ☛ We also say **weigh on sb's mind**: *That problem has been weighing on my mind for a long time.*
weigh sb up to try and find out what a person is like so that you can form an opinion
☆ **weight¹** /weɪt/ noun **1** [U] the heaviness of sth or the amount that it weighs, especially as measured in kilos, etc: *In two months her weight has increased to 65 kilos.* ○ *I need to lose weight before my holidays* (= become thinner and less heavy). ○ *He's put on weight* (= got fatter). ○ *The weight of the snow broke the branch.* **2** [C] a piece of metal with a certain heaviness that can be used to weigh an amount, especially using scales. Weights are also used by athletes when they are training or in the sport of weightlifting: *a 500-gram weight* **3** [C] a heavy object: *The doctor has told me not to lift heavy weights.* **4** [sing] the worry that is caused by a problem: *Telling her the truth took a weight off his mind.*
(IDIOMS) **carry weight** ⇨ CARRY
pull your weight ⇨ PULL¹
weightless adj having no weight, especially when travelling in space —**weightlessness** noun [U]
weighty adj (**weightier**; **weightiest**) serious and important: *a weighty question*
'weightlifting noun [U] a sport in which heavy metal objects are lifted
weight² /weɪt/ verb [T] **1 weight sth (down) (with sth)** to hold sth down with a heavy object or objects: *to weight down a fishing net* **2** (usually passive) to organize sth so that a particular person or group has an advantage/disadvantage: *The system is weighted in favour of people with children.*
weir /wɪə(r)/ noun [C] a type of wall that is built across a river to stop or change the direction of the flow of water
weird /wɪəd/ adj **1** strange and frightening: *a weird noise* **2** (*informal*) not normal: *weird clothes, ideas, etc*
☆ **welcome** /'welkəm/ adj **1** received with pleasure; giving pleasure: *You're always welcome here.* ○ *welcome news* **2 welcome to sth/to do sth** allowed to do sth: *You're welcome to use our swimming-pool.* **3** we say that sb is welcome to sth if we do not want it ourselves: *Take the car if you want. You're welcome to it. It's always breaking down.*
(IDIOMS) **make sb welcome** to receive sb in a friendly way
you're welcome you don't need to thank me: *'Thank you for your help.' 'You're welcome.'*
welcome interj (an expression used for greet-

p	b	t	d	k	g	tʃ	dʒ	f	v	θ	ð
pen	bad	tea	did	cat	got	chin	June	fall	van	thin	then

ing a person who is arriving at a place): *Welcome to London!* ○ *Welcome home!*

welcome noun [C] a greeting to sb who has arrived: *Let's give a warm welcome to our next guest.*

welcome verb [T] **1** to greet sb when he/she arrives: *The children rushed to the door to welcome their father.* **2** to be pleased about sth and support it: *When I told my parents I wanted to go to university they welcomed the idea.*

weld /weld/ verb [I,T] to join pieces of metal by heating them and pressing them together

☆**welfare** /'welfeə(r)/ noun [U] **1** the good health and happiness of a person or group of people: *The doctor is concerned about the child's welfare.* **2** the help and care that is given to people who have problems with health, money, etc: *education and welfare services* **3** (*US*) = SOCIAL SECURITY

,**welfare 'state** noun [sing] (a country which has) a system organized by a government to help people who have no job, who are ill, etc

well¹ /wel/ noun [C] **1** a deep hole in the ground from which water is obtained: *to draw water from a well* **2** = OIL WELL

well verb [I] **well (out/up)** (used about a liquid) to come to the surface: *Tears welled up in her eyes*

☆**well²** /wel/ adj (**better** /'betə(r)/, **best** /best/) (not before a noun) **1** (looking or feeling) healthy: *'How are you?' 'I'm very well, thanks.'* ○ *This medicine will make you feel better.* ○ *Get well soon* (= written in a card that you send to somebody who is ill). **2** in a satisfactory state: *I hope all is well with you.*

(IDIOMS) **all very well (for sb)** (*informal*) (used for showing that you are not happy or do not agree with sth): *It's all very well for her to criticize* (= it's easy for her to criticize) *but it doesn't help the situation.*

(just) as well (to do sth) (used when you are talking about an action that might stop sth bad happening): *It would be just as well to ask his permission.* ☛ Look at **it is just as well (that)** at **just**.

☆**well³** /wel/ adv (**better** /'betə(r)/, **best** /best/) **1** in a good or satisfactory way: *You speak English very well.* ○ *I hope your work is going well.* ○ *Well done!* (= used when you are praising sb that sb has done) ○ *Did they treat you well?* ○ *The car is running much better since it was serviced.* **2** thoroughly, completely or carefully: *Shake the bottle well before opening.* **3** (used with *can, could, may* or *ought* to show that sth is probably true): *He might well be right.* **4** (used with *can't* and *couldn't* to show that sth is not sensible or reasonable): *I can't very well refuse to help them after all they've done for me.* **5** very much: *They arrived home well past midnight.* ○ *This book is well worth reading.*

(IDIOMS) **as well (as sb/sth)** in addition (to sb/sth): *Can I come as well?* ○ *He's worked in Japan as well as Italy.* ☛ Look at the note at **also**.

augur well/ill for sb/sth ⇨ AUGUR

be well out of sth to be lucky because you are not involved in sth: *They're still arguing, I'm glad we're well out of it.*

bode well/ill (for sb/sth) ⇨ BODE

do well 1 to be successful: *Their daughter has done well at university.* **2** to be getting better (after an illness): *Mr Brown is doing well after his operation.*

jolly well ⇨ JOLLY

may/might (just) as well (used for saying that sth can or should happen, especially when you have no choice): *I may as well tell you the truth – you'll find out anyway.*

mean well ⇨ MEAN¹

very well ⇨ VERY¹

well and truly completely: *We were well and truly lost.*

well/badly off ⇨ OFF¹

well off for sth having plenty of sth: *You're well off for space in your office.*

,**well-'balanced** adj **1** (used about a person) calm and sensible **2** (used about a meal, etc) containing enough of the healthy types of food your body needs: *a well-balanced diet*

,**well-be'haved** adj behaving in a way that most people think is correct

'**well-being** noun [U] a state of being healthy and happy

,**well 'done** adj (used about meat, etc) cooked for a long time

,**well-'dressed** adj wearing attractive and fashionable clothes

,**well-'earned** adj that you deserve, especially because you have been working hard

,**well-'fed** adj having good food regularly

,**well-in'formed** adj knowing a lot about one or several subjects

,**well-'kept** adj looked after very carefully so that it has a tidy appearance

,**well-'known** adj known by a lot of people; famous

,**well-'meaning** adj (used about a person) wanting to be kind or helpful, but often not having this effect

,**well-'meant** adj intended to be kind or helpful but not having this result

,**well-to-'do** adj wealthy; with a lot of money

'**well-wisher** noun [C] somebody who hopes that a person or thing will be successful

☆**well⁴** /wel/ interj **1** (used for showing surprise): *Well, look who's here!* **2** (used for expressing doubt, hesitation, etc): *'Do you like it?' 'Well, I'm not really sure.'* ○ *Her new boyfriend seems, well, a little strange.* **3** (used for showing that you are relieved): *Well, thank goodness you've arrived.* **4** (used when you begin the next part of a story or when you are thinking about what to say next): *Well, the next thing that happened was...* ○ *Well now, let me see...* **5** (*also* **oh well**) (used for showing that there is nothing you can do to change a situation): *Oh well, there's nothing we can do about it.*

we'll /wi:l/ short for WE SHALL, WE WILL

wellington /'welɪŋtən/ (*also* ,**wellington 'boot**, *informal* **welly** /'welɪ/ (*pl* **wellies**)) noun [C] (*Brit*) one of a pair of long rubber boots that you wear to keep your feet and the lower part of your legs dry: *a pair of wellingtons* ☞ picture at **shoe**.

☆**Welsh** /welʃ/ *adj* of Wales, its people or their language: *the Welsh coast* ○ *He's Welsh. He was born in Cardiff.*
Welsh *noun* **1** [U] the language of Wales ☞ Welsh is a Celtic language that English speakers cannot understand unless they have learnt it. **2 the Welsh** [plural] the people of Wales

went *pt* of GO¹
wept *pt, pp* of WEEP
were ⇨ BE
we're /wɪə(r)/ *short for* WE ARE

☆**west** /west/ *noun* [sing] (*abbr* **W**) **1** (*also* **the west**) one of the four main points of the compass; the direction you look towards in order to see the sun set: *Which way is west?* ○ *Rain is spreading from the west.* ○ *There's a road to the west of here.* ☞ picture at **north**. **2 the west; the West** the part of any country, city, etc that lies further towards the west than other parts: *I live in the west of Scotland.* ○ *The climate in the West is much wetter than the East.* **3 the West** the countries of North America and Western Europe

west (*also* **West**) *adj* in or towards the west, or from the west: *West London* ○ *the west wind*
west *adv* to or towards the west: *The island is five miles west of here.* ○ *to travel west*

westerly /'westəlɪ/ *adj* **1** to, towards or in the west: *in a westerly direction* **2** (used about winds) coming from the west

westward /'westwəd/ *adj* towards the west: *in a westward direction* —**westward** (*also* **westwards**) *adv*: *to fly westwards*

'westbound *adj* travelling or leading towards the west: *the westbound carriageway of the motorway*

the 'West Country *noun* [U] the south-west part of Britain

the ,West 'End *noun* [U] (*Brit*) the western part of central London where there are many shops, theatres, cinemas, etc

,**West 'Indian** *noun* [C] a person from the West Indies or whose family was originally from the West Indies

,**West 'Indian** *adj*: *the West Indian cricket team*
the ,West 'Indies *noun* [plural, with sing or pl verb] a group of islands in the Caribbean Sea that consists of the Bahamas, the Antilles and the Leeward and Windward Islands

☆**western** (*also* **Western**) /'westən/ *adj* **1** in or of the west: *the western United States* **2** from or connected with countries of the West: *the Western way of life*

western *noun* [C] a film or book about life in the past in the west of the United States
westerner *noun* [C] a person who was born or who lives in the West
westernize (*also* **westernise**) /-aɪz/ *verb* [T] to make a country or people more like the West, eg in the way people dress and behave: *Young people in our country are becoming westernized through watching American television*

☆**wet** /wet/ *adj* (**wetter**; **wettest**) **1** covered in a liquid, especially water: *wet clothes* ○ *Don't get your feet wet.* ☞ **Moist** means slightly wet. **Damp** is used to describe things that are slightly wet and feel unpleasant because of it: *Don't sit on the grass. It's damp.* **2** (used about the weather, etc) with a lot of rain: *a wet day* **3** (used about paint, etc) not yet dry or hard: *The ink is still wet.* **4** (used about a person) without energy, strength or courage
(IDIOMS) **a wet blanket** (*informal*) a person who spoils other people's fun, especially because he or she will not join in
wet through extremely wet
wet *noun* [sing] **the wet** rainy weather: *Come in out of the wet.*
wet *verb* (*pres part* **wetting** *pt, pp* **wet** or **wetted**) [T] **1** to make sth wet **2** (used especially of young children) to make yourself or your bed, clothes, etc wet by urinating: *Joe wet his trousers this morning.*

'wet suit *noun* [C] a rubber suit that covers the whole of the body, used by underwater swimmers and people doing sports in the water

we've /wiːv/ *short for* WE HAVE
whack /wæk; *US* hwæk/ *verb* [T] (*informal*) to hit sb/sth hard

whale

whale /weɪl; *US* hweɪl/ *noun* [C] a very large animal that lives in the sea and looks like a huge fish (but is, in fact, a mammal)
whaling *noun* [U] hunting whales
wharf /wɔːf; *US* hwɔːrf/ *noun* [C] (*pl* **wharves** /wɔːvz; *US* hwɔːrvz/) a platform made of stone or wood at the side of a river where ships and boats can be tied up

☆**what** /wɒt; *US* hwɒt/ *det, pron* **1** (used for asking for information about sb/sth): *What time is it?* ○ *What kind of music do you like?* ○ *She asked him what he was doing.* ○ *What's their phone number?* ☞ Look at the note at **which**. **2** the things (that); all the...: *What he says is true.* ○ *I believe what he said.* ○ *Is it true what he said?* ○ *I haven't got much, but you can borrow what money I have.* **3** (used for showing surprise, pleasure, etc): *What a beautiful day!* ☞ **What** can also be used alone, to express surprise: *'I've just spent a thousand pounds.' 'What!'*
(IDIOMS) **how/what about...?** ⇨ ABOUT²
what for for what purpose; why: *What's this little switch for?* ○ *What did you say that for?*
what if...? what would happen if...?: *What if the car breaks down?*

☆**whatever** /wɒt'evə(r); *US* hwɒt-/ *adj, pron* **1** any or every; anything or everything: *You can say whatever you like.* ○ *He took whatever*

iː	ɪ	e	æ	ɑː	ɒ	ɔː	ʊ	uː	ʌ
see	sit	ten	hat	arm	got	saw	put	too	cup

help he could get. **2** no matter what: *I still love you, whatever you may think.* ○ *Whatever she says, she doesn't really mean it.* **3** (used for expressing surprise or worry) what: *Whatever's the matter?* ○ *Whatever could have happened to them?*

(IDIOM) **or whatever** (*informal*) or any other or others of a similar kind: *You don't need to wear anything smart – jeans and a sweater or whatever.*

whatever (*also* **whatsoever**) *adv* at all: *I've no reason whatever to doubt him.* ○ *'Any questions?' 'None whatsoever.'*

☆**wheat** /wiːt; *US* hwiːt/ *noun* [U] **1** a type of grain which can be made into flour **2** the plant which produces this grain: *a field of wheat*

☆**wheel** /wiːl; *US* hwiːl/ *noun* **1** [C] a circular object that turns around a rod that is fixed to its centre. Wheels are used to make a car, bicycle, etc move or to make a machine work **2** [usually sing] = STEERING WHEEL: *Her husband was at the wheel when the accident happened* (= he was driving).

wheel *verb* **1** [T] to push along an object that has wheels; to move sb about in/on a vehicle with wheels: *He wheeled his bicycle up the hill.* ○ *She was wheeled back to her bed on a trolley.* **2** [I] to fly round in circles: *Birds wheeled above the ship.* **3** [I] to turn round suddenly: *Eleanor wheeled round, with a look of horror on her face.*

'**wheelbarrow** (*also* **barrow**) *noun* [C] a type of small cart with one wheel, two legs and two handles used for carrying small loads, especially in gardens

'**wheelchair** *noun* [C] a chair with large wheels that a person who cannot walk can move or be moved about in

'**wheelclamp** *verb* [T] = CLAMP(3)

wheeze /wiːz; *US* hwiːz/ *verb* [I] to breathe noisily with a whistling sound, especially if you have a chest illness

☆**when** /wen; *US* hwen/ *adv* **1** at what time: *When did she arrive?* ○ *I don't know when she arrived.* **2** (used for talking about the time at which sth happens or happened): *Sunday is the day when I can relax.* ○ *I last saw her in May, when she was in London.*

when *conj* **1** at or during the time that: *He jumped up when the phone rang.* ○ *When we were walking home we saw an accident.* ☛ Notice that we use the present tense after 'when' if we are talking about a future time: *I'll call you when I'm ready.* **2** since; as; considering that: *Why do you want more money when you've got enough already?* ☛ **When** is used for talking about something that you think will happen, but **if** is used for something you are not sure will happen. Compare: *I'll ask her when she comes* (= you are sure that she will come). ○ *I'll ask her if she comes* (= you are not sure whether she will come or not).

whence /wens; *US* hwens/ *adv* (*old-fashioned*) (from) where: *They returned whence they came.*

☆**whenever** /wen'evə(r); *US* hwen-/ *conj* at any time; no matter when: *You can borrow my car whenever you want.* ○ *Don't worry. You can give it back the next time you see me, or whenever.*

whenever *adv* (used when you are showing that you are surprised or impatient) when: *Whenever did you find time to do all that cooking?* ○ *Whenever are you going to finish?*

☆**where** /weə(r); *US* hweə(r)/ *adv, conj* **1** at, in or to what place or position: *Where can I buy a paper?* ○ *I asked him where he lived.* ○ *Where are you going?* **2** at, in or to a place or a situation: *the town where you were born* ○ *She ran to where they were standing.* ○ *I know where we must go.* ○ *Where possible, you should travel by bus, not taxi.* **3** at which place: *We came to a village, where we stopped for lunch.*

'**whereabouts** *adv* where; in or near what place: *Whereabouts did you lose your purse?*

'**whereabouts** *noun* [U, with sing or pl verb] the place where sb/sth is: *The whereabouts of the stolen painting is/are unknown.*

where'by *adv* (*formal*) by which: *These countries have an agreement whereby foreign visitors can have free medical care.*

whereu'pon *conj* (*formal*) after which: *He fell asleep, whereupon she walked quietly from the room.*

whereas /ˌweər'æz; *US* ˌhweər'æz/ *conj* (used for showing a fact that is different): *He eats meat, whereas she's a vegetarian.*

☆**wherever** /weər'evə(r); *US* hweər-/ *conj* **1** in or to any place: *You can sit wherever you like.* ○ *She comes from Bahia, wherever that is* (= I don't know where it is). **2** everywhere, in all places that: *Wherever I go, he goes.*

wherever *adv* (used for showing surprise): *Wherever did you learn to cook like that?*

(IDIOM) **or wherever** or any other place: *The students might be from Sweden, Denmark or wherever.*

whet /wet; *US* hwet/ *verb* (**whetting; whetted**)

(IDIOM) **whet sb's appetite** to make sb want more of sth: *Our short stay in Dublin whetted our appetite to spend more time there.*

☆**whether** /'weðə(r); *US* 'hweðər/ *conj* **1** (used after verbs like 'ask', 'doubt', 'know', etc) if: *He asked me whether we would be coming to the party.* **2** (used for expressing a choice or doubt between two or more possibilities): *I can't make up my mind whether to go or not.* ○ *There was some doubt as to whether she should go.* ☛ **Whether** and **if** can both be used in sense 1. Only **whether** can be used before 'to' + verb: *Have you decided whether to accept the offer yet?* Only **whether** can be used after a preposition: *the problem of whether to accept the offer.*

(IDIOM) **whether or not** (used to say that sth will be true in either of the situations that are mentioned): *We shall play on Saturday whether it rains or not.* ○ *Whether or not it rains, we shall play on Saturday.*

whew = PHEW

☆**which** /wɪtʃ; *US* hwɪtʃ/ *det, pron* **1** (used in questions when there are a number of people or things to choose from): *Which cake would you like?* ○ *Which hand do you write with?* ○ *Which is your bag?* ○ *She asked me which colour I preferred.* ○ *I can't remember which of the boys is the older.* ☛ **Which** or **what**? We use **which** when there is only a limited group to choose from: *Which car is yours? The Ford or the*

ɜː	ə	eɪ	əʊ	aɪ	aʊ	ɔɪ	ɪə	eə	ʊə
fur	ago	pay	home	five	now	join	near	hair	pure

Volvo? We use **what** when the group is not limited: *What car would you choose, if you could have any one you wanted?* **2** (used for saying what thing or things you are talking about): *We need a car which is reliable.* ○ *Did you see the article which Jenny wrote?* ○ (*formal*) *The situation in which he found himself was very difficult.* ☛ In less formal English we would write: *The situation which he found himself in was very difficult.* Often the 'which' is left out: *The situation he found himself in...* **3** (used for giving more information about a thing or animal): *His best film, which won several awards, was about the life of Gandhi.* ☛ Note that there is a comma before 'which' and at the end of the part of the sentence which it introduces. **4** (used for making a comment on what has just been said): *We had to wait 16 hours for our plane, which was really annoying.* ☛ Note that there is a comma before 'which'.

☆ **whichever** /wɪtʃ'evə(r); *US* hwɪtʃ-/ *det, pron* **1** any person or thing: *You can choose whichever book you want.* **2** (used for expressing surprise): which: *Whichever way did you come?*

whiff /wɪf; *US* hwɪf/ *noun* [sing] a smell which only lasts for a short time: *a whiff of perfume*

☆ **while¹** /waɪl; *US* hwaɪl/ (*also* **whilst** /waɪlst; *US* hwaɪlst/) *conj* **1** during the time that; when: *He always phones while we're having lunch.* **2** at the same time as: *He always listens to the radio while he's driving to work.* **3** (*formal*) (used when you are contrasting two ideas): *Some countries are rich, while others are extremely poor.*

☆ **while²** /waɪl; *US* hwaɪl/ *noun* [sing] a period of time (usually short): *Let's sit down here for a while.*

(IDIOMS) **once in a while** ⇨ ONCE
worth sb's while ⇨ WORTH
while *verb*
(PHRASAL VERB) **while sth away** to pass time in a lazy or relaxed way: *We whiled away the evening chatting and listening to music.*

whim /wɪm; *US* hwɪm/ *noun* [C] a sudden idea or desire to do sth (often sth that is not sensible)

whimper /'wɪmpə(r); *US* 'hwɪ-/ *verb* [I] to cry softly, especially with fear or pain —**whimper** *noun* [C]

whine /waɪn; *US* hwaɪn/ *verb* **1** [I] to make a long high unpleasant sound: *The dog is whining to go out.* **2** [I,T] to complain about sth in an annoying way: *The children were whining all afternoon.* —**whine** *noun* [C]

whip¹ /wɪp; *US* hwɪp/ *noun* [C] **1** a long thin piece of leather, etc with a handle, that is used for making animals go faster and for hitting people as a punishment **2** an official of a political party who makes sure that all members vote in important debates in Parliament

whip² /wɪp; *US* hwɪp/ *verb* (**whipping**; **whipped**) **1** [T] to hit a person or animal with a whip **2** [T] to mix the white part of an egg, cream, etc until it is light and stiff: *whipped cream* **3** [T] (*Brit informal*) to steal sth: *Somebody's whipped my sweater!* **4** [I,T] (*informal*) to move quickly or suddenly; to make sth move in this way: *He whipped out a pen and made a note of the number.*

(PHRASAL VERB) **whip sth up 1** to cause a strong emotion: *to whip up excitement* **2** (*informal*) to prepare food quickly: *to whip up a quick snack*

whir (*especially US*) = WHIRR

whirl /wɜːl; *US* hw-/ *verb* [I,T] to move round very quickly; to make sb/sth move in this way: *The dancers whirled round the room.* ○ *The wind whirled the leaves round and round.* ○ (*figurative*) *I couldn't sleep. My mind was whirling after all the excitement.*

whirl *noun* [sing] **1** the act or sound of whirling: *the whirl of the helicopter's blades* **2** a state of confusion: *My head's in a whirl – I'm so excited.*

(IDIOM) **give sth a whirl** to try sth

whirlpool /'wɜːlpuːl; *US* hw-/ *noun* [C] a place in a river or the sea where the water moves quickly round and round

whirlwind /'wɜːlwɪnd; *US* hw-/ *noun* [C] a very strong wind that forms a tall column of air moving round and round in a circle as it travels across the land or the sea ☛ Look at the note at **storm**.

whirr (*especially US* **whir**) /wɜː(r); *US* hw-/ *verb* [I] to make a continuous low sound: *The noise of the fan whirring kept me awake.* —**whirr** (*especially US* **whir**) *noun* [C, usually sing]

whisk /wɪsk; *US* hw-/ *noun* [C] a tool that you use for beating the white part of an egg, cream, etc

whisk *verb* [T] **1** to move sb/sth quickly: *The prince was whisked away in a black limousine.* **2** to beat eggs, cream, etc very quickly with a whisk

whisker /'wɪskə(r); *US* 'hwɪ-/ *noun* **1** **whiskers** [plural] the hair that is growing on a man's face **2** [C] one of the long hairs that grow near the mouth of a mouse, cat, etc ☛ picture at **cat**.

whisky /'wɪski; *US* 'hwɪ-/ *noun* (*pl* **whiskies**) **1** [U] a strong alcoholic drink that is made from grain: *Scotch whisky* **2** [C] a glass of whisky ☛ In the USA and Ireland the spelling is **whiskey**.

☆ **whisper** /'wɪspə(r); *US* 'hwɪ-/ *verb* [I,T] to speak very quietly to sb, so that other people cannot hear what you are saying —**whisper** *noun* [C]: *to speak in a whisper*

☆ **whistle** /'wɪsl; *US* 'hwɪ-/ *noun* [C] **1** the long high sound that you make when you force air out between your lips **2** a simple musical instrument that produces a long high sound: *The referee blew his whistle to stop the game.*

whistle *verb* **1** [I,T] to make sounds by forcing air out between your lips or through a whistle: *The girl was whistling as she walked down the street.* ○ *He whistled a tune to himself.* ○ *The referee whistled and the game was over.* **2** [I] to make a sound like a whistle: *A bullet whistled past his head* (= moved quickly, with the sound of a whistle).

Whit /wɪt; *US* hwɪt/ *noun* [U] = WHITSUN

☆ **white¹** /waɪt; *US* hwaɪt/ *adj* **1** of the very light colour of snow or milk: *an old lady with white hair* ○ *white coffee* (= with milk) **2** (used about a person) having pale skin, of European origin

3 white (with sth) (used about a person) very pale because of illness, fear, etc: *to be white with shock*
(IDIOMS) **black and white** ⇨ BLACK²
in black and white ⇨ BLACK²

,white-'collar *adj* white-collar work is done in an office not a factory, and white-collar workers are people who work in an office

,white 'elephant *noun* [sing] something that you do not need or that is not useful

,white 'lie *noun* [C] a lie that is not very harmful or serious

,White 'Paper *noun* [C] (*Brit*) an official government report on a particular subject that will later be discussed in Parliament

'whitewash *noun* [U] a white liquid that you use for painting walls

'whitewash *verb* [T] **1** to paint whitewash on a wall **2** to try to hide sth bad or wrong that you have done

,white 'wine *noun* [U] wine made from green grapes, that is clear or of a very pale yellow colour ☛ Look at **red wine** and **rosé**.

☆ **white²** /waɪt; *US* hwaɪt/ *noun* **1** [U] white colour, paint, etc: *She was dressed in white.* **2** [C] a person with white skin: *Blacks and Whites in South Africa* **3** [C,U] the part of an egg that turns white when it is cooked ☛ The yellow part of an egg is the **yolk**. picture at **egg**. **4** [C] the white part of the eye

Whitsun /'wɪtsn; *US* 'hwɪ-/ (*also* **Whit**) *noun* [sing] the seventh Sunday after Easter and the days close to it

whiz (*also* **whizz**) /wɪz; *US* hwɪz/ *verb* [I] (**whizz**ing; **whizz**ed) (*informal*) to move very quickly, often making a high continuous sound: *The racing cars went whizzing by.*

☆ **who** /huː/ *pron* **1** (used in questions to ask sb's name, etc): *Who did this?* ○ *Who did you meet at the party?* ○ *Who did you go with?* **2** (used in reported questions and after certain verbs): *She wondered who he was.* ○ *I can't remember who I asked to do this.* **3** (used for saying which person or what kind of person you are talking about): *I like people who say what they think.* ○ *That's the man who I met at Ann's party.* ○ *The woman who I work for is very nice.* ☛ In the last two examples (= when 'who' is the object, or when it is used with a preposition) 'who' can be left out: *That's the man I met at Ann's party.* ○ *The woman I work for is very nice.* **4** used for giving extra information about sb: *My mother, who's over 80, still drives a car.* ☛ Look at the note at **whom**.

who'd /huːd/ *short for* WHO HAD, WHO WOULD

☆ **whoever** /huː'evə(r)/ *pron* **1** the person who: *Whoever is responsible will have to pay for the damage.* ○ *I want to speak to whoever is in charge.* **2** it does not matter who: *I don't want to see anybody – whoever it is.* **3** (used for expressing surprise) who: *Whoever could be phoning so late at night?*

☆ **whole** /həʊl/ *adj* **1** complete; full: *We drank a whole bottle of wine.* ○ *a whole month's holiday* **2** not broken or cut: *Snakes swallow their prey whole* (= in one piece).

whole *noun* [sing] **1** all that there is of sth: *I spent the whole of the morning cooking.* **2** a thing that is complete or full: *Two halves make a whole.*
(IDIOMS) **as a whole** as one complete thing or unit: *This is true in Britain, but also in Europe as a whole.*

on the whole generally, but not true in every case: *On the whole I think it's a very good idea.*

wholly /'həʊlli/ *adv* completely; fully: *The government is not wholly to blame for the situation.*

'wholefood *noun* [U] food that does not contain artificial substances and chemicals and that is as natural as possible

,whole'hearted *adj* complete and without doubt: *to give sb your wholehearted support*

,whole'heartedly *adv*: *We wholeheartedly agree with you.*

'wholemeal *adj* (made from) flour that contains all the grain: *wholemeal bread*

wholesale /'həʊlseɪl/ *adj, adv* **1** connected with buying and selling goods in large quantities: *They get all their building materials wholesale.* **2** (usually about sth bad) very great; on a very large scale: *the wholesale destruction of the rainforests*

wholesome /'həʊlsəm/ *adj* **1** good for your health: *simple wholesome food* **2** (used about a person) looking clean and attractive **3** having a moral effect that is good

who'll /huːl/ *short for* WHO WILL

wholly ⇨ WHOLE

☆ **whom** /huːm/ *pron* (*formal*) **1** (used in questions as the object form of 'who' to ask sb's name, etc): *Whom did you meet there?* ○ *To whom did you give the money?* **2** (used as the object form of 'who' in reported questions and after certain verbs): *He asked me whom I had met.* ○ *I realized to whom I had been speaking.* **3** (used for saying which person or what kind of person the object of a verb or preposition is): *A gentleman whom I had never met sat down beside me.* **4** (used for giving extra information about the object of a verb or preposition): *This is my wife, to whom I owe everything.* ☛ The use of **whom** instead of **who** as the object pronoun or the pronoun after prepositions is very formal. We usually express a sentence such as: *He asked me with whom I had discussed it.'* as *'He asked me who I had discussed it with.'* (Note the position of the preposition at the end.)

whooping cough /'huːpɪŋ kɒf/ *noun* [U] a serious disease, especially of children, in which they have a bad cough and make a loud noise when they breathe in after coughing

whoops /wʊps/ *interj* (*informal*) (used when you have, or nearly have, a small accident): *Whoops! I nearly dropped the cup.*

whoosh /wʊʃ/ *verb* [I] to move very fast, with the sound of air rushing

whore /hɔː(r)/ *noun* [C] (*old-fashioned*) = PROSTITUTE

who're /'huːə(r)/ *short for* WHO ARE

who's /huːz/ *short for* WHO IS, WHO HAS

☆ **whose** /huːz/ *det, pron* **1** (used in questions when you are asking who sth belongs to) of whom?: *Whose car is that?* ○ *That's a nice coat – I wonder whose it is.* **2** of whom; of which:

That's the boy whose mother has just died. o *a firm whose most famous product is chocolate*

who've /huːv/ *short for* WHO HAVE

☆ **why** /waɪ; *US* hwaɪ/ *adv* for what reason: *Why was she so late?* o *I wonder why they went.* o *'I'm not staying any longer.' 'Why not?'* o *Can you tell me the reason why you are so unhappy?* (IDIOMS) **why ever** (used to show that you are surprised or angry): *Why ever didn't you phone?*
why not (used for making or agreeing to a suggestion): *Why not get fish and chips tonight?*

wick /wɪk/ *noun* [C] the piece of string in the middle of a candle ☛ picture at **candle**.

☆ **wicked** /'wɪkɪd/ *adj* **1** morally bad; evil: *The man was described as weak and foolish but not wicked.* ☛ Look at the note at **evil**. **2** liking to annoy other people in a way that is not serious: *a wicked sense of humour* —**wickedly** *adv* —**wickedness** *noun* [U]

☆ **wide** /waɪd/ *adj* **1** measuring a large amount from one side or edge to the other: *The road was not wide enough for two cars to pass.* o *a wide river* ☛ Look at the note at **broad**. **2** measuring a particular amount from one side or edge to the other: *The box was only 20 centimetres wide.* o *How wide is the river?* **3** covering a large area or range: *You're the nicest person in the whole wide world!* o *This shop sells a wide range of goods.* **4** fully open: *The children's eyes were wide with excitement.* **5** not near what you wanted to touch or hit: *His first serve was wide* (eg in tennis).
wide *adv* as far or as much as possible; completely: *Open your mouth wide.* o *wide awake* o *a wide-open door*

widely *adv* **1** to a large degree; a lot: *Their opinions differ widely.* **2** over a large area or range: *Steve travelled widely in his youth.*

widen /'waɪdn/ *verb* [I,T] to become wider; to make sth wider

wide-'ranging *adj* covering a large area or many subjects: *a wide-ranging discussion*

'widespread *adj* found or happening over a large area; affecting a large number of people: *The storm has caused widespread damage.*

☆ **widow** /'wɪdəʊ/ *noun* [C] a woman whose husband has died and who has not married again
widowed /'wɪdəʊd/ *adj* being a widow or widower: *She's been widowed for ten years now.*

☆ **widower** /'wɪdəʊə(r)/ *noun* [C] a man whose wife has died and who has not married again

☆ **width** /wɪdθ/ *noun* **1** [C,U] the amount that sth measures from one side or edge to the other: *The room is eight metres in width.* o *The carpet is available in two different widths.* ☛ picture at **length**. **2** [C] the distance from one side of a swimming-pool to the other

wield /wiːld/ *verb* [T] to hold and use a weapon: *Some of the men were wielding knives.*

wiener /'wiːnə(r)/ *noun* [C] (*US*) = FRANKFURTER

☆ **wife** /waɪf/ *noun* [C] (*pl* **wives** /waɪvz/) the woman to whom a man is married

wig /wɪɡ/ *noun* [C] a covering made of real or false hair that you wear on your head, because you are bald or because you want to cover up your own hair

wiggle /'wɪɡl/ *verb* [I,T] (*informal*) to move from side to side with small quick movements; to make sth do this: *Can you wiggle your ears?* —**wiggle** *noun* [C] (*informal*): *to walk with a wiggle*

wigwam /'wɪɡwæm; *US* -wɑːm/ *noun* [C] a type of tent that was used by North American Indians

☆ **wild** /waɪld/ *adj* **1** living or growing in natural conditions, not looked after by people: *wild animals* **2** (used about an area of land) not lived on, farmed, etc: *the wild mountain scenery of Wales* **3** (used about the weather) stormy, with strong winds: *It was a wild night last night.* **4** (used about a person or his/her behaviour or emotions) not controlled; rather mad: *The crowd went wild with excitement.* o *He had a wild look in his eyes.* **5 wild (about sb/sth)** (*informal*) liking sb/sth very much: *I'm not wild about their new house.* **6** not carefully done, planned or thought about: *She made rather a wild guess.*
wild *noun* **1 the wild** [sing] natural areas, (= not on farms, in zoos, etc): *the thrill of seeing elephants in the wild* **2 the wilds** [plural] places that are far away from towns: *They live somewhere out in the wilds.*
wildly *adv* in a wild way: *to rush about wildly* —**wildness** *noun* [U]

'wildlife *noun* [U] wild birds, plants, animals, etc

wilderness /'wɪldənɪs/ *noun* [C, usually sing] **1** an area of land with very few signs of human life: *The Antarctic is the last great wilderness.* **2** a place where plants are growing in an uncontrolled way

wilful (*US also* **willful**) /'wɪlfl/ *adj* **1** done on purpose, eg to hurt or damage sb/sth: *wilful damage* **2** doing exactly what you want, no matter what other people think or say —**wilfully** /-fəli/ *adv*

☆ **will¹** /wɪl/ *modal verb* (*short form* **'ll**; *negative* **will not**; *short form* **won't** /wəʊnt/) **1** (used in forming the future tenses): *He will be here soon.* o *I'm sure you'll pass your exam.* o *I'll be sitting on the beach this time next week.* o *Next Sunday, she will have been in England for a year.* **2** (used for showing that sb is willing to do sth, or that sth is able to do sth): *'We need some more milk.' 'OK, I'll get it.'* o *Why won't you tell me where you were last night?* o *I'll carry your case for you.* o *My car won't start.* **3** (used for asking sb to do sth): *Will you sit down, please?* **4** (used for offering sth to sb): *Will you have a cup of tea?* **5** (used for talking about sth annoying that sb always or very often does): *He will keep interrupting me when I'm trying to work.* **6** (used for saying that you think sth is probably true): *That will be the postman at the door.*

will² /wɪl/ *verb* [T] to use the power of your mind to do sth or to make sth happen: *He willed himself to carry on to the end of the race.*

☆ **will³** /wɪl/ *noun* **1** [C,U] the power of the mind to choose what actions to take: *Both her children have got very strong wills.* o *My father seems to have lost the will to live.* **2** [sing] what sb wants or desires: *My mother doesn't want to*

iː	ɪ	e	æ	ɑː	ɒ	ɔː	ʊ	uː	ʌ
see	sit	ten	hat	arm	got	saw	put	too	cup

sell the house and I don't want to go against her will. **3** [C] a legal document in which you write down who should have your money and property after your death: *Have you made a will?* o *Gran left us some money in her will.*
(IDIOM) **of your own free will** ⇨ FREE¹
-willed (in compounds) having a will(1) of a particular type: *strong-willed*
☆ **willing** /'wɪlɪŋ/ *adj* **1** (not before a noun) prepared to do sth; having no objection to doing sth: *Are you willing to help us?* o *I'm not willing to take any risks.* **2** ready or eager: *a willing helper* —**willingly** *adv* —**willingness** *noun* [U,sing]
willow /'wɪləʊ/ (*also* **'willow tree**) *noun* [C] a tree with thin branches and long thin leaves that grows near water
will-power /'wɪlpaʊə(r)/ *noun* [U] strength of mind; the ability to keep trying to succeed, even when sth is difficult: *It takes a lot of will-power to give up smoking.*
wilt /wɪlt/ *verb* [I] (used about a plant or flower) to bend and start to die, because of heat or lack of water
wily /'waɪli/ *adj* (**wilier**; **wiliest**) clever at getting what you want
wimp /wɪmp/ *noun* [C] (*informal*) a weak person —**wimpish** *adj*
☆ **win** /wɪn/ *verb* (*pres part* **winning**; *pt, pp* **won** /wʌn/) **1** [I,T] to be the best, first or strongest in a race, game, competition, battle, election, etc: *to win a game, match, race, etc* o *Murphy won and Lewis was second.* o *I never win at table-tennis.* o *Which party do you think will win the next election?* **2** [T] to get sth as a result of success in a competition, race, etc: *How much did you win?* o *Who won the gold medal?* o *Labour won the seat from the Conservatives* (= in an election). ☛ Note that we **earn** (not **win**) money at our job: *I earn £15 000 a year.* **3** [T] to get sth by hard work, great effort, etc: *Her brilliant performance won her a great deal of praise.* o *to win support for a plan*
(IDIOMS) **win/lose the toss** ⇨ TOSS
you can't win (*informal*) there is no way of being completely successful or of pleasing everybody: *Whatever you do you will upset somebody. You can't win.*
(PHRASAL VERB) **win sb over/round (to sth)** to persuade sb to support or agree with you
win *noun* [C] an act of winning a competition, game, race, etc: *We have had two wins and a draw so far this season.*
winner *noun* [C] a person or animal that wins a competition, game, race, etc: *And the winner is...* —**winning** *adj*: *The winning ticket is number 65.*
wince /wɪns/ *verb* [I] to make a sudden quick movement (usually twisting the muscles of the face) because of a sharp pain or sth unpleasant
winch /wɪntʃ/ *noun* [C] a machine that lifts or pulls heavy objects by using a thick chain, etc that winds round and round a drum
winch *verb* [T] to lift or pull sb/sth using a winch: *The injured climber was winched up into a helicopter.*
☆ **wind¹** /wɪnd/ *noun* **1** [C,U] (*also* **the wind**) air

that is moving across the surface of the earth: *There was a strong wind blowing.* o *A gust of wind blew his hat off.* o *high winds* o *a cold north wind* **2** [U] the breath that you need for doing exercise or playing a musical instrument: *She stopped running to get her wind back.* **3** [U] air that you swallow when you are eating or drinking; gas that is formed in your stomach
(IDIOM) **get wind of sth** to hear about sth that is secret
windy *adj* (**windier**; **windiest**) with a lot of wind: *a windy day*
'windfall *noun* [C] an unexpected gift or piece of good luck
'wind instrument *noun* [C] a musical instrument that you play by blowing through it
'windmill *noun* [C] a tall building with long arms (**sails**) that stick out from it and turn in the wind. Windmills are used for grinding corn, producing electricity, etc

windmill

— sail

'windpipe *noun* [C] the tube that takes air from the throat to the lungs
'windscreen (*US* **'windshield**) *noun* [C] the window in the front of a car, etc
'windscreen wiper (*also* **wiper**; *US* **'windshield wiper**) *noun* [C] one of the two moving arms (**blades**) that remove water, snow, etc from the windscreen
'windsurf *verb* [I] to move through water standing on a special board with a sail ☛ We usually say **go windsurfing**: *Have you ever been windsurfing?*

windsurfing

'windsurfer (*also* **sailboard**) *noun* [C] **1** a board with a sail that you stand on as it moves over the surface of the water, driven by the wind **2** a person who rides on a board like this

windsurfer (*also* sailboard)

'windsurfing *noun* [U] the sport of riding on a windsurfer
'windswept *adj* **1** (used about a place) that often has strong winds: *a windswept coastline* **2** looking untidy because you have been in a strong wind: *windswept hair*
wind² /wɪnd/ *verb* [T] to cause sb to have difficulty in breathing: *The punch in the stomach winded her.*
☆ **wind³** /waɪnd/ *verb* (*pt, pp* **wound** /waʊnd/) **1** [T] to wrap sth long round sth else several times: *Wind the string round your finger or the balloon will fly away.* **2** [T] to make sth work or move by turning a key, handle, etc: *He wound*

ɜː	ə	eɪ	əʊ	aɪ	aʊ	ɔɪ	ɪə	eə	ʊə
fur	ago	pay	home	five	now	join	near	hair	pure

the car window down and shouted at the other driver. ○ Wind the tape on a bit to the next song. **3** [I] (used about a road, path, etc) to have a lot of bends or curves in it: *The path winds down the cliff to the sea.*

(PHRASAL VERBS) **wind down** (about a person) to rest and relax after a period of hard work, worry, etc ☞ Look at **unwind**.

wind up to be in a place at the end of a journey or in a particular situation after other things have happened: *We wound up in quite a nice hotel near Calais.* ○ *You'll wind up failing your exams if you go on like this.*

wind sth up to finish, stop or close sth: *The company was losing money and was soon wound up.*

winding *adj* with bends or curves in it: *a winding road through the hills*

☆ **window** /'wɪndəʊ/ *noun* [C] **1** the opening in a building, car, etc that you can see through and that lets light in. A window usually has glass in it: *Open the window. It's hot in here.* ○ *I always keep the downstairs windows closed at night.* ○ *a shop window* ○ *I always try and get a window seat* (= next to a window on a plane). **2** the glass in a window: *to break a window* ○ *These windows need cleaning.* **3** an area on a computer screen that has a particular type of information in it

'**window-pane** *noun* [C] one piece of glass in a window

'**window-shopping** *noun* [U] looking at things in shop windows without intending to buy anything

'**window-sill** (*also* '**window-ledge**) *noun* [C] the shelf at the bottom of a window in a building, either inside or outside ☞ picture at **curtain**.

windy ⇒ WIND¹

☆ **wine** /waɪn/ *noun* [C,U] an alcoholic drink that is made from grapes (or sometimes other fruits): *red/white/rosé wine* ○ *sweet/dry wine* ○ *German wines*

'**wine bar** *noun* [C] a place where you can go to drink wine and have sth to eat

☆ **wing** /wɪŋ/ *noun* **1** [C] one of the two parts that a bird, insect, etc uses for flying ☞ picture at **bird**. **2** [C] one of the two long parts that stick out from the side of an aeroplane and support it in the air **3** [C] a part of a building that sticks out from the main part or that was added on to the main part: *the maternity wing of the hospital* **4** [C] (*US* **fender**) the part of the outside of a car, etc that covers the top of the wheels **5** [C, usually sing] a group of people in a political party that have particular beliefs or opinions: *the right wing of the Conservative Party* ☞ Look at **left-wing** and **right-wing**. **6** [C] (in football, etc) the part at each side of the area where the game is played: *to play on the wing* **7** [C] (*also* **winger**) (in football, etc) a person who plays in an attacking position at one of the sides of the field **8 the wings** [plural] (in a theatre) the area at the sides of the stage where you cannot be seen by the audience

wink /wɪŋk/ *verb* [I] **wink (at sb)** to close and open one eye very quickly, usually as a private signal to sb ☞ Look at **blink**. —**wink** *noun* [C]: *to give sb a wink* ○ *I didn't sleep a wink* (= not at all).

winner, winning ⇒ WIN

☆ **winter** /'wɪntə(r)/ *noun* [C,U] the coldest season of the year between autumn and spring: *It snows a lot here in winter.* ○ *a cold winter's day* ○ *We went skiing in France last winter.* ○ *the Winter Olympics* —**wintry** /'wɪntri/ *adj*: *wintry weather* ○ *a wintry wind*

,**winter 'sports** *noun* [plural] sports which take place on snow or ice, eg skiing and skating

'**wintertime** *noun* [U] the period or season of winter

☆ **wipe** /waɪp/ *verb* [T] **1** to clean or dry sth by rubbing it with a cloth, piece of paper, etc: *Wipe your hands on the towel.* ○ *to wipe your nose on a handkerchief* ○ *Could you wipe the table, please?* ☞ Look at the note at **clean²**. **2 wipe sth from/off sth**; **wipe sth away/off/up** to remove sth by wiping(1): *Wipe the dirt off your shoes.* ○ *He wiped the sweat from his forehead.* ○ *Wipe up the milk you spilled, please.*

(PHRASAL VERB) **wipe sth out** to destroy sth completely: *Whole villages were wiped out in the bombing raids.*

wipe *noun* [C] the act of wiping: *He gave the table a quick wipe.* —**wiper** *noun* [C] = WINDSCREEN WIPER

☆ **wire** /'waɪə(r)/ *noun* [C,U] **1** a long thin piece of metal like strong string that is used for fastening things or in fences, cages, etc: *a piece of wire* ○ *barbed wire* ○ *a wire fence* **2** a piece of wire that is used to carry electricity

wire *verb* [T] **1** to fasten or join two things together using wire **2 wire sth (up)** to connect sth to a supply of electricity by using wires

wiring /'waɪərɪŋ/ *noun* [U] the system of wires that supplies electricity to rooms in a building

wireless /'waɪəlɪs/ *noun* [C,U] (*old-fashioned*) communication by radio; a piece of equipment for communicating by radio

wiry /'waɪəri/ *adj* (**wirier**; **wiriest**) (used about a person) small and thin but strong

☆ **wisdom** /'wɪzdəm/ *noun* [U] the quality of being wise; the ability to make sensible decisions and judgements because of your knowledge or experience: *Athena was the goddess of wisdom.* ○ *I doubt the wisdom of taking a decision too early* (= I do not think that it is a good idea).

'**wisdom tooth** *noun* [C] (*pl* **wisdom teeth**) one of the four teeth at the back of your mouth that appear when you are about 20 years old

☆ **wise** /waɪz/ *adj* having or showing the knowledge or experience to make good or sensible decisions or judgements: *a wise choice* ○ *It would be wiser to wait for a few days.* ○ *a wise old man* —**wisely** *adv*

☆ **wish** /wɪʃ/ *verb* **1** [T] **wish (that)** (often with a verb in the past tense) to want sth that cannot now happen or that probably will not happen: *I wish (that) I had listened more carefully.* ○ *I wish (that) I knew what was going to happen.* ○ *My father wishes (that) he had gone to university.* ○ *I wish I could help you.* ○ Note that in formal English we use **were** instead of **was**

p	b	t	d	k	g	tʃ	dʒ	f	v	θ	ð
pen	**bad**	**tea**	**did**	**cat**	**got**	**chin**	**June**	**fall**	**van**	**thin**	**then**

with 'I' or 'he/she': *I wish I were rich.* ○ *She wishes she were in a different class.* **2** [I] **wish for sth** to say to yourself that you want sth that can only happen by good luck or magic: *She closed her eyes and wished for her mother to get better.* **3** [T] **wish (to do sth)** (*formal*) to want to do sth: *I wish to make a complaint about one of the doctors.* **4** [T] to say that you hope sb will have sth; to say sth as a greeting: *I rang him up to wish him a happy birthday.* ○ *We wish you all the best for your future career.*

wish *noun* **1** [C] a feeling that you want sth: *a wish for peace* ○ *I have no wish to see her ever again.* ○ *Doctors should respect the patient's wishes.* **2** [C] when you make a wish, you say to yourself secretly that you want to have sth or that you want sth to happen, and you hope that it will: *The prince was granted three wishes by the fairy.* ○ *My wish came true* (= I got what I asked for). **3 wishes** [plural] a hope that sb will be happy or have good luck: *Please give your parents my best wishes.* ○ *Best Wishes* (= at the end of a letter)

wishful 'thinking *noun* [U] ideas that are based on what you would like, not on facts

wisp /wɪsp/ *noun* [C] **1** a small thin bunch of hair, grass, etc **2** a small amount of smoke

wistful /'wɪstfl/ *adj* feeling or showing sadness because you cannot have what you want: *a wistful sigh* —**wistfully** /-fəli/ *adv*

wit /wɪt/ *noun* [U] **1** the ability to use words in a clever and amusing way **2** (*also* **wits** [plural]) cleverness; intelligence: *The game of chess is essentially a battle of wits.*

(IDIOMS) **at your wits' end** not knowing what to do or say because you are so worried

keep your wits about you to be ready to act in a difficult situation

-witted (in compounds) having a particular type of intelligence: *quick-witted*

witty *adj* (**wittier; wittiest**) clever and amusing; using words in a clever way: *a very witty speech* —**wittily** *adv*

witch /wɪtʃ/ *noun* [C] (in former times and in stories) a woman who is thought to have magic powers that she uses to do bad things. Pictures of witches in stories show them wearing a black cloak and a tall pointed hat. ☞ Look at **wizard**.

'witchcraft *noun* [U] the use of magic powers to do bad things

☆ **with** /wɪð; wɪθ/ *prep* **1** in the company or presence of sb/sth: *I live with my parents.* ○ *Are you coming with us?* ○ *I talked about the problem with my tutor.* ○ *Does this tie go with this shirt?* ○ *Could you put this book with the others?* **2** in the care of sb: *We left the keys with the neighbours.* **3** having or carrying sth: *a girl with red hair* ○ *a house with a garden* ○ *the man with a suitcase* **4** using sth: *Cut it with a knife.* ○ *I did it with his help.* **5** (used for expressing what fills, covers, etc sth): *Fill the bowl with water.* **6** against: *He's always arguing with his brother.* ○ *I usually play tennis with my sister.* **7** agreeing with or supporting: *We've got everybody with us on this issue.* **8** because of or as a result of sth: *We were shivering with cold.* **9** (used for expressing how sth happens or is shown): *Open this parcel with care.* ○ *to greet sb with a smile* **10** towards, concerning or compared with sb/sth: *Is he angry with us?* ○ *There's a problem with my visa.* ○ *Compared with Canada, England has mild winters.* **11** including: *With wine, the meal cost £25.* **12** at the same time as: *I can't concentrate with you watching me all the time.* **13** because of: *With all the problems we've got, we're not going to finish on time.*

(IDIOM) **be with sb** to be able to follow what sb is saying: *I'm sorry, I'm not quite with you. Say it again.*

☆ **withdraw** /wɪð'drɔː/ *verb* (*pt* **withdrew** /-'druː/; *pp* **withdrawn** /-'drɔːn/) **1** [I,T] **withdraw (sb/sth) (from sth)** (to cause sb/sth) to move back or away: *The troops withdrew from the town.* **2** [T] to remove sth or take sth away: *The suspect yoghurt has been withdrawn from the shops.* ○ *to withdraw an offer, a statement, etc* **3** [T] to take money out of a bank account: *I'd like to withdraw a thousand pounds, please.* ☞ Look at **deposit**. **4** [I] to decide not to take part in sth: *Jackson withdrew from the race at the last minute.*

withdrawal /-'drɔːəl/ *noun* **1** [C,U] moving sth back or away: *the withdrawal of troops from the war zone* **2** [C] the amount of money that you take out of your bank account **3** [U] the act of stopping doing sth, especially taking a drug: *When he gave up alcohol he suffered severe withdrawal symptoms.*

withdrawn *adj* (used about a person) very quiet and not wanting to talk to other people

wither /'wɪðə(r)/ *verb* [I,T] **wither (away)** **1** (used about plants) to become dry and die; to make a plant do this: *The plants withered in the hot sun.* **2** to become weaker, until it disappears: *This type of industry will wither away in the years to come.*

withering /'wɪðərɪŋ/ *adj* done to make sb feel silly or ashamed: *a withering look*

withhold /wɪð'həʊld/ *verb* [T] (*pt*, *pp* **withheld** /-'held/) (*formal*) **withhold sth (from sb/sth)** to refuse to give sth: *to withhold information from the police*

☆ **within** /wɪ'ðɪn/ *prep* **1** in a period not longer than a particular length of time: *I'll be back within an hour.* **2 within sth (of sth)** not further than a particular distance from sth: *The house is within three minutes' walk of the station.* **3** not outside the limits or range of sb/sth: *Each department must keep within its budget.* **4** (*formal*) inside sb/sth: *The anger was still there deep within him.*

within *adv* inside: *Cleaner required. Apply within.*

☆ **without** /wɪ'ðaʊt/ *prep* **1** not having, showing or being with sb/sth: *Don't go out without a coat on.* ○ *Pam drinks her coffee without milk.* ○ *After three days without sleep he was exhausted.* ○ *He spoke without much enthusiasm.* ○ *Can you see without your glasses?* ○ *Don't leave without me.* **2** (used with a verb in the *-ing* form to mean 'not'): *She left without saying goodbye.*

withstand /wɪð'stænd/ *verb* [T] (*pt*, *pp* **withstood** /-'stʊd/) (*formal*) to be strong enough not to break, give up, be damaged, etc: *The* troops were too weak to withstand another attack.

☆ **witness** /'wɪtnɪs/ noun [C] **1** (also **eyewitness**) a person who sees sth happen and who can tell other people about it later: *There were two witnesses to the accident.* **2** a person who appears in a court of law to say what he/she has seen or what he/she knows about sb/sth: *Each witness was cross-examined.* ○ *a witness for the defence/prosecution* **3** a person who sees sb sign an official document and who then signs it himself/herself
(IDIOM) **bear witness (to sth)** ⇨ BEAR²
witness verb [T] **1** to see sth happen and to be able to tell other people about it later: *to witness a murder* **2** to see sb sign an official document and then sign it yourself: *to witness a will*
'witness-box (US **'witness-stand**) noun [C] the place in a court of law where a witness stands when he/she is giving evidence

witty ⇨ WIT
wives pl of WIFE
wizard /'wɪzəd/ noun [C] (in stories) a man who is believed to have magic powers ☞ Look at **witch**.
wobble /'wɒbl/ verb [I,T] to move from side to side in an unsteady way; to make sb/sth do this: *Put something under the leg of the table. It's wobbling.* ○ *Stop wobbling the desk. I can't write.* —**wobbly** /'wɒbli/ adj (informal): *a wobbly table*
wok /wɒk/ noun [C] a large pan that is shaped like a bowl and used for cooking Chinese food ☞ picture at **pan**.
woke pt of WAKE¹
woken pp of WAKE¹
wolf /wʊlf/ noun [C] (pl **wolves** /wʊlvz/) a wild animal that looks like a dog and that lives and hunts in a group (**pack**)
☆ **woman** /'wʊmən/ noun [C] (pl **women** /'wɪmɪn/) an adult female person: *men, women and children* ○ *a single/married/divorced woman* ○ *Would you prefer to see a woman doctor?*
-woman (in compounds) a woman who does a particular activity: *a businesswoman*
womanhood noun [U] the state of being a woman
womanly adj of or like a woman
womb /wuːm/ noun [C] the part of a woman or female animal where a baby grows before it is born
won pt, pp of WIN
☆ **wonder** /'wʌndə(r)/ verb **1** [I,T] to want to know sth; to ask yourself questions about sth: *I wonder what the new teacher will be like.* ○ *He hadn't heard from Julia for a week and he began to wonder if she was all right.* ○ *I wonder who that woman over there is.* ○ *It was something that she had been wondering about for a long time.* ○ *Sometimes I wonder how they manage to live on the amount he earns.* **2** [I,T] **wonder (at sth)** to feel great surprise or admiration: *We wondered at the speed with which he worked.* ○ *'She was very angry.' 'I don't wonder* (= I'm not surprised).* *She had a right to be.* **3** [T] (used when you are asking sb politely to do sth): *I wonder if you could help me.*

wonder noun **1** [U] a feeling of surprise and admiration: *They could do nothing but stand in wonder at the sight.* **2** [C] something that causes you to feel surprise or admiration: *the wonders of modern technology*
(IDIOMS) **it's a wonder (that)**... it's surprising that...: *It's a wonder we managed to get here on time, with all the traffic.*
no wonder it is not surprising: *You've been out every evening this week. No wonder you're tired.*
wonderful /-fl/ adj very good; giving great pleasure: *What wonderful weather!* ○ *It's a wonderful opportunity.* ○ *It's wonderful to see you again.* —**wonderfully** /-fəli/ adv
won't short for WILL NOT
☆ **wood** /wʊd/ noun **1** [U] the hard material that the trunk and branches of trees are made of: *He chopped some wood for the fire.* ○ *Most furniture is made of wood.* **2** [C] a type of wood: *Pine is a soft wood.* **3** [C] (often plural) an area of land that is covered with trees. A wood is smaller than a forest: *a walk in the woods*
(IDIOM) **touch wood** ⇨ TOUCH¹
wooded adj (used about an area of land) having a lot of trees growing on it: *a heavily wooded valley*
wooden /'wʊdn/ adj made of wood: *wooden toys*
'woodland /-lənd/ noun [U] land that has a lot of trees growing on it: *woodland birds*
'woodwind /-wɪnd/ noun [sing, with sing or pl verb] the set of musical instruments that are made of wood and that you play by blowing into them
'woodwork noun [U] the parts of a building that are made of wood, (= the doors, stairs, etc)
woof /wʊf/ noun [C] (informal) (used for describing the sound (**a bark**) that a dog makes)
☆ **wool** /wʊl/ noun [U] **1** the soft thick hair of sheep, goats, etc **2** thick thread or cloth that is made from wool: *The sweater is 50% wool and 50% acrylic.* ○ *knitting wool* ☞ picture at **knit**. Look at **cotton wool**.
woollen (US **woolen**) /'wʊlən/ adj made of wool: *a warm woollen jumper*
woolly (US also **wooly**) /'wʊli/ adj of or like wool: *The dog had a thick woolly coat.* ○ *long woolly socks*
☆ **word** /wɜːd/ noun **1** [C] a sound or letter or group of sounds or letters that expresses a particular meaning: *What's the Greek word for 'computer'?* ○ *Several words are spelt wrong.* ○ *There are five letters in the word 'apple'.* **2** [C] a short statement or conversation: *Could I have a word with you in private?* ○ *a few words of thanks* ○ *Don't say a word about this to anyone.* **3** [sing] a promise: *I give you my word that I won't let you down.*
(IDIOMS) **a dirty word** ⇨ DIRTY¹
get a word in edgeways to interrupt when sb else is talking so that you can say sth yourself
have, etc the last word ⇨ LAST¹
in other words ⇨ OTHER
put in a (good) word for sb to say sth good about sb to sb else: *If you could put in a good*

iː	ɪ	e	æ	ɑː	ɒ	ɔː	ʊ	uː	ʌ
see	sit	ten	hat	arm	got	saw	put	too	cup

word for me I might stand a better chance of getting the job.
take sb's word for it to believe what sb says without any proof
word for word 1 repeating sth exactly: *Sharon repeated word for word what he had told her.* **2** (in a translation) dealing with each word separately, not looking at the general meaning: *a word-for-word translation*
word verb [T] (often passive) to choose carefully the words that you use to express sth: *The statement was carefully worded so that nobody would be offended by it.*
wording noun [sing] the words that you use to express sth: *The wording of the contract was vague.*
word-'perfect adj able to say sth that you have learnt from memory, without making a mistake
'word processing noun [sing] using a word processor: *We've got a computer but I only use it for word processing.*
'word processor noun [C] a type of small computer that you can use for writing letters, reports, etc. You can correct or change what you have written before you print it out.
wore pt of WEAR¹
☆ **work¹** /wɜːk/ noun **1** [U] something that requires physical or mental effort. You usually do work because you feel you have to, not for pleasure: *Her success is due to sheer hard work.* ○ *Ron never does a stroke of work.* ○ *Much of the heavy work on farms is now done by machines.* ○ *There is still a lot of work to be done.* **2** [U] what you do to earn money; the place where you go to earn money: *It is very difficult to find work in this city.* ○ *out of work* (= without a job) ○ *When do you start work?* ○ *I go to work at 8 o'clock.* ○ *The people at work gave me some flowers for my birthday.*

☛ **Work** is an uncountable noun. In some contexts we must use **job**: *I've found work at the hospital.* ○ *I've got a new job at the hospital.* **Employment** is the state of having a paid job and is more formal and official than **work** or **job**. It is an uncountable noun: *Many married women are in part-time employment.* **Occupation** is the word used on forms to ask what you are or what job you do: *Occupation: student. Occupation: bus driver.* A **profession** is a job that requires special training and higher education: *the medical profession.* A **trade** is a job that you do with your hands and that requires special skill: *He's a carpenter by trade.*

3 [U] something that you are working on or have produced: *a piece of written work* ○ *The teacher marked their work.* ○ *Is this all your own work?* ○ *an exhibition of the work of two young photographers* **4** [C] a book, painting, piece of music, etc: *an early work by Picasso* ○ *the complete works of Shakespeare* **5 works** [plural] the act of building or repairing sth: *Danger! Road-works ahead.* **6 works** [C, with sing or pl verb] a factory: *The steelworks is/are closing down.*
(IDIOM) **get/go/set to work (on sth)** to begin; to make a start (on sth)

'workbook noun [C] a book with questions and exercises in it that you use when you are studying sth
'workforce noun [C, with sing or pl verb] **1** the total number of people who work in a company, factory, etc **2** the total number of people in a country who are able to work: *Ten per cent of the workforce is unemployed.*
'workload noun [C] the amount of work that you have to do
'workman /'wɜːkmən/ noun [C] (pl **workmen**) a man who works with his hands, especially at building or making things
'workmanlike adj of or like a good workman
'workmanship noun [U] the skill that a workman needs or uses to do or make sth well
,work of 'art noun [C] (pl **works of art**) a painting, book, piece of music, etc of high quality
'workout noun [C] a period of physical exercise, eg when you are training for a sport or keeping fit
'worksheet noun [C] a piece of paper with questions or exercises on it that you use when you are studying sth
'workshop noun [C] **1** a place where things are made or repaired **2** a time when a group of people meet and discuss or learn more about a particular subject
'worktop (also **'work surface**) noun [C] a flat surface in a kitchen, etc that you use for preparing food, etc on
☆ **work²** /wɜːk/ verb **1** [I,T] to do sth which needs physical or mental effort; to do a job, especially in order to earn money: *My teacher said that I wouldn't pass the exam unless I worked harder.* ○ *I've been working in the garden all day.* ○ *They are working to improve health care in the Third World.* ○ *She's working for a large firm in Glasgow.* ○ *I'd like to work as a newspaper reporter.* ○ *He worked till he was 65, then he retired.* ○ *Doctors often work extremely long hours.* **2** [I] (used about a machine, etc) to do what it is meant to do, correctly; to function: *Our telephone hasn't been working for several days.* ○ *Can you show me how the photocopier works?* **3** [I] to have the result or effect that you want; to be successful: *Your idea sounds good but I don't think it will really work.* **4** [T] to make yourself/sb/sth work; to use or operate: *He works all his employees very hard.* ○ *Do you know how to work the fax machine?* **5** [I,T] to produce a particular effect; to help sth to happen: *His reputation as a hard worker had obviously worked in his favour.* **6** [I,T] to move to a new position or state: *Where's the screwdriver? The hinges on the gate have worked loose.* ○ *We worked our way round to the little beach by climbing over the rocks.*
(IDIOM) **work to rule** ⇨ RULE
(PHRASAL VERBS) **work out 1** to develop or progress, especially in a good way: *I hope things work out for you.* **2** to do physical exercises in order to keep your body fit: *We work out to music at my exercise class.*
work out (at) to come to a particular result or total after everything has been calculated: *The holiday worked out at around £300 each.*

ɜː	ə	eɪ	əʊ	aɪ	aʊ	ɔɪ	ɪə	eə	ʊə
fur	ago	pay	home	five	now	join	near	hair	pure

work sb out to understand sb: *I've never been able to work her out.*

work sth out 1 to find the answer to sth; to solve sth: *I can't work out how to do this.* **2** to calculate sth: *I worked out the total cost.* **3** to plan sth: *Have you worked out the route through France?*

work up to sth to develop or progress to sth: *Start with 15 minutes' exercise and gradually work up to 30.*

work sb/yourself up (into sth) to make sb/yourself become angry, excited, upset, etc: *He had worked himself up into a state of anxiety about his interview.*

workable /'wɜːkəbl/ *adj* that can be used or that can operate in an efficient way ☞ The opposite is **unworkable**.

☆ **worker** /'wɜːkə(r)/ *noun* [C] **1** (often in compounds) a person who works, especially one who does a particular type of job or belongs to a certain group of people: *factory workers* ○ *an office worker* ○ *immigrant workers* **2** a person who is employed in a business, etc especially one who does physical work: *manual workers* ○ *Workers' representatives will meet management today to discuss the pay dispute.* **3** a person who works in a particular way: *a slow worker*

☆ **working** /'wɜːkɪŋ/ *adj* (only *before* a noun) **1** employed; having a job: *the problems of child-care for working parents* **2** connected with your job: *He stayed with the same company for the whole of his working life.* ○ *The company offers excellent working conditions.* **3** good enough to be used, although it could be improved: *We are looking for someone with a working knowledge of French.*

(IDIOM) **in working order** ⇨ ORDER¹

workings *noun* [plural] the way in which a machine, an organization, etc operates: *It's very difficult to understand the workings of the legal system.*

the 'working class *noun* [C] (*also* **the 'working classes**) the group of people in a society who usually do physical work especially in industry, and earn weekly wages: *unemployment among the working class* ○ *a working-class area* ○ *a working-class family*

☆ **world** /wɜːld/ *noun* **1 the world** [sing] the earth with all its countries and people: *I took a year off work to travel round the world.* ○ *a map of the world* ○ *changes in the world's climate* ○ *the most beautiful place in the world* ○ *English is a world language* (= used all over the world). **2** [sing] a particular part of the earth: *the western world* ○ *the English-speaking world* ○ *the Third World* **3** [sing] the life and activities of people on earth; their experience: *It is hard to imagine what the world of our grandchildren will be like.* ○ *It's time you learned something about the real world!* ○ *the modern world* **4** [C] (often in compounds) a particular area of activity or group of people or things: *the world of sport* ○ *the medical world* ○ *the animal world* ○ *the natural world* **5** [C] a planet with life on it: *Do you believe there are other worlds out there, like ours?* **6** [sing] everybody: *The whole world seemed to know the news before me!*

(IDIOMS) **the outside world** people, places, activities, etc that are beyond the area where you live and your everyday experience

think the world of sb/sth ⇨ THINK¹

a/the world of good (*informal*) a great deal of good; a real benefit: *The holiday has done her the world of good.*

worldly *adj* **1** connected with ordinary life, not with the spirit: *He left all his worldly possessions to his nephew.* **2** having a lot of experience and knowledge of life and people: *a sophisticated and worldly man*

,**world-'famous** *adj* known all over the world: *a world-famous writer*

,**world 'war** *noun* [C] a war that involves a lot of important countries: *the Second World War*

,**world'wide** *adj, adv* (happening) in the whole world: *The situation has caused worldwide concern.* ○ *The product will be marketed worldwide.*

worm

☆ **worm** /wɜːm/ *noun* [C] **1** a small animal with a long thin body and no bones or legs: *an earthworm* **2** a worm that lives inside a person or an animal and may cause disease

worm *verb*

(PHRASAL VERBS) **worm your way/yourself along, through, etc** to move slowly or with difficulty in the direction mentioned, perhaps by crawling or by moving in between a lot of people or things: *I managed to worm my way through the crowd.*

worm your way/yourself into sth to win sb's trust, respect or affection, perhaps dishonestly, especially in order to obtain sth you want

worn *pp* of WEAR¹

worn-out /,wɔːn 'aʊt/ *adj* **1** too old or damaged to use any more: *a worn-out sweater* **2** extremely tired: *I'm worn-out. I think I'll go to bed early.*

☆ **worry** /'wʌri/ *verb* (*pres part* **worrying**; *3rd pers sing pres* **worries**; *pt, pp* **worried**) **1** [I] **worry (about sb/sth)** to be anxious (about sb, a problem, an event, etc): *'Don't worry, Mum,' said Peter, 'I won't be home late.'* ○ *There's nothing to worry about.* ○ *He worries if I don't phone every week-end.* **2** [T] **worry sb/yourself (about sb/sth)** to make sb/yourself anxious (about sb/sth): *You look depressed. What's worrying you?* ○ *She worried herself sick when he was away in the army.* **3** [T] **worry sb (with sth)** to bother or disturb sb: *I'm sorry to worry you with my problems but I really do need some advice.*

worried *adj* **worried (about sb/sth)**; **worried (that...)** anxious or unhappy: *Don't look so worried. Everything will be all right.* ○ *I'm worried about Jane.* ○ *We were worried stiff* (= extremely worried) *that you might have had an accident.*

worry *noun* (*pl* **worries**) **1** [U] an anxious state or feeling: *His son has caused him a lot of* worry recently. **2** [C] something that makes you worry; a problem: *financial worries*

worrying *adj* that makes you worry: *a worrying situation*

☆ **worse** /wɜːs/ *adj* (the comparative of *bad*) **1** not as good as sth else: *The weather in March was worse than in February.* ○ *The food at school seems to be getting worse and worse.* **2** (not before a noun) more ill; less well: *The doctors say that he's getting worse.*

(IDIOMS) **be none the worse (for sth)** to be unhurt or undamaged by sth

make matters/things worse to make a situation, problem, etc even more difficult or dangerous than before

the worse for wear (*informal*) damaged; not in good condition: *This suitcase looks a bit the worse for wear.*

worse luck! (*informal*) unfortunately: *The dentist says I need three fillings, worse luck!*

worse *adv* (the comparative of *badly*) less well: *She speaks German even worse than I do.*

worse *noun* [U] something that is worse: *The situation was already bad but there was worse to come.*

worsen /ˈwɜːsn/ *verb* [I,T] to become worse or to make sth worse: *Relations between the two countries have worsened.*

☆ **worship** /ˈwɜːʃɪp/ *noun* [U] praying to and showing respect for God or a god: *Different religions have different forms of worship.* ○ *A church is a place of worship.*

worship *verb* (worshi**pp**ing; worshi**pp**ed; *US* worshi**p**ing; worshi**p**ed) **1** [I,T] to pray to and show respect for God or a god: *People travel from all over the world to worship at this shrine.* ○ *In primitive societies people worshipped the sun.* **2** [T] to love or admire sb/sth very much: *She worshipped her husband.* —**worshipper** (*US* **worshiper**) *noun* [C]

☆ **worst** /wɜːst/ *adj* (the superlative of *bad*) the least pleasant or suitable: *It's been the worst winter that I can remember.*

worst *adv* (the superlative of *badly*) least well: *A lot of the children behaved badly but my son behaved worst of all!*

worst *noun* [sing] **the worst** something that is the least satisfactory or desirable: *My parents always expect the worst if I'm late.*

(IDIOMS) **at (the) worst** if the worst happens or if you consider sb/sth in the worst way: *The problem doesn't look too serious. At worst we'll have to make a few small changes.*

if the worst comes to the worst if the worst possible situation develops

☆ **worth** /wɜːθ/ *adj* **1** having a particular value (in money): *'How much is that house worth?' 'It must be worth at least £200 000.'* **2 worth doing, etc** (used as a way of recommending or advising): *That museum's really worth visiting if you have time.* ○ *It's already four o'clock. It's not worth going shopping now.* ☛ We can say either: *It isn't worth repairing the car* OR: *The car isn't worth repairing.*

(IDIOMS) **get your money's worth** ⇨ MONEY

worth it enjoyable or useful to do or have, even if it means extra cost, effort, etc: *Don't bother cooking a big meal. It isn't worth it – we're not hungry.*

worth sb's while helpful, useful or interesting to sb

worth *noun* [U] **1** value or usefulness: *She has proved her worth as a member of the team.* **2** the amount of sth that the money mentioned will buy: *ten pounds' worth of petrol* **3** the amount of sth that will last for the time mentioned: *two days' worth of food*

worthless *adj* **1** having no value or use: *It's worthless – it's only a bit of plastic!* **2** (used about a person) having bad qualities

worthwhile /ˌwɜːθˈwaɪl/ *adj* enjoyable, useful or satisfying enough to be worth the cost or effort: *Working for so little money just isn't worthwhile.* ○ *Medicine is a very worthwhile career.*

☆ **worthy** /ˈwɜːði/ *adj* (**worthier; worthiest**) **1 worthy of sth/to do sth** good enough for sth, or deserving sth: *The scheme is worthy of our support.* ○ *He felt he was not worthy to accept such responsibility.* **2** deserving respect or consideration: *a worthy leader* ○ *a worthy cause*

☆ **would** /wəd/ *strong form* /wʊd/ *modal verb* (*short form* **'d**; *negative* **would not**; *short form* **wouldn't** /ˈwʊdnt/) **1** (used when talking about the result of an event that you imagine): *He would be delighted if you went to see him.* ○ *She'd be stupid not to accept.* ○ *I would have done more, if I'd had the time.* **2** (used as the past form of 'will' when you report what sb says or thinks): *They said that they would help us.* ○ *She didn't think that he would do a thing like that.* **3** (used for asking sb politely to do sth): *Would you come this way, please?* **4** (used with 'like' or 'love' as a way of asking or saying what sb wants): *Would you like to come with us?* ○ *I'd love a piece of cake.* **5** to be willing to do sth: *She just wouldn't do what I asked her.* **6** (used after 'wish'): *I wish the sun would come out.* **7** (used for talking about things that often happened in the past): *When he was young he would often walk in these woods.* **8** (used for commenting on behaviour that is typical): *You would say that. You always support him.* **9** (used when you are giving your opinion): *I'd say she's about 40.*

☆ **wound¹** /wuːnd/ *noun* [C] an injury to part of your body, especially a cut, often one received in fighting: *Bathe and bandage the wound.* ○ *a bullet wound* ○ *The wound is healing well.*

wound *verb* [T] (usually passive) **1** to injure sb's body with a weapon: *He was wounded in the leg during the war.* ☛ Look at the note at **hurt**. **2** (*formal*) to hurt sb's feelings deeply: *I was wounded by his criticism.*

the wounded *noun* [plural] wounded people: *the sick and the wounded*

wound² *pt, pp* of WIND³

wove *pt* of WEAVE

woven *pp* of WEAVE

wow /waʊ/ *interj* (*informal*) (used for expressing how much you admire or are pleasantly surprised by sth): *Wow! What a beautiful boat!*

wrangle /ˈræŋgl/ *noun* [C] a noisy or complicated argument

---

s	z	ʃ	ʒ	h	m	n	ŋ	l	r	j	w
so	zoo	she	vision	how	man	no	sing	leg	red	yes	wet

wrangle *verb* [I] **wrangle (with sb) (about/over sth)** to argue in a noisy or angry way

☆ **wrap** /ræp/ *verb* [T] (wra**pp**ing; wra**pp**ed) **1 wrap sth (up) (in sth)** to put paper or cloth around sb/sth as a cover: *to wrap up a present* ○ *The baby was found wrapped in a blanket, on the hospital doorstep.* **2 wrap sth round/around sb/sth** to tie sth such as paper or cloth around an object or a part of the body: *The man had a bandage wrapped round his head.*
(IDIOM) **be wrapped up in sth** to be deeply involved and interested in sb/sth: *They were completely wrapped up in each other. They didn't notice I was there.*
(PHRASAL VERB) **wrap (sb/yourself) up** to put warm clothes on (sb/yourself)

wrapper *noun* [C] a piece of paper or plastic which covers a sweet, a book, etc

wrapping *noun* [C,U] paper or cloth that is used for covering or packing sth: *Remove the outer wrapping before heating the pie.*

'**wrapping paper** *noun* [U] paper which is used for wrapping presents: *a sheet of wrapping paper*

wrath /rɒθ; *US* ræθ/ *noun* [U] (*old-fashioned formal*) very great anger

wreak /riːk/ *verb* [T] **wreak sth (on sb/sth)** to carry out or cause sth (a punishment, damage, etc): *The storm wreaked havoc (= great damage) in the forest.*

wreath /riːθ/ *noun* [C] (*pl* **wreaths** /riːðz/) a circle of flowers and leaves, especially one that you put on sb's grave

wreck /rek/ *noun* **1** [C] a ship that has sunk or been badly damaged at sea: *Divers searched the wreck.* **2** [U] the damage or destruction of sth, especially a ship at sea: *the wreck of the Titanic* **3** [C] a car, plane, etc which has been badly damaged, especially in an accident: *The car was a wreck but the lorry escaped almost without damage.* **4** [C, usually sing] (*informal*) a person or thing that is in a very bad condition: *a nervous wreck*

wreck *verb* [T] to destroy, damage or spoil sth completely: *Vandals had wrecked the village hall.* ○ *A fishing boat was wrecked in the storms.* ○ *The strike wrecked all our holiday plans.*

wreckage /'rekɪdʒ/ *noun* [U] the broken pieces of sth that has been wrecked

wrench /rentʃ/ *verb* [T] **1 wrench sb/sth (away, off, etc)** to pull or turn sb/sth strongly and suddenly: *He wrenched the wheel to the left and stopped the car on the grass.* ○ (*figurative*) *The film was so exciting that I could hardly wrench myself away.* **2** to injure your ankle, shoulder, etc by turning it suddenly

wrench *noun* **1** [C] a sudden, violent pull or turn: *With a wrench I managed to open the door.* **2** [sing] an occasion when you feel very sad because you have to leave sb/sth **3** [C] (*US*) = SPANNER

wrestle /'resl/ *verb* [I] **1** to fight by trying to get hold of your opponent's body and throw him/her to the ground. People wrestle as a sport. **2 wrestle with sth** to try hard to find an answer to sth; to struggle

wrestler /'reslə(r)/ *noun* [C] a person who wrestles as a sport

wrestling /'reslɪŋ/ *noun* [U] a sport in which two people fight and try to throw each other to the ground: *a wrestling match*

wretch /retʃ/ *noun* [C] (*old-fashioned*) a poor, unhappy person: *The poor wretch was clearly starving.*

wretched /'retʃɪd/ *adj* **1** very unhappy; miserable **2** (*informal*) (used for expressing anger): *That wretched dog has chewed up my slippers again!*

wriggle /'rɪɡl/ *verb* [I,T] **1** to move about, or to move a part of your body, with short, quick movements, especially from side to side: *Sit still and stop wriggling about!* ○ *She wriggled her fingers about in the hot sand.* **2** to move in the direction mentioned by making quick, turning movements: *The worm wriggled back into the soil.*
(PHRASAL VERB) **wriggle out of sth/out of doing sth** (*informal*) to avoid sth by making clever excuses: *It's your turn to wash up – you can't wriggle out of it this time!*

wring /rɪŋ/ *verb* [T] (*pt, pp* **wrung** /rʌŋ/) **wring sth (out)** to press and squeeze sth in order to remove water from it

,**wringing 'wet** *adj* very wet indeed

wrinkle /'rɪŋkl/ *noun* [C] a small line in sth, often one on the skin of your face which you get as you grow older

wrinkle *verb* [I,T] to form wrinkles (in sth): *She wrinkled her nose at the smell.* —**wrinkled** /'rɪŋkld/ *adj: an old lady with a wrinkled face*

☆ **wrist** /rɪst/ *noun* [C] the part of your body where your arm joins your hand ☛ picture on page A8.

'**wrist-watch** *noun* [C] a watch on a strap which you wear round your wrist

writ /rɪt/ *noun* [C] a legal order to do or not to do sth, given by a court of law or a person in authority

☆ **write** /raɪt/ *verb* (*pt* **wrote** /rəʊt/; *pp* **written** /'rɪtn/) **1** [I,T] to make words, letters, etc, especially on paper, using a pen, pencil, etc: *Some children can read and write before going to school.* ○ *I can't write with this pen.* ○ *Write your name and address on the back of your cheque.* **2** [T] to create a book, story, song, etc and write it on paper: *Tolstoy wrote 'War and Peace'.* ○ *He wrote his wife a poem.* ○ *Who wrote the music for that film?* **3** [I,T] to write and send a letter, etc to sb: *Have you written to your mother?* ○ *I'm writing to thank you for the birthday present you sent me.* ○ *She wrote that they were all well and would be home soon.* ○ *They wrote last week, asking us to spend Christmas with them.* ○ *I've written a letter to my son.* ○ *I've written my son a letter.* ○ *I've written to him.* ☛ In US English we can say: *I've written him.* **4** [T] **write sth (out) (for sb)** to fill or complete a form, cheque, document, etc with the necessary information: *I wrote out a cheque for £10.* ○ *The doctor quickly wrote a prescription for me.*
(PHRASAL VERBS) **write back (to sb)** to send a reply to sb

write sth down to write sth on paper, especially so that you can remember it

iː	ɪ	e	æ	ɑː	ɒ	ɔː	ʊ	uː	ʌ
see	sit	ten	hat	arm	got	saw	put	too	cup

write in (to sb/sth) (for sth) to write a letter to an organization, etc to order sth, give an opinion, etc

write off/away (to sb/sth) (for sth) to write a letter to an organization, etc to order sth or ask for sth

write sb/sth off to accept or decide that sb/sth will not be successful or useful: *Don't write him off yet. He could still win.*

write sth off to accept that you will not get back an amount of money you have lost or spent: *to write off a debt*

write sth out to write the whole of sth on paper: *Have you written out the poem in your exercise book?*

write sth up to write sth in a complete and final form, often using notes that you have made: *to write up lecture notes*

written *adj* expressed on paper; not just spoken: *a written agreement* o *a written test and an oral test*

'write-off *noun* [C] a thing, especially a vehicle, that is so badly damaged that it is not worth repairing

☆ **writer** /ˈraɪtə(r)/ *noun* [C] a person who writes, especially one whose job is to write books, stories, etc

writhe /raɪð/ *verb* [I] to turn and roll your body about: *She lay writhing in pain.*

☆ **writing** /ˈraɪtɪŋ/ *noun* [U] **1** words that have been written or printed; the way a person writes: *This card's got no writing inside. You can put your own message.* o *I can't read your writing, it's too small.* **2** the books, etc that sb has written or the style in which sb writes: *Love is a common theme in his early writing.* o *Her writing lacks realism.* **3** the activity or job of writing books, etc: *It's difficult to earn much money from writing.*

(IDIOM) **in writing** in written form: *I'll confirm the offer in writing next week.*

'writing-paper *noun* [U] paper for writing letters on: *writing-paper and envelopes*

written *pp* of WRITE

☆ **wrong**¹ /rɒŋ; *US* rɔːŋ/ *adj* **1** not true or not correct; not right: *the wrong answer* o *What you said was quite wrong.* o *You've got the wrong number* (= on the telephone). **2** not the best; not suitable; not right: *That's the wrong way to hold the bat.* o *I think she married the wrong man.* **3** (not before a noun) **wrong (with sb/sth)** not as it should be; not working properly: *You look upset. Is something wrong?* o *What's wrong with the car this time?* o *She's got something wrong with her leg.* **4 wrong (to do sth)** bad or against the law; not good or right: *The man said that he had done nothing wrong.* o *I think it was wrong of us not to invite him.*

(IDIOMS) **get on the right/wrong side of sb** ⇨ SIDE

get (hold of) the wrong end of the stick (*informal*) to misunderstand completely what has been said: *You must have got the wrong end of the stick. We're not going there, they are coming here.*

on the right/wrong track ⇨ TRACK

wrong *verb* [T] to do sth to sb which is bad or unfair: *I wronged her when I said she was lying.*

wrongful /-fl/ *adj* (*formal*) (only before a noun) not fair, not legal or not moral: *wrongful dismissal (from a job)*

wrongly *adv* in a wrong or mistaken way: *This letter's been wrongly addressed.* o *She claimed, quite wrongly, that the handbag was hers.* ☛ The adverb **wrong** is used after a verb or the object of a verb, especially in conversation: *He's spelt my name wrong.* The adverb **wrongly** is especially used before a past participle or a verb: *My name's been wrongly spelt.*

wrong² /rɒŋ; *US* rɔːŋ/ *adv* in an incorrect way; not right: *I always pronounce that word wrong.*

(IDIOMS) **get sb wrong** (*informal*) to misunderstand sb: *Don't get me wrong! I don't dislike him.*

go wrong 1 to make a mistake: *I'm afraid we've gone wrong. We should have taken the other road.* **2** to stop working properly or to stop developing well: *The freezer's gone wrong and all the food has defrosted.* o *Everything's gone wrong today.*

wrong³ /rɒŋ; *US* rɔːŋ/ *noun* **1** [U] what is bad or against the law: *Children quickly learn the difference between right and wrong.* **2** [C] an action or situation which is not fair: *A terrible wrong has been done. Those men should never have gone to prison.*

(IDIOM) **in the wrong** responsible for sth bad that has happened

wrote *pt* of WRITE

wrung *pt, pp* of WRING

wry /raɪ/ *adj* expressing a mixture of disappointment and amusement: *'Never mind,'* she said with a wry grin. *'At least we got one vote.'* —**wryly** *adv*

Xx

X, x /eks/ noun [C] (pl **X's**; **x's**) the twenty-fourth letter of the English alphabet: *'Xylophone' begins with (an) 'X'.* ☞ **X** is used by teachers to show that an answer is wrong. It is also used instead of the name of a person if you do not know or do not want to say the name: *Mr and Mrs X.* At the end of a letter it stands for a kiss: *Lots of love, Mary XX*.

xenophobia noun [U] fear or hatred of foreigners —**xenophobic** adj

Xerox /'zɪərɒks/ noun [C] (trade mark) **1** a machine that produces photocopies **2** a photocopy produced by such a machine: *a Xerox of the letter* —**xerox** verb [T]

Xmas /'krɪsməs; 'eksməs/ noun [C,U] (informal) (used as a short form, especially in writing) Christmas: *a Happy Xmas to all our customers*

X-ray /'eksreɪ/ noun [C] **1** [usually pl] a kind of radiation that makes it possible to see inside solid objects (eg the human body) so that they can be examined and a photograph of them can be made **2** a photograph that is made with an X-ray machine: *The X-ray showed that the bone was not broken.* —**X-ray** verb [T]: *She had her chest X-rayed.*

xylophone /'zaɪləfəʊn/ noun [C] a musical instrument that consists of a row of wooden or metal bars of different lengths. You play it by hitting these bars with a small hammer.

Yy

Y, y /waɪ/ noun [C] (pl **Y's**; **y's**) the twenty-fifth letter of the English alphabet: *'Yawn begins with (a) 'Y'.*

yacht /jɒt/ noun [C] **1** a boat with sails used for pleasure: *a yacht race* ☞ picture at **boat**. **2** a large boat with a motor, used for pleasure: *The harbour was full of millionaires' yachts.*

yachting noun [U] the activity or sport of sailing a yacht

'yachtsman /-smən/ noun [C] (pl **-men** /-smən/; feminine **yachtswoman**) a person who sails a yacht in races or for pleasure: *a round-the-world yachtsman*

Yank /jæŋk/ noun (informal) a word used in Britain for a person from the USA ☞ This word is considered rather rude.

yank /jæŋk/ verb [I,T] (informal) to pull with a sudden quick movement and with great force: *She yanked at the door handle and it came off in her hand.* —**yank** noun [C]

yap /jæp/ verb [I] (ya**pp**ing; ya**pp**ed) (used about dogs, especially small ones) to bark in an excited way, making short high noises

☆ **yard¹** /jɑːd/ noun [C] **1** an area usually of concrete or stone with a wall or fence around it, next to or round a building: *I walked through a yard to get to the back door of the office.* ○ *The children were playing in the school yard.* ○ *a farmyard* ☞ Look at **courtyard** and **church**-yard. **2** (US) = GARDEN **3** an area, usually without a roof, used for a particular type of work or purpose: *a shipyard* ○ *a builder's yard* ☞ In British English the piece of land belonging to a house is a **garden** if it has grass, flowers, etc and a **yard** if it is made of concrete or stone. In American English this piece of land is a **yard** whether it has grass or not, but if it is large and also has grass it can be called a garden.

☆ **yard²** /jɑːd/ noun [C] (abbr **yd**) a measure of length; 0·914 of a metre. There are 3 feet (or 36 inches) in a yard: *How do you buy carpet here? By the yard or by the metre?*

yardstick /'jɑːdstɪk/ noun [C] a standard by which things can be compared: *Exam results should not be the only yardstick by which pupils are judged.*

yarn /jɑːn/ noun **1** [U] thread (usually of wool or cotton) that is used for knitting, etc **2** [C] (informal) a story that sb tells, especially one that is exaggerated

☆ **yawn** /jɔːn/ verb [I] **1** to open your mouth wide and breathe in deeply, especially when you are tired or bored: *'I've only just got up,' she said, yawning.* ○ *I kept yawning all through the lecture.* **2** (used about a hole, etc) to be wide open: *a yawning hole in the ground where the bomb*

p	b	t	d	k	g	tʃ	dʒ	f	v	θ	ð
pen	bad	tea	did	cat	got	chin	June	fall	van	thin	then

had exploded —**yawn** noun [C]: 'How much longer will it take?' he said with a yawn.

yeah /jeə/ interj (informal) yes

☆ **year** /jɪə(r); jɜ:(r)/ noun **1** [C] the time it takes the earth to go once round the sun, about 365 days **2** [C] (also **'calendar year**) the period from 1 January to 31 December, 365 or 366 days divided into 12 months or 52 weeks: last year/ this year/next year ○ The population of the country will be 70 million by the year 2000. ○ We go to France at this time every year. ○ Interest is paid on this account once a year. ○ the year before last/the year after next ○ a leap year (= one that has 366 days) ○ the New Year (= the first days of January) **3** [C] any period of 12 months, measured from any point: It's been several years since I last saw him. ○ She worked here for twenty years. ○ He left school just over a year ago. ○ In a year's time, you'll be old enough to vote. ○ They've been living in Spain for the last few years. **4** [C] a period of a year in connection with schools, the business world, etc: The school year runs from September to July. ○ the financial year **5** [C] (used in connection with the age of sb/sth) a period of 12 months: He's ten years old today. ○ a six-year-old daughter ○ This car is nearly five years old. ○ The company is now in its fifth year. ☛ Note that you say: He's ten or: He's ten years old but NOT: He's ten years. Look at the note at **age**. **6 years** [plural] a long time: It happened years ago.

(IDIOMS) **all year round** for the whole year: Most of the hotels are open all year round.

donkey's years ⇨ DONKEY

year after year every year for many years

yearly adj, adv (happening) every year or once a year: a yearly pay increase ○ The conference is held yearly in Sligo.

yearn /jɜ:n/ verb [I] **yearn (for sb/sth)**; **yearn (to do sth)** to want sb/sth very much, especially sth that you cannot have —**yearning** noun [C,U]

yeast /ji:st/ noun [U] a substance used for making bread rise and for making beer, wine, etc

yell /jel/ verb [I,T] to shout very loudly, often because you are angry, excited or in pain: There's no need to yell at me, I can hear you perfectly well. —**yell** noun [C]

☆ **yellow** /'jeləʊ/ adj having the colour of lemons or butter: dark/light yellow ○ a bright/pale yellow dress

yellow noun [C,U] the colour yellow; something that has the colour yellow: a bright shade of yellow ○ the yellows and browns of the autumn leaves

yellowish adj rather yellow

,**yellow 'card** noun [C] (used in football) a card that the referee shows to a player as a warning that he/she will be sent off the field if he/she behaves badly again ☛ Look at **red card**.

,**yellow 'line** noun [C] a yellow line at the side of a road to show that you must not park there

Yellow 'Pages noun [plural] (trade mark) a telephone book (on yellow paper) that lists all the business companies, etc in a certain area, in sections according to the goods or services they provide

yelp /jelp/ noun [C] a sudden short cry, especially of pain, fear or excitement —**yelp** verb [I]

☆ **yes** /jes/ interj **1** (used when answering a question to which another possible answer is 'no'): 'Are you having a good time?' 'Yes thank you' ○ I asked him if he wanted to come and he said yes. **2** (used for saying that a statement is correct or for agreeing with one): 'You spend far too much money.' 'Yes, you're right.' **3** (used when agreeing to a request): 'May I sit here?' 'Yes, of course.' **4** (used when accepting an offer): 'More coffee?' 'Yes, please.' **5** (used for showing you have heard sb or will do what they ask): 'Waiter!' 'Yes, madam.' **6** (used when saying that a negative statement that sb has made is not true): 'You don't care about anyone but yourself.' 'Yes I do.'

yes noun [C] (pl **yeses** /'jesɪz/) an answer, statement or vote of 'yes'

☆ **yesterday** /'jestədi; -deɪ/ adv, noun [C,U] (on) the day before today: Did you watch the film on TV yesterday? ○ yesterday morning/afternoon/ evening ○ I posted the form the day before yesterday (= if I am speaking on Wednesday, I posted it on Monday). ○ Did it really happen three weeks ago? It seems like only yesterday. ○ Have you still got yesterday's paper? ○ Yesterday was the best day I've had for ages. ○ I spent the whole of yesterday walking round the shops.

☆ **yet** /jet/ adv **1** (used with negative verbs or in questions for talking about sth that has not happened but that you expect to happen): We haven't had any serious problems yet. ○ Has it stopped raining yet? ○ There was a pile of work on my desk which I hadn't yet done. ○ I haven't seen that film ☛ In American English: I didn't see that film yet. **2** (used with negative verbs) now; as early as this: You don't have to leave yet – your train isn't for another hour. **3** (used especially with may or might) at some time in the future: With a bit of luck, they may win yet. **4** (used after a period of time) longer: She isn't all that old, she'll live for years yet. **5** (used with comparatives or 'another' to emphasize the size or amount of sth): I'm already busy and now I've been given yet more work to do. **6** (used with superlatives) until and including now/then; so far: This is her best film yet. **7** but; in spite of that: Their plan was simple yet successful.

(IDIOMS) **as yet** until now: As yet little is known about the disease.

yet again (used for emphasizing how often sth happens) once more: I don't want to discuss this yet again!

yet to do, etc if you have yet to do sth, it means that you have not done it (but may possibly do it in the future): The final decision has yet to be made.

yet conj but (when sth is surprising after the first part of the statement): He seems pleasant, yet there's something about him I don't like.

yield /ji:ld/ verb **1** [T] to produce crops, profits or results: How much wheat does each field yield? ○ Did the experiment yield any new information? **2** [I] **yield (to sb/sth)** (formal) to stop resisting sb/sth (so that you do what sb

s	z	ʃ	ʒ	h	m	n	ŋ	l	r	j	w
so	zoo	she	vision	how	man	no	sing	leg	red	yes	wet

has demanded): *The government refused to yield to the hostage takers' demands.* ☞ **Give in** is less formal. **3** [T] to allow sb to have control of sth that you were controlling: *The army has yielded power to the rebels.* **4** [I] **yield to sth** to be replaced by sth, especially sth newer: *Old-fashioned methods have yielded to new technology.* **5** [I] to bend or break: *The dam finally yielded under the weight of the water.* **6** [I] **yield (to sb/sth)** to allow other traffic to go first or to join the road in front of you: *You have to yield to traffic from the left here.* ☞ In senses 4, 5 and 6, **give way** is more common. **Yield** is the usual American word in sense 6.

▸ **yield** *noun* [C] the amount that is produced: *Wheat yields were down 5% this year.* ○ *This investment has an annual yield of 12%.*

yob /jɒb/ *noun* [C] (*also* **yobbo** /'jɒbəʊ/ (*pl* **yobbos**) (*Brit slang*) a boy or young man who behaves badly in public

yoga /'jəʊgə/ *noun* [U] a system of exercises for the body, based on Hindu philosophy. Yoga helps you control and relax both your mind and your body.

yoghurt (*also* **yogurt**) /'jɒgət; *US* 'jəʊgərt/ *noun* [C,U] a slightly sour, thick liquid food made from milk with bacteria added to it

yoke /jəʊk/ *noun* [C] a piece of wood fixed across the necks of two animals when they are pulling a cart, etc: (*figurative*) *the yoke of slavery*

yolk /jəʊk/ *noun* [C,U] the yellow part in the middle of an egg: *He ate the yolk and left the white.* ☞ picture at **egg**.

yonks /jɒŋks/ *noun* [U] (*informal*) a very long time: *I haven't been to the theatre for yonks.*

☆ **you** /juː/ *pron* **1** (used as the subject or object of a verb, or after a preposition) the person or people being spoken or written to: *You can play the guitar, can't you?* ○ *I've told you about this before.* ○ *Bring your photos with you.* **2** (used with a noun, adjective or phrase when calling sb sth): *You fool! What do you think you're doing?* **3** a person (not a particular one); people in general: *You don't see many tourists here at this time of year.* ○ *The more you earn, the more tax you pay.* ☞ **One** has the same meaning but is much more formal: *One tries to help as much as one can.*

you-all /'juːɔːl/ *pron* (used in the Southern USA) you

you'd /juːd/ *short for* YOU HAD, YOU WOULD

you'll /juːl/ *short for* YOU WILL

☆ **young** /jʌŋ/ *adj* (**younger** /-ŋgə(r)/, **youngest** /-ŋgɪst/) not having lived or existed for very long: *They have two young children.* ○ *The film is about the United States, when it was still a young nation.* ○ *young plants* ○ *I'm a year younger than her.* ○ *My father was the youngest of eight children.* ○ *young fashion* (= for young people)

(IDIOM) **young at heart** behaving or thinking like a young person, even if you are not young

young *noun* [plural] **1** young animals: *Swans will attack to protect their young.* **2 the young** young people when you are thinking about them as a group: *The young of today are the adults of tomorrow.*

youngish *adj* quite young

youngster /-stə(r)/ *noun* [C] a young person: *There is very little entertainment for youngsters in this town.*

☆ **your** /jɔː(r); *US* jʊər/ *det* **1** belonging to or connected with the person or people being spoken to: *What's your flat like?* ○ *Thanks for all your help.* ○ *How old are your children now?* ○ *It would be helpful if you could all give me your addresses.* **2** belonging to or connected with people in general: *When your life is as busy as mine, you have little time to relax.* **3** (used for saying that sth is well-known to people in general): *So this is your typical English pub, is it?* **4** (*also* **Your**) (used in some titles): *your Majesty*

yours /jɔːz; *US* jʊərz/ *pron* **1** belonging to or connected with you: *Is this bag yours or mine?* ○ *I was talking to a friend of yours the other day.* **2 Yours** (used at the end of a letter): *Yours sincerely...* ○ *Yours faithfully...* ○ *Yours truly...* ○ *Yours...*

you're /jʊə(r); jɔː(r)/ *short for* YOU ARE

☆ **yourself** /jɔː'self; *US* jʊər'self/ *pron* (*pl* **yourselves** /-'selvz/) **1** (used as the object of a verb or preposition when you are speaking to sb and talking about this person/these people doing an action and also being affected by it): *Be careful or you'll hurt yourself.* ○ *Here's some money. Buy yourselves a present.* ○ *You're always talking about yourself!* **2** (used for emphasis): *You yourself told me there was a problem last week.* ○ *Did you repair the car yourselves?* (= or did sb else do it for you?) **3** in your normal state; healthy: *You don't look yourself today.*

(IDIOM) **by yourself/yourselves 1** alone: *Do you live by yourself?* **2** without help: *You can't cook dinner for ten people by yourself. Let me help you.*

☆ **youth** /juːθ/ *noun* (*pl* **youths** /juːðz/) **1** [U] the period of your life when you are young, especially the time between being a child and an adult: *He was quite a good sportsman in his youth.* **2** [U] the fact or state of being young: *I think that his youth will be a disadvantage in this job.* **3** [C] a young person (usually a young man, and often one that you do not have a good opinion of): *There were gangs of youths standing around on the street corners.* **4 the youth** [plural, with sing or pl verb] young people as a group: *What kind of future does/do the youth of this country have?*

youthful /-fl/ *adj* **1** having the qualities that are typical of young people: *She was nearly fifty but still full of youthful enthusiasm.* **2** young or relatively young: *a piece of music by the youthful Mozart*

'youth hostel *noun* [C] a type of cheap and simple hotel which people (especially young people) can stay at when they are travelling around on holiday

you've /juːv/ *short for* YOU HAVE

yo-yo /'jəʊjəʊ/ *noun* [C] (*pl* **yo-yos**) a toy which is a round piece of wood or plastic with a string round the middle. You put the string

iː	ɪ	e	æ	ɑː	ɒ	ɔː	ʊ	uː	ʌ
see	sit	ten	hat	arm	got	saw	put	too	cup

round your finger and can make the yo-yo go up and down it.

yuck /jʌk/ *interj* (*informal*) (used for saying that you think sth is very unpleasant): *Oh no, not cabbage! Yuck!*

yucky *adj* (**yuckier**; **yuckiest**) (*informal*) disgusting; very unpleasant; horrible: *What a yucky colour!*

yummy /'jʌmɪ/ *adj* (**yummier**; **yummiest**) (*informal*) tasting very good; delicious

yuppy (*also* **yuppie**) /'jʌpɪ/ *noun* [C] (*pl* **yuppies**) a successful young professional person who earns a lot of money and spends it on fashionable things

Zz

Z, z /zed; *US* ziː/ *noun* [C] (*pl* **Z's**; **z's**) the twenty-sixth letter of the English alphabet: *'Zero' begins with (a) 'Z'.* ☛ Note the different US pronunciation

zany /'zeɪnɪ/ *adj* funny in an unusual and crazy way: *a zany comedian*

zap /zæp/ *verb* [T] (**zap**ping; **zap**ped) (*informal*) to kill sb, usually with a gun or other weapon: *It's a computer game where you have to zap aliens with a laser.*

zeal /ziːl/ *noun* [U] (*formal*) great energy or enthusiasm: *religious zeal*

zealous /'zeləs/ *adj* using great energy and enthusiasm —**zealously** *adv*

zebra /'zebrə; *US* 'ziːbrə/ *noun* [C] (*pl* **zebra** or **zebras**) an African wild animal that looks like a horse, with black and white stripes all over its body

,zebra 'crossing *noun* [C] (*Brit*) a place where the road is marked with black and white lines to show that people can cross in safety because cars must stop there to let them over

☆ **zero** /'zɪərəʊ/ *pron* **1** 0; one less than one; nought **2** freezing point; 0°C: *The temperature is likely to fall to five below zero* (= -5°C). **3** nothing at all; none at all: *My chances of passing the exam are zero.* ☛ The figure **0** has several different names in British English. **Zero** is most commonly used in scientific or technical contexts. **Nil** is most commonly used in scores in sport (when spoken). **Nought** is used when referring to the figure **0** as part of a number: *a million is one followed by six noughts.* **O** (pronounced 'oh') is most commonly used when speaking numbers such as telephone or bus numbers.

zest /zest/ *noun* [U,sing] **zest (for sth)** a feeling of excitement, pleasure and interest: *She is a very active person, with a great zest for life.*

zigzag /'zɪɡzæɡ/ *noun* [C] a line with left and right turns, one after the other at sharp angles: *a zigzag path down the cliff* ○ *curtains with a zigzag pattern* ☛ picture at **pattern**. —**zigzag** *verb* [I] (zigza**gg**ing; zigza**gg**ed): *We took a road that zigzagged through the mountains.*

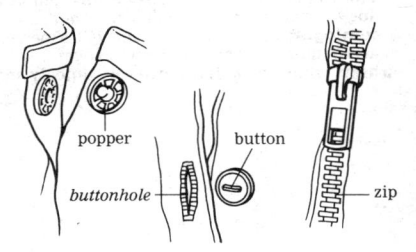

☆ **zip** /zɪp/ *noun* [C] (*also* **'zip-fastener**; *especially US* **zipper**) a device for fastening clothes, bags, etc which consists of two rows of metal or plastic teeth, one on each side of an opening. You can join these rows together to close the opening: *Your zip's undone!* ○ *Do your zip up.*

zip *verb* [T] (**zip**ping; **zip**ped) **zip sth (up)** to fasten sth with a zip: *There was so much in the bag that it was difficult to zip it up.*

Zip code /'zɪp kəʊd/ *noun* [C] (*US*) = POSTCODE

zodiac /'zəʊdɪæk/ *noun* [sing] **the zodiac** a diagram of the positions of the planets and stars, which is divided into twelve equal parts (**signs**) ☛ picture on next page.

☛ The signs of the zodiac are used in **astrology** and **horoscopes** (often called **The Stars**) in newspapers and magazines. People often refer to the signs and to the influence that they think these have on a person's personality and future: *Which sign of the zodiac are you?* ○ *I'm (a) Leo.*

zone /zəʊn/ *noun* [C] an area that is different from those around it eg because sth special happens there: *the war zone* ○ *We're crossing into a new time zone.*

ɜː	ə	eɪ	əʊ	aɪ	aʊ	ɔɪ	ɪə	eə	ʊə
fur	ago	pay	home	five	now	join	near	hair	pure

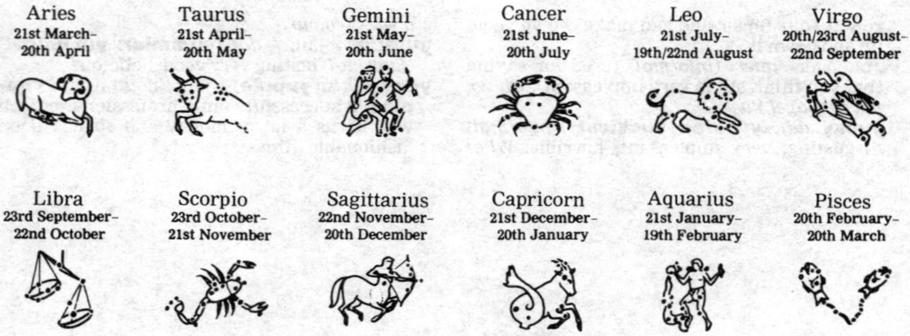

Aries	Taurus	Gemini	Cancer	Leo	Virgo
21st March–20th April	21st April–20th May	21st May–20th June	21st June–20th July	21st July–19th/22nd August	20th/23rd August–22nd September

Libra	Scorpio	Sagittarius	Capricorn	Aquarius	Pisces
23rd September–22nd October	23rd October–21st November	22nd November–20th December	21st December–20th January	21st January–19th February	20th February–20th March

signs of the zodiac

zoo /zu:/ noun [C] (pl **zoos**) (also formal **zo-ological 'gardens**) a park where many kinds of living (especially wild) animals are kept so that people can look at them: *to go to the zoo* ○ *She thinks that it's wrong to keep animals in zoos.*

zoology /zəʊ'ɒlədʒi/ noun [U] the scientific study of animals ☛ Look at **botany** and **biology**. —**zoological** /ˌzəʊə'lɒdʒɪkl/ adj **zoologist** /zəʊ'ɒlədʒɪst/ noun [C] a person who studies or is an expert on zoology

zoom /zu:m/ verb [I] to move very quickly and with a loud noise: *A motor cycle zoomed past.* (PHRASAL VERB) **zoom in (on sb/sth)** to make an object that you are filming appear bigger by using a special lens: *The camera zoomed in on a face in the crowd.*

'zoom lens noun [C] a camera lens that can make an object being photographed appear gradually bigger or smaller so that it seems to be getting closer or further away

zucchini /zʊ'ki:ni/ noun [C] (pl **zucchini**; **zucchinis**) (especially US) = COURGETTE

APPENDIX 1
Irregular verbs

APPENDIX 2
Expressions with numbers

APPENDIX 3
Common first names

APPENDIX 4
Abbreviations

APPENDIX 5
Geographical names and maps

APPENDIX 1

Irregular Verbs

In this list you will find the infinitive form of the verb followed by the past tense and the past participle. Where two forms are given, look up the verb in the main part of the dictionary to see whether there is a difference in meaning.

Infinitive	Past Tense	Past Participle
arise	arose	arisen
awake	awoke	awoken
be	was/were	been
bear	bore	borne
beat	beat	beaten
become	became	become
befall	befell	befallen
begin	began	begun
bend	bent	bent
bet	bet, betted	bet, betted
bid	bid, bade	bid, bidden
bind	bound	bound
bite	bit	bitten
bleed	bled	bled
blow	blew	blown, blowed
break	broke	broken
breed	bred	bred
bring	brought	brought
broadcast	broadcast	broadcast
build	built	built
burn	burnt, burned	burnt, burned
burst	burst	burst
bust	bust, busted	bust, busted
buy	bought	bought
cast	cast	cast
catch	caught	caught
choose	chose	chosen
cling	clung	clung
come	came	come
cost	cost	cost
creep	crept	crept
cut	cut	cut
deal	dealt	dealt
dig	dug	dug
dive	dived; (US) dove	dived
do	did	done
draw	drew	drawn
dream	dreamt, dreamed	dreamt, dreamed
drink	drank	drunk
drive	drove	driven
dwell	dwelt, dwelled	dwelt, dwelled
eat	ate	eaten
fall	fell	fallen
feed	fed	fed

feel	felt	felt
fight	fought	fought
find	found	found
flee	fled	fled
fling	flung	flung
fly	flew	flown
forbid	forbade, forbad	forbidden
forecast	forecast, forecasted	forecast, forecasted
foresee	foresaw	foreseen
foretell	foretold	foretold
forget	forgot	forgotten
forgive	forgave	forgiven
forsake	forsook	forsaken
freeze	froze	frozen
get	got	got; (*US*) gotten
give	gave	given
go	went	gone
grind	ground	ground
grow	grew	grown
hang	hung, hanged	hung, hanged
have	had	had
hear	heard	heard
hew	hewed	hewed, hewn
hide	hid	hidden
hit	hit	hit
hold	held	held
hurt	hurt	hurt
input	input, inputted	input, inputted
keep	kept	kept
kneel	knelt; (*esp US*) kneeled	knelt; (*esp US*) kneeled
know	knew	known
lay	laid	laid
lead	led	led
lean	leant, leaned	leant, leaned
leap	leapt, leaped	leapt, leaped
learn	learnt, learned	learnt, learned
leave	left	left
lend	lent	lent
let	let	let
lie²	lay	lain
light	lighted, lit	lighted, lit
lose	lost	lost
make	made	made
mean	meant	meant
meet	met	met
mislay	mislaid	mislaid
mislead	misled	misled
misread	misread	misread
misspell	misspelt, misspelled	misspelt, misspelled
mistake	mistook	mistaken
misunderstand	misunderstood	misunderstood
mow	mowed	mown, mowed
outdo	outdid	outdone
outgrow	outgrew	outgrown
overcome	overcame	overcome
overdo	overdid	overdone
overhang	overhung	overhung
overhear	overheard	overheard
override	overrode	overridden
overrun	overran	overrun
oversee	oversaw	overseen
oversleep	overslept	overslept
overtake	overtook	overtaken
overthrow	overthrew	overthrown
pay	paid	paid

prove	proved	proved; (US) proven
put	put	put
quit	quit, quitted	quit, quitted
read	read	read
rebuild	rebuilt	rebuilt
repay	repaid	repaid
rewrite	rewrote	rewritten
rid	rid	rid
ride	rode	ridden
ring	rang	rung
rise	rose	risen
run	ran	run
saw	sawed	sawn; (US) sawed
say	said	said
see	saw	seen
seek	sought	sought
sell	sold	sold
send	sent	sent
set	set	set
sew	sewed	sewn, sewed
shake	shook	shaken
shear	sheared	shorn, sheared
shed	shed	shed
shine	shone	shone
shoe	shod	shod
shoot	shot	shot
show	showed	shown, showed
shrink	shrank, shrunk	shrunk
shut	shut	shut
sing	sang	sung
sink	sank	sunk
sit	sat	sat
slay	slew	slain
sleep	slept	slept
slide	slid	slid
sling	slung	slung
slink	slunk	slunk
slit	slit	slit
smell	smelt, smelled	smelt, smelled
sow	sowed	sown, sowed
speak	spoke	spoken
speed	sped, speeded	sped, speeded
spell	spelt, spelled	spelt, spelled
spend	spent	spent
spill	spilt, spilled	spilt, spilled
spin	spun	spun
spit	spat; (US also) spit	spat; (US also) spit
split	split	split
spoil	spoilt, spoiled	spoilt, spoiled
spread	spread	spread
spring	sprang	sprung
stand	stood	stood
steal	stole	stolen
stick	stuck	stuck
sting	stung	stung
stink	stank, stunk	stunk
stride	strode	stridden
strike	struck	struck
string	strung	strung
strive	strove	striven
swear	swore	sworn
sweep	swept	swept
swell	swelled	swollen, swelled
swim	swam	swum
swing	swung	swung

take	took	taken
teach	taught	taught
tear	tore	torn
tell	told	told
think	thought	thought
thrive	thrived, throve	thrived
throw	threw	thrown
thrust	thrust	thrust
tread	trod	trodden, trod
undercut	undercut	undercut
undergo	underwent	undergone
underpay	underpaid	underpaid
understand	understood	understood
undertake	undertook	undertaken
undo	undid	undone
unwind	unwound	unwound
uphold	upheld	upheld
upset	upset	upset
wake	woke	woken
wear	wore	worn
weave	wove, weaved	woven, weaved
weep	wept	wept
wet	wet, wetted	wet, wetted
win	won	won
wind[3]	wound	wound
withdraw	withdrew	withdrawn
withhold	withheld	withheld
withstand	withstood	withstood
wring	wrung	wrung
write	wrote	written

APPENDIX 2

Expressions using Numbers

The Numbers

1	one	1st	first
2	two	2nd	second
3	three	3rd	third
4	four	4th	fourth
5	five	5th	fifth
6	six	6th	sixth
7	seven	7th	seventh
8	eight	8th	eighth
9	nine	9th	ninth
10	ten	10th	tenth
11	eleven	11th	eleventh
12	twelve	12th	twelfth
13	thirteen	13th	thirteenth
14	fourteen	14th	fourteenth
15	fifteen	15th	fifteenth
16	sixteen	16th	sixteenth
17	seventeen	17th	seventeenth
18	eighteen	18th	eighteenth
19	nineteen	19th	nineteenth
20	twenty	20th	twentieth
21	twenty-one	21st	twenty-first
22	twenty-two	22nd	twenty-second
30	thirty	30th	thirtieth
40	forty	40th	fortieth
50	fifty	50th	fiftieth
60	sixty	60th	sixtieth
70	seventy	70th	seventieth
80	eighty	80th	eightieth
90	ninety	90th	ninetieth
100	a/one hundred	100th	hundredth
101	a/one hundred and one	101st	hundred and first
200	two hundred	200th	two hundredth
1 000	a/one thousand	1 000th	thousandth
10 000	ten thousand	10 000th	ten thousandth
100 000	a/one hundred thousand	100 000th	hundred thousandth
1 000 000	a/one million	1 000 000th	millionth

Examples:

528: five hundred and twenty-eight ○ *2 976: two thousand, nine hundred and seventy-six* ○ *50 439: fifty thousand, four hundred and thirty-nine*

Note A small space or a comma is used to separate the 'thousands', eg *25 000* or *25,000*. For the use of the point (.) in decimals, look at the next section. In numbers such as *100* or *1 000*, we can say 'one hundred' or 'a hundred', 'one thousand' or 'a thousand'. In conversation, it is more usual to say 'a' unless we want to stress that it is *one* and not *two*, for example. O can be said as 'nought', 'zero', 'nothing' or 'o'. In the following sections you will see the most usual way of saying it in each type of expression.

Fractions and decimals

½	a half	⅓	a/one third
¼	a quarter	⅖	two fifths
⅛	an/one eighth	⁷⁄₁₂	seven twelfths
¹⁄₁₀	a/one tenth	1½	one and a half
¹⁄₁₆	a/one sixteenth	2⅜	two and three eighths

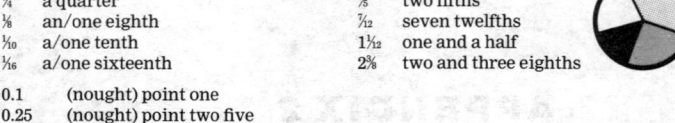

0.1	(nought) point one
0.25	(nought) point two five
0.33	(nought) point three three
1.75	one point seven five
3.976	three point nine seven six

Mathematical Expressions

+ plus
− minus
× times *or* multiplied by
÷ divided by
= equals
% per cent

3^2 three squared

5^3 five cubed

6^{10} six to the power of ten

Examples:

$6 + 9 = 15$ *six plus nine equals* (or *is*) *fifteen*
$5 \times 6 = 30$ *five times six equals thirty* or *five sixes are thirty* or
five multiplied by six is thirty

75% *(seventy-five per cent) of the class passed the test.*

Weight

	GB/US	Metric
	1 ounce (oz)	= 28.35 grams (g)
16 ounces	= 1 pound (lb)	= 0.454 kilogram (kg)
14 pounds	= 1 stone (st)	= 6.356 kilograms
112 pounds	= 1 hundredweight (cwt)	= 50.8 kilograms
20 hundredweight	= 1 ton (t)	= 1.016 tonnes

Examples:

The baby weighed 7lb 4oz (seven pounds four ounces).
For this recipe you need 500g (five hundred grams) of flour.

Note In the United States, the hundredweight is equal to 100 pounds and the ton is calculated as 2 000lb or 0.907 tonne. The stone is not used, so where in Britain you would hear '*She weighs eight stone ten*', an American would say '*She weighs 122 pounds.*'

Length

	GB/US	Metric
	1 inch (in)	= 25.4 millimetres (mm)
12 inches	= 1 foot (ft)	= 30.48 centimetres (cm)
3 feet	= 1 yard (yd)	= 0.914 metre (m)
1 760 yards	= 1 mile	= 1.609 kilometres (km)

Examples:

Height: 5 ft 9 in (five foot nine or five feet nine)

The hotel is 30 yds (thirty yards) from the beach.

The car was doing 50 mph (fifty miles per hour).

The room is 11' × 9'6" (eleven feet by nine feet six or eleven foot by nine foot six).

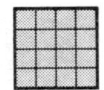

Area

	GB/US	Metric
	1 square inch (sq in)	= 6.452 square centimetres
144 square inches	= 1 square foot (sq ft)	= 929.03 square centimetres
9 square feet	= 1 square yard (sq yd)	= 0.836 square metre
4840 square yards	= 1 acre	= 0.405 hectare
640 acres	= 1 square mile	= 2.59 square kilometres or 259 hectares

Examples:

They have a 200-acre farm.

The fire destroyed 40 square miles of woodland.

Capacity

	GB	US	Metric
20 fluid ounces (fl oz)	= 1 pint (pt)	= 1.201 pints	= 0.568 litre (l)
2 pints	= 1 quart (qt)	= 1.201 quarts	= 1.136 litres
4 quarts	= 1 gallon (gall)	= 1.201 gallons	= 4.546 litres

Examples:

I asked the milkman to leave three pints of milk.

The petrol tank holds 40 litres.

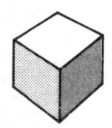

Cubic Measure

	GB/US	Metric
	1 cubic inch (cu in)	= 16.39 cubic centimetres (cc)
1728 cubic inches	= 1 cubic foot (cu ft)	= 0.028 cubic metre (m^3)
27 cubic feet	= 1 cubic yard	= 0.765 cubic metre

Example:

The car has a 1200 cc engine.

Times

	In conversation	*In official language*
06.00	six o'clock	(o) six hundred (hours)
06.05	five past six	(o) six o five
06.10	ten past six	(o) six ten
06.15	(a) quarter past six	(o) six fifteen
06.20	twenty past six	(o) six twenty
06.30	half past six	(o) six thirty
06.35	twenty-five to seven	(o) six thirty-five

06.40	twenty to seven	(o) six forty
06.45	(a) quarter to seven	(o) six forty-five
06.50	ten to seven	(o) six fifty
06.55	five to seven	(o) six fifty-five
10.12	twelve minutes past ten	ten twelve
13.10	ten past one	thirteen ten
19.56	four minutes to eight	nineteen fifty-six

US English: In American English, **after** is sometimes used instead of 'past' and **of** instead of 'to'.

Note In conversation, we do not usually use the twenty-four hour clock. If we need to make it clear that we mean 06.00, not 18.00, we can say 'six o'clock in the morning'. For 22.00, we can say 'ten o'clock in the evening'; for 15.30 'half past three in the afternoon'. In slightly more formal language, we use 'am' for times before midday and 'pm' for times after midday.

Examples:

The train leaves at 06.56.

Something woke me at two o'clock in the morning.

Office hours are 9 am to 4.30 pm.

Dates

Dates can be written in numbers or in numbers and words:

15/4/93 (*US* 4/15/93)   15 April 1993   April 15th, 1993 (*esp US*)

and can be said as:
April the fifteenth, nineteen ninety-three

or

the fifteenth of April, nineteen ninety-three
(In American English, April fifteenth).

Examples:

Her birthday is 9th April (April the ninth/the ninth of April).

The restaurant will be closed May 3 – June 1 (from May the third to June the first).

Temperature

Although in Britain temperatures are officially measured in degrees Celsius, many people still use the Fahrenheit scale in conversation, and this is common in the United States except in scientific use. To convert Fahrenheit to Celsius, subtract 32 from the number, then multiply by 5 and divide by 9:

$68°F - 32 = 36 \times 5 = 180 \div 9 = 20°C$

Examples:

Water freezes at 32°F and boils at 212°F.

The maximum temperature this afternoon will be 68°.

Overnight, temperatures below zero are expected, possibly reaching –10 (minus ten) before morning.

He's got a temperature of 101°. I think he's got flu.

Money

GB

	Amount	Coin/Note
1p	a penny (one p)	a penny
2p	two pence (two p)	a two-pence piece
5p	five pence (five p)	a five-pence piece
10p	ten pence (ten p)	a ten-pence piece
20p	twenty pence (twenty p)	a twenty-pence piece
50p	fifty pence (fifty p)	a fifty-pence piece
£1	a pound	a pound (coin)
£5	five pounds	a five-pound note
£10	ten pounds	a ten-pound note

Note Informal ways of saying the amounts of money are given in brackets.

Examples:

£5.75: five pounds seventy-five o *25p: twenty-five pence (or p)*

The apples are 65p a pound. o *We pay £250 a month in rent.*

US

	Amount	Coin/Note
1¢	one cent	a penny
5¢	five cents	a nickel
10¢	ten cents	a dime
25¢	twenty-five cents	a quarter
$1.00	one dollar	a dollar bill

Examples:

$3.35: Three dollars thirty-five o *59¢: fifty-nine cents* o *Do you have a quarter for the phone?* o *The apartment costs $500 (five hundred dollars) a month.*

Telephone Numbers

When we talk about telephone numbers, we say each number separately, often breaking a long series up into groups of about three, eg: *295013:*

two nine five – o one three.

59433 can be said as *five nine four three three* or *five nine four double-three*.

If you are calling a number in a different town, you have to use the 'area code' before the number:

01865 is the code for Oxford.

If you are phoning somebody in a large firm, you can ask for their *extension number*.

(01865) 56767 × 4840 (extension 4840)

APPENDIX 3

Common First Names

Female Names

Alison /ˈælɪsn/
Amanda (Mandy) /əˈmændə/ /ˈmændɪ/
Angela /ˈændʒələ/
Ann, Anne /æn/
Barbara /ˈbɑːbrə/
Carol, Caroline /ˈkærəl/ /ˈkærəlaɪn/
Catherine, Katherine /ˈkæθrɪn/
Christine /ˈkrɪstiːn/
Clare /kleə(r)/
Deborah /ˈdebərə/
Diana /daɪˈænə/
Dorothy /ˈdɒrəθɪ/
Elaine /ɪˈleɪn/
Elizabeth (Liz) /ɪˈlɪzəbəθ/ /lɪz/
Emma /ˈemə/
Fiona /fɪˈəʊnə/
Gillian /ˈdʒɪliən/
Helen /ˈhelən/
Isobel /ˈɪzəbel/
Jacqueline (Jackie) /ˈdʒækəlɪn/ /ˈdʒækɪ/
Jane /dʒeɪn/
Jennifer (Jenny) /ˈdʒenɪfə(r)/ /ˈdʒenɪ/
Joanna, Joanne /dʒəʊˈænə/ /dʒəʊˈæn/
Judith /ˈdʒuːdɪθ/
Julia, Julie /ˈdʒuːliə/ /ˈdʒuːlɪ/
Karen /ˈkærən/
Linda /ˈlɪndə/
Lynn /lɪn/
Margaret /ˈmɑːgrɪt/
Mary /ˈmeərɪ/
Michelle /mɪˈʃel/
Nicola /ˈnɪkələ/
Pamela /ˈpæmələ/
Patricia (Pat) /pəˈtrɪʃə/ /pæt/
Penelope (Penny) /pəˈneləpɪ/ /ˈpenɪ/
Rachel /ˈreɪtʃl/
Rebecca (Becky) /rɪˈbekə/ /ˈbekɪ/
Ruth /ruːθ/
Sally /ˈsælɪ/
Samantha /səˈmænθə/
Sandra /ˈsɑːndrə; US ˈsæn-/
Sarah /ˈseərə/
Sharon /ˈʃærən/
Sheila /ˈʃiːlə/
Susan (Sue) /ˈsuːzn/ /suː/
Theresa /təˈriːzə/
Tracy, Tracey /ˈtreɪsɪ/
Victoria (Vicky) /vɪkˈtɔːrɪə/ /ˈvɪkɪ/
Wendy /ˈwendɪ/
Yvonne /ɪˈvɒn/

Male Names

Adam /ˈædəm/
Alan /ˈælən/
Andrew /ˈændruː/
Anthony (Tony) /ˈæntənɪ/ /ˈtəʊnɪ/
Benjamin /ˈbendʒəmɪn/
Brian /ˈbraɪən/
Charles /tʃɑːlz/
Christopher /ˈkrɪstəfə(r)/
Darren /ˈdærən/
David /ˈdeɪvɪd/
Douglas /ˈdʌgləs/
Edward (Ted) /ˈedwəd/ /ted/
Frank /fræŋk/
Frederick /ˈfredrɪk/
Geoffrey /ˈdʒefrɪ/
George /dʒɔːdʒ/
Graham /ˈgreɪəm/
Henry (Harry) /ˈhenrɪ/ /ˈhærɪ/
Hugh /hjuː/
Ian /ˈiːən/
James (Jim) /dʒeɪmz/ /dʒɪm/
Jason /ˈdʒeɪsn/
Jeremy /ˈdʒerəmɪ/
John /dʒɒn/
Jonathan /ˈdʒɒnəθən/
Joseph /ˈdʒəʊzɪf/
Keith /kiːθ/
Kevin /ˈkevɪn/
Malcolm /ˈmælkəm/
Mark /mɑːk/
Martin /ˈmɑːtɪn; US ˈmɑːrtn/
Matthew /ˈmæθjuː/
Michael (Mike) /ˈmaɪkl/ /maɪk/
Neil /niːl/
Nicholas /ˈnɪkələs/
Nigel /ˈnaɪdʒl/
Patrick /ˈpætrɪk/
Paul /pɔːl/
Peter /ˈpiːtə(r)/
Philip /ˈfɪlɪp/
Richard (Dick) /ˈrɪtʃəd/ /dɪk/
Robert (Bob) /ˈrɒbət/ /bɒb/
Roger /ˈrɒdʒə(r)/
Sean /ʃɔːn/
Simon /ˈsaɪmən/
Stephen, Steven /ˈstiːvn/
Stuart, Stewart /ˈstjuːət/
Thomas /ˈtɒməs/
Timothy /ˈtɪməθɪ/
William (Bill) /ˈwɪliəm, also ˈwɪljəm/ /bɪl/

APPENDIX 4

Abbreviations

This is a list of abbreviations that are common in English. If they are often used in speech, the pronunciation is also given. Many of these abbreviations can also be written with a full stop (.) marking where a word has been shortened.

AA /ˌeɪ 'eɪ/ (*Brit*) Automobile Association; an organization for motorists. If you are a member of the AA and your car breaks down, you can phone them and they will send someone to help you.
abbr (*also* **abbrev**) abbreviation
AD /ˌeɪ 'diː/ anno domini; used in dates for showing the number of years after the time when Christians believe Jesus Christ was born: *AD 44*
AGM /ˌeɪ dʒiː 'em/ (*esp Brit*) Annual General Meeting
AM /ˌeɪ 'em/ amplitude modulation; one of the systems of broadcasting radio signals
am (*US* **AM**) /ˌeɪ 'em/ before midday: *10 am* (= 10 o'clock in the morning)
anon /ə'nɒn/ (used to show that we do not know who the author of a piece of price is) anonymous
approx approximate; approximately
Apr April: *2 Apr 1993*
arr arrives: *arr York 07.15*
ASA /ˌeɪ es 'eɪ/ American Standards Association; used for indicating the speed of a camera film: *100 ASA*
asap /ˌeɪ es eɪ 'piː/ as soon as possible
Assoc (*also* **assoc**) association
Asst (*also* **asst**) assistant
Aug August: *10 Aug 1957*
Ave Avenue: *26 Elm Ave*

b born: *J S Bach, b 1685*
BA /ˌbiː 'eɪ/ Bachelor of Arts; the degree that you receive when you complete a university or college course in an arts subject
B and B (*also* **b and b**) /ˌbiː ən 'biː/ bed and breakfast; a type of accommodation, often in private houses. The price includes a room for the night and breakfast.
BBC /ˌbiː biː 'siː/ British Broadcasting Corporation; one of the national radio and television companies in Britain: *a BBC documentary* o *watch a programme on BBC 1*
BC /ˌbiː 'siː/ before Christ; used in dates to show the number of years before the time when Christians believe Jesus Christ was born: *300 BC*
BEd /ˌbiː 'ed/ Bachelor of Education; a degree in education for people who want to be teachers and do not already have a degree in a particular subject
bk (*pl* **bks**) book
BR /ˌbiː 'ɑː(r)/ British Rail

Bros (used in the name of companies) Brothers: *Wentworth Bros Ltd*
BSc /ˌbiː es 'siː/ Bachelor of Science; the degree that you receive when you complete a university or college course in a science subject
BST /ˌbiː es 'tiː/ British Summer Time; the system used in Britain between March and October, when clocks are put one hour ahead of Greenwich Mean Time
BTEC /'biː tek/ (*Brit*) Business and Technology Education Council; an organization which offers qualifications for young people who have left secondary school and want to train in commercial or technical subjects

C Celsius; centigrade: *Water freezes at 0°C.*
c (before dates) about, approximately: *c 1770*
CALL /kæl/ computer-assisted language learning
Capt Captain; a rank in the British and American armies
CBI /ˌsiː biː 'aɪ/ Confederation of British Industry; the employers' association
cc /ˌsiː 'siː/ cubic centimetre(s): *a 1200cc engine*
CD-ROM /ˌsiː diː 'rɒm/ compact disc read-only memory; a compact disc which can be used in a computer and which has a lot of information recorded on it. The information cannot be changed or removed.
cf /ˌsiː 'ef/ compare
ch (*also* **chap**) chapter
CIA /ˌsiː aɪ 'eɪ/ (*US*) Central Intelligence Agency; the US government organization that tries to discover secret political and military information about other countries
cl centilitre(s)
cm centimetre(s)
Co 1 company: *W Smith and Co* **2** county: *Co Down*
c/o /ˌsiː 'əʊ/ (used for addressing a letter to somebody who is staying at another person's house) care of: *Mr Peter Boyes, c/o Mr and Mrs B. Jay*
C of E /ˌsiː əv 'iː/ Church of England
Col Colonel; a rank in the British and American armies
Con (*also* **Cons**) (*in British politics*) Conservative
cont (*also* **contd**) continued: *cont on p 91*
Corp (*US*) Corporation: *West Coast Motor Corporation*
cu cubic: *a volume of 3 cu ft*

cv /ˌsiː ˈviː/ curriculum vitae; a short account of your education and work experience, often used when you are applying for a new job
cwt hundredweight; a measure of weight, about 50.8 kg

d died: *W A Mozart, d 1791*
Dec December: *5 Dec 1992*
Dem (*in US politics*) Democrat; Democratic (Party)
dep departs: *dep London 15.32*
Dept department: *Sales Dept* ○ *Dept of History*
Dip diploma
DIY /ˌdiː aɪ ˈwaɪ/ (*Brit informal*) do it yourself; the activity of making and repairing things yourself around your home: *a DIY expert* ○ *a DIY shop* (= where you can buy materials for DIY)
DJ /ˌdiː ˈdʒeɪ/ disc jockey; a person whose job is to play and introduce pop music on the radio or in a disco
doz dozen
Dr doctor: *Dr Anne Walker* ○ *Dr Smith*

E east(ern): *E Asia*
ea each
EAP /ˌiː eɪ ˈpiː/ English for Academic Purposes
EC /ˌiːˈsiː/ European Community
ed edited by; edition; editor
EFL /ˌiː ef ˈel/ English as a Foreign Language
eg /ˌiː ˈdʒiː/ for example: *popular sports, eg football, tennis, swimming*
ELT /ˌiː el ˈtiː/ English Language Teaching (to non-native speakers)
enc (*also* **encl**) (used at the end of a business letter to show that there is sth else in the envelope with the letter) enclosed
ESL /ˌiː es ˈel/ English as a Second Language
ESP /ˌiː es ˈpiː/ English for Specific/Special Purposes; the teaching of English to people who need it for a special reason, such as scientific study, engineering, etc
esp especially
Esq (*formal, esp Brit*) Esquire; used when you are writing a man's name and address on an envelope: *Andrew Kent, Esq.* This is rather old-fashioned and many people now prefer to write *Mr Andrew Kent*.
etc etcetera; and so on, and other things of a similar kind: *sandwiches, biscuits, cakes, etc*
ext extension number of a telephone: *ext 3492*

F Fahrenheit: *Water freezes at 32°F.*
f (*also* **fem**) female; feminine
FA /ˌef ˈeɪ/ (*Brit*) Football Association: *the FA Cup*
FBI /ˌef biː ˈaɪ/ (*US*) Federal Bureau of Investigation; the section of the US Justice Department which investigates crimes that are against federal law, such as bank robbery and terrorism
FC (*Brit*) Football Club: *Everton FC*
Feb February: *18 Feb 1993*
ff (used to indicate that sth starts on a particular page or line and continues for several pages or lines more): *British Politics, p10ff*
FIFA /ˈfiːfə/ International Association Football Federation
fig 1 figure, illustration: *See diagram at fig 2.* **2** figurative(ly)
fl oz fluid ounce(s); a measure of liquid, about 0.028 litre

FM /ˌef ˈem/ frequency modulation; one of the systems of broadcasting radio signals
Fri Friday: *Fri 27 May*
ft foot, feet; a measure of length, about 30.5 cm: *a room 10 ft by 6 ft*

g (*also* **gr** *or* **gm**) gram(s)
gall gallon(s); a measure of liquid, about 4.54 litres
Gen General; a rank in the British and American armies
GB /ˌdʒiː ˈbiː/ Great Britain
GCSE /ˌdʒiː siː es ˈiː/ (*Brit*) General Certificate of Secondary Education; an examination that schoolchildren in England, Wales and Northern Ireland take when they are about sixteen. They often take GCSEs in five or more subjects. For Scottish examinations, look at **SCE**.
GMT /ˌdʒiː em ˈtiː/ Greenwich Mean Time; the time system that is used in Britain during the winter and for calculating the time in other parts of the world
GP /ˌdʒiː ˈpiː/ general practitioner; a doctor who treats all types of illnesses and works in a practice in a town or village, not in a hospital
Gt Great: *Gt Yarmouth*

ha hectare(s)
HGV /ˌeɪtʃ dʒiː ˈviː/ (*Brit*) heavy goods vehicle, such as a lorry: *have an HGV licence*
HIV /ˌeɪtʃ aɪ ˈviː/ human immunodeficiency virus; the virus that is believed to cause AIDS
HM His/Her Majesty: *HM the Queen*
HMS /ˌeɪtʃ em ˈes/ (*Brit*) (for ships in the British Royal Navy) Her/His Majesty's Ship: *HMS Apollo*
Hon 1 Honorary (used to show that sb holds a position without being paid for it): *Hon President* **2** Honourable: a title for Members of Parliament, some high officials and the children of some noblemen
Hons Honours (in Bachelor degrees): *John North BSc (Hons)*
HP /ˌeɪtʃ ˈpiː/ (*Brit*) hire purchase
hp /ˌeɪtʃ ˈpiː/ horsepower (of an engine)
HQ /ˌeɪtʃ ˈkjuː/ headquarters
hr (*pl* **hrs**) hour: *journey time: 3 hrs 15 min*
Hz hertz; (used in radio) a measure of frequency, one cycle per second

ID /ˌaɪ ˈdiː/ (*informal*) identification; identity: *an ID card*
ie /ˌaɪ ˈiː/ that is; in other words: *deciduous trees, ie those which lose their leaves in autumn*
IMF /ˌaɪ em ˈef/ International Monetary Fund
in inch(es); a measure of length, about 2.54 cm: *4 in × 2 in* ○ *He is 6 ft 2 in tall.*
Inc (*also* **inc**) (*US*) Incorporated: *Manhattan Drugstores Inc*
incl including; inclusive: *total £59.00 incl tax*
IOU /ˌaɪ əʊ ˈjuː/ I owe you; a piece of paper that you sign showing that you owe sb some money
IPA /ˌaɪ piː ˈeɪ/ International Phonetic Alphabet
IQ /ˌaɪ ˈkjuː/ intelligence quotient; a measure of a person's intelligence: *have a high/low IQ* ○ *an IQ of 120*
IRA /ˌaɪ ɑːr ˈeɪ/ Irish Republican Army: *a member of the IRA* ○ *an IRA attack*
ISBN /ˌaɪ es biː ˈen/ International Standard Book Number

IT /ˌaɪ ˈtiː/ (*computing*) Information Technology

ITV /ˌaɪ tiː ˈviː/ (*Brit*) Independent Television; the group of independent television companies that are paid for by advertising: *watch a film on ITV* ○ *an ITV documentary*

Jan January: *1 Jan 1993*

Jnr (*also* **Jr**, **Jun**) (*esp US*) Junior: *Samuel P Carson, Jnr* (= the son, not the father of the same name)

Jul July: *4 Jul 1955*

Jun June: *10 Jun 1830*

K /keɪ/ (*informal*) one thousand: *She earns 22K* (= £22 000) *a year*.

kg kilogram(s): *weight 10kg*

kHz kilohertz (used in radio) a measure of frequency

km kilometre(s): *a 10km walk* ○ *distance to beach 2 km*

kph /ˌkeɪ piː ˈeɪtʃ/ kilometres per hour

kW (*also* **kw**) kilowatt(s): *a 2 kw electric heater*

L 1 (*Brit*) (on a car, etc) learner-driver: *L-plates* 2 large (size)

l 1 left 2 line 3 litre(s)

Lab (*in British politics*) Labour (party): *Tom Black (Lab)*

lb pound(s); a measurement of weight, about 454g

Lib Dem (*in British politics*) Liberal Democrat: *David Stone (Lib Dem)*

Lieut (*also* **Lt**) Lieutenant; a rank in the British and American armies and navies and in the American police force

LP /ˌel ˈpiː/ long-playing record: *Which song do you like best on their new LP?*

Ltd (*Brit*) Limited (used about private companies): *Pierce and Co Ltd*

M /em/ 1 (*also* **med**) medium (size) 2 (*Brit*) motorway: *heavy traffic on the M25*

m 1 male 2 (*also* **masc**) masculine (gender) 3 metre(s): *a 500m race* 4 million(s): *population: 10m*

MA /ˌem ˈeɪ/ Master of Arts; a second qualification that you receive when you complete a more advanced course or piece of research in an arts subject at university or college

Mar March: *17 Mar 1956*

masc masculine

max /mæks/ maximum: *max temp 21°*

MBA /ˌem biː ˈeɪ/ Master of Business Administration; an advanced university degree in business

MD /ˌem ˈdiː/ Doctor of Medicine

MEP /ˌem iː ˈpiː/ Member of the European Parliament

Messrs /ˈmesəz/ (used as the plural of *Mr* before a list of men's names and before names of business firms): *Messrs Smith, Brown and Robinson* ○ *Messrs T Brown and Co*

mg milligram(s)

MHz megahertz (used in radio) a measure of frequency

min 1 minimum: *min temp 2°* 2 minute(s): *fastest time: 6 min*

misc miscellaneous

ml millilitre(s): *contents 75ml*

mm millimetre(s): *rainfall: 6mm* ○ *a 35mm camera*

Mon Monday: *Mon 6 June*

MOT /ˌem əʊ ˈtiː/ (*Brit*) 1 Ministry of Transport 2 (*also* **MOT test**) a test to make sure that vehicles over a certain age are safe to drive: *My car failed its MOT.*

MP /ˌem ˈpiː/ (*esp Brit*) Member of Parliament

mpg /ˌem piː ˈdʒiː/ miles per gallon: *This car does 40 mpg* (= you can drive 40 miles on one gallon of petrol).

mph /ˌem piː ˈeɪtʃ/ miles per hour: *a 70 mph speed limit*

Mr /ˈmɪstə(r)/ (used as a title before the name of a man): *Mr (Robert) Hurst* ○ *Mr and Mrs Hurst*

Mrs /ˈmɪsɪz/ (used as a title before the name of a married woman): *Mrs (Jane) Allen*

Ms /mɪz/ (used as a title before the name of a woman, either married or unmarried): *Ms (Emma) Gregg*

MSc /ˌem es ˈsiː/ Master of Science: a second qualification that you receive when you complete a more advanced course or piece of research in a science subject at university or college

Mt Mount: *Mt Everest*

mth (*US* **mo**) (*pl* **mths** *US* **mos**) month: *6 mths old*

N (*US also* **No**) north(ern): *N Yorkshire*

n (grammar) noun

NATO (*also* **Nato**) /ˈneɪtəʊ/ North Atlantic Treaty Organization; a group of European countries, Canada and the USA, who agree to give each other military help if necessary

NB (*also* **nb**) /ˌen ˈbiː/ (used before a written note) take special notice of: *NB There is an extra charge for reservations.*

NE north-east: *NE Scotland*

neg negative

NHS /ˌen eɪtʃ ˈes/ (*Brit*) National Health Service

No (*also* **no** or, in US, symbol **#**) (*plural* **Nos**, **nos**) number: *No 10 Downing Street* ○ *tel no 51236*

Nov November: *17 Nov 1992*

nr near: *Masham, nr Ripon, Yorks*

NW north-west(ern): *NW Australia*

OAP /ˌəʊ eɪ ˈpiː/ (*Brit*) old-age pensioner

Oct October: *13 Oct 1960*

OPEC /ˈəʊpek/ Organization of Petroleum Exporting Countries

opp opposite

oz ounce(s); a measure of weight, about 28.35g: *Add 4 oz flour.*

P (on a road sign) parking

p 1 (*pl* **pp**) page: *See p 94* ○ *pp 63–96* 2 /piː/ (*Brit informal*) penny, pence: *a 24p stamp*

PA /ˌpiː ˈeɪ/ personal assistant

pa per annum; in or for a year: *salary £15 000 pa*

p and p /ˌpiː ən ˈpiː/ (*Brit*) postage and packing: *price: £29 incl p and p*

par (*also* **para**) paragraph

PC /ˌpiː ˈsiː/ (*pl* **PCs**) (*Brit*) 1 personal computer 2 police constable

PE /ˌpiː ˈiː/ physical education: *a PE lesson*

PG /ˌpiː ˈdʒiː/ (*Brit*) (used about films in which there are scenes that are unsuitable for children) parental guidance

PhD /ˌpiː eɪtʃ ˈdiː/ Doctor of Philosophy; an advanced university degree that you receive when you complete a piece of research into a special subject: *She has a PhD in History.* o *Malcolm Crofts PhD*

PIN /pɪn/ (*also* **PIN number**) personal identification number; a secret number that you use with a special card to get money from a cash machine

pkt packet

pl (*grammar*) plural

PLC (*also* **plc**) /ˌpiː el ˈsiː/ (*Brit*) Public Limited Company: *Lloyd's Bank PLC*

pm /ˌpiː ˈem/ (*US* **PM**) after midday: *2 pm* (= 2 o'clock in the afternoon) o *11.30 pm* (= 11.30 in the evening)

PO /ˌpiː ˈəʊ/ Post Office

pop population: *pop 12 m*

pp 1 pages **2** /ˌpiː ˈpiː/ (*before a signature*) on behalf of: *pp J Symonds* (signed, for example, by his secretary in his absence)

PR /ˌpiː ˈɑː(r)/ public relations: *It's good PR* (= it improves people's impression of the firm).

pr (*pls* **prs**) pair

Pres President

PS (*also* **ps**) /ˌpiː ˈes/ (used for adding sth to the end of a letter) postscript: *Love from Tessa. PS I'll bring the car.*

pt (*pl* **pts**) **1** pint; a measure of liquid, about 0.568 litre: *2 pts milk* **2** point: *The winner scored 10 pts.* **3** part

PTO (*also* **pto**) /ˌpiː tiː ˈəʊ/ (at the bottom of a page) please turn over

Q question: *Qs 1–5 are compulsory.*

qt quart(s); a measure of liquid, about 1.136 litres

R river: *R Thames*

r right

RAC /ˌɑːr eɪ ˈsiː/ (*Brit*) Royal Automobile Club; an organization for motorists. If you are a member of the RAC and your car breaks down, you can phone them and they will send someone to help you.

RAF /ˌɑːr eɪ ˈef/ (*Brit*) Royal Air Force

Rd road

ref /ref/ reference: *ref no 3456*

Rep (*in US politics*) **1** Representative (in Congress) **2** Republican (Party)

Rev (*also* **Revd**) Reverend; the title of a Christian priest

RIP /ˌɑːr aɪ ˈpiː/ (used on graves, etc) rest in peace

rm room

RN /ˌɑːr ˈen/ (*Brit*) Royal Navy: *Capt R Wood RN*

rpm /ˌɑː piː ˈem/ revolutions per minute: *engine speed 2 500 rpm*

RSVP /ˌɑːr es viː ˈpiː/ (used on invitations) please reply

Rt Hon Right Honourable: a title for Cabinet ministers and some members of the nobility

S 1 small (size) **2** (*US also* **So**) south(ern): *S Yorkshire*

sae /ˌes eɪ ˈiː/ stamped addressed envelope: *enclose sae for reply*

Sat Saturday: *Sat 2 May*

SCE /ˌes siː ˈiː/ Scottish Certificate of Education. Pupils in Scotland take the SCE at Standard grade at the age of about 16 and at Higher grade at about 17. Those who wish to continue to study some subjects can take the Certificate of Sixth Year Studies (CSYS).

SE south-east(ern): *SE Asia*

Sen 1 Senator **2** (*also* **Snr, Sr**) Senior: *John F Davis Sen* (= the father, not the son of the same name)

Sept September: *2 Sept 1920*

Sgt sergeant; a rank in the British and American armies and police forces

Soc Society: *Amateur Dramatic Soc*

Sq Square: *6 Hanover Sq*

sq square (measurement): *10 sq cm*

St 1 Saint: *St Peter* **2** street: *20 Clifford St*

st (*Brit*) stone; a measure of weight, about 6.356 kg

STD /ˌes tiː ˈdiː/ **1** (*Brit*) subscriber trunk dialling; the system by which you can make long-distance telephone calls direct **2** sexually transmitted disease

Sun Sunday: *Sun 5 April*

SW south-west(ern): *SW Australia*

t (*US* **tn**) ton(s); tonne(s): *5t coal*

TB /ˌtiː ˈbiː/ tuberculosis

tbsp tablespoonful(s): *Add 3 tbsp sugar.*

TEFL /ˈtefl/ Teaching English as a Foreign Language

tel telephone (number): *tel 0865-56767*

temp temperature: *temp 15°C*

TESL /ˈtesl/ Teaching English as a Second Language

Thur (*also* **Thurs**) Thursday: *Thurs 26 June*

TOEFL /ˈtəʊfl/ (*US*) Test of English as a Foreign Language; the examination for foreign students who want to study at an American university

trans translated (by)

tsp teaspoonful(s): *Add 1 tsp salt.*

TUC /ˌtiː juː ˈsiː/ Trades Union Congress; the association of British trades unions

Tue (*also* **Tues**) Tuesday: *Tues 9 March*

TV /ˌtiː ˈviː/ television (set)

U /juː/ (*Brit*) (used about films that are suitable for anyone, including children) universal

UEFA /juːˈiːfə/ Union of European Football Associations: *the UEFA cup*

UFO (*also* **ufo**) /ˌjuːef ˈəʊ/ *or* /ˈjuːfəʊ/ unidentified flying object, especially a flying saucer

UHT /ˌjuː eɪtʃ ˈtiː/ ultra heat treated; used about dairy products that are treated to last longer: *UHT milk*

UK /ˌjuː ˈkeɪ/ United Kingdom; England, Scotland, Wales and N Ireland: *a UK citizen*

UN /ˌjuː ˈen/ United Nations: *the UN secretary general*

Univ University

UNO /ˈjuːnəʊ/ United Nations Organization

US /ˌjuː ˈes/ United States (of America): *the US Secretary of State*

USA /ˌjuː es ˈeɪ/ United States of America: *in the USA*

USSR /ˌjuː es es ˈɑː(r)/ (until 1991) Union of Soviet Socialist Republics

V volt(s): *a 9V battery*

v 1 (*pl* **vv**) verse **2** (*also* **v.**) versus; against: *Liverpool vs Everton: match postponed* **3** (*informal*) very: *v good*

VAT (*also* **Vat**) /ˌviː eɪ ˈtiː/ *or* /væt/ value added tax: *prices include VAT*

VCR /ˌviː siː ˈɑː(r)/ video cassette recorder
VDU /ˌviː diː ˈjuː/ (*computing*) visual display unit: *a VDU operator*
VIP /ˌviː aɪ ˈpiː/ (*informal*) very important person: *the VIP lounge at the airport* ○ *give someone the VIP treatment* (= treat sb especially well)
viz /vɪz/ (*often read out as* 'namely') that is to say; in other words
vol 1 (*pl* **vols**) volume: *The Complete Works of Byron, Vol 2* 2 volume: *vol 333 ml*
VSO /ˌviː es ˈəʊ/ (*Brit*) Voluntary Service Overseas; a scheme for young people to work in developing countries
W 1 watt(s): *a 60W light bulb* 2 west(ern): *W Cumbria*

WC /ˌdʌblju ˈsiː/ water closet; toilet
Wed Wednesday: *Wed 4 May*
wk 1 (*pl* **wks**) week 2 work
WP word processing; word processor: *WP skills necessary*
wt weight: *net wt 454 g*
XL /ˌeks ˈel/ extra large (size)
yd (*pl* **yds**) yard, a measure of length; about 0.914m
YHA /ˌwaɪ eɪtʃ ˈeɪ/ (*Brit*) Youth Hostels Association
yr (*pl* **yrs**) year

APPENDIX 5

Geographical Names and Maps

The British Isles

1. Belfast
2. Newtownabbey
3. Carrickfergus
4. Castlereagh
5. North Down
6. Ards
7. Down
8. Newry & Mourne
9. Banbridge
10. Lisburn
11. Craigavon
12. Armagh
13. Dungannon
14. Fermanagh
15. Omagh
16. Cookstown
17. Magherafelt
18. Strabane
19. Derry
20. Limavady
21. Coleraine
22. Ballymoney
23. Moyle
24. Ballymena
25. Larne
26. Antrim

The Counties of England

Avon /ˈeɪvən/
Bedfordshire /ˈbedfədʃə(r)/
Berkshire /ˈbɑːkʃə(r)/
Buckinghamshire /ˈbʌkɪŋəmʃə(r)/
Cambridgeshire /ˈkeɪmbrɪdʒʃə(r)/
Cheshire /ˈtʃeʃə(r)/
Cleveland /ˈkliːvlənd/
Cornwall /ˈkɔːnwəl/
Cumbria /ˈkʌmbrɪə/
Derbyshire /ˈdɑːbɪʃə(r)/
Devon /ˈdevən/
Dorset /ˈdɔːsɪt/
Durham /ˈdʌrəm/
East Sussex /ˌiːst ˈsʌsɪks/
Essex /ˈesɪks/
Gloucestershire /ˈglɒstəʃə(r)/
Greater London /ˌgreɪtə ˈlʌndən/
Greater Manchester /ˌgreɪtə ˈmæntʃəstə(r)/
Hampshire /ˈhæmpʃə(r)/
Hereford and Worcester /ˌherɪfəd ənd ˈwʊstə(r)/
Hertfordshire /ˈhɑːtfədʃə(r)/
Humberside /ˈhʌmbəsaɪd/
Isle of Wight /ˌaɪl əv ˈwaɪt/
Kent /kent/
Lancashire /ˈlæŋkəʃə(r)/
Leicestershire /ˈlestəʃə(r)
Lincolnshire /ˈlɪŋkənʃə(r)/
Merseyside /ˈmɜːzɪsaɪd/
Norfolk /ˈnɔːfək/
North Yorkshire /ˌnɔːθ ˈjɔːkʃə(r)/
Northamptonshire /nɔːˈθæmptənʃə(r)/
Northumberland /nɔːˈθʌmbələnd/
Nottinghamshire /ˈnɒtɪŋəmʃə(r)/
Oxfordshire /ˈɒksfədʃə(r)/
Shropshire /ˈʃrɒpʃə(r)/
Somerset /ˈsʌməset/
South Yorkshire /ˌsaʊθ ˈjɔːkʃə(r)/
Staffordshire /ˈstæfədʃə(r)/
Suffolk /ˈsʌfək/
Surrey /ˈsʌrɪ/
Tyne and Wear /ˌtaɪn ənd ˈwɪə(r)/
Warwickshire /ˈwɒrɪkʃə(r)/
West Midlands /ˌwest ˈmɪdləndz/
West Sussex /ˌwest ˈsʌsɪks/
West Yorkshire /ˌwest ˈjɔːkʃə(r)/
Wiltshire /ˈwɪltʃə(r)/

The Regions of Scotland

Borders /ˈbɔːdəz/
Central /ˈsentrəl/
Dumfries and Galloway /dʌmˌfriːs ənd ˈgæləweɪ/
Fife /faɪf/
Grampian /ˈgræmpɪən/
Highland /ˈhaɪlənd/
Lothian /ˈləʊðɪən/
Orkney Islands /ˈɔːknɪ aɪləndz/
Shetland Islands /ˈʃetlənd aɪləndz/
Strathclyde /ˌstræθˈklaɪd/
Tayside /ˈteɪsaɪd/
Western Isles /ˌwestən ˈaɪls/

The Counties of Wales

Clwyd /ˈkluːɪd/
Dyfed /ˈdʌvɪd/
Gwent /gwent/
Gwynedd /ˈgwɪneð/
Mid Glamorgan /ˌmɪd gləˈmɔːgən/
Powys /ˈpaʊɪs/
South Glamorgan /ˌsaʊθ gləˈmɔːgən/
West Glamorgan /ˌwest gləˈmɔːgən/

The Districts of Northern Ireland

Antrim /ˈæntrɪm/
Ards /ɑːdz/
Armagh /ɑːˈmɑː/
Ballymena /ˌbælɪˈmiːnə/
Ballymoney /ˌbælɪˈmʌnɪ/
Banbridge /ˈbænbrɪdʒ/
Belfast /ˈbelfɑːst/
Carrickfergus /ˌkærɪkˈfɜːgəs/
Castlereagh /ˈkɑːslreɪ/
Coleraine /ˈkəʊləreɪn/
Cookstown /ˈkʊkstaʊn/
Craigavon /kreɪgˈævən/
Derry /ˈderɪ/
Down /daʊn/
Dungannon /dʌŋˈgænən/
Fermanagh /fəˈmænə/
Larne /lɑːn/
Limavady /ˌlɪməˈvædɪ/
Lisburn /ˈlɪzbən/
Magherafelt /ˈmækerəfelt/
Moyle /mɔɪl/
Newry and Mourne /ˌnjʊərɪ ənd ˈmɔːn/
Newtownabbey /ˌnjuːtnˈæbɪ/
North Down /ˌnɔːθ ˈdaʊn/
Omagh /əʊˈmɑː/
Strabane /strəˈbæn/

North America
ALASKA
0 500 km
Arctic Ocean
Hudson Bay
YUKON
NORTHWEST TERRITORIES
CANADA
BRITISH COLUMBIA
ALBERTA
SASKATCHEWAN
MANITOBA
ONTARIO
QUEBEC
NEWFOUNDLAND
PRINCE EDWARD ISLAND
NEW BRUNSWICK
NOVA SCOTIA
WASHINGTON
OREGON
MONTANA
IDAHO
WYOMING
NORTH DAKOTA
SOUTH DAKOTA
MINNESOTA
WISCONSIN
MICHIGAN
NEBRASKA
IOWA
UNITED STATES
NEVADA
CALIFORNIA
UTAH
COLORADO
KANSAS
MISSOURI
ILLINOIS
INDIANA
OHIO
PENNSYLVANIA
NEW YORK
VERMONT
NEW HAMPSHIRE
MAINE
MASSACHUSETTS
CONNECTICUT
RHODE ISLAND
NEW JERSEY
DELAWARE
MARYLAND
D.C.
WEST VIRGINIA
VIRGINIA
KENTUCKY
TENNESSEE
NORTH CAROLINA
SOUTH CAROLINA
ARIZONA
NEW MEXICO
OKLAHOMA
ARKANSAS
TEXAS
LOUISIANA
MISSISSIPPI
ALABAMA
GEORGIA
FLORIDA
Atlantic Ocean
0 500 1000 km
Pacific Ocean
Gulf of Mexico
HAWAII
0 250 km
Caribbean Sea

The States of the United States

Alabama /ˌæləˈbæmə/
Alaska /əˈlæskə/
Arizona /ˌærɪˈzəʊnə/
Arkansas /ˈɑːkənsɔː/
California /ˌkælɪˈfɔːnɪə/
Colorado /ˌkɒləˈrɑːdəʊ/
Connecticut /kəˈnetɪkət/
Delaware /ˈdeləweə(r)/
Florida /ˈflɒrɪdə/
Georgia /ˈdʒɔːdʒə/
Hawaii /həˈwaɪɪ/
Idaho /ˈaɪdəhəʊ/
Illinois /ˌɪlɪˈnɔɪ/
Indiana /ˌɪndɪˈænə/
Iowa /ˈaɪəwə/
Kansas /ˈkænzəs, ˈkænsəs/
Kentucky /kenˈtʌkɪ/
Louisiana /luːˌiːzɪˈænə/
Maine /meɪn/
Maryland /ˈmeərɪlænd/
Massachusetts /ˌmæsəˈtʃuːsɪts/
Michigan /ˈmɪʃɪɡən/
Minnesota /ˌmɪnɪˈsəʊtə/
Mississippi /ˌmɪsɪˈsɪpɪ/
Missouri /mɪˈzʊrɪ/
Montana /mɒnˈtænə/
Nebraska /nəˈbræskə/
Nevada /nəˈvɑːdə/
New Hampshire /ˌnjuː ˈhæmpʃə(r)/
New Jersey /ˌnjuː ˈdʒɜːzɪ/
New Mexico /ˌnjuː ˈmeksɪkəʊ/
New York /ˌnjuː ˈjɔːk/
North Carolina /ˌnɔːθ kærəˈlaɪnə/
North Dakota /ˌnɔːθ dəˈkəʊtə/
Ohio /əʊˈhaɪəʊ/
Oklahoma /ˌəʊkləˈhəʊmə/
Oregon /ˈɒrɪɡən/
Pennsylvania /ˌpensəlˈveɪnɪə/
Rhode Island /ˌrəʊd ˈaɪlənd/
South Carolina /ˌsaʊθ kærəˈlaɪnə/
South Dakota /ˌsaʊθ dəˈkəʊtə/
Tennessee /ˌtenəˈsiː/
Texas /ˈteksəs/
Utah /ˈjuːtɑː/
Vermont /vɜːˈmɒnt/
Virginia /vəˈdʒɪnɪə/
Washington /ˈwɒʃɪŋtən/
West Virginia /ˌwest vəˈdʒɪnɪə/
Wisconsin /wɪsˈkɒnsɪn/
Wyoming /waɪˈəʊmɪŋ/

The Provinces and Territories of Canada

Alberta /ælˈbɜːtə/
British Columbia /ˌbrɪtɪʃ kəˈlʌmbɪə/
Manitoba /ˌmænɪˈtəʊbə/
New Brunswick /ˌnjuː ˈbrʌnzwɪk/
Newfoundland /ˈnjuːfəndlənd/
Northwest territories /ˌnɔːθwest ˈterətrɪz/
Nova Scotia /ˌnəʊvə ˈskəʌʃə/
Ontario /ɒnˈteərɪəʊ/
Prince Edward Island /ˌprɪns ˈedwəd aɪlənd/
Quebec /kwɪˈbek/
Saskatchewan /səsˈkæʃəwən/
Yukon Territory /ˈjuːkɒn ˈterətrɪ/

Australia and New Zealand

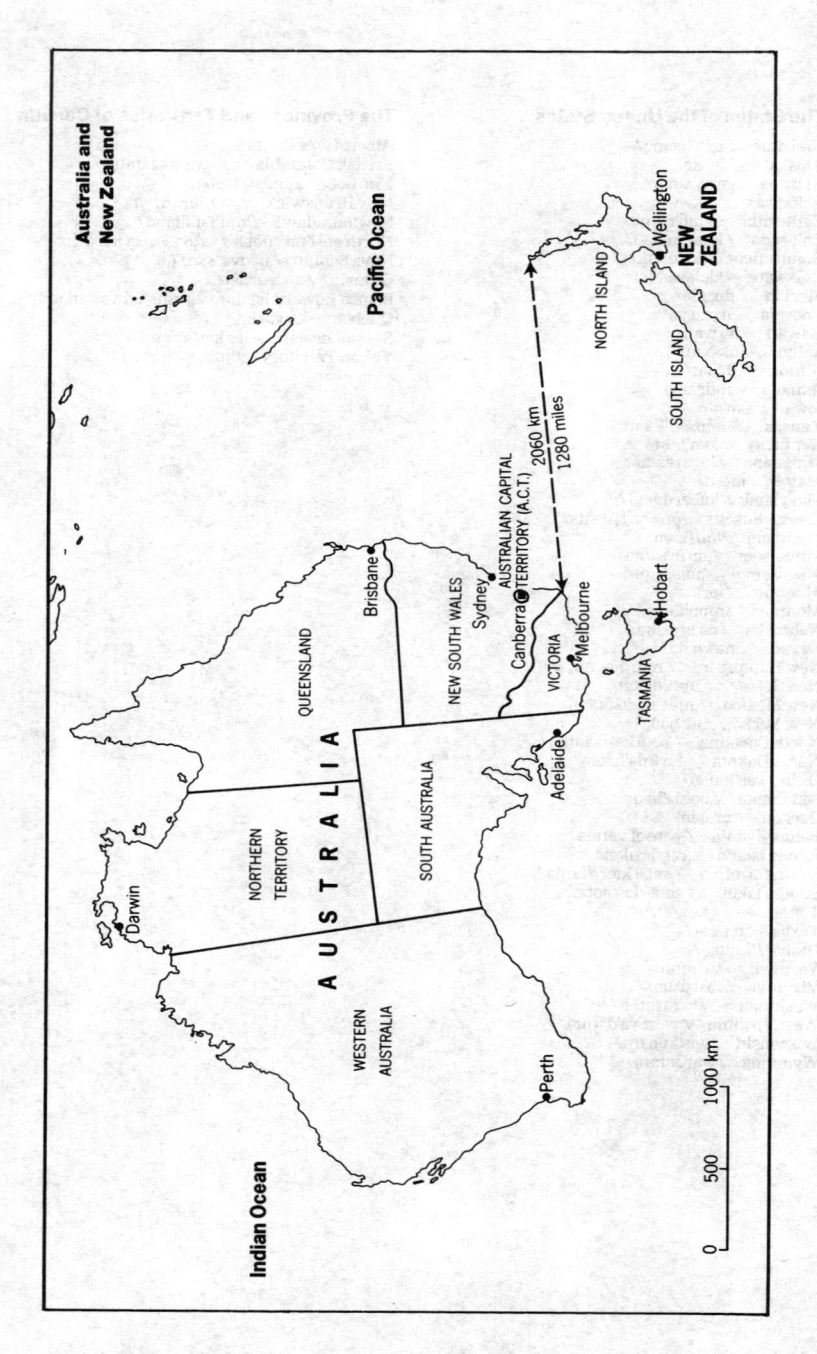

Indian Ocean

Pacific Ocean

Darwin

WESTERN AUSTRALIA

NORTHERN TERRITORY

QUEENSLAND

Brisbane

SOUTH AUSTRALIA

NEW SOUTH WALES

Sydney

A U S T R A L I A

Perth

Adelaide

AUSTRALIAN CAPITAL TERRITORY (A.C.T.)
Canberra

VICTORIA

Melbourne

TASMANIA

Hobart

2060 km
1280 miles

NORTH ISLAND

Wellington

NEW ZEALAND

SOUTH ISLAND

0   500   1000 km

Geographical names

This list shows the English spelling and pronunciation of geographical names and the adjectives that go with them. If there are different words for the adjective and the person, both are given, eg **Denmark: Danish; Dane**.

To make the plural of a word for a person from a particular country, add **-s**, except for **Swiss** and words ending in **-ese** (such as *Japanese*), which stay the same, and for words that end in **-man** or **-woman**, which change to **-men** or **-women**, eg *three Frenchmen; two Englishwomen*.

If there is a different word for all the people as a group, this is given in brackets:
France: French; Frenchman, Frenchwoman (the French).

Inclusion in this list does not imply status as a sovereign nation.

Noun	Adjective; Person
Afghanistan /æfˈgænɪstɑːn; US -stæn/	Afghan /ˈæfgæn/; Afghani /æfˈgænɪ/; Afghanistani /æfˈgænɪstɑːnɪ; US -stænɪ/
Africa /ˈæfrɪkə/	African /ˈæfrɪkən/
Albania /ælˈbeɪnɪə/	Albanian /ælˈbeɪnɪən/
Algeria /ælˈdʒɪərɪə/	Algerian /ælˈdʒɪərɪən/
America /əˈmerɪkə/	American /əˈmerɪkən/
Andorra /ænˈdɔːrə/	Andorran /ænˈdɔːrən/
Angola /æŋˈgəʊlə/	Angolan /æŋˈgəʊlən/
Anguilla /æŋˈgwɪlə/	Anguillan /æŋˈgwɪlən/
Antigua /ænˈtiːgə/	Antiguan /ænˈtiːgən/
Argentina /ˌɑːdʒənˈtiːnə/, the Argentine /ˈɑːdʒəntaɪn/	Argentinian /ˌɑːdʒənˈtɪnɪən/; Argentine /ˈɑːdʒəntaɪn/
Armenia /ɑːˈmiːnɪə/	Armenian /ɑːˈmiːnɪən/
Asia /ˈeɪʃə/	Asian /ˈeɪʃn/
Australasia /ˌɒstrəˈleɪʃə/	Australasian /ˌɒstrəˈleɪʃn/
Australia /ɒˈstreɪlɪə; US ɔːˈs-/	Australian /ɒˈstreɪlɪən; US ɔːˈs-/
Austria /ˈɒstrɪə; US ˈɔːs-/	Austrian /ˈɒstrɪən; US ˈɔːs-/
Azerbaijan /ˌæzəbaɪˈdʒɑːn/	Azerbaijani /ˌæzəbaɪˈdʒɑːnɪ/ Azeri /əˈzeərɪ/
(the) Bahamas /bəˈhɑːməz; US -ˈheɪm-/	Bahamian /bəˈheɪmɪən/
Bahrain, Bahrein /bɑːˈreɪn/	Bahraini, Bahreini /bɑːˈreɪnɪ/
Bangladesh /ˌbæŋgləˈdeʃ/	Bangladeshi /ˌbæŋgləˈdeʃɪ/
Barbados /bɑːˈbeɪdɒs/	Barbadian /bɑːˈbeɪdɪən/
Belarus /ˈbelərʊs/	Belorussian /ˌbeləˈrʌʃn/
Belgium /ˈbeldʒəm/	Belgian /ˈbeldʒən/
Belize /beˈliːz/	Belizean /beˈliːzɪən/
Benin /beˈniːn/	Beninese /ˌbenɪˈniːz/
Bermuda /bəˈmjuːdə/	Bermudan /bəˈmjuːdən/
Bhutan /buːˈtɑːn/	Bhutani /buːˈtɑːnɪ/; Bhutanese /ˌbuːtɑːˈniːz/
Bolivia /bəˈlɪvɪə/	Bolivian /bəˈlɪvɪən/
Bosnia-Herzegovina /ˌbɒznɪə ˌhɜːtsəgəˈviːnə/	Bosnian /ˈbɒznɪən/
Botswana /bɒtˈswɑːnə/	Botswanan /bɒtˈswɑːnən/
Brazil /brəˈzɪl/	Brazilian /brəˈzɪlɪən/
Britain ⇨ Great Britain	
Brunei /ˈbruːnaɪ/	Brunei, Bruneian /bruːˈnaɪən/
Bulgaria /bʌlˈgeərɪə/	Bulgarian /bʌlˈgeərɪən/
Burkina /bɜːˈkiːnə/	Burkinese /bɜːkɪˈniːz/
Burma /ˈbɜːmə/	Burmese /ˌbɜːˈmiːz/
Burundi /bʊˈrʊndɪ/	Burundian /bʊˈrʊndɪən/
Cambodia /kæmˈbəʊdɪə/	Cambodian /kæmˈbəʊdɪən/
Cameroon /ˌkæməˈruːn/	Cameroonian /ˌkæməˈruːnɪən/
Canada /ˈkænədə/	Canadian /kəˈneɪdɪən/
Cape Verde Islands /ˌkeɪp ˈvɜːd aɪləndz/	
Central African Republic /ˌsentrəl ˌæfrɪkən rɪˈpʌblɪk/	
Chad /tʃæd/	Chadian /ˈtʃædɪən/
Chile /ˈtʃɪlɪ/	Chilean /ˈtʃɪlɪən/
China /ˈtʃaɪnə/	Chinese /ˌtʃaɪˈniːz/
Colombia /kəˈlɒmbɪə/	Colombian /kəˈlɒmbɪən/
Comoros /ˈkɒmərəʊz/	
Congo /ˈkɒŋgəʊ/	Congolese /ˌkɒŋgəˈliːz/
Costa Rica /ˌkɒstə ˈriːkə/	Costa Rican /ˌkɒstə ˈriːkən/
Croatia /krəʊˈeɪʃə/	Croatian /krəʊˈeɪʃən/
Cuba /ˈkjuːbə/	Cuban /ˈkjuːbən/
Cyprus /ˈsaɪprəs/	Cypriot /ˈsɪprɪət/

Noun	Adjective; Person
Czech Republic /ˌtʃek rɪˈpʌblɪk/	Czech /tʃek/
Denmark /ˈdenmɑːk/	Danish /ˈdeɪnɪʃ/; Dane /deɪn/
Djibouti /dʒɪˈbuːtɪ/	Djiboutian /dʒɪˈbuːtɪən/
Dominica /dəˈmɪnɪkə; ˌdɒmɪˈniːkə/	Dominican /dəˈmɪnɪkən/
(the) Dominican Republic /dəˌmɪnɪkən rɪˈpʌblɪk/	Dominican /dəˈmɪnɪkən/
Ecuador /ˈekwədɔː(r)/	Ecuadorian /ˌekwəˈdɔːrɪən/
Egypt /ˈiːdʒɪpt/	Egyptian /ɪˈdʒɪpʃn/
El Salvador /el ˈsælvədɔː(r)/	Salvadorean /ˌsælvəˈdɔːrɪən/
England /ˈɪŋglənd/	English /ˈɪŋglɪʃ/; Englishman /ˈɪŋglɪʃmən/, Englishwoman /ˈɪŋglɪʃwʊmən/ (the English)
Equatorial Guinea /ˌekwəˌtɔːrɪəl ˈgɪnɪ/	Equatorial Guinean /ˌekwəˌtɔːrɪəl ˈgɪnɪən/
Eritrea /ˌerɪˈtreɪə/	Eritrean /ˌerɪˈtreɪən/
Estonia /eˈstəʊnɪə/	Estonian /eˈstəʊnɪən/
Ethiopia /ˌiːθɪˈəʊpɪə/	Ethiopian /ˌiːθɪˈəʊpɪən/
Europe /ˈjʊərəp/	European /ˌjʊərəˈpɪən/
Fiji /ˌfiːˈdʒiː; US ˈfiːdʒiː/	Fijian /ˌfiːˈdʒiːən; US ˈfiːdʒɪən/
Finland /ˈfɪnlənd/	Finnish /ˈfɪnɪʃ/; Finn /fɪn/
France /frɑːns; US fræns/	French /frentʃ/; Frenchman /ˈfrentʃmən/, Frenchwoman /ˈfrentʃwʊmən/ (the French)
Gabon /gæˈbɒn/	Gabonese /ˌgæbəˈniːz/
(the) Gambia /ˈgæmbɪə/	Gambian /ˈgæmbɪən/
Germany /ˈdʒɜːmənɪ/	German /ˈdʒɜːmən/
Georgia /ˈdʒɔːdʒə/	Georgian /ˈdʒɔːdʒən/
Ghana /ˈgɑːnə/	Ghanaian /gɑːˈneɪən/
Gibraltar /dʒɪˈbrɔːltə(r)/	Gibraltarian /ˌdʒɪbrɔːˈlteərɪən/
Great Britain /ˌgreɪt ˈbrɪtn/	British /ˈbrɪtɪʃ/; Briton /ˈbrɪtn/ (the British)
Greece /griːs/	Greek /griːk/
Grenada /grɪˈneɪdə/	Grenadian /grɪˈneɪdɪən/
Guatemala /ˌgwɑːtəˈmɑːlə/	Guatemalan /ˌgwɑːtəˈmɑːlən/
Guinea /ˈgɪnɪ/	Guinean /ˈgɪnɪən/
Guinea Bissau /ˌgɪnɪ brˈsaʊ/	
Guyana /gaɪˈænə/	Guyanese /ˌgaɪəˈniːz/
Haiti /ˈheɪtɪ/	Haitian /ˈheɪʃn/
Honduras /hɒnˈdjʊərəs; US -ˈdʊə-/	Honduran /hɒnˈdjʊərən; US -ˈdʊə-/
Hong Kong /ˌhɒŋ ˈkɒŋ/	
Hungary /ˈhʌŋgərɪ/	Hungarian /hʌŋˈgeərɪən/
Iceland /ˈaɪslənd/	Icelandic /aɪsˈlændɪk/; Icelander /ˈaɪsləndə(r)/
India /ˈɪndɪə/	Indian /ˈɪndɪən/
Indonesia /ˌɪndəˈniːzɪə; US -ˈniːʒə/	Indonesian /ˌɪndəˈniːzɪən; US -ʒn/
Iran /ɪˈrɑːn/	Iranian /ɪˈreɪnɪən/
Iraq /ɪˈrɑːkɪ/	Iraqi /ɪˈrɑːkɪ/
(the Republic of) Ireland /ˈaɪələnd/ (also Eire /ˈeərə/)	Irish /ˈaɪərɪʃ/; Irishman /ˈaɪərɪʃmən/, Irishwoman /ˈaɪərɪʃwʊmən/ (the Irish)
Israel /ˈɪzreɪl/	Israeli /ɪzˈreɪlɪ/
Italy /ˈɪtəlɪ/	Italian /ɪˈtælɪən/
Ivory Coast /ˌaɪvərɪ ˈkəʊst/	Ivorian /ˌaɪˈvɔːrɪən/
Jamaica /dʒəˈmeɪkə/	Jamaican /dʒəˈmeɪkən/
Japan /dʒəˈpæn/	Japanese /ˌdʒæpəˈniːz/
Java /ˈdʒɑːvə/	Javanese /ˌdʒɑːvəˈniːz/
Jordan /ˈdʒɔːdn/	Jordanian /dʒɔːˈdeɪnɪən/
Kazakhstan /ˌkæzækˈstɑːn/	Kazakh /kæˈzæk/
Kenya /ˈkenjə; US ˈkiːnjə/	Kenyan /ˈkenjən; US ˈkiːnjən/
Kirgyzstan /ˌkɪəgɪˈstɑːn/	Kirgyz /kɪəˈgiːz/
Kiribati /ˌkɪrɪˈbɑːtɪ/	
Korea /kəˈrɪə/: North Korea South Korea	North Korean /ˌnɔːθ kəˈrɪən/ South Korean /ˌsaʊθ kəˈrɪən/
Kuwait /kʊˈweɪt; US -ˈwaɪt/	Kuwaiti /kʊˈweɪtɪ; US kʊˈwaɪtɪ/
Laos /ˈlɑːɒs/	Laotian /ˈlɑːʊʃn; US leɪˈəʊʃn/
Latvia /ˈlætvɪə/	Latvian /ˈlætvɪən/
Lebanon /ˈlebənən; US -nɒn/	Lebanese /ˌlebəˈniːz/
Lesotho /ləˈsuːtuː/	Sotho /ˈsuːtuː/; (person: Mosotho /məˈsuːtuː/; people: Basotho /bəˈsuːtuː/)
Liberia /laɪˈbɪərɪə/	Liberian /laɪˈbɪərɪən/
Libya /ˈlɪbɪə/	Libyan /ˈlɪbɪən/
Liechtenstein /ˈlɪktənstaɪn/	Liechtenstein; Liechtensteiner /ˈlɪktənstaɪnə(r)/
Lithuania /ˌlɪθjuːˈeɪnɪə/	Lithuanian /ˌlɪθjuːˈeɪnɪən/
Luxembourg /ˈlʌksəmbɜːg/	Luxembourg; Luxembourger /ˈlʌksəmbɜːgə(r)/

Noun	Adjective; Person
Macedonia (former Yugoslav republic) /ˌmæsəˈdəʊnɪə/	Macedonian /ˌmæsəˈdəʊnɪən/
Madagascar /ˌmædəˈɡæskə(r)/	Madagascan /ˌmædəɡæskən/; Malagasy /ˌmæləˈɡæsɪ/
Malawi /məˈlɑːwɪ/	Malawian /məˈlɑːwɪən/
Malaysia /məˈleɪzɪə; US -ˈleɪʒə/	Malaysian /məˈleɪzɪən; US -ˈleɪʒn/
Maldives /ˈmɔːldiːvz/	
Mali /ˈmɑːlɪ/	Malian /ˈmɑːlɪən/
Malta /ˈmɔːltə/	Maltese /mɔːlˈtiːz/
Mauritania /ˌmɒrɪˈteɪnɪə; US ˌmɔːr-/	Mauritanian /ˌmɒrɪˈteɪnɪən; US ˌmɔːr-/
Mauritius /məˈrɪʃəs; US mɔː-/	Mauritian /məˈrɪʃn; US mɔː-/
Mexico /ˈmeksɪkəʊ/	Mexican /ˈmeksɪkən/
Micronesia /ˌmaɪkrəʊˈniːzɪə; US -ˈniːʒə/	Micronesian /ˌmaɪkrəʊˈniːzɪən; US -ˈniːʒən/
Moldova /mɒldˈəʊvə/	Moldovan /mɒldˈəʊvən/
Monaco /ˈmɒnəkəʊ/	Monegasque /ˌmɒnəˈɡæsk/
Mongolia /mɒŋˈɡəʊlɪə/	Mongolian /mɒŋˈɡəʊlɪən/; Mongol /ˈmɒŋɡl/
Montserrat /ˌmɒntsəˈræt/	Montserratian /ˌmɒntsəˈræʃn/
Morocco /məˈrɒkəʊ/	Moroccan /məˈrɒkən/
Mozambique /ˌməʊzæmˈbiːk/	Mozambiquean /ˌməʊzæmˈbiːkən/
Myanmar /ˌmiːænˈmɑː(r)/ (formerly Burma)	Myanmar /ˌmiːænˈmɑː(r)/
Namibia /nəˈmɪbɪə/	Namibian /nəˈmɪbɪən/
Nauru /ˈnaʊruː/	Nauruan /naʊˈruːən/
Nepal /nɪˈpɔːl/	Nepalese /ˌnepəˈliːz/
(the) Netherlands /ˈneðələndz/	Dutch /dʌtʃ/; Dutchman /ˈdʌtʃmən/, Dutchwoman /ˈdʌtʃwʊmən/ (the Dutch)
New Zealand /ˌnjuːˈziːlənd; US ˌnuː-/	New Zealand; New Zealander /ˌnjuːˈziːləndə(r); US ˌnuː-/
Nicaragua /ˌnɪkəˈræɡjʊə; US -ˈrɑːɡwə/	Nicaraguan /ˌnɪkəˈræɡjʊən; US -ˈrɑːɡwən/
Niger /niːˈʒeə(r)/	Nigerien /niːˈʒeərɪən/
Nigeria /naɪˈdʒɪərɪə/	Nigerian /naɪˈdʒɪərɪən/
North Korea ⇨ Korea	
Northern Ireland /ˌnɔːðən ˈaɪələnd/	Northern Irish /ˌnɔːðən ˈaɪərɪʃ/ (adj only)
Norway /ˈnɔːweɪ/	Norwegian /nɔːˈwiːdʒən/
Oman /əʊˈmɑːn/	Omani /əʊˈmɑːnɪ/
Pakistan /ˌpɑːkɪˈstɑːn; US ˈpækɪstæn/	Pakistani /ˌpɑːkɪˈstɑːnɪ; US ˌpækɪˈstænɪ/
Palestine /ˈpæləstaɪn/	Palestinian /ˌpæləˈstɪnɪən/
Panama /ˈpænəmɑː/	Panamanian /ˌpænəˈmeɪnɪən/
Papua New Guinea /ˌpæpʊə ˌnjuː ˈɡɪnɪ; US -ˌnuː-/	Papuan /ˈpæpʊən/
Paraguay /ˈpærəɡwaɪ; US -ɡweɪ/	Paraguayan /ˌpærəˈɡwaɪən; US -ˈɡweɪən/
Peru /pəˈruː/	Peruvian /pəˈruːvɪən/
(the) Philippines /ˈfɪlɪpiːnz/	Philippine /ˈfɪlɪpiːn/; Filipino /ˌfɪlɪˈpiːnəʊ/
Poland /ˈpəʊlənd/	Polish /ˈpəʊlɪʃ/; Pole /pəʊl/
Portugal /ˈpɔːtʃʊɡl/	Portuguese /ˌpɔːtʃʊˈɡiːz/
Puerto Rico /ˌpwɜːtəʊ ˈriːkəʊ/	Puerto Rican /ˌpwɜːtəʊ ˈriːkən/
Qatar /ˈkʌtɑː(r)/	Qatari /kʌˈtɑːrɪ/
Romania /ruːˈmeɪnɪə/	Romanian /ruːˈmeɪnɪən/
Russia /ˈrʌʃə/	Russian /ˈrʌʃn/
Rwanda /rʊˈændə/	Rwandan /rʊˈændən/
St Kitts and Nevis /snt ˌkɪts ən ˈnevɪs; US ˌseɪnt/	
St Lucia /snt ˈluːʃə; US ˌseɪnt/	
St Vincent /snt ˈvɪnsnt/ US ˌseɪnt/	
Samoa ⇨ Western Samoa	
San Marino /ˌsæn məˈriːnəʊ/	San Marinese /ˌsæn ˌmærɪˈniːz/
Sao Tomé and Principe /ˌsaʊ təˌmeɪ ən ˈprɪnsɪpeɪ/	
Saudi Arabia /ˌsaʊdɪ əˈreɪbɪə/	Saudi /ˈsaʊdɪ/; Saudi Arabian /ˌsaʊdɪ əˈreɪbɪən/
Scotland /ˈskɒtlənd/	Scottish /ˈskɒtɪʃ/; Scot /skɒt/, Scotsman /ˈskɒtsmən/, Scotswoman /ˈskɒtswʊmən/ (the Scots)
Senegal /ˌsenɪˈɡɔːl/	Senegalese /ˌsenɪɡəˈliːz/
(the) Seychelles /seɪˈʃelz/	Seychellois /seɪʃelˈwɑː/
Sierra Leone /sɪˌerə lɪˈəʊn/	Sierra Leonean /sɪˌerə lɪˈəʊnɪən/
Singapore /ˌsɪŋəˈpɔː(r)/	Singaporean /ˌsɪŋəˈpɔːrɪən/
Slovakia /sləʊˈvækɪə/	Slovak /ˈsləʊvæk/
Slovenia /sləʊˈviːnɪə/	Slovene /ˈsləʊviːn/; Slovenian /sləʊˈviːnɪən/
(the) Solomon Islands /ˈsɒləmən aɪləndz/	
Somalia /səˈmɑːlɪə/	Somali /səˈmɑːlɪ/
South Africa /ˌsaʊθ ˈæfrɪkə/	South African /ˌsaʊθ ˈæfrɪkən/
South Korea ⇨ Korea	

Noun	Adjective; Person
Spain /speɪn/	Spanish /ˈspænɪʃ/; Spaniard /ˈspænɪəd/ (the Spanish)
Sri Lanka /ˌsriːˈlæŋkə/	Sri Lankan /ˌsriːˈlæŋkən/
Sudan /suːˈdɑːn/	Sudanese /ˌsuːdəˈniːz/
Sumatra /sʊˈmɑːtrə/	Sumatran /sʊˈmɑːtrən/
Surinam /ˌsʊərɪˈnæm/	Surinamese /ˌsʊərɪnæˈmiːz/
Swaziland /ˈswɑːzɪlænd/	Swazi /ˈswɑːzɪ/
Sweden /ˈswiːdn/	Swedish /ˈswiːdɪʃ/; Swede /swiːd/
Switzerland /ˈswɪtsələnd/	Swiss /swɪs/ (the Swiss)
Syria /ˈsɪrɪə/	Syrian /ˈsɪrɪən/
Tahiti /tɑːˈhiːtɪ/	Tahitian /tɑːˈhiːʃn/
Tajikistan /tæˈdʒiːkɪstɑːn/	Tajik /tæˈdʒɪk/
Taiwan /taɪˈwɑːn/	Taiwanese /ˌtaɪwəˈniːz/
Tanzania /ˌtænzəˈnɪə/	Tanzanian /ˌtænzəˈnɪən/
Thailand /ˈtaɪlænd/ (*formerly* Siam)	Thai /taɪ/
Tibet /tɪˈbet/	Tibetan /tɪˈbetn/
Timor, East /ˌiːst ˈtiːmɔː(r)/	Timorese /ˌtiːmɔːˈriːz/
Togo /ˈtəʊgəʊ/	Togolese /ˌtəʊgəˈliːz/
Tonga /ˈtɒŋə/, *also* ˈtɒŋgə/	Tongan /ˈtɒŋən, *also* ˈtɒŋgən/
Trinidad /ˈtrɪnɪdæd/ and Tobago /təˈbeɪgəʊ/	Trinidadian /ˌtrɪnɪˈdædɪən/; Tobagan /təˈbeɪgən/; Tobagonian /ˌtəʊbəˈgəʊnɪən/
Tunisia /tjuːˈnɪzɪə; *US* tuːˈnɪʒə/	Tunisian /tjuːˈnɪzɪən; *US* tuːˈnɪʒən/
Turkey /ˈtɜːkɪ/	Turkish /ˈtɜːkɪʃ/; Turk /tɜːk/
Turkmenistan /tɜːkˈmiːnɪstɑːn/	Turkmen /ˈtɜːkmen/
Tuvalu /ˌtuːvɑːˈluː/	Tuvaluan /ˌtuːvɑːˈluːən/
Uganda /juːˈgændə/	Ugandan /juːˈgændən/
Ukraine /juːˈkreɪn/	Ukrainian /juːˈkreɪnɪən/
United Arab Emirates /juːˌnaɪtɪd ˌærəb ˈemɪrəts/	
(the) United Kingdom /juːˌnaɪtɪd ˈkɪŋdəm/	British /ˈbrɪtɪʃ/; Briton /ˈbrɪtn/ (the British)
(the) United States of America /juːˌnaɪtɪd ˌsteɪts əv əˈmerɪkə/	American /əˈmerɪkən/
Uruguay /ˈjʊərəgwaɪ; *US* -gweɪ/	Uruguayan /ˌjʊərəˈgwaɪən; *US* -ˈgweɪən/
Uzbekistan /ʊzˈbekɪstɑːn/	Uzbek /ˈʊzbek/
Vanuatu /ˌvænuːˈætuː/	
Vatican City /ˌvætɪkən ˈsɪtɪ/	
Venezuela /ˌvenɪˈzweɪlə/	Venezuelan /ˌvenɪˈzweɪlən/
Vietnam /ˌvjetˈnæm; *US* -ˈnɑːm/	Vietnamese /ˌvjetnəˈmiːz/
Wales /weɪlz/	Welsh /welʃ/; Welshman /ˈwelʃmən/, Welshwoman /ˈwelʃwʊmən/ (the Welsh)
(the) West Indies /ˌwest ˈɪndɪz/	West Indian /ˌwest ˈɪndɪən/
Western Samoa /ˌwestən səˈməʊə/	Samoan /səˈməʊən/
(the Republic of) Yemen /ˈjemən/	Yemeni /ˈjemənɪ/
Yugoslavia /ˌjuːgəʊˈslɑːvɪə/	Yugoslavian /ˌjuːgəʊˈslɑːvɪən/; Yugoslav /ˈjuːgəʊslɑːv/
Zaire /zɑːˈɪə(r)/	Zairean /zɑːˈɪərɪən/
Zambia /ˈzæmbɪə/	Zambian /ˈzæmbɪən/
Zimbabwe /zɪmˈbɑːbwɪ/	Zimbabwean /zɪmˈbɑːbwɪən/

Pronunciation

If two pronunciations for one word are given, both are acceptable. The first form given is considered to be more common. A word that is pronounced very differently in American English has the American pronunciation given after a *US* label.

address /əˈdres; *US* ˈædres/

/ - / A hyphen is used in alternative pronunciations when only part of the pronunciation changes. The part that remains the same is replaced by the hyphen.

attitude /ˈætɪtjuːd; *US* -tuːd/

/ ˈ / This mark shows that the syllable after it is said with more force (stress) than the other syllables in the word or group of words. For example *any* /ˈenɪ/ has a stress on the first syllable; *depend* /dɪˈpend/ has a stress on the second syllable.

/ ˌ / This mark shows that a syllable is said with more force than other syllables in a word but with a stress that is not as strong as for those syllables marked /ˈ/. So in the word *pronunciation* /prəˌnʌnsɪˈeɪʃn/ the main stress is on the syllable /ˈeɪʃn/ and the secondary stress is on the syllable /ˌnʌn/.

(r) In spoken British English an *r* at the end of a written word (either as the final letter or in an *-re* ending as in *fire*) is not sounded unless another word that begins with a vowel sound follows. For example, the *r* is not heard in *His car was sold* but it is heard in *His car isn't old*. To show this, words which end in *r* or *re* have (r) at the end of the phonetic spelling in the dictionary.

car /kɑː(r)/

In American English the /r/ is sounded whenever it occurs in the spelling of a word.

Strong and weak forms

Some very common words, eg *an, as, that, of* have two or more pronunciations: a *strong* form and one or more *weak* forms. In speech the weak forms are more common. For example *from* is /frəm/ in *He comes from Spain*. The strong form occurs when the word comes at the end of a sentence or it is given special emphasis. For example *from* is /frɒm/ in *The ˌpresent's not ˈfrom John, it's ˈfor him*.

Pronunciation in derivatives and compounds

Many **derivatives** are formed by adding a suffix to the end of a word. These are pronounced by simply saying the suffix after the word. For example *slowly* /ˈsləʊlɪ/ is said by joining the suffix *-ly* /lɪ/ to the word *slow* /sləʊ/.

However, where there is doubt about how a derivative is pronounced, the phonetic spelling is given. The part that remains the same is represented by a hyphen.

mournful /-fl/; mournfully /-fəlɪ/

In **compounds** (made up of two or more words) the pronunciation of the individual words is not repeated. The dictionary shows how the compound is stressed by using the marks /ˈ/ and /ˌ/. In ˈ*bus-stop* the stress is on the first word. In ˌ*jacket po*ˈ*tato* the secondary stress is on the first syllable of *jacket* and the main stress is on the second syllable of *potato*.